W9-AEM-596

NORTH CAROLINA
STATE BOARD OF COMMUNITY COLLEGES
LIBRARIES
STANLY COMMUNITY COLLEGE

ENCYCLOPEDIA
OF
WORLD CRIME

ENCYCLOPEDIA OF WORLD CRIME

Criminal Justice, Criminology, and Law Enforcement

Volume I
A-C

Jay Robert Nash

CrimeBooks, Inc.
Wilmette, IL 1989

Publisher and **Editor-in-Chief**: Jay Robert Nash; **Associate Publisher** and **Executive Editor**: Oksana L. Creighton; **Managing Editor**: Joseph Anthony Reich (Production/Database/CD-ROM Services); **Senior Editors**: Jim McCormick, Richard C. Lindberg, Jennifer Harris, Richard E. Stark, Jean Blashfield Black; **Associate Editors**: Cordelia Maloney, Michael Steele, Marck L. Bailey, Kristina Lawson, Todd C. Schuett, Laura McKee, Bill Young, Pamela Jameson, Madeleine Avirov, Eric Murphy, Jeff Carlson, Mary Anne Maloney, Julie Witcoff; **Art Director**: Curtis W. Randell; **Art Consultants**: Cathy Anetsberger-Edens, Wm. O. Boze Harz; **Art Production Assistant**: Doreen J. Kozak; **Assistant Editors**: Marydeanne Wildman, John Leacock, Lawrence Eric Buhl, Marcy Firmiss, Constance Kuehn, David Foe, Amy Schroeder, Vincent M. Tornatore, John A. Koehlinger, Andrew D. Schmit, Leslie A. Krampf, Bennett H. Merens, Garrett M. Derner, Carol Hanson, Annie C. Higgins, Joni Overton, Clifford Tarrance; **Research Director**: Melanie L. Wallis; **Assistant Research Director**: Doreen J. Kozak; **Research** and **Editorial Assistants**: Chad R. Well, Timothy A. Walsh, Andrea Nash, Carmel Carroll, Celia Carroll, Kymber Whitney, Inga Johnson, Martha Keefe, Leslie Haines, Paul Addee, Daniel P. Bakula, Darryl Fox, Aaron Epstein; **Bureau Chief** (Washington, D.C.): John E. Vetter; **Foreign Correspondents**: Paul Allen (Paris); Roger Madden (London); David Halliday (Berlin); G. Caetani (Rome); **Editorial Consultants**: Mitchel H. Tobin (Legal Editorial), Robert A. Janet (Law Enforcement).

Business Group: Judith A. Nash, Business Director and Associate Publisher; Patrice Tracy, Business and Sales Manager; Cordelia Maloney, Publicity and Promotion; **Consultants**: Robert Lee Ganchiff, Associate Publisher/Finance; Marc Davis, Advertising and Marketing; George C. de Kay, Publishing and Distribution; E. Leonard Rubin, David Canmann, Legal; **Associate Publishers**: Stanley Ralph Ross, Lawrence Ferguson, Barbara Browne Cramer, Marc B. Benson, Robert D. and Claudette Endacott, Peter Barrett, Lynn C. Maddox, James Baxter, Robert Champion, Helen Creighton, James Creighton.

Editorial and **Sales Offices**: CrimeBooks, Inc., 1213 Wilmette Avenue, Wilmette, IL 60091-2557. Telephone: 1-708-251-8350. FAX: 1-708-251-5289.

Library of Congress Catalog Card Number: 88-92729
ISBN:0-923582-00-2 ENCYCLOPEDIA OF WORLD CRIME
    (6 Vols.)
    0-923582-01-0 ENCYCLOPEDIA OF WORLD CRIME,
    Vol. I (A-C)

Printed in the United States
First Edition

1 2 3 4 5 6 7 8 9 10

INTRODUCTION

Until the publication of the *Encyclopedia of World Crime*, no single source offered detailed, comprehensive information in the international fields of crime, criminal justice, criminology, and law enforcement. The need for such a comprehensive biographical and historical encyclopedia of crime is evidenced by the high rate of public concern and inquiry, stemming from drastic increases in all levels of crime. Where assassination, mass murder, and terrorist acts had been occasional or rare in previous generations, such criminal acts have now become alarmingly commonplace. Certainly the increase in population within the last sixty years has brought about a commensurate increase in crime. (In 1930 there were approximately 130 million persons in the U.S., and that number has almost doubled in the last sixty years.) There are, however, many other factors contributing to the high increase in crime, including the ability of professional criminals to plea-bargain serious, even capital, offenses to receive lesser or minimum sentences—a flagrant misuse of the present-day prosecution and judicial systems in many U.S. states. In addition, the break-down of the American family unit, the considerable defection from organized religions, the rise in drug use and the resulting criminal activities on the part of addicts feeding insidious habits, and the overall decline of respect for law and order have made crime a day-to-day, mainstream problem, particularly in the low-income, poorly educated segments of the population, which directly touches every third person in the U.S.

The aim of the *Encyclopedia of World Crime* is to present the complete historical perspective of crime, from ancient times to the present. More than 50,000 entries within this six-volume work, stemming from more than thirty years of research, range from Biblical times through 1988. (This is a continuity series encyclopedia, offering annual editions, the year 1989 to be covered in CrimeBooks' 1990 Annual.) The international scope of this work encompasses all countries and continents, presenting the most notable and important international criminal cases, persons, places, and events, as well as important persons in the fields of law enforcement, criminal justice, the judiciary, criminology, identification systems, forensic medicine, pathology, penology, and criminal psychiatry and psychology (more case history studies than have ever before been assembled in any one source). Moreover, this work provides thousands of entries dealing with works of drama, fiction, film, poetry, and song, explaining the real-life role models for such works.

The most difficult problem in assembling data for this encyclopedia has been to define dates and substantiate facts, especially for deep historical entries, cases that were, in their own eras, thinly supported by accurate or traceable records. In many instances, historical records were destroyed by various disasters or were ruined through neglect or theft. This left incomplete information which necessitated the reconstruction of cases and facts through the most exacting literary detection, culling information from myriad but reliable sources. In the case of contemporary accounts and entries, all available law enforcement, judicial, criminal justice, and other sources of information were contacted worldwide. (See ACKNOWLEDGEMENTS, page iii.)

This research caused the assembling and organization of the largest, most comprehensive private collection of criminal files known to exist, files in the form of newspaper and periodical clippings, trial transcripts, interviews, and correspondence, at the core of which is the author's personal thirty-year collection. These original files were expanded by our professional research staff and continue to be expanded and defined on a daily basis. Supporting this information is undoubtedly the most comprehensive private crime library available. The staff experts of CrimeBooks, Inc., daily examine the publications of the international and professional press and extract from these sources significant crime information, tracking and updating all important cases, biographical profiles,

and events in the field. (In addition, more than 4,000 photos and illustrations appear in these pages, visual material gathered from historical sources, periodical/newspaper archives, and the author's personal collection of three decades, offering a startling historical view of criminal history.)

The author has personally selected each and every entry in the biographical volumes and the Dictionary of the *Encyclopedia of World Crime*. Selection of entries has been made according to various criteria: those who are historically prominent within their own era, those who have remained significant from their era to the present, and those who may not have been prominent in their own era but whose cases are important firsts or lend insight into the times in which they lived. Moreover, events and places that have historical significance in the field of crime have been included. To encompass all known criminals would have been an impossibility because of space, but generally all noteworthy historical and contemporary persons have been included.

Readers searching for more information than what a particular entry might yield will find, following most entries, a reference paragraph citing further works dealing with the subject, often the most complete bibliographic citations available (hundreds of reference citations follow such entries as Billy the Kid, Jack the Ripper, Abraham Lincoln, and others). This work thusly provides one-stop research on entries that heretofore have been all but impossible to document. These abbreviated bibliographic citations can be found as full bibliographic entries in the Bibliography appearing in the Index Volume (Vol. VI), which offers more than 25,000 entries, the largest single bibliography assembled in this field. The Index Volume also contains a comprehensive subject index and proper name index. It should be noted that general categories, from Arson to Western Outlaws and Gunmen, because of their massive compilations and chronologies, appear in Supplements (Vol. IV). (See HOW TO USE THIS ENCYCLOPEDIA, page v.)

Opinions and value judgments on the part of the author are based on the best research and information available, even in speculative situations, but such editorial decisions have been kept to a minimum and applied only where it is believed that the reader seeks such conclusions. The facts basically speak for themselves and, for the most part, speculation and conclusion is left to the reader. The subject matter of this work is inherently dramatic and sensational and receives no editorial emphasis. Under no circumstance does the editorial position of this work seek to glorify or enhance the image of criminals, but it does attempt to profile the criminal in realistic terms that accurately show personal background, social influence, *modus operandi*, public reaction, law enforcement response, and legal and judicial perspectives.

Here then is a one-of-a-kind encyclopedic work which allows the general reader and researcher alike to incisively view the whole of the world's criminal past and present. More than ten million words profile criminals and those law enforcement persons who combatted them throughout the centuries, the criminal lawyers and government attorneys who represented and prosecuted them, the courts that judged and sentenced them—a vast, dark universe of mankind, that, hopefully, this work will illuminate and define. This savage landscape has been mapped to provide the reader with a revealing, sometimes fierce, geography that has been, until now, largely unchartered. The reader will also find within these pages the struggling presence of good and evil from one generation to the next, measured by a human morality seeking justice and truth. And that quest, not unlike the noble hunt for the Grail, provides the essential goal of this work.

Jay Robert Nash
Chicago, Ill., 1989

ACKNOWLEDGEMENTS

Grateful acknowledgement is given to the thousands of persons who, over the years, have assisted the author and, in recent years, CrimeBooks, Inc., in obtaining valuable source information, research materials of all kinds, photos, illustrations, trial reports, and tracts. Without the splendid and wonderful cooperation of these persons and organizations, this work would not have come into existence. Organizations deserving special recognition in this area include correctional facilities, criminal investigation agencies, government offices, historical societies, libraries, newspaper and other media, and police departments worldwide.

Some of the most helpful include:

CORRECTIONAL FACILITIES: Alabama Dept. of Corrections (Montgomery, Ala.); Arizona Dept. of Corrections (Phoenix, Ariz., Jo Stephens); Baystate Correctional Center (Norfolk, Mass., Deodato Arruda); Bureau of Prisons (Washington, D.C., Helen Butler, Tina Cloyd); California Dept. of Corrections (Sacramento, Calif., Lisa Korb); Connecticut Dept. of Correction (Hartford, Conn.); Delaware Dept. of Correction (Smyrna, Del., Kathryn Pippin); District of Columbia Dept. of Corrections (Washington, D.C., Pat Wheeler); Federal Bureau of Prisons - North Central Region (Kansas City, Mo.) Florida Dept. of Corrections (Tallahassee, Fla.); Georgia Dept. of Corrections (Atlanta, Ga.); Illinois Dept. of Corrections (Springfield, Ill.); Indiana Dept. of Corrections (Indianapolis, Ind.); Kansas Dept. of Corrections (Topeka, Kan., Thomas J. Sloan); Kentucky Corrections Cabinet Dept. of Adult Correctional Institutions; Lackawanna County Prison (Scranton, Pa.); Maryland Dept. of Public Safety and Correctional Services; Massachusetts Dept. of Probations and Records (Boston, Mass.); Minnesota Dept. of Corrections (St. Paul, Minn.); Missouri Dept. of Corrections and Human Resources; Nevada Dept. of Prisons (Carson City, Nev.); New York State Dept. of Corrections (Albany, N.Y., Kelly Priess); New Jersey Dept. of Corrections (Trenton, N.J.); North Carolina Dept. of Corrections (Raleigh, N.C., David Guth); Ohio Department of Rehabilitation and Correction (Columbus, Ohio); Oklahoma Dept. of Corrections (Oklahoma City, Okla., Michelle Matthews); Olmstead County (Minn.), Dept. of Corrections; Pennsylvania Dept. of Corrections (Harrisburg, Pa., Kenneth G. Robinson); South Carolina Dept. of Corrections (Columbia, S.C., Judy Bode); Tennessee Dept. of Correction (Nashville, Tenn., William C. Haynes, Jr.); Texas Dept. of Corrections (Huntsville, Texas); U.S. Medical Center for Federal Prisoners (Springfield, Ill.); Leavenworth (Kan.) Penitentiary; Marion (Ill.) Penitentiary; Utah Dept. of Corrections (Salt Lake City, Utah).

COURT OFFICIALS: Nell E. Anderson (Clerk of the District Court, Teller County, Cripple Creek, Colo.); Tom Bigbee (Record Planning Commission, Canton, Ala.); C. Edward Bourassa (Register of Probate, Hillsborough County Probate Court, Nashua, N.H.); Richard P. Brinker (Clerk, Probate Division of Circuit Court of Miami, Fla.); Arlene D. Connors (Deputy Register in Probate, Milwaukee County, Milwaukee, Wis.); John J. Corcoran (Acting County Clerk, Los Angeles, Calif.); Susan Cottrell (Deputy, San Diego, Calif.); Virginia Crane (Deputy Court Clerk, Neptune, N.J.); John T. Curry (Circuit Clerk, Probate Division, Macon County, Ill.); Director of Licensing, Public Service Level, Minneapolis, Minn.; B.J. Dunavant (Clerk of the Probate Court, Shelby County, Memphis, Tenn.); Bremer Ehrler (Clerk, Jefferson County Court, Probate Division, Louisvile, Ky.); C. Fatni (Record Clerk, Surrogate's Court, Kings County, N.Y.); Mildred Fulton (County Clerk, Cherokee County, Rusk, Tex.); Mildred Gonder (Deputy Clerk, Probate Court, New Albany, Ind.); Harriet L. Gosnell (Trust Officer, Peoples Bank of Bloomington, Ill.); Jackie Griffin (Chief Deputy, Ellis County, Tex.); Carole J. Hals (Deputy Clerk, County Court, Probate Division, Stark, Minn.); James B. Kelley, Jr. (Register, Probate Court, Taunton, Mass.); Julia Kowrak (Register of Wills, City Hall, Philadelphia, Pa.); Leland Larrison (Clerk, Probate Court, Terre Haute, Ind.); Madelina S. Marting (Deputy Clerk, Putnam County, N.J.); Sarah Montjoy (Deputy Clerk, Jefferson County Court, Probate Division, Louisville, Ky.); Olmsted County Court, Probate Division (Minn.); Carl M. Olsen (Deputy Clerk, San Francisco, Calif.); Mrs. Lana J. Olson (Register of Probate, Luce County, Newberry, Mich.); Lorna Pierce (Secretary to Judge Donald Gunn, Probate Court of St. Louis, Mo.); Probate Court, Port Arthur, Texas, Probate Court; Providence, R.I., Probate Court ; Willaim J. Regan (Judge of the Surrogates Court, Buffalo, N.Y.); Elisabeth F. Sachse (Deputy Clerk of court, Baton Rouge, La.); St. Joseph County Health Department (South Bend, Ind.); San Mateo County Sheriff's Office (Hall of Justice, Redwood City, Calif.); Joan R. Saunder (Deputy Register of Wills, Clerk of the Probate; Division, Washington, D.C.); Jean Smith (Deputy Clerk of Court, Watonwan County, St. James, Minn.); Nancy M. Spaulding (Chief Clerk, Schoharie, N.Y.); Storey County (Nev.) Probate Clerk; Surrogates Court of Essex, N.J.; Irene Thuringer (Deputy Clerk, Probate Dept., Pima County, Tucson, Ariz.); John M. Walker (Chief of Public Services, Los Angeles, Calif.); David M. Warren (Assistant Chief Deputy, Probate Courts Department, Harris County, Houston, Tex.); R.D. Zumwalt (County Clerk, San Diego, Calif.).

CRIMINAL INVESTIGATION AGENCIES: Atlanta, Ga., U.S. Attorney's Office; Boston, Mass., U.S. Attorney's Office; Boston, Mass., District Attorney's Office; Brooklyn (N.Y.) District Attorney's Office; Bryan, Texas, District Attorney's Office (Bill Turner); Chicago, Ill., U.S. Attorney's Office; Columbus, Ohio, U.S. Attorney's Office; Cook County State's Attorney's Office (Chicago, Ill., Merle Aguilar); Cook County State's Attorney-Criminal Records Dept., (Chicago, Ill.); Danville, Ill. U.S. Attorney's Office (Rick Cox); Denver, Colo., District Attorney's Office (Dave Heckenbach, Assisant D.A.); Ft. Smith, Ark., District Attorney's Office (Steven Snyder, Assistant D.A.); Franklin County Prosecutor's Office (Columbus, Ohio, Thomas Tornabene); Geneva, Ill., State's Attorney's Office; Hamilton County (Ohio) Prosecutor's Office; Lee County State's Attorney's Office (Ft. Myers, Fla.); Livingston County, Ill., District Attorney's Office; Los Angeles City Attorney's Office (Mike Qualls); Los Angeles, Calif., District Attorney's Office (Grace Denton); Manhattan District Attorney's Office (New York, N.Y.); Montgomery County District Attorney's Office (Cheltenham, Pa.); New Bedford, Mass., District Attorney's Office; New Orleans, La., U.S. Attorney's Office; Reno, Nev., District Attorney's Office; San Jose, Calif., District Attorney's Office; Shiawassee City, Mich., District Attorney's Office; Suffolk County (N.Y.) Assistant District Attorney's Office (Jermyn Ray); Westchester County District Attorney's Office (N.Y.); Will County State's Attorney's Office (Joliet, Ill.).

GOVERNMENT OFFICES: Camden County (N.C.) Clerk's Office; Crown Point, Ind., Mayor's Office; Dept. of Treasury, Public Affairs Office (Washington, D.C., Robert R. Snow); FBI, Special Productions Branch (Washington, D.C., Melanie McElhinney); Federal Bureau of Investigations (Washington, D.C.); Hamilton County Clerk's Office (Cincinnati, Ohio); Municipal References & Resource Center of New York City (New York, N.Y., Devra Zetlan); Shiawassee County (Mich.) Clerk's Office; Tallahassee, Fla., City Clerk's Office (Becky Pippin); U.S. Information Agency (Washington, D.C., Scott Righetti).

HISTORICAL SOCIETIES: Anoka (Minn.) County Historical Society; Arizona State Historical Society (Tuscon, Ariz.); Blair County Historical Society (Altoona, Pa., Sylva L. Emerson, Curator); California Historical Society (Los Angeles, Calif., Peter Evans); Chicago Historical Society; Colorado State Historical Society (Denver, Colo.); Connecticut Historical Society (Hartford, Conn.); Detroit Historical Society; Historical Society of Pennsylvania (Philadelphia, Pa.); Historical Society of Pennsylvania (Pittsburgh, Pa.); Illinois Historical Society (Chicago, Ill.); Illinois State Historical Society (Springfield, Ill.); Kansas State Historical Society (Topeka, Kan.); Kentucky Historical Society (Frankfort, Ky.); Massachusetts Historical Society (Boston, Mass.); Minnesota Historical Society (St. Paul, Minn.); Missouri State Historical Society (Columbia, Mo.); New Jersey Historical Society (Newark, N.J.); New York Historical Society (New York, N.Y., Mariam Touba); Oregon Historical Society (Portland, Ore.); Virginia Historical Society (Richmond, Va.); Wyoming State Historical Society (Cheyenne, Wyo.).

LIBRARIES: Alachua County Library District (Gainesville, Fla., Phillis Filer); Boston Public Library; Bridgeport Public Library (Bridgeport, Conn., Louise Minervino); Broward County Library (Ft. Lauderdale, Fla., Juanita Alpuche, Allison M. Ellis); California State Library (Sacramento, Calif.); Chicago Public Library (Chicago, Ill.); Columbia University Law Library (New York, N.Y.); Denver Public Library (Denver, Colo., James H. Davis, Picture Librarian); Detroit Public Library; Drug Enforcement Administration Library (Washington, D.C., Edith A. Crutchfield); Harvard Law School Library (Cambridge, Mass.); Illinois State Library (Springfield, Ill.); Indiana State Library (Indianapolis, Ind.); John Crerar Library (Chicago, Ill.); Library of Congress (Washington, D.C., Dan Burney); Metropolitan Library System (Oklahoma City, Okla.); Monroe County Law Library (Monroe, Mich., Judge Sullivan); New Orleans Public Library (New Orleans, La.); New York City Public Library (New York, N.Y.); New York State Law Library (Albany, N.Y.); Newberry Library (Chicago, Ill.); North Carolina State Library (Raleigh, N.C.); Northwestern University Law Library (Chicago, Ill.); Scotland Yard Library (London, England); Special Collections Library, Northwestern University (Evanston, Ill., Russell Maylone); University of California Library (Berkeley, Calif., William F. Roberts, Reference Librarian); University of Chicago Library (Chicago, Ill.); University of Missouri Law Library (Columbia, Mo.); University of Missouri Library (Columbia, Mo.); University of Oklahoma (Norman, Okla., Jack D. Haley, Assistant Curator, Western History Collections); University of Wisconsin Criminal Justice Reference and Information Center (Madison, Wis., Sue L. Center, Dir.); Wisconsin Dept. of Justice, Law Library (Madison, Wis., Michael F. Bemis); Yale University Law Library (New Haven, Conn., Robert E. Brooks, Reference; Jo Anne Giammattei, Acquisitions).

MISSING PERSONS BUREAUS: Chicago Police Dept. (Chicago, Ill., Lts. Bill Bodner, John Doyle, Bill Frost); New York Police Department (New York, N.Y., Detective John Griffin).

NEWSPAPERS/MEDIA: *Adam Smith's Money World* (New York, N.Y., Anne Hansen); Albuquerque (N.M.) *Journal;* Arizona *Daily Star* (Tucson, Ariz.); Arizona *Republic* (Phoenix, Ariz.); Arkansas *Democrat* (Booneville, Ark.); Atlanta (Ga.) *Constitution* (Diane Hunter); Baltimore (Md.) *Sun*; Bangor (Maine) *Daily News;* Boston (Mass.) *Herald* (Betsy Warrior); Boston (Mass.) *Globe* (William Boles); Capital News Service (Los Angeles, Calif., Jerry Goldberg); Charleston (W. Va.) *Gazette* (Ron Miller); *Chicago Sun Times* (Chicago, Ill.); *Chicago Tribune* (Chicago, Ill.); Cincinatti (Ohio) *Enquirer, Clarion-Ledger* (Jackson, Miss.); Cleveland (Ohio) *Plain Dealer* (Eileen M. Lentz); *Daily Northwestern* (Oshkosh, Wis.); *Daily Oklahoman* (Oklahoma City, Okla.); Dallas (Texas) *Morning News;* Dayton (Ohio) *Daily News;* Detroit (Mich.) *Free Press;* Detroit (Mich.) *News;* Gallatin (Tenn.) *Examiner* (John Cannon); Greenville (S.C.) *News;* Houston (Texas) *Post;* Houston (Texas) *Chronicle* (Sherry Abrams); Indianapolis (Ind.) *Star* (Nadine Moore); Japan *Times* (Tokyo, Japan, Shigeo Shimada); Las Vegas (Nev.) *Sun* (Jenny Scarantino); Los Angeles (Calif.) *Times* (Renée Nembhard); Louisville (Ky.) *Courier-Journal* (Patrick Chapman); Miami (Fla.) *Herald* (Liz Donovan, Nora Paul); *Morning Call* (Allentown, Pa., Lynn M. Dubbs); New York (N.Y.) *Daily News* (Faigi Rosenthal); New York (N.Y.) *Times* (Tom Wicker); *Newsday* (Garden City, N.Y., Elizabeth Whisnant); Omaha (Neb.) *World Herald;* Philadelphia (Pa.) *Inquirer;* Pittsburgh (Pa.) *Post Gazette;* Portland (Ore.) *Oregonian* (Sandra Macomber); *Press Telegram* (Long Beach, Calif., George Choma); Providence (R.I.) *Journal;* Reno (Nev.) *Gazette-Journal* (Carole Keith, Nan Spina); *Rocky Mountain News* (Denver, Colo.); St. Louis (Mo.) *Post-Dispatch* (Mike Marler); Salt Lake *Tribune* (Salt Lake City, Utah); San Antonio (Texas) *Express-News* (Judy Zipp); San Diego (Calif.) *Union;* San Francisco (Calif.) *Chronicle* (Nikki Bengal); San Francisco (Calif.) *Examiner;* Seattle (Wash.) *Times;* Seattle (Wash.) *Post-Intelligencer;* Selma (Ala.) *Times Journal* (Nicki Davis Maud); *Spokesman-Review* (Spokane, Wash.); Tampa *Tribune* (Tampa Bay, Fla.); *The State* (Columbia, S.C., Dargan Richards); *Times News* (Cumberland, Md., Linda Shuck); Topeka (Kan.) *Capital-Journal;* Trenton (N.J.) *Times;* Tucson (Ariz.) *Daily Citizen;* Tulsa (Okla.) *Daily World;* Wichita (Kan.) *Eagle Beacon;* Winnipeg *Free Press* (Winnipeg, Manitoba, Canada); WTEN-TV (Albany, N.Y., David A. Lamb).

POLICE DEPARTMENTS: Aurora (Ill.) Police Dept.; Baltimore (Md.) Police Dept. (Dennis S. Hill, Dir. Public Info. Div.); Boston (Mass.) Police Dept. (Allison Woodhouse, Research & Analysis); Brooklyn Organized Crime Strike Force (Brooklyn, N.Y.); Chicago (Ill.) Police Dept. (Dennis Bingham, Public Information; Tina Vicini, Dir. News Affair Div.); Chicago (Ill.) Police Dept. Academy (Sgt. Anthony Consieldi); Dallas (Texas) Police Dept. (Capt. J.E. Ferguson); Deerfield (Ill.) Police Dept. (Richard Brandt, Chief of Police, Thomas A. Creighton, Youth Dir.); Indianapolis (Ind.) Police Dept. (Maj. Robert L. Snow); Los Angeles (Calif.) Police Dept. (Stephen F. Hatfield, Public Information Dir.); Metropolitan Police Dept. (St. Louis, Mo.); Miami (Fla.) Police Dept. (Maj. Dean De Jong); Minneapolis (Minn.) Police Dept. (Ted Faul, Deputy Chief of Services; J.E. Bender, Officer); New Scotland Yard (London, England, Annette Eastgate, Robin Goodfellow, Steve Wilmot); Oshkosh (Wis.) Police Dept.; Pennsylvania State Police Troop H; Philadelphia (Penn.) Police Dept. (Mary Ann Edmunds); Portland (Ore.) Police Dept. (Candy Hill Turay); San Diego (Calif.) Police Dept. (Pliny Castanien); Washington, D.C. Police Dept.

NON-GOVERNMENT AGENCIES: Alcatraz Ferry (San Francisco, Calif.); Chicago Crime Commission (Chicago, Ill.).

OTHER CONTRIBUTORS: American Red Cross (Washington, D.C., Margaret O'Connor); Amnesty Int'l (New York, N.Y., Janice Christianson); Chinese Consulate's Office (New York, N.Y.); Joseph Dillman - Registered Pharmacist (Libertyville, Ill.); Japanese Consulate's Office (Chicago, Ill.); Korean Consulate's Office (Chicago, Ill.); Yuri Morozov, Translator; Northwestern University Language Dept. (Evanston, Ill., Rolf Erickson); Anthony J. Pellicano, Private Detective (Los Angeles, Calif.); Pinkerton's, Inc. (New York, N.Y., G.F. O'Neill); Salvation Army (Chicago, Ill., Col. Lloyd Robb); Seaman's Institute of New York City (New York, N.Y., Barbara Clauson).

HOW TO USE THIS ENCYCLOPEDIA

ALPHABETICAL ORDER

Each entry name in the *Encyclopedia of World Crime* is bold-faced and listed alphabetically. Biographical entries are alphabetized by the subject's last name. Everything preceding the comma is treated as a unit when alphabetizing. Hyphens, diacritical marks, periods following initials, and spaces do not influence its alphabetization. For example, **La Pietra** follows **Lang**, and **Black Bart** follows **Black, Robert**. Names with prefixes such as **de**, **von**, or **le** are listed under the most common form of the name, such as **de Gaulle, Charles** and **Ribbentrop, Joachim von**. Names beginning in **Mc** or **M'** are treated as if spelled **Mac**; thus **McManus, Fred** appears before **MacMichael, Sir Harold**. Asian names, in which the family name comes first, are alphabetized by the family name, omitting the comma. Identical names are alphabetized chronologically. Monarchs commonly known by one name, such as **Elizabeth I** or **Louis XIV**, are usually listed under that name only and would precede an identically spelled surname in entry order. Entries with numbers or abbreviations in them are alphabetized as though spelled out. When an entry heading refers to an event rather than to a person, it is alphabetized according to the first key word in the commonly used title, as in **Popish Plot** or **King Ranch Murders**. When the names of two or more people head an entry, it is usually alphabetized according to the most prominent person's last name.

ENTRY HEADINGS

Appearing in boldface type at the beginning of each *Encyclopedia of World Crime* entry is the name by which that entry is most commonly known. Entries are categorized alphabetically under the name of the offender, criminal event, or the professional in the field of crime. If a crime remains unsolved, the entry is found under the victim's name, and is denoted by the abbreviation **unsolv.** in parentheses immediately preceding the crime category. Other entries appearing under the victim's name include **assassinations**; thus, information concerning the assassination of President Abraham Lincoln would be found under Lincoln and not John Wilkes Booth. The royal or political title or military rank held by the assassination victim precedes the category abbreviation. Parenthetical remarks immediately following an entry name indicate an alternate spelling, that person's original or maiden name, or the entry's alias if preceded by **AKA:**. These names also appear in boldface.

Following the name are **date(s)** relevant to that entry. The letter **b.** preceding the date signifies that only the person's date of birth is known, while the letter **d.** signifies that only the person's date of death is known. The letter **c.** (circa) signifies that the date which immediately follows is approximate. In some cases **prom.** (prominent) is used to denote the year(s) in which that entry was noteworthy. All years B.C. are designated as such.

In a number of entries the phrase **Case of** follows the date, designating that the person named was tried for the crime which follows but found Not Guilty.

The **country** designation in each entry heading refers to the country in which the crime was committed or the country in which persons in the field of crime are known professionally. The country is named as it was known at the time the crime was committed; thus, Russia is referenced prior to the Russian Revolution, while U.S.S.R. is used for crimes committed since that time. Entries where crimes are committed in more than three countries or committed on the high seas are designated as Int'l (International).

The last piece of information contained in the Entry Heading is the **crime category**, designating the crime(s) the subject was convicted of, or the professional field of crime with which the subject is associated. For persons wrongly convicted of a crime, prior to the crime category is the designation **(wrong. convict.)**. If however, the subject's conviction was overturned on a legal technicality or there is some doubt as to his actual innocence, then the designation **(wrong. convict.?)** is used. In some cases a question mark may follow the crime category. This denotes that there is uncertainty as to whether the crime in question actually occurred; e.g., **mur.?**, might denote that there is some doubt as to whether a person was killed, committed suicide, or died from other causes.

A number of entries may include more than one person if the criminals or professionals worked together. When the relevant dates of a **multiple name entry** coincide, one date will follow the last person named in the entry heading.

REFERENCES

After each **Encyclopedia of World Crime** entry, the references used in compiling it are cited. The abbreviation **CBA** denotes **CrimeBooks Archives**. Other sources are cited in four categories: nonfiction, fiction, drama, and film. Nonfiction works are listed first, alphabetically by the author's last name. If two or more works by the same author are used, the second and all following citations are indicated by a blank line and are alphabetized by the first word (ignoring articles A, An, The). If a source is anonymous, this is indicated in parentheses after the title. Sources without a specific author (pamphlets, reports, tracts, trial transcripts, compilations, etc.) are listed alphabetically by the title. Plays based on a case appear after **(DRAMA)** and are listed alphabetically by author. Fictional accounts of a case appear alphabetically by author after **(FICTION)**. Films based on the case appear after **(FILM)**, and are listed chronologically, each title followed by the year of its U.S. release. Silent films are denoted by the letters preceding the year of release. Often alternate titles **(alt. title)** of films follow U.S. titles in parentheses.

Cross references immediately following an entry refer the reader to entries containing additional information relevant to the case, person, place, or event being consulted. Direct references are also used frequently throughout the volumes to lead the readers from a well known name (alias, victim, event) to the name under which that entry appears **(Bonney, William H.,** See: **Billy the Kid)**.

KEY TO ABBREVIATIONS USED IN THE *ENCYCLOPEDIA OF WORLD CRIME*

2d lt.	= second lieutenant
abduc.	= abduction
abor.	= abortion
accom.	= accomplices
adm.	= admiral
adult.	= adultery
Afg.	= Afghanistan
Ala.	= Alabama
Alb.	= Albania
Alg.	= Algeria
Arg.	= Argentina

Ariz.	= Arizona		forg.	= forgery
Ark.	= Arkansas		Fr.	= France
assass.	= assassination		Ga.	= Georgia
asslt.	= assault		gamb.	= gambling, gambler
asslt.&bat.	= assault and battery		gen.	= general
attempt.	= attempted		geno.	= genocide
atty. gen.	= attorney general		Ger.	= Germany
Aus.	= Australia		Gr.	= Greece
Aust.	= Austria		Guat.	= Guatemala
banish.	= banishment		harass.	= harassment
Bav.	= Bavaria		her.	= heresy
Belg.	= Belgium		hijack.	= hijacking
Ber.	= Bermuda		Hond.	= Honduras
big.	= bigamy		host.	= hostage
blk.	= blackmail		Hung.	= Hungary
Bol.	= Bolivia		Ice.	= Iceland
bomb.	= bombing		Ill.	= Illinois
boot.	= bootlegging		impris.	= imprisoned
Braz.	= Brazil		Ind.	= Indiana
brib.	= bribery		Indo.	= Indonesia
Brit.	= Britain/England including Wales		Int'l.	= International
Bul.	= Bulgaria		Ire.	= Ireland
burg.	= burglary		Isr.	= Israel
Calif.	= California		Jam.	= Jamaica
can.	= cannibalism		Jor.	= Jordan
Can.	= Canada		jur.	= jurist
cap. pun.	= capital punishment		Kan.	= Kansas
capt.	= captain		kid.	= kidnapper, kidnapping
coin.	= coining		Kor.	= Korea
col.	= colonel		Ky.	= Kentucky
Col.	= Columbia		La.	= Louisiana
Colo.	= Colorado		law enfor. off.	= law enforcement officer or official
comdr.	= commander		Leb.	= Lebanon
Conn.	= Connecticut		loot.	= looting
consp.	= conspiracy		lt.	= lieutenant
cont./ct.	= contempt of court		lt. col.	= lieutenant colonel
corr.	= corruption		lt. comdr.	= lieutenant commander
Cos.	= Costa Rica		lt. gen.	= lieutenant general
count.	= counterfeiting		lt. gov.	= lieutenant governor
cpl.	= corporal		Lux.	= Luxemburg
crim. insan.	= criminal insanity		lynch.	= lynching
crim. just.	= criminal justice		Mac.	= Macedonia
crim. law.	= criminal lawyer		maj.	= major
crim. neg.	= criminal negligence		mansl.	= manslaughter
crime preven.	= crime prevention		Mass.	= Massachusetts
crime&punish.	= crime and punishment		Md.	= Maryland
criminol.	= criminologist or criminology		med. mal.	= medical malpractice
ct. mar.	= court-martial		Mex.	= Mexico
Czech.	= Czechoslovakia		Mich.	= Michigan
Del.	= Delaware		Mid. East	= Middle East
del.	= delinquency		milit.	= military
Den.	= Denmark		milit. des.	= military desertion
det.	= detective		Minn.	= Minnesota
Dom.	= Dominican Republic		Miss.	= Mississippi
Dr.	= doctor		miss. per.	= missing persons
duel.	= dueling		Mo.	= Missouri
Ecu.	= Ecuador		mob vio.	= mob violence
El Sal.	= El Salvador		Mont.	= Montana
embez.	= embezzlement		Mor.	= Morocco
emp.	= emperor or empress		mur.	= murder, murderer
esc.	= escape		mut.	= mutiny
esp.	= espionage		mutil.	= mutilation
Eth.	= Ethiopia		N. Zea.	= New Zealand
euth.	= euthanasia		N.C.	= North Carolina
execut.	= executioner		N.D.	= North Dakota
extor.	= extortion, extortionist		N.H.	= New Hampshire
fenc.	= fencing		N.J.	= New Jersey
Fin.	= Finland		N.M.	= New Mexico
fing. ident.	= fingerprint identification		N.Y.	= New York
Fla.	= Florida		Neb.	= Nebraska

necro.	= necrophilia		toxicol.	= toxicologist
Neth.	= Netherlands		treas.	= treason
Nev.	= Nevada		Tun.	= Tunisia
Nic.	= Nicaragua		Turk.	= Turkey
Nig.	= Nigeria		U.A.E.	= United Arab Emirates
Nor.	= Norway		U.K.	= United Kingdom
obsc.	= obscenity		U.S.	= United States of America
Okla.	= Oklahoma		U.S.S.R.	= Union of Soviet Socialist Republics (after 1918)
Ore.	= Oregon		unsolv.	= unsolved
org. crime	= organized crime		Urug.	= Uruguay
P.R.	= Puerto Rico		Va.	= Virginia
Pa.	= Pennsylvania		vandal.	= vandalism
Pak.	= Pakistan		Venez.	= Venezuela
Pan.	= Panama		vice dist.	= vice district
Para.	= Paraguay		vict.	= victim
path.	= pathologist		Viet.	= Vietnam
penal col.	= penal colonies		vigil.	= vigilantism
penol.	= penology, penologist		Vt.	= Vermont
Per.	= Persia		W.Va.	= West Virginia
perj.	= perjury		Wash.	= Washington
Phil.	= Philippines		west. gunman	= western gunman
pick.	= pickpocket		west. lawman	= western lawman
pir.	= piracy		west. outl.	= western outlaw
Pol.	= Poland		wh. slav.	= white slavery
pol.	= police		Wis.	= Wisconsin
pol. mal.	= police malpractice		Wyo.	= Wyoming
polit.	= politician		Yug.	= Yugoslavia
polit. corr.	= political corruption			
poly.	= polygamy			
porn.	= pornography			
Port.	= Portugal			
pres.	= president			
pris.	= prison			
prof.	= professor			
prohib.	= prohibition			
pros.	= prostitution			
R.I.	= Rhode Island			
rack.	= racketeering			
rebel.	= rebellion			
rev.	= reverend			
rob.	= robbery			
Rom.	= Romania			
Roman.	= Roman Empire			
Rus.	= Russia (prior to 1918)			
S. Afri.	= South Africa			
S.C.	= South Carolina			
S.D.	= South Dakota			
sab.	= sabotage			
Saud.	= Saudi Arabia			
Scot.	= Scotland			
sec. firm	= security firm			
secret crim. soc.	= secret criminal societies			
secret soc.	= secret society			
Sen.	= Senegal			
sgt.	= sergeant			
Si.	= Sicily			
Sing.	= Singapore			
skyjack.	= skyjacking			
sland.	= slander			
smug.	= smuggling			
sod.	= sodomy			
Sri.	= Sri Lanka			
Sudan	= Sudan			
suic.	= suicide			
supt.	= superintendent			
Swed.	= Sweden			
Switz.	= Switzerland			
Tai.	= Taiwan			
Tan.	= Tanzania			
tax evas.	= tax evasion			
Tenn.	= Tennessee			
terr.	= terrorism, terrorist			
Thai.	= Thailand			
tort.	= torture			

TYPES OF ENTRIES

Biographical; case studies; celebrated trials; criminal secret organizations; direct references; historic and current techniques in police science; historical events and places; literary fiction based on criminals or crime events; unsolved crimes.

DICTIONARY

More than 20,000 terms used in America, U.K., and elsewhere by the underworld and law enforcement, from ancient times to the present, are listed in a dictionary (Vol. V).

TYPES OF SUPPLEMENTS

VOL. IV: Arson; Assassination; Bombing; Burglary; Capital Punishment; Computer Crime; Detectives, Notable; Drugs; Dueling; Firearms and Ballistics; Forensic Sciences, Notable Experts; Fraud; Hijacking; Identification Systems; Kidnapping; Looting; Lynching and Vigilantism; Mob Violence (Riots); Organized Crime; Police; Prisons; Robbery; Skyjacking; Terrorism; Toxicology; War Crimes and Criminals; Western Lawmen; Western Outlaws and Gunmen.

DICTIONARY (VOL. V): International Acronyms for Prominent Organizations and Operations; U.S. Correctional Systems; Landmark U.S. Crime Legislation; Landmark U.S. Federal and State Court Decisions; U.S. Correctional Systems; U.S. Crime Commissions; U.S. Federal Bureau of Investigation Offices by City.

INDEX

The index contains the following: Bibliography; Subject Index; Proper Name Index.

A

Abahai, 1592-1643, China, emperor, mur. Chinese emperor who killed his brothers and competitors, conquered Inner Mongolia and Korea, raided northern China, started the Ch'ing dynasty and began the conquest of the Ming dynasty. REF.: *CBA.*

Abancourt, Charles Xavier Joseph deFranqueville d', 1758-92, Fr., milit. Minister of war, killed in the 1792 massacre at the Versailles Palace. REF.: *CBA.*

Abarca de Bolea, 1718-98, Spain, gen., rebel. Spanish general who became prime interior minister in 1792 and was banished in 1794 for his opposition to the war with France. REF.: *CBA.*

Abbandando, Frank (AKA: **The Dasher**), 1910-42, U.S., org. crime-mur. One of the most feared of professional killers, Abbandando worked from the late 1920s and through the 1930s as a hired killer for Murder, Inc. and as the chief lieutenant of Harry "Happy" Maione, rackets boss of Ocean Hill, N.Y. He fell early into street crime and while still in his teens was often arrested for extorting money from small shop owners under the threat of burning down their buildings. Abbandando was sent to several reform schools and while at the Elmira (N.Y.) Reformatory he proved to be a speedy second baseman, so quick on his feet that he was nicknamed "The Dasher."

Hardened and unconscionable by his early twenties, Abbandando worked with

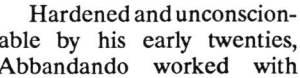

Frank "The Dasher" Abbandando, hired killer for Murder, Inc.

Maione in establishing gambling and loan-sharking rackets. In 1931, they and fellow gangsters joined forces with Abe "Kid Twist" Reles, in battling the Shapiro Brothers of neighboring Brownsville to take control of the rackets there. To that end Abbandando, Maione, Reles, and others shot Meyer and Irving Shapiro to death in 1931 and murdered the remaining Shapiro brother, Willie, in 1934. With the rise of this new gang, dubbed Brooklyn, Inc., Manhattan gangsters, overseeing vast empires of gambling, prostitution, and bootlegging, converted this fledgling organization into what later became known as Murder, Inc., a troop of ruthless killers who would murder anyone at the orders of the bosses, Louis Capone and his boss, Albert Anastasia, the later acting as a supervisor to their gruesome assignments. Above Anastasia was Louis "Lepke" Buchalter, one of the designers of the U.S. national crime syndicate.

Abbandando was given dozens of murder assignments over a ten-year period and he obeyed orders without question, killing as many as forty or more persons who were earmarked by mob bosses for eradication. He asked no questions, along with the others, and happily pocketed the average $500 fee for each murder. The killer purchased a flashy wardrobe (he was partial to blue suits with broad stripes and red ties) and expensive roadsters. He would drive through the Brownsville and Ocean Hill neighborhoods, selecting young females to rape. When later asked about this at his murder trial, Abbandando grew indignant, denying he had ever raped anyone. A prosecutor pointed out one instance where the killer had all but admitted the sexual attack. Abbandando's reply was typical: "Well, that one doesn't count really—I married the girl later."

In 1940, Reles, the street boss of Murder, Inc., was arrested and charged with an old murder. Fearing that some of his cohorts, also picked up at the same time, might talk, Reles himself offered to turn informer and spewed forth a seemingly endless litany of brutal murder—scores of killings—performed by the lethal troops of Murder, Inc., not the least of whom were Frank

Abbandando and Harry Maione. Both Abbandando and Maione were arrested and charged with slaying George "Whitey" Rudnick in a Brownsville, N.Y., garage on the night of May 25, 1937.

As Abbandando and Maione stared daggers at their former boss, Reles related how they and he, along with others, murdered Rudnick, a loan shark whom they suspected of talking to the police. In horrific detail, Reles described the killers stabbing the victim sixty-three times with ice picks, strangling him, and then crushing his head with a meat cleaver. Abbandando and Maione cursed Reles in court but denied having anything to do with any kind of murders when they took the witness stand. Abbandando's conduct was consistent with his brutal, unrepentant nature. At one point he leaned close to presiding Judge Franklin W. Taylor and snarled a whispering threat of death. Judge Taylor was not a man to be intimidated, having announced at the beginning of this sensational trial, "The skull and crossbones of the underworld must come down." To Abbandando's threat, Judge Taylor merely ordered an armed officer to stand between him and the defendant until the killer finished his testimony.

The prosecution confronted Abbandando with his gruesome record, pointing out that he and others had attacked New York police officer Hampton Ferguson in 1928, kicking and beating him senseless before other officers arrived to arrest them. (This was the offense for which Abbandando was sent to Elmira Reformatory, ironically sentenced at that time by the very Judge Taylor who was now presiding over his murder trial.) A series of killings were laid at Abbandando's door but he denied having anything to do with them. It was pointed out that he, Maione, and Vito Gurino had shot to death one Felice Esposito on Feb. 9, 1939, simply because Esposito had agreed to testify in a long-ago murder case; he had witnessed the killing of Vincenzo Manzi by a gangster named Anthony Catone in 1922. Abbandando and others were assigned to kill this man because mob bosses reasoned that if Esposito had been willing to testify seventeen years earlier he might talk again.

Prosecutor Burton Turkus described how Abbandando, on Aug. 23, 1939, along with Vito Gurino and Leo Tocci, kidnapped a 17-year-old girl from a Brownsville bar and gang-raped her in a nearby hotel. Turkus outlined how Abbandando and others extorted thousands of dollars each month from the East New York Bakers Association and Local 138 of the Teamster's Union. The recitation of rapes, murders, and extortion went on for hours. To all of this Abbandando shrugged ignorance, saying he could not hear what the prosecution was saying: "I'm not deaf, I just don't hear so good."

But the killer heard the names (and for the first time in any courtroom) of Louis "Lepke" Buchalter and Joe Adonis (Joseph Doto), who were reigning kingpins of the national crime syndicate at the time. Abbandando was particularly upset, outwardly annoyed, when he was linked to the infamous and ruthless killer Albert Anastasia who was Reles' boss. "I never heard of Albert Anastasia!" he shouted, so loud that he could be heard in the hallway beyond the courtroom, perhaps to assure Anastasia's eavesdropping goons that he had no intention of informing on the boss as Reles had done. But Abbandando went even further, playing the indignant citizen by adding, "How—how could you couple my name in the same breath?"

When he finished testifying, Abbandando gave the press section an oafish grin, as if to say that he considered the murder trial a waste of his time. In fact, he had predicted that no jury would find him or his friend Maione guilty of anything, so confident was the killer in the influence of his bosses Anastasia, Buchalter, and Adonis to "fix" the decision. At the beginning of the trial the killer had boasted, "I'm gonna be eatin' spaghetti at home on Sunday."

The jury had another menu in mind, returning a verdict of first-degree murder against Abbandando and Maione for killing Rudnick. Though the court of appeals later overturned this verdict, both men were retried and found guilty, being sentenced to death. When they were finally shipped to Sing Sing to await execution in the electric chair, Abbandando was his smug self, telling reporters, "I'm gonna miss the first night ball game of the season." His attitude did not change right up to the time he walked into the chamber housing the electric chair on Feb. 19, 1942. He was grimly silent as the black hood was lowered over his staring coal-black eyes and jutting jaw.

Abbandando's body was returned to Brooklyn for burial, services being held at the Church of Our Lady of Loretto. Upon emerging from these services, Rocco Abbandando, the mass killer's brother, spotted a news photographer taking photos and charged at him, knocking him down and wrecking his equipment. The scene was in keeping with the kind of violent life led by Frank Abbandando. See: **Adonis, Joseph; Anastasia, Albert; Buchalter, Louis; Maione, Harry; Murder, Inc.; Reles, Abe; Shapiro Brothers.**

REF.: Carpozi, *Bugsy; CBA;* Fried, *The Rise and Fall of the Jewish Gangster in America;* Gosch, *The Last Testament of Lucky Luciano;* Jennings, *We Only Kill Each Other;* Nash, *Bloodletters and Badmen;* Peterson, *The Mob;* Pileggi, *Wiseguy;* Sann, *Kill the Dutchman!;* Turkus, *Murder, Inc.*

Abbas I, 1813-54, Egypt, pasha, assass. Became Pasha of Egypt in 1849 and was murdered by slaves. REF.: *CBA.*

Abbatemarco, Frank (AKA: Frankie Shots), d.1959, U.S., org. crime. Abbatemarco was an elderly policy bank operator in New York, part of the Mafia family run by Joseph Profaci. The numbers operator was compelled, as were all others in his illegal field, to pay "taxes" to his superiors but, owing to losses, he fell in arrears. His boss, Profaci, insisted that $50,000 in "back taxes"—protection money—be paid in the spring of 1959, and when the elderly Abbatemarco failed to pay, he was shot to death by Profaci gunmen.

This occurance was no exception in the day-to-day violence of the syndicate, except that it irked the unpredictable members of the Gallo Gang, which nominally operated under the directives of the Profaci Family, particularly since Tony Abbatemarco, son of the murder victim (who had, incidentally, served in the Third Marine Division on Guam during WWII), belonged to the Gallo gang and was also reportedly marked for murder by the Profaci faction and for no other reason than his father's fatal tardiness in paying mob dues. Joseph "Crazy Joe" Gallo considered the Profaci demands unreasonable, took some Profaci lieutenants hostage, and made his own demands, all of which set off the bloody Gallo-Profaci War in New York. See: **Gallo, Joseph; Gallo-Profaci War; Profaci, Joseph.**

REF.: *CBA;* Cook, *Mafia!;* Demaris, *The Last Mafioso;* Gage, *Mafia, USA;* Martin, *Revolt in the Mafia;* Nash, *Bloodletters and Badmen;* Teresa, *My Life in the Mafia.*

Abberline, Frederick George, 1843-1929, Brit., law enfor. off. Detective-Inspector Abberline, a methodical but conscientious Scotland Yard officer, was in direct charge of the investigation of the Jack the Ripper murders in London in 1888. This officer received much criticism later for his handling of the Ripper atrocities, it being claimed that he was not as aggressive as he should have been and that, possibly, he actually helped to cover up the true identity of the mass murderer. The most concise and unembellished reports about the five (out of a possible seven or even nine) murders attributed to the Ripper were furnished by Abberline, who provided exacting details concerning the discovery and conditions of the bodies, personally interviewing the investigating constables who discovered the much-mutilated corpses.

Though Abberline never wrote a book of memoirs or put his hand to any missives other than his Scotland Yard reports for the Metropolitan Police regarding the Ripper killings, he did advance, in quoted comments, two theories which were later upheld by some of the many theorists on the still-captivating case. At one time, while conferring with constables walking the Whitechapel beats where the murders mostly occurred, Abberline suggested rather casually that the Ripper might be a woman—a mid-wife—particularly in the case of Marie Kelly, the last authentic Ripper victim. She was three months pregnant at the time of her monstrous end at the hands of the maniac and it was thought that she had called in a midwife to examine her. Some speculated that this mad midwife could have left Kelly's miserable lodgings undetected and even with blood-spattered clothes gone without notice since passersby were used to seeing midwives with blood-stained skirts.

The second theory attributed to Abberline came with the arrest of George Chapman (real name Severin Klosowski) in 1903 for poisoning several women to death. The arresting officer was none other than Inspector George Godley who had worked with Abberline in the Ripper investigations fifteen years earlier. At the time of Chapman's arrest, Abberline, then retired, met with Godley and was quoted as telling him, "So you've got Jack the Ripper at last!" Those who have opted to select Chapman as the best candidate for the Ripper seized upon this Abberline quote to support their theory, pointing out to skeptics that Chapman altered his modus operandi. Instead of slitting his victims' throats and disemboweling them as he had done in 1888, Chapman shrewdly changed his murderous ways, later poisoning his victims, to avoid detection. Others emphasize the Abberline quote signifies this officer's further muddling of the case, purposely planting a false suspicion to continue misleading sleuths from the real identity of the Ripper. These theorists insist that Abberline, acting under direct orders from his superior, Superintendent Sir Charles Warren of the Metropolitan Police, covered up the known facts about the real killer or killers. These Ripperologists insist that Abberline, along with other high officials—perhaps even Queen Victoria herself—knew that the heir to the throne, the Duke of Clarence, was the mad fiend lurking through White-chapel to murder pathetic prostitutes.

Much of this speculation is based upon Abberline's handling of what later came to be known as the Cleveland Street Scandal in July 1889, some months after the Ripper killings allegedly ceased. A homosexual brothel was located at 19 Cleveland Street in the Whitechapel area and to this address flocked wealthy patrons and even certain dissolute members of the nobility. It was later claimed that the Duke of Clarence had often visited here to indulge his considerable perversions. When Abberline learned of the type of clientele the establishment entertained, he and other high-ranking officials covered up the operation, keeping the place under observation for months without acting, allowing the owner and his customers to vanish before closing in on a single pimp and a few of the impoverished boys in the area. This theory has it that minimum charges and sentences were meted out to only two minor players in the scandal and important information about the brothel and its patrons vanished. Much of this cannot be supported with documentation at this late date and remains only speculation.

One story had it that Abberline was the unnamed Scotland Yard inspector contacted by the medium Robert James Lees who had seen the Ripper in a vision. Lees then led the inspector to the home of the killer, a resplendent mansion on the East End of London, a home that belonged to none other than Sir William Gull, Queen Victoria's personal physician. This tale remains, as do many of the wilder Ripper theories, in the realm of the fantastic.

It is pointed out by criminal historians that Abberline, either out of guilty conscience or from pressure from nervous superiors fearing that he might reveal his dangerous information if he continued in his post, suddenly resigned and went into early retirement at age forty-six, immediately after police files on the Cleveland Street Scandal were closed. Even more curious is a report Abberline filed during the Ripper investigation which deals with the only eyewitness as to the true identity of Jack the Ripper. The witness, one George Hutchinson, was personally interviewed by Abberline who took his rather lengthy statement and detailed description of the man who picked up Marie (or Mary) Kelly, the last Ripper victim. Hutchinson was never called back by Abberline or any other police officer to identify any of the Ripper suspects, at least it is not known if he ever made such an identification.

Many doubts and speculations concerning the Ripper could have been clarified by Abberline, but he chose to remain silent in quiet retirement for forty years until his death on Dec. 10, 1929, going to his grave without personal comment. This soft-spoken policeman remains today almost as much an enigma as Jack the Ripper himself. See: **Chapman, George; Godley, George; Gull, Sir William; Jack the Ripper; Lees, Robert James; Warren, Sir Charles.**

REF.: Adam, *Trial of George Chapman;* Archer, *Ghost Detectives;* Barnard, *The Harlot Killer;* Baron, *Sickert; CBA;* Cobb, *Critical Years at the Yard;* Cullen, *Autumn of Terror;* Farson, *Jack the Ripper;* Harrison, *Clarence;* Hyde, *The Life of Sir Edward Carson;* Jones, *The Ripper File;* Knight, *Jack the Ripper, The Final Solution;* McCormick, *The Identity of Jack the Ripper;* Matters, *The Mystery of Jack the Ripper;* Rumbelow, *The Complete Jack the Ripper;* Spiering, *Prince Jack;* Stewart, *Jack the Ripper, A New Theory;* Whitelaw, *Corpus Delicti;* Whittington-Egan, *A Casebook on Jack the Ripper;* Williams, *The Life of General Sir Charles Warren.*

Abbershaw (Abershaw), Lewis Jeremiah, 1773-95, Brit., rob. One of the last active highwaymen in England, Abbershaw was born to a middle-class family at Kingston-on-Thames. At seventeen he was an accomplished driver (postilion) of commercial coaches known as post-chaises. He soon realized that most of his passengers carried considerable sums of money and he organized a group of drivers who fed him information on wealthy passengers traveling on routes through Putney Heath and Wimbledon Commons. There he would lay in wait with one or two accomplices, stop the coaches, and rob their passengers at pistol point.

Nicknamed Jerry, Abbershaw proved to be an excellent horseman, though not the equal to his most notorious protégé, Richard Ferguson, later known as Galloping Dick. For five years, this high-spirited and often humorous highwayman robbed coaches and travelers on horseback at will, escaping numerous pursuits. Police were hard pressed to track Abbershaw down since his accomplices were unknown and he lived a frugal, cautious life, refusing to have any long-standing liaison with females, visiting only prostitutes on rare occasions. Abbershaw lived in a rambling inn near Saffron Hill which British police, then known as the Bow Street Runners, vainly searched. The inn was known as the "Old House on West Street" and it was a labyrinth of secret wall panels and hidden trap doors through which its criminal inhabitants could easily escape when officers began pounding on the heavy front door.

Abbershaw prided himself in his gentlemanly manners when conducting his robberies, politely relieving passengers of their purses but never taking a lady's jewels. On one occasion he became ill in the middle of a robbery and had to be led away by one of his men who took him to the Bald Faced Stag Inn and sent for a doctor from nearby Kingston. After the physician had treated him, Abbershaw suggested he send one of his men with the doctor to see him safely home, adding that "it is a very dark and lonesome journey." The doctor snorted his disdain for dangers such as highwaymen and replied, "I thank you but I fear no man on the road, no, not even Jerry Abbershaw himself!" This story so amused Abbershaw that he never tired of telling it to any of his fellow thieves.

During one robbery, a gust of wind blew Abbershaw's mask upward and revealed his face to the youthful driver of the coach. Later Abbershaw and two men visited an inn where the driver was stopping. The young driver, over tankards of ale, told Abbershaw that he admired his nerve and soon became a member of the band. This new recruit was Richard Ferguson who remained as a driver for some time, feeding Abbershaw important information on gold shipments and prospective victims traveling on the line. He would later prove to be one of the greatest horsemen in England and, following Abbershaw's execution, become his country's most infamous highwayman.

The frustrated police who failed to run down Abbershaw and his men, offered generous rewards for the highwayman's head.

An informant, some later claimed a member of Abbershaw's own band, reported that Abbershaw could be found at the Three Brewers Inn in Southwark. Policemen David Price and Bernard Turner arrived at the inn just as Abbershaw was sitting down to dinner. As they approached him, the highwayman jumped to his feet with two pistols in his hands and fired at both men. One ball went through Price's head, killing him instantly while Turner was shot and wounded. Though Abbershaw managed to escape the trap at the inn, he was captured a short time later and went on trial July 30, 1795, at Croydon in Surrey. The prosecution recited Abbershaw's long list of robberies and brought the wounded policeman, Turner, to testify against him. Other witnesses to the shooting of Price came forward and the highwayman was quickly convicted and sentenced to death.

Abbershaw's conduct in court puzzled many for he showed every sign of being bored until hearing the court pronounce him Guilty. Then he exploded and shouted at the judge, "Am I to be murdered because of the testimony of one witness?" The judge immediately placed the black cap upon his head, indicating that he intended to pronounce the death sentence. Abbershaw contemptuously placed his own hat on his head, mimicking the judge. Officers had to handcuff him and tie him around the arms to lead him from the dock as he became violently abusive to both judge and jury.

All through his trial the highwayman showed a cynical disregard for his fate and, at one time, while on his way to court, stuck his head out of the coach as it was passing Kennington Common, the place of public execution, and snorted to his guards, "Don't you believe I will be twisted (hanged) on this pretty spot by Saturday?"

British highwayman Jerry Abbershaw, left on cart, en route to his hanging, 1795.

No females visited Abbershaw while he awaited execution but several of his friends from his coach-driving days did appear to bring him food and drink. One left a basket of black cherries and Abbershaw used the juice from these berries to draw upon the white walls of his cell a series of pictures which formed a graphic history of his crimes, showing him holding up coaches and in one such picture he portrayed himself pointing a pistol at a coach driver and from his mouth the words, shown in a balloon, "Damn your eyes, stop!"

On Aug. 3, 1795, Abbershaw was taken by open cart to the gallows at Kennington Common where thousands came to witness his execution. The highwayman appeared to be enjoying his own notoriety, chatting with many of his friends in the crowd, even as he gingerly scaled the gallows stairs. He wore his shirt open at the chest and once upon the scaffold, kicked off his shoes, casually explaining to spectators that his mother once said that he would "die in his shoes" and he wished to disprove her prophecy of meeting an ignominious end. With that he placed a flower in his mouth and, smiling, nodded for the executioner to perform his gruesome chore. Executed with Abbershaw was John Little, who had murdered two spinsters at Kew to obtain their considerable property.

Following Abbershaw's spectacular hanging, the highwayman's body was taken to Putney Bottom where it was gibbeted. Hours later, Bow Street police became alarmed when seeing thousands of Londoners begin the journey to view the infamous remains of the highwayman amid rumors that his confederates planned to steal the remains and bury the body in a secret place. A large contingent of Bow Street police were sent that night to stand beneath the swinging heels of Jerry Abbershaw to make sure the corpse was not taken away and buried in a place of honor. See: **Ferguson, Richard.**

REF.: *CBA; The Newgate Calendar;* Pringle, *Stand and Deliver;* Scott, *The Concise Encyclopedia of Crime and Criminals;* Smith, *A Complete History of the Lives and Robberies of the Most Notorious Highwaymen, Footpads, Shoplifts & Cheats of Both Sexes.*

Abbott, Austin, 1831-96, U.S., lawyer. Collaborated with his brother Benjamin Abbott to produce legal compendiums (1855-70) and later wrote similar works independently (1873-95). REF.: *CBA.*

Abbott, Benjamin Vaughan, 1830-90, U.S., lawyer-writer. Drafted New York Penal Code in 1860s which is the basis of present law. In 1870 he was appointed as a commissioner to revise U.S. Statutes. REF.: *CBA.*

Burton W. Abbott   **Stephanie Bryan**

Abbott, Burton W., 1928-57, U.S., kid.-mur. Killer of a 14-year-old, Stephanie Bryan, in San Francisco in 1955, Abbott first appeared to police as an unlikely sex murderer. The San Francisco native attended the University of California, majored in accounting, and, at an early age, married an older woman and had a small son to whom he was ostensibly devoted. He dressed neatly and lived comfortably on a large pension from service-related injuries. Abbott had served in the U.S. Army during WWII, never leaving his Kentucky base since he suffered double pneumonia which activated a latent tuberculosis. A lung and five ribs had been removed. Using the G.I. bill following the war, Abbott entered college and became what was later described as a "professional student," stretching courses over many years, indulging in endless intellectual debates with his professors and fellow students, visiting student hangouts, and chatting with young college girls until running off to visit his wife at work. In his off hours, Abbott sought out talented chess players to best in his favorite game. He dabbled in little-known recipes and liked to think of himself as an expert chef, preparing special dishes for his wife. Whenever they could get away, the Abbotts left their Almeda home and drove 300 miles north to the Trinity Mountains where they had a small cabin. Burton often went alone on such journeys, staying at the cabin to hunt and fish and mostly contemplate life, or so he later told police investigators.

All seemed well in the comfortable, middle-class life of Burton Abbott until the night of July 15, 1955. Georgia Abbott was

entertaining guests that evening, Otto and Leona Dezman. Mrs. Abbott worked in Leona Dezman's beauty parlor as a beautician. Talk turned to the play Georgia Abbott was writing and suddenly she decided to check some storage boxes in the basement to see if she had material for costuming the amateur drama. Inside a box in a basement corner Georgia Abbott found a wallet which contained photos of school children, a half-written letter penned to a boy in a teenage scrawl, and the identification card of one Stephanie Bryan. Mrs. Abbott was trembling as she went upstairs to show her discovery to the Dezmans and her husband.

"Isn't this the girl who disappeared?" she asked her husband. Burton Abbott stared at the identification card with a quizzical look and said nothing. Stephanie Bryan had been in the news since she vanished on Apr. 28, 1955, after walking a schoolmate home; the girl was last seen walking past the Hotel Claremont in Berkeley and some hazy reports given later to police described a teenage girl struggling with a handsome young man in a car parked nearby. The police of Country Costa County and Berkeley had been conducting a massive hunt for the girl and had only turned up Stephanie's French textbook in a distant canyon.

After Otto Dezman looked at the wallet, he immediately called police and detectives were soon questioning the Abbotts who could offer no explanations. Burton Abbott seemed so unconcerned that he sat at his chessboard, moving pieces about, as if figuring new moves to create a checkmate was more important than the missing girl. Police left that night only to return first thing the next morning. While they conducted an exhaustive search of the Abbott basement, Burton Abbott sat quietly in an upstairs bedroom working on a crossword puzzle. Officers took shovels to the earthen floor of Abbott's basement and dug up the girl's bra, her glasses, and some of her school books. When confronted with these items, Abbott showed no signs of nervousness, never flinching when telling the police that his garage had been recently used as polling place and any of the dozens of strangers who were then present could have buried these items. Again, even with such incriminating evidence, the police seemed unwilling to arrest Abbott on suspicion. After all, they had no body.

Then there was Abbott's reserved demeanor and an air of innocence that convinced the Berkeley police and the local district attorney that he knew nothing of Stephanie Bryan's fate. He freely took a lie detector test in Berkeley and this was labelled "inconclusive." Abbott stuck by his story—that he could not have been with Stephanie on the day of her disappearance since he was at his cabin in the Trinity Mountains for the opening of the fishing season. He was released.

It did occur to some investigators to search the area around the Abbott cabin in the Trinity Mountains. By the time two men, a newsman and local hunter, Harold Jackson, arrived at the scene, they discovered the cabin burned down. They were told that some drunken lumbermen had torched the cabin after hearing that the Abbotts might be involved with the missing teenager; they were superstitious, investigators were told, since the cabin had played a peripheral part in another murder in 1948, and thought the place best destroyed. Jackson nevertheless unleashed his bloodhounds and, 335 feet above the cabin, on the side of a steep ridge, the dogs found a shallow grave. Inside of it was the badly decomposed corpse of Stephanie Bryan. Since bears and bobcats had been at the body and the weather had done its worst to destroy what was left, coroner's pathologists identified the girl through the clothing she was wearing. The girl's panties had been tied about her throat but her death was not attributed to strangulation but from many severe blows to the head that almost crushed her skull.

Burton Abbott was arrested and charged with killing Stephanie Bryan, held in the Alameda County Jail in Oakland. He went on trial Jan. 19, 1956, before Judge Charles Wade Snook. There was no question of Abbott's sanity; he had allowed psychiatrists to examine him and was pronounced sane. His only defense was his alibi of having been at his mountain retreat when Stephanie Bryan disappeared; that he could not have been in the Trinity Mountains and in Berkeley at the same time. Proving that alibi was something else. Several of Abbott's acquaintances swore he was in a restaurant or tavern in the resort area on the night of Apr. 28, 1955, not in Berkeley. Others contradicted this claim, saying he did not appear until the morning of April 29. District Attorney J. Fred Coakley was aggressive, some said ferocious, in his prosecution of Abbott, tearing at his cabin alibi by presenting not a portrait of a shy, sickly man interested in only intellectual pursuits, but a psychopathic killer who lurked beneath an exterior which he purposely postured as weak and timid. In fact, Abbott, shortly after the trial began, pleaded his illness and requested that he be removed to a hospital for treatment; this was denied.

Newsmen learned that police had dug up a long history of sexual misconduct by Abbott, that he reportedly had preyed upon young girls for a number of years, and that they had received a complaint from a 13-year-old girl some time *after* Stephanie Bryan had disappeared. A Berkeley housewife claimed that Abbott had, three years earlier, followed her home, flirting with her. The woman at the time was thirty-eight and Abbott was twenty. Newsmen and police concluded that this would fit in with Abbott's penchant for older women. Abbott himself responded to this story by blurting an indignant denial, "She is absolutely false. I cannot explain how she could have said such a thing. I'm not in the habit of following women." When asked if he ever followed any woman, Abbott replied, "Yes, my wife!"

Not once did Abbott ever show emotion in court as his attorneys, Harold Hove and Stanley Whitney energetically sought to save him from the gas chamber. He was implacable and unperturbed, even when the prosecution heaped upon him the most damning accusations. Though Abbott was charged with kidnapping and murder, the prosecution had earlier on concluded that he sought no ransom from Stephanie's well-to-do parents. He was, in the mind of Alameda County's assistant district attorney, Folger Emerson, a sexual deviant who had killed the girl lest she inform the world that he had molested her. Said Emerson, "If ever there was a crime that fitted the punishment of death, this is it. Stephanie Bryan's body was too decomposed to tell whether or not she was violated, but the evidence shows that the original intent of the defendant when he kidnapped her was to commit a sex crime. In all probability he raped her."

The defense fought back, logically pointing out that Abbott, sickly, weighing only 130 pounds, would have found it impossible to rape and kill this girl and then carry her 105-pound body 335 feet up the side of steep mountainside to bury her remains. Exactly, countered the prosecution; Abbott was so emotionally charged with his sexual thrill-killing that he did find the energy to do so and it was suggested that he could have led the girl alive to the place of her burial and then killed her, bludgeoning her to death and leaving her for the forest predators.

As the court battle was waged, jury members kept glancing to Abbott, who, for a week, showed not a flicker of anger at his dogged accusers, displayed no shock at the death of the victim, evinced no dismay at his own predicament. This posture was interpreted by many as arrogance, the kind of willful superiority found in many a psychopathic killer in the past and not a bit unlike the intellectual murderer Richard Loeb, killer of Bobby Franks in Chicago in 1924.

Yet, in his cell, Abbott tried to explain to authorities the reason for his ice like behavior. "There is no reason to be immature and jump up and down and yell," he said. "After all, I've spent several years in the hospital and have learned to keep myself under control while looking death in the eye." Character witnesses for Abbott spoke about his gentility, his love for his son, his devotion to his wife. Georgia Abbott explained how Abbott was called Bud, after the popular comedian of Abbott and Costello fame, and that all who knew him thought of him as considerate and peace-loving. "Bud is gentle and kind and good," Georgia Abbott insisted. "No woman could ask any more of a husband and I am not easy to live with." She went on to point out her husband's

astrological virtues, compared to her own aggressive birth sign. "I am Leo born. I am the lion. He is an Aquarius, the gentle one."

To his lawyers visiting him in his cell, Abbott did show emotion, asking them to tell his wife that he had remembered her birthday and that this was the first time in seven years that he had not celebrated the event with her. "Please tell her I am thinking about her," he said tearfully. Also, with tears welling up in his eyes, Abbott said in his cell to his attorneys, "All I want to say is that I didn't do this." To a reporter, also with Abbott in his cell, the accused man said in a quavering voice, "Each night as I lie on my jail cell bunk, I pray that the person who did this thing gets caught."

No one saw Burton Abbott kidnap or kill Stephanie Bryan, this the prosecution admitted. Such direct evidence was not available, but other evidence which would subsequently damn the cool and collected Abbott was supplied by Dr. Paul L. Kirk, from the criminological department of the University of California. Kirk testified that he had collected hairs and fibers from Abbott's Chevrolet, the car in which the state claimed Abbott kidnapped Stephanie Bryan. The criminologist showed how he had compared and matched the fibers from the car to the victim's sweater, and two hairs found in Abbott's car matched the hairs of the victim's head. Human blood was found, though only pinpoints, in Abbott's car also, but Kirk admitted this could not be matched to that of Stephanie's.

Defense attorneys brought forth their own forensic witness, Lowell Bradford, who headed the Santa Clara County crime laboratory. Bradford tried to show how the hairs could have come from other sources, but in the end it was Kirk who was believed. The forensic evidence, the flimsy alibi, the seemingly indifferent attitude on the part of the accused, all of this added up to a jury verdict of Guilty on Jan. 25, 1956.

Abbott did not break down. A short time later, back in his cell, he said to reporters, "I guess the jurors feel they're correct, but they're wrong. That's all there is to it. They are wrong, wrong, wrong."

The death sentence was passed and Abbott was scheduled to die in the gas chamber at San Quentin on Mar. 15, 1957. His family and friends conducted a desperate campaign to find the real killer, still believing in Abbott's innocence. They placed ads in local papers, offering $2,500 in rewards for identification of the real killer. No one responded.

Abbott's lawyers fought hard for stays of execution, petitioning State Supreme Court Justice William O. Douglas and California Attorney General (later governor) Edmund G. Brown, both avowed foes of capital punishment. Both men denied the appeals. Abbott remained stoic, awaiting the end. A few days before he was scheduled to die, the prisoner was visited in his cell by San Quentin's resident psychiatrist, Dr. David Schmidt, who again asked him about the murder. Abbott shook his head and said, "I can't admit it, Doc. Think of what it would do to my mother. She could not take it." This oblique admission of guilt, revealed some time after Abbott's execution, created a political storm which took some years to abate.

The prisoner's last hours were whiled away reading magazines, and the condemned man did not eat a hearty meal, as the saying goes. Abbott made out a fussy, detailed list of items for his last meal, specifying that he wanted "cocktail sauce, not tartar sauce" to adorn one dish and that his salad be made up of "principally romaine lettuce with vinegar and oil dressing."

Abbott showed no nervousness when he was led to the gas chamber on Mar. 15, 1957. He sat down calmly and Warden Harley O. Teets ordered the execution to proceed. The phone in the room outside the gas chamber rang and at the other end was an aide of Governor Goodwin Knight. "Can you stop it?" the aide asked Teets. "No," replied the warden. "Too late. The gas has already been released." At 11:25 a.m., Burton Abbott was pronounced dead. The request for a stay of execution, it was later explained, was only for one hour, but the reason for that hour's stay was never explained.

The condemned man's body, as was his request, was sent to the University of California where the corpse was to be used for medical experiments and the eyes used for cornea transplants. Abbott's small son was deprived of his father's veteran's life insurance of $10,000 because of the execution; Abbott had told everyone that at least he could leave his boy something to cover college expenses through the policy. Georgia Abbott changed her name and her son's name and left the state. It was her conduct, many later pointed out, that put her husband in the gas chamber.

After finding the damning wallet in the basement, why did she blurt out her discovery when she knew its serious implications, that such a find on the premises of her home would certainly involve her husband if not herself? Some criminal historians have suggested that Mrs. Abbott purposely did this to throw suspicion on her husband. Others claimed that she merely did a simple-minded thing, an unconscious act. Still others suggest that Mrs. Abbott's declaration of her discovery in front of houseguests was to embarrass her husband and his proclivity for sexual deviance, unaware that such aberrant behavior had actually led to the girl's murder.

Convicted rapist Caryl Chessman, who befriended Abbott in San Quentin while he himself awaited execution, later claimed that Abbott had admitted that Stephanie Bryan had been killed "by someone very close to him," and that he had taken the body to the mountains to bury it to protect that person. Chessman's deserved reputation for lying, however, lends little credence to this tale.

Perhaps even more puzzling than Mrs. Abbott's oddball behavior on the night of her basement discovery is the fact that Abbott kept the effects of his victim on his premises. Some criminologists later proposed that he intended to distribute her possessions all over Alameda County to confuse police—such as dropping the French textbook in the remote canyon—and that his wife uncovered the belongings before he could distribute the rest of them. Another theory which has some support in the historical behavior of psychopathic killers is that Abbott had committed, like Richard Loeb, an intellectual crime, a perfect murder, which would hold little interest for him unless he jeopardize himself by allowing certain clues to lead toward him, but not surround him, with guilt. Like the game of chess he so admired and played well, the idea was to let the police think he was the killer, and then, with an absence of real proof (the body itself) to establish his heinous act and to secure a conviction, he, Burton Abbott would escape the ultimate checkmate and win the game. Such strange machinations on the part of killers is not unknown. Murderer Richard Loeb thought the police to be his intellectual inferiors and mocked their search for him by actually volunteering to help them in that search, offering clues to the identity of the killer, presenting a psychological profile of the killer to investigators, daring them, as it were, to see beyond the obvious and to have the nerve, his kind of nerve, to accuse him, the real killer, and then prove it. See: **Chessman, Caryl; Leopold, Nathan, and Loeb, Richard.**

REF.: Boucher, *The Quality of Murder; CBA;* Davis, *Assignment San Quentin;* deFord, *Murderers Sane and Mad;* McComas, *The Graveside Companion;* Nash, *Bloodletters and Badmen;* Williams, *Due Process.*

Abbott, Jack Henry (AKA: Jack Eastman), 1944- , U.S., mur. A man who spent most of his adult life in prison, Abbott committed his first murder in 1966 and, after novelist Norman Mailer worked for his release, killed a second time in 1981. At first, this convict, dedicated wholly to violence, was celebrated by New York's literati for penning a prison journal successfully published by Random House. Like many another criminal before him, Abbott, upon his 1981 release, was adopted by such literary lights as Norman Mailer, his sponsor, and Jerzy Kosinski. He was invited to smart cocktail parties where the rich and famous fawned over him. He was heralded as a "great writer" and an "insightful philosopher." But what Jack Henry Abbott really was, always had been, was a man who would kill anyone over the slightest annoy-

ance. This he did, at the height of his brief literary fame, oblivious to his so-called rehabilitation: a cold-blooded, conscious murder that proved how dangerous it really was for amateur criminologists to meddle with crime.

A habitual criminal, Abbott spent all but nine months of his adult life in prison. He was convicted of forgery, bank robbery, and murder. In 1953, at age nine, Abbott proved so incorrigible in foster homes that he was sent to reform school in Utah. Released at age eighteen, Abbott was arrested and convicted of passing bad checks and sent to Utah State Penitentiary where he killed a fellow inmate in 1966. Tried for this murder, Abbott claimed self-defense, that he had been the victim of a violent homosexual attack. When that ploy did not appear to affect the court, Abbott assumed the role of the lunatic, throwing a pitcher of water at the judge and claiming insanity. A court psychiatrist examined him and reported that Abbott was fit to stand trial. He was sentenced to fourteen years.

In 1971, Abbott escaped from Utah State Penitentiary and was at large for six weeks, during which time he robbed a Denver bank and, upon his recapture, became a federal prisoner. While serving time in a maximum security prison, Abbott read voraciously, consuming scores of books on philosophy, enmeshing himself in the credos of Karl Marx and becoming an avowed Marxist. Abbott read a 1977 newspaper story about Norman Mailer writing a book (*The Executioner's Song*) on Gary Gilmore, who was condemned for murder and awaiting execution in Utah State Penitentiary. Mailer, like his New York contemporary, Truman Capote, was suddenly departing mainstream literature to enter the world of criminology.

It was to Mailer, a powerful influence in the media, that Abbott began addressing his letters, which were fifteen-page, hand-written missives to the author. The clever Abbott, obviously realizing that Mailer was a complete novice in perceiving prison life, offered to aid him in that understanding by detailing his own experiences as a long-term, "state-raised" prisoner.

He intrigued the author by spewing forth tales of dark violence, writing in a clinically descriptive style reminiscent of Mailer's own early works, particularly certain passages from *The Naked and the Dead,* which had certainly not gone unnoticed in Abbott's endless rummaging through prison libraries. The prisoner's literary nightmares described fourteen years of solitary confinement: unbelievable cruelty on the part of prison guards who beat him, tortured him with antipsychotic drugs, sadistically gassed him, starved him so that he was forced to eat cockroaches in his cell to survive, and placed him in strip-and-search cells where he had to stand naked, chained by one arm to his bed.

Abbott's relentless correspondence fed on hatred and violence, intriguing an author whose own interest in violence had always been intense. Mailer took Abbott's letters to the editors of the elitist *New York Review of Books,* and, at his urging in June 1980, an article praising Abbott's writing style appeared in that publication, along with a sample of the letters. This article was read with great interest by Errol McDonald, an editor at Random House. Within two months, McDonald had placed Abbott under a book contract which called for a $12,000 advance, and began organizing the killer's book, which was entitled *In the Belly of the Beast.* Almost immediately, Abbott began to energetically lobby for a parole. The Federal Bureau of Prisons made the first step easier by returning Abbott to Utah State Penitentiary to serve out his remaining time there. Once inside the walls of that institution, an automatic parole was considered. Mailer and others were influential, if not decisive, in their pleas that Abbott be released. Mailer wrote to the parole board that Abbott was really "a powerful and important American writer," urging a positive decision and offering the killer a job as his research assistant. McDonald, the Random House editor, also wrote to prison authorities, saying that he believed Abbott "could support himself as a professional writer if he were released from prison and that he could very well have a bright future."

The parole campaign was successful and Abbott was released

on June 5, 1981, transferred from prison to a halfway house in Manhattan's Lower East Side. When the killer's plane arrived in New York, Norman Mailer was on hand to greet him. Almost at the same time, reviews of Abbott's recently released book gushed torrents of praise upon the killer. Wrote Colgate University Professor Terrence Des Pres in the New York *Times* Book Section: "...awesome, brilliant, perversely ingenious; its impact is indelible and, as an articulation of penal nightmare it is completely compelling." New York's literati welcomed the killer with warm embraces, celebrating his published achievement with a number of cocktail parties and smart gatherings at which Abbott was lionized. Great things were predicted for him. He would become a literary giant of the century. His books would be read as credo by anyone needing to know about prison life. Moreover, some even said, Abbott represented the new wave of American literature and was, in fact, its leader. Other than Mailer, many New York literary lions heaped praise on Abbott's work, and these included the brilliant writer Jerzy Kosinski of *Being There* fame. (Kosinski would later regret endorsing the lethal Abbott, being one of the few in the clique of the killer's admirers who later concluded that the Abbott episode was a fraud, likening the literary laurels placed upon Abbott's head to the literati's support of the Black Panthers in the 1960s.)

Abbott worked briefly for Mailer by doing some scanty research, but he spent most of his time drifting aimlessly about the city, a misplaced creature who paradoxically spent time with the elite and powerful of New York one hour, and the next walking about the worst area of the city, the Lower East Side, peopled with prostitutes, pimps, drug pushers, and hardened criminals like himself. Besides Mailer and Kosinski, Abbott found himself in the company of such sterling personalities as author Jean Malaquais, literary agent Scott Meredith, and Robert Silvers, editor of the *New York Review of Books*. He impressed them to no end with his knowledge of Sartre and Camus, existentialists like himself, he said. He knew just what names and quotations would lure these Establishment personalities closer to his web, manipulating them with ease, calling loudly for entrees from their own menus, chewing voraciously upon the fat of their own philosophical beliefs, and thanking them for allowing him, Jack Henry Abbott, convicted killer, to dine at their table.

Surrounded by the protecting arms of New York's literary sachems, Abbott undoubtedly felt that his future was secure. Now he lobbied discreetly for an even loftier position, one which would afford him continuous recognition and financial support, not as a reformed criminal but as a misunderstood literary giant. He expected his new friends to arrange a fellowship for him at the prestigious MacDowell Colony for accomplished artists in picturesque Petersborough, N.H. Here he would preside over the novice writer, the impressionable artist, dictating the thoughts of youthful, adoring followers. None of this, thankfully, was to be.

On the morning of July 18, 1981, Abbott, accompanied by two women, entered a small, all-night eatery, the BiniBon, on Second Avenue and Fifth Street. It was 5 a.m. After Abbott and the women took their seats, 22-year-old Richard Adan, a struggling Cuban-born actor working as a waiter, approached the table to take their order. Adan had recently appeared on public TV in Spain in a series of dramatic roles that had given his career a boost. His newly completed play about the Lower East Side was soon to be produced by an experimental stage group and the youth, known always to be polite and pleasant, was looking eagerly forward to a blossoming career in the theater. Adan had recently married a young choreographer-actress whose father had given him a job as a waiter in his restaurant so the young couple could make ends meet.

Abbott asked Adan where the washroom was located. Adan, according to customers in the restaurant, courteously explained that it was an employee-only washroom and that insurance restrictions prevented customers from using it. Abbott became incensed and began using abusive language. According to witnesses, Adan asked him to go outside with him to try to settle the argument so as not to disturb the other customers. Abbott later claimed that Adan was threatening him, but it was Abbott who did the threatening. Once outside the restaurant, Abbott drew a knife with a medium-length blade and with one powerful thrust, drove the blade into Adan's heart. Another waiter, just at that moment, looked out of one of the restaurant's windows to see the young waiter jumping up and down, gushing blood. Abbott then returned to one of the women with him, college student Susan Roxas, and shouted, "Let's get out of here. I just killed a man!"

With that, Jack Henry Abbott, acclaimed author, vanished. It is revealing to quote Abbott's own work, where he describes how he knifed a fellow prisoner to death fifteen years earlier, a methodical, cold-blooded act that was duplicated with the same precision in his 1981 murder of Richard Adan: "The enemy is smiling and chatting away about something. He thinks you're his fool; he trusts you. You see the spot. It's a target between the second and third button on his shirt. As you calmly talk and smile, you move your left foot to the side to step across his right-side body length. A light pivot toward him with your right shoulder and the world turns upside down; you have sunk the knife to its hilt into the middle of his chest."

For two months Abbott eluded police and federal agents who were searching for him nationwide. Using the considerable advances from his book, Abbott managed to get to Mexico and hole up near the Guatemalan border; but after some weeks, not being able to speak Spanish or find work that would cloak his activities, he moved back to the U.S., to Louisiana. He was spotted in the Latin Quarter of New Orleans several times but whenever officers appeared, he had just departed his lodgings, almost as if he had been informed that authorities were closing in on him. Investigators interviewed the prostitutes of the Quarter and one streetwalker identified Abbott's photo, telling police that the much-wanted killer was looking for work in the Louisiana oil fields. Officers tracked the elusive killer through the oil towns of Algiers, Harvey, and Marrero, searching through the murky bunkhouses where hundreds of nameless itinerant workers lived, but at every turn they missed their man, sometimes only by minutes. Abbott seemed to have a sixth sense about lawmen closing in on him and would, according to fellow workers, suddenly quit whatever he was doing, grab his meager belongings, and depart. In mid-September 1981, New York Police Detective William Majeski, who had arrived at the BoniBon restaurant after the Adan killing to take charge of the investigation and had trailed Abbott with other officers to New Orleans, learned that the fugitive was using a social security card with the alias of Jack Eastman.

Abbott had selected an anonymous world into which he hoped to disappear. The boom town oil fields of Louisiana collected thousands of roughnecks and roustabouts, many with criminal records, men like Abbott, who sought obscurity. Mixing with these tough, taciturn men were illegal aliens from Mexico, refugees from Vietnam, the flotsam and jetsam of the world, as it were, men who worked for $4 an hour, sixteen hours a day, and paid a third of their salary to the company to sleep in filthy bunkhouses and eat from open-air canteens. The rest of their money they would give to the whores who visited these camps in droves.

On Sept. 23, 1981, following a tip from Detective Carl Parsiola of St. Mary's Parish, James Riley, an intelligence agent of the sheriff's department, accompanied by Dan Dossett of the Morgan City Police, and other officers, located Abbott working in the fields of the Ramos Oil Company. He was unloading pipe from trucks that clogged the roads. Overhead helicopters buzzed about on company work and the nearby bayous belched smoke from tugs pulling freight. Where years before there had been wilderness, this area was now cluttered with humanity and the officers were concerned that their man would once again escape. Carefully, Riley, Dossett, and the others moved toward Abbott, pretending to be workers. When they saw him raise his arms to comb his hair, the lawmen rushed forward, eight shotguns leveled at him.

Abbott was ordered to keep his hands in the air as officers moved forward to handcuff him. He said nothing, remaining motionless, offering no resistance. He wore cheap blue jeans and a T-shirt that were coated with oil; his boots were crusted with caked oil and were falling apart. Returned to New York and held at Riker's Island, Abbott was tried before Judge Irving Lang of the Manhattan State Supreme Court. He was defended by criminal attorney Ivan Fisher and prosecuted by James Fogel. Early on, Abbott displayed anxiety and nervousness, a pose unlike his earlier aloof attitudes.

In his own words, Abbott characterized the death of Adan as the result of a "tragic misunderstanding," a literary understatement without parallel. He went on to explain that he acted in self-defense, believing that Adan intended to attack him, the same plea that Abbott had employed when stabbing a fellow prison inmate to death in 1966. To that claim, a spectator in court rose and shouted, "You intended to do it, you scum!" This cry came from Henry Howard, the father-in-law of the dead Adan. Judge Lang ordered Howard removed from court, but he waited outside the courtroom throughout the trial, frustrated by his inability to see justice done.

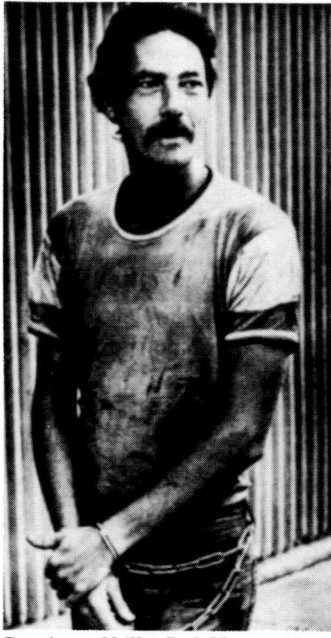

Convict and killer Jack Henry Abbott, chained in Louisiana and en route to his 1981 murder trial.

The prosecution provided several witnesses, but one, Wayne Larsen, a 35-year-old Vietnam veteran, proved damning to Abbott's self-defense tactic. Larsen was standing at the corner of Second Avenue and Fifth Street and watched as Abbott attacked Adan. He testified that Adan was walking away from Abbott when Abbott drew his knife and raised it. He recalled that when Abbott struck Adan there was an impacting sound that "still rings in my ears." Even though Adan was mortally wounded and helpless, Abbott, according to Larsen, acted as if he had merely scratched his victim, cursing Adan and screaming, "Do you still want to continue this?" Adan had made no move toward Abbott and, according to Larsen, was trying to back away from his assailant. Abbott "made a beeline" for the back-pedaling Adan and lunged forward to make sure he killed his man and, in Larsen's words, Abbott's knife blow to Adan's chest was so powerful "that the hair swung back on his (Abbott's) head."

Abbott sat trembling in court, clutching a handkerchief. He wore glasses and his hair was combed in a meticulous pompadour. Immediately following Larsen's testimony, Abbott asked that he be allowed to leave the courtroom. "The testimony was extremely upsetting to him, reliving the event," lawyer Fisher later stated. Abbott's request was granted, although the paradox was evident. Abbott had graphically described his murder of another human being without a gnat-sting of remorse in his best-selling book but he was visibly upset by the retelling of his murder of Adan.

The victim, however, was offered up by Abbott to be not Adan, but Abbott. He again recited the litany of his prison sufferings, the endless abuse that was heaped upon him by an unthinking, inhumane prison system, the very rationale that had brought about his much-influenced parole. Abbott wanted it both ways, first to be released from prison for what the prison system had done to him, then excused from another murder outside of prison and shielded from being returned to that system because of what the prison system had done. If nothing else, Abbott was certainly angling for a minimum sentence, after having been found

guilty of first degree manslaughter.

Prosecutor Fogel was having none of it, calling for a maximum sentence, a life term. "This is a killer," Fogel argued before the bench, "a killer by habit, a killer by inclination, a killer by philosophy, and a killer by desire."

Fisher clung to Abbott's own lifelong defense, stating that his client had been warped by a lifetime of prison. "He was mistreated for so long and so horrible a way. If it was, in fact, the poison of prison that brought about these events, how can it be urged that a lot more is the cure?"

Judge Lang had earlier ruled that Abbott's previous convictions had qualified him as a "persistent violent felon." When he asked the defendant if he had anything to say before sentence was pronounced, Abbott mumbled, "No." Judge Lang then stated that the conviction of Abbott was in part "an indictment of a prison system which brutalized instead of rehabilitating...It's perfectly clear that the defendant could not cope with the reality of a non-prison existence." Judge Lang then sentenced Abbott to fifteen years to life, a minimum sentence. He would be returned to Utah State Penitentiary to serve out his remaining eight years for earlier convictions before serving the New York sentence of fifteen years.

Norman Mailer went before the court and implored leniency, stating, "Culture is worth a little risk. A major sentence would destroy him." Even though Abbott did not receive the maximum sentence, Mailer, following the sentencing, was disgruntled, saying that Judge Lang's sentence was so long as to be "killing." Complained the 59-year-old author, "At the point he gets out, he'll be as old as I am now." Adan's father-in-law, Henry Howard, heard the news of the sentence and was filled with rage. "In twenty-four years," he said, "Jack Abbott will be back on the street and he will kill again. Why are his rights better than Richard Adan's rights?"

This was a question answered obliquely and rather callously by Abbott's attorney, Ivan Fisher, who was quoted as saying, in responding to questions about Adan's family being entitled to the profits from Abbott's book (then estimated to be about $500,000), "If you kill a brain surgeon you're in much more trouble than if you kill a waiter working nights at the BiniBon Restaurant. That's not my judgment, that's the law."

Before being led back to prison, Abbott, through Fisher, announced plans to sue the State of New York for $10 million for "the mental anguish and threats to his life" while he was a prisoner on Riker's Island. Meanwhile, Abbott's book soared to bestseller status, selling more than 40,000 hardbound copies through Random House. At the time, dramatic rights to Abbott's savage tale had been purchased by a film company headed by comic Alan King in the amount of $250,000. See: **Gilmore, Gary; Mailer, Norman.**

REF.: Abbott, *In the Belly of the Beast; CBA;* Mailer, *The Executioner's Song;* Wilson, *Encyclopedia of Modern Murder.*

Abbott, Sir **John Joseph Caldwell,** Can., lawyer-polit. Dean of law at McGill University from 1855-80, mayor of Montreal from 1887-89, and prime minister of Canada from 1891-92. REF.: *CBA.*

Abbott, Robert Sengstacke, 1868-1940, U.S., publisher. Founder of the Chicago *Defender* in 1905, a newspaper covering the black community, and leader of a campaign against lynching. REF.: *CBA.*

Abd al-Aziz, 1830-76, Ottoman Empire, assass. or suic. Sultan of Ottoman Empire from 1861-76. When he failed to put down a revolt in Bosnia and Herzegovina in 1875 he was deposed and subsequently either assassinated or committed suicide. REF.: *CBA.*

Abd Allah (Abd Allah ibn al-Husayn), 1882-1951, Jor., king, assass. Became king when Jordan gained independence in 1946, occupied the West Bank of the Jordan River in 1948, and annexed it in 1950. He was assassinated by a Palestinian nationalist. REF.: *CBA.*

Abdallah, Georges Ibrahim, 1952- , Fr., terr.-mur. Because of repeated terrorist attacks in Paris, terrorist leader Abdallah was tried and convicted under highly unusual circumstances in a 1987 French trial. Abdallah, a 35-year-old Lebanese Christian, had been convicted of complicity on Jan. 18, 1982, in the killing of Lieutenant Colonel Charles R. Ray, U.S. deputy military attaché in Paris; in the unsuccessful 1984 assassination attempt against Robert O. Homme, then U.S. consul general in Strasbourg; and in the murder of Israeli diplomat Yacov Barisimantov in 1982. Publicly claiming responsibility for these and other attacks in both France and Italy was the Lebanese Armed Revolutionary Factions, or FARL; Abdallah was known to police as FARL's leader. When the terrorist was arrested in October 1984, several waves of bombings occurred in Paris, leaving eleven people dead and more than 150 injured, as FARL demanded Abdallah's release.

In a landmark case in February 1987, Abdallah was tried in Paris by a panel of judges, rather than by a jury, under a new antiterrorist law passed in France in December 1986. The law was in response to jurors dropping out of a case against a suspected member of a French urban-guerrilla group, Direct Action (the jurors had received threats that "proletarian justice" would be dealt them if they convicted the guerrilla suspect). Judges traveled to and from court in armor-plated cars under police escort and were guarded around the clock. The regular security police force of twenty-five hundred was reinforced by another one thousand officers from the provinces. Gendarmes were posted at railroad stations, department stores, and other crowded locations. Threats against the judges had been made by Direct Action and by a Liberation of Armenia group that said it would renew bomb attacks unless Abdallah was released. The terrorist was brought into the courthouse through an underground entrance, and a helicopter circled over the courthouse throughout the trial.

Abdallah's lawyer, Jacques Verges, called several previous members of France's Socialist government as witnesses, because they had reneged on a promise to release Abdallah in exchange for Sidney Peyrolles, director of the French Cultural Center in Tripoli, Lebanon, who had been kidnapped in 1985. Verges argued for acquittal, claiming that there was not enough evidence against Abdallah. Georges Kiejman, a French lawyer representing the U.S., asked for a severe sentence that would send a statement to terrorists that France was not a sanctuary for them. Prosecutor Pierre Baechlin, in his closing arguments, pleaded "with a heavy heart" for a light sentence of not more than ten years to avoid making France a hostage to terrorism. After debating for about seventy minutes the seven-member panel of judges sentenced Abdallah to life in prison for complicity in the murders. REF.: *CBA*.

Abdinoor, George (AKA: **The Sheik**), prom. 1934, U.S., (unsolv.) mur. A four-time offender traded information about the murder of George Abdinoor in exchange for reduction of an automatic sentence of life imprisonment. Prior to his sentencing in a Brooklyn court, Harvey Bistany asked for permission to speak to the judge in his chambers, claiming he had knowledge of the murder of Abdinoor. Bistany explained that in January 1934 he was standing on the corner of Atlantic Avenue and Henry Street in Brooklyn when a gangster known as The Turk came by and told him he had just killed Abdinoor. The Turk, a counterfeiter, then asked Bistany to help him carry the body to his car, explaining that the FBI was after him and he wanted to drive the corpse to Abdinoor's hometown of Lawrence, Mass. Bistany, refusing to get involved, remained in the area and later watched The Turk carry the body out of a doorway and dump it into the back seat of his car.

In June, six months later, according to Bistany, he and two other men were invited by The Turk to drive with him to the horse races in New Hampshire. A few miles short of their destination The Turk asked the others to get out and take a bus, saying he and Bistany had some business in Lawrence, and would join them later. He drove on with Bistany to a deserted house on the outskirts of Lawrence. Alone inside for half an hour, The Turk said upon his return: "That's where I buried the goddam rat. I buried him in the cellar there. I went in to see if everything was all right. I'll leave him there a few more months."

After Bistany's confession and an investigation by Lieutenant Flanagan of the homicide squad, Abdinoor's body was exhumed. A positive identification of The Sheik's pen, comb, and nail file was made by his brother, Elias Abdinoor, and an autopsy revealed a .38-caliber, soft-lead revolver bullet in his neck. The Turk was never found.
REF.: *CBA;* Marten, *The Doctor Looks At Murder.*

Abduh, Muhammad, 1849-1905, Egypt, jur. Exiled from Egypt for participating in Urabi Pasha's rebellion in 1882. He later returned and was appointed judge in National Courts of First Instance in 1888 and to the Court of Appeal in 1891. He became mufti of Egypt in 1899. REF.: *CBA.*

Abdullah, Mohammed (Joseph Howk, Jr.), 1939- , U.S., mur. An avaricious reader since early childhood, Howk graduated at the head of his high school class at age fifteen. Though brilliant, he was a much disturbed boy, later claiming racial differences in his family caused him to develop deep mental trauma, his mother being black, his father white. His 140-plus IQ did not balance with the many irrational acts he committed, attempting to hang himself at age nine, trying to burn down his parents' Long Beach, Calif., home at age sixteen.

At that time Howk was taken to the Camarillo State Hospital and was diagnosed schizoid after extensive examinations. Although therapy was recommended, no psychiatric treatments were undertaken. The boy experimented with various religions, finally becoming a Catholic. He dropped this in favor of embracing the Nazi credo at age fifteen. He argued with his teachers over Aryan supremacy until he quit Long Beach City College since the school philosophy was at odds with his own. By seventeen Howk had discarded his ardent Nazi beliefs and dedicated himself to Mohammedanism. He was now a radical follower of Islam and changed his name to Mohammed Abdullah.

When Abdullah entered the University of California at Berkeley in 1958, he advertised his chosen religion, wearing a fez at all times and spouting Islamic credos, practicing Islamic customs. In one of the many coffee shops that catered to the waning beatnik clans, Abdullah met 34-year-old Martin Horowitz, a social dropout, an eccentric drifter who himself had psychiatric problems. Horowitz shared his offbeat philosophies with Abdullah who tagged along after his mentor until meeting statuesque Sonja Lillian Hoff, another student at Berkeley, majoring in home economics with her eye on future social work. The attractive girl was utterly fascinated with minority groups and Abdullah and his strange ways intrigued her.

The couple fell in love but Abdullah's jittery possessiveness soon disturbed the relationship. He could not stand to see the girl even talking to other male students. Abdullah told Sonja about his obsessive love for her and she showed considerable understanding, too much for her own good. After seeing the girl in casual conversation with another male student, Abdullah wrote in his diary (on Apr. 6, 1960), "Tonight I tried to kill myself but Sonja put herself between my knife and my throat." He added, "Next time I suspect her of liking another man, I shall kill her quickly and without warning."

Abdullah did catch the girl with another man but only threatened to murder her. So alarmed was the girl that this time she contacted police and Abdullah was ordered off campus. The girl began dating an Iranian student and Abdullah again threatened to kill her. She left Berkeley but made the error of returning to work a summer job. Abdullah saw her working in a restaurant as a waitress and implored her to come to his apartment for a reconciliation. (He had secretly planned, as noted in his diary, to lure her to the apartment where he would slit her throat and then commit suicide.) The girl told Abdullah never to contact her again.

Going to his one friend, Horowitz, Abdullah obtained a loaded .38-caliber pistol. Horowitz later stated that he loaned the weapon to his friend to "soothe his tensions," but later still, Abdullah claimed he purchased the weapon himself. Armed, the incensed

Abdullah went to the Berkeley library on July 13, 1960, and typed a letter explaining his pain at being rejected and how he intended to murder Sonja Hoff, "I have stolen a pistol to kill my beloved and myself." He then approached the girl as she was studying and asked her to step outside. She agreed, an inexplicable move on her part in that she was once again being confronted by a man who had repeatedly threatened to kill her.

On the steps of the library, Abdullah yanked forth his pistol and, without a word to the girl he loved, shot Sonja Hoff in the head. She died instantly. Abdullah stood over her for some minutes while students and passersby stood riveted in shock. He fired another bullet at the prone girl but it missed. Then he calmly put the gun to his own head and fired a bullet into his skull.

The killer, however, survived even though the bullet remained lodged in his brain. He was blinded in one eye but was well enough by Jan. 3, 1961, to stand trial for murder. Abdullah was quickly found Guilty and was sentenced to die in San Quentin's gas chamber. Horowitz, the willing hand who had provided the murder weapon, was also tried and was convicted of manslaughter. When a ten-year sentence was pronounced, Horowitz went to pieces, sobbing wildly in court.

Mohammed Abdullah was a happy man as he awaited execution, telling his prison guards that he was sure Allah would give him Sonja once they were united in the hereafter. This heavenly reward was, however, denied to the zealot killer when California's Governor Brown commuted the sentence to life imprisonment without parole. The governor's reason was that Abdullah had been insane throughout his life.

REF.: Boucher, *The Quality of Murder; CBA;* Nash, *Bloodletters and Badmen.*

Abel, c.1218-52, Den., king, mur. Became king of Denmark after deposing his brother Erik by murdering him in 1250. After ruling for two years he was killed in an attack on Frisians. REF.: *CBA.*

Abercromby, James, 1776-1858, Brit., jur. The first Baron Dunfermline, he became judge advocate general in 1827, master of the mint in 1834, and speaker of the House of Commons from 1835-39. REF.: *CBA.*

Aberdeen Witches, prom. 1600s, Brit., witchcraft. The *Demonology* of King James, published in 1597, was a treatise that inspired a rash of witchcraft trials in Aberdeen, resulting in the burning of twenty-four men and women. Those accused were said to have been dancing with the devil around the town cross, casting spells on animals, souring milk, causing married men to commit adultery, and handing out love charms made of bent pennies tied in cloth. Janet Wishart, an elderly woman, was indicted for casting a spell on Alexander Thomson, who claimed to have suffered alternately from shivering and sweating. Wishart was accused of causing the death of Andrew Webster, of casting the "evil eye" to cause several other deaths, of raising storms by throwing out live coals, of creating nightmares through the medium of mysterious cats, and of dismembering a corpse on the gallows. She was burned along with another woman at a cost of £11, 10 shillings, which covered the cost of the "peat, tar barrels, and coals," and the executioner's fees.

Several other witches were identified by an accused witch who prolonged her life by turning in others. She claimed to have been at a large gathering in Atholl where she had seen more than two thousand witches, and so was able to reveal what marks each had been given by the devil. Many witches were tried by being forced to swim with their thumbs and large toes bound together; when they were cast into the water in this way, "they floated always above," drowning and thus proving to the people of that time that they were witches.

REF.: Adam, *Witch, Warlock and Magician; CBA;* Linton, *Witch Stories;* Robbins, *The Encyclopedia of Witchcraft.*

Abetz, Otto, 1903-58, Ger., graft-war crimes. An ardent proponent of French culture, Abetz' Francophile interests led him to the position of Nazi high commissioner of occupied France and ambassador to Vichy. As a young man, Abetz was intrigued by French culture. Working in the German youth movement, he studied French literature and language (eventually marrying a French woman, Suzanne de Brouckère), found patrons to support German-French youth congresses, and assisted in the publication of a Franco-German magazine at Stuttgart. Abetz became socially and economically successful, creating an appearance of "deepest sincerity."

As Hitler's power grew, Abetz' background made him a prime candidate for a political position, and in 1934, with expenses paid by the Nazis, he went to Paris to subsidize pro-German writers and ingratiate himself with industrialists and politicians. In 1939, France expelled him as the suspected chief of the Nazi Fifth Column. But in 1940 he returned—this time in uniform—as ambassador of the Third Reich, high commissioner of occupied France, and ambassador to Vichy. In 1943 he lost his position as French ambassador and was captured at the end of the war when he left his hideout in Switzerland.

Abetz was arrested in October 1945 in occupied Germany, and tried in Paris for crimes committed during the German occupation, including complicity in maltreatment of Jews and French military officers and looting of French art treasures. Found guilty at the Palais de Justice in front of a military tribunal in July 1949, Abetz was sentenced to twenty years of hard labor. Released from prison five years later, the one-time top German political agent in France went on to make his living as a freelance economics writer.

Abetz, who began his political career as a pacifist, was described by his friend, the noted French writer Jules Romain: "The problems of the time haunted him to the point of destroying his serenity of mind." On May 6, 1958, Abetz and his wife were killed in a head on collision in Bonn, Germany. He was fifty-five years old. REF.: *CBA.*

Abimelech, Biblical, mur. According to the Bible he murdered sixty-nine of his brothers, leaving only one, Jotham, alive, and appointed himself king of Shechem. REF.: *CBA.*

Abinger, Edward, 1858-1929, Brit., lawyer. Famous for his defense of Steinie Morrison who was tried and convicted in 1911 for the murder of Leon Beron. In his book, *Forty Years At The Bar,* Abinger insisted that Morrison was innocent and claimed he had been convicted on slight evidence. REF.: *CBA.*

Ableiges, Jacques d', prom. 1389, Fr., legal compiler. Compiled collection of laws known as *Grand Coutumier de France* or *Coutumier de Charles VI.* REF.: *CBA.*

Abner, 11th Cent. B.C., Isr., comdr. Army commander in chief during the Reign of Saul. After Saul's death he opposed David and was killed by David's commander, Joab. REF.: *CBA.*

Abokka, 1860s, Nig. Delta, Afr., pir. This self-styled black pirate, calling himself the Superintendent of River Traffic, preyed upon whites newly entering the delta region, kidnapping them and holding them for ransom. One of Abokka's great prizes was Samuel Crowther, the first African bishop sent into the area by the Anglican Church Missionary Society. The pirate exchanged the much-vexed missionary for several thousand bags of beads and cowrie shells. Abokka's transgressions were halted in the late 1860s by British gunboats steaming up the Congo, destroying the jungle hideouts where the pirate and his men lay in ambush.

REF.: *CBA;* Mitchell, *Pirates.*

Abolitionist Riot, 1834, U.S., mob vio. At times, Isaiah Rynders, New York political boss and rabble-rouser, called in the dregs of the Five Points to do his riotous bidding and, in the summer of 1834, a crowd of hoodlums and harlots went berserk in its blind rage against abolitionists, notably Arthur Tappan. The riot actually began in the Bowery Theater where actor Edwin Forrest was appearing in *Metamora.* Forrest was loudly berated for acting in a play that would benefit the manager, an Englishman named Farren.

Forrest attempted to quell the rioters, who busied themselves with tearing out the theater seats and ripping the heavy drapes on the walls. He was hooted into silence, and then the mobsters put on their own strange play, a piece of gabble that supported black slavery. Squads of police were sent to the Bowery Theater and broke inside. Full-scale rioting ensued, but the watchmen managed to drive the thugs into the street. Once outside, the gangs did not disperse, but one of them clanged a large bell, shouting: "On to Arthur Tappan's." Carrying torches, the wave of gangsters moved off in the direction of the abolitionist's home. Somehow, the mob became confused and ended its march on Rose Street (which now squats in the dingy shadows of the Brooklyn Bridge), welling up before the wrong house, the then-elegant home of Lewis Tappan, Arthur's brother.

The more discerning members of the crowd pointed out that they were actually assembled in front of the home of silk merchant Lewis Tappan, while his brother Arthur's home was elsewhere. This bit of street wisdom was ignored by the riot-lusting hoodlums who tore ahead into the beautiful Tappan residence.

Gangsters knocked down the servants and swarmed into all the rooms, breaking the priceless furniture and throwing the splinters into the street where the debris was torched. Screeching, painted whores tore down tapestries and slashed them with long knives. Everything was destroyed—chairs, sofas, mirrors, chandeliers, glassware. One giant thug reached up to a wall and ripped away an exquisite painting. He was just about to put his foot through the canvas when a prostitute recognized the face in the picture and screamed: "It is Washington!" The gangster took the painting to the street. He held it up before one of the fires. The whore ran up and shouted once again: "Damn you, can't you see, it's Washington! For God's sake, *don't burn Washington!*"

The Old Bowery Theater, scene of the Abolitionist Riot of 1834.

The imploring cry somehow struck the patriotic fancy of the cretinous mob, and the refrain was picked up by rasping, screaming dozens: *"For God's sake, don't burn Washington! For God's sake, don't burn Washington!"*

Forming a solemn line, the Five Points mobsters and their vamps passed with gentle caresses the painting of Washington hand-over-hand to a nearby house, and it was placed on a veranda where a score of thugs guarded it. The mob then resumed its total sack of the Tappan residence.

The dull pounding of feet heralded the approach of a squadron of police, and the mobsters turned from their wrecking and looting. Picking up the hundreds of bricks torn from the walls of the Tappan home, the mobsters hurled these in a killing shower at the first ranks of the police, momentarily stopping them. Next, waves of riot-crazed whores advanced, hurling cushions and bedding which had been ignited. These flaming sheets descended into the police files and set the clothes of many on fire. The

determined watch still pressed forward, and the gangsters and their molls were eventually driven from the area after a four-hour fight.

Rynders was not present at this riot, but some reports have it that he secretly gloated over having caused his gang leaders to begin the uproar in the Bowery Theater. There was no secret about his flagrant promotion of the Astor Place riots in 1849. By then, the sinister captain's power was fully entrenched and his strong-arm bullies did as they pleased in the city of New York. Rynders, using the most absurd of excuses, maneuvered his dim-witted legions into riot merely as a gesture of his immense power. City officials never forgot the captain's little exercise, and opposition to his mandates hardly existed for a decade following the riots he inspired. See: **Astor Place Riots**.

REF.: Asbury, *The Gangs of New York;* Barnard, *Forty Years at the Five Points;* Brace, *The Dangerous Classes of New York; CBA;* Headley, *The Great Riots of New York, 1712 to 1873;* Martin, *Secrets of the Great City;* Rees, *The Life of Edwin Forrest;* Werner, *Tammany Hall.*

About the Murder of the Clergyman's Mistress, 1931, novel by Anthony Abbot. This work is based upon the unsolved double murder in the Hall-Mills Case (U.S., 1922). See: **Hall-Mills Case**. REF.: *CBA.*

Abrahams, M., prom. 1890s, Brit., mur. An error of judgment may have cost a rookie policeman the capture of the infamous Jack the Ripper and presaged his own murder years later. Thompson, a young officer on his first night patrol—a beat in London's Chambers Street area—watched as a man suddenly appeared outside Swallow Gardens and, seeing the officer, turned and ran in the opposite direction. Instead of following, Thompson stepped into the gardens and nearly tripped over the mutilated body of Frances Coles, the victim of a Jack the Ripper-type killing. For years this mistake in judgment preyed on Thompson. He feared it to be a foreboding of evil.

Several years later, on another night duty beat, Thompson was patrolling the Commercial Road, the site of a coffee stall frequented by violence. On orders to prevent loitering, he told a young man, Mr. Abrahams, to stop annoying a woman at the stall and move on. An argument ensued. Abrahams moved away and turned around with a knife. Thompson approached, but in seconds fell to the ground, stabbed in the neck.

"Hold him! He has stabbed me!" Thompson cried, clutching Abraham's collar, gripping him so tightly while losing consciousness that it took two officers to pry him loose. Thompson died in the street. Abrahams was carted away with minor bruises. At the trial, Abrahams' defense attorney, C.F. Gill, claimed that his client was injured before the stabbing, and the charge against Abrahams was consequently reduced from first-degree murder to manslaughter. Abrahams died in prison. See: **Jack the Ripper**.

REF.: *CBA;* Thompson, *The Story of Scotland Yard;* Wensley, *Forty Years Of Scotland Yard.*

Abrams, Albert, 1863-1924, U.S., fraud. One of the most spectacular medical quacks of the twentieth century, Abrams became a millionaire claiming that his electrical gadgets could cure any fatal disease, from cancer to syphilis. Contributing mightily to his success was a gullible public that believed anything possible in the infant age of radio and the harnessing of electricity.

On the surface, Dr. Abrams appeared to be an accomplished physician, obtaining his medical degree from the University of Heidelberg in 1882, or claiming to have received his degree there. He also studied at Portland University and, according to his own entry in Who's Who, did research studies in London, Berlin, Vienna, and Paris, the very seats of higher knowledge. By 1893, Abrams was a professor of pathology at the Cooper Medical College in San Francisco and there penned some sensible if not enlightening books which caused no one alarm. In one of these tomes the good doctor wrote: "The physician is allowed to think he knows it all, but the quack, ungoverned by conscience, is permitted to know he knows it all; and with a fertile mental field for humbuggery, truth can never successfully compete with untruth." With these words, Dr. Abrams outlined his own plans to jump feet first into wholesale quackery.

The signs of the doctor's decision to abandon the ethics of his profession were evident some time earlier when he informed students in his course of physical diagnosis that they could attend a far more interesting lecture each evening. This was his own course, devoid of the school's endorsement, for which he charged $200 a head and in which Abrams spewed forth a puzzling new theory of medicine. When school officials learned of the doctor's side practice, he was promptly fired from his position. His answer was to set up his own clinic and quickly write and publish several books, including *Self-Poisoning, Diagnostic-Therapeutics,* and *Spinal Therapeutics,* all in 1909. These and other works described the doctor's amazing new theories which he labelled "Spondylotherapy."

It was all quite simple, really. Dr. Abrams could, by percussing (tapping) the spine or abdomen, determine any kind of disease. He could also, he insisted, by his particular method of tapping, cure those serious diseases. The AMA Journal reviewed Abrams' books and critically scalped them, but the doctor altered the reviews to make them sound praiseworthy and placed them into advertisements for not only his books but to sell-out lectures in San Francisco and in other major cities where he went on tour. To him flocked a horde of other quacks, humbugs, fakes, and doctors whose naivete was as rampant as their curiosity. For years Abrams advanced his oddball diagnostic theories, making substantial sums.

Albert Abrams, quack creator of cure-all medicine.

With the coming of early-day radio, mainly the crystal-set, Abrams capitalized upon the public fascination with electronic waves. "The spirit of the age is radio," wrote Abrams, "and we can use radio in diagnosis." The medium opened up great new financial opportunities to the inventive quack and he quickly produced a startling new invention, a very secret machine which could harness radio waves and produce instant and life-saving diagnoses. He labelled his machine the Dynamizer, into which he would place a piece of filter paper which carried a drop of blood from a patient. The patient, then stripped to the waist, reclined with a wire from the Dynamizer fixed to the patient's head with an electrode. The patient at all times, Dr. Abrams demanded without ever giving an explanation, must be facing *west.* He would then begin percussing (tapping) on the patient's spine or abdomen and quickly diagnose the person's ailment. These miraculous determinations the doctor labelled: "Electronic Reactions of Abrams" or ERA.

To startled audiences packing his lectures, Abrams made an impressive appearance, an imposing figure with a Van Dyke beard (a "torpedo beard" as H.L. Mencken once described it) and a pince-nez from which dangled a long black ribbon. He spoke with great confidence and every articulated phrase rang with authority. Patiently, the doctor explained that every ailment had its own "vibratory rate," which, through careful use of his sensitive machine and subtle tapping, he and only he could interpret and thus define. In this way, Dr. Abrams could diagnose tuberculosis, cancer, syphilis, all manner of serious diseases. At each lecture, which often netted Abrams more than $2,000, the doctor added more and more revelations produced by his Dynamizer and his magical tapping. He could not only determine diseases through his machines and procedures, but could tell the religion practiced by the patient, but only if his subjects were Catholic, Jewish, Protestant, Methodist, Theosophist, or Seventh Day Adventist.

Thousands now flocked to see this miracle man of medicine

and buy his books, as well as buy his hermetically sealed machines and lease the all-important Oscilloclast, a new invention that, when properly applied to the patient, could actually cure anyone of any kind of deadly disease or ailment. By 1920, Abrams was doing a land-office business in selling and leasing his machines to hundreds of radio-wave-using quacks. Thousands of believers flocked to receive his cure from eye-rolling disciples. Abrams then announced an even more startling discovery.

He could now dispense with the use of the dried splotch of blood from a patient. All that was really needed was the patient's autograph. From that signature, Abrams, with the help of his marvelous Dynamizer and amazing Oscilloclast, could diagnose any disease. More importantly, Abrams could now interpret the diseases of the great departed by medically examining their signatures. After some important experimentation, Dr. Abrams announced to the world that he had electronically examined the signatures of Edgar Allan Poe, Dr. Samuel Johnson, Oscar Wilde, Samuel Pepys, and even the great Henry Wadsworth Longfellow and, without an exception, all of these distinguished gentlemen had been suffering from death-dealing syphilis! In Poe's case, he had also suffered severe dipsomania.

Sanity, however, had not abandoned the true medical world. Doubting physicians soon began testing Abrams and his machines. Against his expressed orders, one of his Dynamizers was opened and inside was found nothing more than a jumble of madly scrambled wires attached to rheostats and electrodes that formed no logical pattern or design. Blood samples were sent to Abrams from across the country, along with substantial payments for his priceless diagnoses. One Michigan physician sent a blood sample he said came from a young woman; it was really that of healthy male guinea pig. Abrams shot back a report that the young woman was suffering from "cancer to the amount of six ohms." He added that the poor wretch also had a streptococcic infection of her left fallopian tube and another infection of the left frontal sinus. Abrams was trapped by another doctor who sent a blood sample from a rooster who was diagnosed to have cancer, diabetes, malaria, and venereal diseases.

Yet Abrams had arrived with such impact that he was now considered to be a great diagnostic authority, even though AMA experts were quietly investigating his preposterous claims. In an important paternity case, Abrams and his incredible machines were consulted. He reported that his tappings and vibratory discoveries without question proved that the man was indeed the father of the infant in question. Prominent citizens came forth to sing the praises of this new medical magician, including the widely-read Upton Sinclair, author of such important social works as *The Jungle.*

Sinclair wrote glowingly of Abrams as a man who could bring cures to all the world's diseases, stating in *Book of Life:* "So is opened to our eyes a wonderful vision of a new race, purified and made fit for life...Take my advice, whoever you may be that are suffering, and find out about this new work and help make it known to the world." Nothing daunted Sinclair's almost fanatical belief in Abrams, even after the AMA openly labelled the tapping doctor an utter quack. "He has made the most revolutionary discovery of this or any other age," Sinclair wrote in answer to the AMA. "I venture to stake whatever reputation I ever hope to have that he has discovered the great secret of the diagnosis and cure of all major diseases. He has proved it by diagnosing with taps of his own sensitive fingertips over fifteen thousand people, and my investigation convinces me that he has cured over ninety-five percent."

The AMA brought forth its findings and thoroughly denounced Abrams as a charlatan, but the doctor was by then beyond the reach of exposure. At the age of sixty, Dr. Albert Abrams caught pneumonia and promptly died on Jan. 13, 1924, leaving an estate of more than $2 million. Though the insides of Dr. Abram's phony Dynamizer boxes were opened and showed to be nothing more than a network of crazy-quilt wiring, the unwashed believers remained loyal, thousands of disciples insisting upon the validity of the machines and the tapping procedures, as well as tens of other thousands who claimed to have been cured by ERA. Author Upton Sinclair remained one of these to his dying days.

Sinclair, in later writings, declared that the doctor's final diagnoses had been incorrect because of the proliferation of radio. When he began, Sinclair pointed out, Abrams had the airwaves to himself and his results were pure and absolute. But then came, Sinclair wrote, "complex vibrations of I know not how many radio stations" and these cluttered ERA operations and doomed the Abrams procedures to failure. All these radio stations really killed off the great doctor, said Sinclair, so that "the old man died, literally, of his bewilderment and chagrin."

REF.: *CBA;* Fishbein, *Fads and Quackery in Healing;* ____, *A History of the American Medical Association;* ____, *The Medical Follies;* Gardner, *Fads and Fallacies in the Name of Science;* Mencken, *Prejudices* (Sixth Series); Sinclair, *Book of Life;* Young, *The Medical Messiahs.*

Abrams, Michael (AKA: **Big Mike**), prom. 1890s, U.S., drugs-rob.-mur. Abrams was a giant thug who terrorized New York's Chinatown for a decade. He had operated opium dens on Pell Street and later became a "loggygow" or guide for whites slumming through Chinatown. Big Mike also served as a stall or steerer for a vicious gang of white pickpockets who preyed upon wealthy Chinese merchants. He would accost a rich Chinese businessman on the street, attracting his attention while his confederates picked the pockets of the jostled victim. If any of these hapless merchants complained or cast a suspicion in his direction, Abrams beat the victim to a bloody pulp. On one occasion, he stood over a pickpocket victim who had dared to infer that Abrams was part of the gang that had robbed him. Police arrived to see Big Mike's knuckles skinned and bloody but they arrested the Chinese businessman instead, accepting Abrams' story that the Chinaman had attacked *him.*

Big Mike hired his fists to the highest bidder and often went into Chinatown to attack any merchant who failed to pay off local extortionists. The Chinese had little protection from the police who seldom patrolled Chinatown and so they depended upon local tongs to look after their interests. Abrams ignored the tong leaders and bragged throughout the district how he had killed no less than ten Chinamen. Three of these victims, he boasted, were decapitated by Big Mike who used his clasp knife to slice off their heads. A Hip Sing hatchet man named Sassy Sam became incensed with Abrams' insults and, after downing a bottle of hot rice wine, attacked Big Mike in the middle of Pell Street with a long sword. Abrams took one look at the tong killer and ran down the street, Sam in pursuit, losing much of his fearsome image.

In vengeance, Abrams sought out Hip Sing leader Ling Tchen, dragged him into a Chinatown alley and cut off his head, carrying this blood-dripping trophy through the area to cast fear into the hearts of any Chinaman who dared oppose him. The hierarchy of the Hip Sings met in secret and put into effect a murder scheme to eliminate the white menace. A short time later, Big Mike Abrams was found dead in his room. He had been gassed to death. Knowing Abrams never opened the window to his room (and had, in fact, nailed it shut to prevent intruders from getting to him during his sleep), Hip Sing assassins crept down the upstairs hallway of his boarding house. They fixed a small tube to a gas jet in the hallway and inserted this through the keyhole of Big Mike's room once they knew he was inside sleeping. Then they turned on the gas. The fierce Abrams was found the next day, quite dead, much to the relief of the residents of Chinatown.

REF.: Asbury, *The Gangs of New York; CBA.*

Abrams, Sam, prom. 1920s, U.S., fraud. Abrams took out a large insurance policy before he went swimming at Rockaway, N.Y., in Spring 1928; his clothes were found on the beach some hours later after he had been reported missing by his wife and was presumably washed out to sea. Insurance investigators visited Mrs. Abrams in her Manhattan apartment and became suspicious since she appeared hysterical *before* she had been informed of her husband's probable death. The insurance settlement was withheld pending an investigation which ended some months later in Montreal, Can. Following a collision between two cars in that city, one of the drivers was knocked unconscious and taken to a hospital where authorities found many newspaper clippings concerned with the supposed drowning of Sam Abrams. The accident victim was later identified as Abrams, and he was arrested and later sent to prison for insurance fraud.

REF.: *CBA;* Nash, *Almanac of World Crime;* ____, *Among the Missing.*

Abscam, 1980-82, U.S., graft. In February of 1980, a story of political corruption in the U.S. made headlines nationwide. Before it was over, seven members of Congress would be convicted of accepting bribes and conspiring against the government. John M. Murphy, (D., N.Y.) chairman of the House Merchant Marine and Fisheries Committee, was the first to be indicted in the scandal that would come to be known as Abscam, an acronym for Abdul Enterprises scam. Murphy was alleged to have taken a $50,000 cash bribe from an FBI agent posing as an Arab sheik. At a meeting at the Hilton Inn at Kennedy International Airport in late 1979 Murphy and his associates were videotaped by hidden cameras as they discussed payoffs and made arrangements with the bogus sheik. In exchange for a loan of between $70 and $80 million, Murphy promised the sheik (convicted con man Mel Weinberg) help in gaining political asylum and some 25 percent of the return on a merger between a large shipping firm and the Puerto Rican Maritime Authority, a merger whose regulatory approval Murphy promised to arrange (FBI agents posing as Arab businessmen were told by Representative Michael Myers (D., Pa.) that Myers would "introduce a bill before Congress or intervene with the Department of State"). Other congressmen implicated in the bribe scandal included Senator Harrison A. Williams, Jr. (D., N.J.) and Representatives John W. Jenrette, Jr. (D., S.C.), Richard Kelly (R., Fla.), Michael Myers (D., Pa.), Raymond Lederer (D., Pa.), and Frank Thompson, Jr. (D., N.J.).

When the story first broke, Murphy called it "lies, damn lies." When implicated in the scandal, Jenrette denied any wrongdoing and said he would willingly turn over his records to federal prosecutors. Businessman John Stowe, a vending machine salesman used by the FBI, delivered a $50,000 bribe to Jenrette, but Jenrette claimed to have merely accepted a $10,000 loan from Stowe. A unanimous vote of the House Ethics and Judiciary Committee opposed a resolution demanding that the Justice Department turn over all of its evidence within thirty days.

The FBI front for the undercover investigation involved giving Richard Muffaletto, a New York contractor, the use of $6 million to set up the Olympic Construction Company in July 1978. He established the business, and let FBI agents pose as company employees. Muffaletto also established a credit portfolio that enabled him to obtain bonding needed to win more than $8 million in government contracts, and a secret seventy-five page contract with the FBI allowed him to keep about $100,000 "seed money."

In August 1980 it was discovered that four of the Abscam tape recordings made by undercover agents had been lost or stolen. The first conviction in Abscam, at the end of August 1980, was of Myers on charges of bribery-conspiracy. Chief U.S. District Court Prosecutor Thomas P. Puccio said the verdict justified the FBI's "sting" tactics in public corruption investigations, and thought the use of videotape in such cases would set a trend. Forewoman of the jury, Nancy Biedry, agreed. "If that's what it takes to get to the bottom of it, to really find out, then maybe that's necessary," she said. Critics of the "sting" contended that the tactic constituted legal entrapment.

Myers and Jenrette were convicted, followed by Murphy and Thompson in December 1980. The latter two were found guilty of conspiracy, with Thompson also convicted of bribery for accepting $50,000 from the undercover agents. Murphy had served nine terms in Congress and Thompson thirteen. Myers, Jenrette, and Thompson lost their bids for reelection.

Lederer and Kelly were also convicted of corruption charges.

Williams, who had served in the Senate for twenty-two years, went on trial on March 31, 1981, charged with having used his position to obtain government contracts to benefit a mine in Virginia in which he had concealed interests, and with promising to help one of the bogus sheiks to enter and remain in the U.S.. In return, the sheik was supposed to lend $100 million dollars to the mining enterprise.

Other defendants in the last Abscam trial included Angelo Errichetti, mayor of Camden, N.J., and George Katz, a businessman and Democratic party fund raiser. All defendants denied the charges. Williams was convicted in May of 1981 on nine counts of bribery and conspiracy, and sentenced to a three-year jail term, becoming the first senator in fifty-nine years to be convicted in office. He resigned from his post in March 1982 to avoid being expelled from office, and began serving his sentence in January 1984.

REF.: *CBA*; Tully, *Inside the FBI*.

Absolom, prom. c.1000 B.C., Isr., reb.-mur. The third and favorite son of King David, Absolom, ambitious and covetous of the throne, thought to kill his brothers in order to improve his chances of succession. Handsome and popular, Absolom sought to win the hearts of the people by publically insisting upon social reforms, but secretly he plotted to usurp David. Through his servants, Absolom arranged the murder of his brother Amnon and fled Jerusalem. He returned when David was absent and Ahithophel, courtier and counselor to King David, sought to better his position by secretly advising Absolom to revolt against his father and assume the throne. Joab, the military commander, also sided with the prince, but both supporters were incensed when they were denied command of Absolom's army, which was to attack the forces of David. Ahithophel retired to his native town of Gilon where he hanged himself, and Joab quit the pretender and returned to David, being given an army command. Joab met Absolom's army which was commanded by Amasa and soundly defeated the pretender's forces.

Absolom fled from the battle scene, in the forest of Ephraim, riding a mule. Not looking, he struck a low-level oak branch and his long hair was caught up in the branches, so that he dangled in mid-air, the mule going out from under him. Absolom struggled to free himself to no avail and was recognized by a passerby who pointed out the pretender to Joab who arrived in a chariot. Joab, who had once sworn loyalty to Absolom, solemnly marched up to the pretender and stabbed him three times in the heart. When the news of Absolom's death was brought to David, the king wept and uttered his classic expression of paternal grief: "O, my son Absolom, my son, my son Absolom! Would I had died instead of you, O Absolom, my son, my son!" John Dryden produced a political satire in verse entitled *Absolom and Achitophel* (1681). William Faulkner took the title of his novel, *Absolom, Absolom!* (1936) from the story of Absolom in the Old Testament, as did Howard Spring, in a novel he entitled *My Son, My Son!*, (1938).

REF.: *CBA*; Bible, *II Samuel, 15-18*.

Abu Eain, Ziyad, 1960- , Isr., terr. Suspected of participating in a 1979 Israeli bombing attack, the Palestinian national spent two years in the U.S. after being charged, hoping not to be extradited back to Israel. A suspect in the May 14, 1979, bombing of a crowded Tiberias, Israel, marketplace, an explosion that left two boys dead and thirty-six people wounded, Abu Eain was arrested at his sister's home in Chicago on Aug. 20, 1979, by FBI agents. He then spent two years in the Chicago Metropolitan Correctional Center fighting an Israeli extradition request on the grounds that the charges against him were political and he would not be fairly tried in Israel. During one of his seven appeals hearings, U.S. Atty. Thomas P. Sullivan argued in favor of Abu Eain's extradition, citing a confession by Jamal Yasin, an alleged member of Al-Fatah, the guerrilla army of the Palestinian Liberation Organization. Yasin's confession stated that he had given Abu Eain the bomb, warning him that Israeli authorities were closing in on them. Authorities claimed that the terrorist

then set the bomb off, and flew immediately to Chicago to escape the consequences. Sullivan called the attack "a cowardly act with no notice given."

On Oct. 13, 1981, the U.S. Supreme Court refused to hear Abu Eain's case, and the Arab terrorist was extradited sixty days later, on Dec. 12, 1981. According to the State Department, the U.S. had been "formally assured by the Government of Israel that the crimes charged against Abu Eain—murder, attempted murder, and causing bodily harm with aggravating intent—are common criminal charges which will be tried in an ordinary civilian court." In January 1982 Abu Eain pleaded Not Guilty to setting the bomb. He was tried in Tel Aviv, convicted of murder and attempted murder on June 17, 1982, and sentenced a few hours later to life imprisonment. On Jan. 25, 1984, Arab attorneys for Abu Eain accused Israel of jeopardizing the Palestinian Liberation Organization's future prisoner exchanges with their country by not releasing all those listed in a negotiation agreement that was supposed to have included Abu Eain. Israel insisted Abu Eain's name was not on the list presented by the International Red Cross. REF.: *CBA*.

Abu Hanifah (al-Numan ibn Thabit), 699-767, Iraq, jur. Founded the Hanafite school of Muslim law. REF.: *CBA*.

Abu Khaled, Nasser Mohammed Ali, 1950- , Kuw., skyjack. On June 6, 1977, in Beirut, 27-year-old Abu Khaled was carried aboard a Lebanon Middle East Airways' Boeing 707 airliner bound for Baghdad, Iraq. Because he was an invalid, he was not given the routine security search. On board the flight were 105 other passengers and a crew of ten. As the flight neared its end Abu Khaled wheeled himself along the aisle and held up the pilot with a small pistol and a hand grenade, demanding to be flown to Kuwait. According to passenger Kamel Dawi, Abu Khaled had told him, "I am a sick man and I am forced to do this. I need the money." When the plane landed in Kuwait, the hijacker demanded a $5 million ransom. Joining airport officials in the negotiations were the ambassadors of Lebanon and Iraq. Security forces began making plans to capture the man, under the direction of Kuwait's interior and defense minister Sheik Saad el-Abudlla el Sabah.

After almost eight hours of negotiations the Kuwait Information Ministry announced that Abu Khaled had agreed to surrender, on the promise of safe conduct out of the country. Commandos, disguised as mechanics, then boarded the plane and, with the help of two airline stewards, seized Abu Khaled. He fired a shot from his pistol but no one was hurt. Abu Khaled was brought down the plane's ramp with his hands tied behind his back. Tried and sentenced to prison, he was later released by the Kuwaiti government on the orders of Nasser Mohammed Ali Abu Khalid, on humanitarian grounds, because of his ill health on Aug. 28, 1977. REF.: *CBA*.

Accardi, Settimo (AKA: Big Sam), 1902- , U.S., org. crime. Once a big-time Mafia enforcer, narcotics distributor, and smuggler who knew every major racketeer in the U.S., Accardi was extradited from his native Italy to America carrying his personal possessions in a brown paper bag. Accardi, known to be one of the major importers of heroin into the U.S., controlled the rackets in northern New Jersey for years, and was a leader of organized crime in the New York area as well. During WWI he was in the business of gas-stamp black-marketeering. As an enforcer, he kept other gangsters in line, punishing those who strayed outside the Mafia's strict control. Though never indicted for murder, he was a suspect in several gangland slayings.

Several times arrested on charges of atrocious assault and battery, Accardi pleaded guilty in June 1951 when he and sixteen others were accused of running a 600-gallon-a-day still in midtown Manhattan. He was serving a sentence of one year and one day in a federal prison when the Internal Revenue Service filed jeopardy tax assessments of $159,363 against him. On July 10, 1953, Federal Judge Richard Hartshorne revoked Accardi's U.S. citizenship on the grounds that the 53-year-old gang leader had committed fraud by withholding information about four of his previous arrests and convictions. Accardi had admitted to two arrests at the naturalization hearing, and at the revocation hearing said he could not have been expected to tell immigration authorities about all of his undisclosed criminal record because it would have been a violation of his Fifth Amendment rights to do so.

Arrested again in 1955 in Newark, N.J., for violations of federal narcotics laws, Accardi jumped his $92,500 bond on Sept. 28, 1955, and fled to Italy, smuggling narcotics from there into the U.S. and Canada, and living for a while in Toronto, directing heroin traffic into the U.S.. Five years later the U.S. government located the racketeer, but it took another three years to bring him back. He was traced to Turin, where he was posing as a fruit merchant. A presidential warrant for his arrest was issued in 1960. In April, 1963, he was arrested in Italy. On Nov. 12, 1963, Accardi was flown back to New York City to answer the federal narcotics charges. Accardi's bail of $500,000 was a record for federal court. The once powerful and feared Mafia leader was arraigned on narcotic conspiracy and bail jumping charges and tried and convicted. On Aug. 25, 1964 Judge John M. Cannella sentenced him to a fifteen-year federal prison term and a $16,000 fine. REF.: *CBA*.

Accardo, Anthony Joseph (AKA: Batters; Big Tuna; Joe Batters; Joe Batty), 1906- , U.S., org. crime. Accardo, a product of the Capone era, rose through the ranks as have all leaders of the U.S. Mafia-syndicate, beginning as a ruthless gunman and enforcer for Scarface as early as 1922 at the age of sixteen. He is presently chairman of the board of the Chicago Mafia-syndicate, although he is in semi-retirement in Palm Springs, Calif. Son of a Sicilian shoemaker, Accardo was born in Chicago on Mar. 28, 1906. At the age of fifteen he received his first police citation, a traffic violation. The following year he was a runner and errand boy for the Torrio-Capone gang, working alongside another young ambitious gangster named Felice De Lucia, who was later known as Paul "The Waiter" Ricca. Both Accardo and Ricca would, at the death of Frank "The Enforcer" Nitti in 1943, run the Chicago mob together with Ricca as the undisputed boss of bosses.

During the mid-1920s, Accardo earned his fierce sobriquet, Joe Batters, because of his ability to wield a baseball bat on those who displeased his bosses, mostly loan-shark victims who failed to make their weekly payments, and truculent bar owners who did not sell enough of the Torrio-Capone brew during Prohibition. He was also known to use a pistol and machine gun with expert effect. Accardo was regularly arrested during the 1920s for serious offenses and, throughout his career in organized crime, he ran up a string of twenty-seven arrests for carrying concealed weapons, gambling, extortion, kidnapping, and murder. Witnesses to the various mob murders committed by Accardo, according to police reports, disappeared before the gunman could be prosecuted. By the late 1920s, Accardo had been loaned out to Claude Maddox, who ran the Circus Gang of bootleggers and labor terrorists, a satellite of the Capone gang.

Accardo had become so well known in underworld circles as a loyal and fearless gunman that Capone selected him as one of his personal bodyguards, and he worked under the direction of Frank Nitti and, sometimes, Machine Gun Jack McGurn. It was Accardo's job, as a front-line bodyguard, to stop anyone from invading Capone's headquarters, the Lexington Hotel. Throughout 1928, Accardo was observed by detectives as he sat in the lobby of this hotel with a machine gun in his lap. No policeman thought to walk up to the gangster and arrest him for displaying such lethal rapid-fire weapons but Capone, at the time, owned most of Chicago's judges and police.

When Capone decided to eliminate the gang led by George "Bugs" Moran on Chicago's north side in 1929, he employed Claude Maddox and Accardo to help set up the St. Valentine's Day Massacre. The car used by the killers, later disguised as a CPD detective squad car, was rented by a man who gave his name as James Morton and police later speculated that this man had been Accardo. The car was kept in a garage rented by another man who gave an address which was later proved to be owned by Maddox. Though some reports claim that Accardo was one of the machine gun killers at the Massacre, the evidence proves otherwise, although he undoubtedly helped McGurn to plan the killing of Moran's seven men.

As Capone began to settle old scores at the close of the 1920s, he used Accardo more and more as his special enforcer. He was listed as a prime suspect in the murders of Joseph Aiello (helping Scarface who personally killed Aiello), Jack Zuta, and Michael "Mike de Pike" Heitler. In 1931, the Chicago Crime Commission named Accardo as one of the top twenty-eight public enemies in that city. When Capone went to prison for income tax evasion, his empire in Chicago was run by his lieutenants: Nitti, Guzik, and the Fischetti brothers. Beneath these mob leaders, the second level of enforcers, including Accardo, Ricca, and a young psychopathic killer named Sam "Momo" Giancana, solidified their own positions by overseeing Capone's many rackets. Accardo concentrated on gambling, supervising Capone-established clubs, but adding more gaming operations which remained in his exclusive, rapidly expanding domain, mostly in Chicago's twenty-eighth ward.

Utilizing Capone's ideas of investing illegal money into legitimate enterprises, Accardo, who had amassed a sizable amount of money from his gambling enterprises, put capital into many honest businesses. He invested in trucking firms, hotels, coal and lumber companies, restaurants, travel agencies, and currency exchanges. As the old guard of the Capone Gang died or went into retirement, the fortunes of Accardo improved, along with that of his friend Ricca. When Frank Nitti committed suicide in 1943 rather than face a long prison term for tax evasion, Ricca, though in federal prison at the time, assumed leadership of the Chicago Mafia-syndicate. Accardo never shared power with Ricca, as some reports have it. Ricca was always senior in authority to Accardo until the time of Ricca's death in 1972, and Accardo always deferred to "The Waiter" on all important decisions.

When Paul Ricca was finishing a prison term for tax evasion, Accardo made several trips to Leavenworth to get his marching orders from the boss. On one occasion, in 1945, as revealed by U.S. Senator Estes Kefauver, Accardo accompanied Ricca's tax lawyer, Eugene Bernstein, on a trip to the federal penitentiary. Accardo, using Bernstein as a cover, signed the prison visitor register as Joseph Bulger, a Chicago attorney and one-time president of the Italo-American National Union (Unione Siciliane). In this disguise, Accardo met with Ricca to take orders on mob operations, as well as to make arrangements in paying off the tax debts of Ricca and Louis "Little New York" Campagna, another aging Capone lieutenant, in order to facilitate the release of these two gangsters.

Following Ricca's release, Accardo was rewarded for his loyalty and obedience by being given the Chicago gambling operations, which included all gambling in northern Indiana. In addition to controlling dozens of gambling dens and parlors, Accardo operated a few luxurious dens outright in the 1950s such as a sprawling den on north Clark Street, which Accardo owned with Mel Clark. The den was a full-fledged wire service operation with direct wires to all the nation's racetracks giving instant results. Accardo soon ordered Clark to depart for greener pastures which he did without argument, being replaced by Bernard Korshak, brother of underworld attorney Sidney Korshak. This operation alone, according to one estimate, netted Accardo about $25,000 each day or $7.5 million a year.

By 1950, Accardo was virtual master of all gambling in Chicago, except for the enormous policy racket controlled by Big Jim Martin, who operated in tandem with George D. Kells, alderman of the Twenty-eighth Ward. These men had for years operated a sprawling gambling operation, paying a percentage of the take to the syndicate. Ricca suddenly decided that the mob should have all the profits and ordered Kells and Martin to go to work for the syndicate as paid employees. Both men balked at the idea and Accardo, the then-top enforcer of the mob, was ordered by Ricca to get rid of the pair. Accardo, in turn, called in John "Jackie the Lackie" Cerone, one of his most trusted hitmen.

Cerone, on Nov. 15, 1950, went after Big Jim Martin with a

shotgun, wounding him. The gunman later complained that the ammunition he had been forced to use in his haste was "old stuff" or he would have certainly accomplished his assignment and killed Martin. The shooting was nevertheless effective. Martin immediately sold everything he had in Chicago and relocated in Los Angeles. Alderman Kells did not wait for a visit from madman Cerone. He packed his wife and belongings and drove off to Florida, telling local newsmen that he had to seek warmer climes because his wife was ill. Accardo's domain was now unbroken to the city limits in all directions from the lake. His minions controlled more than 10,000 gambling outlets, chiefly for policy, in newstands, bars, and cigar stores, adding many more millions to the syndicate coffers each year.

The power Accardo wielded in the early 1950s was certainly equal to that of Capone in the Roaring Twenties. Chicago's fearless Judge John H. Lyle, one of the few magistrates the mob never bought, recalled the deep influence Accardo exercised in Chicago's city government, "Reading a newspaper story in 1951, I felt tempted to glance at the dateline to make sure the calendar had not been turned back to the Prohibition days. Accardo had been picked up for questioning. A lower court judge made a night trip to police headquarters and ordered the gang leader freed after permitting him to sign his own bond...In court the next day, the judge discharged him. Despite criticism by the Chicago Crime Commission and the Chicago Bar Association, the Democratic organization reslated the judge and as 1960 began he was still on the bench."

As Accardo grew richer, his tastes and ambitions expanded. He no longer wished to live in a confining hotel suite or apartment. He longed for the respectability of the suburbs. One of his old associates, the brainy Murray "The Camel" Humphreys, a devout apartment dweller, told Accardo that "smart money doesn't go to the suburbs. You and your family will stick out like a sore thumb and the feds will always know exactly where you are. Bad idea, Tony." But Accardo wanted what every other successful American achieved, a spacious home in a crime-free suburb with verdant lawns and tall trees. He insisted upon it, and what Accardo insisted upon, he got. The gang boss began shopping about but his inquiries through operatives met with rebuffs from certain real estate agencies when they learned that the notorious Accardo was the real client. Finally, Accardo managed to buy a sprawling estate in River Forest which he purchased for $150,000 cash and loaded the place with the most expensive furniture and decorations available.

One of Accardo's most treasured possessions was a $10,000 black onyx bathtub in which he could luxuriate as he organized his daily syndicate operations, a stogie in one hand and a pen and pencil in the other, as he scribbled his ciphered orders on a little writing board overhanging the tub. The crime boss added a twenty-room Miami, Fla., mansion to his possessions in 1960, a spread estimated—at that time—to be worth more than $300,000. Again, the mob boss spent lavishly on furniture and decorations and, again, his bathrooms were splendors to behold. One visitor to the Miami mansion later expressed surprise to see the sink in one bathroom held up by four legs of solid gold. (The River Forest home was sold in 1978 for about $480,000, indicating that Accardo was also a shrewd real estate investor, having made more than $300,000 on his original purchase. At that time, new pressure from the FBI was added; in one raid on Accardo's River Forest home, agents discovered $275,000 in cash. Such embarrassing discoveries caused the crime boss to leave the suburb and take up almost permanent residence in his Palm Springs estate.)

The millions rolled in and the Chicago syndicate had no peers, supported completely by the reigning politicians, particularly the clout-conscious members of the Kelly-Nash political machine. Chicago was a wide-open town for gambling and prostitution, this being an age when drug use was at a minimum and usually confined to the black ghettos, considered even by the syndicate as a "dirty habit." Ricca went into semiretirement in the mid-1950s, although Accardo continued to confer with him on all

important matters. Then Accardo fell afoul of the same people who had imprisoned his mentor, Al Capone. IRS agents began to probe deeply into his fabulous income and he was indicted for tax evasion. In 1960 he was convicted and sentenced to six years in prison and fined $15,000. But the conviction was later overturned by the U.S. Circuit Court of Appeals sitting in Chicago because of so-called "prejudicial" newspaper publicity that had occurred during Accardo's trial. He was a free man and could go on to boast, as he does to this day, that he never spent a night in jail, even though Accardo had been cited for contempt in the Kefauver Hearings in 1950-51 and had taken the Fifth Amendment 172 times before the McClellan Committee.

Accardo's most serious internecine problems evolved out of his tax evasion charges. He began to glean too much publicity for the syndicate at the time, which made Ricca nervous. The Waiter decided that Tony Accardo should step, not down but out, of the limelight in 1956, decreeing that a better day-to-day boss of the syndicate would be Sam "Momo" Giancana, a loud-mouthed, tough gunman who ruthlessly killed his way to prominence and who had for some years been Ricca's secret, personal enforcer, eliminating those Ricca chose to kill without conferring with Accardo. It remains unclear exactly how Giancana took over control of the syndicate from Accardo during this confusing period of time, as confusing for the mob as it was for the federal agents who doggedly kept surveillance on Accardo's River Forest home. One story has it that Ricca called Accardo and shocked his longtime sub-boss, stating he should step aside for Giancana until the tax evasion charges were settled. Accardo told Ricca no; he had no intentions of giving up his power. The next night, some time in 1956, Giancana, with Ricca's knowledge and approval, appeared at Accardo's home and fired six bullets from his .45-caliber pistol through the door, then calmly walked to his car and drove away, clearly a message that the next time, the bullets would be inside of Accardo, instead of his front door.

Giancana took over and Accardo stepped aside, concentrating on his tax problems. But Momo Giancana proved to be a serious error in judgment for Paul "The Waiter" Ricca. Giancana was a flashy braggart who loved to be seen in public with celebrities such as Phyllis McGuire of the singing McGuire Sisters. He snarled threats and brags to newsmen and loved to read about himself as the kingpin of Chicago crime. Momo was the archetypal gangster in the shiny sharkskin suit, dark sunglasses and snap-brim hat (although Momo had the persistent bad taste to wear white socks). Tony Accardo must have secretly relished Ricca's mistake in picking Giancana as the front man as he whiled away his time, awaiting appeals to his tax conviction by traveling about the country, buying up real estate in California, Arizona, Florida, Nevada, and South America. On one occasion, while fishing in the Florida Keys, Accardo returned in his chartered boat with a huge marlin, next to which he proudly posed at dockside. Chicago newsman Ray Brennan, who had been sent to the Keys to do a story on the idling Accardo, took a photo of Accardo and the marlin and promptly dubbed the exiled crime boss "Big Tuna" Accardo. The name clung to Accardo as it does to this day, absurd as it was, and certainly less apt than Joe Batters. Neither sobriquet has ever been uttered to Accardo's face, even in jest.

Giancana, as the shrewd Ricca had planned, served Accardo well. Federal authorities began to pay more attention to him than Accardo, which was Ricca's scheme from the start. Accardo continued to make all the top-level decisions while Giancana took the heat. When Accardo's tax conviction was overturned in 1960, he went on playing "dead" as the top don of Chicago but systematically continued to pull the strings, especially after Ricca retired in 1968; Ricca would die of natural causes in 1972, leaving Accardo in complete control, although Giancana was the line boss of all Chicago operations. Federal agents began, by the early 1970s, to follow Giancana everywhere. They parked night and day outside of his home and followed the crime boss wherever he went by car, plane, or rail, just down the block or across the country. They photographed him incessantly and bugged restaurants where

1976: Chicago crime boss (1) Tony Accardo, celebrating with his top lieutenants: (2) Joseph Amato, (3) Joseph "Little Caesar" DiVarco, now dead, (4) James Torello, now dead, (5) Joseph Lombardo, in prison, (6) "Jackie the Lackey" Cerone, in prison, (7) Alfred Pilotto, in prison, (8) Vincent Solano, (9) Dominic Di Bella, now dead, (10) Joseph Aiuppa, in prison.

"Joe Batters" Accardo, Capone enforcer, 1927.

Accardo in the late 1940s, underboss to Paul "The Waiter" Ricca

Accardo in 1965 when he was supreme gang boss in Chicago.

Sam Giancana, who briefly deposed Accardo, murdered in 1975.

he met with other gangsters such as Milwaukee Phil Alderisio, one of his top enforcers.

The constant surveillance drove the normally hotheaded Giancana into frenzied tirades. To escape his dogged pursuers, Giancana began to travel to both coasts, then to Mexico. He could not, however, escape. Finally, after another trip to Mexico, Giancana returned to Chicago, weary of the constant federal pressure. He acted as if he were still in charge of the syndicate but his power had waned and most of his most trusted aides had been systematically eliminated by Accardo allies. Giancana was a liability to the mob and was murdered in his own home on June 19, 1975, while he was frying sausages for a late-night snack. His killer was never found.

Accardo resumed control of the Chicago syndicate with Joey Aiuppa, his strong second-in-command. Other "young turk" mobsters moved up through the ranks during the late 1970s and into the 1980s. There were many aspirants to mob leadership, including the ambitious Tony Spilotro, who was suspected of having killed Giancana to qualify for boss status, but Accardo picked his successor carefully. By 1989, Big Tuna Accardo had permanently retired to his estate in Palm Springs, Calif., leaving in charge Sam Anthony Scarlisi, a wily, low-profile mobster, who is in charge of all daily syndicate operations. Gus Alex, a longtime Accardo associate, also in semiretirement at age seventy-three, acts as Scarlisi's senior adviser. Aiuppa and Cerone, in prison at this writing, both exercise from their cells considerable influence over operations in the western suburbs of Chicago. Yet, Accardo, at age eighty-three, is still consulted long distance on all urgent mob matters, for he remains chairman of the board. His word is still law in the Chicago underworld which works with but has never been controlled by the national syndicate headed by the five traditional Mafia families in New York. See: **Aiello, Joseph; Aiuppa, Joseph John; Alderisio, Felix Anthony; Alex, Gus; Capone, Alphonse; Cerone, John Phillip, Sr.; Circus Gang; Giancana, Sam; Heitler, Michael; Humphreys, Murray; Lyle, John H.; McGurn, Jack; Maddox, Claude; Moran, George; Nitti, Frank; Ricca, Paul; St. Valentine's Day Massacre; Scarlisi, Sam Anthony; Spilotro, Anthony; Zuta, Jack.**

REF.: Alsop, *The Bootleggers;* Asbury, *Gem of the Prairie; CBA;* Cohen, *In My Own Words;* Cook, *The FBI Nobody Knows;* ____, *Mafia!;* Demaris, *Captive City;* ____, *The Last Mafioso;* Eisenberg, *Meyer Lansky;* Fortenay, *Estes Kefauver;* Freemantle, *The Fix, Inside the World Drug Trade;* Fried, *The Rise and Fall of the Jewish Gangster in America;* Friendly and Goldfarb, *Crime and Publicity;* Giancana, *Mafia Princess;* Gosch, *The Last Testament of Lucky Luciano;* Halper, *The Chicago Crime Book;* Katz, *Uncle Frank, The Biography of Frank Costello;* Kefauver, *Crime in America;* Kilian, *Who Runs Chicago?;* Kirby and Renner, *Mafia Enforcer;* Kobler, *Capone;* Lait and Mortimer, *Chicago Confidential;* Lyle, *The Dry and Lawless Years;* McClellan, *Crime without Punishment;* Maclean, *Pictorial History of the Mafia;* McPhaul, *Johnny Torrio;* Maas, *The Valachi Papers;* Martin, *Revolt in the Mafia;* Messick, *Secret File;* Morgan, *Prince of Crime;* Nash, *Bloodletters and Badmen;* ____, *Citizen Hoover;* ____, *People to See;* Overstreet, *The FBI in Our Open Society;* Pasley, *Al Capone;* Peterson, *Barbarians in Our Midst;* ____, *The Mob;* Reid, *The Grim Reapers, The Anatomy of Organized Crime in America;* Royko, *Boss;* Smith, *Syndicate City, The Chicago Crime Cartel;* Teresa, *My Life in the Mafia;* Tyler, *Organized Crime in America;* Ungar, *FBI;* Wendt and Kogan, *Lords of the Levee;* Wicker, *Investigating the FBI.*

Accetturo, Anthony, 1938- , U.S., org. crime. From his home in Hollywood, Fla., Anthony Accetturo directs the activities of the remaining members of the Thomas Lucchese crime family still active in New Jersey. In 1970, Accetturo was forced to flee his home in Livingston, N.J., when a federal grand jury began investigating his involvement in Newark gambling operations. In February 1973, he was named in a five-count indictment that charged six top-ranking Mafiosi from the New York area with loan sharking and extortion. Accetturo was arrested in Miami, and bail was set at $100,000.

The reputed "boss" of the Lucchese interests got into trouble with the government in 1976, when he was ordered to appear before a grand jury in New Jersey. His attorneys fended off extradition attempts after citing their client's poor health. After nine years of eluding the feds, Anthony Accetturo was ordered jailed on Oct. 18, 1985, by Judge Harold Ackerman of the District Court in Manhattan, on the grounds that he posed a threat to government witnesses and the public at large. Accetturo and three of his associates were accused of exercising physical intimidation to promote the interests of their Mafia-fronted business, Taccetta Group Enterprises. The twelve-count indictment listed Accetturo, his underboss Michael Taccetta, and top enforcers Michael Perna and Thomas Riccardi as the principles in a credit-card and wire-fraud scheme. A request for a stay of sentence was immediately filed by their attorneys. At present Tony Accetturo still resides in Florida awaiting a further outcome of his lengthy legal battles with the government. See: **Lucchese, Thomas.** REF.: *CBA.*

Accolti, Benedetto, 1415-66, Italy, jur. Chancellor of the Florentine Republic in 1459. REF.: *CBA.*

Accoramboni, Vittoria, c.1557-85, Ital., (unsolv.) mur. Italian noblewoman whose first husband was murdered in 1581 so that she could marry the powerful Orsini, Duca di Bracciano. When her second husband died Orsini's relatives conspired to murder the hapless Vittoria Accoramboni in 1585.

REF.: *CBA;* (DRAMA) Webster, *The White Devil or Vittoria Corombona.*

Accorso, Francesco (Accorso, Franciscus), c.1185-c.1260, Italy, jur. Father of jurist of same name. REF.: *CBA.*

Accorso, Francesco (Accorso, Franciscus), 1225-93, Italy, jur. Son of jurist of same name. REF.: *CBA.*

Acevedo, Louis, 1956- , U.S., mur. Acevedo and Shelley Sperling had been a couple throughout their teen-age years. But when the 18-year-old honor roll student went away to Marist College in Poughkeepsie, N.Y., her life began to change and she decided to end the relationship. Acevedo, however, would not accept the rejection. In September 1974 she agreed to meet him at a waterworks next to the campus, expecting a final talk. Instead, Acevedo struck her with a brick, fracturing her skull and severely injuring the hand she used to protect herself. He was charged with felony assault and released on $10,000 bail. Later, after a grand jury indicted him for attempted murder, he remained free on the same bail.

College authorities told a terrified Sperling to "phone for help" if Acevedo ever confronted her on campus, and security guards at Marist College were alerted to watch out for him. The former boyfriend, who worked as a part-time therapy aide at an institution for the mentally retarded, kept a gun in his locker. That fact, known to several of his acquaintances and friends, went unreported. On Feb. 18, 1975, Acevedo waited for Sperling outside the college cafeteria. When she saw him, she ran to a telephone and was dialing for help when he shot her dead. REF.: *CBA.*

Achew, James, prom. 1930s, Case of, Brit., mur. Living at Notting Hill, London, Achew had an abiding jealousy of his common-law wife, Sybil da Costa. He was forever accusing her of infidelity without, as the evidence later showed, any real grounds. On Nov. 24, 1929, near dawn, Achew slashed the sleeping woman's throat, killing her. He then tried to cut his own throat and when that proved unsuccessful, he stuck his head in the oven and turned on the gas. Neighbors smelled the gas and Achew was saved to stand trial. Achew was tried before Justice Avory and prosecuted by Eustace Fulton. Defense counsel made much of Achew's delusion, which led him to murder da Costa.

Supporting the presence of insanity, but only in Achew's unbalanced jealousy, was Dr. William Riddle Watson, the chief medical officer of Brixton Prison where Achew was being held. Watson testified that Achew had "no other delusion" except that of believing da Costa was unfaithful to him. He added that, "I do not think the one he had could have been entertained by a perfectly sane man." Avory instructed the jury that Achew's obsession or delusion did not warrant the special verdict of "Guilty, but insane." The jury promptly found Achew Guilty and he received a death sentence. On Feb. 10, 1930, the condemned man was reprieved from the gallows and sent to Broadmoor Criminal Lunatic Asylum, later renamed Broadmoor Institution. The medical and legal views of insanity in this case were obviously at odds but the fact that Achew was ultimately sent to Broadmoor meant that in hindsight the court agreed with Watson's conclusions.

REF.: *CBA*; Lang, *Mr. Justice Avory*; Shew, *A Second Companion to Murder.*

Achey, John Henry, 1833-79, U.S., mur. Achey, a 45-year-old native of Indianapolis, Ind., was a professional sporting man with no particular trade outside of his not very successful adventures in gambling. His father was an inveterate drinker and the son seems to have been one, too. Having recently come into a $2,000 to $3,000 inheritance from his mother's estate, Achey promptly went through most of it. He used the remaining $300 to set up a bank for faro, a then-popular card game, at the Occidental Hotel, joining George Leggett in this escapade. Leggett, who came from a respectable family of local gentlemen farmers, had inherited most of his money and made the rest on slick and polished gambling schemes, establishing himself as a first-class, highly successful gambler.

A few weeks after the opening of the faro bank, Achey, returning from the opera with his wife, was told that a man from Cincinnati, known only as Doc, had won about $600 from the bank in Achey's absence. According to Achey, in an interview given to the Indianapolis *Sentinel,* Leggett then invited Achey to play poker with him and Doc. Achey played, losing $225 and getting drunk in the process. When he realized the game was fixed he accused his companions. He later claimed to have found out that Leggett, Doc, and a man named Brown were hustling him, and that Doc had been called in via a telegraph wire from Ohio for that purpose. Achey nonetheless continued to play, later saying he had lost $875, which left him penniless.

The next day, July 16, 1878, the broke and hungry Achey, seeing Leggett in front of the St. Cloud Hotel, asked him for $25, saying he would "call it square and never bother him any more." Leggett laughed and threatened his former partner with a pistol. The grudge between the men had apparently been building for some time, because, as Achey explained, he then went to his hotel room and got a Smith & Wesson pistol he had "purchased a few days since just on purpose to kill him with." Finding Leggett entering the Chapin & Gore's fancy grocery establishment on North Illinois Street, Achey approached him, calling out, "George, I am now ready for you, draw your gun!" Leggett turned and was shot in the abdomen. He ran to the rear of the store, then back to the front door, passing Achey and deflecting the hand that held the pistol. Achey tried to shoot him several more times, but the gun would not go off. Leggett ran into a nearby shoe store, falling on the threshold as he exclaimed, "I've got my death shot!" Achey walked down the street and was arrested a block or two away by officer Taylor Edwards. Leggett died ten minutes later.

Achey pleaded guilty to the murder charge, later trying to get off by saying it had not been premeditated. Six months after the killing, on Jan. 29, 1879, a large and boisterous crowd, held back by an eighty-member police force, gathered to watch him hang along with another convicted criminal, William Merrick. Achey, who had lost more than forty pounds during his imprisonment, said, as he was dressing to go to his execution, "Well, I'll make a respectable looking corpse, anyhow. I'm ready, bring on the rope."

REF.: *CBA*; Reed, *In Prison and On the Scaffold.*

Acid Bath Murders, See: **Haigh, George John.**

Acker, George, d.1860, U.S., mur. After drinking liquor which had been made of wormwood alcohol, Acker went berserk and murdered Isaac Gordon of Morris County, N.J., in October 1859. Acker was hanged the following year and a local chemist, Dr. Cox, made much of Acker's drinking of adulterated liquor, claiming that this was the reason for the murder, a theory that did nothing to alter Acker's execution.

REF.: *CBA*; *Life and Confession of George Acker, the Murderer of Isaac Gordon.*

Ackerman, prom. 1840s, U.S., count. An elderly counterfeiter spent several years carefully teaching his skills to the younger generation, including his two daughters.

Ackerman, an expert counterfeiter, spent the latter years of his life in Indianapolis passing on to young people his special abilities in the art of making false money. His two daughters, Martha and Almiranda were helpers in his trade, working diligently to assist him until his sudden death.

REF.: Bloom, *Money Of Their Own; CBA.*

Ackerman, Bradley, 1964- , U.S., mur. Ackerman and Julie Alban had grown up in the same affluent neighborhood; their families lived across the street from each other. On June 8, 1988, after they had dated for about ten months, Ackerman asked her to marry him. She refused. Later that evening, as Alban lay sleeping in her parents' home, Ackerman entered her bedroom and shot her in the back. He then shot himself but later recovered from his wound. Alban was paralyzed for life.

Ackerman, the stepson of Daniel Ridder, chairman of the Long Beach *Press-Telegram*, was tried for first-degree murder. Defense counsel, Anthony Murray, arguing that his client was severely depressed over both a recent $30,000 gambling debt and failure to fulfill his early promise as a tennis player, reported Ackerman had taken thirty pills in an attempt to kill himself. Kenneth Lamb, the deputy district attorney who tried the case, told jurors that Ackerman's precision in firing the .38-caliber pistol did not indicate that he was suffering from a Valium blackout, and said the rejected suitor had invented that defense to escape responsibility. Ackerman was found guilty of a willful, premeditated attempt at first-degree murder and sentenced to life imprisonment. Lamb called the verdict "justified," pointing out that Ackerman had sentenced Alban to "death and, failing that, he sentenced her to life in a wheelchair." REF.: *CBA.*

Ackerman, James Waldo, 1926-84, U.S., jur. Lawyer who served as state's attorney of Sangamon County from 1956-60, which includes Springfield, Ill. He was a member of the committee that drafted pattern jury instructions for use in Illinois criminal trials from 1960-66 and in 1976 he became a member of the committee that revised those instructions. He was appointed to the federal bench in 1976 by President Ford. REF.: *CBA.*

Acton, Thomas, prom. 1720s, Case of, Brit., mur. In 1729, a turnkey at Marshalsea Prison, Thomas Acton, was brought to trial four times under charges of having murdered four prisoners under his supervision. A former butcher, Acton was a brutish type, unthinking and sadistic, who enjoyed the miseries of his prisoners and went out of his way to ridicule and shame them. He thought nothing of bringing dying prisoners before him while he entertained guests in his quarters so that these starving, half-conscious wrecks could provide amusement. The trials were held at Kingston, Surrey, with Barton Carter presiding, all taking place in August 1729. The first prisoner Acton was accused of murdering was Thomas Bliss, who had reportedly attempted to escape and was mercilessly beaten by Acton and thrown into the prison's worst solitary cells, the Strong Room. Here, at Acton's orders, Bliss was chained and had no bed or straw. The cell was completely dark, without fresh air, and always damp. Acton was accused of having ordered Bliss to his quarters one day to amuse visitors. He had an iron skullcap placed upon the almost unconscious man, an iron collar placed about his neck, and iron thumbscrews applied to his hands, all of these instruments of torture having been recently found in an ancient prison storage room by Acton, who wanted to see how they worked.

Bliss managed to survive this maltreatment and other tortures and flogging, being released Mar. 25, 1727, but his condition was so poor that his teeth had rotted and he had to beg relatives to chew his meat for him at meals. Such was Bliss' sickly state, all created by the brutal Acton, witnesses claimed, and that he died long before his time. Acton and his own witnesses sneered at these claims, stating that Bliss lived for seven months after being released from prison and that he had taken to heavy drink which brought on a cold and subsequent death. Sir John Darnell, who supervised Marshalsea Prison, stepped forward as a witness to his chief turnkey's good character. Darnell interjected his august presence into all four of Acton's trials to influence the court in its decision, each time testifying as to the sterling qualities of his chief jailer. Before the first trial concluded, one witness, a nobleman friend of Darnell's, stated that he thought Acton was really unfit to be a jailer because Acton was simply too compassionate! Acton was acquitted of any wrongdoing in the death of Thomas Bliss.

The next three trials were all as brief as the first; the second being a charge against Acton for murdering another prisoner, John Bromfield, who had talked back to the turnkey and was promptly beaten with whips, chained, and confined in an area described as "no larger than a coffin." Three months after Bromfield had been placed in Acton's care, in June 1725, the prisoner was dead. Acton shrugged and said the man caught jaundice and died, an act of God, not his. Sir John Darnell again stepped forward to illustrate the great qualities of Acton. The jury again acquitted the jailer. Another prisoner, Robert Newton, also incurred the jailer's displeasure and was thrown into a cell, chained to the wall and subjected to incessant bites from scores of rats infesting the cell. He died a short time after his release. Acton claimed that the man fell ill after being released and this was none of his doing. Sir John Darnell pooh-poohed the Newton death and continued his praise for Acton. The jury acquitted the jailer. James Thompson, the fourth prisoner Acton was accused of murdering, arrived at Marshalsea in 1726 suffering from acute diabetes. Despite his condition, Acton ordered him chained and thrown into a cell where his left side mortified. When another jailer came to Acton and told him that Thompson might die, Acton was quoted as saying, "Damn him, let him lie there and perish!" Thompson died some days later. Acton's sole defense against this strongest of cases was to claim that he was compelled to keep Thompson in a solitary cell since his diabetes caused him "to stink" which offended the other prisoners. Again, Sir John Darnell stepped to the witness stand to extoll the virtues of his most compassionate jailer. The jury acquitted Acton for a fourth and final time.

Protocol and mandatory procedure were ignored in the cases of the four dead prisoners; no inquests were held upon their deaths, which was legally required. Darnell's powerful presence at the Acton trials were blantant exercises of influence by a dreaded authority no jury member of that day would dare to challenge. Worse, Acton was widely known to be an abusive, bestial person with no regard for human life but his heinous actions, if not purposely murderous, were ignored so as not to embarrass Darnell and others of higher authority. The Acton trials illuminate a dark era of flagrant injustice where power and position dictated legal decisions and upheld an oppressive penal system designed to break, if not destroy, the prisoners in its charge, rather than reconstruct and rehabilitate.

REF.: Birkenhead, *Famous Trials of History; CBA.*

Actor's Blood, 1936, a short-story collection by Ben Hecht. This volume contains a story, "The Mystery of the Fabulous Laundryman," which is based on the unsolved murder of Isadore Fink (U.S., 1930). See: **Fink, Isadore.** REF.: *CBA.*

Adachi, Mineichiro, 1869-1934, Japan, jur. President of the International Court of Justice at The Hague from 1931-33. REF.: *CBA.*

Adalbero, d.989, Frankish, archbishop. Archbishop of Reims from 969. He plotted against Lothair's attempts to recapture Lorraine and in 987 declared the Frankish crown elective rather than hereditary. He subsequently gave support to Hugh Capet, then crowned him in 987. REF.: *CBA.*

Adalbero (AKA: **the Old Traitor**), d.1030, Frankish, treas. Bishop of Laon from 977. He plotted with Otto III of Germany against the Frankish throne in 993 and in 998 led an unsuccessful revolt. REF.: *CBA.*

Adaloald, 602-c.626, Italy, mur. Son of King Agilulf who ascended to the throne and led a campaign of murder against Lombard chiefs before he was deposed and murdered. REF.: *CBA.*

Adam, Juliette, 1836-1936, Fr., writer. Novelist who founded and edited *La Nouvelle Revue* (1879). Her second husband was Antonio-Edmund Adam, prefect of the Paris Police during the Franco-Prussian War. REF.: *CBA.*

Adam, Quirin François Lucien, 1833-1900, Fr., jur. Language scholar and lawyer who authored studies of American Indian language. REF.: *CBA.*

Adami, John George, 1862-1926, Brit., pathologist. Author of *Principles of Pathology* (1908). REF.: *CBA.*

Adamic, Louis, 1913-51, U.S., suic.-mur.? A Yugoslavian nationalist who came to America at age fourteen, Adamic became a successful and prominent U.S. writer. At age thirty-eight, he was found dead in his 100-year-old New Jersey farmhouse. Adamic arrived in the U.S. in 1927 and worked as a newsboy, then became a soldier, a sailor, a factory worker, and a restaurant helper. Turning to writing, he based one of his books, *Laughing in the Jungle*, on his experiences as a hobo, and produced several others about politics and the immigrant's status in America. *The Native's Return*, written after he visited his beloved Yugoslavia on a Guggenheim Fellowship, was his first bestseller. He then moved to an old farmhouse in Riegelsville, N.J., continuing as a supporter of the head of Yugoslavia, Marshall Tito, and campaigning briefly for American Progressive Party candidate Henry Wallace in the 1948 U.S. election. Adamic's name came up that same year before the House Un-American Activities Committee, when he was accused of membership in left-wing organizations. Neighbors said the Adamics had become reclusive over the last few years; their house appeared to be locked up and deserted. In fact, Adamic and his wife had moved to California, apparently after threats as a result of his work over a three-year period on a book called *The Eagle and the Roots*, a study promoting Yugoslavia as a bastion of democracy holding out against encroaching Russian Communism. The book was said to be critical of both Russia and the U.S., and was an ardent defense of Tito. Anton Smole, Yugoslav correspondent in San Francisco and a longtime friend, said Adamic had told him of several threats, including one in California when two men stopped him on the street, demanding to see his new book. When the author refused he was beaten unconscious. He moved back to New Jersey shortly thereafter, without his wife, and continued the final work on his book for six weeks.

On Sept. 4, 1951, a paper-mill technician on his way to work at 4 a.m. noticed a glare in the New Jersey hills near Adamic's farmhouse. When fireman arrived from two miles away, the farmhouse garage and studio had burned to the ground. The firemen put out the fire and went inside, discovering a litter of oily rags in the unswept rooms and an unburned wall of the garage soaked with oil. In a second-floor bedroom they found Adamic's body, a .22 Mossberg rifle lying in his lap, and a single bullet wound above his right ear. A Hunterdon County medical examiner returned a tentative verdict of suicide.

Police investigated the possibility of murder, based on threats Adamic had told Smoles and other friends about, demanding he quit work on his last book. According to Adamic's brother-in-law, Harold Sanders, Adamic's wife thought the death was suicide. Sanders said, "He was working too hard, was upset by world conditions, and was under great stress." The FBI investigated the case briefly, dropping it when no angles were found to follow up on. On Aug. 7, 1957, a rusty tin box containing $12,350 in disintegrating large-denomination bills was found in the walls of the burned farmhouse. The package, wrapped in brown paper, had "1950" written on it. At the time of Adamic's death his wife estimated the value of his estate at $5,000. Based on the date and the fact that Adamic had built the wall in which the box was discovered, it is believed that the author had hidden the money. REF.: *CBA.*

Adams, Albert J., 1841-1906, U.S., gamb. Adams began as a runner for Zachariah Simmons, a New Englander who resettled in New York City following the Civil War and, with his three brothers, took over the policy (or numbers) rackets which had been abandoned by Reuben Parsons and John Frink, gambling bosses who had gone on to better things. Adams, who had been born in Rhode Island, first appeared in New York City in 1871, working as a brakeman for the New Haven Railroad. He soon found easier, more lucrative employ as a runner for Simmons. Adams was a quick learner, seeing how Simmons had developed an empire built on policy, one that eventually stretched into twenty cities and made him so many millions that he personally backed the rigged Kentucky state lottery to make more untold millions. It was also apparent to Adams that without political protection Simmons could never have operated. The policy king gave the local political power, Tammany, a fifth of all the enormous profits that rolled in from the gullible players who were addicted to the nickel-and-dime game which was nothing more than a miniature lottery, based on winning numbers ostensibly drawn in Kentucky.

By the late 1870s, Adams secured Simmons' permission to open a few cheap gambling dens and some policy shops of his own. This soon spread to dozens, then hundreds of gambling outlets which Adams directly controlled but was prudent enough to allow the venal members of Tammany to share in his gambling spoils. Adams went even further and made Tammany sachem Shang Draper a partner in several Faro banks, and this splinter gambling enterprise mushroomed to almost 500 cheap Faro banks, which poured a fortune into Adams' pockets. When Simmons and his brothers departed for greener pastures, the policy racket was left wholly in Adams' nickel-clutching hands. He stepped up the game by opening up hundreds of additional outlets throughout Manhattan and for more than twenty years, he was the absolute monarch of policy. Adams, for all his fabulous wealth—an estimated $100 million in profits over two decades—had the deserved reputation as one of the greatest cheapskates in New York. He paid his hundreds of employees slave wages, never tipped, never contributed to charity, and never gave a single possession away, except umbrellas. He would use an umbrella only once, believing superstitiously that it was unlucky to open one a second time after it had been rained upon.

Only a few of Adams' associates could tolerate this closed-mouth, mean-minded gambler. Other than Draper and some other lowlife gamblers, Adams could only call Big Bill Devery, chief of police for New York from 1898 until that post was replaced by that of a commissioner in 1901. Devery, of course, received an enormous cut of Adams' profits for keeping his policemen from raiding the Adams bucket shops, policy outlets, and gambling dens which, by the turn of the century, numbered in the thousands. With so many millions at his disposal, Adams began to invest in legitimate businesses and purchased more than $10 million in prime Manhattan real estate (which would be worth one hundred times that amount today), including a fabulous mansion on East Sixty-ninth Street. To improve his shoddy public image, Adams hired a publicity agent to spread circulars about the city designed to generate widespread respect for his business acumen but really produced little more than guffaws and jeers from the press and Adams' peers. One such circular read: "Al Adams is like unto Andrew Carnegie in that, being a marvelously successful businessman himself, he has drawn around him a corps of men almost equally brilliant as himself, not the least of whom are his four sons."

The circular neglected to state that Adams' sons disliked him. Two of them were educated at Harvard and Heidelberg universities and went on to become successful lawyers who seldom, if ever, mentioned their father's name. Another son was so incensed about his father's illegitimate enterprises when learning of them that he attacked the old man in the foyer of the mansion. Adams had his son arrested and saw to it that the youth spent six months in jail in 1904. By then Albert J. Adams had been exposed for the corrupt gambler and policy racketeer that he was. Reformers making up the Society for the Prevention of Crime, inspired by the leadership of Reverend Charles E. Parkhurst, and better

known as the Parkhurst Society, selected Adams as the most infamous crime czar in New York and spent months collecting information on his widespread operations, taking this to the crusading New York *World* which published lengthy exposés on Adams, noting that he owned two breweries, more than 100 saloons, hundreds of gambling dens, bordellos, and controlled almost all the rackets from the Battery to 110th Street—almost all of Manhattan.

Policy king of NYC Albert Adams, center, on his way to Sing Sing.

Through the efforts of the *World*, Adams was brought to trial in June 1902, and convicted of running illegal gambling enterprises. While awaiting sentence, Adams, instead of going to jail, moved into the finest suite of rooms at the Waldorf-Astoria, with two deputy sheriffs living in adjoining rooms, a privilege that had, in the past, only been extended to the likes of the convicted Tammany potentate William Marcy "Boss" Tweed. Adams had acted as if he would never be convicted, and even after he had been found guilty he believed that somehow his political friends would see to it that he never served a day in jail. He had grossly overestimated the willingness of his Tammany associates to continue linking their fortune to his, especially after the press had utterly shown him to be a money-grabbing crime boss. Tammany ignored Adams and allowed him to be sentenced in 1903 without a whimper of protest. The policy king was fined a paltry $1,000 for his gambling transgressions and sentenced to between a year and eighteen months in prison. The shocked Adams was sent to Sing Sing on Apr. 27, 1903, where he gave his age as sixty-two and stated that his occupation was "a gentleman."

Upon his release on Oct. 1, 1906, Adams returned home to his mansion where he was confronted by one of his sons, the one he later sent to prison for attacking him. His wife of thirty years turned her back on him, as did the few social friends he had made. Adams moved out of his luxurious mansion and took a suite of rooms in the Hotel Ansonia where he made plans to open up a chain of bucket shops that would operate his policy rackets throughout fifty American cities. Yet, Adams' era had ended and tough, new gangs now took over the gambling and bordellos of Manhattan, gangsters like Paul Kelly, Big Jack Zelig, Kid Twist

Zwerbach. The bucket-shop chain idea collapsed and Adams, despite his millions, lived a lonely, wretched life, one of utter disgrace that finally drove him, on Oct. 1, 1906, to lock the doors of his hotel suite at the Ansonia and put a revolver to his head. With one shot, Albert J. Adams blew out his brains.

Policy in New York went into decline. Bob Mott, who had been the king of policy in Chicago, arrived in New York a short time after Adams committed suicide and tried to keep the Adams empire intact but the reformers successfully closed down most of the policy operations by 1908 and by WWI, the policy rackets had become trivial in the many illegal gambling operations controlled by the modern-day gangsters. Not until Stephanie St. Clair and other blacks revitalized policy in Harlem in the early 1920s, the racket then known as numbers, did Policy make a comeback. At this time it became so lucrative that it attracted the attention of bootlegger Dutch Schultz who moved into Harlem and took over the numbers racket, beating and killing the blacks into submission and taking over what, by 1932, had once again become a multimillion-dollar racket. See: **Draper, Shang; Frink, John; Parkhurst, Charles E.; Parsons, Reuben; St. Clair, Stephanie; Schultz, Dutch; Simmons, Zachariah.**

REF.: Addy, *Dutch Schultz;* Asbury, *Sucker's Progress;* Campbell, *Darkness and Daylight, or Lights and Shadows of New York; CBA;* Chafetz, *Play the Devil;* Crapsey, *The Nether Side of New York;* Crockett, *Peacocks on Parade;* Drzazga, *Wheels of Fortune;* Every, *Sins of New York;* Gibson, *Fine Art of Swindling,* Peterson, *The Mob;* Sann, *Kill the Dutchman;* Werner, *Tammany Hall.*

Adams, Caleb, 1785-1803, U.S., mur. At age eighteen Caleb Adams lived hand-to-mouth as an odd-job worker in Windham, Conn. Five-year-old Oliver Woodworth took to following Adams about the streets, asking him incessant questions. Adams inexplicably turned on the boy and crushed his head with an axe, then slit the boy's throat with a knife in full view of many witnesses. He lamely explained that Woodworth "annoyed" him. After a speedy trial, Adams was hanged on Nov. 29, 1803, but not before the Reverend Elijah Waterman gave a bombastic speech about Adams' dissolute life as a "street boy." While standing on the scaffold next to the penitent Adams, the minister recited, for more than an hour, every offense committed by the condemned youth, including the theft of 25 cents.

REF.: *CBA;* Nash, *Bloodletters and Badmen;* Waterman, *A Sermon Preached at Windham.*

Adams, Dick, d.1713, Brit., rob. Raised by respectable parents in Gloucestershire, Adams had the benefit of education wherein he learned to read and write at an early age. He also received tutoring in the keeping of accounts. With his special skills, Adams was hired as a purchasing agent or servant for a duchess living in St. James' Palace, London. He performed his chores dutifully for some years before taking up petty larceny. On one occasion, he invited a merchant of rare silks to bring his best samples to his employer so she could inspect the wares. When the merchant arrived at the duchess' manor house, Adams met him and told him that he should leave the goods, and his employer would inspect them at her leisure. This had not been an uncommon practice by the duchess with previous purchases. The merchant, however, waited for several hours only to learn that the silks he had left with Adams had vanished with the sly bookkeeper. Some days later the merchant encountered Adams on a crowded street and collared him, demanding the return of his silks or a payment of their worth, approximately £200. Adams pointed out the bishop of London who was just then passing in a litter and claimed that the bishop was his uncle and that if Adams could only have a few words with him, Adams would arrange to have the merchant paid. The merchant agreed, and Adams boldly hailed the bishop's litter. His manner was that of a nobleman, as was his attire, and the bishop deigned to speak with someone whom he thought to be a man of distinction, like himself. At that point, the story goes, Adams explained that his friend the merchant was having some vexing thoughts about religion and would appreciate any enlightening remarks the bishop would bestow upon him at a later date at the bishop's residence. The flattered bishop motioned the merchant to him and told the man that he was to come to his residence the next day and he would receive every satisfaction. With that, the merchant allowed Adams to go on his way, thinking he would collect his debt later.

Before the merchant visited the bishop on the following day, the audacious Adams went to the man's shop and borrowed some money, telling the merchant to add this to the amount he would collect from his uncle. The merchant gladly gave Adams a large sum of money and then went to see the bishop. When he presented his bill to the bishop, the clergyman became indignant and said that he understood the man was visiting him to have certain religious questions answered. "But your nephew assured me you would stand his debt." "What?" cried the bishop. "That man is no nephew of mine." The two men glared at each other for some moments until the absurdity of their situation, and the utter capriciousness of Adams caused them to burst into laughter. This is but one of many anecdotes told about the amusing and enterprising Adams who later took up the role of highwayman. His colorful and humorous ways did not change, even though he had taken to the road and robbery.

Like most of his peers, Adams presented himself to his victims like a gentleman, mixing his demands for their jewelry and gold with chivalrous comments and exhibiting the lofty airs of a nobleman. He never took anything as would an outright thief, but merely, as he put it, "borrowed" the jewels and furs of the ladies he robbed, promising to return them later, should they meet again. On another occasion, or another canard, Adams, in company with some other highwaymen, supposedly robbed a nobleman of a silver snuff box, a gold watch, and a purse bulging with gold coins. As the nobleman began to ride off, Adams surveyed his victim's coat, which was much finer than his own, and rode back to the nobleman, demanding that he exchange coats. Stripped of his fine garment, the nobleman again rode off wearing Adams' rather threadbare coat. But when Adams and his cohorts met to divide the loot, Adams realized that in switching his old coat for that of the nobleman's, he had returned all the stolen goods which he slipped into the pockets of his old coat. So angry were his fellow highwaymen that they threatened to beat Adams senseless until he promised never to make such blunders in the future.

Adams was successful for a brief period of time, but later met a victim who did not simply accept his fate after being robbed. The victim rode to a nearby inn, collected a party of men, armed himself, and raced after Adams. The group caught up with the highwayman, who was leisurely ambling down a lane while counting his loot. A wild chase ensued as Adams "made a running fight of it in shooting, Tartar-like, behind him." Adams shot one pursuer out of his saddle, but the group of fast riders finally overtook him and returned him to a magistrate. He was held at Newgate Prison while being tried. He was convicted and sentenced to death, highway robbery then being a capital offense in England. The shadow of the gallows did not seem to affect the condemned man. Up to the very moment he was taken to Tyburn in Mar. 1713, Dick Adams displayed a pleasant and cheerful attitude, whistling and singing the newest songs in vogue, mixing this tuneful posture with a great number of prayers uttered loudly in his cell. Most of the thousands who witnessed this highwayman hang agreed that he died "devout of spirit."

REF.: *CBA;* Hayward, *Lives of the Most Remarkable Criminals;* Hibbert, *Highwayman;* Pringle, *Stand and Deliver;* Smith, *A Complete History of the Lives and Robberies of the Most Notorious Highwaymen, Footpads, Shoplifts & Cheats of Both Sexes;* Villette, *Annals of Newgate.*

Adams, Eddie (W.J. Wallace), 1887-1921, U.S., rob.-mur. Adams, born in Hutchinson, Kan., lived a normal life during his early years, despite the fact that his father died when he was young and his mother remarried. While in his teens, Adams dropped out of school and attended barber college, becoming a barber in Wichita. Into his shop one day stepped John Callahan, the town's criminal Fagin. Callahan flashed a roll of big bills and hinted of greater fortunes to be made illegally.

Adams, who continued to use his real name of W.J. Wallace and kept his job as a barber, went to work at night carrying illegal liquor shipments from Missouri into Kansas under Callahan's direction. He would pick up carloads of booze in Joplin, Mo., and then drive into Kansas, using back roads mapped out by Callahan here the less-than-vigilant revenue agents or lawmen, annoyed by the state's prohibition laws (put into effect four decades before the enactment of the Volstead Act in 1919), would not be present.

The money Adams made was substantial, but the apprentice crook refused to quit his barbershop position, retaining his name of Wallace by day and becoming Eddie Adams, criminal—at night—a true and increasingly terrible enactment of the Jekyll-Hyde story. He met through Callahan many another criminal, including the notorious outlaw Al Spencer, who later told Callahan that Adams, the name he always used when associating with the underworld, "has no scruples."

Such perception from a bank robber like Spencer was not unusual in that Spencer was in the mold of the traditional western outlaw, ruled by a set of unwritten laws: you did not, as an outlaw, rob or injure women or children, and you never killed a defenseless man. Adams—and he expressed his thoughts on the matter regularly—had no reservations in taking human life—anyone's life—in the act of committing a crime. Adams later proved his point with a mindless and horrific display of wanton violence.

Moreover, Adams developed a taste for all things dissolute while in his early twenties and, having the money from his illegal bootlegging, he indulged in his pleasures to the point of exhaustion. First, Adams married a Wichita girl, using his real name of Wallace, but he soon proved himself unfaithful to her and when the girl learned of his bootlegging, she left him. Adams reacted indifferently to this loss and plunged wholeheartedly into whoring, particularly at a Wichita bordello run by Nellie Miles, who also operated a dope-smuggling ring with her husband Clyde Miles. Both of these notorious smugglers later caused the undoing of their partner in crime and super fence, John Callahan, Adams' tutor.

Because of his whoring, Adams contracted a venereal disease that plagued him the rest of his life. His growing dependency upon heroin proved to be a costly pastime and Adams took on more and more criminal assignments from Callahan to pay for his pleasures. He soon graduated to burglary, fencing his stolen goods through Callahan, and then went on to armed robbery. Here Adams felt he needed aid, and Callahan quickly provided it in the form of the three wild Majors brothers, Dudley, Roy, and Ray.

This foursome began by robbing small-town banks in Kansas, Iowa, Nebraska, and even as far south as Oklahoma, just after WWI. Adams, emboldened by the success of his gang, decided to raid into the lucrative state of Missouri, which was then held tightly in the political grip of the Pendergast Machine. He and the Majors brothers burst into a posh gambling den in the spring of 1920, looting the Kansas City players. Several of the dice players, however, whipped out guns and began firing at the Kansas bandits, wounding Roy and Ray Majors. Adams and his henchmen returned fire, killing one of the gamblers and wounding two others before fleeing. But Adams and the two wounded Majors brothers were captured, with Dudley Majors making good his escape.

Police quickly filed murder charges against the bandits and both Majors brothers were sent to prison for five years each, the badly wounded Roy Majors dying in prison a short time later. (Ray Majors was later released, committed several more robberies, and wound up in the Kansas State Penitentiary at Lansing where he would also die behind bars. His brother Dudley would also serve several long prison terms for robbery.)

Eddie Adams was found guilty of being the actual killer of the gambler and was given a life sentence. On his way to the Missouri prison, Adams managed to hoodwink his guards and escape. On board a speeding train, Adams asked to be unshackled so he could use the washroom. Once inside the washroom, Adams broke the small window and worked his way through the opening, holding

onto an outside railing and then dropping himself onto the roadbed when the train slowed at a curve. Uninjured, he began running into the deep night, heading for his native Kansas.

Although there was a great deal of publicity regarding the spectacular escape, none of the travelers who picked up the hitch-hiking Adams suspected that the ragged, dirty character sitting next to them was the much-wanted robber and killer. Once back in Wichita, Adams raced straight to his criminal mentor Callahan and obtained a gun and a car. He drove off in search of a bank to rob and found one in Cullison, Kan. In his haste, however, Adams recklessly drove off the road near Pratt, Kan.

Police found Adams hiding under a nearby bridge after deserting his wrecked car. He was taken without a fight and sent to the state penitentiary, this time to serve out his sentence. In prison, Adams quickly befriended other thieves, bank robbers like himself. (It is axiomatic that types of criminals in prison form cliques based upon the status of their criminal reputations, con men and bank robbers being the princes of the prison.)

Adams impressed Frank Foster, D.C. Brown, and George Weisberger with his criminal exploits, bragging to them that he not only robbed more than two dozen banks but had robbed two different trains alone, the latter a fabrication. (Again, within the ranks of bank robbers, the man who had robbed a train was considered to be most spectacular, worthy of criminal honors and respect from fellow convicts.)

Much of Adams' embellishments were taken from the life of old-time outlaw Al Spencer, whom he had met briefly through Callahan in Wichita. What most impressed Foster and the others were the tales Adams spun about his "solid gold" contacts in Wichita. The authorities in that town were "in the palm of my hand," he said. He could commit any kind of crime and return to Wichita, and the police, to whom he paid considerable "protection" money, he said, would not only look the other way when he passed them in the streets but would contact him if any out-of-town lawmen came looking for him, even concealing Adams in safe hideouts.

Much of what Adams said was true but that truth evaporated when Wichita cleaned house and got rid of its corrupt police officials, putting tough-minded S.W. Zickefoose in charge of all detectives. The new chief of detectives immediately went to Callahan and informed him that all deals were off and that if Callahan or any of his associates were caught committing even the smallest infraction they would be run into the station house and charged. The pickpockets, burglars, and armed thugs who had been infesting the town up to that time were scooped off the streets of Wichita, and law and order was officially restored. All of this took place while Adams bided his time in the Lansing penitentiary.

Working with Foster, Brown, and Weisberger, Adams concocted a scheme as wild as his robberies. He and the others secretly built a ladder in sections which they hid in various workshops of the penitentiary. Then, on the night of Aug. 13, 1921, Adams and Foster, the latter having considerable electrical knowledge, grounded the current in the central electric plant of the penitentiary, throwing the entire place into utter darkness. The escape party quickly assembled the sectional ladder, raced to a wall, and slipped over the side.

Adams had planned well, for outside the penitentiary walls waited a fast car with Billy Fintelman at the wheel. Fintelman, who had earned medals as a courageous doughboy during WWI and had turned to crime to make fast money, had been sent to the penitentiary to pick up the escapees by Wichita crime boss Callahan.

The police dragnet turned up the escape car, abandoned after it had run out of gas. Hours later, a haggard D.C. Brown was found stumbling along a deserted roadway. But he was the only one of the escaped convicts bagged by the police. Adams, Foster, and Weisberger headed straight for Wichita where Callahan warned the wanted men that the town was no longer safe. Nevertheless, Nellie Miles put the trio up at her bordello. Adams lived like a cornered rat, afraid to go out during the day and screaming invectives at the law. He decided that he wanted to see an old girlfriend, a young lady he had met before embarking upon his criminal career. He sent word to her, asking that she meet him. The girl sent back a note rebuffing Adams; the rejection made him go berserk. When Adams learned that the girl was seeing a local policeman, he haunted the man's beat and shot A.L. Young to death one night while the officer was making his rounds.

Then, with Foster and Weisberger at his side, the mentally unbalanced Adams launched a vicious crime wave, looting the Kansas banks at Rose Hill and Haysville. In the latter holdup, Adams was leaving the bank when he suddenly stopped before a harmless old man, James Krievell. For no reason at all (Krievell neither uttered a word nor made a move toward Adams during the robbery) Adams brought his pistol crashing down on the skull of the 82-year-old man. Krievell would later die from this injury.

The gang struck several banks in Missouri and then moved back into Iowa, robbing the bank in Osceola, Iowa, on Oct. 19, 1921. After fleeing the town, the robbers, Fintelman now serving as the wheelman, pulled over to the side of a dirt road. So confident were they that pursuit would be impossible, the thieves decided to take a nap. They were less than twelve miles from the bank they had just robbed. A farmer, C.W. Jones, discovered the bandits sleeping in their car and went for the police. Sheriff West and two deputies, Charles Eaton and John Miller, accompanied by Jones, crept up on the car.

It was the ever-alert Adams who heard the posse approaching and jumped from the car first, firing at the lawmen. His first shot struck farmer Jones and killed him. The other bandits leapt from the car, firing, wounding all the posse men and sending Sheriff West running. They laughed as they drove off the lawmen but soon began cursing when they discovered that bullets from the lawmen had shattered their car's mechanism.

The gang, unscathed, calmly walked to the sheriff's car which was parked nearby, got in, and drove off, leaving the wounded men moaning for help on the road. Police swarming through the county found the sheriff's car abandoned the next morning in Mound City, Kan., where the terror gang had again escaped in another stolen car. In nearby Muscotah, Kan., the gang robbed a dozen stores and then escaped in yet another stolen car.

Adams felt he was now invincible, telling his henchmen that no lawman alive could stop him, capture him, or even wound him in a gun fight. He thought of himself as a traditional outlaw, as famous as the Daltons or Bill Doolin, or even Al Spencer. As the gang approached Newton, Kan., Adams got the opportunity to prove his point. He spotted a sheriff's car in front of him and ordered Fintelman to overtake the deputies ahead of them. The sheriff's car was pulled over and Adams forced two deputies into the road at gunpoint. He stole their weapons, money, and handcuffs, set fire to their car, and then climbed back into the gang car, ordering Fintelman to drive off.

On Nov. 5, 1921, Eddie Adams set about proving his brag that he was a "big-time train robber." He and his gang stopped the Santa Fe's famous Super Chief outside of Ottawa, Kan., taking $35,000 from the mail car. Again, Adams returned to Wichita, staying with Nellie Miles. Wichita detectives suspected that the bandit might be hiding at the Miles bordello, but every time the place was searched the police came away empty-handed. During these searches, Adams was silently sitting in a small hidden room behind a fake wall, a room built by Clyde and Nellie Miles years earlier, where Wichita VIPs could hide from police during occasional raids.

Only at night could Adams venture forth from the bordello, and this caused him frustration and eventual anger which spilled over on the night of Nov. 20, 1921. He told Nellie Miles that he was giving a "party on wheels," and soon two cars, loaded with gangsters and whores, were heading for a roadhouse outside of Wichita. Adams was in one car with Nellie Miles, two of her girls, Foster, and George J. Macfarline, a Wichita thug, who was at the wheel. Fintelman and his wife were in the other car with Weisberger, another local hoodlum, P.D. Orcutt, and two prostitutes.

As the cars roared along the roadway, two motorcycle officers, Bob Fitzpatrick and Rudolph La Croix, noted the speeding autos and gave chase. The officers pulled alongside the car carrying Adams and motioned to driver Macfarline to pull over. He did. Fitzpatrick got off his cycle and walked casually to the car, leaning down to check the occupants. Smiling, Adams reached across Macfarline's chest and fired pointblank into Fitzpatrick's face, killing the officer immediately. "Step on the gas!" he yelled to Macfarline. "Get us out of here fast!"

The car roared away but La Croix did not give pursuit, pausing to attend to Fitzpatrick. Adams ordered the car stopped some miles down the road and told the women to get out, threatening that he would kill anyone who talked. He, Macfarline, and Foster then drove south into the wilds of Cowley County, which had been Bill Doolin's refuge in another century. Later that night the gang stopped at a farm owned by George Oldham. Rousing the farmer, Adams demanded that he sell them some gas for the car. Oldham agreed and went into the barn to get some gas from a barrel stored there. When he emerged he saw Adams getting into the farmer's car and went over to ask what Adams was doing. Adams grinned maniacally at Oldham, drew his gun, and shot the farmer dead.

Adams then heard what he thought were car engines. Believing the posses were closing in on him, he ordered everyone to escape through the nearby fields. After some time, Adams and Foster returned to their car but Macfarline did not return, having gotten lost. Adams and Foster drove off without him.

Macfarline trekked on foot to the small town of Akron, Kan., and there bought a ticket to the town of Gordon, twenty miles up the line. Exhausted, he lay down on a bench in the waiting station and fell asleep. The station master in a nearby office heard Macfarline talking clearly in his sleep. He stepped out into the waiting room where only Macfarline was present. Listening, he heard the hoodlum relate in his sleep the killing of Wichita policeman Fitzpatrick. The station master alerted police up the line.

When the train arrived, Macfarline got on board but was alarmed when the train did not stop at Gordon. He was told by the conductor that Gordon was not a scheduled stop for that train, and he would have to get off further up the line at Augusta, which he did. No sooner had Macfarline alighted when he was arrested by Police Chief W.A. Marshal and other officers. The train had been ordered not to stop at Gordon since it lacked a sufficient police force and to go on to Augusta. Actually, the Gordon cops wanted no part of the man on the train, thinking the sleep-babbling gangster was Adams. It was Marshal, as the officers spoke long distance that night, who agreed to arrest the outlaw in Augusta, and the special train stop was arranged.

Macfarline was turned over to Wichita police and he quickly told everything he knew about the bloodthirsty Adams, saying that the killer was expected at his house in Wichita later that day. Two officers, W.W. Wright and Ray "Tommy" Casner, were sent to the house to await the bank robber. They found it empty and waited for six hours until their vigilance was rewarded.

A car drew up in front of the house. The officers peered through the small door windows of the house to identify Fintelman at the wheel. Getting out of the car was a pleasant-looking young man. "That's Adams!" Wright said, and immediately he ran up the stairs. Casner stood his ground, a shotgun in his hand.

Adams opened the door and Casner stood before him, the sawed-off shotgun leveled at the bank robber. "Come on in," Casner said to Adams.

Then the killer did the unexpected. Instead of surrendering, Adams leaped forward, grabbing the shotgun's barrel, and pushing it to one side. At that moment, Casner squeezed the trigger but was shocked to realize he had not flipped the safety off the gun and it did not fire.

Casner panicked and dashed past the killer, reaching for his pistol, stumbling off the porch just as Adams aimed and fired the shotgun (*he* was careful to flip off the safety). Casner took the load of buckshot in the buttocks as he fell off the porch, a happy accident in that if he had remained upright he would certainly have been killed. Casner bolted across the lawn as Adams jumped after him. Adams, too, fell off the narrow porch so that by the time he righted himself to fire at the officer, Casner was out of sight. Adams and Fintelman fled.

When the embarrassed Casner was found and taken to the hospital, he reported his humiliating experience in detail. Wichita prosecutor Guy Wertz and several detectives immediately drove to the Macfarline house and found an unperturbed officer Wright sitting in the living room, gun in hand, creaking back and forth in a rocking chair.

Wright was asked if anyone was in the house, and he casually replied that he did not know. He was ordered to draw his gun and help conduct a search of the house. Wright's uniform, the officers observed, was covered with lint. Upstairs, the prosecutor looked under a bed and forced Wright to look with him. There was an outline in the dust beneath the bed which clearly showed where Wright had hidden when he left his partner Casner to face Adams alone. Wright was later removed from the Wichita Police Department for his cowardice.

Quickly the gang members and their prostitute girlfriends, including the infamous Nellie Miles, were picked up, first Fintelman, then Weisberger. The members told police the details of all the killings, pointing the finger at ringleader Adams.

Eddie Adams and Frank Foster, at this time, were hiding in an attic room, watching from a window, counting the police cars moving about the streets below. Though Foster urged Adams to flee, the slender killer told his henchman that they must wait for the right time and that time would be the funeral of officer Fitzpatrick. Adams reasoned rightly that most of the Wichita police force would be in attendance at the funeral and he chose that very moment to attempt his escape from the city. He appeared alone at a rent-a-car garage and selected a car. As one attendant filled the tank, another garage employee, scanning a wanted poster for the notorious Eddie Adams, recognized Adams as the stranger in the garage. The attendant called police.

Three detectives, Ed Bowman, D.C. Stuckey, and Charles Hoffman, raced to the garage and ran into the building just as Adams was getting into the car. Hoffman and Adams immediately recognized each other; Hoffman had arrested Adams when he was a rather innocent youth named W.J. Wallace.

Adams remained cool, stating calmly, "How are you, Mr. Hoffman. Come here. I'd like to talk to you."

Hoffman approached the car where Adams was standing. Suddenly, the killer drew his revolver. But before he could fire, Hoffman jumped forward, locking his arms around the killer, trying to take the revolver.

Stuckey and Bowman drew their guns but could not fire for fear of hitting Hoffman. The two detectives watched helplessly as Adams and Hoffman struggled for the revolver which Adams worked barrel-forward against Hoffman's chest, pulling the trigger.

Hoffman fell backward, mortally wounded, but managed to drag the bank robber with him to the floor. Adams jerked free, stood up, and nervelessly aimed his revolver at Bowman, shooting him in the stomach and sending the heavyset detective to the floor.

Stuckey, who had taken a defensive position behind a post in garage, aimed at the snarling killer and fired just as Bowman fired his weapon from a prone position. Before Adams could fire again, he was struck in the mouth by Stuckey's bullet and in the head by the bullet fired by Bowman. The bullet to the head caught Adams in the middle of an unfinished word. The detectives watched this one-man crime wave stand stiffly for a few seconds; then his body swayed and collapsed to the grease-stained floor. Eddie Adams, also known as W.J. Wallace, slayer of six men, was dead.

The bandit was buried two days later and hundreds of curious Wichita residents lined up to view his body. Officer Hoffman was also buried that day and only a score of mourners attended. Detective Bowman recovered from his wound. Frank Foster stole a car some days later and fled to St. Joseph, Mo., where he was captured. He was sent to Lansing for life. The rest of the Adams gang, Fintelman, Weisberger, and Macfarline, also received long prison terms. The wild nightmare created by Eddie Adams was over.

Ironically, the man who had created Adams, John Callahan, remained at large. Boldly, he even attended Adams' funeral, remarking to police detectives, "He was a nice kid before he went wrong."

REF.: *CBA;* Gish, *American Bandits;* Wellman, *A Dynasty of Outlaws.*

Adams, George, 1784-1844, U.S., jur. Began his career as a lawyer in Kentucky in 1810, then served in the lower House of the Kentucky Legislature 1811-14. In 1825 he moved to Mississippi where he served as attorney general from 1828-29. He served as the U.S. district attorney for Mississippi from 1838-42 and was appointed to the federal bench by President Andrew Jackson in 1936. REF.: *CBA.*

Adams, James, 1937-84, U.S., mur. When his indefinite stay of execution was overturned by the U.S. Supreme Court, James Adams became the first black to die in Florida's electric chair in twenty years. Convicted in 1973 of beating a rancher to death with a poker, James Adams had been in the Starke, Fla. prison for ten years awaiting execution. On Mar. 9, 1983, the high court voted 5 to 4 to overturn an indefinite stay of execution just handed down by the 11th U.S. Circuit Court of Appeals in Atlanta. After reviewing new evidence, Florida Governor Bob Graham agreed that Adams should be electrocuted as scheduled. Adams' attorneys immediately applied to the Atlanta appeals court for another delay for their 47-year-old client.

Justice Thurgood Marshall issued a three-page dissent criticizing the order that lifted the execution stay, blasting his colleagues for the "haste and confusion surrounding this decision" and saying that the court "simply (had) not sufficient time with which to consider responsibly the issues posed by this case." Adams was executed on May 10, 1984. REF.: *CBA.*

Adams, Jani, 1948- , U.S., Case of, mur. Because she used gallows humor to deflect the stress of nursing the terminally ill, a Las Vegas nurse was accused of causing the death of one of her patients and a grand jury indicted her on an open murder charge. On Mar. 13, 1980, newspapers nationwide reported allegations that nurses and other employees at the Sunrise Hospital in Las Vegas were making bets on how long their patients would live, and that life-support equipment may have been tampered with to stack the odds. At least six deaths were reportedly under investigation. The next day, four hospital workers from the intensive care night shift were suspended with pay and the hospital's executive director, David Brandsness, defended his employees, saying, "Their professionalism, their morality, their integrity are all being brought into question." On March 23 reports of an "Angel of Death," a nurse supposed to have shut off life-support systems of six patients, killing them, made headlines with Jani Adams, thirty-two, one of the suspended workers, the main suspect. She and her boyfriend, Bernard Deters, thirty-nine, hired San Francisco attorney Melvin Belli to represent her.

The investigations were headed by District Attorney Robert Miller. Early reports of betting on deaths were rescinded; new plans to exhume six bodies were under consideration. Authorities charged Adams with tampering with the oxygen supply of Vincent Fraser—a terminally ill, 51-year-old patient who had recently died—when one of Adams' co-workers claimed to have seen her tampering with valves at Fraser's bedside. Adams denied the charges, saying, "He's lying. I don't know why, but he's lying."

In early April Adams was indicted by a Clark County grand jury on a murder charge. By mid-April twenty-one persons had testified before the jury and Adams had been accused of saying, "Come on, Marian, die" to one patient, and joking to another nurse, "You just don't know how to kill people off." Fraser's wife,

Bertha, testified that her dying husband kept pointing to his respirator and shaking. "He was nervous about something," she said.

Adams continued to deny all allegations and, abruptly, the case collapsed. District Judge Michael Weller dismissed it for lack of evidence, and the district attorney made no appeal. Adams couldn't get a job for the next five months. A June 1980 article in *People* magazine revealed that the jury that indicted Adams saw only small portions of Fraser's extensive medical records, and were not informed that he suffered from both a peptic ulcer and chronic cirrhosis of the liver, and that five doctors had judged his case as terminal. As of May 1981, Adams was employed at another hospital, again in the intensive care unit. She would not name the hospital. REF.: *CBA*.

Adams, John (AKA: **Alexander Smith**), c.1760-1829, Brit., mutiny. Took part in the mutiny aboard *H.M.S. Bounty* in 1789, after which he and eight other sailors founded a colony on Pitcairn Island in Tahiti. See: **Mutiny on the Bounty**. REF.: *CBA*.

Adams, Dr. John Bodkin, prom. 1957, Brit., Case of, mur. A sensation was created in the British press when a middle-aged physician was accused of hastening the deaths of his elderly patients to benefit himself financially. Dr. Adams had been practicing for three decades in the small, wealthy seaside resort town of Eastbourne when rumors of poisonings and probes into wills and reports of drug sales began to circulate. Adams was known for his gentle, attentive manner. For years he had met his patients at the station on their arrival from nearby London, taking them for soothing drives in the country, and holding their hands as they lay bedridden. But police received notes, some anonymous and some from irate relatives, suggesting—with no evidence—that Adams had expedited the deaths of some of his patients. Conjecture over the death of Edith Alice Morrell, an 81-year-old woman whose son gave Dr. Adams her old Rolls Royce and a chest of family silver in gratitude for his care in his mother's final days, caused Scotland Yard to assign Detective Herbert (The Count) Hannam, a homicide specialist, to investigate.

At a hearing to determine whether Adams should be tried for murder, a prosecutor for the Crown maintained that Morrell had not died of a stroke but had been "poisoned by drugs which Dr. Adams administered." Prosecutor Melford Stevenson declared that Adams stood to gain financially from the deaths of a wealthy couple who had been his patients, Alfred John Hullett, seventy-one, and his 50-year-old wife, Gertrude Hullett, who died four months after her spouse in 1956. Evidence against Adams included the fact that he had cashed a £1,000 check made out to him by Mrs. Hullett and asked to have it cleared quickly, and that he had ordered a post mortem done on his patient shortly before she died. Although Gertrude Hullett died of an overdose of barbiturates, a coroner's inquest deemed her death a suicide. Adams was said to have prescribed drugs to a dying woman who had no need for them.

During the three-week trial, which began in April 1957 in the court of Mr. Justice Devlin, Adams sat quietly, taking copious notes to give to his attorneys, while Prosecuting Atty. Gen. Sir Reginald Manningham-Buller called in scores of experts to testify as to whether or not the heroin, morphine, and paraldehyde Adams had prescribed for Morrell had hastened her death. In one of the longest murder trials in the history of the Old Bailey, even Adams himself was moved to asked in bewilderment, "Can you prove it was murder?" A leading British authority on morphine and heroin, Dr. Arthur Henry Douthwaite, concluded that Adams intended to "terminate her life," while Dr. Michael George Corbett Ashby declared that the possibility of death by natural causes "cannot be ruled out." The jury took less than an hour to find Adams Not Guilty. Adams was reported to have sold the story of his case to the *Daily Express* for $14,000.

REF.: *CBA;* Furneaux, *Famous Criminal Cases;* Simpson, *Forty Years of Murder.*

Adams, Kitty, d.1899, U.S., pros.-rob. One of the worst hellions to ever inhabit Chicago's red light district—the Levee—

Kitty Adams first came to the attention of the police in 1880 when she was arrested with a pickpocket named George Shine whom she claimed was her husband. A white woman, Kitty thereafter was seen mostly in the company of black lovers who secured for her a position in a black brothel south of the Levee. This dangerous area was called Coon Hollow because so many blacks lived in and patronized the area. Her black pimp taught her the art of using the razor and Adams kept one inside the bosom of her dress, pulling this out whenever her temper flared. One of her many black lovers displeased her so Adams lopped off his ears. On another occasion she fell to arguing with the driver of a scavenger wagon and ended the confrontation by slicing a six-inch gash in one of his horses, mortally wounding the animal.

In 1886, Adams located a shack inside the Levee and established a streetside crib from which she plied her trade. Often as not, Adams earned much more money as a footpad, robbing husky men on the street at razor-point. She took a partner named Jennie Clark and these two worked together as successful robbers. Clark was a young, attractive redhead who picked up salivating customers and then steered them into dark alleys. There, Adams would be waiting and jump on the victim's back, holding the razor to his throat and demanding all his money and valuables. Clark would pocket the loot and leave, while Adams stayed behind to club the victim's head to make sure that he was unconscious and unable to pursue her and her partner. Those she left unmolested were afraid to complain to police since they would have to admit they had been patronizing a whore, and then, again, there was the question of their manhood being challenged by a woman. Adams was the terror of the Levee from 1886 to 1893, and Chicago police estimated that she had committed no less than 800 robberies during this period.

One indignant man, however, did testify against Adams in 1893, and she was convicted of armed robbery and sent to the women's prison adjacent to the main state prison in Joliet, Ill., for five years. No sooner was Adams locked in her cell than Jennie Clark began to petition Governor John P. Altgeld for her release, stating that Adams was dying of tuberculosis. Altgeld, known as a fair-minded humanitarian, ordered an investigation into the matter. When Kitty Adams appeared before the Board of Pardons, she began to spit up blood and the alarmed members of the board immediately granted her release. She had brought about this timely demonstration by puncturing her gums with toothpicks so that her mouth was full of blood when she entered the hearing room, and all she had to do was cough a few times to convince the blood-flecked board members that her ailment was genuine.

Upon her release, Adams went straight back to the Levee where she and Clark resumed their robberies. Both were arrested in August 1896, for taking $5 from an old man. Only Clark appeared for trial, Adams having skipped on her bail. She could have saved herself the trouble. Clark appeared before Judge James Goggin, one of the most eccentric jurists ever to sit on a bench. Goggin heard the case with a frown which he directed toward the prosecution. Then he made a decision that became one of the most notorious on record, admonishing the old man, telling him and the local district attorney that "any man who goes into the Levee deserves to be robbed" and that the robbers should not be punished. He released Clark and the fugitive warrant for Adams was dropped. Adams and Clark went back to their vicious trade, but in 1898, Adams was again arrested and this time she was given a long prison term in Joliet. The Chicago police were finally rid of "The Terror of State Street," as Adams had come to be known. Her fate was grimly ironic in that Adams died the following year inside her prison cell. The cause of death was tuberculosis. See: **Altgeld, John P.**

REF.: Asbury, *Gem of the Prairie; CBA;* Wooldridge, *Hands Up!.*

Adams, Louis, prom. 1932, U.S., mur. The crowning of Mark Adams as "King of all the Gypsies in the World" was to be a festive celebration. In December 1931, Adams, a farmer in California's San Fernando Valley, invited an army of Gypsy fortune tellers, silversmiths, and card readers from across the U.S., to witness his coronation and feast on barbecued steer. The week-long party came to an abrupt end, however, when Mark's brother Louis Adams murdered his estranged wife from Chicago in front of their nine children. Despondent over their recent separation, Louis decided to take matters into his own hands. He was immediately arrested and jailed. REF.: *CBA*.

Adams, Mary, d.1702, Brit., pros.-rob. Born in Reading, Berkshire, Mary Adams came from humble beginnings and became a servant for a local grocer while in her early teens. Her employer's son some time later had an affair with the girl which resulted in a child. The grocer, who believed his son to be the father, supported Mary until she delivered the baby but she was then dismissed and traveled to London. Here she married twice, but both husbands, when learning that she was having affairs, abandoned her. Adams took on several wealthy, married lovers, blackmailing them for sizeable amounts which were paid when she threatened to inform their wives of their blatant infidelities.

For some time Adams lived in high style on Wych Street, able to afford the best clothing and conveniences from her blackmailing schemes, but she soon ran out of victims when her notoriety branded her a dangerous woman. Adams lost her funds and moved into a handsome bordello as the star boarder as she was far away the most beautiful prostitute the madam could offer her aristocratic customers. Not content with the high fees paid for her bedroom services and resenting the percentage she had to pay the madam for each customer, Adams took to robbing the pockets of her patrons while they slept. She was evicted from the bordello and sank to the level of streetwalking a short time later.

One evening in 1702, Adams picked up a wealthy gentleman in Covent Garden and took him to a low brothel where she picked his pocket when he fell asleep. The man, unlike most other victims fearing to identify themselves, went to the police about the matter and Adams was arrested a few days later. She had many times earlier been accused of such pickpocketing but had always been released for lack of evidence. This time she was convicted on the victim's bold testimony and sentenced to death, her crime then being a capital offense in England.

While awaiting the execution, Adams was given a large cell in the Old Bailey where she was allowed to entertain many of her former customers who brought her food and wine. She entertained these gentlemen sexually and was paid handsomely, earning enough money to purchase a stunning, custom-made mourning gown in which to go to her execution. Taken to the hanging tree at Tyburn on June 16, 1702, Mary Adams seemed unconcerned about her fate, chatting with the cart driver taking her to the place of execution and, even with the rope around her neck, shaking out the wrinkles of her gown. Hundreds of citizens, including scores of Adams' former patrons, attended the public hanging and they applauded the doomed Mary's handsome appearance. Following her death, Adams was given a lavish funeral, one paid for by several of her former lovers.
REF.: *CBA*; Nash, *Look for the Woman*; *Newgate Calendar*.

Adams, Millicent, 1942- , U.S., mur. Socialite Millicent Adams, a post-debutante Bryn Mawr student, raised in upper-class comfort in Philadelphia, Pa., met engineering student Axel Schmidt and killed him when he jilted her for another more socially prominent woman. Schmidt was certainly a dedicated social climber, and his cruel treatment of Adams caused her first to think of suicide, or so she later claimed. But her destructive plan was one that evolved out of practice, not whim, since she bought a St. Bernard, took it to an unused servant's room in her family home and shot it with a .22-caliber Smith & Wesson which she had recently purchased. This scenario was enacted, it was later reported, to make sure that the weapon would work on its intended victim, herself.

Yet, when Adams went to bed with Schmidt for the last time in October 1962, the scorned woman turned the gun on Schmidt, not herself, shooting and killing him with a single, well-aimed bullet. Attorneys for Adams claimed that she had suffered a fit of temporary insanity. Adams pled guilty to manslaughter, but

there was a condition. If the court gave her a ten-year probational sentence, Adams would commit herself to a mental health center. The court surprisingly accepted this arrangement.

Adams gave birth to a child, Lisa, whose father was the man she had slain and she was allowed to visit the girl on weekends. At the end of three years, Adams was released and labelled "rehabilitated." She relocated to the West Coast where she moved in with wealthy relatives. Millicent Adams did not pay dearly for committing homicide; some might have labelled it a slight inconvenience for having done away with a trifling lover.
REF.: *CBA*; Nash, *Look for the Woman*.

Adams, Dr. Moses, prom. 1810s, Case of, U.S., mur. Dr. Moses Adams, who was also the sheriff of Hancock County, Maine, was accused of killing his wife by striking her in the neck with an ax and severing her jugular vein. The murder of Mary Adams occurred in Ellsworth, Maine, on May 12, 1815, and the body was found, it was estimated, about an hour after the killing. Mary Adams' body, discovered by a neighbor, was lying in bed, cold, the ax next to her, and the blood on the blade dry. Moses Adams, who was not present in the house when the body was found, was indicted on June 15, 1815, his trial taking place the following day. No motive for the murder could be established, and the case against Adams was so thinly circumstantial that a jury took only two hours to find him Not Guilty. The murder was never solved. Many Ellsworth residents, however, remained convinced that Adams, who had left his home on official business, secretly returned to murder his spouse with whom he had been arguing for several weeks.
REF.: Bullfinch, *The Trial of Moses Adams*; *CBA*.

Adams, Nick (Nicholas Adamshock), 1931-68, U.S., (unsolv.) mur.? He was a Hollywood actor who had struggled through some difficult times but whose career was on the upswing, so there was no apparent reason to suspect suicide when Adams' body was found at his Coldwater Canyon home in Los Angeles. Born to a Ukranian coal miner in poverty-stricken Appalachia, Adams changed his ethnic name, Adamshock, at the start of a show business career. A Coast Guardsman when *Mr. Roberts* was filmed at a Burbank, Calif., studio, Adams joined a group of sailor extras and took part in the shoot. He became a close friend of James Dean while playing a small role in *Rebel Without a Cause*. Dean's untimely death devastated Adams, who followed in Dean's tracks by imitating his delinquent style, even getting arrested nine times for reckless driving in one year.

Actor Nick Adams whose death in 1968 raised the specter of murder.

Then Adams met and married Carol Nugent and settled down to become a family man, fathering two children. He also starred in a successful television series, *The Rebel*, and worked steadily for two years. When the series was canceled, Adams went into a downward spiral, struggling to find even small parts, and eventually separating from and then divorcing Nugent. A painful battle for the children followed, with the actor winning custody. Soon after, he began getting movie roles again.

Adams had just returned from location work in Mexico and was on his way to start a film in Rome, when he called his close friend and attorney, Erwin Roeder, to arrange to meet for dinner. When the always punctual Adams did not show up for the Feb. 7, 1968 appointment, Roeder went to his friend's house and found him dead, sitting upright against a bedroom wall. According to a coroner's report, Adams had received sometime the night before a thirty-cubic-centimeter dose of paraldehyde, a powerful tranquilizer. Though the dose was not in itself lethal, it had been ingested in combination with "sedatives and other drugs" which had been found in Adams' body. A small amount of paraldehyde had been prescribed for Adams a few months earlier, but no trace of the drug could be found anywhere in his house—no empty prescription bottles or pills—nothing that might have held paraldehyde. Also there were no syringes or any other way the drug could have entered his body except by an oral dose, and, according to the coroner's testimony, the amount ingested would have caused immediate unconsciousness. Adams had just won custody of his children, and his career was improving for the better. The cause of his death remains a mystery.

REF.: *CBA;* Wolf, *Fallen Angels.*

Adams, Randall Dale, 1949-   , U.S., (wrong. convict.) mur. Adams is one who can say with conviction that a movie not only changed his life but saved it as well. On Nov. 28, 1976, Adams, a 27-year-old drifter from Ohio, hitched a ride with David Ray Harris, sixteen, a sociopathic teenager with a criminal record of assaults and theft. The two spent the day together smoking marijuana and drinking beer, later taking in a drive-in movie. Then, according to Adams, Harris dropped him off at the Comfort Motel, angry at the older man for not putting him up for the night. Harris, however, would later testify that the two continued to drive around the Dallas streets.

At 12:30 a.m. police officer Robert Wood, twenty-seven, and his partner, Teresa Turko, twenty-four, stopped a blue car to tell the driver to turn on his headlights. Turko stayed in the police car, sipping a milk shake. Wood walked up to the car and was killed by five bullets shot at point-blank range from a .22-caliber revolver. His murder remained unsolved for more than a month, when clues led police to Harris, then living in the small town of Vidor, Texas, where he had bragged to friends that he had "offed that pig in Dallas." Harris admitted that the murder weapon was a gun he stole from his father, and that he had been in the blue car, which he had stolen in Vidor, but he claimed that it was Adams who murdered Wood. Five months later, Adams, who had no criminal record, was convicted on the testimony of Harris and three eyewitnesses. Sentenced to die, he spent four years on Death Row, and escaped execution by only ten days in 1979, when Supreme Court Justice Lewis Powell intervened. In 1980 his sentence was commuted to life imprisonment on a technicality. He was transferred to the Eastham Unit Prison.

In 1985, Errol Morris, a documentary filmmaker who sometimes worked as a private detective, began research for a Public Broadcasting System film on Dallas psychiatrist Dr. James Grigson, popularly known as "Doctor Death" for his frequent diagnoses of murder suspects in death penalty cases. One of Grigson's clients was Adams. Morris began a three-year involvement in the case, logging over 200 interviews, including several with Harris and with three surprise witnesses, making a movie, *The Thin Blue Line,* in the process.

In Morris' first interview with Harris, the then 25-year-old told the filmmaker that he would never forget the look in the police officer's eyes as he walked up to the car. According to his testimony in court, Harris claimed he had been slumped down in the back seat when the shooting occurred. Other witnesses, particularly Emily Miller, gave testimony that conflicted with earlier statements. She said she had picked Adams out of a lineup, but, at a 1987 federal hearing, admitted she had picked out someone else and that a police officer had pointed Adams out to her later. Harris told the filmmaker on tape, "I know for a fact that Adams didn't do it. I'm the one that was there, so I should know." In September 1988, as Adams continued to serve a life sentence and wait for the case to be reopened, Harris said in a television interview that he had been alone in the car and had fired five shots. Because he was on Death Row for a subsequent murder by that time, his testimony would have meant little in court.

In November 1988, Harris, called as a witness at a hearing to reopen the case, admitted that his finger was on the trigger when the policeman was shot. The Death Row convict also explained that former Assistant District Attorney Doug Mulder, prosecutor at the 1976 trial, had promised him that he would "take care of" other criminal charges pending against Harris at that time in exchange for his testimony. In *The Thin Blue Line,* Harris goes into detail, explaining how he rehearsed his testimony extensively with lawyers. Appellate judges decided that prosecutor Mulder suppressed evidence and knowingly allowed perjured testimony at the trial. Following the December hearing, District Judge Larry Baraka said Adams did not receive a fair trial and wrote a letter supporting parole and recommending that the conviction be set aside.

On Mar. 1, 1989, the Texas Court of Criminal Appeals overturned Adams' conviction. When Adams was finally released, the wrongly convicted man, asked if he was bitter, replied: "I've had thirteen years taken from my life. Can the state replace that?" He will not be retried. On Apr. 6, 1989, Assistant Dallas County prosecutor Winfield Scott, who assisted in prosecuting Adams, was fired by District Attorney John Vance over "disagreements about the case." REF.: *CBA.*

Adams, William Nelson, 1902-   , Brit., mur. The case of 17-year-old William Adams and his murder of 60-year-old George Jones, is more than a curious one. On the evening of June 10, 1919, Adams, who had befriended the older man who had given him lodging in his room and bought him meals and drinks, was drinking with Jones and another man, Charlie Smith, in a Tooting pub. The trio left the pub late that night en route to Sutton when Adams stabbed Jones six times with a shoemaker's awl, three times in the throat and three times in the chest. Jones was later found half alive, wearing only his trousers and vest, his shirt wrapped awkwardly about his chest and neck as if someone had attempted to stop the flow of blood. Jones lived for three days and told police that he had no idea why Adams would want to hurt him, saying, "I had done nothing to him."

When Adams was finally arrested, he told another story, one with bizarre implications. He admitted that Jones had taken him in but had requested that Adams perform a special service in gratitude for his kindness—that the youth kill him. "I've done you a good turn," Adams quoted Jones as having said. "Now you do one for me. Will you kill me?" Adams went on to say that Jones was "worried out of his life" because he was facing a tax bill he could not pay. Adams said he would think about it and did, waiting a week until attacking Jones at the victim's own request in a Sutton park. He described how Jones removed his coat and hat, lying on the grass and handing the awl to Jones, saying, "The best way is to stab me in the left side of the neck."

Adams more or less hesitated but Jones kept urging him on. Charlie Smith, a man never found by police, watched the whole strange scene without participating. Finally, Adams worked up his nerve, he claimed, and stabbed the victim several times, but then tried to staunch the flow of blood by wrapping Jones's shirt around his wounds. He then took the victim's money and left the scene with Smith. Jones died on June 13, 1919, and Adams was charged with committing a homicide he labelled a "murder by request." The jury listening to Adam's odd story at the Guildford Assizes in July 1919, dismissed the cry of the defendant that he was "only trying to oblige the old gentleman" and found him Guilty. Adams was sentenced to death, but Edward Shortt, then Home Secretary, commuted the prisoner's sentence to life imprisonment.

REF.: Berrett, *When I Was At Scotland Yard; CBA;* Shew, *A Second Companion to Murder.*

Adamson, John Harvey, 1944- , U.S., mur. When an investigative reporter with information on Arizona land fraud and rampant underworld corruption in that state was killed by a car bomb in Phoenix in 1976, a $100,000 special prosecution fund was established to investigate the slaying. Adamson, a 32-year-old former tow-truck operator and sometime dog breeder, phoned Pulitzer prize-nominated investigative reporter Don Bolles on June

2, 1976, to say he would give Bolles information linking top Arizona Republicans to land fraud schemes. When Bolles rushed over to meet Adamson at the Phoenix Hotel, he found he had apparently been stood up. Returning to his car, the reporter was blown up by a crude dynamite bomb that exploded as he got into the vehicle.

Hanging on for eleven days and through six operations, losing both legs and his right arm, Bolles died on June 13, 1976. His last words were: "Mafia...Emprise ...They finally got me...John Adamson, find him." Two hours later, Adamson was arrested and charged with murder. At a preliminary hearing held under strict security on June 21 at the Maricopa County Superior Court, Adamson pleaded Not Guilty. The prosecution's two main witnesses were Robert Lettiere, an ex-convict who described driving to a parking lot with Adamson to look for Bolles' car five days before the fatal bombing, and Gail Owens, a former girlfriend of Adamson's who had been with

Investigative reporter Don Bolles, murdered for his news probes.

him when he bought a remote control device which he described as a gift for friend.

After a series of delays, including mistrials and moving the trial site due to pretrial publicity, Adamson pleaded guilty to planting the bomb. He escaped the death penalty in exchange for testimony against Max Dunlap and James Robison. According to Adamson, Dunlap, a wealthy contractor, and Robison, a plumber, detonated the bomb with a remote control radio transmitter used in model airplanes. Dunlap had also promised to help Adamson escape to Mexico after the killing, and to take care of his wife and child. Millionaire Arizona landowner and businessman Kemper Marley, Sr., angry about an article Bolles had written about Marley's alleged troubles with the law in 1942, found his name linked with Dunlap in Adamson's testimony. Dunlap and Robison were convicted of the murder of Bolles and were sentenced to death on Jan. 10, 1977, in Maricopa County Superior Court. Adamson is serving a twenty-year sentence for his part in the crime.

John Harvey Adamson, found guilty of Bolles' murder.

On Feb. 1, 1980, the Arizona Supreme Court overturned the convictions of Dunlap and Robison, on the grounds they were denied their constitutional right to face their accuser, Adamson. The Court further stated that Adamson had refused to answer certain questions and that the trial judge, Howard Thompson, had erred by denying a motion of the defense to strike all of Adamson's related testimony after Thompson declined to force him to answer.

In November 1980 Adamson was sentenced to die in the gas chamber for Bolles' murder. During the new proceedings, Adamson said in a shaking voice that he had fulfilled his agreement to testify against people who once were close associates and that was "a personal punishment far greater than any court could impose." In December 1988 a federal appeals court overturned Adamson's death sentence. The U.S. Court of Appeals for the

Ninth Circuit in San Francisco ruled that Adamson had been improperly sentenced by the Arizona Supreme Court because the trial judge had initially ruled that a prison term was the appropriate sentence for the murder. Later, the court imposed the death penalty only after Adamson violated a plea agreement requiring him to testify against Robison and Dunlap. The death penalty, the court said, also violated the right to a jury trial by allowing the judge to decide whether murder is a capital crime.

REF.: *CBA;* Wendland, *The Arizona Project.*

Adamson, Joy, See: **Ekai, Paul Wakwaro.**

Adcox, Dr. Robert, prom. 1920s, U.S., fraud. When a *St. Louis Star* reporter was assigned to establish a false identity and infiltrate a diploma mill scheme, he spent about five months and $3,000 to uncover the fraud. Dr. Adcox was a well-known St. Louis physician thought to be involved in the business of selling educational and medical degrees. In August 1923 the *Star* assigned Harry Thompson Brundige, a young reporter, to get a job as a salesman that would allow him to circulate freely in the city, and to break into the world of diplomas-by-mail. Brundige dropped his last name to become Harry Thompson, got a job as a coal salesman, and moved in next door to Adcock in Springfield, Mo., rapidly becoming friendly with his neighbor by pretending to come to him as a patient. When Brundige admired the doctor's lifestyle, Adcox invited him, for a price, to become a doctor, too. "If you are willing to spend your $1,000 to become a doctor, you are as good as a doctor right now," he said. The next day they left for Kansas City to visit Dr. Ralph A. Voight in Kansas City, who told Thompson that he could get him a high school diploma, three years credit from a medical school, and enrollment in the senior year course at Dr. R. Alexander's Kansas City College of Medicine and Surgery. After eight months of school, Thompson would get a diploma and be a full-fledged doctor, for a total fee, Voight explained, of $1,000.

After a series of cryptically coded telegrams announcing funds received, increases in costs, and various delays of high school diplomas and other licenses, Thompson met Voight again at the end of September, telling him he had decided not to go to school at all and insisted on receiving his diploma and license anyway. On Oct. 3, Voight gave the reporter a medical diploma and a license to practice in the state of Tennessee, making him "Harry Thompson, M.D." Thompson then decided to become a chiropractor, so Adcox and Voight arranged a meeting with Dr. Florence F. Baars. After two hours and twenty-two minutes and about $39.50 for fees and books, Thompson completed his studies. Another $89.50 for an adjusting table and spinal charts, and two additional hours of instruction prepared Thompson for his future career.

A few weeks later, he received his high school certificate by mail from the state superintendant of public instruction in Missouri and his Doctor of Medicine Degree from the National University of Arts and Sciences in St. Louis. On Oct. 15, 1923, the *St. Louis Dispatch* published the first of Brundige's articles and police arrested Voight, Adcox, Alexander, and Professor W.P. Sachs, a former examiner of Missouri schools. Sachs, who had been in the business of selling diplomas for eleven years, said he had sold around 5,000 bogus documents, mostly doctor's licenses. Voight explained that many of the degrees were purchased from the widows of recently deceased doctors who needed the cash. REF.: *CBA.*

Addicks, John Edward O'Sullivan, 1841-1919, U.S., graft. Businessman who attempted to win election as a U.S. Senator from Delaware through corrupt means but was defeated in 1906. His company eventually went into receivership and there were charges of fraud. REF.: *CBA.*

Addington, Sir Anthony, 1713-90, Brit., physician-toxicol. Addington's chief claim to historic fame in the annals of crime involved the Blandy case where he was called upon, as bad luck would have it for the murderess, Mary Blandy, to examine wealthy British attorney Francis Blandy who had been ailing for some time. Addington had been quietly studying poisons and their effects on humans for years, and he quickly suspected Blandy of being systematically poisoned by his daughter. It was he, long before Blandy died, who pointedly remarked to Miss Blandy that she would be in considerable trouble should her parent perish. When Blandy did die, Addington listed the cause as poisoning and volunteered his services to the prosecution.

In the year 1752, toxicology was an infant science and no one from that medical realm had ever provided testimony in a British murder case. Yet the courts accepted Addington's offer which it undoubtedly looked upon as an experiment rather than as evidence from an expert witness. Addington, in court, provided a rather crude but effective demonstration in proving that Mary Blandy had indeed poisoned her father with arsenic sent to her by her lover, Captain William Cranstoun, a conniving rake whose only designs were for Mary's considerable dowry. Of course, the physician had no way of examining the victim's organs to determine contents of poison nor did any chemical tests then exist by which it could be proved that the powder Mary admitted dumping into her father's port was aresenic; she called it a "love philtre" used to soften her father's heart toward Cranstoun whom he had rejected as an acceptable suitor.

But Addington's simple demonstration was nevertheless electrifying. He stated emphatically that the dregs from Mary's philtre and some grains found in the victim's remains were identical in color, both white for white arsenic. He also tasted both samples, a few grains each, by dropping this on his tongue while court spectators gasped. Both, insisted Addington, tasted alike. But there was more. Addington produced a white-hot iron (some reports claim it was a poker, even more dramatic accounts insist it was a sword, as in sword of vengeance). As judge, jury, the crowd, and Mary Blandy herself, stared in shock, Addington held up some grains taken from her father's body and threw these upon the searing iron. The grains sizzled and gave off a small cloud of smoke. He then held up grains taken from Mary's philtre and did likewise. Again a small puff of smoke. In both instances, the same powerful smell permeated the court, an evil smelling garlicky odor which all present instantly realized was identical. It was a stench that made British legal history. At the end of his demonstration, Addington triumphantly proclaimed, "Never have I observed two things in nature more alike!" Mostly on the strength of this sensational performance, Mary Blandy was convicted, sentenced to death and sent to the gallows on Apr. 6, 1852. Though it would be many decades before toxicologists would refine the primative methods of Addington (later knighted), forensic medicine became a permanent fixture in criminal trials. See: **Blandy, Mary.**

REF.: *CBA*; Kobler, *Some Like It Gory*; Nash, *Look for the Woman*; Roughead, *Tales of the Criminous.*

Addison, Jack, b.c.1688-1711, Brit., asslt.-rob. He could not continue to work as a butcher and keep the woman he loved in the luxury she desired, so Addison turned to crime to please Kate Speed, known in the village of Lambeth as a prostitute and thief. He then committed some of the most daring robberies of his time, victimizing both rich and poor alike. His victims' only consolation was the knowledge that they had lost their money to a thief with a wry sense of humor and an appreciation of the absurd.

One day Addison robbed a minister of five guineas on the road between Westbourne Green and Paddington. "Sir, if you can tell me what part of speech your gold is, I'll return it all," said Addison, enjoying the joke. After some thought, the parson said it had to be a noun substantive. "No, no," Addison laughed. "You are out now. I perceive you are a no good grammarian, for where your gold is at present it is a noun adjective, because it can neither be seen, felt, heard, nor understood." With that, Addison fled.

After fifty-six successful robberies—all committed on foot— Addison was betrayed by Will Jewel, a highwayman serving time at the Marshalsea Prison in Southwark. This poetic footpad, who had spun endless verses for his victims, was arrested in 1711. He was tried, condemned to death according to the prevailing law for robbery, and hanged at Tyburn on Mar. 23, 1711.

REF.: *CBA;* Smith, *Highwaymen.*

Addonizio, Hugh J., prom. 1960s, U.S., polit. corr.-org. crime. Addonizio was the mayor of Newark, N.J., who was convicted on conspiracy charges wherein he took kickbacks from Mafia bosses who controlled his city (not to mention the state) with his more-than-nodding approval. In the late 1960s, the FBI, conducting a widespread investigation into Mafia-syndicate operations in New Jersey, planted scores of wires in the offices of the state's leading crime bosses. When a federal judge ordered that the Bureau make the tapes taken from these wires public, Addonizio's involvement with the Mafia became evidently clear.

One taped conversation snared by FBI agents involved Mafia boss Angelo De Carlo and his lieutenant, Joseph De Benedictis. De Carlo was overheard to tell De Benedictis: "Hughie (Addonizio) helped us along. He gave us the city." In return for allowing the mob to operate freely in Newark, Addonizio received kickbacks from the state's crime cartel, as well as received the dubious benefit of the Mafia's electioneering. Rival candidates who were running against Addonizio were scared off, one of them told by De Carlo: "I'll be the guy to break your legs!"

Crooked Newark, N.J. mayor Hugh Addonizio, left, with actress Sophia Loren and unknown friend at a Washington, D.C. party.

Addonizio, mayor of the thirteenth largest city in America, had served fourteen years in Congress, which caused the shock of his constituents to run deep. He and a dozen other public officials were indicted by a grand jury that charged Addonizio and others had shared $1.5 million in kickbacks extorted by Mafia thugs from contractors doing business with the city of Newark. Federal prosecutor Frederick B. Lacey stated: "The plunder was unmatched by anything in my experience." In his summation to the jury hearing Addonizio's case, Lacey said the Newark mayor and hid co-defendants had practiced "cold-blooded, calculating, contemptuous corruption."

The Newark mayor was convicted before Federal District Judge George H. Barlow, who described Addonizio's blatant graft as that of a "monumental proportion that tore at the very heart of our civilized society and our form of representative government...The corruption disclosed here is compounded by the frightening alliance of criminal elements and public officials." He sentenced Addonizio to ten years imprisonment. The mayor appealed but lost and began serving his sentence in 1972. Others caught in the 1969 FBI taping dragnet included Thomas J. Whelan, mayor of Jersey City, who was convicted of conspiring with Mafia figures to extort money from firms doing business with the city and county governments of New Jersey, and John R. Armellino, mayor of

West New York City, N.J., who was convicted and sentenced to four years in prison for protecting the gambling operations of the Mafia.

REF.: *CBA; Gage, Mafia, USA.*

Adler, Friedrich, See: **Stürgkh, Karl von.**

Adler, John (AKA: Jakey, Jakie), prom. 1910s-20s, U.S., org. crime-pros. Adler had long been associated with Chicago's red light district as a panderer and pimp until he became a lieutenant under the command of Big Jim Colisimo. From 1909 to the end of the 1920s, Adler was a contact man between the brothel operators of Chicago and the police and politicians. He received enormous amounts of cash and split this with the mob boss of the day, first Colisimo, then Torrio, then Capone, sending payoffs to politicians who protected the Levee district and the police who seldom made raids and, even then, only token sorties into the vice area. Adler later invested some of his considerable forture in the nightclub business but became the prey of other gangsters who, in the 1920s, took to kidnapping wealthy underworld figures and holding them for enormous ransom payments as in the case of George Jean "Big Frenchy" DeMange in New York. Adler and his partner Sapho Jo Lawro, proprietors of the Midnight Frolics Cafe in Chicago, were abducted by members of the O'Donnell Gang (southside) and taken blindfolded to a boarding house in early May 1927. Here Adler and Lawro were each chained to a bed in the same room for five days, their captors pistol-whipping them until they agreed to pay $100,000 for their release. The nightclub owners did not report the extortion and kidnapping to police since the pair had "done something shady themselves and dared not appeal" to authorities, according to one report. See: **Capone, Alphonse; Colosimo, James; Madden, Owen; O'Donnell Gang** (southside); **Torrio, John.** REF.: *CBA.*

Adler, Lydia, b.1704, Brit., mur. Ill-tempered since childhood, Adler became the fourth wife of merchant John Adler and not a moment's peace did they share, forever battling through knock-down brawls in which Lydia always bested her bruised husband. Big-boned and muscular, Mrs. Adler was able to throw her husband to the ground where she liberally applied her boots to his stomach. During one such encounter, John Adler was so severely wounded by his wife that he was taken to the hospital. He railed against his brutal spouse, calling on the police to arrest the woman. Adler lingered in pain for twelve days, then died on June 23, 1744, his last cry being, "Do you have the warrant yet?" A few hours later the warrant for Lydia Adler was issued and she was quickly tried at the Old Bailey.

It appeared that the woman would be found guilty and promptly hanged until a physician, Dr. Goodman, testified that John Adler was already suffering from a hernia condition and that blows from his wife's boot did not necessarily cause his death, although the doctor did not say whether or not the original rupture was caused by the boot-stomping Lydia. Mrs. Adler was convicted of manslaughter and met a relatively lenient punishment. She was branded on the hand as a common scold and sent on her way.

REF.: *CBA; Nash, Look for the Woman.*

Adler, Polly (Pearl), 1900-62, U.S., pros. The name of Polly Adler and prostitution in the U.S. were synonymous for more than twenty years. She was the most infamous madam in New York City, identified as such by the celebrated Seabury Investigations of the 1930s. Yet, aside from some brief thirty-day stints in jail, Adler suffered little at the hands of the law. In fact, thanks to her police contacts and considerable payoffs, she flourished, protected by police sworn to close operations such as hers. Born Pearl Adler in Yanow, Rus., near the Polish border on Apr. 16, 1900, Adler immigrated to the U.S. at an early age and was working in a factory before WWI. In 1920, after being a dime-a-dance girl for some years, Adler opened her first bordello—a small apartment. Her business stemmed from Broadway gigolos and stagedoor johnnies, and her staff consisted of three girls and two servants. So good was business that Adler soon moved into another apartment, then another, each one more lavishly furnished

than the last, until her most celebrated brothel was located in the posh Fifties.

Except for a brief episode in 1921, when she attempted to "go legitimate" by opening a lingerie shop (losing $6,000 and most of her stock to slick shoplifters), Adler would remain in prostitution until her retirement in 1944. Many celebrities, from Harry Richman to Wallace Beery (social friends only, according to Adler's memoirs, *A House Is Not a Home*) paid homage to the queen of bordellos. Throughout the Roaring Twenties, Adler was known in inner circles as the madam of the "safest house" in New York. She was likened to the fame of nightclub hostess Texas Guinan and took pride in offering beautiful girls—culled from nightclub choruses and Broadway shows—to wealthy, socialite clients, movie stars, and political sachems. Male customers were assured with certificates from doctors that their female companions for the evening were free of venereal diseases.

New York Madam Pearl Adler.

One of Adler's most insatiable customers was the notorious beer baron, Dutch Schultz (Arthur Fleggenheimer) who visited her West 54th Street bordello at least twice a week, despite the fact that he was married and supported two mistresses. Even when a police dragnet was thrown throughout the state of New York in 1934 for Schultz, he casually called on the much protected Adler and her beauteous ladies. So at home was he is this bordello that Adler once returned from shopping in the early afternoon one day to find the fierce bootlegger sitting in her spacious kitchen, munching on a chicken leg and reading Fred Pasley's biography of Al Capone. When quizzed about his reading habits, Schultz snorted, put down the book and told Adler, "I'm learning how not to make the kind of moves that put this guy in the can."

In the late 1920s, Adler, along with all other substantial brothel madams were recruited into the prostitutional empire built by Charles "Lucky" Luciano. The top crime boss and one of the original organizers of the U.S. crime syndicate began organizing coast-to-coast brothel operations as early as 1928, paying off police and politicians for protection and getting fifty percent of all income from the bordellos he controlled—including Adler's operation. Hundreds of pimps in New York City alone were under his direction and only the wealthiest of these were sent to Adler's operation or that of Gay Orlova's. Luciano denied to his dying day that he ever had anything to do with operating the American bordello empire. He was merely a customer, he claimed. "I done a lot of things in my life," he once said, "but I never had nothin' to do with makin' money outa whores...I didn't have time for a wife. Besides, I always figured that someday I was gonna wind up on a slab and I didn't want to leave a widow and kids cryin' over me. So when I wanted to get some, I used to turn to Gay Orlova or Polly Adler."

Adler, for her part, even when pressured by the Seabury investigators in the early 1930s, refused to even name Luciano as her boss, let alone a customer. Her silence was rewarded by Luciano with a larger percentage of the profits and certainly her life since the vice lord's scores of goons had orders to murder any girl in the organization cooperating with investigators. In 1935, however, vice raids throughout the city brought Polly into a police station crammed with hundreds of her sisters in the trade. The subsequent vice investigations caused Luciano's downfall and sensationalized Adler's name, even though she would only receive a thirty-day term. Luciano received a long prison term. It was

Polly's notorious black book, seized in the raid, that showed the police and political backing she received, along with the names of scores of her famous clients who habitually called—as did Luciano—her phone number, LExington 2-1099, to order up her girls.

Once exposed, Adler's fortunes began to dip, and she experienced regular harrassment and numerous arrests until she decided to retire with her considerable fortunes which were supplemented with royalties from her best-selling autobiography published in 1950. In this less-than-lurid and surprisingly proper book, Adler whitewashed her vice activities, stating: "I didn't invent sex, nobody had to come to my apartment who didn't want to. I was really doing them a favor." The queen of the brothels died on June 10, 1962. See: **Luciano, Charles; Schultz, Dutch; Seabury Investigations.**

REF.: Adler, *A House Is Not a Home;* CBA; Feder, *The Luciano Story;* Gosch, *The Last Testament of Lucky Luciano;* Henriques, *Prostitution in Europe and the Americas;* Mitgang, *The Man Who Rode the Tiger;* Nash, *Hustlers and Con Men;* ____, *Look for the Woman;* Powell, *Ninety Times Guilty;* Sann, *Kill the Dutchman!;* ____, *The Lawless Decade;* (FILM) *A House Is Not a Home,* 1964.

Adomeit, Kurt, 1953-   , and **Adomeit, Ursula, (Ursula Richter),** 1952-   , Ger., mur. Not much rippled the surface of life in Meppen—a dot on the map of West Germany—until July 1, 1975, when Kurt Adomeit led the local police to a shallow grave that held the remains of a man he had murdered nearly three years before. On June 6, 1972, Ursula Richter reported her husband, George Richter, missing. An ex-con then awaiting trial for burglary, Richter married Ursula when she was thirteen and would beat her at the slightest provocation. They had four daughters by the time she was twenty and, to make ends meet, took in boarders, one of whom was Kurt Adomeit.

Adomeit and Ursula became lovers, and knowing Richter would never consent to a divorce, soon hatched a plot to kill him. First, Ursula slipped several sleeping pills into his tea. No reaction. Then she increased the dosage. Still nothing. Then she and Adomeit tried rat poison, which only elicited from Richter an uncharacteristic compliment on the seasoning of that night's supper. Drastic measures were called for. So on the night of May 13, 1972, when Ursula was certain Richter was asleep, she summoned Adomeit to bludgeon the man over the head with a hatchet and later bury him in the Esterfield Forest.

Ursula later divorced her husband for desertion and married Adomeit. Soon after, however, on the day Adomeit began serving a sentence at Osnabrueck Jail on a charge of fraud, Ursula began bringing new lovers home. Hearing the news from a cellmate at Osnabrueck, Adomeit wasted no time getting to the police, once he was out of jail, to expose the skeleton of husband number one. Because of Georg Richter's brutality, the courts were lenient with Ursula and Adomeit. On Nov. 12, 1975, they each received ten years imprisonment within the terms of the juvenile code under which they had been tried. REF.: *CBA.*

Adonis, Joseph (Guiseppe Antonio Doto, AKA: Joey A. Adone; Joe Arosa; James Arosa; Joe DeMio), 1902-72, U.S., org. crime. For three decades Joe Adonis was one of the most powerful crime figures in America, a member of the board of the national syndicate in New York, one whose influence and status was equal to Charles "Lucky" Luciano, Vito Genovese, Carlo Gambino and Louis "Lepke" Buchalter. Through bootlegging, gambling, extortion, bribery, prostitution, and murder, along with widespread investments in legitimate businesses, Adonis became many times a millionaire. He was also vain about his dark good looks and envisioned himself the prototype of the Latin lovers popular on the silent screen. (Actor George Raft, who had driven beer trucks for New York mobsters in the early 1920s, and had met Adonis, was so taken with his style of dress, posture, and attitudes that he mimicked the gangster effectively for the screen, taking on Adonis' personality to portray the tough guy.) Adonis was a thief to his bone marrow. Even after this crime kingpin had accumulated a gigantic fortune, he could not resist the temptation to involve

himself in cheap jewelry heists, such was his insatiable lust to commit a crime.

Born on Nov. 22, 1902, in the small town of Montemarano, Italy, near Naples, Adonis immigrated to the U.S. in 1915, entering the country illegally. (Another story has it that Adonis immigrated to the U.S. with his parents, and his father forgot to take out citizenship papers for his infant son, an error that would proved disastrous for Adonis in later life.) He lived in the poorest section of Brooklyn where he began his career in crime, from petty theft to extortion of shopkeepers and armed robbery. In his criminal pursuits, Adonis met another young thug with high ambitions, Charles "Lucky" Luciano whom Adonis befriended and would later serve with unswerving loyalty. Both youths involved themselves in petty rackets, especially prostitution, pimping for a few whores while establishing cheap gambling dens. Adonis was an aggressive womanizer and, in 1922, when one young, attractive female refused his advances, Adonis raped her. He was later arrested for this crime but Adonis by that time had enlisted in the Brooklyn gang headed by the powerful Frankie Yale. Through Yale's lawyers, Adonis was freed.

It is unclear how Adonis changed his name. One story has it that one of his prostitutes stated that he was so handsome that he "looked like a young Adonis." Another story has it that Adonis was browsing through a magazine and came upon a reference of Adonis of Greek mythology and adopted the name himself. As soon as his criminal pursuits began to pay off, Adonis lavished upon himself an expensive wardrobe of custom-tailored tight-fitting suits. He was forever combing his pomaded hair and primping before mirrors. On one occasion, Luciano caught Adonis combing his dark thick hair before a mirror and said: "Who do you think you are, Rudolph Valentino?" Adonis turned around with a snarl he had begun to perfect, along with a whisper which slipped from the side of his mouth, and replied, "For looks, that guy's a bum!"

With the dawn of Prohibition, dozens of punk gangsters suddenly became overnight millionaires and underworld power-houses as they leaped headlong into the new racket of bootlegging. Adonis was one of these. He had been offered a huge shipment of smuggled liquor by another rising bootlegger named Irving Wexler, later known as Waxey Gordon, at cut-rate prices. Luciano put up the original investment monies, about $35,000, and both Adonis and Luciano traveled by train to Philadelphia to make the deal and pick up the shipment. (Luciano had borrowed the money from Meyer Lansky and Benjamin "Bugsy" Siegel of the Bug and Meyer Mob, and Frank Costello, all rising young mobsters.) With the profits of this booze shipment, Luciano and Adonis went into the bootlegging business on their own in Brooklyn and branched out into Manhattan, although they continued to serve their Mafia masters. Adonis served Frankie Yale as an enforcer for his rackets in Brooklyn and Luciano went to work for the then boss of bosses in New York, Joe "The Boss" Masseria.

The showy gangster, who quickly became known as Joey A., developed his own gang of bootleggers which began to serve the show crowd along the Great White Way and this gang soon became known as the Broadway Mob. Adonis affected the role of the gentleman bootlegger, dressing nattily and speaking with a cultured accent which he picked up from the high society patrons who purchased his expensive liquor. He also invested his money in an old-fashioned restaurant called Joe's Italian Kitchen which served the best in Italian cuisine and catered to local politicians. Waiters served these customers envelopes filled with cash which were placed beneath their plates. The politicians would, without comment, pocket the payments and thus went on to the payroll of Joe Adonis who thereafter was known as "Mr. Fix." He paid off judges, police captains, the sachems of city hall, and, in return, went unmolested by police when he and his men operated their wide-open rackets. On those rare occasions when Adonis was arrested, he was quickly released. His restaurant patrons included Francis J. Quayle, sheriff of Brooklyn, later fire commissioner for New York; Brooklyn undersheriff James J. Ambro; Judge David

Adonis under arrest, 1956.

Adonis testifying before the Kefauver Committee.

NYPD photo of Joe Adonis, rising crime boss, 1937.

New York crime czar Adonis, on board the luxury liner *SS Conti Biancamano*, being deported back to Italy, 1956.

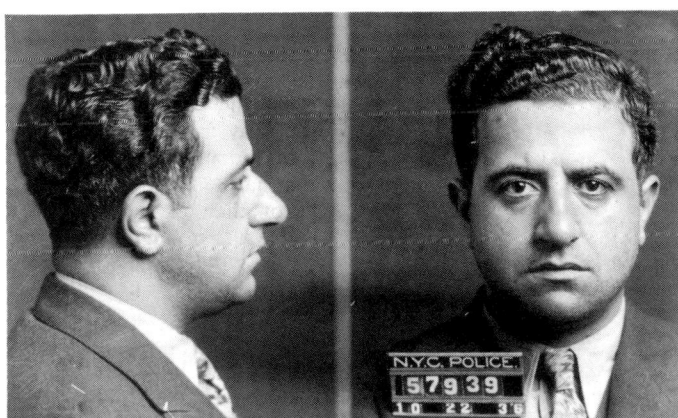

Fierce killer Albert Anastasia who headed Murder, Inc. and enforced Adonis' edicts.

Joe "The Boss" Masseria, murdered by Adonis and three others in 1931.

NYPD photo of Frank Costello, Adonis' underboss.

I. Malbin; James V. Mangano, who later became sheriff of Kings County; and Patrick J. Diamond, Democratic district leader of the Eighth Assembly District, Adonis' area.

Adonis would spread his influence throughout the entire New York City area so that most of the local politicians and high-ranking police officials were, in one way or another, on his payroll. He shared his political influence with Luciano, Lansky, Siegel, and Buchalter so that their many rackets were protected by the scores of bribed government officials. Years later, before the Kefauver Committee investigating racketeering in the U.S., Ambro testified that Irwin Steingut, who became Democratic minority leader in the state senate, was a frequent visitor to Joe's Italian Kitchen as was William O'Dwyer, who was to prosecute members of Murder, Inc. a decade later and subsequently become mayor of New York. Ambro stated that O'Dwyer's entire political career was arranged at the tables of Adonis' restaurant.

By the early 1930s, Adonis, not yet thirty, was gleaning an estimated $10 million a year from his rackets. He began to invest heavily in legitimate businesses, buying several swanky restaurants along the Atlantic coastline, acquiring two huge liquor distributing dealerships (this after Prohibition was repealed and drinking liquor became legal), and three auto agencies. As the cash rolled in from both legal and illegal operations, Adonis kept expanding into the legitimate world, buying controlling interest in the Automotive Conveying Company, of Cliffside Park, N.J. This firm, as Joey A. learned before buying most of the company's stock, had a monopoly on distributing all new cars produced in the Ford Motor plant in Edgewater, N.J. Adonis' firm, using huge trailers, had the exclusive distribution of Ford cars to the states of Connecticut, Delaware, District of Columbia, Massachusetts, New Jersey, New York, Pennsylvania, Vermont, and Virginia. This firm was paid more than $8 million by Ford for delivering its cars from 1932 to 1949, the lion share of the profits going into the pockets of Joe Adonis. The gangster also purchased several cigarette vending machine companies and, to insure his success, ordered wholesale hijacking of cigarette trucks. From 1934 to 1937 his gangsters stole more than $6 million in cigarettes which were placed into Adonis' machines for 100 percent profit.

Though Joey A. made so much money from his various rackets and legal enterprises that he spent most of his time trying to hide it from the prying eyes of the IRS, he nevertheless found time to attend to mob business and the duties that accompanied his position on the board of directors of the national syndicate, the nation-wide crime cartel he, Luciano, and others established in the late 1920s. One of these chores, which established Adonis as one of the new leaders of the embryonic national syndicate, was the murder of an old-fashioned mob leader, Joe "The Boss" Masseria, on Apr. 15, 1931. Adonis' friend Luciano, who had worked for Masseria, decided to desert his mob sponsor to effect a truce with Salvatore Maranzano, a Sicilian boss who intended to kill off all opposition and consolidate all the New York mobs under his direct command, becoming the boss of bosses. Luciano would then assume leadership of Masseria's far-flung rackets and be in a position to kill Maranzano later and assume total mob leadership. This was the first step in establishing the national crime cartel he envisioned with selected peers—including Adonis.

Luciano lured Masseria to one of his favorite restaurants, Scarpato's, which was not incidentally located in Coney Island, Brooklyn. This was squarely in territory which Adonis controlled. On the night of the murder, Luciano dined late with Joe the Boss, stalling until the restaurant was almost empty, then excused himself and retreated to the washroom where he locked the door and sat down to await the results of his planning. Within minutes, as Masseria forked down some last rolls of linguine and clam sauce, four men entered Scarpato's. The manager and employees had vanished and the foursome approached Joe the Boss who looked up and smiled, giving them a friendly wave for he knew them all as young, successful gangsters. They were Joe Adonis, Vito Genovese, Albert Anastasia and Benjamin "Bugsy" Siegel. Without a word to Masseria, each man withdrew a pistol and fired almost point blank into the head of Joe the Boss who crashed forward into his linguine. Anastasia stepped behind the bent, bleeding figure and fired another shot into the back of Masseria's head, the *coup de grace*. The four men pocketed their weapons and walked leisurely out of Scarpato's.

Luciano waited until police arrived before stepping from the washroom to insist that Masseria was his good friend and that he had been washing his hands when the killing took place. He was not charged. By helping Luciano eliminate his superior, Adonis, along with the others, secured a place on the board of Luciano's national crime cartel, established that year. This was certainly not Adonis' first murder; he had, by police estimates, killed more than twenty men in mob wars during the 1920s. He would order the deaths of dozens more in the crime wars to follow, although most of the official killings committed by the syndicate were carried out by Murder, Inc., which was controlled by Anastasia who worked under the direction of Louis "Lepke" Buchalter.

Just as Luciano had to eradicate his superior to take over New York prostitution, gambling, and narcotics, Adonis had to deal with his nominal boss of Brooklyn, Little Augie Pisano who had ruled Brooklyn under the old Mafia regime during the 1920s. But with the death of Masseria, Pisano, who had been a satellite for Joe the Boss, realized that his crime boss days were numbered in Brooklyn. Adonis met with Pisano and suggested that Florida would be an ideal area for permanent retirement, reminding Pisano that he had purchased control of a swanky hotel there. Pisano nodded and said that he would be leaving for Miami soon. In 1933, Little Augie departed Brooklyn to oversee his Miami hotel, leaving what remained of his rackets to Adonis. Joey A., although he set up several lavish living quarters in New York and New Jersey, continued to operate his crime empire from Joe's Italian Kitchen, in the back of which, protected by steel entrance doors, alarms, and heavily armed guards, could be found his richly appointed offices. Here Adonis met with other members of the syndicate, his lieutenants in planning and operating his rackets, and held court over unruly members of his mob, meting out punishments and, if served well, rewarding his hoodlums with cash and possessions.

All narcotics traffic in Brooklyn was controlled by Adonis from 1933 until his deportation in 1956. A levy was placed against all heroin and opium shipments, and fifty percent of all sales went into Joey A.'s coffers. Ever the thug, Adonis kept tabs on all those purchasing expensive cars through his car agencies. Anyone planning to buy a Cadillac was designated as a likely candidate for extortion, and many of these car buyers received phone messages that informed them that the caller knew that the potential car buyer was planning to spend $10,000 on a new car and could afford to pay another $10,000 to prevent his home or office from being blown up or his children kidnapped. These victims were invariably Italian or Sicilian who had grown up with the tactics of the Black Hand extortion practices of the turn of the century and they took such threats seriously. Most paid without informing the police. Those who did complain to the police wound up talking to officers already on Adonis' payroll, for the most part, and received no protection. The result was that the informant was either brutally beaten or sometimes killed.

When Luciano was convicted of extortion, prostitution, and racketeering in 1936, Adonis was appointed the caretaker of his dominion, and Joey A. loyally kept watch over Charlie Lucky's enterprises, securing millions annually for his boyhood chum and dutifully banking these enormous profits in U.S. and foreign banks under aliases. The Luciano operations were actually run by Frank Costello but it was Adonis' duty to make sure that Costello turned over Luciano's share. With Anastasia and his killer legions of Murder, Inc. to back him up, Adonis was never questioned by Costello when monthly payments were made to Luciano's coffers. Moreover, Luciano had early on established another deep friendship with Meyer Lansky, the shrewd, low-profiled Jewish gangster who was the financial adviser to the national crime syndicate. "Cooperate with Meyer," were the last words uttered by Luciano to Adonis before Charlie Lucky went off to prison.

Although Adonis kept faith with Luciano, his natural avariciousness caused him to look southward with greedy eyes to New Jersey which was the province of Abner "Longy" Zwillman, a Prohibition-type bootlegger who had run the rackets in the state for years along with the Moretti Brothers, Willie and Solly. Joey A., and his enforcer, Anastasia, invited themselves to New Jersey, and here Adonis made a deal with Zwillman and the Moretti Brothers. He would finance the establishment of dozens of swank casinos and they would protect these operations from police interference, having local cops in most smaller communities on their payroll. In return, the New Jersey gangsters would get a slice of the spoils. Adonis bankrolled millions to establish scores of lavish gambling dens inside of old warehouses which were left shabby on the outside but with remodeled interiors that made high society patrons gasp with appreciation when entering. The inside of these casinos were appointed with rich tapestries, carpets, and dining areas serviced by waiters in tuxedoes and cigarette girls as attractive and alluring as could be found in the best nightclubs on Broadway. Adonis simply moved New York style and decor to New Jersey and his operations blossomed. Hundreds of thrill-seeking high rollers were driven by limousines to these casinos for a night's outing where they would gladly drop tens of thousands of dollars at roulette and blackjack tables. The casinos, which Adonis began opening in 1942, brought many more millions each year to his accounts.

FBI agents later investigating Adonis' far-flung rackets estimated that he and his junior partner, Willie Moretti, were gleaning $100,000 a week from one casino alone in West Patterson, N.J. The total amount each year from the casinos, the vast bookmaking operations Adonis controlled in New York and New Jersey, and the policy or numbers games he also partially controlled in both areas may have yielded as much as $100 million each year. One restaurant, Duke's Restaurant in Cliffside Park, reportedly designed by Adonis himself, a resplendent place with chandeliers and imported carpets, served as Joey A.'s New Jersey headquarters from 1944 until the gangster's deportation. By that time, New York authorities had exposed Murder, Inc., particularly through the detailed confessions of Abe "Kid Twist" Reles. Anastasia's murder troop had fallen apart, leaving Adonis' Brooklyn operations vulnerable to both the law and the covetous invasion of gangsters under the direction of Vito Genovese. (It was Reles who pinpointed Adonis as one of the most powerful crime czars in America when he stated, "Cross Joey Adonis and you cross the national combination!" Up to that time Adonis had been thought of in law enforcement circles as a successful Broadway racketeer, no more.) Adonis felt it safer to be in New Jersey and moved there permanently, allowing Genovese to eliminate, one after another, his former associates, including the feared Anastasia.

Yet the law reached out to Adonis when he was brought before the Kefauver Committee where he repeatedly refused to answer questions concerning his racketeering, endlessly taking the Fifth Amendment. The canny gangster kingpin did make one mistake, however, by stating that he had been born in Pasaic, N.J. in 1901. Adonis returned to his gambling empire, but his exposé by Kefauver caused New Jersey authorities to finally bring gambling charges against Joey A. He was tried, found Guilty, and sentenced to two to three years in the state prison at Trenton. The law was still not through with him. Officials checked Adonis' background and found that he had been born in Italy and had never become an American citizen. Adonis tried to make deals with the government, but his deportation to his native Italy was ordered by U.S. Attorney General Herbert Brownell, Jr. on Aug. 5, 1953. The wily gangster spent a fortune on expensive lawyers who delayed this action until Jan. 3, 1956, when Joe Adonis, nee Guiseppe Doto, was escorted aboard the luxury liner SS Conte Biancamano where he entered a suite of rooms usually reserved for royalty. He sailed for Italy in style, with many millions of dollars and a swanky villa outside Milan waiting for him. Before the ship sailed, newsmen interviewed the rags-to-riches syndicate

chieftain, asking him if he intended to visit with Lucky Luciano, who had also been deported to Italy some years earlier. With a blank expression on his still darkly handsome face the mass killer snapped, "I have no plans to look him up and I hope he doesn't look me up."

It was later speculated that Luciano and Adonis had fallen out over Adonis' failure to check the ruthless takeover of New York rackets and the killing off of old Luciano stalwarts by Genovese killers, something else Adonis did nothing to prevent. Although the two men did not meet, according to records, throughout their exiles in Italy, Adonis did attend Luciano's funeral in 1962, after the crime czar died at the Naples airport while greeting an American film producer who planned to make a movie about him. Adonis requested permission to attend the funeral of his boyhood friend and was allowed to go to Naples. He appeared, teary-eyed, carrying a floral wreath which read in true gangster tradition: "Goodbye, old pal." Adonis, alone, but living in wealth, was not again heard from until 1972. At the time, Italian police making widespread arrests against all known Mafia figures, dragged Adonis from his posh Milan living quarters and took him to a remote hillside location for questioning. It was reported that he died of a heart attack during this unorthodox if not justifiable interrogation. What remained of the reportedly vast fortune Adonis had secreted away on the continent was never revealed. One New York detective who had waged war against Adonis and his army of goons during the palmy days of these early day crime moguls remarked, "The millions Joey A. took out of the county didn't do him a damned bit of good in the end. He waded through blood to get it and he croaked with empty pockets in a dirty shack." See: **Anastasia, Albert; Costello, Frank; Genovese, Vito; Lansky, Meyer; Luciano, Charles; Maranzano, Salvatore; Masseria, Guiseppe; Moretti, Willie; Murder, Inc.; O'Dwyer, William; Pisano, Augie; Reles, Abraham; Siegel, Benjamin; Zwillman, Abner.**

REF.: Albini, *The American Mafia;* Allsop, *The Bootleggers;* Anderson, *The Business of Organized Crime;* Blumenthal, *Last Days of the Sicilians;* Bonanno, *A Man of Honor;* Browning and Gerassi, *The American Way of Crime;* Campbell, *The Luciano Project;* Carpozi, *Bugsy;* CBA; Chandler, *Brothers in Blood;* Cohen, *In My Own Words;* Cook, *The FBI Nobody Knows;* ____, *Mafia!;* Cressey, *Theft of the Nation;* Dewey, *Twenty Against the Underworld;* Eisenberg, *Meyer Lansky, Mogul of the Mob;* Feder, *The Luciano Story;* Frasca, *King of Crime;* Fried, *The Rise and Fall of the Jewish Gangster in America;* Gage, *The Mafia is not an Equal Opportunity Employer;* ____, *Mafia, U.S.A.;* Gorman, *Kefauver: A Political Biography;* Gosch, *The Last Testament of Lucky Luciano;* Jennings, *We Only Kill Each Other;* Katcher, *The Big Bankroll;* Katz, *Uncle Frank;* Kefauver, *Crime in America;* Kobler, *Capone;* Lewis, *The Honored Society;* Lyle, *The Dry and Lawless Years;* McClellan, *Crime Without Punishment;* McPhaul, *Johnny Torrio;* Maas, *The Valachi Papers;* Maclean, *A Pictorial History of the Mafia;* Martin, *Revolt in the Mafia;* Messick, *Lansky;* ____, *The Private Lives of Public Enemies;* ____, *Secret File;* ____, *Silent Syndicate;* ____ and Goldblatt, *The Mobs and the Mafia;* Nash, *Almanac of World Crime;* ____, *Bloodletters and Badmen;* Nelli, *The Business of Crime;* Peterson, *Barbarians in Our Midst;* ____, *The Mob;* Pileggi, *Wiseguy;* Reid, *The Grim Reapers;* ____, *Mafia;* Reppetto, *The Blue Parade;* Sann, *Kill the Dutchman!;* Schlesinger, *Robert Kennedy and His Times;* Smith, *Syndicate City;* Thompson and Raymond, *Gang Rule in New York;* Tully, *Treasury Agent;* Turkus and Feder, *Murder, Inc.;* Wicker, *Investigating the FBI;* Wolf and DiMona, *Frank Costello, Prime Minister of the Underworld.*

Adshead, John, 1741-72, and **Alsworth, Benjamin,** 1743-72, Brit., burg. These two professional criminals were, for a short period of time, the most successful burglars in London. Of the pair, Adshead was the leader. He had been born in Northamptonshire, England, and before he was twenty, Adshead moved to London where he became a footman, later a gunsmith. To support his expensive tastes, Adshead took to housebreaking. His success at this enterprise also earned him a wide reputation among the fences through which he resold his stolen merchandise, and he became nervous, thinking he might be betrayed to the police. Adshead moved to Bristol where he looted the home of a jeweler which brought him £150. With the proceeds, Adshead opened a pub but this failed. He went back to burglarizing homes, becoming rich.

Expensive clothes and fine living enthralled Adshead, though he continued to live in poverty-stricken areas of London and did not seek the company of cultured people. He desired this lifestyle so that he could feed his ego on the ignorant admiration of his impoverished drinking companions. One of these was a former soldier, Benjamin Alsworth, who had a large family and was unemployed. Alsworth asked Adshead how he could afford to dress in such sartorial style, and the older man told him that he had inherited money from a wealthy uncle, recently deceased. When the ex-soldier asked for a loan of four guineas, Adshead said he did not possess such a sum but smiled and told Alsworth that he could teach him how to "obtain a hundred pounds in an hour."

Burglar Adshead and his partner Benjamin Alsworth pleading with a magistrate at St. Gile's Watch House, London, 1772.

At first Alsworth thought his friend was joking, but Adshead spoke seriously and long about the rewards awaiting the cautious, accomplished burglar. He later took Alsworth to his rooms and there patiently taught him the methods of burglary. Soon the two were housebreaking throughout London and amassing a considerable fortune. They became so complacent that the burglars began to openly carry their loot from the houses they robbed. On the night of May 18, 1772, Adshead and Alsworth burglarized the large house of Mrs. Bellamy on Newman Street and Oxford Road, blithely shouldering huge bundles of stolen silk and other expensive prizes. A watchman called out to them and Adshead dropped his bundle, fleeing into the darkness. Alsworth, the greedier of the pair, held on to his package and was quickly overtaken and arrested. Adshead was arrested by another watchman a short time later and both men were taken before Justice Cox.

Adshead quietly explained that the stolen goods really belonged to him and his friend, that, when detained by the watchmen, they had been in the act of removing these items from their own lodgings so the landlord would not claim them for back rent. Justice Cox, suspicious because the men would not name the address of their lodgings, had them detained. When the Bellamy household awoke that morning and servants discovered the house had been robbed, handbills were immediately printed on orders of the family and these were sent throughout London, particularly to the police stations and magistrate courts. (This was the most effective method of detecting stolen property in that early day. A printed inventory of stolen items described in handbills was compared by watchmen and magistrats to goods found on suspicious persons being detained. A thief and the items he had stolen could thus be identified.)

When authorities realized that the Bellamy inventory of stolen household goods and those in possession of Adshead and Alsworth were one in the same, the two men were arrested and, in June 1772, were tried at the Old Bailey and quickly convicted of theft. Adshead begged the court to be lenient, pointing out that he was still a young man and was willing to change his ways. The dim-witted Alsworth said nothing. As was the draconian sentencing of that time for theft, both men were condemned to be hanged. Adshead, while awaiting execution with Alsworth at Newgate Prison, was penitent to the point of being slavish. On July 8, 1772, both men were taken to Tyburn to be hanged. Before going through the trap, both burglars confessed their crimes openly and cautioned the thousands who had come to see them hang what perils lay in wait for those who took up their evil professions.
REF.: *CBA; Newgate Calendar.*

Adwan, Kamal, 1936-73, Fr., assass. A 37-year-old leader of the Arab political terrorist group Al Fatah, Adwan was assassinated by an Israeli terrorist organization pledged to meeting violence with violence. Adwan was one of the prominent members of the Palestine Liberation Organization (PLO) in the early 1970s. He had been in charge of the information department of the Al Fatah, building cells on the Israeli-occupied West Bank. On Apr. 9, 1973, he went to Beirut, the center of many recent commando actions, along with two other Al Fatah leaders, Mohammed Yusuf Najjar, a founder of the terrorist group and Kamal Nasser, a PLO spokesman. The Wrath of God, a Zionist terrorist group, broke into the closely defended apartment buildings at Rue de Verdun, where the Arab leaders were staying, silently and quickly murdering three guards. Then the hit teams entered the three apartments in the two buildings. When Adwan tried to defend himself with a Kalashnikov assault rifle—a symbol of the Palestinian revolution—he was shot down in front of his wife. In the other apartments, Najjar died as his bedroom was sprayed with submachine gun fire, and Nasser was killed at his writing desk. The Israeli teams withdrew from the scene without being detected, taking off into the night.
REF.: Bell, *Assasssin!; CBA.*

Aegidi, Ludwig Karl, 1825-1901, Ger., jur. Politician and publicist. REF.: *CBA.*

Aeronauts in the New York World, 1897, U.S., fraud. The May 14, 1897, edition of the *New York World* carried a lead story of an aerial balloon crash off the coast of Sandy Hook and the daring rescue of the two aeronauts from the Atlantic.

Doubting the truth of the story, the *New York Sun,* a competing paper, set out to investigate. They learned that at the time of the alleged crash, the aeronauts in question were home, warm and dry, on West Twenty-fifth Street. The story, they found, was a hoax cooked up by a press agent. When the fraud was made public, however, the press agent was nowhere to be found. REF.: *CBA.*

Aethelheard (Ethehard; Adelard; Edelred), d.805, Mercia, prelate. Elected archbishop of Canterbury in 791 but exiled after death of King Offa in 796 and then restored in 798. REF.: *CBA.*

Aethelstan (Athelstan), d.939, Mercia, king. Ascended to kingship of Mercia in 924 and eventually ruled all of England. He issued codes of law, especially pertaining to larceny and corruption. REF.: *CBA.*

Aetius (AKA: the Atheist, the Ungodly), c.366, Syria, her. A prelate considered a heretic and banished by Constantius II in 359, but brought back two years later by Julian and appointed as a bishop. REF.: *CBA.*

Aetius, Flavius, c.396-454, Roman., treas. Famous for his victory over Attila the Hun in 451. Three years later he was put to death by Roman Emperor Valentinian III. REF.: *CBA.*

Afer, Domitius, c.59, Roman., orator. Considered by some to be the best orator of his day. He was famous for his prosecution of Claudia Pulchra and once saved himself from being prosecuted by flattering Caligula. REF.: *CBA.*

Affaire des Poisons, L', 1907, a play by Victorien Sardou. This mammoth historical drama in five acts is set at the time of Louis XIV and draws heavily from the murderous careers of two French poisoners, Marie de Brinvilliers (Fr., 1676) and Catherine De-shayes, known as La Voison. See: **Brinvilliers, Marie de**; **De-shayes, Catherine**. REF.: *CBA*.

Afra, Saint, prom. 303-313, Gr., pros. Although Afra repudiated her past when she converted to Christianity, Rome under Emperor Diocletian would not let her forget her former life as a prostitute. Persecuted and finally killed for refusing to submit to the will of the emperor, her body and those of three other prostitutes were displayed and publicly ridiculed. REF.: *CBA*.

Afrikaner-Broederbond, 1918-pres., S. Afri., secret soc. This nationalist society, which exists today in South Africa, with less than 10,000 members vowing to fight to the death to preserve the white rule of apartheid, was originally formed as an Afrikaans cultural society, but by the mid-1930s, this society, culling members from only the elite in power, had as its secret aim to rule South Africa, after breaking away from English-speaking South Africans and the British Commonwealth. The South African language and customs would be all Boer if the society had its way. Up until 1938, the Afrikaner-Broederbond sought peaceful methods by which to gain political control of the country, but with the rise of the Nazis in Europe, the society, particularly through a splinter group called the Ossewabrandwag, took on Nazi racist credos. From this period of time through the early 1940s, the society was proscribed by the government of Jan Christian Smuts. It was the ex-Boer general himself who labelled the society subversive in 1944; Smuts outlawed the organization for a time and issued orders that no government employee could take its oath. He quite naturally feared that society members, unknown to him, would secretly take power. It was during this hazardous period of time that the Afrikaner-Broederbond could be considered a secret criminal society.

At that time, more than 400,000 Afrikaners were reportedly members of the bond, which operated on a paramilitary basis much like the German bunds in the U.S. shortly before WWII. This force in South Africa by 1940 outnumbered the regular army much as had Ernst Röhm's Brownshirts (the SA) outnumbered the German army when Hitler came to power in 1933. When Hitler began to lose his war, the growth of the then Nazi-oriented Afrikaner-Broederbond ceased. Membership declined after the war, and the society began to dwindle by the 1960s. In 1964, the South African government appointed a one-man commission to examine the aims and makeup of the society. The commission reported that the Afrikaner-Broederbond could no longer be considered subversive, nor was it a threat to the government and the morals of the public.

The society continues today, but is only a small fraction of what it once was. A potential member must meet certain requirements: the applicant must be male, white, Afrikaans-speaking, Protestant, and over the age of twenty-five. In a simple ceremony, the applicant vows never to reveal the identity of other members, nor any of the society's discussions, documents, plans, or procedures. The society today states that its members are "mission-conscious Afrikaners who desire to represent and serve the best that is in our nation." This minority group is nevertheless the hardcore citizenry of South Africa that holds intact the widely-condemned practice of apartheid, still rigidly enforced.

REF.: *CBA*; MacKenzie, *Secret Societies*; Webster, *Secret Societies and Subversive Movements*.

After House, The, 1914, a novel by Mary Roberts Rinehart. This work proved to be so convincing to certain powerful U.S. officials that its fiction became accepted as fact and caused a convicted murderer to be released from prison. Rinehart dealt with the slaughter of Captain Charles I. Nash, his wife Laura, and a seaman, August W. Blomberg by first mate Thomas Mead Chambers Bram aboard the ship *Herbert Fuller* (U.S., 1896). Though Bram had been convicted on strong evidence and had served nineteen years of a life sentence in the U.S. Atlanta Penitentiary, he was pardoned in 1917 by President Woodrow Wilson. Former President Theodore Roosevelt, who first read the Rinehart book, urged Wilson to accept Rinehart's theories.

Wilson, after reading the book, was sufficiently persuaded to pardon Burn. The mystery writer believed, without much evidence to support her claims, that the real killer, Charles Brown, another crew member whom she calls "Charlie Jones," suddenly went berserk and killed the Nash couple and Blomberg. See: **Bram, Thomas Mead Chambers**. REF.: *CBA*.

After the Fact, 1935, a novel by Alan Brock. Profiled in fiction is the mysterious and unsolved Luard murder case (Brit., 1908), the character of General Rouleau being drawn almost wholly from the hapless Major-General Charles Edward Luard. See: **Luard, Caroline**. REF.: *CBA*.

Agar, Edward, See: **Great Gold Robbery, The**.

Agenda Murder, The, See: **Walker, Ernest Albert**.

Agnew, Spiro, prom. 1970s, U.S., graft-tax evas. An associate of Spiro Agnew was convicted of violating campaign laws, and a taxpayer's lawsuit was brought against Agnew and two more associates as corruption charges against the former U.S. vice president multiplied. On Dec. 21, 1976, June Green, a federal judge, refused to release U.S. Justice Department documents related to a criminal investigation of the one-time vice president, saying the files were part of an ongoing investigation in the indictment of Maryland governor Martin Mandel and would only be released when that case was concluded.

Vice President Spiro Agnew.

On Mar. 11, 1977, J. Walter Jones Jr., a Maryland banker known as Agnew's middleman, pleaded guilty to soliciting an illegal $15,000 campaign contribution from the Singer Corporation in 1972 for Agnew campaigns in Baltimore and Maryland. In March 1977 Jones was sentenced to three months in prison and a $5,000 fine for campaign law violations. A week later, the U.S. Court of Appeals refused to intervene in a suit that accused Agnew of violating probation terms imposed after he pleaded no contest to income-tax evasion charges. In June 1980 an Annapolis, Md. court ruled that the confessions of Jerome B. Wolff and I.H. Hammerman 2d could be introduced as evidence in a taxpayer's lawsuit against Agnew and two other men. Wolff and Hammerman claimed to have shared bribes with Agnew. The then four-year-old lawsuit against Agnew ordered him to pay about $200,000 to the Maryland state treasury. Agnew consistently denied accepting bribes, admitting only to some $29,000 in federal income tax liability. For this he was fined $10,000, placed on three years' probation, and was later disbarred as a lawyer.

REF.: *CBA*; Dean, *Blind Ambition*; Demaris, *The Director*; ____, *Dirty Business*; Fields, *High Crimes and Misdemeanors*; Ford, *A Time to Heal*; Hartmann, *Palace Politics*; Messick, *The Politics of Prosecution*; Nash, *Citizen Hoover*; Powers, *Secrecy and Power*; Sullivan, *The Bureau*; Toledano, *J. Edgar Hoover*; Wicker, *Investigating the FBI*.

Agostini, Antonio (The Pajama Girl Murder), Aus., mur. An Italian immigrant working in Sydney, Agostini was married to an assertive, hard-drinking Englishwoman, Linda Platt in 1930. The couple lived a meager existence on Agostini's small salary. He worked at odd jobs, mostly in restaurants as a waiter, and his income, or the lack of it, caused his wife to drink heavily and, according to Agostini's later statements, become abusive. To improve their lifestyle the couple moved to Melbourne where Linda Platt Agostini was last seen alive in August 1934. After that she vanished. When her friends or relatives inquired about her, Agostini merely shrugged, saying that she had run off with a lover. This raised few eyebrows for Mrs. Agostini, an attractive woman with a voluptuous figure, was known to play the field even after her marriage.

On Sept. 1, 1934, a farmer cleaning a culvert six miles from

Albury (located between Melbourne and Sydney) found the body of a young woman. She was badly burned and her head showed vicious head wounds. Her curvacious body was adorned with only pajamas embroidered with a Chinese dragon. When coroner physicians examined the corpse closer they quickly discovered a bullet wound below the right eye. Parts of the skull had been dealt severe blows so that the bone had collapsed. There were burns over the body which conformed with the patches of oil discovered at the burial site. Someone had murdered this woman and then had attempted to destroy the body by soaking it in oil and burning it.

The corpse was first identified by no less than six people as Mrs. Anna Philomena Morgan Coots, the wife of a Sydney writer who had been reported missing. The medical examiners and the police were content to label the body such, and marked the "Coots" murder as unsolved, yet there was some doubt among the

Antonio Agostini, wife killer.

authorities as to the real identity of the dead woman, particularly when Mrs. Coots' mother, Mrs. Jeanette Routledge, viewed the corpse and stated, "I am certain that this is not my daughter." Mrs. Coots' grandmother, her landlady, and several close friends insisted otherwise, that, indeed, the corpse was Anna Coots. Authorities decided not to bury the murder victim under that name. They would wait for developments and other leads. The corpse was placed in a metal coffin which was filled with a special preservative, formalin, an aqueous solution of formaldehyde which will provide indefinite preservation of organic tissues. The body was stored in a basement area of Sydney University's Pathological Museum and there it waited until the police decided whether or not to bury it. The wait lasted for ten years.

During that time a curious police sergeant named King came to visit the corpse and peer at it as it swam in the formalin. (One report had it that the streetcars rumbling by outside caused the corpse to "bob like an apple" in the preservative fluid.) King reported to his superiors that he believed the woman was none other than a friend of his wife's, Linda Platt Agostini, someone the Kings had not seen since early 1931. He was sure of his identification, however, because of the unusually shaped ears on the corpse. They were pointed and had no lobes, something King had noticed about Mrs. Agostini when first meeting her. King made his statement in 1938 at a second inquest which was publicized. An amateur sleuth and medical criminologist, Dr. Palmer Benbow, decided to investigate. He convinced authorities to allow him to examine the corpse and the scanty evidence unearthed by the police.

There was not much to examine—the corpse, wrinkling in formalin, a bag which had been soaked with oil, a piece of toweling. When peering at the toweling under his microscope, Benbow noticed something the police had not discovered or, if they had, had ignored. There were laundry marks on the towel. These marks led the doctor to a shack outside of Albury and there he found an old bed with a metal frame which had been painted. Benbow matched flecks of paint from the frame of this bed to those found on the corpse, and matched fibres from a woolen blanket he found to those found in the dead woman's hair. He began interviewing residents in the area but suddenly Dr. Benbow's one-man investigation came to an abrupt halt. He later claimed that police had obstructed his work and that witnesses suddenly had nothing more to say to him after being visited by

certain authorities. Oddly, Benbow's half-completed investigation aimed itself at establishing the corpse as that of Anna Morgan Coots, not Linda Agostini.

Edith Flemington, Linda's mother through an earlier marriage, had been contacted as early as 1935 when her daughter reportedly ran away to blissful oblivion with an unknown lover. For almost ten years Mrs. Flemington had been writing authorties around the world from her home in Littlehampton, Sussex, England, trying to find her daughter or her daughter's remains. The police in Sydney had sent her a photo of the corpse in the preservative fluid, but she had originally denied the remains as being that of her daughter. (Formalin usually causes the body to shrink and wrinkles to appear on the face, slightly disfiguring features.) But Mrs. Flemington did recognize the photo of the pajamas the dead woman had been wearing, yellow silk pajamas with a green dragon embroidered on the back which, Mrs. Flemington later recalled, had been given to Linda by her sister as a wedding gift.

Mrs. Flemington wrote many letters to the Sydney police describing her daughter and how she had clerked in London stores, been a movie usher and a hairdresser on the Red Star Line which is how she wound up in Australia. She wrote about her son-in-law, Agostini, and how he was not a "reliable type," a would-be silk merchant and part-time waiter, how, on one occasion, instead of buying her daughter an engagement ring, Agostini bought her a one-passage home which Linda never used. In her last letter to the Sydney police, Mrs. Flemington said that though she had failed to recognize the body in the formalin as her daughter she had had strange dreams as of late, seeing her daughter "afloat" in a dark, small area.

Then, in March 1944, Antonio Agostini, who had been interred in an alien prison camp during the war, came under suspicion once again. W.J. Mackay, the newly-appointed police commissioner for New South Wales, intended to clear up the matter once and for all. He had read Mrs. Flemington's last letter and examined the yellowing notes of Dr. Benbow. Mackay, leafing through the thick police files, noticed the name of a dentist who had worked on Linda's teeth, but oddly enough, the dentist had not been asked to compare his charts of Linda Agostini with the teeth of the dead woman. The dentist was called in and the teeth were compared. There was no doubt in the dentist's mind that the deceased was his former patient.

Linda Agostini, the victim known as The Pajama Girl.

Mackay next ordered physicians to take the corpse from the formalin bath and reconstruct it as best as possible. Then he brought in friends and relatives of both Mrs. Coots and Mrs. Agostini. The identification for Mrs. Agostini was the strongest, and Agostini was brought from his prison camp.

The short, balding, and near-sighted Agostini had been interrogated in 1935 by police who had accepted his story about his wife running off with another man. Mackay disregarded that tale and began to pump the little waiter. He soon changed his story. Yes, the pickled corpse was the late Mrs. Agostini, the little man admitted. He added, as he casually chain-smoked in front of the commissioner, that he had killed his wife but not intentionally. On Aug. 28, 1934 they both went to bed drunk but Linda woke up before dawn, he said. She was raving about another woman coming to see him at the restaurant where he worked. (Agostini insisted that his wife was jealous of him to the point of being neurotic.) Somehow she had gotten hold of a gun and was waving it at Agostini, he said, and he tried to take it away from her. In the struggle the gun went off and she was killed by the fatal shot. He panicked

Dr. Palmer Benbow

and attempted to carry the body downstairs, but it fell from his grasp and during its fall the terrible wounds to the head were inflicted on the stairs. He then drove out to the culvert and stuffed the body inside.

Much of Agostini's statements didn't make sense. If the death was accidental why had he attempted to burn the corpse beyond recognition. Agostini insisted that he had not done so, that, perhaps some other person finding the corpse had tried to burn it so as not to be blamed for a murder. More revealing was the report from the original examining physicians who stated that the head wounds found on the body were made *before* the bullet had been fired and that the blows to the skull caused the actual death of Linda Agostini. This, of course, pointed to a beating administered by Agostini. He was charged with murdering his wife and placed on trial on June 9, 1944. No matter how much the prosecution pressured Agostini, the little man would not budge. The killing was accidental, he insisted.

The jury undoubtedly believed the quiet little waiter. Agostini was convicted of manslaughter and sent to serve a six-year sentence at hard labor. He was released in 1950 and was promptly deported to his native Italy where he disappeared. By that time, the body of Linda Platt Agostini had finally found rest, having been buried in July 1944, in Melbourne's Preston Cemetery. There are those today who still insist that the corpse is that of Mrs. Coots who was never found and that there were actually *two murders* occuring on the same day and in the same area. One of the killers was brought to justice and the other, since only one corpse was unearthed, remained at large and unknown.

REF.: *CBA;* Clegg, *Return Your Verdict;* Kelly, *The Charge is Murder.*

Agra Double Murder, See: **Fullam, Augusta Fairfield.**

Agrippina (Agrippina the Younger), c.15-59 A.D., Rome, mur. Daughter of Agrippina the Elder (Vipsania Agrippina), Agrippina the Younger proved to be one of the most murderous women in the history of the Roman Empire. She had been born into a life of intrigue and conspiracy. Her mother had been banished to Pandataria by Emperor Tiberius who mistrusted her and there, in 33 A.D., she died of starvation which may have been arranged by the Emperor. Her daughter, Agrippina the Younger, learned much from

Agrippinna the Elder.

her mother's ignoble death and vowed to secure power at all costs. This she did through sexual prowess, conspiracy, and many murders which she personally carried out. Born in Oppidum Ubiorum, later named Colonia Agrippina after her (modern day Cologne), Agrippina married young, wedding Domitius Ahenobar-

bus by whom she had a son, Nero, later emperor. Agrippina's first husband died, cause not recorded but her second husband, Passienus Crispus, was poisoned by her in 49 A.D. so she could be free to marry her uncle, Emperor Claudius, and become Empress of Rome, a position Agrippina sought since childhood.

Claudius had had little luck with women. One wife, Messalina, had been so profligate (she has been correctly described as a maniacal sadist and an insatiable nymphomaniac) that he ordered her executed in 48 A.D. Agrippina, realizing that her uncle was now without an empress, poisoned her own husband, Crispus, and seduced her uncle, who married her the following year. Agrippina soon began a campaign that would place her son Nero on the throne—eliminating all contenders, including those courtiers who might advise Claudius against naming Nero his heir. One of these was Scribonius, a court astrologer who hinted to the emperor of Agrippina's conspiratorial ways. The Empress harangued her husband into banishing the astrologer who, a short time later, either committed suicide, or, most likely, was murdered by agents sent by Agrippina. When proconsul Statilius Taurus opposed Nero as an heir, Agrippina accused him of crimes against the state and had him indicted by the senate. Rather than face a public trial the statesman committed suicide.

Woe to the women who thought to replace the power-clutching Agrippina. Lollia Paulina, the divorced wife of the dead Caligula, an alluring siren who caught the eye of the womanizing Claudius, was accused of misdeeds and committed suicide. Domitia Lepida, another sensual rival who drew the Emperor's attention, found herself accused of crimes she did not commit. She did take her own life, however, as was then the apparent custom, but thought she would be vindicated. A mock trial produced the Agrippina's desired effect. Domitia Lepida was condemned and executed.

In 54 A.D., fearing that Claudius might change his mind about having Nero succeed him, Agrippina personally prepared a dish of mushrooms for the Emperor, his favorite dish, and served this to him, laced with poison. He survived the attack but was violently ill. (Another version of this murder story has Claudius served the poisoned dish by his official taster, the eunuch Halotus, under the direction of Agrippina.) Claudius was then given an enema, according to one report, supervised by Agrippina, which was dosed with colocynth juice (derived from a wild Palestinian gourd), and this finally

Agrippina the Younger.

killed the 64-year-old Emperor on Oct. 13, 54 A.D. By then Agrippina had already paved the way for her son Nero to assume the throne. Upon the succession of Nero, Agrippina felt that she alone now ruled the Roman Empire. For some time, her son listened and followed her counsel but he later ignored her advice and became one of the most hedonistic, vice-bloated, blood-drenched tyrants in all history. That he was insane toward the end was a certainty. When she began to lose control of Nero, Agrippina agreed to his most perverse desire in order to regain her power, maintaining an incestuous relationship with him, particularly when they traveled together in a closed litter, according to one account which stated that "the state of his clothes when he emerged proved it."

Nero could no longer tolerate his mother's overbearing attitude and directives. He stripped her of her Roman and German guards. He secretly ordered pimps and prostitutes to sail past her riverside estate in Rome and shout insults and obscenities at her throughout the night. She, in turn, threatened him and grew violent in his presence so that Nero's natural cowardice and fear drove him to desperation; he planned his mother's death. First he attempted to have her poisoned but this failed on three separate occasions, with the wily Agrippina learning of the poison ahead of time and taking the proper antidote. Then Nero tried to lure his mother into a room that had been rigged so that the walls and ceilings would collapse upon her and crush her to death but she evaded this murder plan. Next, Nero placed his mother on board a ship that had been tampered with, one that would sink once in deep water. The ship did sink but the athletic Agrippina swam to shore and safety. Nero finally gave up and sent assassins to murder his mother. They were successful. Nero visited her corpse at her retreat at Baiae to make sure she was indeed dead. He stood next to her corpse, gulping down goblets of wine and fondling her legs and arms, showing the body to his friends and discussing the good and bad parts of Agrippina's anatomy, a disgusting and disrespectful display never equaled by Nero's most flagrant peers. The murder of his mother haunted Nero until his dying days and many in his vice-ridden coterie were convinced that Agrippina's ghost drove the emperor mad. Alive, the thought would have pleased this lethal lady to no end. See: **Claudius**; **Nero**.

REF.: Africa, *Rome of the Caesars;* Balsdon, *The Romans, The People and Their Civilization; CBA;* Charles-Picard, *Augustus and Nero;* Charlesworthy, *Cambridge Ancient History;* Robinson, *History of Rome;* Suetonius, *The Twelve Caesars;* Tacitus, *The Annals.*

Aguayo, Robert, 1959-   , U.S., org. crime counselor. After growing up and surviving in one of Los Angeles' most dangerous gang-run neighborhoods, Robert Aguayo decided to work in his community to help turn teenagers away from violence. In 1987, Aguayo, twenty-eight, had been working as a counselor in Latino Echo Park for four years. He had grown up in the neighborhood, an angry, intelligent boy who embraced gang life as a way of joining his peer group. Having had counseling himself as a teen, Aguayo looked at his file and saw he was headed for long term jail. In 1977, attending junior college, he accidentally shot a member of another gang while defending a relative who had been attacked. When Aguayo was released after a year in jail he enrolled at California State University in Los Angeles, receiving a bachelor's degree in psychology in 1986.

For nine years Aguayo has served on the staff of El Centro del Pueblo, the same group that once counseled him, helping teens and their families get job training and advice. Aguayo solicits donations of tickets to sports and arts events, hoping to give gang members a view of other worlds and life options. "People don't join gangs to be murderers or thieves, but because they need to belong," he explains. Aguayo knows that some he counsels may not survive the violence in their communities. In 1986 Robert Garibay, of the Diamond Street gang, came to Aguayo for help, and cut down on drugs, working hard to improve his grades at school and to change his life. In November 1987 Garibay, intending to mockingly scare off some local kids, brought out a gun and started waving it around, slipping and fatally wounding himself. REF.: *CBA.*

Agueci Brothers, prom. 1950s-60s, Can.-U.S., org. crime. Albert and Vito Agueci were born in Sicily and migrated to Canada where they peddled narcotics on a grand scale for Mafia boss Stefano Magaddino, headquartered in Buffalo and controlling huge narcotics trafficking throughout western New York, the Ohio Valley, and Toronto, Can. At first, the brothers operated a bakery in Toronto which was only a front for their heroin trafficking. They were not content with their lucrative racket, however, and wanted to branch out into the U.S. With Magaddino's permission, the Aguecis branched out and were soon selling narcotics in the Buffalo area. They were maverick mobsters and went so far as to peddle dope in New York City where they were arrested on July 20, 1961. It fell to Mafia boss Magaddino to provide bail for his dope peddlers, but he ignored them and Albert Agueci's wife finally managed to provide bail for her husband. Albert Agueci felt that he had been betrayed by Magaddino and set out to murder the Mafia chief. He failed; Agueci's body was found horribly mutilated in a field outside of Rochester, N.Y., on Nov. 23, 1961. His hand had been tied behind his back and he had been strangled with a long cord. Agueci's jaw was broken and his

teeth had been kicked out. One of Magaddino's killers had taken great care to inflict pain upon the victim before strangling him, cutting off the meaty portions of his body, then dousing the victim with gasoline and igniting it. The ghastly murder was a signal to any others who thought to take vengeance on a Mafia don.

The brutal message was not lost on Vito Agueci. He was convicted of narcotics peddling and sent to the federal penitentiary in Atlanta where he met Joseph Valachi, a henchman of Vito Genovese who was also serving time in Atlanta. Agueci wangled a meeting with Genovese and swore that he would avenge his brother which alarmed Don Vito who, in turn, goaded Valachi to murder Agueci. Instead, Valachi believed, with Agueci whispering in his ear, that Genovese wanted to get rid of him. Paranoid, Valachi killed a prisoner he thought was a Genovese man who had been planning to kill him. He murdered the wrong prisoner and received a life sentence. Realizing that he had been victimized by the scheming Genovese, Valachi began to inform on the Mafia families, a famous litany that revealed the modern-day operations of the Cosa Nostra, detailing its broad international operations and its ruling dons. The Valachi revelations brought down the powerful Magaddino which, in the end, served the vendetta purposes of Vito Agueci. See: **Cosa Nostra**; **Genovese, Vito**; **Magaddino, Stefano**; **Valachi, Joseph**.

REF.: *CBA;* Cook, *Mafia!;* Frasca, *King of Crime;* Maas, *The Valachi Papers;* Overstreet, *The FBI in Our Open Society;* Peterson, *The Mob;* Reid, *The Grim Reapers.*

Aguesseau, Henri François d' (Daguesseau), 1668-1751, Fr., jur. Served three terms as Chancellor of France from 1717-18, 1720-22, and 1737-50 under Louis XV. He helped to codify French law and court procedures. REF.: *CBA.*

Aguilar, Robert Peter, b.1931-   , U.S., jur. Trial lawyer who co-authored "The Segregation Decisions and the Resulting Problems on Enforcement" which appeared in the *Hastings Law Journal* (1958). In 1980 he was appointed to a federal judgeship in northern California by President Jimmy Carter. REF.: *CBA.*

Agustin, Antonio (Antonius Augustinus), 1517-86, Spain, jur.-prelate. Papal nuncio to Queen Mary Tudor in 1545, archbishop of Tarragona in 1576, and author of *Emendationum et opinionum libri IV ad Modestinum* (1567). REF.: *CBA.*

Ah Chai, prom.1954-57, China, org. crime-kid. Secret societies of gangsters who extorted money by schemes against and kidnappings of wealthy businessmen, were powerful forces of crime in Singapore and Hong Kong in the 1950s. Ah Chai ran a small import-export firm by day in Singapore, but after hours he was the leader of a secret society known as the "18 Group", which initiated its members with bizarre rituals of oaths and animal sacrifices. Their prime targets were prosperous businessmen, whom they would watch carefully to figure out their schedules and habits, then kidnap and hold in animal pens in rural areas outside Singapore while they waited for their families to deliver ransoms. Payoffs for these abductions averaged about $200,000 each. Over a period of about 3 years Ah Chai and his gang collected a total of $3.74 million, which he invested in land, apartment houses, and small businesses. Police had difficulty catching the criminals because victims were too frightened of retribution to go to them.

In October 1957, a wealthy tailor named Ng Sen Choy left his Wing Loong Road estate in a chauffeur-driven limousine, accompanied by his wife and grandson. As they turned out of the driveway a black Hillman Minx car blocked their path. Two gunmen jumped into the limousine, knocked out the chauffeur, pulled a bag over Choy's head and dragged him into the Minx, saying to Mrs. Choy, "You will hear from us soon." The gangsters, who had counted on Mrs. Choy being too frightened to call the police, were surprised minutes later when they were chased by squad cars. Two gangsters escaped. One, wounded and captured, talked enough to lead Inspector B.W.F. Goodrich of the Singapore Criminal Investigation Department to check out a small import-export company near Raffles Place.

One of the three workers in the office was Ah Chai, but the police had no proof to arrest him. Learning that one of Ah Chai's office workers was a drug addict who had once been fined $1,000 for illegal possession of opium, they searched the office and discovered morphine and a syringe in the man's desk. They jailed him and his morphine cravings eventually caused him to talk. Ah Chai was arrested, tried, and executed for his crimes. REF.: *CBA*.

Ahaziah, prom. c.844 B.C., Judah, king, assass. King of Judah for approximately one year, then assassinated by Jehu and succeeded by Athaliah. REF.: *CBA*.

Ahearn, Danny, prom. 1930-40s, U.S., mur. Growing up on New York's Lower East Side, Danny Ahearn admired gangsters, studied them carefully, and then joined their ranks as a teenager. Although Ahearn had extensive experience as a robber, gambler, and con man, his main profession was killing for hire. Arrested in New York twenty-two times on major charges, Ahearn was released twenty times. Tried twice for murder, he was released both times for lack of evidence. Reportedly after his final arrest, he gave a long, detailed interview in which he described the techniques and etiquettes of his trade. "For a man to commit murder," he explained, "he's got to have no heart." He advised professional assassins to have patience, study their intended victims carefully, keep a cool head, and stay on good terms with the police, reasoning that "They got to make a buck. They're human, too. Treat 'em nice. Then, if you get into trouble you may be able to do business with 'em." Ahearn recommended several standard murder methods such as placing dynamite in the starter of the victim's car or blowing up his house. Women were useful to lure the victims to isolated areas, or to get the target in compromising positions in bedrooms where they would be easy prey. He emphasized working with the police and making connections with them to set up favorable conditions for favors and exchanges.

When hired to kill a woman, Ahearn advised romancing her in nightclubs, then taking her to her apartment and gaining her confidence and affection, so one could later invite her on a vacation, perhaps in the mountains. To avoid trouble, the killer should make sure she writes a letter to her family saying she is going away. Every day of the vacation, he advised, dig part of a ditch in the woods. When the grave is finished, take her for a walk in the woods, knock her on the head, and bury her alive, Ahearn suggests. He suggested that a killer always carry around some poison in order to be prepared, and try, when possible, to leave a gun planted on the victim's body, because, he said, "Police don't interest themselves too much in the case where gangsters are killed."

REF.: *CBA*; Hamilton, *Men of the Underworld*.

Ahlers, Nicolaus Emil Herman Adolph, prom. 1900s, Case of, Brit., treas. Ahlers worked for the German Consul-General in London, holding the position of German consul in Sunderland. At the outbreak of WWI he was arrested for "High Treason with the Statute of King Edward III (1351) in that he adhered to the King's enemies in his realm giving to them aid and comfort in his realm." Ahlers was so charged because he was not only acting as an official of the German government but had committed treason since he had become a naturalized British subject in 1905 and, through his acts, was therefore betraying his country, England, which had just gone to war with Germany. In his defense Ahlers contended that he merely followed instructions from the German Consul in London by sending the following message to Germans then residing in England, in anticipation of war being declared: "All able-bodied men from the age of seventeen to forty-five must try to find their way to Germany."

This message was sent to German reservists in England. Hostilities were officially declared by England at 11 p.m. on Aug. 4, 1914, and Ahler's messages were sent out as late as Aug. 5. Ahlers insisted that he did not learn about the British declaration of war until Aug. 6, 1914, and when he did he immediately ceased sending the messages. He added that only eight German reservists received the messages and were given money by him to return to Germany. Public feeling at the time of Ahlers arrest was so intense that the court chose to split hairs and place Ahlers on trial in December 1914. Justice Shearman thought very little of the prosecution's case and instructed the jury that in his opinion, Ahlers was Not Guilty. The jury, however, full of patriotic zeal, convicted the accused. Under the existing and ancient laws of treason, Shearman had no choice but to sentence Ahlers to death. In appeal however, Lord Reading presiding as Lord Chief Justice, studied the summation by Justice Shearman in the original trial and the judge's favorable remarks toward the accused. These played a large part in saving Ahlers from the gallows. The conviction was quashed and Ahlers was released.

REF.: *CBA*; Humphreys, *A Book of Trials*.

Ahlstedt, Gustave (AKA: **Gustav Arkill**), Case of, U.S., burg. On June 12, 1908, Daniel Donohue, a gripman on San Francisco's Powell Street railway line, reported his wife, Alice, missing. Later that summer, on Aug. 28, her remains were found buried beneath the floorboards of the Western Furniture Factory on Sixty-fourth Street in Oakland. Beside her clothing was a garden spade, later linked to Gustave Arkill, a neighbor of the Donohue's, whose real name was Gustave Ahlstedt. Although the spade was positively identified as Arkill's, he did not emerge as a prime suspect until police found Alice Donohue's handkerchief in his pocket.

Regardless of whether Arkill murdered Alice, his behavior before she disappeared was less than exemplary. Allegedly, Arkill tried to poison his first wife by placing strychnine in her coffee. Then in 1902, he shot and killed his second wife's lover on Folsom Street—a crime for which he was acquitted.

Alice Donohue, unlike Arkill had no such luck, even after death. On Sept. 3, 1908, the morning *Call* revealed that Alice Donohue, formerly Alice Steward, married Daniel Donohue while still married to another man in Pennsylvania. In fact the newspaper stated that she had had many men before Donohue.

This news came as quite a shock to Donohue, who had been a suspect for the murder when he tried to collect on her life insurance policy. After hearing the news, Donohue shot himself. As for Ahlstedt, he was exonerated and no one was ever formally charged with the murder. See: **Donohue, Alice.**

REF.: *CBA*; Duke, *Celebrated Criminal Cases of America*.

Ahmad Baba (Abu al-Abbas Ahmad ibn Ahmad al-Takruri al-Massufi) 1556-1627, Sudan, jur. Known for his biographical dictionary of jurists of Maliki school of Islamic law and for his legal opinions. He was held in Marrakesh from 1594-1603 after being exiled from his native Timbuktu. REF.: *CBA*.

Ahmad Khan, Sir Sayyid, 1817-98, India, jur. Sayid Ahmad Khan served in the East India Company judicial department from 1841-76. He founded several schools and a reform journal. REF.: *CBA*.

Ahmada, See: **Karume, Abeid.**

Ahmet, Pasa Bursali, prom. 1497, Turk., jur. Teacher, writer, and poet who served Ottoman Sultan Mehmet II as a judge and a tutor beginning in 1451. He also served under Bayezid II. REF.: *CBA*.

Ahrens, Heinrich, 1808-74, Ger., jur. and writer of philosophy. REF.: *CBA*.

Ahumada, Danny, prom.1975, U.S., asslt. A family feud that began eleven years earlier led to a shoot-out in a cornfield when the next generation had grown old enough to continue their parents' fight. In January 1964 two friends from a Casa Blanca, Calif., barrio neighborhood had several drinks together before getting into a fight in a parking lot with two brothers-in-law wielding tire irons. John Ahumada ended up critically injured; he survived, seriously disabled. The Lozano brothers, Roman and Marcos, were tried and imprisoned for assault with a deadly weapon. The feud lay dormant for almost twelve years. By then, Richard Lozano and Danny Ahumada had grown old enough to continue their fathers' bad blood.

In 1975, an atmosphere of tension and hostility reigned in the barrio, with Chicano militants deriding police as "the Anglo-dominant society." In August 1975, sniping and harassment in a cornfield rapidly escalated into guerrilla warfare, with five people wounded. Ahumada and Larry Romero were arrested for shooting at a police officer. By Christmas 1976 the families were killing each other, taking pot shots from passing cars. Ahumada was shot twice at point-blank range with a .22-caliber pistol, somehow surviving the attack but, like his father, severely disabled.

The feud has continued, with cooling-off periods that would last for weeks or months. A longtime resident of the Southern California Mexican-American neighborhoods explained, "They're in no hurry. In the barrio, people say, 'Todo se paga.' Everything is paid." Others say the underlying motive is drugs, connected with two Mexican prison gangs, the Mexican Mafia and Nuestro Familia, who struggle over control of narcotic sales in Casa Blanca Many arrests are made, but few cases come to court, and there are even fewer convictions. A deputy district attorney noted, "This is the usual situation where twenty people see the killing and all of them say, 'I didn't see it.'" New generations continue to grow up to murder each other.

REF.: CBA; Trillin, *Killings*.

Aiello, Joseph, 1891-1930, U.S., org. crime. The Aiello family constituted the last serious threat to Al Capone and his control of all bootlegging activities in Chicago in the late 1920s, following the elimination of the Moran gang by Capone gunmen at the infamous St. Valentine's Day Massacre in 1929. Raised in Milwaukee, Wis., the Aiello brothers, Joseph, Dominick, Andrew, and Antonio moved to Chicago. At the beginning of Prohibition, the brothers began a small-time bootlegging operation on the near west side of Chicago, working under the leadership of the Genna brothers. When the Gennas were eliminated by the Irish gangsters under the command of Dion O'Bannion and George "Bugs" Moran in the late 1920s, Aiello joined forces with Moran and others to defy Capone.

Joseph Aiello who tried to kill Capone and was murdered.

Both Capone and Aiello coveted control of the Unione Sicilone, the Sicilian fraternal organization that overlorded all illegal operations conducted by the Italian-Sicilian gangsters. Several killings occured in the battle for the presidency of the Unione Sicilione. Capone himself could not assume this position being a Neopolitan Italian but he hand-picked the Sicilians to occupy the post, including his good friend, Tony Lombardo. Aiello, who had run for the office himself and had been repeatedly denied the presidency, decided to eliminate his competition. He and two others followed Lombardo and his two bodyguards down the street in Chicago on Sept. 7, 1928. When they reached State and Madison streets, considered to be the world's busiest corner at that time, Lombardo and his men, Joseph Lolordo and Joseph Ferraro, were crushed to a standstill by the enormous crowds. Two men pushed through the throng and, at a distance of two feet, put pistols to the back of Lombardo's head and fired point blank. Lombardo was dead on his feet—his head blown off by dum-dum bullets.

Aiello and his aide then fired at the bodyguards, hitting Ferraro in the spine and downing him. Lolordo pulled his own gun but had difficulty getting through the crowd as the killers fled. When he finally broke through to the street, Lolordo was clubbed unconscious by a traffic cop who thought he had captured Lombardo's murderer. Capone was told by Lombardo's bodyguards that they "thought" they had seen Joey and Dominick Aiello in the crowd but Scarface decided to bide his time. He placed Pasqualino "Patsy" Lolordo, the older brother of Lombardo's bodyguard, on the Unione throne. Aiello, by this time, was working with Moran's gang hand-in-glove to unseat Capone which caused Scarface to mark Aiello for death.

Aiello and his men struck first. He and two of his brothers caught up with a Lolordo aide, Peter Rizzito, as he stepped from his Milton Street store and shot him to death. Capone roared back, sending his gunmen into Aiello territory in September 1928, wounding Antonio Aiello and a henchman in one raid and shot and killed four other Aiello gunmen in the weeks to follow. Joe Aiello was not one to back down from Capone and his obviously superior forces. (Scarface could muster, if necessary, more than 1,000 gunmen from his own forces and those of his dozens of satellite gangs.) Aiello and two Moran gunmen, Frank and Pete Gusenburg, called on Lolordo on the afternoon of Jan. 8, 1929.

Lolordo, who thought Aiello a friend, especially since he was one of the directors of the Unione Sicilione, invited him and his two friends into the parlor of his North Side home. As Mrs. Lolordo did her ironing in the kitchen, her husband entertained his friends, pouring whiskey and indulging in loud toasts to each other. Mrs. Lolordo heard loud laughter and back-slapping but at 4 p.m., when a car horn blew loudly outside the house (a prearranged signal, no doubt, that the trio's getaway car was ready), several gunshots roared inside the parlor. Mrs. Lolordo raced into the parlor to see Aiello and his two friends walk solemnly out the front door. One of the men turned and gave her an indifferent glance, then dropped a pistol to the floor before leaving. On the floor, his entire face shot away so that he was unrecognizable except to his wife was Pasqualino Lolordo, dead. Mrs. Lolordo slipped a pillow under the shattered head of her husband and then called police. Later, when Aiello and twenty of his men were lined up before her at a police show-up, the widow Lolordo could not recognize any of the men as her husband's murderers, or, at least, that is what she claimed.

For a time it appeared as if Joe Aiello was a gangland force to be reckoned with; Aiello himself thought he was as crafty as Capone and equal to him in military strategy. He had, within the space of six months, eliminated two of Capone's Unione Sicilione allies, and had gone unscathed. Next he went after Capone himself, giving Scarface's personal chef $10,000 to dump prussic acid in Capone's soup. The chef backed out at the last minute, telling his chief of the plot while tears streamed down his face. Capone allowed the man to live but changed his kitchen help immediately. Scarface was next told that Aiello had placed a $50,000 bounty on him for anyone bold enough to kill Capone. Said Capone to his then top bodyguard, Louis "Little New York" Campagna (who slept outside of Capone's bedroom on a cot with two loaded automatics in his hands every night), "Nobody puts a price on my head and lives!"

Capone arranged for Aiello to be brought into Police Detective Headquarters on North Dearborn Street to answer some questions on a recent murder. Once Aiello had surrendered and was undergoing interrogation, eight cabs arrived in front of the police station and more than twenty men, led by Campagna, alighted. Boldly, these Capone hoodlums, brandished pistols and automatics and the officers outside of the building immediately arrested them and threw them into cells. This, of course, was their plan all along, even though detectives at first thought the gunmen planned to lay siege to the building. Placed in a cell next to Aiello, Campagna began to threaten him. Police listened in to the conversation between Campagna and Aiello.

"Give me just fifteen days," Aiello begged, "just fifteen days and I will sell my stores and house and leave everything in your hands. Think of my wife and baby and let me go."

"You dirty rat," spat back Campagna. "You started this and we're going to finish it. You're as good as dead!"

Aiello did leave town after being released and his brothers' bootleg domain began to dwindle. Dominick Aiello was shot to death and the Aiello gang quickly lost its effectiveness. When Joe Aiello returned to Chicago he found his power eroded and his gang disheartened. Capone dogged his steps for three years. Scarface had notified Aiello that he had broken his promise never to return to Chicago and was at the top of Capone's deathlist. Aiello was a determined sort, however, and was still lured by the presidency of the Unione Siciliane; he lobbied once more for the job and was elected to the post in late 1929. Aiello ordered the more than 1500 Sicilian alky cookers to cease making home-made whiskey for Capone which caused Scarface to assign more than a dozen men to the exclusive task of killing Aiello and his men. The gang boss managed to evade Capone's gunners until Oct. 23, 1930. On that day Aiello emerged from the home of one of his minions, Pasquale Prestigiocomo, alias Presto. Two cars parked across the street suddenly blazed with machine gun fire and Aiello toppled dead to the pavement.

REF.: Asbury, *Gem of the Prairie*; Bonanno, *A Man of Honor*; Burns, *The One-Way Ride*; *CBA*; Eisenberg, *Meyer Lansky*; Gosch, *The Last Testament of Lucky Luciano*; Kobler, *Capone*; Lyle, *The Dry and Lawless Years*; McPhaul, *Johnny Torrio*; Maas, *The Valachi Papers*; Maclean, *Pictorial History of the Mafia*; Morgan, *Prince of Crime*; Murray, *The Legacy of Al Capone*; Nash, *Bloodletters and Badmen*; Pasley, *Al Capone*; ____, *Muscling In*; Peterson, *Barbarians in Our Midst*; ____, *The Mob*; Smith, *Syndicate City*; Spiering, *The Man Who Got Capone*; Sullivan, *Chicago Surrenders*; ____, *Rattling the Cup on Chicago Crime*.

Aikney, Thomas, See: **Broadingham, Elizabeth.**

Ainsworth, Ernest Albert Harrison, prom. 1896, and **Bernard, Henry Peter,** prom. 1896, and **Kaye, William Henry,** prom. 1896, and **Brinsmead, Thomas Edward,** prom. 1896, Brit., fraud. The respected old firm of Brinsmead & Sons had manufactured fine hand-crafted pianos in England for more than fifty years. In 1894, Thomas Edward Brinsmead and his two sons, relatives of the founder, worked as laborers in the factory in Kentish Town. When the founder, John Brinsmead discovered that they were manufacturing their own pianos on the side, he dismissed them.

Thomas Brinsmead decided to go into business for himself at Camden Town, using the thinly disguised name of "T.E. Brinsmead & Sons, Ltd." The company went public in July 1896, offering 20,000 shares at £5 each, even though it owned no factory, no durable goods, and no machinery. To lure investors into the operation, Brinsmead and his associates pasted a billboard to the wall of a building and called it a factory and brought in scores of workmen to pose as piano craftsmen. Brinsmead even purchased several pianos from a warehouse in Islington and advertised them as his own product. The prospectus and a financial newspaper called the *Investor* grossly exagerated the number of orders the company received within the first nine months.

The company folded in 1896, having produced only eighty-three instruments. A financial panic that year forced the owners to liquidate, and the perpetrators of the swindle were tried at the Old Bailey before Justice Phillimore. Thomas Brinsmead was charged with using the family name fraudulently, thereby injuring the reputation of a past employer. He received a lengthy prison sentence of hard labor. Ernest Ainsworth and Henry Bernard, two of the principals in the corporation were sentenced to five years of penal servitude.

REF.: *CBA*; Nicholls, *Crime Within the Square Mile*.

Ainsworth, Robert Andrew, Jr., 1910-81, U.S., jur. Lawyer who was appointed federal judge in the District Court of Louisiana in 1961 by President John F. Kennedy. REF.: *CBA*.

Ainsworth, William Harrison, 1805-82, Brit., writer. Considered to be the first author of "crime-fiction history," Ainsworth made a fortune romanticizing the careers of high-waymen, particularly Dick Turpin (Brit., 1702-24). His novels about brigands and outlaws often outsold the works of such esteemed contemporaries as Charles Dickens. The author unabashedly admitted his admiration for the criminal culprits he elevated to glory. "I always had a strange passion for high-waymen," Ainsworth wrote in the preface to *Rookwood* (1834), his first best-seller, "and have listened by the hour to their exploits, as narrated to me by my father, and especially to those of 'daunt-less Dick' that 'chief minion of the moon'... Turpin was the hero of my boyhood." Turpin, who was in reality a vicious thief, was reshaped into a folk hero by Ainsworth, especially at the con-clusion of *Rookwood* where Turpin makes his dramatic ride to York on Black Bess.

That historic ride in fiction has enthralled children for 150 years since it first appeared in print. The author never seemed to tire in telling how he wrote the passages under the spell of a high-wayman he had created from the shell of a mean-spirited outlaw of a century earlier. "The Ride to York," said Ainsworth, "was completed in one day and one night...a hundred ordinary novel pages in less than twenty-four hours...From the moment I got Turpin on the high road till I landed him at York, I wrote on and on without the slightest sense of effort...Well, I do remember the fever into which I was thrown during the time of composition. My pen literally galloped over the pages. So thoroughly did I identify myself with the highwayman, that, once started, I found it impossible to halt...In his company I mounted the hillside, dashed through the bustling village, swept over the desolate heath, threaded the silent street, plunged into the eddying stream, and kept an onward course, without pause, without hinderance, without fatigue. With him I shouted, sang, laughed, exulted, wept..."

The mythical Turpin of Ainsworth's fertile imagination took root in reality and over the decades, all the villages dotting the Great North Road from Tottenham to York provided so-called historic markers to show that the master rogue Turpin did indeed race through their ways on the gallant Black Bess, a mare whose fame grew as wide as its rider. Yet the truth is that Dick Turpin never rode to York. The mare's carefully preserved hoofprints, the tankard from which Turpin refreshed his steed with strong ale, the overhanging sign of an inn knocked from its hinges by the arm-flailing horseman, all these outlaw artifacts shown to legend-hungry tourists today are as fictional in their claims as was Ainsworth's Turpin.

Ainsworth followed up the enormous success of *Rookwood* with a novel about another highwayman, Jack Sheppard. The book soared to instant best-seller status. Charles Dickens' masterpiece, *Oliver Twist* (1837-39), published at the same time as *Jack Shep-pard* (1839), was eclipsed in sales by the Ainsworth book. These popular works made Ainsworth a wealthy man, despite the fact that England's leading critics and writers, such as William Thack-eray, utterly condemned his books as immoral. To be sure, the author had his defenders, but his success gave vent to a host of imitation works, especially a plethora of plays about the high-wayman, Jack Sheppard. A year after the publication of *Jack Sheppard*, a valet, Francois Benjamin Courvoisier, murdered his master, Lord William Russell in Park Lane. The courteous killer claimed that he had been inspired to slash his 72-year-old employ-er to death after seeing a play about Jack Sheppard only a few nights earlier. This admission caused Lord Joseph Chamberlain to refuse the issuing of any further licenses for plays with the outlaw's name in the title.

The imitative crime of Courvoisier notwithstanding, Ainsworth's success as a novelist of crime fiction continued unabated; he died at age seventy-seven, rich, famous, and comfortable, never having shown a quiver of regret for having distorted dark and terrible creatures into gallent and enviable men. Books authored: *Rookwood* (1834); *Jack Sheppard* (1839); *St. Paul's* (1841); *Guy Fawkes* (1841); *Windsor Castle* (1843); *The Flitch of Bacon* (1854); *Boscobel* (1872), and thirty-two other novels, many of these being illustrated by noted caricaturist George Cruikshank. See: **Shep-pard, Jack; Turpin, Dick.**

REF.: *CBA*; Hibbert, *Highwaymen*.

Airing in a Closed Carriage, 1943, a novel by Joseph Shearing. This work of fiction is based upon the controversial Maybrick poisoning case (Brit., 1889). See: **Maybrick, Florence.** REF.: *CBA*.

Aitchison, Lord (Craigie Mason Aitchison), 1882-1941, Scot., lawyer-polit. Scottish lawyer known for his successful defense of John Donald Merrett who in 1927 was charged with the murder of his mother. He was also successful in his appeal on behalf of Oscar Slater who had served almost twenty years after being wrongly convicted for the murder of Marion Gilchrist. He served as lord justice clerk from 1933 until his death and while in office presided over the murder trials of Jeannie Donald, James Boyd

Kirkwood, John M'Guigan, and Margaret McMillan. REF.: *CBA*.

Aiuppa, Joseph (AKA: **Doves, Joe O'Brien**), 1907- , U.S., org. crime. Long a power in Chicago's Mafia-syndicate, Aiuppa, born on Dec. 1, 1907, in Chicago, began his criminal career as a muscleman and gunner for the Capone mob in 1935, heading the goon squad in Cicero, Ill. His job was then primarily to protect the Capone stronghold of the Hawthorn Hotel in Cicero, and Aiuppa could be seen guarding the entrance at all hours displaying a variety of weapons, from machine guns to automatic pistols. (His overlord for several decades, Tony Accardo, began the same way, as a strong-arm bodyguard who sat in the foyer of the Capone-controlled Lexington Hotel in Chicago.) By 1970 Aiuppa had risen high in the Chicago mob and became the owner of the hotel, renaming it the Towne Hotel, along with the Turf Lounge, which adjoined the hotel. This became, during the 1970s, the chief rendezvous for the bosses of the Chicago syndicate.

Joseph "Doves" Aiuppa, Chicago underboss of the syndicate.

The place also housed a notorious gambling den which proved to be one of the most impregnable gaming rooms ever encountered by raiding police and FBI agents. In a 1970 raid, police and FBI agents went into the basement of the Turf Lounge, tapped on walls, and found a panel which opened into an empty room. There was a steel trapdoor in the floor which was bolted from below. Swinging sledgehammers and picks the officers broke through the trapdoor, letting themselves into another subterranean room. They followed an underground passage which led to yet another steel door. Again the officers labored with sledgehammers until battering down this door. Inside they found an elaborate dice game operation with four men conduting the gambling. At the moment that the door collapsed, dozens of men poured past the officers and others escaped through several underground passageways which had obviously been designed as escape routes. This underground labyrinth had been designed by none other than Aiuppa, a man who took precautions.

Though Aiuppa, from the days of Frank Nitti, controlled the mob's operations in Cicero and the western suburbs of Chicago, he was always a number two or three man in the hierarchy of the Outfit. His nominal boss was Gus Alex, who, along with Murray "The Camel" Humphreys, supplied the brains for the mob. Aiuppa was a thick-witted thug who marble-mouthed his way through life. Even when taking the Fifth Amendment fifty-six times when testifying before the McClellan Committee, he fumbled the brief statement he had to repeat. Gus Alex provided a card with the words to be read, but Aiuppa managed to garble even that —causing Alex no end of frustration.

Aiuppa has always been considered to be one of the more violent members of the Chicago Outfit, having been arrested more than a dozen times for bribery, gambling, assault with intent to kill, and was the suspect in several murders. He was convicted of Contempt of Congress in 1951 when testifying before the Kefauver Committee, a conviction later reversed. Aiuppa served a year in jail for failing to register gambling devices. He was also convicted

in Fort Scott, Kan., in 1962, and jailed for three months for illegally transporting 562 mourning doves from Kansas to Illinois. This last incident earned Aiuppa his strange sobriquet of "Doves" Aiuppa.

The gangster long fancied himself a gentleman hunter, and he encouraged his fellow mobsters to take out their aggressions on the fowl of the earth, holding hunting parties throughout the Midwest. He and some fellow gangsters drove to Kansas during the bird hunting season in 1962 and there blasted more than 1400 birds, mostly mourning doves, from the skies when the legal limit was twenty-four. Officers arrested Aiuppa in his car when he crossed the Illinois line with the hundreds of illegal dead birds in his trunk. He was returned to Kansas where he was convicted before a federal judge who stated that Aiuppa's attack on the birds was nothing short of "unconscionable slaughter." Aiuppa persisted in his bird hunting, establishing the loftily-entitled Yorkshire Quail Club in Kankakee County, to the west of Chicago, enrolling dozens of high-ranking Mafia-syndicate members from around the country as members. The club's hunting permits were issued by the Illinois Department of Conservation, but these were later revoked when Aiuppa was revealed to be the president of the club.

Though Aiuppa has always specialized in gambling, his vast Cicero operations have concentrated over the decades on flesh-peddling and scores of lounges and strip joints where the customers were traditionally given knock-out drops in their drinks. Later, the wealthy customer would find himself in a cheap hotel room with a prositute sitting next to him and one of Aiuppa's gunsels waving blank checks the customer had supposedly signed while drunk, payment for booze and women. Demands at gunpoint would be made for the checks to be converted to cash within an hour or, as was the case of a wealthy doctor, the drugged customer would find himself "in a trunk." This variation of the old badger game brought an estimated $500,000 a year into the Aiuppa-syndicate coffers. The prostitution itself produced twice that amount in Cicero alone each year with gambling operations exceeding $2 million each year.

Aiuppa has also dominated all the bartenders, waitress, and waiter unions in Cicero, for years cutting large chunks of the dues from their unions for syndicate profit. This mob boss was allowed to partake of rackets in Chicago proper, particularly in the area of female flesh, in a bordello or hotel room or on film. He and his goons, including top gun James "Turk" Torello, moved in on the adult film and bookstores of Chicago in 1976, attempting to take over all these stores, including a large chain operated by Paul M. Gonsky. One report has it that when Gonsky refused to turn over his pornographic operations to Aiuppa and company he was marked for death. Gonsky was shot to death on Sept. 21, 1976.

The fencing of stolen goods is also supervised by Aiuppa's organization and woe to the thief who refuses to sell his loot through syndicate channels. In Spring 1978, six professional burglars looted several jewelry stores of gems reported to be worth millions but refused to fence the jewels through Aiuppa's fencing operation. All six were killed. One of Aiuppa's exterminators was reported to be 47-year-old Gerald "Ding Dong" Carusiello of Melrose Park, Ill. Carusiello, who had long been Aiuppa's chauffeur, was the chief executioner of the burglars. He himself was murdered on Sept. 18, 1979, as he stood begging his killers not to shoot him at a construction site in Addison, Ill. Residents heard him scream and plead for several minutes before seven bullets were pumped into him. Carusiello simply knew too much about the wholesale slaughter of the burglars and his loyalty to Aiuppa meant nothing to the liability such information posed.

Information has always meant much to Aiuppa. During the late 1960s and early 1970s, he spent an alleged fortune to obtain sheriff's reports on mob activities by buying an informant, Richard Cain, who wore a wire into police headquarters and that of the Cook County Sheriff's offices to record intelligence that was being gathered on the syndicate. Cain, then a deputy sheriff, dutifully reported back to Aiuppa and others so they were forwarned on any impending raids against their whorehouses and gambling dens. Aiuppa reportedly paid as much as $2,500 a month to Cain for this information. Cain was later suspected of leading a double life in that he was selling information to both the police and the syndicate, and for this betrayal the mob had him exterminated in 1973. It was speculated that Cain, who had become an open aide to mob leader Sam Giancana, whose power was waning and who was opposed by Aiuppa, was murdered as a message to Giancana that none of his own people were safe under his shaky authority.

Mob allegiance also meant nothing in Chicago after the execution of syndicate leader Sam "Momo" Giancana in 1975. At that time Tony Accardo resumed full leadership of the Outfit, having gone into self-imposed exile for ten years. Following Giancana's death, Aiuppa's star rose, and he became the chief enforcer for Accardo but never made top level policy decisions. His job was to deal with insurgent mobsters lusting after Giancana's vacated position. Such a one was Anthony Spilotro, a Chicago syndicate hitman credited with murdering twenty-five persons. Spilotro went on to become the Chicago mob's representative in Las Vegas, returning regularly to the Windy City with hundreds of thousands of dollars skimmed by various casino operators, the cut of the Outfit in return for its initial investments in certain casinos. When a goodly portion of this monthly payoff dropped off, it was naturally concluded that Spilotro was skimming a portion for himself. Spilotro and his younger brother Michael disappeared in 1986, and they were both later found beaten to death in an Indiana ditch. A short distance away was a farm owned by none other than Joey Aiuppa. In prison at this writing, Aiuppa is still a force in mob activities, his control over Cicero operations maintained from his cell, although Aiuppa's men still answer to the overall Chicago boss Sam Anthony Scarlisi. See: **Accardo, Anthony Joseph; Cain, Richard; Giancana, Sam; Scarlisi, Sam Anthony; Spilotro, Anthony.**

REF.: *CBA;* Demaris, *Captive City;* ____, *The Last Mafioso;* Kefauver, *Crime in America;* Kilian, *Who Runs Chicago?;* Kobler, *Capone;* McClellan, *Crime without Punishment;* McPhaul, *Johnny Torrio;* Maclean, *Pictorial History of the Mafia;* Morgan, *Prince of Crime;* Nash, *Bloodletters and Badmen;* ____, *People to See;* Peterson, *Barbarians in Our Midst;* Reid, *The Grim Reapers;* Schlesinger, *Robert Kennedy and His Times;* Smith, *Syndicate City;* Ungar, *FBI.*

Aix-en-Provence Nuns, prom. 1605-1611, Fr., witchcraft. A high-strung young noblewoman and an attractive parish priest formed the basis for rampant accusations of witchcraft that centered on the Aix-en-Provence convent. Madeleine de Demandolx was born into a wealthy aristocratic Provençal family. She was an excitable and deeply religious girl who, as a 12-year-old in 1605, went to live in the Ursuline convent of Aix-en-Provence, a convent made up of just six nuns, all nobly born. Sent back home when she became severely depressed after two years away from her family, Madeleine was cheered by her friendship with Father Louis Gaufridi, whose good looks and playful nature made him a popular parish priest, particularly at ease with women. The 14-year-old girl fell in love with the 34-year-old priest who often came to visit her. Local gossip caused Mother Catherine de Gaumer, head of the convent at Marseilles, to warn Madeleine's mother and Gaufridi about the dangers of the relationship. In 1607 Madeleine again entered the convent, this time as a novice. Confessing Gaufridi's intimacies with her to Gaumer, she was transferred to a convent at Aix where Gaufridi could not visit her. Within a year or so Madeleine, now sixteen or seventeen, began to have severe cramps and seizures and, in December 1609, she smashed a crucifix during confession. The convent's elderly priest, Father Romillon, exorcised the girl, whose hysterical convulsions and periodic speechlessness had now spread to three other nuns. By Easter 1610 Gaufridi was questioned by Romillon; the younger priest denied sexual relations although Madeleine continued to accuse him under secret exorcisms that went on for another year. Other nuns continued to be affected, notably Sister Louise Capeau, or Capelle, who, apparently jealous of Madeleine's notoriety, tried to rival her in hysterics.

Romillon brought both girls to Sebastian Michaëlis, the famous elderly Grand Inquisitor in Avignon, who publicly exorcised them at the shrine of St. Mary Magdalene at Ste-Baume. Several other exorcisms ensued. On December 30, 1610, Gaufridi was brought to Ste-Baume and jailed, later to be returned to his parish for lack of evidence against him. He appealed to the Pope and the Bishop of Marseilles to suppress the Ursuline convents and stop the jailings of the Ste-Baume nuns. Madeleine was exhibiting severe manic depressive behavior by this time. When the case came to the civil courts in February 1611, Inquisitor Michaëlis brought political forces into play in his efforts to prosecute Gaufridi. The two young nuns often went into fits in court, with Madeleine occasionally becoming coherent, confessing that her accusations were "all imaginings, illusions, and not a word of truth in them." She also fainted several times for love of Gaufridi, sometimes acting out erotic behavior in court, other times showing stigmata on her body, continually contradicting her own testimony, becoming deeply depressed, and twice attempting suicide.

Gaufridi was interrogated and, when his body was shaved and he was judged to show marks of the devil, he reluctantly confessed. Michaëlis printed a bogus confession ascribed to Gaufridi. The court ignored the parish priest's later retraction and found him guilty of magic, sorcery, idolatry, and fornication. On April 30, 1611, he was tortured at great length, strangled, and then burned at the stake. The next day, according to the chronicle of the Ursuline convent, Madeleine de Demandolx was cured. Capeau, on the other hand, was not, and her accusations were directly responsible for the burning of a blind girl and for further witchcraft indictments at the convents of St. Claire's at Aix and St. Bridget's at Lille. Madeleine would be accused two more times of consorting with the devil, in 1642, when she was forty-nine, and again in 1652, when she was ordered to pay a heavy fine and sentenced to life imprisonment. In 1662 she was released in custody of a relative in Chateauviex, where she died on Dec. 20, 1670, at the age of seventy-seven.

REF.: Calmeil, *De la Folie;* Cauzons, *La Magie et la Sorcellerie en France; CBA;* Garinet, *Historie de la Magie en France;* Michaelis, *The Admirable History of the Possession and Conversion of a Penitent Woman;* Robbins, *The Encyclopedia of Witchcraft.*

Aizawa, Sabura, See: **Nagata, Tetsuzan.**

Akerman, Alexander, 1869-1948, U.S., jur. U.S. attorney for the Southern District of Georgia from 1912-14 and appointed federal judge in the Southern District of Florida from 1929 by President Calvin Coolidge. REF.: *CBA.*

Akerman, Amos Tappan, 1821-80, U.S., lawyer. Born in Portsmouth, N.H., practiced law in Georgia, and became a member of the Confederate Army during the Civil War. He later served as attorney general under President Ulysses S. Grant from 1870-71 when he resigned under pressure brought by railroad interests after he rejected their claim to certain government land. REF.: *CBA.*

Akhmedov, Akhmed I., prom. 1988, U.S.S.R., mob vio.-mur. Riots against Armenians in Russia left at least thirty-two people dead when a mob descended on apartment buildings, setting some on fire. On Feb. 28, 1988, a violent mob gathered in the Armenian community in the Azerbaijan city of Sumgait. As tension increased, Akhmedov grabbed a megaphone and shouted, "Kill the Armenians!" then led the raging crowd as they stormed seventeen apartment buildings, killing seven people and burning some of them alive. Soviet officials released the information that thirty-two people had been murdered in the ethnic riots, twenty-six of them ethnic Armenians. The Armenians estimated the toll as much higher. Rioting resulted from the republic of Armenia's demands for the acquisition of the Azerbaijan district of Nagorno-Karabakh, which has a mostly Armenian population. The Kremlin rejected the demand. On Oct. 18, Akhmedov went on trial. He received the first death penalty to be issued by the Soviet courts in connection with the riots. REF.: *CBA.*

Akulonis, Peter, prom. 1953, U.S., mur. A quiet, reserved man who did chores for his elderly mother and worked hard for his livelihood, Akulonis came unravelled one day and murdered his entire family. As a youth in Lawrence, Maine, Akulonis was a troubled poor boy, partly deaf, with some facial paralysis, who rebelled by committing acts of petty crime. In the 1930s he changed his ways, marrying, fathering two sons, and becoming a hard-working boilermaker in a tank works. For years Akulonis kept to himself, raising his family. A co-worker talked about the factory: "The noise in here drives you bugs after a while, but he never come off his machine to talk to anybody. He was a bandit for work." Around the Christmas holiday of 1952, things began to change for Akulonis. He sat alone at lunch, complaining once to a friend with a new car, "How can you afford that when I drive a pile of junk? All I do is work and go home...I'm not getting anything out of life." He asked another man at the shop if he thought he was "crazy or something," and soon he began picking fights. Finally he quit and started to drink.

In mid-April Akulonis went to his four-room apartment in the afternoon, picked up a carpenter's ax, and killed his wife with a single blow, turning then on his 4-year-old son, Michael, whom he brutally murdered and mutilated. Going to his brother Alphonse's house, the killer herded his mother and two young nephews into a room and hacked them to death. When the brother returned, Akulonis met him in the kitchen and killed him too. Picking up his 11-year-old son, Peter, Jr., at school, Akulonis drove the boy to some nearby woods, then shot him in the face with a .22 rifle, newly purchased from Sears Roebuck and Co. He returned to his car—a recent loan from his remaining brother Raymond—and drove it to the Cambridge factory where Raymond worked. Raymond got behind the wheel while Akulonis sat in the back. Two other workers along for the ride said they noticed nothing unusual about his behavior. The police, called by Alphonse's widow, were waiting at Raymond's house when the car pulled up. As the officers leaped out of their car, Akulonis shot Raymond through the head, then turned the rifle on himself. A note found in his pocket read, "I love Michael more than life. I loved Mom, Paul, Jimmy, Sis, Peter, Ray." REF.: *CBA*.

Ala-Din Mujahid, d.1378, India, sultan, assass. Sultan from 1375 until assassinated by his cousin Daud. REF.: *CBA*.

Ala ud-Din Muhammad Khalji, d.1316, India, sultan, assass. See: **Jalal al-Din**. REF.: *CBA*.

Alamgir II (Azizal-Din Alamgir), 1699-1759, India., emperor, assass. Mogul emperor of India from 1754 until assassinated. REF.: *CBA*.

Alarcon, Arthur Lawrence, b.1925-   , U.S., jur. Judge in the Los Angeles Superior Court from 1964-78, served on the California Court of Appeals from 1978-79, and appointed federal judge in the Ninth Circuit Court by President Jimmy Carter.

Alarcon, Nestor Mencias, prom. c.1970, Mex., mur. Nestor Alarcon, a 26-year-old Mexican peasant, was hired to kill Isabel Garcia by his employer, Señora Martinez Anguilar. Garcia was having an affair with Señora Anguilar's husband. Señora Anguilar first paid a witchdoctor to put a spell on Isabel Garcia, but when this failed to end the affair she offered Alarcon fifty-five pesos to kill the woman. "That's a lot of money for a man like me," he said later. He hacked Garcia to death with a machete, then turned on her 9-year-old daughter.

Police had closed the books on the case when Alarcon drew attention to himself by leaving town. He was picked up for routine questioning and confessed to murdering Garcia. He told police that Señora Anguilar put him up to it, but reneged on her part of the agreement after learning that Alarcon had also killed the girl. Alarcon later said he committed the murder because he felt obligated to carry out the orders of his employer. REF.: *CBA*.

Albanese, Charles, 1937-   , U.S., mur. In the fall of 1980 Fox Lake, a popular vacation spot near Chicago, was shocked by the deaths of two elderly residents, the first of many over the next sixteen months in a bizarre scheme to seize control of the estates of two wealthy families. If the plan succeeded, Charles Albanese, a prominent Chicago-area businessman driven to obtain wealth and power, would inherit the estates. But first he had to poison up to six of his relatives.

In August 1980 he implemented his heinous plan. Mary Lambert, the 87-year-old grandmother of Albanese's wife Virginia, died of an apparent heart attack on Aug. 6. Twelve days later Virginia's mother, 69-year-old Marion K. Mueller, died the same way. Described as healthy women, their sudden death within two weeks panicked friends and family into believing their local water supply was contaminated. Tests of the water proved negative.

Virginia Albanese inherited $150,000 from the two deceased. An investigation into the deaths uncovered that in May Charles Albanese had persuaded Lambert to leave her estate to her daughter Mueller in the event of her death, aware that his wife would receive the inheritance when Mueller died, and that she had previously willed her property to him.

The deaths were reinvestigated in 1981 when, on May 16, Charles' father, 69-year-old Michael J. Albanese Sr., died of an unknown illness. His death left the family-owned trophy company and an estate worth $267,373 to his sons, Charles and Michael A. Albanese Jr., and would revert to Charles at the death of Michael Jr. In addition, Michael Sr. left his wife Clare a $200,000 life insurance policy paid in full at the time of his death. Should she die, Charles would become her beneficiary.

Authorities reopened the cases of Lambert and Mueller when they learned that all three dead persons were related and that the junior Albanese was ill with symptoms his father had shown before his death. An inquiry into the death of the senior Albanese finally showed signs of arsenic in his system. Doctors examined Michael Jr. and found arsenic as well. The bodies of Lambert and Mueller, exhumed and autopsied, also showed arsenic in their systems. All of the evidence by now pointed to Charles Albanese, who was in line to inherit more than half a million dollars from both families.

Police took Albanese into custody as he, his wife, and his mother were leaving for a vacation in Jamaica. Police feared the two women would have been murdered there as they were the only remaining barriers to the wealth Albanese sought. A jury convicted Albanese on three counts of murder in the poisoning deaths of Mary Lambert, Marion Mueller, and Michael Albanese Sr. Sentenced to death, he awaits punishment on death row. Albanese and his lawyers have appealed the sentence and on Sept. 29, 1988, the Illinois Supreme Court denied their appeal and scheduled Albanese to die in the electric chair on Jan. 25, 1989. REF.: *CBA*.

Alberding, Heinrich, prom. 1928, Ger., fraud-mur. Heinrich Alberding, a 32-year-old businessman from Fulda, West Germany, attempted to fake his own death in order to collect on two life insurance policies valued at 60,000 marks. Alberding was last seen on Jan. 1, 1928, when he left home in order to attend a theatrical performance in Frankfurt. A month later, police received a letter from the missing man. He said he was being held prisoner by a pair of international drug dealers who abducted him on the way to Frankfurt, and that he managed to drop the letter out a window.

In the event of his death, Alberding instructed the police to look in the right sleeve of his jacket for a note. Seven months later on Aug. 23, 1928, a skeleton was found in the woods of Saalfeld with the jacket described in the note. A wristwatch engraved H. Alberding seemed to confirm the identity of the deceased.

However, Professor Ernst Giese, Director of the Institute of Forensic Medicine at the University of Jena, concluded that the skeleton was not of a man in his early thirties, but one much younger. The spinal column was that of a robust 20-year-old. A facial reconstruction clearly showed that the deceased was definitely not Alberding. In 1934, the Fulda police raided Alberding's home and found him hiding under his bed. He was tried, convicted, and sentenced to die for the murder of an unidentified man.

REF.: *CBA*; Thorwald, *The Century of the Detective*.

Alberic I, d.925, Roman., emperor, assass. Emperor of Rome who was assassinated by his own people. REF.: *CBA*.

Albert I, c.1250-1308, Ger., king, assass. King from 1298 until assassinated by his nephew John the Parricide. REF.: *CBA*.

Alberto, Raymond, prom. 1940s-50s, Fr., fraud. Alberto led a ring of shrewd confidence men on the Riviera during the late 1940s, and when he heard that an ultra-conservative French millionaire was overly concerned about Communists taking over France, he set in action an impossible but extremely lucrative scheme. The 27-year-old Baron Scipion du Roure de Beruyère, who had vast real estate holdings in Bagnois-sur-Cêze and villas at Cap d'Antibes, made the mistake of voicing his concerns about the Communists to a hustler named Aimé Gaillard who, a short time later, introduced the baron to Raymond, who claimed that he was an inspector of the French Border Police. Raymond, as he sat with the Baron in one of his luxurious villas sipping cool drinks, confided to the nobleman that France, indeed, was in serious peril of a Communist takeover. He went on to add that the French intelligence service was in dire straits financially until it was voted new government funds and the delay would cause France to miss the opportunity to obtain priceless uranium which the country needed for its atomic weaponry.

French flimflammers, left to right, Louis Gagliardoni, Marius Carlicchi, and Raymond Alberto, laughing up their uranium scam at their trial.

Patriotic to the core, du Roure offered to finance the purchase of the uranium which he believed was being smuggled into France from Germany. He began to advance hundreds of thousands of francs to Alberto and his men, receiving what he thought were sealed shipments of uranium which, he, in turn, passed on to what he thought were French intelligence agents. He did this to serve his country and believed that he had to continue operating secretly so as not to alert the traitorous Communist members of France's Chamber of Deputies. For almost two years, Baron du Roure dumped $342,842 into the hands of the con men, but he eventually grew restless, asking if there would ever be an end to the purchase and clandestine delivery of the uranium shipments. Alberto concluded that his sucker had been bilked up to a point where the ring now risked exposure. He informed the baron that his services were no longer needed and that the government would soon be returning his money with considerable interest. Moreover, added Alberto, France intended to award du Roure with the distinguished Legion of Honor medal.

When the list of official recepients of this award was announced on Dec. 31, 1952, and the baron found that his name was not on it, du Roure angrily called the Deuxième Bureau, France's official intelligence agency, and complained that he had been insulted, that he had given his efforts and money to save his country from the Communists and now, though promised, he was not to be recognized by France. The baron was told that no Inspector Alberto existed. Du Roure mentioned several other French officers of the Bureau, but he was told that these men did not exist either. Realizing, finally, that he had been mulcted, the baron went to authorities and told them where he had buried the secret uranium shipments. These were first examined with Geiger counters and then opened to reveal packages of sand and others with tap water.

The con ring, however, exposed itself when several of its members began to spend lavishly, and Alberto was tracked down as were Louis Gagliardoni, who had impersonated a general of French intelligence named Combaluzier, and Marius Carlicchi, who had pretended to be another intelligence officer, Colonel Berthier. All three confidence men were tried in Paris and, as the ridiculous swindle was unraveled the presiding judge had to stifle laughter at the scheme. "I congratulate you on your imagination," the magistrate told Alberto, "but how were you able to tell the baron such stupendous tales without ever laughing?" Alberto shrugged as he stood before the bench and replied, "He just believed everything." Alberto and Carlicchi were sentenced to four years in prison in June 1953, and Cagliardoni received eighteen months. Go-between Galliard was found harmless but he reveled in the baron's gullibility. "The baron was my pearl," he told a reporter, "and let me tell you, a man's got to crack a lot of oysters before he finds a pearl like that."

REF.: *CBA;* Nash, *Hustlers and Con Men*.

Albinus, c.524, Roman., polit., treas. Served as senator, consul, and patrician under King Theodoric and convicted of treason for corresponding with Eastern Emperor Justin I; executed with Boethius and Symmachus. REF.: *CBA*.

Alboin, d.573, Italy, king, (unsolv.) mur. King of the Lombards from c.565 until he was murdered, supposedly at the hand of his wife. REF.: *CBA*.

Alcatraz, 1933-63, U.S., prison. No other American prison was so dreaded by U.S. criminals, particularly in the 1930s-40s as was Alcatraz, better known as the Rock. For three decades this island strongly projected the image of a lonely, maximum-security prison from which no prisoner could hope to escape. No one was ever paroled from Alcatraz and most left the Rock in a pine coffin. Those who did attempt to escape faced the impossible currents of San Francisco Bay, police boats, and hostile forces on every side where land could be seen if not reached. Alcatraz was very much like the French penal colony on Devil's Island off Cayenne, Fr. Guiana, which served as France's maximum-security penal colony, a place where the most ruthless, incorrigible criminals resigned themselves to penal oblivion. It was because of Alcatraz's distant location, bastion-like appearance, and utter inaccessibility, that the place was chosen to house America's super criminals. The place held the same kind of apprehensions for those who first glimpsed its barren landscape in their exploration of the New World.

The Spanish, first to explore the California coastline, did not enter San Francisco Bay until Aug. 5, 1775, when Lieutenant Don Juan Manuel de Avala, sailed his ship, the *San Carlos*, into the bay. The rocky island in the bay offered sheer cliffs and an uninviting landscape with no true anchorage. The Spanish sailed by the island, noting that it was covered with thousands of pelicans and called the place Isla de Alcatraces, Island of Pelicans. Though the Spanish populated the Bay Area, Alcatraz remained uninhabited. In 1846, Pio Pico, the last Mexican governor of California, granted the sale of the island to Julian Workman, providing that Workman cause a permanent light on the island to warn ships of its existence. Up to that time, Alcatraz was nothing more than a navigational hazard. Workman did little or nothing with the island and never did erect the expected lighthouse. After some legal disputes over the island's ownership, Alcatraz passed into the possession of the U.S. through an executive order by President Millard Fillmore in 1850. The Army Engineer Corps erected a lantern-operated lighthouse 160 feet above sea level on Alcatraz in 1854.

Four years later the island was fortified with three heavy gun batteries and an artillary company. It became Fort Alcatraz and from its vantage place in the middle of the bay, its batteries could sweep away any enemy daring to challenge its guns and those of the facing forts in San Francisco and Marin. The island, however, was difficult to supply because of the treacherous currents in the waters separating Alcatraz from San Francisco by more than a mile and a still longer distance to Marin and other parts of the

Bay Area. It had an obvious purpose to American military commanders other than that of a fortress. Military prisoners were kept at Alcatraz in the tradition of other lonely, rugged islands that had been used as prisons in the past. In addition to France's Devil's Island, there were many traditional island prisons around the world: Fort Drum, the U.S. military prison in the Dry Tortugas; Russia's Solovetskiye Island in the White Sea; Italy's Lipari Island off the northern coast of Sicily. During the early period of the American Civil War, Alcatraz was used to house Confederate prisoners. The first of these were seventeen Confederate privateers led by Asbury Harpending who attempted to arm the schooner, *J.M. Chapman*, and prey upon Union shipping.

By 1868 U.S. military authorities designated Alcatraz as an army prison for incorrigible soldiers, deserters and, during the Indian wars of the 1870s and 1880s, the most troublesome Indian chiefs such as Kae-te-na, one of Geronimo's most dreaded lieutenants. During the Spanish-American War, U.S. Army deserters were imprisoned on the island but they were soon crowded by Spanish troops captured in the Philippines. American troops invalided home from the Philippines later recuperated from dysentary and other tropical ailments on the island. In 1906, when the jails of San Francisco were demolished by the quake and fire that consumed the city, prisoners were transferred to the un-damaged island. Military prisoners were again held on the island after engineers built a concrete and steel blockhouse to hold them. Hundreds of deserters and other U.S. military personnel, along with German spies, were imprisoned on Alcatraz during WWI, including Franz Bopp, German general consul in San Francisco who had been convicted of espionage in 1918. During the 1920s, the number of military prisoners dwindled down to a meager few.

At the dawn of the 1930s and the Great Depression, America was faced with a tidal wave of crime led by organized gangsters in the cities and hordes of farm boys turned bank robbers. The era of the public enemy caused U.S. Attorney General Homer S. Cummings to look about for a place to establish America's premier maximum-security prison. He chose Alcatraz in 1933, even though its buildings had fallen into ruin. Here the toughest, the most notorious of America's criminals would be held in maximum-security and allowed minimum privileges. Through an act of Congress, Alcatraz was officially designated as a U.S. penitentiary and turned over to the U.S. Department of Justice which was given a budget to build an impregnable prison from which no criminal could escape. Alcatraz and other prisons fell under the jurisdiction of the newly established Federal Bureau of Prisons. Seven of the island's twelve acres were designed as the prison compound. Prison employees would occupy residences and recreational areas in the remaining five acres. Four cell blocks, A, B, C, and D were constructed on the foundations of existing military buildings. A block was built over the old army barracks and was thought to be the least secure of the cell blocks and thus was rarely used. B and C blocks were interior cell blocks with three aisles through them, the center aisle nicknamed by the convicts as "Broadway," the outer aisles called "Michigan Boulevard" and "Seedy Street" since it connected C block with D block. B and C blocks housed 324 cells and D block, built in 1939-40 to replace the dungeon-like solitary confinement cells exisiting under the old army barracks, offered forty-two cells for the most incorrigible prisoners.

The dining room or mess hall for the prison was at the northwestern end of the main cellhouse. At the southeastern end of the island could be found the lighthouse, the administrative building, the main gate entrance and beyond that, the arsenal which was manned twenty-four hours a day by guards and was protected by heavy concrete and steel plate, along with bulletproof glass. The prison guard force was made up of 100 men, specially trained for their positions, half of whom were required to live on the island in Alcatraz's duplex apartment buildings which comfortably housed fifty families. To the northwest on the island was the powerhouse and pumping station. Since Alcatraz had no fresh

water supply, water boats and barges had to regularly make trips to the Rock each week. Food and other supplies were also ferried to the Rock, all heavily guarded to prevent against prisoners secreting themselves on these supply boats.

Other than one prisoner, Martin Sobel, none of Alcatraz's prisoners were sent directly to this penitentiary following convictions and sentences in court. All of the Rock's inmates were sent from other federal prisons after they had proved impossible to handle. Alcatraz was the end of the line for such recidivist inmates. The trouble-makers, malcontents, and escape artists of Leavenworth, Atlanta, McNeil Island, and Lewisburg were selected as ideal prisoners for Alcatraz, and these were shipped in the early 1930s by sealed prison trains to the Rock. There were never more than 300 inmates on Alcatraz at a single time; there was one guard for every three prisoners. As the prison became publicized, almost from its official opening in August 1934, with newspaper and magazine writers spinning instant myths about the Rock, and screenwriters embellishing the wildest of rumors, Alcatraz took on a mystique of the invincible. No prisoner, no matter how fierce or how clever he might be, could conquer the Rock. Myths by the score sprang up, many encouraged by authorities to plant further dread in the hearts of criminals.

One myth was that prisoners could never swim to the mainland from Alcatraz because the man-eating sharks would devour them before they paddled thirty feet from the Rock. Though sharks are common in San Francisco Bay, no man-eaters of any note have been recorded. There were never any dungeons used on the Rock except those few cells below the waterline which had been part of the army barracks foundations. These were solitary confinement cells that were dark and dank but were not overrun with rats and could not have passed for any European-type dungeon. Inmates who could not be controlled were sent to these cells for three to four days and were kept on a 1200-calorie-a-day ration, never given merely bread and water. Prisoners at Alcatraz who were sent to these dark solitary confinement cells were chained to the walls, guards using the chains that had been installed by the army decades earlier. These underground cells were held unconstitutional by a San Francisco judge in 1939 who labeled their use as "cruel and unusual punishment." At that time, plans were made to complete D block as the special place of solitary confinement for unruly Alcatraz prisoners.

Other myths persisted. The floors were not highly waxed so that prisoners trying "to run" would "go straight on their butts," as one newsman put it. Although the prison was kept clean at all times, such floor conditions would also send the guards skidding about. Another preposterous newspaper claim had it that the entire prison was kept at an even 70-degree heat so that any prisoner attempting to escape would be shocked into unconsciousness by the freezing bay waters. The Rock was thought to be the dead end for any federal prisoners unlucky enough to be sent there. Yet this was far from the case. About forty prisoners were received at Alcatraz each year and the same number of prisoners were transferred to other federal penitentiaries; many of these transfers were in preparation of parole from other federal insitutions. This was to maintain an unrelenting image that was fostered more by J. Edgar Hoover of the FBI than the Federal Bureau of Prisons over which he held great influence during his tenure. Some prisoners at the Rock actually petitioned the government to *stay* in Alcatraz, rather than be sent to a less restrictive federal penitentiary since prisoners on the Rock did not share cells but had their own to themselves and preferred not to re-enter prison systems with dense populations.

In the early years of Alcatraz, prison authorities attempted to have the Rock live up to its reputation as "the toughest can in the world." Guards were instructed to shoot to kill first and ask questions later if ever confronted with what they thought was a life-threatening situation. They were told that they were dealing with the most desperate criminals in America; inmates who should be shown no mercy, no human kindness. These men were beyond rehabilitation, droned many federal authorities, not the least of

San Francisco with Alcatraz, above right, squatting in the treacherous waters of the Bay.

Alcatraz in 1862 when the Rock was used as an army fort guarding San Francisco Bay.

The first trainload of prisoners, including Al Capone, arriving by barge, docks on Alcatraz Island, 1934.

The building of D block which housed the solitary confinement cells, designed for the worst criminals in America.

Cell blocks A, B, D, top, left to right; C block opening to recreation yard at bottom.

whom was the severe and uncompromising J. Edgar Hoover. The FBI chief had made his views quite clear on the matter of rehabilitation, stating, "There is no possibility of wiping out crime by trying to reform criminals. The house has been burned down. The tree has felt the blow of the ax and has fallen in the forest. The house cannot be re-erected, nor can the tree again point its leaves to the sky."

In the early years of Alcatraz, prisoner movement was kept to a minimum. Convicts were locked in their cells fourteen hours a day, seven days a week. Morning inspection was always at 6:30 a.m. A head count of all inmates in their cells was made. The prisoners stepped out of their cells at command and marched silently to the mess hall where they were given breakfast. At command, prisoners were ordered to stop eating and march back to their cells. The convicts were then marched single file to the small yard for a brief exercise period and then they were assigned to their daily work in the industrial shops. They were marched to the industrial shops and worked until 11:30 a.m. Convicts were then whistled to a stop and marched back to their cells for a head count. They were then marched to the mess hall for lunch which ended promptly at 1 p.m. Convicts then marched back to work. At 5 p.m. the inmates were marched to the mess hall for dinner. At 6:30 p.m. another single file march back to the cell ended with prisoners locked inside their cells and another head count taken. At 9:30 p.m., lights were turned out. This regimen was repeated day in and day out without change—ever.

Prisoners each had their own cells, each cell being five feet wide, nine feet deep, and seven feet high. It contained a bunk, a wash basin, a toilet, and a single shelf. Guards were present everywhere and could see into almost all cells from vantage points of catwalks and strategically positioned towers. All mail was censored and then retyped so a prisoner never saw an original letter sent to him. Visitors were allowed once a month but they had to face a heavy-plated glass window and talk through phones. Guards listened in on all conversations. Visitors had to pass through a metal detector system which would go off with loud bells if the visitor carried anything metallic. When Al Capone's mother arrived to visit her crime czar son, a resident of Alcatraz from 1934 to 1939, the detectors went off and the elderly Mrs. Capone was taken to a room by a female staff worker and ordered to strip. Her girdle was found to have metal stays and she was ordered to leave it behind when visiting her son. So upset and embarrassed was Mrs. Capone that, upon seeing her errant son, she burst into a loud harangue in her native tongue, Italian, demanding that her son do something about her being insulted. (One of those officials listening in on the phone understood Italian.) Speaking a foreign language to a prisoner was also prohibited, as Mrs. Capone was informed, which further added to her embarrassment. Following this visit, the elderly Mrs. Capone never returned to the Rock to see her son. May Capone, the crime boss' wife, was allowed the special privilege of seeing her husband on back-to-back days. Normal visitations permitted only once a month visits but for those who traveled great distances, such as May Capone, who lived in Florida, two visits were permitted, the last day of a month and the first day of the next.

Unlike other federal prisons, convicts could not earn privileges or reduced time through an honor or "good behavior" system and no trustee system existed. The good behavior system, however, was later modified and inmates with exemplary records could considerably reduce their sentences. A code of silence was strictly enforced in the prison's early years. Silence was maintained at all times, day and night. Talking without guard approval was not allowed within the prison mess hall, the library, the showers, workshops, or barbershop. Inmates like James Henry "Blackie" Audett and Alvin "Creepy" Karpis who were serving long prison terms, developed what they called "silent speak," moving their lips silently while others learned to read lip movements. By the early 1940s, however, the silent system was somewhat relaxed.

Much has been said about the brutal treatment given prisoners on the Rock. It was claimed that unruly inmates thrown into the "hole" (solitary confinement) were hosed down with powerful water hoses, the pressure knocking them into walls. It was claimed that inmates were put into straitjackets and beaten with billy clubs and rubber truncheons. It was claimed that prisoners were tied to stakes and whipped into unconsciousness. None of this was ever proven to be true, although straitjackets were used on special occasions. These occasions involved prisoners who seemed to go berserk and attacked guards, many of these inmates feigning mental illness so they could be transferred to a federal correction facility for the criminally insane. The usual inmate tactic was to inveigle one of the guards into his cell and attack him, knowing that the backup guard would enter when the inmate's back was turned and knock him out, usually with a blackjack, a weapon which was not government issue. Once the inmate was down, he was put into a straitjacket and taken to solitary confinement. Medical examiners would later determine whether or not the inmate was truly insane and deserved transfer.

The exercise yard was available to prisoners on weekends and here they played handball and softball, only a hit over the wall did not mean a home run but an out. A gardener who worked outside the wall usually stood waiting for the homers and threw the ball back as there was a limited supply. Inmates had a favorite game called "name that ship." One prisoner would sit on the highest of the stairs in the yard and peer over the wall to the Golden Gate, sighting a ship and describing its shape and estimated tonnage. Others below him would then have to guess the name of the ship. These game players recognized most of the ships that sailed in and out of San Francisco Bay over the years, studying the freighters, cruise ships, and military ships in reference books on ships in the prison library. Movies were occasionally shown and, though there were some knifings and fistfights through the years during this special treat time, the inmates were invariably well behaved when films were shown (never prison or crime films). If a prisoner made a disturbance, most of the other inmates would shout him down as they became incensed if the movie was halted and this privilege denied them.

Severe punishments, invariably long stretches in solitary confinement, awaited anyone caught in homosexual activity. Prisoners were safe from sexual assault in their private cells, but attacks occurred regularly in the basement of the kitchen and the shower stalls where guards who interfered with such activity risked being knifed or attacked by several inmates at one time. Because of the strict regimen at Alcatraz, constant head counts, and religious monitoring of convicts, such sexual practices were kept to a minimum. Contraband, alcohol, and drugs, were also closely screened. The most potent home brew made by prisoners came from the saving of raisins and the fermentation of same, a long, involved process that produced a minimal and decidedly unsavory alcoholic beverage.

Every detail to assure security was attended to with great care. Prisoners through the years attempted to saw through the bars of their cells but always met with failure. It was thought that two types of metals had been used in the making of Alcatraz's bars, the outside metal being casehardened inside and out and the inside being a round steel bar, but following the closing of the Rock the bars were examined and it was learned that the bars, originally installed in 1934, were made of solid steel and next to impossible to saw through since they were not hollow, as was the case with most other prisons. Anything that could be used as a weapon was carefully counted and guarded. Prisoners were allowed to shave in their cells, a double-edged razor placed on the lip of each cell by guards, along with a small piece of leather for sharpening. If a prisoner did not return the razor to the lip within a half hour, at 7 p.m., he was usually put into solitary confinement. No inmate ever attempted a real suicide with the razors handed out, but a few did manage to draw enough blood to convince prison authorities that they required mental attention at the Springfield, Mo., facility, the true aim of most of these prisoners being a transfer to that institution.

No television was ever permitted in any Alcatraz cell during

Convicts filing into the dining hall; they stood at their tables until they were filled, then sat down in unison; there was no talking and above the heads of the inmates were gas bombs in case of riot.

Alcatraz inmates filing through the "snitch box," a metal detector which pinpointed homemade weapons.

The exercise yard adjoining C block where convicts sat on the high steps and peered across the Bay to see San Francisco change through the decades.

The solitary confinement cells of D block.

A cell in solitary confinement.

the TV era, and no inmates were given newspapers or radios. A limited number of magazines, usually those approved by Hoover through the Bureau of Prisons (periodicals catering to sports enthusiasts or family magazines such as *The Saturday Evening Post*) were allowed to circulate through the cells. The prison did have a large library, about 15,000 books, most of which had been left by the U.S. Army and were rather archaic editions, although all of Zane Grey's western novels were present, along with the adventure yarns of Jack London. No literature concerning sex, violence, or crime was present. After WWII, inmates could subscribe to certain publications, particularly *Life, Newsweek,* and *Time* magazines. The convict who could not read was left with next to nothing to do in his cell between 6:30 p.m. and 9:30 p.m. when the lights went out. The most popular material sought in the library had to do with criminal law; dozens of inmates studied the law and became cellhouse lawyers, writing countless writs and petitions, looking for errors in trial transcripts, and seeking new court dates for themselves and other inmates who paid them for their research. Several Alcatraz inmates became as expert in criminal law as practicing attorneys, although their petitions were seldom granted a favorable hearing by the courts.

For years prisoners around the U.S. heard that the worst food served to inmates anywhere could be found at Alcatraz, but in truth the food was invariably above average, although it was, by nature of limited budgets, repetitive and unimaginative. A typical meal served: Frankfurters, chili, potatoes, sauerkraut, carrots, pudding, rolls, and tea. In the early days of the prison, no knives were given inmates but later convicts were allowed to use knives, forks, and spoons, all of which had to be accounted for before and after each meal. One strict rule in the mess hall was that each convict had to eat every bit of food he put on his plate. If a convict attempted to leave the dining room with food on his plate he was disciplined. The mess hall was tightly guarded as it was the one place where the entire population might rise up in open revolt. To prevent this from happening, guards were stationed at strategic points so they could watch everyone, and gas pellets had been installed in the ceiling. These could be dropped on the inmates if any disturbances ever broke out. They did not.

The worst hazard to inmates concerning their food involved truculent cooks who sometimes dosed the food with soap chips or other contaminants. This required the guards to sample each tray of food being served. These tasting exercises were usually assigned to guards with the least seniority and caused them considerable apprehension as they would be the first to be poisoned if any cook decided to doctor the food with lethal substances. Such an event never occurred, much to the relief of the rookie guards. The guards themselves were under almost as much regimentation as the convicts. They could not speak to convicts, unless giving them orders. They had to stand long, lonely watches in the outside towers and walkways, in bitter cold nights when the bay winds sailed through their thin uniforms. They were not allowed radios in the towers and any guard caught with one was subject to instant dismissal. Guards failing to report for duty on time or taking too many sick days were subject to dismissal, and any guard refusing an order from a superior could be fired instantly.

Four wardens governed the Rock during its existence as a federal penitentiary. These were James A. Johnston, 1934-48; Edwin B. Swope, 1948-55; Paul J. Madigan, 1955-61; and Olin G. Blackwell, 1961-63. Of these, Johnston, who had been the warden at Folsom State Prison in California, became Alcatraz' first warden. Johnston had retired from penology and had become a banker. When U.S. Attorney General Homer Cummings selected Alcatraz as the top federal penitentiary in 1933, he asked Johnston to take over control. Johnston was fairly well liked by the guards and inmates alike, a fair man who believed in rehabilitation. He allowed, for instance, Robert Stroud, who later became known as "The Birdman of Alcatraz," to study ornithology in his cell but Stroud never kept birds in his cell at any time when on the Rock. (He had kept birds in his cells, two interconnecting cells, when

a prisoner at Leavenworth.) Swope, on the other hand, was a hardliner, much more in keeping with J. Edgar Hoover's concepts of running prisons. He allowed prisoners only the bare privileges and, in fact, deprived Stroud of his books on birds and took away Stroud's manuscripts and written studies on bird diseases and remedies, a great disservice to ornithology, according to some experts. Madigan and Blackwell were caretaker officials, distant from their staffs and concerned chiefly with running a tight ship.

The most notorious prisoners held on Alcatraz were those who arrived with a great deal of publicity in August 1934. These convicts, removed from several federal prisons as incorrigibles, traveled in three sealed prison cars, a train that roared across the U.S. with its window shades bolted shut, its prisoners not knowing where they were headed, as newsreel photographers filmed the train's progress from one town to the next as it raced westward. The sealed train to Alcatraz was a J. Edgar Hoover publicity stunt to accent the impregnability and mystique of Alcatraz. All the public enemies Hoover could round up and ship to the Rock at this time further enhanced the image of a triumphant Department of Justice and sent an effective message to gangland that a similar fate awaited any criminal who thought himself above the power of the law and the arm of the FBI. It was, at that naive time in America, a very impressive move which gleaned enormous publicity for the G-Men. That first train trip was portrayed in a 1937 Hollywood film, *The Last Gangster*, with Edward G. Robinson enacting a crime czar based on Al Capone, one of the occupants of that first train to Alcatraz. The convicts in the film joke about their unknown destination and jeer at their guards. They boast of escape and their own invincibility but they become edgy as their trip continues westward. Finally, they feel the train cars floating on board the barge taking them out into San Francisco Bay. The bolted shades are released and the prisoners, including the bragging crime boss Robinson, stare pop-eyed at the looming island of Alcatraz. "The Rock!" screams one of the convicts who all echo their instant panic and terror of the place through frantic shouts which dwindle to moans and then vacant stares. All are desolated by their destiny, resigned to their impossible situation. Their destination is Alcatraz, the Rock. Their fate is sealed.

Capone, jailed for income tax evasion, had originally been sent to the federal penitentiary at Atlanta but he soon enlisted an army of stooges in that institution and was waited on hand and foot. He enjoyed immense privileges and his cells were fitted out like luxurious hotel suites. Moreover, he actually continued to run his broad-based rackets in Chicago from his prison cell. To curtail Capone's activities, as well as subject his powerful image to that of a mere prisoner, this most notorious of convicts was the first to be put aboard the Alcatraz train. Also on that train was George "Machine Gun" Kelly, the notorious kidnapper of Oklahoma oilman Charles Urschel, robber and escape artist Charles Berta, Floyd Hamilton of the Barrow gang. More public enemies would join this infamous bunch, Arthur "Dock" Barker, Alvin "Creepy" Karpis, Basil "The Owl" Banghart of the Roger Touhy gang, train robber Roy Gardner, John Paul Chase of the Dillinger gang, and, of course, the reclusive killer and bird expert, Robert Stroud.

At Alcatraz, all of these infamous gangsters, killers, kidnappers, and thieves were no more than numbers. Capone, who became AZ85, did try to exert his influence a few times and was rebuffed by the prisoners. He was more than once attacked by those who had belonged to Chicago gangs he had ruthlessly tried to eliminate in the 1920s. On one occasion Capone, who endlessly practiced on his guitar, became incensed at another prisoner who insulted him and broke his guitar over the prisoner's head, an act unseen by guards which allowed him to go unpunished. On another occasion, friends of the prisoner struck by Capone attacked the gang chief and beat him so severely that Capone was placed in solitary confinement to protect him against the other prisoners. For the most part the crime czar was docile and obedient, seldom disobeying orders or breaking rules.

During the infrequent work strikes, Capone invariably refused to stop his work or leave his post in the laundry which incurred the wrath of other inmates. "I have to protect my skin if I'm gonna get outa here alive," Capone once told guards. He was removed from the laundry and sent to the showers to clean up. Here, on June 23, 1935, a Texas bank robber, Jim Lucas, a hardcase convict who hated Capone for his refusal to join in the strikes, stole a pair of scissors from the barbershop and crept up behind the crime czar, driving the scissors into his back. Capone spent a week recovering in the prison clinic while Lucas went into solitary confinement. James Bennett, head of the Bureau of Prisons, visited Alcatraz in 1937, and he asked to see Capone. The crime boss told Bennett that he was getting along "all right...Capone can take care of himself. But I shouldn't be here. I'm here because of my reputation, because there's such a misunderstanding about me. People don't know the things I've done to be helpful." He mentioned his free soup kitchens in Chicago during the early part of the Depression and how he had settled newspaper strikes.

On Feb. 5, 1938, Capone, who had by then been given duties with the library, handing out magazines to inmates in their cells, was found wandering about the mess hall, wearing his pea jacket, his eyes vacant, spittle drooling down his chin, pointing meaninglessly to a barred window. Then he began to vomit. Guards took him to the clinic. His spine was tapped and the fluid analyzed. Capone was suffering from the advanced stages of syphilis and had developed paresis of the brain. A short time later he became partly paralyzed. Having served most of his ten-year sentence, Capone was removed from the Rock on Jan. 6, 1939, taken to the Federal Correction Institution at Terminal Island near Los Angeles where he was given medical attention. He was later transferred to the Lewisburg, Pa., Correctional Facility and released from there in November to be in and out of hospitals until his death in 1947.

During its thirty-year existence as a federal penitentiary, Alcatraz saw many escape attempts. Thirty-six men in all tried to vanquish the Rock. Of these twenty-six were recaptured, seven were shot, one was known to have drowned and six were never found. These do not include the suicide attempts, the most dedicated of which belonged to counterfeiter John Standig who jumped off a train taking him to Alcatraz but was delivered intact. He later attempted suicide on the Rock and failed again, later telling another convict, "If you ever get out of here, tell them I wasn't trying to escape. I was trying to kill myself." An ex-G.I., Jimmy Groves, was sent to Alcatraz for raping the daughter of an Army officer. He slashed the arteries of both arms soon after arriving at the Rock but several transfusions saved his life. Joe Bowers, inmate AZ210, a German-born thief, was imprisoned on Alcatraz and promptly smashed his glasses in his cell and cut his throat with the jagged edges. He was saved only to make an escape attempt in 1936 that was nothing more than another suicide attempt, one that succeeded, or so it was later reported.

Bowers had struck a guard and had been put into solitary but many convicts insisted that he was unbalanced and really deserved to be at the Springfield, Mo., facility. When released from solitary confinement in April 1936, Bowers was put to work on the garbage detail and this meant that he hauled garbage to the incinerator which was located just inside a high cyclone fence that circled the prison area. The fence was set in a cement footing which extended beyond the fence at one point where there was then a sheer drop of eighty feet to the jagged rocks below at the water's edge. Here, dozens of seagulls gathered to be fed the scraps Bowers salvaged from the garbage. Sometimes Bowers would throw scraps through the fence to the ledge beyond and when this area got to be messy one of the guards, according to James Henry "Blackie" Audett, ordered Bowers to clean off the ledge beyond the fence. Bowers attempted to clean the area by shoving a broom handle through the fence and when this was ineffective, he decided to climb the fence, drop to the other side, and sweep the area, or, at least, that was a later theory. Guards insisted

Bowers was really attempting to escape the Rock at this point.

When Bowers began to climb the fence, the guard in the tower spotted him and ordered him to stop. He fired a warning shot from his powerful 30.06 rifle but Bowers kept climbing. Just as Bowers was at the top of the fence, straddling it, the guard fired again, a bullet that smashed into Bowers' head, killing him. His body toppled over the fence, hit the cement ledge, and rolled off, falling eighty feet to the rocks below. The most commonly accepted story by guards and inmates alike was that Bowers really wasn't attempting to escape but was trying to commit suicide, an attempt that was this time successful. Others, like Audett, who apparently witnessed the shooting to some degree, held another view. Wrote Audett years later, "The records said he was killed while trying to escape. Joe didn't want to escape. His mind was so far gone he had about forgot there was any place else but the Rock and his seagulls." Bowers was the first to allegedly escape but certainly not the last.

The first serious escape attempt from the Rock was made by two hardened criminals, Theodore "Sunny Boy" Cole and Ralph Roe, bank robbers who had arrived at Alcatraz in October 1935. From that moment on the two inmates planned their escape after getting jobs in the mat shop at the north end of the island. The two were responsible for disposing of excess rubber materials, including old tires, used in the mat shop, and these they cleverly threw over a twenty-foot cliff to the rocks at the river's edge. After several months the area at the bottom of the cliff was so thick that it would easily break anyone's fall. Cole somehow managed to secret a Stillson wrench in the machine shop which adjoined the mat shop and, on the fog-bound night of Dec. 16, 1937, he and Roe decided to make their break. That afternoon, Cole retrieved the wrench and Roe, a burly inmate, smashed out the glass of a mat shop window, then clasped the wrench around an eighteen-inch iron bar, inserting this between two steel bars of the window, front and back, and then exerting his considerable strength to break one of the bars. Both men slipped through the narrow opening and then dropped onto the rubber debris below.

No one ever saw the pair again. It was theorized that Roe and Cole made water wings out of their pants and then pushed into the water, attempting to reach Angel Island, the nearest landfall. That barren little island was thoroughly searched and nothing of the inmates was found. Alvin Karpis, who reported later that he had been working in the mat shop with others and witnessed the escape, stated that Roe and Cole each carried two square five-gallon gas cans, the tops welded shut, and with handles on them and that these self-styled buoys were successfully used to get them to the mainland. Most authorities believed that the two men drowned in the dangerous currents of the bay, but still others insisted that the bank robbers, who had more than an estimated $200,000 in stolen, secreted money waiting for them, got to the mainland and vanished. No one wanted to believe this latter story more than inmates nurturing the idea of a similar escape. Through the next twenty-five years, the *possibility* of this pair's successful escape, became the daydreams of other would-be escape artists. Karpis stated that Roe and Cole made their way to South America via Mexico and that they taunted Warden Johnston for years by sending him a yearly Christmas card signed "Ted and Ralph." Karpis later stated that he witnessed both Roe and Cole from the mat shop window as they were pulled beneath the waters by the strong current and that they drowned. His paradoxical statements further muddled the mystery of these two men, perhaps purposely so in that Karpis made these remarks at a time when both escapees could have been alive and in hiding somewhere.

The next serious attempt to escape from Alcatraz, albeit a senseless one that seemed to be a spur-of-the-moment decision by three desperate convicts, occurred on May 23, 1938. Actually, the convicts planned the breakout for months in advance but it was a short-sighted scheme that allowed them to get to the roof of the factory and inside a gun tower, but they had not made a plan that would get them off the island. The three inmates were Tom Limerick, who had robbed banks and kidnapped people in

Nebraska and Iowa and was serving life; Texas bank robber Jimmy Lucas who was serving a thirty-year term and had stabbed Al Capone; and Rufus Franklin, serving thirty years for bank robbery and who was still wanted for murder by the state of Alabama. These men all worked in the factory and they got into the filing room, attempting to bend back the bars of the single window with a device made of two-by-fours. At that moment, Royal C. Cline, a towering senior guard who was much hated by the convicts for his brutality, entered the filing room. One of the convicts, it was never determined which one, jumped the six-foot-four-inch guard from behind, smashing a claw hammer four times into the back of his head, opening his skull and killing him. The convicts then dragged Cline's body to a corner of the room, broke one of the bars on the windows and climbed to the factory roof after cutting away some strands of barbed wire with a pliars.

Though it was a bright, sunny day, neither guard in the two towers that overlooked the area saw the convicts on the roof. Lucas, Limerick, and Franklin made their way across the roof toward a guard tower at the end of a catwalk leading from the roof. They had noticed in the past how the guards on hot days would leave the door to the tower open so they thought to merely rush down the catwalk, get into the tower, overpower the guard, and then, one by one, shoot down the other guards with the weapons found in the tower and somehow blast their way to the dock and the police launch which would take them to San Francisco.

As the trio of convicts raced toward the guard tower, they skidded to a stop, seeing that the glass door to the tower was closed. A substitute guard, Harold Stites, was in the tower and he had followed the regulations by keeping the door closed, in spite of the intense heat. The convicts, stymied, began throwing stones and pieces of metal they had brought along to use as saps, hoping to break the glass of the locked door and get at Stites. A piece of metal shattered the glass and struck the guard on the knee. He stood for a moment with his drawn .45-caliber automatic at his side. Then Limerick rushed the door, throwing more pieces of metal. Stites aimed his weapon carefully and fired two shots, the first striking Limerick in the right eye, killing him. He fell off the roof but his body was caught by the barbed wire at its edge and he sprawled there, a grotesgue form, blood spilling downward to the walkway below from his ghastly wound. Franklin attacked the tower from another direction and Stites shot him in the shoulder with his 30.06 rifle. Franklin fell, also trapped in the barbed wire at the roof's edge. He tried to throw a hammer he carried but could not find the strength; the hammer fell uselessly to the walkway below. Lucas, the bragging leader of the trio, saw his friends shot and down on the roof and he raced to the other side where a guard named Stewart met him, rifle pointed at his head. "Hold it right there," Stewart ordered and Lucas meekly surrendered. Lucas and Franklin were later tried for the killing of Cline and received life sentences.

One of those who thought constantly of escape was the sullen and fierce Arthur "Dock" Barker, last of the deadly Barker brothers who had kidnapped and robbed their way across the Midwest during the 1930s, inspired by a corrupt mother, Ma Barker, who had died with her son Freddie in a to-the-death shootout in a Florida resort in 1935. Following the deaths of his mother and brother, Dock Barker was picked up on a Chicago street, surprisingly with no weapon. He was sent to Alcatraz where he kept mostly to himself, even avoiding his former gangland associate, Alvin "Creepy" Karpis, but then Karpis had been his brother Freddie's lover; both were homosexuals, as were Karpis' Alcatraz friends. Barker was not. He cultivated a few friendships with hardcase inmates, but in the end he opted to try his breakout with four homosexual bandits, kidnappers Dale Stamphill and William Rufe McCain, both serving life terms, Henry Young, a bank robber serving twenty years, and William Martin, a postal robber serving twenty-five years.

Barker originally asked Karpis to join him in his escape attempt, explaining that he and the others intended to purposely break prison rules so that they could be thrown into the solitary confinement cells in D block, then unfinished and lightly guarded. The locks were imperfect and were easily picked on the solitary confinement cells. They would make their break from this area which was also seldom patrolled. He had no plan once they reached the water's edge. Karpis proposed that they slug the guards in the D block area, capture their guns, and then take Warden Johnston hostage with his wife, calling the doctor, and then ordering up the prison launch which would ostensibly take Mrs. Johnston to San Francisco with a reported "burst appendix." They would all escape in the launch, insisted Karpis. Barker rejected this plan as too complicated and Karpis refused to merely jump into the water and make a swim for it.

On Jan. 13, 1939, the five men led by Barker, without Karpis, all of whom having been confined in D block for various prison infractions, managed to pick the locks of their cells, break through a prison window by spreading two bars with a homemade device and then slip into a foggy night, groping their way to the water's edge. The men were not missed for three hours and then, as hundreds of convicts awaited the outcome, the prison population suddenly heard the rapid fire of machine gun bursts. This gunfire was let loose by prison guards in the launch which had been searching the shoreline. Its spotlights picked up Stamphill and Barker on the shoreline as they desperately sought to tie some driftwood together to make a raft. Bullets from police machine guns smashed into their legs. Barker was moving about violently in pain and one of the guards, according to Stamphill, shouted from the boat, "If that s.o.b. moves, shoot him in the head!" Barker reportedly twitched in agony from his wounds and this was enough of an excuse for guards to let loose another burst of gunfire which struck Barker in the back of the head. He still lived, however, and was dragged back to the little hospital where a blood transfusion was attempted. Barker, in his last moment of life, decided he was better off dead, and he roared at the guards and hospital attendants, then pulled the tubes from his arms and died at 5:45 p.m.

Four more convicts attempted a wild breakout on May 21, 1941. These included recently arrived bank robbers Joseph Paul Cretzer, his brother-in-law and partner in crime, Arnold Thomas Kyle, both serving life terms for murder, bank robber Lloyd Barkdoll and, according to authorities, Sam Richard Shockley, bank robber and kidnapper. Cretzer and Shockley would be key figures in the most notorious and bloody breakout attempt at the Rock in 1946. The four convicts attacked the guards in the mat shop, the same area which saw the escape attempt of Roe and Cole four years earlier. Four guards were overpowered and tied up, along with other convicts in the shop so that the inmates not participating in the breakout would not be blamed. Cretzer and the others attempted to saw the bars of the shop windows with a hacksaw. The plan was a simple one. Once the convicts broke through the shop window they would slip down to the rocks below and would be picked up by Edna Kyle who had rented a speedboat for that day.

The plan called for Edna Kyle to take the speedboat to a spot between Alcatraz and Angel Island and there pretend to go fishing, watching the island shore for the appearance of her husband, brother, and other prisoners through binoculars. Once they appeared, Edna was to race the speedboat to the shores of Alcatraz, pick up the escapees, and speed to San Francisco where a fast car, guns, and money awaited them. As the men worked with files and the hacksaw at the stubborn steel bars of the window, Cretzer kept scanning the bay, looking for Edna and the speedboat. He saw nothing but the usual afternoon commercial shipping sliding by in the churning bay. "Don't worry, Joe," Kyle told his brother-in-law. "You can count on Kay. She'll be there." The convicts slaved away at the bars, grinding and sawing until their bodies dripped with sweat but they made no headway against the solid steel bars. (These bars had replaced those that had given way under the force applied by Roe and Cole.) Using grinders and saws, the escaping convicts worked for more than an hour

NOTORIOUS ALCATRAZ INMATES

Chicago crime czar Al Capone, above left, became one of the first inmates at Alcatraz in 1934; Kidnapper George "Machine Gun" Kelly, right, talked of escaping Alcatraz by balloon before being transferred to Leavenworth where he died.

Alvin "Creepy" Karpis, above left, served almost all his time on Alcatraz and refused to take part in any escape attempts, though he aided those who tried to break out; Robert Stroud, the celebrated "Birdman of Alcatraz," right, spent most of his time in the Rock's solitary confinement block.

John Paul Chase, left, was a dreaded member of the Dillinger-Nelson gang, but he cowered with nightmares in his cell on the Rock; Basil "The Owl" Banghart, right, a member of the Touhy gang, stopped trying to escape prison when he arrived at Alcatraz.

SOME WHO TRIED TO ESCAPE

Ralph Roe, left, and Theodore "Sunny Boy" Cole, right, were the first to make a serious attempt to escape the Rock in 1935; they got into the bay and were never seen again.

Arthur "Dock" Barker, left, of the notorious Barker gang, got to the water's edge fo the Rock in a 1939 breakout before being cut down by machine gun bullets; bank robber James Boarman, right, died in a futile 1943 attempt to escape Alcatraz.

Joe Bowers, left, was shot to death in a 1936 escape attempt, but some said it was suicide; Rufus "Whitey" Franklin, right, who was involved in several escape attempts from the Rock, did not participate in the 1946 blastout since his friends could not get him out of his solitary confinement cell.

without success.

Captain Paul Madigan, one of the guards tied up by the escapees, quietly began to reason with the convicts, telling them that the mid-afternoon headcount would soon reveal their breakout attempt and that the mat shop would quickly be surrounded with squads of men with rapid-fire weapons. They stood no chance at all, he reminded them, and pointed out that the grinders they were using on the bars were not made to cut through such steel. The bars, Madigan explained, were made with tool-resistent steel. "Why not give up voluntarily before anything serious happens?" Madigan asked.

Kyle realized the hopelessness of their situation and took the tough Cretzer aside, saying to him, "Joe, we're getting deader every minute. We'll come again, wait and see."

Cretzer threw down the grinder in his hand, cursing and condemning Edna Kyle. "Cut 'em loose!" Barkdoll began cutting the ropes that bound the guards. Then Cretzer moaned, "Women —can't count on 'em, not even your own wife!" He surrendered along with Barkdoll and Kyle. Schockley was also later taken into custody and all were thrown into solitary confinement. It was later learned by Kyle and Cretzer that Edna Kyle Cretzer had not deserted the escapees. She had been stopped in San Francisco by vice cops just as she was about to rent the speedboat and, while the convicts made their futile attack against the bars of the mat shop window, she resided in a cell in the city jail.

Barkdoll later asked to see Captain Madigan while in solitary confinement and Madigan visited him there. "What the hell you got Schockley locked up for?" Barkdoll asked him. "He was tied up with the others, don't you remember? We used your knife to cut him loose." Madigan, still confused by the incident, nodded, "I do remember him being tied up but who was the fourth convict?" Madigan reported this to Warden Johnston who ordered Shockley released from solitary confinement and the fourth convict was never identified, although Alvin Karpis later claimed that it was Floyd Hamilton, who slipped back to his work detail undetected before the officers in the mat shop were cut loose.

Mass breakouts at Alcatraz were less likely to succeed, according to Warden Johnston who believed that "I thought there was more of a chance of a lone wolf escaping," in that he could more easily be overlooked in the headcount. This was the conviction of John R. Bayless, a Missouri bank robber serving twenty-five years. On Sept. 15, 1941, Bayless, working with other prisoners on a garbage detail which had to work on the wharf outside the prison walls, noticed the sudden fog engulfing the wharf, so thick that it was next to impossible to see a human form five feet distant. He slipped off the wharf, ran down a path to the water, stripped, and dove in. He was missed almost immediately and guards found him floundering the the sea. He was ordered to climb out of the water and he did so, vomiting salt water. Tried in San Francisco, Bayless attempted to escape in court but a burly bailiff knocked him unconscious. Five years were added to his sentence.

The mat shop, which had been the scene of two serious escape attempts, was closed down by 1943 and was used as a storage shed where work details were brought under heavy guard and spent time breaking up concrete blocks. It was here that yet another attempt to escape by four prisoners was made on Apr. 13, 1943.

Floyd Hamilton, who had attempted an escape with Joseph Paul Cretzer and others in 1941, along with Fred Hunter, a robber and kidnapper serving twenty-five years; Harold Brest, kidnapper and robber serving fifty years; and James Boarman, serving twenty years for bank robbery, overpowered a guard and jumped into the water, desperately attempting to swim across the bay. Coast guard and police launches, as well as squads of armed guards on shore quickly rounded them up but not before Boarman was shot in the head while in the water. Police attempted to fish his body from the water with a hook, but the corpse sank before it could be brought on board a launch. Brest was taken from the water and Hamilton and Hunter were later caught in a small cave on the island.

Perhaps the most imaginative escape attempt made at the Rock, until that of the Anglin brothers and Frank Morris in 1962, was enacted by John K. Giles, on July 31, 1945. Giles, then fifty, was a lone-wolf convict who had a shrewd and calculating mind. Giles had a bad back which prevented him from heavy work so he was assigned the task of sweeping the dock and tending to the flower beds outside the prison area. At the time convicts in the laundry were working around the clock handling the U.S. Army laundry from the mainland, which was considered a patriotic duty in wartime. Giles, who had long planned his clever escape, helped to unload bags and bags of military clothes from the steamers bringing the laundry to Alcatraz and, piece by piece, he stole enough items to make up a complete uniform of a technical sergeant, secreting these pieces of clothing in an unused dockside building.

At the time the steamer *General Coxe* was laying phone cable from San Francisco to the Rock with army personnel on board. When the *Coxe* docked on July 31, Giles, wearing the sergeant's uniform beneath his prison coveralls, simply went behind a dockside building, took off the coveralls, and marched on board the steamer, clipboard in hand, pretending to be part of the military crew, taking notes on its manifest. The *Coxe* left Alcatraz, heading for Angel Island to lay more cable. About a hour later guards taking the routine headcount, noticed Giles was missing and reported this to Warden Johnston, along with their belief that he had to be aboard the ship. Guards from the Rock jumped into a speedboat and caught up with the *Coxe* as it was about to sail for San Francisco. All of the soldiers on board were lined up and ordered to stand to attention. Guards went down the line and there, at the end, at precise military attention, stood John K. Giles, looking every inch the soldier he was impersonating. A guard clasped handcuffs on the convict and said, "All right, *sergeant*, step out of line." Giles was returned to Alcatraz and had another five years added to his sentence.

The following year saw the worst escape attempt in the history of Alcatraz, one that was undoubtedly doomed from its beginning, even in the minds of the desperate convicts involved. It was more like a rebellion which led to many deaths and a full-scale battle where police from the mainland, along with Marines, and even warships were brought into action. The convicts involved with the Battle of Alcatraz, as it was later dubbed by the press, were the worst in the prison. John Paul Cretzer was undoubtedly the organizer of this open revolt. He had thought of nothing but escape since his arrival on the Rock and had been foiled in one attempt in 1941 for which he spent a long period of time in solitary confinement, and it was here that he racked his brain for a plan to make another, final, certainly suicidal, attempt to gain his freedom. The men who first put Cretzer's mad plan into action was Marvin Franklin Hubbard and Bernard Paul Coy.

An Alabama gunman and holdup artist, Hubbard had committed several robberies at the age of seventeen. He had been captured and locked up in the Alabama State Prison but then escaped. Captured again, he was put into the Jasper, Ala., jail but he escaped again, this time beating a warder senseless and looting the jail's arsenal of a machine gun and three revolvers before fleeing. Joining with another bandit, Hubbard committed dozens of robberies in Alabama and Tennessee for a decade, until a posse surrounded him and his partner in a remote Tennessee cabin. The partner attempted to give himself up and Hubbard, a man of black-and-white perspectives, promptly shot him as he was running toward officers. Lawmen, who thought the partner was firing at them, opened up, killing the partner. Then Hubbard held the posse off for many hours, moving from window to window of the cabin, firing at the posse surrounding him. Hit many times, the wounded Hubbard was finally captured but only after he was out of ammunition. This time Hubbard went to the U.S. penitentiary in Atlanta but after his continued plotting to escape from there, authorities shipped him to the Rock as an incorrigible recidivist. Hubbard worked in the kitchen in off hours when most of the rest of the convicts were either on work detail or in their cells. He

1946: Alcatraz under siege, above, as smoke from mortars and bazookas curls about the island; a bomb explodes against the wall of D block, left; San Francisco police rush by launch to the embattled island, right; troops landing on the Rock, below, left; newsmen on board boats off the island clamor for stories, below, right.

was a pivotal cog in the machinery of Cretzer's escape plans. At the time of the breakout, Hubbard was one of two convicts with some freedom of movement who could enact Cretzer's plan. The other was Bernard Paul Coy.

Coy, in his mid-forties, had been a problem child, throwing wild tantrums at age three, stealing pennies from his mother's purse at age five, expelled from a one-room schoolhouse at age six for attacking the teacher. He was a product of poverty-stricken Kentucky hill people; his common-law parents were uneducated and uncaring. After his sister was born, Coy's mother, frightened and submissive of her callous husband, ignored him. Coy's father only paid attention to him when he misbehaved, habitually kicking and cuffing him. By nine Coy was stealing automobile parts and he had a police record by age ten. In 1931 Coy tried to rob a Kentucky bank but was arrested and sent to the state penitentiary. Upon his release he teamed up with another hard case, Delber Stiles and the pair robbed several banks which culminated in the holdup of the Bank of New Haven, Ky., in March 1939; the pair took a little more than $2,000, but they were both captured a short time later after a cashier identified Coy as the man who placed a shotgun to his head while Stiles grabbed the cash. The pair escaped, however, and hid out in a cave but made the mistake of building a large fire, the smoke from which led a large posse to the camp. Both Coy and Stiles received twenty-five-year sentences and were sent to the U.S. penitentiary in Atlanta, having committed federal offenses in robbing a bank (by then a federal offense) and transporting a stolen car across a state line.

Coy, a withdrawn type with an above-average intelligence, resented prison and proved to be incorrigible in Atlanta. He got into fights with other prisoners and planned escapes. He was finally sent to Alcatraz. There he seldom fraternized with other prisoners, concentrating on any books he could find in the Rock's library that dealt with criminal law and psychology. He wrote several petitions to have his case reviewed, insisting that his consecutive sentences were unlawful. He prepared an elaborate writ of habeas corpus but his petition was denied in March 1942. From that moment on, Coy thought of nothing but escape. "Now I got nothing to lose," he told Cretzer who had sought his friendship, believing Coy was a man who would fight to the death once committed to his plan. He was right. Coy was, like Hubbard, in a good position to put the escape plan into action, having the freedom of C and D blocks as a library worker who disbursed magazines to convicts locked in their cells. These duties, however, were confined to mornings and Cretzer had planned an afternoon break. To that end, Coy asked that he be let out of his cell in the afternoons to mop up the aisles in the cell blocks, explaining to guards that "it helps me pass the time better than being in my cell." He was given the cleaning duties.

The object was to overpower the two guards in C block, William Miller, unarmed at at the door leading from the kitchen area and Bert Burch, who manned the gun gallery which, through a caged catwalk, crossed into D block. At 1:40 p.m. on May 2, 1946, Hubbard left the kitchen and arrived at the C block door where Miller searched him. While Miller was thus occupied, Coy slipped up behind him and struck him from behind while Hubbard beat him. Once down, Miller was threatened with death if he cried out. Hubbard held a knife he had stolen from the kitchen against the guard's throat while Coy tied him up and then rifled his pockets, finding the keys to the C block cells. Miller was dragged to the last cell in C block and locked inside of it. He realized that the key the convicts really wanted was the one to the door that led to the recreation area but he flushed this down the toilet in the cell. Meanwhile Coy and Hubbard raced to Cretzer's cell and released the mastermind of the break.

Cretzer ordered Coy to elimiate Burch. The lean, lanky Coy monkey-climbed the cage wires up to the gun gallery where, using a homemade bar spreader, managed to squeeze into the gallery. When Burch returned from his rounds of D block, Coy jumped him on the catwalk, knocking him senseless and tying him up with wire brought along for that purpose. He then took Burch's .45-

caliber revolver and twenty-one rounds and a Springfield rifle with fifty rounds. These were the only weapons found in the gallery. Burch was left tied on the floor of the gun gallery while Coy threw down the revolver to Cretzer and then entered D block through the catwalk and aimed the rifle at Officer Corwin, ordering him to open the steel ground floor between C block and the D block isolation area. He did and Cretzer entered brandishing the revolver, ordering Corwin to open the solitary confinement cells on the main floor of D block, but the guard explained that he could not do so since the locks on these cells were controlled electronically. Cretzer cursed and demanded that his good friend Rufus "Whitey" Franklin be released. But there was no way Franklin could be freed so twelve men in the second tier of D block were let loose. When they saw Coy with the rifle and Cretzer with the revolver, one of them shouted, "The cons have taken over the joint! Let's go!" Several ran into C block but then decided to go back to their cells when they realized that the escapees did not have access to the recreation yard and were penned inside C and D blocks. Others decided to throw in with the escapees, especially Samuel Richard Shockley, kidnapper and bank robber, who was serving a life sentence.

Shockley was known as Crazy Sam. Shockley had an IQ of 68 and was considered one of the most dangerous convicts on the Rock. At age forty-one in 1946, Shockley had been diagnosed as suffering from an undefined "mental illness." After being sent to Leavenworth, Shockley's behavior had been erratic, first friendly and outgoing, then surly and withdrawn, subject to screaming outbursts. He had been sent on to Alcatraz and was present there to participate in Cretzer's abortive 1941 escape attempt. Cretzer had hand-picked Shockley as one of his henchmen because of his willingness to please the aggressive, decisive Cretzer. On the Rock he was thought to be certifiable. He would erupt at times to scream and yell, set fire to his bedding, and hurl objects at guards from his cell. He had, on many occasions, been placed in a straitjacket and confined in the hospital, tied down to a bed as he raved and babbled about how he heard voices telling him to destroy the authorities. He also claimed that he felt sensations along his spinal column, and he explained in detail to officials that he knew that these sensations were the result of unseen rays directed at his head and spine, sent out by a distant machine operated by an organization Shockley labeled "The Public of Health." Said Shockley, "These rays are sent out to people like me who have strange illnesses. I do believe they help me a lot, these rays." Whenever Shockley talked of such things to Cretzer, the worldly, sardonic killer, would turn away from his stooge and put his fingers between his teeth and bite down to keep from laughing. Then, suppressing his natural urge to mock Shockley, Cretzer would pat the near-cretinous henchman on the back and remark, "You keep thinking about those rays, Sam. They're burning off all the junk you've collected in your mind."

When Cretzer let Shockley out of his cell on the upper tier of D block, the stooge was ready to follow his mentor anywhere and to the death. Ironically, it was only a matter of a few weeks before Shockley was scheduled to be sent off to the mental ward in Springfield, Mo., to serve out his life sentence in much more pleasant surroundings. That meant nothing to Shockley who had resolved to do whatever his friend "Dutch" Cretzer said, to enact any plan. But Cretzer had no plan after discovering that he could not unlock the door to the recreation yard where he thought to free the entire convict population and, the limited number of guards overwhelmed with controlling hundreds of prisoners running all over the island, slip away with a select group in the police launch. Those involved in the planned escape, however, had to get out of C block and into A block, the old army barracks, beneath which, Cretzer and Coy believed, were old tunnels dug by the Spanish and sealed off by the Army years ago. They would find the sealed tunnels, break through the barrier and then follow the tunnel that led to the dock and the police launch. But to achieve that end, the group had to get into the recreation yard, kill the tower guards, and then get to A block. But Officer Miller had gotten rid of the one key that would allow the group to get out of C block. Now the "Spanish Tunnel" plan was a bust (there never were any such tunnels; the convicts had created them in their desperate dreams of escape). All Cretzer could do was free those convicts he thought would be most loyal in a standoff battle with authorities which might gain some time to develop a new escape plan.

The next man let loose by Cretzer was Miran Edgar "Buddy" Thompson, thirty-six, who was serving two consecutive 99-year terms for kidnapping and murder. He had robbed and killed his way through Alabama, Mississippi, and Texas and had escaped from eight different jails and prisons before being sent to Leavenworth for kidnapping. He was taken from his cell there and extradited to Texas where he was convicted of murdering a police officer years earlier and then he was sent on to Alcatraz, arriving on the Rock on Nov. 22, 1945. Tough, taciturn, and ready to do anything, Thompson was quickly recruited for Cretzer's mass breakout.

Coy had done some recruiting of his own. The first convict he let out of his cell was Clarence Victor Carnes, also called Joe and The Choctaw Kid. Carnes was a full-blooded Indian of Choctaw parents, born in the hills of eastern Oklahoma in 1927. He lived in nomadic squalor as a child, his parents moving regularly as his father sought work. He was a street child and was soon in trouble, breaking into a school canteen at the age of eight to steal candy. While a teenager, Carnes entered Golden Gloves and proved to be a top flight welterweight, but he was also a ganglead-er who did not hesitate to commit violent crimes. He and a friend, Cecil Berry, both fifteen, entered a service station in Atoka, Okla., in 1942. Carnes held a pistol in his hand and ordered attendant W.M. Weyland to turn over his cash. Weyland dove for the gun and it went off, killing him. Carnes and Berry were scooped up by police inside of an hour and Carnes was charged with murder.

Only a short time after being jailed, Carnes and Berry attacked an unsuspecting trusty, knocked him senseless, and escaped with a stolen gun. Bloodhounds led a posse to the boys twelve hours later and Carnes pleaded Guilty in court, receiving a life sentence on Oct. 26, 1943. Carnes was sent to the Oklahoma State Reformatory but he, Fred Newel, and Julian Blankenship fled a quarry where they were breaking up rocks for gravel. They abducted a farmer and drove his car across the state line into Texas. When they realized they had broken a federal law, they tied the farmer to a tree and raced back toward Oklahoma (or so Carnes later claimed), driving the car off a bridge. They stole another car and were captured in Boise City, Okla. Carnes was convicted under the Lindbergh Kidnapping Law and given another ninety-nine years. Sent to Leavenworth, Carnes proved to be an unruly prisoner who could not be disciplined. He was shipped off to Alcatraz. He arrived on the Rock on July 6, 1945, at age eighteen, the youngest convict ever to serve time in Alcatraz.

These six men then, Cretzer, Coy, Hubbard, Shockley, Thompson, and Carnes were the men who would wage war with Alcatraz. Once let loose the prisoners attempted to formulate a new escape plan. First they placed the guards all in cell 403. Cretzer kept the revolver and Coy, Thompson, and Hubbard took turns handling the rifle. Carnes carried a homemade knife made from hard plastic and honed razor-sharp. Shockley somehow found a heavy wrench to wield but the other convicts were loath to let him handle the firearms, even Cretzer, his mentor. They felt that he was so unpredictable that he might turn the weapons on them. At this point, Cretzer, searching everywhere for the key to the recreation area, went past several open cells, asking convicts if they wanted to join in the mutiny. Louis Fleish, one of the leader's of Detroit's dreaded Purple Mob, told Cretzer it was useless to try to escape by blasting their way out. They would all be gunned down. Cretzer told him to shut up. Then Fleish said to Coy, "You know you can't get off this rock. Go back to your cell before the other screws get wise and gun you down."

Coy yelled at him, "Dummy up, big shot! I'm getting out. You

want to come along, okay. Otherwise, stay the hell out of our way!"

Fleish closed the door of his cell. To another convict in the next cell he said, "Guys like that are always doing it the hard way. They'll all be dead before the sun goes down, and a lot of other poor, ignorant bastards will die with them." The man in the next cell, a wise, old lifer, agreed and lay back on his bunk. He was Robert Stroud, the infamous Birdman of Alcatraz.

One by one guards entered C block and were confronted by Cretzer and Hubbard or Coy holding guns on them. These were officers Bristow, Lageson, Stucker, and Burdette. These four guards were thrown into cell 403 with Miller and Corwin. Captain Henry Weinhold and three officers, Simpson, Baker, and Sundstrom, heard from an informant that there was some sort of fight between prisoners in C block and they rushed from the kitchen into the block where the mutineers quickly subdued them and pushed them into cell 403. This cell was so crowded with captured guards that Simpson and Baker were put into cell 402. As each one of these officers were taken prisoner, Shockley tried to beat them with his wrench, and he managed to strike Weinhold several times in the head and back before Hubbard shoved him away, saying, "Stop that, you make me nervous." The dim-witted Shockley pouted and said, childlike, "Well, that guy knocked me down and kicked me when he threw me into the hole!" Coy ordered Weinhold to strip. He then put on the guard captain's uniform.

While Cretzer held the revolver on the officers in cell 403, Shockley went inside and began beating the guards, striking their heads, lusting for blood. Cretzer asked them repeatedly where the key was that would open the door to the recreation area. None replied and Shockley went on beating them until he stood dripping sweat, panting. He stepped outside the cell and then tried to attack Fleish, calling him a guard-lover. Cretzer stopped him, soothing, "Sam, calm down, you know he ain't no fink."

The break had been in progress for more than thirty minutes and still the alarm whistles and sirens had not gone off, clearly indicating to Cretzer and Coy that they still held the element of surprise and might possibly effect some sort of escape. They frantically searched for the missing key to the recreation yard and then Coy realized that Officer Miller must have tried to flush it down the toilet. He went into cell 403, shoved aside the guards huddled there and reached his long, bony arm into the toilet, groping frantically about, telling Cretzer that the key had probably not been flushed down the S neck of the toilet, it being too heavy. He was right. Coy fished the key out of the pipe and jubilantly ran to the recreation door. Before Cretzer opened it, Coy and Hubbard told him to wait. They wanted to get into the kitchen where they could better see the tower guards. Coy told Cretzer that he would "knock off" the tower guards first so that they could not fire on them when they ran into the recreation area. He and Hubbard dashed for the kitchen. Here they smashed out a glass and Coy rested the Springfield rifle against the ledge, aiming at James Comerford, the guard in the dock tower which was actually below the windows of the main prison from where Coy was perched.

Coy fired a single shot that whizzed past Comerford and the guard instinctively dropped to the floor of the tower. Associate Warden Miller, who was nearby, also flattened to the floor, telling Comerford, "Don't move. Let who ever is doing that shooting, think he's killed you." Miller passed the word to the other tower guards to do the same and, as Coy's shots rang out, the guards all dropped down, appearing to their would-be killer that they had been killed. In the kitchen, Coy and Hubbard squealed with glee at the sight of the falling guards, believing that Coy had killed seven officers with seven shots. Hubbard congratulated Coy on his marksmanship. Coy bragged that he had been the best hunter in his home town, that he had an eye like an eagle. Then Carnes appeared in the kitchen, yelling to them that the key retrieved from the toilet would not open the recreation area door. Coy and Hubbard rushed back to find Cretzer, Thompson, and Shockley struggling to turn the key in the lock. Cretzer finally pulled it out, walked up to Coy, and dropped the key is his hand, saying, "Bernie, we can't get the damned thing opened. I think the lock is jammed for keeps." Cretzer walked past a window and stared out into the bay, saying almost to himself, "I guess we've had it—Frisco is farther away than ever."

Associate Warden E. J. Miller, after seeing the tower guards shot at, ran up the path to the main prison and entered C block. As he was heading down the main aisle called Broadway he saw what appeared to be Captain Weinhold turn the corner at the end of C block, approaching him with his head downward, his cap pushed forward so that he could not see the man's face. As Miller approached the uniformed man, he suddenly stopped. The man raised his head. It was Bernard Coy who suddenly swung a rifle upward and aimed it at him. "Coy!" shouted Miller, "what the hell is going on here?" He did not wait for a reply but turned about and began to run toward the door at the end of the block. Coy's bullets whizzed past him. The gas billy club Miller was carrying dropped from his grasp, bounced on the hard floor and exploded, burning his face horribly. But Miller kept running until he turned a corner, a bullet just missing him and striking the wall.

By this time Warden Johnston received a call from a tower guard who explained that he could not reach any of the guards in C block and that someone from that block had been shooting at the tower guards. Johnston ordered the siren turned on, as well as the work whistles. All available guards were to assemble at the armory. Johnston notified the Coast Guard and the San Francisco Police, asking them to stand by to lend assistance. San Francisco and the towns surrounding the bay already knew that something serious was happening on the Rock as its sirens wailed across the waters.

By then Coy was back at the recreation area door, pulling the key out of the jammed lock. "That's it," he sighed. "Our luck just ran out. We ain't going nowhere now."

A moment later Associate Warden Miller ran into Johnston's office, his badly burned face alarming his superior. Miller explained that he had thrown his gas billy at Coy and it had bounced back at him, exploding, a not altogether correct statement. In the confusion, Warden Johnston received contradictory information about the breakout. He did not know how many convicts were involved, how many of his guards were being held hostage, and especially how many weapons and what kind had fallen into the hands of prisoners. By checking weapons inventory in the west gun gallery, it was quickly determined by Associate Warden Miller that the convicts had a pistol and a rifle but one report to Johnston emphatically insisted that the convicts had gotten their hands on a machine gun. "One thing is certain," Johnston told his officers, "they do have firearms and one is probably a machine gun. Yes, after thinking through events, I am absolutely convinced that an inmate has a machine gun in the cellhouse. Our situation is desperate." After a long silence, Johnston announced to his staff, "Gentlemen, the tradition of secrecy which has enveloped us all these years will now have to end. As much as I hate to do it, I've got to tell the nation what has happened." Johnston prepared a telegram which he ordered sent to all newspapers, radio broadcasters, and press associations in the northern California. It read, "Serious trouble. Convict has machine gun in cellhouse. Have issued riot call. Placed armed guards at strategic locations. Many of our officers are imprisoned in cellhouse. Cannot tell extent of injuries suffered by our officers or amount of damage done. We will give you more information later in the day as we regain control."

With that alarming message sent and spread within the hour through the world by a headline-seeking press, Johnston had hit the panic button. His ignorance of the situation and lack of communication with any officers in C block caused him to exaggerate a serious but not overwhelming convict revolution. He believed that at least seventy-five inmates were involved in the breakout. The truth was that only six convicts were actively attempting to escape and none had a machine gun. The only

weapons the convicts ever possessed in the Battle of Alcatraz was a pistol and a rifle. Johnston, quite naturally, took no chances. He wired his good friend Warden Duffy at San Quentin for backup guards and sharpshooters. He also asked for riot officers from the San Francisco Police and alerted the Coast Guard to send all their available cutters to patrol the waters around the island, having more marksmen stationed on these ships ready to shoot any convicts who got to the water's edge.

Johnston also sent out emergency calls for physicians and nurses to stand by to handle the wounded in Bay Area hospitals. A few minutes later he received a call from General Joseph Stillwell, in charge of the military in the area, who called Johnston from his Treasure Island headquarters as soon as he heard of the breakout. The tough, battle-hardened general, known as "Vinegar Joe," asked Johnston if he needed help and the warden responded immediately by saying, "Yes, general, most certainly. We are very short-handed. If you could send us ten or fifteen men to help guard the prisoners who have not become involved in the escape, I would appreciate it very much." Stillwell said he would be sending U.S. Marines within the hour and that he would personally arrive on the Rock the next day to see what assistance he could render.

Within the hour, scores of newsmen who had been barred from the island for twelve years since Alcatraz' official opening as a federal penitentiary, cameramen in tow, raced for the San Francisco docks, commandeering any kind of boat that would take them into the bay. Dozens of these small craft would circle the embattled island for forty-eight hours, getting in the way of Coast Guard and military vessels, in a desperate attempt to get the story. The Siege of Alcatraz not only involved the convicts and their keepers but a siege of press people who likened the uprising to a full-scale military battle and, lacking any real facts, exploded reality into nightmare. Radio Station KGO went on the air with the following report, "A bloody uprising is underway on Alcatraz Island. Rampaging convicts have stormed and captured the prison arsenal. Prison officers have been slaughtered. Armed prisoners are overrunning the island. Women and children, families of the prison employees, are in desperate peril. The warden has sent out a call for help to all military and police agencies. A desperate emergency confronts everyone in the San Francisco Bay Area."

Hearing this report, Lieutenant Philip Bergen, one of Alcatraz's off-duty officers, quickly called the island and amazingly got through. He was told that the situation was serious but not as grave as reports would have it. Bergen was ordered to go to Dock 4 and wait there with all other available off-duty Alcatraz officers. A Coast Guard boat would pick them up; they were needed on the island. Bergen went to the dock and was joined there by officers Harry Cochrane, John Wright, and Norman Anthony. All had been enjoying a day off but headed for the docks as soon as they heard the news of the uprising. As the officers waited for the Coast Guard cutter, they could see small puffs of smoke on the island and hear occasional pistol and rifle shots. The siren wailed mournfully across the waters to them. Thousands of citizens raced to the docks in San Francisco to view the spectacle and thousands more lined the shore of Marin across the bay. Coast Guard cutters could be seen racing about the bay, and the little boats crowded with press people bobbed crazily between them.

When the Coast Guard cutter carrying Bergen and the other officers arrived at the Alcatraz dock, Lieutenant Emil Rychner was there to greet them, ordering them to help the guards squatting in the towers. Officer Anthony swayed unevenly as he stepped on the dock. He had been making the rounds of the San Francisco bars on his day off and was tipsy. Rychner took one look at the unsteady Anthony and then asked of Bergen, "Why did you bring this drunk over here? He'll be of no use to us." Bergen shrugged, "We just couldn't stop him." Anthony was taken to the bachelor officer's quarters where he would sleep through the siege.

Meanwhile, inside of C and D blocks, the convicts involved in the uprising had more or less resigned themselves to a suicidal

THE SIX WHO BATTLED THE ROCK IN 1946

Ringleaders of the 1946 blastout, Joseph Paul Cretzer, left, and Bernard Coy, right, both dedicated killers.

Marvin Franklin Hubbard, left, helped plan the 1946 breakout; Miran Edgar Thompson, right, urged Cretzer to murder the captured guards.

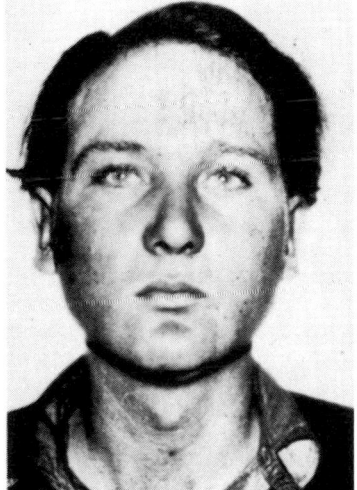
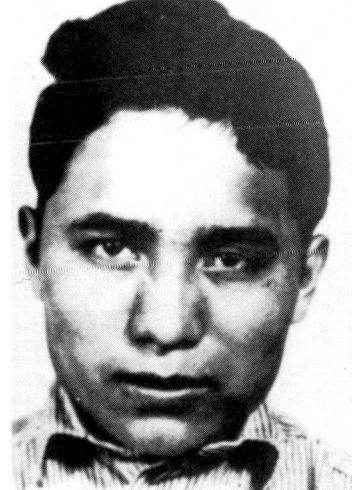

Samuel Richard Shockley, left, a berserk inmate, demanded the deaths of guards and finally got his way; Clarence Victor Carnes tried to save some of the guards from Cretzer's bullets.

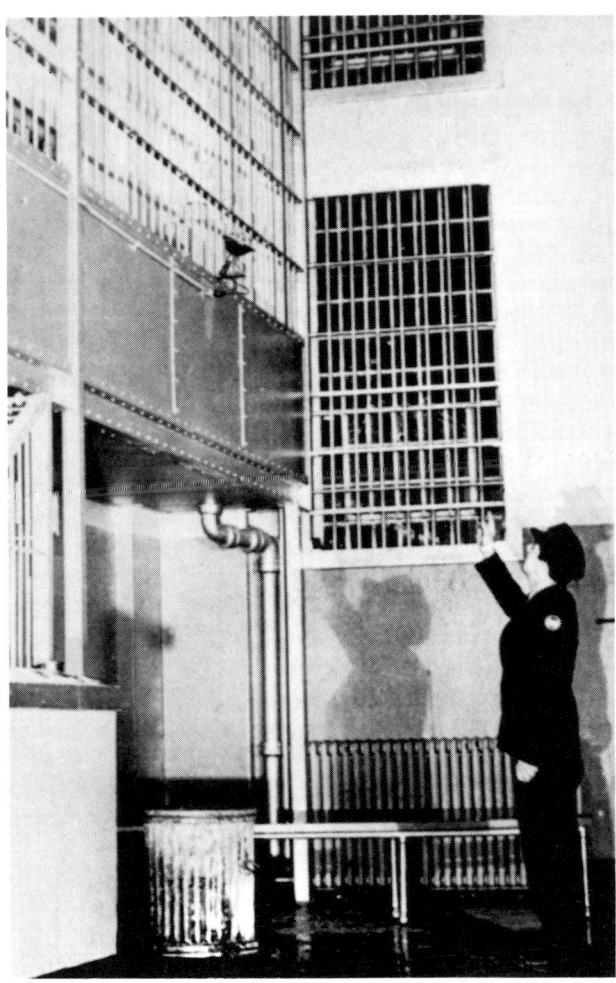

Above, guard points to where Bernard Coy monkey-climbed his way to the gun gallery and used a homemade "bar-spreader" to wriggle through the bars and overpower the guard on duty; below, the road tower where guards crouched to avoid the rifle fire of Coy and Hubbard.

attempt to kill off as many guards as they could before they themselves were killed. While Coy stood guard in an upper tier between D and C block, trying to pick off guards in the towers, Cretzer and the others stood outside of cells 402 and 403, wondering how to use their captives. The berserk Shockley ranted for their deaths, screaming at Cretzer to turn the pistol on the guards, especially Captain Weinhold. "If you try to shoot it out, you'll all be killed, Joe," Weinhold told Cretzer. "You haven't a chance. Just think about it for a moment. Don't throw your life away."

Shockley stood outside the cell spitting wrath, "Shut up, you lousy screw! You beat me up when I burned my cell last time! I hate your guts!"

Cretzer moved close to the cell as Weinhold stood up. "You think we'll all be killed, Captain?" A strange, crooked smile played on the ringleader's face.

"You hear that siren, don't you, Joe?" Weinhold said. "Everybody else for miles around can hear it, too. By this time this prison is ringed by guns. What can you do with a single pistol?"

"We can hold them off, Joe!" shouted Shockley.

"Don't listen to that screwball, Joe," Weinhold told Cretzer. "Think for yourself."

"I'm thinking that there'll be lots more killed here today besides us, Captain," Cretzer answered in a low voice.

"Kill them all, Joe!" screamed Shockley. He pointed to Weinhold. "Especially him. He took my shoes. He made me go without shoes, Joe!" With that, convulsed with rage, Shockley took off his shoes and socks and threw them at Weinhold.

Cretzer stood staring at Weinhold and the other officers, seeming to weigh his fate and obviously enjoying his role as a man who could give or take life. Carnes and Thompson stood next to him. Carnes sensed that Cretzer had made up his mind to kill all the officers and he stated, "Don't hurt them, Joe. They didn't give us any trouble."

Thompson, as hardboiled as Cretzer and Coy, sneered at Carnes, then turned to Cretzer and said, "Hell, go on and kill every s.o.b. in there. We don't want no witnesses. They'll put us all in the gas chamber."

Weinhold and the other officers moved back into the cells as Cretzer smiled and said to them, "It's funny as hell, us arguing what to do with you screws. Yesterday you was arguing about how to handle us."

Shockley screamed, "They'd hang us if they got the chance, Joe, hang us, hang us! Kill them, Joe, kill them all!"

Hubbard, as desperate a killer as the rest, had said nothing. He stood there shaking his head. Cretzer looked at Hubbard, as if to seek approval for what he was about to do. "We don't need no hostages, do we, Marv?"

"Wrong. A deal is always possible, Joe, if you have something to bargain with."

"They're pretty good guys, Joe, why kill them?" Carnes put in.

Shockley was beside himself, jumping up and down, his face twitching, his arms jerking about. He suddenly tried to grab the pistol out of Cretzer's hand, shouting, "Give me that iron! If you ain't got the guts to kill 'em, I'll show you how easy it is!"

Cretzer shoved Shockley away from him but kept the pistol trained on the officers in cell 402. He was no longer looking at Weinhold but narrowed his eyes in a glare to Officer William Miller, the guard who had tried to get rid of the key to the recreation area. "You sank our damn boat, Miller," Cretzer told the guard. "You hid that damned key!"

"Kill him, kill him, kill him!" Shockley chanted. He seemed to be in a daze and a slight foam appeared on his lips. "Shoot, shoot, shoot!"

Then all of the memories of Alcatraz Joseph "Dutch" Cretzer had nurtured with his hate and fear of the prison gushed from his snarling mouth, "Weinhold, you and your goons are gonna kill us in the end anyway. That's nothin' new. You put the tag on a lot of other cons—Bowers, Cole and Roe, Limerick, Dock Barker, that kid Jim Boarman. You ain't gonna be here, any of you, to see it happen to us!" Cretzer's voice was a growl, as he rested the

pistol on the cross bar of the cell.

Weinhold and other officers retreated to the back of the tiny cell. Cretzer fired the .45 once, the bullet smashing into Weinhold's chest, its impact slamming him into the cell wall. Weinhold fell, rolling under the bunk. Next it was Miller's turn. The guard was struck by a bullet in the right arm and he fell among the other guards. The killer's next two bullets took down officers Burdette and Bristow. Then Cretzer shot guards Corwin and Lageson. As he fired in deliberately aimed shots, Cretzer breathed heavily as if he were winded following a long run, but there was nothing hysterical in his actions. He was methodical as he emptied his first clip of bullets. Once all the guards were down in the first cell, Cretzer moved to the second, adding another clip to the .45. Again, breathing heavily, Cretzer rested the pistol on the cross bar to steady his aim and fired three shots, striking officer Simpson in the abdomen and officer Baker in the leg. They fell to the floor as Sundstrom went with them, the bullet intended for him striking the wall harmlessly.

All the wounded guards remained still in their contorted prone positions, pretending to be dead. Hubbard, Shockley, Carnes, and Thompson stared at the carnage in the dark cells (the overhead lights had been smashed by the guards to afford the killers as little vision of them as possible). Blood from the wounds of the guards ran in small rivers out of the cells into the aisle at the feet of the rebel convicts. Then Shockley saw an arm move and called to Cretzer who was sauntering away from what he thought were seven murdered Alcatraz guards. "Joe—here's one screw that ain't dead yet!"

Cretzer returned to peer into the cell. He said, "Well, it's my friend, Mr. Lageson."

"Friend, hell!" screamed Shockley. "He's gonna go to court and squeal like the others."

"I'm not your enemy, Joe," Lageson said weakly. "Take it easy. Sam knows I never did anything to hurt him."

There was the sound of sincere regret in Cretzer's voice as he said, "I'm truly sorry to do this, Mr. Lageson. You ain't so bad a guy but like Sam says, we can't have anyone alive to put the finger on us." He fired at Lageson's head. The bullet creased the guard's scalp, causing his face to run with blood. Lageson passed out and appeared to be dead. All the convicts then left the scene, except Carnes who stood staring in shock at the butchered guards.

Lageson came to for a moment. He inched a pencil out of his breast pocket and wrote down the names of the convicts involved in the uprising, as if leaving a dying message for the outside world so the killers would later be identified. He wrote on the wall of the cell the names of Cretzer, Coy, Carnes, Hubbard, Thompson, and Shockley. Around the names of Cretzer, Coy, and Hubbard, Lageson drew circles, to indicate that these were the real ringleaders and after Cretzer's name he placed a checkmark, to indicate that "Dutch Joe" was the mastermind of the break and the killer of the guards. Then Lageson passed out once more.

Lieutenant Bergen quickly organized a group of officers attempting to rescue the hostages. They entered D block from the west gun gallery and were immediately fired upon by Cretzer and Coy who had anticipated the guards would attack from that direction. Returning fire, the officers managed to work their way down the route to the gun gallery where they found Burch tied up. They released him but Cretzer now had a good view of the officers as he darted in and out of the door connecting C and D blocks. His aim was much better than when he shot the guards in the cells. He managed to hit officer Harold Stites as he stood up to fire. He fired again and wounded Oldham in the right arm. Cretzer fired once more and hit Officer Richberger in the leg. Coy, who was on the top tier of D block suddenly opened up with the rifle and his struck Officer Cochrane in the shoulder, the bullet tearing across Cochrane's back. The officers retreated with their wounded but the courageous Bergen stayed behind, lying flat on the gun gallery floor, holding a phone, and reporting to Warden Johnston the movements of the prisoners.

By the time the guards of his group returned to Johnston's

office, Stites has passed out. A doctor examined him as he lay on Johnston's couch, then turned to the warden and reported, "This man is dead." Stites, who had almost single-handedly stopped a break in 1938, killing Tom Limerick, was now himself dead at the hands of the convicts. (It was later claimed that Cretzer and Coy could not fail to hit their marks since the officers were bunched up and had exposed themselves. Moreover, it was claimed, that in their crouching position along the gun gallery, the officers had unleashed their own return fire and in this wild police barrage, Stites had been struck by a bullet from one of his fellow officers.) Guard William A. Miller was also dead. The tough old officer had managed to first hide the key to the recreation yard and then substitute another which was fished out of the toilet in the cell where he had been held hostage (which is why it did not work in the door when Coy and Cretzer battled with it). The guards pretending to be dead in the hostage cells after Cretzer shot them believed Miller was only superficially wounded. Since none of them dared utter a word, they believed Miller was also feigning death. He was mortally wounded, however, and bravely refused to cry out to his fellow officers. He simply bled to death on the floor of the cell where he was crumpled together with the other guards.

Associate Warden Miller, no relation to William A. Miller, organized another rescue group of fourteen officers, all volunteers, and this group entered the prison area through the library corridor between C and D block. They heard Sundstrom calling out to them, telling them they were in cells 402 and 403. Miller and his men groped their way along since it was now almost night and the cell blocks were dark, the lights having been turned off. Miller and the others moved along under the overhanging galleries and were shot at repeatedly by Cretzer and the others who were now on top of C block and shooting down on them but their aim was blocked by the overhanging tiers under which the officers moved. As five or six officers kept up return fire, Miller led the rest to the cells where the hostages were held. They released them all, dragging the wounded back with them in their retreat from the cell block.

By then the guards outside were pouring rifle fire into both C and D blocks, along with occasional gas grenades, but the convicts had obtained gas masks in the gun gallery and were able to move about freely during the periodic gas attacks. Those not taking part in the break remained in their cells, most under their bunks, their mattresses over them to protect them from the rifle fire from outside. They soaked towels in their tiny sinks and kept these over their faces to ward off the effects of the gas that floated about in pockets throughout both blocks.

Warden Johnston was finally getting a better picture of the uprising and he now knew that the inmates only had two weapons. By simple calculation of the bullets fired at the hostages, out the windows at the guards in the towers and at the invading guards going in and out of C and D block, he realized that the convicts were low on ammunition. The walls and towers of Alcatraz had been depleted of men, but this was soon remedied when squads of Marines landed on the island and manned the outside walls and towers, relieving the exhausted guards who had been on duty without sleep for almost twenty-four hours. It was the same with the convicts, except that desperation kept them wide-eyed and alert. Guards were moving into D block in greater numbers and occasionally spraying the areas of D block where they thought the escapees might be.

There were only three convicts now who continued the forlorn revolt, the three toughest of the lot, Cretzer, Coy, and Hubbard. They had all voiced their willingness to die rather than be taken alive. Cretzer believed that he had murdered all the hostages and Coy was convinced that he had shot and killed at least six guards in the tower. Hubbard, who had fired the rifle several times, also believed that he had murdered at least two or three of the officers who had first entered the western gun gallery. They knew what the penalty would be; if captured they would be tried and sentenced to death, and none of them relished the idea of walking

into the gas chamber at San Quentin. (Contrary to popular belief, no execution facilities were present at Alcatraz and no one in the island prison's history was ever executed on the Rock.) Carnes had left the rebels after Cretzer shot the guards, returning to his cell to await the consequences. Thompson, a wily killer, told the others he was going to search for a weapon, but this was only an excuse to depart from the more dedicated escapees. He knew now that the break was hopeless. Thompson returned to his cell and hid in its darkest corner. Shockley was useless to Cretzer now. He had served as a murderous Iago in encouraging Cretzer to slay the hostages. He was in the way and was acting so erratically that Cretzer gave him some money he had taken from one of the guards and told him to slip back to D block and give it to Whitey Franklin. Shockley, his eyes rolling, his lips quivering, moved away in the darkness, promising to return once he finished his errand.

Hubbard turned to Cretzer and told him, "That bedbug won't come back. He'll just wander back to his cell and hide."

Cretzer replied, "Yeah, I know. But he's better out of the way. No lunatics can help us now."

As they talked in whispers, the convicts in their cells nearby could hear them but said nothing believing that the ringleaders were now kill crazy and would shoot anyone who made a noise.

Coy said nothing for a long time and then snapped, "So Shockley is crazy, huh, and we're all sane?" He then launched into a tirade against Cretzer for using up most of his ammunition.

"I had to use up some bullets on the guards, didn't I? What did you expect me to do—knock 'em off with spit? Besides, I didn't see you trying to save any bullets for that rifle when you were popping those guys out of the towers, Bernie."

"All right, Joe, all right. I just wanted more bullets to kill more screws with."

The next morning found the guards no nearer to quelling the uprising than the day before. Cretzer, Coy, and Hubbard still controlled both blocks and ran back and forth between them, firing occasional shots from the windows at the tower guards and soldiers outside to let them know that it would be dangerous to attempt to rush the prison. But the trio knew that they would have to find a secure hiding place where they could survive the onslaught of a mass attack. They found it in a shallow tunnel which was midway in C block under the concrete floor. The escapees would crawl into the tunnel then dart out occasionally to fire at the guards. At 5:30 a.m. Johnston ordered gas bombs dropped down ventilator shafts that led to the tunnel. Rifle grenades were then fired throughout the morning from the lawn, blowing holes into D block which guards and the Marines, along with newly-arrived Army troops, raked with machine gun fire. Smoke from the gas bombs and grenades and later from motor shells lobbed into D block caused the entire island to be surrounded with billowing clouds of smoke. To the tens of thousands of spectators lining the shorelines of the bar area and in hundreds of boats floating in the bay, the sound of explosions and the sight of the intense, curling smoke, convinced them that a full-scale battle was going on and most believed that the entire prison population had broken free, taken over the arsenal, and that General Stillwell had landed at least a regiment of troops to battle the berserk prisoners. When two destroyers were seen approaching the Island it was believed that all guards, civilians, and military personnel would be withdrawn and the U.S. Navy would simply level the entire island, killing every prisoner on Alcatraz.

Stillwell, along with his long-time military associate, General Frank Merrill, did arrive on the Rock, asking if they could be of any assistance. After Warden Johnston explained how he had positioned his guards and the military personnel that had landed throughout the night, the generals commended him, Stillwell telling him that "you're like a general in the field and you seem to have the situation under control." Stillwell then looked over the D block objective and told Johnston that the blockbuster bombs that had been delivered to the Rock during the night were much too destructive for his needs and recommended use of only the anti-tank shells to blow a hole in D block. Johnston concurred with this plan and several antitank shells were used to tear great gaps in the thick walls of D block.

Inside the tunnel, Coy counted his bullets. He had twenty-five left. Cretzer had four. When he heard the explosions above them, Cretzer cursed. "What's that?" he asked nervously.

"Dynamite," Coy volunteered.

"That ain't dynamite," Hubbard said. "They're using grenades on us!"

This shocked Cretzer. "I never thought they would do something like that. Using those army guys against us. We ain't like the Nazis. I never thought they would do a thing like that."

Coy reassured Hubbard and Cretzer that no matter how many gas bombs and grenades were dropped down the ventilator shafts, they were all safe in the tunnel since no ventilators led to it. He explained that the concrete slab floor above them was at least two or three feet thick and that the entire prison would have to be blown up before anyone could get to them. Their conversation was overhead by convicts in the cells above them through small pipes that ran from the cells to the tunnel. Coy was finally heard to say, "We're in the best damned bomb shelter on this rock."

The battle raged on into Saturday morning until Johnston decided that it was time to "get the prisoners." Above the skies of Alcatraz U.S. Army planes buzzed, and it was thought by newsmen in the boats still scurrying about the harbor, that the Rock was to be bombed. On shore, in parks that gave full view of the battle, thousands of early morning spectators gaped at the island. One enterprising hustler roped off some prized viewing areas in a park and was charging $1 for one hour's viewing. He had placed a homemade sign on a tree which read:

See this spectacular riot!
Mothers! See who might have been your son!
Watch them try to escape and get killed in action!
It will leave you breathless!
One hour for one dollar.

Other enterprising businessmen cashed in on the siege of the Rock, including a local theater owner who immediately ordered a print of a 1938 film, *King of Alcatraz*, a B-film made in 1938. Although it had nothing to do with the 1946 film, the movie was hyped in Saturday morning newspapers as telling the whole story of the prison, implying that it did relate recent events, but only the most naive of filmgoers believed this claim. The movie, however, did big box office business. Tens of thousands of Bay Area residents, however, including phalanxes of children now free of school hours, flocked to the waterfronts and hills surrounding the bay to witness the rest of the battle. The battle, however, was one-sided now since the three convicts had holed up in their small tunnel and all the gunfire, mortar shells, and antitank missiles were being sent into the shambles of D block. Newsmen were desperate for any kind of news from the Rock and this was scant. Warden Johnston had overreacted in his contact with the press and was now being labeled an alarmist, according to some reports. Major H.W. Thompson, who commanded the heavy weapons company of the 97th Division, was buttonholed by newsmen on a boat off the island. Thompson was studying the Rock through his binoculars and told newsmen that grenades, bazooka shells, and mortars had been used against D block, explaining that the steel fragments from these explosives would encompass a sixty-foot radius. He went on to state in an oblique criticism of Johnston that the warden was considering using even heavier explosives, even though these new bombs would certainly collapse the thick walls of D block and allow all the prisoners inside to escape onto the island.

First, Warden Johnston wanted to make sure exactly where the three rebel convicts were located. He wasn't so sure that one or more were not hiding in D block. Before ordering the final assault, he asked Lieutenant Bergen who was still lying in the gun gallery there to tell him over the phone if the block was clear of the gunmen. Bergen had no way of really telling but the information he was seeking came from the oldest convict on the Rock,

the 58-year-old Birdman of Alcatraz, Robert Stroud. He and twenty-five other convicts on D block had withstood the police and army barrage, huddling in their opened cells with nothing but their thin mattresses to protect them against the constant rapid-fire from rifles and machine guns and the explosions from gas bombs, grenades, bazookas, and mortars. All about these terrified, hungry prisoners was the debris of the battle. The explosions had caused the plumbing to burst and the main pipes to open to sea water. Water had shot upward through the pipes during the bombings so that huge pools had spread throughout the main floor and the two tiers housing the isolation cells. Shards of glass, twisted metal, and shattered slabs of concrete lay everywhere. All the lights in D block had been turned off and the prisoners having no part in the uprising merely waited in the gloom, expecting to die at any time.

Stroud, a withdrawn, solemn man, had the dubious distinction of having served more time in isolation than any convict in U.S. history. In addition to being a flagrant homosexual in his earlier years, prison authorities considered him one of the most dangerous federal prisoners in custody, a cold-blooded murderer. Yet he possessed a brilliant mind and an obsession for the study of birds. As a self-taught ornithologist, Stroud had kept birds in his prison cells at Leavenworth where he studied them with crude laboratory equipment, and he had written an immensely popular 500-page book, *Digest of Bird Diseases*. Looking about D block, Stroud concluded that another massive assault would take his life and that of the other twenty-five convicts in the block. Early Saturday morning, May 4, 1946, the last day of the siege, Stroud had counted more than 400 bullets and explosives smashing into D block. He had had enough. Stroud, in his stocking feet, crouched as he moved cautiously along the second tier of D block, working his way toward the stairs so that he could get close to the gun gallery where he knew Lieutenant Bergen and the other officers were huddled. When another bomb exploded in D block, Stroud ducked into cell 15. He was close to the stairs and the gun gallery at this position and he shouted, "This is Stroud speaking! What I say is the truth and I will back every word with my life! There is no gun in D block. What you are trying to do is pure murder."

"I know it's you, Stroud," Bergen called back. "I wish I could believe you but the evidence is against you."

Another guard shouted, "Shut up, you lying old bastard! You cons had your fun and now you can't take it! We're going to blow the block down and I hope you go with it!"

"What do I care!" Stroud shouted back. "I'm an old man. Spent my whole life in these outhouses. You're not beating me out of anything. If you have to kill somebody, I'll step out of here and give you the chance."

Bergen, one of the most sensible of the frustrated guards, replied, "Take it easy, Stroud. You'll live to write some more books."

"There are twenty-five men in here innocent of any part of this nightmare," Stroud said.

More bombs began to explode in D block and Bergen shouted to Stroud, "Keep your heads down." Stroud and Bergen exchanged more remarks and Stroud more or less told Bergen that the trio of killers were not to be found in D block but near the ventilator systems, pinpointing the tunnel where Cretzer, Coy, and Hubbard were hiding. He asked Bergen to stop the shelling into D block as several convicts were already wounded. Bergen later called out to Stroud that the shelling would stop shortly and by 1 p.m. the barrage ended.

At that time, Johnston and his officers realized that Cretzer, Coy, and Hubbard were definitely holed up in the C block cutoff tunnel, and he resolved to bomb them out by dropping explosives onto the floor. The murderous trio in the tunnel crawled about the piping there, trying to find the most secure place to repel an attack which would come through a small door. Several officers led by Associate Warden Miller had already thrown open this door and fired wildly into the shallow tunnel and the convicts had fired back. Grenades had been dropped down pipes and had burst, the

AFTERMATH OF THE 1946 BLASTOUT

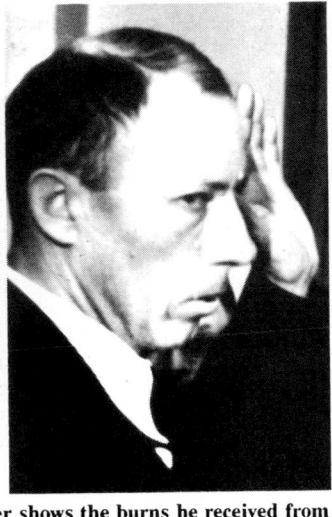

Above left, Associate Warden Miller shows the burns he received from an exploding gas billy during the 1946 breakout; right, Officer Harold Stites, was killed in the gun battle for the gun gallery.

Prison lieutenant Philip Bergen who led several heroic attacks against the armed convicts during the breakout attempt.

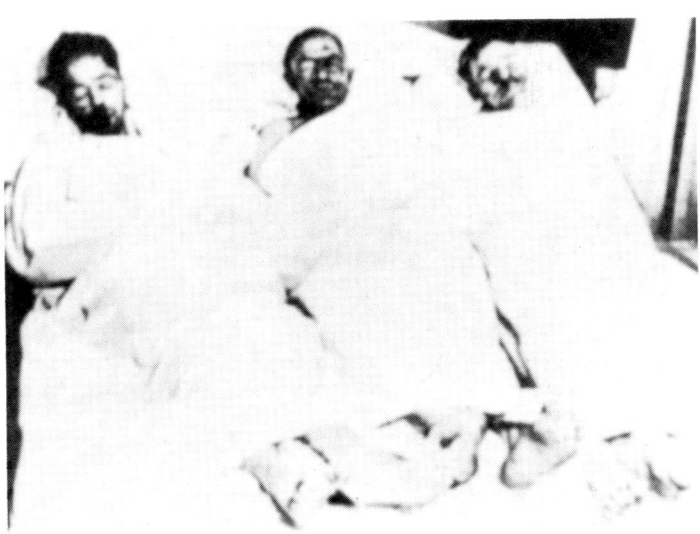

The names of the six convicts involved in the blastout were written down on the cell wall of one of the captured guards who thought he was dying from his wounds; he encircled the names of the ringleaders.

End of the rebellion: The bullet-ridden bodies of Hubbard, Coy, and Cretzer lie in the prison hospital, awaiting burial.

The utility corridor between C and D blocks where Cretzer, Coy, and Hubbard made their last stand against the bombs and machine gun fire.

Thompson, Carnes, and Shockley are led in chains to their trial for the murder of Alcatraz guards; Thompson and Shockley went to the gas chamber.

shrapnel from the grenades and the metal from the pipes fragmenting the entire tunnel and striking the convicts. All of them were suffering from wounds but were determined to die rather than surrender. Coy built a little barricade before the door from the debris in the tunnel. Water and muck was ankle deep and Hubbard groped fruitlessly about in the slop looking for the homemade knife he had taken from Carnes. Hubbard could be heard to tell the others, "I just want one more (guard) before I die!"

Marine Officer Buckner supervised the dropping of grenades down the ventilator shafts to where they would explode in the untility corridor or tunnel where the convicts crouched. He later told reporters, "We cut a hole through the cellblock roof and lowered grenades. It was easy lowering grenades down the cell vents on strings. I must have lowered 500. They each would go off at different levels, depending on how long the string was. With a second string, I'd pull the pin. Duck soup. They shattered the vents to pieces. I also fired my antitank grenades right down the roof holes. My intent was to riddle a kind of concrete culvert or conduit where the cons were hiding. We'd drop a few grenades at each end of the block and give them a little time to run for this culvert. Then I'd fire the rifle grenades."

Finally Assocate Warden Miller and a dozen heavily armed guards threw open the door to the utility tunnel. The place was dark but in the beam of their powerful flashlights, the guards could see that the corridor was a complete shambles. Raw sewage flowed through it several feet deep. It smelled of cordite and smoke from bombs still curled ominously out to the guards. The place was riddled with bomb fragments and gun blasts which the guards had been pouring into the corridor every time they opened and closed the door. Miller shouted a warning that could have come out of the mouth of Samuel Goldwyn, "This is your last chance! Get out here or you're going to spend the rest of your lives dead!"

Silence was his only answer. Miller then turned to his men and said, "Let 'em have it all!" The guards, some kneeling, some crouching above them, others standing above the second row, jammed together to form three rows, firing their shotguns and machine guns into the corridor, later called "Death Corridor." The roar was heard throughout C and D blocks, and it continued until all the officers were completely out of ammunition. "Let's go in and dig 'em out," Miller said. The officers stepped into the corridor. The first body found was that of Coy. He was still wearing Weinhold's uniform, and in his arm he cradled the rifle which had a live round in the chamber. He was in a sitting position behind his shattered barricade. His arms were still flexed upward and were frozen by rigor mortis. Rifle bullets had torn through his neck, cheek, left ear, and right shoulder. He was dragged out.

Cretzer was found next. He too was found wearing a guard's coat, and he was in a firing position, although the pistol had slipped from his grasp and was found behind some pipes. He had three bullets left when he had received a mortal wound, a rifle bullet through his skull which had blown the back part of his brain all over the corridor. Cretzer's body was also cold with rigor mortis setting in but Hubbard's corpse, found at the back of the corridor, was still warm. He had received two shots in the head which had almost been blown off his torso.

After the ringleaders were taken to the morgue, a search for the other three convicts involved in the uprising was immediately conducted by Associate Warden Miller. He did not have to look hard to find Carnes in his cell. He ordered him to stand outside of his cell and strip. Naked, Carnes was taken to A block and thrown into one of the old dungeon-like cells. "If he makes a false move, blow his rotten head off," Miller told the guards leading Carnes away from his B block cell.

Shockley was found in D block, cringing in the back of his cell. Miller ordered him onto the tier walkway. "I ain't done nothin'," he claimed. He looked about him to see other prisoners glaring at him from their cells and then, twitching, Shockley lied, "We

been here all the time, ain't we fellas?" The other prisoners said nothing to support his falsehood.

Miller was having none of it. "You rat," Miller told him, "we know you helped to kill those officers. Admit it, or I'll kick your teeth in!"

Shockley made a furtive move to sidestep Miller and his officers and he was slammed into the wall. "Honest," he whined, "I'm innocent. I was no friend of theirs."

Miller shoved him into the arms of two officers and ordered them to take Shockley to the A block solitary cells. Shockley hobbled off the tier, barefoot, the broken glass on the floor gouging his feet and causing them to bleed. Next, Miller marched to Thompson's cell and ordered him step outside and strip. "But I ain't done nothin'" Thompson snarled.

"Quit lying, you bastard," Miller said, his hate for this conniving convict intense. "If you keep lying, you'll take a dive off this tier, so help me. I know what went on, Thompson. You were the one who didn't want any witnesses, remember? Well, we have witnesses, and they're gonna send you to the gas chamber."

The prison staff were busy feeding the starving convicts but Carnes, Thompson, and Shockley were given only a few crackers and some water. Johnston busied himself by answering a barrage of questions from newsmen. He assured them that the uprising was over. Two guards, William Miller and Harold Stites, were dead. The ringleaders of the uprising, Cretzer, Coy, and Hubbard, were dead. One other prisoner and fourteen guards had been wounded. Johnston reported that guards and military personnel had poured thousands of rounds into D and C blocks during the siege. The warden detailed the weapons used to put down the uprising: shotguns, tear gas launchers, Sprinfield rifles, Garand M-1 rifles, .45-caliber pistols, Thompson submachine guns, carbines, fragmentation grenades, phosphorous grenades, rifle grenades. He did not specify the use of mortars and bazookas by the military, but these weapons were in clear evidence during the battle.

Johnston did not mention the many bizarre episodes occurring during the siege, how James Henry "Blackie" Audett went on making pot after pot of coffee for both the attackers and the besieged convicts, how the drunken guard Norman Anthony, a political appointee, got loose from the guard's bachelor quarters after arriving on the Rock and, while the battle raged, drunkenly marched up and down on the lawn between the crossfire, a rifle perched on his shoulder, until guards risked their lives to tackle him and drag him away. Johnston announced that FBI agents were already on the Rock interviewing guards and prisoners alike, and he felt that the result of these interrogations would lead to murder indictments for Shockley, Thompson, and Carnes.

The FBI agents who did interview almost everyone who was on the Rock during the battle did provide enough evidence against the three living convicts to bring them to that indictment but the other convicts provided agents with nothing. As one agent later remarked, "We encountered a wall of silence as cold and hard as the walls of a cellblock." Shockley, Thompson, and Carnes were tried on Nov. 20, 1946, all charged with the murder of William Miller. (They were not charged with the killing of Stites as it was clear that this murder was committed by either Coy, Hubbard, or Cretzer.) Stroud contributed $200 to the defense of the trio, money he had earned from his book royalties. For fourteen weeks a jury heard the government and defense arguments. Then, on Dec. 22, 1946, the jury found all three Guilty of Miller's murder but recommended mercy for Carnes. Testimony revealed that Carnes, though he took part in the uprising, had tried to save the lives of the guards, a mitigating factor in his receiving a life sentence instead of death. It was death for Shockley and Thompson. Carnes was returned to the Rock and Shockley and Thompson were sent to San Quentin to await execution in the gas chamber.

After almost two years of appeals, time ran out for the condemned pair. On Dec. 2, 1948, both were sent to San Quentin's gas chamber. Thompson had accumulated a great number

THE ALMOST-PERFECT ESCAPE

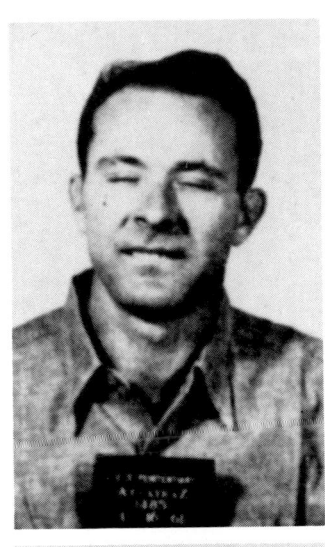

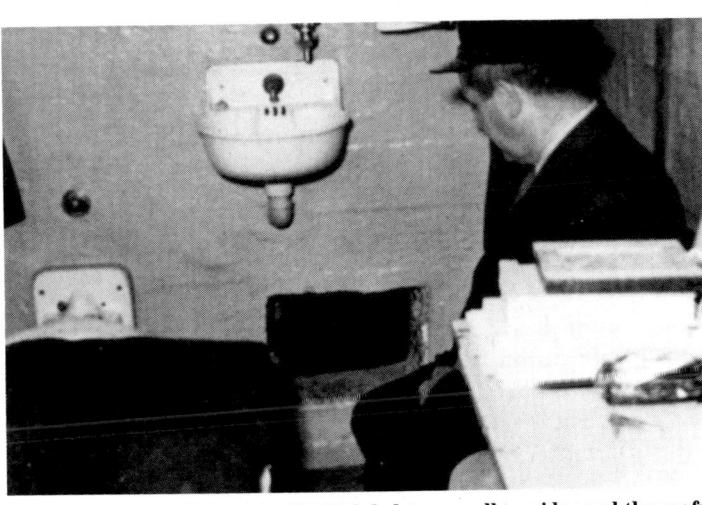

Hole chiseled out of Morris' cell which led to a small corridor and the roof; the three escapees used spoons as digging tools.

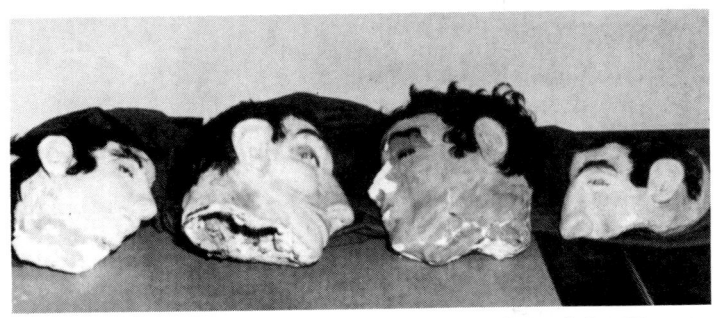

Dummy heads created by convicts which they used on their pillows to convince guards they were in their bunks; the plaster of Paris was obtained for them by Alvin Karpis and the Anglin brothers, who worked in the prison barber shop and took hair cuttings to affix to the plaster heads.

The three clever convicts who engineered the last escape from Alcatraz, so well executed that it may have succeeded: top, Clarence Anglin; middle, John Anglin; bottom, the brains behind it all, Frank Lee Morris.

The dummy head resting on a pillow in Frank Morris' cell; when a guard pulled on it the head rolled onto the floor and the guard became hysterical, thinking someone had decapitated an inmate.

of law books and had feverishly filed petition after petition to save his life. Shockley had done nothing, believing that the authorities would not execute an insane man, although he was judged to be sane. On the last night of his life, Thompson nibbled at a chicken dinner but ate two banana cream pies three hours apart. Shortly before he was to die, he nervously sipped some coffee but choked on some orange juice. Shockley slept almost to the time of his execution. He awoke and wolfed down a large breakfast consisting of bacon and eggs, toast, coffee, and orange juice. Just before he was escorted to the gas chamber, Thompson insisted that "I was in my cell throughout the whole damned thing." In a last letter to his wife, Thompson had written, "I know I've been involved with crime all my life. I've hardened to it. Maybe it's because I ain't had any education, any chance for a decent way of living. Maybe if I had been trained to work at something, I wouldn't have been so bad."

Both men were taken from their death cells and escorted to an elevator which took them six floors upward. They were both placed in the gas chamber which held two chairs and each was secured by ten straps to the chair. As a guard was strapping Shockley into the chair the killer spat at him. Outside the octagonal, apple-green gas chamber with its seven windows (two side windows with venetian blinds pulled so condemned prisoners cannot see their executioners), witnesses took their places. The door was closed and locked. Just before the gas pellets were dropped, Thompson turned to Shockley and said something but his words were not heard. In twelve minutes, both men were pronounced dead by San Quentin physician Dr. L.I. Stanley.

Following the bloody 1946 uprising, additional safeguards were taken. Intercoms were placed at strategic positions so that guards could be reached within seconds. Bulletproof armor plating was placed over the gun galleries. It was pointed out by Warden Johnston and his successors that although the country's top maximum-security prison had been sorely tested, the Rock remained invulnerable to escape. Convicts, however, kept testing that reputation. One of these was Huron Ted Walters, an Oklahoma bandit who had been imprisoned with Floyd Hamilton for bank robbery and was serving thirty years on the Rock. Walters worked in the laundry and he devised a lone-wolf escape which he put into action in August 1948. One day, after the guards had taken the afternoon head count, Walters slipped out of an unlocked door carrying several empty bleach containers. These were large containers and Walters strapped them together, intending to float on them to the mainland. He tripped when he neared a cliff, however, and tumbled downward to be knocked unconscious on the rocks below. Guards looking for him about an hour later found Walters stumbling about dazed and bleeding from many cuts. He was wearing only his shorts. In the distance, borne by the currents and floating out to sea were the empty bleach containers.

The attempts continued in the 1950s. In July 1956, murderer Floyd Wilson, serving life, slipped away from a work detail and made it to the shoreline where he attempted to lash driftwood and debris into some sort of a raft. He was found twelve hours later hiding between the rocks without ever having gone into the water. In September 1958, Clyde Johnson, bank robber and kidnapper who had been Public Enemy Number One and is serving a fifty-year sentence, and postal robber Walter Burgett, serving twenty-five years, escaped work detail and plunged into the water using a raincoat with its sleeves tied as makeshift water wings. When the air collapsed Burgett sank. Johnson was located hiding on the rocks. Burgett's bloated body, or what was left of it, was found some weeks later, floating near the Marin shore. Crabs had eaten away his face and limbs. Johnson later told Alvin Karpis that he watched Burgett go into the water, waiting "to see which way the current carried him before I went in myself. Then, as if a huge shark nabbed him from below, he went down like a rock in the swift undertow. I'd been crazy to follow him out there."

The next break attempt is the most serious in the history of Alcatraz. To many penologists and crime experts this break may have been successful. The fact that the three dedicated convicts who enacted the break were never seen again gave rise to the belief that the Rock was not invincible. Frank Morris and brothers Clarence and John Anglin, all robbers serving long terms, planned their break with another inmate named West, almost from the time they arrived on the Rock in 1960. Sometime in early 1962, the Anglins approached Alvin Karpis who worked in the library and asked if he could provide them with some plaster of Paris. He said he would contact a friend who worked in the hospital and he later smuggled plaster of Paris to them. The Anglins worked in the barbershop as barbers and they gathered cuttings from the same heads over the months, their own and that of Morris and West. They secreted spoons out of the mess hall and used these after lights out to patiently gouge out larger openings around the tiny ventilators in their cells, making fake walls to cover the holes when they were absent from their cells.

When these convicts went to the recreation yard they carried with them the debris from their digging from the night before, depositing small amounts on the concrete floor of the yard, walking over it until it was ground down enough for the heavy winds from the bay to blow it away. Alvin Karpis disputed the story about the stolen spoons, saying upon his release that the escapees actually worked in the utility corridors behind their cells, making repairs to the floors there, having to use jackhammers to destroy the old floor which was then being replaced and that the escapees actually knocked holes out behind their own cells and that the guards saw nothing because they refused to check the corridors because it was too dusty, all these details later covered up by the Alcatraz administrators.

The convicts also obtained art supplies and somehow obtained a woman's makeup kit. After months of careful digging, the convicts decided to escape on the night of June 11, 1962. Following lights out at 9:30 p.m., the Anglins and Morris crawled through the holes; West, however, had not scraped away enough of the wall around the ventilator and he could not squeeze through the opening. He covered it up and went back to his cot and tried to sleep. The other three convicts worked their way up a ventilator shaft to the top of the cell block. Here they managed to pry aside a bar and slip through the roof skylight. Once on the roof, Morris and the Anglins slipped across to an unguarded wall and lowered themselves. They had brought along rubber raincoats which they intended to inflate (according to West's later admissions) and use these as rafts. They intended to get to Angel Island where they planned to steal a boat and then row to Marin County. There, West later stated, they would steal a car and head north to a place where the robbers had allegedly hidden anywhere from $100,000 to $250,000 from previous robberies. This money was to be used to take the trio out of the country and into permanent hiding.

During the night of this escape, guards patrolling the cell block shined their flashlights into each cell to make sure prisoners were asleep in their bunks. Nothing seemed amiss in the cells of Morris and the Anglins. The next morning Officer Bartlett could not seem to rouse the three convicts. He shouted at them but none stirred. Bartlett reached through the bars of two of the cells and jerked the pillows (the convicts slept with their heads facing the bars of their cells). When seeing no movement, Bartlett pulled at the hair on the head of the convict in the third cell and, with a yank, the head separated from what appeared to be the body bulking beneath the blankets. The head rolled onto the floor and Bartlett gave out a scream of terror that echoed throughout the cellblock. He staggered back on the tier and almost fell over the railing, shouting to other guards who came on the run, "Someone has cut this guy's head off!"

The cells of Morris and John and Thomas Anglin were opened and the heads were examined. They were fake heads, well made with plaster of Paris, hair on the scalps taken from the barber shop and even hair on the eyebrow area. The heads were almost works of art, carefully put together and closely resembling their makers. West later explained how the convicts had labored by matchlight for minutes at a time between bunk checks during the night to construct the heads, keeping these in the holes they had dug out of the ventilator areas until the night of the escape. No trace of the three escaped convicts was ever found, although rumors persist to this day that some of Morris' effects were, indeed, found on Angel Island, confirming in the minds of some that the trio made it to that spot, their first destination that eventually took them into oblivion. It was Karpis' belief that the trio effected a permanent escape.

The next night following the escape, the news broadcast from San Francisco was suddenly cut off by the front office and when the report went dead over the intercom, the convicts throughout all the cellblocks rightly assumed that a news flash announcing the escape was being censored. The entire prison erupted in wild cheering. Officially, Morris and the Anglins were listed as missing, presumed drowned in the treacherous bay currents but privately many in the U.S. Bureau of Prisons believed that the Rock had finally been conquered. Then an even more dramatic escape occurred on Dec. 16, 1962. At that time two prisoners, John Paul Scott, a bank robber serving thirty years and Daryl Parker, a bank robber serving fifty years, slipped through the bars of the basement window in the prison kitchen where they worked. They had worked at weakening a single bar for months, employing a serrated spatula and some waxed twine coated with scouring powder as an abrasive for cutting. Once on the roof, Scott and Parker crawled over the roof of another building and let themselves down to ground level by use of stolen electric cords. They reached the shoreline just as the alarm siren sounded.

Quickly inflating surgical rubber gloves stolen from the hospital, the convicts tied these about their legs, arms and waists and then dove into the water. Parker splashed furiously after Scott who was a good swimmer but Parker could make no more distance than 100 yards. Here he clung to some rock outcroppings called Little Alcatraz and waited for the police boat to pick him up. With Scott it was a different matter. Strong and in good physical shape (he had constantly exercised for this challenge), Scott kept swimming for the main current and once it had caught him up, he floated and swam in the direction of Fort Point near the Golden Gate Bridge. His intention was originally to swim to the Aquatic Park straight across the bay in San Francisco. No one would challenge a man rising from the waters here, he correctly reasoned since he knew that cold water swimmers were always in that area. The distance to the Aquatic Park was about a mile and a half but the current swept Scott far beyond his goal, taking him three miles to Fort Point. When he reached this spot, Scott crawled onto the rocks, then fell unconscious, completely exhausted.

Police searching the shoreline spotted Scott lying at the base of a twenty-foot retaining wall and ropes were dropped and fixed around his waist. He was hauled up and put into an ambulance, half dead. Scott came to and exclaimed, "I made it, didn't I. I beat the Rock!" An officer replied, "And you're going right back there." The feat of John Paul Scott shocked and alarmed federal authorities more than all the previous escape attempts in that it proved that a prisoner could actually survive the eight to ten-knot currents of the bay and could manage to reach the mainland areas. Escape from Alcatraz was now possible in the eyes of the world and the mystery of the escape-proof island was finally shattered. Alcatraz as a prison had other problems, almost insurmountable, according to penologists and structural engineers.

The bombs that had been hurled during the wild 1946 breakout attempt had caused thousands of hairline cracks in the huge steel beams that supported D block and part of C block. The walls had been considerably weakened by the incessant mortar and grenade explosions. It was estimated that it would take more than $5 million to make incomplete repairs. It was also estimated that it would continue to cost $30,000 a year to support each prisoner on the Rock. Moreover, U.S. Attorney General Robert Kennedy seriously questioned the viability of retaining Alcatraz as America's top maximum-security federal prison. It was during the Kennedy Administration that paroles from Alcatraz increased to an all-

time high. Kennedy and his friend Byron R. "Whizzer" White had a deep interest in Alcatraz, and after Kennedy appointed White to the criminal division, White made a tour of the Rock. When visiting the laundry, he requested two pair of prison denims with the name "Alcatraz" sewn on the pockets. "When we're up in Cape Cod playing touch football, we'll wear these," White told the laundry workers.

End of the Rock, May 15, 1963; the last twenty-seven prisoners march to the dock as Alcatraz is officially closed.

Expenses in supplying food and fresh water, along with myriad other supplies for Alcatraz soared and the very image of Alcatraz as a place of total punishment was no longer in keeping with the more modern philosophy of rehabilitation. The beliefs of no-compromise law enforcement officers such as J. Edgar Hoover were considered antiquated, and it was really the confrontation between punishment and rehabilitation that brought Hoover and Kennedy into open battle. For many years it was thought in certain quarters, that Alcatraz was no more than J. Edgar Hoover's private prison preserve where those criminals caught in his FBI net were kept almost as one might keep a trophy room. It was not by accident that the most notorious criminals of the 1930s, particularly Karpis, Kelly, Harvey Bailey, and other bank robbers and kidnappers who came under the severe and abiding scrutiny of Hoover remained on the Rock long after they would have normally been rotated to other less austere federal prisons. Robert Kennedy made the decision to close Alcatraz in 1963, believing that the sprawling federal penitentiary at Marion, Ill., which had been constructed on a 1250-acre reservation, could better replace the Rock as the nation's top maximum-security prison. On May 15, 1963, Alcatraz Island Prison was officially closed.

On that day the last twenty-seven federal prisoners were removed in leg irons and chains from the Rock. Notorious inmates such as Alvin Karpis, Clarence Carnes, and James Henry Audett had been moved to other federal institutions earlier. Carnes, who died in 1987, was not one of the last prisoners off the Rock. He had been removed on Jan. 16, 1963, to undergo a gall bladder operation in the Springfield, Ill., facility. He was later transferred to Leavenworth and subsequently paroled. The highest registered number given to a convict was 1041 when the prison closed.

The once invulnerable island lay empty and decaying for some time, occupied at times by local Indian tribes and serving mostly as a tourist attraction for the boatloads of curious visitors to San Franciso. In 1964, the Rock was made into a national park, part of the 43,770-acre Golden Gate National Recreation Area. Alcatraz, of course, was more of a symbol than the vast prison it was thought to have been; no more than one percent of the entire federal prison population ever lived on the Rock. As a prison where inmates were secure, Alcatraz probably has no equal. It was a showpiece prison, however, one that served as a threat rather than a remedy to the most incorrigible American criminals, and one that now takes its place in the annals of the dreaded world prisons of the past. It still reminds visitors to the Bay Area of its awesome history, for its presence in the middle of San Francisco Bay is inescapable, its crumbling buildings, catwalks, and walls symbolizing desolation and doom. See: **Audett, James Henry; Bailey, Harvey; Banghart, Basil; Barker Brothers; Berta, Charles; Blackwell, Olin G.; Capone, Alphonse; Chase, John Paul; Cretzer, Joseph Paul; Cummings, Homer S.; Gardner, Roy; Hamilton, Floyd; Hoover, J. Edgar; Johnston, James A.; Karpis, Alvin; Kelly, George; Madigan, Paul J.; Stroud, Robert; Swope, Edwin B.; Walters, Huron Ted.**

REF.: Audett, *Rap Sheet;* Bennett, *I Chose Prison;* Bruce, *Escape from Alcatraz; CBA;* Cooper, *Ten Thousand Public Enemies;* DeNevi, *Alcatraz '46;* Dorman, *The Secret Service Story;* Ellis, *Alcatraz Number 1172;* Gaddis, *The Birdman of Alcatraz;* Gardner, *Hellcatraz, The Rock of Despair;* Godwin, *Alcatraz, 1868-1963;* Heaney, *Inside the Walls of Alcatraz;* Hoover, *Persons in Hiding;* Howard, *Six Against the Rock;* Johnston, *Alcatraz Island Prison;* Karpis, *On the Rock;* Kobler, *Capone;* Mensch, *Alcatraz;* Nash, *Bloodletters and Badmen;* Powers, *Secrecy and Power;* Schlesinger, *Robert Kennedy and His Times;* Tully, *Treasury Agent; The United States Penitentiary of Alcatraz, California;* Whitehead, *The FBI Story;* (FILM) *Alcatraz Island,* 1937; *The Last Gangster,* 1937; *King of Alcatraz,* 1938; *Federal Man-Hunt,* 1939; *The House Across the Bay,* 1940; *Seven Miles From Alcatraz,* 1942; *Train To ALcatraz,* 1948; *Al Capone,* 1959; *Birdman of Alcatraz,* 1962; *Capone,* 1975; *Escape from Alcatraz,* 1979; *Experiment Alcatraz,* 1986.

Alciati, Andrea, 1492-1550, Italy, jur. Author of legal works who was well known for his historical perspective on Roman law. REF.: *CBA.*

Alcibiades, c.450-404 B.C., Gr., (unsolv.) mur. Brilliant but arrogant, the noted Athenian general and politician had no use for democracy, terming it an "acknowledged folly." A friend of Socrates, Alcibiades was educated in the home of Pericles and from this distinguished speaker developed his near mesmerizing ability to persuade the politicians of Greece to follow his advice. He convinced Athens to break with Sparta and make alliances elsewhere. He became a general and led an expedition against Syracuse in 415 B.C. but was recalled when accused of desecrating a sacred statue of Hermes. The irreverent Alcibiades sidestepped this trumpery and switched sides, fleeing to Sparta where he encouraged the Ionians to revolt against Athens. He later decided that the Spartans were not worth his intellectual effort and he conspired against them to aid the Athenians, winning back for Athens many lost provinces and regaining the favor of Athens where he returned in 407 B.C.

When the Athenians were defeated at Notium, their general, Alcibiades, was labeled a traitor in that he had returned to his errant, disloyal ways, secretly working for the enemy. He fled to Phrygia where assassins sent by his old enemies in Sparta found him and murdered him. The colorful Alcibiades is briefly treated in William Shakespeare's *Timon of Athens,* appears in Plato's dialogs, *The Phaedo* and the *Symposium,* and is caricatured by Aristophanes in *The Clouds.*

REF.: Andrewes, *The Greek Tyrants; CBA;* Jászi and Lewis, *Against the Tyrant;* McLaren, *The Greeek Political Experience;* Robinson, *History of Greece.*

Alcott, John James, 1925-53, Brit., mur. The murder for which Alcott was executed was much contested by his defense counsel who maintained that the killer was insane or, at least, a hysteric who had no idea that he was taking a human life. Though little is known of Alcott's early life, he later admitted that as a youth he got along poorly with his father. When his father later went into the army and served overseas during WWII, Alcott would go into the British countryside and wander for days, living off vegetables filched from farms, and sitting by small fires at night, brooding about his father. During Alcott's trial for murder in 1952, his defense counsel claimed that these early-day wanderings and remorse over an absent father were that of a mentally unbalanced child. The portrait was not unlike one drawn by Viennese psychoanalyst, Dr. Wilhelm Stekel, who had years earlier typified such conduct as that of the neurotic whom he labelled "the unconscious criminal." Stekel claimed that boys resentful of harsh fathers often harbor a secret and deep death wish for such parents. In the case of Alcott, the inference was made, he substituted other victims for his father, killing without conscience, without social sense, without a concept of law and order.

Alcott's teenage years were uneventful except that he did buy a bicycle he knew was stolen and for this offense was sent to a correctional school where he became a model student. He later stole a bicycle and then decided not to keep it, selling it. The sale brought him to the attention of the police and he was returned to the school for a short period. No other illegal incidents occurred in the young man's life until he was sent to Germany after enlisting in the British Army. He later claimed he suffered a series of blackouts while in the service, one following a minor traffic accident. Following the accident, he found himself wandering about the German countryside and being joined by a nomadic Czech who was trying to reach France. The pair stopped at a small lodging house where a night watchman offered them coffee then, inexplicably, according to Alcott, whirled about and threw the scalding coffee at the uniformed Alcott, screaming, "You English bastards take a man's last drink!"

Alcott jumped at the watchman, smashing his face with his fists while, according to Alcott, his Czech friend leapt forward with an empty whiskey bottle in one hand and a fire extinguisher in the other and crashed both of these down upon the watchman's head, sending him unconscious to the floor. The Czech, Alcott stated, hated all Germans after having spent years in a concentration camp during WWII. Both men fled the lodging house, unaware that the watchman was dead. They were picked up a few days later and Alcott was tried before a court-martial, charged with murder. He was found Guilty but, strangely enough, received a pardon and was discharged from the British Army under the term "Services No Longer Required," a discharge invariably reserved for those with poor military records. The reason why Alcott was pardoned for this murder was never explained, and no amount of prodding from civil authorities could later produce information on the murder from army officials.

After resuming civilian life, Alcott became a fireman and married, living quietly at Hither Green. In early August 1952, Alcott and his wife planned to vacation in France. Alcott told his wife that he would pick up his holiday pay but he traveled to Aldershot where he took a room in a boarding house and spent several days shopping for clothes in the area and visiting the station house at Ash Vale Station. There he introduced himself to the railway clerk, Geoffrey Dean, age twenty-eight, married and with a small child, telling Dean that he was a fellow railway worker. He returned to talk to Dean several times and undoubtedly noticed the considerable sums of money from fares that Dean periodically counted and stored in the station house safe. Shortly before 8 p.m. on Aug. 22, 1952, Dean turned over tickets and a date stamp to a night porter and told him he would be staying a little later in the office to perform some cleanup work. The station door was locked and a sign on the door told customers to purchase tickets from the porter. An army sergeant went to the door and heard what he later described as scuffling noises and the voices of two men talking. He read the sign and went in search of the night porter. About an hour later another porter noticed a light on in the station office and knocked at the door. He got no response and looked into the window to see Dean sprawled on the floor, blood seeping from his body. Police were called, broke in the door, and found the murdered Dean with more than twenty stab wounds, several in the heart, the lungs, and even in his legs. Powerful blows had actually crushed some of the victim's bones. The safe was standing open and approximately £168 had been stolen.

Police began a thorough search of all the inns and boarding houses in the area, asking about strangers. One boarding house yielded an empty first-floor room where a young man had stayed. Found was a jacket with blood stains and in the pockets a wallet containing two ten-shilling notes which had blood spots and, most revealing, a passport bearing the name of John James Alcott. Police were posted at the house and some hours later they arrested Alcott as soon as he entered his room. He took little time in showing officers a chimney where he had hidden a knife in a leather sheaf. Inside his pockets were documents from the station house safe and £109. Alcott seemed blasé about being charged with Dean's murder, and all during the time he awaited trial he concerned himself with his wife's welfare and how she would manage financially without him.

At his trial, held at Surrey Assizes in Kingston on Nov. 18, 1952, Alcott showed a strange indifference to his predicament while his lawyers argued that he was certainly insane. He himself claimed that he had suffered another blackout, like those he had experienced in his military service and that the victim, as far as he could remember, was "a decent fellow." He didn't know why he was in Aldershot or why he went to the station house or why he suddenly murdered a man he had been having pleasant conversations with for several days. He explained that he must have blacked out because when he "came to" he was holding the bloody knife and the stolen money and realized that he was in trouble and that is why he hid the murder weapon. Alcott told the court that he "had gone berserk." Why then, if he had only a blind and inexplicable urge to murder had he taken the money, Alcott was asked. "Perhaps I did it because it had been there staring me in the face," he replied. "I could have taken two or three pounds at any time I had liked without his knowing it. It would have been easy, looking back at it."

The prosecution, however, presented a convincing argument that all of Alcott's blackouts, his loss of memory, and insane acts were feigned, that all of this was a back-up plan should he be caught after committing a premeditated robbery and murder. It was shown how Alcott visited the station house a day before the murder and placed a call from there to another station house to inquire about the health of a fellow railway worker who had been accidentally scalded by hot cinders Alcott himself had been shoveling weeks earlier. He told Dean at the time of this call —which was to establish himself as a fellow railway worker to be trusted—that he expected a return call at the station house which would let him know about the injured worker. This was his ruse to excuse a return to the station house the following evening. Moreover, Alcott had purchased an entire new set of clothes —from coat, pants, shirt, to shoes—and these he intended to wear when fleeing the area after the robbery-murder, dumping the "murder clothes." The bloody pants and shoes Alcott had been wearing were found in bushes near the boarding house, and it was reported that these were the very items Alcott was hiding just before he was arrested on his return to the boarding house to retrieve his bloody jacket in order to hide it elsewhere.

The murder weapon was the knife Alcott had hidden in the chimney, one which he had purchased in Aldershot for the very purpose of killing Dean. He later claimed that he had bought the knife as a gift for a young brother and just happened to have the weapon in his pocket when he suffered his impulse to kill the station clerk. The jury did not accept the posture of insanity, nor did the accused man's background conform to the McNaghten Rules on insanity. Alcott was convicted of murder and Mr. Justice Finnemore sentenced him to death. Alcott's relentless attorneys doggedly sought to appeal the case on grounds of insanity. Their request for appeal was denied and Alcott was executed on Jan. 2, 1953.

REF.: *CBA;* Neustatter, *The Mind of the Murderer;* Whitbread, *The Railway Policeman.*

Chicago police photo showing Charles Nicoletti, left, and Felix "Milwaukee Phil" Alderisio, one of the most feared syndicate killers of the 1960s.

Alderisio, Felix Anthony (Felice Antonio Alderizo, AKA: Milwaukee Phil; Phil Aldonese; Phil Alderiso; Phillip Aldi; Phil Gato; Felix Alerise; Alderist; Aldresse; Aldrise; Phil Elderise), 1912-71, U.S., org. crime. Alderisio was one of the most feared professional killers in the Chicago syndicate for more than three decades, and is credited with at least fourteen murders which he fulfilled under contract from his syndicate bosses, chiefly Sam "Momo" Giancana. Alderisio began his career in crime while in his teens, arrested for vagrancy while hanging about the Lexington Hotel in Chicago; he was waiting to see one of Al Capone's lieutenants in hopes of getting a job as a messenger. He got it and began working his way up the ladder of ill-fame, graduating to strong-arm work with Capone's goon squads and later working as a payoff man for Jake "Greasy Thumb" Guzik, delivering money to police officers and judges on Capone's payroll. He would continue in this capacity as a payoff man for the mob throughout his career.

Alderisio's chief value to the Chicago mob was that of an enforcer in the 1950s-60s. He and his working partner, Charles Nicoletti, were picked up many times by police on suspicion of murder but always managed to escape conviction. A typical arrest for Alderisio and Nicoletti occurred in 1962 when police found the pair in a black car parked on a lonely Chicago street. All dressed in black, they were crouching on the floor. Police later described the auto as a "hit" car which had been rigged with special switches that turned off the front and rear lights so as to avoid detection by trailing police cars. A secret compartment in the back seat was fixed with clamps to hold shotguns, rifles, and pistols. On this occasion, Alderisio and Nicoletti told detectives that they were "waiting for a friend" who, undoubtedly, was fortunate that the police appeared before he did.

In addition to the murder contracts Milwaukee Phil completed with unerring accuracy, usually employing a pistol or shotgun, Alderisio was permitted by Mafia-syndicate bosses to direct a team of cat burglars in Chicago's Gold Coast area. These burglars specialized in looting the homes of the super rich and high society, filching mostly rare gems and expensive jewelry which was, in turn, fenced through syndicate-owned jewelry stores and wholesalers.

Alderisio practiced every kind of felony in his lifetime, having early been arrested for burglary in 1929. Dozens of arrests followed for assault and battery, gambling, racketeering, loan-sharking, hijacking, bombing, narcotics, counterfeiting, bootlegging, extortion, bribery, and murder. Through the syndicate's solid connections with Chicago government, the killer was seldom brought to trial. Alderisio lived on Chestnut Street in the heart of the posh Gold Coast, right among the neighbors his burglars regularly victimized. He owned interests in several Rush Street nightclubs, as well as bordellos, restaurants, striptease parlors, small hotels, and meat-packing firms that catered special cuts to the best restaurants in Chicago.

Alderisio's troop was responsible from 1950 through the late 1960s for collecting kickbacks from North Side restaurants and nightclubs, as well as serving as the bagmen for all the bookmaking operations on the city's North Side, and delivering millions each week to the offices of Giancana and other mob bosses. Working directly under Giancana and, later, Gus Alex, Alderisio was named as part of the Mafia-syndicate hierarchy in the early 1960s. He appeared before the McClellan Committee where he took the Fifth Amendment twenty-three times. Collecting a fortune through his lucrative crime post as an underboss, Alderisio lived a rather strange and solitary life. He was seldom seen socializing, unlike the other mob bosses, and took long trips in the 1950s and 1960s to Turkey, Greece, and Italy. Some reports state that these jaunts to the Old World were business trips and that Alderisio was establishing new channels through which heroin could be funneled into the U.S. Midwest. But it is a certainty that part of these long vacations were motivated by Alderisio's obsession with antiquity. He would, when in Greece, spend hours wandering through ancient ruins, photographing them, sitting on the debris of centuries and contemplating a past he barely understood.

On one occasion, when returning from Greece and Italy, Alderisio met with the lunatic crime boss, Sam Giancana in a nightclub which had been bugged by police and FBI agents. As the pair sat in the bugged booth, Giancana silently listened to Alderisio ramble on for twenty minutes about the ancient ruins. Finally, Giancana, who was then nearing the end of his rope with constant police and FBI surveillance, exploded at his startled hit man, yelling, "Phil, goddamnit! Ruins? I got coppers coming out of my eyeballs and you sit there telling me about ruins! Listen to me, Phil, listen real good! Ruins ain't garbage! Forget about them goddamn ruins!" From that moment on, Alderisio's attitude toward his boss Giancana was strictly business. Milwaukee Phil continued his trips to the Old World but he kept his thoughts to himself. Alderisio was finally arrested for extortion and sent to prison where he died in 1971. See: **Alex, Gus; Capone, Alphonse; Giancana, Sam; Guzik, Jake.**

REF.: *CBA;* Demaris, *Captive City;* ____, *The Last Mafioso;* Kilian, *Who Runs Chicago?;* Nash, *Almanac of World Crime;* ____, *Bloodletters and Badmen;* ____, *People to See;* Reid, *The Grim Reapers.*

Alderman, James Horace, 1880-1929, U.S., mur. Known as the "King of the Rum Runners," Alderman, a south Florida bootlegger, was convicted of murdering two members of the U.S. Coast Guard and a U.S. Secret Service agent when a Coast Guard cutter stopped his bootlegging ship on the east coast of the Florida peninsula on Aug. 7, 1927. As the three men lunged at him to take him into custody, Alderman fired, killing all three. Alderman, forty-eight, appeared before U.S. District Court Judge Henry D. Clayton in January 1929. He was convicted and sentenced to hang. An appeal to the U.S. Supreme Court and a request for clemency from President Herbert Hoover were both denied.

Federal authorities asked Broward County officials to execute Alderman at the county jail. Although they wanted only to use the facilities of the county and not its personnel, their request was denied. It was the opinion of county officials that Alderman should be executed on federal land because he was sentenced in a federal court. A massive gallows was quickly erected in a Coast Guard hangar near Fort Lauderdale, Fla. Secrecy shrouded Alderman's execution, and reporters were banned. It was a rare event at the time for the federal government to impose the penalty of capital punishment. REF.: *CBA.*

Aldridge, Alfred Scott, prom. 1929-31, U.S., mur. As a result of the 1929 trial of Alfred Aldridge, a black man charged with the murder of a white police officer, lawyers were given the right to dismiss prospective jurors during the selection of the jury based on their racial prejudice.

Represented by court-appointed attorney James Reilly, Aldridge was charged with the murder of police officer Harry J. MacDonald. To ensure that his client received a fair trial, Reilly asked prospective jurors if they were prejudiced toward blacks. The presiding judge maintained that his questions were improper, prohibited him from continuing, and quickly began the trial. In the end, Aldridge was convicted and sentenced to death. Reilly immediately appealed to the U.S. Supreme Court.

Just one week before Aldridge was to be executed, the high court barred his execution and saved him from death. The court maintained that lawyers have the right to ask questions regarding a prospective juror's beliefs on race in order to protect their own client's inherent right to a fair trial. For the first time, lawyers won the right to reject jurors based on their racial prejudice. REF.: *CBA.*

Aleksandrov, Todor, 1881-1924, Macedonia, terr. Leader of the separatist group Internal Macedonian Revolutionary Organization from 1920-24 and head of a terrorist campaign against the Bulgarian and Yugoslavian governments. REF.: *CBA.*

Alekseyev, prom. 1970s, U.S.S.R., mur. Alekseyev is one of only a handful of Soviet murderers to be identified in the Western press. The state-run newspaper *Izvestia* reported his apprehension at a railroad depot in Sochi, where he was identified from a circular distributed throughout the country. The sergeant who arrested the killer was personally congratulated by a state minister and promoted to lieutenant.

REF.: *CBA;* Chalidze, *Criminal Russia.*

Aleman, Harry (AKA: The Hook), 1940- , U.S., rob.-org. crime-extor. During the 1970s the top enforcer and private "collection agent" for the Chicago mob and their extensive loan sharking empire, Harry Aleman, emerged in 1975 as the prime suspect in the unsolved murder of Mafia chieftain Sam (Momo) Giancana. There was not enough evidence, however, to send him to jail for this or any one of the other five gangland killings Aleman was alleged to have participated in.

Aleman's prestige and influence in mob circles followed on the heels of his marriage to the niece of top Chicago crime boss Joseph Ferriola. This clout showed itself in Aleman's 1977 acquittal for the murder of Chicago Teamster's Union steward William Logan, following rumors that top investigators, prosecutors, witnesses, and the presiding judge had received death threats from organized crime figures.

During the two-day bench trial held before Circuit Court Judge Frank J. Wilson, eyewitness testimony was given by Robert Lowe, who identified Aleman as the man who shot down Logan on Sept. 27, 1972, after the victim failed to provide shipping information to facilitate the mob's plan to hijack Teamster trucks. In return for his cooperation, Lowe was given a new identity and relocated out of Chicago under the Witness Protection Program.

Though Aleman escaped imprisonment this time, he was not so lucky a year later when a federal court convicted him of masterminding a series of home invasions. He served nearly eleven years of a thirty-year sentence at the Marion, Ill., Atlanta, Ga., Oxford, Wis., and Milan, Mich., correctional facilities before being paroled on Apr. 28, 1989. As a condition of parole, Aleman was required to begin work as an $8-an-hour laborer at a South Side warehouse. See: **Ferriola, Joseph.** REF.: *CBA.*

Aleman, Sgt. **Luis Antonio Colindres,** and **Canales,** Pvt. **Daniel,** and **Contreras,** Pvt. **Francisco Orlando,** and **Moreno,** Pvt. **Jose Roberto,** and **Palacios,** Pvt. **Carlos Joaquin Contreras,** prom.

1980s, El Sal., mur. Discovery on Dec. 4, 1980 of the bodies of three U.S. nuns and a church worker who had been raped and murdered two days earlier, not only strained relations between the U.S. and El Salvador, but also led to a possible coverup by Salvadorian military officials.

Almost two years later, Nov. 15, 1982, five men were indicted on charges of murdering New York nuns Maura Clarke, 49, and Ita Ford, 40, a 41-year-old nun Dorothy Kazel, and 27-year-old layworker Jean Donovan, both of Cleveland. A year and a half would pass before the five former guardsmen were found guilty of aggravated homicide, aggravated destruction of property, and theft by a jury of three men and two women on May 24, 1984. The five defendants were Sgt. Luis Antonio Colindres Aleman, and privates Daniel Canales, Francisco Orlando Contreras, Jose Roberto Moreno, and Carlos Joaquin Contreras Palacios. All were sentenced to thirty years in prison.

A coverup of the crime, reportedly revealed to Salvadorian officials by Aleman, may have been instigated by then national guard head Gen. Carlos Eugenio Vides Casanova, according to the U.S. government. REF.: *CBA*.

Alessandri Palma, Arturo, b.1895, Chile, lawyer. Served two terms as president of Chile from 1920-25 and 1932-38. He was forced out of office in the first term as a result of the 1924 depression and a revolt by the army. REF.: *CBA*.

Alessandri Rodriguez, Arturo, b.1895, Chile, lawyer. Legal writer and son of President Palma Alessandri. REF.: *CBA*.

Alex, Gus (AKA: **Sam Taylor; Paul Benson; Gus Johnson; John Alex; Gussie; Shotgun; Slim; The Muscle; Mr. Ryan**), 1916-   , U.S., org. crime. A protégé of Capone lieutenant Jake "Greasy Thumb" Guzik, Alex was born in Chicago on Apr. 1, 1916. His police record began in 1930, and he was named as the killer of at least five persons. Two individuals identified Alex as their assailant in deathbed statements; three others, victims of extortion, claimed that Alex had sent them death threats and all three were later murdered. Better educated than most of his gangland peers in Chicago, Alex dropped out of high school after completing tenth grade, going to work for the Capone gang, chiefly serving Guzik. He soon learned the technique of bribing government officials, which was Guzik's specialty in securing mob protection. From that point on, by the mid-1940s, Alex was the liaison man with

Suave North Side rackets boss, Gus Alex, long a member of the Chicago syndicate.

city hall. He was rewarded with the lucrative Loop rackets, including all gambling and prostitution, especially the call girl racket working out of the best downtown hotels, at one point estimated to return to syndicate coffers more than $1 million a month, some of the extraordinarily attractive call girls demanding and getting $500 to $1,000 per trick.

When appearing before the McClellan Committee, Alex took the Fifth Amendment thirty-nine times. He has been described as "one of the wiliest and slickest crooks" of the Chicago Outfit, and he has proved this repeatedly by remaining the number two or three man in the Chicago syndicate for more than three decades, surviving the reigns of Paul "The Waiter" Ricca, Anthony Accardo, Sam Giancana, and again, Accardo. For a number of years Alex made annual trips to Switzerland, ostensibly to ski the alpine slopes, but this of course was a ruse, as U.S. officials pointed out to Swiss authorities. His real purpose for visiting the country was as a bagman making enormous deposits in unnum-

bered Swiss bank accounts on behalf of the mob. Swiss authorities banned him from the country for ten years, despite pleas from such august American citizens as U.S. Senator Everett Dirksen from Illinois and Congressman William L. Dawson to allow Alex to continue his "sporting trips."

During the 1970s and 1980s, Alex consolidated his political influence in Chicago and in the state capital in Springfield so that he became an invaluable asset to the Outfit, one who would not be considered for retirement or replacement. He is, at this writing, sharing the number two spot in command of the Chicago syndicate with Joseph Aiuppa (in prison at this writing), with Sam Scarlisi in charge of day-to-day operations and Accardo supervising him from not-too-far-away Palm Springs, Calif. See: **Accardo, Anthony; Aiuppa, Joseph; Giancana, Sam; Guzik, Jake; Ricca, Paul; Scarlisi, Sam Anthony.**

REF.: *CBA*; Demaris, *Captive City;* ____, *The Last Mafioso;* Gage, *The Mafia is not an Equal Opportunity Employer;* Kilian, *Who Runs Chicago?;* Kobler, *Capone;* McClellan, *Crime without Punishment;* Nash, *Bloodletters and Badmen;* ____, *People to See;* Peterson, *The Mob;* Reid, *The Grim Reapers;* Royko, *Boss.*

Alex, Michael (AKA: **Death House Mike**), 1912-39, U.S., rob.-mur. On the night of Feb. 26, 1931, Frank E. Pendlebury, operator of a small delicatessen and grocery in Elmhurst, Long Island, N.Y., was shot and killed by four young men robbing his store. When the four youths entered the store, one of them asked for some ham sandwiches. Pendlebury began slicing the ham but was quickly interrupted when the youth pulled a gun and shouted, "Up with them, this is a stickup!" Pendlebury was a burly man, standing over six feet, and he was not used to taking orders from anyone. He threw down his kitchen knife and began struggling with the first youth. Mrs. Pendlebury rushed from the rear room and threw her arms around her husband, screaming, "What do you want with my husband? He has done nothing to you. He doesn't do nothing to anyone."

Then Mrs. Pendlebury heard one of the youths with a gun say, "Wait a minute, lady, we'll finish it." With that he fired a shot that hit Pendlebury in the neck, sending him crashing to the floor. The victim told his wife to "get the police—phone police headquarters." The youths cleaned out the till and fled. Police arrived to find Pendlebury dead and slim clues present. They found a pearl-gray fedora and no witnesses. The hat led nowhere. The only evidence obtained was the .32-caliber bullet removed from the victim, but this caliber bullet was commonly used. The case appeared to be at a standstill until Officer Theofil Galkowski, stationed at the Long Island side of the Queensboro Bridge, noticed four young men in a car who seemed to be behaving suspiciously on the night of Apr. 21, 1931. He and other officers gave chase and cornered the car in which they found two .32-caliber and one .38-caliber pistols. Three of the four men proved to be habitual criminals, according to their fingerprints, and it was quickly proved that the men had just come from robbing a delicatessen when apprehended. Arrested were Julius Siratka, alias Dominick Scifio, also called "Fat," age twenty-four, Walter Borowsky, age twenty-three, and Mike Roadick, age twenty. Another man in the car named Platinachek was released.

All three men were interrogated about the Pendlebury robbery and murder. They were taken to the Pendlebury store and the murder was reenacted while Mrs. Pendlebury remained in the back room. She came forward and pointed to Siratka and said, "Didn't you say to me, 'Wait a minute, lady, we'll finish it'?" Siratka replied, "Yes." When Siratka was returned to a precinct station, he quickly signed a confession, naming his other two friends, Borowsky and Roadick, along with Michael Alex, as his accomplices in the Pendlebury crime. He stated that it was Alex who had actually fired the shot that killed the grocer. Borowsky and Roadick also signed confessions which, for the most part, agreed with Siratka's version of the crime. Roadick added, "I am no squealer, but that is what happened as long as they (Borowsky and Siratka) have told you."

Michael Alex was not to be found, however, having left his

lodgings as soon as he heard that his friends had been arrested. He was a small man whose physical makeup resembled that of a mouse, standing no more than five feet, three inches, weighing no more than 130 pounds, and having a drawn, dark look with large bulging eyes. He was, however, not stupid, but a cunning street punk who had survived in the streets as a thief and petty racketeer since adolescence. He had seldom held a job, working periodically as a pushcart peddler or loader in a local vegetable market.

Though a grand jury indicted all four men, the district attorney, James T. Hallinan, decided to try the first three in the absence of Alex. This proved to be the first mistake in a series of blunders committed by authorities that allowed Michael Alex to escape the electric chair for more than seven years and become celebrated as a man who could not be executed for a crime everyone knew he had committed. His cohorts, at their trial, insisted that Alex was the real murderer of Pendlebury, but this did not help their own case which was heard before Judge Frank F. Adel in Long Island City. All three men were found Guilty and sentenced to be executed. A few days later, Alex was found and arrested.

He was interrogated in an all-night session and taken to the scene of the crime where Mrs. Pendlebury identified him as the killer of her husband. Alex later confessed to killing the grocer and was brought before Judge Adel the next day. Before the astonished judge, a number of newsmen, and officers, Alex suddenly tore off his coat and shirt, turning and bending his back to the judge and saying, "This is the reason I admitted I shot Pendlebury." Judge Adel and others in the court could not help but see the black-and-blue-marks criss-crossing Alex's back. He claimed that detectives Erbacher and Chenkin had beaten him mercilessly for twenty-four hours, using rubber hoses and kicking him in the stomach and legs, areas which also produced welts and abrasions. The newspapers were full of Alex's self-styled martyrdom, despite the denials from the detectives that they ever put a foot to the man's body.

By the time Alex went to trial, his fellow killers had already been sent to the electric chair on Mar. 31, 1932, despite pleas that they be kept alive until they could testify against Alex. Governor Franklin Delano Roosevelt turned down this request without comment, which further vexed the prosecution in the Alex trials to come. Joseph V. Loscalzo, appointed to prosecute Alex by the new Queens County district attorney, Charles S. Colden, employed the confessions of the executed trio in the killing, as well as Alex's own confession, in attempting to convict. The penniless Alex was defended by two able court-appointed lawyers, Richard J. Barry and David M. Wolfe. Both energetically fought for their client, and it was an obviously uphill battle against a very opinioned Judge Thomas Downs. It was Downs who would preside at five separate trials of Michael Alex, all dealing with the Pendlebury killing, and each one of them a judicial disaster, owing much to the truculence and interference of Judge Downs himself.

Downs had been a successful criminal trial lawyer who was deeply involved in Queens County politics long before he was elected a Queens County judge in 1931. When he assumed the bench in 1932, he began to display an unorthodox posture, particularly in the Alex case where, throughout all five trials, he was obviously biased on the part of the prosecution. He constantly made gratuitous remarks about the conduct of defense counsel that were quite apart from the rules of conduct. Moreover, he interposed himself, such was his ego and sense of superiority in the knowledge of criminal cases and the criminal mind, during the examination of witnesses, actually taking over the interrogation of witnesses, much to the chagrin of prosecutor and defense counsel alike. Worse for the state's case, Downs consistently refused to allow any mention of Alex's claim of being beaten up by the police which produced his alleged "forced confession." This claim had been a matter of record before the arraigning Judge Adel but Downs chose to ignore it.

Though a jury found Alex Guilty and Downs sentenced him to death, Alex's lawyers had much to present to the court of appeals while their client awaited execution in Sing Sing on Death

Row. It was here that Alex began to earn his nickname "Death House Mike," one that made him a prison legend. The court of appeals overturned Downs' decision and the conviction in the first trial and Alex was tried again, removed from Sing Sing after spending nine months on Death Row, and placed in Queens County Jail. The second trial, in February 1933, ended with a hung jury. Alex was kept in the Queens County Jail while prosecutors prepared for a third trial which took place on May 22, 1933. Again the jury could not agree and reported to Judge Downs that they stood eight to four for acquittal. Alex began to believe that he would escape the electric chair. The third trial was uneventful, a repeat of the second, except for detectives removing Alex's brother from the spectator section because he was carrying five stink bombs which he planned to explode if the jury returned a conviction against his brother.

The fourth trial began on Jan. 15, 1934, and this time the jurors did agree: Alex was Guilty. Again Judge Downs sentenced the convicted man to death, stating he would sit down in Sing Sing's electric chair on on Mar. 4, 1934. While their client gloomily returned to the Death House, Alex's lawyers, now headed by a shrewd criminal attorney, Joseph Lonardo, again returned to the court of appeals, pointing out the many irregularities practiced by Judge Downs, citing again and again how Downs took over the examination of witnesses and passed obviously biased remarks throughout the proceedings, and that his instructions to the jury were full of judicial errors.

The court of appeals overturned Downs once again and Alex, although the indictment for murder in the Pendlebury case was still active, was released on $5,000 bail, becoming the first convict ever to have been in Sing Sing's Death House and left it alive —twice. He had also earned the dubious distinction of being the first person to be released on bail while a first-degree murder indictment was still charged against him. Alex strutted triumphantly before the press. Asked if he thought authorities would continue to bring him to trial in the Pendlebury shooting, Alex smirked and snorted, "There ain't gonna be no new trial. The law's on my side and they know it." Alex went on to state that all was forgiven, however; that he held no grudges and intended to follow the straight and narrow road from now on. His 17-year-old sister Kathryn and his younger brother John stood listening to their brother mouth his meaningless promises to obey the law. John Alex, a short time later, held up a Bronx restaurant and was arrested and thrown into the Bronx Jail. Sister Kathryn visited him and smuggled a gun to John who promptly attempted to escape. In a wild shooting spree, he shot out the eye of a jailer before being subdued and charged with felonious assault, prison escape, and other offenses, added to the restaurant robbery. He was later convicted and sent to Attica Prison to serve twenty to thirty years for the robbery and ten to twenty years for assault. Kathryn Alex received an indeterminate sentence at Westfield Farms Prison. She was later paroled.

Obtaining an honest job was, of course, out of the question for Michael Alex. He immediately gathered a gang of thugs and began extorting money from shops in his neighborhood. He was arrested in early 1937 for brawling and being drunk and disorderly, but he was released. A short time later he was caught red-handed with others as they were beating a garage owner who had refused to pay protection money to them. He was again released but in early 1938 detectives discovered that Alex had left his home and jumped bail. Judge Downs signed a warrant for his arrest. Before Alex could be picked up, he and two others attacked and held up salesman Jack Ehrlich on the evening of Dec. 18, 1937. When the victim resisted having his watch stolen by Alex, the killer shouted, as he had with Pendlebury, "Let's finish it!" With that Alex fired a bullet into Ehrlich, killing him. Unlike the Pendlebury killing, there were many witnesses to the crime and these came forward after Alex was arrested to testify that he was one of the men hiding in a hallway where Ehrlich had been killed. But before Alex could be brought to trial for the Bronx killing of Ehrlich, he was turned over to Queens to be tried a fifth time for the Pendlebury slaying.

The fifth trial was as disastrous for the state as the previous four. Early on, Detective Erbacher was relating Alex's original confession, repeating hearsay statements on the part of the defendant. Alex's lawyers immediately objected on the grounds that this testimony was extremely prejudicial, insisting that Judge Downs declare a mistrial. The demand caught Downs unawares. He appeared so startled and most likely extremely apprehensive that he would once again be reversed by the upper court that he surprisingly agreed with the defense attorneys, stating, "I deem it such prejudicial error that the motion for a mistrial is granted."

Smiling, Alex left the courtroom believing he could not be touched by the law for whatever offense he committed. He was quickly indicted, however, for the murder of the salesman Ehrlich. The witnesses intrepidly came forward and pointed Alex out in court. Although family members testified that Alex was at home at the time of the Ehrlich murder, the jury convicted the killer and he was once again sentenced to death. Alex's date with the electric chair was on Feb. 23, 1939. This appointment he would keep. While awaiting execution in Sing Sing's Death House, the diminutive killer wasted away with worry after he came to believe that he actually would die in the electric chair. His weight dropped to about 100 pounds and he chain-smoked from morning to night.

"Do something, do something," is all Alex could nervously repeat to the family members who visited him. They were powerless, of course. To his lawyer, Joseph Lonardo, Alex imploringly wrote, "You did it before. Can you do it again?" The attorney had saved Alex twice from the electric chair, but he realized that there were no grounds for a real appeal as the Ehrlich trial had been impeccable. Lonardo did plead with the then-Governor Lehmkan but no commutation was forthcoming.

On the night of Feb. 23, 1939, Alex entered Sing Sing's death chamber, sagging weakly as he clung to the arm of the Catholic prison chaplain, Reverend John P. McCaffrey. The visitor section was jam-packed with forty-one witnesses (usually only a dozen or so were permitted). Reporters who had built up Death House Mike's reputation as "tough" and that "he could take it," were shocked to see the quivering little gangster sob and cry. As he reached the chair he screamed like a baby, "God Almighty, prove to them that I didn't do it. Why do they accuse me. Why, oh why, do they blame me?" He was gasping, tears running down his cheeks. "Oh, please, God above in the heavens, I'm innocent! They've accused me of something I never did. I never even saw Ehrlich killed. Please give me a chance and I know they'll find the guilty party." Guards held him and tried to sit him down in the chair, but he broke free and leapt forward toward the startled visitors, pointing at them and shouting, "Look at those people watching me! They know I'm innocent!"

Sing Sing's executioner, Robert G. Elliott, directed the guards to place Alex into the chair and ordered them to place the electrodes and straps around his arms, legs, chest, and stomach. Alex was still screaming for God to help him when Elliott threw the switch and electricity coursed through the gunman's body, cutting off his hysterical screaming from beneath the black cap that had been placed over his head. He was dead within seconds and the saga of Death House Mike was over. Grim debris floated in his wake. Alex had set many a record with his seemingly endless trials which had cost the state more than $100,000. His own robbery murders had netted him less than $30. The exchange was inequitable. Alex had spent twenty-two months on Death Row during his three stays while awaiting execution, an all-time record. He had seen thirty-five men go to the electric chair during that time. Only one man watched Alex go to his death, a black murderer who became so terrified that he would be left alone on Death Row after Alex's execution that he had to be sedated.

The worst part of the entire Alex episode was the fact that he was a blatant murderer that the state could not convict because of its own blunderings and miscalculations, allowing him to be released to kill again. Here legal technicalities, an egocentric judge, and a bungling system conspired unwittingly to allow a vicious killer to walk the streets in search of additional victims, not unlike the careers of British killers John Alcott and John Merrett. See: **Alcott, John James; Merrett, John Donald.**

REF.: *CBA*; Elliott, *Agent of Death*; Seagle, *Acquitted of Murder*.

Alexander, prom. 1782, Rus., prince, assass. It is believed that Prince Alexander, son of Peter the Great, Czar of Russia, was poisoned while in prison on a charge of *lèse-majesté* at the citadel of St. Paul and St. Peter. During his incarceration, Alexander allegedly became ill, and a soldier in his father's army, Marshal Viede, ordered Henry Bruce—one of Alexander's attendants—to explain to a local pharmacist the severity of Alexander's condition. To establish a sense of urgency, Viede followed Bruce to the pharmacy and told the pharmicist, known as Beer, that the medication must be prepared quickly as Alexander was suffering from a stroke.

The Prince died at 5 p.m., several hours after the medicine was administered. Before his death, he suffered massive convulsions and other symptoms that resembled stomach poisoning, but before his funeral his father, Czar Peter, ordered his son's internal organs destroyed before the body was placed in its coffin.

The question of Peter's guilt in the death of his son has long been in debate by historians. That he felt Alexander was plotting either his overthrow or abdication, is fairly certain. Peter had a deep-rooted distrust of all his advisors, as well as family members. He had been deceived, when assuming the throne of Russia, by his early-day counselors into believing that his country was a thriving, happy country and not until he personally investigated the poverty and near-starvation existence of his people did Peter learn the true state of affairs. From that point, Peter the Great was a man who suspected plots, lies, and conspiracies at every turn, especially in his own household which had fostered an overly ambitious son, Alexander.

REF.: *CBA*; Thompson, *Poison and Poisoners*.

Alexander I (Karageorgevic), 1888-1934, Yug., king, assass. The 1934 murder of Alexander, King of Yugoslavia (1921-34), as he landed at Marseilles on a state visit to France, has been popularly thought to have been an assassination engineered by Croatian fanatics. The killing of French foreign minister Jean Louis Barthou, who was riding in the same car with King Alexander, was thought to have been accidental; he was merely in the way of the assassin's bullets and perished alongside the intended victim. Yet a careful examination of the involved plot to murder the Yugoslavian ruler reveals that those behind it comprised more than a group of Croatian terrorists; the real financiers and strategists of this double assassination, aimed equally at Foreign Minister Barthou, could be found in Berlin and in Rome.

In 1921, Alexander became king of a polyglot nation after the death of his father, Peter Karageorgevic. His father had assumed the throne of Serbia following the assassination of King Alexander Obrenovic and Queen Draga in 1903, a slaughterhouse murder brought about by Dragutin Dimitrijevic, who led his fellow officers of the secret Black Hand Society into the Belgrade palace to boldly murder the Obrenovics. The aim of the fanatics in the Serbian army corps was to place upon the throne a strong pro-Serbian monarch which had been found in Peter Karageorgevic. His son, Alexander Karageorgevic, was equally pro-Serbian, but just as Alexander Obrenovic's undoing had been brought about because of his anti-Serbian attitudes, Alexander Karageorgevic would be marked for death because he promoted Serbian nationalism. Croatian zealots would see to that.

When Alexander inherited the Karageorgevic throne he was no longer merely the king of the Serbs; that country had gone out of existence in 1918 following WWI, having been amalgamated into a sprawling new country called Yugoslavia, which included the old kingdoms of Serbia, Croatia-Slavonia, Montenegro, Bosnia, and Herzegovina. These old countries were now welded into one nation, though its people were culturally and religiously divergent, and radically so. Serbia had been an independent nation for almost a century and had for decades resisted being absorbed into the lethargic Austro-Hungarian Empire that dissolved when the Central Powers collapsed in 1918. It fiercely protected its nationalism and only accepted incorporation into Yugoslavia because King Alexander remained staunchly Serbian in outlook and policy. The Croats, however, had lived long under the governorship of Austria and had enjoyed economic luxury compared to their other Slavic neighbors. Customs and traditions sharply varied between the Serbs and Croats. Serbia was largely Greek Orthodox while Croatia followed the Roman Catholic Church. These two countries shared the same language but their alphabets differed drastically, Serbia employing the Cyrillic alphabet, Croatia that of the Latin.

At all levels of leadership —political, educational, business—the Croats and Serbs were dedicated to each other's subjugation, insisting that their cultures and traditions dominate the new Yugoslavia. Alexander consistently sided with Serbian aims and he was despised by many right-wing Croatians who formed a secret terrorist society of a paramilitary nature which was called Ustacha, a latter-day counterpoint organization to Serbia's now defunct Black Hand Society. Its leader, called "Poglavnik" (a synonym for

King Alexander of Yugoslavia, with French Foreign Minister Louis Barthou, moments before both were assassinated in Marseilles, 1934.

Duce or Fuehrer) was a squinty-eyed nationalist fanatic named Dr. Ante Pavelic who had dedicated himself for years to the destruction of the Karageorgevic dynasty. In the mid-1920s, Croats and Serbs clashed violently, even in the Yugoslavian Parliament. In 1928, several Croat leaders were shot to death by invading Serbian terrorists as they sat in their parliament seats. This bloody outburst caused Alexander to dissolve that political body and assume dictatorial powers. From that moment on Ante Pavelic and his Ustacha followers planned to murder the monarch at the first opportunity.

The Nazi hierarchy in Germany and Mussolini in Rome also had no love for the Yugoslavian ruler and particularly hated the 72-year-old Barthou, who was part of France's old guard which included such foes of facism as Cleenceau and Poincaré. For a decade Barthou had sought to strengthen France's position against the Axis powers of Germany, Italy, Hungary, establishing pacts and agreements with Czechoslovakia, Rumania, and the upstart Yugoslavia, all of these Eastern European countries forming a sort of geographical buffer against the aims of Hitler and Mussolini. Where Alexander was an avowed foe of Nazi Germany—although he paid lip service to Hitler—Barthou actively sought to isolate Germany, as had his political predecessors. For this reason *both* men were marked for murder when it was announced that Alexander would make a state visit to France, to be greeted personally by Barthou, in October 1934.

The moment Dr. Pavelic learned of this visit, intended to cement even further Yugoslavian-French relations, he called several top assassins of his Ustacha to Yanka Puszta, a small Hungarian village on the Yugoslavian border. Hungary and Italy, supporting the pro-fascist Ustacha movement, allowed this terrorist group to establish several paramilitary sites in their border territory and even funded their operations. In Berlin, Ustacha agents were welcomed and received the specific financial support of Heinrich Himmler, head of the dreaded SS. The Berlin-based Croatian newspaper, *Independent Croatian State*, regularly published its fascist propaganda and on Aug. 16, 1934, even called for the murder of King Alexander.

Some time in September 1934, several dedicated Ustacha members arrived in Yanka Puszta. These included Mio Krajl, Yvan Raitch, and Zvonimir Pospechil who drew the winning black

cubes from a bag offered to more than forty partisans. The others, receiving the white cubes, were dismissed and this strange death lottery was over. The three winners later admitted at their trials that they knew they were to be sent on a mission to kill an enemy of the Ustacha but had no idea who that person or persons might be. They asked no questions, such was their fanatic dedication to their cause. The three men were sent to Budapest where they were issued false Hungarian passports. They were joined by Eugen Kvaternik, the Ustacha leader in Berlin and a personal friend of Himmler's. Kvaternik introduced the three assassins to a strange, dark-complexioned man he called Velitchko, a Bulgarian known to be an intimate of Dr. Pavelic and a member of a long-established terrorist group known as the BMPO, a revolutionary Macedonian organization.

Kvaternik assembled these men in a small hotel room and produced a single-paged document, passing this around. It read, "Execute without discussion whatever will be ordered by the bearer." It was signed "The Poglavnik," which was the code name for Ustacha's leader, Dr. Pavelic. The group obediently crossed the Swiss border with Kvaternik, going to Lausanne. Here the assassins discarded their Hungarian passports and were given Czech passports by Kvaternik, who was by then using the alias of Eugen Kramer; the others were also employing aliases. Arriving at the Hôtel des Palmiers, they introduced themselves as Czech businessmen. Here Kvaternik explained their mission. They were to go to Paris where they would meet Ustacha members whose job it was to smuggle into France the necessary weapons and bombs to accomplish their task.

The five men filtered across the border and took up residences in small Paris hotels. Kvaternik studied the local papers and marked editions that described the forthcoming state visit of King Alexander, noting that the monarch would arrive aboard the Yugoslavian cruiser, *Dubrovnik*, which was scheduled to reach Marseilles on Oct. 9, 1934. Alexander would be met by Foreign Minister Barthou, and, following a parade, board a special train to travel to Paris where he would meet with the president of the French Republic. Alexander, accompanied by Barthou, would attend a grand fete at the historic Versailles palace. By then the conspirators were told the identities of their victims: King Alexander and Louis Barthou. Since the known schedule for both men put them first in Marseilles, then in Versailles, Raitch and Pospechil were sent to Versailles, in case the first group missed the targets in Marseilles.

King Alexander and Barthou were shot only seconds before this photo was taken; the officer on horseback is shown bringing his sword down upon the assassin's head.

Kvaternik, Krajl, and Velitchko then took the train to Marseilles but got off at Avignon, going to a small hotel where the threesome met two people, a man who called himself simply Petar and a "beautiful blonde woman" who never gave her name. These two carried suitcases filled with weapons and bombs, and these items were handed out to Kvaternik, Krajl, and Velitchko. From Avignon, Petar, accompanied by Krajl, Velitchko, and the mysterious blonde woman, took the train to Marseilles. Kvaternik crossed back into Switzerland. Before departing Avignon, Kvaternik made a point of telling everyone, "Petar is the boss, the man we all have to obey." Once in Marseilles, Petar checked Alexander's schedule again in the newspapers and bought a map of the city, outlining in it the exact parade route Alexander would take when arriving in Marseilles. Petar led the conspirators along the sweeping La Cannebière, which was the city's equivalent of New York's Fifth Avenue, careful to point out certain areas of this street to Krajl and Velitchko. It would be here that these men would stand in the crowds greeting Alexander and hurl their bombs and fire their pistols.

Police routinely began to investigate "suspicious characters" in the port city as a matter of policy in preparation for the state visit. They concentrated on the small hotels which catered to foreigners, and as soon as Petar was aware of detectives inspecting hotel registers, he ordered his group out of the city. All of them took a train to Aix-en-Provence, which was only an hour's distance from Marseilles, and here they waited out the police search. (It was later suggested that Petar had received a warning of the police sweep from someone in French security. Given the criticism later heaped upon the Sûreté Nationale, the French State Police, for the lack of protection afforded Alexander and Barthou, the possibility of a police collaborator working with the assassins certainly existed.) Petar and his people stayed out of Marseilles until the morning of Oct. 9, 1934. At dawn Petar held a last-minute conference with Krajl and Velitchko and then he and the blonde woman vanished. Krajl and Velitchko, each heavily armed with pistols and bombs, took a bus to Marseilles which arrived just as the Yugoslavian cruiser, *Dubrovnik*, steamed into the harbor.

A vedette boat took Alexander from the cruiser to the Quai des Belges, where Barthou warmly greeted the Yugoslavian sovereign, escorting him to a waiting open-air touring car which would take Alexander to the prefecture for an official city welcome. It was a little after 4 p.m. when the small entourage climbed into the lone touring car, Alexander sitting in the back seat, Barthou at his side. Sitting just in front of Alexander was French general Alfonse Georges. Accompanying the touring car was a platoon of French cavalrymen; a French officer on horseback with saber drawn rode on each side of the touring car, mounted officers in front and behind the slowly moving auto. The crowds along the parade route were thick and a police line held them back as they enthusiastically greeted the king and Barthou.

As the touring car turned onto La Cannebière with its posh shops and affluent citizens, the ovation for the cortege increased in tempo, friendly cheers that caused Alexander to smile at the warm greeting. He waved at the thousands pressing against the sagging police cordon, then turned to Barthou and Georges and said, "It is a great pleasure to be once more in France." These were the last words he would ever speak. At that moment, Colonel Poillet, who was riding alongside the car, saw a man break through the police line, holding something in his hand. Poillet mistook the object in the man's hands for a camera and shook his head, saying, almost offhandedly to the driver of the touring car, "Another of those damned photographers..."

But Poillet was tragically mistaken. The running man was Velitchko and he held a gun in his hands. In a matter of seconds he had leaped upon the running board of the slow-moving touring car, aimed the weapon at Alexander, and began firing. Two bullets entered the king's chest and he slid downward in the car seat, dying. Another bullet struck Barthou and severed an artery. He would bleed to death before proper medical attention was given to him. General Georges, who had been looking the other way when the assassin leaped upon the running board, turned and tried to grapple with the gunman who was leaning into the car and shouting incoherently. In the struggle, Georges was hit by no less than four bullets. He would take six months to recover from his wounds.

The killer, Velitchko, seemed to be intent on killing everyone in the car and took no pains to flee the scene, hanging onto the car and systematically firing every round in his eight-shot weapon. He was struggling to free another gun inside a coat pocket when Colonel Poillet wheeled his horse about and began hacking away at the killer with his sabre. Poillet struck Velitchko several times on the back and head, finally driving him off the running board of the car, which had come to a halt. The crowds broke through the police line and began attacking the assassin, as well as several others whom spectators suspected of being part of the plot. Velitchko finally fell unconscious to the pavement, bleeding from several sabre cuts received at the hand of Colonel Poillet. Police grabbed him and hurried him off to a hospital where he remained in a coma for several hours. There Velitchko died without ever regaining consciousness.

Alexander I of Yugoslavia was by then dead; he had died within minutes after being mortally wounded in the car. Barthou was dead an hour later. The assassins had accomplished their task with amazing ease and two of fascism's most ardent foes had been eliminated in a matter of minutes. Inside the coat pockets of the

King Alexander dying in the back of his touring car on a Marseilles street.

assassin, police found the second unused gun and two bombs, along with a fake Czech passport that identified him as Peter Kaleman, a businessman from Agram. The body was carefully inspected and on the dead man's arm was found a fearsome tattoo showing a skull and crossbones and Bulgarian words that meant "liberty or death." Beneath this were the initials BMPO, which stood for the Bulgarian terrorist group to which the dead man belonged. The name of Vlada Chernozamsky was later attributed to the assassin, and it was claimed that Chernozamsky had been the personal bodyguard of Ante Pavelic, a fanatical follower who knew that he stood no chance of surviving the attempt on Alexander's life and was willing to lay down his own life to achieve the goals of the Ustacha, which is exactly what he did. Exactly who the assassin was has never been fully determined.

The other conspirators were quickly rounded up. Krajl, who had been in the crowd and watched as Velitchko ran to the touring car and killed Alexander and Barthou, had fled the city, returning to Avignon and rejoining Pospechil and Raitch. The three then attempted to cross the Swiss-French border but were identified as having been with the assassin and were arrested and returned to Paris for trial. Each received life sentences and Dr. Pavelic, Kvaternik, and a Croatian terrorist named Bersevic, who commanded the Hungarian-based Ustacha camp at Yank Puszta, were tried in absentia and condemned to death, although none were ever brought to justice. As he was taken from the courtroom, Pospechil struggled with his guards and shouted to the spectators, "Hail Ante Pavelic, our leader! Hail the Free Croatia!

Down with the hangman!" Krajl and Prospechil died in prison before Hitler's armies occupied France in 1940, but Raitch was paroled in 1941 and returned to his native Croatia. Two years later he was murdered, reportedly by Gestapo agents.

This murder in 1943 was paradoxical in that Raitch and his group had done a great service to the Nazis when killing not only Alexander but the arch foe of Germany, Louis Barthou. Yet, the murder made sense in one regard; had the group acted on behalf of Himmler's SS, it was to Himmler's best interests to have anyone connected with this subversive act disappear, especially when it was later learned that Raitch intended to tell certain confidantes the real purpose for the assassination, that the conspirators meant to kill Barthou as much as Alexander. It should be remembered that when Velitchko fired his first two shots which killed Alexander, he had the opportunity to flee and save his own life. Yet he determinedly lingered long enough to fire one or more bullets into Barthou. The foreign minister had certainly been designated for death, not by the Croatian group but by Petar who disappeared with the mysterious blonde. Petar's identity and nationality were never determined, but one could easily surmise that he was not Slavic at all, but German, and that he had arrived from Germany, his *native* country, to which he returned after sending Krajl and Velitchko to perform the assassination.

Vlada Chernozamsky, alias Velitchko, left, killer of King Alexander and Louis Barthou, and, right, his mentor, terrorist leader Ante Pavelic.

The position which Barthou occupied was crucial to Hitler's aims and his replacement was none other than Pierre Laval whose foreign policies were decidedly pro-German, although this was not revealed until after 1940 when Laval came out into the open as a Berlin stooge. (He would later be executed as a collaborator and turncoat, one of the key French officials who made it possible for Hitler to take over France.) At the time, little was said about the poor, almost nonexistent protection given Alexander and Barthou, an old-fashioned honor guard of mounted troops instead of motorcycle guards and armed guards inside cars in front and back of the touring car carrying the dignitaries as was then the custom. The Sûreté Nationale came under heavy scrutiny later, particularly its Marseilles chief, Superintendent Cal, who was later called to testify but begged off on grounds of illness.

Following the conviction of the main conspirators who had revealed the existence of the Ustacha in Hungary and Italy, both of those countries were officially rebuked for harboring terrorists groups but nothing more came of the obvious participation in the plot by Admiral Miklos Horthy of Hungary and Benito Mussolini of Italy. Adolf Hitler, of course, was delighted when hearing that Alexander and Barthou had been killed. He reveled in the slaying of Louis Barthou. Another bitter enemy of Nazi Germany had been eliminated, paving the way for the French traitor Laval to assume the role of foreign minister and secretly further Nazi goals. The pistol shots fired in Marseilles in 1934 did not simply con-

stitute the mad wrath of a fanatical minority, as investigators of that day suggested. These gun blasts were dictated in Berlin as part of Hitler's insidious, overall step-by-step plan to conquer Europe. Ironically, Himmler directly benefitted from the dual assassination. When he learned that a newsreel photographer had filmed the entire killing episode on the Marseilles street, he obtained this footage and studied it for hours so that he could best learn how to provide complete protection for Hitler at his public appearances.

The Croatian catalyst of these events, Dr. Ante Pavelic, employed the Ustacha as a potent fifth column in aiding the Germans to overrun Yugoslavia in 1941 and, as a reward from his Nazi masters, he was made dictator of Croatia with Kvaternik as his second-in-command. These two were responsible for wholesale massacres and genocide for more than four years, under the titular leadership of Prince Paul, who acted as regent of Yugoslavia for young King Peter. Paul was decidedly pro-Nazi and brought his country into the Axis alliance as soon as he assumed the throne. See: **Alexander I (Obrenovic); Pavelic, Dr. Ante; Ustacha, The.**

REF.: Black, *The Establishment of Constitutional Government in Bulgaria;* Bornstein, *The Politics of Murder;* Byrnes, *Yugoslavia; CBA;* Dellin, *Bulgaria;* Dragnich, *Tito's Promised Land: Yugoslavia;* Hoffman, *The Balkans in Transition;* Hoptner, *Yugoslavia in Crisis, 1934-1941;* Hurwood, *Society and the Assassin;* Jelavich, *The Balkans;* Lederer, *Yugoslavia at the Paris Peace Conference;* Lesberg, *Assassination in Our Time;* Logio, *Bulgaria Past and Present;* Macartney and Palmer, *Independent Eastern Europe;* Paine, *The Assassin's World;* Riess, *Total Espionage;* Seton-Watson, *Eastern Europe Between the Wars, 1918-1941;* ____, *The Southern Slav Question and the Hapsburg Monarchy;* Skendi, *Albania;* Stavrianos, *The Balkans Since 1453;* Tomasevich, *Peasants, Politics and Economic Change in Yugoslavia;* Williams, *Heyday for Assassins;* Wolff, *The Balkans in Our Times.*

Alexander I (Obrenovic), 1876-1903, Serb., king, assass. The murder of the last Obrenovic ruler of Serbia by officers of his own army in the infant years of the century was marked by merciless barbarity and heralded a series of European regicides that ultimately led to WWI. When King Alexander (1889-1903) and his morganatic wife Queen Draga were hunted down like wild animals in their own Belgrade palace and slaughtered, the assassinations sent shock waves through every throne room on the continent. The killings were fat with Balkan intrigue, bizarre characters, and the kind of swashbuckling adventures that were usually found in the novels of Anthony Hope and P.C. Wren. Hot political passion, mixed with no little alcohol, flowed in the veins of the assassins on the night of June 10-11, 1903, but even though their bloody act appeared to be wildly impetuous, the seeds of these murders had been planted decades earlier.

The Obrenovic dynasty had never taken deep roots in Serbia. Founded in 1815 by Prince Milos and having a succession of dissolute rulers whose reigns were interrupted by usurping kings from the rival Karageorgevic dynasty, the Obrenovic monarchs were typified by King Milan (1882-1889). Milan lived an extravagant lifestyle, all but bankrupting the government coffers in search of royal pleasures. He had been pampered and spoiled as a child, his parents rearing him in the swank hotels of Paris and Vienna. His education was neglected and he knew little about Serbian customs and history and cared less. At nineteen, Milan fell in love with a ravishing odalisque Russian, Nathalie Keshko, the daughter of a lowly ranked officer. Ignoring his own Serbian parliament and public, he married her. Nathalie loathed him, going to the alter only because her father ordered her to do so.

The contempt Queen Nathalie felt for Milan was evident in their everyday life; she presented him with sneers and insults at every opportunity, even when he sought desperately to please her.

Learning that lilies of the valley were the queen's favorite flower, Milan ordered an entire valley planted with the lilies, bringing his voluptuous bride to the spot when the valley was in full bloom. Queen Nathalie flew into a rage at the sight of the lilies, screaming that her husband was flagrantly extravagant. The couple battled incessantly, and in public, so that Serbians everywhere were genuinely shocked to learn that their seething sovereigns had actually managed to produce a child, Alexander, born on Aug. 14, 1876. Almost from that moment on, Queen Nathalie began traveling with her son, visiting the capitals of Europe on supposed state visits, but her real motive for leaving Serbia was to escape a husband she detested. Milan, for his part, reacted by taking as a mistress a Greek woman of the court who was later described by one historian as "ugly but intelligent."

Milan's disastrous marriage was equalled by his miserable leadership of Serbia. At the age of twenty-one, he led his armies against the Turks and was so soundly defeated that it took Queen Nathalie's plea to the Russian czar to intervene before Milan and his battered legions could be extricated from Macedonia. Though Russian, Nathalie was held in high esteem by her Serbian subjects; she had personally nursed the wounded during the Turkish wars, and regularly visited orphanages and poorhouses to relieve the suffering with gifts of food and money. Her husband, on the other hand, ignored his country's economic plight and indulged in one affair after another, turning the white Belgrade Palace into a house of assignation. Worse, he intrigued with the Austrians with whom most Serbians shared no love.

When his son was about to begin his education, Milan insisted that the boy have Austrian tutors, but Queen Nathalie rejected this notion, demanding and getting Russian tutors for her son.

Milan later accused his wife of turning his son's affections from him and began to devise ways of divorcing his queen. Nathalie then resumed her travels with her son, and Milan, pressured with threats of invasion from powerful Austro-Hungary, became preoccupied with the political menace of the dual monarchy. He signed one treaty after another that either gave away pieces of Serbia to neighboring powers or allowed more powerful nations to dictate the Serbian economy. In 1881, Milan made a secret treaty with Austria which more or less allowed that country to run the affairs of Serbia in exchange for a promise of military assistance in the event of another war with Turkey or even Bulgaria, then Russia's most militant vassal in the

King Alexander I of Serbia, a doomed monarch.

Balkans. For years thereafter, the Austrian military attaché in Belgrade could be seen entering the royal palace to give Milan his orders for the day.

Frustrated at the political trap he had built for himself and angered over his estrangement from Queen Nathalie, Milan intensified his verbal assaults upon his wife. On one occasion, after the couple had screamed vile insults at each other, Nathalie swept up little Alexander and fled to Wiesbaden. Milan accused her of kidnapping his heir and had the German police arrest her and return mother and son to Belgrade. The king decided to rid himself of Nathalie once and for all by entrapping her in what would appear to be an adulterous relationship with none other than the bishop of Belgrade, a devoted friend of the queen's. He summoned the prelate to the palace in the name of his queen and then barged into a room where Nathalie and the bishop were holding an innocent conversation. Milan, who had brought intimates with him as witnesses to "this shameless scene," accused the queen and the prelate of having sexual relations. Queen Nathalie, enraged, announced that from that day forth she would have nothing more to do with Milan and left the country with 12-

year-old Alexander to live in exile.

The reaction of the Serbian people was to demand Milan's abdication, and some extremists talked of "dethronement" which meant the enactment of a coup that would place Peter Karageorgevic upon the throne. Yet, in this day of whispering treason and naive political groups that met in secret without organized plans and leaders, such talk was considered harmless. Milan, however, galvanized public hatred for him by talking once more of a war with Bulgaria. He had, in 1886, taken his militaristic fling in that direction, leading Serbian armies into Bulgaria only to be utterly defeated and return home in complete disgrace.

Money lenders from all points of Europe where Milan had left his useless checks began to demand payments for the king's excesses. The treasury was almost empty, the king was talking of another war sure to end in failure, and he lived the life of a degenerate, having exiled his wife and little heir. Serbians took to the streets to demand reform and Milan, now fearing for his crown, gushed promises of establishing a liberal Parliament where the voice of his subjects would be heard, and of lavishing freedoms and wealth upon a people who had known only oppression and privation. Students ran through the streets of Belgrade, demanding either Queen Nathalie return to rule Serbia or Peter Karageorgevic take the throne. Police arrived and bloody riots ensued. Milan, pressured by the liberal government he had installed, abdicated in favor of his son Alexander in 1889, the boy ruling through three regents.

These regents were all Milan henchmen, two inept generals and a political boss, whose responsibility it was to rear 12-year-old Alexander to virtuous manhood and kingship. Milan had also left strict orders that Queen Nathalie was never to be permitted into the Belgrade palace to see her son. The boy, of course, was ignored by his protectors and grew up lonely and friendless in a sprawling palace without parents; only a few elderly servants guided him through adolescence. Queen Nathalie played the part of the victimized mother. She returned to Belgrade and took an apartment near the palace. It was reported that she would regularly go to the palace gates and longingly look up to the windows to catch a glimpse of her son and would later lean from the balcony of her rooms to watch King Alexander go down the street in his carriage when on his daily outing.

Nathalie's blatant display of the wronged woman image merely evoked contempt from the sophisticated political leaders, but her interference with national affairs caused swift action. The deposed queen began spreading secret information about Milan's clandestine treaties to members of the foreign press which embarrassed Serbian leaders. The regents ordered her to leave the country. Police officials escorted Nathalie to the train station where she was carried on the night express to exile in Hungary. She later petitioned the government for funds and these were supplied so that she could live in luxury at an estate in Biarritz. Milan was living in luxury outside the country, and these two ex-sovereigns were costing the country millions each year, but the attitude was that it was better to pay these volatile people to stay out of Serbia than to let them be close enough to the throne to influence the young King Alexander.

Exactly who was influencing Alexander during his teens is uncertain but young officers in the palace guard, who harbored radical ideas about Serbian nationalism and the recoupment of the country's pride and status, had the young monarch's ear, no doubt. Alexander admired his soldier bodyguards and delighted in wearing the ornate uniform of the palace guard. He was not an impressive youth, short, thick-torsoed, with long arms and spindly legs. His eyesight was poor and he lacked physical endurance, even though, as a child, his occasional British tutor, Stephen Bonsal, had taught him how to swim in a small lake outside Belgrade. (The boy was so proud of this achievement that he informed his servants that the regents need not worry about his physical education, that "you can tell them that the King can swim!")

Just after his seventeenth birthday, Alexander felt he had no further need to tell the regents anything. He called the three regents and the members of his cabinet to the palace, and, while the third course of a sumptuous dinner was being served, Alexander stood up and stated with surprisingly great authority, "Gentlemen, it is announced to all the garrisons in Serbia, to all the authorities, and to all the people, and I announce it here to you, that I declare myself of full age, and I now take the government of the country into my own hands. I thank you, my regents, for your services, of which I now relieve you. I thank you also, gentlemen of the Cabinet, for your services, of which you are relieved also. You will not be allowed to leave this palace tonight. You can remain here as my guests but, if not, then as my prisoners."

For a moment the regents and cabinet members were stunned into silence. Then they rose up full of threats and protests, moving toward Alexander. A military aide stepped forward and drew his sword, holding it outward. The regents and cabinet members froze. A door to the dining hall opened and a full company of palace guards stood at the ready, guns with bayonets fixed to them held high. Alexander showed no emotion as he moved to a doorway, then he turned and said calmly, "I leave you in charge of Lieutenant Colonel Tyirich, whose orders you will obey while I go to the army to administer the oath of fidelity." With that, the boy king was gone, hurrying on horseback to the barracks of the regiments quartered around Belgrade and proclaiming his accession to the Serbian throne. The troops, thinking this would mean reform and a stronger Serbia, endorsed Alexander to a man, vowing allegiance to the monarch. The next morning the fired Regents and Cabinet members were driven through the streets of Belgrade to view hundreds of placards and banners proclaiming Alexander I the ruler of the land. The teenage king then paraded through the streets to accept the adoring cheers of his subjects who looked upon him as a leader with the strength of a Richard the Lion-Hearted.

Alexander appointed a new cabinet the next day and reconstructed the Parliament so that all members were radical nationalists dedicated to reestablishing Serbia as a strong and independent nation. Oddly, the boy king would never again act with such decisive authority, except when dissolving a progressive parliament and firing enlightened cabinet members a year later when he reverted to typical Obrenovic personality, assuming full powers and curtailing Serbian freedoms of speech and press and instituting a dictatorial monarchy. He had originally been under the sway of young militarists in his palace guard, but this soon changed when he took control. He also replaced the officers close to the throne, and substituted slavish guards who had no personal ambitions in the running of the country.

For years, Serbia stumbled along with a king who preferred to play at politics, dally with foreign princesses eyeing his throne, and generally ignore the welfare of his subjects. He resumed his allegiance to his mother whom he had ignored during the regency years and paid regular visits to her estates in Biarritz between 1894 and 1897. Meanwhile, his father, still loyal to Austrian interests, sought to strengthen ties with the dual monarchy by arranging a marriage between his son and Austrian or German princesses. This was not to be. Queen Nathalie had turned Alexander's head toward the East and Russia.

The young king emulated the czar, the total image of the autocrat, even to adopting the military dress and customs of the Russian monarch. When European royalty was bending to the will of democratic government, Alexander continued in the old traditions of supreme rule. Such archaic positions could be held in Germany by the kaiser and in Russia by the czar; their subjects had never known democratic freedoms and were kept ignorant of personal freedoms, but the Serbia of Alexander had seen much reform, had tasted the independence of thought and speech for twenty years and began to resent a king that dragged it back to feudal times.

It was while on a visit to Queen Nathalie that Alexander met and fell in love with one of her ladies-in-waiting, Draga Mashin

(nee Lunyewitza), the widow of a Serbian nobleman, an engineer of some note, who had been in his father's court. The widow Mashin was thirty-seven, ten years older than Alexander, when they met on the sands of Biarritz where the king spent most of the time when visiting his mother. Swimming remained one of his few physical pleasures. Draga was not a ravishing beauty but somewhat thickset and her face was full with a prominent chin. Her most remarkable feature were riveting eyes, large, dark, and commanding.

Draga's past was cluttered with a string of lovers whom she had rejected after losing interest in them. She was an intelligent, well-read woman who was also a brilliant conversationalist. She was diplomatic and manipulative, sharing Queen Nathalie's ardent admiration for anything Russian. That she dominated Alexander there is no doubt; he forced his way into her bed chamber in Biarritz but she ordered him to leave and, by his own later admission, he meekly obeyed. It was suggested that Alexander suffered from physical defects that left him sexually ineffective so that he was naturally attracted to Draga, a woman who represented intellectual rather than carnal companionship.

When Queen Nathalie discovered a love letter from her son to Draga she dismissed her lady-in-waiting and flew into a rage, accusing Alexander of trifling with a commoner, a low-born creature whose only aim was to sit on the Serbian throne, a position Nathalie could no longer claim. From that moment on, Alexander would have nothing more to do with his mother. He returned to Belgrade, imploring Draga to go with him. She refused to become his palace mistress but did take a small home near the palace, and it was here that the couple met regularly. It was an open scandal which Alexander ignored. The slander blathered in the streets was rampant. It was said that Draga had made the king her sex slave and that

Alexander and his tempestuous mistress, Draga, who defied the Serbian government and married.

she was a thoroughly immoral woman, that she had even poisoned her husband to please former King Milan since the husband had been plotting against Milan and that she had even become Milan's mistress. Now Alexander had taken up with his father's concubine.

Little of this vicious gossip was true; Draga came from a respectable family and had had the misfortune to marry a drunk who died in her arms of alcoholic seizure. Her fortunes were so low at age eighteen that she was without food or shelter until Queen Nathalie took pity on her and financed her education, later making her a lady-in-waiting and her chief confidant. Draga had never shared Milan's bed; the former king despised Draga as his wife's closest supporter. It is a fact that during her years at court in the Milan reign Draga took many lovers. It was also true that her father had died in an insane asylum. None of the gossip seemed to bother Alexander, who continued to pay his devoted attention to Draga.

Austrian authorities began to get nervous over the Alexander-Mashin relationship, knowing well that Draga's political sympathies lay with Russia and that she loathed the Austrian influence exercised over the Serbian throne. Officials arrived from Vienna early in the summer of 1900 and more or less ordered Alexander to quit his mistress and marry an Austrian princess who had been selected by Milan. Stubbornly, Alexander replied that he would marry whom he pleased and he promptly announced to the world that his bride to be was Draga Mashin. Moreover, he stated that he would make this woman queen of Serbia.

The Serbian government was in an uproar and Alexander's ministers threatened to quit en masse. Go ahead, he told them. He could always appoint new ministers. Two of these cabinet ministers went to Draga's home and told her that if she did not leave the country immediately, she would be kidnapped and taken to Hungary. The woman agreed to go, but said she would not leave without her belongings and ordered her maids to slowly and carefully pack everything she owned. This, of course, was a stall. One of the maids slipped from the house, unseen by the ministers and their guards, and brought word to Draga's two brothers, both military officers. They, in turn, informed the king, and Alexander appeared at Draga's home a short time later to rescue her from her would-be kidnappers, returning her to the palace where he immediately slipped a diamond ring on her finger and announced his engagement to the world. They were married on Aug. 5, 1900, with Alexander telling his many critics, "I am king and I can marry whomever I please."

His father, Milan, had been serving as commander-in-chief of the Serbian army at Alexander's request. The king had established his father in this position to further insult his mother after the queen had dared to interfere with his affair with Draga. Milan, however, saw in Serbia's new queen nothing more than an extension of the wife he hated and he left the country in disgust.

Rumors about the couple, chiefly the queen, continued to flourish, one lurid scandal heaped upon another. Reports had it that Alexander was impotent and that Draga was barren; there would be no Obrenovic heir to the Serbian throne. Others had it that the couple shared a platonic relationship and practiced weird sexual relations with strangers. Coupled to this was the very real economic collapse of Serbia. The radical elements that controlled the parliament spent so freely that the annual deficit was bloated and national debt was doubled.

More anger-consuming to the Serbs was the report that the childless Obrenovics planned to name Draga's brother Nikodiye as heir to the throne. When the cabinet heard this, its members were in an uproar and the chief minister, General Tzintzar-Markovic, Serbia's prime minister, went to Alexander and confirmed the rumor. Members of the cabinet arrived to also confront the king. Alexander met with them and at his side was Queen Draga. She was asked to leave the meeting chamber by cabinet members, but Alexander insisted that his wife be present. General Tzintzar-Markovic warned Alexander that there would be a revolution if he and the Queen persisted in making Draga's 24-year-old brother heir to the throne. He implored the couple to make this proposal to the Skupshtina (parliament), adding that "in default of direct heirs, the representatives of the people have the right to say who shall succeed to the throne."

Alexander exploded, shouting at his prime minister, "I am the king and I can do as I please!"

"But the will of the people should also be consulted," replied Tzintzar-Markovic.

Queen Draga placed a maternalistic hand on Alexander's arm, stared widely at the cabinet ministers, her huge dark eyes flashing, and said in a firm voice, "The King's will is supreme!" With that, Draga turned her back on the ministers, leading Alexander by the hand as if he were a little boy. The couple left the room without another word, their stunned ministers standing speechless and helpless.

Riots broke out when it was confirmed that Alexander and Draga planned to foist the queen's brother into the Obrenovic line. Police were called out and several people were killed. The army, which had so far held out allegiance to Alexander, was no longer a dependable ally to the throne. Many officers had grown to hate Alexander for neglecting the army financially and politically. A cadre of young officers headed by Captain Dragutin Dimitrijevic had formed a secret nationalistic society called *Ukendinjenje ili Smrt* (later to be known as *Narodna Odbrana* and the Black Hand Society). For two years, since Alexander had married the despised commoner Draga, these officers had met in secret cells, planning to rid Serbia of the Obrenovics and return

the Karageorgevic monarchy as their country's rulers. To this end, several members had contacted Peter Karageorgevic and asked if he would accept the throne should events occur to make such a succession possible. Peter agreed but had no idea, or, at least, this is what he and others later claimed, what the Serbian officers meant by "should events occur." It was the thinking of Dimitrijevic and others that the Karageorgevics would allow the army to take its rightful place as the leadership body of the nation and that this long-ago exiled monarchy would once more lead Serbia back to power and status in the Balkans.

Queen Draga of Serbia, a much-hated monarch.

The officer clique numbered about ninety members, although some later stated that there were as many as 150 members devoted to the plot to murder the Obrenovics. They waited for the best opportunity to strike, one where the people would support their actions. This came in May 1903 when the general elections were proved to have been rigged and controlled by Alexander's puppets. Prime Minister Tzintzar-Markovic went to Alexander and begged to resign his post, telling the irritated king that the government was a complete failure. Alexander asked him to postpone his resignation until a successor could be found.

That night, in what seemed to be a defiant and pompous act, Alexander, Draga, and members of the queen's family showed themselves to passersby by sitting on the main balcony to listen to the military band play in the gardens below. Angry voices shouted insults to the sovereigns, who either pretended not to hear them or ignored the epithets. As the evening wore on the Obrenovic monarchs continued to sit aloofly on their royal perch, including Draga's sisters and brothers, all of whom had been involved in the plot to install Draga's brother as a designated heir, and their mere presence incensed the passing crowds.

On this balmy Wednesday evening, June 10, 1903, as Alexander and Draga sat defiantly on their royal balcony, dozens of army officers from many regiments entered Belgrade to attend a secret meeting, called there by the leader of their secret society, Captain Dragutin Dimitrijevic. The officers came mostly from the Sixth Regiment and included some high-ranking military leaders: Colonel Maumovic, personal aide to Alexander, Colonel Mishic, commander of the Sixth Regiment, and Colonel Alexander Mashin, Queen Draga's brother-in-law who hated Draga, insisting that she had caused the death of his brother, alternately claiming that she had broken his heart and caused the ill health which brought about his death, or had simply poisoned him.

At 11 p.m. that night, about eighty officers met in small groups at pubs, beer gardens, and in the Officer's Club, all these sites close to the Belgrade palace which was called the Old Palace, or the Konac, a two-story yellow brick structure boasting magnificent gardens and gilt-painted railings which fronted on King Milan Street, a wide thoroughfare shaded by beautiful chestnut trees. At the nearby Helimagdan Gardens a group of about twenty officers sat drinking and talking passionately. Dimitrijevic and a larger group of officers were sitting at tables in the rathskeller of a hotel called the Serbian Crown, consuming a great amount of liquor. Dimitrijevic poured drink after drink for Colonel Mashin until that officer's hatred for his sister-in-law, the queen, demonstrated itself with table-smashing rage. Mashin declared that he would lead the officers into the palace that night and execute the offensive monarchs.

The scene took on an almost surrealistic image as the officers got drunk and began to sing ballads. Dimitrijevic stood up and led his men in a frenzied dance which was known as "Queen Draga's Kola," one where the officers locked their arms about each other's shoulders and shuffled right and left in a spinning circle. Their laughter was loud and their singing even louder; they appeared jubilant, as if celebrating a great military victory. While these sinister festivities took place, the Obrenovics retired for the evening. Alexander had had premonitions about impending assassination, but he felt such threats would come only from a civilian source. He trusted the army implicitly, having recently stated, "I am not afraid of revolutions. If anyone rebels against me I am ready to meet him with sword in hand at the head of my faithful army." The Queen was less confident, worrying over many unsigned notes she had received which warned her of possible assassination attempts. Draga put on a brave face but it was only just that. Only a few days earlier she had said, "I am tired of all these mysterious warnings. Everyday we are told that people are coming to assassinate us in the Palace. It is easy to talk like that, but the cowards have not the courage to come and make the attempt." But only one day before the Dimitrijevic forces met in Belgrade, Queen Draga had written to a friend, "I am haunted by a dreadful presentiment."

Much would later be made of a famous British medium, a Mrs. Burchell, who had held a celebrated séance at Gatti's Restaurant in London on Mar. 20, 1903, almost three months before the assassinations, and attended by many important literary and political personages, including W.T. Stead, editor of *The Review of Reviews*. Mrs. Burchell at that time predicted the murder of Alexander and Draga with amazing exactitude as to details, time, and the identities of the killers. Stead was so impressed that he recorded the seance in detail and sent this description to King Alexander by registered mail. The monarch received the frightening report with disdain, remarking that he had "no interest in the supernatural."

Shortly before midnight, Colonel Mashin left the group of officers at the Serbian Crown and rode his horse at breakneck speed to Palilula Barracks, outside of Belgrade, to awaken the troops of the Seventh Regiment and announce to them that he was the newly appointed commander of the Danubian division. He then stated that the regiment would immediately march on the Old Palace where the hated Queen Draga would be arrested and escorted from the country. Alexander had come to his senses at last, Mashin declared, and had decided to divorce and exile the queen and thereby rid himself of a corrupting influence that had all but wrecked Serbia. As Mashin and his troops began marching toward Belgrade, other conspirators met in the city to quickly organize their forces. A captain named Panapotovic, who was the king's adjutant, met with Dimitrijevic and turned over the keys to the gates that led to the gardens of the Konac. About forty officers proceeded to the Konac Palace, letting themselves into the sprawling gardens.

Inside the palace the guard garrison was posted haphazardly at doorways and beside inner gates. The guard commander, Captain Panayotovic, was sprawled unconscious on a sofa, having been given drugged wine by his aide, Lieutenant Zivkovic, who was part of the plot. Zivkovic, hearing the group of officers in the gardens, unlocked the inner gate and allowed Dimitrijevic and the rest to enter. Several soldiers of the palace guard heard the noise and rushed forward, guns drawn.

"Throw down your arms!" ordered Dimitrijevic, but the guards were loyal to Alexander and leveled their weapons at the conspirators who fired a pistol volley, shooting down four soldiers. The firing brought the groggy Captain Panayotovic out of his stupor. He drew his pistol and rushed at the conspirators, firing blindly. He was shot down. The conspirators rushed forward to

huge double iron doors, bolted from within and leading to the inner Konac palace. They had brought everything needed, including dynamite, and this they used to blow the doors from their hinges, a great explosion that went off at precisely 12:30 a.m. and was heard throughout Belgrade. As the doors collapsed, Colonel Maumovic, one of the conspirators who had returned earlier to the palace to prepare for the invasion, staggered forward to greet his fellow conspirators. He had apparently been on the other side of the door trying to unlock it when it had been dynamited from the other side. The explosion had knocked out all the electricity in the palace, and this caused the conspirators to blindly enter the Konac. One of them thought Maumovic to be a loyal guard and shot and killed him by accident as the assassins rushed inside.

Queen Draga's boudoir where the assassins wrecked the furniture and tapped on walls for secret hiding places in their search for the royal couple.

Alexander and Draga were alerted to the intrusion at the sound of the inner iron doors being dynamited, and they immediately hid themselves in a secret dressing room which led from the Queen's bedroom suite. Meanwhile, loyal guards tried to stop the conspirators as they raced down gloomy hallways, groping in the dark and unsure of their footing. A Captain Milkovic rushed at them with his pistol barking and was shot to death. Up large marble stairs ran the conspirators, looking for the royal chamber. At the head of the stairs stood Lieutenant Lavar Petrovic, one of Alexander's most trusted aides. He held a sword in one hand and a pistol in another. For a moment the forty some officers looked up in the dim light to see this lone guardsman face them. Petrovic, a much decorated officer, would not yield when he was ordered to step aside. There was hesitancy, even on the part of the scheming Dimitrijevic, to shoot down this brave officer. He was asked to step aside so that justice could be done and Serbia saved from Queen Draga's catastrophic plans. Petrovic shouted, "Back! Back!" He then advanced alone down the stairs toward them, firing his pistol and lashing out with his sword. A dozen pistols in the hands of the conspirators fired back and Petrovic collapsed dead, rolling down the stairs.

In the streets outside the palace all was chaos. Dozens of policemen had run to the Konac when hearing the dynamite explode, thinking anarchists were at work. They fired at large crowds gathered outside the palace on King Milan Street and were shocked to see members of the crowd firing back at them, wounding several gendarmes. Then the police realized that the crowds were troops of the Seventh Regiment which had just arrived under Colonel Mashin's command. A Captain Kostic rode toward the police and told them they were to return to the police station and that the troops had been called by Alexander to put down a coup d'etat. Mollified, the police withdrew.

Dimitrijevic and his men were beginning to panic inside the palace. Without any light it became impossible to locate their victims. Conspirators ran throughout the palace in their desperate search for Alexander and Draga, combing the cavernous cellars, racing through the ornate dining halls, and crashing through locked doors of bedrooms they found empty. One of the officers sent his aide outside to collect candles and the conspirators sat down, exhausted and frustrated, to wait for light. The entire plot had turned into a lurid melodrama, a comic Balkan opera. At last candles were brought and the officers, flickering candles held high, went through the labyrinthine halls of the upper floor of the palace, seeking the queen's chamber.

An old man, one of Draga's servants, stood next to a large door at the end of one hallway and, as soon as he saw the officers turn into the corridor, fired a pistol. The bullet found its mark, striking Dimitrijevic in the leg. The old man was wounded but kept alive. The officers dragged him through one room after another until he admitted that the conspirators were in the queen's bedroom. The assassins tore the place to pieces, looking under the bed, behind dressing screens, but they found nothing. Dragging the old servant with them, they went from chamber to chamber, finding no one. Alexander and Draga were present, however, standing together terrified as they listened to the assassins stalk them, crashing and breaking the queen's exquisite furniture in her bedchamber. At the sound of the dynamite going off, the king and queen, dressed scantily, had jumped from their bed and run into Draga's little sewing room which, in the dim light from the candles, the conspirators found impossible to locate. The room was only seven feet long and a few feet wide. Ironically, on the floor was an iron grating which led to a secret escape passage which King Milan had had built years earlier but one which Alexander had had bricked up, thinking he would never have occasion to use it. The door to this room could not be easily seen even in bright daylight, it being flush with the wall, covered with the same rose-tinted wallpaper that adorned the entire bedroom. There was no handle or doorknob to this door; one had to slip a few fingers behind a wallpaper seam to slip the latch.

For more than ninety minutes the king and queen had stood in terror, listening to their pursuers curse the darkness, smashing furniture, firing random pistol shots in frustration. And outside the queen's bedroom, slumped on the hallway floor, was Captain Dimitrijevic. When his men failed to find the monarchs, he mumbled something about "utter failure," and slowly raised his pistol, placing this in his mouth. The coup was about to collapse, or so Dimitrijevic thought, and he did not intend to be arrested and face a firing squad.

At that moment, the old servant was brought again into the queen's chamber and was told that he would be killed instantly if he did not reveal the hiding place of Alexander and Draga. The old man pointed shakily to the wall where the closet was located. Officers with axes then began to chop up the wall. It can be speculated that had Alexander and Draga remained silent their hiding place might not have been discovered after all and that the conspirators would have been forced to withdraw at dawn. But they made the fatal error of deciding to seek help by shouting from the closet window that faced King Milan Street. Alexander, some say Draga, stepped to the window and saw some troops in the street and an officer on horseback commanding them. A call went out to the officer to save them, that assassins were at their door. The officer was none other than Captain Kostic and his answer was to draw his revolver and fire a shot that almost struck Alexander.

Kostic then raced inside the palace and into the queen's chamber to tell the conspirators where to chop with their axes. At that moment, Dimitrijevic took the pistol from his mouth and stood up, hobbling into the bedroom. Before the closet door was split wide by the axes, it slowly opened and Alexander and Draga stepped forth. It was later reported that just as the axe struck the closet door, the monarchs were promised safety if they would come forth. The officers, holding their glittering candles high, lowered their pistols and shrank back in the darkness. It was a bizarre sight, Alexander dressed in plain trousers and a red silk shirt. Draga, who had been naked when the couple took flight, had tried to dress herself properly in the tiny closet, but looked ridiculous. She wore a petticoat, white silk stays, and one yellow stocking.

There are several versions of what next occurred. One report had it that an officer stepped forth and demanded that Alexander abdicate because he had "dishonored the throne by wedding a public prostitute." This same report states that Alexander's response was to produce a hidden pistol and shoot the officer dead with a bullet that found his heart. This caused the other officers to fire their weapons and shoot down the royal couple. Another version has it that when the monarchs stepped from the closet, Alexander asked, "What do you want? And what of your oath of fidelity to me?"

Draga's secret dressing room where the king and queen hid, half-dressed, until they brought the assassins to them by their cries for help.

The conspirators said nothing, staring in silence at their haughty sovereign. Finally, Dimitrijevic hobbled forward with his pistol drawn and shouted, "What are you standing gaping at? Here's our oath of fidelity to him!" With that he fired point blank into both Alexander and Draga.

Falling into Draga's arms, Alexander cried out, "Mito, Mito, how could you do this to me?" At that moment, he thought, quite mistakenly, that his favorite general Tzintzar-Markovic was behind the assassination, Mito being Alexander's familiar name for the general. Oddly, Tzintzar-Markovic had himself been killed by other conspirators only a few hours earlier. Queen Drago lived for only a few seconds after Alexander died in her arms. Dimitrijevic shot her also and his fellow conspirators emptied their guns into the fallen bodies.

Such was their rage, the assassins then withdrew their swords and hacked the bodies to pieces, slashing their faces, disemboweling them, nearly severing their limbs. Some of the officers shrank from this barbaric orgy, begging the others to stop, but the leading conspirators did not stop their bloody amputations until they were completely spent. Dimitrijevic, ever the cunning schemer, ordered the bodies to be thrown out the closet window and into the garden where the troops below could see that the monarchs had been slain and that the coup was a success.

The bodies were lifted up and thrown down into the gardens while the conspirators shouted from the window, "Long live Peter Karageorgevic, King of Serbia!" One story has it that King Alexander was not killed outright, that he had only been wounded by the pistol fire and when his body was thrown from the closet window, he came to life and clung to the window sill, crying out for someone to save him and that his fingers were chopped off by the assassins so that he fell into the gardens where troops below bayoneted him to death.

Before leaving the queen's bedchamber, the officers wrecked it, tearing at the wallpaper, slashing the Arabian carpet, smashing the ornate bookcase and tables, then looting Draga's jewelry before they stumbled outside to celebrate their "victory." More than fifty other victims had been slain in the bloody coup, including two of Draga's brothers and key officers who had tried to rally troops in going to the aid of the doomed Obrenovics.

At dawn, with a light rain falling, passersby on King Milan Street viewed the gruesome remains of the monarchs, whose bodies had been purposely left out in the open as a symbol of the coup. The Russian minister who had watched events from his Legation building just across the street from the palace, emerged and walked solemnly across the street. Here he faced Colonel Mashin, who was in charge of the milling troops. "For God's sake," pleaded Minister Tcharikoff, "carry them into the palace. Do not leave them here in the rain exposed to the public gaze."

Mashin appeared to think about the suggestion for some time, then he nodded and ordered palace servants to hose down the bodies which had been stripped of all clothing and were lying naked on the lawn. After being washed the bodies were wrapped in sheets and taken into the palace and put onto two tables in the main receiving hall. That night two doctors performed a post mortem on the corpses, noting that Alexander had been wounded more than thirty times and Draga twice that amount. The physicians, obviously seeking to curry favor with the new regime, reported that they had inspected Alexander's brain and that they had concluded from their discoveries that the last of the Obrenovics had been "completely mad," and that Draga had been "incapable of having children." The bodies were then placed in simple wooden coffins and placed on a cart used for condemned murderers, suicides, and smallpox victims and driven to the old St. Mark Cemetery. Here they were buried in plain graves over which two wooden markers were placed. These read: "Alexander Obrenovic" and "Draga Obrenovic."

Leaders of the coup later awarded themselves handsome payments for having killed the sovereigns, and most were elevated to higher rank when Peter Karageorgevic returned from exile in Geneva to be sworn in as Peter I. Dragutin Dimitrijevic, who had planned the regicides with careful detail, was named chief of intelligence of the Serbian general staff and would later rise to the rank of general. He would go on to become known in the inner circles of terrorism as Europe's master assassin, responsible for dozens of assassination attempts, including the killing of Francis Ferdinand at Sarajevo at the hands of a Serbian zealot into whose hands Dimitrijevic had placed a pistol and a bomb. See: **Alexander I (Karageorgevic); Black Hand Society; Dimitrijevic, Dragutin; Francis Ferdinand.**

REF: Bell, *Assassin!*; Buranelli, *Spy/Counter-Spy; CBA;* Hardman, *The Rise and Fall of The Hapsburg Monarchy;* Hrbelianovitch, *The Serbian People;* Jelavich, *The Balkans;* Johnson, *Famous Assassinations of History;* Macartney, *The Hapsburg Empire;* Mijatovich, *A Royal Tragedy; Assassination of King Alexander and Queen Draga of Serbia;* Paine, *The Assassin's World;* Rowan, *Secret Service;* Stavrianos, *The Balkans Since 1453;* Steele, *The Hapsburg Monarchy;* Temperley, *History of Serbia;* Vivien, *The Serbian Tragedy;* von Ranke, *A History of Serbia and the Serbian Revolution;* Vucinich, *Serbia Between East and West;* Waring, *Serbia;* Webster, *Secret Societies and Subversive Movements;* West, *Black Lamb and Gray Falcon;* Williams, *Heyday for Assassins;* Wilson, *Belgrade: The White City of Death.*

Alexander II (Alexander Nicholas Romanov), 1818-81, Russ., czar, assass. Son of Czar Nicholas I, Alexander assumed the throne in 1855. Unlike his forebears, Alexander was a cultured, refined ruler who had received an excellent education and shared Western views and policies, although he still insisted upon supreme rule in Russia. He was the great reformer, establishing a court system in Russia and improving the judicial laws. In 1861, he freed the serfs through a special edict which won for him the name Great Emancipator. Alexander founded schools and ordered the building of a comprehensive railroad system across the vast Russian landscape. He established effective political and governmental administrations and encouraged a university system which ironically became the hotbed of opposition to his reign. The more education and liberal policies Alexander granted to his people the more unrest his policies sowed. The students of the radical left formed nihilist parties (the word nihilism first appears in a Turgenev novel, *Fathers and Sons,* and means literally "nothing," the political aim of nihilists being to bring down all authority and leave nothing standing in its place).

Nihilist students were undoubtedly behind the first of many

assassination attempts made against Alexander during his 26-year-reign. This occurred in 1861 when an unknown assailant fired a single bullet into his passing coach and missed the Czar. The early nihilists, however, were little more than debating societies with no real organization behind them.

One of their number, a student disgruntled at their endless polemical arguments, decided to act on his own. He was Dimitri Karakozov, a sickly young man who was described by his contemporaries as "emotionally unbalanced." Other reports have it that Karakozov had been dismissed from his political group, which had been named *Hell,* as wholly unreliable. This group later claimed, perhaps in self-protective hindsight, that Karakozov had been publicly disowned by the organization and that he had been labelled "crazy." Karakozov told his student friends that, "I have decided to destroy the wicked Czar and die for my beloved people." No one took him seriously.

Ever since 1862, when the student movement, loose as it was, began in Russia, radical liberals advocated the assassination of Alexander II, even boldly calling for the murder

Czar Alexander II of Russia; he endured seemingly endless attempts on his life.

in their clandestine, sporadically issued pamphlets and newspapers. Plots abounded and two conspiracies formed to murder the Czar were uncovered by authorities in 1862 and 1863 but nothing came of them. There had been student disturbances that had turned into near-riots and mounted Cossack troops had been employed to disband demonstrators. Students were further incensed when many of the more unruly ones were inducted into the army to remove them from political activities.

Karakozov announced to his friends in 1866 that he planned to do more about the situation than publish pamphlets. He purchased an old pistol and then began traveling between Moscow and St. Petersburg, tracking the Czar's movements. Alexander was a man of fixed habits and next to impossible to properly guard. He insisted upon walking in the open streets without escort, believing that no one really wanted to kill him. He knew, and rightly so, that the peasants, the vast majority of the Russian people, regarded him reverentially. He was almost a holy, living icon to the masses of people to whom he had granted freedom, although his abolishment of serfdom in Russia did little to alleviate the tremendous tax and work burdens the peasants continued to bear.

Alexander often stopped on his daily walks to greet and talk to peasants he met. This Karakozov witnessed personally as he watched his prey take walks through the summer garden outside the Winter Palace in St. Petersburg; the Czar strolling by the Neva quays, in front of the Marble Palace and the equally regal-looking British Embassy. Disguised as a peasant, wearing a bright red workman's shirt, Karakozov, on Apr. 14, 1866, saw Alexander step from the gates of the Winter Palace and begin his morning constitutional. When perhaps no more than twenty paces from the Czar, Karakozov whipped out his ancient pistol and took steady aim at Alexander, who had his back to the assassin. Just at that moment a peasant named Komisaroff, a cap maker by trade, raced up to Karakozov and smashed his arm upward at the very moment he fired. As a result, Karakozov's shot missed and his bullet went wild.

As guards rushed forward to subdue the would-be assassin, Alexander turned and realized what had happened. Typical of his character, he walked up to Karakozov, asking him why he would

Alexander II, while riding in a carriage with Napoleon III in Paris on June 6, 1867, was shot at by a Polish assassin named Berezovski, shown under arrest at right; Napoleon used the incident to take bows standing in the carriage, top left.

want to kill him. The student sneered and then spat out, "Because you refused to give the land to the people."

The miraculous survival of the czar, his supporters were quick to point out, was due to the actions of a one-time serf, the peasant Komisaroff, who represented the true sentiments of Russians everywhere—that their czar was loved and respected and they would never permit political lunatics to take his life. A chapel dedicated to St. Alexander Nevsky was later erected on the spot of the failed assassination to commemorate Alexander's narrow escape. Above its doorway, in gold lettering, was placed the following inscription: "Touch not mine annointed."

That the peasant class indeed supported the Czar was widely demonstrated. American Ambassador Clay reported later how the bonds between the Emperor and his people were strong and deep. After hearing of the Czar's escape, countless numbers of people from St. Petersburg and from the surrounding countryside flocked into the city. Wrote Ambassador Clay, "Thousands assembled at the Winter Palace and hurrahed until his Majesty showed himself again and again on the balcony...they camped there all night and the next day." The upper-class citizenry were in shock and university scholars and poets lamented Karakozov's attempt at regicide. The shot fired by the unbalanced student, according to the poet Tiutchev, "laid us all low in dust and shame."

Karakozov and another conspirator were both condemned to death and more than thirty others, students active in Karakozov's political group, were rounded up and sent to prison for life, named as co-conspirators. The would-be assassin mounted the stairs of a gallows in September and a black hood was placed over his head. The rope was then lowered and tightened about his neck. He was, however, at the very last second before the trap was sprung open, reprieved and sent to life at hard labor. The attitude of the liberal czar with such forward-looking programs abruptly changed from that moment. He ordered one repressive measure after another in the next year, almost cancelling the many reforms he had brought into being. Count Alexander Suvorov, the even-tempered governor-general of St. Petersburg who had been known for his kindly attitude toward dissidents, was dismissed and replaced by the severe General F. Trepov, a martinet police

official who immediately sent his police and Cossacks to disband all political organizations, student gatherings, and intellectual meetings of any kind, arresting thousands who were beaten and imprisoned. (Trepov himself would be the target of an assassin twelve years later.) A.V. Golovnin, the liberal minister of education, was ousted and replaced by the stern Dmitry Tolstoy who had opposed all of Alexander's reform measures, including the emancipation of the serfs.

Under Tolstoy, the university students found an insufferable intellectual dictator who eliminated any courses that dealt with contemporary thought and problems. Governmental and social studies were outlawed, as were any political courses. Tolstoy ordered Russian educators to concentrate on classic languages. All Russian students attending foreign universities were ordered to return immediately to Russia. He would not have Russian youth contaminated by Western thought and culture. He would stifle and suppress any thought that contributed to criticism of the regime, any notion of questioning the Romanov dynasty and its "divine right" to rule. Tolstoy's edicts and actions brought just the opposite results he desired. The returning students brought with them the ideals of Western educators and political thinking that would eventually change the course of Russian history and eradicate the Romanovs. They formed thousands of secret political groups, established several secret "cells" of forbidden intellectual discussion, and planted the seeds of Marxism and Communism.

Alexander's own governors and ministers, at his insistence, assured through their repressive programs the ultimate destiny of their sovereign—assassination. "Our worst enemies," wrote one of his more liberal advisers, "are neither nihilists nor Poles but the so-called statesmen who turn people into nihilists and malcontents (and) try to undermine justice." No ruler in the last two centuries was so doggedly pursued year after year by dedicated killers. His popular name, Czar Liberator, was changed to that of Doomed Emperor. Alexander knew his days were numbered but he continued to rule with an even tighter hand, determined to preserve the Romanov dynasty for his heirs. In the more than dozen real plots and attempts against his life, Alexander seldom rcacted openly, almost accepting as a tradition of his office the constant threat to his life. When the attacks increased during the late 1870s, he once blurted his true, innermost feelings, almost shouting to a minister, "Am I a wild beast that they should hound me to death?"

For the most part the Czar placed his care in the hands of God, stating more than once that the Almighty would determine his fate, not a revolutionary assassin. This was the case in 1867 when Alexander was on an official state visit to Emperor Napoleon III of France. The gathering of royalty in Paris at this time was stunning. The kings of Belgium and Prussia were in attendance, as was Bismarck, the Iron Chancellor. Paris was bedecked with colorful flags and decorations and Alexander, far from the cold climes of his native land, relaxed for one of the first times in his reign. He and Napoleon appeared regularly in public and, on June 6, 1867, they rode together, along with Alexander's sons, in an open coach through the Bois de Boulogne, where enormous crowds pressed against the military guards attempting to hold them back so that the road narrowed to a wavering lane and compelled the coach to travel at walking speed.

Suddenly a Pole named Berezovski jumped into the road holding a pistol and fired at Alexander. (The Poles, then under Russian dominance, had been much repressed by Alexander's regime.) It seemed, given the short distance of fire, that the assassin could not miss, but his bullet passed through the nostrils of a horse ridden by one of the French guards and went sailing between Alexander and Napoleon, harming neither monarch. Berezovski fired once more but his pistol blew up and completely shattered his arm. The wounded horse snorted in the direction of the coach and splattered both autocrats and the Czar's two sons with blood. Alexander remained almost motionless, his face without expression, his gaze intent upon the would-be assassin who was being dragged away by guards. Napoleon, on the other hand, being the demonstrative person he was, seized the moment to prove his bravery. He stood up in the carriage and displayed his blood-coated uniform, waving to the crowds, smiling broadly, as if he had just then returned triumphant from some astounding battlefield victory. He reveled in his survival. His face flushed red, his eyes danced, and adrenaline laced his words as he turned, grinning, to Alexander and roared, "Sire! We have been under fire together!"

The misfired assassination in Paris, as German archives revealed decades later, could have been prevented altogether. Bismarck's chief of German intelligence, Wilhelm Stieber, learned of the planned attempt on Alexander's life some weeks before Berezovski fired his wild shot. He informed Bismarck, who ordered him to hold his information from the French until the very last moment so it would appear that Germany was rushing to the rescue of the death-marked czar with a last minute discovery. Stieber did reportedly alert the French police *before* the attack by Berezovski, and they rounded up some of Berezovski's co-conspirators but lost the assailant in the crowds at the Bois de Boulogne and did not discover his presence until after he had made his attempt on Alexander's life.

Alexander's reaction, upon leaving Paris, was to privately condemn Napoleon for his grandstanding and apparent unconcern for his, the czar's, safety, as well as pretending that the assassin's bullet was indescriminately meant for either of them. That bullet, like many fired after it, had but one target, Alexander II of Russia. By 1877, the secret political societies in Russia numbered in the thousands but almost all of them were splinter groups with diverse aims and without central leadership. Some wanted to merely print seditious pamphlets calling for the peasants to rebel, a specious exercise in that the peasant class was the most supportive of the dynasty. Some revolutionaries insisted upon resistance to arrest, effecting the escape of political prisoners, and generally disturbing police activities; most of these tactics amounted to no more than idle talk and were seldom, if ever, put into practice. The major political group at this time was an organization called Land and Liberty (*Zemlya i Volya*). Police swept through the political cells

and arrested 193 politically active students, putting them on trial. Most of these accused traitors were later released after a trial lasting from October 1877 to January 1878.

The day following the end of the show trial, Jan. 28, 1878, a young radical student, Vera Ivanovna Zasulich, brushed past guards flanking the entrace to the office of General Trepov, head of the St. Petersburg police. Pushing her way through a crowd of petitioners, Zasulich marched up to Trepov, drew a pistol from her coat, and shot the general several times point blank. Trepov, though severely wounded, survived. Zasulich was put on trial, not as a political prisoner in the usual closed court, but as a felon in open court. The courtroom was thronged with students and middle-class spectators who roared their approval on Mar. 31, 1878, when Zasulich was found Not Guilty. The young woman was swept outside the courthouse. As police closed in to rearrest her, the crowds pushed the officers away, trampling them. Zasulich escaped in the confusion and was soon smuggled out of the country, becoming the first heroine of the revolutionary movement.

Emboldened by Zasulich's assassination attempt, young revolutionaries began adopting her measures. Police officials were shot in Kiev and on Aug. 4, 1878, Serge Kravchinsky, editor of *Land and Liberty*, the official revolutionary newspaper in St. Petersburg, along with another nihilist, lay in wait for General Mezentsov, director of the counter-revolutionary Third Section, a dreaded secret-police group. Spotting Mezentsov on a crowded street, Kravchinsky ran up to him and repeatedly stabbed the general until he fell dead at his feet. He and his accomplice then leaped into a cart pulled by a noted racehorse, and galloped to freedom as guards on foot vainly attempted to follow.

Alexander ordered more reprisals and, in turn, the revolutionaries continued their violent attacks on his officials. On Feb. 21, 1879, Prince Dimitri Kropotkin, governor general of Kharkov and a cousin of anarchist Prince Peter Kropotkin, was murdered by revolutionaries. General Drenteln, who had succeeded to Trepov's police post in St. Petersburg, was attacked but survived. Several revolutionaries were then executed. This see-saw violence between Land and Liberty and the czar's forces continued until April 1879 when the executive committee of Land and Liberty met to resolve to murder the czar at all costs. Still the committee could not agree upon a specific assassination plan. The dilemma was resolved by Alexander Konstantinovich Solevev, a schoolteacher from Toropetz in the Pskoff district. Solevev announced that he and he alone would kill Alexander.

Again the revolutionaries studied the czar's movements and, incredible after so many attempts had been made on his life, he continued to travel about St. Petersburg with a light escort of guards, often exposing himself in public. On Apr. 14, 1879, Solevev put on a military cap and coat and the the type of boots usually worn by cavalry officers. He boldly approached the coach in which the czar sat as it waited in front of the palace of Prince Gottschkov, his secretary of state. Solevev marched solemnly toward Alexander and appeared to be a retired army officer in his disguise, impressing the guards with such an official bearing that they did not challenge him. He stopped some feet from the coach and came to attention, saluting the czar. Alexander returned his salute and at that moment Solevev drew a pistol and began firing at the czar. He fired four times but his aim was miserable, none of the shots striking the sovereign. Again, one of Alexander's loyal peasants came to the rescue, reportedly a heavyset milkwoman who was just then making a delivery to the palace. She leaped forward and grabbed Solevev by the arm, causing his fifth shot to go wild and stike one of the guards rushing foward. The enraged schoolteacher, helpless with the large woman shoving one hand into his face, bit her finger almost to the bone, but she would not release him until guards surrounded the assassin and clubbed him to the ground.

Alexander peered motionless from the coach to see Solevev reach inside his coat pocket and shirt and produce two capsules which had been fastened under his armpits with wax. He swallowed these poisoned capsules but an antidote was quickly given to him which saved Solevev's life. He was later tried and convicted and, on May 28, 1879, Solevev was taken to a public gallows and hanged before a large, silent throng. The group known as Land and Liberty began to break up, mostly because certain members such as Andre Zhelyabov insisted that the czar be killed at all costs, while others argued for the nonviolent ways of old. Zhelyabov's new group, called People's Will, began to make fantastic attempts to murder Alexander. When it was learned that the czar would be landing in Odessa, a member of the group, Solomon Wittenberg, was caught while attempting to mine the harbor. He was hanged.

Zhelyabov now employed an explosives expert, Nicolai Kibalchick, to arrange the planting of mines beneath the rail routes traveled by the czar. Kibalchick manufactured 100 kilograms of dynamite and placed this into cylinders which were planted in tunnels north of Odessa, but it was later learned that the czar's police had changed the route he would take when returning from the Crimea in November 1979. Several hundred conspirators under Zhelyabov's direction dug a 150-foot tunnel under the tracks south of the Moscow station and waited for the czar's two trains to pass. The first train, they learned, was filled with Alexander's retinue, and the second train would carry the czar. The first train was allowed to go through unmolested but, as the second train approached on the night of Nov. 18, 1879, Zhelyabov ordered the charge to be set off just as the imperial car passed over the tracks. At approximately 10 p.m., the train roared over the planted mine which was exploded, setting off a roar that was heard in downtown Moscow.

One coach was utterly destroyed, blown to splinters. Seven more cars derailed and plunged off the embankment, catching fire. There were many casualties but the czar was not injured. In fact, he was not even on this train. Shrewdly, his guards had suspected just such a ploy by the revolutionaries after finding the abandoned dynamite cylinders north of Odessa and, at the last minute, had switched the two trains, sending the czar on ahead of the baggage train which followed. It was the baggage train that was dynamited, an explosion the czar himself heard just as he alighted from his imperial train which had arrived in Moscow. The failed attempt to kill Alexander only spurred the People's Will onward. Zhelyabov, whose identity was known to the police and who was hunted everywhere, managed to elude his hunters and go on planning the death of Alexander.

At that time a volunteer came forward, one Stepan Khalturin, who was a carpenter in the Winter Palace and whose current assignment was to repair the ceiling in the basement beneath the grand dining room, the Yellow Hall. Khalturin offered to smuggle enough explosives into the Winter Palace to blow up the entire royal family as they sat down to dinner. Zhelyabov excitedly approved of the plan and the carpenter began to take small amounts of dynamite into the palace, secreting this in a basement flue beneath the dining room. Khalturin's comings and goings went unchallenged as he was a familiar figure in the palace, often seen with hammer in hand as he walked through the long, ornate hallways. On one occasion, Khalturin opened a door to a study and there stood the czar, his back to the carpenter. Alexander stood motionless, reading a document. Khalturin fingered the heavy hammer in his hand and realized that all he need do is take a few steps forward and, with one blow, bring the hammer down upon the czar's head to crush his skull and kill him. But the carpenter could not move; his feet were riveted to the floor, or so he later claimed, and he could not bring himself to murder the czar in such a fashion. He quietly backed out, closing the door, and went back to ferreting his dynamite in the basement.

On Feb. 17, 1880, with more than fifty kilograms of dynamite planted in the basement, Zhelyabov gave the order to blow up the imperial family. The time device attached to the dynamite was set to go off at exactly 6:30 p.m. that night, precisely when the entire family, with Alexander at the head of the table, would be seated in the Yellow Hall. But this time, the religiously kept

routine the revolutionaries counted on was disrupted. The royal family was entertaining a guest that evening, Prince Alexander of Hesse-Darmstadt, the czar's brother-in-law who was late, and dinner was postponed for a half hour. Khalturin, who had set the charge for 6:30, left the palace a few minutes prior to the explosion. He stood off some distance from the palace and awaited the results of his dynamite smuggling. At 6:32 p.m., there was a terrific explosion that blew out the French windows of the Yellow Hall, belching yellow flames following. The floor of the dining hall collapsed and the ceiling, walls, and trappings were shredded.

The czar was just that moment leading his family toward the wing housing the Yellow Hall, walking with Prince Alexander down a corridor which was soon filled with smoke and fumes. Chandeliers collapsed, walls sagged, and the lights of the great Winter Palace flickered and then went out. Hundreds of screaming servants raced to the dining hall to find two of their number dead, blown to pieces just as they were making the final table arrangements. Candles were lighted and in the eerie, flickering light of these tapers, held by the quivering hands of trembling servants, the czar and his officers inspected the awful damage. The worst was discovered in the basement where a company of hand-picked Finnish guards were billeted in underground corridors. Sixty-seven guards were dug out of the rubble that night, nineteen of them dead.

The czar, on foot, after a first bomb had disabled one of his sleds, is mortally wounded by a second bomb, March 1, 1881.

One of Alexander's sons told his father that the explosion might have been caused by gas fumes. The czar patted his son's shoulder and replied sagely, "Oh, no, I know what it is." Later it was learned that the czar had found on his plate each morning at breakfast a note warning him that he would not live to see Mar. 2, 1880, the twenty-fifth anniversary of his accession to the Russian throne. (How these notes were so boldly planted has never been explained; some suggest that the carpenter Khalturin had placed the notes, almost as a way of alerting the czar to the danger in the basement, proving his reluctance to actually murder Alexander and his family; others claim that the notes were placed by one of the servants, many of whom belonged to secret revolutionary societies.) On Mar. 20, 1880, Alexander, accompanied by his two sons, attended the funeral of the loyal Finnish guards. The czar was now an ill man. The latest assassination attempt had sapped his resolve and drained his strength. His features were strained and his face pale, bloodless. He seemed to be on the verge of nervous collapse.

The Winter Palace was next to impossible to secure. The four-story sprawling structure with its many wings and galleries fronted on the Neva and was flanked by the Hermitage Museum and the Admiralty building. Access to the Winter Palace was easily gained by those in the street and it was not unusual to see ordinary citizens taking rather loosely arranged tours of the building while members of the royal family were present. It is little wonder then that the czar regularly discovered death threats on small notes stuffed into his clothes, on his writing desk inside his private apartments, even in his bath. On one occasion he pulled a handkerchief from a morning coat which was covered with explosive powder that ignited and severely damaged his eyesight.

Alexander was by then resigned to his violent fate. He told his confidants that it was his job as emperor to face all perils, as a soldier to remain at his post. He could not desert, he could not surrender. To make sure that his family members remained safe, howwever, Alexander ordered that none were to accompany him on any train journeys or carriage rides. He openly defied the terrorists, or invited them to do their worst, continuing as he did to walk alone about the palace areas, a single guard some distance away, or ride about St. Petersburg in an open droshky with a lone Cossack riding on horseback nearby. Zhelyabov once again studied Alexander's routine and prepared to murder the monarch on Sunday, Mar. 13, 1881, knowing that every Sunday the czar visited the Michael Riding school on that day. The agents of the People's Will tracked the czar regularly on these Sunday excursions, marking all the various routes his carriage took. Zhelyabov then set his people busy tunneling beneath several streets, Little Sadovya Street which was between Engineers Square and Nevsky Prospekt where the riding school was located, and other routes such as the Stone Bridge and Little Garden Street. Four bomb throwers were selected and trained in the art of tossing bombs that would explode upon impact. (These were ingenious devices of nitroglycerine packed in thick glass.)

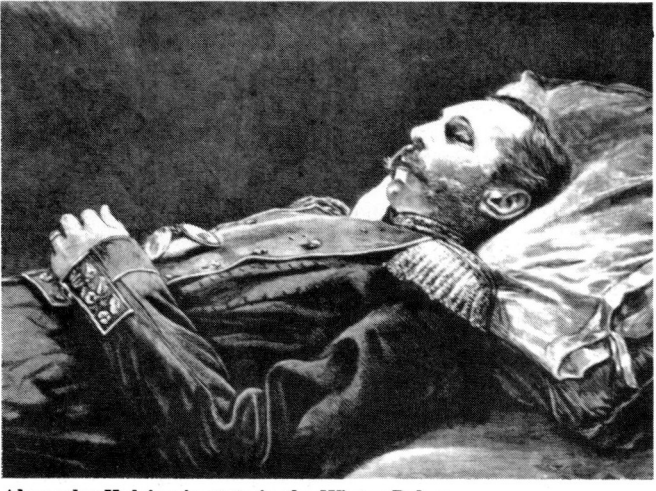

Alexander II, lying in state in the Winter Palace.

The bomb throwers' meeting at the headquarters of the People's Will on Vasili Ostrov Street consisted of Ignaty Grinevitsky, a 26-year-old engineering student; Ivan Yemelyanov, a 20-year-old cabinetmaker; Timofey Mikhailov, a 21-year-old boilermaker; and a student, 19-year-old Nikolai Rysakov. Directing their training was Sophia Perovsky, Zhelyabov's blonde mistress, a 26-year-old fanatical revolutionary utterly dedicated to the task of assassination. Kibalchick, the bomb-maker, constructed the mines placed beneath the streets and the nitro bombs to be thrown by hand. The work of these fanatics went on uninterrupted but police were aware of the plot and agents soon began to close in on the conspirators. They were under the personal direction of a gifted administrator, Count Michael Loris-Melikov. This strange but effective minister, newly appointed to counteract terrorism in Russia following the Winter Palace explosion, had proved himself brilliant on the battlefield as an inspired general. He was decidedly liberal and Alexander gave him a free hand in liberating Russia of murdering fanatics.

To that end, Loris-Melikov, an Armenian by birth, reestablished a free press, opened the schools, returned independence to local government and slackened censorship. Moreover, he prepared legislation for Alexander which would give Russia a constitution which included representation in a parliamentary form where all classes could find an effective political voice. Alexander was returning full circle to the political ideals of his youth, abandoning the repressive measures he had invoked for decades, deciding that persecution of his people brought nothing but revolutionary resolve. Within six months the widespread revolutionary activities dwindled, then almost ceased. Fewer shipments of arms and explosives arrived in St. Petersburg and soon Loris-Melikov was able to report to Alexander that revolution in Russia was nothing more than a "faint murmur." The Zhelyabov group, however, remained at large, its general activities outlined to the czar.

Then, through the network of police spies, the group was pinpointed and two of its members were arrested. A day later, Feb. 27, 1881, police captured Zhelyabov himself and threw him into a cell to await trial. When Alexander was told the news of this arrest, he openly expressed his relief. Now he felt that he and his family would be safe, at least for a little while. The time of safety would last only two days. On Mar. 1, 1881, Alexander planned to sign Loris-Melikov's constitution into law which would be published the following day. This news came to Sophia Perovsky and gave her great cause for alarm. She was determined to murder the czar before he could sign a document that would seem to nullify all the reasons for the revolution she and her lover Zhelyabov had advocated. She and the People's Will would save Russia, not Alexander II. She ordered her bomb-throwers into the streets on the morning of Mar. 1, 1881. They took up their positions along the Catherine Canal route, the very route Alexander's sleigh invariably took each Sunday.

At the Winter Palace the czar kissed his wife goodbye and promised her that he would be careful to take an alternate route on his return from the riding school. Before leaving, however, he received Loris-Melikov who begged him not to leave the palace that day, reporting that he had personally interviewed the terrorist Zhelyabov who had bragged to him that the czar would still be killed, despite the fact that he had been jailed, that his organization was powerful and could still reach out and finish the task he had assigned to it. Alexander thought for a moment, then dismissed his minister's fears as groundless; the terrorist was in jail, the threat was over. He went to his waiting sleigh which was now accompanied by another sleigh carrying Colonel Dvorzhitsky, district chief of police, whom Loris-Melikov had ordered to accompany the czar, along with a special escort of Cossacks.

The party went along its usual route, the sleighs moving fast down the Catherine Canal passageway, the czar waving to those on the street. Most waved back, including the very bomb-throwers positioned along the narrow passageway. They had been ordered not to throw their infernal machines at Alexander until he returned from the riding school. The czar made his brief visit to the school, then, en route home, stopped to see his favorite cousin, Grand Duchess Catherine, leaving her palace after sipping half a cup of tea. But, inexplicably, his small caravan did not return to the Winter Palace via another route but came back the same way along the Catherine Canal street, a move that Sophia Perovsky either fortunately guessed or knew about in advance through one of the palace servants.

There were now three sledges, another police sledge having joined the czar's retinue. Cossacks rode in front and behind the sledges as they moved swiftly across the snow-covered street. Along the street were some police officers, soldiers off duty, and several civilians. Alexander noticed a delivery boy walking down the street with a basket of bread on his head. At the first position where a bomb thrower was to step forward none existed. Timofey Mikhailov had watched the czar's sled sail past him at 1 p.m., thought about the task assigned to him by the order-barking Perovsky, and gave up the notion of killing the czar. He went home, taking his homemade bomb with him. But the other three assassins stuck to their posts and it was Rysakov who first ran forward with his bomb just as the czar's sleigh came opposite the Kojushni Bridge, hurling the explosive which landed behind Alexander's sled. He barely missed his target but the back of the

Czar's sled was shattered and the window smashed. Two Cossacks on horseback were sent crashing to the ground, the horses dead, one Cossack dying. The boy with the bread basket was blown into a wall, mortally wounded. A huge blue cloud of earth, snow, and splinters curled upward.

Alexander stepped from his sleigh with only a slight cut on his hand. It appeared that he once more miraculously survived another assassination, that he could not be killed. Colonel Dvorzhitsky stopped his own sled and rushed to the czar who appeared slightly dazed. He begged Alexander to get into the second sled and move quickly to the Winter Palace. The czar agreed but lingered to make sure that the wounded delivery boy and the injured Cossack were given medical attention. Police officers had thrown Rysakov against a wall, pinioning his arms. A crowd gathered and many tried to help the czar to the police sled. A Cossack officer urged Colonel Dvorzhitsky to remove the czar quickly form the scene, saying, "Colonel, the crowd is too great, we ought to get him away." Reportedly, someone in the crowd shouted, "Thank God, the czar is saved!"

At that moment Grinevitsky leaped forward, shouting, "It's too early to thank God!" and threw his bomb directly beneath the legs of the czar. It went off with a terrific explosion that left Alexander crumpled into the snow, his legs shattered, one almost severed at the thigh, great gouts of blood from his wounds spurting onto the snow. More than twenty people in the crowd had been killed, including Grinevitsky. Dozens of people rushed forward through the smoke, stepping over bodies to help the badly wounded Dvorzhitsky pick up what remained of the dying Alexander. Grand Duke Michael, hearing the explosion, raced to the scene and found his brother mortally wounded. The Grand Duke grabbed a cap from a bystander and placed this on Alexander's head to shield him from view. Leaning close, Michael said, "Alexander, can you hear me?"

The czar, barely alive, replied, "Yes, I hear you." Then a Captain Novikov suggested that the czar be removed to a nearby house, but Alexander, in a faint whisper, was heard to say, "To the palace...carry me to the palace...to die there."

The police sleds had been wrecked by the second explosion and a hired sleigh was ordered up; with Grand Duke Michael lifting the remains of his brother to this sleigh, the royal party proceeded to the Winter Palace. Helping the Grand Duke lift the mortally wounded emperor to this sleigh were several citizens. One of them was Yemelyanov, one of the bomb-throwers who had lost his nerve. He helped to carry the czar to the sleigh, his bomb looking like an innocuous package, still tucked beneath his arm. Then he too went home.

Arriving at the Winter Palace, royal guardsmen carried the dying czar up the marble stairs to his apartments, leaving black drops of blood in a long trail. Alexander was placed on a couch and all the members of the royal family were called to pay their final respects. The heir apparent, Alexander III, stood weeping, his broad shoulders heaving, at the foot of the couch. Among the sobbing children there gathered stood a 13-year-old boy in a sailor suit, Nicholas, who would never forget this traumatic scene and who himself, as Nicholas II, would also face assassination as the last of the Romanov czars in the next century. The family surgeon examined Alexander, who never regained consciousness. Inside of an hour the doctor turned to the family and announced, "The Emperor is dead."

Alexander III, who would never trust his people and never relent in his war against a rising tide of revolutionaries, then walked solemnly from the room. Nicholas watched his father and mother step from the palace, watched them embrace, and then saw his father salute the full regiment of guardsmen that had been drawn up around the Winter Palace, guns at the ready, bayonets fixed. With that, Alexander III saluted his men, leaped into a carriage and drove off "accompanied by a whole regiment of Don Cossacks, in attack formation, their red lances shining brightly in the last rays of a crimson March sunset." But by then there was no one to attack. All of those responsible for the murder of

Alexander II had been arrested.

Before their trial, Rysakov turned informer, detailing the entire operations of the People's Will. He, Zhelyabov, Mikhailov, Kibalchick, and Perovsky were tried and condemned. On Apr. 3, 1881, these five were taken in open tumbrils from their prison cells, all wearing placards reading "Regicide." They were driven to Semenovsky Square where gallows had been erected. An estimated 200,000 people had gathered there to witness the execution of the assassins.

Execution of the assassins of Alexander II.

Perovsky, Zhelyabov, Mikhailov, and Kilbalchick embraced and kissed each other in farewell. They all ignored the traitor Rysakov. Within ten minutes they were all hanged and placed in wooden coffins to be taken to unmarked graves. It was the end of the People's Will and, for the most part, any serious revolutionary activity in Russia for some years to come. A small splinter group of the People's Will remained dormant for six years but surfaced in 1887 only to be rounded up by police before they could throw any bombs. Among this group, executed by the authorities, was Alexander Ulyanov, who shouted from the scaffold, "Long live the People's Will!" Watching him die was his 17-year-old brother, Vladimir, who later exclaimed, "I swear I will revenge myself on them!" This boy would later be known to history as V.I. Lenin. See: **Lenin, V.I.; Nicholas II.**

REF.: Adams, *Imperial Russia After 1861;* Almedingen, *The Emperor Alexander II;* ____, *The Romanovs, Three Centuries of an Ill-Fated Dynasty;* Avrich, *The Russian Anarchists;* Bell, *Assassin, The Theory and Practice of Political Violence;* Berdiaev, *The Origins of Russian Bolshevism;* Black, *Aspects of Social Change Since 1861: The Transformation of Russian Society;* Byrnes, *Pobedonostsev, His Life and Thought;* CBA; Clarkson, *A History of Russia;* Crotty, *Assassination and the Political Order;* Dallin, *A Documentary History of Communism;* Dmytryshyn, *Imperial Russia, A Source Book, 1700-1917;* Ellison, *History of Russia;* Emmons, *The Russian Landed Gentry and the Peasant Emancipation of 1861;* Florinsky, *Russia: A History and an Interpretation;* Footman, *Red Prelude: The Life of the Russian Terrorist Zhelyabov;* Graham, *The Life of Alexander II, Tsar of Russia;* Haimson, *The Russian Marxists and the Origins of Bolshevism;* Hecht, *Russian Radicals Look to America;* Hurwood, *Society and the Assassin;* Hyams, *Killing No Murder;* Johnson, *Famous Assassinations;* Joyneville, *Life of Alexander of Russia;* Karpovich, *Imperial Russia;* Keep, *The Rise of Social Democracy in Russia;* Kirchner, *A History of Russia;* Kluchevski, *A History of Russia;* Kravchinsky, *Underground Russia;* Laferte, *Alexandre II;* Massie, *Nicholas and Alexandra;* Lawrence, *A History of Russia;* Lerroy-Beaulieu, *The Empire of the Tsars;* Mazour, *Russia, Tsarist and Communist;* Mendel, *Dilemmas of Progress in Tsarist Russia: Legal Marxism and Legal Populism;* Miliukov, *History of Russia, Reforms, Reactions, Revolutions* (Vol III); ____, *Outlines of Russian Culture;* Mirskii, *Russia, A Social History;* Mosse, *Alexander II and the Modernization of Russia;* Nechkina, *Russia in the Nineteenth Century;*

Paleologue, *The Tragic Romance of Alexander II*; Pares, *The Fall of the Russian Monarchy, A Study of the Evidence*; ___, *A History of Russia*; Platonov, *History of Russia*; Pokrovskii, *History of Russia*; Pushkarev, *The Emergence of Modern Russia, 1801-1917*; Riasanovsky, *A History of Russia*; Robinson, *Rural Russia Under the Old Regime: A History of the Landlord-Peasant World and a Prologue to the Peasant Revolution of 1917*; Rowan, *Secret Service, 33 Centuries of Espionage*; Seton-Watson, *The Russian Empire, 1801-1917*; Spector, *Introduction to Russian History and Culture*; Stepniak, *Underground Russia*; Sumner, *A Short History of Russia*; Tompkins, *Russia Through the Ages*; Venturi, *Roots of Revolution*; Vernadsky, *A History of Russia*; Vucinich, *The Peasant in Nineteenth Century Russia*; Wallace, *Russia*; Walsh, *The Fall of the Russian Empire*; Walsh, *Russia and the Soviet Union*; Williams, *Heyday for Assassins*; Wolfe, *Three Who Made a Revolution*; Wren, *The Course of Russian History*; Yarmolinsky, *Road to Revolution: A Century of Russian Radicalism*; Zilliacus, *The Russian Revolutionary Movement*.

Alexander, Frank, 1954- , and **Alexander, Harald**, 1931- , Canary Is., mur. The Alexanders, a reclusive German family, were religious fanatics who believed that only a select few of their religious cult were free of Satan's control and that all others were instruments of the Devil to be purged by violence if the "chosen one" of their cult so decreed. This is exactly what happened to the Alexanders in 1970 when 16-year-old Frank Alexander decided that his mother and sisters were possessed of the Devil and had to be murdered. A horrific slaughter followed in which Frank and his equally zealous father Harald destroyed their loved ones in the name of God. Their grisly acts they later excused as part of their religious beliefs.

The Alexanders had originated in Dresden and later moved to Hamburg where Harald Alexander became the ardent disciple of George Riehle, a religious zealot who was, in turn, the self-designated leader of the Lorber Society. Jacob Lorber (1800-64) had founded this religious group in the early part of the nineteenth century, a severe spiritual organization that taught unflinching self-denial and upheld the beliefs that all non-members were basically evil. Riehle became a member of this small sect, which never numbered more than a few hundred members through the decades, and sometime in the 1930s, Riehle came to believe that he was the Prophet of God. Alexander met Riehle in Hamburg when the old man was dying and nursed him through his last days. When Riehle died, Alexander announced to his wife that he had inherited the mantle of the Lorber Society leadership. Dagmar Alexander, equally possessed of her husband's single-minded beliefs, accepted him in his self-appointed role.

When their son Frank was born, Harald Alexander told his wife that their son was now the Prophet of God and that his every whim had to be observed and obeyed. As the boy grew up he was served by his family members—his older sister Marina, his younger twin sisters Sabine and Petra, and his parents—as if he were a potentate. They responded to his every whim, until Frank Alexander dictated their every movement. The boy, when reaching his teens, decided that he could never "pollute" himself with the bodies of women outside of their small sect. He informed his father that he would have sex with his mother and older sister and such incestuous relations became commonplace within the Alexander household, the father not only agreeing to such practices but encouraging his son to have sex with his wife and daughters at any time, often joining with Frank as they both assaulted Dagmar Alexander or the older sister, Marina. The women accepted their roles as sex objects in the belief that they were serving the Prophet of God, Frank Alexander.

Such bizarre practices soon brought them to the attention of the the Hamburg police, especially when the younger sisters began to talk about them to the few friends they had. To avoid police investigation into their activities, the Alexanders moved to a reclusive society, one far apart from the rest of the world—the Canary Islands—relocating to a small apartment at 37 Calle Jesus Nazareno in Santa Cruz, the capital of Tenerife.

Neighbors soon noted that the family remained aloof and its members seldom ventured out of the apartment. Harald Alexan-

der was forever playing a small organ that had been left to him by George Riehle. For ten months the family occupied the small flat without incident, the girls and Frank supporting the family with low-paying jobs—the girls working as domestics and Frank as a shipping clerk, though he kept irregular hours.

Then, on Dec. 22, 1970, Harald and Frank Alexander appeared in the villa occupied by Dr. Walter Trenkler, asking to see 15-year-old Sabine Alexander. Trenkler found the girl in the kitchen preparing a meal for the family and told her that her father and brother were on the patio waiting to see her. She went to them and Trenkler, to his amazement and shock, heard Harald Alexander say to his daughter, "Sabine, dear, we wanted you to know at once that Frank and I have just finished killing your mother and your sisters."

Religious zealots, Frank and Harald Alexander, at their mental hearing; they had slaughtered family members because they were "unclean."

The girl took her father's hand and put it to her cheek and replied, "I'm sure you've done what you thought necessary."

Dr. Trenkler stood in shock for a moment, staring at the Alexanders. Harald Alexander caught Trenkler's stare and said matter-of-factly, "Ah, you've overheard. We've killed my wife and other daughters. It was the hour of killing." The horrified physician then looked over the father and son carefully. What he originally thought was mud and dirt on their clothes, the result of laboring he imagined, was not what covered them from head to foot. It was human blood, gore that smeared their clothes and faces and hands, dried and caking in the hot sun of the courtyard where they stood.

Even more frightening was the conduct of the Alexanders. There was nothing secretive or sinister about them. They were calm and reported their gruesome acts as if nothing was amiss, that the killings they had just announced were perfectly acceptable. Trenkler asked the Alexanders to wait. He raced into the villa and called the police.

Officers quickly arrived and took the Alexanders into custody while Detective Inspector Juan Hernandez and Detective Sergeant Manuel Perera went to the Alexander flat, accompanied by a police physician, and forced open the door. They stepped into a place of carnage; all of the dishes, clothing, papers, including passports and family documents, had been torn to pieces. Everything was in shreds. The apartment was coated with blood–ceilings, walls, floors. In the middle of the living room floor were the mutilated bodies of the two daughters, 18-year-old Marina, and 15-year-old Petra. Their breasts and private parts had been hacked away and nailed to one of the walls. The older girl had been disemboweled. In the bedroom was found the remains of 39-year-old Dagmar Alexander, also horribly mutilated, her breasts and privates also hacked away. Her heart had been cut out, bound on a cord and this was nailed to the wall. The place was a grisly slaughterhouse running blood, a sight so overwhelming that even the hardened officers grew sick to their stomachs.

The Alexanders, at the local police station, freely admitted the gruesome murders. Frank Alexander, called "The Prophet" by his father, related how he was in the bedroom when Dagmar entered it. "I saw that Mother was looking at me and I had the feeling that it was not permitted for her to look at me in this manner. I therefore took the clotheshanger and struck her over the head. After I struck her several times she fell over and lost consciousness. Father had gone to the living room to play the organ and I also went there. First I struck Marina on the head with the hanger, and after she lost consciousness, I struck Petra. Father continued to play the organ and praise Jesus, but when I began to remove the offending parts, he came to help me." Harald Alexander supported every heinous detail of his son's statements, saying that the sex organs of his wife and daughters were "offending parts," and had to be removed, adding that the women in the household had expected the "hour of killing" at any time, that the family had discussed this "holy time" and its eventuality and that the women accepted their role as human sacrifice for The Prophet, Frank Alexander. Both Frank and Harald Alexander then stated that they felt no guilt, that this was all part of their religious beliefs, that women were unclean and had to be purified by killing. They claimed that their victims had been released into heaven through their murders and they even celebrated their grisly acts by playing the organ, both taking turns, and singing hymns after slaughtering the females of their household.

Psychiatrists examined the father and son and concluded that they were both unfit to stand trial. Both were committed to an asylum for the criminally insane where they presently reside, neither, at last report, responding to any kind of treatment and both convinced, still, that the slaughter of their family members was a purification act in keeping with their religious beliefs. Both men still believe that they are being persecuted for their beliefs and neither has expressed one thought of guilt. Harald Alexander continues to address his son Frank as "The Prophet." Sabine Alexander, the surviving female member of the family, begged authorities to send her to the asylum with her brother and father but this was rejected. She was sent to a convent where she still resides, refusing to live in the outside world. REF.: CBA.

Alexander, George Forest, 1882-1948, U.S., jur. Appointed as federal judge to the Alabama Territory District Court three times by President Franklin D. Roosevelt in 1934, 1938, and 1942. He served as U.S. marshal from 1917-21 and as chairman of the Commission on Federal Relations of the Western Parole and Probation Association from 1936-38. REF.: CBA.

Alexander, Lee, 1928- , U.S., extor.-polit. corr. Alexander was the highly visible and well-respected mayor of Syracuse, N.Y., until 1988 when he was sentenced to serve ten years in prison for extortion. He had received national prominence in the 1970s when he took up the cause to save the nation's cities. During his sixteen-year political career, this fallen mayor had received accolades from his peers who six times elected him to serve as president of the National Conference of Democratic Mayors and once as president of the U.S. Conference of Mayors.

Alexander was indicted on July 16, 1987, after a special grand jury investigation into a scandal of political corruption and misuse of campaign funds that shocked the city. On Mar. 24, 1988, Federal District Court Judge Thomas J. McAvoy handed Alexander a ten-year sentence and ordered $100,000 paid in restitution to the city of Syracuse for his involvement in racketeering, conspiracy to obstruct a government investigation, and tax evasion. Alexander explained that his crimes began innocently as a means of raising campaign contributions, but that he began using the

money for private purposes when his political activities started to deplete his family's assets, "robbing them of their future security." McAvoy also sentenced seven other men involved in Mayor Alexander's kickback scandal. REF.: CBA.

Alexandra, Empress of Russia, See: Nicholas II.

Al Fatah, See: Arafat, Yasir.

Alfonso of Aragon, d.1500, Ital., assass. Alfonso of Aragon, son of Alfonso II, King of Naples, was violently murdered by an assassin on July 15, 1500, his dramatic death occurring during a Papal celebration at St. Peter's Basilica. It was believed that a group of mercenaries was sent, probably by Cesare Borgia, to assassinate Alfonso, who stumbled into the large crowd gathered before the Pope clinging to an open wound in his bloody chest. Alfonso collapsed at the feet of the pontiff and was immediately taken into the church to a room behind the Pope's chambers. His wife and sister tended his wounds during the evening and believed that he would recover. The following morning, Alfonso was found dead, strangled with a rope.

REF.: CBA; Thompson, *Poison and Poisoners.*

Alford, William, prom. 1899, U.S., Case of, mur. Alford was a transplanted southerner living in Los Angeles, Calif., in 1898 when he met prominent lawyer Jay E. Hunter, whom he would later be tried for murdering. Hunter hired Alford to repair some plumbing in his home, and Alford, described as an honest man and a hard worker, accepted the job. Upon finishing, he presented Hunter with a bill of $102 for his services, but Hunter refused to pay.

After several attempts by Alford to collect, he sued Hunter, and the judge ordered Hunter to pay the handyman for his work. Hunter, who failed to show up in court for the trial, denying that he had ever employed Alford, still refused, so Alford devised a smear campaign to ruin Hunter's image in the community. He quickly had several handbills printed stating, "Jay E. Hunter Does Not Pay His Debts." Alford intended to spread the handbills throughout Los Angeles, but first would show one to Hunter in a final attempt to collect from him.

Outside Hunter's plush law office, the two men quarreled loudly. The argument became violent, and a shot was fired. When Hunter's colleagues arrived, they saw Alford holding a smoking pistol standing over the bleeding body of Hunter on the floor, Hunter's walking cane in pieces. Hunter died two days later of peritonitis, an infection caused by the bullet wound. Alford was immediately charged with first-degree murder, and the city's leading citizens hired former law professor Stephen M. White to prosecute him. Earl Rogers, one of White's former students, volunteered to represent Alford who was unable to secure counsel.

The dramatic trial began in 1899 and continued over several days. The battle pitted student against teacher, and both were determined to win. Each side paraded a succession of witnesses whose testimony supported the counselors' arguments. Rogers maintained that Hunter repeatedly struck Alford with his cane before the handyman fell to the floor, cowering below the enraged attorney. Fearing for his life, Alford pulled out a gun and shot Hunter who was bent over beating him with the half of his cane that he still held in his hand, the other half having broken off and rolled across the floor. To support this case of self-defense, Rogers displayed the intestines of the dead man as evidence.

Shock rippled through the courtroom when Hunter's internal organs were brought in. Medical testimony on them proved that the bullet shot from Alford's gun was fired upward at Hunter, entered his body below the naval, and traveled down through the intestines. The bullet would not have had the same trajectory had it been fired as the prosecution maintained. A few minutes later, the jury returned a verdict of Not Guilty. William Alford was cleared of all charges and Earl Rogers had beaten his mentor.

REF.: CBA; Wolf, *Fallen Angels.*

Alfred, Duke of Edinburgh, prom. 1868, Aus., (attempt.) assass. The attempted assassination of Alfred, Duke of Edinburgh, on Mar. 12, 1868, was the first assassination attempt in the history of the colony. The murder attempt occurred in the Sydney suburb of Clontarf where an Irishman named Mr. O'Farrell shot Alfredin the back. The Duke lived, and O'Farrell was subsequently executed for the crime.

REF.: *CBA*; Paine, *The Assassins' World*.

Alger, Cyrus, 1781-1856, U.S., firearms designer. Inventor who improved gun barrel of the rifle. REF.: *CBA*.

Ali (Ali ibn Abi Talib), c.600-61, Islamic empire, caliph, assass. Son-in-law of Muhammad. He became one of Muhammad's first converts and later, the fourth caliph, reigning as spiritual leader of Islam from 656 until his assassination by members of the Kharijite sect at Kufa. REF.: *CBA*.

Ali (Ali Pasha AKA: The Lion of Janina), 1741-1822, Turk., pasha, assass. Pasha of Janina from 1788, he came to power through the use of murder. He was assassinated on order of Sultan Mahmud II. REF.: *CBA*.

Aliwoli, Jamaljah, c.1936- , U.S., attempt. mur. On Mar. 29, 1988, Aliwoli led Chicago police on a chase that ended with three officers severely wounded and a 44-year-old mother immortalized as a heroine. While on routine patrol, officers Daniel B. Duffy and Gregory F. Matura noticed a taxicab driving erratically along a South Side street. They pulled the vehicle over, and the 52-year-old driver, Aliwoli, stepped out of the cab and walked away from the vehicle, leaving two puzzled passengers inside. When Duffy and Matura attempted to detain him, he pulled a .357 Magnum handgun from beneath his coat and fired at the rookie officers. The terrified passengers fled the cab as officer Duffy slumped to the ground. Matura, his hand wounded in an attempt to grab the gun from Aliwoli, squeezed off twelve rounds before ducking into an alley to reload. Aliwoli shot the helpless Duffy once again and turned in search of Matura.

As the cab driver stalked the policeman, a 44-year-old mother, Anne Claxton, stopped her car to assist Duffy, who had crawled to the security of a van parked nearby. Claxton stood between Aliwoli, holding his big gun, blocking Duffy from his view. Aliwoli asked Claxton where Duffy had gone. Told that she did not know, Aliwoli jumped back into his cab. Claxton, a black woman, had just saved Duffy, a white policeman, from imminent death, and she also succeeded, however briefly, in breaking the color barrier in this often prejudiced city.

As the cab sped off, police in squad cars pursued. They dodged bullets fired at them from the cab, and a third policeman, Dennis R. Mertz was wounded. The chase ended when Aliwoli crashed into an apartment building several blocks from where Duffy lay bleeding on the street. After a final gun battle, police took Aliwoli into custody. They later learned that during the 1970s he had served a six-year prison sentence for the attempted murder of two police officers.

Aliwoli was convicted in 1989 of three counts of attempted murder. The ex-convict received a sixty-year sentence for the attempted murder of officer Duffy and two 30-year sentences for the attempted murders of officers Matura and Mertz. Aliwoli, currently serving his sentences at Stateville Penitentiary in Joliet, Ill., is appealing the decision. REF.: *CBA*.

Allaway, Edward Charles, 1939- , Case of, U.S., mur. Armed with a .22-caliber semiautomatic rifle purchased a week earlier at a K-Mart, Edward Allaway entered the library building of California State University at Fullerton one day in July 1976. He searched the basement and ground floor, firing at co-workers whom he accused of "messing around with (his) wife," Bonnie, twenty-two. Allaway killed seven people and wounded two others before police subdued him.

Allaway who worked as a janitor at the library, was unable to cope with his wife's decision to end the marriage. He was arraigned on seven counts of murder at the Orange County Courthouse in Santa Ana.

The prosecutor asked for the death penalty, and in the subsequent trial Allaway was found Guilty of six counts of first-degree murder, one count of second-degree murder, and two counts of assault with a deadly weapon. However, the jury could not decide whether Edward Allaway was sane at the time of the shootings.

Their deadlock threw the case into the hands of the judge, who declared him Not Guilty by reason of insanity. Allaway was committed to the Atascadero State Hospital, where he awaits further psychiatric review. REF.: *CBA*.

Allaway, Thomas Henry, 1886-1922, Brit., mur. Allaway was an avaricious chauffeur for a Mr. Sutton in Bournemouth, a thoroughly unscrupulous character who chiseled his employer out of every dime he could manage. On one occasion, Allaway was told to purchase four new tires for Sutton's green-gray limousine. He purchased three new Dunlop-Magnums and one used tire, a Michelin. This bit of niggardly cheating was to be the scheming chauffeur's undoing, one that eventually helped to send him to the gallows. In addition to defrauding his employer, Allaway was a secret sex pervert who preyed upon women seeking work in the advertising columns of the London newspapers. He read one advertisement placed by Irene Wilkins, the unmarried daughter of a London lawyer and a cook by profession, who

Thomas Allaway enticed Irene Wilkins to her murder through misspelled telegrams.

lived in Streatham. She placed an ad in the Dec. 22, 1921, edition of the *Morning Post*, and received the same day a telegram with misspellings which asked her to take a train to Bournemouth where she would be picked up by limousine and taken to the estate of her new employer, who signed the telegram "Wood." Wilkins wired back to the postal station in Bournemouth that she would arrive on the 4:30 p.m. train.

The body of Irene Wilkins was discovered the next day outside of Bournemouth. She had been killed by heavy blows to her head with what may have been a hammer. Police found her body lying in a field with her clothes disarranged. A later examination revealed that she had not been raped and it was speculated that the killer, who had taken none of the woman's little money and small valuables, intended only to rape her but was probably frightened off when she put up a struggle and killed her instead, then fled.

On the road near the field, officers found tire tracks which bore the discernable tread marks of the distinctive Dunlop-Magnums. They began to check all cars with these tires in the area. When news of the murder broke, several persons came forward to give information to the police. Frank Humphris had been on the train to Bournemouth and had noticed Wilkens alight and get into the green-gray limousine. He informed police but nothing was done with his information. He later saw the car again in Bournemouth and wrote down the license plate and passed this on to police but, again, nothing was done with this helpful data. A month later, the post office clerk who had taken the telegrams from the killer went to the police with an identification of the man. He later followed the sender home, giving the address to the police as well. Still, officers did not follow up on this information.

Then Thomas Allaway stole his employer's checkbook and forged several checks, fleeing the area. He was traced to Reading and arrested on Apr. 27, 1922, for forgery. Now the police acted on the information provided by Humphris and the postal clerk, who identified Allaway as the man who had sent several telegrams to women in an apparent attempt to lure them to Bournemouth. The handwriting on the telegram sent to Irene Wilkins by Allaway was matched to the checks he forged, along with other writings and, by then, the police had matched the tire tracks near the murder site to the Dunlop-Mangnums on the car Allaway was driving. Allaway's consistent misspellings of certain words were also to damn his case, as these, appearing in many of his handwriting samples, were matched to the murder telegram. He was tried for murdering Irene Wilkins at Winchester in July 1922 before Justice Horace Avory and prosecuted by Thomas Inskip. Although the defense counsel attempted to prove an alibi for the time of the murder, the weight of evidence seemed overwhelming to the jury, which found Allaway guilty after an hour's deliberation.

Asked if he had anything to say as he stood in the dock and awaited the sentence of the court, Allaway replied, "I am innocent of the crime, absolutely." Allaway waited until all hope for reprieve was gone before he confessed to having murdered Irene Wilkins, but he gave no motive which was obviously rape. Allaway was untroubled as he awaited his execution, sleeping soundly in his cell and eating all of his meals. He put on ten pounds before going to the hangman at Winchester Prison on Aug. 19, 1922. John Ellis, the executioner, who was normally quite professional in his work, botched the job so that when Allaway shot downward into the pit, the misapplied rope failed to break his neck and he thrashed about for some minutes as he slowly strangled to death. At a later inquest, the prison physician was asked if Allaway's death had been instantaneous and he replied with classic understatement, "Almost."

REF.: Atholl, *Shadow of the Gallows;* Brock, *A Casebook of Crime;* Brookes, *Murder in Fact and Fiction;* Butler, *Murderer's England; CBA;* Ellis, *Blackmailers and Co.;* Firmin, *Crime Man;* Goodman, *Posts-Mortem, The Correspondence of Murder;* Gribble, *Clues That Spelled Guilty;* Hoskins, *The Almost Escaped;* Humphreys, *Seven Murderers;* Jackson, *Mr. Justice Avory;* Lang, *Mr. Justice Avory;* Laurence, *Extraordinary Crimes;* Logan, *Rope, Knife and Chair;* O'Donnell, *The Trials of Mr. Justice Avory;* Shew, *A Second Companion to Murder;* Shore, *Crime and Its Detection;* Wilson, *Encyclopedia of Murder;* Woodland, *Assize Pageant.*

Allee, Alfred Y., 1855-96, U.S., law enfor. off. Allee, born in DeWitt County, Texas, was appointed deputy sheriff of Karnes County, Texas, in 1882 and in that year he reportedly shot a robbery suspect but was later charged with murder. Some claimed that Allee was merely settling an old score. He was acquitted.

Allee was made deputy sheriff of Frio County, Texas, and a short time later he began arguing with another deputy named Rhodes about who was faster on the draw. Both men drew their weapons and Allee, firing two six-guns, pumped eight bullets into Rhodes, four finding the victim's heart. Amazingly, Allee was again acquitted of murder, some friendly witnesses insisting that Rhodes drew first.

Much was said of Allee's ability to shoot down prisoners already cowed and victims unprepared for his lightning temper and fast draw, but the lawman proved his mettle in September 1888, when he was

Western lawman Alfred Allee seldom took prisoners.

assigned to track down the wild, vicious train- and bank-robber Brack Cornett. The outlaw had evaded a posse of Texas Rangers and was heading for Arizona when he was intercepted by Allee, who had trailed him across the prairie. In a pitched gun battle, both men raced their horses toward each other. Using two guns, they blazed away at each other as they rode forward. Allee's aim was good and Cornett was shot dead from the saddle.

Allee's temper was short and his hatred for blacks pronounced. Once, when boarding a train, it was alleged, a black porter shoved him back down the stairs when he ordered the porter out of his way. Allee fell backward, grabbed a rail outside the sleeping car to balance himself, and then jerked himself back up the stairs; a pistol in his hand barked once and sent a bullet into the porter's

heart. He was quickly acquitted in a trial where statements were made about blacks who "don't know their place." The explosive peace officer escaped death many times, but his own violent past caught up with him in Laredo, Texas, on Aug. 19, 1896, when he was stabbed in a barroom brawl, dying almost instantly. See: **Cornett, Brack.**

REF.: Bartholomew, *The Biographical Album of Western Gunfighters; CBA;* Stephens, *Tribute to a Ranger, Captain Y Allee.*

Allen, Brenda, b.c.1913- , U.S., pros. Allen was a Los Angeles madame who for years had operated one of the city's swankiest brothels. Her career ended when a vice squad began an investigation into her business, unaware that it would expose the department's own corruption and bring about the downfall of several officers, including the chief of police. Leading the investigation was Sergeant Charles Stoker who bugged telephone wires in Allen's brothel and allegedly overheard incriminating conversations between Allen and another member of the vice squad, Sergeant Elmer Jackson. Stoker heard Jackson call in to work from the brothel, and later listened as Jackson apologized to Allen for a recent raid. The whorehouse was immediately raided again. Convicted of prostitution and sentenced to prison, Allen won temporary release in 1949 to testify to a grand jury on alleged police corruption.

Allen told the special court that since opening her business, she had been paying for police protection with weekly bribes to Jackson and Stoker. Both officers denied her charge, but were transferred out of the city, along with six others. Shortly thereafter, Police Chief C.B. Horrall abruptly retired. REF.: *CBA.*

Allen, Charles (AKA: **Big Time Charlie**), prom. 1910s, U.S., pros. Allen had, by his own boasting, great adventures in the Alaskan gold strikes and in Mexico, riding and scouting for Pancho Villa in his wars against dictators Diaz and Huerta. He appeared in the Denver area about 1916 and soon became rich by managing hundreds of whores as a master pimp. His method was to addict young girls to heroin and opium and then place them in the lowly cribs and bordellos he owned, paying them slave wages which were mostly in the form of dope. Within a period of four years, it was estimated that Allen accumulated more than $1 million from his prostitution empire, at least half of this paid to local authorities who allowed him to operate without interference. Prostitution was one thing, according to the liberal-minded officials of Denver, but hard drugs could not be tolerated, and when Allen made moves to begin wholesale distribution of drugs throughout the community, police cracked down on him. His home was raided in 1919 and large quantities of heroin and opium were seized. He was sent to Leavenworth to serve five years for illegal drug trafficking, which smashed his prostitution racket.

REF.: *CBA;* Nash, *Almanac of World Crime.*

Allen, Edward H.B., 1908- , Case of, U.S., mur. The 1931 murder of Francis A. Donaldson III rocked Philadelphia's social elite and splintered the family of accused murderer Allen with the release of violent resentment and charges of sexual impropriety. On the evening of Nov. 9, 1931, 23-year-old Allen shot Donaldson —his sister's lover—in what appeared to be an act of vengeance against a man he had long-standing resentment toward, a man who he believed had seduced his 18-year-old sister.

Allen's six-day trial began on Feb 1, 1932. In his defense, Allen maintained that he had murdered Donaldson in self-defense even though he had driven six miles to retrieve the shotgun used in the crime. The prosecution introduced Allen's confession to police officers on the night of the murder and produced evidence of his hatred for his childhood acquaintance. On Feb. 6, the ten-man, two-woman jury acquitted Allen of willful homicide, eliciting rousing applause from courtroom spectators. REF.: *CBA.*

Allen, Elisha Hunt, 1804-83, U.S., lawyer-polit. Admitted to the Massachusetts Bar in 1826, Allen later moved to Maine and served in state House of Representatives from 1835-1940. He also served in the U.S. House of Representatives from 1841-43 and in the Massachusetts House of Representatives in 1849. He was U.S. Consul to Hawaii from 1850-57 and chancellor and chief justice of Hawaii from 1857-76. He was Hawaiian minister in Washington D.C. from 1876 until his death i 1883. REF.: *CBA*.

Allen, Florence Ellinwood, 1884-1966, U.S., jur. Began the first of two terms on the Ohio Supreme Court in 1922, becoming the first woman to be a state supreme court justice. She was appointed to the Sixth Circuit District Court by President Franklin D. Roosevelt in 1934. REF.: *CBA*.

Allen, Floyd, d.1913, U.S., mur. The Allens of Carroll County, Va., had long been a potent force in local politics, a huge clan whose history stretched back to the American Revolution. Family members owned large tracts of land, and since the American Civil War the Allens were considered to be the leading citizens of the area. They possessed a fierce pride in their history and their place in the community, no more so than Floyd Allen, who became the patriarch of the clan by the turn of the century. A Democrat, Allen boasted that no Republican ever bested him at the ballot box or with fists. He had held a number of public offices and felt that his family prestige and his own self-inflated image put him above the law. Allen reveled in his political clout. On one occasion, in 1904, after he had been sentenced to jail for one hour after striking a lawman, Allen refused to enter a cell, sending a runner to the governor, who immediately issued a pardon. He was forever knocking down deputy sheriffs and other officials who disagreed with his blunt, brutal tactics, a violent habit that blossomed into mass murder in 1912.

It was Allen's intractable conviction that not only was *he* above the law but so too were all of his relatives. Two of his nephews, the fatherless Edwards boys, got into a bloody fight at school and, after seriously injuring several other students, fled. A small posse made up of Allen enemies tracked the boys to North Carolina and arrested them, bringing them back into Virginia. They were met by Floyd Allen and several of his more hardened back-county relatives, gun toters all, who ordered the posse members to release the Edwards boys, stating that the lawmen had no right to make arrests across the state line which was, in fact, the truth. The posse members hurled insults at the Allens and a battle ensued where guns were fired and punches were thrown. Although no one was killed, several men on both sides were badly injured. Floyd Allen was indicted for assault and battery and held for trial at the Carroll County Courthouse in Hillsville, Va.

There were three trials, the last ending on Mar. 13, 1912. In the last trial, since Allen's influence was so broad, jurors from faraway counties were brought in to judge the case. On Mar. 14, 1912, Floyd Allen was to hear the verdict of the jury. He took no chances. Allen summoned the most truculent of his clan members to pack the courtroom the following day and scores of Allens filed into the court, many with pistols hidden inside their coats and pants pockets. Allen himself was not searched since he was thought too important a person to be treated as a common criminal. Inside of Allen's large sweater were two pistols. He sat grim-faced at the defendant's table with his attorney, Judge Bolen, a former local magistrate who had battled hard for Allen's vindication. On the bench was Judge Thornton L. Massie. At the prosecution table sat state's attorney Commonwealth Foster, an avowed enemy of the Allen clan, as was Sheriff Webb and most of his deputies who ringed the courtroom. The jury foreman, C.L. Howell, was asked for the verdict and Howell passed the written verdict to Judge Massie who read it aloud without emotion, "Guilty as charged in the indictment—one year in the penitentiary."

Allen stiffened in his chair, gripping the armrests so tightly that his knuckles showed white. His attorney, Judge Bolen, reached over to him and patted him on the shoulder, saying, "Take it easy, Floyd. There are better days ahead."

"I'm going to take it calm," Allen replied in a low voice as he stared at clerk Goad who handed the judge's order to the sheriff. "I just hate it on account of my two boys," the clan chief added.

"The sheriff will take charge of the prisoner," Judge Massie ordered. Sheriff Webb and several deputies began to approach Allen, who then stood up and fumbled with the buttons of his sweater.

"Gentlemen," Floyd Allen solemnly announced, "I don't aim to go." He then whipped out two pistols and the rest of the Allen clan produced guns. The firing commenced, filling the entire courtroom with clouds of black smoke. Panic seized the large crowd which bolted *en masse* for the doorway. The sheriff and his deputies returned fire, blasting away at Floyd Allen, Sidna Allen, and Floyd's son Claude, who fired their weapons resolutely at the deputies, the jury, and the judge. Allen took special aim at the prosecuting attorney, Commonwealth Foster, who had expected trouble and had armed himself. Foster, holding up a heavy law book in front of his face, traded shots with Floyd Allen as he retreated to a door leading to back rooms.

The crowd was in a frenzy to escape the bloody shootout. People knocked each other down and trampled upon one another. Chairs and benches crashed backward as the spectators scurried, scrambled, clawed their way toward the exits. Several fell, wounded in the murderous crossfire. Little Bettie Ayers, an Allen witness, ran screaming toward an exit, yelling, "Let me out of here!" A bullet slapped into her back, knocking her down. Judge Massie had watched in horror as his courtroom was turned into a slaughter pen. He suddenly slumped forward on the bench, blood spreading out in front of him from a chest wound. Attorney Foster was struck several times by bullets as he emptied his guns in the direction of Floyd Allen, as did Deputy Queensberry who fired round after round from his .25-caliber pistol from the jury room doorway. Allen reeled backward, hit in the thigh, so that he crashed through the railing which broke and he fell on top of his lawyer, Judge Bolen. Cried Bolen, "For God's sake, get off me before they kill me shooting at you!" Allen got to his feet and then raced toward an exit. He turned to fire at clerk Goad who was shooting at him. Sidna and Claude Allen fired at the clerk who was hit by eleven bullets, one going into his open mouth, chipping a tooth and smashing out of the back of his neck. Goad, however, continued to fire back.

"I'm hit bad," Floyd Allen cried out to Sidna Allen, taking a gun from him since he was out of bullets and firing as he ran from the courtroom and down the steps to his horse which was tied up to a nearby railing. Before he could mount, however, Allen stepped on a rock and broke that part of his leg which had already been splintered by a bullet. The intense pain caused him to beg relatives to help him mount his horse. Once in the saddle, Floyd Allen briefly fainted and then, coming to, told relatives to bring a carriage. He was put into a carriage and taken down the street to Burnett's stable where he was removed and placed on the ground; his relatives believed Allen was dying. It began to rain. At the courthouse, clerk Goad, bleeding from his many wounds, hid behind one of the towering pillars of the building and traded shots with Sidna Allen who was hiding behind another.

Inside the courtroom, Judge Massie was dying. With his last breath he told juror Daniel Thomas, "Sidna Allen shot me...Give me a drink...Tell my wife..." By the time Judge Bolen reached him Massie was dead. Inside the juror's room, on a couch where he had collapsed, was Attorney Foster. He had been hit in the head and blood drenched the floor where he was lying. His wife rushed to the room just as he let the automatic in his hand fall to the floor. He was dead. When they lifted his large body to take it to the morgue, dozens of bullets spilled from his pockets. Commonwealth Foster had expected a battle with the Allens and he had gotten it. Sheriff Webb was also dead, his body riddled with bullets; in death he clenched between his teeth a toothpick. Little Bettie Ayers was mortally wounded. She died the next day, as did a juror named Fowler. Five were dead or dying in the courthouse and sixteen others were wounded, many of these just barely clinging to life until medical help was summoned and saved their lives.

The Allen clan fled as the courthouse was surrounded by scores of deputies who had been appointed in just this eventuality. A dozen deputies, guns drawn, then marched down the street to Burnett's stable where Floyd Allen lay in the rain, blood coating his pants. Staring down at his father was Victor Allen, who had taken no part in the shoot out. "This thing hurts me," Victor told his father. "I've always tried to do right."

"I made my peace with my God about seven years gone," Floyd Allen said, looking up at his son, "and methinks I see him now."

Victor Allen shook his head and replied, "No–it's the devil that you see."

The Allens were rounded up and both Floyd Allen and his son Claude were convicted of murder and were executed in 1913, both going to the electric chair—first the father, then the son. Sidna Allen was convicted and sentenced to fifteen years but was pardoned in 1926 by Governor Harry Byrd. Victor Allen was acquitted.

REF.: Botkin, *A Treasury of Southern Folklore; CBA;* DuBose, *Virginia and the Virginia Country.*

Allen, George E. (AKA: **Dr. Jesse Fairchild Adams**), 1920- , U.S., fraud-impersonation. Allen served as the chief physician of the Tennessee Department of Corrections for thirteen months before investigators learned that he was an imposter. Allen, as Dr. Jesse Fairchild Adams, was hired on Aug. 7, 1978, to head the state's inmate medical program where he treated convicts and supervised a staff of seventy, including six doctors, until an anonymous tip claiming he was not really a doctor began an investigation that led to his arrest in September 1979.

Allen, an aquaintance of the actual Dr. Adams, a retired Navy surgeon, was charged with six counts of practicing medicine without a license. On July 18, 1980, he was convicted and sentenced to one to four years for fraud. Allen served over two and a half years and was released on Feb. 8, 1983. REF.: *CBA.*

Early day New York vice lord John Allen leading his prostitutes in a drunken prayer meeting.

Allen, John, b.1828, U.S., pros. Allen operated from 1850 through 1880 a so-called dance hall that was nothing more than a sprawling whorehouse, one of the most patronized bordellos in New York City and the hub of criminal activities in the notorious Fourth Ward. Raised in upper New York State, John Allen came from wealthy parents, and his three brothers were ministers, two being Presbyterian and the other Baptist. The "way of the cloth" was the career his parents had chosen for him. Allen dutifully attended the Union Theological Seminary for a while, but suddenly quit and, with his young wife, moved into the teeming Fourth Ward where he opened, in 1850, a dance house at 304 Water Street.

The place became the most infamous dive in New York. The dance girls were heavily painted prostitutes, and they not only solicited every man who stepped onto the dance floor with them, but thought nothing of offering their services in a nearby open booth rather than take the trouble to walk upstairs to their miserable cribs. Herbert Asbury describes these energetic harlots, usually twenty in number, as wearing "low black bodices of satin, scarlet skirts and stockings, and red-topped boots with bells affixed to the ankles." The girls would shake these bells wildly to indicate to Allen that a customer had agreed to do more than clod-hop upon the rickety floor. Allen thusly never lost count of the number of men his whores entertained sexually.

Writing for *Packard's Monthly,* Oliver Dyar labeled Allen "the wickedest man in New York," and Allen lived up to the sobriquet with boozy enthusiasm. Alcoholic, Allen was drunk most hours of the day, sobering when the necessity arose to select new prostitutes for his harem, count out his illegal profits, or sermonize his unwholesome employees. (Several girls who worked for Allen were from respectable families, and had been compromised by his swarm of pimps and ensnared into whoredom through blackmail and even threats of murder; one of these unfortunates was the daughter of the lieutenant-governor of a New England state.)

The sanctimonious Allen was addicted to his own kind of peculiar religion as much as he was to booze, and he never lost an opportunity to introduce spiritual matter to his errant workers and patrons. Every day at noon, an hour before he opened his hall, Allen would gather his sirens, bartenders, swampers, pimps, and pickpockets and, standing upon his long bar, read loudly to them from the Bible, furry-tonguing the Scriptures while gesticulating with his arms.

In each upstairs crib, Allen had placed a Bible, and his harlots were expected to read several passages a day, ready to answer his short quizzes on the holy words. Religious newspapers like the *Observer* and the *Independent,* along with hymn books of all kinds, were scattered throughout the dancing, drinking, and fornicating areas. At about 3:00 each morning, Allen would stagger drunkenly through his expansive dive and collect customers and workers alike. He would then lead them in a rousing hymn entitled, "There is Rest for the Weary" (a favorite of the prostitutes).

Squads of policemen on patrol would stand perplexed outside of Allen's at these times, wincing and gritting as their ears were assailed by shriek and scream, giving out in unison:

> There is rest for the weary,
> There is rest for you.
> On the other side of Jordan,
> In the sweet fields of Eden,
> Where the Tree of Life is blooming,
> There is rest for you.

The Reverend A.C. Arnold heard of Allen's hypocritical religious tirades and interpreted the fierce sanctimoniousness of his boarders as a sign that these craven creatures were redeemable. He led a half dozen clerics and dozens of fervent followers into the dive one midnight and held a six-hour revival meeting. Allen, so drunk that he could hardly raise his head from his own bar to protest at the ruination of his business, eventually joined in by blubbering out a few unintelligible psalms.

Several of the girls "got religion" and ran away. Customers, embarrassed, slunk to other bordellos. The religious leaders returned time and again. Allen's trade went to pieces. The reverend always waited until Allen was totally immobilized by drink before asking him for permission to hold one of his meetings. This was promptly at midnight, or shortly thereafter, when the skin trade was most brisk, and Allen invariably, helplessly, muttered his approval. The onslaught of the religious reformers appeared to overwhelm Allen, and his place was shut down for what first appeared to be inexplicable reasons. Some days later, Allen posted a notice on his locked door which read:

THIS DANCE HOUSE IS CLOSED
No gentlemen admitted unless accompanied by
their wives, who wish to employ Magdalenes
as servants.

The following week, regular Sunday services ensued in Allen's dance hall, and the Fourth Ward reeled under the shock of its most wicked denizen embracing the pure ways of the devout. Further, the crowds spilling out from Allen's dive, most being middle-class people coming to gape at a den of iniquity, began to inspect, out of curiosity, the premises of other dives. To the amazement of New Yorkers everywhere, revival and temperance meetings began occurring in other disreputable places, such as Kit Burns' Sportsmen's Hall, and the dives owned by Tommy Hadden and Bill Slocum.

Burns' pit, where dogs were set against one another in to-the-death battles while heavy betting took place, became a popular attraction for the crowds attending religious services. On such occasions, according to the New York *World*, Burns would stand outside and curse the missionaries for not "hurrying up" with their proceedings. The hooligan owner was quoted as saying: "I'm damned if some of the people that come here oughtn't be clubbed. A fellow 'ud think they had never seen a dog-pit before. I must be damned good looking to have so many fine fellows looking at me."

But it was all sham, as the investigative work of the New York *Times* subsequently pointed out. In an angry exposé, the *Times* reported how Allen had neither returned to the faith of his family, nor reformed his ways by some sudden rekindling of religion. He had secretly made a deal with the reformers to rent out his dance hall for a full month, receiving from the clergymen $350 as rent. John Allen's business had fallen off anyway as a result of the religious invasion of his sinful sanctum, and it seemed a logical way for him to recoup his losses. Drunk or not, Allen remained until death a shrewd businessman, accumulating $100,000 in cold cash and five times that much in real estate holdings.

The *Times* informed its readers: "As for the other men's reformation, that is as absolutely a piece of humbuggery as Allen's. Tommy Hadden is playing the pious with the hope of being secured from trial before the court of General Sessions for having recently shanghaied a Brooklynite, and also in consideration of a handsome moneyed arrangement with his employers—similar to that of Allen. Kit Burns' rat pit will be opened for religious services on Monday next; but the public need not be deceived in the matter of his reformation. His motive, like that of the others, is to make money, and, be it known, he is to receive at the rate of $150 per month, for the use of his pit for an hour every day.

"Slocum desired prayers at the Howard Mission on Sunday last, but it is understood that he is not to be lionized because the missionaries are not willing to pay him a high enough rental for his hall. As for the general movement carried on in Water Street, under the false pretense that these men have voluntarily and from purely religious motives, offered their saloons for public worship, and have, themselves, determined to reform, very little more need be said. The daily prayer meetings are nothing more than assemblages of religious people from among the higher grades of society, in what were once low dance halls.

"There is an unusual amount of interest displayed at these meetings and much good, doubtless, has been accomplished thereby, but it is also a fact that there are but a few, and sometimes none, of the wretched women, or ruffianly vicious men, of that neighborhood present. Those classes are not reached at all, and it is false to say that a revival is going on among them. The character of the audiences and the exercises are similar to that of a noon meeting at the Fulton Street Church."

Their quick-money scheme revealed, Allen, Burns, Hadden, and Slocum resumed their prostitution operations with vigor. The Fourth Ward legions of thugs and Jezebels laughed up their collective sleeve, and religious leaders turned elsewhere to save souls.

REF.: Asbury, *Gangs of New York; Asmodeus in New York* (Anon.); Barnes, *The Metropolitan Police;* Brace, *The Dangerous Classes of New York; CBA;* Costello, *Our Police Protectors; Hot Corn* (Anon.); Lewis, *The Apaches of New York;* Moss, *The American Metropolis;* Myers, *History of Tammany Hall;* Parkhurst, *My Forty Years in New York; The Volcano Under the City* (Anon.); Walling, *Recollections of a New York Chief of Police.*

Allen, John Edward, (AKA: the Mad Parson), 1912- , Brit., mur. Allen, twice committed to a mental institution by the time he was twenty-five, brutally murdered 17-month-old Kathleen Diana Lucy Woodward on Oct. 21, 1937. While employed as an assistant chef at the Lamb Hotel in Burford, Oxfordshire, he befriended the Woodward family and often played with the child, whom he had taken for a walk on the day she disappeared. When her body was later found lying beside a road, she had been strangled with a clothes-line. Her hand still clutched the two pennies Allen had given her. Two days later, Allen surrendered to authorities and was charged with murder.

On Nov. 6, 1937, Allen was convicted of the murder and remanded to psychiatric care at the Broadmoor Asylum where he joined an entertainment group—The Broadhumoorists—which performed comedy shows for the inmates. Ten years later, Allen escaped from Broadmoor dressed as a cleric—his Broadhumoorists costume. He was recaptured two years later, but while free he became known in the press as the Mad Parson. On Sept. 18, 1951, Allen, at the age of thirty-nine, was released from the asylum.

REF.: Butler, *Murderers' England; CBA.*

Allen, Joseph, d.1909, U.S., mur. Allen joined with Jesse West in saloon operations and later a booming cattle business throughout Oklahoma, developing a bitter feud with cattle baron A.A. Bobbitt. When Allen and West could not best Bobbitt, they hired a professional killer, Jim Miller, to murder the cattle baron. Bobbitt's riddled body was found on Feb. 26, 1909, and Allen, West, Miller, and another confederate, Berry B. Burrell, who had "spotted" Bobbitt for Miller, were arrested. While awaiting trial in Ada, Okla., Allen imported a prominent criminal attorney, Moman Pruiett, who seldom lost a defense case. (His record later showed that Pruiett won 303 acquittals out of 343 murder cases where he acted as the defense attorney.) The consensus of opinion in Ada had it that the old Texas killer-for-hire and his employers would get off. A mob of more than forty men broke the prisoners from the local jail on Apr. 19, 1909, dragged the four accused men to a nearby livery stable and, after a few words which condemned the conspirators, promptly lynched all four men. Miller, who insisted that he by hanged with his hat on, was undoubtedly the most dangerous killer in Texas, Oklahoma, and New Mexico. He bragged with his last words that he had murdered fifty-one men. The vigilantes who executed this murderous band were never brought to justice. See: **Bobbitt, A.A.; Miller, James B.**

REF.: Bartholomew, *A Biographical Album of Western Gunfighters;* Biles, *The Early History of Ada; CBA;* Mann, *Four Years in the Governor's Mansion in Virginia;* Pruiett, *Momanb Pruiett, Criminal Lawyer;* Shirley, *Shotgun for Hire, The Story of "Deacon" Jim Miller, Killer of Pat Garrett.*

Allen, Kenneth, 1943- , U.S., mur. In December 1978, 24-year-old Allen engaged up to twenty-five Chicago police officers in a gunfight at his South Side apartment which eventually led to his slaying two undercover officers on a Chicago street three months later. Police arrived at Allen's apartment shortly after his girlfriend, Bianca Smith, reported a quarrel between herself and Allen, who would not allow her to remove property from their shared home. Allen held police at bay for nineteen hours with an arsenal of weapons—high-powered magnum revolvers, semi-automatic pistols, and a hand-held M-16 rifle—until his arrest that evening.

Three months later, on Mar. 3, 1979, Chicago plainclothes narcotics officers William P. Bosak and Roger Van Schaik were gunned down in daylight after stopping a car suspected of carrying drugs. Heavily armed men in the car opened fire on the officers as Allen arrived and fired on them from the opposite direction. Witnesses claimed that one wounded officer, bleeding on the ground, pleaded for his life as Allen pumped three more shots into his body. Additional officers responded to the shooting and gave chase to Allen's automobile, which slammed into a Chicago Transit Authority bus and three police cars before coming to a halt. Allen fled and was captured seven blocks away.

Allen was charged with the murder of the officers and held in custody without bond. He later pleaded guilty, explaining in court that the murders were a case of mistaken identity. He was found Guilty and sentenced to death in the Illinois electric chair. In 1980, he filed a plea to the state supreme court requesting that any appeal of his conviction be denied and that he be put to death immediately. No reasons for the plea were given, but the court ruled that every death penalty conviction receives an automatic appeal. REF.: *CBA*.

Allen, Lizzie (Ellen Williams), 1839-96, U.S., pros. Allen appeared in Chicago in 1858, leaving a proper middle-class home in Milwaukee, Wis., with the dedicated intent of becoming the most famous madam in the Midwest. She was attractive, ambitious, and eighteen years old. She became a much-desired inmate of Mother Herrick's posh brothel Prairie Queen and, in 1865, moved to The Senate where she was also much in demand. Allen was so popular that she was allowed to keep more than half of all payments from her high-society customers and this she hoarded until she had enough money to open her own bordello on Wells Street in 1869, a small three-girl establishment that was furnished in high style. The Chicago Fire of 1871 destroyed the place but Allen had saved enough money to erect a two-story brothel on Congress Street which became an institution and gave great competition to the queen of vice, Carrie Watson. Allen maintained between twenty-five and thirty alluring sirens at her establishment, which was tastefully furnished and attracted the carriage trade. Allen would remain at this location for almost twenty years, accumulating a fortune. She specialized in offering young girls; half of her inmates were reported to be under the age of eighteen.

In 1878, Allen met a young clerk while shopping at Marshall Field's Emporium, a handsome, clever fellow named Christopher Columbus Crabb who was then earning $14 a week. Allen took a liking to him and Crabb became her lover. By the mid-1880s, Crabb took to managing Allen's extensive holdings, about ten brothels and many tracts of land and homes she rented on the North Side of Chicago. Allen introduced Crabb to another madam, Mollie Fitch, and he also managed her properties. When Mollie Fitch died, she left $150,000 to Crabb in a will that some believed had been altered by Crabb. Using some of this cash but mostly money put up by Allen, about $150,000, the couple built an imposing mansion of twenty-four rooms on Lake View Avenue, but police prevented them from turning this distinguished address into a whorehouse and the couple simply maintained a residence here, replete with six servants and several liveried carriages. Allen reasoned that if she could not establish the most prestigious brothel on Lake View Avenue, she would build it elsewhere.

To that end, in 1890, she and Crabb invested $125,000 in a new double-front, two-story structure on South Dearborn Street, in the heart of the Red Light district. It was sumptuous and offered the most sophisticated prostitutes in Chicago. Allen called it The House of Mirrors and it became the most famous bordello in the city, its reputation drawing tycoons and social lions from New York, Philadelphia, and New Orleans. For six years, Lizzie Allen reigned at this address, some saying that she had surpassed even the celebrated Carrie Watson in reputation. In 1896, Allen grew ill and decided, after thirty-eight years in prostitution, that she would retire to her mansion and art collection. She leased The House of Mirrors to Effie Hankins and retreated to her mansion. Four years later Hankins would sell the place to two enterprising ladies, Ada and Minna Everleigh, who would turn this bordello into the most luxurious and famous in the world. In March 1896, Allen signed over all her earthly properties to her man Crabb and died on Sept. 2, 1896, leaving Crabb, whom Mayor Carter Harrison called "an imposing rooster," with an enormous fortune, estimated to be between $300,000 and $1 million. Allen was buried in Rosehill Cemetery. Upon her tombstone, carved according to her wishes, was the inscription: "Perpetual Ease." See: **Crabb, Christopher Columbus; Everleigh Sisters; Prairie Queen; The Senate; Watson, Carrie.**

REF.: Asbury, *Gem of the Prairie;* Casey, *Chicago, Medium Rare; CBA;* Currey, *Chicago, Its History and Its Builders;* Dedmon, *Fabulous Chicago;* Drago, *Notorious Ladies of the Frontier;* Flynn, *History of the Chicago Police;* Hamilton, *The Epic of Chicago;* Harrison, *Stormy Years;* Lewis and Smith, *Chicago, The History of Its Reputation;* Nash, *Look for the Woman;* ____, *People to See;* Reckless, *Vice in Chicago;* Stead, *If Christ Came to Chicago;* Steffens, *Shame of the Cities;* Van Every, *Sins of America;* Washburn, *Come Into My Parlor;* Wendt and Kogan, *Lords of the Levee;* Wilson, *Chicago and Its Cesspools of Vice and Infamy;* Zorbaugh, *The Gold Coast and the Slum.*

Allen, Margaret, 1906-49, Brit., mur. The murder of 68-year-old Nancy Ellen Chadwick by Margaret Allen in 1948 was a motiveless and mindless act which still baffles criminologists to this day. Allen, the product of an immense family—she was the twentieth child of twenty-two offsprings—had always denied her own femininity. Everything about her was masculine and she preferred the company of burly male workers in Rawtenstall, Lancashire, England. At an early age, Allen took on jobs that usually went to males. She loaded coal, repaired houses, even became a bus driver. She was fired from this last position for abusing passengers—shoving and cuffing them if they did not take their seats fast enough.

Short and stocky, Allen, in 1935, checked into a hospital and had a "delicate" operation performed, one, she later confided to a friend, which changed her "from a woman to a man." Allen then made no pretense about her turnabout sexual role, cutting her hair short, donning male clothes, drinking with roustabout workers in bars. She had no female friends, except for Mrs. Annie Cook, and this relationship evaporated when Allen, while on vacation with Mrs. Cook, proposed a sexual bout which was promptly rejected by the offended Mrs. Cook.

Margaret Allen murdered an old woman out of whim and went to the gallows.

Allen next invested her savings in the purchase of a delapidated building that once served as Rawtenstall's police headquarters, situated on the town's main street, Bacup Road. To this house Mrs. Nancy Ellen Chadwick, a drifter, came to knock on the door on Aug. 28, 1948, dragging all her earthly belongings in an old sack. Her body was found inside that sack the next day, her head crushed by what police later determined to be a coal hammer, the face coated with ashes.

Detectives had a relatively easy job tracing the victim to Allen since a bloodstained path led directly to Allen's home. Moreover, the suspect went out of her way to encourage Scotland Yard inspectors to arrest her. She dogged their footsteps and stood about, hands thrust into her trousers, staring at them as they inspected the area. At one point, she rushed up to a detective and pulled at his sleeve and pointed to the nearby river. "Look, there's something there!" The object floating in the river was Mrs. Chadwick's knitting bag which officers found empty of the money the victim was alleged to have carried in it.

But still she was not charged. Margaret Allen then barged into the local pub, swilled down several beers, wiped her chin, and bellowed, "I was the last person to see the old woman!" She, like many an arrogant criminal before her, was openly challenging the police to make a case against her. (A similar case where the killer's ego insisted he actually lead the police to his door to challenge the police to make a case against him, was that of the haughty Richard Loeb, of the notorious Leopold and Loeb of Chicago, who thought to commit the perfect murder as an intellectual exercise.)

By late August, however, Scotland Yard sleuths had already gathered enough evidence to convict Allen of the Chadwick murder, matching hairs from the head of the victim to Allen's clothing and discovering in Allen's house several effects of the victim. It only remained for Allen to confess her crime. This she did after inspectors came to her door on Sept. 1, 1948. When formally charged, Margaret Allen smiled and admitted killing the old woman. "I was in a funny mood," she said out of the corner of a crooked smile. "She seemed to insist on coming in (to the house). I just happened to look around and saw a hammer in the kitchen. On the spur of the moment I hit her. She gave me a shout and that seemed to start me off more and I hit her a few times, I don't know how many." She gave no other explanation. Margaret Allen had killed an old woman on a whim.

After a five-hour trial, Allen was found Guilty, despite her counsel's feeble attempt to prove her insane. She was sentenced to death. Her old friend, Mrs. Cook, got together a petition to ask for a commutation but only 162 people in the town of almost 30,000 signed the document. Margaret Allen didn't seem to care. She acted, in her last hours at Strangeways Prison, as if the whole matter was nothing more than an inconvenience. She complained about her cell's lack of creature comforts and when she was brought the last meal she had requested, a plate of scrambled eggs, she kicked it out of the jailer's hands, splattering the food onto the wall of the cell and sneering, "At least no one else will enjoy that meal!" Without a word, Margaret Allen stomped up the stairs of the scaffold on the morning of Jan. 12, 1949, and was hanged on schedule. See: **Leopold, Nathan.**

REF.: Butler, *Murderer's England*; *CBA*; Heppenstall, *The Sex War and Others*; Hibbert, *The Roots of Evil*; Hugget, *Daughters of Cain*; Nash, *Look for the Woman*; O'Donnell, *Should Women Hang?*; Shew, *A Second Companion to Murder*; Wilson, *Encyclopedia of Murder*; ____, *Murderess.*

Allen, Ned (AKA: **"Bull Run"**), prom. c.1890s, U.S., wh. slav. Allen was the proprietor of Hell's Kitchen—one of San Francisco's most notorius brothels—until he was murdered. The flamboyant Allen enslaved as many as forty French and Spanish women at Hell's Kitchen, some as young as fourteen, who, drugged and intoxicated, were forced to perform for the male clientele dressed in the house's "uniform"—red jacket, black stockings, garter, and red slippers. Once drunk, the women would engage customers in sex, and after they had passed out, their bodies would be savagely abused during sexual frenzies that often included more than one man.

Ned Allen's life ended while he drank and caroused at another Barbary Coast hangout, the Clover Club. He started an argument with habitual criminal and pimp Bart Freel, who used a small knife to stab Allen to death. Freel received a ten-year sentence, but rid the city of one of its most notorious villains.

REF.: *CBA*; Drago, *Notorious Ladies of the Frontier.*

Allen, Peggy, Case of, U.S., mur. In August 1968, Peggy Allen, mother of five, was charged with the murder of her alcoholic and abusive husband in their small frame house in rural North Carolina. She told authorites that her husband had gone on a drinking rampage and had smashed furniture throughout the house and threatened to kill her and their children. To protect the children, Allen said she shot her husband in the head with a rifle while he lay on a couch. On the advice of her attorney, Allen pleaded guilty to manslaughter and a trial date was scheduled. After an investigation prompted by a slew of mail in Allen's favor to the governor's office, she won a suspended sentence and was freed on her own recognizance. Her son Bobby, grateful that his mother would not go to prison, thanked her for shooting his father. REF.: *CBA.*

Allen, Peter Anthony, 1943-64, and **Evans, Gwynne Owen (John Robson Welby)**, 1940-64, Brit., mur. Both Allen and Evans were milkmen and thugs who committed small robberies in Liverpool and had, since their teens, been in trouble with police. On the night of Apr. 6-7, 1964, John Alan West, a 53-year-old laundry driver, was attacked by Allen and Evans as he interrupted their robbery of his small house. They stabbed West several times and struck him on the head many times, crushing his skull, before running outside and driving away with Allen's wife in the car. (She had gone along for the ride, not knowing, she later claimed, what the two men were planning.) Police, who had been summoned by a neighbor, found Evans' raincoat and a girl's phone number inside one of its pockets, along with other items that led them to pick up Evans forty-eight hours later.

West's watch was found on Evans, who immediately claimed that Allen had done all the hitting and stabbing and was responsible for West's death. He merely "took a few things." Allen put the blame for the murder on Evans, but admitted that the car the killers had used on the murder night had been stolen in another part of Liverpool. Both men were tried at Manchester Crown Court in June 1964 and little defense could be offered. The only question in the court's mind was who actually did the killing, Allen or Evans. A jury quickly decided that both men were Guilty and they were condemned. The distinction these two thugs held in the annals of crime was not the sordid murder they committed but the fact that they were the last two to hang in England before capital punishment was abolished by a bill originally introduced in Parliament in 1956, one finally passed ten years later where hanging was suspended. Both men were executed on Aug. 13, 1964, but in separate prisons—Allen in Liverpool's Walton Prison, Evans at Strangeways Prison in Manchester.

REF.: *CBA*; Jones, *The Last Two to Hang*; Potter, *The Art of Hanging.*

Allen, Roger, prom. 1737, Case of, Brit., riot. A prohibition act outlawed the sale and distribution of gin in 1736, and met with great opposition from the working classes of London. In January 1737, an angry mob gathered in front of the Thrift Street, Soho home of Sir Thomas de Veil, one of the proponents of the Gin Act, who was harboring a pair of informants. The mob, led by Roger Allen, demanded that de Veil release the men so that they could be dealt with. Fearing for their lives, Sir Thomas refused. The Bow Street Runners arrested Allen and read the Proclamation Against Riots to the throng. At de Veil's insistence, Allen was tried in May 1738. He was acquitted on a plea of insanity and released, to the delight of the cheering mob that had gathered outside the court building.

REF.: Armitage, *Bow Street Runners*; *CBA.*

Allen, Stuart Buckner, 1929-c.1947, Case of, U.S., mur. Stuart Buckner Allen, the adopted son of Reverend James S. Allen, minister at Christ Episcopal Church in St. Joseph, Mo., murdered 59-year-old church sexton, John Frank in April 1947, because he had an urge to kill someone.

On the day of the murder, Frank was working in the basement of the church when 15-year-old Allen asked him for a hammer. With the hammer he beat Frank to death, then picked up an electric drill and bored holes in the corpse's neck, abdomen, and groin. After his arrest, Allen told police that he killed Frank on a whim and that he had had previous urges to kill. It was rumored, though never substantiated, that Allen's parents allowed him to vivisect chickens.

Allen was found Not Guilty by reason of insanity and was sentenced to Missouri State Hospital for the mentally insane in Fulton, Mo., by Judge Duval Smith. He was eventually released from the hospital, though he had escaped several times. Upon his release, he attended Kansas University and died several years later. See: **William Heirens**. REF.: *CBA.*

Allen, William Joshua, 1829-1901, U.S., jur. Prosecuting attorney for the state of Illinois who was appointed federal judge in the Southern District of that state by President Grover Cleveland in 1887. REF.: *CBA.*

Allen, William O'Meara, 1847-67, **Gould, William**, d.1867, and **Larkin, Michael** d.1867, (AKA: **The Three Fenians**), Brit., mur. Massive crime waves rolled across Ireland and England during the 1860s, prompting officials to discuss imposing harsher penalties on individuals who broke the law. Hundreds of citizens demonstrated against capital punishment, and mob violence erupted in 1866. In the years following Fenian insurrections swept the urban areas of the two island nations. On Sept. 17, 1876, police Sergeant Charles Brett was murdered in Manchester, England, when Allen, Larkin, and Gould attacked a prison van to free two of their Irish comrades. Allen fired the fatal shot but all three men were found guilty of the murder. Outraged at their conviction, a mob of 12,000 persons gathered in Manchester on the day of their execution. The government, fearing a riot, called in the military to quell the crowd's anger. The Three Fenians were hanged as scheduled on Nov. 23, 1867.

REF.: *CBA;* Cobb, *Murdered On Duty.*

Allende Gossens, Dr. **Salvador,** 1908-1973, Chile, pres., assass.? The military coup in Chile led by General Ugarte Augusto Pinochet and others in 1973 culminated in the death of Chile's Marxist president, Salvador Allende (1970-1973). Political controversy continues to surround the death of Allende, especially whether he took his own life on Sept. 11-12, 1973, or was summarily executed on Pinochet's orders by troops. During the coup, Allende and some of his most trusted bodyguards and advisers remained in Santiago's presidential residence, Le Moneda Palace. It was later claimed and supported by Allende's wife Hortensia Bussi Allende that President Allende, rather than be taken prisoner, killed himself. Yet other reports have it that Allende was machine-gunned to death by troops invading the palace and still another claim, inconclusive, insists that Allende was assassinated by CIA agents on orders from U.S. officials who thought Allende, a staunch Communist supporter, was dangerous to American interests in the Western Hemisphere.

News of the revolt against his regime reached Allende early in the morning of Sept. 11, 1973. He learned that Navy personnel at Valparaiso and truckloads of armed sailors were en route to Santiago. He attempted to call his military commanders with no success. At 6:30 a.m., Allende called Orlando Letelier, one of his most trusted ministers, and informed him of the uprising, telling him: "The carabineros are the only units that respond. The other commanders-in-chief don't answer the phone. Pinochet doesn't answer." He asked Letelier to find out what he could about the revolt and later ordered his minister to take over the Defense Ministry before troops overran the building in Santiago, but by then it was too late. Pinochet's troops were in full control of the city, except for Le Moneda Palace.

The palace was held by Allende's loyal forces until 3 p.m. They had fought bitterly for control of the building, the symbol of power, and one report had it that the military junta had to resort to bombing the palace with planes. Troops from the garrison stationed at Tacna overran the palace a little after 3 p.m. and it was at this time, according to one report, that "Allende was killed by a burst of machine gun fire." This claim was later hotly contested by officials in the U.S. and in Chile who insisted Allende blew his brains out with an automatic just as the Tacna Regiment stormed into Le Moneda Palace. This latter claim was, at first, endorsed by Mrs. Hortensia Allende, but she repudiated her statements made in Chile after flying to exile in Mexico. There she stated that her husband had been assassinated, a murder decreed by the right-wing military junta conducting the successful coup. The most outspoken critic of the regime, Letelier, who survived his own execution, insisted that Allende had been executed. Letelier left Chile following the 1973 coup but was later assassinated in Washington, D.C. in 1976. See: **Letelier, Orlando.**

REF.: Agee, *Inside the Company; CBA;* Dinges and Landau, *Assassination on Embassy Row.*

Allers, Katherine, prom. 1922, U.S., fraud-arson. Katherine Allers was a stately, middle-aged Brooklyn woman who tried but failed to bilk an insurance company with a fraudulent fire claim. On Mar. 22, 1922, at a city real-estate auction in Brooklyn, N.Y., Allers purchased a run-down mansion on East 53rd Street and Avenue M in the Flatlands section. The city stipulated, however, that she clear the property within thirty days to make way for a roadway about to go through.

Allers insured the house for $5,000 and the furniture for $2,500 before setting two separate fires with kerosene-soaked rags and a candle. Appearing before Supreme Court Justice Harry Lewis in Brooklyn, she accused Fire Marshal Brophy of offering to split the insurance money in exchange for a confession.

Judge Lewis rebuked Allers for giving false and malicious testimony. He then sentenced her to five to ten years in the Auburn Prison. REF.: *CBA.*

Alley, Leavitt, prom. 1872, Case of, U.S., mur. On Nov. 6, 1872, an employee of the Cambridge Gas Works noticed a barrel floating down the Charles River. He jumped into a rowboat and paddled to retrieve the barrel but, just as he was about to tie it to the boat, he shrank back in horror. Sticking out of the barrel was a human hand. Another barrel later discovered on shore revealed the hideous remains of a dismembered corpse, which was later identified as that of Abijah Ellis, a Boston merchant. Leavitt Alley was arrested a short time later and charged with killing Ellis on Nov. 5, 1872. The owner of a livery stable, Alley, it was known, had had dealings with Ellis and owed him a considerable amount of money. At Alley's trial it was proved that he had purchased an ax only a a few days before Ellis' murder and it was this instrument, the prosecution claimed, that was used to smash the victim's skull four times, as well as dismember the corpse. Moreover, testimony by Alley's teenage son revealed that Alley had blood on his shirt on the night of Ellis' death.

Alley's attorneys claimed that the blood had come from one of Alley's ailing horses. A great deal of time was spent on testimony regarding the difference between the blood of humans and horses, with medical authorities offering their involved theories. The prosecution, however, could not produce Alley's bloody shirt. Witnesses came forward to state that loud noises were heard in Alley's stable on the night of the murder but no eyewitnesses to the actual murder could be found. The prosecution then attempted to prove that the barrels in which the chopped-up remains were found had belonged to Alley, but this evidence was inconclusive. The defense sought, at the opening of the trial, to convince the jury that dismembering a corpse did not constitute murder in the first degree, Alley's lawyers early on believing that their client stood little chance of acquittal. The prosecution's case, however, was thinly constructed on circumstantial evidence, and the case against Alley collapsed when the jury returned a verdict of Not Guilty. The murder of Abijah Ellis remained unsolved.

REF.: *CBA;* Fiske, *Report of the Trial of Leavitt Alley.*

Allingham, Margery Louise, 1904-66, Brit., writer. Wrote a series of detective novels, beginning with *Crime at Black Dudley* (1928). She created the fictional detective Albert Campion. REF.: *CBA.*

Allison, Charles, prom. 1870s-80s, U.S., west. law enforc. off.-outl. The Nevada-born Allison became a deputy sheriff in Conjos County, Colo., but he soon turned against his own profession and organized a vicious band of outlaws that preyed almost exclusively on stages traveling the rough roads of Colorado and New Mexico. Allison flourished during the 1870s, accused of several murders in connection with his robberies. He was captured in 1881 by Sheriff Matt Kyle but escaped. A reward for $1,000 was placed on Allison's head, a considerable sum for those days, and this prompted a clever, relentless Denver detective, Frank Hyatt, to track down Allison and four of his men, capturing the band in an Albuquerque, N.M., livery stable while they slept. Allison was sent to the Colorado State Prison for thirty-seven years, served ten, and was released in 1890. He was last seen tending bar in a Butte, Mont., saloon.

REF.: Brown, *An Empire of Silver; CBA.*

Allison, James, d. 1898, Can., mur. On Aug. 9, 1897, Allison, while working as a hired hand on a farm near Galt, Ontario, murdered his employer, Emma Orr, and buried her body in a shallow grave. Following a three-day search for the missing woman, volunteers found the body buried near some swampland on the family farm. Orr had been severely beaten with a sharp object and killed with a shotgun. It is believed that Allison sexually abused the woman he had lusted for previous to the murder.

On Aug. 19, Allison was formally charged and a trial date was set for early the following year. After an extensive trial which included a re-creation of the crime, Allison was found Guilty of murder and sentenced to death. The young man was hanged on Feb. 4, 1898.

REF.: Campbell, *A Century of Crime; CBA.*

Allison, Robert A. (Clay), 1840-87, U.S., west. gunman. That Clay Allison was unbalanced from an early age there was no doubt. He had a mean streak running to his marrow and a seething anger that seemed never to abate. His clubfoot and a condition that was occasionally diagnosed as "epileptic" may have contributed to his mercurial temper. Allison worked on his parents' farm near Waynesboro, Tenn., until he was twenty-one. Immediately upon the outbreak of the Civil War, he enlisted in the Confederate Army and went off willingly to fight for the South. His clubfoot did not seem to hamper his ability to perform active duty. He saw action in several battles but was sent home in March 1862 to recuperate from wounds that seemed more mental than physical, a Confederate doctor stating that Allison was suffering from a condition that was "partly epileptic and partly maniacal." He had reportedly threatened to shoot his superiors following one battle because they refused to pursue and execute retreating Union troops.

Quick-draw gunman Clay Allison, killer of a half dozen men.

A short time later, Allison got the chance to vent his anger on one Union soldier, a corporal of the Third Illinois Cavalry who rode onto the Allison farm and announced to Allison's mother that he intended to take everything valuable on the premises. Clay went to a closet, got out a gun, and promptly shot the Union soldier dead. Following the end of the war, Allison, his two brothers, Monroe and John, his sister Mary, and her husband, Lewis Coleman, migrated to Texas. While Allison was waiting to take a ferry across the Red River, he became incensed when ferryman Zachary Colbert tried to double-charge them. Allison beat up Colbert and left him unconscious while the family took the ferry across the Red, paying nothing.

Once in Texas, Allison signed on with several cattle barons as a cowboy, helping to blaze the Goodnight-Loving Trail through Texas, New Mexico, and Colorado in 1866. He became an expert, tough cowhand, working first for Oliver Loving and Charles Goodnight, then for cattle barons M.L. Dalton and Isaac Lacy. He drove a huge herd of cattle to New Mexico in 1870 and demanded as pay 300 head of cattle. With this small herd Allison began his own ranch near Cimarron, N.M., which was soon lucrative. It was on October 7 of that year that Allison's true savagery emerged. Allison brooded about a locally convicted murderer, Charles Kennedy, while drinking heavily in the saloon at Elizabethtown. He stirred up sentiment against Kennedy and then led a lynch mob across the street to the jail. Allison and others battered down the door, knocked the deputies senseless, and dragged Kennedy screaming from his cell. He was taken to a local slaughterhouse where Allison and others not only lynched Kennedy but mutilated his corpse with the huge knives employed for butchering cattle. Allison then cut the body down and, using an ax, decapitated the corpse and jammed the head on a pole, riding with this gory trophy all the way to Henry Lambert's saloon in Cimarron where Allison put the head on display.

Those who befriended Allison stayed fiercely loyal to the gunman. His enemies, on the other hand, not only hated him but vowed to kill him whenever the opportunity arose. One of these was gunslinger Chunk Colbert who had secretly planned to kill Allison ever since Clay beat up his uncle Zachary some nine years earlier at the Red River crossing. Colbert rode into Cimarron and challenged Allison to a horse race. Both men rode their horses wildly and the race wound up in a dead heat. They decided to rest up at the Clifton House, an inn near Allison's ranch. Both men sat down to eat large dinners. (One madcap Western historian went so far as to state that the two men eyeballed each

other intently while they stirred their coffee with the barrels of their six-guns.) They talked amiably, but Allison noticed Colbert reach for his cup of coffee with one hand and his pistol with another. Before Colbert could lift the six-gun beyond the rim of the table, Allison tipped his chair backward, falling toward the floor which caused Colbert to hurry his shot which, in turn, plowed into the table top. As he fell backward, however, the cool-under-fire Allison aimed a single shot that smashed into Colbert's head, going in above the right eye and killing the gunman.

After Colbert was buried behind the Clifton House, someone asked Allison why he would sit down to dinner with a man he knew intended to kill him. Quipped the sardonic gunman, "Because I didn't want to send a man to hell on an empty stomach." Charles Cooper, a friend of Colbert's who had been present at the shoot out, did not take part in the gunfight, but he stated to friends that he would settle matters with Allison later. On Jan. 19, 1874, Cooper was seen riding toward Cimarron and then was never seen again. It was widely believed that Allison killed Cooper and buried the body on the prairie. Two years later, the gunman would be charged with murdering Cooper but the prosecution could produce no body nor any evidence that Allison committed the crime; the gunman was released.

As time passed, Clay Allison earned the reputation of a mad gunfighter who feared no one and could be counted on to do the unexpected. It was reported that Allison, totally drunk, stepped from a saloon in Canadian, Texas, wearing nothing but his ten-gallon hat, his boots, and his six-guns, to march up and down the main street challenging any and all to face him. There were no takers. Another report had the gunman and a drinking companion, Mason T. Bowman, stripping to their underwear and dancing wildly about a saloon and then shooting up the floor at each's others feet to quicken the pace without bloodying a single toe.

On Oct. 30, 1875, Allison took part in another lynching, helping to hang one Cruz Vega, under arrest for murder in Colfax County, N.M. As Vega was dragged to a telegraph pole by Allison and others, he shouted out that he was not the killer, but that the murder he stood accused of had been committed by Manuel Cardenas. It mattered not to Allison and his friends. Cruz was strung up and while he slowly strangled to death the compassionate Allison shot him in the back "to put the poor Mex out of his misery." The gunman then had the body taken down; he tied the end of the lynch rope to his saddle and rode through the streets, dragging the body outside of town, over rocks and heavy brush, until the face was unrecognizable. He left Vega's body to rot in the desert.

Cruz's employer, rancher and feared gunman Francisco Pancho Griego, showed up in Cimarron on Nov. 1, 1875, asking for Allison. With him were Luis Vega, the 18-year-old son of the lynch mob victim, and Griego's partner, Florencio Donahue. Allison boldly confronted the trio outside the St. James Hotel and suggested they step inside the bar to talk things over. The men had a few drinks and seemed to talk amiably. Then Griego motioned to a corner of the bar and he and Allison walked to the spot. As Allison turned he saw that Griego had removed his large sombrero and had begun to fan himself, an uncommon gesture on one of the coldest nights of the year. Allison had also prepared for treachery with a trick of his own; having palmed a small pistol, he fired this weapon as soon as Griego's sombrero stopped at his gunbelt. The lights in the saloon suddenly went out (thanks to a friend of Allison's), and when the lamp was next lit the body of Francisco Pancho Griego was seen sprawled on the floor, a bullet in his heart. Allison had disappeared.

Colfax County citizens began a campaign to get rid of the lethal Allison, urging the editor of the Cimarron *News and Press* to write some scathing articles about the New Mexico badman. One of the those behind the publicity campaign was none other than Allison's own brother-in-law, Lewis Coleman. The gunman's response to this civic campaign to run him out of the territory was to ride into Cimarron and wreck the entire offices of the *News and Press*, putting it out of business. Though Allison's neighbors were nervous about his presence, total strangers living in towns Allison visited on his trail drives were positively traumatized when he and his cowboys rode into town. Such was the situation when Clay and John Allison appeared in Las Animas, Colo., on the night of Dec. 21, 1876. They had just sold a herd of cattle and were looking to entertain themselves, at the expense of the local citizenry, of course.

Spotting festivities in progress at the Olympic Dance Hall, the Allison brothers stomped inside and began dancing with the wives of local merchants, both of them almost drunk and impolitely stepping upon the toes of their partners. Town constable and deputy sheriff Charles Faber quietly walked up to the Allisons and asked them to check their six-guns but they ignored him. Faber stepped outside and quickly deputized two men, getting a shotgun and returning to the dance hall. Just as he entered, someone shouted, "Look out!" John Allison, who was still attempting to dance with a cringing local lady, spun around, appearing to draw his gun. Faber let loose with a blast from one of the shotgun barrels. Clay Allison, who was at the bar and had his back to the scene, wheeled around with his pistols in his hands (he usually wore one gun but on occasion wore two). As John Allison received a load of buckshot in his chest and arm, Clay fired four deliberate shots at Faber, hitting him only once, but this shot ripped through the deputy's chest, killing him. As Faber fell, his shotgun went off once more, the second barrel of buckshot slamming into John Allison's leg, sending the brother toppling to the floor. (As was the case with most Western shootouts, all this gunfire took only a few seconds to occur.)

Allison then chased the two deputies outside, firing at them as they ran for their lives down the street, escaping uninjured in the darkness. Returning to the hall, Allison went to his brother and then called for a doctor. He reached over to Faber's fallen body and yanked the bloody corpse next to the semi-conscious John Allison, telling his brother, "Look here, this man is dead, John, not to worry, vengeance is ours! Not to worry."

John Allison eventually recovered from his wounds and Clay Allison managed to escape punishment by proving self-defense. This shootout spread the reputation of Allison far and wide through the hell holes and cow towns. Legends about the fierce gunman began to appear in the penny dreadfuls and police gazettes of the East where Allison was portrayed as the most dangerous gunman of the Old West, a man who outdrew and backed down the most esteemed of lawmen, including the venerable Wyatt Earp and deadly Wild Bill Hickok. Of course, these stories were apocryphal and only occurred in the fertile brains of writers who never crossed the Mississippi.

To the citizens of Colfax County, however, Allison was infamous enough. He found that few in the area wished to befriend him, or, worse, do business with him. Losing money on cattle he could not sell, Allison moved to greener territory, buying a ranch in Hemphill County, Texas. There he married and his wife gave birth to two girls, Patsy, born a cripple, and Clay, who was born after Allison's strange, premature death. The gunman seemed to temper a bit and began to avoid confrontations with other gunfighters. His fortunes rising once more, Allison bought another ranch in Lincoln County, N.M., and here he developed considerable herds. On one trail drive to Wyoming, Allison stopped off in Cheyenne, so the tale goes, where he went to a local dentist with a howling toothache. The dentist, learning the identity of his patient, nervously worked on the wrong tooth. Allison pushed his hand away and went to another dentist, who filled the right cavity. So incensed was Allison at the first dentist's ineptitude that he raced back to the first man, strapped him into his own chair, and yanked out the dentist's front tooth. He intended to pull every one of his teeth but a rescuing crowd heard the dentist's screams and pulled Allison away before he could do more damage. There is little support for this story, in fact, and none for the tale which graphically described how Allison, forced to share a room with another gunman one night, shot his room-

mate for snoring too loudly.

Allison's end was ignominious and grimly ironic. On July 1, 1887, Allison was returning from Pecos, Texas, where he purchased supplies for his ranch. Apparently he had been drinking, for about forty miles from Pecos, the gunfighter toppled from the buckboard he was driving and fell beneath the wheel of the heavily laden wagon. The horses jerked forward and the wheel crushed Allison's head, almost decapitating him, which caused some to later recall how Allison had severed the head of the killer Kennedy seventeen years earlier. It was said, following Allison's death, that he was heading toward a rendezvous where he planned to murder his neighbor, John McCullough, with whom he had had a recent argument, but this was mere fiction. The contemporary tale-tellers of Allison's era could not accept a mundane end for one of the worst killers of the West. Fate, they would have it, intervened to prevent the gunman from claiming one more victim.

Historians later estimated that the six-foot, blue-eyed gunman had shot and killed *at least* fifteen men during his notorious career. Shortly before his death, Allison told a newsman, "I never killed a man who didn't need it." He then added that in all his gunfights he was merely "protecting the property holders of the country from thieves, outlaws, and murderers." He could have numbered himself among these miscreants, for Allison was no simple rancher with a hair trigger. Throughout his days on the range he practiced wholesale rustling of cattle and horses. On one occasion, he even attempted to steal a herd of army mules but the stubborn beasts would have none of him. He fell from his horse amidst the herd, and they began kicking him. He actually drew his gun, frothing with rage and intent upon shooting several of the mules, but he received another kick and the gun accidentally went off, sending a bullet into Allison's good foot. This caused him to add pressure to the clubfoot, increasing a lifelong pain and creating a permanent limp. Allison used a cane after that until the very day of his death. See: **Earp, Wyatt; Hickok, James Butler.**

REF.: American Guide Series, *New Mexico, A Guide to the Colorful State*; Archambeau, *Old Tascosa*; Ball, *The United States Marshals of New Mexico and Arizona Territories, 1846-1912*; Bartholomew, *Some Western Gunfighters*; Botkin, *A Treasury of Western Folklore*; Breihan, *Great Gunfighters of the West*; Brent, *Great Western Heroes*; Bronson, *Red Blooded*; Buffum, *Smith of Bear City*; Casey, *The Texas Border and Some Borderlineres*; CBA; Chapel, *Guns of the Old West*; Chrisman, *Lost Trails of the Cimarron*; Clark, *Clay Allison of the Washita*; Claussen, *Cimarron —"Last of the Frontier"*; Cleveland, *No Life for a Lady*; ____, *Satan's Paradise*; Coe, *Frontier Fighter*; Coolidge, *Fighting Men of the West*; Cox, *Luke Short and His Era*; Crocchiola, *Clay Allison*; Culley, *Cattle, Horses & Men of the Western Range*; Dobie, *The Flavor of Texas*; Elman, *Fired in Anger*; Erwin, *The Southwest of John H. Slaughter*; Farber, *Texas with Guns*; ____, *Those Texans*; Fitzpatrick, *This is New Mexico*; Hall-Quest, *Wyatt Earp, Marshal of the Old West*; Hendricks, *The Bad Man of the West*; Hertzog, *A Directory of New Mexico Desperadoes*; Hogan, *The Life and Death of Clay Allison*; Holloway, *Texas Gun Lore*; Horan, *The Wild Bunch*; Hubbs, *Robert Clay Allison, Gentleman Gunfighter*; Hunter and Rose, *The Album of Gunfighters*; Keleher, *Maxwell Land Grant*; ____, *Violence in Lincoln County*; Knight, *Wild Bill Hickok*; Lake, *Wyatt Earp, Frontier Marshal*; ____, *The Far Southwest*; Looney, *Haunted Highways*; McCarty, *The Enchanted West*; ____, *The Gunfighters*; Miller and Snell, *Why the West was Wild*; Monaghan, *The Book of the American West*; Myers, *Doc Holliday*; ____, *The Last Chance, Tombstone's Early Years*; *History of New Mexico*; Nash, *Bloodletters and Badmen*; O'Connor, *Bat Masterson*; Oden, *Early Days on the Texas-New Mexico Plains*; Otero, *My Life on the Frontier*; Pearson, *The Maxwell Land Grant*; Penfield, *Western Sheriffs and Marshals*; Phares, *Bible in Pocket, Gun in Hand*; Porter, *Pencilings of An Early Western Pioneer*; Raine, *Guns of the Frontier*; Rascoe, *Some Western Treasures*; Sabin, *Wild Men of the Wild West*; Sandoz, *The Cattlemen*; Schoenberger, *Gunfighters*; Sims, *Guntoters I Have Known*; Siringo, *Riata and Spurs*; Small, *The Best of the True West*; Stanley, *Clay Allison*; ____, *Dave Rudabaugh, Border Ruffian*; ____, *Desperadoes of New Mexico*; ____, *The Elizabethtown (N.M.) Story*; ____, *Fort Bascom*; ____, *Fort Union*; ____, *The Grant that Maxwell Bought*; ____, *One Half Mile from*

Heaven; ____, *The Otero (N.M.) Story;* ____, *The Private War of Ike Stockton;* Streeter, *Man with A Gun;* Taylor, *Taylor's Thrilling Tales of Texas;* Thompson, *Clayton;* Vestal, *Queen of the Cowtowns, Dodge City;* Ward, *Cimarron Saga;* Waters, *A Gallery of Western Bad Men;* Wellman, *The Blazing Southwest;* White, *Trigger Fingers.*

Allnutt, William Newton, b.1835, Brit., theft-mur. Compelled by "an inner voice," 12-year-old William Allnutt tried and failed until, by poisoning, he succeeded in killing his grandfather. Orphaned at the age of ten, Allnutt was sent to a boarding school, and later, when the regimentation of school life had taken its toll, to the London suburb of Hackney, the home of his 73-year-old grandfather, Samuel Nelme. Revered as the deputy chairman of the Hackney Board of Guardians, and thought by some to be the last hope for the brilliant, troubled boy, Nelme was a stern disciplinarian. On Oct. 20, 1847, however, Nelme went too far. He hit William a little too hard, and William struck back. Not physically, not that day, nor the next, but in a few incidents no one could explain.

One day a bullet whizzed by the old man's head while he was walking in the garden. William claimed to have witnessed a stranger scale the wall of the garden, but there was no one else present to corroborate his story. Later, William's schoolmaster told his mother that the boy had brought a small pistol to school. Allnutt then stole a quantity of rat poison from a locked bureau drawer in Mr. Nelme's study. He sprinkled arsenic into the sugar bowl, knowing that his grandfather was partial to sweets. At the same time, William had predicted his grandfather's imminent demise to Maria, the housemaid.

On Oct. 26, 1847, William fulfilled his prediction. Nine days later he was arrested for the theft of seventy guineas and a watch which belonged to his grandfather. When an inquest into Nelme's death revealed arsenic in the stomach, William confessed to the murder. On Nov. 21, three days after he was sentenced to die, William gave penance to the prison chaplain and wrote an impassioned, moving letter to his mother, begging forgiveness from God and his accusers. William Allnutt's death sentence was commuted. He was believed to have spent the remainder of his days in prison. REF.: *CBA;* Wilson, *Children Who Kill.*

Allred, James V, 1899-1959, U.S., jur. Served as attorney general of Texas from 1931-35 and as Texas governor from 1935-39. In 1938 he was nominated twice as federal judge for the southern district of Texas by President Franklin D. Roosevelt and again in 1949 by President Harry S. Truman. REF.: *CBA.*

All the King's Men, 1946, a novel by Robert Penn Warren. This excellent work of fiction analyzes the rise and fall of a political despot in the American Deep South and is wholly based on the mercurial career of Huey Long, who is called Willie Stark in Warren's novel. The assassination of the Kingfish (U.S., 1935) is grimly depicted but the assassin is given a sympathetic character that dangerously borders on the excusable. Oddly, this was the fourth novel based on the histrionic Long but proved to be the most durable and effective. The others, detailed elsewhere in the text, are *A Lion is in the Streets* by Andrea Locke Langley, *Number One* by John Dos Passos, and *Sun in Capricorn* by Hamilton Basso. The Warren novel was produced as a powerful film in 1949, directed by Robert Rossen and starring Broderick Crawford as the Long character, rendering a truly memorable performance which deservedly won for him an Academy Award. Shepperd Strudwick gives a sensitive essay of the assassin, a young, intellectual doctor. See: **Long, Huey Pierce.** REF.: *CBA.*

All This and Heaven Too, a novel by Rachel Field. This work of fiction, a grand soap opera which was almost as popular in its day as *Gone With the Wind,* is based on the wife-murder committed by the Duke de Praslin (Fr., 1848). An excellent film based on this book and by the same title, offered Bette Davis and Charles Boyer (as a much more sympathetic duke than the one in real life) as the star-crossed lovers in 1940. See: **de Praslin, Duke.** REF.: *CBA.*

Allweiss, David, 1952- , U.S., rob.-rape-mur. In 1975, David Allweiss, a 21-year-old New York writer, was convicted of a series of rape-robberies and a violent murder which occurred on Manhattan's East Side two years earlier. In the fall of 1973 Allweiss committed several sexual attacks within a small area of the city. He would gain entrance to his victim's apartment and flash a knife, forcing the women into sex after wrapping a pair of pantyhose around their necks. On Oct. 10, 1973, Allweiss, having been previously arrested on sex charges, turned himself in for the long string of rapes. He was quickly arraigned and released. Less than two weeks later the dead body of Carol Hoffman was found on the floor of her East Side apartment. A pair of pantyhose were tied around her neck and a small knife was lodged in her stomach.

Allweiss was arrested, but refused to confess. On the advice of his attorney he decided to plea-bargain as the prosecution had little evidence to convict him on a charge of murder. The process continued for two years, but finally stalled in 1975 when the prosecution was allowed to introduce Allweiss' previous crimes as evidence in court to establish a pattern to his criminal actions. The evidence proved damaging to Allweiss, who was found Guilty of second-degree murder. The judge awarded Allweiss two consecutive sentences—eighteen years for the rapes and twenty-five years-to-life for the murder of Carol Hoffman. As a result, Allweiss is ineligible for parole until the year 2019, when he would be sixty-seven years old. REF.: *CBA.*

Almarez, Stella Delores, 1951- , U.S., mur. On June 18, 1980, in despair over her failed marriage, Stella Almarez of Norfolk, Neb., brutally slashed the throats of her two infant daughters and then shot down her older girls, ages seven and ten. Failing in her suicide attempt, Mrs. Almarez was arrested the next day and arraigned on a murder charge. In November 1980 she was found Not Guilty by reason of insanity by a Madison County jury and was committed to the Lincoln Regional Center for hospitalization. The controversial verdict led to sweeping changes in state law. As a result, the burden of proof that a person was insane at the time they committed a murder shifted from the prosecution to the defense. It is now up to the defense counsel to prove that his or her client was insane at the time they murdered.

A second noteworthy change involved the disposition of defendants remanded over to the custody of mental health facilities, like the one in Lincoln. During Mrs. Almarez' five-year stay at the regional center, she was permitted to work outside the hospital. A revision of the legal codes, however, required that each inmate be reviewed annually to determine their mental fitness before being permitted to wander off the grounds. Also, an inmate could only be released after hospital officials received a written order from the judge.

Released in 1985, Stella Almarez was the first Nebraska patient to be affected by this new ruling. Judge Merritt Warren of the Madison County District Court, declaring Almarez no longer a danger to herself or society, ordered her unconditionally released on Oct. 2, 1985. REF.: *CBA.*

***Almdijk* Case,** 1949, U.S., smug. This landmark case involving the U.S. Customs Service effectively halted the smuggling of carbon black—a substance controlled by the U.S. Commerce Department—to Warsaw Pact countries through second and third-party intermediaries. In March 1949, U.S. Customs agent Al Scharff was notified by sources of the illegal movement of the industrial material across the Texas border into Mexico. Carbon black, used in the manufacture of paint, automobile tires, and war material, is strictly regulated by the U.S. and is not permitted to be shipped to any unfriendly governments especially those in the Soviet-allied Eastern Block.

Scharff tracked the movement of the 600-ton shipment from Laredo, Tex. to Tampico, Mexico, where it was loaded aboard a Holland-America Line ship, the *S.S. Almdijk,* en route to Amsterdam, where Scharff expected the cargo would be diverted to the Soviet Union. While it was at port in Houston, Scharff and other U.S. officials boarded the *S.S. Almdijk* and seized its cargo, including the shipment of carbon black. Alexander Danon, a Mexico City businessman who had purchased the material from its U.S. manufacturer, became furious at their actions and the Amsterdam recipient threatened to bring a suit in U.S. court against the Customs Service for its action.

Danon refused several invitations from the U.S. attorney general's office to come to the U.S. and testify on his own behalf, knowing that he would probably lose the case and be sentenced to jail for smuggling contraband. As a result, the U.S. attorney general's office resolved the issue by consent decree and ordered Danon and his backers to pay freight charges to the Dutch line and to finance costs incurred by the U.S. Customs Service when it unloaded the freighter's cargo. The carbon black was released on the stipulation that it not be sent behind the Iron Curtain.

REF.: *CBA;* Roark, *Coin of Contraband.*

Almer, Jack (AKA: **Jack Averill; Red Jack**), d.1883, U.S., rob.-mur. Almer was chief of the Red Jack gang that preyed on Arizona stagecoaches during the early 1880s, particularly active along the San Pedro River. The gang held up the Globe stage on Aug. 10, 1883, near Riverside. When the Wells Fargo guard insisted that the stage was not carrying any gold, and showed signs of resisting the robbers, a female passenger jumped from the stage, lifting her skirts high and bellowing in a decidedly bass voice that he was a liar. It was Almer, disguised as a female passenger, dark veil and all. In that impossible impersonation Almer had witnessed the gold being placed under a seat on the stage and thus signaled his men to move in when the stagecoach passed a spot where the gang was waiting. The guard went for his gun and Almer reached inside his skirt and pulled his own six-gun, shooting the Wells Fargo man dead. The gang took $2,800 in gold and bills and fled. Sheriff Bob Paul organized a strong posse and hunted the Red Jack gang down one by one. Paul and his men unearthed Almer hiding near Wilcox, Ariz., on Oct. 4, 1883, and shot him to pieces when he tried to battle his way to freedom.

REF.: Bartholomew, *The Biographical Album of Western Gunfighters; CBA.*

Almodovar, Anibal (AKA: **Terry**), 1916-43, U.S., mur. Almodovar was a Puerto Rican sailor living in New York City, a ladies' man who did as he pleased with his girlfriends and his 23-year-old wife, Louise Petecca Almodovar, a waitress who met the handsome, dashing Almodovar, whom she called Terry, at the Rhumba Palace in Manhattan. After dancing with him, she fell in love and the two were married a short time later. Only a few weeks went by before Louise accused Terry Almodovar of seeing other women. He exploded and then moved out. A short time later, Louise called Terry and asked to meet with him, to see if they could patch up their differences. Almodovar arranged to meet his wife in Central Park. There, near 110th Street in the tall grass, is where police found Louise Almodovar's body on Nov. 2, 1942. She had been strangled. The waitress had apparently struggled with her killer; the sleeve of her jacket had been torn from the shoulder. Chief medical examiner, Dr. Thomas A. Gonzales, determined that the killer had murdered with expertise: "The killer did not throttle her by placing both hands around her neck. He did it with two fingers from each hand, placing them on the windpipe. The larynx was only slightly fractured."

Until the dead woman was identified, police thought she had been killed by park thugs, but then they received reports on Terry Almodovar's marriage to the girl, and their breakup over his womanizing and violent streaks of temper. He was arrested on suspicion. Almodovar's clothing was turned over to Dr. Alexander O. Gettler, chief toxicologist of the medical examiner's office. Dr. Gottler found seeds of various types of grass in Almodovar's trouser cuffs and these he passed on to Dr. Joseph J. Copeland, professor of botany and biology at City College. Meanwhile, Terry Almodovar confessed that he had met with his wife in Central Park, and when Louise began to accuse him of seeing other women, he lost control and strangled her to death. He later recanted this confession, saying that he had been coerced into making the admission. When he was brought to trial, however, the killer never for an instant thought he would be convicted by some seeds of grass.

Almodovar was placed on trial on Feb. 24, 1943, before Judge George L. Donnellan. The prosecution presented an impressive array of forensic evidence; the botanical evidence provided clearly placed Almodovar at the scene of the murder. Dr. Copeland testified in court that he had examined the seeds of grass found in Almodovar's trouser cuffs and that he had determined these to be a rare species (*Plantago canceolata, Panicum dichotomiflorum, Eleusine indica*) which could be found only in the area of Central Park where Louise Almodovar had been killed. No other spot in New York City had this rare form of grass which had been planted at the murder site for experimental reasons. Copeland, at the request of police to head off Almodovar's expected alibis, also emphatically stated that this type of grass could only be found in two spots in Long Island and three small areas of Westchester County. Copeland went on to add that the grass seeds in Almodovar's trouser cuffs had matured only within a week or so of the time of the murder, which clearly placed the killer at the murder site. The jury returned a verdict of Guilty and Almodovar was sentenced to death, going to the electric chair in 1943. The Almodovar conviction stands as a hallmark in scientific research dealing with a murder case.

REF.: Block, *Science vs Crime; CBA;* Radin, *12 Against the Law;* Thorwald, *Crime and Science.*

Almon, John, 1737-1805, Brit., writer. Wrote political pamphlets. He was prosecuted but acquitted for his pamphlet "Juries and Libels" published in 1765. Later, after being sent to prison for libel, he fled the country. REF.: *CBA.*

Almond, James Lindsay, Jr, 1898-1986, U.S., jur. Attorney general of Virginia from 1948-57 and governor of Virginia from 1958-62. He was appointed as a federal judge in the Court of Customs and Patent Appeals by President John F. Kennedy in 1962. REF.: *CBA.*

Almy, Frank C., d.1892, U.S., burg.-mur. A professional burglar who used the alias of George Abbott, Almy was apprehended for several thefts in New England and sentenced to fifteen years in the New Hampshire State Prison. He escaped and worked as a farm laborer near Hanover, N.H., where he met attractive Christie Warden. When the young woman rebuffed his marriage proposal, Almy killed her. Hundreds of local residents joined posses in search of Almy who, ironically, hid himself in the Warden barn for more than a month before being discovered. He was executed the following year following his confession and a quick trial.

REF.: *CBA; Life, Trial and Confession of Frank C. Almy;* Nash, *Bloodletters and Badmen.*

Alo, Vincent (AKA: **Jimmy Blue Eyes**), prom. 1940s-60s, U.S., org. crime. Alo was a henchman of Lucky Luciano's, working as a liaison man between politicians in Luciano's pocket and the boss of bosses. Alo's sobriquet is curious. He was called Jimmy Blue Eyes but his eyes were brown. Alo was the Mafia connection with the syndicate's banker, Meyer Lansky. It was thought that Luciano assigned Alo as a watchdog over Lansky to make sure that the banker kept the ledgers straight in dealing with the billions of dollars the national crime cartel took in each year. This was not the case; Alo was designated by Luciano to provide protection to Lansky in the event any maverick mobster thought to kidnap the mob banker and hold him for ransom. By 1929 Alo was not only Lansky's bodyguard but his close friend. When Lansky's child was born a cripple in 1930, it was Alo who took the shaken Lansky to a Boston hideout and sat with him for almost a week as the normally abstinent Lansky drank himself into a stupor, then cleaned him up, and drove him home to Manhattan. In later years, Alo moved to Hollywood, Fla., where he bought a lavish home for $100,000; the mansion was only ten miles distant from Lansky's modest Miami Beach bungalow. He met with Lansky almost daily to discuss mob business and carry reports back to the Mafia factions. Alo became particularly indebted to Lansky in the late 1930s when the syndicate banker cut Alo in on lucrative gambling concessions Lansky had established in Cuba through his close association with dictator Fulgencio Batista. These enterprises made Alo a millionaire.

During the syndicate heyday in America in the early 1950s, Alo joined with Adonis, Lansky, Mert Wertheimer, (a member of Detroit's Purple Gang), and millionaire syndicate gambler Frank Erickson in establishing the lavish Colonial Inn Casino in Hallandale, Fla., an operation which provided side money for its owners, about $700,000 a year, but these were the *declared* profits. Huge profits in stolen securities, however, were made by Alo, Lansky, Carlos Marcello (Mafia boss of New Orleans), Angelo DeCarlo of New Jersey, Angelo Bruno of Philadelphia, and Lansky's Bahamian contact, Louis Chesler. From 1958 to 1962 more than $50 million a year went into syndicate pockets from enormous thefts of Wall Street securities. These stolen securities later found their way to Swiss banks, according to one federal report. It was estimated that Alo's cut of this theft operation brought him more than $25 million, since he provided many of the thieves who looted the offices of Wall Street brokers.

Alo was later named by Joe Adonis as the overlord for his Brooklyn Mafia family and he actively promoted prositution, narcotics peddling, and gambling in this crime-ridden area. Although Alo kept a low profile in his go-between chores, he was nevertheless brought before the Crime Committee headed by Senator Estes Kefauver and labelled a dangerous and important figure within the hierarchy of the national crime cartel. In his efforts to send Meyer Lansky to jail in 1970, Robert M. Morgenthau, U.S. attorney for the southern district of New York, failed to glean enough evidence against the crafty syndicate banker. He did, however, manage to convict Alo for obstruction of justice and send him to prison, a term most believed was being served by a sacrificial lamb. See: **Lansky, Meyer; Luciano, Charles.**

REF.: *CBA;* Cook, *Mafia!;* Demaris, *The Last Mafioso;* Eisenberg, *Meyer Lansky;* Gage, *Mafia, U.S.A.;* Katz, *Uncle Frank;* Kefauver, *Crime in America;* Maas, *The Valachi Papers;* Martin, *Revolt in the Mafia;* Messick, *Lansky;* ____, *Secret File;* ____, and Goldblatt, *The Mobs and the Mafia;* Nash, *Bloodletters and Badmen;* Peterson, *The Mob;* Reid, *The Grim Reapers;* Teresa, *My Life in the Mafia;* Wicker, *Investigating the FBI.*

Alphonse (AKA: Alphonse de France), 1220-71, Fr., count, host. Son of Louis VIII and brother of Louis IX for whom he stood hostage in 1250. He died during the Eighth Crusade. REF.: *CBA.*

Alsopp, Gunnar, 1843-87, U.S., suic.-mur. Alsopp was a hermit farmer who lived outside of Billings, Mont. He had migrated to the area some time in the late 1860s, following the American Civil War. Little is known of his background, except that his small farm yielded few crops, and he earned money as a wheelwright on occasion, fixing the wagons and carriages of neighboring farmers. One such farmer was Frank Newall, a notorious tightwad who argued with Alsopp about money he owed him for repairing a large wagon. Alsopp brooded over the unpaid debt and then, on the night of Aug. 12, 1887, rode to the Newall farm and, according to the only surviving member of the family, kicked open the front door of the house and entered with two pistols blazing, shooting down Frank Newall, his wife Alice, their three grown sons, and two daughters. As wounded family members writhed on the floor, the berserk Alsopp reloaded his two guns and then walked calmly about the rooms and fired more bullets into the prone family members. Little Billy Newall, five, was sprawled beneath the bodies of his mother and father and was thereby saved from death.

Thinking he had killed the entire family, Alsopp stepped outside, only to see the six farmhands streaming from the bunkhouse up the road. He pulled his rifle from a scabbard affixed to his wagon and knelt down, shooting each and every farmhand who approached him. One, Jim Davis, got close enough with a shotgun to let loose a blast which tore away the top of the seat of Alsopp's wagon but he, too, was shot down and killed, a bullet in his head. Alsopp had killed all six farm hands, walking along the roadway and checking to make sure they were dead, firing bullets into their heads with a pistol. All of this was witnessed by Billy Newall, who had crawled out from beneath the bodies of his parents and run to a window of the farmhouse. He watched

as the madman climbed into his wagon and rode solemnly away in the night. Little Billy then ran to a neighboring farmhouse and aroused the family there. The next day a posse of more than fifty men rode to Alsopp's farm. They did not bother to call out for his surrender, but merely peppered his house, barn, and outhouse with hundreds of shots before a few of their more courageous members entered the house. They found the bloodthirsty farmer slumped in the corner of his bedroom. He had been dead long before the posse opened up its barrage, having killed himself with a single bullet from a pistol still gripped in his hand, presumably only a few hours after he returned home from the Newall farmhouse slaughter. At his side lawmen found some old tintype photos, one of a family which could have been the killer's, another of an attractive young woman, and a third of Alsopp, in the uniform of the Prussian Guards wearing chevrons which gave him the rank of sergeant.

REF.: *CBA; A Debt Paid in Full, The Mass Killing of the Newall Family and Their Hired Hands;* Newall, *All My People Gone; The Tragedy at the Newall Farm.*

Alsworth, Benjamin, See: **Adshead, John.**

Altamira y Crevea, Rafael, b.1866, Spain, jur. Authored works on Spanish history and law. REF.: *CBA.*

Alterie, Louis (Leland Varain, AKA: Two-Gun), 1886-1935, U.S., org. crime. Alterie was a devoted O'Bannion gunman during the Chicago bootleg wars and is credited with killing at least twenty rival gangsters in various shoot-outs. His background is sketchy and, depending on the stories one believed, he was more adventurer than gangster. Alterie was reported to have been born in either Los Angeles or Denver, and at one time in the early 1900s he boxed professionally under the name of Kid Haynes. Another story has it that he joined the Denver Police Department where his derring-do caused him to rise to the rank of lieutenant. This story is doubtful since Alterie's lifelong bent was on the wrong side of the law. He was first reported to be in Chicago in 1922 when arrested with Terry Druggan, head of the Valley Gang. Both men were charged with robbing $50,000 in jewelry from two local citizens. Although the thieves were clearly seen by their victims, when it came time to try Alterie and Druggan, the witnesses lost their

"Two-Gun" Louis Alterie challenged Capone gunmen to shoot it out at noon on Chicago's busiest corner.

memories and could identify no one.

War hero and early-day bootlegger Samuel J. "Nails" Morton befriended Alterie some time later and introduced him to his friend, charming gangland boss Dion O'Bannion, one-time choir boy turned arch gangster and killer. O'Bannion and his mostly Irish mob controlled the North Side of Chicago and Alterie was invited to participate in the rich spoils. He was told to organize several unions and went about this chore with happy alacrity, slugging and beating union leaders into electing him and other O'Bannionites as presidents for life. One of these organizations, The Theatrical and Building Janitors' Union, made Alterie its president for life, after he and several O'Bannionites pistol-whipped its leaders into a quick election. From this and other union rackets, Alterie gleaned an estimated $50,000 a month after giving O'Bannion his split. Within a year Alterie was rich and he began to purchase property: apartment buildings, nightclubs, restaurants, a few small theaters. He even bought a 3,000-acre ranch outside of Gypsum, Colo., which later served as a retreat from the gang wars and a hideout for fugitives.

Alterie was often called upon to lend a hand to O'Bannion's lieutenants in their ongoing bootleg wars with the West Side Genna Brothers, the Druggan-Lake Valley Gang, the West Side O'Donnell Brothers and, of course, Capone. He is credited with inventing the one-way ride, taking a Philadelphia gangster, Johnny Dougherty, alias Duffy, for a car ride in 1923 with O'Bannion at his side. Dougherty was an independent bootlegger who had tried to muscle in on O'Bannion's territory, which earned him two bullets in the head. (The dubious honor of creating the one-way ride, however, goes to Earl "Hymie" Weiss, another O'Bannion sub-chief. Weiss took a hijacker named Steve Wisniewski for a ride in 1921, shooting him, and dumping his body on a city street, in Torrio-Capone territory.)

Though he could not claim to have rendered the first one way ride, Alterie did invent the ambush murder wherein he would rent an apartment close to the home or office of an intended victim. He would make sure that the apartment was on the second floor and faced the street, usually directly across from the home of the gangster marked for murder. Before the apartment windows, Alterie would set up several .50-caliber machine guns, stolen from U.S. Army arsenals, and await the victim's arrival. Numerous O'Bannion enemies were dispatched through this ambush technique which Alterie undoubtedly learned from his exposure to the lore of backshooting and drygulching of outlaws in the Old West when riding about his Colorado ranch. In the fall, at the opening of the deer season, Alterie would invite O'Bannion, Moran, and Weiss to join him and his pal Nails Morton in riding about the ranch and potshooting at hapless deer. They were an odd-looking lot in those palmy days of the early 1920s, big city gangsters donning ten-gallon hats and riding about on spirited horses, hunting deer instead of men. On such occasions Alterie employed his usual *three* guns (two .38's with maple-wood handles and a snub-nosed revolver) to shoot at the frightened deer.

Alterie is also credited as being the only gangster during the Roaring 20s to personally execute a horse. His friend Morton had learned to ride horses at Alterie's Colorado ranch and, when returning to Chicago, he took up the habit of renting a horse to ride along the Lincoln Park Bridle Path on the North Side. Morton, a gentleman on the surface, would don a riding derby, jodphurs, and high boots before trotting his horse along the path each day. One day in May 1923, Morton had the bad luck to rent a vicious bucker who threw him onto the bridle path, then kicked the gangster's brains out. When hearing the news Alterie went berserk and drove directly to the stable. He rented the same animal, galloped it to a remote spot, then dismounted. Taking out his two .38's, Alterie blasted the animal to death and exclaimed, "Take that! No horse can kill a pal of mine and get away with it!" He later called the stable and told the owner, "We taught that damn horse of yours a lesson. If you want the saddle, go and get it!"

The bright lights attracted Alterie, as well as his boss, O'Bannion. Both men delighted in attending the theater, but where O'Bannion would go home following the performance, Alterie and his gunsels would then indulge in marathon nightclubbing. On one occasion, Alterie and a henchman, Johnny Phillips, whooped into the Northern Lights Café. They gulped down several bottles of ersatz champagne and then Phillips made a lunge for the singer performing on the tiny stage, Dorothy Kressner. When Kressner rebuffed Phillips, the gangster began to cuff her about the stage floor with Alterie shouting encouragement. Police were called and two officers charged inside but made the mistake of keeping their weapons in their holsters. Alterie and Phillips pulled their guns and forced the cops to march out of the place with their hands in the air. Another patrolman, Officer Frank Sobel, waiting in a squad car outside, spotted the gangsters frog-marching his partners from the speakeasy and drew his own weapon.

When Alterie spotted Sobel pointing his weapon at him he opened fire, as did Phillips. The other two cops, who had been disarmed by the gangsters, dove for the pavement. Several shots were fired by the gangsters and Sobel, who bravely returned their

fire. Alterie, sobering quickly, motioned to Phillips to run for it. He raced down the street with his henchman behind him. Sobel ran after them, ordering them to stop. Phillips turned and took aim at the officer but Sobel got off a shot that killed the gangster. Alterie turned a corner and escaped. He was never charged, let alone brought to trial. None of O'Bannion's top lieutenants were molested by the police during the boss' lifetime. O'Bannion paid enormous graft to Chicago's political powers, including judges, police captains, and aldermen, as well as Mayor William "Big Bill" Thompson, one of the most venal politicians in American history. He also delivered several important wards into the Republican camp each election. O'Bannion and his boys, including the erstwhile Alterie, could do no wrong in the eyes of the law which were seldom open.

The highly protected O'Bannion mob began to erode, however, when O'Bannion was murdered in his flower shop in 1924 by three Capone gunmen who arrived to ostensibly pick up some floral wreaths for a funeral. So enraged was Alterie at this killing—known as the "handshake murder" in that the killers shook O'Bannion's hands to keep them away from the three guns he wore—that he swore open vengeance on his boss' killers. Alterie had been called in for interrogation by the incorruptible Police Captain John Stege, and Stege's office was swarming with newsmen who wanted to know what Alterie intended to do to the killers of Dion O'Bannion. Alterie, a handsome, black-haired man, tall and broad-shouldered, wearing a custom-tailored suit and a boiled shirt, jutted his jaw and swelled his chest. "If those cowardly rats have any guts they'll meet me at noon at State and Madison and we'll shoot it out." Stege was so incensed at this proposal of Western style vigilantism that he slapped Alterie's face. The gangster only gave him a grin, then walked free when his lawyer arrived with a writ of habeas corpus.

At O'Bannion's funeral some days later, and against the wishes of other O'Bannionites, Weiss and Moran, Alterie once more played to the press, standing in front of his boss' flower-bedecked bier and, with tears streaming over and down his apple cheeks, told reporters, "I have no idea who killed Deanie, but I would die smiling if only I had the chance to meet the guys who did, any time and any place they mention and I would get at least two or three of them before they got me. If I knew who killed Deanie, I'd shoot it out with the gang of killers before the sun rose in the morning and some of us, maybe all of us, would be lying on slabs in the undertaker's place."

These incendiary remarks, when printed in the daily press, caused Mayor Deever, a reform man who had replaced Mayor Thompson for one term, to call his own press conference, stating to reporters that Alterie's remarks branded Chicago as a savage killing ground. "Are we still abiding by the code of the dark ages?" he asked in shock. Deever ordered police to crack down on Alterie and the North Side mob. When police raids occurred against Weiss-Moran speakeasies and gambling dens, Moran blamed Alterie. "You're getting us in bad with the boys downtown. You talk too much. Beat it to that ranch of yours and stay there."

Alterie departed Chicago in the mid-1920s but made periodic visits to the Windy City to keep his hand dipping into the union coffers which he continued to control. The gang wars raged on. Weiss was murdered, then Moran's gang was mostly wiped out in 1929 at the St. Valentine's Day Massacre. Capone himself was eventually undone by receiving a tax evasion conviction and sent to prison. Alterie kept returning to Chicago; he let it be known that the old days were, for him, dead and gone. Frank Nitti and other Capone sub-chiefs led him to believe that all was forgiven. The Western gangster was allowed to continue his union rackets, but in 1935 he was called by the federal government as a witness in the tax evasion trial of Ralph "Bottles" Capone, one of Scarface's brothers. At first Alterie could remember nothing but when told he would be facing a perjury charge, he changed his mind and suddenly recalled important information the prosecution was seeking.

Not long after that, on July 18, 1935, Alterie left his Chicago apartment with his wife, en route to his union offices. After taking only twenty paces down the street, Louis "Two-Gun" Alterie suddenly heard an ancient, deadly sound from his own past, the lethal chatter of machine guns. The 49-year-old gangster turned, instinctively reaching for a pistol that was not there, and the spray of machine gun bullets tore through his body, sending him mortally wounded to the sidewalk. Mrs. Alterie, who was some steps behind her husband, ran to the fallen gangster and cradled his head in her arms. Alterie looked up at her and murmured, "I can't help it, Bambino, but I'm going." He died a moment later.

Investigating officers some hours later discovered the machine gun nest. It was situated in two bay windows in a second-story apartment facing the street. Two machine guns were still in place, empty cartridges littering the floor. The man who had rented the room was gone, one who had given the name of Sullivan. The mysterious roomer was never found nor were any of the other killers who manned the machine guns. Alterie's murder remains unsolved and served as an ironic reminder of the carnage he had helped to create. He had been shot from ambush in the exact manner that Alterie himself had employed when gunning down others in his heyday of beer and blood. See: **Capone, Alphonse; Moran, George; Morton, Samuel J.; O'Bannion, Charles Dion; Weiss, Earl.**

REF.: Asbury, *Gem of the Prairie;* Burns, *The One-Way Ride; CBA;* Fried, *The Rise and Fall of the Jewish Gangster in America;* Kobler, *Capone;* Landesco, *Organized Crime in Chicago;* Lyle, *The Dry and Lawless Years;* Lynch, *Criminals and Politicians;* McPhaul, *Johnny Torrio;* Nash, *Bloodletters and Badmen;* Pasley, *Al Capone;* ____, *Muscling In;* Sullivan, *Chicago Surrenders;* ____, *Rattling the Cup on Chicago Crime.*

Altgeld, John Peter, 1847-1902, U.S., polit. A champion of human rights, the German-born Altgeld was the first Democratic governor of Illinois (1892-96) since the Civil War, and he aroused tremendous opposition to his pardoning of three conspirators involved in the Haymarket Riot (U.S., 1886). He also vigorously opposed the sending of federal troops to break a strike at the Pullman works. In the instance of pardoning the Haymarket rioters, Altgeld set a precedent in that his pardon was based on his conviction that the imprisoned men were wholly innocent and that his pardon was not one of clemency based upon a presumption of guilt. The Haymarket Riot, as it was called, occurred in Chicago on May 4, 1886, while a crowd of workingmen listened to radical speakers demand better wages and jobs. Police intervened and a bomb was tossed, killing one officer on the spot and wounding six others who later died. Several workers in the crowd of 3,000 had been killed and many wounded.

The 180 police officers at the scene, under the command of Captain John "Clubber" Bonfield, reacted violently, clubbing and shooting workers at random. Some of the workers were armed and returned fire but the crowd dispersed rapidly. Almost all of Chicago's leading radicals were later arrested. Of these, ten men were charged with inciting to riot and murder. Four, August Spies, Albert Parsons, George Engel, and Adolph Fischer, were sentenced to death and hanged on Nov. 11, 1887.

Altgeld was, about that time, elected to the superior court but as a judge he remained silent about the Haymarket case. Four years later he was elected governor of Illinois and he immediately began to study the trial records, an exhaustive investigation that revealed gross prejudice and improprieties by the presiding judge, Joseph Easton Gary. He resolved to set part of the matter straight by pardoning the remaining three men who had been languishing in prison. These were Michael Schwab, Samuel Fielden, and Oscar Neebe. Another defendant under a death sentence, Louis Lingg, had committed suicide in his cell before his scheduled execution. Altgeld, writing an 18,000-word executive order entitled *Reasons for Pardoning,* set Schwab, Fielden, and Neebe free on June 26, 1893. His argument was either the defendants were innocent or guilty and that he could not free guilty men as an act of political generosity. He determined that they were innocent.

This heroic decision caused Altgeld his political career, as he well knew it would. He was attacked by the press across the nation, scathing editorials condemning him as an anarchist and traitor stemming from newspapers in Detroit, New York, Chicago, Philadelphia. Chicago's conservative city fathers, who had held up Judge Gary as a champion of law and order and a bastion of American ideals, were incensed that Altgeld would describe him as a bigot. Some of these leaders insisted that Altgeld's only motivation for the pardon was to seek revenge on Judge Gary for an 1889 decision where Gary had reversed a judgment in the amount of $26,000 which was to be paid to Altgeld by the city of Chicago for damage to Market Street property owned by Altgeld. But the real reason for Altgeld's pardoning of the three accused men, as history has proven, was his determination to uphold justice at any cost, including his own political and professional career.

Before issuing his pardon, Altgeld had remarked to the great Chicago criminal lawyer, Clarence Darrow, "If I pardon the Haymarket anarchists, from that day on I will be a dead man." Following the release of Schwab, Fielden, and Neebe, Altgeld's career all but collapsed. He ran for the governorship in 1896 and was soundly defeated by Chicago's monied class. Labor suffered equally at the loss of Altgeld, with workers losing their eight-hour day and the reforms Altgeld and others had worked hard to establish. Altgeld was not quite finished, seeking the mayor's office in 1899 as an independent candidate. He polled only one sixth of the available vote and then retired to private law practice. He lost most of his property, and business reverses made him almost a pauper in 1902 when he joined the law offices of his friend, Clarence Darrow. Following a speech on Mar. 12, 1902, at the Joliet Theater where he defended the Boers then attempting to stave off subjugation by the British in South Africa, Altgeld suffered a cerebral hemorrhage and died six hours later in a small hotel room.

Clarence Darrow was on hand at the train station to receive the body shipped from Joliet, Ill. The body lay in state at the Chicago Public Library Building for two days while tens of thousands filed past the bier. Darrow gave one of the most moving speeches of his career during the funeral services, stating, "In the days now passed, John P. Altgeld, our loving chief, in scorn and derision was called John Pardon Altgeld by those who would destroy his power. We who stand today around his bier and mourn the brave and loving friend are glad to adopt this name." (Darrow, of course, was a celebrated agnostic which explained the posture of his following remarks.) "If, in the infinite economy of nature, there shall be another land where crooked paths shall be made straight, where heaven's justice shall review the judgments of the earth—if there shall be a great, wise, humane judge, before whom the sons of men shall come, we can hope for nothing better for ourselves than to pass into the infinite presence as the comrades and friends of John Pardon Altgeld, who opened the prison doors and set the captives free." See: **Darrow, Clarence; Haymarket Riot.**

REF.: Altgeld, *Live Questions;* ____, *Our Penal Machinery and Its Victims;* Barnard, *Eagle Forgotten: The Life of John Peter Altgeld;* Browne, *Altgeld of Illinois;* Browning and Gerassi, *The American Way of Crime; CBA;* Darrow, *The Story of My Life;* David, *The History of the Haymarket Affair;* Dedman, *Fabulous Chicago;* Farr, *Chicago;* Ginger, *Altgeld's America;* Harrison, *Stormy Years;* Kennedy, *Profiles in Courage;* Kunstler, *The Case for Courage;* Lewis and Smith, *Chicago, The History of Its Reputation;* Nash, *People to See;* Stone, *Clarence Darrow for the Defense;* Tierney, *Darrow;* Weinberg, *Clarence Darrow;* Whitlock, *Forty Years of It;* (FICTION) Fast, *The American: A Middle Western Legend;* Marshall, *Ordeal by Glory.*

Althers, Mr., U.S., wh. slav. Althers, while living in San Francisco, Calif., proposed marriage to an 18-year-old woman in an attempt to sell her into white slavery. The young woman, who had just arrived in Northern California, was living with her older sister when she met Althers. He proposed marriage, but before they wed he drugged the girl with alcohol and took her to a local lodging house, intending to sell her to a white slaver in nearby

Oakland. The woman escaped and Althers was arrested. He was later convicted of trafficking in the white slave business and sentenced to a term of five years in the state penitentiary.

REF.: *CBA*; Roe, *Great War*.

Alvarez, and Killorain, Japonica Jack, 1826-1910, and **Brown, Arthur, and Barnett, Mr., Peru,** fraud-rob.-mur. In 1849 this group of four thieves, led by the Spaniard, Alvarez, swindled the priests at the church at Pisco out of a vast treasure, reportedly stolen from the Incas. The gang then buried the loot on a deserted island in the Tuamotu chain in the South Pacific after which they set sail for Australia with a plan to pose as shipwrecked mariners and meet a contact who would sail back to the island with them. Upon arrival, their contact failed to show up at the meeting site. Alvarez and Barnett were killed by natives, and Brown and Killorain, while engaged in a fight, killed three men and were sentenced to twenty years in jail. Brown died in prison and Killorain never made it back to the island.

Just before his death, Killorain related their story to author Charles Edward Howe who prompted the French government to grant permits to explore the waters around the islands. Searchers never uncovered the stolen treasure which may still be hidden somewhere in the Tuamotus.

REF.: *CBA*; Furneaux, *True Mysteries*.

Alvarez, Louis, 1941- , **Charles Horton,** 1940- , **Leroy Birch,** 1939- , and **Leoncio DeLeon,** 1941- , U.S., gang mur. Alvarez, Horton, Birch, and DeLeon were members of an eighteen-member racially-mixed gang known as the Egyptian Dragons who savagely beat 15-year-old Michael Farmer to death in New York City in 1957. Farmer, a polio victim, was beaten and stabbed in Manhattan's High Bridge Park on July 30, 1957. Seven of the Dragons were arrested on charges of murdering the boy, while the remaining eleven were apprehended and transferred to juvenile facilities to be held as delinquents.

Testimony and evidence exhibited during the fourteen-week trial of the seven youths painted the 17-year-old Alvarez as the ringleader in the slaying and marked him as the individual who fatally stabbed Farmer. Eighteen-year-old Horton was believed to have been the one who brutally beat the boy with a machete. The all-male jury retired to deliberate on their verdict on Apr. 15, 1958. Twenty-four hours later they found Alvarez and Horton guilty of second-degree murder, and Birch and DeLeon guilty of second-degree manslaughter. Three other members of the gang, Richard Hills, John McCarthy, and George Melendez were acquitted.

On May 28, 1958, General Sessions Judge Irwin D. Davidson sentenced the four youths to prison terms ranging from five years to life. Alvarez and Horton received the mandatory sentence of twenty years to life. Nineteen-year-old Birch received the maximum of seven-and-a-half years to fifteen years, while 17-year-old DeLeon was sentenced to five to fifteen years. REF.: *CBA*.

Alvarez, Raul López, 1959- , Mex., kid.-torture-mur. This former member of the Guadalajara homicide squad kidnapped, tortured, and murdered a U.S. drug enforcement agent and his pilot, dumping their bodies near Guadalajara. DEA agent Enrique Camarena Salazar and his pilot Alfredo Zavala Avelar disappeared from Mexico in 1985. Their brutally beaten bodies were later found near Guadalajara. Alvarez was one of three individuals in the employ of Mexican drug lord Rafael Caro Quintero who were charged in the slayings. The 26-year-old ex-police officer, aided by Rene Martin Verdugo-Urquidez and Jesus Felix-Guiterrez, was ordered by Quintero to eliminate the two men after they had been investigating him for drug trafficking.

On Oct. 29, 1988, Alvarez was sentenced in Los Angeles, Calif., by Federal District Judge Edward Rafeedie to serve one life term, four consecutive sixty-year terms, and one ten-year term to run concurrently. Jurors found Alvarez guilty after viewing a video-tape of him confessing to the killings and explaining the torture methods used on the two men. Rafeedie ordered that Alvarez be ineligible for parole consideration until after he has served at least sixty years of his 240-year sentence. REF.: *CBA*.

Alvarez de Toledo, Fernando, 1507-82, Spain, comdr. Soldier who in command in the Tunisian campaign of 1535 and later, commander of the imperial armies. In 1567 he was sent to the Netherlands by Philip II where he is believed to have executed 18,000 people, including Count Egmont and Count van Hoorne through his Council of Troubles, also known as the "Council of Blood" because he sanctioned atrocities committed by his army. REF.: *CBA*.

Alvarez-Qurioga, Roman, 1945- , **Alvarez-Quiroga, Juliana,** 1946- , **Alvarez-Qurioga, Roman Jr.,** 1971- , Case of, U.S., drug traffic. On Sept. 28, 1988, Roman Alvarez-Qurioga and his family were charged with possession of a controlled substance with the intent to distribute after they were pulled over by Illinois State Police near Pontiac, Ill., for exceeding the speed limit by three miles an hour. Roman Alvarez-Qurioga was issued tickets for speeding and improper lane usage after which a search of their station wagon uncovered 160 pounds of cocaine valued at between $7 and $12 million stashed under the roof head liner of the car. The drug bust was one of the largest in Illinois outside of Chicago and surrounding Cook County.

Alvarez-Quiroga and his wife Juliana were arraigned on federal charges while their son, Roman Jr., will face trial as an adult on similar state charges. Roman Sr. was held without bond while his wife and son were set free on their own recognizance. On Dec. 1, 1988, the Houston family appeared before Judge Harold Frobish who dismissed the charges against them. REF.: *CBA*.

Alverson, Leonard, prom. 1890s, U.S., (wrong. convict.) rob. A cowboy working at Cushey's ranch in Cochise County, Ariz., Alverson and three other wranglers were suddenly arrested by a hard-riding posse on Dec. 13, 1897. Alverson and two of the other cowboys were quickly convicted of robbing the SP Sunshine Special train at Stein's Pass, N.M., on Dec. 9, 1897. This robbery had been particularly bloody with the agent of the mail car killed by the gang, one gang member also killed, and another wounded during a wild gun battle. There had been five members of the holdup gang, three escaping. It was assumed, without a great deal of evidence, that Alverson was the leader of the holdup gang, since he bore a resemblance to the leader. He, Ed Cullen, and Dave Atkins were all given long sentences at the Santa Fe Prison.

In 1899, the notorious train, bank, and stagecoach robber, Thomas "Black Jack" Ketchum, having some occasional noble thoughts while awaiting execution for robbery, sent a letter from prison to President William McKinley in which he admitted that he and some others were wholly responsible for the murderous robbery of the Sunshine Special in 1897. Said Ketchum, "William Carver, Sam Ketchum, Bronco Bill, and I did the job. I have given my attorney these names and a list of what was taken and where same can be found. I make this statement realizing that my end is fast approaching and I very soon must meet my Maker." Alverson and the other two men were released with apologies but no compensation. See: Ketchum, Thomas.

REF.: Bartholomew, *The Biographical Album of Western Gunfighters*; *CBA*; Nash, *Bloodletters and Badmen*.

Alverstone, Viscount (Richard Everard Webster), 1842-1915, Brit., jur. Served three four-year terms as attorney general between 1885 and 1900. He was lord chief justice of England from 1900-13 and presided over many murder trials, including those of Herbert John Bennett, Horace Rayner, Madar Lal Dhingra, and Hawley Harvey Crippen. REF.: *CBA*.

Alves de Lima y Silva, Luis Duque de Caxias, 1803-80, Braz., soldier. In charge of the military police in Rio de Janeiro from 1831. REF.: *CBA*.

Alvord, Burton, 1866-c.1910, U.S., law enfor. off.-west. outl. Moving west with his father, a justice of the peace, Alvord settled in Tombstone, Ariz., where, as a teenager, he found a job as a stable hand at the O.K. Corral. Shortly after he began work there, Alvord witnessed one of the most spectacular gunfights of the Old West, the showdown shoot-out between the Earp-Holliday clan and the Clanton-McLowery outlaws, a bullet-spitting incident that would remain with him for the remainder of his days. Though he was only fifteen at the time of this legendary gun battle on Oct. 26, 1881, Alvord watched carefully as the Earps bested the outlaws by their cool composure and deliberate aim, a hallmark that was to be Alvord's adopted character when acting as a lawman or an outlaw.

At age twenty in 1886, Alvord was selected as a deputy by John Slaughter, the newly-elected sheriff of Cochise County. Slaughter had already seen the mettle of this young man a year earlier when Alvord had been challenged by a local Tombstone tough ubiquitously named "Six-shooter Jimmy." Both men had gone for their guns and Alvord had killed his opponent with one deliberately-aimed shot. From 1886 to 1890 Alvord served as Slaughter's back-up man in many a shoot-out with outlaws, rustlers, and gunmen of all kinds. Alvord accompanied Slaughter and another deputy, Cesario

Western lawman turned outlaw, Burt Alvord.

Lucero, in May 1888, in a pursuit after three Mexican train robbers, tracking these men down to their camp near the Whetstone Mountains one night. The lawmen found the thieves sleeping in their blankets around a smoldering campfire and ordered them to surrender. The three bandits dove for their guns and a pitched battle took plance in which one of the train robbers was shot. When he fell, the other two men meekly surrendered.

A month later, in the same area, on May 7, 1888, Alvord helped Slaughter capture three more Mexican bandits. Again, the lawmen crept up on their prey at night and caught the robbers asleep. A gun battle ensued and one of the bandits was killed, another wounded, the unharmed bandit surrendered quickly. The wounded Mexican, however, managed to escape. The following year, in February of 1889, Alvord began to slip from his role as the ramrod tough deputy. He began drinking heavily and frequently mixed with the outlaw element that drifted into Tombstone. On one occasion, Alvord got drunk with two surly cowboys named Fortino and Fuller, the threesome then in a private house near Slaughter's residence. Fuller exploded over a remark made by Fortino and seized Alvord's six-gun, shooting Fortino to death with it. The deputy was too drunk to stop Fuller at the time. When Slaughter arrived and learned of his deputy's involvement and how Alvord's own weapon was used in a killing, the sheriff exploded, verbally chastising Alvord in front of dozens of witnesses. The deputy was put on notice; either he mended his ways or he would be an unemployed lawman.

Alvord soured on Slaughter and Tombstone following this incident and he moved to Fairbank, Ariz., in the early 1890s where he became the town constable. His drinking and cavorting with known criminals soon caused town fathers to ask for his resignation and Alvord move on to Wilcox, Ariz., where he was made the town constable. He continued to drink heavily and most of the young outlaws labelled him a hopeless alcoholic from whom they had nothing to fear. One such gunman was Billy King, a rough-and-tumble cowboy who harassed Wilcox one day in 1898. Alvord appeared and ordered King to put up his gun and stop racing his horse up and down the main street. King gave the constable a winning smile and suggested that the two "settle matters over drinks" in the nearby saloon. Alvord and King went to the saloon and belted down a few drinks, but the cowboy grew sullen and threatening so Alvord asked him to step outside. As soon as King went through the back door of the saloon, Alvord drew his pistol and fired every bullet in his gun into King's face, killing him

instantly. Burt Alvord was not a man to waste time.

By the turn of the century Alvord had given up on keeping the peace. He would rather break it and join with the outlaws he had befriended over the years. He had physically changed into a dour-faced man with a bald head and a black beard; his dark eyes were full of anger and menace. For some years he led a band of ruthless train robbers. He was arrested first in 1900 and then in 1903 when he and his sidekick, Billy Stiles, were imprisoned. Both men managed to escape after Stiles was made a trustee at the Tombstone Jail and stole the keys to the lockup, allowing him to set Alvord free. Alvord, then much wanted, reasoned that the best way to effect a permanent escape was to play dead. He and Stiles located two corpses (they either killed two Mexicans or unearthed them from recent graves) and sent these bodies to Tombstone in sealed coffins, spreading the word that the pine boxes contained the wanted outlaws, Burt Alvord and Billy Stiles. The ruse failed, however, when suspicious lawmen broke open the coffins and found the ripening bodies of the Mexicans.

Arizona rangers set off in grim pursuit of Alvord and Stiles, locating the pair at their secret camp near Nigger Head Gap, Mex. The rangers ignored international law and crossed the border into Mexico to confront the two bad men. Both Alvord and Stiles went for their guns and both were wounded in the battle, Alvord shot twice in the leg, Stiles in the arm. Alvord was immobilized and could not reach his horse while Stiles managed to get into the saddle and ride wildly out of the trap, escaping. The rangers took Alvord into custody and he was sent to the Arizona prison at Yuma, serving two years for robbery. He was released in 1906 and decided that he would leave the American west forever, seeking his fortune in Central America. He was later reported to be in Venezuala and Honduras and, as late as 1910, the year he was presumed to have died, seen working as a canal employee in Panama. See: **Earp, Wyatt; Holliday, John H.; Slaughter, John Horton; Stiles, William Larkin.**

REF.: American Guide Series, *Arizona, A State Guide;* Axford, *Around Western Campfires;* Bakarich, *Gunsmoke;* ____, *There's Treasure in Our Hills;* Bartholomew, *Kill or Be Killed;* Block, *Great Train Robberies of the West;* Breihan, *Great Gunfighters of the West;* ____, *Great Lawmen of the West;* Brent, *Great Western Heroes;* Burns, *Tombstone, An Iliad of the Southwest; CBA;* Chisholm, *Brewery Gulch;* Erwin, *The Southwest of John H. Slaughter;* Gregg, *Drums of Yesterday;* Haley, *Jeff Milton, A Good Man with A Gun;* Holloway, *Texas Gun Lore;* Hughes, *South from Tombstone;* Hunt, *Cap Mossman;* Hunter and Rose, *The Album of Gunfighters;* Johnson, *Famous Lawmen of the Old West;* King, *Main Line;* McCarty, *The Enchanted West;* McCool, *So Said the Coroner;* Martin, *Tombstone's Epitaph;* Miller, *Arizona, The Last Frontier;* ____, *The Arizona Story;* Penfield, *Dig Here!;* ____, *Western Sheriffs and Marshals;* Raine, *Famous Sheriffs and Western Outlaws;* ____, *Forty-five Caliber Law;* Ringgold, *Frontier Days in the Southwest;* Rynning, *Gun Notches;* Schultz, *Southwestern Town, The Story of Wilcox, Arizona;* Shirley, *Buckskin and Spurs;* Small, *The Best of True West;* Sonnichsen, *Billy King's Tombstone;* Walters, *Tombstone's Yesterdays;* Waltrip, *Cowboys and Cattlemen;* Way, *Frontier Arizona.*

Amado, Christian, 1961- , U.S., wrong. convict. On Feb. 4, 1980, a man pulled a shotgun from underneath his coat and shot 28-year-old George Sneed while he waited on the porch of a friend's Boston apartment building. The man convicted of the crime was 21-year-old Christian Amado, identified by a witness by a photograph as resembling the man he had seen murder Sneed. The witness testified on the stand, however, that Christian Amado was positively not the murderer, although Amado and the man in the photograph were one and the same. Amado was convicted of first- degree murder on Oct. 29, 1980, in Suffolk County Superior Court.

Two years later his defense attorney, appealing the 1980 decision before the Massachusetts Supreme Court, won an acquittal for his client who, justices ruled, was convicted on insufficient evidence. Christian Amado was released in 1982. REF.: *CBA.*

Amalasuntha (or **Amalasuentha** or **Amalaswintha**), 498-535,

Tuscany, queen, assass. Daughter of Theodoric, king of the Ostrogoths, Amalasuntha was left with two children at the death of her husband, Eutharic and she succeeded her father as co-regent (526-35) of Tuscany with her cousin, Theodahad. The ruthless Theodahad, attempting to take the empire for himself after finding Amlasuntha intractable in holding the throne for her son, sent assassins to his cousin's palace and there the queen, trapped in her bath, was murdered in 535. Eastern Emperor Justinian, who had signed an alliance with Amalasuntha, used her murder as a pretext to have his Byzantine forces invade Italy, which saw the ruination of Theodahad's armies and lands, and indirectly brought about his own assassination. See: **Theodahad**.

REF.: *CBA;* Diehl, *Cambridge Medieval History;* Seville, *History of the Kings of the Goths.*

Amar, Judy (AKA: Judy Love), 1948- , U.S., burg. Born in rural Arkansas as Judy Love, Amar became the ruling queen of Florida's sneak thieves in the 1980s when she broke into posh homes and stole between $3 million and $6 million worth of property over a five-year period. Amar moved to South Florida where she hoped to live an extravagant life quite the opposite of her life on the family farm. She worked as a prostitute for more than ten years before meeting her third husband, Jesus Avila, who was wanted for questioning in the 1982 slayings of two people outside a Miami nightclub. Avila introduced her to the real wealth of the underworld when they began working together, robbing homes first in Dade County, then moving up the coast to Palm Beach and Boca Raton.

Amar eventually struck out on her own, making a name for herself by the time she was apprehended in 1984. She made a full confession to several burglaries but was released to undergo a hysterectomy. She immediately skipped town.

Palm Beach County Detective Ron Tomassi finally caught her in 1987 after a rash of burglaries in Boca Del Mar, Fla., and a tip from a drug dealer who often supplied Amar with cocaine financed with the stolen property. Amar was convicted on thirty-three counts of burglary and grand theft and sentenced to ten years in prison. REF.: *CBA.*

Amasa, Biblical, Isr., capt., assass. Captain of Absolom's army, assassinated by Joab. REF.: *CBA.*

Amati, Giovanna, c.1970s Case of, Italy, kid. Amati, the 18-year-old daughter of an Italian theater owner, was kidnapped and held for fifty-four days until her father paid a $2.1 million ransom for her safe return. She later assisted in the successful apprehension of one of her captors whom she had fallen in love with during her ordeal. After her release, the man, known only as "Daniel," sent her two dozen roses as a token of his affection. It is not known whether she agreed or was coerced into laying the trap for her lover outside a theater in the Via Barberini, but she pleaded with Italian officers to free "Daniel" who was immediately taken into custody.

REF.: *CBA;* Moorehead, *Hostage To Fortune.*

Amatuna, Samuel Samuzzo (AKA: Samoots), 1899-1925, U.S., org. crime. A product of Little Italy in Chicago, Amatuna began his criminal career in his teens as a messenger for the murderous Genna brothers. The Gennas controlled a vast empire of alky cookers and provided the Torrio-Capone Gang with much of its home-made liquor supply. Amatuna proved his mettle to the Gennas by administering beatings to any of the Sicilians whose production fell short of expectations. Moreover, he was adept with a knife and pistol and would fearlessly attack anyone who dared criticize the ruthless Gennas. Amatuna was made the personal bodyguard of Angelo Genna in 1920, and he also served as a strong-arm thug, fixing election returns. The Gennas, in the early 1920s, concerned themselves chiefly with wresting political control of their own territory and fought tooth and nail to take over the Nineteenth Ward. This ward, called the Bloody Nineteenth, was the center of all illegal activities for the Gennas. The area had changed drastically in thirty years, from a predominantly Irish neighborhood to a new melting pot that teemed with newly arrived Italian and Sicilian immigrants.

John Powers had been the alderman of the Nineteenth Ward since 1888, ruling the district for almost forty years. But his Irish constituency had dwindled, and the flood of Italians and Sicilians into the area caused one of their own, Anthony D'Andrea to demand political representation and he went after it with armed thugs. Not all Italians and Sicilians felt D'Andrea was the best man to represent their people. Powers had proven to be a good alderman and he received support from many of the ward's non-Irish residents. Frank Lombardi was one of these. This loyal Powers supporter entered a saloon on Taylor Street on Feb. 21, 1916, and was shot dead by a dark-featured, nattily dressed youth who fled and was never apprehended. According to one report, the killer was Amatuna who, at age seventeen, earned the right to Genna mob status by killing his first man. The Gennas, of course, wanted D'Andrea as the alderman to further strengthen their position with police and the courts. When Prohibition began the Gennas quickly went into the liquor production and bootlegging business but continued to battle the Powers faction.

Chicago gangster Samoots Amatuna, loyal to the Genna brothers unto death.

The Gennas set off a bomb on the alderman's front porch on Sept. 28, 1920, and it was Amatuna who reputedly lit the fuse. The blast caused considerable damage but no injuries. It was a warning which the feisty Powers refused to recognize. The alderman surrounded his house with armed guards and a bevy of private detectives, shotguns in their hands, marched solemnly around buildings where Powers held his political meetings in preparation for the hotly contested 1921 election which pitted once again, D'Andrea and Powers against each other. Several more bombs were exploded in front of homes owned by supporters of each man but no one was killed. Powers narrowly won the election which caused Angelo Genna to go crazy. He vowed that Paul Labriola, a Powers man and a bailiff for the municipal court, would pay for his support of Powers, figuring that the narrow win of only 435 votes were Italians and Sicilians Labriola had convinced to vote for Powers.

On Mar. 9, 1921, Labriola was shot to death by three men who were later identified as Angelo Genna and his two top aides, Amatuna and Frank "Don Chick" Gambino. Only Genna and Gambino were indicted for the killing but they were later released for lack of evidence. The killing was attributed to D'Andrea but he was merely a Genna stooge, one whom the brothers engineered into the presidency of the Unione Siciliane, the organization that controlled the thousands of Sicilian alky cookers. Amatuna had killed Labriola, and he had also dispatched Harry Raimondi and Gaetano Esposito, two more allies of Powers. Amatuna was the strong-arm link between both the Unione Siciliane and the alky cookers. He grew rich and powerful under the Genna banner and by the time Amatuna was twenty-five he had accounts in several banks and interest in a dozen businesses. He was a dandy, wearing more than $40,000 in diamond studs and cufflinks when attending the opera with Angelo Genna and other nineteenth ward gangsters.

Amatuna possessed a musically correct tenor voice and would unexpectedly break into song to please his gun-toting friends. To allow himself a showcase for his own singing and short violin compositions, Amatuna bought the Bluebird Café on Halsted

Street and held court here almost every night, singing, playing his violin and providing good Sicilian cuisine. The place was a popular eatery for those who enjoyed good food, red wine, and a singing gangster. Amatuna never wore his two guns inside of his restaurant. "No one can shoot me in here," he once proudly told newsmen. "The place is full of my friends. Any guy who would hurt me here would be torn apart by my patrons."

Samoots, as he was called by his friends, indulged his fancies at every opportunity. He owned three dozen tailor-made suits and hundreds of monogrammed shirts which were his pride and joy. When a laundry dared to return one of his shirts with a scorch mark, the gangster went crazy, leaping out of bed and racing after the horse-drawn laundry wagon. Half-dressed and with two pistols in his hands, Amatuna raged at the driver and leveled one of his guns at the man. A crowd had assembled and Amatuna had the presence of mind to look about. He saw a beat patrolman standing at the edge of the crowd, waiting. Instead of shooting the cowering wagon driver, Samoots confined his rage to the horse, shooting the animal dead, then walking silently back to his home. The beat cop in the crowd, obviously on the Genna payroll, did nothing.

This oddball gangster amused himself and entertained his neighbors in the summer evenings by opening the windows of his apartment and playing one tune after another on his violin; he had learned to play the instrument as a boy under his mother's constant encouragement. His boss, Angelo Genna, called Bloody Angelo because of the dozens of men he had killed, would drop by the apartment and listen to Samoots play for hours. Then, being the utilitarian he was, Genna decided to put Amatuna's musical talents to work for him. He would join the Musician's Union and take it over. "Aww, boss, that'll take too long," Amatuna replied. "Me and the boys will pay them horn-tooters a visit, one visit, and take the joint over." Amatuna's top two torpedoes, Abraham "Bummy" Goldstein (who ran a wildcat distillery and was sometimes called Pete the Peddler) and Eddie Zion (who had interests in several roadhouses in northern Cook County), accompanied him to the Musician's Union headquarters the next day. They all carried violin cases and when they marched into the offices they opened the cases and produced guns. When union officials ordered them off the premises, Amatuna and his men opened fire, wounding one union official but failing to kill anyone; they fled at the sound of police whistles.

Following the killing of Angelo Genna in May 1925, the Genna gang disintegrated but Amatuna tried to keep the family power intact. He walked into the Unione Siciliane headquarters with Goldstein and Zion at his side and told everyone that he was the new president. He held the office for only a short time. On the evening of Nov. 13, 1925, Amatuna prepared to attend a performance of *Aida* at the Auditorium Theater with his betrothed, Rose Pecorara, part of the Mike Merlo family (Merlo had been a power in the Italian-Sicilian community, having run the Unione Siciliane for many years before his death in 1924). Amatuna, as was his habit before attending any social function, went to a barbershop owned by Isadore Paul on Roosevelt Road for a manicure and shave. He appeared alone in the shop, his bodyguards Goldstein and Zion absent. Amatuna was dressed in his evening wear—a tuxedo with long tails—and he glistened with diamonds. When the barber asked about Samoots' missing "friends," Amatuna shrugged, telling him that he could not reach them that day.

The gang boss sat down in the chair and, as a hot towel was applied to his face, two men entered the shop and drew guns. The manicurist screamed and fell to the floor. Amatuna leaped up, drawing his own gun and hid behind one of the barber chairs. The two gunmen opened fire as did Samoots. His shots went wild but two bullets from the gunmen struck the young gangster in the chest, and he pitched forward mortally wounded as his killers escaped.

Amatuna was rushed to the hospital where he begged a priest to bring his beloved Rose to his bedside. He wanted to be married before dying. The girl was brought to Samoots' deathbed and the priest began the ceremony but before Amatuna could say "I do," he lapsed into unconsciouness and then, within minutes, took the long slide into death.

Amatuna's attackers were identified as Vincent "The Schemer" Drucci and Jim Doherty, both of the Weiss-Moran mob who had been mortal enemies of the Gennas. The driver of the getaway car which waited outside the barber shop was identified as Frank Gusenberg, also a Weiss gunman. None of these men were ever brought to trial. Amatuna's bodyguards, Goldstein and Zion, whose conspicuous absence from the barbershop had been noted, were either paid to stay away from the scene, it was claimed, or had defected to the Weiss-Moran gang and had helped to set up their boss. (Surviving Genna brothers insisted that Amatuna's death was assured when Samoots ignored the policy of only hiring Sicilians as bodyguards, with Mike Genna hissing, "Them Jew boys only work for themselves and they will always side with the Irish in the end.") Both Zion and Goldstein were killed a short time later, Zion, on November 17, after returning home from Amatuna's funeral and Goldstein, on Nov. 30, 1925. Two killers spotted Bummy in a drugstore and, having no weapon of their own with which to dispatch the marked man, grabbed a shotgun from an unmanned detective car nearby and used this to blow away the last of Amatuna's men.

Dead at twenty-six, Samuel Samuzzo Amatuna, was not to rest in his adopted country. His body was dug up after an elaborate funeral ceremony and shipped back to his native village of Pogallo, Sicily, where it was interred with great pomp by his family. He was considered a local hero since he sent much of his racket money to his relatives in Sicily, much of this ill-gotten loot having been used to repair the local church which had for centuries been in ruins. Though the citizens of Chicago's Little Italy paid lip service to the accomplishments of Amatuna and to his generosity to the local inhabitants, few were really sorry to see him go to his death. Hundreds of elderly Sicilians slaving over their alky boilers had been beaten unconscious by the ambitious Amatuna for not meeting their quotas of cheap liquor. Dozens more lay in cemeteries where bullets from Samoots' guns had sent them. Because of the manner in which Samoots Amatuna went to his Maker, it became general policy among barbers to never again fully cover the face of any client with a hot towel and always keep their barber chairs facing the front door so that anyone entering the shop could be seen and identified. See: **Capone, Alphonse; Drucci, Vincent; Genna Brothers; Unione Siciliane.**

REF.: Asbury, *Gem of the Prairie*; Burns, *The One-Way Ride*; *CBA*; Kobler, *Capone*; Landesco, *Organized Crime in Chicago*; Murray, *The Legacy of Al Capone*; Nash, *Bloodletters and Badmen*; Pasley, *Al Capone*; ____, *Muscling In*; Sullivan, *Chicago Surrenders*; ____, *Rattling the Cup on Chicago Crime*.

Amaziah (Amasias), c.780 B.C., Judah, ruler, assass. King of Judah, c. 800-c. 783 B.C. He was captured and taken prisoner by Joash, King of Israel, and assassinated at Lachish. REF.: *CBA*.

Amberg, Joseph C., 1892-35, and **Amberg, Louis** (AKA: **Pretty**), 1899-35, U.S., org. crime. The Ambergs were loansharks, bootleggers dope peddlers, and extortionists, both of them killers accredited with at least twenty murders in their territory of Brownsville, a near-poverty area of Brooklyn, which the brothers terrorized for a decade. Immigrating from Russia with their parents, the Amberg boys (there were two more—Oscar and Hyman, known as "Hymie the Rat"), helped their father peddle fruit through the streets before they reached their teens. They were street-hardened early and when in their teens, Joe and Louis took to petty protection rackets, telling shopkeepers that if they did not pay them a weekly stipend, their shops might catch fire or be blown to pieces by an accidentally tossed bomb.

Louis Amberg was the loudest and most fierce of the brothers. He was called Pretty, an ironic sobriquet because he was one of the ugliest hoodlums to ever walk the streets of Brooklyn. A mean streak in Pretty Amberg ran to his core. He terrorized citizens in restaurants, on the sidewalk, anywhere he made human contact. A small, stocky man, Pretty had to prove that he was bigger than his fellow human beings and this meant that he would knock an innocent person into the gutter as he strolled through his haunts, or saunter into a restaurant where he would sweep food-filled plates from the tables of dining guests, then sneer and tell them to "order something else." He and his brother Joe were known as "six for five" loansharks. They would loan $5 to a juice victim and demand $6 within one week. If anyone failed to pay they had their arms or legs broken by Pretty Amberg who delighted in such chores. He was a walking arsenal, usually carrying three guns, a knife, and brass knuckles. When the Amberg rackets slowed down, Pretty hired out as a gunman to Dutch Schultz.

The end of NYC ganster Joe Amberg, dead in foreground, and his chauffeur, ambushed by Murder, Inc. killers.

The powerhouse syndicate in Brooklyn headed by Joe Adonis and backed up by Albert Anastasia's killer squads of Murder, Inc. paid little attention to the brutal Ambergs, believing their rackets to be petty and of no significance to syndicate coffers. But the Ambergs began to flourish in the early 1930s when money was short and they reaped a fortune through their loan-sharking activities. With some of their considerable profits they bought a large Brooklyn laundry and insisted that every restaurant in the area (except, of course, Adonis' infamous Joe's Italian Kitchen) use their services to clean tablecloths, napkins, and the like. Those who were reluctant to sign up were approached by Pretty who invariably told them, "You know, we got a lot of laundry bags at the shop. You don't sign up with us, you're gonna be in one of them bags." (This story reached the ears of Damon Runyon who used the laundry bag threat in one of his stories.)

Until Prohibition was repealed, the Ambergs did a large business in peddling bootleg hootch in Brooklyn, using the same strong-arm tactics in forcing huge orders from saloon keepers. The Ambergs got rich and their reputation spread to such Manhattan bootleggers as Owney "The Killer" Madden who, upon meeting Pretty, told him he had never been in Brownsville. Amberg's unthinking response was to tell Madden that if he ever came into his territory he would kill him. Pretty Amberg took pains to insult most of the leaders of gangland. He met the deadly Jack "Legs" Diamond and told him that if he ever dared to enter Brownsville, he would kill him and his entire family and friends. Dutch Schultz, in the early 1930s, eyed the lucrative Amberg operations and told his one-time gunman Pretty that he was thinking of becoming an Amberg partner. Amberg patted the side of his tight-fitting, pin-striped suit where a hidden pistol bulged and said, "The first thing you'll see in my area is this gun, Dutch,

and it'll be the last thing you see."

Such brazen attitudes finally caused the Ambergs to run afoul of the newly-established national syndicate. Anastasia's men were asked to settle a cafeteria strike in Brownsville in 1933. Abe "Kid Twist" Reles, a vicious killer who had murdered dozens of men by his own later admissions, stepped into the union-management fray and ordered the union men to go back to their serving trays or "you'll be drowned in your own soup." The strike abruptly ended and Reles demanded $8,500 from management which was paid. When Pretty Amberg heard of this payment he exploded, demanding half the payment since he controlled the cafeteria employee's union. Reles refused and the argument was brought before the syndicate board. At a meeting in Joe Adonis' restaurant, Joe's Italian Kitchen, Benjamin "Bugsy" Siegel, one of the syndicate's original board members, held court on the matter. Also present but silent as Siegel presided were Lucky Luciano, Albert Ansastasia, Adonis, and Louis Capone (no relation to Al Capone) who was Lepke Buchalter's representative. Reles sat to the side as Amberg strutted into the back room to present his case. He did not request the money; he demanded it. Siegel listened patiently, then turned to Reles and said, "Give him the money, Abe." Reles paid Amberg the money.

When Pretty left the room, Reles, his fleshy face flushed with reddening anger, blurted to Siegel, "Why did you do that, Ben? He didn't do nothin' to make that dough!"

Siegel smiled slightly and said, "I'm just giving that little runt some rope. He'll hang himself with it one of these days."

The Ambergs came to the end of their rope in 1935. In that year, Joe Amberg, along with Jack Elliott and Frank Tietlebaum, murdered Hyman "Hymie" Kazner, a one-time Waxey Gordon gunman who was in the employ of the fearsome Albert Anastasia. Amberg and the others put Kazner into a laundry bag and dumped his body into a sewer system but the body somehow floated into the Canarsie River. When it was found, Anastasia exploded, demanding retribution. Joe Amberg was brought to Siegel's office and was grilled for more then ten hours until he admitted the murder, giving obscure reasons for the "hit." Only hours after Amberg was released, a top level summit meeting was held. Siegel and Adonis voted to allow Amberg to live since he worked some of their Brooklyn rackets for them, but Anastasia insisted that he be murdered, along with Elliott and Tietlebaum, the latter being a Lepke Buchalter gunman. But Louis Capone, Lepke's man, agreed with Anastasia that such rampant freelance killings could not be tolerated. Adonis and Siegel, after much arguing, relented and gave their approval for the murder of Amberg.

Capone, after consulting with Anastasia, summoned three Murder, Inc. killers, Harry "Happy" Maione, Alexander "Red" Alpert, and Philip "Philly" Mangano, the latter a brother of Vincent Mangano who was later to head one of the five powerful New York Mafia families. Mangano had a special reason to get rid of Joe Amberg since he and Anastasia owned some Brooklyn laundries that vied for business with the Amberg operations. On Sept. 30, 1935, the three killers, following directions delivered by Louis Capone and supervised by Siegel, lured Amberg to a Brooklyn garage. Murder, Inc. was economy minded; killing spots were selected for convenience but not always with thought of repercussion. The garage was half-owned by Murder, Inc.'s worst killer, Harry "Pittsburgh Phil" Strauss, although Strauss was not present during this murder. (It is amazing that Strauss, a known owner of the murder site, was not brought in for questioning later.) Amberg, who thought he was about to meet with syndicate bigshots to develop new territory for his increasing narcotics trade, arrived at the garage in his limousine, driven by chauffeur Mannie Kessler. As soon as the limo entered the garage, its huge door slid shut and Maione, a sinister joker, stepped forward, opening the back door with a flourish as would a doorman.

Amberg stepped out and looked about. "Where is Joey A. and Ben Siegel?"

Maione answered him by pulling out his revolver, saying, "Right here, Joe."

He, Mangano, and Alpert, all holding guns, shoved the mob boss to a wall of the garage. Maione ordered Kessler out of the car, too, and then pushed him to the wall so that both men faced the naked bricks. Then he, Alpert, and Mangano opened fire, emptying their revolvers into the two men who toppled backward, the backs of their heads blown away. They lay silent on the garage floor, and their killers jumped back quickly so that the rush of blood would not soil their shoes. Maione stared at the rivulets of blood flowing into a water drain and said, "Pep (the mob's name for Strauss) ain't gonna like his garage all messed up like this."

The three killers then fled the garage. Mangano was so excited by the murder that he ran the wrong way down the street, so that he could not locate the getaway car. Maione stood in the middle of the dark street, shouting after him, "Philly! Hey, Philly! Over here, this way!" Mangano turned around and managed to get into the car as Alpert moved it out into the street. A beat cop, however, had already peeked into the garage, saw the slain men, and fired a shot at the fleeing car. The bullet sailed through both back windows of the large sedan and struck no one. The three killers in the car were all destined for violent deaths themselves. Seven months later, Alpert would be murdered by Abe "Kid Twist" Reles, Martin "Bugsy" Goldstein, and Anthony "Dukey" Maffetore. In 1942, because of testimony given by Reles, Maione's one-time associate in Murder, Inc., Happy would go to the electric chair for his many murders. Philip Mangano would be murdered in 1951 for betraying the Agueci Brothers. (Even those who supervised the Amberg slayings would die in similar fashion, Louis Capone going to the electric chair in 1944 with his boss, Lepke, and handsome Bugsy Siegel being shot to death in the Beverly Hills home of his mistress, Virginia Hill, in 1947.)

Next it was the turn of Frankie Teitlebaum. He was shot down twelve days after Joe Amberg and Mannie Kessler. His body was stuffed into a trunk and left beneath a Manhattan bridge. Police later concluded that his killers had erred, that by placing the body in a trunk, they could not fit it into a sewer opening and were left to deposit the trunk in the most convenient spot.

Jack Elliott, who had operated as a freelance gunman and protector of businessmen threatened with ransom kidnapping, was the most feared of the three men who had been marked for murder because of Hymie Kazner's death. The killers of Murder, Inc. stalked him for weeks and finally caught the gangster in his car on the Hackensack Flats in New Jersey. They took away Elliott's two guns, then locked him in his car and set the auto on fire, pumping bullets into it for half an hour. None of bullets struck their victim, a coroner later determined. Elliott roasted to death.

Louis Amberg was enraged at the murder of his brother, Joe. In the Hollywood tradition of the snarling gangster, Pretty Amberg sent out the word to gangland that he would "have the heads of everyone involved in killing my brother. I know the bums behind it. I'm gonna get Capone and Pep!" He had passed a sentence of death on Louis Capone and Harry "Pittsburgh Phil" Strauss. Anastasia took this remark to his boss, Lepke Buchalter, who, in turn, summoned his chief enforcer, Emmanuel "Mendy" Weiss, asking him how to deal with the cunning Pretty Amberg. Said Weiss, "Pretty won't go with nobody but me. He likes me. I'll steer him. He'll never get wise." Weiss, pretending to sympathize with Amberg over the loss of his brother, suggested that he and Pretty have dinner and drinks at a nightclub owned by one of his friends. When Amberg expressed caution about leaving Brooklyn, his home territory, Weiss assured him that the club they would visit was near the plaza leading to the Williamsburg Bridge which stretched over the East River. The club was in Brooklyn, just barely.

On Oct. 23, 1935, Weiss picked up Amberg and the two of them drove to the club. When they stepped into the office of the club's owner, several Murder, Inc. goons jumped Amberg and strapped him to a chair. Amberg let out a stream of cursewords

in Weiss' direction but Mendy had no time to dally with Pretty Amberg. He had more important chores to perform in New Jersey, for on the same day, Weiss drove to New Jersey and met with Charlie "The Bug" Workman and another man, went to the Palace Chop House in Newark, and there shot Dutch Schultz and three of his men, the Dutchman dying some hours later. (This was a murder decreed by the syndicate board and had nothing to do with Amberg. Schultz had defied the board and had gone ahead with plans to murder New York District Attorney Thomas E. Dewey who had been bringing pressure on the Dutchman's rackets. It was felt by Luciano and Lepke Buchalter that Schultz dead would serve them better than a murdered government official, a killing that would certainly bring them all down.)

Pretty Amberg's killers were never named by Reles or other Murder, Inc. informers, but police detectives guessed that his slaughterhouse killing had been performed by Pittsburgh Phil Strauss, Happy Maione, and Frank "The Dasher" Abbandando. The killers exercised a deep wrath for Amberg in torturing him to death. His body was literally sliced off in pieces, all the meaty areas cut out as one might carve a turkey breast. They also used an ax on Amberg, chopping away at his arms, legs, torso. When his killers tired of Pretty's screams they ended their grisly chore by blowing off the back of his head with a shotgun blast. Still the killers were not done with their victim. Such was there hatred for Pretty Amberg that the troop of killers decided to make him a spectacle in death. His bloody corpse was tossed into the back of a car which was driven to a secluded area near the Brooklyn Navy Yard. The killers summoned a dozen of their friends and the prostitutes who serviced the gang to join them in "some fun with Pretty," as they put it. As the gang stood around the car holding the hacked up remains of Amberg, more Murder, Inc. members arrived in a small van and carried many cans of gasoline to the auto, which was doused with the gas. Five women of the gang then drew lots to see who would be the one to ignite the gas-soaked car. An attractive blonde picked the shortest matchstick and laughed as she lit it and threw it onto the car which blazed up. The killers and their women then stepped back and admired their handiwork, applauding, some toasting the gruesome bonfire with champagne they had brought along for the occasion. Kid Twist Reles later stated that it had been decided on the day of Pretty Amberg's death, the troop of killers would elect a "Miss Murder, Inc." which was the woman who won the right to torch the car. "Yeah," grunted the brutal Reles in his later statements, "it was Ladies Night."

With the deaths of Joe and Louis, the Amberg gang fell to pieces. The remaining brothers fled for their lives. Oscar Amberg, it was later claimed, was abducted by Murder, Inc. goons and buried alive. One later story had it that Pretty Amberg and Dutch Schultz had coincidentally put out separate murder contracts on each other, both filled on the same day. As previously stated, however, these were unrelated killings that merely happened to occur on the same day, although gangland, always in search of lethal myths that perpetuated the fierce image of the American gangster, insisted that Amberg and Schultz "cancelled each other out." See: **Abbandando, Frank; Adonis, Joe; Agueci Brothers; Anastasia, Albert; Buchalter, Louis; Gordon, Waxey; Luciano, Charles; Maione, Harry; Mangano, Vincent; Reles, Abraham; Schultz, Dutch; Siegel, Benjamin; Strauss, Harry; Weiss, Emmanuel; Workman, Charles.**

REF.: Addy, *The Dutch Schultz Story;* Carpozi, *Bugsy; CBA;* Fried, *The Rise and Fall of the Jewish Gangster in America;* Jennings, *We Only Kill Each Other;* McPhaul, *Johnny Torrio;* Nash, *Bloodletters and Badmen;* Sann, *Kill the Dutchman!;* Thompson and Raymond, *Gang Rule in New York;* Turkus and Feder, *Murder, Inc.*

Ambuhl, John E., b.1891, U.S., police chief. A member of the Indianapolis, Ind., police force for thirty-five years, John E. Ambuhl retired in 1961 as captain of police. He began his career on Jan. 4, 1926, when he was hired as secretary to then Police Chief Johnson. Ambuhl held several positions within the department and was promoted to chief of police on Jan. 1, 1952—a position he held until January 1956 when he was reassigned as inspector of police. On June 17, 1957, Ambuhl was promoted to captain of police and served the city of Indianapolis until his retirement at the age of sixty-nine on Jan. 17, 1961. REF.: *CBA*.

Ameer Ali, Syed (Sayyid Amir Ali), 1849-1928, India, jur. Judge of the high court of Calcutta until 1904 when he retired and moved to England. In 1909 he was appointed Indian judge to Privy Council. REF.: *CBA*.

Amen, John Harlan, prom. 1942, U.S., lawyer. Amen was the special prosecutor in a 1942 case that uncovered widespread corruption within the Brooklyn, N.Y., police force. Amen charged forty-nine police officers with accepting $1 million in bribes from bookmakers as protection money for their illegal gambling operations. A special investigative squad filmed the policemen accepting the money, which they used for extravagant purchases including motorboats, summer homes, automobiles, and $1,000 furs for their wives. REF.: *CBA*.

Amerbach, Basilius, 1533-91, Ger., jur. REF.: *CBA*.

Amerbach, Bonifacius, c.1496-1562, Switz., jur. REF.: *CBA*.

American: A Middle Western Legend, The, 1946, a novel by Howard Fast. The protagonist for this novel is Governor John Altgeld of Illinois, who, amidst a storm of life-threatening protest, pardoned surviving Haymarket rioters (U.S., 1886). See: **Altgeld, John Peter; Haymarket Riot**. REF.: *CBA*.

American Medical Association, prom. 1941, U.S., antitrust violation. In 1941, the American Medical Association (AMA) and its Washington, D.C., branch—the District Medical Society—were convicted of violating the Sherman Antitrust Act when a jury found that the health organization acted illegally when, in 1939, it barred members from consulting or practicing medicine on patients enrolled in group health plans. In 1939, the AMA took action against Group Health Association, (GHA) Inc., a family health-care plan organized by 2,500 government employees in 1938. GHA hired nine physicians to provide medical care to its members for an annual fee of less than $50. The AMA, opposed to group medical care, refused to allow its members to treat GHA patients and barred those same patients from treatment at AMA certified hospitals. In addition the organization expelled Dr. Mario Victor Scandiffio, a GHA doctor, and forced the resignation of another AMA physician from the GHA payroll.

During the two-and-a-half year trial, the court heard testimony from several GHA patients. One man, suffering from acute appendicitis, was refused treatment by his GHA doctor. An elderly woman, after having been hit by an automobile, was required to leave the AMA certified hospital she was taken to because her GHA doctor was not allowed to treat her there. In April 1941, the court found the AMA and its Washington branch in violation of the Sherman Antitrust Act, while the doctors were acquitted. REF.: *CBA*.

American Tragedy, An, 1925, a novel by Theodore Dreiser. This classic work was wholly drawn from the short and murderous life of Chester Gillette who murdered his unwanted girl friend, Grace Brown (U.S., 1906). Dreiser was a reporter covering the trial at the time and a great amount of the actual trial transcript found its way, verbatim, into his novel. Two films and two plays were based upon the Dreiser work. One play, by Patrick Kearney (1926) used the title of the novel. See: **Gillette, Chester**. REF.: *CBA*.

American Tragedy, An, 1931, a film directed by the great Hollywood stylist, Josef von Sternberg. This picture was based upon the Theodore Dreiser novel of the same name, which was, in turn, based upon killer Chester Gillette (U.S., 1906). The film faithfully followed the novel with an anxious Phillips Holmes portraying the youthful murderer. *A Place in the Sun* was its remake. See: **Gillette, Chester**. REF.: *CBA*.

Amerman, Max, b.1923, U.S. mur. Calling itself the "Sweetest Town on Earth," Medina, Ohio proved to be anything but that on the night of Oct. 5, 1950, when Harold Mast was murdered on the back porch of his farmhouse. Mast was shot in the back with a bullet from a twelve-gauge shotgun just before entering the home Amerman was leasing to him. As no one saw his assailant, suspicion soon fell on Amerman who was in love with the dead man's wife, Randi Mast. Amerman had paid for the woman's parents to come to the United States from Germany, allowed the Masts to lease his luxurious farm very inexpensively, and often attempted to have sexual intercourse with Mrs. Mast.

At the time of the murder, however, Amerman was in New Jersey, giving him a solid alibi which was doubted only after questioning 17-year-old Jerry Killinger. Killinger and Amerman, ten years the teen's senior, had a very close friendship, so close that Killinger would not divulge what he knew about Mast's killing. When police confronted Amerman with knowledge of this friendship, he admitted to having arranged for Killinger to shoot Mast so that he could marry Mrs. Mast. Killinger then confessed to pulling the trigger. The day before Killinger turned eighteen, Nov. 16, 1950, the jury found him guilty of murder without recommendation for mercy. He was sentenced to be electrocuted at the Ohio State Penitentiary in Columbus, as was Amerman after he pled guilty to first degree murder in January 1951.

REF.: *CBA*; Radin, *Headline Crimes of the Year*.

Amery, John, d.1946, Brit., treas. Amery was an ardent anti-Communist. In 1937, his neo-fascist political convictions led him to Spain where he fought on the side of Generalissimo Francisco Franco Nationalist forces. Amery was the son of Leopold Amery, a brilliant orator in the House of Commons whose stirring speech led to the downfall of the Chamberlain government in 1940. Educated at the finest schools, John Amery was in many ways a product of his class and the times in which he lived—the impassioned 1930s—when the flower of English youth embraced the great political causes. Unlike so many other members of his generation who were opposed to fascism, Amery embraced the doctrine. His hatred of Russia bordered on obsession.

With the explosion of WWII, Amery, who was marooned in Vichy France and unable to return home, was used by the Nazi puppets to spread anti-British propaganda. Taken to Berlin in 1943, he gave a series of radio broadcasts urging his countrymen to enter into a negotiated peace with the Germans and to unite against the common enemy, the Russians.

Amery toured German POW camps to recruit British soldiers for his St. George's Legion to fight on the Russian front *with* the German army. There were few volunteers. At the end of the war he was captured by the Russian Partisans and turned over to the Americans who released him into the custody of the British.

In one of the showcase trials of the post-war period, Amery was indicted for treason and placed before the aging jurist, Sir Travers Humphreys. He pleaded guilty to all charges in a surprise move that confounded the legal experts. Amery seemingly had a death wish. The death sentence was passed and Amery was hanged despite strong protests from members of the Labor Party, who had stood in opposition to the man's father on many far-reaching issues over the years.

REF.: Burt, *Commander Burt of Scotland Yard*; *CBA*.

Ames, James Barr, 1846-1910, U.S., prof. Dean of Harvard Law School from 1895 until his death. REF.: *CBA*.

Amiel, Jean, 1922- , Fr., mur. On June 23, 1959, in Perpignan, France, English instructor Amiel accidentally shot 16-year-old Alain Rolland in the head as the boy ran with a group of friends from Amiel's home after dropping firecrackers through the letter slot in the front door. Amiel raced to the window to see who the perpetrators were after hearing the explosions in the hallway. According to him, he shot one round from his revolver randomly out the window to frighten the boys. The bullet accidentally hit Rolland in the back of the head and killed him instantly.

A jury convicted Amiel of murder, but the judge, believing Amiel's story, gave him a sentence of only two years and a damage assessment of 3 million francs for the family of the slain youth. The short sentence angered the Rolland family and many citizens so strongly that when Amiel was taken to prison, authorities secreted his wife and daughter out of town, fearing for their safety.

Tragedy for the Rolland family struck again when the boy's

father, Eugène Rolland, committed suicide. He left a note saying, "I am going to join Alain." REF.: *CBA*.

Amili, al-, Muhammad ibn Husayn Baha al-Din, (AKA: Shaykh Baha), c.1546-c.1622, Iran, jur. Chief judge of the Islamic court of law at Isfahan under Shah Abbas I. He also wrote on legal issues. REF.: *CBA*.

Amin, al-, c.785-813, caliph, assass. Son and successor of Harun al-Rashid, he was caliph of Abbasid dynasty. When opposed by his brother al-Mamum, he surrendered, and was murdered for surrendering. REF.: *CBA*.

Amin, Idi (Idi Amin Dada Oumee), 1928-   , Uganda, pres., mur. For eight years Idi Amin ruled the East African nation of Uganda with an iron fist. To his subjects, the swaggering 6-foot-4 strong man in the military uniform was a popular hero, having driven out 55,000 to 80,000 Asians-the bulk of Uganda's professional class. The rest of the world, however, viewed Idi Amin somewhat differently. Behind the mask of false bravado and superficial concern for the impoverished Ugandan peasants lurked a dangerous, unpredictable madman who instigated some of the worst atrocities in that nation's history.

Born in the village of Koboko in the West Nile region to a poor farmer in the Kakwa tribe, Amin as a boy tended goats and worked in the fields. His formal education ending with the fourth grade, Amin acquired whatever else he learned from the army, serving with the Eleventh East African Division of the King's African Rifles. During WWII he fought in Burma as an infantryman.

Having found a career in the military, Amin's advancement was swift, if not meteoric: from corporal to sergeant-major to "effendi" —a rank created by the British army for non-commissioned officers singled out to receive commissions—to deputy commander of Uganda's army and air force by 1964. Meanwhile, Amin had reigned as Uganda's heavyweight champion from 1951-60 and had received special military training in Britain and Israel—a country he would angrily denounce as a Zionist enemy of Uganda's four million Muslims.

Amin counted among his closest friends Dr. Milton Obote, appointed prime minister in 1962. During his friend's tenure Amin became one of Uganda's most powerful men, despite charges of misappropriating $350,000 in gold and ivory earmarked to buy arms and ammunition to assist Congolese rebels against General Joseph Mobutu.

Responding to these charges, Obote crushed all Ugandan dissidents who demanded Amin's ouster. He arrested five Cabinet ministers and suspended the Constitution on Feb. 24, 1966. Two days later, the barrel-chested strongman was rewarded for his faithful "service" to the prime minister with a promotion. Amin was placed in charge of the combined armed forces and ordered to suppress the tribal kingdoms, which had enjoyed a degree of autonomy under the old regimes. When the Baganda people revolted against totalitarian rule, Amin was sent in to brutally crush all local opposition.

Prime Minister Obote's political shift to the left in the autumn of 1969 led to increasing discord between the military and the government. Dr. Obote began to distrust Amin, and took steps to strip him of a large measure of power. The secret police were placed under the control of Inspector General E.W. Oryema, and a contingency of Langi tribesmen. In September 1970, Idi Amin was sent to Egypt to attend the funeral of Gamal Nasser, which provided Obote with an opportunity to consolidate his power at the expense of his vacationing general. When Amin returned he found that his prestige and influence over the government had vanished, and there were reports that he was placed under house arrest. Idi Amin's political survival, and indeed his very life, depended on his response to this threat.

While Obote was attending a diplomatic conference in Singapore, Amin staged a bloodless coup on Jan. 25, 1971. Promising free and fair elections for all, he proclaimed himself the ruler of Uganda. The government, he said, "would be guided by a firm belief in the equality and brotherhood of man, and in peace and goodwill to all." Amin promised that there would be no purges or scapegoats in the new order, but contradicted these statements by suspending political meetings and open debates as his first official act. He abolished the Ugandan parliament on Feb. 2, 1971, and appointed an eighteen-member cabinet to uphold the one-man, one-rule doctrine of Idi Amin. Three weeks later he promoted himself to full general and was proclaimed president by the military. The farcical promises of free and open elections were words without meaning.

The first few months of the new government were characterized by prosperity and political harmony. Great Britain recognized Amin as the rightful leader of his nation and the *New York Times* praised the general's "deftness in the political field" and his "skill in dealing with people." By mid-1971 the large budget deficit Amin had inherited from his predecessor coupled with a wild defense-spending program plunged the nation into a severe depression. The army massacred 4,000 to 5,000 Langi and Acholi tribesmen who opposed Amin's stern policies, and scores of Christian refugees fled across the border into Kenya and Tanzania after Amin, a Muslim, decided to crush religious dissent.

In 1972 Amin severed ties with his former ally Israel to affirm his allegiance to the Arab world. Explaining that he could "understand why Hitler killed millions of Jews," Amin expelled 500 Israeli technocrats working in Uganda. These actions foreshadowed his controversial decision, on Aug. 5, 1972, to expel thousands of Indians and Pakistanis with British passports, the backbone of the middle class. With the departure of the Asians, the fragile fiber that held together the Ugandan economy was largely gone. Commenting on the turn of events, the *New York Times* reported that "dissidents, real or potential, are dragged screaming from the bar or cafe...; bodies of well-known former citizens are washed up on the shores of... lakes; swaggering glazed-eyed soldiery waylay and molest tourists."

Within a year Uganda had become an outlaw nation, thanks to Amin and his private gang of thugs known as the State Research Bureau (SRB). They were a sadistic blend of criminal outcasts and ex-soldiers who roamed the towns and villages murdering at will. In the diplomatic realm, the dictator's favorite ploy was to threaten and blackmail foreign powers to gain recognition. When the London government broke off relations with Amin, several hundred British citizens were barred from leaving the country until they each wrote a letter expressing their gratitude toward the president for the "kindly" way in which they were treated.

The self-styled President for Life extracted loyalty oaths from Europeans trapped in Uganda. On bended knee, they were forced to pledge unswerving loyalty to the man the western journalists unaffectionately labeled "Big Daddy." All the while, his dreaded secret police dragged off political opponents in the middle of the night, and tortured and killed an estimated 250,000 civilians.

The severed heads of his most prominent victims were carefully arranged on the shelves of a freezer in Amin's house. In moments of extreme megalomania the hulking dictator would open the door and preach to them about the evils of political dissent. Questions were raised among world leaders about the general's sanity. Those who recalled Amin's earlier pilgrimage to Mecca described how the first rainfall in the holy city in over a half century convinced Amin he was the new Muslim prophet. Journalist David Martin, who covered Amin during those turbulent years, offered a more realistic assessment. "He seized power in January 1971 to survive. He has killed ever since for that same reason." The Amin regime was censured by President Jimmy Carter for its callous and inhumane treatment of career diplomats, prompting a war of words between the United States and Uganda and an ugly hostage incident that threatened to escalate into armed conflict in the spring of 1977. The aircraft carrier U.S.S. *Enterprise* was positioned near the African coast in an effort to intimidate Amin to release U.S. citizens trapped inside Uganda's borders.

Terrorist situations were nothing new to Big Daddy. He was

humiliated by Israeli commandos who freed a jetliner of hostages at the Entebbe Airport in the spring of 1976. When U.S. actor Godfrey Cambridge died after portraying Amin during the filming of the television version of the celebrated Entebbe raid, Amin cited this as a "good example of punishment by God."

Amin survived at least ten attempted coups by political opponents before he was eventually toppled in April 1979 by the combined military forces of Tanzania and exiled leader Milton Obote. He fled to Libya, but was sent on his way eight months later by Colonel Muammar Gaddafi, who declared him an undesirable. Amin was by this time a political outcast who traveled through the Middle East with his four wives under an assumed name. He lived for a time in Saudi Arabia before being expelled in January 1989. After failing in his attempt to re-enter Uganda, Amin was allowed to return to Saudi Arabia as an exile on Feb. 8, 1989, under the condition that he cease his political activities. See: **Entebbe**.

REF.: Bell, *Assassin!; CBA;* Demaris, *Brothers in Blood;* Dobson and Payne, *Counterattack;* _____, *The Terrorists;* Hacker, *Terror and Terrorism in Our Times;* Liston, *Terrorism;* O'Ballance, *Language of Violence;* Schreiber, *Terrorists and World Order.*

Ammon, Robert A. (AKA: **Colonel**) prom. 1899, and **Miller, William F.**, prom. 1899, U.S., fraud. In 1899, a down-and-out Wall Street hanger-on named William Miller engineered a financial swindle that netted $430,000. But by the time Miller went to prison, his partner, "Colonel" Robert Ammon, had seen to it that he barely had a dime to show for it.

Miller rented a suite of offices on Floyd Street, Brooklyn, in February 1899. He printed handbills and circulars soliciting funds for investment. Promising inside information on hot stock tips, the sham business grew and prospered. The Franklin Syndicate, as Miller called the firm, attracted investors from across the United States and Canada.

Miller sent interest checks to the out-of-towners to ensure their continued support. When the Franklin Syndicate grew too large for Miller to handle by himself, he hired two business agents, Rudolph Guenther and Edward Schlessinger, who in turn introduced him to one of New York's cracker-jack lawyers, the self-styled "colonel," Robert A. Ammon.

Ammon, a veteran of the bucket shop racket, took charge. He incorporated the business and placed $100,000 in a certificate of deposit with Wells Fargo. By this time there were rumors that Miller was running a green goods game, and that the Franklin Syndicate was little more than an elaborate swindle. This was true, of course, but Ammon hotly denied the allegations and demanded retractions from the papers.

At the Boston office, investors staged a run on the bank, taking home $28,000 in Franklin Syndicate cash. In New York, the police were closing in. Ammon advised Schlessinger to flee to Canada, while he cleverly tucked away $30,500 with Wells Fargo. But in order for the state to prosecute, it had to prove that this was the same money Miller stole from his customers.

William Miller was brought back to New York and prosecuted by Kings County District Attorney John Clark on the strength of Ammon's testimony. Meanwhile, Schlessinger absconded to Europe with $175,000 and lived the life of a high roller.

Miller, by this time penniless, was convicted and sent to Sing Sing for ten years. While in prison, he was persuaded by the district attorney to give evidence against Ammon. His story was convincing, and Ammon was convicted, despite his plea that he had acted only as Miller's counsel and was therefore somehow immune. Miller served half his sentence before Governor Frank Wayland Higgins of New York pardoned him. Ammon went to Sing Sing, where he used his money and influence to gain privileged treatment. REF.: *CBA*.

Amos (AKA: **Fox**), prom. 1810, Brit., pros. Under the British penal code set forth by Henry VIII in 1533, homosexuality was a statutory offense punishable by severe penalties, including death. On July 9, 1810, the Bow Street Runners, under the direction of James Read, raided the White Swan public house in the Clare Market. The White Swan was a notorious rendezvous for homosexuals. Twenty-three patrons arrested in the raid were remanded to St. Clement Dane's watch house. Several weeks later, the White Swan was raided a second time when regiment drummers named Mann and White complained they had been accosted there by Ensign Hepburn.

The landlord of the Swan was a man named Amos. Along with several of his customers, Amos was arrested and sentenced to stand in the pillory at the Haymarket. The men were taken by cart from the Old Bailey yard to the pillory. On the way, they were pelted with mud. After they were placed in the stocks, taunting citizens hurled dead cats and dogs, potatoes, and other vile objects at them. On the way back to prison, they were whipped by the driver of the cart. One man was so severely injured during his hour in the stocks that the *Morning Herald* reported it was unlikely he would live. REF.: *CBA*.

Amsler, Joseph C., 1940- , and **Keenan, Barry W.**, 1940- , and **Irwin, John W.**, 1921- , U.S., kid. Frank Sinatra Jr. was finishing dinner in his Lake Tahoe, Calif., motel room on Dec. 8, 1963, when he heard a knock on the door. John Foss, a sideman in the Tommy Dorsey band, answered it. "We have a package for Mr. Sinatra," the stranger said. Before Foss could reply, three men burst into the room and ordered him to get dressed while they bound and gagged the trumpet player. At gunpoint, the son of the singer and world famous movie star was led into a waiting car bound for the gang's hideout in the Los Angeles suburb of Canoga Park. The car sped away into the snow-packed Sierra mountains.

Foss broke free minutes after he was bound. He notified the county sheriff, and soon an army of FBI agents descended on the Tahoe area. Fearing for his life, young Sinatra advised his abductors of the best way to avoid roadblocks. He said that it would be easy to fool the police by saying, "We've been to a party and had too much to drink."

Seven ransom calls were placed to Frank Sinatra Sr., who was preparing to begin work on his latest movie, *Robin and the Seven Hoods.* The singer was ordered to fly to Los Angeles to finalize the "drop"—$240,000 in small, unmarked bills to be delivered to a Texaco gas station on Sepulveda Boulevard in a brown paper bag. Before the kidnappers got hold of the money, Frank Sinatra Jr. persuaded them to release him. By this time he had struck up a quasi-friendship with the three men, none of whom were professional criminals. "It's too bad we couldn't have met under different circumstances," he told John Irwin, a 42-year-old house painter from Hollywood. Irving's two accomplices, 23-year-old Barry Keenan and Joseph Amsler, also 23, were novices. Amsler was a professional boxer and electronics technician from Playa del Ray, and Keenan the son of a Los Angeles stockbroker who attended high school with Frank Sinatra's eldest daughter Nancy. All three seemed more frightened than their victim, who bid farewell to them on Dec. 18 near Roscomare Road, two miles from his mother's home in Bel Air. Before Sinatra Jr. left, he advised his captors to pull up to a side of the road where it was dark, so he would not be able to read the license plate on the car.

Sinatra Jr. was picked up on the highway by policeman George Jones in an unmarked car. He drove the boy to his mother's house past a throng of reporters. Three days later the kidnappers were picked up by FBI men at scattered sites in the Los Angeles metro area. Irwin was arrested at Imperial Beach, where he had stashed away $47,938 of the ransom money. The FBI found $168,927 in the Culver City apartment rented to Amsler.

Speculation mounted that this was nothing more than a cleverly staged publicity stunt designed to promote Sinatra's sagging show business career, an argument used by defense attorneys who were later cited for perjury after they induced their clients to testify about a fourth accomplice, a man named "Wes." During the trial, which commenced in Los Angeles in January 1964, Amsler and Irwin both mentioned this mysterious figure, believed to be William Westley Wood, a Marine Corps veteran who had been convicted of mail fraud in Florida. After questioning Wood at length, the FBI said that he had no direct role in the affair. The trial lasted three months. Assistant U.S. District Attorney Thomas Sheridan summoned seventy-four witnesses. The defense called only nine.

On Mar. 7, 1964, U.S. District Judge William East sentenced Keenan and Amsler to provisional maximum terms of life imprisonment. Irwin was acquitted on one of the six counts of abduction—that of having participated in the actual kidnapping. He received seventy-five years for the other five counts brought against him. East praised the jury for its work, noting that "everybody (on the defense was) lying to protect themselves." Frank Sinatra Sr. was understandably pleased. "The jury has rendered a just verdict, and we are happy that they and the court were not confused by the false statements and innuendos made during the trial, and elaborated on by the press," he said. REF.: *CBA.*

Amuso, Victor, 1934-   , U.S., org. crime. Amuso was a "foot soldier" in the service of New York mobster Joey Gallo before switching his allegiance to the powerful Carlo Gambino crime family in the early 1970s.

On Dec. 21, 1972, Amuso was arrested outside the infamous "House on Morgan Avenue," used to front the "Bronx Connection," a kickback scheme in which prison paroles were sold to inmates for upwards of $20,000. The building belonged to Richard Curro, a 38-year-old city corrections officer who acted as the broker between the mob and the prison inmates. Amuso, a resident of Brooklyn, was carrying a switchblade and a file folder of stolen parole documents at the time of his arrest.

Five years later, on May 30, 1977, the Brooklyn mobster was arrested in a drug trafficking scheme involving the smuggling of large quantities of heroin from the Far East. At the time of the arrest Amuso and two of his accomplices were carrying with them three pounds of heroin. REF.: *CBA.*

Ananda VII (Ananda Mihidal), 1926-46, Siam, king, (unsolv.) assass. Born to Prince Mahidol and a commoner named Sangwala, Ananda was raised in Switzerland, his mother fleeing court intrigues against her because of her commoner background. When the king was overthrown in 1938, Ananda was proclaimed King of Siam (later Thailand) and returned to assume the throne with a board of regents ruling in his stead. He presided at massive parades, state affairs, and religious rites, all of which served to confuse his young mind. His mother persuaded the regents to allow the young king to continue his education in Switzerland and, upon returning to Lausanne, the boy told newsmen, "I don't think it's much fun to be king. I would rather stay here and play with my electric trains."

During WWII, Ananda remained in Switzerland while Siam was occupied by Japanese troops, its tiny army resisting only one day before surrendering. The country was ruled by a Japanese puppet, Marshal Phibul Songgram, later tried as a war criminal. Following the war, in 1945, Ananda was invited to return to Siam and assume the throne which he did at age nineteen. The king was decidedly democratic and alarmed advisers that he intended to turn Siam into a republic within a few years, abdicating the throne. Later reports indicate that die-hard monarchists or members of the Communist party, poisoned the king on June 7, 1946. He was ill for two days but recovered. He weakly sat up in bed on the morning of June 9, 1946, to take some medicine. At 9 a.m., a shot rang out in the royal bedchamber and when guards rushed inside they found the 20-year-old king. He was lying on the floor, a bullet hole in his head. His mother arrived and held him in her arms until court physicians arrived to pronounce Ananda dead.

At first officials insisted that Ananda had died accidentally while inspecting an automatic which had gone off, killing him. The statement was absurd and obviously designed to cover up what had been a clear-cut case of assassination. Ananda could hardly sit up in his bed on the day of his death, let alone get out of bed and suddenly begin to fondle his gun collection. He was an expert with weapons and would never have handled a gun in such a fashion where he would have shot himself. More than a dozen physicians inspected the wound and announced, indeed, that

the king had been murdered. Investigations went on for a year without results being announced.

One-time war criminal Songgram led a bloodless coup on Nov. 8, 1947, and took control of the government, stating that Nai Pridi, the so-called Siamese patriot who had thrown him out of office and invited Ananda to assume the throne in 1945, was the real culprit. Pridi, who had fled the country upon Songgram's return, was secretly a Communist who had installed Ananda on the throne to subsequently dispose of him and more easily take over the country, according to Songgram.

Young King Ananda of Siam, with his brother Pumipol, was invited to the throne only to be assassinated.

The new leader of Siam vowed to track down Ananda's killers and began a liberal program to democratize the country, changing its name from Siam to Thailand and using Ananda's murder to purge the country of his political enemies. Scores of "suspects" where arrested and wound up rotting in prison cells or were shot to death "while attempting to escape." The purge went on for nine years, culminating in 1955 with the arrest of the two royal pages who had been outside Ananda's chamber on the morning of the killing. These two men, officials stated, were responsible for the assassination of the king. They were summarily tied to crosses and machine gunned to death. Justice had been done, announced the regime. Songgram's opponents, however, insisted that he had ordered Ananda's death so that he could then step in and pretend to be the savior of the nation, while solidifying his own position by eradicating all important resistence. The real killers of King Ananda of Siam, however, were never officially identified. See: **Songgram, Phibul.**

REF.: *CBA;* Godwin, *Killers Unknown;* Nash, *Almanac of World Crime;* _____, *Open Files;* Simpson, *Forty Years of Murder;* Sparrow, *The Great Assassins.*

Anargeros, Sophie (AKA: **Sandra Peterson; Sophie Peterson; Mrs. Wally Hamilton**), 1931-   , U.S. mur. For a girl whose own mother placed her in a juvenile delinquent school, and who was termed by a probation officer as "hell bent," Sophia Anargeros, by the age of fifteen, was already destined for a life of crime.

On her release from the school, Anargeros left her home town of Somerville, Mass., just outside Boston, changed her first name to Sandra, and headed west to Reno, Nev. She spent the next couple of years working for gambling establishments and similar businesses attracting customers. Anargeros was married briefly in Southern California, just long enough to gain another name, Sandra Peterson.

During the winter of 1950, Anargeros took up a new profession—stealing from Texas motorists whom she induced into offering her a ride. She soon teamed up with a 14-year-old girl, in whose house the hitchhiker-thief had been living. The two lure a male driver into the back seat of the car and rather than submit to sex, they would rob him at gunpoint, then order him to drive off or simply leave him on the roadside and drive off in his car. However, not all of their crimes were successful.

One driver, Lewis Patterson, resisted being robbed, and for his efforts received two bullet wounds, one in his side and one in the chest, that killed him. Anargeros and her accomplice tried in vain to escape pursuit—buying bus tickets headed in the opposite direction from which they were traveling, though returning the tickets later, and even dyeing the color of their hair.

The two were arrested in San Angelo, Tex., Anargeros confessed that she had killed the man, but only in self-defense after he had tried to rape her—a claim that the younger girl's statement repudiated, resulting in a charge of murder against Anargeros. After four days, a jury found her guilty of murder with malice on Jan. 20, 1951, for which she received a sentence of two life terms, serving just over ten years—under the name of Sophie Peterson—before she was pardoned on Dec. 19, 1961.

REF.: *CBA*; Radin, *Headline Crimes of the Year*.

Anastasia, Albert (Umberto Anastasio, AKA: Lord High Executioner; The Mad Hatter; Big Al), 1903-57, U.S., org. crime. One of the most ruthless killers of American organized crime, Anastasia was the mob's top exterminator. He personally murdered at least fifty or more persons but was responsible, as head of Murder, Inc., the syndicate's execution squad located in Brooklyn, N.Y., for the killing of hundreds, perhaps thousands of victims for four decades. He was of middle height and carried extra weight that was mostly muscle since he worked out regularly. His hands were enormous and anyone hit with his fists invariably reported broken bones. His face was fleshy. A large nose boomed over thin lips and Anastasia's eyes, usually narrowed to a suspicious squint, seemed to dart about wildly when he became excited—and this was usually before he ordered someone murdered.

Shortly before WWI, in 1917, Anastasia and his nine brothers immigrated from Italy to the United States the 14-year-old Albert slipping onto a Brooklyn dock in the dead of night, without shoes, and hiding with a relative until he could find work. A strapping boy, Anastasia was given a job on the docks and was a longshoreman by age sixteen, working alongside his brother Anthony. Anastasia was also active in a brutal Brooklyn gang which preyed on women, robbing and raping them. Early on he decided to change his name from Anastasio to Anastasia to avoid bringing shame upon his family and being identified with them when he was mentioned in newspapers as a gangster, or so the story goes. But his brother Tony kept the original family name and went on to become one of the leading racketeers controlling the Brooklyn docks twenty years later, working under the direction of his bully-boy brother Albert.

Anastasia quickly came under the wing of Brooklyn gang boss, Joe Adonis, and it was through Adonis and his fabulous bootleg wealth that Anastasia was able to set up his own fledgling gang of bootleggers and killers at the dawn of Prohibition. By this time, Anastasia had been credited with killing at least five men in gangland wars over bootleg territory in Brooklyn. He made a mistake, however, when he boldly murdered a fellow longshoreman, one Joe Torino in 1920, in a dispute over the right to unload ships with precious cargoes. There were several witnesses to this killing where the powerful Anastasia stabbed and strangled his victim. He was convicted and sentenced to death. Anastasia lingered on death row in Sing Sing for eighteen months but he won a new trial when the witnesses reversed their statements and, when the witnesses suddenly vanished, the thug-killer was released. Of course, Anastasia's gang members saw to it that the witnesses disappeared.

Upon his release, Anastasia became Adonis' right-hand enforcer, threatening and beating up saloon keepers who were reluctant to peddle Adonis beer and liquor, extorting money from local shopkeepers for protection, and organizing the longshoremen into unions which came early under gangster control. In addition,

Anastasia put together a group of killers in the late 1920s. The utterly ruthless thugs formed the gang which later became known as Murder, Inc. Anastasia invented a whole new vocabulary for his killers so that when they spoke in public or over the phone references to their murders would be misunderstood. A "contract" was an agreement to murder someone, the victim was a "hit," and members of the killer group belonged to "the troop." Anastasia's killers were the most cold-blooded executioners in American criminal annals and they included Harry "Pittsburgh Phil" Strauss, Harry "Happy" Maione, Abe "Kid Twist" Reles, Frank "The Dasher" Abbandando, Seymour "Blue Jaw" Magoon, Martin "Bugsy" Goldstein, and Allie Tannenbaum. These men were recruited early in their careers as apprentice bootleggers and strong-arm thugs who had small gangs later integrated into the Adonis combine.

Though Anastasia's top bosses in years to come—Adonis, Luciano, Lucchese, Mangano—were either Sicilian or, like himself, Italian, Anastasia paid his allegiance to Louis "Lepke" Buchalter, the shrewd Jewish gangster who, with Jacob "Gurrah" Shapiro, had taken over the garment workers' unions and who supervised Anastasia's stranglehold on the stevedore unions. He was also enamored of other Jewish gangsters, Meyer Lansky and his sleek strong-arm lieutenant, Benjamin "Bugsy" Siegel. The Jewish killers in Murder, Inc., Strauss, Tannenbaum, and others were recommended by Lepke who was Anastasia's nominal boss when it came to the overall operations of the group. Anastasia's loyalty and dedication to Lepke, later caused the Sicilian-Italian faction of the syndicate to consider Anastasia a maverick and untrustworthy as a member of their inner circle.

Anastasia was a key member of the national crime cartel from its inception. He was present at the historic 1929 Atlantic City convention of mobsters from all over the United States. Anastasia was also involved in the deadly Castellammarese War in New York between the gangland factions of Joe "The Boss" Masseria and Salvatore Maranzano. Though he fought with the Masseria side, Anastasia was one of the four gangsters who killed Joe the Boss in Coney Island in 1931, and it was he that administered the *coup de grace* to Masseria while his fellow murderers, Bugsy Siegel, Vito Genovese, and Joe Adonis stood by admiringly, the killing performed at Luciano's orders. This display of cold-blooded willingness to murder established, for Anastasia, a fearsome reputation among his own peers, one which implanted respect and apprehension among them.

There was no one Anastasia feared on either side of the law. When Dutch Schultz went before the syndicate board in 1935 and insisted that New York District Attorney Thomas E. Dewey be murdered because of the legal pressure he was exerting on the Dutchman's illegal enterprises, Anastasia listened intently. He then staked out Dewey's Fifth Avenue apartment for four days, posing as a loving father, walking up and down the block with a small child he borrowed for the job, either pushing the child in a baby carriage or having the small boy peddle next to him on a tricycle, according to varying reports. Anastasia later reported to the syndicate leaders that Dewey was poorly guarded and that he could be murdered "without too much trouble."

It never occurred to the killer that murdering Dewey would bring down incredible heat upon the newly born syndicate. Anastasia approached the idea as merely another job and he had satisfied himself that it could be accomplished. His limited vision proved to be the very reason why he was always held in disdain by the hierarchy of the national crime cartel. Yet he was essential to the syndicate as its chief enforcer and because he wielded such dangerous power through his control of Murder, Inc., he held syndicate boss status throughout his life. Schultz's plan to kill Dewey did not materialize, however; he himself was murdered on orders of Lepke Buchalter, the nominal chairman of the syndicate board.

Anastasia's devotion to Lepke was almost childlike. He thought Buchalter was an intellectual genius, the cleverest man on the syndicate board, and he took it upon himself to protect the diminutive Lepke at all costs. When both New York and federal officers were searching for Buchalter in the late 1930s, it was Anastasia who provided him a hidden sanctuary through his Murder, Inc. associates. But it was also Anastasia who convinced Lepke to turn himself into authorities, telling Buchalter that a deal had been made where Lepke would serve time in a federal prison and not be turned over to New York to face a murder charge and possible electrocution in Sing Sing which is exactly what happened to Buchalter in 1944. It was later claimed that Anastasia had been told by other syndicate leaders, chiefly Luciano, who at the time was in prison, that the prolonged search for Lepke had caused too much police heat on syndicate operations and that Buchalter should be persuaded, by a man he would trust, to turn himself in. That man, of course, was Anastasia, who, some believe, knew that once Buchalter was in federal custody he would be turned over to New York authorities and eventually go to the electric chair, a fate decreed by Lucianio who resented Lepke's authority and feared his power through Anastasia.

In 1940, when Brooklyn District Attorney Burton B. Turkus suddenly found several members of Murder, Inc. willing to turn state's evidence, Anastasia, too, went into hiding. Reles and others implicated him in several murders and named him as their boss in their murder-for-profit organization. Albert Tannenbaum stated to Turkus that Anastasia ran afoul of a crusading longshoreman named Peter Panto, who had begun a campaign to clean up the Brooklyn waterfront in 1939, and an enraged Anastasia personally garroted and buried the labor leader in quicklime. Tannebaum instructed Turkus where to find the body which was dug up in Lyndhurst, N.J. Tannenbaum's statements were supported by Kid Twist. Reles, however, never lived long enough to testify in court against Anastasia. He was pushed to his death in 1942 from a six-story hotel room window of the Half Moon Hotel in Coney Island. At this time, Albert Anastasia went into even deeper hiding, finding a place where no police official would ever think to look for him, the U.S. Army.

The arch killer enlisted in the army in 1942 both to avoid Turkus' investigators as well as to sidestep any future move to have him deported to his native Italy. Though his criminal record and gangster background was well known, Anastasia was nevertheless accepted by the army and he was attached to the Eighty-Eighth Division at Camp Forrest, Tenn., where he rose to the rank of sergeant. Because of his army service, Anastasia was allowed to become a naturalized citizen in 1943, thus making sure he could never be sent out of the country. Contrary to gangland belief that Albert Anastasia was sent overseas where he saw action and became a hero under gunfire, the syndicate boss remained in the United States throughout the duration of the war. Though his unit went overseas, Anastasia reportely bribed some minor officials and was allowed to remain behind at Town Gap, Pa., where he supervised a small army transporation center. Following the war, Anastasia paraded about Brooklyn in his uniform, sporting medals he had purchased in a pawnshop and hinting darkly of the many heroic deeds he had performed on the battlefield. Nothing could be further from the truth. He was, as in civilian life, a coward who was terrified of facing an armed, alert enemy. The myth that Anastasia was a war hero was perpetuated by his henchmen, and even his enemies in the Mafia-syndicate, such as Vito Genovese, came to believe the fabricated war stories.

To create a legitimate front for his dock racketeering, Anastasia had his brother Tony hire him as a foreman in the late 1940s. He made a few brief appearances along the Brooklyn docks to grunt a few orders and then returned to supervising his lucrative gambling, narcotics, and prostitution operations which Anastasia had extended into New Jersey where he would eventually relocate. Much of the crime empire Anastasia ruled, as one of the five Mafia family members in New York, was inherited from Luciano. The broad territories in Manhattan and Brooklyn that Luciano had once overlorded, fell under the authority of Philip and Vincent Mangano after Luciano was deported to Italy in 1946. Frank Costello was the underboss of this Mafia family, a position

Vito Genovese had held in the early 1930s until he fled to Sicily in 1934 to avoid a murder charge. He had returned to the United States following WWII and schemed to recover his former position but he had to contend with Anastasia who looked with a covetous eye on the Mangano domain. First, Anastasia ordered Philip Mangano murdered on Apr. 19, 1951, and when Vincent Mangano disappeared later in that year, Anastasia took over. (He is credited with having abducted Mangano who was tortured for information about his operations and murdered once he talked.) This was not done without Luciano's approval. Although Luciano had been deported to his native Italy after WWI, he was still the top member of the American syndicate, ruling from his Italian exile. When Luciano secretly left Italy in 1949 and visited Cuba, a steady stream of American gangsters flew to Havana to pay homage to the boss of bosses. Anastasia appeared and held a secret conference with Luciano, and it was at this time, federal agents believe, that Luciano gave his approval for the elimination of Vincent Mangano. Anastasia would never have eradicated a Mafia family boss without the blessing of the boss of bosses.

As a Mafia don, however, Anastasia displayed an erratic, explosive nature and found it impossible to check his mercurial, murderous temperament. When watching a TV news show one day in 1952, Anastasia saw Arnold Schuster, an amateur sleuth who had identified the much-wanted bank robber Willie "The Actor" Sutton on a New York subway and informed police which had led to Sutton's arrest. While Schuster was being interviewed, Anastasia leaped from his chair and shouted to his goons, "I can't stand squealers! Hit that guy!" Schuster was murdered, according to the orders of the Mad Hatter, on Mar. 8, 1952. When news of this mob murder reached the ears of Vito Genovese, the calculating Mafia don began to spread the word that Anastasia was unstable, a thug murderer who did not deserve the high rank he had achieved in the syndicate. Genovese also wooed the loyalties of Carlo Gambino, who served as Anastasia's underboss and Gambino, in turn, persuaded his good friend Joseph Profaci, a Mafia family boss, to oppose Anastasia at every turn, siding with Genovese.

Standing between these factions, however, was Frank Costello, the so-called Prime Minister of Organized Crime. Costello was the financial guardian of Luciano's old rackets and an avowed enemy of the scheming Don Vito. Genovese spread the word that Anastasia had attempted to bully his way into controlling some of the lucrative gambling casinos in Cuba which were controlled by Meyer Lansky and Frank Costello who were in league with the then military dictator of the island, Fulgencio Batista. The Mad Hatter had been rebuffed and was now plotting against his former ally, Costello, claimed Genovese. Then on the night of May 14, 1957, Costello was entering his swank Manhattan apartment building when a lumbering, fat young hoodlum, later identified as Vincent "The Chin" Gigante, stood outside the building and shouted at the gang chief from some thirty yards distant, "This is for you, Frank!" With that he fired a single shot and then fled. The bullet grazed Costello's head but he survived. Gigante was identified by the doorman of the apartment building but was later tried and acquitted when Costello refused to identify him as his would-be killer. The word through Mafia enclaves had it that this had been the work of Anastasia; that he had hired Gigante, a Greenwich Village thug, paying him $500 to murder Costello, but that Gigante had botched the job.

Costello himself believed this tale and agreed with Genovese and other Mafia dons that the Mad Hatter had to be eliminated. It was Genovese, of course, who had hired Gigante, instructing him to purposely miss Costello so that the gang chief could legitimately seek and get his vengeance against Anastasia. That vengeance was reaped shortly after 10:15 a.m. on Oct. 25, 1957, when Anastasia walked into the barbershop of New York's Park Sheraton Hotel. He waved at the shop owner Arthur Grasso as he sat down in the deep leather of chair four. Joe Bocchino, who had been cropping Anastasia's short, curly hair for years, covered him with the candy striped barber's cloth and began to clip at the

Albert Anastasia, the "Mad Hatter" of the Mafia.

Arnold Schuster turned in a bank robber and Anastasia ordered him murdered.

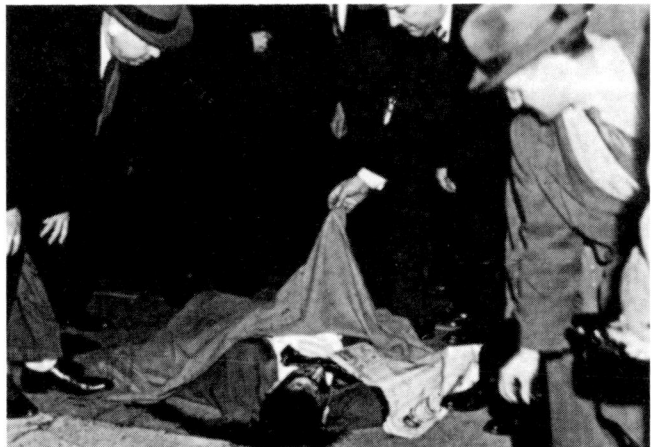

The body of Arnold Schuster, killed for being a good citizen.

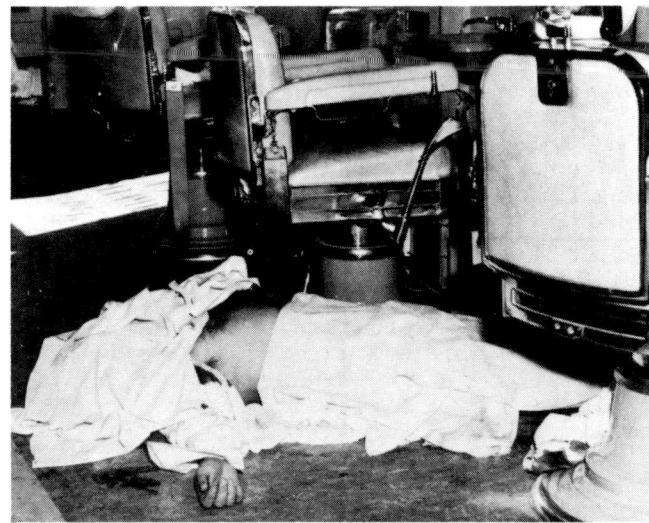

The most feared killer of the Mafia lies dead, Oct. 25, 1957, in a Manhattan barber shop.

Anastasia, underboss to Lepke, directed Murder, Inc.; shown here with his lawyer.

Anastasia's body being carried out of the Park Sheraton Hotel.

gang boss' hair while a manicurist sat next to the chair and worked on the Mad Hatter's fingernails. Jimmy, the shoeshine boy, began to slap brown polish on the gangster's wing-tipped shoes. Two short, squat men wearing fedoras and aviator sun glasses then entered the shop and pulled .38-caliber revolvers, waving the shop people away from chair four. As they scattered in fright, both men began to blast at the seated figure.

Anastasia had been dozing in the chair, his eyes closed. They popped open just before the first shot was fired. The gang boss raised his left hand as if to shield his head from the bullet which tore through the palm. Two more bullets smashed his left wrist and entered his hip. Anastasia let out a roar and struggled to get out of the chair, reaching, some reports later said, for a gun that he no longer wore. Bullets crashed into the barber's shelf in front of the chair, splintering bottles of hair tonic. Another bullet struck Anastasia in the back as he stood upright for a moment, the barber's cloth still clinging to him. He sank to the floor, and one of the gunmen calmly walked up to the prone figure and fired a bullet into the back of his head, a *coup de grace* identical to the shot Anastasia had fired into the head of Joe "The Boss" Masseria in 1931. Their gruesome task completed, the two gunmen raced for the door and vanished. They were never apprehended, but gangland consensus had it that the murder had been carried out by Larry and Joe Gallo who had received a "contract" from Don Vito Genovese.

There was no typical mobster funeral for Albert Anastasia, with massive floral wreaths and a long motorcade of limousines packed with black-suited gangsters. The ceremony was simple and was attended by his family members, including his union-mobster brother Tony. Anastasia's wife Elsa, who married the arch killer in 1937 at age nineteen after moving from Canada to New York, refused to believe any of the terrible stories about her wealthy husband. She insisted that he was a good family man who worked hard to support his family and maintain their lavish home in Fort Lee, N.J. Mrs. Anastasia claimed that her dutiful husband never drank, only smoked cigarettes and that he was usually home by 9 p.m. He often took the children to see movies, she said, and liked to take the family to visit the homes of friends. "I never heard him say a bad word in front of me or the children," Elsa Anastasia told one writer. "He never spoke roughly. He used to go to church with me every Sunday. He gave generously to the church...Now he's not even buried in consecrated ground." The Anastasia family sold its U.S. holdings and changed their name, moving to Canada. The same day Anastasia collapsed into the cuttings of his own hair, Vito Genovese took over the old Luciano Mafia family, through underboss Carlo Gambino, telling Frank Costello that he was permanently retired. See: **Abbandando, Frank; Adonis, Joe; Anastasio, Anthony; Batista, Fulgencio; Buchalter, Louis; Costello, Frank; Dewey, Thomas E.; Gallo Brothers; Gambino, Carlo; Genovese, Vito; Gigante, Vincent; Lansky, Meyer; Luciano, Charles; Maione, Harry; Mangano, Vincent; Maranzano, Salvatore; Masseria, Joseph; Profaci, Joseph; Reles, Abraham; Schultz, Dutch; Schuster, Arnold; Siegel, Benjamin; Sutton, Willie; Strauss, Harry; Turkus, Burton B.**

REF.: Alexander, *The Pizza Connection;* Asbury, *Sucker's Progress;* Bonanno, *A Man of Honor;* Browning and Gerassi, *The American Way of Crime;* Campbell, *The Luciano Project;* Carpozi, *Bugsy; CBA;* Cohen, *In My Own Words;* Cook, *The FBI Nobody Knows;* ____, *Mafia!;* Cressey, *Theft of the Nation;* Demaris, *The Last Mafioso;* Eisenberg, *Meyer Lansky, Mogul of the Mob;* Feder, *The Luciano Story;* Fortenay, *Estes Kefauver;* Frasca, *King of Crime;* Fried, *The Rise and Fall of the Jewish Gangster in America;* Gage, *The Mafia is not an Equal Opportunity Employer;* ____, *Mafia, U.S.A.;* Gosch, *The Last Testament of Lucky Luciano;* Greenhaw, *Flying High, Inside Big Time Drug Smuggling;* Jennings, *We Only Kill Each Other;* Katcher, *The Big Bankroll;* Katz, *Uncle Frank;* Kefauver, *Crime in America;* McClellan, *Crime Without Punishment;* McPhaul, *Johnny Torrio;* Maas, *The Valachi Papers;* Maclean, *A Pictorial History of the Mafia;* Martin, *Revolt in the Mafia;* Messick, *Lansky;* ____, *Secret File;* ____, and Goldblatt, *The Mobs and the Mafia;* Nash, *Almanac of World Crime;* ____, *Bloodletters and Badmen;* ____, *Open Files;* Navasky, *Kennedy Justice;* Peterson, *The Mob;* Reid, *The Grim Reapers;* ____, *Mafia;* Sann, *Kill the Dutchman!;* Schlesinger, *Robert Kennedy and His Times;* Teresa, *My Life in the Mafia;* Tully, *Treasury Agent;* Turkus and Feder, *Murder, Inc.;* Wicker, *Investigating the FBI;* Wolf and DiMona, *Frank Costello, Prime Minister of the Underworld;* (FILM) *Murder, Inc.,* 1960; *Lepke,* 1975.

Anastasio, Anthony (AKA: Tough Tony), 1906-63, U.S., org. crime. Brother of syndicate chieftan Albert Anastasia, Tough Tony took control of the astoundingly lucrative Brooklyn docks through the International Longshoremen's Association for which

Brooklyn waterfront boss Tony Anastasio.

he was a vice president and head of the powerful Local 1814. Through Anastasio's iron grip of this union, millions of dollars each year were funneled into syndicate coffers from kickbacks on dues, stolen merchandise from precious cargoes, and payoffs from many shipping companies. Tough Tony ruled the great shipping port for three decades through the mere threat of his brother Albert, head of Murder, Inc. It was claimed that he could wreck the country's imports and exports if he so desired and even cause sabotage to important ships to make a Mafia point. One story, a canard, has it that boss of bosses Lucky Luciano, imprisoned in Dannemora during WWII, the most severe prison in New York, wanted a transfer to a more relaxed penal institution. When his request was denied, he ordered Albert Anastasia to talk to his brother.

Tough Tony then arranged for the French luxury liner, *Normandie,* to be blown up so that federal authorities would quickly realize that Luciano could, in the tradition of Cagliostro, "afflict as well as heal." Because of the explosion, the tale goes on, Luciano was transferred to more comfortable prison surroundings. Nothing could be further from the truth. An exhaustive investigation concerning the *Normandie's* explosion which caused the ship to capsize at its mooring docks failed to support this story, one that Anastasio himself spread to undoubtedly increase his own lethal prestige.

Anastasio was the first to identify his brother's body after Albert was slain at the Park Sheraton Hotel in 1957. He then rushed to Frank Costello where newsmen later found both men sobbing and embracing each other, dispelling any notion that Costello had ordered the killing of Anastasia. Tough Tony Anastasio's influence along the New York docks waned after his brother's mob execution but he was allowed to hold on to his position by Vito Genovese, who had been behind Anastasia's murder. Tough Tony Anastasio died of natural causes in 1963. See: **Anastasia, Albert; Costello, Frank, Genovese, Vito; Luciano, Charles.**

REF.: Bonanno, *A Man of Honor; CBA;* Cook, *Mafia!;* Feder, *The Luciano Story;* Frasca, *King of Crime;* Gosch, *The Last Testament of Lucky Luciano;* Katz, *Uncle Frank;* Kefauver, *Crime in America;* McClellan, *Crime Without Punishment;* Peterson, *The Mob;* Wolf and DiMona, *Frank Costello, Prime Minister of the Underworld;* (FILM), *On the Waterfront,* 1954.

Anastay, Lieutenant, d.1892, Fr., mur. As a second lieutenant in the French army, Anastay was convicted of murder and guillotined in Paris at the Roquette Prison in 1892. Prior to his execution the officer wrote a novel, *The Genesis of a Crime,* detailing the crime he committed with himself as the hero. He asked that a doctor be present at his decapitation so that questions of the afterworld could be asked of his recently severed head. No doctor was present.

REF.: *CBA;* Laurence, *A History of Capital Punishment.*

Anatomist, The, 1931, a play by James Bridie (Osborne Henry Mavor). This drama is based upon the unorthodox medical practices of Dr. James Knox and presents those two gruesome ghouls, Burke and Hare (Scot., 1828-29). See: **Burke, William**. REF.: *CBA*.

Anchisi, René, and **Guillemenot, Adolphe**, and **Sauvageot, Serge**, prom. 1932, Fr., burg.-mur. A loaf of bread intercepted by a jailer in eastern France resulted in the conviction of three men, charged with housebreaking for the murder of an Englishman living in Paris. Inside the loaf of bread, passed between the three prisoners who did not as yet know what crime they had been charged with, was a note which read, "Don't forget you were not in Paris September 16." The note, siezed in December 1932, alluded to the unsolved murder of Donald Ross, whose body was discovered Sept. 17, 1932. Following seven hours of third-degree interrogation, two of the burglars, Adolphe Guillemenot and Serge Sauvageot confessed, while René Anchisi claimed to know nothing about the crime.

The burglars admitted that they had taken a very drunk Ross home on the evening of September 15. Ross invited them in for a drink, and after he fell asleep the burglars ransacked the home, later tying up Ross when he awoke, but claiming they had not killed him. No evidence of alcohol was found in the dead man's body, though the test may have been performed too late for accuracy—one of several mistakes the police made in their investigation, including failure to notice a pair of glasses in the apartrment which did not belong to Ross. At the crime scene, a number of carpets and pieces of furniture were missing, though several valuables were left behind, which led to the belief that the murder was committed by German agents against a former member of British intelligence, which Ross was.

As the investigation continued, the three suspects were tried and convicted for burglary in November 1933, Anchisi receiving eight years servitude in a penal colony, Guillemenot and Sauvageot each sentenced to twelve years. After sentencing, the burglars were charged with Ross' murder and the trial began in May 1935. Evidence against the three was slim, excepting the confessions they made—confessions which may have been obtained illegally and which refuted the conclusion that Ross had no alcohol in his body. There even were witnesses who claimed to have seen Ross alive the morning after the burglars had left him tied up. Nevertheless, a jury found the three guilty of murder and sentenced them to twenty years of penal servitude in French Guiana. On hearing the verdict, Anchisi, who had to be physically restrained, shouted, "We'll never forget your 'mugs.' You'll hear from us when we get back from Guiana."

REF.: *CBA*; Greenwall, *They Were Murdered In France*.

Anckarsvard, Carl Henrik, 1782-1865, Swed., consp. Swedish politician who was one of the leaders of the coup d'etat against King Gustav IV in 1809. REF.: *CBA*.

Anderson, Aldon Junior, b.1917- , U.S., jur. District attorney of Utah from 1953-57 and appointed federal judge in Utah District Court by President Richard M. Nixon in 1971. REF.: *CBA*.

Anderson, Alexander, 1820-58, U.S., rape-mur. Mary Ann Ream entered the small cottage of Conrad Garber in Manheim, Mass., on the night of Dec. 15, 1857, looking for her mother-in-law, Elizabeth Ream, who was visiting her next-door neighbor, Mrs. Anna Garber. The daughter-in-law followed a trail of blood that ran from the kitchen to a back room where she discovered the bodies of Mrs. Garber and Mrs. Ream. Both women had been beaten about the head and their throats had been cut from ear to ear. The elderly women, a coroner quickly concluded, had also been raped. Detectives concluded that the women had been sitting in the front sitting room, when they were knocked down by blows from a club and hatchet and then dragged into the back room where "they were violated," then murdered. A short time later police officers Baker, Huffnagle, and Kuhns spotted two men on Middle Street, described in reports as "a Negro and a mulatto speaking the German language." They were Alexander Anderson, a black, and Henry Richards, a half-caste, both of them chimney sweeps who had been working in the area of the Garber cottage.

Blood was found on Richards' shirt and he and Anderson were taken to police headquarters and ordered to disrobe. More blood was found and the two men were charged with the double rape-murders. Anderson was placed on trial for the murder of Mrs. Garber on Dec. 21, 1858. The Manheim courtroom was so tightly packed that the overflow crowd had to stand on tiptoe to see anything, and a quick-acting concessionaire sold boxes upon which spectators could stand. Three judges, Hayes, Long, and Brinton, heard this spectacular case. Anderson was defended by M. Harris who argued that the prosecution's case was entirely circumstantial. However, the jury was impressed by the claim that one of Anderson's shoes, left at the scene of the crime, had blood on it which matched blood found on his clothes. Anderson was found guilty of first-degree murder. The following day, Harris tried to defend Richards by claiming that Anderson had committed the murders and Richards was but a simple-minded accomplice. Richards was, nevertheless, found guilty. Both men were sentenced to be hanged on Apr. 9, 1858.

Anderson, born in Lancaster, Pa., on Dec. 16, 1820, had spent most of his childhood and teenage years in the Lancaster poorhouse, following the deaths of his parents. As a small boy, he committed petty crimes which escalated in later years to burglary and robbery. He had served a number of prison terms. Richards had also served two terms for larceny. Only Anderson confessed to the rape-murders before both men were led to the scaffold on execution day. Authorities were dismayed because the rainy weather kept public attendance down to a few hundred spectators, and at least two thousand had been expected to bolster the town's commerce. One entrepreneur, however, erected a large platform on the lot adjoining the execution grounds and he charged more than 100 persons $1 each to witness the double hanging. Anderson prayed aloud before stepping onto the trapdoor while Richards visibly shook as the rope was placed about his neck. Both men were sent through the trap a few minutes after noon. Physicians examining the bodies of both men following the executions reported that Anderson had "discharged both bladder and bowels" and that "considerable seminal fluids" had been emitted by the condemned man at the time of death. The publisher of the only record of this murder and trial, claimed that all proceeds would go to the wife and orphaned children of Alexander Anderson.

REF.: *CBA*; Rockafield, *The Manheim Tragedy, A Complete History of Mrs. Garber and Mrs. Ream with the Only Authentic Life and Confession of Alexander Anderson*.

Anderson, Allen Leroy, 1943- , U.S., forg.-theft-burg.-mur. Capital punishment does not deter all criminals, but for Anderson it was the one punishment he painstakingly avoided, though he was unable to escape a sentence of life imprisonment. Earlier in his life, Anderson had spent eleven years behind bars for forgery, auto theft, and burglary before his parole to a Seattle, Wash., halfway house in January 1976. While there he had a homosexual relationship with a fellow inmate, who rejected him six months later and possibly led to the violence that followed.

Anderson, on June 1, 1976, stole credit cards and a car from the halfway house director and headed across the country committing crimes in twenty or more states during the next five months. Eight murders were believed committed by Anderson, though he confessed to only two. Of the eight, seven victims were shot in the back of the head. Anderson did not murder all the witnesses to his crimes. Once in Richland, Iowa he let the family who surprised him as he robbed their home live, but only after ordering them to sit on the bathroom floor as he stood over them continually cocking and uncocking his gun.

When he was finally apprehended by Los Angeles police on October 28, Anderson was driving a van and trailer he stole from a man he had bludgeoned to death in Chowchilla, Calif. According to the public defender for Anderson, Lester Gendron, "The death penalty was the only thing he worried about." Upon learning that there was no such punishment in California, Anderson pled guilty, and even pled the same, after waiving extradition, to a murder on Aug. 10, 1976, in Northfield, Minn. He was sentenced to life imprisonment on August 10, 1976, at Stillwater State Prison and will be eligible for parole Dec. 14, 1993. REF.: *CBA*.

Anderson, Bella, See: **Barrow, George.**

Anderson, Billy Dean (AKA: **The Mountain Man**), c.1944-79, U.S. rob.-attempted mur. Although eluding capture by hiding in the hills of Tennessee near the Kentucky border for almost five years, Anderson was finally tracked down by federal agents who shot and killed him when he resisted arrest. After serving time for shooting a Tennessee state trooper in 1962, Anderson earned himself a place on the FBI's ten most-wanted list on Jan. 21, 1975. While attempting to rob a nightclub near Jamestown, Tenn. in December 1973, he shot and seriously wounded a deputy sheriff from Fentress County, Tenn. That same year he allegedly robbed a bank near Mooreland, Ind., and was still at large following his escape from maximum security at the Morgan County, Tenn. jail on Aug. 6, 1974.

Anderson was returning from visiting his mother in Pall Mall, Tenn. on July 7, 1979, to his hiding place among the caves and hills when ten to fifteen FBI agents surprised him. He was shot and killed by an agent when he raised a loaded .22-caliber rifle. The fugitive was also armed with two loaded pistols and additional ammunition. REF.: *CBA*.

Anderson, Clifford, c.1937-   , U.S., mur. Twice in his life Anderson took vengeance upon the man who fired him from his job, the second time fatally shooting his boss and a co-worker. Anderson, who had previously stabbed his employer when fired from a job in California, was working as a janitor in the building where he lived on Chicago's Near North Side when he killed the two men on Sept. 5, 1978. Three days after losing the job, Anderson left his apartment carrying a .25-caliber pistol, with which he shot building engineer Mack Sutton, fifty-seven, in the face, and then walked into the office of the building's manager, Robert Williams, forty-one, and shot him.

A jury took three hours and fifteen minutes on Oct. 26, 1981, to return a verdict of Guilty for two counts each of murder and armed violence. He was condemned to death but the sentence was reduced to life imprisonment on Apr. 12, 1989, when the courts reversed and remanded the earlier decision. Anderson is being held at the Pontiac Correctional Center in Pontiac, Ill. REF.: *CBA*.

Anderson, David L. (AKA: **Billy Wilson; Buffalo Billy**), 1862-1918, U.S., count.-rob.-mur. Born in Ohio, Anderson moved to Texas at an early age with his family. He became a cowboy at an early age and when he was eighteen he resettled in White Oaks, N.M., where he ran a small livery stable. There he was known as Billy Wilson. Anderson sold his stable in 1880 to a sharper who reportedly paid him off in counterfeit bills. When Anderson began to pass these bills they were identified as bogus currency and he was arrested and indicted. Skipping bail, Anderson fled and joined the band of Billy the Kid. On the night of Nov. 29-30, 1881, a sheriff's posse trapped the Kid and Wilson, shooting the horses out from under both men, but the resourceful outlaws managed to escape on foot in the dark.

The Kid and Anderson then joined with Dave Rudabaugh and, obtaining fresh mounts, boldly rode into White Oaks where they spotted Deputy James Redman who had been part of the posse that had attacked them the night before. All three men opened fire on Redman who had the presence of mind to run for cover, escaping injury. At the sound of this gunfire, dozens of well-armed citizens appeared on the street and began firing at the three outlaws who promptly galloped out of town. The following night a posse tracked the three men to the ranch house of Jim Great-house where they opened negotiations with the outlaws in arranging their surrender. Billy the Kid agreed to exchange Greathouse, then ostensibly a hostage, for posse leader Jim Carlyle. It was Carlyle's reasoning that, once inside the ranch house, he would persuade the Kid, Anderson, and Rudabaugh to surrender. The posse waited for some time and then witnessed Carlyle's body crashing through a window, three bullets having

been pumped into the deputy. While the posse members stood in shock, the outlaws made their getaway. The frustrated possemen vented their wrath on the ranch house, burning it to the ground.

A later story had it that Anderson had tried to reason with the Kid when Carlyle stepped inside the Greathouse building, saying that he had no important charge against him and that he would rather surrender. The Kid talked him out of that and a short time later cold-bloodedly turned and shot Carlyle three times and then smashed his body through the window. Pat Garrett, who would later become famous for shooting down Billy the Kid, then assumed command of the posses in the area, searching for the gang. The lawman set a trap for the gang near Fort Sumner, N.M., and, with a number of deputies, waited for the outlaws to appear. On Dec. 19, 1880, the Kid, Anderson, Rudabaugh, Charlie Bowdre, Tom O'Folliard, and Tom Pickett appeared on the road leading to the old hospital. Garrett, Lon Chambers, and several other deputies suddenly leaped from cover, with Garrett ordering the outlaws to halt. But the possemen did not wait for the outlaws to respond to Garrett's command. Posse members opened fire on Pickett and O'Folliard, who were riding in front, and shot them from their saddles. Rudabaugh's horse collapsed, killed in the hail of bullets but Rudabaugh managed to jump onto the horse ridden by Anderson and escaped with the Kid and Bowdre.

Trapped later by Garrett and a large posse at Stinking Springs, Anderson surrendered his six-gun to the lawman, and it was later alleged that this very weapon was used by Garrett to kill Billy the Kid. Anderson was tried for murder and robbery and was convicted in 1881, sent to the prison at Santa Fe, N.M. He managed to escape and flee to Texas where he lived under his real name, Anderson. For years, Anderson lived quietly in Sanderson, Tex., a town begun in 1880 by a relative. He married and raised a family, operating the Old Cottage Bar. He became so popular that Anderson was elected sheriff in 1905 and he proved himself to be an upstanding lawman, keeping the peace with a resolute, steady hand. By that time, Anderson's outlaw career as Billy Wilson was known to authorities and, because of his years of faithful service to the law, men like Pat Garrett had successfully moved to have old charges against him dropped.

The violent past, however, caught up with Anderson on June 14, 1918, when he was asked to go to the train station in Sanderson to quell a disturbance. At the depot he found a drunken cowboy named Ed Valentine whom he knew. Anderson felt he could reason with the rowdy who had been drunkenly brandishing his pistol. But when Anderson arrived the young cowboy ran to a shed and refused to come out. Sheriff Anderson stepped in front of the opened door and called into the darkness for Valentine to come out. A single shot came out of the gloom and pierced Anderson's chest. He fell mortally wounded, dying within an hour. So incensed were local residents by this senseless killing that Valentine was quickly seized and lynched. See: **Billy the Kid; Garrett, Patrick Floyd.**

REF.: Bechdolt, *Tales of the Old Timers;* Breihan, *Great Gunfighters of the West;* ____, *Great Lawmen of the West;* Brent, *Great Western Heroes;* Brothers, *Billy the Kid;* ____, *A Pecos Pioneer;* CBA; Coe, *Frontier Fighter;* Cunningham, *Triggernometry;* Fitzpatrick, *This is New Mexico;* Forrest, *Arizona's Dark and Bloody Ground;* Fulton, *Maurice Garland Fulton's History of the Lincoln County War;* Gard, *Frontier Justice;* Garrett, *The Authentic Life of Billy the Kid;* Hamlin, *The True Story of Billy the Kid;* Hendricks, *The Bad Man of the West;* Hendron, *The Story of Billy the Kid;* Hening, *George Curry;* Holloway, *Texas Gun Lore;* Horan and Sann, *Pictorial History of the Wild West;* Hough, *The Story of the Outlaw;* Hunt, *The Tragic Days of Billy the Kid;* Hutchinson and Mullin, *Whiskey Jim and A Kid Named Billie;* Keleher, *The Fabulous Frontier;* ____, *Violence in Lincoln County;* King, *Wranglin' the Past;* Metz, *Pat Garrett;* Moore, *The West;* O'Connor, *Pat Garrett;* Otero, *My Life on the Frontier;* ____, *The Real Billy the Kid;* Siringo, *History of "Billy the Kid";* Stanley, *Dave Rudabaugh, Border Ruffian;* ____, *Seven Rivers;* Sterling, *Famous Western Outlaw-Sheriff Battles;* Wellman, *The Trampling Herd.*

Anderson, Don Benny, 1940- , U.S., kid. As leader of an anti-abortion ring, Anderson tried to close down an abortion clinic by abducting the clinic's owner and the owner's wife. The attempted kidnappings on Aug. 12, 1982, of Dr. Hector Zevallos and his wife from their home in Edwardsville, Ill., not far from St. Louis, Mo., resulted in a sentence of thirty years imprisonment for Anderson, for interfering with interstate commerce—since the Hope Clinic for Women in Granite City, Ill. engaged in interstate commerce—and a twelve year-term for conspiring to commit such a crime. The sentences are to be served consecutively.

At his trial on Feb. 10, 1983, Anderson made a fifteen-minute speech prior to sentencing, in which he said, "This trial is a mockery and a sham," and then recited the Lord's Prayer. Two members of Anderson's group, the Army of God, pled guilty to aiding their fellow Texan in the attempted kidnappings. These were 20-year-old Matthew M. Moore and his brother, 18-year-old Wayne Moore. Anderson is serving his prison term in the Federal Correctional Institution at Memphis, Tenn., and will be eligible for parole in November 1992. REF.: *CBA*.

Anderson, George Weston, 1861-1938, U.S., jur. U.S. district attorney from 1914-17 and appointed federal judge to the First Circuit Court by President Woodrow Wilson in 1918. REF.: *CBA*.

Anderson, Harry, prom. 1891, Case of, U.S., burg. In an attempt to escape from the Chicago patrolman who caught him while leaving the home of a tailor by the side window, Anderson pulled out a razor while stooping to tie his shoe. Officer C.R. Woolridge prevented the escape by hitting Anderson on the head with his nightstick, handcuffing him, and then bringing him in. Anderson and another man had allegedly broken into the house of a tailor on the night of May 27, 1891, and were busy tying up a bundle of items when the tailor's daughter saw them and they fled without any goods. The case against Anderson, who had earlier served time in Joliet State Penitentiary for burglary, was dismissed when the girl was unable to identify him.

REF.: *CBA*; Wooldridge, *Hands Up*.

Anderson, Hugh, d.1873, U.S., west. gunman-duel. Texas cowboy Anderson was part of a trail herd that moved from Saledo, Tex., to Newton, Kan., in 1871. While on the trail he and several other cowhands were asked to hunt down a killer named Juan Bideno, and this gunman was tracked to Bluff City, Kan., where he was killed by Texas gunslinger John Wesley Hardin. Upon arriving in Newton, Anderson learned that his good friend and gambler William Bailey had been shot to death by a rough-and-tumble railroad foreman, Mike McCluskie, who had left town following the killing. Anderson and his friends let it be known that they intended to seek revenge on McCluskie when, if ever, he returned to Newton. McCluskie returned to Newton on Aug. 20, 1871, and Anderson immediately went after him as the burly railroad foreman sat playing faro in Perry Tuttle's Dance Hall.

Without waiting for McCluskie to make his move, Anderson raced up to him, swore, and pumped several shots into the foreman before he could draw his gun. This set off one of the wildest gun battles ever witnessed in the West, later called the Newton General Massacre. Anderson had made good his boast; he had killed McCluskie but had been severely wounded and, before he could be arrested, the quick-triggered cowboy was spirited out of town by friends who tended his wounds. Two years later, in June 1973, McCluskie's brother, Arthur McCluskie, who had been looking for Anderson, arrived in Medicine Lodge, Kan. Anderson was tending bar at Harding's Trading Post. A man named Richards who had helped McCluskie locate Anderson, went into Harding's bar and told Anderson that Arthur McCluskie was outside waiting to settle the score over the killing of his brother, giving Anderson a choice of knives or guns. Anderson chose guns, asking Harding to be his second in a duel that was very formal for the Old West. He then closed the bar, telling grumbling patrons that he had "a chore to do" and would be back in a few minutes. He never returned.

Once outside, Hugh Anderson stood back to back with Arthur McCluskie, walked twenty paces and, at the command, turned around and fired reapeatedly, as did his opponent. A crowd in the hundreds had gathered around the blood fight and were making loud wagers as the first shots went wild. Then McCluskie's second bullet found its mark, smashing into Anderson's arm and breaking it. The cowboy-bartender sank to his knees in pain, attempting to stop the flow of blood from an artery. He then aimed at McCluskie with his good hand and his bullet smashed into McCluskie's mouth. McCluskie spat out gobs of blood and broken teeth and fired again, advancing on Anderson. With deliberate aim, Anderson fired twice more, his bullets striking McCluskie in the leg and the stomach. Now McCluskie crashed to the ground and appeared to be dying. He worked himself to a kneeling position and fired another shot at Anderson, striking him in the abdomen. Anderson pitched backward, gasping for air.

Both men appeared to be dying but McCluskie show some signs of life, pulling out a knife and then crawling painfully to his foe where he sank the knife to the hilt in Anderson's side. At the same moment, Anderson, his own knife in his hand, swiped McCluskie's neck, cutting his throat. Both men then collapsed and died within seconds of each other. The gamblers collected their wagers and the bodies were dragged off for a quick burial. Harding, who had seconded Anderson, showed remarkable restraint in this duel. When both men were shot to the ground and before they pulled their knives, many in the crowd began to step forward to stop the battle but Harding, holding a shotgun, warned them not to interfere, allowing the combatants to kill each other, according to the rules they had agreed upon. See: **Hardin, John Wesley; Newton General Massacre**.

REF.: *CBA*; Miller and Snell, *Great Gunfighters of the Kansas Cowtowns*; O'Neal, *Encyclopedia of Western Gunfighters*; Rosa, *The Gunfighter*; Yost, *Medicine Lodge*.

Anderson, Joseph, 1757-1837, U.S., jur. U.S. senator from Tennessee from 1797-1815 and comptroller of the U.S. Treasury from 1815-36. REF.: *CBA*.

Anderson, Judith Mae, See: **Cook, Barry**.

Anderson, Leroy Gene (Larry Gene Anderson), 1952- , U.S., rob.-mur. Usually murderers leave behind bits and pieces of evidence. Anderson left behind his name, address, and signature at the pawnshop where he killed his last murder victim. Anderson's first victim was Jack Edward Brooks, a 62-year-old night watchman for the Polk Vocational Technical Center in Eaton Park, Fla., who was shot twice in the head with a .22-caliber automatic rifle on July 3, 1970, and then robbed. His next victim was 70-year-old Lavon Aikens, whom he robbed of, among other things, a gold watch and a .32-caliber gun with which Anderson murdered his third and final victim.

The owner of Knight's Swap Shop, 52-year-old James R. Knight, was killed by Anderson just fifteen days after the first murder. He shot Knight with the gun he had stolen from Aikens, and then fled. Anderson, however, forgot he had signed his name in the pawnbroker's ledger after selling Knight the .22-caliber weapon he had used in the first two murders and the gold watch he stole from his second victim.

Police easily found Anderson a few miles away in his trailer, and also discovered in the killer's car two more guns, more than one thousand rounds of ammunition, and blood-soaked money—the damaged money possibly accounting for Anderson's pawning of his rifle and the gold watch. Anderson pled guilty and was sentenced to life in prison on Jan. 26, 1971. He later escaped but was captured and sentenced on May 30, 1972, to an additional two years, which will run consecutively into his previous sentence, as will the two years he received on Oct. 5, 1973, for illegal possession of a weapon. The killer is eligible for parole in 2019. REF.: *CBA*.

Anderson, Levi E., c.1889-1975, U.S. (unsolv.) mur. An informant's tip and a resulting autopsy led to the discovery that Anderson had not died of natural causes. The autopsy revealed that the 86-year-old Chicago man had been choked and beaten to death, just as the informant had told police.

Suspected in murdering the WWI U.S. Navy veteran was 23-year-old Eddie Turner, whom police said had forced Anderson to give him money. Turner is thought to have killed Anderson with the man's own cane by pressing it against his throat while demanding the money. Anderson bequeathed $8,000 to the U.S. government which his will stated had "been very good to me." REF.: *CBA*.

Anderson, Lucious, 1848-73, U.S., suic.-mur. Born outside of Brattleboro, Vt., Lucious Anderson was the spoiled son of a prosperous farmer. Anderson was often truant, took to torturing small animals, and, in his teens, he stole money from his father's strongbox. In 1869, his parents died of influenza and he inherited the sprawling farm worked by six hired hands whom he browbeat until they grew to hate him. Anderson began to drink heavily, hiring and firing his employees, believing all intended to do him harm. In the spring of 1873, Anderson hired Rufus Jellico, a towering man of enormous strength. The dimwitted Jellico turned out to be lazy and shiftless and ignored Anderson's orders. On the morning of May 16, 1873, Anderson told Jellico to clean the hogpen. Jellico snorted: "Rufus don't clean no hogpen. Rufus break the back of anyone who tells him to clean hogs."

The paranoid Anderson raced inside his house, retrieved a rifle and ran up to Jellico, firing a shot that killed him. The other workers arrived to hear Anderson babbling a story about how Jellico tried to kill him. One of the workers went for the sheriff, while Anderson retreated to the large farmhouse to drink drink. An hour later, the workers outside heard a shot and ran inside to find Anderson dead on the floor. He had shot himself. Sheriff W.L. Munsey arrived to find the dead farmer with his diary clutched in his hand, the last entry reading: "My hired hands killed Rufus Jellico and I believe they are going to come in here and shoot me, too." No workers were arrested, and Anderson was credited with the Jellico murder.

REF.: *CBA; The Murder and Suicide at the Anderson Farm, A Strange Tale of a Demented Mind*.

Anderson, Percy Charles, d.1935, Brit., mur. Edith Drew-Bear's body was discovered floating in a water tank by Brighton police on Nov. 25, 1934, but neither drowning nor the five bullets in her back and head had caused death. She had been strangled with a silk scarf wound tightly under her chin, according to Sir Bernard Spilsbury, who conducted the postmortem two days later.

The attack on the 21-year-old movie theater usher was characterized during the trial of her murderer, Anderson, as maniacal, a point the defense tried to use in proving that Anderson was not guilty by reason of insanity. Spilsbury noted that the bullets were fired from a .22-caliber gun—presumably a Walden Safety Revolver which was never recovered—and thus had not seriously wounded the victim, but had likely induced unconsciousness before she was choked to death and then dumped in the water tank.

When arrested, Anderson was carrying poison, ammonia chloride, and zinc chloride, and possessed in his room bullets identical to those found in Drew-Bear's body. He admitted quarreling with Drew-Bear but beyond that remembered nothing. In March 1935 he pled insanity to the charge but was nevertheless convicted of murder and executed at Wandsworth.

REF.: Browne, *The Scalpel of Scotland Yard; CBA*.

Anderson, Perry L. Jr., 1944-   , U.S. law enf. off. After serving in the U.S. Army from 1964-67, including one year of duty in Vietnam, where he won the Bronze Star for meritorious service, Anderson joined the Miami Police Department on Feb. 24, 1969. Before his appointment as Chief of Police on July 15, 1988, he had served as sergeant, lieutenant, major, deputy chief, and assistant chief. He is a graduate of the Southern Police Institute at the University of Louisville. REF.: *CBA*.

Anderson, Reese, prom. 1880s, U.S., vigil. Anderson was a cowboy who worked for the Granville Stuart ranch in Montana. When the nearby area, known as the Lower Judith Basin, welled up with scores of bandits and robbers in 1884, Anderson volunteered to lead two dozen of Stuart's cowhands in a vigilante sweep of the area. Anderson and his men rode into the hideout area between the Musselshell and Judith rivers and surprised the outlaws, capturing and hanging twenty-three horse thieves caught red-handed with stolen herds. REF.: *CBA*.

Anderson, Robert, and **Fleming,** prom. 20th Cent., Fr., theft. Had it not been for the insolent treatment two U.S. civilians gave the owner of a Bordeaux, France, jewelry store that was later burglarized, neither the local police nor the U.S. military stationed there would have solved the crime. Anderson and Fleming, who had visited the jeweler's a few days before the crime to look the place over—they asked the owner to show them diamonds kept in the safe and then angrily left—did a remarkable job in avoiding arrest until a woman was observed wearing a platinum watch taken from the jeweler's. Following her led to Anderson and eventually to a co-worker named Fleming.

A close watch was kept over the pair. On the night they planned to divide the jewels and go to Spain, the authorities were ready. When fourteen U.S. military personnel surrounded the shack that housed the burglars, Anderson and Fleming surrendered. They pled guilty and were sentenced to ten years at Fort Leavenworth. REF.: *CBA; Russell, Adventures of the D.C.I.*

Anderson, Robert Palmer, 1906-78, U.S., jur. Public defender of New London County, Conn. from 1936-47. Appointed federal judge in Connecticut District Court in 1954 by President Dwight D. Eisenhower. REF.: *CBA*.

Anderson, Scott L., prom. 1870s, U.S., west. gunman. Scotty Anderson was a fearless guard for the Northwestern Stage amd Transportation Company, guarding the firm's considerable gold shipments in the Dakotas. One particular run, the Deadwood-Pierre, S.D., was plagued by a bold band of bandits headed by an ex-company guard, Boston Joe. Several guards had been killed and more than $50,000 in gold shipments stolen. Anderson, a tough, unflinching hard case who carried two shotguns along with three pistols, was hired as chief guard to protect this run. On his first assignment, Anderson and four guards, heavily armed and protecting more than $100,000 in gold, took the Deadwood-Pierre stage which was stopped by Boston Joe and his gang near Deadman's Creek. The bandits and guards opened up on each other, blazing away as the stage made a run for it. Boston Joe and his men dashed after it, firing as they attempted to catch the stage. Anderson, though wounded several times, managed to kill Boston Joe. The other guards shot three of the remaining outlaws dead in their saddles before two of the guards were killed and the driver wounded. Anderson brought the stage in safely to Pierre to report the end of the outlaw band.

REF.: Bartholomew, *The Biographical Album of Western Gunfighters; CBA*.

Anderson, Terry, 1947-   , Leb. Case of, abduc. Anderson, the Associated Press' Middle East bureau chief, is the record-holder of an unenviable title: the hostage held longest of fourteen foreign hostages held captive in Lebanon. Anderson's ordeal began on March 16, 1985, when his car was stopped and three men abducted him at gunpoint. His captors have been identified as members of a pro-Iranian Shiite Muslim group known as the Islamic Jihad, which means "Islamic Holy War." During his captivity Anderson has had four birthdays and has missed all of his youngest daughter's birthdays, a girl who was born after his capture. A fellow hostage, who has since been released, said the last remark Anderson made to him was, "Promise me one thing. I'm never forgotten." If alive, Anderson is still a hostage as of this printing. REF.: *CBA*.

Anderson, Thomas Weldon (AKA: **Atherstone**), d.1910, Brit., (unsolv.) mur. Anderson was a successful, middle-aged actor who used the name of Atherstone when trooping the boards. He lived with his mistress on Prince of Wales Road in Battersea Park, London, separated from his wife for more than ten years. The actor had two teenage sons who visited him often and were treated by the mistress as her own boys. But in early 1910, Anderson quarreled with his woman and left, taking up residence elsewhere. His 17-year-old son, however, kept a dinner engagement with the mistress, one that had been established weeks earlier, on the night of June 16, 1910. They were interrupted by a noise in the backyard, two gunshots. They ran outside to see a short, powerfully-built man hurl himself over the brick wall leading to an alley. They turned to see a figure crouched next to the door of an empty basement apartment. This turned out to be the body of Thomas Weldon Anderson. He had been shot in the head with two bullets and was quite dead.

The case baffled police then as it does today. Anderson, who had told his son that he would not be attending the dinner, was found wearing slippers and his boots were in a bag on top the mantlepiece of the empty basement apartment. In one of Anderson's pockets was found an 18-inch strip of cable. It was later conjectured that Anderson had entered the basement apartment secretly, put on his slippers so as not to arouse his mistress and prepared to murder her with the cable. Yet Anderson's love for his son was well known and he would never had done anything to jeopardize the boy's life. Also, he was not by nature a violent man and had little or nothing to fear from the mistress. The little man who killed Anderson was never found. The killer was estimated to be no more than five foot three inches, according to witnesses who saw him clamber off the brick wall and disappear down a dark street near the river. It was thought that he might have been a burglar who accidentally stumbled upon Anderson while attempting to rob the basement apartment, yet no professional burglar would have bothered with an obviously empty flat. Police failed to provide a motive for the killing, let alone a suspect. The Anderson case remains one of the more intriguing of unsolved murders in the history of London.

REF.: *CBA;* Lambton, *Echoes of Causes Celebres;* Nash, *Open Files;* Shew, *A Companion to Murder;* Villiers, *Riddles of Crime.*

Anderson, William (AKA: Bloody Bill), 1837-64, U.S., mur. Born in Jefferson County, Mo., on Feb. 2, 1837, Anderson enlisted in the guerilla band of William Clarke Quantrill, a Confederate group, in 1863, having operated with his own guerilla band since the beginning of the Civil War. Often as not, this most fierce of Quantrill's raiders, operated with his own band of men, about sixty-five strong. Anderson was feared throughout the border states of Missouri-Kansas as an out-and-out killer—aptly nick-named Bloody Bill—who preferred to murder anyone with Union sympathies. While Quantrill would earn his notoriety at the sacking and burning of Lawrence, Kan., Anderson's annihilation of Centralia, Kan., in 1864 would make his name synonymous with murder.

This fierce killer who, like his men wore his hair long and unkempt, postured as a Confederate soldier, but he and his men, in reality, were most often nothing more than raiding plunderers of small, defenseless towns. Contemporary accounts reported that Anderson's three sisters had all died when the building where they were being guarded by Union troops caught on fire. Anderson claimed that his sisters had been brutally raped and then locked in the building which was then purposely torched, and this was the reason why he showed no mercy to Union troops and sympathizers. Most historians, however, agreed that Anderson was simply a bloodlusting lunatic who enjoyed inflicting pain and death. Jim Cummins, who later rode with Jesse James and had been a member of Quantrill's legions during the war, later stated that Anderson was "the most desperate man I ever met." Union forces operating in Missouri and Kansas were grimly aware of the fact that Anderson never took prisoners but always shot captives out-of-hand. This was never more in evidence than during Bloody Bill's raid on Centralia.

While attempting to join up with regular Confederate Army troops under the command of General Sterling Price, Anderson and about seventy men swooped down on Centralia on Sept. 27, 1864. As soon as the local merchants recognized the savage looking Anderson and his ragged troops with their long, tangled hair and filthy long dusters, they realized they were at the mercy of the worst guerilla raider of the war. The shopkeepers and their families fled their homes and stores into the open county. Several women were dragged back and raped by Anderson's men while

others set fire to the entire town and executed those they thought were Union supporters. Whiskey barrels were located in one store and Anderson and his men gulped down great quantities of this raw alcohol, using their shoes as cups.

Anderson, checking the train schedules at the depot, realized that a train was scheduled to pass through Centralia at noon that day and he ordered a huge barricade built across the tracks. At noon a passenger train was forced by the barricade to stop at Centralia. Its passengers were herded onto the depot platform, including twenty-six Union soldiers under the command of a Lieutenant Peters, men who had been furloughed and were en route to St. Joseph, Mo. Peters, recognizing Anderson from a train window and realizing that the guerilla leader was known to murder any Union officers, threw a blanket over himself, jumped from the train, and attempted to hide beneath the platform of the burning depot.

Civil War guerilla "Bloody Bill" Anderson committed mass murder at Centralia, Kan., in 1864.

The guerilla chieftan spotted the cowardly officer and yelled to his men, "Pull that bastard out of there!" Peters was dragged from beneath the platform and, as Anderson approached him, guns in hands, broke free and tried to run for his life. Anderson took careful aim and fired six bullets into him, killing Peters. He then ordered the remaining twenty-six Union troopers lined up in an open field. All knew of Anderson's no quarter policy and that he had given his men strict orders to kill all Union prisoners. Most fell on their knees to pray or beg sobbingly for mercy. Anderson paraded up and down in front of them, bristling with guns. (He was a walking and riding arsenal, usually with four Navy Colt pistols in his waistband, four rifles on his horse, a sabre, a hatchet, and a bag of pistols wrapped around the horn of his saddle.)

Anderson ignored the pleas from the troopers that their lives be spared. He stopped, stuck a cigar in his mouth and lighted this, then asked softly, "Boys, do you have a sergeant in your ranks?" None of the men answered, all fearing that anyone admitting to the rank of sergeant would be tortured. Anderson repeated his question calmly several times, indicating that if the Union troops cooperated, their lives would be spared. Finally, Sergeant Thomas M. Goodman stepped forward, admitting his rank. "Fine," smiled Anderson around his cigar. "We'll use you to exchange for one of my men that the damned Yankees have caught." Goodman was ushered out of line. The guerilla chieftan than withdrew two of his Colts and went down the line, firing until the chambers of both guns were empty. He took two more pistols and emptied these and then two more, until all twenty-six Union soldiers had been murdered in cold blood.

Goodman would later escape to tell the tale of Anderson's brutal slaughter but by that time the guerillas had already ridden off to attack Union troops elsewhere. While in Texas some weeks later, Anderson married a young girl and brought her back to Ray County, Mo., settling briefly in a small farmhouse before riding off once more to lead his men in more murderous raids. Anderson's bloody crimes were halted, however, on Oct. 27, 1864, when, at the head of his guerilla column, riding near Orrick, Mo., he was ambushed by Union troops under the command of Captain S.P. Cox. Anderson was struck by dozens of bullets and was dead in his saddle. His men fought wildly to retrieve his body but were driven off. Anderson's corpse was taken to Richmond, Mo., where it was propped up in a chair and a pistol placed in its dead hand and then photographed. A few minutes later, Union soldiers, full of hatred for this butcher, cut off Anderson's head and impaled it on a telegraph pole and placed at the entrance of the town to assure one and all that the terrible guerilla leader was indeed dead. His carcass was then tied to a rope and dragged up and down the streets, before the remains were dumped into an unmarked grave at the outskirts of town.

It was later claimed that Anderson was not killed at the Orrick ambush and that another man, a look-alike, was killed and that Anderson changed his name and escaped to Oklahoma where he ran a saloon for several years in Erin Springs. Another report has it that the mass killer went to Texas after the war and settled in Salt Creek, Brown County, where he lived peacefully under an alias for sixty years. Some credibility was attached to this last story in that a man bearing a slight resemblance to Anderson died in Salt Creek on Nov. 2, 1927. On the table next to his deathbed was found an ancient photograph of three young women who were later identified as Anderson's long-dead sisters. See: **Quantrill, William Clarke.**

REF.: Bartholomew, *The Album of Western Gunfighters;* Breihan, *The Killer Legions of Quantrill;* ____, *Quantrill and His Civil War Guerilas; CBA;* Connelley, *Quantrill and the Border Wars;* Cummins, *Jim Cummins' Book;* Edwards, *Noted Guerillas, or the Warfare of the Border;* Garwood, *Crossroads of America;* Nash, *Bloodletters and Badmen;* Rosa, *The Gunfighter.*

Anderson, William, prom. 1870s, U.S., west. gunman. Anderson was a drunken gunman who lived in Delano, the vice district of Wichita, during the 1870s. He was forever getting into trouble with the law and, in the spring of 1873, he was involved in a violent argument in a Wichita livery stable. He pulled a gun, as did others, and a brief shootout occurred where one of Anderson's shots smashed into the forehead of a passerby, killing him. The death was ruled accidental and Anderson was released. A short time later, on Oct. 27, 1873, Anderson was lounging inside of Rowdy Joe Lowe's Delano bar when an enraged cowhand named Red Beard burst into the bar. He had been jilted by one of the saloon girls, Annie Franklin, and he sought revenge, pulling his gun and shooting the girl in the stomach. Lowe let loose with his shotgun and blasted Beard who fired back as he staggered outside. In the exchange of bullets, Anderson was caught in the crossfire, taking a load of buckshot in the head which caused him to become permanently blind. Anderson spent the rest of his days sitting outside cowtown saloons, hat in hand, begging coins.

REF.: *CBA;* Miller and Snell, *Great Gunfighters of the Kansas Cowtowns;* O'Neal, *Encyclopedia of Western Gunfighters.*

Anderson, William H., d.1878, U.S., west. law enfor. off. Anderson, born in Illinois, moved as a youth to Texas and served in the Confederate Army during the Civil War, later deserting to serve with an Illinois regiment. He moved back to Texas following the war and was appointed a U.S. deputy marshal, a post he served with distinction, having a reputation as an expert marksman. He invariably captured any felon he sought out. In 1878 he was ordered to track down outlaw Bill Collins, last surviving member of the Joel Collins outlaw band. Doggedly trailing the Collins brother through several states, Anderson finally cornered his man in Manitoba, Can. Outside the small hamlet of Pembina, both Anderson and Collins shot it out, killing each other. Anderson's body was returned to Texas for burial and his family was given the considerable reward that had been placed on Collins' head.

REF.: Bartholomew, *The Biographical Album of Western Gunfighters; CBA.*

Andre, Major John, See: **Arnold, Benedict.**

Andre Cornelis, 1887, a novel by Paul Bourget. The involved murder scheme of the Peltzer Brothers (Belg., 1882) serves as inspirational background material in this work of fiction. See: **Peltzer Brothers.** REF.: *CBA.*

Andrew (Andrey Yuryevich Bogolyubsky), c.1111-74, Rus., prince, assass. Succeeded his father as prince of Rostov-Suzdal in 1157. In 1169, he conquered Kiev and was named grand prince of Vladimir. He was later assassinated by nobles. REF.: *CBA.*

Andrew, Robert, prom. 1870s, U.S., west. law. enfor. off. An Oklahoma lawman and detective, Andrew was responsible for discovering the hideout of the Doolin gang. This resulted in the Ingalls, Okla., raid on Sept. 1, 1893, and the capture of many members of that band. See: **Doolin, William.** REF.: *CBA.*

Andrew of Carniola (Andrew of Kraina), d.1484, Slavic, bishop, consp.-suic. Became bishop of Carniola in 1476. After he failed to be appointed cardinal in 1478 he denounced Pope Sixtus IV and attempted to have him formally indicted at a council he convened in Basel. When this attempt failed, he was imprisoned, then allegedly committed suicide. REF.: *CBA.*

Andrews, Dorothy Ann, 1941- , U.S. mur. Garnering forty-one ribbons at the 1979 Shiawassee County Free Fair was what made Andrews "Homemaker of the Year" at the Michigan State Fair that year. Shooting to death her 28-year-old husband, Terry Andrews, was not what a prize-winning homemaker should do.

Andrews shot her husband twice with a .22-caliber rifle in the lower jaw while he slept on Nov. 15, 1981, and he died four days later. The 40-year-old woman, confined to a wheelchair from multiple sclerosis which she contracted in 1976, pled guilty to voluntary manslaughter at her second trial held on Mar. 23, 1984, after the first trial ended in a hung jury on Oct. 18, 1982. She was sentenced to sixty months probation, required to pay $1,000 in court costs, and enter a mental health treatment program. Andrews was discharged from probation supervision on Oct. 16, 1987. REF.: *CBA.*

Andrews, Joseph, d.1769, U.S., pir.-mur. A violent, alcoholic seaman, Andrews signed aboard the schooner *Polly* and set sail for the West Indies in August 1766. Andrews soon persuaded two other crew members, William Harris and a seaman named Johnson to kill Captain Duryee and other crewmen and passengers, seize the cargo, and sell it off at St. Kitts. As the ship approached St. Christopher, with Harris at the helm, Johnson crept up on the Captain who was asleep on a hencoop on deck and killed him with one blow from an axe. Andrews went from cabin to cabin below deck and murdered the first mate and three passengers—one a small boy. The mutineers then dumped the bodies overboard. When the vessel arrived at St. Kitts and the mutinous pirates attempted to sell their stolen cargo, they were revealed as mass murderers. Harris fled and vanished but Andrews was seized and returned to New York where he was tried and convicted on May 17, 1769.

While awaiting execution for piracy and murder, Andrews made a full confession to clergymen visiting him in his cell. On May 23, 1769, he was taken to a beachfront area and, before a large throng, shouted out a weepy speech of self-condemnation, and was hanged while thousands cheered. Andrews' body was later taken to Bedloe's Island where it was hung in chains and left to rot. Johnson, the third mutineer-pirate, was later caught in the West Indies, and he was taken to Eustatia where, after a one-hour trial, was broken on the wheel.

REF.: *An Account of the Trial of Joseph Andrews; CBA; The Last Dying Speech and Confession of Joseph Andrews; A Narrative of Part of the Life of Joseph Andrews.*

Andrews, Lowell Lee (AKA: The Nicest Boy in Wolcott), c.1940-59, U.S. mur. Referred to as "the nicest boy" in his hometown of Wolcott, Kan., by the local newspaper, Andrews did anything but live up to it when he attempted to fulfill his secret dream of becoming a hired gun in Chicago. Andrews, at the age of eighteen, weighed 300 pounds, wore horn-rimmed glasses, never drank alcohol, never dated, regularly went to church, and was an honor student. But because he needed money for the trip to Chicago to see his dream through, Andrews decided to kill his sister and parents and sell the property owned by his well-off farming family.

While his family watched television, he entered the parlor carrying an automatic rifle and revolver and shot his sister between the eyes, his mother three times, and his father twice, before reloading, since the first round failed to kill his parents. He confessed the killings to his pastor a few days later. He was found

Guilty of murder, despite being diagnosed as schizophrenic, sentenced, and hanged at Leavenworth Prison. REF.: *CBA*.

Andrews, Mary, d.1721, Brit., tort. In 1721, Mary Andrews' British jailers forced a confession from her by means of a ghastly torture introduced in 1714 at the end of Queen Anne's reign to replace *peine forte et dure*, commonly known as pressing to death. A prisoner who refused to confess would have his thumbs tied with a cord, then twisted until the agony was unbearable. Thumb screwing was practiced in open court, and became a spectator sport for the gallery. In Mary Andrews' case, the cord snapped three times before she confessed. She was sentenced to death. REF.: *CBA*.

Andrews, Milton Franklin (AKA: **Brush, Curtis,** and others), d.1905, U.S., rob.-asslt.-suic.-mur. The literally hard head of former steeplechase rider Friday Ellis proved to be the downfall of robber and murderer Andrews. When a bloodied and semiconscious Friday Ellis was discovered on a Berkeley, Calif., street on Oct. 11, 1905, the search for the killer began. Ellis told the police that Andrews had boasted of killing a woman, who turned out to be Mrs. Bessie Bouton. Bouton had traveled with Andrews as his wife and her charred body with a bullet in the back of her head was discovered on Dec. 16, 1904. Police learned that Andrews could only drink malted milk because of a stomach problem.

Police soon heard about a woman purchasing large quantities of malted milk in San Francisco. The woman Eda Little, who, as Andrews' accomplice also posed as Mrs. Brush, was followed to an apartment and after police announced themselves two shots were heard. Inside the apartment they found Andrews and Little dead, apparently each shot in the forehead by Andrews. Further evidence linked Andrews to the murder at New Britain, Conn., on Aug. 2, 1904, of Eugene J. Bosworth, who had been robbed of hundreds of dollars and whose skull had been crushed.

In a confession found in Little's stocking, Andrews wrote of the attack on Ellis, "I did not know at the time that he had a gorilla's skull or I would have used a pile driver."

REF.: *CBA*; Duke, *Celebrated Criminal Cases of America*.

Andrews, Samuel M., prom. 1868, Case of, U.S., mur. Andrews had been named in the will of Cornelius Holmes, one of the wealthiest residents of Kingston, Mass. On May 26, 1868, Andrews beat Holmes to death by hurling heavy stones at his head. In a rather sensational trail, beginning on Dec. 11, 1868, Andrews' defense attorney entered a plea of "transitory" insanity and self-defense. On the witness stand, Andrews insisted that Holmes was a violent homosexual and that he had to fend off an attempted act of sodomy by Holmes by crushing the victim's head with stones. He had, at the time, gone out of his mind, Andrews claimed. The insanity pleading was successful; Andrews was found guilty but sent to an asylum.

REF.: *CBA*; Davis, *Report of the Trial of Samuel M. Andrews*; *Full Report of the Trial of Samuel M. Andrews*; *Trial of Samuel M. Andrews*.

Andrews, Thomas, prom. 1760s, Case of, Brit., rape. Powerful friends saved him from the gallows, but for this rapist of Smithfield disgrace and scandal cost him the respect of his tightly knit community. Andrews kept a public house at Pye Corner. In 1761 an unemployed servant named John Finnimore asked the innkeeper to help him find a job. This Andrews could not do, but he offered to provide Finnimore with lodging for the night. Finnimore declined, saying he had a room in the Red Lion Court near Saint Sepulchre's church.

The next night Finnimore returned to accept Andrews' generous offer, for he had lost his room at the Red Lion. Andrews said the inn was presently full but since his wife was away Finnimore could share his bed, an arrangement Finnimore accepted. At 1 a.m. the last of the ale house crowd left the inn. What passed between the two men during the night is conjecture, but Finnimore departed early in the morning in great haste. He went to the constable and a warrant for Andrews' arrest was drawn up. The constable, disgusted by Finnimore's story, had both men jailed until Sir Robert Ladbroke, the sitting alderman of Guildhall, could sort out the details. Andrews was brought to trial at the Old Bailey on a charge of homosexual rape based on the vivid testimony of Finnimore, and the jury found him guilty and sentenced him to die. There was no doubt in the minds of the jury and the townspeople of Andrews' guilt. In their minds he was a perverse fiend worthy of death, the prevailing judgment on homosexuals in the 18th Century. But in this instance, Andrews' powerful friends secured a pardon for him. He was discharged from Newgate prison in July 1761. REF.: *CBA*.

REF.: *CBA*; Mitchell, *The Newgate Calendar*.

Andreyev, Leonid Nikolayevich (Andreev, Leonid Nikolaevich), 1871-1919, Rus., lawyer-writer. Lawyer and police reporter who wrote realistic novels and short stories including "The Seven Who Were Hanged" (1909). Opposed to the revolution, he fled to Finland in 1917 and died there, impoverished. REF.: *CBA*.

Andronicus I Comnenus, c.1110-85, Roman, emperor., assass. Grandson of Alexius I Comnenus, he was regent for Emperor Alexius II whom he killed in 1183. During his short reign he tried to eliminate the power of the nobles. He was eventually overthrown by Issac Angelus and killed by a mob. REF.: *CBA*.

Andros, Sir Edmund, 1637-1714, Brit., polit. Appointed colonial governor of the province of New York in 1674. When the New England colonies were united in 1686 as the "Dominion of New England," he was appointed governor. The colonies revolted and imprisoned him, charging that he interfered with their rights and customs. He was sent back to England for a hearing but charges were never pressed. He later returned to the colonies and served as governor of Virginia from 1692-97. REF.: *CBA*.

Angel, 1947, a play by Mary Hayley Bell. This drama, produced in Liverpool, England, is based on Constance Kent's murder of her small half-brother Francis (Brit., 1860). See: **Kent, Constance**. REF.: *CBA*.

Angell, Joseph Kinnicutt, 1794-1857, U.S., lawyer-legal writer. REF.: *CBA*.

Angelos, Anthony G., 1926- , U.S., fraud. Following the collapse of the Des Plaines (Ill.) Bank in March 1981, investigators learned that the bank's president from 1977 to 1980, Anthony G. Angelos, had defrauded the bank of more than $5 million over a two-year period. Angelos and his associate, John Voyiatzis, were indicted on thirty-two counts, including bribery, mail and wire fraud, and racketeering. Angelos received $50,000 to $90,000 in kickbacks on loans he negotiated, and fraudulently transferred $2.4 million from a British bank in Nairobi, Kenya, to the Des Plaines Bank. In a plea bargain, Angelos admitted his guilt to one count each of mail fraud and bank fraud in exchange for the government dropping the remaining thirty counts. U.S. District Judge Stanley J. Roszkowski sentenced Angelos to five years in prison on Mar. 21, 1984.

Illinois governor Dan Walker at one time nominated Angelos to be state director of insurance, but withdrew the name amid allegations that the job was offered in repayment of Angelos' $50,000 contribution to the governor's campaign. REF.: *CBA*.

Anger, Roger, See: **Guay, Albert**.

Angiulo, Gennaro J., 1919- , U.S., org. crime. Beginning as a lowly runner for the numbers racket in Boston, Angiulo rose through the ranks of the Mafia-syndicate, first endorsed for positions of authority by New England boss Raymond Patriarca, then permitted to establish his own Boston policy ring under boss Joseph Lombardo. When Lombardo was succeeded by Philip Bruccola, Angiulo rose to a number two position. Bruccola, facing federal heat for income tax evasion, fled to Sicily and Angiulo took over as boss of the Boston syndicate by default. He was challenged in this position by Ilario Zannino but Patriarca, ruling New England from Providence, R.I., gave Angiulo the nod and he was acknowledged as the boss, Zannino becoming his reluctant second-in-command.

It was a shaky dynasty that Angiulo ruled with Zannino balking at his every command. When Patriarca died in 1984, Angiulo lay claim to the entire New England area but he was contested in this by the truculent Zannino who, to secure the Boston fiefdom for himself, backed Raymond J. Patriarca, Jr. as the new boss of bosses for New England. After a summit meeting attended by several Mafia-syndicate members representing the East Coast, Patriarca was given New England to rule. He, in turn, named Zannino as his chief lieutenant and boss of Boston, demoting the ambitious Angiulo to a common soldier. Angiulo's problems increased in the mid-1980s when federal racketeering charges were brought against him. He was convicted and sent to prison to serve a forty-five-year term in 1986.

REF.: *CBA;* Peterson, *The Mob;* Teresa, *My Life in the Mafia.*

Anglin, Francis Alexander, 1865-1933, Can., jur. Served on the Canadian Supreme Court from 1909-33. REF.: *CBA.*

Angry Brigade, The (Barker, John; Creek, Hilary Anne; Greenfield, James; Mendleson, Anna), prom. 1971, Brit., terr. One of the first and most dangerous terrorist organizations in England was responsible for at least twenty-five bombings in less than a year, though not once costing a life. Not only did this fanatical group lead to an increase in acts of terrorism in and around London, but led also to the creation of the Bomb Squad at Scotland Yard.

The Angry Brigade, as the terrorists called themselves in a communiqué claiming responsibility for the explosions, said, "Our attack is violent. Our violence is organized...Where two or three revolutionaries use organized violence to attack the class system there is The Angry Brigade." Attacks were committed against property and not people; the homes of government officials and businesses especially catering to extravagances were prime targets.

Police finally caught up with the brigade's leaders during a raid on Aug. 20, 1971, where an automatic pistol, two submachine guns, eighty-one rounds of ammunition, and thirty-three cartridges of explosives were found in the apartment shared by 23-year-olds John Barker, James Greenfield, and Anna Mendleson, and 22-year-old Hilary Anne Creek. Justice James presided over the trial of the four, taking great pains to seat a nonpolitical and unbiased jury. They were found guilty and sentenced to ten years in prison.

The sentence was followed by one last brigade communiqué, number fourteen, by those still at large, which read, "Sooner or later they will be freed. Sooner or later you will hear from us again."

REF.: Borrell, *Crime In Britain Today; CBA.*

Ankarström, See: **Gustavus III.**

An Lushan (K'ang, AKA: Hsiung Wu, Yen La Wang), 703-57, China, emperor, assass. Chinese general who launched a rebellion in 755, proclaimed himself emperor in 756 and was assassinated the following year by a slave who conspired with his son. REF.: *CBA.*

Ann Arbor Murders, See: **Narcisco, Filipina B.**

Annee, Paul A., 1942- , U.S. law enf. off. The current Chief of Police of the Indianapolis, Ind., Police Department, Annee, has been a member of the city's force since Sept. 20, 1965. Through the years he has served as patrolman, detective sergeant, lieutenant, deputy chief, and captain, a position he held for almost five years before receiving appointment as chief on Aug. 29, 1986. REF.: *CBA.*

Annenberg, Moses L., 1878-1942, U.S., org. crime. Annenberg, and his brother Max, raised on Chicago's South Side, began their varied careers as circulation thugs for the Chicago *Tribune* and were later hired away by William Randolph Hearst to peddle his newspapers, the *Examiner* and the *American,* no matter the cost. Moses organized an army of killer thugs who burned newstands, beat up, and even killed distribution managers in their circulation wars with the *Tribune* which became particularly violent between 1910 and 1911. Working for Annenberg, who became Hearst's circulation manager in 1904, were a bevy of apprentice hoodlums who later became the most feared gunmen in Chicago. Annenberg ran a school for assault and battery and many of his circulation boosters refused to stop at murder. Among these were such terrors as Charles Dion O'Bannion, George "Bugs" Moran and Frank McErlane, the latter having the dubious honor of using a machine gun in the Chicago gang wars for the first time.

Moses Annenberg was a man of great ambition and was so

effective at his bully-boy circulation chores that Hearst paid him a hefty salary and ignored Annenberg's other business interests. He patterned himself after Hearst and thought of himself as another publishing giant. In 1922, with money he reportedly "borrowed" from his friend, Johnny Torrio, Annenberg bought the *Daily Racing Form* and did so well with this tip sheet that he quit Hearst four years later, deciding to establish his own print empire. He would later purchase the New York *Morning Telegraph* and still later buy the lucrative periodicals, *Screen Guide* and *Radio Guide.* Throughout the late 1920s and 1930s, Annenberg acquired other publications, including the powerful Philadelphia *Inquirer.* The company that pumped endless millions into Annenberg's pockets, however, was Nation-Wide News Service, which Annenberg formed with syndicate gambler, Frank Erickson who represented Meyer Lansky, Lucky Luciano, and Frank Costello in all national gambling interests. Annenberg came to meet these leaders of the national crime cartel when attending the first syndicate summit meeting in Atlantic City in 1929, brought along to represent gambling interests by his good friend, Al Capone. It was at this meeting that Annenberg, through Capone, outlined how

Moses Annenberg became one of the world's richest men by organizing a wire service for the early-day crime cartel. He went to prison for income-tax evasion in 1939.

the syndicate would control the racing results from all the tracks across the nation through Nation-Wide.

This service established a monopoly on racing results from all the tracks in America, through AT&T wires, funneling this information to hundreds of cities in the U.S. and all the thousands of syndicate controlled bookmaking operations, gambling dens, and poolrooms throughout the country. Nation-Wide charged large fees for its use and so many millions poured into Annenberg's coffers that he became one of America's wealthiest citizens. Shrewd as he was, Annenberg, like Capone before him, felt he owed the government nothing for his grand fortune and was charged, along with his son Walter, with income tax evasion in 1939. It was claimed by federal authorities that Moses had paid only a few hundred dollars in income tax in 1932 when his detected income demanded a payment of more than $300,000. Prosecutors stated that he owed more than $1.5 million in tax payments for the year 1936 and had paid less than a third of that amount. Almost $10 million was owed by Annenberg, according to the federal government. In return for government lawyers dropping the case against his son Walter, who had pleaded not guilty, Annenberg walked into court with a guilty plea. He was sentenced to three years in prison. He happily paid the $9.5 million.

Annenberg's power waned after his conviction, although his personal fortune continued to grow to what some have estimated to be the fourth or fifth largest family fortune in America. His Nation-Wide News Service was replaced by the Continental Press Service run by James M. Ragen who would be murdered in 1946 by the mob for his intractable stance on sharing certain profits of his enormous returns from Continental. Annenberg, on the other hand, served his time and retired in Babylonian luxury. His son.

Walter Annenberg, a supporter of Republican causes, was named as ambassador to England by his good friend, President Richard Nixon. The Annenberg fortune remains intact today, built upon the bones of illegal gambling. See: Capone, Alphonse; Costello, Frank; Erickson, Frank; Lansky, Meyer; Luciano, Charles; McErlane, Frank; O'Bannion, Charles Dion; Ragen, James M.; Torrio, John.

REF.: Andrews, *Battle for Chicago*; Asbury, *Gem of the Prairie*; Browning and Gerassi, *The American Way of Crime*; Carlson, *Hearst*; *CBA*; Gies, *The Colonel of Chicago*; Hynd, *The Giant Killers*; Kobler, *Capone*; Lindberg, *Chicago Ragtime*; Lundberg, *Imperial Hearst*; McPhaul, *Deadlines and Monkeyshines*; Messick, *Secret File*; Nash, *Bloodletters and Badmen*; ____, *People to See*; Older, *William Randolph Hearst*; Pasley, *Al Capone, The Story of A Self-Made Man*; ____, *Muscling In*; Reppetto, *The Blue Parade*; Reuter, *Disorganized Crime*; Smith, *Syndicate City*; Sullivan, *Chicago Surrenders*; ____, *Rattling the Cup on Chicago Crime*; Swanberg, *Citizen Hearst*; Tebbel, *The Life and Good Times of William Randolph Hearst*; Waldrop, *McCormick of Chicago*; Wendt, *Chicago Tribune*; Winkler, *W.R. Hearst, An American Phenomenon*; ____, *William Randolph Hearst, A New Appraisal*.

Annesley, Richard, Case of, Ire., kid. As the only son of Baron Altham of Dunmaine in Ireland, James Annesley would have been the heir to his father's barony and the earldom of Anglesey, that is, unless his father had not quarreled with the boy's mother and grown to despise the boy.

The hatred increased when Altham's brother, Richard Annesley moved to Dunmaine and plotted with the baron to kill James. The 9-year-old ran off to Dublin to escape his fate and remained in hiding until the death of his father. But not long afterward he suddenly disappeared—an occurrence many blamed on his uncle—and was not heard from again for eleven years.

During those years James had been a slave in a Guiana sugar plantation but he now returned to claim the title of baron and earl. While awaiting his suit, James accidentally killed a poacher, a crime which actually helped his cause, because his uncle tried to bribe a peasant to say he witnessed the murder. When the bribery attempt was revealed, the charge was dropped and the rightful heir, James Annesley, won his suit.

REF.: *CBA*; Stevens, *From Clue To Dock*.

Anno (Hanno), c.1010-75, Ger., archbishop, assass. As Archbishop of Cologne, led an uprising of princes against the regency of Agnes of Poitou, abducted her son King Henry IV, and usurped the regency. He was assassinated in 1075 and canonized as a saint in 1183. REF.: *CBA*.

Annunziata, Joseph, and **Simonelli, Neil**, prom. 1942, U.S., mur. A rash of violence against New York City teachers, including beatings and rock peltings, reached a crowning point when a Brooklyn high school teacher was shot to death by two students in October 1942.

Annunziata and Simonelli returned to their school with a revolver after being reproached by their mathematics teacher for smoking in the bathroom, and had then ordered them to leave. The boys shot the teacher in the back, leaving him to die in the school corridor. Annunziata and Simonelli were convicted of murder and sentenced in December 1942 to fifty years imprisonment at the Sing Sing Correctional Facility. REF.: *CBA*.

Ansaldi, Marius, prom. 1950s, Fr., drugs. Through the combined efforts of French and U.S. agents, a major supplier of drugs in France was caught red-handed. During a drug bust in 1950, U.S. narcotics agents picked up the trail of Ansaldi in Paris and soon had an undercover agent, John C. Cusack, negotiating a deal for heroin with Ansaldi when the drug dealer disappeared. Cusack handed the case over to Commissaire Hugues of the French Sûreté. Hugues located a member of Ansaldi's gang and carefully watched his movements until he led him to Ansaldi.

At just the right moment, Hugues and eight of his men burst in on Ansaldi's operation at a villa in Montgeron, actually seizing Ansaldi and two chemists manufacturing drugs. Ansaldi and his gang, including Antoine Bergeret, who was picked up later, were convicted and sent to the Melun penitentiary.

REF.: *CBA*; Goodman, *Villainy Unlimited*.

Ansegis (Ansegisus), 770-c.833, Fr., abbot, saint. Abbot of Fontanelle from 823, he wrote *Quatuor Libri Capitularium Regum Francorum*, a collection of the laws and decrees of Charlemagne and Louis le Debonnaire. Completed in 827, the collection is commonly known as *Capitularies*. REF.: *CBA*.

Ansell, Mary Ann, 1877-99, Brit., mur. Ansell was a domestic servant in London who tried to cash in on a £22 insurance policy she held on her half-witted sister Caroline by sending a cake poisoned with phosphorus to her at the Leavesden Asylum in Watford where she was confined. The dim-witted Caroline who was devoted to her older sister Mary, shrieked with joy when the cake arrived and she shared it with some friends. A short time later the girl died in agony and her friends were deathly ill. Mary Ansell immediately drew suspicion upon herself when she refused to let doctors perform an autopsy on her sister. Physicians, however, were able to pump the contents out of the victim's stomach and determine that she had been poisoned with phosphorus. Ansell by then had aggressively sought payment from the insurance company holding the policy on her sister's life and this, coupled to her previous actions, caused her to be arrested and charged with murder.

She denied having sent the cake but the package was traced to her. When it was proved that she had purchased the phosphorus, Ansell insisted that it was to rid her apartment of rats. "I am as innocent a girl as ever was born," she cried out when jailed, pending trial. She appeared before Justice Matthew in June 1899 and was quickly convicted after a jury was presented with the overwhelming evidence against her. Mary Ansell was hanged before a large throng on July 19, 1899, at St. Albans Prison. She fainted several times en route to the scaffold and had to be half-carried to the hangman. When the rope was placed about her neck, she shouted, "Oh, my God in Heaven! Lord have mercy on my soul!" She fainted again, sagging unconscious but held upright by the rope. The trap was quickly pulled and she shot downward to death.

REF.: Atholl, *Shadow of the Gallows*; Butler, *Murderer's England*; *CBA*; Nash, *Look for the Woman*.

Anselmi, Albert, and **Scalise, John**, prom. 1920s, U.S., org. crime. The Sicilian born Anselmi and Scalise were partners in crime from boyhood. They had begun their criminal careers while in their teens in Marsala, Si., and it was there, in 1920, that the pair murdered a high-ranking official and fled to the U.S., going to Chicago. Here the terrible Genna Brothers sheltered them and hired them to enforce the sale of their miserable home-grown liquor, awful swill made in hundreds of Sicilian homes in crude alky cookers. The Gennas, six brothers in all, were allied with the Torrio-Capone gang which controlled the great South Side of Chicago. With Anselmi and Scalise as their top guns, the Genna liquor revenues soared. The murderous pair had a series of quirks that made them standouts among the army of goons and thugs that infested Chicago at the time, not the least of which was their deep-seated belief that by rubbing bullets with garlic, their victims would die of gangrene if they survived the bullet itself. This practice soon spread throughout gangland, although garlic produced no such results.

The Gennas were mortal enemies of the powerful North Side Irish gang run by the colorful Charles Dion "Deanie" O'Bannion. The two gangs were forever battling over territory on the Near North Side, each attempting to control the flow of Prohibition liquor in the area. And each gang had taken its toll on the other in numerous shootings up the end of 1924. O'Bannion had often showed his hatred for the Gennas, even in front of his tenuous allies, Johnny Torrio and Al Capone. He was finally marked for death by the Gennas. Torrio and Capone gave their approval for the Irishman's execution. The event allowing this cautious gangster to be approached by his avowed enemies was the death of the peace-loving Mike Merlo, long president of the influential Unione Siciliane which controlled the huge alky-making operations of Chicago. Merlo died of natural causes on Nov. 8, 1924, and national president of the Unione, Frankie Yale, a potent New York crime boss, arrived in Chicago to pay his respects. He named Angelo Genna as the new Chicago president of the Unione.

John Scalise and Albert Anselmi, the worst killers on Capone's payroll.

Merlo had, while alive, forbidden open warfare with O'Bannion and the Sicilian gangsters but now that Angelo Genna controlled the Unione, O'Bannion's execution was quickly planned, and it fell to Anselmi and Scalise to perform the deed. They were joined by none other than gang boss Yale, who agreed to be part of O'Bannion's murder to show his support of the Gennas. O'Bannion owned a flower shop on North State Street, across from Holy Name Cathedral. He had been reaping great profits from Merlo's death. The Unione had ordered thousands of dollars of floral wreaths for Merlo's funeral and floral ensembles had been ordered by Torrio ($10,000 worth) and Capone ($8,000). Doing such a land office business with his enemies caused the florist-gangster to overlook the presence of hated Sicilians in his shop. He had just finished several expensive floral pieces ordered by the Unione on the morning of Nov. 10, 1924, when three men entered his shop.

"Hello, boys," he was overheard to say to them by his black janitor, William Crutchfield who was in the back room sweeping the floor. O'Bannion smiled and walked toward the men, holding out his hand and saying, "Have you come for Mike Merlo's flowers?" The three men approached the Irishman slowly, knowing that he always carried three guns and was the deadliest shootist in Chicago with more than twenty-five murders to his credit. The tall man in the middle was Yale and he was flanked by Anselmi and Scalise. Yale held out his hand, took O'Bannion's and said, "Yes, we've come for the flowers." Yale then yanked the unsuspecting O'Bannion toward him so that he could pinion his arms at his side, preventing the Irish gangster from reaching for the guns in his specially made pockets. Anselmi and Scalise pulled revolvers and fired almost point blank into O'Bannion. Five bullets crashed into him before Yale let go, sending the gangster into a display of his own flowers. Anselmi kneeled and fired point blank into the gangster's head. Then the three men ran from the shop and jumped into a waiting Jewett sedan which roared off down State Street. This was the first so-called "handshake murder" which was invented by Anselmi and Scalise, practitioners of methodical murder.

Though no one was charged in the O'Bannion murder, the Cook County coroner wrote on the margin of his official report, "Slayers not apprehended. John Scalise and Albert Anselmi and Frank Yale suspected." Police stopped Yale at the LaSalle Street railway station just before he was about to board his New York-bound train. He was asked if he knew anything about the O'Bannion slaying. He shrugged and stated, "I came for Mike Merlo's funeral." With that he was released. Police detectives recalled at the time that Yale had also been visiting Chicago in

1920 when "Big Jim" Colosimo had been murdered. The killing of O'Bannion was the worst error in gangster judgment the Gennas could make. It galvanized the Irish mob under the determined leadership of crafty Earl "Hymie" Weiss, who vowed to take revenge on the Gennas. He did, causing the clan to be nearly exterminated within three years. During this "Bootleg Battle of the Marne," as the Weiss wars were dubbed by local newsmen, Hymie approached Capone with an offer to end the gang war, saying in 1926 that he and his men would stop invading Capone bootleg territory (by then Torrio had departed, having almost been killed in an ambush arranged by Weiss and Moran). There was only one condition. Capone had to turn over the killers of O'Bannion, Anselmi and Scalise, to allow Weiss to execute them. Snarled Capone, "I wouldn't do that to a yellow dog!"

Weiss had earlier attempted to persuade Sam "Samoots" Amatuna, a Genna ally, to betray Anselmi and Scalise to his men. Amatuna pretended to go along but tipped Mike Genna to an ambush where George "Bugs" Moran and Vincent "The Schemer" Drucci waited in a parked car. On June 13, 1925, Genna, accompanied by Anselmi and Scalise, raced past the car containing Moran and Drucci, letting loose several shotgun blasts and wounding the surprised North Siders. Moran and Drucci dragged themselves to a hospital where they spent several weeks mending and vowing revenge on Amatuna whom they would later arrange to have murdered. Meanwhile, Mike Genna gunned his car down Western Avenue and struck a truck at Fifty-ninth Street. A police car with four officers had been racing after the Genna car and when it crashed, the officers drove up behind the disabled auto. The three gangsters tumbled out of the car as Officer Michael Conway stepped out of the patrol car, saying to them, "Why didn't you stop? Didn't you hear our gong?"

Their answer was three shotgun blasts which immediately killed Officers Harold Olson and Charles Walsh. Conway was wounded and William Sweeney, the only officer unhurt, pulled his revolver and began shooting at the gangsters. When their weapons were emptied, Anselmi and Scalise raced down the street, Genna into an alley where he yanked forth a revolver and exchanged fire with the pursuing Sweeney. One of Sweeney's shots pierced Genna's leg, severing an artery. He smashed out a basement window and was later found cowering in the basement, trying to stop the flow of blood. He was dragged to an ambulance where his last mortal act was to kick an attendant in the face as he lay dying on a stretcher, shouting, "Take that, you s.o.b."

Anselmi and Scalise had, meanwhile, run down Fifty-ninth Street and into a dry goods store, demanding to buy new hats to replace the ones they had lost. They were running sweat and mixing their English with rapid-fire Sicilian which alarmed the proprietor, Edward Issigson, who had heard the gun battle and told them he would sell them nothing. The pair spied a passing trolley car and ran outside. Issigson ran to the street and stopped a patrol car, telling the officers that two suspicious men had just jumped onto the trolley car. Officers dragged them off the back platform and both men were later booked for the murder of officers Walsh and Olson. "These men will go straight to the gallows," announced State's Attorney Robert E. Crowe. He assigned his assistant, William McSwiggin, to prosecute the pair. McSwiggin would later be murdered along with a West Side gangster by none other than Al Capone himself, wielding a submachine gun from a moving auto.

It was later revealed that the death of Mike Genna had been providential in that Anselmi and Scalise had already defected from the Genna clan and gone over to Capone, who had ordered Mike Genna killed by them. It was their plan to first waylay the ambushers Moran and Drucci and then drive Genna to a secluded spot and murder him, blaming his death on the North Siders. Officer Sweeney's bullet did the job for them. Ironically, as Genna drove the getaway car from the spot where Moran and Drucci had been wounded he was really taking himself for a one-way ride.

On Oct. 5, 1925, Anselmi and Scalise went on trial for the

murder of the Officers Walsh and Olson. Death threats by the dozens had been sent to the the many eye-witnesses to the murders, even the jury members and the presiding judge. Detective Sweeney was the star witness and a day before he was scheduled to testify his home was blown to pieces by a bomb. He nevertheless testified against the murderous pair who, by that time, were credited with no less than fifty murders since their arrival in Chicago five years earlier. McSwiggin doggedly prosecuted the killers and made a telling case against them. The killers were defended by the all-refined Michael J. Ahern, Capone's top criminal lawyer. He had no real defense for his clients who had been caught red-handed and had been identified by several witnesses as the two men who fired shotgun blasts into Olson and Walsh. Ahern's address to the jury startled the court in its blatant assertions in the taking of human life. Said Ahern to the jury, "If a policeman detains you, even for a moment, against your will, you are not guilty of murder, but only of manslaughter. If the policeman uses force of arms, you may kill him in self-defense and emerge from the law unscathed." The shrewd lawyer had provided a way out for the much-threatened jury members, several of whom were then under police protection at their own requests. The jury found Anselmi and Scalise Guilty of manslaughter and the pair received fourteen-year prison sentences.

Scalise and Anselmi, under arrest in 1925 after a wild shootout with Chicago policmen; they killed two officers and managed to escape legal punishment through Capone's clout.

Anselmi and Scalise served only a few months of their fourteen-year sentences in Joliet State Prison before the Illinois Supreme Court responded to their lawyer's argument that they had not received a fair trial. Both men were released on $25,000 bail to await a new trial. At the trial Scalise admitted he fired only one bullet. Lawyers for the pair argued that the two men were only defending themselves against "unwarranted police aggression." Anselmi and Scalise were acquitted. The killers strolled from the courtroom to be embraced and their hands pumped by a bevy of Capone's gunsels. Mrs. Walsh, wife of one of the slain detectives, stood at the courtroom door, her face pale. She stated, "My husband and his friend were killed by these men who now have a crowd waiting to shake their hand. I give up."

The killer pair went to work for their benefactor Capone with a vengeance, slaying countless bootleg enemies. They are credited, along with Tony Accardo, Frank Nitti, and "Machine Gun" Jack McGurn with murdering Capone nemesis Hymie Weiss and were, in 1929, the machine gunners who mowed down the seven men of the Bugs Moran gang at the infamous St. Valentine's Day Massacre. But the pair fed on their own ambition. Though they received staggering salaries as Capone's two top gunmen, more than $100,000 a year each, they sought to improve their lot by usurping Scarface himself. Both men had been arrested after the St. Valentine's Day Massacre as prime suspects, but before they could be tried in a court of law, Capone himself found them guilty of treason and carried out his own sentence, death.

Both Anselmi and Scalise, Sicilians to the core, secretly met with the new president of the Chicago Unione Siciliane, Joseph "Hop Toad" Guinta, a suave glad-hander who believed he could wrest control of the $60-million-a-year bootleg empire from Capone, using his two best gunman to kill Scarface. Guinta, a former ally of Frankie Yale's, was a Brooklyn-born thug who arrived in Chicago in 1925. The plot was all Sicilian, one where the Italian Capone would be eliminated by his own men. Scalise was named by Guinta as the top enforcer for the Unione Siciliane, and he bragged in front of Capone lieutenants, "I'm the big shot now, not Al. It all falls to me and Albert." Guinta thought of himself as the brains behind the new combine. He had risen slowly in the Unione, slavishly serving one president after another until he himself became the top man in the Unione. He enjoyed hob-nobbing with society nightclubbers and was usually seen in tuxedo and white spats, attending the theatre, the opera, and the best supper clubs. He was so socially active that mobmen nick-named him "Hop Toad."

Capone's most loyal bodyguard, Frank Rio, learned of the plot and warned Scarface who, at first, refused to believe that his two best executioners would turn on him after he had paid a fortune to rig their trials and make them rich men. Rio insisted and Capone then devised a test. Early in May 1929, Capone invited Anselmi and Scalise to dine with him at his armed fortress, the Hawthorn Inn in Cicero. At dinner, according to plan, Rio argued with Capone and then slapped the boss' face and marched out of the place. Two days later Anselmi and Scalise met with Rio and told him that Capone was ungrateful for the service rendered to him by such loyal men as Rio. The bodyguard cursed Scarface and swore he would teach him a lesson.

Joseph "Hop Toad" Guinta joined with Anselmi and Scalise in trying to depose Capone; all three were killed by Scarface.

Anselmi then told him that their good friend, Joseph Aiello, an avowed foe of Capone's, had offered $50,000 to anyone who killed Scarface. Guinta joined the group and the four men spent days at a resort where they plotted Capone's extermination, Rio actively taking part. When Rio left he vowed that he would kill Capone himself. He went straight to his boss and reported what had happened.

On the night of May 7, 1929, Capone summoned Guinta, Anselmi, and Scalise to the Hawthorn Inn where he rendered them a small banquet which was packed with his top gunmen, including Machine Gun Jack McGurn, Sam "Golfbag" Hunt, William Jack "Three-fingered" White, Frank "The Enforcer" Nitti, and Frank Rio. Capone reportedly made a speech about loyalty, then stepped up behind the three guests of honor and was handed a sawed-off baseball bat. He crashed this down on the heads of all three men, crushing their skulls. As the trio sat in bloody, dead heaps at the table, their faces resting in plates of pasta, Capone took a revolver and fired a single shot into the heads of the traitors. He ordered the bodies taken away. In a back room of the hotel, seven or eight goons went to work on the corpses, also using baseball bats and large pieces of lumber. They broke every bone in the bodies of Anselmi, Scalise, and Guinta before the bodies were taken to a remote spot across the state line in Indiana near Wolf Lake, outside of the town of Hammond. Scalise and Guinta were left in the car, Anselmi was dragged off about twenty feet and dumped into a ditch. The bodies of Anselmi and Scalise were shipped back to Sicily for burial while Guinta was buried in Chicago's Mount Carmel Cemetary, only a few plots away from Charles Dion O'Bannion and Angelo Genna, mortal enemies in life, companions in death. See: **Accardo, Anthony; Aiello, Joseph; Amatuna, Samuel Samuzzo; Capone, Alphonse; Drucci, Vincent; Genna Brothers; McGurn, Jack; McSwiggin, William; Moran, George; Nitti, Frank; O'Bannion, Charles Dion; Torrio, John; Weiss, Earl; Yale, Frank.**

REF.: Allen, *Merchants of Menace*; Allsop, *The Bootleggers*; Asbury, *Gem of the Prairie*; Burns, *The One-Way Ride*; *CBA*; Farr, *Chicago*; Halper, *The Chicago Crime Book*; Kobler, *Capone*; Lyle, *The Dry and Lawless Years*; McPhaul, *Deadlines and Monkeyshines*; ____, *Johnny Torrio*; Murray, *The Legacy of Al Capone*; Nash, *Bloodletters and Badmen*; Pasley, *Al Capone*; ____, *Muscling In*; Smith, *Syndicate City*; Sullivan, *Chicago Surrenders*; ____, *Rattling the Cup on Chicago Crime*.

Anslinger, Harry Jacob, 1892-1975, U.S., law enfor. off. Anslinger was one of the preeminent law enforcement officers of the 20th century, noted for his relentless pursuit of drug traffickers and career criminals. As the first United States Commissioner of Narcotics, in the early 1930s Anslinger identified a national organized crime syndicate that oversaw gambling, prostitution, and the flow of illegal drugs and liquor to U.S. cities. FBI Director J.Edgar Hoover hotly denied the existence of such a criminal conspiracy. By the 1960s, however, the facts were undeniable and even Hoover had to admit that the Mafia existed.

Anslinger was born in Altoona, Pa., and was attending Pennsylvania State College in 1914 when war broke out in Europe. When the United States entered the conflict in 1917, Anslinger went to work for the Ordnance Division of the War Department, in Washington, D.C. He later held diplomatic posts in the Netherlands, Germany, Venezuela, and the Bahamas, where he became acutely aware of the drug menace beginning to permeate the United States.

Anslinger returned to Washington in 1926 after five years abroad to become Chief of the Division of Foreign Control with the Treasury Department, representing the United States at the Conference on Suppression of Smuggling in London, 1926. By 1929 he was a recognized expert on the smuggling of illegal liquor into the United States.

Anslinger received a law degree in 1930, and shortly after was appointed the first U.S. Commissioner of Narcotics, a position he held through five presidencies. His uncompromising stance against drugs drew criticism from the American Medical Association and other regulatory agencies more concerned with treatment than with punishment. Anslinger considered drug addiction a problem for criminal law enforcement. He urged medical treatment for addicts, but offered no sympathy to those who committed crimes to satisfy their habits.

Anslinger's hand-picked agents in the Bureau of Narcotics were burly, incorruptible men who used any means, legal or not, to bust a drug ring. In one celebrated raid in Hammond, Ind., in 1968, three carloads of agents descended on a drug den with baseball bats, breaking limbs and shattering knee caps. Anslinger was actually feared in the underworld.

In the 1930s, Hoover resented the attention Amslinger got for his prosecution of New York mobster Charles (Lucky) Luciano. There was no criminal syndicate, Hoover argued. While the FBI director focused on the dustbowl bank robbers of the plains states and the Southwest, Anslinger compiled impressive lists of big-city racketeers in the narcotics trade. But no one believed that a criminal cartel actually existed.

The effect of marijuana on youth obsessed Harry Anslinger. His article "Marijuana: Assassin of Youth" appeared in the July 1937 issue of *American Magazine*. As a result, the Marijuana Tax Act was passed the same year, and the cannabis plant was banished from general medical use and stricken from the official record of the *Pharmacopoeia of the United States of America*. Anslinger said, "The answer to the problem is simple—get rid of drugs, pushers, and users. Period." He urged passage of the Uniform State Narcotic Acts, and by 1950 most states had adopted the law or similar measures.

In 1942, the Narcotics Bureau turned its attention to the Japanese opium trade. Anslinger found proof that Japan had violated trade agreements and promoted opium addiction in Manchuria and China before the outbreak of WWII. "Wherever the Japanese army goes, the drug traffic follows," he said. Responding to the dangers of illegal opium reaching U.S. shores, the Coast Guard and the Bureau of Customs joined the Narcotics Bureau to hunt down West Coast traffickers.

During the war, Anslinger built a stockpile of medicinal drugs for distribution to the armed services. The drugs were kept in the Treasury Department's gold vaults in Washington, D.C.

Anslinger was appointed U.S. Representative to the United Nations Commission on Narcotic Drugs, June 6, 1946, where he worked to increase cooperation among international police agencies seeking to curb drug traffic.

Harry Anslinger retired in 1962 after thirty-two years as Commissioner of Narcotics. He died on Nov. 14, 1975, at his home in Holidaysburg, Pa. See: **Hoover, J. Edgar; Luciano, Charles (Lucky); Lansky, Meyer.**

REF.: Abel, *Marijuana, The First Twelve Thousand Years*; Anslinger, *The Murderers*; _____, *The Protectors*; Campbell, *The Luciano Project*; *CBA*; Coles, *Drugs and Youth*; Cressey, *Theft of the Nation*; Demaris, *The Director*; Eisenberg, *Meyer Lansky*; Feder, *The Luciano Story*; Freemantle, *The Fix, Inside the World Drug Trade*; Gosch, *The Last Testament of Lucky Luciano*; Greenshaw, *Flying High, Inside Big Time Drug Smuggling*; Grinspoon, *Marijuana Reconsidered*; Katcher, *The Big Bankroll*; McClellan, *Crime Without Punishment*; Martin, *Revolt in the Mafia*; Messick, *Lansky*; Morgan, *Drugs in America*; Nash, *Citizen Hoover*; Ottenberg, *The Federal Investigators*; Reid, *The Grim Reapers*; Reppetto, *The Blue Parade*; Schlesinger, *Robert Kennedy and His Times*; Shannon, *Desperadoes*; Sullivan, *The Bureau*; Tully, *Treasury Agent*; Ungar, *FBI*; Wicker, *Investigating the FBI*; Wilson, *The Investigators*.

Anson, Sir **William Reynell,** 1843-1914, Brit., jur. Author of *The Principles of the English Law of Contract* (1879) and *The Law and Custom of the Constitution*, parts one and two (1886 and 1892). REF.: *CBA*.

Anstis, Thomas, d.1723, Brit., pir. As formidable a pirate as ever lived, Anstis shipped out from Providence, R.I., aboard the *Buck Sloop* in 1718. During the course of the voyage he conspired with six other men to become pirates. They then seized control of their vessel and raised the flag of the Jolly Roger. One of the men, Captain Bartholomew Roberts, after a series of daring adventures separated from Anstis on Apr. 18, 1721, to plunder the West Indies.

Anstis sped toward Bermuda where he sighted a fast ship called the *Morning Star*, bound from Guinea to the Carolinas laden with treasure. Anstis captured the vessel and outfitted it with thirty-two pieces of cannon. John Fenn, a gunner, was placed in charge, and with a full complement of arms and men the two pirate ships sailed the coastal waters in search of booty. Dissension broke out among the crewmen, however. Some had never wanted to be pirates so they sent a petition to the king asking pardon on grounds that they had been impressed into duty by Roberts and Anstis.

The pirate crew retired to a small island near Cuba where, for nine months, subsisting on turtle and fish, the crew awaited a reply from England. In August 1722, disappointed that their plea had been ignored, they sailed off again. When they arrived at the Grand Caimenes, the *Morning Star* ran aground and the survivors were rescued by Captain Anstis who, under sail again, saw that they were being pursued by two fast British naval ships, the *Hector* and the *Adventure*. Cannon fire dogged Anstis's every move through waters roiling from a gale. Eventually Anstis abandoned his ship and fled to an island.

The *Hector* landed on the island a short time later. The British captured forty of Anstis's men who told their captors about their petition to the king. Meanwhile, Anstis escaped in his brigantine. At the Bay of Honduras he cleaned up and refitted the vessel, and then, with John Fenn, set sail in December 1722 for the rich harvests of the Bahama Islands. They soon captured an Irish sloop called the *Antelope* and sailed it to the island of Tobago in April 1723 where it was to be outfitted for duty as a privateer.

But then an English man-of-war called the *Winchelsea* sailed into port. Caught off guard, the pirates burned their ship and fled into the countryside. Anstis again evaded his pursuers, but the British had succeeded in ending his reign of piracy, and soon ended the pirate's life, killing him as he lay in his hammock. Most of the remaining crew surrendered at the Dutch settlement of Curacco and were granted amnesty. The rest, including Fenn, were tried and executed in accordance with British maritime law. See: **Roberts, Bartholomew.**

REF: Botting, *The Pirates; CBA;* Gosse, *History of the Pirates.*

Anthimus of Iberia, d.1716, Rom., bishop, treas. Romanian bishop and writer who was executed for anti-Turkish nationalist sympathies. REF.: *CBA.*

Anthony, James, d.1814, U.S., mur. Anthony, a hatter, harbored a deep resentment for Joseph Green, a fellow merchant in Rutland, Vt., often commenting that Green was a rogue. On Feb. 14, 1814, Green disappeared and a hunt for him led authorities to Anthony's shop. Green's bloody clothes were found hidden in the shop beneath a small furnace and the body of the victim was uncovered two days later, buried beneath a woodpile in Anthony's yard. Anthony was tried on Mar. 2, 1814, before Judges Nathaniel Chipman, Daniel Ferrand, and Jonathan H. Hubbard. He was defended by the chief judge's son, Daniel Chipman and Rollin C. Mallary, but these lawyers were hard-pressed to mount a reasonable defense in that the evidence against their client appeared to be overwhelming. In his own defense, Anthony claimed that he had been present when Green was beaten and then strangled to death but that another person, who remained unidentified, did the actual murder.

At first the prisoner claimed that the blood found on his shirt and underwear was the result of his falling down a flight of stairs which caused a nosebleed. Later, Anthony admitted that he held down Green's kicking feet as he was killed so that "he would not kick over a bunk or make a noise." The prosecution provided a number of witnesses who testified that Anthony had long held a grudge over a business deal with Green. Thomas Miller stated that Anthony had said that "such fellows" as Green "ought not to live." The jury returned from its deliberations within five minutes and found Anthony Guilty. He was hanged a few weeks later.

REF.: *CBA; Facts Relating to the Murder of Joseph Green; Trial of James Anthony for the Murder of Joseph Green.*

Anthony, Raymond, 1914- , U.S., skyjack. An unemployed used car salesman who had been hitting the bottle, Anthony was a native of Baltimore who boarded an Eastern Airlines Boeing 727 en route to Miami on June 26, 1969. He was wearing shorts and sandals when he boarded the plane and was in an obvious state of drunkenness, according to most reports. Once the plane was aloft, Anthony produced a pocketknife and forced a flight attendant to take him to the cockpit. There he babbled almost incoherent threats as he ordered the pilot to fly immediately to Cuba, which he did. Fidel Castro's government in Cuba welcomed Anthony with open arms and released the Eastern Airlines crew of seven and the plane's ninety-six passengers who returned safely to the U.S. Anthony then sobered up and began to lobby Castro's

officials for permission to return to the U.S. He wrote his sister in Baltimore that he wanted to come home. By July 1969, six Americans had skyjacked planes to Cuba; all were returned to the U.S. in November 1969. These included Thomas Boynton of Kalamazoo, Mich., who skyjacked a small plane on Feb. 18, 1968; Thomas George Washington, who skyjacked an Eastern Airline plane on Dec. 19, 1968, in Philadelphia; Ronald T. Bohle, who skyjacked an Eastern flight on Jan. 9, 1969; Robert L. Sandlin, who skyjacked a Delta Airlines plane in Dallas on March 17, 1969; and Joseph Calvin Crawford who diverted a Continental Airlines flight from El Paso, Texas, on July 26, 1969.

Raymond Anthony was one of the first U.S. skyjackers, a drunk with a penknife who ordered a crew to fly him to Cuba.

Most of these skyjackers were unemployed, and Washington took along his small daughter. All these men faced criminal charges when returning to the U.S. Raymond Anthony was tried and convicted of skyjacking, although his laywer defended his client by attempting to put the blame on a credit card company which had sent Anthony an unsolicited credit card. After receiving the card, Anthony immediately got drunk, charged his airfare, and jumped on board the Miami-bound Eastern flight which he skyjacked to Cuba, almost out of whim, remembering the many recent skyjackings of Cuban-bound planes. Anthony was sentenced in Baltimore on Oct. 5, 1970, before Judge Alexander Harvey II. Judge Harvey summed up Anthony's offense as being "the tragic case of an alcoholic whose life is a failure at the age of fifty-six." This did not prevent Judge Alexander from sentencing Anthony to a stiff fifteen years in prison in order to signal other potential skyjackers that the court would deal severely with similar offenses. Judge Alexander then took to task the flight crew of the skyjacked Eastern airline, stating that he could not understand why the crew had meekly obeyed "the drunken orders of a little man holding a penknife." See: **Bohle, Ronald T.: Boynton, Thomas; Washington, Thomas George.** REF.: *CBA.*

Antigonus I, c.135-104 B.C., Judea, king. assass. Co-regent with his brother Aristobulus from 105 B.C. until he was assassinated as part of a conspiracy. REF.: *CBA.*

Antiochus II (Antiochus Theos), 286-247 B.C., Syria, king, assass. Son of Antiochus II, he directed an unproductive war against Ptolemy II from 260-52. After forcing the tyrant Timarchus from Miletus in 258 he was given the name "Theos" which means "the divine." He was supposedly poisoned by Laodice, the first of his two wives. REF.: *CBA.*

Antiochus V (Antiochus Eupator), 173-162 B.C., Syria, king, assass. Son of Antiochus IV, he reigned as king from 163-62 under the regency of Lysias. He was overthrown by his cousin Demetrius I Soter and assassinated at age eleven. REF.: *CBA.*

Antiochus VIII, d.96 B.C., Syria, king. Joint ruler with his mother from 125-21, sole ruler from 121-115, then forced to share the realm with Antiochus IX. See: **Cleopatra Thea.** REF.: *CBA.*

Antipater (Antipater the Idumaean), d.43 B.C., Judea, procurator, assass. Father of Herod the Great, he first became influential in Judea after Pompey took Jerusalem in 63. With Pompey's decline he befriended Caesar and aided him in Alexandria. He was subsequently rewarded with Roman citizenship and the office of Procurator of Judea where he served from 47 until his assassination. REF.: *CBA.*

Antipater, d.4 B.C., Judea, prince, consp.-treas. Son of Herod the Great, he organized the execution of his half-brothers Alexander and Aristobulus in an attempt to become king. He was later convicted of plotting against his father and executed. REF.: *CBA.*

Antiquis Murder, See: **Jenkins, Charles Henry.**

Antoine, Joseph, prom. 1828, Case of, U.S., mur. Francis C. Jenkerson, age seven, and Samuel Field, age eleven, disappeared from their Providence, R.I., homes on July 26, 1828, and their bodies were found three weeks later, buried in a sandbank. Antoine, and Johan and Joanna Wohlfahrt, were arrested a short time later, charged with murdering the two boys. Following a hearing the trio were released since no substantial evidence could be produced against them. Antoine and the Wohlfahrts had spoken critically of the two boys who had gotten into mischief about their homes which had brought them under suspicion. The case was left in a muddled condition, authorities stating that the boys might have met accidental death but this did not explain why their bodies had been buried.

REF.: *CBA; Examination of Joseph Antoine, Johan Fransoeis Wohlfahrt and Joanna Susan Wohlfahrt; True and Faithful Account of the Most Material Circumstances Attending the Mysterious Disappearance of Samuel Field and Francis C. Jenkerson.*

Antone, Anthony, 1918-84, U.S., mur. Convicted of arranging the death of a former police officer, Antone became the first man executed (since the United States reinstated the death penalty) who did not actually kill the victim. Antone gave a hired killer a gun and paid him to kill Richard Cloud, a former Tampa, Fla., policeman known as "Super Cop" who then, in 1975, was in pursuit of an underworld drug czar, though he had earlier been fired from the police force for beating prisoners. Antone claimed his innocence to the murder and said he was being persecuted because he was a Sicilian.

Antone's execution on Jan. 26, 1984, was witnessed by forty-seven persons and protested by some forty others outside the prison. It was the third execution in Florida and the twelfth in the United States since capital punishment was made legal in 1976. At age sixty-six, Antone was the oldest inmate on Florida's death row before his electrocution. The U.S. Supreme Court denied his request for a stay of execution by a vote of seven to two the evening before his death. His last words were taken from Jesus Christ on the cross, "Forgive them Father, for in their ignorance they know not what they do." REF.: *CBA.*

Antonia, Claudia, d.66 A.D., Roman., assass. Daughter of Roman Emperor Claudius, she was killed by Nero. REF.: *CBA.*

Antoniewicz, Joseph, and **Hallowell, William A.,** and **Parks, Edward H.,** prom. 1952-68, U.S., (wrong. convict.) mur. Following a 1952 conviction for felony murder, to which Antoniewicz, Hallowell, and Parks had all pled guilty, the three youths—all under eighteen years old at the time of their arrest—spent sixteen years on life sentences in prison before the decision was overturned.

Judge Edmund B. Spaeth Jr. ordered the release of Antoniewicz, Hallowell, and Parks on Feb. 13, 1968, after testimony from a Philadelphia medical examiner who said the man killed had died of coronary heart disease and not from an attack by the youths during a robbery nine days earlier. REF.: *CBA.*

Antonini, Theresa (Theresa Marschall), 1785-1809, Ger., rob.-mur. Born and bred in Berlin, Theresa Marschall was exposed early to a life of crime. Her family was made up of professional thieves and all her young beaus pursued criminal ways, including a handsome young Sicilian named Antonini, whom she married at a young age. The couple successfully robbed the coaches of wealthy travelers throughout Austria and southern Germany, especially Bavaria. They were caught on several occasions and imprisoned together but always managed to either convince authorities of their innocence or bribe their way to freedom.

In November 1809 the pair took passage in a coach carrying Dorothea Blankenfeld, a rich woman who, they learned from a servant, had sewn more than 2,000 talers into the stays of her corset and carried many jewels hidden on her person. Antonini

made many plans on how to murder the woman but these continually fell through as the trip progressed. Finally, when the coach stopped at an inn in Maitingen, Bav., the Antoninis simply invaded the woman's room after dosing her soup with laudenum which left the victim unconscious. They sat on the woman's bed thinking of ways to kill her—such as dropping molten lead into her eyes, a typical idea from the vicious-minded Theresa. When her husband failed to melt a spoon for that purpose, Theresa grabbed a poker and began to crash this down on the victim's head. Dorothea Blankenfeld, however, proved too strong, and awoke, screaming to be spared. Theresa kept hitting her but her blows were ineffective. Antonini grabbed the poker and crashed it down on the victim's head so that he crushed the skull. The killers, with the help of Theresa's 15-year-old brother Carl, pocketed the woman's valuables and then bundled up the body in a sack, taking this with them the next morning when boarding the coach, pretending that this was part of their luggage. The innkeeper, who had noticed two women arrive the previous night and only one depart, rushed to the room that had been occupied by Dorothea Blankenfeld and found it splattered with blood—the floor, the walls, all drenched with gore. He flashed the alarm and a company of dragoons set out after the coach, catching up with it before the Antoninis could toss their bloody sack onto the side of the road, which had been their plan in disposing of the body.

The trio arrived in Nuremberg for trial. Their only defense was a feeble claim that they had discovered the Blankenfeld woman murdered in her bed, and they had smuggled the body out of the inn so they would not be suspected of the terrible deed. Carl Marschall collapsed under interrogation, confessing his guilt in the killing but pointing out that his sister and brother-in-law performed the actual murder. Next Theresa confessed but she said her husband did the killing. Antonini would admit to nothing. He and Theresa were condemned to the headsman's block and young Carl Marschall was given fifteen years in prison. Antonini escaped execution by starving himself to death in his cell, but the beautiful, lethal Theresa kept her appointment with the headsman. She was dragged to the block by a rope tied about her hands, screaming for mercy. A black hood was placed about her head but she continued to beg the executioner to free her, that she would reward him with untold fortunes from her stolen loot, that she would offer her body to him. The giant headsman did not reply, only swinging the axe in a large looping movement which severed the killer's head with one blow.

REF.: *CBA; Nash, Look for the Woman.*

Antonio, Maurice, d.1852, U.S., mur. Antonio lived with a common law wife whom he shared with another Portugese laborer, Ignacio Teixeira Pinto, the trio living in a small farm house near Gates, N.Y. The neighbors never really knew which man was the real husband of the woman. When the two men fell to arguing over her, Antonio beat Pinto to death and buried his body beneath the floorboards of a corncrib where it was later discovered. Antonio was charged with the killing and convicted. Before he was hanged on June 3, 1852, Antonio admitted the murder and pointed out that Pinto had every right to the woman since he was her lawful husband.

REF.: *CBA; Trial of Maurice Antonio.*

Antonius, Marcus, 143-87 B.C., Roman., orator, assass. Follower of Sulla, he was executed by order of Cinna and Marius. REF.: *CBA.*

Antrim, Henry (Kid Antrim, William Antrim), See: **Billy the Kid.**

Anything for a Quiet Life, 1942, novel by A.A. Avery. This work of fiction is based upon the notorious career of super stock swindler, Philip Musica, also known as F. Donald Coster, and his huge but empty firm of McKesson and Robbins (U.S., 1920s-1930s). See: **Musica, Philip.** REF.: *CBA.*

Anytus, prom. 399 B.C., Athens, polit. Athenian politician primarily responsible for the prosecution, conviction, and condemnation of Socrates on charges of "corruption of the young." REF.: *CBA.*

Anzalone, Theodore V., c.1925-   , Case of, U.S., polit. corr. Although the conviction of Theodore V. Anzalone for illegal currency transactions was later reversed, the case eventually led to a strengthening of the law that failed to penalize him. While working as a close aide for Boston mayor Kevin H. White, Anzalone allegedly converted $100,000 cash into twelve bank checks to buy municipal bonds to place in a bank account for the mayor's mother, Patricia White. He also is alleged to have disguised currency transactions to avoid their being reported by banks, as federal law requires all cash transactions over $10,000 to be reported to the Internal Revenue Service. Found Guilty on both counts, Anzalone became the eleventh member of White's administration or political organization to be convicted on charges of fraud or extortion.

In 1985, the First Circuit Court of Appeals reversed the decision, stating that the law Anzalone allegedly violated was too vague. Because of this decision, the U.S. Congress incorporated what became known as the Anzalone Statute into the Anti-Drug Abuse Act of 1986, which prohibits someone from structuring amounts of cash larger than $10,000 into smaller amounts to avoid the law. REF.: *CBA*.

Anzilotti, Dionisio, b.1869, Italy, jur. President of the Permanent Court of International Justice from 1928-30. REF.: *CBA*.

Apacalo, Anthony, 1867-c.1904, U.S., org. crime. One of the earliest organizers of criminal activities in New York, Apacalo migrated from Sicily in 1881, settling in the Five Points where he later operated a string of fruit and vegetable stores and stands. By the 1890s, Apacalo was using his stores as fronts for the fencing of a flood of stolen goods which, unlike the secularized gangs of the day, he accepted from any and all gangs and independent thieves. Apacalo became a millionaire many times over, according to one report, by the time he was thirty, and he financed the careers of apprentice gangsters such as Paul Kelley, who later became the supreme crime czar of Five Points, financing Kelley's first restaurants but remaining his secret partner.

Though he was often suspected early in his criminal career as being a Black Hander, Apacalo was one of the leading Mafia figures in New York City by 1897. His name appears on special police reports of the day, but no evidence was ever brought into court against him. Apacalo was never arrested or charged with an illegal act, but he was suspected of being involved in at least ten killings, murders he ordered his henchmen to perform when tribute was not forthcoming from Mafia dominated merchants. He was a secretive person in private life, having several residences but no family. One account stated that Apacalo, who had hired English tutors to improve his speech and cultural advisers to heighten his knowledge of world literature and music, traveled, at the turn of the century, to upstate New York where he married the beautiful daughter of a wealthy landowner and maintained a mansion and a vast estate near Syracuse which he visited regularly, thus explaining his long absences from his Manhattan offices.

It has been estimated that this early-day crime boss invested more than $1 million in illegal enterprises, from lavish gambling dens to sumptuous bordellos, backing others willing to take public bows and remaining a secret partner who received forty percent of all the fabulous profits. Apacalo never gave up his role as the city's master fence, the continuous source of his bloated fortune. He concentrated in rare uncut gems taken from jewelry merchants, along with similar priceless items stolen from the homes of the rich along Fifth and Park avenues. One story has it that Apacalo, along with his blonde wife, attended a high society party in Syracuse where he lived under a different name, and was introduced to a visiting social grande dame from New York City whose diamond and emerald necklace Apacalo had received in a shipment of stolen items. He had kept the necklace and had the stones reset in a different pattern and this necklace was being worn around the neck of his wife when the couple met the victim from whom it had been looted. The victim reportedly complimented Apacalo's wife on the exquisite necklace her thoughtful husband had bestowed upon her.

In Febuary 1904, Anthony Apacalo sold his legitimate holdings, some to his protégé Kelly, and left the rackets that had so enriched him. A report a month later had it that a body floating in the East River was identified as the crime boss but police refused to accept the corpse as that of the Mafia don. One Mafia watcher, Detective Joseph Petrosino, speculated that Apacalo, whom Petrosino described as "one of the most clever criminals in America," had ordered the murder of a nondescript hoodlum and had planted documents on the body which would identify the corpse as the crime boss, before the body was tossed into the East River. REF.: *CBA*.

Apache Kid (Zenogalache, AKA: The Crazy One), b.1867, U.S., west. outl. Next to Geronimo, the most fierce and feared Apache of the old Southwest was the Apache Kid, the son of Toga-de-chuz, a chief who was murdered by a rival for the Kid's mother. The boy, who was never known by any other name than the Apache Kid to whites, but whose Apache name was Zenogalache, waited many years before taking his revenge, eventually murdering his father's killer near the Aravaipo River. At an early age the orphaned Kid was taken in at the San Carlos Indian Agency, N.M. Here the famous cavalry scout, Al Sieber, educated the boy and taught him the use of firearms and the codes of the military, later getting the Apache Kid an appointment as the first sergeant of the Apache Government Scouts which were under the command of the U.S. Cavalry. The Scouts served as agency policemen who made arrests among their own people.

The Apache Kid, terror of the Southwest.

Following the murder of the old Indian who had killed the Kid's father, Sieber ordered the Apache Kid into San Carlos. He appeared with ten of his heavily armed men. When Sieber told other Indian policemen to take the group to the guardhouse, the Kid ordered his men to fire on Sieber and he was wounded in the leg before the band rode pell-mell from the agency. There was a price on the Kid's head ever after. In addition to the military, several scouts and gunmen joined in the hunt for the Kid, and this included the famous Tom Horn, later hanged for murder. The Kid and his band, increased to about thirty, rode for the Mexican border and en route stole a herd of horses from the Atchley Ranch near Table Mountain, killed a trapper in his cabin, one Bill Diehl, and tortured and murdered rancher Mike Grace as they moved southward.

For two years the Kid and his men eluded capture but were finally taken and sentenced to death following a quick trial. The Kid insisted that he was innocent of the Diehl and Grace killings, that others in his band had done the deeds. His plea reached President Grover Cleveland's ears and the chief executive granted him a pardon. But as soon as he was released, the Kid led another band on bloody raids through the territory, stopping freight wagons, murdering the drivers and taking the goods. Sheriff Glenn Reynolds of Gila County, Ariz., led a huge posse after the Kid and managed to capture him. This time the Kid was sent to prison for seven years. However, en route to the Yuma Prison, on Nov. 1, 1889, the guards and their six prisoners camped near Riverside in the Pinal Mountains. The Kid and his men broke free and murdered his guards, Reynolds, and Bill Holmes. Another guard, Eugene Middleton, badly wounded, survived the Kid's wrath and limped into Globe, Ariz., to tell authorities how the Kid escaped after murdering the guards while they slept.

After six of the Kid's band were captured and two were hanged (the other four committed suicide by strangling each other with their loin cloths while in their cell the morning before the execution), the Kid went on a murder rampage, killing several settlers. He attacked a prairie schooner in which a woman, her young son, and an infant were travelling to meet the woman's husband. The Kid stopped the covered wagon, shot the woman and boy to death but oddly spared the infant. This crime incensed the military and civilian population and hundreds set out to hunt down the killer Indian. One scout named Dupont abruptly came across the Kid on a trail in the Catalinas. Both men had single shot rifles and paused, staring at each other. Neither wanted to waste one shot and be at the mercy of the other so they dismounted, sat on rocks through the long day, glaring at each other while the sun beat down upon them. At dusk, the Kid stood up and grunted, "Me leaving." With that the killer mounted his horse and rode off while Dupont heaved a heavy sigh of relief.

For several years the Kid and a small band of renegade Apache followers raided ranches and freight lines throughout New Mexico, Arizona, and northern Mexico, hiding out in the Mexican Sierra Madre mountains. A price of $5,000 was placed on the Apache Kid's head but no one ever claimed the reward. Edward A. Clark, who had been the partner of Bill Diehl, continued to live on his horse ranch which the Kid raided several times, the last attack occuring in 1894 when the Kid and his men surrounded the ranch house and lay siege to Clark, his new partner, John Scanlon, and a visiting Englishman named Mercer. When night fell, Clark slipped out of the house and worked his way to the corral where he saw two Indians leading away his favorite horse. He fired two shots and in the morning found the body of a squaw, the Kid's wife. He also found a trail of blood leading from the spot where the woman's corpse sprawled. Clark followed the trail of blood but it petered out in the rocks of the high hills. "It was the Kid all right," Clark later claimed. "He crawled away to die somewhere, I know."

Supporting Clark's theory was a sudden silence from the Apache Kid. No more ranches were raided or settlers and freightman killed. The outlaw's trail ceased to exist. One account by Mrs. Tom Charles insists that a posse led by Charles Anderson trapped the Kid near Kingston on Sept. 10, 1905, and shot him dead. Some later reports had it that the Apache Kid simply retired to his mountain hideout in Mexico and lived well into the twentieth century, dying of consumption sometime around 1910. This claim has never been substantiated. See: **Horn, Tom.**

REF.: Applegate, *Native Tales of New Mexico*; Argall, *Outlawry and Justice in Old Arizona*; Botkin, *Folk-Say*; _____, *A Treasury of Western Folklore*; Bronson, *The Vanguard*; Brophy, *Arizona Sketch Book*; Burgess, *Bisbee Not So Long Ago*; CBA; Charles, *Tales of the Tularosa*; Chisholm, *Brewery Gulch*; Day, *Gene Rhodes, Cowboy*; Dobie, *Apache Gold and Yaqui Silver*; Erwin, *The Southwest of John H. Slaughter*; Forrest, *Arizona's Dark and Bloody Ground*; _____, *Lone War Trail of Apache Kid*; Ganzhorn, *I've Killed Men*; Hayes, *Apache Vengeance*; _____, *Sheriff Thompson's Day—Turbulence in the Arizona Territory*; Hearn, *Killing of Apache Kid*; Hendricks, *The Bad Man of the West*; Horan, *The Great American West*; _____, and Sann, *Pictorial History of the Wild West*; Hutchinson, *The Life and Personal Life of Eutene Manlove Rhodes*; Kemp, *Cow Dust and Saddle Leather*; Kent, *Reminescences of Outdoor Life*; Kuykendall, *Ghost Riders of the Mogollon*; Lee, *These Also Served*; Liggett, *My Seventy-five Years Along the Mexican Border*; Marshall, *The Wham Paymaster Robbery*; Matthews, *Interwovern, A Pioneer Chronicle*; Miller, *Arizona, The Last Frontier*; _____, *The Arizona Story*; Monaghan, *The Book of the American West*; Murdock, *Arizona Characters in Silhouette*; Nash, *Bloodletters and Badmen*; Penfield, *Western Sheriffs and Marshals*; Quinn, *War-Paint and Powder Horn*; Raines, *Famous Sheriffs and Western Outlaws*; Ringgold, *Frontier Days in the Southwest*; Rose, *Prehistoric and Historic Gila County*; Santee, *Apache Land*; Schmitt, *The Settlers' West*; Scott, *Some Memories of A Soldier*; Sonnichsen, *Tularosa, Last of the Frontier West*; Sparks, *The Apache Kid*; Thrapp, *Al Sieber, Chief of Scouts*; Way, *Sgt. Fred Platten's Ten Years on the Trail of the Redskins*; Wilson, *An Unwritten Story*.

Apalachin Conference, 1957, U.S., org. crime. Three weeks after the slaying of Mafia-syndicate kingpin Albert Anastasia, about sixty of the top syndicate leaders from around the U.S. met at the country estate of Joseph M. Barbara near Apalachin, N.Y. Barbara, the president of the Canada Dry Bottling Company of Endicott, N.Y., was born in Castellammare, Si., in 1905. He had migratred to the U.S. in 1921 and had been active in the rackets from the mid-1920s. (Unlike some of his rather careless contemporaries, Barbara had had the presence of mind to become a citizen in 1927, thus preventing his deportation back to Sicily in the future.) He had been a suspect in murder cases in 1932 and 1933 but he was never officially charged. Barbara's only conviction occured in 1944 when he was convicted of possessing 300,000 pounds of illegal sugar. He had been under surveillance for a number of years, especially after New York State Police had observed several syndicate members visiting Barbara in 1956, the same year in which Barbara held meetings with Joseph Bonanno, John Bonventre, and Frank Garofolo in Binghamton, N.Y.

When state police learned that Barbara was making reservations for several men in the Apalachin area, two state policemen, Police Sergeant Edgar D. Croswell and Trooper Vincent Vasisko, accompanied by two federal agents of the Alchohol-Tobacco Tax Unit, decided to investigate. These officers drove onto the Barbara estate on Nov. 14, 1957. As soon as the officers were spotted by the mob men in Barbara's large house, they broke wildly to escape what they thought would be a mass arrest. Some of the men ran to cars parked nearby and roared off down several roads leading from the rural estate. Others, dressed in expensively tailored suits, men in their sixties and seventies, ran shakily, wobbly-legged, through the fields and into the woods, tearing their clothes with the underbrush as they ran. Roadblocks were set up and many of the men were stopped in their cars or picked up as they wandered, panting, out of the woods. All of the "conventioneers" (Barbara announced that the meeting was a small Canada Dry convention) carried thick wads of cash, some as much as $10,000, but no wallets, although drivers of the cars produced a driver's license which they all carried in their shirt pockets.

When the identities of those in attendance was made public, the roster was a shocking who's who of the New York Mafia-syndicate. Barbara's brief guests included Vito Genovese, Carlo Gambino, Joseph Bonanno, Joseph Profaci, Joseph Magliocco, Gerardo (Jerry) Catena, Natale Joseph Evola, Michele Miranda, Carmine Lombardozzi, John Ormento, Joseph Riccobono, Paul Castellano, Alfred Rava. Some of those present had traveled considerable distances and represented far flung fiefdoms of the syndicate. These included Santo Trafficante, Jr., then running a casino for the mob in Havana, Cuba, and later the crime boss of Florida; Gabriel Mannarino from Pennsylvania; Frank DiSimone, head of the Los Angeles Mafia; James Civello, boss of the Dallas syndicate; James Colletti, Colorado crime boss; Frank Zito, boss of southern Illinois; John Scalish, Cleveland's Mafia overlord; Joseph Ida, crime czar of Philadelphia. Chicago had been represented by Sam Giancana, but Momo had managed to elude police in the woodlands and somehow escape the dragnet, according to one reliable report. The panic exhibited by these men during the impromptu raid caused Cosa Nostra informant Joseph Valachi to sneeringly remark, "If soldiers (low-level mobsters) got arrested in a meet like that, you can imagine what the bosses would have done. There they are, running through the woods like rabbits, throwing away money so they won't be caught with a lot of cash, and some of them throwing away guns. So who are they kidding when they say we got to respect them?"

Though none of those notorious crime bosses were charged after they had been discovered fleeing the Barbara estate, their names were made public and headlines across the country shouted speculations of the summit meeting of the Mafia. The reasons for the meeting, according to Joe Valachi and others, had to do with the pecking order of the national syndicate, chiefly the restructuring of the five New York families. Carlo Gambino, who had been the underboss to the murdered Albert Anastasia, was to be officially recognized as the head of the Anastasia family.

The sprawling estate of Joseph Barbara in Apalachin, N.Y., where sixty-five of America's top Mafia-syndicate leaders met on November 14, 1957, all of them scattering down roads and into woods when police arrived.

MAFIA MEETING: APALACHIN, N.Y., 1957

Fleeing into the woods was Mafia don Vito Genovese, left, followed by fellow New York crime bosses Joseph Profaci, middle, and Joseph "Joe Bananas" Bonanno, right.

Running wildly to escape the police dragnet thrown around the Barbara estate were, left to right, Chicago boss Sam "Momo" Giancana; the host of the crime conference, Joseph Barbara; New York Mafia don Joseph Magliocco; Nat Evola.

He had conspired with his lieutenant, Joseph (Joe Bandy) Biondo to have Anastasia killed, one account stated, responding to pressure from Vito Genovese who wanted Anastasia out of the way so that he could exercise supreme gang rule in New York. Furthermore, the enclave members were present to annoint Genovese himself as a Mafia family head and absolve him of planning Anastasia's killing which concerned no one in Apalachin anyway since all present feared or hated the kill-crazy Anastasia.

Anthony Anastasio, the slain Anastasia's brother (the difference in spelling had been intentional by Anastasia, to protect his family's good name, he once claimed), angered over the killing, informed Justice Department officials that the bosses had met in Apalachin to establish a hit list of disobedient soldiers, as well as a discussion on whether or not to murder several federal narcotics agents who had been making life difficult for the syndicate. Though a vote was never taken—the state police interrupted the procedures—it was felt by most of the older Mafia leaders, the majority present in Barbara's home, that narcotics was ruining the structure of the long-established crime cartel and bringing federal and local police heat down upon other lucrative rackets that would have been otherwise left alone. Many of the older dons thought to actually outlaw drug traffic and to put out a standing order that anyone in the syndicate peddling drugs would be killed. This report, however, is more in keeping with the mythical Mafia as portrayed in the film *The Godfather* than the money-lusting, conscienceless group that met in Apalachin.

The Apalachin enclave did achieve one dramatic effect. The U.S. public became acutely aware of organized crime, and the impetus of the event caused many governmental committees to be established which probed into crime cartel activities. American citizens who had thought that gangsters had disappeared with Prohibition or into Warner Brother mobster films realized that organized crime was bigger and deadlier than ever, every major American city linked to another through an organization that was almost as well financed as the federal government, and one which was more deadly than the independent gangsters of the 1930s. See: **Anastasia, Albert; Anastasio, Anthony; Atlantic City Conference; Bonanno, Joseph; Catena, Gerardo; DiSimone, Frank; Gambino, Carlo; Genovese, Vito; Giancana, Sam; Havana Conference; Magliocco, Joseph; Miranda, Michele; Profaci, Joseph; Riccobono, Joseph; Scalish, John; Trafficante, Santo; Zito, Frank.**

REF.: Bonanno, *A Man of Honor;* Browning and Gerassi, *The American Way of Crime;* CBA; Cook, *The FBI Nobody Knows;* ____, *Mafia!;* Cressey, *Theft of the Nation;* Davis, *Mafia Kingfish;* Demaris, *The Director;* ____, *Captive City;* ___, *The Last Mafioso;* Eisenberg, *Meyer Lansky, Mogul of the Mob;* Frasca, *King of Crime;* Gage, *The Mafia is not an Equal Opportunity Employer;* ____, *Mafia, USA;* Katz, *Uncle Frank;* Kobler, *Capone;* Lyle, *The Dry and Lawless Years;* McClellan, *Crime Without Punishment;* McPhaul, *Johnny Torrio;* Maas, *The Valachi Papers;* Martin, *Revolt in the Mafia;* Messick and Goldblatt, *The Mobs and the Mafia;* Nash, *Bloodletters and Badmen;* ____, *Citizen Hoover;* Navasky, *Kennedy Justice;* Ottenberg, *The Federal Investigators;* Peterson, *The Mob;* Powers, *Secrecy and Power;* Reid, *The Grim Reapers;* Sullivan, *The Bureau;* Teresa, *My Life in the Mafia;* Tully, *Treasury Agent;* Ungar, *FBI;* Wicker, *Investigating the FBI;* Wolf and DiMona, *Frank Costello, Prime Minister of the Underworld.*

Apis, See: **Dimitrijevic, Dragutin.**

Apollodorus of Damascus, prom. 150, Gr., architect, assass. Admired by Emperor Trajan, he designed the Forum Trajanum at Rome and the triumphal arches at Ancona and Benevento. He fell out of favor, was banished, and killed by Emperor Hadrian. REF.: *CBA.*

Aponte, Héctor Escudero, and **Lopez, Jose Francisco Rivera,** and **Rivera, Armando Jimenez,** prom. 1987, Pu. Ric., arson-mur. What turned out to be the second worst hotel fire in United States history, killing ninety-seven people, was meant to have been only a small blaze, according to the man who set the Dupont Plaza Hotel on fire New Year's Eve 1987. Héctor Escudero Aponte, a 35-year-old hotel maintenance man, ignited a can of cooking fuel

while an accomplice, 29-year-old bartender assistant Armando Jimenez Rivera, shielded him from observation after giving Aponte the fuel. The two were incited to commit the arson by 40-year-old bartender Jose Francisco Rivera Lopez. All three men were members of the Teamsters Union that had called a strike for New Year's Day. The union denied involvment in the case, and no evidence exists to dispute their claim.

Federal judge Jose Fuste handed down stiffer sentences than sought by prosecutors, who said there had been no intention of murdering anyone. Aponte, who pled guilty to arson and murder in the death of 49-year-old Secret Service agent Manuel de Jesus Marrero Otero, was sentenced to two concurrent terms of ninety-nine years in prison. Lopez also received a sentence of ninety-nine years, while Rivera was given seventy-five years.

Commonwealth Court then handed down sentences for the same crimes to be served concurrently with the federal convictions. Lopez was given twenty-five years for each of the ninety-six counts of second-degree murder, while Rivera received twenty-four years on the same count. Each was also sentenced to eighteen years imprisonment for arson and five years imprisonment for conspiracy, to run concurrently. REF.: *CBA.*

Aposhian, Dalbert, 1926-33, U.S., (unsolv.) mur. In the opinion of veteran San Diego chief of detectives Harry Kelly, the disappearance and brutal murder of 7-year-old Aposhian in July 1933 was the most diabolical crime he had ever seen. The case was the sixth unsolved San Diego murder in two years, but in many ways the most horrifying. Dalbert was the eldest of three children born to Mr. and Mrs. George Aposhian, who owned a small shop not far from San Diego Bay. A bright boy, he wanted to be an artist when he grew up. His dreams ended when he mysteriously disappeared on July 18 after leaving his father's store to play with a neighbor boy.

Aposhian's sexually abused body was found a week later in the bay about 100 feet off a pier, where it had floated for about seventy-two hours. Chief Harry Raymond of the San Diego police ordered an extensive manhunt for the killer, described in the press as a sexual degenerate for his brutal assault on the boy and his wanton disfigurement of the boy's face.

There were very few leads. For a time the police suspected a rooming house drifter named Horace Patterson who had left behind a bloodstained towel in the bathroom of a Seventh Avenue flophouse. The results of a chemical analysis of the towel could not support an indictment. A taxicab driver reported seeing a frightened, tearful boy matching Dalbert's description walking near Second Avenue and Broadway. He spoke with the youngster who explained that he had come to San Diego from Pasadena to visit an aunt. The cabby then drove away.

The police turned to the riff-raff who frequented the San Diego waterfront. An old salt known as "Stogies" told a strange story that everyone dismissed as a hallucination. In it, a little boy was attacked by a male pervert and dumped in the water. But "Stogies" died before the police could learn the identity of the stranger. And with his death went the last hope of catching the vicious killer of Dalbert Aposhian. REF.: *CBA.*

Appel, Hans, 1940-   , Case of, Ger., mur. A hard-working stonemason in his youth, Appel had worked hard to become a great success in life, owning a large construction company in Frankfurt by the time he was thirty-four. He was happily married to Renate Poeschke, a woman ten years his junior. She was a devoted mother to their only child and two children from Appel's former marriage. Appel could deny her nothing, especially when she told him her brother Jurgen Poeschke had left East Germany and had no where to live. He told her it would be all right if Jurgen moved in with them until he got a job. After a sixteen-year separation Renate was overjoyed to see her brother. Appel did not realize how delighted his wife was until he returned home one night from work in 1974, and his 6-year-old daughter Claudia told him that "Mummy and Uncle Jurgen were in bed all afternoon and they were naked."

Apple could not believe it; he first suspected that Jurgen was an old lover of Renate's but, after checking with immigration, the fact that he was Renate's brother was confirmed. He confronted the pair and they freely admitted that they had slept together. Appel threw Jurgen out of his house and his wife followed her brother. Appel still could not believe that his beautiful wife was involved in an incestuous relationship. He picked up Renate's other brother, Dieter, and drove from Frankfurt to Wiesbaden. En route he asked Dieter if it was true that his brother Jurgen and his sister Renate slept with each other. Dieter shrugged and said that it was not only true but that he, too, had slept with Renate many times, that he and his brother had been making love to their sister since they were teenagers. At that time, something in Appel snapped. He pulled out a gun and shot Dieter Poeschke dead, later dumping his body in a ditch along the roadway.

When Dieter's body was later found it was traced to Renate and then to her husband. Hans Appel did not deny the murder but told his story openly to a Frankfurt court on July 29, 1974. He was given a twenty-one-month prison sentence which was limited to a short period of time until the businessman could arrange bail pending an appeal. He later won the appeal when charges were dropped by Renate and Jurgen. Charges against these two accusing them with incest were then dropped by the police. REF.: *CBA*.

Applegate, Everett, See: **Creighton, Mary Frances**.

Appleton, John, c.1855, Brit., mur. On Mar. 28, 1905, John Appleton, in a drunken stupor, confessed to police that he and Joseph Earnshaw, had robbed and killed a man, later identified as William Ledger, near Newcastle in July 1882. Having no other evidence to go on—records showed the crime remained unsolved—the police believed Appleton and arrested him. Earnshaw, apparently, had since died.

Appleton was tried at the Durham Assizes in July 1905, where he recanted his confession, stating he had only read of the murder. He was convicted and sentenced to death, but the sentence was later commuted to life due to the peculiar circumstances of the case.

REF.: *CBA; Shew, Second Companion To Murder; Smith-Hughes, Unfair Comment*.

Appo, Quimby (Lee Ah Bow), 1814-1912, U.S., mur. One of the most bizarre prisoners ever to be jailed in the New York Tombs was its first Chinese inmate, the berserk killer, Lee Ah Bow, known to the police as Quimby Appo. He was not, as some historians have claimed, the first Chinese in New York. The first Chinese settlers were those artisans stranded when their showboat, the junk *Ki Ying*, caught fire while docked in the East River. These homeless Chinese took lodging on Mott Street between Pell and Chatham, and the area became New York's Chinatown. Appo, a murderer by temperament, arrived in New York from California as the personal slave of a landed gentleman. This was more than seven years after the Ki Ying group took up residence.

In no time at all, the unbalanced Appo attempted to kill a shopkeeper. He was booked for attempted murder in the summer of 1840. Female missionaries visited Appo in his cell, and he became their prime target for conversion to Christianity. With their help, Appo was released. In the next twenty years, the "Chinese Devilman" or "Devil Appo," as the press dubbed him, was arrested at least a dozen times for assaults and attempts to commit homicide. On Mar. 9, 1859, Appo attacked three women in his boarding house. One of these females was his mistress, who made the mistake of serving him a cold dinner. He stabbed her. When another woman rushed into the apartment, Appo drove a dirk into her heart.

Racing down a back stairs, Appo's escape route was blocked by the stout landlady. She turned her back on him and he promptly stabbed her in the buttock. Police arrived and carted the Devilman off to The Tombs, where he was scheduled to hang for murder. The persistent missionaries mounted a campaign to save their religious pet and convinced authorities to reduce his sentence to seven years, which he served in constant anger. He would bite the hands of jailers as they shoved his food through the bars. He screamed for hours on end. He spat at Warden Fallon and tried to claw anyone who recklessly got too close to his cell. Somehow, Appo's savage behavior only further endeared him to the missionaries.

Upon his release, the Devilman promptly stabbed his landlady, Lizzie Williams. Through a lawyer provided by the missionaries, Appo was again released. There was no end to the liberties Appo took with his fellow creatures. Drunk one day in 1872, the Devilman dug up a large cobblestone from the street and crashed it down upon the head of one John Linkowski. With one blow, the diminutive Chinese had dashed the man's brains out. Again, he was thrown into the Tombs, and again the religious zealots got him released. Appo was about to take up the cross, they doggedly insisted.

Instead, Appo took up another dirk and drove it into Cork Maggie, a Bowery whore. Since she survived the attack, the missionaries pointed out to police, there was no sense in prosecuting. The Devilman was not even taken into custody. A year later, on Oct. 21, 1876, this fierce little man jumped up from a card game and plunged a dagger several times into the chest of one John Kelly, whom he accused of cheating him. This time, authorities sent Appo to Matteawan, the state prison for the insane, the same prison which later housed the notorious train robber Oliver Curtis Perry and millionaire murderer Harry K. Thaw.

The Devilman never left this prison. He would endlessly stare from his cell window and, upon seeing the searchlight of the Hudson River Nightboat, would scream: "Here comes my diamond!" Officials at the institute reported that Appo "believes that he has grand hotels, palaces, servants and horses outside the asylum; that he is King of the World and Omnipotent, the Second God; commands the wind and the sun; that Tom Sharkey and General Coxey are his military staff and that he must suffer for Ireland." The Devilman suffered for ninety-eight years before being buried on the grounds at Matteawan on June 23, 1912.

REF.: *CBA; Sutton, The New York Tombs, Its Secrets and Mysteries*.

Approved School Breakout, The, 1947, Brit., mur. At an Approved School in the British Midlands, ten teenaged boys plotted the murder of their hated headmaster. According to the plan, on Feb. 15 they would break into his home, steal some ammunition, shoot him, and escape with the car.

The plan went awry, however, when a teacher named Hopkins entered the washroom as the boys were loading their stolen rifles. The leader of the group spun around, firing two shots into the teacher. Then all the boys fled, abandoning their plans for the headmaster.

Within five hours of the shooting all five were captured. They pled Guilty to conspiracy and murder, but their lawyer, citing insanity, argued for leniency. The judge weighed the evidence before sentencing two 16-year-olds to three years in prison. One 15-year-old who conspired to kill the headmaster was sent to another Approved School, and the other boys were held pending a psychiatric evaluation under the terms of the Mental Deficiency Act.

REF.: *CBA; Wilson, Children Who Kill*.

Aquino, Benigno S., Jr., (AKA: Ninoy), c.1932-83, Case of, Phil., assass. As leader of the opposition to Philippine president Ferdinand Marcos, Benigno Aquino was clearly the leading contender for the presidency before he was gunned down upon returning to his homeland from exile.

Aquino became the Philippines' youngest mayor at twenty-two, its youngest governor at twenty-nine, and its youngest senator at thirty-four. In 1972, when Aquino was forty, Marcos declared martial law, thus extending his term as president beyond the country's constitutional limit. At that time, Marcos had Aquino arrested and convicted of murder, rape, illegal possession of firearms, and subversion. Aquino was sentenced to die, but spent more than seven years in prison on the specious charges. In 1980, Marcos allowed Aquino to have heart surgery in the United States, where he stayed for three years.

Upon his arrival at Manila International Airport on Aug. 21, 1983, Aquino was escorted off the plane by three soldiers, while two others prevented anyone else from leaving the plane. Within thirty seconds Aquino had been shot in the head, and his guards had shot his alleged assassin, Rolando Galman, seven or eight times. Aquino's body was removed immediately.

Aquino's friends had begged him not to return to the Philippines. Aquino replied, "I'm committed to return. If fate falls that I should be killed, so be it." Aquino often referred to Filipino patriot José Rizal, who was shot by a Spanish firing squad upon returning from exile in 1896, igniting the Philippine war of independence.

A tape recording of the assassination clearly indicates that someone ordered the shooting. One witness claims that he saw Aquino shot before he reached the ground, refuting the government's claim that he was shot on the ground by Galman. The government maintained that it was not involved in the murder, though Aquino was surrounded by five guards when he was shot.

Political experts believe it unlikely that Marcos actually ordered the killing, but they suspect factions particularly loyal to the president, especially the army under the leadership of General Fabian Ver. The government conducted an investigation of the assassination but its validity is doubtful. Aquino's wife, the Philippines' current president Corazon Aquino, refused to allow exhumation of her husband's corpse for further examination. REF.: *CBA*.

Arafa, Sidi Mohammed ben Moulay, prom. 1953, Morocco, sultan, att.-assass. Allal ben Abdallah was a young Moroccan nationalist opposed to the government of Arafa, a colonial puppet of the occupying French. When Sultan Arafa signed into law a decree which transferred a large measure of political power to a French-run administrative council, the 28-year-old former house painter decided to kill the man he felt had dealt a severe blow to his country's liberation movement.

Ben Abdallah got his chance in September 1953, the morning after the decree became law. Accompanied by imperial guards, Sultan Arafa mounted his prized steed for a short ride to the mosque where he was to offer his morning prayer. When he arrived at the shrine, the usual throng of well-wishers pushed and shoved their way close to the royal entourage for a better view. Ben Abdallah revved the engine of his rusting model-A Ford, parked near the wall of the mosque, and raced directly at the Moroccan ruler at forty miles per hour.

A young Frenchman named Robert King leaped on the running board of the dilapidated roadster in an attempt to subdue the assassin before he killed the sultan and innocent bystanders. Ben Abdallah pulled out a butcher knife as the automobile careened wildly toward the royal party. King was stabbed in the shoulder but his valiant effort allowed the sultan a few extra seconds to dismount his horse unharmed. The car crashed into the riderless horse just as imperial guards opened fire. Allal ben Abdallah fell to the ground, his body riddled with bullets. Turning to an aide, the nervous sultan whispered: "*sibismaken*," meaning "no harm done." However, the horse had to be put to sleep after sustaining a leg injury. REF.: *CBA*.

Arafat, Yasir, 1929-   , (AKA: **Abu Amar**), Mid. East, terr. Since the Six-Day War between the Arab states and Israel ended in June 1967, Yasir Arafat has been the recognized leader of a Palestinian "government in exile." As the head of Al Fatah and the Palestine Liberation Organization (PLO), Arafat has spent his entire adult life working for the creation of a homeland for his people after their expulsion during the creation of the modern state of Israel in 1948. To achieve these aims, Arafat has sanctioned commando raids, airline hijackings, and other acts of deliberate terror which have undermined the Palestinian cause and earned universal condemnation from the western press.

Arafat was born to a prominent family in Jerusalem in 1929. However, much of the family fortune was lost in legal entanglements in the Egyptian courts. During the 1948 crisis, Arafat ran guns and ammunition to the Arabs. His family became refugees

in Gaza after Israel's founding. After the war he emigrated to Cairo where he studied engineering at Faud I (Cairo) University. He also became a trained leader of the militant Palestinian student factions which harassed the British regiments at the Suez Canal in 1951-52. After receiving his degree, Arafat attended the Egyptian military academy and graduated as a commissioned officer knowledgeable in the use of high explosives. In 1956 he served as a demolitions expert in the Egyptian struggle against the French and British at Port Said and Abu Kabir.

Shortly afterward, Arafat returned to private life in Kuwait as a civil engineer in the public works department. In the late 1950s he edited *Our Palestine*, a nationalistic magazine espousing Palestinian autonomy. Using the alias Abu Amar, he personally trained Arab boys from the refugee camps for dangerous commando missions behind Israeli lines. In the mid-1950s, Arafat helped found Al Fatah, short for Harakat al Tahrir al-Falastin, or Movement for the Liberation of Palestine. Al Fatah was a wholly independent organization that swore allegiance to no single Arab state, but claimed to represent all of them against their common enemy, Israel. In 1965 Arafat left his government job in Kuwait to assume command of Al Assifa (the Storm), the military units of the Al Fatah. At a conference of the Arab League in 1964, the PLO was officially founded. In time it would become the chief representative for the Palestinian cause with Yasir Arafat emerging as the leader of the organization. Until then, President Gamal Nasser of Egypt kept the PLO in check.

Arafat believed that independence could be achieved only through armed conflict. By 1969, the year that Al Fatah gained control of the PLO with Arafat as its executive chairman, arms and money were arriving daily from other Arab nations. The PLO used guerilla tactics against Israeli military installations and settlements. Unable to win a direct military victory, their strategy was to promote political instability in the region, in the belief that continued tension between Israel and its neighbors was essential to a final victory. Operating from ten commando bases in Jordan and Lebanon, the PLO staged covert raids against the Israelis, which usually resulted in swift retaliatory strikes against the PLO.

Arafat has always maintained that he was working for the creation of a Palestinian state that would provide equality for Moslems, Christians, and Jews. Yet his refusal to work for a negotiated peace with the Israelis contributed to serious rifts within his own organization. In what came to be known as "Black September", King Hussein of Jordan began to expel PLO guerrillas in 1970. A civil war erupted between the Jordanians and the PLO rebels, which ended in a negotiated settlement on Sept. 27. An extremist faction within the PLO named itself Black September and claimed responsibility for the murder of U.S. Ambassador Cleo Noel in Khartoum in 1973. The high point of Arafat's career came in 1974 when the Arab League declared him "the sole legitimate representative" of the Palestinian people. But in the following years, unity gave way to bitter factionalism.

In May 1983 a rebel group led by Abu Mousa broke away from the PLO and sought haven in Syria. President Hafez Assad welcomed the group because he was eager to play his own hand against Arafat. The credibility of the Palestinian leader was further undermined among certain factions of his own people when he announced on Nov. 15, 1988, that the PLO would grant implied recognition to Israel. At the same time, Arafat declared a free and independent state of Palestine on the Israeli-occupied West Bank and Gaza Strip.

The United States refused Arafat's application for a visa to address the United Nations General Assembly in New York. In handing down its controversial decision on Nov. 24, 1988, the U.S. State Department cited "ample evidence" of Arafat's sanctioning of terrorism, including his close association with Abu Abbas, a member of the PLO executive committee held responsible for the murder of U.S. citizen Leon Klinghoffer aboard the Italian cruise ship *Achille Lauro* in 1985. Arafat not only knew about these terrorist actions, but condoned them. The actions of the PLO in this regard were in opposition to the Cairo declaration of November 1985, in which Arafat foreswore the use of terrorism as a political tool.

The 1988 decision not to admit Yasir Arafat to the United States angered many who felt sympathy for the "intifadah" in the occupied territories. The U.N. General Assembly has condemned Israel's "persistent policies and practices violating the human rights of Palestinians." The resolution must have pleased Arafat, who, at sixty, showed a willingness to take his place in the world community. A lifelong bachelor, the PLO leader once explained that he had "married a woman called Palestine."

REF.: *CBA; Clutterbuck, Guerrillas and Terrorists; Demaris, Brothers In Blood; ____, The International Terrorist Network; Dobson and Payne, The Terrorists; Hacker, Crusaders, Criminals, Crazies, Terror and Terrorism In Our Time; Maas, Manhunt; O'Ballance, Language of Violence; Schreiber, The Ultimate Weapon, Terrorists and World Order.*

Araluce, Juan Maria de, 1917-76, Spain, polit., (unsolv.) assass. Following the death of Spanish dictator Generalissimo Francisco Franco in 1975, a period of political turmoil ensued, characterized by armed attacks against prominent members of the rightist government. A separatist movement known as the Basque Nation and Freedom (ETA) sought political independence for their people living in the northern part of the country. To achieve its aim, the Marxist radicals waged a terrorist war against the conservative regime of King Juan Carlos and his prime minister Adolfo Suarez Gonzalez, who ruled the government in the first months after Franco's death.

It was this group that claimed responsibility for the bloody noontime assassination of Araluce, a high-ranking member of the Council of the Realm on Oct. 4, 1976. Araluce favored moderation, and had worked hard to restore freedoms long denied to the Basque peoples under the forty-year rule of Franco. The Council of the Realm is an advisory body to the king concerned with political appointments.

The unknown assassins waited in ambush near Araluce's home on the Avenida de Espana in San Sebastian. Accompanied by a chauffeur and three armed bodyguards, the 59-year-old president of the council of the Basque province of Guipuzcoa exited his limousine on the crowded thoroughfare. As he reached his doorstep, a solitary gunman emerged from the shadows and raked the automobile with a blast of machine gun fire. Araluce and his bodyguards were killed instantly. The chauffeur died eight hours later.

Three men climbed into a white car and sped away in the confusion and were never found. Later that day an anonymous phone call was received by a newspaper in San Sebastian. The callers identified themselves as members of the extremist ETA-V, headed by Miguel Angel Apalategui Ayerbe, who had carried out the kidnapping and murder of a wealthy Basque industrialist several months earlier though paid informants later disputed this claim. However, the execution was sloppy, and not up to the standards of the highly skilled but cold-blooded faction. The Communist Party was responsible for the outrage, many said.

The French border was sealed off and a house-to-house search was conducted in San Sebastian with little success. Araluce was buried in the Valley of the Fallen, as the government assured the people that it would continue to press ahead with its plan to institute badly-needed Democratic reforms in Spain. REF.: *CBA.*

Aram, Eugene, 1704-59, Brit., mur. An accomplished scholar and philologist, Aram was expert in the Latin, Greek, Hebrew, and Celtic languages. He was also a thief and a murderer. His case is all the more intriguing in that he was not tried for his capital crime until fourteen years after he committed it. Aram was born in Ramsgill in the West Riding of Yorkshire. His father was a gardner on the Newby estate of Sir Edward Blackett. Aram was self-taught, with some help from the tutors of the Blacketts, and was able to rise to the position of schoolmaster at Knaresborough by 1734. He had married Anna Spence in 1731 and the couple produced seven children, a family that kept the schoolmaster on the brink of bankruptcy from year to year. His frustation at making ends meet, some historians claim, soured Aram's otherwise

poetic, gentle nature and caused him to be overly strict with his students, some of whom later describing him as a "stern disciplinarian."

To pick up extra money, Aram enlisted the aid of a disreputable character named Richard Houseman, a sometimes weaver, and the two of them practiced petty thievery at night. He also obtained stolen goods with several other thieves, including Henry Terry, a gamekeeper in the area, and Francis Iles, a receiver of stolen goods who fenced these purloined items in areas as far away as Scotland. Another friend of Aram's at the time was a wealthy shoemaker, Daniel Clark whose wife had inherited considerable wealth. Clark shared with Aram a deep interest in books, botany and gardening. On the night of Feb. 7, 1745, Clark, along with a considerable quanitity of expensive goods—velvets, plate (which may have been stolen from neighborhood households), and other rare

Eugene Aram, an educated killer.

items—and most of his wife's dowery of £200, disappeared. A short time later Aram and his friends were arrested on suspicion of having had some of Clark's goods but were released for lack of evidence. Aram grew desperate and fled to London, leaving his large family to fend for itself. He changed his name and took teaching positions where he tutored wealthy children in Latin. He later moved to Middlesex and still later to King's Lynn, Norfolk.

Had it not been for a strange quirk of fate, Eugene Aram's name might have been lost to criminal posterity. Workman digging at Thistle Hill near Knaresborough found some human bones on Aug. 1, 1758. These were presumed to be Clark's remains and a frenzied effort was made to locate all of the missing man's friends, including Houseman and Aram, both of whom having been seen with the victim on the night of his disappearance by a local innkeeper, William Triton. Houseman was located but he denied having had anything to do with Clark. The bones found by the workmen later proved not to be the remains of Clark and Houseman was released. Then some old plate that had been in Clark's possession was located and traced to Houseman who was arrested once again. This time Aram's old confederate confessed but put the blame for Clark's murder on Aram, telling authorities that he and Aram had taken the shoemaker to St. Robert's Cave where Aram struck Clark several times on the head and breast and killed him. Houseman then led officials to the cave where the skeletal remains were found and accepted as that of Clark. Still Aram was at large.

The schoolteacher, however, had the misfortune to meet a resident of Knaresborough who was visiting King's Lynn and recognized him. The man, John Barker, was no ordinary traveler but a constable living in Knaresborough who had known both Aram and Clark. He arrested Aram and returned him to Knaresborough. En route, Aram denied ever having known Clark, a serious mistake in that his friendship with Clark was well known, and Barker's testimony later in court about Aram's denial in having known Clark further damned the schoolteacher's cause. When arriving in Knaresborough and appearing before Magistrate Thornton, Aram denied his guilt and tried to shift the blame for Clark's death onto Houseman and Terry, but Houseman had already turned state's evidence for the Crown and his version of events was what the prosecution accepted and used against Aram. The schoolteacher, along with Terry and Houseman, were jailed at York Prison on Aug. 21, 1758, and remained there pending trial until the following year when Aram was brought to the York Assiazes on Aug. 3, 1759, before Justice Noel, prosecuted by

Fletcher Norton, K.C., a relentless advocate for the Crown. Aram conducted his own defense and he did a brilliant job of it.

Houseman again described in detail how Aram murdered Clark, and other witnesses were systematically paraded before the court by the prosecution to prove that Aram had possessed, following Clark's disappearance, a considerable amount of money which he used to pay outstanding bills; money, it was assumed, he had taken from Clark after beating him to death. Aram countered by stating that the bones found in St. Andrew's Cave could be those of anyone, that no one could positively identify these remains as that of Clark, Houseman's claims notwithstanding. He also cited many cases where men who supposedly had vanished later returned. Exhibiting his knowledge of history, Aram cited the many battles that had been fought over the centuries about St. Andrew's Cave and that the remains Housemen had held up as that of Clark could have been those of a fallen warrior ages ago. He also claimed that on the night of Clark's disappearance, he was deathly ill. He claimed that an illness at the time of the so-called murder had left him "so macerated, so enfeebled that I was reduced to crutches." He could not prove this, however, even through the testimony of his deserted wife Anna whose statements about him were ambiguous at best.

Aram depended upon his intellectual stature in presenting his case, portraying himself as a man of high intelligence and emotional sensibility. In an eloquent presentation of his own character he stated, "I concerted not schemes of fraud, projected not violence, injured no man's person or property. My days were honestly laborious and my nights intensely studious." No man living such a purposeful life could, he stated, "plunge into the very depth of profligacy, precipitately...Mankind is never corrupted at once. Villainy is always progressive." (In uttering these lofty words, Aram could have been speaking for many a modern-day criminologist advocating social and economic environment as the chief causes of crime.) He was no thief, no murderer, Aram insisted but had been so labeled by thieves and murderers eager to save their own necks, chiefly Houseman and, to some degree, Terry, who testified against Aram when Aram implicated him in Clark's disappearance. He was a victim of circumstance, the schoolteacher claimed with great passion and alliterative pleading. He left his case with the good conscience of the court.

The jury, however, had heard testimony from authorities who quoted Aram's many contradictory statements. No, he did not known Houseman, Terry, Clark. Well, yes, he knew them but they were not his associates. Yes, he had some dealings with them but only brief encounters of no importance. In the end, he was found Guilty and was sentenced to be hanged. Aram stood in the dock listening to his death sentence with a calm attitude and a slight smile on his face. He made no comment as he was led off to prison to await the executioner. The night before Aram was scheduled to hang, the schoolteacher somehow obtained a razor and attempted to cut his throat in his cell, but a warder interrupted him and saved him for the scaffold. On Aug. 6, 1759, Eugene Aram ate a small breakfast and then received in his cell two clergymen who attempted to spiritually console him. He confessed the murder of Clark to them, according to one account, but still claimed that Houseman, who had escaped the gallows through his testimony, was equally guilty. Contradictory to the end, Aram then began his old claim that the skeleton found was that of some person other than Clark. "What became of Clark's body?" he asked one of the clergymen.

"I'll tell you what became of it," the cleric reportedly replied. "You and Houseman dragged it into the cave, stripped and buried it there, brought away his clothes and burned them at your own house." Aram stood up and faced the cell wall, ordering the clergymen to leave him alone. A short time later he was publicly hanged outside the gates of York, going to his death with composure. His body was then taken to Knaresborough on Aug. 7, 1759, where it was gibbeted in chains and the corpse left to rot and then mummify for many years so that thousands of travelers passed the hideous remains along the main road to be reminded of the sins of Eugene Aram. One fanciful tale has it that the schoolteacher's widow visited the hanging spot daily, picking up the bones of her once beloved spouse as they fell to earth one by one, burying these in a secret grave and that it took her a decade to collect all the remains. A local doctor later went to the site and cut off the head or what was left of it and the skull was later exhibited in the Royal College of Surgeons in London.

This brilliant murderer found his way into literature other than the criminous. Thomas Hood eulogized the errant schoolteacher in a lengthy poem entitled "The Dream of Eugene Aram," which was later quoted at great length by England's most infamous felon of the nineteenth century, Charles Peace. This master criminal would recite its seemingly endless stanzas when in his cups, astounding his fellow thieves who sat mesmerized in pubs, listening to Peace rattle off Hood's fanciful portrait of Aram the murderer and equating Aram, in the sense of criminal history, to that of any distinguished historical figure. To Peace, Eugene Aram was as important as King Richard the Lionhearted, an ancient idol which spurred Peace on to his own heinous acts and led him to the same end, the gallows. See: **Peace, Charles.**

REF.: Birkenhead, *Famous Trials of History;* Birmingham, *Murder Most Foul;* Boucher, *The Pocket Book of True Crime Stories;* Butler, *Murderer's England; CBA;* Hunt, *Dictionary of Rogues;* Kingston, *Dramatic Days at the Old Bailey;* Mitchell, *The Newgate Calendar;* Scott, *The Concise Encyclopedia of Crime and Criminals;* Watson, *The Trial of Eugene Aram;* Wilson, *Encyclopedia of Murder;* (FICTION) Bulwer-Lytton, *Eugene Aram.*

Aramburu, Pedro Eugenio, d.1970, Arg., kid.-assass. Major General Aramburu rose from the peasant class of Basque Argentina to become provisional president of his country when the corrupt military dictatorship of Juan D. Perón collapsed in September 1955. He led the military revolt, five years in the making, that ultimately toppled the popular Perón and forced him into self-imposed exile in Madrid. Placing himself at the head of the ruling junta in November 1955, Aramburu restored the liberal-democratic 1853 constitution and allowed the press a freedom long denied by Perón.

In 1958 Aramburu was forced to retire following his defeat for re-election. Despite notable reforms, widespread opposition rose to his hard-line policy regarding the Perónists, many of whom were shot, imprisoned, or exiled during his three-year rule. One of his closest friends, General Juan José Valle, was executed because of his past support of Perón and his involvement in an aborted 1956 coup d'état.

The supporters of Valle never forgave nor forgot what Aramburu had done to their leader, and they waited fourteen years for revenge. On May 29, 1970, an underground guerrilla group calling itself the "Juan José Valle Command" kidnapped Aramburu. They advised president Juan Carlos Onganía that their revolutionary court had sentenced the general to death in retaliation for the life of Valle and twenty-seven of his followers. True to their word, the group executed the stern-faced former president and left his body in the basement of a farmhouse 300 miles west of Buenos Aires where it was found on July 17.

Three days later a man identified as Hector Arturo Diaz shot himself in the head when military police broke into his home to question him about the kidnapping. In a September gun battle in the capital city, two more suspected Valle commandos were killed during a fifteen-minute shootout with police. While the country teetered toward another civil war, President Ongania reinstituted the death penalty for all convicted kidnappers and pressed ahead with the investigation into Aramburu's murder.

Five suspects, including a Roman Catholic priest, were eventually arrested and tried for the murder. On Dec. 16, 1970, a panel of three judges returned a guilty verdict against three of the defendants, a 27-year-old television script writer, Carlos Maguid, was sentenced to eighteen years in prison, the priest, Father Alberto Carbone, let off with a two-year suspended sentence, and student leader Ignacio Velez, who received thirty-two months. REF.: *CBA.*

Arango, Doroteo, See: **Villa, Francesco Pancho.**

Aranguren, William, (AKA: **Desquite**), prom. 1960s, Col., mur. More than 2,000 policemen and soldiers along with aircraft scoured the Colombian hills in search of the *banditi* responsible for the August 1963 massacre of forty-two civilians. The *banditi* was William Aranguren, a former army private who failed his exams in military police school. When he was denied the chance to become a government soldier, Aranguren organized a rebel band and retreated to the mountains where he planned quasi-military campaigns against unarmed civilians. Wearing the uniform of an army captain, the bandit leader personally supervised ambushes against unsuspecting travelers.

In western Colombia his band of forty desperadoes swooped down on a passing car, and three passengers were taken to a roadside hideout and held captive. The outlaws returned to the highway where they stopped a bus and herded the passengers at gunpoint back to the house. Aranguren ordered his guerrillas to take the prisoners' valuables and kill all the men. The forty-two male prisoners were beaten and hacked to pieces with machetes in what police described as one of the worst massacres in Colombia in fifteen years. The renegade activity of Aranguren and his gang was the fallout of a long and pointless civil war between conservative and liberal political factions dating back to 1948.

A formal truce between the two parties had been declared in 1957, but this did not discourage bandits like Aranguren from robbing and murdering for profit in the name of "liberation." As the funeral procession for the victims of the bus massacre wound its way through the streets of Manzanares, the survivors remembered Aranguren had issued the ominous warning: "It will happen again." REF.: *CBA.*

Arason, Jon, c.1484-1550, Ice., bishop, assass. Bishop of Holar, he was the last Catholic bishop in Iceland. When he opposed the imposition of Lutheranism and seized the See of the Lutheran Bishop Marteinn, he was arrested and then beheaded. REF.: *CBA.*

Araujo, Jaime, prom. 1980s, U.S., smug.-org. crime. Araujo was a one-time drug kingpin whose gang of heroin smugglers earned him an estimated $33 million from narcotics transactions. Before he was sentenced to prison for thirty-five years, Araujo invested $1.5 million of his earnings in valuable U.S. real-estate.

Under federal statutes enacted in 1970, the government was empowered to seize the assets of major drug traffickers in addition to assessing them fines. In the case of Araujo, he was forced to pay the government $1.2 million, but only $260,000 worth of his personal property was confiscated by drug enforcement agents. REF.: *CBA.*

Arbenz Guzman, Jacobo, 1913-71, Guat., polit., consp. Took part in the coup d'etat against dictator Jorge Ubico in 1944. Served as minister of war from 1949-50 and as president of Guatemala from 1950-54. REF.: *CBA.*

Arbin, Eric von, See: **Kreuger, Alexander.**

Arboleda, Julio, 1817-c.1862, col., pres., assass. Columbian poet who was leader of the revolt of 1856. He assumed the office of president in 1860 and was assassinated approximately two years later. REF.: *CBA.*

Arbuckle, Roscoe Conkling (AKA: **Fatty**), 1887-1933, Case of, U.S., rape-mur. In the infant years of Hollywood, Arbuckle was the most popular comedian in America, loved wider and deeper than even the immortal Charlie Chaplin. He was a fat man—enormous, some said obese—with a fish-mouth smile that punched open twinkling eyes. Arbuckle was the highest paid actor in the country during his heyday, at $5,000 a week, and the world was his, until lust and/or passion overcame reason and led to a charge of murder.

Born in Smith Center, Kan., on Mar. 24, 1887, and christened Roscoe Conkling Arbuckle after a right-wing Republican politician (even though his father, William, was an ardent Democrat), Arbuckle weighed fourteen pounds at birth. His weight would always be a problem and, at the zenith of the Virginia Rappe scandal that destroyed his film career, it would be the cause of an indictment of first-degree murder.

The Arbuckle family moved to California, settling in Santa Ana in 1888. William Goodrich Arbuckle was a rigid taskmaster, demanding that his four children work at early ages. Roscoe, whom the neighborhood aptly dubbed "Fatty," began working before he was ten. His father, who roamed about California in search of quick fortunes, would return home to regularly beat him and the other children for no apparent reasons.

Fatty was hanging about the stage entrance of a local Santa Ana theater in 1895 when Frank Bacon, whose troupe was appearing in a revue entitled "Turned Up," approached him with an offer. He told the 8-year-old Arbuckle that the child who was supposed to play a pickaninny had not arrived. Bacon offered him the job for fifty cents. Fatty accepted and remained in show business, in one form or another, for the rest of his life.

Following the death of his mother, Fatty drifted about, working as a dishwasher and busboy in a hotel once owned by his father in Watsonville. Then he moved on to San Jose and Santa Clara where he briefly attended high school, spending most of his time singing and dancing in local theaters for prize money.

By 1904, Arbuckle, who had a lilting tenor voice, was singing for good money in San Francisco cafes. He was in the city when the great 1906 quake struck and, along with thousands of others fleeing the fire that followed the earthquake, was ordered at bayonet point by troops rushing into the city to clear away debris.

In the next few years, Fatty worked cafes and burlesque houses, appearing as an in-between-acts singer. He married a fellow performer, Minta Durfee, when both were appearing in Long Beach, Calif., in 1908. A year later, Fatty drifted into Hollywood to pick up odd jobs in the blossoming motion picture industry. He began at Selig Studios, performing burlesque routines in one-reel comedies, working on and off for four years, until he moved to Mack Sennett Studios where he became a star by late 1913 in the unforgettable Keystone comedies.

Roscoe "Fatty" Arbuckle was an overnight sensation, as they liked to say in Hollywood. Americans responded to his clowning and mugging with overwhelming approval. Often teamed with the brilliant Mabel Normand, Arbuckle ran up a staggering succession of hits—*Fatty and the Heiress, Fatty's Wine Party, Mabel and Fatty's Wash Day, Fatty and Mabel Adrift*—more than 120 films. By 1920 he was making feature-length films for Famous Players-Lasky and earning a staggering $5,000 a week. He lived as his girth suggested—high, wide, and handsome—and, despite his marriage to Minta, gave full vent to his carnal desires, which were almost incessant.

Arbuckle soon became known in Hollywood as a man who would chase (and catch) any girl, particularly young starlets. He often boasted to his friends and co-workers of his conquests, especially one-night stands where he satiated himself in record time. He once remarked to his boss Mack Sennett: "If there weren't beautiful women in the world I wouldn't want to live."

He was also a heavy drinker when alone, which was seldom. After leaving Minta in 1916, he would sit in his posh Hollywood mansion and write gushing missives to his wife. One, written in 1921, read: "Love is a whisper, a scene, a delicate thing, unable to survive when crowded with words and people and actions. Apart, I adore you and my love for you is rich and growing." But Fatty's love grew in all directions and was lavished upon any woman who returned his leer with a smile. One of these was Virginia Rappe (pronounced rap-pay), a starlet who had attracted Fatty's roving eye in 1918 when she attended a party celebrating the completion of one of Arbuckle's films.

The comedian was immediately taken with the 24-year-old actress, toasting her eloquently with the words: "To the loveliest woman of them all. May she prosper!" He then insisted Rappe have every dance with him. Virginia complained to her escort and fiancé Henry Lehrman, a film director, that Fatty was holding her too tightly on the dance floor.

"It probably just seems that way because he's so fat," laughed Lehrman who had helmed many of Arbuckle's films and, as one of the top Mack Sennett directors, had also directed several Charlie Chaplin films, having studied under the master director David Wark Griffith.

Yet, throughout the night, Rappe continued her complaints that Arbuckle was grabbing her indelicately. "He's fresh," she said to Lehrman, and finally convinced her fiancé to take her home. Arbuckle, however, never forgot the beautiful raven-haired actress and at every opportunity made a heavy pass at her. She ignored him.

Later, in 1918, when Virginia Rappe was labeled by the press as "one of the best dressed girls in the movies," Arbuckle sent her a gold watch around which was wrapped a note asking her to star in one of his movies. She refused politely, stating that she preferred to make her own way, and shortly thereafter received a starring role in a movie entitled *Twilight Baby*. She went on to make *The Punch of the Irish* and several other silent films that were successful.

Going it on her own was not unusual for Rappe. From childhood she had had to fend for herself. Born in New York in 1894 (some reports say 1896), Virginia was the fatherless daughter of a show girl named Mabel Rapp; Virginia added the "e" in 1913 when she was working as a commercial model in Chicago. When she was eleven, Virginia Rappe's mother died and she moved to Chicago to be raised somewhat haphazardly by an elderly grandmother. (In a blistering and blatantly unfair portrait drawn by David Yallop in *The Day the Laughter Stopped*, Mabel Rapp was labeled a "prostitute"; Yallop states that Virginia, when she arrived in Hollywood, "tended to strip at a party after she had had something to drink," and that she and her fiancé Henry Lehrman "both had a venereal disease." All of these remarks by Yallop were inexcusable, in that Yallop's work, rabidly in support of Arbuckle, is a repulsive whitewash that pays slavish homage to the comedian's film work and portrays his character as ethical and moral, which it seldom was.

The early life of Virginia Rappe was scarred by tragedy. At seventeen, when she was a popular model in Chicago—"her figure is nothing less than spectacular," remarked one admirer—Virginia became engaged to John Sample, a well-known sculptor but an artist whose mental balance was slightly off-center. For no apparent reason, Sample gave a party one night on the roof of his apartment building where he exhibited his work. Rappe was not present to see the 44-year-old Sample smilingly down a drink, walk to the edge of the roof, and dive headfirst to his death. The motive for this bizarre suicide was never established. Virginia was hysterical for weeks.

Virginia left to see friends and relatives on the West Coast in 1915, just at the time of the San Francisco Exposition. By then Rappe had established herself as a fashion designer, and friends like Sidi Spreckles introduced her to high society buyers. Within months, she opened a shop and was earning $4,000 a year as a dress designer. Virginia then met Robert Moscovitz, the wealthy son of a dress-manufacturing dynasty, and became engaged for a second time. One night, as the pair left a theater, a trolley car skidded off its tracks and crashed onto the sidewalk where they were walking. Robert was pinned beneath the wreckage, his back broken. He died a few months later. Rappe, who had suffered a brain concussion after being struck by flying debris, slowly recovered. She left San Francisco in remorse, telling a friend that she would never return to a city where so much unhappiness had engulfed her. But she would return in 1921, and she would die in San Francisco at the hands of the most popular comic in America, as many would later swear through gritting teeth.

Moving to Los Angeles in 1917, Virginia went to live with her aunt, Mrs. Joan Deltag, at 504 North Wilton Place. She became morose and lost weight, dropping from her normal 125 pounds to 108. She went sleepless; dark circles swelled beneath her flashing dark eyes. As a way of explanation, Rappe told her aunt: "I'm a jinx. As soon as I love a man something terrible happens to him." The next man in her life, however, Henry Lehrman, would escape the fate of her first two lovers.

Lehrman, during a War Bond party, spotted the attractive girl and asked her to dance. The successful film director held her in his arms and said with dramatic flair: "My God, you're the most beautiful woman in the world. Your beauty reaches out and pulls me inextricably into the trap." Such a line was straight from a title card of one of Lehrman's silent movies, but it worked its charm on Rappe, who soon became the director's fiancé.

At first, Rappe worked as an extra in silent films, most of which were Lehrman's, but then she began getting small parts on her own. In early 1918, Virginia's sweet face adorned the sheet music of the widely popular song, "Let Me Call You Sweetheart," and her face was suddenly known throughout the country. Then she was named "The Best Dressed Girl in Pictures" and feature parts rolled in, followed by the starring roles. She was a success and still very much in love with Henry Lehrman.

Lehrman and Rappe planned marriage or, specifically, Rappe did. The director took her on a shopping tour of Los Angeles jewelry stores one day, purchasing gifts for her as well as an expensive tiger-eye stone surrounded by diamond chips in a death's head ring. This Lehrman bought as a birthday gift for his friend, Wallace Reid. Lehrman's extravagance led to an argument, and the director and actress briefly separated. He went to New York on business.

Virginia decided to enjoy the ensuing Labor Day weekend (Sept. 2-5, 1921) by motoring to San Francisco with her agent, Al Semnacher and his girlfriend, Bambina Maude Delmont Montgomery, a shapely unemployed actress who had recently been divorced. (Bambina was later charged with bigamy, having two husbands at the same time, James Hopper and Cassius Clay Woods, the latter an accused embezzler.)

The trio checked in to the Palace Hotel and Rappe busied herself with ordering dresses from a seamstress she knew. Roscoe Arbuckle was also in San Francisco, staying at the St. Francis with his friends, actor Lowell Sherman and director Fred Fischbach, in a suite of rooms. Arbuckle was in an expansive mood and decided to throw a party, ordering liquor from a bootlegger named Jack Lawrence and having minions like Fischbach spread the word that he wanted to see glamorous people, especially attractive women. When Fatty heard that Virginia Rappe was staying at the Palace, he asked Lowell Sherman to contact her so she would know about the party he was throwing on Sept. 5, 1921 in suite 1219-21 at the St. Francis.

At least that is one story of how the wild Arbuckle bash began. Another more sinister tale relates how Arbuckle insidiously set up the entire trip to seduce an unwitting Virginia Rappe. Leo Guild, in *The Fatty Arbuckle Case*, recalls in exacting detail how Arbuckle ran into Bambina Delmont in a drugstore and, knowing her boyfriend Semnacher was Rappe's agent, gave Delmont several hundred dollars to finance the trip to San Francisco. Arbuckle knew that Lehrman was in New York and while the director was away thought to pluck the plum he had so long coveted. Delmont, who had had several one-night stands with Arbuckle, went along with the sneaky proposition to inveigle Rappe to San Francisco on Arbuckle's promise to find a role for her in one of his forthcoming movies.

The truth of this story is as hazy as the events that took place in Arbuckle's noisy, crammed suite during the late morning of Sept. 5. It is known that Fatty and Lowell Sherman walked about the three-room suite in pajamas and bathrobes, drinking with several guests, including show girls Zey Prevon and Dollie Clark. Arbuckle looked terrible on this Monday morning. He had greeted Labor Day with sleepless, bright pink eyes and a runny nose, the side effects of too much drink and not having gone to bed since Saturday. He made constant trips to a bridge table in the center of the room which was laden with bottles of liquor and glasses as bellhops lugged ice buckets into the large reception room. (Just how much liquor was stored in Arbuckle's suite during this alcoholic revel is uncertain. One report has more than twenty gallons of hard booze constantly available through the amenable bootlegger Jack Lawrence who, in spite of its highly

Hollywood comic Fatty Arbuckle was the biggest box office attraction in the early 1920s.

Roly-poly Arbuckle was notorious for his womanizing.

Arbuckle sitting on the running board of his $25,000 Pierce-Arrow which had its own toilet and bar.

Virginia Rappe, the prettiest starlet coveted by Arbuckle; she resisted his advances repeatedly, being engaged to another.

A composite shot showing Arbuckle and Virginia; Hearst artists also did photo overlays to put a cigar in Arbuckle's mouth and a glass and bottle of gin in his hands.

Another clever Hearst composite showing Arbuckle behind bars which were superimposed over a photo of the comedian.

unlawful presence under Prohibition laws, boldly had his liquor deliveries to Arbuckle's suite brought straight through the front door of the St. Francis, employing a dozen bellboys to carry the bottle-clinking loads.)

The fat man was in a sour mood as he looked about the suite and saw that Virginia Rappe, the whole purpose of his visit to San Francisco, was not present. Lowell Sherman went into his bedroom and got dressed, suggesting that Fatty do the same, telling Arbuckle that more guests would be arriving soon. Arbuckle snorted his disdain for propriety and remained in his striped pajamas and maroon robe. He poured himself a stiff drink and turned on the heterodyne tube radio to pick up news from Los Angeles. This contraption was considered a scientific marvel in those days, a radio that could receive a signal more than 500 miles distant.

Then, impulsively, Fatty went to the phone and called Al Semnacher at the Palace Hotel, reportedly snorting to the Hollywood agent: "Well, you s.o.b.—we got a party going here. Where are you? Are the girls here?"

"The girls are here," Semnacher replied, adding that Rappe and Delmont were sleeping.

Fatty ordered Semnacher to bring the girls to his suite. "I got a lot of deadheads at this party. We need some fresh blood."

Zey Prevon was standing near to Arbuckle and quipped: "If it's blood you want, how about cutting your throat?"

Semnacher told Arbuckle that he would try to wake the girls and get them over to the party. He wasn't sure that he could convince Virginia to attend. Arbuckle told him that if he couldn't bring Virginia Rappe, he (Arbuckle) would go to the Palace and get her. He then hung up, grabbed a heavy telephone directory, and flung it angrily across the reception room of the suite.

Al Semnacher awakened Bambina and told her that it was urgent for both of their careers that she convince Virginia to go to Fatty's party. Delmont, clever woman that she was, did not mention Arbuckle's name directly to the actress, merely stating that they should visit some of the smart dress shops in the St. Francis Hotel and perhaps they could "drop by a party being held in the hotel."

"What party?" inquired Rappe.

"Oh, a lot of people from Hollywood."

Virginia shrugged and said she wanted to visit the shops. "Maybe we won't even go to the party," she said.

Once at the St. Francis shops, Virginia complained to Bambina that one of her shoes was pinching her foot. The scheming show girl saw her opportunity and said: "Why don't we look in on the party and it'll give you a chance to rest your feet?"

Rappe took the suggestion, saying that she would only stay for a few minutes. It was precisely 11:55 a.m. when Semnacher ushered Bambina and Virginia into Arbuckle's suite. Lowell Sherman greeted them, showing the trio into the spacious sitting area which, minutes before, had been cleaned and where a new bar had been set up. Fatty had shaved, but remained in his pajamas and robe. He was looking out the open window when Virginia and the others came in, his broad backside turned to their view. Suddenly he spun about, smiling his porcine smile and approached Virginia Rappe, who showed surprise at seeing him.

He nodded to Al and Bambina, then lavishly stated to Virginia: "How wonderful to see you—welcome to earthquake heaven." He turned quickly to Fred Fischbach and ordered the director to make Virginia a drink. Fischbach dutifully made a screwdriver (then called an "orange blossom"), orange juice and gin, for the actress, who sipped it as she sat down. When Arbuckle heard that a shoe was pinching her, he made a show of massaging Virginia's foot to her embarrassment.

More guests arrived; there would be at least thirty persons in the reception room and the two bedrooms as the party went into high gear. Many of these revelers were show business types, mostly show girls, including May Fellows, Mabel Pearson, Maud Parsons, Effie McMorrine, and many prominent San Francisco bigwigs. Within the hour Arbuckle noticed the liquor supply

dwindling and rang up his favorite bellhop, a young man he called "Tom-Tom," telling him to get another load of alcohol to his suite quickly. "There's no Prohibition in here," he laughed.

Dollie Clark talked with Rappe briefly about her desires to be a movie actress while Arbuckle stood by attentively, ignoring most of his other guests. At this time, the washrooms, one off each of the two bedrooms of the suite, were in constant use. The extra bottles of liquor and ice were kept in both bathrooms and, with the great amount of drinks being consumed, the guests were running back and forth between the reception room and the washrooms.

Bambina Delmont complained to Lowell Sherman that she had gotten a terrible headache from the bootleg hootch. Sherman told her that he had the perfect remedy—"tomato juice, a sure cure. We have it handy." He led her into a bathroom, poured the juice and, just as Bambina was about to drink it, Fischbach came through the half-open door, tipping the glass and spilling the contents down the front of Bambina's dress. Her scream brought several guests on the run, including a furrier's wife who was in attendance with her wealthy husband. The woman assured Delmont that she could remove the stain "with a little lemon juice and hot water."

Bambina was persuaded to remove her dress and put on Lowell Sherman's bathrobe which was several sizes too big for her, exposing much of the show girl's large breasts, while her dress was put on an open window sill to dry in the hot sun. Virginia was annoyed at having to wait for the dress to dry; she wanted to leave the party and told Semnacher so. When Arbuckle heard this, he offered the actress another drink. "No," Virginia told him. "Alcohol gets me dizzy quickly and I haven't eaten."

"I know what you're thinking," Fatty told the woman he coveted. "If I seem to be pushing drinks at you it's only because I'm a good host." He then told her he would order her some food from room service. Virginia asked for kippers and coffee.

Arbuckle ordered the food and also asked that a Victrola be sent up to the twelfth-floor suite, which was soon filled with the sounds of such popular ballads as "On the Gin Gin Ginny Shore" and "Three O'Clock in the Morning."

While couples began to dance, the fat comedian became annoyed when a tall show girl, Alice Blake, made a point of his corpulence. "You aren't so fat," she giggled.

Arbuckle pretended indifference, saying: "I'm going to take my weight down to two-fifty (from 266 pounds)." He then cracked: "But it will ruin my career." Although Arbuckle's weight was the reason for his slapstick comedy success, he secretly hated the idea of being overweight. He once told an intimate: "Nobody, but nobody likes a fat man!"

At a little after 2 p.m., the party began to thin out. Al Semnacher took Alice Blake to an afternoon rehearsal and returned in minutes. Fred Fischbach left to scout a beach area for a new movie he was directing. Alice Blake returned within a half hour to tell everyone that her rehearsal had been cancelled, and she headed with determination to the bar area.

Virginia Rappe grew more impatient to leave, constantly asking Delmont, who was getting tipsy, if her dress was still wet. Rappe turned to see Arbuckle hovering nearby. She looked at him as if for the first time and said: "Roscoe, isn't it customary that you dress a bit more formally when entertaining?"

Arbuckle looked about the room at the bevy of tippling show girls, politicians, and businessmen and sneered: "For those pigs this *is* formal wear."

"You're despicable," said Virginia Rappe and moved away, urging Bambina to get into her dress, wet or dry. The show girl was getting somewhat drunk, dancing about the room to expose her body through the gaping robe Lowell Sherman had draped about her. "I'm in no hurry," she said to Virginia. "Why don't you have some fun?"

Semnacher was taken aside by Arbuckle and they whispered momentarily. Then the agent approached Rappe and said: "Arbuckle says he's truly sorry for what he said."

"He's awful," retorted Virginia.

"Just take it easy," the agent cooed. "We'll be leaving soon."

At about 2:30 p.m. another show girl, Betty Campbell, arrived wearing a seductive, extremely low-cut gown. Lowell Sherman, a notorious Hollywood rake, made a beeline for her and promptly attempted to seduce Campbell in one of the bathrooms.

Tom-Tom the bellhop arrived with Virginia's kippers but, unseen by the actress, Arbuckle took them into the bathroom off his bedroom and put them on a shelf, winking at Fred Fischbach, who laughed at the meaning. Fischbach became quite drunk and began parading about the reception room with a lamp shade on his head, a lame gag by 1921, which no one thought funny.

Bambina Delmont was particularly unimpressed. She had had a half dozen drinks and suddenly announced to one and all: "This is a dull party!" She ran into Arbuckle's room and, minutes later, emerged wearing another set of the comedian's baggy pajamas. She bowed to the applause of the guests and then, putting on a record, went into a snaky harem dance, kicking up her heels so that the pajamas billowed and fluttered. Guests encouraged her by clapping with the beat of the music, and Delmont's dance became more and more frenetic until she appeared to be a whirling dervish, panting, sweating, then almost collapsing at the end of the dance. "It's hot," she said, wiping away the perspiration on her forehead. With that she ripped away the top of the pajamas and threw them down. She wore nothing underneath and exposed her large breasts haughtily.

Arbuckle grinned. "Okay! Now we have a real party!" he shouted.

Bambina began another dance and Fatty grabbed her and danced wildly with her, his heavy body actually shaking the furniture.

"Take it off, Fatty!" someone shouted.

"No, only the girls undress," he shouted back, still dancing with Delmont and trying to untie the strings of the pajama bottoms she wore.

Delmont pushed away his hands. "Stop that, you idiot! I've got panties on underneath and there's a hole in them."

Arbuckle spun away, pouring another drink while Delmont considered dropping the pajama bottoms in her dance, which she eventually did. One of the male guests objected and to spite him, Bambina began to lower her panties, hole and all. The male guest told her: "Keep that up and the police will be raiding this place and arrest you for indecent exposure." Bambina Delmont ignored him, further slipping down the panties and shouting to the boozy crowd: "I've got the greatest figure in the world. I'm built!"

The man slapped her in the face and the show girl stopped her striptease act, bursting into tears. Another show girl, perhaps Alice Blake, no one remembered for sure, dashed forward and slapped the man. He quickly walked to the door of the suite, saying "to hell with all of you," and went out with a slam.

Virginia Rappe wanted to leave but she had to visit the washroom first; however, every time she went to either washroom she found them occupied. At about 3:20 p.m., Rappe made another attempt, walking toward room 1221, the room occupied by Lowell Sherman. She appeared ill, woozy from the alcohol she had consumed, an estimated three drinks. Some later said that she appeared in a hypnotized state, that she had a chronic bladder problem. The bootleg booze was later blamed for Virginia's groggy condition. The bad liquor had already made several guests ill.

As Virginia walked across the reception room, Arbuckle moved quickly to her side, took her hand and whispered something, steering her into his own bedroom. Bambina Delmont, standing close by, later swore that Arbuckle said something like: "I've waited five years for this and now I've got you." He slid his hand about her waist and gave her a slight shove into the bedroom with his free hand. Oddly, Virginia voiced no objection to his manner.

Once inside the bedroom with the actress, Arbuckle turned to the other guests and winked. Then he slammed the door and locked it. At least this was the story Delmont and others later

told to police and partially supported in court. Arbuckle and his friends were later to sharply disagree. The comedian, according to this version, went into his bedroom to find Rappe kneeling on the floor of his bathroom, vomiting. He said that he picked her up, put her on his bed and watched, horrified, as she went into agonized writhing, before summoning help.

The most believable story was the first—that Arbuckle did lead Rappe into bedroom 1219, his room, and locked the door in front of several guests. The guests watched the door fascinated, imagining the assignation taking place behind it between the promising actress and the Paramount funnyman whose new contract brought him $3 million a year.

Bambina Delmont and others later claimed that instead of moans of ecstacy, what was heard within fifteen to twenty minutes were Virginia Rappe's shrieks of pain—loud piercing screams. Before the outcry—Virginia was distinctly heard to scream "I'm dying"—Bambina slipped into pajamas again and put her ear to the door. She said to Lowell Sherman standing nearby: "What are they doing in there?"

Sherman laughed and told her the couple were making love. At this time, Dollie Clark took a phone call from the desk; the manager warned her that there was too much noise coming from the suite and asked that the guests quiet down. Dollie promised that they would "bring it down to a college roar" and hung up.

Delmont, according to her later testimony to police, took off a shoe and began pounding on the door, saying: "Let me in—Arbuckle—come out of there—let her alone—she's a good girl!" Then came the screams and the words, "I'm dying, I'm dying!" Bambina later insisted that, with her ear to the door, she heard Virginia also scream: "He's killing me!"

It was plain to many of the guests that the party had taken a sour turn, that Arbuckle's conduct was not only improper but frightening. Many began to slip out of the suite, hurrying down the hall to the elevators, some even taking the stairs to the ground level.

Arbuckle refused to answer the door, apparently ignoring Delmont's persistent knocking and calling. Zey Prevon also called for him to come out, and when no response came Zey began to cry. Virginia's screaming finally subsided. Within minutes, Arbuckle opened the door, his pajamas in disarray. He was wearing Virginia Rappe's Panama hat at a crazy angle in an attempt to be funny. His fleshy face was bright pink and he dripped sweat. He walked to the open window to get some air and then gestured to the bedroom, saying: "Go in and get her dressed and take her back to the Palace. She's no fun—she makes too much noise!"

Zey and Bambina rushed into the bedroom to find Virginia frothing at the mouth. She was half lying on the bed, her clothes in disorder, and she was tearing wildly at her clothes, screaming: "I'm hurt! I'm dying! I know I'm dying!" She tore away her dress, her shirtwaist, her stockings and garters, flinging these items in all directions as she screamed, while Delmont and Prevon tried to calm her. A sleeve dangled on the frantic actress' arm and Arbuckle, who had walked back into the bedroom, tried to make light of the traumatic situation by reaching forward and tugging hard at the fragment of dress, snorting: "All right, if you want that off, I'll take it off for you!"

"Stop that, Roscoe," Zey Prevon said, pushing Fatty's arm away, "she's sick, can't you see that?"

She's not sick—just putting it on," Arbuckle huffed.

He walked casually into the reception room to talk with other nervous guests while Rappe continued screaming. Zey Prevon, Alice Blake, and Bambina Delmont, all of whom were nearly intoxicated, suggested myriad home remedies to help the distraught actress. It was thought that if she were stood on her head her pains would cease and Fred Fischbach, a large man, responded to the suggestion by jumping on the bed and grabbing Virginia by the ankles, yanking her nude body upside down. Her screams stopped momentarily, then she appeared to pass out.

Next, the women tried to revive Rappe by placing her in a tub of ice water. She was given bicarbonate of soda mixed with water, but the actress disgorged this. Ice cubes wrapped in towels were placed on her head and abdomen, which is where she said she felt the stabbing pains. Nothing worked and finally a house doctor was called.

Virginia Rappe was carried to another room of the hotel where Dr. Olav Kaarboe briefly examined her and stated to Bambina, who was by then sober, that Virginia simply had had too much to drink. But the actress' condition worsened in the ensuing hours while Arbuckle's wild party continued. At 7 p.m., Dr. Arthur Beardslee, another hotel physician, was called by Delmont. Rappe was in great pain and screaming. Dr. Beardslee examined her closely. Beardslee was later to testify: "I knew I was dealing with a surgical abdomen. It was self-evident. It was an abdomen which would require surgical interference. An operative case." Yet, strangely, the doctor prescribed no medicine, did not suggest Virginia be removed to a hospital and, in fact, did absolutely nothing for her.

Virginia went through excruciating pain, unable to keep down any of the food given to her. The next day, she was half out of her mind. A nurse, Jean Jameson, was called in to care for the actress. At one point, the nurse was later to testify, the actress became lucid and told her that Arbuckle had raped her. "She thought Arbuckle had thrown himself upon her," Jameson later said.

For two more days, Virginia Rappe lay in a bed in the St. Francis Hotel. Another doctor, Melville Rumwell, who had examined Rappe several times, acted in the manner of his predecessors. He did nothing for the girl. This kind of medical indifference caused nurse Vera Cumberland (who had replaced nurse Jameson) to quit her post. She stated that the conduct of the doctors was inexcusable. (It was later claimed that the physicians had been paid off by Arbuckle or his friends or studio bosses to allow Virginia to quietly die). Cumberland also stated later that Rappe who had bruises on her arms and legs, said that Arbuckle had sexually assaulted her. She was replaced by a third nurse, Martha Hamilton. Not until Sept. 8, when Virginia's condition deteriorated drastically, did Dr. Rumwell order her removed to the Wakefield Sanatorium, but it was hopeless. Virginia Rappe, while her close friend Sidi Spreckles held her in her arms, died on Sept. 9, 1921 at 1:30 p.m. The cause of death was ambiguously listed by Dr. Rumwell, who later stated that a bag of pus had been ruptured and this had caused inflammation and poisoning of the actress' system. The pus may have been the result of gonorrhea, yet Virginia denied ever having any such venereal disease.

Arbuckle's supporters later proposed an impossible theory of what really caused Virginia Rappe's death—nothing, of course, that had anything to do with the lascivious comic. The actress, insisted the comedian's boosters, had died of an illegal abortion. She was pregnant at the time of the party and complications had set in during her consumption of *three* drinks, which is why she was finally removed to Wakefield, a maternity hospital. Wakefield did specialize in maternity cases but was also a general hospital in close proximity to the St. Francis Hotel; it had been chosen by Dr. Rumwell merely as a matter of convenience.

Medically it was almost a certainty, according to the later testimony of physicians, that external pressure had caused mortal injuries to Virginia Rappe which resulted in her death. Her bladder was distended by her intake of alcohol at the party, and she could not relieve herself since the bathrooms in the suite were constantly occupied. Her bladder, officials later stated, was ruptured by the heavyset Arbuckle when he raped her. (Arbuckle was cited as having attacked Virginia *twice* or more, and then sadistically using a bottle on her.)

A postmortem operation was conducted on Virginia Rappe, and it was easily determined that her bladder, which was removed and placed in a specimen jar, had been ruptured and that she had died of peritonitis.

On the day of this autopsy, Roscoe "Fatty" Arbuckle was in Los Angeles. He had taken the steamer *Harvard* back to his home town. Before leaving San Francisco on Thursday, Sept. 8, the day before Virginia Rappe's death, he placed a call to Bambina Delmont and asked how Virginia was doing.

"She is very ill," replied Bambina. "I'm praying."

"I'm leaving for Los Angeles tomorrow morning," he told her. "Virginia will be all right. If anything goes wrong, you have my number. Call me. Send all the bills to Anger." (Lou Anger was Arbuckle's agent; Anger took twenty percent of the comedian's fat income instead of the usual ten percent. Anger spent as much time paying off for Fatty's sexual indiscretions in the past as he had negotiating Arbuckle's handsome studio contracts.)

On the Friday of Virginia Rappe's death, Roscoe received a call from Sid Grauman. His newest film, *Gasoline Gus*, had opened days before at Grauman's Egyptian Theater to critical raves, and it had just broken all box office records. Fatty was elated. He held a conference that afternoon with Paramount executive James Cruze to plan his next big movie.

The report of the autopsy of Rappe's corpse was released, and soon San Francisco reporters had the full but varied story of the wild Arbuckle party at the St. Francis. Bambina Delmont was tracked down by newsmen. She was still at the St. Francis, suffering from nervous exhaustion, but she held an interview while in bed. She told her story of how Arbuckle took Rappe into his room and attacked her. "Virginia was a good girl and I know that she had led a clean life." Bambina sobbed. "I know it is my duty to see this thing through."

"What kind of man is Roscoe Arbuckle to do what you say he did?" one reporter queried.

"The brute!" yelled Delmont. "I don't see why such men are permitted to live." Within hours the press screamed its blearing headlines—trumpet calls that heralded the end of Fatty's posh Hollywood career and announced the most sordid scandal ever to come out of the sexual cesspool that was then Hollywood. "FATTY ARBUCKLE SOUGHT IN ORGY DEATH" was only one of the headlines electrifying readers across the nation. The Hearst press became particularly vicious in its attacks on Arbuckle as months went by.

It was 10:30 p.m., Friday night, Sept. 9, 1921, when Arbuckle's butler answered the door of Fatty's mansion and was overrun by a host of yelling Los Angeles reporters. Fatty put down the script for his next movie, which he had been reading in his well-stocked library, and went into the reception area. "Boys, boys," he said with a broad smile. "What in hell's name is going on?"

They barraged Fatty with questions, while telling him that Virginia Rappe had died and that Bambina Delmont, Alice Blake, and others attending his party had accused him of raping and killing the actress.

"Did you rape her outright or did she lead you on?" asked one reporter.

"Who was at the orgy you gave?"

"It's being said that you paid off the San Francisco police, doctors, everybody, to keep this thing quiet. What about it?"

Arbuckle was at first stunned. His florid face flushed dark red as he stood before the reporters petrified. Then, slowly, he explained how he had driven up to San Francisco in his $25,000 custom-built Pierce Arrow with Fred Fischbach and Lowell Sherman, and he detailed his activities on Saturday and Sunday. He then said that there had been no wild party, only a few friends getting together socially and having a few drinks (ignoring the fact that Prohibition was in effect and that he had flagrantly broken the law.) He then presented an entirely fabricated story, a boldface lie, of the events in San Francisco: "Shortly before noon Monday, a friend of Mr. Fischbach's, with us in the apartment, remarked that he had seen Miss Rappe at the Palace and desired to meet her, as he wished her to model some gowns for him. I told him that I knew her, and would make the introduction. She readily consented to come to the St. Francis.

"After meeting the man, we had a few drinks. Miss Rappe had one or two drinks. She went into the other room of the apartment

Arbuckle at his first trial, seated, with his lawyer Frank Dominguez; the overweight lawyer was selected so that Arbuckle would not look so obese.

Arbuckle testifying for his life; the bedroom door from his hotel suite is propped up behind his chair.

Arbuckle and lawyer Dominguez only moments before he was charged with murder.

Bambina Maude Delmont, star witness against Arbuckle in the Rappe case.

Fatty working as a director of short subjects, his before-camera career ruined; he used the alias of William Goodrich for his directorial credits.

and began tearing her clothes from her body and screaming." (Roscoe could not recall the name of the friend and, as time went by, his memory of the San Francisco debacle grew dimmer and dimmer until he had changed his story in court at least four times.)

"The other woman (Zey Prevon)," Fatty went on, regaining his composure, "and Miss Delmont, and a companion (Alice Blake) rushed into the room. They put Miss Rappe into a tub of cold water. She cried out that gas had formed around her heart (this was never heard by anyone), that she couldn't breathe. I engaged another room in the hotel and moved her there. Then a physician was called; after he had reported that she had quieted down, Mr. Sherman and I went into the dining room and danced the rest of the evening."

To explain Bambina's vitriolic attacks in naming him as the cause of Virginia's death, Arbuckle said: "Miss Delmont came back into my room after Miss Rappe was put to bed and began to get hilarious. I chased her out and suppose she is sore at me for that."

The attacks on Delmont's credibility would increase, and decades later it was claimed that the show girl had set up Arbuckle, tried to blackmail him for a crime he never committed and, when he refused to pay off, vengefully charged him with raping and murdering Virginia Rappe when the actress had merely died of a chronic bladder disorder. All of this was and is nonsense. Bambina and the other show girls had nothing whatsoever to gain and everything to lose by attacking the most affluent comedian in America at the time and incurring the wrath of his powerful millionaire bosses who could be counted on to go to any length to protect Fatty's career and their very lucrative investment—his films.

Arbuckle's statements to the press first mollified officials and the news community, but the next day two San Francisco theater managers quietly replaced two successful Arbuckle films with two other movies. It was a subtle move that would change to a landslide within months.

To cover himself, Arbuckle was advised by Paramount executives to contact the San Francisco police. He called and was asked to return to the Bay city for routine questioning. Early Saturday morning, Sept. 10, 1921, Arbuckle, his agent Lou Anger, his lawyer Frank Dominguez and, oddly enough, Rappe's agent, Al Semnacher, got into Fatty's Pierce-Arrow and began the long drive up the Coast highway. (Semnacher's presence, commanded by movie moguls, was window dressing, making it appear that if Virginia's agent was at Arbuckle's side at this time, the comedian was guiltless.)

By the time the party reached the Hall of Justice in San Francisco on Saturday night, mass hysteria over "the beast" Arbuckle had been whipped up by the local press. The comedian was greeted angrily by four detectives and two assistant district attorneys, Milton U'ren and Isador Golden. Dominguez, the lawyer, was physically kept away from his client, Arbuckle, who was removed to a private room where, for three hours, he was mercilessly grilled, city attorneys waving statements signed by Bambina Delmont and Alice Blake, among others, in front of Fatty's nose. The unnerved comedian was finally allowed to step outside into the hall where his lawyer cautioned him to remain silent. Then, while an army of reporters and news photographers hovered with cameras ready, city attorney U'ren burst through a door and pointed his finger at Arbuckle, thundering: "You are under arrest on a charge of murder!"

Minutes later the assistant D.A. told the press: "Roscoe Arbuckle had been charged under that section of the penal code that provides that a life taken in a rape or attempted rape is considered murder."

To this, Duncan Matheson, San Francisco chief of detectives, added: "Neither I nor Mr. U'ren nor Chief of Police (Daniel) O'Brien feel that any man, whether he be Fatty Arbuckle or anyone else, can come into this city and commit that kind of offense. The evidence shows that an attack was made on the girl."

At that moment, Arbuckle was on the fifth floor, where the 34-year-old comedian was booked on a charge of first-degree murder. He was then placed in Cell 12 and the key was turned. The onslaught against Fatty increased in tempo when film director Henry Lehrman, grief-stricken at the death of his fiancé, consented to meet with New York reporters at 25 West 51st Street where he was staying on business when news reached him that Virginia Rappe had died in San Francisco.

Lehrman had received reports of the St. Francis party from some who had been in attendance and from Sidi Spreckles. He had read the newspaper accounts, and by the time he faced thirty or more reporters he was livid with rage against the comedian, shouting: "I could not face Arbuckle! I would kill him! If he wants to live he had better be punished." Lehrman, who was walking about the room as he talked, suddenly stopped and flashed his cufflinks in the reporters' faces. They read an inscription which stated: "To Henry. My first and last sacred love. Virginia."

Dabbing his eyes with a handkerchief, the director was asked if he was about to go to California to take a closer look at the case. "My prayer is that justice be done. I don't want to go to the Coast now. I could not face Arbuckle." He held up a signed photo of Virginia Rappe and a copy of an affidavit of Jean Jameson, the nurse who said she heard Virginia charge Fatty with raping her. "She said she blamed Arbuckle for her injuries and wanted him punished," said the director.

He then became weighted down with the thought of Virginia's death, sighing: "That is just like Virginia. She had the most remarkable determination. She would rise from the dead to defend her person from indignity. Before she died, she kept on saying, 'Don't tell Henry, don't tell Henry.' That means one thing. She had lost the battle she made to defend herself."

Someone made the mistake of asking Lehrman what he personally thought of the comedian. Raged the director: "Arbuckle is a beast! I directed him for a year-and-a-half. I finally had to tell him if he didn't keep out of the women's dressing room, I would see that he was through. He boasted to me that he had torn the clothing from an unwilling girl and outraged her...That's what comes of taking vulgarians from the gutter and giving them enormous salaries and making idols of them. Arbuckle came into the pictures nine years ago. He was a bar boy in a San Francisco saloon. Not a bartender, a bar boy—one of those who wash glasses and clean cuspidors.

"Such people don't know how to get a kick out of life, except in a beastly way. They are a disgrace to the film business. They are the ones that resort to cocaine and the opium needle and who participate in orgies that surpass the orgies of degenerate Rome. They should be swept out of the motion picture business!"

Lehrman paused dramatically, then, after stating how he had not left his New York hotel suite since receiving the wire announcing his fiancé's death, he warned the newsmen: "Arbuckle has powerful friends, and much influence and money will be used to save him." As if taking a cue from one of his own melodramas, Lehrman sank to his knees in front of the newsmen, clasped his hands together, and gazed pleadingly upward while tears welled in his eyes. He said: "God, give me justice!"

The Lehrman interview swept the country into a violent anti-Arbuckle mood and few comedians dared to publicly make a stand for him. Mack Sennett gave a press interview in which he pointed to Fatty's high moral character. Said Sennett: "I never knew him to be mixed up in any brawls or to do an ungentlemanly thing toward any girl. He was a kind, good-natured fat man and a good comic." The slip Sennett made in this statement was obvious to the most unsophisticated reporter. He used the word *was*, putting Fatty's career and character in the past tense.

Undoubtedly, Sennett and Sid Grauman and others who attempted to come to Fatty's rescue had millions involved in Arbuckle's films and their statements were logically mixtures of personal loyalty and box office profits. Adolf Zukor, head of Paramount, and other movie potentates, however, had already written Fatty off when the news of the San Francisco party exploded into headlines. At first the studio went ahead, releasing Arbuckle's latest films, but the protest against Fatty, coming from women's groups and the clergy across the land, grew to a thunder-clapping storm that demanded his career be obliterated. He was a blight on the minds of the children who had laughed at his comedies, a national disgrace, this lascivious beast who hid behind the clown's mask. Arbuckle's films were cancelled, present and future films dumped, scrapped. Paramount later paid him off, giving Fatty part of the money due him under his contract.

While awaiting trial, Fatty was pilloried by the newspapers which reported his hideous conduct, and gossip mongers stated that he had used a champagne or Coca-Cola bottle not once, but twice, on his victim and that he had also employed a jagged piece of ice. Later, during the first Arbuckle trial, Assistant District Attorney U'Ren was to scoff at the defense counsel's portrait of Arbuckle as a simple comic who was innocent of the charges; a simple comic who made the children of America laugh. "Oh, if the children of America could have seen Roscoe Arbuckle put ice in the private parts of Virginia Rappe," U'Ren had intoned sarcastically, "how they and their mothers would have laughed with glee! Oh, my friends, this man who makes the world laugh—who makes the world laugh. Thank God, he will never make the world laugh again."

There were three trials in all, the first beginning on Nov. 18, 1921, when Fatty went on trial for rape-murder. The district attorney, Matthew Brady, stated at the onset that "powerful influences are working behind the scenes on my witnesses. Bribery is rampant." He related how Paramount chief Adolf Zukor had called him, telling him he had millions at stake in the case, and asked that the case be quashed. Brady reported that he had hung up on Zukor. Other millionaire Hollywood producers tried vainly to reduce the murder charge to manslaughter, Brady said, but to no avail.

Much of Brady's claims seemed to be supported when examining the conduct of the state's three witnesses. Bambina Delmont never took the witness stand, despite the fact that she was the complaining witness, although her affidavit damning Arbuckle was read in court. Alice Blake and Zey Prevon's testimonies became weaker and weaker through all three of the Arbuckle trials, from 1921 through 1922. Officials in the district attorney's office told the press that the witnesses were being bought off and that some of the jurors were being bribed. The first trial ended with a hung jury, with ten jurors in favor of acquittal and two against. A mistrial was declared. A second trial had the jurors in favor of conviction, ten to two. A third trial resulted in acquittal, but the hard-fought battle had cost Arbuckle his mansion on Adams Street in Los Angeles and his fleet of expensive roadsters. His lawyer's fees—defense counsels had mounted what the press termed "a million dollar defense"—had obliterated the fat man's bank accounts.

By the time Arbuckle walked free from court, he was a forgotten man. His films were banished and those intrepid souls who dared to show an Arbuckle film risked riot. One Wyoming theater-owner who showed an Arbuckle comedy was attacked by dozens of cowboys who stormed into his theater, some on horseback, shot up the screen, and ruined the theater.

Fatty mistakenly believed that he would be able to return to films after his third trial. The jurors of this trial put together a statement read by their foreman: "Acquittal is not enough for Roscoe Arbuckle. We feel that a great injustice had been done him. We feel it was only our plain duty to give him that exonera-tion, under the evidence, for there was not the slightest proof adduced to connect him in any way with the commission of the crime." The statement could have been written by Paramount's publicity department. Arbuckle's attitude was one of jubilation and triumph. All would be forgotten and he could get on with his multi-million dollar career, he undoubtedly thought when he issued his own statement: "I deeply appreciate the clear picture my legal counsel prepared for the jury and I thank the jurors from the bottom of my heart for their verdict. As for the American public, I pray they will accept the verdict as my vindication."

The American public did not accept Arbuckle as being innocent. Even though the state had failed to provide enough evidence against him, particularly in the form of eyewitnesses who drastically changed their stories, the verdict only meant that Arbuckle could not be proven guilty on the evidence available. He was nevertheless universally condemned.

Jesse Lasky and other Paramount executives called Arbuckle to a meeting at the studio some days after his acquittal. They were frightened, Lasky explained, of going ahead with any of Fatty's movies, at least for the moment. Lasky suggested Arbuckle take a three- or four-month European tour, a vacation "to let things die down." Arbuckle reluctantly agreed, but it proved to be a mistake. His absence from the U.S. and the screen only reaffirmed in the minds of his eighty million fans that his studio did not believe him innocent. He lost his following in droves.

Paramount spent a good deal of money trying to untarnish Fatty's image, establishing Arbuckle Day in places like Mount Vernon, N.Y. These celebrations were filmed, but most of those cheering encouragement were local people paid as extras.

When Fatty did return to Los Angeles he gave a lavish party for the movie community and bigwigs and stars turned out in great numbers. Even Marion Davies, the mistress of William Randolph Hearst, was in attendance to toast his health and wish him well, ironic in that Hearst had turned his papers loose on Arbuckle in an obvious attempt to wreck his career.

In spite of its show of support, the Hollywood hierarchy turned its back on Arbuckle. Will Hays was appointed by studio heads to clean up Hollywood's image inside of films and out. The Hays office, largely established because of Fatty's tainted conduct, became sort of a censorship board of what could or could not appear in films. Its influence spread throughout the community, unofficially regulating the private conduct of those who made millions via the silver screen.

When Paramount dumped Fatty, he began directing grade B films under the alias of William Goodrich, using his father's first and middle names, to earn a living. His close friend, Buster Keaton, one of the few who remained loyal to him during his long slide downward, suggested humorously that Fatty use the alias of "Will B. Good." Fatty did not laugh. Nobody laughed at the roly-poly comic for eleven years, until Warner Brothers signed him up to do some short comedies. These shorts were released in 1933, but no one found Fatty funny anymore. His brand of slapstick humor had long ago faded.

Arbuckle slipped even further, being arrested several times for drunk driving. On one occasion, he reportedly tossed a bottle from his car and laughed at the approaching cop with the line "there goes the evidence." It was claimed that he had thrown the bottle he had used on Virginia Rappe out of the twelfth floor of the St. Francis Hotel during the night of the wild party, a bottle, incidentally, Dashiell Hammett, as a Pinkerton agent assigned to the case at the time, took months to look for without success. (The Pinkerton Agency had been hired by the defense to dig up dirt on Virginia Rappe and her friends. Hammett, out of curiosi-ty, rooted about looking for clues and evidence that might prove the comedian guilty, although he later publicly stated that they thought Arbuckle was being framed by the local authorities. His attitude at the time of his investigation was that of a bemused spectator. At one point, Hammett was sitting in the lobby of the Plaza, when the comedian, going through his second trial, entered the hotel. "He came into the lobby," Hammett later wrote. "He looked at me and I at him. His eyes were the eyes of a man who expected to be regarded as a monster but he was not yet inured to it. I made my gaze as contemptuous as I could. He glared at me, went to the elevator still glaring.")

On the night of June 28, 1933, Roscoe Fatty Arbuckle ate dinner with some friends and his third wife, Addie McPhail (his second marriage to Doris Deane ended in divorce when he failed to make a comeback). He and Addie returned to their hotel room and Arbuckle slid beneath the sheets laughing uproariously about some joke told earlier at dinner. He fell silent. The 46-year-old comedian was pronounced dead of a heart attack at 2:15 a.m. the following morning.

Arbuckle's body lay in state at Campbell's Funeral Parlor in New York, the same establishment that had held services for Rudolph Valentino some years earlier when thousands of flappers came to near riot in their grief over losing The Great Lover. Strangely enough, many thousands filed past Fatty's flower-covered bier, the largest audience he had drawn in a decade. In its obituary of the comic, The New York Herald-Tribune inquired: "Did Roscoe Arbuckle rape and murder Virginia Rappe in a Hotel St. Francis room in San Francisco? We don't know. But if he didn't, life gave him a raw deal."

What life did to the dead Virginia Rappe was much worse. She was labeled a whore and slut by Fatty's defense lawyers at his trials. As Arbuckle slowly inched forward into a cult comic long years after his death, the image of Virginia Rappe blurred into utter obscurity; she was only a "difficulty" Fatty once encountered. Vilified in death, then forgotten, was the fate of Virginia Rappe who received no deal, fair or otherwise, from the living.

REF.: Anger, *Hollywood Babylon;* Blesh, *Keaton;* Brownlow, *The Parade's Gone By;* Canfield, *God in Hollywood;* Cantor, *My Life Is In Your Hands;* Carr, *Hollywood Tragedy;* CBA; Chaplin, *My Autobiography;* Durgnant, *The Crazy Mirror: Hollywood Comedy and the American Image;* Edmonds, *Hollywood R.I.P.;* Fowler, *Father Goose: The Story of Mack Sennett;* ____, *Goodnight, Sweet Prince: The Life and Times of John Barrymore;* Gifford, *Chaplin;* Gish, *The Movies, Mr. Griffith and Me;* Goldwyn, *Behind the Screen;* Goodman, *The Fifty Year Decline and Fall of Hollywood;* Green and Laurie, *Show Biz;* Guild, *The Fatty Arbuckle Case;* Guiles, *Marion Davies;* Gussow, *Don't Say Yes Until I Finish Talking: A Biography of Darryl F. Zanuck;* Hays, *The Memoirs of Will Hays;* Johnson, *Dashiell Hammett, A Life;* Keaton, *My Wonderful World of Slapstick;* Lahue, *Clown Princes and Court Jesters: Some Great Comics of the Silent Screen;* ____, *Dreams for Sale: The Rise and Fall of the Triangle Film Corporation;* ____, *Kops and Custards: The Legend of Keystone Films;* ____, *Mack Sennett's Keystone: The Man, the Myth and the Comedies;* ____, *Motion Picture Pioneer: The Selig Polyscope Company;* Lasky, *I Blow My Own Horn;* Lee, *Those Scandalous Sheets of Hollywood;* Loos, *A Girl Like I;* MacGowan, *Behind the Screen;* Milner, *Sex on Celluloid;* Nolan, *Hammett;* Nuetzel, *Whodunit? Hollywood Style;* O'Dell, *Griffith and the Rise of Hollywood;* Radin, *Crimes of Passion;* Randall, *Censorship of the Movies;* Robinson, *The Great Funnies;* ____, *Hollywood in the Twenties;* St. Johns, *Final Verdict;* Sann, *The Lawless Decade;* Scott, *The Concise Encyclopedia of Crime and Criminals;* Sennett and Shipp, *King of Comedy;* Thomas, *Selznick;* ____, *Thalberg;* Yallop, *The Day the Laughter Stopped;* Zukor, *The Public is Never Wrong.*

Archdeacon of Stow, (AKA: **Canon and Precentor of Lincoln Cathedral**), prom. 1920, Brit., adult. In the spring of 1920 the cathedral town of Peterborough, England, was scandalized by the behavior of the esteemed Archdeacon of Stow, who was observed by several eyewitnesses to have engaged in an adulterous union at the Bull Hotel. He was cast out of his many holy offices and publicly ostracized by the church hierarchy.

At the time, the 61-year-old churchman and father of several children was highly regarded by his parishioners. The woman seen with him was wearing a blue dress, but no one could say with certainty who she was. The Archdeacon would say only that the woman was an invention of his enemies, the Vicar of Appleby Magna and the Rector of Nether Seale, men who had been trying to destroy him for years. The court found him Guilty of adultery.

REF.: CBA; Pearson, *More Studies in Murder.*

Archer, C.E., See: **Great Gold Robbery, The.**

Archer Brothers, prom. 1880s, U.S., west. outl. The Archer Brothers of Indiana were the scourage of Orange and Marion counties for several decades, bandits who regularly robbed stagecoaches, trains, and travelers, escaping back to their homes where relatives and friends protected them against arrest. The Archer clan operted in much the same fashion as had the Reno Brothers of Indiana two decades earlier, robbing when low on

funds, then resuming the ostensibly respectable roles of farmers and shopkeepers. The nominal leader of the holdup gang was Thomas Archer and his brothers included Morton, John, and Samuel. All four brothers were finally caught by possemen in March 1886. Vigilantes hanged Tom, Mort, and John without trial. Sam Archer, the youngest of the gang, was held for trial and, following a speedy conviction for robbery and murder, was officially hanged on July 10, 1886. See: **Reno Brothers.**

REF.: Bartholomew, *The Biographical Album of Western Gunfighters;* CBA.

Archer-Gilligan, Amelia (AKA: **Sister Amy**), 1869-1928, U.S., mur. Archer-Gilligan, or Sister Amy, as she was called by the charges of her nursing home in Windsor, Conn., was a marrying murderer who had the dubious distinction of being blessed by the unwitting relatives of her victims. Establishing a nursing home in Windsor in 1901, Archer-Gilligan began taking in old men whom she promptly married after their wills had been signed over to her. Five of these unsuspecting elderly gentlemen perished soon after the nuptials, all of them poisoned, it was later determined, over a period of fourteen years. In addition to these victims, Sister Amy also murdered at least a dozen other persons, elderly women who were entrusted to her nursing home, but only after each had drawn up new wills which made her the sole beneficiary. Relatives incredibly approved of such measures after listening to Sister Amy tell them that it was the only way in which she could be compensated for taking care of the old people since her monthly rates were bargain cheap. Of course, the patients did not live long enough to cause a severe drain on Sister Amy's coffers. Usually a new patient at Sister Amy's home lasted but a few short months before Archer-Gilligan helped them into eternity by poisoning their food. A few she suffocated with pillows and chalked up their deaths to heart failure, the death certificates signed by a senile doctor who merely wrote down the causes of death as Sister Amy described them.

This convenient murder factory became suspect when a relative learned that an elderly aunt had died only a few days after she had been placed in Sister Amy's home and only hours after the woman's will had been signed over to Sister Amy. The relative did some investigating and then went to officials to prove that the death rate at the Archer-Gilligan home was ten times higher than at other homes for the aged. Police placed an undercover agent in the home who witnessed the scheming Sister Amy administering poison to some of the patients. Archer-Gilligan was arrested by the policewoman and was tried and convicted of murder in 1914, sent to Weathersfield Prison to serve a life term. She began to have nervous fits and, after she tried to poison the warden and several turnkeys, Sister Amy Archer-Gilligan was sent to an insane asylum, kept in a padded, locked cell until 1928 when she died.

REF.: CBA; Furneaux, *The Medical Murderer;* Hynd, *Murder, Mahem and Mystery;* Nash, *Look for the Woman;* Robinson, *Science Catches the Criminal;* Smith, *Famous American Poison Mysteries;* Wilson, *Encyclopedia of Murder.*

Archer-Shee, George, 1895-1914, Case of, Brit., rob. In 1908, George Archer-Shee was a 13-year-old schoolboy at the Royal Naval College at Osborne on the Isle of Wight. He came from a distinguished family whose aim it was to have George serve as a Navy officer. The boy was handsome, bright, and polite and nothing in his past suggested a criminal bent. Yet, George was accused of stealing a five shilling postal order from the locker of another cadet, Terence Back, and cashing it at the school's post office where clerk Clara Tucker handled the transaction. The boy was summarily dismissed from the school following a brief investigation. His father, Martin Archer-Shee, a respected banker, could not believe his son was a thief and traveled to Osborne to confront his son before removing him from the college as authorities had requested. Archer-Shee, ac-companied by George's half-brother, Major Martin, met with the boy and asked him if he had stolen the postal order. George did not hesitate to give his father a positive "no." The was enough for Martin Archer-Shee.

Although the boy had to be removed from the school, Martin

Archer-Shee hired one of the most famous legal minds in England and Ireland, Sir Edward Carson, to seek justice for his son. Carson, after battling to prove that Archer-Shee had the right to a trial (not as a servant of the Crown being enrolled at the Royal Naval College but as a citizen of England), took the case to the King's Bench Division of the High Court where he argued against the equally brilliant Sir Rufus Isaacs who sought to prevent exoneration of George Archer-Shee. If the boy was innocent, the Admiralty had itself faltered and wrongly accused a helpless youth, the kind of tyrannical act that could disgrace the government itself. Carson, during the hearing, tactfully defended his young client while gently interrogating Clara Tucker, the postmistress who admitted to him that "all these cadets were very much alike." In short, she could not identify the youth who had

The falsely accused British Naval cadet, George Archer-Shee.

cashed the postal order, and there were no real grounds for George's dismissal. After an exhausting battle with Isaacs, the representative of the government rose in his chair and addressed the bench. Said Isaacs, "I say now on behalf of the Admiralty that I accept the statement of George Archer-Shee that he did not write the name on the postal order, and did not cash it, and consequently that he is innocent."

This was one of Edward Carson's greatest victories, a moral triumph in that he had taken on the government itself and caused the powerful Admiralty to admit that it had maligned an innocent boy by rashly and unfairly judging him guilty out of hand. The boy's badly mauled reputation was restored and he was wholly vindicated, although he had lost two years schooling and did not reapply to the Royal Naval College. The government awarded his father £7120 compensation for costs. George Archer-Shee lived only another four years, volunteering for duty when England went into WWI. He was one of the first to fall, killed at the tender age of nineteen on the bloody battlefield at Ypres. The Rattigan play, based on George Archer-Shee, is somewhat misleading in that it injects a suspicion of the boy's guilt after the court has pronounced him innocent, which certainly was not true in the real case.

REF.: CBA; Woollcott, Long, Long Ago; (DRAMA) Rattigan, The Winslow Boy; (FILM) The Winslow Boy, 1950.

Arcine, James, (James Arcene), d.1885, and **Parchmeal, William,** U.S., rob.-mur. To avoid the gallows James Arcine told the presiding judge at Fort Smith, Ark., that he was only ten years old when he shot and killed Henry Feigel, a Swedish laborer. If true, Arcine is the only person in the United States to be executed for a crime committed when he was so young. Arcine and a friend, William Parchmeal, were Cherokee Indians living near the U.S. Army base at Fort Smith. On Nov. 25, 1872, Henry Feigel set out from Talequah, capital of the Cherokee Nation, en route to Fort Gibson. He carried all he owned over his shoulder and just 25 cents in his pocket.

Two miles out of town Feigel was overtaken by Arcine who fired four bullets into him before finishing the job with a large stone. Parchmeal later claimed he stood helplessly by, fearing Arcine would kill him if he intervened. The killer removed Feigel's boots which had been half-soled before he set out on his ill-fated hike. Arcine later would boast that he had stolen them from a dead man. Feigel's body was found in a thicket the next day. Though Arcine and Parchmeal were strongly suspected, no arrests were made and the affair was forgotten for the next thirteen years.

In 1884 the case attracted the attention of Deputy U.S. Marshal Andrews, who uncovered new evidence that established their guilt. After his arrest, Arcine told the authorities that he was thirty-three years old, which appears to be true. Parchmeal confessed to Andrews and led him to the exact spot where the killing had occurred. His attempt to secure leniency from the court failed. Parchmeal's confession had only served to place the noose squarely around his and Arcine's necks. An appeal was made directly to President Chester Arthur, who refused them clemency. June 26, 1885 was set as the date of execution. The two convicted murderers prayed and sang in the Cherokee language up to the minute they were led to the gallows. REF.: CBA.

Ardashir III (Artaxerxes III), 621-30, Per., king, assass. Elevated to the throne at the age of seven in 628 after the assassination of Khosrau II. Assassinated at the age of nine. REF.: CBA.

Arden, Alice, 1516-51, Brit., mur. Though born into bluebloods, Alice Arden conducted her private life like a common streetwalker. Arden was the stepdaughter of Sir Edward North whose father had won world renown as the translator of Plutarch. Her husband, Thomas Arden was wealthy and of the gentleman class who gave his wife every comfort, moving her into a large mansion in Faversham, England, in 1544. Alice, however, betrayed his trust at every opportunity to see her lover, Richard Mosby (or Mosbie), a lowly tailor who had once been a servant in the North household and who had maintained a sexual liaison with Alice since seducing her when she was but a teenager. Arden, on the other hand, was a man twice her age, one who was retiring and considerably less passionate than the interloper Mosby. Alice tired of her husband and made plans to kill him so that she could spend the rest of her days with the ardent Mosby.

Unlike most wives with murder on their minds, Alice Arden made no secret of her desire to get rid of her husband. She solicited ideas from known enemies of Thomas Arden. There were many. One such was a painter named Clark who proposed that he paint Alice on a large canvas, this portrait to hang in Arden's bedroom. He would temper the oil with poison and when Arden retired he would breath in the poison fumes emanating from the canvas and die in his sleep. The fumes would be gone by morning, Clark promised, and thus the murder weapon would vanish. Alice told Clark that such a plan was to risky. A servant might enter the room and breath the fumes or she herself might die of the deadly oils while sitting for the portrait. No, Clark's plan would not do. She preferred a more direct approach. Alice went to a man named Green who hated Thomas Arden since having been bested in a land dispute. Alice offered him £10 if he would provide two men who would kill her husband. Green, in turn, hired two local Faversham ruffians named Shakebag and Black Will to perform the deed. On Feb. 15, 1551, Mosby invited Thomas Arden to a game of backgammon, making sure that the victim's back was to a large closet. (Shakebag and Black Will had been hiding in Arden's huge mansion for some time with Alice providing them with food and drink until the opportunity to kill her husband presented itself.) As Arden and Mosby began playing, Mosby suddenly shouted, "And now, sir, I may take you if I will!"

"Take me which way?" replied Arden, puzzled at the sudden outburst, not realizing that this was the signal to the assassins to strike. Black Will leaped from the closet and began to strangle Arden with a towel. Mosby grabbed a heavy pressing iron and brought this down upon Arden's head several times. He fell dead to the floor and the killers, aided by a servant named Michael, dragged the body into the counting room. He came to life again and Black Will smashed him on the head, a killing blow. But Alice Arden wanted to make sure. She rushed into the room with a long knife and plunged this several times into her husband's chest. The body was then taken out into a nearby field and left there. Alice then sent out word by some servants to the local townspeople that her husband had not returned to dinner and that

154

she was worried that he might have been attacked by highwaymen which were then plaguing the area. Villagers carrying torches conducted a search of the fields and Arden's body was discovered hacked to pieces.

Alice was confident that the local authorities would conclude that Arden had been the victim of highwaymen. She neglected to see, however, that her plan was impossible from the beginning due to its inept execution. Bloody carpet hairs covered the shoes of the victim and a trail of blood led from the mansion to the garden. It was obvious to the local mayor that Arden had not been killed on the lonely road but inside his own house and his body dragged outside. A search of the grounds around the mansion unearthed the bloody towel and knife used to murder Arden. The Mayor bluntly told Alice that he suspected her of having a hand in her husband's demise. Alice became indignant, replying archly, "I would you should know that I am no such woman!"

Alice Arden and cohorts murdering her husband, 1551.

Then the Mayor showed her the bloody towel and the gore-coated knife. Alice Arden trembled for a moment in silence, then confessed to the murder, dramatically taking the bloody towel and pressing it to her face, moaning, "Oh, the blood of God, help for this blood that I shed!" Mosby was found in his room, pretending to be asleep. He was awakened and accused of the killing. Boldly he denied committing the crime which was equally stupid in that his hose and purse were still covered with his victim's blood. Green, the man who had supplied the killers, fled with Black Will and Shakebag. Black Will was captured near Flushing and hanged. Shakebag, who had only stood by as a lookout during the murder, was hunted down near Southwark and run through by swords in the hands of his pursuers. The killing of a high born person in England at that time was intolerable and the rage of the authorities was expressed by wholesale arrests and executions, even of the innocent such as one of Alice Arden's maidservants who was burned at the stake. George Bradshaw, who had carried messages between Alice and Mosby, not knowing their contents, was seized and instantly hanged. Adam Fowl, who ran a local inn, the Fleur de Lys, was strapped to the underside of a horse and taken to London where he was thrown into the darkest dungeon of Marhalsea Prison. His crime had been serving two tankards of ale to Alice and Mosby when they stopped at his inn during one of their clandestine meetings.

The servant Michael was hanged in chains at Faversham while Mosby and his sister Susan, who had helped in the murder plot, were taken to Smithfield and both of them hanged at the same time. Alice Arden found no quick relief at the end of a rope. She was made into a spectacle and served as a warning to any other rebellious wives who thought to murder their husbands. She was taken to Canterbury and, after thousands of spectators had been assembled, rode to the stake in an open cart on Mar. 14, 1551. She was tied to a stake and then slowly burned to death while the great throng dinned catcalls and insults into her ears just before her torturous death.

REF.: Bierstadt, *Curious Trials and Criminal Cases*; Butler, *Murderer's England*; CBA; Nash, *Look for the Woman*.

Ardlamount Mystery, The, See: **Monson, A.J.**

Arensdorf, John, prom. 1888, Case of, U.S., mur. Reverend George C. Haddock, a fiery clergyman who had been leading a one-man anti-saloon crusade in Sioux City, Iowa, entered the saloon and brewery owned by Arensdorf on Aug. 3, 1886. He launched into a hell fire temperance speech which not only upset the startled customers but enraged Arensdorf and his employees. Suddenly, someone fired a pistol and Haddock fell dead to the barroom floor. The smoking pistol was on the bar next to Arensdorf and he was later arrested and charged with murder. In a speedy trial Arensdorf was acquitted by a jury which included a number of his regular customers. The brewer immediately adjourned to his saloon where he held a victory celebration with "drinks on the house," an event that would have added greatly to the spiritual mortification of the lately departed Reverend George Haddock.

REF.: *CBA; The Defense; Who Killed Haddock? The Famous Arensdorf Case.*

Argentine Political Violence, 1976, Arg., bomb.-mur. By year's end, the death count in Argentina stood at 1,476. A published statement from the Argentine ministry condemned the bloodshed, and attributed the year-long genocide to "the insanity of irrational groups...they want to disrupt the national peace and tranquility."

The problem began in March 1976 when a military coup ousted President Isabel Martinez de Perón. The ensuing struggle between leftist guerrillas and right-wing death squads culminated in a bloody orgy on Aug. 20, when ten bomb blasts rocked Buenos Aires, and forty-seven mangled bodies were found ten to fifteen miles outside the city. All of the victims had been gunned down execution-style, and were believed to have been rebel sympathizers.

On New Year's Eve twenty-seven guerrillas were killed in separate incidents, which brought the curtain down on the bloodiest year to date in Argentina's long and storied history. REF.: *CBA.*

Ariberto da Antimiano (AKA: Heribert of Antimiano), d.1045, Italy, archbishop, consp. Archbishop of Milan from 1018. He led his armies in the service of the Holy Roman Empire but was arrested in 1037 by Emperor Conrad II. Escaped and returned to Milan where he defied Conrad, leading to his exile from 1040-44 after a revolt of commoners. REF.: *CBA.*

Aristobulus, d.6 B.C., Palestine, treas. Heir of Herod by his second wife Marianne the Hasmonaean, he was accused of treason by his father and executed along with his brother Alexander. REF.: *CBA.*

Aristobulus III, d.42 B.C., Cappadocia, king, assass. After reigning as king from 51 B.C., he was put to death by Cassius after taking Pompey's side against Caesar. REF.: *CBA.*

Aristogiton, See: **Hipparchus.**

Arizona Rangers, 1901-10, U.S., law enfor. agency. The Arizona Rangers were formed just after the turn of the century to assist local lawmen in the state who were overwhelmed by the number of criminals infesting the state. Arizona was then making the transition from Old West traditions to modern statehood, employing new police techniques that had yet to take hold. Desperadoes were still being chased on horseback at this time and the days of the posse, the vigilante, and the rangers were on the wane. The rangers were, neverless, a potent factor in fighting crime. Headed by the celebrated Captain Burton C. Mossman, the Arizona Rangers formed the nucleus of what later became the modern-day state police, as did the Texas Rangers. Though the organization saw only a decade of life, the Arizona Rangers became a legendary organization which tracked down numerous public enemies on horseback such as the vicious gunman Augustin Chacon and lawman-turned-outlaw Burt Alvord. See: **Alvord, Burton; Chacon, Augustin; Mossman, Burton C.**

REF.: American Guide Series: *Arizona, A State Guide*; Argall, *History of Arizona Territory*; ____, *Outlawry and Justice in Old Arizona*; Briggs, *Arizona and New Mexico*; Brophy, *Arizona Sketch Book*; CBA; Coolidge, *Arizona Cowboys*; Forrest, *Arizona's Dark and Bloody Ground*; Lockwood,

Arizona Characters; McClintock, *Arizona Prehistoric;* Martin, *An Arizona Chronology;* Miller, *Arizona, The Last Frontier;* ____, *Arizona Cavalcade;* ____, *The Arizona Story;* Murdock, *Arizona Characters in Silhouette;* Sexton, *The Arizona Sheriff.*

Arjun (Arjun Mal), 1563-1606, India, guru-martyr. Fifth Guru of the Sikh religion from 1581 until death. He was persecuted by Emperor Jahangir and became the first martyr of Sikhism. REF.: *CBA.*

Arkansas Tom, See: **Daugherty, Roy.**

Arlington, Josie, 1864-1914, U.S., pros. One of the most celebrated madams in New Orleans for a quarter of a century, Josie Arlington is looked upon today, even by respectable citizens of New Orleans, as a distinguished historical resident of that city, legends about her inspiring poetry and song. Arlington is remembered for being one of the strongest supporters of early-day jazz and its musicians.

THE STAG ✦ ✦
712-714 Gravier Street

ARLINGTON ✦ ✦
110-114 N. Rampart Street

THE ARLINGTON ANNEX ✦ ✦
Corner Basin and Customhouse Streets

T. C. ANDERSON, Proprietor. ✦ ✦ ✦   NEW ORLEANS

An advertisement for Josie Arlington's brothels in New Orleans, fronted by her sometimes partner, Tom Anderson.

At the very vortex of sex in New Orleans during Storeyville's heyday was the palatial brothel lorded over by the moody, volatile Arlington. Born Josie Deubler in the city about 1864, this hotheaded strumpet became the mistress of a gambler and rake named Philip Lobrano, alias Schwarz. For nine years, while she hustled in the bagnios along Customhouse Street, Arlington always returned to her lover each night, bringing with her the proceeds of her nocturnal assignations. In those days, Josie used the last name of Alton, and she was a terror in the brothel, ready to fight customers and her sister whores at the drop of a silk slipper.

Arlington's worst fight occurred in 1886 when she took on a behemoth black whore named Beulah Ripley. The brawl lasted almost an hour, the two hellions savagely clawing, biting, scratching, and hair-pulling. Beulah ultimately gave up and crawled from the scene missing an ear and her lower lip, which Josie had unceremoniously ripped and chewed away. Arlington's vanity in this encounter suffered a mortal blow. Beulah Ripley had yanked almost every hair out of Josie's head, compelling the courtesan to wear a wig for the remainder of her days.

The brawling was not confined to the street, but occurred in all rooms of Josie Arlington's emporium, the most serious havoc taking place on Nov. 2, 1890. Arlington's lover, Lobrano, in an attempt to break up the melee involving twenty screaming prostitutes and their bewildered customers, shot and killed Josie's brother, Peter Deubler, one of the many relatives Josie Arlington kept on her payroll and who was considered by Lobrano as the leading scavenger of that "flock of vultures." Acquitted twice for the killing, Lobrano found Josie's door permanently locked to him and he disappeared.

Such chaotic incidents seemed to sober the hellion, and Arlington suddenly fired all of her wildcats and hired "nothing but the most elegant of ladies, refined, tasteful." Madame Lobrano d'Arlington, as Josie called herself by 1890, came to present, through the pages of the *Mascot* and the *Blue Book*, women she claimed were of European royalty. (These privately printed periodicals discreetly advertised the wonders and wares of New Orleans bordellos.) Her first baroness, Arlington insisted, was a member of the Czar's court, direct from St. Petersburg. It was quickly revealed in 1895 that the baroness, one La Belle Stewart, was no blue blood, but a snake dancer who had doubled as a whore during the Chicago World's Fair in 1893. Undaunted, Josie continued to publicize many of her inmates as fallen aristocrats, and her emporium on Customhouse Street thrived with the best business and richest gentlemen ever to saunter across the invisible boundaries of Storeyville.

Tens of thousands of dollars flowed into Josie Arlington's private coffers and most, including her silent partner and protector, Tom Anderson, thought her a near-millionaire. She acted like it, building a resplendent mansion on Esplanade Avenue. Her servants and coachmen were richly liveried. On every finger of her hands sparkled diamonds, rubies, emeralds, sapphires. Life was sweet then for the queen strumpet. Society, although some upper-crust holdouts still snooted, for the most part accepted Arlington as a New Orleans institution. Madame lived the part with regal bearing.

The fun went out of Josie Arlington's life in 1905, when a flash fire crackled through her bordello. She barely managed to escape the flames. She suffered minor burns and her expensive wig was burned from her head. Josie bore the spiritual mortification of being jeered as she raced through the streets in her singed tatters with the hoots of "Hey, baldie!" in her ears.

She was beset with dark moods after that blaze. Thoughts of death never left her, and in her morbid fascination with her own demise, Josie began systematically inspecting each and every graveyard in the city, looking for her appropriate resting place. She found the right spot in the Metarie Cemetery. Here, she had an $8,000 vault constructed. The tomb boasted red marble. There were two enormous flambeaux at the top of the monument, and in the back, chiseled deep, was a gigantic cross. The door to the tomb was solid copper and, as Arlington directed, upon it was a *bas-relief* of a figure of a woman kneeling, her arms encompassing flowers.

Arlington took to visiting her tomb each day and would sit silent inside the murky confines, rummaging through her own thoughts. Her bordello business boomed, even though Josie had relocated to Tom Anderson's Arlington Annex in 1905, following the fire, but it held little interest for the last of the great madams. From 1909 until her death in 1914, Josie Arlington lived like a hermit in her Esplanade mansion, seeing only a few old friends and looked after by her niece. She was fifty at her death on Feb. 14, 1914, and her passing seemed to serve as a signal that raucous Storeyville was at an end.

Three years later, the Army and Navy, then frenetically preparing men to send to France and the attritional trenches of WWI, established several military installations in and about New Orleans, then an important embarkation port. Enacting an old regulation that prohibited the existence of places of prostitution within a five-mile radius of military sites, Storeyville was promptly and utterly closed down by the Navy. Vice crumbled. Gamblers went broke. Pimps shot themselves for lack of business, and the army of scarlet women slipped like ghosts from the city.

Yet, for decades later one red light would still be lit. On the road alongside the Metarie Cemetery stood a red traffic light. Its amber glow at night freakishly reflected upon Josie Arlington's tomb, striking the two flambeaux at such an angle as to suggest that New Orleans was honoring Josie Arlington, its most celebrated madam, with an eternal flame. For years, until it was removed, visitors, jazz men, and small boys stood gaping at the strange red light above the tomb as it went on and off, on and off, beckoning. See: **Storeyville.**

REF.: Asbury, *The French Quarter;* Blue Book, The, *A List of Madams;* Cable, *Old Creole Days;* Carter, *The Past is Prelude: New Orleans, 1718-1968;* Castellanos, *New Orleans as It Was;* CBA; Curtis, *New Orleans;* Dabney, *One Hundred Years: The Story of the Times-Picayune from Its Founding to 1940;* Fremaux, *New Orleans Characters;* Huber, *The*

New Orleans Tomb; King, *New Orleans, The Place and Its People;* Laughlin, *New Orleans and Its Living Past;* Longstreet, *Sportin' House;* Parkhill, *The Wildest of the West;* Richey, *The New Orleans Book;* Rose, *New Orleans Jazz;* Sinclair, *The Port of New Orleans;* Szarkowski, *E. J. Bellocq: Storeyville Portraits, Photographs from the New Orleans Red-Light District, Circa 1912;* Tinker, *Creole City, Its Past and Its People.*

Arlosoroff, Dr. **Chaim,** d.c.1934, Isr., assass. During the British occupation of Palestine, many prominent Jewish leaders like Arlosoroff believed that cooperation with His Majesty's government was necessary to ensure the peaceful establishment of a national homeland. This view was challenged by radical Zionist factions who believed there could be no Jewish homeland so long as Britain clung to its Mandatory Power in the region.

Arlosoroff was also a Zionist, but he did not share the extreme views of some of his colleagues. While walking along a beach in Tel Aviv with his wife, he was gunned down by an unknown assassin carrying what was at first believed to be a Browning automatic. The British arrested an Arab nationalist who confessed to the crime, but later recanted. Three members of the Revisionist Party also were detained. One was released outright, a second man was acquitted, and the third—a young Zionist named Abraham Stavsky—was charged with murder.

Stavsky was identified in court by Mrs. Arlosoroff, who said she recognized the murder weapon. The gun was sent to Robert Churchill in London, who concluded that it was a rare Nagant revolver, the kind manufactured and used by the Russians around 1901. This prompted speculation in the media that the killer was a Bolshevik sympathizer.

The trial proceedings lasted eleven months. Stavsky was convicted of murder by a lower court, but the verdict was overturned in two appeal trials on the grounds that Palestinian law required that a wife's testimony be corroborated by an independent witness. No one came forward and Stavsky was acquitted. When the Jewish state was founded in 1948 the young Zionist was killed on board the S.S. *Altalena* when it was blown up in the Israeli harbor. REF.: *CBA;* Hastings, *The Other Mr. Churchill.*

Armadale, 1865, a novel by Wilkie Collins. This work profiles a character named "Mrs. Oldershaw" who is based, in fact, on the notorious Sarah Rachel Russell Levison, best known as Madame Rachel (Brit., 1860s-70s), procuress and blackmailer who perfected the Badger Game. See: **Leverson, Sarah Rachel Russell.** REF.: *CBA.*

Armagnac, Bernard VII d'. d.1418, Fr., law enfor. off., assass. Leader of the Orleanist party which battled the Burgundians during the reign of Charles VI. He served as constable of France in 1415 and was killed by a mob in 1418 when Burgundians gained control of Paris. REF.: *CBA.*

Armistead, Norma Jean, 1930-   , U.S., mur. In October 1974, Nurse Armistead of the Kaiser Hospital in Los Angeles quietly sneaked into the medical records section where she scribbled an entry into the ledger, a false pregnancy, her own. It was unusual but not impossible that a childless 44-year-old woman should suddenly become pregnant. There were more than a few sneering comments made by hospital personnel, but soon the matter was forgotten.

On May 15, 1975, Armistead paid a social call on 28-year-old Kathryn Viramontes in her Van Nuys apartment. The younger woman was completing her own term of pregnancy when she was suddenly accosted by knife-wielding Armistead, who was not interested in the family valuables or any cash hidden about the house. She slashed her victim in the throat and then performed a crude but successful caesarean section to extricate the living infant from the womb of the dead woman. Armistead checked herself into the hospital a few hours later and informed the doctors that she had given birth to the boy prematurely at home. It was not long afterward that the true facts of this bizarre murder came to light.

A jury later convicted Norma Jean of first-degree murder after declaring her to be legally sane when she took the knife to Viramontes. REF.: *CBA.*

Armour, John Douglas, 1830-1903, Can., jur. Justice of the Canadian Supreme Court in 1902. REF.: *CBA.*

Armour, Joseph, 1967-   , U.S., mur. In October 1988, a jury in Cook County, Ill., convicted Armour of murder after the ex-convict beat 27-year-old Ronald Turner to death during a street fight on the South Side of Chicago. Armour seized a machete and hacked off the ear of his hapless victim before fleeing along 52nd Street. The senseless, mean-spirited crime blended into the tapestry of life and death on the tough ghetto streets of the city.

An 11-year-old boy who lived among the street gangs that infest the South Side bravely identified the killer to officials from the state's attorney's office. Armour was arrested, tried, and sentenced to forty years in prison by Judge James Heyda of the Criminal Court on Nov. 15, 1988. REF.: *CBA.*

Mr. and Mrs. Herbert Armstrong; the major fed his wife poison.

Armstrong, Herbert Rowse, 1870-1922, Brit., mur. Major Herbert Rowse Armstrong was a small, mousey-looking man whose wife Katherine Mary Armstrong henpecked him from morning to night. Armstrong had been a major during WWI and he insisted that he be addressed by the rank with which he retired. The only authority he really possessed was titular and his dominating wife stripped him of even that by ridiculing his military experiences. The couple lived comfortably with their three children in a cottage in Cusop Dingle closed to the border of Wales-England. The quiet and dignified Armstrong worked as a solicitor in the Welsh town of Hay-on-Wye. When Katherine Armstrong wasn't picking at her husband's habits, she was complaining about her constantly failing health as do most dedicated hypochondriacs. To neighbors and friends Armstrong appeared to take the constant nagging and scolding with good-natured tolerance but he secretly seethed at the humiliation heaped upon him by his unbearable wife, so much so that he put into action a plan he was sure would allow him to get away with murder.

In the spring of 1920, Armstrong began spending all his extra time killing weeds about his cottage area, purchasing considerable quantities of arsenic to eliminate the unwanted growth. In July of that year, Mrs. Armstrong made out a will in which she left all her earthly possessions to her mild-mannered husband. Some weeks later, Katherine Armstrong was having so many delusions and visions that she was removed to an asylum where she was certified as insane. While his wife languished in the asylum, Armstrong began taking short vacation trips to London and, when at home, made a great show of practicing his hobby of weed-killing. At the turn of the year, Mrs. Armstrong made an amazing recovery which allowed her to return home but she soon grew ill and, on Feb. 22, 1921, she succumbed to illness. The cause of death was attributed to a combination of heart disease and gastritis. Major Armstrong grieved briefly, entering a terse comment in his diary, "K died."

Armstrong seemed to take his wife's death with relative calm. In fact, in the months that followed, his normally withdrawn personality seemed to grow more aggressive. He took many vacations to London and suddenly took a great interest in his lackluster business, going after clients with confirmed zeal. His chief rival in the town of Hay was a solicitor named Oswald Norman Martin who received in the mail a box of chocolates from an unknown person. Martin thought this to be a small favor from one of his clients who wished to remain anonymous and he later served the chocolates to a dinner guest who became violently ill only minutes later. The chocolates were turned over to a toxicologist who determined that they had been injected with arsenic. The solicitor was baffled as to who might send him such a lethal gift. On Oct. 26, 1921, in response to an invitation, Martin went to Armstrong's home to take tea. Armstrong chatted casually while the two men sipped their tea, then reached for a buttered scone on a nearby plate but instead of eating this himself, handed it to his guest, saying, "excuse my fingers." The crude manner of serving was overlooked by Martin who attributed such conduct as typical of an aging bachelor who had just been widowed. He ate the scone and was later violently ill.

Dr. Thomas Hincks, who had attended Armstrong's wife and had had reservations about the manner of her death, was summoned to Martin's home to treat the ailing solicitor. Hincks was concerned over Martin's erratic pulse which would not be the normal result of stomach disease. He sent a sample of the solicitor's urine to a clinic for analysis and received a report that it contained a substantial amount of arsenic. Police, now suspicious of Armstrong after reading reports from Dr. Hincks, encouraged the badly frightened Martin to continue his acquaintence with Armstrong. Martin was sent a barrage of invitations from Armstrong to have another tea with him but he nervously found one excuse after another to postpone the lethal appointment. When the solicitor could stand the game no more, he insisted that the police act. Investigators had been attempting to put a case together against the polite little major but were unsure of their case. They finally gave Martin relief by arresting Armstrong on Dec. 31, 1921, charging him with the attempted murder of Martin. A short time later, detectives obtained permission to exhume Mrs. Armstrong's body which was carefully examined by Scotland Yard's forensic bloodhound, Dr. Bernard Spilsbury, who found the remains of Katherine Armstrong filled with arsenic.

Armstrong was now charged with his wife's murder, in addition to his attempt on Martin's life, and placed on trial on Apr. 3, 1922, at the Hereford Assizes, appearing before Justice Darling and prosecuted by Attorney General Sir Ernest Pollock. Sir Henry Curtis-Bennett, one of the ablest criminal lawyers in England, defended Major Armstrong with the argument that Mrs. Armstrong had committed suicide by taking arsenic, such was her mental condition at the end. This claim was countered by Pollock when he produced a nurse who had been present at Katherine Armstrong's deathbed and quoted the victim in court as having said, "I have everything to live for—my husband and my children." This was not the comment of a suicidally bent woman. Further, Armstrong, who conducted himself with impressive ease while in the dock, seemed to incur the emnity of Justice Darling who personally questioned the diminuative major several times. The most damning evidence was a packet of arsenic which had been found on Armstrong by officers who arrested him and from whom he appeared to be hiding the poison. He later claimed that this was but a small packet of poison he had put together, blending poison and other substances, to kill dandalions. Police found twenty packets of arsenic which Armstrong had put together which puzzlied Lord Darling and he inquired why the major would take the trouble to make separate doses of the poison instead of merely sprinkling the arsenic throughout the weedy area.

"I really do not know," Armstrong replied to Justice Darling. "At the time it seemed the most convenient way of doing it." His indecisive response further damned the solicitor in the eyes of those who believed him guilty of killing his wife. Moreover, only nineteen dandalion's were counted in the weed patch and Arm-

strong had prepared twenty packets of poison. It was assumed that the extra packet was to be used on Armstrong's rival, Oswald Martin. Also weighing heavily against the major was the testimony of a physician testifying for the prosecution who insisted that he had examined Armstrong and that the prim-and-proper major was suffering from advance stages of a venereal disease which he had apparently contracted following his wife's death. This evidence doomed the man in the dock perhaps more than anything else since he had postured himself as a man of high morals and great scruples. Armstrong was found Guilty and sentenced to death; hanged on May 31, 1922.

The Armstrong case reminded the public of another sensational murder trial against another solicitor, Harold Greenwood, also from Wales, who was charged with poisoning his wife with arsenic in 1920, but who had been acquitted. It was speculated during Armstrong's trial that he had read about the Greenwood acquittal and believed that he could poison his own wife and, if charged, would be released as had Greenwood, convinced that his social position, his military rank, and his occupation as a solicitor would put him above suspicion, beyond conviction. Ironically, Greenwood wrote a series of articles for *John Bull* magazine during Armstrong's trial in which Greenwood described in bemoaning detail of what it was like to be tried for murder. If indeed, Armstrong had been inspired by reading about the Greenwood case a year before he murdered his wife, he may have dug deeper into the history of murder and located the case of Cordelia Botkin who mailed poisoned chocolates to one of her rivals twenty-some years earlier in America. Botkin's murder ploy may have also inspired Armstrong to dispose of his business rival, the hapless Oswald Martin. See: **Botkin, Cordelia**; **Greenwood, Harold**; **Spilsbury, Sir Bernard**.

REF.: Barker, *Lord Darling's Famous Cases*; Bosanquet, *The Oxford Circuit*; Browne, *The Rise of Scotland Yard*; _____ and Tullett, *The Scalpel of Scotland Yard*; CBA; Cuthbert, *Science and the Detection of Crime*; Deardon, *Some Cases of Sir Bernard Spilsbury and Others*; Glaister, *The Power of Poison*; Graham, *Lord Darling and His Famous Trials*; Grice, *Great Cases of Sir Henry Curtis Bennett, K.C.*; Gross, *Masterpieces of Murder*; Haestier, *Dead Men Tell Tales*; Jackson, *Case for the Prosecution*; Lambton, *Thou Shalt Do No Murder*; Lawrence, *A History of Capital Punishment*; Logan, *Wilful Murder*; *Notable British Trials*; Odell, *Exhumation of a Murder*; Pearson, *Instigation of the Devil*; _____, *More Studies in Murder*; Randall, *The Famous Cases of Sir Bernard Spilsbury*; Rowland, *Murder Revisited*; Russell, *Best Murder Cases*; Shew, *A Companion to Murder*; Shore, *Crime and Its Detection*; Speer, *The Secret History of Great Crimes*; Thompson, *Poisons and Poisoners*; Townsend, *Black Cap, Murder Will Out*; Tullett, *Strictly Murder*; Walker-Smith, *The Life of Lord Darling*; Wensley, *Forty Years of Scotland Yard*; Wilcox, *The Detective-Physician*; Wilson, *Encyclopedia of Murder*; (FICTION) Huxley, *Mortal Coils* ("The Gioconda Smile"); Meadows, *Friday Market*.

Armstrong, John, d.1528, Brit., rob. Armstrong headed a huge gang of bandits near the Scottish border in the 1520s, virtually controlling the area in spite of the efforts of King James V (of Scotland) to eliminate the thieves who preyed upon countless travelers and small towns. The wily Armstrong grew so bold as to propose through emmissaries that the king enlist his services and that of his men to suppress the widespread brigandage which he, Armstrong, himself was practicing, one of the earliest incidents on record of the "protection" racket. King James agreed to meet with Armstrong and when the bandit chieftan arrived at the rendezvous with a small retinue, the king's men overpowered the bandit chief and his followers. They were all promtly hanged. Armstrong has since become the subject of many ballads in which he is portrayed, ironically enough, as a victim of injustice.

REF.: Bailey, *The Fatal Chance*; CBA; Furneaux, *Famous Criminal Cases*; Simpson, *Forty Years of Murder*.

Armstrong, John, 1931- , Case of, Brit., mur. Armstrong, a medical attendant in the Royal Navy, who lived with his family at Gosport, near Portsmouth, was convicted in 1956 of murdering his 5-month-old child Terence, originally charged with dosing him with Seconal. The child died on July 22, 1955, and it was originally thought that he had swallowed some poisoned berries that his older sister had eaten, the sister having recovered. Red skins from the berries were supposedly found in the baby's windpipe and stomach. After the child was buried, detectives continued their investigation because the erratic behavior of the parents aroused their suspicions. The red skins were sent to the Forensic Laboratory of Scotland Yard were they were determined to be the gelatin shells of the drug Seconal. The child's body was exhumed and an autopsy confirmed the presence of Seconal. Detectives learned that the medical cabinet in the Navy clinic where Armstrong worked had previously been broken into and some Seconal capsules taken. The Armstrongs denied ever having Seconal in the house and a coroner's inquest left the death with an open verdict.

The Armstrongs with the child John Armstrong was convicted of killing.

On July 24, 1956, Mrs. Armstrong, who had since separated from her husband, told police that, indeed, her husband had kept Seconal in the house and that he had been taking the capsules in order to sleep. She added that she would be willing to give further evidence if any action was taken against her estranged husband. Police were suspicious of Janet Armstrong's statements, asking her if these comments did not stem from any bitterness she had toward him. She denied speaking out of anger, adding that she asked her husband following the baby's death if he had given Terence any Seconal and said that he replied, "How do I know you have not?" She then confessed that she threw out the Seconal in the house at her husband's instructions and did not inform police because "I was frightened what my husband would do to me if I did, and I wanted to save him getting into trouble." It was known to the police that Janet Armstrong was angry at not being given an official separation order by a magistrate's court from her husband whom she claimed had beaten her repeatedly. Out of pique, it was thought, she had called Inspector Gates at New Scotland Yard and suddenly recalled having the Seconals in her house.

Though motive for the murder of the child was vague, Attorney General Sir Reginald Manningham-Buller personally charged both Armstrongs with murdering their child and they were tried at Winchester before Justice Pilcher. The trial consisted of vicious attacks on each other by the Armstrongs, replete with lies and heavily laced with seething hatred. The fact that the Armstrongs had lost an earlier child, Philip, who had died in March 1954 at age three months, reportedly of pneumonia, gave vent to the idea that the young couple simply eradicated their unwanted children whom they found difficult to support on Armstrong's meager salary. Manningham-Buller was dogged in his prosecution, but Mrs. Armstrong's attorney, the wiley Norman Skelhorn, using the statements of prosecution witnesses, established a pattern for Mrs.

Armstrong's inability to dose her child with Seconal. The case was known as a "cutthroat defense" wherein each defendant accused the other of the murder. When Justice Pilcher summed up the case for the jury he instructed members that they did not have to find *both* of the accused Guilty or Not Guilty, leaving open the possibility of finding one of the parties guilty, an option readily seized upon by a jury that took only forty-five minutes to reach a decision. Armstrong was found Guilty and his wife Not Guilty. John Armstrong was sentenced to death but later reprieved. This case was the first significant murder in which dangerous drugs played a direct role and one where toxicology became a key factor.

REF.: Bailey, *The Fatal Chance; CBA;* Furneaux, *Famous Crimes No.4;* Jones, *My Own Case;* Simpson, *Forty Years of Murder;* Thorwald, *The Century of the Detective.*

Armstrong, John Barclay, 1850-1913, U.S., west. law enfor. off. Born in McMennville, Tenn., in January 1850, Armstrong, son of a dentist, left home at an early age and drifted about the southwest until reaching Austin, Texas, in 1870 where he married and began life as a rancher, raising a large family of seven children. Armstrong was an early advocate of law and order and to that end, joined the Travis Rifles in 1871, this group being a paramilitary organization put together to combat rampant lawlessness in Texas. In 1875, Armstrong enlisted with the Texas Rangers and became one of its most famous members, first serving under L.H. McNely where he quickly reached the rank of sergeant because of his excellent service. So dedicated was Armstrong and so fearless in battling outlaws when accompanying his superior that he was dubbed "McNely's Bulldog."

On Oct. 1, 1876, Armstrong and a company of rangers cornered a band of rustlers and outlaws near Espinoza Lake. Several outlaws escaped but four of them elected to shoot it out and all were killed by Armstrong and his men. Another two rustlers were later shot by a small contingent of Armstrong's command. Armstrong and another ranger, Leroy Deggs, were assigned to arrest John Mayfield, a rancher who had been charged with murder and on whose head a considerable reward had been placed. On Dec. 7, 1876, Armstrong and Deggs rode to Mayfield's ranch in Wilson County, Tex. They found their man in a corral and Armstrong told Mayfield that he was under arrrest. He laughed and reached for his gun. The lawmen pulled their pistols and shot the rancher dead. A dozen ranchhands came running and threatened to kill the two rangers if they attempted to take the body with them. Armstrong and Deggs thoughtfully withdrew without the corpse which was later buried secretly to prevent Armstrong from collecting the reward.

The next man Armstrong went after was the most wanted outlaw of his day, as well as the fastest and most feared gunslinger of the era, John Wesley Hardin. A $4000 reward had been posted for Hardin's arrest for murder. The ranger spent months tracking the elusive Hardin, learning that the outlaw was somewhere in the Gulf State area. The trail led him to Florida where, on Aug. 23, 1877, Armstrong learned that Hardin would be on a train stopping at Pensacola. Though he had no actual authority in the area, Armstrong appointed a few local men as deputies and boarded the train when it arrived.

A large, burly man with an intent gaze and an unswerving nature, Armstrong intended to take Hardin dead or alive and told his nervous deputies to walk behind him as he marched through the coaches, looking for his prey. Armstrong spotted Hardin sitting in a coach seat with a member of his gang, Jim Mann. Three other heavily armed Hardin associates sat in nearby seats. Armstrong motioned for his deputies to sit apart from him and he took a seat directly across from Hardin and Mann while the train idled in the station. (At the time Armstrong was limping and using a cane, having accidentally shot himself in the leg while cleaning a pistol, and this image of being crippled thoroughly disarmed Hardin's normally accute suspicions.) Slowly, Armstrong drew forth his long-barreled .45-caliber pistol, put this in his lap, then stood up and aimed it at Hardin and Mann. "I am a ranger and you are both under arrest," Armstrong calmly announced.

"Surrender your weapons."

Hardin jerked his head back, exclaiming, "Texas, by God!" He reached for his pistol but in his awkward effort to stand up from the cramped train seat, Hardin hooked the long barrel in his suspenders. While he was struggling to untangle himself, his partner, 19-year-old Mann, drew his pistol and fired across the aisle at Armstrong, blowing the ranger's stetson from his head, missing his scalp by half an inch. Armstrong stood up wobbly-legged, balancing his bad leg with his cane in one hand and with the other carefully, cooly aimed his six-gun, firing one shot which plowed into Mann's chest. The young outlaw dove head first out the open train window, got to his feet, took a few steps down the station platform and then crashed downward, dead.

Texas Ranger Armstrong, who captured John Wesley Hardin.

Hardin by then was on his feet, still struggling to release the hammer of his weapon from his suspenders. In frustration he kicked Armstrong in the chest and sent the lawman reeling backward down the aisle. The ranger got to his feet and jumped forward, bringing his gun butt down on Hardin's head several times, pistol-whipping him into unconsciousness. During this entire incident, which lasted no more than a few minutes, Hardin's three other outlaw companions sat frozen in their seats. With Hardin down and unconscious, Armstrong turned to them and quietly asked for their guns. They turned them over meekly, and Armstrong took the entire gang into custody, later delivering them to Texas authorities. This time the ranger did collect the reward and used the $4000 to purchase more than 50,000 acres of cattle land in Willacy County, Tex., calling his spread the XIT ranch, one of the largest at that time.

Armstrong did not retire from the rangers, however, but continued to battle outlaws such as King Fisher, cleaning out that rustler baron's operations in South Texas and rising to the rank of captain. This most respected of rangers retired in 1882 to attend to his lucrative cattle ranch. He accepted the post of U.S. marshal for his area for a brief period, then returned to his ranch. He maintained a large crew of cowhands and rigidly bossed their work, much as he had when operating as a Texas Ranger. One cowboy, a truculent sort, refused to take Armstrong's harsh order on Nov. 18, 1908, and shot his boss out of his saddle. (The cowboy was later sent to prison for attempted murder.) Armstrong survived this attack as he had so many others and died peacefully in his bed on his ranch, May 1, 1913. See: **Hardin, John Wesley.**

REF.: Bartholomew, *The Biographical Album of Western Gunfighters*; *CBA*; Cunningham, *Triggernometry*; Gard, *Frontier Justice*; Gillett, *Six Years with the Texas Rangers*; Hardin, *The Life of John Wesley Hardin*; Hendricks, *The Bad Man of the West*; Holloway, *Texas Gun Lore*; Jennings, *A Texas Ranger*; Nash, *Bloodletters and Badmen*; Nordyke, *John Wesley Hardin, Texas Gunman*; O'Neal, *Encyclopedia of Western Gunfighters*; Raymond, *Captain Lee Hall*; Rosa, *The Gunfighter*; Sonnichsen, *The Grave of John Wesley Hardin*; ____, *I'll Die Before I'll Run*; Webb, *Texas Rangers*.

Armstrong, Karelton Lewis, prom. 1970s, U.S., bomb.-mur. A member of the radical SDS, Armstrong and others, ostensibly as an act of "political expression," planted and set off a bomb in the mathematics building of the University of Wisconsin in Madison in August 1970. The resulting explosion killed Robert Fassnacht, a 33-year-old physicist and father of three children, as well as wounding several others. Armstrong was placed on the FBI's Most Wanted list in 1970 and was sought nationwide for two years for sabotage, destruction of government buildings, and conspiracy to commit murder. He was captured in Toronto, Can., in 1972 and pleaded guilty to second-degree murder. Radical leader Daniel Ellsberg tried to convince the court to free the murderer but Armstrong nevertheless received a twenty-three-year sentence in the penitentiary. He was released in 1979.

REF.: *CBA*; Nash, *Almanac of World Crime*.

Armstrong, Thomas Jefferson, 1841-61, U.S., rob.-mur. Armstrong went to work for his brother-in-law Robert Stinson when he was just a boy. Stinson owned a large carpet manufacturing concern on Front Street in Philadelphia during the Civil War. The carpeting trade was lucrative and Stinson had many competitors, among them 55-year-old Robert Crawford, who owned a factory nearby.

On May 21, 1860, Crawford approached Armstrong with a business proposition. He asked the 19-year-old weaver if he would sell small quantities of his brother-in-law's yarn directly to him at a discounted price. Armstrong agreed to the illegal transaction, realizing that the yarn which wholesaled at fifty cents a pound would probably not be missed by Stinson if he was careful. The arrangement continued for several months right up to the time Crawford was found murdered in the streets.

Caught up as he was before the murder in the sale of stolen merchandise, Armstrong knew he risked exposure and a likely jail sentence. When James Hollingsworth arrived at the Stinson warehouse on Sept. 20, Armstrong was cautious. He knew the man had an unsavory reputation in the community, but he also realized that he himself was knee-deep in crime. Armstrong decided he had no alternative but to go along with the scheme when Hollingsworth proposed that he act as middleman in the sale of a large quantity of rug yarn to a prospective buyer. For locating an interested party, Armstrong was promised $10 of the $100 purchase price.

"I told him to return about dinner time," Armstrong said. "I then went over to Crawford's factory a short distance away from Stinson's. I supposed the yarn had been stolen, but I did not tell Crawford so. I thought he might infer that fact for himself. He said he was willing to buy it as he wanted to make a spec."

Crawford gave Armstrong $2 to hire a rig to transport the rug yarn from one warehouse to another. At the appointed hour the next day, Armstrong picked up Hollingsworth, his assistant John Schindler, and Crawford near the corner of Fourth and Girard. There was a smell of liquor on their breath, and the mood seemed convivial. The older men passed the bottle back and forth but Armstrong declined. He had not touched a drop in nearly four years.

Hollingsworth directed Tom to drive on, not sure of where they were headed. Crawford had left his wife and family at seven that night with $88 in his pocket to buy some material for his business, so he was in no mood to be a party to a "fool's errand." His patience wearing thin, he accused Schindler and Hollingsworth of treachery, going so far as to imply that the merchandise was stolen. In the back of the carriage the three men engaged in a fistfight while Armstrong drove on.

Near the Germantown Road, James Hollingsworth struck Crawford over the head with a heavy blunt object. He and Schindler beat him senseless and then there was a gunshot. They dropped the body on the side of Diamond Street near Hancock and Clinton. Armstrong was warned to keep silent about the matter or risk reprisal. He returned the wagon to the Laurel Street stables where the hostler noted, with alarm, blood on the seat. Two days later the rug weaver was arrested and charged with first-degree murder after his two companions were exonerated.

When the trial of Armstrong began in Philadelphia on Jan. 7, 1861, the city was divided in its opinion on his guilt or innocence. Armstrong emphatically denied killing Crawford, and he pleaded not guilty. But the testimony of the livery man and several eyewitnesses who heard the screams of the dying man but saw only the driver Armstrong, was enough to convict him. Sergeant E.K.

Tryon of the Eleventh District, the first to arrive on the murder scene, said he had observed two men, one he believed to have been the defendant.

Armstrong was found Guilty and sentenced to death on Feb. 25, 1861, by Judge Joseph Allison. He bolted up from his seat in the courtroom to remind the judge that he had just convicted an innocent man. "You may take my life, but not my clear conscience! Thank God I am innocent," he cried. However, the gun used to kill Crawford was traced back to Armstrong, and that was all the evidence the jury needed.

Up to the moment of his execution on Aug. 9, 1861, Armstrong's calm demeanor shocked even the most hardened jailers and crime reporters. Just before the white cloth bag was placed over his head, he showed no remorse or guilt. "Gentlemen, I again bid you farewell," he said. "I die at peace with all the world." Outside the prison walls several thousand people milled about, waiting for the executioner's final words: "It is done." REF.: *CBA.*

Armwood, George, 1909-33, U.S., lynch. Armwood was the twenty-first black man to be lynched by an angry mob of whites in 1933. His crime was rape, and his victim was a 71-year-old Maryland woman named Mary Denston who was walking down a lonely country highway near Kingston in October 1933. The toothless old woman was grabbed from behind and raped in the bushes. Later that day, 24-year-old Armwood was arrested by the state police and taken to Baltimore, where racial animosity did not run nearly so high as it did on the Maryland eastern shore. But the police had not counted on the intervention of the Somerset County Prosecutor John Robins and Judge Robert Duer. The pair ordered the illiterate black man who signed his name with an "X" remanded to their jurisdiction to answer charges.

Armwood was taken to a small jail in Princess Anne where local townsmen had already gathered to plan a lynch party. Alerted to the growing danger, Governor Albert Cabell Ritchie ordered troopers to the jail to reinforce a small band of lawmen standing guard outside the cells. By nightfall, the reinforcements had not arrived and only thirteen police officers stood between Armwood and death.

Judge Duer sat down to a leisurely dinner and was slow to react to reports of a lynch mob growing outside the local jail. The sheriff had been absent from his office all afternoon, and when he returned that night he found the jail under siege. There was little he or anyone else could do—or wanted to do—at this point to prevent a murder.

The jailhouse was stormed, and Armwood was taken from his cell to an oak tree near Duer's residence. The kicking and beating Armwood had suffered while being dragged the short distance to the hanging tree resulted in his death. Still, the mob was not placated. The body was doused in gasoline on the courthouse steps and set on fire. "Here's what we do on the eastern shore!" said one.

Judge Duer, Prosecutor Robins, and even Governor Ritchie were held accountable for the assault, which occurred as a result of their inaction. The *Baltimore Sun* reminded the elected officials that the people "will not tolerate dodging of responsibility." But in this case the sentiments of the backwoods folk were clearly with the mob. "Investigation?" said the sheriff of Somerset County. "Well, boys, I was in the thick of that affair. I looked right in the faces of some of that mob and I didn't recognize a soul—not a single soul. I bet they were from down Virginia way." The hanging rope was presented to Mary Denston's son as a souvenir. He was a Philadelphia policeman. REF.: *CBA.*

Arnas, Mr., b.1921, Indo., adult.-mur. Arnas was a 35-year-old laborer who worked in a glass factory in Djakarta, Indonesia, when he murdered his wife and four children one night in 1956. He was a simple man whose only passion in life seemed to be his pretty young mistress Dahlia. One day Dahlia demanded that Arnas prove that his love was genuine. "But what can I do?" he protested. "Kill your wife and children," she answered coldly. "Then I will know you love me." If this would make his Dahlia

happy, Arnas decided, he would gladly do it.

The bottlemaker located a hatchet, and on a rainy, thundering night killed the children and his wife. The murder weapon he dropped down a well and then he fled the city. His blood-soaked shirt later was found among Dahlia's personal things. Dahlia's mother told police of her daughter's terrible demands, and not long afterward, Arnas was arrested and charged with murder. Two years later Arnas remained behind bars awaiting trial despite conclusive evidence of his guilt. "We are still investigating the case," explained a police officer familiar with the killer and the crime.

REF.: *CBA;* Whitehead, *Journey Into Crime.*

Arnet, Richard, d.1728, Brit., executioner. Arnet served as the London hangman from c.1717 until his death.

REF.: Bleackley, *Hangmen of England; CBA.*

Arnold, Andrew J., prom. 1910s, U.S., wh. slav. Arnold led a group of vicious white slavers in Manhattan during the early 1910s, preying upon young girls who thought to establish careers in modeling. He sent his emmissaries to Central Park where, posing as photographers, they would pick up attractive young girls with the promise of paying them for short modeling stints. One of these girls was Anna Standroup who was accosted in Central Park in April 1914, by Leo Kirschner who told her he would give her $50 for some harmless photographic posing in his studio. She agreed and they went to his studio on 149th Street where Anna posed for some innocent shots. Kirschner then told Anna that they would have to go to another address where she would receive her pay. He took her to an apartment on 124th Street, which was a bordello run by Madam Ruth Waller. There Anna Standroup was stripped of her clothes and held captive for many months, raped repeatedly by many men. She was told that if she attempted to escape, she would be killed and if she did manage to get to the police the resulting publicity would ruin her family's good name. Police received a tip that Waller was running a whorehouse at the 124th Street address and raided the place, finding Standroup and other girls who had been forced into prostitution. Waller, Kirschner, and the man who financed this and other operations of its kind, Andrew J. Arnold, were arrested and later received long prison terms.

REF.: *CBA;* Nash, *Among the Missing.*

Arnold, Benedict, 1741-1801, U.S., treas. To all Americans treason and the name of Benedict Arnold are synonymous. Few citizens of the U.S. today realize that Arnold was also one of the greatest heroes of the American Revolution up to the time he attempted to sell out his country in 1780. An adventurer, Arnold was one of the first to organize a company of New England minutemen, serving with distinction from the first moment of hostilities between the colonies and the British Crown. Born in Norwich, Conn., on Jan. 14, 1741, Arnold lived a fantasy life as a boy. His father was a drunken failure, and to compensate for the shame he felt, the youth invented a heroic image for himself and attempted to mold this into a reality by running off to fight in the French and Indian War at age seventeen. He deserted a year later and at age nineteen returned to his homestead in Norwich, having learned that his parents had both died. He auctioned off all the family belongings and set up a shop in New Haven where he sold potions and medicines of dubious value, giving himself the title of Dr. Arnold. The store was really a front for smuggled goods Arnold secretly bought from West Indies pirates.

By 1767, Arnold was a rich man, living in a resplendent house on Water Street. He married Margaret Mansfield, the attractive daughter of the town's High Sheriff. She bore him three sons. At the time of the Boston Massacre, Arnold was in the West Indies but he returned to join a company of militia and raised his voice loudly against British tyranny. When the Revolution broke out at Lexington and Concord on April 19, 1775, Arnold, by then elected captain of his militia company, marched his men to battle. By May 3, 1775, Arnold had been commissioned a colonel and had raised 400 volunteers to fight the British troops. In September

1775, the Continental Congress appointed George Washington commander-in-chief of the American armies. Washington, knowing of Arnold's zeal and his knowledge of Quebec during the French and Indian Wars, ordered Arnold to attack the British-held city. Hundreds of revolutionary volunteers flocked to Arnold's banner, including a youthful Aaron Burr, who would himself be tried for treason in 1807.

In a forced march through blizzard conditions, Arnold's 700 men reached Quebec, joining with 300 men under the command of Richard Montgomery, a former British officer, the two forces attacking the fortress on the wintry night of Dec. 20, 1775. Montgomery was killed in the first charge; only Arnold and thirty men made it into the city but a withering fire greeted them

Benedict Arnold, America's most infamous traitor.

which cut down Arnold. His leg was shattered with a minnie ball and he had to be dragged back by Daniel Morgan and others. The Quebec expedition failed but Arnold had fought valiantly and his reputation as a fierce commander soon spread throughout the Continental Army. Washington appreciated his young subordinate but mistrusted Arnold's impetuous judgment. When Arnold returned he found that his wife had died and his fortune had evaporated.

Arnold's volatile temperament had created many enemies for him in the political arena. He was accused of misdirecting his command at Quebec and even attacked for his unorthodox raid on Fort Ticonderoga. So upset was Arnold that he thought to resign his commission, but was persuaded not to do so by Washington himself. It was to the good fortune of the Continental Army that Arnold remained at his post. On Oct. 17, 1777, 5,000 of the best British troops in the colonies were mauled into surrender by a small American army under the command of Arnold and other generals. It was Arnold who led one heroic charge against these crack British regulars until Gentleman Johnny Burgoyne, their commander, formally surrendered his sword. It was one of the worst defeats ever suffered by a British army. Arnold never received recognition for his contribution to this great victory which caused him to smolder with deep resentment.

In Philadelphia, General Arnold met and fell in love with beautiful Margaret Peggy Shippen whose blueblood family members were politically divided. She was a decided Tory, secretly expressing her sympathies for the British and, following her marriage to Arnold, she worked on the American general, persuading him to think favorably about his once-avowed enemy. Arnold was considerably disabled by his wounds and he limped about Philadelphia in charge of a paper command. He was finally offered a command in the field, but by then Arnold, deprived of his full pay by hostile politicians in Congress and insulted on the streets of Philadelphia, decided the go over to the enemy. Arnold begged off Washington's battle assignment and was given command of West Point. By then he had been corresponding with British commanders through Major John Andre, a friend of his wife's, and stated that he would turn over West Point to the British for a payment of £20,000. He met Andre secretly at Stony Point on Sept. 21, 1780, to finalize plans for the betrayal of West Point. Arnold gave Andre signed papers that would ostensibly get him through the American lines; the British major, to hide his uniform, wore a long cloak. A short time after he left Arnold, Andre was arrested by American forces.

Hearing of this, Arnold panicked and fled to the British lines. Andre, a noble and dignified officer, was tried and condemned to death. The handsome, 29-year-old Andre was hanged on Oct.

2, 1780. Arnold was made a general in the British Army, fought in some lesser engagements and, following the defeat of the British, took refuge in England where his wife Peggy later joined him. King George III consulted with Arnold about American affairs and the traitor was given a small pension as a retired British brigadier general; he also received £6,315 for his betrayal, not the £20,000 he had originally demanded. Arnold lived miserably in London, scorned by the British as a turncoat and hated in America where his name had turned into a curse. He died in London on June 14, 1801, with his wife Peggy at his side. His last request was that he be buried in his old American army uniform. Almost sixty-three years later, a short story by Edward Everett Hale, entitled "The Man Without A County," was published in the December 1863 issue of the *Atlantic Monthly*. The story concerned a man who had cursed his country and was compelled to live in exile ever after. Most historians agreed that the article, written by the grandnephew of Nathan Hale, one of America's greatest heroes, was based upon America's most notorious traitor, Benedict Arnold.

REF.: Billias, *George Washington's Generals;* Callahan, *Daniel Morgan, Ranger of the Revolution; CBA;* Clinton, *The American Rebellion;* Flexner, *The Traitor and the Spy;* Jensen, *The Founding of A Nation;* Locke, *The Birth of America;* Nickerson, *The Turning Point of the Revolution;* Prescott, *The American Revolution;* Robson, *The American Revolution in Its Political and Military Aspects;* Roberts, *March to Quebec, Journals of the Members of Arnold's Expedition;* Smith, *Our Struggle for the Fourteenth Colony;* Van Doren, *Secret History of the American Revolution;* Wallace, *Appeal to Arms: A Military History of the American Revolution;* ____, *Traitorous Hero: The Life and Fortunes of Benedict Arnold.*

Arnold, Dorothy Harriet Camille, 1885-1910, U.S., miss. pers.-mur. The heiress to a sizeable Manhattan fortune and the niece of U.S. Supreme Court Justice Rufus Peckham, Dorothy Arnold went shopping on Dec. 12, 1910, and was never seen again. The chunky but attractive Arnold was dressed at the height of fashion, wearing an ankle-length coat over an expensive dress that dropped to the ankles of her high-buttoned shoes. She carried a fox fur muffler and $36 which she had drawn from her bank account in order to buy a dress for the forthcoming debut of her younger sister. She wore a Baker hat—an enormous wide-brimmed hat bedecked with artificial flowers which was the fashion rage of the era. When Arnold failed to return home, an alarm went out and, when police were unable to locate her, the New York press stepped up its speculations about her disappearance, uncovering a playboy lover who had been seeing Arnold, one George Griscom, a much-married man.

Griscom was reported to have been on a vacation in Florence, Italy, at the time of Dorothy Arnold's disappearance and when he returned to New York he made a great show of trying to find the missing girl, placing "Come Home" ads in the papers, the tone being that Arnold had vanished voluntarily. No one ever saw the young woman again, however. Her father, Francis Arnold, spent more than $100,000 on detectives who followed false leads, on information that was both specious and the work of pranksters. There were letters by the thousands that insisted that Arnold was in the Honduras working in a brothel, the captive of white slavers; that she ran away to Honolulu to be with a handsome young man from a high-society family.

A self-styled supernaturalist insisted that on the day that Arnold vanished a beautiful white swan appeared out of nowhere in the Central Park Lagoon; this person insisted that the 25-year-old woman had been transformed into a beautiful bird. Even this absurd "information" was purchased by Francis Arnold, so desperate was he to find his lost daughter. Arnold came to believe, without ever volunteering information, that his daughter had been murdered around 1916 when a Rhode Island convict insisted that he had been paid $150 to dig a grave in the cellar of a house near West Point. The man who had paid the convict was described as a wealthy New Yorker who matched the description of George Griscom. The convict stated that the woman he buried had died on the table of a quack abortionist and that the young man had her body secretly buried to cover "his sins." Police dug up several cellars in West Point but unearthed no body.

Dorothy Arnold, the girl in the Baker hat, below, who vanished in 1910; her father posted rewards and police blanketed New York with wanted posters, like that at right.

At right, the mysterious George Griscom, Dorothy's playboy lover.

John H. Ayers, police captain and chief of the city's Missing Person's Bureau, gave a speech to some students in 1921 in which he stated that he knew exactly what had happened to Dorothy Arnold but he could not reveal the details of her "terrible fate." Though grilled repeatedly by newsmen over the years, Ayers consistently refused to explain his remarks. Francis Arnold died in 1922, leaving nothing to his missing daughter, believing that she had been killed. His will stated, "I have made no provision for my beloved daughter, Dorothy H.C. Arnold, as I am satisfied that she is not alive."

REF.: *CBA;* Livingston, *The Murdered and Missing;* Nash, *Among the Missing;* Smith, *Mysteries of the Missing;* Sutherland, *Ten Real Murder Mysteries Never Solved!.*

Arnold, Joseph, (AKA: **Joseph Aranyos; Jeremy Voltaire; Jerry Voltaire; Jerry Boltaire; Jack Moore; Big Joe**), 1917-   , fenc.-rob.-org. crime. Arnold was arrested for auto theft when he was only twelve years old. By the time he graduated into organized crime, this professional extortionist and criminal fence had received three sentences for operating an interstate stolen-auto ring and loan-sharking.

In 1939 Arnold resided in New York City where he operated a jewelry store on Maiden Lane. That same year a Philadelphia society matron named Mrs. Henry Breyer was robbed of her jewels, estimated to be worth in excess of $125,000. Arnold obliged the four men who robbed her by purchasing their loot for $20,000. On Dec. 2, 1942, Judge Owen W. Bohan sentenced Big Joe to a term of nine months in consideration of his guilty plea and a request from the Municipal Parole Board that the court affix a definite term.

Arnold drifted into Chicago where he became the chauffeur and bodyguard for Jimmy Allegretti, North Side mob boss responsible for syndicate gambling and vice activities. The white-haired, paunchy mobster cultivated some useful political connec-

tions in the 38th Ward, fronting his criminal operations under the guise of Shirts Unlimited, a State Street retail store. REF.: *CBA.*

Arnold, Louise, prom. 1923, U.S., mur. Arnold was a poor Czech immigrant who settled in Manhattan before WWI. To support her three sons following the death of her husband Frederick in 1911, she took a job cutting and wrapping cigars in the back room of the American Exchange Cigar Company on Third Avenue.

Mrs. Arnold had a boyfriend, Vincent Calevacca, a night watchman near the City College of New York, who told Louise he was a widower who lived alone. They began to keep company. Not long afterward the widow professed her love for him. Fearing a scandal and sensitive to the neighbors' gossip, Mrs. Arnold pressed him for a commitment. "Are you going to marry me as you said?" she asked him one day. "Please do. Everybody is talking about us."

Calevacca stalled—he was never interested in marrying Louise because he already had two wives, one in New Jersey, another in Jamaica. When he confessed his polygamy on July 5, 1923, Mrs. Arnold rushed at him with a bread knife she had concealed in a candy bag. "He sprang at me trying to get the knife and I stabbed at him wildly," she later told police. "He screamed and I turned and ran down the hall, he screaming and staggering behind me. It was terrible." Vincent collapsed a few seconds later. The neighbors who had talked about their illicit affair for weeks now had something new and more terrible to gossip about.

Detectives pieced the details of the crime together through the sworn statements of Sadie Kelly, a probation officer who had spoken with Calevacca from time to time about Mrs. Arnold. "This woman will kill me yet!" he told her on at least one occasion. "I told her once that I was a widower, but since I told her I'm married and have a wife and family, she swore she was going to get me."

The victim's family was located in Lodi, N.J. He had eight children who were comfortably maintained by the money their father earned working as a night watchman. When the court learned of Calevacca's double life, Mrs. Arnold was spared the death penalty. She pleaded guilty to a reduced charge of man-slaughter and was sent to prison at Auburn. REF.: *CBA.*

Arnold, Philip, 1829-73, and **Slack, John,** prom. 1870s, U.S., fraud. Philip Arnold and John Slack had the distinction of being the only two confidence men to ever successfully salt a diamond mine in the U.S., a scam that fleeced the pockets of some of America's richest men. In the summer of 1871, both Arnold and Slack went to the offices of George Roberts, a mining promoter, showing him a sack of dia-monds, emeralds, and rubies, saying that they had dis-covered a high plateau in Wyoming which was loaded with every known rare gem in the world. This occurred, of course, at a time when lapi-dary experts were extremely limited in their ability to de-termine the value of true gems. The jewels left by Ar-nold and Slack were valued at being worth more than $300,000, even though the con men had spent only $20,000 in buying industrial gems to use as their lure. Arnold and

Con men Philip Arnold and John Slack are portrayed as dangerous snakes; the flimflammers bilked millionaires for a fortune with a phony diamond.

Slack asked the mining promoter if he thought he might be able to put together a financial group to invest in developing the diamond field they had found. They were willing, of course, to give controlling interest in the field to the investors; they were but simple farmers and prospectors who sought only to make a "reasonable profit" from their discovery. Roberts contacted more than a dozen multimillionaires, including William C. Ralston, president of the Bank of California; General George H. Dodge, August Belmont, Henry Seligman, General George P. McClellan, General Samuel L. Barlow, and General Benjamin F. Butler. Baron Rothschild got involved through his U.S. representative and London millionaires Asbury Harpending, William Lent, and Alfred Rubery also asked to invest. It was an "insider's" investment, one which would reap untold billions in rare gems.

The con men passed several tests set for them by the investment consortium, taking representatives of the millionaires to the Wyoming field—blindfolded for the last part of the trip on muleback—where they were shown a plateau of 6,500 feet which they had salted with another $50,000 in industrial gems Arnold had purchased in Antwerp. The represerative was allowed to fill a sack full of the gems and cart this back to civilization where such distinguished jewelers as Charles Lewis Tiffany turned them over to their inexpert lapidaries who pronounced them priceless. The consortium coughed up $100,000 as a down payment to Arnold and Slack and continued to give them similar amounts regularly over the next two years to develop the field, holding a claim on the area. Of course neither Arnold nor Slack developed anything, except their own bank accounts. They pocketed at least $500,000 in payments from the consortium before departing the West. Slack was never seen again but Arnold boldly returned to his native Elizabethtown, Ky., where he bought an estate. When the bilked millionaires discovered that they had been conned, most of them kept quiet, lest the world mock them for their greed and lack of common sense, let alone the shabby business acumen they had displayed.

One of the suckers, William Lent, did admit to having been taken in this preposterous scam and filed suit, which is how the details of the impossible fraud came to light. There was little chance of Lent winning his suit since Arnold would be tried in his home town where his friends admired him for suckering some of the world's richest men. He nevertheless refunded about $150,000 to Lent to get rid of the suit. Arnold was still left with about $250,000. This money went to his head, however, and he soon had visions of becoming an international fiancier himself. To that end he opened a bank in Elizabethtown but his financial glory was short-lived. An enraged banking competitor let loose a blast from a shotgun into Arnold's back as he strolled down the street one day, and the con man died a short time later from these wounds, coupled with pneumonia.

REF.: *CBA*; Gibson, *The Fine Art of Swindling*; Mehling, *Scandalous Scamps*; Nash, *Hustlers and Con Men, An Anecdotal History of the Confidence Man and His Games*.

Arnold, Samuel, See: **Lincoln, Abraham.**

Arnold, Stephen, b.1775, U.S., mur. A teacher in Cooperstown, N.Y., Arnold was intolerant of any student who made mistakes, exploding with invective against any child who failed to provide him with the correct answer to a question. His brother left his 6-year-old daughter with Arnold for a short time and the severe teacher put her through exhaustive tests. When the girl, Betsy Van Amburgh by name, could not pronounce the word "gig," Arnold went berserk and beat the child to death with a club. He was later apprehended in Pittsburgh, Pa., and returned to New York to be tried before James Kent, chief justice of the state supreme court. (Kent's *Commentaries on American Law*, published 1826-30, would be a standard reference work for more than a century.)

Arnold's 1805 trial was brief; he was quickly convicted and sentenced to hang, being brought to the scaffold in Cooperstown with great pomp—a battalion of infantry and a company of artillery leading the way. Thousands gathered to see the school teacher hang, but the crowd was disappointed by the local sheriff who, at the last moment, produced a reprieve from the governor. The sheriff later stated that he wanted the killer to feel the great fear of death as part of his punishment. Arnold was later judged insane and released.

REF.: *A Brief Relation of the Cruel Murder of Betsy Van Amburgh*; *CBA*; *Life and Confession of Arnold*; *The Trial of Stephen Arnold*.

Arnold, Thurman Wesley, 1891-1969, U.S., jur. Assistant attorney general of the United States from 1938-43, prosecuting over two hundred antitrust cases. He also served as judge on the U.S. Court of Appeals for the District of Columbia from 1943-45. REF.: *CBA*.

Arnstein (Arndstein), Jules W. (AKA: Nicky; Nick Arnold; Nicholas Arnold; Wallace Ames; John Adams; J. Willard Adair), prom. 1910s-20s, U.S., fraud-rob. Arnstein was a dapper, handsome crook who wore Bond Street clothes, ate in the best restaurants, and stayed in the finest hotels in America and Europe. He liked everyone to think that he was an international gambler, encouraging the romantic image he had of himself, especially in the women who loved him. One of these was the Broadway comedienne, Fannie Brice, who squandered her fortune on him and his worthless ways. He was arrogant, selfish, and vain as a strutting peacock, but full of color and had a great sense of offbeat humor. Coupled with his intriguing personality, Arnstein's image was expanded by the notorious and flamboyant characters about him, his financial backer, Arnold Rothstein, whom he admired and followed into gambling disaster and his celebrated lawyer, William J. Fallon, "The Great Mouthpiece" for America's most infamous criminals, not the least of whom was Arnstein.

Gambling, the obsession that was to grip Arnstein all his life, was utterly foreign to his hard-working, middle class parents, immigrants who struggled to maintain repectability. His father, a Jew born in Berlin, fought gallantly in the Franco-Prussian War of 1870 and was decorated several times. He later immigrated to the U.S., settling in New York. Arnstein's mother was Dutch, reared in the Episcopal Church and when she married his father, it was agreed that the family would attend St. Joseph's Epicopal Church in New York City. The gambler proudly told his friends in later years that he was a communicant in the church through his teens, adding, "No boy could have been brought up with more love and care than was I, and I always have loved the beautiful things of life—beautiful pictures, good books, and birds and flowers. My fondness for gambling, however, led me to live a life rather apart from my family. It is one of the penalties I have payed for my fondness for the cards, the dice, and the horses."

Arnstein, in addition to sharping transatlantic passengers at cards on luxury liners, beginning about 1910, was a deft confidence man, mulcting victims in a variety of con games. His first arrest was one of an international nature. In 1912, Arnstein bilked an American businessman, William E. Shinks, of Springfield, Mass., out of $15,000 but fled to London. There, with dyed blonde hair, he and some others busied themselves in fleecing British bluebloods. He was arrested in London for the Shinks scam by two New York detectives, Barney Flood and Joseph Riley. The detectives had gone to London to arrest two American racketeers who had eluded their handcuffs after posting a $100,000 bail in the British courts. Flood and Riley then received a cable to arrest Arnstein on the Shinks job. The detectives found their man at the Savoy, living royally and calling himself James Wilfred Adair. When they approached him in the hotel foyer, Arnstein, affecting a British accent, "Raaly, this is a surprise. You quite have the advawntage of me, don't you know. I really cawn't say that I evah saw you befoah."

"Cut the act, Arnstein," Flood told him; he had met Arnstein years earlier when busting up crap and poker games in New York. "You're going back to the States with us."

Arnstein maintained his phony identity and accent all the way back to the U.S. on board a luxury liner and right into a New York court where he managed to post $25,000 bail (provided by his father who thought his son could do no wrong). Arnstein's lawyer, William Fallon, tried mightily to wiggle his client out of a conviction in the Shinks case but the prosecution by District Attorney Charles S. Whitman was doggedly effective and Arnstein was eventually convicted, being sentenced to serve two years in Sing Sing by Judge Otto Rosalsky. Arnstein arrived at Sing Sing on Mar. 18, 1916, and became a model prisoner of trusty status. Whitman, then governor, pardoned him on July 16, 1917, with almost nine months taken off the con man's sentence.

The short time Arnstein spent in Sing Sing was due to his powerful friends, both criminal and political. He was a friend and sometimes employee of Mr. Big, Arnold Rothstein, and the client of William J. Fallon whose political links to local and state politicians were strong. Moreover, Arnstein had met the internationally celebrated Ziegfeld comedy star Fannie Brice in London in December 1913 when Brice was starring at the London Palladium. For propriety's sake, the comedienne later claimed she met Arnstein in Baltimore in 1914. She was married to hotel and barbershop owner Frank White whom she divorced in 1913. Arnstein was also married, having wed Carrie Greenthal on May 5, 1906. While Arnstein was a prisoner at Sing Sing, Fannie visited him as often as permitted, spending a fortune in fees to Fallon to get him out. She reportedly sold a good deal of her jewelry, getting only $20,000 for gems that were worth ten times that amount, to keep Arnstein comfortable in prison.

Fannie Brice, a fool for love, also had to deal with Arnstein's estranged wife who filed a $100,000 suit against her for alienation of affection. Fannie paid her off and she and Arnstein were married in Brooklyn, date uncertain. The couple settled down and produced two handsome children. Arnstein told a reporter, "I love a home, a fireside. I think of my wife waiting for me, with the children and my heart warms. A wife and children, and the future to look forward together." While Arnstein played the family man to the press, he continued his liaisons with the underworld, often becoming the front man in enormous white collar robberies. He appeared to mastermind these robberies on Wall Street, particularly those of negotiable bonds, but the man who pulled the strings was his idol, Rothstein. "I have a gambler's heart," Arnstein once confided in a friend. "It is a great thrill to me to play a game. One of the biggest kicks I ever got was when I saw Arnold Rothstein lose $500,000 once on the turn of a card without a sign of emotion."

It was Rothstein who was undoubtedly behind the theft of $5 million in Liberty Bond thefts which began in 1918. Messengers carrying these bonds from one Wall Street broker to another, as forms of collateral on various investments, were provided with no security guards and the runners were easily held up. The bonding houses which insured the bonds for the broker were the real losers, having to shoulder the loss. Police began to tail the messengers but this proved an almost fruitless task in that there were so many messengers picking up Liberty Bonds by the scores and at all hours without notice, that officers found it impossible to keep track of the deliveries. Finally, on Feb. 2, 1920, police followed a messenger from Parrish and Company on Broadway and interrupted seven men who, minutes later, were in the act of holding up the runner at gunpoint. Among the seven stickup men was Joseph Gluck, a man with a long history of assault and armed robbery. He was the acknowledged ringleader of the holdup gang but Gluck refused to talk, insisting that he would wait to hear from his lawyer. Neither his lawyer nor his bail bondsman appeared and Gluck languished in the Tombs.

Incensed at being ignored by his bosses, Gluck made a deal with the district attorney, getting a suspended sentence for informing on the top people in the bond theft ring. These included Nick Cohen whom Gluck said recruited him for the robbery band and Cohen's underboss, William Furey, his liaison to Cohen. Only once, Gluck said, did he get a glance at the man he called "Mr. Arnold, the mastermind" of the bond robberies. It was to Arnold that the bonds were delivered and he, in turn, fenced them for half of their worth, Gluck surmised, keeping the lion's share of the profits for himself. (The truth was that Arnstein turned over more than $5 million in stolen bonds to his mentor, Rothstein, and received one-fifth on the dollar, a considerable amount but from which he had to fund the entire robbery ring.) At first police thought that the mysterious "Mr. Arnold" was none other than the notorious gambler Arnold Rothstein, but when pictures of Rothstein were shown to Gluck the bandit shook his head. He described "Mr. Arnold" as tall,

handsome, slendor, very sophisticated with a handsomely waxed mustache that was slightly turned up at the ends. This fit the description of Nicky Arnstein and Gluck nodded instantly when shown Arnstein's photos. An all-points bulletin was issued to arrest Arnstein. But the dapper gambler knew all about Gluck and the non-stop confessions he made to the police. Cohen and Furey, who had also been arrested, joined with Gluck in identifying Arnstein as the boss of the bond thefts.

Arnstein was nowhere to be found. Fannie Brice told detectives that her husband was off somewhere playing cards. When told that her husband was the mastermind behind the bond thefts, Fannie laughed uproariously. "Nicky? My Nicky?" she told detectives. "Nicky Arnstein couldn't mastermind an electric light bulb into a socket!" To Fannie Brice, Nicky Arnstein was a sweet, ineffectual gambler, a charming man who was fun to be with, a tender-hearted husband who doted upon their children. She would cling to her romantic image of Arnstein until the day of her death in 1951, saying many years after they had divorced, still in love with the rogue, "He stood for manners, education, good breeding, and an extraordinary gift for dreaming." No, certainly, her Nicky could never have been behind the notorious Wall Street robberies.

The fugitive was far from New York at this time, having gone to Pittsburgh and registered at a posh hotel to wait for a deal to be made by his lawyer Fallon. He still had Arnold Rothstein behind him and was confident that he would never serve another day in prison. Rothstein continued to support his colorful lieutenant, calling in Fallon and ordering him to establish bail for the missing Arnstein. Fallon began negotiating for his client Arnstein. Officials insisted that a $100,000 bail be set but Fallon argued them down to $60,000. When this was arranged, Arnstein slipped into New York City in May 1920 and, in keeping with his whimsical nature, suggested that he turn himself into the police in a spectacular fashion. He, Fannie Brice, Rothstein, and William J. Fallon got into Rothstein's blue Cadillac Laudelet and drove it behind the tail end of the annual police parade, driving down Fifth Avenue to take cheers and waves from thousands of spectators, including many dignitaries on the reviewing stand, among them the police commissioner and the mayor. The car pulled up in front of a fashionable speakeasy owned by Thomas E. Foley, Big Tom of Tammany fame. Rothstein and Arnstein went across the street to the Criminal Courts Building to arrange Nicky's bail while Fannie Brice, Fallon, Donald Henderson Clarke, a newsman friendly to the Arnsteins, and bondsman Harold Norris, stepped into Foley's for some drinks.

When Fallon later looked out the window of the saloon, he saw that Rothstein's expensive car was gone, stolen. He turned to Foley's manager, Michael N. Delagi and told him that Rothstein would have his head for allowing his Cadillac to be stolen. The much-frightened Delagi immediately got on the phone and made several cars, saying that the car stolen from in front of Foley's place belonged to Mr. Big. The vehicle reappeared within thirty minutes. Inside of it was the notorious Edward "Monk" Eastman, and three of his goons. Eastman was apologetic, saying his boys had no idea that the car belonged to Mr. Rothstein. "You was lucky callin' so quick," Eastman added, since the car was already in a garage and a crew was about to dismantle it and sell its expensive parts. (Eastman, once an underworld powerhouse, would be murdered only seven months later.)

Fallon made legal history in his defense of Arnstein, telling his client to refuse to answer the court's questions on the grounds that "they would tend to incriminate and degrade" him. He carried this argument all the way to the U.S. Supreme Court where the court agreed with Fallon, upholding the rights of an accused under the Fifth Amendment. It was the Arnstein case that set the precedent for all witnesses who were to later "take the Fifth." Fallon had more tricks up his sleeve. He insisted that his client be tried in a federal court in Washington, D.C., since his client could not get a fair trial in New York where prejudice ran high against him. Of course, the real reason was that Fallon knew Arnstein, with

Gambler and ladies' man Nicky Arnstein with his friend and hard-drinking lawyer, William J. Fallon (left); Arnold Rothstein (middle), known as "The Big Bankroll," was the man Arnstein admired most; Arnstein (right) after his release from prison.

The romance of Nicky Arnstein and Fannie Brice was a chaotic one—he was an incessant gambler and she a hard-working Ziegfeld Follies star; they are shown at left in 1920 when Arnstein was charged with engineering the theft of millions in Liberty Bonds; at bottom Nicky and Fannie with their two children, a happy family that later broke apart when Brice sued for divorce on grounds of adultery; Brice at right with comedian Bob Hope, doing her interpretation of "Baby Snooks" of radio fame.

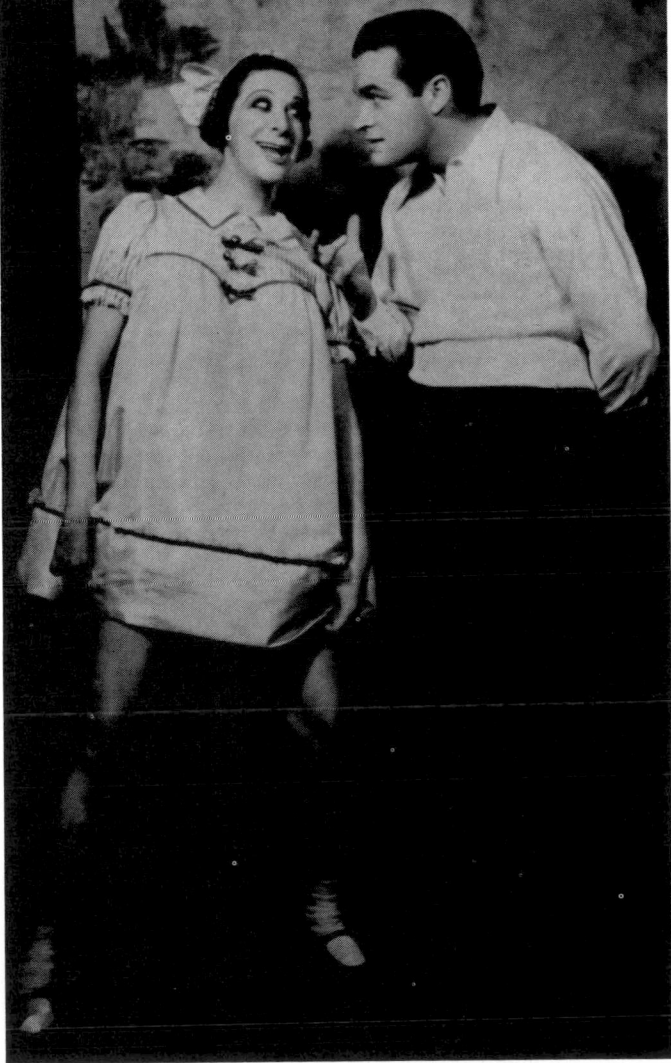

several eye-witnesses testifying against him, stood no chance of acquittal. In New York the minimum penalty for robbery was twenty-five years but the same offense in federal court could only bring a 2-year sentence. Once tried in the federal court, New York had to drop charges against Arnstein so as not to violate the "double jeopardy" rule of the Constitution. Arnstein was convicted of the bond robberies and sent to Leavenworth on May 16, 1924. He emerged a free man on Dec. 21, 1925, having served only a year and a half. Again, faithful Fannie Brice was waiting for him.

The marriage, however, was worn out with Arnstein's antics. He abused Fannie mercilessly, telling her that her most popular song, "My Man," made people think she was singing about him and that the lyrics condemned him as an insensitive brute. When she had her Roman nose changed to a Grecian nose (by plastic surgeon Dr. Harry Schierson), he told her she was now so beautiful that it made him feel insecure. But it was Arnstein's insatiable gambling and philandering with other women that undid the strong emotional ties Fannie Brice had wrapped about their union. She finally divorced the errant Arnstein in 1927 on grounds of adultery, stating that she had found her husband with another woman in a Chicago hotel room. The films based on the Brice-Arnstein relationship were, of course, highly fictional. Nicky Arnstein was therein portrayed as a man of considerable depth and intelligence. He was nothing more than a cheap crook with a thin veneer of urbane manners glossing over a wholly larcenous nature. Only Fannie Brice saw Nicky Arnstein as someone worthwhile and when she left him, he was exposed for the opportunist he was. He lived out his life in obscurity in southern California. See: **Eastman, Monk; Fallon, William J.; Rothstein, Arnold.**

REF.: *CBA;* Churchill, *A Pictorial History of American Crime;* Clarke, *In the Reign of Rothstein;* Farnsworth, *The Ziegfeld Follies;* Fowler, *The Great Mouthpiece;* Katcher, *The Big Bankroll;* Peterson, *The Mob;* Sann, *The Lawless Decade;* Thompson and Raymond, *Gang Rule in New York;* (FICTION) Wilstach, *Under Cover Man;* (FILM) *Funny Girl,* 1968; *Funny Lady,* 1975.

Aronowitz, Joseph, and **Klein, Philip,** and **Levy, Jack,** prom. 1940s, U.S., brib.-gamb. In late 1948, Aronowitz called David Shapiro, the co-captain of the George Washington University basketball team, telling him that they should meet out of "mutual benefit." Shapiro had never met Aronowitz but agreed to meet with the gambler. After the meeting, Sharpiro went to the police, telling detectives that Aronowitz offered him large amounts of money if he would arrange to shave points when playing games with teams having little chance of beating Washington. The detectives told Shapiro to play a waiting game and pretend he was interested in the deal. The gamblers then invited the basketball star to a New Year's Eve party and offered him $1,000 to shave his points in the game against Manhattan College, to be played on Jan. 4, 1949, in Madison Square Garden. Shapiro, according to plan, insisted that the gamblers pay his "uncle" on the night of the game. Aronowitz, Philip Klein, and a bigshot Florida gambler, Jack Levy, agreed and paid the "uncle" who turned out to be a detective. The trio were all arrested, convicted and given long prison terms. Shapiro and his teammates went on to score a stunning victory over Manhattan College. This incident was but a prelude to the massive inroads other gamblers made into bribing college basketball stars into shaving points in the 1950-51 season. See: **Basketball Scandals, 1951.**

REF.: *CBA;* Danforth, *The D.A.'s Man.*

Arpels, Claude, prom. 1977, U.S. fraud. On Mar. 3, 1977, Arpels, president of Van Cleef & Arpels, an exclusive jewelry store on Fifth Avenue, was indicted in Manhattan Federal District Court for offering "gratuities" to IRS agents. The four-count indictment accused Arpels of providing agent Ellis Iversen with an emerald ring, two expensive wristwatches, and a diamond brooch valued at $1,400 during an audit of tax returns conducted in 1973-74. According to company vice president Robert Sullivan, the store had not received "one cent of advantage" on their tax returns, but had been repeatedly shaken down by crooked IRS

agents during a fourteen-month period. "We went along due to harassment," he said.

Iversen pleaded guilty to having conspired to receive illegal gifts from Van Cleef and other merchants, and was sentenced to three months in prison. He was subsequently discharged from the IRS. Arpels and the company controller, Al I. Schwartz, also entered a guilty plea. Schwartz was assessed a $2,500 fine. REF.: *CBA.*

Arraj, Alfred Albert, b.1906- , U.S., jur. Member of the Joint Committee on Judicial Ethics from 1973 and appointed federal judge for the Colorado District Court by President Dwight D. Eisenhower in 1957. REF.: *CBA.*

Arran Murder, The, See: **Laurie, John Watson.**

Arras Witches, 1459-91, Fr., witchcraft. Pierre le Broussart was the church's emissary to Arras, France, assigned to ferret out religious heretics belonging to the Vaudois and Waldensian sects, and also all those suspected of practicing the black arts. In 1460 the Inquisitor seized and arrested a townswoman named Deniselle Grenières who was tortured into revealing the names of five other people engaged in witchcraft.

The charges against the accused were outlined by a local chronicler named Jacques du Clercq who told of men and women who were mysteriously transported to the "devil's banquet" where they were forced to engage in carnal orgies with Satan. Two theologians who studied the case recommended mercy since there was no evidence of murder or desecration of holy objects. Le Broussart ignored their counsel and advice, and had Grenières and the four women belonging to the Vaudois sect dressed in heretic's clothing, taken to the stake on May 9, 1460, and set on fire. Oblivious to their screams, the Inquisitor stood solemnly by relating the crimes of the accused. The witches had flown about the countryside on *baguettes* (brooms) he said, and had engaged in wild bacchanalia with demons.

The witch hunt did not end there. Du Clercq recorded in his journal that "many notable persons were imprisoned as well as lesser folk, crazy women and others who were so horribly tortured and so terribly tormented that some admitted they had done exactly what was charged." Some of the wealthier townspeople who were arrested and imprisoned by the Inquisition were able to buy their freedom. Others were not so lucky.

By the end of the year business conditions in the town of Arras had suffered badly. Le Broussart was censured by the Archbishop of Rheims and the Bishop of Arras, Jean Jouffroy, who dismissed the remaining witchcraft cases. The affair ended on July 10, 1491, when the Parliament of Paris decided that the Inquisitor had acted "in error and against the order and dignity of justice." Prayers were solicited for the unfortunate victims forced to walk on fire and swallow vinegar to test their guilt or innocence.

REF.: *CBA;* Limborch, *Historia Inquisitionis;* Raviart, *Sorcières et Possédées;* Robbins, *Encyclopedia of Witchcraft;* Summers, *The Geography of Witchcraft.*

Arrhidaeus, d.317 B.C., Macedonia, king, assass. Son of Philip II of Macedon, he was elected king of Macedonia in 323 B.C. by Alexander the Great's soldiers after Alexander died of a fever in Babylon. He was executed in 317 on the order of Alexander's mother, Olympias. REF.: *CBA.*

Arria, d.42 A.D., Roman., suic. Wife of Caccina Paetus who was sentenced to death for conspiring against Emperor Claudius. Not wanting to outlive her husband, she stabbed herself, then handing him the dagger, said, "It doesn't hurt." REF.: *CBA.*

Arriaga, Manual Jose de, 1842-1917, Port., pres.-writer. Portuguese poet and legal writer who took an active role in the revolution that overthrew King Manuel in 1910 and established the republic. He was elected president in 1911 and resigned in 1915. REF.: *CBA.*

Arridy, Joseph, c.1915-39, and **Aguilar, Frank,** c.1903-37, U.S., asslt.-rape-mur. In somber tones, District Attorney French L. Taylor assured the frantic residents of Pueblo, Colo., that he would not allow the defendant's history of mental illness to stand in the way of a murder conviction. The community demanded no less. There was even talk of lynching Joseph Arridy for the senseless murder of 15-year-old Dorothy Drain. Not much was known about Arridy before the murder. He had spent most of his life in an insane asylum at Grand Junction, Colo. On Aug. 8, 1936, the thin-faced, 21-year-old escaped from the institution. He hopped a freight train for Colorado Springs where he assaulted a 20-year-old woman who barely escaped with her life. The attack occurred near a railroad underpass.

Arridy continued on to Pueblo where, on the night of Aug. 15, he broke into the home of Vernon Drain, a foreman for the Works Progress Administration (WPA). Drain and his wife had made plans to attend a local dance, leaving their two daughters, Dorothy and Barbara, home by themselves. The Drains left their home at 11 p.m. Both girls were asleep. The police speculated that Arridy and an accomplice named Frank Aguilar entered the home between midnight and 3 a.m. Stone Avenue was a quiet neighborhood where citizens left their doors unlocked at night. Nobody could conceive of the horrible crime Arridy and Aguilar were about to commit.

The two men entered through the front door, going through the darkened house with the help of matches. They found the two sisters sleeping in a bedroom. While Aguilar looked on, Arridy raped Dorothy before killing her with a dull hatchet. Twelve-year-old Barbara miraculously survived the ordeal, though she remained in a coma for thirteen days. "Assault was the motive in this case," theorized police chief Arthur Grady. "There was no robbery connected with it. The girls were asleep." Arridy would later say the assaults were done out of meanness and he felt sorry.

The police had only a few clues to work with, but a massive dragnet commenced. Pueblo had not experienced anything like this in years. Nervous parents kept their children indoors, and for the first time the houses on Stone Street were bolted shut. Every law enforcement agency in southern Colorado was mobilized, and bloodhounds were brought in from Canon City to assist in the search. Arridy later told the police he hid in the dusty attic of his mother's home just two blocks from the site of the murder. When Mrs. Arridy discovered bloodstained clothing, she allegedly turned him out of the house with $1 in his pocket. When his parents were questioned by police, however, they said they had not seen their son in more than three years. A search of the attic tended to corroborate their contention.

Arridy fled to Cheyenne, where he was captured by special agents of the Union Pacific railroad. He confessed, implicating Aguilar who was also employed by the WPA. "I intend to file murder charges against both," Taylor said. The arrest of Arridy and Aguilar closed out a sordid chapter of Pueblo history. The two killers were executed in Colorado two years apart. Aguilar, perhaps because he was judged sane, was the first to go on Aug. 13, 1937. Arridy followed on Jan. 6, 1939. REF.: *CBA*.

Arrington, George W., 1844-1923, U.S., west. law enfor. off. One of the greatest Texas Rangers on record, Arrington was born in Greensboro, Ala., on Dec. 23, 1844, and fought for the Confederacy in Mosby's Raiders. Following the Civil War, Arrington joined other Confederate soldiers and went to Mexico, offering his services to the doomed Emperor Maximilian and then moved on to seek adventure in Central America before returning to the U.S. in 1867. He eventually moved to Texas and joined the Texas Rangers in the early 1870s, fast rising through the ranks until he was appointed a captain. Arrington's territory was the Panhandle of Texas, then one of the worst nightmares for any lawmen. The area was overrun with hostile Indians and hundreds of hardcase outlaws who would rather shoot it out than talk truce. Whenever Arrington and his company of twenty men went out in sweeps to capture outlaws, fugitives by the scores were either captured or killed. In one month alone, July 1878, Arrington and his company rounded up forty men, half of these having separate murder charges against them.

As a captain of the rangers, Arrington proved himself fearless. Often as not, if his men were on duty elsewhere, he would go after several desperadoes alone and invariably bring in two or three rustlers. He was as tough as any outlaw on the plains, and his

strict discipline was applied to his own men. Whenever he caught one of his own rangers tipsy he would order him locked up as a common drunk. Arrington was living proof that the Rangers, like the Mounties, always got their man. He would track fugitives to both ends of the continent. He trailed one wealthy cattle rustler all the way to New England, returning him to Texas secretly. Arrington knew that the wealthy fugitive would have lawyers waiting in each state through which they would travel so he purposely changed trains at regular intervals and stayed in hotels using aliases for himself and his captive.

Arrington left the Rangers in the early 1880s and became sheriff of Wheeler County, a post he kept for eight years before retiring to his Rocking Chair Ranch in 1890. The old lawman came out of retirement briefly to become sheriff for the same county in 1894 and during this time he was confronted by six tough drunken cowboys in a local saloon who dared him to throw them into jail. Arrington had a small jail and no deputy so he did the next best thing. He handcuffed the six men to the bar rail and held them in custody for twenty-four uncomfortable hours, until all promised to leave town without creating further disturbances. Arrington died on his ranch, Mar. 31, 1923.

REF.: Bartholomew, *The Biographical Album of Western Gunfighters;* CBA; Gillett, *Six Years with the Texas Rangers;* Webb, *The Texas Rangers.*

Arrington, Marie Dean, 1935- , U.S., mur. In his capacity as the public defender of Leesburg, Fla., Robert Pierce was well acquainted with Arrington. He represented her teen-aged son and daughter when they stood trial for armed robbery and forgery in 1968. The outcome of these two separate trials did not please Arrington—herself an ex-convict who was free on bond while awaiting sentencing for the shooting death of her husband in 1964.

The anger the black woman felt toward the public defender festered until Apr. 22, 1968, when she put on her best new outfit and took a cab down to Pierce's private office. To her dismay, the object of her vendetta was not in, just a 37-year-old secretary, Vivian Ritter. Later that afternoon Pierce returned to find Ritter gone. It was not like her to just walk out. Never once during her thirteen-year employment had the pretty brunette done such a thing. The police were immediately notified. Within hours several witnesses volunteered the information that Ritter and an unidentified black woman had been observed leaving the building together, but they were not walking side by side. It was quickly surmised that Ritter had been forcibly taken from the building, perhaps at the gunpoint.

Six days later the shotgunned remains of Ritter were found. There was strong evidence that suggested she had been senselessly tortured before her death. Arrington was picked up shortly afterward by Florida police. She was convicted of first-degree murder in the slaying of Ritter and sentenced to die in the electric chair. A twenty-year prison sentence for the 1964 murder of her husband was tacked on by the courts.

Before her execution could be carried out, Arrington escaped from the women's prison in Lowell, Fla., on Mar. 1, 1969. Her name was added to the FBI's Most Wanted List and she remained a fugitive for nearly three years. There was some talk in Leesburg that a vigilante group located Marie Dean and had taken her into the swamps where Vivian Ritter was avenged. This was not the case, however. The murderer was captured in New Orleans in 1972 by FBI agents. REF.: *CBA*.

Arrison, William, 1826-55, U.S., bomb.-mur. Arrison's father was a veteran of the War of 1812. When he received his discharge, he moved his family to Delaware County, Ohio, where his son William was born in 1826. The Arrisons were a family of farmers, and young William was brought up to respect the land. He received his early education in Quincy, Ill., but when the 1848 California gold rush began he abandoned his studies and a future career in agriculture to move west and seek his fortune.

After a few years Arrison returned from California to study medicine at the Cincinnati College of Medicine and Surgery. While there, he worked as a house surgeon at the Marine Hospital, a facility run by Superintendent Isaac Allison, who frequently clashed with Arrison over trifling matters, usually related to money. On one occasion Arrison had loaned the older man a small sum of cash which was never repaid. Arrison's roommate, Dr. Thomas Cummings, was a party to a particularly bitter quarrel between the two men one night in May 1854.

Allison demanded that Arrison pay him for a medical book he had recently purchased—he had gone out of his way to find the volume and expected compensation. Arrison objected to the price, saying he could get it much cheaper. "You are a knave and a coward!" Allison shouted. Blows were struck, but the student was no match for the superintendent, who thrashed him about the face and head. When it was over Arrison lifted himself off the floor and said, "Cummings, I have got a great notion to kill."

He brooded about the matter for nearly a month before deciding to go to Adderly's drug store and buy gunpowder. In his boarding house Arrison constructed a wooden box which he lined with leaden bullets and slugs. If opened, the triggering mechanism disengaged and the bullets would instantly strike the victim. Arrison's ingenuity, coupled with his extensive knowledge of firearms, served him well in this instance.

After the infernal device was assembled, Arrison carefully wrapped it in paper and twine and then summoned a delivery boy named King, who took it to Charles Jackson near the hospital at Western Row and Longworth the night of June 26, 1854.

Jackson and Cummings examined the attached card and shook the box. They concluded it must be something of great value, not realizing fully the extent of their friend's anger toward Allison. The package was shown to Mrs. Allison. "I suppose here is a present for you," said Dr. Joseph Baker, who received the box from Jackson. She smiled and took the package into an adjoining room. Five minutes later a loud explosion was heard from the upstairs chamber of the hospital. Allison's wife emerged from the room, dazed and bleeding, her dress on fire but quickly extinguished by Dr. Baker. Her husband however, was riddled with bullets in the stomach and thighs and was barely alive. Allison was removed to an operating room where he died later that night.

Arrison was arrested and charged with premeditated murder. His trial began in the Criminal Court of Cincinnati on Dec. 11. Nine days later a verdict of Guilty was returned by the jury. Attorneys for Arrison put forward a motion for a new trial, but it was overruled by Judge Flinn. On Dec. 23 the doctor was sentenced to hang. REF.: *CBA*.

Arroyo, Miguel, 1924- , U.S., (wrong. convict.) mur. Arroyo owned a small grocery in the tough Bedford-Stuyvesant neighborhood of Brooklyn, an area plagued by gang warfare between rival Puerto Ricans and blacks who fought for control of the "turf." Edward Davis, a 15-year-old, was killed outside the store during a street fight on Sept. 19, 1964. Based on shaky eyewitness reports and the fact that his grocery had recently been burglarized by young hooligans, Arroyo was arrested the next day. He was indicted for manslaughter in December and convicted by a jury on May 12, 1965.

Nearly two years later some new facts came to light which absolved Arroyo. Defense witnesses were re-examined, and they were unanimous in their opinion that the killer was 25-year-old Jose Velasquez, who had recently been picked up for narcotics possession. On July 21, 1966, the stockily built young drifter who listed his residence on 85th Street, New York, was arrested in the Manhattan Criminal Court building after his drug charge was dropped.

Harry Gittleson, the presiding judge at the time of Arroyo's conviction, approved an application for a new trial. Arroyo was released on parole without having to post bail, and formally cleared on July 25. "I was persuaded that there was a sharp doubt whether this man was properly convicted and I sent word to District Attorney Aaron Koota asking that a further investigation be made," Gittleson explained. "I couldn't escape the conclusion that three young women testifying for Mr. Arroyo were telling the truth." REF.: *CBA*.

Arsenault, Henry (Henry Powell), 1927- , U.S., rob.-mur.

In 1955 Powell killed a Newton, Mass. lawyer during a home invasion. He was convicted of first-degree murder and sentenced to die in the electric chair. A half-hour before his scheduled appointment with the executioner, Powell's sentence was commuted to life in prison. Given a second chance in life, he promised to devote the remainder of his days to counseling wayward youths headed for trouble.

True to his word, Powell addressed a number of high school groups in the greater Boston area. He appeared on various national talk shows, and founded the Project Youth Juvenile Counseling Program. By 1979 he claimed to have personally counseled 50,000 minors.

He was a trusted inmate of the Bay State Center in Norfolk, and had always returned to prison following his unchaperoned speaking engagements at the local community centers. In 1979 Powell married and on March 13 of that year he mysteriously vanished.

"It makes no sense," said Larry Parnell, a member of the state corrections department. "I was very shocked to hear it." So was everybody else. The story made the national news wires, but it was a tempest in a teapot. Four days later Powell surfaced. At present, he remains in detention at the Bay State Center, a quiet, reserved individual who continues to make good on a promise made thirty-five years earlier. REF.: *CBA*.

Arses (Xerxes III), prom. 337 B.C., Pers., king, assass. Son of Artaxerxes III, appointed king of Persia in 338 and ruled for two years until he was killed by the eunuch Bagoas. REF.: *CBA*.

Arsinoe III, d.c.205 B.C., Egypt, assass. Daughter of Ptolemy III Euergetes, sister of Ptolemy IV Philopator, and mother of Ptolemy V Epiphanes. She was executed on order of her brother. REF.: *CBA*.

Arsinoe IV, d.41 B.C., Egypt, assass. Daughter of King Ptolemy XI Auletes and sister of Cleopatra. She was captured and led through the streets of Rome, then executed on order of Antony. REF.: *CBA*.

Arson, See: **Supplements**, Vol IV.

Artabanus (AKA: Ardaban) d.c.464 B.C., Pers., minister, assass. Minister to Xerxes I whom he assassinated in 465. He either killed Darius himself or convinced Artaxerxes I to do so. In the confusion following their deaths he ruled Achaemenia until he was assassinated by Artaxerxes. REF.: *CBA*.

Artavasdes III, prom. 40 B.C., Arm., king, assass. King of Armenia from c.55 to 34. He succeeded his father Tigranes I the Great, then abandoned the Roman Empire and gave his allegiance to the Kingdom of Parthia. When Mark Antony's Roman army invaded the second time, Artavasdes was captured, taken to Alexandria, and executed by Cleopatra. REF.: *CBA*.

Artaxerxes III (O'chus), d.338 B.C., Pers., king, assass. Son of Artaxerxes II, he succeeded to the throne in 359 B.C. and immediately murdered most of his relatives. Repeated attempts to conquer Egypt were defeated until 343. He was killed by a eunuch, Bagoas, an Egyptian who had become his chief advisor. REF.: *CBA*.

Arthur, 1393-1458, Brittany, law enfor. off., banish. Son of John IV the Valiant, he was captured at Agincourt, then imprisoned in England from 1415-20. In 1425 he was appointed constable of France and took control of the French Army. He was banished from the French court from 1427-32. During a portion of that time he fought under Joan of Arc. REF.: *CBA*.

Arthur, Charles, prom. 1911, Brit., burg.-asslt. Described by the London papers as "an English desperado", 31-year-old Arthur was sentenced to a life of penal servitude by Justice Grantham in 1911 for shooting wildly at a policeman during a burglary. Before a second bullet could find its mark, Arthur's aim was deflected by a woman in the street. The penalty was harsh, but as Robert Churchill observed, it was "lucky for him that he missed." The defendant pleaded his own case. Arthur had decided to forego paying legal fees, perhaps believing that no barrister could present his case more eloquently than he.

REF.: *CBA*; Hastings, *The Other Mr. Churchill*.

Artukovic, Andrija (AKA: **Alois Anich, the Butcher of the Balkans**) 1900- , Yugo., war crim.-geno. Shortly after German troops arrived in Yugoslavia in 1941, a puppet government headed by fascist sympathizer Ante Pavelic was established and the systematic transportation of Jews and Serbs to Nazi death camps in the East began. Artukovic rose to power quickly in the new order, finally appointed minister of the interior and given full responsibility for eliminating 750,000 Serbians and 20,000 Jews residing in the "Independent State of Croatia."

Pavelic and Artukovic employed some of the most atrocious techniques of genocide known to the modern world, for example, contests among the elite corps of secret police known as the Ustashi to see who could sever the most human heads in a short time. This infamy earned Artukovic the nickname "Butcher of the Balkans." In 1948 Artukovic entered the United States illegally, using the pseudonym Alois Anich. He traveled to Surfside, Calif., where he went into business with his brother who owned a road building and construction firm.

Artukovic's Nazi past was not fully revealed until 1951 when the Yugoslavian government asked the United States to deport him for the murders of an estimated 1,239 civilians. A long court battle followed as the former fascist leader fought tenaciously to avoid extradition. In 1959 U.S. Commissioner Theodore Hocke issued a decree protecting Artukovic from those seeking his deportation, on the grounds that the charges were "political in character" and issued by a repressive Communist regime. Then the thick filefolder containing sensitive information about the accused mysteriously disappeared from a suburb in Los Angeles, prompting speculation that Artukovic had powerful friends in the CIA and the U.S. State Department who granted him asylum in return for information.

"I am innocent. I have done nothing to warrant this persecution in America," he said in his defense. "Never did I think such a thing could happen in this wonderful country."

The years passed, and the controversy was still not resolved. Following an unsuccessful 1967 plot to kidnap Artukovic and spirit him away to a jail in Yugoslavia, a wall was constructed around his home south of Long Beach. Rarely was he seen by his neighbors. He was fearful that Israeli agents might drag him off in the night.

In December 1975 Representative Elizabeth Holtzman of New York requested the Immigration and Naturalization Service to re-open the matter and consider rescinding the stay of extradition order, issued in 1959. "The longer everybody waits the better it is for Artukovic," a congressional aide said. "I mean the guy is already 76, and his health is failing, and I doubt Yugoslavia wants to put a body on trial." REF.: *CBA.*

Arvenitakis, Takos, prom. 1870, Gr., kid.-mur. The kidnapping of prominent westerners by outlaw bands of the Mid-East and Mediterranean regions may be said to date back to 1870, the year that Takos Arvenitakis and his renegade horde were loose on the Greek frontier.

A former soldier who had seen action against the Turks, Arvenitakis and his outlaw brigands seized and held for ransom a party of British travelers who had set out from Athens to explore the ancient battlefield at Marathon. The British Legation at Athens had granted permission to tour the site. The entourage was composed of Lord and Lady Muncaster, Frederick Vyner, the younger brother of Lady de Grey, and several others. They set forth on Apr. 9, 1870, and were provided an armed escort to guard against the brigands active in the uninhabited regions. They were joined by a complement of twelve policemen from Marathon on the return trip to Athens. This only slowed the party down, and provided the bandits with the opportunity they were seeking.

The guards were killed by thirty of Arvenitakis' men in a brief and bloody skirmish. The British travelers were seized and held for a million drachmas. Lady Muncaster was set free and told to deliver the ransom demand to the government. As a sign of good faith, her husband was subsequently released. The Ionian Bank in Athens paid the demand, but then the rebel leader increased the stakes. He asked for a general pardon and safe passage for his men. The Greeks granted permission for the brigands to flee into Turkey, but Takos soon came to the conclusion that he was being duped. The Turks would just as soon see him dead than safe in their country with ill-gotten loot.

When the bandit leader found out that Greek soldiers were on his heels, he put to death Vyner and two members of the party. Eventually the troops overtook the guerilla band. Six of the bandits were captured and many more were wounded. Takos, however, eluded his captors and fled into the hills. When Queen Victoria learned of the outrage, she demanded that Greece be dealt with sternly. This idea was rejected by Prime Minister Gladstone, who kept a cool head during the debate. As a result, the queen held him in disfavor for many weeks afterward.
REF.: *CBA;* Messick, *Kidnapping.*

Asbury, Herbert, 1891-1963, U.S., crime writer. Born in Farmington, Mo., Asbury became one of the top true-fact crime writers of the first half of the twentieth century. He served in France during WWI and, as a working journalist, was on the staff of the New York *Sun* (1916-20), New York *Herald* (1920-24), and New York *Herald Tribune* (1924 on). The son of a clergyman, Asbury fell heir to a plethora of unpublished material gathered by reformers within his own family, reports on the old-time vice districts and nineteenth century gangsters of New York, Chicago, New Orleans, and San Francisco. He put this priceless material to excellent use, coupling to it his own extensive research to produce a number of classic books concerned with American crime. These include his classic study of the nineteenth century gangsters, *The Gangs of New York* (1928), early-day crime and criminals in San Francisco, *The Barbary Coast* (1933), the brothels and madams of New Orleans in *The French Quarter* (1936), nineteenth century gambling and gamblers in *Sucker's Progress* (1938), early-day crime in Chicago in *Gem of the Prairie* (1940), and a lively history of Prohibition in *The Great Illusion* (1950). Asbury wrote a number of other crime-related books which include the biography of Bishop Francis Asbury, *A Methodist Saint* (1927), the biography of temperance leader, Carry Nation, *Carry Nation* (1929), and *The Golden Flood* (1942). He also authored two crime novels, *The Devil of Pei-Ling* (1927) and *The Tick of the Clock* (1928).
REF.: *CBA;* Nash, *Hustlers and Con Men.*

Aschoff, Karl Albert Ludwig, 1866-1942, Ger., path. REF.: *CBA.*

As for the Woman, 1939, a novel by Francis Iles (pseudonym for Anthony Berkeley Cox). This work is wholly based on the Edith Thompson case (Brit., 1922). See: **Thompson, Edith**. REF.: *CBA.*

Ashby, James, d.1853, U.S., gamb. Ashby was an usual sharper in that he preyed almost exclusively on his fellow gamblers, plying his tricks on the Mississippi in the heyday of the riverboats. He worked with a young man made up to look like the worst kind of country jake, ostensibly a dimwitted fellow, accompanied by his senile father who was dressed in derelict clothing and worked a discordant, out-of-tune fiddle. The father, of course, was Ashby, who would hover about the table where his son had been inveigled into a crooked game of cards. He would play the fiddle in fits of inspiration and then pause, saying he could no longer remember the tune he had begun. The young man, however, won against the best of the riverboat sharpers, this being attributed to "beginner's luck." The real reason for such marvelous fortune was Ashby's irregular fiddling. He would spot an opponent's hand and signal to his "son" what the player was holding through a few notes he played. Ashby was quite successful with this scam for a number of years until the act began to wear thin and too many gamblers began to recognize the old man. He quit the riverboats and resettled in St. Louis where he ran the largest Faro bank. Ashby grew to be a wealthy man and he adorned himself in the finest clothes. His fingers shone with huge rings bearing large jewels, and diamonds bedecked his brocaded vest; he wore gold bracelets, earrings. James Ashby was a walking Christmas tree, and when he died, his fellow gamblers said that he literally crushed the life out of himself with the weight of so much gold and so many gems.

REF.: Asbury, *Sucker's Progress*; Canfield, *Gambling and Card-Sharpers' Tricks Exposed*; *CBA*; Devol, *Forty Years a Gambler on the Mississippi*; Green, *Gambling Exposed*; Nash, *Hustlers and Con Men*; Richardson, *Beyond the Mississippi*.

Ashcroft, David, 1769-1817, and **Ashcroft, James**, 1764-1817, and **Ashcroft, James, Jr.**, 1685-1817, and **Holden, William**, 1770-1817, and **Robinson, John**, b.1764, Brit., rob.-mur. Thomas Littlewood was a fairly well-to-do shopkeeper in Salford, Manchester. On the outskirts of the Lancaster-Manchester Road he owned a spacious country house where he resided with his wife, and two boarders: an elderly woman named Mrs. Marsden, and a 20-year-old girl, Hannah Partington.

One day in early August 1817, Littlewood was alerted to some possible danger his family might be in by Harriet Towel, who had just paid a social call on her friend Hannah. She found the doors locked, and had observed Mrs. Marsden bent over in her kitchen chair. Mr. Littlewood entered through the window. He found Mrs. Marsden and Hannah dead in the kitchen and £160 missing from the house. They had been assaulted with a poker and a meat cleaver, and the entire house had been ransacked for valuables.

The police arrested five suspicious-looking men who had been seen lurking about the Crown and Anchor Inn on Hilton Street. On the day of the murders the three Ashcrofts and their confederate, William Holden, were observed near the Littlewood family home. The large roll of bank notes these men later flashed in the nearby alehouses convinced the police they had committed the crimes.

The men were arrested and brought before a jury which returned a verdict of guilty against all of them except Robinson, who was acquitted. Littlewood was not acquainted in any way with the murderous Ashcrofts. They were common laboring men, weavers by trade. Their decision to rob the home of Littlewood was based on hearsay information that a large amount of money could be found inside. The four convicted men were hanged on Sept. 8, 1817.

REF.: Butler, *Murderers' England*; *CBA*.

Ashe, Richard (AKA: Frank Butler), 1858-97, Aust., mur. Richard Ashe was a cold, plodding killer who never deviated from his time-tested methods of murder. In the 1890s he selected his victims by running a newspaper ad in the Sydney, Aust., *Morning Herald*: "Experienced miner wanted as mate to visit Blue Mountains prospecting."

Each time he ran this ad, he was sure to get a number of responses from hungry, unemployed men. Ashe would select the applicant that best suited his needs and would strike out for the Blue Mountains. When the victim began to dig, Ashe would pull out his revolver and shoot the man in the back. After the body had been covered up sufficiently, he would take all the victim's possessions and return to Sydney to run the ad again. In 1896, he murdered at least three men this way: a sea captain named Lee Weller, a man named Arthur Preston, and another known only as Burgess.

Each time he returned to the city, he gave the last name of his most recent victim as his own. In November 1896, using the Weller's name, Ashe boarded the *Swanhilda* at Newcastle and set sail for San Francisco, where perhaps he planned to re-introduce his prospecting murder racket. The killer was well acquainted with the country. In his earlier wayfaring days, Ashe had journeyed to the United States from Britain via South America to join the army. He deserted once he found the military life not to his liking.

Thirteen days after he left Australia, the police identified the remains of the real Lee Weller in a desolate spot outside Glenbrook township. By this time they were on to Ashe, and had reconstructed his movements up to the time he set sail for America. The San Francisco police were notified, and a detective was sent to the United States to capture Ashe. On Jan. 21, extradition papers were signed in Washington, D.C. The San

Francisco police were put on alert, and the captain of the vessel was intercepted and notified. The *Swanhilda* passed under the Golden Gate Bridge and Ashe prepared to land. He did not know that a full complement of police and customs agents were ready for him. He was picked out by detectives as he stood in line for a routine medical examination aboard the ship.

During the full month required to finalize extradition proceedings, Ashe became somewhat of a local hero to San Franciscans. There were a number of women who offered to visit him in jail and bring him gifts. He played on their sympathies by twice attempting suicide, failing each time. By the time Ashe again reached Australia he was a horrible sight, barely able to speak after attempting to slice open his throat with the ragged edge of a tobacco can. The jury was unmoved by the spectacle and convicted him of murder. He was hanged on July 16, 1897.

REF.: *CBA*; Gribble, *Compelled To Kill*; Gurr, *Famous Australasian Cases*.

Ashford, Mary, See: Thornton, Abraham.

Ashikaga Yoshiaki, 1537-97, Japan, shogun, banish. Last shogun in his line, serving from 1568-73. He was installed, deposed, and banished by Oda Nobunaga. REF.: *CBA*.

Ashley, Andrew, 1958-61, U.S. (unsolv.) kid.-mur. North Buffalo, N.Y., was a city plagued by a rash of kidnappings in the summer of 1961. Nervous parents reminded their children to be wary of strangers, mindful of the tragic fate that befell Andy Ashley, a blonde-haired 3-year-old boy found floating in the Delaware Park lake early in July.

A local psychiatrist theorized that the assailant might have been a woman. "This is the reaction of a person who has become extremely jealous, perhaps as a result of the loss of her own child," he said. Police had little to go on. An emotionally disturbed teenager named Chyrel Julia was taken into custody on three different occasions. The 15-year-old maintained a diary that alluded to the Ashley kidnapping, but police were never sure whether she was directly responsible for the abduction. Meanwhile the residents of North Buffalo made sure that their children were safely in bed at nightfall. REF.: *CBA*.

Ashline, Roy, prom. 1920s, and **Ladd, Bucky**, prom. 1920s, and **Racicot, Sam**, prom. 1920s, U.S., boot.-rob. During Prohibition, Ladd's father was the supervisor of customs near the Canadian-U.S. border. His responsibility was to confiscate Canadian liquor smuggled into New York state. The seized liquor was stored in a customs house and kept under lock and key.

Ladd, who did not share his father's sentiments concerning the "dry law," stole his father's key to the warehouse and made a duplicate which he used to admit his gang. They stole twenty-two cases of whiskey earmarked for medicinal use at area hospitals and sold them in Plattsburgh, N.Y., for top dollar. Roy, Sam, and Bucky raided the customs house three more times. Federal agents changed the locks but neglected to seal the overhead transom which permitted the cat-like bootleggers to gain admittance. The choice whiskeys were sold to New Rochelle cafes and speakeasys, with no one the wiser. Suspicion fell on the custom's agents assigned to duty in the area, but they were as baffled as the prohibition agents.

Years later Racicot explained how the youthful bootleggers stole the booze. But by this time he was living in Canada, immune from U.S. prosecution.

REF.: *CBA*; Everest, *Rum Across the Border*.

Ashton, John, d.1814, Brit., rob. While awaiting execution at Newgate in 1814 on a charge of highway robbery, John Ashton went completely mad. A few moments before the noose could be affixed to his neck, Ashton ran up the steps to the scaffold dancing and shouting, "Look at me! I am Lord Wellington!" Appalled by the spectacle, the Reverend Mr. Cotton attempted to carry on with the last rites.

Ashton continued to prance about as the hangman prepared him for the drop. The trap kicked open and Ashton fell, but in an instant he bounced back up to the platform and shouted, "What do you think of me now? Am I not Lord Wellington now?"

After a brief struggle the executioner pushed the deranged man back down. This time Ashton did not survive the drop.

REF.: *CBA*; Hibbert, *Highwaymen*.

Ashwell, Thomas, (AKA: **Charles R. Jefferson; Thomas McBride Cochran; T.J. Whitney; Herbert Goddard**), 1910-40 , U.S., asslt.-kid.-rape-mur. The Hollywood dream factory of the 1930s was a powerful lure for many impoverished schoolgirls coming of age during the Great Depression. Fan magazines and movie marquees created the illusion. Con men pandered to these dreams. To please a fast-talking talent agent, a star-struck girl would believe almost any lie if it carried with it the promise of fame and riches.

Thomas Ashwell was a cog in the publicity mill, a bit player on the fringe of show business who cleverly disguised his criminal past with a cloak of respectability. The grandson of a Presbyterian minister in Eustice, Fla., his first brush with the law occurred in 1925 when he was sent to a Pennsylvania reform school on a charge of criminal assault. There he involved himself in a small theater group, and on his parole in 1930 passed himself off as a script writer for radio and the screen.

In 1936 he directed a production of *The Bishop Misbehaves* for the West Palm Beach city recreation department and showed promise. From there he went to Miami where he became district director for a federal theater project, a government-sponsored program for unemployed actors, producers, and choreographers.

Ashwell's self-assured manner and charm fooled a number of star-struck girls who believed that he could might help them. In Denver he married a young woman named Beth Collar. Because he had no money, she hocked a diamond ring to secure the necessary cash to purchase a gold band. He promised her a leading role in his secret plan for an experimental theater that would revolutionize show business. "All the people who met him thought he was a very fine person," she later recalled.

Her dreams turned to dust when Ashwell deserted her to return to Miami on July 30, 1939. Using various aliases, he presented himself as a Hollywood talent scout interested in locating fresh faces for a project he was working on. Through Bob Nolan, a former associate at WLW radio in Cincinnati, Ashwell met 17-year-old Francis Dunn and her 19-year-old friend Jean Bolton. Impressed with their good looks and naiveté, Ashwell told them he had arranged to take them to West Palm Beach where he would have publicity photos taken.

Fearing that the FBI was on to him, Ashwell left Miami with the two women in great haste on August 7. After stopping to eat, he drove them to a secluded spot near the intra-coastal canal off Boca Raton. There he admitted that he wasn't what he pretended to be, and brandished a gun at the two frightened women before driving off the main road. When he stopped the car, he led Jean Bolton to a tree where he bound and gagged her. But Francis Dunn was the real object of his attentions. He had criminally attacked her several times during their fifty mile excursion out of Miami. Now, enraged by something she had said, Ashwell struck her with a pistol butt and dragged her a short distance off the road and out of the view of Jean Bolton. Then the failed actor brutally killed her.

Only wit and cunning saved Jean Bolton. She tricked Ashwell into allowing her to call her family to ask for a second car that killer could use to flee to California. Instead of her aunt arriving with the getaway car as Ashwell was led to believe she would, the Boca Raton police turned up. Clad in a sports shirt and a pair of Bermuda shorts, Ashwell admitted to Sheriff W. H. Lawrence of West Palm Beach that he had killed the girl with a hammer, because, as he explained, "She said something bad about Jocelyn," a former sweetheart.

From across the country reports and inquiries began arriving about other crimes allegedly committed by Ashwell. Director J. Edgar Hoover of the FBI assailed the parole system for allowing Ashwell to walk the streets after serving only four years of the twenty-year sentence he had received in Pennsylvania. This time though, there was no escape. Ashwell was tried, convicted, and

executed in the electric chair on July 29, 1940. His stage and screen career ended before it had even begun. REF.: *CBA*.

Askew, Anne, 1521-46, Brit., martyr, her.-treas.-tort. Askew was burned at the stake in the parish of St. Bartholomew's in Smithfield, along with four men, all charged with religious treason. The young woman was not Catholic, but she had renounced an edict of Henry VIII which required all English subjects to recognize the king as the rightful head of the church. Anne was also accused of heresy for denying the Eucharistic doctrine, and suspected of harboring fugitive priests. She defiantly told the Lord Chancellor that she only regretted *not* having had the chance to assist them in their flight from the king's vengeance.

When she refused to recant her heresy, Askew was placed on the rack and tortured until she was unable to walk or stand without assistance. At the fiery stake, the Lord Mayor offered her a royal pardon if she would agree to acknowledge her crime against king and country. She refused and the flame was lit. Then a great clap of thunder sounded, followed by a rainstorm. Those who witnessed this tragedy concluded that the heavens had opened up to receive Anne and her fellow sufferers.

REF.: *CBA*; O'Donnell, *Should Women Hang?*

Aspar, Flavius Ardaburius, d.471, Italy, gen., mur. After the death of Emperor Marcian, who had appointed him patrician, he arranged for Leo I to ascend to the throne in 457. He was killed as part of a conspiracy between Isaurians and Leo. REF.: *CBA*.

Aspasia, b.c.470-410 B.C., Gr., pros. Born in Miletus, Aspasia was renowned throughout Greece for her beauty and charm. She became the mistress of the Athenian statesman and ruler Pericles in the 5th century B.C. When Pericles decided to divorce his wife for a woman reputed to be a brothel keeper, the royal court was scandalized, and poets and sages of Athens circulated rumors that Aspasia procured women of easy virtue for the enjoyment of her new husband.

When the Peloponnesian War began in 431 B.C., some maintained that the cause was two pretty young consorts who had been spirited away by the Megarians. These charges led to more scandal.

For years Aspasia suffered public humiliation every time she showed herself at theaters or the marketplace. When Pericles entered a period of decline, government ministers seized the opportunity to put her on trial for treason and only an impassioned plea from her eloquent, revered husband before the courts saved her from death. Aspasia was acquitted and allowed to return to her proper place in Greek society. When Pericles died in 429 B.C., she became the mistress of Lysicles. By this time, however, she had been virtually forgotten. She lived out her final days in peace.

REF.: Bullough, *Prostitution*; *CBA*.

Aspen, Marvin E., b.1934, U.S., jur. Draftsman of the Illinois Criminal Code (1959-60) and assistant state's attorney for Illinois from 1960-63. He was appointed federal judge to the northern district of Illinois by President Jimmy Carter. REF.: *CBA*.

Asquith of Bishopstone, Lord (Cyril Asquith), 1890-1954, Brit., jur. Fourth son of Prime Minister Herbert Asquith, he was appointed to the King's Bench Division of the High Court in 1938, and presided over several notable murder trials, including those of Gordon Frederick Cummins, Sidney George Paul, Derek Lees-Smith, and Harold Dorien Trevor. In 1946 he was appointed a lord justice of appeal and in 1951, a lord of appeal. REF.: *CBA*.

Assassination, See: **Supplements,** Vol. IV.

Assassins, See: **Order of the Assassins.**

Asser, prom. 1918, Brit., mur. On a cold night in January 1918, a young Canadian army corporal named Dunkin stationed at a military base in Warminster was shot to death in his bunk. Next to the bed investigators found a .303 Lee-Enfield rifle they believed was a suicide weapon. Yet when they examined the gun's barrel, there were no fingerprints to indicate that Dunkin had pulled the trigger.

Sir Bernard Spilsbury was summoned by the local police and the military to help solve the case. After considering the trajectory of the shot, Spilsbury concluded that the only way the corporal could have pulled the trigger was with the muzzle pressed against his cheek. Lying on the cot as he was, Dunkin could not possibly have fired the gun from the estimated distance of five inches. Therefore suicide was ruled out as the cause of death. The police continued their investigation until they located the murderer—an army private named Asser who had entered the quonset hut while Dunkin was asleep. See: **Spilsbury, Bernard.** REF.: *CBA.*

Asser, Tobias Michael Carel, 1838-1913, Neth., jur. Statesman and author of works on international law who was the co-recipient of the Nobel Peace Prize in 1911. REF.: *CBA.*

Astor Place Riots, 1849, U.S., mob. vio. The petty jealousy between two actors spurred the bloody Astor Place riots into being, with New York's political intriguer, Isaiah Rynders, nudging the rioters into action almost as an afterthought. The crafty Rynders knew full well of the hatred Edwin Forrest and William C. Macready had for each other. When both actors were to open in the Astor Place Opera House and the Broadway Theater on the same night, May 7, 1849, each to perform his version of *Macbeth*, Rynders used the opportunity to stir up nationalistic hatreds, manipulating the swollen Irish population of the city in tirades against the English.

The British tragedian, Macready, was the object of Rynders' wrath. The violently anti-British Rynders and hundreds of his rowdies forced their way into the Astor Place Opera House, taking the seats of those who had purchased tickets. Long before the play was to begin, Rynders and his mobsters began stamping their feet and shouting anti-British phrases. Theater managers summoned police as Mrs. Pope, who was to play Lady Macbeth, peeped through the curtains to see the thugs in an uproar and beseeched one theater operator, "My God, Mr. Hackett, what is the matter? Are we to be murdered tonight?"

Macready was fearless. He ordered the curtain raised and he promptly sallied into his performance. The dazzling set and bright lights of the stage initially startled the gangsters into silence. Macready was cheered by those in the boxes, but the orchestra and gallery, where Rynders' minion sat, erupted in jeers and catcalls. The actor could not be heard, and he angrily faced the audience, folding his arms in contempt, waiting for the tumult to fade. It did not.

The uproar continued and increased. Macready then, peacock-proud, haughtily walked along the stage, sneering at his detractors. The din increased. The actor tried to shout down the crowd, but this only accelerated the verbal rage of the thugs. Not one of the Macready's silvery words was heard. He motioned Lady Macbeth onto the stage, thinking that the toughs would traditionally respect the presence of a woman. The abuse not only continued when the distraught Mrs. Pope appeared, but became more vile.

"English whore!" the gangsters shouted. "Pig! Slut! Vermin!"

Mrs. Pope ran from the stage, blushing, it was reported, "even through the rouge on her face."

The full fury of the mob then turned back to Macready. "English fool! Get off the stage!" Rynders stood for a moment on a seat and yelled: "Three cheers for Ned Forrest!" A chair was hurled onto the stage and it smashed to bits at Macready's feet. Rotten eggs and tomatoes showered down on the actor. More chairs were hurled, some barely missing Macready. He was finally led from the stage just as Rynders' mobsters began to wreck the theater.

The manager, minutes later, attempted to inform the audience that the actor had fled to his hotel, thinking this would prevent his theater from being destroyed. He could not be heard. The desperate man obtained a board and chalked upon it the words, *Macready has left the theater!* He walked up and down the stage through a hailstorm of eggs and chair splinters, showing the sign, and this produced gales of laughter from the rioters. The object of their hatred absent, the thugs began to leave the theater. Once in the street, nervous groups of watchmen sighed in relief as the mob broke up and groups of rioters sauntered off to their drinking dens to toast another British defeat.

Three days later, Macready was induced by the more civilized elements of the city, including Washington Irving and John Jacob Astor, to once more attempt his *Macbeth*. Authorities promised the actor and his troupe protection, further insuring the actors' safety by selling tickets exclusively to Macready supporters.

Rynders was having none of this. He drew up an inflammatory poster and had hundreds of these printed and placed in strategic spots in the city. The incendiary proclamation read:

WORKINGMEN!
SHALL AMERICANS OR ENGLISH RULE IN THIS CITY?
The crew of the British steamer have threatened all
Americans who shall dare to offer their opinions
this night at the
ENGLISH ARISTOCRATIC OPERA HOUSE
WORKINGMEN! FREEMEN!
STAND UP TO YOUR LAWFUL RIGHTS!

The second appearance of Macready in *Macbeth* at the Astor Place Opera House on May 10 was a repeat of the first riot, but much worse. Squads of police rounded up the first groups of gangsters who arrived at the theater. Inexplicably, these rowdies were not taken to precinct jails or the Tombs, but were locked up in the basement of the theater. As more and more hoodlums arrived, their long columns trailing out of the Five Points, the police retreated. Those thugs in the theater basement set fire to the building and pandemonium was again let loose.

As Macready once more fled to his hotel without bothering to change his costume, a regiment of National Guards appeared in Astor Place. The rioters ran to a huge pile of paving stones next to the theater and began to hurl these at the advancing troops. Scores of soldiers fell to the street, knocked unconscious by the stones.

Recorder Talmadge scurried up to General Hall, who was in command of the dwindling troops. "You must order your men to fire," Talmadge told Hall. "It is a terrible alternative, but there is no other."

"Well," Hall fumed, "the National Guards will not stand and be pounded to death with stones...nearly one-third of the force is already disabled."

General Hall tried once more to reason with the wavering lines of rioters. A broad-chested thug marched up to the officer and jutted his face into Hall's. "Fire and be damned!" yelled the hoodlum. "Fire, if you dare—take the life of a freeborn American for a bloody British actor!" He ripped open his shirt and puffed out his beefy chest at the troopers, who nervously glanced at their commander. Just then, a paving stone struck an officer and shouts of "Hit 'em again!" filled the air.

Hall spun about. "Elevate your weapons!" he ordered his men. The line of troopers aimed their pieces over the heads of the menacing rioters. "Fire!" The volley rolled out and above the crowd. Instead of frightening the mob, the harmless volley encouraged many to think that the soldiers were using blanks. A powerfully built hoodlum jumped to the front ranks of the mob and shouted, "C'mon, boys! They have blank cartridges and leather flints!" He began to charge forward and hundreds followed on the run.

At the command, the soldiers closed ranks and leveled their weapons directly at the oncoming mob. They held their fire until the mobsters were so close that "their muzzles almost touched the hearts of the men." Then they let loose a volley that scythed down scores of cursing rioters. Those unharmed in the swaying mob saw the bloody bodies of others crumpled in their midst, and the child's play was no more. The mob shrank back, receding further and further into the dark street. Then they rallied. Scores picked up paving stones and these flew in a flurry against the troopers.

General Hall, his face washed with blood from a head wound, stood at the first rank of his soldiers and shouted: "Ready! Aim! Fire!" The second volley was more lethal than the first, dozens of groaning rioters sent crashing to the street, gripping their bodies where wounds gushed blood.

As the troops prepared to deliver yet another volley, more soldiers arrived with two cannons. These were trained on the retreating mobsters. Yet the rioters refused to quit Astor Place. Agitators encouraged them to charge the soldiers. Hall and other officers ordered the troops to fire, and another volley was sent into the crowd.

Although the riot was all but over, the military took no chances. Two regiments at full strength now formed separate lines and, as the rioters limped off, the soldiers sent two more volleys at them, both fired at the same time but in different directions—one down Lafayette Place, the other along Eighth Street. These killing bursts were unnecessary. The mob was already broken and survivors were hobbling home.

Out of the 10,000 to 15,000 rioters, twenty-two had been killed and thirty more wounded. Several innocent bystanders had been hit by random bullets. Some estimates of the dead and wounded were twice that of the numbers officially released.

Rynders had seen the whole thing, lurking in the shadows at the rear ranks of the mob. He had sent forth agitators at the right moment to impel the mob forward against the soldiers. He had seen his riot-inspired thugs broken and had departed just before the mob had been finally smashed. Hours later, Rynders sat in the Arena, his favorite pub, and smirked: "Well, we taught them a lesson." Just what lesson he had in mind was never specified.

To the portly war hero, General Winfield Scott, who was residing on Second Avenue almost opposite Astor Place, the riot was traumatic. At hearing the first shots, the General sent out servants to discover what was the matter. More shots caused him to send out more servants. His wife watched him pace nervously back and forth in his study. "Why, General," Mrs. Scott finally blurted, "you are frightened!"

Scott turned to her with bristling indignation. "Am I a man to be frightened, madam? It is *volley* firing, madam, *volley* firing! They are shooting down American citizens!" Just what kind of citizens, Scott had no way of knowing.

REF.: *Account of the Terrific and Fatal Riot at the New York Astor Place Opera House* (Anon.); Asbury, *The Gangs of New York*; Bales, *Tiger in the Streets*; Barnard, *Forty Years at the Five Points*; Booth, *History of the City of New York*; Brace, *The Dangerous Classes of New York*; CBA; Headley, *The Great Riots of New York, 1712-1873*; Heaps, *Riots, U.S.A.*; Minnigerode, *The Fabulous Forties*; Moody, *The Astor Place Riot*; Moss, *The American Metropolis*; Mott, *The New York of Yesterday*; Rees, *The Life of Edwin Forrest*; Stone, *History of New York City*; Wilson, *Memorial History of New York City*.

Atahaulpa, d.1533, king, Peru, kid.-assass. After Spanish soldiers found some Incas poling a raft laden with gold and silver objects encrusted with rare gems along the coast of Peru in 1527, plans were made to invade the Incan empire. The man selected for what became a brutal slaughter of an entire people was conquistadore Francisco Pizarro who had been subjugating the natives of the New World for thirty years in the name of Spain. He was the illegitimate son of Colonel Gonzalo Pizarro from Truxillo in Estremadura, Spain. He was utterly ruthless in his search for riches. His expedition left Panama in 1530, landed in Peru, and immediately murdered a local chieftan to subdue natives surrounding his Pacific base. He then marched inland with 168 men, about a third of these mounted on horseback. He carried with him guns and a few small cannons, weapons that would make his small army equal to the thousands of natives who might oppose him.

Peru at that time was ruled by an Incan lord called Huayna-Capac who died of disease and left his lucrative empire to his two sons, Atahaulpa and Huascar who immediately set their armies against each other in a struggle for the throne. Atahaulpa had received reports of the Spanish expedition and how they had killed his chief with a strange new weapon that struck down opponents at great distances. He had no weapon that could cope with such lethal wonders. To placate the invader, Atahaulpa agreed to meet with Pizarro in the town of Cajamarca. Pizarro arrived at the town first and hid his soldiers in houses about the main square, awaiting the Incan ruler with only a handful of troops and Friar Vincent de Valverde, a Dominican priest who had been sent by the king of Spain as the "protector" of the Indians. Atahaulpa arrived with a huge army which camped outside of the town. He entered Cajamarca with ten thousand unarmed natives and eighty of these carried him on his huge litter.

Friar Valverde greeted the ruler and told him through an interpreter that he was making him a present of the Bible, the great book of Christianity. Atahaulpa, puzzled at the gift, examined the Bible. Having never seen a book before, it meant little to him. The Incan god was represented by the sun and all signs and directives were interpreted by the sun's activities. Atahaulpa threw the Bible to the ground which enraged Friar Valverde. He screamed to Pizarro that the heathens must be punished for desecrating the good book. The conquistadore needed an excuse to unleash his troops, and the Bible incident, which may be a canard, was enough for him to give his orders to open fire on the unarmed Incans. The slaughter of Atahaulpa's people was devastating and went on for hours, with an estimated 7,000 natives murdered in the sprawling town square of Cajamarca. Atahualpa had been spared; Pizarro and a few of his men grabbed the Incan ruler at the first outbreak of gunfire, shielding him.

The king was later taken to a small temple and held captive. When Atahaulpa saw how the Spanish tore through the town, desperately looking for loot, he thought to buy himself free of captivity by offering his own ransom. He told Pizarro that he would fill a room in the prison where he was kept and Pizarro shrewdly picked out the largest room, one which was 22-by-17-feet. Atahaulpa sent out runners to strip the temples and palaces of his kingdom and return with gold, silver, and rare gems. This they did, bringing mile-long caravans to Cajamarca where Pizarro began to fill the room, emptying the gold and silver from jugs and jars so that the room would hold more. Finally, the room was crammed from floor to ceiling with more than twenty-two tons of gold and twelve tons of silver worth £3 million.

Meanwhile, although a captive, Atahaulpa continued to rule his land and gave orders for his brother Huascar to be murdered along with two half-brothers; assassins performed the killings and Atahaulpa was now supreme ruler of the Incas, at least in name. By then Pizarro's men had conquered Quito, Atahaulpa's stronghold and were marching on the captial of Cuzco. When a report reached Pizarro that an enormous Incan army was approaching Cajamarco to rescue Atahaulpa, the Spanish general suddenly put the Incan ruler on trial for treason. Atahaulpa was quickly convicted and then tied to a stake on July 26, 1533. He was told that unless he gave up his heathen ways and converted instantly to Christianity, he would be burned alive. Atahaulpa agreed to become a Christian. He was then baptised, taking the name Francisco in honor of Pizarro. As soon as the ceremony was over, several Spanish soldiers stepped forth, grabbed the king and held him while one of Pizarro's executioners threw a leather cord about the neck of Atahaulpa and garrotted him to death. Pizarro's ruthless kidnapping for ransom and murder of Atahaulpa caused a storm of protest from the king of Spain, who objected to a royal peer being murdered, and the governor of Panama condemned Pizarro's actions, adding that Atahaulpa was an innocent victim who had "never harmed a single Spaniard." All the protest meant nothing in the end; the riches Pizarro shipped back from the New World left his sovereign and superiors salivating for more. They quickly forgave him for his murderous ways.

REF.: Baudin, *Daily Life in Peru Under the Last Incas*; ____, *A Socialist Empire, The Incas of Peru*; CBA; Mason, *The Ancient Civilizations of Peru*; Messick and Goldblatt, *Kidnapping*; Nash, *Almanac of World Crime*; Prescott, *Histories: The Rise and Decline of the Spanish Empire*; Stewart, *Native Peoples of South America*; Von Hagen, *The Ancient Sun Kingdoms of the Americas*; ____, *The Incas, People of the Sun*; *The World's Most Infamous Crimes and Criminals*.

Ataulphus (**Atawulf** or **Ataulf**), d.415, king, assass. King of

Visigoths who succeeded his brother-in-law Alaric in 410. He withdrew his army from Italy into Gaul, made an alliance with Emperor Honorius, and married the emperor's half-sister, Galla Placidia. After leading his army into Spain he was assassinated at Barcelona. REF.: *CBA*.

Atchison, David Rice, 1807-86, U.S., jur. Served as U.S. judge from 1841-43 and as U.S. senator from Missouri from 1843-56. He was serving as president pro tem of the Senate on March 4, 1849, the day that Zachary Taylor refused to be inaugurated as president because it was Sunday. Some hold that as a result, Atchison was president for that day. REF.: *CBA*.

Texas Ranger Ira Aten, one of the most dedicated and tough lawmen in the Southwest.

Aten, Ira, 1863-1953, U.S., west. law enfor. off. Born in Illinois on Sept. 3, 1863, Aten moved with his family when a child to Round Rock, Texas, where his father had a small farm and traveled the Bible belt as a Methodist minister. As a youth, Aten and his brothers Edwin (b.1871) and Franklin (b.1860), were exposed to the rough and tumble westerners inhabiting and visiting their community, from wild cowboys to dedicated gunslingers and bandits. In 1878, when Ira was only fifteen, he and his brothers saw Sam Bass, the infamous outlaw, brought into Round Rock, mortally wounded after a gun battle with a posse following a robbery. His father, the Reverend Mr. Aten, was called to Bass' deathbed where he gave him spiritual aid in his last moments and heard the outlaws's last words. ("Let me go—the world is bobbing around," slipped from Sam Bass' mouth before he died.) From that moment on, Ira Aten vowed that he would never follow the path of the gunman but would become a champion for law and order, promising his father that he would join the Texas Rangers as soon as he was of age. Aten went on to become one of the most respected rangers in the Lone Star State.

Known to lawmen then as an expert marksman, Aten joined Company D, Frontier Battalion of the Texas Rangers, serving under Captain L.P. Sieker in March 1883. He had just turned twenty and was immediately assigned to cover the most dangerous territory in Texas, the border along the Rio Grande which was awash with rustlers running stolen cattle from Texas into Mexico. At the Rio Grande River in March 1884, Aten accompanied Sieker and five other rangers in a sweep of the area. About eighty miles south of Laredo, the rangers came upon a gang of rustlers who immediately tried to escape across the border. Sieker, Aten, and Ben Reilly rode ahead of the other rangers and cut the outlaws off from reaching the Mexican border. In a running

gunfight, Sieker was hit by a bullet in the heart, toppling dead from his horse. Reilly received a blast in the thigh and was also shot from the saddle. This left Aten to attack the two outlaws alone. Pumping his Winchester, the Ranger shot one bandit in the shoulder, the other in the hand and, joined by the remaining Rangers, brought the wounded outlaws to the Webb County Jail but were themselves arrested and thrown into jail and the outlaws released. This was the doing of Sheriff Dario Gozalez, a corrupt lawman who was in the pay of the rustlers. Aten and the other Rangers spent three weeks in the Webb County Jail before being released.

In 1887 Aten, who had been promoted quickly to the rank of corporal and then sergeant in the Rangers, was assigned to track down the much-wanted outlaw, Judd Roberts who had escaped from the San Antonio Jail. In April 1887, Aten learned that Roberts would be visiting a ranch in Williamson County and he lay in wait for the outlaw. As Roberts arrived, Aten jumped from behind his cover and ordered him to surrender. The outlaw drew his gun and fired off several wild shots which missed the resolute Aten. The Ranger took careful aim, fired one shot and blasted the six-gun out of Roberts' hand. The outlaw, however, spurred his horse around and escaped. Aten cornered Roberts two months later in June when he rightly guessed that Roberts would attack rancher John Hughes of Liberty Hill, Burnet County, Texas, Hughes had earlier made an enemy of the outlaw. When Roberts arrived at the ranch in the dead of night, creeping up to a window, gun in hand, ostensibly to murder Hughes, Aten stepped from the darkness and told Roberts he was under arrest. The outlaw fired a shot which whizzed past Aten and the lawman returned fire, again wounding the outlaw in his shooting hand. Roberts ran to his horse and again escaped.

Hughes, realizing that the vengeful Roberts would return, offered his services to Aten in tracking down the outlaw and the two men set off on a month-long chase after Roberts, one that took them through the Texas Panhandle. There, on a small ranch where Roberts was known to have a sweetheart, Aten and Hughes trapped the killer. Roberts ran from the ranch house, his girl friend running after him. Instead of surrendering, Roberts again chose the gun and fired blindly at Aten and Hughes. Both returned fire and Roberts fell to earth with six bullets in him; his sweetheart cradled him in her arms until he died minutes later. It was at this time that Aten persuaded Hughes to join the Texas Rangers. He did, becoming one of its valued members for twenty-eight years.

Aten was a sergeant of the Rangers when he led Hughes, Bass Outlaw and Sheriff Will Terry after the cattle-rustling Alvin and Will Odle, two brothers known for their lethal gunfights. On Dec. 25, 1889, the lawmen cornered the brothers near Vance, Texas, as they were running stolen cattle by moonlight. In the resulting gunfight both Odle boys were killed. Aten then retired from the Rangers and was promptly appointed sheriff of Fort Bend County which was plagued by a Democrat-Republican political fight later known as the Jaybird-Woodpecker War, one which involved Texans attempting to eradicate the last of the carpetbag politicians left over from the Civil War. Aten and his deputies soon put a stop to the wholesale shootings that took several lives, and the lawman is credited with halting this deadly Texas feud.

The next year, 1891, Aten bought a small ranch near Dimmitt, Texas, and was soon opposing two conniving brothers, Andrew and Hugh McClelland. The McClellands had migrated from Tennessee and intended to win election to high office and then set a land-grabbing scheme in motion. Aten's small but important ranch was part of the scheme. During a heated election for county judge, Andrew McClelland, a lawyer by trade, addressed a large crowd in Dimmitt. Aten, who had campaigned against McClelland, was in the crowd and the lawyer singled out the ex-Ranger, calling him a liar and a crook. After the election, which resulted in McClelland's defeat, Aten went to Dimmitt and told McClelland to arm himself so that he could avenge his honor. The lawyer went to a hardware store while Aten waited in the street.

In minutes McClelland leaped into the street with two new .45-caliber pistols in his hands, both spitting bullets in Aten's direction. Aten fired one shot which shattered McClelland's arm. The lawyer collapsed but managed to get off another shot which harmlessly chewed up some dust between Aten's feet. He was carried off by friends as Aten holstered his weapon.

No sooner had the ex-lawman put away his pistol than a bullet sang past Aten's face, one fired by the other McClelland brother, Hugh. Aten drew his weapon once more as Hugh McClelland ducked behind a wooden shack. Aten fired through the thin boards twice, wounding the other brother who was also carried away to the doctor's office. Aten then turned himself in to local authorities. The McClelland brothers survived and Aten was released as having fired in self-defense. Aten, who retired officially as a captain of the Texas Rangers, was elected sheriff of Castro County in 1893 and served well for almost a year, rounding up rustlers and bandits with regularity. He became known for his humane treatment of prisoners as well as his ability to take fugitives alive, this mostly due to his ability to shoot weapons out of the hands of his prey.

In 1895 Aten quit his sheriff's post and permanently retired to the position of superintendent of 600,000 acres of XIT ranchland, a job he held until 1904. He then moved his wife and five children to the Imperial Valley in California to raise oranges, dying in Burlingame on Aug. 6, 1953, at age ninety-one. Both Aten's brothers Edwin and Franklin also became members of the Texas Rangers. In Edwin's case it was a no-choice decision. Edwin shot and killed a card cheat who drew a pistol and tried to murder him. His brother Ira arrested him and gave him only one option. Either he would go to jail and stand trial or become a Texas Ranger. He chose the latter and went on to become an excellent lawmen, responsible for the arrest of dozens of rustlers along the Rio Grande when serving with Captain Frank Jones of Company D, at Alpine, Texas. As fearless as his brother Ira, Edwin Aten crossed many times into Mexico in pursuit of the dreaded Jesús Mariá Olguin and his gunfighter sons. Edwin Aten was with the redoubtable Captain Jones when they and other Rangers pursued Olguin into Mexico in June 1893 which ended in a wild gunfight that claimed the life of Jones. Franklin Lincoln Aten, the oldest of the Aten brothers, never served as a lawman, content to remain a beekeeper all his days. Like his brothers he lived a long life; he was more than 100 when he died. See: **Bass, Samuel; Hughes, John; Jaybird-Woodpecker War; Jones, Frank; Judd, Robert; Outlaw, Bass.**

REF.: Bartholomew, *The Biographical Album of Western Gunfighters*; *CBA*; Gard, *Frontier Justice*; ____, *Rawhide Texas*; Holloway, *Texas Gun Lore*; Hunter, *The Moving Finger*; Hunter and Rose, *The Album of Gunfighters*; Martin, *Border Boss, Captain John R. Hughes, Texas Ranger*; Preece, *Lone Star Man—Ira Aten*; Sonnichsen, *I'll Die Before I'll Run*; Sterling, *Trails and Trials of A Texas Ranger*; Webb, *The Texas Rangers*.

Athaliah (Athalia), d.836 B.C., Judah, queen, assass. Wife of King Jehoram and the mother of King Ahaziah. Upon her son's death she usurped the throne and murdered all of her grandsons except Joash who later became king. She was killed in a revolt. REF.: *CBA*.

Athens, Lamia of, (AKA: Venus Lamia, Lamia), prom. c.294, B.C., Gr., pros. Lamia was one of the exotic dancing girls of Egypt who became the consort to King Ptolemy. The famed Greek biographer Plutarch later described her as a "vampire" who engaged in blood orgies. The description was perhaps born out of personal malice for this woman who rose from prostitute to the entertainer of two powerful rulers of the ancient world. When Ptolemy died, Lamia took up with King Demetrius of Macedonia, who levied a burdensome tax on his people to pay for the large quantity of soap she used in her bath. A temple was built in Athens to glorify her memory, and she became popularly known as Venus Lamia to her many admirers.

REF.: Bullough, *Prostitution*; *CBA*.

Athens Airport Massacre, 1973, See: **Black September**

Athoe, Thomas, Sr., 1665-1723, and **Athoe, Thomas, Jr.**, 1699-1723, Brit., asslt.-mur. Athoe, Sr. was not the kind to easily forgive or forget an insult. He was the mayor of Tenby, his son the village bailiff—two men to be feared and respected. This was something George Merchant and his brother Thomas would not do though they were nephews of the elder Athoe. Ill feeling had existed between the relatives for some time concerning a division of property rights.

Believing that George Merchant had cheated his family out of its rightful claims, Athoe, Sr. told his attorney that while he would not press the matter against the Merchants in court, he would assuredly "pay them in their own coin." On Nov. 23, 1722, an agricultural fair was held near Tenby. The Athoes and the Merchants attended, and a quarrel broke out between the two families over their ancient grudge. When the fair ended late that night, the Athoes, seething with anger, learned from an innkeeper where the Merchants had gone. Armed with this information, they jumped on their horses and pursued their enemies.

The Merchants had stopped to rest at a place called Holloway's Water. Here, overtaken by the Athoes, they attempted to hide behind the bridge, but were easily detected by the noise of their horses. Armed with bludgeons, Athoe, Jr. shouted, "I owe thee a pass, and now thou shalt have it!" The Merchants' pleas for mercy fell were ignored. George was strangled from behind. His murder was later recounted by the townsmen with horror, for in a fit of rage the younger Athoe had bitten off the poor man's nose. Thomas Merchant was severely beaten and left for dead, but luckily a passer-by saw him lying in the roadway and took him to a nearby house, where a surgeon attended to his wounds.

The elder Athoe was arrested. His son fled to Ireland, where, through political intervention, he was seized and remanded back to Hereford where both men were indicted on Mar. 19, 1723, for murder. In his weak condition, the surviving Merchant recounted the events of that night to a jury. In June the Court of the King's Bench pronounced the death sentence on the Athoes. On July 5, 1723, the tearful son was comforted by his father as they were led out to the hanging tree. "Lord have mercy upon us!" were the final words of the murderous father and son.

REF.: *CBA*; Mitchell, *The Newgate Calendar*.

Atkin, Lord (Richard Atkin), 1867-1944, Brit., jur. Appointed to the King's Bench Division of the High Court in 1913, presiding over many murder trials including those of David Greenwood and John Starchfield. He was promoted to lord justice of appeal and, lord of appeal in ordinary, and later died in office. REF.: *CBA*.

Atkins, Charles A., 1954-   , and **Hack, William S.**, prom. 1988, U.S., consp.-fraud. Known as the "boy wonder of the tax shelters," Charles Atkins enticed a number of prominent investors from the entertainment industry to sink their money into limited partnerships that involved "tax straddles"—whereby certain financial transactions would show accelerated losses to come out ahead through fraudulent tax deductions filed with the IRS. "Every year they would keep deferring the tax," explained Prosecutor Stuart Abrams, "they'd enter into new losses to wipe out the income that would roll forward."

Among the Hollywood celebrities who fell for the scheme were actors Lorne Greene and Sidney Poitier, producer Norman Lear, the late artist Andy Warhol, and Laurence Tisch, president and chief executive officer of CBS, Inc. The total amount of losses generated through these nonexistent transactions totaled $1.1 billion. The investors in turn reported $350 million in tax deductions. Defense attorneys for Securities Groups, an umbrella organization created by Atkins, argued that U.S. tax laws drafted between 1978 and 1983 were vague in nature and did not clearly define what constituted an improper transaction. "The practices of which these people were convicted were widespread on Wall Street, sufficiently widespread that people did not view them as criminal," said Attorney Paul Grand.

The government called it one of the largest cases of tax-shelter fraud in U.S. history. On Dec. 10, 1987, Atkins and two associates, William S. Hack and Ernest Grunebaum, were found Guilty on a twenty-eight count indictment charging them with conspiracy and fraud. On Mar. 11, 1988, Judge Morris Lasker of the Federal District Court in Manhattan sentenced Atkins to two years in prison to be followed by four years of community service. He appealed his sentence. Hack received four months, and Grunebaum was released with a six-month suspended sentence. The verdict was called "surprising" by Robert Romano, a civil attorney in Manhattan who noted that the government had dealt harshly with similar offenders in the past.   REF.: *CBA*.

Atkins, David Adkins, David, b. 1875, U.S., (wrong. convict.) rob. A cowboy who worked ranches in Arizona and Texas, Atkins was identified for a robbery later admitted to be the work of Thomas "Black Jack" Ketchum. After Ketchum confessed to the 1897 train robbery at Steins Pass, N.M., stating that he committed the crime where the express guard was murdered, Atkins was released, along with Leonard Alverson, also convicted and sentenced with Atkins for the same crime. Atkins had also been convicted and sentenced for the murder of a man in Tom Green County, Texas, which was later proved to be the work of Bill Carver, a member of Butch Cassidy's Wild Bunch. See: **Alverson, Leonard; Carver, William; Ketchum, Thomas**.
REF.: Bartholomew, *A Biographical Album of Western Gunfighters*; *CBA*.

Atkinson, Sir Cyril, b.1874, Brit., jur. King's counsel in 1913 and judge of the High Court in 1933. In his 15 years on the bench he presided over many murder trials including those of Thomas Joseph Davidson and Udham Singh. REF.: *CBA*.

Atkinson, George Wesley, 1845-1925, U.S., jur. Agent for the Internal Revenue Service from 1876-80, U.S. marshal from 1881-85, and appointed federal judge on the Court of Claims by President Theodore Roosevelt in 1905. He published *After the Moonshiners* (1879) and *Handbook for Revenue Officers* (1880). REF.: *CBA*.

Atkinson, Isaac, 1614-40, Brit., rob.-mur. Afforded all the advantages of the privileged class, young Atkinson chose to squander it away for the life of a footpad. His father was a prosperous nobleman who maintained a posh country estate in Farringdon, Berkshire. When Isaac turned sixteen, he was sent to Oxford University where he led a dissolute life, preferring the company of prostitutes and ale house rabble-rousers to serious academic study. In disgust his father asked him, "Are not you now a lying son of a whore?" To which he replied, "My mother knows best, father."

His university career terminated, Atkinson turned to robbery and larceny. One night he came upon the home of a wealthy earl. Taking a ladder from the adjacent scaffolding, he climbed to the second floor bedchamber, where he overheard a discussion between the earl and his wife. The couple were debating the wisdom of hiring a physician to attend to the woman who was believed to be incapable of bearing a child. "I vow, madam, I have £500 lying over the bed's tester which I would give with all my heart to a surgeon who could rectify a mistake which Nature hath made with you," the earl promised.

The next day when the earl and his servants had gone off on a hunt, Isaac presented himself at the lady's door, passing himself off as a physician. With the calm, assured manner of a skilled confidence man he explained that he had been summoned by the earl to attend to the delicate matter. "Why then, do your work as soon as you please, sir, and I'll pay you according to his lordship's orders," she said. Whereupon Isaac had sex with the woman and then ordered her to lie still for two hours so that the operation would not be spoiled. With the £500 he fled to London, where, by his own estimate, he robbed 160 lawyers in an eight-month period.

Atkinson's brief but spectacular crime spree ended near Turnham Green, when he provoked a market woman he had tried to rob. She alerted a local innkeeper, who organized a posse. Atkinson was trapped in a field outside of town, but before he could be taken he shot and killed four of his pursuers. He was arrested, taken to Newgate, and sentenced to be hanged. He went to the gallows at Tyburn in 1640 with complete scorn and mockery for all those who had caused his demise.
REF.: *CBA*; Pringle, *Stand And Deliver*, Smith, *Highwaymen*.

Atkyns, Sir Edward, 1587-1669, Brit., jur. Defended Prynne on libel charges that resulted from the publication of *Histriomastix*. REF.: *CBA*.

Atlanta Bond Theft, 1904, U.S., rob. In 1904 a gang of thieves smuggled $50,000 worth of bonds and securities from a large financial institution in downtown Atlanta. At the time they believed that the bank was not a member of the American Banker's Association, which was a client of the Pinkerton Detective Agency. When the robbers learned of their folly, the stolen bonds were returned and the leader of the gang placed an urgent telephone call to the agency to apologize for any inconvenience they might have caused.
REF.: *CBA*; Hamilton, *Men of the Underworld*.

Atlanta Children Murders, See: **Williams, Wayne B.**

Atlantic City Boardwalk Case, c.1900s, U.S., polit. corr. For years the corrupt city fathers of Atlantic City, N.J., dug their hands deep in the public trough, skimming tens of thousands of dollars a year in graft money from building contractors. The rapacious politicians would award contracts to low bidders, and then charge the city for padded "expenses." Particularly hard hit were resort hotel owners who were assessed exorbitant tax rates for the privilege of operating near the famed boardwalk.

The local political machine brought in armies of "repeaters"— men paid to vote twice for machine candidates. Good-government advocates and the beleaguered hotel men had their hands tied. In desperation they called the Burns Detective Agency to see what could be done. Agent Raymond Schindler, who was assigned to the case, devised an elaborate "sting" operation fronted by his associate Edward Reed, whom he considered to be "one of the greatest experts in roping and finesse" he had ever met.

Reed told the politicians of the absolute necessity of paving the boardwalk with concrete, convincing them of the long-term cost savings, which, of course, meant no savings at all to the taxpayers. The half-million dollar return would line the pockets of the city hall grafters and the construction engineers.

One by one the parties to the scheme met with Reed in his hotel suite at the Waldorf Astoria in New York, and a second hotel in Trenton, N.J. What these grafters did not know was that agents were using a hidden dictograph in the adjacent rooms to record their words, the first time this device was used in a large criminal case. Based on the printed transcripts, and the money passed between Reed and the victims of his "sting," the crooked politicians were arrested and their stranglehold on the city was permanently ended.
REF.: *CBA*; Hughes, *The Complete Detective*.

Atlantic City Conference, 1929, U.S., org. crime. The first enclave of U.S. crime bosses occurred in Atlantic City, N.J., in early May 1929. Much has been written about this first Mafia-syndicate convention, and an equal amount of dashing verbiage speculated on the real reasons for the get-together of several dozen crime czars from all of the great cities (except the then undeveloped far West). Several of the more cerebral mob mentors developed the idea of creating a national crime cartel by the mid-1920s, not the least of whom was Chicago's evil genius, Johnny Torrio. Torrio, as early as 1920, when he assumed mob leadership in Chicago following the death of Big Jim Colosimo, had attempted to quell the battling gangs of Chicago, divide up the city into sacrosanct territories where the gangsters could peddle their bootleg booze without being harrassed by other gangs. The volatile nature of the gangs—the sharp divisions created between them by national and cultural heritage—had doomed Torrio's twisted dream of organized crime. But young, shrewd criminals in the East, where Torrio relocated after being nearly shot to death in 1924, eagerly listened to his theories about a share-the-wealth program where all the gangs of the U.S. would follow certain rules established by a hierarchy of bosses or an executive board of the national combination, he called it.

Torrio's ideas were wholeheartedly embraced by the diplomatic

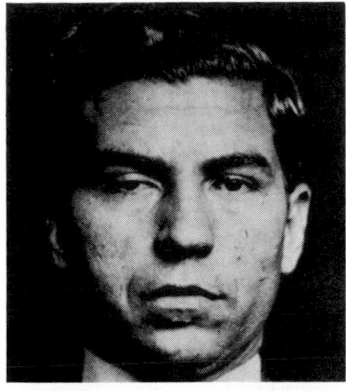

CRIME CONFERENCE, ATLANTIC CITY, 1929

The first crime cartel conference, in May 1929, brought the top gangsters from all over the U.S. to Atlantic City, N.J., the meeting called by one-time Chicago crime boss, Johnny Torrio, mentor to Al Capone (above) and on Capone's behalf. From New York came (left-hand column) Charles "Lucky" Luciano, Joe Adonis, and Albert Anastasia.   Moses Annenberg, Capone-sponsored wire service operator (bottom left-hand column), was the man everyone wanted to meet; he was setting up a multi-milliondollar wire system for their national bookie operations. Also present was Frank Costello (bottom center), who helped negotiate territories where the Annenberg wire service would be franchised.   Meyer Lansky (top, third column) financed national tie-ups to the Annenberg wire service on behalf of the newly-established crime syndicate. Torrio (right-hand center), acted as chairman of the board.   Waxey Gordon, one of the most powerful bootleggers on the East Coast (bottom, third column), contributed $300,000 to the Annenberg setup.

bootlegger and gambling boss of New York, Frank Costello. They also appealed to the business instincts of prostitution and dope king Charles "Lucky" Luciano and his associates, Joe Adonis, Albert Anastasia, Vincent Mangano and Frank Scalise. Luciano and his confederates had had enough, they said, of the wild shootout ways of their own superiors, Joe "The Boss" Masseria and Salvatore Maranzano. They wanted to organize to be the first to do so, and thus assure themselves of the lion's share of controlled rackets and the most lucrative territories for those rackets. Endorsing the idea of a national syndicate was Louis "Lepke" Buchalter, who had organized the garment worker's unions so that he controlled their dues, salaries and received enormous kickbacks from the manufacturers employing tens of thousands of workers. His good friend and that of Luciano, Meyer Lansky, looked upon the organization of a national crime syndicate as sound business which would keep black ink on the books.

Lansky's trip to Atlantic City had a twofold purpose. He had just wed Anna Citron of Hoboken, N.J. His presence in Atlantic City was to enjoy his honeymoon and help form the national crime syndicate. The New York delegation was made up of Luciano, Buchalter, Lansky, Costello, Adonis, Anastasia, Scalise, Mangano, Frank Erickson (who had inherited the gambling empire of the recently slain Arnold Rothstein), and the unpredictable numbers king and bootlegger from Brooklyn, Dutch Schultz. From Cleveland came Moe Dalitz and Louis Rothkopf. The boss of Boston, Charles "King" Solomon was present. Detroit's Purple Gang was represented by Joe Bernstein. Crime kingpin of Kansas City, Johnny Lazia, arrived. From Philadelphia came Waxey Gordon, Max "Boo-Boo" Hoff, and Nig Rosen. Willie Moretti and Abner "Longy" Zwillman represented New Jersey. Host of the convention was Atlantic City crime boss Enoch L. "Nucky" Johnson, a swaggering giant who booked his contemporaies into the best hotels along the Boardwalk. The most powerful of the crime bosses in the U.S. then, of course, was Al Capone, who traveled to Atlantic City with a large retinue. His one-time boss and mentor, Johnny Torrio, had invited Scarface to attend.

Torrio, the elder statesman of crime in America at the time, it was later said, *ordered* Capone to attend the Atlantic City enclave but nothing could be further from the truth. No one, including the deposed Torrio, was in a position to order Capone to do anything. Capone was one of the bosses who asked for the meeting. He shared the ideas of Lansky, Costello, and Luciano in organizing the rackets on a country-wide basis to prevent the endless invasion of his Midwestern territory by outside gangs.

Capone arrived with Jake "Greasy Thumb" Guzik, Frank "The Enforcer" Nitti, and his bodyguard, Frank Rio. He also brought along one of the real reasons for having the enclave, his good friend Moses Annenberg, who owned the *Daily Racing Form*, read across the country by every horse gambler following the results at every racetrack. Capone and Annenberg had conceived of a way in which a national crime cartel could control horse-betting results throughout the nation, achieved by Annenberg's newly-formed Nationwide News Service which Capone bankrolled. This service would send over AT&T wires all the results from every track, only seconds after each race had been run, and feed this information to every betting parlor, poolroom, and gambling den in America. The offer to establish this service for the crime cartel required the approval of the various crime bosses who controlled those countless gaming areas in their respective cities. Frank Erickson, representing the gambling interests of the East Coast, was, of course, all for embracing the idea which would see the city crime bosses all subscribing to the services and seeing to it that only *their* gambling dens would receive this service, thus establishing a multi-million dollar (each month) monopoly. Of course, Annenberg, along with Capone, would receive the lion's share of the profits of the service. (Annenberg's vast fortune, estimated to be the fifth largest in the world before his death, stemmed from the gambling service monopoly he financed through Capone.)

This was the centerpiece of discussion at the Atlantic City Conference, a plan that was universally adopted and one that

established gambling as the first syndicated national vice to be promoted by the new crime cartel. Luciano, a master pimp and vice lord of prostitution in New York, then advocated the establishment of running whores on an interstate basis through various cities where the brothels were also to be organized by local crime bosses with dues kicked back to the cartel to continue funding operations. This proposal was met with lukewarm reception from many of those attending the conference which was held in several hotels, meetings being changed from one room to another each day to avoid detection from local police. The story that these crime moguls held all their discussions on the beaches of Atlantic City to avoid being overheard is completely false, a canard that was embellished to the ridiculous by certain inept researchers and writers who claimed that Capone, Luciano, et al removed their shoes and socks, rolled up the legs of their trousers, and actually waded to knee-deep water to hold their highly confidential discussions.

Another falsehood perpetuated by one crime writer after another and even endorsed by Lucky Luciano in his so-called "memoirs" (after *he* had read the story in various printed forms) was that the Atlantic City meeting had been arranged to curb Al Capone's lust for blood. Capone was to recieve orders from the other bosses to cease his gang wars in Chicago and get himself arrested to appease national and local lawmen who were unnerved by Capone's recent slaughter of the Moran gang some months earlier at the St. Valentine's Day Massacre in 1929. One report had it that Torrio, who had once been Capone's sponsor and boss in Chicago before retiring with gunshot wounds from the Moran gang, actually ordered Capone to get himself arrested or, as he darkly hinted, be exterminated. This story was as absurd as the beach-wading tale. Capone was one of those who called for the conference in order to establish Annenberg's wire service one which would enrich every gangster attending by millions. It would have been economic suicide for any of these bosses to slavishly embrace the Annenberg-Capone gambling plan in one minute and to order the most powerful crime czar in America, on the other hand, to get himself arrested. It is certain that had anyone attending the conference even suggested such a thing to Capone that person would have had to deal with the wrath of all attending, a rage that would have naturally stemmed from those realizing that profits from the Capone-Annenberg scheme would be short-lived should the volatile Capone be insulted. The embryonic syndicate then, as it is now, concerned itself with only one thing—profits. Nothing was allowed to stand in the way of making their illegal millions.

The story about ordering Scarface to get himself arrested was constructed in hindsight of Capone's arrest in Philadelphia a short time later, one that was arranged by Capone himself, so that he and his bodyguard, Frank Rio, were discovered to be carrying concealed weapons, thus violating a local law which they freely admitted. Both Capone and Rio were given a year in jail, being released on Mar. 17, 1930. Capone had called two Philadelphia detectives who had visited his Palm Island, Fla., estate some months earlier, James "Shooey" Malone and John Creedon. Capone informed Malone that he and Rio would be emerging from a movie house in downtown Philadelphia and gave the detective the exact time. The detectives were waiting for him when he stepped to the street, discovered both Capone and Rio were carrying .38-caliber revolvers and placed them under arrest. They were quickly arraigned before Judge John E. Walsh of the criminal division of Philadelphia's municipal court, pleaded guilty and received their sentence. From arrest to imprisonment, only sixteen hours elapsed. Before Capone went smilingly to prison, he told Philadelphia's Director of Public Safety Samuel E. Schofield that he was exhausted with the gang killings. He was asked if he hadn't just attended a much publicized meeting of gang leaders from around the country at Atlantic City and Capone said yes, adding that he had told the other crime czars that he wanted the killings stopped and stopped immediately. With that, Al Capone lit a cigar and walked to a police van waiting to take him to a cell equipped with all the modern luxuries and conveniences.

Of course the real reason why Capone arranged his own arrest was to escape the pursuing guns of George "Bugs" Moran who had lost a goodly portion of his North Side gang in February 1929 when Capone's gunners shot down seven Moran men in the St. Valentine's Day Massacre. Moran, in retaliation, put a $100,000 pricetag on Scarface's head, this money to be paid only if the Chicago crime czar was killed. Gunmen lead by Willie Marks and Ted Newberry, top Moran enforcers, had been following Capone all over the East Coast and had even stalked him along the Boardwalk of Atlantic City during the crime summit. This very real fact was known to Capone who believed that the only place he would really be safe at the time was in jail which is why he arranged to be arrested by his friends Malone and Creedon. Though in prison, Capone continued to run the Chicago rackets as well as enjoy the added millions of dollars of profit that began to flow from Annenberg's wire service, one that had been installed in every nationwide betting parlor and gambling den by the time Scarface stepped out of Eastern Penitentiary. The Atlantic City Conference did more than establish a nationwide gambling syndicate. The conference galvanized the the gangs of America into a powerful single unit which was directed by a board of governors whose collective word was law, whose decisions were sacrosanct, and whose influence would affect every American, in one form or another, for generations to come. See: **Adonis, Joe; Anastasia, Albert; Annenberg, Moses; Apalachin Conference; Buchalter, Louis; Capone, Alphonse; Costello, Frank; Dalitz, Moe; Erickson, Frank; Gordon, Waxey; Guzik, Jake; Havana Conference; Hoff, Max; Johnson, Enoch; Lazia, John; Luciano, Charles; Mangano, Vincent; Maranzano, Salvatore; Masseria, Joesph; Moran, George; Moretti, Willie; Purple Gang; Rothkopf, Louis; St. Valentine's Day Massacre; Schultz, Dutch; Solomon, Charles; Torrio, John; Zwillman, Abner.**

REF.: *CBA;* Addy, *The Dutch Schultz Story; CBA;* Feder, *The Luciano Story;* Fried, *The Rise and Fall of the Jewish Gangster in America;* Gage, *Mafia, USA;* Gosch, *The Last Testament of Lucky Luciano;* Katz, *Uncle Frank;* Kefauver, *Crime in America;* Kobler, *Capone;* McPhaul, *Johnny Torrio;* Messick and Goldblatt, *The Mobs and the Mafia;* Murray, *The Legacy of Al Capone;* Nash, *Bloodletters and Badmen; ____, Citizen Hoover;* Pasley, *Al Capone;* Peterson, *Barbarians in Our Midst; ____, The Mob;* Wicker, *Investigating the FBI;* Wolf and DiMona, *Frank Costello, Prime Minister of the Underworld.*

Attardi, Alphonse (AKA: **the Peacemaker**), b.c.1892, U.S., drugs-org. crime. Attardi was an informer living in a dingy, rat-infested flat on New York's Lower East Side in the early 1950s. Known to his former Mafia associates as the Peacemaker, Attardi had taken a bum rap in Houston and gone to prison while many of his friends went free. When he got out of prison, a bank had foreclosed on his small olive oil importing business on Christie Street in New York, and his wife, the one joy in his life, soon died.

Agents from the Treasury Department visited him in 1952 to see if he would become an informer. The aging mobster told Agent O'Carroll that he was out of the drug trade. All he had left, he said, was his life and a little room off of Delancey Street. "I can't do it," he said. "I'd be dead if I worked for you." O'Carroll left his card and told him to think it over.

Six months later a need for money prompted Attardi to make the phone call, and he agreed to work with the agents. His job was to introduce an undercover agent to some friends involved in the drug trade. Joe Tremoglie, who was fluent in Italian, was chosen to work with Attardi. In the next ten months the undercover agent met several of the major drug traffickers and capos working the Lower East Side, including Benny Bellanca and Pietro Beddia, who were put under heavy police surveillance. These men soon were snared in an all-encompassing net woven by Treasury agents and Attardi, the Peacemaker, collected his $5,000 reward and took his new girlfriend out of the country.

REF.: *CBA;* Whitehead, *Border Guard.*

Attebery, Ira (Attebury), 1915-79, U.S., suic.-mur. For three years, Attebery regularly attended the annual Battle of the Flowers Parade in San Antonio, capping off a week-long fiesta celebration. The 64-year-old retired trucker lived in a small trailer park not far from the parade route, and tended to keep to himself. "I thought it was strange that he went to parades since he had little to do with people," said Kate Copeland, the manager of the trailer park where Attebery lived until he went berserk on Apr. 27, 1979. "He was a loner," she added.

The self-styled parade afficionado lined up, by police estimate, six automatic rifles and enough bullet clips to supply a military arsenal. Near the intersection of Broadway and Grayson, Attebery began firing wildly into a crowd of 4,500 parade spectators through a window in his trailer home. "He would expose himself, fire, and then duck. The total gunfire lasted about thirty minutes, and it was another thirty minutes before we found him dead," said Captain Patrick Nichols of the San Antonio police. To the police officers standing in the middle of the parade route, Attebery yelled "Traitors! Traitors!"

Before he turned the gun on himself, Attebery killed two people and wounded fifty more. Blood samples taken from the dead man's body revealed the presence of the drug PCP, known in the streets as "angel dust," a deadly drug recently banned in Texas because of the unpredictable, occasionally suicidal behavior it brought on in addicts.

Attebery ran berserk under the delusion that the police were chasing him because of a 1971 trucking accident he was involved in that killed two women. On at least one previous occasion he had contacted the police seeking psychiatric help. "I would have been very happy if police had brought the man here," said Robert Pugh, director of the county mental health department. "But unless the man was willing to come and was in violation of a law, the police could not have brought him in." REF.: *CBA.*

Attel, Abe, See: **Rothstein, Arnold.**

Atter, Leonard Vincent, 1929- , Case of, Brit., mur. Robina (Ruby) Bolton was working as a prostitute in Paddington, England at the time of her death on Jan. 13, 1956. Her husband served as her business agent and chauffeur, and would wait in a parked car outside the flat until she had finished working. On Jan. 13, between 8:30 p.m. and 12:30 a.m., Mr. Bolton drove his wife back and forth between Hertford Street, Mayfair, and Westbourne Terrace, Paddington, where she met four different clients.

When Bolton went to pick her up the next morning, he found his wife dead, the victim of a mad slasher. The police arrested Leonard Atter, a 27-year-old clerk, in connection with the crime. Atter admitted to having sexual relations with Bolton the night of the murder, but added a curious sidelight to the case: Ruby Bolton had paid *him* £5 for his sexual favors. "She was very nice," he said. "She made me tea and sandwiches." He denied killing her, though, and said he had left the flat before 3:00 a.m. after Ruby explained that she had another client coming to see her.

The coroner said the death had occurred between midnight and 2:00 a.m. Atter had been with her all that time, and forensic investigators found traces of blood on his clothing during a laboratory test. A copy of *True Detective* magazine containing a story markedly similar to the crime at hand was found in Atter's room. Armed with these facts, the prosecution brought the suspect to trial. Defense attorney A.P. Marshall charged that there was little to go on other than suspicion and rumor, and without proper motive the jury could not be expected to return a guilty verdict. The jurors apparently agreed, and Atter was acquitted of all charges. REF.: *CBA.*

Attia, Joseph Victor Bhamin (AKA: **Jo Le Moko, Marcel Deloffre**), prom. 1947, Fr., rob. In 1938, Joe Attia was sent to the notorious Bataillon d'Afrique in North Africa. It was the last stop for youthful members of the French underworld, a reform school that seemed more like a concentration camp to the inmates. It took brains and endurance to survive the harsh environment. Attia had both. While battling the uncompromising elements and his own rebellious nature, Attia took time out to befriend Pierre Loutrel, known in French criminal circles as Madman Pete. After WWII broke out, the two youthful offenders returned to France where they took widely divergent paths. Madman Pete joined up with Pierre Bony's ruthless French Gestapo to hunt down resistance fighters. Joe Attia fought on the side of the resistance before he was caught by the Gestapo and tortured in 1943. His death sentence was commuted by the Germans and he was sent to the Mauthausen concentration camp in Austria. There Attia instilled courage and hope in the other desperate prisoners who were forced to walk the March of Death, when the Nazis moved the inmates ninety miles in advance of the approaching allies.

Joe Attia was a *dur*, a tough guy who relied on cunning and resource. He also never forgot a friend. After the war, Madman Pete reverted back to his life of crime. He shot and killed his way up and down the French Riviera, taking with him a fortune in gold and currency. During this time Attia was mistakenly identified as a member of the Loutrel gang. This was never the case, but neither can it be said that Attia betrayed his friend to the police. When Madman Pete was shot and killed outside the Hotel des Marroniers in September 1946, Attia fulfilled the dying man's last request by burying his remains on a tiny island not far from Paris.

Attia, whose criminal record included six verdicts of "Not Proven," was forced into hiding by the French police. He fled to Marseilles, where desperate men are known to "disappear," and he assumed the alias of Marcel Deloffre. In July 1947, a special squadron of French police assigned to ferret out the last remnants of Madman Pete's gang swooped down on the theatre district where they located and arrested Joe Attia. He was charged with carrying a forbidden weapon—one of heavy caliber—and was sent to the prison at Aix after refusing to tell the police where Pete was.

Two years later and still in chains, he maintained the wall of silence until Henri Courtois came forward to tell the police what they wanted to hear. Pete's remains were identified by forensic experts, but this did not help Attia. In fact, it had the reverse effect. Jo le Moko, as he was known on his rap sheet, was charged with "illegal detention of a corpse," and was sentenced to seven more years. When he was released in December 1953, Attia was feted with a big dinner by survivors of the concentration camp. Afterward, he bought a bar in Montmartre and settled down with his girlfriend. But the quiet life was definitely not for Attia, dubbed the "gangster that never was." In the late 1950s he joined a gun-running racket operating in Tangiers and was sent back to prison.

REF.: *CBA;* Goodman, *Villainy Unlimited.*

Attica Prison Riot, 1971, U.S., mob vio.-mur. On Sept. 9, 1971, more than 1,000 convicts in the overcrowded, poorly operated Attica Prison, outside of Buffalo, N.Y., took control of the prison compound and portions of the cell blocks, seizing fifty guards and civilian prison employees and holding them hostage while making demands for reform. The rioters set up makeshift tents and living quarters in the open compound, tore apart a cell block and created a state of siege as local and state police responded to the uprising. At the time the prison housed 2,254 convicts and, as many penologists later concurred, was operated with little thought of rehabilitation. Cells were overcrowded, inmates received harsh punishment for the slightest infraction, and petitions asking for changes were routinely ignored, increasing the resentment and hostility of prisoners. The overpowering of the rebelling prisoners at Attica five days after the uprising was accomplished by an army of sheriff's deputies, prison guards, and state troopers, more than 1,500 in all, who opened up a devastating crossfire which not only killed many of the convict ringleaders but, as the evidence later showed, many of the hostages as well.

The Attica disaster was one that could have apparently been avoided had prison officials been more responsive to the increasing unrest by inmates over conditions and had the prisoner petitions for reform been treated with some realistic concern. The uprising was not spontaneous but one that developed over a two-month period. In July 1971, Russell G. Oswald, state commissioner of corrections, received a petition for prison reforms from a prison group calling itself the Attica Liberation Faction. While

Oswald continued to study the petition, on Aug. 22, 1971, Attica prisoners held a silent breakfast protest over the death of George Jackson, a San Quentin prisoner who was shot while attempting to escape. On Sept. 2, Oswald met with Vincent Mancusi, Attica superintendent, and Frank Lott, prisoner representative, promising that reforms would be made some time in the future.

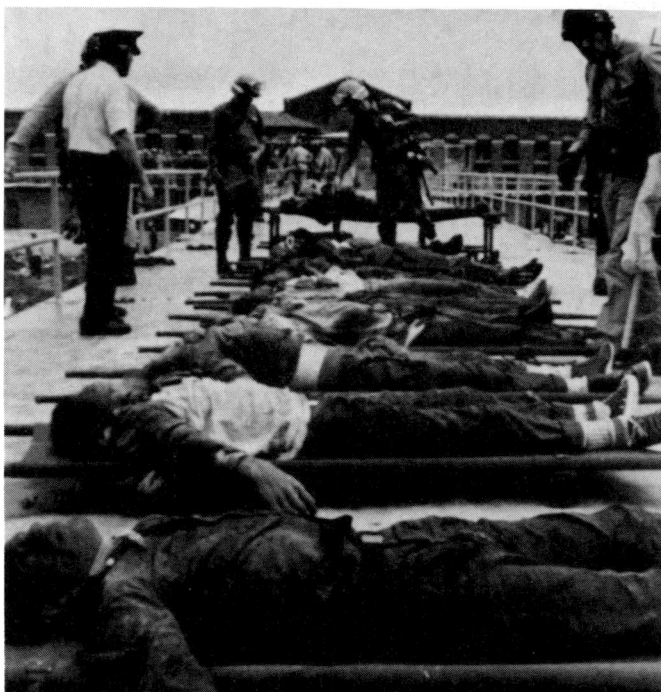

Guards and state police identifying the dead following the police onslaught of rioting inmates in Attica.

Many Attica inmates interpreted Oswald's deliberations as stalling tactics, and resentment among many prisoners was demonstrated on Sept. 8, 1971. Corrections Officer Richard Maroney gave an order to inmates Leroy Dewar and Richard Lamorie. These prisoners reportedly defied him and were then ordered to solitary confinement. As Dewar and Lamorie were being taken to solitary, inmate William Ortiz threw a can of soup at Officer Tom Boyle, striking the guard in the face. Ortiz was also thrown into solitary. On Sept. 9, several inmates managed to free Ortiz from his cell so he could go to the mess hall to have breakfast. When Ortiz was discovered missing from his cell, a squad of guards led by Lt. Robert Curtiss, attempted to put Ortiz back in his cell but this officer and his men were overpowered and knocked unconscious by a group of prisoners. Keys were taken from the guards and the rebelling prisoners unlocked the cells of hundreds of others. The rebellion spread throughout the prison and fifty hostages were quickly taken.

A call for the murdering of the hostages caused several Black Muslim prisoners to appoint themselves the guardians of the hostages. Meanwhile, inmate Roger Champen organized prisoners in the yard. Although Superintendent Mancusi's swift plan to recapture the prison met with partial success in that a portion of the prison was retaken and held by the guards, the inmates became furious with Mancusi for the obvious contempt he showed when negotiating with the inmates for the release of the hostages. Oswald arrived at the prison in the afternoon, but he broke off negotiations with the prisoners the next day when inmates proved intractable in their demands. There were five demands made by the Attica prisoners: 1) Complete amnesty for all rebelling prisoners and guaranteed freedom from "physical, mental, and legal reprisals;" 2) Guarantees that the ringleaders would be released and allowed to escape the U.S. to "a non-imperialistic country;" 3) That the federal authorities take over complete jurisdiction of Attica; 4) That Attica be rebuilt under the direct supervision of the inmates; and 5) That negotiations be conducted on behalf of the prisoners by representatives of the Black Panther Party, the Young Lords, Louis Farrakhan of Muhammed Speaks, William Kunstler, criminal lawyer, Tom Wicker of the New York Times, and others.

Headed by mostly black inmates, the rebellion was both short-sighted and self-serving on the part of ringleaders. Many of those requested to represent the prisoners arrived at Attica and attempted to conciliate matters, but the voices of so many varied negotiators, all with their own political aims in mind, served to confuse matters and heighten an already lethal situation. The demands of the prisoners became so outrageous that Oswald and other officials felt that it was no use to continue discussions, especially when prisoners insisted that Mancusi be removed immediately. Outside negotiators pressured Governor Nelson Rockefeller's representative to have the governor come to Attica and negotiate directly with the inmates. Oswald, seeing that the prisoners were assuming a more menacing stance toward the hostages, called the governor and asked him to come to Attica but Rockefeller refused. On Sept. 13, when prisoners refused a number of concessions made by Oswald, hundreds of guards, state and local police formed for an attack. The hostages were dragged out to an open walkway where they stood blindfolded while the most savage of the rebelling inmates held knives to their thoats. It was at this moment, authorities believing that the hostages were about to be massacred, that the order was given to assault the main body of rebelling prisoners.

The massive assault saw hundreds of officers advancing on D Yard, blasting away with indiscriminate fire that mowed down both hostages and inmates alike. Following the attack, it was determined that police had killed twenty-nine inmates and ten hostages, wounding eighty-five other inmates, three hostages, and a state trooper. The police attack was universally condemned by press and authorities alike, although the prisoners in their death-threatening position with the hostages certainly provoked the senseless assault. Twenty officers were held responsible for the attack but the New York governor, in 1976, announced that no disciplinary action would be taken against them. He also, to balance the ledger and "close the book" on the Attica riot, pardoned seven former prisoners involved in riot and communted the sentence of an eighth inmate. The Attica Prison riot remains as one of the most bloody and purposeless slaughters in the history of American penology.

REF.: *CBA*; Wicker, *A Time to Die*.

Atto Adalbert, d.988, Canossa, count. Rescued Adelaide, the widow of Lothair II, from prison in 951, provoking attack by Berengar II whom he repulsed. He was appointed count of Canossa by Emperor Otto I in 962. REF.: *CBA*.

Attrill, Mabel Lucy, prom. 1940, Brit., mur. In 1940 Attrill shotgunned to death a 65-year-old man named Frank Cave near Ventnor. It was one of many murder cases investigated by the esteemed British pathologist Sir Bernard Spilsbury.

REF.: Butler, *Murderers' England*; *CBA*.

Attwood, Sheila, 1940-51, Brit., Case of, mur. British police were still trying to piece together the facts surrounding the murders of 7-year-old Christine Butcher of Windsor, and Brenda Goddard, six, when they learned that a third child—Sheila Attwood of Kings Standing, Birmingham—had just been found dead in a garden near her parents' home on Aug. 2, 1951. Sheila had suffered the same fate as the two other girls. She had been strangled, but not raped. Nine days before the body turned up in the hedge, the foster mother of the Goddard girl received an anonymous letter, which read: "I want to say how sorry I am for what I did to your daughter. I don't know what made me do it, but it is too late now. But I can say within the next two weeks they will find my body somewhere." A postscript said there might be another murder within that two weeks.

The day after that "other" murder, 33-year-old Horace Carter of Caversham Road was arrested and charged with the murder of Attwood. In court he described how the crime was carried out, along with a lot of nonsensical testimony, such as wondering how

much insurance money he would collect if his neck were to be "stretched." After pleading Not Guilty to the charges, he was declared legally insane.

REF.: *CBA*; Harrison, *Criminal Calendar II*.

Atwell, prom. 1850s, Brit., forg.-burg. Atwell was a petty thief recruited by forger James Saward, better known as "Jim the Penman," after Atwell burgled an ironworker's shop and delivered some checks and bank drafts to Saward for duplication. Atwell was given an assumed name and assigned the job of courier between the bank and the Penman. He remained a member of the gang for months, but finally was arrested on the east coast of England when a branch of Barclay's Bank became suspicious of a number of transactions made through a client named Whitney. The slippery "Penman" fled to London but was picked up on Oxford Street and was tried at the Old Bailey on Mar. 5, 1857. Atwell turned Queen's evidence against his former employer, and received a reduced sentence of penal servitude. See: **Jim the Penman**.

REF.: *CBA*; Twyman, *The Best Laid Plans*.

Atwell, William Hawley, 1869-1961, U.S., jur. Served as U.S. attorney for the Northern District of Texas from 1898-1913 and appointed to the federal bench for the same district by President Warren G.Harding in 1923. He published *Atwell's Federal Criminal Law and Procedure*, *Charges to Jurors*, and an autobiography. REF.: *CBA*.

Atzerodt, George A., See: **Lincoln, Abraham**.

Aubray, Marie Madeleine, See: **Brinvilliers, Marie**.

Auburn Prison Riots, 1929, U.S., mob viol. Called the "prison without walls," and touted for its liberal policy of convict self-government, the Auburn Prison in New York, overcrowded by more than 500 men, was like a barrel of dynamite waiting to explode. On July 29, 1929, armed convicts at Auburn seized ammunition and riot guns and held the prison at siege for five hours.

Inspiration for three films and several books, the first of the two Auburn Prison Riots happened just one week after riots at Clinton Prison in Dannemora, N.Y. Known as "Siberia" to the gangster underworld, Clinton blew up in a vicious revolt, resulting in the deaths of three inmates, injuries to guards and prisoners, and damages of about $200,000. About 1,300 inmates had rioted just after breakfast, beating two guards, setting fire to buildings, and storming the walls. The riot was in part the reaction of prisoners who had demanded new potatoes instead of old for their meals, and wanted a full day off on Sundays; both requests had been refused. Prisoners were overcome after about five hours when guards and state troopers overwhelmed them with machine and riot guns, tear gas, and hand grenades.

Although there had been no official statement about the riots, Auburn Prison inmates knew of the uprising, and guards at Auburn were concerned over the possibility of a similar situation. With a capacity of 1,226, Auburn had been overcrowded since January 1928 with 1,517 inmates; by June 1929, the numbers had risen to 1,750. Just days before the Auburn riot, State Prison Commissioners W.W. Nicholson and Colbert A. Bennett had urged that Auburn be abandoned. Plans for the construction of a new prison were already underway.

At around 11:00 a.m. on July 28, 1929, the arsenal of the Auburn Prison was seized by 1,700 convicts who stormed the prison walls, rushing from the main corridor into the prison yard, shooting four guards, and setting fire to several buildings. The desperate rush for freedom began an hour later, and was believed to have been planned from the outside as well as by the Auburn convicts. A guard, Wallace, opening the door in response to the trusty's signal, was besieged by about fifty-five prisoners who beat him unconscious. Joined by 100 or more prisoners, they raced down the hall, shooting another guard, Merle Osborne, and throwing acid in his face. They grabbed his keys to unlock the arsenal and seized guns and ammunition. The guard at the main gate, Ryther, fell wounded as prisoners ran along the wall, dodging fire for twenty or thirty feet in their maniacal efforts to escape.

Four dropped to the street; escaping in stolen cars were Arthur Barry, Joseph Caprico, Steve Pawlak, and George Small; all had been convicted of robbery or burglary.

From burning shops prisoners grabbed shovels, pickaxes, and knives, as snipers fired on guards. Two prisoners, Joseph Cirrongone and George Wright, were killed in the melee. Cirrongone was shot in the eye by a sniper while cooking in the prison kitchen, and Wright was shot in the surge of 1,700 rioters, led by a trusty, from the main hall to the yard. State troopers from three local companies of the New York National Guard's 108th Infantry were called in to assist the 150 prison guards as they held the raging convicts at bay. Troopers, armed with pistols and covered by machine guns, dropped from the high walls into the mass of rioting men to help guards drive prisoners away from makeshift barricades, breaking up groups and forcing convicts back into their cells.

Firemen were hampered in their efforts to put out the flames by prisoners who hacked at the hoses with butcher knives and axes from the prison kitchen. Destroyed in the fires were the machine shop, the furniture plant, the kitchen, the cane shop, and an old wing scheduled to be torn down, as well as the building in which the prison documents were kept, destroying all records of criminal identification. Damage was later estimated at $250,000. Because the power plant had been put out of commission, electricians strung up wires for searchlights.

Warden Edgar S. Jennings pronounced the situation under control after five hours of mayhem. Eight hundred armed men, many of them civilians, stood watch over the prison that night, as convicts were taken into the chapel and corridors of the main building. As soon as Commissioner Whalen received news of the uprising, he ordered heavy guards placed on all other New York prisons. As Warden Jennings surveyed the damage at Auburn, he was greeted by jeers and catcalls from the prisoners.

A total of eleven inmates had escaped, with Cornelius Lynch and Joseph Wojciechowaki returning. Lynch, who had served as a private under Warden Jennings' command during WWI, returned on his own volition on Aug. 5, 1929; Wojciechowaki was captured in Cleveland, Ohio, on August 1. The total damage in the July riot was estimated at between $450,000 and $470,000.

On Nov. 13, 1929, escaped convict George Small was captured after a gun battle with police in Brooklyn in which a bystander was killed. On Nov. 28, six convicts were convicted of rioting by a County Court held before Judge Edgar S. Mosher. Steve Pawlak, Joseph Bravata, Joseph Phillips, William Force, Chester Orysiak, and Hugh Bennett were found Guilty of leading the uprising. Force and Pawlak both refused to give their statements of previous convictions; all six prisoners had been brought to court under extra heavy guard. With Mosher's Nov. 30 sentencing of several of the convicts (Pawlak, Bravata and Force were up on additional charges as four time offenders), it seemed that the Auburn Prison Riot troubles were accounted for, and justice had been served.

At 11:00 a.m. on Dec. 11, 1929, fifty men, in solitary confinement for their part in the July riot, were discovered armed in a corridor by the prison chaplain. Father Donald Cleary pleaded with the convicts in vain to disarm. The men had handcuffed six guards and forced them back to the cells to free the other prisoners. Capturing Warden Jennings as he returned to his office, the desperate men manacled him, holding him hostage as they waited for Henry Sullivan, leader of the group, to report back on the number of guards at the main gate. George A. Durnford, the head keeper, was shot and killed when he tried to escape. Other guards were wounded as they ran to see what was happening. A scribbled message saying, "For God's sake, give them what they want," signed with Warden Jennings name, was delivered to State Trooper Captain Stephen McGrath, stationed at the prison's gate. Commanding one of his men over the screaming sirens to go telephone the commissioner of correction at Albany, McGrath received the reply from Acting Governor Herbert H. Lehman: "The Warden will have to take his chances. There will be no compromise."

Troopers attempted to fool the prisoners by ordering three cars pulled up to the main gates. McGrath asked Father Cleary to tell the prisoners that the troopers would capitulate to their demands for safe conduct out of the prison in order to save the lives of the warden and the other captive guards. Unaware of the strategy, Father Cleary relayed the message. Barricading themselves behind cars, trees, and fences, troopers watched as leaders Sullivan and Perry Johnson, sprinting for freedom, were mowed down by a hail of bullets. McGrath ordered the charge, with tear gas bombs to smoke the men out from barricades. For the rest of the day, National Guard units mobilized, with 1,500 armed men gathered for the attack, as sniper fire continued at Auburn. With orders to shoot to kill, militiamen formed a cordon around the jail, and troopers stormed the prison. At 5:30 p.m. the convicts who refused to surrender were shot down as they opened fire on the troops. Lunging out of clouds of tear gas, convicts clawed at the yard wall, climbing over each other's backs in a futile grab for freedom, then racing back inside the cell block.

By nightfall, the machine guns were silent. Troopers positioned their machine guns. Lifer Steve Pawlak stood up behind the last barricade, snarling, "Go to hell." Troopers opened fire, and the six remaining rebels fell dead. Nine guards and prisoners had been killed, including Pawlak, Johnson, Sullivan, Alexander Tucholker, another lifer; Stephen Sporney, Luke J. Bonnell, James Biancrasi, and Ernest Pavesi. Scores of convicts and guards had been wounded.

Searches for hidden weapons were underway by the next morning. On Dec. 13, Governor Franklin Delano Roosevelt appointed a special trial term of the Cayuga County court to bring swift justice to the seven surviving ringleaders of the second Auburn Prison riot. The Department of Corrections in Albany initiated an investigation to determine the cause of the rioting, and District Attorney Benn Kenyon announced his intention of asking for murder indictments for those responsible for Head Keeper Durnford's murder. In a radio address, Superintendent of Federal Prisons Sanford Bates called for federal leadership in penal affairs, describing the overcrowded conditions that had helped precipitate the 1929 riots at Auburn, Dannemora, and Colorado's Canyon Prison as "intolerable."

The three week trial of the Auburn convicts indicted for murder ended on Feb. 15, 1930. Three were found Guilty of first degree murder, and three were acquitted by a jury that deliberated for twenty-two hours. Sentenced to die in the electric chair for the murder of convict Sullivan were Jesse Thomas, Claude Udwin, and William Force. Acquitted of murder, but tried later for assault were Frank Leagan, Leo Lewis, and Albert Cassidy. All six of the defendants responded to the verdicts with sneers. Acquitted of the murder charge in a separate Mar. 12, 1930, trial was Max Becker, who fainted when he heard the verdict, then recovered to deliver a beaming speech of thanks to the jury. Becker was later sentenced to an additional twelve years, added to his thirty-year term for burglary, for attempting to escape in May 1929. The sentences of Terrence Reilly and Verne Gore, who had fought on the side of the law and saved the lives of fellow inmates during the riots, were commuted by Governor Roosevelt on June 20, 1930. Udwin, Force, and Thomas were executed at Sing Sing Prison on Aug. 28, 1930. Two of the escaped convicts, George Small and Arthur Barry, were acquitted on Dec. 24, 1932, of charges of rioting. Convicted on Feb. 16, 1933, of escaping during the July riot, Small listened to Judge Kennard Underwood announce the verdict, then responded, "Once I bet right." See: **Alcatraz; Attica; Clinton Prison Riot; Ohio State Penitentiary.**

REF.: *CBA;* Fox, *Violence Behind Bars*' Mitford, *Kind & Unusual Punishment;* (FILM), *The Big House*, 1930; *The Last Mile*, 1959.

Audett, James Henry (AKA: **Blackie**), 1902-79, U.S., boot.-smug.-rob. Audett was one of the last of the Dillinger gang members, not closely identified with Public Enemy Number One since he was a "free-lance" gangster who worked with many bank-robbing gangs of the early 1930s. Born in Calgary, Alberta, Can.,

Audett ran away from home as a teenager and went to work for the railroads in Washington State, later moving to Oregon. He served in France during WWI and, upon his return to the U.S., took up bootlegging as a way of life. When Audett's wife and children were killed in an auto accident, he attacked the driver of the other car, a wealthy Portland, Ore., resident, Walter Pierce. After Pierce was acquitted of a manslaughter charge (driving while drunk), Audett almost killed Pierce and received a six-week sentence, his first incarceration.

During Prohibition, Audett became a top bootlegger, working with Oregon gangsters Irv Wilks, Joe Parsell, and Albert Moore. He also ran a smuggling operation wherein he brought in illegal Chinese to Portland and other cities and received $300 a head. In 1926, Audett kidnapped a crooked plainclothes cop, Sergeant Staten, a go-between for Audett's bootlegging mob and the authorities. Staten took pay from Audett to keep local Portland police from raiding Audett's

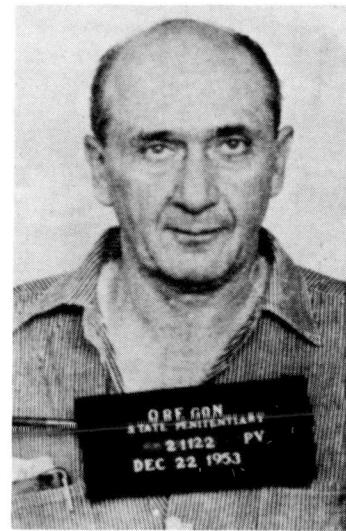

James Henry "Blackie" Audett, who was sent to Alcatraz *twice.*

warehouses, but when the bootlegger learned that the detective was also informing officials on some of Audett's gang members, he kidnapped the policeman and cut off his ear. Squint Miller, one of Audett's men, mailed the ear to the U.S. attorney in Portland, with a note that read: "If you keep sending these damned stoolpigeons after us, the next time we're going to send you a head!"

Staten escaped and later informed on Audett, who was sent to the U.S. Federal Penitentiary at McNeil Island for kidnapping. Audett escaped and fled east. He met Jake Fleagle in Denver and joined the notorious Fleagle bank-robbing gang, operating in several western states throughout 1927. He was arrested for bank robbery and was thrown into the McCook County, Neb., jail, sharing a cell with another infamous bank robber, Earl Thayer, who had been robbing banks and trains since 1912. Both men escaped from the McCook Jail by overpowering a trusty and stealing a police car. Thayer fled to Mexico and Audett to Chicago where he teamed up with Al Sutton, a celebrated safecracker. One safe the pair opened yielded $26,000. Audett and Sutton cracked so many safes within a few months' time that Al Capone, crime czar of the city, called them into his Lexington Hotel offices and ordered them to leave the city because "you guys are bringing too much heat down on my boys and you ain't splitting much with me."

Audett left for France, his pockets bulging with more than $100,000 in stolen loot. He was arrested in Marseilles by French police who identified him from a fugitive warrant poster, and shipped him back to the U.S. where he was then sent to the federal penitentiary at Leavenworth to serve out his original sentence, plus an additional sentence for escaping from McNeil Island. He shared a cell with the notorious Frank Nash, a southwestern bandit with strong ties to the corrupt Pendergast Machine. When Nash got out of Leavenworth, he persuaded Johnny Lazia, Pendergast's crime boss of Kansas City, to use his political influence to obtain Audett's release. In 1930, Audett was paroled through the Pendergast-Lazia connection, and he went to work for Lazia, helping to rig elections for the Pendergast Machine. It was Audett's job to keep "repeaters" voting and to make sure all Kansas City prostitutes voted several times each. He also destroyed ballot boxes and threatened citizens suspected of voting against Boss Tom Pendergast.

Audett also served as a lieutenant of Lazia's in controlling the crime boss' many lucrative gambling operations. He took a mistress, a hard-boiled woman named Gladys Carlson, who was later executed for murdering two Chicago policemen. Audett was also given special chores by Lazia such as delivering payoffs to politicians all over the U.S. Audett later claimed that he delivered hundreds of thousands of dollars in cash to such distinguished politicians as U.S. Senator William McAdoo of California, governor Huey Long of Louisiana, and Big Bill Thompson, mayor of Chicago; these politicians were paid to help effect local and federal legislation that was favorable to Pendergast interests throughout the U.S.

In 1933 Lazia appointed Audett as a bodyguard for Mary McElroy, the attractive daughter of Kansas City manager and Pendergast crony, Henry McElroy. Mary McElroy had been kidnapped by four apprentice kidnappers in 1933, a gang headed by Walter McGee. She was held for two days before the ransom had been paid and later testified at the trials of the kidnappers. McGee drew a death sentence which caused Mary to plead for his life (his sentence was commuted to life), an act which caused reporters to spread the story that Mary had fallen in love with her kidnapper. Audett later insisted that this was the case. Mary was obsessed with gangsters long before her celebrated kidnapping, having been exposed to the Lazia crowd through her crooked father. It was Mary McElroy who called Audett in June 1933 after *she* had gotten an inside tip from Lazia, and told Audett that machine gunners would be taking a federal prisoner away from FBI agents and other lawmen when a train carrying Frank Nash arrived in Kansas City's Union Station. "She knew it was going to happen," Audett later stated. "She knew from Lazia, Pendergast, and McElroy. She looked upon me as a big brother. She took me down to the Union Station to keep me out of trouble, so she'd know I was with her, just sitting in the car with her, not on the platform with all that shooting."

Audett and McElroy sat in the parking lot of Union Station on June 19, 1933. As if witnessing a blood sport, both watched four men alight from two cars and begin firing at lawmen and their prisoner after they got off a train, killing three police officers and an FBI agent, along with the prisoner they sought to free, Frank Nash. Audett named the killers as Verne Miller and Maurice and Homer Denning. He also stated that William "Solly" Weissman was present but Weissman was dead by that time, killed by an underworld associate. Another Weissman, Solly's younger brother, George, was probably the other man. The slaughter, later dubbed by newsmen as the Kansas City Massacre, shocked the nation and brought abrupt action by federal authorities. Because the FBI agents had been unarmed in this shootout, federal legislation was quickly enacted so that Hoover's agents were authorized to carry weapons. J. Edgar Hoover insisted later and to the end of his days that Charles Arthur "Pretty Boy" Floyd and his sidekick, Adam Richetti, were the killers in the Kansas City Massacre. His agents tracked down Floyd in 1934, killing him in Ohio. Richetti was later executed for the crime, protesting his innocence to the end.

By early 1934, with Lazia's power on the wane in Kansas City, Audett aligned himself with independent bank-robbing gangs then terrorizing the Midwest, particularly those headed by the Barker Brothers and John Dillinger. He participated in several bank robberies with Dillinger in May and June 1934 but, according to Audett, "federal heat" was so intense that Public Enemy Number One, Dillinger, devised a plan to effect a permanent escape. Through his lawyer, Louis Piquett, Audett, and others, Dillinger reportedly paid a "double" to take his place, an unsuspecting nonentity named James Lawrence, who believed that, if arrested, he would be released after being able to prove his true identity. This was the same man shot down and killed at the Biograph Theater on July 22, 1934, and claimed to be Dillinger, according to Audett and the author of this work.

Audett stated that, following the Biograph shooting, he drove the real Dillinger to the West Coast where Dillinger married and settled down, first in Oregon, later in California, living to a ripe old age. It was also in 1934 that Audett was arrested and convicted of bank robbery, and sent to Alcatraz. He was later paroled and sent back to the Rock, one of the few men to ever bear two numbers in Alcatraz. Again paroled, Audett found it impossible to live the "straight life." In 1974, he and an 81-year-old accomplice held up a Seattle bank. Blackie Audett was seventy at the time. He was sent to Leavenworth, then, with failing health, to the federal correctional facility in Lexington, Ky. He was finally paroled to the author's custody in June 1979 and died two months later, after revealing his role in the Dillinger escape. Book authored: *Rap Sheet.* See: **Alcatraz; Capone, Alphonse; Barker Brothers; Dillinger, John Herbert; Fleagle Gang; Floyd, Charles Arthur; Hoover, J. Edgar; Kansas City Massacre; Lazia, John; McGee, Walter; Nash, Frank; Pendergast Machine; Thayer, Earl; Weissman, William.**

REF.: Audett, *Rap Sheet; CBA;* Clayton, *Union Station Massacre;* Karpis, *On The Rock;* Louderback, *The Bad One;* Nash, *The Dillinger Dossier.*

Auersperg, Johann Weikhart, 1615-77, Aust., polit. Austrian diplomat who helped negotiate the Peace of Westphalia in 1648. He was banished to Carniola in 1669 by Leopold I. REF.: *CBA.*

Augsburg, Afra of, prom. 1st cent., Turk., Saint, pros. Afra of Augsburg was canonized as a Christian martyr during the Roman persecutions. She was a prostitute from Cyprus who opened a brothel frequented by church dignitaries who adjured the fallen women to renounce their ways. According to legend, Afra and the women she employed in the bordello abandoned harlotry in order to embrace Christianity.

REF.: *CBA;* Henriques, *Prostitution.*

Augustine, Robert, d.1863, U.S., west. gunman. In 1863, a tough cowboy named Robert Augustine got drunk and went amuck in San Antonio, Texas, stepping from a saloon with pistols in hand and then riding pell-mell up and down the main streets "hurrahing" the town. This was a form of amusement in the Old West where bored cowboys and gunmen would race back and forth along the streets of a town, shooting his guns wildly in the air and, often as not, destroying windows and occasionaly shooting anyone so foolish as to appear in the streets during the "hurrah." When Augustine finally ran out of ammunition, he was apprehended and locked up in the Bat Cave Jail.

When Augustine was brought to trial he presented an unorthodox defense which was one of the most terrifying and effective in the annals of the Old West. The vicious cowboy reportedly had an early-day camera brought into the courtroom and ordered the photographer to take a photo of the judge and jury. Snarled Augustine, "I'm taking a photograph of you all. I want your faces so impressed in my brain that I shall not forget and if you convict me, I'll get out and make every one of you bite the dust! And that counts for you, too, Judge!" With these death-threat words ringing in their ears, the jury acquitted Augustine and the judge released him immediately. A few days later a group of vigilantes led by Asa Mitchell, grabbed the truculent Augustine, dragged him to a chinaberry tree and promptly hanged him.

REF.: Bartholomew, *A Biographical Album of Western Gunfighters; CBA.*

Aulisio, Joseph, 1966- , U.S., mur. Aulisio liked to tinker with automobiles. His friends and schoolmates expected him to become a mechanic, like many other high school boys in the small town of Old Forge, Lackawanna County, Pa. By all accounts, he was a model student, loyal, obedient, and helpful, according to his principal Walter Ermolovich, who also knew the boy's father Robert, a biology teacher in the school.

Problems started when the Aulisios' youngest child died in its third month. Relations between family members became strained, ending in the parents' divorce. Joseph's school work declined, and he began cutting classes. He grew sullen and withdrawn, to the dismay of his parents, still engaged in the bitter divorce suit. His unhappiness finally culminated in murder on July 26, 1981, when the dark-haired youth abducted 8-year-old Cheryl Ziemba and her

brother Christopher Ziemba, four, from their home on the outskirts of Scranton. Two days later their bodies were found in an abandoned strip mine, shotgunned to death.

Aulisio was found guilty of first-degree murder and sentenced to die in the electric chair, which caused protest among opponents of capital punishment. "We're reading more and more about vicious crimes by younger and younger people," countered Judge James Walsh of the Lackawanna County Common Pleas Court. "Incidents like that are causing a lot of people to say that if they are guilty of adult criminal activity they should be subject to adult punishment." In 1982 Aulisio was the youngest offender to sit on death row in a U.S. prison. During the long appeals process he was transferred to the State Correctional Institution at Huntingdon where he currently resides. REF.: *CBA.*

Ault, Maude, b.1891, and **Ault, Robert Eugene,** b.1910, U.S., fraud. Ault and her grown son Robert owned a filling station near Decatur, Ill. before the onset of the Great Depression. Like many small business people with big dreams, Ault believed her pot of gold was just around the corner if only the right break came her way.

One day in 1930 she decided to take matters in hand. With her son at her side, she drove to River Forest, a Chicago suburb, where she told her brother Lorenson Bandy about a certain bootlegger named Max Orendorff who was incarcerated in the federal penitentiary in Atlanta. The mysterious Orendorff made his millions with Al Capone after the Chicago gangster rose to prominence in 1925, according to Ault. If there was a way to free Max from prison, he would make them all rich. Intrigued, Bandy agreed to do what he could.

Several trips allegedly were made to Atlanta before the news came out that Max had been freed. Then he died, leaving oil lands and real estate valued at $50 million to the Aults—provided Bandy could recruit "investors" to put up money to defray the legal expenses of selling the assets. Letters were sent out to prominent U.S. citizens promising a 200 to 1 return on every dollar invested. Such public figures as crime-fighter Thomas Dewey, Judge Harlan Stone of the Supreme Court, and Winthrop Aldrich of the Chase Manhattan Bank were advertised as investors by the Ault's "solicitor" James Cleary, who never existed.

And neither did millionaire bootlegger Max Orendorff; Robert Ault and his mother had perpetrated a colossal hoax. They were charged with mail fraud in March 1930. Banker Aldrich traveled to Danville, Ill. to testify that he never in his life had the pleasure of making Mrs. Ault's acquaintance. The conniving pair were found Guilty, sentenced to ten years in prison, and fined $3,000 each. REF.: *CBA.*

Aunay, Pierre, and **Leani, Jean,** prom. 1930s, Fr., drug smug.- org. crime. The great drug bust went bad, leaving two sadder but wiser international police detectives with egg on their faces. Two Corsican gangsters, Pierre Aunay and his associate, Jean Leani, sold American cigarettes in the French black market until they were swindled by U.S. gangsters. They next turned their attention closer to home, to the lucrative French drug connection extending from the Turkish poppy fields to the port of Marseilles.

Charles Syracuse and his assistant John Andréa decided to lay a trap for the two smugglers. Posing as wealthy American racketeers, they enlisted the help of a middleman named Roger Olivié who put them in touch with Aunay. For three kilos of cocaine, the two detectives agreed to pay six million francs at a meeting at the Hotel Ruhl. Listening devices were set up in an adjacent room, monitored by Commissioner Hugues of the Paris police. Just before the deal went through, Aunay and Leani began speaking French to Andréa. In previous discussions, the gangsters had conversed in Italian with the undercover officer. This clever ploy, designed to flush out the inexperienced narcotics agents, caught Charles Syracuse off guard.

Aunay pointed a gun at Andréa, as they slipped out of the room with the six million francs in hand. A police officer in the downstairs lounge fortunately had the good sense to record the license plate of their Peugeot sedan as Aunay joined Leani and they drove off. The car was spotted the next day in Cannes, and the offenders arrested. But all they had left was three million francs. The rest of the government's money had mysteriously disappeared. The parcels of cocaine when examined contained only icing sugar. The guns were only toys, purchased in a local shop. "We left them in the big ashtray in the hall of the hotel on our way out," said Aunay. Both the firearm and drug charges were dropped, and all that Hugues could hold them on was a charge of theft. Charles Syracuse returned to Rome where, at last report, he purchased a French language book.

REF.: *CBA; Goodman, Villainy Unlimited.*

Aung San, c.1914-47, Burma, rebel, assass. Leader of the revolutionary group Dombama Asi-ayone. He fled to Japan but later returned to Burma with the invading Japanese Army in 1941. He then led the Burma Independence Army against British forces and was named minister of defense in the puppet government established by the occupying Japanese. In 1945 supported the allies and in 1947 he negotiated an agreement with Clement Atlee for the independence of Burma. His assassination was ordered by his rival U Saw. REF.: *CBA.*

Aurelian (Lucius Domitius Aurelianus), c.212-75, Roman., emperor, assass. Rose from a common soldier through the military ranks and elected emperor by the Roman Army in 270. Credited with restoring the Roman Empire to power, he defeated Palmyra in 273, destroyed the city, brought Queen Zenobia to Rome as a prisoner, and reconquered Egypt that same year. In 274 he took Gaul and Britain from Tetricus, a pretender to the throne, and began building the fortification walls of Rome. He was ssassinated by a conspiracy of his own officers. REF.: *CBA.*

Aurelio, Thomas A., prom. 1945-53, U.S., jur., graft-org. crime. The influence of the Cosa Nostra is pervasive, in this case extending to the state Supreme Court. Aurelio secured his nomination to the court largely through the efforts of New York crime boss Frank Costello. After his appointment went through, he called the mobster at his home to thank him. The conversation was recorded by FBI agents, and it went like this:

Aurelio: "Good morning, Francesco. How are you? And thanks for everything."

Costello: "Congratulations. It went over perfect. When I tell you everything is in the bag, you can rest assured."

Aurelio: "It was perfect. Arthur Klein did the nominating. First me, then Gavagan, then Peck. It was fine."

Costello: "That's fine...Well, we will have to get together, you, your Mrs. and myself, and have dinner some night real soon."

Aurelio: "That would be fine, but right now I want to assure you of my loyalty for all you have done. It's undying."

REF.: *CBA; Hibbert, The Roots of Evil.*

Auriol, Joseph, (Abbé Auriol), b.1852, Fr., mur. Joseph Auriol entered the priesthood for all the wrong reasons. At the age of sixteen, the impoverished youth who resided near the French-Spanish border went to hear the Abbé Pompidor speak to his congregation at Prades. Swept up in the brilliant oratory, Auriol decided that he would become a priest like the Abbé Pompidor, and escape the grinding poverty of his youth.

His uncle endorsed the idea. Garda, as the man was known, had been caring for young Joseph since his father was sent to prison some years before. Auriol had some misgivings, but talked himself into taking the vows. In 1880, after nearly a decade of administering to his parishioners at various outlying villages, Abbé Auriol was sent to Nohédes where he befriended two prosperous old ladies named Rose Fonda and Marie Fonda, who had blessed the church with many financial endowments over the years.

He rewarded their kindnesses by digging up roots and herbs which he passed off as healing drugs designed to cure their physical ailments. At the same time, the priest became enchanted with a 22-year-old school teacher named Alexandrine Vernet, and it was not long before he had broken his vows with this woman. The ensuing scandal forced Auriol to make other arrangements. He moved his mistress to a neighboring village before deciding to quit the priesthood forever. It was now 1881, and the soon-to-be defrocked priest needed money to finance his contemplated move to Spain, and his future life with Alexandrine. To this end, he decided to poison the elderly sisters with the deadly hellebore root he picked in the mountains.

On July 18, Marie was struck by a sudden and violent illness while she ate her breakfast. She died an hour later, leaving all her property to her sister. The next week Rose made a will bequeathing her entire estate to Abbé Auriol. On July 30 she too died, after drinking some tea specially prepared by the kindly priest. An anonymous letter written to the authorities at Prades accused Auriol of the murders. When he was arrested, his pockets contained a vial of prussic acid and 11,000 francs. Yet, when the bodies of the sisters were exhumed, no trace of poison could be found. The doctors could not say with certainty whether the women had met with an untimely death.

Nearly a month passed. In solitary confinement, the priest finally acknowledged his guilt and confessed the crime to the police and the parishioners who had trusted him. He later retracted the confession, but it did not stave off the impending criminal action brought against him. He was found Guilty of the two murders, but the jury attached extenuating circumstances to their verdict. Auriol escaped the guillotine but received a sentence of hard labor for life. The jurors were apparently impressed by his honesty and willingness to renounce the priesthood before deciding to commit murder.

REF.: *CBA; Irving, Studies of French Criminals of the Nineteenth Century.*

Aurobindo, Sri, 1872-1950, India, consp. Philosopher and poet who was imprisoned in his youth for nationalist activities and later fled to French Pondicerry. REF.: *CBA.*

Austin, Alice, and **Simmons, Ted,** and **Scott, Ira,** prom. 1930s, U.S., bomb.-mur. Alice and Earl Austin of Hardin County, Ill., were in the middle of a bitter divorce. Earl Austin was suing Alice for desertion; she had run away with a local swain, Ted Simmons. Alice countersued Earl, charging him with adultery, and named Lacene McDowell as the other woman. The divorce action raged on until Alice Austin decided that waiting for drawn-out divorce proceedings to bring her a proper financial settlement was a waste of time. She and her lover, Ted Simmons, thinking to cash in on a life insurance policy on Earl Austin's life (still signed over to Alice), planned to murder the estranged husband. They plotted his death in many schemes but finally went to Ira Scott, a farmer with a knack for putting mechanical things together—in this case a bomb—requested by his two eager clients. Scott fashioned an infernal machine and placed this in Earl Austin's car.

On Mar. 20, 1939, Earl Austin and Lacene McDowell got into Earl's car to go for a drive along the rural roads of Hardin County. An hour later a terrific explosion rocked the car as it sped along, blowing away the floorboards and sending the car careening off the road and into a ditch. Both Earl Austin and Lacene McDowell were blown skyward at the moment of the blast, flying more than twenty feet into the air. Austin was dead within seconds but Miss McDowell, with one leg blown off, managed to linger for an hour. She remained unconscious and could tell State's Attorney Clarence E. Soward nothing before she died. Soward, however, was aware of the violent divorce action between Austin and his wife Alice and knew that Alice's sweetheart, Simmons, had openly threatened Earl Austin. He interviewed both Alice and Ted Simmons. Both expressed their profound regrets at the deaths of Earl Austin and McDowell, adding that they were with a group of people when the car blew up. The matter rested in limbo for some weeks until police received a tip that a local farmer, Ira Scott, had been acting nervously when going into town to buy some grain. Scott had purchased more items than his meager earnings would normally allow which also aroused suspicions.

When Scott was confronted by Soward, he broke down immediately, blurting, "I didn't mean to (kill them). I didn't know that there was going to be anybody in the car. Alice and Ted Simmons gave me fifty dollars to bomb it for the insurance. They didn't tell me that there would be anyone in it." He went on to say that he thought Alice and Ted wanted to collect insurance on the *car*, an implausible statement. Further, if no one was to be in the car, Scott failed to adequetly explain why he had set the timing device of the bomb on a delayed mechanism so that it would only go off after the car had been driven for about an hour after it had been started. His statements were downright idiotic in that his defense was built upon the car being driven by itself. By his own admission, Scott had run the fuse from the dynamite back into the exhaust manifold and this would have been impossible to ignite unless someone was indeed driving the auto. Simmons and Austin continued to deny their guilt when all three were later tried. All were found Guilty and each received a fourteen-year sentence.

REF.: *CBA;* Cohen, *100 True Crime Stories;* Nash, *Almanac of World Crime;* ____, *Murder, America.*

Austin, Edward, Dr., prom. 1839, Brit., libel. The libel case against Austin was tried before Justice Vaughan in the Court of the Common Pleas in 1839. The plaintiff was Dr. Ventris Field, who practiced in the town of Rotherhithe for nearly eighteen years. In 1838 a letter was circulated among the Poor Law Commissioners complaining of a certain medical doctor (Austin) who was negligent in his duty to a pregnant woman named Mrs. Daly. The anonymous communication prompted a board of inquiry, which deeply wounded Austin, who blindly accused Field of authoring the letter.

Austin wrote his own letter to the board, accusing Field of malpractice in a similar case. "My silence in the case of a murderous operation performed by him on a Mrs. Elizabeth Mason in Staples Rents has been the means of screening him probably from criminal proceedings, certainly from universal disgust and the opprobrium of every medical man." Field was incensed by the accusation, and sued Austin.

It was demonstrated that Mrs. Mason suffered from an ovarian cyst, and despite the valiant efforts of Ventris Field she died. There was little anyone could do at that point. The jury considered the evidence and returned a verdict of Guilty against Austin. He was ordered to pay the plaintiff £100.

REF.: *CBA;* Parry, *Some Famous Medical Trials.*

Austin, John, d.1783, Brit., asslt.-rob. Austin was the last British felon to be publicly hanged at Tyburn Hill. He walked to his execution on Nov. 7, 1783 to pay for the murder of John Spicer, whom he robbed and stabbed. Austin appeared composed as he made the final trek from Newgate to Tyburn, begging forgiveness from the hundreds of people who turned out to witness this final gallows execution.

The public spectacle of Tyburn hangings created terrible congestion on the roadways. When local business began to suffer the courts ordered that all persons convicted of capital offenses in London and Middlesex County be hanged on the scaffold in front of Newgate Prison. "The age is running mad over innovations," said author Samuel Johnson, who favored preservation of the old ways.

REF.: Bleackley, *Hangmen of England; CBA;* Potter, *The Art of Hanging.*

Austin, John, 1790-1859, Brit., jur. Law professor and author who wrote *Province of Jurisprudence Determined* and *Lectures on Jurisprudence.* REF.: *CBA.*

Austin, Richard Bevan, b.1901, U.S., jur. Assistant state's attorney for Cook County, Ill. in 1933, and first assistant state's attorney and acting state's attorney from 1947-48. He served as special prosecutor for Cook County from 1951-52 and first assistant state's attorney from 1952-53. He was elected judge of the Superior Court for the county of Cook in 1953 and re-elected in 1959. In 1969 he was appointed to the federal bench for the Northern District of Illinois by President John F. Kennedy in 1961. REF.: *CBA.*

Austin, Tom, d.1694, Brit., rob.-mur. Austin was born in Devonshire to hard-working farmers who left him the entire estate upon their deaths. The farm yielded an annual income of £80, not a princely sum, but enough to sustain his wife who had contributed an £800 dowry to the marriage.

Within four years, his taste for high living had corrupted Tom Austin. His farm was mortgaged away, and he had to resort to beggary in order to feed his family. Desperate, he committed his first serious crime. On the road between Wellington and Taunton Dene he held up Sir Zachary Wilmot for the sum of 46 guineas and a silver sword. When the nobleman resisted, he was shot dead. Austin quickly spent the loot and then set upon his own uncle.

Finding the uncle away from home, he killed the man's wife and her five small children with a hatchet. This brutality yielded Austin only £60. Later, his wife asked about the bloodstains on his clothing. Cursing her, Austin slit his wife's throat. He next went after his own two children, but irony worked against Tom Austin. His uncle stumbled upon the grisly scene just as Tom had killed the youngsters. The sheriff was summoned, and Austin was jailed in Exeter and hanged in August 1694. Before he died he spotted a peasant woman selling some curds. "I wish I could have a pennyworth of them before I am hanged," he said to the executioner. "Because I know not when I shall eat any again."

REF.: *CBA;* Hibbert, *Highwaymen;* Smith, *Highwaymen.*

Autullo, Dante, Jr., U.S., 1956- , Case of, drug traffick. A suspected drug kingpin, Autullo owned a pizzeria in Orland Park, Ill., a suburb south of Chicago. The pizza parlor and his bar in nearby Worth were the preferred meeting places for drug traffickers planning million-dollar cocaine deals.

On July 26, 1988, U.S. marshals confiscated both establishments as part of an ongoing investigation by the IRS and the Drug Enforcement Administration. Under a 1984 federal statute, drug enforcement agencies were empowered to seize property used for the sale and distribution of narcotics. "We heard rumors that the place the pizza parlor was a coke den ever since it opened last fall," explained Bryant Harris, who owned a convenience store across the street from the pizza parlor.

The restaurant and the bar were valued in excess of $1 million dollars. The owner, Autullo, previously had been indicted in Will County, Ill. for possession of cocaine with intention to distribute. Autullo listed a personal income of less than $10,000 a year on his 1986 federal income taxes, yet when investigators searched his $225,000 home in Lockport in 1987, they seized cars, diamonds, a boat, and jewelry worth more than a million dollars. Questioned by Will County officials in June 1987, Autullo confessed to selling 60 kilograms of cocaine with a monthly return of $175,000.

On Jan. 23, 1989 Judge Michael Orenic of the Circuit Court of Will County dismissed all charges against Autullo. REF.: *CBA.*

Auxonne Nuns, prom. 1660-62, Fr., witchcraft. In 1660 an Ursuline nun in Auxonne, France, was accused of bewitching a young priest and eight other sisters into committing lesbian and heterosexual acts inside the walls of the convent. Sister St. Colombe was charged with witchcraft on Oct. 28, 1660. Eight other nuns, including Mother Superior Barbara Buvée, accused the unfortunate young woman of practicing the devil's work, which they claimed caused the alleged orgies.

Father Nouvelet, the young parish priest, blamed his sexual affair with Marie Borthon on witchcraft and conducted an exorcism in the chapel to cleanse the nuns of their alleged possession. At the time the priest claimed to have observed amazing sights, which he believed to be demonic in nature. When the Mother Superior voiced her opposition to the exorcisms, she was accused of witchcraft and brought before the Parliament of Dijon.

The inquiry continued until August 1662 when the charges were dismissed. Sister St. Colombe, who had remained in solitary confinement, was transferred to another convent. Independently hired physicians visited the convent on a regular basis, concluding that the whole affair had been a fraud. A final report, issued on June 15, 1662, stated: "...in all their acts, whether bodily or mental, the nuns have never displayed any legitimate or convincing sign of true demoniacal possession." REF.: *CBA.*

Avarne, b.1891, Case of, Brit., abor. Avarne first became acquainted with his patient, a woman pregnant for the second time, on May 27, 1933. The father was a retired hotel owner who had maintained the girl as his mistress for nearly seven years. Once before, in 1926, she had carried this man's child and was given money and sent to Southampton to complete her term of pregnancy.

This second time, though, the hotel man felt obliged to help her out of the predicament and sent her to Avarne. The doctor never intimated that he would perform an illegal abortion. Instead he prescribed a mild bromide and sent her to a rest home to deliver the child. In her fifth month complications arose. The patient complained of hemorrhaging and stomach pain.

On July 27 a cesarian section was performed to save the baby. Avarne was not present, and only later discovered that the child had been born dead. Since the mother entered the home in seemingly perfect health, suspicion of inducing an abortion was cast on the doctor. The girl recovered, but Avarne was arrested by Centenier Foster, prefect of police, pending an investigation by the eminent British pathologist, Sir Bernard Spilsbury and a battery of doctors.

Spilsbury was convinced that Avarne was guilty as charged. The other physicians dissented, stating that it was a fetal death and nothing more. The trial was held in Jersey. A twenty-four man jury was empaneled to consider the evidence. After a short trial it acquitted Avarne. The sensational trial attracted a crowd of 7,000 who lined the town square. When the verdict was read, a bonfire was lit, and the doctor was carried out of the courthouse on the shoulders of his supporters. Meanwhile, Sir Bernard retreated to London, refusing to acknowledge the presence of the defense counsel who sailed back on the same packet boat. See: **Spilsbury, Bernard**.

REF.: *CBA*; Smith, *Mostly Murder*.

Averill, James (Jim), and **Watson, Ella**, d.1889, U.S., west rob.-gunman-lynch. The bloody Johnson County War in Wyoming was largely precipitated by the gruesome fates of gunman-rancher Jim Averill and his buxom paramour, Ella Watson, better known as Cattle Kate. Averill's background is sketchy, though it was claimed by contemporary historians that he was either a graduate of Yale or Cornell. He arrived at Sweetwater, Wyo., in late 1887, just when the powerful Wyoming Stock Growers' Association was planning to wipe out the newly arrived hordes of immigrant settlers who had streamed into the area to cultivate the rich land for farms. The ranges were soon fenced off with barbed wire, and the classic battle for land was waged between settlers and small ranchers lined up against the cattle barons.

Shortly after arriving, Averill bought a small ranch and established a combination store-saloon-post office. The approximately eighty residents of Sweetwater soon elected him justice of the peace and Averill's reign over this little frontier dynasty led him to believe that he could defy the ruthless cattle barons headed by Albert Bothwell. He began complaining to authorities about the encroachments of the cattlemen and was bitterly opposed to the Maverick Act which the Association had forced into existence. The wealthy cattlemen, who owned Wyoming's governor and most of its state senators, ordered the new law which allowed all unbranded calves to become the property of the Association. Thus, the thousands of stray cattle, no matter who rightfully owned them, went into the pens of the cattle barons. Men like Bothwell also coveted the entire Wyoming range and those who refused to sell their claims to the cattlemen were either run out of the territory or murdered by gunmen like Frank Canton, a glorified stockman's detective who was nothing more than killer for hire.

While the range battles expanded, Averill was besieged by his saloon customers to provide some female companionship for their amusement. He remembered a voluptuous woman named Ella Watson whom Averill had met in Rawlins. Watson was the daughter of a wealthy farmer in Smith County, Kan., and by the time she was eighteen she had already been married and separated from her husband. (Whether or not she was ever divorced is still unanswered, but she later claimed that her marriage was ruined because of her spouse's "infidelity.") Ella Watson was known to many men other than Averill, having earned her living as a prostitute in Denver, Cheyenne, and Rawlins. Averill penned her a purple-prosed letter, asking her to join him, ostensibly as his lover. She replied that she was on her way. It was later suggested that Watson was lured to Sweetwater by Averill on the promise of marriage and that when she arrived, penniless and with nowhere else to go, he made her his concubine and then the communal sexual property of the small ranchers who supported his store and saloon. Watson soon established a claim for a spread adjoining that of Averill's and she ordered stock pens built on her land since she took as pay for her sexual favors in the form of cattle. Thus this statuesque, tough woman earned the sobriquet of Cattle Kate.

Jim Averill, gunman and cattle rustler who was hanged with his sweetheart Ella Watson, 1889.

Kate was a tall, big-boned woman whose stamina with her cowboy lovers was legendary. She rode horses as would a man, never side-saddle, and was quite frank in her spoken ambitions to amass a cattle fortune, believing that Averill, whom she truly loved, would marry her and they would together establish a powerful cattle empire on their own. Watson remains somewhat of an enigma to this day, described as feminine and demure by her relatives and friends and as a hellion by the press and her enemies. The Cheyenne *Mail Leader*, for instance, reported that she was "of a robust physique, a dark devil in the saddle, handy with a six-shooter and a Winchester, and an expert with a branding iron." This unflattering profile was written following Kate's brutal demise as a way of supporting the cattlemen's claim that Kate rebranded and penned the cattle Averill stole from the cattle barons in preparation for resale. Watson's father described her in a contradictory statement, "She was a little girl, between one hundred and sixty to one hundred and eighty pounds."

Averill's attitude toward Watson was one of economics. He considered Kate a good investment, and the maverick cattle he and his men, including foreman Frank Buchanan, rounded up on the range, were brought to Kate's pens and there branded with Averill's own brand before being shipped to eastern markets. The cattlemen in the area were incensed with Averill's free-and-easy ways with their livestock, but they took little direct action. Averill was usually surrounded by several gunmen and Buchanan, an expert with rifle and shotgun, seemed always to be at his side. He was himself an expert gunman and had shot several men in the past. One of these, a man named Johnson, quarreled with Averill and the rancher shot him dead. Before turning himself in for this shooting, Averill wrote the local judge a flowery letter in which he claimed self defense, a missive that caused his later release. It was Averill's talent with pen and paper that eventually brought about his demise. In the spring of 1889 he began to write to several local newspapers, venting his spleen on the cattlemen and branding them thieves and killers, after the Association made claim to his own spread. He also expressed indignant anger over the stockmen's claim that his partner Kate was running a "hog ranch." She was a respected cattle rancher, Averill insisted.

The cattlemen suffered greatly during the 1888 blizzards which depleted their herds but the cattle in Kate's pens seemed to increase and she and Averill were growing rich. Averill began buying expensive clothes, gold cufflinks, and watch chains and he even sent off for imported cigars while he took Kate on shopping trips to Denver where she bought new dresses by the dozen. Kate thought to make her burden less by returning from Denver with another girl who was to satisfy her crude customers. Instead the poor girl almost died at the hands of a drunken Jim Averill who attacked her, then tied her to a wagon and left her to the savage elements. She was found the next morning half frozen to death. Sobering, Averill apologized (some said only after Kate leveled a shotgun at him) and gave the girl a generous amount of money.

Meanwhile, Averill and his men kept rounding up range strays, branding them, and shipping them off to market. At the same time, Averill kept up his barrage against the Association by writing letters to local papers. The Cheyenne *Weekly Mail* published his most bitter attack on the stockmen on Apr. 7, 1889, a letter that caused gunman Frank Canton to insist that Averill and his prostitute partner be eradicated. Adding fuel to this idea was an incident occuring in early June of that year. A cattleman rode to Watson's pens and identified some of his own cattle, asking Kate where she obtained them. Averill gave his usual laconic reply, "I bought them." The cattleman accused her of buying stolen cattle and Watson raced into her cabin and returned with a Winchester. The cattleman promised he would return and lay claim to his calves, then rode quickly away while Kate resolutely aimed her rifle in his direction.

A short time later a herd of cows belonging to Bothwell was raided by Averill, Buchanan, and others and the calves cut out and driven to Kate's pens (or so the story was later related by Association supporters). To keep the mothers from trailing behind the calves, Averill and his men slew the cattle and this bloody trail was followed almost to Watson's pens by cowboys working for Bothwell. When informed of this raid, Bothwell exploded, declaring that he would take the law into his own hands. First, Bothwell sent a spy to the Averill-Watson ranches and this man reported that he watched the pair get drunk at Kate's house. Thinking the couple would be suffering from hangovers and be easily caught off-guard, Bothwell, on July 20, 1889, ordered twenty of his best gun hands to follow him to the Sweetwater claims. The cattlemen first stopped at Watson's ranch. One report had it that both Watson and Averill were found in drunken stupors, "sitting next to a crude fireplace, the room clouded with tobacco smoke, a whiskey bottle and glasses on the table and firearms within easy reach." The facts are otherwise.

The cattlemen found Watson alone, returning from the outhouse in a skimpy nightgown. She tried to run into the ranch house but gunmen stopped her and dragged her before Bothwell who motioned to a wagon the posse had brought along. "You're going to Rawlins," he said, indicating that Watson and Averill would be brought before the law in that town and charged with rustling. Cattle Kate's reply was typically female, "I can't go to Rawlins. I don't have a new dress." Bothwell ordered her into the wagon and the big woman was lifted up and tossed onto the rough planks of the wagon which was then whipped on to Averill's place. There gunmen surrounded Averill's store-saloon and ordered him to step outside. He stepped outside, blinking at the bright sunlight. Bothwell lied in telling Averill that a warrant for his arrest had been posted and he was being taken to Rawlins. Unarmed, Averill, in his shirtsleeves, was grabbed and thrown into the wagon. They sat together wholly unconcerned about their fate, joking and laughing, making fun of the men who rode silently next to the wagon.

The taunting by Averill and Watson only seemed to strengthen the resolve of the possemen who rode to a small canyon through which snaked the Sweetwater River. Ropes were placed around the necks of the two captives and they were led over rocks to the water's edge. One of the possemen told Kate that they intended to drown her and Averill in the river. She looked at the shallow stream and laughed; it was still a joke to her. "Hell, there ain't enough water in there to give you hogbacks a bath!" she snorted. While the possemen hesitated, Averill's foreman, Frank Buchanan, who had followed the posse's trail, stood on a cliff looking down

on the party. He began firing at the possemen but the return fire was so withering that he was forced to flee.

This attack bolstered the possemen and they quickly led Averill and Watson to a split cottonwood tree, threw the ropes over the limbs and then ordered them to jump from rocks on which they were perched. An idiotic grin clung to Averill's face; he believed the vigilantes were continuing their joke. Watson, however, suddenly realized that this grim exercise was real. They were about to be hanged. She punched out wildly at the men around her and tried to remove the tightly drawn noose from around her neck. Two men held her arms while a cattleman stepped forward and casually kicked Averill's legs out from under him, sending him into space. Watson screamed and was then pushed off the rock where she stood. So eager were the cattlemen to lynch the pair that they had forgotten to tie the hands of their victims and both Averill and Watson clawed at the nooses that slowly strangled them. According to a report appearing in the Casper *Mail*, "the kicking and writhing of those people was awful to witness."

"Cattle Kate" Watson on horseback, alongside the pens holding the herds of stolen cattle for which she and Jim Averill were hanged by vigilantes.

It took quite a while for the couple to die. Finally, their bodies went limp as their eyes bulged hideously and bloody foam dripped from their mouths. The cattlemen left them dangling from the cottonwood tree and slowly rode away. Some of the members of this posse later regretted the double lynching, saying that they only meant "to frighten" Averill and Watson but the charade went too far. Others claimed that had Buchanan not fired on them the couple would have been taken to authorities and charged with cattle rustling. But these were merely tales designed to absolve the guilty, others claimed and that the whole incident was nothing more than premeditated murder, that Averill and Watson were respectable ranchers and had stolen no cattle at all. They were murdered because they would not give up their land to the covetous cattlemen.

Two days later the bodies of Averill and Watson were cut down and opinion quickly turned against the Association and its lynch-bent members, the Casper *Mail* demanding retribution and angrily asking in an editorial, "Is human life held at no value whatever?" Kate's father, Thomas Watson, arrived in Rawlins to claim his daughter's body, telling reporters that the cattlemen were liars, that his child was incapable of cattle rustling. "She never branded a hoof or threw a rope," he insisted. A dark stranger wearing two guns rode into Rawlins and buried Averill. He was identified as Averill's brother, and he busied himself for some time in rounding up witnesses against the possemen. Six of those who had been part of the lynch mob were subsequently arrested, but the process was a farce from the beginning. Rawlins authorities were in the pockets of the Association, and these six defendants were permitted to sign each other's bail bond. None were convicted. The deaths of Jim Averill and Cattle Kate did serve, however, to inspire homesteaders and small ranchers to stand up to the Association and a full-scale bloody range war erupted in Johnson County. Inside that death-filled turmoil, Frank Buchanan disappeared, presumed murdered by Frank Canton on behalf of the cattlemen. One of the more intriguing stories concerning the legends that gathered about Averill and Watson is that the couple produced a son, Thomas Averill, or so one Thomas Averill later claimed. He stated that he was five when the possemen arrived at his mother's cabin and that they shot him in the throat and left him for dead. He was raised by Indians and went on to work in many Wild West shows where he was known as Buffalo Vernon. When the Johnson County War ground down, Cattle Kate's small cabin was sold at auction for a mere $14.19, purchased by one of the possemen who had put the nooses around the necks of Jim Averill and Cattle Kate Watson. See: **Canton, Frank; Johnson County War.**

REF.: Adams, *The Best of the American Cowboy;* Aikman, *Calamity Jane and the Lady Wildcats;* Atherton, *The Cattle Kings;* Bard, *Cattle Wrangler;* Bartholomew, *The Biographical Album of Western Gunfighters;* Beals, *American Earth;* Beebe, *The American West;* Brown and Schmitt, *Trail Driving Days;* Brown, *The Plainsmen of the Yellowstone;* Burt, *The Diary of A Dude Wrangler;* ____, *Powder River; CBA;* Chatterton, *Yesterday's Wyoming;* Clay, *My Life on the Range;* Cushman, *The Great North Trail;* Flagg, *A Review of the Cattle Business in Johnson County;* Frink, *Cow Country Cavalcade;* Gage, *The Johnson County War;* Gard, *Frontier Justice;* Guernsey, *Wyoming Cowboy Days;* Horan, *The Authentic Wild West, The Outlaws;* ____, *Desperate Women;* ____ and Sann, *Pictorial History of the Wild West;* Larson, *History of Wyoming;* Lloyd, *The Invaders;* Mazzulla, *Outlaw Album;* Miller, *Shady Ladies of the West;* Mokler, *History of Natrona County, Wyoming;* Monaghan, *The Legend of Tom Horn;* ____, *The Book of the American West;* Moore, *Souls and Saddlebags;* Nash, *Bloodletters and Badmen;* Paine, *Tom Horn, Man of the West;* Parkhill, *Wildest of the West;* Pence, *Ghost Towns of the West;* Penrose, *The Johnson County War;* ____, *The Rustler Business;* Rennert, *The Cowboy;* Rollinson, *Wyoming Cattle Trails;* Rosa, *The Gunfighter;* ____ and May, *Gun Law;* Sandoz, *The Cattlemen;* ____, *Love Song of the Plains;* Smith, *The War on Powder River;* Waller, *Last of the Great Western Train Robbers;* Wilhelm, *Cavalcade of Hooves and Horns.*

Avery, d.1712, Brit., rob. Born in Oxfordshire, Avery was apprenticed at a young age to a London bricklayer. There was no chance for easy money in this line of work, though by all appearances, he was a successful young tradesman. Originally, he disguised his thieving activities from his wife, but eventually gave up all pretenses about the life of crime he had undertaken. Avery galloped pell-mell through the English countryside in search of victims. Once, while on his way to Surrey, he stopped a fish merchant. Engaging the proprietor in a harmless dialogue, he said that he, too, was a fisherman of sorts: "Ay, I'm something towards it, for every finger I have is a fishhook."

"Indeed, I don't apprehend your meaning, sir," the fishmonger replied. By way of explanation, Avery pulled out his pistols. "You see now my meaning may soon be apprehended," he replied, "for there's not a finger on either of my hands but will catch gold or silver without any bait at all." Avery took £20 from the startled merchant and fled to London. He continued his robbing, remembering the words of one of his victims who said, "the hangman is the only bait to catch such devils as you," for robbery was still punishable by death in Britain at that time. Not long after this, Avery was seized by the sheriff, sent to Newgate, and hanged at Tyburn on Jan. 31, 1712 for his many crimes.

REF.: *CBA;* Smith, *Highwaymen.*

Avery, Rev. Ephraim K., prom. 1832, Case of, U.S., mur. In December 1832, Sarah Maria Cornell of Tiverton, R.I., was found hanging from a haystack frame with what appeared to be a suicide note found neaby. It read, "If I should be missing, enquire of the Rev. Mr. Avery of Bristol—he will know where I am." This led authorities to arrest the Reverend Ephraim Avery and begin one of the most sensational U.S. murder cases in the early nineteenth century. Avery was further incriminated by the fact that he had been only a short distance away when the tragic Cornell died and he could only explain his presence in the vicinity by saying that he had been wandering about the countryside on that chilling December day for no reason at all. Despite all this, local magistrates were obviously influenced by Avery's clergyman status, and the charges against him were dismissed.

A local publication depicted Avery as strangling his sweetheart, Sarah Cornell, though the clergyman was acquitted.

An examination of Cornell's body proved her to be five months pregnant, and it was then generally assumed that Avery was the father of the unborn child and that to hide his sexual indiscretions with Cornell he hanged the poor soul and passed off her death as a suicide. The press and the public clamored for Avery's capture. Fearing that he would be lynched, the minister fled to Rindge, N.H., where he was later found hiding under an assumed name. He was returned to stand trial before the state supreme court of Rhode Island in what was a record for that time—twenty-seven days—in which 196 witnesses tesitified for and against him. In the end, Avery was acquitted for lack of solid evidence, although he was condemned at large for killing Sarah Cornell and such was his notorious reputation that his days as a clergyman were ended and he sought and found total obscurity.

REF.: Adams, *Report on the Trial of Ephraim K. Avery; Brief and Impartial Narrative of the Life of Sarah Maria Cornell; CBA; The Correct, Full and Impartial Report of the Trial of Rev. Ephraim K. Avery;* Drury, *A Report on the Examination of Rev. Ephraim K. Avery; Explanation of the Circumstances Connected with the Death of Sarah Maria Cornell; A Facsimile of the Letters Produced at the Trial of Rev. Ephraim K. Avery;* Hallett *The Arguments of Counsel in the Close in the Trial of Rev. Ephraim K. Avery;* Harnden, *Narrative of the Apprehension in Rindge, N.H. of the Rev. E.K. Avery;* Hildreth, *A Report on the Trial of Ephraim K. Avery;* Nash, *Almanac of World Crime; Particulars of the Cruel Seduction and Horrid Murder of Sarah M. Cornell;* Staples, *A Correct Report on the Examination of the Rev. Ephraim K. Avery; Strictures on the Case of Ephraim K. Avery; The Terrible Haystack Murder; The Trial at Large of the Rev. Ephraim K. Avery; The Trial of Rev. Ephraim K. Avery; Trial of Rev. Mr. Avery; A Vindication of the Result of the Trial of Rev. Ephraim K. Avery;* Williams, *Fall River, An Authentic Narrative.*

Avery, John (Long Ben), See: **Every, Henry.**

Avery, Peter, 1668-1712, Brit., rob. Avery was an uneducated family man, a London bricklayer by trade who worked long hours and remained utterly devoted to his family, having many children upon whom he doted. For many years Avery provided an above-average income which benefited his family greatly, allowing his wife and children to dress well, and live in better quarters than most in his line of work. Everyone marvelled at Avery's devotion to his family and an almost inhuman dedication to his work. But most of Avery's income did not derive from industrious bricklaying.

At night, with his family asleep, like the Jekyll-Hyde character of Deacon Brodie a century later in Scotland, Avery dressed, quietly left his lodgings, went to a livery stable, and rode into the countryside around London to prey upon night travelers as a masked highwayman. Peculiarly demonstrating a strange loyalty to his peer group, Avery did not rob tradesmen, except for fishmongers whom he had disliked since childhood, having been beaten by one for taking a fish from a stall. Most of his victims were wealthy merchants, and he had little patience with truculent victims. If any protested handing over his purse and jewels, Avery immediately shot dead the victim's horse and quickly terrified him into cooperating.

Against his better judgment, or so he later claimed, Avery took on a partner after many years of robbery, a man named Waterman whose oafish ways and careless manner soon caused both men to be apprehended. They were taken to Newgate where, after a speedy trial, they were condemned. Waterman appealed and was reprieved but Avery had no such luck, his petitions to Queen Anne being ignored. He was much embittered when he was taken to Tyburn on Jan. 31, 1713, and hanged before a large throng.

REF.: *CBA; The Newgate Calendar;* Smith, *A Complete History of the Lives and Robberies of the Most Notorious Highwaymen, Footpads, Shoplifts & Cheats of Both Sexes.*

Avery, William H., See: **Millington, Frank** and **Mary.**

Avidius Cassius, Gaius, d.175, Roman., comdr., assass. Commander of all Roman forces in the East. In 175, upon hearing the false rumor that Emperor Marcus Aurelius had died, he proclaimed himself emperor. He was later assassinated by one of his soldiers. REF.: *CBA.*

Avinain, Charles (Avignon, Charles), 1799-1867, Fr., mur. Avinain had a long criminal career which trailed back to 1833, with convictions for highway robbery and burglary with violent assault. He had been sent to Cayenne in French Guiana for a number of years, and when returning to Paris, he became a butcher. A tall, powerful man, even in his sixties, Avinain terrified his family who had separated from him after his imprisonment in Cayenne, and they stayed away from him, even though one of his daughters, a milliner, lived only a few blocks from her father's butcher shop. In the spring of 1867, all Paris was shocked at the number of dismembered bodies that began to turn up, floating in the Seine. The exact number of bodies were never fully recorded, undoubtedly since it was difficult to determine what parts belonged to what corpses, but it was estimated that at least twenty bodies were fished out of the Seine in the first seven months of 1867.

The police were baffled, having no way to identify the slain bodies, except to report that all the victims had been men. The shrewd Chief Claude of the Sûreté took pains to examine the grisly remains of the bodies, consulting with the police surgeon who informed him that the victims had all been strong men who worked with their hands, and their well-developed leg muscles led the doctor to believe that they were all farmers who had worked for years in the fields. He added, "The murderer of these men has at some time or another, served in a convict hospital and has either watched or assisted in surgical operations and autopsies. Furthermore, I am of the opinion that, by trade, he is a butcher. He has obviously been used to cutting up the carcases of animals for food." The surgeon pointed out the precision cuts at the joint areas of the corpses, similar to those made by butchers when slaughtering animals.

Claude began to inspect the records of all known criminals who had served in prison hospitals and came up with a number of suspects but he narrowed these down to a few who were presently occupied in Paris as butchers. Then he began to make the rounds, interviewing these butchers and their families. He learned from Avinain's wife and daughter that they seldom, if ever, saw Charles Avinain who kept to himself. By then, Claude had determined the identity of two of the victims. They had both been farmers, one named Désiré Duguet (whose stumpy severed hands were identified by his son who had come to Paris looking for this father) and Vincent Lecompte (identified in a similar manner). Both farmers had traveled to Paris from nearby farms to sell their loads of hay. Claude next investigated a row of huts near the Seine which were owned by the butcher Charles Avinain who had been, Claude had also learned, an assistant in the medical center at Cayenne. Inside of these huts Claude found the stolen loads of hay, along with other personal effects of the victims. The floors of the huts were stained with dried blood. It was then obvious to Claude that Avinain, his primary suspect, had been murdering farmers to steal, and later sell, their loads of hay in the marketplace at La Chapelle. Checking in the market area, he was told that Avinain had, indeed, met with the farmers and promised to buy their hay at greater prices than others offered and that the farmers had driven off with the butcher.

Accompanied by a detective, Chief Claude then went to the shop operated by Avinain on the Avenue Montaigne. He pounded on the door which flew open to reveal an old but towering man in a shaggy white beard. He was a giant, close to seven feet tall and was obviously still powerful, despite his years. The intrepid Claude took a few steps into the shop, shouting, "Surrender, you!" To his astonishment, Avinain vanished right before his eyes, taking two steps to his right and and then sinking straight through the floor. When Claude stepped further into the shop he could see an open trapdoor that led downward into a dark passageway that connected with the sewers of Paris. Lighting a torch, the police chief and his aide groped their way into the sewers, clinging to a narrow ledge used by the sewer inspectors, but there were no hand or foot rails and both men almost fell into the filthy waters rushing past them. They heard Avinain cursing them in the darkness as he moved ahead of them, apparently trying to reach another exit. Claude ordered his aide to return the way they had come and alert gendarmes to cover all the sewer exits in the vicinity. The brave Claude then went on alone, following the mass murderer. Claude continued into the sewers after the giant, whose curses echoed after him down the arched tunnels of the sewers, its walls glistening with moisture, the fumes from its foul waters creating an overpowering stench. The detective slipped and nearly fell into the waters several times as enormous rats ran squealing between his legs. (The scene would no doubt have inspired Hugo to write this desperate scene into his classic crime novel, *Les Misérable,* had he not written it five years earlier in 1862. Some sleuths of the day claimed that Avinain had read the novel by Victor Hugo and this had inspired *him* to cut a trapdoor in his shop's floor and break through to the sewer wall as a way of escape should he be trapped by authorities. It was later shown, however, that Avinain used the sewer passage to carry bodies from his shop and into the sewers which linked him to the huts along the Seine where he dragged the bodies, cut them to pieces, and deposited the remains in the river, believing that these would disappear.)

The giant killer worked his way through the many tunnels of the sewer system but he found at every exit a group of gendarmes waiting for him and so he went on and on through the frightening labyrinthe, Claude doggedly following him, ordering him to surrender. (This scene, too, had a place in filmic history, used by Orson Welles in his grim escape attempt of Harry Lime in *The Third Man.*) In desperation, the monstrous killer burst through a manhole cover, drawing up his huge frame to street level only to be surrounded by seven gendarmes who flailed their nightsticks at him, but Avinain put up a Hurculean fight. He knocked two gendarmes unconscious with his hamhock fists, using them as clubs. He broke the jaw of a third gendarme and kicked in the ribs of another. Finally, exhausted, he was subdued, held to the ground just as Claude emerged from the sewers, brushing away the filth covering his clothes. Claude knelt to the monster and asked him if he had murdered the farmers. The glinty eyed Avinain roared a curse at him before he was dragged away.

During his trial the butcher was arrogant and impudent before the court. When the magistrate asked him how he had 'cut up' the bodies of his victims, Avinain gave the judge a contemptuous sneer and then said, "Pardon me, monsieur, do not say 'cut up.' Say dissected." He showed no remorse at his many murders and seemed proud that he had earned the sobriquet "The Terror of the Seine." At the end of the trial, Avinain boasted, "I killed these men in order to rob them and I have nothing to regret." He was more concerned with how he would be remembered by the world after he had been executed. His reputation as a professional multiple murderer was dear to him. "I do not wish it to be said, however," Avinain instructed the court, "that I 'dismembered' my victims. I did nothing of the sort. I 'dissected' them in a decent and proper manner. I am not a bungler." On the morning of his execution, Avinain requested that he be buried next to Lemaire, a particularly repugnant and vicious murderer who had recently been condemned for murdering his own father by slicing him to pieces. "Really," said Avinain on the way to guillotine, "he is the only man I have ever admired." The mass killer was placed on a specially made plank to accomodate his giant body and then slipped forward so that his huge head rested in the hollow beneath the blade directly above his neck. A moment before the blade fell, the sinister Avinain grinned at those witnessing his execution and shouted, "Never confess!"

REF.: *CBA;* Logan, *Masters of Crime;* Nash, *Almanac of World Crime;* Whitelaw, *Corpus Delecti.*

Avory, Sir **Horace Edmund (AKA: The Acid Drop, The Hanging Judge, Old Horace),** 1851-1935, Brit., jur. Served for 25 years on the King's Bench Division of the High Court and during that time presided over 163 murder trials including those of Edith Bingham, Edward Hopwood, Browne and Kennedy, Thomas Allaway, and Patrick Mahon. He was considered a fair but severe judge who demanded strict adherence to the legal code. Sentenced many murderers to death. REF.: *CBA.*

Avril, Robert, 1911- , Fr., mur. Avril, a common laborer with a miserable childhood, habitually attacked and raped women and, eventually, the attacks turned into murder. On Aug. 28, 1955, the body of a young woman was found in some tall grass off the roadway near the small village of Picquigny, between Amiens and Abbeville in northern France. The victim's clothes were in disarray and a band of white on her suntanned wrist showed police that the woman's wristwatch had been stolen. An English-made bicycle was found nearby along with some clothing that had been torn out of the bag fixed to the bicycle's rack. A check of the area disclosed that a 23-year-old school teacher named Janet Marshall from Nottingham, England, had registered in a nearby youth hostel the previous evening. The body was identified as Marshall and a search for her killer ensued. Police discovered that Marshall had stopped at a cafe in Picquigny on the morning of August 26 to have breakfast. Detectives, led by Inspector Henri Van Asche, concluded that the woman had been waylaid by one of the common laborers who worked in the area and they interrogated several men without charging anyone. Local residents described one particular laborer who had a brutal face and had been seen to watch Janet Marshall as she pedalled out of the village of Picquigny. A composite sketch was made of the man and this was circulated throughout the area. The circular also mentioned an unusual detail concerning this laborer; he was missing three fingers on his left hand.

Five months after the murder of Janet Marshall, Robert Avril, a 44-year-old laborer, was arrested, charged with stealing a bicycle. He was brought before Judge Jean DeTraux in Amiens. The judge took one look at Avril and then remembered the police composite that had been circulated in the Marshall slaying. He looked at the composite and realized that it bore an amazing resemblance to the man who stood before him. He asked Avril

to hold up his left hand. Three fingers were missing. DeTraux asked Avril where he was on Aug. 26, 1955, and the laborer quickly, all too quickly for the judge, replied that he had been visiting his sister in Sucy-in-Brie. DeTraux also knew from police reports that Janet Marshall's German-made camera, along with her wristwatch, had been taken following her murder. When police visited Avril's sister she said that her brother had visited at the end of August and had left a camera with her. This proved to be Marshall's camera. Moreover, articles of clothing belonging to the victim were found in Avril's lodging. He was interrogated and confessed to murdering the school teacher, saying that he, at first, only thought to have sex with her but then he strangled her with a piece of string when she resisted. He insisted that he did not rape the woman but fled from the scene, stealing her watch, camera, and some small pieces of clothing.

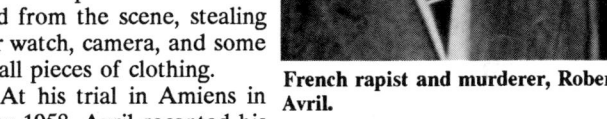

French rapist and murderer, Robert Avril.

At his trial in Amiens in May 1958, Avril recanted his original confession and was allowed to play to the sympathy of the jury by relating in detail his sad childhood. He described how he had lost his fingers at age seven in an accident, how his mother died when he was still a child, and that his father committed suicide after it was revealed that he had had incestuous relations with Avril's older sister. In court, Avril also insisted that he had left Janet Marshall in an unconscious condition, that she was not dead and that someone else probably came along and murdered her after he fled. Against these self-defensive statements stood Avril's long history of attacks on women. In April 1944, Avril had stopped along a roadway to help 22-year-old Madeleine Thiery remove some dust from her eye. He had then dragged her into some woods, raped her, and stole three pounds of butter from her. In June 1944 Avril attacked a 19-year-old girl and the following month he attacked and raped another 19-year-old girl and a 56-year-old woman, then another young girl some days later, this last victim escaping before Avril could drag her into a clump of bushes. In all these attacks, the victims had been on bicycles which Avril kicked out from under them as they pedaled past him, disabling them so that he could easily drag them off and compel them to have sex with him. He was arrested for these rapes in 1944 but not convicted until 1946 when Avril was sentenced to ten years of hard labor. He was released in 1951 and resumed his attacks on helpless women, culminating in his murder of Janet Marshall.

Every piece of evidence in the Avril case pointed to the man's guilt, and it was further claimed by the presiding judge, Jean Bourdon, that Avril had denounced members of the Resistance to the dreaded Gestapo during the Nazi occupation of France. This was vehemently denied by the accused. Inspector Van Asche testified that Avril, when first arrested, told police, "I killed her (Janet Marshall) without meaning to." Though the energetic Public Prosecutor Max Dussert argued long and hard for a death sentence, Avril escaped the guillotine. The jury deliberated his case for thirty-five minutes and then returned a verdict of Guilty "with extenuating circumstances," meaning that Avril's awful childhood had contributed mightily to his attitude toward women, and he was therefore not wholly responsible for his awful murder of young Janet Marshall. The killer was sentenced to life at hard labor with no chance of parole.

REF.: *CBA;* Furneaux, *Famous Criminal Cases;* Greenwall, *They were*

Murdered in France; Heppenstall, *The Sex War and Others;* Wilkinson, *Behind the Face of Crime.*

Avvakum Petrovich, c.1621-82, Rus., clergy, executed. Leader in the revolt against the reforms of the Russian Orthodox liturgy made by Patriarch Nikon. He was exiled, imprisoned, and then burned at the stake. REF.: *CBA.*

Axilrod, Dr. Arnold Asher, prom. 1955, U.S., rape-mur. Axilrod was a distinguished member of the Minneapolis, Minn., social community, active in civic and charitable affairs. He was also one of the most successful dentists in town, along with being a sexual deviate who drugged his patients, then raped them. In the case of Mrs. Mary Moon-
en, Dr. Axilrod went further.
He murdered his patient and
dumped her body, like so
much garbage, along a roadway. Mrs. Moonen, an attractive 21-year-old Minneapolis
housewife, was married to
Matthias Moonen, a soldier
who had been in Korea for
several months. Her body was
found on Apr. 23, 1955, in
Lake of the Isles, a fashionable Minneapolis district. The
woman had been strangled,
but her purse, found next to
her, had not been touched so
police ruled out robbery. A
pathologist determined that

Dr. Arnold Axilrod drugged and raped his patients, a practice that led to murder.

she had not been raped but that she had had sexual intercourse with a man a short time before her murder. Police began the tedious rounds of interviewing all who knew the slain woman. One of these was Mary Moonen's sister, Mrs. Donald Newton.

Mrs. Newton could offer detectives no information until one of them mentioned her sister had told a friend she had a dental appointment the day before her body was found. Mrs. Newton then stated that her sister was probably seeing Dr. Arnold Asher Axilrod, one of the city's most prominent dentists. She added that Axilrod had been her dentist, too, but that she no longer went to him. When asked why, Mrs. Newton slowly revealed that she felt uncomfortable in the dentist's company, that Axilrod had once given her a pill that knocked her out for two hours and when she came to Axilrod was standing over her and talking suggestively to her. "At first I thought he was kidding." When Axilrod made a pass on the next visit, Mrs. Newton decided to stop going to him, although she recommended the dentist to her sister—even after that.

Axilrod was arrested and confessed to the murder of Mrs. Moonen, according to police, but he later reneged on his state-ments and emphatically denied ever having raped Mrs. Moonen after drugging her. He did use pills that sedated patients, he explained, but this was to deaden nerves in sensitive teeth he was working on. He admitted that a few patients were rendered unconscious by these pills but such instances were extremely rare. Police began to look deeper into Axilrod's background and discovered that they had had a complaint against him three year's earlier when a 17-year-old girl had phoned police, not leaving her name, to complain that Dr. Axilrod had given her a knockout pill and that she had awakened hours later on his office couch. After Axilrod's arrest and impending trial was announced, more than twenty women came forward to state that they, too, had been drugged by the dentist and wound up on his couch. The local papers made much of this in their sensational stories, writing reams of copy about Dr. Axilrod's "love pills."

The dentist steadfastly denied any wrongdoing but the police produced his original statements to detectives in court. Axilrod had initially admitted that Mrs. Moonen had come to him, claiming that she was pregnant (which she was, according to a doctor treating her) and that she had insisted that he was the

father of her unborn child and something had to be done about it. He told her to wait in his car, that he would drive her home. In the car, Dr. Axilrod said, they quarreled and he suddenly blacked out. "I guess I did it," he was quoted by police. "No one else was there." It was a case of who did the jury believe, Axilrod or the police? Prosecuting Attorney George M. Scott, drew a severe portrait of a scheming pervert who drugged his unsuspect-ing patients so that he could rape them. Jury members accepted the police version and convicted the dentist of manslaughter. On Nov. 3, 1955, Dr. Axilrod was sentenced to between five and twenty years in prison.

REF.: *CBA;* Wilson, *Encyclopedia of Murder.*

Ax Man of New Orleans, prom. 1910s, U.S., (unsolv.) mur. The bloody fiend who murdered with abandon in New Orleans for almost a decade terrorized the entire city and seemed to operate without concern of apprehension or identification since he was seen in the act of his brutal murders many times. Yet the Ax Man of New Orleans, as he is known in criminal history, remains a mythical and evil figure who escaped punishment. The Ax Man first struck in 1911, chopping to death three Italian grocers named Schiambras, Cruti, and Rosetti. He established a modus operandi which never varied in the years to come, chiseling out panels of the back doors leading to rear rooms where the grocers slept behind their shops. In each of the 1911 killings, the murderer had used an ax to slash and crush the heads of his victims. The killer was not heard from again until the night of May 23, 1918, when he chiseled out the panel of a rear door and entered the bedroom of Mr. and Mrs. Joseph Maggio, grocers, attacking them in their sleep, crashing his ax so forcefully down on the head of Mrs. Maggio that he decapitated her. He struck her husband several times and then slit his throat with a razor. The Ax Man then fled, but Maggio was still alive and tried to speak, making strange, gurgling noises which finally brought his two brothers Jake and Andrew on the run from another room. By the time police arrived, Joseph Maggio was dead. Officers found a blood-drenched ax on the back stairs of the grocery and a gore-crusted razor in the bedroom. Again, no clues could be found to lead them to the killer.

Without evidence, the frustrated police arrested the surviving Maggio brothers and charged them with the killings, but they released the pair when the psychopathic killer struck again on June 28, 1918, when another grocer, Louis Besumer was attacked by a maniac who struck him several times on the head with an ax, along with his common-law wife, Mrs. Harriet Lowe, who was gashed about the head several times. The couple survived and, having no other suspects, arrested Besumer and released the Maggio brothers. Mrs. Lowe told police that she "long felt that Mr. Besumer is a German spy." Her comments, of course, were related to German spies then reportedly active in New Orleans, working on behalf of Germany, then at war with the U.S. But all this proved ridiculous when, on Aug. 5, 1918, the Ax Man struck again, attacking Mrs. Edward Scheider, the wife of another grocer. Though the killer struck her several times in the head with his ax, the woman survived and gave birth to a healthy baby some days later. She described her assailant as a tall, powerfully built man who hit her several glancing blows while she slept and then fled in the dark. Police then released Besumer.

The city was in an uproar. A giant headline in the *Times-Picayune* asked, "Is An Axman at Large in New Orleans?" Police had the answer to that on Aug. 10, 1918, when Joseph Romano was attacked by an ax-wielding assailant while he slept in the back of his store. His two nieces responded to the commotion, throwing open the bedroom door to see a tall, heavyset man fleeing through a window, leaving his bloody ax on the floor. Romano lingered for a few hours but was unable to communicate anything to detectives. He was a rare exception in the ax man's list of victims in that he was a barber, not a grocer. Again, police found that the killer had gained access to Romano's room by breaking out a panel in the back door. The killings continued into the next year with a bloody attack on the Cortimiglia family. Here the ax man attacked both Charles Cortimiglia and his wife Rose, furiously crashing his ax down on their heads several times and, despite Mrs. Cortimiglia's pleas, splitting wide the head of their infant girl, who slept in a nearby crib, before fleeing. The adult Cortimiglias survived. The death of her child so unhinged Mrs. Cortimiglia that she blindly accused Frank Jordano, a competitive nearby grocer, of being the killer. Jordano was arrested and later put on trial, convicted, and condemned to death solely on Rose Cortimiglia's accusations. Mrs. Cortimiglia later told authorities that she had lied about Jordano and he was released only a short time before he was scheduled to hang.

Meanwhile, the Ax Man began sending messages to the local papers. One was received by the *Times-Picayune* which was dated "from Hell," and was signed "The AXMAN." The letter writer said he was a devil and that he would again visit New Orleans on Mar. 19, 1919, and would go on a killing spree that the police were powerless to stop. He added that he would not enter any house where jazz music was playing; he said that he loved jazz music and would not molest anyone who shared his tastes. On the appointed day, the city of New Orleans rocked with jazz. Gramophones and jazz records were worn out during the night of Mar. 19, as frenzied citizens thought to ward off the evil one by placating him with his favorite brand of music. The Ax Man, as police predicted, did not appear. Authorities had early on claimed that the message sent to the *Times-Picayune* was no more than the workings of a prankster, one who was emulating the grim messages sent to London papers thirty-some years earlier by the notorious Jack the Ripper.

Steve Boca, another grocer, was attacked on Aug. 10, 1919, his head severely gashed, but he managed to survive his assailant whom he described as a tall white man, heavyset, and extremely powerful. The madman seemed to be everywhere. The police doubled patrols in areas where the Ax Man had previously struck only to find attacks occuring in other parts of the city.

William Carlson, a pharmacist, was awakened by a noise at the back door that led to his bedroom on the night of Sept. 2, 1919. He saw a chisel poke through a panel of the door and immediately jumped from his bed, retrieving a pistol he had recently purchased for just this eventuality. Carlson fired twice through the door and saw the chisel fall through the hole in the door. He heard heavy footsteps retreating through the back yard.

Sarah Laumann, while sleeping in her bed, was suddenly struck several times by an ax on the night of Sept. 3, 1919. She survived with horrible wounds and could not describe her attacker.

On Oct. 27, 1919, Michele Pepitone was sleeping in the rear of his father's grocery when he was attacked and murdered by the Ax Man. This was the worst of the Ax Man's attacks in that the killer spent a good deal of time chopping his victim's head to pieces so that Pepitone was totally unrecognizable. His widow later insisted that this death was Mafia related, that her husband was the son of Pietro Pepitone, who had killed Paul DiCristina, a black hander, in 1909, rather than submit to extortion. (DiCristina had been a powerful Mafia don in Sicily and the U.S., the one who arranged for the murder of NYPD Lieutenant Joseph Petrosino in Palermo in 1909.) The killer of Michele Pepitone, said the widow, thought he was killing the father who had taken DiCristina's life, and enacting the revenge demanded by vendetta. She insisted that her husband had been killed by a Mafia killer named Joseph "Doc" Mumfre. In an elaborate scheme, Mrs. Pepitone later married Angelo Albano whom she knew was a friend of Mumfre's and moved with Albano to Los Angeles. There, Mumfre visited Albano and tried to extort money from him. When Albano refused, he vanished in October 1921. Mrs. Pepitone-Albano went to police and told her story about Mumfre being the Ax Man of New Orleans but she was not believed. A few days later Mrs. Pepitone-Albano waited for Mumfre to walk down an alleyway. When he arrived she stepped forth, dressed all in black, and shot him dead. She was convicted of second-degree murder and sent to prison for ten years, released in 1925. Though she continued to claim that Mumfre was the Ax Man who

had terrorized New Orleans, the multiple killer was officially listed as being at large, a human monster of mystery. See: **Mumfre, Joseph; Petrosino, Joseph**.

REF.: *CBA*; Nash, *Open Files;* Reid, *Mafia;* Tallant, *Ready to Hang;* Wilson, *Encylopedia of Murder*.

Ayala, Samuel, prom. 1977, and **Profit, William**, prom. 1977, and **Walls, James** Jr., prom. 1977, U.S., rob.-mur. The Watsons and the Minters were the best of friends, living near each other in Lewisboro, N.Y., a posh white-collar suburb in Westchester County. Ralph and Sheila Watson purchased their wooden two-story home on Smithridge Road in 1971. Bonnie Minter and her husband David lived on West Lane. Their children were too young to walk by themselves, so the two mothers frequently drove them back and forth to play together.

This arrangement continued until Mar. 3, 1977, when the occupants of a mysterious blue van that had been lurking about the community for weeks broke into the Watson home shortly before nightfall. Three men, identified as William Profit, Samuel Ayala, and James Walls pointed a gun at the four children, warning them to keep quiet. Bonnie Minter and Sheila Watson were taken to an upstairs bedroom, where they were shot eleven times at close range. The spacious colonial house was ransacked as the burglars removed electronic equipment, a typewriter, a TV and other items difficult to trace. The four children were moved into a second floor room, but were not injured by the murderers.

Two days later Profit and Ayala were picked up in Norwalk, Conn. Walls was arrested outside Boston and extradited back to White Plains to face criminal indictment. In a fifteen-to-seventeen count indictment, the three defendants were charged with felony murder, grand larceny, burglary, and possession of weapons. Walls pleaded guilty and was sentenced to twenty-five years to life on Nov. 30, 1977. Ayala and Profit, who had committed the actual murders, were tried by a jury that found them guilty of second-degree murder. On Feb. 22, 1978, Judge Richard Darongo sentenced them to a maximum term of fifty years each for the unprovoked slaying of the two Lewisboro women. REF.: *CBA*.

Aycock, Charles, prom. 1920s, U.S., fraud. Aycock was a blatant quack who sold a bogus medicine called Tuberclecide which he claimed would provide a complete cure for tuberculosis, especially in children. Aycock's medicine consisted of creosote carbonate and little else, yet he peddled endless quantities of this useless "cure-all" from 1918 to 1928 without legal restraint, even though there were dozens of court hearings about the drug and Aycock's total lack of medical qualifications. In one of his many booklets, distributed by the tens of thousands, Aycock claimed that Tuberclecide was one of "the greatest inventions of modern times that have benefited mankind." Especially cruel was the fact that this wholly ineffective elixir was sold at considerable cost to tens of thousands of parents desperate to help their children who were stricken with tuberculosis and found it did nothing to aid the victims. Physicians called in to condemn the phony drug were so ambiguous in their evaluations that the courts found it impossible to condemn the drug or its promoter.

Aycock, in his own defense, pretended it was a miracle which had cured his own tuberculosis, and he was merely trying to help mankind, at a slight fee, of course. "I am like Jesus Christ opening the eyes of the blind," he stated, full of pretended innocence, at one hearing, "and when critics asked how it was done, he said, 'I do not know. I was blind but now I see.' That is all I can say. I took it and I got well. That is all I know." Finally, a federal circuit court decreed in 1928 that it agreed with the U.S. Postmaster General, that Tuberclecide was absolutely useless and that Aycock's promotion and selling of this quack medicine was a fraud. Aycock, however, ceased his sale of Tuberclecide and retired on the vast riches it had brought him.

REF.: *CBA*; Nash, *Almanac of World Crime;* _____, *Hustlers and Con Men;* Young, *The Medical Messiahs*.

Ayliffe, John, Esq., d.1759, Brit., forg. John Ayliffe emerged as a popular folk hero in England in the remaining days before his scheduled execution on Nov. 19, 1759. His crime was embezzlement, and the prosecutor in the case was Baron Henry Fox, a member of the House of Commons, who was recently appointed paymaster general where he was said to have amassed a personal fortune.

The people believed Ayliffe was the victim of a private grudge carried to the fullest extreme by the wily Fox. Because he led an interesting but profligate life, Ayliffe became the dashing and ribald hero, and Fox the cunning villain of this English melodrama. REF.: Bleackley, *Hangmen of England; CBA.*

Azana y Diaz, Manuel, 1880-1940, Spain, pres., consp. Played an active role in the overthrow of Alfonso XIII in 1931. He served as minister of war for the new government, then as premier for a short time until he was arrested and imprisoned. He was eventually released to serve as premier again and then became president of Spain from 1936 until Franco's victory in 1939 forced him into exile in France. REF.: *CBA.*

Azo (Azzo or **Azolinus Porcius),** c.1150-c.1230, Italy, jur. Law professor who wrote *Summa Codicis* and *Apparatus ad Codicem.* REF.: *CBA.*

Azuni, Domenico Alberto, 1749-1827, Sardinia, jur.-writer. REF.: *CBA.*

Azzone, c.1150-1230, Italy, jur. Professor and author who was leader of the Bolognese School of Jurists and wrote summaries of Roman law. REF.: *CBA.*

B

Baader-Meinhof Gang, 1967-77, Ger., terror. For almost a decade, West Germany was to suffer a seemingly endless series of horrible bombings, murders, robberies, and kidnappings created by the Baader-Meinhof (B-M) gang. Its members were utterly ruthless, without conscience, and dedicated to the destruction of a system that had weaned them in comfort and security. Its leaders, Andreas Baader and Ulrike Meinhof, did not spring from impoverished gutter-life, but evolved from Germany's middle-class during that country's greatest economic post-WWII boom. Inspired by certain left-wing educators, the gang members represented Hitler's early-day Nazi party in reverse. Although its philosophy was of the radical left, its tactics were identical to that of the Nazi Brownshirts of the 1920s. The gang employed terror to achieve its ends and, for a time, was so effective that German political and business leaders were compelled to barricade themselves in their own homes, which had been turned into armed fortresses.

Just as the Nazis used as a rallying point the "martyrdom" of Horst Wessel (a vicious Nazi thug killed in a 1930 street brawl), the university students who later formed the Baader-Meinhof gang were galvanized by the death of an obscure West German student, Benno Ohnesorg. On June 2, 1967, the Shah of Iran was welcomed in Berlin by the West German government, setting off protests from the student left. Among the students jeering and throwing eggs and tomatoes at the Shah's passing motorcade was Ulrike Meinhof, self-styled political journalist and devout Marxist. She would later become the guiding light of the terrorist gang that would bear her name.

This demonstration was one of the worst riots Germany had seen in decades. Police, alerted to possible violent demonstrations, overreacted to the students pelting the Shah's motorcade with rotten fruit and rocks. They employed the "liver-sausage" tactic, sealing both sides of the student group, which stretched for several blocks, forcing the students to flee at the ends and, as they burst forth, attacking them with rubber truncheons and nightsticks. The main body of students fled wildly down a narrow passageway, Krumme Strasse. The police, hot on their heels, overtook many of them, beat them to the ground, and fell on top of them as more police in the rear rushed forward to run over those who had fallen. The students in the lead of this rushing mob suddenly saw masses of police in front of them and realized they were trapped. They turned and began to battle the police behind them.

In the free-for-all, one plainclothes officer, Sergeant Karl-Heinz Kurras, panicked when he was pushed about, and drew his service revolver. He fired a single shot, and the crowd froze into silence and inertia. A young man with dark hair and a scraggly mustache lay dead in the narrow street. The police and crowd, stunned by the slaying, gathered in a large circle to look down at the fallen student, 26-year-old Benno Ohnesorg. He was married, his wife was pregnant, and he had never before participated in a political demonstration. He had joined other students to hoot and jeer the Shah because he thought "it would be fun." Now he was dead, a martyr to a cause he knew nothing about. Ulrike Meinhof, on the other hand, knew much about what had just occurred. She was the editor-in-chief and top political columnist for a weekly leftist publication, *Konkret,* and in her role as propagandist, she had written about the Shah's forthcoming Berlin visit with a pen that dripped acid. Her diatribe against the Persian ruler had been read by mostly university students, who answered Meinhof's call-to-arms, as it were, and gathered to protest the Shah's presence in Germany. Many in the crowd of students were diehard Marxists like Meinhof, but just as many were apolitical, such as the dead Ohnesorg, who had by his untimely death become a *cause célèbre.*

Two students in that rock-throwing crowd met the day of the protest over the Shah's arrival—the spoiled, well-to-do academic playboy, Berndt Andreas Baader, and a tall, blonde student, Gudrun Ensslin, a fanatical communist. The two bumped into each other as they ran from the police, and made their introductions as they huddled in a doorway while the crowds streamed past them. Baader was born in Munich on May 6, 1943. His father was killed fighting for Hitler's Germany on the Russian front. His mother raised the boy with syrupy affection. He was doted upon by a host of other female relatives. When he reached his twenties, Baader, a handsome but lazy sort, sought the companionship of dominating females. He drove expensive sports cars and dressed in the latest fashion, but when meeting any strong-willed female he displayed a weakness and an almost slavish attitude. In 1963, Baader moved to Berlin and took up with an artist, Ellinor Michel, living with her and her husband in a *menage a trois* arrangement. Michel had his child, Suse, without any comment from her husband.

Baader then met Ensslin, a white-faced, shrill-voiced fanatic who followed the strict Communist party dogma. She was deeply attracted to the handsome Baader and found, for the first time in her life, something other than politics that interested her. They went to live in Michel's studio and there began a sexual liaison that caused the artist to throw the pair out. Baader left his own child without a word, and Ensslin abandoned her own son, Felix, and her husband, Bernard Vesper. It was Vesper who had indoctrinated Gudrun Ensslin into leftist causes. The daughter of an Evangelical pastor, born in 1940 (she was three years older than Baader), Ensslin had studied in America for a year, concluding that Americans were naive when it came to politics. She drifted through Tubingen University and then the Free University in Berlin. Ensslin had no regard for public or private morality. She slept with whomever attracted her attention and, when her son was only a few months old, happily agreed to appear in a pornographic film, *Das Abonnement.* When this film was later shown in German theaters, Ensslin proudly took her friends to see her sexually cavorting on the screen.

After being evicted from Michel's studio, the pair went to Frankfurt, where Ensslin had many friends among the violently leftist university students who habitually beat up other students who disagreed with their politics. Baader had no political fixation; he was merely along for the ride with Ensslin. She, on the other hand, was more stringent and violent than most of her Frankfurt friends, urging them to rise up against the government, kill its elected officials, and take power so that German ties to the "imperialistic" United States could be severed. She would sit in cafes and sweep glasses and bottles off tables, screaming in an earsplitting voice that action had to be taken immediately. She and Baader lived with students belonging to the newly created SDS (*Sozialisticher Deutscher Studenbund*), but had to keep moving from one small apartment to another. Ensslin's constant shrieking about action and her incessant "hysterical nagging" so annoyed her friends that they found it impossible to tolerate her and her fawning boyfriend for more than a few days.

After picking up a couple of other political nomads, Thorwald Proll and Horst Sohnlein, Baader and Ensslin drifted from cafes to back rooms for days, deciding how to strike out at the Establishment they—or at least Ensslin—so hated. After deciding that two epitomes of the capitalistic society were the huge department stores, the Kaufhof and the Schneider, Ensslin insisted that these places be destroyed. She obtained some hashish and bought some pamphlets describing how to build incendiary bombs. Proll purchased all the necessary equipment and chemicals and put these together. Then the four revolutionaries set out to begin the so-called "People's War" on Apr. 3, 1968; proper acts of revenge, they called it, for the slaying of Ohnesorg, a young man they never knew. They entered the department stores, half-drugged, wearing filthy clothes, bumping into furniture displays, and knocking over mannequins. The foursome could hardly have been more conspicuous. They managed to secrete their fire bombs, and staggered outside to sit in a nearby cafe and wait for the fires to begin. (Another historical parallel is clearly seen when remembering the Reichstag fire of Feb. 27, 1933, when the Nazis torched their own government building and blamed the communists in order to unite Germany with the Nazi cause.)

Gudrun Ensslin could not contain herself; she wanted the world to know she had set the fires and started the revolution. She went to a phone booth and called the German Press Agency, shrilly telling a startled editor: "Soon there will be flames in the Schneider and the Kaufhof. It's a political act of revenge." She hung up, of course, without leaving her name. While the fires blazed and hundreds ran to the fiery scene, following the wailing fire engines, the four arsonists sat in the cafe nearby, gleefully watching the terror, joking and getting drunk. The fires started in the toy departments of the stores (what better symbolism than to strike at the heart of middle-class childhood, thought these student thugs), but the blaze was quickly extinguished, and investigators found one of Proll's bombs intact. They began to make inquiries, and soon the four terrorists were identified. Found in Proll's car were the makings of bombs and, on the careless Ensslin, the written formula for creating an incendiary bomb which she had copied out of a pamphlet.

All four were identified by department store employees who particularly recalled seeing Gudrun Ensslin. One woman, with a frown of disgust on her face, said as she picked Ensslin out of a police lineup: "You could not forget her—she has the same rat's tails hairdo, the one with the sunken eyes and the flat chest. That's her." The foursome faced trial on Oct. 13, 1968, charged with arson. The men were unruly and boisterous in court, refusing to comply with regulations and insulting the judge. Sohnlein repeatedly tried to punch the court guards and had to be restrained. When the judge called Baader's name, Proll stood up, knowing the judge did not know who Baader was, impersonating his friend.

"You were born in 1943?" asked the judge.

"No," Proll smugly replied, "I was born in 1789."

"You do start off with a lot of nonsense," said the judge, refusing to be ruffled by the adolescent behavior, the same kind of posture that was displayed during the trial of the so-called Chicago Seven at about the same time.

The trail was a farce. Ensslin remained mute, slumped in her chair at the defense table. Baader sneered and made inane remarks while Proll and Sohnlein shouted communist slogans. The foursome had no defense and knew it, opting for idiocy and any form of outlandish behavior that allowed them to heap ridicule upon the court. Toward the end of the proceedings, Ensslin made a grandstand play for the role of heroine by admitting the arson she had committed. Baader chimed in, also taking responsibility. Both of them insisted that Sohnlein and Proll were innocent. All were convicted, but instead of receiving maximum sentences of six years, as the prosecution strongly demanded, the four arsonists were each sentenced to three years imprisonment.

Baader did not take well to prison life. He brooded long and soon caused his fellow inmates to dislike and distrust him. Once, while trying to strike up a conversation with another prisoner in the yard during exercise period, Baader told the man that he had been sent to prison for trying to burn down a department store to protest the Vietnam war and to bring down capitalism. For a moment the prisoner stared at Baader, then blurted: "That's the most idiotic thing I ever heard." Baader contented himself by writing heroic letters to communist students outside the prison walls, playing the part of political martyr. His mother, Anneliese Baader, believed him to be a victim of society and said so, writing one letter after another to authorities to protest the "cruel" treatment of her son.

Ensslin's mother was even more expressive, stating: "It would be better for Gudrun to be shot before she shot someone else...her life is destroyed." Gudrun Ensslin was all the more arrogant in prison after learning that leftist students had elevated her and her boyfriend to the status of proletarian heroes. She thought of herself as the leader of a great cause, a person who had already left her unforgettable mark on posterity. "We do not want to be merely a page in cultural history," she snapped at a prison psychiatrist when he asked Ensslin what she hoped to achieve through terrorist acts. The examining physician realized that Ensslin was emotionally dependent upon Baader, hated herself for it and resented him so that, in revenge for the weakness he imposed upon her, led him into political mayhem and personal disaster.

Lawyers for the apprentice arsonists were able to obtain temporary releases for the foursome after they had each served fourteen months. They were set free on June 13, 1969 to await an appeal that would not be heard until the following November. Baader and Ensslin emerged to find themselves hailed as spectacular heroes by the student leftists who urged them to lead them in an open revolution against the government. Most of these radicals were members of the SDS. Instead, Baader, Ensslin, and Proll escaped to France and lived in hiding, supplied with money by Proll's sister, Astrid. When the money ran out, Baader returned alone to Germany, first to Munich, then to Berlin, reveling in the many wanted posters he saw which showed his picture and offered a small reward for this "escaped felon."

In Berlin, Baader was given shelter by an SDS acquaintance, Ulrike Meinhof, who had become his most ardent admirer, publicizing his heroic stand against imperialism and the government. Meinhof, like Ensslin, hated all authority. She no longer posed as a journalist, but was now a full-fledged revolutionary bent on the destruction of western democracy. Meinhof was born on Oct. 7, 1934 in Oldenburg, Lower Saxony; her parents were both art historians. Like Baader, she lost her father at a tender age, being only five when he died. Her mother died when she was fourteen. Her mother's closest friend, Renate Riemeck, a leftist educator, took the child under her wing and raised her, instilling in Meinhof a basic contempt for any politics other than the radical left.

At age twenty-three, Meinhof was studying sociology at Munster University, and it was here she began demonstrating against nuclear weapons, NATO, and, especially, the U.S. She was noticed by Klaus Roehl, who published a leftist newspaper, *Konkret*. Meinhof was soon writing the most radical columns in the paper. Roehl lived with Meinhof and later married her after he made the paper a success by mixing leftist politics with sex. The couple drove about in expensive cars and lived in a luxurious home. Meinhof gave birth to twin daughters and then managed to get a TV program, on which she carefully espoused her left-leaning politics. All was well in her world until she found Roehl with another woman and divorced him, ending a seven-year marriage. Meinhof now sought to edify only herself. She packed her daughters Bettina and Regine off to a boarding house and went to live with student radicals in Berlin. There she participated in the Shah of Iran riot and later became a fanatical supporter of Andreas Baader when he went to jail for his ineffectual arson job in Frankfurt.

When Baader jumped bail, fled to France, and returned to Germany, Ulrike Meinhof welcomed him into her apartment with open arms. To her, he was the Lenin of their small but determined group of revolutionaries. Baader, however, was recognized when he went to a cemetery to dig up some hidden weapons, and was promptly sent back to prison. Meinhof, joined by the gaunt and sinister Ensslin, decided to set their idol free. Ensslin left the others little choice, crying and raging about how she could not live without "Baby." Meinhof learned that Baader was taken out of Tegel Prison on certain days to do research at the German Institute for Social Questions, a small library in Dahlem. (The trusting tolerance of the radical left by the government at that time was positively mystifying.) She and several others entered the library on May 14, 1970 and, producing submachine guns, shot the place to pieces, wounding two guards and injuring several library workers and patrons. Baader fled the library with Meinhof at his side and the two, with Ensslin goading them on, embarked upon a terror spree that brought about the worst crime wave in recent German history.

THE BAADER-MEINHOF TERRORIST GANG

Andreas Baader

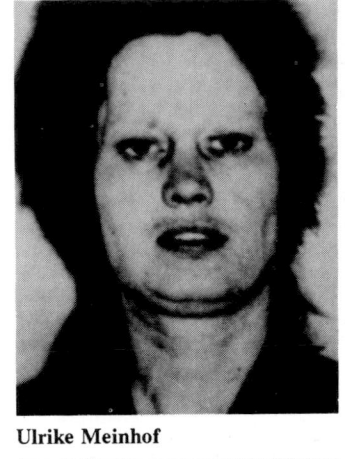

Ulrike Meinhof

Gudrun Ensslin

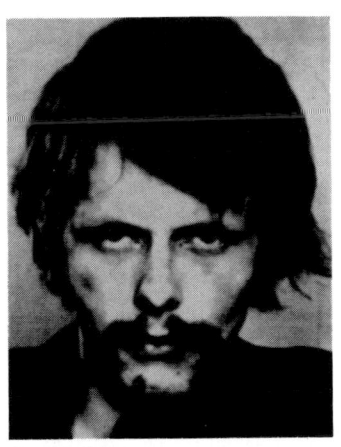

Jan-Carl Raspe

Holger Meins

Irmgard Möller

Ralf Reinders

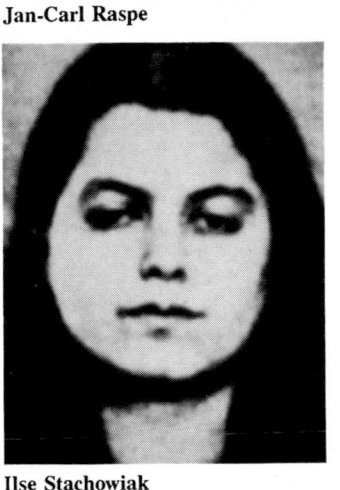

Ilse Stachowiak

Ingeborg Barz

Klaus Jünschke

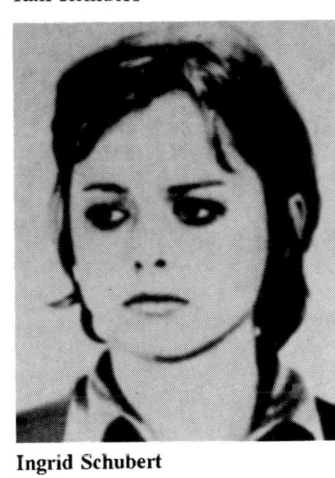

Ingrid Schubert

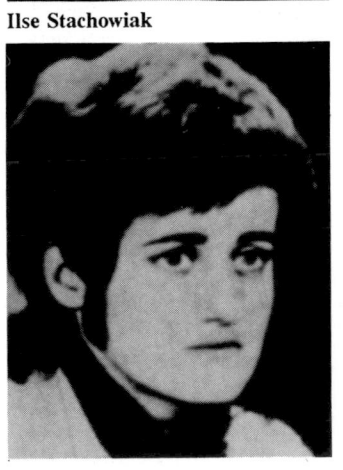

Astrid Proll

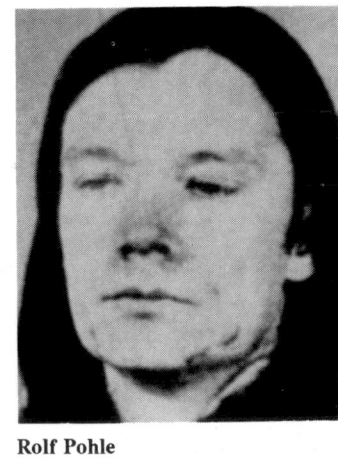

Rolf Pohle

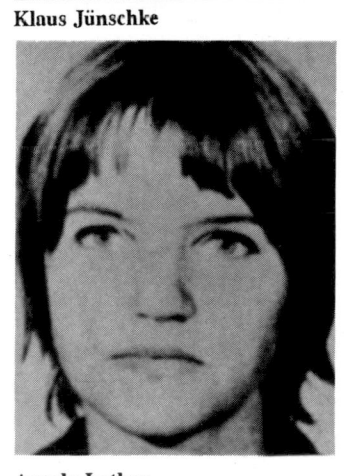

Angela Luther

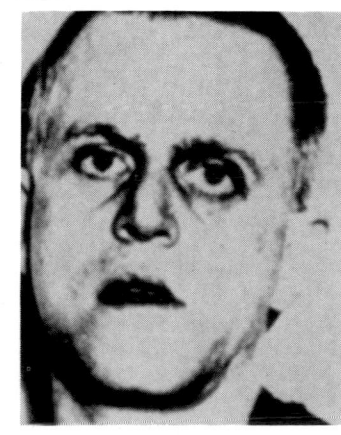

Hans-Jürgen Bäcker

Intellectual encouragement was offered by Horst Mahler, Baader's defense attorney during his arson trial and founder of the radical Red Army Faction, a terrorist underground organization dedicated to violently undermining the German government. To learn the techniques and tactics of terrorism from Palestinian terrorists, Mahler arranged for fake passports for himself, Baader, Meinhof, Ensslin, and others, all of them traveling under assumed names to Beirut, where Mahler had contacts with high-ranking members of the PFLP (Popular Front for the Liberation of Palestine). They were to undergo training as urban guerrillas. The Germans proved to be adept with weapons, but Baader and some of the other German males refused to participate in the commando training course. Baader arrogantly told his Palestinian teachers that it was not necessary for him to crawl through the mud of an infiltration course to be an expert urban guerrilla.

The women, however, were enthusiastic learners and proved to have extraordinary skill with weapons. Meinhof, Ensslin, and other females in the German group amazed their Arab instructors with their keen-eyed marksmanship. Meinhof and Ensslin were delighted to roll their bodies out of moving autos and risk being blown up by dashing through minefields. In later studies of the Baader-Meinhof group it was aptly pointed out that such physical prowess on the part of the lady terrorists was in keeping with the total female domination of the German terrorist gang. The males in the group had all been dominated from childhood by females, and they had selected as sexual partners women who were their intellectual superiors. The Arabs were soon disgusted with the Germans, who refused to take their terrorist education seriously. Baader, for instance, was forever taking his group off to Beirut movie theaters where he and the others would sit like small children, captivated by Hollywood westerns and spy thrillers. Baader thought of himself as a latter-day Marlon Brando and was delighted whenever Ensslin and Meinhof called him by the movie star's name.

The group next moved to a tough PFLP training camp in Jordan, but they argued once more with their Arab teachers. Peter Homann, one of Meinhof's past lovers, was present with the group in Jordan and later told the German press that the Palestinians had no use for their German comrades, expressing particular disdain for Baader, whom Homann labeled "a coward, performing the whole revolt to cover up his cowardice; they wouldn't even take him on patrol." The one course taught by the Palestinians which captured the complete attention of the Germans was the one dealing with bank robbery. The Germans were told that bank robbery was the easiest way to finance any expensive terrorist activity. They would soon put these techniques to use in their native land.

Returning to Berlin with arms and the know-how to use them, the German terrorists began robbing banks with alacrity in Fall 1970. Some days the group, led by Mahler, robbed as many as three banks. The gang amassed a small fortune, tens of thousands of marks, but Mahler hoarded the loot, warning all that to spend too freely would draw the attention of the police. Mahler, the one-time lawyer, now played at being a secret agent, wearing grotesque disguises—false noses, bright red toupees to cover his baldness, phony beards, and mustaches. Police were not fooled. They tracked him down and cornered him in October 1970 while he was returning to his apartment. They were waiting for him inside his flat when he unlocked the door. Stepping inside, Mahler saw twelve policemen pointing their pistols at him. He acted surprised, telling the police that "this must some mistake." One of the officers smirked and asked Mahler for his identification papers. Mahler produced identity cards that said he was Gunter Uhlig.

Another officer stepped close to the errant lawyer and yanked the cheap red wig from the top of his head, saying: "Do you still imagine that we can't recognize you, Herr Mahler?"

Mahler bowed, playing out his self-imagined part of adventurer, replying: "My compliments, gentlemen."

After a quick trial, Mahler was sent to prison for fourteen years. None in the terror gang mourned his loss; he was thought by then to be an inept intellectual who talked and talked about revolution, but failed to create a workable plan to bring down the government. He preferred to rob banks and hide the spoils for a rainy day. Meinhof took over the leadership of the gang, recruiting members mostly from the radical SDS. The gang began to increase in numbers, so that by 1971 there were more than 150 in its ranks with chapters in Berlin, Frankfurt, and Munich. The bank robberies went on and each raid became more bloody, Meinhof encouraging her followers to "kill the pigs" who offered the slightest resistance, referring to policemen.

On Jan. 15, 1971, the gang burst into two banks in Kassel at the same time, looting the vaults. The haul was considerable, and with this Meinhof purchased an enormous quantity of arms from the Arab terrorist organization, Al Fatah. These weapons included boxes of automatic rifles, machine pistols, and boxes of ammunition. Also added to the gang were newly recruited members of a bizarre radical group called SPK, Socialist Patients' Collection, all mental patients organized by their equally unbalanced doctor, Wolfgang Huber, a physician at the Psychiatric-Neurological Clinic at the University of Heidelberg. Huber had originally organized his patients as a political force against the university doctors controlling the clinic in order to force the faculty to give them unlimited access to drugs. As a result, Huber and his charges were thrown out of the clinic and the whole crazy lot of them joined Meinhof. With the infusion of these lunatics into the gang, the killings began in earnest.

Gang members were ordered to steal cars, obtain weapons—even from police arsenals—and investigate banks that contained large amounts of money so that these could be robbed. From Spring 1971 no road in Germany was safe from these gang members. Petra Schelm, a 21-year-old hairdresser, accompanied by drug addict Werne Hoppe, had stolen a BMW (the gang's favorite car) and were stopped by two policemen at a roadblock outside of Hamburg on July 15, 1971. The two were ordered out of the car. Hoppe leaped to the roadway, firing at the police who returned fire. Hoppe, realizing his position was hopeless, threw away his weapon and ran down the road. Schelm, who had been personally trained by Meinhof, also emptied a pistol at police, then threw the weapon down when it was empty. She stood in the middle of the road for some moments, glassy-eyed. Schelm carried a coat over one arm, and the police, motioning for her to walk toward them, told her to drop the coat. She did; beneath it she held a Firebird Parabellum (all members were armed with this weapon). She began firing again, advancing on police. One of the officers answered with a spray of machinegun fire, and Schelm fell dead to the pavement. Hoppe was caught an hour later by officers in a helicopter who swooped from the sky and jumped on top of him as he was running down the road. He was sent to prison.

Schelm was made into another leftist cult hero by Meinhof who ordered all gang members not known to police to attend her funeral. Fifty radical students arrived to place a red flag on the girl's casket, which was promptly removed by police, who took pictures of all in attendance. Police intensified their efforts to round up gang members, but had little luck as the leftists were hidden in the homes of well-to-do radicals. Those police found on the roads offered stiff resistance. Two officers were shot when investigating a suspiciously parked car on Sept. 25, 1971 on the Freiburg-Basel motorway. The assailants were die-hard Baader-Meinhof protégés, Margrit Schiller and Holger Meins. Both escaped. (In almost every encounter, police realized that the gang members traveled in twos and threes, but a woman, always a woman, was at the wheel of the car and was the obvious leader. The woman would be the one to bark out orders to her male companions, shrieking at them to open fire on police. It was also noted that in almost every confrontation with the B-M gang, its members appeared to be in a drugged state. Meinhof, it was later reported, issued daily rations of hashish to members.)

Schiller was cornered on a Hamburg street on Oct. 22, 1971,

but she pulled a pistol from her handbag and emptied it into a policeman named Schmid, killing him at point-blank range. As other police closed in, Schiller fled and escaped through a park. Police were in pursuit, but they were halted by a withering fusillade from rapid-fire weapons operated by three of Schiller's companions who apparently were to meet her in the park. The next morning, police spotted a tall blonde-haired woman making a call in a phone booth. As she stepped out, they demanded she show them her identity papers. She gave them a crooked smile and produced the papers, which said she was Dorte Gerlach. As the officers looked at the papers, the 23-year-old blonde ran her hands across her chest and stuck out her tongue, rolling this around full lips. She leaned close to one of the officers and whispered a price in his ear, pretending to be a common prostitute.

One of the officers opened her bag and found a fully-loaded 9-mm-caliber pistol; she was promptly arrested and put into a police car where she screamed foul language at the officers. Schiller, who would later claim that others in her group had shot and killed the policeman Schmid, was sent to prison, given a twenty-seven-month sentence. She would be released in 1973, only to be rearrested the following year for subversive activities. Schiller represented the most lethal element of the B-M gang as she was an original member of the offshoot SPK from the Heidelberg asylum.

But there were always plenty of new recruits to the hazy cause of the Baader-Meinhof gang. Wolfgang Grundmann, accompanied by his attractive, blonde mistress, Ingeborg Barz, joined the gang in November 1971 and were immediately assigned by Meinhof to look over a fat bank in Kaiserslauten, thirty-five miles from Heidelberg. Barz was no revolutionary, just a secretary who had worked for the Berlin Telephone Company who had fallen in love with a dedicated Marxist, Grundmann. She involved herself with the B-M group because she thought the terrorists were "exciting people who knew how to have thrills." Since Barz looked the most presentable of the Heidelberg contingent and spoke well, she was sent to a branch of the Bavarian Mortgage and Exchange Bank in Kaiserslauten to check on its security. On Dec. 10, 1971 Barz entered the bank and hung about a counter, pretending to fill out lottery forms. Her overlong visit caused many to take notice of her.

Twelve days later, on Dec. 22, 1971, a man entered this bank, went to a counter and placed a tape recorder on it. He looked about, seeming to study every person in the bank. There were no guards present. Then he hit a button on the tape recorder that instantly blasted forth ear-deafening rock music. This was the signal to the gang that it was safe to enter. Three people rushed into the bank holding automatic weapons. They wore anoraks and knitted balaclava helmets that covered their faces and left only sinister-looking slits for their eyes. One of them shouted: "Raid! Hands up! To the wall!" When some of the customers began to talk nervously, the robber screamed: "Silence!"

One of the gang stayed at the door, holding a submachine gun on the customers and employees. The other three, also waving submachine guns, leaped over the counters and scooped up the cash from the tellers' cages; one of them went to the vault with a bank officer and order him to open it. At this time, a 32-year-old policeman, Herbert Schoner, noticed a minibus illegally parked in front of the bank, and he walked across the street, telling the driver to move the vehicle. As he stepped behind the bus, the driver threw the vehicle into reverse and almost crushed Schoner into the car behind. Schoner leaped out of the way and ran to the driver's side of the bus, gun drawn, ordering the driver out. The driver fired several shots from a pistol through the window. Schoner was hit in the neck with one bullet, and his face was covered with blood from the cuts received from the flying glass. He fell to the pavement, but managed to fire three shots at the driver of the minibus as he was crawled toward what he thought was the safety of the bank doorway. As Schoner pushed the bank door open, one of the gang members, sitting on a counter covering

the customers with his submachine gun, casually swung about, took deliberate aim, and fired a short burst into Schoner. The policeman fell back through the door, into the street, dead. He was the father of two small children.

When Schoner collapsed, the gang members inside the bank abandoned the safe, which was not yet opened by the fiddling bank officer, and ran from the bank with briefcases stuffed with money from the tellers' cages. They leapt into the minibus and roared off down the street. Police alarms went off in two nearby stations, but when the officers tried to drive out of the stations, they found both exits blocked by a Volkswagen 1300 and an Alfa Romeo, preventing them from giving chase. Of course, these vehicles had been strategically parked by B-M gang members for that purpose. One witness in the bank later identified the man with the tape recorder as Klaus Jünschke, one of the mental patients under Dr. Huber's care and one of the most ardent members of SPK. (Huber was no longer directing his patients in the ways of terrorism, having been arrested and jailed on July 7, 1971.)

On Dec. 28, detectives found the hideout in Kaiserslauten that had been used by the gang members while they planned the bank robbery. The terrorists had fled but it was an obvious B-M lair. The place was littered with soiled mattresses, bomb-making paraphernalia, revolutionary pamphlets, and some old clothes. Several grams of hashish were found in a teacup, and three sets of fingerprints were identified as being that of Jünschke, Ingeborg Barz, and Wolfgang Grundmann. Also found was a note, written in Meinhof's handwriting, which stated "Fat One 1330," an obvious reference to the Volkswagen that had been parked in front of one of the police station exits.

The press was soon featuring the robbery-murder with such headlines as "BAADER-MEINHOF MURDERS ON." Alarmed at the wanton killings that were taking place across Germany, Chancellor Willy Brandt addressed the nation in a special television address. He warned the terrorists that the government would do everything in its power to suppress its activities, saying: "The free democracy which we have built from the ruins of dictatorship and war must not be understood as a weak state." He asked citizens to cooperate with the police in combating the plague of terrorists.

One of those who watched Brandt on TV was Ingeborg Barz. She came from a well-to-do family and had been with Grundmann for about four months. The "thrills" she had sought had turned into bloody murder and she was now frightened for her life. She had expressed her horror at the killing of Schoner to other members who warned her that revolutionaries must have no conscience about killing their enemies. Barz then decided to escape the terrorist gang, calling her mother in Berlin and telling her that she was innocent of any terrorist activities. "I have nothing to do with them here," she emphasized, referring to the group in the Kaiserslauten-Heidelberg area. Barz made the mistake of talking to her fellow terrorists before leaving their company. She was reminded that she had taken an oath to the gang, that she could never desert their cause, and to do so would mean death. Barz was then put on the phone to talk to Meinhof who was in a Berlin hideout. Meinhof ordered Barz to drive to a remote spot on the Rhine riverbed near Ludwigshaven. She and Meinhof, the gang leader promised her, would work something out so she could leave the gang without disgrace.

Barz, full of confidence in her leader, drove to the rendezvous spot, but when she got out of her car she looked around to see not Ulrike Meinhof, but Andreas Baader. According to gang member Gerhard Muller, who was later captured, Meinhof had sentenced Barz to death for wanting to leave the group, and the female killer had sent Baader to murder the girl. Baader struck Barz on the head with a blunt instrument, crushing her skull. He then rolled her body into the river with some weights affixed to her ankles, before driving off in his stolen Alfa Romeo. The body, however, surfaced in July 1973 and was identified. Meinhof's purpose here was to hold the gang members together; if she could not do it with her own rhetoric, she would do it under threat of death. Barz was the example she sought and it proved effective. No other gang members left the group, except by police capture.

This was the case for Barz's boyfriend, Grundmann, who had merely shrugged when he was told that his "chicken-hearted" girlfriend had to be killed. The terrorist had moved to Hamburg where he was staying with Manfred Grashof—an avowed anarchist. Both men had been planning, under instructions from Meinhof, to blow up several government buildings. The gang was now entering its ultimate revolutionary stage, the mass bombings of buildings. Police, however, received a tip as to the location of the Hamburg hideout, and, on Mar. 2, 1972, appeared before the apartment door. Five officers, guns drawn, greeted Grundmann when he answered their knock. One of the officers ordered: "Hands up! Police!"

Grundmann shrank back, hands high and quivering, screaming: "Stop! Don't shoot! We're unarmed!"

The anarchist Grashof, however, had no intentions of surrendering. Standing behind Grundmann, hidden from the sight of the officers, he grabbed a machine pistol and opened up just as Grundmann dove for the floor. His bullets smashed into the officer in charge who later died of his wounds. The other officers returned fire and shot Grashof. Grundmann and the wounded Grashof were jailed and later imprisoned, Grundmann being released in October 1976. This shootout alerted the entire B-M gang, which had moved into the Hamburg area. They split up into small groups, scattering all over Germany. Their Hamburg hideouts were later discovered and the fingerprints of Baader, Meinhof, Ensslin, Holger Meins, and Jan-Carl Raspe were identified. Raspe was a particularly brutal radical, the most vicious of the bunch who enjoyed killing and even had a gunsmith construct a special stock on his submachine gun so that he could grip it more firmly.

Meinhof and her mentor Ensslin were enraged that they had been driven out of Hamburg. They decided to step up their terrorist acts by planting powerful bombs in factories, government office buildings, and military posts—especially those where American troops were quartered. To create the bombs, explosive experts under Raspe's direction, set up a small factory and began to produce large pipe bombs. Bomb expert Dierk Ferdinand Hoff constructed the bombs by hand and, on May 11, 1972, Ensslin, Baader, Meinhof, and Raspe planted three of these pipe bombs in American Army's Fifth Corps headquarters in Frankfurt. The group somehow accessed the entrance to the post and placed three packages, wrapped as gifts, with flowers placed on top of the boxes, in a large phone booth area.

As the smiling, joking group left the post, heading for a vacation in France, the bombs went off, one terrific explosion after another. Thirteen U.S. soldiers near the phone booth area were flattened by the blast. In addition, Lieutenant-Colonel Paul Abel Bloomquist, thirty-nine, who was walking to his car, was struck by a bomb fragment. He collapsed and bled to death before help could reach him. Bloomquist had been highly decorated for services in Vietnam; he left a widow and two children. (When the terrorists learned that they had murdered an American officer, they bought expensive champagne and celebrated.) The blast caused damages of more than $1 million, and American post commanders put every U.S. station in Germany on alert. No one, orders stipulated, would be admitted again to a U.S. post without proper identification and rechecking of that identification.

Yet security at the U.S. Army Supreme Headquarters in Heidelberg still proved vulnerable. A woman drove through the gates of this post on May 24, 1972, parking her car in the lot. She had been admitted because her car possessed USA-EUR green plates, those issued to American personnel; these plates had obviously been stolen from one of any number of American cars parked about the city. At 6 p.m., with the parking lot beginning to fill up with U.S. military personnel en route to their homes, the car blew up, a terrific blast that instantly tore two American officers to pieces. Standing next to the parked car containing the

bombs were Captain Clyde Bonner, twenty-nine, father of two, and Ronald Woodward, father of three. Following the blast which injured several other servicemen, there was not enough left of Bonner and Woodward to gather any kind of identification. As had been the case following the Frankfurt blast, a female, most likely Meinhof, called the German Press Agency and claimed responsibility for the explosion, saying it was created by the Red Army faction in retaliation for the martyrdom of Schelm and as an expression of opposition to the Vietnam War. In the name of this slain murderess, Meinhof ordered bombs to be exploded in the Augsburg police station. This occurred on May 12, 1972, after two females of the gang, Irmgard Möller and Angela Luther, walked into the station and casually left two suitcases laden with bombs which went off minutes later, causing the roof to collapse and five policemen to be seriously injured. Schelm was also "honored" by an explosion in the parking lot of the State Criminal Investigation Offices in Munich also on May 12, 1972, when sixty cars where blown up and the office building badly damaged. Three days later Baader, Meins, and Raspe located the Karlsruhe residence of federal judge Wolfgang Buddenburg, and planted a bomb in his Volkswagen. Judge Buddenburg had signed the arrest warrants for all the Baader-Meinhof criminals. The judge, however, did not use his car on May 15, 1972. Instead, his wife, Gerta Buddenburg, got into the car, and it blew up in her face. She miraculously survived but was a cripple for life. The bombings went on and on while the vexed authorities chased shadows, barely missing gang members time and again when raiding suspected hideouts. Rewards amounting to hundreds of thousands of dollars were placed on the heads of all the B-M leaders, but few dared to inform on these blood-lusting killers.

Government leaders and prominent businessmen were to be assassinated and their families blown up, announced Meinhof through phone calls. In response, the Ministry of Defense and the Federal Chancellery were ringed with troops, barricades were put up, and the homes of every important German politician and business leader were assigned police protection. VIP figures were told not to leave their homes until the Baader-Meinhof gang was rounded up. But the probability of this happening was doubtful; the underground terrorist network through Germany was now widespread and well-financed through robberies that had provided millions for the gang. They could insulate themselves against identification by remaining mobile and anonymous, being able to afford to pay their way for endless hideouts, fast cars, arms, and ammunition. Then, on June 1, 1972, the Baader-Meinhof Commission of the Frankfurt police received a phone call from an anonymous tipster who is identified to this day only as "an old-age pensioner."

The caller explained that there was a bomb factory in a garage on the north side of Frankfurt and gave police the address. The caller said that the garage was stored from floor to ceiling with "gas cylinders" which were brought to the garage by "young people driving ostentatiously big cars." Special plainclothes police squads rushed to the site and found the bomb factory. The place held hundreds of lethal explosive devices, a small arsenal of weapons and ammunition, and boxes of revolutionary literature. Bomb experts dismantled the explosive devices while the area was ringed with police in various disguises. Many of the policemen were dressed as common gardeners, busying themselves with mowing lawns and trimming hedges while they kept watch on the garage. Early the following morning, a lilac Porsche roared through the deserted streets of Frankfurt and came to a roaring stop near the garage. Three young men alighted, one staying near the car.

The other two men entered the garage. Police, hundreds of them creeping forward behind bushes, trees, and rooftops, closed in on the man next to the car. In a few minutes he noticed officers moving through some nearby shrubs, and he began to run down the middle of the street, pulling a pistol and firing blindly behind him. Dozens of officers converged on the young man once his gun was empty. He was tackled and held down. He was Jan-Carl Raspe, one of the important B-M leaders.

Ulrike Meinhof and protégé Irene Goergens, 1969.

Bomb damage, U.S. Army headquarters, Frankfurt, 1972.

German embassy, Stockholm, burning, 1975.

USAEUR barracks, Heidelberg, after bombing, 1972.

Holger Meins under arrest in Frankfurt, June 1972.

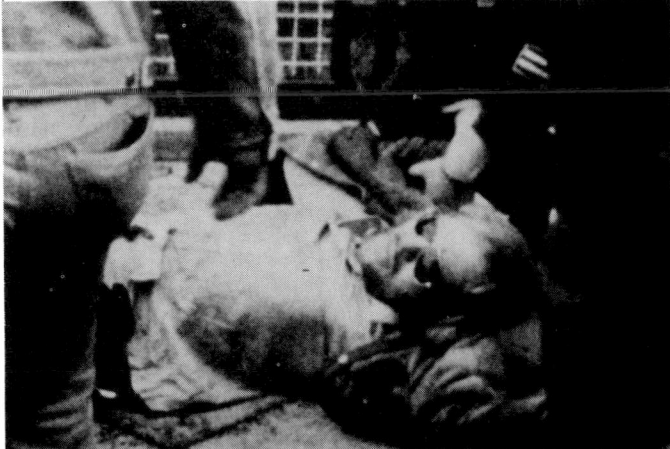

Andreas Baader, arrested, Frankfurt, June 1972

Ulrike Meinhof, imprisoned, 1975.

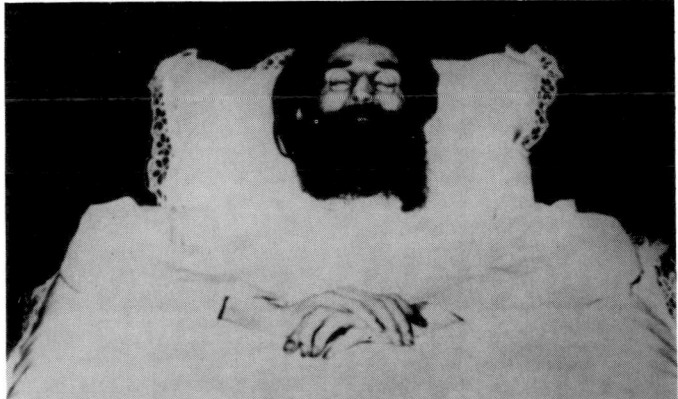

Holger Meins, dead, 1974.

Inside the garage were Andreas Baader and Holger Meins. They stood petrified for a moment while hearing the shooting outside, Raspe trying to draw the police away from them. They opened the garage door slightly to see police swarming through the alleyway. Baader and Meins quickly barricaded the garage door and tried to use some of the bombs but found that they had been made useless. By then tear gas shells were smashing through the windows. An armored car rolled down the alleyway. Gasping, Baader and Meins threw the tear gas canisters outside so that the alleyway was a smoky channel. An officer talked to the trapped terrorists through a bullhorn: "Come out one at a time. Nothing will happen to you. Think of your life. You are still young."

Baader opened the door a crack. He could be seen smoking a cigarette and putting bullets into his pistol. He then took careful aim at a policeman on a rooftop, but another officer fired first, the bullet smashing into the door and then slamming into the terrorist's leg. Howling with pain, Baader retreated to the rear of the garage. A few minutes later, Holger Meins stuck his head out the door and begged the police not to shoot him, that he was going to surrender. The officers were taking no chances. They remembered the coat-over-the-arm trick practiced by the fanatic Petra Schelm. Holger was ordered to strip. He removed all his clothes, except his underpants, then hobbled outside. He had been grazed in the leg. When officers pinioned his arms behind his back, Holger screamed in fright, begging police not to hurt him.

"Who is still in the garage?" police asked Holger.

"Andreas," he snorted.

Television cameras had by then arrived at the scene, and Holger was photographed in all his embarrassing nakedness. Police wasted no more time. A dozen officers advanced to the garage doors and threw them open. Baader lay in the back of the garage, holding his bleeding leg. He wore expensive, tailor-made clothes and dark glasses. Next to him on the floor was his pistol. As the officers walked toward him he made no move to pick up the weapon. He was lifted up, dragged out of the garage, and thrown onto a stretcher while the cameras caught it all. "You are all swine!" the terrorist gang leader screamed. A high-ranking officer walked forward and spoke to the sergeant who had dragged Baader from the garage, asking him: "Have you searched him for weapons?" Just at that moment a pistol slipped from Baader's pocket and fell off the edge of the stretcher, which was being lifted into an ambulance. Baader was rushed to a hospital where he was given a blood transfusion. Then he was put into a cell.

The top members of the terror gang were falling one by one into the hands of the authorities. Next came Gudrun Ensslin. She walked into a Hamburg boutique to try on a coat, setting aside her own jacket. The saleslady, placing the jacket on a chair, noticed how heavy it was and then saw a gun sticking out of a pocket. She called police and Ensslin was taken without a battle. She was whisked off to a jail cell. Only Ulrike Meinhof was still at large. A week later, police in Hanover received a tip that Meinhof was staying in the apartment of a leftist teacher. Officers surrounded the place and then knocked on the door. A woman with straggly dark hair and hollow circles and dark bags under her eyes answered. She was unarmed. Police did not ask her name. Officers grabbed her and pulled her arms behind her back to fasten handcuffs. She struggled and screamed foul names at them. As she was dragged to the patrol wagon the woman kept yelling "you pigs! you pigs! you pigs!" Police knew that they had captured Ulrike Meinhof.

Found on Meinhof was a note from Ensslin, which had been smuggled out of the prison holding Ensslin only two days earlier. It read: "Mac is on holiday, four weeks, to be spent there." This was, police concluded, a reference to a notorious British terrorist, Iain MacLeod, who had become the arms supplier for the B-M gang. MacLeod was tracked down to a Stuttgart apartment. When police came to his door, he opened it for a moment then slammed it shut in their faces. Officers were taking no more chances. They instantly opened up with machine guns, firing through the door. On the other side, with gun in hand, MacLeod fell dead.

Other radical members of the gang still remained, and they sent dire messages to authorities, threatening wholesale destruction of the government if their leaders were placed on trial. For two years the government put off the trial, building a bomb-proof courtroom in Stammheim. Gang members meanwhile searched their own ranks for traitors, suspecting that some member had tipped police as to the whereabouts of their leaders. They settled on 20-year-old Ulrich Schmucker who had been found sleeping inside a car loaded with bombs on May 7, 1972, by police and who was later released. Gang members were convinced Schmucker was guilty of treason, since he gave no reason for his release. A mock trial was held, and he was found guilty of collaborating with "the pigs." His close friend, Gotz Tilgener, who had brought Schmucker into the organization, was ordered to shoot him. Tilgener refused, telling his comrades that "you have gone too far." Someone else in the gang, on June 4, 1974, then shot Schmucker, and his body was dumped in Grunwald Park in Berlin. (Some claim that Schmucker was actually taken to a remote spot, tied to a tree, and shot by a firing squad of eight B-M members.) A B-M member called authorities to inform them that Schmucker had been "liquidated" because he had been "an instrument of the class enemy." It was later reported that the real reason for Schmucker's execution was because he had informed authorities of a 1972 bomb plot by B-M members who planned to blow up the Turkish Embassy in Bonn in retaliation for the execution of three Turkish terrorists. Tilgener, the member who had refused to kill his friend, was found dead a short time later, his death attributed to a combination of drugs and alcohol, but murder was never ruled out. Inside his apartment were found dozens of death-threat letters from B-M members.

Gang members inside prison cells proved as ruthless with their own lives as they had been with others, when they freely roamed the German landscape. Holger Meins refused to eat anything and went on a hunger strike. He denied himself food and then water, dying on Nov. 9, 1974. His death must be avenged, Meinhof demanded in a note smuggled from her prison cell to her still-faithful members on the outside. A week later the meaning of her cryptic note was understood. Her followers performed a brutal assassination in revenge for Meins' death.

Gunter von Drenkmann, president of the West German Supreme Court, was celebrating his sixty-fourth birthday in his Berlin home on Nov. 17, 1974. His doorbell rang, and the judge was called to the doorway by a servant who told him that a group of "nice young men" were there to present him with a birthday gift. The judge stood in the doorway as several young men all offered him small bouquets of flowers. He smiled. Then the young men dropped the flowers and showed the guns they had been holding beneath the flowers. They emptied the weapons into the judge who fell dead in the doorway. Oddly, Drenkmann had never tried any of the Baader-Meinhof gang. Next, B-M terrorists kidnapped 52-year-old Peter Lorenz as he was driving to his Berlin office. Lorenz was head of the Christian Democrat party and was the most popular candidate for mayor of Berlin. He was placed in a cell and guarded by masked terrorists who demanded that six terrorists be released. One of these was a B-M leader, Horst Mahler, who refused to leave his cell. The other five were members of an offshoot terrorist organization, which had splintered from the B-M gang and had been earlier arrested and imprisoned. The kidnappers did not ask for Baader, Meinhof, or Ensslin, apparently believing that they were better off in jail as martyrs to the cause. The Lorenz kidnapping had been organized by Ralf Reinders, Fritz Teufel, and Angela Luther, now seeking to establish their own terrorist group. Reinders was later identified as one of the young men who shot Judge Drenkmann.

Photos of Lorenz were taken of him in his cell and sent to authorities who were told that he would be killed unless their demands were met. Five terrorists were taken from their cells and flown from West Berlin to Frankfurt, where a Boeing 707 flew them to Aden. The terrorists were given 20,000 marks each before departing. It was a great defeat for the German government. Still, the government planned to put Baader, Meinhof, and Ensslin on trial, and as the date approached their loyal followers schemed to find a way to have them released. On Apr. 24, 1975, several terrorists broke into the West German Embassy in Stockholm, Swed. All of these fanatics were later identified as part of Huber's "crazy brigade," the communist mental patients. Taken prisoner was Ambassador Dietrich Stocker and several other diplomats. The terrorists announced that if Baader, Meinhof, Ensslin, and twenty-three other B-M terrorists then in prison cells were not released, given $500,000, and flown out of the country, the diplomats would be killed one-by-one.

When no answer from the Bonn government was forthcoming, the military attache, Lieutenant-Colonel Andreas Baron von Mirbach, was taken to the head of the stairs (the terrorists were barricaded on the fourth floor of the building, negotiating with authorities on the third floor) and shot several times, his body thrown down the stairs. One of the killers laughed and told the police waiting below that the Bonn government would agree to terms now. The killers fully expected the German government to cave in as it had in the Lorenz affair. But a short while later, Swedish police called up the stairs to the terrorists that Bonn had replied to their demands, and the answer was no. The terrorists were in shock. German chancellor Helmut Schmidt refused to negotiate with them. He and his government had had enough of the Baader-Meinhof gang. Then the terrorists received a message from the Swedish minister of justice, offering to let them leave the country unharmed if they would release the remaining hostages. The terrorists answered this proposal by shooting another diplomat, a helpless, near-enfeebled 64-year-old man, leaving his corpse half-dangling out a fourth-floor window. Still Bonn would not budge.

The Swedish authorities planned to attack the place with tear gas shells, followed by a massive assault by troops but, shortly before 10 p.m., the terrorists capitulated, sending out the remaining hostages. They themselves elected to commit mass suicide. At midnight, the building was rocked by a terrific explosion which collapsed the floors of the building. Among the ruins was found the leader of the embassy raid, Ulrich Wessel, who had inherited millions of dollars but was nevertheless a dedicated Marxist. He was dead. Five other terrorists hobbled from the ruins, including Hanna-Elise Krabbe, Karl-Heinz Dellwo, Lutz Taufer, Bernd Maria Rossner, and Siegfried Hausner who died five days later from a crushed skull.

Nothing now could stop the trial of Baader, Meinhof, Ensslin, and Raspe. They appeared in court on May 21, 1975. The court building was an armed camp surrounded by gun-bearing troops. Machine guns were mounted on rooftops surrounding the building, and close-circuit TV cameras scanned the streets for blocks around. The stakes were high. Either these terrorists would be justly convicted or the government would collapse. The trial was uneventful, except for the incessant outbursts from the defendants. Hundreds of pages, listing more than 600 capital offenses committed by the defendants, constituted the charges. For a year the prosecution presented its litany of murders, bombings, torture, robberies. On May 4, 1976, tired of the proceedings and still wishing to take the limelight from the others, Ensslin confessed to having caused three of the four murder-bombings with which the group was charged.

This confession so upset Meinhof that, on the night of May 9, 1976, she tore a towel into strips and used this to make a crude rope. She fastened the rope to the window bars of her cell, stood on a chair and, placed the noose around her neck. She jumped from the chair and hours later guards found her dangling, quite dead, her tongue, black and drooling, sticking from a mouth that had almost cut it in two when her jaw had obviously clamped shut. She was given a huge funeral on May 15, 1976, in West Berlin, which more than 4,000 radical students attended, many of them wearing masks so they could not be identified by police.

The killings went on. On Apr. 7, 1977, Siegfried Buback, chief federal prosecutor for West Germany, was shot to death while driving down a street in Karlsruhe. Still this did not stop the action of the court. On Apr. 28, 1977, Baader, Ensslin, and Raspe were all found Guilty of several murder counts and dozens of murder attempts. They were sentenced to life imprisonment. The killings went on still. B-M terrorists tried to kidnap Dr. Jurgen Ponto, head of the Dresden Bank, thinking to ransom him for the jailed terrorists. But Ponto resisted his abductors who shot him dead on July 30, 1977, when he opened the door of his Frankfurt home. Again, the terrorists used the flowers-in-hand technique to get Ponto to come to the door. He was really responding to one of the callers in particular, his own goddaughter, Susanne Albrecht, who stood with the killers holding a gun under her own bunch of flowers. Unknown to Ponto, she had become the mistress of SPK killer Karl-Heinz Dellwo, who had been captured after the embassy attack in Sweden.

Next the terrorists kidnapped Dr. Hans Martin Schleyer, one of the country's top industrialists, killing three of Schleyer's bodyguards and his chauffeur before taking him captive. They again demanded the release of Baader, Ensslin, and Raspe. The Bonn government stalled for time as its police conducted a desperate search for the kidnap victim. The terrorists released photos that showed Schleyer in a state of near-collapse, but Bonn still refused to meet their demands. The terrorists asked for help from their Arab brothers in the PFLP. On Oct. 13, 1977, an Arab splinter group from the PFLP promptly seized a Lufthansa airliner en route from Majorca to Frankfurt and held its passengers captive, demanding that the Baader group be released from prison, along with several Arab terrorists then in prison. Also, they demanded $15 million and an uninterrupted flight to a Middle Eastern destination. The plane was shuttled about from airport to airport while Bonn refused to admit defeat. In Aden, the terrorists shot and killed the pilot, Jurgen Schumann, after forcing him to kneel in front of his passengers. They threw his body from the plane and said they would kill more if their demands were not met. After flying to Mogadishu, the terrorists made more threats and demands. They were answered by a contingent of German commandos from the Grenzschutz Gruppe 9 who, with the permission of the Somali government, stormed the plane and shot it out with the Arab killers. Three of the four terrorists were killed, the fourth wounded. All eighty-six passengers were released, only one being slightly wounded. None of the German soldiers were wounded. It was a smashing victory for governmental law and order. Raspe, who had a secret transmitter hidden in his cell, learned of the terrorist defeat and somehow managed to have two guns smuggled into prison. Baader used one of them to blow out his brains, and Raspe used the other to kill himself. Ensslin followed Meinhof's lead and hanged herself in her cell.

In retaliation for these deaths, the few remaining B-M terrorists killed Schleyer, whose body was later found in the trunk of a car which had been parked in Mulhouse, Fr. Some of his slayers were later caught and given prison sentences. This was the last significant criminal act by the Baader-Meinhof terrorist gang, which soon went out of existence as a viable force in world terrorism. The German nightmare, which had lasted a decade, was finally over.

REF.: Adorno, *The Authoritarian Personality; Der Baader-Meinhof Report;* Becker, *Hitler's Children, The Story of the Baader-Meinhof Terrorist Gang;* Bunn, *German Politics and the Spiegel Affair: A Case Study of the Bonn System;* Carr, *The Angry Brigade;* CBA; Clutterbuck, *Guerrillas and Terrorists;* Cockburn, *Student Power;* Debray, *Che's Guerilla War;* Demaris, *Brothers In Blood: The International Terrorist Network;* Dobson, *Black September: Its Short, Violent History;* ____ and Payne, *Counterattack, The West's Battle Against the Terrorists;* ____, *The Terrorists, Their Weapons, Leaders and Tactics;* Godwin, *Murder U.S.A.;* Goode, *Affluent Revolutionaries: A Portrait of the New Left;* Grosser, *Germany in Our Time;* Habermas, *Protestbewegung und Hochschulreform;* ____, *Toward a Rational Society: Student Protest, Science and Politics;* Hacker, *Crusaders, Criminals, Crazies, Terror and Terrorism in Our Time;* Horchem, *Extremisten in einer selbsbewussten Demokratie;* Hunt, *On the Spot;* Laqueur,

Terrorism; _____ and Alexander, *The Terrorism Reader;* Liston, *Terrorism;* Moorehead, *Hostage to Fortune, A Study in Kidnapping in the World Today;* Nash, *Look for the Woman;* O'Ballance, *Language of Violence, The Blood Politics of Terrorism;* _____, *Terror in Ireland, The Heritage of Hate;* Parry, *Terrorism, From Robespierre to Arafat;* Röhl, *Fünf Finger sind keine Faust;* Schreiber, *The Ultimate Weapon: Terrorists and World Order;* Sloan, *Simulating Terrorism;* Sterling, *The Terror Network, The Secret War of International Terrorism;* Wilson, *Encyclopedia of Modern Murder;* (FILM) *Germany in Autumn,* 1978; *Stammheim,* 1986.

Babcock, Miner, 1796-1816, U.S., mur. On June 21, 1815, 19-year-old Miner Babcock was arrested for the murder of his mother's lover, a black man named London. London had lived with Babcock's mother in their Connecticut home for six years following her husband's death in 1809.

On the morning of June 21, Babcock overheard London and his mother quarreling. According to Babcock, he attempted to stop the fight but instead became involved. The argument turned violent, and London attacked him, Babcock said, explaining that to protect himself, he stabbed London in the stomach. While in jail at Norwich, Conn., Babcock confessed to the stabbing but maintained he had not intended to kill.

Babcock was first tried on Oct. 11, but the verdict was thrown out because it was discovered that one juror did not meet the legal requirements to judge the case. He was tried again in January 1816, found guilty, and sentenced to death. Babcock was hanged before a large crowd at the Norwich gallows on June 6, 1816. REF.: *CBA.*

Babel, Isaac Emmanuilovich, 1894-1941, Rus., writer. Exiled to Siberia by the Soviet government in 1937. REF.: *CBA.*

Babeuf, Francois Emile (Francois Emile Baboeuf, Gracchus Babeuf), 1760-97, Fr., consp.-suic. Espoused an agrarian communistic doctrine known as "Babouvism" to the French peasants who were in open revolt. Believing that the French Revolution had not developed along the lines of his own radical theory of a classless society, he hatched a wild plot to overthrow the Directory in 1796 and restore the 1793 Constitution. He was eventually betrayed by one of his associates, apprehended, and sentenced to die at the guillotine. Before the scheduled hour of the execution, he killed himself with a knife. REF.: *CBA.*

Babington, Anthony, 1561-86, Brit., consp. Led a Catholic conspiracy swayed by cleric John Ballard to overthrow Queen Elizabeth and place Mary Queen of Scots on the English throne. The plan failed when the secretary to Elizabeth, Sir Francis Walshingham, informed the queen of his discovery of incriminating letters from Mary approving the assassination. The queen had Mary Stuart, Ballard, Babington, and eleven others executed in London. See: **Ballard, John.** REF.: *CBA.*

Baby-Face Nelson, See: **Nelson, George.**

Baca, Elfego, 1865-1945, U.S., west. law enfor. off. Born in Socorro, N.M., Elfego Baca moved to Kansas with his family while in his teens. His father got into an argument with two cowboys in 1882 and shot both of them dead which caused him to receive a long prison sentence. The family moved back to Socorro where Baca worked in a store. He nevertheless harbored visions of becoming a lawman and a man who, like his father, was not afraid to use a gun. To that end he purchased a mail-order lawman's badge and two six-guns which he wore proudly. In October of 1884, a cowboy named McCarty got drunk in Frisco, N.M., where Baca was working. McCarty began to "hurrah" the town, picking Mexicans as his targets, causing many of these hapless people to "dance" to the music of his bullets. Baca rushed to the scene and, pinning on his badge, the self-styled lawman arrested McCarty after drawing his two guns. He marched the tipsy cowboy to the town square where he informed citizens that he would take McCarty to Socorro where he would be tried for disturbing the peace.

At that moment, more cowboys led by their foreman, a man named Perham, arrived in the plaza and demanded that McCarty be released. Perham and McCarty, citizens informed Baca, both worked for the largest rancher in the area, Tom Slaughter, a man unused to having his cowboys arrested without his approval. Baca shrugged and then told Perham that he would count to three and if they did not leave the plaza he would start shooting. Without waiting for a response, Baca rapidly counted to three and then opened fire on the cowboys, wounding one in the knee. Another one of Baca's shots struck the horse Perham was riding, causing the animal to crash to earth, mortally injuring Perham.

Elfego Baca in old age.

Citizens led by J.H. Cook then approached Baca and convinced him to turn his prisoner over to a local justice of the peace. McCarty was fined $50 for disturbing the peace and Baca's sense of justice was served. He stated that he intended to leave for Socorro the next day, but when he began to leave town he suddenly faced more than eighty well-armed cowboys under the command of Tom Slaughter.

It was never determined who fired the first shot, but suddenly Baca was blazing away with both six-guns at the entire Slaughter band. He turned and darted down an alleyway to a small Mexican hut which was made of poles and mud, ordering the small family inside to escape. Just as they did so, Slaughter's men surrounded the hut and began to fire at it, riddling the walls and door. Baca crouched low and fired through the eighteen-inch opening beneath the door, his bullets smacking into Jim Herne as he rushed the hut with rifle in hand. Herne died in the dusty street outside the hut, his body dragged away by a dozen cowboys pouring a deadly barrage into the hut. Slaughter's men lay siege to the small building, hour after hour pouring tremendous fusillades into the walls of the hut so that the hail of bullets literally tore away the walls and cut the wooden door to shreds. Baca occasionally returned fire and his aim proved to be deadly accurate. One cowboy after another fell wounded by Baca's pinpoint firing. The Slaughter people finally strung ropes between buildings and placed blankets over these so they could walk about freely without Baca picking them off.

Slaughter's men, using shotguns and buffalo guns, poured several volleys into the roof of the hut at sundown, causing the roof to collapse. It took Baca two hours to dig himself out from under the debris. He continued to fire back at his antagonists. At midnight some of Slaughter's men worked their way close enough to the hut to hurl a lighted stick of dynamite which blew away half of the hut, but Baca remained uninjured, having crouched in an undamaged corner of the building. Again he rose to fire at the cowboys, managing to wound two or three more. At dawn, Baca was seen to calmly cook his breakfast in the ruins of the hut which brought cheers and applause from the many Mexican spectators viewing the battle from afar. Still, the Slaughter cowboys were determined to ferret out the upstart Baca. Some of their more inventive numbers ripped out some heavy cookstoves from nearby buildings and used these as metal shields, moving them across the open ground around the half-demolished hut, but Baca picked off those behind them, creasing the skull of one cowboy and winging another in the arm. The cowboys gave up the idea of trying to rush the 19-year-old "deputy sheriff."

Before the Slaughter group unleashed another barrage, Cook, a deputy sheriff named Ross and Francisquito Naranjo approached the hut under a flag of truce and persuaded Baca to surrender, promising that he would be delivered safely to the authorities in

Socorro. He agreed, but only if he could keep his guns. Amazingly, this was agreed to by the Slaughter band, who apparently had been instilled with a great deal of respect for the sharpshooting Baca. More than thirty cowboys escorted Baca to Socorro but the cowboys rode in front of a buckboard in which Baca sat with Cook and Ross. Throughout the journey to Socorro, Baca kept his guns trained on his captors lest they go back on the promise he had been made.

In Socorro, the evidence was heard. Four men had been killed by Baca and at least ten other cowboys had been wounded by the self-styled lawman. Yet his heroic defense of the hut so impressed the court, along with its belief that Baca was acting in self-defense, that he was acquitted in two hotly-argued murder trials. Following his release, this survivor of New Mexico's most famous gunfight sought many public offices and was generally elected by landslides. He served as deputy sheriff, county sheriff, mayor of Socorro, school superintendent, and district attorney. He narrowly missed being elected to the governorship. Baca, although he rarely drew his gun as a lawman, was, because of the legendary Frisco fight, the most feared gunman in the territory. At age fifty he was again called upon to draw his six-guns.

In 1915, Baca was approached by an old enemy, Celestino Otero, who accosted the aging lawman as he stepped from the Paso del Norte Hotel in El Paso. Otero and some of his henchmen jumped out of a car and Otero pulled a revolver. He fired at Baca but the shot went wild. Baca drew both six-guns and fired a bullet from each, both striking Otero in the chest and killing him immediately. Baca was again tried for murder and acquitted. In 1919, Baca was again elected sheriff of Socorro County. Upon taking office, he went through all the wanted circulars of his own and neighboring counties and then wrote letters to these wanted felons, demanding that they immediately turn themselves in or he would strap on his six-guns and bring them back head down over a saddle. Such was Baca's fierce reputation that a half dozen of the most deadly outlaws in the area came meekly to Socorro to surrender to the famous sheriff. He died at age eighty in Albuquerque, N.M., in 1945.

REF.: American Guide Series, *New Mexico, A Guide to the Colorful State*; Bartholomew, *The Biographical Album of Western Gunfighters*; Beck, *New Mexico*; Beckett, *Baca's Battle*; Botkin, *A Treasury of Western Folklore*; Callon, *Las Vegas, New Mexico*; *CBA*; Cook, *Fifty Years on the Old Frontier*; ____, *Longhorn Cowboy*; Crichton, *Law and Order, Ltd.*; Fergusson, *Erna Fergusson's Albuquerque*; ____, *Rio Grande*; French, *Some Recollections of a Western Ranchman*; Haley, *Jeff Milton, A Good Man with A Gun*; Hendricks, *The Bad Man of the West*; Hening, *George Curry*; Hertzog, *Old Town Albuquerque*; Hutchinson, *The Life and Personal Writings of Eugene Manlove Rhodes*; Keleher, *The Fabulous Frontier*; Kemp and Dykes, *Cow Dust and Saddle Leather*; La Farge, *Santa Fe*; La Follette, *Eight Notches*; Looney, *Haunted Highways*; O'Connor, *Pat Garrett*; O'Neal, *Encyclopedia of Western Gunfighters*; Otero, *My Nine Years as Governor of the Territory of New Mexico*; Schaefer, *Heroes Without Glory*; Stanley, *The Duke City*; ____, *Socorro, The Oasis*; Ward, *Cimarron Saga*.

Bacchus, d.c.303, Roman, treas. While serving in Syrian army, he angered Emperor Maximillian by refusing to worship Jupiter, the supreme Roman god. His death by torture was commemorated in both Eastern and Western churches. REF.: *CBA*.

Bacchus, Thomas, and **Roberts, Samuel**, d.1772, Brit., coin. Thomas Bacchus learned the art of coining from his father William, who organized a gang of counterfeiters in Southwark. Samuel Roberts, a baker by trade, was so hopelessly in debt that he acted as agent for the Bacchus gang when the time came to dispose of the counterfeit money. The baker and the coin maker were sold out by a third accomplice and were arrested and brought before Sir John Fielding. Thomas Bacchus and Sam Roberts were hanged at Tyburn on May 21, 1772.

REF.: Armitage, *Bow Street Runners*; *CBA*; Potter, *The Art of Hanging*.

Bache, Benjamin Franklin, 1769-98, U.S., libel. Arrested and imprisoned in 1798 for politically opposing Federalist President John Adams. He wrote inflammatory editorials in his newspaper, the Philadelphia *General Advertiser*, also known as *Aurora*. He was later released on parole as were many other anti-Federalists when Thomas Jefferson entered the White House in 1801. REF.: *CBA*.

Bachelet, Vittorio, 1924-80, Italy, jur. Bachelet, Italian lecturer and judge, was gunned down by two unknown assassins as he walked out of the political science building on the campus of Rome University on Feb. 12, 1980. Bachelet, vice-president of Italy's judges' association, was shot eight times by two anonymous attackers, a woman in a gabardine suit and a bearded man. The murdered jurist had been an associate of former Italian Prime Minister Aldo Moro who was kidnapped and killed two years earlier. Both slayings may have been the work of the Red Brigades—a terrorist organization formed in part by Marxist philosopher and lecturer at the University of Padua, Antonio Negri. See: **Moro, Aldo; Red Brigades.** REF.: *CBA*.

Bachelor, Brett Allen, 1958- , U.S., (wrong. convict.) mur. Bachelor was sentenced in 1979 to serve 15 years for the brutal strangulation murder of a 75-year-old apartment manager in Hyde Park, Fla. During the trial, Bachelor pleaded with the court, saying, "Please, I'm innocent. You should believe me. I'm innocent." In July 1980, Circuit Court Judge Arden Mays Merckle ordered Bachelor released from prison, where he had served eight months of a 15-year sentence.

Bachelor was released when, during a second trial of co-defendant Kenneth Mullins, also indicted in the 1978 murder, evidence introduced showed that a key witness had mistakenly identified Bachelor as the killer. Bachelor was freed on his own recognizance, and both he and Mullins were acquitted of all charges. REF.: *CBA*.

Bachofen, Johann Jakob, 1815-87, Switz., jur. He sat on the Basil Court from 1842-66. REF.: *CBA*.

Backshall, Josephine, 1935-74, Brit., (unsolv.) mur. In the fall of 1974, Backshall, a 39-year-old mother of three, placed a classified advertisement in a local Essex County newspaper seeking part-time employment. Her ad stated that she had banking and typing experience but was willing to consider anything. A few days later, after an offer of employment, Backshall was dead.

Shortly after placing the ad, Backshall received a telephone call from a man asking to photograph her to promote a new line of cosmetics. The attractive middle-aged woman, excited at the prospect of modeling, arranged to meet the man the following week. After she drove fifteen miles to Witham, Essex, from her home in Maldon, the man failed to show up. During the next two weeks she received two more phone calls and arranged two more appointments, which the man failed to keep. The two finally met at Backshall's home, where the man shot a series of photos and agreed to pay Backshall £100 for her work. On Oct. 29, 1974, she received another call from the man and arranged yet another meeting for that evening. Three days later, Backshall's body was found in a shallow pond. Her hands had been bound and she had been strangled to death.

After spending more than 100,000 man-hours on the investigation, police still had no clues. They believed the man's first name may have been either Pete or Dave and his last name either Thomson or Johnson, although he may not have used his actual name, and that he may have driven a blue Ford. From forensics reports, they determined that her killer took her for her last meal to a Chinese restaurant, since medical examiners found traces of alcohol and the remains of Chinese food in Backshall's digestive system. Only one witness, an employee of the Fountain public house in Good Easter, Essex, saw Backshall and her killer at the bar, but was unable to give police a good description of the man.

Police believe Backshall's murderer answered her ad, which he perceived as a solicitation of prostitution. Stating in the copy that she would "consider anything" led police to believe that the murder was triggered by lust, although no definite motive has ever been determined. REF.: *CBA*.

Bacon, Francis (First Baron Verulum), 1561-1626, Brit., polit. corr. In 1601, helped convict the Earl of Essex of high treason. Appointed attorney general in 1613, he confessed to receiving bribes for various chicanery suits. He paid a fine of £40,000 and was cast out of Parliament. Within a year he was pardoned by the king and his money refunded. He is known for philosophical writings and legal writings including: *Maxims of the Law* (1630). REF.: *CBA*.

Bacon, Sir Nicholas, 1509-79, Brit., jur. Father of Francis Bacon, he maintained the great seal under Queen Elizabeth. REF.: *CBA*.

Bacon, Roger, c.1220-94, Brit., witchcraft-her. Experimented with alchemy, optics, and the practical application of gunpowder. His scientific work aroused the jealousy of his colleagues and the suspicions of the Church. The Franciscans had him removed from Oxford and imprisoned in Paris prison in 1257 for practicing religious heresy and black magic. REF.: *CBA*.

Bacon's Rebellion, 1676, U.S., mob vio. Nathaniel Bacon (1647-76), who had immigrated to Virginia from England in 1663, became the vocal leader of hundreds of pioneers being plagued by constant Indian attacks. Bacon and others sought aid from Virginia governor William Berkeley, but this venal and corrupt official, along with other members of the Virginia govenment, was disinclined to lend such help. He and others had profited considerably through the sale of weapons and ammunition to the Indians. Berkeley also supported an unjust local tobacco monopoly and had generally shown a haughty and unconcerned attitude toward the settlers of his dominion. Bacon, himself a member of Virginia's ruling class, was a dynamic speaker and a man of action. Without governmental approval, Bacon led a punitive expedition against the Indians which caused Berkeley to brand him a rebel.

After a reconciliation, Bacon was readmitted to acceptable Virginia society, but this idealistic young freedom fighter insisted that Berkeley and the government institute political and social reforms, that all settlers be educated at public expense, and that militia be assigned to protect all frontier outposts. This enraged the arrogant, mercurial Berkeley, who again labelled Bacon a rebel. Bacon's response was an indignant outburst of eloquence: "It vexes me to the heart that while I am hunting the wolves and tigers that destroy our lambs, I should myself be pursued as a savage. Shall persons wholly devoted to their king and country—men hazarding their lives against the public enemy—deserve the appellation of rebels and traitors? The whole country is witness to our peaceable behavior. But those in authority, how have they obtained their estates? Have they not devoured the common treasure? What arts, what sciences, what schools have they promoted? I appeal to the king and parliament where the cause of the people will be heard impartially."

In this last belief, Bacon was wrong. King Charles II was as indifferent to the welfare of his colonial subjects as was his representative, Berkeley. In 1676, the governor assembled a huge force and marched against Bacon, but was unsuccessful in tracking down his wiley pioneers in the wildness. A short time later, Bacon led 400 of his toughest frontiersmen into Jamestown and demanded immediate social reform and military protection for their families against Indian raids. Bacon's men surrounded the state house, poking muskets through every window, aiming at those in the assembly. Governor Berkeley dramatically ran outside and tore open his shirt, baring his breast and shouting: "Here! Shoot me! Before God, shoot!"

Bacon waved off several men willing to perform this deed, saying to Berkeley: "No, it may please Your Honor, we will not hurt a hair of your head, nor of any other man's. We are come for a commission to save our lives from the Indians." With that, he marched into the assembly and lectured its frightened members for some time. But the government leaders regained their aristocratic composure and flatly denied Bacon and his men any promise of military aid, nor would they permit him to again lead his own men against the Indians. Bacon and his men, incensed,

lit torches and raced about Jamestown, setting fire to each and every building. William Drummond, one of Bacon's ablest lieutenants, set fire to his own fine house to demonstrate his loyalty to the popular cause. The entire town was burned to the ground, not a house left standing.

Following the destruction of Jamestown, Bacon was declared a traitor and a price was put on his head, as well as those who followed him. Berkeley raised a small army and tracked down most of the rebels, hanging twenty-three of them. Bacon escaped the hangman, however, having died on Oct. 26, 1676, of dysentery. The cause for which he fought quickly collapsed without his leadership. Berkeley demonstrated a wild blood-lust for revenge by insisting that every male on the frontier be executed, and even his own assembly had to pass legislation to stop the wholesale hangings, ordering the governor to "spill no more blood." Said one of the officials: "Had we let him (Berkeley) alone, he would have hanged half the country." In England, upon hearing of the mass executions, Charles II remarked in his typical lofty air: "The old fool has hanged more people in that naked country than I did here for the murder of my father."

REF.: Archer, *Riot! A History of Mob Action in the United States;* Brown, *Strain of Violence;* Bruce, *Economic History of Virginia in the Seventeenth Century;* ____, *Social Life in the Seventeenth Century; CBA;* Craven, *The Southern Colonies in the Seventeenth Century, 1607-1689;* Hofstadter and Wallace, *American Violence;* Kraus, *The United States to 1865;* Smith, *Seventeenth Century America;* Washburn, *The Governor and the Rebel: A History of Bacon's Rebellion in Virginia;* Wertenbaker, *Torchbearer of the Revolution: The Story of Bacon's Rebellion and Its Leader;* ____, *Virginia Under the Stuarts.*

Badalamenti, Gaetano, prom. 1970s, Si., org. crime. One of the kingpins of the Sicilian Mafia, Gaetano Badalamenti controlled the narcotics traffic from the Middle East into Europe, especially Germany, operating out of a Hamburg headquarters. He was one of the most powerful Mafia figures in recent times, sitting on the ruling board of the Mafia in Palermo, Si. Badalamenti was one of the seventy-five top Mafia figures rounded up in a massive 1974 dragnet and, even though the public prosecutor had asked for his acquittal, was convicted of conspiracy and extortion and sent to prison for six years. His brother Joseph was also a member of the Mafia hierarchy during this time.

REF.: Alexander, *The Pizza Connection;* Blumenthal, *Last Days of the Sicilians; CBA;* Falzone, *Historie de la Mafia;* Hesse, *Mafia;* Servadio, *Mafioso.*

Badby, John, d.1410, Brit., her. Burned at the stake for denying transubstantiation. REF.: *CBA*.

Baekeland, Antony, 1946-81, Brit., mur. Barbara Baekeland's relationship with her son Antony bordered on obsession. On Nov. 17, 1972, Tony murdered his adoring mother at their lavish London penthouse.

Antony Baekeland, great grandson of the "father of modern plastics" and heir to the family fortune, was a troubled youth with homosexual tendencies. When he was twenty-one his parents separated. While living with his mother, Tony began experimenting with LSD. After he stabbed Barbara in the London penthouse, he placed an order for Chinese food just as the Chelsea detectives arrived. His trial began at the Old Bailey on June 6, 1973, and it was a sensational one, highlighted by rumors of incest between Barbara and her son. Witnesses told how the former movie star desired to "cure" her son of his homosexuality. Tony Baekeland, was convicted of manslaughter under the "diminished responsibility" statute in British law. He was sent to Broadmoor, where he remained for the next seven years. In July 1980, Tony was discharged from custody and flown to New York to live with his grandmother Nina Fraser Daly. A week later, Baekeland assaulted the elderly woman with a knife because she refused to "quit nagging him." Mrs. Daly survived the attack, but criminal charges were filed, and once again the young heir found himself behind bars, this time on Riker's Island. It was there that Tony Baekeland ended his life, on Mar. 21, 1981.

REF.: *CBA;* Robins, *Savage Grace.*

Baer, Frank, prom. 1888, U.S., arson. Frank Baer was a mill owner living in Greensburg, Pa., who decided to eliminate his competition by torching two rival mills. There was no loss of life, but the damage was so complete that the two mill owners were forced into bankruptcy. Baer's self-designed monopoly was short-lived. His accomplice, William Richardson, angrily went to the police and informed on Baer after the mill owner refused to pay him the full amount promised for Richardson's aid in burning down the mills. Baer was quickly arrested, tried, and convicted, given a six-year sentence. Richardson, ironically, was also convicted and given an eight-year prison term.

REF.: *CBA;* Nash, *Almanac of World Crime.*

Baer, George Frederick, 1842-1914, U.S., lawyer. In the great railroad strike of 1902 which paralyzed major coal shipments across the United States, he led the opposition to the United Mine Workers of America. REF.: *CBA.*

Báez, Buenaventura, 1810-84, Dom., consp. Led a revolt against the Haitian government in 1843. He was president of the Dominican Republic at various times, spending a total of fifteen years in office, but frequently exiled during his fifty year career. REF.: *CBA.*

Baez, Cecilio, 1862-1941, Para., lawyer. President of Paraguay in 1906. REF.: *CBA.*

Bagg, Arthur Richard, 1914- , S. Afri., mur. On Nov. 23, 1937, Arthur Richard Bagg, a 23-year-old South African, savagely stabbed his 17-year-old lover in a fit of jealousy and rage and later dumped her mutilated body under a viaduct on Oaklands Atholl Road outside Johannesburg. He was taken in for questioning several days after the partially-clothed body of Marjorie Patricia Rosebrook was found stabbed twice in the breast with a small knife.

Bagg became a prime suspect three days later when, during questioning, his accounts of his activities on the day of Rosebrook's murder did not correspond to those given by witnesses who had seen the two lovers together that day. After several attempts by Sub-Inspector U.R. Boberg to compel him to tell the truth, Bagg finally broke down and confessed to the murder. He later re-enacted the events of that day, taking detectives to the site of the crime and explaining his actions in detail.

Although Bagg had confessed, police were unable to locate the murder weapon and several articles of clothing missing from the dead girl's body. They repeatedly scoured the sites where Bagg claimed he disposed of them, but turned up nothing. After threatening to search his house, Bagg agreed to lead police to the missing items.

Bagg, described as somewhat eccentric, was an artist interested in mysticism and the occult. Unknown to anyone was his special affinity for the legendary vampire, Count Dracula. Bagg worshipped him and frequently conducted ritualistic services in his honor. He led police to the site of these rituals—a secret earthen chamber located below the floor of his bedroom. A trapdoor hidden underneath the linoleum provided access to the chamber, where police discovered the murder weapon and the missing blood-stained clothing. In addition, they found a piece of leather with writing carved into it: "I hereby befile (sic) the living God and serve only the Dark One, Dracula; to serve him faithfully so I may become one of his faithful servants." It was signed by Bagg.

Bagg's trial began on Feb. 28, 1938. During his testimony, he changed his confession and claimed the girl had committed suicide and that he was covering up for her with his earlier confession. The jury failed to believe him, and, after slightly less than two hours of deliberation, they returned a verdict of Guilty. Justice Saul Solomon sentenced Bagg to death, the maximum punishment for his crime, but this was later reduced to life imprisonment based on psychiatric evaluations of his mental state. Bagg was released in 1947 after serving only nine years of his sentence.

REF.: Bennett, *Too Late For Tears; CBA.*

Bagoas, prom. 4th Cent. B.C., Per., assass. Court attendant to Artaxerxes III. In 338 B.C., he assassinated the king and installed Arses on the throne. Two years later he killed Arses

who was succeeded by Darius. Darius had him executed after he learned that he was also targeted for death. See: **Artaxerxes; Arses.** REF.: *CBA.*

Bahadur Shah II (Muhammed Bahadur Shah), c.1775-1862, India, treas. Ruled the Mughal kingdom from 1837-58. He was the nominal head of his country, propped up by the British East India Company who controlled internal policy making. During the Sepoy Mutiny of 1857, the rebel troops compelled him to participate in the revolt. He was captured by the British in 1858 and sentenced to life imprisonment. He died at Rangoon. REF.: *CBA.*

Bahuti, al (Bahuti al-Misri), d.1641, Egypt, lawyer. One of the last advocates of the Hanbali school of Islamic law in Egypt. REF.: *CBA.*

Bailes, Marie Ellen, 1902-08, Brit., (unsolv.) mur. Marie Bailes was returning to her home at Islington in North London after leaving St. John's Catholic School on May 30, 1908. She never arrived. The next morning a nervous man was seen to enter a restroom near St. George's road. He carried with him a large package which he left inside the room. When he left, an attendant opened the package to discover the body of the Bailes girl, her throat slit. The attendant gave a good description of the man, but police, despite a lengthy and exhaustive search, were unable to find the killer.

REF.: *CBA;* McNaghten, *Days of My Years;* Nash, *Open Files;* Savage, *Savage of the Yard;* Shew, *A Second Companion to Murder.*

Bailey, Adonijah, d.1825, U.S., mur. Adonijah Bailey lived with Jeremiah W. Pollock and when he learned that his roommate had a cache of gold coins, Bailey crushed Pollock's head with an ax and robbed him, hiding his body in the nearby woods. Pollock was reported missing on Oct. 23, 1824, and a search party began to look for him, finding his buried corpse on Nov. 3. Bailey was immediately accused of the murder and was tried at Brooklyn, Conn., for three days, Jan. 13-15, 1825, which resulted in a conviction. Unwilling to await the executioner, Bailey hanged himself in his cell a short time later.

REF.: *CBA; Report on the Trial of Adonijah Bailey.*

Bailey, Benjamin, 1773-98, U.S., mur. Jost Follhaber, a wandering peddler, encountered Benjamin Bailey near Machonoy Mountain, Pa., and joined the traveller, telling him he was a hunter, his sole purpose being to rob Follhaber. He did rob the peddler at gunpoint, once the pair reached the top of the mountain on Aug. 11, 1797, but, as Bailey later admitted, he feared that the incensed Follhaber would later identify him to authorities so, almost as an afterthought, Bailey shot the man, then struck him repeatedly with his tomahawk. The trial, along with the jury's deliberation, lasted twenty hours non-stop before Bailey was convicted. Bailey was executed on Jan. 6, 1798, at Reading, Pa.

REF.: *CBA; The Confession of Benjamin Bailey.*

Bailey, F(rancis). Lee, 1933- , U.S., crim. law. One of the most successful and effective criminal lawyers practicing in the U.S., F. Lee Bailey is less eccentric and demonstrative than many of his contemporaries. He is noted for his excellent pretrial preparation and the selection of jury members, winning them over often before the trial begins. Since passing the bar in Massachusetts, Bailey has risen through the legal ranks to become one of the most sought after lawyers of this era. Of course, much of Bailey's reputation has been built upon sensational cases where, for the most part, he emerged triumphant. One of his first significant cases, one already lost, was that of Dr. Sam Sheppard, who had been convicted of murdering his wife. Bailey won the physician a new trial and managed to get his client released. He was successful in defending Captain Ernest L. Medina, who stood accused (and universally condemned by the press and most of the public) for reportedly ordering the My Lai Massacre of Vietnamese civilians and, in a remarkable display of legal maneuvering, managed to have Albert DeSalvo, the Boston Strangler, tried on non-capital charges. Bailey was equally victorious in defending those who stood accused of the Great Mail Robbery which occurred on Aug. 14, 1962, on a Cape Cod highway in Massachusetts, a theft that netted the robbers more than $1.5 million.

Not all of Bailey's efforts were rewarded with wins. He lost the case for Patricia Hearst and one of the two sensational trials of Dr. Carl Coppolino. He ran into great difficulties, including an indictment against himself, in the Glen W. Turner case, one where Turner, a whirlwind entrepreneur, stood accused of illegally manipulating his companies in a labyrinthine pyramiding scheme. Yet Bailey, a cool head under fire, has found unique ways to undermine the presence and image of his opponents. In one murder case where the death penalty was almost assured, Bailey managed to get the prosecuting attorneys to smile before a jury and then rebuked his adversaries for treating a serious case with frivolity and mirth. His jury selections have proven to be masterful, and he invariably saves his clients' necks in cases most would consider hopeless by establishing a rapport with one or more

F. Lee Bailey

jurors. In one of the Coppolino cases, he portrayed his client as "stepping out of line" a little but no more and he found a potential juror who admitted that he, too, "stepped out of line" once in a while, a fact that did not make him a murderer. Bailey managed to select this man and played so successfully to him that when it came time for the jury to deliberate the case, the juror dragged his chair away from the rest of the jury, informing them: "I vote Not Guilty. Call me when the rest of you are ready to agree with me."

Much of the criticism leveled at Bailey can be attributed, at least among his peers, to jealousy, for he attracts enormous press coverage with almost every case he accepts. Moreover, Bailey is among the elite of criminal lawyers, demanding and receiving enormous fees. He practices his own eccentricities when dealing with difficult cases where jury selection is all-important. At such times, Bailey employs a hypnotist to advise him on various prospective jurors, particularly women, telling the lawyer that certain females will be more or less responsive to his questions by the way they crossed their legs under his questioning. Bailey has been called a "headhunter" and a "maverick" by critics who nevertheless hold him in grudging high esteem. See: **Coppolino, Carl; DeSalvo, Albert; Great Mail Robbery; Hearst, Patricia; Medina, Ernest; Sheppard, Samuel; Turner, Glen W.**

REF.: Alexander, *Anyone's Daughter;* Bailey, *The Defense Never Rests;* ____, *For the Defense; CBA;* Coppolino, *The Crime That Never Was;* Moscow, *Every Secret Thing;* Pollock, *Dr. Sam;* Zuckerman, *Vengeance Is Mine.*

Bailey, George Arthur, d.1921, Brit., mur. The January 1921 murder trial of George Arthur Bailey was the first murder trial in England in which women served on a jury. After the four-day trial was over, the three women jurors helped convict Bailey for the poisoning murder of his wife. He was sentenced to death and executed on Mar. 2, 1921.

REF.: *CBA;* Shew, *A Companion To Murder.*

Bailey, Harvey John (AKA: **Old Harve, Tom Brennan, Thompson**), 1887-1979, U.S., rob.-kid. Known as "Old Harve" because of his prematurely gray hair, Bailey was a professional bank robber whose reputation was deep and vast within the ranks of the underworld, particularly among the independent bank robbers of the 1920s and early 1930s. Bailey was not initially a dedicated criminal but a family man who had been raised in a good family. He had little formal education and began working as a railroad fireman in 1905 when only sixteen. He was a burly youth who stayed out of trouble, earned his pay and made regular deposits in a savings account. In 1918, Bailey was drafted and sent to France where he served with distinction. Upon his return, like so many other veterans, he embarked upon a new career as a bootlegger, taking advantage of the liquor demand created by Prohibition.

John Pendergast, the brother of Boss Tom Pendergast of Kansas City, had warehoused enormous quantities of liquor just before the Volstead Act was enacted. In 1920, Pendergast recruited a number of reliable men to run this booze to small towns in the Midwest, selecting Bailey as one of his runners. Bailey began running illegal liquor to Tulsa, Okla., St. Joseph, Mo., and Council Bluffs, Iowa. He prospered and, by then, had married and had two sons, buying a large farm in Sullivan County, Mo. Bailey enjoyed the considerable cash his bootlegging produced, buying a large black Buick which was his pride and joy. He made the mistake of loaning this car to four thieves who botched a robbery in Maryville, Mo., and got caught. Bailey was indicted for allowing the thieves to use his car and, after posting a $2,000 bond, he fled.

Bailey next tried his hand at bank burglary, joining with a few other safecrackers in night raids on banks in Iowa and North Dakota but the take was small and Bailey, as he would do so many times in the future, gave up crime as a way of making a living, moving his family to Ottumwa, Iowa, where he bought a small farm and lived under the alias of Tom Brennan. The farm yielded little income and Bailey was soon joining old underworld friends in planning bank robberies. He, Alvin Johnston, Nick "Chaw Jimmie" Traynor, and "Dude" Richardson struck a Des Moines, Iowa, bank in the summer of 1922 and drove away with $12,000 in cash. This was considerable loot in those days, and Bailey soon concluded that bank robbing offered the most profitable opportunities. Along with Jimmie "The Wolf" Lindon and Curly Santle, Bailey, on Sept. 28, 1922, robbed the Hamilton County Bank of Cincinnati, speeding off with two suitcases full of cash and negotiable bonds. When the thieves opened the cases they gasped. Their take was a staggering $265,000. News of this gigantic robbery soon spread through the network of bank robbers in the Midwest, and Bailey's name became famous for "making the big heist."

For this reason, James Ripley and others invited Bailey to join them in one of the boldest robberies in American history up to that time, the holdup of the U.S. Mint in Denver. Bailey later claimed that he was not present during this astounding daylight raid which netted the robbers between $200,000 and $500,000 in cash. Bailey insisted that he had been called to the side of his brother Jim, who was deathly ill, just before the raid was made on the mint and missed the Denver robbery, but his statements may have been tempered by the fact that a guard had been killed in the robbery (along with one of the bandits who died later, according to one report) and Bailey would not have admitted to a crime where a life was taken. He did admit that Alvin Johnston, one of the bandits in the Denver raid, contacted him and asked him to fence the hot money. This Bailey did, earning a large portion of the take.

With more than $85,000 from his share of this robbery and other holdups, Bailey moved his family to the Maywood section of Chicago. There he invested in two service stations with a few junior partners and decided to go straight. At first the stations flourished and Bailey, who tinkered with inventions and learned carpentry as a youth, developed the first car conveyor system in a washing and polishing operation that soon brought in considerable profits. When business fell off in 1925, Bailey and an apprentice bank robber, Ed Fitzgerald, who admired Bailey's reputation as a bank caser or planner, drove to a small Iowa bank and, with two others, robbed it. Said Bailey later: "We got about four thousand dollars and my share was nine hundred. It was a long way to drive for that kind of money."

Bailey, living with his family in Chicago under the alias of Ben Bloom, continued to make bank robbery sorties throughout the 1920s. He joined Alvin Johnston, Slim Jones, and two Peoria bandits in robbing a bank in LaPorte, Ind., on Nov. 12, 1926, taking $140,000. Three weeks later, Bailey planned the robbery of the Olmsted County Bank and Trust in Rochester, Minn., storming into the bank with Alvin Johnston, Ed Fitzgerald, Slim Jones, and Larry DeVol, taking $30,000. Next, Bailey cased the Farmer's National Bank of Vinton, Iowa, robbing it with the same gang on Aug. 19, 1927, stealing $70,000. Bailey spent less time with his service stations and more time concentrating on bank robberies. He was a methodical thief, first determining sizeable amounts each bank would contain through his contact with Eddie Bentz, a specialist in bank casing, then going to the proposed robbery area, driving along the back roads, or "cat roads," as the thieves of that day called them, to determine whether or not clear escape routes were open and pursuing police could be eluded.

The bank robberies rolled on. The gang robbed the Whitney Loan and Trust Company of Atlantic City, Iowa, in the summer of 1928, taking $55,000 in cash and Liberty Bonds. The gang was joined by a towering thief named Homer Wilson, an old friend of Bailey's, who presented a problem during the getaway in that he was so tall, about six feet, eight inches, that he barely squeezed into the getaway car. On Dec. 18, the gang robbed the bank in Sturgis, Minn., getting away with $80,000. Five days later, the same gang, Bailey leading them, raided a bank in Clinton, Ind., stealing $52,000. This bank robbing band proved to be the most successful in the Midwest during the late 1920s. Bailey and his men looted banks with relative ease and little or no gunplay, accumulating more than $1 million. Bailey's share was well over $100,000 which he promptly placed in a savings account in Calumet City, Ill.

So successful was Bailey that legitimate business held no interest for him; he also craved the excitement the robberies brought him and by 1929 he had sold his service stations and lived exclusively from his bank robberies. He and his gang robbed the bank in Cherokee, Iowa, and in the summer of 1929, the same band stormed into the little bank in Estherville, Iowa, but the take was only $2,000. Bailey was annoyed with Fitzgerald and Devol for brandishing a machine gun and a shotgun at local residents while waiting in the street for the rest of the gang to emerge from the bank. He once more decided to retire, but Black Friday in October brought the

Bank robber Harvey Bailey.

stock market crash and banks subsequently collapsed in the resulting panic, including the bank in which Bailey had put his stolen money. With about $40,000 he had placed in a safety deposit box, Bailey again moved his family to Kenosha County, Wis., where he bought a small farm, intending to wait out the oncoming Depression.

Bailey's farm was a failure, and he was soon back planning bank robberies. With two professional bank robbers, Thomas Holden and Francis Keating, who had recently escaped from the U.S. penitentiary in Leavenworth, Kan., Bailey planned another bank job in Willmar, Minn. Holden and Keating recruited a young bootlegger who had just been released from Leavenworth, a man named Barnes who had provided them with faked passes which allowed Holden and Keating to walk out of Leavenworth.

Barnes changed his name to Kelly and was later to be known as the infamous Machine Gun Kelly. Another bandit named Sammy Stein was added to the roster and the five men struck the bank on July 15, 1930, taking $70,000. This time, everything seemed to go wrong. Unlike most of the previous bank robberies planned by Bailey where no local police were present, Willmar boasted several deputies who began firing on the getaway car as soon as it roared away from the bank. Stein, sitting in the back seat, took a bullet in the back of the head. The gang later buried his body outside of Rochester, Minn.

The Willmar raid proved to be near disastrous for Bailey, a cautious, clever thief who traditionally attempted to avoid violence. He felt his gang members were, for the most part, bumbling amateurs and decided to replace his roster of heist men. With Holden soliciting new talent, Bailey enlisted the aid of Howard Phillips, an ex-sheriff from South Dakota named Verne Miller, and Fred Barker, a young gunman who came from a family of thieves—one of the four dreaded Barker brothers. This band struck the Ottumwa (Iowa) Savings Bank on Sept. 9, 1930, taking an estimated $100,000. Following the robbery, Bailey and others used information supplied to them by the master bank caser, Eddie Bentz, to strike the Lincoln National Bank in Lincoln, Neb., on Sept. 17, 1930. The loot amounted to the largest haul taken in the history of U.S. robbery up to that time, a staggering $2,654,700 in negotiable securities and $24,000 in cash. Involved in this cleverly planned robbery was Eddie Bentz, Ed Fitzgerald, and Harvey Bailey, although Bailey insisted that he was in Minneapolis at the time of the robbery and his participation consisted of arranging to peddle the stolen securities for Fitzgerald which subsequently brought 50¢ on the dollar. The robbery was so devastating to the Lincoln Bank that it was forced to close its doors forever. This robbery established Bailey as the supreme bank robber in the U.S. among his underworld peers, and he was deluged with offers from lone bandits and large-scale robbery bands to work with him.

Bailey began selecting his men from the what was thought to be the cream of bank robbers. He planned the robbery of the Sherman Central Bank in Texas, meeting in Dallas with George "Machine Gun" Kelly, Verne Miller, Frank Nash, and a getaway driver named Dutch Joe. Bailey had some harsh words for Kelly who, at first insisted that his ambitious, attractive wife, Kathryn Shannon Kelly, be present at the meeting. No, Bailey told him; he never allowed women to be part of any of his planning. "Things always go wrong when women are involved," Bailey told Kelly who reluctantly returned to his red-haired wife and informed her that she would be no part of masterminding the Sherman, Texas, raid. A firebrand and egotist, Kathryn Kelly exploded, raging against Bailey, but she allowed her cowed husband to participate in the Texas robbery since they were both broke. (Kelly, in fact, had borrowed $1,000 from Bailey when agreeing to go on the raid.) The sharply-featured Kathryn Kelly, who would later be portrayed as an evil genius by J. Edgar Hoover after the Kellys kidnapped Oklahoma oil baron Charles Urschel in 1933, thought of herself as one of the greatest criminal minds of the century. She had shaped her husband's underworld career and had promoted his bogus reputation as a fierce gunman, labeling him "Machine Gun," and encouraging his annoyed peers to use this moniker when referring to Kelly. Her ruthless ambition and vainglorious self-perception would later lead the Kellys into ultimate disaster.

The raid on the Sherman bank, occurring in 1931, netted the thieves about $40,000 and Bailey took the lion's share since he had cased this bank and planned the escape routes the gang employed when making their getaway along the county back roads. Kathryn Kelly was so disappointed with her husband's share of the loot that she ordered Kelly not to repay the $1,000 he had borrowed from Bailey. This irked Bailey, who vowed he would never again invite the Kellys to participate in any bank robbery he organized. Bailey then moved to Kansas City, living in an expensive apartment. The town was then totally controlled by Johnny Lazia, underworld boss for the Pendergast political machine, and it served as a haven for scores of high-living, free-spending bank robbers, including Keating and Holden, Fred Barker, and his lover, Alvin Karpis, later to be known as "Creepy," Charles Arthur "Pretty Boy" Floyd, Larry DeVol, and Frank Nash.

The gangsters lived well, spending most of their time in the best nightclubs and restaurants. In good weather, Bailey, Holden, and Keating, golf enthusiasts, attired themselves in the finest knickers and sweaters and played the links. They bought expensive new cars, the finest wardrobes, and glittering jewels for their wives and sweethearts. The country may have been sinking ever deeper into the widening chasm of Depression, but these men lived like rajahs. Whenever the money began to run out, they merely planned another bank robbery and refilled their coffers. The banks selected for such looting, of course, were invariably small institutions in rural areas which were guarded lightly or not at all. The laws of the day allowed bank robbers to raid a bank in one state and escape to another without state authorities having the right to pursue them. Bank robbing was not then a federal offense. Because of Bailey and others like him, federal laws would later be enacted to allow agents of the FBI to pursue this wily quarry from state to state and eventually track down the super bandits of the 1930s, as the press had dubbed them.

Bailey next began to plan the robbery of the bank in Fort Scott, Kan., but he found that by including Fred Barker, Karpis, and their friend Larry DeVol, he had invited trouble. Barker, now living with Karpis and Ma Barker, a crusty old harridan, began to strut about, insisting that he approve of any plan Bailey made. He also insisted that his mother receive a "cut" of the loot, although she made but few comments about the organization of such raids. Bailey went along with Barker since his group now constituted most of the required manpower. The Fort Scott raid, on June 17, 1932, proved to be a near disaster, thanks to the maniacal Freddie Barker. The gang included Bailey, Holden, Phil Courtney, and the "wild ones"—Barker, DeVol, and Karpis. Holden parked a big Hudson touring car a block away from the bank to avoid the suspicions of local police (Bailey insisted that a getaway car never be parked directly in front of the bank). The other five men went into the bank, and as soon as a teller spotted the weapons in their hands he hit the alarm button.

When Barker heard the alarm he went berserk, screaming: "I'm gonna shoot everyone in this place!" Bailey calmed him down while Courtney, DeVol, and Karpis systematically looted the tellers' cages, taking between $32,000 and $47,000, according to later varying estimates. Then Bailey stepped into the street and waved for Holden to bring on the Hudson. When the big car roared to the front of the bank, the gangsters began to get into the auto, but Karpis paused to peer down the street. "Look at that!" He pointed to several police officers running toward the bank, all heavily armed. "Grab these girls!" Barker shouted and he and DeVol and Karpis dragged three females employed by the bank, placing them on the running boards of the car as it sped off. "It's only for a few miles," Bailey told one woman who appeared traumatized. The captives began screaming hysterically when Barker, seeing a motorcycle cop pursuing them, leaned out of a window with a machine gun and fired several bursts which missed the officer but stopped pursuit. The captives were released some miles outside of Fort Scott.

The robbery at Fort Scott jangled Bailey's nerves, and he told Holden, Keating, and Frank Nash—old pros at looting banks for decades—that he would never again "work with such crazy people" as Fred Barker. The Barkers and their seedy mother were the dregs of the independent bank robbers of the day, according to Bailey, and he regretted ever involving himself with them and with the Kellys. "That kind of heat burned everybody," he said years later. Bailey was also angered over the fact that Barker had insisted upon dividing the money taken from the Fort Scott bank and, after he had awarded himself and his own men, DeVol and Karpis, with extra portions, he cut out a wad of bills "for Ma, because she had some ideas about how to pull this one off."

Barker handed Bailey only $4,000, a pittance compared to what he was used to receiving. A patient man, Bailey said nothing, took his share and went back to his quiet life. Some weeks later, while he, Holden, Keating and Nash were about to tee off at the Old Mission Golf Course in Kansas City, detectives, who had traced their cars, arrested the four gangster golfers who were members of the club. They surrendered without resistance.

Bailey was convicted of the Fort Scott robbery and sent to Kansas State Penitentiary with a ten-to-twenty-year sentence. He was not to remain there long. On May 31, 1933, Bailey escaped the penitentiary with four Oklahoma bandits, Wilbur Underhill, known as the "Tri-State Terror," Bob Brady, Ed Davis, and Jim Clark. The Oklahoma outlaws headed for the Cookson Hills, but Bailey had decided to quit crime. He had enough loot hidden in the southwest to make a permanent exit, and he headed for Mexico. He bought a used car and drove leisurely toward Texas but was stopped by a police roadblock; shooting his way out, he was wounded in the leg. Bailey headed for Paradise, Texas, and the Shannon Ranch, a hideout for fugitives. The ranch was owned and operated by R.G. "Boss" Shannon who was none other than Kathryn Kelly's stepfather. When Bailey arrived, still bleeding from his leg wound, he was astounded to find the Kellys present on the ranch. It was his bad luck to discover that the Kellys had just kidnapped oil man Charles F. Urschel in a badly planned scheme hatched by Kathryn Kelly. Urschel was on the premises, still being held while the Kellys negotiated a $200,000 ransom, when Bailey arrived. He was given a bed in a small shack and told that he could stay as long as it took his wound to heal.

Some days later the Kellys received their ransom payment and Urschel was taken away and later released unharmed. Their confederate in this kidnapping, Albert Bates, returned to the ranch with some of the ransom money which he gave to Shannon and his wife. He then discovered Bailey still recovering from his wound. "Listen, Harve," he told Bailey, "This place is hot. I told the others to get out. Why didn't you go with them?" Bailey pointed to his shattered leg, explaining that the wound was taking a long time to heal and that he could not drive a car. Bates tossed $500 on the bed, where Bailey reclined, and headed for the door, saying nervously: "Take that and go and see a doctor. You better get running, Harve. The Law is right behind me!"

On the hot morning of Aug. 12, 1933, Bailey hobbled out of his cottage and moved to the front porch of the main Shannon house. He sat back in a rocker with a rifle across the arms of the chair and fell asleep as the flies buzzed over his head. Some time later he was awakened with a tug and a sharp order: "Wake up, Harvey!" He opened his eyes to see FBI agent Gus T. Jones, one of those who had arrested him at the golf course in Kansas City. Jones stood holding an automatic to the bank robber's head, saying: "If you try for that gun, I'll riddle you." Bailey shrugged and handed the agent the gun, stating: "I'm here alone. You've got me."

Jones and other agents present removed the rifle and then helped Bailey to his feet, "Harvey Bailey," one of them said to the tired old bank robber, "caught snoozing in a rocker."

Bailey gave him a thin smile and said: "Well, a fellow's got to sleep some time."

Found on Bailey was more than $1,200, including the $500 Bates had given him. This loan turned out to be a lifelong curse in that the cash was part of the Urschel ransom money paid to the Kellys. Now Bailey was charged with kidnapping the Oklahoma oilman, as well as escaping from prison. The ranch was swarming with FBI men and local officers. The Shannons were rounded up and Urschel himself was present to identify them as part of the kidnapping gang. Bailey, despite his protests, was charged with kidnapping Urschel and was taken to Dallas where he was put into the "escape-proof" Dallas County Jail, a towering building in those days. Bailey was housed on the tenth floor of this building in a special holding cell where he awaited trial. He struck up a rapport with a dim-witted deputy sheriff, Thomas L. Manion, who was in awe of Bailey and reveled in Bailey's tales of his robberies. Bailey told him he had fortunes hidden and promised that if Manion helped him escape he would cut him in on a goodly share of his loot, plus part of the take from his next three bank robberies. Manion agreed and smuggled a hacksaw to Bailey who began working on a single bar through the night of Sept. 3-4, 1933.

When Manion checked on his progress, he found that the prisoner was having difficulty so the deputy sheriff took turns with Bailey as they worked on the bar. Finally, Manion, tiring, retrieved a Stillson wrench, handing this to Bailey. "Here," he told the prisoner, "this ought to do it." Bailey was able to snap the bar with the wrench and get into the hallway. He took Manion's gun and, en route to the elevator, locked up six guards. Then he took the elevator to the sixth floor and there, at gunpoint, forced Deputy Sheriff Nicholas Tresp, to escort him to the jail's garage where the two drove away in one of the fast sheriff's cars. Bailey dropped Tresp off some miles later and began driving east toward the Cookson Hills. (An almost identical escape would be made by John Dillinger in 1934 when Public Enemy Number One fled the "escape-proof" jail in Crown Point, Ind.)

Hundreds of law men were in pursuit of Bailey whose escape had captured national headlines. Approaching Ardmore, Okla., Bailey saw the roadblock and turned his car about. Two dozen cars packed with more than 100 men gave chase, the officers firing wildly with submachine guns and shotguns so that Bailey's car was riddled. The gas tank was hit and, without exploding, the gas escaped. Bailey, miraculously escaping injury, drove the car to a halt as it ran out of gas. The old bandit was dragged from the car and put into chains, shackled hand and foot, and taken back to Dallas. (Manion, for aiding Bailey in his escape, later drew a long prison sentence.) When placed in another cell which was watched day and night, Bailey was asked by a guard: "What did you think you would prove, Harvey?"

"That I could get out," replied Bailey, but it would be the last prison break for the notorious bandit. He would spend most of the rest of life behind bars, ironically for a crime he did not commit. He refused to testify against the Kellys, Shannons, and Bates and was convicted with them for kidnapping Charles Urschel. Receiving a life sentence, he was sent to Alcatraz, one of that dreaded prison's first inmates, along with Al Capone and other "big shots" of the underworld. He stayed on the rock for twelve years. On Aug. 11, 1946, Bailey was transferred to Leavenworth and, from there, to Seagoville, Texas—a minimum-security institution. When paroled in 1962, Bailey was met by Kansas officers who returned him to the Kansas State Penitentiary where he was to serve more time for his 1933 escape with the Underhill gang.

On March 31, 1965, Bailey was finally released. He went to work in Joplin, Mo., as a cabinet maker. He retired in 1969 when he could no longer work because of failing health. Bailey's first wife divorced him in 1948 while he was still in Leavenworth but he remarried in 1966, wedding the widow of Herbert Farmer, who had been part of the 1930s underworld, an armorer who supplied bandits with automatic weapons. Farmer had been sent to Alcatraz for his association with several gunmen connected with the Kansas City Massacre of 1933. Following a series of kidney ailments, Harvey Bailey died in Joplin on Mar. 1, 1979. To his dying day, Bailey cursed the name of J. Edgar Hoover, blaming the FBI chief for falsely imprisoning him for the Urschel kidnapping. See: **Alcatraz; Barker Brothers; Bentz, Edward; Hoover, J. Edgar; Kelly, George; Nash, Frank; Underhill, Wilbur.**

REF.: Alix, *Ransom Kidnapping in America;* Audett, *Rap Sheet; CBA;* Clayton, *Union Station Massacre;* Cooper, *Ten Thousand Public Enemies;* Dorsett, *The Pendergast Machine;* Edge, *Run the Cat Roads;* Gish, *American Bandits;* Graves, *Oklahoma Outlaws;* Hamilton, *Men of the Underworld;* Hoover, *Persons in Hiding;* Hynd, *Murder, Mayhem and Mystery;* Johnston, *Alcatraz Island Prison;* Karpis, *The Alvin Karpis Story;* _____, *On the Rock;* Kobler, *Capone;* Louderback, *The Bad Ones;* Messick, *Kidnapping, The Illustrated History;* Nash, *Bloodletters and Badmen;* Powers, *Secrecy and Power;* Reddig, *Tom's Town;* Toland, *The Dillinger* *Days;* Wellman, *A Dynasty of Western Outlaws;* Whitehead, *The FBI Story.*

Bailey, James Warren, 1943- , and **Riley, Irvin George,** 1961- , and **Whyte, James Albert,** 1960- , U.S., kid.-mur. For three years James Bailey kept the freezer in the basement of his North Tampa, Fla., home firmly locked. The two Bailey children, Diane May, fourteen, and James, Jr., eighteen, were told to beware the consequences of touching it.

Curiosity finally overcame the threats, and on Mar. 6, 1988, Diane and a friend jimmied open the freezer with a screwdriver. They recoiled in horror as the lid opened, revealing the severed head and torso of a woman. Diane frantically called her older brother James, who said he had known about the body but had decided to say nothing, fearing reprisal from his father. The police were summoned and a warrant for the arrest of 45-year-old suspected drug pusher James Warren Bailey was sworn.

In addition to his teenaged children, Bailey shared his Richmere Street home with his girlfriend, Betty Pearl Watts, and her son Timothy. Amidst the garbage and dirty laundry, a cache of guns was found and seized by police.

The corpse was identified as that of Kimberly Ann Hanlon, a 29-year-old prostitute who had been picked up by the North Tampa Police in 1983. She had become involved with Bailey, whose gang of small-time drug dealers included Irvin George Riley and James Albert Whyte. Hanlon, suspected of filching drug profits, was taken to Bailey's home where she was bound, gagged, raped, and shot in the back of her head. The body was dissected with a power tool and locked in the freezer, where it remained for the next three years.

Because the state could not establish aggravating circumstances supporting the death penalty, Bailey was sentenced to three consecutive life terms. Judge Richard A. Lazzara, when criticized for his leniency, responded that "no matter how the community feels about Mr. Bailey for what he did to her, I have to follow the law and that's what I am going to do."

Irvin Riley was convicted of kidnapping and rape on Jan. 28, 1989, and given the same sentence as Bailey. The third defendant, James Whyte, received twenty-five years' probation in exchange for turning state's evidence against his two confederates. REF.: *CBA.*

Bailey, Norman Percival, d.1924, Brit., suic. Major Bailey was a distinguished officer in the British military during WWI, after which, traumatized by the horrors of the war, he suffered from depression and recurring nightmares that forced him to relive the war. On Dec. 7, 1923, Bailey's wife was found shot and stabbed to death in the bedroom of their home in Hove. Bailey had disappeared. Six months later, his body was found floating in the Thames River with a bullet wound in the head and an army revolver in his clothing.

The case of his mysterious death went to trial without a suspect, the purpose being to determine whether Bailey committed suicide or was murdered. Attorney Sir Bernard Spilsbury, maintained that Bailey had killed himself in response to severe depression he had been fighting for some time. Spilsbury maintained that Bailey, an expert swimmer, jumped into the river and shot himself in the head while in the water. Testimony from the medical examiner supported this assumption and further explained that it would be nearly impossible for a man to first shoot himself and then plunge into the river.

The jury, taking Bailey's current mental state into consideration, ruled that the death was a suicide that resulted from combat-induced depression. The death of Mrs. Bailey remains a mystery.

REF.: *CBA;* Townsend, *Black Cap Murder Will Out.*

Bailey, Raymond (AKA: **Ray Carter**), d.1958, Aus., mur. Raymond Bailey was driving a DeSoto sedan with his wife on the Alice Springs-Port Augusta Highway in South Australia on Dec. 6, 1957. In the middle of the night, Bailey left his caravan, carrying with him a Huntsman single-shot rifle. He used it on Thyra Bowman, her 15-year-old daughter Wendy, and their friend Tom Whelan, who had set up camp for the night in the wilderness.

The Bowmans were on their way to Adelaide when they were

overtaken by Bailey. Their bodies were located by an aerial search party looking for their missing automobile. Near their campfire several .22-caliber shell casings were found which matched the rifle found in Bailey's possession. In Kulgera, several eyewitnesses reported seeing a DeSoto sedan. The car was spotted on Jan. 21, 1958, by Constable Glen Hallahan at Mount Isa in Queensland.

When questioned by police, Bailey said his name was Carter. He could not, however, explain a concealed .32-caliber handgun sewn under the front seat of his car. The suspect finally confessed to the shootings, but changed his story four times. Bailey was extradited to Adelaide and tried for murder. Deliberations opened on May 12, 1958, Sir Geoffrey Reed presiding. Less than eight days later the jury returned a verdict of Guilty. The death sentence was imposed within minutes, and Bailey was executed at the Adelaide Jail on June 24.

REF.: *CBA; Clegg, Return Your Verdict.*

Bailey, Reese, prom. 1936, U.S., rob. Known as the "Robin Hood of North Carolina," Bailey had had a long career of robbing banks before a gun battle with federal agents in Chillicothe, Ohio, ended in his capture. He participated in his last great heist in 1935 when he and several others joined forces to rob the Rosalia State Bank in Rosalia, Wash.

To divert the attention of the citizens of the small town, the bank robbers set a nearby house ablaze. As police and citizens ran to the burning structure, the robbers walked into the bank wearing Mexican hats, garish clothing, and makeup. An accomplice waited outside near the getaway car, clothed in a long dress and armed with a shotgun. Word quickly spread to the volunteer firefighters that the bank was being robbed and Marshal Bert Lemley rushed to the bank. When he arrived he was quickly gunned down by the dress-clad wheelman.

Once Lemley was shot, the bank robbers ran out of the bank taking cashier Matt Elliot hostage. As they sped away, squad cars pursued, and to facilitate their escape, the robbers threw roofing nails from the broken rear window of the getaway car which punctured the tires of the pursuing officers' car. The thieves made a clean getaway and later pushed hostage Elliot out of the speeding car.

Federal investigators believed the robbery was organized by Reese Bailey, a known criminal who had employed the same techniques in previous robberies. In November 1936, he was tracked to a rented farm in Chillicothe after he had applied for license renewal on his automobile in nearby Waverly. On Nov. 26, 1936, federal agents cornered Bailey on the farm, where he was wounded in a shootout and taken into custody.

Bailey was tried and convicted for attacking the officers, receiving a sentence of twenty years in Alcatraz. For his part in the Rosalia bank robbery, he was sentenced to life in prison.

REF.: *CBA; Cohen, One Hundred True Crime Stories.*

Bailey, Robert Ballard, prom. 1950, U.S., (wrong. convict) mur. Bailey was convicted in 1950 for the murder of a West Virginia housewife. In 1960, the governor of West Virginia granted Bailey a pardon after he was ruled innocent.

After his conviction, Bailey, who had already served two prison terms in a West Virginia penitentiary, appealed the decision all the way to the U.S. Supreme Court. The high court denied his request for appeal and he was sentenced to be the first to die in the state's new electric chair. Just two days before Bailey's scheduled execution, prison warden Orel Skeen granted him a reprieve from death row, as he believed Bailey was innocent. With the assistance of attorney Erle Stanley Gardner, Skeen succeeded in winning a pardon for the convicted man, who was freed after serving ten years for a crime he did not commit.

REF.: *CBA; Gardner, Court of Last Resort.*

Bailey, Robert Taylor (AKA: **James Lofton**), 1922-45, U.S., rape-mur. Dorothy Braun had been warned by her widowed mother not to pick up hitchhikers along the road. The 32-year-old social worker from Kenosha, Wis. assured her that she and her girlfriend, Neil Pietrangeli would do no such thing, "unless he's a soldier."

After spending the Labor Day weekend in Kenosha, the two women were returning to their jobs in the central part of the state. Mrs. Anna Braun had urged them to take a bus rather than drive, but the green 1941 coupe was barely a year old, and the late summer weather was ideal for a drive. At the outset of their journey, Braun and Pietrangeli had $110 in cash and a $10 check issued to Braun.

When the two reached the outskirts of Sparta in the early morning, they spotted a hitchhiker wearing a U.S. army uniform. The man, Robert Bailey, had a long history of burglary and larceny. He had spent six months on a Mississippi road gang but escaped to join the army. A violent, dangerous psychopath, Bailey had deserted the army twice and was carrying a stolen .45-caliber army revolver when Braun and Pietrangeli picked him up. He leaped into their car and ordered the two to drive to a wooded area outside of town, where he forced them to remove their clothing and raped them. He then shot Pietrangeli and dragged her body into the brush, then fired two shots into Braun and left her at the side of the road, fleeing with the car.

An hour later a passing milkman, Alick Chambers, spotted her in the ditch. She was barely able to reconstruct the terrible events before dying of her wounds in the private office of a local doctor. Bailey meanwhile drove west into Le Sueur, Minn., where he cashed Braun's check at a local bank. He endorsed the check in her name, listing his army serial number.

Bailey continued on through Minneapolis. In the small town of Anoka, thirteen miles north of the city, a waitress in a roadside diner served him a cup of coffee, commenting on the tragedy, which by this time was front-page news. "It's too bad they don't seem to be able to catch those fellows from Wisconsin," she said. Bailey's face turned white. When he dropped a nickel on the counter, hurried out of the diner and drove away, the waitress recognized the green coupe from newspaper descriptions.

Bailey was apprehended in California and returned to Wisconsin to stand trial. He pleaded guilty to a charge of murder on Sept. 29, 1942, and was sentenced to life imprisonment at the state correctional facility at Waupun. On July 5, 1945, he died from what doctors described as a low-grade cerebral hemorrhage. The body was transported back to Bailey's family home in Hattiesburg, Miss., for burial. REF.: *CBA.*

Bailhache, Sir **Clement Meacher,** 1856-1924, Brit., jur. Bailhache as solicitor, then barrister of civil matters. He was appointed judge of the King's Bench, Division of the High Court from 1912 until his death in a boating accident in 1924. He was the presiding judge in the Thomas Clanwaring and Arthur Beard murder cases. REF.: *CBA.*

Baillie of Jerviswood (Robert Baillie), d.1684, Scot., consp. Led nationalist movement to overthrow Anglican domination and establish the Scottish Presbyterian Church. In 1683, he journeyed to London where the Duke of Monmouth and Lord Russell implicated him in the Rye House Plot against King Charles II. He was hanged in Edinburgh in 1684. REF.: *CBA.*

Bailly, Jean Sylvain, 1736-93, Fr., treas. Astronomer and political leader who set aside his scientific studies of Halley's Comet to serve as mayor of Paris and President of States-General in 1789. He imposed martial law on the French people, quickly fell from popularity, and was guillotined. REF.: *CBA.*

Bain, John, b.1868, U.S., fraud. Bain was a self-made man who acquired a fortune from a chain of twelve Chicago banks he founded. In June 1932, he was convicted on charges of defrauding depositors when all twelve banks failed with only $300,000 left in reserves to pay the 150,000 depositors a total of $13 million owed to them.

The crash occurred after several years of bad investments, shaky real estate ventures, and juggled assets caught up with the banker. Bain was sentenced to one to five years in prison. REF.: *CBA.*

Bain, Robert Owen (AKA: **Roger O. Billings, Ralph O. Boswell, Ralph O. Bosworth, R.O. Brewster,** and **R.O. Brigham**), prom. 1900s, U.S., rob.-forg.-embezz. Bain led detectives on a four-year search and evaded capture for embezzling more than $28,000 in funds from two companies before his chance meeting with William J. Burns agent, Detective Ray Schindler, in a New York City store. Schindler, manager of the New York City office of the Burns agency, was hired by the American Bankers Association after Bain skipped town with almost $10,000 he had stolen from an inactive savings account drawn on the Chicago bank where he worked.

Over a four-year period, Bain embezzled corporate funds totaling $10,000 from the Chicago bank, and an additional $18,000 from a Chicago steel company. He also forged several hundred dollars in stolen checks drawn on the account of the steel company and stole $6,500 from his wife and mother-in-law. After a long police search and hours of stakeouts, Bain was taken into custody by New York City policemen after Schindler wrestled him to the floor of the Rogers Peet store. Schindler happened upon Bain after a failed setup attempt using Evelyn Saunders, who had slept with Bain but had also been robbed by him when he stole several expensive items from her jewelry collection. The stolen jewelry was found in his possession, and he was arrested on charges of theft.

Bain was convicted and sentenced to prison for jewel theft. On his release, he was to immediately go to trial for embezzlement, but his wealthy parents agreed to an out-of-court settlement, and the American Bankers Association dropped the charges.

REF.: *CBA*; Hughes, *The Complete Detective*.

Baird, P.C., d.1928, U.S., lawman. P.C. Baird served with the Texas Rangers and rose to the rank of sergeant in Company D, Frontier Battalion. Baird and two other Rangers encountered several fence-cutters near the Greer ranch near Green Lake on July 29, 1884, the offenders being known outlaws. When the Rangers ordered these men, about five in number, to surrender, the outlaws fired on them. In the return fire, Baird shot and killed John Bailey, also known as John Mason. A Ranger was wounded in the gunfight but all the outlaws were captured. Baird was elected sheriff of Mason County in 1888 and in the following year, a gunfight broke out in Mason inside Garner's Saloon. Baird and a deputy raced down the street to investigate, and at that moment, two brothers, Jesse and John Simmons stepped from the saloon with shotguns blazing at the lawmen. Baird and his deputy stood calmly in the middle of the street and took aim at the brothers who were advancing on them, both in an obvious state of drunkenness. Baird fired a single shot which hit John Simmons, killing him, and his deputy dispatched Jesse Simmons. Baird served as sheriff of Mason County through 1898 and then retired. He died on Mar. 9, 1928, in San Antonio, Texas.

REF.: Bartholomew, *A Biographical Album of Western Gunfighters*; *CBA*.

Bakaris, Saleh Abdullah (AKA: Hag Saleh), prom. 1965-69, Yemen, mur. During the last years of British colonial rule in the Middle-Eastern nation of Yemen, Saleh Bakaris led a team of hired assassins in a guerilla war with the Marxist National Liberation Front. The NLF sought to expel the British forcibly, which they did in 1969. The new political leaders placed Bakaris in charge of "security forces." When he failed to show proper enthusiasm for the new government, he too was assassinated.

REF.: Bell, *Assassin!*; *CBA*.

Baker, Dr. Abner, Jr., d.1845, U.S., mur. The murder of Daniel Bates by Dr. Abner Baker arose from a long-standing feud between the Baker-Bates families of Kentucky. Baker encountered Bates, his brother-in-law, on the street in Cumberland, Ky., and, after the two arch enemies exchanged a few heated words, Bates began to walk off. Dr. Baker withdrew his pistol and fired pointblank into Bates' back, killing him. After a quick hearing, packed with Baker allies, the doctor was released, judged insane. He immediately went into hiding and the Bates family, hearing of the murder and the obviously rigged judicial decision, posted wanted flyers throughout the county offering a sizable reward for the capture of Dr. Baker.

A Baker clan meeting was held and patriarchs of the family decided that it was a matter of family honor that their kinsman be cleared of all charges at a formal trial. Dr. Baker was turned over to authorities and he was immediately put on trial. The Baker strategy backfired, for a jury not only found Baker Guilty of first-degree murder, but he was judged sane enough to be executed. Despite a menacing uproar from the Baker clan, filled with weighty petitions and letters begging officials to pardon Dr. Baker, the volatile physician was hanged on Oct. 3, 1845.

REF.: *CBA*; Crozier, *Life and Trial of Dr. Abner Baker, Jr.*

Baker, Andrew, 1978-88, U.S., drug. Ten-year-old Andrew Baker was described as a healthy child and a nice boy. So when he died while swimming as a result of cocaine consumption, citizens in his hometown of Joliet, Ill., were shocked. In April 1988, while swimming, Baker passed out and drowned as a result of a fungus that had grown in the boy's heart from the use of cocaine. A coroner's investigation revealed that the boy had used or been given drugs several times, including shortly before his death. Should they apprehend the dealer who supplied the cocaine, the state's attorney's office will consider pressing murder charges. REF.: *CBA*.

Baker, A.Y., prom. 19th Cent., U.S., fraud-tax evas. Known as the "Millionaire Sheriff," Hidalgo County, Texas, Sheriff A.Y. Baker and several cronies defrauded county residents of more than $6 million by siphoning profits from expensive public improvement programs. Baker eventually was sentenced to prison for income tax evasion.

REF.: *CBA*; Hynd, *The Giant Killers*.

Baker, Cullen Montgomery, 1835-69, U.S., west. outl. Baker was born in Weekly County, Tenn., on June 22, 1835, the son of a poor farmer who took his family to Cass County (later Davis County), Texas, in 1839. The boy grew up dirt poor and, because of his homespun trousers and bare feet, was the butt of jokes by other boys. Slender, sallow-faced Baker finally fought back, beating the biggest boy in the area. Baker was a lonely, withdrawn boy who read books of knights and ancient heroes and dreamed of becoming a valiant westerner who would command respect. He obtained an old pistol at age twelve and began practicing a quick draw from his waistband. He then acquired a rusty but workable rifle and practiced shooting each day with both weapons, becoming an expert marksman by the time he was fifteen—the age when he took his first long drink of whiskey. When in his teenage cups, the drunken boy would challenge adults who annoyed him to "go for your guns." But Baker's reputation of being a crack shot caused all to back away from him. This encouraged a growing braggart personality that boasted of great deeds never accomplished. On one occasion, just for the sadistic joy it gave him, Baker pulled his pistol on an old man and terrorized him in a local town, driving the old man from the city limits and laughing hilariously.

At the age of nineteen, Baker ordered all the youths in the area to stage a mock cowboys-and-Indians battle—a wild melée in which he was struck in the head with a tomahawk and knocked unconscious. The blow seemed to bring Baker to his senses as he lay in bed for several weeks recovering. He told his parents that he had been a fool, that someone would eventually come along and best him at his own vicious games and he would wind up dead. He vowed to reform. Some weeks later, in January 1854, still wearing a head bandage, Baker married 17-year-old Jane Petty and he settled down to quiet farming. But he soon tired of this routine and took up his old ways of violence. He forced other teenagers to carry him on their shoulders through the towns while he drove them on by pecking at their heads with knives or slamming the butt of his pistol against the sides of their heads. One youngster named Stallcup, an orphan, received the brunt of Baker's bullying. Baker chased him about with a whip on an August day in 1854, lashing the terrified child. His guardian brought suit against Baker and a farmer named Bailey, who had witnessed the whipping, testified in court against Baker who was heavily fined, warned to mind his manners, and sent on his way.

Baker showed up at Bailey's house an hour after the trial, his pistol tucked into his waistband. He called Bailey outside and the farmer stepped onto his porch, a pistol in his hand, limp at his side. "So you'd talk against me, huh, Bailey," Baker said with a sneer. "Well, you got a gun. Use it while you got the chance!" The farmer hesitated for a moment, then yanked the pistol upward and fired a quick shot that whizzed past Baker's head. Baker drew his weapon and fired two shots, one hitting Bailey in the chest, the other in the head, propelling him backward through his front door so that he fell dead in front of his horrified family. Baker rode quickly away and was absent from Cass County, hiding out with relatives in Perry County, Ark., for almost two years. He took his ugly nature with him to Arkansas where he stabbed to death a man named Wartham in an argument about horses. Baker returned to Cass County in 1856 but fled when he learned that he was still wanted to face murder charges in the killing of Bailey. After another two years in Arkansas, Baker once more returned to Texas, but only to retrieve his wife and daughter, resettling them in Arkansas. His wife died on July 2, 1860, and Baker took their child to Sulphur County, Texas, and the home of Hubbard Petty, his daughter's grandfather, leaving the child in the old man's care. He never saw his daughter again.

Authorities in Perry County, Ark., pressed charges against Baker for the Wartham killing and he fled back to Cass County, Texas, where officials dropped murder charges against him for the killing of Bailey. Baker told one and all he was through with killing, that he was a reformed man, but it was an old story. A local belle, Martha Foster, fell in love with Baker and they were married on July 1, 1862. A short time later, Baker was conscripted into the Confederate Army and sent to Little Rock, Ark., to serve with his company. He was a poor soldier, often absent without leave, returning to Texas to ostensibly visit his wife and family but in reality to escape the discipline of army life. Finally, Baker refused to return to his company, settling near Spanish Bluffs, Ark., on a small farm, stating that he was growing corn for the Confederacy, a much more important role than soldiering since the South needed food. The area was occupied by northern troops under the command of Captain F.S. Dodge in Spring 1864. These Union soldiers were all blacks, which incensed the southerners in the area, particularly Baker, who hated Negroes. Three black soldiers and a sergeant entered the local saloon at Spanish Bluffs where they saw a single customer at the bar. It was Baker, wearing a broad Confederate hat. The sergeant demanded identification papers from Baker and he turned with a gun in his hand, shooting the sergeant and then the other three soldiers.

Now Baker was wanted by both sides, by the Confederate Army as a deserter and by the Union forces as a killer. He fled to Little Rock, which had also been occupied by northern troops, and there took the oath of allegiance and joined the Union Army using a false name and claiming that he had been a Confederate officer. Ironically, he was placed in charge of a company of black troops. He deserted the Union Army and returned to Texas, staying with his uncle, Tom Young. By late 1864, Texas was overrun with deserters from both armies, and these freebooters roamed the countryside as bandits. Baker fell in with one group and soon became their leader, robbing farmers trying to flee the area as they crossed the Saline River. He looted farms and ranches throughout the territory.

One story, perhaps apocryphal, has Baker and his band of thieves rustling a great herd of cattle, including livestock taken from a widow named Drew, near Jefferson. Baker stopped at Mrs. Drew's farm where she told him that robbers had just taken her herd. She offered Baker a substantial reward if he could find the rustlers and deal with them, returning her cattle. He promised to do what he could, pretending to be shocked at the wholesale robbery. A short time later, Baker caught up with his band, ordering them to separate the Drew cattle from the rest, and these were driven back to the Drew ranch where Baker received a cash reward which was more than what he and his men would have realized had they sold off the stolen cattle elsewhere.

When the war ended, Baker, to avoid arrest for his many robberies, moved to the Sulphur River area in southwestern Arkansas where he became the manager of the Line Ferry, settling down for a while with his wife Martha, who took ill and died on Mar. 1, 1866. Baker seemed to have truly loved his second wife; he was grief-stricken for weeks, even making a lifelike effigy of her which he adorned with her clothes and placed upon his front porch for all the neighbors to see. He was finally persuaded to remove this mannequin in the interest of good taste. Baker later proposed to Bell Foster, his dead wife's 16-year-old sister, but she rejected him in favor of local schoolteacher, Thomas Orr. Baker later picked a fight with Orr and cracked the teacher's head with a tree limb. He later went to Orr's small school and ridiculed Orr before his students, cursing him and threatening to shoot his head "off from your shoulders!" So bitter was Baker at being rejected by Bell Foster that he continued to plague the teacher, who had a crippled arm, with threats, writing Orr letters in which he promised to beat or shoot the teacher if he ever found out that Orr missed any classes.

By early 1867, Baker had returned to Cass County, Texas, where he continued to make a nuisance of himself, exercising his bullyboy tactics at every opportunity. On June 1, 1867, Baker arrived at the Rowden store and, finding it locked, broke inside and took whatever goods he wanted. Before he rode away, Mrs. Rowden arrived and asked him what he was doing. Baker told her he would pay for the goods later. When Rowden returned and heard from his wife how Baker had helped himself to his provisions, the shopkeeper rode to Baker's small ranch and demanded payment. He carried a shotgun at his side. "Sure, I'll pay you in a few days," Baker told him. On June 5, 1867, Baker appeared at Rowden's store and called the storekeeper outside. Mrs. Rowden and her children begged Rowden not to go outside, knowing the fierce reputation of Cullen Baker. Rowden nevertheless grabbed his shotgun and stepped onto the porch of his store.

"What do you mean by speaking so disrespectfully to me?" Baker shouted to Rowden.

"I'm sure I never meant to do such a thing," Rowden replied.

Before another word could be uttered, Baker whipped out his six-gun and fired four shots into the store owner. He was hit in the chest by all four bullets and fell forward, dead. Baker returned home to hear some days later that citizens in the area were organizing a huge posse to arrest him for the Rowden killing. He sent a message to town stating that he would kill anyone who attempted to bring him to trial over a "fair fight," pointing out that Rowden had been armed with a shotgun. Texas was still occupied by Union troops at the time and the Union commander at Jefferson, Texas, sent a patrol to Pett's Ferry, where Baker was staying, to arrest the gunman. A sergeant and a private found Baker at the ferry and asked him his name.

"It's Johnson," Baker lied, "but what in hell makes you so particular?"

"We thought you might be Cullen Baker," the sergeant told him, fingering his pistol, "the man we are searching for. From your weapons and the way you're dressed, I am inclined to believe you are Baker." The sergeant, a fearless type, pulled his pistol but before he could level it at Baker, the gunman whipped out his own six-gun and blazed off four shots, all of which struck the sergeant, blowing him off the saddle, dead. The private lashed his horse about and raced back to the detachment to report the killing.

Baker fled, going down river and hiding in Bowie County, but troops scouring the area for him, encircled his hiding place the next day. Baker, realizing that he had no chance against a company of soldiers, began to shout: "Charge them, boys! Charge them!" The soldiers, believing that they were facing a large band of outlaws led by Baker, fled in panic. Some days later, a small group of soldiers encountered Baker riding a mule and a gunfight erupted. Baker shot one of the soldiers dead before the rest of the troopers took flight. On Oct. 10, 1867, Baker stopped a Union supply wagon escorted by a four-man patrol. The driver reached for his pistol but Baker shot him dead and drove off the other soldiers with withering gunfire. He then stole the supply wagon.

Baker was now a much-wanted man with a $1,000 reward posted for his capture, dead or alive.

More than 600 soldiers were assigned to track the outlaw down and these troopers fanned out in small contingents throughout the territory. One, led by Captain Kirkham, found Baker in Boston, Texas. Baker, seeing he was surrounded by at least two dozen heavily-armed troopers, boldly marched up to Captain Kirkham and said: "I'm Cullen Baker. You looking for me?"

Kirkham went for his pistol but Baker's lightning draw produced his pistol first which barked and sent a single bullet into Kirkham's head, killing him instantly. Before Kirkham's men could react, Baker jumped on his horse and raced out of town. In November 1868, Baker organized another outlaw band which raided farms and ranches along the Red River and ranged as far as Sevier and Little River counties in Arkansas. Baker and his men, in one raid, shot and killed two government agents named Andrews and Willis. When Baker received news that more than a thousand troopers were searching for him, he stole an officer's uniform and impersonated a Union captain, requesting and receiving supplies from local farmers, saying that his troops needed fresh supplies in their search for the notorious outlaw, Cullen Baker.

With the troopers and lawmen of two states looking for him, Baker took to writing letters to local newspapers in which he attempted to justify his actions, portraying himself a victim of the Civil War, a defender of the white man's rights against black carpetbaggers, and that he would willingly submit himself to the justice of "unbiased men" if any could be found who were not influenced by the lies spread throughout Texas and Arkansas about him. Baker then rode back to the Foster home, still seething about Bell Foster, who had since married Thomas Orr. He and his men surrounded the Foster home and Baker demanded that his ex-father-in-law turn Orr over to him. Foster did so, on the promise that the crippled school teacher would not be harmed. It was Baker's sadistic intention to show Bell that he could do what he pleased with her ineffectual husband. He forced the teacher to ride behind one of his men with a rope affixed about his neck, the end of which Baker held in his hand as he rode ahead. He stopped a few miles away and tied the rope around the limb of dogwood tree, then ordered the man behind whom Orr was riding to spur his horse onward, leaving the teacher dangling.

Baker and his men rode on, but the bandit chief had second thoughts about losing his best rope. He turned to one of his men and shouted: "Cut down that wretch and drag him away! And bring me that rope!" Orr was cut down and left for dead as the band rode away. But Orr miraculously survived his own hanging and vowed to track down his tormentor. On Jan. 6, 1869, Orr, with three others, followed Baker and an accomplice to a hideout in southeastern Arkansas, coming upon the two men just as they were squatting next to a fire, having lunch. Orr and the others did not call out to the outlaws to surrender, knowing what their answer would be. The teacher and his companions rode down on Baker and his henchman with their six-guns blazing, shooting both men dead on the spot. Orr found that his old adversary was a walking arsenal. Strapped to his side was a double-barrelled shotgun. Baker was also wearing four six-guns, three derringers, and six knives. Also found on Baker's corpse was a carefully kept packet of newspaper clippings which described him as "the Arkansas brigand," and the most feared gunman in the Lone Star State who had spread "a reign of terror in Texas." Many historians have portrayed Baker as a soft-spoken southern gentlemen who was compelled to take up the gun, although he kept his scruples intact and was a gentleman when treating with women and children. He was anything but this, a vicious gunman, an immoral, ruthless killer, a man who despised culture and education. His death at the hands of a meek-mannered school teacher was poetic justice indeed.

REF.: Bartholomew, *Cullen Baker;* _____, *The Biographical Album of Western Gunfighters;* Bivens, *Memoirs;* Breihan, *Great Gunfighters of the West; CBA;* Cunningham, *Triggernometry;* Holloway, *Texas Gun Lore;* O'Neal, *Encyclopedia of Western Gunfighters;* Orr, *Life of the Notorious Desperado, Cullen Baker, From His Childhood to His Death, with a Full Account of the Murders He Committed;* Ray, *Murder at the Corners;* Ripley, *They Died With Their Boots On;* Steen, *The Texas News;* Taylor, *Bill Longley and His Wild Career;* Waters, *A Gallery of Western Bad Men;* Webb, *The Handbook of Texas.*

Baker, Frederick, 1838-67, Brit., mur. Baker met three small girls—8-year-old Minnie Warner, 7-year-old Lizzie Adams, and 8-year-old Fanny Adams—while they played in a meadow near Alton, Hampshire, on Aug. 24, 1867. Baker gave Minnie and Lizzie three halfpence each to spend on candy. He also paid Fanny three halfpence to go with him for a walk to a nearby field. Later that evening the little girl's head was found lying in a bloody pool in that field. Her body had been dismembered, and her limbs and internal organs strewn haphazardly throughout the area. About the time the girl's eyeballs were found floating in a nearby river, Baker was seen talking to a friend over a beer in a local pub.

Minnie Warner later identified Baker as the man who had given them the money and he was taken into custody. A search of his home turned up several items of evidence: blood stained clothing, two small knives, and, most damaging of all, a diary. In the entry dated Aug. 24, Baker had written, "Killed a young girl. It was fine and hot."

Baker's diary proved to be the most damaging piece of evidence introduced during his trial. The jury immediately found him Guilty and sentenced him to death. Baker was executed at Winchester prison in December. REF.: *CBA.*

George Baker (Father Divine) with wife Edna.

Baker, George (AKA: **Father Divine**), c.1882-1965, U.S., fraud. George Baker's origins are hazy but it is fairly certain that he was not, as he once claimed, "combusted one day in 1900 on the corner of Seventh Avenue and 134th Street in Harlem." He was born about 1882 in the South, most probably Georgia, where he worked on a plantation as a young man. He later worked as a gardener for $3 a week. He met a traveling preacher named Samuel Harris and learned the art of addressing crowds, particularly at black hallelujah gatherings. Shrewd and cunning far beyond the gullible nature of his own people, Baker soon realized that he could manipulate audiences better than his employer. In 1914, he struck out on his own, appearing in backwater Georgia counties where he boomed: "I be God, you be God, drop your yoke of bondage." He announced that he was The Messenger, or John Doe, alias God, or God in the Sunship Degree. This gobbledygook went over well with his naive followers whose deep poverty and lack of education caused them to rush to his side, embracing whatever philosophy he cared to spew forth.

Baker, who was now called Father Divine, appealed mostly to female blacks whose "yoke of bondage" consisted of cooking and cleaning for their husbands, a burden they wished to abandon. Scores of husbands quickly filed complaints against Father Divine for fraud and, in 1915, ironically coinciding with the rebirth of the Ku Klux Klan in Georgia, a Georgia court convicted him. Rather than imprison and make a local martyr out of him, the court ordered Father Divine to leave the state. He departed with a number of followers, mostly female, including a new and personable wife named Peninah. The cult arrived in New York and settled in Sayville, Long Island, where he established a rollicking commune. Every Sunday his wife, an excellent cook, prepared a sumptuous feast of fried chicken, ribs, stew, mashed potatoes, vegetables of all varieties, and mountains of homemade ice cream. The Sunday meetings conducted by Father Divine were half lecture and half feast, and soon scores of blacks from the depressed areas of the Bronx and Brooklyn flocked to Long Island to see the new preacher.

Father Divine's message to them was simple. If they did exactly as he told them, they would live forever, never die, and have eternal happiness and wealth beyond their wildest imaginations. He established dormitories for men and women and sent them out to work as cheap labor gangs. In return for their keep and Peninah's cooking, the followers gave almost all their income to Father Divine. He grew rich and his cult expanded to the point where local residents began to complain about his revival meetings and general operations, charging fraud and disturbing the peace. Official charges were finally brought against Father Divine who faced trial on May 24, 1932, standing before Judge Lewis J. Smith. The defendant and his followers promised terrible retribution if the Messenger was punished, but Judge Smith ignored these threats and, after conviction, sentenced Father Divine to a year in jail and fined him $500. Four days later, although he was in good health, 50-year-old Judge Smith died. Father Divine seized upon this happenstance and said loudly in his cell: "I hated to do it," clearly implying that, as God, he had been instrumental in Judge Smith's departure from this world.

This "miracle" caused hundreds of disbelievers to embrace Father Divine's patchy religion. When he moved to Harlem in 1933, he was overwhelmed with destitute followers. Already wealthy from his Long Island operation, Father Divine purchased several run-down boarding houses, calling these "Heavens," and moved his flock into them. His organization grew over the years until Father Divine was one of the most powerful and influential residents of Harlem, a man who decided elections and decreed how much money each follower had to tithe to his church each year. He was many times a millionaire before he died but he had, according to many of his followers, betrayed the cult and his people in his absolute greed for money. Moreover, Father Divine abandoned his first black wife and two more before marrying a white Canadian blonde, Edna Rose Ritchings, whom he renamed Sweet Angel.

Father Divine kept from his people the fact that his first wife, Peninah, died of cancer. Mortal death had been banished by Father Divine and to admit its reality was to destroy his ministry. He explained to his disgruntled followers that his wife, Sweet Angel, was the reincarnation of his first spouse, Peninah. Though he claimed he owned nothing, that everything was owned by the ministry (this, of course, to avoid IRS problems), Father Divine lived like a king while his followers continued to wear threadbare clothing and feast only at his Sunday banquets. He and Sweet Angel traveled about in Rolls Royce limousines, living in luxury suites of hotels in New York and Philadelphia owned by the ministry. They wore fur coats and were waited upon by a thirty-person staff.

Father Divine claimed to have millions of followers but there were apparently never more than 50,000 believers at a given time. Their utter devotion to him as God, however, assured him with a life of ease and comfort. He died, contrary to his own supernatural dictates, in 1965, as he lay in his four-poster bed, pink silk sheets about his corpulent body. Following his death, the ministry fell off considerably to a handful of diehard believers.

REF.: *CBA;* Hunt, *Dictionary of Rogues;* McKelway, *True Tales From the Annals of Crime and Rascality.*

Baker, James, 1856-86, and **Rudge, Anthony Benjamin,** 1840-86, and **John Martin,** 1852-86, Brit., rob.-mur. During the fall of 1885, Baker, Rudge, and Martin engaged in a spree of robbery and violence that culminated in the death of one police officer and the wounding of two others. The three gang members pulled their final heist on Oct. 28, 1885, in Cumberland when they stole £400 of jewelry from the private collection of Lady Graham. Once the items were found missing, a bulletin went out to police throughout the area and the robbers were cornered near Kingstown.

Resisting the officers with a volley of gunshots, they injured two of the policemen in the fray. The robbers escaped and were approached by Constable Joseph Byrnes at Gosling Dyke. Byrnes attempted to capture the burglars, but they shot him in the head and dumped the dying man in a nearby field.

Police began a county-wide manhunt for the murderers, and Baker, Martin, and Rudge were soon captured. The three were convicted and sentenced to death for the murder of Byrnes. At the gallows, Martin confessed to the murder, but all three were hanged for the crime on Mar. 8, 1886.

REF.: *CBA;* Whitbread, *The Railway Policemen.*

Baker, Joseph (Boulanger), b.1800, U.S., pir.-mur. Joseph Baker, a Canadian, signed on board the merchant schooner *Eliza,* sailing from Philadelphia to the West Indies. Once on the high seas, Baker put into effect his mutinous plans, which he had earlier outlined to two other seamen, Peter LaCroix and Joseph Berrouse. These three, during a night watch, crept up on the first mate and threw him into the sea after a fierce struggle. When Captain William Wheland heard the commotion, he dashed from his cabin. Baker wounded him and made him prisoner. The greedy eyes the mutineers had cast upon the ship's cargo had blinded them to the fact that none of them knew how to navigate the ship to a safe port where they could sell the goods on board.

Captain Wheland, a shrewd judge of his captors, promised that he would sail the ship to "the Spanish Main" where the mutineers could join fellow pirates. Baker nodded agreement, telling Wheland that he could live long enough to get the ship to a safe haven. He told LaCroix and Berrouse that he intended to cut the Captain's throat once they were in sight of land. None of this intrigue was lost on Wheland who patiently waited for his opportunity. It came when LaCroix and Berrouse were below decks, taking inventory of the stock they had stolen. A single hatchway led to the hold and Wheland closed and locked this, trapping two of his enemies. Baker was at the wheel and Wheland managed to sneak up behind him with an ax which he used to chase the suddenly terrified Baker to the mainmast, ordering him to climb into the rigging where he could keep an eye on him. Baker dutifully climbed to the highest perch and there, obedient to the shouted orders of Captain Wheland, lashed himself to the mast.

Through heavy seas, the *Eliza* made her way southwest. Single-handedly, in what must be a record of heroic endurance, Captain Wheland, who tied himself to the wheel, sailed his vessel for fourteen days. He hardly slept while keeping an eye on the cargo hold door, listening to LaCroix and Berrouse bang uselessly away at the bolt, shouting promises and threats. And up in the rigging sat the truculent Baker, food and drink sent up to him by rope, pleading with Wheland to let him come down and alternately cursing and threatening him. Wheland sailed into St. Kitts, exhausted but triumphant, turning over the mutineers to U.S. Navy officials who returned the murderous trio to Philadelphia on board the U.S. *Ganges,* a sloop of war.

Once in Philadelphia, the mutineers were tried for murder and piracy, both capital offenses, before the Circuit Court of the U.S. on Apr. 21-25, 1800, all three men being found Guilty and sentenced to death. Baker, LaCroix, and Berrouse were hanged on May 9, 1800, in Philadelphia before thousands of citizens who made it a day of celebration.

REF.: *CBA; The Confession of Joseph Baker; The Last Words and Dying Confession of the Three Pirates; A Narrative of the Horrid Murder & Piracy Committed on Board the Schooner Eliza, of Philadelphia, on the High Seas by Three Foreigners.*

Baker, Louis, See: **Poole, Bill.**

Baker, Mary (Mary Wilcox, AKA: Caraboo), 1795-1865, Brit., fraud. Eighteen-year-old Wilcox ran away from her Devon home searching for the good life. While in London, working as a maid, she met her husband, who later left her to travel to the Orient. Before he went away, he explained to Mary what the Orient was like—its various cultures, customary dress, and many languages. Mary later used this knowledge to acquire fare for travel to the U.S. by defrauding Samuel Worrall of several pounds.

Mary passed herself off to Worrall as an Oriental princess named Caraboo, from the land of Javasu. She said she had arrived in London after being kidnapped by pirates and had escaped by jumping from their ship while it was anchored in the English Channel. Worrall found her story so fascinating that he related her tragedy to a friend who used her as a subject for an article which gave the Javasu princess national notoriety.

Soon a woman from Bristol contacted Worrall to say that she had also been duped by Caraboo. Baker was set up by Worrall with the woman's help. Once her ruse was exposed, she gave a full confession, explaining that she was trying to secure £5 to travel to America. The wealthy Worrall paid her fare to the U.S., but she returned to England in 1824. Mary Baker died in 1865 at the age of seventy. REF.: *CBA.*

Baker, Newton Diehl, 1871-1937, U.S., lawyer. Mayor of Cleveland from 1912-16, and secretary of war under President Woodrow Wilson. REF.: *CBA.*

Baker, Rosetta, 1865-1930, U.S., (unsolv.) mur. Sixty-nine-year-old Baker had become quite a businesswoman since her divorce from her husband. By 1930, she had acquired several apartment buildings in San Francisco's fashionable Nob Hill area and was a prominent figure in the community. Baker had for years employed Liu Fook, a 62-year-old Hong Kong native, to clean and maintain her buildings, and it was Fook who was charged with her murder.

Arriving for work on the morning of Dec. 8, 1930, Fook found Baker's brutally beaten and strangled body lying on her bedroom floor. He ran screaming into the hallway, alerting neighbors. Police investigators determined that Baker had been robbed, as a large sum of money and several items of jewelry had been stolen from the apartment. They charged Fook with the murder after finding several clues at the scene that linked him to the crime. Fook's arrest divided the city, with a majority of the Chinese population rallying behind him in support.

During the trial, Fook maintained his innocence under a barrage of attacks from the prosecuting attorney, who introduced several items of evidence that appeared damaging to the janitor's defense, including his disdain for Baker's lifestyle. Baker had an affinity for young men, and testimony from witnesses revealed she had fired Fook several times for his insistence that she stop her affairs with these men. The lawyer also explained how investigators had found shredded remnants of Fook's clothing at the scene and scratches on the floor that were matched to his shoes.

On Mar. 18, 1931, the jury delivered its verdict after only twenty-one minutes of deliberation. The jury found Fook Not Guilty. He was released, and clamoring crowds of supporters cheered the decision. Four days later, Fook left San Francisco aboard a ship en route to Hong Kong where he was reunited with his Chinese wife.

REF.: *CBA; Rodell, San Francisco Murders.*

Baker, Valentine, prom. 1875, Brit., asslt. In June 1875, while riding on the London and South Western Railway, Colonel Baker, an officer in the British military, sexually assaulted a woman in her compartment until her screams for help were answered. He was taken into custody when the train stopped at Waterloo. After a trial, Baker was sentenced to one year in prison and fined £500. He was forced to resign from the military, but upon his release joined the Turkish military under the Sultan of Turkey.

REF.: *CBA; Whitbread, The Railway Policemen.*

Baker, William Eli, 1873-1954, U.S., jur. Prosecuting attorney for Randolph County, W. Va., from 1900-12. He was appointed federal judge of the Northern District of West Virginia by President Warren G. Harding in 1921. REF.: *CBA.*

Baker Estate Swindle, 1866-1936, Can.-U.S., fraud. The Baker Estate Swindle centered about a fabulous inheritance for almost anyone named Baker who might have been related to Jacob Baker, a wealthy Philadelphia landowner who died in 1839. According to this scheme, anyone named Baker, Becker, or Barker were entitled to land that occupied the center of Philadelphia and was worth between $1 billion and $3 billion. This incredibly wealthy area, the con men who operated this scheme pointed out, included Independence Hall, the Pennsylvania Railroad Station, Benjamin Franklin's grave, and the Liberty Bell—some of America's most hallowed and historical sites. The scheme was begun as early as 1866 in Ontario, Can., where sharpers gleaned a fortune from suckers named Baker who contributed vast sums for legal fees in the battle to free the real estate from local and state control. The scheme was reborn in the late 1880s and at the turn of the century.

William Cameron Morrow Smith

The most flagrant operator of the Baker Estate Swindle was William Cameron Morrow Smith, who took in millions of dollars from gullible investors named Baker. These investors received monthly reports on bogus legal battles in Philadelphia and throughout Pennsylvania as valiant attorneys (who never existed) took on the state legislature in their incessant war to win back for everyone named Baker, Becker, or Barker that which was rightfully theirs. The scheme was particularly effective in the towns of Altooner, Johnstown, and Pittsburgh, Pa., where Smith and his many agents were most active. Alfred T. Hawksworth, an intrepid postal inspector who spent twenty years gathering evidence on the Smith clan, finally had Smith and twenty-eight of his confederates brought to trial in 1936. The 70-year-old Smith, it was proved, had mulcted more than 3,000 people named Baker, Barker, and Becker (even a few named Beck) into contributing more than $4 million to his heroic legal fight. He was given a long prison term and died later in his cell, still writing letters to gullible marks to contribute to *his* legal battle to win a pardon and go on with his crusade to free the property of Jacob Baker from a dogged and nameless probate court.

REF.: *CBA; MacDougall, Hoaxes; Nash, Hustlers and Con Men, An Anecdotal History of the Confidence Man and His Games.*

Bakht Khan, c.1797-1859, India, mut. Former member of the British army who led the Sepoy Mutiny in 1857. After establishing a rebel government, he was driven from Delhi and killed in battle. REF.: *CBA.*

Balboa, Vasco Núñez de, 1475-1517, Spain, treas. Discovered the Pacific Ocean and settled vast areas of the Caribbean on behalf of Spain. He was accused of sedition, stemming from political disputes with the governor of Panama, and was tried, condemned, and executed. REF.: *CBA.*

Baldivieso, Enrique, 1901-   , Bol., lawyer. Teacher of constitutional law who founded the Socialist party in 1936, and served as vice president of Bolivia in 1938. REF.: *CBA.*

Baldridge, Adam, prom. 1685, Madagascar, pir. Adam Baldridge established his pirate headquarters on the islet St. Mary's off Madagascar in 1685 after killing a man in Jamaica. He built a large, imposing fort overlooking warehouses and an inland waterway used by other pirate vessels and merchant ships of all nations. The fort was protected by forty cannon and was virtually impregnable.

Baldridge decided which ships would pass in and out of St. Mary's harbor unmolested. He subdued the local tribes, and natives appealed to Baldridge to arbitrate their disputes, which he did for an exorbitant price.

Within a few years, the port became a haven for Mediterranean pirates. Baldridge supplied their ships, exacting a large toll for his services. Baldridge lived an extravagant life, enjoying his riches and comforts, including a harem of island girls. He was forced to flee to the British colonies in North America in 1697 when the natives discovered he had sold a group of their countrymen into slavery. REF.: Botting, *The Pirates; CBA.*

Baldwin, Alexander White, 1835-69, U.S., jur. Prosecuting attorney for Storey County, Nev., in 1859. He was appointed judge of the District Court of Nevada by President Abraham Lincoln in 1865. REF.: *CBA.*

Baldwin, Henry, 1780-1844, U.S., jur. Member of the House of Representatives from 1817-22, and appointed associate justice of the Supreme Court in 1830, following the death of Associate Justice Bushrod Washington. Serving until 1844, Justice Baldwin upheld the pro-slavery position during his tenure of office. REF.: *CBA.*

Baldwin, James Harris, 1876-1944, U.S., jur. U.S. attorney of Butte, Mont., from 1917-19. Appointed to the bench of the District Court of Montana in 1935 by President Franklin D. Roosevelt. REF.: *CBA.*

Baldwin, Marlene "Brandy", 1941- , U.S., pros. Baldwin was arrested on Dec. 7, 1979, during a raid on a house of prostitution she operated in the posh Forest Hills neighborhood of San Francisco. She was tried and convicted of pandering and sentenced to serve ninety days at the Convent of the Good Shepherd. When questioned about her crime she replied, "I want to put it to rest and write a book about my life." REF.: *CBA.*

Baldwin, Robert, 1804-58, Can., jur. Attorney general of Upper Canada in 1842 and from 1848-51. During that time he significantly revised Canada's judicial system. REF.: *CBA.*

Baldwin, Roger Nash, 1884-1981, U.S., criminol. Roger Baldwin was a specialist in juvenile delinquency and founded the National Civil Liberties Bureau, the forerunner of the present-day ACLU, for which he later served as a director from 1917-50, and national chairman from 1950-55. REF.: *CBA.*

Baldwin, Simeon Eben, 1840-1927, U.S., jur. Chief justice of the Connecticut Supreme Court from 1907-10, and governor of Connecticut from 1910-14. REF.: *CBA.*

Baldwin, Thurman (AKA: Skeeter, Balding, Jack Pipkin), b.1867, U.S., west. outl. Thurman Baldwin worked in Oklahoma as a cowboy and joined the Bill Cook gang in the early 1890s and participated in the gang's many robberies. He was at large for some months after the Cooks were rounded up in 1894-95, but was captured in late 1895 outside of Wichita Falls by Texas Rangers Bob McClure, W.J.L. Sullivan, and W.J. McCauley, along with two other lesser lights of the Cook gang, Jess Snyder and Will Farris. Baldwin, who admitted to having committed some robberies with the Cooks, was tried for robbery before Judge Isaac Parker who sentenced him to thirty years, as severe a sentence as possible for his crimes. Parker, who was known as "The Hanging Judge,"

Thurman "Skeeter" Baldwin

stated that it was not his intention to sentence Baldwin so severely for his crimes of robbery but that he did so because he believed such "severe sentences deter others" from committing similar offenses. Baldwin, a tall, rangy man of few words but one who possessed a considerable sense of humor, replied: "This is a helluva court for a man to plead guilty in." He served ten years and, following his release, is presumed to have led an exemplary life since no criminal record exists beyond that time nor any other trace of the last of the Bill Cook gang.

REF.: Bartholomew, *The Biographical Album of Western Gunfighters; CBA;* Horan and Sann, *Pictorial History of the Wild West;* Hunter, *Peregrinations of a Pioneer Printer;* Hunter and Rose, *The Album of Gunfighters;* Shirley, *Henry Starr, Last of the Real Badmen;* ____ , *Law West of Fort Smith;* Sullivan, *Twelve Years in the Saddle for Law and Order on the Frontiers of Texas;* Wellman, *A Dynasty of Western Outlaws.*

Baleka, Patrick, 1959- , and **Hlomuka, Oupa**, 1953- , and **Motselane, Geoff**, 1947- , Case of, S. Afri., treas. On Nov. 17, 1988, Baleka, Hlomuka, and Motselane were acquitted of treason at the end of the three-and-a-half-year trial of sixteen members of South Africa's largest anti-apartheid organization, the United Democratic Front. The activists were jailed in 1984 and charged with treason, terrorism, murder, and subversion for their part in the violent uprising against the South African government's organized policy of racial discrimination known as apartheid. Baleka, Hlomaku, and Motselane had been denied bail throughout the trial and had already served forty months in a Pretoria prison when they were acquitted. REF.: *CBA.*

Balewa, Sir Abubakar Tafewa, 1912-66, Nigeria, prime minister, assass. Led Nigeria to independence in 1961, and became the country's first prime minister from 1957-66. He was killed in a military coup. REF.: *CBA.*

Balfour, Alexander, 1687-1752, Scot., mur.-escape. Returning from his university studies at St. Andrews for a brief holiday, Balfour became infatuated with his sisters' tutor, a young woman named Anne Robertson who his father had recently hired. Noticing his son's behavior, Lord Burleigh discharged the woman. Alexander was scheduled to make his grand tour of the Continent and his father did not want a commoner interfering with his plans.

During his travels around Europe, Balfour sent Robertson a long, passionate letter saying he would kill any man she married. The tutor paid little heed, marrying a man named Syme. When the lovesick young man returned months later, he traced Robertson to Innerkeithing, where she now lived with her husband and a new child. Balfour, enraged at this betrayal, shot Syme through the heart.

Balfour was arrested several days later and sentenced to death. Before the scheduled execution, Balfour's sister arrived at the prison and secretly exchanged places with him. Disguised in a women's clothing, Balfour escaped in a carriage which stood outside Edinburgh. Balfour's sister was released and, through the intervention of Lord Burleigh, Balfour was granted a royal pardon. He eventually inherited his father's estate, and fifty years later was still in good health and enjoying all the rights and privileges of the family title, proving that in some cases, infamy can go unpunished.

REF.: *CBA;* Mitchell, *Newgate Calendar II.*

Balfour, Jabez Spencer, 1843-1912, Brit., fraud. Balfour's parents were moderately successful people who provided an above-average education for their son and a way of life that was at the edge of the upper crust, one that gave him a sense of superiority and opulence. His father was a minor official for the Ways and Means Office of the House of Commons and his mother was an author of some repute, writing two popular purple-prosed works entitled *Women of Scripture* and *Moral Heroism.* She was able, from the sales of these works, to give her son an education in France and Germany. While in his early twenties, Balfour became a member of parliamentary agents and soon rose to become the director of Lands Allotment Ltd., an appointment, which he later admitted "took me quite by surprise."

Mouthing idealism, Balfour became a self-appointed champion

of the little man in England, vowing that he would bring financially depressed people better housing and a brighter future. These lofty promises got him elected as a Liberal representative to Parliament. This occurred during a period when the small property owner made advances in acquisitions and, as head of the Balfour Group, the enterprising Balfour encouraged investments in Lands Allotment Ltd. and the Liberator Building Society which, under his leadership, increased its holdings from £15,000 in 1867 to £750,000 in 1888. Hotels and homes were built by the firm but profits were largely on paper only and few dividends ever declared, most of the money going into Balfour's own pockets. Balfour showed profits through the sale of land and buildings from one company to another, all of which he controlled or owned, a sort of Peter-to-Paul swindle which was made complicated and almost impenetrable through a labyrinth of documents and deeds.

British super swindler Jabez Balfour portrayed as Napoléon.

A financial panic in 1892 caused investors to make universal withdrawals against the Liberator Building Society, demands the firm could not meet since it held mostly paper assets. The Society collapsed and more than 25,000 people were financially ruined, the very constituents Balfour represented in Parliament. Instead of attempting to explain his position, Balfour fled to Argentina and successfully avoided extradition for three years. During this period, the government assigned a small army of accountants and land experts to examine the miasmic records of the Balfour Group, and by the time Balfour was returned to England in 1895, enough evidence was at hand to convict him of fraud on Nov. 28, 1895. He was sentenced to fourteen years in prison and there drew upon his family talent of writing, producing an excellent record of his incarceration entitled *My Prison Life*, which produced enough sales to make Balfour somewhat comfortable in his old age.

REF.: Balfour, *My Prison Life;* Browne, *The Rise of Scotland Yard; CBA;* Dilnot, *The Real Detective;* Kingston, *Dramatic Days at the Old Bailey;* Marjoribanks, *For the Defense, The Life of Sir Edward Marshall Hall;* Scott, *Concise Encyclopedia of Crime and Criminals;* Symons, *A Pictorial History of Crime;* Woodhall, *Secrets of Scotland Yard.*

Balgar, Robert L. (AKA: **Albert B. Danton, Roger Dilton, Ronald Smith**), prom. 1920-42, U.S., fenc.-fraud-pris. esc. Balgar was first arrested in the early 1920s for mail fraud. While serving seven years at Leavenworth for the crime, he was released to testify in a Chicago trial, but before he arrived in court, he escaped via a restroom in his brother's law offices.

Balgar was a fugitive for the next twenty-two years. After fleeing Chicago, he went to Montreal, Can. and later Europe where he was joined by his longtime girlfriend Rosie Niktin. They married and traveled extensively, eventually returning to the U.S. where he opened a collection agency in Los Angeles from which he fled when FBI agents closed in on him and his wife masquerading as Mr. and Mrs. Albert B. Danton.

Balgar was finally apprehended in New York City where he opened yet another collection agency under the name of Ronald Smith. FBI agents had received a tip on his whereabouts from an acquaintance in Florida, where he and Rosie often vacationed. Twenty-two years after his escape, federal agents confronted Smith at his office, where Balgar finally surrendered to the officers, saying, "It's been a long time, gentlemen." REF.: *CBA.*

Balistrieri, Frank P., 1918- , U.S., consp.-org. crime. As he stood before Judge Terence T. Evans awaiting sentence on extortion and bookmaking charges, Frank Balistrieri, the reputed boss of mob operations in Milwaukee, Wisc., denied all allegations of wrongdoing. "The first time I heard the word Mafia was when I read it in the newspapers," he said. But on May 30, 1984, he was sentenced to thirteen years in federal prison and fined $30,000. A month earlier his two lawyer sons Joseph, forty-three, and John, thirty-five, were found Guilty of extorting money from a vending machine businessman in 1978.

In September 1983, Frank Balistrieri and his sons were indicted along with other ranking organized crime figures from Chicago, Cleveland, and Kansas City on charges of skimming more than $2 million in profits from the Stardust and Fremont hotel-casinos in Las Vegas. It was the first time that investigators had successfully linked mob leaders in four different states.

The casinos were fronted by Allen Glick, an ambitious "boy wonder" from San Diego who arrived in Las Vegas in 1974 and began borrowing from the Central States Teamster's Pension Fund to finance the purchase of the hotels. It was alleged that the 32-year-old Glick had received $162 million from the Teamsters in return for certain guarantees that the mob would be allowed to skim future profits from his Vegas operations. The conspiracy began on Mar. 20, 1974, when Nicholas Civella and Carl DeLuna of the Kansas City family met with Balistrieri to discuss the operation. Then Balistrieri met with Glick alone to secure an option on Argent Corporation. Allen Glick agreed to sell half the corporation to Balistrieri's sons for the trifling sum of $25,000 because, as was pointed out by the mobster, "he had an obligation arising from assistance to Glick in obtaining a pension fund commitment in the amount of $62.75 million."

On Dec. 31, 1985, Balestrieri pleaded guilty to two of eight counts of conspiracy before U.S. District Judge Joseph Stevens, Jr. in Kansas City. The government agreed to drop six charges in return for a guilty plea on the more serious charge of attempting to conceal ownership of the casino and skimming its profits and one count of interstate travel to aid racketeering. He was immediately sentenced to ten years in prison and fined $20,000. The prison term was to run concurrently with the thirteen-year sentence handed down in Milwaukee in 1984. Balistrieri's failing health was the main reason given for his surprise plea of guilty. REF.: *CBA.*

Ball, Ebenezer, d.1811, U.S., count.-mur. Ball was a notorious counterfeiter in rural Washington County, Maine, who had a number of arrests, all made by the local constable, John Tilston Downes. When learning that Ball was flooding the countryside with more bogus money, Downes rode out to Ball's home on Jan. 28, 1811. Ball greeted Downes and his two deputies, Isaac Parker and Stephen Dyer, with a gun in his hand, shouting at Downes: "By God, if you advance another step, I will blow you through!" Downes took that fatal step and Ball shot him in the abdomen. Ball was then seized by Parker and Dyer while Downes quickly bled to death. Both deputies testified at Ball's trial on June 22,

1811, stating that Ball intended to murder the constable. Ball's lawyers, who had pleaded him not guilty before Judge Sewell, argued that the gun Ball brandished had a broken lock and was a useless weapon; they claimed that the gun, long in disuse, had gone off accidentally. The jury was convinced of Ball's guilt through the damning testimony of Parker and Dyer and he was convicted and executed later that year.

REF.: *CBA; The Trial of Ebenezer Ball.*

Ball, Edward, 1917- , Ire., mur. Though the body of 55-year-old Vera Ball was never found, her son Edward was tried and convicted of her murder. Mrs. Ball was the wife of a Dublin physician. Following their separation, she lived with her 19-year-old son in Boosterstown, a suburb of Dublin. On the morning of Feb. 18, 1936, a newspaper delivery man stopped to investigate an automobile parked on an odd angle in Shankill, County Dublin. He found traces of blood on the front seat.

Identifying the car as belonging to Mrs. Ball, police went to the Boosterstwon home. Here they were greeted by Edward Ball, who said he had last seen his mother the previous evening. Police searched the house, turning up several items of bloody clothing and discovering a large stain on his mother's bedroom rug, none of which Ball could explain. When pressed further, he said his mother had suffered a recent bout of depression and had killed herself with a straight razor. Ball said he found her dead in her room, took the body to Shankill, and threw it into the sea.

His explanation did not convince the police, however, and Ball was charged with murdering his mother. Police believed he used a hatchet found in the garden, covered with blood. He was convicted of murder, but the jury also declared him insane. The judge ordered Ball detained at the discretion of the local governor-general.

REF.: *CBA; Deale, Memorable Irish Trials.*

Ball, Eli, prom. 1919, U.S., mur. On Feb. 19, 1919, Ball murdered his sister Lilly Billings, and her husband Abe Billings, as they tried to remove furniture from the rural Kentucky home that had been willed to him by his sister Nell Washam, when she died the previous year. Lilly Billings maintained that she was entitled to some of the farm's furnishings, as it had all been inherited from the family by Nell when her parents died. Ball served several years in a state penitentiary for the murders, but was released to return to the homestead in Bear River Valley, Ky.

REF.: *CBA; Montell, Killings.*

Ball, George (AKA: George Sumner), 1892-1914, Brit., mur. The 22-year-old Ball worked as a clerk in the shop of John Bradfield in Liverpool. He was assisted by a dim-witted 18-year-old, Samuel Angeles Eltoft. Manager of the shop was 40-year-old Christine Catherine Bradfield, a hard taskmaster who was known to neighbors as a kindly person. She tolerated no nonsense in the shop which sold tarpaulins manufactured by her brother John and she was forever prodding Ball, who was known as George Sumner by his employers. On the night of Dec. 10, 1913, Walter Musker Eaves, a ship's steward who was waiting for his girlfriend in Old Hall Street and who was standing directly in front of Bradfield's, suddenly had his new hat knocked off his head when one of the shop's shutters blew off. The shop appeared

Murderer George Ball.

dark but within a few minutes Eltoft appeared and picked up the shutter. Eaves showed him his hat and demanded that he be paid for the damage done to his bowler by the shutter. Eltoft politely asked him to wait and soon emerged with Ball who courteously

paid Eaves two shillings for the creases made in the hat.

Eaves was still in Old Hall Street when, a short time later, both Ball and Eltoft appeared, pushing a tarpaulin-covered cart with considerable effort up the street, and disappearing around the corner. The next day Eaves read a newspaper report about a woman's body being found in the Leeds-Liverpool canal by a bargeman who had fished the body, sewn into a sack, out of the canal. The steward went to the police who had just escorted John Bradfield from the morgue. Bradfield had also responded to the newspaper report when his sister had failed to return home from the shop and he had identified the body, telling officers that he had no idea who would want to murder his sister.

Christine Bradfield

Detective Inspector Duckworth of the Criminal Investigation Department (CID), after interviewing neighbors and shop customers, realized that the only real suspects in the case were the two clerks, Ball and Eltoft. He decided to interview Eltoft first, realizing, when John Bradfield talked about the pair, that the younger clerk was impressionable and gullible. He waited until late on the night of Dec. 11, 1913, then forced his way into Eltoft's room, startling the youth and grilling him so intensely that Eltoft blurted out the fact that his superior, George Ball, had bludgeoned Christine Bradfield to death. He hated her for her constant nagging and, after she ordered him to do something, Ball had suddenly exploded and crushed the woman's head with an iron pipe, forcing Eltoft to help him dispose of the body. Duckworth, placing Eltoft under arrest, then raced to Bell's boarding house but the young man had fled. His landlady later stated that Ball had returned home the night before and she had noticed bloody scratches on his face. He told her that he had received the injuries at the shop where he worked, adding: "It's a rotten business."

The scratches, coupled with some of Eltoft's confusing statements later given in court, suggested that Ball had raped the spinster in a back room of the shop and she had scratched his face; in retaliation he had struck her on the head with the pipe.

The Liverpool police, despite a desperate search for Ball, were unable to locate him. Duckworth was struck with an inspiration. He was a movie fan who believed that the movie theaters springing up all over Liverpool could be of great service to the police in tracking down Ball. He had the fugitive's photograph shown on all the screens of the theaters between features, running beneath the photo a title card reading: "GEORGE BALL, WANTED FOR MURDER, REWARD." This was the first time that movies had been used in tracking down a wanted criminal, and the technique proved effective. Ball, who had moved and disguised himself, was identified by someone who had seen his photo in one of the theaters as he left a football match on Dec. 20, 1913. He was immediately arrested and tried in February 1914 at the Liverpool Assizes, Justice Atkin presiding. He was defended by Sir Alfred Tobin, who had been the lawyer for the notorious wife-killer, Dr. Hawley Harvey Crippen. Prosecuting was Sir Gordon Hewart.

The trial was one-sided with Hewart utterly destroying the testimony of the nervous Ball who rattled off a fantastic story about "a tall chap with a dark brown mustache" who sprang from behind a pile of tarpaulins in the shop just before closing and attacked Christine Bradfield, killing her, then held a revolver on Ball and Eltoft, telling them that if they did not dispose of the body for him, he would kill them both. Hewart shredded this tale quickly, asking Ball why, when he went to the street to pay Eaves for the destruction of his hat, he did not ask the burly steward for help since, according to Ball's own testimony, the killer was still in the shop at the time. Ball could only mutter: "I was afraid." Moreover, Hewart pointed out that the victim had been carefully sewn into a tarpaulin sack with a system of stitching that was peculiar to the method used by Ball.

The jury returned a Guilty verdict, and Ball, as he was being dragged away by four warders, cried out: "I am innocent! Innocent!" He was sentenced to death and his dull-minded accomplice Eltoft was given a four-year prison sentence. When realizing that there would be no appeals or commutations, Ball confessed the murder of Christine Bradfield to the Bishop of Liverpool only hours before he was hanged at Walton Prison on Feb. 26, 1914. See: **Crippen, Dr. Hawley Harvey.**

REF.: Butler, *Murderers' England; CBA;* Deans, *Notable Trials, Difficult Cases;* Duke, *The Stroke of Murder;* Ellis, *Black Fame;* Kingston, *Dramatic Days at the Old Bailey;* Kobler, *Some Like It Gory;* Shew, *A Second Companion to Murder.*

Ball, Ian, 1948- , Brit., attempt. kid.-attempt. mur. The 26-year-old Ball, described as shy by neighbors and friends, shocked England when he attempted to kidnap Princess Anne for a £3 million ransom. On the evening of Mar. 20, 1974, Ball drove his Ford Escort through an intersection, blocking the path of the royal limousine Princess Anne and husband Mark Phillips were riding in on their way to Buckingham Palace.

Brandishing a .38-caliber pistol and .22-caliber revolver, Ball gunned down Anne's bodyguard, Inspector James Beaton, chauffeur, Alex Callender, reporter Brian Mc-Connell, and police Constable Michael Hill before fleeing

Ian Ball

into nearby St. James's Park where he was captured by police Constable Peter Edmunds. Ball was sentenced for an unspecified amount of time to the high-security Rampton Hospital for the criminally insane.

REF.: Borrell, *Crime In Britain Today; CBA;* Messick, *Kidnapping.*

Ball, John, d.1381, Brit., treas. Ringleader of Wat Tyler's peasant revolt, which demanded an end to serfdom. He was put to death in the presence of Richard II for his role in this affair. REF.: *CBA.*

Ball, Joseph (Joe), 1894-1938, U.S., suic.-mur. Joseph Ball was a serial killer who murdered perhaps as many as twenty-five women. All of his victims were young and beautiful. Though Ball took their possessions and whatever money they had when he murdered his victims, his motive was love. He killed one woman after another, including his second and third wives, so that he would be able to devote his time to his next paramour. To Joe Ball, these murders were not without a utilitarian end; he chopped up his victims and fed them piecemeal to the five pet alligators he kept in a foul-smelling pool behind his inappropriately named gin mill, The Sociable Inn, located near Elmendorf, Texas. This Lone Star native was educated at the University of Texas but he found legitimate pursuits uninteresting and, at the dawn of Prohibition in 1920, he became a bootlegger, amassing a considerable fortune.

The young bootlegger worked hard at his illegal profession which confused his friends who knew that his wealthy family had offered Ball any number of lucrative positions in its vast holdings in cattle and commerce. He had turned all this down to go his own way. He bought a house in Elmendorf and operated out of here during the 1920s, selling flavored alcohol at $5 a gallon. Though the house was modern, Ball lived without the benefit of a cleaning lady, and he was always in an unkempt condition. He padded about in a dirty bathrobe when clients called to buy liquor and he spent most of his time in bed with beautiful young women, a bottle of booze, and a plate of fried chicken on the bed table at all times. His only greeting to customers was: "Got the cash?" When the client produced the necessary money, Ball whistled to his black handyman to bring forth the liquor shipment. Often as not the uncaring Ball returned to his bed and the arms of his lover, continuing his lovemaking, oblivious to the gaze of his caller.

Ball was a large, big-boned man, well over six feet, who was muscular but overweight, thanks to his ravenous eating habits. He was expert with a revolver and carried one with him at all times, on occasions whipping out this weapon and firing a practice shot or two to impress witnesses with his marksmanship. In the late 1920s, Ball opened his crudely appointed saloon, The Sociable Club, about fifty feet back from U.S. Highway 181. He developed a liking for alligators and bought five, placing them in a large cement pool behind his club. He would, after a night of drinking, take his best customers outside and amuse them by throwing large chunks of meat into the pool and hoot and holler as the roaring beasts jawed the food, their thrashing tails violently churning the murky water.

For the more sadistic of his friends, Ball arranged his own little horror shows. He kept stray dogs and cats in a pen near the pool and he would take these poor creatures out of the pen and hold them over the pool, teasing the always hungry reptiles and terrifying the animals. Tiring of the game, Ball would throw the strays into the pool where they would be torn apart by the alligators. As he brutalized these animals, he himself became more and more brutal. He shouted instead of talked and threatened anyone who disagreed with him. Yet Ball managed to keep employed a steady stream of beautiful barmaids, radiant young ladies he reportedly paid extremely well and all of whom, it was said, became his mistresses. These women came and went with alacrity which aroused the suspicions of a local constable and neighbor of Ball's, especially when such favorites as Hazel Brown and Minnie Mae Gotthardt disappeared.

When asked by the constable why the girls had suddenly vanished, Ball exploded and pulled his revolver, shoving this into the constable's face and threatening to kill him if he went on probing into his affairs. The constable, afraid for his life, did not report the incident. This was not the case with Texas Ranger Lee Miller. When relatives asked police to investigate the disappearance of Hazel Brown in the fall of 1938, Miller and several deputies went to Ball's roadhouse. They entered the Sociable Inn on Sept. 24, 1938. Ball greeted them affably and then asked if they wanted some beers. "No, Joe, we're here to have you answer some questions about Hazel Brown."

The saloon keeper shrugged and then walked behind the bar. "Then, I'll pour one for myself." Instead of pouring a beer, Ball went to the cash register and opened the bottom drawer. He pulled out a revolver and the officers, thinking he was about to fire at them, pulled out their own guns and aimed these at Ball. The saloon owner gave them a crooked grin, then put the revolver to his temple and squeezed the trigger, blowing off the top of his head. Later, the deputies found hunks of human flesh floating in a water barrel behind the house, and in the pool where the alligators swirled, there was a trace of blood. Clifford Wheeler, the terrified handyman who worked for Ball, admitted that his employer had murdered many young women and two of his own wives, that he had witnessed Ball shoot one of his wives and his subsequent chopping up of her body and the feeding of her remains to his alligators. Wheeler said he did not dare say a word to authorities about Ball since his employer said he would kill him. He was given a four-year prison sentence as an accessory to murder.

No clear number of Ball's victims was ever recorded but it was estimated that Joe Ball killed at least twenty women. Most of these young women had been impregnated by the killer and he murdered and dismembered them when they began to demand that he marry them. He did marry two of his victims, but he tired of these ladies and dispatched them to the alligator pool. "Joe, he weren't no marrying man," Wheeler told police.

REF.: *CBA*; Holmes, *Serial Murder*; Nash, *Murder, America*; Radin, *Crimes of Passion*; Wilson, *Encyclopedia of Murder*.

Ball, William Weekly, prom. 1850s-60s, Case of, Brit., mur. A resident of Ringstead, Northamptonshire, Ball jilted the local beauty, Lydia Atley, who disappeared on July 22, 1850. Joseph Groom reported overhearing Atley telling Ball, as she walked with him in his large orchard: "I've got the idea that you intend killing me, isn't that so?" In her conversation with the wealthy Ball, Atley revealed that she was pregnant and that her lover Ball was the father. An argument broke out and another local resident, John Hill, also walking about that night near the Ball estate, saw the couple and reported that Atley had shouted at Ball: "It's yours, I tell you, yours and no one else's!" These were the last words ever heard from Lydia Atley. She was not seen again. Ball was questioned by authorities, but the rich landowner denied all knowledge of Atley's whereabouts.

Ditchdiggers working in the area fourteen years later uncovered a skeleton that was identified as the remains of Lydia Atley from a missing tooth on the left side of the mouth. Ball was charged with murdering the young woman and secretly burying her body. His lawyers pointed out that several persons, according to medical records, had had a tooth pulled from the left side of the mouth. Ball's attorneys then illustrated how the area where the remains were found was a traditional burying spot of nomadic gypsies and that the skeleton was, in all probability, that of a dead gypsy. After a short deliberation, the jury sided with the defense and Ball was released, but the consensus of the town was that Ball, after having made the hapless woman pregnant, had killed Atley to avoid having to marry her. He was openly branded a murderer, an image that held until his dying day. Ball seemed to encourage this scurrilous reputation by taking long nightly strolls through the gypsy burial ground and pausing long near the spot where the skeleton had been found.

REF.: *CBA*; Nash, *Among the Missing*.

Ballad of Reading Gaol, The, a poem by Oscar Wilde. This prosaic but profound literary work was based on Charles Wooldridge, ex-trooper of the Royal Horse Guards who had murdered his wife (Brit., 1896) and was hanged for the crime. Wilde, who was a fellow prisoner with Wooldridge at Reading, so empathized with the plight of the withdrawn Wooldridge that he immortalized the condemned man's fate with the theme that "each man kills the thing he loves." This best read of Wilde's now mostly forgotten work indicted the prison and social order of the day: "the vilest deeds, like poison weeds, bloom well in prison air." See: **Wilde, Oscar; Wooldridge, Charles Thomas**. REF.: *CBA*.

Ballantine, William, 1812-87, Brit., lawyer. Prosecutor of murderer Franz Muller in 1864. In 1871, he supported Arthur Orton who became the infamous Tichborne Claimant. See: **Muller, Franz, Tichborne Claimant**. REF.: *CBA*.

Ballard, Guy, d.1939, U.S., fraud. Ballard and his wife engineered one of the largest swindles of the 1930s when they promoted themselves as the earthly missionaries of St. Germain during the whirlwind "Great I Am" tour then crisscrossing the nation. Ballard claimed that he had met St. Germain at the top of California's Mt. Shasta, and that this patron saint of the occult instructed him to spread his gospel of immortal life throughout the U.S. Ballard added that all believers, in return for "love gifts," would win immortality upon their death. "Love gifts" were to be presented to St. Germain through the Ballards—his sole human disciples—and the gifts were to include anything of value, especially U.S. currency. Believers in the "Great I Am" were also forbidden to own pets, eat meat, or touch onions, and they were instructed by St. Germain to remain clean and never wear soiled underwear or have body odor.

After five years of preaching the gospel according to St. Germain, the Ballards had acquired over three million followers and amassed huge sums of money from "love gifts" and a complete line of St. Germain souvenirs, inspirational items, and books from the St. Germain Press which published the teachings of their patron saint.

Guy Ballard died in 1939, but failed to reappear and prove his immortality as St. Germain had promised. His wife continued the charade for six months until she was arrested and sentenced to one year in prison for mail fraud. She was also indicted on charges of tax evasion, and eventually paid the U.S. Internal Revenue Service a total of $104,943.63 in back taxes. REF.: *CBA*.

Ballard, John, d.1586, Brit., consp. Conceived the Babington Plot against Queen Elizabeth. Put to death along with eleven co-conspirators. See: **Babington, Anthony**. REF.: *CBA*

Ballew, Stephen Merris, d.1871, U.S., mur. An adventurer and thief, Ballew got a job as a horse wrangler on the Golden farm in Quincy, Ill. He convinced the family that he was an expert horse trader, and he and James P. Golden set out for Texas on a horse-buying expedition in the fall of 1870. Ballew returned alone with a wild tale of the young Golden vanishing with the purse for the purchase of horses. He was so convincing and endearing to James' sister that he was not only believed but the sister married him. Ballew then busied himself with making secret arrangements to have the Golden property turned over to his custody. Before these sinister plans came to fruition, the body of James Golden was found in Collin County, Texas. It was proved that Ballew murdered Golden on Oct. 21, 1870, hidden the body, and taken the Golden money. During a turbulent trial, Ballew was convicted and sentenced to death. He was hanged in 1871.

REF.: *CBA*; Dudley, *The Climax in Crime of the Nineteenth Century, Being an Authentic History of the Trial, Conviction and Execution of Stephen Merris Ballew*.

Ballistics, See: **Supplements**, Vol. IV.

Ballou, Sidney Miller, 1870-1929, U.S., jur. Judge of the Supreme Court of Hawaii, appointed by President Theodore Roosevelt in 1907 and served until 1909. In 1897, he compiled the Civil and Penal Laws of Hawaii from codes first published in 1869. They were adopted by Congress when Hawaii was admitted as a territory in 1897. REF.: *CBA*.

Balsamo, Joseph, See: **Cagliostro, Count**.

Balta, José, 1814-72, Peru, pres., assass. President of Peru from 1868-72. He became president after leading a revolt in 1868 which toppled the government of Mariano Prado. He was assassinated by army mutineers in 1872 after he attempted to nullify the results of a popular election. REF.: *CBA*.

Baltes, Mark, 1958-86, Case of, U.S., mur. Twenty-six-year-old Baltes was struck and killed by a hit-and-run driver on South Ocean Boulevard in Palm Beach, Fla., on the evening of Mar. 8, 1986. Defense attorney Barry Krischer knows who the murderer is, but the law has yet to bring him to court.

Baltes, having just gotten out of his fiancée's car after an argument exacerbated by alcohol, staggered along South Ocean Boulevard as his girlfriend Beth Miller drove away. Miller never saw Baltes alive again because shortly after she left him beside the road, he was killed by a light-colored Buick Riviera that dragged his body along the pavement for sixty feet without slowing down. Baltes was killed instantly.

The following day, Krischer contacted authorities, claiming to represent the hit-and-run driver. The driver was willing to turn him or herself in to authorities in return for punishment no stronger than probation. The state's prosecutor immediately denied the request. After two-and-a-half years of investigation, police have turned up no clues and in September 1988 the Baltes family filed a $6 million lawsuit against the unknown defendant in the hope they could win court approval to force Krischer to reveal his client's name.

In October 1988, the Baltes family lost its case. State circuit court Judge Timothy Poulton ruled that Krischer was fully within the law and did not have to reveal the name of the driver who had sought his counsel. Poulton explained that Florida laws regulating attorney-client privileges do not require Krischer to provide this type of information to the grieving family members. The West Palm Beach, Fla., police keep the Baltes case open in hope that new clues will identify the hit-and-run driver. REF.: *CBA*.

Baltimore, Lord Frederick, and **Griffenburg, Elizabeth,** and **Harvey, Anne,** prom. 1768, Case of, Brit., abduc.-rape. During his lifetime, Lord Baltimore did little to uphold the honor and integrity of the family name, which extended back to the time of George Calvert, founder of Maryland in 1632.

Frederic Baltimore was a wealthy idler who had little use for the religious beliefs of the peasants and shopkeepers residing near his family home in Epsom. His consuming interest was the pleasure of the flesh, and the village offered him an abundant supply of women. Fascinated by stories of Turkish sultans who kept a bevy of women in their harems, Baltimore traveled to Constantinople, reconstructing a sultan's seraglio upon his return. He assigned the task of procuring young women to Anne Harvey, an employee, and Elizabeth Griffenburg, the wife of a local physician.

Sarah Woodcock being brought to Lord Baltimore.

In November 1767, Baltimore made the acquaintance of Sarah Woodcock, who ran a milliner's shop in nearby Tower Hill. After visiting her store, Baltimore decided he must have her in his harem. He instructed Harvey, an engaging hostess, to lure Woodcock to her home. As Harvey and Woodcock chatted, a townsman named Isaac Isaacs came to the door, explaining that a wealthy woman insisted upon seeing Woodcock that afternoon. "The lady wants a great many things and will be a very good customer to you," said Isaacs. The lady in question was, in fact, Lord Baltimore, who promptly took Woodcock prisoner in his London home. Woodcock, however, was determined not to be violated, and after two days Baltimore had still not succeeded in his goal. Changing his methods, the paramour told her he would take her to her father. Instead, his coachmen drove Baltimore and Sarah to a private country estate, where she was raped.

Meanwhile, Woodcock's disappearance had been discovered. Suspecting treachery, a young man named Davis spied the captive Woodcock at Baltimore's country estate. A legal writ demanding her release was then delivered to the house. Baltimore and his two female accomplices were arrested on charges of seduction and rape. Baltimore's defense was that the young woman could have escaped or made her presence known at any time. Furthermore, he claimed, he was not violent and that the publicity surrounding the case was punishment enough for the alleged crime. Lord Baltimore swore to the truth of his story before the

King's Bench at Kingston, Surrey. After ninety minutes of deliberation, the jury returned a verdict of Not Guilty, supporting Baltimore's claim that Woodcock was not an entirely unwilling participant.

REF.: *CBA;* Henriquez, *Prostitution;* Mitchell, *Newgate Calendar I;* ____, *Newgate Calendar II.*

Balue, Jean, c.1421-91, Fr., consp. Jean Balue was appointed cardinal in 1467 by King Louis XI, after which Balue was imprisoned for conspiring with Charles the Bold against the monarch. REF.: *CBA*.

Ba Maw, 1893-1977, Burma, consp. Supported the separation of his country from India. He served as Burma's first prime minister from 1937-39 and led the puppet government during the Japanese occupation. He was imprisoned from 1940-42. REF.: *CBA*.

Bamberg Witch Trials, 1609-33, Ger., witchcraft. More than 900 people were murdered in Bamberg, Germany, during a twenty-four-year period in the early 1600s. The Bishop of Bamberg, Johann Gottfried von Aschhausen, was responsible for the deaths of 300 persons beginning in 1609. On his orders, these people were jailed, tortured, and convicted of witchcraft In 1622, Bishop Gottfried Johann Georg II Fuchs von Dornheim replaced von Aschhausen and slaughtered up to 600 people.

During this twenty-four-year reign of terror in Bamberg, several small prisons were constructed specifically for witches. In these jails, prisoners were tortured with thumbscrews, leg vises, strappado, and other bizarre methods that included scalding lime baths and the *Schnur,* a method that entailed tying a rope around a victim's neck, then pulling the rope back and forth to create friction that would cut into the skin, eventually sawing the bones in half.

Hundreds fled Bamberg relating horror stories of the atrocities they had witnessed or escaped. They maintained that the judicial system had run amok and that people were being unjustly convicted. Emperor Ferdinand II intervened in an attempt to provide true justice but was unable to end the holocaust. It was not until 1633, when Bishop Fuchs von Dornheim died, that the witchcraft murders came to a halt.

REF.: *CBA;* Lea, *Materials Toward a History of Witchcraft;* Summers, *The Geography of Witchcraft;* Wilson, *Witches.*

Bambrick, Thomas, d.1916, U.S., (wrong. convict.) mur. On Oct. 7, 1916, Bambrick was executed in the electric chair at Sing Sing Prison in Ossining, N.Y., but prison warden Thomas Mott Osborne was convinced that he died an innocent man. Bambrick was convicted in 1915 of the murder of New York City police officer George Dapping in September 1915. Evidence was uncovered after his conviction that convinced the warden that Bambrick was innocent but that he knew the actual murderer and had refused to reveal his identity and risk being known as a "squealer." REF.: *CBA.*

Banana War, 1964-69, U.S., org. crime. This Mafia war was fought in New York City and was instigated by Joseph C. Bonnano, head of one of the city's five Mafia families. Bonnano sought to take over most of the New York rackets by ousting through execution or pressure the old 1930s ganglords, chiefly Thomas "Three-Finger Brown" Lucchese and Carlo Gambino, allying himself with Joseph Magliocco and Joseph Colombo, one-time enforcer for the Joe Profaci family. It was Colombo's job to kill Lucchese and Gambino but his attempts failed and he himself, under the guise of being killed in a racial murder, was shot down during a New York City rally.

When Bonnano moved to take over Mafia-syndicate operations in Buffalo, N.Y., his thugs attacked the goons controlled by Stefano Magaddino, and in Los Angeles, where Bonnano's men tried to unseat the powerful Frank DiSimone, a top level meeting of the national crime cartel was held and it was decided to kidnap Bonnano. He was abducted on Oct. 21, 1964, by two gunmen who grabbed him on Park Avenue. It was thought that Bonnano, known as "Joe Bananas," had received the customary "one-way ride" and had been executed, his body dumped into the Hudson

River wearing the traditional "cement overshoes."

Magaddino's men, however, had kidnapped Bonnano and taken him to Buffalo where he was held pending a decision of life or death from the ruling crime czars. Magaddino, who was Bonnano's cousin, argued that by killing Bonnano a bloodbath would ensue for years. This had already begun when Gaspar DiGregoria had been installed in Bonnano's old position, splitting that Mafia family and causing several shootouts. Bonnano promised that he would retire to Arizona and devote himself exclusively to his interests in the West if he were released. He was set free but he did not keep his word, renewing the war in New York which led to several gun battles and, after five years, eight men murdered and scores wounded on both sides. A heart attack in 1968 caused Bonnano to retreat to his Tucson, Ariz., home and, without his direction, the war ground down. It came to an abrupt halt after a bomb exploded in the lavish Bonnano home in Tucson. Carmine "The Cigar" Galante, a one-time enforcer for Bonnano who had been serving a long prison term, emerged from prison and attempted briefly in the 1970s to take over the old Bonnano rackets in New York. He was shot to death, ending the last serious internecine war of the American Mafia-syndicate. See: **Apalachin Conference; Bonnano, Joseph; Colombo, Joseph, Sr.; DiSimone, Frank; Galante, Carmine; Gambino, Carlo; Lucchese, Thomas; Magaddino, Stefano; Magliocco, Joseph; Profaci, Joseph.**
REF.: Bonnano, *A Man of Honor; CBA;* Demaris, *The Last Mafioso;* Martin, *Revolt in the Mafia;* Messick and Goldblatt, *The Mobs and the Mafia;* Nash, *Bloodletters and Badmen;* Peterson, *The Mob;* Reuter, *Disorganized Crime;* Sondern, *Brotherhood of Evil, The Mafia.*

Bandaranaike, Solomon West Ridgeway Dias, 1899-1959, Ceylon, prime minister, assass. Founded the nationalist Sri Lanka Freedom Party in 1952. As prime minister of Ceylon from 1956-59, he maintained a strict neutralist foreign policy. He was eventually assassinated. REF.: *CBA.*

Banda Singh Bahadur (Lachman Das or Lachman Dev or Madho Das), 1670-1716, India, treas. Leader of Sikh troops during the overthrow of the Mughal empire. He was later captured and tortured to death by enemy troops in the fall of Gurdas Nangol. REF.: *CBA.*

Bandera, Stefan, d.1959, Ger., assass. Bandera, leader of the Ukranian Nationalists—an organization that opposed Soviet annexation of the Ukraine during WWII—was found dead outside his Munich apartment in 1959. His death was ruled a suicide until 1961 when Soviet agent Bogdan Nikolaevich Stachinsky defected to the West and confessed to the murder of Bandera and a second Ukranian Nationalist, Lev Rebet.

Stachinsky, while an agent for the Soviet secret police, assassinated both Ukrainians with a new Soviet-made weapon—a double-barreled pistol that fired cyanide pellets. Stachinsky explained to German authorities that he murdered Bandera and Rebet, although Rebet's murder was just a test to see if the cyanide gun would work, and that Bandera was his main target.

Following his assignment to East Berlin after the murder, Stachinsky's German girlfriend became pregnant, and they secretly married. Stachinsky's Soviet superiors were infuriated by his actions, and he fled to West Berlin fearing for his family's safety, knowing that he faced life imprisonment in West Germany for the assassinations. REF.: *CBA.*

Bandiera, Attilo, c.1811-44, Italy, treas. Leader, with his brother Emilio, of an unsuccessful revolt against Austrian rule in the kingdom of Naples from 1819-44. He was betrayed by a confidante, tried, and executed as an insurgent. REF.: *CBA.*

B & O Railroad Strike, 1877, U.S., riot. The great Railroad Strike of 1877 began in Martinsburg, W. Va., and spread rapidly westward. A by-product of the industrial age, it was the first large-scale labor upheaval in the U.S., brought on by a bleak economic picture and the insensitivity of railroad management. In 1873, the U.S. suffered a major depression. Unemployment rose, and the resulting decline in trade with the emerging West forced the railroad companies to take corrective measures. In 1877, they imposed an across-the-board pay cut of ten percent, while doubling the number of cars per train. This was viewed as yet another corporate attempt to break the spirit of the workers.

On July 17, 1877, disgruntled workmen at the Martinsburg terminal of the Baltimore & Ohio Line began a strike that would effectively shut down railroad commerce in the U.S. The state militia was called upon to clear the tracks at Cumberland, Md., but, in sympathy with the workers, they refused to do so. The Baltimore militia was summoned, but large groups of workers and local residents prevented their train from leaving the station. Twelve were killed in the shooting that followed, and the B & O station was burned to the ground. The bloodshed was repeated in Pittsburgh, where the local militia refused to bear arms against their fellow citizens. When the Philadelphia contingency, commanded by Major General Robert Brinton, arrived on the scene, they were greeted by rioters armed with stones and firearms.

The militia fired into the crowd, killing ten people and wounding seventy. Angry workers drove the soldiers into the roundhouse and set it on fire. The troops escaped through a hail of gunfire. Afterward, the crowd destroyed some 104 locomotives, the depot, and 2,152 cars. The strike spread to Chicago and other Midwestern cities and towns, forcing President Rutherford Hayes to call up 75,000 army volunteers to quell the rioting. The army ended the disruptions within two weeks. The employees were not yet unionized, and were therefore unable to negotiate their demands for better working conditions. After great loss of life and numerous reports of army "massacres," the strike collapsed. The newspapers of the day saw the strike as an attempt to imitate the Paris Commune of 1871, and bitterly denounced the strikers. "Rioters are worse than mad dogs!" complained the *Independent,* a religious periodical. The 1877 Railroad Strike started a labor war through which workers eventually won the eight-hour workday and a recognition of the legitimacy of the trade union movement. See: **Haymarket Riot.**
REF.: Bruce, *1877, Year of Violence; CBA;* Hofstadter and Wallace, *American Violence;* Sloan, *Our Violent Past.*

Bang, Else Wille, 1899- , Den., euth. Bang poisoned her mother in December 1931 to end her suffering as she slowly died from an incurable disease. Against the wishes of family members, Bang confessed to a Danish judge that she gave her mother, the Baroness von Deuben, a fatal dose of her regular medication to save her soul from eternal damnation. Bang explained that the dying woman had previously failed in a suicide attempt, and, believing that individuals who take their own lives are damned, she assumed the responsibility and administered the poison.

At the time of Bang's confession, Denmark had passed legislation approving leniency for those accused of murder if the victim had asked for help in bringing about the death. This new law did not apply in Bang's case as it was not scheduled to go into effect until 1933. As a result, the judge ordered the body exhumed for investigation and remanded Bang into the custody of a mental hospital for psychiatric evaluation. REF.: *CBA.*

Banghart, Basil (AKA: The Owl), prom. 1930s, U.S., pris. esc.-rob. Banghart, whose criminal record dated back to 1925, was an armed robber specializing in raiding postal mail trucks, his modus operandi similar to that of Roy Gardner. Banghart was also widely known during his day as a "super slippery escape artist," in the words of Warden James A. Johnston of Alcatraz. Because of his oversized head and large, staring eyes, Banghart had been dubbed "The Owl." He was sentenced to the federal penitentiary at Atlanta in 1927, but he escaped. Arrested in Pittsburgh, Pa., in October 1928, Banghart escaped from the custody of a U.S. marshal. Arrested in Knoxville, Tenn., and charged with auto theft, Banghart, in February 1930, escaped again. In 1932 Banghart was arrested for armed robbery but, while awaiting trial, he grabbed a guard's gun, shot the man, and escaped the Detroit, Mich., jail.

The Owl was a free-lance triggerman who worked with several Midwestern robbery gangs through the early 1930s. He was always the "hot man," the man who held guards or robbery victims at bay with, usually, a machine gun. This was the case with the spectacular mail truck robbery in Charlotte, N.C., on Nov. 15, 1933. The mail truck had just pulled out of the train station depot carrying $100,000 in $5 bills, en route to the Federal Reserve Bank of Charlotte, when two cars full of heavily-armed men blocked its way, bringing it to a halt. Four men jumped out of the car. Banghart, wielding a submachine gun, ordered the two guards out of the truck and he held them captive against a wall while his three companions brought an acetylene torch and cut through the heavy bolts of the back of the truck (the back of the truck was locked, and the only key to the rear doors was kept at the destination point).

Once the bolts on the doors had been cut away, a task that took the two men working the torches no more than a few minutes, five mail sacks carrying the cash were thrown into a sedan and the gang piled into the one car and sped off, leaving the other car behind. Fingerprint experts went over this car, which had been stolen from a Charlotte resident, but it was clean and no clues to the identity of the robbers turned up until a few days later when Walter Wearn, brother of the mayor of Charlotte, informed police that four men and a woman had moved into an expensive apartment building next to his home and had acted suspiciously, disappearing on the day of the robbery. The apartment was checked, found to be in disarray, as if its occupants had hurriedly departed. Clothing, food, ammunition for machine guns, and eleven empty beer bottles were found.

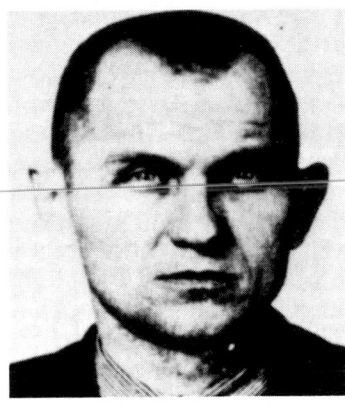

Basil "The Owl" Banghart

Chief Detective Littlejohn, on a hunch, sent the beer bottles to Charlotte fingerprint expert J.B. Earl, who managed to get a set of prints off one bottle and send copies to all major police departments. He soon got a response from the Bureau of Identification of the Chicago Police Department. Its fingerprint expert, Tom Laffey, comparing the prints from the beer bottle with those of armed robbers with the same modus operandi as that of the postal truck thieves, matched them with that of Charles "Ice Wagon" Connors (real name Lawrence Collins) and Louis "Dutch Louie" Schmidt. This amazing scientific sleuthing finally led to the capture of the Banghart gang. Since Connors and Schmidt were known members of the Banghart Gang, federal and local authorities concentrated on searching for these men. The Owl and Isaac "Hill-Billy" Costner, two more members of the robbery gang, were located in Baltimore on Feb. 11, 1934, traced to an expensive apartment building through the license plates on a car Banghart had been driving. The Owl was taken without a fight as he emerged from the building, despite the loud protests of his neighbors to police; they insisted that Banghart, who had been living there under an alias, was too much a gentleman and too wealthy to be considered a gangster.

Inside the apartment police found two machine guns, two high-powered rifles, several revolvers, two false mustaches, and $12,500 of the Charlotte mail robbery. Banghart was jailed, pending trial, while FBI agents occupied the apartment and waited for other gang members to show up. A few days later an agent answered a knock on the door. Standing before him in shock was Isaac Costner, who was immediately arrested. Costner and Schmidt were convicted and sent to the Atlanta federal penitentiary, but Banghart, who was tried in the Jake "The Barber" Factor kidnapping, was given a ninety-nine-year term in Joliet, Ill., along with Roger "The Terrible" Touhy. (The Factor kidnapping was a fraud, engineered by Factor on behalf of Chicago crime czar Al Capone, who wanted to get rid of his bootlegging competitor Touhy and his friend Factor obliged him. Ironically, Banghart, who had but

a passing relationship with Touhy, went to prison for a crime he did not commit.) In addition to the term Banghart drew in Illinois, he was given a thirty-six-year federal sentence, to be served after he had finished his Illinois sentence.

Banghart vowed that he would escape once more and, with Touhy and two others, made good his brag on Oct. 9, 1942. Using guns that had been smuggled to them, Banghart, Touhy, and others shot a guard and got over the prison wall, running to a nearby roadway where a fast car awaited them. The FBI took over the case, using the federal sentence Banghart had received, to establish jurisdiction. FBI Director J. Edgar Hoover personally supervised the hunt for Banghart, via phone with his Chicago Bureau, where, on Dec. 29, 1942, the fugitives were located in a North Side apartment house. A wild shootout ended with two gang members killed and Banghart and Touhy once more in custody. Touhy, who had no federal convictions against him, was sent back to Joliet. (Touhy would not be released until 1958 when a federal judge announced that he had been convicted for a crime "that never happened" and he would be shot to death a short time after being released, gunned down by members of the old Capone mob.)

There would be no more escapes for Banghart. He was shipped off to Alcatraz where he would spend the rest of his days, pensively brooding about his past and endlessly planning but never executing his "big time break" from The Rock. Though involved in violent crimes for most of life, Banghart, as an examination on the Rock indicated, was an interesting exception to the traditional profiles of such criminals. According to Alcatraz psychiatrist Dr. R.M. Ritchey, Banghart was "well oriented, no disturbances of consciousness. Intellectually he shows normal responses with a high I.Q. of 107. He was more modest than reports about him seem to indicate. There is no evidence of any mental abnormality and he is not psychotic." Banghart was a practical robber of the day. To him, robbery and escapes, daring or not, were all part of the so-called profession he had chosen early for himself. To fellow Alcatraz prisoner Alvin Karpis, Banghart once stated: "I grew up with guns. They didn't make me feel powerful but I knew that I could get my way by having one in my hand. Robbery was my job and I was good at it for some time and then it blew up in my face as I knew it would. The day will come when I will have too much of an identity and then there won't be any place I can go. I ran out of space once they knew who I was, once I made the "big time" and had all the cops and feds after me. The job was over. I was out of work." See: **Alcatraz; Capone, Alphonse; Factor, Jake; Touhy, Roger.**

REF.: *CBA;* Cooper, *Ten Thousand Public Enemies;* Demaris, *Captive City;* Edge, *Run the Cat Roads;* Heaney, *Inside the Walls of Alcatraz;* Johnston, *Alcatraz Island Prison;* Karpis, *On the Rock;* Nash, *Almanac of World Crime;* ____, *Bloodletters and Badmen;* Robinson, *Science Catches the Criminal;* Toland, *The Dillinger Days;* Touhy, *The Stolen Years.*

Bangkok Legless Drug Smuggler, prom. 1978, Thai., drug traffic. Drug traffickers have forever engineered unique methods to smuggle controlled substances across international borders. In Bangkok, Thai., in 1978, a 45-year-old man from Düsseldorf, Germany, was apprehended for smuggling two pounds of morphine inside his artificial limbs. He was jailed for five years for trafficking in drugs. REF.: *CBA.*

Bangladesh Independence War Atrocities, 1971, Bangladesh, war crimes. When British rule of the Indian Subcontinent ended in 1948, two independent nations remained, divided by religion: predominantly Hindu India and Muslim Pakistan. But Pakistan itself was divided. West Pakistan was the home of the Punjabi aristocracy and the seat of government, while hundreds of miles away on the other side of India, East Pakistan was populated by Bengalis and produced jute, the country's major cash crop. In 1971, the Bengalis' frustration with their exploitation by West Pakistan exploded in a civil war that turned East Pakistan into the independent nation of Bangladesh.

As unrest grew in East Pakistan in early 1971, Pakistani president Yahya Khan determined to hold the region at all costs.

His army terrorized the Bengali populace, and on Mar. 26 brutally attacked the University of Dacca, home of East Pakistan's intellectual elite. Tanks levelled dormitories and other buildings, killing students, faculty, and their families. But the repression only stiffened Bengali resistance. On Apr. 1, citizens of Jessore in East Pakistan rounded up small groups of Punjabis living there and paraded them to the city's center where they beat, hacked, and shot them to death. The army stepped up its campaign, hoping to put down the rebellion before the May monsoons made fighting impossible. But, largely due to help from Prime Minister Indira Gandhi of India, within the year the Bengalis achieved their goal and the "Bengal Nation," Bangla Desh, was born. See: **Gandhi, Indira**. REF.: *CBA*.

Banister, Christopher, c.1658-c.1718, Brit., asslt.-rob.-mur. After serving as a gunsmith's apprentice in Devonshire, Christopher Banister left the trade to work as a court bailiff, an occupation which provided endless opportunity to swindle and bribe prisoners. When he was discharged by the Master of the Ordnance for stealing from royal commissaries, Banister opened a pawnshop. Catering to the poor, he charged fifty percent on any sums they borrowed, quickly building a tidy profit.

In 1712, Banister murdered a local constable who had presented a writ for the arrest of Powel Revel, a prostitute who was sharing Banister's bed. His ill-gotten fortune secured him an official pardon, and Banister soon resumed his criminal ways.

Banister practiced a variety of techniques for robbing people. One of the most brutal of these was the hook-pole lay, which involved assaulting horseback riders with a long, hooked stick, often injuring the victims severely.

Children and old people were Banister's favorite targets to swindle. The kid-lay was a swindle that he particularly enjoyed. This involved sending a child on an errand while he watched over the child's parcels. When the child returned, Banister would be gone with the packages.

The law finally caught up with Banister in 1718 when he tried to steal a muslin hood, valued at a mere four shillings, from Dorothy Thompson, a London woman. For this petty thievery Banister was committed to Newgate and tried at the Old Bailey in February, 1719. As robbery was punishable by death, the jury agreed that Banister should hang at Tyburn for his many crimes. He was conveyed by coach to the hanging ground on Mar. 23, 1719, unrepentant to the end.

REF.: *CBA*; Smith, *Highwaymen*.

Banister, Debra, 1955-   , U.S., mur. In the mid-1980s, rural Florida housewife Banister became the mastermind of two familial murders that shocked the residents of Gainesville, Fla. In 1984, 29-year-old Banister, a bank employee at the Gainesville Sun Bank, was in her second marriage, a marriage she considered inadequate. Her husband, Joe Banister, could not give her what she wanted or needed, according to Debra, and she was looking for something better. Debra's sister, Marlene Sims, had also been divorced and was remarried. In 1984, Marlene was deeply involved in a custody battle over her two children from her previous marriage to Cecil Batie. One day she told her sister she wished Cecil were dead, and that's when Debra referred her to *Soldier of Fortune* magazine.

Marlene Sims read the classified advertisement in the magazine offering the services of a mercenary who would go anywhere and do anything for the right price. Banister telephoned the Atlanta phone number in the ad and arranged an appointment with Vietnam veteran-turned-truck driver John Wayne Hearn. Hearn agreed to kill Sims' ex-husband for $10,000, and he took a special interest in Banister. A torrid affair followed their first meeting at a Georgia restaurant.

To raise the money to pay for the murder, Banister and Sims concocted a scheme to bilk their grandmother's insurance company out of several thousand dollars, enough to cover Hearn's fees. They chauffeured their grandmother to Gainesville, returned to their rural home-town, and burned her house to the ground. With the insurance money, they paid Hearn his fee and on Jan. 6, 1985,

he fired two shots into Cecil Batie as he slept on the couch in his living room.

Banister's affair with Hearn continued and she suggested that he kill her husband Joe so she and the mercenary could spend their lives together. Hearn agreed, and he shot Banister with his own rifle as he drove along a rural Florida road in his pickup truck on Feb. 2. Hearn later attended Joe Banister's funeral and, thinking himself an amateur photographer, took photographs at the ceremony.

When authorities learned that the two murdered men were relatives in the same family, they began to investigate Sims and Banister. Authorities subpoenaed telephone bills and once they linked them to Hearn and the mercenary ad in *Soldier of Fortune*, Hearn became their prime suspect. About the same time, Hearn received a telephone call from Robert Vanoy Black of Bryan, Texas, asking him to murder his wife, Sandra. Banister persuaded Hearn to take him up on his offer, and Hearn traveled to Texas and murdered Sandra Black in her home for $10,000.

When he returned to Florida, authorities took him into custody and he confessed to all three murders. On Apr. 15, a Bradford County, Fla., grand jury indicted Hearn and Banister on charges of first-degree murder in the death of Joe Banister. Two months later, Hearn and Banister were charged with the murder of Cecil Batie by Alachua County authorities. Several other members of the Sims family were also named for complicity, including Banister's sister Marlene.

To avoid the death penalty, Hearn turned state's evidence in the trials of Banister and Sims in return for a sentence of life imprisonment. In August 1986, Banister was convicted of second-degree murder in the death of her husband and sentenced to 17 years in prison. Both Banister and Sims received sentences of 30 years for their part in the death of Cecil Batie, with Banister to serve her second sentence concurrently. Hearn traveled once again to Texas to testify against Robert Black, who was charged with murdering his wife. The family of Sandra Black slapped a $107 million gross negligence suit against *Soldier of Fortune* magazine. Prosecutors believe that with good behavior, Debra Banister could be released in 1995. REF.: *CBA*.

Baniszewski, Gertrude Wright, 1929-   , U.S., child abuse-mur. A native of Indianapolis, Gertrude Baniszewski lived with her three children Stephanie, Paula, and Johnny, surviving on a meager income that forced her to take in children for the summer to earn extra money. In 1965, Baniszewski agreed to board Sylvia Likens, sixteen, and her sister Jennie, fifteen. Jennie Likens would be no problem, the housewife believed since she was crippled and could get about very little. The parents of the two sisters worked in a circus and paid Baniszewski $20 a week to take care of their children. During the first week of their stay, the two girls were fed little, receiving a few slices of toast in the morning and no lunch. A bowl of soup was

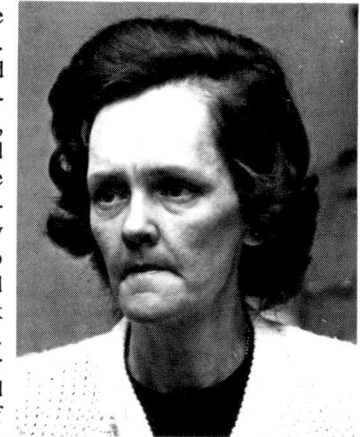
Gertrude Baniszewski

their only supper. At the end of the first week, Baniszewski dragged both girls to an upstairs room of the house and mercilessly beat them, screaming that she was boarding them "for nothin'!"

The hardened housewife, though receiving weekly payments from the Likens parents, resented having the two girls in her home and cursed them whenever they were in her presence. A deep-seated streak of sadism began to manifest itself whenever she was near them; she struck out at them, hitting them so hard that her hands stung from the impact, she later admitted. She reserved her most sadistic treatment for the older girl, Sylvia, whom she beat regularly and then took to paddling on the bare buttocks with a board that left scars. Baniszewski then began encouraging neighborhood children and her own offspring to beat the poor girl, who begged them to stop without relief. The housewife then ordered the other children to put out burning cigarettes on the girl's arms and hands. One of Baniszewski's children, Paula, whipped into a frenzy of hatred by her mother, beat Sylvia so hard that she broke her hand which had to be put into a cast. The Baniszewski girl then used the cast to beat Sylvia on the head.

Baniszewski then decided that Sylvia Likens was a whore and tied her up in the basement, releasing her only to beat her and then force her to dance naked in front of other children. Directing a dim-witted neighborhood boy, Ricky Hobbs, needles were heated and used to brand the girl's stomach with the words: "I am a prostitute and proud of it." This horrible torture completed, Baniszewski then released the full fiendish fury of her nature, beating the girl, slamming her head against the basement wall with such force that Sylvia Likens died from the blow. The housewife panicked and called police, telling them that Sylvia had run off with a gang of boys, then returned and was mutilated and killed by them; she had found the poor girl in her basement. Her children repeated this story to investigating officer Melvin Dixon. As Dixon was about to leave, Jennie Likens hobbled forward and whispered to him: "Get me out of here and I'll tell you the whole story."

The officer took the girl away and quickly learned the truth about the vicious Gertrude Baniszewski. She was charged with murder and convicted, given a life sentence. Baniszewski won a new trial on appeal but was again convicted and sent back to prison to serve out a life term. In all of the many interviews conducted with this murdering sadist, the housewife has but one excuse for her slaying of a defenseless girl left in her care: "I had to teach her a lesson."

REF.: *CBA;* Nash, *Bloodletters and Badmen;* ____, *Look For The Woman.*

Bankes, Sir John, 1589-1644, Brit., jur. Attorney general of the British Crown from 1634-40, and chief justice of the Common Pleas from 1640-44. REF.: *CBA.*

Bankhead, John Hollis, 1872-1946, U.S., lawyer. Three-term senator from Alabama from 1931-49. REF.: *CBA.*

Bank of Taiwan Scandal, 1927-38, Case of, Japan, fraud. Charges of stock fraud leveled at cabinet members of Japanese Prime Minister Makato Saito led to the end of his two-year reign over the island nation. In May 1934, eight members of Saito's cabinet were indicted on charges of purchasing stock in a Japanese corporation, Imperial Rayon, and selling it to friends below market value.

The stock buys came after Saito's government saved the country's largest bank, the Bank of Taiwan, from financial ruin. With government help, the Bank of Taiwan acquired the assets of the Imperial Rayon Company. In return, the bank secretly sold Rayon stock to the Vice Minister of Finance, Hideo Kuroda, and seven other members of Saito's cabinet. The scandal, once exposed, resulted in the resignation of Saito, Kuroda, and all remaining cabinet members. Saito never faced trial because Japanese military officers assassinated him in February 1936.

The remaining defendants stood trial and were acquitted of all charges in 1938. REF.: *CBA.*

Bank Riot, Baltimore, 1835, U.S., riot. The Bank of Maryland collapsed on Mar. 24, 1834, resulting in a loss of between two and three million dollars, and leaving many angry depositors bankrupt. While residents waited for the directors to make amends, pamphlets were published accusing the bank of swindling the people of Baltimore.

A mob gathered in Monument Square on Aug. 6, 1835, three days after the publication of the latest incendiary pamphlet. After breaking a few windows, the crowd dispersed at the mayor's request. But rumors of an impending riot persisted, prompting Mayor Jesse Hunt to organize a private militia on Aug. 8. That night, rioters sacked a house and confronted the militia. At least ten people were killed and 100 wounded in the ensuing violence. The arrested rioters were released the next day on the mayor's orders, after others invaded Hunt's home and looted the parlor. The next night, the militia stood by as mobs sacked the houses of the bank trustees. The wife of one trustee diverted the crowd by pleading that she, and not her husband, owned the house. The riot was over by Aug. 10, when 85-year-old General Samuel Smith raised a citizen's vigilante group to end the anarchy.

REF.: *CBA;* Hofstadter and Wallace, *American Violence.*

Banks, prom. 1700s, Brit., execut. Banks was appointed as a public hangman on Nov. 12, 1717, and began his service the following month. His most notable execution came at Tyburn gallows on Mar. 17, 1718, when he oversaw the execution of the Marquis de Paleotti, who had been convicted of murdering one of his servants.

It is not known when Banks ended his career, but it is believed that either he or his successor Richard Arnet executed John Price at Bunhill Fields on May 31, 1718, and Jack Sheppard at Newgate in February 1724.

REF.: Bleackley, *Hangman of England; CBA.*

Banks, Alf, and **Edward Hicks,** prom. 1919, Case of, U.S., mur. Banks and Hicks were two of fifty-one blacks convicted of murder after a 1919 racial uprising near Elaine, Ark., ended in the death of five whites and 200 blacks. Banks, Hicks, and ten other rioters were originally charged with first-degree murder and sentenced to death. Following the trial, the decision was reversed because of a technicality and Banks and five of his co-defendants were retried and once again found Guilty and sentenced to death. The Arkansas State Supreme Court once again reversed the decisions of the lower courts, and in 1923 all of the men who had stood trial for murder were freed. REF.: *CBA.*

Banks, Jerry, 1951-81, U.S., suic.-mur. Having recently been released from death row, Banks murdered his estranged wife and turned the .38-caliber pistol on himself following an argument the couple had had regarding their impending divorce. Virginia Banks, was found dead in her McDonough, Ga., home on Mar. 30, 1981, four days before her divorce from her husband would have been finalized.

Banks had recently been released from a Georgia penitentiary where he had served six years on death row for the 1974 murders of a high school band director and a 19-year-old student. Banks was released on Dec. 22, 1980, after the state supreme court overturned his conviction based on the testimony of a previously silent witness. Banks was believed to have been distraught about his divorce and the fact that his estranged wife, Virginia, had been awarded custody of their three children. In 1983, Henry County, Ga., paid $150,000 to the three Banks children in a suit filed against the county for its mishandling of the case. REF.: *CBA.*

Banks, John, d.1806, U.S., mur. John Banks, a resident of New York City, was a violent alcoholic who had trouble keeping any kind of job. He was vicious with his friends and brutal toward his wife, Margaret, who was also a habitual drunk. Banks was forever complaining about her miserable housekeeping and the awful meals she served him. He returned home one night to find her in an alcoholic stupor. Ordering her to sober up and brown some peanuts he had brought, he said he would return shortly and that she was to have supper ready. When he did return, Margaret Banks gave him "pot liquor" instead of his coffee, no peanuts, roasted or otherwise, and not a morsel to eat.

Enraged, Banks produced some eggs he had obtained and when he ordered his wife to cook them, she smashed them on the floor. Banks exploded, grabbed a fire shovel and brought this down on his wife's head. She was still alive, so he slit her throat. When he sobered up, Banks made a report to police and was promptly arrested and tried on May 29, 1806. His derogatory descriptions of his late wife's shortcomings, including repeated statements about how he gave Margaret Banks every penny he earned, did not mollify the jury. Banks was convicted and was hanged on July 11, 1806; he went to the scaffold still complaining about his wife's terrible cooking.

REF.: *An Authentic Account of the Trial of John Banks for the Murder of His Wife, Margaret Banks; CBA; A Full and Particular Narrative of the Life, Character and Conduct of John Banks;* Nash, *Bloodletters and Badmen.*

Bankston, Clinton, Jr. (AKA: **Junebug**), 1971-   , U.S., mur. When it happened, everyone who knew him expressed the greatest surprise. "This all did shock me. He didn't seem the type," said Agnes Freeman, a neighbor in the Nellie B. Apartments of Athens, Ga., northeast of Atlanta. Clinton Bankston lived with his mother in this deteriorating section of Athens, an area of high unemployment and gang activity. Bankston was a high-school dropout who spent most of his time riveted to his television. His perceptions of the world were shaped by the images of violence on prime-time television.

On Aug. 15, 1987, Bankston committed a real-life crime so horrible and senseless that its barbarity eclipsed anything law enforcement officers of this small Georgia city had ever encountered.

Robbery was foremost in Bankston's mind when he entered the home of Sally Nathanson in the fashionable Carr's Hill section of Athens. Nathanson and her visiting sister, Ann Orr Morris, who lived in an adjacent house, were found dead. Her 22-year-old adopted daughter, Helen Nathanson, was later found lying dead in one of the bedrooms by police investigators. All three had been savagely butchered with a hatchet.

The mutilated bodies could be positively identified only through the efforts of the state crime lab in Atlanta. Athens Police Chief Everett Price conducted a thorough investigation and was able to link the murders of the three women to a similar crime committed against two elderly people the previous April. Items belonging to the earlier murder victims, Glenn and Rachel Sutton, had been found in the Bankston apartment. Bankston was arrested on Sunday morning near his grandmother's house on Moreland Avenue.

District Attorney Harry Gordon urged the courts to try the 16-year-old Bankston as an adult for the murders of five people. The Supreme Court of Georgia, however, ruled that underage offenders convicted of murder could not receive the death penalty. Bankston pleaded guilty, citing insanity as his defense. On his seventeenth birthday, the quiet boy who liked to ride around the neighborhood on his bicycle received five consecutive life sentences. REF.: *CBA.*

Banning, C. Michael, 1944-88, U.S., (unsolv.) mur. C. Michael Banning, forty-three, was found stabbed to death in his Hammond, Ind., law office on Feb. 23, 1988. Banning's secretary, Debbe Cole, twenty-three, was beaten but survived the assault. Three men were seen leaving the office about 11:30 a.m., minutes after the stabbing.

Before entering private practice, where he generally handled divorce cases, Banning served as an assistant Lake County prosecutor from 1979 to 1981. His office had been bombed three years earlier on Feb. 3, 1985. Hammond police, along with the U.S. Bureau of Alcohol, Tobacco and Firearms, turned up no evidence after a six-month investigation. REF.: *CBA.*

Bannon, Charles, 1909-31, U.S., mur. In 1931, Bannon became only the eighth white man to be lynched in North Dakota following his slaying of a rural family of six. Bannon worked as a hired hand on the farm of A.E. Haven near Shafer, N.D. In February 1930, Bannon slaughtered the six-member Haven family and buried their bodies in the barn. He continued to live on the farm for nine months during which time the murdered family was not missed. Bannon was apprehended in November when he attempted to sell some of the Haven livestock at a local market. He was questioned in the family's disappearance and, after the bodies were found, charged with their murders. Bannon was lynched in February 1931. REF.: *CBA.*

Bantz, Gideon D., b.1854, U.S., jur. Attorney for the territory of New Mexico. He was appointed federal judge of the territorial court of New Mexico by President Grover Cleveland in 1895. REF.: *CBA.*

Banuolo, Donna, and **Woodfield, Lawrence,** prom. 1981, U.S., fraud. Banuolo and her boyfriend, Woodfield, were charged with fraud in 1980 when a Circuit Court judge in Chicago ruled that the couple had bilked a senile widow out of her $100,000 life savings which the woman had received after the death of her husband in 1977.

During their trial, Banuolo explained that she was using the money to help Mrs. Timo Joutsen secure legal counsel to handle her financial affairs following the sudden death of her 75-year-old husband. Mrs. Joutsen, suffering from senility since 1971, willingly gave the money to Banuolo who first deposited it into a joint savings account and later transferred it into Woodfield's personal checking account. The judge found them Guilty and ordered the couple to repay the entire $100,000. REF.: *CBA.*

Baptist, Michael, 1955-   , and **Lawrence, Lenox,** 1957-   , and **Lindsay, Wayne,** 1957-   , U.S., mur. Baptist, Lawrence, and Lindsay are three Chicago youths convicted of murdering two teenagers and wounding another to prevent them from testifying in the murder trial of 16-year-old Elijah Baptist, the younger brother of Michael. Murdered were 19-year-old Henry Carter and 16-year-old Leslie Scott, witnesses in the upcoming trial of Elijah who had been convicted of killing a grocery clerk on the city's south side.

Testimony from 17-year-old Leo Carter, wounded in the incident, proved damaging to the defense. After only three hours of deliberation, the jury returned a Guilty verdict. On Nov. 15, 1976, presiding Judge Albert S. Porter sentenced the youths to serve 250-500 years each in an Illinois penitentiary after hearing evidence in what he called "the most vicious, heinous case" he ever presided over. REF.: *CBA.*

Bar, Karl Ludwig von, 1836-1913, Ger., jur. Author of scholarly papers on German and international law. REF.: *CBA.*

Barabbas (Bar Abbas), prom. 33 A.D., Case of, Isr., rebel. Brought before the Roman Governor Pontius Pilate, Barabbas was freed while Jesus of Nazareth was condemned to die on the cross. According to the Gospels of Matthew, Mark, and John, it was the custom of the Romans to release a political prisoner during the time of the Passover. But other sources suggest this practice may have been particular to Pilate. The choice of which of the two men to save was allegedly left to the people. The assembled throng demanded that Barabbas be released.

Little factual information is known about Barabbas. John called him a "robber," perhaps indicating that he was actually a political insurgent. Historians have suggested that Jesus' entry into Jerusalem during the Passover was accompanied by a riot, and that Barabbas may have been arrested by Roman officials as a revolutionary. Luke says Barabbas was arrested "for a certain insurrection made in the city and for murder was cast into prison."

The name Barabbas, if written as the two words "Bar" and "Abbas," means the son of a "father" or scholar of the law. The name also appears as "Jesus Barabbas" in various Biblical texts. Perhaps Barabbas was a follower of Jesus whom the Romans mistook for the prophet.

REF.: *CBA;* Furneaux, *True Mysteries; Matt. xxvii 15-26; Mark xv 6-15; Luke xxiii 16-25; John xviii, 39-40.*

Barany, Serge, and **Marcucci, Noël,** prom. 1960s, Fr., rob.-mur. Barany was in his late thirties when he embarked on a bank-robbing career with Marcucci, a paroled ex-convict from the Tulle prison. The pair traveled from mainland France to Corsica where they shot and killed the proprietor of a local hotel. Three days later they robbed a post office at Noailles and fled by train from Cahors.

A gendarme pursued them and during an exchange of gunfire on board the train, the policeman was killed, presumably by Barany who was later identified by a passenger. At the trial of the two felons, Barany admitted to firing the gun, but said he intended only to scare off the gendarme, not kill him. Marcucci emphatically denied his role in the killing, but was convicted along with Barany. Both men were sentenced to die after the court rejected a plea for a new trial.

REF.: *CBA*; Heppenstall, *The Sex War and Others.*

Barba Hernández, Javier, d.1986, Mex., drugs-org. crime. The Guadalajara Drug Cartel, known as La Familia, hired Javier Barba Hernández to help them fight their war against the Mexican Federales and the U.S. Drug Enforcement Agency (DEA). Barba Hernández also brought to the cartel political ties he cultivated when he practiced law in Jalisco.

The lawyer-turned-gangster served as warlord for three ranking members of La Familia: Ernesto Fonseca Carrillo, Rafael Caro Quintero, and Miguel Angel Félix Gallardo. The DEA believed he drove the bodies of two Americans named John Walker and Alberto Radelat to their gravesite. Cáro Quintero's gangsters mistakenly killed the Spanish-speaking tourists in a Guadalajara seafood restaurant on Jan. 30, 1985, believing they were undercover DEA agents.

On Nov. 17, 1986, the Federales killed Barba Hernández in a shootout in Mazatlán. The DEA had been anxious to question Hernández about the unsolved February 1985 murder of their agent, Enrique Camarena. It was known that Barba Hernández had accompanied Fonseca Carrillo to the villa where Camarena was held prisoner before he was slain. The Federales explained that they had been "forced" to kill Barba Hernández, but they refused to release hair and fingerprint samples to the DEA. The U.S. government strongly suspected a cover-up by the Mexicans. See: **Cáro Quintero, Rafael; Camerena, Enrique.**

REF.: *CBA*; Shannon, *Desperados.*

Barbara, Joseph M., Sr., 1905-59, U.S., org. crime. Joseph Barbara is best known as the host of the notorious Apalachin Mafia Conference in 1957 where his lavish 60-acre estate briefly housed the most notorious crime bosses of America. Immigrating from Sicily in 1921, Barbara worked for the Buffalo, N.Y., Mafia family as a hit man, executing rival gangsters as far away as Pennsylvania. He was taken into custody during the 1930s on a number of murder charges, but no case was ever made against him. He and three of his goons were accused of murdering rival bootlegger Sam Wichner in 1933; police stated that Barbara invited Wichner to his home to divide up territory and there Barbara, an ape-like creature with powerful hands, personally strangled Wichner to death.

The only conviction suffered by Barbara occured in 1946 when he was found Guilty of illegally acquiring 300,000 pounds of sugar. Following this conviction, Barbara became a distributor for soft drinks in upstate New York, owning many franchises which had suspiciously fallen under his control. He had a heart attack in 1956, and this was used as an excuse for the Apalachin Conference, occurring the following year, purportedly a gathering of old companions visiting a sick friend. The break up of the conference by lawmen brought Barbara to national attention, and he was ordered to testify before the State Investigation Commission of New York, relative to Mafia activities. His lawyers delayed Barbara's appearance by pleading that their client was too ill to testify, that he could suffer another fatal heart attack at any moment, an event that occurred in June 1959. See: **Apalachin Conference.**

REF.: Bonnano, *A Man of Honor*; *CBA*; Cressey, *Theft of the Nation*; Demaris, *The Director*; Eisenberg, Dan, and Landau, *Meyer Lansky*; Gage, *Mafia, USA*; ____, *The Mafia is not an Equal Opportunity Employer*; Gosch and Hammer, *The Last Testament of Lucky Luciano*; Hibbert, *Roots of Evil*; Katz, *Uncle Frank*; Kobler, *Capone*; McClellan, *Crime without Punishment*; McPhaul, *Johnny Torrio*; Maas, *The Valachi Papers*; Martin, *Revolt in the Mafia*; Messick, *Lansky*; Navasky, *Kennedy Justice*; Overstreet, *The FBI in Our Open Society*; Peterson, *The Mob*; Reid, *The Grim Reapers*; Servadio, *Mafioso*; Ungar, *FBI*; Velie, *Desperate Bargain*; Wicker, *Investigating the FBI.*

Barbaro, Anthony F., 1957-75, Case of, U.S., suic.-mur. Barbaro was a member of the National Honor Society and the recent recipient of a college scholarship when he turned against society with a vengeance. On Dec. 30, 1974, the 17-year-old senior at Olean High School in Little Valley, N.Y., positioned himself on a third floor loft where he took aim at passers-by with a high-

powered rifle he had learned to use while practicing with the school rifle team. A classmate later recalled that Anthony had talked about "holing up" in the school armory.

A school janitor, an employee of the local power company, and a woman seated in her automobile were cut down in the deadly hail of fire. Eleven other persons were wounded before young Barbaro was taken by police. He was later indicted for second-degree murder, first-degree assault, and first-degree reckless endangerment.

The moon-faced youth pleaded innocent by reason of insanity, but was declared to be competent to stand trial following a psychiatric examination. On Nov. 1, 1975, the day before the case was to go to trial in Cattaragus County, Barbaro hanged himself in his jail cell using a bedsheet. He left behind three suicide notes, one expressing regret that he would no longer be able to play chess with his jailer, Sheriff Charles Hill. REF.: *CBA.*

The piratical Barbarossa brothers.

Barbarossa I (Arouj or Horush or Koruk, AKA: Redbeard), c.1473-1518, Turk., pir. One of two sea-roving pirate brothers who raided Italian, Spanish, and French shipping for the Mamelukes, Barbarossa I pillaged indiscriminately. In 1504, two heavily-laden treasure ships of the Vatican were sent from Genoa to Rome, and when they became separated, a small, fast ship, captained by Barbarossa I intercepted the second ship and attacked it. After subduing the Vatican crew, the Turks stripped off their own garb and put on the uniforms of the captives. They quickly overtook the first Vatican ship and signaled for it to rendezvous. When the second ship caught up with the first, the disguised pirates quickly overwhelmed the Vatican crew. Barbarossa I then sailed with an enormous booty to Tunis, where the pirate chief, called Redbeard, gave half of the loot to the Emir for protection which was gladly given. But Barbarossa, who had lost one hand in his pirate battles, had no intention of sharing power with the Emir and, at an audience with the potentate, casually reached out with his one good hand and strangled his host to death, immediately proclaiming himself Emir.

Incensed at the increased raids conducted by Barbarossa I against his ships, Charles I of Spain ordered a huge armada with 10,000 men to storm Tunis and the Turkish pirates, along with their Arab allies, were slaughtered. Barbarossa I was trapped in the Emir's palace and there scores of Spanish soldiers cut the pirate to pieces. It was this brother's terrible reputation that tainted the image of his surviving sibling, and most historians have profiled both Barbarossa brothers as fierce, merciless beasts who murdered at whim and showed not a bit of mercy to their victims. Both wore the sobriquet Redbeard but the most infamous of the pair was certainly Barbarossa I. See: **Barbarossa II.**

REF.: *CBA; Cabal, Piracy and Pirates;* Course, *Pirates of the Eastern Seas;* Earle, *Corsairs of Malta and Barbary;* Fisher, *Barbaray Legend: War, Trade and Piracy in North Africa, 1415-1830;* Forester, *The Barbary Pirates;* Innes, *The Book of Pirates;* Masefield, *On the Spanish Main;* Mitchell, *Pirates;* Moorehead, *Hostages to Fortune;* Ormerod, *Piracy in the Ancient World;* Williams, *Captains Outrageous: Seven Centuries of Piracy.*

Barbarossa II (Khizr, Khair ed-Din or Khaireddin or Chaireddin, AKA: Redbeard), c.1466-1546, Turk., pir. Upon the death of his brother, Barbarossa I, Khizr, or Barbarossa II, went to Selim I, the Sultan of Turkey, and asked that he provide an army to retake Tunis from the Spanish, stating that he would make the land a present to Turkey in return. The armies and navy were provided and Barbarossa II retook all the lost lands of Tunis and was made deputy ruler in 1516 by Selim I. For more than thirty years Barbarossa controlled the Mediterranean Sea with his hordes of Turkish and Arabic pirates, becoming as famous as Atilla the Hun or Hannibal. His ships looted almost every coastal town from Spain to the Black Sea and, since he considered his raids part of a Holy War against Christians, he was inclined to show little mercy to prisoners. Those too young or old, those unfit for work as slaves, were butchered by his pirates; the rest of a town's inhabitants, thousands, were sold into slavery.

Barbarossa II, who was also known as Redbeard, heard that the Duchess of Trajetto was a rare beauty and the pirate decided she would make an excellent gift for Selim I. He raided the city of Calabria with a mighty fleet of sixty ships, but found that the Duchess, warned in advance of Redbeard's intentions, had escaped her seaside villa in her nightgown, riding her horse to death to reach safety. When she returned to Calabria, she found the city in ruins, most of the inhabitants murdered, crucified—as was Barbarossa's favorite method of execution—or taken off into slavery. The pirate, in his rage at not capturing the duchess, had burned the city to the ground. This incident pointed to the world the barbarous nature of the Turkish pirate. Yet, the same man took an 18-year-old Italian girl prisoner, so the story goes, when besieging Reggio. Instead of sending the beautiful girl to one of his many harems, the pirate, who had fallen in love with the girl, begged her to marry him, saying he would abandon the siege of her city if she consented. She did, and Barbarossa retired to his magnificent palace in Constantinople, living into his sixties in wedded bliss. He was far from the hedonistic, cruel tyrant the world thought him to be when he died in bed in 1546. By this time, Barbarossa had given up the black flag and sword and had become a scholar, learning several languages and becoming a patron of the arts. He did not die, as popular history has it, through sexual overindulgence with a bevy of his harem ladies surrounding him. He died with his Italian wife at his side and a book in his hands. See: **Barbarossa I.**

REF.: Cabal, *Piracy and Pirates; CBA;* Chatterton, *The Romance of Piracy;* Course, *Pirates of the Eastern Seas;* Earle, *Corsairs of Malta and Barbary;* Ellms, *The Pirates' Own Book;* Fisher, *Barbary Legend: War, Trade and Piracy in North Africa, 1419-1830;* Forester, *The Barbary Pirates;* Innes, *The Book of Pirates;* Lydon, *Pirates, Privateers and Profits;* Masefield, *On the Spanish Main;* Mitchell, *Pirates;* Moorehead, *Hostages to Fortune;* Ormerod, *Piracy in the Ancient World;* Tenenti, *Piracy and the Decline of Venice;* Williams, *Captains Outrageous: Seven Centuries of Piracy;* Woodbury, *The Great Days of Piracy.*

Barbaroux, Charles Jean Marie, 1767-94, Fr., treas. Member of the moderate Girondist group who voted at the Convention with the faction that demanded that King Louis XVI be put to death. Because of his opposition to the policies of Robespierre and the more extreme Jacobins, he was declared an enemy of the state and executed along with many other Girondists in 1794. REF.: *CBA.*

Barbato, Joseph, b.1892, U.S., (wrong. convict.) mur. Judge James M. Barrett of the Bronx County Court offered some timely advice to Barbato just before he set the convicted murderer free on Nov. 26, 1930: "Tomorrow is Thanksgiving Day and you ought to pray to God. You have much to be thankful for."

The 38-year-old killer had good reason to count his blessings. He had been convicted of murdering Mrs. Julia Musso Quintieri in her Bronx rooming house on Sept. 15, 1929, after she rejected his sexual advances. In December a jury convicted him of first degree murder. Barrett sentenced him to death, and off to Sing Sing Barbato went to await the electric chair. Then in July the Court of Appeals ruled the conviction invalid because the police coerced a four-word confession out of Barbato. A doctor who examined the defendant concluded that he had been beaten by police while in custody. Assistant District Attorney Solomon Boneparth put forward a motion requesting Barbato's release, which was accepted and acted upon by Judge Barrett. REF.: *CBA.*

Barbe, Gilbert Warren, See: **Schwartz, Charles Henry.**

Barber, Ann, d.1821, Brit., mur. Barber was sentenced to die in York, on Aug. 10, 1821, for poisoning her husband with arsenic she had secured from a local druggist. She went to her death on the gallows three days later in a state of near hysteria. It was the largest public gathering to watch an execution in York up to that time.

REF.: *CBA;* Poynter, *Forgotten Crimes.*

Barber, Arthur, 1941- , U.S., (wrong. convict.) mur. A Bronx man named Arthur Barber was arrested, tried, and convicted for the murder of Elijah Williams, which occurred on Dec. 19, 1965. Williams was a bookie and numbers runner with whom Barber had quarreled.

A jury convicted Barber of first-degree murder despite evidence that the police had conducted their interrogation in a brutal, shocking manner, questioning him for an extended period of time without arraignment, denying him permission to call an attorney, and neglecting to advise him of his right to remain silent lest he incriminate himself. His conviction was upheld in the appeals courts, and Barber began serving his sentence. He clung to the faint hope that the federal courts might free him, but as the years passed the chances grew remote.

Ten years later, on Sept. 10, 1975, Federal Judge Constance Baker Motley ruled that the actions of the police at the time constituted a "pattern of lawlessness which shocks the conscience." In a twenty-page opinion, Motley cited evidence that Barber had been arrested without probable cause and beaten by police. She ordered his immediate release if the state was unable to schedule a trial within sixty days. REF.: *CBA.*

Barber, Orion Metcalf, 1857-1930, U.S., jur. Served as state's attorney in Bennington County, Vt., from 1886-87, and appointed associate judge of the U.S. Court of Customs Appeals in 1910-28 by President William Howard Taft. REF.: *CBA.*

Barber, Ronald L., prom. 1972, U.S., rob. When Barber and six of his accomplices broke into the vaults of the Laguna Niguel branch of the United California Bank on the weekend of Mar. 24, 1972, they probably never dreamed that the Internal Revenue Service would demand its share of the loot.

A portion of the stolen money and valuables were later found in Ohio, but $1.4 million was still outstanding eight years later. Barber was arrested and sentenced to prison on charges of conspiracy and larceny. After release, he settled down to a quiet life in Anaheim, Calif., believing this episode of his life was over.

Then the IRS began investigating his tax claims for 1972. They ordered him to pay taxes on $200,000, which they believed to be Barber's share of the take. In Tax Court, he claimed he never received any of the money. Notwithstanding this claim, Barber was ordered to pay the IRS its due regardless of whether or not he actually received the money. The decision was handed down by Judge William H. Quealy. Officials at the Tax Court conceded that Barber might be allowed by the IRS to pay his debt in small amounts in the absence of fraud. REF.: *CBA*.

Barber, Susan, prom. 1981, Brit., mur. Barber was an Essex housewife engaged in a torrid love affair with her husband's best friend in May 1981. Her lover's name was Richard Collins, and the tryst had gone on for nearly eight months before the cuckolded husband came home unexpectedly one day to find them both in his bed. Michael Barber reacted violently. He beat his wife and threw Collins out of the house. But this did not cool his wife's ardor.

The next day Susan slipped a deadly weed poison known as Gramoxone into his steak and kidney pie. In small doses, Gramoxone is deadly to humans. Death is brought on by fibrosis of the lungs, which makes breathing all but impossible.

Michael Barber was admitted to Hammersmith Hospital in London where he was diagnosed as suffering from pneumonia and kidney failure. Upon further examination doctors concluded that Barber was afflicted with Goodpasture's Syndrome, a rare nervous disorder. After he died, a pathologist named David Evans conducted the postmortem. He was not convinced that the cause of death was natural. Blood samples were taken and sent over to the National Poisons Unit and to the company which had manufactured the weed killer. A trace of paraquat, a toxic herbicide, was found in each instance. Based on this chemical analysis, Mrs. Barber and Richard Collins were arrested in April 1982 and charged with murder. Collins received two years' imprisonment, and Susan Barber, who by this time was no longer interested in her former boyfriend, received a life sentence.

REF.: *CBA*; Wilson, *Encyclopedia of Modern Murder*.

Barbera, J. Anthony, prom. 1931, U.S., (wrong. convict.) rob. Anthony Huegler and his wife Emma owned a small delicatessen-grocery on Reid Avenue in Brooklyn. They were fearful but hard working people who kept only small amounts of cash in their drawer. A sinister looking young man with a cap pulled down over his face entered the store on Feb. 5, 1931, and held up the couple at gunpoint. He left the store with $70 taken out of the till. The police combed the neighborhood for a suspect matching the description provided by the Hueglers. Based on the sketchy information provided, Barbera was arrested on suspicion because he had been observed in the neighborhood for several days, and a gun found in his car provided the police with enough circumstantial evidence needed to sustain an arrest. Barbera protested that he had nothing to do with the holdup. He had taken his fiance to a movie theater on Myrtle Avenue that night, twelve miles from the Brooklyn delicatessen.

A Kings County Grand Jury returned a first-degree robbery indictment against Barbera. The case was heard by Judge A.I. Nova on Mar. 24 and 25, 1931. Despite compelling evidence from defense witnesses who corroborated the young man's alibi, the jury believed the Hueglers, who admitted that the robber had the cap pulled low over his face. Barbera was found Guilty.

While awaiting sentencing, the police arrested a second man, Harold Sorenson, who had a long record of delicatessen robberies. District Attorney William F.X. Geoghan was satisfied that Sorenson—not Barbera—committed the robbery when Sorenson related the exact words spoken by Mrs. Huegler in the store. On Mar. 30, 1931, Sorenson's confession was read to Judge Nova. Barbera was freed minutes before his scheduled sentencing.

REF.: Borchard, *Convicting the Innocent*; *CBA*.

Barberi, Maria, b.1872, Case of, U.S., mur. A native of southern Italy who migrated to the U.S. in 1892, Maria Barberi was a plumpish, homely young woman who had the misfortune 7to meet a dedicated rake, Domenico Cataldo, a fellow resident of New York's Little Italy. Though warned by her father against such philanderers as Cataldo, Barberi moved in with the man and performed all the chores and duties of any wife, except that Cataldo refused to marry his mistress. This preyed upon the mind of Maria Barberi, she being a Catholic and expecting her man to do the "right" thing. Cataldo had originally lured her into his lodgings on Thirteenth Street by promising marriage but, by April

1895, the gambling and hard-drinking Cataldo not only openly refused to marry the woman, he made fun of her repeated requests to walk down the aisle. "Only pigs marry!" he sneered one day before a group of his card-playing friends. Barberi had followed him to a bar where she overhead Cataldo regaling his friends with his refusal to marry her.

Barberi asked him pointblank if they would ever marry and Cataldo mocked her, saying through a laugh: "You get that mother of yours to give me $200 and maybe I'll marry you." He then paused as his snickering friends looked on and added: "But I don't believe in it. Like I told you, Maria, only pigs marry." Barberi stood behind her man thinking, first starting to move away, then turning back to place her arms about Cataldo from behind, as if to embrace him. As she did so she produced an old razor and, with one quick move, she cut his throat, almost from ear to ear. The stricken man, eyes bulging in shock, leaped up, staggered down the length of the bar, and stumbled outside. He lay on the pavement and looked up pleadingly to passersby who thought him drunk. To one stranger who seemed to stop and stare down at him in curiosity, Cataldo croaked his last two words: "I die." He was dead by the time a police wagon arrived to pick up his body. Maria Barberi, who never for an instant denied having killed her brutal lover, was charged with murder and tried before Judge John W. Goff, a severe and unstinting jurist.

Eyewitness testimony, coupled with Barberi's own admissions in faulty English, brought in a verdict of Guilty and, to the shock of the court, Goff later sentenced Maria Barberi to death. No woman had ever been electrocuted and this prospect so horrified the sob sisters of the yellow press that they mounted a campaign to win Barberi a new trial. While she awaited her death in Sing Sing's Death House, Maria received hundreds of letters from supporters. Six men proposed marriage, while another wrote to New York governor Levi Parsons Morton that if his train fare from Fort Scott, Kan., was paid, he would gladly travel to Sing Sing and sit in the electric chair instead of Barberi. Leading feminists joined the crusade to save Barberi, led by such social lions as Contessa di Brazza Savargon, who demanded the woman be released, that she had killed a man who had ruined her reputation and honor. The governor of Arkansas and most state representatives sent a petition to Governor Morton, demanding Barberi's release or at least a commutation for life imprisonment. The Italo-American League of Texas held a convention at the Griswold Hotel in New London, Conn., and then delivered a demand for reprieve to Morton.

It was the corps of sob sisters, however, who daily bleated their pleas and demands for Maria that finally wore down Governor Morton with such printed ditties as:

> Swift as a flash a glitter blade
>   Across his throat she drew,
> 'By you,' she shrieked, 'I've been
>   betrayed:
>   This vengeance is my due!'
> Behold her now, a wounded dove,
>   A native of a clime
> Where hearts are melted soon with love
>   And maddened soon to crime.

Governor Morton finally relented and ordered a new trial for Barberi, who was removed from Sing Sing to the Tombs in Manhattan and there, in her cell, placed a birdcage which housed her pet canary, newly acquired from a male admirer. She called the bird Cicillo and talked to it constantly, especially when the many female members of the press visited her. Upon their arrival, Maria would begin to chatter to her canary: "Tell me, Cicillo, tell me, little one, will they really kill your Maria?" The sob sisters labeled the convicted killer "The Tombs Angel," and described how she "prayed in the light of a solitary sunbeam falling on the cold stones of her cell."

On Nov. 16, 1896, defense lawyers Friend, House, and Grossman were quick to pick up the "persecution" theme, stating that Barberi had been driven to murder by a callous and ruthless man who had been evil incarnate. They also claimed that she was the victim of "physical epilepsy," that she could not control her impulsive action to slit Cataldo's throat. Moreover, they chimed the statements of the sob sisters who had universally condemned phrenologists who had studied Barberi's head and pronounced her a "murderous type." Countered the sob sisters: "Is Maria a degenerate?" They went on to demean the shaky science of phrenology wherein such "alienists" determined a person's evils on the basis of their physical appearance and proportions, an unpredictable and rather arbitrary extension of the criminal measurement identification system established by Alphonse Bertillon. One phrenologist, Dr. Hrdlicka, provided charts of Barberi's skull with his drawings and annotations affixed to it, stating that her physical proportions definitely pointed to her being a "confirmed lunatic." This defense witness found himself in deep trouble when the prosecutors quickly produced several unlabeled charts of human skulls, which Hrdlicka pronounced "abnormal." Prosecuting attorneys gloated when stating that the charts of the skulls they had provided belonged to none other than President Grover Cleveland, George Vanderbilt, and the presiding judge at Barberi's trial, Henry Alger Gildersleeve.

The Tombs, where Maria Barberi was imprisoned.

To support their pleading of "physical epilepsy," Barberi's attorneys brought forth one of her uncles who admitted that, after having a few drinks in a bar, he would lose control of his body, begin stripping off his clothes, and then run down streets naked. A neighbor, Angelo Piscopo, testified that Barberi had fits all the time, and when asked to described these fits, Piscopo suddenly tore at his clothes and gyrated, quivered, and performed what could be best described as a St. Vitus Dance which caused several women in the jammed courtroom to faint dead away. Barberi's mother then testified that her poor daughter was subject to "fits" since childhood and, when pressed by Assistant District Attorney McIntyre, the mother herself suffered what appeared to be a fit, crying out: "Oh, my head!" When Barberi herself took the stand she told, in broken English, a tale of being given something to drink by that cad Cataldo and when she awoke she found herself "to be ruined, all the reputation gone bad in bed with him." She added that she was plagued with constant head-aches. "Sometimes I feel a great machine in my head," she moaned, "and the pain is so great that I cannot stand it. Some-times I have dreams where there are cats jumping all over me, scratching, scratching."

Prosecutor McIntyre was more than solicitous with Barberi, allowing her to repeatedly kiss his hand before he cross-examined her. At one point, Barberi said to him: "Oh, don't do anything to me...I prayed for you the night they took me to Sing Sing." McIntyre comforted her when she began to cry and soothed her when he put his questions to her ever so gently. Barberi told him

that she never intended to kill Cataldo, that she meant to commit suicide if he refused once more to marry her. The jury was baffled by most of what they heard at this trial and its members were undoubtedly swayed by the emotional performance of the defendant. On Dec. 10, 1895, the jury retired and took fifty minutes to decide that Maria Barberi was innocent, returning a verdict of Not Guilty. A great cheer went up in the courtroom, and McIntyre smiled happily at not having sent this woman to her death. He kissed Barberi's hand and said: "I never doubted for an instant, my dear, that you were a good, honest girl." This was one of the most amazing double-faced performances by any prosecuting attorney in the annals of criminal justice. Barberi hugged and kissed her attorneys and anyone else she could grab in the milling throng. She triumphantly returned to the Tombs where, followed by a bevy of sob sisters, she playfully pounded on the door of the dreaded jail with a fleshy hand, shouting: "Let me in, let me in!" She wanted to retrieve her pet canary Cicillo. With bird in hand, Maria Barberi left the Tombs, waving triumphantly to the sob sisters who had saved her and allowed her to slip into a reportedly long and anonymous life.

REF.: *CBA;* Gross, *Masterpieces of Murder;* Nash, *Look for the Woman;* ___ , *Murder, America;* Pearson, *More Studies in Murder.*

Barbican, James, prom. 1920s, U.S., boot. Barbican joined the ranks of the rumrunners in 1924. He prospered in an industry whose very existence was based on bribery and intimidation of public officials. The bootlegger depended on the rumrunner to convey his liquor to the distributor. As a rumrunner, Barbican relied on the inherent greed of the police and prohibition agents assigned to enforce the Volstead Act. He understood just how much money to offer a corrupt policeman to pass through a town or a precinct, unmolested.

The amount of the Barbican's bribes varied from $50 to $200, the trick being not to give too much or too little. In one case, a gullible law-enforcement officer was deceived into thinking he had been rewarded with a thick wad of bills, when all there was in the rubber-banded roll was a twenty wrapped around nineteen ones.

REF.: *CBA;* Hamilton, *Men of the Underworld.*

Barbie, Klaus (AKA: the Butcher of Lyons, Klaus Altmann), 1913- , Fr., war crimes. Memories of the German occupation and the mass extermination of French Jews were dramatically re-kindled in a courtroom in Lyons, France, on May 11, 1987, when former Gestapo chief Barbie finally went to trial for crimes against humanity.

Barbie was an unrepentant Nazi. Between 1943-44 he served the Third Reich as the Section Four leader of the Lyons Gestapo unit. He later described himself as a minor functionary, but this belied the larger role he played in sending hundreds of innocent people to concentration camps. In the remote village of Izieu in southern France, for example, Barbie rounded up forty-four Jewish children on Apr. 6, 1944, and forced them into the back of a truck which took them straight to the death camps.

Barbie claimed that his job was to hunt down French Resis-tance fighters, not kill Jews. But in both roles he was equally successful. In 1943 Barbie arrested Jean Moulin, the right-hand man to Gen. Charles de Gaulle, who commanded the Free French in exile. Moulin was on a secret mission when he was seized and tortured to death. Barbie was condemned for this action during a trial conducted in absentia in 1954.

When the Nazis surrendered to the allies in 1945, Barbie remained in Europe, allegedly protected by U.S. intelligence officers. With an exit visa, granted on Feb. 21, 1951, he slipped out of Europe that year to take up residence in Bolivia. Using the name of Klaus Altmann, the former Nazi lived in South America until his expulsion early in 1983. Surprising political developments in Bolivia, coupled with the determined efforts of two Nazi hunters named Serge Klarsfeld and his wife Beate to find their man, resulted in Barbie's extradition back to France where he went on trial.

The "Butcher of Lyons" threatened to rip the cover off long-suppressed allegations of massive collaboration between former members of the Resistance and Nazi officials in Lyons, which prompted concern among certain high-ranking government officials. However, there was no scandal and Barbie was convicted of war crimes as everyone expected. Judge André Cerdini sentenced him to life in prison on July 4, 1987. He showed no visible emotion, only repeating, as he did throughout the trial, that he carried out orders like any good soldier. France had long since abolished the death penalty, so Barbie, who had caused the deaths of so many, was fortunate to escape with his life. REF.: *CBA*.

Barbosa, Ruy, 1849-1923, Braz., lawyer. Helped draft the 1890 Constitution. REF.: *CBA*.

Barbot, John, d.1753, W. Indies, duel-mur. Barbot qualified for the bar in 1749, but had incurred such a large public debt that his father decided to send him off to the British colonial possession, St. Christopher's, in the West Indies.

It was not the kind of life the fun-loving young lawyer had imagined for himself, but he made the best of it by striking up a friendship with another professional man his own age, Dr. James Webbe. Through the doctor's connections, Barbot built up a small commercial business within three years, earning £800 per annum.

In 1752 Dr. Webbe was badly in debt. His estate at Bridgewaters was seized and put up for public auction. The sale of the estate was handled by Matthew Mills. The bidding was sluggish, but for inexplicable reasons Barbot put up £2,200, a sum of money he did not have. His colleagues stood by as Mills awarded the estate to Barbot conditioned on his ability to pay within thirty days. When it became clear to Mills that Barbot could not produce this sum in that time, the two men decided to settle by dueling. Barbot suggested a lonely beach front at Frigate's Bay. Mills was agreeable. Shortly after midnight on Nov. 26, 1752, they met on the beach, armed with pistols. There were no witnesses to the affair, only the islanders who were not admitted into British colonial courts.

Therefore Barbot could claim that he was nowhere near the site when the body of Mills was found the next day. The townspeople suspected otherwise. Had he admitted to his role in the duel, the courts might have spared his life. Witnesses came forward to say that they had seen John Barbot, but only from a distance. Based on this testimony, the jury rejected his argument that he had been looking over some pistols in Dr. Webbe's garden the night of the murder. They found Barbot guilty and he was executed on Jan. 20, 1753 at Basseterre. REF.: *CBA*.

Barbour, Oliver Lorenzo, 1811-89, U.S., lawyer. Compiled a sixty-seven volume log of *Reports of Cases in Law and Equity in the Supreme Court of the State of New York*, covering the years 1847-77, a document also known as *Barbour's Supreme Court Reports*. REF.: *CBA*.

Barbour, Philip Pendleton, 1783-1841, U.S., jur. Elected to the House of Representatives from 1814-25, served as Speaker of the House from 1821-23, then as state judge, General Court for the Eastern District of Virginia from 1825-27, and as U.S. district judge, Court of Eastern Virginia from 1830-36. He was appointed associate justice of the U.S. Supreme Court in 1836 to replace Justice Gabriel Duvall. While sitting on the Bench, his decisions tended to reflect the Democratic shift of the country, characterized by President Andrew Jackson who had nominated him. REF.: *CBA*.

Barclay, Sir George, prom. 1696, Brit., consp. Intrigued against King William III who reigned as sole sovereign following the death of Mary, daughter of the Duke of York. He was put to death in 1696 for his involvement in an unsuccessful assassination plot. REF.: *CBA*.

Barclay, Margaret, d.1618, Scot., witchcraft. Barclay lived with her husband Archibald Dean in the town of Irvine, county of Ayrshire. She did not get along with her in-laws so she went before the church court seeking arbitration in a domestic quarrel. Church officials advised her to forget about the matter and try to reconcile the differences in an amicable way. Margaret was not satisfied with this advice and continued to speak out against her in-laws.

When the brother-in-law left for France in the company of the town provost Andrew Tran, Margaret said she hoped the ship would sink to the bottom of the sea and the crabs would eat them up. It was said in anger, but there was little reason to believe that Margaret Barclay had engaged in any deliberate sabotage. But when a passing tramp named John Stewart reported that a vessel had sunk near Padstow, England, Barclay was accused of witchcraft. Stewart was taken to prison where he confessed under torture that Barclay had sought his aid against "such persons as had done her wrong."

According to Stewart she had fashioned a waxen model of the ship her brother-in-law sailed on, and an image of Provost Tran. The demonic ceremony was witnessed by a local townswoman named Isobel Insh and her young daughter who told of a dog emitting a strong light from its mouth which permitted Barclay to go about her work.

Stewart, Insh, and Barclay were subjected to unspeakable tortures. John Stewart committed suicide in his jail cell shortly before the trial began. Isobel Insh escaped to the church belfry but fell off the roof and died. The accused witch Barclay was placed in a stock, and heavy iron bars were placed across her legs until she pleaded for mercy. "All I have confessed was in agony of torture, and before God, all I have spoken is false and untrue," she said. A court of elders convicted her of witchcraft. She was strangled and burned at the stake.

REF.: *CBA;* Robbins, *The Encyclopedia of Witchcraft and Demonology;* Scott, *Letters on Demonology and Witchcraft*.

Barclay, Robert, 1648-90, Scot., her. Governor of New Jersey from 1682-88, and the author of a religious treatise. He was imprisoned on several occasions for his opposition to both Calvinism and Catholicism. REF.: *CBA*.

Bar Cocheba, Simon (Simon Bar Kokba or Simon Bar Coziba), d.135, Isr., assass. Hebrew leader of an unsuccessful revolt against Emperor Hadrian who tried to Romanize Judea 132-35. He was killed in the village of Bethar, near Caesarea. After the uprising was put down, thousands of Hebrew men, women, and children were sold into slavery. The remaining inhabitants dispersed throughout Asia Minor and Africa, marking the final exodus of the Jews from their homeland until the founding of Israel in 1948. REF.: *CBA*.

Bard, Guy Kurtz, 1895-1953, U.S., jur. Judge of the Eastern District Court of Pennsylvania, appointed by President Franklin D. Roosevelt in 1939. He previously served as an attorney for the U.S. Justice Department from 1934-37, and as special assistant to the attorney general in 1937. REF.: *CBA*.

Bardas, d.866, Byzantium, assass. Brother of Empress Theodora. He served as her co-regent during the rule of his nephew Michael III. He was betrayed and killed by Michael and Basil the Macedonian whom he helped rise to power. REF.: *CBA*.

Bardlett, William, 1951- , U.S., mur. Without an apparent reason a 25-year-old elevator repair man named William Bardlett borrowed his sister's .22-caliber pistol and killed three family members on Nov. 25, 1976. The Thanksgiving Day tragedy on Chicago's West Side was a grim reminder of the random violence plaguing big city ghettos.

In this case Bardlett murdered two nephews, 9-year-old Dwayne, and 2-year-old Cecil Jr., and his brother-in-law Cecil White, Sr. White and the two boys had gone to the Bardlett home to share a Thanksgiving dinner, believing that William was at work. Bardlett burst into the Harding Avenue apartment and shot White and his son before fleeing. Police later found the revolver underneath the body of the 2-year-old and spent shell casings strewn around the apartment. Officers from the Shakespeare Avenue Police District arrested the suspect at his sister's residence when he stumbled in without warning during a routine interrogation.

Bardlett was brought before Judge William Cousins on Nov. 28, 1978, and charged with murder. He was declared unfit for trial, and the case continued. He appeared before Cousins again on May 29, 1979, and was remanded to the Department of Mental

Health for a fitness hearing. On Nov. 6, Cousins ruled him Not Guilty by reason of insanity in a bench trial. However, in a separate ruling handed down on Dec. 17, the court found the defendant not in need of hospital treatment but decided that he should visit the Isaac Ray Center for periodic mental health checkups. William Bardlett was back on the streets. REF.: *CBA*.

Barère de Vieuzac, Bertrand, 1755-1841, Fr., assass. Member of States-General in 1789 and of the National Convention in 1792. He was the chief propagandist for Robespierre during the Reign of Terror, which earned him the nickname *Anacreon of the Guillotine*. His power and influence waned when the French people tired of the Committee of Public Safety and the butchery practiced by its leader, Robespierre. In 1794, he escaped to Bordeaux to work as a secret agent for Napoléon. During the Restoration he was proscribed for regicide, but granted general amnesty in 1830. REF.: *CBA*.

Baretti, Joseph (Giuseppe Marc Antonio Baretti, AKA: Aristarco Scannabue), 1719-89, Case of, Brit., mur. Born in Turin, Italy, Baretti was a respected man of letters whose many admirers included Dr. Samuel Johnson.

As a young man, Baretti was forced to earn a living after gambling away his inheritance. In 1750, he settled in England, where he taught Italian. Three years later, he published a treatise defending Italian poetry against the criticisms of the French philosopher Voltaire. Baretti attracted the attention of Dr. Johnson, who encouraged him to continue publishing his writing. Travelling Europe, Baretti became famous, especially in Italy, where he was criticized for publishing a paper satirizing Italian traditions.

An unfortunate altercation with the law occurred on Oct. 6, 1769, a few months after Baretti's return to England. At 4 p.m. he left the Royal Academy in Soho to retrieve some letters from the Orange Coffee House. Baretti was physically and verbally assaulted by two peasant women in the Haymarket, an area populated by tradesmen, laborers, and petty criminals. His accent made them think he was a Frenchman, which increased their vehemence. Believing the women to be in distress, Evan Morgan and other men appeared and also began assaulting Baretti, who managed to escape, turning to confront his pursuers with a small penknife. Shouting, "Murder! Murder!" he stabbed Evan Morgan in self-defense.

Baretti was arrested on a charge of willful murder and tried at the Old Bailey in November 1769. Dr. Johnson and other prominent men testified to the integrity of their compatriot, adding that assaults occurred with regularity in the Haymarket. To his own and his learned acquaintances' relief, Baretti was acquitted of all charges.

REF.: *CBA;* Mitchell, *Newgate Calendar II*.

Barfield, Velma Margie, 1933-84, U.S., forg.-mur. Barfield became the first woman to be executed in the U.S. in twenty-two years on Nov. 2, 1984. The 51-year-old former Sunday School teacher from St. Pauls, N.C., was convicted in 1978 for poisoning her male companion, Stuart Taylor, and her mother with arsenic. At the trial Velma Barfield claimed a drug dependency led her to murder after she had forged a $300 check drawn on Taylor's bank account.

Barfield sat on Death Row for ten years, before exhausting her last appeals. On June 13, 1984, Judge Robert L. Farmer set an August date for execution, which was later postponed until Nov. 2. REF.: *CBA*.

Barginde, Sigrid, 1894-1981, U.S., (unsolv.) mur. At first detectives from the Chicago Police Department did not believe Sigrid Barginde when she told them that "strangers" were invading her home each night to rob and beat her. The frail, partly deaf woman lived in a modest brick bungalow in the Roseland community on Chicago's far South Side.

Early in 1981 detectives from the nearby Kensington station received the first of a series of calls from Barginde, who complained that three people, a man, a woman, and a child, hit her on the head and locked her in a closet while they rifled through her home for money and valuables. Patrol Officers Bill Melmine and Larry Viles examined the house, but found no signs of forced entry. Police and social workers concluded that she may have been suffering from delusions, brought on by poor vision, hearing, and diminished mental capacities. Barginde's persistent claim that the phone was tapped and her house bugged seemed too far-fetched to be true. A phone company repairman determined that pieces of the receiver had been forcibly removed, however. The police believed that the elderly woman may have mistakenly tampered with the phone herself.

Her frantic calls to the police continued until June 26, 1981, when she was found dead in her home. Traces of blood had soaked through the bed and the pillow, suggesting murder. Though her hands were tied in front of her, the Cook County Medical Examiner's office ruled Barginde's death a heart attack. Dr. Wayne Carver, a pathologist who conducted the autopsy, believed the attack was brought on by emotional stress or by physical over-exertion. Regarding murder, Carver said, "We have found no such evidence in this case. We have found no link between a possible break-in and her death." By this time, however, police conceded that her earlier reports of unknown burglars breaking and entering the house were probably true. The case was officially closed on Sept. 30, 1981, after Cook County Probate Judge Arthur Perivolidis ordered all of the victim's records turned over to surviving family members. In a letter dated Sept. 4, Mrs. Ingvelde Evans, sister of the deceased, said that Carver's assertion that Sigrid had tied her own hands "stretches the limit's of one's credulity." REF.: *CBA*.

Barhytt, Charles (AKA: Charles Thompson), prom. 1899, U.S., burg. Barhytt told Chicago police he was a naval recruiting officer assigned to the Masonic Temple when he was arrested at the end of December 1899. A check of police records at the identification bureau revealed that he was a notorious midwestern burglar who had been arrested once before, in 1895, and sent to the Pontiac Reformatory.

Shortly before the Christmas holiday in 1899, Detective Clifton Rodman Wooldridge, one of the ablest in the department, found out from a saloon waitress named Jennie Love that the J. Goldenberg furniture house on State Street was about to be robbed by a disgruntled former employee named Joseph Neponuck, who had worked as a shipping clerk shortly before being discharged for pilferage and general dishonesty.

The burglary was committed on Dec. 20 and three expensive rugs were left at Love's Clark Street saloon for pickup by the unsuspecting burglars. By prior agreement, Wooldridge called on Jennie the next day, but she was not on the premises. Her housekeeper had been instructed to release the merchandise to the plainclothes detective, however, and this was done at once. She further provided a description of Neponuck's accomplice, a young man wearing a white woolen sweater.

That night Wooldridge located Neponuck at his home. Charles Barhytt was found hiding in the adjoining washroom, and both men were taken to Love's place and identified. Protesting that he was just an innocent Navy recruiter, Barhytt's Bertillon records were examined, as was the file record of the earlier 1895 case. The suspect confessed and led police to the hiding place where the remaining loot was stashed. Barhytt was convicted on Feb. 20, 1900, and sentenced to the penitentiary by Judge Jonas Hutchinson. His friend Neponuck was freed when Barhytt admitted that he had planned and carried out the crime alone.

REF.: *CBA;* Wooldridge, *Hands Up!*

Barker, and Hughes, prom. 1887, Brit., Case of, disturb. the peace. An unusual case was brought before the Recorder of Brighton in 1887, involving a fraudulent religious cult and two men who tried to stop the larceny but were accused of a crime themselves.

Barker and Hughes stormed in on a meeting of the "Army of the Lord" one night, attempting to expose the minister, a man named Wood, as a charlatan. Wood had bilked an old woman out of £2,500, and dozens of other townspeople had lost similar amounts. However, when they burst into the tent, Barker and Hughes discovered to their dismay that an orderly prayer meeting was going on in which the participants were reading from the gospel of St. Mark.

Barker and Hughes were arrested under an obscure 1812 statute that made it a crime to disrupt a religious meeting. They enlisted the famous barrister Marshall Hall to represent them before the court. Hall delivered an impassioned oration, in which he exposed Wood, known to his followers as "King Solomon," as a fraud. Barker and Hughes were acquitted by the jury at the Old Bailey.

REF.: *CBA;* Marjoribanks, *For the Defense, The Life of Sir Edward Marshall Hall.*

Barker Brothers, prom. 1930s, U.S., rob.-mur. The Barker clan, four brothers coddled in crime by a mean-minded harridan of a mother, Ma Barker, were undoubtedly the most vicious, murderous bandits to plague banks, lawmen, and kidnap victims in the Midwest during the early 1930s. Each of the Barker brothers, with the possible exception of Arthur, was a psychological and social misfit, thanks to their brutal upbringing by a woman who taught them that crime was their heritage and laws were made to be broken. The Barkers, when at their zenith, proved to be an elusive gang, one that operated erratically, and were wholly unpredictable. Its members, usually led by Fred and Arthur, were seasoned bank robbers for the most part, and they came and went as various raids were planned. As many as thirty or forty men were later identified as having participated in one Barker robbery or another. This terror gang remained fairly anonymous until the Barkers decided to momentarily quit bank robbing and begin kidnapping millionaires, a rash and ill-chosen enterprise that suddenly brought them national press attention and caused their identities to be pinpointed.

What confused police hunting the Barkers was the inconsistency of their operations. The gang members would conduct a sophisticated robbery on one hand where the bank to be robbed was surveyed carefully, its financial holdings determined and safe entries and exits from the bank meticulously planned, getting away with staggering amounts of money. On the other hand the Barkers would randomly pull petty stickups for a few hundred dollars. Unknown to the police was the character of Fred and, on occasion, Arthur Barker, one which caused them to seize any kind of opportunity to commit a crime, no matter how paltry. They were thugs at heart who associated with seasoned criminals like Harvey Bailey, Frank Nash, and the Holden-Keating gangs which really planned and executed the more spectacular crimes which involved the Barkers but were not of their creation. The periodic spurts of bloodletting committed by the Barkers was due to the neurotic nature of the brothers, especially Freddie, who was certainly unbalanced if not legally certifiable as insane; insanity had coursed through the blood of the Barkers for generations and their mother was often described as "touched" by family friends.

The reason why the gang could so completely disappear after committing an infamous crime was to be found in their political associates, particularly those in so-called "safe" cities like St. Paul, Minn., Kansas City, Mo., and Hot Springs, Ark., cities that were then controlled by corrupt administrations and equally venal police departments which allowed wanted fugitives to establish comfortable havens in their towns, for a price, of course. The authorities in these cities insisted on only one rule which bound these gangsters. They were never to commit crimes in the "safe" cities. Kansas City was the most notorious of these, controlled by the Pendergast Machine and underworld Kansas City boss, Johnny Lazia. When Harvey Bailey, Thomas Holden, Francis Keating, and Frank Nash were arrested at a golf course in Kansas City it was not by local police but by FBI agents who avoided seeking the help of local officers, thinking rightly that the gangsters would be contacted by friendly officers and thereby evade capture.

Unlike most of the independent bank robbing bands of the Midwest at the time—those led by John Dillinger, Charles Arthur "Pretty Boy" Floyd, George "Baby Face" Nelson—the Barkers maintained close relationships with high ranking members of organized crime in the cities. The gang, from 1931 to 1935, reaped enormous profits from its illegal operations, robberies, kidnappings, and burglaries, several million dollars and a goodly portion of this money was used to pay off not only corrupt officials but city crime czars who controlled those officials, in return for protection against arrest and prosecution.

The much publicized core of the gang, of course was Ma Barker, who was heralded by FBI promoters, once she was identified, as a criminal mastermind who planned all the robberies and kidnappings enacted by her ruthless sons. She was profiled in the press as an evil genius who had no regard for life and who had developed sources of information on banks and police at high governmental levels which she had corrupted with enormous payoffs. The FBI position was based upon the fact that Ma Barker was always present with the chief members of the gang and moved with them as they roamed from Minnesota to Texas, from Nebraska to Illinois. (The Barkers never raided in Indiana as that state was the established province of John Dillinger and his super gang.) The only reason for Ma Barker's persistent presence with the gang, J. Edgar Hoover rationalized, was that she was its guiding light, its director of operations, a shrewd, calculating female who successfully matched wits with the best of law enforcement agencies and officials. This was far from reality.

Ma Barker (1872-1935) was born Arizona Donnie Clark, near Springfield, Mo., in the foothills of the Ozarks. One of her most oft-repeated memories was seeing Jesse James and his gang ride through Carthage, Mo., one day and she became enthralled with the outlaw bands of the West, so struck was she by the image of the tall, handsome bandit. In 1892, she was absorbed by the exploits of the Dalton gang which was shot to pieces that year in Coffeyville, Kan., while trying to rob two banks simultaneously. It was also in 1892 that "Arrie," as she preferred to be called, married George Barker, a common laborer. The couple settled down in Aurora, Mo., where they produced four errant sons, Herman (1894-1927), Lloyd (1896-1949), Arthur (1899-1939), and Fred (1902-35). All of them lived by the gun and died violent deaths, as did their mother. The boys grew up with no thought for formal education, as had been the case with their uneducated mother. They were seldom in school, and before they were teenagers they were charged with fighting, damaging private property, and committing petty thievery. When neighbors and authorities complained to Ma, she exploded, defending her sons against all accusations, saying "they are good boys and mind me. You mind your own business."

George Barker was an ineffectual husband and father who invariably bowed to his wife's decisions. When officials approached him to explain his sons' actions, Barker would shrug and say: "You'll have to talk with Mother. She handles the boys." Later, after he had left his volatile wife and her killer brood, Barker would say: "She'd pack up those boys and take them to Sunday School every week and I don't know why. Because when I tried to straighten them up, she'd fly into me. She never would let me do with them what I wanted to." When churchgoers began to criticize the wild actions of her sons to Ma, she quit the church. Her boys could do no wrong, she said. Ma insisted that the family move to Webb City, Mo., where her boys would stand a better chance of growing up without being persecuted. When Herman Barker, the first of the boys to get into serious trouble, was picked up for petty thievery in 1910, Ma Barker raced to the Webb City police station and there exploded in a tirade against shocked officers. She told them they were persecuting Herman and that she would go to the governor of the state and get them all kicked off the force if they did not release her son immediately. They did. Herman was arrested in 1915 for highway robbery, and again Ma Barker managed to get him released. "My boys are marked," she told neighbors as the family prepared to move again, this time to Tulsa, Okla. "The police here (in Webb City) won't ever stop picking on my boys."

It was the same story in Tulsa where the Barker boys were

regularly picked up by police for fighting, stealing and damaging property. Always, Ma Barker appeared before authorities and, through tantrums, tears, and promises, managed to get them released. They would never do it again. They are just active boys, a little wild, that's all. But it was Ma Barker who set the example her boys so diligently followed. By 1915, her Tulsa home became a haven for the most notorious fugitives in the Southwest. Wanted train and bank robbers Al Spencer, Frank Nash, Earl Thayer, Ray Terrill, Francis Keating, and Thomas Holden all hid in Ma Barker's home at one time or another. Her sons saw an endless parade of armed men sitting about the place, drinking, playing cards, bragging of their crimes which inspired the brothers to believe that there was glamour and adventure in such pursuits—notions their own mother wholeheartedly embraced. She held these men up to her sons as admirable and worthy of imitation, undoubtedly clutching her childhood image of border bandits and seeing these latter day outlaws as reincarnations of Jesse James and the Younger Brothers.

When they were teenagers, the boys began carrying guns and committing small-time holdups. They all belonged to the Central Gang in Tulsa and they planned the robberies of grocery stores and small shops. In 1922, Lloyd was the first to enter the "big time" by attempting to hold up a post office. He was caught, and this time nothing Ma Barker could do or say would save her son from prison. Lloyd Barker was convicted and sent to Leavenworth for twenty-five years. He would serve all his time and be released in 1947, the only brother to survive the Barker crime wave. The diminutive Arthur, called Dock (or Doc), who stood only five feet, three inches, was the next to run afoul of the law. He had run up a string of arrests since 1918 for stealing cars and for robberies. Just after Lloyd was sent to Leavenworth, Dock Barker was convicted of murdering a night watchman in a Tulsa Hospital which had been robbed of a drug shipment. He was sent to the Oklahoma State Prison to serve a life sentence. Dock insisted that he never committed this crime, and his mother backed this tale up by convincing a 20-year-old apprentice bandit named Volney Davis to later claim he committed the crime. Dock Barker did, indeed, steal the drugs and commit the murder; he was a morphine addict, a habit he picked up from one of his mother's star boarders, Ray Terrill.

The youngest of the clan, Fred Barker, was also busy during the 1920s, committing many wild holdups and being arrested and briefly jailed. His mother always managed to bail him out but Fred finally drew a ten-to-fifteen-year sentence for armed robbery and was sent to the Kansas State Penitentiary in Lansing. There he met youthful but dedicated robbers such as himself, befriending Larry DeVol, Volney Davis, and a young Canadian thief named Alvin "Creepy" Karpis. It was reported later that Barker and Karpis, who shared a cell together, became so intimate that they became lovers. Said James Henry "Blackie" Audett years later: "All them Barkers, except Dock, were homosexuals and there ain't nothin' worse than a homosexual bank robber and killer. You see, if one of them saw a cop coming at them with a weapon they would shoot to kill 'cause they thought their lover might be bumped off. They was protecting their lovers, as well as themselves. Freddie killed a lot of people later to save his sweetheart Karpis and it was the same way with Karpis who said he never killed anyone but he did, plenty, I saw him do it when I was with that gang for a short time. They were all kill-crazy lovers."

Audett later claimed that homosexual practices were common in the Barker family and that here again the boys took their cue from Ma who was an erratic heterosexual but was also at times a pronounced lesbian. "Hell, Freddie and Karpis spent most of their time, when not knocking over banks, running around trying to find young girls for Ma. This was when they was hiding out in northern Minnesota where they had a lodge all to themselves. The boys would bring the girls to Ma and when the old lady was through with them she would tell Freddie and "Creepy" Karpis to get rid of them and those two crackpots would just up and kill these poor girls and dump their bodies into the lakes nearby.

God, there were bodies of young girls floating all over those Minnesota lakes because of crazy old Ma Barker. Disgusting; the whole bunch of them made me so sick that I only went on two jobs with them. They couldn't keep regulars in the gang because of the way they lived.

"Dock didn't go for any of that. He lived apart from his brother Fred and Ma. He had a girl, maybe a wife, nobody knew for sure. Dock steered clear of Freddie when he could and said little when they planned their jobs. He knew his brother was crazy and would kill anyone, except Ma. Dock walked into a room by accident once and found Fred and Karpis in bed together and Fred fired a shot at him, his own brother, that just barely missed him. That's how Freddie was all right, a fag nut. When Karpis tried to change his looks later by going to a plastic surgeon who botched the job, Freddie took one look at his sweetheart and got sick. Freddie called him "Creepy" after that and the name stuck. The surgeon made Karpis look like a monster, and I think that the hot love Fred had for Karpis cooled real fast after that. No one could work with the Barkers for long. Old Harve Bailey did the Fort Scott job with them and told me later that he would never go with them again. 'Those guys like killing people,' he told me, 'makes 'em feel like bigshots. They're punks.' Well, they might not have been as strange and crazy as Clyde Barrow and that little ugly witch friend of his, Bonnie Parker, but they were nuts enough to scare the hell out of anyone."

Herman Barker was the next brother to go to prison. He joined Ray Terrill of the Kimes-Terrill gang in robbing several banks is the Midwest but the two were captured following a Missouri bank raid. The reason for this was Terrill's implementation of a unique if not prompt bank robbery technique that Terrill had picked up from his one-time partner, Matt Kimes. This involved dragging a small, moveable safe from the bank, lifting it into a truck by a pulley system and then opening it later at leisure. When Barker and Terrill took too much time hauling away the safe, a posse caught up with them and took them prisoners. Herman Barker managed to escape but was wounded. He, like all of his brothers had done, limped back home to Ma Barker in Tulsa where she tended his wound and encouraged him to try simpler methods of robbing banks. Herman decided to stick to robbing stores which offered less resistance than banks but even here his luck ran out. On Sept. 18, 1927, Barker robbed a store in Newton, Kan., but a local police officer, J.E. Marshall exchanged shots with Barker as he sped out of town. Marshall died of his wounds and the next day Herman Barker was found dead in his car which was in a ditch outside of Wichita. It appeared that he pulled over after being wounded by Marshall's bullet and decided to end it all, putting a bullet into his own brain.

For almost four years Ma Barker lived without her sons. Herman was dead, and Lloyd, Arthur, and Freddie were in prison. Her husband, George Barker, had already left her. She took up with a dapper but penniless bill poster, Arthur Dunlop, a man in his sixties with a drinking problem, but he was better than no man at all. Ma spent most of her time writing petitions to governors, begging for the release of her sons, tearfully claiming that they were her sole support and that she would surely die of starvation without their financial aid. Her deluge of letters, petitions, and demands finally paid off when Freddie Barker, along with his cellmate Alvin Karpis, were paroled from the Kansas State Penitentiary on Mar. 20, 1931. He and Karpis immediately went about the job of supporting Ma Barker by burglarizing several clothing stores in Missouri and Kansas. They dutifully brought their loot back to Ma who fenced the stolen goods through her Tulsa contacts. Karpis was treated by Ma as an adopted son, urging him to take what he wanted in life.

Karpis later stated: "What I wanted was big automobiles like rich people had and everything like that. I didn't see how I was going to get them by making a fool of myself and working all my life." Whatever Fred Barker decided they would do, Karpis agreed to do, from robbery to kidnapping and, if necessary, murder. Ma Barker's active role in the gang that these two eventually put to-

Herman, Arthur (Dock), and Freddie Barker.

Ma Barker with paramour Arthur Dunlop.

Ma and lover Dunlop.

Barker gangsters Larry DeVol and Alvin Karpis.

Volney Davis

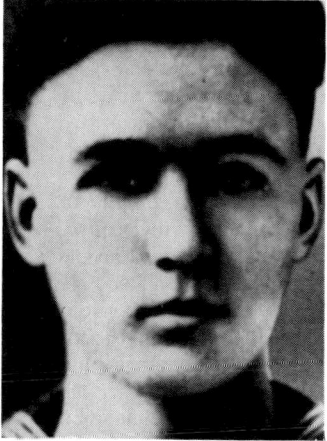

Byron "Monty" Bolton

Edna Murray

Fred Goetz (Shotgun Zeigler)

Crime boss Harry Sawyer

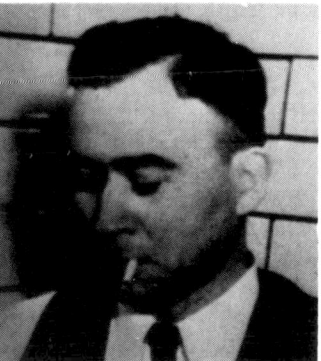

"Lapland Willie" Weaver

gether has long been in debate. She was portrayed by J. Edgar Hoover in later years as "an animal mother of the she-wolf type" who had been, because of Herman's suicide, transformed "to a veritable beast of prey." According to the FBI, Ma Barker was, indeed, the brains of the gang but Karpis later insisted that she was nothing more than a mumbling, fat old lady to whom Fred Barker was pathologically devoted. Harvey Bailey, who participated in the 1932 Fort Scott bank robbery with the Barkers, later supported Karpis' claims, saying that Ma Barker, who was never arrested in her life, had no role in gang activities, let alone planning its raids. Said Bailey in later years: "The old woman couldn't plan breakfast. When we'd sit down to plan a bank job, she'd go into the other room and listen to Amos and Andy, or hillbilly music on the radio. She just went along with Freddie because she had no choice. Freddie loved his mother and wouldn't leave her to fend for herself."

The Barkers decided that Tulsa would not do as a hub of their robbery activities; they decided they needed a hideout much more remote and inaccessible. Ma and Freddie bought a ramshackle farmhouse near Koskonong, Mo., which Karpis, who was skilled in mechanics, rigged an elaborate electronic system which warned the occupants of anyone entering the front gate area by ringing alarm bells throughout the house. From this house Fred Barker and Karpis, who then lived under the aliases of Dunn and Hamilton, made sorties into Missouri, Kansas, Arkansas, and Oklahoma. In July 1931, Barker and Karpis robbed a store in West Plains, Mo., without mishap but two days later Sheriff C.R. Kelly spotted both men sitting in their car, sorting out loot from the robbery. He pulled his gun but Barker and Karpis shot him down and left Kelly dead in the road. The Barkers quickly deserted the Koskonong hideout, leaving trunks of clothing and letters—the thin, shoddy memorabilia of the Barker clan. In her haste, Ma left the family Bible, old dolls she had collected as a child, and the faded report cards of her wayward sons from schools in southern Missouri—all showing poor grades. Also found by searching lawmen were letters to Ma from her sons sent from prison, all claiming innocence, professing reform, and expressing their deep affection for the mother who was mostly responsible for sending them behind bars.

The family moved to Kansas City, and within a few months Fred Barker, Karpis, Bill Weaver, and James Wilson robbed the Mountain View, Mo., bank of $7,000. With this stake, the gang moved to another "safe" city, St. Paul, Minn. Here the gang was offered a haven by crime boss Jack Peifer who ran a sprawling nightclub known as Hollyhocks. In this place, and in The Green Lantern, owned by Harry Sawyer (alias Sandlovich), another St. Paul crime kingpin, the Barkers planned wholesale hijackings of clothing, cars, and cigarettes by the truckloads, delivering these goods to Peifer and Sawyer who fenced them and kept the gang in walkabout money through the fall of 1931. The gang members increased as Barker cronies were paroled or escaped from southwestern prisons. These included Volney Davis, who first went to prison for stealing a pair of shoes, and who had gone to prison with Dock Barker for robbery and murder, and William Weaver, an Arkansas gunman who had known Fred Barker and Karpis in the Kansas State Penitentiary at Lansing. Weaver was known as "Lapland Willie" and "Phoenix Donald." Both Davis and Weaver would wind up in Alcatraz, serving life sentences for their roles in the Barker gang kidnapping of Edward G. Bremer (Weaver would drop dead of a heart attack while working in the Rock's laundry in 1954).

Gang members that came and went read like a who's who of the underworld. Seasoned bank robbers Harvey Bailey, Frank Nash, Thomas Holden, and Francis Keating joined the Barkers for bank raids. Lawrence "Larry" DeVol, a vicious gunman later killed in a holdup, enlisted, as did an ex-motorcycle cop named Phil Courtney; Fred Goetz (alias Shotgun Ziegler) who reportedly had a hand in the 1929 St. Valentine's Day Massacre and who would later be killed by Moran gangsters while trying to start his car on a Chicago street; Gus Winkler, who, like Goetz, would also

be killed by Chicago gangsters; Earl Christman who would be mortally wounded in the Barker robbery of the Fairbury bank raid of 1933 and be buried secretly by the gang in Kansas City; Homer "Big Potatoes" Wilson who had robbed banks for twenty years without ever being apprehended. Others included Charles J. Fitzgerald, Monty Bolton, Harry Campbell, Jess Doyle, James Wilson, Tommy Gannon, Isidore Blumenthal (Kid Cann), Tom Philbin, Russell Gibson, and Tommy Banks.

The gang also brought along its women friends, gun molls in the parlance of the day's press and these included Davis' flamboyant and felonious girl friend, Edna "The Kissing Bandit" Murray who had escaped from the Missouri State Penitentiary. Paula Harmon, a friend of Fred Barker's, was sometimes present, but this was not a sexual relationship since Fred maintained a lover's relationship with Karpis. These and other women were not welcomed by Ma Barker who hated any females present within the framework of the gang. They were soon driven out at her urging. Also eliminated was Arthur V. Dunlop, who had been drinking heavily in the winter of 1931-32. He had complained constantly about the incessant moving about by the Barkers and then, when in his cups, began bragging about how he knew about "big jobs" the gang would be pulling soon. Ma Barker had tired of the old man and told Freddie to "get rid of him." Dunlop disappeared but his body was later found floating the icy waters of Lake Freasted in northern Wisconsin.

According to Karpis, Jack Peifer ordered five of his gangsters to take Dunlop "for a ride." They shot him several times, then threw him into the lake. "Peifer's guys bumped off the old man as kind of a return favor to us," Karpis later said. The "return favor" had to do with the work the Barkers had been doing for Peifer, yet it is most probable that Karpis lied and that he and Fred Barker themselves murdered the old man. They seldom left such chores to others, particularly since Fred Barker hated the old man and enjoyed taking lives. He and Karpis had proved that when on a raid in Pocaholtas, Ark., in November 1931. Chief of Police Manley Jackson had stopped their car just outside of that town and they got him to turn around, then shot him five times in the back, killing him.

Barker tired of the small robberies done for the Peifer-Sawyer axis, and he and Karpis went on an impulse bank robbery and brought away considerable cash. Barker and Karpis, accompanied by William Weaver and Larry DeVol, robbed a branch of the Northwestern Bank of Minneapolis in November 1931. The haul was staggering: $81,000 in cash and $185,000 in bonds, a raid that convinced Fred Barker that bank robbery would be his chief occupation in years to come. In the early winter of 1932, accompanied by Larry DeVol, William Weaver, and a few others, Barker and Karpis robbed banks in Redwood Falls, Minn., Flandreau, S.D., and Beloit, Wis. The loot was small but steady. They planned bigger robberies. In May 1932, along with Harvey Bailey, Larry DeVol, and Phil Courtney, Barker and Karpis held up the bank in Fort Scott, Kan., taking $47,000. Barker almost killed several policemen who tried to follow the gang as it sped out of town; he ordered several female bank employees to stand on the running boards of the getaway car so that police would not shoot at the escaping band, an act of violence that caused Bailey to swear off the Barkers for life.

Fred Barker, with Jess Doyle, Frank Nash, Earl Christman, and Alvin Karpis, raided the Cloud County Bank at Concordia, Kan., on July 25, 1932, looting the safe and tellers' cages of a staggering $250,000. It was said by some reporters later that Ma Barker had actually cased this bank, visiting the bank some weeks in advance and pretending to be a wealthy Oklahoma oil woman, telling the bank officials that she was thinking of buying a home in Concordia and moving there. Of course, she would be making substantial deposits but, she asked, was the bank safe from the marauding bank robbers plaguing the Midwest. The officials, according to this account, bent over backwards to show Ma Barker how their alarm system worked, where it was hooked up to a wire that led to the local police station and where their armed guards were positioned. When the gang entered this bank a few weeks later, they knew exactly where to cut the alarm system and quickly disarmed the guards.

Given the emphatic denials by surviving gang members later of Ma Barker's role as "the brains" of the Barker gang, it seems unlikely that uneducated, frumpish Ma could have convinced anyone that she was a law-abiding business woman. Yet she did have a flair for the dramatic and a cunning knowledge of human nature that had molded her streetwise sons, and such an impersonation may not have been beyond her abilities. Harvey Bailey and Alvin Karpis may have portrayed Ma Barker as an ineffectual, mumbling old lady to protect their own images of shrewd desperadoes who planned and enacted their own robberies. It was more likely that the Concordia bank job was planned by the mastermind of the era, Eddie Bentz, who had robbed the Denver Mint in 1922 and had since become the bank planner for almost every important bank robbing band in the Midwest—from the Dillinger gang to the Barkers.

On Sept. 27, 1932, Ma Barker's incessant stream of begging letters to the Governor of Oklahoma paid off; William H. "Alfalfa Bill" Murray granted her son Arthur a parole, an act that would cost several police officers their lives and cause the loss of hundreds of thousands of dollars on the part of bank depositors and kidnap victims. No sooner was Dock back with the Barker brood when plans were made to rob the Third Northwestern Bank of Minneapolis. On this raid, occuring Dec. 16, 1932, were both Fred and Dock Barker, Karpis, Verne Miller, Jess Doyle, Bill Weaver, and Larry DeVol. It was bloody. Police arrived just as the gang emerged from the bank and both Barker brothers and Karpis opened up with their machine guns, killing two officers and wounding a civilian crouching in the street. The take here was small, only $20,000 which caused the gang members to argue about the split. As usual Fred Barker decided the issue by holding a gun in one hand and grabbing what he wanted of the loot with the other.

The next bank robbery, again reportedly planned by master bank caser Eddie Bentz, but some accounts insist Ma Barker did the casing and planning, was the Fairbury, Neb., bank. The gang, which included Ma, Dock, and Fred Barker, Jess Doyle, Frank Nash, Alvin Karpis, and Earl Christman, first wintered in Reno, Nev., enjoying life with the profits of their most recent bank jobs. In April 1933, the gang looted the Fairbury bank of $151,350, another gigantic haul. This robbery was not without violence. Officials of the bank resisted Fred Barker's orders to open the safe at first and Barker went crazy, screaming and shooting into the ceiling. When the bank president still balked, Barker shot him in the leg. Then, as the safe was being opened, one of the bank guards dove for a gun on a counter, and he fired at Earl Christman, mortally wounding him. Both Barker brothers and Karpis opened fire on the guard, killing him. The gang dragged Christman and the loot from the bank to waiting cars and sped out of town, but Christman would be robbing no more banks. He was taken to Verne Miller's Kansas City hideout and died there, raving about riches he would never spend.

The Barkers quit Kansas City and returned to their safe hideout in St. Paul, Minn., on May 29, 1933. Both Fred and Dock Barker met with the city's crime boss, Harry Sawyer, who took them to Jack Peifer's nightclub, Hollyhocks. There they met Fred Goetz, known in underworld circles as Shotgun Ziegler, a man so well-dressed and with such cultured bearing that he appeared to be an upstanding businessman from Chicago. In reality, he was the wayward son of an uppercrust Chicago family who had enlisted in the infant U.S. Air Corps during WWI and had served heroically. He had attended the University of Illinois, School of Engineering, but had run afoul of the law in 1925 when he was arrested for raping a 7-year-old girl. He was also reportedly one of the machine gunners at the 1929 St. Valentine's Day Massacre. Goetz, Sawyer, and Peifer had an idea. They proposed that the Barker gang kidnap a wealthy St. Paul brewer, William A. Hamm. Peifer insisted that Hamm's people would gladly pay $100,000 in

cash for his release. The Barkers jumped at the idea and, after enlisting Karpis, Goetz, Monty Bolton, and Charles J. Fitzgerald, they put the plan into action.

On June 15, 1933, Hamm left his brewery and began to walk to his nearby home on Cable Avenue. He was approached by two men who shoved him into the back seat of a waiting car which sped off. Hamm was held face down on the floor of the car with a gun to the back of his neck. He was given a ransom note and ordered to sign it; the note demanded a payment of $100,000. One of the kidnappers asked who Hamm thought would be the best go-between and the brewer replied that William W. Dunn, sales manager for the brewery would be the best choice. He signed the note which ordered payment and this was later delivered to Dunn. But first Dunn received a call from Alvin Karpis who told him on the phone: "I want to talk to you and I want you to listen to what I am going to say and don't butt in. We have Mr. Hamm. We want you to get $100,000 in fives, tens, and twenty-dollar bills. And see that they aren't marked. If you tell a soul about this or call the police it will be too bad for you and you will never see Hamm again."

When the caller hung up without allowing Dunn to say a word, the sales manager thought at first the call had been a prank. Then, when the note was delivered, Dunn informed the Hamm family and Hamm's mother insisted that the St. Paul police be called in. Meanwhile, the Barkers and Karpis drove Hamm to Bensenville, Ill. En route, a pair of goggles stuffed with cotton were placed over his eyes so he could not see and Hamm was allowed to sit upright for the long ride. When the car arrived at its destination, a door was opened and the brewer felt the icy cold hand of a woman grab his and lead him into a house, up some stairs, and into a small furnished room where he was ordered to keep his back to the door or be shot to death.

Dunn then received a note from the kidnappers, at his St. Paul home, delivered by a taxi driver. Police detectives closed in on the driver who nervously explained that he had been paid by a "young fellow to deliver the note." He said he had no idea what the note contained. The driver was released. The note was a preliminary outline of how the Hamm ransom would be delivered. A short time later, another note arrived at Dunn's home, this also from the kidnappers. The note stated that the kidnappers had trailed the cab driver and had seen the detectives close in; Dunn was informed that he was "not too smart," and that if he continued to have the police involved, Hamm would be killed.

Hamm meanwhile was kept blindfolded and only Fred Goetz talked to him, although his meals were served to him by what Hamm later described as a heavyset woman (the boards beneath her steps creaked when she walked), ostensibly Ma Barker police later concluded when the Barker-Karpis gang was identified as the real kidnappers. Goetz and Hamm chatted about Franklin D. Roosevelt and various beers. Hamm told his kidnapper that when the labels were removed from the bottles he could not tell one beer from another. Said Goetz: "You know I'm a man with a champagne appetite and a beer income." Goetz continued to inform the prisoner about the negotiations but the brewer grew nervous when Goetz snarled at one point: "They're very slow at the other end."

When the brewer had to go to the washroom, he told his captors and Goetz left the room, telling Hamm that the door was open and that he was to walk blindfolded down the hall. He was allowed to take off his goggles when in the washroom but was told that if he emerged without them a guard stationed in the hallway would cut him in half with a burst from his machine gun. Goetz took Hamm's hand and placed it on the barrel of a machine gun to convince him of the threat. On June 17, 1933, the ransom was paid, thrown alongside a roadway by Dunn after he passed a car which blinked its headlights. In Bensenville, some hours later, Goetz entered Hamm's room and told him: "Take off all your clothes and face the wall!" The brewer obeyed, thinking he was going to be murdered and that the gang wanted to bury him without traceable possessions. Instead a razor and a clean shirt were thrown upon the bed and Hamm was told to clean up. "The ransom's been paid," Goetz said laconically. "You're going home."

A short time later, Hamm was again led to a car by the cold-handed woman, and he spent ten hours in a long drive north. Near Wyoming, Minn., the car was stopped and Hamm was ordered to get out. He stood by the side of roadway still wearing his goggles. Alvin Karpis told him: "We're going to get some sandwiches and coffee. Wait here. We're coming back for you." Hamm stood there for almost an hour and then carefully removed his goggles. He was standing in the dark on a country road, alone with only a distant light from a farmhouse to guide him back to civilization. Upon Hamm's return, he was met with a crowd of newsmen; the kidnapping had made national headlines. He was asked what the kidnappers told him before he was released. "They said that if I ever want anything or if they can ever do anything for me to just let them know."

"Did they give you a forwarding address?" asked one reporter facetiously.

"No," smiled Hamm. "They neglected to do that."

The Roger Touhy gang of Chicago would later be rounded up and mistakenly charged by the Department of Justice with the Hamm kidnapping and no one in the Barker-Karpis gang thought to inform authorities otherwise. Its members were too busy planning the next criminal escapade. This was another raid in which lives were lost. The Barker brothers, Karpis, DeVol, and Fitzgerald attacked the Swift Company in South St. Paul, Minn., on Aug. 15, 1933, taking a $30,000 payroll. When two local policemen answered calls for help and started to pursue the two cars in which the gang sped away, machine gun fire killed one officer and wounded another. The gang became more daring, and no robbery was beyond their imagination, no matter the risks. They had successfully escaped from police for almost two years, losing only a few members of the gang.

When Fred Goetz proposed robbing a federal reserve mail truck in Chicago, most of the gang agreed to go on the raid. Only Karpis hung back, telling the others that it was too risky to pull a raid in Chicago, that there were too many police officers to deal with and that the crime would cause the federal agents to be on their trail. The Barkers went ahead with the robbery, joined by Goetz, William Weaver, and Monty Bolton, a hothead with a trigger finger. The raid was a disaster. After stopping the truck and throwing several sacks of what the gang thought was a money shipment into their getaway car, two policemen raced toward the truck, firing their revolvers. Bolton gave a shriek of joy and let loose a burst from his machine gun. The bloodlusting killer instantly killed patrolman Miles A. Cunningham and wounded the other officer before leaping upon the running board of the getaway car which raced off.

Dock Barker, before the gang arrived at its hideout in one of the northern suburbs, tore through the mailbags and found nothing but useless mail and no money. "There's nothing here at all," he told Fred Barker. Fred turned to Goetz, shoving an automatic under his chin. "We almost got killed, the whole bunch of us because of you're nutty idea. I ought to blow that empty head of yours apart!"

"You grabbed the wrong bags," Goetz told him with quivering lips. "Not my fault."

Dock Barker finally managed to calm his psychopathic brother who ordered the car stopped before it reached the Chicago city limits. He shoved Goetz out of the car. "We don't know you anymore. Get lost!"

Ma Barker reportedly chastised her sons for following the hairbrain schemes of Fred Goetz, telling them that they should stick to bank robbery and, in particular, kidnapping—enterprises that paid more than mail trucks. With that, the gang sat down and planned another kidnapping. This time, on Jan. 17, 1934, the gang abducted wealthy St. Paul bank president Edward George Bremer. The banker dropped his 8-year-old daughter at school that morning and began driving to his office, a daily routine that was seldom interrupted. When he brought his car to a halt before

a stop sign, the door of the car was thrown open and an arm thrust toward him holding a gun to his head. "Don't move or I'll kill you," a voice ordered.

The gang followed the same procedures enacted in their kidnapping of Hamm. Goggles stuffed with cotton were placed over Bremer's eyes after he was transferred to another car, and he was ordered to sign a ransom note demanding $200,000 for his safe return. The contact man was Walter Magee, a friend of the Bremer family. Bremer was again taken to the Bensenville, Ill., hideout and held prisoner. He had initially put up a brief struggle and had been pistol whipped. There were cuts on his face and his leg was bruised when one of the kidnappers had slammed a car door on it. In his room, Dock Barker gave Bremer some hot water and a towel and was told to clean up his minor cuts. "It could have been worse," Barker told his captive. If you hadn't put up a fuss you wouldn't have got them (the cuts)."

Unlike the Hamm kidnapping, the Bremer family did not cooperate with police or federal agents, although there were so many mishaps in delivering the ransom money that the Barkers thought police had been contacted. To allay their suspicions, 65-year-old Adolph Bremer called an amazing press conference to state: "I am sorry that the impression has been spread that information (about the kidnapping) has been given to the police. Whatever information has been given out has been against my will, and has created, through the newspapers, a wrong impression...We want to get Eddie back home safe."

Fred Barker remained in St. Paul, attempting first to deal through Magee, then H.T. Nippert, another Bremer family friend, but several ransom delivery arrangements were abandoned when police seemed to be closing in. Days, then weeks passed with the ransom still out of reach. Fred Barker finally exploded and jumped in his car, driving at high speeds all the way to Illinois, shouting at Karpis all the way that he would kill Bremer as soon as he got to Bensenville. Karpis feebly tried to calm him down but gave up, knowing Fred Barker's mercurial temperment took him to mental rages that reason could not reach. When arriving in Bensenville, Fred jumped from the car with two automatics in his hands and raced into the hideout. He ran up the stairs yelling that he was "gonna croak that damned Bremer right now!" At the top of the stairs stood his diminuative older brother Dock.

"What's the matter, Freddie?" Dock said in a quiet voice.

"That stinking banker, I'm gonna cook that bird right now. His friends are just stalling for time so the cops can pick up our trail. Get out of my way, Dock."

The older brother did not move; he stood resolutely in front of his kill-crazy brother and then said: "The man in that room down the hall is worth $200,000, Freddie. Alive, we've got to prove he's still alive or they'll never pay the money."

Fred tried to shove his brother aside: "I don't care about the money. I don't like the guy. He goes."

Dock Barker stepped aside and then uttered the name he knew would bring his brother to his senses: "Sure, blow his brains out but you know what Ma will think about that. Besides, she's up there alone and needs you. If the cops close in up there she won't have anyone in front of her." The mere mention of his mother seemed to calm the killer; Fred Barker's pathological devotion to his mother overrode any thoughts in his troubled mind and his brother Dock knew it. Fred turned around, pocketed his automatics and returned to St. Paul to continue arrangements to pick up the ransom money. (Dock Barker was also devoted to his mother, but was less demonstrative in his loyalty to Ma than Fred. Dock had suffered from severe headaches since childhood, headaches so devastating that it took his mother's soothing hands to rub away the pain; even as an adult Dock would sit next to his mother as she massaged his aching forehead, talking to him about what a great man he was until the nerve-shattering pain left him. Such bizarre scenes were employed in the motion picture *White Heat*, a shocking 1949 film in which James Cagney plays a maniacal gangster named Arthur Cody Jarrett, an almost identical portrayal of Arthur Dock Barker).

William W. Dunn and William A. Hamm (top left), and home of Barthol Mey where Hamm was reportedly kept prisoner (top right) by the Barker gang. House where kidnap victim Edward G. Bremer was held captive (left), and Bremer (right).

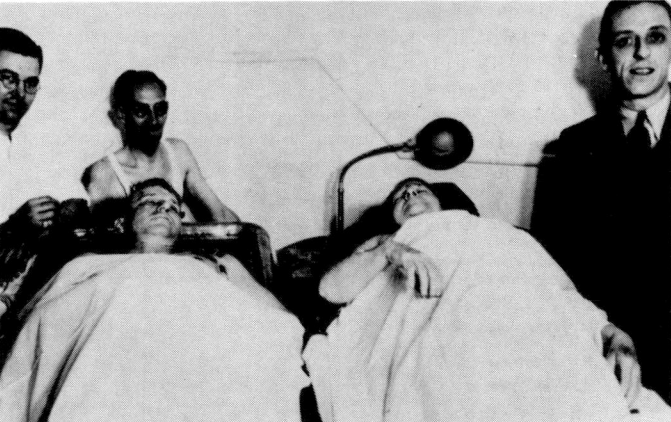

Lake Weir, Florida, after the seige.

Freddie and Ma Barker in the morgue, 1935.

The Barker arsenal at the Florida cottage.

FBI super agent Melvin Purvis.

Weeks went by and Bremer became nervous. At one point Dock Barker gave him a glass of beer. The blindfolded man held up the glass and toasted his kidnapper. "Well, pardner, here's to you." Barker sipped his beer, then said: "This thing is stretching out a helluva lot longer than we expected. It won't be too long before you crack up." Barker then told Bremer that he would have to be chained to his bed at night, but he apologized for the inconvenience. As he was chaining up Bremer that night, Barker said almost in a whisper: "Would it relieve your mind if you believed me when I tell you that I will make sure that you will be returned home safely."

"I'll take your word," Bremer said. "Let's shake on it." He held out his hand, groping blindly for Barker's.

The gangster replied: "Let's just say we did. I don't want you to feel my hands."

The trouble in arranging the pay-off for Bremer was Harry Sawyer. The crime boss had fallen on hard times. His rackets had diminished with the coming of the Great Depression and the gangs were paying him less and less for protection. Moreover, he had helped plan the Bremer kidnapping but had bungled a half dozen ransom deliveries. Ma Barker, according to one report, finally stepped in and insisted that Alvin Karpis handle the pay-off arrangements. Karpis had a Catholic priest deliver a note to Magee which told the recepient to pack $200,000 in five-, ten-, and twenty-dollar bills in a suitcase. He was then to drive to Farmington, Minn., and wait for the Rochester bus which would arrive at 9:15 p.m. He was to follow this bus on its route until he saw four red lights on a hill and he was then to place the suitcase alongside the road and drive off. Magee followed instructions and, on Feb. 7, 1934, the ransom money was delivered.

At the same moment, the kidnappers in Bensenville fell to arguing. Three of them were drinking heavily and the banker overheard one of them insist that "Bremer be bumped. The whole thing has busted wide open." Then Bremer heard Dock Barker say: "No, I gave Ed my word. He took it and it's not going to be broken. I'm running the show." A short time later, Barker came into Bremer's room and told the blind-folded man: "The money has been paid. We're taking you home." He then added a comment that Bremer later thought curious: "Ed, if you ever get into trouble and we're at large, we'll help you, no matter what." As Barker helped Bremer into his coat and began taking him to a car for the return trip home, he said: "Another mob offered us $50,000 for you, now that we're finished with you. They think they can get another $100,000 out of your people." Bremer sagged in the back seat of the car but Barker quickly added: "We turned them down."

Bremer was driven to a lonely spot near Rochester, Minn., and Dock Barker asked him to get out of the car and count to fifteen before removing his blindfold. Bremer began to count but a voice, not Barker's, shouted: "We haven't left yet. Start counting over again, slow." The banker heard the car begin to move off and then stop. He felt sure that the kidnappers had decided to kill him. He heard Barker's voice shout: "Drive on, dammit!" Then the car moved off and Bremer waited until he could no longer hear its motor. The exhausted banker managed to hobble off to a nearby farmhouse and was soon back with his family. Through Bremer's descriptions of sounds and names overhead, along with his estimation of distances he had traveled while being transported by the kidnappers, police and federal agents were able to piece together, for the first time, a profile of the Barker-Karpis gang. Soon its members, through police informants, began to be known. Moreover, the gang had been sloppy, some of its members leaving fingerprints on gasoline cans and a flashlight dropped at the site of the ransom pickup. One by one, the gang members were identified. Soon photos of Dock and Fred Barker, Alvin Karpis, and others began appearing in FBI wanted posters and between the covers of *Liberty* and *True Detective* magazines.

Desperate to change their appearances, Karpis and Fred Barker went to an underworld physician, Dr. Joseph P. "Doc" Moran who specialized in plastic surgery and the alleged eradication of fin-

gerprints. Moran, who maintained offices on Irving Park Boulevard in Chicago, had served a stiff sentence in Joliet Prison for performing illegal abortions on prostitutes working for the Capone brothels. Moran was also an alcoholic who informed Barker and Karpis that not only could he alter their appearances so drastically that no one would ever recognize them but that he could also help to fence the Bremer ransom money. The Barker gang had had little trouble in disposing of the Hamm ransom money; they had unloaded the money in Reno at a loss of only five percent, realizing $95,000. But the Bremer case had brought so much heat from police that normal laundering contacts had refused to handle the ransom money. In desperation, the gang turned to such irresponsible braggarts as Doc Moran to wash the money.

Moran was half drunk when he operated on Barker and Karpis. He injected them with heavy doses of morphine, working on their noses and chins, slicing away fat and tucking folds of skin behind their ears to draw the skin tight over their faces. He scraped their fingertips with a scalpel after freezing them with cocaine. "He sharpened the ends of my fingers the way you'd sharpen a pencil," Karpis later lamented. Both were left with horrible scars, especially Karpis whom Barker dubbed "Creepy" because of his new, grotesque appearance. Barker's thumbs swelled up after they became infected and Ma Barker spent hours nursing him back to health. Moran had been paid $1,250 for the operations but it had been badly botched; both gangsters had been changed little in physical appearance except, in Dock Barker's words, "they were now twice as ugly as when they started." The pain in Fred Barker's hands was so intense that, at one point, he screamed: "I'm gonna kill that guy Moran as soon as I can hold a gun!"

Barker refrained from murdering the doctor, however, continuing to believe the drunken doctor's claims that he could wash the Bremer ransom money. Moran did obtain a small percentage of washed money for the Barkers through a contact man, Russell "Slim Gray" Gibson, who funneled the ransom cash to Chicago politician John J. "Boss" McLaughlin. He returned about ten percent in usable money. McLaughlin tried to pass some of this money and was arrested by the FBI while still holding some of the Bremer cash. This so unnerved the Barkers that the gang left Chicago and moved to Toledo, taking Moran with them. There the doctor, only in his thirties but looking twice that age because of his alcoholism, began to drink night and day. The Toledo mob, headed by Peter Licavoli, offered the Barkers protection (for a price) and while Moran was drinking in one of saloons operated by this mob, he was overheard to loudly tell a prostitute that he could make a fortune by turning in the much-wanted Barkers. "I've got this gang right in the hollow of my hand," he gloated. "Right here." He held up his cupped hand. "In the hollow of my hand!"

The Barker brothers heard about this boast and, in early August 1934, took Moran for a ride. Fred Barker later told Karpis: "Dock and me shot the s.o.b. Anybody who talks to whores is too dangerous to live. We dug a hole in Michigan and dropped him in and covered the hole with lime. I don't think anybody's gonna come across Doc Moran again." (This underworld plastic surgeon was later obliquely profiled in several crime films, including *High Sierra* and *Dark Passage*.) Following the killing of Doc Moran, the Barkers met in Chicago and decided to split up; the gang would scatter and later meet to plan another robbery. Dock took an apartment in Chicago. Fred and Ma Barker traveled to the deep south and finally rented a rural house in Oklawaha, Fla., which overlooked Lake Weir. Karpis and other members of the gang visited them here. They lay about on the beach and Fred Barker and Karpis hunted alligators when in the mood to fire their submachine guns. They would kill a pig and then drag its corpse trailing blood behind their boat, luring the alligators and then spraying these hapless beasts with .45-caliber slugs.

Dock promised to visit his brother and mother after they sent him a map which had the Lake Weir area circled in ink. But Barker never went south. On the night of Jan. 8, 1935, a dozen

FBI agents led by Melvin Purvis surrounded Barker's apartment in Chicago. They had been tipped to the gangster's hideout by Russell "Slim Gray" Gibson, who had made a deal with the agents after being picked up on a drug charge. Gibson himself had been released but when officers went to his room to further interrogate him, Gibson pulled a gun and was shot to death. Dock Barker was, at that moment, taking a walk down the block, an evening constitutional that seldom varied. He had been planning to visit his mother and brother soon. Suddenly, a half dozen FBI agents surrounded him, pointing automatics and submachine guns at him. "Put 'em up, Dock," an agent barked, "you're under arrest." Barker slowly put his hands in the air. Melvin Purvis, agent in charge, stepped forth and frisked the gangster. "Where's your gun?" Purvis asked him. Dock Barker smirked and said: "Home and ain't that a helluva place for it?"

Barker was hustled to FBI headquarters where, for many hours, he was incessantly grilled; the agents wanted to know the whereabouts of his mother and brother Fred. The glinty-eyed gangster would say nothing. Purvis studied the hardened bank robber and kidnapper and later wrote: "He sat in a chair, his jaw clenched, and looked straight ahead. He was not impressive-looking. Only his eyes told the story of an innate savagery." Except for trips to the washroom, Barker was handcuffed to that chair in Purvis' office for eight days and nights, sagging with exhaustion but he remained silent, asking for nothing; he did not beg sleep, food, or silence. Dock Barker had been there before; he had had years of police interrogations, grillings, third degrees. He had spent more than a decade behind prison bars. This was not a man who talked to authorities; only the underworld would ever hear his opinions, learn in fragments his knowledge, know whatever secrets he cared to divulge. To those on the side of the law, his sworn enemies, he offered only silence.

Purvis and his men got lucky, however. In searching Barker's apartment they found a map of Florida with the area around Oklawaha. Squads of FBI agents soon located the Lake Weir House. Fourteen agents, accompanied by local and state police, surrounded the lakeside house on Jan. 16, 1935. The Barkers were told to come out, "one by one, hands over your heads." They had no idea how many persons were in the house. One story has it that an inspector actually knocked on the door and Ma Barker opened it a crack, her eyes narrowed, her jaw set. When she was told to surrender she reportedly snarled: "To hell with you, all of you!" Then she slammed the door and shouted to her loyal son Fred: "Let the damned feds have it! Shoot!" This, of course, was the FBI story as told by J. Edgar Hoover's personal publicist, Courtney Riley Cooper. However, there is no doubt that Ma Barker was not the enfeebled, mindless, muttering old woman depicted by gang members Harvey Bailey and Alvin Karpis. At the end, she was a fierce killer who was seen at an upstairs window of the Lake Weir house and, in her capable hands was a gas-operated automatic rifle which she fired like an expert at agents and officers crouching behind cars and trees. Her son Freddie fired a submachine gun, blasting away at everthing that moved in front of the house that served as their fortress. It was Ma who was heard to yell at the beginning of this vicious gun battle: "All right, go ahead!"

For forty-five minutes the battle raged with FBI agents pumpings hundreds of bullets into the house until it was rented with holes. Yet the Barkers fought on, knowing the battle was futile and they would die at their posts. The agents and officers actually ran out of ammunition during the gunfight, being forced to send for more from a Jacksonville armory. When the firefight resumed, the lawmen began firing teargas bombs through the windows of the cottage and soon the place was gushing smoke and gas. Yet through it, the diehard Barkers continued to fire at the officers. Finally, there was silence from the house. The agents waited, then they brought forth Willie Woodbury, a black handyman who worked for the Barkers. Woodbury was ordered to go into the house and check on their quarry. The handyman timidly went forward and slowly entered the house, calling out to his

employers. There was no answer. In a few minutes he emerged from the house and shouted from the porch: "Dey's hear, boss. Dey's dead." (This is quoted verbatim from the writing of FBI agent Melvin Purvis.)

Upstairs at one window, agents found Fred Barker dead, clutching an automatic with fourteen bullets in him. Next to him was an empty submachine gun. At another window lay Ma Barker, dead with three bullets in her body, one through the heart, this mortal wound later claimed to be self-inflicted. Some claimed that it was to be expected that Ma would opt for suicide, the same self-inflicted fate chosen by her son Herman. The rifle still clutched in her hand still held fifty-four of its ninety-four rounds of ammunition. Hundreds of empty shell casings littered the floor about her to clearly indicate that she had reloaded several times. More than $10,000 in clean cash was found in her handbag, along with a card from Dock in Chicago, mailed two weeks earlier, stating: "See you soon."

Of the Barker-Karpis gang only Karpis and some lesser gangsters were still at large. Dock Barker was sent to prison for life for the Hamm and Bremer kidnappings, and he died in 1939 while attempting to escape from Alcatraz. The surviving Barker son, Lloyd, was released from prison in 1947 but was killed by his wife in 1949. All the bodies of the Barkers eventually wound up in a small cemetery near Welch, Okla., on the ramshackle filling station operated by old George Barker, the father and husband of the deceased. Occasionally a traveller would stop, have the old man fill up his tank and then spot a clump of untended graves on a nearby hillside. When the traveler asked about the graves, George Barker would say, almost in a whisper: "That's Ma and the boys." See: **Alcatraz; Audett, James Henry; Bailey, Harvey; Goetz, Fred; Hoover, J. Edgar; Karpis, Alvin; Kimes-Terrill Gang; Lazia, John; Licavoli, Peter; Miller, Verne; Purvis, Melvin; St. Valentine's Day Massacre; Spencer, Al.**

REF.: Alix, *Ransom Kidnapping in America;* Audett, *Rap Sheet;* CBA; Cooper, *Ten Thousand Public Enemies;* deFord, *The Real Ma Barker;* Demaris, *The Director;* DeNevi, *Alcatraz '46;* Edge, *Run the Cat Roads;* Gaddis, *Birdman of Alcatraz;* Gardner, *Hellcatraz, The Rock of Despair;* Gish, *American Bandits;* Godwin, *Alcatraz, 1868-1963;* Heaney, *Inside the Walls of Alcatraz;* Hoover, *Persons in Hiding;* Johnston, *Alcatraz Island Prison;* Karpis, *The Alvin Karpis Story;* _____, *On the Rock;* Kobler, *Capone;* Louderback, *The Bad Ones;* Messick and Goldblatt, *Kidnapping, The Illustrated History;* Mensch, *Alcatraz;* Moorehead, *Hostages to Fortune;* Nash, *Almanac of World Crime;* _____, *Bloodletters and Badmen;* _____, *Citizen Hoover;* _____, *The Dillinger Dossier;* _____, *Look for the Woman;* Powers, *Secrecy and Power;* Purvis, *American Agent;* Reddig, *Tom's Town;* Reppetto, *The Blue Parade;* Rudensky, *The Gonif;* Sullivan, *The Bureau, My Thirty Years in Hoover's FBI;* Symons, *A Pictorial History of Crime;* Thorwald, *Century of the Detective;* Toland, *The Dillinger Days;* Toledano, *J. Edgar Hoover;* Touhy, *The Stolen Years;* Ungar, *FBI;* Wellman, *A Dynasty of Western Outlaws;* Whitehead, *The FBI Story;* Wicker, *Investigating the FBI;* (FILM) *Queen of the Mob,* 1940; *White Heat,* 1949; *The FBI Story,* 1959; *Ma Barker's Killer Brood,* 1960; *Bloody Mama,* 1970.

Barkley, Clinton (AKA: **Bill Bowen**), prom. 1870s, U.S., west. outl. Clinton Barkley was a Texas gunman who was wanted for murder in 1873, and sought the help of his brother-in-law, Merritt Horrell, of the five battling Horrell Brothers. Horrell promised Barkley that if he came to Lampasas, Texas, Horrell home territory, he would be defended against any lawmen by Horrell guns. As soon as Barkley arrived in Lampasas, a local murder warrant was issued for his arrest and, on Mar. 19, 1873, Captain Thomas Williams, accompanied by three officers, entered Jerry Scott's Matador Saloon in Lampasas, knowing Barkley and the Horrells were inside. The minute Williams and his men stepped through the swinging doors, Barkley, Martin, Tom, and Sam Horrell, along with saloon owner Scott, opened fire with their six-guns. Williams and two of his men dropped to the floor dead while the third deputy returned fire as he backed out of the saloon, his shots wounding Martin and Tom Horrell.

Martin Horrell, who had been taken to a relative's home in Lampasas after being shot, was arrested, along with saloon owner

Scott, both jailed in Georgetown to await trial for murder. A few days later, the Horrells roared into Georgetown and stood guard in front of the jail while Barkley calmly got off his horse with a sledgehammer and assaulted the jail door. Enraged citizens began pot-shooting at the outlaws, slightly wounding Barkley in the shoulder, but he kept swinging the sledgehammer at the door and the Horrells returned fire, wounding lawyer, A.S. Fisher, which caused the rest of the citizens to put up their guns. Barkley broke down the jail door and the Horrells rushed inside, rescuing Martin Horrell and Scott.

Barkley continued to serve the Horrells throughout the bloody Horrell-Higgins war. He was a member of the Horrell faction that raided a Higgins line camp in June 1877, rustling some cattle and shooting down two of Higgins' cowhands. On June 14, 1877, Tom, Martin, and Sam Horrell, accompanied by Barkley, his brother Tom, and two other Horrell men, ran into a Higgins group headed by John Pinckney Calhoun Higgins, his top aide, Bill Wren, his brother-in-law, Frank Mitchell, and half a dozen other Higgins men. Both sides went for their guns and a wild shootout ensued. Wren was wounded by Barkley and the Horrells shot and killed Mitchell. Citizens managed to persuade the gunmen to call a truce which ended the battle. More than a dozen Higgins men sought revenge the following month, July 1877, by boldly attacking the Horrell ranch. For two days, the ranch house was peppered incessantly by the Higgins faction, managing to severely wound two Horrell men before Pink Higgins called off the attack. Barkley was badly unnerved by this last battle and decided to quit the gunslinger business. He packed up his belongings and quietly rode away and out of western history. See: **Horrell-Higgins War.**

REF.: *CBA;* Gillett, *Six Years with the Texas Rangers;* O'Neal, *Encyclopedia of Western Gunfighters;* Webb, *Texas Rangers.*

Barlow, Kenneth, 1919- , Brit., mur. Elizabeth Barlow was pronounced dead in her bathroom on May 3, 1957, by a doctor called to her home at Thornbury Crescent, Bradford. He had been summoned by Kenneth Barlow, Elizabeth's husband, who told the physician that he discovered his wife in the bathtub, her head beneath the water. He had tried artificial respiration, he said, but it did no good. At first authorities believed that the dead woman, known to be ill and in a weakened condition, had suffered an accidental death, but the doctor who first examined the body took note that the dead woman's eyes were dilated. Also, at a later postmortem, several injection marks on the buttocks of the corpse were detected. Officials found hypodermic syringes in the Barlow residence, but this was not considered unusual since Barlow was a male nurse.

Barlow and wife Elizabeth.

Police were suspicious from the beginning, noting that the pajamas Barlow had been wearing when the doctor arrived were not wet, in spite of his claim of seizing the dripping body and giving it artificial respiration. Also, detectives calculated, a drowning person would make some sort of splashing movement that would soak the floor about the bathtub, but the floor was dry when the doctor first arrived. Barlow was charged with murdering his wife, but he insisted that he loved her, saying that he did not have a reason in the world to kill her. (It was later learned that Barlow's first wife had died less than two years earlier at the young age of thirty-three, but her death had been attributed to natural causes; this death was never revealed in Barlow's trial.)

At Barlow's trial before Justice Diplock at the Leeds Assizes, the most damning statements came from Harry Stork, who had

worked with Barlow two years earlier. He recalled how Barlow had boasted of discovering the perfect murder weapon, an injection of insulin which would quickly be dissolved in the bloodstream and be undetectable. Moreover, authorities at St. Luke's Hospital in Huddersfield where Barlow worked, reported that three ampoules of ergotamine had been discovered missing from the medical supplies. Involved statements from medical authorities then argued whether or not insulin was injected into the dead woman, although some traces were found in the body, according to one report. The defense, headed by Bernard Gillis, countered that Elizabeth Barlow, realizing that she was drowning, and in a state of utter panic, released a massive discharge of insulin into her own bloodstream. The prosecution made short work of this preposterous and obviously desperate claim by quickly proving that, for the dead woman to have done so, her pancreas would have had to produce in seconds more than 15,000 units, a physical impossibility.

It was Barlow's own darkly jocular talk with patients and nurses about the perfect murder that eventually brought him down. In addition to Stork, a nurse named Waterhouse at East Riding General Hospital, told the court how Barlow explained that insulin could kill a person with a trace. Barlow had also told a patient, Arthur Evans, then at Northfield Sanitorium in Driffield, Yorkshire, where Barlow was then working, that he could inject insulin into someone and that no one would ever know that this was the cause of death since it could not be traced. The jury stayed out for only a short while before returning to find Barlow Guilty. He was sent to prison for life.

REF.: *CBA;* Furneaux, *Famous Criminal Cases #5;* Heppenstall, *The Sex War and Others;* Hoskins, *The Sound of Murder;* Rowland, *Poisoner in the Dock;* Thorwald, *The Century of the Detective;* ____, *Proof of Poison;* Wilson, *Encyclopedia of Murder.*

Barlow, Silas, prom. 1876, Brit., mur. Barlow met Eliza Soper about a year after his wife passed away. The widower was employed by the South-Western Railway in Britain, and earned a substantial income. In August 1876, Soper, with an infant, rented rooms in a lodging house on Leopold Street in Vauxhall. The landlady, Mrs. Wilson, noticed that her tenant frequently took a man in. This man was her husband, Silas Barlow, she explained.

Several weeks passed. Mrs. Wilson thought nothing more of the arrangement until Eliza pounded on her door on Sept. 3. She was weak, groggy, and unable to stand. The day before Barlow had administered a deadly dose of Battle's Vermin Killer into her glass of sarsaparilla. The light blue powder contained strychnia, which is fatal to humans.

Eliza recovered from her "illness" a few days later. Barlow had failed to give her enough of the poison to make the drink lethal, an oversight he corrected a week later. On Sunday, he knocked at Mrs. Wilson's door to report that his wife had suffered two more convulsive "fits." Doctor James Miller was summoned but Eliza Soper had already slipped into unconsciousness. She died the next day. The young child was also murdered, the body found five days later floating in the river near Battersea.

Barlow was put on trial before Justice Denman on Nov. 27, 1876, at the Central Criminal Court. It was established that the defendant had purchased the pesticide at a small shop on the Vauxhall Road. Small traces of strychnia were found in Soper's body. Barlow was convicted of murder and put to death on Dec. 2, 1876, for the murders of Mrs. Soper and her child.

REF.: Browne, *Trials For Murder By Poisoning; CBA.*

Barmash, Soloman, d.1902, and **Barmash, William,** prom. 1902, and **Bernstein, Hyman,** prom. 1902, and **Bernstein, Philip,** prom. 1902, Brit., forg. Soloman Barmash was a master currency forger who taught his son the trade, but in 1893 their business was abruptly halted when the Crown sentenced both to penal servitude. When the elder Barmash was released some years later, he took up the career of cigar merchant and lived a quiet, honest life until he met an international swindler and forger named Jacob Schmidt.

The crafty Schmidt demonstrated to Barmash his considerable

skills in duplicating the tricky watermark on currency notes. Satisfied that Schmidt's work could stand the test, Barmash assembled a gang of money-passers and set up the German in a flat in a North London suburb where he printed more than 450 notes in three denominations. Barmash purchased a second-hand press for six guineas. Discarded plates were tossed into the Portsmouth Harbor, just in case the police began snooping around.

When Schmidt completed his work, Barmash sent his son William, the slippery con-man Hyman Bernstein, and another man named Stern to the U.S. to pass the counterfeit bills. Things did not go well, however. Treasury agents arrested young William, who had more than £10,000 with him, and Bernstein fled to South Africa. William Barmash returned to Britain with the remaining notes smuggled past customs in a cigar box.

In December 1902 the forgers were taken into custody and put on trial at the Old Bailey. The Barmashes volunteered enough information for the Crown to build a case against the rest of the gang. Soloman Barmash, hoping to earn a reduced sentence, pleaded guilty. But before the final verdict was read, someone—their identity was never established—slipped a small handgun, concealed in a steak and kidney pie, into Barmash's cell, which he used to commit suicide.

Philip Bernstein, whose brother had initiated the forgery, received twenty years in penal servitude. William Barmash was given ten years. "Hymy" was arrested in Cape Town and sent back to London where he was sentenced in May 1903 to ten years, thanks to his brother, who had provided the Crown with enough information to track him down. Fourteen other men with reduced roles in the conspiracy received short prison sentences, thus ending one of the greatest forgery cases in the annals of British crime.

REF.: *CBA*; Nicholls, *Crime Within the Square Mile*.

Barmat Scandal, 1919-25, Ger., polit. corr. Gustav Adolf Bauer was a member of the German Reichstag from 1912-33. In 1919, he was named chancellor until he was forced to step down the next year in the midst of a securities scandal that rocked the foundations of the shaky German republic.

The Ministry of Posts maintained control of some of the largest cash reserves in the country. In 1919 a portion of these assets were invested in a brokerage house owned by a firm called Barmat Brothers. In return for its money the government received securities of dubious value. In 1924 Barmat Brothers declared itself insolvent. The resulting losses sustained by the republic were in excess of $15 million and the Prussian State Bank lost millions more. The Bauer coalition, already under attack from the right, was assailed in the *Lokal Anzeiger*, the newspaper that revealed the exchange of graft money between the former chancellor and Barmat Brothers.

The Barmats were arrested and leading Socialist members of the Reichstag were forced to resign, including Dr. Anton Höfle, the former Minister of Ports. The scandal mirrored the deeper fiscal problems facing Germany in the post-war period, and provided the new Nazi coalition with added propaganda with which to mount an attack against the Weimar Republic. REF.: *CBA*.

Barnave, Antoine Pierre Joseph Marie, 1761-93, Fr., treas. Member of States General and the National Assembly in 1789. He was guillotined in 1793 for advocating a moderate constitutional government and corresponding with the king. REF.: *CBA*.

Barnes, Earle, prom. 1914, U.S., forg. In a case of mistaken identity, a cashier from a large Boston department store named Herbert Andrews was tried and convicted on seventeen counts of passing bad checks. A Suffolk County jury accepted the sworn testimony of seventeen witnesses who positively identified him as the man who had written the checks. Based on their testimony the cashier was found guilty on Feb. 26, 1914, and sentenced in May to fourteen months in prison on Deer Island.

The bad checks kept reappearing, however, even with Andrews behind bars. Suspicion swung to Earle Barnes, a Denver man who posed as a visiting socialite living on Nantasket Beach. He lived extravagantly, writing checks that came back with the terse explanation "no account."

Barnes was arrested on June 12, 1914. Given the overwhelming evidence of guilt and the pile of bad checks bearing his handwriting, Barnes confessed to Captain Armstrong of the Boston Police Department. He was arraigned two days later and pleaded guilty to the same judge who had sentenced Andrews.

Barnes' plea was admitted, and he received a sentence of eighteen months at Deer Island. One mystery remained unsolved: why seventeen witnesses had been so quick to identify Herbert Andrews, who did not resemble Earle Barnes in any way.

REF.: Borchard, *Convicting the Innocent; CBA*.

Barnes, George, See: **Kelly, George**.

Barnes, Harry Elmer, b.1889, U.S., penol.-writer. Teacher and writer, Barnes produced a wealth of useful literature in penology, his major works being *Evaluation of Penology in Pennsylvania*, *The Story of Punishment*, and *Prisons in War Time*. REF.: *CBA*.

Barnes, Leroy (AKA: **Nicky**), 1933- , U.S., drugs-org. crime. Barnes, a black born in Harlem, became a drug pusher early in life and drew a sentence for drug trafficking. While in New York's Green Haven Prison, he befriended Mafia chieftan Joseph "Crazy Joe" Gallo. When both men were released, Gallo formed an alliance with Barnes, financing him and setting him up as the largest drug dealer in Harlem. Barnes became a multi-millionaire, cutting the Gallo Brothers in for a huge slice of the drug profits. As the so-called "King of Harlem," Barnes carried as much as $100,000 in his pockets and owned so many expensive cars that police could not tail them all while keeping him under constant surveillance. Because of Barnes' incredible affluence, there arose a myth about him becoming head of the so-called Black Mafia, an image that Barnes encouraged, even though he was never anything more than a vassal to the Gallos and, subsequently, to other Italian-Sicilian masters.

IRS investigators tried for years to put Barnes in prison for tax evasion, but the crafty drug czar claimed "miscellaneous" income and paid more than $250,000 on these ambiguous earnings, a claim the IRS found next to impossible to disprove. Finally, in 1978, Barnes was caught red-handed on a drug peddling charge, drawing a fine of $125,000 and a term of life imprisonment. Barnes, while serving his time, had repeatedly offered to turn in any and all former associates in his drug peddling in return for release, but he has offered no information of any import and remains behind bars. Though he claimed to have a "Sicilian connection" which funneled drugs straight to Harlem and his operation, Barnes could never prove such an affiliation since it never existed. The Mafia-syndicate, an all-white operation at the hierarchy, has no minority members on its board of directors. See: **Black Mafia**. REF.: *CBA*.

Barnes, Peter, 1907-40, and **Richards, James**, 1910-40, Brit., bomb.-mur. A new wave of Irish Republican Army terrorism hit Britain in 1939-40. This latest move to gain political independence for the six counties in Northern Ireland came about as a result of the "S Plan," a radical plot to create chaos in the streets. Manchester, Birmingham, London, Liverpool, and Coventry were targeted for random acts of bombing and terror. However, the plan did not receive the sanction of Irish Prime Minister Eamon de Valera, himself a former IRA member who favored political separation, but only through peaceful means. De Valera had outlawed IRA activity in his country.

This did not deter Peter Barnes and James Richards from carrying out a bombing in the streets of Coventry on Aug. 25, 1939. Barnes and Richards took up lodging with Joseph Hewitt, a tinsmith, and his family. The three men then constructed a bombing device, and hid their supplies in a hole under the stairs in Hewitt's house.

On Aug. 22, Barnes and Richards purchased a bicycle from the Halford Cycle Company. The final pieces of the bomb were assembled two days later, placed in the carrier basket on the bike which was taken to Broadgate in Coventry, and left alongside a parked car. The bomb went off at 2:32 p.m., with devastating effect. Five people died including Elsie Anscll, whom the plotters were eventually charged with murdering.

It was easy for the police to trace the bombers. A registration number on the bicycle was salvaged, and traces of potassium chlorate were later found at the Clara Street residence. Barnes, Richards, the Hewitts and Mrs O'Hara, Hewitt's mother-in-law, were charged with murder under the 1883 Explosive Substances Act. Their trial began in Birmingham on Dec. 11, 1939.

Mrs. O'Hara and her family were acquitted. The two IRA men, Barnes and Richards, were convicted and hanged at Winson Green Prison in Birmingham on Feb. 7, 1940. In Dublin a thousand protestors carried black flags through the streets in honor of the martyred IRA men. Prime Minister De Valera, who once spent time in a British prison for burning the Union Jack, said the IRA program of direct action would hinder Northern Ireland in its struggle for independence but would strengthen his people's resolve.

REF.: Burt, *Commander Burt of the Scotland Yard; CBA;* Wilson, *Encyclopedia of Murder.*

Barnes, Robert, 1495-1540, Brit., her. Jailed by Cardinal Thomas Wolsey in 1526 for his work with the Protestant church. He escaped and fled to Europe to meet with Martin Luther. When he returned to England he was burned for religious heresy under the terms of the Six Articles. REF.: *CBA.*

Barnes, Seaborn (Seaborne or **Seab** or **Sebe, AKA: Nubbins Colt),** 1853-78, U.S., west. outl. Born in Tarrant County in north Texas, Barnes was an illiterate hardcase who went to work as a cowboy in his early teens. His father, a lawman, died while Barnes was a small child and his widowed mother moved with her five children to Handley, Texas, a few miles from Fort Worth. There Barnes and his family lived off the charity of relatives and the boy grew up embittered over being a have-not. He went to work early, lacking any kind of education, cooking for local ranchers. He also worked briefly as a potter in Denton County. When he was only seventeen, Barnes was jailed for a year in Fort Worth over a shooting. He did not hold his liquor well and was involved in many barroom fights. He was arrested several times for assault and was jailed in 1874 in Calahan County, but he escaped wearing his leg irons. Hobbling across the street from the jail, Barnes forced the local blacksmith to hack off the shackles before he fled on a stolen horse. He joined Sam Bass, already a notorious Nebraska bandit who arrived in the Fort Worth-Dallas area in 1878. Barnes became Bass' most loyal lieutenant, following the bandit chief in several desperate holdups in the spring of 1878. Others in the band included Thomas Spotswood, Arkansas Johnson, Frank Jackson, Henry Underwood, Sam Pipes, and Albert Herndon.

Barnes participated in all the train robberies Bass engineered, helping to rob the Texas Central at Allen Station on Feb. 22, 1878, stopping a train on the same line at Hutchins, Texas, on Mar. 18, looting the mail car of a Texas and Pacific train near Eagle Ford on Apr. 4 and stopping a train of the same line at Mesquite on Apr. 10. It was during this last robbery that the Bass gang met strong opposition. As they approached the mail car a tremendous fusillade was unleashed by citizens in the passenger cars, along with guards who were escorting some captives to prison and armed railway detectives. Several of the gang were wounded, Barnes being the worst hit. Three bullets struck his right leg and one punctured the left. Barnes barely managed to mount his horse and gallop off with the rest of the gang.

Following the spate of train robberies, which netted the gang little more than $1,000, the Texas Rangers and local lawmen by the score began searching for the outlaws. A large posse led by Texas Ranger captain June Peak and Sheriff W.F. Eagan, cornered the Bass gang near Salt Creek in Wise County on June 13, 1878. A terrific gun battle ensued in which Arkansas Johnson was killed and others were wounded. Bass, Barnes, and others managed to escape on foot after the posse captured their horses. They slipped by the posse during the night, reached a nearby farm where they stole some horses, and then escaped. The gang, now down to Bass, Barnes, Frank Jackson, and Jim Murphy, planned to rob the

bank at Round Rock, Texas, on Sept. 20, 1878. Murphy had secretly agreed to inform on the gang some time earlier to extricate his family from felony charges. He informed the local contingent of the Texas Rangers of the impending raid on Round Rock and when the gang rode into town a day earlier than the planned bank robbery to survey the town, the Rangers were waiting for them, trapping them in a local store as they were buying tobacco.

Barnes was approached in Koppel's Store by Deputy Sheriffs Morris Moore and Ellis Grimes. Grimes noticed a bulge beneath Barnes' coat. He put his hand on Barnes' shoulder, telling him that there was a local ordinance against carrying firearms. "Are you armed, young man?", Grimes asked Barnes from behind his back. Barnes turned, reaching beneath his coat, and pulling forth his pistol which he fired. Grimes fell backward, dead. Deputy Moore returned fire but he was hit several times by shots from Bass and Jackson. Murphy was not present, having told Bass that he would look around town to see "if the Rangers were about." The trio fled the store but a hail of bullets slammed into them from the guns of a half dozen Rangers and lawmen running toward the outlaws. Barnes tried to untether his horse but Ranger Dick Ware, who had not expected the outlaws until the next day and had been in the barbershop, raced to the street with lather on his face. He drew his weapon and fired only once, but his bullet struck Seaborn Barnes square in the forehead and killed him instantly.

Jackson and Bass galloped from the scene. Bass was by then mortally wounded and died a short time later. Jackson made a permanent escape. Murphy, the traitor, identified Barnes by the four bullet wounds in his legs.

Barnes was buried next to his bandit chieftan, and on his tombstone read the words: "He was right bower (sea anchor) to Sam Bass." See: **Bass, Sam; Jackson, Frank.**

REF.: Bartholomew, *The Biographical Album of Western Gunfighters;* Bates, *History and Reminescences of Denton County;* Breihan, *Badmen of Frontier Days;* ____, *Outlaws of the Old West;* Brent, *Great Western Heroes;* Brown, *Sam Bass and Company;* Casey, *The Texas Border and Some Borderliners;* Castleman, *Sam Bass, The Train Robber; CBA;* Chilton, *The Book of the West;* Clark, *Then Came the Railroads;* Cowling, *Geography of Denton County;* Cunningham, *Triggernometry;* Fallwell, *The Texas Rangers;* Farrow, *Troublesome Times in Texas;* Gard, *Sam Bass;* Grisham, *Tame the Reckless Wind, The Life and Legends of Sam Bass;* Hendricks, *The Bad Man of the West;* Hogg, *Authentic History of Sam Bass and His Gang;* Holloway, *Texas Gun Lore;* Horan, *Pictorial History of the Wild West;* ____, *The Wild Bunch;* Hullah, *The Train Robber's Career;* Hutchinson, *The Life and Personal Reminescences of Eugene Manlove Rhodes;* McGiffin, *Ten Tall Texans;* Martin, *A Sketch of Sam Bass, the Bandit;* O'Neal, *Encyclopedia of Western Gunfighters;* Penfield, *Dig Here!;* Raymond, *Captain Lee Hall of Texas;* Rennert, *Western Outlaws;* Roberts, *Rangers and Sovereignty;* Sterling, *Famous Western Outlaw-Sheriff Battles;* Webb, *The Texas Rangers.*

Barnes, Stanley Nelson, 1900- , U.S., jur. Fellow of the American Institute of Forensic Medicine. President Dwight D. Eisenhower appointed him judge of the Ninth Circuit Court in 1956. He and S. Chesterfield Oppenheim published *Report of the Attorney General's National Committee to Study the Anti-trust Laws* (1956). REF.: *CBA.*

Barneveldt, Jan van Olden (Johan van Oldenbarnevelt or **Jan van Olden Barneveld),** 1547-1619, Neth., treas. Called the "Father of Dutch Independence," he participated in the Netherlands' 1568 revolt against Spain, and helped frame the Triple Alliance with England and France against Spain in 1596. In 1618, he was illegally arrested for subversion and treason, tried without legal counsel, and beheaded in 1619. REF.: *CBA.*

Barney, Elvira Dolores, 1905-36, Case of, Brit., mur. Elvira Dolores Barney was a rich, spoiled woman who had had everything since birth. Her father, Sir John Mullens, had given Barney everything in life and by the time she was in her twenties, she had become the epitome of the wealthy flapper. She was a heavy drinker, gave wild parties in her exclusive London townhouse, and followed the hedonist lifestyle typified by Evelyn Waugh in works like *Vile Bodies*. Barney's husband left her in 1930, but she continued her unstable and dissolute life, taking a lover, 24-year-old unemployed dress designer, Michael Scott Stephen, a gigolo, really, who lived off of rich women and was almost three years younger than Barney. Their love affair was tempestuous. First the couple would make passionate, non-stop love, the next night Scott would be banished to a couch in the living room of the Barney townhouse for some insult he had hurled at Barney. Their arguments were notorious, sometimes lasting for hours, from late at night until the next morning. The neighbors heard them roaring and the crash of broken glass and tumbling furniture was commonplace. All that ended early in the morning of May 31, 1932.

Playgirl Elvira Barney.

At that hour Dr. Thomas Durrant, a highly esteemed London doctor, arrived at the Barney house, answering a desperate summons from Barney. When he entered the living room he saw Stephen on the floor with a revolver in his left hand. "He can't be dead!" Barney shrieked, "He can't be! He wanted to tell you himself...I love him so... He wanted to see you to tell you it was an accident." Suddenly, Barney made a move toward the gun, shouting: "Let me die, let me die—I want to kill myself!" Dr. Durrant stepped on the revolver to stop her from picking it up. The doctor placed the nearly hysterical woman in a chair, and she finally told him, through sobs, a disjointed story of how she and Stephen had argued and how he had picked up the revolver from beneath a cushion where it was hidden. They had struggled for the weapon and it had gone off, the bullet striking him. "As we were struggling together—he wanted to take it away, and I wanted to get it back—it went off. Our hands were together–his hands and mine."

Detective-Inspector Winter arrived and looked about the townhouse, noting that the bed had been slept in by two people and that there was a bullet hole in the wall near the bed. He asked Barney to accompany him to the station. She refused, ordering him to leave the premises. Then she shouted: "I'll teach you to put me in a cell, you foul swine!" When her parents arrived, however, Barney calmed down and went to the station where she repeated what she had told Dr. Durrant. She was then allowed to return to her parents' posh townhouse in Belgrave Square. On June 3, 1932 she was arrested and charged with murder. She was tried at the Central Criminal Court on July 5, 1932, before Justice Travers Humphreys. Prosecuting was Sir Percival Clarke and defending was the celebrated Patrick Hastings, who initially refused to handle Barney's case. His wife, however, felt sorry for the parents of the accused woman, saying that their good names would be ruined unless their daughter was acquitted. Hastings took the case reluctantly but defended his client with his usual brilliance.

Neighbors who testified at the trial only served to confuse the court. One stated that she heard two shots fired, another heard five shots. Dr. Durrant testified that Barney's affection for her dead lover seemed sincere, reporting that she kissed the corpse several times. The quarrel had been about another woman, some witnesses stated, but Barney denied this, saying that Stephen had threatened to leave her for other reasons and that she had threatened to kill herself if he left. He had struggled with her over the gun to prevent her from committing suicide. Hastings pointed out that the .32-caliber revolver had a hair trigger and no safety catch, making it easy for the weapon to go off accidentally. At another dramatic point, the astute defense counsel, recalling an earlier witness claiming that Barney had fired a weapon with her left hand, suddenly ordered his client to "Pick up that revolver, Barney!" Instinctively, his client picked it up with her *right* hand.

Hastings dealt with forensic experts deftly in this trial, getting the famous pathologist, Bernard Spilsbury, to admit that the bullet received by Stephen might have been fired by the dead man but at an awkward angle. Robert Churchill, the ballistics and weaponry expert for the prosecution, emphatically insisted that it would be next to impossible for the victim to have accidentally killed himself with the revolver since it required an abnormal amount of strength to pull the trigger on this particular weapon. Hastings picked up the revolver and toyed with it as he cross-examined Churchill, casually clicking the trigger as he put his questions, drawing forth low laughter from the gallery, as he off-handedly demonstrated how easy it was to pull the trigger of this weapon. (It was later said that Hastings had exerted so much strength in his show of easy manipulation of that trigger that he almost broke a finger but made it appear that firing the weapon was child's play.)

In his impassioned summation, Hastings addressed the jury with: "I am not going to beg for mercy and a lenient view of what has happened. I stand here and I claim that on the evidence Mrs. Barney is entitled, as of right, to a verdict in her favor. She is a young woman with the whole of her life before her. I beg you to remember that I ask you as a matter of justice and of right, that you should say 'Not Guilty.'" The jury deliberated for one hour and fifty minutes before returning a verdict of Not Guilty. When Barney emerged from the Old Bailey, a great crowd awaited her and she was cheered wildly as she drove off with her parents in their chauffeur-driven limousine. A short while later Elvira Barney, who had survived one of the most sensational murder trials of her era, moved to Paris and lived a haunted, lonely life, dying in her luxurious apartment four years later.

REF.: Browne, *The Scalpel of Scotland Yard*; ____, *Sir Bernard Spilsbury: His Life and Cases*; CBA; Furneaux, *They Died By The Gun*; Hastings, M., *The Other Mr. Churchill*; Hastings, Patricia, *The Life of Patrick Hastings*; Hastings, Sir Patrick, *Autobiography*; ____, *Cases In Court*; Hyde, *Sir Patrick Hastings*; ____, *United in Crime*; Jacobs, *Aspects of Murder*; Lustgarten, *Defender's Triumph*; ____, *The Murder and the Trial*; Rowland, *Criminal Files, Celebrated Trials*; Russell, *Best Murder Cases*; Shew, *A Companion to Murder*; Thorwald, *The Century of the Detective*; Vanstone, *A Man In Plain Clothes*; Wilson, *Encyclopedia of Murder*.

Baron, Joseph Octavius, 1820-38, U.S., mur. Octavius Baron was the son of a Montreal watchmaker, who had immigrated to Canada from Bordeaux, France. By the age of sixteen, Baron amassed a large debt through his profligate activities. To flee the son's creditors, the watchmeaker moved his growing family across the border into New York. They settled in Rochester where it was hoped the boy would learn a useful trade. Instead, Octavius found the billiard parlors, saloons, and sporting houses in the Rochester "tenderloin" more to his liking.

William Lyman was a commercial agent employed by Horace Hooker, who, in 1837, owned a small railroad line operating out of Rochester. Large sums of money frequently passed through his hands. The notes were sent by the Connecticut River Banking Company on a weekly basis to Lyman's attention at the railroad office. This information was conveyed to Baron by two of his friends, Peter Fluett and a man named Bennett who induced him to rob Lyman. "They have heaps of money there," Fluett said. For several days Baron followed Lyman home to determine the best locale for the crime.

Shortly after 9 p.m., on Oct. 23, Baron waylaid Lyman near Andrews, Clinton, and Franklin Streets and neighborhood residents later testified they heard shots ring out. Lyman, who was in the habit of carrying the money home with him each night, was found dead in the street the next day, his money gone. The shot was fired by Baron but it was Bennett who counted the fat roll of bills. After the killing, they went to the U.S. Hotel, where most of the proceeds were split three ways. The remaining sum was wrapped in a handkerchief and put in a woodpile for safe-keeping.

Witnesses were produced who linked Baron to the killing based on the clothing he wore that night. He was arrested by the Rochester police and charged with murder. During interrogation, Baron changed his story several times, first accusing Fluett of pulling the trigger, then Bennett.

Finally, though, Baron was the only member of the gang to stand trial for the murder. His trial began on May 29, 1838, before a panel of three judges and a twelve-man jury. An impressive array of witnesses testified to having seen the flash of a gun on the dark October night, while others told of hearing gunshots from their homes. Baron's earlier confession was admitted into evidence, as shaky as it may have seemed to the defense.

On June 7, the jury returned a verdict of Guilty. Baron assumed a cold air, defiantly maintaining his innocence. He restated his alibi, the one he had given throughout the trial —Bennett fired the pistol, Fluett stole the money from the dead man's pockets, and all Baron did was hold onto the money for safekeeping. The fact that this was a complete reversal of his original confession influenced the jury to return its Guilty verdict. The court sentenced Octavius Baron to hang on July 25, 1838.

REF.: *An Awful Warning to the Youth of America, Report of the Trial of Octavius Baron; CBA.*

Barrack, Margaret, and **Duncan, Mary,** and **Shinney, Janet,** prom. 1759, Scot., rob. On May 31, 1759, by the sentence of the Magistrates of Aberdeen, Scotland, three local women, Barrack, Duncan, and Shinney, were exhibited in the public square with a rope tied around their necks and a placard affixed to the bosom of their dresses proclaiming their guilt. For a period of twenty-four hours, the women were ordered to stand in the Market Cross before being led away on a cart to the outskirts of town from which they were permanently banished. Shinney, Barrack, and Duncan had been found Guilty of stealing small quantities of tea and sugar from a local merchant.

REF.: Andrews, *Old-Time Punishments; CBA.*

Barré, Aime Thomas (AKA: Emile Gérard), 1853-78, and **Lebiez, Paul,** 1853-78, and **Morin, Léontine,** prom. 1878, Fr., mur. In a crime markedly similar to the fictional murder of Alena Ivarovna in Fyodor Dostoevski's *Crime and Punishment,* two young medical students living in Paris decided to kill an old woman who, they thought, had lived too long. "She's an old miser," Lebiez said. "What right has she to hoard up her gold when there are many others who could put it to some use?"

Aime Barré was a promising student who won top academic awards at the Lycée in Angers, where he met his future associate in crime, Paul Lebiez. Like Barré, Lebiez displayed a natural aptitude toward science, especially anatomy. When his friend's money problems became grave in the early winter months of 1878, Lebiez put him up to murder. A wealthy old woman named Mme. Gillet, who lived in a room on the Rue de Paradis-Poissoniére, had earlier refused Barré's request for a loan, though she possessed roughly £500 in negotiable securities, more than enough to help Barré settle his accounts with his creditors, among them a couple of shop girls he had defrauded.

When she refused the loan, Barré and Lebiez decided to murder her. They invited her up to their apartment in the Rue d'Hauteville, where Lebiez stabbed her through the heart and Barré struck her over the head with a hammer. The body was cut up and wrapped in parcels which were taken to a rooming house belonging to a woman named Mme. Jeanson on Mar. 23, 1878.

Barré registered under the name of Emile Gérard. The mysterious bundles were discovered by Jeanson on Apr. 6. At first the police treated them as a practical joke, but they soon were convinced that the remains were those of the missing old woman. Barré was identified by Jeanson as being the same Mr. Gérard who had rented the room some weeks earlier. A handwriting analysis conducted by the magistrate confirmed Jeanson's accusation.

Barré and Lebiez were tried for murder at the Cour d'Assises in Paris in July 1878. Léontine Morin, Barré's mistress, was charged with receiving stolen goods. After only a day of deliberation, a verdict of Guilty was returned against the two murderers. Morin was given three years' imprisonment for her role in the crime.

Before their execution on the guillotine on Sept. 7, Lebiez explained that the only reason he wanted to see the woman dead was so he could get enough money to purchase a new microscope to help him in his scientific studies.

REF.: *CBA;* Irving, *Studies of French Criminals of the Nineteenth Century.*

Barreda Laos, Felipe, prom. 1930s, Peru, lawyer. Peruvian delegate to the Permanent Court of International Justice at the Hague. REF.: *CBA.*

Barrena, Juan, prom. 1930s-40s, Mex., fraud. Juan Barrena was an expert practitioner of the Spanish Prisoner con game. He would rope a wealthy American tourist traveling in Mexico, and, after ingratiating himself, would sorrowfully explain that his sister (sometimes it would be a cousin), a woman of incredible wealth, had been wrongly imprisoned and if she could only be released she would gladly turn over half her fortune to any benefactor bringing about her freedom. Barrena came equipped with all the convincing tools of this ancient and successful con game, providing cleverly faked documents to support the prisoner's identity and bank account statements that would stun any stock broker. The sucker would then begin to pay out sums to Barrena in exchange for the prisoner's fortune, a bleeding process that usually went on for a few weeks (thus making this game one of the Big Cons, in that it took considerable time to mulct the victim, as compared with the short con such as the pigeon-drop where the mark is taken within a few hours).

Barrena was usually assisted by towering, hatchet-faced Camilo Vasquez, who enacted the part of the head jailor in charge of the lady Barrena was trying to free, a greedy penologist who kept insisting that more and more money be paid by the mark. When the sucker appeared to grow suspicious or believe he was overextending himself, the two con men would promise to deliver the prisoner the next night. Invariably, the sucker would be waiting in his car to spirit the beautiful and grateful prisoner away but, of course, she would never appear and Barrena and Vasquez would disappear. So flagrantly tireless were these two con men in the working of the Spanish Prisoner game that they were eventually identified by Mexican police in 1941 and, were delivered to San Francisco authorities by two cooperative Mexican detectives without the benefit of a then existing extradition treaty between the U.S. and Mexico. Both men were tried in San Francisco and given long prison sentences for bilking one embarrassed American businessman out of thousands of dollars.

The Mexican press, however, roared its indignation at the human hijacking of Barrena and Vasquez; one newspaper, *Excelsior,* indicting American authorities for its part in the extralegal abduction of the two con men, which had been labeled out and out kidnapping. Moreover, this publication applauded the con men by stating they had been correcting an uneven balance of money between the U.S. and Mexico and had exposed greedy Americans willing to break the law for a cut of an illegal pie. "If you study the problem purely and strictly from the point of view of justice," editorialized *Excelsior,* "Vasquez and Barrena are nothing more than two patriots—two ingenious helpers of morality...They worked to level the balance of exchange so perniciously weighted in favor of the powerful speakers of English.

They are helpers of morality because they dedicated themselves to the noble task of punishing all secretly immoral persons —defaulters without courage." This high-minded bombast, of course, has been the historic defense of all confidence men everywhere whenever their frauds have been exposed. It did Barrena and Vasquez little good as they were ushered away to serve their time in San Quentin.

REF.: *CBA*; Nash, *Hustlers and Con Men*.

Barrett, Edward, 1900-77, U.S., polit. corr. Eddie Barrett was a powerful cog in the Democratic political machine that ruled Chicago for half a century. Born and reared in the ethnic Irish neighborhoods of Chicago's south side, Barrett entered politics in the early 1930s when Mayor Anton Cermak and Democratic party boss Pat Nash, forged a "machine" that would last in one form or another until the 1980s. When Richard J. Daley was elected mayor in 1955, Barrett began a five-term reign as Cook County Clerk, a position that wielded enormous graft potential.

For seventeen years Daley and Barrett were synonymous with Democratic politics in Chicago. However, by the 1970s the mayor, his machine, and an army of party hacks and ward healers were under attack by younger, more progressive elements just attaining political maturity.

In September 1972, Barrett became one of the first victims of the reformers when a federal grand jury indicted him on charges of receiving $180,000 in kickbacks from a manufacturing company in Pennsylvania that sold voting machines to Cook County. He was found guilty in 1973 and sentenced to a three-year term in the penitentiary. He never served a day, due to a long appeals process and his poor health. He was granted parole, his pension and office were taken away. Barrett died in 1977. REF.: *CBA*.

Barrett, George, d.1936, U.S., mur. Mistaking a government agent for a rival clan member, Barrett opened fire with a gun on a warm summer day in 1935. The murderous mountain man from the backwoods of Kentucky first came to the attention of the federal authorities in 1932 when he killed his aging mother, and then beat his sister to death using the butt of a rifle. That same year he engaged in a five-hour shooting orgy with another hill family he had been feuding with for months.

In 1935 George Barrett was overtaken by G-men after accidentally killing agent Nelson Klein at West College Corner, Ind. The FBI was searching for Barrett in connection with a stolen car scheme he had masterminded. When the Kentucky feuder was taken into custody he was barely alive—his brother-in-law had shot out one of his eyes, and the G-men had fired a volley of slugs into his legs. Despite his wounds, U.S. District Judge Robert C. Baltzell ordered the defendant hanged at the Marion County Jail in March 1936, the first man sentenced to death under a recently enacted statute that mandated capital punishment for anyone convicted of killing a federal officer. Baltzell expressed the hope that God would show mercy on the convicted man's soul. "I think He will, your honor," Barrett smirked.

Indiana was in a dilemma concerning Barrett. Death by hanging was abolished in 1913 when the electric chair was adopted for use in its prison system. The federal government had to supply the equipment, but there was no one left in the state who knew how to carry out a hanging successfully.

An Illinois farmer named Phil Hanna volunteered his services. It was a personal hobby, he explained. Ever since he had witnessed a bungled hanging as a boy, Hanna had practiced the technique on straw dummies. He developed what he called a foolproof method for disposing of felons. Satisfied that they had found the right man, officials hired Hanna was hired to do the job.

Minutes before the appointed hour of execution, Hanna chatted with Barrett. A deputy sheriff released the trap door and Barrett died ten minutes later. REF.: *CBA*.

Barrett, James Emmett, 1922- , U.S., jur. Prosecuting attorney in Lusk, Wyo., from 1950-63 and appointed judge of the Tenth Circuit Court by President Richard M. Nixon in 1971. REF.: *CBA*.

Barrett, Michael, 1841-68, Brit., mur. Barrett was a Fenian who was convicted of setting off the notorious Clerkenwell Prison explosion on the night of Dec. 13, 1867, by shooting into a barrel of gunpowder which blew up a wall of the prison. The blast killed six persons and wounded dozens of others, six of whom later died. The motive for this mass murder was to affect the escape of two Fenians imprisoned behind Clerkenwell's walls. Though the handsome, young Irishman insisted that he had never been near Clerkenwell at the time of the explosion, he was convicted and sentenced to hang, the last person to be publicly hanged in England, on May 26, 1868. There was some doubt about Barrett's guilt and there were a number of high-standing protestors against this last public execution, but it was carried off before several thouand persons who had gathered before Newgate Prison to witness the event, including hundreds of children.

When William Calcraft appeared on the scaffold with the prisoner there was wild cheering from the throng that soon changed to hisses and booing but Barrett ignored the crowd, praying fervently with a priest who stood at his side. He said nothing to executioner Calcraft as the black hood was placed over his head and then the noose tightened about his neck. He was sent through the trap moments later and died quickly, but Calcraft and his assistants took their time cutting Barrett's body down which angered many of those in the crowd who lingered behind, hoping to get some of the dead man's clothes as souvenirs. So incensed were some spectators that they threatened Calcraft and he speedily cut down the body and dragged it into the prison before anyone could lay hands on it.

REF.: Andrews, *Old-Time Punishments;* Bishop, *Executions;* Brock, *A Casebook of Crime;* Browne, *The Rise of Scotland Yard;* CBA; Cooper, *The Lesson of the Scaffold;* Duff, *A New Handbook on Hanging;* Laurence, *A History of Capital Punishment;* Potter, *The Art of Hanging;* Thomson, *The Story of Scotland Yard*.

Barrett, Thomas, 1803-45, U.S., mur. Barrett got drunk on the night of Feb. 18, 1844, and staggered into the wrong house in Luneberg, Mass., or at least that was his later version at his trial, and came upon 70-year-old Mrs. M. Houghton, raping her and then strangling her to conceal the murder. Barrett was promptly convicted at Worcester, Mass., and was hanged there on Jan. 3, 1845.

REF.: *CBA; Trial and Execution of Thomas Barrett.*

Barrett, Will, prom. 1925, U.S., forg. Will Barrett was arrested in Nashville, Tenn., in January 1925 for passing forged checks. He confessed to robbing the village postmaster of Priors, Polk County, Ga., on Sept. 15, 1923, a crime which had resulted in the wrongful conviction and imprisonment of Hugh Lee.

A handwriting comparison convinced detectives that Barrett had signed both sets of forged checks recovered from Nashville and Polk County. Will Barrett, an escapee from the Alabama Penitentiary, was brought to trial in the U.S. District Court, northern Georgia on Feb. 9, 1925. He pleaded guilty and was sentenced to three-and-a-half years in the Atlanta Penitentiary. See: **Lee, Hugh C.**

REF.: Borchard, *Convicting the Innocent; CBA.*

Barrie, Peter C. (AKA: Paddie Barrie), prom. 1930s, U.S., fraud. Of the many race track frauds involving doctored thorough-breds over the years, Barrie stands out as one of the most ingenious of all turf swindlers.

Though his parents were Irish, Peter Barrie was born in Edinburgh, Scotland. He went to work at the stables of Lady Mary Cameron, a wealthy woman who lived outside Edinburgh. At the time, a spotted gray mare with no racing value took up valuable space in the stable, and Lady Cameron was anxious to unload it for whatever she could get. Barrie offered her $85, which she accepted. A few days later Barrie returned with a splendid-looking race horse which he offered to Cameron for $1,400. The bay-colored steed was feisty and ready to run, according to its trainer. The deal was consummated and Barrie left with his money. A few days later colored dye began to run off the horse. The $85 purchase had been made up to look like a prize race horse through narcotics and cheap dye.

Barrie moved to the U.S. where his talents were recognized by the gambling syndicates who paid him $5,000 each time he "doped" a mount that successfully won or lost, depending on the gangsters' strategy at the moment. Pinkerton detectives arrested him at Hialeah and tried to have him deported. However, he jumped bail and remained at large for two years, during which time he perpetrated his greatest swindle.

At Havre de Grace on Oct. 3, 1931, Barrie bought a prized three-year old stallion named Aknahton for $4,300. From a nearby stable he bought a sorrel named Shem who had yet to enter the winner's circle. With the time-tested methods used on Lady Cameron, Barrie made up Aknahton to look like Shem and entered the horse in the first race on the last day, at 52-1 odds. Needless to say, the horse won the event by a commanding four lengths. The heavy wagering returned Barrie and his bookie friends an estimated $1 million. As a result, the Jockey Club asked the Pinkerton Agency to devise a foolproof system of horse identification to prevent a similar deception. Each new horse now receives a number tattoo on the inner upper lip.

Barrie was apprehended by the Pinkertons—two years after he jumped bail—and deported.

REF.: *CBA;* Horan, *The Pinkertons;* Williams, *The Super Crooks.*

Barrington, Daines, 1727-1800, Brit., jur. Son of John Shute Barrington and author of *Observations on the Statutes* (1766). REF.: *CBA.*

Barrington, George, b.1755, Brit., rob. As a schoolboy, Barrington showed a natural bent toward crime. When his schoolmaster beat the lad for what he considered unjust cause, he ran away to the city where he was taught the art of pickpocketing by a troop of touring actors.

After the actors were arrested, George Barrington left for England where he used a variety of clever disguises to throw unsuspecting victims off guard. He assumed a fine air and his undeniable charm served him well at theaters and public receptions, prime locations for a master pickpocket. Arrested twice for theft, he was sentenced to hard labor on board the rotting hulks of prison ships moored on the Thames. He was released a year later, apprehended again, and sentenced to five years' labor. His stay in prison was short this time, as an aristocrat secured Barrington's release on the condition that he leave the country.

Barrington was apprehended a third time in London and sentenced to a seven-year term to be served in Australia. Fortune smiled on him when the other convicts planned a mutiny. Believing that would be folly, he talked them out of it and was given freedom as his reward. In Australia he became a new man, serving the Crown as Superintendent of Convicts and High Constable. He later wrote about his experiences in the highly acclaimed *Voyage to Botany Bay.*

REF.: *CBA;* Hunt, *Dictionary of Rogues.*

Barrington, John Shute (First Viscount), 1678-1734, Brit., lawyer. First Viscount Barrington who, as Emissary to Scotland in 1705, won Presbyterian support for a union with England. REF.: *CBA.*

Barriobero, Eduardo, 1876-1939, Spain, rebel.-mur. Regarded as a champion of the underdog and the politically oppressed, Barriobero was shot by a firing squad on Feb. 10, 1939, after being adjudged Guilty of crimes against the state by the rightist government of Generalissimo Francisco Franco.

Eduardo Barriobero was a deputy in the Spanish Parliament before the outbreak of the Spanish Civil War of 1936. Widely known for his advocacy of left-wing causes, he was a member of a dwindling minority of Spanish Federalists opposed to Franco's fascist insurgents. He became the first high-ranking republican leader seized by the nationalist forces in Barcelona, in February 1939. He was accused of extorting money from wealthy nationalist sympathizers at the outbreak of the revolution in 1936, and was charged with the wholesale murder of one hundred rightists while presiding over the People's Tribunal. In a thirteen-count indictment against the aging leader, it was alleged that Barriobero

deposited the extorted money into his own private account with the Credit Lyonnais in Lyons, France.

"You have always been anti-national, unpatriotic, and un-Spanish," accused the prosecutor, Captain Jose Rodríguez.

"I am an old man and I know my time is near," Barriobero replied to his accusers. "I may have been guilty of common crimes, but I am not guilty of capital crimes. If I took sums of money through fines it was to keep up revolutionary appearances among my comrades. I am not an anarchist. I am a radical anti-clerical Freemason." REF.: *CBA.*

Barrios, Jacinto Girón, 1928-82, and **Carague, Manuel Ren,** 1927-82, Guat., (unsolv.) assass. Within a twenty-four hour period two Guatemalan mayors were gunned down in the streets of their villages in attacks that may have been politically inspired. Mayor Manuel Ren Carague was shot by unknown assassins as he walked toward the marketplace of Chichicastenango on Feb. 7, 1982.

A day earlier, Jacinto Girón Barrios, fifty-four, mayor of San Pedro Jocopilas, was killed while with a family member, 36-year-old Margarita Alicia Girén. No official explanation was given for the random violence, which also claimed the lives of eighteen other persons outside Santa Cruz del Quiché during that same bloody weekend. REF.: *CBA.*

Barroso, Gustavo, b.1888, Braz., lawyer. Author of numerous books including *Herois e Bandidos* (1917). REF.: *CBA.*

Barrow, Clyde Champion, 1909-34, and **Parker, Bonnie,** 1910-34, U.S., rob.-mur. Clyde Barrow and his petite gun moll mistress Bonnie Parker were nothing like the characters portrayed in the film *Bonnie and Clyde.* They were illiterate, unfeeling killers with vicious, cunning personalities, and at all times they expressed the nature of gila monsters. These two, joined by equally brutal Buck Barrow (Clyde's brother), Ray Hamilton, and other southwestern bandits of the early 1930s, spread terror through Texas, Oklahoma, Kansas, Missouri, and other states, stealing penny ante amounts and earning a reputation as utterly lethal killers who enjoyed taking lives. Lawmen quickly learned that to attempt to reason with them was to invite death. For a period of about two years, 1932-34, the Barrow gang, never more than five or six members, became the terror of the Southwest. They preyed upon small store owners, filling stations, and travelers driving along remote roads. They lived in the country for the most part, renting small, cheap cabins, often sleeping in the cars they stole. They were vagrant thiefs with high-powered weapons and, contrary to popular belief, they were never cult heroes to the hill people and squalid farmers who made up their heritage. Bonnie and Clyde preyed upon these poor tenant farmers as much as they attacked and robbed middle-class shopkeepers. They were universally hated, unlike Charles Arthur Floyd from Oklahoma and John Dillinger from Indiana, by their own kind, as well as the police.

The reckless manner in which the Barrows operated, their utter disregard for the law, and their contempt for their own violent ends, which they reveled in predicting, pointed to only one rationale that held the band together—they intended to be killed as they had killed, with the gun, inside a storm of violence. In short, the Barrows were fanatically suicidal. Both Clyde and Bonnie recorded their almost every movement together, taking photographs of each other in menacing poses, writing long letters to their families in which they portrayed themselves as persecuted, misunderstood, young people and sending even longer missives (and even poems) to the newspapers—letters that glorified their robberies and attempted to exonerate their killings. Bonnie mooned over the image of being hunted like an animal and she profiled the vicious Clyde Barrow in her awkward poetry as a heroic outsider who had been driven to crime, who had been forced to commit horrible murders and robberies. It was all an act, of course, played out for the press, which thrived on publicity-seeking killers like Bonnie and Clyde. The black part of the legend was all true.

Clyde was an expert killer who practiced his marksmanship every day he lived outside of prison, firing all manner of weapons: submachine guns, shotguns, rifles, automatics, and revolvers. He

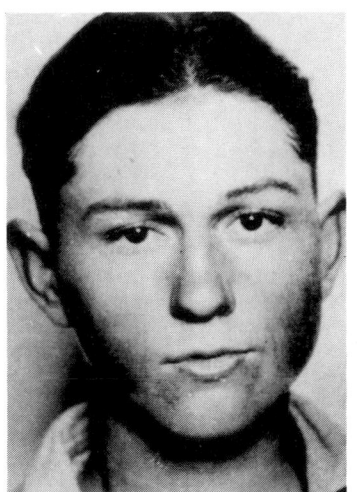

Clyde in his teens.

Ray Hamilton

Bonnie gets the drop on Clyde, 1934.

Bonnie with cigar and revolver, 1934.

Clyde Barrow armed to the teeth.

taught Bonnie Parker to fire all these weapons too, and she, in turn, devised a special trick pocket for Clyde, one where his right trouser was zippered so that he could carry a sawed-off shotgun next to his leg and then, employing the break-away zipper, whip the gun out and fire in one motion. This gun-loving pair appeared in 1932 in the Joplin, Mo., home of Herbert Farmer, an armorer for the bank robbers of that day, asking to look at new Browning Automatic Rifles (BARs) which Farmer had recently stolen from a U.S. Army arsenal. Present at the time was James Henry "Blackie" Audett, who watched as Bonnie and Clyde clutched the new BARs Farmer handed them. "They sat there with gleaming eyes," Audett later recalled, "stroking and fondling those big guns like they were holding their own children. Spit dripped a little bit from the side of Clyde's mouth and Bonnie was purring like a cat in heat. They were nuts, these two punks, real bad killers. Herb (Farmer) knew it, I knew it, and everybody in the business knew it." Indiana bandit John Dillinger expressed the universal underworld opinion of Bonnie and Clyde one day in 1933 when he read of one of their bank robberies (for $1,500, the largest robbery they ever committed), in which the two thiefs shot up the bank and everybody in it. "They're a couple of snot-nosed punks." said Dillinger. "They're giving bank robbing a bad name."

Poverty was at the core of Clyde Barrow's life, always had been, and even in his robbing heyday the most paltry sums disdained by other gangsters of the era were appealing to this nickel-and-dime thief. Born in Teleco, Texas, on Mar. 24, 1909, Clyde was one of eight children, and early on he aped his older brother Ivan Marvin Barrow, called Buck, a troubled and unruly boy who taught Clyde how to steal turkeys and later cars. By the age of ten, Clyde was impossible for his parents to handle; he was an incorrigible petty thief, a runaway, and a truant whom they placed in the Harris County School for boys.

Roy Thornton

When released as a teenager, Clyde joined the Square Root Gang in Houston, committing small burglaries with Ray Hamilton and Frank Clause. One of his thefts included a beat-up saxophone which Clyde practiced on endlessly, much to the annoyance of the other gang members. The Square Rooters spent most of their active evening hours rolling drunks and stealing cars. Clyde called this "high livin'" and taught himself to drive with expert ability.

In 1928, Clyde began robbing gas stations and lunch counters in the Dallas area with his brother Buck, but this crime spree was short-lived. The boys, speeding along a road near Denton, Texas, ran straight into a police blockade and tried to shoot their way out to freedom. Clyde, already an expert driver, was at the wheel, and Buck jumped on the running board of their sedan, firing at police. When Clyde spun the car around, Buck received several police bullets in the arm and legs and fell off the crazily spinning car. Clyde gunned the engine and escaped down the road but Buck was captured and convicted of armed robbery, given five years in Eastham Prison Farm.

In January 1930, after robbing a few stores, Clyde walked into Marco's Cafe in Dallas and ordered a hamburger, so the most popular story goes. He took one look at the 22-year-old, blonde-haired waitress and asked her for a date. She was Bonnie Parker, standing only five feet, born in Rowena, Texas, on Oct. 1, 1910, the daughter of a bricklayer. (Clyde Barrow, like most of the super bandits of the 1930s, the Barker Brothers, Dillinger, Baby-Face Nelson, was a man of small stature, just barely five-foot-six, and he later bragged to friends that "Bonnie is just the right size for a man like me.") Parker was married to a convict named

Roy Thornton, who was serving a ninety-nine-year term in Eastham for murder, but she dated regularly, and once she began to see the neurotic Clyde she moved into a small furnished room in Dallas with him. (The fact that Bonnie had Thornton's initials tattooed on her thigh never bothered Clyde.) She was enthralled by Clyde's fierce temperament and thrilled at the sight of the guns he wore beneath his suitcoat. According to Bonnie's mother, Clyde did not meet Bonnie at Marco's Cafe but at the home of a girlfriend who knew Clyde. He took her on wild rides into the country and there showed her how he could shoot the head off a fast-flying quail. He placed cards in the crevices of farm fences and shot the pips out of them, then cut them in half with automatic fire. They spent hours together practicing their marksmanship, and Bonnie soon became an expert with automatics, pistols, and submachine guns.

Bonnie Parker's diaries in the late 1920s reveal a young woman who had been abandoned by a professional thief, worked her humdrum waitress job, and spent her off-hours in movie theaters where she enjoyed romantic films—most of them silent since "talkies" did not arrive in Texas theaters until about 1930. Her diaries are repetitive and filled with one or two lines for each day, tiresome lines that summed up her empty life. On Jan. 10, 1928, she wrote: "Blue as usual. Not a darn thing to do. Don't know a darn thing." The following day she wrote: "Haven't been anywhere this week. Why don't something happen." The next day she wrote: "Blue as hell tonight." The next: "Sure am blue. Everything has gone wrong today. Why don't something happen. What a life!" The next: "Not doing anything tonite." The next: "Stayed home tonight. Nothing particular happened." The next: "Went to a Chocolate Shop today...Sure am blue tonight. Have been crying. I wish I could see Roy." Bonnie Parker had been living a weary, hopeless existence and Clyde Barrow was her escape into excitement, high drama, and a full, if dangerous, life. Robbery and murder went hand-in-hand with her fantasies of escape. Anything was preferable to the life she had been living, even an early grave. She found that committing robberies brought her instant thrills and gratification.

There were robberies, a lot of them. Mostly Bonnie drove the car and Clyde ran into cafes or grocery stores, quickly cleaning out the till while holding proprietors and customers at bay with a shotgun or a pistol. He would then dash outside and leap into the already moving car Bonnie was driving. Often the bandit would stand on the running board and fire his weapons into the air as the car shot down the main street of a one-horse town, imitating the cowboys of old who would "hurrah" a town by riding up and down the streets on their pintos, firing their six-guns into the air. It was all a lark to Clyde Barrow, but to Bonnie Parker these exploits were high drama which she associated with Clyde's pronounced manhood. In this she was mistaken for Clyde was almost indifferent to heterosexual relationships. He preferred young men, admitting to Bonnie that he had become addicted to homosexual practices while in the reformatory, although Clyde and Parker did maintain an on-and-off sexual relationship that was satisfying to neither. When they took young men into the gang, such as W.D. Jones and Henry Methvin, it was understood that both Bonnie and Clyde would have relationships with these apprentice bandits.

Sometime in early 1930, Bonnie and Clyde robbed a Waco, Texas, store and Clyde left his fingerprints behind. He was identified and tracked down to the Dallas apartment. When officers burst through the door they found Clyde embracing Bonnie on the couch, kissing her. They were both drunk. Clyde stood up wobbly-legged, reaching to his shoulder-holster, but it was empty. He had removed his pistol. Police dashed forward and pinned his arms, dragging him out as he shouted: "All you want is me! She's got nothin' to do with nothin'!" Clyde was convicted of robbery and given a two-year sentence in the Waco jail but he was not behind bars for long. After Clyde heard that his brother Buck had escaped the Eastham Prison Farm he sent word to Bonnie to visit him in the Waco jail and "bring me a pickmeup." His reference was to a gun. In the first week of March 1930, Bonnie arrived at the jail and smuggled a .38-caliber Colt with a Bisley handle so thin it could be slipped through the bars of Clyde's cell. This was strapped to Bonnie's thigh, and when the guard was not looking she passed the weapon to Clyde.

Clyde forced his way out of the Waco jail that night and stole a car, driving northward. He abandoned the car, stole another, and repeated this process several times until jumping a freight train. He was arrested in the freight yard of Middleton, Ohio, as he jumped from a cattle car. Clyde was sent to Eastham Prison Farm, which was appropriately dubbed "The Burning Hell" by prisoners. Brutal punishments were inflicted upon inmates here, and the truculent was beaten with whips and placed upon the "barrel cavalry," forced to sit atop a pickle barrel for hours in the burning sun until he collapsed from heat exhaustion. Still, he continued to break the rules, organizing a crap game. One of the big losers was convict Ed Crowder who complained to guards that was the "gambling boss" of the yard. Clyde was punished again, this time placed in the heat box—a narrow box in a sun-baked yard where he was compelled to stand upright for hours, sucking in the stifling air inside the box. When released, Clyde grabbed a lead pipe and crushed Ed Crowder's head, a murder officials did not attribute to Clyde until after his violent death.

Like Ma Barker, who deluged authorities with petitions for the release of her four imprisoned sons, Cummie Barrow was forever writing letters begging the release of either Clyde or Buck Barrow. She was finally successful in persuading Texas Governor Ross Sterling to release Clyde on Feb. 2, 1932. When Clyde stepped from the prison farm, his parole in his hand, Bonnie was waiting for him. "I'll die before I ever go back into a place like that," he told her. "I'll go with you," she vowed. They stole a car a few days later but were seen driving off and police were soon on their trail, closing in on them at Mabank, Texas, where, in the wild pursuit, Clyde lost control of the car and crashed into a tree. As he had done with his brother Buck years earlier, jumped from the car, running across the open fields, leaving Bonnie to be captured by police. She was jailed for three months at Kaufman, Texas, but on her release she went straight back to Clyde and they resumed their robbery career.

Before Parker was released, Clyde, accompanied by Ray Hamilton, robbed the Sims Oil Company of a $300 payroll in Dallas on Mar. 25, 1932. A short time later, Clyde alone entered a small jewelry store in Hillsboro, Texas, and asked 65-year-old John M. Bucher to show him some costume jewelry. He pulled a gun and robbed Bucher of forty dollars, but when Bucher put up a struggle Clyde shot and killed him. In May 1932, Clyde, with Hamilton and Frank Clause, drove through the Lufkin, Texas, area, robbing a half-dozen filling stations. On May 12, 1932, went into a Dallas liquor store, ordered a bottle and then held up the place, taking $76 from the till. (Even though Prohibition was still in effect, Texas, for the most part, ignored the dry federal law and openly sold liquor.) Clyde then drove to Atoka, Okla., and there, on Aug. 5, 1932, was found by two officers as he lurked in the shadows outside of a barn dance. He was carrying two automatics and intended to rob the ticket taker. Sheriff C.G. Maxwell and Deputy Eugene Moore approached and asked him what he was doing. "You better step out into the light, boy, so I can see what you're all about," Maxwell told Clyde. Clyde drew both his automatics and began firing almost point blank at the two officers, who collapsed dead.

On Aug. 20, 1932, Clyde and others robbed the Neuhoff Packing Co. in Dallas of $1,100, and some hours later he met with Bonnie Parker, who had just been released from jail. They traveled to Carlsbad, N.M., with Ray Hamilton, and en route they were stopped by Sheriff Joe Johns. Instead of killing the lawman, the killers amused themselves by taking the officer captive, handcuffing him with his own cuffs and verbally abusing him on a long trip back through Texas, dropping him off near San Antonio on Aug. 13, 1932. "Tell your people that we ain't a bunch of nutty killers, sheriff," Clyde told him. "Just down home people

tryin' to get through this damned Depression with a few bones." Bonnie stripped the sheriff of his badge and said, as the car moved off: "I'll just keep this souvenir of our meeting, good-looking."

Sheriff Johns alerted local authorities who threw up roadblocks in three counties. The Barrows encountered one roadblock on Aug. 14, 1932, outside of Wharton, Texas, but managed to drive around it, firing their weapons into a crowd of policemen. In September 1932, Clyde and Hamilton raided the National Guard Armory in Fort Worth, Texas, removing many boxes of ammunition, automatic rifles, submachine guns, pistols, and shotguns. Using some of this high-powered weaponry, the gang strode into the Abilene State Bank on Oct. 8, 1932, taking $1,400. Two days later, Clyde halted his stolen car in front of a grocery store owned by Howard Hall in Sherman, Texas, in the Red River Valley. Though he had ample funds to pay for the goods he ordered Hall to pack, the cheap-minded Clyde pulled a gun and reached into the till to take $50. Hall, a butcher, dove over the counter at him wielding a cleaver. Clyde shot him twice through the head, killing him. The gang stole another car and headed into Missouri. In Oronogo, Mo., on Nov. 14, 1932, the gang robbed the local bank of a mere $200. Bonnie and Clyde got physically ill when counting the meager stolen money. Then they started back for Texas, homesick, determined to see their family members.

Bonnie in one of Clyde's stolen cars, 1932.

They slept like gypsies, mostly on the seats of their cars, seldom bathed, and once in a while treated themselves to the thin luxury of a tourist cabin with running water. They ate cold sandwiches but sometimes stopped at picnic grounds where they roasted hot dogs over open fires—their favorite meal. While driving back to Texas to visit with Bonnie's mother, the couple stopped their stolen car in a gas station and began chatting with the naive attendant, William Daniel Jones, impressing him with their bragging stories of the banks they had robbed. They invited the gullible Jones to join them and he agreed, giving them the money in the till and jumping into the back seat. That night Bonnie slept with both men and continued to ravage Jones, according to his later statements. (Jones claimed that Bonnie Parker was an insatiable nymphomaniac who demanded sex of him four or five times a day and at all hours. Clyde, Jones said, in describing his "eighteen months of hell," also attacked him sexually on occasions. He insisted that he took part in their robberies and killings only because they ordered him to do so at the point of a gun, threatening to kill him if he did not continue his slavish obedience. At night, Jones said, he was tied up with chains to the wheels of the stolen cars they drove.)

When visiting her mother at a remote farm, Bonnie was told by family and friends that police were watching the Parker home day and night and a similar vigil was kept on the house. There was a reward of $250 on Clyde's head, dead or alive—a reward commensurate with the kinds of robberies he had committed. The Barrows were told to stay on the roads and not come home again. They committed more small robberies and, on Dec. 23, 1932, the car in which they were riding blew a tire outside of Temple, Texas. The trio walked to town and Clyde picked out a Ford V-8 and jumped the cable wires to start it. Bonnie and Jones jumped into the back seat just as the car owner, Doyle Johnson, came running from his house to protest. Clyde pulled out his automatics and emptied them into Johnson, killing him. "How stupid can a person be," snorted Clyde as he drove off. "Would you die for a car, W.D.?" he asked the hapless Jones. "No, sure wouldn't," replied the captive gang member.

By this time, Ray Hamilton had quit the gang and struck out on his own, robbing a few banks but his luck ran out in a few months. "You'll get caught and I'll have to get you out of prison," Clyde had warned him. "You ain't as smart as I am." Hamilton teamed up with Gene O'Dare to rob the Carmine State Bank at LaGrange, Texas, on Nov. 9, 1932, and, with gunman Les Stewart at his side, robbed the Cedar Hill State Bank in Dallas of $1,800 on Dec. 25, 1932. This last robbery yielded more money than Hamilton had ever taken with Bonnie and Clyde, and he sent them a gloating postcard via Bonnie's relatives which read "my score is higher than anything you got for the year." But just as Clyde had predicted, Hamilton was picked up by police. He went to a Dallas whorehouse and there bragged about his recent bank robberies; an enterprising madam turned him into the police to pick up a few hundred dollars in reward money. Hamilton was quickly tried and given 263 years in Eastham. While awaiting transfer to the prison, Hamilton sent out a desperate plea to Clyde Barrow to free him, this information leaked through an elaborate prison grapevine system which Clyde had established through prison and jail trustees and inmates being released and those being imprisoned. (He sent small gifts of cash, usually no more than $5 or $10, or sometimes cartons of cigarettes to his informants, but in the hard days of the Depression this was considered generous and it produced quick information.)

Clyde received a terse message from Ray Hamilton: "Get me out!" To that end, he planned to visit Hamilton's sister, Mrs. Lillie McBride, a Dallas resident, and organize through her a jailbreak for Hamilton. Meanwhile, Hamilton's partner on the Cedar Hill robbery, Les Stewart, had robbed another bank in Grapevine, Texas, on Dec. 31, 1932, with Odell Chandless. Stewart had been captured by the Texas Rangers and told them that his partner on the Grapevine job, Chandless, would be visiting Mrs. McBride on the night of Jan. 6, 1933, coincidentally the very night that Clyde Barrow had made arrangements to go to the McBride house. Rangers and Dallas police officers were lying in wait at the house, expecting Chandless, not Clyde, when the Barrows arrived. That night Clyde drove past the house twice, telling Bonnie that "there's something wrong here. I don't know what it is, just a feeling I get and when I get that feeling I'm usually right." He parked the car in front of the McBride house and told Jones to keep the motor running. He slipped a sawed-off shotgun into this specially made zippered pants pocket and told Bonnie to grab a Browning Automatic Rifle and cover him. She poked it through a side window of the car while Clyde cautiously went up the stairs of the front porch.

The house was packed with Texas Rangers and local policeman. When Ranger J.F. Vannoy heard Clyde's footsteps on the porch he ordered the 18-year-old Mrs. McBride to answer the door. She started for the door but just then Clyde, outside, responding to his "feeling," jumped back off the porch and fired his shotgun, blasting out an upstairs window, the shards of glass falling on F.T. Bradberry, a deputy sheriff who had been crouching beneath the sill. Vannoy and his men let loose a deafening barrage from the doors and windows of the house as Clyde back-pedaled toward the waiting car. Deputy Malcolm Davis, who had run out the back door and around the house, faced Clyde as he was about to get into the car. "Hold on there," Davis shouted and aimed his revolver at Clyde who fired the other barrel of his twelve-guage shotgun, the load of buckshot catching the sheriff in the chest, blowing him flat and dead to the ground. Meanwhile, Bonnie peppered the house with withering fire from her BAR as Clyde jumped into the car and Jones gunned the auto down the street. As the gang made its escape, Bonnie, who had a pathological fascination for Clyde's ruthless ability to murder, cooed a compliment to him: "Why, honey, you never miss, do you? You cut that lawman clean in half with one barrel!"

By the time the Dallas police were able to seal off the city and check every car going and coming, searching every known criminal haunt, the Barrows were driving through Oklahoma. The gang then went into Missouri and, near Springfield, Clyde, who was at the wheel of another stolen car, spotted motorcycle cop Thomas Persell. He told Jones and Bonnie to hold on and purposely raced the car to more than 100 m.p.h., roaring past the state trooper. Persell gave pursuit and, on a barren stretch of roadway, Clyde roared to a stop, causing Persell to halt so quickly that his motorcycle sailed from beneath him. The incensed Persell stood up and then marched toward the car. As he got near, Clyde, grinning, opened the car door and pointed a submachine gun at him. The state trooper was taken hostage and dropped off a hundred miles distant, unharmed and stripped of his gun. He was told by Bonnie to get into a "new line of work where you won't meet such dangerous people as us."

Bonnie Parker reveled in her role of female bandit, taking great joy in not only defying the law but ridiculing its representatives, deriving a sense of power and place which had never been hers before joining Clyde . She had established, finally, evil or not, an identity of her own. She was a celebrity and did all she could to perpetuate the image of the gun-tough mob girl who kept pace with her frantic killer-lover. In snapshots of themselves later left behind and published throughout the nation's press, the Barrows purposely projected a fierce image. They posed with an amazing array of weaponry and Bonnie was the ham of the lot, mugging for the Kodak on one occasion while holding a rifle on Clyde, "getting the drop on him" so to speak, as he held his hands skyward in mock submission, a snake-like grin on his face. Another time, Bonnie jammed one of Clyde's cigars in her mouth, leaned on the headlight of a car, put her leg up on the bumper and glared menacingly at the camera, a revolver clutched in her other hand which rested on a hip, as if reaching into a holster to fast-draw any opponent who dared to meet her in mortal combat. The picture presented an image upholding the traditions of a gunslinger's Old West that had long vanished, except in the minds of the historically and socially retarded Texas citizens belonging to Bonnie and Clyde's uneducated class. To them, nothing had changed in five decades; it was still a matter of outlaw and posse, of daring bandits and relentless lawmen.

It was a game, lethal and terminal, that the Barrows played, and in their sprawling, crude world of wide-open spaces where cars had replaced horses and rapid-fire weapons were substituted for six-guns, they looked forward to death with self-indulgent heroics, employing a rationale for their criminal careers not dissimilar to that of the old western outlaws. Jesse James and his band successfully claimed that they had been driven into banditry for having fought on the losing side of the Civil War; Bonnie and Clyde used the Depression and heartless bankers foreclosing on farms and shops as their excuse to strike back against authority. To themselves they were American frontier heroes, pathfinders of a new and violent age to be admired. Bonnie, especially, craved with murderous lust her place in history and made sure that a photographic record would be left behind to mark her distinctive contribution to American crime. There were times, however, haggard and briefly coming to grips with the terrible reality she had created for herself, that Bonnie saw that reality in all its gory detail. Following the publication of the photo showing her with the cigar in her mouth, she became pensive and later called herself "stupid" for having portrayed herself as a brutal gun moll, even though the photo had been taken in jest. She tried to repudiate the image later by telling Police Chief Percy Boyd, one of the gang's many hostages: "Tell the public that I don't smoke cigars. It's the bunk."

The gang got an unexpected jolt of support through the offices of the governor of Texas. Mrs. Miriam A. "Ma" Ferguson, who had held the office earlier, was re-elected to the governorship; she was an arch liberal who felt that the best way to reform recidivist criminals was to let them loose in open society where they could earn their keep, hold their heads high, and become useful citizens. To this end, she patiently listened to the plaintive pleas of Blanche Barrow, Buck's wife, who had hitchhiked with her three children to the state capital and there, with her children tearfully begging to see their imprisoned father once more, Blanche convinced "Ma" Ferguson to pardon her errant husband who had certainly learned his lesson. ("Buck won't do no more robbing, honest. His letters, look at 'em, are full of promises to be a hard-working man if he can only get out and back to supporting me and these here poor little ones who are orphans without him. We're starvin' without my man, governor. I know that as a woman you know what it means for a wife to be without her man to take care of the family.")

Ma Ferguson knew all right, or said she did. When serving an earlier term as governor of Texas, Mrs. Ferguson had issued more than 2,000 pardons to convicts, most of these being serious criminal hardcases who came back to plague the state's hard-pressed lawmen. The Texas Rangers were particularly opposed to Governor Ferguson, many in that famed law enforcement organization

Buck Barrow

openly denounced her pardoning practices. Frank Hamer, the very man who tracked down Bonnie and Clyde after relentlessly pursuing them for more than 100 days, resigned his position with the Texas Rangers as soon as Ma Ferguson took office. Ivan Marvin Buck Barrow, one of the worst criminals in Texas, walked out of the Huntsville Prison on Mar. 20, 1933, holding a full pardon from Governor Ferguson. He stayed in Dallas for a week while his wife Blanche gave birth to her fourth child, and then the couple placed their children with relatives and stole a car, driving madly to catch up with brother Clyde.

Once Buck and Blanche joined Bonnie, Clyde, and Jones, the five went on a quick robbery spree through early April 1933, robbing a jewelry store in Neosho, Mo., looting a federal armory in Springfield, Mo., and sticking up a loan office in Kansas City, Kan., getting small amounts. Theirs was a hit-and-run modus operandi, striking quickly, almost impulsively whenever they needed lunch money. They made no plans. They struck, ran, struck again, and ran again, living in their stolen cars, always on the move, racing through the Southwest and backtracking on their well-known routes. Buck came to Clyde and told him that his wife Blanche was still "a little delicate" after giving birth to their fourth child and that she was not used to living out in the open. He wanted to rent a small place where the gang could rest up and Blanche could recuperate. Clyde did not like the idea but agreed to "hole up a short time but not for long or the laws will be on us and we'll all be dead." The gang rented a small four-room apartment above a garage in Freeman's Grove Addition, a suburb of Joplin, Mo. This place had been recommended as a "safe hideout" by Herbert Farmer.

The Barrows relaxed for the first time in years, having about $1,000 from recent robberies. They stayed inside the three rooms, Bonnie and Clyde in one bedroom, occasionally joined by Jones who normally slept on a couch in the living room, Buck and Blanche in the other bedroom. They sat in the kitchen to eat their meals and spent the evenings in the tiny living room playing cards and looking over the hundreds of photos they had taken of each other. The gang ordered food from a local grocery store by phone and the delivery boy found it strange that he was never allowed into the apartment. The petite blonde woman opened the door only a crack to slip his money to him and told him to leave the packages outside the door. The delivery boy was the nephew of a local lawman and he mentioned these strange clients to the uncle who, in turn, contacted State Trooper G.B. Kahler. Sergeant Kahler, after learning that the residents in the garage apartment were driving a car with Texas license plates, concluded that the occupants were bootleggers running an illegal liquor operation. On April 13, 1933, he enlisted the aid of two detectives on the Joplin, Mo., police department, a highway patrolman, and a constable, then led the four men in a raid on the place.

As Kahler and his men were driving down Oak Ridge Drive toward the apartment, Clyde, standing in the garage with Jones where they were checking on the big stolen Marmon car, dropped a wrench. He had one of his "feelings" and told Jones to close the doors of the garage. Upstairs, Blanche was cooking, Buck was sitting in his undershirt reading a newspaper, and Bonnie was laboring over a long poem which she had entitled "The Story of Suicide Sal." She had just completed the poem when two police cars turned into the alleyway leading to the garage, one parking at the front of the alleyway, the other swinging into it and blocking the one-way escape route.

Wes Harryman, a Newton County constable, got out of the lead car with a pistol in his hand and advanced on the garage. The door of the garage creaked open a crack and Clyde poked a shotgun through it, firing at the same time that Harryman squeezed off a round from his revolver. The shotgun blast took off the top of his head. Joplin police detective Harry L. McGinnis ran forward from the first car, firing his pistol but he was felled by another blast from Clyde's shotgun—the load shattering his right arm so that it hung in strands from the elbow, ripping into the right side of his head and neck, exploding arteries. He fell to the pavement and bled to death in minutes. McGinnis' partner, Detective Thomas DeGraff, who had been in the lead car, took cover behind the car blocking the alley and began firing his automatic in the direction of the garage but he came under withering fire from a submachine gun fired from the upstairs window of the apartment. Buck Barrow was spraying the entire alley with bullets. Bonnie stood at another window firing two revolvers, shrieking in delight. Blanche Barrow, exposed for the first time to gunfire, stood in the middle of the living room, traumatized and staring in shock.

The doors of the garage suddenly burst wide and Jones leaped outside, rapidly firing a Browning Automatic Rifle. DeGraff retreated down the alley. Then Jones reached the detective car blocking the alley and released the brake. Just as he finished, a shot from Kahler at the mouth of the alley slammed into Jones' head. He clutched the bleeding wound, a grazing shot, and staggered back to the garage, calling out Clyde's name. Buck dashed out into the alley, firing the submachine gun. He pushed the detective car, its front wheels perched on a rise in the alley and the car coasted backward as Buck fired around it at Kahler, Patrolmen Grammer and DeGraff fired back but had to jump out of the way as the detective car crashed through the other car, knocking it sideways and opening the escape route, then bouncing across the street and slamming into a tree. To the lawmen's surprise, Blanche Barrow, screaming hysterically, followed the driverless car down the alleyway. She ran madly into the street and down the block. "Let her go," Kahler ordered. "We want the men."

At that moment, the Marmon roared out of the garage with Clyde at the wheel, Buck firing the submachine gun from a window, Bonnie firing her revolvers from another and Jones lying wounded in the back seat. It sailed down the driveway, swerved into the street and roared down the block where it paused for a moment while Buck reached out and pulled his wife into the car. It then raced off down the street and was soon out of sight. McGinnis and Harryman were dead by the time an ambulance arrived. Inside the gang's apartment, police found a huge arsenal of revolvers, automatics, submachine guns, shotguns, and dozens of boxes of ammunition. They also found photos of all the gang members and these soon broke on the front pages of the nation's newspapers. Along with letters to family members, lawmen found Bonnie Parker's poem, "The Story of Suicide Sal." It was unfinished but newspapers delighted in printing it, a curious bit of doggerel loaded with self-justification and prophetic doom, a poem that caused Bonnie's mother to later state: "I realize that I am not learned in such matters, but to my inner consciousness there seemed to be a strange and terrifying change in the mind of my child." It read:

THE STORY OF SUICIDE SAL

We each of us have a good alibi
For being down here in the joint;
But few of them are really justified,
If you get right down to the point.

You have heard of a woman's glory
Being spent on a downright cur.
Still you can't always judge the story
As true being told by her.

As long as I stayed on the island
And heard confidence tales from the gals,
There was only one interesting and truthful,
It was the story of Suicide Sal.

Now Sal was a gal of rare beauty,
Though her features were somewhat tough,
She never once faltered from duty,
To play on the up and up.

Sal told me this tale on the evening
Before she was turned out free,
And I'll do my best to relate it,
Just as she told it to me.

I was born on a ranch in Wyoming,
Not treated like Helen of Troy,
Was taught that rods were rulers,
And ranked with greasy cowboys.

Then I left my home for the city
To play in its mad dizzy whirl,
Not knowing how little of pity
It holds for a country girl.

The raid at Joplin had interrupted Bonnie's composition but when the newspapers got hold of the poem and published it, Bonnie gleefully bought all the papers she could find that carried her down-home sonnets and was suddenly inspired to new literary heights. She now wrote the end of her poem, no longer disguising herself or Clyde Barrow, her bandit lover. She would clutch her infamy now, and blurt to the world her bold story, taking a defiant and doomed stance. She wrote herself and Clyde into the annals of crime with the finish of her prose poem, ranking herself and Clyde with the most notorious criminals in American history. She was, thanks to the press, an instant tradition, a fiery legend that would burn bright beyond the laws she and Clyde had broken. Bonnie worked day and night to write the finish of her "masterwork" and then mailed copies of this to newspapers. The end of her tale read:

You have heard the story of Jesse James,
Of how he lived and died.
If you are still in need of something to read.
Here's the story of Bonnie and Clyde.

Now Bonnie and Clyde are the Barrow gang.
I'm sure you have all read
How they rob and steal,
And how those who squeal,
Are usually found dying or dead.

There are lots of untruths to their write-ups.
They are not so merciless as that;
They hate all the laws,
The stool-pigeons, spotters and rats.

If a policeman is killed in Dallas
And they have no clues to guide–
If they can't find a fiend,
They just wipe the slate clean,
And hang it on Bonnie and Clyde.

If they try to act like citizens,
And rent them a nice little flat,
About the third night they are invited to fight,
By a submachine gun, rat-tat-tat.

A newsboy once said to his buddy:
"I wish old Clyde would get jumped;
"In these awful hard times,
"We'd make a few dimes
"If five or six cops would get bumped."

They class them as cold-blooded killers,
They say they are heartless and mean.
But I say this with pride,
That once I knew Clyde
When he was honest and upright and clean.

But the law fooled around,
Kept tracking them down,
And locking them up in a cell,
Till he said to me,
"I will never be free,
"So I will meet a few of them in hell."

The road was so dimly lighted
There were no highway signs to guide,
But they made up their minds
If the roads were all blind
They wouldn't give up till they died.

The road gets dimmer and dimmer,
Sometimes you can hardly see,
Still it's fight man to man,
And do all you can,
For they know they can never be free.

They don't think they are too tough or desperate.
They know the law always wins,
They have been shot at before
But they do not ignore
That death is the wages of sin.

From heartbreaks some people have suffered.
From weariness some people have died,
But take it all in all,

Our troubles are small,
Till we get like Bonnie and Clyde.

Some day they will go down together,
And they will bury them side by side.
To a few it means grief,
To the law it's relief,
But it's death to Bonnie and Clyde.

If the publication of this work caused Bonnie to strut and Clyde to hold her up to gang members as a "talented writer", the poem incensed the honest, hardworking lawmen of the many states that sought these killers, spurring them on to capture them. What enraged lawmen equally were newsmen and publicity people who had made these "criminal vultures" folk heroes. Newspapers, particularly those in the Midwest, graphically detailed what they termed "The Battle of Joplin," portraying the gang members not as the berserk murderers they were but as daring bandits who somehow were deserving of grudging respect because of their ferocity and determination to escape. The gang members began to believe in their own image. In Ruston, La., on Apr. 27, 1933, Clyde stole a Ford V-8, one of the fastest cars on the road and his favorite, causing its owner, H.D. Darby, to race after the auto. Instead of killing Darby, Clyde took him prisoner, along with his girlfriend, Sophie Stone. The gang took the couple along with them and Darby quickly recognized the blonde-haired girl wearing a beret as Bonnie Parker. The couple sat in frozen terror, expecting to be murdered any minute, but, after driving 125 miles, Clyde stopped the car near Magnolia, Ark., and let the couple out. Bonnie asked Darby what he did for a living and when he told her he was an undertaker, she said: "Well, if I ever get killed, I hope you'll take care of me."

The gang went on robbing, concentrating on small banks, roaming as far north as Indiana, where they robbed the Lucerne State Bank of $300 on May 8, 1933. The Barrows drove further north into strange territory, robbing the First State Bank of Okabena, Minn., on May 16, 1933. Here they took away $1,500 and, for the Barrows, this was a young fortune. They traveled all the way back to Texas without robbing anyone. When arriving in Alma, Texas, on June 22, 1933, the gang went straight to a small bank and robbed it of a few hundred dollars. The next day they held up a Piggly-Wiggly store in Fayetteville, Texas. Following this penny-ante robbery, Clyde brazenly drove once more through Alma, going past the bank the gang had robbed two days earlier. The town marshal, H.D. Humphrey, spotted the Ford V-8 bearing the same license plates as the car used in the bank robbery. He pursued the car with Deputy A.M. Salyars at his side.

Clyde was cut off by another car in this chase and crashed into it, causing the Ford to explode into flames. Humphrey and Salyars drew their guns and walked slowly forward, believing everyone in the Ford was dead, burned to death. Then Clyde and Buck Barrow, hiding on the other side of the car, opened up on the officers with a BAR and a shotgun. The valiant officers kept advancing, exchanging gunfire with the bandits until Humphrey fell wounded to the road. Salyars took cover behind a barn, reloading and firing at the Barrows, who scurried to the police car. Clyde stopped in the road and knelt beside the stricken Humphrey. "I ought to finish you right now," he told the marshal. "Go ahead," Humphrey said weakly, "I think you've already killed me anyway." Clyde left him in the road and climbed into the police car which roared away, even though Deputy Salyars fired several shots into it. Marshal Humphrey died four days later of his wounds.

The police car gave out some miles down the road and the brothers, who had left Jones, Bonnie, and Blanche elsewhere, headed into the hills on foot. They tried to steal a car from a widow but she refused to give them the keys to her jalopy, even though Clyde beat her with his fists and Buck whipped her with chains found in her cabin. They left the woman's farm only seconds ahead of a 200-man posse combing the brush for the bandits. Clyde and Buck somehow made it back to Fort Smith, Ark., where they joined the others and, after stealing another car, drove to Oklahoma. From there they headed into Missouri and, near Platte City, the gang rented two cabins in the Red Crown Cabin Camp. They bought food from the manager, Delbert Crabtree, and he became suspicious when he was repeatedly paid with nickels, dimes, and quarters, believing the guests were petty thieves. He notified state police who asked for descriptions of the guests. They concluded it was the Barrow gang, and the small change they were using had come from a rash of filling station holdups the Barrows had recently committed.

A small army of lawmen was put together in Kansas City and more than 100 state troopers, local sheriffs, deputies, constables, even an armored car with a searchlight were rushed to the camp area. One of the lawmen went to one of the cabins and knocked on the door. "We are law officers and want to talk to you," he said to the occupants.

"Just one minute while I get dressed," a female voice said politely. It was Bonnie Parker. Jones, who had been sleeping with Bonnie, slipped out of a side door of the cabin and got behind the wheel of a car parked between the two cabins. The officer banged on the door once more and Bonnie said: "The men are on the other side."

"You had better come out," the officer said.

Clyde and Buck Barrow had been alerted and had armed themselves. They crouched next to the car in which Jones sat. All three men were armed with shotguns and submachine guns. "Let 'em have it!" shouted Clyde and the bandits opened a withering fire that mowed down Deputy George Highfill, his legs blown away, Sheriff Holt Coffee, struck in the neck, and his son Clarence, hit in the head. A bullet struck the horn in the armored car and it gave a steady blast which disoriented the possemen surrounding the cabin area. Some thought it was a signal to charge and these officers were quickly cut down by the blazing weapons fired by Clyde and Buck. The officers retreated. Then, as Jones revved the motor of the car, Buck Barrow came dashing out of one of the cabins with two automatics in his hands, both blazing. Behind him came Bonnie and Blanche, holding mattresses to shield them against the withering fire from the possemen. The car, with Clyde standing on the running board and firing a submachine gun, jumped forward out of the area between the cabins. Just as Buck, Bonnie, and Blanche were about to get into the car a bullet slammed into Buck Barrow's head. The women grabbed him as he sagged toward the ground and dragged him into the back seat of the car. Jones, a cap pulled low over his face, gunned the car through the lines of the posse as Clyde kept firing at the officers.

As the car careened past, the posse members raked it with hundreds of shells, blowing out the windows and almost knocking the doors from their hinges. Yet the car kept going, bumped over open land, swerved onto a road that led to Platte City, and roared off in the darkness. In the back seat of the car Blanche was screaming that she had been hit and that Buck was dying. Everyone except Jones was wounded. Bonnie had been grazed by a bullet along her right ribs. Clyde had a scalp wound where a bullet had grazed his head. Blanche's eyes had been cut by the window glass which had dissolved under the possemen's hail of bullets. She could hardly see and was in terrible agony. Her husband, however, was in the worst shape; Buck Barrow had received a bullet through his right temple and it had gone out of the left side of his head. The gang, when stopping the car near Hoover, Mo., looked him over under the glare of flashlight and Jones whispered to Bonnie: "I think he's done for."

Since they were road people, they had nowhere to go to seek medical aid. Unlike the Barkers or the Dillinger gang, they had no underworld contacts that could lead them to physicians willing to doctor bandits. They had little or no money for such expensive support. The gang did what it had done for Jones when he was previously wounded; they took out their small first-aid kit and doctored their wounded. It was apparent, however, that Buck

Dexter, Iowa, July 24, 1933: A posse has just swarmed over the Barrow gang—the hysterical Blanche, in sunglasses to left, is held by lawmen, while Buck Barrow, at right, kneeling on the ground in his underwear, is mortally wounded; Bonnie and Clyde escaped.

Barrow would die of his wounds unless he were taken to a hospital. Hundreds of lawmen were seeking the Barrows. Posses swarmed through five states hunting them. A motorist driving along a lonely road in Mount Ayr, Iowa, drove past a battered car parked in a ditch. He saw a man lying in the back seat, a bloody bandage over his head. Two men and two women were squatting next to the road, huddled over a small fire. They were burning bloody bandages. The motorist reported the sighting and soon more than 1,000 lawmen and possemen were converging on a woodland area between Dexter and Redfield, Iowa.

This report caused more than 200 lawmen and deputies to converge on the woods near Dexter. The National Guard was called in and hundreds of local citizens carrying shotguns and hunting rifles joined the searchers. On July 24, 1933, John Love, a farmer and a member of the local vigilante group, spotted two cars driving into a deserted amusement park area. Love hid behind thick brush and watched as two women and three men got out of the cars and began building a campfire. He crept off to notify authorities; his description of the cars and people matched that of the gang and the army of hunters moved cautiously toward the amusement park. The lawmen quietly surrounded the area, cautioned by Sheriff C.A. Knee of Adel, Iowa, that any sudden rush would scare off the prey; they were a crafty lot and Knee ordered his men to move up on the gang by going from tree to tree and that no one was to fire until he gave the order.

When the possemen came to the clearing, they lay down in the thick underbrush and trained more than 400 guns on the group. Bonnie was making coffee over an open fire and Blanche, wearing riding breeches and boots, her injured eyes covered with dark glasses, was frying eggs. Buck, who was miraculously recovering from his head wound, sat on the running board of one of the cars. Next to him sat Jones, chatting. Clyde stood watching the women,

smoking a cigarette, glancing about, turning his head slowly to scan the woods that ringed the clearing, always the sentinel.

Suddenly, Clyde stood ramrod stiff as he saw a movement in the trees. He shouted: "The law's coming!" and dove for a shotgun. Bonnie dumped the coffee into the fire which gave up a cloud of steam and she and the others picked up weapons. The next moment the area was raked by a lethal shower of bullets, an incredible fusillade that slammed into the cars from every side.

"Start the car, start the car!" yelled Clyde to Jones as he fired the shotgun but, as Jones leaped for one of the cars, he was struck by a load of buckshot and fell, stunned, to the ground. Clyde shoved him into the back seat and slipped behind the wheel while Bonnie ran around the other side and jumped into the car.

With a roar, Clyde drove bumpily over the open ground. The possemen concentrated their fire on the racing car which seemed to change directions every second, riddling its windows and doors with hundreds of bullets. A bullet smacked into Clyde's arm but he kept control of the wheel, driving crazily around in a circle, attempting to find a way out, but he was faced by almost a solid sheet of fire from hundreds of guns. The car hit a tree stump and the trio tumbled out of it, racing to the second car and then driving a short distance before a storm of bullets blew the car to shreds. The windows literally exploded and the bumpers were shot off, the hood so riddled with bullet holes that it looked like a giant sieve. Again, Clyde, Bonnie, and Jones slid out of the car and then raced toward the only portion of woods that offered no wall of fire, dashing into the thick underbrush and disappearing.

Still in the clearing, hiding behind a tree stump, were Buck and Blanche Barrow. They clutched automatics and Buck, again bleeding from his head wound, fired off clips rapidly and in almost all directions as the possemen left the woods and began advancing on the stump, pouring volley after volley into it. Buck was heard above the din to curse the lawmen as he fired at them, wounding several. He was hit twice but kept firing as Blanche, hysterical and screaming, methodically reloaded the automatics for him. Buck fired off the clip, then threw Blanche the automatic and took the other with the fresh clip in it. The battle raged on for several minutes but the remaining Barrows were doomed. Buck was hit another four times, in the arms and chest, and he suddenly sagged forward, vomiting blood. Sheriff Knee signaled to his men to cease fire. "They're down!" he shouted. A national guardsman, accompanied by Dr. H.W. Keller, rushed forward to see Buck on all fours, blood seeping from his wounds and gushing from his mouth. He still clutched an automatic and tried to raise this to fire once more but the guardsman kicked it out of his feeble grasp. Buck rolled over as Blanche, now held kicking and struggling by officers, screamed: "Don't cry, Daddy! Don't die, Daddy! Don't die!"

Ivan Marvin Buck Barrow would die, however, five days later in Kings Daughters Hospital at Perry, Iowa, too weak to survive the seven wounds in his body. Blanche Barrow, who would be sent to prison for ten years for her part in the Dexter battle, hated Clyde for deserting his brother. "He promised he would never do that," she told officials later when in custody. "He vowed he would never desert his brother and he left him to die like a dog. Clyde will roast in hell for that." Thoughts of escape, not hell, occupied the mind of Clyde Barrow when he, Jones, and Bonnie broke into the woods around the killing grounds of the clearing. At that time, all three of the remaining gang members were wounded, Clyde in the arm, Jones also in the arm, and Bonnie in the fleshy part of her back where she had received a load of buckshot. They moved through the dense woods which were loaded with lawmen, heading toward a stream that skirted the park. They appeared trapped, surrounded by what was later estimated to be at least 400 to 500 lawmen, guardsmen, and armed vigilantes. According to one eyewitness report they "fought desperately each step through the woods, darting from brush clump to brush clump. They made difficult targets and they were shooting with deadly accuracy."

When the trio found the stream, they struggled down an embankment and crossed the waist-high water slowly. They reached the other side where a steep embankment met them and beyond that was a huge cornfield. As they struggled up the embankment, dozens of possemen broke through the woods behind them, standing atop the opposite embankment and firing down at the fleeing bandits. Bonnie was hit and fell. The possemen cheered. Clyde tried to lift her up, but his wounded arm was limp, and Jones pushed him up the embankment, then, in a hail of bullets, went back for Bonnie, lifting her up and carrying her to the embankment. He was a perfect target as bullets smacked into the red earth around him. His head suddenly jerked to one side and Jones appeared to be hit by a bullet which caused the possemen to give out another cheer but Jones kept going and soon all three fugitives disappeared into the high cornfield. "I ain't goin' in there after 'em," one vigilante said. The others quickly agreed; the outlaws could lie in wait and shoot down any one of them that tried to cross the stream or easily hit them as they walked into the high corn.

Sheriff Knee ordered a ring of 100 men to surround the cornfield, but by that time the bandits had already run through the corn, left the far side of the field, and had stolen a farmer's Plymouth sedan, roaring northward. Airplanes were called in to search the area and one plane, followed by a column of cars which was headed by an armored car, spotted the Plymouth kicking up dust on a country road as it raced along at high speeds. The plane dipped its wings to indicate where the fugitives were, and the column of cars containing fifty lawmen roared ahead, trying to cut off the Plymouth at a crossroad near Guthrie Center but, by the time the lawmen reached the intersection, they had only a moment to unleash a volley of fire at the car which roared past them. The bandits made good their escape, heading for Minnesota, a state, Clyde reasoned, where lawmen were least likely to look for the Southwestern bandits. Bonnie recovered from her minor gunshot wound, but she had been burned badly during one escape and she suffered for months. Her face had been scarred and she looked twice her real age.

The Barrows stayed on the road, living like bums, afraid to even show their faces in a small town for a quick robbery. They stole clothing from the clotheslines of farms and food from the fields. Barely surviving on raw vegetables was not what Jones had envisioned when joining Bonnie and Clyde. In October he managed to slip away from the deadly pair and hop a freight to Texas, where he was quickly arrested. He confessed to robbery but put all the murders on Bonnie and Clyde, seemingly happy to be in custody. Jones rattled off a lengthy account of his experiences with the Barrows and his statements were greedily published by newspapers and detective magazines. Bonnie and Clyde were also homesick for Texas and managed to meet with Bonnie's parents near Grand Prairie where a strange family picnic was held. Throughout the homecoming, all Bonnie talked about with her mother was her own funeral and how she wanted to be buried next to Clyde "after the laws kill us."

After running for a few weeks, Bonnie insisted that she and Clyde return to Dallas to see their parents on Thanksgiving. Dallas sheriff Smoot Schmid had learned of the Grand Prairie meeting and assigned detectives to follow the mothers of both bandits. When the parents were spotted driving toward Fort Worth, Schmid ordered a posse to follow them, leading to a lonely road where they hid in bushes, watching the two mothers who sat in a car. Suddenly another car approached from the opposite direction. In it were Bonnie and Clyde. But Clyde, again following his instincts, did not slow down, driving by the car in which the two mothers sat waiting, picnic baskets full of turkey and trimmings in the back seat of their car. After Clyde's auto traveled a short distance down the road, Schmid's possemen opened fire, raking the car and pumping seventeen bullets into it. They aimed low at the tires but missed. Their bullets, however, plowed through the doors and struck both bandits in the legs. These were minor wounds that quickly healed. Clyde was nevertheless incensed that his mother's life had been placed in jeopardy. He sent a note to Sheriff Schmid which informed the lawman that if "a hair of my mother's head is ever harmed you will pay with your life." He added that he would not send anyone else to kill Schmid; he would personally murder the lawman.

This daring threat was learned by Ray Hamilton, Clyde's old partner, who had been sending requests to Clyde via the prison grapevine that he break him out of Eastham. From the moment Hamilton entered Eastham, Hamilton had bragged how he would be broken out of the place. Hamilton told Warden B.B. Monzingo that "I won't be here long. Clyde Barrow won't let me lie around no prison farm." When Clyde received word once again that Hamilton wanted to break

Ray Hamilton just before Clyde arranged his prison escape.

out, he arranged for three .45-caliber automatics to be placed in a large clump of brush where he knew Hamilton would be working with a road gang from the prison on Jan. 16, 1934. On that day, Hamilton, along with Joe Palmer and Henry Methvin, Hilton Bybee and J.B. French, found the guns at the appointed spot and turned on their guards. Hamilton shot and mortally wounded Major E.M. Crowson, who was in charge of the road gang, when the officer tried to run Hamilton down with his horse. Other guards were knocked off or shot off their horses as the five prisoners fled through a dense wood. When they emerged on the other side of the woods they saw Bonnie and Clyde waiting for them with two cars. The convicts piled into the cars as Bonnie and Clyde sprayed the woods with submachine gun and BAR fire, although they hit no one since there were no guards pursuing the fugitives. Bybee and French were let out of the cars some miles distant from Eastham; they wanted to strike out on their own. French was recaptured the next day, and Bybee was picked up in Amarillo the next week.

On Jan. 20, 1934, the gang, now swollen by the three escaped convicts, robbed the bank in Lancaster, Texas, taking a small amount. The Barrow gang was the most sought-after group of criminals in the country, considered more dangerous than the Barkers or the John Dillinger gang. Clyde was already credited with killing between fifteen to twenty persons, and lawmen knew he would not hesitate to murder at any time. The Barrow gang had broken several federal laws in recent months, new laws that made driving a stolen car across a state line and bank robbery federal offenses. Now the FBI joined in the pursuit of the gang. All normal havens were denied Bonnie and Clyde. When the gang showed up at the home of one of Hamilton's relatives, the bandits were told to "keep goin', there's no place for you here." They were surrounded by thousands of possemen, militia, vigilantes, and national guardsmen, all closing the ring. The bandits fled into the sprawling 2,500 square miles of wilderness that made up the Cookson Hills which had been a traditional hiding place for outlaws since the days of Belle Starr.

Lawmen did not bother to enter the Cookson Hills; it was unchartered for the most part and, other than wilderness trails, no network of roads traversed the rugged terrain. It was well known to lawmen that the inhabitants of the Hills were sympathetic to criminals, especially their own kind, feeding and hiding such men as Wilbur Underhill, Bob Brady, the Kimes-Terrill boys, and, especially the local folk hero, Charles Arthur "Pretty Boy" Floyd. When Floyd learned that the Barrows had entered his private sanctuary, he sent word to the natives to avoid the gang members: "Don't feed them, don't give them shelter. Sic the law on them if you can. The Barrows are rattlesnakes and have nothing to do with our people." Moreover, Oklahoma authorities grew incensed when lawmen from other states pointed to the Cookson Hills as a natural haven for outlaws from other states.

The gang had entered the Hills at Muskogee and were camping out in that area, according to one report received by officials. An enormous army was then put together, several National Guard units, state police, FBI agents, sheriffs, constables, and vigilantes— more than 1,000 men—this force entering the Cookson Hills in a determined search for the Barrow gang on Feb. 17, 1934. This was the largest force ever assembled in U.S. history with the expressed purpose of tracking down a single band of outlaws. All the searchers had but one order: Find the Barrows and kill them all—shoot to kill. Torrential rain fell as the search parties entered the Hills and soon even the largest search parties were fumbling through the thick brush and dense woods, themselves lost and bogged down. The old roads turned to quagmires which sucked the hundreds of police and military cars to a stop. The rain turned to snow. The Hills echoed with erratic machine gun fire, the booming of shotguns. This usually meant that some driver had failed to stop his car when ordered, and posses were signaling that suspicious characters had been sighted. All of the outlaws then hiding in the Hills fled along narrow, little-known escape routes, including Floyd and members of the Ford Bradshaw gang. The Barrows roared out of the Hills and eluded the dragnet, listening to the officers signaling each other with gunfire so they knew where their pursuers were located. The massive dragnet did scoop up a dozen outlaws but all of them were "small-timers."

Heading northward, the Barrows struck small banks in Michigan, Iowa, and Indiana, small banks in small towns with little to offer the robbers except a few hundred dollars. These banks, like almost all raided by the Barrows, were teetering on the brink of bankruptcy, so hard hit were they by the Great Depression.

Most of the small banks struck by the Barrows were family operated and contained the meager savings of farmers and local shopkeepers, all of whom were suffering during the Depression. When these banks were robbed, they collapsed and the loss often caused the foreclosures of shops and farms, there then being no federal insurance to cover deposits. The gang began to fall apart in the spring of 1934. Joe Palmer developed stomach ulcers and left to return home to his eventual capture and imprisonment. Ray Hamilton argued with Clyde about Bonnie's split of the loot and left to return to Texas. Henry Methvin, a quiet youth from Louisiana who was identical to Jones in his slavish devotion to Bonnie and Clyde, stayed on with the murderous pair.

Texas by this time had had enough of its homegrown crime wave. When Major Crowson died of the wound he received from Hamilton during the Eastham break, lawmen lobbied officials for a "Wanted Dead" reward to be posted for Bonnie and Clyde. A storm of political debate erupted in the state legislature over the proposed reward. "You are about to do in cold blood what a mob does in the heat of passion," argued Representative T.H. McGregor. Congressman George Winningham jumped to his feet, stating: "I place Barrow and his gang beyond the category of human beings. You are talking about according a trial to a beast. I say give him the same chance he gave those he murdered. Shoot him down like the mad dog he is!" The more moderate members of the legislature had their way and a "Wanted Dead or Alive" reward of $2,500 was issued. None of these measures would work with Clyde Barrow, reasoned Lee Simmons, head of the Texas prison system. He called in one of the toughest lawmen in Texas to deal with the Barrows, Frank Hamer, who had been a Texas Ranger for twenty years until resigning his position in protest over the election of Ma Ferguson, the pardon-granting governor.

Grapevine, Texas, Apr. 1, 1934: Bonnie and Clyde murdered two motorcycle cops on this spot when their picnic was interrupted.

Hamer, considered the fastest draw in the state, a man who had killed sixty-five outlaws in his dedicated career, was given the assignment of hunting down Bonnie and Clyde. He took to the road, living exactly the way Bonnie and Clyde did, sleeping in his car, checking their routes and learning that Clyde basically followed a pattern, going as far east as Louisiana and then doubling back into Texas, driving north in a large loop through Missouri and Kansas, then, when leaving Texas, driving again east through Oklahoma and Arkansas. Hamer learned every habit and routine of Bonnie and Clyde, including the fact that they had picked up a white rabbit and kept it as a pet, buying it lettuce when Clyde stopped to buy his Bull Durham roll-your-own cigarettes. Hamer barely missed his quarry in Texarkana, and, again, in Shreveport. He came upon their campsite at Wichita Falls so nearly missing them that their campfire was still smoldering. Then, in the spring of 1934, the trail vanished.

The Barrows had gone into hiding on the farm of Ivan Methvin, Henry's father, located in Bienville Parish, La. Here they healed old wounds, ate chicken and corn, and played cards, much to the chagrin of Henry's father, who wanted his son to give up his life of crime. Bonnie and Clyde talked of nothing but death and how it would come to them. They decided to return to Texas

W.D. Jones, an unwilling Barrow accomplice.

The riddled death car and the curious.

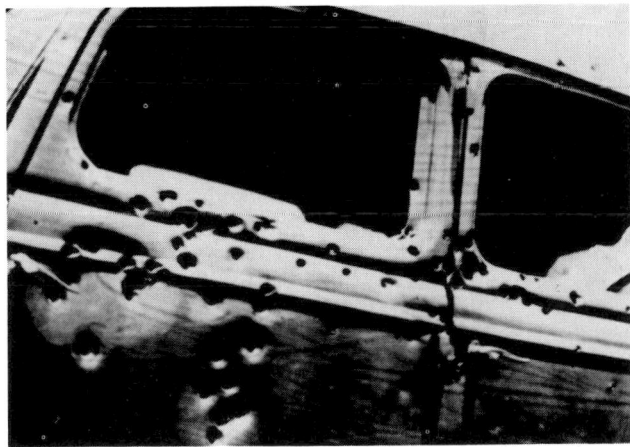

Hundreds of bullets pierced the death car.

The posse that shot Bonnie and Clyde.

Clyde met death with his shoes off.

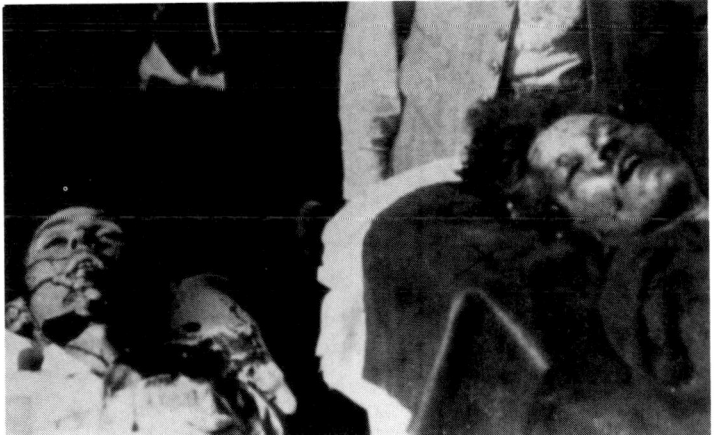

Clyde and Bonnie in the morgue, 1934.

one more time to see their relatives and they drove to a rendez-vous near Grapevine, Texas, on Apr. 1, 1934, to meet with Bonnie's sister. Just as the three were playing with Bonnie's pet rabbit, two motorcycle cops, E.B. Wheeler and H.D. Murphy, rode past, giving the trio a suspicious once-over. The two patrolmen rode to a rise in the road and turned around, going back toward Bonnie and Clyde. As they slowly drew up to the parked car, Clyde reached into the car and grabbed a shotgun. He unloaded a barrel into each officer, almost at point blank range, killing both of them. Neither Murphy nor Wheeler, men in their early twenties, ever had a chance to go for their guns. This double killing caused Clyde Barrow to be made Public Enemy Number One in Texas.

Once again in Oklahoma, Clyde stole a Plymouth but the car, with Bonnie and Methvin inside, got stuck in the mud. Clyde saw a farmer approaching and tried to flag the car down, but the farmer saw the weapons stacked on the back seat of the car and kept going. He reported what he had seen to Police Chief Percy Boyd of Commerce, Okla., and he and Constable Cal Campbell drove to the site where the Plymouth was still mired. Both officers drew their guns and cautiously approached the car but Clyde jumped out from behind the auto holding a Browning Automatic Rifle. Campbell, a fast-draw artist, whipped out his pistol and fired before Clyde could react but his shot missed. Clyde shot Campbell in the chest, knocking him backward, a mortal wound. He then spun about and blasted Chief Boyd into the mud. Bonnie and Methvin appeared and they picked up Boyd and put him into the car, dressing his minor wound. Campbell was dead. As they drove along, the gang members casually talked to Boyd as if nothing had happened. Then Clyde said to Boyd: "I'm sorry I killed the old man but I had to. He shot at me." They released Boyd near Prescott, Kan.

Federal and state lawmen were not closing in on the Barrows. Frank Hamer had learned, as had FBI agent L.A. Kindell, that the third member of the gang was Henry Methvin and that his father owned a farm in Bienville Parish, La. Both men met while they were independently attempting to pinpoint the gang's hideout. They then enlisted the aid of Henderson Jordan, sheriff of Acadia, La., the town closest to the Methvin farm. The three lawmen went to Ivan Methvin, who admitted that his son was a member of the Barrow gang but he refused to work with them, stating: "I've got my boy to think about." In a few weeks he returned to the lawmen, offering to help, stating that Bonnie and Clyde had forced him and his son to leave his farm and move to a cabin in the back woods near Gibsland, La. The father made a deal with the lawmen, one which Governor Ferguson agreed to: if he helped the officers capture Bonnie and Clyde, his son would receive a pardon for his involvement with the bandits.

Ivan Methvin told his son about the plan and Henry, long weary of running with the bandits, agreed to slip away from the pair when they went shopping the next day in Shreveport. When the trio arrived in Shreveport, Henry Methvin told Clyde he was going to buy a shirt and disappeared through the back door of a small clothing store. Bonnie and Clyde thought he had gotten lost and returned to the backwoods cabin where, with Henry's father, they waited for him to return but he did not. Clyde thought that Henry might have gotten "mixed up" and had returned to another house the gang had rented as an auxiliary hideout. Clyde turned to the sweating Ivan Methvin and told him: "You better check on it. We'll meet you on the road between Sailes and Gibsland tomorrow morning at nine." The pair left to stay in the rented house and, as soon as they were gone, Methvin called Sheriff Jordan who could not reach FBI agent Kindell since he was out of town. But he did manage to contact Frank Hamer who immediately rounded up his own men, M.B. "Manny" Gault, an ex-Ranger like himself, and two tough Dallas sheriff's deputies, Ted Hinton and Bob Alcorn. These four men, along with Sheriff Jordan and his deputy, Paul M. Oakley, made up the posse that would bring an end to Bonnie and Clyde.

The lawmen drove along the road that evening selecting a spot where a high embankment on one side offered a perfect field of fire. They drove out to the spot, which was between Sailes and Gibsland, near Mt. Lebanon, parking their cars behind the embankment so they could not be seen from the road. It was 3 a.m., May 23, 1934. The lawmen were heavily armed and sighted up and down the roadway as soon as dawn broke. Hamer and Jordan held automatic shotguns, Gault and Alcorn had Winchester repeaters, Hinton, a Browning Automatic Rifle, and Oakley, a submachine gun. At about 8 a.m., Ivan Methvin appeared driving his truck which Jordan flagged down and told him to park alongside the roadway and to remove a tire as if he had a flat. He did so and nervously fiddled about with the wheel, looking anxiously up the road for Bonnie and Clyde.

"I want to take these two alive," Sheriff Jordan told the other men, "but, if they reach for their guns, let them have it." Frank Hamer had been told something else by Lee Simmons, chief of the Texas Prison System: "I don't care how long it takes. I'll back you to the limit. I'd be foolish to tell you how to do your job, but the way I look at it, the best thing to do is to put them on the spot, know you are right, and shoot everybody in sight." At 9 a.m., a few cars passed but failed to stop as Methvin kept his frustrating vigil and the lawmen behind the brush at the top of the embankment gripped their weapons tightly. Then, at 9:15 a.m., a fast-moving Ford V-8 appeared at the top of a distant rise in the road and sped toward the truck where Methvin waited. Clyde was at the wheel, wearing dark glasses and driving in his socks. Bonnie sat beside him wearing a new red dress and red shoes she had purchased in Terre Haute, Ind., some weeks earlier. She was eating a sandwich. Under Bonnie's front seat were fifteen stolen license plates (these were changed each day to avoid detection) and behind her, in the back seat and on the floor, was an arsenal consisting of eleven pistols, a revolver, a shotgun, three Browning Automatic Rifles, and more than 2,000 rounds of ammunition. Bonnie's makeup case sat on top of the weapons and so did Clyde's saxophone. He had been practicing this long-forgotten instrument, the first item he had ever stolen; sheet music was strewn on the floor of the back seat.

Clyde brought the car to a halt a few yards away from Methvin's truck. They were directly in front of the place of ambush. "Got a flat?" Clyde asked Methvin, sticking his head out of the car window. Methvin nodded. "Did you find Henry?" Clyde asked him. Methvin shook his head. He then asked: "Do you have a drink of water?"

"Sure," Bonnie said and reached for a thermos.

At that moment a truck carrying black farm laborers was rumbling down the road toward the ambush site. Methvin panicked and dove beneath his truck. The perplexed Bonnie and Clyde gaped in wonder at Methvin's bizarre action. Jordan, wanting to get it over with before the truck with the blacks passed between the officers and the Barrows, shouted: "Put 'em up, Clyde! You're covered!"

Clyde shifted into first gear, grabbed a shotgun, and began to swing the car door open almost in one sweeping movement. Bonnie suddenly had a pistol in her hand. The lawmen let loose a terrifying fusillade which poured into the V-8, peppering the car over and over again, like heavy rain falling, a thunderous blast of rapid-fire weapons that caught the bandits full force, riddling the outlaws. The stream of fire was so thick and intense that it slashed Clyde Barrow's tie in half and tore his suitcoat from his body. Bonnie's dress was cut from her shoulders by the withering fire, and both bodies hopped and bounced about under the impact of the stream of bullets, a literal "dance of death" as if both were puppets being jerked about by a berserk manipulator. They spoke no final farewells to each other. There was no time. They never got to fire a shot, much to the gratitude of their lawmen foes. They died bloody, their bodies ripped to pieces, much like their many victims over the last two years.

Clyde's foot slipped off the clutch pedal, and the car, still in low gear, ground ahead, bouncing into a ditch and stopping. The lawmen continued to spray the car with almost every round of ammunition they had. After four minutes of this incredible barrage, Sheriff Jordan waved his men to cease fire. Hamer looked at his watch. It was 9:20 a.m. He stood up on the embankment and then walked down slowly to the car, water steaming from its burst radiator. Gault shouted to him: "Be careful—they may not be dead." The awful reputation of these two bandits, legendary in their own day, had caused the lawmen to be cautious, even after pumping 167 slugs breast-high into the car. Hamer checked the occupants of the car and turned: "They're dead, both of them." (Hamer refused all later financial offers to appear in public and talk about the taking of Bonnie and Clyde. He received $180 a month while tracking down Bonnie and Clyde, but the state of Texas refused to pay him $14 in phone bills during his time on the case because Hamer neglected to keep receipts.)

The role of the Methvins was not revealed for several decades since they feared reprisal for betraying Bonnie and Clyde. From the moment Bonnie and Clyde were killed, crowds came running to view the carnage and collect souvenirs. The blacks in the truck jumped down after the shooting ceased and collected empty cartridges for souvenirs. As the death car was being towed to Arcadia with the bodies still in it, crowds appeared along the roadway, women wiping the blood from the bodies on handkerchiefs and scarfs for souvenirs. The bodies, still bleeding, were put on two slabs in an Arcadia undertaking parlor and the weapons found in the back seat of the car were piled on top of the bodies. The residents who gathered in a great crowd before the parlor were then allowed inside one by one to view the bodies, at a charge of $1 per head.

The killing of Bonnie and Clyde was front page news around the world. The New York *Herald* stated that "society is glad that Louisiana rubbed them both out." Yet the legends about these two bandits expanded long before they had been buried, not as Bonnie wished, together, but separately, Clyde in a Dallas cemetery next to his gunman brother Buck, Bonnie in Fish Trap Cemetery some miles from her killer lover. Her body was later moved to Crown Hill Memorial Park Cemetery to prevent souvenir hunters from despoiling her tombstone. Few attended Clyde's funeral but Bonnie Parker's interment drew large crowds. As her body was lowered into the ground a quartet sang "Beautiful Isle of Somewhere."

Many who had associated with Bonnie and Clyde, including Mrs. Cummie Barrow and some of Bonnie's relatives, served various sentences for "aiding and abetting" the bandits. Ray Hamilton and Joe Palmer were recaptured and sentenced to death for killing Major Crowson. Both made a spectacular escape from the Death House at Huntsville in July 1934, but they were again captured and put to death. Henry Methvin, despite the deal his father had worked out for him, was sentenced to death in Oklahoma for the murder of Constable Campbell, but his sentence was later commuted to life and he was paroled in 1942.

The pulp magazines continued to keep the legend of Bonnie and Clyde alive for several decades, aided by Hollywood which churned out several films allegedly based on their lives, the best of which is Fritz Lang's *You Only Live Once*. The 1967 film, *Bonnie and Clyde*, though an excellent period production that captured the mood and flavor of the Depression-ridden era, did little or nothing to accurately portray these two desperate killers, providing a rationale for their actions that even the cunning Bonnie and Clyde could never imagine. They were shown to be admired and supported by the poor people of their day which, of course, was a blatant misrepresentation; they preyed upon and injured these very people at every turn. They were shown to have momentary thoughts of honor and peform some acts of charity and compassion. In one scene Clyde is shown returning money to a farmer in a bank he is robbing ("We only want the bank's money."), a *beau geste* that was really performed by John Dillinger when he robbed the Greencastle bank in Indiana. Such an act was unthinkable on the part of Bonnie and Clyde, both hypocritical fakers who were more accurately described by Ray Hamilton, one of their own gang members, stating before his execution:

"Bonnie and Clyde? They loved to kill people, see blood run. That's how they got their kicks. They were dirty people. Her breath was awful and Clyde never took a bath. They smelled bad all the time. They'd steal the pennies off a dead man's eyes."

The image given to the world, one that the uninformed too readily accepted, was that of two persecuted lovers who were forced into banditry and death by a cruel and unthinking society. They were killers, both of them, without conscience, without mercy, wholly unlike the image the Parker family attempted to project by placing the following inscription (not her own) on Bonnie's tombstone:

As the flowers are all made sweeter
By the sunshine and the dew,
So this old world is made brighter
By the lives of folks like you.

See: **Audett, James Henry; Dillinger, John Herbert; Floyd, Charles Arthur; Hamer, Frank; Underhill, Wilbur.**
REF.: Audett, *Rap Sheet;* Boar, *The World's Most Infamous Murders;* Cawelti, *Focus on Bonnie and Clyde; CBA;* Cooper, *Ten Thousand Public Enemies;* Demaris, *The Director;* Edge, *Run the Cat Roads;* Fortune, *The True Story of Bonnie and Clyde;* Gish, *American Bandits;* Godwin, *Murder U.S.A.;* Hoover, *Persons in Hiding;* Jenkins and Frost, *I'm Frank Hamer, The Life of a Texas Peace Officer;* Kobler, *Some Like It Gory;* Louderback, *The Bad Ones;* Nash, *Almanac of World Crime;* ____, *Bloodletters and Badmen;* ____, *The Dillinger Dossier;* ____, *Look for the Woman;* Reddig, *Tom's Town;* Reppetto, *The Blue Parade;* Rogers, *The Lusty Texas of Dallas;* Toland, *The Dillinger Days;* Toledano, *J. Edgar Hoover;* Ungar, *FBI;* Webb, *The Texas Rangers;* Wellman, *A Dynasty of Western Outlaws;* Wicker, *Investigating the FBI;* (FILM) *You Only Live Once,* 1937; *Gun Crazy,* 1949; *They Live by Night,* 1949; *The Bonnie Parker Story,* 1958; *Bonnie and Clyde,* 1967; *The Other Side of Bonnie and Clyde,* 1968; *Killers Three,* 1968; *Thieves Like Us,* 1978.

Barrow, George, b.1871, and **Barrow, Addie,** prom. 1899, and **Anderson, Bella,** prom. 1899, U.S., kid. When 20-month-old Marion Clarke disappeared from her New York home on May 21, 1899, it was a kidnapping reminiscent of the famous Charley Ross case of 1874. The New York *Times* recalled with horror the unsolved abduction of Ross, a case which attained national prominence in its day.

This time there would be a happy ending. The kidnapping scheme was conceived by 28-year-old George Barrow, an Arkansas man who fled to New York City after various scrapes at home with the law. Barrow and his wife Addie hired a governess named Bella Anderson whose task it was to locate prospective kidnap victims, hire herself out to the victim's family, and then carry off the infant while the ransom demand was drawn up by Barrow.

The Clarke family was not a wealthy one, so Barrow's demand was modest, only $300. The abduction prompted an outpouring of sympathy for the family. The New York *World* offered a $1,000 reward, and, not to be outdone, the *Journal* posted $2,000. On June 2 the child was spotted by a grocer in Garnerville, N.Y. The Barrows were arrested, and the baby was brought back to New York amidst throngs of cheering well-wishers. At a performance of the play, *The Man In the Moon*, comedian Sam Bernard stepped off the stage to inform the audience of the safe return of Marion.

Nurse Anderson testified against her employers at the trial, explaining that the Barrows planned a series of these kidnappings across the country, receiving for her cooperation a reduced sentence of four years. Barrow was given a term of fourteen years and ten months' hard labor at Sing Sing. Addie Barrow was sentenced to twelve years and ten months, closing out one of the most lurid kidnapping cases of the nineteenth century.
REF.: Alix, *Ransom Kidnapping In America; CBA;* Nash, *Open Files.*

Barrow, Henry (or **Barrowe**), d.1593, Brit., her. Founder of the Congregationalist Church. He was imprisoned in 1586 for renouncing the authority of clerical leaders and hanged at Tyburn for his seditious writings. REF.: *CBA.*

Barrows, Ralph Edward, prom. 1949, U.S., mansl. Barrows was known in New York's homosexual community of the late 1940s as violent and sadistic. At the age of fourteen he ran a bordello out of his Manhattan studio apartment, often beating the young female inmates senseless. Ralph Barrows' stock in trade, however, became the midtown, and Lower East Side homosexuals he seduced and robbed.

In need of quick cash, Barrows drifted into a West 45th Street cafe on the night of Feb. 12, 1949. There he met a quiet-looking businessman from Toronto, Canada who introduced himself as Cameron McKeller, representative of a liquor importing firm and a guest at the elegant Waldorf-Astoria Hotel. Ever obliging, Barrows volunteered to take McKeller back to his room after he had imbibed too much. There, Barrows viciously assaulted the visitor and stomped him to death. A wrist watch and the cash in the dead man's wallet, modest by all accounts, were Barrows' take. He made one mistake, though. A book of matches bearing the address of the West 45th Street Cafe was left behind.

A cocktail waitress remembered that two men had been drinking shots all evening. She promised to notify detectives if the suspect returned—which he did—the next day. Ten minutes later the police had their man in custody.

Assistant District Attorney Harold Birns prosecuted the case but failed to secure an indictment of first-degree murder since premeditation and robbery had not been clearly established as motives. At best, Barrows could be sent away for manslaughter if his lawyers failed to present an adequate defense.

Meanwhile, officials from the District Attorney's office continued their investigation, touring the homosexual bars of Manhattan, and questioning patrons about Ralph Barrows. The natural reluctance of the men to cooperate with the law stymied Birns. It was generally conceded that the killer was a sadistic bully, but beyond that no hard facts supported a first-degree murder charge.

A letter from a Herbert Diether Jr. told of overhearing Barrows' plan to "pick up a queer and rob him," but the author of this note could not be found. The defendant was brought to trial later that summer and was sentenced to twenty to thirty years in Sing Sing on the original charge of manslaughter.

REF.: *CBA*; Danforth, *The D.A.'s Man.*

Barrows, Samuel June, 1845-1909, U.S., reformer. Prison reformer who influenced the passage of New York State's first probationary and parole laws. REF.: *CBA.*

Barry, Arthur (AKA: Toomer), b.1890, U.S., burg.-rob. A notorious second-story burglar, Arthur Barry specialized in looting the homes of the wealthy along the Eastern seaboard during the 1920s. He reportedly stole more than $2 million in cash and jewelry from the homes of the first Mrs. Clarence Mackay, Joshua Cosden, and Mr. and Mrs. Jesse Livermore. While burglarizing the Livermore bedroom, Barry was discovered by Mrs. Livermore. He ordered her at gunpoint to sit down and be quiet while he scooped up her jewelry. When Mrs. Livermore nervously groped for a cigarette, the suave Barry lit it for her. When he was about to take one of her favorite rings, she asked that he leave it with her, telling the burglar that it was her good luck piece. Barry handed her the ring and went on his way. Caught in 1928, Barry was sent to Auburn Prison to serve a long prison term, but during the 1929 riots at the prison, he managed to escape.

Barry was at large for more than three years, laying low and posing as a windshield-wiper salesman, occasionally casing and robbing one of the great estates in New Jersey and then retreating to a modest home in Newton, N.J., where he lived under the name of Toomer. Detectives finally trailed Barry to his bungalow after he fenced some stolen jewelry. He was captured through a ruse where a news dealer went to his home to complain about his not paying his bill. As Barry stepped onto the porch of his home, a dozen detectives rushed forth, pinning his arms. A gun was found in his pocket and another loaded revolver in his windshield-wiper sample case. He was sent back to Auburn to serve out his long sentence, another lengthy term added for his 1929 escape and the burglaries and robberies committed during his time at large.

REF.: *CBA*; Hunt, *Dictionary of Rogues*; Wade, *Great Hoaxes*

and Famous Imposters.

Barry, Jeanne du (Jeanne Bècu), 1743-93, Fr., treas. Contributed to the fall of the Duc de Choiseul in 1770. At the onset of the Revolution she assisted French emigres, and was eventually guillotined by the Revolutionary Tribunal. REF.: *CBA.*

Barry, Marion, prom. 1980-87, U.S., polit. corr. In 1979 Barry was elected mayor of Washington, D.C., for the first time. Through three scandal-ridden terms in office, he continued to poll large majorities in re-election campaigns. In November 1986 Marion Barry garnered sixty-one percent of the popular vote amidst allegations of widespread graft and corruption in city departments.

Eleven top city officials were convicted of corruption between 1979 and 1987, including Ivanhoe Donaldson, deputy mayor of economic development. A close personal friend of the mayor, Donaldson pleaded guilty to cheating the city out of $200,000 through bogus building contracts and various kickbacks. In May of 1987, U.S. Attorney Joseph diGenova wrapped up a seventeen-month probe into fraud and bribery schemes that affected virtually every city office. "It's easier to get your name in the paper by announcing a probe against my administration than by doing anything substantive," the mayor shot back.

Compounding Barry's problems were charges that his girlfriend, Karen Johnson, supplied him with cocaine, and that a top aide, David Rivers, had been marked by the FBI as a probable drug distributor. Another friend and former city employee Charles Lewis, was indicted on drug charges. Meanwhile, Barry's approval rating remained high among low income people and minorities, comprising the bulk of the inner-city population. REF.: *CBA.*

Barry, Mary Ann, 1855-74, Brit., theft-mur. A thief from childhood, Mary Ann Barrett lived in London with her common-law husband, Edwin Bailey, also a thief. When their only child was born, both parents neglected it, then decided that the infant, when less than a year old, was a nuisance. They killed the child and were discovered trying to dispose of the remains. Both were condemned and hanged with another prisoner, Edwin Butt, who had strangled his sweetheart in a fit of jealous rage. This triple execution was a rare occurrence, and drew thousands to witness the end of the three criminals.

REF.: *CBA*; Nash, *Look for the Woman*; O'Donnell, *Should Women Hang?*

Barry, Sir Redmond, 1813-80, Ire., jur. First solicitor general of Victoria, Aus. in 1851. REF.: *CBA.*

Barry, Richard (AKA: W.H. Ford, John Derby), prom. 1924, U.S., burg.-forg. Irving Greenwald was walking through New York's financial district one day in March 1924 when a postal inspector tapped him on the shoulder and asked if he happened to be J.C. Alderman. Assured that he was not, the postal inspector nevertheless insisted he come down to headquarters on a charge of passing forged money orders. Someone named Alderman had stolen a stack of blank money orders from a Buffalo postal sub-station in January, and had been spending them in New York City department stores.

Greenwald said he had no knowledge of the transactions, but was identified by store clerks. On Apr. 11, 1924, he was indicted for passing forged money orders. On the advice of his attorney, J. Joseph Lilly, Greenwald entered a plea of guilty on Apr. 14. After a one-day trial, Irving Greenwald was found Guilty and sentenced to seven-and-a-half years at the Atlanta Federal Penitentiary.

After he was incarcerated, more stolen money orders began turning up in Philadelphia and New York. Richard Barry, who operated under several aliases, was arrested and brought before the clerks who had originally fingered Greenwald. The two men did not resemble each other in the least. All but one of the witnesses quickly pointed out Barry as the forger.

On June 23, 1924, he pleaded guilty to passing forged money orders and was sentenced to three years in the Atlanta Federal Penitentiary. On Aug. 7, Greenwald was granted a full and unconditional pardon by President Calvin Coolidge.

REF.: Borchard, *Convicting the Innocent; CBA.*

Barsi, Jozsef, 1933-88, U.S., mur.-suic. In a tragic, real-life enactment of a television drama, 11-year-old actress Judith Barsi and her mother Maria were shot to death in their West Hills, Calif., home on July 27, 1988. The killer was the girl's father, 55-year-old Jozsef Barsi who took his own life afterward. Judith had portrayed the daughter of Jeffrey MacDonald in the 1984 TV adaptation of Joe McGinniss' best selling book *Fatal Vision.* MacDonald was convicted of murdering his entire family while under the influence of drugs. REF.: *CBA.*

Barstow, Ralph Gordon, prom. 1940, Case of, Brit., mur. Barstow married Mary in 1937 when she was only sixteen. The couple lived with his parents in Preston where she bore a child. Then, when the war clouds gathered over Europe, Ralph Barstow was called into service where he learned from an acquaintance that his wife had begun an extra-marital affair with an army lieutenant.

Barstow brooded over this matter for some time. In a moment of pique he told a friend, "When I go home, I will bump her off!"

After he regained his composure, Barstow persuaded his wife to leave their home in Preston and live with him near the base at Cheltenham. While en route to their destination they missed their train in Birmingham, and took a room in Edgbaston. On Nov. 14, 1940, a man in an adjacent room heard a shot ring out. Barstow ran excitedly out of his room saying he had accidentally shot his wife. He told police investigators he was cleaning his rifle when the bullet in the breech discharged.

Recalling his earlier threats to kill his wife, the Crown indicted him on murder charges. Pathologist Robert Churchill was summoned to give expert testimony. He explained that the rifle was in the same position at the time the shot was fired as it would have been if Barstow were unloading. The prosecutor, Maurice Healy, concurred with Churchill and moved to have the case dismissed. The shooting of Mrs. Barstow was officially ruled an accident.

REF.: *CBA;* Hastings, *The Other Mr. Churchill.*

The elegant French pirate Jean Bart.

Bart, Jean, c.1651-1702, Fr., pir. Jean Bart was a French privateer from Dunkirk who operated with the secret commission of King Louis XIV. He was a gentleman pirate, elegantly attired and insisting upon the normal rules of warfare when his squadrons overwhelmed Dutch vessels and destroyed the Dutch herring fleets. He took enormous spoils but did not seek the normally ruthless reprisals of those in his trade when offered resistance. Bart was after loot to send to his king, not slaves. The prisoners captured by his well-disciplined men were treated with consideration and put ashore at the first landfall. If Bart demonstrated any great failing, it was his vanity. He dressed in ornate clothes, strutting about the deck of his flagship, peacock-proud. He dined on the best plate and was adamant that his top mates display the proper table manners, hardly the image of the raw, uncouth pirate the world had come to dread. After Bart's successful raids against the forts near Newcastle-on-Tyne, he was officially acknowledged

by Louis XIV, and, in 1697, was given the command of a royal fleet. He died a much respected captain of the French Royal Fleet, known for his courage, despite his early occupation as a desperate corsair.

REF.: Cabal, *Piracy and Pirates; CBA;* Chatterton, *The Romance of Piracy;* Gosse, *The Pirates' Who's Who;* Innes, *The Book of Pirates;* Lydon, *Pirates, Privateers and Profits;* Pringle, *Jolly Roger;* Russell, *The French Corsairs;* Williams, *Captains Outrageous;* Woodbury, *The Great Days of Piracy.*

Bartels, John R., Jr., 1934-   , U.S., law enfor. off. John Bartels received his law degree from Harvard University in 1960. Before accepting a post as Assistant U.S. Attorney for the Southern District of New York in 1964, he had been engaged in private law practice for three years.

Bartels served as chief of the Justice Department's New Jersey Organized Crime Strike Force, 1969-71. During this time he received several major awards, including the Department of Justice Award for Distinguished Service in 1970 and the Federal Criminal Investigator's Association Man of the Year Award a year later.

On Sept. 11, 1973, President Richard Nixon named the 38-year-old lawyer administrator of drug enforcement. The position was created by the Reorganization Plan of 1973 which established the Drug Enforcement Administration (DEA) within the Department of Justice. Bartels began his new job with some prior experience in drug law enforcement, since he had served as Deputy Special Assistant Attorney General and Deputy Director of the Office for Drug Abuse Law Enforcement since 1972. REF.: *CBA.*

Barter, Richard (AKA: Rattlesnake Dick, Dick Woods), 1834-59, U.S., west. outl. Richard Barter was born in Quebec, Can., (some reports state England), the son of a British officer. He migrated to California during the Gold Rush days and, not finding gold, decided to steal his fortune, beginning with rustling horses. Barter was not successful, being captured and imprisoned for two years. Upon his release he formed another gang made up of Cy and George Skinner and some others. In 1856, Barter learned from a drunken mining engineer that large gold shipments were being sent down Trinity Mountain from the mines of Yreka. Barter sent George Skinner and three others to intercept the gold shipment which was packed on mules. Skinner accomplished the task easily, stopping the gold shipment outside of Nevada City, holding guns on the muleskinners who meekly turned over more than $80,000 in gold bullion. Skinner and his men did not have to fire a shot. They made off with the shipment to keep a rendezvous with Barter and Cy Skinner. But Rattlesnake Dick did not keep the appointment; he and Skinner had been jailed for stealing mules.

Barter immediately sought out George Skinner to obtain his share of the gold shipment robbery, an enormous amount for those days. But George Skinner was already dead. Skinner had found it next to impossible to take the heavy gold shipment down the mountain passes without fresh mules, so he buried most of the stolen gold and headed for Folsom to meet Barter. He and his confederates were intercepted by Wells Fargo detectives who shot and killed him in a wild gun battle. His confederates fled. Barter and Cy Skinner spent weeks trying to find the gold and then gave up. (This treasure is still being unsuccessfully sought.) Barter went back to robbing stagecoaches but his luck soon ran out. Sheriff J. Boggs trapped Barter and Skinner in a mountain pass near Auburn, Calif., on the night of July 11, 1859. Boggs fired one bullet which entered the heart of Rattlesnake Dick, killing him instantly. Skinner was wounded, taken into custody, and later given a long prison sentence.

REF.: Angel, *History of Placer County, California;* Bartholomew, *The Biographical Album of Western Gunfighters;* Block, *Great Stagecoach Robbers of the West; CBA;* Fisher and Holmes, *Gold Rushes and Mining Camps of the Early American West;* Hemphill, *Down the Motherlode;* Horan and Sann, *Pictorial History of the Wild West;* Hungerford, *Wells Fargo;* Jackson, *Anybody's Gold;* ____, *Bad Company;* ____, *Tintypes in Gold;* Johnston, *Lost and Living Cities of the California Gold Rush;* Nash, *Blood-*

letters and Badmen; Shippey, *It's An Old California Custom.*

Barthélemy, Emanuel, d.1855, Brit., duel.-mur. His stock in trade was political insurrection. Emanuel Barthélemy came of age in France during a period of upheaval and change and believed in the ideals of the 1789 French Revolution, which he found sadly lacking in the government after the restoration of the monarchy in 1814. Opposed to King Louis XVIII and everything he stood for, Barthélemy shot and killed one of the royal gendarmes. He was sent to prison but was granted a reprieve after the July 1830 revolution brought Louis Philippe to power.

In 1848 Louis Napoléon annointed himself Napoléon III, and drove many revolutionary exiles including Barthélemy out of the country. The political refugees formed a small colony in Egham, Middlesex, Britain. There, Bathélemy took an active part in the leadership of the community, asserting himself through bullying tactics and intimidation. In 1852 he challenged a French naval officer named Cournet to a duel to settle once and for all who should lead the exiles.

The duelists assembled at Englefield Green with pistols. What Cournet did not know was that Barthélemy and his friends had tampered with his weapon the night before. Given the right to fire the first shot, the navy man's gun discharged harmlessly into the air. With a customary flair for the dramatic, Barthélemy graciously offered to forego his turn if his opponent would agree to finish the duel with swords. Cournet, a well-bred gentleman, declined. Barthélemy took aim, fired, and Cournet fell in his tracks. It was clearly a case of murder but not until the Surrey assizes convened was the plot laid bare. However, the jury ruled the duel had been fought fairly. Barthélemy was acquitted.

In 1854 the celebrated revolutionary met a young English-woman claiming to be the daughter of wealthy salesman George Moore, whom, she avowed, had badly mistreated her, and was planning to deny her dowry. Barthélemy visited him in his apartment to straighten out the matter.

The father refused to concede anything, even after he was threatened with exposure and public ridicule, for it was law that a bride should have a dowry. Angry words passed between the two which ended in the death of Moore. A servant threw open the door and screamed to passersby. In a panic, Barthélemy fled down the stairs but was intercepted by a police officer named Collard and the two men fought in the hallway. Barthélemy drew out a pistol and fired two shots into Collard, who then lingered a few days but eventually died of his wounds. By the time the struggle ended, the police had arrived on the scene to take the assailant into custody.

The trial began at the Old Bailey in 1854. The defense was unable to locate or identify the mysterious "daughter" to whom Barthélemy claimed to be engaged—she was never to be seen again. Many believed she had been recruited for purposes of blackmailing Moore. Since Moore kept large sums of cash in his home the prosecution contended that Barthélemy's motive was robbery, pure and simple.

The jury accepted this logic and returned a Guilty verdict. Barthélemy walked to the gallows on Jan. 22, 1855. He did not fear death he said, only the prospect of having his clothes and personal belongings publicly exhibited at Mme. Tussaud's Wax Museum in London.

REF.: *CBA;* Kingston, *Remarkable Rogues.*

Barthou, Jean Louis, See: **Alexander I (Karageorgevic).**

Bartlett, Adelaide (Adelaide Blanche de la Tremouille), b.1856, Case of, Brit., mur. The Bartlett murder case was undoubtedly the strangest in nineteenth century England, involving a murder by liquid chloroform and a family where affairs between members were acknowledged. Adelaide Bartlett had been born in Orleans, the illegitimate child of a French mother with little background and an English father whose wealth was considerable. The father raised the girl, sending her to good schools in England and presenting her to Edwin Bartlett, a successful 30-year-old grocer who lived in Pimlico. Bartlett met Adelaide in the home of his brother Charles and later, her father paid the fussy grocer a considerable amount of money to marry his daughter, the wedding taking place on Apr. 9, 1875. Adelaide was a beautiful, dark-eyed, curly haired girl of nineteen, eleven years younger than her strict and demanding husband whom she never loved. The marriage was anything but normal. Bartlett refused to take his new bride to bed to consummate the marriage and immediately objected to his wife's lack of education. She was poorly read, he complained to his family, and knew nothing of the history of the world. He sent her off to school to improve her mind, first for a year in a school in Stoke-Newington, then two years in a convent in Belgium.

Adelaide Bartlett and her husband Edwin.

When Adelaide returned to England, she moved into Bartlett's home at Herne Hill, Pimlico. Her husband spent almost all his waking hours supervising the many groceries he owned in the London suburbs. Lonely, ignored, and seeking companionship, Adelaide turned to Charles Bartlett, her husband's brother and they had a brief affair, or at least that was the story spread by Edwin's father, an old crank who hated Adelaide. He had refused to attend his son's wedding to "the foreigner," and had constantly criticized the marriage, not meeting his daughter-in-law until she returned from Belgium, almost three years after her marriage to his son. When Edwin heard about the so-called affair, he exploded and sent his solicitor to his father, demanding that the old man sign a document where he retracted his scandalous statements and apologized. The couple lived in apparent peace until 1871, when Adelaide became pregnant. Bartlett, as big a skinflint as his father, refused to have a doctor deliver the baby, saying that they were "expensive charlatans" and that a nurse would do. He hired Annie Walker, a rather inexperienced nurse who was terrified when the baby was born and, feeling helpless, begged Bartlett to send for an experienced physician. The husband refused and the child was delivered stillborn. Adelaide was placed in a dangerous position, enduring considerable pain. It was later stated that she almost died as a result of the medical inattention.

Adelaide Bartlett, following this horrifying experience, refused to have another child and began to resist her husband's sexual advances. Bartlett, it later appeared, had a large, almost insatiable appetite for sex, so his wife's refusal to go to bed with him caused endless arguments and consistent hostility between the couple.

So successful had Bartlett become that, in 1885, he was able to buy a new home at Merton Abbey, near Wimbledon. The Bartletts attended a Wesleyan church on High Street and here met the handsome, 27-year-old Reverend George Dyson. They soon became friends and Bartlett asked the engaging Dyson to privately tutor his wife in history, mathematics, and Latin. During the course of these private lessons, Dyson seduced the more-than-willing Adelaide, and a love affair ensued. Bartlett seemed oblivious to the affair and even made out a new will on Sept. 3, 1885, leaving most of his estate to his wife. He later called on Dyson and told him that if anything happened to him, Dyson and his wife "may come together." Dyson replied that he thought he was getting too fond of Bartlett's wife—his last attempt at decency—but the naive husband merely pooh-poohed such notions.

The couple then moved again to Pimlico to a small living quarters where Dyson was invited to visit at all kinds of strange hours. Bartlett bought him a lounging coat and slippers and the three seemed to be inseparable, a *ménage à trois,* either through intent on the part of an oddball husband or one of innocent friendship. It was the latter story that everyone was asked to believe during Adelaide's sensational trial. The scenes at this homestead witnessed by servants, however, suggest anything but innocence. Adelaide was seen to rest her head on Dyson's knee while sitting at his feet on the floor, or on his shoulder as if in a half-swoon, while the two stood together, often in Bartlett's presence. Then Adelaide was seen to be reading medical books and those dealing with pharmaceutical supplies. She explained to Dyson, according to her later statements, that her husband had a strange and incurable illness and was not expected to live very long.

On Dec. 10, 1885, Bartlett grew ill and Dr. Alfred Leach was called in to examine him, finding the grocer stricken with severe diarrhea. Dr. Leach noted that Bartlett was extremely nervous and that his gums were inflamed, as if he had taken a large dose of mercury, the use of which in that primitive medical era was applied to the dreaded syphilis. Bartlett shrugged at all of this and told Leach that he had received a large sample pill at one of his shops and took it. Perhaps it contained mercury, perhaps not, he did not know. Such mindless ingestion of strange pills was typical of Bartlett's wildly erratic conduct toward the end of his life. Bartlett did admit that he had fits of depression, had insomnia, and sometimes fell to uncontrollable crying. "I believe I am going to die," he told Dr. Leach, adding that his friends and relatives had not been kind to his wife. Adelaide, who was present, blurted excitely: "Doctor, Mr. Bartlett's friends will accuse me of poisoning him if he does not get better."

This statement shocked Dr. Leach, but before he could react, Bartlett asked him to bring in another doctor "for the protection of my wife." A Dr. Dudley was brought in as a consultant and he found the patient tired and depressed but neither physician could find any symptoms of disease and prescribed rest and fresh air. They gave him a tonic and a mild sedative, but before the physicians left Adelaide said to them: "What's the use? He will walk around the room like a ghost. He will not sleep unless I sit and hold his toe." This last remark raised the eyebrows of both doctors, but then much of what the Bartletts said was odd if not outright bizarre. Bartlett's next complaint was equally strange; he claimed worms were eating up his insides and wriggling up his throat. Some of his teeth were extracted but he continued to rave about the worms inside of him. The doctors purged him with santonin, sulphate of soda, epsom salts and two globules of croton oil.

On Dec. 26, 1885, Adelaide's lover Dyson paid the couple a visit and walked Adelaide to the post office, where she mailed a few letters. At this time she asked Dyson to get her some chloroform, saying that she sometimes used this to help Bartlett sleep. She said she would sprinkle a few drops on his pillow or one of her handkerchiefs and put this near his head. Dyson asked her why she did not obtain the chloroform from Dr. Leach. Her answer was that the physician did not want to entrust her with drugs, but she insisted that she knew what she was doing. She gave Dyson a sovereign to pay for the chloroform. One of the letters Adelaide had mailed that day was to her father-in-law. Again, as was her habit, she had spoken her mind and told the old man that she wished to "be friends with you, but you must place yourself on the same footing as other persons—that is to say that you are welcome here when I invite you, and at no other time. You seem to forget that I have not been in bed for thirteen days, and consequently am too tired to speak to visitors. I am sorry to speak so plainly, but I wish you to understand that I have not forgotten nor forgiven the past."

Dyson, meanwhile, purchased chloroform for Adelaide, telling a local chemist that he wanted it to "remove grease stains from his coat." He obtained four small bottles of chloroform at different times and transferred the contents of these to one large bottle, taking the label of one of the small bottles and placing it on the larger one; it read: "Chloroform, Poison." On Dec. 29, Dyson took the chloroform to Adelaide. He found Bartlett up and about, claiming to feel much better. Adelaide complained about having to sit up in a chair all night every night for two weeks, holding Edwin Barrett's toe and that she feared that Barrett's relatives would accuse her of not nursing her husband properly. Dyson suggested she employ a nurse and she turned to him, snapping: "You don't trust me!" Dyson immeidately apologized.

Bartlett's jaw became inflamed and his condition worsened. Dr. Leach ordered another tooth extracted on Dec. 31, 1885. With Adelaide at his side, Barrett sat in the dentist's chair while Dr. Leach administered nitrous oxide gas before the dentist pulled another tooth. The dentist noticed that the four sockets where the previous teeth had been pulled were infected and remarked: "This looks very much like necrosis setting in." The comment did not alarm Barrett who ate that evening with a ravenous appetite, consuming a jugged hare, several helpings of oysters, bread and butter, mango chutney, and cake. Barrett ordered the maid, Alice Fulcher, to make him a large haddock for breakfast, New Year's Day, and was so excited at the prospect of eating it that he asked the maid to wake him up an hour earlier than usual so he could eat his favorite fish. Mrs. Caroline Doggett, the landlord's wife, arrived and Bartlett told her that he was feeling so good that he thought he might go to the seaside for some fresh air in the near future.

Adelaide Bartlett ignored this remark and began talking to Mrs. Doggett about chloroform, asking the woman if she had ever used it, and then explaining quickly that she usually used ten drops on a pillow next to her husband so he could sleep. Then she asked if Mrs. Doggett thought twelve drops might not be too much. The woman had no idea what Adelaide was talking about. Bartlett went to sleep about 12:30 a.m. and for the next three and a half hours the so-called "Pimlico Mystery" occurred. At 4 a.m., Adelaide was at the maid's door, pounding and saying: "Alice, I want you to go for Dr. Leach. I think Mr. Bartlett is dead." By the time Dr. Leach, accompanied by the landlord Mr. Doggett, arrived at 85 Claverton Street, the room they entered was cozy, warmed by a large fire. Bartlett's body was cold, as if he had been dead for three or more hours, but there was no sign of convulsions. He had a peaceful look on his face. There was no smell on his lips but Dr. Leach noticed that the smell of brandy was on the dead man's chest, as if someone had tried to pour brandy down his throat.

Through sobs, Adelaide said she had fallen asleep in the chair at the foot of her husband's bed as usual, holding his toe, as usual, and that she had nodded off while hearing Bartlett snore deeply. Then she said she woke up with a cramp in her arm. She said she noticed that her husband's face was buried in a pillow and she tried to turn him over, then realized he was dead. She told Dr. Leach that she had rubbed her husband's chest with brandy and tried to pour some down his throat to revive him but this had failed. "What can he be dead of, Doctor?" asked Adelaide.

"I don't know," Dr. Leach replied. "Could he have got prussic acid?"

Adelaide then gave a response significant to the case: "Oh, no. He could have got at no poison without my knowledge."

Then Dr. Leach and Doggett looked over the room carefully, noting that the head of Bartlett's bed was next to the mantle shelf where a small glass stood; this was three-quarters full of brandy but, according to Doggett, it smelled of ether or perhaps some other kind of drug. On a nearby stand was a small bottle labeled "Chlorodyne." Adelaide volunteered: "I have given him nothing." She then said that she had rubbed Bartlett's sore gums with chlorodyne but that he had not swallowed any of it. Adelaide then told Dr. Leach to perform any kind of post-mortem operations and spare no expense. "We are all interested in knowing the cause of death," she said.

Several doctors were called in for the post-mortem, including one hired by Bartlett's father who snooped around the Bartlett home. He heard about Dr. Leach's question concerning prussic acid and kissed the dead lips of his son to see if he could detect this substance; he could not. Dr. Green and other physicians performed an autopsy and Green later stated that when he opened Bartlett's stomach it was as if he had just opened a fresh bottle of chloroform, so strong was the odor of chloroform in the room. Still, the doctors could find no cause of death for Edwin Bartlett. Mrs. Bartlett left a short time later to visit friends but departed without her bags. Her father-in-law had her searched before she left and when she returned, she later testified, she found the bottle of chloroform Dyson had given her and threw it out the window. Dyson later met with her and nervously asked her whether or not she had used the chloroform. She told him to forget about it but he persisted and she stamped her foot and shouted: "Oh, damn the chloroform!" Dyson then tried to back quickly out of their relationship, saying that he would like to have back all his letters and poems that he had sent to Adelaide. She responded by tearing these up and handing them back in pieces. Adelaide added that it didn't matter since she had either made copies of everything he had written or committed the missives to memory. One of Dyson's love poems read:

> Who is it that hath burst the door,
> Unclosed the heart that shut before
> And set her queen-like on her throne,
> And made its homage all her own?—
> My Birdie

An inquest was held on Feb. 11, 1886, and Dr. Leach repeated the remarks made to him by Adelaide Bartlett, including statements which drew great suspicion to her. She had told the doctor that a day or so before her husband's death she had decided to tell him that she was using chloroform to get him to sleep, sprinkling it on his pillow or on a handkerchief kept by his face. She said she showed her husband the bottle of chloroform and that he raised no objections and put it on the mantle shelf next to the bed. The next day she removed the bottle, Adelaide said, but she added cryptically: "I did not know if he used any of it." The implication Adelaide made, of course, was that her weird husband, subject to all manner of oddball behavior, *drank* the chloroform (perhaps to demolish the worms he said he felt crawling up his throat), and that this might have been the reason why the doctors performing the autopsy on his body were overwhelmed by the strong odor of chloroform emitting from his stomach when he was opened up. At the same inquest, Reverend Dyson stated that he had obtained the chloroform for Adelaide at her request and that he had secretly purchased small amounts. He added—and this was a damning statement to his now chilly ex-lover—that Adelaide had referred to the purchase of the chloroform, following her husband's death, with a comment that was a near-admission of guilt: "If you do not incriminate me, you may be perfectly sure that I will not incriminate you."

When the inquest closed on Feb. 18, 1886, Adelaide Bartlett was charged with her husband's murder and Dyson with being an accessory before the fact. Their trial opened at the Old Bailey on Apr. 12, 1886. Publicity about the case had been rampant and there was standing room only in the courtroom. So large was the turnout of spectators that special sections of seats were built in the court. Justice Wills presided and Sir Charles Russell, who would become chief counsel for defense in the sensational Maybrick case three years later, led the prosecution. Dyson was defended by Sir Frank Lockwood and Adelaide Bartlett was championed by one of the most remarkable defense attorneys in British jurisprudence, Sir Edward Clarke, who, nine years earlier, had defended Patrick Staunton in a celebrated murder trial.

Dyson sat in the dock with Adelaide, but they did not look at each other and sat as far away from each other as the space would permit. There was no conversation; all the love they had expressed for each other had vanished. In the vacuum replacing their fleeting affection was a chilly indifference to each other. They appeared as strangers in the dock. Russell was the first to speak, surprising the defense by stating that the crown had no case to present against Dyson and asked that he be dismissed. No sooner was this granted than Reverend George Dyson, one-time paramour of Adelaide Bartlett, leaped to his feet and bolted from the dock, leaving Adelaide alone in the dock to face her accusers. Russell insisted that the scheming wife had long planned to murder her husband and used his illness as the pretext to systematically dose him with chloroform, getting him groggy enough on the night of Dec. 31, 1885, to pour a great quantity of chloroform down his throat and kill him. Clarke countered that for the medically unskilled Adelaide, using the chloroform as Russell suggested was impossible, and he obliquely stated that the unpredictable Bartlett had himself swallowed the caustic substance, committing suicide.

The trial of Adelaide Bartlett, April 1886.

The elder Mr. Bartlett took the stand to repeat his old slanders that Adelaide slept with his other son, Charles, and that she was a thief, forging Edwin's last will so that she inherited everything. He appeared vicious and vindictive and was not a convincing witness for the prosecution. Dyson was brought back but his testimony was thin and of little use to the prosecution, except for the remarks he had made at the inquest, which he repeated in a whining voice. Dr. Leach was one of the pivotal witnesses. He brought notes to court and consulted them hurriedly as each question was asked, a nervous and frustrated man. Judge Wills repeatedly asked him to calm down. Leach repeated Adelaide's statements about her husband having the chloroform which made her appear guilty.

Yet, during cross-examination by Clarke, Dr. Leach drew a portrait of Edwin Bartlett that convinced one and all that his patient was anything but sane. He told of visiting Bartlett one day and his patient said: "I could not sleep. I was nervous and restless. When I saw my wife asleep in the chair, I got up and went and stood over her like this." Dr. Leach spread his arms wide and stood up to demonstrate Bartlett's pose. "I was like this for two hours," he went on quoting Bartlett, "and I felt the vital force being drawn from her to me! I felt it going through my fingertips and after that I laid down and slept." He added that his patient also told him that he and Adelaide were under mesmeric influences. Edwin Bartlett, it appeared from Dr. Leach's remarkable statements, could sap his wife's energy for his own weak body through some method of hypnosis. "My patient was one of the most extraordinary men I ever had to deal with," said the doctor, "though a very pleasant and nice man." He was asked by Clarke if he thought his patient was insane. "At one time I did and I tried to find the key to it," Leach replied, but he did not elaborate.

Then the prosecution brought in its star witness, Dr. Thomas Stevenson, an internationally celebrated toxicologist who was professor of medical jurisprudence at Guy's Hospital. Stevenson, who had performed the autopsy on Bartlett, reported that he found enough chloroform in the stomach—more than eleven grams—to kill anyone. Clarke asked Stevenson if there had ever been a case where chloroform had been used to murder anyone and the doctor had to admit that there was none. Clarke, who had, of course, consulted his own medical experts, asked Stevenson if the brain of the deceased appeared normal and the physician said yes, adding, after being prodded by Clarke, that if chloroform had been inhaled by Bartlett, the cerebral ventricles of his brain would show evidence of this, and the post-mortem had shown that this was not the case. Clarke went on systematically demolishing the prosecution's forensic case, getting Stevenson to admit that it would be extremely difficult to pour liquid chloroform down a sleeping man's throat since it might get into the windpipe. Also the caustic nature of chloroform would cause so much pain as to compel the man to scream and alarm the neighbors who were downstairs drinking New Year's punch at the time Bartlett went into his death sleep. A crucial part of Clarke's cross-examination of Stevenson involved the damage chloroform would do to Bartlett's throat. The following questions and answers undid the prosecution:

Q.: If the patient got into such a state of insensibility as not to reject it, it would go down his windpipe and burn that?

A.: Some of it might.

Q.: If it did so, it would leave its traces?

A.: I should expect to find traces.

Stevenson admitted that he found no traces of the burns that chloroform would make if poured down Bartlett's throat, either internal traces or burns about the mouth which would be evident.

At that time, present laws prohibited Adelaide Bartlett from testifying on her own behalf, which was just as well, in the estimation of Clarke, even though she could have made a statement from the dock. Clarke wisely chose to keep his client silent. In his brilliant summation, once he had worked the forensic evidence to his position, Clarke insisted that the unbalanced Bartlett had intended to commit suicide and leave his wife in the loving hands of George Dyson. Said Clarke: "He (Bartlett) drank it off quickly...there were no burns in the mouth and throat...no vomiting or outcries...Mr. Bartlett went to sleep peacefully...Here was no scientific miracle worked by a grocer's wife."

Russell had missed an opportunity to earlier introduce the theory that Adelaide had given her husband the chloroform in his brandy. When he did try to present this theory, Clarke strongly objected, stating that it was too late to introduce this new theory and the court supported him. The prosecution had erred in concentrating its case on the theory that the chloroform had been administered by inhalation and orally which had proven to be a medical impossibility. It desperately attempted to change its position to having the chloroform disguised in brandy at the last minute, a move too late to be effective. It was a devastating blow from which the prosecution could not recover. Russell and his experts had stepped into the forensic trap subtly established by Clarke wherein the prosecution insisted upon a murder method for which there was no evidence. The jury took only two hours to deliberate before returning the verdict it was compelled to choose. Adelaide Bartlett, her eyes closed and supported in a half-comatose state by two female warders, stood in the dock to hear the verdict: "Although we think that there is the gravest suspicion attaching to the prisoner, we do not think there is sufficient evidence to show how or by whom the chloroform was administered." A verdict of Not Guilty was read. Adelaide suddenly came to life, standing erect, a loud gasp coming from her. The court exploded into loud commotion while Clarke, exhausted, sat at the defense table, placed his head in his hands

and, for the only time in his illustrious career, cried out of jubilation and triumph.

The prisoner was free and though she was legally innocent, her peers considered her guilty. There was just no way of proving that she had murdered her husband. She left the dock a free woman with Bartlett's considerable fortune at her command, but she also departed with a reputation in ruin. She would live out her life as a marked poisoner. Ever the proper Victorian, Adelaide wrote elaborate letters expressing her thanks to the warden of Clerkenwell Prison where she had been confined, to Dr. Stevenson, thanking him later for a letter she had received from him in which he concurred with the verdict, and one addressed to the man who had undoubtedly saved her from the gallows, Edward Clarke, stating: "Forgive me for not earlier expressing my heartfelt gratitude to you. I feel I owe my life to your earnest efforts, and though I cannot put into words the feelings that fill my heart, you will understand all that my pen fails to express to you. Your kind looks toward me (in court) cheered me very much, for I felt that you believed me innocent. I have heard many eloquent Jesuits preach, but I never listened to anything finer than your speech."

The Bartlett case, however, remained one of the great, if not classic, murder mysteries of the nineteenth century. To this day, few question Edwin Bartlett's murder. The abiding puzzlement, the imperceptible method of his demise, remains the nagging question, summed up jocularly immediately after Adelaide Bartlett's trial by the noted surgeon, Sir James Paget: "Now that she's acquitted, she should tell us, in the interests of science, how she did it." See: **Maybrick, Florence; Staunton Family.**

REF.: Altick, *Victorian Studies in Scarlet;* Beal, *The Trial of Adelaide Bartlett for Murder;* Birmingham, *Murder Most Foul;* Bridges, *Poison and Adelaide Bartlett;* CBA; Cole, *The Anatomy of Murder;* Dunbar, *Blood in the Parlor;* Glaister, *The Power of Poison;* Gwynn, *Did Adelaide Bartlett...?;* Hartman, *Victorian Murderesses;* Humphreys, *Criminal Days;* Kingston, *Dramatic Days at the Old Bailey;* Lambton, *Echoes of Cause Celebres;* Lustgarten, *Defender's Triumph;* ____, *The Murder and the Trial;* Moiseiwitsch, *Five Famous Trials;* Morland, *Background to Murder;* Notable British Trials; Pearce, *Unsolved Murder Mysteries;* Roughead, *Famous Crimes;* Rowland, *Poisoner in the Dock;* Simpson, *The Anatomy of Murder;* Thompson, *Poison Mysteries Unsolved;* ____, *Poisons and Poisoners;* Villiers, *Riddles of Crime;* Walker-Smith, *The Life and Famous Cases of Sir Edward Clarke;* Wilson, *Encyclopedia of Murder.*

Bartlett, Ara, b.1824, U.S., jur. State's attorney of Kankakee, Ill., in 1860. He was appointed judge of the Dakota Territory in 1864 by President Abraham Lincoln and re-appointed in 1865. REF.: *CBA.*

Bartlett, Helen, prom. 1959, U.S., mur. After her first husband died in 1940, Helen met Alfred Babin. They were married during the war and lived together until his death in 1956. Helen Babin discovered his body. She notified the police, explaining that she had found him in his bath lying face down. During the day, she said, Alfred had been drinking heavily. The coroner reported that Mrs. Babin's story was indeed true because a large quantity of whiskey had been found in his stomach. Husband number two left behind a $69,000 insurance policy.

During her short period of grief, Babin met 69-year-old Wright Bartlett, a veteran with an assured income of disability payments, who was recuperating from a long illness at the Veterans Hospital. They were married in 1959, and, at his wife's suggestion, Bartlett agreed to go on a long honeymoon to Texas and Florida. By this time insurance investigators became suspicious of Helen's motives—she had recently insured her husband's life in excess of $110,000.

Several months later the newlyweds returned to Buffalo, where Bartlett complained of poor health. He explained that his wife had fed him sandwiches instead of the hot meals to which he had been accustomed. By this time police had entered the case. Under heavy questioning Helen Bartlett admitted to murdering her second husband, Babin, by holding his head under water in the bathtub. REF.: *CBA.*

Bartlett, Josiah, 1729-95, U.S., jur. Chief justice of the Superior Court of New Hampshire from 1788-90, and a signer of the Declaration of Independence. REF.: *CBA*.

Bartlett, William, prom. 1928, Brit., mur. In 1928, William Bartlett, whose body was racked with tuberculosis, married his cousin Marjorie. The former shoemaker with one wooden leg agreed to invest his savings in a business venture with his bride and so, with £300—the sum total of their combined worth—Mr. and Mrs. Bartlett opened a small confectionery store in London. The business suffered reversals, and Bartlett, not a stable man, lapsed into deep depression. Physical and mental problems had plagued him for much of his life.

Bartlett's anxieties finally drove him to murder on Oct. 26, 1928. Confessing his crime, he told the police at Paddington Green that he had no memory of the events, but was brought to his senses when their bed crashed to the flooor and he saw his murdered wife. When the case went to trial Bartlett was found Guilty but was adjudged insane.

REF.: Butler, *Murderers' England; CBA*.

Bartley, Alvis R. (AKA: **The Mountain Man**), 1934-79, U.S., burg.-rob.-attempt. mur. Alvis Bartley was born in the Bear River Valley of Kentucky, and it was there that he died in 1979. But in the early 1960s Bartley was wanted in California, Indiana, Ohio, and Kentucky on charges of armed robbery. Despite the partial paralysis caused by a 1962 shootout with law enforcement officials, Bartley eascaped from several jails, making him a hero back home in Bear Valley. People believed there was no jail secure enough for Alvis Bartley.

In December 1973 he was arrested for shooting a deputy sheriff in Morgan County, Tenn., but escaped the following August through an eighteen-inch hole bored in a metal plate. The FBI added Bartley's name to their Ten Most Wanted list. For the next five years he eluded the fifty agents assigned to the case.

The chase ended on July 7, 1979, when FBI men, assisted by local lawmen, staked out his home near the Fountain-Trundle county line in Kentucky. Bartley was on his way back to his hideout in the caves when FBI agents shot him, ending the life of a man the hill people called "a good old country boy who would give you the shirt off of his back."

REF.: *CBA*; Montell, *Killings*.

Bartolus (**Bartolo** or **Bartolo of Saxoferrato**), 1314-57, Italy, jur. Professor at Pisa and author of many legal treatises including *On Procedure, On Evidence,* and *Commentary on the Code of Justinian*. REF.: *CBA*.

Barton, Andrew, d.1511, Scot., pir. Andrew Barton was a Scottish adventurer and naval officer who was commissioned a privateer by James IV and proved himself so courageous and resourceful that, with just a small fleet, cleared the Scottish coast of hordes of invading Flemish pirates in 1506. He impressed his sovereign by sending him several barrels filled with the heads of the pirates he and his crewmen had killed. Barton was, in turn, labeled a pirate by King Henry VIII whose officers killed him during a wild naval battle. The Scottish captain was later lauded in the seaman's ballad, *Sir Andrew Barton*.

REF.: Cabal, *Piracy and Pirates; CBA*; Innes, *The Book of Pirates*; Mitchell, *Pirates*; Williams, *Captains Courageous: Seven Centuries of Piracy*.

Barton, Bert, prom. 1924, U.S., boot. Bert Barton, a rumrunner, received his illegal liquor from a distributor and manufacturer, then conveyed it to persons interested in selling intoxicants in violation of the Volstead Act. Such was the nature of smuggling in the Roaring Twenties.

In 1924 Barton met a millionaire rancher from San Antonio at a private party given for the local oil men—Barton had sold liquor to the hotel where the gala affair was held. In June he turned up at the millionaire's 25,000-acre ranch, intimating that he could get his hands on some quality liquor in a hurry. To show his good faith Barton delivered several cases of gin to the ranch before moving the remainder of his load into a warehouse in San Antonio.

When fifty cases of gin mysteriously disappeared from the warehouse, Barton accused the rancher's employees and cowpokes

of stealing them. The owner of the ranch investigated and discovered that the allegation was true, promptly returning the missing liquor to Barton. By this time, however, customs officials were alerted to the presence of a large schooner named the *Charles Buckingham* moored in Matagorda Bay containing 3,000 bottles of Cuban liquor brought in from New Orleans.

Agent Al Scharff quizzed all the known liquor smugglers in the area and learned that the rancher was vitally interested in the vessel. The region was now too hot for Barton, who fled, leaving others to hold the bag. The rancher was convicted of violating the prohibition laws and was fined $1,000. Outraged by what he perceived to be a gross injustice, the powerful rancher filed a $15,000 libel suit against the San Antonio *Daily Express* which had given the case sensational treatment in its morning editions.

A lower court upheld the claim and the rancher won the case. However, the state supreme court reversed the judgment on June 9, 1926, citing the inherent freedom of the press to make public comment on issues of vital concern.

REF.: *CBA*; Roark, *The Coin of Contraband*.

Barton, Sir Edmund, 1849-1920, Aus., jur. Attorney general from 1891-93, and judge of the Australian High Court from 1903-20. REF.: *CBA*.

Barton, Elizabeth (AKA: **Fair Maid of Kent, Holy Maid of Kent**), 1506-34, Brit., her.-witchcraft. Afflicted with a nervous condition and a sporadic skin ailment, Elizabeth Barton's unpredictable ailments were interpreted in 1520 as manifestations of supernatural power. Born of peasant parents, Barton, at the age of fourteen, was taken in by an innkeeper at Ashford, Kent, where she displayed uncontrollable fits and said she saw visions. She predicted the death of one of the innkeeper's children, a prophesy which came lamentably true (although the child was ill before the prediction). At nineteen, Barton slipped into a trance for a week, and, while so possessed, delivered esoteric diatribes on sin, virtue and the Ten Commandments. It was thought that she was controlled by the Holy Ghost, and even King Henry VIII, after hearing stories about the girl, sent Sir Thomas More to investigate. More visited Barton and reported later to Henry that she had no spectacular powers.

The witchcraft trial of Elizabeth Barton.

But others were more apt to believe in Barton's powers. After she moved into the rectory of John Cobb at Aldington, Elizabeth Barton was visited by Archbishop Warham of Canterbury who became quickly convinced that she was a holy seer. He endorsed her divine powers, saying to doubters that he would "not hide the goodness of the works of God." Miracles were attributed to the maid: Women who could not suckle their infants suddenly were bursting with milk, altar candles gave birth to flames when Barton pointed at them, and the ill and crippled were restored to health after she laid hands upon them. Barton was sent to the convent of St. Sepulchre's at Canterbury, where she convinced the nuns of her purity and her powers of prophesy. She became a novitiate. On one occasion, supposedly before 3,000 people, Barton, dressed in a nun's habit, lay in a trance for three hours before a statue of the Blessed Virgin. She spoke in strange voices, describing the joys of heaven and the torments of hell.

Thousands flocked to her; she became a symbol of goodness, and scores of tracts and books were written of her, describing her as "The Fair Maid of Kent," "The Holy Nun of Kent," and "The

Holy Maid of Kent." She became, however, in the accounts of some historians, a tool in the hands of nobles opposed to Henry, particularly the Marchioness of Exeter, the countess of Salisbury, the Bishop of Rochester, and others. These high-born persons subtly convinced Barton to render prophecies against Henry, critical of his treatment of Queen Catherine and damning him for his association with Anne Boleyn. Elizabeth Barton then assumed a regal attitude, one where she openly forbade the king to divorce Catherine and she said that if Pope Clement VI permitted the divorce he would die. Henry would die within seven months after divorcing Catherine, Barton insisted. She went even further, announcing publicly that Henry "is like Saul. He will never be king in the eyes of God." When Henry drove through Canterbury, Elizabeth Barton stood in the way of his coach, warning him that he was putting his soul in peril and was courting the tortures of hell. Henry ignored her.

Worse for Barton, she aligned herself with Henry's political foes, especially Wolsey, and this incurred the emnity of Thomas Cromwell who sent Cranmer (later to become Archbishop of Canterbury) to interview the young woman. Cranmer reported that "she never had visions in all her life. All that she ever said was feigned of her own imagination, only to satisfy those who resorted to her and to obtain worldly gain." Barton was charged with heresy and witchcraft. Cranmer obtained a confession from her in which Barton said that she was an imposter and that she had been possessed by Satan, a confession she repeated after being taken from London Tower to Tyburn where she was tied to a stake. As the faggots piled about her were torched, Barton admitted her guilt but cried out that "to say the truth, I am not so much to blame considering that it is well known to these learned men that I am a poor wench without learning..." She gave out a shriek as the flames consumed her. According to Henry's direct order, Barton's head was severed from her body and buried separately from the rest of her remains.

REF.: *CBA*; Notestein, *A History of Witchcraft in England*; O'Donnell, *Should Women Hang?*; Potter, *The Art of Hanging*.

Barton, John Evert, 1924- , U.S., rape-mur. He blamed his crime on an alcohol-induced mental lapse. There was no denying that Navy seaman John Barton was a hard drinker. The 19-year-old veteran of the Pacific Theatre was assigned to the Naval Operating Base at Terminal Island outside Los Angeles. On Oct. 5, 1943, he had spent the better part of the day consuming liquor in a seamy waterfront bar in San Pedro. At 11 p.m. Barton left the saloon in search of action.

At a nearby bus stop stood 18-year-old Gladys Pearcy, on her way home from work. She had worked as a telephone operator since her June graduation from San Pedro High School. Her brother was also a Navy man, serving in the southwest Pacific.

The dark-haired young woman looked enticing to the drunken sailor, but she rejected his advances. He followed her home, but she continued to resist. Barton threw her down, dragged the semi-conscious woman into a school playground at Twelfth and Cabrillo, and raped her, pounding her head against a wall. She died of a basal skull fracture. He left the nude body in the school's grandstand, but as he realized the severity of what he had done, Barton felt compelled to confess.

At 3 a.m., he banged on the door of San Pedro resident Henry Muller, who called the police. "I knew something like this would happen to me sometime," Barton sobbed. He led the police to the Pearcy's battered body. At the inquest, the victim's stepfather, who had identified her body, tried to attack Barton, but was restrained by police officers. Barton made no comment, save that he was the father of a four-month-old baby.

Given his age and lack of criminal history, Barton was spared the death penalty. He served time in San Quentin from Jan. 6, 1944, until he was paroled in 1968. On June 25 of that year he received a full pardon from then-governor Ronald Reagan. REF.: *CBA*.

Barton, Mary, 1665-1715, Brit., asslt.-rob.-mur. Barton turned to crime after her parents forbade her to marry her sweetheart, who, grief-stricken, poisoned himself. Barton's father, a prosperous druggist from York, regretted his refusal when his daughter fled to London.

Mary Barton secured a job with a bodice-maker and became pregnant by the owner's apprentice. Several months later, the drunken apprentice was drowned while trying to cross the Thames River on horseback. Having no use for a pregnant woman, the merchant sent Barton away. She became a prostitute, then a pick-pocket, earning a reputation as a highly skilled thief.

Barton met a member of the footguards named Bird, who acted as her accomplice while posing as her husband. One day, a potential victim attempted to seize Mary in order to have her arrested, but was assaulted by Bird. The next night the man returned with a constable, who arrested the pair for assault and robbery. Barton was spared the hangman's noose, but Bird was executed at Tyburn in 1692.

Changing specialties, Barton practiced shoplifting in the countryside of Derby, Lincoln, and Nottingham for nearly eight years until she was arrested and condemned to death. Pregnant once again, Barton was sent to jail, not the gallows. When King William III granted general amnesty to many criminals, Barton was reprieved, resuming her life of crime with increased violence.

One day Barton entered the home of a tavern keeper with her gang of strong-arm men. Unable to find the couple's cache of hidden money, they trussed the tavenkeeper and his wife together, securing a frightened kitten to the man's groin. When the tortured merchant revealed the location of his money, Barton and her companions fled with the cash.

Barton's gang also attacked a local author, setting fire to his manuscripts when he denied having any money. Bound and gagged, the man died among his books as his house caught fire.

Mary was seized in Bedfordshire in 1715. Receiving the mandatory death penalty for robbery and murder, she was hanged at the Bedford jail in 1715.

REF.: *CBA*; Smith, *Highwaymen*.

Barwell, Sir **Henry Newman**, b.1877, Aus., jur. Attorney general of South Australia from 1920-24, and agent general for the same region from 1928-33. REF.: *CBA*

Barwick, Charles, 1908- , and **Burton, Reginald**, prom. 1930, Brit., rob. At the stroke of midnight on St. Valentine's Day, 1930, two young automobile thieves named Charles Barwick and Reginald Burton drove up to a jeweler's store on St. Swithin's Lane. Using housebreakers' tools, they smashed in a display window but just before they were to flee with a handful of jewels, a policeman came on the scene.

They jumped back in the car and drove straight for the policeman who ducked into a doorway. Continuing at a breakneck speed, the unsuccessful bandits knocked down a city postman before crashing into the front of the Bank of England, an ironic ending to an ill-fated caper. Barwick was later sentenced to three and a half years in penal servitude. For his part in the "smash-and-grab game" Burton received three years at hard labor.

REF.: *CBA*; Nicholls, *Crime Within the Square Mile*.

Bas, Marvin J., 1905-50, U.S., (unsolv.) org. crime.-assass. Two public officials were gunned down the same night in Chicago because of their alleged connections to organized crime. Marvin Bas, a lawyer and politician, had promised to open a searching investigation into gambling activities in suburban Cook County under the auspices of the Republican nominee for sheriff, John Babb.

As he walked along Orchard Street on the city's North Side, two syndicate gunmen emerged from the car and fired a shot into Bas' head at close range, killing him instantly. The killers were never found despite the presence of two eyewitnesses and Bas became yet another victim of Chicago gangland violence. Whether the lawyer's hands were entirely "clean" is a matter of speculation since the state's attorney's office conducted a mysterious raid and seized his private files against the wishes of his widow.

The other was William Drury, a former Chicago police captain with rumored mob ties who had recently opened a detective

agency to catch gangsters. Drury was gunned down in an alley in back of his Addison Street residence the same night Bas died, Sept. 25, 1950. Both men were scheduled to appear before the Sen. Estes Kefauver Rackets Committee scheduled to begin its preliminary investigation into the workings of the Chicago mob in December. See: **Drury, William.**
REF.: *CBA,* Harrison, *Criminal Calendar II.*

Basasiri, al (Abù al-Harith Arslàn al-Muzaffar), d.1060, Iraq, assass. A Buyid dynasty military commander, who with Arab cooperation, attempted to seize control of Baghdad in 1059. He was murdered by Seljuq Turks led by Toghrul Beg. REF.: *CBA.*

Bashold, Joanne, 1952-   , Case of, U.S., child abuse. Joanne Bashold grew up in a quiet little town in mid-America. Kirtland, Ohio, with its winding country roads, provided a stark contrast to the crime and poverty of New York's Harlem section, where Joanne took up residence in January 1976.

According to her foster parents, Jack and Peg Bashold, their adopted daughter was "in a world of her own," uncomfortable around her peers and quietly withdrawn with her books and animals. She seemed almost incapable of returning her parents' affection and was alienated from boys. After graduating from high school, Joanne worked a number of odd jobs, but found nothing to her liking. To the dismay of her parents, she moved to Cleveland in 1972 where she rented a shabby apartment on East Ninth Street, deep in the heart of the city, an area infested with drunks and drug dealers. "I told her I couldn't understand why she was living there," Peg Bashold said. "I told her she'd get killed."

After she moved to New York in 1973, Joanne lost contact with her mother. She lived in Manhattan for several years, working for tip money and spare change, but never once did she turn to her parents for a loan. In 1976 she moved to a rat-infested apartment in Harlem with no furniture except a single folding chair. Most disturbing to social workers in the welfare department and at Bellevue Hospital was her total self-reliance in the face of personal misery. "She could have had psychological counseling, budget counseling, a caseworker visit her home," a representative from the Human Resources Administration said.

On Sept. 2, 1976, Joanne called her home in Ohio to tell her family she had given birth to a girl. The news shocked the family. Joanne had not said a word about the matter before and was remembered as a girl who had always rejected the advances of boys and men. Then tragedy struck. Four days after Joanne's release from the hospital, her half-starved German shepherd killed and devoured her baby while she was away.

Bashold was brought before Judge Hyman Solniker facing charges of negligent homicide. After a cursory investigation of her background by District Attorney Robert Morgenthau, it was decided not to prosecute her. "The defendant had never been involved in a similar situation and had no reason to know this tragedy would occur," he said. The child was buried on Sept. 22, and funeral costs paid for by the New York Social Services Department. Vowing not to return to Ohio, Joanne went to live with her cousin in the fashionable SoHo district of Manhattan, where she was comforted by the prayers and wishes of strangers who sent her money in excess of $2,000. REF.: *CBA.*

Basile, Tobia, b.1809, Italy, rob.-mur. The legendary Tobia Basile spent most of his adult life in prison, imprisoned in 1860 for murder. He was one of the Neapolitan leaders of the criminal secret society, the Camorra, a family federation of criminals who protected each other and exercised great influence in elections throughout southern Italy, particularly in Naples and Calabria, having close ties with the Mafia in Sicily. Basile reportedly trained legions of Camorristas while serving out his long sentence, teaching them the arts of thievery, murder, and extortion, a sort of Italian Fagin with a much more sinister intent. (The Camorra was born in the prison systems of southern Italy and inmates serving long terms were considered to be the grand masters of the society whose job it was to pass on the secrets and methods of the Camorra to worthy young prisoners.)

Released in 1890, Basile supposedly returned to a nagging wife he eliminated by walling her up alive and then departing his homestead. Her body was found later with every indication that she had lived for several days, clawing hopelessly at the freshly layed bricks sealing her inside a two-foot passageway, screaming, while her husband slept on the other side of wall before deciding to pack up his belongings and disappear. REF.: *CBA.*

Basketball Scandal, 1951, U.S., brib. The great basketball swindles of 1951 actually began a few years earlier, when a one-time New York jeweler who traded in black-market gold and fancied himself a gambling genius, Salvatore Sollazzo, contacted Edward Gard, backcourtman for Long Island University. After wining and dining Gard, Sollazzo offered him $1,000 to shave points on a game. The basketball star accepted, and not only did Gard cut down the spread of points in one game (allowing Sollazzo and others to beat the odds-making bookies by making bets inside of a set spread of points), but the basketball player solicited others on his team to join him, missing a few passes here and there, losing the ball, and failing to garner rebounds, so that LIU won, but not by the score the odds makers in the newspapers had set. It was deft and clever, and the system soon spread throughout the great basketball teams of the time—City College of New York, Kentucky, Toledo, Manhattan, and Bradley, until the greatest college players, heroes to millions, were taking bribes to shave points or throw games.

Sollazzo was an unlikely mastermind in setting this corrupt system into action. Immigrating with his family from Palermo, Si., in 1906 when he was less than two years old, Sollazzo's beginnings were less than impressive. He worked as an apprentice to his father, a jeweler, after leaving school in the eighth grade in 1919. Ten years later, when his father died, Sollazzo took over his father's Brooklyn store which went bankrupt within a year. To feed his wife and children, the jeweler began selling cheap gems door-to-door and then selling gems that he did not own, which brought about his first arrest.

The charge against him was dismissed, but a short time later he was again arrested, this time for a much more serious offense. Sollazzo had been a lookout for a gang of armed robbers who botched a jewelry firm heist in Manhattan. He was given seven years in Sing Sing; the sentence would have been more severe, but Sollazzo was able to prove that he had not been armed as had his fellow thieves. As a model prisoner, the failed jeweler was paroled in five years.

Working again as a jewelry salesman, Sollazzo, in 1940, opened another shop, specializing in the making of birthstone and wedding rings. It was at this time that he bought, for next to nothing, a large amount of platinum, which was then not in demand and relatively inexpensive.

A few years later, platinum became a rare ware material that shot the price of the precious metal sky-high, and Sollazzo sold off his stored platinum for a great deal of money, which he used to open up another store. Within a few more years, he was one of the largest makers of wedding rings in the U.S., with scores of workers on his payroll and a gross income of more than $1 million a year.

Even though he had become prosperous beyond his wildest dreams, the lure of the illicit beckoned and Sollazzo responded with alacrity. He fixed his books and cheated Uncle Sam out of $500,000 in taxes, according to Charles Rosen, writing in *Scandals of 51.* He began to gamble heavily, chiefly betting the horses, losing large sums of money on whimsical bets—an easy mark for any racetrack tout.

Divorced by this time, Sollazzo remarried. His second wife, Jeanne, was a long-legged, raven-haired beauty, who had once been a chorus girl in a Philadelphia nightclub. She would later play hostess to the basketball players visiting Sollazzo's swanky Manhattan apartment. One of these visitors was Eddie Gard. It was Gard who later brought fellow LIU players Dick Feurtado and Sherman White into the crooked setup, with players receiving between $500 and $2,000 per game to either shave points or out-

and-out dump a game. Sherman White, at the time, was one of the outstanding players of the era. The rationale used to convince the All-American White was the same used on other superstars like Alex Groza, Ralph Beard, Gene Melchiorre—"everybody's doing it, why not you? Why shouldn't you have some extra money?"

The important point was that each player was told by Gard, Sollazzo, and others that "you don't have to lose, only shave a few points." This way, each athlete felt he wasn't really compromising himself or his teammates; he and they would win, but the score would not be so staggering.

Even CCNY went into the trick bag opened by Sollazzo and others, the entire starting five—Eddie Warner, Floyd Lane, Al Roth, Irwin Dambrot, and Eddie Roman—managed by Mr. Basketball himself, Nat Holman. The shaving, dumping, and fixing was rampant in the 1949-50 and 1950-51 seasons, until one youth, Junius Kellogg, a six-foot-eight player for Manhattan, was approached by Hank Poppe, one of the captains of the Manhattan team a year earlier, a hustler who had already graduated and was busy snaring up-and-coming players like Kellogg into the fix for a cut of the payoff and sure-winning bets.

Poppe met Kellogg in a parking lot and offered him $1,000 to make sure Manhattan lost to De Paul University in an upcoming game. Kellogg said no, but Poppe told him to "think it over," and said he would contact the new black player soon. Kellogg did think it over, but instead of accepting the bribe he went to his team's coach, Ken Norton, and told him everything. Norton, in turn, informed school authorities, who contacted the Bronx District Attorney's office. Detectives interrogated Kellogg extensively and then told him to pretend to play along with Poppe, which he did. Poppe told him that "All you have to do is control the margin of the victory...Everyone's doing it, everywhere, all over the country. The pros too. But...don't stink up the joint. Make it look like you're trying."

Kellogg played his worst game against De Paul, who was figured to lose by ten points. They lost by only three, and this made winners of Poppe and his associates. Poppe was arrested some hours later at home and immediately implicated three New York gamblers, Cornelius Kelleher and Benjamin and Irving Schwartzberg, the brothers being bookmakers and acting as the setup men. All of the gamblers were quickly rounded up and jailed. In this instance, the Manhattan fix had been established not by Sollazzo, but by Kelleher.

Even before these arrests, fans across the country had noticed the sloppy play of their champions—the seemingly intentional bad passes and lame rebounds, the weak set shots and haphazard defenses. By the time the 1951 college basketball scandal broke, fans across the country were regularly shouting "Fix!" and "Dump!" during most games. The pay off system had become a national disgrace, one which caused Ken Norton later to state: "This racket is not purely local. I loathe the whole stinking business. I can't believe that gamblers got next to my kids."

In many respects, however, the college system of treating athletes as special students was the beginning of the massive bribe-taking. In recruiting potential basketball stars for colleges and universities, especially those who looked as if they might turn into superstars, students were offered free room and board and pocket money and, worst of all, the entrance requirements or academic standards for students were lowered drastically. In many instances, basketball stars did not study at all and were given academic tests a 10-year-old could easily field. This system of pampering athletes mightily contributed to an attitude on the part of players that, if they could pick up any extra money by merely shaving points from the total score of a game and still win that game, they were merely taking the system that supported them a logical step further, or at least that was the rationalization.

The Manhattan exposé quickly led to intensified investigations across the country into the rampant basketball fixing. Particularly effective was Frank S. Hogan, district attorney for New York City. Players came forward in twos and threes to confess their

parts in the fixing. Perhaps the most shocking admissions came from ex-All-Americans (their titles were stripped from them) Lou Groza, probably the greatest player of his time, and Ralph Beard of Kentucky. Both Groza and Beard had been members of the 1948 U.S. Olympic squad. When Groza was taken into custody he moaned: "Someday when I'm gray—when this thing is done and I've lived it down, I'd like to tell the whole story about what it's all been like—about recruiting." Added Ralph Beard: "Recruiting—that's the start of it. How they went out and got us to play. It got so big. We got big, too big."

Bradley's top star, Gene Melchiorre—his cover name with the gamblers was "Squeaky" because of the narrow margins of victory he was able to manipulate through his clever playing—admitted that he had dumped and fixed games throughout the 1950-51 season. Melchiorre confessed that he had received for one game $4,000 from a payoff man in a Chicago motel lobby, which he dispersed to fellow players Fred Schlictman ($500), Aaron Preece ($1,000), and Jim Kelly ($500). This payment was for shaving the Bradley-Oregon State game on Dec. 7, 1950. Bradley was a heavy favorite to win over Oregon State. There was a ten-point spread in the betting odds favoring Bradley, and all Melchiorre and the others had to do was to make sure that their team won by a close margin, which they did, the final score being 77 to 74.

This kind of shaving made fortunes for gamblers like Sollazzo, who reaped millions from the $15 million in illegal bets made daily in the country. It was obvious to investigators that the gamblers, in paying off Melchiorre and his like with only $4,000 bribes, were reserving for themselves incredible fortunes. On the Bradley-Oregon State game alone, the gamblers fixing the game took the bookies for more than $200,000.

Said one of the bribed players: "When the point spread is big enough—say, eight to twelve points—a small group of players can control the points without the slightest danger of being detected by their coach or even their own teammates. Matter of fact, a couple of really smart operators can win the game for their team—grab off the headlines as the stars of the game—and still make the score come out the way the gamblers want it!"

This was supported by the shocked coaches of the teams involved. Coach Fordy Anderson of Bradley stated: "I've studied the movies of the Oregon State game at least twenty times and can't find a single play which indicates the kids weren't giving their best efforts every second."

Hank Fisher, the radio broadcaster who had announced the game, declared: "In a stretch of more than 100 games, I hardly took my eyes off the ball, and in all that time I never saw a movement by a Bradley player—against Oregon State or any other opponent—which looked suspicious."

Many of the players were convicted and given suspended sentences, then barred forever from the game. Some of the gamblers were convicted and sent to prison. Salvatore Sollazzo, the jeweler who had made too good, went to prison for twelve years.

The sportscasters and sportswriters of the nation went into a frenzy, then shock, over the great scandal. Said Irving Marsh of the New York *Herald Tribune*: "Basketball is through as a big time sport." Of course, this pessimistic view proved to be utterly wrong, but the infamous, nationwide fixing of the sport did institute strong safeguards against such corruption from again flourishing, especially at the recruiting level. Academic requirements for players were raised and the favors for players abandoned; but it was a decade before the game lost an odor stronger than the sweat of its bounding players.

REF.: *CBA*; Rosen, *Scandals of '51*.

Basque Witches, prom. 1609, Fr., witchcraft. Pierre de Lancre was the author of *Tableau*, a 1612 pamphlet which attempted to convince religious skeptics about the authenticity of witchcraft and the female practitioners of the black arts. He was sent by the king to the Basque-speaking regions of Guienne near the Spanish frontier to investigate claims of witchcraft.

In the town of Labourd, de Lancre claimed that a majority of the 30,000 residents were witches, their possession beginning years earlier when Christian missionaries cast out the devils in Japan and the Far East. These demons relocated in Labourd where nearly 12,000 of them pranced in orgiastic meetings in the public square near Hendaye.

De Lancre extracted confessions from several of the accused witches through torture and brutal inquisition. A published account of the confession of 17-year-old Marie Dindarte told how the devil had visited her on Sept. 27, 1609. With a special ointment covering her body, she allegedly gained the power to fly through the air. Sexual escapades with demons were given credence by De Lancre, who ordered wholesale burnings. Bishop Bertrand d'Echaux put his professional career on the line when he saved five priests accused of conducting a black mass. Further, he denounced the hysteria and demanded an immediate end to the witchhunt.

Riots broke out in the streets of Labourd when 5,000 fisherman returned from a long journey to Newfoundland only to find their loved ones sacrificed as witches. De Lancre became universally hated for his persecutions and complained of a black mass conducted in his own room on Sept. 24, 1609. REF.: *CBA*.

Bass, Dr. Andrew, prom. 1930s, U.S., fraud-mur. Dr. Andrew Bass of Columbia, Mo., believed he had a foolproof scheme to swindle an insurance company. First he selected a victim, William Folta of St. Louis, a man for whom he had negotiated the sale of a farm. Next he recruited a stooge, a down-and-out car mechanic named William Pearlman, of Columbia.

The plan, as he related it to the mechanic, was simple. Pearlman would pose as Folta and travel around the local area getting to know people while Bass took out a large insurance policy on Folta's life. At the opportune moment, Folta would be killed and the beneficiary, Folta's mother, would become the immediate suspect. Bass said he would find someone to murder and he would plant suitable identification on the victim. The mother, Mrs. Mary Folta, would be arrested while he and Pearlman walked off with a cool $200,000 in insurance money. However, Bass neglected to mention that he had no intention of splitting this money with the gullible Pearlman.

For his troubles, Pearlman received three bullet holes in the head and was left by the side of a road near Bentonville, Ark., an identification card found in the wallet listing him as William Folta of St. Louis. When the mother was brought down to identify the remains, she insisted the body was not her son's, though there was a resemblance.

Dr. Bass was contacted and he explained that he had just sold 3,000 acres of farmland—later declared to be almost worthless—to Folta for $215,000. This struck the insurance company and Mrs. Folta as odd, it being the same amount of life insurance recently taken out by the deceased. The mother's insistence that the murdered man was not her son flew in the face of a murder-conspiracy theory.

Dr. Bass's insistence that the mother claim the body of her son and thus take over the recently sold farmland sent police back to the real estate office to review the history of the transaction. When it was revealed that Folta had put up $200,000 in life insurance policies as security, Bass was arrested on suspicion. The next day the body of "Folta" was identified by Pearl Powell as that of Pearlman. Dr. Bass' car was found in Kansas City. Inside was a box of .38 shells and traces of blood were detected in the front seat of the car. It was an open-and-shut case from the standpoint of the prosecution. Dr. Bass raised a few eyebrows by pleading guilty to the charges but it was a brilliant ploy. By acknowledging his guilt he avoided a certain rendezvous with the electric chair and received instead a life sentence at the Tucker Farm State Penitentiary.

REF.: *CBA; Cohen, One Hundred True Crime Stories.*

Bass, Samuel (Sam), 1851-78, U.S., west. outl. The lore and legend of Sam Bass became a permanent part of Texas history almost before this daring outlaw met his early end by the tool of his trade, the six-gun. In his short criminal career—a span of

about four years—Bass managed to rob stagecoaches, trains, and banks with lightning speed, committing holdups with such alacrity that the lawmen of several states began hunting him as one of the most infamous desperadoes of the Old West. He seemed to be everywhere, from the Black Hills to the Texas Panhandle. Unlike most Texas outlaws, Bass was not a homegrown bad man. He was born in Mitchell, Ind., near Woodville, on July 21, 1851. His parents died when Sam was a small child, one of ten children in the Bass family. The children were sent to relatives to be raised and it was Sam's bad luck to be put in the care of a tight-lipped, skinflinted uncle, David Sheeks. The uncle denied his small nephew any sort of education, compelling the boy to work his farm as soon as he was strong enough to fetch and carry. Throughout his youth Bass knew nothing but work, first slaving for his uncle and later working as a millhand and teamster. At the age of eighteen in 1869, Bass built a raft

Sam Bass at age sixteen.

and floated down the Mississippi to St. Louis. From there he drifted to Rosedale, Miss., where he worked for a year.

There was nothing revealed in Bass' background or steady personality that indicated a bent for crime. In 1870, Bass, working as a teamster, drove some supplies to Denton, Texas. He stayed on in Denton to work for the local sheriff, W.F. "Dad" Eagan, who ran a supply company. It was Eagan who would later spend months trying to capture Bass when he turned outlaw. In the beginning, Bass proved to be a thrifty, hardworking employee who followed his uncle's tightwad practices, refusing to ever pay more than $5 for a suit, and when making deliveries, Eagan had to remind young Sam to make sure that he fed the horses regularly rather than keeping them on short rations to save money. With his hard-earned savings, Bass bought a sorrel mare, a fast horse he entered in several races. The mare won on several occasions and Bass collected enough from bets to quit Eagan.

With money in his pocket, Bass began to drink in the local saloons, befriending such rowdies as Henry Underwood. One hot day in 1875, Bass and Underwood bought melons which they attempted to slice apart. Bass dropped his melon, causing a group of young blacks standing nearby to hoot and jeer at the pair. Bass and Underwood began to stone the blacks, which caused Denton's Sheriff Gerren to place them under arrest. Both men jumped on their horses and raced out of town. Gerren swore out warrants against them. For this prosaic offense, Sam Bass became an outlaw. Underwood, born in 1846, also in Indiana, had fought with Jennison's Jayhawkers against Quantrill's guerrillas and was both mean-streaked and criminally inclined, influencing the naive Bass against a law-abiding life. Following their escape from Sheriff Gerren, Bass and Underwood split up, Underwood riding to southwest Texas where he had a small ranch and an upstanding wife. Bass rode to San Antonio. There Bass met Joel (Joe) Collins, a hell-raiser who came from a fine San Antonio family. Both invested their money in a small herd of cattle which they drove north, making a considerable profit from its sale in Sidney, Neb. A cowboy and gunman, Jack Davis, befriended Bass and Collins in a local saloon and suggested that they could make a fortune in a boomtown called Deadwood, in South Dakota. The pair invested their money in a freight company there but later sold out to invest in a mine which did not pay off.

Bass and Collins decided to take what they wanted. They recruited a number of freight handlers who had worked for them, most of them fast-draw gunmen, which included Tom Nixon, Bill Heffridge, Jack Davis, and James Berry. The bandits robbed seven Deadwood stages in the Black Hills area between 1876 and

1877 but they quit this line of robbery after stopping one stage filled with heavily armed guards who let loose a deadly barrage in their direction. Bass and Collins returned fire before riding off, leaving the stage driver dead in his seat. These robberies had not proved lucrative, the band taking in only small amounts of money. Jack Davis, a California bandit, suggested that the gang attack a Union Pacific train, saying that these trains carried huge gold shipments from the West, consigned to Wells Fargo and routed to eastern banks. Collins perfected a plan to rob the Union Pacific train at Ogallala, Neb. The group, which included Bass, Collins, Nixon, Davis, Heffridge, and Berry, arrived in Ogallala, but Collins thought too many people were present and decided that the band would attack at Big Springs, Neb. Here, on Sept. 19, 1877, the band boarded the train at 10 p.m. at a water station, taking more than $60,000 in newly minted twenty-dollar gold pieces from the mail car, being shipped from the Denver Mint. They took an additional $1,300 from the startled passengers, and $450 from the mail car safe. (It should be noted that Bass and his men *did* rob the passengers of this train, contrary to denials from so-called western experts, whereas the gang led by Bass later in Texas did not have time to rob passengers on the trains they robbed.)

Sam Bass, standing left; J.E. Gardner, right; seated, unknown and Joel Collins (with gun).

The gang split up following the robbery, going in pairs in separate directions, knowing that the enormity of the theft would soon bring posses down on them. Joel Collins and Bill Heffridge followed the Kansas Pacific Railroad line and were overtaken on Sept. 26, 1877, by a huge posse led by Sheriff Bardsley near Buffalo Station. Both outlaws decided to make a fight of it and were killed. About $25,000 in twenty-dollar gold pieces was found in Collins' saddlebags. In the middle of October, Berry was trapped and wounded in a gunfight with officers who surrounded his Mexico, Mo., home. He told lawmen the details of the Big Springs robbery and gave them the names of his fellow bandits, saying that he believed Tom Nixon had boarded a train headed for Chicago and from there intended to return to his native Canada. Authorities in Texas refused to believe this story and

arrested Henry Underwood, whom they believed to be one of the Big Springs bandits, using the alias of Tom Nixon. Underwood was innocent of the crime, as authorities later learned. Nixon, who had been a blacksmith by trade, utterly disappeared with about $10,000 in gold pieces.

Following the breakup of the first gang, Bass, now emulating his boyhood heroes, the Reno Brothers of Indiana, first to rob trains in the U.S., gathered about him a new group of bandits with the intent of robbing Texas trains. These new recruits included Seaborn Barnes, a tough western gunman, Frank Jackson, Tom Spotswood, Henry Underwood, Arkansas Tom Johnson, all hardcases, and, at the end, Jim Murphy, a novice thief from a clan of thieves whose disloyalty to Bass was to equal in legend the betrayal of Jesse James by the notorious Ford Brothers. With Barnes, Spotswood, Jackson, and Underwood, Bass went back to robbing stages, stopping a coach outside of Mary's Creek, near Fort Worth, in October 1877, but the take of $43 was so miserable that the bandits quit stagecoach robbery altogether. They would concentrate on Texas trains, Bass vowed.

The gang stopped the Houston & Texas Central express at Allen Station on Feb. 22, 1878, taking $1,280. The raid was committed by Bass, Spotswood, Barnes, Jackson, and Underwood, who stopped another flyer of the same line at Hutchins on Mar. 18. The same group struck the Texas and Pacific line on Apr. 4, at Eagle Ford, robbing the safe in the mail car. On Apr. 10, 1878, the bandits attacked a Texas and Pacific express while it was stopped at Mesquite, but here they ran into serious trouble for the first time. The train was loaded with convicts en route to prison and their heavily armed guards opened fire on the outlaws from windows as soon as they appeared. Passengers and train employees also grabbed guns and let loose a withering barrage that wounded several gang members. Seaborn Barnes was struck once in the left thigh and three times in the right leg. Grabbing what little loot they could, the bandits leaped on their horses and escaped without losing a man. Barnes recovered from his wounds within a few weeks. (These rather hurriedly planned train robberies netted the gang about $1,500 each; Bass did not have the special kind of information Jack Davis had brought to him about west-to-east gold shipments in the Big Springs robbery and lacked the effective tactics employed by Joel Collins, whom many still believe to be the real brains of the first Sam Bass gang.)

The four train robberies committed by the Bass gang so alarmed authorities in the Dallas-Fort Worth area that an army of lawmen assembled in the region—sheriffs, deputies, bounty hunters, and local militia, hundreds of heavily armed men all looking for the most notorious outlaw in Texas, Sam Bass. He was an elusive quarry, however, moving from one remote hideout to another in Denton County. Since the Texas Rangers were short-handed in the area, a company of thirty men was organized under the command of one-time deputy sheriff, city marshal June Peak, who at the time was recorder for the city of Dallas. Peak was a determined, hard-riding lawman; he promised that he would bring in the Bass gang dead or alive. Meanwhile, Bass and his men hid out in the dense, vast Elm and Hickory Bottoms, an enormous swamp area where, as one newsman of the day described it, "the foliage is dense—the vines hang in masses and it is not good daylight until 12 noon." Bass and Underwood knew these bottoms well, having gone hunting and fishing here years earlier.

Ranger Peak, now a captain in the force, with thirty men, accompanied by a large posse, under the command of Sheriff W.F. Eagan, Bass' old employer, were combing the back areas of Wise County on June 12-13, 1878, when they encountered the Bass gang camped at Salt Creek. The outlaws were cooking breakfast in the pre-dawn hours when the lawmen rode down on them, firing as they came. Arkansas Tom Johnson pulled two six-guns and picked off three riders far ahead of the posse as they splashed across the creek but other Rangers behind these wounded men riddled Johnson, who collapsed in a heap, dead. Bass and the others returned fire but then realized that they were hopelessly outnumbered, and they scrambled up a small gorge to retrieve their horses. They found that the Rangers and Eagan's men had cut them off, having captured their mounts. The outlaws slipped into a long gulley and fled on foot. Later they stole some horses from a nearby ranch and made good their escape. This escape so enraged state officials that rewards were increased for each gang member, particularly Bass.

The gang was reported to be in five different counties in a single day, which caused Rangers and lawmen to ride about in a confused search. But on May 21, 1878, a break in the manhunt appeared in the form of James W. Murphy, who, along with his father, Henderson Murphy, had been charged with harboring the Bass gang and faced certain imprisonment. Jim Murphy approached Captain Peak with a proposition. He would deliver the Bass gang if charges against him and his father were dropped. Authorities agreed to the deal. Murphy then joined the gang as a full-fledged member, waiting for an opportunity to betray Bass and his men. Several traps were set but the wily outlaws always managed to slip from the grasp of the lawmen. Murphy was present with the gang held a meeting and decided to rob the bank at Round Rock, Texas, on July 20, 1878. He managed to write a letter to Major John B. Jones of the Rangers, telling him that the bandits would raid Round Rock on July 20, and "for God's sake" to get there first with his men.

Jones sent a large contingent to Round Rock, telling them to expect Bass and his men on July 20. Unexpectedly, Bass and the others decided to go into the town a day before the planned robbery "to look things over." Both Davis and Murphy had looked over the small town twice earlier. Jackson said he thought there were too many cowboys at Round Rock and that they might be lawmen waiting to spring a trap. Murphy told him that some large cattle herds had just been driven into the area and that explained the presence of so many gun-carrying men. On July 19, 1878, all four bandits rode into town to make sure everything was safe for the robbery planned for the next day. The town was divided into Old Round Rock and Newtown, where new buildings had mushroomed because of the cattle boom, and this is where the bank, fat with cash, was located. As the gang passed through Old Round Rock, Murphy, looking for a

Sam Bass shortly before the fatal Round Rock raid.

chance to separate himself from the doomed gang, said to Bass: "I think I'll look around here to see that things are safe, maybe buy some grub for the horses." Bass nodded in his direction. The others rode into Newtown and tied their horses up in an alley next to Koppel's store which was next to the bank. Bass, Barnes, and Jackson walked into the store to buy some tobacco.

The Rangers, include Major Jones, were spread about the town, not expecting the outlaw band until the next day. Murphy, in Old Round Rock, desperately searched for lawmen to inform them that the gang had arrived earlier than expected. Meanwhile, Sheriff Hoke Grimes and his deputy, Morris Moore, spotted the three men going into Koppel's store and followed them inside. All three men were wearing long coats with suspicious bulges beneath them. Grimes, not thinking that the visitors were members of the Bass gang, believed they were wearing concealed weapons and this was against a local ordinance. He stepped up behind Seaborn Barnes and put a friendly hand on the outlaw's shoulder, saying: "You

wearing a six-gun, son?" Barnes tore open his coat and whipped out his pistol, turning and firing, blasting two bullets into the startled sheriff, who died on his feet. Before he fell, Bass and Jackson shot Grimes four more times and sent two bullets into Moore's lungs. The deputy got off one shot before collapsing, the bullet ripping through Bass' hand. The three men dashed to the street and turned the corner to the alley, going for their horses.

At the first sound of gunfire, Rangers flew to the street. Major Jones saw the three gunmen turn the corner and shouted for his men to attack them. A dozen rangers and other lawmen converged on the alley, firing as they ran, with the outlaws firing back. Ranger Dick Ware had been having a shave in the barbershop and at the first shots in the store, he jumped from the barber's chair still wearing the striped bib around his neck, his face coated with lather. He ran with two guns in his hands and when he turned the corner into the alley, he saw the bandits trying to mount their skittish horses. Barnes had one foot in the saddle when he saw Ware, twisting about to take aim with his pistol. But Ware came to a dead stop and fired deliberately, hitting the outlaw square in the forehead and killing him. Seaborn Barnes fell into the alleyway, dead. Bass was struggling with his horse, the animal moving about wildly, frightened by the gunfire. A Ranger knelt at the mouth of the alley and fired. Bass groaned as the shot tore into his back and burst through his chest. Another shot from a second Ranger shattered his arm. Frank Jackson, unhurt, returned fire, driving the Rangers back somewhat into the street as he went to the bandit chief and helped his leader into the saddle. Holding the reins of Bass' horse, Jackson spurred his horse out of the back of the alley and down another street.

Murphy, who had taken refuge in a doorway in Old Round Rock, crouched low to see Jackson and Bass gallop past him down the street. He later stated: "I was sitting in a door at Old Round Rock as they came by, and Frank was holding Bass on his horse. Bass looked pale and sickly, and his hand was bleeding and he seemed to be working cartridges into his pistol. Jackson looked at me, as much as to say, 'Jim, save yourself if you can.' I then saw Major Jones go by and hallooed to him, but he did not hear me." Murphy went to Newtown and identified the body of Seaborn Barnes by pointing out the four bullet wounds the outlaw had received during the shootout at the abortive Mesquite robbery. At first the crowd of irate citizens thought to lynch Murphy as one of the outlaws but Major Jones returned, his horse spent in pursuit of the fleeing Bass and Jackson, and ordered the crowd to let Murphy go. All charges against Murphy were later dropped and he was given a large reward, but Murphy's name became synonymous with traitor. Even members of the valiant Texas Rangers condemned Murphy for his betrayal of Bass. Captain Jesse Lee Hall described Murphy as "a veritable Judas in every sense of the word."

Frank Jackson, with a superficial wound in his shoulder, managed to steer Bass' horse for several miles. Near Bushy Creek, Bass asked to stop. His saddle was coated with blood from his terrible back and chest wound and he told Jackson he could not go on. Jackson helped him from his horse and put him beneath a shady tree. "Go on, Frank," Bass told his last lieutenant. "I'm finished but you get going before the law gets here." Jackson argued with him, telling him that he would bind up his chief's wounds and they would make their escape. Bass said he was too badly wounded and then ordered Jackson to flee, telling him to take all the gold in his saddle bags. Jackson complied and rode away. He returned briefly to Denton, Texas, and then rode on and out of history, completely vanishing.

Bass was found by Jones and other Rangers that night. As the Rangers approached him, Bass held up his uninjured arm and said weakly: "Don't shoot. I am the man you are looking for. I am Sam Bass." The Rangers noticed that the outlaw had torn his shirt to pieces in order to bandage his awful chest wound which still seeped blood. Bass was carried back to Round Rock where a Dr. Cochran tended to his wounds but gave no hope that the bandit chieftain would survive. Major Jones sat by the outlaw's deathbed, questioning him about past robberies but he got little or no information from Sam Bass. At one point Bass told Jones: "It's agin my profession to blow (inform) on my pals! If a man knows anything, he ought to die with it in him." On the morning of July 21, 1878, Bass' twenty-seventh birthday, the outlaw still thought he might recuperate and asked Dr. Cochran about his chances. The physician minced no words, telling Bass that "the end is very near." Bass nodded and replied: "Let me go." A few moments later he said: "The world is bobbing around." These were the last words of Sam Bass. He was buried in a grave next to Seaborn Barnes in the little Round Rock cemetery.

Following the death of Sam Bass, the man who betrayed him, Jim Murphy, lived a nightmare existence. The 200-pound Murphy, who wore a red mustache and chin beard and whose small blue eyes seemed watery and darted everywhere at once, lived in mortal fear that Frank Jackson or some other friend of Sam Bass would seek him out and kill him. He claimed to have received word that Jackson was looking for him. Murphy spent most of his time holed up in a small room in Round Rock, writing lengthy letters to Major Jones, begging him to protect him against possible killers, phantom outlaws that so plagued Murphy that he asked to sleep in the small jail, being locked inside a cell at night with two six-guns next to his sleeping form. Finally, on June 7, 1879, Murphy could no longer bear the strain. He swallowed poison and died. See: **Barnes, Seaborn; Hall, Jesse Lee; Reno Brothers.**

REF.: Allen, *The Real Book of the Texas Rangers;* American Guide Series, *Texas, A Guide to the Lone Star State;* Baird, *Bronc Buster and Trail Driver;* Ball, *The United States Marshals of New Mexico and Arizona Territories;* Bates, *History and Reminiscences of Denton County;* Billings, *The Owlhoot Trail;* Blacker, *The Old West in Fact;* Block, *Great Stagecoach Robbers of the West;* ____, *Great Train Robberies of the West;* Botkin, *A Treasury of American Folklore;* ____, *A Treasury of Western Folklore;* Branch, *The Cowboy and His Interpreters;* Breihan, *Badmen of Frontier Days;* Brent, *Great Western Heroes;* Bridwell, *The Life and Adventures of Robert McKemie;* Bruce, *Banister Was There;* Burt, *American Murder Ballads;* Bushick, *Glamorous Days;* Carson, *The Union Pacific;* Casey, *The Black Hills and Their Incredible Characters;* ____, *The Texas Border and Some Borderliners;* Castleman, *Sam Bass, The Train Robber;* ____, *The Texas Rangers;* CBA; Chapel, *Guns of the Old West;* Chilton, *The Book of the West;* Chrisman, *Fifty Years on the Owl Hoot Trail;* ____, *Lost Trails of the Cimmaron;* Clark, *Then Came the Railroads;* Clarke, *The Palo Pinto Story;* Coolidge, *Fighting Men of the West;* Cowling, *Geography of Denton County;* Cunningham, *Famous in the West;* ____, *Triggernometry;* *The Dalton Brothers and Their Astounding Career in Crime* (Anon.); Dalton, *Under the Black Flag;* DeArment, *Bat Masterson, The Man and the Legend;* Delony, *40 Years A Peace Officer;* Donaghey, *Autobiographical Sketch of George W. Donaghey;* Donald, *Outlaws of the Border;* Drago, *Outlaws on Horseback;* ____, *Wild, Wooly & Wicked;* Durham, *The Negro Cowboys;* Emery, *Court of the Damned;* Erwin, *The Southwest of John H. Slaughter;* Fallwell, *The Texas Rangers;* Farber, *Texans With Guns;* Farrow, *Troublesome Times in Texas;* Finger, *The Distant Prize;* Fitzpatrick, *This is New Mexico;* Flannery, *John Hunton's Diary;* Fletcher, *The Wayward Horseman;* Frantz and Choate, *The American Cowboy;* Fry, *Historical Episodes of Denton;* Gard, *The Chisholm Trail;* ____, *Fabulous Quarter Horse;* ____, *Frontier Justice;* ____, *Rawhide Texas;* ____, *Sam Bass;* Gardner, *The Old Wild West;* Gay, *Into the Setting Sun;* Gillett, *Six Years With the Texas Rangers;* Grant, *The Cowboy Encyclopedia;* Grisham, *Tame the Reckless Wind;* Hafen and Young, *Fort Laramie and the Pageant of the West;* Haley, *Jeff Milton, A Good Man With A Gun;* Hamner, *Light'n Hitch;* Harlow, *Old Waybills;* Henderson, *100 Years in Montague County, Texas;* Hendricks, *The Bad Man of the West;* Hendrix, *If I Can Do It On Horseback;* Hicks, *Belle Starr and Her Pearl;* Hogg, *Authentic History of Sam Bass and His Gang;* Holbrook, *The Story of American Railroads;* Holland, *The Double Log Cabin;* ____, *The Man and His Monument;* Holloway, *Texas Gun Lore;* Horan, *Desperate Men;* ____, *The Great American West;* ____, *The Pinkertons;* ____, and Sann, *Pictorial History of the Wild West;* Horton, *History of Jack County;* Hough, *The Story of the Outlaw;* House, *City of Flaming Adventure;* ____, *Cowtown Columnist;* ____, *Texas Treasure Chest;* Hudson, *Andy Adams, His Life and Writings;* Hullah, *The Train Robber's Career, A Life of Sam Bass;* Hunt, *Bluebonnets*

and Blood; Hunter and Rose, *The Album of Gunfighters;* Hunter, *The Moving Finger;* Hutchinson, *The Life & Personal Writings of Eugene Manlove Rhodes;* Hutto, *The Dallas Story;* Hyer, *The Land of Beginning Again;* Jennings, *A Texas Ranger;* Kelly, *The Sky Was Their Roof;* Kemp, *Cow Dust and Saddle Leather;* King, *Mavericks;* Lackey, *Stories of the Texas Rangers;* Lieberson, *The Columbia Records Legacy Collection;* Logue, *Tumbleweeds;* Loomis, *Bushwhacker;* Love, *The Rise and Fall of Jesse James;* McCarty, *The Enchanted West;* McGiffin, *Ten Tall Texans;* McKennon, *Iron Men;* Martin, *A Sketch of Sam Bass;* Martin, *Border Boss;* Masterson, *The Katy Railroad and the Last Frontier;* Miller and Snell, *Why the West Was Wild;* Miller, *Pioneering North Texas;* Monagham (ed.), *The Book of the American West;* Monroe, *San Juan Silver;* Nash, *Bloodletters and Badmen;* Nordyke, *John Wesley Hardin;* North, *The Saga of the Cowboy;* O'Neal, *Encyclopedia of Western Gunfighters;* ____, *They Die But Once;* Paine, *Texas Ben Thompson;* Parker, *Gold in the Black Hills;* Peak, *A Ranger of Commerce;* Penfield, *Dig Here!;* ____, *Western Sheriffs and Marshals;* Perry, *Texas, A World in Itself;* Prather, *Come Listen to My Tale;* Preece, *The Dalton Gang;* ____, *Living Pioneers;* ____, *Lone Star Man;* Raine, *Guns of the Frontier;* Ray, *Down in the Cross Timbers;* Raymond, *Captain Lee Hall of Texas;* Rennert, *Western Outlaws;* Richardson, *Adventuring With A Purpose;* Ridings, *The Chisholm Trail;* Riegel, *America Moves West;* Ringgold, *Frontier Days in the Southwest;* Roberts, *Rangers and Sovereignty;* Rogers, *The Lusty Texans of Dallas;* Rosa, *The Gunfighter, Man or Myth?;* Santerre, *Dallas' First Hundred Years;* Scott, *Such Outlaws as Jesse James;* Shirley, *Heck Thomas, Frontier Marshal;* ____, *Six Gun and Silver Star;* ____, *Toughest of Them All;* Simpson, *Llano Estacado;* Siringo, *Riata and Spurs;* Small, *The Best of True West;* Sorenson, *Hands Up!;* ____, *The Story of Omaha;* Spring, *The Cheyenne and Black Hills State and Express Routes;* Stambaugh, *A History of Collin County, Texas;* Stanley, *Jim Courtright, Two Gun Marshal of Fort Worth;* Steen, *The Texas News;* Sterling, *Famous Western Outlaw-Sheriff Battles;* Sterling, *Trails and Trials of A Texas Ranger;* Sutton, *Hands Up!;* Terrell, *The Terrells;* Thorp, *Story of the Southwestern Cowboy;* Tilghman, *Marshal of the Last Frontier;* ____, *Outlaw Days;* Triplett, *The Life, Times, and Treacherous Death of Jesse James;* Tyler, *The History of Bell County;* Waters, *A Gallery of Western Bandits;* Watson, *A Century of Gunmen;* Webb, *The Handbook of Texas;* ____, *The Story of the Texas Rangers;* ____, *The Texas Rangers, A Century of Frontier Defense;* White, *Texas, An Informal Biography;* ____, *Trigger Fingers;* Wilhelm, *Texas, Yesterday and Tomorrow;* Williams, *The Black Hills;* Winther, *The Transportation Frontier;* Yost, *The Call of the Range;* Younger, *True Facts of the Lives of America's Most Notorious Outlaws;* (FILM), *Calamity Jane and Sam Bass,* 1949.

Bassett, Charles, prom. 1870s-90s, U.S., law enfor. off. Charles Bassett, a steady, level-headed officer who seldom displayed any kind of alarm no matter the crisis, became the first sheriff of Ford County and Dodge City, Kan., on June 5, 1873, and later served for many years as the town marshal. It was Bassett who appointed Wyatt Earp a deputy marshal. He was present at many confrontations between lawmen and outlaws, as well as shootouts between local residents. Bassett was not really a gunman but an officer who generally backed up such men as Ed and Bat Masterson and the Earp Brothers. Bassett helped Earp track down James "Spike" Kennedy, killer of beautiful Dodge City showgirl Dora Hand in 1878. It was Bassett who disarmed Cock-Eyed Frank Loving after his famous lethal duel in Dodge City with Levi Richardson on Apr. 5, 1879. On that occasion, the smoke still curling from the barrel of Loving's gun, Bassett arrived at the scene and calmly walked up to Loving without drawing his own gun. He reached out and took Loving's six-gun which was pointed at his chest, and then arrested him. Through the 1880s and 1890s Bassett served consistently as a lawman until his retirement shortly before the turn of the century. See: **Earp Brothers; Kennedy, James; Masterson, Edward J.; Masterson, William Barclay; Richardson, Levi.**

REF.: *CBA;* DeArment, *Bat Masterson, The Man and the Legend;* Faulk, *Dodge City;* Horan, *The Authentic Wild West, The Lawmen;* Nash, *Bloodletters and Badmen;* Raine, *Famous Sheriffs and Western Outlaws;* Rosa, *The Gunfighter, Man or Myth?;* ____, and May, *Gun Law.*

Bassi, Ugo, 1801-49, Italy, consp. Chaplain who served Garibaldi in 1848. He was captured by the Austrians near

Comacchio, tortured, and killed in 1849. REF.: *CBA*.

Bassville, Nicolas-Jean Hugou de, 1753-93, Fr., assass. Assassinated by an Italian partisan during anti-French demonstrations while serving in the foreign service of the Revolutionary Government assigned to Naples. REF.: *CBA*.

Basta, Giorgio, 1550-1607, Rom., consp. Soldier in the Transylvanian Army who plotted the death of Prince Michael the Brave of Wallachia in 1601. He then assumed command of the Hapsburg troops occupying his country. REF.: *CBA*.

Bastard Verdict, 1931, a novel by Winifred Duke. Harold Greenwood, who stood accused of murdering his wife in a sensational trial (Brit., 1919), serves as the role model for this work of fiction. See: **Greenwood, Harold**. REF.: *CBA*.

Bastendorf, Severin, prom. 1876, Brit., perj. Hannah Dobbs was a domestic servant accused of murdering an elderly spinster named Miss Hacker in October 1876. The remains were found in the coal cellar of Hacker's building three years later. Because the evidence against Dobbs was largely circumstantial, she was acquitted in July 1879, ending a three-year ordeal.

The sensational press published an account of the murder, describing how Dobbs had sold certain items of clothing belonging to Hacker to local people. The publication went on to say that a man named Severin Bastendorf was the actual murderer, repeating an earlier allegation Dobbs had made during the trial. Bastendorf was Dobbs' employer and rumored to be her lover.

Outraged by these insinuations, Bastendorf sued the publisher for libel. Although he won the libel case, he was later convicted of perjury for his testimony concerning his relationship with Dobbs. He was sentenced to a year in prison.

REF.: Brock, *A Casebook of Crime*; *CBA*.

Bastianini, Giovanni, d.1868, Italy, forg. Giovanni Bastianini might have become one of the world's great sculptors if he had concentrated on producing original work instead of cheap imitations of the Renaissance masters. In his time, though, some of Bastianini's best terracotta forgeries were exhibited in London's famed Victoria and Albert Museum.

REF.: *CBA; MacDougall, Hoaxes.*

The storming of the Bastille, July 14, 1789.

Bastille, 1340-1789, Fr., prison. The ancient Bastille was part of the fortifications of fourteenth century Paris, an architectual outcropping of the walls built to resist invaders, first known as The Bastille of St. Antoine, the word "Bastille" of Roman origin and meaning loosely a temporary fort built to resist sieges. The fortress was rebuilt many times but the first stones of the Bastille that would later be used as a dreaded prison were laid in 1370. Hugues Aubriot, with a commission from Charles V, designed the Bastille as it was later remembered, a square fort in Paris with towers at all four angles. Charles VI ordered the Bastille enlarged, adding four more towers, the structure taking on the

design of a parallelogram. Except for a few modifications, this was the essential structure attacked by revolutionaries in 1789.

The storming of the Bastille on July 14, 1789, France's independence day, seems to have been a rather arbitrary action. Camille Desmoulins, a colleague of Danton's, claimed responsibility for the attack on the Bastille. Prior to this several peaceful citizen's groups had approached Governor de Launay, who commanded the small garrison at the Bastille, requesting that he turn over all the powder stored in the dungeons. A loyalist, he refused, adamantly intent on holding the fortress in the name of the king. He had politely informed the revolutionaries that they would be fired upon if they attempted to break into the historic prison which represented the long tyranny of the French monarchy, a symbol of political oppression. The Bastille had long been a prison where political foes of the French kings were sent to rot and die.

Desmoulins, drinking with his friends in the gardens of the Palais Royal, was suddenly inspired to mount a table and exhorted the massive crowds to storm the Bastille. "The people were struck by my enthusiasm and by my eager bearing," Desmoulins later stated. "They surrounded me and urged me to mount a table. In a moment I had six thousand people around me." Within the hour there were an estimated 20,000 persons—some reports had it three times that number—attacking the weakly-held fortress. The battle lasted for about two hours. De Launay could not depress the huge cannons on the walls since these had marine mountings and were designed to fire at those laying siege beyond the walls of Paris but a cannonade from the streets blew holes in the walls of the old prison. The guards inside, mostly elderly pensioners, returned a solid fire that took the lives of eighty-three revolutionaries trying to swim the moat and wounded an equal number.

De Launay resisted surrender during a brief truce but his own men insisted that he wave the white flag and he capitulated. The drawbridge was lowered and the revolutionaries stormed inside the ancient prison where they summarily slew de Launay and all the guards, then went searching for political prisoners to free. There were none. Only seven prisoners were found, four forgers, two madmen and a nobleman who had been convicted of incest. The king was powerless to prevent the fall of the Bastille since the French guards had gone over to the revolutionaries and the foreign mercenaries sent to relieve the brief siege were slaughtered by the huge crowds. The revolutionaries roamed for weeks through the vast caverns of the ancient prison, tearing down walls behind which they found scores of chained skeletons, the remains of prisoners who had been walled up alive; huge blocks of concrete with enormous chains embedded in them; torture tables and racks; whips, and all the devices of ancient tortures. The Bastille was later torn down for the most part and the key to its main gate sent to George Washington in America; he kept the key on a table in the foyer of his home.

REF.: Alger, *Paris in 1789-94*; Carlyle, *The French Revolution*; *CBA*; Claretie, *Camille et Lucile Desmoulins*; Gaxotte, *The French Revolution*; Griffiths, *The World's Famous Prisons (Early French Prisons)*; Lofts and Weiner, *Eternal France*; Loomis, *Paris in the Terror*; Morton, *Camille Desmoulins*; Taine, *The French Revolution*; Thompson, *The French Revolution*; Webster, *The French Revolution, A Study in Democracy*.

Bastwick, Dr. John, 1593-1654, Brit., libel. Bastwick was a victim of the English Star Chamber, the system of law by which a dissenter or enemy of the crown could be tried and convicted on hearsay and without benefit of counsel. During the reign of King Charles I (1625-49), the Court of the Star Chamber was at the height of its powers and was particularly harsh with Presbyterians who dared to speak out against the Catholic church.

In 1637 Dr. John Bastwick published an inflammatory pamphlet titled *Elenchus Religionis Papistic* which assailed the church hierarchy. The king's counsel attempted to have him tried for high treason, but the judges decided that he should only answer for charges of libel.

Bastwick debated that matters of Divinity could not be arbitrated by the king's emissaries, and that he was being dealt with unfairly. His arguments were rejected and he was ordered to pay £5,000 and to lose his ears. When this was done, the doctor was transported to prison in the Scilly Isles which his wife was forbidden to visit.

In 1640 the Long Parliament reversed this earlier judgment against Bastwick. He was ordered released and compensated for the indignities he had suffered from his persecutors. A year later, Star Chamber proceedings were outlawed and they were never revived. See: **Charles I, King.** REF.: *CBA.*

American troops in the 1942 Bataan Death March.

Bataan Death March, 1942, Phil.-Japan, war crimes. The American-Filipino defense of the Bataan Penninsula during WWII lasted more than three months, from January to Apr. 9, 1942, at which time U.S. General Edward P. King surrendered his Allied Commmand to Imperial Japanese forces. The defense of Bataan was heroic and legendary. General Douglas MacArthur, in overall command of about 70,000 U.S. and Filipino troops, at the beginning of WWII in the Pacific, planned to delay the Japanese juggernaut sweeping through the Pacific. He and his men did exactly that, forcing the invaders to use their best troops and most modern equipment for more than three months while giving the U.S. and its allies enough time to build up forces and equipment to strike back against a barbaric war machine that had been put in motion by Emperor Hirohito.

MacArthur directed the battle of Bataan until President Franklin D. Roosevelt, to save this war hero from capture, ordered him to escape from his headquarters on the island fortress of Corregidor in Manila Bay, sending him to command troops in Australia. His successor, Lieutenant General Jonathan Wainwright, following MacArthur's dictates, ordered his field commander, General King, to fight to the death. General King, by early April 1942, saw no reason to sacrifice more than 12,000 U.S. troops and about 58,000 Filipino troops. These gaunt men, with little or no ammunition, were dying of disease and malnutrition. There was practically no food to feed them and they barely had the strength to stand up in their foxholes and repel the well-fed, well-equipped crack Japanese divisions that daily overran their positions. King disobeyed Wainwright's order and surrendered the Luzon force on Apr. 9, 1942, to officers under the command of Japanese General Masaharu Homma. He asked that his troops be given gas for trucks so that his wounded and sick could be conveyed to prison camps.

The response to this request by a Japanese officer through an interpreter was: "Surrender must be unconditional!"

"Will our troops be well treated?" King asked.

"We are not barbarians!" snapped the Japanese officer.

The capitulation of the U.S. Army and Philippine Constabulary on Luzon in 1942 marked the worst defeat ever suffered by U.S.

forces in any war and comprised the largest body of troops ever surrendered by a U.S. command. Only hours after King's surrender, the atrocities began. Thousands of U.S. and Filipino soldiers were disarmed and then stripped of their personal belongings. If any prisoner was found to have Japanese souvenirs, flags, weapons, or the like, he was immediately shot, the captors believing that the prisoners had earlier stripped these items from dead Japanese soldiers.

In ragged lines, the starving U.S. and Filipino troops were forced to march from Mariveles to the town of San Fernando, a distance of sixty miles. Shoes were taken from many prisoners who were forced to walk barefoot. Hats and helmets were taken from the prisoners so that they baked bareheaded in the blinding sun. They were prodded, shoved and pushed at bayonet point by Japanese guards who had received orders to kill off as many prisoners as possible before they reached the prisons that would hold them for the duration of the war.

A few Japanese commanders refused to order their troops to murder prisoners, unless they received written orders from Colonel Masanobu Tsuji, the merciless staff officer who implemented the lethal march. No written orders were ever issued, only verbal communiques, but Japanese officers who refused to carry out these orders were treated with disdain by their peers and seldom received promotions in the future. Most complied with Tsuji's command after they received phone calls from him or his aides, who informed the commanders that this order came from Imperial headquarters. Behind Tsuji's verbal order stood the designers of the Death March, Major General Wachi Takaji, General Homma's chief of staff, who had created the incident of the Marco Polo Bridge in 1937 which Japan used as a pretext to invade Manchuria; Lieutenant General Mudaguchi Renya, who had commanded the Japanese invasion force at the Marco Polo Bridge; and Major General Cho Isamu, a ruthless murderer responsible for the rape of Nanking in 1937.

Japanese rank and file soldiers, however, needed few officers to order them to their gruesome tasks. They willingly cuffed and beat the helpless prisoners as they made their agonizing way along the dusty roads toward San Fernando, careful not to openly murder the helpless Americans and Filipinos. Once they had knocked their victims to the ground and had them in a dazed position, they *then* bayoneted or shot them to death, claiming that the prisoners did not respond to orders to get back into line and were therefore guilty of disobedience and trying to escape. Attempts at escape were encouraged by the Japanese. They forced prisoners to march past farms laden with food and fresh water, continuing to starve the marchers, but allowed them to drink from polluted carabao wallows or privy spillovers, which caused intestinal diseases which later killed the prisoners.

As truckloads of Japanese troops raced past the staggering prisoners, going in the opposite direction toward the coast in prepartion of attacks on Corregidor which was still holding out, Japanese soliders leaned over the rails of the trucks and swung the butts of their rifles against the helpless Americans and Filipinos, knocked them down, crushing the skulls of others and killing them. As the Death March progressed day after day, the dead began to litter the roads and adjacent fields. When reports of the march reached the ears of Filipinos in the towns lining the route of the doomed prisoners, women, children, and old men in these towns crowded against the moving line of prisoners, giving them water, fruits, vegetables, even money. Some of these civilians were grabbed by Japanese guards and knocked senseless, bayoneted, or shot to death. But still the brave Filipino civilians continued to risk their lives to help the forlorn prisoners.

The guards relished their roles as executioners. Many of them spoke English well and told the Americans that they were being mistreated because they had surrendered and were therefore cowards and not worthy of humane treatment, that, because they had disgraced themselves as soldiers by surrendering, they were not entitled to be treated as normal prisoners of war, an insane logic with only one other meaning: one could only be respected as a solider if one had died in battle. All of this double-talk was no more than another form of punishment administered by a nation that had adopted sadism and cruelty as acceptable conduct for victors who had triumphed over "inferior races."

The thousands of Japanese guards who committed countless and unspeakable atrocities throughout the many days of the Death March acted with impunity, knowing that their superiors would not rebuke them. In fact, Japanese officers stood by in silence while their men disemboweled living prisoners and strung their entrails along farm fences, laughing maniacally as they did so. Other prisoners who did not move fast enough for some Japanese officers where immediately branded as deserters and were beheaded in the middle of the road. Their heads were then mounted on fence posts as symbols of Japanese authority.

In some of the small towns along the torturous route the wealthy Filipino fathers of some of the prisoners pulled their sons out of the prisoner lines and bargained with their Japanese guards, paying enormous amounts of money to have their sons released to them. In more than one instance, heroic young Filipinos, most of them belonging to the famed Philippine Scouts, refused to be ransomed from the prisoner ranks by their own fathers, saying, even though many of these haggard men were close to death, they would share the fate of their American comrades in arms.

The Japanese guards marched the prisoners in groups of thirty or forty with a space of perhaps a quarter mile between them, so that the prisoners coming from the rear could not see the atrocities being committed to the group ahead. If prisoners turned around to see what had happened to the men in their group they were knocked down and invariably bayoneted to death. The killing went on for almost ten days, concluding, for the most part, on Apr. 20, 1942. Once the half-dead survivors of the Death March reached San Fernando, thousands were herded into boxcars and shipped to Camp O'Donnell. They were packed so tightly in these cars that only the strongest survived, all standing through the ordeal, hundreds dying in the incredibly hot, stench-permeated boxcars. Thousands more would die in the so-called internment camps at Cabanatuan, Davao, Bilibid Prison, and other camps. They would be beaten, tortured, starved, or they would die of disease and wounds. Only about 4,000 U.S. veterans of Bataan survived the war.

Of the 12,000 U.S. soldiers in the March, close to 3,000 died at the vicious, vindictive hands of their Japanese guards. More than 8,000 Filipinos met the same fate. This nerve-shattering, mindless, and barbaric act by the Japanese stamped their culture as coercive, inhumane, and wholly uncivilized, staining this nation's honor for generations to come. The Bataan Death March historically ranks with the most perverse war crimes committed in any age, from the Black Hole of Calcutta of the Sepoy Rebellion to the nightmare extermination camps of Hitler's obscene Third Reich. Following the surrender of Japan in 1945, war crime trials were held in Manila and other Asian cities which saw the conviction of many of those responsible for the Bataan Death March and other atrocities. Among those convicted and executed for this monstrous mass murder was Japanese General Homma. His emperor, Hirohito, was ultimately the chief architect for the Death March and countless other offenses against humanity, although this most insidious of war-mongering leaders never shouldered a bit of responsibility for his acts, escaping, as he had planned from the beginning, behind his dynastic shield and the sanctuary of the Shinto religion which then looked upon him as a god. See: **Hirohito, Emperor; Homma, Masaharu.**

REF.: Abraham, *Ghost of Bataan Speaks;* Beloti, *Corregidor, Saga of a Fortress;* Benedict, *The Chrysanthemum and the Sword;* Bergamini, *Japan's Imperial Conspiracy;* Borton, *Japan's Modern Century;* Boyle, *Yanks Don't Cry;* Brougher, *South to Bataan, North to Mukden;* Brown, *Bilibid Prison; CBA;* Coleman, *Bataan and Beyond;* Craigie, *Behind the Japanese Mask;* Dyess, *The Dyess Story;* Emerson, *Guest of the Emperor;* Falk, *Bataan, The March of Death;* Fortier, *life of a POW Under the Japanese;* Hawkins, *Never Say Die;* Johnson, *Hour of Redemption: The Ranger Raid on Cabanatuan;* Kenworthy, *The Tiger of Malaya, The Inside Story of the Japanese Atrocities;* Kerr, *Surrender & Survival, The Experience of American POWs in the Pacific, 1941-1945;* Knox, *Death March, The Survivors of Bataan;* Lory, *Japan's Military Masters: The Army in Japanese Life;* McCracken, *Very Soon Now, Joe;* McGee, *Rice and Salt;* Miller, *Bataan Uncensored;* Moody, *Reprieve from Hell;* Morton, *The Fall of the Philippines;* Rutherford, *Fall of the Philippines;* Schultz, *Hero of Bataan: The Story of Jonathan M. Wainwright;* Smith, *Triumph in the Philippines;* Stewart, *Give Us This Day;* Toland, *But Not in Shame;* ____, *The Rising Sun: The Decline and Fall of the Japanese Empire;* Vance, *Doomed Garrison—The Philippines (A POW Story);* Wainwright, *General Wainwright's Story;* Weinstein, *Barbed Wire Surgeon.*

Batcheller, George Sherman, 1837-1908, U.S., jur. U.S. judge and member of the international tribunal for the legal administration of Egypt from 1876-85 and 1898-1908. REF.: *CBA.*

Bateman, Dr. Charles, d.1685, Brit., consp.-treas. Dr. Charles Batemen resided in the parish of St. Dunstan, in London, at the time of the Monmouth Rebellion in 1685. Politically active, he had fought hard for the passage of the Exclusion Bill designed to thwart James, the Duke of York from succeeding his brother Charles II, as king. James Scott, the Duke of Monmouth, was the favored candidate of the exclusionists, but he was ruthlessly crushed at the battle of Sedgemoor on July 6, 1685, and his followers were rounded up and put on trial for treason in what came to be known as the Bloody Assizes. Judge George Jeffreys, 1st Baron, conducted the proceedings. Jeffreys earned a reputation as a stone-cold executioner rather than an impartial jurist for his work during the treason trials when more than 300 people were sentenced to death.

Bateman was arrested as a traitor against the crown and accused of participating in the Rye House Plot to assassinate Charles. He had not fought with Scott at Sedgemoor, however, and his role in the Rye House Affair was inconsequential. However, a witness named Thomas Lee was brought forward and testified that Bateman was a willing participant in a plan to seize the King, the Tower of London, Whitehall, and Savoy. Lee and several other key witnesses for the prosecution feared for their lives and were willing to offer false testimony in the hope of securing a reprieve.

The most highly skilled barristers appeared for the crown, but Bateman was denied counsel, as were all defendants accused of treason at that time—a ruling eventually overturned during the reign of William and Mary. The outcome of Bateman's treason trial was almost a foregone conclusion, though favorable witnesses for the defense were finally admitted.

Jeffreys sentenced the defendant to hang at Tyburn and then to be disemboweled. Bateman was a victim of the times he lived in. But so, too, was George Jeffreys. When King James II was overthrown, the judge attempted to flee England, but was seized and imprisoned in the Tower of London where he died in 1689. See: **Rye House Plot.**

REF.: *CBA;* Parry, *Some Famous Medical Trials.*

Bateman, Mary (Mary Harker, AKA: The Yorkshire Witch), 1768-1809, Brit., witchcraft-mur. Born of Yorkshire, England, parents, Mary Bateman began thieving at the age of five, stealing her father's clothing and hiding these to exchange for other items with neighbor children. In 1778, she moved to Leeds where she became a seamstress, but she spent most of her time telling simple-minded customers that she was a seeress and possessed powers that would bring them good fortune. She told fortunes and was well paid for it. She later married a hard-working laborer, John Bateman, who was devoted to his wife but was repeatedly milked of his money by her. One day Bateman appeared at the plant where her husband worked and sobbingly handed him a letter she had received that said his father was on his deathbed. John Bateman borrowed money and traveled to Thirsk where he found his father, the town crier, hard at work and in perfect health. When he returned to his home in Leeds, Bateman found his wife in their dwelling, sitting on a single pillow. The rest of the house was stripped of every piece of furniture, sold off, Bateman said, because she had gotten into some unexplained trouble and had to "buy her way out of it."

John Bateman did not object; he had long believed his wife was a witch with great powers and it was dangerous to incur her wrath. Though she was a known thief, the authorities in Leeds did nothing to interfere with Bateman's merciless schemes of self-enrichment. When a fire all but destroyed a large plant in Leeds, Bateman went door-to-door in the poorest district in town, begging foodstuffs and linen, supposedly for the workers who had lost their jobs in the burned out plant and for their destitute families. She sold off the contributions and kept the money for herself. Bateman was not reported for this shameful deed since most believed she would retaliate with her powerful witchcraft. Then Bateman turned her witchcraft into profit by selling off love potions, charms, and prophecies. Sometimes she resorted to direct extortion, telling victims to give her gold pieces or their loved ones would be kidnapped or killed, according to her visions, of course, tableaus of the future she could turn around by applying her powerful magic.

Mary Bateman and her demons, according to a contemporary artist.

Two gullible natives, William and Rebecca Perigo, came to Bateman and said that Rebecca's breasts suffered from a condition called "flacking" which a sinister neighbor had caused by putting a curse upon her. Bateman countered with her own magic and Mrs. Perigo grew better, which endeared Bateman to the artless Perigos. She continued to milk the couple by selling them charms and potions. She decided to rob them of their entire savings and possessions by simply poisoning them with a pudding heavily laced with arsenic. Rebecca died but William Perigo survived. Ignoring Bateman's dictates to never consult with any physician and to seek only her help, Perigo, on Oct. 19, 1808, went to Dr. Thomas Chorley who told him he was being poisoned with arsenic. The gullible man suddenly came to his senses and raced home to check two pillowcases Mary Bateman had "charmed." The witch had told Perigo to place all his guinea notes inside the pillows and that she would place a protective spell on the pillows to keep them safe from robbers. When Perigo tore open the pillowcases he found his money gone and useless paper in their place. He confronted Mary Bateman who shouted: "You've opened them too soon and ruined the spell, causing the money to turn into useless paper."

Perigo went to Constable Driffield and set up a trap for the Yorkshire Witch. He later met her at the Leeds and Liverpool Canal Bank where she was sitting on a tree stump. Hiding nearby was the constable, waiting to overhear their conversation. Bateman apparently spotted the constable and when Perigo arrived she immediately accused *him* of poisoning her, vomiting and then screaming: "The bottle which you gave me has almost poisoned me!...I would scorn to give a dog such a bottle!" Constable Driffield, however, was not taken in. He stepped from the bushes and placed the woman under arrest, charging her with theft, witchcraft, and murder. A search of the Bateman house later unearthed all the Perigo possessions Bateman had stolen, as well as a huge supply of various poisons.

In a quick trial, Bateman was convicted of extortion, witchcraft, and murder; she was sentenced to death. Before her execution, Bateman went on with her thieving ways, taking the last pennies from condemned prisoners while promising that reprieves and pardons would soon be granted through the powers of her magic. She was allowed to keep her small child with her while she awaited execution, which occurred on Mar. 20, 1809. She quietly kissed her child farewell and walked stoically to the scaffold where thousands came to see her die. Mary Bateman, before she went through the trap, shrieked that she was innocent. Her end served to help the needy in an ironic twist of fate. Mary Bateman's blackened, bloated body was displayed for those who wished to gaze upon the remains of the Yorkshire Witch. They were charged a modest sum and this money was given to charity. Later, the most superstitious of these spectators paid even more money to strip pieces of blackened skin from the corpse. They intended to use these grisly souvenirs as charms to ward off evil witches such as Mary Batemen.

REF.: Atholl, *Shadow of the Gallows;* Butler, *Murderer's England; CBA; The Extraordinary Life and Character of Mary Bateman, The Yorkshire Witch;* Hyson, *Sixty Famous Trials;* Nash, *Look for the Woman;* O'Donnell, *Should Women Hang?;* Potter, *The Art of Hanging;* Robbins, *The Encyclopedia of Witchcraft and Demonology;* Wilson, *Encyclopedia of Murder.*

Bates, Albert, See: **Bailey, Harvey; Kelly, George.**

Bates, Edward, 1793-1869, U.S., atty. gen. Circuit prosecuting attorney in 1818, state's attorney in 1820, member of the U.S. House of Representatives from 1827-29, and attorney general under President Abraham Lincoln from 1861-64. He resigned in protest of Lincoln's war policies which he believed impinged upon constitutional guarantees. REF.: *CBA.*

Bathory, Elizabeth (or **Batory**), 1560-1614, Hung., mur. Married at fifteen to Count Ferencz Nâdasdy, countess Elizabeth Bathory lived in regal splendor inside the Castle Csejthe. Waited on hand and foot, Bathory occupied her teenage years with pleasures of the flesh and toward her twentieth year she began to display a decided taste for sadistic punishment. Her husband, while fighting the Turks, the story goes, found a rare manuscript on ancient tortures and the countess read this crusty document with avid interest which later turned to fascination. She was also obsessed with flagellation, a trait learned from an unbalanced aunt, and ordered her servants to whip her for long, painful periods. The countess was an attractive woman, dark and sensuous, and she took many lovers while her husband was still alive. Upon his death in 1604, Bathory's mind seemed to snap. She slept erratically, ordered her servants to walk about naked, and developed an unpredictable appetite, demanding that she be served only exotic fruits from the Middle East. When a servant girl dared to bring her some commonplace apples, the countess flew into a rage and struck the girl, cutting the flesh with a large ring. Some blood splashed on her face and when she wiped it off she became convinced that her aging complexion in that spot had suddenly been revitalized, made youthful again.

With this discovery, the countess believed that eternal youth could be obtained if she bathed in the fresh virgin's blood. To this end, Bathory ordered her palace guardsmen to scour the countryside and bring her peasant girls who, upon being proved virgins, were slain, their blood drained into a hot bath in which the countess submerged herself every morning. It was reported that, like the legendary Dracula, Bathory turned vampire and actually sucked the blood out of her victims, but this was never supported even by her most lunatic aides, especially the cruel Dorotta Szentes, who was known as Dorka. For years the countess bathed in her human blood but the rejuvenation process was evident only in her demented self-perception. Her followers, fearing for their own lives, did her bidding, murdered girls by the scores to satisfy her maniacal whim, and buried the bodies through the old underground passages of the castle.

Bathory, in one grim moment of reality, saw herself as the aging crone she was and screamed to Dorka that it was the *quality* of blood that was missing. She was bathing in the gore of inferior humans and suddenly seized upon the idea that only the blood of aristocrats could return her youth. She devised a scheme to snare the young daughters of her peers, telling bluebloods throughout Hungary that she would take under her tutorship twenty-five of the prettiest daughters of aristocrats and teach them in the ways of social graces. Since Bathory was one of the richest and most powerful persons in the country and her horrific deeds had been secret, many members of the lower nobility seized this opportunity as a way of advancing their own positions, and sent their daughters to this monster in 1609.

At first Bathory pretended to conduct classes in manners and etiquette but she would have the girls murdered one by one in their beds as they slept and then butchered for her gory bath. Her most trusted servants, however, grew careless and, instead of burying the bodies in the castle caverns, simply tossed the corpses over the castle wall where peasants soon discovered and identified them. (It was conjectured that the servants intentionally made the murders apparent in order to bring Bathory's sins to public view.)

Once the murders became known a great outcry against the countess caused the arrest of her most trusted aides, Dorka, a male servant, and a captain of the palace guard. Bathory herself, under Hungarian law, could not be arrested or tried for common murder since she was a member of ranking royalty and therefore immune from criminal prosecution. Her servants were found Guilty and burned alive at the stake for their awful slayings, but this did not appease an increasingly hostile populace which demanded punishment of Countess Bathory so vociferously that the government feared open rebellion. To sidestep laws that protected the lunatic Bathory, the Hungarian Parliament convened and passed a special law which permitted authorities to bring her to trial.

Countess Bathory was convicted of murdering scores of young girls (the count was staggering, between 600 and 750), but since she could not, under any legal circumstances, be executed in any prescribed manner, she was sent to her suite in the castle and walled up in these rooms. She was fed through an opening in the brick wall and managed to survive in her isolated castle tower for more than three years until she died screaming to be released. When the wall was broken down and officials stepped inside the suite, they beheld, as one described "a creature so hideous as to make Evil itself cringe." See: **Vlad Dracul; Vlad Tepes.**

REF.: Boar, *The World's Most Infamous Murders;* CBA; Godwin, *Murder U.S.A.;* Nash, *Almanac of World Crime;* _____, *Look for the Woman;* (FILM), *The Devil's Wedding Night,* 1973; *Mamma Dracula,* 1980.

Bathtub Murder, The, 1933, a novel by Mabel Dana Lyon and Josephine Hughston. The Lamson case serves as the inspiration for this fictional work in which the authors actually employ the prosecutor's closing speech in David Lamson's trial. See: **Lamson, David.** REF.: *CBA.*

Bathurst, Benjamin, 1784-1809, Brit., (unsolv.) mur. Benjamin Bathurst was seemingly destined for a career in the British foreign service, for his father was the Bishop of Norwich and he was related to Earl Bathurst, who held various cabinet posts in the late eighteenth century. On his graduation from Oxford, the young man was assigned to serve as Secretary of Legation in Stockholm, Sweden, and in 1809 he was sent to the Court of Vienna to represent the crown as an envoy, a high honor for one so young.

He arrived in Austria at the precise moment of that country's defeat at the hands of Napoléon's armies. The British embassy was ordered closed by the conquering emperor, and all diplomats were expelled immediately. Bathurst complied, and the driver of his coach proceeded through Prussia en route to Hamburg where Bathurst would secure safe passage by boat to England.

Accompanied by his personal valet, Ilbert, and a representative of the Prussian government named Krause, Bathurst stopped in the little town of Perleberg on Nov. 25, 1809. The village was situated on the road between Berlin and Hamburg, and it was here that the British envoy mysteriously disappeared after fearing for his safety for several days. At the little inn where he stopped for the night, Bathurst appealed to the town major Captain von Klitzing for protection.

He was given assurances that the Prussian government would cooperate fully and provide protection, but Bathurst was not placated. He decided to continue on, foregoing his earlier decision to spend the night in Perleberg. Shortly before his departure, he vanished. The town was searched without avail. Later, two women gathering firewood in the forest stumbled upon

a pair of men's trousers containing tattered portions of a letter written by Bathurst to his wife, explaining his anxiety over his safety.

A sizable reward was offered by the Prussian government, which feared an international incident. Emperor Napoléon granted Bathurst's young wife safe conduct through the war-torn lands to search for her missing husband, but nothing came of it. Years passed and still no clue turned up. When Bathurst's name was mentioned in conversation, most conceded that he had been murdered by Napoléon's agents. No one could provide a better explanation until some workmen uncovered a skeleton of a man in a house they were tearing down in Perleberg in 1852.

The building had once been owned by a waiter named Martins who worked at the inn where Bathurst had stayed. The presence of a hatchet wound in the skull, and the absence of clothing lent credence to the theory that the skeleton was Bathurst. Villagers remembered that Martins had presented his daughters with a large dowry of £150 when they married. Bathurst had a comparable sum of money with him when he disappeared. Still others maintained that the envoy died in one of Napoléon's dank prisons and was buried beneath a stone floor. The mystery is unsolved.

REF.: *CBA;* Hyde, *United In Crime;* Stevens, *From Clue to Dock.*

Batista, Fulgencio (Fulgencio Batista y Zaldivar), 1901-73, Cuba, org. crime. Fulgencio Batista began as a lowly private in the Cuban national army (1921-33), rising to the rank of sergeant. He led a coup that overthrew dictator Cépedes in 1933 when he was made a colonel and commander of the Cuban constitutional army, remaining the country's military strong man for the next twenty-five years. He was dictator of the country from 1933, controlling the civil government and the military, holding the title of president (1940-44), then retiring. Batista returned to power in 1952, leading a military coup. It was at this time that he formed an alliance with the U.S. crime syndicate. Meyer Lanksy, who had established strong ties with Batista in the early 1930s in setting up lavish gambling casinos (from which Batista took a huge part of the take) in Havana, remained the dictator's lifelong friend. Batista turned over virtual control of all gambling in Cuba to the syndicate, under

Cuban dictator Fulgencio Batista.

Lansky's direction. He was given more than a third of the profits from these syndicate-financed casinos, millions of dollars that Batista secreted in Swiss accounts. One report has it that Lansky invited Batista to his Havana hotel room some time in the mid-1930s and opened up a suitcase filled with more than $5 million, handed it to the Cuban strongman, and told him: "This is our earnest money for the gambling franchise in Havana." From that moment on, Lansky ran the gambling. Many other U.S. gangsters attempted to muscle into this fabulously lucrative enterprise, including Carlos Marcello, Santo Trafficante, Jr., and Albert Anastasia, but they were all told by Batista that "the little man must give his approval before you step on the island." Lansky, of course, had no intentions of following such a regulation.

In 1959, with the revolution of Fidel Castro sweeping everything before it, Batista and his high-ranking officers fled Cuba, taking millions more with them. Leaving at the same time was Meyer Lansky, who ordered several of his minions in the casino to remain behind and see if they could cut a deal with Castro in continuing the syndicate's gambling enterprises in Havana. The answer was abrupt and surprising. Castro, who had played a cat-and-mouse game with the U.S. until he was in total power, suddenly announced that he was a die-hard communist and not at all interested in capitalism, including the casinos, which he immediately ordered demolished. It was the end of the syndicate's most lucrative gambling operations until it began to make huge inroads into the Las Vegas casinos. Batista lived in lavish exile until his death in 1973. While in exile, he met with Lansky from time to time in Florida where the two discussed the possibility of retaking Cuba and reestablishing the casinos, an event that never took place. See: **Lansky, Meyer; Marcello, Carlos; Trafficante, Santo, Jr.**

REF.: *CBA;* Eisenberg and Landau, *Meyer Lansky;* Fried, *The Rise and Fall of the Jewish Gangster in America;* Katz, *Uncle Frank;* Messick, *Lansky;* ____, *Syndicate In the Sun;* Morgan, *Prince of Crime.*

Battaglia, Alfredo, 1967- , Case of, Italy, kid. Thirteen-year-old Alfredo Battaglia was kidnapped on Oct. 30, 1979, as he walked home from school in the town of Bovalino, Italy. His father, a wealthy jeweler, paid a $300,000 ransom. The boy was held captive for nearly four months until he was finally released on a lonely stretch of highway outside Reggio Calabria on Feb. 23, 1980. As a reward for "being a good boy," his abductors gave him $360. Battaglia was reported to be in good health. REF.: *CBA.*

Battaglia, Frank J., prom. 1980s, U.S., law enfor. off. Frank Battaglia was a forty-year veteran of the Baltimore Police Department when Mayor William Donald Schaefer appointed him commissioner on Sept. 1, 1981.

In 1959 the chief received the Sunpapers Policeman of the Year Award for having implemented the "Battaglia Plan." Other noteworthy commendations followed. He won two presidential citations, from Gerald Ford in 1976 and from Jimmy Carter three years later. REF.: *CBA.*

Battaglia, Giuseppe, and **Guarna, Domenico,** and **Danis, Benjamin,** and **Lev, William,** and **Rider, Theodore,** prom. 1957, U.S., smug. Giuseppe Battaglia arrived in the U.S. from Milan, Italy, in 1952 to open a clothing import business. The number of American tourists who visited his haberdashery in the old country had convinced him that there was a market in the U.S. for imported Italian clothing.

He went into business with his friend and partner Domenico Guarna, an arrangement that allowed Battaglia to call on retail establishments across the country and overseas while Guarna tended the store in New York. From time to time Battaglia returned to his native land to buy the latest fashion lines from top Italian manufacturers. In each instance he sailed to and from the port of New York, paying his import duties on merchandise without question.

Inspector Benjamin Danis became acquainted with Battaglia in 1954 after he inspected his luggage and reviewed his customs declarations for irregularities. Danis implied that he might allow the Italian to bring additional items into the country, over and above what was listed on the sheet, without paying the dues. "I can give you some tips that will help you in clearing customs," he promised.

Battaglia invited Danis to stop by his shop and pick out some fancy ties for himself. After accepting this gift and a $20 bill to go with it, Danis laid it on the line. "I can arrange to handle the inspection of your baggage," he said. "I won't ask any questions if all your merchandise is not listed on the declarations."

Battaglia calculated that his potential savings would be considerable, and so he readily agreed to the scheme. In the next three years $147,613 worth of Italian clothing entered the country illegally and Battaglia, Danis, and two other customs inspectors, William Lev and Theodore Rider, had bilked the government out of $56,600 in duties.

The arrangement would have continued had not the Customs Special Agency Service been tipped off by Battaglia's angry competitors whose prices he severely undercut. When Guarna

returned from Italy on Oct. 1, 1957, aboard the *Cristoforo Colombo,* the special agents of the Rackets Squad and Dave Cardoza of the customs office were lying in wait.

Battaglia and his partner were arrested, fined $15,000, and given five years' probation. Inspectors Lev and Danis were sentenced to three years in prison. Lev was fined $2,500—exactly half of what he had received from the clothing smugglers over a three-year period.

REF.: *CBA;* Whitehead, *Border Guard.*

Battaglia, Samuel (AKA: **Teets**), 1908-73, U.S., org. crime. A member of the old 42 Gang of Chicago, along with Sam "Momo" Giancana, Samuel Battaglia joined Capone's bulging ranks of gangsters in 1924 and by the late 1930s had risen high in the Chicago syndicate, specializing in loan-sharking. By the 1950s, Battaglia, a strong arm thug who would run up more than two dozen arrests for burglary, robbery, and murder (a suspect in seven homicides), emerged as one of the top syndicate leaders in Chicago, and was thought to be the logical successor to Sam Giancana. An uneducated thug, Battaglia held court in the back room of the Casa Madrid restaurant, having juice victims behind on their payments brought to him. He would decide whether the loan-shark sucker would be beaten or even killed. (If anyone dared challenge his decisions, Battaglia would roar a line for which he was nicknamed: "Shaddup or I'll bust ya in da teets (teeth)!"

When testifying before the McClellan Committee, Battaglia took the Fifth Amendment sixty times (not because he might implicate himself, some said, but because his diction was so poor that he would appear to be the moron he really was). Vying with Battaglia for the top mob position in Chicago in the 1960s were Sam Giancana, Sam DeStefano and Fiore "Fifi" Buccieri. By that time, Tony Accardo, the reigning mob kingpin appeared to be on the wane. Battaglia lost out when, in 1967, he was convicted of extortion and sent to prison for fifteen years. Giancana took over the Chicago Outfit while Battaglia spent his life behind bars. He died in 1973, along with Buccieri and DeStefano. Giancana himself was killed in 1975 and Accardo, who had never really been out of power, resumed the leadership of the Chicago Mafia-syndicate. See: **Accardo, Anthony Joseph; Buccieri, Fiore; DeStefano, Samuel; Giancana, Samuel.**

REF.: *CBA;* Cressy, *Theft of the Nation;* Demaris, *Captive City;* Gage, *The Mafia is not an Equal Opportunity Employer;* Nash, *Bloodletters and Badmen;* Overstreet, *The FBI in Our Open Society.*

Batters, Joe, See: **Accardo, Anthony Joseph.**

Batthyany, Lajos, c.1806-49, Hung., treas. Leader of the 1845 independence movement and premier of the first ministry in 1848. He was arrested and executed by the Austrians a year after taking office. REF.: *CBA.*

Battice, Earl Leo, b.1903, U.S., mur. A four-masted schooner named the *Kingsway* set sail from Perth Amboy, N.J., in 1926, bound for the Gold Coast of Africa where the skipper was to deliver a load of lumber. The *Kingsway,* a rusting, barnacle-infested hulk, was manned by a sullen, suspicious-looking crew and a captain named Lawry who lost control of his men.

The ship dropped anchor in Puerto Rico. Lawry went ashore and recruited a 23-year-old mulatto named Earl Battice who signed on as a cook. Battice insisted on taking his wife Lucia on the long voyage, but Lawry said no, reasoning that one woman among a crew of men would cause trouble. Battice refused to compromise and at length the captain, with trepidation, agreed to hire them both.

What Lawry did not realize was that his cook never intended to bring his wife aboard. It was his mistress Emilia Zamot, a poor Creole girl from the streets of San Juan that he wanted to take with him. The jealous wife got wind of this scheme, however, and drove the Creole from the ship.

The *Kingsway* slipped out of the harbor of San Juan on Dec. 15. Battice proved to be an excellent cook and his wife a pleasing addition to the crew. But after several weeks, Lucia became enamored with the burly German engineer Waldemar Karl Badke, whom everyone feared. They began conducting an affair, flagrantly, and without regard for the cuckolded mulatto cook.

The situation became intolerable for Battice, but there was little he could do. His fellow crewmen held him in low regard, and the captain was powerless to intervene, for Badke was feared and respected, and any attempt to thwart him might end in mutiny. Both captain and cook were effectively emasculated by the time the ship approached Monrovia.

Battice finally took matters into his own hands. On Feb. 4, 1927, he seized a razor and assaulted his wife in the storeroom where she was with Badke. It was a surprising gesture from one as docile and timid as Battice. The other crew members now felt some grudging respect for their cook, who was placed in irons by Captain Lawry. Lucia lingered on for seven days before succumbing to her wounds, but during that time, she confided to the captain that Battice had planned her murder in Puerto Rico. When she finally died, her body was dropped over the side of the ship.

Lawry completed his business in Monrovia and headed back to the U.S. amidst growing fears among the crewmen that Battice had placed a deadly curse over them all. Four men became violently ill from the food prepared by the new cook, an African tribesman named Codgo.

Lawry removed Battice's leg irons and returned him to the kitchen. The *Kingsway* reached the coast of the U.S. in August 1927. The year-long voyage, filled with so many perils, had at last ended and Battice was arrested and tried for second-degree murder. He received a ten-year sentence at the Federal Penitentiary in Atlanta.

REF.: *CBA;* Jackson, *The Portable Murder Book.*

Battisti, Cesare, 1875-1916, Italy, treas. Criticized the Austrian dictatorship in the pages of his newspaper *Il Popolo*. He fled to Italy in 1914 to join the Alpine chasseurs but was wounded, captured, and executed as a traitor by the Austrians. REF.: *CBA.*

Battus, John, 1785-1804, U.S., rape-mur. John Battus, a mulatto, attacked 14-year-old Salome Talbott in Canton, Mass., killing her after she threatened to expose him as a rapist. He confessed to the crime shortly after the body was discovered and, following a speedy trial, was hanged at Dedham, Mass., on Nov. 8, 1804.

REF.: *CBA; The Confession of John Battus.*

Bauer, William Joseph, 1926-   , U.S., jur. State's attorney for the Eighteenth Circuit Du Page County, Ill., from 1964-70, and U.S. attorney for Northern Illinois from 1970-71. He was appointed judge of the Court of the Northern District of Illinois by President Richard M. Nixon in 1971, and named to sit on the bench of the Seventh Circuit Court by President Gerald Ford in 1974. REF.: *CBA.*

Bauerdorf, Georgette, 1924-44, U.S., (unsolv.) mur. In 1944, Georgette Bauerdorf worked as a canteen hostess. She didn't need the money; her wealthy father, New York oil millionaire George F. Bauerdorf, kept an apartment for her at 8493 Fountain Avenue, just off Los Angeles' Sunset Boulevard. Bauerdorf thought life as a canteen junior hostess was romantic, and kept a diary describing her flirtations with servicemen. On Oct. 11, 1944, she went to work anticipating a rendezvous with her latest beau, Private Jerry Brown, in El Paso, Texas. Although she had an altercation with a soldier who wanted to dance with her against her wishes, Bauerdorf completed her shift, ate dinner, and returned to her apartment without further incident.

In the small hours of the morning, however, Bauerdorf was attacked and killed. Her partially clad body was found in her bathtub the next day. Police were not certain whether the killer had followed her home or entered through an upstairs window. The murderer had suffocated Bauerdorf with a towel and fled, taking only the car keys. The next day, the stolen auto, a 1936 coupe, was found ten miles away where the driver had ran out of gas.

The Bauerdorf murder remains a puzzle. The servicemen mentioned in her diary were investigated, but no viable leads have ever been discovered. REF.: *CBA.*

Bauf, Richard, c.1673-1702, Ire., rob.-mur. Little is known about the early life of Richard Bauf, one of the most notorious highwaymen in the history of the British Empire. His daring escapades might have never occurred if an Irish judge had exercised compassion early in the boy's life.

When Bauf was twelve, his parents were sentenced to hang from the highest "cross-timber" for robbery and murder. The judge, ignoring the boy's protests, ordered young Bauf to serve as executioner.

Left alone in the world, the young orphan picked pockets at country fairs, churches, and public meetings to earn a living. He later became a "grumet," or sneak-thief, entering the upper chambers of noblemen's houses and stealing gold, silver, and fine linens.

As a grown man, Dick Bauf became infamous as a highwayman. His familiar call of "stand and deliver" struck terror into many travelers. Bauf was indiscriminate in choosing his victims. One day he stopped General Richard Ingoldsby, supreme commander of the Irish military forces. When Ingoldsby refused to surrender his money, Bauf shot his horse, his footman, and groomsman. The general finally surrendered, but offered a reward of £500 for Bauf's arrest.

Fortune seekers from across the kingdom attempted to earn the reward. Bauf captured ten of these men, bound them inside a deserted country barn, and lit a fire in the hay. He then fled to Scotland, where he was eventually captured by an angry husband whose wife he had slept with. Bauf was sent back to Ireland to stand trial, where he unsuccessfully offered the government £5,000 in exchange for his freedom. On May 15, 1702, the cunning highwayman was hanged in chains on the Mount of Barnsmoor in Ulster.

REF.: *CBA;* Smith, *Highwaymen.*

Baugh, Andrew T., prom. 1880s, U.S., west. outl. A former Confederate officer, Andrew T. Baugh turned to cattle rustling in Georgia in the 1870s, and the early 1880s, he moved to Texas where he and a small band of rustlers continued to steal cattle. Baugh was captured in Texas by a posse of cowboys who interrupted Baugh and his men as they were driving a stolen herd of cows toward Mexico. He was hanged in 1885.

REF.: Bartholomew, *The Biographical Album of Western Gunfighters; CBA.*

Bauman, Arnold, 1914-   , U.S., jur. District attorney of New York County, N.Y., from 1945-47, U.S. attorney of the Southern District of New York from 1953-55, member of the Committee on Criminal Law, and appointed judge of the Court of the Southern District of New York by President Richard M. Nixon in 1971. REF.: *CBA.*

Baumes, Caleb Howard, 1863-1937, U.S., lawyer. Chairman of a New York joint legislative committee to draft revisions to the criminal codes and penal laws. Through his efforts several statutes were passed, notably the *Baumes Law* (1926), which mandated life imprisonment for those convicted of a felony or certain misdemeanors for the fourth time. REF.: *CBA.*

Baxter, Jeannie, b.1889, Case of, Brit., mansl. In his opening remarks to the jury the esteemed British lawyer Marshall Hall compared the life and times of young Jeannie Baxter to those of a character out of French fiction. "The pen of Zola and the brush of Hogarth" would be needed to adequately describe the facts in the case, he said.

The facts were these. In 1913 Baxter lived on Maida Vail, London, with her six-year-old daughter. She had an older lover who lived in the North Country, a married man who maintained her comfortably. At a London night club she met Julian Bernard Hall, a dashing young rake who lived near Piccadilly and loved the social scene. A former aviator who had flirted with death many times, he was also a hopeless drunk who played with guns when the mood suited him.

One night Jeannie's two lovers confronted each other in her small London flat. The staid, reserved man from the North Country reluctantly agreed to settle matters with pistols. Hall proposed that they light a cigarette and extinguish the lights in the flat in order to make it a "sporting" event. After several wild shots were fired, Baxter cried out for it to end. She then agreed to Hall's surprising marriage proposal and sent her other suitor away.

The fast-living playboy made many promises he could not keep, among them, the wedding date, Apr. 15, 1913, which passed by quietly without notice by Hall. The next day the distraught Baxter turned up at his Denman Street apartment, reminding him of his broken promise. They quarreled, and Hall pulled a pistol from the drawer, challenging her to take it from him.

She jarred the weapon loose from his grasp, and reached for it as it skittered across the floor. "I saw him bend down to pick up the revolver," she later told the jury. "I snatched it up and fired four times on the ceiling as rapidly as I could. I then rushed to the door and shouted, 'Jack has been shot'." Her lover was dead, and Baxter was charged with murder. Lawyer Hall pushed for an acquittal, but the jury found her Guilty of a reduced charge of manslaughter. She was given a three-year prison sentence.

REF.: Bowker, *Behind the Bar*; CBA; Hastings, *The Other Mr. Churchill*; Marjoribanks, *For The Defense, The Life of Sir Edward Marshall Hall*; Shew, *A Companion to Murder*.

Baxter, Richard, 1615-91, Brit., libel. Puritan, author, and religious reformer. He urged leniency for Charles I who faced execution in 1649 and argued for the rights of dissenters to remain in the Church of England. He was imprisoned by Chief Justice George Jeffreys for libeling the church in his published work *Paraphrase on the New Testament*. REF.: CBA.

Baxwell, James, prom. 20th Cent., Gibraltar, (wrong. convict.) mur. Baxwell was a middle-aged widower who lived with his pretty young daughter Betty on Gibraltar. They lived a life of comfort and ease, until William Katt, a business rival of Baxwell, began courting Betty in spite of her father's objections. When the young man asked to marry her, the father said no.

"I refuse your request," he said. "And lest you should entertain false hopes, permit me to add that no matter what happens I will not change my mind." James Baxwell soon showed he was a man of his word.

The situation became desperate when he decided to move back to London. Before the plans were drawn up, however, the girl mysteriously disappeared. By now the community was aware of the intransigence of the father. There was a great deal of suspicion on the part of the local people that Baxwell murdered his daughter and hid the body in a nearby cave he used for storage. When fragments of her torn dress were found, Baxwell was indicted for murder. The poignant testimony of Katt aroused considerable sympathy and helped seal the doom of the father.

Baxwell's persistent claim that he was innocent failed to move the jury, which returned a Guilty verdict. Seconds before the execution by hanging, Katt emerged from the crowd of onlookers with a startling confession. Torn by guilt, the young businessman cried that Betty was alive and was hidden away by their mutual agreement. Baxwell was cut down, but the shock was too much for his heart. He collapsed and died from coronary failure. Betty came out of hiding and entered a convent. Katt was sentenced to penal servitude.

REF.: CBA; Ellis, *Black Fame*.

Bayan, prom. 14th Cent., Mongolia, polit. corr. Instituted stringent anti-Chinese policies upon assuming control of the government from Emperor Togon-Timur. His desire to exterminate the Chinese race led to bloody revolts. He was deposed in 1339. REF.: CBA.

Bayard, James Asheton, 1767-1815, U.S., lawyer. Member of Congress from 1797-1813. REF.: CBA.

Bayer, Widow, d.1879, Fr., (unsolv.) mur. An elderly woman who ran a shop where she sold butter and eggs, the Widow Bayer was found murdered on May 30, 1879. Paris police found the widow strangled and the shop robbed. Her body bore bruises that had come, police concluded, from repeated kicks from someone wearing shoes without heels. Inspector Alfred Morain suspected a couple named Ka, who lived area, of having done the deed, especially since the man wore shoes without heels. Both man and wife had been seen in or about the shop only hours before the Widow Bayer was found dead but evidence that could bring about an arrest, let alone a conviction, was lacking. Morain found satisfaction in reporting later that "the woman died of congestion in a gutter at Les Halles" and that "the man was later shut up in a lunatic asylum."

REF.: CBA; Morain, *The Underworld of Paris*; Nash, *Open Files*.

Baylanch, Autry, 1894-1925, and **Baylanch, Jes**, b.1897, and **Baylanch, Gee**, b.1872, U.S., boot.-rape-mur. Deep in the Rutherford Mountains in Kentucky, the hill people still talk about Gee Baylanch and his brawling, hard-drinking clan. During the 1920s, the lawless family sold moonshine and killed anyone who tried to stop them.

When a neighbor of the Baylanches named Bing Tarter began to encroach on their whiskey-making empire, Gee volunteered to be deputized. In the company of Deputy Cleo Parks they gunned down Tarter in cold blood, a crime the mountain people did not forgive.

The Baylanch boys, Autry and Jes, grew up in Brake County. Jes raped the pretty young wife of Nuland Merton one night, and, fearing Jes might come back, the outraged husband of the victim maintained a bedside vigil, armed with a shotgun.

"I've heard it said that back there on the mountain if they found somebody riding a pretty nice horse they'd just dump his body over that cliff and take his horse," recalled one neighbor. The Baylanches were mean-spirited feudists, part of a wild, unrestrained, lawless class of people who casually thumbed their noses at society's conventions.

REF.: CBA; Montell, *Killings*.

Baylanch, Oren, 1904-30, U.S., mur. The son of Frank Baylanch and a cousin of the infamous hill clan, young Oren Baylanch showed early signs that he would live a quiet life. But, like his notorious family he loved the taste of liquor and the company of loose women. Baylanch lived near Brownsville, Ky. His favorite haunt on a Saturday night was Trish Pannings' whorehouse, located in Hemp Hollow.

On Oct. 4, 1930, Oren and five friends paid a call on the Pannings establishment to select a few women for their evening's entertainment. The men quarreled over one of the women and in the brawl that followed, Oren killed Ben Talbot, to whom he was distantly related, and was then shot dead by the man's brother, Lug. Oren and Ben were buried side by side in the Baylanch family plot. Lug Talbot was convicted of voluntary manslaughter and sent to the Kentucky State Penitentiary for fifteen years. After his release he committed suicide. See: **Baylanch, Autry**.

REF.: CBA; Montell, *Killings*.

Bayle, Blodwen, 1932- , Case of, Brit., mur. In the town of Swansea, Wales, lived a shy, withdrawn housewife named Blodwen Bayle. Her husband Frank was a philandering n'er-do-well who carried on an affair with his young secretary Doreen Soupton while Blodwen cared for her three teenaged daughters from a prior marriage, Susan, Sarah, and Sheila.

Frank had married Blodwen in 1959, with her parents' approval, because he seemed like a responsible, caring man. They were fooled. When Bayle tired of her he began dating other women openly and without regard for the feelings of his stepdaughters. Blodwen's marital problems worsened. She began counseling sessions with her church vicar, meeting him once a week. After some trepidation she confessed a deep secret to him one day in 1978. Her husband Frank had sexually seduced the three girls, she said, and since they were over the age of eighteen, and had not been coerced, she believed there was little to do but remain silent about it. "But Frank ran away with Miss Soupton," the churchman said, reiterating what everyone in Swansea believed when Bayle dropped out of sight in September 1975.

"No," Blodwen said. "Doreen Soupton simply left town to take another job. I told everyone that Frank had gone with her. But it wasn't true. Frank is lying somewhere at the bottom of the

Bristol Channel, or what is left of him by now. It's been over two and a half years."

Soft-spoken Blodwen had put fifty sleeping pills in his evening meal, and then when she was satisfied that his pulse had stopped, she dumped him over the side of a cliff. A jury was so moved by her plight that the 47-year-old mother was found innocent because of extenuating circumstances.

REF.: *CBA*; Dunning, *The Arbor House Treasury of True Crime*.

Bayley, James, and **Reynolds, Thomas**, prom. 1736, Brit., vandal. James Bayley and another man, Thomas Reynolds, were indicted at the Old Bailey on Apr. 10, 1736, for tearing down a tollgate at Ledbury. This act of vandalism was punishable under the terms of the Black Act which made it a capital offense to appear in disguise bearing arms. Reynolds was hanged, but Bayley earned a reprieve.

REF.: *CBA*; Mencken, *By The Neck*.

Bayly, William Alfred, 1906-34, N. Zea., mur. Ever since William Bayly's father sold his farm in Ruawaro, N. Zea., to Samuel Pender Lakey, there had been bad blood. Then Bayly bought property next to the Lakey dairy farm and moved in. At first their petty disputes involved land boundaries and sheep-grazing rights, but over the years the problems took on more serious overtones. "You won't see the next season out, Lakey!" Bayly threatened on one occasion.

The threat was not an idle one. On Oct. 16, 1933, Mrs. Christobel Lakey was found floating face-down in a duck pond. Her husband had disappeared, and Bayly volunteered a possible solution to the police. He said that the couple had been quarreling a lot lately, and that Samuel had probably murdered his wife and then run away. The police were suspicious. They searched William Bayly's property and uncovered evidence of a body. Bone fragments were scattered piecemeal on the farm. They also found Lakey's watch and cigarette lighter. Blood in Bayly's tool shed was clear evidence of recent foul play.

Despite his denials, Bayly was found Guilty of murder in a month-long trial in Auckland. He was executed at the Mount Eden jail on July 30, 1934, just a few days after his twenty-eighth birthday.

REF.: *CBA*; Simpson, *The Anatomy of Murder*; Rowland, *More Criminal Files*; Wilson, *Encyclopedia of Murder*.

Baynes, Andrew, c.1685-1711, Brit., rob. Baynes was so unsuccessful at housebreaking that he decided he had to change careers. Twice arrested and convicted of breaking and entering, he was reprieved both times. The second robbery was committed in the home of the Earl of Westmoreland, from which Baynes stole fine damask curtains, Parliamentary robes, and gold medallions valued at £500. Only his willingness to return the merchandise saved him from the gallows.

Andrew Baynes then became a "footpad," or robber of pedestrians. His favorite method was to stop a victim, steal his belongings, and tie him to a tree naked. Once he and his gang stopped a tailor named Archer near Highgate. Baynes knew him well, since the tailor had recently mended one of his garments. When Archer reminded him of their acquaintance, Baynes leveled a pistol at him and replied, "Yes. I know you well enough, and therefore I'm resolved to send you home like a gentleman, for you shall have no money in your pockets." Baynes bound him to a tree and set his bulldog upon him.

Near Kentish Town, Baynes and his fellow travelers stopped three Quaker women. They had only twelve shillings and two guineas among them. The men stripped the women, bound them to a tree, and prepared to rape them. Baynes, however, stopped them. "The spirit moves me to show no favor here to these female hypocrites," he said haughtily, "who we'll leave in the dark till their own light conducts them to a better place." It was perhaps the only time Baynes exhibited any degree of compassion for his victims. The courts were not inclined to show Baynes any compassion. Robbery was an offense punishable by death, and Baynes was hanged at Tyburn in 1711.

REF.: *CBA*; Smith, *Highwaymen*.

Bazelon, David L., 1909- , U.S., jur. Member of the board of directors of the National Council on Crime and Delinquency. Author of many scholarly papers dealing with criminal justice including *The Imperative to Punish* and *Beyond Control of the Juvenile Court*. He was appointed judge of the Circuit Court in Washington, D.C., by President Harry S. Truman in 1949. REF.: *CBA*.

Beach, Lewis U., d.1885, U.S., mur. Though he confessed to the murder just after his wife was brutally slain, Lewis Beach later retracted his statement, offering no other story to explain the extensive incriminating evidence or his earlier admission of guilt.

On Apr. 7, 1884, Beach, an Altoona, Pa., surgeon, walked into the house of his brother-in-law, Levi Knott, at 6:30 a.m. to say, "Levi, Mary is dead. I have killed her. You will find her down there lying in her blood. You may shoot me if you like." Deciding to first deliver his relative to the police to be locked up, Knott stopped on the way at the home of another sister, Mrs. Willis Fleck, to tell her the news. Mrs. Fleck then went alone to her sister's residence and discovered the badly mutilated corpse. The front door, walls, and floors of the parlor and bedroom were splattered with blood, indicating the fierce and prolonged struggle that had taken place. Near the head, which was almost severed from the body, were two surgeon's knives, ten and five inches long, and a kitchen cleaver. The imprint of the murdered woman's hand was found on the front door near the latch, probably made when she attempted to reach the street to get help. The fatal wound was a thirteen-inch gash in her neck, with numerous other cuts on her hands and arms.

The Altoona mayor, Mr. Howard, had been sworn in to hear Beach's first official confession, and testified at the trial that the doctor said he and his wife had had a mild argument during the night and that at about five o'clock he had awakened to find her with a knife sticking out of her throat. In his efforts to remove it he had enlarged the wound. The jury visited the accused in his cell and heard the doctor repeat the story he had told Howard, denying that he had admitted his guilt to Knott. Beach explained that his wife had said to him, "Dearie, I am dying," and claimed he had no idea how the knives got out of his case. He said he had no trousers on at the time of the murder. Evidence at the trial included those trousers, heavily stained with his wife's blood. The jury found him Guilty of the slaying and he was executed by hanging in Hollidaysburg, Pa., on Feb. 12, 1885, in front of a large crowd of spectators. REF.: *CBA*.

Beadle, William, d.1783, U.S., suic.-mur. The fact that farmer William Beadle of Wethersfield, Mass., was not in his right mind, was evident from his behavior in the last five years of his life. The man was given to sullen periods of long silence, and when he did speak, his words formed an almost incoherent babble. He made a hardscrabble living but seldom complained. He began to take an ax and a carving knife to bed with him at night, fingering the edge of the knife for several minutes in pensive silence. His wife Lydia was apparently a trusting soul since she raised no objections to her husband's eccentric behavior nor did she feel any apprehensions, although she described her spouse's actions to a few friends.

At dawn on Dec. 11, 1873, William Beadle awoke next to his implements of death and, before his family awakened, went from bed to bed, killing his four children and then his wife. He then slit his own throat.

REF.: *CBA*; Marsh, *The Great Sin and Danger of Striving with God*; *A Narrative of the Life of William Beadle*; Nash, *Bloodletters and Badmen*.

Beagles, David Ervin, prom. 1971, U.S., rape-mur. On Feb. 8, 1969, at about 10:20 p.m., a couple driving just outside Tallahassee, Fla., saw a woman staggering toward them, badly beaten and screaming for help. Fearful of getting involved, the couple drove away and called the police. Officers, headed by Sheriff Raymond Hamlin, Jr. and Lt. Larry Campbell arrived on the scene eleven minutes later, finding a parked Mustang and, in the bushes, a woman's purse, its contents intact. Twenty yards away they found a shallow, newly dug grave containing the still warm body of 30-year-old Betty Jean Houston, her face bruised and battered as a result of gunshot wounds from a .22-caliber automatic. She also had been severely beaten and grotesquely mutilated with a heavy glass insulator that lay nearby. The police sent for information on the Mustang's license plates, dusted the car for prints, and examined a small train case they found in the back seat. From a racing track form and train ticket stubs marked "Jacksonville to Tallahassee," they reasoned that Houston had gone out of town to the sports event, then began hitchhiking home from the train station. She had been picked up and taken to a deserted lane in the woods where she was raped and beaten and left for dead, but she somehow had managed to get up and stumble to the highway. The Mustang's license number belonged to David Beagles.

Sheriff Hamlin remembered Beagles as a man he had captured and helped convict in the 1959 gang-rape of a Tallahassee college student. Sentenced to life imprisonment in 1959, his exemplary behavior in jail had won him a parole in 1967. Now, two years later, Hamlin arrested Beagles again, this time on a charge of first-degree murder. After leaving his supposedly dead victim, Beagles had returned to gather up and dispose of her clothing, and, finding her still alive, had killed her. He had almost finished burying her when he saw police approaching and ran off. Beagles was apprehended in River Junction, Fla., and sentenced, again, to life in the Florida State Prison on Oct. 17, 1969. REF.: *CBA*.

Beal, Fred Erwin, b.1896, U.S., mob vio.-mur. A prolonged strike at a North Carolina textile mill in 1929 led to a fight in the night that left the local police chief dead and three of his officers wounded.

Fred Beal was one of many Gastonia, N.C., workers long dissatisfied with conditions at the textile mill. He had joined the Communist party and participated in a strike that had gone on for months. There was deep ill-will between the strikers and the police, and, on the night of June 7, 1929, a fight broke out in the dark. When it was over Gastonia Chief of Police Orville F. Aderholt was dead and three policemen were wounded. Of fifty persons arrested, sixteen were brought to trial. Charged with murder and conspiracy were thirteen men and three women, most of them students. A crowd of 200 spectators—mostly women with babies—mill workers and students came to sit in the 90-degree heat to hear the proceedings. The trial was moved to Charlotte as defense counsel Tom P. Jimison requested that the trial be moved from the atmosphere of vengeance and tension that pervaded Gastonia, exemplified at one point when a mob in Charlotte began shouting, "Get Tom Jimison and string him up!"

The courtroom theatrics were covered in the national press. One exhibit of the prosecution, headed by John G. Carpenter, involved a large cart wheeled before the jurors. When the covering was taken off, a life-sized wax dummy of the murdered police chief was revealed. Perhaps as a result of tactics like this, one of the jurymen, Joseph Campbell, broke down, was judged by a doctor to be suffering from "acute emotional insanity," and was removed to a padded cell.

A new trial opened before the same judge, Justice Victor Maurice Barnhill, in late September, following a mistrial. The prosecution had reduced the charges to second-degree murder, and there were now only nine defendants instead of the original sixteen. Beal, who had been hailed by the Communist press as a hero, denied his political principles, claiming he had been on the floor of a shack when Aderholt was shot. Prosecutor Carpenter exhorted the jurors to remember that the union headquarters in Gastonia was "not a cross section of hell, but a whole section of hell! There was immorality there. Yes, *immorality*! Hugging and kissing in public." After an hour of deliberation the jury found Beal and his six co-defendants Guilty as charged. Judge Barnhill sentenced Beal and three defendants to serve seventeen to twenty years in the North Carolina State Prison. REF.: *CBA*.

Beale, George P., and **Baker, George**, prom. 1865, U.S., rob.-mur. Both George Beale and George Baker were professional thieves who heard that Daniel Delaney kept large amounts of money in his home in Salem, Ore. On the night of Jan. 9, 1865,

Beale and Baker went to Delaney's home, and while Beale called Delaney from his house, Baker lay in ambush and shot Delaney as he emerged. Both men ransacked the house and stole what money was there. Before leaving the premises, Baker, the blood lust upon him, spotted Delaney's dog barking in the yard and shot and killed the animal, too. Suspicions were aroused when the two men began to spend money freely in a local tavern and were seen wearing some clothes the victim was known to have owned. Following the discovery of Delaney's corpse, both Beale and Baker were arrested just as they were about to leave town. They were tried, convicted, and hanged in Salem on May 17, 1865.

REF.: *CBA; Confessions of George P. Beale and George Baker*.

Beall, Edward (AKA: The Black Prince), prom. 1895-1900, Brit., fraud. A solicitor who became part of a banking scheme that defrauded the public out of more than £30,000, Beall claimed he was merely a conduit for the cash.

Known as The Black Prince, he rode in a fancy coach with four black horses, Edward Beall, a solicitor for twenty years, was arrested along with cohorts William James Carruthers Wain, a civil engineer, Thomas Lambert, a director, and Charles Singleton, a financial agent, in June 1899. The charges were issuing a false prospectus, conspiracy to fraud, making false returns, and obtaining money and securities under false pretenses. In 1893 the four men had opened The London and Scottish Banking and Discount Corporation, Ltd., a supposedly international firm that existed mostly on paper. Claiming a capitalization of £102,000, the company advertised a prospectus offering founders' shares for sale, and placed ads in prestigious financial magazines. Describing themselves as a bank of good position and standing, offering a variety of appealing investments and guarantees, the company circulated pamphlets and faked profits to declare dividends, ultimately bilking investors of more than £30,000. Their subsidiary companies included the British Steam and the London Refuse Steam companies, and part of their assets consisted of a patented dust destruction process which purported to turn household and street garbage into electricity without burning a pound of coal. When civil suits against them reached huge proportions, they were finally arrested and tried.

In the fifteen-day trial that took place at the Old Bailey before Mr. Justice Channel and a jury, Beall said he was only the "conduit pipe" for the passage of money. Channel said he was the brains of the operation and Singleton's work amounted to "frequently signing his name." Only Lambert was acquitted. Beall's solicitor's license was revoked when he was found Guilty, along with Singleton and Wain. Beall disappeared from business dealings for several years, resurfacing again in 1904 to be prosecuted for inciting a clerk to steal papers from a city solicitor's office, papers he intended to use for a blackmailing scheme. In 1914 Beall again was arrested for conspiracy to extort money—with four other men, he had blackmailed directors and company promoters into paying him for not publishing defamatory articles in a financial journal he controlled. Justice Darling sentenced Beall to five years of penal servitude.

REF.: *CBA*; Marjoribanks, *For the Defense, The Life of Sir Edward Marshall Hall*; Nicholls, *Crime Within the Square Mile*.

Beall, John Yates, 1835-65, U.S., treas. Seized in Canada in 1864 as a Confederate spy, he was executed on the gallows by the Union army. REF.: *CBA*.

Beamer, George N., 1904-74, U.S., jur. Prosecuting attorney in South Bend, Ind., from 1939-41 and attorney general of Indiana from 1943-44. He was appointed judge of the court of the Northern District of Indiana by President John F. Kennedy in 1962. REF.: *CBA*.

Bean, Harold Walter, 1939-   , U.S., mur. Describing his scheme to get rid of a wealthy elderly widow, Harold Walter Bean told a cohort, "We've added another round to our bag of tricks... Murder."

Dorothy Polulach, an 81-year-old widow, lived quietly as a recluse in her expensive South West Side Chicago home, which was barricaded with locks and elaborate security systems to protect her costly antiques and jewelry. One afternoon in mid-February 1981, a man in priest's garb stopped to talk with her as she shoveled snow off her front walk, suggesting that a lady her age should have help, and offering to bring someone to assist her soon. On Feb. 17 the priest returned with a companion. Recognizing the one man, Polulach let them in. Bean, disguised as a priest, began to beat the elderly woman, who fought back. His accomplice, Robert Byron, also called "Spook," quickly filled his briefcase with jewelry and ransacked the house for other valuables, for the killing was intended to look like a robbery. Bean knocked Polulach down, then handcuffed her and dragged her upstairs, shackling her ankles and breaking her glasses before putting a .38-caliber pistol to her head and shooting her twice. Her body was discovered three days later by Phyllis Mahl and her husband. Mahl called Polulach's stepdaughter, Ann Polulach Walters, in Fort Lauderdale, Fla., to tell her of her stepmother's death. Though Walters appeared shocked, actually she had hired Bean to murder Polulach as she would inherit as much as $750,000 and the Polulach home when her father's second wife died.

Detectives Tom Ptak and Mike Duffin took over the case. Mahl told them that Walters was exhibiting strange behavior, like hiding pastries at the funeral services and finding mysterious messages in the wake register. Then a man named Jimmy Steele was heard to brag in a Cicero tavern about the slaying, saying the victim had been shot twice in the head—information only the killer could know. Ptak and Duffin questioned Steele, learning that he was the stepson of Harold Bean. Steele then confessed that he had rented the priest's outfit for Bean and had heard him talking to an attorney about Walter's potential inheritance. Bean, a master of disguise and a criminal since he was sixteen, had once hidden from the FBI for six years. With these leads, the detectives went to visit Walters, now enmeshed in witchcraft rituals to exorcise her murdered stepmother's spirit, and asked her to look at some mug shots, including one of Bean.

Walters' response was, "You know the whole thing, don't you?" She and her husband, Wayne Walters, confessed and were charged with murder and conspiracy on Apr. 5, 1981. Bean was arrested in a remote area of the Palos Hills Forest Preserve on Apr. 25, and Byron soon after, charged with helping Bean break into the Polulach home. Robert Danny Egan, who drove the getaway car, testified against Byron and Bean and received a seven-year prison term for his part in the crime. In October 1981 Bean and Byron were convicted of murder and sentenced by Judge James M. Bailey to die in the electric chair. Walters pleaded guilty to plotting the murder and was sentenced to 25 years in prison. Wayne Walters received a seven-year prison sentence for conspiracy. REF.: *CBA*.

Bean, Robert M., prom. 1890s, U.S., mur. Robert Bean and Samuel Hagar, an engineer, were part of a political argument involving several men in Nashville, Tenn. The argument erupted into a brawl and Bean began shooting at Hagar who fired back in what became a gun battle along the street, with both men running down several blocks firing at each other. Hagar was hit five times and died of his wounds. At his trial in 1893, Bean insisted that he was only trying to stop the argument. The first trial ended with a hung jury. At a second trial, Bean's role of peacemaker was not accepted by the jury and he was convicted of second-degree murder, and sentenced to twenty years at hard labor.

REF.: *CBA; Speech of Noah W. Cooper in the Bean Murder Case.*

Bean, Roy, c.1823-1903, U.S., jur. Nothing was orthodox about Roy Bean, and little in his life qualified him to sit in judgment of others, yet this uneducated, colorful, and contrary man set himself up as the only "law West of the Pecos" in Langtry, Texas, and ruled this dust-blown hamlet with harshness and humor for twenty years. Bean's background was hazy at best, but it is known that he was born about 1823 in a crude cabin along the Ohio River in Mason County, Ky. His parents, Francis and Anna Bean, were uneducated hill people who barely scraped a living from the wildness and young Roy, having little, soon developed a taste for the finer things of life. His brothers, Sam and Josh, left home

first, Sam going to Mexico where he later fought in the Mexican-American War and, still later, settling in Dona Ana County, N.M., becoming its first sheriff. Josh went further, traveling to California where he became the first mayor of San Diego. He was murdered in 1852. Roy Bean left the hardscrabble life in Kentucky while in his teens, seeking his fortune in Mexico with his brother Sam.

Judge Roy Bean, the only "Law West of the Pecos."

Both arrived in Chihuahua in 1848 and there got into an argument with a drunken Mexican cowboy who reportedly drew a knife of young Roy, who pulled a pistol and, with one shot, drilled a bullet into his antagonist's forehead. To the Americans in Chihuahua the killing was self-defense, but local authorities labeled Bean's shooting murder and Roy fled to California where he worked for his brother Josh briefly, ran a saloon, joined the California Rangers and, when his brother was slain in 1852, fled once more, this time going to Mesilla, N. M. Roy later told the tale that he had fought a duel on horseback in San Diego and left that town after killing his opponent. He also said, some years later, that he stole a beautiful Spanish girl from her Mexican lover near the Mission of San Gabriel outside Los Angeles. The boyfriend and his friends supposedly lynched Roy Bean for his transgressions and left him to dangle but he was cut down by the sweetheart and escaped with rope burns around his neck.

During the Civil War, Bean organized a guerilla band which he dubbed The Free Rovers, a group of scavengers that ostensibly robbed from wealthy landowners and converted the loot into supplies for the Confederacy. Bean's group, however, was considered to be nothing more than a band of rustlers and robbers who stole in the name of the southern cause. Following the war, Bean moved to San Antonio, Texas, where, for eighteen years, he enmeshed himself in a myriad of money-producing schemes that produced little or no money. He worked as a butcher, a dairy operator, a saloon-keeper, and a freighter. Bean was in and out of court so often, pressing claims and mostly losing, that he became a regular fixture in the San Antonio courthouse. In the course of his many suits, the unschooled, almost illiterate Bean learned much about the law, knowledge he would later put to effective use. During this long dry spell, Bean wed a child-bride, Virginia Chavez. After bearing two sons and two daughters for the hard-drinking, easy living Bean, Virginia left her failed husband.

Bean, however, saw the advance of the railroads as his opportunity and he followed the railhead as it worked across West Texas, first at Vinagaroon where he was appointed a justice of the peace by the drunken road-gang workers he befriended and who were impressed with Bean's law-spouting speeches. When Vinagaroon died, Bean moved on with the Southern Pacific, getting off at a desolate spot called Langtry. Here Bean established his little empire that was to win him fame across the state of Texas and earn him a lasting, if curious, lore as one of the strangest judges of the West. Bean later claimed that he named the tiny town of Langtry, a half-dozen broken down shacks that butted up against the rail line, after the popular British actress. Bean saw a picture of the "Jersey Lily" in a magazine and exclaimed: "By gobs, what a purty critter!" He kept the magazine clipping until the day he died, nailing it to the wall of his saloon where it faded and yellowed year after year.

Armed with a copy of the Revised Statutes of Texas, 1879 edition, Bean got himself appointed justice of the peace in Langtry on Aug. 2, 1882, occupying a twenty-by-fourteen-foot shack adorned with signs that read: "Judge Roy Bean, Notary Public," "Justice of the Peace," "Law West of the Pecos," and "Ice Beer." The place was entitled with another prominent sign, reading: "The Jersey Lilly," named after Bean's heart-throb, Lily Langtry. The sign was misspelled by a illiterate sign-painter who worked off one of Bean's notorious fines by painting the signs while drunk.

Bean's actions as a judge became more and more eccentric. He once found a body with forty dollars in gold and a pistol in one of the dead man's pockets. He fined the corpse forty dollars for carrying a concealed weapon and pocketed the money. Bean would officiate at any occasion, for a price, of course. He charged $2 for inquests, and there were many of these in Langtry where everyone carried weapons and fired first and talked later, if anyone was left alive to talk. For weddings and divorces, Bean charged $5 for each ceremony. He had no right, of course, to grant divorces and when challenged on one of these actions, he snorted: "I guess I got a right to unmarry 'em if it don't take." His wedding ceremonies were somber affairs and Bean usually rushed through the traditional rites. When he finished he would invariably stare long and hard at the groom and state: "And may God have mercy on your soul," a comment usually reserved for those who had been condemned to death.

Judge Bean, sitting on porch wearing sombrero, trying a horse thief at Langtry, Texas, 1900.

The judge was as concerned about selling his liquor as he was about dispensing justice. Before any important court hearing, Bean would suggest that everyone buy "a good snort" to liven up the proceedings. Though he was supposedly loved by children and animals, Bean was a harsh man with a dark humor who favored white citizens and considered all others worthless. On one occasion a railroad worker who had shot a Chinese laborer was brought before him. Bean leafed through his one law book briefly and then looked up and said: "There ain't a damned law here that says it's illegal to shoot a Chinaman! Defendant is discharged."

Of course, Bean bent over backwards for anyone who worked for the railroad since the Southern Pacific made a regular stop at his small town. The railroad was the only source of supplies and business, especially when trains stopped long enough to allow passengers to visit The Jersey Lilly, and buy a few drinks. The inside of the place was part saloon and part court with a small back room where Bean slept. If any customer got drunk in the courtroom area instead of the saloon, Bean promptly fined the offender.

Lily Langtry remained Bean's lifelong obsession. No one could bring up her name in his ramshackled saloon without buying a drink and toasting her picture which was behind the bar. When the actress toured America in 1888, Bean traveled to a San Antonio theater to see her, wearing his best suit and a battered top hat, paying a staggering price for a front-row customer. He sat bug-eyed throughout the performance but did not have the courage to visit the actress backstage later. When Bean returned to tell his tale of seeing the actress, he called for a week-long celebration. The judge's reign was interrupted twice, in 1886 and in 1896 when elections he claimed were rigged put others in his place. Bean, however, continued to win the post of justice of the peace and by the turn of the century his legendary character and judicial decisions had reached eastward, drawing hundreds of visitors to the dusty town of Langtry just to get a glimpse of Bean sitting on the porch of his establishment, meting out justice to drunks, wife-beaters, and rowdies.

Even Lily Langtry finally came to visit the famous judge in 1903 but her most ardent fan was by then dead. Bean had gone into San Antonio on Mar. 15, 1903, where he witnessed a cockfight in the Mexican quarter. So aroused by the blood sport was he that he went on an extended bender and was taken back to his shack in Langtry in an almost comatose state. He lingered in his back room for some hours, unable to recognize his own son, Sam, who had ridden a horse to death to get to his father's deathbed. He died on Mar. 16, 1903. Toward the end of the year, Lily Langtry alighted from a passenger train and toured Bean's miserable shack, which still bore her picture over the bar. The natives gave her the judge's pet bear which had been chained for years to Bean's bed, but the animal ran off once it was released. Then Lily was given the judge's revolver which she took home with her to England where she placed it on a mantle to remind her of the "strange little man in America" who loved her and who never met her.

Bean was buried in Del Rio, Texas, with little pomp. His children were present and his daughter, fifty years later, objected to the critical stories about her father, stating in his defense: "The only thing about Papa that anybody could object to was that he was a Republican and favored a high tariff...He was a wonderfully kind, good and gentle father...And he was a honest, fair and impartial judge." Judge Roy Bean was also one of the most unusual jurists ever seen in the annals of the West.

REF.: Anderson, *History of New Mexico*; Bancroft, *History of California*, Vol 6; Bartholomew, *The Biographical Album of Western Gunfighters*; Bell, *Reminiscences of a Ranger*; _____, *On the Old West Coast*; Burns, *The Robin Hood of El Dorado*; Bushick, *Glamorous Days*; CBA; Chabot, *With the Makers of San Antonio*; Clift, *History of Maysville and Mason County*; Horan and Sann, *Pictorial History of the Wild West*; James, *Frontier and Pioneer Recollections of Early Days in San Antonio and West Texas*; Langtry, *The Days I Knew*; Lloyd, *Law West of the Pecos*; McDaniel, *Vinagaroon*; Mills, *Forty Years at El Paso*; Raht, *The Romance of the Davis Mountains and the Big Bend County*; Rosa and May, *Gun Law*; Santleben, *A Texas Pioneer*; Smythe, *History of San Diego*; Sonnichsen, *The Story of Roy Bean, Law West of the Pecos*; (FILM), *The Westerner*, 1940; *The Life and Times of Judge Roy Bean*, 1972.

Bean, Sawney (or **Beane**, AKA: **Cunningham, Sandy**), prom. 1430s, Scot., can.-mur. Bean, born in Edinburgh to poor parents, grew up despising the hard work his father performed as a ditcher. He grew up a petty thief and in his youth seduced a girl but refused to marry her. The girl's parents brought charges and Bean fled with the girl to the wilds of the Scottish coast, settling in an enormous cave near Galloway. He fathered several children and they, in incestuous turn, fathered more children until forty-eight of the clan were living in the caverns along the rocky coastline. They preyed on strangers traveling the roads for decades, killing them for their belongings, but this did not come to the attention of the authorities since the Bean family dragged away the corpses and cannibalized them. Though scores of travelers vanished, search parties found no trace of the missing people.

Scottish cannibal and mass murderer Sawney Bean.

Then, in 1435, Bean and several of his family members attacked a man and woman traveling on the main road toward Edinburgh. They overtook the cart and attacked the couple, knocking them senseless with clubs. Just as they were disemboweling the woman, a large group of cavalrymen thundered down the road and interrupted the blood-soaked cannibals. There was a pitched battle and the Beans were finally driven off but not pursued. The captain of the king's guard feared that he would be overwhelmed by the sheer numbers of the cannibals and he reported back to King James IV. The king mustered an army of more than 500 men, infantry and cavalry, and he led this contingent into the foul-smelling Galloway caverns where the troops subdued the fierce Bean family but only at the cost of twenty soldiers.

The caverns were huge and stretched on for several miles, offering their own fresh water supply in the the form of small pools. In each cavern the soldiers found mounds of clothing, jewelry, implements, parts of carts and carriages—the loot of many lifetimes—taken from the Bean victims. Also, to their horror, the troops found scores of bodies, or pieces of bodies, cured like hams or strung up like sides of beef, male and female, adult and child. The main cave was a giant butcher shop where human cadavers had been dismembered, smoked, salted, and hung out to dry in preparation for the next meal. King James ordered the entire clan brought back to Leith in chains. Once there, Bean and his family were summarily sentenced to death for their heinous crimes. Thousands watched as the Bean family members were led into the main square. Here the males were butchered as they had butchered, having their genitals, hands, and feet cut off and allowed to bleed to death in front of their women. Then three great fires were built and the women were thrown alive into the roaring blazes to perish in screaming agony.

REF.: *CBA*; Howe, *Scoundrels, Fiends and Human Monsters*; Nash,

Almanac of World Crime; Wilson, *Encyclopedia of Murder.*

Bean, Thomas Lee, 1945- , U.S., rape-mur. Thomas Bean was not a normal boy. "The kid seemed to have a mean streak in him. He used to tear birds apart and make my kid sick," recalled Mrs. Hugo Cavilli, a one-time neighbor of the Bean family in Reno, Nev. "A normal boy just doesn't go around doing that sort of thing."

Bean was a neglected child shuttled around the country by his nomadic parents who had a hard time making ends meet. His father, Elza Bean, was a traveling salesman who claimed to be an ordained minister of the Nazarene Church but was, for the most part, a ne'er-do-well without a congregation.

In 1961 Bean was sent to a youth reformatory in Elko, Nev., for criminally assaulting a young woman in Salt Lake City, Utah. Upon his release a year later, Bean was unable to establish any relationships with women. He lurked about the neighborhood near his Reno home, pilfering women's underclothing from clotheslines in order to attain gratification for his insatiable but perverted sex drive. As he later admitted: "It's been a childhood dream to rape a girl... I have always wanted to kill." On the night of Apr. 5, 1963, his fantasy became a grisly reality.

The victim was 24-year-old Sonja McCaskie, a divorced mother of two who had represented England in the 1960 Olympics at Squaw Valley. Sonja was shy and withdrawn, but was a proficient downhill ski instructor at Slide Mountain. She enjoyed jazz, classical music, and literary works, but, by contrast, her slayer was barely literate.

Bean was drawn to McCaskie's brick duplex apartment on Yuri Avenue in Reno shortly after midnight. He had never met Sonja, but noticed the laundry which she had hung to dry before retiring for the evening. Finding the door unlocked, Bean entered, armed with a butcher knife and a spool of baling rope. McCaskie awoke and pleaded for mercy, hoping that the attacker would spare the life of a working mother. Bean, in a trance, was uninterested in the woman's plight. He killed her and spent the next five and a half hours disemboweling the corpse.

Police discovered McCaskie's remains when the babysitter of her year-old son became alarmed at her disappearance. The crime appalled even the most seasoned police officers on the Reno force. Chief Elmer Briscoe took three men into custody, including a University of Nebraska professor whom Sonja had named in a paternity suit. Polygraph tests failed to incriminate these men.

Hugo Cavelli, recalling Bean's passion for expensive European cars, notified the district attorney when he discovered McCaskie had driven a TR-3 sportscar. Nine days after discovery of the body, Bean was arrested. At the police station he broke loose and fled, pursued by police officers firing guns. Recaptured, Bean asked regretfully, "Why didn't you kill me?"

He admitted his guilt, reconstructing his movements on the night of the murder for the district attorney and a court reporter. Bean was convicted of murder and sentenced to death, remaining on Nevada's Death Row for years. Before his appeals were exhausted, the Supreme Court abolished the death penalty. In 1980, after nearly seventeen years in prison, Bean remained in maximum security, his request for parole denied by a unanimous vote. REF.: *CBA*.

Beard, Arthur, prom. 1919, Brit., mur. A notable criminal trial involved night watchman Arthur Beard, who raped and strangled 13-year-old Ivy Lydia Wood on July 25, 1919, in Hyde, Cheshire.

On Oct. 6, 1919, Justice Clement Meagher Bailhache sentenced Beard to death. An appeal was immediately filed, and the verdict in the first trial was overturned on the grounds that Beard was incapable of forming the intention to murder because of his severe state of drunkeness at the time of the assault. "Malice afore-thought" was therefore absent, and the court ordered the charge reduced to manslaughter.

The Crown was displeased with the verdict, and Lord Hewart and Sir Charles Matthews, brought the matter before the House of Lords. Lord Frederick Edwin Birkenhead, Lord Haldane, and

Lord Reading reversed the judgment on Mar. 5, 1920. The judges argued that Beard had not been too drunk to rape the child. Lord Birkenhead re-established the original charge of murder but ruled that Beard could not be executed. The prisoner began serving a life sentence.

REF.: *CBA;* Neil, *Man-Hunters of Scotland Yard;* O'Donnell, *Cavalcade of Justice;* Shew, *A Companion to Murder.*

Beard, Edward T., c.1828-73, U.S., west. gunman. Raised with wealth and education, Edward Beard married and produced three children in Beardstown (named after his father), Ill. Without any explanation, Beard suddenly left his family and went West in 1861, becoming a notorious rowdy and gunman in California, Oregon, and Arizona. When he heard of the cattle boom in Kansas, Beard moved to Wichita and opened a notorious dance hall in nearby Delano, a hangout for soldiers stationed nearby. On June 3, 1873, one drunken soldier argued with a prostitute named Emma Stanley over her price for the night, and fired a bullet into her leg. Beard leaped over the bar and ran toward the group of soldiers, blindly firing his six-gun. He shot one soldier in the throat and another in the leg, neither being the culprit who escaped out a back door and deserted the army that night. Two nights later, thirty troopers sought revenge by invading Beard's dance hall and shooting up the place, wounding a gambler named Charles Leshhart, shooting Emma Stanley in the other leg, and wounding another dance hall girl. Before retreating, the soldiers torched the dance hall and then watched from the street, cheering as it burned to the ground.

After rebuilding his dance hall, Beard was immediately at odds with the dreaded gunman Rowdy Joe Lowe, who had built a saloon next to Beard's (winning in a race to see who could build a dance hall first). On Oct. 27, 1873, Beard, drinking heavily, accused one of his prostitutes, Jo DeMerritt, of stealing from him. DeMerritt threw a bottle at him and fled next door to Lowe's saloon. The drunken Beard followed her, staggered into Lowe's, and in the smoke-filled place mistook another prostitute, Annie Franklin, as being DeMerritt. He fired a shot which struck the woman in the stomach. Lowe then grabbed a shotgun and exchanged shots with Beard. Lowe's shot missed but Beard's bullet grazed Lowe's neck. A stray bullet struck and wounded Bill Anderson who was standing at the bar.

Beard fled and Lowe, as drunk as his quarry, went after him. Both men, mounted on horses and racing out of town, had a running gunfight. Lowe caught up with Beard near the river bridge and emptied his shotgun into him, then rode back to town where he turned himself in to the sheriff. Beard was found critically wounded in the arm and thigh, loaded with buckshot. He clung to life for two weeks, but through loss of blood died on Nov. 11, 1873. See: **Lowe, Joseph.**

REF.: *CBA;* Drago, *Wild, Woolly & Wicked;* Miller and Snell, *Great Gunfighters of the Kansas Cowtowns;* O'Neal, *Encyclopedia of Western Gunfighters.*

Beard, Joe, See: **Purvis, Will.**

Beard, Red, prom. 1870s, U.S., pros. In a lawless area outside a Kansas town limits, two men struggled to dominate the prostitution trade. Red Beard was an educated man who competed with the crude, tough Joe Lowe for the business of cowboys in their rival dance hall saloons with second-floor brothels in Delano, a settlement that sprang up around the cattle runs across the Arkansas River near Wichita, Kan. Cattle would be held for three or four days in stockyards there before they were put on railroad cars. The cowboys waited with them, getting paid and spending freely before they hit the trail again. Beard's place was known as the more sophisticated of the two, based in part on the fact that when one of Beard's women died, he buried her in a cemetery, while Lowe buried a woman who had committed suicide in his back yard. Lowe was a drunk who would fly into wild rages, and was controlled only by his even-tempered wife, Kate Lowe, apparently a calculating businesswoman. Lowe was reputed to have murdered several men, including Jim Sweet, a gambler whose place was known as "the swiftest joint in Kansas," and, during peak

trail-driving seasons, pulled in as much as $1,000 a week, a large sum in those days.

REF.: *CBA;* Drago, *Notorious Ladies of the Frontier.*

America's first skyjackers, Cody and Leon Bearden.

Bearden, Leon, 1923- , U.S., skyjack. An unhappy and chronically dissatisfied criminal decided he was tired of the U.S. and, wanting to go to Cuba and renounce his citizenship, took his 16-year-old son with him to skyjack a plane.

On Aug. 3, 1961, Leon Bearden and his son, Cody Bearden, boarded a Boeing 707 jetliner in Phoenix, Ariz. An unemployed car salesman from Coolidge, Ariz., the elder Bearden had a twenty-year criminal record that included prison terms for forgery, robbery, and grand theft. At about 1:30 a.m., when the jetliner was airborne, the two, armed with pistols, walked to the cockpit and Leon told the pilot, Captain Byron Rickards, as he held a .38-caliber gun against his head, "We are going to take this plane to Cuba. Alter your course 45 degrees to the south." Rickards, who had been in another skyjack in 1931 in Peru, stalled for time by saying he did not have enough fuel to make the trip and would have to stop in El Paso. Bearden agreed, and Rickards radioed a message so that by the time he landed in Texas, police, border patrolmen, and FBI agents were waiting at the International Airport.

Because it was assumed that the skyjackers were Castro henchmen, President John F. Kennedy was kept informed about the situation. When a pregnant woman grew hysterical, the elder Bearden took four passengers and the crew as hostages and allowed the other sixty-one passengers to leave. After several hours, while the ground crew dawdled, Bearden fired a bullet between one of the hostage's feet, saying again that he intended to take off. Fuel tanks were quickly filled and, as the plane taxied, lawmen rushed out of hiding places in a motorcade and poured machine-gun fire into the undercarriage of the plane, flattening its tires and knocking out an engine. FBI agent Francis Crosby boarded the jetliner to negotiate. Bearden threatened to kill himself and one of the hostages knocked the criminal out with a surprise punch. The plane had been under siege for ten hours. The Beardens were charged with kidnapping, transporting a plane, and obstructing commerce by robbery. On Oct. 18, 1961, Bearden was found Guilty in U.S. District Court of violating three federal laws. Cody had pleaded guilty to his part in the skyjacking and was sentenced to a correctional institution until he was 21. On Oct. 31, 1961, Leon Bearden was sentenced to life imprisonment. REF.: *CBA*.

Bear River Tom, See: **Smith, Thomas J.**

Beary, Doug, prom. 1860s, U.S., mur. Doug Beary, a native of Fountain County, Ky., joined one of the many bands of guerrillas and bushwhackers who terrorized the elderly, women, and children left at home during the war. A Unionist, he opposed the Confederate guerrilla bands in and around the Bear River area, pillaging, robbing, and murdering. His victims included soldiers home on leave and people who sympathized with the South. Ambush killings were so frequent that people often did not attend funerals for fear of being murdered themselves. According to a local historian, "These guerrillas developed into savage warriors, and anarchy was the law of the land." William Brownlow, governor of Tennessee, commissioned Claborne Beary on Apr. 1, 1868, to lead a small company that would put an end to the violence. In June 1864, Beary's Union guerrillas attacked and killed Jeff Bede, the leader of a rival gang known as the Bede or Bear gang. See: **Bede Gang.**
REF.: *CBA; Montell, Killings.*

Beasley, Milton (AKA: Art Norris, Duke, Mel Norris), 1933- , U.S., org. crime-mur. Hired by drug pushers to murder an informer, Beasley insisted he had never heard of his victim and seemed confident that he would not be convicted of the killing.

Defying the code of the underworld, Bill Green turned government informer against the large-scale organized crime narcotics ring in which he had been involved. On Aug. 10, 1961, he was found dead in his car in Las Vegas, Nev., with two .25-caliber bullet wounds in his head. The California Bureau of Narcotics assigned agents John Warner and George E. Ohlson to track down his killer, with permission to go out of state in their search. In Nevada City, Nev., Green's neighbor, Mary Courtney, told them she had heard unusual noises the night he was killed, and gave a description of two men fleeing the scene in different cars. The only other clue the agents had was a single smudged fingerprint found on Green's car door. Interviewing people who had known the victim, Warner and Ohlson talked to a man who casually revealed information about some gamblers including an acquaintance of the dead man, someone "he called 'Duke,' or something like it." Through a police teletype that went out to cities in both Nevada and California, the agents checked the so-called "nickname file" and came up with Milton Beasley. He had been arrested in the Oakland area on drug charges and later was released.

Warner and Ohlson returned to Los Angeles while Oakland detectives kept a watch on Beasley. Interviewing him at a bar, Warner was told by Duke, "I never heard of this guy Green. And about some rube talkin' about me in Vegas, I never was in that lousy burg." Evidence, however, began to pile up against Beasley. The fingerprint on Green's car door matched Beasley's police file prints; a positive identification was made by Green's mother—who gasped when she looked at his photo—and underworld sources explained that a man named Duke had been hired to kill Green for $5,000. A Las Vegas contact told the agents that Beasley was seen just before the slaying with a girl known as a drug addict, and that he had shown her a .25-caliber automatic pistol, boasting, "I'm the guy who's going to use this here and I'm going to make plenty of dough out of it." Beasley, usually out of funds, had purchased a Cadillac, paying cash for it, the day after the killing, and had gone to a Los Angeles hotel to talk to a clerk to establish his residence there on the day Green was slain.

With the additional testimony of a narcotics ringleader named Patterson, who testified in court that he had been part of a conspiracy to murder Green and had hired Beasley for the job, Duke was tried in February 1964, found Guilty of first-degree murder, and sentenced by Judge John Mowbray to life without possibility of parole in the Nevada State Penitentiary.
REF.: Block, *Fifteen Clues; CBA.*

Beaton, David (David Bethune), 1494-1546, Scot., mur. Led a faction seeking political alliance with France at the expense of England. He instigated a ruthless persecution of Protestants in 1539 after succeeding his uncle David Beaton as archbishop of St. Andrews. While serving as Chancellor of Scotland in 1546 he had Reformation preacher George Wishart burned at the stake on the charge of religious heresy. Followers of Wishart, Norman Leslie and William Kirkealdy, murdered him in revenge. REF.: *CBA.*

Beatson, John, d.1802, and **Whalley, William,** d.1802, Brit., rob. A father and son team were among the last of the British highwaymen to be publicly hanged. Their robbery of the Royal Mail Coach near East Grinstead on July 20, 1801, closed a colorful era of English crime. John Beatson and his adopted son William Whalley were arrested at Knutsford, Cheshire, after they drew attention to themselves by mistreating their horse.

Found in their possession were gold, jewelry and banknotes worth £1,700. The trial of Beatson and Whalley began at Horsham on Mar. 29, 1802. The father claimed that his son had no part in the affair, but the argument failed to save him. John Beatson and his adopted son were hanged on Apr. 7, 1802, before 3,000 spectators.

REF.: *CBA; Pringle, Stand and Deliver.*

Beattie, Charlton Reid, 1869-1925, U.S., jur. District attorney in New Orleans, La., from 1909-18. He was appointed judge of the court of the Eastern District of Louisiana by President Calvin Coolidge in 1925. REF.: *CBA.*

Beattie, Henry Clay, 1884-1911, U.S., mur. In 1911, the city of Richmond, Va., was rocked with news of a bloody slaying five miles outside the city. Henry Clay Beattie, on the night of July 18, arrived at the home of Thomas E. Owen, which was off the Midlothian turnpike. Breathlessly, he pointed to his open auto. The Owens moved cautiously to the car. In the back seat they saw Mrs. Louise Beattie. The top of her head had been blown off.

Beattie told police that he and his wife had been stopped by a tall highwayman who waved a gun in their faces. The bearded man had shouted at them: "You had better run over me...You have got all the road!" or, at least, that's what Beattie claimed the man said. Beattie tried to drive around the tall highwayman, he said, but the man raised his weapon and fired just as the car passed him. Mrs. Beattie was killed instantly by the blast and the killer fled, howling through the nearby woods. Or had he been laughing? Beattie couldn't remember, he told police. The gun? Beattie remembered stopping the car, running after the man, and wresting the weapon from him before the murderer escaped. He couldn't recall where he had thrown the gun.

Mrs. Beattie was buried before the coroner's jury could make up its mind about her demise. That was decided by Detective L.L. Scherer, who found the murder weapon alongside the C&O Railroad tracks. Tracing its sale, Scherer discovered that a Paul Beattie had purchased the gun for H.C. Beattie. The husband was quickly arrested and tried for the murder of his wife.

Beattie emphatically denied his guilt, although a staggering case had been built against him. Even after he was sentenced to die in the electric chair, the convicted man refused to admit to the slaying. The 27-year-old was led into the death room on Nov. 24, 1911, still mumbling about the tall, bewhiskered highwayman who had murdered his wife. (It was eventually learned that Beattie had been a student of the Old West and that he had described a photo of Jesse James which was kept in his album of gunslingers.)

Not until he was executed was the truth learned from Beattie himself. His religious advisors, the Reverends J.J. Fix and Benjamin Dennis, provided newsmen with Beattie's handwritten confession which they had witnessed the day before his electrocution. It read:

"I, Henry Clay Beattie, Jr., desirous of standing right before God and man, do on this, the 23rd day of November, 1911, confess my guilt of the crime charged against me. Much that was published concerning the details was not true, but the awful fact, without the harrowing circumstances, remains. For this action I am truly sorry, and believing that I am at peace with God and am soon to pass into His presence, this statement is made." REF.: *CBA*.

Beauchamp, Jereboam O., 1803-26, U.S., mur. Jereboam Beauchamp was a young southern attorney who was inspired by any gesture of honor that typified the antebellum South, particularly when it came to defending a lady's virtue. He was only twenty-one and foppishly naive when meeting Ann Cooke, a 38-year-old Virginia belle. She captivated him so that he was at the mercy of any whim that urged her emotions. Beauchamp proposed marriage and Ann Cooke graciously accepted, but she insisted that before the nuptials, her beau perform a slight service for her. She had been degraded by Colonel Solomon P. Sharp, a member of the Kentucky House of Representatives. He had made her his mistress, seduced and impregnated her, then, after finding and marrying another, abandoned her. Ann Cooke demanded that her honor be avenged and that Beauchamp meet the blackguard Sharp on the field of honor. The youth mumbled something about taking vengeance in the near future. The couple married but Sharp remained a festering sore in their relationship. Two years later, Sharp became a focal point in a heated election. Ann Cooke Beauchamp not only reminded her husband of his long-ago promise to wreak havoc on the rake who had seduced her (she never gave birth to Sharp's child, or any child, according to available records). Moreover, she revealed Sharp's sins against her to Sharp's political enemies who publicly used the seduction as an issue, thus compelling Beauchamp to take some sort of action.

The young attorney challenged Sharp to a duel but the savvy politician was disinclined to fight and ignored the challenge. Enraged at this further insult, Beauchamp visited the colonel's estates some nights later. He wore a red hood over his head to avoid recognition and when Sharp answered his front door, Beauchamp plunged a knife several times into his chest, killing the politician. His killer then fled, but he was identified as he tore the hood from his head. Some days later, Beauchamp was arrested and charged with murdering Sharp. He was thrown into a dungeon-like prison in Frankfurt, Ky., and here Ann visited him, gushing gratitude for satisfying the debt of honor due her tarnished reputation.

In May 1826, Beauchamp was tried, convicted, and sentenced to death in the Frankfurt Circuit Court, his execution fixed for July 7, 1826. Before this date, Ann visited her condemned husband and mixed some poison with their tea, but their desired deaths were not forthcoming. Both became sick and were nursed back to health. On the day of the hanging all Frankfurt turned out to view the execution. Ann was allowed to say her goodbyes to Beauchamp and share his last meal of tea and chipped beef. Although she had already attempted to complete a suicide pact with her husband earlier, jailors gave no thought to searching her. She had smuggled a long knife into the cell and, after the couple finished dining they took turns stabbing each other. Ann died of her wounds in Beauchamp's arms.

Jail guards rushed into the cell to find Ann's bloody corpse and Beauchamp clinging to the body, several wounds in his stomach. "Tell my father that my wife and myself are going straight to Heaven—we are dying!" Authorities concluded, however, that the condemned man was enough alive to hang, and he was pulled out of the jail while dragging his wife's corpse with him. Beauchamp was placed in a closed carriage with the corpse, both wrapped in a blood-soaked blanket. He cried out to the dead woman in his arms: "Farewell, child of sorrow. For you I have lived, for you I die!" Thousands of spectators who were picnicking on the grounds around the gallows in an open field shouted their anger at not seeing the condemned man displayed in an open cart as was the custom of the day.

When the carriage came to a stop in the shadow of the gallows, Beauchamp, almost in a dead faint from loss of blood, had to be carried half-conscious up the long stairs leading to the high gallows. A band struck up a popular air, "Bonaparte's Retreat From Moscow," which the condemned man had asked to be played days earlier. A black hood was placed over Beauchamp's head, the rope around his neck, and he stood there for seemingly endless minutes while a local preacher condemned his soul to hell. Then the hangman kicked the lever controlling the trapdoor and Jereboam O. Beauchamp fell into space and death.

Both Ann and Jereboam Beauchamp were buried in the same grave with a huge sandstone marker upon which was enscribed a melancholy poem penned by Ann Beauchamp while sitting with her beloved in the Frankfurt jail. It read, in part:

> He heard her tale of matchless woe
> And burning for revenge he rose
> And layed her base seducer low
> And struck dismay to virtue's foes.

The Beauchamp suicide-execution has since become Kentucky folklore, embellished far beyond the real facts, which of themselves remain spectacular enough.

REF.: *The Beauchamp Tragedy; CBA; The Confession of Jereboam O. Beauchamp;* Dana and Thomas, *Beauchamp's Trial; The Kentucky Tragedy; Letters of Ann Cooke; The Life of Jereboam O. Beauchamp;* Nash, *Bloodletters and Badmen; The Trial of Jereboam O. Beauchamp; Vindication of the Character of the Late Col. Solomon P. Sharp.*

Beauchamp, Richard de (Earl of Warwick), 1382-1439, Brit., treas. Participated in the overthrow of Richard II in 1387. He was imprisoned in 1397 for treason but released by order of Henry IV. REF.: *CBA*.

Beaufort, François (Duc de Vendome), 1616-69, Fr., consp. Conspired against Cardinal Richelieu in 1642 which resulted in a five year imprisonment from 1643-48. He was killed in action in 1669 while serving in the Royal Navy. REF.: *CBA*.

Beaufort, Henry (Third Duke of Somerset), 1436-64, Brit., treas. Member of an English noble family dating back to the 1390s. His army was defeated by the Yorkists in 1460 and he was captured and beheaded four years later. REF.: *CBA*.

Beauharnais, Alexandre Vicomte de, 1760-94, Fr., treas. Fought in the American Revolution and later served the French revolutionary government as deputy of nobility to States-General. During the Reign of Terror he was accused of surrendering the French armies at Mainz to the Prussians without just cause. In 1794, he was executed at the guillotine. REF.: *CBA*.

Beauharnais, Hortense de (Eugénie-Hortense de Beauharnais), 1783-1837, Fr., consp. Daughter of Alexander Beaharnais. She married Louis Bonaparte, King of Holland, and was mother of Charles-Louis, (Napoleon III). She was banished from France in 1815 because of her role in various political intrigues. REF.: *CBA*.

Beaumanoir, Philippe de Rémi, c.1246-96, Fr., jur. Author of *Coutumes de Beauvoisis,* a study of old French law. REF.: *CBA*.

Beaumont, Campbell Eben, 1883-1954, U.S., jur. Assistant district attorney of Fresno County, Calif., from 1918-21, and district attorney of Fresno, Calif., in 1921. He was appointed to the federal bench of the Southern District of California by President Franklin D. Roosevelt in 1939. REF: *CBA*.

Beaumont, Robert de (Earl of Leicester), 1104-68, Brit., jur. Chief Justice of England jointly with Richard de Lucy from 1153-66. He was counselor to William II and Henry I. REF.: *CBA*.

Bebel, August, 1840-1913, Ger., treas. Co-founded the Social Democratic Party. In 1872, he was imprisoned along with Wilhelm Liebknecht for plotting high treason against Germany and Saxony a year after securing a seat in the newly formed Reichstag. REF.: *CBA*.

Beccaria (Cesare Bonesana or Marchese di Beccaria), c.1735-94, Italy, jur. Professor of law and economics at Milan. Beccaria argued for an end to capital punishment and confiscation of property. His ideas about judicial reform were published in 1764 as *Tratto dei Delitti e delle Pene*. REF.: *CBA*.

Bechtle, Louis Charles, 1927-   , U.S., jur. Assistant U.S. attorney and chief of the Criminal Division in Philadelphia, Pa., from 1957-59, and U.S. attorney of the Department of Justice in Philadelphia, Pa., from 1969-72. He was appointed judge of the court of the Eastern District of Pennsylvania by President Richard M. Nixon in 1972. REF.: *CBA*.

Adolph Beck and his double, William Thomas; Beck served time for Thomas' crimes.

Beck, Adolph, 1841-1909, Brit., (wrong. convict.) fraud. The classic case of mistaken identity is that of Adolph Beck, a sometimes clerical worker who led a nomadic life, living at times in Norway, South America, and England. Although he could be classified as a drifter, Beck was certainly no criminal, yet he was so firmly identified as such by a number of witnesses that he was sent to prison for crimes he did not commit while his almost exact double remained at large to go on defrauding and stealing.

In late November 1896, Beck was walking down Victoria Street when Ottilie Meisonnier, a language teacher, stared at him as he passed beneath the street lamps. She walked up to Beck and held on to his arm, demanding the return of two wrist watches and some rings. "You stole my jewelry and I want it back!" she insisted. Beck tried to pull away but the determined woman clung to him. He managed to yank his arm free and then, spotting a constable, walked up to the policeman and asked him to deal with the drunken woman who was accosting him. The teacher explained that Beck was a thief, having bilked her out of her jewelry two weeks earlier. The constable took both Beck and Meisonnier to the Rochester Row Police Station.

There the teacher explained how Beck had approached her in early November, tipping his hat to her and addressing her as Lady Everton. When realizing his mistake, he had told Meisonnier how much she resembled the beautiful noblewoman, one of his peer group. Beck, continued the teacher, had mentioned his vast estate in Lincolnshire, his six gardeners, and his friendship with Lord Salisbury, then prime minister of England. The two of them had gone off to a restaurant where Beck had told the naive teacher that he had been smitten by her and insisted she travel the Riviera with him on his yacht. Her clothes and jewelry, he had said, would not do, however, as the couple would travel through "high social stratas." Beck had given her a check for forty pounds and told her to buy some new clothes. He then took her two wrist watches and some rings, saying that he would have these refitted with better mountings. He arranged to meet her later but never arrived at the rendezvous. His check, of course, was worthless,

and Meisonnier realized that she had been victimized in one of the oldest confidence games practiced.

Beck was put into a lineup and Meisonnier once again positively identified him as the swindler. In addition, several other women came forward and were equally sure that Beck was the same man who had worked a similar fraud on them. Two policemen then identified Beck as a thief and con man named John Smith whom they had repeatedly arrested in the past. A handwriting expert named Gurrin (who would later offer wrong comparisons and testimony in the case of George Edalji, another wrongly convicted man) testified that, after examining the bogus check written by the swindler and Beck's handwriting, they were one and the same. Though he protested his innocence, Beck was brought before a judge who recognized him as the man named Smith, someone he had sent to prison before. Beck was sent to prison for seven years and even given Smith's old prison number. To seal his fate, Beck was *positively* identified as Smith when his Bertillon measurements were compared with that of Smith. One discrepancy existed which authorities dismissed as a clerical error. The Smith records showed that Smith had been circumcised but Beck had not.

After serving five years, Beck was released. Again, while walking down a London street three years later, a young woman ran up to him, calling for the police, telling constables that Beck had swindled her out of her jewelry. Once more, after being *positively* identified by eyewitnesses, Beck was tried and convicted. While he was waiting to be sentenced, Detective Inspector John Kane heard of another swindler who had been using the same methods as Smith and he visited this man in a detention cell. When Kane took a look at this man he stepped back in shock. The prisoner, whose real name was Wilhelm Mayer, was the exact double of Adolph Beck and he had been using the aliases William Thomas and John Smith for years. It was quickly proven that Mayer was the real culprit and committed all the crimes for which Beck had been accused and for which he had served five years of his life. Mayer was sent to prison and Beck released with apologies. In compensation for his five years' imprisonment, Beck was awarded £5,000 by the government, but so embittered and dissolute was he by the time he received this money that he spent it wastefully, dying in the gutter in 1909. See: **Doyle, Arthur Conan; Edalji, George.**

REF.: Borchard, *Convicting the Innocent;* Browne, *The Rise of Scotland Yard; CBA;* Cuthbert, *Science and the Detection of Crime;* Fabian, *Fabian of the Yard;* Hibbert, *The Roots of Evil;* Humphreys, *Criminal Days;* Nordon, *Conan Doyle;* Stevens, *From Clue to Dock;* Symons, *A Pictorial History of Crime;* Thompson, *The Story of Scotland Yard;* Thorwald, *The Century of the Detective.*

Beck, David, prom. 1950s, U.S., corr.-tax evas. As president of the powerful and rich International Brotherhood of Teamsters union, with 1.5 million members, David Beck lavished wealth upon himself, milking the union funds and pocketing enormous amounts of cash. He built for himself from these funds a posh Seattle estate, replete with waterfalls and movie projection rooms. Beck later resold this estate to his own union and then affixed a Teamster resolution wherein he would be able to live on the estate rent-free for the duration of his life. It is not known how many millions Beck stole from his union coffers but investigations directed by a youthful Robert Kennedy for the McClellan Committee revealed the labor leader was filching great amounts of money. Committee investigators determined that nothing Beck owned in the way of clothing had been purchased with his own money. The Teamsters bought his socks and even his bow ties. Before appearing before the Senate Select Committee on Improper Activities in the Labor or Management Field, Beck announced to reporters: "I have nothing to fear. My record is an open book." He then took the Fifth Amendment more than 200 times when answering the questions put to him by McClellan and others.

The McClellan Committee exposure ruined Dave Beck, who had headed the Teamsters since 1952, and James R. Hoffa replaced him in 1958. Hoffa had nothing but contempt for Beck, once stating: "Dave Beck? Hell, I was running it (the Teamster's union) while he was playing big shot. He never knew the score." Beck attempted to repay some of the money he stole from his union, returning about $370,000, but he was nevertheless convicted of income tax evasion and was given a long prison term.

Powerful union leader Dave Beck who was toppled from his Teamster's throne after looting union funds.

When he was released he still enjoyed a lifetime pension of $50,000 a year from the Teamsters. Treasury agents still insisted that Beck pay $1.3 million in back taxes and that the IRS had the right to seize any and all property of the disgraced union leader. Secretary of the Treasury John B. Connolly, under President Richard Nixon, put a hold on Beck's debt to the government in 1971. This moratorium was approved by Nixon, who later received the wholehearted backing of the Teamsters.

REF.: *CBA;* Demaris, *The Director;* Gage, *Mafia, U.S.A.*

Beck, Dieter, prom. 1960s, Ger., rape-mur. If a cab driver had come forth with his testimony regarding a killing, the murders of two other women in a seven-year period might have been prevented.

On Apr. 8, 1961, a shoe factory worker on his way to his job came across the corpse of a woman lying in a ditch near the Rehme, Germany, railway station. The victim, 23-year-old Ingrid Kanike, had been raped and strangled, according to a coroner's report, at around midnight on Apr. 7. A local woman, Kanike habitually went to the movies on Friday evenings in nearby Minden, returning by train and taking a cab to her home. Fifteen or twenty people who had been on the midnight train were questioned, as were six local cab drivers, all married, middle-aged men. None had been employed by the cab company for less than eight years. There were no clues or suspects and the case remained unsolved. Four years later, on May 25, 1965, a landlady in the city of Herford, eight miles from Rehme, suspected her missing boarder of skipping out on the rent. She entered the boarder's apartment to find that Ursula Fritz had been dead for ten days, and like Kanike, Fritz had been raped and strangled. A month later police arrested Gerd Simmon, a 34-year-old unemployed butcher, when he tried to rape a 14-year-old girl near the Rehme railway station. A crowd formed to lynch the man they assumed to be the sex murderer of Kanike and Fritz. But when police inspectors Anton Jech and Heidel interrogated Simmon he freely admitted being a criminal who had served several years

in jail for attempted rapes, but repeatedly denied having committed any murders. When Jech and Heidel showed a photo of Simmon to Fritz's landlady and coworkers, no one identified him.

In a routine cross-referencing with the earlier murder, the Herford inspectors discovered that one of the cabdrivers told a different story when he was questioned a second time. Jech and Heidel called in August Fennel, who admitted that he had given Kanike a ride, recognizing her as a local woman he had driven before. The night of her death, he said, she got into his cab with a good-looking man of about thirty, who told him to stop the cab and let them out in the spot where the body was found the next day. The couple, he said, "seemed friendly enough together." Fennel was unable to identify any of the passengers from the 12:07 Minden train, but four were suspects, based on their age and appearance. One was later eliminated—he had been in the hospital at the time of Kanike's murder. With no further evidence, police could only wait.

On Feb. 29, 1968, the body of 21-year-old Anneliese Herschel was found on the railway tracks. She too had been raped and strangled. In her pocket was a matchbook from the Igloo Bar in Bielefeld. Discovering that Herschel had been with a man the night she was killed, Sergeant Max Kramer brought photographs of the three suspects to the Igloo and obtained three positive identifications of Dieter Beck. When picked up by police at his home Beck said, "I'm glad it's over. I didn't want to kill those girls. It's just something that comes over me and then I can't help myself. I'll confess to the murders, but I don't want to talk about it."

At his trial, Beck's many girlfriends described him as a satisfactory lover, with the peculiar habit of pretending to strangle them as they made love. The trial lasted from June 22-26, 1969. Beck was found guilty of premeditated murder on all three counts and sentenced to three terms of life imprisonment.

REF.: *CBA;* Dunning, *The Arbor House Treasury of True Crime.*

Beck, Douglas, 1927-77, U.S., suic.-mur. A doting father despondent over losing custody rights murdered his teenaged daughter and then shot himself.

Douglas Beck, fifty, a former school teacher and self-employed engineer, had weekend custody of his only child, 13-year-old Rebecca Beck. Divorced for nine years, Beck had been engaged in an ongoing battle to obtain full custody rights, a fight he had recently lost to Erma Beck, his ex-wife. Over the Memorial Day weekend the father and daughter had gone on a camping trip and on their return the following Monday, Rebecca phoned her mother to ask permission to stay another night with her father. When the girl did not return as scheduled to her mother's home on Tuesday afternoon, the parent phoned Beck's house and got no answer. She went to the apartment and saw her ex-husband's car still on the street, and called the police. The two bodies were found side by side in a North Side Chicago apartment. Beck apparently had waited until his daughter fell asleep, then put the barrel of a .25-caliber automatic to her head and pulled the trigger once. He then lay down next to her and fired the gun at his own head. Police found three unaddressed letters Beck had written to his father, a minister, and his ex-wife, describing his despondency over the custody decision. REF.: *CBA.*

Beck, H.O. (AKA: Ole, Edward Welch), d.1912, U.S., west. rob. Beck was an old-time western train and stagecoach robber who had been serving time with Ben Kilpatrick, the "Tall Texan" of Wild Bunch fame. Both men were released from federal prison in early 1912 and immediately planned a train robbery of the Southern Pacific's *Sunset Express* in a remote desert spot. They boarded the train at Dryden, Texas, a small water stop, on Mar. 13, 1912, and attempted to rob the Wells Fargo car of its cargo of $65,000, but the guard, David A. Troutsdale, attacked both men, killing Beck and Kilpatrick and delivering their bodies to officials at the next stop as if he were casually dropping off some mailbags. See: **Kilpatrick, Benjamin.**

REF.: Beebe and Clegg, *U.S. West, The Story of Wells Fargo; CBA; Fulcher, The Way I Heard It;* Horan, *The Authentic American West, The*

Outlaws; Kelly, *The Outlaw Trail;* Rennert, *Western Outlaws.*

Beck, James Montgomery, 1861-1936, U.S., lawyer. Assistant attorney general from 1900-03, and a member of the House of Representatives from 1927-34. Books authored: *The Evidence in the Case* (1914), *The Constitution of the United States* (1922), and *May It Please the Court* (1930). REF.: *CBA.*

Beck, Martha Julie (or Jule), 1921-51, and **Fernandez, Raymond Martinez** (AKA: **Charles Martin**), 1914-51, (AKA: **The Lonely Hearts Killers**), U.S., big.-fraud-mur. Fernandez, born in Hawaii of Spanish parents, was an adventurous youth who reportedly served with British Intelligence during WWII, winning commendations. He was wounded in the head in 1945, an injury that altered his personality from sanguine to phlegmatic, according to one report, and sent him on a criminal career in which he bilked well-to-do widows out of their savings after proposing marriage. He was tall and thin, covering his almost-bald head with a cheap black wig. But the love-desperate women who fell for his pedestrian pitch of woo, thought of him as an irresistible Latin lover. In the words of one newsman: "He was a rather seedy Charles Boyer." Fernandez found his victims in the then-popular lonely hearts clubs or through the lonely hearts columns of newspapers. He even married several women, having one family in Spain, another in the U.S., and reportedly others still in Mexico and Canada.

Lonely hearts killers Martha Beck and Raymond Fernandez joke with guard.

One of the lovelorn ads Fernandez answered turned out to have been placed by Mrs. Martha Beck, a registered nurse who ran a home for crippled children in Pensacola, Fla. When the sleazy Lothario arrived on Mrs. Beck's front door in 1947, he was taken aback by the obese woman standing before him. She welcomed him with open arms and Fernandez the con, for some inexplicable reason, man fell in love with the unattractive Martha. Mrs. Beck, who had been divorced since 1944, lavished attention on Fernandez who confessed his swindling ways to her. To his surprise, she not only approved of his crooked pursuits but asked to be part of his widow-bilking schemes. The couple traveled northward, stopping in cities along the way to answer lonely hearts advertisements and mulct the love-sick widows.

Their usual procedure was for Fernandez to woo and win the lovelorn lady and, during the course of a brief courtship, introduce Beck as his sister. Then, following the wedding, Beck would move in with the newlyweds, and the looting of savings and jewelry quickly ensued. Most of the women, more than 100 of them, were in their late fifties or sixties, but Beck could not bear to be in the same house with Fernandez and a new wife, knowing he was making love to another woman. Her jealousy grew whenever the victim was young and attractive, such was the case with Mrs.

Delphine Dowling of Grand Rapids, Mich. Mrs. Dowling, twenty-eight, had a 2-year-old daughter, Rainelle, and was apprehensive of Fernandez, allowing him and his "sister" to move into her home but delaying the nuptials with her newly found Latin lover until she was convinced her spouse-to-be was sincere. Beck found it impossible to sleep in the next room while her own man was on the other side of the wall with a younger, more attractive woman. They would not wait for the wedding ceremonies, Beck told the docile Fernandez. Mrs. Dowling and her daughter had to go. Both disappeared in January 1949.

Neighbors noticing the absence of Mrs. Dowling and her daughter, called police and when officers arrived at the Dowling residence, Beck and Fernandez calmly invited them inside, telling them they had no idea where Mrs. Dowling and her child and gone. Police thought the pair looked suspicious and insisted that the home be searched. Beck shrugged and Fernandez waved them into the parlor. Investigators found a fresh patch of cement on the floor of the basement. "It's the size of a grave," said one officer and they soon unearthed the bodies of mother and child. The Lonely Hearts Killers, as Beck and Fernandez were quickly dubbed by the press, collapsed immediately, freely admitting the murders and then bragging that there were as many as seventeen other victims they had killed. Beck, glorying in her publicity, explained that she dosed Mrs. Dowling with sleeping pills, but the young woman was strong enough to resist the drugs and Fernandez shot her in the head. They originally did not plan to murder the little girl. When she cried for her mother, Martha Beck said, as if displaying her humanity, they bought her a dog. But the child continued to whine so Martha dragged her into the bathroom, filled the tub, and held her beneath the water until she drowned.

Fernandez and Beck, of course, were well aware of the fact that the state of Michigan had no death penalty and undoubtedly reasoned that they would be imprisoned and later be paroled, in spite of their heinous crimes. (This was the same tactic earlier employed by Fred R. "Killer" Burke, one of the machine gunners at the 1929 St. Valentine's Day Massacre.) With that comforting thought in mind, the pair bragged about their other murders. "I'm no average killer," Fernandez boasted. "I only got five hundred off the Dowling woman," he said disappointedly, "but take Mrs. Jane Thompson, I took six thousand off of her." He explained how he married Thompson and took her to Spain where he murdered her, poisoning her with digitalis. He then returned to the U.S. to explain that he and his poor wife had been in a train wreck and she had been killed. The Thompson family did not bother to check if there had been such a wreck; they merely took his word for it. Fernandez was so convincing a liar that he moved in with Thompson's mother, Mrs. Wilson, wooed and bilked her and then murdered her, too.

Throughout the long confession, Beck was at Fernandez' side, chuckling perversely as he droned his litany of murder. She found it all amusing but was solicitous of her lover. When he began to sweat, he removed his cheap wig. Beck reached over to pat his bald pate dry with her handkerchief, thickly scented with cheap perfume. Then she urged him to continue, as if she were a child begging for a tale to be completed. Fernandez recalled a Mrs. Myrtle Young. He took her to Chicago in 1948 on their honeymoon. He laughed and said: "Poor woman, she died of over-exertion." Beck could no longer allow Fernandez to hog the limelight. She blurted out her own confessions rapidly, her heavy jewels jiggling as she rattled off murder after murder. One she vividly recalled—there were so many that taxed her memory—involved Mrs. Janet Fay of Manhattan. She and Fernandez had already taken the 66-year-old woman's last cent, but she was murdered anyway, only because Beck's jealousy exploded when the old woman cried out for Fernandez as the couple was leaving Fay's apartment.

Beck was incensed at Fay's display of affection for her man, and she grabbed a hammer and smashed it down on Fay's head, crushing her skull. Then Beck said in her best child's voice: "I turned to Raymond and said, 'look what I've done,' and then he strangled her with a scarf." Beck explained that although she had already murdered Fay, Fernandez, out of his deep love for Martha, insisted on taking part in the killing by strangling the lifeless corpse. Both killers were amazed when the state of Michigan abruptly allowed them to be extradited to New York to stand trial for their self-admitted slaying of Mrs. Fay—New York still had the death penalty. Both defendants were tried before Judge Ferdinand Pecora, pleading not guilty by reason of insanity. Psychiatrists examining both of them reported them sane and the trial went ahead. On one occasion, when Beck was being brought into court, she broke away from her female guards and lifted the startled Fernandez out of his chair, kissing him on the mouth and neck and cheeks. She had to be pried loose, screaming: "I love him! I do love him and I always will!"

A jury quickly convicted the pair and Judge Pecora sentenced them to death, their execution to be held on Aug. 22, 1949, at Sing Sing. While awaiting the electric chair, the couple exchanged love letters, sent between the male and female cellblocks. When Beck heard that Fernandez was regaling his fellow prisoners in death row with her eccentric behavior, she exploded, sending him the following message:

> You are a double-crossing, two-timing skunk. I learn now that you have been doing quite a bit of talking to everyone. It's nice to learn what a terrible, murderous person I am, while you are such a misunderstood, white-haired boy, caught in the clutches of a female vampire. It is also nice to know that all the love letters you wrote 'from the heart' were written with a hand shaking with laughter at me for being such a gullible fool as to believe them. Don't waste your time or energy trying to hide from view in church from now on, for I won't even look your way—the halo over your righteous head might blind me. May God have mercy on your soul.

M.J. Beck

Through appeals filed by their lawyers, Beck and Fernandez managed to postpone their date with the electric chair until Mar. 8, 1951. Fernandez ordered a large meal but, with his death only a few hours away, he could not eat it. He did smoke a long Havana cigar down to a small stub. Then he handed a note to one of the guards, saying that these words would be his last utterances on earth. The note, later widely published, read:

> People want to know whether I still love Martha. But of course I do. I want to shout it out. I love Martha. What do the public know about love?

Martha Beck, who was tired of being portrayed as a flabby, fat woman, told a female guard that she would show the world what kind of woman she was; she would resist ordering a feast for her last meal. That said, she ordered fried chicken and fried potatoes and a salad—a double order of each. She announced that she still loved Raymond Fernandez. There existed at Sing Sing a tradition that when two persons were to be executed, the weakest was to be sent to the chair first. This was Fernandez. He was half-carried to the electric chair by several guards and was in a state of nervous collapse when the switch was thrown. Martha Beck followed, walking on her own, confident, smiling as she almost threw her great bulk into the chair. See: **Burke, Fred R.**

REF.: Boar, *The World's Most Infamous Murders;* Brown, *Introduction to Murder;* CBA; Goodman, *Posts-Mortem: The Correspondence of Murder;* Hyde, *United in Crime;* Nash, *Look for the Woman;* ____, *Murder, America;* Reynolds, *Murder 'Round the World;* Rowan, *Famous American Crimes;* Sanders, *Murder Behind the Bright Lights;* Scott, *Concise Encyclopedia of Crime and Criminals;* Wilson, *Encyclopedia of Murder.*

Beck, Robert (AKA: Iceberg Slim), 1918- , U.S., pros. One of the most famous pimps in the Midwest, Beck used a combination of cajoling and psychology to control hundreds of women.

Born in Chicago in 1918, Robert Beck, better known as Iceberg Slim, chronicled his career in prostitution in *Pimp: The Story of My Life.* Soliciting and selling sex mostly in Chicago from the late 1930s to around 1961, Beck took up writing as a second career. Acknowledging that pimping has changed because "women have changed," Beck claimed in 1973 that drugs, women's liberation, and changing sexual mores had affected the business of selling sex. Television and luxury cars, he explained, also made women more aware of the opulence in the world, causing them to be more difficult to impress and control. Many younger pimps, Beck added, used harder drugs like heroin as a means of manipulating the women. Beck's other books include the biography of a con man, *Trick Baby,* the story of a homosexual queen, *Mama Black Widow,* and a collection of essays, *The Naked Soul of Iceberg Slim.* By the early 1970s, Beck achieved success as a lecturer in the Los Angeles area, speaking at high schools and colleges about the degradations of street life. REF.: *CBA.*

Beck, Sophie, b.1850, U.S., fraud. Sophie Beck was a small-time confidence trickster in New York who finally hit upon a swindle that netted her a fortune. She moved to Philadelphia and there founded a hollow company she called The Story Cotton Company. Beck advertised widely for investors in a get-rich-quick firm that would somehow corner the cotton market; she promised a fifty percent return on any investor's funds within a short period of time. Within a few months, Beck had taken in more than $1 million. She closed her posh offices, fired her large staff, hired as a front, or, in the parlance of con men, a big store, then sailed for Europe where she changed her name and lived out a long, luxurious life as a grande dame.

REF.: *CBA;* Nash, *Hustlers and Con Men;* ____, *Look for the Woman.*

Becker, Abraham, d.1924, U.S., mur. Abraham Becker murdered his wife Jennie in New York City in 1922, buried her and covered the corpse with alkali. He then claimed that his wife had run off with another man. When her body was discovered, authorities found it difficult to identify the corpse, except that her stomach contained, according to one report, the exact foods Becker had lovingly fed his wife on the night of her disappearance and this fact, along with other evidence, led to Becker's conviction and subsequent execution in 1924.

REF.: *CBA;* Marten, *The Doctor Looks At Murder.*

Becker, Barent, d.1815, U.S., mur. A farmer living near Mayfield, N.Y., Becker Barent decided that his hard-working wife Ann was a burden to him and decided to get rid of her. He offered to make dinner and prepared a stew which he liberally laced with arsenic. Ann Becker was dead within a few hours of consuming her husband's specially prepared dish. After failing to convince authorities that his wife had died of overwork, Becker admitted the murder. He was sent to the gallows on Oct. 6, 1815. From the scaffold, the farmer lectured his friends and relatives about the evil of man, then he led the scores of people who had come to see him die in a hymn he had composed while awaiting the hangman.

REF.: *CBA; Report on the Trial of Barent Becker; The Trial of Barent Becker.*

Becker, Charles (AKA: The Prince of Forgers), prom. 1870s-90s, U.S., forg.-rob. Thought to be one of the most clever forgers of his time and a man with an extensive and profitable criminal career, Becker earned the nickname, the Prince of Forgers.

Operating throughout the U.S., particularly on both coasts, and in Europe, Charles Becker's first major crime was the burglary of the Third National Bank in Baltimore, Md., in 1872, when he and his partners, Joseph Chapman and "Little Joe" Elliott, opened the "Chapman and Elliott Brokerage" offices above the bank in order to tunnel through the floor and drill into the vault below. They fled to Europe with around $50,000 and committed numerous forgeries there before being captured in Smyrna, Turkey, three years later. Tried in Britain, they were sentenced to three years in prison but Becker and Elliott escaped to London, leaving Chapman behind. Becker and Joe Riley later relocated to New York where the two passed a phony check for $64,000 drawn on the Union Trust Company. When arrested, Becker gained immunity for turning state's evidence. His next escapade, for which he eventually served prison time, was to forge a large amount of worthless stock for the Philadelphia and Reading Railroad in Pennsylvania—along with his father-in-law, Clement Hearing, Becker operated a lithograph business in New York, presumably for the purpose of forgery. Becker and Hearing were later convicted of counterfeiting 1,000-franc notes in France and served ten years at Kings County Prison.

On his release Becker took James Creegan as his partner and middleman. They worked throughout the country, defrauding five banks in one day in Omaha, Neb., and pulling in around $100,000 dollars in Pacific Coast ventures with a third partner, Frank Seaver, also known as Frank Dean.

Master forger Charles Becker.

Adding a new partner, Joe McCluskey, their big haul occurred in 1895 when they obtained a draft for $12 from the Crocker-Woolworth Bank and altered the figure to read $22,000 instead. Seaver drove to the Mission Street Bank in San Francisco the next day in a horse and buggy and withdrew the $22,000 in gold, taking it to McCluskey and Creegan to divide. The fraud was discovered on Jan. 4, 1986, when the banks involved tried to balance their accounts. McCluskey and Seaver were arrested in Minneapolis and returned to San Francisco in March 1896. When Becker and Creegan were arrested soon after, they not only denied their guilt but even protested that they were not in California when the crime was committed. Both were found Guilty on Aug. 28, 1896, and sentenced to life in prison. A new trial was granted because of an alleged mistake in instructions to the jury. Creegan confessed before the second trial, then Becker followed suit. The Prince of Forgers was sentenced to seven years in prison, while Creegan was sentenced to two years at Folsom Prison.

REF.: *CBA; Duke, Celebrated Criminal Cases of America; Horan, The Pinkertons.*

Becker, Charles, 1870-1915, U.S., pol. mal.-mur. The image of the crooked cop without conscience, compassion, or remorse for his ruthless acts was devastatingly summed up in the character of Charles Becker, a lieutenant of the New York Police Department. Becker made a fortune by protecting New York City gamblers until he decided one of these sharpers should be killed, and he ordered the murder of Herman Rosenthal. This blatant slaying by hired killers under Becker's command eventually led Becker to the electric chair, but long before that, a decade before, Becker ruled the gambling empire of New York City. His word was law—to break *his* law was to face unendurable punishment, ruination, and early death. Becker, the corrupt cop, came into being not at his source environment, but in the heart of New York City, or, to be exact, in its Tenderloin, the most exciting, dramatic and vice-ridden area of America at the time. This land of payoff and kickback was far from the green, comfortable hills where Charles Becker was born on July 26, 1870. The sixth child of ten, Becker was born in Callicoon Center, N.Y., a hamlet in the foothills of the Catskills in Sullivan County. He was a large boy and did not shirk fights. At home he was truculent and slow to obey his parents. At school he was even slower to complete assignments. Yet his honesty was never questioned and he excelled in athletics and manual labor. By the time he was eighteen, he had developed a tall, powerful body with broad shoulders, massive arms, and enormous hands that, when doubled into fists, were like the flat sides of two stonemason hammers.

At this time Becker bid farewell to his family and rural life, and traveled to New York City to see a German baker who was a friend of his father's. The baker gave him a job and a room above the bakery, which was in the German section of the city in the old Seventh Ward. To the south was the Bowery and to the north was the wealth of Manhattan which beckoned like a beacon fire to the ambitious Becker. After a brief affair with the baker's daughter, which found Becker confronting the baker and being ordered from his establishment, the youth, then nineteen, went to work as a waiter at The Atlantic Gardens, a sprawling beer garden which had once been the pride of the German community, where free music and excellent nickel beer was offered to a generally middle-class patronage. With the ending of the Civil War, this great spa had declined so that by 1889, when Becker went to work there, the place was populated at night by gamblers, thugs from the Bowery, and prostitutes plying their trade. The well-built, no-nonsense Becker found himself knocking the heads of thugs who created disturbances. He soon built a reputation as a man who could best almost any plug-ugly with a mind to starting trouble.

The job of bouncer was offered to Becker, and the 21-year-old accepted, working in another beer garden. Here he became known as a brutal overseer no thug would think to anger. Even the most fierce of the early day New York gangsters such as Edward "Monk" Eastman gave Becker a wide berth. Eastman not only grew to respect the quick-fisted Becker but he befriended him, taking him to his political sponsor, Timothy "Big Tim" Sullivan, the powerful head of Tammany for the entire East Side of Manhattan. Sullivan used Eastman and his fearsome gang as strikebreakers and political strong-arm thugs who made sure that every election was a Tammany triumph. Tammany also dictated the politics for the entire city at that time and Sullivan lived like a czar, making appointments to political and police posts at will and whim. Sullivan sized up Becker as someone above the status of an ordinary thug, a young man with intelligence and street savvy—one who not only would be loyal to Tammany but to Sullivan himself. The police force, Sullivan concluded, was the right spot for Charles Becker. In 1893 Beck paid a $250 fee to Tammany for his appointment to the police force. This was customary and was publicly known and excused, at least by the poltical sachems who ran things, as a way of assuring the fact that men known to the organization, who were screened as good candidates by Tammany and were not strangers with criminal records, were thus brought onto the force. The screening process cost Tammany money and the applicant was merely paying back the organization's investment. Such money was no small investment. At the time, $250 was one-third the yearly pay of an average cop on the NYPD. The force at that time had more than 5,000 men on the streets, all of them white and most of them, like Becker, Catholic.

The type of police officer the NYPD then hired and kept on the force was not very much different than the type of thug who worked for Monk Eastman, except that they wore uniforms and never openly committed theft. Patrolmen were burly, big men who used their long nightsticks to club anyone who got in their way, either innocent citizen or hooligan. Even to ask a question of the beat cop in those days was to risk being poked in the chest with his stick and hustled down the street for bothering an officer of the law. The man who established and maintained this hardboiled attitude was Inspector Alexander "Clubber" Williams, who was infamous for his brutality and ruthless manner. It was the grafting Williams who gave the wide-open vice district its name. He had been serving in a West Side precinct in the 1870s and when he was transferred to the choice area, he remarked to a newsman: "I've been living on chuck steak for a long time. Now I'm gonna get me some of the tenderloin." Williams supervised an area that stretched approximately between Twenty-Third and Forty-fourth streets and between Third and Seventh Avenues, this being the old Twenty-ninth Precinct. Here could be found the best hotels, the finest theaters and restaurants, as well as hundreds of posh gambling dens, lavish bordellos, and vice dens of all sorts, a plum for grafting policemen such as Williams.

During the Lexow Committee Hearings, which began just about

The crooked NYPD Lt. Charles Becker.

Big Tim Sullivan   **Herman "Beansie" Rosenthal**

Bald Jack Rose   **Harry Vallon**

Becker henchman Bridgey Webber, front left.

Sam Schepps   **Gambler Arnold Rothstein**

Big Jack Zelig, gangster.   **Herbert Bayard Swope**

the time Becker joined the force, Inspector Williams was the focal point of the investigation into police graft. Prosecuting counsel John Goff, who, ironically, was to preside over Becker's own first murder trial almost twenty years later, revealed that Williams had more than $250,000 in the bank, owned a mansion and a yacht, and lived like a king. Williams boldly admitted that he took what he liked in the district he controlled and he was later dismissed from the force, though never prosecuted. His was the enduring image that etched itself into the mind of the ambitious Charles Becker. He, too, would someday preside over the Tenderloin and make his own fortune, this he vowed. Long before that time, however, Becker found himself in continuous trouble, so much trouble that he gleaned more press coverage in that day than any other common cop on the force. At first Becker was assigned to the Fulton Street area and later, due to the strings of his mentor, Inspector Williams, moved to the Tenderloin. It was here that he ran headlong into the famous writer, Stephen Crane, who had seen him years earlier on a dark street pounding the face of a helpless prostitute who had failed to pay him off that night.

Crane had established himself as one of America's finest authors the previous year, in 1895, with the publication of *The Red Badge of Courage,* and was the toast of New York at the age of twenty-four. He disdained the literary parties and salons, preferring the company of Bowery lowlifes, bums, and apprentice hoodlums and their women, mostly prostitutes. He had long taken the view that the beat cop in New York was nothing more than a thug in uniform and had been writing a series of articles exposing their grafting, brutal ways, communicating with the new police commissioner, Theodore Roosevelt. On the night of Sept. 15, 1896, Crane found himself at the Broadway Gardens, assigned by the editors of the New York *Journal* to write about the underworld types who crowded the tables there. With him were two streetwalkers of his acquaintance and they were joined by another whore named Dora Clark. At 3 a.m., Crane put one of the girls on a streetcar, and when he returned to the sidewalk, he found the large, lumbering Becker arresting his other two friends for soliciting. Crane stepped forth and said one woman was his wife. Becker, who was later described by Crane as "picturesque as a wolf," then reached out and grabbed the other girl, Dora Clark, arresting only her on charges of prostitution. As he dragged the girl off, Crane protested and Becker smirked, snarling: "You ain't married to both of 'em, are you?"

Rushing to the Tenderloin station house, Crane obtained Becker's name and badge number, then told newsmen that "whatever her character (that of Dora Clark), the arrest was an outrage. The policeman flatly lied!" Crane appeared as a witness for Clark later in court, where Becker insisted that he had seen the woman solicit two men within five minutes. Crane told the presiding magistrate that this was a boldfaced lie, that he had been with the woman for several hours and nothing of the kind happened. Dora Clark then testified that she had been persecuted for several months by Becker and other policemen in the area because she had resisted the advances of a cop named Rosenberg. This officer had solicited sex from Dora and she, thinking he was black because of his swarthy complexion, had replied: "How dare you speak to a decent white woman!" Calling the officer black when he was not was thought by fellow officers to be the worst insult their ranks could receive and Dora Clark had been marked for vengeance.

After listening to the statements, the magistrate, who had recently received a favorable profile by Crane, shocked Becker and dozens of other officers who had lent him support by siding with Crane and accepting his version of the events. Dora Clark was released. Becker had received his first minor setback, but this incident was nothing compared to his next ill-fated news notice. Becker was working the graveyard shift on Sept. 20, 1896, with another officer named Carey when, close to dawn, the two patrolmen saw three men flee from a tobacco shop carrying sacks of loot. They gave chase, shouting for the burglars to halt. Though heavyset, Becker was fast on his feet and he caught up with one of the burglars, bringing him down with one blow from his nightstick. A second burglar outdistanced the pair. Then one of the officers, it was never determined who, shot the third from some distance. This escapade was played up in the press and Becker was hailed as a hero. The dead man, Becker insisted, was a notorious second-story man named John O'Brien. There was talk of giving Becker a commendation and an important promotion until, three days later, the relatives of the slain man identified him as 19-year-old John Fay, a plumber's assistant. Fay had accidentally stepped in the line of fire which both Becker and Carey knew, Fay's family claimed, but they assumed no one would inquire about a dead young man they were passing off as a notorious thief. John Fay's reputation had been tarnished, his relatives said, so that a pair of "gun-happy killers" could make the police force look good in the press. Becker and Carey were suspended for a month and were privately warned by their superiors to make sure of their targets in the future.

By the time Becker returned to his post in the Tenderloin, he was surprised to see Commissioner Roosevelt come into the precinct station to review the men there. He singled out Becker, shook his hand, and commended him for his considerable bravery in taking on thieves face to face but then he turned and told the entire group that they should all be more careful in their treatment of "unfortunate women," that even these fallen angels had the same rights as law-abiding citizens. In this way, without singling Becker out, Theodore Roosevelt had subtly upbraided him, warned him. But Becker was not a man of subtleties. He proved that when he sought out Dora Clark in October 1896 and beat her until he blackened both her eyes and broke her nose. He was stopped by fellow officers from choking her to death. He left her on the sidewalk, warning her that she would "wind up in the river" if she ever again accused a New York cop of anything. But Dora was stubborn and brought charges against Becker. A police hearing was held, the longest on record up to that time, and Becker got off with a casual reprimand.

It appeared to Becker that his political influence through Big Tim Sullivan was not only intact but would protect him against any pesky citizen daring to challenge his authority. On one occasion Becker arrested a society woman whom he accused of soliciting. She turned out to be perfectly innocent, having said goodbye to one of her lawyers on the street after a meeting in his office. Becker, confronted with the testimony of the lawyer, gave the man his usual sneer, refusing to back down and stating: "I know a whore when I see one!" He was reprimanded and sent back to the street where, a short time later, he arrested another woman who approached him and asked directions to the subway. He mumbled something to her she did not understand and she questioned him again. Annoyed, Becker grabbed the poor woman and ran her into the station house, booking her as a common drunk. She turned out to be the wife of a New Jersey manufacturer. This incident caused Becker's superiors to slavishly apologize to both the woman and her influential husband, and even Becker's political sponsor, Big Tim Sullivan, had to step in and persuade the couple not to sue. Sullivan had a quiet talk with his protégé, telling him that he had to be more cautious in the future when arresting women. He had plans for Becker, Sullivan told him, big plans, so it was important that he maintain an unblemished record.

Some time later, however, the easy-to-anger Becker, while on a raid against a gambling house, was shoved by a gambler who boasted of his political influence. Becker, who was alone in the room with the man at the time, pulled a pistol and shot the gambler dead, later claiming that the man pulled a gun. No witnesses were present to contradict him but Becker's superiors again had a quiet talk with him, warning him severely to keep his hand off his gun unless it was absolutely necessary to use it. To make sure that he got the point, Becker was suspended for a month. The hamhock-fisted officer took this time to marry Vivian Atteridge. He had been married briefly in 1905 to a pretty young girl named Mary Mahoney, but she had died nine months later of tuberculosis. The marriage to Atteridge would last until 1905 when Becker would divorce her. Vivian would remarry in 1907, wedding Becker's brother John who was also a member of the NYPD.

In 1901, Becker came under the direct command of Captain Max Schmittberger, the very man who had exposed the corrupt practices of Inspector Alexander Williams. Though Clubber Williams was no longer on the force, he acted as an adviser to Becker, who had long ago embraced the Clubber's philosophy of brute force. Becker, by then a roundsman (one status above patrolman, similar to the rank of corporal), was known by Schmittberger to be a Williams partisan and, as such, was treated coldly and suspiciously by his superior. Schmittberger was thought of as a squealer and a turncoat who had exposed his own people to the Lexow Committee and, as such, many high-rankers on the force wanted to see this man disgraced and deposed. It was with this in mind that Commissioner Bingham and later Commissioner Waldo, who had been told by angry police officials that Schmittberger was corrupt, secretly ordered Becker to dig up evidence that would expose Schmittberger. The police captain knew this, of course, and moved to get rid of Becker by having him transferred to another precinct. After meeting with Williams, Becker filed malfeasance charges against Schmittberger. The enraged captain filed countercharges, but all of these charges were dropped after Commissioner Bingham brought the aggrieved parties together and told them to forget their differences for the sake of the department.

For some time, little was heard of Charles Becker. He must have concluded that the ways of Clubber Williams could do little to advance his career and he maintained a low profile for several years, keeping his record clean. Then, in 1904, Becker suddenly received the department's highest award for heroism which put his name back into the headlines. He had seen a young man in the Hudson River struggling to stay afloat. Fully clothed and without a moment's hesitation, Becker jumped into the river and pulled the man to safety. He turned out to be an unemployed clerk named James Butler who blubbered his thanks to a grinning Becker before newsmen who had conveniently been called to the scene. Butler praised Becker to the newsmen as one of the bravest fellows he had ever seen, explaining that a plank he was walking on gave way and he fell into the River near 10th Street. But it was only a week later when Butler called up the same newsmen and complained that Becker had reneged on his promise. What promise was that, he was asked. Becker, Butler explained, had offered him $15 to jump into the Hudson so that he could jump in after him and appear to be the great hero. But Becker had never paid him the $15 and now Butler was angry at having ruined his only suit for nothing. Becker denied the whole story, laughing at the idea, which he called preposterous. By then he had his medal and a promotion to sergeant.

A short time later, through his Tammany contacts, Becker was promoted to lieutenant and he began to make his moves against the posh gambling and vice dens of the Tenderloin. One story has it that about 1907, Becker made the rounds of all the big time gambling dens and demanded $15 payment a week for himself even though the gamblers explained that they had already paid their "protection" money. After collecting $150, Becker was called into Schmittberger's office and the captain told him to put the money down on his desk, explaining that he knew exactly how much he had collected. Becker tossed the money on the desk and Schmittberger handed him back $15, telling him that that amount was his end, ten per cent, and from that day forward he would be Schmittberger's personal bagman and receive ten percent of everything he collected. Becker the bagman went to work with a vengeance, becoming rich in the course of the next few years. But in 1911, Police Commissioner Rhinelander Waldo decided to crack down on the Tenderloin gamblers after being goaded by scores of enraged reformers objecting to the blatant vice district. Waldo felt that Schmittberger was the core of the rotten apple in the Tenderloin. Years earlier he had, as a Deputy Police Com-

missioner, met with Becker secretly, ordering him to get evidence against Schmittberger, not knowing, of course, that Becker was Schmittberger's bagman and heir apparent to wholesale graft in the precinct. Becker, quite naturally, agreed to the secret investigation, sitting as he was in the catbird's seat, able to provide snippets of information on his captain without ever giving Waldo enough evidence to bring about Schmittberger's removal.

At the same time Becker made himself look good to downtown superiors by appearing to energetically attack the gambling and vice dens by conducting incessant raids against these places. Yet he went on making enormous illicit profits from the gamblers he was protecting, satisfying both Waldo and his protection-paying gambling dens. In 1911 Becker organized and led 203 raids into the Tenderloin where he and his men made 898 arrests which resulted in 103 convictions, a staggering record that outwardly made Becker look like a law enforcement crusader. But what the record also showed, if one dug deeper, were sentences that amounted to next to nothing. Most of the convictions ended in suspended sentences or small fines seldom exceeding $50. Waldo blamed the court system and corrupt judges for such leniency, and to some extent he was correct, since many judges were then, as before and after this golden age of kickbacks and payoffs, on the take. Becker, however, was the man who manipulated these judicial decisions. He simply ordered his men, when appearing in court, to have loss of memory as to the particulars of the raids they conducted. They conveniently misplaced or lost vital evidence that would have assured strong sentences. Faced with this type of shallow prosecution, judges were compelled to issue light sentences. The whole system worked both ways for Charles Becker.

By late 1910 Becker operated autonomously as the head of the gambling squad or, because of the violent manner in which the squad often tore apart gambling dens (those who had been slow to make payoffs), the group known as "the strong-arm squad." His word was law in the Tenderloin by then and he paid nothing to Schmittberger who had been neutralized and later ousted by Big Tim Sullivan. Becker, after minor payoffs to his own officers, split his payoff take only with Big Tim and this further enriched his own coffers by tens of thousands of dollars. To keep the gamblers and vice lords in line, Becker, through Big Tim, employed the worst gang of thugs in New York to perform beatings and even murder, chores too messy for his own corrupt policemen. Monk Eastman had been sent to prison by then, abandoned by Tammany as uncontrollable and had been replaced by Jacob "Big Jack" Zelig (whose real name was William Alberts), a towering, fierce thug who had been Eastman's right-hand man, a gangster which much more cunning than Eastman, one who knew how to keep his organization in line. Zelig and his host of killers worked directly under Becker's orders, going on his payroll but being directed in their nefarious activities by gamblers who took their orders from Becker.

If any of these gangsters ever disobeyed Becker's dictates, he merely had them arrested for violating the Sullivan Law, a law ironically put on the books by none other than Big Tim when, in 1909, he decided to return to the state senate. A disloyal or disobedient gangster would be dragged into court and charged by Becker's minions with carrying concealed firearms, thus violating the Sullivan Law. This carried with it a mandatory eight-year sentence. Of course, when this law went into record, the gangsters never carried firearms unless on the job. Becker got around this by simply having his men provide "throw-away" guns or spare pistols and automatics which were supplied by police officers in quickly convicting a gangster who did not cooperate with the system. Herbert Bayard Swope, later the chief journalist covering the Becker-Rosenthal murder, would later write that "Becker *was* the System. Like Caesar all things were rendered unto Becker in the underworld. Like Briareus he had a hundred arms...and more power in the Department than the Commissioner."

But Becker was not without competition. A number of other lieutenants under his command lusted for his power position and they would do just about anything to come within the good graces of Big Tim Sullivan, the Tammany sachem and real czar of influence and power in New York. Big Tim was many times a millionaire with villas, mansions, yachts, and endless sources of cash; he had been on the take since Boss Croker abandoned his leadership at Tammany in 1901, retiring to the French Riviera with his own millions hustled from the city. Yet Big Tim had no ambitions to retire. He had to have more and more and knew that the Alexandrian philosophy of dividing and controlling his henchmen, Becker included, was the key to the flowing cornucopia of graft. Becker knew this also, that Big Tim would quickly replace him at any time if convenient. So Becker shrewdly began to cultivate certain members of the press as early as 1910, giving crime reporters inside tips on raids and making sure that he and only he received glorification in print. He even went so far as to hire Charles Plitt as his press agent, making sure that the newspapers were informed of his daily activities, or those that made him look like a police hero to the public. Thus for two years up to the Rosenthal killing, he overshadowed almost every policemen in the department, except for the commissioner. This caused Becker to undoubtedly become the most disliked member of the department but he was also the most dangerous. As such, no officer dared to openly criticize or confront him. The specter of Big Tim cast a shadow across every precinct.

Becker's alliances with the press would later backfire on him, although he reaped numerous benefits for a short time from his liaisons with crime beat reporters. In late 1911 a reporter warned Becker that there was a conspiracy within the department to have him framed as a bagman, and Becker, fearing this report was real, went straight to Commissioner Waldo, asking that he be assigned to another position other than heading the "strong-arm" squad. Perhaps by then he had amassed what he considered to be the fortune that would take him comfortably through retirement. Perhaps his meeting with Waldo was nothing more than a fishing expedition. Waldo assured him that he was not being investigated, that he was doing an excellent job, and that he should keep up the good work. Becker went back to being the czar of the Tenderloin. But there was some truth to the reporter's tip. Waldo had been receiving letters from an informant using an alias. One of these letters, received in March 1912, stated: "I would like to have you investigate quietly Lieutenant Becker. He is now collecting more money than Devery (Big Bill Devery, New York's thoroughly corrupt chief of police during the 1890s), and it is well-known to everyone at Police Headquarters. Please do this and you will be surprised at the result."

This letter, incredibly, was sent by Waldo straight to Becker. It was the commissioner's policy, as sort of a naive procedure of fair play, to send such blind accusations to the officers being accused so that they could respond directly. In reality, the officer accused of misconduct was expected to investigate himself and dutifully report on his own wrongdoings. Of course, such officers never found credence in any of these accusations, all of them to the last letter being the work of cranks and malcontents. Becker shrewdly went one step further and returned this letter to Waldo, saying prudently that he was not in a position to react to such a document and that perhaps it would be better if the commissioner were to send this letter on to another person in the department. He knew that such a straightforward response would all the more readily confirm in Waldo's mind that he, Charles Becker, was beyond reproach and nothing more would come of the accusation, which is exactly what happened. Waldo's decision to simply file this and other letters concerning Becker's wholesale graft as crank mail later caused him much embarrassment.

Becker, unlike the high-living Sullivan and former police bigwigs who had taken payoffs with both hands for years, kept a low profile outside of his police duties. He was a conservative and cautious crook, secreting his illegal loot in so many banks that most of his fortune was never fully tracked down, even years after he was executed. He continued to live in a modest apartment at 159th and Edgecomb Avenue with his third wife, Helen, whom he had married in 1905 after his divorce from Vivian Atteridge. Helen was a schoolteacher, born in 1874 and a dedicated educator who went on teaching slow high school learners at P.S. 90 for $1,820 a year, even in 1912 when her husband had amassed a reported $1 to $2 million. As a couple, they enjoyed simple pleasures such as horseback riding and gardening. They planned to build a modest house in the near future. Helen would later defend her husband with a fierce loyalty that saw her pleading for his life right up to the last second, abandoning her pride to prostrate herself before Governor Whiteman, the very man who had convicted her husband. No matter what evidence was later put before her, Helen Becker refused to believe that her husband, whom she called Charlie-Lover (he called her My Queen), ever committed a single illegal act. Charles Becker was an honest man, Helen insisted, a simple man from a large family; she never tired of saying how she, like her husband, came from a family with ten children.

The one indulgence practiced by Becker was taking his grateful wife to the best restaurants in town. They dined with political dynamos and business tycoons who curried Becker's favor. They feasted upon sumptuous meals at Rector's, Sharkey's, Sherry's, Luchow's, and never picked up a check. When going to dinner or an occasional show, the Beckers rode in chauffeur-driven limousines owned by such people as millionaire broker Henry Sternberger. Although Helen Becker did not know them by profession, scores of other men would table-hop to sit with the Beckers and whisper in her husband's ear before then moving off, men glittering with diamonds and full of conspiracy. These were the top Tenderloin gamblers, not the least of whom were young sharpers who had come under the protective arms of Big Tim Sullivan, chiefly Arnold Rothstein and Herman "Beansie" Rosenthal. Sullivan had mentioned these two gamblers by name to Becker, telling him that he felt "paternal" toward both these two young Jewish sharpers and would like to see their careers blossom.

It was not surprising therefore that Becker went out of his way to befriend the more social of the pair, Rosenthal, when meeting him at an Elks' Club Ball on New Year's Eve 1911. At the time, Becker sent Helen home and stayed to get drunk with the pudgy young gambler, or pretended to be drunk, displaying an inordinate amount of affection toward a man he had just met, throwing his bear-like arms around Rosenthal, kissing him on the cheeks several times and then lumbering onto a table and shouting to all his cronies: "Boys, Herman Rosenthal is my best friend and anything he wants, he gets!" He got down and hugged the gambler once more. "Anything in the world for you, Herman. I'll get up at three o'clock in the morning to do you a favor! You can have anything I've got!" Becker then called three of his top officers over and told them: "This is my best pal and you do anything he wants you to do." Becker continued to cultivate this strange new friendship by meeting with Rosenthal at the Lafayette Turkish baths, at the Elks' Club, and various restaurants. In the Turkish baths the hulking Becker would sit, towel-wrapped, next to the chubby, flabby Rosenthal and pump him subtly about the strength of Big Tim's support. Rosenthal told him that Big Tim had authorized a new, posh club, which Rosenthal intended to call The Hester Club, that would be opened shortly. Becker not only promised him protection for this club but went on to tell the gambler that he was "getting hold of a lot of money" through the easy efforts of his strong-arm squad, and that he might be interested in investing in The Hesper Club. Of course, Becker was making a bid to short-cut Big Tim's own investment in the club so that he would be on an equal footing with Sullivan on the interest level of many clubs. Becker's ambition was still white-hot and he undoubtedly thinking of somehow supplanting Big Tim as he had Schmittberger.

Thanks to Providence, Becker did exactly that. In the spring of 1912, Big Tim's dissolute lifestyle caught up with him. He was seized by paresis of the brain, generally caused by long-standing syphilis, and became bedridden, half-conscious most of the time. He was no longer an effective force in New York's system of graft.

Becker, without waiting for approval from Tammany, took over Sullivan's role as soon as he heard his political mentor had fallen ill. Becker immediately leveled an enormous duty on all gambling dens and bordellos, sending his men around to obtain the weekly increase. Some of Becker's police goons arrived at the newly opened Hesper Club where the strong-arm cops were told: "No payoffs here. This is Big Tim's house." True, Sullivan had fronted a good deal of the money Rosenthal had used to establish this lavish gambling den in a three-story brownstone at 104 West 45th Street, just off Sixth Avenue. The place sported thick carpets and heavy, dark drapes, massive furniture, which was the vogue of the era, and the latest gambling wheels, tables, and devices. But, ironically, Becker himself had also invested in the club, giving Rosenthal $1,500 for twenty percent of the profits, a holding a mortgage on all the furniture as well for his small investment. It was his thinking that, despite the profits Rosenthal paid him, he could still enjoy an additional $500-a-week payoff from The Hesper. Rosenthal, however, balked at this double payoff and refused to give Becker's boys a cent.

When Becker heard of this refusal, he met with Big Jack Zelig and ordered the thugmaster to see Rosenthal personally. Zelig went to Rosenthal and told him: "You better pay. Sullivan's out and Becker's the boss now." Rosenthal told Zelig that he was crazy and that he would see Sullivan about it. But Sullivan was dying in bed and Rosenthal found only the boss's politically inept brother Florrie, his nephew Jim, and Frank Farrell lounging in Big Tim's sumptuous office. They had no idea what he should do. They were trying to figure out Big Tim's secretly organized empire themselves and were getting nowhere. The obstinate Rosenthal left, later telling Zelig that he had no intention of giving Becker anything, including the twenty per cent on the investment.

When Becker heard this, he exploded. He roared at Zelig: "Make him pay!" Zelig and some of his goons, "Gyp the Blood" Horowitz, Whitey Lewis, Dago Frank and Lefty Louie, the four men who were to take Rosenthal's life in full view of dozens of stunned witnesses. They grabbed the gambler as he was stepping out of his club one night and beat him unconscious. Still the stubborn gambler refused to pay off. He went back to Big Tim's relatives who told him: "Make a deal with Becker, that's all we can tell you." Rosenthal was beaten. He called Becker and the two men met. Rosenthal complained that his club was new and not doing as well as he had hoped. He needed more time to pay the additional money Becker was demanding. Becker told him he had a month and to make sure he got his percentage, installed one of his cronies in Rosenthal's club. This man was Jack Rose, better known along the Main Stem as Billiard Ball Jack because he did not have a human hair on his shining bald head. Rosenthal had always hated the pugnacious Rose and he found the gambler's permanent presence in his club offensive. He brooded about this until his pent-up rage broke loose in diatribes against New York Police Lieutenant Charles Becker. He began to speak to anyone, everyone, about this "crooked cop," until his incessant carping was heard by the crusading district attorney, Charles Seymour Whitman.

Before Whitman acted on the Rosenthal rumors, Commissioner Waldo received another letter which complained about the blatant operations of a gambling den at 104 West 45th Street, Rosenthal's Hesper Club. This was in Becker's Tenderloin and Waldo called the lieutenant into his office. Here he confronted Becker with the letter, his usual custom, informing him: "I can't understand this could have escaped your attention." Waldo gave Becker a direct order to close The Hesper and keep it closed. This was one letter Becker did not return to the Commissioner. He had no alternative except to comply with orders. He informed Rosenthal that he had to "close you up for a while." Rosenthal protested but Becker was firm. Not only was the Hesper Club closed but, to make sure it remained closed, Becker placed a police guard around the clock in the front room on the main floor. The presence of these cops drove Rosenthal nearly crazy since he lived on the premises and he bitterly complained to any and all who

would listen that it made him and his poor wife feel like prisoners. It was intolerable. He wouldn't stand for it. He would do *something* to show Becker that he could not treat Herman Rosenthal "like a dog."

The presence of the police in his home so enraged the beefy gambler that he began to war with the department. He announced that he would lock out these interlopers and, on one occasion, he slammed the doors and bolted them during a changing of shifts. He stood outside and dared the police to break into his place. The answer came in hours when a crew showed up on West 45th Street with a new hydraulic lift which could tear out the entire door frame. Before permanent damage was done Rosenthal capitulated, running across the street and unlocking the door. As the late spring brought hot weather, Rosenthal threatened to stoke up the furnaces in his building and "roast those cops out of there," but this proved to be an idle boast. Rosenthal's wife, Dora, a buxom and demonstrative woman, nagged her husband incessantly about policemen roaming her home, and every time the shift would change, she would lean out of her third-story bedroom window and shake her fist at the officers changing the guard, shouting that they were violating her home.

When Rosenthal could no longer bear this continuing indignity, he filed harrassment charges against several high-ranking policemen in the department but oddly never mentioned Becker. Although local judges scoffed at the complaints Rosenthal made, the gambler persistently filed new complaints. All of this got back to Becker. Now the crooked cop felt the kind of pressure he had only administered in the past. He became enraged. How dare this gambler create problems for the police and for him? He would not tolerate such defiance. He had Zelig's goons threaten Rosenthal again but the gambler refused to back down. Becker decided then and there that only one course of action was left to him. According to the sensational thirty-eight-page confession later made by Jack Rose, Becker came to him and ordered him to organize the death of Herman "Beansie" Rosenthal. Rose was to employ his fellow gamblers, Harry Vallon (Harry Vallinsky) and Louis Bridgie Webber in organizing Rosenthal's death with Zelig's gunsels. Becker was specific in his command to Rose, telling him: "I want Rosenthal croaked! I want him murdered, shot, his throat cut, any way that will take him off the earth!" Rose told Becker that Zelig and his men might be hesitant to kill a man who was so much in the public eye, a man whose vendetta against the NYPD had put him on the front pages of the daily newspapers. "If those rats don't go along I will find out where they hang out and frame every one of them and send them up the river for carrying concealed weapons!" Becker emphasized that nothing would happen to anyone who killed the man he had marked for murder. "All that's necessary," Becker told Rose, "is to walk right up to where he is and blaze away at him and leave the rest to me. Nothing will happen to anybody that does it. Walk up to him and shoot him before a policeman if you want to and nothing will happen!"

Rose reluctantly set about organizing the murder of Rosenthal but he dragged his feet, as did Webber and Vallon. Becker pursued them like a terrier, at one point shouting that he would frame the gamblers unless they got the job done quickly. "Why isn't he croaked?" Becker would say in his daily phone call to Rose. "Why isn't that man dead yet? You're all a bunch of damned cowards!" He literally hounded the gamblers with threats up to the night when Rosenthal was finally murdered. Only hours before this happened, Becker was on the phone to Rose, saying: "If only that s.o.b. is croaked tonight, how happy I will be, how lovely it will be!" The problem in getting Becker's gruesome job done lay within the ranks of the gamblers who worked at cross-purposes. All of them owned interests in various gambling joints and competed with each other, distrusting each other's motives. All of them would have just as readily put each other on the spot if Becker had asked for *their* deaths. None of them, however, had any love for Rosenthal.

Only a few years earlier Rosenthal and Webber had fought

over gambling territories that brought out their respective gunmen in open warfare. Rosenthal had actually arranged for Webber's murder in 1909, hiring a notorious thug named Spanish Louie (or Louis) to beat Webber to death. Rosenthal had actually watched from a shadowy doorway while this goon nearly beat Webber to death but was interrupted by a patrolman who gave chase to the fleeing Louie. With that, Rosenthal sauntered across the street, pretending to be passing by, and helped Webber to his feet, wiping away the blood pouring from his broken nose with his own handkerchief and telling Webber how awful it was that the streets were no longer safe. The next year Spanish Louie was shot to death from a speeding auto by four gangsters in Webber's employ, these being Christian "Boob" Walker, Harry "Gyp the Blood" Horowitz, Lefty Louie and Whitey Lewis. These were Zelig's boys but the same gunmen were for hire by anyone with money and they often free-lanced for Rosenthal. Still, the gamblers found dozens of excuses for not killing Rosenthal, hoping that Becker would change his mind. Rosenthal didn't aid his own cause by loudly accusing the police of wholesale graft. Not having any success with the local magistrates who refused to indict anyone on his accusations, Rosenthal went to the press, badgering newsmen to print his story of wholesale corruption in the police force. Everyone turned a deaf ear, except a reporter for the *World*, Herbert Bayard Swope. Swope had known Rosenthal for some years; a habitué of Tenderloin casinos, he and Rosenthal had been on more than speaking terms, the gambler steering the reporter to the best play in town, often enough feeding him tips on various horse races. Swope not only listened to Rosenthal but decided to print his affadavit in the *World*. The story that Rosenthal gave Swope was nothing like the tale he had brought to the city magistrates. To Swope the gambler described in detail his relationship with Police Lieutenant Charles Becker, from the very first moment they had met at the Elks' Club on New Year's Eve to the massive payoffs he had made to the crooked cop, along with all the other payoffs Becker was receiving throughout the Tenderloin. Rosenthal named every gambler in on the payoffs, all the police collectors and bagmen, all the backup thugs who did the dirty work for the cops. After the Swope story ran, the most important of his life and the story that would make him into a newspaper magnate, the newsman went after Whitman to make sure the district attorney did his duty. He persuaded Whitman to take Rosenthal's direct statement and bring a grand jury indictment against Becker.

Before Whitman took Rosenthal's deposition, Becker heard of the affidavit in the *World* office and marched to the newspaper with his lawyer. He inspected the document and snarled: "This is a pack of lies!" He turned on his heels and went back to badgering Rose to have Rosenthal killed immediately. Rosenthal was oddly blasé about the lethal peril he had created for himself. "I know I'm a marked man," he told a newsman, "and I've probably signed my own death warrant but I don't care." Despite these words of bravado, Herman Rosenthal cared very much, and he took pains to stay out of his usual haunts, holing up on the third floor of his brownstone. He ventured forth to seek the advice of the rising young gambler, Arnold Rothstein, who offered him money to leave town. Rosenthal said he would never let himself be run out of New York but he later returned to Rothstein, asking for the money. Rothstein turned a cold shoulder to his one-time friend Rosenthal and told him it was "too late to do anything." This meeting with Rothstein occurred on the afternoon of July 15, 1912. Rosenthal thought about Rothstein's remark and decided that there was something more to do. He had earlier stated that "this is a fight to the finish. I know that the whole police department will be against me and that all the gamblers, big and little, will fight me, too, because this means a big investigation that will clean up the city."

Late that day and into the evening, Herman Rosenthal talked for five hours to District Attorney Whitman and key staff members, reiterating everything he had revealed to Swope and promising to reveal even more when brought before a grand jury, if he

lived that long. Whitman promised that if he stayed in his home, he would be all right. The district attorney was the only key official in New York who had no strings to Tammany, having gotten elected without that organization's help. He was the mortal foe of Tammany mayor William Jay Gaynor (who had disavowed his Tammany connection once in office) and especially eschewed the friendships of such sachems as Big Tim Sullivan. A crusader and a tireless reformer, Whitman vowed to use Rosenthal's accusations to clean up the city. Before leaving Whitman's offices that night, however, Rosenthal gave himself little chance of ever appearing before a Grand Jury, telling Whitman: "I may not live to do it. You may never see me again alive." His words, undoubtedly couched for dramatic effect, could not have been more prophetic.

That night, at about 10 p.m., Rosenthal received a phone call from someone he considered important enough to meet later. He told his wife that he would be going out to keep an important rendezvous but he refused to reveal the identity of the man who had called. Dora Rosenthal begged her husband not to go out, reminding him that he was in great danger but Herman Rosenthal somehow felt confident that no one would dare harm him; he had become too public, too well-known. Why, he was on every front page of every newspaper in New York. He had attacked the New York Police Department and the police of the city would never dare let anything happen to him now. His indictment against the NYPD was his insurance policy. He had not reckoned on the ruthless indifference Charles Becker had to such logic.

So confident was Rosenthal that he walked all the way to his meeting place, his favorite hangout, The Metropole Hotel, on 43rd Street, just east of Broadway. The hotel was owned by the Considine Brothers and Big Tim Sullivan, Rosenthal's mentor; nothing could happen to him there, the gambler reasoned. The place was a favorite after-hours haunt for actors, newsmen, gamblers, racetrack touts, and Broadway characters of every stripe. Its bar and restaurant teemed with the most colorful (and often dangerous) people in town, the kind of place Herman Rosenthal loved. As Rosenthal neared the hotel he ran into some gamblers he knew. One of them reached out and said: "Herman, it's not safe for you to be out tonight. Go home. Turn around and go home right now." Rosenthal pulled away and laughed off the warning. He intended to keep his appointment at the Metropole. He turned into the hotel lobby shortly before 1 a.m., July 16, 1912, and as he passed the bustling, jam-packed bar, there was a moment of silence, a strange hush as the scores of drinkers paused for a moment as if to acknowledge the passing of a ghost.

Rosenthal sauntered into the dining room and sat down at his favorite table, and here, too, the crowd stared momentarily at him in a strange awe, not expecting him to be there in the flesh, to be alive at all. From the scores of statements made later and over the years it was evident that everyone in the Metropole, everyone "in the know" in Manhattan, knew that Herman "Beansie" Rosenthal was going to die that night, "go on the spot," as Damon Runyon later put it and he later intimated that he was present in the bar that night. The Metropole was teeming with Runyon characters, the very prototypes who would later people his *Guys and Dolls* and other Broadway tales. Oddly, Rosenthal sat down next to Christian "Boob" Walker, one of the goons who worked for his arch nemesis, Bridgie Webber. Other Webber cronies, Fat Moe Brown and Butch Kitte sat down for a while while Rosenthal ordered a steak and a horse's neck (ginger ale and a lemon twist). The Metropole had a number of unique drinks created by its gambler patrons. Billiard Ball Jack Rose, hated by Rosenthal, had created his own drink which was forever after known as a "Jack Rose," this being a cocktail containing a jigger of applejack, juice of half a lemon, and a half ounce of grenadine, which was all shaken with cracked ice and strained.

When the steak came, Rosenthal wolfed it down, keeping his eye on the door, as if expecting someone to come in at any moment. Boob Walker later stated that "Herman ate as if he could take it with him." Finishing his supper, the gambler excused

The public murder of Rosenthal as depicted in New York's newspapers of the day.

Left: Four killers at a picnic: (top, left to right) Gyp the Blood, Lefty Louie, Dago Frank, and (bottom, seated at right) Whitey Lewis. Top: Gyp the Blood and Lefty Louie at trial; they were condemned to the electric chair.

Judge John W. Goff   D.A. Charles Seymour Whitman   Mrs. Helen Becker   Charles Becker, executed.

himself, got up, and shuffled into the lobby where he bought the latest editions. He was on the front pages bigger than ever. He bought a copy of the *World* which blared the headline: "GAMBLER CHARGES POLICE LIEUTENANT WAS HIS PARTNER." He tucked this under his arm and ambled back to his table in the restaurant which was near one of the large windows that faced the street and still gave Rosenthal a clear view of the front door. He spread the newspaper out in front of him and the other gamblers at his table took one look at the headline and quickly excused themselves. A group of gamblers at the next table stared at him incredulously.

Rosenthal shot his French cuffs blazoned with huge gold links, shoved his chair back so that his stomach bloated forward over a huge gold belt buckle which featured his initials in large letters reading HR, and smirked at his friends sitting at the next table. "What do you think of the papers lately?" he said in a conspiratorial voice. "You boys aren't sore at me, are you?" Rosenthal asked this question without really expecting an answer. One of the gamblers shook his head and said: "Herman, you're a damned fool." Ignoring this remark, Rosenthal ordered a cup of coffee and began to read the newspaper, dwelling on every word that dealt with his accusations. Some of the gamblers sitting nearby who had been whispering among themselves looked up at the entranceway to the dining room and suddenly fell silent. At the doorway was a police detective named William J. File. He glanced about the room and then disappeared into the crowded lobby which, instead of emptying out at that time of the morning, was actually filling up so that standing room was getting scarce. It seemed as if everyone in the know on the Main Stem wanted to be there at the kill, or, at least, that was the image of the thronged Metropole that many writers later created. Other plainclothes NYPD detectives were also on hand that night, and out on the street, no less than six—some said more than a dozen—patrolmen strolled the sidewalk on both sides of the street on the block where the Metropole was located, its bright marquee lights flooding light up and down the street. The public killing of Herman Rosenthal was undoubtedly an event no one wanted to miss. Someone in front of the Metropole, a man in a dark suit and a straw boater, his voice full of authority, began to order the taxicabs parked there to move on and he continued to have the cabs pull away from the entranceway for twenty minutes, until the front of the hotel was completely clear of parked vehicles right up to the moment Herman Rosenthal stepped outside to meet his terrible fate.

Oblivious to his own impending execution, only a half hour away, Rosenthal went on bathing in his press glory. He was the talk of the town and he knew it, reveled in it, glorified in the danger he had brought to his own door. He feared nothing, his expression told everyone; he alone would clean up New York. Even when his arch enemy Bridgie Webber sauntered into the hotel dining room a little after 1:30 a.m., Rosenthal gave him a slight smile. Webber walked casually up to Rosenthal and placed his hand on the pudgy gambler's shoulder, saying affably: "Hello, Herman, how's everything?" Rosenthal nodded and said: "Fine, everything is just fine. How is it by you?" Webber did not reply, merely stood there for a moment, then he patted Rosenthal's shoulder several times, turned around, and walked quickly out of the hotel. This was the signal to waiting gangsters outside who could see through the dining room window which of the diners was to be their victim. Months later, at Becker's prolonged trial, Webber sat calmly in the witness stand and was asked: "When you went to the Metropole, for what purpose did you look for him (Rosenthal)? Was it for the purpose of having him murdered?" The answer was a quiet, unperturbed "Yes, sir." Webber's pat on the shoulder was his kiss of death. After making sure that Rosenthal was at the Metropole, Webber went outside to inform the eight men waiting there, four of them gangsters with guns bulging in their pockets, that their victim was almost ready for the slaughter.

It was almost 2 a.m. when a waiter carrying a tray of dishes

stopped at Rosenthal's table and told him that "there is a man in the lobby who wants to see you." Rosenthal looked through the dining room door to see Harry Vallon, a gambling henchman of Webber's—a man with the face of a bloody hatchet. Vallon stood staring at him, impassive, his hands jammed into his coat pockets. Rosenthal got up and slowly walked up to Vallon in the lobby. "Can you come outside for a minute, Herman? There's someone outside who wants to see you." Vallon asked him. The utterly unsuspecting Rosenthal shrugged and followed Vallon outside into the sultry, steaming night. The heavyset gambler followed Vallon outside to the sidewalk, standing under the bright lights of the Metropole, a perfect target. Vallon suddenly stepped back, out of the light and into the shadows. Several gamblers Rosenthal knew stood nearby, including Dave Mendelsohn, Sigmund Rosenfeld, and Chick Beebe. They stood off in the distance and in the shadows, twenty feet or so from the hotel entrance. Also standing in the shadows talking with cronies was Billiard Ball Jack Rose, talking with another gambling intimate, Sam Schepps. Down the block several uniformed policemen could be seen milling about. The street was crowded but no one seemed to take any notice of a huge 1909 Packard that was idling almost in the middle of the street. A dark, swarthy man sat at the wheel. Four other dark, swarthy men (some reports said five men), all described later as short in stature and dressed in dark suits and wearing soft felt hats, stood in front of the car, forming an arc before the hotel entrance.

One of the men shouted: "Over here, Herman!" Rosenthal, who had lit a cigar when crossing the lobby, squinted into the darkness, unable to identify the man who called out to him with an unfamiliar voice. Rosenthal took a hesitant step forward, saying: "Who's that?" The killers closed in on him, just barely entering the glaring arc lights from the marquee, and five shots rang out, striking Rosenthal at close range (powder burns were to blacken his face). The bullets struck him in the neck, the nose and two in the head. One wild shot struck the door frame of the hotel. Rosenthal, spouting blood, fell dead in the street, the newspapers he had been carrying flying upward and then settling over his crumpled, prostrate body.

Eyewitnesses later claimed that the chief killer, the fierce Gyp the Blood Horowitz, had stepped forward before the fusillade erupted and hailed his victim with the words "Hello, Herman." After Rosenthal collapsed from his lethal wounds, Horowitz leaned over to make sure the gambler was dead, then stood up, and said, "Goodbye, Herman." He then casually stepped over the body and joined his fellow gangsters, getting into the Packard which quickly roared down the street. (One witness swore that Gyp the Blood had sneered at his fallen victim and snorted the word "Gotcha!") Rosenthal lay in the street for some minutes, the many witnesses on the sidewalks frozen in a murder scene motif. In a doorway down the street, some later insisted, mob leader Jack Zelig lit a cigar and walked away from the scene. Then the street exploded with shouts and panic. Police came running from everywhere and witnesses raced to patrolmen to give varied descriptions of the killers and several versions of the license plate on the Packard.

One unlikely witness to this gory murder was none other than the esteemed drama critic for the New York *Times*, Alexander Woollcott, who would later become a best-selling author and remembered for his radio appearances as the Town Crier. Recalling the Rosenthal murder twenty-two years later when writing *While Rome Burns*, Woollcott summed up the livid scene: "I shall always remember the picture of that soft, fat body wilting on the sidewalk with a beer-stained tablecloth serving as its pall. I shall always remember the fish-belly faces of the sibilant crowd which sprung in a twinkling from nowhere, formed like a clout around those clamorous wounds. Just behind me an old timer whispered a comment which I have had more than one occasion to repeat. 'From where I stand,' he said, 'I can see eight murderers.'"

As evidence and the testimony of several gamblers scrambling to save their necks would later prove, there were four murderers, plus the man who ordered the killing, all of whom would later sit down in the electric chair for their blatant display of firearms. The killers and their driver fled down 43rd Street in the large Packard sedan. As the car turned onto Broadway with a squeal of tires, Detective File raced from the hotel, his .38-caliber revolver in his hand. He took a look at Rosenthal's body, the left side of the face blown away, and ordered two patrolmen nearby to follow him. They ran down the street to Broadway where Police Lieutenant Edward Frye met them. The four officers jumped into a cab and order the taxi driver to follow the Packard which was fast disappearing down Broadway. It soon outdistanced the taxi and disappeared. Fortunately, a young, unemployed cabaret singer, Charles Gallagher, had been walking toward the Metropole when the shooting occurred and had the presence of mind to write down the license plate of the car as it sped past him. He later had to argue with policemen to give them the number "NY-41313."

District Attorney Whitman was awakened at home by the indefatigable Swope who told him that his star witness had just been murdered. Whitman climbed out of his pajamas and into street clothes, going immediately to the 47th Street Precinct Station where the body of Rosenthal lay on a slab in the back room. Some minutes after the bleary-eyed Whitman arrived at the station, he turned to see Charles Becker enter. Becker later claimed that he too had been awakened by a newsman giving him the news of the killing and rushed to his own precinct station to verify the slaying. He took one look at the body and then he met the eyes of Charles Whitman glaring at him. For a moment the hardboiled crooked cop tried to stare down the district attorney but Whitman's eyes narrowed to slits of contempt and Becker, without a word, lowered his eyes and turned around, leaving the station quickly. He later met with Rose, Webber, and Vallon to congratulate them on the killing, telling the gamblers that he had just gone to the station house and how "it was a pleasing sight to me to see the squealing Jew lying there, and, if it had not been for the presence of Whitman, I would have cut out his tongue and hung it on the Times Building as a warning to future squealers."

An hour later, Whitman returned home, beside himself with anger over the killing of Rosenthal, telling his wife that "I'm going to get Becker if it's the only thing I ever do. New York is supposed to be the greatest city in the world...But as long as Becker and all those like him are allowed to defy and corrupt every law by which decent people live, New York will never be anything but a human sewer!" He vowed to send the killers, including Becker, to the electric chair. Whitman was greatly aided in his goal by soon receiving word that the license plate of the murder car had been traced to a rental garage. The killers could not have selected a more conspicuous auto to use in New York's most sensational murder of the decade. It had once belonged to the great fighter, John L. Sullivan, and was easily traced. It had been rented by a number of gamblers and these—Vallon, Rose, and Webber—were soon under arrest. They were housed in the Tombs but refused to admit to anything until it appeared quite obvious to them that they, not the actual triggermen, would be charged with the killings.

Rose was the first to crack, giving Whitman his famous thirty-eight-page statement in which he liberally quoted Becker's "Croak Rosenthal" decree. Realizing that Rose was saving his own skin, Webber and Vallon soon joined the chorus, corroborating every damning word Rose said, all, of course, with the promise of immunity extended to them. Through the cooperation of the gamblers, the killers, Harry Gyp the Blood Horowitz, Lefty Louie (Louis Rosenberg), Whitey Lewis (Jacob Seidenschmer) and Dago Frank Cirofici, were all convicted by a jury that took twenty minutes to make up its collective mind on Nov. 19, 1912. All four young killers were electrocuted in Sing Sing on Apr. 14, 1913, a Monday. The previous day, the three Jewish men, Horowitz, Rosenberg, and Seidenschmer, were fed a Passover Dinner prepared in an Ossining hotel, which consisted of stuffed Hudson River bass, chicken soup and macaroons, roast chicken, mashed turnips, matzos, hardboiled eggs, and peaches. All claimed to be innocent, saying that Vallon was the real killer. Dago Frank Cirofici called for a Catholic priest, then later "confessed" to warders, saying that Vallon and Gyp the Blood had done the killing. He was innocent, he claimed, being at home that night. The men swaggered to their deaths, heroes to the underworld in their own weird code, dying without begging for mercy. Their end came long before that of the man who had ordered them on their murderous mission. It took three years for the law to run Charles Becker to ground.

Once the gamblers made their confession, District Attorney Whitman allowed them their freedom, provided they would testify against Becker at his trial which was scheduled for Oct. 7, 1912. Whitman took no chances. Knowing that he must have corroboration for all the damning statements made chiefly by Rose, he brought another gambler named Sam Schepps into the picture. Schepps was assured immunity and confessed his part in the Rosenthal killing which he too claimed was ordered by Lieutenant Becker. The once powerful Becker was by then suspended from the NYPD and had been locked in the Tombs to await trail. His attorney, John F. McIntye, was able and quick-witted, but he was up against an almost predetermined case since the shocking, brutal statements by Rose, which revealed Becker to be nothing more than a bestial and inhuman creature, had been broadly printed in the press. Moreover, Whitman was an eloquent and formidable opponent who was by now imbued with a messianic crusade to rid the world of police corruption and that particular venality was personified by Charles Becker. To Whitman, Becker was evil incarnate and he had taken it upon himself to eradicate this scourge personally. He was no less inspired in seeking this legal goal than was the mythical Sir Perceval who had hunted through the bogs of hell to find the Grail.

For his part, Becker exuded confidence from his prison cell. It was all a frameup, the gamblers had lied to save their own skins, Whitman was using him as a scapegoat in winning the governorship. He told his wife the trial would come to nothing and he would be back on the job before Christmas. What reasonable jury would take the word of such Broadway trash as Vallon, Rose, Webber, and Schepps over that of an upstanding police officer who had received his department's highest commendation for valor? He expected aid from Mayor Gaynor and, of course, his gentle superior, Commissioner Waldo. Yet, curiously, support from these totemic government officials was absent. Also, no one in the department, other than Becker's brother John, by then a lieutenant on the force, had come forward to lend strong support. There was a silence that befell Becker, ominous and knowing. And all but Becker, his blindly loyal wife, and some close relatives, accepted this man's doom.

A quicker death awaited Becker's gangster chieftain Big Jack Zelig. One day before Becker's trial began, Zelig, the most feared thug in New York, was murdered by an obscure goon whose motives were as absurd as the manner he chose to rid the city of a crime czar. Zelig was to testify at Becker's trial; he was listed as a defense witness, but Whitman, as he later stated, intended to have the gangster speak on behalf of the prosecution. If this was known by members of the underworld at the time, the presence of Zelig's killer was not a lone act of an unthinking thug, but a planned killing ordained by the leaders of the system.

Zelig acted in the last moments of his life as if he hadn't a care in the world. On the night of Oct. 5, 1912, Zelig had dropped into Siegel's Coffee House on Second Avenue and there enjoyed the company of a half dozen gangsters under his command. He drank heavily, downing several glasses of gin. He decided to get some air and stepped outside, lit a cigar, and looked about for the two detectives whom he knew had been assigned to watch him—since he was now an important witness in the Becker trial—and also to gather information on his on-going illegal activities. Zelig had been off-handedly grateful for this police surveillance since he knew he had been marked for death by a fierce new rival for his underworld territory, Jack Sirocco.

Although he had been expected to return to his men at Siegel's, Zelig inexplicably strolled a block or so and then, seeing a streetcar going uptown, jumped on board, walked to the back of the car, and squeezed his large frame between an old man and a young woman. As the car moved away from the Fifth Street stop, Zelig noticed from his bench seat a young, tall man racing after the car. He took the cigar out of his mouth and encouraged the passenger to catch up with the car, saying, "C'mon, you can make it, old boy!" The young man reached out, caught the outside handle bar, and swung himself onto the running board of the streetcar. Instead of entering the car, the slightly breathless passenger worked himself behind the last bench on the outside of the car so that he hung from the rear, standing behind Zelig. He reached into his pocket and withdrew a .38-caliber revolver. Zelig and the others in the car were facing the other direction and no one saw the killer place the muzzle of the gun behind Zelig's left ear. He fired one shot. Zelig leaped forward with the impact, his face a mask of blood, crashing to the streetcar floor where his dying body gave one shuddering spasm and went limp. Screaming women and shouting men in the car pointed frantically to the sour-faced killer hanging at the end of the trolley.

The killer wasted no time, leaping from the car as it moved on. His jump was ill-chosen for he landed almost at the foot of a startled patrolman, banging into him, his revolver still in hand. The cop raised his nightstick and instinctively began clubbing the killer until he lay senseless on the sidewalk. He was identified a short time later as 30-year-old Philip "Red Phil" Davidson, who had occasionally worked as a fruit peddler but had a long criminal record as a narcotics pusher, gambler, and white slaver. He laconically told police that he had killed Zelig because the gangster had stolen $400 from him earlier that day. Later Davidson changed his story, saying that he had misstated the amount. Zelig had cheated him out of $18 and that is the reason why he felt compelled to murder the man. Of course, it was all nonsense. Zelig was a wealthy man who gave $20 to bootblacks for a mere shine and would not have spent a second bruising his knuckles over such a paltry amount. Davidson, after a brief trial, was given twenty years in prison and was released in twelve.

Whitman made much of Zelig's killing, claiming that the gangster would prove that Rose and the other gamblers had been telling the truth and that Becker was guilty. McIntyre, for the defense, said that such statements were ridiculous, that Zelig would have proved that Rose, Vallon, and Webber, all sworn enemies of Zelig's, had planned the killing of their worst competitor on their own and had used Zelig's best killers to do it and that Becker had no connection with the Rosenthal murder. It was, however, with Big Jack dead on a morgue slab, a moot issue. Becker's trial went ahead as planned and was over in twelve days.

Judge John Goff, a no-nonsense law-and-order magistrate, argued throughout the trial with defense counsel McIntyre and seemed to show a decided interest in having Becker found guilty. He allowed Whitman every opportunity, and made McIntyre battle himself into illness to make the meagerest point. Goff had long been a conservative foe of political graft and police corruption in New York, challenging the powers of Tammany as early as the 1890s during the Lexow and Mazet hearings. (Goff, during this trial, as was his habit with any other, took his lunch inside his chambers; this consisted exclusively of milk and crackers which he always washed down with a long swig of Irish whiskey.) His conduct was much in question and it drove Becker, outwardly calm during the entire course of the trial, to near rage when talking with his attorney in his Tombs cell. At one conference with McIntyre, Becker shouted at his beleaguered attorney: "Between that judge and your inability to stop the DA, I'm going to fry! I could have done better by myself." He insisted on taking the witness stand to clear himself but McIntyre persuaded him against this, assuring Becker that Goff's high-handed ways would prejudice the case and assure a victory for the defense in the Appeals Court. "It doesn't matter what the jury does," McIntyre told his client "No

conviction will ever survive an appeal."

Becker came to believe that the prosecution's case would not hold up, that the jury would reason that a bunch of murderous gamblers were obviously trying to frame a police officer who had persecuted them. He became so confident that he would be acquitted that he told his wife to wear her best dress on the last day of the trial. They would go to one of the best restaurants in town to celebrate his release. No one was more shocked when he was found Guilty and later sentenced by Goff to reside in Sing Sing where he would later be executed. McIntyre, however, was proved correct. The Appeals Court overruled the conviction, citing Goff's conduct and other discrepancies in the trial. Becker was tried again, and brought back from Death Row to the Tombs.

Judge Samuel Seabury who was as famous as Goff in combating New York corruption, presided over Becker's second trial which began on May 2, 1914, Whitman's choice in that he was more even-handed and careful in his supervision of the trial. Whitman did not want another reversal. Becker had to die in the electric chair and that meant that the second trial must end in a conviction that would be upheld at any judicial level. W. Bourke Cochran, an ex-judge, served as Becker's attorney, but he was no match for Whitman who once more paraded his gamblers before the jury with their inflammatory but utterly memorable testimony. Seabury avoided the pitfalls of Judge Goff and was extremely cautious in his instructions to the jury. On May 22, 1914, the jury took one hour and fifty minutes to convict Charles Becker of the murder of Herman Rosenthal. Becker was later sentenced to die in Sing Sing's electric chair on July 6, 1914. But one appeal after another postponed that date with death.

While Becker and his lawyers fought for his life, Whitman ran for the governor's office and, with the Becker conviction as the single most important achievement in his career to bolster support, he was swept into the Albany mansion with a tremendous Republican landslide on Nov. 3, 1914. Now Becker and his attorneys were faced with seeking Whitman's mercy after all other appeals failed. This Becker found intolerable, saying: "My life has been sacrificed on the altar of Whitman." But, as Becker's final date for execution approached, July 30, 1915, the condemned man found himself writing a pleading letter to the very man who convicted him, begging Whitman to commute his sentence. Whitman, through an aide, stated: "The Governor cannot pardon a man he convicted." Whitman himself, just before the execution, after denying Becker's plea for clemency, said: "As far as Becker's conviction is concerned, there was never a criminal case more perfectly proven in the annals of crime. I have never had any doubt about Becker's guilt. If I had any now I would pardon him."

In a dramatic last minute effort, Mrs. Helen Becker went personally to Governor Whitman and begged for an interview. Whitman, through an aide, agreed to see her but when she appeared at the Governor's mansion in Albany only twelve hours before her husband was to die, she found the governor gone. She learned he was in Peekskill reviewing a military event. She trailed him there only to learn he had gone to Poughkeepsie. She found him at the Nelson House. Here the governor, cornered, as it were, by the desperate wife who had never given up on her husband or lost a second of belief in his innocence, was forced to face Helen Becker who implored him to consider her husband's last plea for a review of his case. Whitman only stood in the center of the Governor's suite, arms clasped behind his back, saying nothing. Mrs. Becker, understanding his silence to be a final refusal, broke down.

Nothing stopped Becker's execution on July 30, 1915. He entered the death room at Sing Sing and stoically, some reporters later stated "arrogantly," approached the electric chair, sitting down while staring ahead, his chin up, his eyes glaring at the twenty-odd witnesses. He repeated the litany being said by the prison chaplain, Father James Curry. The convicted killer looked massive and powerful as he sat in the chair, thick, muscular legs that were exposed at the calf where the trousers had been slit for the electrodes, an expanding chest that breathed evenly. Charles

Becker insisted upon his innocence to the end and decided to show himself unafraid. He held a crucifix and when the first jolt of electricity was thrown into him, 1,850 volts of current, his large body of 215 pounds lurched against the straps with such force that the leather creaked and groaned, almost bursting their anchors. In ten seconds the current was shut off but an examining physician, Dr. Charles Farr, reported that Becker was still alive. Another ten-second jolt was thrown into him. Again his body strained against the straps. The doctor listened again to Becker's heart with his stethoscope and announced that the man was still alive. For a third time the body was given another jolt and this time Dr. Farr, after listening closely for a heartbeat, turned and said: "I pronounce this man dead."

By then the witnesses were exhausted with the shock of Becker's awful death, one that had taken nine minutes and was later considered one of the most "botched" executions in Sing Sing history. The nine minutes had seemed like an eternity to the witnesses, one of whom was a *World* reporter who later wrote: "To those who had sat in the gray-walled room and watched and listened to the rasping sound of the wooden switch lever being thrown backward and forward and had seen the greenish-blue blaze at the victim's head and feet, and the grayish smoke curling away from the scorched flesh, it had seemed an hour." The Crookedest Cop in the World was dead. See: **Lexow Committee**; **Rothstein, Arnold**; **Zelig, Jack**.

REF.: Adams, *A. Woollcott*; Asbury, *The Gangs of New York*; _____, *Sucker's Progress*; *CBA*; Clarke, *In the Reign of Rothstein*; Crane, *The Sins of New York*; Fried, *The Rise and Fall of the Jewish Gangster in America*; Kahn, *The World of Swope*; Katcher, *The Big Bankroll*; Lebrun, *It's Time to Tell*; Logan, *Against the Evidence*; Lynch, *Boss Tweed*; Mackenzie, *World Famous Crimes*; Nash, *Almanac of World Crime*; _____, *Bloodletters and Badmen*; Parkhurst, *Our Fight With Tammany*; Peterson, *The Mob*; Pink, *Gaynor*; Reppetto, *The Blue Parade*; Rodell, *New York Murders*; Root, *One Night in July*; Scott, *Concise Encyclopedia of Crime and Criminals*; Smith, *William Jay Gaynor*; Snyder, *A Treasury of Great Reporting*; Steffans, *Autobiography*; Stoddard, *Master of Manhattan*; Sullivan, *Our Times, Vol. IV, 1909-1914*; Tebbel, *The Life and Good Times of William Randolph Hearst*; Teichmann, *Smart Aleck*; Thompson, *Gang Rule in New York*; Tully, *Era of Elegance*; Werner, *Tammany Hall*; Woollcott, *While Rome Burns*; (FICTION) Crane, *Maggie, A Girl of the Streets*; Rosenberg, *Night Cry*; (FILM), *Manhattan Melodrama*, 1934; *Where the Sidewalk Ends*, 1950.

Becker, Charles (AKA: **Dutchman**), b.1903, U.S., forg.-count. Charles Becker was born a butcher's son in Württemberg, Ger. After a childhood of poverty and hunger, he decided to use his skills as an artist and engraver. In 1924, during the height of the German depression, Becker sailed to the U.S. In 1929 he turned his attention to forgery and counterfeiting. He got a job in a chemical plant where he found the necessary dyes and inks. Becker stole small quantities of the ink and set up his own laboratory in the back of his little flat.

Unlike other counterfeiters, Becker insisted on using authentic paper. He bleached some dollar bills white and turned them into tens so that not even experts could tell the difference. Soon the Dutchman, as he was known to his underworld associates, had exchanged his bogus $10 bills for $50,000 in real cash. Becker then shifted his base of operations to London, where he opened a legitimate brokerage office on Threadneedle Street. With the help of partners Andrew Sawyer and Philip Carter, he bought valid securities with his counterfeit bills at a second phony bokerage firm he had established. Then the securities were assigned to the legitimate operation and resold for genuine currency. Sawyer-Carter. Ltd. became so successful that Becker had to work around the clock counterfeiting £100 and £500 notes to meet demand.

By 1940 Becker had flooded the capitals of Europe with his counterfeit currency, setting off a near panic on foreign investment markets. Becker had counterfeited the French franc, German mark, Italian lire, and British pound. He slipped quietly back into the U.S., but was arrested in Boston in 1947 and convicted of forgery. His American captors knew nothing about the larger swindles he had perpetrated in Europe.
REF.: *CBA*; Wade, *Great Hoaxes and Famous Imposters*.

Becker, Edward, 1933- , U.S., jur. Member of Committee of the Administration of the Probation System and lecturer at the University of Pennsylvania Law School. In 1970, he was appointed judge of the Eastern District Court of Pennsylvania by President Richard M. Nixon and in 1981, he was appointed to serve on the bench of the Third District Court by President Ronald Reagan. REF.: *CBA*.

Becker, John, d.1937, U.S., mur. Katherine Bracken went to work for the Pittsburgh-Shawmut railroad in Jefferson County, Pa., during WWI, when few men remained in the work force. For years she was admired for her diligent, thorough work as a tower operator adjacent to a lonely railroad embankment on the outskirts of Brookville. No one remembered her having taken time for romantic involvement; her job always came first. "We've all known Katie Bracken for years," explained district attorney Robert Morris. "We don't think she had any enemies."

Bracken's virtue proved to be her downfall. On the night of Apr. 10, 1936, her partially clad body was found at the bottom of a thirty-foot embankment by W. Reed Lettie, who was scheduled to relieve her at 9:50 p.m. She had been dragged down the stairs, bleeding from the throat and wrist. Her body was still warm.

Inside the tower, the meager furniture strewn about the room suggested a violent struggle. Blood stained her desk and the train charts she had been examining at the time of her death. An inkwell, surmised to be one of the murder weapons, was found outside the door of the tower.

Sheriff Samuel G. Lowry was stymied in his attempt to identify the killer. A state police dragnet failed to turn up any suspects in the immediate vicinity. After two months there were still no clues, and news of the investigation disappeared from the Pittsburgh *Post-Gazette*. The district attorney's office kept the case open, however, and suspicion eventually fell on John Becker, a temporary night watchman at the nearby Deemer Glass Plant who had falsified his timekeeping records. Investigators determined that on the night of the murder Becker had failed to make his 9 p.m. rounds, covering his tracks by creating a false record of his movements.

After hours of questioning, Becker finally confessed when confronted with an eyewitness to the crime. "I wanted a woman—any woman," he told the prosecutor. "I went over to the tower. Katie Bracken wouldn't have anything to do with me...I got mad. I picked up a glass inkwell and hit her over the head with it three or four times—knocked her almost out, I guess."

Becker was indicted for murder on Aug. 27, 1936. During the trial, he claimed his confession had been obtained under duress but the jury did not believe him. He was found Guilty on Nov. 5, and sent to the electric chair at Rockview Penitentiary, Bellefonte, Pa., in July, 1937. REF.: *CBA*.

Becker, Marie Alexander, b.1877, Belg., mur. A native of Liège, Marie Becker, fifty-three, was a bored housewife, married to a cabinetmaker. While buying vegetables at a street stall in 1932 she was approached by Lambert Beyer, a middle-aged lothario who propositioned her. She accepted without qualifications and was soon involved in a deep love affair, convinced that the only way to recapture her youth was to murder her husband and go on with her girlish affairs. Becker poisoned her spouse with digitalis and, after tiring of Beyer, poisoned him with the same lethal drug. The once proper Becker, much to the shock of neighbors, became a nightlife creature, haunting dance halls and nightclubs, wildly dancing with men half her age. She paid these gigolos to accompany her to her bed and was soon out of money. Becker had opened a dress shop some months earlier from the proceeds of her husband's insurance and, to obtain money for her expensive affairs, she began to poison her female patrons with digitalis, dropping this in a cup of tea in the back of her shop while discussing a new order with a customer. She would steal what money her patrons possessed and then, while the customer was in a drugged condition, manage to get them home where they shortly died of "unknown causes."

The number of murders committed by the homely housewife totaled ten known homicides, but there may have been twice that before Becker was arrested. She brought suspicion to herself when a woman friend casually remarked that her husband was aggravating her so much that she wished he were dead. "If you really mean that," responded the poisoner, "I can supply you with a powder that will leave no trace." The friend went to the police who had long suspected Becker because of the number of her clients who had mysteriously perished after visiting her shop. She was arrested and, while in detention, the bodies of her husband, Beyer, and some of her customers were exhumed and traces of the poison were found.

Mass poisoner Marie Becker.

Witnesses at Becker's trial told how they had seen the killer attend the funerals of her victims, kneeling at gravesides and weeping hysterically. She would later be seen that night doing erotic dances in Liège nightclubs, spending the very money that she had pilfered from her hapless victims. Becker held back nothing at her trial, gloating over the murders and describing with arch disdain the way her victims died. One of her victims, she said, "looked like an angel choked with sauerkraut." Another she described as "dying beautifully, lying flat on her back." Convicted, Marie Becker was sent to prison for life, there being no death penalty in Belgium at that time. She died in prison sometime during WWII.

REF.: *CBA;* Cohen, *100 True Crime Stories;* Nash, *Look for the Woman.*

Becket, Thomas (Thomas A. Becket or Thomas of London), 1117-70, Brit., assass. Born to a merchant father in London, Thomas Becket was educated at Merton Abbey in Surrey and later at Oxford and still later in Paris. His first position was in the sheriff's office in London and here he was noticed by Theobald, Archbishop of Canterbury, a friend of Becket's wealthy father. Becket was assigned to manage various church properties as well as represent the see of Canterbury in the Vatican. Henry II befriended the witty and intellectual Becket, and first appointed him chancellor in 1158, and, in 1162, despite opposition, as Archbishop of Canterbury. Then King Henry attempted to prevail upon Becket to cooperate with him in bringing the clergy under his direct supervision and make church members subject to the laws of the land.

Thomas Becket

Becket saw Henry's move as one that would put the king in supremacy of the Church, even though the Vatican had warned that no secular prince had authority over any Church prelate. Becket would not yield to Henry's desires and later commmands. He had given up the wastrel ways which he had practiced so

assiduously with his sovereign, King Henry, and now Becket had thoroughly reformed his position with religious fervor. He dedicated his life to the preservation of the Catholic Church in England and approached his chores with the zeal of a monk. Rather than obey Henry's orders, Becket fled to France where he remained in exile for seven years. Henry restored Becket to his see in 1170, after a reconciliation had been effected in France.

When Becket returned to England, he assumed his old office as Archbishop of Canterbury but his relationship with Henry was strained. When the king fell ill, Becket excommunicated the Archbishop of York and other bishops who had agreed to Henry's suppression of the Church and its prelates. He went on to excommunicate various nobles who had forsaken their vows to the Church and had sworn allegiance to Henry's edicts concerning the Church. Then Becket himself issued decrees which, in effect, countermanded Henry's religious edicts. Henry, recovering from his illness in Normandy, churlishly remarked that he was disappointed in his closest nobles who had not avenged him on the insolent Becket. Four knights, Reginald Fitzurse, William Tracy, Hugh de Morville, and Richard Briton, next visited Canterbury on Dec. 29, 1170, seeking an audience with the Archbishop.

These knights, seeking revenge against Becket for usurping their monarch's edicts, as well as his excommunication of their own number, arrived at Canterbury with a large troop of soldiers and were themselves heavily armed. The four armored men clanked across the wide floors of the cathedral to the altar where they found Becket. They demanded that he step from the church, but he refused. Tracy tried to drag him from the cathedral but Becket clung to a pillar, then turned and threw his assailant from him. Tracy crashed in heavy metal to the floor, and Fitzurse drew his huge broadsword and swung mightily at Becket but he hit him only a glancing blow, breaking the arm of his cross-bearer, Edward Grim. Then Becket knelt before the altar, his back to his assassins who, wielding their giant swords, crushed his head, spilling his brains upon the cathedral floor. Becket was canonized as a saint in 1172. The spot where Becket was assassinated was later marked as a shrine, although Henry VIII, in his complete break with Rome, plundered the place in 1538, expunging Becket's name from Church records.

REF.: Carey, *Eye-Witness to History; CBA;* Hurwood, *Society and the Assassin;* Johnson, *Famous Assassinations of History;* Melville, *Famous Duels and Assassinations;* Nash, *Almanac of World Crime;* Paine, *The Assassin's World;* Sparrow, *The Great Assassins;* (FILM), *Becket,* 1964; *The Lion In Winter,* 1968.

Beckett, Henry (AKA: Mr. Perry), d.1919, Brit., rob.-mur. A soldier in the British army, Henry Beckett became quite friendly in the spring of 1919 with the Cornish family who lived on Stukley Road at Forest Gate. In April, as the result of his association with a war widow, the family told Beckett not to visit them anymore. About a week later the soldier, low in funds and apparently missing the Cornishes, went to their house when he knew that Walter Cornish, the father, would be at work. As he walked in front of the family home Mrs. Cornish called him in to scold him. Enraged, Beckett grabbed an ax from the scullery and hit her in the head several times, then stabbed her in the throat with a large carving knife to make sure she was dead. He carried the corpse to the back yard and covered it with wood, cutting off the woman's finger to steal her wedding ring. Beckett then went back inside to clean up and to ransack the house for jewelry and trinkets. He waited for about two hours for the Cornish daughters, Marie Cornish and Alice Cornish, to return from school. When six-year-old Marie walked in the door he murdered her with several blows of the ax to her head, tossing her body down to the bottom of the cellar near the stairs. Shortly after, Alice, fifteen, returned home. He murdered her the same way and left her corpse at the top of the cellar stairs. About five minutes later Walter Cornish came in from work and Beckett crept up behind him and hit him several times. When the dying Cornish escaped to the front of the house and called for help, the alarmed killer ran out the back way after hiding the weapon under a rug on the sofa.

Through help from neighbors and other witnesses, Beckett was captured the next day. He made no attempt to deny his guilt, saying, "Well, I may as well tell the truth, it was me that murdered them all." His attorney, Fox Davies, pleaded insanity due to hardships and privations his client had experienced while serving in the Near East, but the robbery motive convinced the jury that Beckett was responsible for his actions. He was judged Guilty and executed by hanging in August 1919.

REF.: Brock, *A Casebook of Crime; CBA;* Neil, *Man-Hunters of Scotland Yard.*

Beckett, Moses, 1873-1979, U.S., (unsolv.) mur. On Nov. 28, 1979, Moses Beckett, 106, had just left the Haven Memorial United Methodist Church in Philadelphia to attend a birthday party following a prayer service for his younger sister, Ella Palmer, who had just turned 104. A gunman drove up to the church, got out of his car, and fired shots from a handgun. The killer then reloaded, fired several more times, and took off. The victims were Beckett, Shade Sherman, sixty-three, and Althea Dunmark, sixty-five. Edward Durrah, seventy-five, was left in critical condition from multiple wounds. The lay leader of the church, Leon Bivens, said, "It looks like it was some sort of a madman with a gun." At another birthday party given for her by neighbors a few days earlier, Palmer had told a guest to "Thank the Lord for life." REF.: *CBA.*

Beckett Sisters, prom. 1800s, U.S., wh. slav. Rose Beckett and Mary Beckett of St. Louis, two attractive teenagers, were abducted by a gang of white slavers headed by Sam Purdy. Taken to Natchez, the girls were sold to bordello operators for $400 and then shipped to a notorious brothel called The Swamp. Carlos White, a religious zealot and reformer, tracked the sisters through the southland and rescued them from their whoremasters, reportedly shooting one thug who tried to prevent the sisters from leaving with White. They were returned to their home and parents in St. Louis while White became a local hero. See: **Purdy, Sam; Swamp, The.** REF.: *CBA.*

Beckford, William, prom. 1780, Brit., fraud. A clever and eccentric art student wrote a book when he was twenty that purported to be about famous painters but was really a fraud.

In 1780 William Beckford, who would later author a famous gothic novel, *Vathek,* wrote *Biographical Memoirs of Extraordinary Painters,* a witty satire inspired by facetious remarks a housekeeper at Fonthill Abbey would make as she led visitors on a tour of paintings by Murillo, Rubens, and other artists. Theoretically to assist her, and more practically to express his negative opinions about various Dutch and Flemish schools of art, Beckford wrote the *Biographical Memoirs* to serve as the housekeeper's guide. Attributing many of the classic masters' works to painters with names like Og of Bason and Blunderbussian of Venice, Beckford created lives as well as names for these nonexistent painters. His hoax was so effective that it fooled many readers, including his housekeeper.

REF.: *CBA;* MacDougall, *Hoaxes.*

Beckwith, John H., d.1879, and **Beckwith, Robert W.,** 1858-78, U.S., west. law enfor. off. Beckwith and his brother Bob were born in New Mexico and were ranchers who were deputies battling the McSween "Regulators" which included Billy the Kid. John and Robert Beckwith were with a group of deputies who stopped rancher John Tunstall on Feb. 18, 1878, killing him, and setting off the infamous Lincoln County (N.M.) war. John Beckwith was involved with a number of shootouts, one, on Aug. 16, 1878, in the home of his hardcase father, Henry, who killed his son-in-law, William Johnson, during a wild argument in the ranch house, a fight where John tried to intervene and was almost shot to death by his own father. On Aug. 26, 1879, Beckwith encountered rustler John Jones stealing some of the Beckwith herd, and both men went for their guns. Beckwith was shot dead from the saddle.

Robert Beckwith operated a cattle ranch with his older brother John in Lincoln County and was deputized in the Lincoln County War, as a member of the Murphy-Dolan faction. Robert accom-

panied six others of the "Seven Rivers Crowd" on Apr. 30, 1878, when, near Lincoln, N.M., they encountered Regulator chief Frank McNab and two of his men, Ab Sanders and Frank Coe who were watering their horses in a stream. McNab and Sanders had already dismounted and they were shot down immediately by Beckwith and the other men, but Coe, still mounted, spurred his horse on while firing at his pursuers. The horse was killed and Coe was arrested. When the Beckwith faction returned to the stream they saw that McNab was still alive, trying to crawl to safety. They shot him to pieces. Sanders, who was left for dead, later recovered.

On July 15-19, 1878, during the siege of Alexander McSween's store, Robert Beckwith, shortly before his twentieth birthday, stepped into clear view and announced to those inside the store that he was a deputy sheriff. He boldly marched to the door of the store, throwing it open and announcing that anyone who gave himself up would go unharmed. The response was a hail of gunfire, one shot smashing Beckwith's wrist, a second plowing into his left eye and killing him. McSween and the others came charging out of the house and McSween was shot to death by Beckwith's companions, falling over young Beckwith's body. See: **Billy the Kid; Lincoln County War.**

REF.: Bartholomew, *Jesse Evans, A Texas Hide-Burner;* Brent, *The Complete and Factual Life of Billy the Kid; CBA;* Coe, *Frontier Fighter;* Cunningham, *Famous in the West;* Cushman, *The Great North Trail;* Fulton, *Maurice Garland Fulton's History of the Lincoln County War;* Garrett, *The Authentic Life of Billy the Kid;* Hamlin, *The True Story of Billy the Kid;* Hening, *George Curry, 1861-1947;* Hertzog, *A Directory of New Mexico Desperadoes;* Holland, *History of Parker County;* Hunt, *The Tragic Days of Billy the Kid;* Keleher, *Violence in Lincoln County;* Klasner, *My Girlhood Among Outlaws;* Monahan, *The Book of the American West;* Nolan, *The Life and Death of John Henry Tunstall;* O'Neal, *Encyclopedia of Western Gunfighters;* Poe, *Buckboard Days;* Siringo, *History of Billy the Kid;* Stanley, *The Seven Rivers;* Steckmesser, *The Western Hero in History and Legend;* Thorp, *Story of the Southwestern Cowboy.*

Beckwith, Oscar F., d.1888, U.S., mur. Beckwith's mind may have been deranged since youth, for his slaughterhouse murder of Simon A. Vanderook of Austerlitz, N.Y., was apparently not accompanied by robbery, only an inexplicable urge to murder. On Jan. 10, 1882, Beckwith stabbed his victim to death then spent hours dismembering the corpse, parts of which he left strewn about the victim's porch and yard, having no concern over being detected. Beckwith was nevertheless tried twice and given a total of six separate death sentences. He was sent to the gallows on Mar. 1, 1888.

REF.: *CBA; The Life and Career of Oscar F. Beckwith.*

Beckwourth, James (AKA: Jim, James Beckwith), 1799-1866, U.S., rob. Son of Jennings Beckwith, an Irish nobleman, and a mulatto slave, James Beckwourth was born in Virginia but was a freed slave by 1822 when he moved west to Missouri where he officially changed his name from Beckwith to Beckwourth. He joined several expeditions through the Rocky Mountains and the Sierras, becoming a famed Indian fighter and scout within the next fifteen years, guiding countless wagon trains to California. He discovered that considerable profit lay in selling horses to the migrant hordes and, to obtain sizeable herds, he and other celebrated mountain men, Pegleg Smith and Old Bill Williams, assembled a huge gang of horse thieves, some reports say more than 150 men, and began raiding ranches throughout California.

This super gang of horse thieves, the most feared in the history of California, looted horses from almost every ranch in middle and southern California in 1840, stripping the horse herds from the San Bernadino and San Gabriel valleys. The gang was pusued by José Antonio Carillo, the Spanish governor, and a small army which trapped the rustlers at Resting Springs. A full scale battle ensued where dozens on both sides were killed and wounded but the amazing Beckwourth managed to fight his way through to freedom, escaping with most of his men and more than 1,000 horses.

The shootout proved too hazardous even for the adventure-seeking Beckwourth and he later gave up horse stealing to take up ranching, storekeeping, and eventually scouting for the army. He served as a guide to Colonel John M. Chivington in 1864 and was part of the Sand Creek Massacre. Two years later, Beckwourth, while trading with Crow Indians, was reportedly poisoned to death by his Indian hosts as he sat at one of their campfires, eating a meal especially prepared for him.

REF.: *CBA;* Horan, *The Great American West.*

Beddingfield, Ann, d.1763, and **Ringe, Richard,** 1744-63, Brit., mur. All the comforts of her estate and her lofty position in the community of Suffolk could not make Beddingfield, wife of farmer John Beddingfield, a happy woman. Her love and passion were directed toward a handsome, 19-year-old servant named Richard Ringe.

Ringe, flattered by Ann Beddingfield's attention, became her lover. An illicit affair was soon not enough, however, so the two lovers decided to kill her husband. Ringe bought poison from a local chemist and mixed it in the man's drinking water. Beddingfield, noticing particles in the bottom of his glass, dumped the water without tasting it.

Frustrated, the two lovers changed methods. When Beddingfield returned from a trip, he discovered his wife had moved her bedclothes into a chambermaid's room. When she refused to return to his bed, Beddingfield went to sleep, but was rudely awakened when Ringe tried to strangle him with a cord. A struggle ensued, but the younger, more agile Ringe succeeded in killing his master. Swearing the chambermaid to secrecy, he left the body to be discovered the next day by another maidservant.

Despite obvious swelling around the corpse's neck, the coroner concluded that the cause of death was natural. The lovers, discovering they were no happier than before, quarreled incessantly and grew to dislike each other.

Upon her discharge, the servant who had witnessed the murder told the story to her parents, who then summoned the sheriff. The pair were arrested and brought before the court, where the coroner testified that the wounds around the dead man's neck had been overlooked as a cause of death. Ringe confessed his guilt but Beddingfield remained silent until the day of her execution.

On Apr. 8, 1763, the two were taken by cart to Rushmore, where Ringe was hanged and Beddingfield burned at the stake. Before the noose was fitted around his neck, Ringe cautioned young men to avoid wicked women and to consider chastity a virtue. It was a lesson which he had learned too late.

REF.: *CBA;* Mitchell, *Newgate Calendar II;* Nash, *Look For the Woman.*

Bede Gang (AKA: **Bear Gang**), prom. 1860s, U.S., mur. The Bede gang was a group of four brothers and a few other rabble-rousers who carried on family grudge fights in the Kentucky area of Bear River. Tennessee Governor William Brownlow commissioned on Apr. 1, 1868, Claborne Beary "to raise, arm, and equip" ten men to curtail the violence caused mostly by the Bede boys. The gang was caught but soon allowed to escape and regroup. A prominent resident of the area wrote a letter of protest to Brownlow, complaining that the local sheriff was "disposed to shield if not to aid and encourage the lawless among us...particularly...Jesse Bede and his immediate associates," adding that the sheriff had not only permitted one of the Bedes to escape, but had even allowed him to keep his arms. The wave of killings—locally referred to as "wars"—perpetrated by the Bede gang kept the area alarmed for years after the war. Families with which the Bedes fought—and often murdered members of—included the Holt, Washam, and Parrigan clans. By around 1875 the feud violence had almost stopped, to be replaced by general destruction perpetrated by men back from the Civil War, which had ended twelve years before.

The Bede brothers included Sherwood (Sherrod) Bede, Jesse (Jes) Bede, Bill Bede, and Poley (Pole) Bede. Sherwood and Jesse were Union guerrillas in a company of independent scouts and continued, with their brother, to have shootouts after the war.

Their mother, "Sukie" Bede, regularly treated their wounds and often contended that she "could have saved President Garfield when he was shot" because she had so much practice at nursing. Poley Bede was one of Kentucky's earliest moonshiners, keeping a whiskey still just above Brownsville, and killing both a lawman and the informer who had led him to his still. Jesse Bede was a notorious hog thief, killing the son of a man from whom he had stolen sixteen of the animals when the youth inappropriately called him "a damned hog thief."

REF.: *CBA;* Montell, *Killings.*

Bedell, Joshua, 1921- , and **Cummings, Samuel,** 1946- , and **Clarke, David K.,** 1923- , and **Davies, Alfred T.,** c.1925- , and **Gardiner, Faikai,** 1921-88, and **Toe, Gbassie,** d.1988, Liberia, witchcraft-abduc.-mur. Harper City is a prosperous, developing coastal town in the West African nation of Liberia. Underlying its modern facade, however, is "African science," commonly known as juju. Despite their modern lifestyles and attitudes, many Liberians still accept the idea of ritualistic human sacrifice as practiced by the juju high priests.

Joshua Bedell was a prominent local mortician who had friends in government willing to help him run for mayor of Harper City. When polls predicted his political defeat, Bedill appealed to Alfred Davies, a former mayor of Harper City believed to possess magical charms. David Clarke, a former Methodist minister and the head of Liberia's ruling party, also approached Davies for help with his aspirations, as did Faikai Gardiner, the town's chief prosecutor, Gbassie Toe, a butcher, and Samuel Cummings, a bank guard.

Davies required human sacrifice to help these men achieve their ambitions. In the book *Witchcraft: European and American,* British anthropologist Geoffrey Parrinder explains: "the purpose of ritual murders is to obtain ingredients for a medicine of invincible power. Hence a human victim, far better than an animal, is chosen."

Cummings selected acquaintances of his own children, 6-year-old Samuel Johnson, Jr. and 7-year-old Emmanuel Dalieh, as sacrificial victims. On Oct. 27, 1986, Samuel and Dalieh were approached during a parade attended by most of the 15,000 residents of Harper City. They were taken to the Davies home, beaten to death with a stick by Toe, and deposited into the Hoffman River after removal of certain body parts.

The arrest of the six men triggered rioting and mob violence in the streets of Harper City. When the case went to trial in the spring of 1988, a change of venue was requested and the trial was moved to Monrovia, the capital. The killers were found guilty and sentenced to death, but their case is still under appeal. In passing sentence, Judge George Tulay noted that "the funniest and most serious aspect" of the case was the defendant's persistent claim that they were Christians. REF.: *CBA.*

Bedell, Penn, prom. 1870s, Case of, U.S., mur. By the 1870s, shootings in Atlanta, Ga., had moved into the streets, and on Mar. 5, 1872, the city's first policeman was killed in the line of duty. M.W. Raspberry had stopped a professional gambler named Penn Bedell, thinking he might have had something to do with the robbery some days earlier of the Fort Valley, Ga., bank. Bedell refused to stop as he sauntered down Decatur Street and Raspberry, an aggressive type, pulled a pistol and aimed it at Bedell, who charged him. The two men struggled and the pistol went off, Raspberry taking a slug in the abdomen. The policeman died two days later. Surprisingly, Bedell was set free, his claim of self-defense upheld. But the gambler was to perish in the same fashion. While out on bail for another offense in February 1874, Bedell was shot to death by one Gaines Chisolm while strolling along Pryor Street. REF.: *CBA.*

Bedford, Gunning, Jr., 1747-1812, U.S., jur. Attorney general of Delaware from 1784-89. Appointed to the district court of Delaware by President George Washington in 1789. REF.: *CBA.*

Bedford Hills Correctional Facility, prom. 1976-81, U.S., penal reform. A New York State prison for women, the institution caused several controversies from the late 1970s to the early 1980s, including a class-action suit to ban male guards.

In November 1976, the prison was investigated by the New York State Commission of Corrections, looking into reports of rampant use of tranquilizing drugs forced on inmates. Seven prisoners had charged they were illegally confined to the Matteawan State Hospital, an institution for the criminally insane, where they were injected with drugs and made to participate in behavior modification programs. Federal Judge Marvin E. Frankel of the Southern District ordered the women transferred back from Matteawan to Bedford Hills Prison. The seven inmates had been detained in the segregation unit for disciplinary infractions, then sent to Matteawan without a judicial hearing. According to investigators, some inmates had become dependent on drugs due to their indiscriminate distribution to prisoners.

In February 1977 Bedford Hills was again in the news. The correctional facility, according to Ruby Ryles of the State Department of Correctional Services, at more than ninety-five percent of its capacity, housed 407 prisoners. A plan under consideration proposed to shift some of the inmates to the nearby men's prison in Buffalo, N.Y. Later that year, in April, several inmates sued in federal court charging that they had been embarrassed, humiliated, and degraded by male guards in their housing units since February, when the guards were posted at clinic, living, and toilet facilities. The plaintiffs charged that they were "unnecessarily and involuntarily exposed in the nude and partially clad to the men guards." Some plaintiffs were of the Muslim faith, which prohibits women from exposing their bodies to any man except their husbands or fathers. Benjamin Ward, a defendant named in the class-action suit, had issued a directive in October 1976 which permitted male officers to fill any job assignments within the prison. Ryles, speaking for the department, said, "We are trying to establish a system where there is no sexual identity of officers." A month later, federal Judge Robert J. Ward ruled that Bedford Hills' medical facilities were "grossly inadequate" and constituted a policy of "deliberate indifference" to the inmates' needs. Sick-call procedures forced prisoners to tell their problems to a nurse who stood behind a barred cashier-type window or a locked door, thus not allowing for a meaningful evaluation of the problem.

In August 1981, the Bedford Hills nursery program for new mothers made news. Operated with state assistance by the Catholic Charities of Brooklyn, the nursery allowed children born after their mothers are sentenced to stay with the inmates for one year. The mother's primary duties were to care for their children and to keep their living quarters clean. Sister Elaine of the Catholic Charities said the nursery has existed "as long as the prison has," since 1933, and is the only one of its kind in the country. REF.: *CBA*.

Bedloe, William, d. 1680, Brit., fraud. Attractive and well-dressed, William Bedloe was popular with women and lived in style, supported by the young wife of an old, very wealthy merchant. When the woman became pregnant, Bedloe sold his coach and valuables and travelled from place to place, avoiding rent payments as he went. His comfortable state was restored by a woman he rescued from debtor's prison by paying her debts. She in turn shared her love and money after she became the mistress of Spain's ambassador to England. Bedloe specialized in providing distinguished family trees for those newly named to a peerage, information which he then used in order to deceive them. Another swindle found him posing as the steward of the just-deceased master of a great house, colecting rents and selling off his property. Bedloe also gambled extensively, often playing with loaded or weighted dice and liked to leave clever poems behind to further insult his victims after he had bilked them.

Joining ranks with the famous imposter Titus Oates, the two concocted evidence against the English Catholics and informed on the alleged conspirators of the Popish Plot, a frameup based on political rivalries and national hysteria. Eleven innocent men were executed as a result of this scandal, and Bedloe became a hero in the Protestant party. The fraud finally revealed, the public demanded vengeance against the libelous informers. Bedloe,

however, while riding on his horse on a hot day, ruptured his gallbladder and died a few days later.
REF.: *CBA*; Hunt, *Dictionary of Rogues*.

Bednarski, Richard Lee, 1970- , U.S., mur. The murder of two gay men became a celebrated case when the presiding judge gave their killer a light sentence partly because the victims were homosexuals.

On May 15, 1988, Richard Bednarski, eighteen, went with nine friends to the Oak Lawn area of Dallas for the purpose of harassing gay men. While standing on a street corner yelling at passersby, Bednarksi persuaded another youth to join him in robbing Tommy Lee Trimble, thirty-four, and Lloyd Griffin, twenty-seven. The four drove to a hilltop clearing in a nearby park, where Bednarski pulled a gun and ordered the older men to disrobe. When they refused Bednarksi shot them both, killing Trimble instantly. Griffin died three days later. At the trial District Judge Jack Hampton, fifty-six, offered several explanations as to why he gave the murderer a thirty-year sentence instead of the maximum life imprisonment. "Those two guys that got killed wouldn't have been killed if they hadn't been cruising the streets picking up teenage boys. I don't much care for queers cruising the streets picking up teenage boys. I've got a teenage boy." Hampton, who had been on the bench for about eight years, said he put prostitutes and gays "at about the same level, and I'd be hard put to give somebody life for killing a prostitute." He would have given Bednarski a harsher sentence if the victims had been, he reasoned, "a couple of housewives out shopping, not hurting anybody." He had rejected the prosecution's request for a life sentence because he did not believe the victims were blameless.

Several human rights groups, including the Texas Civil Liberties Union, filed a complaint with the Texas State Commission against Hampton. Rallies and news conferences urged that Hampton resign. As of this writing, the inquiry is still in progress. REF.: *CBA*.

Bedraja (P'ra P'etraja or Phra Petracha), d.1703, Siam, mur. King of Siam from 1688-1703 who persecuted French and Christian colonialists before cutting off Siam to European trade. He executed the Greek minister of government Constantine Phaulkon. REF.: *CBA*.

Bedreddin (Badr al-Din ibn Qadi Samawna), 1358-1416, Turk., jur. Ottoman theologian whose social doctrines led to the Iznik revolt in 1416. REF.: *CBA*.

Bedstead Suffocations, prom. 1894, Brit., mur. An ingenious device innkeepers could use to profit from unwary guests was presented in Britain in 1894 when *Strand Magazine* illustrated a "suffocating bedstead" consisting of a heavy wooden box which could be lowered over sleeping tenants to trap them in an airless cavity. Presumably while they were dying or after they had died, the enterprising innkeeper could steal their possessions, disposing of the body later. REF.: *CBA*.

Béeche Argüello, Octavio, b.1866, Cos., jur. President of the Supreme Court of Justice in 1935. REF.: *CBA*.

Beecher, Henry Ward, 1813-87, Case of, U.S., adult. Beecher, born in Litchfield, Conn., was the son of Lyman Beecher and was pastor of the Plymouth Congregational Church in Brooklyn, N.Y., from 1847-87. His sister was the noted author, Harriet Beecher Stowe, author of the classic *Uncle Tom's Cabin* (1851-52). He was a hell-storming speaker of stentorian tone, a champion for women's suffrage and one of the leading abolitionists against slavery. Beecher was also one of the most vocal social reformers in New York, thundering against the widespread vice in the city. He led crusades where he and his followers marched through the worst dives of the city, lecturing prostitutes and criminals, pointing at them while he read off their criminal offenses from rap sheets he had obtained from cooperative police officials. He and his dogmatic protégés appeared so regularly at such hellholes as Satan's Circus and Bill Allen's Dance Hall that they were considered regulars, although their presence was for an altogether different purpose than drinking and whoring.

The reformer's social and clergical position and image was

suddenly shattered in 1874 when his leading protégé, Theodore Tilton, charged his mentor with sleeping with his wife. A trial for adultery followed in 1875, and though Beecher was released without a conviction after the jury disagreed, his reputation was forever ruined. Contributing to this earth-shaking scandal was Victoria Woodhull, one-time prostitute, champion of women's rights, and perpetual candidate for the U.S. presidency. It was Woodhull who first learned of the Beecher-Tilton affair (through reformer Elizabeth Cady Staton) and published every lurid detail of the adulterous relationship in her publication, *Woodhull & Clafin's Weekly.*

Woodhull, who had long battled with Beecher for a position in the reform movement, not only provided titilating details of the Beecher scandal each week (through which Tilton claimed he first learned of his wife's infidelity), but insisted that *she* had slept many times with Beecher *and* with Tilton, claiming they were both secret satyrs. Woodhull called Beecher a "poltroon, a coward, and a sneak." Beecher, who had his hands full with Tilton's suit, refused to sue Woodhull, but his friend and fellow reformer, Anthony Comstock, brought obscenity charges against Woodhull and her sister, Tennessee Chaflin, co-publisher of the weekly. Both sisters were jailed on Comstock's complaint, where they spent six months on and off, until tried and pronounced Not Guilty by a jury that was more offended by Beecher's philandering than Woodhull's exposure of it.

Beecher's life was wrecked by the Tilton scandal, although his congregation remained loyal to him. He lost his widespread influence and spent the remaining three years of his life exhaustively giving lectures in which he attempted to vindicate himself. Other than his own followers, few appeared at his lectures, and the reformer died an utter failure of a cerebral hemorrhage on Mar. 8, 1887. See: **Comstock, Anthony; Woodhull, Victoria Clafin Martin.**

REF.: Asbury, *The Gangs of New York*; Beecher, *Lectures to Young Men on Various Important Subjects*; Brown and Leech, *Anthony Comstock*; *CBA*; Dorr, *Susan B. Anthony*; Hibben, *Henry Ward Beecher*; Lutz, *Susan B. Anthony*; Nash, *Zanies*; Sachs, *The Terrible Siren, Victoria Woodhull*; Stowe, *Saints, Sinners and Beechers*.

Beeker, Clifford, prom. 1924-46, U.S., law enfor. off. For twenty-two years, Clifford Beeker served the Indianapolis Police Department in a variety of positions. He was promoted to traffic man in July 1924, transferred to motorcycle man a year and a half later, then switched to first-grade patrolman "to conform with the 1927 budget" in less than one year. He was promoted to detective sergeant six months later, only to be reduced again to first-grade patrolman after six months. Beeker then became detective investigator, a position he held for four years and later he was reassigned, once again, to first-grade patrolman. In December 1941, he became a bailiff and two years later took the rank of lieutenant and was promoted to chief the same day. Two years later he resigned as chief of police to take over as chief of detectives, again on the same day. Beeker resigned as detective inspector on Jan. 16, 1946, to accept another position, presumably not with the police force. REF.: *CBA*.

Beeman, Gary L., 1951-   , Case of, U.S., mur. A thief who was arrested, tried, and convicted for murder adamantly maintained that he was innocent before winning a retrial and acquittal through his own defense.

On Nov. 16, 1975, Robert Perrin, fifty-two, was savagely beaten and murdered in his home in Geneva, Ohio, shot once through the head. A Geneva policeman, Dennis Brown, testified that he saw a man matching the description of 25-year-old Gary Beeman leaving Perrin's home at 5:20 a.m. Beeman was arrested and tried for aggravated murder at the Ashtabula County Court of Common Pleas. His defense counsel, Thomas Shaughnessy, a court-appointed lawyer, maintained that Beeman's companion for part of that evening, Claire Robin Liuzzo, had murdered the older man when Liuzzo became angry at Beeman for failing to carry out their mutual plot to rob Perrin. Prosecuting attorney Ronald Vettel maintained that there was no evidence that anyone but Beeman

had been in Perrin's house that night. On June 4, 1976, Beeman, who had served a three-year term for armed robbery, was convicted on circumstantial evidence of murder, and sentenced to death by Common Pleas Court Judge Roland Pontius.

Arguing for a retrial, Beeman cited the court's decision not to let one witness testify since the defense had not laid the necessary groundwork during cross-examination. Also he had told his lawyer prior to the trial that he wanted to be involved in the questioning and the cross-examination. Beeman further argued that Pontius denied his request to have legal materials made available for him, which he claimed was "discriminatory" since, had he been released on bond or financially well off, he could have had access to the materials. Judge Pontius called Beeman's bond argument "presumptuous." Shaughnessy, asking to be excluded from the appeal case, noted that a question of competency came up between himself and his client. He explained, "It's my opinion it's a vain attempt to go back to court and rehash and rehaggle everything. I instructed Beeman that it was a vain act." Facing death, Beeman continued to lobby until he was granted a retrial in 1978 on the grounds that his right to cross-examine Liuzzo, the prosecutor's main witness, had been unfairly restricted.

At a 1979 retrial, Beeman initially handled his own defense, based on legal studies he had done while in prison, later handing his case over to attorney Albert Purola on the tenth day of the twenty-three-day trial. Beeman and Liuzzo continued throughout the proceedings to accuse each other of the murder. But five witnesses, including Robert Westfall, a former cellmate of Liuzzo's, testified that they had heard Liuzzo admit to the murder. Westfall said that in January 1976, Liuzzo told him he tried to rob a homosexual man, scuffled with him, and shot him in the head. Beeman was acquitted of all charges. Judge Robert L. Ford told Beeman the acquittal did not implicate Liuzzo in the killing. REF.: *CBA*.

Beer Hall Putsch, See: Monica Putsch.

Beggar's Opera, The, 1728, a play by John Gay. This drama of the seamy side of life in London presents an unscrupulous villain named Peachum who is wholly based on the master criminal Jonathan Wild, hanged for organizing London's underworld and supervising all major criminal activities (Brit., 1725). See: **Wild, Jonathan.** REF.: *CBA*.

Behan, John, d.1917, U.S., west. law enfor. off. The Missouri-born Behan arrived in Prescott, Ariz., in the 1860s and, after serving time in the territorial legislature, he became tax collector and sheriff of Yavapai County in 1879. Behan later became deputy to Charles Shibbell, sheriff of Pima County and, notably, Tombstone, an end-of-the-trail hellhole which was dominated by gun-happy cowboys who were more gunmen than cattlemen, including the notorious McLowery and Clanton families of dedicated rustlers. Shibbell, in order to bring some law and order to the town, asked Wyatt Earp and his brothers to become his deputies. The coming of the Earps aggravated Behan and his own followers, who later elected Behan sheriff. It was Behan, a devout Democrat as were the cowboy factions, who became one of Wyatt Earp's most bitter enemies. Earp and his brothers were Republicans and sided with the town elders, the storekeepers, and the saloonkeepers.

Behan was later accused of siding with the gunslinging Clantons and McLowerys, encouraging their outlaw exploits and their eventual confrontation with the Earps in the legendary gunfight at the O.K. Corral in 1881. It was Behan who tried to stop the Earps and Doc Holliday from going down to the Corral when he heard they were about to confront the outlaw Clanton-McLowery faction. He was getting a shave at the time (some reports had him lurking in an alleyway with a shotgun, preparing to backshoot the Earps but deciding against this at the last moment). He allegedly leaped out of the barber chair and raced to the street, lather still on his face, and argued with the Earps briefly, telling them they had no authority to disarm the cowboys at the Corral. Wyatt Earp gave him a menacing look, hand on his holstered gun and told him to step aside. Behan stepped aside and the Earps walked into legend.

Following the gunfight Behan and his faction slowly took control of Tombstone but, by that time, the Earps had moved on. Behan was never anything more than a titular lawman who desired public office and the authority of that office. As sheriff of Tombstone he did manage to keep the peace the Earps had secured but seldom used his guns to quell the rowdy and reckless. He was forced into a gunfight with Dick Tolby some time later, and fired all the shots in his six-gun, hitting Tolby who died later and was buried in the crowded Tombstone cemetery, Boot Hill. Behan still later served as a state clerk and, goaded by friends to uphold a reputation he had slimly earned, joined Theodore Roosevelt's Rough Riders during the Spanish-American War, serving in Cuba, the Philippines, and in China. This record allowed him to secure the position of U.S. treasury agent in El Paso, Texas. Behan died in Tucson in 1917. See: **Earp, Wyatt.**

REF.: Bakarich, *Gunsmoke;* Bartholomew, *Western Hard-Cases;* ____, *Wyatt Earp;* ____, *The Biographical Album of Western Gunfighters;* Bechdolt, *When the West was Young;* Breakenridge, *Helldorado;* Breihan, *Great Lawmen of the West;* Burns, *Tombstone, An Iliad of the Southwest;* *CBA;* Chapel, *Guns of the Old West;* Chilton, *The Book of the West;* Chisholm, *Brewery Gulch;* Clum, *It All Happened in Tombstone;* Cox, *Luke Short and His Era;* Cunningham, *Triggernometry;* Franke, *They Ploughed Up Hell in Old Cochise;* Ganzhorn, *I've Killed Men;* Gardner, *The Old Wild West;* Hall-Quest, *Wyatt Earp, Marshal of the Old West;* Hendricks, *The Bad Man of the West;* Hogan, *The Life and Death of Johnny Ringo;* Holloway, *Texas Gun Lore;* Horan, *The Great American West;* Jaastad, *Man of the West;* Jahns, *The Frontier World of Doc Holliday;* Johnson, *Famous Lawmen of the Old West;* King, *Mavericks;* Koller, *The Fireside Book of Guns;* Lake, *Wyatt Earp, Frontier Marshal;* Martin, *The Earps of Tombstone;* Miller, *Arizona;* Monaghan, *The Book of the American West;* Myers, *Doc Holliday;* O'Connor, *Bat Masterson;* Penfield, *Western Sheriffs and Marshals;* Raine, *Famous Sheriffs and Western Outlaws;* Rickards, *Buckskin Frank Leslie;* Rosa, *The Gunfighter, Man or Myth;* Sterling, *Famous Western Outlaw-Sheriff Battles;* Walters, *Tombstone's Yesterdays;* Way, *The Tombstone Story;* Wellman, *The Trampling Herd;* White, *Bat Masterson;* Wilson, *Out of the West.*

Beheshti, Ayatollah Muhammad, d.1981, Iran, (unsolv.) assass. Counter-revolutionary forces loyal to deposed Iranian president Abolhassan Bani-Sadr were blamed for a June 28, 1981, bombing in Tehran which claimed the life of Ayatollah Beheshti and seventy-three other Islamic leaders.

Beheshti was next in line to succeed Ayatollah Khomeini as leader of the Islamic fundamentalist revolution that overthrew the Shah in 1979. Beheshti, as Iran's justice minister, was responsible for the execution of thousands of political dissidents.

The bombing was the most serious terrorist attack on the Khomeini regime to that time. There were few suriviors, though President Ali Rajai, perhaps the real target of the bombers, escaped unhurt. REF.: *CBA.*

Beidler, John X., 1831-90, U.S., west. vigil. German-born John X. Beidler first came to prominence as a vigilante in Kansas where he single-handedly broke up a gang of cowboys "hurrahing" a town by firing a small howitzer loaded with printer's type into their midst, causing them to pick lead slugs out of their bodies for weeks. Later, when Beidler moved to Montana, he fearlessly led vigilantes without wearing the traditional mask, challenging the friends of those he hanged to seek him out. None did.

A squat, fierce little man with a walrus mustache, Beidler always went armed with a rifle; some said he slept with the weapon. He was so aggres-

Vigilante and lynching expert John X. Beidler.

sive in his lynching of desperadoes and horse thieves that many believed he performed the executions more out of perverse pleasure than as justice-seeking acts of retribution against criminals. It was Beidler who invariably provided his "long rope" for the lynching of captured outlaws. When Helena, Mont., finally established a police force, Beidler and his friends retired, the dogged vigilante becoming a customs inspector for Montana and Idaho, a position he held until his death on Jan. 22, 1890. See: **Slade, Jack.**

REF.: Breihan, *Badmen of Frontier Days;* ____, *Outlaws of the Old West;* Brown and Felton, *The Frontier Years;* Callaway, *Montana's Righteous Hangmen;* *CBA;* Chapel, *Levi's Gallery of Long Guns;* Collins, *Great Western Rides;* ____, *The Hanging of Bad Jack Slade;* Cushman, *The Great North Trail;* Fisher and Holmes, *Gold Rushes and Mining Camps;* Hendricks, *The Bad Man of the West;* Holloway, *Texas Gun Lore;* Horan, *The Great American West;* Hutchens, *One Man's Montana;* Johnson, *Famous Lawmen of the Old West;* Raine, *Guns of the Frontier;* Sabin, *Wild Men of the Wild West;* Sharp, *Whoop-Up Country;* Trinka, *Out Where the West Begins;* Triplett, *Conquering the Wilderness.*

Beihl, Eugen, 1908- , Spain, kid. Freed after twenty-five days in captivity, Eugen Beihl, an honorary West German consul to Spain, had this to say about his Basque kidnappers: "I am no enemy of the Basques. I am even their friend." Beihl was seized on Dec. 1, 1970, by members of the Basque Nation and Liberty, (ETA), a radical separatist group seeking political independence from Spain.

His abduction was in retaliation for the court-martial of fifteen Basques charged with murder and terrorism. The kidnappers threatened to murder Beihl if the government sentenced any of the prisoners to death. However, the diplomat was released before a verdict in the trial was handed down. Beihl's release on Christmas Day was intended to elicit support for the separatist movement, and "to show the world that ETA is not an irresponsible, fanatical, and bloodthirsty band," according to spokesman Telesforo Monzon. He warned, however, that any executions of the political prisoners in Burgos, Spain, would result in further reprisals by the ETA. REF.: *CBA.*

Beiliss, Mendel, prom. 1913, Case of, Rus., mur. Anti-Semitic feelings ran high in Czarist Russia. Right-wing groups like the Union of True Russians blamed the large Jewish population for many of the nation's economic and social ills in the years preceding the 1917 Revolution.

When a young Orthodox Christian boy named Andrei Yushchinsky was found hacked to death outside Kiev on Mar. 20, 1911, the Union of True Russians blamed Mendel Beiliss who worked at a brickworks near the site of the murder. A vindictive neighbor named Shaklovsky mentioned Beiliss' name to the police. The state took two years to assemble its weak case. The prosecution contended that Beiliss dragged the boy from a Jewish hospital, inflicted wounds, and drained his blood. The hard evidence, however, suggested that Vera Cheberyak, a depraved woman with a fondness for young boys, committed the murder.

In October 1913, Mendell Beiliss was found Not Guilty.

REF.: *CBA;* Chalidze, *Criminal Russia.*

Belachheb, Abdelkrim, 1945- , U.S., mur. When a woman in a Texas bar refused the sexual advances of the man she was dancing with, he went out to his car and returned to shoot her, killing six other people at the same time.

Abdelkrim Belachheb, a 39-year-old from Morocco, was at Ianni's Restaurant and Club in North Dallas in the early morning of June 29, 1984. When a woman he was dancing with admonished him for his aggressive behavior by pushing him away, he blew her a kiss, then went to his car and loaded a Smith and Wesson 459 automatic pistol. Returning to the club, he walked over to the woman who was now seated on a barstool and shot her to death. Belachheb again returned to his car, reloaded the gun, walked a second time into the bar, and randomly shot patrons off their barstools, killing five more and critically wounding another, who died at Parkland Memorial Hospital shortly after. According to Sergeant Bill Parker, he then fled in his station wagon, abandoned it after a traffic accident, and walked to the home of Mohammed Benali, about ten miles from the club. The two men spoke in Arabic, according to Benali's friend, Anne Avis, then went to a back room of the house where they sat for about an hour of fasting, honoring the last day of Ramadan, a religious holiday during which Muslims keep a strict fast from sunrise to sunset and refrain from even thoughts of violence. Three hours after the shootings, they called the police, who arrested the killer.

Victims included Marcelle Ford, thirty-two, Frank Parker, forty-nine, Joseph Minasi, thirty-six, Linda Lowe, forty-three, and Janice Smith, forty-six. The police withheld the name of the sixth victim, a woman. Belachhem was tried in the Dallas District County Court of Judge Meier, and convicted on multiple charges of murder and attempted murder. On Nov. 15, 1984, he was sentenced to life imprisonment, and is currently serving his term at the Texas Department of Corrections Prison in Huntsville, Texas. Police spokesman Bob Shaw called the case "the worst multiple killing in the city's history in modern times." REF.: *CBA.*

Beland, Lucy (AKA: **Ma**), d.1941, U.S., drugs. Ma Beland, a mother of six, grew weary of rural life in Texas and insisted that her husband, J.H. Beland, move the family to Fort Worth, Texas, in 1908. She had threatened her husband that unless he could give her the finer things in life, she would send their daughters out to work as prostitutes. Beland, engineer for a cotton-oil gin, used up his savings to satisfy his wife's demands and went broke, leaving the family in 1912 and dying a few years later. Ma Beland, true to her awful word, sent her daughters into prostitution, turning her Fort Worth home into a brothel and center of narcotics distribution.

Ma's children all became either heroin or morphine addicts and her daughter Cora died of a morphine overdose smuggled to her by her own mother while she was in jail, serving a term for prostitution. After the 1914 Harrison Narcotics Act became law, drugs were scarce and Ma's sons, Charles and Joseph Beland, became the top drug peddlers in the Southwest. Beland and her clan became fabulously rich and paid out enormous bribes to officials who protected their widespread operations. The Federal Bureau of Narcotics began to concentrate its energies against the Beland mob in 1930 and, in the following year, obtained enough evidence on the drug clan to send Ma's daughter, Willie Beland, and her husband, Lester James, to prison in 1931. In 1935, FBN agents caught Charles Beland selling drugs and he was given a long term.

Not until 1937 was the infamous Ma Beland herself caught red-handed dealing drugs. An agent walked into her Fort Worth dry goods store and flashed a roll of hundred-dollar bills. The greedy old harridan could not resist the temptation of selling the undercover agent seven ounces of heroin. She was immediately arrested, tried, and given a two-year prison term. She would have received a longer term but the judge in the case, swayed by her feigned image of a kindly grandmother victimized by ruthless federal agents, gave Beland a reduced sentence "because of her advanced years." When released in 1939, Ma Beland returned to aggressively selling drugs but she did not live to enjoy the fruits of further illegal earnings, dying in 1941. Her funeral was lightly attended since most of her relatives were in prison. REF.: *CBA;* Nash, *Look For the Woman.*

Belcastro, James (AKA: **King of the Bombers**), prom. 1920s, U.S., org. crime-bomb.-mur. James Belcastro was an expert at making all sorts of bombs, especially those with long delay mechanisms which allowed him to set these explosives off at great distances. He employed bombs in his widespread Black Hand racket in Chicago's Little Italy where he became rich extorting money from his fellow Italians. Belcastro came to the attention of Al Capone in the early 1920s and he was used by Scarface as his chief terrorist. If a saloonkeeper or bartender proved truculent in refusing to buy Capone beer, instead of that from a rival gangster-owned brewing company, Belcastro was ordered to blow up the saloon. This he did with alacrity, and more than 100 deaths

were attributed to this ruthless bomber during the mid to late 1920s. He was particularly active during the 1927 Chicago primary elections which were later dubbed "The Pineapple Primaries," thanks to Belcastro's lethal handiwork. Belcastro was ordered to make sure that voters cast their ballots for Capone's hand-picked mayoral candidate, William Hale Thompson. To that end, Belcastro and his henchmen set bombs throughout Chicago polling places known to be hostile to Hale's election, exploding these and killing fifteen persons, horribly wounding scores more.

One political opponent, a lawyer named Octavius Granady, was so openly critical of Thompson that he was personally earmarked for murder by Belcastro. On the night of Apr. 10, 1927, Belcastro and three of his men drove past a spot where Granady was talk-

Capone bomb expert James Belcastro.

ing with some friends and opened fire from the fast-moving auto. Their aim was poor and the lawyer dashed to his car, driving off, the mobster car in pursuit. The nervous lawyer lost control of his car which smashed into a tree. When he staggered from the

The results of one of Belcastro's bombs.

wreck, Granady was caught in the glare of the lights from the gangster's car as he roared toward him. Belcastro leaned from the window of the car with a machine gun, as did his men, and fired almost point-blank into Granady, cutting him almost in half. The "King of the Bombers" was arrested and tried for this murder, but witnesses suddenly lost their memories and evidence dwindled to nothing. Belcastro was acquitted. He later rose through the ranks of the Capone mob to become one of its top enforcers. He died peacefully in bed some years later. See: **Capone, Alphonse.**

REF.: Asbury, *Gem of the Prairie; CBA;* Kobler, *Capone;* Nash, *Almanac of World Crime.*

Belcher, Emory Allen, 1923- , U.S., pris. esc. Emory Allen Belcher was convicted in 1951 of a $75 burglary. After his escape, he settled in Orlando, a hundred miles from where he had been jailed. Using his own name, he worked for twenty-six years as a cook and a tile setter, became a family man, and had no further trouble with the law. In May 1977, a computer caught up with Belcher. He spent two days in jail while prosecutors decided whether to try him on the decades-old escape charge. Tom Davidson, assistant state attorney of Hillsborough County, made the announcment on May 27, 1977. "We're not going to prosecute," he said. "We feel justice would not be served." Belcher's clean record since his escape warranted his being allowed to remain free, Davidson explained. Belcher said he was "heartbroken" when arrested, and that he had worried about being caught for the first sixteen years after his escape, but had not thought about it much for the last ten years. Leaving the county jail, Belcher was "greatly relieved." His wife, he said, "always thought I had something hanging over my head. But I never told her what it was." REF.: *CBA*.

Belesme, Robert of (Robert of Belême, Earl of Shrewsbury), prom. 1098, Brit., treas. Supported Robert's Rebellion against William I, revolted against Henry I, and was banished from the realm. Upon his return in 1112, he became the French king's ambassador, but was later seized and imprisoned for life. REF.: *CBA*.

Belew, George Lester, 1913- , U.S., fraud-forg. Apparently a master forger, Belew had limited schooling but an almost limitless ability to commit fraud and deceit.

Born into a farm family in Mt. View, Mo., George Belew's education did not extend beyond grammar school. Nevertheless, he was able to pass himself off in a variety of professions, defrauding a number of people in the process, and repeatedly managing to escape from prisons. At seventeen he was drew a ten-year jail term in the Iowa State Penitentiary for forgery. Within four years, Belew convinced authorities he had reformed and was released on parole. Two months later, in Miami, he forged several checks and was again arrested. Returned to Iowa, he was sentenced to fifteen years for forgery, but managed to be released in just five. Within seven months Belew turned up in Manitoba, Can., was arrested by the Royal Canadian Mounted Police, and sentenced to the Stoney Mountain Penitentiary. For the next several years, Belew practiced his escape techniques as well as his forgery, breaking out of prisons in Phoeniz, Ariz., and Cleveland, Ohio. Following his release from the U.S. Penitentiary on McNeil Island, Wash., Belew spent two years passing bad checks across the U.S. From February 1953 to August 1954, the forger passed through forty-five states, posing as a writer, truck driver, war correspondent, doctor, and military officer. In September 1953, the FBI issued an identification order when a federal grand jury in Fargo, N.D., returned an indictment against Belew.

In August 1954, Belew attempted to pass a check in Hays, Kan., but an astute druggist called the Ellis County sheriff's office. Belew was arrested, but managed to escape again, this time by throwing hot water into the sheriff's face and beating him about the head before fleeing with an accomplice in the sheriff's car. Despite an area-wide manhunt, Belew evaded capture, leaving his accomplice behind. In the following six months, FBI agents continued to receive Belew's bad checks, perplexed that they all held thumb prints that did not match those of the forger. Then in January 1955, Belew was caught again. FBI agents discovered the mysterious "thumb" marks were actually the print of Belew's right big toe. Belew was sentenced to the U.S. Penitentiary at Leavenworth, Kan., and later transferred to the U.S. Federal Hospital in Springfield, Mo., when he contracted tuberculosis. After he recovered, he received a nine-year jail term in Duluth, Minn., where he wrote a poem "Repenting for His Life of Lawlessness," dedicated to "All the Youth of America Who think Crime Will Pay." Whether Belew really had a change of heart or whether the poem is yet another forgery is not clear.

REF.: *CBA*; McGuire, *The Forgers*.

Belknap, William Worth, 1829-90, U.S., polit. corr. Army brigadier general from 1864-65, and secretary of war under President Ulysses S. Grant in 1869. He was implicated in corruption while in office and in 1876, was impeached by the House of Representatives for receiving bribes. REF.: *CBA*.

Bell, George Joseph, 1770-1843, Scot., jur. Brother of Sir Charles Bell. He was professor of law at Edinburgh University in 1822, and a member of a legal committee that drafted the judicature act of 1825. REF.: *CBA*.

Bell, Griffin Boyette, 1918- , U.S., atty. gen. Chairman of the Atlanta Commission on Crime and Juvenile Delinquency from 1965-66. He was appointed to the bench of the Fifth Circuit Court of Appeals by President John F. Kennedy in 1961 serving

until 1976, and became attorney general under President Jimmy Carter in 1977. Authored numerous legal publications including *Toward A More Efficient Federal Appeals System* (1971). REF.: *CBA*.

Bell, Hamilton, prom. 1880s-90s, U.S., west. law enfor. off. Bell followed Bat Masterson as sheriff of Ford County, Kan. He was a rigid, stand-up lawman who seldom drew his guns and was known, after thirty years of law enforcement, as a sheriff who never shot a man nor beat one over the head with a pistol. Still, it was reported that Hamilton Bell took more men into custody, using warrants, than any other lawman of the Old West. He retired about 1911 and, at the age of ninety, was operating a pet shop in Dodge City, selling canaries, his favorite bird. See: **Masterson, William Barclay**.

REF.: Bartholomew, *The Biographical Album of Western Gunfighters; CBA*; Rath, *Early Ford County;* ____, *The Rath Trail*.

Bell, Herman, 1948- , and **Bottom, Anthony**, 1952- , and **Washington, Albert**, 1943- , U.S., mur. Three militant members of the Black Liberation Army shot and killed two policemen outside Colonial Park Houses in Harlem, N.Y., on May 21, 1971. Bell, Washington, and Bottom were tried twice for the murders of Officers Joseph Piagentini and Waverly M. Jones. The first trial ended in a hung jury, but the three men were convicted when the case was brought before the New York Supreme Court on Apr. 10, 1975.

Life sentences were handed down on May 13 by justice Edward J. Greenfield. Herman Bell, and the two co-defendants were hustled back to a holding pen, but someone had smuggled knives, mace, explosive devices, and lock picks to the convicts minutes before they arrived. Defense lawyers contended the items were a plant. After the botched escape attempt, authorities moved the men back to Riker's Island.

For Herman Bell, a self-styled revolutionary previously convicted of bank robbery in San Francisco and scheduled to stand trial for robbery in New Orleans, it was the second time in three months that he had failed to escape from detention. On Feb. 16, Bell pulled a knife-shaped stick on a Riker's Island guard. He obtained the keys to his cell but was quickly subdued by other guards. Shortly afterward prison authorities received notice that five men had left the Tiffany Street Pier in Bronx, N.Y., in a rubber launch and were headed across the East River toward Riker's Island. The rubber craft was eventually found, but the five men had disappeared. REF.: *CBA*.

Bell, James E., 1901-29, U.S., mur. A man with a persecution delusion terrorized the streets of Newark, N.J., during a morning rush hour, killing two people and wounding three others before he committed suicide.

At 9 a.m. on Apr. 2, 1929, Julius Rabinowitz, thirty-eight, a jewelry salesman, was directed to the third floor apartment of James E. Bell by Louise Hooper, a neighbor in the tenement building. Intending to drop off some laundry work for Bell's wife, he knocked on the door. Bell flung it open and fired four shots from an automatic pistol into Rabinowitz's body, then shot him in the head with a shotgun. As he raced down the stairs with a weapon in each hand, Bell called back to Hooper, "Please tell my wife I've killed a man." On the street, Bell fired at a passing car, attracting the attention of 45-year-old William H. Bahrs, a post office clerk who was at home reading. As Bahrs looked out his window, Bell fired, hitting the man in the face and killing a caged canary inside the house. Bahr stumbled to the phone and called the police. Charles Ramsperger, a 51-year-old cashier on his way to work, was Bell's next victim. The crazed killer also wounded Louis Pollack, a 43-year-old store owner, with a random shot.

Patrolman Thomas J. Hackett of the Newark police arrived and Bell shot him as he tried to draw his gun. Hackett then commandeered a taxicab to drive him around the block in an effort to catch Bell from behind. Joined by officer Samuel Cobb, Hackett found Bell dead in the alley, shot through the head with his own bullet. The wounded were rushed to City Hospital, Ramsberger dying on the way. Police found an arsenal of weapons in Bell's apartment, including two swords, a long curved knife, two blackjacks, 100 shotgun cartridges, sixty bullets, and a bag of buckshot.

One of Bell's neighbors, the Reverend Mr. Douglas, told of going to the man's apartment a few days earlier, jokingly calling to him, "I've got a warrant for you." When the excited Bell saw who it was he begged the minister never to do anything like that again, explaining, "I've been persecuted something awful and I'm liable to kill somebody anytime." An autopsy revealed that Bell was suffering from a blood disease. REF.: *CBA*.

Bell, John, 1817-33, Brit., mur. John Bell's father, a religious man, read the Bible daily and sang in the church choir. His mother was an indulgent parent who spoiled John and his 10-year-old brother, James Bell. John, apparently a high-spirited child, had recently been expelled from school for a brief time for threatening to kick his teacher in the shins. Except for this incident, he was not considered a bad boy. In 1831, when John was fourteen, Richard Falkland, the 13-year-old child of a candle maker, disappeared after leaving home to collect his sick father's parish allowance of nine shillings. Ten weeks later his body was discovered in the woods, his throat cut and his features no longer recognizable. When two witnesses said they saw Falkland in the company of the Bell boys, John admitted they had been with him but had left him to return home. James soon broke down, admitting their plan to rob and kill Richard, but blaming his older brother for the murder, saying he himself had only gained one shilling and sixpence from the crime. John Bell confessed shortly after his brother told the story of the murder and showed no emotion during the trial. After only two minutes, and not bothering to leave their box to reach the decision, the jury condemned him to die. He was hanged in front of a crowd of 5,000 people in 1833—the last person under the age of sixteen to be executed in England.
REF.: *CBA*; Mencken, *By the Neck*; Wilson, *Children Who Kill*.

Bell, J.W. (AKA: Lone Bell), d.1881, U.S., west. law enfor. off. J.W. Bell had been a Texas Ranger in the mid-1870s, serving under Captain Dan Roberts in San Saba County, Texas. He later served as a deputy to Pat Garrett who had captured Billy the Kid. He was one of the two guards killed by Billy when the Kid escaped from the jail in Lincoln, N.M., on Apr. 28, 1881, even though he befriended the young outlaw and had been kind and considerate to his prisoner. The other deputy, Robert Ollinger, was also murdered by Billy the Kid as he escaped the jail. See: **Billy the Kid; Garrett, Patrick Floyd.**
REF.: Ball, *Ruidoso*; Bartholomew, *The Biographical Album of Western Gunfighters*; Breihan, *Bad Men of Frontier Days*; Burns, *The Saga of Billy the Kid*; CBA; King, *Wranglin' the Past*; Pannell, *Civil War on the Range*; Rennert, *Western Outlaws*.

Bell, Larry Gene, 1948- , U.S., kid.-mur. The mental problems of convicted murderer Larry Gene Bell dated back to 1975, when he attempted to kidnap two young women in South Carolina using a knife and gun. Bell was apprehended and spent twenty months in prison and the state hospital. Despite warnings from his doctors, in 1979 state officials released Larry Bell.

Sharon Faye Smith, seventeen, disappeared from her family home in Red Bank, S.C., on May 31, 1985. Her body was found in a wooded area behind the Masonic Lodge in Saluda County, S.C. She had been suffocated. In June, the killer called the Smith home nine times to torment the family with vivid descriptions of the rape-murder. He claimed to have given Sharon a choice of gunshot wound, drug overdose, or suffocation. In the last call, made on June 22 to the victim's sister Dawn, Bell alluded to the disappearance of 9-year-old Debra May Helmick, who was kidnapped from her Richland County home and found murdered in nearby Lexington County.

A few days after Bell told Dawn Smith that "God had chosen her to join her sister in death," the killer was arrested and charged with the murders of the two girls. On Feb. 23, 1986, Larry Bell was found Guilty of killing Sharon Smith by a Berkeley County jury after only fifty-five minutes' deliberation. Four days later

he was sentenced to die in the South Carolina electric chair. A second death sentence was imposed on Apr. 2, 1987, by a jury in Pickens County who convicted Bell of the kidnap-murder of Debra Helmick. "The facts of the case were terrible," conceded Defense Attorney Jack Swerling. "Larry Gene Bell's name just brings up those kind of feelings of fear and revenge in people." Court observers said it would probably be years before Bell exhausted his appeals and was actually put to death. REF.: *CBA*.

Bell, Mary Flora, 1957- , Brit., mansl. Mary Bell was only eleven years old when she killed two small boys in Newcastle, England. Children in the Scotswood district of the city began to have serious accidents in the spring of 1968. On May 11, a 3-year-old boy fell from the roof of an air-raid shelter where he had been playing with Mary Bell and another girl named Norma Bell (not related). The boy survived the fall but was seriously injured. The following day, the mothers of three children went to police to complain that Mary Bell had been choking their small boys and girls, all about age six. A constable visited Mary Bell and gave her a lecture about keeping her hands off other children. On May 25, 1968, the night before Mary Bell turned eleven, some boys playing in an abandoned

Child killer Mary Bell.

house found the body of 4-year-old Martin George Brown. No cause of death was apparent and it was concluded he had swallowed some pills he found in a bottle. Later that day Norma Bell's father stopped Mary Bell from choking his 11-year-old daughter; the father had to slap the girl to get her to stop.

On the following day, May 26, a nursery school was broken into and damage was done. Investigating officers discovered a crudely written note laced with misspelled obscenities and a line that read "We did murder Martin Brown." Some days later, Mary Bell went to the Brown house and asked if she could see Martin. The distraught mother told her: "No, dear, Martin is dead." Replied Mary Flora Bell: "I know. I wanted to see him in his coffin." On May 31, police responded to a recently installed alarm in the nursery which had recently been vandalized and found Mary Bell and Norma Bell inside. Both girls swore they had never been in the school before and were sent home with a stern lecture. Mary Bell then began telling people that her friend Norma had killed the Brown child. When she heard that Norma's parents had become incensed over these remarks, Mary Bell ran to her friend's house and pantingly apologized.

On July 31, 1968, 3-year-old Brian Howe disappeared in the Scotswoord area and when a search ensued, Mary Bell told Howe's older sister that she saw the boy playing on concrete blocks in a deserted lot. Searchers found the boy's body near the blocks. The boy had been strangled to death and there were cuts on his stomach and legs. A pathologist reported that the killer could have been a child since little force had been employed in the murder. All the children in the area were then questioned as to their whereabouts on the night of Howe's death. Mary Bell stated that she had been playing near the area where the boy was killed and that she had seen an 8-year-old boy beating Brian and that the older boy was carrying a broken scissors. The boy was interviewed and found to have been somewhere else on the night of the murder. Suspicion was directed toward Mary Bell since no one knew that a pair of broken scissors had been found at the murder site. Norma Bell was then interviewed and she said that she and Mary Bell had walked through the murder area and that Mary Bell had stumbled over the body of the Howe child and then admitted to her that she had killed him.

When Mary Bell was brought into police headquarters for further questioning, she assumed a very adult posture, insisting that she be allowed to contact a solicitor while accusing the police of "brainwashing" her. Norma then informed police that she had been with Mary when Mary Bell killed the boy, but that she had run away when Mary had "gone all funny" and began strangling the child. She returned to see Mary Bell mutilating the corpse with the scissors and with a razor she used to cut the stomach. Norma Bell correctly told police that the razor could be found beneath a rock. Mary retaliated by accusing Norma Bell of the murder. Chief Inspector James Dobson of the CID had for some time suspected Mary Bell of murdering the Brown and Howe boys. He had been watching her for some days and witnessed her strange actions on the day that the body of the Howe boy was removed from his home in a small coffin. "That was when I knew I couldn't risk another day," Dobson later stated. "She stood there laughing, laughing and rubbing her hands. I thought, My God, I've got to bring her in or she'll do another one."

Both Mary Bell and Norma Bell were placed on trial on Dec. 5, 1968, but it was clear early on that Norma Bell was completely under the domination of Mary Bell and that she was innocent of the murders. Mary Bell, who had told a police woman that she wanted to be a nurse so she could stick needles in people and that she "liked hurting people," was found Guilty of manslaughter in both the Brown and Howe cases due to "diminished responsibility." She was sent to Moor Court, an open prison, to serve a life sentence, since no asylum would accept her. She escaped with another inmate for three days in September 1977 but was recaptured within three days. Mary Bell proudly announced that she and the other girl had picked up some boys and that she had lost her virginity. She added that she felt that if she were left at large she could quickly become a useful citizen, a claim that found no support with officials.

Mary Bell's childhood in the impoverished Scotswood area was certainly a potent factor in the making of her murderous personality. Her mother was only seventeen and unmarried when she gave birth. When she did marry, the mother, whose personality was volatile, left Mary alone a great deal of the time and often vanished for days on end. Her father was also gone a great deal of the time, and the Bell home was described as "poorly furnished and dirty." In school, the child was known to be a habitual liar and an exhibitionist, one who liked punishing others. After Mary Bell's imprisonment, her father was sent to prison for robbery.

REF.: Butler, *Murderers' England; CBA;* Heppenstall, *The Sex War & Others;* Lucas, *The Child Killers;* Sereny, *The Case of Mary Bell;* Wilson, *Encyclopedia of Modern Murder;* Wilson, *Children Who Kill.*

Bell, Shirley, 1936-42, U.S., (unsolv.) abduc.-rape-mur. Only 6-year-old Lynn Sage remarked upon the bicyclist riding through the San Bernardino, Calif., streets with a little girl perched atop his handlebars. Turning to his mother, he said, "There goes Shirley Bell with a man on a bicycle, but it is not her father."

When Shirley left for school on Feb. 3, 1942, she was dressed in a new, brightly-colored birthday dress and carried a tin lunchbox and a jump rope. Shortly before the school bell rang at 9 a.m., several witnesses observed Shirley riding away from the school playground. John D. Lewis, a Muscoy rancher, thought it peculiar, but did nothing. "I have three children myself," he explained. "I thought of that because the man and child were going the wrong direction from the school district."

Several eyewitnesses described the bicyclist as clean-shaven, hatless, and approximately thirty years old. Police Chief James Cole and Sheriff Emmett L. Shay concentrated their search for the girl north of the city in the desolate, arid Cajon Wash where only cacti and sagebrush grew. The first clues surfaced twenty-four hours later, following a night of anguish at the Bell household. Officer Lee Robb found a bicycle track and the footprints of a man and a child in the desert near the Muscoy Reservoir.

A mile north the tracks ended with marks indicating a struggle, suggesting to the police that the girl had become suspicious and attempted to flee. Nearby, her bruised body was found half-buried in the sand. Her mangled lunchbox lay several hundred yards away, its contents apparently eaten by the killer. Shirley had been raped and then strangled with her jump rope, the coroner concluded. The sheriff ordered all "known degenerates" arrested and interrogated, then was struck by a thought. When Albert Dyer had killed three young Inglewood children five years ago, he had joined the search party to throw police off the trail. Was it possible that Shirley's killer lingered in the area to assist in the search effort?

News photographs of dozens of onlookers at the murder site were scrutinized. Perhaps the killer stood among the crowd; it was impossible to tell. Shay and Cole retired without ever finding anyone who could positively identify the man who had carried Shirley away in front of all her neighbors. REF.: *CBA.*

Bell, Sydney, prom. 1890, U.S., rob.-mur. On his way home in the early morning hours, a San Francisco man was shot in front of his house by a short man wearing a mask.

At around 1 a.m. on Aug. 17, 1890, Samuel Jacobson staggered into his home and told his family he had been shot in the stomach while getting off a streetcar. A masked man had threatened him with a gun, then shot him before running away. When Jacobson died the next day a .32-caliber bullet was found in his body. Police had few leads, though there was information about a pair of thieves who wore masks, one short, the other tall. A few weeks after the murder, Edward Campbell approached Detectives Hogan and Silvey, intimating that he could provide various kinds of information, apparently trying to earn a few points in exchange for informing. Campbell told the officers that a man named Charles Schmidt was shipping some stolen articles from San Jose to San Francisco. After a watch was set up, police arrested Schmidt and the property was indeed found to be stolen goods. Schmidt, a tall man, confessed to seven robberies he had committed with a short man named Sydney Bell. Campbell, who was tall like Schmidt, was kept under surveillance. When he did not lead the police to Bell, an officer finally told him that they believed Campbell could tell them the true story of the killing. He agreed to confess under the condition that he receive immunity.

Working as a salesman for the Singer Sewing Machine

Robber Sydney Bell.

Company, Campbell had been sent out with Sydney Bell to canvass for sales, and Bell had persuaded him to team up in order to rob pedestrians. The pair had robbed several people when, on the night of Aug. 17, as they met to go out thieving again, Bell showed his partner a .32-caliber pistol and a leaded policeman's club. Campbell said he became nervous and repeatedly protested against committing any more robberies. Bell became angry. As the two rode together on the streetcar around midnight, Bell went up to a young man, Jacobson, and told him to put up his hands. Jacobson grabbed Bell, who then shot him in the stomach. The police arrested Bell when he went to meet Campbell at his home, and Bell admitted to more than sixty-five robberies, but refused to confess to the Jacobson murder.

On Apr. 22, Bell was tried for murder in the Superior Court and was found Guilty on May 7. An appeal and a new trial followed in which Bell was tried for three counts of robbery, to which he pleaded guilty. On Sept. 17, he received a sixty-year sentence. Schmidt, found Guilty of assisting Bell in several robberies, was sentenced to San Quentin Prison but, on the first day there, he committed suicide by swallowing potassium cyanide. For his cooperation with Police, Campbell was set free. Bell served nineteen years of his sentence and was paroled in May 1909.

REF.: *CBA; Duke, Celebrated Criminal Cases of America.*

Bell, Tom (Dr. **Thomas J. Hodges**), 1825-56, U.S., west. outl. Tom Bell, a brilliant Alabama-born surgeon who had served in the U.S Army during the Mexican-American War, turned bandit in 1855 and terrorized the California counties of Yuba, Nev., and Placer about two years after the death of the notorious outlaw, Joachim Murieta. Bell had been raised in Rome, Tenn., and had received a good education. He went on to medical school, then served with the Tennessee Volunteers under Colonel Cheatham in the Mexican-American War. He went West to follow the gold strikes, but he wound up broke and then turned to banditry, looting a San Francisco cabin. He was caught and sent to Angel Island, then a state prison in the middle of San Francisco Bay, where he served a year. Here he met the men who later made up his outlaw band: Bill Gristy, also known as Bill White; Ned Connor, a fierce-looking bandit with long red whiskers, and Jim Smith, an escape artist whose entire body was covered with tattoos.

When released, Bell and these men were joined by Bob Carr who called himself "English Bob", Montague Lyon, also known as "Monte Jack", and Juan Fernandez, a killer and thief wanted in Mexico. Unlike the fierce Murieta, noted for his cruelty to his victims, Bell was often considerate of those he preyed upon and showed them pity when depriving them of their valuables. He and his men robbed stagecoaches but often stopped wagon drivers such as Dutch John who was robbed by Bell and his men near Volcano, Calif. He turned over $30.25; Bell took the cash but returned the coin, telling John to "buy a drink and forget this incident."

A flat nose made Bell easy to remember and this was the first thing his victims described to lawmen seeking him, that and the fact that he was also very handsome, with blue eyes, sandy hair, blond mustache and goatee, a tall man standing well over six feet. Bell was early identified, even by his own men who had the habit of boasting that they were "Tom Bell's men." The band stopped John McMillan, a wagon driver for a mining company, and took more than $3,000 in gold dust from his shipment. He was tied to a tree and blindfolded, but Bell made sure that the bonds were loose and McMillan could free himself within a short time. When the victim removed his blindfold he found that Bell had left him food and a hunting knife so that he could survive in the wilderness.

Lawmen searching for Bell were confounded by his knowledge of which travelers would be carrying gold and money. Then, by interviewing these victims, officers realized that almost all of the victims had been guests at the Western Exchange Hotel or Hog Ranch, located on the main road between Sacramento and Nevada City. The hotel owner, Elizabeth Hood, of course, was being paid by Bell to supply him with information on wealthy travelers and gold shipments. Other innkeepers at the Mountaineer House on Auburn Road and the California House near Marysville, also provided Bell with similar information for a price or a share of the loot stolen. On Mar. 12, 1856, Bell and his band stopped a mule train laden with $21,000 in gold, taking the gold bags, and tying the five drivers to trees, again leaving pocket change with the mining men. When this pack train was stopped, Wells Fargo guard S.T. Barstow had half-pulled his gun when Bell shouted to him: "Stop that! We don't want to kill you but we must have your money." Again, the robber had proved his inclination to avoid bloodshed. This was soon changed with a bloody stagecoach robbery some months later.

Bell and his men were soon rich, but they were hunted by scores of posses and vigilantes throughout northern California. Bell decided that he would make one more "strike" and then go east and resume his career in medicine. He learned that a huge gold shipment of more than $100,000 would be shipped on Aug. 12, 1856, from Camptonville to Marysville. The gold's owner, a man named Rideout, rode ahead on horseback, the stage rumbling behind him, guarded by driver John Greer and messenger Bill Dobson; both cradled shotguns. Bell, ever cautious, planted one of his men on the stage in the disguise of a miner. This man got off the stage at the California House and there signaled to another gang member that the gold was indeed aboard the stage.

Rideout continued leading the stage once it was back on the wilderness road and was soon surrounded by Bell and two other men, Gristy and Carr. Riding up on the stage from behind were Monte Jack, Connor, and Fernandez. The outlaws ordered Greer to bring the stage to a halt but the seasoned driver only whipped them to faster speeds. Infuriated, three of the bandits opened fire on the stagecoach, raking it, and killing a female passenger, Mrs. Tilghman, the wife of a barber in Marysville. A bullet struck her directly in the forehead. Two male passengers cried out when they, too, were wounded. Greer was wounded in the arm but kept hold of the reins while Dobson let loose with his shotgun, then his pistols, blasting Fernandez from his horse and wounding first Bell's horse, then Bell in the arm. The outlaws tried to stop the stage once more at another spot up the road, but Greer whipped his horses past them at such speed that the stationary outlaws could do nothing. When the stagecoach arrived in Marysville, a posse was quickly formed and, headed by Police Captain William King, and Sacramento detectives Robert Harrison and Daniel Gay, went immediately in pursuit of the Bell gang. The posse returned empty-handed.

Bell by this time thought himself immune to capture and he taunted Captain King with letters in which he stated: "Catch me if you can!" Rewards were posted and one citizen recognized a member of the Bell gang, William Carter, who was captured and quickly revealed the hideouts of his fellow outlaws. Detective Harrison and others rounded up the gang members, one by one, each informing on the others. Bill Gristy was identified in Knights Ferry and he was taken prisoner by the local sheriff. He quickly revealed Bell's hideout at Firebaugh's Ferry near the San Joaquin River. On Oct. 4, 1856, a posse led by Judge Belt and Robert Price, overcame the outlaw on the trail and decided not to turn him over to officials but to hang him vigilante style. Bell accepted his fate laconically but asked if he could write two letters, one to his mother, the other to a Mrs. Hood who had harbored him at the Western Exchange Hotel. To his mother the outlaw wrote touchingly:

Dear Mother:

I am about to make my exit to another country. I take this opportunity to write you a few lines. Probably you may never hear from me again. If not, I hope we may meet where parting is no prodigal career in this country, I have always recollected your fond admonitions, and if I had lived up to them, I would not have been in my present position; but, dear Mother, though my fate has been a cruel one, yet I have no one to blame but myself. Give my respects to all my old and youthful friends. Tell them to beware of bad associations, and never to enter into any gambling saloons, for that has been my ruin. If my old grandmother is living, remember me to her. With these remarks, I bid you farewell forever.

Your only boy,
Tom

Possemen came forward with a bottle of whiskey, offering the condemned man a drink. He accepted gratefully, lifting the bottle to his executioners, thanking them for their thoughtfulness. "I have no bitterness toward any one of you," he said. He showed not a bit of nervousness as his hands were tied behind his head and a rope was placed over the limb of a sycamore tree, the other end looped around his neck. He was given a few minutes to pray and this Bell did, lowering his head and quietly saying words only he could hear. He lifted his head and nodded to the possemen as a signal that he was ready. His horse was whipped forward and Tom Bell, California's most dangerous outlaw, swung into space.

REF.: American Guide Series, *California, A Guide to the Golden State*; Banning, *Six Horses*; Bartholomew, *The Biographical Album of Western Gunfighters*; Boggs, *My Playhouse was a Concord Coach*; Block, *Great Stagecoach Robbers of the West*; CBA; Delay, *History of Yuba and Sutter Counties*; Dunlop, *Doctors of the American Frontier*; Fisher and Holmes, *Gold Rushes and Mining Camps of the Early American West*; Goss, *Highwaymen in the Quick Silver Mining Region*; ____, *The Life and Death of a Quicksilver Mine*; Hemphill, *Down the Mother Lode*; Horan, *Desperate Men*; Hungerford, *Wells Fargo*; Jackson, *Anybody's Gold*; ____, *Bad Company*; ____, *Tintypes in Gold*; Lardner, *History of Placer and Nevada Counties*; Sabin, *Wild Men of the Wild West*; Shippey, *It's an Old California Custom*; Stong, *Gold in Them Hills*; Tinkham, *History of San Joaquin County*; Wilcox, *Reminiscences of California Life*; Wilson, *Treasure Express*; Winther, *Via Western Express & Stagecoach*.

Bellamy, Charles, prom. 1717, Brit., pir. Charles Bellamy and his pirate marauders sailed up and down the coast of the Carolinas in the early eighteenth century "making war on the whole world," as he would later put it. Bellamy had a flair for the English language, justifying his actions in the larger context of man's corrupt legal systems, which he neither respected nor observed. "They villify us, the scoundrels do, when there is only this difference: they rob the poor under the cover of the law, forsooth, and we plunder the rich under the protection of our own courage."

By 1718, many pirates, including Ballamy, were forced to flee to safe ports in Madagascar or the Gulf of Guinea.

REF.: Botting, *The Pirates*; CBA; Mitchell, *Pirates*; Rankin, *The Golden Age of Piracy*.

Bellamy, George Anne (Georgiana), c.1731-1788, Brit., pros. An elegant and cultured woman, Bellamy apparently engaged in prostitution for pleasure as well as for profit.

The illegitimate offspring of Lord Tyrawley, George Anne Bellamy was educated in a convent in Boulogne and became a famous actress. She performed at the celebrated Covent Gardens Theater in London, and authored an *Apology* in six volumes in 1785. Her close friends and customers included the well-known actor and theatrical manager, David Garrick, and many other literary and diplomatic figures of English society, including Lord Chesterfield and the British statesman Henry Fox. She also enjoyed the company of virtuous society women, many of whom allowed their daughters to become friendly with this famous and cultured prostitute. REF.: CBA.

Bellamy, Samuel, d.1717, Brit., pir. During the time that Samuel Bellamy served aboard Benjamin Hornigold's pirate ship, not once did the brigands prey upon English shipping. The captain plundered only vessels belonging to the enemies of the Crown—France and Spain. These restrictions were not to the liking of Bellamy and other crewmen.

Captain Hornigold and his loyal crewmembers were put off the vessel, and Bellamy took his place. The new captian sailed first to the West Indies and then up to the Virginia Capes, where his heavily-armed *Whido Galley* captured the *Agnes*, the *Anne of Glasgow*, and the *Tryal* within two months. In April 1717, Bellamy got careless. His men seized a cargo of wine and spirits off the coast of Cape Cod. Instead of guarding the sealed casks, they tore them open and consumed the entire contents. The pirates, in their drunken state, ran the *Whido Galley* ashore. Bellamy and eight of his men were easily captured and brought back to Boston to stand trial. Found Guilty of piracy, Captain Bellamy, along with seven crewmembers, was hanged.

REF.: CBA; Rankin, *The Golden Age of Piracy*.

Belle, Earl, 1932- , U.S., fraud. A native of Pittsburgh, Pa., the 26-year-old, baby-faced Belle was considered at one time the boy wonder of high finance. After establishing his Cornucopia Gold Mines company, Belle's profits soared out of sight, and he

was briefly hailed as one of the most brilliant young businessmen in America. He was interviewed by Mike Wallace and spewed forth a credo worthy of Horatio Alger: "If you claw your way up to success you never have to ask anyone for anything." Belle's clawing, it was later revealed, consisted of taking out one enormous bank loan after another, the last to cover the first and so on, and then, with the participation of a partner, draining the assets of the company. With more than $2 million thus stolen from his own firm, Earl Belle, wizard of American finance, then beat a hasty departure for Rio de Janeiro, Braz. There he resided, successfully resisting all

Boy business wonder and swindler Earl Belle.

attempts at extradition. Belle later confessed from his posh living quarters in Rio that the records of his firm, Cornucopia Gold Mines, were "falsified and quite incomplete." He added that he was "deeply sorry for all the people who have been misled and all the wrongs done." When asked whether or not he deserved to be punished for his swindle, Belle shrugged, smiled and said: "I imagine a permanent exile is punishment enough."

REF.: CBA; Nash, *Hustlers and Con Men*.

Bellenden, Sir John, d.1577, Scot., consp. Lawyer and privy council to Mary Queen of Scots in 1561. He was involved in the plot to kill David Rizzio, court musician and close confidante of Mary. See: **Rizzio, David**. REF.: CBA.

Belli, Melvin, 1907- , U.S., crim. law. Melvin Belli is known as an innovative and imaginative defense counsel whose success in both criminal and civil law has been widespread and, for the last fifty years, he has been the leading exponent of "demonstrative evidence." Belli, a law graduate of Boalt Hall at the University of California in 1933, used this technique in his first significant criminal case, the defense of San Quentin convict Ernest Smith who stood accused of murdering a fellow inmate. Smith insisted that he had killed in self-defense, explaining that every prisoner carried a weapon in prison. The skeptical Belli went to Warden Clinton Duffy of San Quentin who showed him a drawer filled with knives, files, blades of all kinds, homemade by the inmates. Belli borrowed the drawer and brought this into court, spilling the contents on the floor and then picking up the weapons one by one in front of a shocked jury. Smith was acquitted, and Belli had established his "demonstrative evidence" technique, a method he would use effectively with juries for five decades.

Early in his career, during the Depression, Belli took cases for no fee at all, just to get experience. As the years progressed, he became one of the richest and most famous attorneys in the U.S., certainly the most celebrated in San Francisco, where tour guides took pains to point out his home to visitors to the Bay area. Though Belli has defended many criminals such as Mickey Cohen and Jack Ruby (he was criticized for his handling of this case), his chief accomplishments are in the field of civil law where he is known as "The King of Torts." Belli is no paragon of modesty, stating in 1976: "Ask any lawyer or judge; every one of them will tell you I've done more to change trial law on the civil side than anyone in the legislatures ever did or is doing. In forty years I've taken more cases' upstairs (to appellate courts), done more lecturing and written more than any practicing lawyer."

REF.: Belli, *My Life on Trial*; CBA; Cohen, *Mickey Cohen: In My Own Words*; Reid, *The Grim Reapers*.

Bellinger, Charles Byron, 1839-1905, U.S., jur. Prosecuting attorney in Portland, Ore., in 1871. He was appointed judge of the District of Oregon by President Grover Cleveland in 1893. He published *The Codes and Statutes of Oregon* (1902). REF.: CBA.

Bellingham, John, 1673-99, Brit., fraud-mur. As he recalled his criminal adventures from his cell at Newgate Prison, Belling-ham admitted that he deserved punishment. The reprieves he had been given early in his career were not deserved, and actually had inspired him to commit even worse crimes. Now, as he con-templated death, suicide seemed honorable but frightening.

John Bellingham, the son of a justice, was born in Surrey. He had become a criminal at age thirteen, when most of his peers were still learning their lessons. After killing a man on the Brixton Causeway, he had been reprieved by the Surrey assizes. He then specialized in counterfeiting, becoming a skilled penman who could turn a £5 note into £40 and pass it off as genuine.

On Oct. 13, 1699, Bellingham was indicted at the Old Bailey for altering the endorsement of a bank note against Sir John Elwell. More serious were charges of embezzlement and counter-feiting. Facing a possible death sentence, he implicated his accomplice John Arthur and his own brother in a notorious mail robbery, hoping the court would be lenient. He pleaded with Secretary James Vernon of the exchequer office, claiming that information volunteered to a justice could not be used as evidence, but Vernon shook his head. Bellingham would meet a robber's fate upon Tyburn ill.

On the morning of Oct. 27, 1699, he handed his bottle of poison to a clergyman, favoring a quick death by hanging over the painful death of foul poison. REF.: *CBA*.

Bello, Clemente Vazquez, prom. 1932, Cuba, assass. In a time when political assassinations were rampant in Cuba, several of the Cuban president's friends and associates were murdered.

Dr. Clemente Vazquez Bello acted as speaker of the Cuban Senate in 1932 and was a good friend of Gerardo Machado, the country's president. As Bello left his house on a December afternoon in 1932 to drive to the Senate, an open touring car with seven men inside—carrying riot guns—sped toward him. Dozens of bullets struck Bello, more than sixty puncturing his car. The wounded chauffeur managed to drive to the hospital, where Bello died a few hours later. The Machado government quickly retaliated. Within an hour three cars of armed men cornered Dr. Ricardo Dolz, an anti-Machado leader, in his car and attempted to kill him. But their aim was bad and Dolz escaped, hiding out in the Uruguayan Legation, where he was soon joined by Manuel de la Cruz, another leader of the opposition party. Just fifteen minutes after the attack on Dolz, a gunman entered the home of the de Andrade brothers, and killed Gonzalo Freyere de Andrade, a Cuban representative; Leopoldo de Andrade, an engineer; and Guilllermo de Andrade, an attorney. Thirty minutes later assassins shot Dr. Miguel Angel Aguilar, a leader in the unsuccessful anti-Machado uprising. He died the next day.

Just before the funeral of Dr. Bello, detectives inspected the Colon Cemetery where interment was to take place. There they found twenty-three bombs planted near the spot intended for Bello's grave, bombs packed with enough dynamite to blow up a large portion of the cemetery, including those attending the funeral, many of them government officials. REF.: *CBA*.

Belot, Françoise, d.1679, Fr., alchemist. Françoise Belot, not satisfied with poisoning that simply added arsenic to wine or other drinks, experimented with new and more powerful methods. He began his experiments by force-feeding toads arsenic, then putting them in silver chalices, puncturing their heads and finally, crushing them, thus producing a cup that he claimed would kill anyone drinking from it. Throughout this delicate operation, Belot would chant charms to enhance the process. "I know a secret," he explained in his own account, "such that, in doctoring a cup with a toad, and what I put into it, if fifty persons chanced to drink from it afterwards, even if it were washed and rinsed, they would all be done for, and the cup could only be purified by throwing it into a hot fire."

Fearing that someone might think his intentions were evil, Belot added: "After having thus poisoned the cup, I should not try it upon a human being, but upon a dog, and I should entrust the cup to nobody." Renowned for part of his career, Belot's theories and techniques made him quite popular and prosperous,

for a while. He died by torture, broken on the wheel, on June 10, 1679. See: **Armstrong, Herbert Rowse; Black, Edward Ernest; Blandy, Mary; Botkin, Cordelia; Bryant, Charlotte; Cotton, Mary Ann Robson Mowbray; DeMelker, Daisy Louisa; Hoch, Johann Otto; Jegado, Helene; LaFarge, Marie; Maybrick, Florence Elizabeth; Seddon, Frederick Henry; Smith, Madeleine.**
REF.: *CBA*; Thompson, *Poison and Poisoners.*

Belushi, Jim, 1955- , Case of, U.S., asslt.&bat. In July 1987, actor Jim Belushi pleaded innocent to charges of assault and battery in Los Angeles. On Jan. 2, 1987, Belushi had allegedly stopped in the Westwood area to attack Bobby Ray Henson, a pedestrian who spat at the BMW Belushi was driving after the car had passed dangerously close to him. Also in the car was Belushi's 6-year-old son. The then 32-year-old actor did not show up at the arraignment—the charges were denied by his lawyer. Belushi was allowed by Commissioner Joseph Ruffner to remain free without posting bail. Conviction on the charges carried a sentence of up to $12,000 in fines and a possible year in jail.

In October 1987, Henson, who had required thirteen stitches as a result of being knocked to the ground, showed up in court to say he no longer wished to proceed with the case. In a civil compromise, a financial settlement was made with the victim out of court for an undisclosed amount. But, because of the violence of the attack, the city attorney's office objected to the municipal court's dismissal of the case and filed an appeal. That appeal was denied early in 1988. REF.: *CBA*.

Belvin, Paul Augustus, 1943- , Ber., mur. Appealing to a killer's vanity, two Scotland Yard detectives invited him to be an amateur detective and help solve the crime he committed.

On July 4, 1971, at 4:30 a.m., the partly clothed body of Jean Burrows, a 24-year-old British journalist vacationing with her husband in Bermuda, was discovered floating in three feet of water in Hamilton Harbour, a yacht basin for millionaires. The night before, Burrows, her husband, and two other journalists had ridden mopeds home after a dinner date at the popular Hoppin' John's restaurant, but she did not arrive with the others. A post-mortem by Dr. Wenwyon, the local pathologist, revealed that she had been raped, knocked unconscious by a heavy blow to the head, and then drowned by being held under water. Bruises indicated an attempt at strangulation before the drowning. Her moped was hidden three hundred yards from the body in a tall patch of grass. Recruited from Scotland Yard in London to investigate the crime were detectives William Wright and Basil Haddrell. After sending slides and photographs assembled by Wenwyon for analysis in London, the detectives set up house-to-house inquiries and came up with the name of Paul Augustus Belvin, a 28-year-old local man frequently seen in the basin where the body was found. Two witnesses recalled him as the winner of a competition the year before in which he had found a hidden key and won a cash prize, gaining some publicity.

When the detectives called Belvin in for questioning they found him to be clever, with a great deal of information about local gossip and of the area. Wright surprised Haddrell, his superior, by asking Belvin if he would like to be an amateur detective and assist them in the investigation. Belvin eagerly agreed, and then proceeded to act out the entire crime in accurate and precise detail, even leading the detectives to the murder weapon, an iron pipe he had thrown into the sea. Tests on Belvin's clothing proved conclusively that he was the murderer. On Sept. 1, 1971, he confessed. Belvin was found Guilty and sentenced to death, a sentence later commuted to life imprisonment.
REF.: *CBA*; Tullett, *Strictly Murder.*

Bembenek, Lawrencia (Laurie Bembenek), 1959- , U.S., mur. A former policewoman and ex-Playboy bunny was convicted of murdering her husband's former wife because the ex-wife received substantial alimony.

On May 28, 1981, Christine Schultz was shot dead in her home in Milwaukee, Wis. In June, Laurie Bembenek, married to Elfred Schultz, Christine's ex-husband and a former police detective, was charged with the murder. Bembenek had been fired from the police force in September 1980, and Elfred Schultz resigned as a detective in December 1981. Witnesses at the March 1982 trial, said Bembenek, a former Playboy bunny in Lake Geneva, Wis., had talked about having Christine Schultz killed, complaining that her alimony payments were too large. Prosecution witnesses included Schultz's two sons: Shannon Schultz, eight, who testified that the person who came into his room seconds after shooting his mother wore a green jogging suit, and 12-year-old Sean Schultz who remembered the murderer in a loose green army jacket. Four witnesses testified that Bembenek owned a jogging outfit like that described. Hairs from a wig found hidden in Bembenek's apartment matched hairs found near the slain woman's body. Robert Kraemer, assistant district attorney, headed the prosecution's case, portraying Bembenek as a woman addicted to "the fast life," while defense attorney Donald Eisenberg said his client was framed, quoting the Bible and Pope Paul VI in his four hours of closing arguments. Bembenek was found Guilty of first-degree murder and sentenced by Judge Michael Skwierawski to life imprisonment. A large crowd of spectators followed the 15-day trial. REF.: *CBA*.

Bemis, China Polly, d.1933, U.S., pros. The scarcity of women in the old West made it a prime region for importing prostitutes. One of the popular stories from those times are anecdotes about "poker brides"—women won as stakes in gamblers' card games. One story dealt with the Idaho town of Warren, in the rugged, isolated Salmon River country. With a comparatively large population of 3,000 circa 1872, one-third of it Chinese brought to the U.S. to build the first transcontinental railroad and staying to join the mining boom, Warren had few women. Near the Big Salmon, called "the River of No Return" for its inaccessibility—boats guided to nearby Riggins would have no way of getting back by water—Warren's female population con-

China Polly Bemis

sisted of Lapwai Indians and four Chinese prostitutes controlled by "Big Jim."

Not long after the mining boom had died out in Warren, Big Jim succumbed to a heart attack. The four women he had imported from San Francisco were no longer in servitude. One of them, China Polly, opened a small but successful restaurant.

China Polly was allegedly a "poker bride"—a woman won by Charley Bemis in a hand of poker. Others tell a different story. A long-time friend of Polly's, well-informed on Warren history, was Jay Czikek, who related that she fell in love with the gambler Bemis. When he was shot in the face by an Indian who was his rival for Polly's affection, she nursed Bemis back to health, and he responded by giving up gambling and making her his common-law wife. The couple moved to another isolated spot in the area, which came to be known as Bemis Point. There they set up a ranch, were legally married, and stayed together in that spot for fifty-one years, until Bemis' death. Czikek and his wife were her friends all that time. After Bemis' death, for a treat, they took her by boat to Boise to see a big city, but she was so unnerved by electric lights, movies, and radio that she returned to the Bemis Point ranch and lived there alone till she died ten years later, on Nov. 5, 1933.

REF.: *CBA*; Drago, *Notorious Ladies of the Frontier*.

Ben Ali, Ameer (AKA: **Frenchy**), prom. 1891, U.S., mur. A man convicted of a New York City murder on circumstantial evidence was released nine years later and transported to his native Algeria.

At 9 a.m. on Apr. 24, 1891, night clerk Eddie Harrington made

his rounds of Manhattan's sleazy East River Hotel on the Lower East Side, kicking stragglers out of their low-rent rooms. Getting no response when he knocked on the door of Room 31, he opened it with a master key and discovered the mutilated corpse of Carrie Brown, a 60-year-old former actress and regular in the dissolute neighborhood. She had been strangled, slashed with a filed-down cooking knife, and the sign of a cross was carved on her thigh. Police Inspector Thomas Byrnes handled the investigation. The case attracted considerable public interest, in part because the sign of the cross was the mark of London's "Jack The Ripper."

Brown was seen coming into the hotel at around 11 p.m. with a 30-year old blonde male companion of stocky build, described by witnesses as a seafaring man. This man was never found, but another regular at the hotel, Ameer Ben Ali, a dark-haired man, who otherwise matched the description of the killer, was arrested, along with several others for questioning. Ben Ali had spent the night of the murder in Room 33, just across the hall from Room 31 and was known to be an occasional companion of Brown.

Based on the evidence of bloodstains and marks in the hallway between the two rooms and on the door, chair, blanket, and mattress of Room 33, Ben Ali was brought to trial on June 24, 1981. An interpreter translated for the accused, whose grasp of language, including his native Algerian Arabic, was limited and inconsistent. Inspector Byrnes brought in witnesses for the prosecution to prove that Ben Ali had been living a sordid existence and often stayed at the East River Hotel, sometimes wandering from room to room at night. Several experts testified that the bloodstains had come from one body, probably from the abdomen of the murdered woman. When, on July 2, the defense directly asked the confused Ben Ali for the first time if he had killed Brown, the Algerian became hysterical, then pleaded repeatedly for the rest of the trial that he was innocent. Ben Ali was convicted of second-degree murder, indicating a compromise made by the jury. On July 10, 1891, Ben Ali was sentenced to life imprisonment at Sing Sing. Shortly after he began serving this sentence he was transferred to the hospital for the criminally insane at Matteawan.

Rumors that the murderer had boarded a boat bound for the Far East continued to circulate in New York City during the nine years following Ben Ali's conviction. In 1900, an application for a pardon was made on Ben Ali's behalf, based on new evidence that a man answering the killer's description had begun working in New Jersey shortly before the murder and was absent from his home on the night of the killing, disappearing a few days later. In his abandoned room a brass key with a tag reading "31," which matched the keys at the East River Hotel, was found, along with a blood-stained shirt. Governor Benjamin Barker Odell ordered that Ben Ali be released, judging that the new evidence demolished the case against him. The bloodstains found leading to and inside Room 31, the prosecution's main evidence, had been made at the time of the coroner and police visits to the scene of the crime. Ben Ali's sentence was commuted on Apr. 16, 1902, and the French government transported him back to Algeria.

REF.: Borchard, *Convicting the Innocent; CBA*.

Benan Letter, prom. 1910, Ger., hoax. A letter purporting to chronicle the life of Jesus was exposed as a hoax in Germany by two University of Berlin professors.

Published in 1910 in Berlin, the *Benan Letter* supposedly was found near Cairo in 1860. Based on a Greek text that reportedly had been lost, it was discovered by scholar Freiherr von Rabenau, a historian who died in 1879 in Munich. The *Benan Letter* had been edited by Edler von der Planitz, who said he received the manuscript from von Rabenau. The writer, Benan, is supposed to have been converted by Jesus to the Hebrew God, and the letter was said to have been sent to Strato, a private secretary of the Emperor Tiberius.

The letter starts with the discovery of the Christ child by an astronomer, Putiphra, who was later given permission by Joseph and Mary to take Jesus back to Egypt to educate him in philosophy and religion. At twelve, Jesus astounded the best Hebrew scholars with his knowledge. Later, as a young man, he supposedly studied medicine, earning a reputation as a healer. At twenty-six, the letter explains, he had a romantic courtship with the daughter of a rich grain dealer, returned to Palestine just before he turned thirty, and began his missionary work. When Benan returned three years later to find out what had happened to Jesus, he reached Jerusalem on the day of the crucifixion, observing the rising of Christ on Easter Sunday.

The letter was exposed by Dr. Carl Schmidt and Dr. Herman Grapow, both of the University of Berlin, who revealed that all the names and dates were taken from the works of a Münich professor, J.F. Lauth, who died in 1865. They also proved that Rabenau was a fictitious character.

REF.: *CBA; MacDougall, Hoaxes.*

Bender, Tony, See: Strollo, Anthony C.

Bender Family, 1872-73, U.S., mur. The first, most notorious of America's mass murderers, who now oddly enjoy historical significance, at least in the sovereign state of Kansas, were the fierce and enigmatic Benders. Outwardly, this was a typical family of the American frontier, father, mother, daughter, son, all hardworking souls dedicated to the land, innkeepers who sought the common goals of commercial success—enough wealth to provide old age comforts, enough security to weather the storms howling down from the future. Untypical were the methods the Bender Family employed in its mercantile practices, for the real business of the Benders was murder, and their victims, like the wayward wanderers who stumbled upon their own doom at Castle Dracula in far away Transylvania, were travelers seeking food and a bed for the night. This they received cheerfully from their sly hosts, along with an early unmarked grave.

The four Benders appeared for the first time in Labette County, Kan., in Fall 1870. The father, John Bender (some claim his name was William), was a man of about sixty, a primitive immigrant wearing a shaggy beard and possessing large, angry-looking eyes. He was accompanied by an equally robust wife whose first name is not recorded, a woman of fifty, with blue eyes and brown hair, his son John, about twenty-seven, and daughter Kate, age twenty-four. Much was later said of the backgrounds of these four, most reports differing widely. It was later reported that John Bender, Jr., was not a Bender at all, his real name being John Gebhardt, or Liefens, and that he was Mrs. Bender's son from a previous marriage. Whether John Bender was his father or not, the younger man possessed all the traits of the old man. He was surly, sullen, and mean of spirit. His face was later described as having "had the fierce malice of a hyena." His build was slight and across thin, turned-down lips rode a light brown mustache. John Bender spoke broken English, preferring to converse in German, the native tongue of his father. The old man never spoke anything but German, although he would make some guttural-sounding English words when angry, which was most of the time.

Kate Bender, who was later described as a vicious-looking harridan or ravishing beauty, depending upon the sympathies of her ex-lovers and the editorial whims of newsmen in that day, spoke good English but with a slight German accent. Her mother seldom spoke at all, merely followed the grunted orders from the old man, working like a horse from dawn to dusk. Kate, of course, was of chief interest of this band of murderers and by most accounts she was far from ugly, although one report describes her rather brutally as "a large, masculine, red-faced woman." Others profile Kate as a very good looking red-haired girl, statuesque, buxom, with a small waist, slender hips and mesmerizing eyes, full lips and a charming manner, a cross between the subtle sirens of the Nile and the plump Broadway stars of that day. Kate herself might not have been a Bender either, but, as was claimed by some, the mistress of John, Jr. Of this strange family, only Kate possessed a personality remembered long by those who encounted the Benders. Governor Thomas Osborn of Kansas, who issued wanted posters for the family shortly after their horrendous crimes were unearthed, described Kate with some first-hand facts: "Dark

hair and eyes, good looking, well-formed, rather bold in appearance, fluent talker." But when she and the other three members of her cold-hearted clan rolled across the gentle hills of southern Kansas in late 1869, she had no identity to speak of; she was just another homeless pioneer looking for a place to root.

The first resident of Labette County to greet the Benders was a fellow German immigrant, Rudolph Brockmann, who ran a small country grocery store. How he came to know the Benders before they called on him for aid has never been learned. Brockmann had a large land claim and allowed the four strangers riding in a large wagon, all their earthly possessions piled behind, to build a shanty house on his property. They managed to endure a severe winter and moved in the spring to another hastily constructed building. In the following spring of 1871, the Benders selected a site on the main road stretching between the Kansas towns of Cherryvale and Parsons, closer to the former, their single structure squatting seven miles northeast of Cherryvale. The Benders had studied traffic on the road, which was considerable, for along this well-beaten path hundreds of travelers made their way from Fort Scott and the Osage Mission to Independence. Beyond, to the southwest, was the Indian Territory that would later become the state of Oklahoma. The Bender Inn was only eighteen miles from what is now the Kansas-Oklahoma border. The house was a simple affair, one which functioned as living quarters for the four Benders and was designed, with exceeding malice aforethought as later discoveries showed, to offer travelers the comforts of the crude inns of the day. The house was in a hollow, surrounded by plum and cottonwood trees, at the end of long vale in the prairie but it could not be seen at any great distance by those riding along the main road. Near the building was Drum Creek, a small stream seldom more than waist-high deep.

Behind the house the Benders kept hogs and a few cattle in some pens. The house, or inn as it was called, had but one room that passed for two, divided as it was by a large piece of canvas. The first section of the house at the entrance was for travelers who could sit at a large table and eat the meals prepared by Mrs. Bender and Kate. Behind the canvas was the area that functioned as sleeping quarters for the family and guests. In back of the house was also a stable where patrons could keep their horses overnight. In back of that stretched a garden, rather haphazardly kept by the Benders, and an orchard. To their meager ensemble, the Benders added a limited grocery which was nothing more than some shelves against the wall of the first room. They were lined with tinned goods and other supplies which were purchased by overnight guests and some of the Bender neighbors who lived quite a distance from nearby towns and found it convenient to occasionally buy some items from the Benders.

For about a year and a half the Bender Inn was no more than a waystop and its inhabitants aroused no special notice, except that Kate Bender began making a name for herself in many small towns in southern Kansas. Kate had moved into rural society quickly. By Fall 1871 she became the desired partner of young men attending county dances and she proved an excellent dancer. Several young swains later claimed that she was also free and easy with her favors, although so aggressive a sex partner that after one night her lovers gave her up from exhaustion. This was undoubtedly hindsight embellishment, given the monster image of Kate later favored by most portraits. For about a month Kate worked as a waitress in a Cherryvale hotel, but she resigned when male patrons began to make advances, or so she said when quitting. Only Kate of the entire Bender clan could be seen attending church on Sunday and, for a short time, she attended regular Sunday evening meetings.

It was at one of these meetings that Kate Bender announced that she was a genuine medium and that she had the power to call the spirits of the dead to the presence of the living. In fact, she said, her entire family possessed these powers, all of them were spiritualists who had direct contact with the Great Beyond. To prove it, Kate began to give lectures on the subject and hold crude séances where she spoke for those at her table to the "Dear Departed," for a price, of course, and the spirits replied through her to the loved ones still chained to earthly life. So popular did Kate become that she took her act on tour through the local Kansas towns, appearing in theaters which were mostly packed with men eager to hear the secrets of the Beyond. Her success increased her capacities to make one miracle after another, until she began to place advertisements in local newspapers which described her abilities to cure almost every human malady. One advertisement stated: "Professor Miss Kate Bender can heal disease, cure blindness, fits and deafness. Residence: 14 miles east of Independence on the road to Osage Mission. June 18, 1872." In light of what was found at that address later one can only shudder at the thought of the sick and infirm traveling the lonely roads to Kate Bender, seeking relief from physical agonies only to be met by excruciating pain and bloody death.

During the period such advertisements were running, Kate Bender appeared to appreciative audiences in the towns of Parsons, Labette, Oswego, and Chetopa. Men flocked to see her for female lecturers were rare in that day and most men found such appearances shocking. There were occasions when men would shout to Kate across the footlights that she had no business as a woman appearing in public to lecture on any subject, that she was merely using her curing and spiritual talks as guises to stump for obtaining equal rights for women, that she was secretly lobbying for the female vote. If this were the case, of course, Kate Bender should be entered in the female hall of fame honoring the pioneers who struggled for equal rights for women. It was not. Kate fended off such accusations with a winning smile and went on to suggest that those with real interest in employing her powers should visit her at the Bender Inn. There she would put them in touch with the Great Beyond. This claim was more than ironic as events would prove.

In the summer and fall of 1872 the conduct of the Benders began to noticibly change. Kate was off lecturing most of this time but her brother John was absent from the wayside inn for extended periods of time, these being business trips, according to the senior Benders who never explained what business their son was conducting. By fall of that year both Kate and John had returned to the inn and their demeanor from that time on was later reported as decidedly strange. It is guessed with some degree of accuracy that the murder spree in which the family indulged was confined to the six month period between October 1872 and March 1873. What caused the Benders to decide that murder for profit was the best or only course open to them remains a mystery. The decision was made. The murders began.

A man named Wetzell of Independence, Kan., read Kate's running advertisements in a local newspaper and, because he suffered from a nagging and seemingly incurable neuralgia, decided to visit this lady of miracles. Wetzell and a friend named Gordan rode to the Bender Inn in the fall of 1872, where Kate greeted the pair warmly. She examined Wetzell's face closely and told him that she could positively cure him but since it was near dinner time, it would be best that the visitors sit down to a good home cooked meal first. She and Mrs. Bender prepared the meal. While they waited, Wetzel and Gordan were surprised to see old man Bender and his son John enter the inn and stare at them, saying nothing. They seemed to be scrutinizing the height and weight of the travelers. Kate Bender motioned the visitors to sit at the table and this they did, in the only chairs available which had been placed tightly against the canvas partition so that when the two men sat down their heads pushed against the canvas. By then the male Benders had walked behind the partition and were making noises that sounded as if they were dragging some heavy weights toward the canvas.

Just as the meal was being served, Wetzell and Gordan, responding to nervous impulse, stood up and grabbed their plates, telling Kate that they preferred to eat standing up. They stood away from the table, nervously munching their food at a small counter. At that moment all the charm went out of Kate Bender.

Where she had earlier been pleasant and charming, she now sneered viciously at the two travelers; she was now caustic and abusive toward them. "You two have no manners," she told them, "only farm animals eat standing up! Are you gentlemen or beasts of the field?" Neither man made a response. Her eyes widened, her prominent jaw jutted forth and her teeth showed as she spat out her words: "Disgusting! Vile!" She pointed a long finger at Wetzell and, with eyes blazing, shouted: "Cure you? You are not worth a cure!" She turned to Mrs. Bender, who stood in front of the pair, her hands on wide hips, glaring at them. "Look at these beasts," hissed Kate Bender to her mother, "two horses with their snoots in the trough!"

Suddenly, Bender and his son reappeared, coming from behind the canvas, once more staring at the visitors in stony silence. Then they scuffled outside, and Wetzell saw them go into a nearby shanty that passed for a barn where they stood talking, looking back to the inn, as if debating what next to do. Wetzell and Gordan put down their plates, mumbled their thanks for Kate's dubious hospitality and went outside to the road where their carriage was tied. As Gordan got into the carriage, Wetzell drew forth his pistol and kept it by his side, not knowing what to expect from his now demoniac hosts. He later claimed that, at any moment, he thought he would see the father and son come charging out of the barn with weapons aimed at killing him and his friend. Just at that moment two freight wagons en route to Independence came rumbling down the road and Wetzell waved a nervous hello to the drivers, then jumped into the carriage. Gordan whipped the horses to a full gallop so that the travelers were ahead of the wagons. Wetzell turned to look back at the inn. It was now dark but he could see in the doorway, holding a lantern aloft, the Junoesque form of Kate Bender, peering after them; he later swore than he saw her arm go up as she shook a menacing fist in his direction. Both Wetzell and Gordan stopped some miles down the road to discuss what had just happened and concluded that they had been unnecessarily alarmed over the mercurial temperament of a rather tempestuous female and the phlegmatic actions of the Bender males who were, at best, cretinous types with mordant personalities. They marked it off as misadventure and decided to forget the matter. It never occurred to them to notify authorities about the peculiar behavior of the Benders.

Wetzell's escape, one certainly of intuitive compulsion, was not shared by others whose sense of danger was less acute. Most prominent of these was Dr. William H. York, one of the leading citizens of Independence, Kan. Dr. York had been visiting his brother, Colonel A.M. York, who lived in Fort Scott and was one of the richest men in the territory. Moreover, a third brother was a state senator who was considered the most powerful man in southern Kansas. Dr. York left Fort Scott on Mar. 9, 1873, returning to his Independence home. He stopped at Osage Mission and left there on Mar. 10. Outside of Cherryvale, the doctor met some friends on the road and told them he intended to stop at the Bender Inn for his midday meal. York was in a fine humor as he rode off on his expensive horse. He sat on a saddle of the finest leather. His clothes and boots were new and expensive. He also carried with him a considerable amount of money, as much as $1500 some later estimated, and in his vest nestled a gold watch of great value. Dr. York was only two miles from the Bender place when more friends passed him on the road. Again he stated that he would stop at the inn to have some of Kate Bender's "fine stew." It was the the last time anyone ever saw Dr. William York alive.

Days passed, and Dr. York did not arrive home. His family notified the other York brothers and soon both men organized search parties. A dozen detectives were also hired by the Yorks and these men combed the countryside between Fort Scott and Independence. In Independence, Colonel York, who announced that he would spare no expense to find his brother, ran into Wetzell who related his experience at the Bender Inn. He made no claims against the Benders, he said, but their actions had been more than suspicious. On Apr. 3, 1873, a large search party rode to the Bender inn to inquire as to the whereabouts of Dr. York. When they arrived, the Bender family claimed no knowledge of Dr. York; they had never set eyes on him. No amount of questioning by the searchers caused the family to change their story. The detectives rode off, planning to search beyond Cherryvale and the Osage Mission. But all their inquiries led the search back to the Bender Inn where Dr. York's trail vanished. When this was reported in detail to Colonel York, he decided to personally conduct the search.

On Apr. 24, York himself visited the Benders; accompanying him were twelve heavily armed men from Cherryvale. Before this group reached the Bender inn, they came across John Bender the younger. He was sitting alongside the road with a Bible in his hands. York questioned him while still sitting in the saddle, asking once more if he had seen his brother, Dr. York. The reply was startling. Yes, John Bender had seen him. He certainly had stopped at the inn. Bender reported that his sister Kate had prepared a good dinner for the doctor who ate it and then left the inn. Before any more questions could be put to Bender, the young man volunteered some harrowing information. "There are outlaws hereabouts," he told York. "I have been shot at by these people—dangerous men, border ruffians they are, the worst scum of the war." (He referred to those Civil War soldiers who, after the end of the war in 1865, had taken up outlawry along the Kansas border, raiding small villages and robbing unsuspecting travelers.) Colonel York pressed Bender for an explanation: "Why tell us this?" Replied Bender: "You see, sir, your brother, Dr. York, was most likely robbed and killed by the same bandits who sometimes lurk around these places. Find those bandits and you will find the body of your brother most likely."

York and his men then rode on to the inn and there Kate Bender greeted them warmly, telling them that she did remember seeing Dr. York and serving him some stew. Why had she not told the first search party this, she was asked. She had simply forgotten, Kate replied. With that she and her mother served the search party a large meal. One man with York who had been with the first search party, walked up to Kate Bender and held her hand firmly, saying: "You claim to be able to reach the spirit world, do you not?" "That is well known," she replied. "Then contact the spirits now and ask them in which world Dr. York can be found, among the living or the dead." Kate Bender pulled her hand away and shook her head. Colonel York asked her to hold a séance then and there and search the Beyond for his brother. "This I cannot do," replied Kate. "There are too many unbelievers here and the spirits resist giving aid to those who scoff at their powers." She then turned to the detective who had cynically asked her to contact the Other World and said: "If you wish to make such contact with the Beyond, then come back here in five days and come alone. I will take you and your questions into that world and you will have all the answers you require."

Both Bender males then arrived at the inn, and father and son appeared eager to aid York and his men any way they could in finding the lost doctor. It was John Bender the younger who suggested that the entire party drag Drum Creek, pointing out that "this was the place, the Creek, where the bandits shot at me in the past and that is where you will find the body of your brother if he is to be found at all." The men stepped outside and the Benders led them down to the Creek which they dragged for hours with no success. Exhausted, the search party left that evening, convinced that the Benders knew nothing of Dr. York's disappearance. They were a cooperative and compassionate family, even if Mrs. Bender had complained during their stay that "a crowd of men like this should not disturb peaceable people like us." As the York party rode off, only the detective who had toyed with Kate about her spiritualistic powers remained skeptical and suspicious of the Benders. Colonel York asked this young man if he actually planned to return in five days to contact the spirit world through Kate Bender. "Should I undertake that journey," he told the colonel, "I would never return to this world."

The search for the mythical bandits proved fruitless, and by May 5, 1873, York and his detectives were once again back at the Bender Inn, but this time there was no trace of the family. Neighbors had already heard the livestock moaning in pain and had investigated the area a day earlier. They found the Bender livestock mostly dead, hogs and calves having perished from thirst. The family had deserted the place, leaving in a great haste. They had not even bothered to take their cattle and hogs with them, precious property in that hardscrabble era. Colonel York ordered his men to break a padlock that had been placed on the front door of the inn, and this was smashed open. The searchers entered the inn and then stepped back, momentarily overwhelmed by a terrific stench. A short time later they found the inside a shambles, as if the family had packed pell-mell and cleared out in manic desperation. Everywhere they stepped litter and debris greeted them. Even some of Kate's "lecture papers" were found scattered over the floor. (These papers were later carefully examined and in them were found startling statements about "the foulness of man" and how "the murder of the heart" should be explored to "expose the natural instincts of a killer race." Much of this was later attributed to inventive newspapermen enhancing the already colorful character of Kate Bender.)

Searchers soon discovered the source of the powerful stench which had been created by the shuttered windows having been sealed by the departing Benders. A trap door toward the rear of the building was found and opened and a pit six feet deep lay beneath this. At the bottom of the pit was a thick layer of congealed human blood which, in the airless inn, had caused the stench. York and his men began to tear the place apart in their desperate search. The colonel went to the back door of the inn and peered out at a stretch of land near the orchard. This had been plowed and harrowed meticulously by the Benders, but such industry puzzled the young detective who had originally suspected Kate Bender of foul play. He pointed to his much plowed land and said to York who was looking at the same spot: "The Benders did not farm. They grew nothing on their land. Why then plow up the land?" It had rained the night before, and much of the furrows had been washed over, leaving peculiar looking mounds of earth in this plowed patch. Colonel York gasped and then shouted: "Boys, I see graves yonder in the orchard!"

The men raced to the plowed area and began to dig furiously. The first of these graves yielded the much sought-after Dr. William York. His body was badly decomposed but recognizable. The skull had been crushed and the throat slit. Of course, all of York's valuables, including his boots, had been taken by the killers. One after another, seven more graves were opened and bodies removed. These included W.F. McCrotty, a Cedarville resident who had been traveling to Independence to contest a land office case six months earlier. He had undoubtedly stopped at the Bender place for food and sleep and was murdered for his money and belongings. McCrotty was, perhaps the first of the known victims to be killed by the Benders. The next corpse was identified by a small ring the killers overlooked; his body was too badly decomposed to identify. The victim was D. Brown, a horse trader from Cedarville. Henry F. McKenzie, who had disappeared on Dec. 5, 1872, a native of Hamilton County, Ind., who had been traveling to Independence to relocate there with his sister, was next found and identified later by the sister, Mrs. J. Thompson who recognized the dead man's clothing. Then came the body of a man named Longcor and, found beneath his body in the shallow grave, the body of his baby girl. Longcor had lost his wife in late Fall 1872, had buried her body in Cherryvalle, and had then headed for Iowa with his small child, only to stop at the Benders for refreshment and untimely death. Two more bodies were then discovered, both males, but they were so badly decomposed that their identities were never established.

So far there had been eight victims in all, but several more were later added to the Bender tally. Colonel York and his men quickly pieced together the murder method employed by the sinister Benders. Guests were seated at the table in the inn and

The Bender Inn, near Cheeryvale, Kansas, where more than a dozen were murdered, 1871.

John Bender, Sr.

Kate Bender

Posse members digging up the buried victims.

Kate Bender lecturing on spiritualism.

The two-room murder inn.

GOVERNOR'S PROCLAMATION.
$2,000 REWARD

State of Kansas, Executive Department.

WHEREAS, several atrocious murders have been recently committed in Labette County, Kansas, under circumstances which fasten, beyond doubt, the commissions of these crimes upon a family known as the "Bender family," consisting of

JOHN BENDER, about 60 years of age, five feet eight or nine inches in height, German, speaks but little English, dark complexion, no whiskers, and sparely built;

MRS. BENDER, about 50 years of age, rather heavy set, blue eyes, brown hair, German, speaks broken English;

JOHN BENDER, Jr. alias John Gebardt, five feet eight or nine inches in height, slightly built, gray eyes with brownish tint, brown hair, light moustache, no whiskers, about 27 years of age, speaks English with German accent;

KATE BENDER, about 24 years of age, dark hair and eyes, good looking, well formed, rather bold in appearance, fluent talker, speaks good English with very little German accent;

AND WHEREAS, said persons are at large and fugitives from justice, now therefore, I, Thomas A. Osborn, Governor of the State of Kansas, in pursuance of law, do hereby offer a REWARD OF FIVE HUNDRED DOLLARS for the apprehension and delivery to the Sheriff of Labette County, Kansas, of each of the persons above named.

In Testimony Whereof, I have hereunto subscribed my name, and caused the Great Seal of the State to be affixed.

[L. S.]   Done at Topeka, this 17th day of May, 1873.

THOMAS A. OSBORN,
Governor.

By the Governor
W. H. SMALLWOOD,
Secretary of State.

Reward poster for the Bloody Benders.

served a hearty meal. Their chairs were purposely placed so that their heads pressed against the canvas partition separating the one-room inn into two rooms. Behind the canvas curtain stood old man Bender and his son John. As soon as the victims' heads made an impression on the other side of the canvas, the two men would strike the impression with a stonemason's hammer, crushing the skulls. There had been some occasions where, as the investigators reconstructed the Bender modus operandi, the two Bender males had struck two men at the same time with their hammers. With the victim unconscious, Kate and her mother stripped the corpses of their valuables and the men dragged the bodies to the trap door, throwing them into the pit where, to make sure of death, the throats were slit much in the manner of slitting a hog's throat, allowing the pool of blood to build up in the bottom of the pit. This was done often enough in broad daylight, the bodies kept in the pit until the cover of darkness allowed the Benders to drag the bodies outside and bury them in graves where they had furrowed the land. The plowing was meant to hide the outlines of the graves. In the instance of the small Longcor child, a girl of about eighteen months, no marks of violence covered her body. She had merely been thrown down into the shallow grave, her father's corpse placed on top of her and she had been buried alive. This was supported by a local physician who stated that the child had died of suffocation, smothered by the weight of her own dead father. This child killing, more than any of the others, filled the searchers with incredible and unabating rage, causing them to vow vengeance on the mass killers. (If certain reports are to be believed, their consuming vengeance was achieved in a spectacular manner.)

The awful discoveries did not end that terrible day. The next day, May 6, 1873, searchers found another grave near the orchard. This yielded the body of a child which was so decomposed that its sex was difficult to determine but later doctors concluded it was the body of an 8-year-old girl whose bones had been literally pulled from their sockets and crushed by some demented fiend who took a long time to mutilate the flesh. Later, near Drum Creek, the body of a man identified as Jones was found. Again, the head had been crushed, the throat slit. In months to come other bodies in the area were found, twenty in all, but eleven murders were definitely attributed to the Benders who had made their inn a foul slaughterhouse. The discovery of the bodies caused hundreds of citizens from nearby communities to descend upon the inn, and so incensed were these shocked spectators that armed posses were immediately formed. Colonel York offered rewards for the Benders, as did local and state officials. As the armed bands set off in several directions to hunt down the fiends, Colonel York is reported to have shouted in anger and pain: "Boys, find these monsters, if it takes you through the Indian Nation, and finish them!"

Long before the posses rode that far they stopped about a mile from the Bender Inn, at the grocery of Rudolph Brockmann, the first man to help the Benders in Kansas. By then the searchers had discovered that Brockmann had not only helped the Benders settle in the area, but that he and old man Bender had actually been partners in the grocery from 1869 to 1871. He alone would know where these butchering maniacs were, the mob concluded. Brockmann was dragged from his home and mercilessly questioned. He insisted time and again that he knew nothing of the whereabouts of the Benders. Taking Brockmann into the woods about eight miles from his home, the mob pummeled and pushed him about, attempting to get him to provide information about the fleeing fiends, information they believed he possessed. Brockmann shook his head and said he had no idea where the Bender family had gone. Someone brought a rope and placed it about Brockmann's neck. He denied having any knowledge about the wanted killers. He was yanked upward and hanged high until his feet stopped kicking and he was about to die. Then he was lowered and revived; he was given cold coffee to drink so that he could regain his speech. Again the possemen grilled him, but they received the same answer. Brockmann knew nothing. Again

Brockmann was yanked skyward, then brought down when close to death. The half-conscious grocer pleaded with the possemen: "I beg your mercy, please, I knew nothing of these people for months now. I have not seen them." Again he was hanged, brought down, and choked out his ignorance. Once more the rope stretched his neck. He was lowered. He made his denials. A fourth time the grocer was pulled upward by the rope, lowered at the last minute, and he still gasped he knew nothing. This time, with the passion of the mob cooled, he was believed. Some of the searchers insisted that Brockmann did know, but feared the Benders more than the rope, that if he did tell what he knew he felt the Benders would seek him out and torture him before killing him. But most of the possemen were weary of their gruesome chore, and they decided to give Brockmann his life. They rode off, searching down by the bottoms of Drum Creek.

It was here that the body of the man named Jones had been found, his head almost severed from his torso. More than that grisly grave offered evidence of the Benders. Nearby in the snow on the ground, still frozen in spots, were strange marks made by a wagon wheel, one that was obviously out of plumb so that, as it revolved, it made a zig-zag track through the snow. The possemen reasoned that Jones had been killed when the ground in the orchard had been so deeply frozen that a grave could not be dug. The Benders had put the body in their wagon and driven to the Creek, cut a hole in the ice and shoved the body into it. Using the peculiar wagon marks to follow, the possemen followed these tracks southwest toward the Indian Territory. Some hazy reports have it that the Vigilance Committee members did find their quarry and wreaked a horrible vengeance on them, that old man Bender and his son John put up a fight and were riddled with bullets, that Mrs. Bender grabbed an ax and attacked several possemen and she too had to be shot repeatedly like a hard-to-kill viper before dropping dead of wounds and belching curses at her attackers. Kate Bender was saved for the last. She was tied to a small tree and branches were placed around her, as was the custom of putting witches to the torch in earlier centuries. The kindling was torched and the woman was burned alive as she shouted profanities at the possemen in a loud, long shriek that supposedly lingered in their ears for the remainder of their lives.

This tale of vengeance seemed to find support in letters received in 1910 by criminal historian Captain Thomas S. Duke. He had written the chiefs of police in Cherryvale and Independence. J.N. Kramer, Cherryvale's chief of police, informed Duke that "It so happened that my father-in-law's farm joins the Bender farm and that he helped to locate the bodies of the victims. I have often tried to find out from him what became of the Benders, but he only gave me a knowing look and said he guessed they would not bother anyone else. There was a Vigilance Committee formed to locate the Benders, and shortly afterward old man Bender's wagon was found by the roadside riddled with bullets. You will have to guess the rest." D.M. Van Cleve, police chief of Independence, wrote: "In regard to the Bender family I will say that I have lived here forty years, and it is my opinion that they never got away. A Vigilance Committee was formed and some of them are still here, but they will not talk except to say that it would be useless to look for them, and they smile at reports of some of the family having been recently located. The family nearly got my father. He intended to stay there one night, but he became suspicious, and, although they tried to coax him to stay, he hitched up his team and left."

Even in 1910 there were those still alive who had hunted the Benders and who may have been part of the posse that reportedly caught up with the fiends. If they had participated in the summary executions of the four killers, they would have been indictable for murder, even forty years later, there being no statute of limitations on homicide. Under such legal circumstances, no one then or later could be expected to admit having taken a life, even the most despicable lives of the hated Benders. Yet, with the absence of bodies in graves where the world could point with some relief and knowledge that the bloody Benders had finally been tracked down, there remained the many legends that blossomed in the wake of the Bender flight. The story that the family escaped completely remains persistent to this day. One tale has it that the family raced their wagon to Chanute, which was then called New Chicago, and there tied their exhausted horses to a rail and left them, buying train tickets to some unspecified destination in Texas but that the family got off the train at Chetopa to further confuse pursuers and made their way on foot through the Indian Nation to Texas. A wagon matching the Bender vehicle was found in Chanute some days after the bodies were found at the Bender inn. The wagon, some speculated, might have been a ruse, planted by Bender associates to mislead the possemen.

There was a story that the Bender clan had been members of a very large criminal organization that stretched its evil talons through the states of Kansas and Missouri, even into the Indian Nation. This organization specialized in murdering travelers and stealing horses. The Benders were one of many murderous families who settled in lonely places for a few years, killed until discovered and then moved off to resume their dark work elsewhere. One book, *The Five Fiends*, published a year after the Benders fled into oblivion, claimed that Kate Bender was not one but three women, all using the same name, all appearing throughout the southwest in spiritualist lectures and all married to the same man, a satyr and murder maniac who was none other than the cunning John Bender, Jr. Bender the younger, it will be remembered, had taken long and unexplained business trips in Fall 1872, and it was theorized that Bender was really acting as a booking agent for all these women known as Kate, setting their lectures and selecting victims to visit his "sisters" at several murder inns he was then operating. This wild speculation was never proved in fact in that only one Bender murder inn was ever discovered and that was enough for anyone. The author of *The Five Fiends* obviously indulged in colorful fiction, taking pains to protect his identity against criticism by authoring this work anonymously. Such impossible fictional treatments of the Benders have continued through the decades, the most recent being *The Bloody Benders*, which adroitly mixes fact and fiction but comes to a less spectacular conclusion than what is found in *The Five Fiends*, a title which of itself is misleading in that only *four* Benders were ever known to have existed.

Another, final speculation was rendered by John Towers James in *The Benders of Kansas*, one that through a process of elimination, outlined the logical route the Benders used to make their permanent escape. James had them fleeing by train from Thayer, to Humboldt, Kan., switching to another train line which ran to Venita in the Indian Territory and getting onto another railroad line there to take a train to Denison, Texas, where they may have finally vanished forever. There was much to believe in this, the best of the theories regarding the Bender escape route, in that this was the only route that was not covered by the many posses hunting the killers. Four main posses fanned out from Cherryvale after the discovery of the bodies. One posse headed for Thayer, another toward Independence, still another toward Oswego, and a fourth, a party of seven men led by an ex-captain of the Union Army, rode straight into the Indian Territory. The first three parties returned within a week, admitting that the trails they followed led nowhere. The eight men that had crossed into the Indian Territory did not return for quite some time, about two weeks, and when they did return they refused to discuss the Benders. None of them even mentioned the name of the killers, and it was assumed that this was the posse that had caught up with the killers and destroyed them. The silence of these men had been assured, it was claimed, when they discovered more than $7,000 on the Benders when they were caught (some later claimed the amount was as high as $10,000), all blood money taken from their victims. After killing the Benders, it was speculated, the posse members divided the money equally as a sort of bounty payment for their labors, and the possession of this loot further insured their silence once they had returned to Cherryvale.

Still, no amount of dire reports that had the Benders dead could cease the belief that the fiends were alive and well, a belief that became traditionally strong. One of the believers was a self-styled soothsayer and practioner of spiritualistic rites, much like Kate Bender. She was Mrs. Frances McCann, of McPherson, Kan., a small, spare woman with indefatigable energy and a suspicious eye for much wanted felons living under aliases. McCann had dreams each night that revealed marvelous and frightening truths to her about her neighbors, her relatives, and even her employees. One night in 1888 her clairvoyance focused upon Sarah Eliza Davis, the woman who did McCann's washing. McCann's spirits clearly informed her that Sarah Davis was none other than the legendary murderess, Kate Bender, operating under a disguise. For months the dogged spiritualist investigated Sarah Davis and her elderly mother. She traveled through several states looking into the background of the family and haunted their every footstep, watching the Davis family from the distance of their outhouse, where she made nightly notes of their suspicious activities. Then, equipped with what she thought was enough evidence to convict the Davis', McCann went to authorities. She insisted that the Davis women be arrested and tried as the missing murderesses, Mrs. Bender and her daughter Kate.

Although local authorities were inclined to dismiss these accusations, McCann raised such a fuss and Sarah Davis acted in such a manner as to bring suspicion against her that the women were finally arraigned in November 1889 for the murder of Dr. York, sixteen long years after the Benders had vanished. This took place in the Oswego courthouse. Certain officials were convinced that finally the Bender monsters, or, at least two of them, were now in custody, but many of the chief state's witnesses were not so sure, particularly the almost hanged Rudolph Brockmann. He took one look at the Davis women and said no, these were not Mrs. Bender and Kate.

Working in favor of the accused was the fact that they were defended by John Towers James, later to write one of the best books on the Benders and a Judge Webb who had actually dined at the Bender inn in 1873 and managed to survive being killed; he certainly remembered Mrs. Bender and daughter Kate. But Mrs. McCann, who sat at the prosecutor's table and urged the state's attorney to be more aggressive in his questioning of witnesses, relentlessly badgered the court to bring these two monsters to justice. A trial date was set for the two women, but attorney James finally unearthed documentation from the state of Michigan proving that Sarah Davis was exactly who she said she was and her mother was Mrs. Almira Griffith, who had led a dissolute life, had been convicted of manslaughter years earlier, and had served time in prison. This was the reason why the accused women had kept their silence and refused to defend themselves, fearing that the dark past would catch up with them. The trial against Griffith and Davis was abandoned and McCann went back to her crystal ball considerably annoyed. She had, at least, smelled out a felony, even though it had nothing to do with the Benders, and secured for herself, somewhere slightly above crank status, a place in the Bender mythology.

That myth exists to this day. Were the Benders run down and killed? Did they survive to live out their lives in the West under assumed names, the memories of their days filled with the nightmares of their past? No one knows for sure and never will know, unless evidence in the future pinpoints the true facts. Over the early years of this century, several men died, claiming they had been part of the original posse that had tracked down the Benders. They admitted in deathbed confessions that they had killed the Bender family, horribly mutilating their bodies which were then thrown down a well. These deathbed confessions made by a man named Downer in Chicago and a man named Harker in New Mexico in 1909 and 1910 went unsubstantiated, as did a report of an old man arrested for murdering a man in Idaho in 1884. This suspect was thought to be John Bender, Sr. Officers believed that since his victim had been murdered in the modus operandi of the Benders, his skull crushed from behind, and the fact that the old man answered the loose descriptions of John

Bender, Sr., that he was one and the same. He was reportedly shackled by the ankle in his cell and, after somehow obtaining a large knife, the old man tried to cut off his foot in an effort to escape and subsequently bled to death. His remains were later examined by some Kansas residents who had known the old man, but they could not positively make an identification.

The inglorious chronicle of this mass murdering family is preserved on a Kansas State marker outside of present day Cherryvale. It reads: "On the high prairie, a mile northwest, beyond the nearby Mounds which bear their name—the Bender family, John, his wife, son, and daughter Kate—in 1871 built a small house. Partitioned into two rooms by a canvas cloth, it had a table, stove and grocery shelves in front. In back were beds, a sledge hammer, and a trap door above a pit-like cellar. Kate, a self-proclaimed healer and spiritualist, and reported to be a beautiful, voluptuous girl with tigerish grace, was the leading spirit of her murderous family. The house was located on the main road. Travelers stopping for a meal were seated on a bench, backed tight against the canvas. In the next two years several disappeared. When suspicions were finally aroused, in 1873, the Benders fled. A search of their property disclosed eleven bodies buried in the garden, skulls crushed by hammer blows through the canvas. The end of the Benders is not known. The earth seemed to swallow them, as it had their victims."

REF.: Adams, *The Old-Time Cow Hand;* Adleman, *The Bloody Benders;* Baughman, *Kansas in Maps;* Bird, *A Lady's Life in the Rocky Mountains;* Bolitho, *Leviathan;* Booker, *Wildcats in Petticoats;* Boucher, *The Pocket Book of True Crime Stories;* Brown, *The Gentle Tamers;* Butterfield, *The American Past;* Case, *History of Labette County; CBA;* Churchill, *A Pictorial History of American Crime;* Cook, *The Border and the Buffalo;* Curry, *Parson, Labette County, Kansas;* Drago, *Wild, Woolly & Wicked;* Duke, *Celebrated Criminal Cases of America;* Eaton, *Pistol Pete, Veteran of the Old West;* Every, *Sins of America;* Ferris, *The National Survey of Historic Sites and Buildings; The Five Fiends;* Hardy, *Kate Bender, The Kansas Murderess;* Harlow, *Murders Not Quite Solved;* Horan, *Pictorial History of the Wild West;* Humphrey, *Following the Prairie Frontier;* Isely, *Four Centuries in Kansas;* Jackson, *The Portable Murder Book;* James, *The Benders of Kansas;* Klose, *A Concise Study Guide to the American Frontier;* Laut, *Pilgrims of the Santa Fe;* Logue, *Tumbleweeds and Barbed Wire Fences;* Marcy, *Thirty Years of Army Life on the Border;* Masterson, *The Katy Railroad and the Last Frontier;* Monaghan, *The Book of the American West;* Nash, *Bloodletters and Badmen; ____, Look for the Woman;* Orman, *A Room for the Night;* Pearson, *Murder at Smutty Nose;* Rich, *The Heritage of Kansas;* Richmond, *A Nation Moving West;* Rorick, *The Notorious Benders;* Ross, *The Bloody Benders;* Schmitt, *The Settler's West;* Shackleton, *Handbook of Frontier Days of Southeast Kansas;* Shirley, *Toughest of Them All;* Strong, *My Frontier Days & Indian Fights on the Plains of Texas;* Sutton, *A Life Worth Living;* Triplett, *History, Romance and Philosophy of Great American Crimes and Criminals;* Warden, *Thrilling Tales of Kansas;* Wilson, *Encyclopedia of Murder;* York, *The Bender Tragedy.*

Benedict VI, d.974, Italy, pope, assass. Imprisoned and eventually strangled on orders from Crescentius I, leader of the Roman nobility, following the death of Emperor Otto I in 973. He was replaced by Boniface VII, an antipope. REF.: *CBA.*

Benedict, Kirby, 1832-74, U.S., jur. Kirby Benedict was only twenty-two when he was made a judge in Taos, N.M. Shortly after he donned his black robes, he presided at the trial of José Maria Martinez, a convicted murderer. Benedict's sentencing of Martinez on Mar. 22, 1854, remains a classic in western lore: "José Maria Martinez, it is now springtime. In a little while the grass will be springing up green in these beautiful valleys, and on these broad mesas flowers will be blooming. Birds will be singing their sweet carols, and nature will put on her best, most gorgeous and most attractive robes, and life will be pleasant...But none of this for you, José Maria Martinez. When these things come to gladden the senses of men, you will be occupying a space about six by two feet beneath the sod, and the green grass and those beautiful flowers will be growing above your lowly head...And the court was about to add, 'May God have mercy on your soul,' but the court will not assume such responsibility of asking an all-

wise Providence to do which a jury of your peers refused to do. However, if you affect any religious belief...it might be well for you to send for your priest, or your minister, and get from him such consolation as you can. But the court advises you to place no reliance upon anything of the kind. Mr. Sheriff, remove the prisoner." Martinez later escaped but was hunted down by a posse and shot to death on the Pecos River in a pitched battle.

Benedict was a controversial jurist and, when later practicing the law, he ran afoul of powerful persons in New Mexico. He was disbarred in 1872, but a special bill was passed by the legislature allowing him to resume his practice, until the bill was recalled by the opposition and tabled. Benedict settled briefly in Santa Fe, N.M., where he was in a state of constant depression, dying of a heart attack in 1874.

REF.: Bartholomew, *The Biographical Album of Western Gunfighters;* CBA.

Benhadad I (AKA: **Hadadezer**), prom. 854 B.C., Damascus, (unsolv.) mur. Formed a coalition with King Ahab of Israel. He defeated Shalmanesser III of Assyria at Karkar in 854 and was murdered. REF.: *CBA.*

Benintende, Joseph (AKA: **Joe Granza**), and **West, Jack** (AKA: **Zip**), prom. 1950, U.S., bribe.-consp.-org. crime. Joseph Benintende was a Kansas City mobster who had served time for bank robbery prior to his 1953 conviction for bribery and conspiracy. Benintende maintained lavish apartments in New York, Chicago, and Kansas City.

In 1948 the fast-living gangster met Jack "Zip" West, a small-time bookmaker with big ideas. West knew about a basketball point-shaving scheme hatched by two brothers named Nick and Tony Englisis. During the 1949 NCAA Tournament, Nick Englisis had approached three star players of the Bradley University team. If they could hold their final point total below the Las Vegas "line," everyone stood to make a profit, Englisis told the skeptical players, and several members of the Kentucky team were already in on the deal. The players finally agreed, promising for $500 each to rig a tournament game with Bowling Green State University. However, an unheralded Bradley substitute upset the odds by sinking a last minute shot that effectively wiped out the Englisis mob. There was no payoff, just $25 to the corrupted Bradley players as a sign of good faith for the next season.

When the 1950 NCAA Tournament rolled around, Jack West was ready to offer the Englisis brothers a deal. He offered to pay them $1,000 a game for information about the fix engineered by a bookmaker named Klukofsky. West assumed control of the situation on behalf of his boss, Benintende. The point-shaving scheme worked so well that plans were made to fix regular season games on the 1950-51 schedule. The Bradley team received about $4,000 in payoffs for their role in the fix. The story was much the same at Kentucky, where assistant coach Adolph Rupp acted as the point man between the gamblers and the players. By the time the betting scandal became public in April 1951, a third school, Toledo University, was involved. On July 24, assistant district attorneys began interviewing players.

Zip West, Joe Benintende, and Jack Rubenstein (Jack Ruby) entered a guilty plea to charges of conspiracy, bribery, and attempted bribery in a series of sweeping indictments handed down in April 1953. Benintende was sentenced to four to seven years in prison. West received two to three, and Rubenstein, who introduced the "money men" in the deal and who would later shoot Lee Harvey Oswald in Dallas, was sentenced to two to five years. Tony Englisis received a light six-month sentence. His brother Nick was ordered to begin serving an indeterminate sentence. Indictments against the players were dismissed in April 1953, but the integrity of the college game was tarnished. See: **Black Sox Scandal; Kennedy, John F.**

REF.: *CBA;* Danforth, *The D.A.'s Man.*

Benitez, Martin Rivera (AKA: **Big Soul**), prom. 1970s, Mex., mur. A killer for hire, Benitez was a native of Hildago who would murder anyone if the price was right. Between 1969 and 1972, it is estimated by Mexican police that he killed at least fifty persons.

Twelve headless bodies were found in his "morgue," in a woods near his Jazatipan house. Benitez, serving life, explained later that he was so much in demand that lines formed around his house and that to prove that the victims were indeed killed by him, he would cut off the heads and show these to his employers. "I saw nothing wrong in killing for money," the mass murderer said without a bit of remorse. "If I had not done it, someone else would." REF.: *CBA*.

Benito, Don, prom. 1724, Spain, pir. Captain Don Benito of the *Francis de la Vega* plundered merchant shipping off the Virginia Coast. Benito called himself a Spanish knight, but actually received his sailing orders from the governor of Cuba, who had leased the ship to him. His crew was composed of men from Ireland, Spain, France, and England. It was common practice, following the Treaty of Utrecht in 1713, for the Spanish colonial outposts to charter pirate vessels to prey on English shipping in the colonies.
REF.: *CBA; Rankin, The Golden Age of Piracy.*

Benjamin, Judah Philip, 1811-84, U.S., lawyer. U.S. Senator from 1853-61. He served as Confederate attorney general under Jefferson Davis in 1861, secretary of war from 1861-62, and secretary of state from 1862-65. He departed for England in 1865, after an unsuccessful attempt to arm slaves for the Confederate army during the Civil War. He established a private law practice and was appointed Queen's Counsel in 1872. REF.: *CBA*.

Benjamin, Victor H., 1951-80, U.S., drugs. The drugs Victor Benjamin smuggled from Bolivia into Miami, Fla., proved to be lethal when he swallowed them to get through customs.

A 29-year-old California state government employee, Benjamin said he was going to Greece to visit his mother, but went instead to La Paz, Bol., and from there to Miami. As he passed through customs at the Miami International Airport on Jan. 4, 1980, 110 balloons containing cocaine burst inside his body. Benjamin died in a Miami hospital after collapsing at the airport. The assistant Dade County medical examiner, Dr. Donna Brown, said X-rays showed "little packets" in his intestines—cocaine weighing 250 grams and worth up to $100,000 on the street, depending on its purity—inside rubber balloons. Chief Deputy Medical Examiner Dr. Ronald Wright explained, "The bags, or balloons, always do break. Rubber is semipermeable to water. The pressure builds up and they burst." REF.: *CBA*.

Bennett, Benjamin, prom. 1820, U.S., mur. A resident of Saratoga Springs, N.Y., Bennett became incensed when Seth Haskins, an old man, refused to make him a loan for a small amount, and grabbed a tree limb and crushed Haskins' head with it. It was later reported that the old man was hard of hearing and had not really refused the loan, but mumbled that he could not hear what Bennett was saying to him. Bennett, full of remorse, was convicted and sentenced to hang. He embraced religion before the end, and was accompanied to the gallows in June 1820 by so many clergymen that the executioner had to ask several church leaders to step down into the large crowd assembled to see their parishioner hang.
REF.: *An Authentic Report of the Trial of Benjamin Bennett; CBA; The Trial of Benjamin Bennett for the Murder of Seth Haskins.*

Bennett, Edward P., prom. 1880s-90s, U.S., count. Machinist-farmer Edward Bennett, a native of Ensign, Mich., discovered a discrepancy in the federal law which permitted the coining of silver dollars as long as there was sixteen ounces of silver equaling one ounce of gold in the coinage, but that federal coins were actually equaling thirty-two ounces of silver to one of gold. He conformed to the law and earned the difference by issuing his own silver dollars which Bennett minted in the tens of thousands after buying large quantities of silver in bulk rate, making excellent dies and using his own powerful press inside his log cabin. Residents of Michigan knew what coins were Bennett's, but passed them without protest, figuring they were just as good as any issued by the government. Bennett operated until his arrest in 1897 when he received a prison term.
REF.: *Bloom, Money of Their Own; CBA*.

Bennett, Granville Gaylord, 1833-1910, U.S., jur. Territorial governor of Dakota in 1874, assigned the task of revising the codes of law, a project completed in 1875. He was appointed to the Court of the Dakota Territory by President Ulysses S. Grant in 1875. He published a *Report of Cases Argued and Determined in the Supreme Court of the Territory of Dakota* (1889). REF.: *CBA*.

Bennett, Harold Joseph, 1900-   , Brit., theft. On Aug. 24, 1933, 33-year-old Harold Bennett hid in the Geological Museum on Jermyn Street in London until the last of the visitors and staff had departed. Then he filled his pouch with twenty-six sapphires, one beryl, some diamond crystals, and other precious stones valued at £374.

The two night watchmen who patrolled the building discovered the theft at 2:30 a.m. on Aug. 25, a half hour after Bennett had escaped with his loot. On Oct. 17, Bennett tried to sell a large cut zircon to Calipe Casimir on Poland Street, London, to raise enough money for fare to go back to South Africa. Casimir gave him £2 for the stone and the two men agreed to do business again, this time with a quantity of yellow sapphires. Detectives by then had a description of a man seen in the museum three straight days before the robbery, which matched that given by the Poland Street jeweler. Bennett listed a false name on the receipt, but gave his correct address. The police searched his room and found five cut sapphires in a small embroidered bag. Bennett was arrested, taken to the Vine Street police station, and charged with theft and "breaking out" of the museum.

On Nov. 21, he was found Guilty of receiving stolen property, but was acquitted of "breaking out." The criminal court recorder, Sir Ernest Wild, sentenced Bennett to seventeen months at hard labor. REF.: *CBA*.

Bennett, Herbert John, 1880-1901, Brit., mur. By the time he was fifteen, Herbert Bennett was a sneak thief committing petty burglaries. Two years later, when Bennett was a grocer's assistant in Northfleet, Kent, he met music teacher Mary Jane Clark, a woman two years his senior. He ostensibly went to her to learn how to play the violin, and seduced her. They were married at West Ham on July 22, 1897. The two embarked on a series of swindles, with Mrs. Bennett willingly participating. The Bennetts bought up as many old violins as they could find, cleaned them up, and then Bennett sent his wife door to door with a hard luck story about how her husband, a brilliant violinist, had just perished and she was forced to sell his "rare" instrument. Through this scam, the Bennett's built up a nest egg of more than £400. They used this money to purchase a grocery store at Westgate-on-Sea which, after being heavily insured, burned down with all its contents consumed. (The Bennetts had sold off the stock beforehand.) With the insurance money, the Bennetts bought another store at Plumstead, where they lived with their infant girl.

The Bennetts, according to their landlady in Plumstead, argued violently, and one day she heard Mrs. Bennett state: "Herbert, I will follow you for the sake of the baby, and if you are not careful, I can get you fifteen years!"

"I wish you were dead," Bennett roared back, "and if *you* are not careful you soon will be." The Bennetts reportedly sold off their stock in the new store and then settled elsewhere, leaving their creditors in the lurch. In 1900, Bennett moved about quite a bit. There is a report that he traveled to South Africa and became a highly paid spy for the Boers until he came under suspicion and was sent back to England. He did work at the Woolwich Arsenal where he was paid only thirty shillings a week, but Bennett always seemed to have plenty of cash which later gave vent to the rumor that he was a paid spy in the service of a foreign power, taking secret inventory of the arsenal.

Tiring of his wife, Bennett spent a good deal of time in the London clubs, and there he met an attractive parlor maid named Alice Meadows. He told her he was single and then gave her an expensive engagement ring on Aug. 28, 1900. They talked of marrying the following June, and Meadows suggested that a perfect spot for a honeymoon would be Yarmouth. In fact, the couple visited Yarmouth and Ireland on brief vacations. All the while Mary Bennett was living at Bexley Heath, separated from Bennett while he found suitable employment, or that is what he told her to excuse his long absences. On Sept. 14, Bennett visited her and suggested they take a short holiday in Yarmouth. The next day, she registered as a widow named Mrs. Hood in a Yarmouth boarding house run by Mrs. Rudrum, telling her that she had been escorted to Yarmouth by her brother-in-law who was from York and was insanely jealous of her. Mrs. Bennett was still assuming disguises, no doubt to keep creditors or authorities looking for her and her husband off the track, given their years of fraud together. Such impersonations appealed to her in that she thought she was living a romantic life with a dashing young man of enterprise and daring.

While Mrs. Bennett was waiting for her husband to arrive at Yarmouth, he was busy telling Alice Meadows that he could not spend the upcoming weekened with her; he had to go to Gravesend to visit his grandfather who was on his deathbed. Then, on Sept. 22, 1900, Bennett appeared in Yarmouth. At about 11 p.m. that night a spooning couple on the South Beach at Yarmouth saw a couple on a slope above, some thirty feet distant. They appeared to be arguing. Some minutes later they heard the woman cry out softly: "Mercy, mercy." The couple walked up the slope and passed the man who was kneeling or crouching over the woman, and they appeared to be "skylarking." The man looked up at them, but it was too dark for the couple to make out his features. At 11:45 p.m., a man later identified as Herbert Bennett arrived out of wind at the Crown and Anchor Hotel in Yarmouth. He hurriedly explained that he had missed his train to Gorleston and asked for a room. He was up early the next morning and departed as quickly as he had come.

About that time, a boy who worked for a bathing house on South Beach was strolling across the sandy slopes when he found the body of a young woman. Her skirts had been pulled up and her blouse pulled aside to reveal her privates. A mohair bootlace was knotted so tightly about her neck that it was embedded in her flesh. Officials and a later autopsy revealed that the victim had been raped and murdered. She was identified as Mrs. Hood, staying at Mrs. Rudrum's lodgings, but Mrs. Hood was an obvious alias. Police had few clues with which to establish the victim's identity until discovering a laundry mark, the number 599, in her clothes. This was sent out to various laundries, and six weeks later a Bexley Heath laundry reported that the laundry marks belonged to clothes owned by Mrs. Mary Bennett.

It took police little time to hunt down her husband. Bennett was arrested on a Woolwich street on Nov. 6, 1900. In his apartment police found a woman's gold chain, a woman's wig, a man's wig, and a fake mustache. Bennett was charged with murder and tried at the Old Bailey in March 1901 before Lord Alverstone, who had recently become Chief Justice of England, prosecuted by Sir Charles Gill and defended by the celebrated Edward Marshall Hall. The defense position was that Bennett was not in Yarmouth at all during the time of his wife's murder, but in Eltham where he befriended Douglas Sholto Douglas, a manufacturer of specialty items. The two had been together long after the last train for Yarmouth left Eltham. Gill's cross-examination of this witness proved him to be either mistaken or unsure of Bennett's identity. Moreover, the manager of the South Quay Distillery Pub in Yarmouth testified that Bennett was the man who accompanied the victim to his pub on the night of the murder and that he and the victim drank in his pub until closing and then went off in the direction of the beach.

The most damning piece of evidence against Bennett was the gold chain found in his lodgings. Mrs. Rudrum, the Yarmouth landlady, identified the gold chain as having been worn by the victim on the day of her murder. A beach photographer then came forward to identify a photo found in Mrs. Bennett's Yarmouth room, one that he had taken of her in the afternoon before her death. In the photo Mrs. Bennett was wearing the gold necklace, one that seemed to slip around the defense case of

Herbert John Bennett, as tightly fixed as a hangman's noose. Defense counsel Hall argued strenuously that the gold necklace in the photo and the one found in his client's rooms were not the same, stating that the one in the photo was a "rope chain of the Prince of Wales pattern," while the one found in the Bennett apartment was one of a "link variety," but this contention further confused Hall's argument since the photo did not show the gold chain clear enough to determine exactly what type of chain it was.

The evidence was seemingly overwhelming against the accused. It was also stated by a witness that Bennett had appeared in Yarmouth with hair and mustache the color and make of the wig and false mustache found in his rooms. The prosecution carefully built its case, describing how the scheming Bennett had disguised himself, gone to Yarmouth, and murdered a wife he had tired of, making it appear that she had been attacked by a sex maniac. Hall countered that his client had, indeed, lived "a worthless life" but that he was too clever to have murdered his wife in such an obvious manner, leaving clues and a trail back to himself. Hall did not put his client on the stand which, in the eyes of the jury, made it appear that the accused was being shielded against his own possible admissions. It was believed that Hall feared that the cadgy Gill would destroy

The tell-tale locket and chain.

his client under cross-examination, espeically that Bennett would be unable to explain his presence in Eltham that night.

The jury retired and returned a verdict of Guilty inside of thirty-five minutes. Lord Alverstone appeared nervous when delivering the death sentence to Bennett, much more so than the accused, whose demeanor in the dock throughout the trial was one of calm composure. Bennett never once showed any signs of distress, and still proclaimed his innocence when he went to the hangman at Norwich Prison on Mar. 21, 1901. According to tradition, a black flag was hoisted when Bennett went to his death but the flagstaff reportedly broke and many in the crowd before the prison that day felt that this was a sign that Bennett was innocent. The same claim was maintained by attorney Hall throughout his life, the Bennett case being the one that brought him to national prominence. He believed that a sex maniac had murdered his client's wife, and a later incident seemed to point to that conclusion. On July 14, 1912, another woman, Dora May Gray, was found murdered in the same spot in South Beach, Yarmouth, where Mrs. Bennett had been slain, and around her neck was a bootlace, the instrument used to strangle her to death. It was also said at that time that the victim had been slain by a copycat killer employing Bennett's own modus operandi. See: **Alverstone, Viscount; Hall, Edward Marshall.**

REF.: Bowker, *Behind the Bar;* Bresler, *Scales of Justice;* Brock, *A Casebook of Crime;* Butler, *Murderers' England; CBA;* Capon, *The Great Yarmouth Mystery;* Deardon, *Some Cases of Sir Bernard Spilsbury & Others;* Dilnot, *Celebrated Crimes;* Felstead, *Sir Richard Muir;* Gough, *From Kew Observatory to Scotland Yard;* Gribble, *Adventures in Murder;* Jacobs, *Aspects of Murder;* Kingston, *Dramatic Days at the Old Bailey;* Logan, *Great Murder Mysteries;* Marjoribanks, *For the Defense, The Life of Sir Edward Marshall Hall;* Morland, *Hangman's Clutch;* Neustatter, *The Mind of the Murderer;* Shew, *A Companion to Murder;* Shore, *Crime and Its Detection;* Stevens, *From Clue to Dock;* Symons, *A Reasonable Doubt;* Wilson, *An Encyclopedia of Murder.*

Bennett, James Van Benschoten, 1894-1978, U.S., penol. Born in New York, James Bennett was graduated from Brown University in 1918. After serving in the Air Force during WWI, he accepted a Civil Service appointment as assistant investigator for the U.S. Bureau of Efficiency. In 1926, he began his long and distinguished career in penology. As assistant director of the field survey division for a congressional committee looking into employment practices in the nation's penal system, James Bennett prepared a report titled *The Federal Penal and Correctional Problem*, 1929. It became the standard work in the field, outlining the problems facing U.S. penologists with followup recommendations.

From 1937 until 1964, Bennett served as the director of the U.S. Justice Department's Federal Bureau of Prisons, overseeing twenty-six correctional institutions. He believed that criminal rehabilitation could be best achieved through job training for inmates, prisons without bars, and halfway houses. During his term of office he worked hard to enact these reforms, succeeding in substantially reducing recidivism among paroled inmates.

A member of the board of directors of the American Prison Association, the American Bar Association, and the Osborne Association (for prison reform), Bennett also served as secretary of the National Parole Conference. He died on Nov. 19, 1978, at Bethesda, Md. REF: *CBA*.

Bennett, Louis William, prom. 1957-60, U.S., (wrong. convict.) mur. Because of an alcoholic blackout, an Oklahoma man could not be sure he was not guilty of murdering a friend. Rather than risk pleading innocent and facing the death sentence, he pleaded guilty and got life in prison.

Police told Louis William Bennett, an alcoholic, that his fingerprints were found on a doorstop, and that he was believed to be the murderer in the beating death of 70-year-old Fred Ernest in Bartlesville, Okla. Bennett had been on a binge for several days. Unable to recall his actions, he assumed that he had committed the crime and pleaded guilty to manslaughter. Sentenced in July, 1957, by Judge Jesse Worten to a thirty-five year jail term, Bennett later would remember that he had painted the doorstop for Ernest. After Bennett had served three and a half years in jail, Leonard McClain, a Texan sentenced to life at the Huntsville Prison for murder, admitted he had beaten Ernest to death with a hammer ten days before slaying his Dallas landlady. FBI agents then talked with Bennett and used a lie detector to help prove his innocence. The wrongly convicted man was released in December 1960 and given an unconditional pardon by the governor. Bennett left jail to go home to see his mother for Christmas; authorities gave him a bus ticket to Lawton, Okla., a new khaki suit, and a $5 bill. The reprieved man declared, "I am bitter at no one at all."

REF.: *CBA*; Radin, *The Innocents*.

Bennett, Myrtle (Myrtle Adkin, AKA: The Bridge Table Murder), prom. 1929, Case of, U.S., mur. Myrtle Bennett, originally a native of Arkansas, saw her future husband's picture on the desk of a friend and vowed she would some day marry the handsome perfume salesman. When she later spotted John G. Bennett on a train in an officer's uniform during WWI, she accosted him and they were married on Nov. 11, 1919, Armistice Day. The couple moved to Kansas City, Mo., and lived the high life during the Roaring Twenties. On the night of Sept. 29, 1929, the Bennetts were entertaining Charles and Mayme Hofman. After an icebox dinner, the foursome decided not to go to the movies but to play some contract bridge. The first two hours saw the Bennetts win but the Hofmans began to triumph, and, at midnight, Bennett began to deal the last bridge hand of his life. He opened the bidding with one spade. Hofman bid two diamonds and Myrtle Bennett bid four spades. Hofman doubled and the play began. Mrs. Bennett put down her hand and went into the kitchen, she later claimed, to prepare some breakfast for her husband who was off to St. Joseph, Mo., at dawn to sell his perfumes.

When she returned to the bridge table her irate husband, with a losing hand, accused her of overbidding. "You're a bum bridge player," countered Mrs. Bennett. Her husband then slapped her face once, perhaps three or four times, the number of slaps was never accurately determined in court. She reportedly went to the couch and cried while Bennett, so incensed at losing at bridge, stormed about the house, declaring he was leaving for St. Joseph immediately. The Hofmans said nothing but busied themselves by chuckling and toting up their winning scores and the money due them. "No one but a cur would strike a woman in the presence of friends," Myrtle Bennett said to her red-faced spouse. Charles Hofman also reproached his host for striking Mrs. Bennett, which caused Bennett to ask his guests to leave his home immediately. As the Hofmans prepared to make a hasty departure, Mrs. Bennett went out of the room, then returned to the den with a gun in her hand.

"My God, Myrtle," exclaimed Bennett to his wife, "what are you going to do?"

Two bullets whizzed out of the gun, then a brief pause, then two more shots followed. The last two shots struck Bennett. Mrs. Bennett, who was not arrested until authorities could sort out the confused report on the shooting, visited the mortuary the next day where she viewed the in-state remains of her husband, complaining that the mortician had neglected to put a handkerchief in the breast pocket of her husband's suitcoat. As relatives filed past she repeated the same line to all who listened: "Nobody knows but me and my God why I did it." Mrs. Bennett was later arrested but, because of legal maneuvers, not tried until 1931. She was tried before Judge Ralph S. Latshaw and defended by former Senator Jim Reed; Latshaw had presided at the sensational 1909 murder trial of Dr. Bennett Clarke Hyde, who was accused of killing his father-in-law, millionaire Thomas Swope, a founding father of Kansas City. Reed had prosecuted Hyde in a case that smacked of bribery and corruption. Mrs. Bennett was prosecuted by James R. Page.

The trial was a ridiculous farce. Mrs. Bennett took the stand to insist that she was returning to the den with the gun on the night of her husband's tragic demise to pack it in his suitcase so that he would have some protection on the road. She stumbled and the gun went off twice and her husband mistook her intention and raced forward to grab the gun, which went off twice more. Reed demonstrated how the deceased grabbed the weapon and accidentally shot *himself* in the armpit and the back, an achievement which only the the most gifted contortionist could accomplish. Reed's performance was a masterpiece of bathos. He shouted, ranted, and wept openly before the jury as he presented his client's defense, repeating that this would be his last criminal case, and that he would not want to retire with a taste of failure in his mouth. With each crying jag, Mrs. Bennett, as if on cue, joined in with wails of her own. When Page remonstrated with Reed over the sloppy display he was making, Reed sobbed, "I can't help it, I just can't help it...the poor woman!"

Prosecutor Page made a fatal mistake by having its star witness, a relative of the dead man, proscribed by the court. This witness was prevented from testifying by Judge Latshaw who stated that the prosecution had waited to present this person as a rebuttal witness when he should have been presented in direct testimony. The jury found Mrs. Myrtle Bennett Not Guilty but what further shocked readers of this nationwide story was the amazing fact that Mrs. Bennett, who had filed for the life insurance on her husband, was awarded $30,000 following her trial. An anonymous writer for the Kansas City *Star* later summed up the case with the following ditty:

> One spade he bid,
> Poor dud, he is dead,
> She sits in widow's weeds;
> He went down one,
> She got her gun—
> One spade is all he needs.

See: **Hyde, Dr. Bennett Clarke.**
REF.: *CBA*; Reddig, *Tom's Town*; Woollcott, *While Rome Burns*.

Bennett, Olive, 1909-1954, Brit., (unsolv.) mur. A midwife spent the last several weeks of her life meeting a variety of different men, dating often, and drawing large sums of money from her savings. One of her lovers murdered her as well.

In the early morning of Apr. 24, 1954, George Anderson, a groundskeeper at the Holy Trinity graveyard, Stratford-on-Avon, England, discovered a woman's shoe, eyeglasses, and a set of false teeth behind a gravestone. Beyond the churchyard wall he found a brown hat on the edge of the River Avon. A few hours later police lifted the body of Olive Bennett, a 45-year-old midwife, from the river. A resident at the Maternity Home at Tiddington, she was a small woman, and she had been strangled and dumped in the river. A ninety-pound tombstone found three days later was believed used to weigh down the corpse. When police questioned area residents, they learned that Bennett was seen drinking at the Red Horse Hotel, and just before midnight, a waiter observed a couple embracing in the churchyard. He described the man as tall, blonde, and about thirty-five years old. Following names from Bennett's address book and from letters found in her apartment, police questioned her friends and acquaintances, and learned that she had recently gone out with several men and had withdrawn substantial amounts from her savings account.

The River Avon was drained for further evidence, revealing an angora scarf and the contents of Bennett's purse. It was also discovered that a round-trip ticket to Stratford had been issued to a tall, blonde man the night of the murder, and that half of a return ticket to Worcester was not used. Bennett originally came from Worcester. Five married men intimate with the victim were called in by police, but no further evidence was uncovered. A verdict of murder by a person or persons unknown was recorded on July 1, 1954. Bennett's murder remained unsolved.

REF.: *CBA*; Furneaux, *Famous Criminal Cases*.

Bennett, Richard Bedford, 1870-1947, Can., lawyer. Attorney general in 1921, and prime minister from 1930-35. REF.: *CBA*.

Bennigsen, Leonty Leontyevich (Levin August Theophil Bennigsen), 1745-1826, Rus., consp. Russian general related to the British House of Hanover. He entered the military in 1773, fought against the Turks in Poland from 1793-94, and plotted the successful assassination of Emperor Paul I of Russia in 1801. REF.: *CBA*.

Bensinger, Peter B., 1936- , U.S., law enfor. off. Born in Chicago in 1936, Peter Bensinger graduated from Yale in 1958. He is a member of the International Association of Chiefs of Police, the National Council on Crime and Delinquency, the American Correctional Association, and the Illinois Academy of Criminology. As a leader in drug-enforcement administration, Bensinger has been involved in many aspects of law enforcement and crime studies, including task force groups, crime commissions, and the U.S. Department of Justice National Institute of Corrections. He served as director of the Illinois Department of Corrections from 1970-73, executive director of the Chicago Crime Commission from 1973-75, and Administrator of Drug Enforcement from 1976-83, when he retired to work in the private sector with drug testing. REF.: *CBA*.

Benson, Egbert, 1746-1833, U.S., jur. New York attorney general from 1777-89. He was appointed judge of the Second Circuit Court by President John Adams in 1801. REF.: *CBA*.

Benson, Harry, 1866-1917, Brit., fraud. Harry Benson spent a lifetime working confidence games, but not until the sunset of his life did he hit upon a scheme that enriched him beyond his wildest machinations. Released from Parkhurst Prison in March 1914 after having served five years for fraud, Benson had but thirty shillings in his pocket. He was nevertheless an enterprising swindler, and only six weeks later he convinced a naive motor engineer in London to turn his tiny company into a limited firm, wherein Benson began to dupe investors into funding huge engineering projects which never existed. Moreover, Benson began a phony bank, and then a bogus association, The Prisoners' Aid Society, which ostensibly worked for the benefit of wrongly convicted prison inmates. The association, of course, did no such

thing. Benson merely took as many donations as he could collect from liberal and conscientious citizens, pocketed the money, and lived the high life.

As a prison inmate in Parkhurst Prison, Benson had met and talked with the infamous killer Steinie Morrison, slayer of Leon Beron in 1911. There were a number of influential persons who believed Morrison was innocent, and Benson capitalized on this conviction by claiming to begin a fund to set Morrison free. One wealthy socialite was approached by Benson, who stated that he intended to publish a weekly newspaper which would crusade for Morrison's freedom. The gullible woman gave Benson £5,000 to begin his paper and he continued to mulct this naive investor, buying a small farm and hiring ex-convicts to tend to a few sheep. Benson took his investor to this place often to show her how his Prisoners' Aid Society was helping to rehabilitate ex-convicts. He did publish a newspaper of slender volume in which he raved about Morrison's innocence.

Morrison reportedly knew of Benson's crusade on his behalf and sent him messages of encouragement through the prison grapevine, but the celebrated prisoner had no idea that Benson was using him as a gimmick to bilk suckers out of substantial cash. The scheme went on for several years, with Benson taking more than £35,000 from his socialite lady friend for Morrison's release, as well as several times that amount from lawyers, businessmen, and even government officials. He lived in a lavishly decorated apartment, had a country place, and ate in the best restaurants while employing a few hack writers to gush out their diatribes about Morrison and attack the government for all manner of wrongs. Suddenly, when Scotland Yard was completing its investigation of Benson's fraudulent operations and had just obtained warrants for his arrest, the con man fell seriously ill and was taken to a West End clinic. On Oct. 22, 1917, detectives from Scotland Yard visited the clinic to arrest the con man. When they entered his private room they were greeted by a doctor who pointed to a bed containing Harry Benson, con man. He had died only a few minutes earlier.

REF.: *CBA*; Kingston, *A Gallery of Rogues*.

Benson, Henry (Harry, AKA: Comte de Montagu, G.H. Yonge, Count Yonge, J.H. Yonge, Hugh Montgomery, George Washington Morton), b.1848, Brit., fraud. Born of respectable Jewish parents in London, Henry Benson was partly educated in Paris and was a cultured and clever confidence man who began bilking on a high level following the Franco-Prussian War of 1870. He called himself the Count de Montagu when he met the Lord Mayor of London, saying that he was the mayor of the small French town of Chateaudun, which had been nearly demolished in the recent war and he was collecting funds for the poor and needy of his town. The Lord Mayor of London gave him £1,000 but the swindle was soon exposed and, days later, Benson was tried and convicted of fraud and sent to Newgate Prison for a year. He tried to commit suicide in his cell by setting his bed on fire but he only succeeded in burning himself horribly, so much so that he was a cripple

Swindler Henry Benson.

for some years afterwards, having to spend most of his time in a wheelchair.

Released in July 1873, Benson immediately changed his name to J.H. Yonge and used variations on this name while conducting new swindles, chiefly with 23-year-old William Kurr, a clever, young con man who was in the business of setting up dummy companies that dealt in turf betting. Benson enacted the role of a celebrated horserace gambler who claimed he was so successful that whenever he bet on a race the odds dropped on his favorite. In this way, Kurr claimed, they could manipulate odds and produce enormous profits for investors. Thousands of gullible racetrack goers poured money into the fake firms, enriching Benson and Kurr but producing little profit. The swindlers would fold one firm after having sold off its paper assets to another and continue this process so that their gambling company schemes presented an incredible labyrinth of legal documents. To prevent the police from probing too deeply into their affairs, the con men paid off Scotland Yard detectives John Meiklejohn, Nathaniel Druscovitch, William Palmer, and Chief Inspector George Clarke.

These officers came into the bribery circle of Benson and Kurr as early as 1872, when Kurr had cultivated Meiklejohn, who then brought in Druscovitch, who brought in the next officer in need of money. All of these Scotland Yard detectives were in charge of the Continental Branch of Investigation, which dealt with violations of the Betting Act. When warrants for either Kurr or Benson were issued by their irate victims, the officers warned their criminal associates or buried the warrants, receiving considerable payoffs for these efforts. Ben-son, who had recovered from his crippling wounds and was now walking about with the aid of a cane, set up his next victim in Paris—the wealthy Comtesse de Goncourt—who was inveigled into a betting scheme where she expected to make amazing profits. The Comtesse gave Benson and Kurr £1,000 and then another £10,000, believing she would soon be realizing ten times that amount through the bets placed for her by Benson and Kurr.

Instead of being content with this amount, the con men asked the Comtesse for anoth-er £30,000, but she told them that she would have to consult her lawyer for such a large amount. The lawyer, hearing what his client had been up to, contacted the authorities

Opera star Adelina Patti, a Benson victim.

in England. Scotland Yard assigned Druscovitch to run down the con men and he went to Kurr, telling him: "I must arrest some-body." Kurr shrugged and told him to arrest him, believing he could bluff his way out of any charge. Druscovitch refused, believing he and the other Scotland Yard officers would be exposed. But Scotland Yard superiors sent others to arrest Kurr in his pub at Islington. Benson had fled to Rotterdam and Druscovitch was sent after him with orders to arrange extradition of Benson back to England. Ironically, the detective, himself involved in the entire swindling empire of Benson and Kurr, was arresting his criminal boss. Benson and Kurr were placed on trial at the Old Bailey in April 1877 and charged with fraud and forgery. Their bold trail had left considerable evidence which convicted them. Benson was given a fifteen-year prison term, and Kurr, his brother Frederick Kurr, and a man named Bale were given ten-year terms. Others in their elaborate swindling ring also received long sentences.

Following their convictions, as the Scotland Yard detectives feared, both Benson and Kurr turned informers, hoping to lessen their sentences by exposing the police officers who had been on their payroll. Meiklejohn, Druscovitch, and Palmer were all tried

in a police court and found Guilty. Clarke, defended brilliantly by Edward Clarke (not related), was acquitted. An attorney named Froggatt was also found Guilty, and the guilty men were sentenced to two years in prison, mild terms compared to that meted out to Benson and Kurr. These convictions represented the worst scandal to ever invade the otherwise sacrosanct Scotland Yard. Kurr was released a few years later and faded into oblivion, but, when released in 1887, Henry Benson went on to more spectacular swindles, mostly in America.

Benson managed to meet the celebrated Spanish-born coloratu-ra Adelina Patti on board a ship taking her to New York, bowing to her as she was about to disembark. She thought him to be one of the delegation meeting her at the Manhattan dock and allowed him to take her arm, escorting her down the gangplank. To the New York officials greeting the famous singer, Benson appeared to be one of the prima donna's entourage. This, of course, was Benson's intent. He quickly set himself up as Patti's New York agent and he collected a $20,000 advance from Mexican officials who thought they were booking Patti for a concert in Mexico City. Before he could flee, Benson was arrested and thrown into the Tombs. Realizing that he would spend the rest of his life in prison, Henry Benson climbed to the top tier of the Tombs and threw himself downward to his death, finally completing the suicide he had begun almost two decades earlier in Newgate Prison.

REF.: Browne, *The Rise of Scotland Yard*; CBA; Cobb, *Critical Years at the Yard*; Dilnot, *The Real Detective*; Kingston, *Dramatic Days at the Old Bailey*; ____, *A Gallery of Rogues*; Thomson, *The Story of Scotland Yard*; Twyman, *The Best Laid Schemes*; Woodhall, *Secrets of Scotland Yard*.

Benson, Paul, 1918- , U.S., jur. Attorney general of North Dakota from 1954-55. He was appointed to the bench of the District Court of North Dakota by President Richard M. Nixon in 1971. REF.: *CBA*.

Benson, Steven, 1951- , U.S., mur. Threatened with being cut out of his wealthy mother's will, a 34-year-old would-be entrepreneur planted two pipe bombs in her car, murdering two people and severely injuring a third.

Steven Benson was born into money, the son of tobacco tycoon Edward Benson and Margaret, his heiress wife. Gifted at elec-tronics, Steven Benson, at an early age, built a television set, an achievement his mother spoke of proudly. By the time he reached adulthood, however, he had become greedy, unsuccessful at his many business adventures, and twice divorced. Benson spent copious amounts of the family money on small businesses that repeatedly fell apart. After his father died in 1980, Margaret Benson continued to give her eldest son money for his ventures, but when she learned he was lifting funds from the businesses into his own pocket, she threatened to write him out of her will. On July 9, 1985, Benson, then living with his mother and his nephew, Scott, twenty-one, in Naples, Fla., planted two twenty-seven pound bombs in his mother's car. Set off by an electronic device, they killed Scott, Margaret Benson, and severely injured Carol Lynn Kendall, Scott's mother and Steven's sister.

Kendall served as the state's main witness, testifying against her brother. One year after the bombs exploded, Benson was found Guilty of murder and condemned to serve two consecutive life sentences, along with thirty-seven years for attempted murder and arson.

REF.: Andersen, *The Serpent's Tooth*; CBA; Greenya, *Blood Relations*.

Benson Murder Case, The, 1926, a novel by S.S. Van Dine. This gripping mystery uses as its role model Joseph Elwell, whose enigmatic and still unsolved murder (U.S., 1920) continues to baffle experts to this day. A 1930 film, directed by Frank Tuttle, based on the book and using the same title, stars William Powell as the indefatigable Philo Vance. Actor Richard Tucker plays Benson, millionaire womanizer—á la Elwell—shot and killed on his vast estate. The only departure Van Dine took in his novel from the real-life murder is that Vance catches the culprit. See: **Elwell, Joseph P.** REF.: *CBA*.

Bentham, Jeremy, 1748-1832, Brit., jur.-pris. reform. Born at

Houndsditch on Feb. 15, 1748, Jeremy Bentham was a child prodigy of sorts, admitted to Westminster School when he was only seven. At the age of twelve he entered Queen's College at Oxford, and was only fifteen when he took advance studies at Lincoln's Inn. Though he was an intellectual giant with a probing analytical mind, Bentham was also devoid of humor. He was boring and pedantic and fiercely believed in utilitarianism—in fact, he was its philosophical founder. He served briefly as a barrister, representing only one case, before he devoted himself entirely to the study of jurisprudence. His voluminous writing, though he published little, had utilitarianism at its core, an unswerving belief he expressed as "the greatest good to the greatest number which is the measure of right and wrong." Bentham's first significant published work, *Fragment on Government* (1776), vigorously attacked the accepted bible of all British law schools, Blackstone's *Commentaries.* Though this work found approval in high places, British law was not altered through Bentham's utilitarian credo.

Following extensive travels and legal studies, Bentham published *Defense of Usury* (1788). His *Principles of Morals and Legislation* appeared the next year. After a decade of writing about the law, Bentham put together his best known work, *Traités de Législation.* He then embarked on lobbying various countries to adopt his theories of rational

Jeremy Bentham

legislation but found little or no support in the U.S., Germany, or his native land. Though the French much admired Bentham and made him an honorary citizen of the revolutionary new Republic, that country shunned the utilitarian application to its laws. Bentham, when not preoccupied by his legal theories, advanced what he called "moral inventions." These included designs for prisons, particularly his "panopticon." One of Bentham's designs was employed for the building of Millbank Prison in London, a structure universally condemned as ill-conceived. His "panopticon" was adopted, however, by the state of Illinois when it built the state penitentiary at Joliet in 1921, a sterile structure that has proven functional.

Though looked upon today as a pioneer in jurisprudence and penology, Bentham remains a historical oddity, flamboyant and eccentric in his lifetime. He once proposed that the bodies of family members should be stuffed, especially those coming from great estates, and erected along driveways, instead of trees, so that future generations could view their illustrious ancestors each day and so develop an appreciation of their own history. Bentham's own body, according to his will, was mummified following an autopsy, which was performed (during a wild rain and lightning storm) before his surviving friends and relatives—also at his wish. The head was so mutilated that it had to be replaced by a wax duplication, but the original corpse was embalmed, then coated with copal varnish to prevent rot and ward off dampness. The corpse was dressed in Bentham's finest attire and placed in a closet in London's University College, where it is rolled out each year to preside at board meetings. This rather grim tradition was also dictated by Bentham when leaving a considerable amount of money to his college. If he could not convince others to employ the bodies of their relatives for utilitarian purposes, at least his own remains could be put to use, frivolous or not. See: **Joliet State Penitentiary.**

REF.: Atkinson, *Jerry Bentham: His Life and Work;* Bowring, *Complete Works with a Biography; CBA;* Nash, *Zanies;* Reppetto, *The Blue Parade;* Scott, *The Concise Encyclopedia of Crime and Criminals;* Wallas, *Jeremy Bentham.*

Bentinck, William Cavendish, 1774-1839, India, jur. Colonial governor for British Crown of Bengal, India, from 1828-33. During his administration he effected many judicial and financial reforms, suppressed the Thugs, and abolished the suttee. See:

Thugee. REF.: *CBA.*

Bentley, Derek, 1933-53, and **Craig, Christopher,** 1936-   , Brit., rob.-mur. Derek Bentley and Christopher Craig were in the process of robbing a London warehouse on Nov. 2, 1952, when police arrived, called by witnesses who saw the boys breaking into the building. Bentley, nineteen, and Craig, sixteen, took to the roof of the building when the constables rushed up the inside stairs. Bentley, who was armed with brass knuckles and a knife, was quickly subdued by police but Craig, armed with a gun, hid behind an elevator shaft housing. Detective Frederick Fairfax shouted for Craig to surrender. Bentley, according to later police testimony, then yelled to his fellow burglar: "Let 'em have it, Chris!" A bullet whizzed into Fairfax's shoulder. He fell to the floor of the roof but got up when Bentley tried to flee and held on to him. Bentley then told Fairfax: "He's got a Colt .45 and plenty of bloody ammunition." Several other constables appeared on the roof, all unarmed, and they threw bottles, pieces of wood and other objects at Craig but all missed.

Constable Miles advanced on the boy and Craig fired a single shot that hit the policeman square in the forehead, killing him. "I am Craig!" the youth shouted. "You've just given my brother twelve years! Come on you coppers, I'm only sixteen!" Craig's brother, Niven Scott Craig, twenty-six, had only three days before been given a long prison term for armed robbery. Then Bentley said to the officers holding him: "You'll want to look out. He'll blow your heads off." The officers began to take Bentley off the roof and he shouted to his gun-wielding partner: "Look out, Chris, they're taking me down!" This was later interpreted to be another command to Craig to fire once more. Craig did, but he hit no one.

Reports of the gunfight reached the Croydon Police Station and guns were sent to the officers trying to subdue Craig. Fairfax, though wounded, obtained a gun and went after the youth, telling him as he bravely approached Craig: "Drop your gun. I also have one." Craig, hiding behind the elevator shaft housing, shouted back: "Yes, it's a Colt .45! Are you hiding behind a shield? Is it bulletproof? Are we going to have a shooting match? It's just what I like!" With that Craig began firing, as did Fairfax. There were

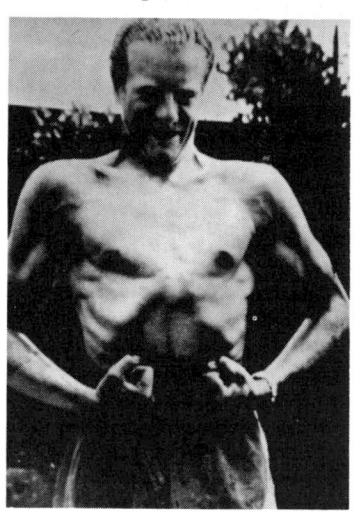

British thief and killer Derek Bentley.

four clicks from Craig's gun and then he said: "There, it's empty!" With that, he turned and leaped straight off the roof, falling twenty feet, his fall broken by several police officers who were standing below. Though severely wounded with a fractured spine and a broken wrist, Craig survived, shouting as they carried him to an ambulance: "I wish I was ____ dead! I wish I had killed the ____ lot!"

Fairfax, a modest officer who always minimized his incredible courage that night, was later given the George Cross for his gallant actions in capturing the killer burglars. Constable Miles, killed by Craig, was posthumously awarded the King's Police Medal for Gallantry. Though this gunfight pointed out to many the need for London's policemen to bear arms, police officers continued to perform their hazardous duties unarmed. The brutal murder of Constable Miles, however, shocked the public and sensationalized the trial of Bentley and Craig at the Old Bailey on Dec. 9, 1952, before Lord Goddard, Lord Chief Justice of England. Christmas Humphreys and J.T. Bass prosecuted, and F.H. Cassel defended Bentley while E.J. Parris defended Craig.

The case for the Crown seemed to be open and shut but, as the trial progressed, police testimony appeared confused, and

Bentley's role as the instigator of Craig's murder of Constable Miles was not clear-cut. Bentley, uneducated and sub-normal, according to psychiatrists, pleaded not guilty to being part of the killing. He claimed that he did not urge his friend to gun down Constable Miles but, when he said "let 'em have it," he meant that Craig was to turn over his gun to the officer. Implausible as this claim appeared, given Bentley's other remarks, it was easily interpreted as a plus for the defense. It was also claimed that the bullet which killed Miles could have been fired by another gun, according to the ambiguous statements of a ballistics expert. Bentley gave a poor showing of himself in the witness box. When Justice Goddard asked Bentley what his intent was on the night of the killing, going about with a knife and brass knuckles, Bentley replied cretinously: "Just to go to Croydon for a ride, sir, just an ordinary ride, just to walk around." Craig did little more than display his hatred for the police once in the witness box. Craig's father testified, stating that he had taught both his sons to shoot weapons but that Christopher had been a retiring boy, one who loved fairy tales read to him as a small child, a youth who lived in a fantasy world.

Both youths were convicted by a jury that took only seventy-five minutes to deliberate their case. Craig, who was underage, was given an indefinite sentence, but Bentley, nineteen, was sentenced to death, despite the fact that the jury recommended mercy. Bentley's lawyers filed appeals but these were denied. Petitions from friends, family members, and many citizens were also ineffective in winning the youth a reprieve. On Jan. 28, 1953, Bentley was hanged at Wandsworth Prison. Following this execution, an avalanche of written protest descended upon the government, which contributed mightily to the subsequent abolition of Great Britain's death penalty.

REF.: Bentley, *My Son's Execution;* Bresler, *Lord Goddard;* Brophy, *The Meaning of Murder; CBA;* Cobb, *Murdered on Duty;* Duff, *A New Handbook on Hanging;* Furneaux, *Famous Criminal Cases/Vol I;* ____, *They Died by the Gun;* Grimshaw, *Lord Goddard, His Career and Cases;* Hibbert, *The Roots of Evil;* Jacobs, *Aspects of Murder; Notable British Trials;* Parris, *Most of My Murders;* Potter, *The Art of Hanging;* Scott, *Scotland Yard;* Smith, *Lord Goddard;* Wilson, *Encyclopedia of Murder;* Yallop, *To Encourage the Others.*

Benton, Wallace, b.1859, Case of, Brit., mur. Wallace Benton owned a tract of land at Tilney St. Lawrence, near King's Inn in Norfolk, England. Financial trouble forced him to mortgage the farm in 1925. Delinquent in his payments and in poor health, Benton was ordered to vacate in 1929. His neighbor, Thomas Henry Williamson, was to take possession of the estate and make any necessary repairs.

In the last few days before the eviction was to take effect, Benton became increasingly despondent and vengeful. On Mar. 21, 1929, he took his rifle and shot Williamson. He later claimed that the gun had discharged accidentally.

Benton was charged with murder and tried at the Norwich Assizes in June 1929. In deteriorating health and nearly blind, Benton apparently did not fully comprehend what was going on around him. The jury found him Guilty, but at the same time issued a strong recommendation for mercy. Justice Travers Humphreys imposed the death sentence, but Benton did not hang. He was issued a court reprieve after an earlier appeal was denied.

REF.: Butler, *Murderers' England; CBA;* Hastings, *The Other Mr. Churchill;* Humphreys, *A Book of Trials;* ____, *Seven Murderers;* Shew, *A Companion to Murder;* Wilson, *Encyclopedia of Murder.*

Bentz, Edward Wilhelm (AKA: Ned Dewey, William Joslyn, Sam Longman, Henry Vaughner, Frederic Wendell, Frank Wilson), b.1896, U.S., rob. Perhaps no bank robber in the twentieth century equalled the daring and intelligence displayed by Eddie Bentz, who planned more bank robberies for more super gangs in the 1920s and 1930s than any other bank caser. Yet Bentz, a phantom robber who plagued state lawmen and FBI agents for more than fifteen years, was wholly unlike any of those bandits he worked with, a man of mystique, literary imagination, culture, and refinement. He was an acrobat, an actor who played many roles, a lover of antiquity, a collector of rare books and coins, a gentle bigamist, and the mastermind behind every major bank robbery in the U.S. for more than a decade. He was a man who prepared for all emergencies, checking every detail of his vocation, bank robbing. Long after he had become a multimillionaire from his enormous shares from robberies he had planned, Bentz went on designing spectacular robberies and even committed some himself "just to keep his hand in."

Born into a farming family, Bentz ran away from home as a youth and fulfilled every boy's dream—he joined a circus. He was a big boy—almost six feet by his mid-teens—and he got a job as a roustabout. From the acrobats he learned how to perform amazing acrobatic tricks, climbing ropes hand-over-hand with rapid movement, vaulting himself twenty to thirty feet into the air from springboards and dropping an equal distance in a harmless fall, swinging with ropes across great distances to land on a tiny spot every time, and scaling walls with ropes and hooks. Bentz, through his prodigious physical exercises, had developed a muscular, trim body that could perform marvelous feats. By that time he had also become a superb character man, for he spent endless hours with the circus clowns who showed him the art of changing his entire appearance with makeup kits. He could alter the shape of his nose and jaw with gum arabic (a trick later employed by Willie "The Actor" Sutton). He knew how to dye his hair and eyebrows to realistic tints. He could effectively assume any kind of posture, from the stooped appearance of an elderly man, shuffling his feet and leaning heavily upon canes, to that of cripples or even the deformed. All of these learned skills Eddie Bentz would later employ to great results in the robbing of banks.

Returning to his Washington state home just before his seventeenth birthday, Bentz embarked on a series of petty thefts that landed him in the state training school at Chehalis, Wash. He quickly escaped by pole-vaulting over a wall. Picked up again for burglary, Bentz was sent to the State Reformatory at Monroe, Wash. Released, he again embarked on a series of robberies that earned him a sentence in the state prison at Walla Walla. He was paroled, violated parole, and was returned to the state prison. Released, Bentz changed his name to Ned Dewey and committed several bank robberies in Wisconsin, New Jersey, Pennsylvania, Indiana, and Washington, moving across the country and enlisting the aid of local bandits. He never revealed his true name to these men, always using aliases. Between short prison terms, Bentz continued to plan bank robberies. He had become an avid reader in and out of prison, and he was soon an expert on banking matters.

Bentz studied banks as closely as he studied classic books and his stamp and coin collections. He read the financial sections of newspapers every day, paying particular attention to the required-by-law statements of banks which reported their holdings in cash and in bonds, as well as other securities. He would also note scheduled transfers of money which were also publicly stated in newspapers—information his fellow bank robbers had never dreamed was publicly available. Bentz would then visit banks he intended to rob or have robbed by others, and noted their security systems, guards (if any), and the availability of local law enforcement officers. He would also "run the roads" leading from the town to determine the best escape routes, charting back roads that interconnected for fifty-mile distances. Bentz would then contact one of the top bank robbing gangs he used and put his plans before them.

This was the method Bentz employed when he went to Harvey Bailey, Jim Ripley, and a few other top bandits in 1922, explaining how the Denver Mint could be robbed. He had been inside the mint impersonating a federal banking inspector and had been shown all of its security procedures. Some weeks later, Bentz reappeared with other bandits and took $500,000 in cash and securities, a staggering theft for that era. Bentz, who had planned the operation with the able assistence of Bailey, an old pro bandit, vowed that he would take less risks in the future and restrict his participation to the planning of bank robberies and not their enactment.

On Sept. 17, 1930, Bentz, Bailey, and others took more than $1 million in cash and bonds from the Lincoln Bank and Trust Company. This clever robbery, one which gutted the bank's assets and forced its permanent closing, was, of course, planned by Eddie Bentz. A guard was killed, causing Bentz to swear he would never again participate in robbing a bank, but he broke his word again and again, always to his own disservice.

For the most part Bentz worked with top bank robbers, gang chieftains who knew him, but the lower echelon had no idea who provided the information on those banks holding large amounts of cash and securities. Sometimes Bentz put together a gang of complete strangers, never revealing his own identity and departing immediately after the splitting up of the loot. He lived a life wholly apart from the bandits of his profession. He kept four separate homes and dozens of comfortable apartments throughout the U.S. In the homes, according to one report, were four separate wives, all women with different personalities—a redhead with an outgoing personality who liked nightclubs and dancing, a stay-at-home brunette, a cool blonde who enjoyed concerts and art museums, and another blonde who was addicted to the outdoor life.

Bentz lived with these women comfortably for many years, presenting himself to them as a sales director who had to be on the move a good deal of the time, or a cattle buyer who had to travel the Southwest to buy herds of cattle, or a mine owner compelled to travel to his many mines. This explained his long absences from each of them, but he religiously kept up correspondence with all of them. He established more fictional backgrounds for himself when renting expensive apartments and befriending the neighbors and managers, so that if inquiries were made by police about any suspicious characters his name would never be brought up. As Bentz himself later explained: "I'm a big, farmerish-looking sort of fellow, sort of easy-going, like to laugh and talk and be chummy with people, and that doesn't match up with their ideas about criminals. And I always liked nice things—went to good shows, stayed at the best hotels, ate at the best places, and was always quiet and gentlemanly about it. People think crooks hide in cellars."

By the early 1930s, Bentz, or the aliases he used with many of the super bank-robbing gangs, found himself planning dozens of robberies for the Barker gang, Charles Arthur "Pretty Boy" Floyd, John Dillinger, the Jake Fleagle gang in the West, Harvey Bailey, and many others. Bentz operated coast-to-coast, his gangs striking in New England one week, in the South the next, in the Midwest and the West in following weeks. Moreover, Bentz grew enormously rich, taking as his share of the robberies all the securities and bonds, often worth three or four times as much as the actual cash taken. To the bandits such securities were useless and they were glad to get rid of them. To Bentz, the bonds and other securities could easily be cashed in almost at their full value. Following a robbery, Bentz would call the president of the bank that had just been looted and inform him that he would return certain securities at eighty percent of their full value, reminding the banker that he knew that the banker had juggled his own books (which he did) and that by recovering the bonds stolen from his bank he could cover some of the funds he, the banker, had embezzled. On other occasions, Bentz would contact insurance executives eager to buy back stolen securities without question in order to keep losses down in their districts. At still other times, Bentz went to unscrupulous attorneys who paid considerable sums for securities and fenced them through their own clients.

The mastermind enjoyed the wealth he accumulated. He bought expensive wardrobes, but his suits were conservative, custom-made by the best tailors. He purchased hand-crafted luggage, tasteful but expensive jewelry, and he continued to indulge in his hobbies of stamp and coin collecting, spending tens of thousands of dollars on his collections each year. He bought entire private libraries and had these shipped to his homes,

antique and rare first editions of the classics which he read at all hours, even taking books with him when casing a bank. Bentz thought of himself as a gentleman thief, and he sneered at the violence embraced by Bonnie and Clyde. When John Dillinger once challenged one of his bank robbery plans, Bentz faced him with a glare and said: "I was in this business for ten years before you ever walked into a bank with a gun in your hand. You're an upstart." Dillinger found Bentz's attitude amusing but the lunatic Fred Barker did not.

Bentz had planned several bank robberies for his old friend Harvey Bailey, including the 1933 Fairbury, Neb., bank raid which was taken over by Fred Barker. When Barker looked over the plan, he asked Bailey who had drawn it up and Bailey told him: "The top man in my profession." Finally, after Barker persistently badgered him for an identity, Bailey mentioned the name of Eddie Bentz. Barker then insisted upon meeting Bentz and when he did he ordered the quiet bank caser to accompany the mob on the Fairbury raid. Bentz reportedly drove the getaway car in order to qualify for his cut of the loot, but he confided to Bailey later that he would never work with the Barkers again. It was during this robbery that a guard was killed. Bentz hated violence and repeatedly claimed that he had planned his robberies so well that there was never any need for gunplay. Yet he never took into account a berserk killer like Freddie Barker.

As the gang escaped pursuing police after this raid, Bentz was identified, and it was this identification which ultimately led to his arrest, an arrest Bentz always attributed to the unreliable Barkers. Bentz left the Midwest for some time in 1934, planning bank robberies in the West, and then moving to the East Coast where he lived with one of his wives in a Manhattan townhouse. He thought of retiring with the identity he had established in New York but he was inevitably drawn to the Midwest to see one of his other wives and also "keep his hand in" by planning a few more bank robberies. After one robbery, police closed in on Bentz. As they drew up in several cars before a Chicago apartment building, a limousine came shooting out of the building's underground parking lot. Officers stopped the limousine, throwing the beams of their flashlights onto the face of a startled chauffeur. He politely explained: "I just received a call from my employer, Dr. Mason, who has an emergency call at Lakeview Hospital and—" He was allowed to drive on. The chauffeur, in full livery, had been Edward Wilhelm Bentz, employing one of his many disguises. FBI agents later learned that Bentz kept at least four limousines parked in several hideouts which he used effectively in making several escapes, sometimes as a chauffeur, sometimes as a banking official with an accomplice pretending to be the chauffeur. Bentz even convinced a southern sheriff that he was a government official hurrying by limousine to the state capital to deliver to the governor a report on the elusive bandit, Eddie Bentz, perfectly affecting a southern accent.

Bentz was a man of many diguises and aliases. He lived with a wife in Chicago as Henry Vaughner, known as a real estate magnate. As Vaughner his hair was jet black and he wore a mustache, thin and trimmed. In Los Angeles he was Sam Longman, a mining expert. In Houston he was Frank Wilson, a cattle buyer. In New York he was William Joslyn, sales director of a firm specializing in imported furs. Tiring of all of these roles, Bentz met a 17-year-old runaway from Milwaukee, Wis., a beautiful young girl to whom he confided his true identity. She was thrilled at meeting a real life bank robber and she became his mistress. Bentz spent months teaching her etiquette and manners. He gave her good books to read and taught her an appreciation of classical music and fine art. He became her Pygmalion and he married her, his fifth and final marriage.

The mastermind decided to settle down and turn his back on his criminal past. He selected New England as the only area where he felt he would not be recognized. He moved with his new wife to Portland, Maine, and there lived as Frederic Wendell. Here he began a small firm, the Ultra Products Company, which manufactured small, inexpensive toys such as lead soldiers and miniature horses and dogs. Bentz found legitimate business demanding and his firm began to falter. His attorney told him that he needed to raise capital but Bentz was on a tight budget. Although Bentz had millions of dollars worth of stolen securities hidden about the country, he could not unearth this illegal treasure for fear of being recognized in his old haunts. Also, he knew any movement of these bonds at this time would bring attention to him. Bentz returned to outright banditry. Calling upon two old-time thieves from his past, Bentz raided the Caledonia National Bank of Danville, Ver., on June 4, 1934, taking more than $7,000 in cash, $8,000 in bonds, and $3,500 in American Express money orders.

The once-careful mastermind had been sloppy in the Danville robbery, leaving a fingerprint that the FBI identified some weeks later as that of Edward Wilhelm Bentz. Witnesses picked him out of rogues' gallery files and his photo was soon on the front pages of American newspapers as one of the most hunted bandits in the country. He shipped his young wife back to Milwaukee and ran from hideout to hideout, but he was always asked to move on. "Federal heat" followed him everywhere and he was too dangerous to harbor. For almost two years, he escaped one police trap after another. Bentz was finally tracked down by FBI agents in Brooklyn on Mar. 13, 1936. He was hiding with a burglar whose own actions tipped agents to Bentz's presence in the apartment. They attacked the place with tear gas and as the shells exploded in the apartment, Bentz dove for a dumbwaiter which led to an upstairs apartment. The small apparatus broke under the weight of his large body and he smashed the top, pulling himself up hand over hand to the next apartment. But agents, hearing the crash of debris in the shaft of the dumbwaiter, raced upstairs, and there captured the white-faced mastermind.

As he was being led away, Bentz calmly stated: "I hope they send me to Alcatraz. All my friends are there." The discipline Bentz had prided himself on seemed to collapse at his trial. He was tired of running, tired of hiding, and no longer took delight in his endless impersonations and cleverly planned robberies. He resigned himself to prison and admitted his many robberies, including the Lincoln bank heist in 1930. He was given a 20-year term and sent to the federal penitentiary in Atlanta. Then he got his wish and was sent to Alcatraz, received on the Rock on May 17, 1936, where he served out his time longing for his private library and his stamps and coins and writing long apologetic letters to five women who had long ago divorced him. See: **Bailey, Harvey; Barker Brothers; Dillinger, John; Fleagle Gang; Floyd, Charles Arthur.**

REF.: *CBA;* Hoover, *Persons in Hiding;* Johnston, *Alcatraz Island Prison;* Nash, *Almanac of World Crime;* Wellman, *A Dynasty of Western Outlaws;* Whitehead, *The FBI Story.*

ben Yair, Eleazer, prom. 73 A.D., Judea, rebel.-geno. When the winds changed in the mountainous region where the city of Masada was situated, the leader of the Zealots took that as an omen that God had turned his back on his people, and ordered a mass suicide.

In 66 A.D. the Jews in Judea rose up against the Roman Empire's occupation, but the rebellion was put down except for a small group of about 1,000 Zealots, who retreated to their natural fortress stronghold called Masada, near the Dead Sea. Masada, dominating the desert region where it stood, was a natural rock formation of steep cliff plateaus with only a narrow and arduous path leading up to it. It had been further strengthened by King Herod, who added a great eighteen-foot-high wall and towers at strategic points. Inside Masada were living quarters and storehouses for food and armaments. Cisterns supplied water, and food could be grown on the summit. Masada was built to withstand a siege for years if necessary. It had been captured from the Romans by the Zealots in a surprise attack in 66 A.D. In 72 A.D., Flavius Silva, the Roman governor, marched a powerful army, the Tenth Legion, to recapture the fortress. Eight camps were set up around Masada, and a ramp of earth constructed to support siege engines. Catapults to throw stones into the fortress

were put in position at the base of the cliffs, and soon they damaged buildings, wounding and killing many of Masada's residents.

By 73 A.D. Silva began to assemble huge war machines on the newly-built ramp. A giant battering-ram cracked the stone walls of the fortress, and a section of Masada's wall gaped open. The Zealots worked all night to fill the hole with timber and earth and, by morning, the Romans tried to batter it again, finding that the ram was not effective against the pliant timber. Silva then ordered his men to hurl flaming torches against the wood, but when the precarious winds of the mountainous region shifted, the Roman soldiers panicked as the fire burned them and their equipment instead of harming the Zealots. Not long after, the wind shifted again.

Masada's leader, Eleazar ben Yair, called his people together. He had decided that the new wind shift signified that God had rejected the Jews, and believed that it was God's will that the Jewish race should be exterminated. His solution was that the Masadans who remained should take their own lives, rather than be captured and tortured or mocked by the Romans. Convincing the besieged Zealots that this would be an act of spiritual atonement, ben Yair instructed every man to go home and kill his wife and children. The men drew lots, and the ten chosen killed their own comrades. The last ten again drew lots. The chosen Zealot had the task of killing the other nine Zealots and making sure that no one was left alive in Masada. When he had finished, he fell on his sword, thus committing suicide.

On Apr. 15, 73 A.D., the Romans marched up the ramp to Masada only to find silence and smoke drifting up from smoldering ruins. Then two women appeared, leading five small children. This group had hidden away, the only witnesses to the carnage at Masada.

REF.: Canning, *50 True Tales of Terror; CBA.*

Ben-Zvi, Itzhak (Isaac Shimshelevich), 1884-1963, Isr., consp. Member of the Knesset from 1949-63, and second prime minister of Israel from 1952-63. He founded the first Hebrew school in British Palestine in 1909, was exiled by the Turks for pro-Zionist activity in 1915, and returned to the region three years later to organize the Jewish Legion with David Ben-Gurion. REF.: *CBA.*

Berberés, Jean, d.1950, Fr., (unsolv.) mur. When a North African gang was foolish enough to try to extort money from an underworld gang lord, the gang's collector was found dead soon after.

In Béziers, France, Henri le Gitan was an underworld gang leader with a reputation for knowing how to get things done. In 1950, one of the North African gangs that worked the Pigalle area thoughtlessly suggested that Gitan should give them protection money. A janitor found the body of Jean Berberés, the gang's collector, dead in front of a fireplace, his corpse filled with bullets in a style of killing favored by Gitan. Although his alibi was successful, police closed down Gitan's popular nightclub, the El Monico, and put him out of work.

REF.: *CBA;* Goodman, *Villainy Unlimited.*

Berdella, Robert, 1949- , U.S., sod.-abduc.-mur. The business card for his shop of the macabre bore the inscription, "I rise from death. I kill death and death kills me." Described by neighbor Kim Sheldon as an "introverted, old hippie type from the sixties," Robert Berdella was in some ways a grim reaper of death. Between July 6, 1984, and Aug. 5, 1987, he imprisoned, tortured, and killed six men to satisfy his sadistic, homosexual cravings, dismembering the bodies and stuffing them in the garbage.

Born in northern Ohio, Berdella drifted into Kansas City, Mo., in 1969 to attend classes at the local art institute. He bought a house in a pleasant, middle-class neighborhood called Westport, and even helped organize a neighborhood watch program.

In the 1970s Berdella opened up Bob's Bizarre Bazaar, a store specializing in the macabre. Replica skulls were sold as gag items, but were quickly taken from the shelves when investigators discovered real skulls buried in Berdella's own backyard.

Berdella's three-year murder spree came to light on Apr. 1,

1988, when police found Christopher Bryson walking the streets wearing only a dog collar around his neck. Six days earlier, the 23-year-old hitchhiker had been picked up, brought to Berdella's house, and bound and gagged in the bedroom. When he refused to submit to sexual acts, Berdella warned him that he would end up in the trash like the others. Bryson eventually escaped by burning his ropes with a book of matches. When police detectives searched the house, they uncovered over 250 explicit Polaroid photographs of the tortured victims. Syringes which Berdella used to inject animal tranquilizers were found along with a diary detailing the dates and times he administered a dosage. In the backyard two human skulls were dug up. Berdella confessed that he had buried the decapitated head of 20-year-old Larry Pearson whom he had tortured for a period of forty-three consecutive days before he died.

The other four victims included Gerald Howell, nineteen, Robert Sheldon, twenty-three, Mark Wallace, twenty, Walter Ferris, twenty-five, and Todd Stoops, age unknown. "Most of the victims had some connection to the gay community, to street hustling, or both," explained Jackson County prosecutor Albert Riederer. Satanism and demonic ritual were ruled out as motives. Berdella's sadistic fantasies were nurtured by a 1965 sex-hostage movie titled *The Collector*, in which a young woman is kidnapped by an introverted butterfly hobbyist and chained in a basement apartment.

It had been years since the Kansas City police had encountered a case of this magnitude. The Berdella case was front-page news for weeks, which only served to hamper the police investigation. A gag order was issued, but the continuing news leaks led to growing tensions between the city police and the prosecutor's office. Complicating matters was the pending election for prosecutor. Riederer was badgered for immediate results by his opponent Carol Coe. At one point, she demanded an interview with Berdella so she "could get him to confess like Perry Mason, so we can put him away."

On Aug. 3, 1988, Berdella pleaded guilty to the felonious restraint and second-degree murder of Larry Pearson, hoping to save himself from the electric chair. Judge Alvin C. Randall was startled by the defendant's admission of guilt, given the circumstantial evidence and the lack of actual eyewitnesses. Because the prosecutors had failed to inform Berdella that they would seek the death penalty, the killer received a reduced maximum sentence of life in prison. On Dec. 20, Berdella confessed to slaying five other men. He received five concurrent life sentences for these crimes.

In prison, Berdella created a trust fund to distribute portions of his estate to the families of the six victims, including the proceeds from the sale of his large collection of antiques. "It's just a step to work toward rehabilitation and getting a governor pardon in twenty years," explained Paul Howell, the disconsolate father of one of the victims. "If I had to describe him in one word, I'd say calculating," added Detective Albert DeValklenaere. REF.: *CBA*.

Berdue, Thomas, prom. 1851, Case of, U.S., asslt. & bat.-rob. Because the people of San Francisco were enraged at the inability of the criminal laws to reduce the amount of crime that came with the gold rush to their city, and because he bore a remarkable resemblance to a notorious criminal, Thomas Berdue almost lost his life.

In 1850, when California had just been admitted to the Union as a state, San Francisco was the scene of gold fever, accompanied by a brutal crime wave of robberies and murder. On Feb. 19, 1891, a shopkeeper, C.J. Jansen, was robbed in his dry goods store of $2,000, severely beaten, and left to die by two assailants. Jansen gave a description of the thieves, one of whom matched that of James Stuart, a thief and murderer from the Australian group of escaped convicts known as the "Sydney men." Within twenty-four hours police had arrested two Australians. One was Robert Windred, apprehended as the accomplice. The other claimed to be Thomas Berdue, although he matched the description of Stuart.

Jansen, still in critical condition, identified Berdue as his attacker. An angry crowd of almost seven thousand people tried to seize the prisoners as they were taken to the police station and attempted it a second time as the mob swelled by another two to three thousand. A popular court was formed, with judge, jury, and counsel, and the prisoners were tried in absentia in the recorder's room of the City Hall. Several more attempts were made to seize the two men, who several times barely escaped public execution.

Windred and Berdue were legally tried on Mar. 14, 1851, with Jansen the main witness for the prosecution. A verdict of Guilty was brought in and the accused was sentenced to fourteen years in the state prison, then immediately sent to Marysville, Calif., to stand trial for the murder of Charles Moore, a man Stuart had been accused of killing. At that trial, several witnesses positively identified Berdue, down to a scar on his right cheek and a stiff middle finger on one hand. Two defense witnesses, however, including a judge who had once tried the criminal, adamantly denied that the man on trial was Stuart.

On July 4, 1851, the prisoner again was found Guilty, and this time sentenced to be hanged. He maintained his innocence throughout the trial. A month earlier, in June, San Francisco businessmen, discontented with law enforcement in their city, formed a Vigilance Committee. On July 1, 1851, a shack had been robbed and a party from the Vigilance Committee picked up a well-dressed, well-spoken man as they searched for their thief. Though he said his name was Willard Stevens, he proved to be James Stuart. Letters were sent to the Marysville prison where Berdue was waiting to be executed. Stuart signed a full confession, admitting to the assault upon Jansen, as well as to several other crimes. Berdue was pardoned by Governor John McDougal, and the Vigilance Committee, hearing that the wrongly convicted man was penniless, collected a fund of $302. Berdue's petition for reimbursement from the state of California for the $4,000 he had spent in his efforts to prove himself innocent was refused on the grounds that "To grant the prayer of the petitioner would establish a precedent which, if carried out in all cases of this kind, would more than exhaust the entire revenue of the State." REF.: *CBA*.

Berenger (AKA: **Berenger of Tours**), c.999-1088, Fr., her. Archdeacon of Angers in 1040. He was excommunicated ten years later by Pope Leo II for rejecting the doctrine of transubstantiation. He was imprisoned by Henry I in 1050, condemned by synod a year later, and forced to sign an orthodox statement in 1054, which he later recanted. REF.: *CBA*.

Bérenger, René, 1830-1915, Fr., jur. Authored the *Bérenger Laws* advocating immunity from prosecution for first offenders. REF.: *CBA*.

Berenguer Gang, prom. 1975, Italy, kid. Many gangs participated in kidnappings in Italy in 1975, a year that saw a total of seventy-seven cases in that country.

The Berenguer gang, its members of Marseilles and Roman descent, was made up of former car thieves and holdup men. Within an eight-month period this gang netted about $5.54 million by kidnapping five wealthy Romans. Unlike Mafia gangs, which are tightly bound by the oath of silence and loyalty taken by all new members at their initiation, gangs like the Berenguers are said to be easier to break, being more vulnerable to leaks and informers.

The style of these non-Mafia groups is distinctive. They hold their victims in apartments in suburbs of big cities, often inside polystyrene cells, with their eyes covered with tape and ears stuffed with cotton, a technique developed after one hostage led police to his kidnappers after he had carefully spent his captive hours keeping a close tally of trains departing and flight patterns of planes overhead.

REF.: *CBA*; Moorehead, *Hostages to Fortune*.

Berenice II, c.269-221 B.C., Egypt, mur. Cyrenese wife of Egyptian king Ptolemy III. An astral constellation, *Coma Berenices*, was named in her honor shortly before she was murdered by her son Ptolemy IV Philapator. REF.: *CBA*.

Berenice III, d.80 B.C., Egypt, queen, assass. Daughter of Egyptian ruler Ptolemy IX. She ascended to the throne in 80 B.C., following the death of her second husband Ptolemy XI, and was killed that same year by Ptolemy Alexander. REF.: *CBA*.

Berenice IV, d.55 B.C., Egypt, mur. Cleopatra's eldest sister who ruled the kingdom from 58-55 B.C. in her father's absence. Berenice was murdered by her father, Ptolemy XII, when he was restored to the throne. REF.: *CBA*.

Berg, Alan, 1934-84, U.S., mur. (vict.) A controversial radio host who described himself as "the last angry man," Berg was murdered for his views by neo-Nazi white supremacists.

A former Chicago lawyer with a reputation for bluntness, Alan Berg once said, "You can never know where the nuts are going to come from. So you live day to day." The host of a daily radio show on Denver station KOA, Berg's program reached nearly a quarter of a million listeners. Calling himself "the man you love to hate," Berg joked about the many death threats he received. On June 18, 1984, Berg was shot to death in his driveway at around midnight. Police found ten .45-caliber shell casings near his corpse. The performer apparently died almost instantly. On Mar. 27, 1985, police arrested Bruce Carroll Pierce in Rossville, Ga., as a suspect. The leader of the Order, a neo-Nazi group found predominantly on the West Coast, Pierce was armed with three pistols and had a van full of bombs, grenades, machine guns, automatic weapons, dynamite, and a crossbow and arrow. The Order, an offshoot of the Church of the Aryan Nation, is an organization accused of staging armored-car robberies, netting about $4 million, to finance violent revolutionary activities. Three other members of the organization also linked to Berg's murder were David Lane, a Denver neo-Nazi leader; Robert Matthews, founder of the Order; and Richard Scutari. Matthews had been burned to death in a thirty-six hour standoff and shootout with FBI agents near Seattle in December 1984. On Mar. 31, 1985, Lane was arrested at a shopping center parking lot in Winston-Salem, N.C. He was also wanted in a counterfeiting case.

On Apr. 11, 1985, the U.S. Justice Department had approved federal prosecution of the Order under a federal racketeering law. Twenty-four people, twelve of the Order, had been arrested in twelve states since September 1984, three months after Berg's death. Of the ten Order members charged with conspiring to overthrow the U.S. government, Lane, Scutari, and Pierce were also accused of the machine-gun murder of Berg, charged with a civil rights violation punishable by life imprisonment. On Dec. 3, 1987, a federal district court jury found Lane and Pierce Guilty of violating Berg's civil rights, and sentenced each to 150 years in prison. Pierce was convicted of shooting the talk show host thirteen times with a submachine gun, and Pierce was convicted of driving the getaway car. Scutari and a fifth defendant, Jean M. Craig, were found Not Guilty of participating in Berg's death. REF.: *CBA*.

Berg, Pamela Sue, 1957- , and **Crain, James**, 1956- , U.S., mansl. Residents of a small town in Illinois reacted to the vicious murder of a five-year-old boy by firebombing the house of the prime suspect.

On Jan. 11, 1981, the body of 5-year-old Alan Madden was found on the floor of his home. An autopsy revealed more than 100 bruises on his body, and all of his major organs were ruptured. Accused of the murder were Madden's mother, 24-year-old Pamela Berg, and her live-in boyfriend, martial arts expert James Crain, twenty-six. While Berg remained jailed, Crain was released on Jan. 16 on a $300,000 bond—his home in Quincy, Ill., had been firebombed in his absence, and authorities received a number of calls threatening his life. Adams County Deputy Sheriff Anthony Grootens said, "Most of them (the calls) say something to the effect that 'If you don't take care of (Crain), we will'." After relatives refused to claim the body, the Madden boy was buried in a donated casket, with policemen serving as pallbearers and strangers putting flowers on his grave.

Berg's trial began on May 5, 1981. According to the testimony of two Quincy police officers, she had broken down after several hours of questioning and admitted that she and Crain had beaten the child for hours the night he died. She said that after an hour of beating Madden, she had turned him over to Crain, who began dropping the boy face down onto his knee for a period of two hours. Saying she realized Crain had gotten "carried away," Berg gave the boy a cold bath to reduce his swelling, then put him on an air register to warm him. At around 2 a.m. she realized that the child's heart had stopped, and said she gave him mouth-to-mouth resuscitation. In her initial statement, Berg told police that of her three children, Alan was accident-prone and that his death was caused by injuries brought on himself. Berg was convicted of involuntary manslaughter two days later, and sentenced to ten years in prison in early June. At Crain's trial in late January 1982, he pleaded for a sentence of five years, saying it would be "plenty to pay for the mistakes I've made." According to Crain, who maintained that Berg had murdered the boy with repeated physical abuse, his mistakes had been moving in with Berg and not knowing what to do to prevent what happened. Circuit Court Judge Edward Dittmeyer sentenced Crain to ten years in jail and a $10,000 fine for his part in the slaying.

Immediately after sentencing, Crain was rearrested and handcuffed, charged with sixty-three counts of public aid fraud and theft. He and Berg were charged with stealing more than $10,000 in public aid benefits in the year preceeding Madden's death. REF.: *CBA*.

Bergdoll, Grover Cleveland, 1893-1966, U.S., draft dodger. A millionaire Philadelphia playboy, Grover Cleveland Bergdoll was drafted into the U.S. Army in 1917 at the beginning of WWI but when he failed to show up at his draft board, he was listed as a deserter and a draft dodger. His mother, Emma Bergdoll, owner of one of the biggest breweries in Philadelphia and many times a millionaire, appeared at the draft board and pointedly told officials that she was against the war with Germany since the Bergdolls were German and had always been good German-Americans. She said: "I will give $1,000 to the Red Cross if Grover does not have to fight. If it were any other country but Germany that he would fight I would be willing for him to go."

Draft dodger Grover Bergdoll.

The draft board told her no exceptions were made and pointed out to her that her son had been a pioneer aviator and was sorely needed in the infant U.S. Army Air Corps. Bergdoll had financed the building of his own biplane in 1912 and had made many record flights, logging almost 800 hours in the air between 1912 and 1914. Mrs. Bergdoll refused to budge and so did the draft board. Bergdoll could not be found and was posted as a fugitive. Wanted Posters by the tens of thousands were distributed throughout the U.S. while Bergdoll was traveling in a cross-country auto race, or so he later claimed, to show that he was unaware of the search for him.

Bergdoll remained at large until 1920 when he was captured. He had been living well, traveling throughout the U.S., spending lavishly on good hotels, food, and clothes, as was his habit, a lifestyle that did not endear him to the hundreds of thousands of doughboys who served in WWI. He was found on Jan. 7, 1920, asleep in his own mansion and police squads had to rescue him from a lynch mob before he could be hanged from a lamppost. He was later tried and quickly convicted. Bergdoll's selection of Harry Weinberger as his attorney could not have been more ill-advised. Weinberger's own image was as unpopular as the clients he had represented in the past, notably the dedicated anarchist-communists Alexander Berkman and Emma Goldman, who had both been recently deported.

Sentenced to five years in prison, Bergdoll escaped by telling the guards who were about to take him to prison that he had a fortune in gold hidden beneath the porch of his sprawling castle-like mansion in Philadelphia. If the guards allowed him to show him the gold, he would share it with them. The guards, of course, would allow him to escape. When the trio arrived at Bergdoll's home, the wiley draft dodger, who stood only five-foot-four, slipped into a pantry and out of a window, once more escaping. (It should be noted that there were 337,649 U.S. draft deserters in WWI, of which 163,738 were caught, and given minor sentences, leaving more than 170,000 men never tried for avoiding military service. An example was made of Bergdoll, many claimed, because of his enormous wealth.)

From the moment Bergdoll went out the window, he led thousands of pursuers in a wild chase that lasted almost twenty years, hiding out in the U.S. and in Europe, flitting back and forth in all manner of disguises. The government spent millions to recapture him and Bergdoll became an unsavory household word in the U.S., forever linked to the words of "slacker" and "coward." Ironically, Bergdoll finally tired of the chase and surrendered to officials on May 27, 1939, when returning from Germany aboard the luxury liner *Bremen*. It was said that he would have stayed in Germany indefinitely had it not been for the fact that Adolf Hitler was about to plunge that country into its second devastating world war within twenty years.

By this time, with the U.S. once more on the eve of war and its patriotism being sorely tested, Bergdoll had become a symbol of the idle rich escaping the duties of the average citizen through influence and wealth. Congress debated Bergdoll's case and President Franklin D. Roosevelt was pressured to make an example of the most infamous draft dodger in U.S. history. He would be granted no amnesty, although this had been extended to all other deserters and draft dodgers. The diminuative millionaire was sent to prison for seven years at hard labor. Bergdoll was released in 1944 but he had been broken in health and spirit, and for the remaining nineteen years of his life, he was a man of little interest or energy. He suffered a mental breakdown and was confined in a psychiatric clinic in Richmond, Va., when he died on Jan. 27, 1966.

REF.: *CBA*; Dell, *The United States Against Bergdoll*.

Berger, Gottlob, b.1897, Ger., war crimes. Gottlob Berger, whose first name means "Praise God," set up the feared Sonderkommando units on behalf of his boss, SS Chief Heinrich Himmler. One of only a handful of men that Himmler addressed on a first-name basis, Berger's specialty was selecting the most attractive Jewish women from the death camps and injecting them with strychnine. According to eyewitnesses, the remains were then boiled into soap.

Arrested by the allies at the end of WWII, Berger was tried at Nuremberg for crimes against humanity. He was charged with rebellion, espionage, and covert activities in European countries targeted by Hitler for invasion. For his sympathetic treatment of American prisoners of war, Berger allegedly received some private assurances of a lesser sentence. Instead the tribunal sentenced the lieutenant general to twenty-five years in prison on Apr. 14, 1949. REF.: *CBA*.

Berger, Joseph, 1908- , and **Klar, Gabriel**, 1906- , U.S., mansl. On Jan. 17, 1937, a testimonial dinner honoring Barney Shapiro, president of the Garment Truckmen's Benevolent Association of New Jersey, was held at the Manhattan Opera House in New York City. The seven hundred guests quieted down when the orchestra stopped playing at around 11:30 p.m. as it was announced that Grover Whalen, head of the New York World's Fair Committee, would address the crowd. When Whalen began his speech, a voice on the other side of the room suddenly started singing *Pennies From Heaven*. Frank Cicero, a 33-year-old truck driver from Stamford, Conn., was having a good time and did not realize Whalen was speaking. Two men at a table nearby glared at Cicero, then moved to his table and a fight broke out. As the

orchestra began to play again, Whalen left the podium, and the brawl escalated into violence. Cicero dropped to the floor, stabbed. By the time Police Inspector Michael F. McDermott arrived with several officers and an ambulance crew six minutes later, he was dead. Counting heads, McDermott found that six persons had escaped the police cordon that went up around the crowd. Four were quickly eliminated as suspects. The remaining guests, Gabriel Klar and Joseph Berger, both of Brooklyn, were already known to the police. But they had already disappeared.

Two days later a call came in to the West 30th Street Police Station. Attorney Jerome Rosenhaus, speaking for his clients, said Klar and Berger were ready to surrender and would meet officers at the Governor Clinton Hotel. The suspects were booked on homicide charges, and tried that June. Rosenhaus claimed that neither had participated in the stabbing, saying the fight was "more of a drunken brawl than anything else." On June 10 the jury found both men Guilty of second-degree manslaughter. Each was sentenced to serve terms of seven and a half to ten years in Sing Sing prison.

REF.: *CBA*; Cohen, *One Hundred True Crime Stories*.

Berger, Meyer, 1893-1966, U.S., writer. As the staff writer for the New York *Times* who covered the nation's crime beat in the 1930s, Meyer Berger proved to be outstanding in his coverage of such gangsters as Dutch Schultz and Al Capone, particularly during Scarface's sensational tax evasion trial in 1931. For stories filed on Capone's mercurial trial, Berger was nominated for a Pulitzer Prize. He later wrote a fascinating report on the murder of Abe "Kid Twist" Reles, one-time member of Murder, Inc., who informed on his fellow murderers. Reles was being held in the Half Moon Hotel in Coney Island in 1942 while rattling off his non-stop testimony against Murder, Inc. killers. Suddenly, Kid Twist went out the window of his hotel room to his death. Berger, reporting the death, absurdly claimed by officials to be a suicide, stood in the window through which Reles went to his death and described the last landscape beheld by Kid Twist. Berger finally won a Pulitzer for his coverage of the mass killing spree committed by berserk WWII veteran Howard Unruh in Camden, N.J., in 1949. REF.: *CBA*.

Berger, Theodor, prom. 1904, Ger., rape-mur. Theodor Berger, a Berlin pimp, lived with his girlfriend Johanna Liebestruth in a dingy flat on the Ackerstrasse for six months. They had known each other for eighteen years, but Berger had always avoided a commitment. Then, after murdering 9-year-old Lucie Berlin, he agreed to marry Liebstruth to save his life.

The headless torso of the girl was found floating in the River Spree on June 11, 1904. The remains were identified as those of Lucie Berlin, who lived downstairs from Berger. When questioned by the police, Berger made a full confession. He said he assaulted Lucie after becoming aroused by the site of her bare legs while she stood on her head for him in the apartment. Johanna was in prison, serving a three-day sentence for prostitution. The pimp explained that he was desperate for a woman by the third day. When the young girl resisted his advances, Berger raped and strangled her and cut her body into small pieces.

Blood samples taken from the remains in the river matched those found in Liebestruth's room. Berger was charged with murder and tried at the Second District Court of Berlin on Dec. 12, 1904. On Dec. 23, Berger was found Guilty of murder. He was sentenced to fifteen years in prison.

REF.: Block, *Science vs Crime*; *CBA*; Thorwald, *Crime and Science*.

Berger, Victor L., 1860-1929, U.S., treas. First Socialist elected to the House of Representatives in 1911. He was found in violation of the Espionage Act in 1918, and sentenced to prison for 20 years on a charge of giving aid and comfort to the enemy during wartime. He was stripped of his house seat, the case went before the Supreme Court, and was overturned in 1921. REF.: *CBA*.

Bergman, Bernard (AKA: **Bernard Leifer**), 1911- , U.S., theft-fraud. A millionaire many times over and a renowned leader in politics and fund-raising, Rabbi Bernard Bergman was convicted of fraud and the theft of almost $3 million in a major nursing home scandal.

One of the most successful fund-raisers for Jewish causes, Bergman made contributions to politicians like Richard Nixon and New York Governor Nelson Rockefeller, and had distributed funds to charitable organizations for years. When Medicaid legislation in the early seventies made nursing homes a highly profitable business—the fastest growing industry in the U.S., outside of computers—Bergman led a criminal syndicate that profited from the elderly, making millions by misappropriating funds, collecting Social Security checks, and stealing money from the deceased and incapacitated. His syndicate had pulled in at least $2 million by the time federal and state agencies began to investigate. With a $25,000 inheritance and other funds never accounted for, Bergman bought buildings in New York and New Jersey. Patients from these homes were later hospitalized in dehydrated, infected states, sometimes in shock and suffering from neglect. Countless others died prematurely in these homes under conditions of squalor and disease. Rockefeller, whose administration was implicated in the corruption that allowed these circumstances to exist, suffered lasting damage to his political career because of these allegations of criminal neglect.

Another political figure implicated in Bergman's scandal was Albert Howard Blumenthal, an Albany Assembly majority leader who was charged in December 1975 with accepting a bribe from Bergman to help him obtain a license to open the Park Crescent Nursing Home. Indicted as an alleged perjurer at the peak of his political career, Blumenthal never regained his reputation, although the charges against him were abruptly dismissed by New York Supreme Court Justice Aloysius J. Melia on Apr. 13, 1976. Special State Prosecutor Charles Hynes also investigated Eugene Hollander, the second largest owner of suspect nursing homes after Bergman. Hollander pleaded guilty to charges of defrauding Medicaid of hundreds of thousands of dollars, promising to make restitution of more than a million dollars and to get out of the nursing home business. When Hollander was sentenced to spend five nights a week in jail for up to six months and was fined $10,000, Bergman pleaded guilty on condition that his wife and son would not be prosecuted. Bergman agreed to make restitution of a quarter of a million dollars when Hynes found out that the Rabbi had bilked Medicaid of $2.5 million, and Bergman finally began to talk, including information about his association with Blumenthal, which he had assiduously withheld. The 64-year-old Bergman was sentenced by Federal Judge Marvin Frankel to four months in prison, creating public outrage at the light treatment of a man who had caused pain, suffering, and even death to thousands. Bergman served his sentence from September 1976 to January 1977 at Allenwood Penitentiary, a minimum-security prison in northern Pennsylvania. See: **Nixon, Richard.**

REF.: *CBA;* Rose, *The World's Greatest Rip-Offs.*

Beria, Lavrenti Pavlovich (or **Beriya,** AKA: **Beria the Butcher**), 1899-1953, U.S.S.R., law enfor. off. A hardcore Bolshevik, Lavrenti Pavlovich Beria was a merciless policeman who headed the dreaded NKVD, the Communist secret police. He had started as a bureaucratic cog in the Bolshevik government of Georgia, becoming head of that state's security police from 1921 to 1931, hand-picked by Josef Stalin, a native of Georgia. Beria, at age eighteen, joined the Bolshevik party in 1917 and participated in the Revolution which brought Lenin, Stalin, and Trotsky to power. Beria served Stalin exclusively, acting as his "fixer" in that he murdered countless political figures Stalin believed to be secretly plotting his downfall. The brutal cop also falsified documents in 1935 to show that Stalin, not Lenin, was the chief architect of the 1917 Revolution.

In 1938 Stalin promoted Beria to chief of Internal Affairs or the NKVD, replacing its chief, Nicolai Yezhov, who vanished but was reportedly strangled to death by Beria. Through the ruthless Beria, Stalin purged thousands of his old comrades who were arrested by Beria's police goon squads, interrogated and tortured, and then were either shipped off to labor camps to die or secretly executed. During WWII, Beria was responsible for scores of atrocities dealing with his political prisoners. As the Germans advanced toward Minsk, Beria ordered the political detention camp in that city destroyed. His policemen machine gunned 10,000 prisoners to death, then blew up their remains with grenades and torched the entire camp so that none of these prisoners would fall into the hands of the Germans, and possibly escape to oppose him and his murderous chief, Stalin.

Lavrenti Beria, head of Stalin's secret police.

Following the war, Stalin enacted a calculated program to eliminate all of the old Bolshevik leaders still alive to consolidate his position as supreme dictator of Russia. Stalin used Beria to oust one Communist leader after another, but then Stalin became apprehensive of his killer cop. At one point, Stalin told his daughter Svetlana, who was staying with Beria and his wife, to leave immediately, saying to her on the phone: "I don't trust Beria. He could use you as a hostage in trying to force me from office." In 1951, Stalin, as he had with all other comrades, turned on his old enforcer, having Beria charged with conspiring with the West as an "imperialist agent." Beria was scheduled for trial, which promised to be another political showcase proving that only Josef Stalin was to be trusted with the safety and future of Communist Russia.

Before this occurred, however, Stalin himself suddenly died in March 1953. Beria was arrested and supposedly tried in secret, then, on Dec. 23, 1953, shot to death by a firing squad in Lubianka Prison. Another report has it that Beria resisted arrest when a special execution squad barged into his NKVD headquarters and that he and several of his top killer cops were shot to death in a firefight. "Beria the Butcher," was, nevertheless, eliminated by the Politburo members who so desperately feared his murderous ambitions. See: **Stalin, Josef.**

REF.: *CBA;* Crankshaw, *Khrushchev Remembers;* Deutscher, *Stalin;* Riasanovsky, *A History of Russia;* Stephan, *The Russian Fascists;* Tolstoy, *Stalin's Secret War;* Walsh, *Russia and the Soviet Union.*

Berkman, Alexander, 1870-1936, U.S., anarchy-attempt. mur. Alexander Berkman was born and raised by Jewish bourgeois parents in Russia, having been a member of the privileged class. He became a radical, then a devout anarchist, migrating to the U.S. in 1890 where he met anarchist leader Emma Goldman, who was then associated with German immigrant Johann Most. Most edited an anarchist weekly, *Freiheit,* a newspaper published in New York that explicitly urged open revolt against the government and advocated the overthrow of capitalism. It detailed to its radical readers how to use dynamite, nitroglycerine, and other explosives in the manufacture of bombs, which were to be used to blow up government and business buildings. Goldman carried on an intellectual and sexual ménage à trois with Most, a deformed man full of constant rage, and the bull-necked fanatic Berkman. These three radicals found their burning cause in the Homestead, Pa., strike by workers of the Carnegie Steel Company in June 1892.

Philanthropist and billionaire Andrew Carnegie could never abide unions and made no secret of it. He wanted to break the unions in his plants, and to that end he and his managers decided to confront the union by announcing a wage cut. Union members marched out. More than 300 non-union workers were hired at Homestead, protected by barbed wire fences and an army of Pinkerton detectives. When the situation threatened to turn violent, Carnegie went to Scotland to fish for salmon, leaving matters in the hands in his general manager, Henry Clay Frick, a hard-headed businessman who vowed to break the union control of Carnegie workers. He stated publicly that he had no intention of rehiring union workers and that union workers presently in Carnegie housing would be evicted unless they went back to work at non-union status. When Berkman heard this, he exploded, shouting to Most and Goldman: "I must go to Homestead!"

Berkman arrived in Homestead, Pa., on July 23, 1892, gaining entrance to Frick's office by stating that he was an agent of a New York employment fund ready to help Carnegie break the union. Frick had his back to the door through which Berkman entered. The Carnegie manager was conferring with John Leishman, vice president of the firm, and he half-turned in his chair to see Berkman suddenly rushing toward him with a pistol in his hand, firing as he came forward. Two bullets smashed into Frick's neck on either side. Leishman jumped up, knocking Berkman's arm upward so that the remaining bullets, fired in rapid succession, went into the ceiling. Leishman and the injured Frick both struggled to pin Berkman to the floor, but the anarchist managed to free one hand and draw a knife, which he plunged into Frick's side and legs seven times before Pinkerton guards rushed into the office and knocked him senseless.

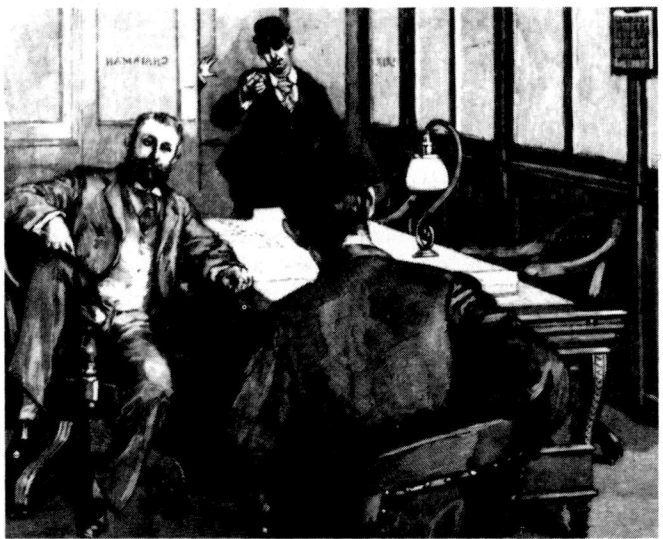

Alexander Berkman attempting to murder Henry Clay Frick.

Frick, who would survive the savage attempted murder, lay bleeding on the floor, half-conscious, whispering: "Let me see his face." He had barely gotten a glimpse of his assailant. When the attack was over Berkman was brought before him. Frick looked up, wiping the blood from his face, then said: "Why, I have never met this man before in my life." He turned to Leishman and said: "Why would this man want to take my life?"

"To take the life of capitalism," snorted Berkman, who struggled vainly to free himself from the grip of the burly guards. He was hurried from the room and, at his trial a short time later, he freely admitted his attack on Frick. He attempted to use his trial as a podium from which to spew forth his anarchistic views, but he was silenced and even prevented from committing suicide in court, which was to be his final political statement. Berkman was given sixteen years in prison. In New York, Johann Most openly denounced Berkman's attempted murder of Frick as "idiotic." He repeated his statements at a giant rally and while he was doing so, Emma Goldman, his one-time lover and political supporter, leaped to her feet, raced to the stage, and there flayed Most with a horsewhip while screaming that he was a traitor. The anarchist movement was shattered forever. From that moment on, American anarchism became nothing more than a small and disorganized force of political malcontents who effected no political change.

Berkman felt betrayed by his colleagues, and wrote angry letters about his confederates, chiefly Most, while he served fourteen years behind bars. Upon his release in 1906, he took up residence with his old lover Emma Goldman, the two of them publishing a small anarchist magazine, *Mother Earth*. In 1917, both vociferously opposed America's entry into WWI. They demonstrated before draft boards and were convicted of obstructing conscription in 1917, sent to prison that year, and released in 1919, only to be deported to their mother country, Russia, on Dec. 2, 1919. Goldman and Berkman were led up the gangplank of the ancient steamer *Buford* which the press had labelled "The Red Ark." Joining the involuntary expatriates were 247 other radicals who had been scooped up in the recent "Red Raids" ordered by U.S. Attorney General A. Mitchell Palmer. William J. Flynn, chief of the Bureau of Investigation, the precursor to the FBI, supervised the deportation proceedings. He thought it a cheery outing and was seen to laugh and joke with his agents, including a young lawyer who had recently joined the bureau, J. Edgar Hoover.

Flynn escorted Berkman on board ship and stood next to him, wagging his finger in his face and telling him never to come back to America or he would be thrown immediately into a cell. Berkman glared at the burly, red-faced Flynn, who suddenly laughed, pulled out a cigar and jammed this into the mouth of the startled Berkman, telling him: "Aww, don't be so glum, you're alive, aren't you? You better enjoy that cigar 'cause you won't get anywhere you're going."

A crowd of dignitaries from Washington, D.C., arrived just before the ship sailed and these politicians waved to Berkman and Goldman, one congressman shouting: "Merry Christmas, Emma!" Goldman thumbed her nose at him and Berkman, incensed at their treatment, screamed to those at dockside as the ship began to pull away: "We'll come back! And when we do, we'll get you bastards!" But Berkman and Goldman never came back. She died in Russia, venerated as a Communist saint. Berkman became disillusioned with communism and relocated to Paris where he haunted bistros and cafes, trying without success to interest strangers in his anarchistic movement. He committed suicide in France on June 28, 1936, little-remembered in America where once he thought to bring about a total revolution. See: **Flynn, William J.; Goldman, Emma; Hoover, J. Edgar; Palmer, A. Mitchell; Red Raids.**

REF.: Avrich, *The Russian Anarchists;* Bell, *Assassin!;* Berkman, *The Bolshevik Myth;* ____, *Now and After; CBA;* Drinnon, *Rebel in Paradise, A Biography of Emma Goldman;* Goldman, *Living My Life;* Laqueur, *Terrorism;* McLellan and Avery, *The Voices of Guns;* Nash, *Citizen Hoover;* Powers, *Secrecy and Power;* Reppetto, *The Blue Parade;* Toledano, *J. Edgar Hoover;* Ungar, *FBI;* Whitehead, *The FBI Story;* Wicker, *Investigating the FBI.*

Berkowitz, David (AKA: Son of Sam), 1953-   , U.S., mur. David Berkowitz, an unbalanced slayer who terrorized New York for more than a year as the "Son of Sam," was born June 1, 1953, the bastard son of a woman who gave him up for adoption. Throughout his miserable life, he had a deep sense of rejection. He grew up shy and terrorized by women. His stepfather, Nat Berkowitz, ran a hardware store in the Bronx and later retired to Florida. His stepson David remained in New York, living on Pine Street in Yonkers. He worked at odd jobs and his room was always littered with garbage. He could not sleep, he complained in letters to his stepfather, because the sound of trucks on the street and a neighbor's barking dog kept him up every night. He became paranoid, insisting that strangers on the street displayed hatred for him and spat at him as he walked past. "The girls call me ugly and they bother me the most," he wrote his stepfather.

On Christmas Eve 1975, Berkowitz attacked two girls with a knife at separate sites. The first girl frightened him off with her wild shrieking, but he plunged the blade into the lung of the second girl, a 15-year-old schoolgirl and left her for dead. She survived. Berkowitz waited seven months before striking again, this time on the night of July 29, 1976. He found two girls, Donna Lauria and Jody Valenti talking in the front seat of a car parked on Buhre Avenue. Calmly taking a gun from a brown paper bag, he fired five shots into them, killing Lauria and wounding Valenti in the leg. Police were baffled—the killer was a person without motive and was thought to be one who killed for thrills. Berkowitz shot and wounded Carl Denaro on the night of Oct. 23, firing through the rear window of his car as Denaro sat with his girlfriend, Rosemary Keenan, in front of a Flushing bar. On Nov. 26, two more girls, Joanne Lomino and Donna DeMasi, sitting on the stoop of a house in the Floral Park section of Queens, were approached by Berkowitz, who began to ask them directions, but stopped in mid-sentence. He pulled his gun from the brown bag and fired blindly, wounding both of them before fleeing. Lomino was paralyzed by a bullet that lodged next to her spine. Other bullets dug out of the wooden stairs of the stoop matched those in the Lauria-Valenti shooting.

Police still had no clue as to the identity of the killer, despite efforts to trace the gun. Then, on Jan. 30, 1977, Berkowitz spotted a young couple necking in a car in Ridgewood. He crept up on the car, took the gun out of the brown paper bag, and fired through the window, one of his bullets striking the head of Christine Freund, who collapsed into the arms of her boyfriend, John Diel. She was pronounced dead a few hours later. On Mar. 8, 1977, Berkowitz walked up to Virginia Voskerichian, an Armenian student he had never met, pulled out his gun, and fired point-blank into the girl's face, killing her as she walked down a Forest Hills street. Witnesses described Berkowitz as about five feet, ten inches tall, with black hair combed straight back. He was described by authorities as "a savage killer" and women were warned to go nowhere alone at night in the city. On Apr. 17, 1977, Berkowitz came upon Valentina Suriani and Alexander Esau, sitting in a parked car in the Bronx, only a short distance from where he had shot Lauria and Va-

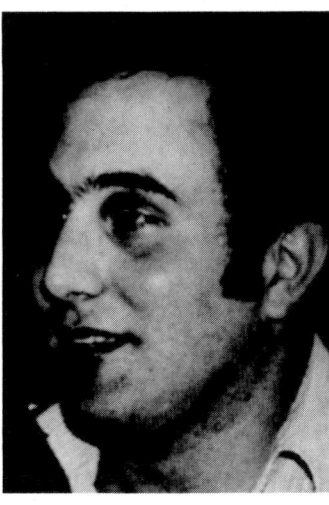

Mass murderer David Berkowitz.

lenti. He shot both of them at close range. Suriani was killed instantly and Esau, with three bullets in his head, died in the hospital some time later.

Following this shooting, a note was found addressed to Police Captain Joseph Borrelli, who had made several statements about the killer to the press. To Borrelli, Berkowitz wrote: "I am deeply hurt by your calling me a weman-hater (sic). I am not. But I am a monster. I am the Son of Sam. I am a little brat...I love to hunt, prowling the streets, looking for fair game...tasty meat...The weman of Queens are prettyist of all." In this letter, Berkowitz, seeming to emulate the letters Jack the Ripper sent to authorities almost a century earlier when prowling the streets of London, claimed that he had been brutalized by his father when he was a child and that he was later ordered by his father to go into the streets and murder. Berkowitz sent a similar letter to New York columnist Jimmy Breslin, who had been writing extensively about the slayer.

Berkowitz struck again on June 26, 1977, shooting Judy Placido and Salvatore Lupo as they sat in a car in a street in Queens. This time Berkowitz had fired quickly and his aim was poor; his victims were only slightly wounded. Berkowitz roamed the streets of the Bronx and Queens looking for victims but police seemed to be everywhere. He went to Brooklyn and, on July 31, 1977, found Stacy Moskowitz and Robert Violante sitting in a car. He fired four shots through the window, killing Moskowitz and blinding Violante. A woman walking her dog saw Berkowitz run to his car and leap in, speeding away. She told police that the car had a parking violation ticket in its windshield. Police checked to find that only four parking tickets had been issued that morning

and the carbon copy of one of these bore the registration number of David Berkowitz of Yonkers. Police Inspector Tim Dowd and others found the car parked near Berkowitz's apartment and waited for him to appear on Aug. 2, 1977. Berkowitz walked toward the car at 10:15 p.m. Dowd stepped forward and said: "Hello, David."

Berkowitz stood still for a moment, then his pudgy face crinkled with his peculiar beamish smile. "Inspector Dowd!" he said, recognizing the officer from his newspaper photos. "You finally got me." He surrendered meekly and later tried to mount a defense of insanity, but psychiatrists testified at Berkowitz's trial that he was faking. The sinister Son of Sam name was an invention of Berkowitz's, taken from his neighbor, Sam Carr. It was Carr's dog who had kept him up nights. He had shot the dog but the animal recovered and it was later claimed by Berkowitz that the dog spoke to him as one of the voices that told him to go out and murder. Berkowitz pleaded guilty to murder charges when he was arraigned on Aug. 23, 1977, and was never tried. He was sentenced to 365 years in prison with no hope of parole. His apartment was later looted by souvenir hunters.

REF.: Boar, *The World's Most Infamous Murders;* Cartel, *Serial Mass Murder;* CBA; Fox, *Mass Murder;* Godwin, *Murder U.S.A.;* Klausner, *Son of Sam;* Lubin, *Good Guys and Bad Guys;* Willeford, *Off The Wall;* Wilson, *Encyclopedia of Modern Murder.*

Berman, Dave (Davie, AKA: **Davie The Jew**), 1903-57, U.S., org. crime. Beginning his career in Sioux City, Iowa, Dave Berman had learned the principles of organized crime by the time he was fourteen years old.

A bright youth, Berman used charm to win the confidence of gamblers in the early 1900s, and was the leader of a gang of crime enforcing teenage toughs by the time he was fourteen, a gang used by gamblers to enforce their domain and collect gambling debts. At sixteen Berman was running his own bootleg operation, in charge of more than twenty distilleries and quickly taking over others until he was the biggest bootlegger in Iowa. He then joined the notorious Purple Gang which operated out of Detroit, supplying Al Capone's speakeasies with Canadian liquor.

Berman's next criminal move was into bank robbing and, by the age of eighteen, he was the leader of his own gang. He landed him in jail for the first time a few days before his twentieth birthday. Although there were several additional arrests for bank robbery, Berman avoided convictions repeatedly by making sure his brother Chickie Berman was in the lineup with him. The two looked so much alike that a positive identification was never made. On May 6, 1927, Berman went to New York City to orchestrate the kidnapping of Abraham Scharlin, a mob bootlegger. Arrested for the kidnapping after a shootout, Berman refused to talk despite weeks of questioning. He was sent to Sing Sing Prison to serve seven and a half years, famous for telling the detective who questioned him, "Hell, the worst I can get is life." On his release in 1934, Berman joined up with the gangsters who had founded Murder, Inc., and was rewarded for not having revealed his connections in the kidnapping by being given, at his request, gambling control of Minneapolis.

In 1944, Berman made the biggest move of his career, shifting to the undeveloped town of Las Vegas to help shape it into a phenomenally lucrative operation, along with famous mob leaders like Lucky Luciano, Meyer Lansky, and Frank Costello. He became known as the ambassador of gambling, working fourteen-hour days in his hotels. Then, in 1950-51, the Kefauver Senate Crime Investigating Committee began to investigate Berman, along with his wealthy associates. Though he was never asked to testify, his daughter Susan Berman, who later wrote a book, *Easy Street,* about her father, remembers kidnap drills and late night "vacations" to Los Angeles. In 1957, at the age of 54, Berman died of natural causes. See: **Purple Gang; Capone, Al; Murder, Inc.; Luciano, Lucky; Lansky, Meyer; Costello, Frank.** REF.: *CBA.*

Berman, Otto (AKA: **Abbadabba**), 1881-1935, U.S., org. crime. An accountant with an incredible capacity for figures, Otto Berman was Dutch Schultz's numbers (policy) controller, handling the books and records of the Dutchman's multimillion-dollar racket, which flourished chiefly in Harlem in the late 1920s and early 1930s. He reportedly received as much as $10,000 each week for his brilliant record keeping, reporting to the Dutchman that the numbers racket was delivering profits of about $500,000 each week. When Schultz, Berman, and two bodyguards, Abe Landau and Lulu Rosenkrantz, were killed on Oct. 23, 1935, in the Palace Chop House in Newark, N.J., the gangsters were in the process of going over Berman's weekly reports. See: **Schultz, Dutch.**

REF.: Campbell, *The Luciano Project; CBA;* Eisenberg and Landau, *Meyer Lansky;* Gosch and Hammer, *The Last Testament of Lucky Luciano;* Maas, *The Valachi Papers;* Peterson, *The Mob;* Pileggi, *Wiseguy;* Sann, *Kill The Dutchman!;* Thompson and Raymond, *Gang Rule in New York.*

Bermondt-Avalov, Pavel Mihailovich, prom. 1919, Rus., fraud. A thief credited with stealing an entire country, Pavel Bermondt-Avalov conceived of fraud on a grand scale.

Bermondt-Avalov was spying for Germany against the Russians in 1917 when, on his way through a forest, he came across a big ammunition depot. Walking over to the Russian sentry, he was challenged and threatened with a rifle. The spy responded by saying, "Idiot, put that down! Get out of my way, you ignorant peasant!" When his fury convinced the sentry that he was a Russian officer, Bermondt-Avalov marched into the camp, banging on the doors and demanding to see the officer in charge. Followed by a line of corporals, he then proceeded to make a tour of inspection of the camp. Once inside a shed full of artillery shells, he hid himself and used a wrench to set off the timing fuse of the shells, then marched out towards the camp entrance. As he passed the sentry again, the ammunition started exploding, and the entire camp was soon destroyed. Bermondt-Avalov's next move was to lead a group of mercenaries into the town of Jelgava, in Latvia, destroying many of its Russian defenders in a ruthless charge of his cavalry. Calling on the commander of the remaining German army faction, Captain Von der Goltz, he offered him his three hundred soldiers. When Goltz said it was money he needed, and that he already had 30,000 men of his own, Bermondt-Avalov promised to get it.

He left for Berlin and there convinced various banks that had mortgages in Latvian territory that it would be to their advantage to invest in keeping Latvia from the Russians to protect their investments. He returned to Goltz in 1919 with a million marks, and a plan to defraud him. In Vienna the Allies were considering how to partition postwar Europe. Bermondt-Avalov, hoping to alarm French premier Georges Clemenceau and U.S. President Woodrow Wilson into removing Goltz, sent a cable to the British telling them that German bankers had sent a million marks to Goltz, who had plans to take over Latvia. On his return to Latvia, Bermondt-Avalov informed Goltz that he had raised a quarter of a million marks, and that the remaining money would soon follow. Goltz, suspicious, sent a letter of inquiry to the Berlin banks. When he received a cable from the banks explaining the fraud, he ordered Bermondt-Avalov tortured. But when a telegram from Allied Headquarters arrived to inform Goltz that he was relieved of his command, and Bermondt-Avalov offered the beaten leader a quarter of a million marks for his army of mercenaries, Goltz signed the soldiers over to him. The new leader marched into Riga, Latvia's capital, and took the city in October 1919, effectively stealing the country from the Bolsheviks, and hoping not to be dislodged by the Allies. But when the French navy shelled Riga and Allied troops overwhelmed the city, he fled, living out the rest of his life as a celebrity for his proficient and grand-scale thievery.

REF.: *CBA;* Gibson, *The Fine Art of Swindling.*

Bernadotte af Wisborg, 1895-1948, Swed. (unsolv.) assass. Count Bernadotte af Wisborg, a descendent of French aristocracy, was the president of Sweden from 1946-48. A popular ruler, he was instrumental in bringing about the Arab-Israeli cease-fire in 1948. But, as United Nations mediator in the region, he was viewed with suspicion and mistrust by the radical Zionist LEHI faction operating outside the government established by David Ben-Gurion. They considered Bernadotte the unwitting tool of

the enemies of Israel, and killed him on Sept. 17, 1948, in Jerusalem.

The Ben-Gurion government feared reprisals. Various LEHI suspects were rounded up, but in the end neither the U.N., Sweden, nor any of the Western nations imposed sanctions, economic or otherwise, against Israel.

REF.: Bell, *Assassin!; CBA.*

Bernard VII (Comte d'Armagnac), d.1418, Fr., (unsolv.) mur. Constable of France who led Armagnac forces in a civil war against the Burgundians. He was in control of the government under Charles VI between 1413-18, and was murdered. REF.: *CBA.*

Bernard, Henry Peter (AKA: **Gyde, Henry Warwick**), and **Bernard, Marcus Edward Septimus,** and **Darby, Walter** (AKA: **Mr. Scott**), prom. 1900s, Brit., fraud. To invest one's money in the City of London Investment Corporation in 1904 was not necessarily a sound proposition, for the company's sole purpose was to collect money for the personal use of Henry Peter Bernard, Marcus Edward Septimus Bernard, and Walter Darby.

Despite having only £70 among them, Darby and the Bernard brothers started up the corporation which that soon had capital amounting to £100,000, of which roughly only £11 would be paid back to investors. These three bankrupt men also encouraged investments in the Welsh Slate Quarries and the North Wales Quarries Ltd., both existing only on paper and producing only £25 worth of slate for billiard tables and tombstones, yet yielding Gyde and Darby £12,000.

The authorities finally caught up with the con artists, though Darby escaped for a year before his arrest in Liverpool. It took two trials at the Old Bailey to convict the Bernards, the first ending in a hung jury, the second, in November 1908, finding the two Guilty after just fifteen minutes of deliberation, for which Marcus Bernard received a year in prison, and his brother five years penal servitude. Both collected about £55,000 in four years of swindles.

Darby was also found Guilty at his trial in March 1909 at the Old Bailey. He, too, was involved in prior swindles, making £60,000 over a two-year period in a debt-collecting scheme. At Darby's trial it was learned that Henry Bernard was the same Bernard in an earlier scheme known as the Brinsmead case. REF.: *CBA.*

Bernard, Mountague, 1820-82, Brit., lawyer. First professor of international law at Oxford from 1859-74. REF.: *CBA.*

Bernardy, Sigoyer de (Marquis de Bernardy), d.1947, Fr., mur. Though placed in an insane asylum during the 1930s—once for claiming to have eaten a missing man whose identification papers were found in his home—Sigoyer de Bernardy managed to obtain his release and became wealthy during WWII by opening a restaurant selling wholesale liquor to German soldiers.

De Bernardy, who called himself a marquis, married Janine Kergot and they had two children. He also had one child by the nursemaid of his children, Irène Lebeau, for which his wife left him in 1944. The court ordered De Bernardy to pay 10,000 francs a month, but an attempt to collect this alimony one month proved to be fatal for Kergot, who disappeared without a trace after going to his home to inquire about the money.

Her disappearance would have remained a mystery if not for letters written by De Bernardy to Lebeau while he was imprisoned after the war for collaborating with the enemy. One letter alluded to a cask which held clothing and jewelry belonging to the missing woman, while another spoke of a red armchair which Lebeau said was the chair Kergot was sitting on when De Bernardy strangled her. De Bernardy claimed he was innocent, stating he had only helped Lebeau conceal the body after she had shot Kergot.

The missing woman's body was discovered in the wine cellar of De Bernardy's warehouse in the Rue de Nuits, but no bullet wound was found. At the joint trial of De Bernardy and Lebeau on Dec. 23, 1946, Lebeau was acquitted but De Bernardy was sentenced to death and guillotined in June 1947.

REF.: *CBA;* Wilson, *Encyclopedia of Murder.*

Bernauer, Agnes, d.1435, Ger., witchcraft. Arrested for witchcraft and drowned in the Danube under orders from Ernest, Duke of Bavaria-Munich after it was revealed that she married his son Albert. REF.: *CBA.*

Berner, John F., 1926- , U.S., law enfor. off. After beginning his career with the St. Louis Police Department as a switchboard operator in February 1943, John F. Berner graduated first in his class from the Police Academy in 1949 and attended Southern Police Institute. He also served as Supervisor of Recruit Training, In-Service Training Supervisor, and Acting Director of Police Academy, as well as the department's Chief of Police from July 24, 1982 to Sept. 28, 1985. REF.: *CBA.*

Berner, Mary, b.c.1898, U.S., (wrong. convict.) fraud. Berner quit her job at an insurance company about the same time that a number of the company's checks disappeared. Fortunately, Emma Lutz later confessed to the crimes for which Mary Berner was wrongly convicted.

A year and a half prior to her arrest in December 1928, a woman fitting Berner's description cashed fraudulent checks, always for amounts less than $50, at approximately sixty banks in the Chicago area. Since Berner had left her job at the same time as some checks were found missing and because she had been positively identified by witnesses, a grand jury found her Guilty. She refused to plead, but the judge entered the guilty plea for her and sentenced her to a year's probation.

Berner never finished her sentence, for in April 1929, Lutz confessed to the charges against Berner and was then tried, convicted, and sentenced to one year in prison.

REF.: Borchard, *Convicting the Innocent; CBA.*

Berner, Mrs. Stewart, prom. 20th Cent., U.S., (unsolv.) mur. When the remains of four bodies were taken from the ruins of the burned-down home of Stewart Berner the first three were identified as that of his wife, Mrs. Stewart Berner, and their two children, but the fourth was not identified as that of Stewart Berner.

Though Stewart was tall and broad, the torso of the corpse thought to be his was considerably smaller and neither Stewart's ring nor his tie-pin were found on it. Investigation into the possible murder and arson revealed that the Berners were not on the best of terms, and that Stewart had told the hostess of Mrs. Berner's bridge club that his wife would not be present the night before the fire, and had informed their laundry lady not to show up the day before as his wife was out of town.

Further inquiry showed that Stewart was having difficulties at work and faced dismissal from his job at the post office and possible imprisonment. The search for Stewart proved fruitless as he disappeared without a trace, thus leaving the question unanswered as to whether he was guilty of murder.

REF.: *CBA;* Whitelaw, *Corpus Delicti.*

Berneri, Camillo, d.1937, Spain, assass. As the acknowledged spiritual leader of Italian anarchism, Camillo Berneri lived in Barcelona, Spain, while Benito Mussolini was in power in Italy. Berneri had been strongly outspoken against the Spanish policy of Soviet leader Joseph Stalin, whose guards, the PSUC, murdered Berneri and tossed his body into a gutter where it was found on May 6, 1937, the morning after his abduction. George Mink, also known as Alfred Herz, an American working for the Soviet Union, was publicly charged by anarchists with organizing the assassination.

REF.: *CBA;* Dewar, *Assassins At Large.*

Bernhardt, R. Jack, 1940- , U.S., fraud. After only seventeen days on the job, stockbroker R. Jack Bernhardt caused the bankruptcy of a 51-year-old brokerage firm and landed himself a ten-year prison sentence.

The Securities and Exchange Commission charged Bernhardt with manipulating stocks, practicing unauthorized trade of his clients' stock, and lying to his clients in an $8 million fraud from June 1976 to February 1977. The Chicago broker had purchased and sold more than 1.3 million shares of Olympia Brewing Company and Stange Company stock without the permission of his customers, while inducing others to buy the stock because of possible takeovers which never happened. He was found Guilty by a jury on twelve counts of securities fraud and nine counts of mail fraud in October 1982.

U.S. District Court judge, Charles P. Kocoras sentenced Bernhardt to ten years' imprisonment, berating the defendant for twenty minutes, saying, "Your weapon in this case was a simple trust, and you abused that trust." REF.: *CBA.*

Bernstein, Charles, b.c.1897, U.S., (wrong. convict.) rob.-mur. At the age of eighteen Bernstein decided to give up a criminal career after spending fourteen months at the Elmira Reformatory for stealing from a New York drugstore. Crime, however, would follow Charles Bernstein, for the conviction remained on his record and eventually led to his conviction for bank robbery and murder, neither of which he committed.

While Bernstein was on a business trip to St. Paul, Minn., a bank robbery was committed the same day in Hopkins, a town just west of the state capital. Police discovered upon looking into hotel guest lists that Bernstein had a prior conviction, so in February 1919, he was arrested in New York and returned to Minnesota for trial. Though many eyewitnesses stated that Bernstein could not have been the robber, he was found Guilty and sentenced to five to forty years in prison. He served nine years at the state prison in Stillwater before his parole in 1928 at the urging of prosecutor Floyd B. Olson, who would later become the state's governor.

Four years later, the unbelievable happened. Bernstein was charged with killing a gambler named Milton W. "Milsie" Henry in Washington, D.C., on Apr. 21, 1932. Henry was shot with five bullets from a sawed-off shotgun while sitting in his car. The man pulling the trigger was observed by government attorney Carroll Rhodes just after the shooting, and the day before by laundry driver James Hughes. Again, though witnesses for the defense outnumbered those for the prosecution, Bernstein lost the trial. He was found Guilty on Mar. 24, 1933, and sentenced to death by electrocution on Oct. 7.

An investigation was opened when it was learned that the testimony of the prosecution's eyewitnesses was suspect. Rhodes had poor eyesight and would have had to look through a tree and a distance of seventy feet to see the killer, if he had even looked out his window—which he told a co-worker he had not—while Hughes apparently had made up his story. Eventually President Franklin D. Roosevelt commuted Bernstein's sentence to life in prison on May 28, 1935, twelve days prior to Bernstein's eighth execution date. On June 13, 1940, Roosevelt commuted the sentence further to time served already, and a full and unconditional pardon was granted by President Harry S. Truman on Apr. 30, 1945.

REF.: *CBA;* Radin, *Innocents.*

Beron, Leon, See: **Morrison, Steinie.**

Berrien, John MacPherson, 1781-1856, U.S., jur. Member of Congress from 1824-29, 1841-45, and 1847-52. He was nominated by President Andrew Jackson to serve as attorney general from 1829-31, and appointed justice of the Georgia Supreme Court in 1845. In 1852, he joined the Know-Nothing Party, a coalition of anti-Catholics opposed to foreign immigration and the abolition of slavery. REF.: *CBA.*

Berrigan, Rev. Daniel J., 1921- , and **Berrigan, Philip F.,** 1923- , U.S. burg.-consp. Arrested a number of times for protests against nuclear weapons and for anti-war demonstrations, the Reverend Daniel J. Berrigan and his brother Philip F. Berrigan, were charged with burglary following one such incident.

After breaking into the General Electric Space Division plant in King of Prussia, Pa., on Sept. 9, 1980, the Berrigan brothers, along with six others, smashed the nose cones of two Minuteman missiles with hammers and then splashed their own blood on documents and tools, an act similar to Philip's splashing blood on the Pentagon building on Dec. 28, 1976, for which he served fifty-seven days in jail. All eight members of the group, which called itself the "Plowshares Eight" after the slogan "Swords to Plowshares" of the Atlantic Life Community peace network, were convicted Mar. 6, 1981, of burglary, conspiracy, and public mischief. The brothers were sentenced to three- to ten-years' imprisonment.

The Berrigans have also visited Ulster, Northern Ire., to lend support to prisoners at Long Kesh and Armagh prisons who are protesting the British government's refusal to recognize them as political prisoners for the crimes they have committed.

Philip Berrigan has been excommunicated from the Catholic Church for marrying. His wife, Elizabeth McAlister, received a prison sentence on July 17, 1984, of two to three years for splashing blood and pounding with a hammer on a B-52 bomber at Griffies Air Force Base in New York on June 13, 1984.

REF.: *CBA*; Demaris, *The Director*; Nash, *Citizen Hoover*; Powers, *Secrecy and Power*; Toledano, *J. Edgar Hoover*.

Berry, Charles Ferdinand Duc de (Charles Ferdinand de Bourbon), 1778-1820, Fr., prince, assass. As the youngest son of King Louis XVIII's brother, Charles X the Comte d'Artois, the Duc de Berry appeared destined to continue the Bourbon dynasty in France as his older brother, the Duc d'Angoulême, had had no children after twenty years of marriage. De Berry was viewed by Royalists as the hope for the future of the monarchy, that is, until his assassination.

The man who would dash the hopes of the Royalists was a 32-year-old political fanatic named Jean Pierre Louvel, who had been planning the destruction of the Bourbons ever since their return from exile in 1814, only postponing his attempt on the king's life at that time because of the warm reception the monarch received at Calais. Louvel obtained work at the royal stables of Versailles in order to carry out his plan against the monarchy by first killing de Berry, whom he saw as the champion of Royalist interests. By carefully stalking his victim, Louvell eventually got his chance.

The assassinated Duc de Berry.

After escorting his pregnant wife, who was feeling ill, to their carriage during an evening at the opera, de Berry turned to go back to the theater when his assailant struck the duke in his right side with a dagger, deeply implanting the weapon. The wound Louvell gave de Berry on Feb. 13, 1820, caused his death early the next morning, but before dying the duke asked the king to pardon his attacker, saddened by the fact that a Frenchman had committed the act. Nevertheless, Louvell was condemned to die after pleading guilty and was guillotined on June 7, 1820.

REF.: *CBA*; Johnson, *Famous Assassinations of History*.

Berry, Charles Henry, 1823-1900, U.S., jur. Attorney general of the Minnesota Territory from 1858-60. He was appointed judge of the territorial court of Idaho in 1888 by President Grover Cleveland. REF.: *CBA*.

Berry, Henri (Duc de Bordeaux, Comte de Chambord), prom. 18th Cent., Fr., assass. Member of the Berry ruling house of central France. He was killed in Paris. REF.: *CBA*.

Berry, James, 1852-1913, Brit., execut. James Berry was born in Heckmondwike, Yorkshire, on Feb. 6, 1852, the son of a well-educated wool merchant. He later worked as a policeman, shopkeeper, lecturer, preacher, and farmer, mostly while he was the official hangman of England and Ireland. He became a policeman at West Riding just after reaching manhood and was seriously wounded in a gang fight, which caused him to cease his duties as a constable. He had met and befriended William Marwood, Britain's official hangman, who showed him the use of his ropes and the methods he employed in executing condemned prisoners. He had also witnessed several hangings performed by William Calcraft, another official executioner. Upon Marwood's

death in 1884, Berry applied for his job and became the official hangman until 1892. He was a sensitive man who was deeply religious and his position caused him considerable anxiety. Berry later stated that he would pray for the souls of those he was about to hang the night before an execution, kneeling for hours in the shadow of the gallows.

Berry took his job seriously and sought to improve the executions he had to perform, making sure the condemned person suffered little. He was the first hangman to establish a system of graduated drops, according to the weight of the condemned person, to ensure that the prisoner's neck was broken instantly. Berry's system was inaugurated shortly after one of his first executions, that of Henry Devlin, who strangled to death horribly because the rope failed to break his neck when he fell through the trap. The executioner dispatched more than 200 condemned prisoners. One of his most nerve-wracking chores was to hang Walter Wood, who was convicted of murdering his wife. Berry and

British executioner James Berry.

Wood had gone to school together and the executioner wept as he sent his old friend through the trap.

The most sensational hanging—or near-hanging—performed by Berry was that of 19-year-old John Lee in February 1885. Three times Lee was placed on the trapdoor of the gallows and Berry yanked at the lever which would release the door but three times the door failed to open. Berry and two assistants jumped up and down on the door but it failed to open while the prisoner stood on it. When Lee was removed the trapdoor sprung open without pressure. This unnerving procedure went on for half an hour but Lee, who had staunchly maintained his innocence, proved to be "the man they could not hang." The warden at Exeter Jail ordered a stop to Lee's execution and he was later reprieved and subsequently freed.

Berry underwent numerous nerve-shattering experiences. When sailing to Ireland to hang convicted killers he had to be protected by guards, as all English hangmen were hated and threatened with death. Before a man named Conway was to be hanged in Liverpool, the condemned man tried to commit suicide by slitting his throat and he was dragged, half-dead, to Berry's rope and hanged. This grisly execution so upset Berry that he resigned his post and became a preacher, lecturing against capital punishment and later stating that he was convinced that he had hanged many innocent persons. See: **Devlin, Henry; Lee, John**.

REF.: Atholl, *The Reluctant Hangman*; ____, *Shadow of the Gallows*; Brock, *A Casebook of Crime*; *CBA*; Duff, *A New Handbook on Hanging*; Hibbert, *The Roots of Evil*; Laurence, *A History of Capital Punishment*; Logan, *Rope, Knife and Chair*; Potter, *The Art of Hanging*; Yeats and Brown, *Escape*.

Berry, John, prom. 1756, and **Egan, James**, d.1756, and **Macdaniel, Stephen**, prom. 1756, and **Salmon, James**, prom. 1756, and **Blee, Mr.**, prom. 1756, Brit., fraud-consp. The profession of thief-taker was like that of a bounty hunter. It often attracted savage, burly men who were themselves on the fringes of the law. John Berry of Hatton Garden was such a man. In 1749 he assembled a gang of thief-takers who, if business was slow, would entice honest men into committing crimes and then have them arrested for the reward money. Berry's fellow thief-takers included Stephen Macdaniel, who kept an inn at Holborn; James Egan, a shoemaker; and James Salmon, who made leather breeches. His other accomplice was a man named Blee, a servant hired to procure likely victims.

The inhabitants of Islington, near London, had posted a reward of £20 for the apprehension of any highwayman perpetrating a crime in the region. Blee located two easy marks for their thief-taking scheme: John Ellis and Peter Kelly, two local pickpockets. Blee induced the two to join a robbery attempt of Salmon. Their resistance was broken down by liquor and the promises of greater rewards to come.

In a planned scene, Blee and his two young friends watched their ostensible victim, John Salmon, drinking in a public house. They followed the drunk Salmon, confronted him at gunpoint, took his breeches, and told Kelly and Ellis that they could sell the breeches to James Egan, who would pay a princely sum for such an item. Egan and Macdaniel then finished the ruse by getting a warrant for the two men's arrest.

When Kelly's things were searched a knife was found. Satisfied that the evidence was convincing, a magistrate committed the two thieves to a jail in Maidstone. While in transit to that city, the prisoners told the sheriff how they had been tricked. Knowing that Blee and Macdaniel were connected in some way, he ordered their arrest. During the hearing, Blee confessed the whole story, supplying minute details that implicated the others.

An indictment was brought against all four, and a verdict of Guilty was passed at the Old Bailey sessions. Since no one in the affair was truly innocent, the judge spared their lives. The men were sentenced to stand in pillories at various locations throughout London. Afterward, all the prisoners were to be locked up inside Newgate for seven years, but Egan never made it.

On Mar. 5, 1756, Salmon and Egan were brought into the open and their heads and arms were locked into the wooden devices. No one, including the constable, had anticipated the anger of the townspeople toward these men. Egan and Salmon were pelted with stones, dead dogs, potatoes, and other items as they stood helpless in the stocks. The authorities tried to intervene but, fearing injury, stood aside and let the crowd have its way with the malefactors. A sharp stone struck Egan on the head, killing him instantly. At this point, the sheriff cancelled the pillory for the other men and jailed them, extending their sentences to compensate for the time they would not be spending on public display. All of them died while in prison.
REF.: *CBA; Newgate Calendar.*

Berryer, Pierre Nicolas, 1757-1841, Fr., lawyer. Legal counsel for Marshal Michel Ney when he was tried for treason in 1815. REF.: *CBA.*

Berta, Charles, prom. 1920s-30s, U.S., rob. Charles Berta was a fearless gunman who specialized in the robbing of postal stations. He was apprehended several times but managed to escape a number of prisons. When finally recaptured, he was labeled an incorrigible recidivist and shipped to Alcatraz with the first trainload of public enemies in 1934. Once on the Rock, however, he adjusted to prison life and became a model prisoner, one of the few who was released directly from Alcatraz in 1949. He had spent more than twenty-four years, on and off, behind bars and was so nervous about entering the free world that he had to be sedated before he was put into the police launch and taken to San Francisco. Once off the island, Berta became a bartender in San Francisco and never again got mixed up in crime. See: **Alcatraz.**
REF.: *CBA; Heaney, Inside the Walls of Alcatraz.*

Bertani, Agostino, 1812-86, Italy, consp. Physician and revolutionary active in the Milan revolt in 1848. He was secretary general of Naples under Garibaldi and member of parliament from 1861-86. He was the spokesman for the radical left-wing factions and published the party's newspaper *La Riforma* (1866). REF.: *CBA.*

Bertelsman, William Odis, 1936- , U.S., jur. Judge of the court of the Eastern District of Kentucky, appointed by President Jimmy Carter in 1979. Authored many scholarly legal papers, including *Libel and Public Men* (1966). REF.: *CBA.*

Berthelier, Philibert, c.1465-1519, Switz., treas. Led the Eidguenot faction in their struggle to remain independent from Geneva and the rule of Charles III, Duke of Savoy. After organizing a splinter group known as Enfants de Geneve in 1515, he was executed by John, Bishop of Geneva, a Savoy puppet. REF.: *CBA.*

Berthier, Emile (AKA: Mad Emile), prom. 1926, Brit., mur. For killing rival French gang leader "Charles the Acrobat" Baladda on Apr. 5, 1926, Emile Berthier was found Guilty but insane a few weeks later at the Old Bailey. Eventually he was transferred into the hands of the French government. This was the first murder case solved by Scotland Yard detective Robert Fabian, whose investigation led to the capture of Berthier, who had shot Baladda in the stomach at the Cochon Club.
REF.: *CBA;* Fabian, *Fabian of the Yard.*

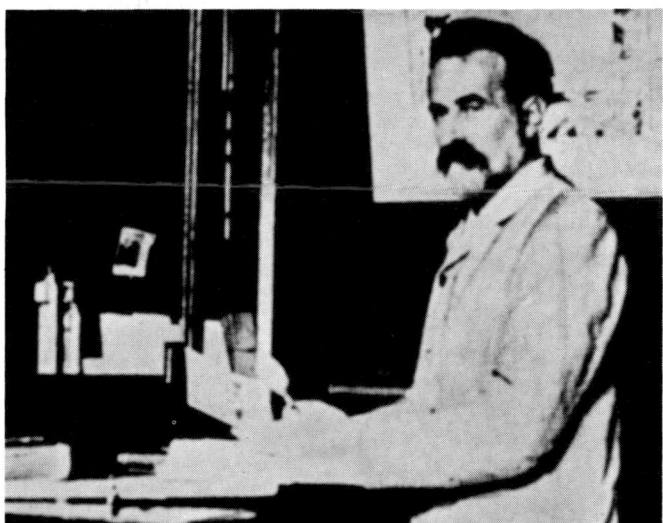

Alphonse Bertillon at the beginning of his spectacular career.

Bertillon, Alphonse, 1853-1914, Fr., criminol. The son of Louis Adolphe Bertillon, Alphonse Bertillon is generally credited with being the creator of what is now generally termed forensic science. His greatest triumph was the establishment of the first universally used criminal identification system, known as the Bertillon Anthropometric System, or *bertillonage.* Bertillon was anything but an inspiring individual. He was sickly as a child and his constitution continued to be frail into adulthood. He also had a sour disposition and was pedantic. Bertillon began his career as a junior filing clerk in the Paris Préfecture of Police where he began to develop a theory not wholly his own, that of creating an exact system of measurements, or anthropometry, which means "man measurements." It was Bertillon's deep-seated belief that any adult could be identified if exact measurements were recorded of that person and later used to compare with measurements taken of a criminal suspect. In 1879, Bertillon drafted a proposal to adopt this ID system and submitted it to the Prefect of Police, Louis Andrieux. It was rejected and Bertillon was told to stop daydreaming and pay attention to his filing chores.

The novice forensic scientist persisted, however, and his break came when, using his measurement system, Bertillon identified a criminal named Martin who had been using the alias of Dupont. The French police slowly adopted Bertillon's measurement system and, in 1892, Bertillon scored a major triumph by identifying one of the most sought-after terrorists on the continent, Claudius Francois Koenigstein, who had been arrested and booked under the name of Ravachol. By pinpointing these two identities as one and the same, Bertillon's ID system was hailed as foolproof and almost universally adopted by most governments as *the* system employed by police. Other than the French, the most ardent followers of *bertillonage* were Italy, Germany, Spain, Russia, and Austria. The American police adopted this system but put it slowly into police and prison procedure, while the British were reluctant to embrace *bertillonage,* pointing out that it required

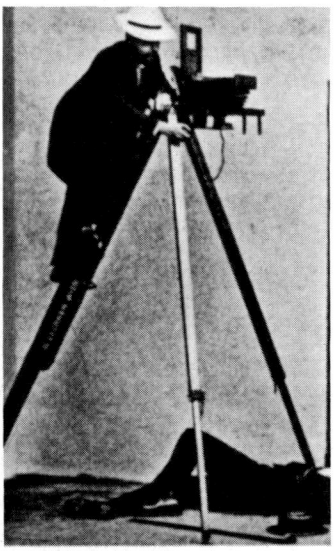

Alphonse Bertillon, and with his camera.

Bertillon photo of a murder scene.

Bertillon photo/measurements of Ravachol.

Bertillon's police photo of himself.

Bertillon being elaborately measured.

A cartoon mocking *bertillonage.*

endless measuring procedures and paperwork. The British looked more optimistically at the development of fingerprinting for the best ID system, although it was untried at the time of Bertillon's system.

Despite challenges from police and discrepancies between known felons who often had the same measurements, Bertillon's *complete* measurement system was hailed as foolproof if all of Bertillon's directives were followed. His fourteen measurements included the circumference of the head and chest, and the length of the arms, legs, feet, fingers, nose, ears, and so on. In addition, Bertillon instituted a system of photographing criminals, which is still employed to this day, in which he insisted that the suspect be photographed with a complete profile and a full head shot, the same distance from the camera, with the same amount of light, and kept in a fixed position which would correspond to the computation of Bertillon's measurement requirements. Bertillon made hundreds of thousands of files with specific measurements of all known criminals and an equal number of photographs taken in France and in other countries.

Having struggled long to establish his ID system, Bertillon was naturally the most severe critic of the newly proposed fingerprint ID system, claiming that it was an inexact science, but he, of course, was proven wrong and lived long enough to see fingerprinting completely replace *bertillonage*. He grudgingly admitted that there was some use to fingerprinting when stating: "My measurements are surer than any fingerprint pattern, but the criminal does not leave his measurements at the scene of the crime." Bertillon did not discredit fingerprinting altogether. In fact, in 1902, he helped the cause of fingerprinting by identifying, with fingerprints alone, a much-wanted felon, Henri Leon Scheffer.

Bertillon was vain to the point of believing himself an expert in all fields of forensic science, claiming that he was also a handwriting expert, and, as such, examined the writings of Alfred Dreyfus, the accused French Army captain. He stated that Dreyfus, indeed, had written a notorious document in which he described French fortifications and equipment, and delivered this to the German government. Dreyfus was convicted and sent to Devil's Island, wrongly convicted on the so-called "evidence" provided by Bertillon. When he was later proved innocent, Bertillon was held in disrepute by many of his fellow criminologists.

By the turn of the century, *bertillonage* began to lose ground to fingerprinting with Bertillon's early advocates going over to "the other side," so to speak. One of Italy's leading criminologists, Professor Ottolenghi, who had championed *bertillonage*, began to endorse the universal use of fingerprinting, embracing the theories and procedures advanced by fingerprinting pioneers Edward Henry, Thomas Galton, Henry Faulds, William Herschel, and, most notably, Juan Vucetich. By early 1913, Bertillon had fallen seriously ill, suffering from incurable pernicious anemia. His doctors told him he would die but Bertillon believed that when he did, his precious ID

Bertillon's first measuring instruments.

system would die with him. For almost a year, he was in terrible physical discomfort, feeling cold at all times, covering himself with blankets and staying in a single Paris room where he kept a stove at white heat around the clock. Bertillon was in a state of constant exhaustion and was losing his sight.

Bertillon photograph of felon Henri-Leon Scheffer, the first man in Europe to be convicted on fingerprint evidence alone.

From all over the world Bertillon received reports that countries were abandoning *bertillonage* for fingerprinting and he became enraged when learning that South American criminologist Juan Vucetich had stated: "I can assure you that in all the years during which we applied the anthropometric system, in spite of all our care, we were unable to prove the indentity of a single person by measurements." Vucetich later visited Bertillon at his home in Paris. Bertillon opened his door and Vucetich put forth his hand. Bertillon said: "Sir, you have tried to do me a great deal of harm!" He slammed the door in Vucetich's face. Bertillon continued to drag himself to his office where he supervised his workers from a chaise longue. He was dying and the French government, which had given him the red ribbon of the Legion of Honor for his creation of *bertillonage*, now wished to confer upon him the rosette that went with it, the additional decoration much desired by Bertillon.

A government representative arrived to tell him that France wished to award him the rosette, but there was one small condition. He must admit his error in judgment regarding the handwriting of Captain Alfred Dreyfus, who had long since been vindicated and had become a hero of the Republic. The obstinate Bertillon shouted from his deathbed: "No! Never! Never!" The rosette was denied him and, wracked with pain and gone blind, Alphonse Bertillon died on Feb. 13, 1914. By that time *bertillonage* was already a thing of the past. See: **Faulds, Henry; Galton, Thomas; Henry, Edward; Herschel, William; Ravachol; Vucetich, Juan.**

REF.: Almados, *Bertillon et Vucetich;* Brookes, *Murder in Fact and Fiction; CBA;* Griffiths, *Mysteries of the Police and Crime;* Irving, *Studies of French Criminals of the Nineteenth Century;* Kingston, *A Gallery of Rogues;* Mitchell, *Science and the Criminal;* Morain, *The Underworld of Paris;* Reiss, *Portrait Parlé;* Reppetto, *The Blue Parade;* Rhodes, *Alphonse Bertillon, Father of Scientific Detection;* Scott, *The Concise Encyclopedia of Crime and Criminals;* Stockis, *Alphonse Bertillon;* Thomson, *The Story of Scotland Yard;* Thorwald, *The Century of the Detective;* ____, *Crime and Science;* Whitehead, *The FBI Story;* Williams, *Heyday for Assassins;* Woodhall, *Secrets of Scotland Yard.*

Bertin, Pierre, See: **Buffalo Bill House.**

Bertram, Charles Julius, 1723-65, Den., fraud. As an English teacher at the Danish Royal Naval Academy in Copenhagen, Charles Julius Bertram reputedly discovered a genuine Fourteenth Century manuscript in 1747. The manuscript, *De Situ Britanniae,* gave a description of Britain during the Roman Empire and included an ancient map, all of which mislead historians for 119 years.

Dr. William Stukeley, the London Society of Antiquaries' first secretary, espoused the authenticity of the document Bertram claimed was written by Richard of Cirencester and that he discovered in an archive. Belief in the hoax greatly affected historical writing—various maps were altered and a work by Bertram supplanted the *Itinerarium* by Antonus—and it was not until 1866 that exposure of the fake was revealed.

REF.: *CBA;* MacDougall, *Hoaxes.*

Bertrams, Carl H., 1956- , and **Shelhamer, Richard K.,** 1949- , and **Ayling, George Y.,** 1951- , U.S., fraud. Salesmen at the Chicago office of First Commodities Corporation of Boston were told not to "worry about the customers. Just sell and get the money in here," according to one broker. It was a tactic that eventually brought in $3.2 million before the company folded in 1987 due to FBI investigations and investor lawsuits.

Carl H. Bertrams, Richard K. Shelhamer, and George Y. Ayling pled guilty on Dec. 15, 1988, to two counts of mail fraud as part of a plea-bargaining agreement in which the salemen would provide further information regarding the swindle. High-pressure sales pitches were made by the three, and others, which included false statements of the effects Russian troop movements would have on commodities, and misleading clients into believing the corporation had "a multi-million dollar research department, when, in fact, Bertrams knew...the research department was composed of one person."

Bertrams and Shelhamer each received five years' probation and a sixty-day sentence in a halfway house which ended June 30, 1989, while Ayling was sentenced only to five years' probation. REF.: *CBA.*

Bertrand, Delphine, b.c.1890, U.S., (wrong. convict.) mur. Because she did not want to have her sexual wantonness made public, Bertrand confessed to a murder she did not commit.

Delphine Bertrand told police that on the night her supposed fiancé, James Streeto, was killed—Dec. 24, 1943—she was tied up in a bedroom during the beating and stabbing. Her story, however, did not seem plausible. The marks on her wrist were not those of an alleged three-hour struggle to free herself, a bullet was found under the left armpit of Streeto, though no gunshot was mentioned, and an autopsy revealed he had eaten a large meal, not a light one as Bertrand claimed.

At that point, her story changed completely as she confessed to murdering Streeto after the two had fought over his refusal to marry her, though she still failed to mention the bullet wound. She pled guilty to a charge of manslaughter on Apr. 11, 1944, and was sentenced to from ten to fifteen years at the women's correctional facility in Niantic, Conn.

Two years later, the case that police Captain Leo Carroll thought was unfinished finally ended. Carroll learned that three men were in the cottage the night of the murder, two of them admitting it after their arrest and pleading guilty in July 1946. The third man had been in the bedroom with Bertrand, though not as a captor but as a lover. Bertrand, who was released, said she would rather have been known as a murderer than a loose woman. She was subsequently deported to her native Canada when news of the illegal alien's scandal spread.

REF.: *CBA;* Radin, *The Innocents.*

Bertrand, Francois, prom. 1849, Case of, Fr., graverobbing. In 1849, 24-year-old French army sergeant Francois Bertrand, was caught red-handed rifling fresh graves at the Picpus Cemetery in Paris and was placed under arrest. Bertrand was tried for graverobbing and molesting corpses, answering charges with a shocking confession in which he lucidly admitted engaging in this practice for many years. Bertrand detailed his many perversions since childhood when, at the age of nine, he began to imagine himself in a room of voluptuous adult women whom he ravished as corpses. As a young man he carried on normal sexual relationships with women and was considered a bit of a Don Juan, but was always formally correct and polite when in the company of females. It was only when passing cemeteries that he underwent a type of sexual seizure wherein he was compelled to dig up corpses and violate them sexually, later taking to violently mutilating and disemboweling corpses. Bertrand, who was sent to an asylum for the criminally insane, became the first classic case of violent necrophiliac perversion which some analysts have called necro-sadism.

Bertrand admitted, in his somewhat bragging confession, that he suffered severe headaches, dryness of the throat, and uncontrolled physical trembling before and during his necrophiliac acts but, once sexually relieved, all these symptoms vanished. He, like other flagrant violators of the dead who were tried in the nineteenth century, (such as Victor Ardisson and Henri Blot) said he felt tremendous apprehension about being discovered and lived in great fear, but after committing his atrocious acts he had little or no remorse. Afflicted with a similar perverse compulsion, coupled to the actual killing of women before coitus could be performed, was mass-murderer Earle Nelson, labeled by the sensation-seeking press of the 1920s as "The Gorilla Murderer." See: **Nelson, Earle Leonard.**

REF.: *CBA;* Ellis, *Studies in the Psychology of Sex,* Vol III; Krafт-Ebing, *Psychopathia Sexualis;* Masters and Lea, *Perverse Crimes in History;* (FICTION) Endore, *The Werewolf of Paris.*

Bertrand, Louis, b.1840, Aus., mur. Henry Kinder was a bank teller in Sidney, Aus. He lived with his wife Helen and their children in the fashionable suburb of Sydney Harbor. His apparent suicide attempt on Oct. 1, 1865, came as a shock to the community. He lived for four more days, with a gunshot wound in his head. After his death, the coroner returned a shocking verdict. Henry Kinder died from poison in his system, not from the self-inflicted wound.

The police learned that Helen Kinder was having an affair with Louis Bertrand, a man of unstable temperament. When Bertrand was brought in for questioning he was already serving time in jail for using threatening language. Bertrand had planned to divorce his wife, and had persuaded Helen to agree to the murder of her husband. The shooting occurred in the Kinder home on Oct. 1. Jane Bertrand was in the kitchen with Helen Kinder when they heard the gunshot. Louis and Henry were together in the next room, and the court never established who pulled the trigger. Kinder was still alive four days later, and his health was improving, until he drank a glass of milk containing a fatal dose of belladona. Louis Bertrand had allegedly forced his wife to mix the poison.

The case against Louis Bertrand and Helen Kinder opened in Sydney on Dec. 18. Bertrand's diary, which established the veracity of the rumors about marital infidelity, was introduced by the prosecution. With Henry Kinder out of the way, Bertrand would have been free to marry Helen. Jane Bertrand was apparently an unwitting dupe of the bizarre scheme hatched by her husband, and was freed before the case went to trial. Helen Kinder was acquitted because she had fallen under the "spell" of the wily murderer, and was not entirely to blame for what had happened.

Helen later returned to her home in New Zealand and went to work as a barmaid. As for Louis Bertrand, he was found Guilty of murder and sentenced to hang. The verdict was later vacated under appeal to the Supreme Court. The conduct of the presiding judge in the trial was not beyond reproach. He had passed the death sentence, yet at the same time expressed remorse for the defendant and had implied that the verdict was unjust.

While the Legislative Assembly of New South Wales pondered the case, a doctor found Bertrand to be insane and ordered him committed to the asylum at Parramatta.

REF.: *CBA;* Simpson, *The Anatomy of Murder.*

Bertucci, Clarence V., 1921- , U.S., mur. The war was over. For the German prisoners still confined in the POW camp at Salina, Utah, in July 1945, all that remained was the long trip home to begin their lives anew. Located 150 miles south of Salt Lake City, Camp Salina received hundreds of Nazi prisoners during the war without incident. By day the buses transported the men to Sevier and Sanpete counties where they picked beets under the direction of U.S. Army personnel. It was a quiet, if not dull, existence for both POWs and GIs during the closing months of WWII.

All this changed on July 8, when in a moment of mental duress 23-year-old Army private Clarence Bertucci seized a .30-caliber air-cooled machine gun perched atop a guard tower and began strafing the tents of the sleeping German prisoners.

Bertucci, who had been confined to the stockade on three occasions for insubordination and desertion, was scheduled to report for duty at Tower One at midnight. At 11 p.m. he shared a few beers in town with some local Salina girls before grabbing a quick cup of coffee at an all-night diner near the camp.

It was a cool, cloudless night as Bertucci climbed the guard tower and took over the gun. He looked out across the tent city where 250 Germans slept. He loaded 250 rounds into the weapon. Then, for the next fifteen seconds, he riddled forty-three tents from left to right as frantic prisoners scurried for cover. Wakened abruptly, Lieutenant Albert Cornell ran to the tower and ordered Bertucci to cease firing. He did, because all the ammo in the machine gun had been discharged. Corporal Delmire Butts charged up the ladder to bring him down from his post.

When all the tents were checked, eight Germans had been killed and twenty more wounded. The victims were laid to rest at Fort Douglas and accorded a proper military funeral. For the rest of the prison-camp population unhurt in the hail of bullets, there were more beets to pick. Colonel Arthur Ericsson, commanding officer of the Army Services Forces POW camp at Ogden, refused their request for a two-day layoff. "We declined the request on the grounds that it would be better for them to work than to stay idle," he said.

When questioned by an investigating board, Bertucci showed no remorse for what he had done. He said he hated Germans, and he wanted to kill them. The tedium of a noncombat assignment had apparently been too much for this young soldier. "Something must have happened to him," explained his mystified mother upon hearing the news.

On Aug. 18, a panel of medical officers and psychiatrists at Bushnell General Hospital concluded that Bertucci was "mentally unbalanced." Five days later he was granted a discharge from the Army and sent to Mason General Hospital, Brentwood, Long Island, N.Y., for further tests and evaluation.

Back home in New Orleans, his thirteen brothers and sisters recalled that shy, withdrawn Clarence had acted strangely when he returned on a furlough from England in 1944. After he left for his tour of duty in the Utah desert, they discovered a cryptic message penciled on a doorsill. It read: "Live and let live." REF.: *CBA*.

Berwid, Adam, prom. 20th Cent., U.S., mur. The law which requires the Office of Mental Health in New York to notify all potential victims and law enforcement offices prior to the release of mental patients considered dangerous was enacted as a result of a murder committed by Adam Berwid. It was, however, enacted too late to save the murderer's ex-wife.

Although Berwid was considered dangerous and had even threatened to kill his former wife, he was still issued a twenty-four hour pass to leave the Long Island, N.Y., state hospital. Not long after his departure the last words of Berwid's ex-wife were screamed over the phone to a police operator, "He's killing me!" Her murder created such a stir that the state legislature quickly passed a bill designed to prevent similar crimes.
REF.: *CBA*; Lubin, *Good Guys, Bad Guys*.

Berwinski, Ryszard Wincenty, 1819-79, consp. Poet and critic of the state. He was imprisoned twice before being permanently exiled to Constantinople. REF.: *CBA*.

Besant, Annie, and **Bradlaugh, Charles**, prom. 1877, Brit., obsc. Before the end of the 19th Century a great outcry arose against the publication of information about contraceptives, so it did not take long for a bookseller to be found Guilty of selling obscene literature for carrying Knowlton's *Fruits of Philosophy*. Nor did it take long for Annie Besant and Charles Bradlaugh to be arrested for selling the same book though they were fully aware of the previous conviction.

Besant and Bradlaugh and their Free Thought Publishing Company announced plans to sell the forty-year-old book without illustrations, hoping to inform people about birth control but not offend anyone. Sir Alexander Cockburn, the judge at their trial,

called the obscenity charge ridiculous, but the jury found the book to be "calculated to corrupt public morals," did not find such morals in the defendants. Cockburn determined this to be a Guilty verdict, but would have dismissed Besant and Bradlaugh without punishment if not for a comment made by Besant.

In a speech prior to sentencing, Besant said she and Bradlaugh would continue to publish the book. Her statement resulted in Cockburn's handing down a sentence of two to six months in prison and a fine of £200 for each publisher. This conviction was quashed on appeal because the indictment was determined to be groundless. Besant later established the Malthusian League, which promoted complete freedom in discussing contraception.
REF.: Bullough, *Prostitution; CBA*.

Besnard, Marie Joséphine Phillippine Davaillaud, b.1896, Case of, Fr., mur. Thanks to local gossips in the provincial area of Loudun, Vienne, Fr., Marie Besnard, an obviously disturbed widow, was accused of murdering her husband, Léon Besnard and several others, including her 87-year-old mother. A postmistress, Madame Pintou, spread the story that Léon Besnard had confided to her before his death, on Oct. 25, 1947, that his wife was poisoning him to death. The story had it that Marie, a sexually frustrated housewife who had taken up with a German farm worker named Dietz, killed her husband to be with her lover, a man thirty years her junior. Thirteen bodies, including that of her two dead husbands and her mother, were dug up and a great deal of arsenic was found in all of

Gossip brought about the prolonged murder trial of Marie Besnard.

the bodies. Mrs. Besnard was arrested on July 21, 1949.

Besnard was not placed on trial until Feb. 20, 1952, since the government took eighteen months digging up and examining Besnard relatives. She was found Guilty of illegally collecting annuity payments for one of her dead relatives and forging a signature on the receipts. She was sentenced to two years in prison and fined 50,000 francs but this was only a way in which to imprison the woman while the government built up its murder case against what they thought was an arch killer. All the bodies, dug up year after year and examined and re-examined possessed enough arsenic to kill hundreds of people, or so said the most learned toxicologists in France. These so-called experts, however, were inexcusably inept and, while the Besnard case dragged on for twelve years, endlessly argued their forensic theories. It was proven eventually that the very soil of the cemetery where the bodies were buried contained a great deal of arsenic which had worked its way *into* the bodies, a toxicological condition often existing in certain types of soil. After what is probably one of the longest murder trials on record, if not the longest, Marie Besnard was released on Dec. 12, 1961, for lack of evidence.
REF.: *CBA*; Heppenstall, *The Sex War and Others*; Rowan, *Famous European Crimes*; Thorwald, *The Century of the Detective*.

Bessarabian Gang, prom. 1902, Brit., mur. During one of the frequent and violent skirmishes between rival London gangs—the Bessarabians, comprised mainly of Russian immigrants, and the Odessians—an Odessian named Brodovitch was stabbed to death in October 1902. Barnett Brozishewski was apprehended immediately, Max "Kid McCoy" Moses was arrested three days later, and Samuel Oreman turned himself in. All were leaders of the Bessarabians.

The trial of the gang leaders, all finally convicted of manslaughter, was conducted by Justice Bigham, who sentenced Brozishewski to six months of hard labor, Moses to ten years of penal servitude, and Oreman to five years of penal servitude. Earlier that year,

Moses and Brozishewski had been arrested and charged, along with Joseph Weinstein, with violent highway robbery though no trial or conviction ever occurred.

REF.: *CBA;* Wensley, *Forty Years of Scotland Yard.*

Bessarabo, Charles, See: **Myrtal, Hera.**

Bessus, d.c.329 B.C., Sogdiana, mur. Political ruler of Sogdiana and Bactria. He consolidated his holdings by murdering Darius in 330 B.C. to become King Artaxerxes IV. He was captured and executed for regicide after trying to oppose Alexander the Great. See: **Darius III.** REF.: *CBA.*

Best, Alton Alonzo, 1956- , U.S., sod.-mur. When Alton Best was led away to prison to begin serving an 18-year sentence for the murder of 20-year-old nursing aid Janice Elaine Morton, defense attorney Neal Kravitz noted with a tinge of sadness, "Mr. Best is a really nice, thoughtful, nonviolent man who did something horrible because of his drug use. It is sad. It really is a tragedy." But many others would not agree.

What the baffled Washington, D.C., detectives do not know is just how many more deaths the "nice, thoughtful" drug user may have been responsible for. Between Dec. 13, 1986, and Jan. 12, 1987, five badly mangled bodies were found in a remote wooded area near the Bradbury Recreation Center in Suitland, in Prince George's County, Md. Janice Morton's body was found on Jan. 15, 1987, a couple of miles away. All six of the victims were poor, young, black women and they had all been sodomized.

Alonzo Best, a groundskeeper for the National Park Service on winter furlough, had a record of violent crime dating back to Dec. 1981 when he kidnapped and robbed two young women, but the charges were later dropped. In 1983 he was arrested and convicted for possessing PCP and two years later was convicted of mail fraud. At the time of his arrest for murder, he had several arrests for drug possession.

On Jan. 15, 1987, Best drove a black van belonging to his nephew, D.C. policeman William Armah, into an alley near 414 Eastern Avenue, in the northeast section of the District of Columbia. There he deposited the severely lacerated body of Janice Morton, who was twelve weeks pregnant when she died. Her body was found a few hours later by a witness who identified Best as the man who had left a large item in the alley. The hunt for the black van started. Later that afternoon, Best returned the van to his nephew, who discovered bloodstains in the rear. Best told him that the blood was from an injured friend he had taken to a hospital.

Janice Morton's mother had reported her disappearance to police, though she had not seen her daughter for nearly eighteen days. The body was not identified for another twelve days, when Morton's employer recognized the sketch in the newspaper. A search of the Morton residence turned up an address book and the name of an acquaintance who was able to link the killer to the victim.

Strangely enough, two days before Best was apprehended, the now-famous black van was pulled over by Prince George's County police, but the officer neglected to search the vehicle because the driver showed police credentials. Best, beside his nephew, must have thought he was safe, but he was finally arrested on Jan. 30 1987. The van was located in a repair shop, and the bloodstains were found. The police soon learned that Armah and Best had shared an apartment near Suitland prior to the murders of the five women. They also found that Best had tenous links to at least three of the women found at Suitland. But the evidence connecting Best to those murders stopped there.

Prosecutors presented the court with a seemingly airtight case against Best for the murder of Janice Morton. Best pleaded guilty to second-degree murder in exchange for the government's agreement to drop first-degree and rape charges. There was no chance of securing a death sentence against Best because capital punishment had long been abolished in Washington, D.C. Judge Reggie Walton of the D.C. Superior Court sentenced Best to fifteen years to life, with an additional forty months to five years for sodomy. If Best had chosen to dump the body a few hundred feet away, he would have been in Maryland, where capital punishment exists. REF.: *CBA.*

Best, Robert Henry, 1896-1952, U.S., treas. After spending more than eighteen years in Vienna reporting for United Press, Robert Henry Best began broadcasting propaganda for the Nazis during WWII, espousing his hatred of Communism, Jews, and the New Deal, radio broadcasts which led to his being branded a traitor.

Best, who had teamed with William "Lord Haw Haw" Joyce—hanged in England for treason after the war—and Douglas Chandler—convicted of treason in the U.S.—was arrested by British troops and returned to America where he was tried in Boston for treason. He was found Guilty by a jury on Apr. 16, 1948, after evidence showed that he had told a Nazi radio official of his willingness to betray his country to fight communism. Assistant U.S. Attorney General T. Vincent Quinn sought the death penalty, but Federal Judge Francis J. W. Ford sentenced Best to life imprisonment and fined him $10,000.

Best, who claimed his trial was conducted unfairly, appealed to the Circuit Court of Appeals which on July 6, 1950 upheld the trial court's decision. He later appealed to the U.S. Supreme Court, which refused to hear the case on Feb. 26, 1951. While appealing, Best was held in the Suffolk County Jail in Boston, but later served his time in the U.S. Medical Center for Federal Prisoners in Springfield, Mo., where he died of a cerebral hemorrhage, one of many he experienced the last two years of his life. REF.: *CBA.*

Betancourt, Rómulo, 1908-81, Venez., pres., attempt. assass. Imprisoned or exiled numerous times for his liberal convictions, Rómulo Betancourt founded the Acción Democrática party in 1941 and was one of the leaders of a military coup that deposed General Angarita in 1945. Betancourt was named president of the ruling junta that same year. In 1948, he was exiled only to return nine years later to assume the presidency of Venezuela in 1959.

An attempt made on on President Betancourt's life proved to be unsuccessful but resulted in the death of two people and sanctions against the man held responsible. On June 24, 1960, Betancourt's presidential car was thrown onto the grassy median of the divided Avenida de los Próceres in Caracas as it passed a parked 1954 green Oldsmobile and sixty pounds of ammonium-nitrate dynamite in the car was detonated by remote control. The explosion flung shards of shrapnel through the air, killing a bystander and presidential aide Colonel Ramón Armas Peréz, who died later, and caused the president's car to burst into flames, resulting in first-degree burns on the face and hands of Betancourt.

Evidence not destroyed by the blast quickly led to the capture of those who set off the bomb. Juan Manuel Sanoja, calling himself a Venezuelan general, directed three other conspirators in planting the bomb, but it was Col. John Abbes Garcia, following the orders of Dominican Republic dictator Rafael Leonidas Trujillo, who masterminded the plot. Trujillo was found Guilty by the Organization of American States, whose sentence included an end to diplomatic ties with other American nations above the consular level and economic sanctions, beginning with an arms embargo. REF.: *CBA.*

Betchel, Lawrence, prom. 20th Cent., Case of, U.S., mur. During a fight between a Philippine war veteran and a fellow member of the U.S. National Guard in San Francisco, Lawrence Betchel shot and killed the veteran, Frank Riordan. Betchel, who shot Riordan when he grabbed for his rifle and bayonet, claimed that he acted in self defense because Riordan was attempting to disarm a soldier, Randolph Merriwether, who Riordan apparently had called a "tin soldier," instigating the fight. He was nevertheless arrested and charged with murder, though the district attorney asked Judge Cook to dismiss the case, which he did.

REF.: *CBA;* Duke, *Celebrated Criminal Cases of America.*

Bethea, Rainey, 1914-36, U.S., mur. Rainey Bethea, a black killer of a 70-year-old white woman, was the last person to be publicly hanged in the U.S. More than 20,000 persons, almost all of them white, assembled in Owensboro, Ky. Only moments after Bethea dropped through the trap, the huge, cheering throng surged forward and began stripping away parts of the condemned man's clothing, but doctors, fighting to listen to Bethea's heart, announced he was still alive. Police pushed back the wild souvenir hunters while Bethea slowly strangled to death for another fifteen minutes. He was finally pronounced dead and the crowd was allowed to tear away the dead man's remaining shreds of clothes. REF.: *CBA*.

Bethell, Richard (First Baron Westbury), 1800-73, Brit., jur. Attorney general from 1856-58. He was a strong advocate of legal reform and codification. REF.: *CBA*.

Bethmann-Hollweg, Moritz August von, 1795-1877, Ger., jur. Member of the upper chamber from 1849-52, and the lower chamber from 1852-55. REF.: *CBA*.

Beto, Joseph Anthony, 1945-   , and **Zamp, Jerome**, 1947-   , U.S., mur. It took three months and a search as far away as New Orleans, La., before the killers of Dr. Hans Wachtel were caught.

Wachtel was shot twice in the head on Feb. 2, 1977, while sitting in his car parked outside his South Side Chicago apartment. The 67-year-old doctor was the chairman of the obstetrics-gynecology department at Woodlawn Hospital. His assailants were Joseph Anthony Beto, who was arrested May 13, and Jerome Zamp, arrested in New Orleans two days later.

Both were found Guilty of murder and sentenced by Judge Barbaro to spend from 200 to 300 years in prison. Others were sought and arrested for the crime but no other convictions were made. REF.: *CBA*.

Betti, Ugo, 1892-1953, Italy, jur. Magistrate from 1920-30, and served as judge from 1930-44. REF.: *CBA*.

Betts, Samuel Rossiter, 1786-1869, U.S., jur. Legal scholar who served as district attorney in Orange County, N.Y., from 1820-23. He was appointed judge of the court of the Southern District of New York by President John Quincy Adams in 1826. REF.: *CBA*.

Bevan, Catherine, 1680-1731, U.S., mur. Mrs. Catherine Bevan, wife of a rich farmer in Delaware, began an affair with her 60-year-old husband's servant, Peter Murphy, a man twenty-five years her junior, and then decided to kill her spouse so she could live with her young lover. She poisoned her husband's coffee but it seemed to have no affect so Murphy beat Henry Bevan unconscious with a tree limb while Catherine strangled him to death with her best handkerchief. Murphy hastily built a wooden coffin and placed the victim's corpse within, nailing the lid shut. Catherine announced that her husband had died of a fit and held a brief ceremony, but a local judge grew suspicious when the body was not shown to mourners as was the custom. He ordered the coffin opened and Bevan's battered body soon revealed the true nature of his death.

Only an hour after Mrs. Bevan and Murphy were arrested, the young lover confessed to the murder, blaming the woman, saying he was a pawn in her clutches. Both were convicted of murder and sentenced to death. Their executions were held before a large crowd on June 10, 1731. Murphy was hanged but the unfaithful, murderous Catherine was put through a special ordeal. She received the same sentence that had been given British murderess Catherine Hayes five years earlier. She was to be strangled to death while tied to a stake and then her body burned beyond recognition. After the screaming, pleading woman was tied to a stake surrounded with wood, a rope with a slip knot was placed about her neck and the executioner stood some twenty feet distant, holding the other end of the rope. He ordered the kindling about the miserable woman ignited, and while the flames shot up, he yanked on the rope to strangle her. The flames rose too quickly, however, and the rope was quickly burned away before it could do its work. Catherine Bevan was burned alive, enduring excruciating pain, suffering the only such execution ever meted out in the U.S. See: **Hayes, Catherine**.

REF.: *CBA*; Nash, *Look for the Woman*.

Bevan, Gerard Lee (AKA: **Leon Vernier**), prom. 1922, Brit., fraud. After rising to the top of one of England's most prestigious brokerage firms Gerard Lee Bevan decided to try his hand in the insurance business, a decision which led to his downfall and to the collapse of a 144-year-old brokerage house.

As the senior of five broker partners at Ellis & Company, Bevan had capital of £108,000 in 1919, more than enough to afford the £20,000 deposit required by the Board of Trade to enter the insurance business. In issuing false balance sheets which made it appear that his companies had enormous assets—one asset was listed at £319,523 but only £133,000 was secured, and another balance sheet, in 1921, listed total assets for one company at £2,890,391 when actually £1,318,864 was still—Bevan single-handedly cleaned out the coffers of Ellis & Company. By January 1922 when the parent company to Bevan's insurance endeavors realized he had been issuing false balance sheets and prospectuses, and had committed fraudulent conversions, Ellis & Co. had, in reality, been insolvent for three years.

While the investigation continued, Bevan fled London, just ahead of a warrant for his arrest, leaving the country by plane on Feb. 8, 1922. Authorities finally caught up with him in Vienna, though then he had dyed his hair, grown a beard, and changed his name to Leon Vernier of Lille, Belgium. He was returned to the Old Bailey where he stood trial in November 1922. He was found Guilty by a jury and sentenced by Justice Avory to seven years' imprisonment and five years of penal servitude to be served concurrently.

REF.: *CBA*; Nicholls, *Crime Within the Square Mile*.

Bew, William, d.1689, Brit., rob. Will Bew was the brother of Captain Bew, a highwayman who had been killed by the thief-takers at Knightsbridge. This tragedy planted in Will Bew's mind a firm resolve never to be taken. And for a time he operated as a highwayman in the Bristol countryside without the slightest interference from the sheriff. Will Bew was just luckier and cleverer than most robbers.

However, things eventually became hot for Bew in England, and he fled to Paris to practice thieving. In the parish of St. Denis, he learned that an archbishop was being buried in an expensive pontifical robe. Imagining that he might find other untold riches in the tomb, Will Bew hid in the graveyard until nightfall. As he began to remove the heavy slab covering the tomb, he was caught by a gang of grave-robbers who felt they had prior claim to the grave.

Will was ordered to continue working while the robbers sat idly by. When the grave was open, he removed a valuable silver cross and the ornate robe, which the gang claimed, but Will managed to pocket a ruby ring. The robber gang demanded that he look further, and as he did so, the heavy slab closed over him.

Will Bew might have died there if not for an extraordinary turn of luck. A second grave-robbing gang removed the stone so that they too might rifle the contents of the tomb. At an opportune moment, Bew flew out of the grave, making such a frightful noise that the robbers could only think that they had unloosed the devil himself, and they fled.

With his ruby in hand, Will left the graveyard to buy new clothes for the return trip to England. Back in his native land, he continued his profession for years before being taken at the Red Lion Tavern in Brentford. No longer lucky, Will Bew joined his brother in death when he was hanged at Tyburn on Apr. 17, 1689.

REF.: *CBA*; Smith, *Highwaymen*.

Bey, Enver, and **Bey, Djevet**, and **Bey, Talaat**, prom. 1915-18, Turk. tort.-rape-mur. Rather than put an end to the senseless massacre of Armenians committed by Sultan Abdul Hamid II, who they overthrew in 1908, Young Turk leaders continued to kill innocent people accused of aiding the Russians during WWI. Enver Bey in 1915 ordered his brother-in-law Djevet Bey to annihilate the Christian Armenians, which Djevet promptly did, shooting people from more than eighty villages, after first raping the women and torturing the men—one official confessing he "delved into the records of the Spanish Inquisition and adopted all the suggestions found there."

The killing did not end there. During a forced march across the Syrian desert, only 150 of 18,000 Armenians survived the seventy-day journey to Aleppo. Enver accepted complete responsibility, while co-leader Talaat Bey felt that even more Armenians should be exterminated. All three fled Turkey in November 1918, denounced nationwide for allying themselves with the Germans during the war and profiting from the sale of food during a famine. REF.: *CBA*.

Bhutto, Zulfikar Ali, 1928-79, Pakistan, (wrong. convict.?) mur. Following the overthrow of the Pakistani government—amid political strife caused by accusations of corruption in the government and a lopsided victory during elections on Mar. 7, 1977—the ousted prime minister, Zulfikar Ali Bhutto, was tried, convicted, and sentenced to die by firing squad for allegedly ordering the assassination of a political foe.

Bhutto, who came to power in 1971 after the end of the war with India, had been prime minister of Pakistan since 1974 when he ended martial law. With opposition to his rule growing, a military coup led by General Mohammed Zia ul-Haq took place on July 5, 1977. Zia Ul-Haq had Bhutto imprisoned in September and tried for the murder of Nawab Mohammad Ahmed Khan, who was machine-gunned to death Nov. 11, 1974, during an attempt on the life of his son, Ahmad Raza Kasuri, who opposed Bhutto.

The former prime minister was found Guilty of murder—charges of political corruption and electoral fraud were subsequently set aside—on Mar. 18, 1978, mainly on the testimony of Bhutto's director of security, Masood Mahmud, who was held captive for two months before confessing with a promise of immunity. According to Bhutto, Mahmud's confession and testimony was "dishonest and utterly unreliable." Also considered by many to be dishonest were the entire proceedings, because Zia Ul-Haq apparently influenced the decision of the jury. An appeal of the conviction was turned down on Feb. 6, 1979, by the Pakistan Supreme Court which upheld the lower court's decision.

Death by hanging was substituted for a firing squad and Bhutto, along with the men he allegedly ordered to commit the crime—Mian Mohammed Appas, Arrad Iqbal, Rana Isti Khar, and Guylam Mustafa—was executed on Apr. 4, 1979. Tara Masih, at the time Pakistan's first and only hangman since Pakistan became a nation, said of Bhutto, "He was the only man I hanged who I was convinced was an innocent man." REF.: *CBA*.

Biaggi, Mario, 1917- , and **Biaggi, Richard,** 1949- , U.S., tax evas.-bribe.-fraud. After spending ten terms as a Democrat from New York in the U.S. Congress, Mario Biaggi was found Guilty in the Wedtech corruption scandal of bribery, conspiracy, extortion, fraud, perjury, and tax evasion, for which U.S. District Judge Constance Baker Motley sentenced him to eight years in prison on Nov. 18, 1988. Biaggi's son, Richard, who stood trial with his father in September 1987, was convicted of bribery, fraud, and tax evasion, for which he received a two-year sentence. The elder Biaggi is serving his sentence at the U.S. penitentiary in Leavenworth, Kan. and is scheduled for release on Apr. 10, 1991. REF.: *CBA*.

Bialek, Robert, d.1956, Ger., (unsolv.) kid.-mur. In 1928, while still in his teens, Robert Bialek joined the communist youth movement in Breslau, Ger. During the war, the Gestapo arrested him as a subversive, but released him after he promised to refrain from political work. After the war, Bialek rose to prominence in the new political order. The East German government named him secretary for the Saxon Communist Party, and later inspector general in the dreaded Volkspolizei, or "People's Police."

During the Cold War, Bialek split with party leaders, especially the first secretary of the Socialist Unity Party, Walter Ulbricht. He was demoted to the position of "culture director." In 1953, Moscow's decision not to pay bonuses to German railroad workers alienated Bialek still further.

Tipped off that the government was about to arrest and charge him with fomenting the June 1953 Berlin revolt, he defected to the West. Robert Bialek entered the Marienfels refugee center in West Berlin on Aug. 27, 1953. He was welcomed with open arms, and encouraged to engage in counterintelligence activities against the East Germans. For the next year Bialek was the radio voice of the West, broadcasting anti-Communist tirades into the Soviet bloc.

In February 1956 Bialek disappeared. East German agents were believed to have killed him. Paul Drzewiecki, his niece Christina, and Herbert Hellwiig invited Bialek to a West Berlin flat one night in November to discuss the news from the East. Drzewiecki invited Bialek back the next night to celebrate his birthday, but Bialek was suddenly taken ill. He was carried into a taxi and driven away, never to be seen again. REF.: *CBA*.

Kenneth Bianchi   **Angelo Buono**

Bianchi, Kenneth (AKA: **The Hillside Strangler, Steve Walker, Anthony D'Amato, Nicholas Fontana, Billy**), 1952- , and **Buono, Angelo, Jr.,** 1935- , U.S., sod.-tort.-rape-mur. These two bestial killers slew ten young women and girls who were mostly part-time prostitutes, murdering them from 1977 to 1979 in Angelo Buono, Jr.'s home in Glendale, Calif., committing the slayings attributed to the Hillside Strangler. Kenneth Bianchi, who had been born in Rochester, N.Y., and had been raised by foster parents, arrived in Los Angeles in 1977 to stay with his cousin Buono, a street-tough sub-normal creature who was always trying to prove his manhood and authority. He reveled in being Italian and flew the Italian flag 24-hours-a-day from a flagpole on the grounds of his house. He ran an upholstery business out of his garage and was already parading prostitutes through his home by the time Bianchi arrived. One night, as the cousins sat about drinking beer, they speculated as to what it might be like to murder someone.

They started their mass murder spree by killing Elissa Teresa Kastin, twenty-one, on Oct. 6, 1977, dumping her naked body near Chevy Chase Drive in Glendale. Their next victim was 19-year-old Yolanda Washington; her body was found on the slopes of the distinguished Forest Lawn Cemetery, the resting place of movie stars, on the night of Oct. 18, 1977. The body was naked, cleaned by the killers so as to leave no clues, and posed in a lascivious position. Bianchi and Buono went on to murder eight more women. On Oct. 31, 1977, the naked body of 15-year-old Judith Lynn Miller was found on a hillside next to the road in Glendale. She had been raped, sodomized, and strangled to death. Her wrists, ankles, and neck bore the marks of the ropes that had bound her, as was the case with the Washington woman and those victims to come. Bianchi and Buono, to show their contempt for lawmen looking for them, made sure that this body and the others had been cleaned, leaving no clues whatsoever, but placed the corpses in spots where they could easily be found and usually close to police stations, as if to thumb their noses at police.

On Nov. 20, 1977, the killers slew three more, Kristina Weckler, twenty; Dolores Cepeda, twelve; and Sonja Johnson, fourteen, dumping the nude body of Weckler on a slope in Highland Park and the corpses of Cepeda and Johnson in Elysian Park. They killed Jane Evelyn King, twenty-eight, on Nov. 23, 1977, dumping her body at the off-ramp of the southbound Golden State Freeway. On Nov. 29, 1977, Bianchi and Buono murdered Lauren Rae Wagner, eighteen, placing her naked body on Cliff Drive in Glassell Park. Next, on Dec. 14, 1977, police found the naked body of Kimberly Diane Martin, eighteen. The intensity of the murders slackened but, on Feb. 17, 1978, Cindy Lee Hudspeth's naked body was found in the trunk of a car which had been driven off Angeles Crest Highway. The killings had all been committed in Buono's home and the bodies dumped in a rough circle around that house.

Police announced regularly that they were closing in on the Hillside Strangler and that several "good" suspects had been pulled in for questioning, but when the killings stopped, police had little to say and less to investigate, their special team of investigators reassigned to other chores. Los Angeles detectives were perplexed when the killings suddenly ended. The reason for this was hygiene. Bianchi left Buono's home because of the filthy conditions there, going to Bellingham, Wash., where, in January 1979, he raped and strangled to death with a cord two college women, Karen Mandic and Diane Wilder, packing the bodies into the trunk of Mandic's car. Following a missing persons report, these bodies were found and Bianchi came under suspicion as having been seen with one of the women shortly before her disappearance.

Ironically, Bianchi was working as a security guard and had applied for a job with the Bellingham police department. (He had also applied for a job with the Los Angeles Police Department and, in fact, had gone along on a few rides with officers in Los Angeles while the Hillside Strangler was being sought.) Bianchi, who had steeped himself in psychiatric studies, played a game with doctors examining him, pretending, it was later reported, to have a split personality, or many personalities, one of which being the killer of the women. He claimed that he had blackouts and could not remember his actions. He presented all the symptoms of someone unbalanced, out of control, legally insane. His act, however, did not work, and he was charged with the murder of the two Bellingham women. Then Bianchi offered prosecutors a deal; he would turn over his cousin Buono, the real Hillside Strangler, he said, if he were removed to California and did not have to face the death penalty in Washington, that of hanging. Washington authorities agreed to the deal, as long as Bianchi pleaded guilty. He did and received a life sentence, then was shipped to California to testify against his brutal cousin, Buono, after which he would serve his time in a California prison, one less austere and rigid than Washington's Walla Walla Prison.

On Bianchi's statements, Buono was charged with murder but Bianchi, who had fooled six Washington state psychiatrists into labeling him legally insane, now could not testify against Buono since he was a lunatic. Yet it was shown that he had planned his "insanity" position years earlier, reading endless studies on psychiatry and particularly studying the novels, *Sybil* and *The Three Faces of Eve*, preparing for his own positioning of multiple personalities, a psychological profile he assumed when confronted with the Washington murders. Bianchi had gone so far as to claim he had a degree in psychiatry and was about to actually open up a practice in Los Angeles before going off to Washington. Bianchi also had faked being hypnotized, according to most reports, when being examined in Washington, and then released his other "identities," claiming that these personalities had done the horrible murders with his beast-like cousin Buono.

Bianchi nevertheless gave a complete profile of the murders he committed with Buono once back in Los Angeles, describing how he and Buono drove about in Buono's car, using fake badges to identify themselves to young women as policemen, ordering them into Buono's auto, which they passed off as an unmarked police car. Once the women were in the car, they were taken to Buono's home, tortured, forced to have sex with both of them, and then tied up and murdered, usually strangled, although the killers experimented with injections and other murder methods that proved unsuccessful. Then the murderers fastidiously washed their victims and dumped their naked bodies at remote spots.

Buono was arrested in 1979 after Bianchi's Washington conviction, and he was eventually tried on Nov. 16, 1981. A grueling two years passed during which more than 400 witnesses were heard, 55,000 pages of trial transcript were compiled, and millions of dollars were spent to convict Buono. A jury, more than two years later, convicted him of nine counts of murder on Nov. 14, 1983. The trial was aptly labeled a "judicial extravaganza" by the press, one in which Buono insisted, in court and out, that he was innocent of the murders his cousin claimed he had performed. (He had been extremely thorough in cleaning up his home after Bianchi left, not one fingerprint of the victims, not even his own, could be found by police, although a single eyelash belonging to one of the victims was unearthed and a few strands of fiber from one of Buono's chairs was found on one of the bodies.) A surprise prosecution witness was 27-year-old Catherine Lorre who identified both Bianchi and Buono as the two men who had stopped her on a Hollywood street in 1977, saying they were detectives and demanding her identification. She had shown her driver's license and next to it, Bianchi saw a photo of her as a little girl sitting on her father's lap, her father being the famous character actor of films, Peter Lorre. Bianchi later admitted that he had let Lorre go because he feared that murdering the child of a celebrity would bring more police heat down upon him and Buono.

Judge Ronald George, who had refused to drop charges against Buono "for lack of evidence," as asked by the prosecution during the initial stages of his trial when it felt it would lose the case altogether, had conducted a fair and impartial trial for more than two years. He pronounced sentence on Angelo Buono, Jr. on Jan. 9, 1984, giving him life imprisonment without possibility of parole. Bianchi, against his clever designs, was ordered sent back to Walla Walla Prison to serve out a life sentence, parole not available until the year 2005. Stated Judge George after sentencing: "I'm sure Mr. Buono and Mr. Bianchi, that you will only get your thrills by reliving over and over the tortures and murders of your victims, being incapable as I believe you to be, of ever feeling any remorse."

REF.: Cartel, *Serial Mass Murderers; CBA;* Levin and Fox, *Mass Murder;* Schwartz, *The Hillside Strangler;* ____, *A Murderer's Mind;* Wolf and Mader, *Fallen Angels.*

Biase, Anthony Joseph, prom. 1950s, U.S., org. crime. Anthony Biase, born in 1908, was arrested many times in the 1930s for bookmaking, burglary, and theft in the Rocky Mountain states, and he later developed gambling interests in operations in Los Angeles, San Francisco, and Las Vegas. When Vito Genovese made his move to take over the Mafia families of New York in 1957, and also extend his influence to the western states, Biase became a Genovese ally. He became the head of Mafia-syndicate operations in Denver, Colo., after his associate, Anthony Marcella, was convicted of narcotics violations and sent to prison for forty years.

REF.: *CBA;* Nash, *Bloodletters and Badmen;* Reid, *The Grim Reapers;* Wyden, *The Hired Killers.*

Bibb, Charles Scott, 1801-32, U.S., jur. Prosecuting attorney in Franklin County, Ky., from 1826-32. He was appointed judge of the territorial court of Arkansas by President Andrew Jackson in 1832. REF.: *CBA.*

Bibeau, John T., prom. 1932, U.S., mur. It is said to be bad luck when a black cat crosses one's path. For Alfred Elliot it was bad luck when a black cat chanced to sit on Bibeau's chair.

John T. Bibeau, who had been living with Elliot and his wife for a number of years, had a fear of black cats and became enraged when one sat in his dinner chair on Oct. 20, 1932. Bibeau insulted Mary Elliot which led to Elliot to beat up his friend, and file a complaint against him with the police. Bibeau was arrested and later moved out of the house, located outside Seattle in Tolt, Wash.

Bibeau returned to the ranch house on Nov. 26, 1932, to retrieve his belongings. After Elliot refused to admit him, he shot through a window and hit Elliot in the stomach. Elliot died ten days later. At his trial for murder, Bibeau's attorneys pled insanity for the man who sat throughout the proceedings with a ghastly grin on his face, but the jury was not amused and found him Guilty with a recommendation for life imprisonment.

REF.: *CBA;* Cohen, *One Hundred True Crime Stories.*

Bichel, Andreas, 1770-1808, Ger., mur. Bavarian born Andreas Bichel moved to the town of Regendorf in the early 1800s and there set up a curio shop while passing himself off as a clairvoyant. He made little money but saw an opportunity to get rich by murdering and robbing lone females traveling from town to town. He would convince these gullible young women that he could only read their future if they were absolutely motionless and to make sure of that he would, with their naive permission, tie them to a chair. Stepping behind each victim, he would sever the spinal cord then reach over the shoulder to plunge a long knife into a lung, killing the victim quickly. He took whatever money these women carried, stripping their bodies of clothes and cheap jewelry, which he later sold, and then burying them in a woodshed located behind his home.

This systematic murderer flourished for a number of years without suspicion directed toward him since he was careful not to molest local persons. Then, in 1808, the sister of Catherine Seidel appeared in Regendorf in search of the missing woman. The sister visited several shops and noticed at the local tailor shop a skirt which had been worn by Catherine. She asked about it and was told that Andreas Bichel had sold it to the tailor. The Seidel woman reported this to the police who went to Bichel's house to make inquiries. Bichel was visibly shaken at their questions and a search of his home was made; piles of female clothing were found and a large box containing jewelry taken from Bichel's murder victims over the years. Officers searched the grounds and, responding to a powerful stench, began digging in the shed behind the house, finding the bodies—more than fifty of them.

Convicted and sentenced to death in 1808, Bichel was visited in his cell by a priest a few hours before he was to go to his death. "You have committed horrible crimes against humanity," the priest intoned. "I have come to hear your repentence for these bloody deeds."

"Do not tell me of repentence," snapped Bichel through sneering lips, "but tell me if the dead can tear and injure."

Then the prisoner was taken to the executioner and broken at the wheel. He was placed face up on a wheel and tied so tightly that the cords broke his flesh and then the executioner, wielding a sledgehammer, broke every bone in his body before beheading him.

REF.: *CBA;* Nash, *Almanac of World Crime;* Wilson, *Encyclopedia of Murder.*

Bickerstaff, Benjamin F., d.1869, U.S., west. outl. A native of Sulphur Springs, Hopkins County, Texas, Benjamin Bickerstaff served in the Civil War as a guerrilla, and, following the war, he turned outlaw. While traveling in Louisiana in 1867, Bickerstaff murdered a freed slave who spoke defiantly to him. He then went back to Sulphur Springs and raised an outlaw band of about twenty men, raiding Union supply depots and killing many federal troops who were part of the Army of Occupation after the war. Bickerstaff was looked upon as a local hero, but he was nothing more than a bandit who used public animosity toward Union troops as an excuse for his criminal operations.

So effective were Bickerstaff's men in sacking federal warehouses and ambushing Union patrols, that three full companies were moved into Hopkins County and "forts" were established throughout the area around Sulphur Springs in an attempt to capture the band. A $1,000 reward was placed on Bickerstaff's head, dead or alive, but no local residents would think to turn the bandit into authorities, let alone shoot him down. This attitude

changed a few years later when Bickerstaff and his men turned on Texans, shooting and robbing citizens at will. When Bickerstaff and his men roared into the town of Alvarado, Johnson County, on the night of Apr. 5, 1869, the gang "hurrahed" the town by firing weapons into the air and some into the store windows. Irate citizens spilled into the street heavily armed, warned in advance of the arrival of the gang, and gunned down several members, including Bickerstaff who was shot dead from his horse by a load of buckshot from a shotgun fired almost point blank into his face.

REF.: Bartholomew, *The Biographical Album of Western Gunfighters;* CBA.

Bickford, James Madison, b.1833, and **Cook, Thomas,** b.1836, U.S., mur. While driving horses along the Hopkinton and Port Kent Turnpike in upstate New York on June 6, 1853, 28-year-old John B. Secor was shot with a rifle ball causing him to fall from his horse before his death. Wright Van Tassel left his fallen partner and chased after the horses which had run off.

As the body lay in the road, James Madison Bickford apparently stole Secor's watch and pocketbook, items found only fifteen feet from where Bickford was arrested the next day for shooting Secor. Upon this evidence he was brought to trial on July 19, 1854, and convicted of murder. Bickford's servant Thomas Cook, who confessed to being with Bickford at the time his master shot Secor, was found Guilty of aiding and abetting Bickford, and was recommended to mercy by the governor. Bickford was sentenced to be hanged on Sept. 22, 1854. REF.: *CBA.*

Bickford, Mary Ann (or Maria), See: **Tirrell, Albert John.**

Bicycle Squad, 1895-1934, law enfor. group. With the coming of the "steam carriages," as they were termed by New York's then-Police Commissioner Theodore Roosevelt, a special police squad on bicycles were assigned to run down "speedsters" traveling at the dizzying speed of 30 mph. The police on bicycles increased in numbers over the years to more than 150 but by the 1920s, the squad was thought to be archaic and ineffective. The Bicycle Squad was nevertheless kept in operation, almost as a curiosity, until it was abandoned in 1934 and the hundreds of bicycles auctioned off to poor children in impoverished areas. REF.: *CBA.*

Biddings, Robert, 1954- , U.S., rob.-kid.-rape. The persistence shown by the parents of a rape victim in Columbus, Ohio, led to the arrest of Robert Biddings, believed responsible for at least sixty rapes.

On Aug. 5, 1988, Biddings attempted to rape the mother of a June 1987 rape victim in the same area where he attacked her daughter. The young woman's parents had staked out the spot for nearly a year to try to catch him if he struck again. The woman's husband drew a gun on Biddings, who was holding a gun to his wife's head, and yelled, "Freeze! Police!" Biddings fled, but not before the couple recorded the license plate number of his car.

Biddings, who became known as the "handcuff rapist" for using handcuffs on earlier victims, was charged and tried for attacking nineteen women in Columbus from 1984 to 1988. The jury found him Guilty on May 26, 1989, on forty counts of rape, kidnapping, and aggravated robbery. He was sentenced on May 31 to 484 to 955 years in prison, plus life, in addition to fifteen years for gun violations. For similar crimes committed in Cincinnati—amounting to seventy-three counts—he pleaded Guilty. As of this writing, Robert Biddings awaits sentencing for the crimes committed. REF.: *CBA.*

Biddle, Ed, and **Biddle, Jack,** and **Dorman, Frank,** and **Wilcox, Jennie,** and **Wright, Jessie,** prom. 1901, U.S., rob.-pris. esc. Twenty-seven burglaries occurred in Pittsburgh in early 1901. Police believed they were the work of the same criminal gang. Their suspicions were confirmed on the morning of Apr. 12 when the gang shot and killed Thomas Kahney, the owner of a grocery store.

That same morning, Police Inspector Robert Gray learned that the suspects were holed up in a house on Fulton Street. Police officers encircled the house, began to force their way in, and in the ensuing shootout, Detective Patrick Fitzgerald was killed. The gang members surrendered quietly, and were identified as Ed and Jack Biddle, Frank Dorman, and female accomplices Jennie Wilcox and Jessie Wright. The Biddles were convicted of murder and sentenced to hang on Dec. 12, 1901. Dorman received a life sentence and the two women were acquitted.

The Biddle brothers were remanded to the custody of Warden Peter Soffel at the Allegheny County Jail in Pittsburgh to await execution. Shortly before daylight on the morning of Jan. 30, 1902, Ed Biddle asked Guard James McGeary for medical help. He said that his brother had become very ill overnight. When McGeary returned with the medicine that Biddle had requested, he discovered that the brothers had sawed through the bars. They pointed guns in the faces of the guards, threw one over a railing onto a concrete floor, shot another, and walked out of the jail.

When he recovered his composure, the warden explained that it was probably his wife who smuggled weapons to the brothers. She had developed an infatuation with Ed Biddle. Mrs. Soffel and the Biddles were located the next day, Jan. 31, 1902, at the home of J.J. Stevens in Mount Chestnut, Pa. They attempted to escape in a sleigh, but were stopped by rifle shots after refusing to surrender. John and Ed Biddle were shot, and died the next day at the Butler, Pa., hospital. Mrs. Soffel, wounded in the chest, expressed a desire to die, but did not.

She was tried for aiding and abetting a prison escape, and received a two-year sentence. Upon her release the warden's wife became an actress, but her performance was abruptly halted by the authorities. She went into seclusion and tried to earn a living making dresses. She died on Aug. 30, 1909, at the West Pennsylvania Hospital. Her story was brought to the screen in 1984 with Diane Keaton in the leading role of *Mrs. Soffel*.

REF.: *CBA; Duke, Celebrated Criminal Cases of America.*

Biddle, Francis Bevereley, 1886-1968, U.S., jur. Francis Biddle was a successful corporate lawyer from Philadelphia when he was called on to accept a judgeship on the U.S. Circuit Court of Appeals in 1939. The Third Circuit Court proved to be a springboard to national office. In 1940 the immigration and naturalization offices were transferred to the Department of Justice. Biddle was asked to coordinate the work with other branches of the department and earned a reputation as somewhat of a hardliner against individuals suspected of seditious activity against the government. In August 1941, the supporters of labor leader Harry Bridges accused Biddle of authorizing the FBI to conduct wire taps on his phone.

On Sept. 3, 1941, Biddle was confirmed by the U.S. Congress as the nation's fifty-eighth attorney general. He served until the end of WWII, at which time he accepted appointment to the bench of the Nuremberg War Crimes Tribunal. See: **Bridges, Harry.**

REF.: *CBA; Demaris, The Director; Nash, Citizen Hoover; Powers, Secrecy and Power; Toledano, J. Edgar Hoover; Whitehead, The FBI Story; Wicker, Investigating the FBI.*

Biddle, John, 1615-62, Brit., her. Known as the father of English Unitarianism. He was imprisoned for the first time in 1644 for publishing *Twelve Arguments Against the Deity of the Holy Ghost.* In 1655, he was banished by Oliver Cromwell in order to escape execution for heresy, but was arrested again after he returned three years later. REF.: *CBA.*

Bideno, Juan, d.1871, U.S., west. outl. Mexican-born Juan Bideno worked as a cowboy but was known as a fast-gun and hired out for killings, one report has it. In June 1871, Bideno signed on to a cattle drive from Texas to the railhead at Abilene, Kan. The trail boss was 22-year-old Billy Cohron, who noticed Bideno's slack work and called him on it several times, leading to hard words between the pair. As the herd crossed the Cottonwood River in Kansas on July 5, 1871, Cohron and Bideno again fell to arguing and then went for their guns. Bideno shot the youthful trail boss dead and fled, riding south toward Texas.

A self-appointed posse of cowboys tracked the killer to Bluff Creek, Kan. The four men following Bideno were John Cohron, the victim's brother, Hugh Anderson, Jim Rodgers, and a young Texan who would later be known as the fastest gun in the West, John Wesley Hardin. Several different stories of Hardin's gunfight with Bideno exist. According to one, Bideno was just mounting his horse when Hardin and the others rode into town and Hardin challenged the killer. Both men then rode at a full gallop down the street toward each other blazing away with their six-guns and that Hardin sent a bullet into Bideno's heart.

Another story reported how Cohron, Anderson, and Rodgers surrounded the cafe where Bideno was eating and Hardin went inside alone. As Hardin approached Bideno's table he told him that he had been deputized to arrest him and that if he surrendered to him he would not be hurt. The Mexican gunman dropped his knife and fork, leaned back in his chair so that his holsters were free and went for his guns. Hardin, walking solemnly across the room, pulled his six-gun with lightning speed and drilled a bullet into Bideno's brain, instantly killing the outlaw. See: **Hardin, John Wesley.**

REF.: *CBA; Nash, Bloodletters and Badmen; Nordyke, John Wesley Hardin, Texas Gunman; Raine, Famous Sheriffs and Western Outlaws; Rosa, The Gunfighter; Schoenberger, Gunfighters; Streeter, Prairie Trails and Cow Towns.*

Bidwell Brothers, See: **Great Bank of England Forgery.**

Biebusch, Frederick, b.1823, U.S., count. One of the great U.S. counterfeiters of the 19th Century, Beibusch emigrated from Germany in 1844 and moved to St. Louis, Mo., where he made his fortune. Extremely wealthy, Frederick Biebusch was arrested fifty-one times before he was convicted, once serving five months of a ten-year sentence in 1865 before being pardoned by the governor, who was influenced by a number of Biebusch's friends—friends indebted to the counterfeiter.

Biebusch was known for evading the law—as his conviction record shows—often paying witnesses for the prosecution to leave town before testifying, or bribing prosecutors to dismiss a case. After his final arrest in 1870, letters from U.S. Secret Service members were discovered in his home that mentioned their desire to help him with any legal matters if payment was forthcoming.

REF.: Bloom, *Money of Their Own; CBA.*

Biegenwald, Richard F., 1941- , U.S., mur. There is no honor among thieves. Richard Biegenwald, a sadistic killer from Asbury Park, N.J., realized this too late in the game. He also learned a valuable lesson in human nature: what you say in an unguarded moment can return to haunt you. While serving time in prison for killing during a holdup, Biegenwald made the acquaintance of Dherran Fitzgerald. Later, when both men were released, they decided to share an apartment together with Biegenwald's wife in Point Pleasant, N.J. Biegenwald took Fitzgerald into his confidence and revealed the sordid details of five different murders he had committed between 1981 and 1983.

Biegenwald had a long record of violent crime dating back to 1958, when he murdered New Jersey municipal prosecutor Stephen Sladowski during a grocery store holdup. The victim's wife urged the courts to spare the life of the young killer, with the tearful explanation that there had been too much bloodshed already. In 1959 the 19-year-old was sentenced to life in prison. He was twice denied parole and had been disciplined on several occasions before gaining release in 1975.

His next brush with the law occurred in 1980 when he violated his parole by moving to Teaneck, N.J. That same year he was implicated in a Staten Island rape case. The charges were dropped, but Biegenwald found himself behind bars at Rahway State prison until his discharge was granted in February 1981. There he met Dherran Fitzgerald.

Acting on a tip from Fitzgerald, investigators searched a lonely spot off Route 35 in Ocean Township where the remains of 18-year-old Camden resident Anna M. Olesiewicz were found. The girl had been missing since Aug. 28, 1982, when she was lured into Biegenwald's car to share a marijuana cigarette. After driving aimlessly through Asbury Park, he shot her four times in the head with a small-caliber handgun.

Fitzgerald and Biegenwald were arrested in their Asbury Park apartment on Jan. 22, 1983, eight days after the body was discovered. An arsenal of handguns, grenades, shotguns, and silencers were found along with a cache of illegal drugs. Monmouth County Prosecutor Alexander D. Lehrer followed up on Fitzgerald's tip and other pieces of evidence that led him to two unmarked graves in the quiet Charleston section of Staten Island where Biegenwald had disposed of the bodies of 17-year-old Maria Ciallella of Brick Township, N.J., and William J. Ward, a 34-year-old hoodlum who had tried to hire Biegenwald to perform a contract hit. The Ciallella woman was found in the backyard of a frame house belonging to Biegenwald's mother. She had been abducted on Halloween night, 1981, while walking home on Route 88. The killer had fired two shots into her head, then disposed of the remains in his own backyard.

The bodies of two other teenaged girls, 17-year-old Betsy Bacon and 17-year-old Deborah Osborne, were uncovered in two Jersey sites. Forensic experts identified the remains through dental charts. Deborah Osborne had been abducted at the Idle Hour Tavern in Point Pleasant, near a motel where she had been working as a chambermaid. Police theorized that she had left the tavern and hitched a ride with Biegenwald.

A sixth victim, 57-year-old convict John P. Petrone, was linked to Biegenwald when it was learned that the two men had become friends in prison. Petrone was silenced when Biegenwald suspected him of being a police informer.

Staten Island District Attorney Richard D. Murphy raised the possibility that the full extent of Biegenwald's crimes might never be known. Investigators continued to comb the areas adjacent to the grave sites but found only a few animal bones.

On Dec. 7, 1983, Biegenwald was convicted of murdering Anna M. Olesiewicz. He became the second New Jersey man to be sentenced to die by lethal injection under the newly reinstated death penalty, which took effect three weeks before he fired the first fatal shots. He sat on Death Row for more than three years, until Mar. 5, 1987, when the New Jersey Supreme Court ruled in a 6-1 decision that the law was constitutional, but that in Biegenwald's case the death sentence should be overturned because of grave errors in the sentencing hearing. The court upheld his conviction but ordered that a new sentencing hearing be scheduled to determine if he should be executed or sentenced to prison for life.

On Jan. 23, 1989, a jury in Freehold, N.J. deliberated for six hours before deciding that Biegenwald should be executed. The defense attorneys urged leniency, on the grounds that the defendant's sociopathic behavior should be carefully analyzed. The jury rejected this argument, and Judge Patrick McGann set Mar. 15 as Biegenwald's date of execution. The date was automatically postponed pending a mandatory Supreme Court review. REF.: CBA.

Biehler, Robert Leroy, prom. 1977, U.S., mur. Robert Leroy Biehler, the man who desired to be known as "the pimp of San Fernando Valley," was sentenced to life imprisonment in 1977 for murdering a female roller-derby skater, a 15-year-old boy and his mother, and their neighbor. California Superior Court Judge Peetris had wanted to preclude the possibility of early parole for Biehler by giving the killer a death sentence or at least consecutive sentences for each of the for murders, but, due to the state of Claifornia's Sentencing Law of 1976, Judge Peetris was unable to do so.

REF.: CBA; Godwin, Murder U.S.A.

Bielaski, Alexander Bruce, 1883-1964, U.S., law enfor. off. As head of the United State's federal law branch Alexander Bruce Bielaski uncovered German propaganda during WWI and later helped enforce Prohibition laws, but he was also known as a victim.

A year after earning a law degree at George Washington University in 1904 Bielaski joined the Justice Department, rising to the top of the Bureau of Investigation—which later became the Federal Bureau of Investigation—on Apr. 30, 1912. At a Senate

hearing on Dec. 6, 1918, Bielaski provided the government with information concerning wartime German propaganda activities in the U.S.

After retiring from the bureau at the end of the war, Bielaski entered private practice though his name was kept before the public when he was kidnapped in 1922 at Cuernavaca, Mexico. He escaped three days afterward. Bielaski admitted to using government money in 1926 when he operated the Bridge Whist Club, a phony speakeasy designed to ensnare bootleggers, which it did. He defended his actions, pointing out that his decoy played a major role in the apprehension of the William V. Dwyer liquor gang. Bielaski retired again in 1927. REF.: CBA.

Alexander Bruce Bielaski

Bière, Marie, prom. 1800s, Case of, Fr., attempt. mur. Promised a marriage in the near future, Marie Bière, an accomplished soprano, willingly became the mistress of the man she loved, Robert Gentien. Soon she became pregnant, and rather than incure the wrath of his parents, or more likely to have to deal with a family, Gentien persuaded Bière, an accomplished soprano, to move to Paris from their seaside resort at Biarritz.

In Paris Bière lived in virtual poverty, without much food or clothing for her infant daughter, and with little help from Gentien. The child soon died and, with its death, all love for Gentien faded from Bière, who decided to kill him and then herself, thus reuniting in death the family she never had. Her attempt to kill him failed as neither of two bullets greatly wounded Gentien. After hearing the sad love story her diary had to tell, the jury found her Not Guilty of attempted murder and she was freed.

REF.: CBA; Gribble, Adventures In Murder.

Bierut, Boleslaw, 1892-1956, U.S.S.R., consp. Communist supporter who was imprisoned in Soviet jails for various political crimes between 1938-43. After the war he helped the Russians consolidate their rule in eastern Europe, serving as president of Poland from 1945-52, and premier from 1952-54. REF.: CBA.

Biggin Hill Robbery, 1950, Brit., rob. On Sept. 27, 1950, Thomas Temple of Biggin Hill, England, was awakened by the sound of a burglar alarm in his shop next door to his home. Temple called the police, who conducted a thorough search of the premises. Two assailants sprung from the shadows and shot an officer in the neck. One of the burglars then fled the building, with Temple in pursuit. The fleeing robber ran right into the arms of the police outside. Thomas Temple returned to the wounded constable to lend assistance. Finding the second burglar attacking the fallen officer, Temple picked up the policeman's truncheon, drove off the gunman and stayed at the wounded man's side until help arrived. For this, Temple received the coveted Binney Medal, given to private citizens who exhibit bravery in the face of grave danger.

REF.: CBA; Scott, Scotland Yard.

Biggs, Ronald, See: **Great Train Robbery, The**.

Bigland, Reuben, prom. 1922, Brit., libel-blk. By purposely getting himself arrested and charged with committing a crime, Bigland, from the witness stand at his own trial, accomplished the conviction and downfall of Horatio Bottomley.

As a publisher from Birmingham, Reuben Bigland had been well-acquainted with Bottomley since 1912, even lending him money from time to time. On one occasion Bottomley, rather than repay Bigland £500 he owed him, agreed to rig a game called the "War Stock Combination," where people bought tickets in the hopes of winning prizes. Third prize was £1,000, which Bigland won, an arrangement Bottomley made to procure Bigland's help in other schemes, including the rigging of a court case. Bigland cooperated for a time, but decided to end Bottomley's deceit by attacking him in a pamphlet.

Bigland wrote the libelous article merely to provoke a suit by Bottomley, a suit that went to trial Jan. 23, 1922, at the Old Bailey, but was dismissed when the prosecutor said the Crown would not offer evidence. Bottomley proved unlucky in a second trial against Bigland, this one for attempted extortion of Bottomley in November 1920. Bottomley claimed that Bigland had persuaded three men to force Bottomley to pay him money or have unflattering pamphlets about him printed.

In defending Bigland at the Shropshire Assizes on Feb, 17, 1922, A.S. Comyns Carr allowed Bigland to take the stand and tell his story of the wrongdoings of Bottomley, wrongdoings which neither the prosecution nor Bottomley, who was present, attempted to refute. Following the recommendation given by Darling the jury retired for only three minutes before determining that Bigland was Not Guilty. See: **Bottomley, Horatio.**
REF.: Barker, *Lord Darling's Famous Cases; CBA;* Lustgarten, *Story of Crime.*

Big Mail Robbery (AKA: **The Big Job**), 1952, Brit., (unsolv.) rob. One of the greatest robberies in the history of London took place on May 21, 1952, and to this date remains unsolved, or at least unproved.

The Big Mail Robbery was committed with a great deal of planning and care, not only prior to the heist but after the crime was complete. A total of £287,000 in cash was stolen from a post office mail van when it stopped at Newcastle Street in London at 4:17 a.m. Within seven minutes three postal workers had been overpowered and eight bandits had driven off, one in a car that had stopped in front of the van, three in the van itself, and four in a car that pulled up behind the van. Eighteen of thirty-one mail bags were taken from the vehicle and placed in a van awaiting the postal van's arrival. This van, which was equipped with false sides to conceal the money, was parked on the street at Spitalfields Market and left there for a day before the robbery and the process of changing the bank notes into untraceable bills was begun.

Discovery of the robbers was almost impossible as they left behind only a pair of bolt cutters, a raincoat, and various other objects without even the trace of a fingerprint. Thorough searches made by Scotland Yard in the months following the crime turned up nothing, nor could investigators find anyone willing to talk about the robbery, so well covered were the gang's tracks. Eventually the police, led by Chief Superintendent Robert Lee, came to know the names of at least twelve of the men involved, including the leader, but because there was no proof other than money traced to the robbery, no convictions have been made. REF.: *CBA.*

Bigot, François, 1703-c.1777, Fr., fraud. Commissary of Louisbourg, Nova Scotia, from 1739-44. He undermined the colonial government through fraud, deceit, and treachery and the colony eventually fell to the British. Upon his return to France he was tried, imprisoned, and banished. REF.: *CBA.*

Big Sue (AKA: **The Turtle**), prom. 1812, U.S., pros. A huge black woman, Big Sue weighed more than 350 pounds and operated the first around-the-clock brothel in New York City, opening its doors in 1812 on Arch Street. Big Sue's approach to inducing customers into her low dive was a direct one. She merely thundered into the street, grabbed male passersby, and dragged them into her single-story bordello, literally hurling these patrons into the arms of her waiting girls.
REF.: *CBA;* Nash, *Almanac of World Crime.*

Bilansky, Ann (Mary Ann Evards Wright), 1820-60, U.S., mur. Ann Bilansky of St. Paul, Minn., fell in love with her handsome, young nephew, John Walker, and decided to get rid of her husband Stanislaus, a saloonkeeper. Her murder plan was made without thought of detection, apparently, since she loudly complained to neighbors that her elderly husband was a nuisance and she would be glad if he died. Some days later Ann Bilansky

served her husband some soup heavily dosed with arsenic. The death of Mr. Bilansky alarmed one of the neighbors, Mrs. Lucinda Kilpatrick, who had repeatedly heard Mrs. Bilansky's complaints about her husband. Two nights after Bilansky was buried (and Ann was already in the arms of her nephew), Mrs. Kilpatrick woke up out of a sound sleep and then awakened her husband, telling him that she had just dreamed about Ann Bilansky and in her dream she saw Mrs. Bilansky poisoning her husband.

Kilpatrick went to the police with his wife's story, adding what Mrs. Bilansky had said about her recently departed spouse. Authorities ordered the exhumation of Bilansky's body and it was found loaded with arsenic. Mrs. Bilansky and Walker were arrested but the nephew, a hard-working carpenter, proved that he was busy with customers in his shop at the time Mrs. Bilansky prepared the fatal meal for her husband. He was released for lack of evidence and Mrs. Bilansky was placed on trial. Quickly convicted, she was sentenced to death.

On Mar. 23, 1860, Ann Bilansky was escorted up the stairs of a high scaffold as a huge throng witnessed her last moments. She was indignant at the prospect of being hanged and spat at the executioner: "How can you stain your hands by putting that rope around my neck?" The hangman apologetically told her that he was doing his job. She nodded and then said: "Be sure my face is well covered." He placed a black cap over her face, placed her on the trap, slipped the noose about her neck, and then pulled the lever which opened the trapdoor and sent the poisoner to her death. Ann Bilansky was the only woman ever hanged in the history of Minnesota.
REF.: *CBA;* Nash, *Look for the Woman;* ____, *Murder, America.*

Bilger, George, 1917- , and **Sheeler, Rudolph,** c.1912- , U.S. (wrong. convict.) mur. Not only did the Philadelphia police arrest the wrong man for the murder of a fellow officer, but after shooting to death the actual killer in a gunfight they arrested and beat a confession out of an innocent man.

Patrolman James T. Morrow, working in plain clothes, tracking down a robber who had killed John Canham and wounded another victim, Mrs. May Baxendale, was himself shot in the back three times and killed on Nov. 23, 1936. Joseph Broderick, the first man police tried forcing a confession from, was released when it was revealed how the police obtained the confession. In May 1937 police arrested George Bilger, whom Morrow had been tailing, and he readily confessed, accusing a patrolman as his accomplice. At his trial in June 1937, he was found Guilty, but the decision was set aside because Judge Harry S. McDevitt did not feel Bilger told the truth. A second trial found the defendant Guilty and he was sentenced to life in prison, while the patrolman was exonerated of collusion.

The robbery spree continued even with Bilger behind bars, and on Sept. 12, 1938, schoolteacher Edward Tamkin was killed. Police learned that the killer was Jack Batton, whose real name was Jack Howard, and on Feb. 6, 1939, they shot Howard who died before he could be questioned. Howard need not have been questioned. The guns he possessed were proof enough that he had killed Canham, Morrow, and Tamkin, but the police wanted a living killer to stand trial, because Bilger appeared innocent and his trial had blackened another officer's name.

Unfortunately for Rudolph Sheeler he was just what the police wanted. By visiting the same patient in the hospital as Howard had, Sheeler connected himself with the killer and he was promptly arrested. It did not matter that the patient was Sheeler's sister, all that mattered was that he confess. To make sure a confession was obtained, the police booked Sheeler under a false name and proceeded to beat a story to their liking out of him, which he gave after his wife finally discovered his whereabouts and a lawyer procured a writ of habeas corpus. He recanted his confession at his arraignment, but after further beatings and fear of more he finally pled guilty. This plea did not match his confession, so the police rewrote it. The three trial judges accepted it without question at his trial on Mar. 29, 1939. Bilger was pardoned and placed in a mental hospital.

Twelve years after his trial and sentence to life imprisonment Sheeler was finally cleared of the charge when discovery was made of the forced confession, complete with its numerous inconsistencies with the murder in question, and the fact that Sheeler was in New York at the time of the murder. On May 1, 1951, Sheeler was found innocent and later six police officers were suspended for their involvement in the case.

REF.: *CBA; Radin, The Innocents.*

Billaud-Varenne, Jean-Nicolas, 1756-1819, Fr., terror. Politically active during French Revolution as member of the Jacobin club from 1789, of the Commune from 1792, and the Committee of Public Safety in 1793. He helped bring about the downfall of Robespierre in 1794, and was tried as a political terrorist and sentenced to penal servitude in Cayenne, French Guiana, in 1795. He refused amnesty from Napoléon, but was released to Haiti in 1816. REF.: *CBA.*

Billee, John, and **Willis, Thomas,** d.1890, U.S., west. outl. After robbing and murdering W.P. Williams and burying his body in a ravine in Oklahoma's Kiamichi Mountains on Apr. 12, 1888, John Billee and Thomas Willis were apprehended by three deputies, Will Ayers, James Wilkerson and Perry DuVall. While en route back to Fort Smith, Oklahoma Territory, for trial, the three lawmen and the two prisoners bedded down in a deserted cabin near Muskogee, Okla. During the night, Billee managed to free one hand from the handcuffs which bound him to one of the deputies and reached for the deputy's gun. He shot Ayers, DuVall, and Wilkerson, wounding them, but Wilkerson managed to wound the outlaw before Billee made good his escape. All three wounded deputies, embarrassed at being jumped, were publicly denounced when they delivered their prisoners to Fort Smith. Billee and Willis were convicted of murder and sentenced to death. After several legal delays, they were both hanged at Fort Smith on Jan. 16, 1890.

REF.: *CBA; Shirley, Law West of Fort Smith.*

Billik, Herman (AKA: **Professor Billik**), b.c.1857, U.S., mur. When the family of Chicago milkman Martin Vzral began dying off one by one of a strange stomach illness, gossip soon pointed to a strange sorcerer who had visited the family and Vzral's widow. Upon the widow's death the magician was arrested and later convicted of killing six members of the Vzral family.

Not long after Vzral consulted a seer, Herman Billik, who assured him a prosperous life, he became ill and died on Mar. 27, 1905. In the same manner death occurred for the milkman's 22-year-old daughter, Mary, on July 28; the next youngest daughter, Tilly, on Dec. 22, 1905; 18-year-old Rose on Aug. 26, 1906; and 12-year-old Ella on Nov. 30, 1906. Each death provided the widow and mother, Rose Vzral, with insurance money, which led to rumors spreading far enough to reach the police and Billik, who apparently persuaded Rose to commit suicide with poison just before the police arrived.

Police arrested Billik and charged him with the murder of all six Vzrals, especially after exhumation and autopsies of the bodies revealed that arsenic poisoning had caused their deaths. At the trial Billik admitted to conning the Vzrals out of money but not to murdering them; nor could the prosecution prove that he had ever purchased or possessed arsenic. The jury, however, still found the evidence damning enough to return a verdict of Guilty on July 18, 1907, and Billik was sentenced to death. This sentence was never carried out, as it was learned that the milkman's surviving son, Jersolobat Vzral, had perjured himself at Billik's trial, and later that the father-in-law of Vzral's eldest daughter, Emma Vzral Niemann, had also died of arsenic poisoning, adding to the rumor that someone close to the family had killed the Vzrals. After a sixth stay of execution Billik's sentence was commuted to life imprisonment by Governor Charles Samuel Deneen on Jan. 22, 1909. See: **Blandy, Mary; Cotton, Mary Ann Robson Mowbray; DeMelker, Daisy Louisa; Jegado, Helene; LaFarge, Marie; Smith, Madeleine.**

REF.: *CBA; Smith, Famous American Poison Mysteries.*

Billings, Warren K., See: **Mooney, Thomas J.**

Billingsley, Fred, and **Billingsley, Logan,** prom. 1916, U.S., boot. After enactment of the Washington state legislature's prohibition of alcohol on Jan. 1, 1916, brothers Fred and Logan Billingsley opened the Stewart Street Pharmacy in Seattle. The two had already quit their bootlegging operation in Oklahoma, where Prohibition had been in effect for four years, when they began dispensing liquor for so-called medical reasons in Seattle. Their business grew until liquor was pouring in from California, Canada, and Cuba, angering a rival gang led by a former police officer Jack Marquett, and resulting in a number of battles, until all three men were imprisoned in 1917.

REF.: *CBA; Kobler, Ardent Spirits.*

Billington, James (**Joshua Billington**), 1833-1900, Brit., execut. Although employed as a hairdresser in Farnworth, Britain, when he performed his first hanging in 1884, James Billington soon became quite adept at the practice and was named as the official executioner for Yorkshire at Armley Jail, a post he held for seven years before replacing James Berry as the hangman for the city of London.

Billington studied his craft well, working on ways to reduce the amount of time necessary to carry out an execution. By using a double-buckle strap instead of the straps and belt previously used, Billington could have a condemned man pinioned in half a minute rather than a minute and one half. Of the executions he performed, the most notable were Joseph Canning, Walter Horsford, Louise Massett, Patrick M'Kenna, Mr. Milson, James Canham Read, and Neil Cream.

At the execution of Cream, the famous poisoner was in the midst of shouting something from under the white hood he wore when Billington pulled the lever releasing the trap. Cream may have been alluding to the unsolved Jack the Ripper murders when he yelled, "I am Jack..." before the rope cut short his speech. Later Billington remarked, "If I had only known he was going to speak I should have waited for the end of the sentence."

REF.: *CBA; Laurence, A History of Capital Punishment.*

Billington, John, d.1630, U.S., mur. John Billington reserved a historical niche for himself in American history by becoming the country's first official murderer. He arrived with the original band of Pilgrims on the *Mayflower* in 1620, landing at Plymouth Rock. Billington and his family were unlike the other Pilgrims to the New Land and had caused the leaders of this adventuresome band no end of vexation. He had committed some criminal offenses in England, and he and his clan traveled to America more to escape the prying eyes of law enforcement officials than to practice an unpopular religion. On the trip over, Billington loudly complained about the accomodations for himself and family, swearing at every opportunity. His churlish behavior and foul tongue finally brought down the wrath of Captain Miles Standish who ordered Billington's neck and feet tied together for a day, placing him on display on the maindeck as an example of a sinner deserving corporal punishment.

Such demonstrative treatment did nothing to curb Billington's bilious attitude. After the Pilgrims established their first colony, Billington continued to make a nuisance of himself. He avoided work and was labeled a slacker, punished repeatedly by being put into the stocks. He started arguments with church elders and threatened to attack those who disagreed with his notions of how the New Land should be developed. It was Billington's idea to let his fellow settlers clear and plough the land. John Billington would then farm it, he said. He was not made for hard labor. One of his bitterest enemies was John Newcomen who had many times denounced Billington in church as lagging behind on his work, spreading gossip and lies about his neighbors. The two men had come to blows on several occasions and Newcomen had bested Billington.

In 1630, a decade after the founding of the Pilgrim settlement, John Billington's seething anger at Newcomen finally spilled over into murder. He stalked his neighbor for several days, noting the paths Newcomen took through the woods when hunting game. A few days later Billington hid behind a rock along the route Newcomen always took, and when his foe appeared on the path, he fired his blunderbuss almost point blank into Newcomen who died instantly from the blast. When Newcomen's body was discovered hours later, Billington was the first man suspected.

Arrested, he was quickly tried and convicted. His fellow Pilgrims sentenced him to be hanged. Billington was not only hanged but his corpse was left to rot from a tree, until it fell to pieces. His skull was reportedly nailed to the tree until it became petrified, a grim reminder of what awaited any of those Pilgrims who thought to stray from a law-abiding life. Oddly, thousands of Americans doggedly lay claim to being related to Billington, irrespective of his infamous place in history, such is the desire of these citizens to establish their own historical identity.

REF.: Boucher, *The Quality of Murder*; CBA; Nash, *Bloodletters and Badmen*.

Billy the Kid (William H. Bonney, AKA: Henry Antrim, Kid Antrim, William Antrim, Henry McCarty), 1859-81, U.S., west. outl. Next to Jesse Woodson James, no other outlaw of the American Old West still captures the imagination and near-obsession of the public than Billy the Kid, a lethal phenomenon who killed, according to legend if not record, twenty-one men before his twenty-first birthday. This famed bad man was reportedly born in New York City on Nov. 23, 1859, the son of William and Kathleen (or Catherine) McCarty Bonney, and named William H. Bonney. Another story has it that he was born on Sept. 17, 1859, as Patrick Henry McCarty to Catherine and Patrick McCarty. And still another account has it that he was born in Indiana to Joseph McCarty of Cass County. The first report seems to be the most reliable, especially since the Kid used the name of William H. Bonney, signing his letters as such. Yet a reliable account has Mrs. Bonney or McCarty living in Indianapolis, Ind., with William Antrim and moving west with him and her two sons, Henry and Joseph in 1870, settling first in Wichita, Kan., where Mrs. Bonney ran a laundry and dabbled in small real estate holdings. One report has it that the family lived for a while in the newly establish town of Coffeyville, Kan., and it was here that Billy first got into trouble, arrested for pilfering butter and other items from a local store.

Mrs. McCarty-Bonney decided to move to the Southwest with Antrim, marrying him in Sante Fe, N.M., on Mar. 1, 1873. The Antrims, along with the two boys, Henry (Billy) and Joseph, to Silver City where Antrim became a miner and Mrs. Antrim ran a small boarding house. Always a sickly, frail woman, Mrs. Antrim died on Sept. 16, 1874, after a short illness. Billy was then about fifteen and did not get along with his stepfather, William Antrim, who thought the boy was a troublemaker as he had been in some minor scrapes in Silver City where he went to school and did odd jobs. He and another youth, George "Sombrero Jack" Shaffer, stole some clothes from a Chinese laundry, mostly as a prank, and were arrested. Billy, rather than face the wrath of his stern stepfather, left town, drifting about Arizona, performing odd jobs on ranches and in small towns.

It was during this loosely recorded period of wandering that the Kid supposedly shot his first man. One account claimed he killed an unknown gunman in Coffeyville even before he and his family left that town and, a few years later, shot and killed three Apache braves near the Chiracachua Reservation, killed a blacksmith in Fort Bowie, three cardsharps in Mexico, two more Indians in the Guadalupe Mountains, and so on. It is known that he was first called the Kid in 1877 when he got into an argument with Irish blacksmith Frank P. Cahill at Camp Grant, Ariz., on Aug. 17, 1877. The blacksmith who was in a saloon owned by George Adkins, called Billy a pimp, slapped the Kid's face, and threw him to the floor. The Kid realized he was no match for the burly Cahill and he immediately drew his six-gun as the blacksmith came toward him, firing a single shot that mortally wounded Cahill who died the following day. Billy was locked up in the post guardhouse but he escaped and began running.

This was the first recorded killing by Billy the Kid, official or not. Not until the outbreak of the Lincoln County War in New Mexico did the Kid's guns claim known victims. The first and second of these were Frank Baker and Billy Morton. These two men, with others, stopped the gentleman English rancher J.H. Tunstall while he was driving his buckboard along a lonely road and shot him to death. Billy, who worked for Tunstall and had been almost adopted by him, vowed that he would kill every man responsible for Tunstall's death. He had wandered into Lincoln County in late 1875 and was hired as a ranch hand by the Murphy-Dolan forces. L.G. Murphy and J.J. Dolan owned giant ranches in Lincoln County and were in mortal combat with other ranchers for water rights and grazing land, chiefly Alexander McSween and John Tunstall who were supported by the greatest cattle baron of that day, John Chisum.

Billy spent most of his time rustling Chisum's cattle from the sprawling Jinglebob Ranch and turning these over to Murphy who sold them to Mexican and Indian buyers. By accident, the Kid met John Tunstall, a cultured, kingly man who became the father figure Billy never had. The Kid went to work with him, idolizing Tunstall and his gentlemanly ways, trying to emulate his mentor's style and sense of nobility. Tunstall thought the Kid showed promise and was later quoted as having said of Billy: "That's the finest lad I ever met. He's a revelation to me every day and would do anything on earth to please me. I'm going to make a man of that boy yet."

Tunstall's plan for Billy never materialized. On Feb. 18, 1878, he was stopped on the road by a group of gunmen who had been deputized by Sheriff William Brady, a Murphy-Dolan backer. This band included many of Billy's former friends before he had switched sides in the Lincoln County War, including Billy Morton, Jesse Evans, Jim McDaniel, and Frank Baker. These so-called deputies informed Tunstall that they were going to take part of his herd, cattle which they claimed belonged to Murphy. Tunstall objected, pointing out that all his cattle were branded and if they checked the brands, they would see for themselves that Murphy could not lay claim to them. Evans and the others drew their guns and ordered Tunstall to surrender. He got out of his buckboard and handed over his gun, saying: "I don't want bloodshed." As he was handing Evans his gun, Evans fired a bullet into the helpless man who pitched downward to the road. Billy Morton then cruelly fired a bullet into Tunstall's head, killing him.

When the Kid heard the news of Tunstall's death he said: "He was the only man who ever treated me kindly, like I was free born and white." He then gritted his teeth and said in a rage: "I'll get every s.o.b. who helped kill John if it's the last thing I ever do." This remark was passed along to the members of the Murphy-Dolan clan and many of its members became apprehensive, knowing that Billy the Kid was a single-minded man who would ride miles out of his way to confront an enemy, and that his marksmanship was unfailing, starting with a fast draw no one had beat to date. The Kid at this time was not an impressive looking fellow. He stood about five-feet-ten-inches tall, had a receding chin, an overbite that made him appear to have exaggerated buck teeth, and narrow, squinting eyes of icy blue that were piercing to look into, eyes that seemed to dart about nervously whenever danger was near. He was a clever killer, an expert bushwacker who would not hesitate to shoot from ambush, fire a bullet into an enemy's back, or sneak up on an adversary in the middle of the night with a knife and dispatch his man without a second of sorrow.

The first to feel the bite of Billy's bullets were Billy Morton and Frank Baker. When the Kid heard that Richard M. "Dick" Brewer had been sworn in as a special constable to arrest Tunstall's killers, he joined the group of "regulators," being sworn in as a deputy. After several days of searching, on Mar. 6, 1878, Brewer's posse found a group of riders about six miles from the Rio Pecos. The band rode off, breaking up in small groups, with Brewer's men in hot pursuit. The Kid raced after Morton and Baker, firing his six-gun and Winchester as he rode. He ran both men down after their horses collapsed and took them prisoner, but he vowed to kill both men. The prisoners were taken to the

Chisum ranch and, on Mar. 9, 1878, the Kid was a member of the regulators removing the prisoners to Lincoln. The party stopped at Roswell, about five miles from Chisum's ranch so Morton could mail a letter. Morton told the postmaster there, M.A. Upson, to notify his relatives if any harm came to him. Upson asked him if he thought the posse taking him and Baker to Lincoln would injure them. Morton said that the posse had promised John Chisum to deliver the prisoners safely to authorities in Lincoln and he trusted their word.

At that point, William McCloskey, one of the regulators, stepped forward, having heard the conversation between Morton and Upson, saying to Morton: "Billy, if harm comes to you two, they will have to kill me first." The posse rode off, the Kid and Charlie Bowdre in the lead, some distance in front of the posse and its prisoners, looking out for Murphy-Dolan men who might try to release Morton and Baker. Then rode Morton and Baker with McCloskey and John Middleton right behind them. Following were Dick Brewer, Henry Brown, Frank McNab, Sam Smith, Jim French, J.G. Skurlock, and Fred Wayt. The posse and its prisoners never reached Lincoln.

On Mar. 11, 1878, McNab appeared in Roswell and reported that Morton and Baker had tried to escape, pulling McCloskey's guns from their scabbard and killing him, and then being shot to death by the posse. This was later proven to be a lie. The posse, with the exception of McCloskey, had apparently agreed to kill the prisoners. It was unclear whether or not the Kid and Bowdre knew of this plan which may have been developed as the posse rode along, the men in the rear making the decision. McNab, a short time after the posse had left Roswell, near a spot called the Black Water Holes (also called Steel Springs), rode up to McCloskey and put a six-gun to his head, saying: "You are the s.o.b. whose got to die before harm can come to these fellows, are you?" He fired, blowing out McCloskey's brains, his corpse falling from the horse. Morton and Baker, realizing they were marked for execution, then spurred their horses on and the Kid, turning to see them flee, pursued them, overtaking them, and firing two bullets which killed them both.

The posse split up, McNab returning to Chisum's ranch where he worked, the others going off to separate destinations. The bodies of McCloskey, who was thought to be in league with the prisoners, Morton, and Baker were left where they fell and were later buried by Mexican sheepherders. The Kid went to Lincoln, working for McSween. Later, he heard that Andrew L. "Buckshot" Roberts, a dedicated Murphy-Dolan man, was hunting him and the other killers of Morton and Baker. Brewer got together his regulators, including the Kid, and sought out Roberts, finding him in early April 1878 at Blazer's Saw Mill, about forty miles south of Lincoln. As the regulators rode into the area, Roberts, on horseback, saw them, and bravely charged them alone on horseback, firing his Winchester as he rode. Roberts was a western hardcase of incredible courage. He had been a soldier and had been in many gunfights. He was a crack shot with his Winchester and equally accurate with his six guns. As Roberts raced forward, he sent a rifle bullet whizzing past the Kid's head. Billy jumped from his horse and fired a shot that struck Roberts in the abdomen, but the tough old gunfighter managed to dismount, grab his guns, and take refuge in an outhouse. The regulators peppered the outhouse with dozens of shots and it appeared that Roberts had been killed. Brewer stood up and began to advance on the tiny building when Roberts thrust his Winchester through a hole and fired, his bullet crashing through Brewer's head, killing him. Roberts' Winchester barked again and this time Charley Bowdre was seriously wounded in the side, but his heavy cartridge belt had deflected the bullet and saved his life. Again the regulators riddled the outhouse, this time hitting Roberts several times, mortally wounding him. He died clutching his Winchester.

The Kid, now that Brewer was dead, vowed to continue his purge of the Murphy-Dolan faction. To this end he sought out Sheriff William Brady and his deputies George Hindman and J.B. Matthews. The Kid and Matthews had already confronted each other on the streets of Lincoln and Matthews had avoided a gunfight by slipping into a building and hiding. On Apr. 1, 1878, the Kid and five of his friends rode unseen into Lincoln and hid behind an adobe wall. They cut holes in the wall through which they could see the entire main street, with a view of the courthouse and through which they could fire their weapons. A short time later Sheriff Brady, Hindman, and Matthews appeared on the street, all carrying rifles and six-guns. As soon as they came under the Kid's guns he and his companions opened fire from their ambush. Brady fell dead with several bullets in him. Hindman fell next to him, mortally wounded. Matthews raced to a row of buildings and took refuge. The Kid ran to the fallen lawmen, intent on taking Brady's weapons, but when he picked up Brady's rifle, Matthews fired a shot that blew it out of his hand, the bullet grazing Billy's side. He retreated to the adobe wall and then the Kid's party saddled up and rode out of Lincoln. The Kid's brutal ambush of Brady and Hindman was one of the most ruthless, cowardly murders ever committed in the territory and it lost Billy the support of many who, up to that time, had backed him.

With the deaths of Brady and Hindman, the count of those killed by Billy the Kid, depending on whose count one accepted, had reached seventeen. He would kill five more men before he himself was slain by a man he had known for years, a friend at one time, a lawman only at the time he fired his fatal shot into the Kid. Following Brady's murder, George "Dad" Peppin became the new sheriff of Lincoln and he put together a large force to capture the Kid who made himself available to Peppin and his men by visiting McSween in his large Lincoln mansion with fourteen men. They barricaded the place and were soon surrounded by Peppin and about forty of the toughest gunfighters in the territory. Marion Turner, a Roswell merchant who had once been aligned with Chisum but had gone over to the Murphy-Dolan faction, had control of Peppin's posse and ordered it to open fire on the McSween mansion. This occurred on July 15, 1878. The gun battle raged for five days before a truce was called.

Turner then called out to the bullet-ridden mansion that he had warrants for the Kid and his men, charging them with the murder of Sheriff Brady and Deputy Hindman. There was a moment's silence, then Billy shouted back: "We too, have warrants for you and all your gang which we will serve on you hot from the muzzles of our guns!" The fight again ensued. The Turner-Peppin forces aided by a company of U.S. infantry commanded by Lieutenant Colonel Nathan Augustus Monroe Dudley, made a shambles of the mansion, but the occupants fired back at their attackers with vigor and many were wounded on both sides. Colonel Dudley threatened to fire his two field cannons at the house, reducing it to rubble unless the Kid's forces surrendered, but the guns remained silent. The battle was witnessed by several newsmen who later wrote fabulous, untrue reports. One had it that Mrs. McSween "encouraged her wild garrison by playing inspiring airs on her piano, and singing rousing battle songs until the besieging party, getting the range of the piano from the sound, shot it to pieces with their heavy rifles." This, of course, was nonsense. Mrs. McSween and three other females left the house before the battle commenced.

One of the Mexicans inside the McSween house, exhausted with the battle, called out that those inside the mansion would surrender, but the Kid leaped across the room and knocked him senseless with his gunbutt. Outside, the call had been heard and Robert Beckwith approached the kitchen door of the house, with John Jones next to him. He called out for McSween as he stood in the open doorway. Billy sent a bullet into his skull, killing Beckwith instantly. Jones was also shot as the Kid shouted to his comrades: "Come on!" With that, Billy, two guns blazing in his hands, jumped over Beckwith's body, followed by his friends, as they made their mass escape, hundreds of bullets smashing into the building around them. The Kid miraculously fought his way through the lines of besiegers, wounding several, and made it to the nearby river, plunging in and getting to the other side where

Billy the Kid

Susan McSween

Catherine Bonney Antrim

John Tunstall

Richard Brewer

William Antrim

Alexander McSween

Tom O'Folliard

he was covered by high reeds. His friends, including Tom O'Folliard, followed and most were wounded. McSween refused to desert his home. He stepped into the yard and was shot to death, nine bullets entering his body.

The Lincoln County War was the disgrace of New Mexico and President Rutherford B. Hayes replaced Governor Axtell with Lew Wallace. As the new territorial governor, Wallace resolved to bring the bloody war to an end. He announced that a general amnesty was in effect for all those involved in the war, except for those who had been charged with murder. This meant Billy the Kid. But the Kid had cleverly seen his chance to escape murder warrants some time earlier. He had witnessed the killing of Huston Chapman, a lawyer for the McSween faction, who was shot down in cold blood on the streets of Lincoln by William Matthews, William Campbell, and James Dolan, but he had not gone for his guns. He went instead to Governor Wallace, offering to turn state's evidence against the three killers in exchange for a full pardon.

Wallace met with the Kid on Mar. 17, 1789. Billy walked into the home of John Wilson, holding a Winchester and a six-gun, asking if Wallace was there. Governor Wallace stood up and was shocked to see a slender boy with only a faint stubble of beard, finding it hard to believe that the Kid was the most feared gunman in the West. Wallace said that if he surrendered and testified against Matthews and the others in the Chapman killing he would receive a full pardon. Billy said he did not like the idea of surrendering; it appear that he was a coward. He would be arrested then, Wallace volunteered, a fake arrest but one that would convince everyone that the Kid had put up a fight. The arrest was made and the Kid testified against the killers, so much enjoying the widespread publicity he received that he talked non-stop about all the outlaws in the territory, providing details on their rustling and thieving activities, thus breaking the code of silence binding all criminals. But he was Billy the Kid and he reveled in his black fame; he did as he pleased.

Part of the bargain the Kid made with Governor Wallace was to stand trial for the murder of Brady and Hindman. Wallace had promised that Billy would be set free but the Kid grew uneasy waiting for his day in court and suddenly decided to leave his loosely guarded confines in the back of a store, simply ambling to the street where he mounted someone else's horse and rode away, going to see his friends at Fort Sumner. Here he ran into Texas gunman Joe Grant who had told anyone who would listen that he intended to make his reputation by gunning down Billy the Kid. The Kid had also heard the story and, when meeting Grant, told him how much he admired Grant's expensive six-gun, asking if he could inspect it. Grant foolishing handed over the gun and Billy reportedly turned the cylinder to three empty chambers. A short time later, after the Kid had returned the gun, Grant and Billy squared off and fired at each other. Grant's gun only clicked as he fired an empty chamber but Billy's shot killed the ambitious Grant on the spot, or, at least, that is the story still told.

Billy and his gang were surrounded in a ranch house some time later by a posse and the Kid asked for a truce to negotiate. Gunman Jimmy Carlyle stepped from cover to talk and the Kid shot him down. When Carlyle was killed, the rest of the posse fled in terror, and the Kid and his men rode away without interference. It seemed as if New Mexico was to be forever plagued by the gunplay of Billy the Kid. That changed in 1880 when Pat Garrett was made sheriff of Lincoln County. He had known the Kid well; they had both ridden for the Maxwell ranch and had played cards and gotten drunk together on their days off. There was a deep and genuine friendship between them, but that too changed when Garrett put on his badge. He had been ordered to capture the Kid at all costs by Governor Wallace, who had placed a $500 reward on the Kid's head for not keeping his promise to stand trial for the Brady killing.

Garrett lost no time forming a posse and setting a trap for the Kid and his band on Dec. 18, 1880. With more than a dozen men laying in wait with him, Garrett, who had received a tip that the Kid and his men would be approaching Fort Sumner, saw Tom O'Folliard riding point for the gang and opened fire. O'Folliard was hit and his horse bolted but the mortally wounded O'Folliard turned about and limped back to Garrett. Blood gushed from O'Folliard's chest and the gunman said to Garrett: "Don't shoot again, Garrett, I'm killed." Garrett told him to dismount but O'Folliard said he could not, that he was dying and needed help to get off his horse. The Kid and his friends fled. O'Folliard died about an hour later.

The Kid and his men were now on the run and Garrett pursued them relentlessly, finally cornering the band in a deserted farmhouse near Stinking Springs on Dec. 21, 1881. Inside of the house were Billy, Charlie Bowdre, Dave Rudabaugh, Tom Pickett and Billy Wilson, the Kid's closest friends and most ardent followers. The lanky Garrett stepped out from cover in the moonlight and called for the gang to surrender. The Kid's response was typical; he fired off several shots, attempting to kill his one-time friend. Garrett and his men, about twenty strong, opened up a withering fire on the farmhouse. When Bowdre crossed in front of an open window he was hit in the chest and let out a piercing scream. "I'm killed, Billy, they killed me," he said as he crouched in the one-room farmhouse.

Billy stood Bowdre up and shoved him to the door, ruthlessly telling his friend: "They have murdered you, Charlie, but you can get revenge! Go out there and kill some of the s.o.b.'s before you go!" With that, the Kid swung the door open and shoved his friend Bowdre out into a hail of bullets. Bowdre lifted his six-gun but did not have the strength to fire. He was hit several more times and fell face forward, saying: "I wish...I wish...I wish..." Then he died and his body rotted there as Garrett and his men kept up the siege for two days. The Kid and his men, starving and panting for water, surrendered and were taken to Santa Fe. Here the Kid sent a letter to Governor Wallace, reminding him of his promise to pardon him. Wallace refused to answer, telling newsmen that the Kid reneged on *his* promise to stand trial for the murder of Sheriff Brady. There would be no pardon.

With great fanfare, the Kid was taken to Mesilla, N.M., where he was tried before Judge Warren Bristol for killing Andrew "Buckshot" Roberts. He was convicted and Judge Bristol, a stern, unrelenting jurist, sentenced the Kid to death, telling the stoic Billy that he would hang "until you are dead, dead, dead!" The Kid reportedly yelled back: "And you can go to hell, hell, hell!" While awaiting execution, the Kid gave expansive interviews to eager newsmen, posing as a persecuted victim in the one-sided Lincoln County War, telling reporters: "I expect to be lynched. It's wrong that I should be the only one to suffer the extreme penalties of the law." He went on to complain that he was being singled out for punishment where there were many others more deserving of the hangman's rope. He was removed to Lincoln to await execution by two of Garrett's top deputies, J.W. Bell and Robert Ollinger. On the trip, Ollinger, who had been a Murphy-Dolan henchman during the Lincoln County War, made no secret of his hatred for the Kid. Once the Kid was locked up in the old courthouse in Lincoln, Ollinger kept prodding Billy with the butt of his shotgun whenever the Kid had to go to the washroom, saying: "I can save you from the hangman, Kid. Just make a run for it...I'd love to put a load of buckshot in your back...give it to you the way you gave it to Sheriff Brady!"

Billy said nothing, only took the punishment, biding his time. Bell, on several occasions, told Olliger to stop persecuting the Kid. His kindness toward Billy caused the Kid to become friendly with the deputy but this was only an act. He was determined to escape and he would kill anyone who got in his way, including the gentle deputy. On Apr. 28, 1881, Billy asked Bell to help him to the latrine which was down the stairs and in back of the courthouse. As he was hobbling toward the stairs en route to the outhouse, Bell close by, the Kid knocked Bell down with his shoulder and hopped quickly into Garrett's gun room which was only a few feet away, grabbing a pistol. Bell came running into

Pat Garrett (on white horse) brings in Billy the Kid.

Deputy Bob Ollinger.

The Kid escaped from the Lincoln County Courthouse.

Governor Lew Wallace.

Pat Garrett, left, with friends.

The grave of Billy the Kid and pals.

the room and saw the gun in the Kid's hands, pleading with him to put it down. "Sorry, Bell," said the Kid and shot the deputy dead. He then hobbled over to the outside second-story balcony with a loaded shotgun and waited for Bob Ollinger whom he knew would come running at the sound of the shot that killed Bell.

Ollinger, who had been drinking in a nearby saloon, soon appeared, running toward the court house. "Hello, Bob," a friendly voice called out, and Ollinger looked up to see Billy on the balcony, a shotgun aimed straight at his head. Juggling the weapon and the heavy manacles about his wrists, the Kid pulled back both hammers of the shotgun as Ollinger stood petrified in the middle of the street. Billy let loose both barrels at the hated Ollinger and the lawman was blown twenty feet into the ruts of the road, his head almost blown away. The Kid hobbled down the stairs and stopped a handyman, ordering him to get an ax. Then the handyman was ordered to chop off the manacles from the Kid's ankles and wrists, which he did. Billy gathered several pistols, a Winchester, and the shotgun, went to the street and mounted a horse tethered to a hitching post outside the courtroom. He rode up to the spot where Ollinger's body lay and dropped the shotgun next to it. To startled witnesses gaping at him, Billy the Kid, ever the limelighter, swept off his wide hat and waved it, shouting: "Adios, amigos!" Then he galloped out of town as the news of his spectacular escape was flashed across the country.

Such daring caused local residents to believe that Billy the Kid, who escaped the noose two weeks before his scheduled execution, would never be brought to justice. Garrett vowed he would get the Kid and spent three months tracking him all over New Mexico. Finally, on the night of July 14, 1881, he rode onto the old Maxwell ranch where he and the Kid had worked and spent many happy hours together. The Kid was visiting a young Mexican woman at the ranch and stepped out of a bedroom, into the moonlight, when he heard the hoofbeats of horses outside. Garrett, meanwhile, had entered the large ranch house, gone down a corridor and entered the darkened bedroom. The Kid stood outside in the shadows, calling in a loud whisper in Spanish: "Quien es?...Quien es?...Quien es?" (Who is it?) When no one answered, the Kid stepped back through the outside door to the bedroom, he turned to see his old friend Garrett holding a gun on him. The Kid was armed, according to Garrett's later report: "He came there (into the bedroom) armed with a pistol and a knife expressly to kill me if he could. I had no alternative but to kill him or suffer death at his hands." Two shots rang out and Billy the Kid, living legend, fell to the bedroom floor dead. Garrett's first shot struck the outlaw in the heart and killed him instantly, the second shot going wild.

Possemen who had accompanied Garrett to the ranch and who nervously waited in the shadows outside were shocked to see Garrett suddenly dash outside, yelling triumphantly: "I killed the Kid! I killed the Kid!" He stood outside the ranch house for some time, trembling and saying nothing. Then he went back into the bedroom where Deluvina Maxwell, the pretty woman the Kid had come to see, held the lifeless body of the killer boy in her arms. She looked up at Garrett, accusing the lawman of shooting her lover in the back, adding with a sneer: "You didn't have the nerve to kill him face to face."

As with most of the Kid's story, his death remained a subject of heated controversy for decades and still causes endless debate. Did Garrett, one time friend of the outlaw, murder the youthful gunman when his back was turned? Was Billy armed? It did not matter in 1881. Garrett was hailed, for the most part, as a hero, even though murder charges were brought against him. He was acquitted by a coroner's jury who ruled the shooting of Billy the Kid "justifiable homicide." The $500 reward was not paid to Garrett for some time. In fact, a special act by the territorial legislature had to be passed before Garrett collected the reward. Billy the Kid, who died four months before his twenty-second birthday, was first buried at the Maxwell ranch in clothes that were too large for his slender body. Deluvina Maxwell placed a cross over his grave with a marker stating "Duerme bien, Querido." (Sleep well, beloved.)

Souvenir hunters, however, soon arrived and the grave was despoiled many times until the body was removed to the common grave at Fort Sumner where Billy the Kid was buried with his two best friends, Tom O'Folliard and Charlie Bowdre, who had died for their outlaw chief. The stone over this grave bore the names of its three occupants and the word "Pals." Garrett went on to fame but little reward. He had a small ranch and employee problems. On Feb. 28, 1908, he was shot to death by an angry tenant rancher who felt Garrett had cheated him out of wages. Of the two, Billy the Kid's name became the most remembered and attached to it is a strange lore that has somehow overshadowed the true nature of this ruthless killer, one that will not admit to his cold-blooded murders, his total disregard for humanity, his utter lack of mercy. In this twisted legend of the Old West, the Kid's victims are not human beings but notches on a gun, twenty-one of them. See: **Bell, J.W.; Garrett, Patrick Floyd; Lincoln County War.**

REF.: Adams, *A Fitting Death for Billy the Kid*; Adler, *Billy the Kid, A Case Study in Epic Origins*; Alldredge, *Cowboys and Coyotes*; American Guide Series, *New Mexico, A Guide to the Colorful State*; Anderson, *History of New Mexico*; Argall, *Outlawry and Justice in Old Arizona*; Atherton, *The Cattle Kings*; Axford, *Around Western Campfires*; Baca, *We Fed Them Cactus*; Bailey, *When New Mexico Was Young*; Ball, *Ma'am Jones of the Pecos*; ____, *Ruidoso, The Last Frontier*; Bancroft, *Works of Hubert Howe Bancroft*, Vol. XVII; Bartholomew, *Jesse Evans*; Benton, *Cow by the Tail*; Bishop, *Old Mexico and Her Lost Provinces*; Blacker, *The Old West in Fact*; Botkin, *A Treasury of American Folklore*; ____, *A Treasury of Western Folklore*; Boylan, *The Old Lincoln County Courthouse*; Boynton, *The Rediscovery of the Frontier*; Branch, *Westward*; Breihan, *Badmen of Frontier Days*; ____, *Great Lawmen of the West*; ____, *Outlaws of the Old West*; Brent, *The Complete and Factual Life of Billy the Kid*; Brothers, *Billy the Kid*; ____, *A Pecos Pioneer*; Brown, *Trail Driving Days*; Buffum, *Smith of Bear City*; Burns, *The Saga of Billy the Kid*; Burt, *American Murder Ballads*; Callison, *Bill Jones of Paradise Valley, Oklahoma*; Callon, *Las Vegas, New Mexico*; Calvin, *Sky Determines*; Cannon, *Toward the Setting Sun*; Carr, *The West Is Still Wild*; Carson, *The Union Pacific, Hell on Wheels*; Casey, *The Texas Border and Some Borderliners*; CBA; Chapel, *Guns of the Old West*; ____, *Levi's Gallery of Western Guns and Gunfighters*; Charles, *More Tales of Talarosa*; Chilton, *The Book of the West*; Cleaveland, *No Life for a Lady*; Coan, *A History of New Mexico*; Coe, *Frontier Fighter*; ____, *Ranch on the Ruidoso*; Coleman, *From Mustanger to Lawyer*; Collison, *Life in the Saddle*; Cook, *Fifty Years on the Old Frontier*; ____, *Longhorn Cowboy*; ____, *The Border and the Buffalo*; Coolidge, *Fighting Men of the West*; Corle, *Desert Country*; Cox, *Luke Short and His Era*; Crawford, *The West of the Texas Kid*; Crichton, *Law and Order*; Cunningham, *Famous in the West*; ____, *Triggernometry*; Cushman, *The Great North Trail*; Daggett, *Billy LeRoy, The Colorado Bandit*; Day, *Gene Rhodes, Cowboy*; Debo, *The Cowman's Southwest*; Dils, *Horny Toad Man*; Dobie, *Cow People*; ____, *Guide to Life and Literature of the Southwest*; ____, *A Vaquero of the Brush Country*; ____, *Southwestern Lore*; Doctor, *Shotguns on Sunday*; Douglas, *Cattle Kings of Texas*; Drago, *Great American Cattle Trails*; ____, *Outlaws on Horseback*; ____, *Red River Valley*; ____, *Wild, Woolly & Wicked*; Dunlop, *Doctors of the American Frontier*; Durham, *The Negro Cowboy*; Ealy, *Water in a Thirsty Land*; Erwin, *The Southwest of John H. Slaughter*; Evans, *Adventures of the Great Crimebusters*; ____, *Long John Dunn of Taos*; Fable, *Billy the Kid*; Farber, *Texans with Guns*; Fergusson, *Murder & Mystery in New Mexico*; ____, *Our Southwest*; Fierman, *Billy the Kid, The Cowboy Outlaw*; Finger, *Adventures Under Sapphire Skies*; ____, *The Distant Prize*; Fisher, *Gold Rushes and Mining Camps*; Fishwick, *American Heroes*; Fitzpatrick, *This Is New Mexico*; Florin, *Ghost Town Album*; Forrest, *Arizona's Dark and Bloody Ground*; Foster-Harris, *The Look of the Old West*; Frantz, *The American Cowboy*; Fraser, *Seven Years on the Pacific Slope*; Freeman, *Prose and Poetry of the Live Stock Industry of the United States*; French, *Gray Shadows*; Fridge, *History of the Chisum War*; Fulton, *Maurice Garland Fulton's History of the Lincoln County War*; ____, *New Mexico's Old Chronicle*; ____, *Roswell in Its Early Years*; Gage, *The Mafia Is Not An Equal Opportunity Employer*; Gann, *Tread* of the Longhorns; Gard, *The Chisholm Trail*; ____, *Frontier Justice*; Gardner, *The Old Wild West*; Garrett, *The Authentic Life of Billy the Kid*; Gaylord, *Handgunner's Guide*; Gibson, *The Life and Death of Colonel Albert Jennings*; Gish, *American Bandits*; Grant, *The Cowboy Encyclopedia*; Gregg, *Drums of Yesterday*; Gregory, *True Wild West Stories*; Grey, *Seeking a Fortune in America*; Griffis, *Tahan*; Griggs, *History of Mesilla Valley*; Guyer, *Pioneer Life in West Texas*; Hadfield, *Picturesque Rogues*; Haley, *Charles Goodnight*; ____, *George W. Littlefield*; ____, *Jeff Milton, A Good Man With a Gun*; ____, *Jim East, Trail Hand and Cowboy*; ____, *The XIT Ranch of Texas*; Hall, *History of the State of Colorado*; Hamilton, *Wagon Days on Red River*; Hamlin, *The True Story of Billy the Kid*; Hamner, *Short Grass and Longhorns*; Harkey, *Mean as Hell*; Harrison, *Hell Holes and Hangings*; Hart, *Old Forts of the Southwest*; Heermans, *Thirteen Stories*; Hendricks, *The Bad Man of the West*; Hendrix, *If I Can Do It on Horseback*; Hendron, *The Story of Billy the Kid*; Hening, *George Curry, 1861-1947*; Hertzog, *Little Known Facts About Billy the Kid*; ____, *Old Town Albuquerque*; Hicks, *Belle Starr and Her Pearl*; Holloway, *Texas Gun Lore*; Hopper, *Famous Texas Landmarks*; Horan, *Desperate Men*; ____, *The Great American West*; ____ and Sann, *Pictorial History of the Wild West*; Horn, *New Mexico's Troubled Years*; Hough, *The Story of the Cowboy*; ____, *The Story of the Outlaw*; House, *Cowtown Columnist*; Howard, *This Is the West*; Howe, *Timberleg of the Diamond Tail*; Hoyt, *A Frontier Doctor*; Hudson and Maxwell, *The Sunny Slopes of Long Ago*; Hughes, *Oklahoma Charley*; Hunt, *The Tragic Days of Billy the Kid*; Hunter, *The Trail Drivers of Texas*; ____ and Rose, *The Album of Gunfighters*; Hutchinson, *Another Verdict for Oliver Lee*; ____, *The Life and Personal Writings of Eugene Manlove Rhodes*; ____, *The Rhodes Reader*; ____ and Mullin, *Whiskey Jim and a Kid Named Billy*; Hyde, *Billy the Kid and the Old Regime in the Southwest*; Jahns, *The Frontier World of Doc Holliday*; James, *Frontier and Pioneer Recollections of Early Days in San Antonio and West Texas*; Jenkinson, *Ghost Towns of New Mexico*; Johnson, *Famous Lawmen of the Old West*; Johnson, *Wagon Yard*; Kane, *100 Years Ago With the Law and the Outlaw*; Keith, *Sixguns by Keith*; Keleher, *The Fabulous Frontier*; ____, *Maxwell Land Grant*; ____, *Violence in Lincoln County*; Kelly, *Flowing Stream*; Kelly, *The Sky Was Their Roof*; Kemp, *Cow Dust and Saddle Leather*; Kent, *Reminiscences of Outdoor Life*; King, *Mavericks*; ____, *Pioneer Western Empire Builders*; ____, *Wranglin' the Past*; Klasner, *My Girlhood Among Outlaws*; Knight, *Wild Bill Hickok*; Koller, *The American Gun*; ____, *The Fireside Book of Guns*; Koop, *Billy the Kid*; Kuykendall, *Ghost Riders of the Mogollon*; La Croix, *Billy the Kid*; La Farge, *Santa Fe*; Lake, *He Carried a Six Shooter*; ____, *Wyatt Earp*; Lamar, *The Far Southwest*; Lathrop, *Tales of Western Kansas*; Laughlin, *Caballeros*; Lavender, *The Big Divide*; Leckie, *The Buffalo Soldiers*; Lewis, *The True Life of Billy the Kid*; Lewis, *It Takes All Kinds*; Logue, *Under Texas and Border Skies*; Long, *Piñon County*; Looney, *Haunted Highways*; Lord, *Frontier Dust*; Love, *The Life and Adventures of Nat Love*; Lovell, *The Personalized History of Otero County*; Lynon, *The Wild, Wild West*; McCallum, *The Enchanted West*; ____, *Maverick Town*; ____, *The Wire That Fenced the West*; McGeeney, *Down at Stein's Pass*; McIntire, *Early Days in Texas*; McKee, *"Ben Hur" Wallace*; McKennon, *Iron Men*; Madison, *The Big Bend Country of Texas*; Mangan, *Bordertown*; Marshall, *Santa Fe, The Railroad That Built the Empire*; Martin, *Border Boss*; Masterson, *The Tenderfoot's Turn*; Maynard, *Oklahoma Panhandle*; Mazula, *Brass Checks and Red Lights*; ____, *Outlaw Album*; Metz, *John Selman, Texas Gunfighter*; Michelson, *Mankillers at Close Range*; Miller, *Ranch Life in Southern Kansas and the Indian Territory*; Miller, *Pioneering North*; Miller, *Early Days in the Wild West*; Monaghan, *The Book of the American West*; ____, *The Legend of Tom Horn*; Monroe, *San Juan Silver*; Moore, *The West*; Moss, *Rough and Tumble*; Mullin, *The Boyhood of Billy the Kid*; ____, *A Chronology of the Lincoln County War*; Myers, *Doc Holliday*; Nahm, *Las Vegas and Uncle Joe*; Nash, *Almanac of World Crime*; ____, *Bloodletters and Badmen*; Neal, *Captive Mountain Waters*; Neider, *The Great West*; Nicholl, *Observations of a Ranch Woman*; Nolan, *The Life and Death of John Henry Tunstall*; Nolen, *Galloping Down the Texas Trail*; Nordyke, *John Wesley Hardin*; North, *The Saga of the Cowboy*; Nye, *Pistols for Hire*; O'Bryne, *Pike's Peak or Bust*; O'Connor, *Pat Garrett, A Biography of the Famous Marshal and the Killer of Billy the Kid*; O'Neal, *Encyclopedia of Western Gunfighters*; O'Neal, *They Die But Once*; Otero, *My Life on the Frontier*; ____, *My Nine Years as Governor of the Territory of New Mexico*; ____, *The Real Billy the Kid*; Parrish, *Coffins, Cactus and Cowboys*; Parson, *A Courier of New Mexico*; Peavy, *Charles A. Siringo*; Peck, *Southwest Roundup*; Penfield, *Western Sheriffs and Marshals*; Poe, *The Death of Billy the Kid*; Poe, *Buckboard Days*; Poldevaart, *Black-Robed Justice*; Preece, *The Dalton Gang*; ____, *Lone Star Man*; Price, *Death Comes to Billy the Kid*; Prince, *A Concise History of New Mexico*; Raine, *Famous Sheriffs and Western Outlaws*; ____, *Guns of the Frontier*; ____ and Barnes, *Cattle*; Rascoe, *Belle Starr*; Rascoe, *Some Western Treasures*; Rennert, *The Cowboy*; ____, *Western Outlaws*; Rhodes, *The Hired Man on Horseback*; Richardson, *Two Guns, Arizona*; Rickards, *Charles Littlepage Ballard, Southwesterner*; Ridings, *The Chisholm Trail*; Riegel, *America Moves West*; Ringgold, *Frontier Days in the Southwest*; Rister, *Outlaws and Vigilantes of the Southern Plains*; Rittenhouse, *The Man Who Owned Too Much*; Robertson, *Famous Bandits*; Rockwell, *New Frontier*; Rolt-Wheeler, *The Book of Cowboys*; Rosa, *The Gunfighter, Man or Myth?*; ____ and May, *Gun Law*; Ruth, *Great Days in the West*; Rutledge, *A Few Stirring Events in the Life of Col. Dick Rutledge*; Sabin, *Wild Men of the Wild West*; Sandoz, *The Cattlemen, From the Rio Grande Across the Marias*; Sands, *Lost Pony Tracks*; Scanland, *The Life of Pat F. Garrett*; Schaefer, *Heroes Without Glory*; Schesinger, *The Rise of the City, 1878-1898*; Scobee, *Fort Davis, Texas*; ____, *Old Fort Davis*; Scott, *Such Outlaws as Jesse James*; Segale, *At the End of the Santa Fe Trail*; Shackleford, *Gunfighters of the Old West*; Shinkle, *Reminiscences of Roswell Pioneers*; Shipman, *Letters, Past and Present*; ____, *Taming the Big Bend*; Shumard, *The Ballad and History of Billy the Kid*; Siringo, *A Cowboy Detective*; ____, *History of Billy the Kid*; ____, *The Lone Star Cowboy*; ____, *Riata and Spurs*; ____, *A Texas Cowboy*; Sonnichsen, *Alias Billy the Kid*; ____, *I'll Die Before I'll Run*; ____, *Outlaw*; ____, *Ten Texas Feuds*; ____, *Tularosa*; Stanley, *Antochico*; ____, *Clay Allison*; ____, *Dave Rudabaugh, Border Ruffian*; ____, *Desperadoes of New Mexico*; ____, *The Duke City*; ____, *Fort Bascom*; ____, *The Las Vegas Story*; ____, *The Lincoln (N.M.) Story*; ____, *The Mogollon (N.M.) Story*; ____, *The Private War of Ike Stockton*; ____, *The Seven Rivers (N.M.) Story*; ____, *The White Oakes (N.M.) Story*; Steckmesser, *The Western Hero in History and Legend*; Steen, *The Texas News*; Sterling, *Famous Western Outlaw-Sheriff Battles*; Stone, *Twenty-four Years A Cowboy*; Stover, *Son-of-a-Gun Stew*; Sullivan, *The L.S. Brand*; Sutherland, *Out Where the West Be-Grins*; Sutton, *Hands Up!*; Swan, *Frontier Days*; Taylor, *Taylor's Thrilling Tales of Texas*; Taylor, *Colorado, South of the Border*; Taylor, *The Chisholm Trail and Other Routes*; Thompson, *They Were Open Range Days*; Thompson, *Clayton*; Thorp, *Story of the Southwestern Cowboy*; Timmons, *Twilight on the Range*; Tolbert, *An Informal History of Texas*; Townsend, *The Tenderfoot in New Mexico*; Turner, *Avery Turner*; ____, *These High Plains*; Twitchell, *The Leading Facts of New Mexico History*; Van Doren, *An Autobiography of America*; Wallace, *Cattle Kings of the Staked Plains*; Waller, *Last of the Great Western Train Robbers*; Walters, *Tombstone's Yesterdays*; Waltrip, *Cowboys and Cattlemen*; Ward, *Bits of Silver*; Waters, *A Gallery of Western Badmen*; Watson, *A Century of Gunmen*; Weadock, *Dust of the Desert*; Wellman, *The Blazing Southwest*; ____, *A Dynasty of Western Outlaws*; ____, *Glory, God and Gold*; ____, *The Trampling Herd*; West, *Billy the Kid*; White, *The Autobiography of A Durable Sinner*; ____, *Lead and Likker*; ____, *Trigger Fingers*; Wilhelm, *Cavalcade of Hooves and Horns*; Williams, *A City of Refuge*; ____, *The Old New Mexico*; ____, *Pioneer Surveyor, Frontier Lawyer*; Williams and Pepper, *The Mysterious West*; Wilson, *Out of the West*; Winn, *The Madacam Trail*; Woods, *Ghost Towns*; Wooten, *Women Tell the Story of the Southwest*; Young, *True Stories of Old Houston and Houstonians*; (FILM) *Billy the Kid*, 1930; *Billy the Kid Returns*, 1938; *Billy the Kid in Texas*, 1940; *Billy the Kid*, 1941; *Billy the Kid in Santa Fe*, 1941; *Billy the Kid Wanted*, 1941; *Billy the Kid's Fighting Pals*, 1941; *Billy the Kid's Range War*, 1941; *Billy the Kid's Roundup*, 1941; *Billy the Kid Trapped*, 1942; *Law and Order*, 1942; *The Mysterious Rider*, 1942; *The Kid Rides Again*, 1943; *The Outlaw*, 1943; *Western Cyclone*, 1943; *Overland Riders*, 1946; *Return of the Badmen*, 1948; *Son of Billy the Kid*, 1949; *I Shot Billy the Kid*, 1950; *The Kid from Texas*, 1950; *Captive of Billy the Kid*, 1952; *The Law vs Billy the Kid*, 1952; *Last of the Desperadoes*, 1956; *The Parson and the Outlaw*, 1957; *The Left-Handed Gun*, 1958; *One-Eyed Jacks*, 1961; *The Outlaw Is Coming*, 1965; *Billy the Kid vs Dracula*, 1966; *The Man Who Killed Billy the Kid*, 1967; *A Few Bullets More*, 1968; *Chisum*, 1970; *The Last Movie*, 1971; *Dirty Little Billy*, 1972; *Pat Garrett and Billy the Kid*, 1973; *Young Guns*, 1988.

Bilney, Thomas (Thomas Bylney), c.1495-1531, Brit., her. Considered saintly prayer and religious artifacts as image worship. He was convicted of heresy and burned at the stake. REF.: *CBA*.

Bim Boom Gang, prom. 1920s, U.S., org. crime. This Chicago-based gang, operating on the near southside of the city, was noted for its robberies of warehouses containing expensive furs and federal storehouses containing whiskey impounded at the beginning of Prohibition. Bim Boom gang members were constantly at war with such gangs as the Thistles, the Deadshots, and a particularly violent gang of petty thieves led by Danny O'Hara. The Bim Booms lay one claim to underworld history in that its members began loading rock salt in its shotguns. During gang battles, members would fire this unusual ammunition at opponents who, when hit with it, would become paralyzed. Several killings were attributed to the Bim Booms from 1921 to 1930. The gang died out with the coming of the Depression.
REF.: *CBA*; Kobler, *Capone*; Nash, *Bloodletters and Badmen*; Reid, *The Grim Reapers*; Thrasher, *The Gang*.

Binaggio, Charles, 1909-50, U.S., org. crime. The successor to Johnny Lazia, crime boss of Kansas City, Mo., under Boss Pendergast, the Texas-born Binaggio arrived in Kansas City in 1932. Having committed robberies and burglaries in Denver, Binaggio went to work for Lazia as a strong-arm thug protecting lucrative gambling operations. He moved up the Lazia hierarchy and by 1934 was one of Lazia's chief lieutenants, in charge of the boss' protection, which utterly failed when Lazia was shot to death. It was later reported that Binaggio had conspired to have his boss killed so he could take over the multimillion-dollar rackets in Kansas City. When the Mafia-syndicate expanded westward after WWII, Binaggio resisted demands that he share with the national crime cartel the profits from his many lucrative rackets. He and his bodyguard, Charles Gargotta, were trapped in their headquarters, The First District Democratic Club, on Apr. 6, 1950, and shot to death, each receiving four bullets in the head. Their killers were never identified. See: **Lazia, John.**
REF.: *CBA*; Lait and Mortimer, *Chicago Confidential*; McPhaul, *Johnny Torrio*; Peterson, *The Mob*; Smith, *Syndicate City*; Turkus, *Murder, Inc.*

Binder, Aaron M., 1928- , and **Celani, Frederick George,** 1949- , U.S., fraud-rack. A high-tech engineering firm appeared to be a wise investment for a number of television stars, but when profits came to a standstill, investors were told to write off the investment as a loss on their tax returns, losses which took almost $7 million in taxes from the U.S. government.

The fraudulent firm was run by Aaron M. Binder and Frederick George Celani, both from California, who bilked $14 million from investors, claiming that the money would be spent on research and development. In reality, no research was done and the con artists spent more than $1 million of the investment money. Binder and Celani created tax shelters for their clients, who could claim losses when actually the only loss that took place was their initial investment.

Both men were indicted on numerous charges and found Guilty in July 1985 of racketeering, mail and wire fraud, and related charges. Binder was sentenced to ten years in prison and Celani, fifteen. REF.: *CBA*.

Bingham, Edward Franklin, 1828-1907, U.S., jur. Prosecuting attorney in McArthur, Ohio, from 1850-55. He was appointed judge of the Supreme Court (now district court) of Washington, D.C. by President Grover Cleveland in 1887. REF.: *CBA*.

Bingham, Richard John (7th Earl of Lucan, AKA: Lucky), b.c.1935, Case of, Brit., attempt. mur.-mur. On Nov. 7, 1974, Veronica, Countess of Lucan, who had been separated from her husband for eighteen months, watched a television program in a second-floor room of her London home. Her three children were sleeping upstairs. Sitting with her employer was 29-year-old governess, Sandra Rivett. Rivett, who was about the same size as the countess, went downstairs to make a cup of tea at about 9:15 p.m. when a man attacked her with a lead pipe. When the countess went to check on Rivett, she interrupted the killer, who

was putting Rivett's body into a canvas bag. She later said she recognized the killer as her husband, Richard John Bingham, who then turned on her and tried to kill her by wrapping the chain of a pendant around her neck and shoving several fingers down her throat. Then he picked up the pipe again and struck her with the weapon. Lady Lucan broke away and ran to a pub, 100 yards from her home. The woman collapsed and was taken to the hospital where she was treated for shock and injuries. An hour and a half later, her husband visited a friend in Sussex where he wrote two letters to his brother-in-law concerning financial matters and his version of the attack. Bingham wanted his 7-year-old son to attend Eton House and he wanted his children to be "told the truth," when they were older. He also said that he had been standing outside his wife's home when, upon seeing an intruder assault Lady Lucan, he rushed inside the house to help her. Bingham, a reputed gambler in debt, left the Sussex home about 1:30 that morning and police located the car he was driving at Newhaven later in the day, a port that has a ferry traveling to France. Police issued warrants for Bingham's arrest five days after the attacks. Initially, police scoured England, France, and Haiti, but were unable to locate Bingham. He was later charged in absentia with murder, the first person to be charged under that method in 200 years. In June 1975, at a coroner's inquest, a jury found that Rivett had been murdered by Bingham, but he has never been found and tried. REF.: *CBA*.

Bingham, Theodore, c.1858-1934, U.S., law enfor. off. Brigadier General Theodore Bingham reigned as New York's police commissioner for three-and-a-half stormy years. His tenure of office was characterized by frequent clashes with Mayor George B. McClellan, the Tammany Hall political organization that attempted to guide his hand in appointments and patronage, and members of the rank-and-file who deeply resented Bingham's authoritarian policies.

General Bingham was appointed commissioner Jan. 1, 1906. His difficulty was in implementing reforms. Bingham hoped to divorce political interference from day-to-day police work. In May 1907, he shifted every powerful police captain in the city, effectively severing the ties to Tammany Hall which had been nurtured over many years.

NYPD Commissioner Bingham.

The so-called "Bingham Bill" temporarily ended the rule of the bosses and established the commissioner as the real head of the department. His harsh measures to insure honesty and forthrightness in the ranks did not always meet with the approval of the captains. In October 1907, Bingham was arrested at headquarters and forced to post bail when one of the fired captains filed a law suit against him.

The controversy grew in April 1908 when Bingham, exasperated by the constraints of the system, expressed the wish that forty aging police captains who refused to retire would die. Notable reformers and clergymen like Dr. Charles Parkhurst decried his insensitivity. The beginning of the end occurred on Feb. 27, 1909, when Commissioner Bingham addressed the City Club of New York. He described the metropolis as the "dirtiest place on this earthly footstool." In June, Supreme Court Justice William J. Gaynor demanded that Mayor McClellan fire Bingham at once after the commissioner refused to comply with a ruling that prohibited the police from posting photographs of men not convicted of a crime in the "Rogues Gallery." The case involved a 19-year-old man named George B. Duffy who had been branded a felon by virtue of his picture appearing in the gallery. Unhappy policemen joined the fight to oust Bingham. Mayor McClellan at first supported Bingham, but when Bingham refused to institute the changes that would clear Duffy, the mayor had no choice left but to fire the chief.

Bingham was discharged on July 2, 1909. His place was taken by Deputy Commissioner William Baker, but Bingham did not give up the fight so easily. He filed a libel suit against Justice Gaynor, who eventually apologized for his indiscreet remarks. A movement began to re-appoint Bingham commissioner in 1915, under the politically independent "fusion" ticket which had been swept into City Hall. By this time, however, the ex-chief was employed by the city bridge department. Bingham died on Sept. 4, 1934, at his summer home in Chester, Novia Scotia after a long illness. He was seventy-six. REF.: *CBA*.

Bingham Family Poisonings, 1911, Brit., (unsolv.) mur. Members of the Bingham family had long been custodians of historic Lancaster Castle. After serving as caretaker of the castle for more than thirty years, William Hodgson Bingham died in January 1911. James Bingham, William's son, was then appointed caretaker, and he asked his sister Margaret to take on the job of housekeeper. She died a short time after assuming this position and was replaced by Edith Agnes Bingham, half sister to James. Edith Bingham, however, proved to be an irritable and uncooperative member of the staff and James Bingham planned to replace her. On Aug. 12, 1911, two days before Edith's replacement was due to arrive at the castle, James sat down to a steak dinner prepared by his half sister and promptly died.

Suspicious officials inspected the bodies of all three recently deceased Binghams and found considerable amounts of arsenic in the corpses. Edith Bingham was quickly charged and tried in the very castle where the untimely deaths had occurred. The prosecution insisted that she had murdered her relatives with white arsenic which was available to her, stored in the castle to kill weeds. The motive given for the killings was a small inheritance which would be paid to Edith Bingham once all her family members were dead. The defense adroitly pointed out that there was not a bit of evidence to indicate that Edith had administered poison to her relatives. The jury took only twenty minutes to find her Not Guilty. The Bingham family poisonings remain unsolved to this day.

REF.: *CBA*; Jackson, *Mr. Justice Avory*; Nash, *Open Files*; Shew, *A Companion to Murder*; Thompson, *Poison Mysteries Unsolved*.

Binney, Horace, 1780-1875, U.S., lawyer. Member of the House of Representatives from 1833-35. He published numerous legal papers and edited *Reports of Cases Adjudged in the Supreme Court of Pennsylvania* (1809-15). REF.: *CBA*.

Binns, Bartholomew, prom. 1880s, Brit., execut. The appointment of Bartholomew Binns, the immediate predecessor to James Berry, to the position of hangman for London was short-lived due to his inability to properly hang condemned prisoners.

Following a hanging in March 1884, at Liverpool, one of Binns' last, the prison's governor remarked that "Binns had no idea how to do his work satisfactorily," referring to the prisoner's dying fifteen minutes after the drop occurred. After Binns was dismissed, the sheriffs chose Berry for the position. The House of Lords worked unsuccessfully to make the executioner's office official in order to ensure the executioners were properly trained. See: **Berry, James**.

REF.: Atholl, *The Reluctant Hangman*; *CBA*.

Binnya Dala, d.1774, Burma, assass. Last ruler of the Mon Kingdom of lower Burma. He commanded a large military expedition into Upper Burma in 1751, killing the Toungoo king. In 1757, he was deposed by Alaungpaya and was held prisoner until his execution. REF.: *CBA*.

Bintel, Joe (AKA: **Fat Joe**), prom. 20th Cent., U.S., (unsolv.) mur. Bintel made a living by providing New York City felons with bail money. He also died as a result of his profession.

Joe Bintel would bail only professional criminals or those closely tied with the underworld, relying on a code of honor that those he bailed out would show up for court and not run off, a code which worked to everyone's satisfaction until the state of New York passed a law requiring life imprisonment for people convicted of a fourth felony. Since many of Bintel's clients fit this classification, they would run rather than appear for trial. To avoid losing his money, Bintel began to turn them in secretly. Eventually the felons learned of his snitching, and Bintel wound up with a bullet in the back of his head.

REF.: Carey, *Memoirs of a Murder Man*; *CBA*.

Bioff, William Morris, 1900-55, U.S., org. crime. With a record that stretched back to the age of ten, William Bioff practiced almost every known felony, from prostitution to burglary. He began as a pimp for street whores in the Levee, Chicago's most notorious vice district. Bioff went to work for the Guzik brothers, Harry and Jake, notorious procurers. Jake Guzik was Al Capone's chief financial adviser and through him, Bioff met Scarface and subsequently, his successor, Frank "The Enforcer" Nitti. It was Nitti who assigned Bioff the task of enforcing the edicts of mob-backed George Browne, who became president of the International Alliance of Theatrical Stage Employees and Motion Picture Operators. Both Bioff and Browne, through various extortions of the motion picture industry studios, made millions for the syndicate as well as themselves.

Mob extortionist Willie Bioff.

Bioff extorted money from every major producer in Hollywood and in New York, paying particular attention to the booth operators in movie houses. He told producers that they must install *two* operators in each booth, but producers claimed that they would go broke under such a union arrangement. Bioff

Bioff blown to pieces after informing on the mob.

compromised, forcing theaters to accept two operators but at a lower scale of pay than originally demanded, and gave an enormous payoff to himself and the mob. Newspapers began a campaign in the late 1930s which exposed the Bioff-Browne association with the film industry, leading to a trial that saw both being convicted of extortion and racketeering, and sentenced to ten years in prison. Bioff and Browne, in return for reduced sentences, agreed to testify against top syndicate mobsters such as Frank Nitti, Phil D'Andrea, Paul "The Waiter" Ricca, Charlie "Cherry Nose" Gioe, John Roselli, and Lou Kaufman, all of whom, except Nitti, went to prison as a result. Nitti, desperate to avoid another jail term and awaiting a tax evasion trial, committed suicide in 1943.

Released from prison, Bioff and Browne fled from the revenge of the syndicate. Browne went deep into hiding and never again surfaced. But Bioff, still craving the gangland limelight, moved to Phoenix, Ariz., and there contributed campaign funds to Barry Goldwater's senatorial war chest. Moreover, he went to work for Gus Greenbaum, manager of the Riviera Casino in Las Vegas, an operation reportedly backed by the very Chicago gangsters Bioff had sent to prison. Chicago mobsters were soon informed of Bioff's presence in Phoenix. On Nov. 4, 1955, Bioff left his home, got into a pickup truck, stepped on the starter and was killed in the resulting explosion. Gus Greenbaum and his wife were later murdered, ostensibly for hiring Bioff. See: **Capone, Alphonse; D'Andrea, Philip; Gioe, Charles; Guzik, Jake; Nitti, Frank; Ricca, Paul; Roselli, John.**

REF.: *CBA;* Demaris, *Captive City;* ____, *The Last Mafioso;* Eisenberg and Landau, *Meyer Lansky;* Fried, *The Rise and Fall of the Jewish Gangster in America;* Gage, *Mafia, U.S.A.;* Kobler, *Capone;* Lait and Mortimer, *Chicago Confidential;* Messick, *Secret File;* Morgan, *Prince of Crime;* Nash, *Almanac of World Crime;* Reid, *The Grim Reapers;* Smith, *Syndicate City;* Velie, *Desperate Bargain, Why Jimmy Hoffa Had to Die.*

Birchall, John Reginald, d.1890, Int'l, fraud-mur. Coming from respectable middle-class parents, John Reginald Birchall was a spoiled and careless young man who did not apply himself at Oxford, giving wine parties instead of studying. He left college in his third year and embarked on a series of petty swindles which led to financial success. Birchall married and lived well in London and in New York, traveling back and forth while enacting land sales swindles. In 1889, Birchall placed several large advertisements in London newspapers in which he sought investors in rich Canadian farms that would bring triple profits to investors in a short time, he claimed. Answering the ads were Frederick Cornwallis Benwell, a wealthy young businessman, and Douglas Pelley, another young man with limited savings to invest. Birchall sold a full partnership in his land development scheme to Benwell for £500. To Pelley, Birchall sold one fifth share in a Canadian farm for £170, explaining that he was to be part of a farm pupil program.

Birchell and his wife, accompanied by Benwell and Pelley, then embarked for New York, sailing on the *Britannic.* Upon their arrival in New York, the group traveled to Buffalo. There Pelley was instructed to stay with Mrs. Birchall while Benwell accompanied Birchall to Princeton, Ontario. In a few days, Birchall returned to Buffalo alone, saying that the prospective farm he was to buy turned out to be a bad investment and that Benwell had decided to drop out of the investment and had left for England. A few days later, on Feb. 21, 1890, two hunters at the edge of the sprawling Blenheim Swamp, a wilderness area in southeastern Ontario near Princeton, found the frozen body of Benwell with two bullets in his head. No identification could be found on the body, except a cigarette holder with the initials F.C.B. Superintendent John Wilson Murray used the newspapers to spread the word of the murder in hopes of identifying the corpse. Some witnesses came forward to report that Birchall, using an alias, had been seen in the area with Benwell.

Birchall, bloated with self-confidence, actually went with his wife to Superintendent Murray and identified the dead man as Benwell, a man he had met by accident on the trip over from England. The con man undoubtedly thought that such a bold move would thoroughly disarm the police, but he made several slips in his conversation with Murray that convinced the detective that he was involved in Benwell's murder. Murray learned that Benwell had been recruited in London by Birchall for his invest-

ment scheme, and then Pelley arrived to report that Birchall had taken him to Niagra Falls after Benwell's murder where Birchall tried twice to kill him. Birchall was charged with murdering Benwell and was tried at Woodstock, Ontario.

Money for Birchall's case was provided by his well-to-do family and a spirited defense was made for him. However, witnesses came forward to state that they had seen Birchall accompanying the victim to the area around Princeton and had heard two shots a short time after the men had gone into the Blenheim Swamp district. Birchall insisted that he was innocent and made such a convincing case for himself that it was thought he would be acquitted. He was nevertheless convicted and sentenced to hang on Nov. 14, 1890, at Woodstock. The condemned man was fastidious to the end, directing his wife to buy a fine flannel shirt, open in front, with a turned-down collar for his execution, along with black cashmere socks and a new collar and tie. Mrs. Birchall, who had originally been charged with her husband, was set free when it was learned that she had no knowledge of her husband's murder schemes (she later returned to London and remarried). When Birchall was hanged on the appointed date, the hangman sent him through the trap with a 350-pound weight attached to his legs, but instead of the condemned man's neck being broken by the rope, the ill-fixed knot caused Birchall to strangle to death for about six minutes.

REF.: Campbell, *A Century of Crime; CBA;* Dilnot, *Great Detectives and Their Methods;* Gribble, *Famous Feats of Detection and Deduction;* ____, *Great Detective Exploits;* Kingston, *A Gallery of Rogues;* ____, *Rogues and Adventuresses;* Laurence, *Extraordinary Crimes;* Liston, *Great Detectives;* Mencken, *By the Neck;* Miller, *Twenty Mortal Murders;* Sanders, *They Caught These Killers;* Taylor, *Gallows Parade.*

Bird, Edward, 1691-1719, Brit., consp.-mur. His father secured for him an ensign's commission in a military regiment, hoping that army life would be rewarding, for Edward Bird showed no singular abilities at school. Away from the combat lines, where he was most comfortable, young Bird proved to be a harsh disciplinarian with his foot soldiers. His swagger and bluster soon disappeared, however, when commanding officers demanded that he advance toward the French troops.

When Bird returned from an expedition in Flanders, his father purchased a lieutenant's commission for him. Then Bird married a kind and noble woman who possessed a considerable fortune. He took up with a prostitute with whom he imagined himself to be in love. After some deliberation, they decided to murder his wife and claim her riches. They mixed a strong dose of laudanum with her tea, then celebrated her demise in a bordello on Silver Street. There, in a riotous moment, Bird killed a servant named Samuel Loxton. The next day, Sept. 25, 1718, Bird was committed to Newgate. The only thing standing in his favor was the shaky testimony of a prostitute. The jury, unimpressed by her defense, sentenced Bird to die.

Bird, who had gone to great lengths to avoid death in the army, was not about to walk to the gallows without a fight. He concocted a fabulous scheme involving an alehouse strumpet named Susannah Cooper, who agreed to pose as Diana Loxton, the deceased's wife. Susannah went before the king and pleaded for the life of Bird, who had agreed to care for her poor, fatherless children. The king, inclined to be lenient, granted Bird clemency on condition that he leave the country when the score was settled.

When the news of the clemency reached the real Diana Loxton, she wrote to the king explaining that the imposter had been picked up near St. James Palace by Edward Bird's father, who offered her a considerable amount of money to pose as the distressed widow.

Convinced that the real Mrs. Loxton was telling the truth, the court reimposed the death sentence on Feb. 16, 1719. Bird attempted to cheat the hangman by poisoning himself, but the dose was not strong enough. He then stabbed himself with a small penknife, but was rescued in the nick of time. Resigned to his fate, Edward Bird walked to the gallows with his head held high. He requested a pinch of snuff and then bowed to the assembled throng. "Gentlemen, I wish your health," he said, and was executed.

REF.: *CBA*; Smith, *Highwaymen.*

Bird, Elijah, prom. 1850s, U.S., mur. On Dec. 1, 1851, Elijah Bird, the scion of a distinguished Atlanta, Ga., family, killed his brother-in-law in a family dispute that eventually had the entire town in an uproar.

John Bird, being one of the large plantation owners in Atlanta, arrived at the Hilburn house in a carriage with his family. Bird went inside the house alone to transact some business with Dr. Nathaniel G. Hilburn, who was married to his daughter. Hilburn suddenly burst outside and ran down the stairs of his home. He appeared deranged. Grabbing an ax, Hilburn shouted: "I'm going to cut the top off that carriage right now!" He swung wildly at the carriage, giving it some sound whacks. Mrs. Bird, inside the carriage and ducking the blows, screamed for Hilburn to stop. The doctor put down the ax and the Bird daughters threw it over a fence. Mrs. Bird then picked up Hilburn's walking stick, which he had dropped, and crashed it down on his head.

"You'll do that, will you?" Hilburn yelled, and lunged for Mrs. Bird. Her son, Elijah, moved more quickly than the half-mad doctor and reached across his mother's shoulder to plunge a 50-cent, double-blade, buckhorn-handled pocketknife into Hilburn's neck, immediately severing an artery. Hilburn bled to death on the walkway in front of his home within five minutes.

Elijah Bird was imprisoned and tried for murder. He was convicted and, on Apr. 14, 1853, Judge Edward Young Hill ordered him hanged, ending with the ominous words: "...until he is dead, dead, dead, and may God have mercy on his soul."

But Bird would never hang; his wealthy father saw to that. John Bird moved heaven and the state legislature to save his son. Through influential friends, the plantation owner had a special bill introduced which allowed for the pardon of his son. The bill passed and Elijah Bird, a condemned murderer, escaped the gallows by a hair and through the fortune of his father. John Bird, however, spent almost every dime he had to free his son, selling off hundreds of the best acres of his plantation.

Atlantans were moved to lynch-mob anger with the pardon of the killer, and several town meetings were held. Before he was apprehended by rabid vigilantes and with the few remaining dollars his father could scrape together, Elijah Bird fled Atlanta in the dead of night, whipping his carriage horses south. He did not stop until he reached Louisiana, where he managed, again with his father's help, to buy a small plantation.

Elijah Bird did not entirely escape the vengeance of man. Several years later, the foreman of his Louisiana plantation was insulted by Bird and, brooding over the curse, casually followed his abrasive employer into a field. Swinging a cane hoe from behind, he split Bird's skull. Slaves found Bird dead in the field before dusk, the hoe still buried in his head. When news of Bird's death arrived in Atlanta, only a few mourned. Some of Hilburn's relatives threw a "vindication party." REF.: *CBA.*

Bird, Jack, 1648-90, Brit., rob.-mur. After deciding that a baker's life was too sedate, Jack Bird left Huntingtonshire in 1673 to join the First Regiment Footguards, commanded by the Duke of Monmouth. He deserted the army and went to Amsterdam, where he was seized and sentenced to hard labor for stealing valuable silk. The labor was taxing, and he became ill from sheer exhaustion.

He survived this ordeal, however, and on his release returned to England, where he became a highwayman. He stole a horse near St. Edmondsbury, Suffolk, and became quite efficient with pistols and sword.

One day, on the road between Gravesend and Chatham, he met a man who seemed to be an easy mark. The intended victim, Joseph Pinnis, had lost both of his hands in a naval battle. When asked to deliver the money he had in his coat pocket, Pinnis told Bird that it was not an easy task for a man with no hands. As the thief reached into the man's pocket, Pinnis grabbed Bird with his stumps and wrestled him to the ground. The fight continued until the driver of a passing dray separated the two combatants and hauled Jack Bird to the jail in Maidstone. He was sentenced to hang but was spared this fate through an act of mercy on the part of the government.

The shame of having been bested by a man without hands failed to keep Jack Bird from life on the road. When a Welsh driver he met a mile out of Acton refused to stand and deliver as commanded, Jack Bird exclaimed, "If a son of a whore once could take me without hands, I shall not venture my carcass within the reach of one that has hands, for fear of another conviction." Thereupon he fired his pistols through the man's head and made off with his eighteen pence.

Jack Bird's life in crime ended unceremoniously. Because he favored the company of prostitutes and pickpockets, he frequently accompanied them on their nocturnal forays into the marketplace. One night he helped a lady friend knock down and rob a man on the Strand. The pair were arrested, but the evidence against Jack Bird was flimsy. However, since he was well-known for his past robberies, the court was inclined to show him no mercy. Like all convicted robbers at that time, Bird was condemned to death. The woman was acquitted. Bird went to the gallows at Tyburn Hill on Mar. 12, 1690. His body was taken to Surgeons' Hall where it was dissected and put on public display.

REF.: *CBA*; Smith, *Highwaymen.*

Bird, Jake, 1901-49, U.S., mur. Jake Bird was convicted of a double ax murder in Tacoma, Wash., and confessed to several other murders while awaiting his execution in prison. Bird was born on Dec. 14, 1901, in Louisiana. He spent his adult years wandering around the country, staying briefly in New York, Maine, Boston, Philadelphia, Chicago, and St. Louis. Though he worked several temporary jobs and found frequent employment with the railroad, he was a professional criminal who burglarized homes wherever he found himself. He spent a total of thirty-one years in prison in Utah, Iowa, and Michigan, all on burglary charges. While in prison, he read law books and learned the strategies and tactics of the legal system. Those investigators who worked on his case remembered Bird as a man who thought little of committing violent acts. A black man, Bird hated both whites and women, and especially loathed white women. He was described by many as sophisticated, calculating, witty, an able conversationalist, and extremely dangerous.

In the early morning hours of Oct. 30, 1947, two police officers, Patrolmen Evan "Skip" Davies and Andres "Tiny" Sabutis, responded to a report of a woman screaming in a neighborhood on South J Street in Tacoma. Approaching the house where the screams originated, Davis saw a man running from the back of the house. He pursued the man and cornered him in an alley. The man was not wearing shoes, and his clothes were spattered with blood. The man charged Davis, who drew his gun and repeatedly struck him over the head. The man drew a knife and slashed the officer's hand. Sabutis arrived and found Davis clubbing the man with his gun. But when he attempted to handcuff him, the knife wielder slashed Sabutis across the back. Enraged by the violence, Davis beat the man around the face until he lay panting on the ground. The officers brought the man back to the home, where they discovered the bodies of Mrs. Bertha Kludt, fifty-two, and Beverly June Kludt, her 17-year-old daughter. The daughter was lying between the bedrooms and the kitchen and her mother lay in one of the bedrooms. Both were beaten and slashed with the blunt end and the blade of an ax. They were dressed in their nightgowns and covered with blood. Police identified the suspect in custody as Jake Bird.

Within a few hours of his arrest, Bird signed a confession to the murders of the Kludt women. He said he had been in Washington only three days when he walked through a residential district seeking a home to burglarize. He found an ax in a nearby shed and took it with him for protection. Finding the back door of the home on South J Street unlocked, he entered the house, took off his shoes, went into one of the bedrooms, and took the purse he found there. As he tried to open the purse in the kitchen, he was startled by Mrs. Kludt, who approached him from behind. Bird threatened her, but told her he only wanted to rob the house. The commotion woke Beverly, who entered the kitchen and jumped on Bird's back. Mrs. Kludt likewise grabbed Bird and began screaming. Bird grabbed his ax and began swinging, knocking the two women down. He could not remember how many times he hit them after that.

Bird's prosecution, however, was not cut and dried. He withdrew his confession shortly after signing it, and claimed he signed it because the police beat him and he feared for his life. Bird claimed that the police cracked his ribs, whipped him around the legs until he had no skin left, and beat him around the face until four of his teeth were knocked out and he required several stitches in his head and face. The police neglected to mark evidence from the scene of the crime, and later had difficulty identifying it. Furthermore, there were no fingerprints, and Bird could be placed only within the vicinity of the crime. Yet, within hours of his arrest, several cities, including Los Angeles, Louisville, Ky., Orlando, Fla., Evanston, Ill., and Kansas City, Kan., indicated that Jake Bird might be involved in one of their unsolved murder cases. According to Bird's later confessions, he participated in more than ten murders throughout the U.S. Police retained the services of Dr. Charles P. Larson, a well-known criminal pathologist. Dr. Larson found brain matter and two blood types in Bird's pants. With this evidence, the prosecution secured Bird's conviction.

At his trial, the jury found Jake Bird Guilty of two counts of first-degree murder after only thirty-five minutes of deliberation. Sentenced on Dec. 6, 1947, Bird addressed the court for the first time when Judge E.D. Hodge asked him if he wished to say anything. Bird pronounced his own ominous sentence. "All of you who have had anything to do with my case will be punished," Bird claimed. "I am putting the Jake Bird hex on you. Mark my words, you will die before I do." With that, Judge Hodge sentenced Bird to be hanged by the neck until dead and scheduled the execution for Jan. 16, 1948. The convicted man began a campaign of legal manipulation and bargain making in order to stay his sentence. His first appeal went unacknowledged by Judge Hodge. Bird then informed Walla Walla Prison officials that he would help them solve ten murders if Governor Mon C. Wallgren granted a stay of execution. The governor agreed to listen to Bird and grant a stay only if he helped clean up unsolved murder cases.

In the presence of undersheriff Joe Karpach, governor's representative Pat Steele, a court reporter, and Warden Smith, Jake confessed for three days. As he was very clever and well-read, he tricked his audience on several occasions, divulging only half-truths. He never claimed ignorance in any area, and twisted sentences and questions to his own ends. Bird was also well-versed in law and understood how to make the most of the little he knew. His stories of two murder cases contained details that secured him one reprieve. One case, from Evanston, Ill., involved the burglary and murder of Lillian Galvin and Edna Sibilski, her maid, on Oct. 22, 1942, in which $31,000 in jewelry and fur coats was stolen. Because of the details Bird knew about this killing, he was granted a sixty-day reprieve on Jan. 16, 1948, only hours before the scheduled hanging. Bird also claimed to have committed several murders in Cleveland which had been attributed to the "Mad Killer." He told in detail how he and an accomplice robbed a man, stabbed him to death, cut off his head, and dumped his body—cut in sections—into Bull Run Creek. They killed several others, making them look like victims of the Mad Killer, who turned out to be a 45-year-old man named Frank Carter. Bird won an appeal on May 20, but the court upheld the previous conviction and sentence. On the day of his second scheduled hanging, Bird won a hearing for a new trial "on order to show cause in the matter of the application for a Writ of Habeas Corpus." Appearing before Judge Sam M. Driver, Bird took the stand for the first time and acted as his own counsel. He claimed he was tortured to obtain a confession, that he was inadequately represented by counsel in his first trial, that his counsel, attorney

J.W. Selden, encouraged the jury to find him guilty, and that the trial judge ignored his appeal. Judge Driver refused to grant a new trial. Twelve hours before his third scheduled hanging, Bird produced a "Certificate of probable cause for appeal to the Court of Appeals in San Francisco." This won him a thirty-day stay of execution, but did not ultimately save him. Chief Judge William Denman denied his appeal. When told of the decision, Bird said "Well, that's too bad." Bird returned to the court where he was originally convicted so that his execution could be rescheduled. On the trip to Tacoma, a guard asked Bird if he had any regrets about the murders he committed. Bird said he regretted only one—a little boy he killed with a rock in Omaha, Neb., because the boy called him a nigger. He claimed it was an accident and that he should not have done it.

Perhaps the strangest aspect of Bird's trial was the hex he placed on those who played an active role in convicting him. The condemned man claimed they would die before him. One month after sentencing Bird, Judge Hodge, who was in excellent health, died of a heart attack. One of Bird's attorneys, J.W. Selden, died on the anniversary of Bird's sentencing. Joe Karpach, who took Bird's three-day confession at Walla Walla, died in January 1948, followed soon after by chief court clerk Ray Scott. One of the officers who took Bird's confession after his arrest, Sherman Lyons, died of a heart attack. The last to die was Arthur A. Stoward, one of Bird's guards at Walla Walla. The strange coincidence of these deaths, however, left Dr. Larson nonplused. "Those six men who did die didn't die of Jake Bird, they died of coronary occlusions," he said."

Jake Bird was hanged on July 15, 1948, twenty months after his conviction. The prison physician pronounced him dead after fourteen minutes. See: **Carter, Frank.**

REF.: *CBA;* McCallum, *Crime Doctor.*

Bird Cage, The, 1880s, U.S., pros.-mur. A hellhole in Tombstone, Ariz., during the 1880s, The Bird Cage was the roaring cowboy town's theater, owned by William and Lottie Hutchinson. It was nothing more than a glorified saloon with boxes that faced the stage and had curtains behind which the Hutchinson prostitutes plied their trade. There were many shootings in this low dive during its sinister heyday and a number of fatalities. Even actors brave enough to appear in this theater were wounded by random gunshots fired by drunken patrons who were displeased with a performance. REF.: *CBA.*

Birdman of Alcatraz, See: **Stroud, Robert Franklin.**

Birger, Charles, 1884-1928, U.S., org. crime. Charles Birger was a product of small-town America, a reckless and ruthless bootlegger who assumed the airs of a Robin Hood in the rural Illinois county of Williamson. This county, in the southern part of the state, had more in common with southern notions of banditry as held in Kentucky and Missouri than in the metropolis of Chicago. Birger, a handsome man of six feet, with a thick head of hair and the swaggering posture of a cavalier, had served in the U.S. cavalry which is where he undoubtedly learned the military tactics he later employed in the bloody bootleg wars of Williamson County. He lived for a while in New York City (some reports had it that he was born there but records indicate otherwise), then returned to the Midwest. Birger moved to Missouri, married, and joined Egan's Rats, a powerful gang that controlled East St. Louis. He later opened a store in southern Illinois and was part of labor gangs that fought the Ku Klux Klan in pitched battles around Herrin. At the dawn of Prohibition, Birger saw a chance to get rich by controlling all illegal liquor distribution in Williamson County. He bought a country estate near Egypt, Ill., which he dubbed Shady Rest, and recruited a small army to his colors.

Battling Birger for control of the bootleg territory were the fierce Shelton Brothers—Carl, Earl, and Bernie—whose gang of forty or fifty dedicated gunmen equalled Birger's own small army. Both gangs, through more than seven years of open warfare, turned Williamson County into a massive killing ground where dozens of persons—gangsters, and innocent citizens alike—were slain. Birger was inventive, buying used gas tank trucks and con-

THE BIRGER-SHELTON BOOTLEG WAR IN ILLINOIS

Illinois gangster Charlie Birger (inset) who boldly posed with his heavily armed gang, sitting atop a car.

One of Birger's armored cars.

Carl Shelton

Earl Shelton

verting these and other trucks into homemade tanks with machine guns mounted inside of them. The Sheltons did the same thing and pitched battles between these weird-looking vehicles were fought up and down the roadways of southern Illinois. The Sheltons went one step further, hiring airplanes and dropping bombs in the vicinity of Birger's stronghold, Shady Rest, attempting to wipe out the entire gang. (This was undoubtedly the only time when aerial warfare was practiced by gangsters attempting to eradicate their rivals.)

Birger was the most public gangster of his day. He sauntered about the streets of Egypt with two pistols on his hips, surrounded with no less than ten rifle-bearing men. He looted arsenals and soon his men were carrying submachine guns. The smiling, dapper gang leader hired professional photographers to take pictures of himself and gang members posing with their awesome weaponry in front of Shady Rest. Birger mailed these photos to the press and to his enemies, the Sheltons, as a way of displaying his power and declaring his intent to control Williamson County. In the first five years of Prohibition, Charlie Birger grew rich, taking in profits of $100,000 a month. He lived well, bought tailor-made clothes in Chicago, sent his small daughters to private schools, and provided his wife with wardrobes, jewels, and new cars. Yet, Birger's bloody reputation was so widespread that his small daughters came home singing songs about him killing people. Birger quietly told his girls that he only killed "bad people."

One of those "bad people," in the estimation of Charlie Birger, was Joe Adams, the owner of a crude roadhouse. Adams, a 300-pound wheeler-dealer, was also the mayor of West City, a small town in Franklin County, just across the Williamson County line. Adams had originally been a Birger ally, helping him to run liquor into Franklin County, but by 1926 Adams had gone over to the Shelton gang. When Birger learned of this he exploded, calling Mrs. Adams and asking her if she had much life insurance on her husband. When she said she had very little, Birger said: "Well, you'd better get a lot more, because we're going to kill him and you'll need it!" Some days later Birger called in two young men who had recently joined his gang, Harry and Elmo Thomasson, ages nineteen and twenty-one. Art Newman, a one-time Shelton gangster who had gone over to Birger when Birger's gang appeared to be winning the Birger-Shelton war, and Ray Hyland, Birger's gun-toting chauffeur, stood next to Birger as he gave the brothers a .38 and a .45. "We've got a job for you two boys," Birger said, "and it's got to be done tomorrow."

"Have you ever killed anyone?" Newman asked the brothers.

"I never had enough against anyone to kill them," replied Harry Thomasson.

"You are the boys to kill Joe Adams," Birger said matter-of-factly. "He don't know you and the law won't suspect you." Birger then told them that Hyland would drive them to West City and point out Adams' house. They would go to the house and if Adams or any of the Shelton gang members answered the door, they were to kill them. If anyone else answered the door, they were to leave and return later, and kill Adams when he appeared.

The brothers arrived at Adams' house on the night of Dec. 12, 1926. Mrs. Adams answered the door and the brothers asked to see Adams, who was sleeping. Adams then came to the door and Harry Thomasson handed him a note which Birger had written, ostensibly a note from Carl Shelton, his mortal bootleg enemy. The note read: "Friend Joe: If you can use these boys, please do so. They are broke and need work. I knew their father. C.S." As Adams read the note, both brothers produced the guns Birger had given them. "I shot him twice with the revolver that was hidden up my sleeve," Harry Thomasson later told police. "Elmo then shot him once. We then ran back to the car where Hyland was waiting and drove away." The next day, the brothers were paid $150 for the murder, $50 for each bullet fired into Mayor Joe Adams. The murder raised a storm of protest in Franklin County, a county that was not controlled by Birger. The local state's attorney began a heated investigation into Adams' murder and Birger was soon pinpointed as the mastermind behind the killing.

Proving murder against the crime boss, however, was a different matter. Charlie Birger did as he pleased, at least in Williamson County. Only a short while after he ordered the murder of Adams, Birger and his men abducted state patrolman Lory Price and his wife Ethel, whom Birger suspected of working with the Sheltons while taking money from him for protecting liquor shipments along highways patrolled by Price, and then arranging for those shipments to be hijacked by the Sheltons. Birger ruthlessly ordered his men to kill Ethel Price, which they did, throwing her body down a mine shaft and covering the opening with timber. Birger then shot the patrolman three times and drove around in a car, the officer bleeding to death in his lap as he looked for a suitable place to dump the body. He told his men that they would help him find another mine shaft to hide the body in or "I'll wipe out the whole lot of you!" He finally dumped the body along a roadside, then drove on to one of his hideouts where he drank with his killer gang until dawn, handing them bonuses for aiding in the murders.

The overconfident Birger never for a moment believed that any of his gang members would betray him after the February 1927 murders of the Price couple. But his ruthlessness in disposing of the patrolman and his wife, and his willingness to take any life, convinced several members that associating with Birger would eventually mean death if he came to believe a member had been disloyal to him. One of these worried henchmen was Harry Thomasson, one of the killers of Joe Adams. When his brother Elmo disappeared in early spring 1927, Thomasson concluded that Charlie Birger had killed him so that there would be no witnesses to his involvement in the Adams murder. Harry was convinced that he was next on Birger's "hit list." He went to Franklin County authorities and told the complete story of the Adams murder. Birger was indicted and ordered to surrender to Franklin County officials. This was but an empty order, however, since Birger was surrounded by an army of gunmen in his hideout near Egypt, Ill., and it would take the National Guard to bring him in.

Birger was tricked into surrendering by Jim Pritchard, sheriff of Franklin County, who called him on the phone and told him he believed that the Sheltons had killed Adams because he was holding out "some of the roadhouse profits from them," a lie which Birger accepted. He then said that if he, Birger, would be good enough to accompany him to Benton, Ill., in Franklin County, "just to answer the warrant," he would be released within a short time and be back in his home. Pritchard told the gang leader that if Birger did this favor for him, he, Pritchard, would be able to help him in his war against the Sheltons. When Pritchard mentioned that Birger would have to spend a night in jail, Birger told him that he would have to take his weapon with him because enemies were everywhere hunting him. Pritchard told him: "You bring any weapon you like, Charlie." Birger, amazingly, agreed to the short stay in Pritchard's jail, saying he had nothing to fear since he had nothing to do with Joe Adams' death.

On Apr. 29, 1927, Sheriff Pritchard arrived at Birger's house to find the gang chief wearing one of his best suits. His wife Bernice tucked a brand new green handkerchief into the breast pocket of his suitcoat. Birger straightened the fresh silk shirt he wore, one with his initials on the inside pocket and adjusted a new green silk tie his wife had just bought for him. Pritchard watched the vain gangster primp before a mirror. Birger asked his wife: "How do I look?"

"Like a movie star, honey," she replied.

"You think I look like anybody special?" Birger asked Pritchard.

"Can't say that I do," said the sheriff.

"Of course not, not with this suit and tie on," Birger said. "But when I wear my clothes from out West, the riding pants and boots, well, folks say that I am the spitting image of Tom Mix, the cowboy movie star."

"Damned if you don't," Pritchard said. "It was the clothes that threw me off."

Bernice Birger served some freshly made hot apple pie and coffee, and Pritchard and Birger ate and chatted. Then the sheriff

Birger smilingly surrenders, left; in court with daughters, center; henchman Art Newman, right.

Joking with his executioners, Birger is shown only moments before being hanged, 1928.

suggested they leave. Birger went to the mantle and grabbed a submachine gun with a full pan of ammunition affixed to it. Charlie Birger spent the night in a cell of the Franklin County Jail, sitting on a chair with the machine gun cradled in his arms. In the morning, Pritchard arrived and asked that Birger leave the gun behind while he kept his date in court to answer the warrant. Birger refused, telling Pritchard that he had too many enemies in the streets, but he promised to give up the weapon just before stepping into the courtroom. Pritchard nodded and escorted the gangster into the street, deputies all around them. As they walked to the courtyard, hundreds of citizens flocked to see the infamous gangster who reveled in the attention. He held out the sub-machine gun for spectators to touch it and then, laughing, tossed a handful of coins to children in his path.

Just before entering the courtroom, Pritchard asked Birger for the submachine gun. Birger turned to him and said: "Yes, sir, a promise is a promise. That's one thing you'll find out about Charlie Birger, Jim. His word is as good as all the tea in China." With that, Birger turned over the weapon and entered the courtroom. As they sat down, Birger waved and smiled to dozens of spectators who called out to him. His happy demeanor changed abruptly when Judge Charles H. Miller ordered deputies to bring in the state's star witness. When Birger saw Harry Thomasson enter the court, his hands manacled, he tried to bolt out of his chair but Pritchard and his deputies poked him with guns, the sheriff grabbing Birger's arm in a vise-like grip, saying: "You try that again, Charlie, and they'll be hanging a man with a broken arm."

Birger realized he had been hoodwinked and he screamed at Pritchard: "You liar!" At his trial, beginning on July 14, 1927, Birger was represented by Robert E. Smith. Tried with him were Art Newman and Ray Hyland, who had already supported Thomasson's testimony and had added information about the Price killings for good measure. Smith's defense of Birger narrowed down to a plea of innocent and Birger's word against the others. Next to Birger sat his wife, eyes downcast, thin lips tightly drawn. His daughters sat next to him, the youngest, Charlene Birger, an innocent-looking wide-eyed child, on his lap. This was, of course, a desperate device by Smith to win sympathy for a client who had lost all credibility through the horrific stories told about him by his own gang members.

Smith realized that the best he could do would be to save his client from execution. In his summation, he fairly shouted at the jury: "Thomasson didn't hang. He received a life sentence and he is the confessed murderer! If I hand you a pistol, would you shoot Charlie Birger if he sits here? If you wouldn't, would you ask the sheriff to do it?" He then turned to Birger and said loud enough for the juror to hear: "Charlie, in a few minutes, your life is going to be taken from my hands and given to these twelve men." Smith then wheeled about abruptly and said: "Gentlemen, Birger's fate rests with you."

After twenty-four hours, on July 26, 1927, the jury returned a Guilty verdict for Birger, Hyland, and Newman. Birger received the death penalty; Hyland and Newman would be sent to prison for life. Hanging, even though it had been abolished by the state on July 1, 1927, had been reserved for Birger since he had ordered the murder of Adams the previous year. The date of his execution was set for Oct. 25, 1927. He received several stays of execution while his attorneys filed desperate appeals. The final date for Birger's hanging, however, was finally fixed for Apr. 19, 1928. Birger decided that he would go out in the image he had maintained throughout his gangster career and in court, tough and fearless. He gave interviews in his death cell while he peered from a window that looked down on the scaffold. On the day of his execution, he looked down at the spectators thronging about the gallows, and laughed, saying: "Never did see so many ugly people in my life." He turned to his guards and laughed again, stating: "They're no better looking than you fellows." To reporters gathered outside his cell he said: "I've been a fool. I didn't think. I've been a heel and no good. I played the game and lost but I'll lose like a man."

Birger ate a Spartan breakfast of gruel, oatmeal, and coffee. The warden offered to get him a catered meal from a nearby restaurant but Birger refused. When he was offered a ham sandwich a little later, the gangster said: "Just this time I'm going to follow the rule of the Jews. I'm going to stick to that to the end, so I can't take it." Birger had been visited by Rabbi J.R. Mazur and had embraced the religion of his childhood. Then he talked of his boyhood in St. Louis, his time in the Army. He looked out of the cell window to see a beautiful spring morning. "Funny thing," the gangster intoned, "I've always got such fun out of life. I liked to live and spend money. Maybe I made it in ways some folks call crooked, but I always worked hard, whatever I went at. Life is awfully sweet. You never know how much you want to live until you come to a fix like this. I shot men in my time but I never shot one who didn't deserve it."

A physician arrived and offered Birger a shot of morphine. He waved it away, saying: "I had a horse that needed a hypo to run. I don't need one to walk out there." He dressed in silk underwear, put on a new tan suit, new brown shoes, a tan shirt, and a striped tie. He walked without aid to the outside stockade where more than 500 persons were jammed into the area. Across the street the rooftops were crowded with more spectators and thousands milled in the streets beyond the stockade walls. As he stepped into the yard and approached the gallows, Birger, smiling broadly, pointed to the many deputies holding machine guns and said: "Looks like the Western Front." He gingerly walked up the thirteen steps to the scaffold platform where several officials stood with the hangman. Birger looked up at a huge elm tree that spread its branches above the stockade wall and said: "Beautiful world!"

Birger looked down at the faces turned up in his direction and shouted with a broad grin on his face: "Good morning!" Those in the first rows nervously replied "Good morning" and then fell silent. Birger continued joking and chatting. The hangman, Phil Hanna of Epworth, Ill., who was about to perform his sixty-second execution, stepped forward and Birger shook his hand and said: "You're a wonderful old boy." The crowd and officials were amazed at Birger's conduct. He appeared happy, almost jubilant, wearing a wide smile that ignored the solemnity of the moment, almost as if the entire event was a charade, a joke, a bad moment in time he could laugh away, and he spoke of the exquisite spring morning as a living, protective thing that could almost reach out and save him, such was the incongruity of its beauty and the horrible fate about to embrace him.

Straps were tied tightly about his ankles, legs, and arms which were pinioned back, but Birger continued to smile and joke with the jittery hangman. He turned to the crowd and said: "I haven't got anything against anybody in the world! I forgive everybody! I can do that because of this wonderful Jewish rabbi." The gangster nodded his head in the direction of Rabbi Masur who stood praying nearby. "That's all." The black cap was placed over his head. From beneath the cap, Charlie Birger said softly: "Goodbye." The trap was sprung and Charlie Birger, the most terrible gangster ever seen in Williamson County, Ill., was dead by 9:43 a.m. See: **Shelton Brothers.**

REF.: *CBA; Bain, War in Illinois;* Mencken, *By the Neck.*

Birger Magnusson II, 1280-1321, Swed., mur. Son of Magnus I and king from 1290-1318. He battled against his brothers for control of the country from 1306-10, and had them imprisoned and eventually killed in 1317. A revolt forced him to flee to Denmark in 1318. REF.: *CBA.*

Birkenhead, First Earl of (Frederick Edwin Smith), 1872-1930, Brit., lawyer. Attorney general in 1915. He was sponsor of the *Law & Property Act* (1922). REF.: *CBA.*

Birkett, Lord Norman, b.1883, Brit., jur. King's Counsel in 1924, member of the House of Commons from 1923-24 and 1929-31, judge of the King's Bench Division of the High Court from 1941-50, member of the Nazi war crimes tribunal at Nüremberg in 1946, and appointed Lord Justice of Appeal from 1950-56. During his career he represented the defense in a number of British murder trials including those of Beatrice Pace, Sarah Hearn, Ethel Major, Dr. Buck Ruxton, and Edward Royal Chaplin. He led the prosecution team against Alfred Arthur Rouse and Frederick Nodder. REF.: *CBA*.

Birmingham Boys, prom. 1920s, Brit., org. crime. As a rival gang to the Italian mob run by Darby Sabini, the Birmingham Boys were constantly at odds with Sabini's gang. Each gang was involved with horse racing and earned a living as bookmakers, often trying to collect money from their rival's customers. This led to violent skirmishes, none of which ever resulted in convictions. During the month of April 1922, a man was clubbed and four others were stabbed in the back, typical of the violence between the two gangs.

REF.: *CBA*; Greeno, *War On the Underworld*.

Biron, Charles de Gontaut (Duc de Biron), 1562-1602, Fr., consp. Military leader known as the Thunderbolt of France who led the armies of Henry IV in 1598. He was beheaded in 1602 for conspiring to overthrow the king and seize the province of Burgundy which he ruled as governor. REF.: *CBA*.

Biron, Ernst Johann (Ernst Johann Bühren, Duke of Kurland), 1690-1772, Ger., mur. Accompanied his lover Empress Anna Ivanova to Russia and became chamberlain, leading the country during her reign from 1730-40. During this period, he executed or banished dozens of political rivals and imagined enemies. Following the death of Anna in 1740, a palace revolt resulted in his own banishment to Siberia from 1741-42. He was restored to the ducal throne of Kurland in 1762 by Catherine the Great, only to abdicate seven years later. REF.: *CBA*.

Biron, Sir **Henry Chartres**, 1863-1940, Brit., jur. Practiced at the Old Bailey, London Sessions, and in the police courts for twenty years. His direct method of advocacy gradually eliminated the rambling styles practiced by English lawyers. In 1906, he became metropolitan magistrate at Old Street and later at other locations. He was promoted to chief metropolitan magistrate following the retirement of Sir John Dickinson. He was involved in the trial of James Stevens. REF.: *CBA*.

Birrell, Lowell McAfee, prom. 1950s, U.S., fraud. Poor from his birth in Wilson, N.Y., on Feb. 5, 1907, Lowell McAfee Birrell possessed a brilliant mind that saw him at the head of his class at Syracuse University and the University of Michigan Law School. He obtained his doctorate of law at the unheard of age of twenty-one, and went on to become the most successful lawyer at the esteemed firm of Cadwalader, Wickersham and Taft. During the 1930s, Birrell became one of New York's most celebrated lawyers and businessmen. After Prohibition's repeal he put together a chain of small breweries into one firm, the Greater New York Breweries, and made a fortune. He appeared to have everything, lavish living quarters, a burgeoning bank account, the high regard of his peers. Yet, lurking deep in Lowell Birrell was the desire to acquire more. His insatiable greed led him into white collar fraud on a giant scale.

Cecil B. Stewart, millionaire broker and insurance underwriter, thought he was about to die in 1944. Birrell, who had met Stewart at a social gathering, told him to consult one of his own doctors who could "shrivel up" Stewart's cancer. Following some consultations, Stewart became convinced that Birrell's physician had eliminated the cancer and gratefully named Birrell as head of his many far-flung companies. A few months later, Stewart promptly died of cancer and Birrell went on a swindling rampage. Using the sound Stewart companies as collateral, Birrell engineered huge loans to buy other firms and then gutted the coffers of those firms, later merging them with healthy companies to hide their hollow shells. Birrell created a fantastic corporate maze that utterly confounded investigators of the Securities and Exchange Commission. The corporate con man established interlocking directorates, foreign agents as company registrants, and these led to even more foreign agents who, in Birrell's name, set up anonymous bank accounts in foreign countries, all of them controlled by Birrell.

A typical Birrell operation was the acquisition of Swan-Finch Oil, a much-respected firm. After Birrell got control of this company he increased its shares from 43,000 to three million, moving its assets to other firms he directed that were about to collapse, thus shoring up his shaky empire. Birrell would boost his stock in the weaker companies by having agents buy up shares of these failing firms near the close of the day, creating a small upward trend the following day. When the stock of one of these empty firms rose to the breaking point, Birrell would quickly sell his stock, reap great profits, and leave his investors taking the loss. With his profits, Birrell lived like a rajah. He never seemed to sleep, giving round-the-clock parties on a lavish scale in his Manhattan apartments or at his palatial Bucks County, Pa., estate. The cream of New York society attended these extravagant fêtes, including such fellow stock swindlers as Serge Rubinstein, who would be mysteriously murdered in his own posh Manhattan apartment in 1955. Birrell was also a notorious womanizer, patronizing high-class prostitutes, including the notorious call girl, Pat Ward, at $500 a night, this expensive flesh supplied by socialite whoremaster Mickey Jelke.

Birrell's illicit success attracted other slick sharpers to his side, including Virgil Dardi and Alexander Guterma who became directors of one of Birrell's once-healthy firms, United Dye and Chemical Corporation. They looted this firm on behalf of Birrell, and Dardi later went to jail for his illegal efforts. Birrell, however, always seemed to escape indictment since he made sure there was no direct trail of documents that would lead to him and provide evidence to convict him. He swaggered about New York nightclubs actually bragging that he was one of the most astute swindlers of his era. One evening a wealthy attorney meeting Birrell in a night spot informed him that he had just invested large sums into one of his firms. Birrell, tipsy on champagne, a blonde under each arm, laughed uproariously and boomed: "You put money into one of my companies? That was a mistake, sir! Nobody makes any money in any of my companies except me!"

Super swindler Lowell Birrell.

New York District Attorney Frank Hogan worked long years assembling enough evidence to convict the bold swindler, and Birrell finally received a subpoena to answer questions about one of his bogus firms in October 1957. He hurriedly packed $3 million in cash (out of the $14 million Hogan later estimated he looted from his firms) and fled to Rio de Janeiro, Brazil. Birrell's records were seized, such as they were, and government accountants spent years trying to figure them out. Meanwhile, the high-living Birrell basked in the warm sun of Rio from a mountaintop retreat, vowing never to return to the U.S. But, inexplicably, he returned in 1963 to face charges of swindling upward of $25 million from gullible investors. Birrell was confident, however, that he would be exonerated, and his subsequent trial soon revealed why he had returned without fear of punishment for his flagrant acts. Judge Inzer B. Wyatt ruled that all the Birrell records that had been taken by government agents had been illegally seized and were therefore inadmissible. The original search warrant issued for these records was so ambiguous as to be meaningless in a court of law, according to Judge Wyatt, a conclusion Birrell's lawyers had already reached when they urged their client to return to the U.S. without fear of conviction.

Birrell smiled broadly through pudgy cheeks as he walked from court, exclaiming to reporters: "The Constitution still prevails!" But government agents did not give up on the super con man and continued their investigations, dragging Birrell through a seven-year nightmare of interrogations, depositions, and court appearances, until they had proved he had illegally used some stock certificates in obtaining a paltry $5,000 loan from the First National Bank of Cincinnati. He was convicted and given a two-year sentence. His many appeals failed, including that with the U.S. Supreme Court, and Birrell went behind bars on Jan. 11, 1972. It took fifteen years of dedicated work on the part of government officials, not to mention millions of dollars in costs, to finally take Lowell McAfee Birrell out of the American business community where he had wreaked financial havoc and wrecked the fortunes of countless investors. See: **Dardi, Virgil; Hogan, Frank; Rubinstein, Serge.**

REF.: *CBA;* Nash, *Hustlers and Con Men;* Ottenberg, *The Federal Investigators.*

Bisbee, Ariz., 1917, U.S., abduc. IWW (Industrial Workers of the World, known as the Wobblies) workers struck the enormous copper mining company, Phelps-Dodge Copper, in Bisbee, Ariz., in 1917. Management refused to negotiate and secretly organized a 1,000-man posse under the command of Sheriff Harry Wheeler. More than 2,000 workers were seized in a midnight raid and herded into waiting cattle cars, which were locked and then shipped across the state line into New Mexico. This proved to be the largest *en masse* abduction in U.S. history, one which effectively broke the back of the IWW in Arizona. Phelps-Dodge was so influential that no legal suits against the firm for this abduction were permitted by the local courts. REF.: *CBA.*

Bisbee, Ariz., Massacre, 1883, U.S., rob.-mur. Five masked outlaws entered Bisbee, Ariz., on the night of Dec. 8, 1883, two of them entering the Goldwater and Castaneda store which was also the depository for considerable cash and gold. Wearing long coats that hid their rifles, the outlaws produced their guns once inside and demanded that all the money be turned over to them. J.C. Tappenier, one of the six Bisbee citizens inside the store when the outlaws entered, reached for his gun and a gunfight ensued which saw Tappenier shot to pieces. When citizens began to run down the street toward the store, the three bandits waiting outside began to fire, fatally shooting a woman and two men. Then the bandits rode out of town, leaving four dead and another dozen persons wounded. The Bisbee Massacre, as the bandit raid was thereafter known, had been planned by John Heath and involved his henchmen, Daniel Kelly, William Delaney, Comer "Red" Sample, James "Tex" Howard, and Daniel Dowd, all of whom were later tracked down and hanged by vigilantes. See: **Heath, John; Kelly, Daniel.**

REF.: Burgess, *Bisbee Not So Long Ago;* Burns, *Tombstone, An Iliad of the Southwest; CBA;* Chisholm, *Brewery Gulch;* Cox, *Luke Short and His Era;* Erwin, *The Southwest of John H. Slaughter;* Franke, *They Ploughed Up Hell;* Ladd, *Eight Ropes to Eternity;* McCool, *So Said the Coroner;* Marshall, *The Wham Paymaster Robbery;* Way, *Frontier Arizona.*

Bischoff, Charles, 1887-1947, U.S., abduc.-mur. For five days in 1931, Cincinnatians waited to hear the fate of Marian McLean, a 6-year-old girl abducted near her tenement home. The case had all the earmarks of familiar tragedy, bringing to mind the unsolved disappearances of three other Cincinnati children: 11-year-old Elizabeth Nolte in 1915, 9-year-old Emily Gump in 1919, and 9-year-old Freda Hornberger in 1921. Two of the three girls were never found. A third was left dead at her parents' doorstep, which prompted speculation that a madman was still loose in the neighborhood.

For nearly a month, Marian had been too sick to go to school. But on Dec. 17 her mother, Mrs. Mildred McLean, a laundress, decided to allow the child to go outside and play. Wearing a blue chinchilla coat, Marian skipped happily out the door and down the street with her playthings. An hour later, she walked over to visit an older boy named Julius Servizzi, who was washing his car.

She laughed when his dog suddenly jumped onto the clean hood with muddy paws. Servizzi shook his head and turned away to clean up the mess, as Marian flitted into a nearby alley, blissfully unaware that a man was watching.

In the next few days, one of the most intensive manhunts in Cincinnati history commenced. Rewards were offered both by police and Hamilton County, but no help was forthcoming. Police intensified their search in the vicinity of the apartment building where Mildred McLean and her daughter lived.

The body was finally discovered on Dec. 22 by Charles Bischoff, a 45-year-old shoemaker, who lived only a few doors from the McLeans. A team of 105 city firefighters were conducting a building-by-building search of the neighborhood when Bischoff burst out of his tenement shouting, "There's a dead child in my cellar!"

Investigators concluded that the girl had been dead for fifteen hours and that the body had been dragged from an adjacent building to conceal it from the approaching firemen. The labyrinth of interconnecting passageways in the crumbling building convinced police that only a man with intimate knowledge of the layout could have moved a body to the spot where Marian's body now lay. Detectives decided that Bischoff was somehow connected with the crime.

Angry neighbors formed tight knots around the Bischoff residence. If the police had lingering doubts about the cobbler's guilt, the neighbors did not. Riot squads were dispatched to West Twelfth Street to disperse the gathering while Mrs. McLean was taken to detective headquarters to identify her daughter's shredded clothing. "I don't see how I can face Christmas," she sobbed. Her estranged husband, living in Phoenix, Ariz., was provided with free airfare to Cincinnati.

Bischoff steadfastly denied his guilt for two weeks, but under the pressure of relentless questioning he finally confessed on Jan. 11, 1932. "I done it and it's done," he said in a tersely worded statement that harbored no remorse. He told police that he had assaulted and gagged the child, then left her to bleed to death in the cellar. She had died of internal hemorrhage. Prosecutor R.N. Gorman ordered excavation of the infamous cellar to determine if the bodies of the other three missing children could be located, but nothing was found.

The grand jury was asked to return a charge of first-degree murder against Bischoff, but he was adjudged mentally incompetent. He was committed to the Lima State Hospital, where he died on Apr. 10, 1947. REF.: *CBA.*

Bishop, Arthur Gary (AKA: **Roger W. Downs, Lynn E. Jones**), 1951-88, U.S., kid.-sex asslt.-mur. Arthur Bishop was born in 1951 in Hinckley, Utah. An honor student and popular teenager, he was also devoutly religious, and later served as a missionary in the Philippines for the Church of Jesus Christ of Latter-day Saints (the Mormons). Things began to go wrong for Bishop in 1974, when the church excommunicated him. He went to work at a Ford dealership in Murray, Utah, but was arrested for embezzling $9,000 by forging the owner's signature on a check. In 1981, Bishop decided to disappear. He ended all contact with his family, and changed his name to Lynn E. Jones, and later, Roger W. Downs. By this time, two small boys had vanished from their homes without a trace.

Alonzo Daniels, four, was playing in the front yard of his Salt Lake City home on Oct. 16, 1979, when he disappeared. His abduction was the first of five that would puzzle police in the next four years. Kim Peterson, eleven, was taken on Nov. 27, 1980, followed by Danny Davis, four, on Oct. 20, 1981; Troy Ward, six, on June 22, 1983; and Graeme Cunningham, thirteen, on July 14, 1983. In the case of Danny Davis, eyewitnesses said they saw a man and a woman leading the boy out of a grocery store. Davis' grandfather was shopping at the time. Kim Peterson had told his parents that he was going to meet a man who wanted to buy his roller skates on a corner near his home. Police found his body in a shallow grave in Cedar Fort, Utah County. The bodies of Danny Davis and Alonzo Daniels were found nearby.

Police wanted Bishop for embezzling $10,000 from Ski Utah, one of his many employers. He was arrested on July 25, 1983, after police questioned him about the disappearance of Graeme Cunningham. They learned that Bishop had been planning a trip to Southern California with the boy the week after he had disappeared. The county sheriff revealed that Bishop had been living in the immediate vicinity at the time of the five murders. Bishop confessed to police, then led investigators to the shallow graves near Cedar Fort, and to a secluded area in Big Cottonwood Canyon where the remains of Troy Ward and Graeme Cunningham were found. There was evidence of sexual assault, and police found explicit sexual photographs at Bishop's residence.

Arthur Gary Bishop was convicted after a six-week trial in 1984 of five counts of first-degree murder, five counts of aggravated kidnapping, two counts of forcible sexual assault, and one count of sexual abuse of a minor. Under Utah law, he could choose death by firing squad or lethal

Sex killer Arthur Bishop.

injection. Bishop chose to take the injection on June 10, 1988. He spent his last moments studying the Book of Mormon, and expressing regret for his crimes.

REF.: *CBA;* Shew, *A Second Companion To Murder.*

Bishop, Arthur Henry, 1907-26, Brit., mur. Arthur Henry Bishop, angry at being fired from his position as hall-boy at the residence of Sir Charles Lloyd, murdered the sleeping Frank Edward Rix on the night of June 7, 1925. Bishop was tried for murder, although his lawyers attempted to have the charge reduced to manslaughter, arguing that Bishop was drunk at the time. Justice Swift sentenced him to death at the Old Bailey after the jury found him Guilty. He was hanged on Aug. 14, 1926.

REF.: Shew, *A Second Companion To Murder; CBA.*

Bishop, Barnell, 1939- , U.S., arson-rob.-mur. In an attempt to destroy evidence of the robbery and murders he had committed, Bishop set fire to the Cantrell Cleaners, but as he fled, he forgot to remove his gun, complete with fingerprints untouched by the flames.

After the cleaners had closed for the night, Barnell Bishop had forced Albert Lizzio, fifty, to open the safe at gunpoint and give him the contents. He then beat Lizzio over the head and attacked his wife, Ida Lizzio, their 14-year-old son John, and an employee of the Lizzios', 45-year-old Jake Wright. Bishop then piled clothing on top of the unconscious victims, doused the piles with cleaning fluid and lighted them. Wright managed to notify the police before being engulfed in flames. He later died from the burns and injuries he suffered.

Bishop, who had been released from a California prison three months before, was arrested the night of the fire and imprisoned once again after being convicted on four counts of first-degree murder, robbery, and arson. On Sept. 26, 1973, he was sentenced to four terms of life imprisonment without possibility of parole, fifteen years for robbery, and ten years for arson, all to run consecutively. REF.: *CBA.*

Bishop, Cameron David, 1942- , U.S., bomb. Cameron David Bishop was placed on the FBI's Ten Most Wanted list on Apr. 15, 1969, for sabotaging defense plant utilities. Bishop was the first "revolutionary" to be so listed. A member of the Students for a Democratic Society (SDS), he was accused of participating in the dynamiting of four power transmission towers in Colorado between Jan. 20-28, 1969. The towers carried power to nearby

government supply plants.

At the time of the bombing Bishop was awaiting trial on charges stemming from a student sit-in at Colorado State University. Bishop remained "underground" until his arrest on Mar. 12, 1975, in East Greenwich, R.I. His car contained a small arsenal of weapons, according to local police.

Bishop was convicted on three counts of sabotage in a Denver courtroom on Sept. 19, 1975, and sentenced to seven years in prison. He became just the third person convicted in peacetime under the terms of the 1918 Sabotage Act. On May 6, 1977, the U.S. Court of Appeals for the Tenth Circuit overturned Bishop's conviction on the grounds that he had not received proper notification that his actions were forbidden under the little-known 1918 statute. President Harry Truman had in 1950 issued a proclamation outlawing certain political activities during a time of national emergency. The court ruled that Bishop could hardly have known the law was still in effect in 1969. REF.: *CBA.*

Bishop, Jesse Walter, c.1933-79, U.S., drugs-rob.-mur. A self-defined professional gunman born in Glasgow, Ky., Jesse Walter Bishop committed his first armed robbery at fifteen in Los Angeles. A Korean War paratrooper, he became addicted to heroin during his tour of duty—apparently after being treated with morphine as treatment for a wound that would earn him a Purple Heart—and was convicted for possession of heroin in 1951. He spent time at Fort Leavenworth, Kan., and was dishonorably discharged. During the next twenty-five years, Bishop would be convicted four times for armed robbery and drug offenses and spend nineteen of those years in prison. Then he held up a Las Vegas casino.

On Dec. 20, 1977, Bishop told a cashier at the El Morocco Hotel casino that he was a robber. Casino employee Larry Thompson and 22-year-old newlywed David Ballard intervened. Ballard, a mechanic from Baltimore, Md., was on his honeymoon, having been married only three hours earlier. Bishop shot Thompson in the stomach, then Ballard in the back as Ballard ran for his life. Thompson was wounded; Ballard later died. Bishop made off with $278 and for the next two days held up motorists on his way out of town—until police roused him from sleep beneath a trailer in Boulder City, Nev. Waiving his right to a jury trial, Bishop pleaded guilty and was sentenced to death.

Bishop welcomed his sentence, which he termed "an occupational hazard," and refused all efforts on his behalf to prevent his execution, which would be the third legal execution in the U.S. since 1967. In January 1977, Gary Gilmore was executed by a Utah firing squad, and in May 1979, John A. Spenkelink was electrocuted at a Florida prison. Bishop's refusal to fight the death penalty, as Gilmore had done, angered groups opposed to capital punishment, who, against the murderer's wishes, tried to intervene. He fired his two Clark County public defenders, Kurt Lenhard and George Franzen, saying they were only in on it for the publicity, and said his death was inevitable. The appeals process, he explained, would continually make his execution date uncertain, and thus was "cruel and inhumane punishment" and "a miscarriage of justice."

Although Henry Schwarzschild, director of the American Civil Liberties Union (ACLU) capital punishment project, argued that the death penalty was a "useless and brutalizing ritual," the ACLU's petition for a commutation to life imprisonment was rejected by the Nevada Pardons Board on Aug. 24, 1979, three days before Bishop's scheduled execution. That same day, the U.S. Ninth Circuit Court of Appeals turned down Stanford University law professor Anthony Amsterdam's plea for a stay of execution. He had argued that Bishop was not mentally fit to refuse an appeal. Also on Aug. 25, U.S. Supreme Court justice William H. Rehnquist ordered a stay of execution.

Rehnquist and the Supreme Court would later reject all further appeals: on Oct. 1 the Court rejected, by a vote of seven to two, an appeal by attorneys Lenhard and Franzen, and by a vote of seven to one, an appeal made by the NAACP Legal Defense Fund Inc. Because Bishop would not allow an appeal, the ACLU appealed the execution on behalf of eleven Nevada taxpayers. Dean Breeze, counsel for the taxpayers, claimed that "spending state money to carry out an unconstitutional act—the execution of Jesse Bishop," should not be permitted. The appeal was rejected by the Nevada Supreme Court on Oct. 20.

As the last of the appeals was being denied, the two-seat gas chamber at the Nevada State Prison near Carson City, dormant since 1961, was being readied. At 12:14 a.m. on Oct. 22, a capsule of cyanide gas was dropped from a tube into a dish of acid. At 12:21 a.m., Bishop was pronounced dead. Before his death, Bishop informed authorities of eighteen others he had killed for hire. And after refusing a last-minute opportunity to appeal, he said, "This is just one more step down the road of life that I've been heading all my life. Let's go." REF.: *CBA*.

Bishop, John, and **Williams, Thomas (AKA: Thomas Head),** d.1831, Brit., mur. Unemployed John Bishop persuaded his son-in-law Thomas Williams to join him in a criminal enterprise first popularized in Edinburgh by Burke and Hare. Their racket was body-snatching and murder. Cadavers, especially those of children, fetched top prices at the London surgical schools in the early nineteenth century.

On Nov. 3, 1831, Bishop and Williams induced a young Italian boy named Carlo Ferrari to follow them to their home at Bethnal Green by promising him work. There, they gave him a glass of rum spiked with laudanum. After ten minutes Carlo fell asleep. Bishop and Williams tied the feet of their victim and lowered him head first into a public well.

Two days later Bishop, Williams, and a barrister's son named May appeared at the dissecting room of King's College in London, where they offered the corpse to the surgeons for twelve guineas. After some haggling, Bishop accepted nine guineas, and delivered the body that afternoon. The doctors became suspicious when they discovered bruises on the body during their preliminary examination. The Bow Street police were summoned, and the trio of murderers were arrested while in a state of drunkeness. Their trial was conducted at the Old Bailey on Dec. 2, 1831. The verdict was Guilty and Chief Justice Tindal sentenced Bishop and Williams to death. May was reprieved at the King's pleasure. Bishop and Williams were hanged on Dec. 6 before a crowd estimated at 30,000.

REF.: Atholl, *Shadow of the Gallow; CBA;* Forster, *Studies In Black and Red;* Logan, *Rope, Knife, and Chair;* Mencken, *By The Neck;* Smith-Hughes, *Eight Studies In Justice;* Turner, *The Inhumanists.*

Bishop, Oliver, prom. 1939, U.S., mur. Only his advanced age saved Oliver Bishop from the Florida electric chair. His crime was murder, and the victims were his son George and his son's fiancée Louise.

In the eyes of the old man, his son was about to commit a mortal sin by marrying a woman to whom he was distantly related. But George and Louise were in love, and they planned to drive from Oliver Bishop's Tampa Bay home to a place where they might procure a license legally. The night before they were scheduled to depart, Bishop went to his woodshed and found a heavy sash weight. He crept into his son's bedroom and crashed the piece of iron down on his skull, killing the young man instantly. Louise was still awake, and when she saw what Bishop had done, she tried to flee through the yard. Bishop caught up with her near the fence and bludgeoned her to death. He buried the bodies in the marshy sand of McKay Bay. Weeks later, on May 28, 1939, a crab fisherman scouring the beach found the remains of the young couple. Police checked the missing persons reports and interviewed the estranged wife of Oliver Bishop at her home in Palmetto Beach. She reported that George and Louise had set out on a trip on Easter weekend and had not sent word of their whereabouts.

The trail led to Oliver Bishop's home in Tampa. Assistant Chief of Detectives Malcolm Beasley connected Bishop to the crime by comparing the mud on his shoes to the sand and silt of McKay Bay. They were the same. Confronted with this evidence, Bishop confessed to his crime. He was indicted for first-degree murder, found Guilty, and sentenced to life in prison. REF.: *CBA.*

Bishop, William Bradford, Jr., 1937-   , U.S., mur. A total mental breakdown was blamed for the slaughter of William Bishop's family on Mar. 1, 1976. Bishop, a rising foreign service officer in the State Department in Washington, D.C., had been a brilliant student, graduating from Yale and serving in Army Intelligence in the early 1960s. He married his childhood sweetheart, Annette Kathryn Weis, the couple producing three sons. In 1965 Bishop joined the State Department and he was quickly promoted with assignments as a foreign service officer in Addis Ababa, Ethiopia; Milan, Italy; and Gaborone, Botswana. Upon his return to Washington, Bishop bought a fashionable home in Bethesda, Md., and settled into Washington assignments at the State Department. By 1976 he was an incurable insomniac, constantly worried over not having had a promotion in five years. He suffered long periods of depression and began seeing a psychiatrist, taking sleeping pills, and even consulting a hypnotist in a desperate attempt to be able to sleep.

Living by the book became a credo to Bishop. He established a weird, unswerving regimen, allowing himself just so many hours in the week to do everything he felt he had to do, so many hours for work, so many hours for watching TV, so many hours to exercise by walking and playing tennis, so many hours with his family, and with his wife. Bishop even allocated exact hours each week in which he would allow himself to get drunk. All of this he entered in a diary, keeping precise notes on his every waking moment. Bishop spent so much time chronicling his every move that, in his own words, he developed an "enormous new capacity for love of self...a whole new confidence and style, an intellectual and moral integrity...the real self." Then the "real self" of Bishop's personality, according to psychiatrists later charting his lethal course, emerged on Mar. 1, 1976. Bishop was last seen at a Texaco service station filling a five-gallon drum of gasoline, chatting happily with attendants. He went home and beat to death his wife, Annette, thirty-seven, three children, William Bradford III, fourteen, Brenton, ten, Geoffrey, five, and mother, Lobelia Bishop, sixty-eight, piling the bodies into his station wagon. He drove to a lonely spot outside of Columbia, N.C., dumped the bodies into a ditch, soaked them with the gasoline from the five-gallon drum, and set them afire—or, that is the way police later reconstructed the mass murder of the Bishop family.

Smoke from the smouldering bodies was seen by some drivers on the road and the bodies were discovered a short time later. But Bishop had disappeared. Two weeks later his abandoned station wagon was found near Gatlinburg, Tenn., in the Great Smoky Mountain range. FBI agents investigating Bishop's disappearance were convinced, and still are to this day, that Bishop, indeed, murdered his family and then vanished. Agents proved that he had used one of his credit cards on Mar. 2, 1976, the day after the murder of his family, in Jacksonville, N.C. On that day the killer bought considerable sporting equipment, as he intended to spend some time in the wilds. He was believed to have entered the Great Smoky Mountain range where he, an experienced camper, could lose anyone following him. Some speculation was made about Bishop going into these wilds to commit suicide but it was reported in July 1978 that Bishop may have been spotted in Sweden and that he could have reached that country through his contacts in the foreign service. Since Bishop was indicted as a federal fugitive, the FBI has not closed its books on this case and agents are still searching for the killer.

The profile of Bishop as a mental case, some officials claim, was one which the murderer invented for himself long before killing his family, a mass murder he had planned long in advance of the so-called breakdown symptoms he later openly manifested, symptoms and actions that were designed to convince psychiatrists that, coupled to his murderous acts, he had become insane. His blind, suicidal trek into the Great Smokies was also made to appear as the unbalanced act of a man who had lost all control and would later die in the wilderness of starvation. All of this was an act, officials state, to persuade police that William Bradford Bishop, Jr. was dead. Some claim that he had met a foreign woman, fallen in love with her, and killed his family to be with her, that he escaped the wilds of the Great Smokies and left the U.S. and is now residing somewhere in a Scandinavian country. Such a devilishly clever plan was not beyond the intellectual scope of Bishop, who prided himself on his mental agility and whose every act was directed by a bloated ego that told him he was capable of achieving any goal in life, even the perfect murder.

REF.: *CBA*; Nash, *Among the Missing*.

Bismarck, Prince, prom. 1870, Case of, Prussia, forg. Though France and Prussia were ready to go to war, it took a forgery to ignite hostilities into violence.

When the Ems dispatch was sent from Wilhelm I of Prussia, it was altered by Prince Bismarck prior to release of the message to the press. Bismarck's altered message, which the prince boasted of changing before the eyes of generals Roon and Moltke, purported that the king had insulted French ambassador Count Vincent Benedetti. This falsehood led to war, as Bismarck hoped it would.

REF.: *CBA*; MacDougall, *Hoaxes*.

Bismarck Hall, 1870s, U.S., wh. slav.-pros.-rob. One of New York's worst hellholes was a subterranean dive called Bismarck Hall, located at Pearl and Chatham streets. The hall had an annex which led into caverns beneath the streets where dozens of young women who had been forced by white slavers into prostitution serviced their drunken customers, charging no more than fifty cents a trick. One report had it that the women had been purchased by the management for a sum that bound them to the hall for a number of years. Female inmates could leave but they had to post a security amount to assure the owners that they would return and, usually this sum of money was so high that most of them could never leave.

In his U.S. tour Grand Duke Alexis of Russia visited this lowly place and, rumor had it, recognized a noblewoman from his own country who had been reduced to waiting tables and offering her sexual favors to customers on occasion. Alexis reportedly bought his country woman back from the owners of the Bismarck and took her back to Russia with him where he restored her to her estates. One of the characters at the Bismarck the Duke found fascinating in a macabre sort of way was a creature called Ludwig the Bloodsucker. Ludwig was a short, fat, florid-faced German with a gigantic head crowned with a thick and unkept forest of black hair. Moreover, hair in great bunches grew out of Ludwig's ears and a tuft of black hair even shot out of the tip of his huge nose. This grotesque barrel-like person "entertained" patrons of the Bismarck Hall by drinking down large goblets of human blood, the source of this gruesome beverage undefined (some said from the morgue).

REF.: Asbury, *The Gangs of New York*; *CBA*.

Bistoni, Ansan (AKA: **M. Albert**), prom. 1950s, Fr., smug. On his return from Havana, Cuba, in October 1956, Ansan Bistoni and his girlfriend, Simone Prévost, received a warm welcome from the police. Undoubtedly Bistoni had a warmer welcome in mind than meeting Commissaire Hugues at Orly airport.

In his absence from France, Bistoni had been found Guilty of drug smuggling and sentenced to five years' imprisonment. Before his deportation from Cuba, Bistoni was involved in smuggling drugs, forgetting that one of his top men, Ignace Mariotti, had been arrested in December 1953, though Mariotti did not forget his fellow Italian countryman.

REF.: *CBA*; Goodman, *Villainy Unlimited*.

Bittaker, Lawrence Sigmond, 1941- , U.S., mur. The man who raped, tortured, and murdered five teenage girls between June and October 1979, in the suburbs of Los Angeles was captured five months after his last attack.

On Apr. 28, 1980, Lawrence Sigmond Bittaker was charged with five counts of murder, ten counts of rape, five counts of kidnapping, three counts for other sex crimes, and one count for conspiracy to commit murder, rape, and kidnapping. The killer

was also charged with illegal possession of tear gas, and for soliciting two other inmates at the county jail to kill 29-year-old Jan Malin, the victim and a witness of his tear gas attack at Manhattan Beach.

After a month of testimony and almost a week of deliberation, Bittaker was found Guilty on Feb. 17, 1981, after California's first televised trial. Roy Lewis Norris agreed to plead guilty for his involvement in the slayings in order to avoid the death penalty. He received forty-five years to life imprisonment. Bittaker was sentenced to death by Torrance (Calif.) Superior Court Judge Thomas W. Fredericks on Mar. 24, 1981, with the added stipulation that should the killer's sentence ever be reduced to life in prison, he would have to serve 199 years and four months. This verdict was challenged in an appeal, but the California Supreme Court upheld Bittaker's death

Mass killer Lawrence Bittaker.

sentence on June 22, 1989. Bittaker is currently awaiting execution at California State Prison in San Quentin.

Bittaker's victims included 13-year-old Jacqueline Leah Lamp and 15-year-old Jackie Gilliam, both from Redondo Beach; 16-year-old Shirley Ledford of Sun Valley; 16-year-old Lucinda Schaefer of Torrance; and 18-year-old Andrea Hall of Tujunga.

REF.: Cartel, *Serial Mass Murderers*; *CBA*.

Bitterman, Chester A., III, 1953-81, Col., (unsolv.) kid.-mur. As a Bible translator working for the Summer Institute of Linguistics in Colombia, 28-year-old Chester A. Bitterman III was accused of being a CIA agent and taken captive by leftist guerrillas who later murdered the U.S. citizen.

Guerrillas who claimed to be members of the April 19 Movement but more likely were part of the splinter group, National Coordination of the Masses, captured Bitterman in Bogota, Columbia, on Jan. 19, 1981. The kidnappers claimed that the institute which employed their hostage was really a CIA front, and that Bitterman would die unless the institute agreed to leave Colombia by Feb. 19.

After holding Bitterman for forty-seven days, their demands unmet, the guerrillas killed him, leaving his bullet-ridden body on an abandoned bus in the country's capital where it was found Mar. 7, 1981, after the kidnappers notified a local radio station. More than fifty people were arrested in connection with the murder. REF.: *CBA*.

Biunno, Vincent Pasquale, 1916- , U.S., jur. Judge of the District Court of New Jersey, appointed by President Richard M. Nixon in 1973. He authored numerous legal texts including a 1967 pamphlet covering the *New Jersey Rules of Evidence, Gann Law Books*. REF.: *CBA*.

Bjorkland, Rosemarie Diane (Penny), 1941- , U.S., mur. A resident of Daly City, Calif., Rosemarie Bjorkland awoke on the morning of Feb. 1, 1959, and told herself, as she related in court: "This is the day I will kill someone. If I meet anyone, that will be it." The 18-year-old girl was obviously in a deranged frame of mind when she took a .38-caliber pistol from her parents' home that day and began wandering through the hills of San Francisco, looking for a person to murder. She found a gardener, August Norry, emptying refuse from his pickup truck on a lonely road. He apparently thought she was stranded and asked if she wanted a lift into town. Penny Bjorkland smiled and thanked him. Then she drew the pistol and emptied it into the hapless father of two children, killing him. She reloaded the weapon and fired another clip of bullets into the dead body, twelve shots in all. Then she climbed into Norry's truck and took it for a thrill ride through the hills.

Police, examining the bullets that killed Norry, noticed they were unusual "wadcutters" used mostly for target practice. They traced the bullets to a gun shop, and its proprietor, Lawrence Schultz, reported that the bullets had been purchased by Penny Bjorkland. She was quickly arrested at her parents' home and

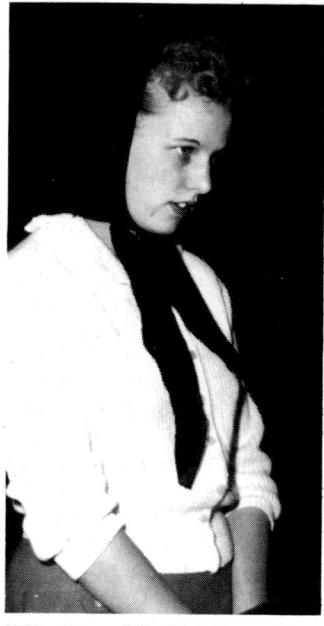
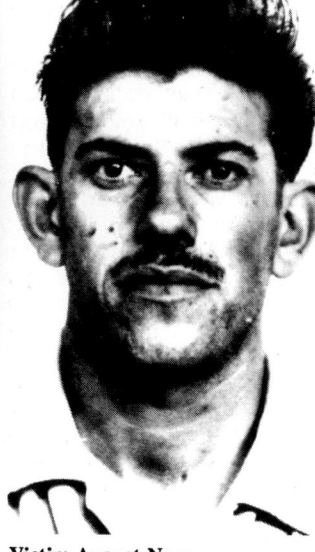

Killer Penny Bjorkland.   **Victim August Norry.**

confessed almost immediately, explaining that all she did was follow a "sudden urge." Bjorkland was tried and convicted. Before she was led away to begin serving a life sentence, Bjorkland shook her head at reporters and said: "This is not what I expected."

REF.: *CBA;* Nash, *Bloodletters and Badmen;* ____, *Look for the Woman.*

Black, Edward Ernest, 1886-1922, Brit., mur. Ed Black, an insurance agent, was married to a woman eighteen years his senior who owned a candy shop in Tregonissey, near St. Austell, Cornwall, at the time of her death on Nov. 11, 1921. Badly in debt and no longer in love with his wife, Black purchased two ounces of rat poison from Timothy White's store in St. Austell, explaining that he planned to kill some pesky rodents.

He added the deadly substance to his wife's breakfast on Oct. 31, 1921. Three days before she died he fled Cornwall to take up residence at Cashin's Temperance Hotel in Liverpool. Mrs. Black died from what physicians believed was gastro-enteritis, an affliction she had suffered from for some time, and for which she received regular medication from her druggist. However, a post-mortem examination carried out by a second doctor dissatisfied with the original diagnosis showed arsenic in her tissues.

Meanwhile, police arrested her estranged husband in the hotel after he failed in an attempt at suicide by cutting his throat. In court, Black called his signature on the poison register at the apothecary a forgery. This defense failed him, and he was convicted and hanged at Exeter on Mar. 24, 1922. See: **Blandy, Mary; Cotton, Mary Ann Robson Dowbray; DeMelker, Daisy Louisa; Jegado, Helene; LaFarge, Marie; and Smith, Madeline.**

REF.: Bresler, *Scales of Justice;* Butler, *Murderers' England; CBA;* Shew, *A Companion To Murder;* Thompson, *Poisons and Poisoners.*

Black, George Barron, 1899-1949, Brit., (unsolv.) rob.-mur. Answering a 999 distress call, Bristol CID officers found Black lying dead on the floor of the Knowle Bank on Jan. 7, 1949. The 50-year-old bank manager had grappled with an unknown robber seen loitering in the lobby for an hour before the hold-up, who then shot him. The gunman fired two more shots at Black before fleeing from the bank with £100 in hand. Two men outside the bank attempted to block his path. A rugby player named Phil

Patten jumped on the running board of the robber's stolen Austin, but fell off as the car swerved around the corner. No one ever saw the robber again, and his car was found abandoned outside town, the gas tank empty.

Eyewitnesses described him as a light-skinned, smartly-dressed business man of about twenty-six years. Donald Twitt, Black's assistant, told police the man announced the stick-up shortly after 3 p.m, and Black tried to tackle him in the lobby. "Hand over the money or you'll get it too!" the robber screamed at Twitt, and ordered him into the washroom just before the getaway.

The police interviewed thousands of people, but found no leads. The robber's identity and his reasons for lingering in the bank for an hour before the robbery remained a mystery. On Apr. 8, the inquest into the death was officially closed.

Posters were displayed all over the country, and an independent investigation was conducted in France, Belgium, Scotland, Wales, Australia, and Ireland, without result.

REF.: *CBA;* Harrison, *Criminal Calendar.*

Black, Hugo La Fayette, 1886-1971, U.S., jur., Hugo La Fayette Black served as police court judge in Birmingham, Ala., from 1911-14, prosecuting attorney in Jefferson County from 1914-17, and was elected Alabama senator from 1927-37. He was appointed associate Supreme Court justice by President Franklin D. Roosevelt in 1937 to succeed Justice William Van Devanter and served until 1971. Black joined the Ku Klux Klan in 1923 and left the group two years later. In a national radio address in 1937, he disavowed all past association with the KKK. In *Brown vs. the Board of Education* (1954), he voted with the majority in declaring racial segregation of public schools to be unconstitutional. REF.: *CBA.*

Hugo L. Black

Black, Isaac (Ike), d.1895, U.S., west. outl. Ike Black was a native of Kansas who drifted to Oklahoma when in his teens and there became a cowboy and, later, a cattle rustler. He became a member of the notorious Doolin Gang in the early 1890s and later joined Zip Wyatt (Dick Yeager) in committing several holdups. On Aug. 1, 1895, Black, Wyatt, and others rode into a posse trap near Skelerton Creek, outside of Sheridan, Okla. The posse, headed by U.S. Marshal W.D. Fossett and Sheriff Bill Banks, opened fire when the outlaws refused to surrender and shot Black from his saddle. He was dead by the time the lawmen reached him. Wyatt was wounded but managed to escape; he was later captured. One of the members of the posse, the son of lawman Fossett, had gone to grade school with Black and he spent considerable time worrying about whether or not his bullets were the ones who killed his boyhood friend. Black's corpse was taken to Canton, Okla., where it was put on display; the morbidly curious paid a dime each to see the dead outlaw stretched out on a wooden plank. See: **Wyatt, Nelson Ellsworth.**

REF.: Barnard, *A Rider of the Cherokee Strip;* Bartholomew, *The Biographical Album of Western Gunfighters; CBA;* Debo, *Prairie City, The Story of An American Community;* Hunter and Rose, *The Album of Gunfighters;* James, *The Cherokee Strip;* ____, *They Had Their Hour;* Nix, *Oklahombres;* Rainey, *The Cherokee Strip;* Shirley, *Toughest of Them All.*

Black, Jack, prom. 1870-1900, U.S., burg. Looking back on a long and prosperous criminal career, Black would always say, "I had no more thought of right or wrong than a wolf that prowls the prairie. I hunted because I was hunted myself, and I showed no consideration for anybody or anything because I knew I would receive none."

Black quit school at age fourteen to work in a Kansas City cigar store which fronted an illegal gambling den in its back rooms. A thirst for adventure and a desire to crack the big time convinced the boy to pack up and hit the railraods. In Denver, arrested on a vagrancy charge, he was sentenced to fifteen days' hard labor on a chain gang.

On the way to begin serving his sentence, Black escaped and remained a fugitive for months, during which time he committed the first in a series of house burglaries which were to become his stock and trade. His partner, Smiler, was shot in the face and died during a foiled robbery attempt. Black was captured the next day and returned to prison where he met his famous sidekick, the Sanctimonious Kid, an accomplished thief, confidence man, and fence, who knew all the back alleys and gaming tables of San Francisco. When the two men were paroled, they headed for San Francisco, where Black gained a first-hand education from the older man. "You read a lot of books about criminals, but forget it all," Sanc told Black. "Take nothing you can't put in your coat pocket. You've got to watch yourself like a fat man on a diet." Words to live by.

After a long, fruitful partnership, the criminal and the apprentice parted ways. The Sanctimonious Kid drifted to Australia where he was hanged for killing a policeman. Black drifted in and out of various U.S. jails and in later years gave up crime altogether, becoming a reporter for the San Francisco *Call*. He published his memoirs in 1926.

REF.: *CBA*; Hamilton, *Men of the Underworld*.

Black, James W., 1795-1813, and **M'Donald, John**, 1793-1813, Scot., rob.-mur. Near the town of Coltbridge, Scotland, lived two young roughnecks named John M'Donald and James Black who decided one day to become highwaymen. They bought pistols from a local gunsmith and proceeded to Calton where they held up 72-year-old William Muirhead on May 12, 1813. After rifling his pockets they shot the old man dead, and leaving the body in the road where it was found that night by a passing coachman.

A local barmaid furnished the police with an accurate description of the two felons. Based on this information they were seized and jailed for robbery and murder. A death sentence followed, passed by the High Court of Judiciary, and a gibbet was constructed on the precise location where Muirhead's body was found. The prisoners were executed on July 12, and carried to a surgical college in full view of curious spectators who lined the road.

REF.: *CBA*; Mencken, *By The Neck*.

Black, Jeremiah Sullivan, 1810-83, U.S., jur. Attorney general under President James Buchanan and secretary of state from 1860-61. He accepted nomination to the U.S. Supreme Court in 1861, but was rejected in Congress by Republicans who considered him soft on the slavery question, and by southerners who remembered that he had urged Buchanan to fortify Fort Sumter prior to the outbreak of hostilities. While serving as attorney general he exposed the California land title frauds, while opposing the doctrine of squatter sovereignty. He served as one of the legal advisors to President Andrew Johnson during the impeachment hearings but withdrew from the case because of personal disagreements. REF.: *CBA*.

Black, Lloyd Llewellyn, 1889-1950, U.S., jur. Lloyd Llewellyn Black had a long legal career in the Pacific Northwest where he served as the prosecuting attorney for Snohomish County, Wash., from 1917-19. He was later appointed federal judge to the court of the Western District of Washington by President Franklin D. Roosevelt in 1939. REF.: *CBA*.

Black, Norman William, 1931- , U.S., jur. Magistrate for the Southern District of Texas from 1976-79. He was appointed judge of the Southern District of Texas by President Jimmy Carter in 1979. REF.: *CBA*.

Black, Robert, 1947- , and **Hearn, John Wayne**, 1945- , U.S., mur. Robert Black, of Bryan, Texas, decided to murder his wife Sandra in order to collect $175,000 from a life insurance policy—money that he planned to use to leave Bryan and run off with his cousin. With this plan in mind, Black responded to a classified advertisement placed in *Soldier of Fortune* Magazine in

1985. The advertisement read:

> Ex-Marines, 67-69 Nam Vets. Ex-DI, weapons specialist—jungle warfare. Pilot. ME. High risk assignments. U.S. or overseas...

John Wayne Hearn, a self-styled "Rambo" and an ex-Marine had placed the ad. Black contacted Hearn and offered him the job of killing his wife for $10,000. Soon thereafter, Sandra Black lay dead, shot twice in the head as she carried groceries into her home. She died instantly.

Robert Black was convicted of first-degree murder on Feb. 26, 1986, in the 85th District Court of Texas and sentenced to die in the electric chair. His conviction is under appeal. That same day, Hearn pleaded guilty and was sentenced to life in prison, with an affirmative finding—meaning that he must serve a minimum of twenty years before being granted a parole hearing. He was then returned to Florida and convicted for an earlier murder.

Meanwhile, attorneys for the family of Sandra Black filed a $22.5 million civil lawsuit against the publishers of *Soldier of Fortune*, charging them with criminal negligence for running a gun-for-hire ad. Defense attorney Larry Thompson defended the magazine's right to publish such material, and pointed out that it did not mention any illegal activity. "It's a very innocuous ad," he said. In March 1988, a federal court in Houston awarded $9.4 million in damages to the victim's family. *Soldier of Fortune* is appealing the award. See: **Banister, Debra.** REF.: *CBA*.

Black, Susan Harrell, 1943- , U.S., jur. Judge of the court of the Middle District of Florida, appointed by President Jimmy Carter in 1979. She authored various legal manuals including *Burden of Proof, the Florida Bar Continuing Legal Education Evidence Manual* (1978) and *Extradition, the Florida Bar Continuing Legal Education Criminal Law Manual* (1978). REF.: *CBA*.

Black Bart (Charles E. Boles, AKA: Charles E. Bolton, T.Z. Spalding), 1832-c.1917, U.S., rob. One of the most unusual stagecoach robbers in American history was an old man known in the annals of the West as Black Bart. He used many aliases, including Charles E. Bolton and Charles E. Boles, the latter, most probably his true name. Bart, in addition to being an expert lone bandit who robbed more than two dozen stages in California in 1877-78, exercised a sardonic brand of humor in the form of doggerel scratched on foolscap and left in the empty strongboxes he looted. He was frivolous and capricious, a jokester whose laughing nature endeared him even to his victims.

The infamous Black Bart.

Bart first struck on a mountain pass called Funk Hill, four miles outside of Copperopolis, Calif., on July 26, 1875. The driver of the Wells Fargo stage, John Shine (later a U.S. marshal and a California state senator), brought up his team short, startled at the strange apparition before him. Bart wore a long, white duster over his clothes, and over his head was a flour sack with holes that had been cut for the eyes. A deep voice commanded: "Throw down the box!" The driver reached beneath his seat and withdrew the Wells Fargo strongbox containing several thousand dollars. He tossed down the wooden box, reinforced with iron bands, which was padlocked. Bart grabbed the box and slipped into a nearby woods. Shine drove off some distance and then stopped the stage, walking back down the road to see a half dozen guns leveled at him from outlaws positioned behind boulders. He stood rock still and then realized the outlaws were not moving. He approached one, and then another boulder, to discover dummies with sticks for guns pointed at him. (Bart accomplished his robberies by pretending to have a large gang positioned behind several large boulders, and when he first stopped the stage, he would call out to his imaginary gang: "If he dares to shoot, give him a solid volley, boys!")

The lone bandit continued to stop Wells Fargo stages with alacrity, always along mountain roads where the driver was compelled to slow down at dangerous curves. (It was later estimated that Bart robbed as much as $18,000 from Wells Fargo stages over the course of four years, striking twenty-nine times.) He left no clues whatsoever, although he did leave a spare gun after one robbery, and he was always extremely courteous to passengers, especially women travelers, refusing to take their jewelry and cash, telling them: "I don't want your money, only Wells Fargo boxes." He made a favorable impression on drivers and passengers alike as a courteous, gentlemanly robber who apparently wanted to avoid a gunfight at all costs. On Aug. 3, 1877, the lone bandit, again appearing in his duster and flour sack, stopped the Arena stagecoach, en route to Duncan's Mill on the Russian River. He took the strongbox and its contents of $300 in cash and a check for a similar amount.

Some days later a posse found the empty box, and inside of it was a note reading:

> I've labored long and hard for bread,
> For honor and for riches
> But on my corns too long you've tred,
> You fine-haired sons-of-bitches.

The stage robber had signed the note with a name that would go down in Western history: "Black Bart, PO-8." The letters and number mystified lawmen as much as the name Black Bart. Tracking posses found no trace of the elusive bandit, and superstition had it that the stage indeed had been robbed by a ghost. For a year the robber was not to be seen. Then, on July 26, 1878, Bart held up another Wells Fargo stage, one traveling between Quincy and Oroville, Calif. Again, he wore the same weird outfit, the long flowing duster and the flour sack, and again, his voice, described as "hollow and deep," ordered the driver to "throw down the box!" This time Bart made off with $379. He also helped himself to a passenger's $200 diamond ring and a gold watch worth $25.

Once more, pursuing lawmen found the empty strongbox with another note which stated:

> Here I lay me down to sleep
> To wait the coming morrow,
> Perhaps success, perhaps defeat
> And everlasting sorrow.
> Yet come what will, I'll try it once,
> My conditions can't be worse,
> And if there's money in that box,
> 'Tis money in my purse.

Again there were no clues to follow. The bandit seemed to have vanished into thin air. Bart himself was responsible for a trail that led nowhere. Wells Fargo drivers noticed that when he stopped a stage, he wore large socks over his boots so that he would leave no heel marks in the dirt to be followed. Moreover, he never used a horse but slipped into the wilderness on foot and thus left no trail of horse tracks. Bart, it was later discovered, was an excellent hiker and outdoorsman who traveled great distances on foot, camping out for weeks to get to and from his robbery sites which he scouted carefully. He used a shotgun most times in his robberies, but not once in all of his many robberies did he ever fire it. As it turned out, he could not have fired the weapon since he never loaded it, or at least that is what he told arresting officers later.

Bart was not a rampant pillager of Wells Fargo. He only robbed stages periodically, sometimes with as much as nine

months' time between robberies, and he later stated that he "took only what was needed when it was needed." Most stagecoach drivers were submissive to Bart, seldom defying him with a cross word and obediently tossing down the strongbox when ordered to do so. This was not the case with hard case George W. Hackett who, on July 13, 1882, was driving a Wells Fargo stage some nine miles outside of Strawberry, Calif. Bart suddenly darted from a boulder and stood in front of the stage, stopping it and leveling a shotgun at Hackett. He politely said: "Please throw down your strongbox." Hackett was not pleased to do so; he reached for a rifle and fired a shot at the bandit. Bart dashed into the woods and vanished, but he received a scalp wound that would leave a permanent scar on the top right side of his forehead.

Robberies became increasingly difficult for Bart, and his last, on Nov. 3, 1883, almost spelled his doom. He stopped another Wells Fargo stage on that day, almost in the exact spot where he robbed the first stagecoach in 1875. A lone rider following the stage, Jimmy Rolleri, fired a shot at Bart as he was dragging the strongbox into the underbrush, and wounded him in the hand. Bart used his handkerchief to wrap around the wound; this was later found with a San Francisco laundry mark on it. The men assigned to track down Black Bart were two shrewd, tough detectives, James B. Hume and Henry Nicholson Morse, one-time sheriff of Alameda County. Harry Morse realized that there were ninety-one laundries in San Francisco, but he set out to visit each one of them and, at Ferguson & Bigg's California Laundry, his search was rewarded with an identity, that of Charles E. Bolton, a mining engineer. Morse and Hume, accompanied by local police, arrested Bolton-Bart in his hotel. He would not admit to being the bandit, and denied that his name was either Charles E. Bolton, the name under which he had been living in San Francisco for years, or his supposedly given name, Charles E. Boles. When booked, he gave his name as T. Z. Spalding.

Found in Bart's hotel room was a Bible which had been given to him by his wife in 1865. It bore the name of Charles E. Boles. He was born and raised in upper New York State and had been a farmer, until he married and moved to Illinois just before the Civil War. He served as a sergeant in 116th Illinois Volunteer Infantry. When his family members died, he moved to California to seek his fortune. He had tried a number of jobs and even tried panning for gold before he turned to stagecoach robbing. With his loot, he had invested in several small businesses which brought him a modest income, but he could not resist the urge to go back to robbing stages when money became short. After days of denying he was the famous Black Bart, the bandit finally admitted that he had committed several robberies of which he stood accused, but only those occurring before 1879—mistakenly believing that the statute of limitations would protect him against prosecution. Bart was convicted and given a six-year prison sentence in San Quentin Prison, arriving there on Nov. 21, 1883.

Bart served about four years and was released on Jan. 21, 1888. By then he had aged considerably, with one ear gone deaf, his eyesight failing, his shoulders stooped, and his hair whitened. His spirit was crushed, and he sought only to escape the newsmen surrounding him when he stepped from the prison gates. He disappeared and was later thought to have returned to his bandit ways, especially since another Wells Fargo stage was robbed on Nov. 14, 1888. The lone bandit left another bit of doggerel that read:

> So here I've stood while wind and rain
> Have set the trees a'sobbin'
> And risked my life for that damned stage
> That wasn't worth the robbin'.

Detective Hume examined the note and compared it with the genuine Black Bart bits of poetry of the past. He declared the new verse a hoax and the work of another man, declaring that he was certain Black Bart had permanently retired. This gave rise to the later notion that Wells Fargo had actually pensioned off the robber on his promise that he would stop no more of its stages, paying him a handsome annuity until his death, which was reported in New York newspapers as being sometime in 1917, although this was never officially confirmed. The last time Detective Jim Hume heard of Black Bart's whereabouts was sometime in 1900, when he received a report that the old man had died in the high California mountains while hunting game. This rather pedestrian end was unacceptable to those who bore the legend of Black Bart into the next century. Writers and reporters had the outlaw living in a hundred different places and robbing stages until Wells Fargo decided to close its last stage routes. Today the legend and reality of Black Bart are almost impossible to separate, which is undoubtedly the way the bandit would have wanted it.

REF.: *American Guide Series, California, A Guide to the Golden State;* Ault, *The Home Book of Western Humor;* Bartholomew, *The Biographical Album of Western Gunfighters;* Beebe, *The American West;* _____ and Clegg, *U.S. West, The Saga of Wells Fargo;* Block, *Great Stagecoach Robbers of the West;* Boggs, *My Playhouse Was a Concorde Coach;* Botkin, *A Treasury of Western Folklore;* Buckbee, *Pioneer Days of Angel's Camp;* CBA; Curran, *Mr. Foley of Salmon;* Cushing, *The Story of Our Post Office;* Dane, *Ghost Town;* Dickson, *San Francisco Is Your Home;* _____, *Tales of San Francisco;* Dillon, *Wells Fargo Detective;* Drury, *California, An Intimate Guide;* Duke, *Celebrated Criminal Cases in America;* Fanning, *Great Crimes of the West;* Finger, *Foot-Loose in the West;* Fisher, *Gold Rushes and Mining Camps of the Early American West;* Gard, *The Great Buffalo Hunt;* Gardner, *The Old Wild West;* Glasscock, *The Golden Highways;* Goethe, *What's In a Name?;* Goss, *The Life and Death of a Quicksilver Mine;* Gray, *Men Who Built the West;* Hansen, *Wild Oat in Eden;* Harlow, *Old Waybills;* Henderson, *Keys to Crookdom;* Hendricks, *The Bad Man of the West;* Holbrook, *Let Them Live;* Horan and Sann, *Pictorial History of the Wild West;* Howard, *This Is the West;* Hubbard, *Building the Heart of an Empire;* Hungerford, *Wells Fargo;* Hunter and Rose, *The Album of Gunfighters;* Issler, *Stevenson at Silverado;* Jackson, *Anybody's Gold;* _____, *Bad Company;* _____, *Tintypes in Gold;* Lewis, *High Sierra Country;* McCarty, *The Enchanted West;* Martin, *Stockton Album Through the Years;* Moak, *The Last of the Mill Creeks and Early Life in California;* Moody, *Stagecoach West;* Murphy, *The Hearts of the West;* Nash, *Bloodletters and Badmen;* Paden, *The Big Oak Flat Road;* Quiett, *Pay Dirt;* Rennert, *Western Outlaws;* Russell, *One Hundred Years in Yosemite;* Sabin, *Wild Men of the Wild West;* Shippey, *It's an Old California Custom;* Sonney, *An American Outlaw;* Stellman, *Mother Lode;* Swan, *Frontier Days;* Tinkham, *History of San Joaquin County;* Torchiana, *California Gringos;* Travers, *California, Romance of Clipper Ships and Gold Rush Days;* Waters, *A Gallery of Western Badmen;* Wilson, *Treasure Express, Epic Days of the Wells Fargo;* Winther, *The Old Oregon Country;* _____, *The Transportation Frontier;* Wood, *Calavaras;* (FICTION) Manning, *The Gold Dragon.*

Blackbeard (Edward Teach, AKA: Tach, Tatch, Thatch), d.1718, Int'l, pir.-mur. No pirate who roamed the open seas in search of booty and conquest ever matched the fierce character of Blackbeard, who was truly a sadistic madman, a bloody butcherer of helpless victims. But he was fair in his insanity, oppressing his crews and peers with the same demoniac punishments as he inflicted upon his enemies and captives. It was later said by revisionist historians that Blackbeard blatantly performed atrocities to establish for himself an image of mercilessness, of ferocity, producing instant terror in those who faced him in combat. The truth was that Blackbeard was deranged and simply enjoyed killing, reveling before his own death in the hundreds of lives he had taken.

Blackbeard was born Edward Teach in either Bristol, England or Jamaica. His brother became a respected artillery officer in the Jamaican army but Blackbeard went to sea early and became a pirate as a youth. His name came from the long, flowing black beard he assiduously cultivated, one which he used to create a bogeyman character. Daniel Defoe described the beard as "that large quantity of hair which like a frightful meteor covered his whole face and frightened America more than any comet." Blackbeard twisted his hair in long strands, adorning it with ribbons, and to further accent his fierce-looking beard he would, before attacking a ship or coastal city, put slow-burning gunner's matches in the ends of his waxed beard strands and in his hat so that he looked like a volcano belching fire and smoke. When going into battle, the pirate put on a glaring red sash and hung six pistols from it. Being ambidextrous, he wielded two swords in combat.

Edward Teach, the notorious Blackbeard the pirate.

To serve with Blackbeard was to risk one's life with enemies and the captain as well. Blackbeard, a giant of a man with seemingly endless stamina and power, was forever testing his crews. He would pick fights with the toughest of his mates and bring the contest almost to death blows. Dozens of his pirates bore facial scars that they had received from Blackbeard's sword or knife point. On one occasion, Blackbeard suspected that one of his crews was planning a mutiny or desertion. He boarded this ship and ordered everyone into a hold where sulphur barrels were stored. "Now," he said with gleaming eyes, "we shall make our own hell!" With that he lit the sulphur and compelled the crew to stay in the hold and inhale the noxious fumes. He laughed wildly as his crew members eventually bolted for the hatch, coughing and choking, their faces streaming tears. He stayed longest in the hold and emerged to call his now submissive followers weaklings.

Captives taken after Blackbeard's crews overwhelmed a ship were usually mistreated. Women were invariably gang raped by his crews, Blackbeard believing that they were a "natural part of the spoils." He forced some of his captives to walk the traditional plank to their own watery graves, and others who looked at him in "an odd fashion" were run through with his sword, or had their eyes poked out or their ears or noses cut off. A few he disemboweled in front of his crews and fed the bloody entrails to sharks following his flagship, *Queen Anne's Revenge,* a forty-gun French frigate which seldom found its equal in high seas combat. Oddly, when capturing a ship, Blackbeard often spared the enemy captain. He would interrogate the crew of the ship he had captured and, if these sailors swore that their captain was a fair man, the captain would be spared, put into a longboat first and shown all the courtesy of a military prisoner. Captains who received a bad report from their crew members were horribly mutilated and then murdered.

Blackbeard earned an undying reputation as the worst buccaneer in pirate history, yet he operated for only about three years before his career was brought to an end. His ships operated out of Ocracoke Inlet in North Carolina. He preyed upon shipping of all nations sailing along the coasts of Virginia and the Carolinas. The pirate operated with impunity because of the connivance of North Carolina governor, Charles Eden and his secretary and collector of customs, Tobias Knight, both of whom secretly protected Blackbeard and shared in all his loot. One report had it that the venal Eden, so thankful for one enormous load of loot, sent Blackbeard a 16-year-old virgin from North Carolina, whom he suggested Blackbeard marry. The pirate turned the girl over to his crew for their sexual pleasures.

Blackbeard in mortal combat with Lt. Maynard.

Blackbeard was so bold that he would sail to the bar outside of Charleston, his favorite hunting ground, and blockade the harbor for ten days to two weeks at a time. Then he would attack and capture any ship that went in or out of the harbor. Charleston governor Robert Johnson begged Eden for help but got none. Then, in 1718, Johnson learned that two men-of-war were anchored as guard ships off the Virginia coast. Johnson asked Virginia governor Alexander Spotswood to send the two warships to attack Blackbeard. Without authority, Governor Spotswood dispatched Lieutenant Maynard and the two men-at-war to the Carolinas with explicit instructions to wipe out the pirates. Maynard sailed his vessels to Ocracoke Inlet and attacked at dawn but ran aground. The smaller man-of-war was nearly blown out of the water as Blackbeard's flagship raked it with a broad-side. But the pirate ship also ran aground, and leaving his own stranded flagship, *H.M.S. Pearl*, Maynard and his crew boarded the *Queen Anne's*

Blackbeard's head swinging from the bowsprit of Lt. Maynard's ship.

Revenge, fighting hand to hand with the pirates, overwhelming them. Just before the enemy came aboard his ship, Blackbeard, undoubtedly realizing that his end was near, seized a huge jug of rum and poured it down his throat, sloppily spilling it down his front. He then roared: "Damnation to all who give or ask for quarter!" He charged into the enemy after firing off his six pistols, swords flailing. Three sailors, including Maynard himself, attacked the giant and ran him through several times with their swords.

To prove that the scourge of the seas was dead, Maynard cut off Blackbeard's ugly head, hanging this grisly trophy from the

bowsprit of his ship so that all the inhabitants of the Virginia coastal towns could see that the pirate was finally dead. Governor Eden exploded and threatened to have Spotswood and Maynard arrested. When this proved futile, Eden tried to punish these gentlemen with legal action but this, also, failed. Eden gave up and also ceased to encourage any other freebooters to plague the coast of the state he had been appointed to protect and preserve. Blackbeard remains in the fierce annals of piracy the most terrifying of his awful breed, a human monster of the high seas who thoroughly enjoyed death and destruction, even his own.

REF.: Boar, *The World's Most Infamous Murders;* Botting, *The Pirates;* Brooke, *Book of Pirates; CBA;* Defoe, *A General History of Pyrates; The Book of Pirates;* Jameson, *Privateering and Piracy in the Colonial Period;* Lee, *Blackbeard the Pirate;* Mitchell, *Pirates;* Rankin, *The Golden Age of Piracy;* Scott, *The Concise Encyclopedia of Crime and Criminals;* Williams, *Captains Outrageous, Seven Centuries of Piracy.*

Blackburn, Duncan (AKA: **Tom Blackburn**), prom. 1870s, U.S., west. outl. Duncan Blackburn was a stagecoach robber who operated around Deadwood, Dakota Territory. He often rode with another outlaw, Jim Wall. Blackburn's activities ceased in 1877 when Boone May, a fierce stagecoach guard, became famous for killing four bandits who had been plaguing the very stage line Blackburn and others had preyed upon. Little is known about this outlaw except a host of rumors. One has it that he had an affair with Calamity Jane who bore him a son and, after serving a long prison term, Blackburn returned to his native Baltimore with this boy, settling down and becoming a prominent businessman.

REF.: Bartholomew, *The Biographical Album of Western Gunfighters;* Bronson, *Red Blooded;* Brown and Willard, *The Black Hills Trails;* Casey, *The Black Hills and Their Incredible Characters; CBA;* Holloway, *Texas Gun Lore;* Lake, *Wyatt Earp, Frontier Marshal;* McClintock, *Pioneer Days in the Black Hills;* Sabin, *Wild Men of the Wild West;* Spring, *The Cheyenne and Black Hills Stage and Express Routes;* Tallent, *The Black Hills.*

Blackburne, Francis, 1782-1867, Ire., lawyer. Attorney general from 1830-34. He presided at the trial of Irish nationalist Smith O'Brien. REF.: *CBA.*

Blackburne, Lancelot, 1658-1743, Brit., pir. Lancelot Blackburne, reputed pirate in the West Indies in 1681, returned home after two years of sailing the Caribbean and later became the archbishop of York. Sir Horace Walpole later wrote: "The jolly old archbishop of York had all the manners of a man of quality, though he had been a buccaneer and was a clergyman; but he retained nothing of his first profession except his seraglio."

REF.: *CBA;* Rankin, *The Golden Age of Piracy.*

Blackburn Murder See: **Griffiths Peter.**

Black Dahlia, The (Elizabeth Ann Short), 1925-47, U.S., (unsolv.) mur. The Black Dahlia case, still unsolved to this day, proved to be one of America's most baffling and sensational murders of the twentieth century. On Jan. 15, 1947, the horribly mutilated body of Elizabeth Ann Short was found in a vacant Los Angeles lot by a woman walking her small child on Norton Street, between Thirty-ninth and Coliseum streets. She literally stumbled over the lower half of the victim's body, which was on the sidewalk, the other half of the torso in the high weeds of the lot. She went, screaming, for the police and soon the nation's headlines blared the skimpy facts of the gruesome killing. Called into the case were veteran detectives Harry "Red" Hansen and Finis Arthur Brown. They would stay on this most vexing case of their careers for many years to come, follow endless leads, listen to countless crackpots confess to the murder, and, in the end, leave the file open and unsolved for generations to come. Hansen would work on the case periodically up to the time of his retirement in 1971.

The corpse the officers saw had been mutilated by a savage fiend, one who had battered the head and slashed the face almost beyond recognition by cutting the mouth at the edges from ear to ear to form a gruesome grin. The killer had made repeated cuts on the thighs, arms, and breasts, and these slashes were both straight and in circles. Scores of cigarette burns marked the flesh. Rope burns found on the hands and feet made it evident that the victim had been tortured for several hours before the maniac finished his grisly work. The initials "B.D." had been carved into one thigh. (These initials stood for Black Dahlia, as police later learned.) The killer had scrubbed the body before depositing it in the empty lot. The detectives noted the killer had meticulously cleaned the body parts with a hard brush, leaving bristles embedded in the flesh. This was undoubtedly done to eliminate any traces of the killer's identity (or, possibly, to satisfy a fetish of some sort).

Identification was impossible except for the victim's fingerprints, which were taken and sent to FBI headquarters in Washington, D.C. Within a short time, the Los Angeles Police Department was sent the results of the Bureau's search through its millions of prints—a card which identified the dead woman as Elizabeth Ann Short, born July 29, 1924, in Hyde Park, Mass., giving her last known address as Santa Barbara, Calif. Once the press learned of this, reporters were sent scurrying through the Los Angeles area to get more background on the victim. One of the more enterprising scribes Bevo Means of the Los Angeles *Herald-Express,* discovered that Short had lived in Long Beach and interviewed Short's former landlady, learning that Short had a peculiar quirk—she always dressed in black. All her shoes were black, her dresses and skirts and blouses were

Elizabeth Short, the celebrated Black Dahlia.

black. She wore a black jade ring at all times and, when her trunk was found, it was learned that all her undergarments were black.

Means talked to the owner of a drugstore in Long Beach and found out that the victim was much admired by all the young men she met at his soda fountain. "Who could forget a beautiful girl like that?" the drugstore owner told Means. "Always in black. The fellows coming in here called her The Black Dahlia." The sobriquet was used by Means in his first story, and the name electrified editors across the country. Soon every newspaper, radio station, and wire service used the arresting name which became household words across the nation. The name Black Dahlia also explained the initials carved on the victim's leg. Detective Hansen soon learned that Short, one of five children, had been raised in near-poverty in Medford, Mass., and had left home in 1942 at age seventeen, going to Los Angeles to seek a career in show business. It was an old story, one enacted thousands of times each week as pretty, young women with no experience headed for Hollywood and wound up taking menial jobs to survive, or, worse, turned to prostitution.

Elizabeth Short made the usual rounds of the film studios and got nowhere. She landed a job at Camp Cooke, working in the post exchange as a hostess, serving coffee and doughnuts to lonely GIs, a position she held through 1944. She was a popular girl, even elected a "Cutie of the Week." She reportedly became engaged to Major Matt Gordon, Jr., an Air Corps officer who was later killed in India. Her life went downhill after that. Short was picked up several times as underage while drinking in Santa Barbara lounges and bars with soldiers, and finally she was shipped back to Massachusetts. She got off the bus before arriving there and returned to Hollywood, where she became a call girl. It was at this time, while earning considerable cash from her occasional "dates," that an assistant producer at one of the studios dubbed her The Black Dahlia, after noticing that she

always wore black. Short was promised many screen tests by her clients, who never kept their word. Forsaking the elusive film contract, Elizabeth Short returned home in 1946 to see her mother. Then she drifted to Florida and later Chicago, working as a cocktail waitress in both cities.

By December 1946, Short had returned to her old haunts in California, just barely avoiding the label of streetwalker. She moved to San Diego and convinced a woman to take her in, telling her that she was a destitute war widow, a story she would repeat many times to gain sympathy, lodging, and money from the kindhearted. In January 1947, Short was back in Long Beach but had resolved to quit prostitution, telling her friends that she was looking for a job and had given up her dreams of becoming a movie star, that all she wanted was to find a good man, to settle down, and to have children. She mentioned that she was deeply in love with a man she referred to only as Red.

A few days later her dissected corpse was found. Hansen began to interview Short's friends, hunting for the elusive boyfriend The Black Dahlia intended to marry. The killer then surfaced indirectly, six days following the murder. He called Jimmy Richardson, city editor of the Los Angeles *Herald-Examiner,* speaking in a voice described by Richardson as "soft and silky." The caller detailed the mutilations made on the corpse to convince Richardson that he, indeed, was the murderer. "I killed her," the caller said. "I'm going to turn myself in but I want to have a little more fun. I want to watch the cops chase me some more." Then he added: "You can expect some souvenirs of Beth Short in the mail." Richardson described the caller as egotistical, proud of the fact that he had eluded police, a personality with a superior attitude. A few days later, as promised, the killer sent the "souvenirs"—Short's birth certificate, her address book with more than seventy names of male clients in it, and a note which had been pieced together from newspaper headlines which read: "Here is Dahlia's Belongings. Letter to follow."

The message sent by the Black Dahlia's killer; the envelope held Elizabeth Short's address book and birth certificate.

Detectives immediately began to run down all the men listed in Short's address book, although they first thought that the killer would not have been so foolish as to send such an item with his own name in it. Later, it was reasoned that the killer, being the vain slayer that he was, could well have had his name in that little black book and had sent it on as a challenge to police to see if they could select him from all the others listed therein. Challenging the police is a game historically played by many criminals, usually by psychopathic killers like the Ax Man of New Orleans, David Berkowitz (Son of Sam), William Heirens, and Jack the Ripper (see entries). Even Richard Loeb, who, with his love slave, Nathan Leopold (see entry), boldly murdered Bobbie Franks, then, with the consummate gall of the megalomaniac, insisted upon helping the police to find the killer, hunting for clues, looking for the body that he himself had hidden. The killer of Elizabeth Short was no different, except he never revealed his true identity and used the phone and the mail to make his presence known and felt.

Following the killer's contact with newsmen, Hansen and other detectives were able to track down Elizabeth Short's trunk, and inside they found many love letters from boyfriends. They began to contact these men in hopes of finding the killer. Meanwhile, as expected by some experts, the killer reneged on his promise to give himself up, sending another postcard, again made up of letters clipped from newspapers which read: "I've changed my mind. You would not give me a square deal. Dahlia killing justified." No more mail arrived from the sender, who police believed to be the real killer. Detectives also believed that one of Short's friends, Robert Manley, who was also known as Red, was a prime suspect. Manley, a 24-year-old married hardware salesman who lived in Huntington Park, had sent a telegram to Short in San Diego only a week before she was murdered. It read: "Be there tomorrow afternoon late. Would like to see you. Red."

Robert Manley, prime suspect in the Black Dahlia case, with his wife Harriet.

When Hansen picked up Manley for questioning, the suspect yelled: "I don't know her! I never met the woman!" Manley did an about-face when being grilled at police headquarters, admitting that he had picked up Short at a San Diego bus station and they had spent the night together in a motel room. He told Hansen that "she had bad scratches on both her arms and above the elbows...She told me that she had a friend who was intensely jealous of her...an Italian with black hair." Manley said that he did not know this person or even his name, only that this man lived in San Diego. Manley told police that he had denied knowing Short at first because he and his wife had been arguing and he did not want to make matters worse by confessing his affair with Short. He went on to state that his night with Short was not pleasant, that she had gotten sick after they had been drinking and he had wound up driving her to Los Angeles and dropped her off at the Biltmore Hotel on Jan. 9, 1947. He swore that this was the last time he had seen her.

Manley was interrogated with considerable intensity by detectives and his whereabouts on the night of the murder were thoroughly checked. He was finally released when police were convinced that he was innocent. The image of the Black Dahlia, however, was to plague Robert Manley. In 1954, he was committed to an insane asylum by his wife who claimed that "he hears noises, writes foolish notes, and has a guilt complex." Police again questioned Manley and went away once again believing that he was innocent of the murder. Dozens of other men were suspected, dragged in for questioning, and "sweated" for hours, but all proved to have solid alibis for the night of the killing.

Psychiatrist J. Paul de River of the Los Angeles Police Department had predicted that the Dahlia case would cause considerable crackpots to confess to the murder, but officials were in no way prepared for the *hundreds* of psychological malcontents who came forward.

One of these was Daniel S. Voorhees, a 33-year-old unemployed waiter who called detectives and screamed over the phone: "I can't stand it any longer! I want to confess to the murder of the Black Dahlia!" He was picked up and, while being driven to headquarters, Voorhees blurted over and over "I killed her, I killed her." Though he signed a confession which stated that he had committed the murder, Voorhees denied ever sending the letter and postcard to newsmen and the police. Some days later Voorhees jumped up in his cell and yelled that he did not kill Short, demanding to see his attorney, adding: "I'm not gonna talk to you anymore. I've talked too much already." Voorhees was later sent to an institution for psychiatric care.

Hansen and his partner Brown answered a report from another self-confessed killer, finding Army corporal Joseph Dumais covered with blood and dozens of newspaper clippings dealing with the Dahlia slaying littering his cheap room. Said Dumais: "It's possible that I could have committed the murder. When I get drunk I get rough with women." His claim did not hold up and he was released. Then John N. Andry, chief pharmacist's mate in the Navy, was arrested by the detectives after he bragged in a Long Beach bar that he had great skill in cutting up bodies. When grilled by police, Andry said: "Well, I'm capable of doing it," but he quickly added that he was "only kidding." Dumais, Andry, and countless others who confessed were questioned by Detectives Hansen and Brown, who always asked pointed questions of the many who confessed, questions to which only the murderer would have the answers, which dealt chiefly with the state of the corpse as it was left in the empty lot and specific mutilations made by the killer. None had the answers.

The case stretched into the macabre over the years. At one point seers and soothsayers who claimed to see the past and future inundated the police department with reports of where to look for the killer and how to employ magic to produce positive results. One caller, a woman phoning long distance, seriously told Detective Hansen to "bury the girl with an egg in her right hand. The killer will then be found in a week. That's the way it works in Alabama!" A photographer insisted that if the police turned over the eyes of the dead girl he would be able to retrieve an image of the killer from the irises, this being an old myth in trapping murderers, a wayward notion that the last vision of the victim, the image of the killer, is forever trapped in the victim's eyes. Then there was the ludicrous. Hansen received a call from a hysterical waitress who reported that two men with guns had just left her restaurant, two ugly-looking thugs who had talked furtively and in suspicious detail over their sandwiches about the Dahlia killing. When she identified her restaurant, Hansen had to suppress a laugh, saying: "That was us! My partner and I ate there today."

In the wake of the Dahlia killing, there followed a series of murders that were not dissimilar in modus operandi. Mary Tate was sexually attacked and strangled to death with a silk stocking only three days after Short's body was found. In February 1947, the mutilated body of Mrs. Jeanne French was found, with obscenities written in lipstick on her stomach. On Mar. 11, 1947, the body of Mrs. Evelyn Winters was discovered, also hacked to pieces. Then police found the body of Rosenda Mondragon, who had also been strangled to death with a silk stocking. Next to be found was Mrs. Dorothy Montgomery, her body left naked and mutilated. Mrs. Laura Trelstad was found beaten to death, her naked body dumped in a vacant area. Detectives believed that at least two of these murders were committed by the same fiend who slaughtered Elizabeth Short, but these murders, like that of Dahlia, remain unsolved to this day.

Captain Jack Donahoe, overall head of the Black Dahlia investigation, developed an unusual theory, coming to believe that the killer was not a man but a *woman,* pointing out that the wounds inflicted on Short's body were similar to those which had been performed by women in other cases. Donahoe believed that the horrible mutilations were done out of the kind of spite a female reserves for a detested rival. Donahoe added that between male and female killers, women were "the deadlier of the species." He also pointed out that Elizabeth Short had spent some time among a lesbian community in Long Beach and may have incurred the wrath of either one or a group of lesbian killers who took their revenge on her for deserting their sexual world. There were few women, however, who confessed to the Dahlia slaying.

A prime suspect, who was arrested in December 1947, was Donal Graeff. This man had taken in a destitute woman, Mrs. Helen Miller, and had attacked her, carving his initials on her hip.

Elizabeth Short's sparsely attended funeral.

Graeff claimed he was drunk at the time of his attack and had no idea of what he was doing. He was dropped as a Dahlia suspect after an extensive investigation into his background. Year after year, the so-called killer continued to come forward. Nine years after the Dahlia murder a New York dishwasher, 44-year-old Ralph von Hiltz adamantly insisted that he knew who the killer of Elizabeth Short was, that he had no part in the killing, but had witnessed the murder and helped the slayer dissect the corpse. He was interrogated, but had no idea of what he was talking about; he was dismissed as another crackpot.

Hansen answered every lead on the case for twenty-five years, no matter how absurd they might have been. He believed, after becoming intimate with every nuance of Elizabeth Short's life, that she may have brought about her own demise. He said: "From all accounts, Elizabeth Short liked to tease men. She probably went too far this time and just set some guy off into a blind berserk rage." Hansen also believed that he "never met the killer face to face. I know he didn't manage to slip through with the other subjects. We considered the possibility of his coming right in, making a confession, then cleverly sidestepping the key question. We watched for that, had taken measures to expose him in that advent. We never underestimated this guy. You'd never believe the amount of checking we did on this case. We followed everything as far as it would go, then we'd turn right around and walk through it all again." The bizarre motive of the killer, as well as his (or her) identity, remains as mysterious and unexplained today as it was on that first shocking day when the shattered remains of The Black Dahlia were found. See: **Ax Man of New Orleans; Berkowitz, David; Heirens, William; Jack the Ripper; Leopold, Nathan, and Loeb, Richard.**

REF.: *CBA;* Gribble, *They Had a Way With Women;* Henderson, *The Super Sleuths;* Nash, *Almanac of World Crime;* ____, *Open Files;* Rice, *45 Murderers;* Rowan, *Famous American Crimes;* Wolf, *Fallen Angels.*

Black Dick, prom. 1810, Brit., rob.-mur. One of the most dangerous and cunning robbers the early Bow Street Runners of London were concerned with was Black Dick. In 1810, Black Dick and two accomplices robbed the Whitehaven Bank of £14,000. He was flushed out by one of Robert Peel's most capable men, Constable Harry Adkins, known to the criminal underworld as the "Little Ferret" for his detective work. Black Dick was taken into custody at Birmingham, but escaped by lowering himself from a jail window with a rope fashioned from by twisting and knotting his bed clothes.

Black Dick was quickly apprehended by Adkins who made sure the felon did not escape a second time. First, though, Adkins beat him on the legs with a stick until he agreed to come quietly. Black Dick was charged with the murder of an executive of the British Linen Company and for taking £900 worth of cloth after his escape from prison.

REF.: Armitage, *Bow Street Runners; CBA.*

Black Doodler, The, prom. 1975, U.S., (unsolv.) mur. The police and the press of San Francisco dubbed this serial killer the "Black Doodler," because he sketched the faces of intended victims prior to their deaths.

The Doodler preyed on members of San Francisco's gay community, primarily concentrated along Castro Street in the city's center. In 1975, he began his bloody knifework. He would entice his victims by first sketching their portraits to flatter them. After engaging in homosexual intercourse, the Doodler would viciously assault each one with a knife.

At least six gay men fell victim to the killer. All of them were white and middle-class. A Stanford psychologist named Philip Zimbardo theorized that the killer was both attracted and repelled by his victims, and said, "It's highly likely that he is someone who may be attracted to the homosexual experience on one level but, at another level, feels a powerful moral outrage toward it."

REF.: *CBA;* Godwin, *Murder U.S.A.*

Black Dragon Society (Kokuryukai), 1901- , Japan, secret crim. soc. For decades Western journalists equated the subversive secret Black Dragon Society with the Mafia of the Orient. Albeit its ranks from the beginning were infested with street criminals in Japan *and* China, but the Society was, from its inception to the present, a revolutionary cell dedicated to Pan-Asianism and the fostering of xenophobia, particularly toward the white race. It was the Black Dragon Society which financed the 1911 revolution in China which overthrew the Manchu Dynasty. Leaders of the Chinese Kuomintang party, including Sun-Yat Sen and Chiang Kai-shek, formulated their party and their concepts of republicanism in the Tokyo headquarters of the Black Dragon Society in 1905.

The name of this secret Asian tong stemmed not from some monster of ancient times but from the Amur River, also called the Black Dragon River, which separates Siberia from Manchuria. The name of this river stood as a symbol of Japan's determination to prevent Russia from extending its frontiers south of the Amur at the turn of the century. Japan, through the Black Dragon Society and its then powerful military and political leaders, employed widespread scare tactics about Russia's expansionist aims in preparation for the war of 1904-05 in which Japan vanquished Russian fleets and, to some extent, the Russian imperialist armies in Manchuria. The founder of this war-mongering society was Ryohei Uchida, a protegé of Mitsuru Toyama, a nationalistic gang leader who had founded an earlier secret organization, the Genoyosha, a group which controlled all illegal rackets in Japan and also advanced the nationalist cause. Toyama was the leader of this society and the mentor to the Black Dragon Society which he manipulated at will through Uchida.

Toyama was, in reality, the crime czar of Japan for more than fifty years, one of the most powerful men in the nation who dictated terms to the politicians as well as the militarists. The Black Dragons were so powerful that Japan's monarchy gave it sideways recognition and its members invariably found their way into the military hierarchy and to high levels of the country's political administrations. Following Japan's victory over Russia in 1905, the Black Dragons lobbied for further attacks against the Czar, advocating a Strike North posture which they did not relinquish until WWII when the militarists elected a Strike South policy, attacking not Russia but China, and U.S. and British territories in the Pacific.

From 1910 to its decline in the late years of WWII, the Society enriched itself through control of the opium trade in Japan and elsewhere, drug traffic directed by Toyama and his minions. The Black Dragons kept power by intimidation, and, when necessary, assassination of those who opposed the Society's aims. When Director Abe of Japan's Political Affairs Bureau of the Foreign Office showed indifference to the Society's program for attacking Russia, he was assassinated on Sept. 5, 1913. A few years later the Society sent one of its youthful adherents to kill Count Kato Takaakira, Japan's foreign minister, an assassination attempt that failed. Toyama's figurehead leader of the Black Dragons, Uchida, spent eighteen months in prison but was never brought to trial for the Kato conspiracy.

The Society was active in blaming the Koreans for the 1923 earthquake-fires that destroyed Tokyo, spreading the word that the Koreans had acted as incendiaries after the quake and were bent on destroying all of Tokyo. The mass slaughter of Koreans that followed were urged, directed and endorsed by the Black Dragons, as a way of persuading jingoistic military commanders to urge an attack on Korea and subsequently Russia, another propaganda measure that was aimed at once again supporting the Society's unswerving goal, the Strike North plan. In the mid-1930s, when Emperor Hirohito sided with the Strike South militarists, the Black Dragons went into decline and even ominous and powerful Toyama was reduced to back-water politicking. He would die in 1944 but the Society still lingers today, but barely alive, nurtured by successful Japanese businessmen who now approach the Society's original military aims as economic conquests of the West. See: **Hirohito, Emperor; Toyama, Mitsuru.**

REF.: Bergamini, *Japan's Imperial Conspiracy;* Byas, *Government by Assassination; CBA;* McNelly, *Politics and Government in Japan;* Morton, *Japan, Its History and Culture;* Mosley, *Hirohito, Emperor of Japan;* Reischauer, *Japan, The Story of a Nation;* ____, *The United States and Japan;* Scalapino, *Democracy and the Party Movement in Prewar Japan;* Toland, *The Rising Sun.*

Blacket, Mary, d.1726, Brit., rob. Mary Blacket was trained as a domestic, but abandoned the profession to marry a sailor. After she gave birth, her husband went to sea. In need of cash, she committed the only crime for which she was ever charged: the highway robbery of William Whittle on Aug. 6, 1726. She took from him a watch valued at £4 and sixpence in cash. Mary claimed that Whittle was mistaken when he identified her as his assailant and she maintained this even on the gallows, but this denial failed, and Mary Blacket was hanged at Tyburn.

REF.: *CBA;* Pringle, *Stand and Deliver.*

Black Hand, 1750-1920s, Int'l., extor. The Black Hand, despite the wild claims of newsmen and yellow journalists to the contrary, was never a formal organization with any kind of national or international ties. The Black Hand was never a society (although a Black Hand Society did exist for hundreds of years in Spain as an organization designed to help the needy and to fight invaders, but died out before 1900; another Black Hand Society originated in Serbia, a secret cabal designed to establish Serbian dominance in the Balkans, see **Black Hand Society** entry). The Black Hand was never tied to any of the real secret societies or criminal conspiracies, such as the Camorra, the Mafia, or the Unione Siciliane, even though many members of these nefarious organizations practiced the sinister ways of the Black Hand. It was simply an extortion racket practiced upon citizens, first in Italy and Sicily as early as the 1750s, and later in the U.S., chiefly affecting Italian-Sicilian immigrants in major metropolitan areas, especially New York, New Orleans, Philadelphia, Detroit, New Orleans, Chicago, St. Louis, Kansas City, and San Francisco.

The racket was prosaic—and deadly. An anonymous Black Hander would threaten various types of violence to extort money from one, usually well-to-do, victim. These threats most often involved kidnapping a family member, threatening to blow up a

business or shop, or to attack, injure, or kill a family member or the recipient of the Black Hand note. These notes were crudely written in broken English (in the U.S.) and boldly demanded a certain amount of money, with specific instructions as to how the cash was to be delivered. The note would usually be decorated with a number of horrific symbols and images—daggers dripping blood, a bomb exploding, a gun smoking at the barrel, a skull and crossbones, a body dangling from a rope tied about the neck. The signature of the sender was invariably a hand imprinted in heavy black ink, thus the sobriquet, *La Mano Nera* (The Black Hand).

A typical Black Hand note, 1900.

During the tidal wave of Italian immigration to the U.S. from 1890-1910, the Black Hand flourished. The leading Black Hander in New York was Ignazio Saietta, called Lupo the Wolf, who ruthlessly extorted money from thousands of gullible, fearful Italian immigrants inhabiting the Little Italy section of Harlem. Saietta extorted tens of thousands of dollars from his victims, killing at least thirty of those who refused to pay up. He simply strangled them in their homes, dragged their corpses outside to his waiting cart, and drove to a livery stable he owned. He then hacked up the bodies, burned parts of them, and buried what would not burn in his backyard. Saietta also loaned himself out as an enforcer to other Black Handers, shooting, stabbing, or beating up victims who had refused to pay. However, he was a dangerous man to hire for these grisly chores; he liked the work too much and often went too far, killing victims who were supposed to live long enough to pay the extortion demanded of them. Saietta, after terrorizing his own people for more than three decades, was arrested for counterfeiting, a profession to which he was obviously ill-suited since he was so handily caught. He was sent to prison for thirty years, but his place was quickly taken by other ambitious Black Handers.

Battling the Black Handers for years was a powerful, 200-pound New York police officer, Lieutenant Joseph Petrosino, who single-handedly made hundreds of arrests of vicious Black Hand extortionists, including the much-feared Saietta. One of the most distinguished Italians consistently victimized by Black Handers was the great Italian tenor Enrico Caruso. Petrosino was brought into the case when Caruso was appearing at the New York Metropolitan Opera House. Caruso had been paying off the Black Handers for years, reportedly $1,000 out of every $10,000 he earned with his marvelous voice. Every time he appeared in New York he would receive Black Hand notes, politely informing him that if he did not pay the demanded extortion, lye, or other corrosive agents would be slipped into his tea or wine. Worse, the Black Handers threatened to kidnap his family members, promising horrible tortures and death. Only through one of Caruso's aides did Petrosino learn of the high-handed extortion. He supposedly tracked down the Black Hander who had been plaguing the singer for years, beat him mercilessly, then, ignoring deportation proceedings, dragged him to a ship sailing for Italy and put him on board. Drawing his service revolver, he told the shaken Black Hander: "If you return to this country, I will blow your brains out. If you ever again bother Mr. Caruso anywhere on earth, I will find you and blow your brains out."

Petrosino received thousands of Black Hand notes each year, threatening his death if he did not desist in seeking out the extortionists. His answer to this was to double his efforts and even establish an all-Italian police squad to deal with the growing Black Hand problem. It was Petrosino who apprehended Enrico Alfano, a powerful member of the New York Camorra and the top Black Hander, after the imprisonment of Saietta. Police in Naples had contacted Petrosino, informing him of a much-wanted fugitive, and enclosed Alfano's photograph. This allowed the tough New York cop to make the Alfano arrest and also gave him the idea to travel to Naples, Italy, and Palermo, Si., to look through all the photos in police files in order to identify the Italian and Sicilian criminals he knew operated in New York and were wanted in their native countries and thus have them deported from the U.S. To that end, Petrosino traveled to Palermo, Si., and was murdered by Mafia killers on Mar. 12, 1909.

The murder of Petrosino created an international furor which caused the Mafia and its practitioners of Black Hand extortion to go underground. The chief of the Mafia and a virulent Black Hander, Paulo Marchese, who had ordered Petrosino's murder in Sicily, left Palermo when local police began to prepare a case against him (at the insistence of U.S. authorities). He changed his name to Paul di Cristina and immigrated to New York. He was recognized as Marchese there and quickly departed for New Orleans where he established himself among the large Italian community as a rich merchant. Di Cristina, however, continued his extortionist ways and was soon boldly sending Black Hand notes to Italian merchants,

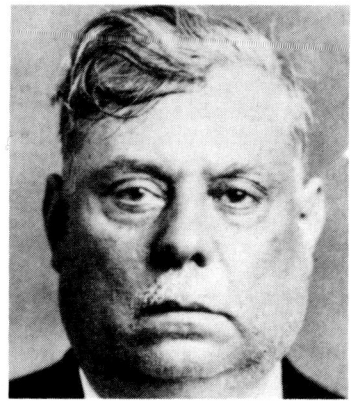

Ignazio Saietta, the most notorious Black Hander in America at the turn of the century.

signing his own name and delivering the notes in person. He felt immune to arrest and no one ever refused to pay whatever he demanded. In late 1909, one stubborn grocer, Pietro Pepitone, told Di Cristina's strong-arm thugs that he would pay no Black Hand money. To convince the boss of his statements, the burly grocer beat one of the Black Handers senseless, throwing him into the street.

Di Cristina decided to settle matters himself. So fearsome was his reputation, he believed, that all he had to do was to appear before Pepitone and repeat his demands to cause the grocer to quickly submit. The Mafia chief, driving a wagon, arrived in front of Pepitone's store. He tethered the horses to a hitching post and walked solemnly up the wooden stairs to the store's porch. Suddenly, Pepitone came through the door of his shop. Di Cristina looked up to see a shotgun in the grocer's hands, the barrel aimed at his head. Before he could utter a word, Pepitone squeezed the triggers of both barrels and Paulo di Cristina's body was blown apart. The grocer, convicted of manslaughter, was sent to prison for twenty years but was released six years later. Pepitone's son, Michele, was murdered in October 1919, while sleeping in the rear of his store. This killing was attributed to the fiend labeled the Ax Man of New Orleans, a mass murderer then plaguing the city, but others said the murder was in reprisal for the slaying of di Cristina ten years earlier.

Kansas City Black Hand activities drastically increased in 1912 with the arrival of master extortionist Joseph "Scarface" DiGiovanni, when he left Sicily for the U.S. (DiGiovanni was born in Palermo in 1888 and was compelled to flee his native city after murdering at least a dozen Black Hand victims.) DiGiovanni, who could not write or speak English, and whose face resembled a raw

steak after he had been horribly disfigured when one of his own stills blew up before him, took over liquor distribution in Kansas City. He also continued his Black Handing operations, using his brother, Peter "Sugarhouse Pete" DiGiovanni, as an enforcer.

These brutal brothers, backed up by a host of thugs, controlled the Italian-Sicilian community in Kansas City for five decades, milking its wealthiest members of hundreds of thousands of dollars through Black Hand extortions. Early in their murderous careers, the DiGiovannis were almost put out of business after twenty of their victims went to the police and reported their extortion racket. The brothers were arrested by Kansas City police detective Louis Olivero in 1915, but before they were tried, Olivero was shot in the back and killed, a bloody message sent to those who thought to testify against the brothers. The Black Hand victims suddenly refused to cooperate further with the police. The DiGiovanni stranglehold on the Italian-Sicilian community in Kansas City did not ease until their power eroded in the 1950s when younger leaders took over the K.C. rackets.

Chicago's criminal history offers a large slice of Black Hand activities, dating back to 1890 and continuing into the early 1920s. Black Handers like James "Sunny Jim" Cosmano and James "King of the Bombers" Belcastro operated freely for decades in Chicago, where Black Hand victims were given only one chance to pay extortion money before being killed. Squandering uncooperative victims through murder was acceptable to them since, in their viewpoint, other extortion victims were plentiful. Thirty-eight truculent Black Hand victims were murdered on one street corner—at Oak and Milton streets in Little Italy—between Jan. 1, 1910, and Mar. 26, 1911. Many of these helpless immigrants were killed by a fearsome character known only as Shotgun Man. He patrolled the area in broad daylight, a shotgun cradled in his arms, looking for those who had refused to meet Black Hand demands.

A typical note sent by a Black Hander came from Joseph Genite who sent the following to a wealthy businessman who lived in Chicago's Little Italy:

Most Gentle Mr. Silvani:

...You will be so good as to send me $2,000 if your life is dear to you. So I beg you warmly to put them (the small bills) on your door within four days. But, if not, I swear this week's time not even the dust of your family will exist. With regards, believe me to be your friend.

Genite was arrested and tried, but when witnesses appeared in court they saw known Black Handers enter the courtroom, stand in the rear, and draw their fingers across their throats, signals that meant all the witnesses would later be killed if they dared to testify against Genite. The accused man was released for lack of evidence. No one testified against him. On other occasions, the signal of death was a red handkerchief drawn slowly from a breast coat pocket and wiped across the forehead, then dropped to the floor. In any event, the would-be witnesses always seemed to get the message and backed off from testifying.

A police sweep of Chicago's Little Italy in 1910 snared more than 200 Italian and Sicilian gangsters, almost all of whom were known Black Handers. Not one was convicted. The notes these murderous men left could not be traced nor identified as having been written by them. All were printed and purposely distorted in English structure so that no writing patterns could be compared by handwriting analysts. One of those notes, unsigned except for an imprint of a black hand, ignored any subtleties:

You got some cash. I need $1,000. You place the $100 bills in an envelope and place it underneath a board in the northeast corner of Sixtyninth Street and Euclid Avenue at eleven o'clock tonight. If you place the money there, you will live. If you don't, you die. If you report this to the police I'll kill you when I get out. They may save your money but they won't save your life.

Legitimate businessmen were not the only victims of the vicious Black Handers. These reckless extortionists levied huge demands against the top racketeers in Chicago, especially Big Jim Colosimo, boss of the Levee (Chicago's vice district at that time) and crime czar of most of the city's South Side. He was plagued by Black Handers, especially after he opened his famous Colosimo's Cafe on Wabash Avenue. Black Handers immediately threatened to blow up the posh cafe, along with all of Colosimo's high society customers, unless he paid off. He did, but then fought back by importing his nephew, Johnny Torrio, from the Five Points gang in New York. Torrio, at age thirty-one, arrived in Chicago in 1909, just in time to receive orders from his uncle to eliminate the Black Handers. More then ten of these extortionists were killed within a month. Sunny Jim Cosmano demanded $10,000 from Colosimo "so your cafe will stay open." Torrio sent out his hit squad to meet Cosmano. The Black Hander thought he was going to receive his money. Instead Torrio's men—Joe Moresco, Joe "Jew Kid" Grabiner, Billy Leathers, "Chicken Harry" Gullett, Mac Fitzpatrick, and W.E. Frazier, the last a gunman Torrio imported from San Francisco—met Cosmano and his men beneath a South Side bridge and shot down the Black Handers. Cosmano was shot in the stomach and nearly died. He recovered and lived long enough to extort others, but he refrained from sending Black Hand notes to fellow gangsters.

NYPD Lt. Joseph Petrosino, implacable foe of the Black Hand.

The business leaders of the Italian community also tried to fight the Black Handers by forming the White Hand Society, a group that tried to identify Black Handers for police and urged immigrants not to respond to extortion demands, but instead to inform on their oppressors. This society even formed its own police force, armed these citizens, and had them patrol the mean streets of Little Italy. Italian business members belonging to the White Hand Society provided considerable funds to prosecute all Black Handers but the slack response on the part of Chicago's political administrations, the harassment of White Handers by Black Handers, and the indifference on the part of most Italian-Sicilian immigrants soon brought the White Hand Society to a standstill. The organization was rendered impotent by a rash of bombings carried out by the maniacal Black Hand gang headed by Sam Cardinelli. Among this gang were brutal killers, such as the mentally retarded giant Frank Campione, and an 18-year-old murderer named Nicholas Viana, who was called "The Choir Boy." This gang was responsible for more than 800 bombings which killed twenty people and wounded hundreds more between 1915 and 1918. Cardinelli, Viana, and Campione were all later convicted of murder and hanged.

Though Prohibition vaulted petty thieves, flesh peddlers, and minor racketeers to crime czar status as they made bootlegging into a multimillion-dollar racket, the Volstead Act inadvertently brought relief to the Italian-Sicilian communities in America. The Black Handers quit the extortion racket to enter bootlegging, and by the mid-1920s, the Black Hand was considered a thing of the criminal past. Many of the bombers, including a new generation of non-Italians, went to work for racketeers, taking over unions through force. One of these was Andrew Kerr, arrested

in 1921 and charged with ordering his killers to bomb dozens of union offices. Kerr not only admitted supervising this wholesale terrorist campaign but boasted that he had the "best bombers in Chicago," naming Con Shea, "Soup" Bartlett, and Jim Sweeney as the elite of his corps.

After Kerr and Sweeney were sent to prison, Joseph Sangerman assumed the position of chief bombing terrorist for the mobs. His berserk lieutenant, George Matrisciano, alias Martini, had been a Black Hander since 1905 and, as Sangerman's chief union terrorist, he reveled in his status of "top bomber." Matrisciano brazenly paraded about Little Italy with two sticks of dynamite jutting from his coat pockets and would stop total strangers to show them with idiot pride a fading newspaper clipping which described him as a "terrorist." Such blatant public displays convinced Sangerman that Matrisciano was a risk to his organization; he ordered the bomber murdered. After Matrisciano was killed, the Black Hand and its techniques all but disappeared in Chicago. See: **Ax Man of New Orleans; Belcastro, James; Petrosino, Joseph.**

REF.: Alix, *Ransom Kidnapping in America;* Asbury, *The Gangs of New York;* ____, *Gem of the Prairie;* ____, *The French Quarter;* Blumenthal, *Last Days of the Sicilians;* Bonanno, *A Man of Honor;* CBA; Cressey, *Theft of the Nation;* Crouse, *Murder Won't Out;* Demaris, *Captive City;* Eisenberg and Landau, *Meyer Lansky;* Fried, *The Rise and Fall of the Jewish Gangster in America;* Gage, *Mafia, USA;* Kahn, *Fraud;* Kobler, *Capone;* Lait and Mortimer, *Chicago Confidential;* Lynch, *Criminals and Politicians;* McPhaul, *Johnny Torrio;* Maas, *The Valachi Papers;* Messick and Goldblatt, *The Mobs and the Mafia;* Morgan, *Prince of Crime;* Nash, *Bloodletters and Badmen;* ____, *Citizen Hoover;* Peterson, *The Mob;* Reid, *The Grim Reapers;* ____, *Mafia;* Reppetto, *The Blue Parade;* Servadio, *Mafioso;* Spiering, *The Man Who Got Capone;* Thrasher, *The Gang;* (FILM), *The Black Hand,* 1950; *Pay or Die,* 1960.

Black Hand Society, 1911-17, Serbia, secret crim. soc. The birth of this military society, secret and utterly nationalistic, was slow to evolve, nurtured by the seeds of Serbian hatred for the political oppressions of the Austro-Hungarian empire. Ever since 1878, when neighboring Bosnia and Herzegovina came under Austrian domination, ardent Serbian nationalists grouped together to form clandestine cells to plot terrorism and assassination against the Austrian government.

Fostered by the local colleges, especially the Belgrade Military Academy, hundreds of Serbian youths formed one secret group after another, from one generation to another, to destroy Austrian authority and work feverishly for Slavic unity. Their goal was to ultimately unite all the Balkan countries under the Serbian banner, but these scattered groups were not effective until the turn of the century, when an impassioned and intelligent young Serbian officer, Dragutin Dimitrijevic, formed a dedicated group of young officers into a nationalist organization called *Ukendinjenje ili Smrt.* At first, members of this secret organization met in local beer halls and mostly plotted bombings and assassinations of the hated Austrian officials in neighboring Bosnia.

Dimitrijevic bought the beer and spent most of his time making speeches to his recruits who, like schoolboys, enthusiastically created sinister-looking emblems to affix to their hidden banners and threatening missives: a death's head, a bomb with lighted fuse, a glass of poison, a dagger dripping blood, and, finally, the symbol of a black hand, an imprint of a hand dipped in black ink and pressed upon a letter sent to anyone suspected of revealing the organization's existence and operations. This symbol, cf course, meant instant death to anyone who betrayed the *Ukendinjenje ili Smrt,* and was, no doubt, borrowed from the long existing Italian extortion racket practiced by the Camorra and known for a century in Italy as the Black Hand. The aim of the Serbian nationalists, however, was not to extort money from hapless victims but to kill or destroy anyone or anything that stood in the way of Slavic unification. "Union or death" was the motto of Dimitrijevic's group which whispered more about blood-curdling plans than they actually enacted.

All this changed, however, in 1903 when fifty or more Serbian officers, fearful that their monarch, King Alexander I (Obrenovic) was going to make secret alliances with Austria through his willful and much disliked wife, Queen Draga, decided to kill their Serbian sovereigns. Dimitrijevic stirred up the anger of his fellow conspirators, plying them with drink and singing patriotic Serbian ballads on the night of June 11, 1903 before leading them into the Belgrade Palace where local guards were shot down and the monarchs, King Alexander and Queen Draga, were ferreted out from a cramped hiding space and executed by Dimitrijevic himself.

This double assassination was all the more hideous in that the killers mutilated their victims and displayed the slashed corpses to the public; the act, gruesome as it was, also established Dimitrijevic and his group as the most powerful organization in Serbia, one that set a new king upon the throne and spread its black gospel throughout the land, formally adopting the title of the Black Hand (officially known as *Narodna Odbrana*). Dimitrijevic's own position was enormously strengthened when the new king, Peter Karageorgevic, through his generals, named the master assassin to a high post in military intelligence. He would later rise to the rank of general and become chief of intelligence of the Serbian General Staff.

Under the guise of instituting seemingly harmless "educational programs" to elevate Slavs to a "higher culture," the Black Hand spread its bloody doctrine of unification through terrorism and murder. From 1911, when the loosely formed *Ukendinjenje ili Smrt* was reorganized into the *Narodna Odbrana* by Dimitrijevic, the Black Hand became a force to be dreaded even by the most powerful governments in Europe, particularly the mighty Austro-Hungarian empire which became the object of the society's deadly wrath as dozens of its provincial officials were shot, bombed and abducted by members of this secret terrorist organization.

The Black Hand served Serbia well during the Balkan Wars of 1912-13, its agents spreading southward to perform sabotage and murder as Serbian boundaries spread into Macedonia. Dimitrijevic, privy to top secrets from the Serbian high command could funnel information to his own sacrosanct society and order death and destruction of anyone he thought to be an enemy of Serbia, irrespective of his government's actual position; he preempted both his prime minister and king to achieve his own political ends. Such was the case in 1914 when Dimitrijevic armed several students of fanatical nationalistic bent and sent them haphazardly to Sarajevo, Bosnia in June, hoping (but not really expecting) that one of them might be lucky enough to kill Austrian archduke Francis Ferdinand. One of these students, ironically an avowed anarchist, Gavrilo Princip, managed to get close enough to the Austrian heir to the throne as he and his wife were riding in an open car and kill both of them, an event that brought about WWI four weeks later.

Few knew that the real culprit that brought about WWI was the sinister Black Hand Society and its evil chief, Dimitrijevic, and long after both the society and its founder were defunct and dead the catalysts remained in obscurity. Dimitrijevic and his co-conspirators continued to flourish during WWI but they became dangerous even to Serbian leaders, or so it was assumed, and Alexander Karageorgevic, prince regent, suddenly, in 1916, ordered the arrest of Dimitrijevic and his top aides and, following a secret trial, had them executed. With them died the dreaded Black Hand Society of Serbia. See: **Alexander I (Obrenovic); Alexander I (Karageorgevic), Dimitrijevic, Dragutin; Ferdinand, Francis; Varesanin, Gen. Marijan.**

REF.: Bell, *Assassin!*; Buranelli, *Spy/Counter-Spy*; *CBA*; Graham, *St. Vitus' Day*; Hardman, *The Rise and Fall of the Hapsburg Monarchy*; Macartney, *The Hapsburg Empire*; Mijatovich, *Serbia of the Serbians*; _____, *A Royal Tragedy*; Rowan, *Secret Service*; Seton-Watson, *Sarajevo*; Strauss, *The Desperate Act, The Assassination of Franz Ferdinand at Sarajevo*; Webster, *Secret Societies and Subversive Movements*; West, *Black Lamb and Gray Falcon*.

Black Hole of Calcutta, 1756-57, India, mur. Founded by the British in 1690, Calcutta, India, was ruled by the East India Company, a venal and exploitative organization that took what it could from the populace in goods and foodstuffs and returned little. The British were overthrown in 1756 by armies under the direction of the nawab of Bengal. His special killer squads herded the badly beaten garrison together and summarily murdered hundreds of helpless men, women, and children. These hapless persons were led in small groups into a dark room where they were slaughtered like cattle, the room later being dubbed the Black Hole of Calcutta. The city was retaken in 1757 by troops commanded by Robert Clive. The killers of the British garrison were hunted down and executed, some by hanging, others by being tied to the front of cannons and blown to pieces. See: **Clive, Robert.** REF.: *CBA*.

Black Jack (Ketchum), See: **Ketchum, Thomas.**

Black Legion, prom. 1930s, U.S., secret crim. soc. A variation on the Ku Klux Klan, the Black Legion was organized in 1933 by Harvey Davis, an employee of Detroit's Public Lighting Commission. Its credo, as were its costumes and paraphernalia, was modeled after the KKK. The Legion operated secretly behind its pseudonym, the Wolverine Republican League, and recruited only those who were white, native-born, and Protestant. Davis established the criteria of the secret organization which was, ostensibly, to defend decency and womanhood in the U.S., a vigilante group that would actively eradicate Jews, blacks, Catholics, communists, and anarchists. The costume of this organization was almost identical to that worn by KKK members, except that their robes and hoods were black.

Initiation rites were founded on an image of terror. Members in good standing stood in a circle wearing their robes while initiates kneeled before them. Members held guns to the heads of the initiates who were ordered to chant a long, rambling oath which, in part, read: "In the name of God and the Devil, one to reward, the other to punish, here, under the black arch of God's avenging symbol...I will exert every possible means in my power for the extermination of the anarchist, the communist, the Roman hierarchy, and their abettors...I will show no mercy, but strike with an avenging arm as long as my breath remains...I pledge... never to betray a comrade, and that I will submit to all the tortures mankind can inflict, rather than reveal a single word of this, my oath."

An exact number of members belonging to the Black Legion was never determined, but most reliable reports show the figure at about 20,000 active dues-paying members. Davis and his henchmen actually made considerable money from the sale of robes, whips, symbolic rings and women's jewelry, along with weapons, knives, and revolvers, charging exorbitant prices for bullets. Davis and others really sought to make the automotive work force in Detroit all-white and Protestant, along with electing officials who abided by Black Legion philosophy. The long standing criminal organization of that city, the Purple Gang, a mixture of Jewish and Italian gangsters, also came under the Black Legion's scrutiny, and many of the gang members were attacked and hospitalized during the Legion's heyday, although the Purples had been rendered ineffective by that time through an aggressive political and law enforcement campaign.

Davis reserved the organization's wrath for his political and racial foes, selecting his first victims in 1935. Police began to turn up bodies of those who had obviously been murdered, but investigators could not give a single reason for the strange homicides. In early 1935, the body of Silas Coleman, a black, was found in a swamp about forty miles from Detroit, his corpse shot several times. John Bielak, a union organizer, was found dead outside of Monroe, Mich., a short time later. His killers had tortured him, slicing his flesh before hacking him to pieces with what seemed to be swords or machetes. Then another union man, Edward Armour, was riddled by gunfire from a passing truck as he walked down a Detroit street. He survived to tell police that he had no idea why a truckload of gunmen would want to murder him.

The killing went on, inexplicably, murders that remained unsolved. Then, in May 1936, a body was found behind the wheel of a car on Gulley Road on Detroit's far West Side. The victim, shot five times, was taken to the morgue where fingerprints were taken and the dead man was shortly identified as one Charles Poole whose only criminal offense was an old vagrancy charge in Kansas City. While detectives stared down at Poole's shot-up remains, believing they had another unsolved murder on their hands, a couple entered the morgue. The man and wife had been summoned to the morgue to identify an accident victim but, as they passed the slab holding the Poole body, they both stopped and gasped. "I know that man," said the wife. "He was a friend of my brother's."

"Who is he to you?" one of the detectives asked the woman.

"We called him Chap," she replied. "But none of us have seen him in a good long while." Then the woman added, almost as an afterthought: "People say that he has been running around with a man named Tennessee Slim."

Mrs. Robert White and Mrs. Harvey Burke told inquiring detectives that Mrs. Poole was in the hospital, about to have a baby. Mrs. Poole and others identified Tennessee Slim as none other than Harvey Davis who was quickly arrested and charged with Poole's murder. While Davis confidently resided in jail, claiming that his lawyer's would soon have him released, detectives swarmed over Detroit, looking for Poole's friends. Detective Jim Havrill found Owen and Marcia Rushing, who had known the murdered man well. Mrs. Rushing was visibly upset while Havrill questioned her and her husband.

"What's your wife hiding, Owen?" Havrill asked Rushing. "See—she's eating her heart out. Don't let her go on like that."

Shaking, Mrs. Rushing suddenly blurted: "We can't tell you! You don't know those people!"

"What people?"

"That...that organization! They kill people who talk. They carry guns and there are thousands and thousands of them. They are like the Ku Klux Klan, only bigger and more awful!"

The Rushings began to talk as did others, and soon the Detroit Police uncovered the story of the Black Legion. They began to make more arrests, capturing Erwin Lee who was carrying a .38-caliber revolver and a blackjack in his pockets, en route to "an assignment." They rushed into John Bannerman's home and found thousands of black silk robes and hoods decorated with skulls and crossbones. Bannerman had tried to burn the robes but there were too many to destroy before police caught him. Then Dayton Dean, one of Davis' cowed followers, was picked up. Dean began to talk and unraveled all the secrets of the Legion. He admitted that he had joined the Ku Klux Klan in 1922 and later moved his allegiance to the Legion when Davis, also a one-time KKK member, began the Legion in 1933. He said that Davis had ordered all the murders in 1935 either for political or racial reasons, but in Poole's case, it was supposedly to avenge a beating Poole had given to his pregnant wife. Dean admitted that he had lured Poole to his death because they had been friends and he and seven others, including Davis, all wearing the black robes of the Legion, drove Poole to a secluded spot outside the city. There, Davis pronounced a death sentence on Poole and all the Legion members fired a bullet into the victim.

Davis was also the man who ordered the death of Silas Coleman, "because he wanted a nigger to shoot," according to Dean, who went on to describe how Davis and others drove Coleman to the swamp outside Detroit and then ordered him to run for his life. As the terrified black man raced into the darkness, the Legion members all pulled out revolvers and used the fleeing Coleman for target practice. "Don't miss!" screamed Davis, "or you may get an extra bullet sent your way." This last remark, quoted by Dean, was typical of Davis, who kept his men together through death threats and constant fear that they too might be marked for execution if they were thought to be disloyal to the Legion, or, more precisely, to Davis. Dean, who learned that he had been put on Davis' "hit list" for informing, went on cooperating with authorities, bravely repeating his testimony in court where Davis and his lieutenants were tried *en masse*. They

were convicted and given life sentences. Dean, because of his state's evidence, received a light sentence. He would later be profiled by Humphrey Bogart in Hollywood's straight-from-the-headlines film production, *The Black Legion*.

With Davis and his top aides in prison, the Black Legion quickly disintegrated. In the late months of 1936, police counted more than 15,000 black robes once worn by dedicated members of the Legion. The robes had been dumped into garbage cans throughout the Detroit area. "The ones that worry me," one detective said, "are the robes that were not thrown away, the ones that went into trunks, chests, closets and attics, the ones that might be worn again." His fears were, thankfully, unfounded. The Black Legion never again surfaced.

REF.: *CBA;* Nash, *Almanac of World Crime;* ____, *Citizen Hoover;* (FILM), *The Black Legion,* 1937; *Nation Aflame,* 1986.

Black Liberation Army, prom. 1971-72, U.S., terror.-mur. The Black Liberation Army (BLA) resorted to a systematic campaign of murder and terror to draw attention to itself. The BLA was a splinter group of the Black Panthers that targeted U.S. police officers for death in the early 1970s.

They struck first on May 21, 1971, in Harlem where two police officers, one white, one black, were gunned down while answering a call for help. Three months later, three black men walked into the Ingleside, Calif., police station and shotgunned the desk sergeant to death before fleeing. Thus the BLA announced their program of death and defiance. Anthony Bottom, Albert Washington, and Herman Bell were arrested and convicted for both attacks.

In January 1972, the BLA was back in New York. Near the corner of Avenue B and Eleventh Street, another black and white patrol team was shot in the streets. Officers Gregory Foster and Rocco Laurie were walking their beat when three men fired on them from behind. One of the BLA members performed a "war dance" over the dead policemen. The next day a message arrived promising a new "spring offensive." The note was signed "The George Jackson Squad of the BLA." After the arrest of Bell, Washington, and Bottom, the BLA began to disintegrate. In its heyday, membership never exceeded 200. Most of the young militants had long criminal records. See: **Bell, Herman; Black Panthers, The.**

REF.: *CBA;* Dobson and Payne, *The Terrorists—Their Weapons, Leaders and Tactics;* Godwin, *Murder U.S.A.;* Laqueur, *Terrorism;* McLellan and Avery, *The Voices of Guns.*

Blackman, William, d.1928, U.S., mur.-lynch. In the little town of Rapides Parishes, La., a young black man made the mistake of gunning down a white deputy sheriff named J. Frank Phillips in June 1928. William Blackman, the killer, was shot and killed immediately afterwards by police officers. This, however, did not satisfy the blood-lust of angry white southerners who went after Blackman's two brothers, Lee and David. The two men were put into protective custody and temporarily moved to the Leesville jail while they awaited transportation to Shreveport.

The sheriff was taking the two by car to the safety of the big city when they were ambushed by a vigilante mob on a country back road a few miles out of town. The Blackman brothers were dragged from the car and shotgunned to death execution style while the law- enforcement officers were ordered to move on. Lee and David Blackman had nothing to do with the murder of Sheriff Phillips but were killed anyway. REF.: *CBA.*

Black Mass, The, prom. 16th-20th Cent., witchcraft. The diabolical celebration of the devil, mentioned as early as 1525 in the accounts of Paulus Grillandus, is for the most part a literary invention that came into vogue when belief in witchcraft declined.

According to legend, the Black Mass was included in the witches' Sabbath, but surviving historical accounts do not refer to a demonic service of any kind. Noted witchhunters of the Inquisition would attempt to lend credence to their accusations by describing devilish parodies of the Holy Mass. In 1611 Father Gaufridi of Aix-en-Provence, France, confessed under torture to making the sign of the cross backward, and mocking the benedic-

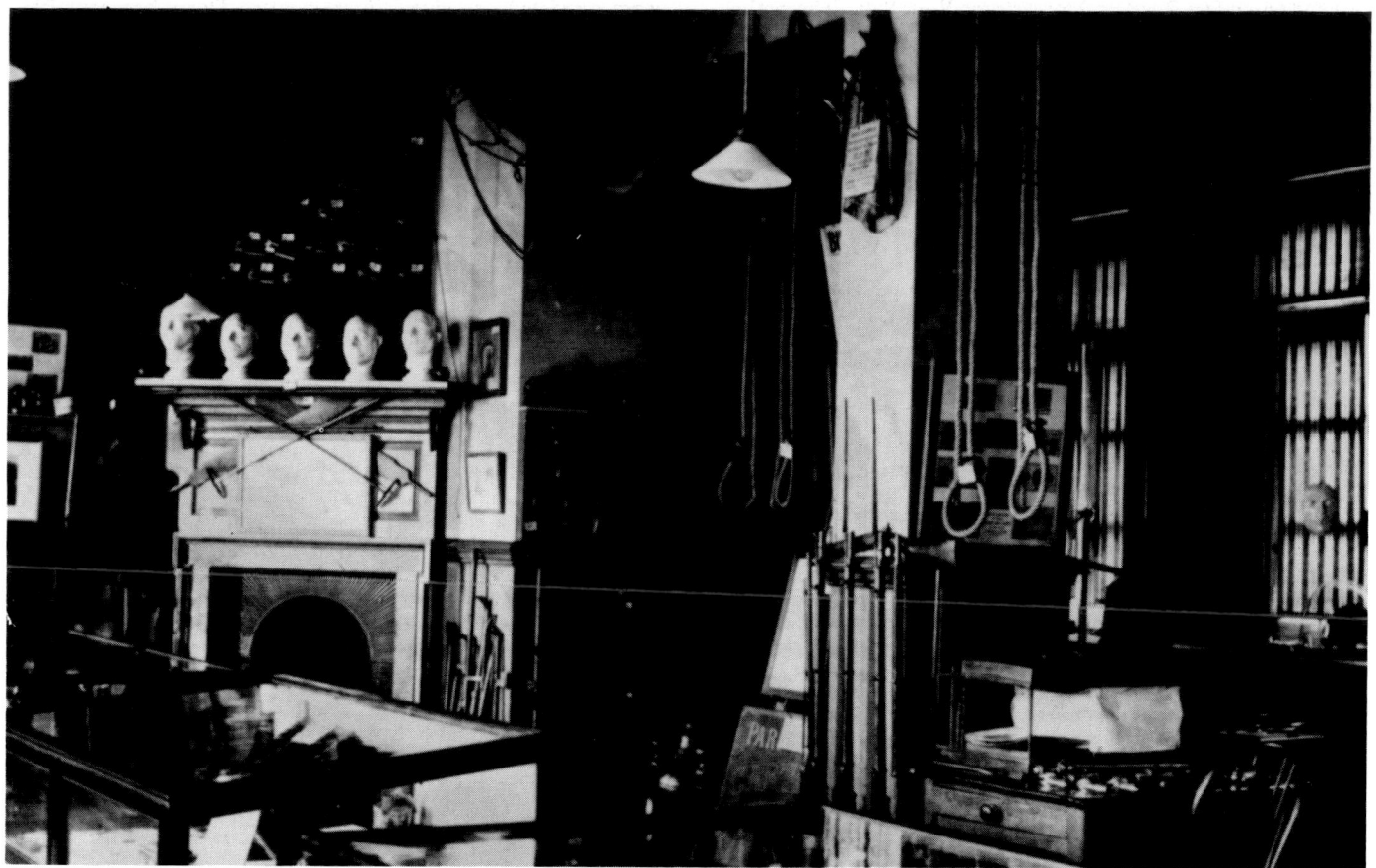

The Black Museum at Scotland Yard; the dangling ropes were used in actual executions.

tion by saying, "Go in the name of the Devil."

In about 1750, the satanic mass was allegedly celebrated by French noblemen in the court of King Louis XIV. Fifty priests were summoned to conduct the blasphemous service which included a liturgy and mass on the prone body of a nude girl. This came to be known as the Chambre Ardente Affair.

The Black Mass was given literary credence in 1791 when the Marquis de Sade published *Justine,* an erotic novel depicting the violation of a young woman representing the Virgin Mary. In more recent times the Black Mass has become of man's relationship to the nether world, and has survived into the modern era. REF.: *CBA;* Huysmans, *Down There;* Rhodes, *The Satanic Mass;* Robbins, *The Encyclopedia of Witchcraft and Demonology;* Wilson, *Witches.*

Blackmun, Harry Andrew, 1908-   , U.S., jur. Received first federal judicial appointment as judge of the U.S. Court of Appeals for the Eighth Circuit from President Dwight D. Eisenhower in 1959. He was appointed U.S. Supreme Court justice in 1970 by President Richard M. Nixon when Justice Abe Fortas resigned. Book authored: *Thoughts About Ethics* (1974). REF.: *CBA.*

Black Museum, The, 1860s-present, Brit., crime museum. Scotland Yard, in the mid-nineteenth century, began to collect the most unusual artifacts of crime and criminals, putting these curios on display for special visitors. Included in the museum are the ingenuous burglary tools used by England's master burglar and murderer, Charles Peace. The curious will also find the knighthood regalia of Sir Roger Casement, executed for treason; the death mask of Heinrich Himmler, the Nazi SS leader and undoubtedly the greatest mass murderer of this or any age; the whips, knives, and other torture instruments used by killer Neville Heath; the murder tools of John Reginald Christie; and a host of murder weapons from famous and unsolved cases, along with ropes used by England's hangmen. REF.: *CBA.*

Black Muslims, prom. 1960s-1970s, U.S., secret soc.-terr.-mur.

The doctrine of "Black Isolationism," which called for total segregation of the races and the founding of a separate black homeland, was first outlined in 1913 by the Prophet Drew Ali and given direction in 1930 by Wallace D. Fard, a Chicago-based religious leader hailed by his followers as the spiritual incarnation of Allah. Professor Fard's fierce nationalistic views coupled with an unbending faith in Islam formed the basis of the movement. The group later became known as Black Muslims from C. Eric Lincoln's 1961 book *Black Muslims In America.* Fard and his disciples sought to promote black pride and separatism, often through violence. In 1934, Fard mysteriously disappeared. He was succeeded by Elijah Muhammad, who proclaimed himself the "Messenger of Allah," and the leader of the Nation of Islam.

Under the direction of Muhammad, Black Muslims reached out to society's disenfranchised: young blacks imprisoned across the U.S. for strong-arm robbery, drugs, and murder. Hardened convicts began to consider themselves "political prisoners" of the system. Such was the case with Malcolm Little, a small-time thief who experienced a religious transformation while in the state prison in Charlestown, Mass. Under the patient tutelage of Elijah Muhammad, Little changed his name to Malcolm X and became the movement's most eloquent speaker before his assassination in 1965.

Muhammad's Nation of Islam recruited extensively from U.S. prisons and urban ghettos, teaching delinquent youths courtesy and respect for the faith, and imbuing them with pride in their cultural heritage. Those Muslims, however, who believed in effecting social change through nonviolent action, who sought peaceful coexistence with white America, were often branded as traitors and subjected to harassment, even death.

In 1974, following the abduction of heiress Patricia Hearst, Black Muslim chapters in Oakland and San Francisco distributed food to thousands of ghetto residents. Hearst's abductors, the Symbionese Liberation Army (SLA), demanded that, as the price for her release, food banks be opened in the Bay Area. The Black Muslims acted as the "managers" of the distribution points in San Francisco, Oakland, and Richmond. Over 13,000 recipients jostled for position, setting off a near riot. To prevent looting of the Muslims' Shabazz Bakery in Oakland, the leaders were forced to deplete the entire storeroom of fish and eggs. The next day the Muslims submitted a bill for $154,000 to the organizers of the drive. A check for $99,026 settled the matter, but the Muslims were not asked to participate in subsequent food campaigns.

During the Hearst kidnapping ordeal, the Muslims robbed Hibernia Bank and allegedly organized a murder cult known as the Death Angels, which was responsible for a series of un-provoked attacks on white San Francisco residents. The city in response organized Operation Zebra. In one week, over-zealous police officers stopped and searched 600 black men. Civil rights groups petitioned the U.S. district court for an injunction to stop the indiscriminate harassment of blacks by police. The courts agreed, and Operation Zebra was forced to cease operations. Meanwhile, four black men were identified and arrested. In March 1976, the second longest trial in California history concluded with the convictions of Larry Craig Green, J.C. Simon, Jesse Lee Cooks, and Manuel Moore. All four were sentenced to life in prison.

By the end of the 1970s, Black Muslims had renounced their former militancy and repudiated the earlier racist teachings of Fard. In May 1985, Wallace D. Muhammad disbanded the American Muslim Mission in order to bring its members into the worldwide Islamic community. A militant faction that refused to accept Wallace Muhammad's new order coalesced under the direction of Louis Farrakhan. See: **Hearst, Patricia; Khaalis, Kalil; Malcolm X; Symbionese Liberation Army**.

REF.: *CBA*; Dobson and Payne, *The Terrorists—Their Weapons, Leaders and Tactics*; Hacker, *Crusaders, Criminals, Crazies: Terror and Terrorism In Our Time*; McLellan, and Avery, *The Voices of Guns*; O'Ballance, *Language of Violence—The Blood Politics of Terrorism*; Powers, *Secrecy and Power*; Schreiber, *The Ultimate Weapon—Terrorists and World Order*; Toledano, *J. Edgar Hoover*; Tully, *Inside the FBI*; Ungar, *FBI*; Wicker, *Investigating the FBI*.

Blackout Ripper, The, See: **Cummings, Gordon**.

Black Panthers, The, prom. 1960s, U.S., terror.-mur. The Civil Rights movement of the 1960s spawned the Black Panther Party, a militant coalition of U.S. blacks bent on changing the system through violent and radical means. Disenchanted members of the Southern Christian Leadership Conference (SCLC) and the Student Nonviolent Coordinating Committee (SNCC) organized the Lowndes County Christian Movement for Human Rights. It was in Lowndes County, Ala., in 1965 that the Jim Crow laws and segregationist policies in place in the South led Stokely Carmichael to coin the watchword of a new generation: Black Power. Bobby Seale and Huey P. Newton founded the revolutionary Black Panther Party in the days and months following the Selma march. The task at hand was to change the squalid living conditions of blacks in Lowndes County and elsewhere, and the attitudes of those blacks living in abject poverty.

As black consciousness was aroused, members of the SNCC organized regional chapters of the Black Panther Party. A national headquarters was opened in Oakland, Calif., and it was there that the Panthers evolved from an essentially non-violent advocacy group to a uniformed paramilitary presence. The Panther manifesto was first spelled out in Eldridge Cleaver's *Soul On Ice*, an indictment of white racism in America. But it was Newton who gave the group its direction. Huey Newton indicted the police as enemies of social change and swore to prevent police brutality in the black community by whatever means possible. As a result, Panther leaders fought several pitched gun battles with police officers.

In 1968 Newton was convicted of voluntary manslaughter for shooting an Oakland police officer. He served twenty-two months in prison before his court-ordered release in 1970. In 1969, police shot Mark Clark and Fred Hampton in an early morning raid at Panther headquarters in Chicago. The police said they were searching for weapons, and their unprovoked attack resulted in conspiracy charges against Cook County State's Attorney Edward Hanrahan. In 1972, Newton announced that henceforth the party would renounce the "rhetoric of the gun" and try to improve conditions for blacks by working within the system. By the time another decade had passed, the Black Panther Party had ceased operations.

In its heyday, the Black Panther Party claimed a membership of 2,000, with regional chapters in thirty cities. In 1968 FBI Director J. Edgar Hoover described the Panthers as the "greatest threat to internal security in the country." Years later, former Black Panther Bobby Rush offered a different assessment of Newton and the movement he founded. "Newton took the lead in transforming the Black Panther Party from one described as a black nationalist organization to one that encompassed groups and issues from across the social spectrum." See: **Hanrahan, Edward; Hoover, J. Edgar; Newton, Huey**.

REF.: Alexander, *The Pizza Connection*; *CBA*; Demaris, *The Director*; Dobson and Payne, *The Terrorists—Their Weapons, Leaders and Tactics*; Gage, *The Mafia Is Not An Equal Opportunity Employer*; Hacker, *Crusaders, Criminals, Crazies: Terror and Terrorism in Our Time*; Haskins, *Street Gangs*; McLellan and Avery, *The Voices of Guns*; Nash, *Citizen Hoover*; Powers, *Secrecy and Power*; Schreiber, *The Ultimate Weapon—Terrorists and World Order*; Sullivan, *The Bureau: My Thirty Years In Hoover's FBI*; Toledano, *J. Edgar Hoover*; Tully, *Inside the FBI*; Ungar, *FBI*; Wicker, *Investigating the FBI*.

Black September Organization, prom. 1970s, Mid. East, bomb.-terror.-mur. The Black September movement, dedicated to the cause of Palestinian liberation through violent means, took its name from the September 1970 war with Jordan in which Palestinian commandos were expelled from the country following a series of airline hijackings. The members of this radical splinter group of Al Fatah carried out a series of terrorist attacks against Israel, its Western allies, and anyone else opposed to the establishment of a Palestinian homeland.

The first victim of Black September was an Arab. Jordanian Prime Minister Wasif Tol was shot and killed outside the Sheraton Hotel in Cairo. On May 13, 1972, three members of the Japanese Red Army, recruited by Black Septembrists, carried out a machine gun attack in the Israeli air terminal at Lod. Twenty-five persons were killed, including eleven Puerto Ricans on a religious pilgrimage to the Holy Land.

Unlike the Jihaz el-Rasd faction of Al Fatah, Black September did not confine its campaign of terror to the Middle East. At the XX Olympiad in Munich on Sept. 5, 1972, eight Syrian-trained commandos scaled a six-foot fence surrounding the Olympic compound. Their target was the dormitory of the Israeli athletes. They planned to take athletes hostage and negotiate the release of fedayeen held in Israel. The eight Black Septembrists demanded to be flown back to the Arab country of their choice, or two athletes would be executed every half-hour.

The German government failed to secure the release of the hostages, and decided to provide the terrorists with safe passage out of the country. Shortly before midnight a helicopter transported the Arabs and nine hostages to the Furstenfeldbruck air base and a waiting jet that was to take them to Cairo. Seconds after the Black Septembrists appeared on the tarmac, German sharpshooters opened fired. The nine athletes were murdered by their captors during the gun battle with West German security forces. Five of the eight Arabs were killed. Three were taken into custody: Kadir el Dnawy, Mohammed Abdullah, and Ibrahim Abd es. The next day Israel launched air attacks against several locations identified as Al Fatah training camps in Syria and Lebanon.

The terrorist war escalated in the year following the Munich massacre. In March 1973 Black September extremists killed American chargé d'affaires Curt Moore in Khartoum, Sudan. See: **Arafat, Yasir**.

REF.: Becker, *Hitler's Children—The Story of the Baader-Meinhof*

Terrorist Gang; CBA; Clutterbuck, Guerrillas and Terrorists; Demaris, Brothers in Blood: The International Terrorist Network; Dobson and Payne, Counterattack—The West's Battle Against the Terrorists; ____, The Terrorists—Their Weapons, Leaders and Tactics; Hacker, Crusaders, Criminals, Crazies: Terror and Terrorism in Our Time; Laqueur, Terrorism; Liston, Terrorism; O'Ballance, Language of Violence—The Blood Politics of Terrorism; Schreiber, The Ultimate Weapon—Terrorists and World Order; (FILM), *Olympic Murders,* (1972); *Black Sunday* (1977).

Black Sox Scandal, 1919, U.S., brib. The scandal that sullied the image of baseball for years and blackened the name of the Chicago White Sox for decades was brought about, in a great part, by the owner of the team, Charles Comiskey. He had spent what for him was a great fortune in putting together a super team, including the great outfielder, Joseph Jefferson "Shoeless Joe" Jackson, who was hitting a whopping .350 in 1919 and who had been called by Walter "Big Train" Johnson, dean of pitchers, "the greatest natural ballplayer I've ever seen." Comiskey paid $31,500 for Jackson, buying him from Cleveland. He had obtained Oscar "Happy" Felsch from the Milwaukee team and had acquired, over a few years, the likes of first baseman Arnold "Chick" Gandil, George "Buck" Weaver, Charles "Swede" Risberg, and the two top pitchers of the era, Claude "Lefty" Williams and superstar Eddie Cicotte. Yet, with all these stars in the White Sox crown, Comiskey penny-pinched the very men who were making a fortune for the club.

The Sox had won the pennant in 1917 with these stalwarts and the incredible pitching of Cicotte, who won twenty-eight games that year. They were equally impressive the following year and, in 1919, overwhelmed the league by winning twenty-nine games. Comiskey, though he had promised his top players bonuses if they turned in good performances, sidestepped this commitment, laughing off the promise when his players confronted him, and, instead, sending them cases of champagne (which he got for next to nothing). Some of the players made extra money by giving tips to the hordes of gamblers that flocked to the park in those days, especially Gandil, who loved these flashy touts, carousing with them in nightclubs late at night, his pockets stuffed with their money after he "tipped" them to what might happen in the next day's game.

Gamblers such as New York's notorious Arnold Rothstein, known as "The Big Bankroll," knew that the team to bet on was the White Sox, as did a host of other shapers, including Joseph "Sport" Sullivan, Billy Maharg, Nat "Brown" Evans, William Thomas "Sleepy Bill" Burns, and the colorful Abe "The Little Champ" Attell. Rumors began to spread through the gambling world that the Sox players were miserable and a goodly number of them might be willing to fix the 1919 World Series. Gandil was the source of information, telling his betting friends that the great slugger, Jackson, was in financial trouble, having made poor business investments and that he did not even have enough money to support his family. (Jackson had earned his sobriquet of "Shoeless Joe" when, while playing for a Greenville, S.C., team as a youngster, he discarded shoes that did not fit him and played a game barefoot. Jackson was illiterate; he could neither read nor write, but none of that mattered to Connie Mack who considered Jackson one of the greatest players who ever played for his Athletics. He consistently ended his seasons with staggering batting averages; in 1911, Jackson batted .408).

Gandil also informed the gamblers that Cicotte had, like Jackson and the others, asked Comiskey repeatedly for raises but that the baseball tycoon merely patted Cicotte on the back and told him that he was making "enough" money as it was, paying him almost $6,000 a year. There had been open arguments in the locker room, Gandil explained, open revolts where the players had to be coaxed on to the field to play by their dynamic manager, William "Kid" Gleason. Player complaints always centered about the same thing, money, or the lack of it. They knew Comiskey was getting rich from the record crowds their brilliant playing produced, and they rightfully concluded that the highhanded boss was refusing to let them join in the profits. Three weeks before

the 1919 World Series was to begin against Cincinnati, Gandil met with Joseph "Sport" Sullivan in Boston's Hotel Buckminster. He told Sullivan that "I think we can put it in the bag," explaining that he would require $10,000 for eight players, $80,000 in all. The players participating would be himself, shortstop Risberg, third baseman Weaver, utility infielder Fred McMullin, Felsch, Jackson, and the two key men in the scheme, pitchers Cicotte and Williams. The pitchers would be hurling two games each, Gandil figured, and that meant that four games of the Series could be fixed so that Cincinnati would win. Sullivan said he would get the payoff money and ordered Gandil to set up the players, saying that Rothstein would be the financial backer.

All the players except Cicotte agreed quickly to the bribe and the fix. Gandil kept working on the talented pitcher who finally relented as the team was traveling by Pullman one night toward Boston. Cicotte had struggled with his conscience and lost. He went to Gandil and said: "Okay, I'll do it for $10,000. Cash. Before the Series begins." Gandil notified Sullivan but the gambler said he was having a hard time raising the cash, that Rothstein thought it a bad risk, that there were too many people involved and one was sure to talk. Meanwhile, Billy Maharg and Bill Burns were able to raise $10,000 on their own, believing that Rothstein would dip into his big bankroll for the balance required. Rothstein hesitated, asking a confederate, Nat Evans, to look into the matter. Abe Attell, once featherweight boxing champion of the world, a high roller who had been present at the meeting between Rothstein and Evans, decided he would advance some of the bribe money.

Gandil received the first $10,000 bribe and slipped this under Cicotte's pillow, believing that the pitcher was the key man in the fix and had to be paid off first. When Cicotte found the money he quickly sewed it into the lining of his best coat which he wore constantly through the next few weeks, despite the hot weather. Rothstein then began advancing huge chunks of the bribe money but informed Cicotte through Attell that he wanted a sign from the great pitcher that the Series, indeed, was fixed. Cicotte was to hit the first Cincinnati batter coming to the plate in the first game. The gamblers withheld the rest of the bribe money until Cicotte did as asked. Though only Cicotte had been bribed, the other seven players, meeting in a hotel room, agreed that they would accept the promise of the gamblers to be paid later and several, like Gandil, borrowed money to bet against their own team. Gandil wrote his wife during the Series: "I have to bet my shoes." Actually, the double-dealing Sullivan had received the bribe money, all of it, from Rothstein but withheld $70,000 to place his own bets on the Series, planning, he later claimed, to pay off the players from his profits.

Cicotte kept his word to Rothstein. When the first Cincinnati player, Maurice Rath, came to the plate, he served him a ball, then struck Rath in the back, sending him to first. Rothstein, watching in the grandstand through binoculars, immediately sent his runners out, placing more than $500,000 on Cincinnati, making heavy side bets with money moguls like Harry Sinclair, the oil baron. Rothstein's enormous bets actually drove down the odds against Cincinnati so that gamblers were, in hours, offering even odds which astounded the uninformed betters who knew Cincinnati, compared to the Sox, had a team that was slightly above average and not expected to win the Series. Cincinnati's poorest batters got hits off Cicotte that first day, even Reds pitcher Dutch Reuther, known to be one of the worst batters in baseball. By the fourth inning, the Reds had a 6-1 lead and Kid Gleason jumped from the Sox dugout to yell at Cicotte: "That's all, dammit, that's all!"

Williams delivered a less than mediocre performance the next day, so that the Reds won easily, but complicating the fix was Sox pitcher Dickie Kerr who pitched the greatest game of his life, winning the third game for the Sox. Cicotte and Williams made sure that their team lost the next two games, 2-0 and 3-0 so that the Reds walked away with the World Series. The playing by the Sox was blatantly amateurish. The team's big bats were silent, the

Charles "Swede" Risberg, tough and mean; he threatened to kill Joe Jackson if he talked about the 1919 World Series fix.

Oscar "Happy" Felsch who went out of his way to make sure that other players got in on the fix.

George "Buck" Weaver insisted to his dying day that he was innocent but never proved it.

Pitcher Claude "Lefty" Williams was responsible for throwing away games in the 1919 World Series.

Arnold "Chick" Gandil, a willing "fixer" of the Series.

Eddie Cicotte threw away his great career for $10,000.

Shoeless Joe Jackson, greatest of them all, also guilty.

William "Kid" Gleason, the honest Sox manager who suspected a fix but was powerless to pick out the guilty players until too late.

Sox owner Charles Comiskey.

Ban Johnson

York Times.

WEDNESDAY, SEPTEMBER 29, 1920. TWO CENTS

EIGHT WHITE SOX PLAYERS ARE INDICTED ON CHARGE OF FIXING 1919 WORLD SERIES; CICOTTE GOT $10,000 AND JACKSON $5,000

Yankee Owners Give Praise to Comiskey And Offer Him Use of Their Whole Team

COMISKEY SUSPENDS THEM

Following the announcement from Chicago yesterday that Owner Charles A. Comiskey had suspended two star pitchers, two regular infielders, his two leading outfielders and one utility player, Colonels Jacob Ruppert and T. L. Huston, owners of the New York Club, put at Comiskey's disposal the entire New York American League Club.

It is not likely, however, that the offer will be accepted. The reason advanced for the unusual offer is that such a grave and unforeseen emergency requires an unusual remedy. An American League rule prevents the transfer of a player from one club to another after July 1 without the asking of waivers, which would give any club in the league an opportunity to get the player. This is the technicality referred to in the message.

The telegram from the Yankee owners to Comiskey read as follows:

Promises to Run Them Out of Baseball if Found Guilty

TWO OF PLAYERS CONFESS

A typical headline in 1920 announcing the shocking story of the World Series fix.

Attorney William J. Fallon, left, and his client, Arnold Rothstein.

Sports writer Ring Lardner had suspicions.

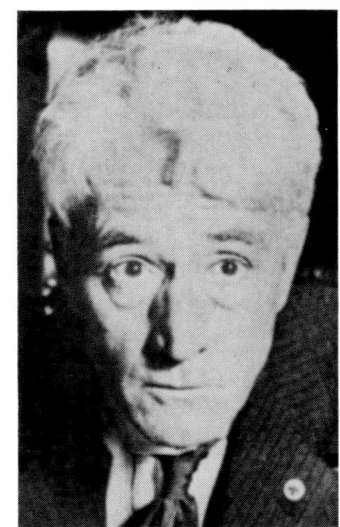

Judge Kenesaw Mountain Landis.

William Maharg, gambler.

Abe Attell, gambler.

Attell when he was a boxing champ.

sharp and aggressive defense crumbled, the pitching vanished. Comiskey was suspicious of his players right from the first botched game and, the next day, he began receiving anonymous reports that his players were throwing the Series. He went to American League chief Ban Johnson and asked him to investigate but Johnson, who harbored grudges against Comiskey over old insults, told the Sox owner that he was nothing more than a spoiled sport, and later told reporters that Comiskey's complaint was "the whelp of a beaten cur."

Comiskey hired detectives to look into the claims of bribery, but they found no evidence to prove this accusation. Sports writer Ring Lardner even snooped about, as did fellow scribe Hugh Fullerton, but whenever these newsmen approached gamblers who had cavorted with them for years and brought up the possibility of a fix, the betting men fell silent. The rumors of the great fix continued, even into 1920 when most of the crooked players returned to the Sox roster and began another season that promised to see the Sox once more in World Series contention. In July of that year, while Lardner was eating in a Manhattan restaurant and gambler's hangout, Dinty Moore's, he heard Abe Attell loudly proclaim that Arnold Rothstein had fixed the World Series of 1919. Lardner had already given up on the notion and when Attell affirmed his claim to his face, the great sports writer snorted: "Who would print that?"

The dogged Comiskey, however, felt he had been cheated and persisted in his efforts to uncover the scandal, arranging through his political associates the convening of a grand jury to investigate the matter. Cicotte was on the verge of a nervous breakdown and Kid Gleason knew it. He persuaded the talented pitcher to go to Comiskey and make a clean breast of it. Cicotte did, sitting before Comiskey and weeping, saying between sobs: "I know what you want to know...I know...I know...Yeah...We were crooked...We were crooked."

Comiskey exploding, jumped up, and shouted at Cicotte: "Don't tell me! Tell the grand jury!"

The pitcher went before the grand jury, telling the whole story, blaming Gandil for setting up the fix with the gamblers. "I've lived a thousand years in the last twelve months...Now, I've lost everything—job, reputation, everything. My friends all bet on the Sox, but I couldn't tell them. I had to double-cross them. I'm through with baseball. I'm going to lose myself if I can and start life all over again." Cicotte said that he had thrown the World Series so he could put $4,000 down on a farm.

Swede Risberg had no intention of admitting his guilt. He was one of the toughest players in baseball, a mean-minded fellow with a ruthless streak in him. Risberg had beaten up fans after games when they dared to criticize his playing. He had threatened other players with beatings if they dared to implicate him in the fix. When Risberg learned that Shoeless Joe Jackson intended to go to the grand jury and confess, he confronted Jackson and, setting his square jaw, squinted his eyes and said: "Just keep your mouth shut, that's all, Joe. I swear to you, I'll kill you if you squawk."

Jackson did talk, in spite of Risberg's threat, saying that he had been paid only $5,000. When officials heard about Risberg's death threat, detectives were assigned to guard Jackson. Shoeless Joe went on to tell reporters: "Now Risberg threatens to bump me off if I squawk...Old Joe Jackson isn't going to jail. But I'm going to get far from my protectors until this thing blows over. Swede is a hard guy." As he left the courtroom, one of the most dramatic scenes in all baseball took place. Scores of young boys who idolized Jackson and who followed him everywhere, were assembled before the fallen champion. One young boy inched forward and held on to Jackson's sleeve, saying with tears in his eyes: "Say it ain't so, Joe, say it ain't so." Fighting back his own tears, the once great Shoeless Joe Jackson, placed his large hand gently on the boy's head for a moment, then choked: "Yes, kid, I'm afraid it is."

A resulting trial saw the eight crooked players acquitted of criminal charges. The jury, highly partisan, carried the eight accused players out of the courtroom on their shoulders but this in no way vindicated their corrupt actions. They were, all of them, finished in baseball. The game would never again be soiled by the likes of such men, vowed the team owners, and a short time later, Judge Kenesaw Mountain Landis was appointed commissioner of baseball. He would rule with an iron hand for many years to come, meting out severe punishments for the slightest infractions committed by any baseball player and this included the private lives of players.

When Babe Ruth's nightlife began to get out of hand in the late 1920s, Landis called him in for a redressing, pointing out to the Yankee slugger that he would destroy the image of baseball for millions of youngsters if he did not curb his nightclubbing and womanizing. Landis, at that time, brought up the scene of the little boy confronting Joe Jackson and telling Ruth that he, the immortal Babe, had overshadowed the terrible deeds of the Black Sox, as they were known for years afterward, but all of that could be undone by his notorious after-hours conduct. "Do you want a little boy pulling on your sleeve, Babe," Landis asked Ruth, "asking you that same question?" The great Babe Ruth, half giant, half child, hung his head and tears streamed down his florid face. "*That* will never happen, Judge, I promise," he said, vowing to reform. It never did. No gambling scandal in baseball equaled the infamy of the Black Sox until Cincinnati's Pete Rose (ironically from the same team that benefited from the 1919 fix) was kicked out of baseball in 1989 for betting on the game.

The only real winner of the infamous 1919 World Series fix was its chief financial backer, Arnold Rothstein, who, represented by attorney William J. Fallon, was brought in for questioning during the trial of the eight players. Nothing could be proved against him and he laughed off the attempt of the prosecution to have him indicted. He nevertheless reaped a reported $4 million profit on the Series fix, a gambling coup that made him the most important fixer and gambler in America. He was also the most powerful underworld figure in the country, the one man who financed national criminal operations a decade before the establishment of the national crime syndicate. See: **Rothstein, Arnold.**

REF.: Asinof, *Eight Men Out;* Axelson, *Commy;* Barrow, *My Fifty Years in Baseball;* Bartlett, *Baseball and Mr. Spalding;* Casey, *Chicago, Medium Rare;* CBA; Chaefetz, *Play the Devil;* Clarke, *In the Reign of Rothstein;* Dedmon, *Fabulous Chicago;* Farrell, *My Baseball Diary;* Fried, *The Rise and Fall of the Jewish Gangster in America;* Gilbert and Bryson, *Chicago and Its Makers;* Gosch and Hammer, *The Last Testament of Lucky Luciano;* Katcher, *The Big Bank Roll: The Life and Times of Arnold Rothstein;* Lewis and Smith, *Chicago, The History of Its Reputation;* Lieb, *Baseball As I Have Known It;* McPhaul, *Deadlines and Monkeyshines;* Mann, *Baseball Confidential;* Mayer and Wade, *Chicago, Growth of a Metropolis;* Meeker, *Chicago With Love;* Merriam, *Chicago;* Messick and Goldblatt, *The Mobs and the Mafia;* Moore, *Dateline Chicago;* Nash, *People to See;* Peterson, *The Mob;* Pierce, *A History of Chicago;* ____, *As Others See Chicago;* Spink, *Judge Landis;* Sullivan, *Our Times;* (FILM) *Eight Men Out,* 1988.

Blackstone, Sir **William,** 1723-80, Brit., jur. Author, lecturer, and judge of the Common Pleas from 1770-80. He wrote *Commentaries on the Common Laws of England* (1765-69). REF.: CBA.

Blackstone Rangers Chicago Check Fraud Case, prom. 1967-68, U.S., fraud. During the late 1960s, a powerful black Chicago street gang known as the Blackstone Rangers operated a fraudulent check operation that diverted $50,000 in federal funds from the government's War On Poverty program to line the pockets of gang chieftains.

The IRS became suspicious after agent Howard C. Doulder conducted a five-week investigation into time sheets and attendance records of certain gang members supposedly attending job-training sessions. A U.S. Senate Permanent Subcommittee on Investigation delved into the activities of the Woodlawn Poverty Organization, created in 1967 by the Rangers and disbanded a year later. The committee determined that $927,241

in funds was granted by the Office of Economic Opportunity to this War on Poverty program.
REF.: *CBA;* Haskins, *Street Gangs;* McGuire, *The Forgers;* Powers, *Secrecy and Power.*

Blackwell, Olin G., prom. 1961-63, U.S., penol. Olin Blackwell succeeded Paul Madigan as warden of Alcatraz Penitentiary on Nov. 26, 1961. Blackwell's tenure was notable for a relaxation of standards. Inmates on the "Rock" were permitted great latitude in the items they were permitted to purchase with the money they earned. It was not unusual to see hardened criminals knitting and crocheting inside their cells. The embroidered items were sold as gifts, and a number of the finer pieces decorated the warden's private office.

The last escape attempt from Alcatraz occurred during the waning days of the Blackwell administration. In December 1962, John Paul Scott and Daryl Parker, who were serving long sentences for bank robbery, sawed through a storage window in the basement using butcher twine soaked with scouring powder. They squeezed through the narrow opening and tried to swim across the Bay. Scott nearly died from exposure near the Golden Gate Bridge. The strong current forced Parker to cling to a large boulder. He was later picked up by Alcatraz guards.

Warden Blackwell said goodbye to the last of the 1,576 prisoners who spent time on the "Rock." These remaining inmates departed for new quarters on Mar. 21, 1963. On May 7, he was appointed warden of the Federal Penitentiary at Lewisburg, Pa. He later served as warden of the fortress-like Atlanta Federal Penitentiary. REF.: *CBA.*

Blair, Eric Arthur (AKA: **George Orwell**), 1903-50, Burma, law enfor. off. Assistant superintendent to the Indian Imperial Police in Burma from 1922-27. Books authored: *Burmese Days* (1935), *Animal Farm* (1944), and *1984* (1949). REF.: *CBA.*

Blair, Jacob Beeson, 1821-1901, U.S., jur. Prosecuting attorney in Ritchie County, Va., from 1845-47 and member of the House of Representatives from 1861-65. He was appointed judge of the territorial court of Wyoming by President Ulysses S. Grant in 1876, and re-appointed by Presidents Hayes in 1880 and Arthur in 1884. REF.: *CBA.*

Blair, John, 1732-1800, U.S., jur. Colonial leader and judge of the first Virginia Court of Appeals from 1780-89, and the Virginia Supreme Court of Appeals in 1789. He was appointed associate Supreme Court justice in 1789 until ill health forced his resignation in 1796. An ardent Federalist, he was one of the five original members of the Supreme Court. REF.: *CBA.*

Blair, Montgomery, 1813-83, U.S., jur. District attorney for Missouri from 1839-41, judge of the Court of Common Pleas from 1845-49, and postmaster general under President Abraham Lincoln from 1861-64. In 1857, he represented Dred Scott, a slave, in an unsuccessful appeal before the Supreme Court for his freedom. See: **Scott, Dred**. REF.: *CBA.*

Blair, William W., d.1824, U.S., jur. District attorney in Frankfort, Ky., from 1823. He was appointed judge of the Territorial Florida Court by President James Monroe in 1824 and died while in office. REF.: *CBA.*

Blaisdell, John, prom. 1822, U.S., mansl. On the evening of Feb. 18, 1822, two farmers named John Blaisdell and John Wadleigh entered the dry goods store of Nathaniel Weeks in Exeter, N.H., to purchase an ax and an ax handle. After paying the merchant, the two men left the store. A short time later, Blaisdell split open the skull of Wadleigh with the white oak ax handle, valued at ten cents. In panic, he tried to cover up his crime by running to the home of a black man named Jude Hall, explaining that his friend Wadleigh had become drunk and gotten into a fight. He was badly injured and in need of help, Blaisdell explained.

Hall found Wadleigh in the road, still alive but barely coherent. When Wadleigh saw Blaisdell standing nearby, he recoiled in horror. This struck Hall as peculiar. Wadleigh was carried to his home, where he died the next day. "Oh that fellow," he whispered to his wife. "Oh Lord, I'm done," were his last words.

The ax handle, stained with unmistakable traces of blood, was found by Charles Parks a week later near the side of the road approaching Cove Bridge. It was identified as having been the property of Blaisdell, who explained that he had cast it aside in order to carry Wadleigh to safety.

The trial began on Sept. 24, 1822, in the Superior Court of Judicature at Exeter. For some time Blaisdell had harbored a grudge against Wadleigh who had taken a lucrative tree-cutting job originally promised to Blaisdell by farmer Joshua Pike. This was the only motive the prosecution could offer for the seemingly unprovoked, unwitnessed killing.

Defense Attorney Ichabod Bartlett exhorted the jury "to beware that you pronounce such a verdict as shall not make wretched the remainder of your lives—such a verdict as shall not inflict pangs in the hour of death."

Grave doubt lingered in the jurors' minds despite a physician's testimony that the blow to the Wadleigh's head could not have been caused by a simple fall or accident. They declared Blaisdell Guilty of manslaughter and sentenced him to hard labor for three years with an additional fifteen days in solitary confinement. REF.: *CBA.*

Blake, Daniel, c.1743-63, Brit., rob.-mur. When he was only twenty years old, Daniel Blake set out for London, where he hoped to find work as a manservant in the house of a well-to-do man. He found employment in the house of Lord Dacre, where his conduct by day was exemplary. By night it was a different story. When off duty, Blake made the acquaintance of women of low character. Needing more money than he was currently making with Lord Dacre, Blake decided to rob Mr. Murcott, the butler in the household. Late one night he entered Murcott's bedchambers, armed with a small knife and a poker. He knocked Murcott out with the poker, then finished the job with the blunt knife. For his troubles he collected twenty guineas from the pocket of the man's coat.

The body was discovered by the porter the next morning, along with the knife Blake had carelessly left behind. When the news of Murcott's untimely death spread to the servants' quarters, Blake was overcome by false grief.

A cloud of suspicion soon fell on Blake, however, when he paid off several old debts the day after the murder. Then the murder weapon was traced to Blake. The former butcher was taken into custody and his confession was read to Sir John Fielding, who committed him to Newgate to stand trial. On Feb. 28, 1763, Blake was found Guilty and sentenced to death, his body to be placed in chains on Hounslow Heath. While awaiting his fate, Blake became repentant. As he faced the avid crowd on his last day, he called to them, "You were all born; but you know not in what manner you shall die. Let my fate warn you to keep the sabbath, and honour your parents."

REF.: *CBA; Newgate Calendar.*

Blake, Edward, 1833-1912, Can., jur. Prime minister of Ontario from 1871-72, and minister of justice from 1875-77. REF.: *CBA.*

Blake, Henry Nichols, 1838-1933, U.S., jur. Attorney for the Montana territory from 1869-71 and district attorney for the first judicial district of Montana from 1886-87. He authored a number of legal papers and summations including *Report of Cases Argued and Determined in the Supreme Court of Montana Territory from December 1868* and *The Revised Codes of Montana of 1907*. He was appointed judge of the territorial court of Montana by President Ulysses S. Grant in 1875 and re-appointed by President Benjamin Harrison in 1889. REF.: *CBA.*

Blake, John (AKA: **Tulsa Jack**), d.1895, U.S., west. outl. A Kansas cowboy during the late 1880s, John Blake moved south to the Oklahoma Territory where he met Bill Doolin and joined his gang, becoming one of Doolin's most loyal and stouthearted followers. He participated in many bank robberies and train robberies committed by the Doolin gang at Perry, Okla., and other places. At the wild gun battle between the Doolin band and lawmen at Ingalls, Okla., on Sept. 1, 1893, Blake shot his way through barricades from a hotel to the stable where the gang's horses were kept, freeing the animals and leading them back to gang members who, along with Blake, mounted them and made good their escape, leaving only gang member Roy Daugherty (Arkansas Tom) who was trapped in a second-story hotel room.

The Doolin gang continued its robbing spree and, on May 20, 1894, the gang robbed the bank in Southwest City, Mo., where Bill Dalton, the only member of the Dalton gang to ride with the Doolins, shot J.C. Seaborn, former state auditor and one of the leading citizens of the state. Seaborn, along with dozens of other citizens, joined the local lawmen in harassing the gang as it attempted to make its escape. Blake was one of these and it was later claimed that his deadly marks-manship was responsible for wounding several vigilantes firing at the gang while it thun-dered down the main street of town. Blake, the most daring of the gang, was the last man out of town, covering the re-treat. Though hundreds of shots were fired at him, he miracu-lously escaped injury.

Tulsa Jack Blake, shown in death.

This was not the case following the gang's robbery of a Rock Island train near Dover, Okla. The Doolin band rode to their hideout on the Cimarron River and encamped. In the early morning of May 5, 1895, a large posse led by the redoubtable lawman Chris Madsen came upon the Doolins as they were asleep in their camp. Tulsa Jack Blake was on guard at the time and, spotting Deputy William Banks sneaking up on the sleeping forms of his fellow bandits, pulled his six-gun and fired at the lawman. The bandits leaped to their feet and a roaring gun battle ensued. Blake continued to exchange shots with deputy Banks and one of Banks' shots struck his cartridge belt, exploding a shell that tore into Blake's stomach, causing a mortal wound. Tulsa Jack died as Bill Doolin and the others leapt into their saddles and splashed across the Cimarron to make their thunderous escape. See: **Clifton, Daniel; Dalton Brothers; Daugherty, Roy; Doolin, William; Newcomb, George; Pierce, Charles; Raidler, William; Weightman, George; West, Richard.**

REF.: Barnard, *A Rider of the Cherokee Strip;* Bartholomew, *The Biographical Album of Western Gunfighters;* Breihan, *Badmen of Frontier Days;* ____, *Great Gunfighters of the West;* Canton, *Frontier Trails;* CBA; Croy, *Trigger Marshal, The Story of Chris Madsen;* Drago, *Outlaws on Horseback;* ____, *Road Agents and Train Robbers;* Graves, *Oklahoma Outlaws;* Hanes, *Bill Doolin, Outlaw;* Harrington, *Hanging Judge;* Holloway, *Texas Gun Lore;* Horan and Sann, *Pictorial History of the Wild West;* Hunter and Rose, *The Album of Gunfighters;* James, *They Had Their Hour;* Jones, *The Experiences of a Deputy U.S. Marshal of the Indian Territory;* Lake, *Under Cover for Wells Fargo;* McGinty, *The Old West;* Miller, *Bill Tilghman, Marshal of the Last Frontier;* Morris, *Oklahoma, Yesterday, Today and Tomorrow;* Newson, *The Life and Practices of the Wild and Modern Indian;* Nix, *Oklahombres;* O'Neal, *Encyclopedia of Western Gunfighters;* Osborn, *Let Freedom Ring;* Raine, *Famous Sheriffs and Western Outlaws;* Shirley, *Heck Thomas, Frontier Marshal;* ____, *Six-Gun and Silver Star;* ____, *Toughest of Them All;* Sutton, *Hands Up!;* Tilghman, *Marshal of the Last Frontier;* ____, *Outlaw Days;* Wellman, *A Dynasty of Western Outlaws.*

Blake, Joseph (AKA: **Blueskin**), d.1724, Brit., rob.-attempt. mur. A drunkard, a ruffian, and a thief, Joseph Blake, better known in London's underworld as Blueskin, had served as a companion to the celebrated highwayman Jack Sheppard. He also worked for the notorious Jonathan Wild who, to the law-abiding world, was the chief law enforcement officer of London, but was really a criminal mastermind who planned countless robberies which thieves like Blueskin performed, turning over most of the loot to Wild. In 1724, the year in which Sheppard was executed,

the shop of a London draper named Kneebone was robbed and Wild was asked to investigate. The thief-taker knew immediately that the robbery was the work of Blueskin and went with Quilt Arnold and others to arrest Blueskin, who first resisted arrest by drawing a knife. When he saw Wild, his secret master, he threw down the knife and was taken to Newgate to stand trial. The robber undoubtedly believed that Wild would later arrange to have him released.

Before his trial, Blueskin asked to see Wild privately and the thief-taker walked up to the shackled thief in the courtyard of the Old Bailey. Wild, who was about to give evidence at Blake's trial, offered Blueskin a drink from his flask. The robber gulped down the rum as Wild attempted to question him about the location of stolen loot Blueskin had hidden, hoping to turn a profit for himself. Blake, thinking Wild might be able to help him avoid the noose, asked him to put in a good word for him at his trial. Wild gave him a smirk and said as he laughed in the ruffian's face: "I can't do that. You're a dead man and will be tucked up (hanged) very speedily."

Blueskin exploded with rage and produced a knife he had hidden on his person, slashing Wild's throat to the windpipe and nearly killing him on the spot. Fortunately for Wild two physicians

Joseph Blake attempts to murder Jonathan Wild.

were present who rushed to his aid and stopped the bleeding, narrowly saving his life. Blueskin was dragged before the court and promptly convicted of robbery and attempted murder, then sent to the gallows, as Wild had promised, robbery then being a capital offense. Wild would soon join him after his double life was exposed. See: **Sheppard, Jack; Wild, Jonathan.**

REF.: *CBA;* Gollomb, *Master Highwaymen;* Hibbert, *Highwaymen;* Postgate, *Murder, Piracy and Treason.*

Blake, Lena, and **Rice, Josie,** prom. 1893, Case of, U.S., rob. On Jan. 23, 1893, a Galveston, Texas, man named Albert Hoyder was waylaid and robbed on Chicago's South Clark Street by two women, Lena Blake and Josie Rice, who were posing as pros-titutes.

Hoyder was unfamiliar with the dangerous Clark Street levee area, infested by footpads, streetwalkers, and confidence men. In town to settle a $42,000 inheritance left him by his uncle, Hoyder was accosted by the women near the Harrison Street police station with over $5,000 in his money belt. The women enticed him into an upstairs room and drugged him with wine.

When he awoke, he discovered that his money was gone. He

reported the theft to the police, who arrested both women. Blake received bail from one of the court hangers-on, and promptly skipped town. Rice confessed fully, telling the judge that her companion had left her just $137. Six months later, Detective Clifton Rodman Wooldridge arrested Blake, but she was discharged for lack of evidence. She claimed that all the stolen money was gone—she had given some of it to her mother to open a restaurant.

REF.: *CBA*; Wooldridge, *Hands Up!*

Blake, Robert, d.1929, U.S., mur. Robert Blake was a condemned prisoner in Texas who was executed in 1929 for murder. Before going to the electric chair, Blake kept a curious chronicle of activities and dialog between other condemned prisoners on Death Row. His remarks, which detail the anxiety of nine condemned men waiting to be put to death, appeared in the July 1929 edition of *The American Mercury* and were later used in the grim prison drama, *The Last Mile*. The prisoners mostly concern themselves with the possibility of a reprieve. When a telegram does arrive for one of the prisoners, he is incensed that it is not from the governor ordering a stay of execution, but from a sheriff asking if he can bring some additional visitors to see the man electrocuted. The prisoners share their last cigars and fruit and endlessly discuss their impending deaths, one stating in forced doggerel:

Why do they pull a black cap over your face
And let it remain until you're dead?
Because the high voltage of electricity
Will make your eyes pop out of your head!

The Death Row area described by Blake in his grim narrative was immediately adjacent to the room housing the electric chair. At the end of his chronicle, Blake states: "These lines are written while Six (referring to the condemned prisoner taken from cell number six) is being strapped into the chair. The door between the death chamber and Death Row is open." He quotes the words of the condemned man which he and the others can hear as Six awaits the current of electricity which will end his life: "I hope that I am the last one who ever sits in this chair. Tell my mother that my last words were of her." Then Blake adds: "The lights go dim as we hear the whine of the motor when the switch is turned on...The lights go dim twice more." One of the prisoners shouts from Death Row: "They're giving him the juice again. Wonder what they're trying to do, cook him?" One of the condemned men says "I won't be able to sleep for a week." Another replies from his cell: "I'm going to sleep now. You'll be able to sleep all right. Forget about it."

One week after writing the above report, Robert Blake himself walked into the dreaded room and sat down in the electric chair to face his own end.

REF.: *CBA*; (DRAMA) Wexley, *The Last Mile*.

Blanche Fury, 1939, a novel by Joseph Shearing. This work of fiction is based on the Rush murders (Brit., 1848). An above-average film noir production directed by Marc Allegret was produced in England in 1948 under the same title, drawing from the Shearing novel. See: **Rush, James**. REF.: *CBA*.

Blanck, Tom, prom. 1894, U.S., burg.-rob. Blanck was born in New York City, but committed his first crime in British Columbia in January 1891 when he held up a stagecoach and stole $4,500, killing the driver when he resisted. Blanck crossed the border a few weeks later but quickly ran afoul of the law after committing a burglary. In Fairhaven, Wash., he killed a policeman, Peter Brugh, as the officer chased him after a robbery.

Without any clear plan the desperado drifted into Helena, Mont., where he killed a bartender and a deputy sheriff who stood in his way. Returning to Washington state on Sept. 30, 1894, Blanck turned his gun on Constable William Jeffrey of Puyallup, when the constable became suspicious of a package dropped by the side of a railroad track. Blanck had run into a nearby building when Jeffrey picked up the bundle containing a .45-caliber

Colt revolver. "Drop that!" commanded Blanck, who snuck up behind Jeffrey. When the constable hesitated he was shot through the heart.

Several days later a Seattle detective arrested the fugitive after a brief gun fight. Blanck confessed to his many crimes, and implicated himself in the shooting death of a Seattle bartender named Charles Bridwell four days after Jeffrey's murder.

In a short trial, the killer was convicted and sentenced to hang. Blanck would not go quietly, however. On Mar. 17, 1895, he pointed what appeared to be a small revolver through the bars at jailkeeper Jerry Yerbury, demanding immediate release for himself and seven felons. When all were safely out the door, Yerbury discovered that the gun was nothing more than a block of wood whittled into the shape of a gun.

The other escaped prisoners were eventually captured and returned to jail. Blanck was overtaken near Orillia, Wash., on Mar. 21, 1895, while holed up in a farmhouse. He battled it out with sheriff's deputies, emptying his revolver. He then emerged from his hiding place, willing to give up, but the law-enforcement officers opened fire anyway. The gunman who blazed a trail of murder across two states and into Canada lay dead from his wounds. The police said they believed Blanck was carrying a concealed gun in his clothing at the time of his surrender. This proved not to be the case.

REF.: *CBA*; Duke, *Celebrated Criminal Cases of America*.

Blanco, Luis Carrero, prom. 1973, Spain, (unsolv.) assass. As the number two man in the right-wing government of Francisco Franco, Admiral Luis Carrero Blanco was responsible for the direction the new Spanish government would take when the aging dictator died. The Basque separatists had waited for years for their chance at political autonomy. As the country showed signs of moving away from its fascist past, the Basque minority radicalized, pushing for an independent state.

A small group of extremists known as the *Euskadi Ta Askatasuna* (ETA), believed the only way to achieve this end was through armed confrontation and terrorist action. The leaders of the group targeted Blanco for death in 1973. He became a hated symbol of an oppressive government. For weeks four ETA leaders burrowed under the streets of Madrid, digging a chamber they would fill with explosives at the opportune moment. Then when Blanco drove by on his regular route to and from the Church of San Francisco de Borja on Serrano Street, the explosives would blow his automobile to the sky. It was a difficult, highly complex operation. The charge would be detonated from a distance, and triggered as the automobile drove directly over the mine.

By Dec. 15, with everything in place, eighty kilos of explosives were brought in from the Basque country. An electronic cable was run underneath the street along the path of the telephone wires. The terrorists waited until Dec. 20 to carry out their plan. With U.S. Secretary of State Henry Kissinger in town, the security in the area had doubled. When things returned to normal on the twentieth, the four Basques went to work. Blanco left the church at 9:30 a.m. and climbed into his Dodge Dart, accompanied by Police Inspector Don Juan Antonio Bueno Fernández and a chauffeur, Don José Luis Pérez Mojeda.

The car wound its way along Serrano Street, slowing down near a double-parked Austin left there by the ETA. A minute later the charge was detonated and the Dart was shot five stories into the air, settling on the rooftop of a nearby terrace, the three occupants dead. With the neighborhood in chaos, the ETA plotters slipped away unobserved. The next day they issued a communique which claimed responsibility for the deed. Though no one was brought to trial for the murder of Blanco, the fascist government had ways of avenging attacks like these. Five years later 28-year-old José Miquel Peñoran was assassinated in the French town of Anglet when he stepped down on his accelerator pedal, his car instantly obliterated. Peñora, a suspected terrorist known by the revolutionary name Argola, probably masterminded the 1973 assassination of the Spanish premier. REF.: *CBA*.

Bland, Theodric, 1776-1846, U.S., jur. Judge of the District

Court of Maryland, appointed by President James Monroe in 1819. He published an appendix on contempt of court cases tried in England and the U.S. which appeared in report form as *An Essay on Constructive Contempt of Court*, written and prepared for George Bourne's *Report of the Case of Baptis Irvine In a Matter of Contempt* (1808). REF.: *CBA*.

Blandig, Albert, d.1849, Brit., big.-suic.-mur. A marrying murderer, Albert Blandig set himself up as a practicing doctor in Liverpool and London, marrying two women. Though he had no medical background or degree, Blandig made a comfortable living serving those in the poverty districts of both cities. He explained his long absences to both wives by saying that medical research took him away. In July 1849, his London wife May discovered the Liverpool wife Jane. Blandig, a normally reserved and calculating person, panicked, poisoning May Blandig with arsenic, then later took his own life when arrest for murder seemed imminent. REF.: *CBA*.

Mary Blandy at the deathbed of her father, whom she had poisoned.

Blandy, Mary, 1719-52, Brit., mur. Mary Blandy was the daughter of wealthy Francis Blandy, a lawyer whose home was in Henley on Thames. She was well educated, a reader of the classics, and her protective father doted upon her. Although he publicly made much of the £10,000 dowry he had settled on his daughter, he also discouraged the many suitors who came forward seeking her hand in marriage. Mary, an intelligent but plain-looking woman, became desperate at the age of twenty-six, feeling that her father's dominant personality would prevent any man from ever walking her to the altar. Then Captain William Henry Cranstoun, son of a Scottish peer, appeared in the area, recruiting for the army. He befriended the Blandy parents who thought him a good match for their daughter, based on their snobbish notion that he was of their "class." Mary was receptive to the idea, even though Cranstoun was almost twice her age.

Cranstoun, who had a wife and two children in Scotland, actively pursued Mary, his eyes more on the dowry than the female. He was invited to stay with the Blandys and lived with them for more than a year, sending desperate letters to his wife, convincing her to sign an agreement whereby she disowned him. When he asked that she also have their marriage annulled, Mrs. Cranstoun absolutely refused, filing suit against her philandering spouse. When Francis Blandy discovered the existence of Cranstoun's wife through legal papers that arrived at his residence, the irate father ordered the rake from his home, denouncing him as an opportunist. Cranstoun first took a mistress and lived near the Blandys to taunt Mary, who was by then hopelessly in love with him. He finally dropped the mistress and returned to Scotland.

Then flowed a series of letters between Cranstoun and Mary Blandy, each pouring out their eternal love for each other. Cranstoun reportedly sent Mary a "love potion" which, he said, would cause her father to be more tender hearted toward him. Mary dosed her father's tea and gruel with this potion, later claiming that Cranstoun had suggested this method of administering the potion. Francis Blandy drank his tea and ate part of his gruel which was finished by some of his servants. All grew ill, with Blandy so stricken that he was bedridden. Doctors were called, among them Anthony Addington, a physician who had been studying the effects of poisons. He could not quite determine Blandy's ailment but suspected that the old man was being poisoned and blatantly told Mary that if her father died, she would undoubtedly be charged with murder.

Francis Blandy never got out of his bed. He worsened daily and, after physicians concluded he would die, Blandy called for his daughter. Mary, suspected by doctors and servants alike for causing her father's condition, pretended ignorance of the cause of her father's illness. Yet, oddly, when visiting her father at his deathbed, Mary begged him to forgive her, which he did, giving her his blessing on Aug. 14, 1751, when he died. Mary's mother died a short time later of natural causes, leaving Mary in total control of her father's vast estate. While she made plans to again see her lover Cranstoun, Mary's fate was being determined by a methodical physician. Dr. Addington convinced authorities, in a precedent-setting move, to allow him to exhume the body of Francis Blandy. Examining the corpse, Addington found white grams of arsenic in the victim's hair and in other parts of the body. By virtue of his discoveries, Mary was charged with murder and tried on Mar. 3, 1752.

Though Mary Blandy was well defended, many witnesses came forward to refute her claims of innocence, testifying that she had personally supervised the preparation of her father's fatal meal. Dr. Addington appeared in court and conducted the first forensic demonstration to prove that Francis Blandy had, indeed, been poisoned by arsenic—a crude but dramatic display that left the jury convinced that Mary had killed her loving father to be with the adventurer Cranstoun. She was found Guilty and then sentenced to be executed by hanging. As the product of the upper class, her execution drew enormous crowds at an open field near Oxford where a scaffold had been purposely erected to tower over the field so that the thousands frolicking and enjoying the grim spectacle could clearly see the hanging from any distance.

On Apr. 6, 1752, Mary Blandy showed great composure while being taken to the scaffold in an open cart, ignoring the jeers and catcalls from the rowdy spectators. She hobbled out of the cart when it reached the scaffold, encumbered by the leg irons she wore beneath her hooped skirt. As she struggled to climb the tall ladder to the platform, ruffians at the foot of the ladder attempted to look beneath her dress. This so unnerved her that when she reached the platform, to preserve her dignity to the last, the condemned woman said to her waiting executioners: "Gentlemen, don't hang me high, for the

Mary Blandy, wearing a leg iron, at her execution in 1752.

sake of decency." After the rope was placed around her neck, Mary Blandy placed a handkerchief over her face. Her body was left to dangle for some time to please the morbid crowd. She was later buried in the Blandy plot next to her parents.

Cranstoun, charged with conspiring to murder Francis Blandy by providing the arsenic used to kill him, fled from Scotland to France before officials could seize him. He took refuge in a monastery where he converted to the Catholic faith and issued statements that insisted upon his innocence. Cranstoun died of illness on Nov. 30, 1752, less than eight months after the love of his life went through the trap at Oxford. It was later revealed that Cranstoun's murder schemes would not have netted him the fortune he thought awaited him. Francis Blandy had lied; there was no £10,000 dowry. He had obviously advertised this fortune to bloat his own image as a rich landowner. His entire estate, it was announced following the deaths of all the Blandys, came to less than £4,000. Once Blandy had publicly stated that great riches awaited the lucky man who married his Mary, he went about the task of having to dissuade any suitor from claiming his daughter, lest his brag about the dowry be proven the lie it was. Thus, indirectly, Francis Blandy brought about his own dire end, and that of a daughter he loved, by creating a murderous greed for a fortune that did not exist. See: **Addington, Sir Anthony**.

REF.: Altick, *Victorian Studies in Scarlet;* Birmingham, *Murder Most Foul;* Brookes, *Murder in Fact and Fiction;* Butler, *Murderer's England;* CBA; de la Torre, *Villainy Detected;* Glaister, *The Power of Poison;* Gross, *Masterpieces of Murder;* Kobler, *Some Like It Gory;* Laurence, *A History of Capital Punishment;* Mencken, *By the Neck;* Mitchell, *The Newgate Calendar;* Nash, *Look for the Woman;* O'Donnell, *Should Women Hang?;* Parry, *Some Famous Medical Trials;* Potter, *The Art of Hanging;* Roughead, *Tales of the Criminous;* Stevens, *From Clue to Dock;* Thompson, *Poison and Poisoners;* Wilson, *Encyclopedia of Murder*.

Blanqui, Auguste (Louis-Auguste Blanqui), 1805-81, Fr., treas. Socialist and revolutionary leader skilled in the technique of military insurgency. He trained a band of guerilla fighters who later became known as Blanquists, and led an unsuccessful military coup in 1839 against King Louis Phillipe resulting in his capture and imprisonment for life. Pardoned in 1848, he resumed his revolutionary activity. In 1870 he led a revolt which placed the Third Republic in power, but Blanqui became quickly disillusioned with their conservative policy. He became the president of the notorious Paris Commune in 1871 which opposed the same government he helped establish. Blanqui spent a total of 33 years behind bars for his role in various political revolts. His theory of dictatorship of the proletariat was later adopted in Marxist ideology by Nikolai Lenin. REF.: *CBA*.

Blanther, Joseph (AKA: Archibald Forbes), 1859-98, U.S., suic.-mur. Joseph Blanther was a decorated Austrian war hero knighted by Emperor Franz Josef on Dec. 12, 1878, for gallantry in battle. For mysterious reasons he retired from the army and departed his native land, arriving in San Francisco Feb. 2, 1896, where he rented a room with the Hogan family who lived on Haight Street.

Blanther arrived in the U.S. with little money. To support himself, he engaged in petty swindles and borrowed small amounts of money from fellow lodgers. Then he met an aging dowager named Mrs. Philipini Langfeldt, a lonely woman who lived on Geary Street and flaunted her meager wealth in a way that suggested she possessed enormous riches.

Blanther was a charmer and Mrs. Langfeldt felt flattered by his fawning attentions. He

Murderer Joseph Blanther.

spoke of his military exploits at length and never missed an opportunity to display his medals, while secretly making plans to murder the lady and steal her jewels.

He got his chance on May 15, 1896. Invited by Langfeldt, Blanther entered her rooming house unobserved, though several of the tenants recalled hearing loud laughter coming from Mrs. Langfeldt's room. The next day a servant named Susie Miller found Mrs. Langfeldt dead in the room, her neck slashed and five of her valuable rings missing. Tenants in the house who knew she had been seeing Blanther reported their suspicions to the police, but he had already left San Francisco by train and assumed an alias Archibald Forbes. The Austrian consulate confirmed for the police that Blanther's military claims were legitimate. The greater mystery was why a distinguished war hero would have fled his country to murder an old woman in the U.S.

The Pinkerton Detective Agency circulated a photo of Blanther found in a Chicago gallery. Nearly two years later, on Mar. 2, 1898, a county official in Meridian, Texas, reported to the local sheriff that the photo strongly resembled the Koppearl schoolmaster, Mr. Forbes. He was taken into custody and jailed pending arraignment. A few hours later his jailers looked into his the cell and found that Blanther had committed suicide. He had swallowed a capsule of potassium cyanide hidden under his hat band. The schoolmaster evidently had prepared himself for just such a day.

REF.: *CBA;* Duke, *Celebrated Criminal Cases of America.*

Blanton, Ray, 1930-   , U.S., polit. corr.-mail fraud-consp.-extor. When Ray Blanton gained the governorship of Tennessee in 1974, he was viewed as a folk hero. The plain-spoken Democrat from southwestern Tennessee grew up in poverty not far from where Sheriff Buford Pusser established a reputation as an incorruptible lawman.

During his gubernatorial campaign Blanton ran on an anti-Watergate, anti-corruption platform. Once in office, though, he evidently believed his position gave him the right to do as he pleased. "I'd say, 'Governor, you can't do that. It's not constitutional'," recalled lobbyist Nelson Biddle. "And I'd get this icy-blue stare and he'd say, 'I *can* do it. I'm the governor.' That would be the end of it."

What Blanton did the night before he left office was sign clemency papers for fifty-two state prisoners including twenty-four convicted murderers. The scheme was hatched by six aides including Blanton's legal counsel Thomas Sisk and William Aubrey Thompson, a former Democratic committeeman in Hamilton County. A highway patrolman and security officer on the governor's staff named Charles Taylor used his position to locate prison inmates willing to pay upwards of $15,000 to secure their release. "These people I'm fronting for have a product to sell," one of the bagmen said, his comments recorded through secret FBI tapes. "This is the only game in town."

The investigation into parole selling came to light on Dec. 18, 1978, when Blanton was subpoenaed by a federal grand jury. The scandal escalated, and the governor was forced out of office in January 1979, three days before the end of his term. Incoming governor Lamar Alexander took office early and immediately put a freeze on the last-minute pardons and commutations Blanton had signed as his last official act.

The ex-governor managed to avoid prison at the time, but was convicted by a federal jury in June 1981 for selling state liquor licenses and skimming twenty per cent of the profits in a cleverly disguised kickback scheme. Blanton and two of his former aides were indicted in a twelve-count indictment charging them with conspiracy, mail fraud, racketeering, and tax evasion.

Summing up the life and career of this controversial public figure, Nelson Biddle recalled, "Governor Blanton was the last of the old southern machine politicians. He played hardball politics. You were loyal to your friends and tough on your enemies, and if you got the votes, then you called the shots." REF.: *CBA*.

Blaskowitz, Johannes, 1883-1948, Ger., war crimes. Field marshal who led the Nazi Eighth Army into Poland in 1939 where he observed the atrocities committed against Jews and Polish dissidents. He issued a protest to Adolf Hitler, but this was not seriously considered by the war crimes tribunal convened after the

German-Japanese surrender. He was accused of butchering civilians and prisoners-of-war in Poland, and faced a possible death sentence. He committed suicide in a Nüremberg prison. REF.: *CBA*.

Blastares, Matthew, prom. 14th Cent., Byzantium, jur. Author of an influential volume setting forth civil and ecclesiastical laws entitled Syntagma kata stoicheion (1335) which was later adopted for use by the Slavic countries. REF.: *CBA*.

Blatchford, Samuel Milford, 1820-93, U.S., jur. Judge of the District Court for the Southern District of New York from 1867-72, appointed by President Andrew Johnson, and judge of the Second Circuit Court of New York in 1878. He was appointed associate Supreme Court justice by President Chester Arthur in 1882 to replace Ward Hunt who resigned. In 1892, he submitted the majority opinion in Counselman vs. Hitchcock which established the precedent that the Fifth Amendment can be waived only if the witness or litigant is guaranteed absolute immunity against all future prosecutions from future actions of a similar nature. He reported extensively on various court decisions over the years, gaining early notoriety with the *Argument of William H. Seward in Defense of William Freeman on His Trial For Murder* (1846). He served as personal secretary to William Seward and then as a partner in his law firm. His opinion concerning the case of François Farey on a writ of habeas corpus, New York 1869, was also published as a legal paper. REF.: *CBA*.

Blazek, Frank, 1906-40, U.S., mur. Born in Austria, Frank Blazek moved to New York City and went to work in the city water works department. He was a brooding intellectual, fond of poetry and classical Viennese music, all of which impressed 16-year-old Virginia Bender. Blazek, twenty-eight, was sophisticated and worldly. They became engaged in 1936 but her parents wanted Virginia to finish her schooling before she married.

During their two-year engagement Blazek's jealousy and possessiveness finally got the best of her. Virginia called off the engagement and moved away. A year later Blazek read in the newspaper about her impending engagement and called her on June 5, 1939, to wish her luck. "Do you mean that?" she asked. "You bet I do," he said. "You're going to need luck."

On June 19 Blazek purchased a hunting knife at an Army-Navy surplus store on 125th Street. He proceeded to her apartment on 137th Street in the Bronx where he stabbed and killed her. Then he covered her with a blanket, because, as he later explained, the sight of blood repulsed him.

Bender's fiancé appeared in the vestibule a short time later and Blazek, peering through a crack in the door, told him to go away. Detective-Captain Glen Armstrong of the Bronx Police was summoned and not long afterwards the Viennese killer was arrested. He confessed to Assistant District Attorney Martin Klaus and was tried, condemned, and executed in the electric chair on Sept. 11, 1940.

REF.: *CBA*; Wilson, *Encyclopedia of Murder*.

Blazes, Albert, d.1926, Case of, U.S., rape-lynch. In Wilson, Ark., a black man named Albert Blazes was accused, based on hearsay evidence, of sexually assaulting a young white woman. Needing a scapegoat, the sheriff and two deputies turned the bloodhounds loose in the fields. Blazes was captured on May 30, 1926, and dragged to a deserted barn where he remained under the watchful eye of the sheriff until a lynch mob arrived. It was another typical southern lynching with one new twist: several members of the lynch mob were women. REF.: *CBA*.

Bleak House, 1852, a novel by Charles Dickens. In this novel Dickens profiles a murderous French maid named Hortense who is undoubtedly based upon Swiss-born Maria Manning, a maid who, with her husband Frederick, murdered a wealthy money lender (Brit., 1847) and was subsequently hanged before more than 50,000 people, with Dickens himself in the crowd recording the traumatic scene. See: **Manning, Frederick and Maria**. REF.: *CBA*.

Blémant, Robert, d.1965, Fr., org. crime.-(unsolv.) mur. Robert Blémant, a former French police superintendent from Marseilles,

abandoned his career in law enforcement to become the right-hand man of organized crime boss Antoine Guérini. When Robert Blémant challenged his benefactor for leadership of the criminal underworld, he was assassinated while sitting behind the wheel of his Mercedes in May 1965.

REF.: *CBA*; Heppenstall, *The Sex War and Others*.

Blennerhassett, Harman, 1765-1831, U.S., consp. In 1805, he schemed with Aaron Burr, James Wilkinson, and others to illegally seize land in Spanish America and establish a separate republic. He was arrested in 1806, but was never tried. See: **Burr, Aaron**. REF.: *CBA*.

Blevins Family, prom. 1880s, U.S., west. outl. The Blevins family, five brothers, assorted cousins and nephews, were deeply involved in the Arizona range war of the 1880s called the Graham-Tewksbury Feud. All were ranchers located in Pleasant Valley, but most of the clan members doubled as hired gunmen, and some of them were dedicated killers like Andy Blevins, who was also known as Andy Cooper. Andy Blevins was a rustler and killer who hired out to the Grahams cattlemen who were battling the sheep herders headed by the Tewksburys. On Sept. 2, 1887, Andy Blevins led some of his brothers and other cattlemen on a night ambush of the Tewksbury sheep camp, shooting clan leaders John Tewksbury and Bill Jacobs in cold blood as the sheepmen went to check on their horses. Mrs. Tewksbury raced from the house to go to her fallen husband, but Andy Blevins fired several shots at her to drive her away. The sheepmen then came under siege from the Blevins faction and later slipped away under the cover of darkness. Andy Blevins was so angry about the other sheepmen eluding him that he allowed some starving hogs to eat the bodies of Tewksbury and Jacobs.

Sheriff Perry Owens, one of the deadliest shots in the West, then gathered a posse and rode out to the Blevins ranch near Holbrook on Sept. 4, 1887. He advanced on the ranch house with a rifle in his hand, apparently intending to serve warrants on Andy Blevins for the murder of Tewksbury and Jacobs. At that moment, Andy Blevins fired at Owens from behind the front door of the ranch house but his shot was wild. Owns fired a rifle shot that smashed into Blevins' chest and sent him reeling backward into the arms of his mother. Then John Blevins, the oldest brother, stepped to the door and fired at Owens; the lawmen's responding fire brought him down, too. Mose Roberts, a brother-in-law of the Blevins, then raced outside, firing rapidly at Owens, but the sheriff brought him down with a single, mortal shot. Next, 16-year-old Sam Houston Blevins charged toward Owens with a blazing sixgun, and the sheriff fired one shot that killed the boy on the spot. Only John Blevins survived this gunfight.

Another brother, Charles Blevins, was shot to death in front of Perkins Store in Holbrook on Sept. 27, 1887, when he opened fire on Sheriff William Mulveron who returned fire and killed him. Hampton Blevins had already been killed on Aug. 10, 1887, in another shootout at the Middleton ranch. Except for John Blevins, the Blevins family members were decimated in the bloody Graham-Tewksbury Feud. John Blevins later became a lawman and helped chase the Apache Kid in 1889 after the Kid had murdered Sheriff Glenn Reynolds. See: **Apache Kid, The; Graham-Tewksbury Feud**.

REF.: Bartholomew, *The Biographical Album of Western Gunfighters*; Breihan, *Great Gunfighters of the West;* ____, *Great Lawmen of the West; CBA;* Coolidge, *Fighting Men of the West;* Drago, *Great Range Wars;* O'Neal, *Encyclopedia of Western Gunfighters;* Raine, *Famous Sheriffs and Western Outlaws*.

Blin, George, prom. 19th Cent., Fr., pris. esc. George Blin employed deception and countless disguises to break free of his jailers. Twenty times police arrested this notorious French criminal, and twenty times he escaped from prison. One time he casually told the arresting detective to expect a social call from him as soon as he was able to get away. The policeman thought no more about the matter until he came home one day and found his house burgled. Blin had left behind a receipt for the money he had stolen.

REF.: *CBA;* Kingston, *A Gallery of Rogues.*

Bliss, George Miles, prom. 1870s, U.S., rob. During the corrupt reign of New York City Mayor William Marcy Tweed, George Bliss organized the city's leading bankrobbers and certain corrupt policemen into a powerful syndicate that shared the spoils of stolen cash and securities.

Bliss and his one-time partner Mark Shinburn came to the attention of U.S. and Canadian police when they robbed a savings bank in Saint Catherines, Ontario, and escaped across Niagara Falls by fastening two clotheslines and three pairs of horse reins around their waists. While the border patrol stood guard on top of the only bridge crossing the treacherous waters, the robbers negotiated their way inch by inch, suspended by girders underneath the bridge. They made it, though the experience was a sobering one and Shinburn decided to retire from the business. With his proceeds from the heist he settled down in Germany where by all accounts he became very successful.

Bliss continued in his criminal ways, elevating bank robbery to a precise science. He invented a tiny lock pick which he dubbed the "Little Joker," for its uncanny ability to open any safe, no matter how tricky the combination. The "Little Joker" soon became the scourge of the New York banking world. Bliss introduced the device to several of the city's top officials, including Boss Tweed who was beginning to feel the heat of reform elements for his years of rapacious rule.

To throw the reformers off the scent, Bliss proposed to the mayor that Detective Jim Irving—a man who would "go along" —be promoted to a captaincy so that the leading bank forgers and robbers, united in a fraternity, could pay a percentage of their take to the police and the corrupt city administration for protection. Sneak thieves soon cavorted around town like princes, decked out in fine evening wear and dining in the luxurious dining rooms of the leading hotels near Broadway.

In 1869 Bliss pulled off the biggest caper of his career, the $2.75 million robbery of the Ocean Bank on Fulton Street. Police officers from Irving on down were paid in excess of $132,300 for their silence and cooperation.

The "Bank Ring" lasted even after Tweed went to jail in 1873. Not until Thomas Byrnes became chief of detectives did the long process of weeding out the grafters begin. By this time Bliss was behind bars for his role in the robbery of the Barre Bank of Vermont.

REF.: *CBA;* Demaris, *Captive City;* Hamilton, *Men of the Underworld.*

Blondel (Blondel de Nesle), prom. 12th Cent., Fr., troubadour. According to legend, he located Richard, Coeur de Lion in a prison by singing a verse of a song they had written together. Richard answered by singing the second verse inside the prison walls. REF.: *CBA.*

Blonger, Louis (Lou), prom. 1890s-1920s, U.S., fraud. A French-Canadian, Louis Blonger migrated to Denver, Colo., where he and his brother Sam opened a rowdy saloon in 1880. Blonger offered gambling of all sorts and platoons of strumpets to service customers. When Denver cleaned up its gambling dens and bordellos, Blonger concentrated on confidence games of all kinds, becoming the bunco king of the Rocky Mountain states. He was assisted by Adolph W. Duff, a wily sharper known as Kid Duffy. Blonger made substantial payoffs to the infant, corrupt Denver Police Department (DPD) and, by the turn of the century, most of the force, including the chief of police, was on his payroll. He was the most powerful man in the city, king of the Denver underworld, with direct phone lines from his office to that of the mayor and the chief of police. There was nothing Blonger could not fix in the city. If any con man in his phalanx of swindlers was caught red-handed, Blonger would simply make a call and the man would be put on a train, returning to Denver when it was safe to do so.

Rules established by Blonger were strictly obeyed by his men. No swindler could pull a "Big Store" game unless Blonger gave his approval and no violence was tolerated. Prominent Denver citizens were to be left alone and visitors to the city were the only suckers his men were allowed to victimize, and these marks could be chosen only after they had been cleared with Blonger and the police department. Blonger spent a good deal of time on the phone with DPD Police Chief Mike Delaney, discussing what victims were or were not

Denver crime boss Lou Blonger.

suitable to be fleeced. Whenever one of Blonger's men violated any of his dictates, he was fined or even banished from the city. After Dick Turner, a deputy sheriff from a small town near Denver, was fleeced in a short con while visiting the city, Blonger upbraided the con man for not getting approval to "take the mark." Then the con man was banished forever from the precincts of Denver.

Blonger's reputation as the top con man of the West was known nationwide in the underworld and hundreds of the most daring and notorious con men in the country flocked to his banners, including the celebrated Joe Furey, Reno Hamlin, Charles Gerber, and the legendary Jefferson Randolph "Soapy" Smith. Furey, who ran a gang of con men of his own, made the mistake in 1920 of fleecing a Texas cattleman and one-time sheriff, J. Frank Norfleet, bilking $45,000 from Norfleet in an investment scheme. When Norfleet discovered that he had been mulcted, he exploded and tracked down every member of the con ring. The classic manhunt eventually caused Blonger's downfall. Because of Norfleet's persistent campaign against the Denver Ring, Blonger, Duff, and dozens of their top con men were rounded up, tried, and sent to prison. See: **Norfleet, J. Frank.**

REF.: *CBA;* Cooper, *Ten Thousand Public Enemies;* Nash, *Hustlers and Con Men;* Van Cise, *Fighting the Underworld.*

Blood, Thomas, c.1618-80, Brit., rob. Born in Ireland, Blood was the son of a blacksmith and his life was full of intrigue and adventure—both real and imagined. During England's Civil War, beginning in 1642, he served in the Parliamentary forces of Cromwell and rose through dashing battle feats to the rank of colonel. He later obtained forfeited estates which gave him a yearly income of £500. He subsequently lost these estates and the lucrative income which turned him into an ardent Republican. He led an abortive coup to overthrow the crown in Ireland by seizing Dublin Castle and capturing the Duke of Ormonde in 1663. Defeated, Blood fled to Holland where he went into hiding. Blood became a legendary conspirator, involved in the plots of the Fifth Monarchy Men in London and the revolutionary Conventeers of Scotland. In 1666, he fought in the battle of Pentland Hills but he managed to escape, as usual. Blood's successive and miraculous escapes from these conspiracies and other misadventures, led most to believe that he had been allowed to flee by government officials who had made a secret pact with him: his freedom in exchange for information about the rebels with whom he worked.

The notorious Colonel Blood.

In 1671, Blood put together the most fantastic plot of his life, the stealing of the British Crown Jewels from the Tower of London. Oliver Cromwell had stolen the jewels in 1649 after Charles I had been executed and, upon their recovery, great care was shown in protecting the royal heirlooms from ever being stolen again. The jewels consisted of crowns, state swords, scepters, orbs—spurs of chivalry which were all in gold and silver and richly ornamented and inlaid with rare gems. These priceless jewels had been placed in the Tower of London with a strong and loyal detachment of guards ordered to protect the jewels around the clock from any thief so bold as to attempt to steal them. That thief was none other than the daring Colonel Blood. In April 1671, Talbot and Dolly Edwards, official caretakers of the jewels who lived in the Martin Tower rooms directly above the heavily guarded jewel room, were approached by a traveling minister and his wife. The Edwards couple were obligated to show the jewels to distinguished visitors, and they conducted a tour of the jewel room for the visiting clergyman and his wife.

The clergyman and his wife befriended the Edwards couple and the minister stated that he knew of a wealthy young man who would be a good suitor for the Edwards' daughter. When next he visited the Tower, the parson promised, he would bring the young man along. The Edwards couple delighted in the prospect of meeting the young man. The parson returned on May 9, 1671, bringing along two friends and telling Edwards that his newphew, the young suitor, would be along shortly. Said the parson: "Until he gets here, why don't we visit the jewel room? My friends are most anxious to see the ensigns of the king." Once inside the jewel room, the parson, who was none other than Colonel Blood, seized the gullible Talbot Edwards while his two friends tried to bind him with ropes. Edwards struggled and Blood pulled out a mallet and struck the caretaker on the head three times, knocking him unconscious. Then a gag was stuffed in Edwards' mouth and he was tied to a pillar.

Blood and his two fellow thieves then began to steal the most valuable jewels in the room. The Colonel used his mallet to smash the largest crown flat so that it would fit in his pouch. The second man slipped the royal orb into a large pocket in his coat. The royal scepter was too long to conceal so the third man quickly filed the scepter into halves and slipped these into the specially made pockets of his cloak. Just as the filing of the scepter was completed, the alarm was given and guards swarmed through the many passageways of the Tower. Blood and his two friends dashed from the jewel room and down flights of stairs, slipping past guards going upward. The guards thought the three men were officials also looking for the thieves. Blood and his men got to the main gate where their horses awaited them, held by a confederate. Mounting, they rode wildly away with a detachment of guards riding after them. The thief carrying the orb found the gold ball too cumbersome to carry and threw it into a large crowd which had assembled along the escape route. Then he dismounted his horse and vanished.

Blood rode on but the leather pouch holding the crown slipped from his saddle horn and he stopped to retrieve it. As he did so, the mounted guards overtook him and there was a wild swordfight which saw Blood disarmed and taken prisoner. He was taken back to the Tower and imprisoned there, along with the other three men. The jewels were recovered and guarded night and day by special soldiers who were stationed inside the jewel room as well as outside. Blood refused to cooperate with his captors, telling them that he would not answer any questions "unless they are put to me by the king himself." When King Charles II was told of this, he was as staggered by the arrogance of Blood's demands as he was by the daring robbery. The king could not resist meeting the adventurer who was expected to be executed.

King Charles went to the Tower and visited with the bold Colonel Blood, listening to his eloquent explanation for attempting the robbery. The amazing thief told the king that in taking the Crown Jewels he was merely retaliating against an oppressive system that had wrongfully deprived him of his estates. Charles was so enthralled by the colorful Blood that he not only reprieved him from the gallows but pardoned him and his companions. The king restored Blood's estates and even awarded the great conspirator with a pension of £300 a year (some said as a bribe to

Blood for not continuing his conspiratorial ways). Charles' generosity did little to curb Blood's appetite for intrigues and plots. He continued to be involved in all manner of conspiracies. When he died on Aug. 24, 1680, Blood was deeply enmeshed in a lawsuit brought against him by the Duke of Buckingham.

REF.: Birkenhead, *Famous Trials of History;* Brock, *A Casebook of Crime; CBA;* Gollomb, *Master Highwaymen;* Hunt, *A Dictionary of Rogues;* Hyams, *Killing No Murder;* Nash, *Almanac of World Crime;* Scott, *The Concise Encyclopedia of Crime and Criminals.*

Bloody Sunday Massacre, 1905, Rus., mob vio. On Sunday, Jan. 22, 1905, thousands of striking workers in St. Petersburg, led by a priest, Father George A. Gapon, filed down the streets of the capital, bearing a petition for the czar. This petition, signed by tens of thousands of workers, listed their grievances and hopes for the future. A peaceful demonstration, the workers, with Gapon at their head, were met by mounted Cossack troops, as well as army units, cadets, and police as they approached the czar's Winter Palace. As the thousands of workers entered the square before the palace, the troops opened fire and ninety-two workers were killed and hundreds wounded, by official count. (The true number was probably three to four times that.) The workers fled in panic.

The massacre did much to damage the credibility of Nicholas II and, more than any event up to that time, galvanized workers into taking a radical stand against the czarist government. Bolsheviks found willing new recruits by the thousands for their cause because of the senseless St. Petersburg slaughter, an act on the part of his troops that Nicholas neither authorized nor knew about, according to most reliable reports. Yet the irreparable political damage was done and, as a result, massive strikes occurred in St. Petersburg, Moscow, Odessa, and elsewhere. The massacre gave vent to more demands from liberal upper class and aristocratic leaders for a constitutional assembly, which came about later in 1905—a further erosion of the czar's absolute powers. Worsening the situation and stigmatizing the czar as inhuman and unfeeling was the fact that he made no public comment denouncing the act of the military as his most able adviser, Count Sergius Witte, had urged. Nicholas believed at the time that, though no order had been given to fire on the workers, he would be casting aspersions on the army if he denounced their actions—a lethal blunder, as the czar would later learn. See: **Bolshevik Riots; Nicholas II.**

REF.: Almedingen, *The Romanovs; CBA;* Dmytryshyn, *Imperial Russia: A Source Book, 1700-1917;* ____, *USSR, A Concise History;* Fischer, *Russian Liberalism;* Florinsky, *Russia: A History and an Interpretation;* Haimson, *The Russian Marxists and the Origins of Bolshevism;* Jorre, *The Soviet Union, The Land and Its People;* Karpovich, *Imperial Russia, 1801-1917;* Kornilov, *Modern Russian History;* Levin, *The Second Duma;* Longworth, *The Cossacks;* Masaryk, *The Spirit of Russia;* Massie, *Nicholas and Alexandra;* Mayor, *The Economic History of Russia;* Meyer, *Leninism;* Miliukov, *History of Russia;* ____, *Russia and Its Crisis;* Miller, *The Economic Development of Russia, 1905-1914;* Pares, *The Fall of the Russian Monarchy;* ____, *Russia and Reform;* Pearlstien, *Revolution in Russia!;* Pushkarev, *The Emergence of Modern Russia, 1801-1917;* Riasanovsky, *A History of Russia;* Seton-Watson, *The Decline of Imperial Russia, 1855-1914;* Tompkins, *The Russian Intelligentsia;* Ulam, *The Bolsheviks;* Venturi, *Roots of Revolution;* Walsh, *Russia and the Soviet Union;* Wolfe, *Three Who Made a Revolution;* Yarmolinsky, *Road to Revolution.*

Bloom, David, 1965- , U.S., embez.-fraud. David Bloom very much wanted to live the fast life along the avenues of the trendy upper West Side of Manhattan. After he graduated from Duke University with a degree in art history, the somber dark-haired youth purchased a deluxe condominium for $830,000 and many rare works of art valued at $5 million. Among items in his collection were paintings by Edward Hopper, John Singer Sargent, and Willem de Kooning. The *New York Times Magazine* and other leading publications profiled young David Bloom, and praised him as an up-and-coming art investor.

What no one knew was that his condo, the art work, and other trappings of Bloom's glamorous life were purchased with other people's money. After completing his college education he had formed his own company which he called the Greater Sutton Investor's Group. Encouraged by his reputed financial acumen, gullible investors, including close friends, parted with $10 million within two years, believing that Bloom would double their money. Instead, he used the funds to live the high life.

U.S. Securities and Exchange officials became suspicious after reading about his exploits in the press. Bloom had donated $20,000 to his alma mater as part of a $1 million pledge to the school. His penchant for showing off helped spring the trap which eventually resulted in his conviction and imprisonment on a charge of mail fraud. Hounded by the SEC, the young investor agreed to an out-of-court settlement with his investors. His paintings, real estate holdings, and various other items from the collection were sold off and the proceeds divided among them. Bloom's attorney, Peter Morrison, argued that his customers actually profited from the transactions, for had he invested their money in stocks as they originally intended him to, all of the money would have been lost in the stock market crash of Oct. 19, 1987. Some of the art work in the collection had appreciated in value during this time.

Two days after Bloom agreed to the settlement he was indicted on one count of mail fraud and one count of securities fraud. In April 1989, U.S. District Judge David Edelstein upheld a sentence of two four-year terms at the federal prison camp in Allenwood, Pa. The harshness of the sentence shocked observers, but the judge pointed out that Bloom had unconscionably bilked his own friends and relatives, while other investment swindlers often victimize nameless, faceless investors. REF.: *CBA*.

Bloom, Ike, d.1930, U.S., pros. Ike Bloom was a notorious white slaver and whoremaster in Chicago who first came to the notice of police when, in 1903, he bought an interest in Freiberg's, the worst bordello in the Levee, the city's red light district. Bloom's partner in this operation was his brother-in-law, Solly Freiberg. This place was for years the worst fleshpot in the city where hundreds of women sauntered through the sprawling rooms, serving drinks with knock-out drops and jackrolling customers in plain sight. Others charged $1 for a quick trip to a crib in the back rooms, with Bloom receiving fifty percent of everything these ignorant, diseased women made. Bloom paid police handsomely to operate without interference, but so many complaints piled up against Freiberg's that the place was repeatedly closed, its liquor license revoked, only to be reinstated when Bloom went to his politician friends with envelopes stuffed with cash.

Freiberg's was closed by Mayor Carter Harrison on Aug. 24, 1914, after he had received a petition signed by more than 18,000 people complaining about the hellhole. Included in the petition were scores of signatures of women who actually worked there. It reopened with the election of William Hale Thompson, who, as mayor, promised that Chicago would be "a wide open town." Bloom became a slavish vassal to crime boss James "Big Jim" Colosimo, boss of the Levee and its myriad whorehouses, gambling dives, and opium dens. In time, Bloom became Big Jim's whoremaster and supervised hundreds of brothels in the city. He became rich in this position and considered himself a bon vivant, always well but loudly tailored, and accompanied by the towering, buxom prostitutes he liked to introduce as his "nieces and wards."

After Colosimo was murdered by a young thug from Brooklyn, Al Capone (at the connivance and with the blessings of Colosimo's nephew, Johnny Torrio), Bloom made one of his last public appearances, delivering the eulogy at Big Jim's funeral. "There wasn't a piker's hair on Big Jim's head," Bloom intoned before a large throng. "Whatever game he played, he shot straight. He wasn't greedy. There could be dozens of others getting theirs. The more the merrier as far as he was concerned. He had what a lot of us haven't got—class! He brought the society swells and the millionaires into the red light district. It helped everybody, and a lot of places kept alive on Colosimo's overflow. Big Jim never bilked a pal or turned down a good guy and he always kept his mouth shut." As a one-time Colosimo crony, Bloom fell into disfavor with Torrio and later with Capone, and was allowed

through the 1920s to operate a few bordellos, but his influence and position had vanished. Bloom grew ill in 1929 and, after having both legs amputated, he died the following year. No one gave a eulogy at his funeral. See: **Capone, Alphonse; Colosimo, James; Torrio, John.**

REF.: Asbury, *Gem of the Prairie; CBA;* Demaris, *Captive City;* Kobler, *Capone;* Lait and Mortimer, *Chicago Confidential;* Landesco, *Organized Crime in Chicago;* McPhaul, *Johnny Torrio;* Reppetto, *The Blue Parade.*

Blot, Henri, prom. 20th Cent., Fr., necro. Twenty-six-year-old Frenchman Henri Blot entered the Saint-Ouen cemetery one night to violate the corpse of a recently deceased ballerina. After completing the sexual act with the remains, he fell into a trance-like state and had to be awakened by cemetery guards the next day. This phenomenon has been observed in other necrophiliacs. In this case Blot, when brought before the magistrate, showed no outward guilt or remorse for what he had done.

REF.: *CBA;* Masters, *Perverse Crimes In History.*

Blount, James Henderson, 1837-1903, U.S., lawyer. While serving as special commissioner to Hawaii in 1893, his investigation revealed that certain Americans had instigated a revolution that toppled the regime of the popular Queen Liliuokalani. This action established Hawaii as a U.S. protectorate. He ordered the U.S. flag lowered to half-mast, a controversial decision which was supported by President Grover Cleveland. REF.: *CBA.*

Blount, John, See: **South Sea Bubble.**

Bluebeard, See: **Landru, Henri Desire.**

Outlaw Blue Duck, with wife Belle Starr.

Blue Duck, prom. 1880s, U.S., west. outl. Blue Duck was a half-breed lover of Belle Starr's who was under a sentence of death for murdering a farmer in the Indian Nations in 1886. Scheduled to die on July 23, 1886, at Fort Smith, Blue Duck was saved through the actions of his common-law wife, Belle Starr, who hired a lawyer. The lawyer managed to get Blue Duck several reprieves and later a commutation to life imprisonment at the federal penitentiary in Menard, Ill. Blue Duck was later paroled, but by then Belle Starr, a horsethief, had been shot and killed. See: **Starr, Belle**.

REF.: Aikman, *Calamity Jane and the Lady Wildcats;* Bartholomew, *The Biographical Album of Western Gunfighters;* CBA; Croy, *Last of the Great Outlaws;* Drago, *Outlaws on Horseback;* ____, *Red River Valley;* Elman, *Fired in Anger;* Glasscock, *Then Came Oil;* Hagen, *Indian Police;* Harman, *Belle Starr;* Harrington, *Hanging Judge;* Hicks, *Belle Starr and Her Pearl;* Holloway, *Texas Gun Lore;* Horan and Sann, *Pictorial History of the Wild West;* Hunter and Rose, *Album of Gunfighters;* Rascoe, *Belle Starr;* Scott, *Belle Starr in Velvet;* Shackleford, *Belle Starr, The Bandit Queen;* Shirley, *Henry Starr, Last of the Real Badmen;* ____, *Law West of Fort Smith;* ____, *Outlaw Queen;* Sutton, *Hands Up!;* White, *Lead and Likker.*

Bluestone, Jesse, prom. 1910, and **Mosenson, Samuel**, b.1885, U.S., wh. slav. Following the passage of the Mann Act in 1910, numerous prosecutions of men and women engaged in the notorious white slave trade took place. One of the most famous trials of that period occurred in November 1910, in Pittsburgh, Pa.

Jesse Bluestone was a Russian immigrant who had lived in the U.S. about nineteen years. Before his conviction on a Mann Act violation he served in the Pennsylvania legislature. "The fact that a man of such character could be elected to help make laws for Pennsylvania is a revelation of the influences which sway our politics and is perhaps explanatory of some of the phenomena of our legislation," declared the Pittsburgh *Dispatch* in an editorial on Nov. 26.

Bluestone's accomplice was Samuel Mosenson, who courted the victim, a young woman named Ethel. Pretending to be wealthy, Mosenson lured Ethel to Cleveland where they were to elope. At the train station in Pittsburgh she was met by Sadie Golden, the owner of a bordello on Second Avenue. Golden told the young woman that Mosenson unexpectedly had gone on ahead, and she was to chaperon the girl to Cleveland where he and Ethel would rendezvous.

They arrived in Cleveland and lingered for several days until her suitor sent word for them to come to Chicago, where he had urgent business. The unsuspecting woman took the train with Golden to Chicago where her money was stolen and she was sold into prostitution at a Dearborn Street bordello in the South Side levee district.

Through cunning and guile, Ethel managed to escape. She made her way back to Pittsburgh and told her story to the police. By this time Golden had fled the country. Mosenson and Bluestone were put on trial and convicted of white slavery on Nov. 24. "Mr. Bluestone came and told me (to marry him)...," the woman sobbed. "He said I would be rich, for he said Sam was rich." See: **Mann, James**.

REF.: *CBA;* Roe, *Great War on White Slavery.*

Bluffstein, Sophie (AKA: **The Golden Hand**), 1854-91, Rus., fraud. A beautiful, dark-haired woman, Sophie Bluffstein married a banker but deserted him when his investments began to fail. With money she had filched from her husband's accounts, Bluffstein posed as a wealthy woman, taking the best suites in the best hotels in Europe. She traveled to Paris, Vienna, London, St. Petersburg, always employing the same type of fraud. Wearing exquisite jewelry and accompanied by liveried servants, Bluffstein would visit the most famous jewelers and select rare and priceless gems. These were delivered to her hotel suites but payment was not demanded. The custom then was, when jewelers dealt with royalty and the wealthy, to wait a discreet period of time, sometimes as much as a week, before presenting the bill, lest they offend the purchaser with crass demands for money. Knowing well this custom, Bluffstein would obtain the gems, then check out of her hotel suite the next day, assuming another identity and going on to another capital of Europe.

Bluffstein was exposed while trying to fleece a jeweler in Smollensk, Rus., her native city. She was thrown into prison, but she quickly seduced the warden, convincing him not only to let her escape but to leave his wife and children and flee with her. She deserted the warden and suddenly became enamored of radical political parties in Russia. While police were sweeping an illegal political gathering, Bluffstein was arrested as a political subversive, and her criminal record was unearthed during interrogation. Bluffstein was sent to Siberia and locked up in Androvsk Prison. So bewitching was Sophie Bluffstein that her jailors were given strict orders never to enter her cell. She was kept handcuffed for more than two years. When released, Bluffstein settled in Vladivostok where she opened a popular inn. She spent the rest of her short days regaling customers with her extravagant confidence games and swindles, dying at the age of thirty-seven in 1891.

REF.: *CBA;* Nash, *Look for the Woman.*

Blum, Robert, 1807-48, Ger., treas. Founder of the German Catholic Movement. He led the leftist student movement and served as vice president of the Frankfurt National Assembly 1848. After delivering a speech in support of the democratic insurgents in Vienna in 1848 he was arrested and shot. REF.: *CBA.*

Blumen, Julius (Julius Busch), b.1896, and **Blumen, Leopold (Ludwig Busch)**, b.1898, U.S., embez. One of the most baffling cases of Samuel T. Maccubbin's long career as an insurance investigator involved two debonair brothers who advertised themselves as wizards in the world of international finance.

Julius and Leopold Blumen were citizens of Poland who arrived in San Francisco in July 1924 seeking employment in the foreign exchange department of several major banks. Under the assumed name of Busch, the brothers presented their credentials to the Bank of Italy where Julius went to work, and the Anglo-California Bank which hired Leopold several weeks later. Their manner was graceful, and their knowledge of foreign currencies was as good as their credentials claimed. Soon they became trusted employees and were assigned major accounts. Slowly the brothers wormed their way into high society where they gained the trust and admiration of the Nob Hill elite. No one suspected that they were embezzlers.

Suddenly, Julius Blumen quit his job after fourteen months, citing salary differences with his supervisor. Leopold followed suit at his bank several weeks later. The bank managers were sorry to see them go, but there was little they could say. Three months later an audit was conducted on Julius' accounts. To the bank examiners' horror numerous false entries and the theft of bonds going back to the beginning of his employment were uncovered.

The same pattern of embezzlement was detected at the Anglo-California Bank where Leopold worked. The stolen bonds and securities collectively totaled $109,000. Their apartments were thoroughly searched but the brothers had decamped months earlier, leaving behind a box of rubbish and several suits with the labels cleverly torn out. The only clue that surfaced during the investigation was the testimony of a baggage handler who recalled shipping the brothers' luggage on the eastbound Southern Pacific Overland train.

In desperation the police turned to Sammy Maccubbin, whose firm, the Fidelity and Deposit Company, was vitally interested in recovering its own losses. Maccubbin returned to the apartment house and demanded to look through the "rubbish" the brothers left behind. The police said they had already done so and found nothing. The insurance man persisted. At the bottom of the carton he found a pair of shoe trees with the name Blumen scratched into the side. Through immigration records the identity of the embezzlers was revealed.

He traced their path eastward through Detroit, Pittsburgh, New York, and across the ocean to Liverpool. In London, Maccubbin interviewed a score of postmen before hitting pay dirt. "Sir, I know where they live," one man said. In the company of Scotland Yard investigators the brothers were arrested on May 1, 1926. More than $60,000 in stolen securities was located in a London bank vault but was only recovered after a lengthy court battle.

On Aug. 13, 1926, the brothers appeared before San Francisco judge Harold Louderbach, pleading guilty to embezzlement. After a trial that lasted through the fall and winter, the Blumens were sentenced to one to ten years in San Quentin. "We just took a chance thinking we could get away with it," Julius said. "We're very sorry now, but I know we should have been sorry beforehand. We have nothing more to say."

REF.: Block, *Fifteen Clues; CBA.*

Blumenfield, Isadore (AKA: **Kid Cann**), prom. 1935, Case of, U.S., mur. Two eyewitnesses swore that Isadore Blumenfield, alias Kid Cann, murdered Walter Liggett in cold blood in December 1935. But Cann was acquitted and the murder remains unsolved.

Liggett, owner and editor of the weekly tabloid *Mid-West American,* was gunned down outside his Minneapolis, Minn., apartment as he returned from work. Although never proved, many believed that Liggett's controversial editorials denouncing ties between the underworld and Minneapolis and Minnesota government officials led to his killing. Liggett's wife, who was in the car with her husband when he was killed, said she saw Kid Cann lean out of a passing car and shoot. A second witness, who was in the alley behind the Liggett's apartment, also identified Cann as the man who fired the deadly shots. Witnesses in Cann's defense, however, said that the accused was at the Artistic Barber Shop at the time, far from the scene of the crime. The jury took little time to find the defendant Not Guilty. REF.: *CBA.*

Blumer, Fred, prom. 1931, U.S., (unsolv.) kid. In April 1931, a prominent brewery executive named Fred Blumer was seized at gunpoint at his office in Monroe, Wis., driven south to an undisclosed location near Freeport, Ill., and held until a $150,000 ransom was paid. The victim was freed but the kidnappers escaped with the money. Investigators believed Blumer's kidnapping was only one in a series of abductions possibly committed by the Al Capone gang in Chicago. Still another theory said that the kidnappers were members of a St. Louis ring, responsible for ten abductions within a year. Whichever the case, the criminals were never identified.

REF.: Alix, *Ransom Kidnapping In America; CBA.*

Bluntschli, Johann Kaspar, 1808-81, Switz., legal scholar. Professor at Zürich from 1833-48, Munich from 1848-61, and Heidelberg in 1861. He was co-founder of the Institute of International Law at Ghent and author of *Allgemeines Staatsrecht* (1852). REF.: *CBA.*

Theodore Boasso (inset, right) illegally married Mary Kuhn (inset, left), and was shot by her.

Boasso, Theodore J., prom. 1880s, U.S., big.-polit. corrupt. Theodore J. Boasso, son of an Italian printer, entered New Orleans politics as a ward healer at an early age, working mightily for the machines of Mayor J. Valsin Guillotte and Governor Samuel D. McEnery. He was first rewarded by being appointed director of the state insane asylum, a post for which he was wholly

unsuited. When Guillotte became mayor in April 1884, Boasso was then named to the New Orleans Police Department as chief of detectives, the position then called chief of aids. Boasso, who already had strong contacts with the New Orleans underworld, began to work in collusion with burglars, confidence men, and armed robbers. Whenever there were complaints, Boasso tried to mollify the complaining witness, even offering bribes to citizens to keep quiet about criminal offenses. In one instance a man from Colorado was bilked out of $400 and Boasso offered him $150 not to prosecute.

The mayor ignored complaints against his chief of aids, and, in fact, went out of his way to publicly support his crooked henchman, attending public fetes and affairs with Boasso. One night in June 1885, Boasso accompanied Mayor Guillotte to the residence of Ambrose Kuhn, a wealthy grocer, where the chief of aids met Kuhn's beautiful twin daughters, becoming enamored of Mary Catherine Kuhn. He began seeing the young Kuhn, lying to her that he was unmarried. He then eloped with the 18-year-old on June 20, 1885, the service conducted by one of his cronies who had no authority to marry anyone. Boasso then showed Mary Catherine Kuhn a fake marriage certificate and she consumated the union with her attentive lover. Kuhn learned of this perverse charade and arrived at the love nest, taking his daughter home with him. When the young woman learned how she had been deceived, she went hunting for Boasso and found him emerging from a saloon with a friend on Anthony Street. She produced a revolver and shot Boasso in the liver and the back.

This was one Boasso scandal Mayor Guillotte could not cover up. His chief of aids recovered and was then promptly tried for bigamy and forging a false marriage certificate. Boasso was convicted and sent to prison, given a fourteen-year sentence. The strutting bigamist served a little less than eight years before Governor Murphy J. Foster pardoned him in 1894. Upon his release, Boasso was given an insignificant political job and soon faded from the public eye.

REF.: Asbury, *The French Quarter; CBA.*

Boatright, Buck, prom. 1890s-1930s, U.S., fraud. A contemporary of the fabulous Joseph "Yellow Kid" Weil, Buck Boatright was a one-time train conductor who turned to confidence games to make his fortune. He was the inventor of a "short" con called The Smack—a short con being a confidence game which took only a short period of time to accomplish. Boatright centered his activities in Kansas and Missouri train depots where he would spot a wealthy sucker and befriend him. He would then appear to inveigle a confederate into a harmless game of matching coins, roping the sucker into the game by whispering to him: "You call heads and I'll call tails. Whichever way, we'll both win and split the take later."

Then Boatright would toss a coin and smack it down hard on top of his hand (thus the name of the game). The three men would then call out their choices of either heads or tails. Within no more than fifteen or twenty minutes, Boatright, who had been collecting all the winnings, would then announce that he had a train to catch and, ostensibly paying off the confederate, would walk off with the sucker to a nearby restaurant to divide their winnings. Just as they were sitting down, the confederate would appear and demand to know if Boatright and the sucker were in league to fleece him. The sucker would grow nervous and deny any collusion, invariably stating that he had just met Boatright.

The confederate, suspicious and irate, would then demand that they prove it by going off in different directions. Boatright would promise to meet the sucker later to split the take but, to mollify the suspicious confederate, he suggested they had best appear to go their separate ways. The sucker would go to the rendezvous suggested by Boatright and, of course, the con man would never appear, joining up with the confederate to split the sucker's winnings.

REF.: *CBA;* Nash, *Hustlers and Con Men.*

Bob, Charles V., b.c.1887, U.S., fraud. Bob may be the only U.S. swindler to appear on the map of the world. When Admiral

Richard Byrd crossed the South Pole in 1929, he named a mountain range in honor of the man who had invested large sums of Byrd's family fortune into what the explorer believed to be "secure" investments.

Charles Bob emerged from nowhere to attain a position of prominence during the stock market boom of the 1920s. Renting a spacious apartment on Fifth Avenue in New York City, he paid for it with money he received dumping worthless mining stocks on small-time investors eager to make a quick killing in the bull market. Bob created a financial house of cards that lured both powerful and obscure men. His picture frequently ran in the rotogravure sections of New York City newspapers alongside that of debutantes, investors, and the Broadway show crowd. He flew across the country in his own plane and lived the life of a high roller until the great stock market crash on Oct. 29, 1929.

Even after the bottom fell out, Bob survived, for he had sold $6 million in worthless stocks just before the market hit bottom. For men like Bob, the easiest way to show a profit during those reckless, speculative years was to report a fictitious loss in a stock deal and then unload actual securities far below the going price. That way a one to three million dollar loss could be reported to the IRS at tax time. REF.: *CBA*.

Bobadilla, Francisco de, d.1502, Spain, consp. Succeeded Christopher Columbus as viceroy of the Indies in 1499. He sent Columbus back to Spain in shackles resulting in his own recall and arrest in 1502. REF.: *CBA*.

Bobbitt, A.A., See: **Miller, Jim.**

Bobrikov, Nikolai Ivanovich, 1839-1904, Rus., assass. Governor general of Finland from 1898-1903. His attempts to develop an alliance with Russia met with strong opposition. He was murdered after gaining control of the country in 1903. REF.: *CBA*.

Count Bocarmé   **Countess Bocarmé**

Bocarmé, Comte **Hippolyte de** (AKA: **Mr. Berent**), 1819-51, Belg., mur. Before his marriage in June 1843, Comte Hippolyte de Bocarmé enjoyed his reputation as a womanizing con man. He lived life to the fullest, but gradually ran out of money to continue in the manner he had become accustomed to, especially after his father died. So he married a daughter of the bourgeoisie—Lydie Fougnies, whose father owned an apothecary shop in Peruwelz. When the elder Fougnies died, de Bocarmé discovered that the old man's estate was worth several thousand francs, and that most of it had been willed to his chronically ill son, Gustave. By this time, de Bocarmé and his wife had squandered their own meager fortune. When they learned of Gustave's im-pending marriage to Demoiselle de Dudzech, they invited him to the Chateau de Bitremont for a holiday.

On the night of Nov. 20, 1850, the count's servants discovered Gustave Fougnies' body in the dining room. Both the body and the floorboards had been washed down in vinegar. On Nov. 22, an autopsy revealed corrosive burns in Fougnies' mouth, throat, and stomach, so his tongue, intestines, and liver were sent for further analysis to Jean Servais Stas, a professor at the École

Royale Militaire. The comte and comtesse were placed under arrest pending the outcome of the tests.

When Stas learned that the comtesse had cleaned the body in vinegar, he immediately suspected foul play, and on Nov. 28, rendered his verdict: death by nicotine poisoning. Then the magistrate of Tournai, Heughebaert, discovered that from Oct. 28 to Nov. 10, the Comte had been washing down tobacco leaves and manufacturing cologne from tobacco juices. Moreover, he had been secretly visiting Professor Loppers in Ghent to learn how vegetable poisons affect human beings. De Bocarmé was particularly interested in learning whether such poisons left any trace in the body. Loppers assured him they did not. On Dec. 2, Stas explained to Heughebaert that there was enough nicotine present in the dead man's system to kill several people.

Police surmised that de Bocarmé had held Gustave down while his wife poured liquor mixed with nicotine poison down her brother's throat. "Just before leaving us, Gustave said he wished to drink our healths," de Bocarmé later testified. "My wife went to fetch a bottle of Madeira from the cupboard. By a lamentable error, such as might occur to anybody, she took one containing nicotine which happened to be on the **Gustave Fougnies** same shelf and filled glasses from it." Gustave put up a struggle before he died, and had splattered the poison across the floor. That explained why the comtesse had been so meticulous in her cleaning on the night of the murder.

The comte and his wife stood trial at the Palais de Justice in Mons on May 27, 1851. They accused each other of carrying out the vile crime, but after a sensational eighteen-day trial, the jury exonerated the comtesse, acceding to the custom of sparing gentlewomen the guillotine. On July 19, 1851, her scheming husband, however, was led by torchlight to the scaffold in Mons. See: **Stas, Jean Servais.**

REF.: *CBA;* Thompson, *Poisons and Poisoners;* Thorwald, *The Century of the Detective;* Wyndham, *Crime On the Continent.*

Boccia, Ferdinand, d.1934, U.S., org. crime. A small-time Brooklyn hoodlum, Ferdinand Boccia's big score consisted of steering a wealthy sucker to Mafia underbosses Vito Genovese and Michele Miranda in 1934. Genovese and Miranda bilked the man out of $50,000 in a crooked card game and another $100,000 in an ancient con game called The Green Goods, one where a box with stolen Treasury Department plates could produce endless $100 bills. Boccia had been promised one third of all the profits from the swindles but Genovese stalled. Then Boccia and William Gallo robbed a store owned by one of Genovese's friends, further vexing the crime boss. When Boccia pressed his claim, Genovese and Miranda gave $200 to another small-time crook, Ernest "The Hawk" Rupolo, and ordered him to kill Boccia. This he did.

Then Genovese decided that Gallo might also be a problem so he gave Rupolo another $175 to kill Boccia's sidekick. Rupolo befriended Gallo and, after the pair had been drinking one night, Rupolo pulled a revolver from his pocket and put it to Gallo's head as the two walked along a lonely street. The gun misfired twice and Gallo asked what Rupolo was doing. The Hawk merely grinned and said he was "playing a joke." Rupolo stopped at a friend's house and found that the revolver's firing pin was bent. He repaired it and caught up with Gallo a short time later, putting the gun to Gallo's head for a third time. When he pulled the trigger, the revolver went off, but Rupolo's aim was poor and only injured Gallo who later testified against the Hawk. Rupolo was sent to prison from nine to twenty years. As the Hawk gathered dust behind bars he grew more and more embittered about Genovese and, ten years later, came forth to inform on Genovese, causing his arrest. The 1934 murder contract Genovese gave out on Ferdinand Boccia backfired, causing Vito Genovese to suffer countless hours of sleepless nights as well as the constant threat of imprisonment or, worse, the electric chair. See: **Genovese, Vito; Miranda, Michele; Rupolo, Ernest.**

REF.: *CBA;* Eisenberg and Landau, *Meyer Lansky;* Gage, *Mafia, USA;* Gosch and Hammer, *The Last Testament of Lucky Luciano;* Katz, *Uncle Frank;* McClellan, *Crime Without Punishment;* Maas, *The Valachi Papers;* Martin, *Revolt in the Mafia;* Peterson, *The Mob;* Reid, *The Grim Reapers.*

Böcking, Eduard, 1802-70, Ger., lawyer. Editor of many highly regarded legal classics. REF.: *CBA.*

Bocskay, István, 1557-1606, Hung., assass. Led a Hungarian uprising against Emperor Rudolph from 1604-06 and secured the Treaty of Vienna in 1606 which guaranteed the religious freedom of Hungarian Protestants. He was poisoned to death. REF.: *CBA.*

Bodawpaya (AKA: Mintayagyi Paya), d.1819, Burma, king, assass. King of Burma from 1782-1819. He was a despotic leader schooled in Buddhist teachings. He overthrew his grand-nephew Maung Maung from the throne and executed him. REF.: *CBA.*

Boddy, Albert, prom. 1937, Brit., mansl. Boddy, a bachelor who lived with his married sister and her husband in High Wycombe two years before the outbreak of WWII, liked to frequent a local pub called the Hour Glass. There he would enjoy a glass of ale and a game of dominoes or darts in the company of a married woman named Mrs. Godby who lived a quarter-mile away.

Boddy professed his love for the woman but she did not give the bricklayer any indication that her feelings were the same. When she agreed to be his partner in a darts tournament to be held the night of Mar. 27, 1937, he was very excited. The night of the tournament she informed him of her change of heart. Someone else would be her partner, she said.

Greatly discouraged by this news, Albert Boddy went to a friend's house to borrow an ancient .410 Belgian folding gun. He then entered the Hour Glass and shot Mrs. Godby at close range. She fell dead instantly, and Boddy dropped his weapon. "I did not intend to kill her," he said in his defense at the trial. "I only meant to kick up a row." He explained that he was drunk at the time and really didn't know what he was doing. Convicted of manslaughter, Boddy was sentenced to three years of hard labor.

REF.: *CBA;* Hasting, *The Other Mr. Churchill.*

Boden, Wayne Clifford (AKA: The Vampire Rapist), prom. 1969-71, Can., rape-mur. Canada's most notorious serial killer of the late 1960s and early 1970s had a breast fixation. This came to light during a murder investigation that stretched from Montreal to Calgary.

Wayne Boden murdered for the first time on July 23, 1968. The victim, 21-year-old Norma Vaillancourt, worked as a schoolteacher in Montreal. Her strangled body carried bite marks on the breasts, but what puzzled police was the apparent absence of a struggle. The victim had an almost serene look on her face, according to an attending pathologist.

Boden committed three more murders of a similar nature in Montreal over the next two years. His victims, Shirley Audette, Marielle Archambault, and Jean Way were professional women who succumbed to Boden's charms. The police deduced they had met their deaths during intercourse. Of the three, only Way had struggled for her life.

Nothing was heard from the killer for several months. He next turned up in Calgary—some 2,500 miles from Montreal—on May 18, 1971. His victim, another schoolteacher, Elizabeth Anne Pourteous, taught at the Browness High School. Her raped and strangled body was found by her apartment building manager. Two of her colleagues reported to police that they had observed Elizabeth earlier in the day in the company of a man driving a blue Mercedes bearing a bumper sticker depicting a steer. Police picked up Boden the next day when the tell-tale car was spotted by them near Pourteous' apartment.

The suspect admitted to knowing the victim, but that was all. However, police linked Boden to the girl through a photograph retrieved from Marielle Archambault's apartment. Then an orthodontist identified the teeth marks as those of the killer.

Wayne Boden was sentenced to four concurrent life sentences. His killings were not premeditated, but the result of an intense sexual obsession with breasts, manifested in violence during sexual intercourse.

REF.: *CBA;* Wilson, *Encyclopedia of Modern Murder.*

Bodenham, Anne, 1573-1653, Brit., witchcraft. Anne Bodenham was servant and mistress to Dr. Lamb, the personal physician to the Duke of Buckingham, and lived with him at his manor. Lamb practiced alchemy and magic on the side, which compelled a superstitious mob to stone him to death in the streets of London in 1640.

Following the death of her benefactor, Bodenham began to capitalize on his name and reputation. She took up residence in Wiltshire where the townspeople of Fisherton Anger looked upon her as a sorceress. Neighbors would frequently ask her to prepare special potions, deliver incantations, and foretell future events. One of her regular clients was the wife of Richard Goddard, a paranoid woman who believed that her two daughters were trying to poison her. Goddard's wife asked Bodenham to prepare a special poison made of dried vervain and dill, which she used unsuccessfully against her daughters.

In 1653, the year of her death, Bodenham began dispensing legal advice to the son-in-law of Richard Goddard. She allegedly called on demonic forces to help her in this endeavor. (The ceremony was described in Nathaniel Crouch's *Kingdom of Darkness,* published thirty-five years later in 1688.) Not long after this, Anne Bodenham's alleged sorcery came to light when Mrs. Goddard's daughters complained that their mother had consulted a witch who prepared a deadly potion to kill them. Ann Styles, a servant girl who acted as the go-between for Bodenham and her customers, verified their claim in order to save herself from the scaffold. She described how her employer changed herself into a black cat, and wrote in the book the names of all who had sold their souls to the devil. To give credence to these accusations, Styles went into fits during the witchcraft trial. Two witch symbols were found on Bodenham's body—the final determinant of her guilt. Anne Bodenham was hanged at Salisbury, Wiltshire, in 1653. REF.: *CBA.*

Bodin, Jean, 1529-96, Fr., writer-witchcraft. A classical scholar born in Angers, France, Jean Bodin became a professor of Roman law at the University of Toulouse. In 1576 *The Republic,* the first of several noteworthy books written by Bodin and published during his lifetime, appeared. However, the volume he is best remembered for was the notorious *Démonomanie,* published in French in 1580 and later translated into Latin.

Though regarded as a liberal, Bodin's book reflected all the superstitious paranoia of the age concerning witchcraft and demonology. It was used as a handbook by judges conducting witch trials, advising them about the best ways to extract confessions through torture and brutal interrogation. Jean Bodin provided the first published definition of a witch, describing her as "one who knowing God's law tries to bring about some act through an agreement with the devil."

Though Bodin's earlier works were condemned by the Inquisition, *Démonomaie* was widely accepted by both Roman Catholics and Calvinists who thought alike when it came to witchcraft. This narrow-minded, prejudicial volume had at least a few detractors in its day. Archbishop Samuel Harsnett assailed Bodin for telling an "unsavory, melancholy and unsavory tale of an egg which a witch sold to an Englishman and by the same transformed him into an ass." REF.: *CBA.*

Bodine, Joseph Lamb, b.1883, U.S., jur. District attorney in New Jersey from 1919-20 before receiving an appointment from President Woodrow Wilson to sit on the bench of the district court of New Jersey in 1920. REF.: *CBA.*

Bodine, Mary (Polly Houseman), b.1807, Case of, U.S., mur.

The crime, known perpetually as the "Staten Island Murder", cost New Yorkers endless hours of debate. Most of the argument was over one hawk-nosed, rail-thin woman named Polly Bodine and how she managed to evade the gallows after murdering her brother's wife and infant child. Murder is the kindest word; her victims were butchered and, since their gruesome deaths were at the hands of a woman of some respectability, the slayings were even more unnerving. The woman Bodine was an odd sort, withdrawn, tightlipped, mincing. At fifteen, she was Polly Houseman and married Andrew Bodine, producing two children, Eliza Ann and Albert. She was never happy with her spouse and began to meet men in clandestine ways, mostly sailors whom she picked up along the small, dark streets slicing away from the docks.

Polly Bodine at her trial.

Bodine discovered his wife's capricious disaffection and a swift separation followed. Polly continued her secret, lightning affairs, and Bodine himself sank into debauchery, becoming, in the words of one account, "blunted in every moral sense...he fell in with a woman much of the same stamp as himself." The equally errant husband, though he was still married to Polly, took his mistress, a Miss Simpson, in official wedlock. A vicious competition between prudishness and hypocrisy, no doubt, caused Polly to call this illegal marriage to the attention of the authorities, who quickly arrested Bodine. He was sent to the state prison for two years for bigamy. On the day of his sentencing, Polly set herself up with a druggist named Waite, whose successful apothecary was at 252 Canal Street. Their union became so strong, that Polly prevailed upon her benefactor to take her son Albert as an apprentice in the store.

She then turned her activities toward self-enrichment. Her brother, George W. Houseman, was a man of considerable means, having made his fortune in the buying and selling of oysters. Polly began to spend more and more time in his Staten Island house, ostensibly helping his wife care for the rather large home and the small infant, newly born to the Housemans. Polly's brother left on an extended business trip to Virginia in early December 1843, asking his sister to help out his small family in his absence. Polly murmured assurance that things would be all right, but on Christmas Eve, everything in George Houseman's life went to ruin.

On that normally festive evening, Staten Island neighbors of the Housemans were alarmed to see flames and smoke gushing from the bedroom windows of the house. A dozen residents ran to the structure, broke through the locked door, and rushed into the flaming bedroom. A newspaper account of the day related the rest of the scene: "Having extinguished the flames, they lifted the mass of ruins formed by the smouldering bed, and there to their astonishment discovered the charred remains of Mrs. Houseman and her infant. Every soul present recoiled with a shudder of unmingled horror, and cause for the nonappearance of the unfortunate woman during the day stood horribly revealed. She had been murdered! There was a red mark around her neck; around her wrists were the fragments of a handkerchief, which from the position of her hands and knees, showed plainly that she had been bound to her sacrifice. A part of her head had been burned away, and nearly all the cranium of the child was consumed to its base; a fragment of the infant's skull, with the scalp and hair attached, was found among the ruins, with the blood on the inner side fresh, proving that the fire had been but the sequel of the 'graceless action of some heavy hand.'"

Polly Bodine was nowhere to be found. Some time later, it was discovered that she was on the 1:50 p.m. boat for Staten Island the day after the discovery of the murder. Either by coincidence or plan, she met her brother, George Houseman, on the ferry; he was just then returning from his business trip. Before he could speak, Polly, known for her lifelong lack of emotional displays, burst into heaving sobs. She then told her brother about the awful fate that had befallen his family. Stunned, Houseman stared at his sister for a long while and then pushed her away, instinctively distrusting her exhibition of sorrow. When she followed, he locked her out of his cabin.

The murder puzzled local police and, at first, they suspected the husband, but Houseman's alibi was perfect. He had been traveling on business appointments in Virginia, and proved it. He told the coroner's jury on Dec. 28 that the killings were probably committed by someone who had learned that he had sold his schooner shortly before his trip and obtained $1,000. That amount, however, was not in his house at the time of the killings; he had given the money to his mother for safekeeping.

Emeline Houseman and her child, the jury concluded, had been killed by a gang of strangers in search of loot. Houseman then dramatically offered the object of their search, the $1,000, as a reward for information leading to the arrest of the killers. With the posting of this reward, the bereaved husband gave a detailed description of the property stolen from his home on the night of the murder. This included silver spoons, a gold watch and chain, Emeline's earrings and breast pin, and an expensive clasp her child had been wearing.

Artist's version of how Polly Bodine murdered and set afire her victims, Mrs. Houseman and her child.

Five New York pawnbrokers responded after looking over this widely distributed list. A woman with the face of a bird and wearing a cloak, hood, and veil had entered the pawnshop of A. Adolphus at 332 William Street on the night of the Houseman slayings. She identified herself as Ellen Henderson of Bergen, N.J., and she pawned a gold watch for $35. This was the same watch Houseman had given to his wife Emeline. The same woman had appeared a short time later in the pawnshop of John J. Levy at 32 East Broadway, where she received $25 for the gold chain that had been attached to Emeline's watch. Immediately after that, she went to a pawnbroker named Davis on Chatham Street, where she pawned some of the Houseman's silver spoons; the remainder of the spoons she pawned at Hart's, a few doors down from Davis' shop. Her last visit that day was at Thompson & Fisher Jewelers at 331 Broadway. Here, the woman exchanged Emeline's earrings, the murdered wife's breast pin, and her child's hair clasp, for cash.

From the collective description given by the pawnbrokers, the woman known as Ellen Henderson from Bergen, N.J. appeared to be Polly Bodine. She was arrested and taken to the Tombs. Three of the pawnbrokers arrived, were shown to her cell, and promptly identified Polly, without question, as the woman who had pawned the Houseman jewels and spoons.

Police learned of Polly's sexual liaison with Waite and they arrested the paramour in his home. In the druggist's coat pocket, officials found a note Polly had written to her lover. It read in part: "Mr. Waite, you can't imagine my troubles, as I slept with Emeline last. I want you to get a soot (sic) of clothes and come to see me with Albert. Close the store—you will be examined on my coming to New York...You and Albert must say that Albert came to the ferry for me and I remained with you all day (the day of the murder), with the exception of going to Spring Street for about ten or fifteen minutes to get a basket mended, went out the next morning about the same length of time, was going to stay some days, but her brother-in-law came to let her know about the accident. I and my son returned to the Island immediately. You will be treated well. We are all worn out with examinations. Your store is going to be searched and other places. Hide the things I left (articles of clothing taken from the Houseman residence) and put them where they cannot be found."

Clearly, Polly was the fiend who had brutally tied up Mrs. Houseman, thrown her onto her bed, along with her infant, and then, according to studies made of the woman's corpse, leaped upon her back and forced her arm upward toward her neck, breaking it. Officials deduced that Polly tortured Mrs. Houseman in such a manner to compel her to tell where the jewelry and silver spoons were hidden. She then slashed the throats of mother and child alike and added, in her murderous fury, dozens of stab wounds to each victim. To obliterate her crime, she then piled flammable materials beneath the bed and set them afire, covering the corpses with heavy quilts to assure the complete burning of the bodies. The quick-moving Houseman neighbors had prevented the fire from consuming the evidence of the slayings. Polly then left Staten Island with her stolen goods, pawned them in New York, and timed her return to the island to coincide with her brother's arrival in order to make it appear that she was visiting the Housemans for the first time in several days, her coming and going on Dec. 24 unnoticed by neighbors.

It appeared that Polly Bodine was an immediate candidate for the gallows, but her lengthy trials, in which her shrewd lawyers availed themselves of her widespread bad publicity, stayed the execution. First tried in June 1844 in Richmond County, Polly went free when one juror held out against the other eleven. According to one report, he refused to condemn the woman "because of his personal opposition to capital punishment, though he subsequently confessed to being convinced of her guilt."

A second trial held in New York resulted in a guilty verdict, but this was reversed by the state supreme court, which ruled that the presiding judge, John W. Edmonds, had overlooked certain legal necessities. "When it was found impossible to panel a full jury," the press related, "since twelve men out of a community of 400,000 persons could not be found who had not already arrived in their own minds as to the guilt of the prisoner," the venue was changed and the accused stood trial for a third time in Poughkeepsie. This was in April 1846, almost two-and-a-half years after the murder had been committed.

In the third trial, the prosecution fumbled hopelessly about, failing even to introduce the testimony of the pawnbrokers, who had identified Polly Bodine as the woman who had taken loans on the stolen Houseman property, as well as the salient point that the hair bracelet received in exchange for such items was found on her person. The confused jury, even though the presiding magistrate, Judge Barculo, instructed the jurors that Polly appeared to be guilty on previously introduced evidence, brought in a verdict of Not Guilty. Polly Bodine was set free, much to the horror and stupefaction of New York as a whole.

The press ranted at the "blockheads of a sheriff's panel" and "the drivelers of the bench" for not finding Polly guilty and moaned long and loud for years to come how the "ghosts of the butchered innocents must forever wander unavenged."

REF.: *CBA; The Early Life and Complete Trial of Mary, Alias Polly Bodine, for the Murder of Emeline Houseman and Her Child; The Life of Andrew Hellman, Alias Adam Horn...To Which is Added a Full Account of the Staten Island Murders;* Van Every, *Sins of New York.*

Bodkin, Sir **Archibald,** 1862-1957, Brit., lawyer. Junior treasury counsel at the Old Bailey from 1892-1908, senior treasury counsel from 1908-1920, and director of public prosecutions from 1920-30. As a prosecutor, he helped establish a legal precedent of presenting all the relevant facts of a case before the court, whether or not they directly related to the defendant. He secured the conviction of many notorious British murderers including George Joseph Smith, known as the Brides of the Bath killer, John Starchfield, and George Chapman. REF.: *CBA.*

Bodkin, John, d.1742, and **Bodkin, Dominick,** d.1742, and **Hogan, John,** d.1742, and **Burke, Mr.,** prom. 1742, Ire., mur. To the residents of Tuam, Ireland, Oliver Bodkin, Esquire, was a kindly old sort, generous in spirit and indulgent of his two sons, born to two different women. The oldest boy, John, was sent to Dublin to study law at the university. However, he found the living arrangements unsuitable and soon returned home to be supported by his father.

Believing that the money due him as the elder son was being withheld by his stepmother, John Bodkin's dislike for his parents festered into hatred. When he heard rumors that his father planned to turn over the entire estate to his younger brother, John planned to kill them all. He enlisted several local ruffians, including his cousin Dominick, a shepherd named John Hogan who tended the family fields, and another man named Burke, who was reputed to be quick with a blade.

When the appointed day arrived, John Bodkin and his thugs, expecting to find his father alone, found his stepmother, his younger brother, a man named Lynch, kitchen maids, and the male servants all in the house with him. Determined not to be put off, Bodkin and his associates massacred everyone inside with sharply honed razors. Even the dogs and cats failed to escape.

When news of the tragedy reached Tuam, suspicion immediately fell on John Bodkin. Taken into custody, he confessed to everything, revealing the names of his accomplices. Dominick had killed five people and John Hogan, two, while John and the man named Burke had finished off the rest.

The three conspirators were tried in Tuam and found Guilty on Mar. 26, 1742. The townsmen extracted revenge by severing John Hogan's head and placing it on the market house. The two Bodkins were gibbeted in sight of the house where they had performed their brutal work.

REF.: *CBA;* Mitchell, *Newgate Calendar II.*

Bodmin Jail Riot, 1827, Brit., riot. In May 1827, a group of Bodmin Jail inmates led by a man named Sowden refused to engage in hard labor unless their demands for better treatment were met. When the men became rowdy and began destroying equipment in the workhouse, a militia from Cornwall was brought in to quell them.

The rebellious prisoners attempted to seize the muskets of the militiamen, but were beaten back and some were taken to separate cells. When Sowden refused the order to begin working the treadmill, he was sentenced to corporal punishment. His fellow inmates were then ordered to work or be punished. Given this choice the men agreed to work and promised obedience. One of the men's demands had been to receive a clean shirt each workday.

REF.: *CBA;* Thomson, *The Story of Scotland Yard.*

Body Snatchers, The, 1885, a novel by Robert Louis Stevenson. Ghouls and graverobbing murderers William Burke and William Hare (Brit., 1828) are the inspiration for this chilling work of fiction. See: **Burke, William.** REF.: *CBA.*

Boe, Nils Andreas, 1913-   , U.S., jur. State's attorney of Minnehaha County, S.D., from 1937-40. He served as a special investigator from 1941-42 and in other state and local offices before receiving an appointment from President Richard M. Nixon to sit on the Customs Court in 1971. REF.: *CBA*.

Boesky, F. Ivan, 1936- , U.S., fraud. For Ivan Boesky, the "king" of Wall Street arbitrage and one of the richest men in the U.S., the price of greed was three years in jail plus $100 million in fines. "He can't earn a living. He is on the verge of bankruptcy," complained Boesky's attorney, Leon Silverman. But some said the fines barely dented Boesky's vast "junk bond" empire. Boesky was one of those who, like characters in Tom Wolfe's novel *Bonfire Of the Vanities,* could control high-yield junk bonds and could consider himself one of the "masters of the universe."

In 1977 Drexel Burnham Lambert, a New York-based investment banking firm, introduced a new generation of high-yield bond funds which paid investors substantial returns to finance risky business ventures. The "junk bond," as it came to be known, catapulted Drexel, a minor player in the late 1970s, to the forefront of the Wall Street community a decade later. The rise of Drexel was fueled by Michael R. Milken, who took a summer job with the firm in 1969 while attending the University of Pennsylvania's Wharton School of Business. In 1978, Milken, a self-made entrepreneur at the age of thirty-one, moved the junk bond business to southern California. He analyzed companies considered "non-investment grade" by the bond rating houses of Wall Street, determined each company's real value, and then carefully reviewed its prospects. Junk bonds, he said, allow "entrepreneurs outside the system to get capital to realize their dreams." His method enabled corporate "raiders" like Ivan Boesky to finance hostile takeovers of large companies. Drexel had revolutionized the marketplace.

At first, other investment firms were suspicious of Drexel's methods. But, within a few years, a merger-and-acquisition frenzy gripped Wall Street, which culminated in the 1988 buyout of RJR Nabisco for $25 billion. Drexel's competitors marveled at the simplicity of the junk bond concept, and soon realized the potential of underwriting and selling these bonds. By 1986, Ivan Boesky, a high-profile Wall Street speculator who specialized in takeover stocks, had siphoned an estimated $400 million from his arbitrage firm, according to his former partners. Of greater concern to the government, who began investigating corrupt practices on Wall Street in 1986, was Boesky's relationship to Drexel. The firm admitted receiving $5.3 million for "advisory services" from Boesky in that year alone. This led to speculation that Milken and his associates were givin Boesky advance information about takeover plans before the information was made public.

With this knowledge, Boesky could buy the target firm's stock, and hold it until the takeover announcement. When the price of the stock jumped at the news of an impending takeover, Boesky could sell it at the inflated price. He then could share the profits with Drexel.

Government investigators discovered the insider-trading ring in 1986 when they received an anonymous tip from South America that Boesky and others were making vast illegal fortunes. The investigation led to Drexel investment banker Dennis Levine, whom the Securities and Exchange Commission (SEC) charged with making $12.6 million on illegal stock trades between 1980 and May 12, 1986, when an indictment against him was handed down. Levine was charged with obstructing justice and attempting to destroy records. On June 5, he implicated Ivan Boesky.

Boesky, the government charged, had entered into a two-year conspiracy with Milken to exchange information about impending takeovers. Boesky secretly agreed to record telephone calls and wear concealed listening devices as a part of a plea-bargaining agreement with government prosecutors, led by U.S. Attorney Rudolph Giuliani.

The undercover surveillance helped catch another big fish: 38-year-old John Mulheren Jr., head of a $25-million-a-year arbitrage firm. After realizing he was caught, Mulheren began acting irrationally. He left his Rumson, N.J., mansion one night in February 1988 armed with a semiautomatic rifle, but was intercepted by police on a tip from his wife. His intention, it seemed, was to kill Boesky.

Meanwhile, Giuliani's office announced a full-scale investigation of Drexel. On Nov. 14, 1986, Boesky agreed to plead guilty to one felony count, and to pay $100 million in penalties. He was formally sentenced to three years in prison on Dec. 18, 1987, by U.S. District Judge Morris E. Lasker, and was ordered to serve his time at a minimum security facility in Lompoc, Calif. The 689-inmate prison was derisively referred to as "Club Fed," because of the comforts provided its well-heeled tenants. At his sentencing, Boesky was contrite. "I am deeply ashamed," he said. "I have spent the last year trying to understand how I veered off course." U.S. Attorney John Carroll praised Boesky for his cooperation and the spirit in which it was given. But critics maintained that the Boesky had made few sacrifices. He still maintained his lavish Manhattan apartment and his Fifth Avenue office, which he used as a "command post" for his lawyers.

The insider trading probe continued, even after Boesky began serving his sentence on Mar. 24, 1988. Michael Milken was forced to resign from Drexel Burnham Lambert after twenty years with the firm. He has since formed his own consulting firm in Los Angeles and awaits trial. On Feb. 20, 1987, Dennis Levine was sentenced to two years in prison and ordered to pay $362,000 in damages. But Giuliani's biggest coup of all was the six-count felony indictment against Drexel charging the firm with mail, wire, and securities fraud, insider trading, and "parking" stocks to hide their true ownership. The SEC said this scheme helped Boesky avoid disclosure requirements on his various stock holdings. The integrity of Drexel, the fifth largest investment firm in the U.S., was further undermined by startling revelations that it had cheated its most valued clients. On Dec. 21, 1988, Drexel agreed to a $650 million out-of-court settlement, of which more than half was to be returned to stockholders and clients. "They've thrown the book at them, almost every violation of the 1934 Securities and Exchange Act," commented Edward Brodsky, a former U.S. Attorney.

The two-and-a-half-year investigation of Wall Street was the most significant since the stock market crash of October 1929, when the nation was plunged into the Great Depression. In the aftermath of that crash, Ferdinand Pecora's independent investigation led to the creation of the SEC, a regulatory agency designed to prevent unethical practices on Wall Street. But the Boesky scandal illustrated that the system was still vulnerable. See: **Levine, Dennis.** REF.: *CBA*.

Boethius, Anicius Manlius Severinus, c.480-c.524, Roman., consp. Philosopher accused of plotting against Theodoric the Great, king of the Ostrogoths. He was wrongly convicted of treason and imprisoned at Pavia in 524. While awaiting his execution he wrote the seminal work of his career, *The Consolation of Philosophy.* REF.: *CBA*.

Boettcher, Charles, II, 1902- , U.S., (unsolv.) kid. Unpaid gambling debts may have been the kidnapper's only motive for abducting Charles Boettcher II, a wealthy investment banker from Denver, Colo., on Feb. 12, 1933.

Taken by car to an unidentified location outside Denver, Boettcher never saw the faces of his abductors because during the long ordeal his eyes remained taped. A ransom demand of $60,000 was paid by the young man's father, banker Charles K. Boettcher. The cash was retrieved by the kidnappers near a railroad culvert outside the city.

Speculation mounted in the press that angry gamblers resorted to kidnapping Boettcher to collect debts owed them. Boettcher senior offered little comment, other than to say that "all obligations were fulfilled." The son was dropped off on a Denver side street shortly after the money pickup. An air-to-ground search began in northern Colorado and southern Wyoming, but the kidnappers eluded capture. See: **Roma, Joe.** REF.: *CBA*.

Boger, Wilhelm, 1907- , Ger., war crimes. In December 1964 at the Frankfort Town Hall, twenty-two former members of the Nazi SS (Elite Guard) went on trial for the systematic murder of Jews, Poles, Russians, and Gypsies at the Auschwitz concentration camp. The defendants were one-time camp custodians who had filtered back into mainstream German society after the war. Their twenty-month trial was to become the longest in German history.

Among the twenty-two accused war criminals was 57-year-old Stuttgart salesman Wilhelm Boger, who 'had served as the chief of the Auschwitz intelligence system. Known as the "hangman of Auschwitz," the Nazi security chief had invented an insidious torture device called the "Boger Swing" in which the victim was bound hand and foot, suspended from a parallel beam, and whipped to insensibility, sometimes death. "We helped those too tired to go on," Boger explained laconically.

Boger and sixteen of his camp associates were sentenced on Aug. 19, 1965, to varying prison terms. The former SS man received a sentence of life in prison. REF.: *CBA*.

Boggie, Clarence Gilmore, prom. 1933-48, U.S., (wrong. convict.) rob.-mur. Twice imprisoned for crimes he never committed, Boggie might have died alone and forgotten in the state penitentiary in Walla Walla, Wash., if not for the intervention of a team of crack crime writers from *Argosy* Magazine and a conscientious clergyman.

Erle Stanley Gardner first conceived the idea of "A Court of Last Resort," a monthly magazine series featuring real life crimes. The first case to be featured in *Argosy* was the most sensational, that of Clarence Boggie, an itinerant lumberjack from Portland who seemed to have a penchant for being in the wrong place at the wrong time.

Gardner first heard of Boggie through the Reverend W.A. Gilbert, a rector at St. Paul's Episcopal Church in Walla Walla who volunteered his time at the local prison. Gilbert maintained that Boggie had served thirteen years for a murder he never committed, following an earlier robbery conviction that eventually was overturned.

Boggie's incredible story began early in the Depression when he camped out at one of the many hobo "jungles" near Portland, Ore. Out of work and penniless, Boggie was sleeping under a bridge when a car sped by overhead. A team of bank robbers tossed a coat out the window which held a large amount of stolen cash. Not knowing this, the lumberjack tried on the coat and found it a perfect fit. Police searching the river bed arrested him when they noticed the familiar coat and he was tried, convicted, and sentenced to prison where he remained for several years before being granted a formal pardon when new facts about the robbery came to light.

Ironically, another coat got him in trouble a second time. On June 26, 1933, an elderly recluse named Moritz Peterson was murdered in his boarding house in Spokane, Wash., by a man believed to have rifled through Peterson's small quonset hut two days earlier in search of valuables. Peterson never mentioned Boggie's name before he died, but the police knew of his presence in Spokane at the time of the murder. Then a convicted Idaho bank robber implicated Boggie in the Peterson murder in return for a promise that he would not be extradited to Washington to face more serious charges.

Several months later police located an overcoat in a small Oregon town Boggie had stayed in following his first parole. When the daughter of the murder victim identified it as having once belonged to her father, the authorities were convinced they had located their man. He was arrested, but only after a long chase by police. By attempting to flee, Boggie had inadvertently played into the hands of the prosecution which contended that if he were innocent, he would not have run away.

Boggie was convicted, based on perjured evidence submitted by the deputy prosecutor and by shaky identification of the overcoat made by Peterson's daughter. He received a life sentence which he began serving in 1935.

Gardner opened his investigation into the Boggie case in 1948. The transcript of the trial was examined by Ed Lehan, a special deputy attorney general who flew out from Washington. He concluded that the evidence submitted could not support a conviction. The wheels of justice then slowly turned and a written report submitted to Governor Monrad Wallgren of Washington gained Boggie a pardon in December 1948.

The actual killer was later identified through eyewitness testimony and a second examination made on the murder weapon. By this time, though, the state declined to prosecute. See: **Gardner, Erle Stanley**.

REF.: *CBA*; Gardner, *Court of Last Resort*.

Boggs, Eli, prom. 1857, China, pir. Boggs was one of the last of the ocean-going pirates. He was active in Hong Kong in the 1850s, plundering the rich cargo of the opium clippers sailing out of China. His cruelty was legendary. It was said that Captain Boggs once cut up the body of a wealthy Chinese merchant and sent the pieces to shore in small buckets to warn those who would have him apprehended.

Eli Boggs was captured following a bloody siege in 1857. The American-born pirate swam for shore after his junk was blown out of the water by enemy pirates. He used a knife to stab his pursuers before he was at last captured.

REF.: *CBA*; Mitchell, *Pirates*.

James Bogle, kidnapper of Willie Whitla.

Bogle, James H., and **Bogle, Helen McDermott** (AKA: **Mr. & Mrs. Boyle; Mr. & Mrs. Jones; Mr. & Mrs. J.H. Walters**), prom. 1909, U.S., kid. James H. Bogle and his wife kidnapped 8-year-old Willie Whitla in Sharon, Pa., on Mar. 18, 1909. Bogle arrived at 9:20 a.m. at the East Ward School in Sharon and told the school's janitor, William Sloss, that he had been sent by Whitla's father to pick up the boy. The janitor went to Willie's teacher, Anna Lewis, who had the boy put on his coat and then escorted him outside to a waiting horse-drawn buggy driven by a heavy set, middle-aged man. As he drove off with the 8-year-old, Miss Lewis began to worry and remarked to Sloss: "I hope that man doesn't kidnap Willie." The unsuspecting boy rode on with Bogle, asking when he would see his father. The kidnapper told him soon and gave him a cheese sandwich. A short time later one of Willie's schoolmates saw the boy leave the buggy and mail a letter.

Whitla's father was a prominent lawyer, James P. Whitla, who was also the brother-in-law of steel tycoon Frank H.Buhl. That night, Willie's worried parents received a ransom note demanding $10,000. The note read: "We have your boy and no harm will come to him if you comply with our instructions. If you give this letter to the newspapers or divulge any of its contents, you will never see your boy again. We demand $10,000 in $20, $10, and $5 bills. If you mark the money or attempt to place counterfeit money you will be sorry. Dead men tell no tales. Neither do dead boys. You may answer at the following addresses: Cleveland *Press*, Youngstown *Vindicator*, Indianapolis *News*, and Pittsburgh *Dispatch* in the personal columns. Answer: "A.A. will do as you requested. J.P.W."

Whitla complied, placing the notice in the newspapers. He informed police that he would not cooperate with any investigation until his son was returned. Then ensued a series of botched meetings arranged for the delivery of the money to the Bogles.

The Hollenden Hotel in Cleveland, where James Whitla was to find his kidnapped son, Willie.

Whitla was told to go to the Flat Iron Park in Ashtabula, Ohio, on Mar. 20, 1909, and deposit the money at a certain spot in the park but no one arrived to pick up the ransom. Another note told him that "a mistake was made in Ashtabula Saturday night." Whitla was then instructed to go to Cleveland by train and go to Dunbar's Drugstore where a note would be waiting for him with more instructions. Once in the drugstore, Whitla picked up another note telling him to go to a candy store operated by a Mrs. Hendricks; he was to leave the money with Mrs. Hendricks, and mark it for the attention of "Hayes." Whitla left the money with the candy store operator who had no idea who he was or who Hayes was. She handed Whitla a note from Hayes in a sealed envelope which told the attorney to go to the Hollenden Hotel in Cleveland and that his boy would be delivered to him within a short time.

The nervous father went to the Hollenden and spent several hours of frantic waiting, pacing the lobby, checking the staircases and the area around the hotel. At 8 p.m., two boys, Edward Mahoney and Thomas Rumsey, got on the Payne Avenue streetcar and recognized Willie Whitla from the photos that had been appearing in the daily newspapers. He seemed to be in a drugged state, and when the boys quizzed him as to his destination, Willie told them that he was going to see his father at the Hollenden Hotel. Oddly, he told them that his name was Jones. The boys saw Patrolman Dewar, get on the car and they pointed Willie out to him. Dewar took Willie to the Hollenden where his frantic father rushed to embrace his son. Willie then told his father that he had been in the custody of "Mr. and Mrs. Jones" who said that

his father had put him in their safekeeping so he would not catch smallpox, then reaching epidemic proportions in the area, and that he was to tell anyone who asked about his identity that his names was Jones. He added that he had been kept in a house where he had to hide under a sink whenever there was a knock at the door because "it might be the doctor to take me to the pesthouse." Willie laughed when he said that "it was fun fooling the doctor." He told his father and police that "Mr. and Mrs. Jones" put him on the trolley car and told him where to get off to reach the Hollenden Hotel.

Willie's return to Sharon by train ended with a triumphant welcome. Thousands greeted him at the depot where bands played and cheering throngs pressed toward the Whitla family to view the boy. Cleveland Police Chief Kohler conducted a massive search of all boarding houses that would match the description given by Willie. His detectives found one house where a man and wife had recently departed in a hurry, the Granger Apartment House on Prospect Avenue. The owners told detectives that the couple had given the names of Mr. and Mrs. J.H. Walters.

A saloon keeper, Pat O'Reilly, then informed police that a young couple had recently been in his place spending money lavishly, almost $30 (a lot of money to spend at that time), buying drinks for everyone in his place, always paying with new $5 bills. The couple police sought were found on Mar. 22, 1909, both drunk in a Cleveland saloon. They gave the name Boyle to Captain Shattuck and Detective Woods who arrested them, and when they arrived in front of the police station, the man tried to break free but Shattuck fired off a shot that stopped him in his tracks. Inside the woman's dress was found $9,848, almost all of the ransom money.

The couple, later identified as James and Helen Bogle, were tried in Mercer, Pa. Mrs. Hendricks, the confectionary store owner, identified Bogle as the man who left the note for Whitla and later picked up the package containing the ransom money. Helen Bogle, a loud-mouthed slattern, had already convicted the pair when they were arrested, bragging to police: "I planned the whole thing." She thought of herself as a criminal mastermind. Willie Whitla testifed in court that Bogle had "whiskers here," pointing to his upper lip to indicate that the kidnapper had worn a mustache when picking him up at his school. A barber, Abner Hancock of Niles, Ohio, testified that he had shaved Bogle's mustache off a few hours after the kidnapping.

Willie Whitla reunited with his family.

Neither Bogle nor his wife offered any kind of defense and both were convicted of kidnapping. On May 11, 1909, Bogle was given a life sentence and his wife was sentenced to twenty-five years' imprisonment. Before being sent to prison, Bogle gave out a story that the idea of kidnapping Willie Whitla originated with Harry Forker, Mrs. Whitla's brother. He said that on the night of June 8, 1895, he found Forker removing papers from the body of Dan Reeble, Jr. on the sidewalk on Federal Street in Youngstown. Bogle went on to state that he had been blackmailing Forker since that time, receiving small amounts until November 1908 when he demanded a final payment of $5,000. Forker told Bogle he did not have that kind of money, according to Bogle, but suggested that Bogle kidnap his nephew, Willie Whitla, and hold him for ransom. Police dismissed Bogle's story as fantastic and produced policeman Michael Donnelly who said that he had known the dead Reeble, and had talked to him only a few minutes before his death. Reeble had gone upstairs and fell from a

Willie's triumphant return to Sharon, Pa., 1909.

second-story window when Officer Donnelly was only 200 feet from the building where Reeble lived. Donnelly stated that Reeble was in the habit of sitting in the open window before retiring and that he probably lost his balance and fell to his death. The officer insisted that no one was near the body when Donnelly rushed up to discover his friend Reeble dead.

REF.: Alix, *Ransom Kidnapping in America; CBA;* Duke, *Celebrated Criminal Cases in America;* Messick and Goldblatt, *Kidnapping;* Nash, *Almanac of World Crime;* ____, *Among the Missing;* ____, *Look for the Woman;* Smith, *Mysteries of the Missing.*

Bogue, Andrew Wendell, 1919- , U.S., jur. Judge advocate general stationed in the U.S. Army at Camp McCoy, Wis., from 1950-52. State's attorney of South Dakota from 1952-54, member of the A.B.A. Committee on Operation of the Jury System, and appointed judge of the District Court of South Dakota by President Richard M. Nixon in 1970. REF.: *CBA.*

Boguet, Henri, c.1550-c.1619, Fr., jur.-demonologist. While serving as chief judge in St. Claude, France, Henri Boguet tortured 8-year-old child named Loyse Maillat who had allegedly been exorcised of demons.

The girl reported that the possession was caused by a woman named Françoise Sécretain. Through torture the judge was able to obtain from her the names of forty other witches—some of whom were burned at the stake.

Henri Boguet was a recognized expert in the black arts. He wrote a landmark treatise called *Discours des Sorciers,* which provides valuable information to modern day scholars about the prevailing attitudes toward witchcraft in sixteenth-century Europe, a publication that went into twelve editions in twenty years. His section on "The Manner of Procedure of a Judge in a Case of Witchcraft" contained seventy articles which codified statutes and court procedures. Members of Boguet's family attempted to suppress publication of the book, but were not successful. REF.: *CBA.*

Bohle, Ronald T., 1948- , U.S., skyjack. Ronald Bohle was one of several young skyjackers who commandeered jetliners to Cuba in the late 1960s and early 1970s. Bohle was a student at Purdue University when, on Jan. 9, 1969, he held a knife to a stewardess aboard an Eastern Airlines jet bound from Miami to

Nassau. He ordered the plane diverted to Havana, Cuba.

At first the Cuban authorities welcomed the American expatriate, but they quickly grew disillusioned and jailed him. In November 1969, Ronald Bohle left Cuba and sailed to Montreal on a freighter. Canadian immigration officials turned him over to the U.S., where he was charged with aircraft piracy. On May 15, 1970, he was sentenced to twenty-five years in prison by District Court Judge Robert Grant in South Bend, Ind. A psychiatrist testified at the trial that Bohle was a schizoid personality whose mental illness resulted from the time he spent on Midway Island while in the U.S. Navy. REF.: *CBA.*

Bohun, Humphrey de, VIII (Third Earl of Essex), 1276-1322, Brit., treas. Member of a noble family founded by a Norman in the 1100s. He was seized in 1314 as a follower of the king at Bannockburn and executed eight years later as a baronial supporter at Boroughbridge. REF.: *CBA.*

Boiardo, Ruggiero (AKA: Richie the Boot), 1891-1984, U.S., org. crime. One of the elder Mafia dons of New Jersey, Ruggiero Boiardo immigated from Italy in 1900, going to Chicago. By 1910 he was a laborer in Newark, N.J. When Prohibition became law, Boiardo became a bootlegger and grew rich and powerful, working with New Jersey crime czar Abner "Longy" Zwillman. In the 1930s, Boiardo entered the numbers racket and soon added to his illegal fortunes. He retired in 1941 after having served only a short term for carrying a concealed weapon, although Boiardo was a suspect in a number of killings. He nevertheless was still deeply involved in loansharking and gambling rackets and remained the crime patriarch of Essex County, N.J., until his death in November 1984. Boiardo was not brought to trial in the 1980s because of his advanced age, although federal authorities felt they had gathered enough evidence to send the don to prison for the rest of his life. See: **Zwillman, Abner.**

REF.: *CBA;* Gage, *Mafia, U.S.A.*

Boise, Reuben Patrick, 1818-1907, U.S., jur. Prosecuting attorney in the territory of Oregon from 1854-55. He received a judicial appointment from President James Buchanan in 1858 and was assigned to the bench of the Oregon Territorial Court. REF.: *CBA.*

Boise, Thomas, d.1864, and **Grogan, Daniel,** d.1864, and **Gibbony, Mortimore,** prom. 1864, U.S., mur. Thomas Boise was a notorious ruffian and drunk who pestered and plagued local residents until, in September 1864, he, Mortimore Gibbony, and Daniel Grogan killed Abraham Deem, a local farmer, who criticized their drunken behavior. Gibbony escaped custody, but Boise and Grogan were convicted and sentenced to death. On the scaffold both men argued that they each had the right to see the other hanged first. To settle the argument, the sheriff tried to hang both men at the same time but the rope broke. Grogan was then hanged while Boise laughed maniacally. The large crowd assembled for this gruesome farce, then cheered as Boise was sent alone to his death through the trap. Gibbony was later caught and hanged.

REF.: *CBA;* Nash, *Bloodletters and Badmen.*

Boise (Idaho) Homosexual Scandal, 1955, U.S., pros. Until December 1955 the capital city of Idaho was regarded as somewhat of a rugged frontier town with a storied past, but an otherwise modern, clean-cut city. Then a private detective named Howard Dice was hired by a concerned parent who suspected that her son and a score of other teen-aged boys belonged to a homosexual prostitution ring.

Dice and the local police interviewed more than 125 youths who admitted they had been hired by older men in the community to engage in various sex acts for a set fee of $5 to $10 per meeting. The money was used, they said, to help pay for automobile maintenance and gasoline. The state of Idaho granted daylight driving permits to fourteen- and fifteen-year-olds at the time.

Several prominent local men, including Joe Moore, vice president of the Idaho National Bank, high school teacher John Calvin Bartlett, and Paris T. Martin, a lawyer, were named in the first wave of indictments. Moore received a seven-year sentence and four other men were given terms ranging from six months to ten years. Dr. John Butler of the Idaho Department of Mental Health urged that a support system for the convicted men be put in place, but Judge Merlin Young who heard the case demurred. "As an adult you have an obligation to the youth of the community," he explained. REF.: *CBA*.

Bojorques, Narciso, and **Chevez, Cleovara**, and **Garcia, Antonio**, and **Ponce, Noratto**, and **Soto, Juan**, and **Vasquez, Tiburcio**, prom. 1860-75, U.S., rob.-arson-mur. Bojorques and his companions were the ringleaders of a gang of Mexican desperados who terrorized the southern portion of California in the 1860s and 1870s. The murderous Bojorques rode north to Alameda in 1863 where he shot down a husband and wife named Golding, and their young child, before setting fire to their ranch house. In 1865 Sheriff Harry Morse engaged Narciso Bojorques in a shootout near San Jose where the bandit was badly wounded. He escaped, but was cornered in Copperopolis, and killed by a western outlaw named One-Eyed Jack.

REF.: *CBA*; Duke, *Celebrated Criminal Cases of America*.

Bokassa, Jean Bedel, 1919- , Bangui, mur. In 1960 France recognized the independence of its former colonial possession Bangui, located in the Central African Republic. At the time, the arid wasteland was a drain on the French economy and many politicians were happy to see it let go.

The Republican government established by France in Bangui was deposed in a bloody coup headed by a tyrannical madman named Jean Bokassa, whose penchant for pomp and royal splendor was exceeded only by his reputation for lunacy. In December 1977 Bokassa crowned himself emperor of the new Central African Republic and invited a score of dignitaries from Europe and all across Africa to witness his coronation, which cost an estimated £10 million.

The forty-eight hour gala was patterned after his great hero, Emperor Napoléon's coronation, which flattered the government of France which generously established a £1 million credit line for Bokassa to purchase a fleet of Mercedes limousines for the royal procession. This took place in a country where only ten percent of the two million population could read or write. Bangui, despite an impressive uranium reserve, was an impoverished country.

Many Western nations refused to send envoys to attend the event as a sign of protest. The U.S. cut off all economic aid to express its displeasure over the policies of the new Napoléon. Those who attended feasted at a lavish table, not knowing that some of their appetizers were human entrails from the bodies of recently executed prisoners.

Two years after Bokassa's coronation the embarrassed French engineered a palace revolt after learning of Bokassa's genocide of Bangui school children. Two hundred youngsters were rounded up by the Imperial Guard after their parents refused a direct order to outfit them in school uniforms they could not afford. Taken to a prison, Bokassa's guards systematically beat the children to death and their remains were fed to the emperor's pet crocodiles.

The deposed African statesman David Dacko was placed in charge of the government by his French protectors when Bokassa visited his ally Colonel Muammar Gaddafi in Libya. The power-mad emperor was exiled to Paris where he opened a boutique that supplied safari suits to African tourists. REF.: *CBA*.

Bolam, Archibald, prom. 1839, Brit., mansl. Joseph Millie, a widower with four children, was employed by Bolam, an officer manager at the Newcastle-upon-Tyne Savings Bank in England. Perhaps believing that his underpaid, overworked employee planned to kill him, Bolam decided to end the unfortunate man's life before he himself became a victim.

On Nov. 17, 1839, the police broke into the inner office of the bank after the volunteer fire brigade extinguished a blaze of mysterious origin. They found Millie lying face down on the floor, his head bashed in and blood everywhere. In the outer office Archibald Bolam lay prostrate on the floor unconscious, his neck cut. Recovering, Bolam said he had dropped in at the bank at

seven that evening to attend to business matters and observed Millie asleep in the office, but before he could say anything, a man with a blackened face jumped him from behind in what was obviously a burglary attempt.

The police questioned this story, because the blood from Bolam's throat ran down his coat in a way that suggested a self-inflicted wound. Large sums of money found in the bank manager's house led police to charge him with pre-meditated murder. Eventually convicted of manslaughter after the judge suggested to the jury that Millie died as a result of a business quarrel, Bolam was exiled from the country.

REF.: Butler, *Murderers' England*; *CBA*; Wilson, *Encyclopedia of Murder*.

Bolber, Morris, and **Favato, Carino** (AKA: **the Philadelphia Witch**), and **Petrillo, Herman**, and **Petrillo, Paul**, prom. 1937, U.S., fraud-mur. During the height of the U.S. Depression, Morris Bolber decided to expand his faith healing racket which netted his gang a tidy sum in the ethnic Italian neighborhoods of Philadelphia.

"Dr. Bolber," as he called himself, recruited a down-and-out tailor named Paul Petrillo and his brother Herman to kill insurable victims. At least thirty people were killed over a five-year period. Bolber, the Petrillos, and a third party to the scheme, Carino Favato, simply slugged their victims over the head with a bag of sand and collected their insurance money. The targets of the swindle were the errant husbands of the women Bolber "treated" during his consultations. It was a neat crime. No trace of violence was visible and the coroner usually reported that death resulted from a massive cerebral hemorrhage.

The infamous "witch" Favato had buried three of her husbands shortly after poisoning them with arsenic. A woman in her early forties with an ugly hooked nose and an eccentric disposition, Favato also was a real baseball fan, frequenting Shibe Park where she cast "spells" on visiting teams that came to town to play the Athletics. She promised Bolber she could put her special talents to good use in the insurance frauds and became his "scout." The Petrillo brothers administered the sandbag, while Bolber raked in the cash.

The whistle was finally blown in 1937 when Herman Petrillo bragged about the killings to an ex-convict named Harrison. The details he revealed were relayed to Detective Sam Ricardo, who by this time was on the gang's trail. Caught in their tracks, the "Philadelphia Witch" and the Petrillos confessed. Bolber and Favato received life sentences. The plodding, murderous Petrillos were executed.

REF.: *CBA*; Hynd, *Murder, Mayhem and Mystery*; Kent, *The Death Doctors*.

Bolding, Jane Francis, 1958- , Case of, U.S., mur. The case of Jane Bolding provided a new wrinkle in U.S. jurisprudence, as legal scholars debated whether it was possible to convict a person solely on statistical probability. "The question is, can statistics ever prove anything beyond a reasonable doubt?" Professor Alan Dershowitz of the Harvard Law School wondered.

Nurse Bolding worked at Prince George's Hospital just outside Washington, D.C. In 1984, patients under her care began to die at an alarming rate. From January of that year until her dismissal on Mar. 7, 1985, a total of eighty-eight cardiac arrests were logged into the records of the evening shift she worked. The figure was three times that of the day and late-night shifts. "The chance of that happening by chance is about one in 100 trillion," said Dr. Jeffrey J. Sacks, an epidemiologist at the Federal Centers for Disease Control. He noted that statistically, only thirty-one heart attacks should have occurred during this time and that Bolding was the attending nurse in 65 per cent of these cases. Several of the patients had exhibited a tendency to suffer recurrent attacks, and were always found to have a high level of potassium in their blood.

Alarmed that there was a silent killer lurking in the hospital, hospital officials contacted Prince George's County Police Chief Michael Flaherty on Mar. 18. A statistical survey revealed that

Bolding's patients were 35 to 96 times more likely to suffer heart attacks than those under the care of other nurses. Fifty-seven patients she had treated had suffered cardiac arrest, compared to five among all her co-workers. Police who took Bolding into custody the next day and grilled her for twenty-two straight hours.

She confessed to having injected potassium chloride into five intensive care patients, killing three instantly. Her actions were purely humanitarian, she explained, and not criminal. Nurse Bolding demonstrated her remorse by writing two letters of apology to the family of one of the victims. Unfazed by compassionate excuses, the court filed a charge of first-degree murder against her in the September 1984 death of 70-year-old Elinor Dickerson. However, this first charge was later dropped for lack of evidence. On Dec. 16, 1985, the county grand jury indicted her on three more counts of first-degree murder and seven counts of assault. The case came before Judge Joseph Casula, who ruled on Jan. 25, 1988, that since the confession had been obtained under extreme duress, her statements were inadmissible. "The police misconduct was a purposeful and flagrant violation of her constitutional rights," Casula said, adding that Bolding had been "illegally detained."

Disappointed prosecutors had to devise a new stratagem to convict the "Killer Angel." Through the federal Centers for Disease Control, prosecutors sifted through a backlog of cases. A study prepared by Dr. Sacks of CDC tended to affirm her guilt, but even the prosecutors conceded that the evidence was purely statistical and inconclusive. No one had witnessed Jane Bolding killing a patient or exhibiting any harmful tendencies. There was no murder weapon. There was not even a ruling from the state medical examiner that a homicide had, in fact, occurred. When Bolding's trial began on May 18, it had all the signs of a malpractice case, not a murder trial. Legal experts expressed the opinion that statistics alone would not be able to sustain a murder conviction in Maryland or any other local jurisdiction. Meanwhile, Bolding's lawyers played their trump card by deciding to let Judge Casula decide her fate instead of a jury. Sitting at the defendant's table, Bolding was surrounded by medical records, hospital procedure manuals, and X-ray charts brought in by her lawyers and estimated to be worth a half-million dollars.

In the heat of June, when temperatures climbed past the 90 degree mark, courtroom procedure became an exercise in frustration for the principals on both sides of the aisle. "Four more degrees and it's cardiac arrest time," quipped defense attorney Fred Joseph.

The long and difficult case ended on June 20, 1988, when Casula acquitted Bolding of murder and attempted murder, noting that the evidence was "insufficient to sustain a conviction." The judge admitted that in his opinion the defense had adequately demonstrated that the heart attacks were brought on by the unauthorized administration of high levels of potassium chloride, and that Nurse Bolding was a significant risk factor for patients suffering from cardiac arrest.

Her acquittal, though anticipated, was no consolation to the surviving family members of the three-year ordeal. "When Martha Moore died, I had no thoughts that anything unusual had happened. But now I'll have to live with this. If she has any decency, any conscience, then she's not free," said Mary Higgs, who recalled that Bolding had predicted her sister's death "It's inevitable," she told Higgs one day. "She's going to die." And she did. REF.: CBA.

Boldt, George Hugo, 1903-84, U.S., jur. Special deputy attorney general of Washington state from 1940-41 and 1946-47. He was special prosecuting attorney in Pierce County from 1948-49 and a member of the Committee on Administration of the Criminal Law from 1959-68. He received a judicial appointment from President Dwight D. Eisenhower to the court of the Western District of Washington in 1953. REF.: CBA.

Boles, Charles E., See: **Black Bart**.

Boleyn, Anne, c.1507-1536, Brit., adult. In 1525, Anne Boleyn, daughter of the Earl of Wiltshire, became the mistress of King Henry VIII. For the next two years, the king's adultery remained a state secret as he considered how to divorce his wife, Catherine of Aragon. Not until Easter of 1533, however, did Henry marry Anne Boleyn, at which time the legal problems posed by his "divorce" from Catherine were being untangled in the courts of Rome. Archbishop Thomas Cranmer pronounced the marriage legal, after which Anne was crowned Queen of England.

Anne's daughter born in September 1533 would later become Queen Elizabeth. But because Anne did not deliver the son and heir Henry so badly wanted, her reign was an unhappy one. On Jan. 29, 1536, she delivered a stillborn child, and in May, she was indicted for adultery and incest with her brother, three men from the privy chamber, and a court musician. The trumped-up charges were based on Henry's desire to be rid of her, and on May 2, 1536, she was taken to the Tower Of London. Anne's uncle, the Duke of Norfolk, arrested her, and testified against her in court. On May 17, the Archbishop of Canterbury declared the marriage invalid, freeing the king to marry Jane Seymour, which he did on May 21, two days after Anne was beheaded. On May 19, 1536, in the presence of assembled nobility on the Tower Green, Anne was beheaded by Rombaud, the notorious executioner of Calais.

Two noblemen had been sent across the English Channel to bring Rombaud to London. Beheading was a form of execution used in Britain only in rare instances. The "block and axe" would be used again, to claim the lives of Mary, Queen of Scots in 1587, the Earl of Essex in 1601, and Sir Walter Raleigh in 1618. REF.: Bishop, Executions; CBA.

Bolgnia, Joseph, and **Scatta, Salvatore**, and **Di Donne, Theodore**, and **Kimmel, Samuel**, and **Zizzio, Domenick**, and **Bruno, Eugene**, prom. 1935, U.S., mur. Edwin Esposito collected coins from ticket agents of the Culver Subway Line, Brooklyn, and performed his job with efficiency for many months.

On Sept. 2, 1935, Esposito left his home bound for the Avenue A station. The fare collector there handed him $240 in coins and Esposito jogged off for his next appointment down the line. Stopped on the platform by two masked bandits who demanded his chamois pouch containing the change, Esposito put up a fight, but was shot dead by one of the thugs who snatched up the bag and dashed for the exit.

The Brooklyn Homicide Squad worked on the case for several weeks and arrested Joseph Bolgnia and five of his gang members after local shopkeepers told police they were being flooded with small change from several men seeking to exchange coins for currency. Bolgnia had a long rap sheet and a big ego and, taken in for questioning, that ego got him in trouble. Resentful of Bolognia's assertion that he was the "brains" behind the operation, Salvatore Scatta claimed he was the toughest of the two. It was not long before District Attorney William Geoghan extracted a full and eager confession out of the pair and the names of the four accomplices.

All six gang members were found guilty of murder by Judge Peter Brancato in one of the shortest, most cut-and-dried cases in the history of New York State. It was the first time six men were sentenced to be executed in the state for taking the life of one person. Before the sentence could be carried out, however, Governor Herbert Lehman commuted the death sentences of gang members DiDonne, Kimmel, Zizzio, and Bruno to life. Bolgnia and Scatta later were executed. REF.: CBA; Kobler, Some Like It Gory.

Bolin, Patty, 1936-76, U.S., suic.-mur. Described by neighbors as a kind, giving woman and "ideal" in all ways, Patty Bolin purchased a .22-caliber pistol on Thanksgiving Day, 1976 with which she murdered her family. The 40-year-old homemaker and mother of four lived in Upper Arlington, a suburb of Columbus, Ohio.

"They were fantastic people," said Mr. and Mrs. Stephen Young, who lived near the Bolins. "There was never anything said or done to indicate that anything like this could ever happen."

That is, until Patty Bolin went on a shooting rampage on Dec. 8, 1976. First she shot and killed her husband, Ronald, forty-three. When daughter Tamela Jean returned from school she turned the gun on her, dropping the 12-year-old in her tracks.

Todd Bolin, nine, was outdoors playing when the shots that killed his sister rang out. His mother called him in, but when he saw what she had done, he ran outside screaming, "she's shooting everyone! She's shooting up the place!" Todd made the mistake of going back in the house to see if there was anything he could do. Bolin shot him dead.

The eldest daughter, Alicia Ann, fifteen, escaped death only because Bolin's pistol misfired three times. "Go to your room," Bolin ordered, but Alicia ran out of the house and called the police. When Patrolman Thomas French arrived it was all over. Bolin had claimed her final victim: herself. REF.: *CBA*.

Bolingbroke, Roger, d.1441, Brit., necromancy. Court astronomer Roger Bolingbroke was accused of sorcery and attempting to conjure up spirits of the deceased in July 1441. Though he renounced his faith in the black arts in the presence of the Archbishop of Canterbury, Bolingbroke was adjudged Guilty by the King's Counsel and hanged and quartered at Tyburn. He claimed that his actions were guided by Elianor Cobham, daughter of Reginald Cobham, Lord of Stirborough. The young woman was convicted of witchcraft, heresy, and treason and was made to offer public penance in the streets of London before beginning a life prison sentence in Chester Castle, Kenilworth.

REF.: *CBA*; Potter, *The Fine Art of Hanging*.

Prison warden Bolland, left, fleecing his prisoners at poker.

Bolland, James, d.1772, Brit., forg.-fraud-extort. It took many years for the British authorities to stop the swindling activities of James Bolland, who used public office to disguise his criminal enterprises.

Bolland realized early that to succeed in crime, one needs a good front. His butcher shop in the Borough of Southwark held no interest for him, so he secured an appointment to the sheriff's office in the county of Surrey. During his years as a merchant, he ingratiated himself with the bailiffs and other low-ranked officers of the court who might do him a favor one day.

Bolland outfitted a house at the foot of Falcon Court in Southwark as a prison. Those he arrested, if he had no reason to send them directly to prison, were forced to pay him room and board at an exorbitant rate, far above those prevailing at other lock-up houses in London and the surrounding counties. With their cash resources disappearing fast, prisoners awaiting their day in court frequently asked to spend the remaining time in the regular city jail rather than pay for the comparative comfort of Bolland's prison and his compulsory, rigged poker games. If a prisoner dared accuse Bolland of cheating at cards, he would take offense and have him committed to the city jail. His infamous

reputation as a crooked bondsman and despotic jailer spread while he lived in luxury.

Also notorious for many frauds, including one for horse theft, he went into bankruptcy, and his business declined. Hoping to restore his fading income, Bolland moved to County Middlesex where he was nominated to be a sheriff's officer. While visiting a billiard hall, Bolland met a man who was seeking the recovery of £300 from a ship captain of the East India company. In return for arresting the debtor, Bolland was promised a handsome reward. He tracked down the captain shortly before he set off for the Indies, and obtained the £300, issuing a receipt for the money. Bolland pocketed the entire amount and told his employer that the captain had eluded capture and was far from England by this time.

Months later a second bailiff was dispatched to find the captain. When he was arrested near Blackwell, he produced the original receipt Bolland issued. A lawsuit was filed for the recovery of the £300 but Bolland could not pay. He was incarcerated at Fleet Street Prison, but soon released by virtue of the insolvency act.

Bolland returned to his former occupation of private jailer which had proved successful for him in Surrey. In his new lockup house, he charged inmates six shillings a day, and those who were unwilling to pay were sent to jail.

Bolland might have continued perpetuating his minor swindles and extortions for years had it not been for his forgery of an endorsement on a bank draft.

The forgery was detected and Bolland was arrested, tried, and sentenced to die, as robbery and fraud were capital offenses at that time. He went to the gallows on Mar. 18, 1772, denying that he had committed a fraud in this instance, though admitting that on at least one occasion he had perhaps swindled someone.

REF.: Armitage, *Bow Street Runners*; *CBA*; Mitchell, *Newgate Calendar*.

Bolles, Don, 1929-76, U.S., mur. (vict.). A prize-winning investigative reporter for the Arizona *Republic,* Don Bolles told friends that he was working on a "Mafia story" in early Spring 1976. In fact, he had been investigating the link between a giant sports conglomerate and the crime syndicate. On June 2, 1976, Bolles got into his car in Phoenix, Ariz., and it promptly blew up. Bolles lost both legs and an arm, then, eleven days later, his life. Before he died, Bolles said that "John Adamson did it," and he was able to talk about the business conglomerate association with the crime cartel and how both were manipulating dog racing in the state. While investigative reporters from all over the U.S. poured into Phoenix to aid police in finding Bolles' killers, detectives went after John Adamson and others who were subsequently convicted of the reporter's murder. See: **Adamson, John.** REF.: *CBA*.

Bollman, Justus Erich, 1769-1820, U.S., consp. Intrigued with Aaron Burr in an ill-fated attempt to cede Spanish lands in the southwest for the purpose of establishing a separate republic. He was imprisoned, but was released by order of the Supreme Court. He revealed Burr's scheme to President Thomas Jefferson in 1807, denying that it was a seditious act of treason against the U.S. He later testified at Burr's trial. See: **Burr, Aaron.** REF.: *CBA*.

Bolo Pascha (or **Bolo Pacha**), d.1918, Fr., esp.-treas. Assumed the name of a German spy and spread defeatist propaganda among the French people, coining the term *Boloism.* He was tried and executed by firing squad in the 1918 for treason. REF.: *CBA*.

Bolshevik Riots, 1905, Rus., riot. Feeding on the general unrest and economic turmoil in czarist Russia after Russia lost its war with Japan in October 1905, Bolshevik leaders aroused public sentiment against the government of Nicholas II and called for a Constituent Assembly to debate sorely needed reforms. On Oct. 30, a general strike in St. Petersburg and an inner-city communication stoppage forced the embattled czar to agree to the demands of the workers. He promised a liberal constitution guaranteeing free speech and personal liberty for all Russian citizens.

When the reforms were slow in being implemented, Bolshevik

leaders encouraged armed skirmishes between peasant workers and czarist troops. In December 1905, from Kronstadt to Sevastopol the economy of the nation ground to a halt as leftist radicals rioted in the streets of Moscow. The disturbances were eventually quelled, however, and the czar succeeded in temporarily placating his subjects by convening the First Duma of the Empire on May 10, 1906.

Meanwhile, the Bolshevik movement, based on the works of Karl Marx, was financing its activities with armed robbery. Vladimir Lenin justified the banditry on the grounds that the Bolsheviks "stole what had been stolen." Under the direction of Semyon Ter-Petrosyan, gangs of revolutionaries robbed the state, daring in 1907 even to rob the post-office coach on Erevan Square in Tbilisi.

REF.: Almedingen, *The Romanovs; CBA;* Chalidze, *Criminal Russia;* Dmytryshyn, *Imperial Russia: A Source Book, 1700-1917;* _____, *USSR, A Concise History;* Fischer, *Russian Liberalism;* Haimson, *The Russian Marxists and the Origins of Bolshevism;* Jorre, *The Soviet Union, The Land and Its People;* Karpovich, *Imperial Russia, 1801-1917;* Kornilov, *Modern Russian History;* Levin, *The Second Duma;* Longworth, *The Cossacks;* Massie, *Nicholas and Alexandra;* Mayor, *The Economic History of Russia;* Meyer, *Leninism;* Miliukov, *History of Russia;* _____, *Russia and Its Crisis;* Miller, *The Economic Development of Russia, 1905-1914;* Pares, *The Fall of the Russian Monarchy;* _____, *Russian and Reform;* Pearlstien, *Revolution in Russia!;* Pushkarev, *The Emergence of Modern Russia, 1801-1917;* Riasanovsky, *A History of Russia;* Seton-Watson, *The Decline of Imperial Russia, 1855-1914;* Tompkins, *Roots of Revolution;* Walsh, *Russia and the Soviet Union;* Wolfe, *Three Who Made a Revolution;* Yarmolinsky, *Road to Revolution.*

Bolt, Nut & Rivet Manufacturer's Association, prom. 1931, U.S., consp.-rack. As secretary of commerce, former president Herbert Hoover compelled U.S. manufacturers of durable goods to standardize gauge and industrial quality.

The immediate beneficiary of this mandate was the bolt, nut, and rivet industry which went from a $3 million loss in 1925, to a $7 million profit in 1930. Certain unscrupulous entrepreneurs within the Bolt, Nut & Rivet Manufacturer's Association had conspired to fix prices within federally mandated guidelines by offering generous discounts and freight equalization for their "preferred" customers, which included Bethlehem Steel and the Pacific Coast Steel Corp. By 1931, the association controlled roughly ninety-five per cent of all the industry's business.

In March of that year Manhattan federal judge Frank Coleman ordered the association dissolved under the terms of the Sherman Anti-Trust Act, charging its members with unfair restraint of trade and price fixing. The association promised that "immediate steps would be taken to organize a new association which would so operate as to be free from any criticism." REF.: *CBA.*

Bolton, Carl E., 1909- , Case of, U.S., asslt. The shots struck Walter Reuther just as he and his wife got up from the dinner table on Apr. 20, 1948. The outspoken president of the United Automobile Workers did not have a clue about the identity of his assailants when interviewed in the hospital the next day. "It could have been management, a Communist, a fascist, or a screwball," he said. "I can't put them in any order." Reuther suffered four hits of .12-gauge buckshot in his chest and right arm. Though serious, the wounds were not fatal and he recovered from the attack.

The search for the gunmen continued for four months, until Carl Bolton, former vice president of a UAW local in Highland Park, Mich., was arrested on Oct. 19. When captured, Bolton was involved with a gang of sneak thieves and small-time crooks who terrorized portions of Indiana and Michigan. The police were tipped off by John Kaliszewski, alias Jack Miller, a former convict who claimed Bolton offered him $15,000 to do away with "a dirty red Communist." When Miller declined, Bolton allegedly promised him a lifetime job in the union.

Miller had a long record of burglary and his untrustworthiness was taken into consideration by the four-man, eight-woman jury that acquitted Bolton of assault on Feb. 24, 1950, in the Record-

er's Court in Wayne County. Meanwhile, Reuther underwent a series of painful operations to restore his shattered right arm. REF.: *CBA.*

Bolton, Charles E., See: **Black Bart.**

Bolton, David, 1938- , and **Ellis, Michael,** 1946- , and **Cohen, Raymond,** 1945- , Brit., rob.-mur. It never occurred to David Bolton that he would be involved in the murder of his associate, dance instructor Janet Williams, when he broke into the swank flat of Michael O'Carroll in Falmouth House, Bayswater, to steal enough money to pay his rent.

The indigent was tantalized by the opulence of O'Carroll's apartment and the man's extravagant lifestyle. By comparison his own prospects were none too good. Bolton had recently lost his job and faced eviction. After attending a party at O'Carroll's, he decided to burglarize the flat and steal jewels worth, in his estimation, £15,000 to £20,000. Needing accomplices, Bolton recruited Michael Ellis, twenty-two, a swimming teacher, and Raymond Cohen, an athletic type who managed a football team.

Bolton and his two partners were admitted to the apartment by O'Carroll's live-in girlfriend, Williams, on Mar. 13, 1968. They bound and gagged her and searched the rooms, finding far less than Bolton expected. When O'Carroll arrived a few minutes later, he was tied up and placed next to Williams. Then the two were strangled after O'Carroll tried to ring the service bell for help. By this time Cohen had left the apartment to fetch O'Carroll's Lancia automobile.

When he learned that Williams and O'Carroll had been killed execution-style, Cohen surrendered to the police, not wanting to be implicated in a murder he did not commit. At the Old Bailey, Justice Sebag Shaw sentenced Ellis and Bolton to life imprisonment for murder and an additional fifteen years for robbery. Cohen, originally charged with murder, got two years for robbery after Ellis' counsel corroborated his version of the events as being true.

REF.: *CBA;* Simpson, *Forty Years of Murder.*

Bolton, John, d.1775, Brit., suic.-mur. When he was honorably discharged from the army in 1763, John Bolton returned to his small country farm near Ackworth to care for his family. For the next five years he led a placid life. Then a seemingly insignificant occurrence set into motion a chain of events that deprived him of his good fortune, his family, and ultimately his life. A 10-year-old girl came to live with the family and work as a maid. Elizabeth Rainbow, the maid, showed signs of becoming very beautiful. Emanuel Bowes, the family's other employee, was a young apprentice who helped with the farm work.

Five years passed and Bolton, taken by Elizabeth's beauty, seduced her, then thought nothing more of it. Several months later, young Elizabeth announced that she was to bear a child. Bolton promised her that all would be right. He purchased medicine from a doctor in York who guaranteed that it would abort an unwanted child.

Bolton ordered Elizabeth to drink the putrid substance, but instead of ending the pregnancy it brought on severe stomach convulsions. Fearful that his wife would find out, he decided to kill Elizabeth and conceal the crime. On Aug. 21, 1774, Mrs. Bolton took the children to a neighbor's house two miles away. The young apprentice was sent away on the pretense of securing medical attention for Bolton's ailing livestock. Bolton led Elizabeth into the musty cellar, where he strangled her with a cord. When Emanuel returned, Bolton had him take some offal into the cellar to absorb some standing water. The boy left and Bolton covered the body with the debris.

When his wife returned, he explained that Elizabeth had run off, as young girls sometimes do. Yet she could not help but notice that her husband seemed uneasy and aloof. The disappearance of Elizabeth Rainbow occasioned much gossip in the village until, after ten days, the constable arrested Bolton and took him to the justice of the peace pending an investigation.

The body was soon discovered, and a charge of willful murder was brought against Bolton following the coroner's inquest.

During the trial, Bolton refused to admit his guilt. In the face of damning evidence and certain execution, he decided to save the hangman a job. On Mar. 29, 1775, Bolton slipped a homemade noose around his neck and hanged himself from a beam in his prison cell at York Castle.

REF.: CBA; Mitchell, *Newgate Calendar*.

Bolton, Mildred Mary, 1886-1943, U.S., mur. From the very beginning, Charles W. Bolton, Jr. realized that he had made a mistake when he asked for Mildred's hand in marriage in 1922. The docile insurance broker from Chicago proved to be no match for the jealous, high-strung woman from Kalamazoo, Mich. The couple moved to Hyde Park, on Chicago's South Side. Charles Bolton commuted to his downtown office every day, and returned at night to face the stern admonitions of his jealous wife. Mildred believed that her dowdy, middle-aged husband was carrying on affairs with the women at the office.

Charles Bolton, victim.   **Mildred Bolton, killer.**

Mildred beat her husband senselessly. When Charles refused to divorce her, his employers delicately suggested that he might want to go into business for himself. He did not and one night Mildred slashed him with a razor. Chicago Police later questioned Mildred at home. Smoking a cigar, her feet up on a table, she casually explained that his "accident" was the result of careless shaving. It was three in the morning.

Charles Bolton finally had enough. He filed for divorce on Jan. 20, 1936. Mildred, however, refused to give up so easily. On June 11, she purchased a revolver and four days later turned up in her husband's downtown office. She rode the elevator to the tenth floor and coolly discharged six bullets into her husband. As he lay in agony on the floor, Mildred said, "Why don't you get up and stop faking?" Charles Bolton died shortly thereafter. Mildred was originally sentenced to death in the electric chair, but Governor Henry Horner commuted her sentence to 199 years at the women's penitentiary in Dwight, Ill. There she died on Aug. 29, 1943, having slashed her wrists with a stolen pair of scissors.

REF.: CBA; Nash, *Look For the Woman; ____, Murder America*.

Bomb, The, 1920, a novel by Frank Norris. This highly speculative work of fiction is based upon the bloody Haymarket Riot (U.S., 1886). See: **Altgeld, John Peter; Haymarket Riot.** REF.: CBA.

Bombay Riots, 1921, India, riot. During an official state visit to India in 1921, Edward VIII, the Prince of Wales, faced rioting mobs in the streets of Bombay. Inspired by the doctrine of passive resistance taught by Mahatma Ghandi, the frenzied populace had been begun its long period of agitation against the British colonial government. The result of this gruesome tragedy: fifty people dead and many more injured.

REF.: CBA; Sparrow, *The Great Assassins*.

Bommarito, Joseph, and **Livecchi, Angelo,** and **Pizzino, Ted,** prom. 1930, Case of, U.S., mur. Broadcasting from the downtown studios of radio station WMBC, Jerry Buckley, a lone voice of civic conscience in 1930's Detroit, railed against the wanton excess

of the crooked municipal government of Mayor Charles Bowles and the notorious Purple Gang, which was pulling the strings.

There was a groundswell of support for a recall of Mayor Bowles, who promised much but did little to eradicate Detroit's powerful crime syndicate. Jerry Buckley at first remained neutral about taking such a radical step as removing a mayor from office. But as the gangland murders mounted (there were ten underworld figures shot in July 1930 alone), the radio announcer jumped on the band wagon. The constant death threats made against him by the underworld did not seem to phase Buckley. "I get twenty threats a day," he said. "There is always someone who says I will be killed." On July 21, 1930, Buckley signed on and told his audience that Mayor Bowles was about to be recalled. The people had spoken. So, too, however, would the crime syndicate.

Shortly after one in the morning, Buckley received a phone call from a woman. She asked if he could come to the lobby of the LaSalle Hotel, where WMBC had its studio. "Okay, it's a date," he said. A few minutes later he took the elevator down to the lobby and sat down in a chair facing the Adelaide Street entrance. Normally a very busy place, the lobby on this particular night was strangely quiet. In fact, there was only one other person present: Jack Klein, a projectionist. Buckley did not notice three men entering the building. The syndicate gunmen emptied their pistols into him, and then fled out the door into a waiting car that drove off down Woodward Avenue.

Police Commissioner Thomas Wilcox, who was part of the Bowles administration, promised to take charge of the investigation, but then left town for four days to attend a convention in Duluth, Minn. The press was outraged. Michigan attorney general Wilbur Bruckner empaneled a grand jury to investigate the matter. A handful of incorruptible police officers led by Lieutenant J.H. Hoffman tailed a gunman named Ted Pizzino to New York, where he was promptly arrested. Two Detroit-area mobsters, Joseph Bommarito and Angelo Livecchi, were arrested and held as accomplices.

The three men were tried before Judge Edward Jeffries, the "white knight," thought incapable of being corrupted by crooked politicians and gangsters. The prosecution believed it had an airtight case as well. Cab driver Gus Reno, the projectionist Jack Klein, and hotel porter Robert Jackson all identified the trio of gunmen. Yet a verdict of Not Guilty was returned. It was conceded that in all likelihood the jurors had been "approached" and witnesses coerced by syndicate interests. Pizzino and Livecchi were later arrested and sentenced to life in prison for the murder of two local drug pushers, but Bommarito remained free.

REF.: CBA; McClellan. *Crime Without Punishment*; Reid, *The Grim Reapers*.

Bompard, Gabrielle, See: **Eyraud, Michael.**

Bompart, Mère, prom. 1770, Fr., wh. slav. To satisfy the prurient sexual tastes of King Louis XV of France, a harem was maintained on the grounds of Versailles. The cost of the "Parc aux Cerfs" to France was estimated at 7 million francs. Procurement of young girls between the ages of nine and eighteen was left to Mère Bompart, described as a fat, aging woman with a robust temperament. Bompart's recruits invariably came from the ranks of the poor, who were anxious to see their daughters attain a position as courtesan to the king.

REF.: CBA; Henriques, *Prostitution*.

Bompensiero, Frank (AKA: Bomp), 1905-77, U.S., org. crime. A shifty, backstabbing character, Frank Bompensiero worked for the mobs in Detroit and later migrated to California where he worked for crime boss Jack Dragna, who sent him to San Diego to organize the numbers and gambling rackets there. Bompensiero became the crime boss of that city until the mid-1960s when, to avoid federal prosecution, he became an FBI informant, providing the Bureau with information on Mafia operations in southern California, including the activities of his own men, it was reported. Although syndicate leaders soon learned that Bompensiero was double-crossing the organization, he was too well guarded and too cautious to put himself in a position where he could be executed. A contract was placed on his life and it was not until February 1977 that two Mafia killers caught up with Bompensiero as he was approaching his posh Pacific Beach apartment. They fired four bullets into his head and escaped. The killers were not found. See: **Dragna Family**.

REF.: *CBA;* Servadio, *The Last Mafioso;* Zuckerman, *Vengeance Is Mine.*

Bonafous, Louis (Frère Léotade), d.c.1850, Fr., mur. During the early morning hours of Apr. 10, 1847, a Toulouse bookbinder named Bertrand Conte paid a business call on the Institute of Christian Brethren to sell some of his recently printed books. His young assistant, Cécile Combettes, was instructed to remain outside while Conte transacted his business. When he came out a short time later, Cécile was gone.

The next day her ravished and beaten body was found in a kneeling position in the St. Aubin cemetery. At first the gendarmerie believed Conte had committed the crime, since he was reputed to be an indiscreet man around young girls. Under questioning he steadfastly denied any knowledge of the crime but told the authorities he had noticed two members of the religious brotherhood lurking near the institute's vestibule just before he stepped inside to do his business. The two brothers whose names were Frère Jubrien and Frère Léotade likewise denied their guilt, but Conte implicated the latter by recalling a promise made to Cécile that he would deliver some rabbits to her garden.

Strands of hay, clover, and fig leaf found on Cécile Combette's dress and on the garb worn by Léotade convinced the jury that he had committed the murder in the hayloft, and had disposed of the body in the cemetery. However, the entire case was riddled with puzzling contradictions. An eyewitness claimed to have observed Conte walk away with his young charge, which if true, would have cleared Bonafous of all charges. A verdict of Guilty with "extenuating circumstances" was returned against the defendant. Frère Léotade was ordered to spend the rest of his days in prison. He died two years after the trial ended in 1848, protesting his guilt to the end.

REF.: *CBA;* Fouquier, *Causes Célèbres;* Pearson, *Instigation of the Devil;* Stephen, *General View of the Criminal Law of England;* Wilson, *Encyclopedia of Murder;* Woodall, *Collection of Reports of Celebrated Trials.*

Police photos of "Joe Bananas" Bonanno.

Bonanno, Joseph (AKA: Joe Bananas), b.1905, U.S., org. crime. Illegally entering the U.S. in 1924 by way of Havana, Cuba, Joseph Bonanno went to Chicago and worked for Al Capone as a bootlegging hijacker and rum runner during the 1920s. When the Castellammarese War broke out in New York City, Bonanno went to New York to work for gang boss Salvatore Maranzano, who was fighting Joe "The Boss" Masseria. Both of these crime czars were battling for control of the Unione Sicilione, a powerful Mafia-controlled union, as well as numerous rackets throughout New York City. It was Bonanno who gave the oath of allegiance to Joseph Valachi in 1930 when he was initiated into the La Cosa Nostra, another name for the Mafia (and one used exclusively by New York members of the Mafia). Following the deaths of both Maranzano and Masseria, Bonanno emerged as a powerful Mafia family boss who controlled a vast loan-sharking and

gambling empire which stretched from Montreal to Haiti.

When federal investigations resulted in imprisonment of his fellow crime bosses, Charles "Lucky" Luciano and Louis "Lepke" Buchalter, Bonanno fled to Sicily in 1938, returning later and becoming a naturalized citizen of the U.S. in 1945. One of Bonanno's specialties, according to most reports, was getting rid of the bodies of those who had been eliminated by the mob. He owned a number of funeral homes and came up with the idea of building coffins with false bottoms. When a legitimate corpse was buried, the coffin also contained, in another area beneath the top layer, the body of a Mafia victim. In this way, the Mafia successfully hid countless bodies over several decades. Bonanno, in addition to his funeral sideline, established a coast-to-coast army of racketeers who operated in New York, Chicago, Las Vegas, and southern California, controlling much of the loan-sharking operations in those areas with the cooperation of local Mafia bosses. Bonanno supplied the cash, the local mob chieftans the muscle to collect the juice loans. Bonanno purchased a luxury home in Tuscon, Ariz., and, in 1953, let it be known to his fellow members of the national crime cartel that he was going into semi-retirement. Yet, for the next ten years, Bonanno consolidated his forces and, in Fall 1964, called his chief New York City enforcer, Joseph Magliocco, startling the fat gunman with an order to kill almost every top crime boss in the U.S., including Frank Di Simone, head of the Mafia in California; Thomas Lucchese, head of the Mafia in New York and New Jersey; Carlo Gambino, head of the Mafia in Brooklyn; and Steven Magaddino, Mafia boss of Buffalo, N.Y.

Magliocco, overweight and suffering from high blood pressure, then called *his* enforcer, Joseph Colombo, Sr. When this Mafia underboss received the order for the mass murder of the top crime czars in the U.S., he pretended to comply but instead went to the men marked for murder, revealing the Bonanno hit list. At a meeting in the swanky New York home of Thomas "Tommy Ryan" Eboli on Sept. 18, 1964, Colombo repeated the orders he had received from Magliocco to Lucchese, Magaddino, and other Mafia chiefs, including Chicago's Sam "Momo" Giancana. Magliocco was summoned and he admitted that Bonanno had given him the orders. He was fined $50,000 for passing on the murder orders and sent on his way. Magliocco was spared since he had "cooperated" with the board of directors who knew he was a man already marked for death; Magliocco died a short time later when his blood pressure exploded. The lethal Giancana immediately lobbied for Bonanno's murder but Lucchese and others who had begun their criminal careers with Bonanno sought to reason with their fellow mob chief.

On the night of Oct. 21, 1964, Bonanno was abducted by his own enforcer, Mike Zaffarano, and two other men as he was about to enter his New York apartment house at Park Avenue and 37th Street, also firing a random shot at Bonanno's lawyer, William P. Maloney, who was with Bonanno at the time. For almost a year, Bonanno was held prisoner by Magaddino in Buffalo, kept in a Catskills retreat. There Bonanno finally promised to retire and turn over his rackets to the other board members of the crime cartel; loansharking, narcotics, and gambling operations in the U.S. estimated to be worth more than $2 billion a year. He was finally released on the proviso that he would leave the country. Bonanno went into self-exile in Haiti for more than a year. Then his son Salvatore was almost killed in a Mafia-style attack in New York. This attack was a violation of the agreement reached between Bonanno and the New York crime bosses. Bonanno ordered men still loyal to his Mafia banners to attack those who had replaced him, especially gunmen working for Paul Sciacca who had been promoted to Bonanno's place on the national board of directors of the syndicate and now headed the Bonanno family. It was Sciacca, Bonanno felt, who had tried to murder his son Salvatore.

The opening battle of what was later called the Bananas War, occurred on the night of Nov. 10, 1967, when a lone gunman, dressed in black and wearing a long coat, walked into the Cypress

Gardens, a Brooklyn restaurant. He pulled out a submachine gun and fired twenty-two .45-caliber slugs at three Sciacca men. Nineteen bullets found their mark, killing James and Tom D'Angelo, and Francisco "Frank the 500" Terelli, who had been eating spaghetti and swallowing chianti wine. The killer strode out of the restaurant unmolested. Peter Crociata, another Sciacca man, was shot in the throat as he was parking his car on a Manhattan street on Mar. 4, 1968. The syndicate fought back; Sciacca ordered the death of Sam Perone four days later. Perone had been one of Bonanno's most loyal aides for more than thirty years and was his son's chauffeur.

Bonanno, back at his Tuscon estate, sent out a message to the syndicate crime bosses: "Next time they hit one of my men, they lose one of their *capos* (chiefs)...first in one family, then in another." He proved his threat some days later when one of his men, wielding a submachine gun, walked into a New York drugstore where Cologero Lo Cicero was sitting at a soda fountain. Lo Cicero, a *capo* for the Joseph Colombo family, turned to have the submachine gun jammed into his face. A burst from the gun made Lo Cicero an unrecognizable corpse. The war waged on for years with at least twenty gangsters on both sides killed and dozens more wounded until a permanent truce was called. Bonanno and his family were allowed to live in peace and he was also permitted to keep control of certain rackets. In return, Bonanno ceased to have his enemies killed. This was the last great war to date between quarrelling Mafia factions in the U.S. In the 1980s, Bonnano wrote a self-serving, whitewashing autobiography which nevertheless admitted to the existence of the Mafia and he was brought before a grand jury to answer questions regarding statements made in his book. When he refused, he was jailed. See: **Capone, Alphonse; Buchalter, Louis; Colombo, Joseph, Sr.; DiSimone, Frank; Gambino, Carlo; Giancano, Sam; Luciano, Charles; Lucchese, Thomas; Magaddino, Steven; Magliocco, Joseph; Maranzano, Salvatore; Masseria, Joseph.**

REF.: Alexander, *The Pizza Connection;* Blumenthal, *Last Days of the Sicilians;* Bonanno, *A Man of Honor; CBA;* Cressey, *Theft of the Nation;* Davis, *Mafia Kingfish;* Demaris, *Captive City;* ____, *The Last Mafioso;* Eisenberg and Landau, *Meyer Lansky;* Fried, *The Rise and Fall of the Jewish Gangster in America;* Gage, *Mafia, USA;* ____, *The Mafia is not an Equal Opportunity Employer;* Gosch and Hammer, *The Last Testament of Lucky Luciano;* Katz, *Uncle Frank;* Kirby and Renner, *Mafia Enforcer;* Kobler, *Capone;* McClellan, *Crime Without Punishment;* Maas, *The Valachi Papers;* Martin, *Revolt in the Mafia;* Messick, *Lansky;* Messick and Goldblatt, *The Mobs and the Mafia;* Nash, *Bloodletters and Badmen;* Navasky, *Kennedy Justice;* Overstreet, *The FBI in Our Open Society;* Peterson, *The Mob;* Reid, *The Grim Reapers;* Reuter, *Disorganized Crime;* Servadio, *Mafioso;* Sondern, *Brotherhood of Evil;* Wicker, *Investigating the FBI;* Zuckerman, *Vengeance is Mine.*

Bonaparte, Charles Joseph, 1851-1921, U.S., atty. gen. Charles Joseph Bonaparte, son of Jerome Bonaparte, grandson of Jerome, King of Westphalia and Elizabeth Bonaparte, and nephew to Napoleon III, was born in Baltimore, Md., and became a practicing lawyer in the U.S. before being appointed U.S. attorney general (1906-09) by President Theodore Roosevelt. At Roosevelt's request, on July 1, 1908, Bonaparte established the first Bureau of Investigation for the detection and prosecution of crimes against the U.S. The Department of Justice had authorized the establishment of such a department as early as 1871, but since this organization was never defined until Roosevelt's era, it came into existence later. The new organization was not officially called the Bureau of Investigation until Stanley Finch became its director on Mar. 16, 1909.

Bonaparte initially put together a small force of twelve accountants, or examiners, who came from the Justice Department and who had been auditing the accounts of U.S. attorneys, marshals, and clerks. They were by no means detectives and had no notion of how to deal with any type of crime except embezzlement, forgery, and other white-collar crimes that fell within their auditing and bookkeeping inspections. Still, Bonaparte's new bureau was the beginning of the FBI. See: **Federal Bureau of Investigation; Hoover, J. Edgar.**

REF.: *CBA;* Kobler, *Capone;* Lowenthal, *The Federal Bureau of Investigation;* Nash, *Citizen Hoover;* Overstreet, *The FBI in Our Open Society;* Powers, *Secrecy and Power;* Toledano, *J. Edgar Hoover;* Ungar, *FBI;* Whitehead, *The FBI Story;* Wicker, *Investigating the FBI.*

Bonaparte, Napoléon, See: **Napoléon I.**

Bonaparte, Pierre-Napoléon, 1815-81, Case of, Fr., mur. Pierre Bonaparte was the rebellious nephew of Emperor Napoléon I, and a constant source of embarrassment in later years to Napoléon III, who had proclaimed the Second Empire in 1852. Pierre spent his early years traveling around Italy, where his father had him arrested for consorting with nationalists. Released in 1831, young Bonaparte journeyed to the U.S. and to Colombia, where he participated in a popular insurrection led by Francisco Santander. Disappointed at not attaining the military rank he thought proper for a Bonaparte, Pierre returned to New York, and from there back to Italy, where he continued to cause trouble.

On May 3, 1836, Bonaparte was arrested in Canino, and was to be transported to a Roman jail. Before this could be accomplished, Pierre fended off thirty police in a wild melee that claimed the life of one arresting officer. He was tried for murder on Sept. 24, and condemned to death, but the sentence was commuted to exile. Pierre spent the next ten years wandering remote areas of Europe before settling in a small Belgian village. The Revolution of 1848 and subsequent rise of Napoléon III brought him back to France, but he quickly proved an embarrassment to the government, especially after he announced his intention to marry his mistress of many years, with whom he had two children.

In 1869, Pierre became embroiled in a fight between two rival publications: *La Ravanche,* an anti-Bonapartist sheet, and *l'Avenir de la Corse,* which supported the regime. On Dec. 30, 1869, Bonaparte wrote a letter congratulating the editors of *l'Avenir de la Corse* on their editorial stance against their competitor. Writing under a pseudonym, the exiled journalist Henri Rochefort replied in his own paper, *la Marseillaise,* that Pierre Bonaparte is in "this category of lame unfortunates" who had sacrificed his republican principles on behalf of the despotic regime of his uncle the emperor. It was a grave affront, and Bonaparte demanded satisfaction in a duel.

Journalist Paschal Grousset, acting independently, demanded that Bonaparte also engage him in the field of honor. Accordingly, he sent his seconds to Bonaparte's home on the afternoon of Jan. 10, 1870. Victor Noir, a youth of twenty-one and aspiring journalist, and Ulric de Fonvielle introduced themselves as the representatives of Monsieur Grousset, handing Bonaparte the message. "I am going to fight with Rochefort," Prince Pierre shouted, "not with one of his hacks!" The impetuous Noir then slapped Bonaparte. Pierre stumbled backward, pulled out his gun and fatally shot the young man. Noir was removed to a nearby house where he died. The murder of Victor Noir jeopardized the already shaky regime of Napoléon III. The Emperor took great pains to distance himself from his bothersome relative, but Paris was indignant.

The murder trial of Pierre Bonaparte began on Mar. 21, 1870, at the Palais de Justice in Tours. Defense attorneys argued that the shooting was carried out to avenge a gross insult. Six days later, the jury returned a verdict of Not Guilty, but the court ordered Prince Pierre to pay 25,000 francs to the Noir family. On Apr. 2, the Emperor scolded Pierre for bringing on a "great scandal" and strongly recommended that Bonaparte leave the country at once. He drifted into obscurity, his financial resources sharply depleted. Pierre Bonaparte died at Versailles in 1881. He was given a simple burial. Ten years later, officials from the Third Republic erected a monument to Victor Noir at the Père Lachaise. The doorman had become a martyr for those opposed to despotic rule.

REF.: *CBA;* Williams, *Manners and Murders In the World of Louis-Napoleon.*

Bond, Hugh Lennox, 1828-93, U.S., jur. Justice of the criminal court of Maryland from 1860-61. He was appointed to the Fourth

Circuit Court of Maryland in 1870 by President Ulysses S. Grant. His decisions against the Ku Klux Klan in South Carolina effectively ended their reign of terror during the post-Civil War period. REF.: *CBA*.

Bond, John C., prom. 1875, Can., forg. In 1874 a clever counterfeiter and forger named John C. Bond fled from Toronto with the proceeds of a $1,500 mortgage in hand. Inspector John Wilson Murray of the Ontario government vowed to take the crook by whatever means necessary.

Learning that Bond's brother worked as a clerk in the post office, Murray posed as a job applicant. Soon the postal manager hired him to work in the mail sorting department where he scanned thousands of pieces of mail, searching for an envelope that matched a sample of Bond's handwriting. After several days he came across a letter postmarked from Evanston, Ill. The peculiar bend in the letter "B" convinced Murray that this was a lead worth pursuing.

Armed with a blurred photograph and a written description of the suspect, Bond traveled to Evanston where he enlisted the help of the local police chief, Carney, in preparing extradition papers. Murray happened upon the forger on an Evanston street, took him into custody, and returned to Toronto on Oct. 16, 1875, to stand trial. He was convicted and sentenced to seven years in prison REF.: Campbell, *A Century of Crime; CBA*.

Bond, Oliver, c.1760-98, Brit., treas. Attempted to establish an independent Irish republic in 1798. He was later convicted and died while in prison. REF.: *CBA*.

Bonesana, Cesare (Marchese de Beccaria), 1738-94, Italy, criminol. An early day criminologist, Cesare Bonesana was a professor of mathematics and, later, a government official whose closest friend was Alessandro Verri, chief warder of the prison in Milan, Italy. Bonesana is associated with the classical theories of criminology and his best known work is *Essay on Crime and Punishment,* published in 1776, in which he affixed mathematics to quantitative methods in the field of criminology. REF.: *CBA*.

Bonhoeffer, Dietrich, 1906-45, Ger., consp. Cleric and strong anti-Nazi, he was arrested, tried, and convicted in 1943 for his involvement in a plot to assassinate Adolf Hitler. He was subsequently executed, but two of his books of philosophy were published posthumously. REF.: *CBA*.

Boniface, Saint (Winfrid, Wynfrith), c.680-755, Brit., mur. Benedictine missionary and archbishop of Mainz in 748. He was known as the Apostle of Germany, and received the sanctions of Pope Gregory to organize the church in Bavaria. He resigned his see in 1754 in order to evangelize West Friesland and destroy the objects of heathen worship. He was killed by an angry mob at Dokkum. REF.: *CBA*.

Bonifacio, Andres, 1863-97, Phil., consp. Led the revolt against Spanish colonial authority on Luzon in 1896 and was replaced as the leader of his people by Emilio Aguinaldo a year later. He attempted to form a rival government but was tried and executed by Aguinaldo. REF.: *CBA*.

Bonilla, Rodrigo Lara, 1944-84, Col., (unsolv.) assass. In apparent retaliation for his vigorous campaign to suppress the Colombian drug traffic, two gunmen riding a motorcycle shot and killed Colombian Justice Minister Rodrigo Lara Bonilla on Apr. 30, 1984.

The machine gun-wielding assassins hit Bonilla as he was driving home through the streets of Bogota. Despite the presence of a police car and an unmarked vehicle driven by his bodyguards, the politician made a relatively easy target.

Bonilla was appointed head of the Ministry by President Belisario Betancur in 1983. On Mar. 10, 1984, his men seized 27,500 pounds of cocaine from a laboratory in the Caquetá Provence with the help of officials from the U.S. Drug Enforcement Agency. The cocaine had an estimated street value of $1.2 billion. Not long after that Bonilla began receiving death threats.

The murder shocked the country and prompted a crackdown against the manufacturers of cocaine. Deep in the jungles of Colombia, large drug plantations began springing up in the mid-

1970s. By the time of Bonilla's death, an estimated 75 per cent of the American supply of cocaine was exported from this small South American country.

Declaring an end to his country's "moral vacations," President Betancur enlisted the military in his fight against the powerful drug traffickers. Meanwhile, police questioned one of the two Bonilla assassins seized following an exchange of gunfire. The man would only say that unknown parties had paid him and his accomplice $20,000 to do away with a high government official. The search for the murder conspirators continued. REF.: *CBA*.

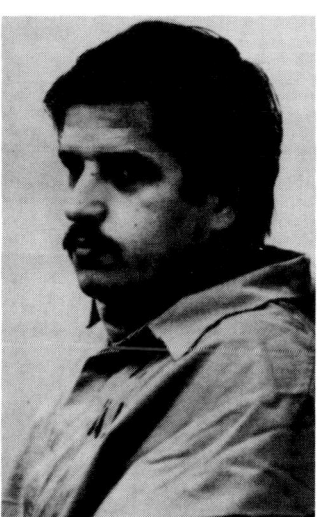 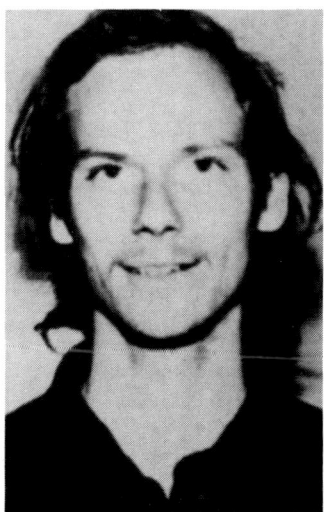

Bonin, "The Freeway Strangler."   Bonin's partner, Vernon Butts.

Bonin, William (AKA: The Freeway Strangler), 1947- , and **Butts, Vernon**, prom. 1980, U.S., asslt.-tort.-mur. Bonin was shuttled in and out of detention homes following his first criminal conviction at the age of ten. His father was a drunk and a gambler, and his doting mother more often than not became the servile victim of her husband's murderous rage. In 1969, the young truck driver from Downey, Calif., was convicted of his first sex crime, charged with molesting five boys. Bonin was sent to Atascadero State Hospital but after two years physicians concluded he was not receptive to treatment. For the next five years William Bonin darted in and out of prison on a variety of sexual offenses. A psychiatrist's report concluded that his homosexual problems were related to his mother's domination during childhood.

By his own estimate, Bonin killed at least twenty-one teen-aged boys between 1978 and 1980. With the help of several willing accomplices including Vernon Butts, Bonin cruised the highways of Los Angeles and Orange County targeting young homosexuals for death. Butts, at first shocked, soon became a willing participant in the killing orgy, which always accompanied "rough sex." "After the first one, I couldn't do anything about it," Butts explained. "He (Bonin) had a hypnotic way about him."

The naked and battered bodies were deposited near the on-off ramps of the Los Angeles freeways. The press quickly dubbed the unknown assailant the "Freeway Strangler." Police from four counties assisted in the investigation which yielded no new clues. Butts grew tired of the game and temporarily dropped out of sight, but this did not deter Bonin who recruited younger, more willing henchmen to help him locate victims. Two of these men, Greg Miley and James Monro, were drifters who wandered into Hollywood where they met Bonin.

Police finally were tipped off to the identity of the "Freeway Strangler" by a 17-year-old youth Bonin tried to enlist as an accomplice. Bonin was arrested in Hollywood after parking his van at a closed gas station.

Charged with fourteen counts of murder, he was arraigned in Los Angeles Superior Court along with Butts who confessed to helping in five of the killings. However, the prosecution lost its star witness when Butts hanged himself in his jail cell. On Mar.

12, 1982, Judge William Keene sentenced the serial killer to death. After the trial ended Bonin admitted that even if he were freed he would continue to kill. "I couldn't stop killing," he said. "It got easier each time."

REF.: Cartel, *Serial Mass Murders; CBA.*

Bonmartini, Countess Linda, b.1873, and **Bonetti, Rosina,** prom. 1902, and **Murri, Tullio,** prom. 1902, and **Naldi, Pio,** prom. 1902, and **Secchi, Dr. Carl,** prom. 1902, Italy, mur. From the beginning of her marriage, Linda Bonmartini complained bitterly about the intellectual capacities of her husband, Count Bonmartini. "My God, would that someone rid me of that soft-brained bigot!" Linda Bonmartini said to her father. Not only were the Count and Countess at odds over political matters (he was a conservative, she was a socialist), but Bonmartini was an unfaithful husband. His numerous infidelities drove Linda into the arms of her former lover Dr. Carlo Secchi, a foppish medical student who provided her with drugs to sedate the Count so they could be together. Tullio Murri, Linda's brother, also disliked the count, and had quarreled with him over money on several occasions. Dr. Secchi and Tullio decided to kill Count Bonmartini. They considered poison, but it was too slow. Tullio would attend to the matter himself, but he needed a decoy.

One night in August 1902, Tullio's beautiful mistress, Rosina Bonetti, lured the Count into the bedroom of his home on the Via Mazzini, Bologna. Expecting a romantic interlude, Bonmartini instead found his wife, her brother, and Dr. Secchi lying in wait. Bonmartini was stabbed repeatedly by the group until he was dead. Hearing of this bloody crime first-hand from his son Tullio, Professor Murri, who held a chair at the university in Bologna, informed the local magistrate, who promptly arrested the conspirators. The trial was held in Turin and on Aug. 11, 1965, after lengthy deliberations, all four were found Guilty. Tullio Murri was sentenced to thirty years' solitary confinement. The countess and Dr. Secchi received ten-year sentences, Rosina Bonetti seven. All the defendants appealed their sentences. Rosina Bonetti's sentence was commuted, but by then she was in an insane asylum. But in 1906, the king, in response to petitions from her influential friends, pardoned Countess Bonmartini.

REF.: *CBA;* Nash, *Look For the Woman;* Sanders, *Murder In the Big Cities.*

Bonne, François de (Duc de Lesdiguières), 1543-1626, Fr., law enfor. off. Joined the Huguenot troops in 1575, and later supported Henry of Navarre. In 1622, he was appointed constable of France. REF.: *CBA.*

Bonner, Antoinette (AKA: The Diamond Queen), 1892-1920, U.S., fraud. Along Jeweler's Row in mid-town Manhattan, Bonner, a poor Romanian immigrant, earned a reputation for having a sharp eye and a sixth sense about the clarity and purity of uncut diamonds. The merchants who bought and sold the precious stones trusted her with portions of their inventory which she personally delivered to clients for their perusal. Bonner always returned the unsold stock.

In 1914 she finally gave in to temptation. With a large quantity of diamonds, Antoinette Bonner absconded to Paris where police arrested her and returned her to New York. She claimed at her trial she had gone to Paris to find buyers for her diamonds. There were wealthy clients, she said, who lived in Paris. No one could prove or disprove this contention so she was freed by the court.

In 1920 the Diamond Queen secretly disposed of uncut stones obtained from several prominent jewelers. But now the police were keeping a close eye on her. A second complaint was filed, and not long afterward the police found Bonner in her office. She looked at the officers coolly before swallowing a lethal dose of poison. The pretty young Romanian dropped dead.

REF.: *CBA;* Kingston, *Dramatic Days at the Old Bailey;* Nash, *Look For the Woman.*

Bonnet, Edward (Ned Bonnet), d.1713, Brit., rob. Men of the cloth held a special fascination for Ned Bonnet, one of England's legendary highwaymen. His confrontations with clergymen on the open road afforded Bonnet a chance to debate the vexing notion of good and evil. With pistols pointed squarely at the chest of his victim, Bonnet usually succeeded in winning his argument.

"Pray sir, keep your breath to cool your porridge and don't talk of religious matters to me," he told an Anabaptist minister on his way to Ely, "for I'll have you know that like all other true-bred gentlemen, I believe nothing at all of religion. Therefore deliver me your money and bestow your laborious cant upon your female auditors."

Forced to live in near-poverty after a tragic fire destroyed his house, his misfortune drove him to London where he soon realized that the fast and easy path to financial solvency was through illegal means. Bonnet joined up with a gang of highwaymen who terrorized the countryside near Cambridgeshire, carrying out over three hundred successful robberies in a short period of time. A skilled horseman, Bonnet decided to leave the gang. Years later Englishmen humorously recalled the time he stopped a young dandy riding in a carriage with a woman known to be a courtesan who attended to the needs of wealthy students at Cambridge University. The pair were having a riotous time as the coach sped on toward its destination.

Bonnet, pistols drawn, stopped the driver and demanded that the young man hand over £6 or face the consequences. When the dandy refused, Bonnet ordered both of them out of the carriage. He ordered them to strip and tied them together by the hands. He then sent the horse and carriage away, forcing the shamed couple to walk back to town without a stitch between them. The student was expelled from the university and the courtesan was sent to jail.

Edward Bonnet continued his activities for several more years. He was betrayed by Zachary Clare, another highwayman, who agreed to tell what he knew about Bonnet in return for clemency. Bonnet was taken at Cambridge and led to jail by a full contingent of five-hundred guards. There was little chance for a reprieve, for robbery carried with it a mandatory death penalty. He was put to death on Mar. 28, 1713, expressing sorrow for the shame he brought to his wife and children.

REF.: *CBA;* Hibbert, *Highwaymen;* Smith, *Highwaymen.*

Bonnet, Jeanne (AKA: Little Frog Catcher), 1841-76, U.S., rob. A tomboy who always wore men's clothing, Jeanne Bonnet was known as Little Frog Catcher; she made her living catching and selling frogs in San Mateo County, Calif. She forsook this meager living in early 1876 and formed an all-female gang of sneak thieves, filching items from local stores. Bonnet's gang members were all former prostitutes from San Francisco bordellos who also donned men's clothing and lived with Bonnet in a shack off Market Street. The gang was short-lived, however, when Bonnet was found dead, a bullet in her heart. Detectives concluded the apprentice thief had been murdered by whoremasters incensed over Bonnet's stealing their women.

REF.: Asbury, *The Barbary Coast; CBA.*

Bonnet, Stede (AKA: Major Bonnet, Captain Edwards, Captain Thomas), d.1718, Brit., pir.-mur. Endowed with a small fortune, a good education, and social rank, Stede Bonnet relinquished these worldly advantages to plunder the coastal waters of the British colonies of North America. His social acquaintances on the island of Barbados, where he resided, believed that a disease of the mind had caused him to become a pirate.

About 1715, Stede Bonnet outfitted a fast sloop with ten guns and seventy men. He named his vessel Revenge, and sailed toward the Virginia Capes, where he soon captured the *Anne,* the *Turbet,* the *Endeavor,* the *Bristol,* and the *Young.*

Within a few months, Bonnet's cargo hold was filled with molasses, clothes, ammunition, rum, and other prizes. But then his own ship was taken by another notorious pirate, Blackbeard (Edward Teach), and Bonnet was forced to serve aboard his ship, Queen Anne's Revenge When Blackbeard lost his ship at Topsail Inlet, Bonnet regained command of his sloop. He sailed to Bathtown, N.C., where he made his peace with the colonial authority, promising to end his crimes against the British. In return for a royal pardon, Bonnet agreed to move against the

Spaniards as a privateer.

Bonnet discovered that Blackbeard had stolen a good part of his provisions. Bent on revenge, Bonnet sailed up and down the Capes but could not locate Blackbeard.

The capture of pirate Stede Bonnet.

Unable to pay a fair exchange rate for necessary goods, Bonnet's crew reverted to piracy. The Revenge plundered every vessel in sight and Bonnet, now called Captain Thomas, became the terror of the British colonies. The South Carolina authorities, alarmed at having a pirate in their midst, enlisted the help of Captain William Rhet, a privateer who placed his two vessels, the *Henry* and the *Sea Nymph,* at the governor's disposal.

The hanging of Bonnet the pirate, 1718.

Bonnet was at last overtaken by Rhet in September 1718 near the coast of Carolina. Bonnet and his crew were put ashore on Sept. 30, near Charlestown. The men were placed under guard by the militia, but Bonnet and David Hariot, one of his men, escaped by bribing one of the sentinels.

Fearing that Bonnet would organize a new pirate band, the governor issued a reward of £700 for his apprehension. Mean-

while, Bonnet had secured a new vessel, but was sorely in need of provisions. He laid anchor at Swillivants Island, off Charlestown. Colonel Rhet learned of Bonnet's whereabouts from the governor, and with a heavily armed band of men, he set out for the island. In a brief flurry of gunfire, Hariot was killed and Bonnet was forced to surrender. On Nov. 6, 1718, the pirate leader was returned to Charlestown where he was put on trial in a Vice-Admiralty Court. Indictments were sworn against Bonnet and thirty-three members of his plundering band. All but four men were found Guilty and sentenced to die. The prisoners declared that their intentions were honorable but that they were driven to piracy by the terrible shortage of provisions.

On Nov. 8, 1718, twenty-two members of the pirate gang were executed at White Point near Charlestown, pursuant to the sentence handed down by Judge Nicholas Trot. In passing sentence on Bonnet, the judge noted the fact that he compounded his crimes by murdering eighteen people. Judge Trot quoted scripture, and expressed the hope that Bonnet was sufficiently repentant. On Nov. 18, Captain Bonnet was hanged. See: **Teach, Edward.**

REF.: Botting, *The Pirates; CBA;* Chatterton, *The Romance of Piracy;* Defoe, *A General History of the Robberies and Murders of the Most Notorious Pirates, 1717-1724;* Ellms, *The Pirates' Own Book;* Gosse, *History of the Pirates I;* Innes, *The Book of Pirates;* Lydon, *Pirates, Privateers and Profits;* Pringle, *Jolly Roger: The Story of the Great Age of Piracy;* Rankin, *The Golden Age of Piracy;* Williams, *Captains Outrageous: Seven Centuries of Piracy.*

Bonneville, Nicolas de, 1760-1828, Fr., consp. President of a Paris district during the outbreak of the revolution in 1789. He was jailed during the Reign of Terror and persecuted by Royalists. Books authored: *Histoire de l'Europe moderne* (1789-92); *De l'esprit des religions* (1791). REF.: *CBA.*

Bonney, Edward W., d.1862, U.S., mur. G.W. Hirsch first arrived in San Francisco in December 1860. With his life savings in hand the French immigrant took a room at the What Cheer House at Sacramento and Leidesdorff Streets. It was here that he met Edward Bonney who persuaded him to invest his money in a small stationery business that was about to open.

Bonney's intentions, however, centered around the $600 cash that belonged to Hirsch. On Jan. 2, 1861, the two men rode out of town in Bonney's carriage. Along a deserted stretch of highway the stationer began pummeling his new partner over the head until he was dead. To disguise the injury, he bandaged the corpse's face and sat it upright next to him.

Bonney drove the carriage along the road, passing many other San Franciscans who were enjoying the cool, pleasant day. Some noticed the bandaged man on the passenger's side but dismissed him as an invalid.

In East Oakland the corpse was abandoned alongside a road after Bonney failed to sever the head with a blunt pocket knife. Two weeks later the decomposed body of Hirsch was located and returned to San Francisco where Bonney supplied the identification. Had he not been so willing to come forward to examine the remains, it is likely that he might have escaped police detection for his conflicting statements and peculiar manner made the police suspicious. Bonney was officially charged with first-degree murder, convicted several months later, and hanged on May 9, 1862.

REF.: *CBA;* Duke, *Celebrated Criminal Cases of America.*

Bonney, Thomas Lee, 1943-   , U.S., mur. Bonney of Chesapeake, Va., told an astonished courtroom that he was not personally responsible for the actions of his nine other "personalities," one of whom shot and killed his 19-year-old daughter Kathy Carol in 1987.

The remains of the young woman were found along the Dismal Swamp Canal in Camden County, N.C., not far from the Virginia state line. When the trial commenced in Pasquotank County in November 1988, District Attorney H.P. Williams painted a picture of a middle-aged man who killed his daughter in a jealous rage. Kathy Carol allegedly was involved with a married man at the time of her death.

Bonney pleaded innocent by reason of insanity, citing a multiple personality disorder he had suffered from for years. During the trial jurors were shown videotapes of the killer, who, under hypnosis, revealed ten different personalities in recorded interviews with Dr. Paul F. Dell, professor of psychiatry at the Eastern Virginia Medical School.

The insanity plea failed and Bonney was convicted of first-degree murder on Nov. 25, 1988. Five days later Judge Paul Wright sentenced the defendant to death in a case that attracted national attention. At present Thomas Lee Bonney remains on death row in North Carolina pending further appeals. REF.: CBA.

Bonney, William, See: **Billy the Kid.**

Bonnie and Clyde, See: **Barrow, Clyde.**

Bonnot Gang, prom. 1910s, Fr., rob.-mur. Jules Joseph Bonnot had been one of the most daring racecar drivers in the early era of autos. He turned anarchist in about 1911 and then decided to form a gang of thieves who would use the car for fast getaways, Bonnot being the first to employ the motorized escape in Europe. (Henry Starr was the first American bandit to use the car in a robbery in the U.S., see entry). On Dec. 21, 1911, Bonnot and others waylaid a bank messenger named Gaby of the Société Générale in Paris' Rue Ordener, shooting him and taking a pouch stuffed with a half million francs, then the equivalent of £25,000 or $200,000, an enormous haul that stunned the French police. They drove off in a Delaunay-Belleville car. The bandits then raided an arsenal on the Grand Boulevard, taking scores of rifles, revolvers, and many boxes of ammunition. As usual, the bandits made their escape in a car driven by race driver and gang leader Bonnot. Following several more robberies where great sums were taken, more than ten thousand reward posters for the gang were distributed throughout Paris and neighboring cities. Prime Minister Poincaré stated: "Bonnot must be brought to justice by whatever means and at whatever cost."

To capture the elusive bandits, the French Garde Mobile, or Flying Squad, also employing cars, were assigned to track down the murderous band. Bonnot, meanwhile, robbed a factory and shot several persons, then motored to Belgium. When Bonnot and his men drove back into Paris, a policeman recognized the Dion-Bouton car in which they were riding and leaped onto the running board as the car sped along. Bonnot and his men fired three bullets into his chest, killing him. The French bandit leader seemed to be emulating the tactics of the American western bandits, except that he used cars instead of horses to make his escapes. Police were aided by author H. Ashton-Wolfe, who ironically specialized in penny dreadful-type books of fanciful tales that claimed to report about real criminals. Ashton-Wolfe had actually employed Bonnot as a chauffeur, and he had had a photo taken of himself in the car and Bonnot at the wheel. This photo was the first to be used in identifying the bandit chieftan.

Since his car had now been identified, Bonnot fielded about for another fast auto and decided to obtain the fast new touring car owned by the Marquis de Rougé. The gang scouted the routes driven by the Marquis, a well-known sporting figure, and, in March 1912, drove their car into the path of the auto driven by the Marquis' chauffeur. They brutally shot the Marquis and the chauffeur to death and threw their bodies into a ditch, abandoning the Dion-Bouton for the touring car. Bonnot, Francois Callemin, and others then drove to Chantilly where they raided the local bank, firing rifles as they entered, killing one clerk and injuring two others. The bandits leaped over the tellers cages and scooped up the money in the drawers, a technique that John Dillinger and others would duplicate in the U.S. two decades later.

Outside the bank, Callemin and others fired their rifles in the air to frighten off the citizens who came running toward the bank at the sound of the first gunfire. The scene was something out of the American West a half century earlier. With Bonnot and his men rushing from the bank, those bandits outside the bank fired wildly into the air and at scurrying citizens, then they all leaped into the touring car and Bonnot jerked the car forward as

if he were in a race, speeding out of town. A policeman fired at the retreating car, wounding Callemin, but this only served to make the bandit angry and he fired a random shot at a motorist traveling in the opposite direction.

The Sûreté Nationale, one of France's four police forces, made an all-out effort to capture the ruthless bandits, assigning hundreds of its men to track down Bonnot. Poincaré announced that Bonnot was "the most dangerous criminal of this century, or the last." A short time later, Bonnot and his men struck again, this time raiding the ancient fortress of Vincennes where they shot one guard and wounded others while looting the arsenal of guns and ammunition. The gang was now hunted everywhere in France, police and even military units on the trail of its members. Bonnot was all bravado and threatened to kill anyone who dared get near him or his men. One of his henchmen, Pierre Garnier wrote challenging letters to the Sûreté. One missive said: "I know that you will get the better of me in the long run. All the strength is on your side. But I will make you pay for it dearly."

In March 1913 Bonnot's top aide, Callemin, was arrested as he peddled down a Paris street on a bicycle. As he was dragged away, the anarchist robber-murderer screamed: "I was ready for you! But you had all the luck! You will find that my three revolvers are all loaded!" A few days later one of the gang members contacted police and told them that they could find Bonnot in his hideout at Choisy-le-Roi, adding: "I hope you get the skunk! He killed one of my best friends." More than 200 policemen and soldiers closed in on the bandit chief's lair, using carts filled with hay and mattresses to approach the house.

As the policemen and troopers moved forward, Bonnot began firing at them, dozens of rounds that killed one man and wounded many others. He ran from window to window firing and screaming oaths, a lethal maniac. The police and troops fired back and the gun battle raged for more than six hours until there was no more gunfire from the house. Cautiously, police crept forward, entered the house and climbed the stairs. They found Bonnot on the floor, hit by four bullets, bleeding to death. He was in a half coma and with his dying breath he cursed the officers staring down at him. Nailed to a wall was a letter he had written during the gun battle. It read: "I am famous. My name is trumpeted to the four corners of the globe and the publicity given to my humble person must make all those people jealous who try in vain to get into the papers. As far as I am concerned, I could well have done without it." He added that certain persons who had harbored him were innocent of his crimes. Police inspecting the bandit's dead body soon realized that Bonnot had inflicted the wound that killed him, committing suicide before he could be taken into custody. Several other gang members chose the same inglorious exit, including a gang member named Carouy who drank prussic acid. Callemin, Soudy, and Monier were tried for murder, found Guilty, and sentenced to the guillotine. They were all beheaded on Apr. 21, 1913. Garnier and another gang member shot it out with police on May 14, 1913, and were killed. The rest of the gang members were quickly rounded up and given long prison terms. It was the end of Bonnot's reign of terror. See: **Starr, Henry.**

REF.: Ashton-Wolfe, *The Underworld; CBA;* Morain, *The Underworld of Paris;* Nash, *Almanac of World Crime; ____, Among the Missing; ____, A Crime Chronology;* Symons, *A PIctorial History of Crime;* Wilson, *Encyclopedia of Murder.*

Bonny, Anne, and **Read, Mary,** prom. 1720, U.S., pir. Anne Bonny was the illegitimate daughter of an Irish lawyer named William Cormac. The attending scandal drove Cormac to the New World where he began a new life with his mistress and infant daughter. Carmac flourished in Charleston, S.C., and bought a large plantation. While in her teens, Anne disappointed her father by running off with an itinerant sailor named James Bonny.

Bonny heard of handsome subsidies paid to fortune hunters in the Bahamas by Governor Woodes Rogers, who was looking for men to track down and capture the pirates that infested the area. With his wife Anne, he traveled to the island in 1716 and worked as a paid informant, picking up scraps of information on

Jules Bonnot   **Pierre Garnier**

Police checking one of Bonnot's cars.

Bonnot at the wheel of a car, 1910.

Using moving barricades to attack Bonnot.

Volunteers firing on Bonnot's hideout.

Police closing in on a Bonnot hideout.

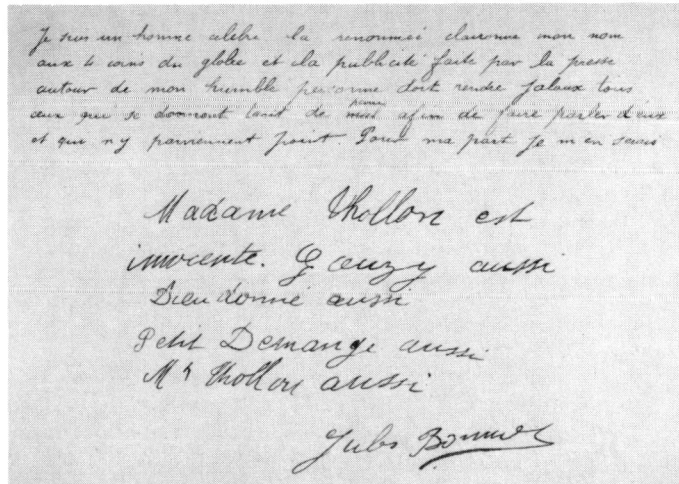

Bonnot's letter, found after the battle.

the waterfront. Anne was disgusted with her husband's seamy line of work and when the opportunity presented itself, she fled New Providence to become a pirate herself. While Bonny investigated the pirates, Anne openly consorted with them.

When Governor Rogers offered an amnesty, pirates by the dozen converged on the island, including "Calico" John Rackham, known for his gaudy striped pants. Rackham noticed Anne and tried to "buy" her divorce from Bonny. The husband refused and reported Rackham's intentions to the governor, who ordered Anne flogged unless she returned to her husband. Instead, Anne went to sea with Rackham. Together they outfitted a pirate ship and went in search of prey.

The fierce female pirates Anne Bonny and Mary Read.

They soon captured a Dutch ship laden with rich cargo and a crew of healthy sailors ready to be impressed into pirate duty. Anne Bonny selected a fair youth she deemed worthy of seduction. The boy turned out to be a girl, Mary Read. Read and Bonny became fast friends. They also acquired an unsavory reputation as two of the most fearsome pirates of the Caribbean until one day in October 1720 when Captain Burnet of the Royal Navy captured their vessel, the *Queen Royal,* as it lay anchored off Jamaica. Rackham was taken along with the rest of the crew to St. Jago de la Vega, where they were tried as pirates. Anne and Mary pleaded pregnancy and escaped the death sentence.

Mary Read died in her prison on Dec. 4, 1820, from a fever before her child was born. Anne Bonny escaped, and was said to have lived to old age on a South Carolina plantation. See: **Bonnet, Stede.**

REF.: Botting, *The Pirates; CBA;* Mitchell, *Pirates;* Nash, *Look For the Woman;* Rankin, *The Golden Age of Piracy;* Scott, *The Concise Encyclopedia of Crime and Criminals.*

Bonomini, Ernesto, c.1902, Fr., assass. In July 1923, noted Italian journalist and proponent of the fascist movement Mr. Bonservizi arrived in Paris to work as a foreign correspondent for the government publication, *Il Popolo d'Italia.* Many Italian exiles believed Bonservizi was a political spy sent by Benito Mussolini to report on the movements of the Paris dissidents. This belief was shared by Ernesto Bonomini, an Italian draft evader and anarchist.

Bonomini left Italy in August 1922 to escape the draft. The serious young revolutionary settled in the Italian colony of Paris where he studiously read the left-wing journals of the day: *L'Humanité, La Libertaire,* and *L'Action Français.* Thus inspired by liberalism, his opposition to Mussolini's brand of fascism grew into an obsession. To better observe Bonservizi and his friends, Bonomini quit a well-paying job in order to work as a waiter at the Passage des Princes restaurant, Bonservizi's favorite meeting place.

Bonomini watched and waited. Then, on Feb. 20, 1924, he crept up beside Bonservizi's table and fired two shots into the side of his head. One week later the Italian correspondent died, which delighted his assassin. "My conscience made me do it," he declared. "I wished to kill the idea rather than the man."

In an emotionally charged courtroom, Maitre Henry Torrès

defended Bonomini as neither a Bolshevik nor a socialist, but as an enemy of dictators. A sympathetic jury returned a Guilty verdict with "extenuating circumstances," and on Oct. 23, 1924, Bonomini was sentenced to eight years at hard labor.

REF.: *CBA;* Heppenstall, *Bluebeard and After;* Morain, *Underworld of Paris.*

Bonsal, Dudley Baldwin, 1906- , U.S., jur. Chairman of the Special Committee on the Federal Loyalty Security Program from 1955-57; member of International Commission of Jurists in Geneva, Switz., from 1953-73; and member of the Committee to Implement the Criminal Justice Act, U.S. Judicial Conference from 1964-79. He received judicial appointment to the Court of the Southern District of New York by President John F. Kennedy in 1961. REF.: *CBA.*

Bontade, Giovanni, 1946-88, Si., org. crime. Mafia chief Giovanni Bontade was a key member of one of the feuding Mafia clans in Sicily during the late 1980s in the bloodiest gangland war in decades, which is still raging at this writing. On Sept. 27, 1988, while Bontade and his wife were at home in their villa outside Palermo, rival gunmen stormed the place, subduing bodyguards and shooting Bontade and his wife Francesca to death. The slaying of the Bontades brought the number of Mafia murders to fourteen at the time. Only a few days earlier a Sicilian judge and his crippled son had been murdered in the all-out vendetta war. REF.: *CBA.*

Bonus Army Riot, 1932, U.S., riot. In 1924, the U.S. Congress passed a bill to award a monetary bonus to veterans of WWI, payable in 1944. But the Great Depression arrived in 1929, leaving many of the veterans unable to provide for their families. Recalling the bonus they had been promised, veterans' groups demanded the payment immediately. From across the nation, former soldiers came to Washington in Spring 1932, hoping to force Congress to authorize immediate payment. By summer, the Bonus Expeditionary Force (BEF) had swelled to 20,000. They lived in squalid little shacks in Washington's Anacostia Flats—"Hoovervilles," to many. The House of Representatives, sympathetic to the soldiers' plight, passed the Bonus Bill on June 15, but, as 12,000 men waited on the steps of the Capitol, the Senate rejected it two days later.

President Herbert Hoover convinced Congress to give the protestors enough money to return home, but only a handful of men accepted the offer. The rest remained in their tent city, contemplating new protests. The president received constant reports that communist agitators were planning an insurrection. Hoover ordered Chief of Police Pelham D. Glassford to clear the area. The veterans refused to move, and two of them were killed. Hoover then ordered General Douglas MacArthur into the area. He decided to make short work of the BEF, despite Hoover's pleas that the situation be handled delicately. Assisted by his adjutant, Dwight D. Eisenhower, and Major George Patton, MacArthur's four troops of cavalry and four infantry companies marched into the riot zone, supported by six tanks.

The army systematically burned the makeshift camps to the ground and hurled tear gas canisters into the ranks of the BEF, blinding an 11-week-old baby and injuring several people. The president was angered by MacArthur's actions, but MacArthur tersely explained that the rioters were "animated by the essence of revolution." Hoover took full responsibility for the incident, which came to symbolize the despair and hopelessness many Americans felt during the Depression. It was soon learned that the leaders of the Bonus Army, notably Walter W. Waters, had organized squads of men to drive out the small faction of Communist Party leaders who had formed the Worker's Ex-Service Men's League to create a disruption.

REF.: Allen, *Since Yesterday;* Bendiner, *Just Around the Corner;* Bernstein, *The Lean Years: A History of the American Worker, 1920-1933; CBA;* Conger, *The Thirties, A Time to Remember;* Ellis, *A Nation in Torment: The Great American Depression, 1929-1939;* Emerson, *Hoover and His Times;* Filler, *The Anxious Years;* Hofstadter and Wallace, *American Violence;* Horan, *The Desperate Years;* Lee, *Douglas MacArthur;*

Schlesinger, *The Crisis of the Old Order, 1919-1933;* Seldes, *The Years of the Locust, 1929-32;* Shannon, *The Great Depression;* Simon, *As We Saw the Thirties;* Wecter, *The Age of the Great Depression, 1929-1941;* Wilbur, *The Hoover Policies;* Wilson, *The American Earthquake;* Wolfe, *Herbert Hoover.*

Bonynge, Paul, prom. 1936, U.S., jur. Paul Bonynge of New York was a plain-speaking, no-nonsense kind of lawyer. When he ran for county judge of Nassau County, Long Island, in 1931 he told the voters that on occasion he had violated the Prohibition laws. Such an admission from a candidate for the judicial bench was tantamount to suicide and he lost the election.

A year later he moderated his public stance by promising never to imprison a man for something he would do himself. This time Bonynge, a cousin of former Republican Congressman Robert William Bonynge, was elected a justice of the New York Supreme Court.

True to his word, the judge upheld his campaign promise. In June 1936, Percy Reed, owner of the Nassau Kennel Club and well-known operator of dog races, asked Justice Bonynge for a favorable ruling on his business. For some time Reed had been harassed by the local authorities for staging a gambling operation under a thinly disguised pretense of "selling" $2 options on the dogs.

Admitting that it was an "ingeniously devised scheme," Bonynge gave the devil his due and awarded the judgment to the plaintiff without costs. "For a generation or more betting at horse races was unlawful," the judge said in his written summation. "After this prolonged burst of morality the Legislature suddenly discovered the need of 'improving the breed of horses,'...restored race track betting by removing the criminal penalties. But let no one suspect that our best citizens repair to Belmont Park and other nearby tracks for the purpose of betting or gambling. Perish the thought, for their minds rest on higher things." REF.: *CBA.*

Boodle Gang, 1850s-60s, U.S., org. crime. Organized in about 1855, this New York gang operated on the Lower West Side and specialized in hijacking food and clothing wagons. By the 1860s, the Boodlers took to robbing bank messengers and used their overburdened carts to block streets so that police could not pursue them. The largest amount stolen from bank messengers was $14,000, taken from a bank clerk in January 1866. This theft caused so much police activity and arrests of Boodle Gang members that the gang dwindled in numbers and later disappeared when the rival, more powerful Potash gang took over its territory.
REF.: Asbury, *The Gangs of New York; CBA.*

Booher, Vernon, d.1929, Can., mur. On July 9, 1928, four murders took place at the Booher farm at Mannville, near Edmonton, Alberta. Police found the bodies of field hands Gabriel Cromby and Bill Rosyk in the bunkhouse, and those of Mrs. Booher and her son Fred inside the house. Booher's son, Vernon Booher, had reported the multiple shootings, but could shed no light on the identity of the likely killer.

The police determined that the four victims had been shot with a .303 rifle belonging to a neighbor, Charles Stephenson, who said the weapon had been stolen from his home the previous Sunday. In desperation, police turned to a Viennese psychic, Dr. Maximilien Langsner, who was credited with solving a recent burglary case in Vancouver through ESP. At the inquest, he stared thoughtfully at Booher. When it was over, he declared with a degree of certainty that Vernon had killed his family, but was unsure of the motive. Langsner then led police to a patch of prairie grass where the murder weapon was buried.

Booher was arrested on July 17, and held as a material witness in the Edmonton Jail. Langsner visited him and ascertained his motive for the murders. Booher had been denied permission to marry the daughter of a local farmer. In anger, he murdered his family. A diminutive woman, Erma Higgins, had witnessed Vernon sneaking out of church that Sunday to steal the rifle from Stephenson. When confronted by Higgins, Vernon broke down and confessed to the killings. The first of Booher's two murder trials began on Sept. 24 at the Supreme Criminal Court of Alberta.

He was convicted of murder and sentenced to be hanged. However, the appellate division of the supreme court granted Booher a new trial because additional evidence had been produced by the defense. The second trial ended on Jan. 23, 1929, with another Guilty verdict. Booher was hanged in the Alberta Jail at Fort Saskatchewan on Apr. 29, 1929.
REF.: *CBA;* Logan, *Rope, Knife, and Chair;* Wilson, *Encyclopedia of Murder.*

Bookie Gang, The, prom. 1945, U.S., burg.-rob.-mur. During the two years they worked together, this odd assortment of second-story men, Prohibition-era rumrunners, and syndicate triggermen successfully pulled off fifty-seven robberies, four burglaries, two auto thefts, and committed at least three murders. The Chicago Bookie Gang raked in several hundred thousand dollars from the various jobs. But as Lawrence (Tiny) Mazzanars sadly recalled, "Dice, horses, women got everything we made—mostly dice."

The men met in prison between 1938-42 while serving time for various crimes committed in Illinois. The leaders of the Bookie Gang were hardened criminals: Virgil Summers, a burglar and house breaker from Downstate Illinois, George (Bugs) Moran, one-time leader of Chicago's infamous North Side gang until Al Capone's torpedoes wiped out his henchmen in the 1929 St. Valentine's Day Massacre, James Joseph Kelly, an ex-convict who had spent half his life in the Joliet Penitentiary for armed robbery, and Richard Todd, a West Side street-corner lounger who had been arrested but never previously convicted.

From the back room of a snack shop at Madison and Paulina streets, the principal members of the Bookie Gang planned their operations over coffee and doughnuts. Their first target: the syndicate-run handbooks and slot machines of Cook and Lake counties, run by Eddie Vogel, former Capone stooge but now the undisputed boss of Chicago gambling operations, a risky undertaking for the syndicate did not appreciate being trifled with. Beginning in August 1945 the gang knocked over syndicate handbooks on the average of one a week.

The harassed leaders of the Chicago outfit were rumored to have posted a $20,000 reward for the Bookie Gang, dead or alive. Also, the gang's well-timed robberies drew unwanted attention to mob gambling operations which led to a police crackdown in the fall of 1945.

Summers, Steve (the Greek) Manos, Renoto Lolli, and Moran and company, quickly served notice that they, too, would not be intimidated. An informant named Eugene Duggan was executed for spilling all he knew to Detective Emil Smicklas of the Chicago Police Department robbery detail. Then two police officers named Charles A. Brady and George Hellstern were shot dead on the North Side on Sept. 2 while investigating a robbery. The Bookie Gang had violated an unwritten law of the underworld: never shoot a policeman.

Realizing this, the gang took steps to punish the offender, Red Smith, who had spent most of his life in jail. Mazzanars and Lolli killed the Irishman for his terrible indiscretion, then buried the body in a vacant suburban field. The first break in the case came when Assistant State's Attorney Alexander Napoli filed murder charges against Mazzanars and Lolli which eventually led to their confessions. Lolli dreamed of retiring from the gang a wealthy man, and planned to take $100,000 and go to small-town America where he would marry his sweetheart. Instead, he received thirty years.

It took several more months of diligent police work on the part of Smicklas and John Alcock to put the Bookie Gang out of business. By April 1946, five of its members were dead. Lolli, Mazzanars, Kelly, and Summers were behind bars. Richard Todd was placed on probation after turning state's evidence, and the once powerful Bugs Moran was sentenced to ten to twenty-five years for armed robbery in Dayton, Ohio (also wanted on release for another bank robbery). See: **Moran, George (Bugs).**
REF.: *CBA;* Hapler, *The Chicago Crime Book.*

Boomerang, 1947, a film directed by Elia Kazan. This motion picture, drawn from a *Reader's Digest* article ("The Perfect Case" by Anthony Abbott), is based upon the unsolved murder case of a Catholic priest, Father Hubert Dahme (U.S., 1924) for which drifter Harold Israel was charged. The film was shot on location in the courts and jail in Stamford, Conn., inspiring a new wave in Hollywood realism. The prosecutor in the film, portrayed by Dana Andrews, is based on a then-young state's attorney, Homer Cummings who went on to become U.S. attorney general in President Franklin D. Roosevelt's first and second administrations. See: **Cummings, Homer Stille; Dahme, Father Hubert; Israel, Harold.** REF.: *CBA.*

Boorn, Jesse, and **Boorn, Stephen,** prom. 1819, Case of, U.S., mur. The Boorn brothers were simple peasant farmers from Manchester, Vt. They had a sister named Sally, who married Russel Colvin, considered by the townsfolk to be an eccentric personality, if not feeble-minded.

It came as no surprise in Manchester when Colvin suddenly disappeared in May 1812. He had the wanderlust in him and had run off before, sometimes staying away for weeks on end. This time, though, Colvin stayed away—for seven years.

In the spring of 1819, Uncle Amos Boorn had a vivid dream. In it he claimed to have spoken with the ghost of Colvin who led him to the precise spot where he was buried. Three times Amos claimed to have received a nocturnal visit from the ghost, and on each occasion the burial spot was always the same, a burned-out silo on the Boorn property.

A few days later a boy and his dog dug up some old bones found near the family home. Recalling that Stephen and Jesse had quarreled with Colvin shortly before he vanished, residents of the town demanded an investigation. The proof of guilt seemed incontrovertible. Jesse was brought to the justice of the peace on Apr. 27, 1819, and examined for four days. He accused Stephen of murdering Colvin and named several likely burial spots where the remains might be found.

Stephen was bound over to the grand jury which returned an indictment for murder, though the bones near the stump were found to be those of an animal. The most damaging testimony came from a convicted forger named Silas Merrill who testified that Jesse had told him about the quarrel. According to Merrill, Stephen had struck the fatal blow and Colvin's body had been buried under the same cellar old Amos had dreamed about.

The case was riddled with hearsay evidence and rumor. The most puzzling aspect was the absence of a body. Despite all this, Jesse and Stephen were convicted of murder on Jan. 28, 1820, and sentenced to death. Jesse's sentence was later commuted to life imprisonment.

As the days moved down to his scheduled execution, Stephen's hopes began to fade. At the last possible moment Colvin was located in New York City. He knew nothing about the plight of his brothers-in-law until a Manchester man named James Whelpley noticed an article in the New York *Evening Post* asking the whereabouts of Colvin, if in fact he was still alive. The story had been placed by friends of the Boorns, who were anxious to stave off a hanging. Colvin returned to his home town. He refused to reconcile his differences with Sally but willingly appeared before the magistrate to help clear his friends Jesse and Stephen. The state's attorney entered a motion of *nolle prosequi*—the case would proceed no further.

REF.: Borchard, *Convicting the Innocent; CBA;* Dempewolff, *Famous Old New England Murders;* Jackson, *The Portable Murder Book;* Pearson, *Studies In Murder.*

Boost, Werner (AKA: The Düsseldorf Doubles Killer), 1928- , Ger., rape-mur. In the years following WWII, Werner Boost earned his living transporting refugees across the East German border. He then moved to Düsseldorf in 1950. On Jan. 7, 1953, Boost and a companion shot a lawyer named Dr. Servé, who sat in a parked car with his male lover. Servé's lover was beaten and robbed.

Two years later, on Oct. 31, 1955, Boost and his accomplice, Franz Lorbach, apparently struck again, this time allegedly taking the lives of a young couple who had just left a Düsseldorf res-

taurant. The battered remains of Thea Kürmann and Friedhelm Behre were found in a water-filled gravel pit. Their skulls had been crushed. The press dubbed the unknown murderer the "Doubles Killer."

On Feb. 7, 1956, a gardener who worked in the village of Lank-Ilverich, outside Düsseldorf, reported his discovery of two charred bodies in a burnt haystack. The night before, someone driving a stolen black Merce-des had raced through the neighborhood minutes before a fire of mysterious origin broke out. Boost allegedly set the fire and committed the murders of Peter Falkenberg and Hildegard Wassing.

Police captured Boost on June 10, 1956, as he crept up on a parked Volkswagen in the woods outside Düsseldorf. Lorbach, who had been taken into custody earlier said that he had been "hypnotized" by Boost into carrying out the "Doubles Murders." Lorbach also said Boost would inject the couples with a sedative and rape the women before killing them. Lorbach re- **German mass killer Werner Boost.**
ceived six years in prison. Werner Boost eventually was convicted of the murder of Dr. Servé. The evidence in the other murders proved inconclusive. He was sentenced to life imprisonment on Dec. 14, 1959.

REF.: *CBA;* Deeley, *The Manhunters*Dunning, *The Arbor House Treasury of Crime;* Heppenstall, *The Sex War and Others;* Thorwald, *Crime and Science;* Wilson, *Encyclopedia of Murder.*

Booth, Arnett, and **Travis, John,** and **Adkins, Orville,** d.1938, U.S., kid.-mur. In November 1937, a 79-year-old physician named Dr. James Seder of Huntington, W. Va., was kidnapped, taken to an abandoned coal mine, and held for twelve days while his three abductors negotiated a $50,000 ransom with his family.

During the period of confinement Seder contracted pneumonia. Before the money was paid he was rescued from the cave, but his fragile health had been greatly endangered by shock and exposure. Just before Seder died, Arnett Booth, John Travis, and Orville Adkins were arrested and charged with using the postal system for extortion. These charges were held in abeyance until the state was able to prosecute the kidnappers for murder. The three men were found Guilty on all charges and hanged in West Virginia on Mar. 21, 1938. They became the first persons to suffer the death penalty in the state's history for the crime of murder as a result of ransom kidnapping.

REF.: Alix, *Ransom Kidnapping In America; CBA.*

Booth, Ernest, prom. 1920s, U.S., burg.-rob. Ernest Booth was a quiet, reflective boy inspired to become a criminal after reading about the exploits of the Artful Dodger in Charles Dickens' *Oliver Twist.* At the age of fifteen, the young Oakland, Calif., bandit perfected what he thought to be a foolproof method of robbery. He would ring the doorbells of his intended victims' homes, and if they were not in, he would enter and make off with the loot.

By his twentieth birthday, Ernest Booth had spent a considerable amount of time in state reformatories for robbery, petty larceny, and check forgery. In Milwaukee, Wis., he organized a car-theft ring, in which the license plates and registration slips from junkyard heaps were switched with automobiles stolen from out of state.

After a stint in the Marines, cut short by his desertion during WWI, Booth returned to the States and was promptly arrested for his many past crimes. He served five years at San Quentin before earning a parole. By this time he had bigger fish to fry. With two confederates, Dan and Buddy, Booth became a bank robber. His biggest job netted him $20,000 and a return trip to prison where he had time to pen his memoirs. His autobiography detailing a criminal's progress was published in 1929. REF.: *CBA;* Hamilton, *Men of the Underworld.*

Booth, Henry (Second Baron Delamere, First Earl of Warrington), 1652-1694, Brit., consp. Charged with complicity in the Rye House Plot of 1683. Two years later he was acquitted of similar charges during Monmouth's Rebellion. He fought for William of Orange in the Glorious Revolution of 1688, and served as chancellor of the exchequer from 1689-90. REF.: *CBA.*

Booth, John Wilkes, See: **Lincoln, Abraham.**

Booth-Clibborn, Catherine, b.1859, Brit., pris. reform. Sister of Ballington Booth and grand-daughter of William Booth, founder of the Salvation Army. She organized branches in Paris and Switzerland and directed the prison work effort in Paris. She wrote *Branded* (1897) and *After Prison, What?* (1903). REF.: *CBA.*

Bootle, William Augustus, 1902- , U.S., lawyer. U.S. attorney assigned to Macon, Ga., from 1929-33, and appointed judge of the Middle District of Georgia in 1954 by President Dwight D. Eisenhower. REF.: *CBA.*

Booze, Eugene P., d. 1939, U.S., (unsolv.) mur. In the black sharecropper town of Mound Bayou, Miss., Republican Party boss Eugene Booze was the wealthiest, most influential citizen, owning thousands of acres of fertile cotton and timberland along with the family home, which his sister-in-law Estelle Montgomery coveted.

The family dispute led to a court action which forbade Estelle from setting foot inside the house. Enraged, she chased her brother-in-law with a butcher knife but was shot dead by two white state police officers.

The crime did not set well with the inhabitants of the small Mississippi town. Late one night in November 1939, Eugene Booze was shot dead in a bloody ambush. Marshal John Thomas could not supply a possible clue as to who might have done such a thing. REF.: *CBA.*

Borah, William Edgar, 1865-1940, U.S., lawyer. Republican senator from Idaho between 1907-40 who was the leader of a movement to prevent the country from joining the League of Nations and the World Court from 1919-1921. REF.: *CBA.*

Borchard, Edwin, 1884-1951, U.S., legal scholar. Recognized authority on international law. He served as law librarian of Congress from 1911-13 and 1914-16, was professor of law at Yale from 1917-50, and served as the U.S. representative to the Committee of Experts for Inter-American Codification of International Law in 1930. REF.: *CBA.*

Borden, Lizzie, 1860-1927, Case of, U.S., mur. It is a wonder that a plump, shy, 32-year-old American spinster from an upperclass family could ever become one of the world's most celebrated murderers, especially when she was acquitted at her sensational 1893 trial and, that the heinous crimes for which she stood accused could have been easily committed by two other persons. Lizzie Borden lived a quiet life in Fall River, Mass., residing in her father's large three-story house on Second Street. It was here, on the sizzling hot day of Aug. 4, 1892, that Andrew Jackson Borden, sixty-nine, and his wife Abby Durfee Gray Borden, sixty-four, were found chopped to death from hatchet blows. Other tenants of the death house at the time of the grisly murders included Lizzie's sister Emma, the family maid and cook, Bridget Sullivan, and John Vinnicum Morse, sixty, brother of the first Mrs. Borden, who had come to visit.

Lizzie's mother, Sarah Morse Borden, had died when Lizzie was a small child and Andrew Borden had quickly remarried in 1865 to Abby Durfee Gray, a kind-hearted, gentle woman who worked as hard in her own home as did the hired help. It was later claimed that Lizzie harbored a deep-seated hatred for this woman who had replaced her own mother in her father's affections, but this could hardly have been the case since Lizzie's mother died when Lizzie was very young and it was Abby Borden who raised the child and who was the only real mother Lizzie ever knew or remembered. In fact, as an adult, Lizzie called Abby "mother," except when angry with her and then, in minor fits of pique, called her "Mrs. Borden." Her sister Emma, an equally retiring spinster, was older than Lizzie, forty-one at the time of the murder, and could have more easily nurtured the deep-rooted resentments of Abby Borden attributed to Lizzie as motives for murder.

Later claims also insisted that Lizzie wanted her stepmother and father dead so she could claim her father's money, or that she was about to be disinherited for obscure reasons and struck quickly to preserve her inheritance. This was all nonsense. Both Lizzie and Emma stood to benefit from their father's will without concern; the will had been written a decade earlier. Andrew Borden had not altered the will nor had he any plans to change it, and this both sisters knew. Moreover, Borden had not only set aside a handsome inheritance for both of his daughters, but he had allocated considerable land and farms for them and both enjoyed above-average allowances from which to freely draw money for clothes and other expenses. As spinsters, the Borden sisters had little to worry about; the present was comfortable and the future secure.

Bridget Sullivan, the hard-working maid in the Borden household, was a closed-mouthed person who literally worked from dawn until dusk, cleaning, cooking three meals a day, and doing the most arduous chores for the large family, albeit Abby Borden helped with the considerable workload. It was Bridget who prepared the heavy meal eaten by the family the night before the killings, one which caused Andrew and Abby Borden to become ill. In fact, Lizzie herself, as well as Bridget, had become slightly sick after dinner, so the later claim that Lizzie had poisoned the food in her first attempt to murder her parents was rejected as nonsense. Some days earlier, Lizzie had tried to purchase prussic acid. She had told the druggist that she wanted the prussic acid to clean a sealskin coat, but the local druggist had refused to sell her the acid. It was said that she nevertheless obtained poison and managed to dose the meal. The Bordens ate from common platters and therefore Lizzie could not be sure which portion would contain the lethal dose, if, indeed, she had opted for this murder plan which, since she also took her own portions from those common platters, could have meant her own death.

John Vinnicum Morse, Lizzie's uncle, visited the family on Aug. 3, 1892, taking the guest room. Early on the day of the murder, Morse left the Borden house to visit friends in Swansea. Emma Borden also left the house, renting a buggy and driving some thirty miles to visit friends in Fairhaven. Lizzie was left in the house with Bridget and her parents. Andrew Borden left the house at about 9 a.m., visiting the downtown bank for which he was president, and making several stops to collect rents from the buildings he owned. He was not a well-liked man by those with whom he did business, known as a penny-pinching landlord who fought over every dollar he earned. He had enemies, it was known, one man arguing so heatedly with Borden a week earlier in the Borden house that he was ordered to leave the premises. Also, the Bordens had, in recent months, suffered a rash of burglaries in their barn, and they had reported a daylight burglary of the house two months before the murders.

Lizzie had nightmares about impending doom because of her father's skinflint reputation and the enemies he had created through his hard business deals. She confided her fears in Alice Russell, telling the neighbor: "I feel that something is hanging over me that I cannot throw off." She felt that her father's enemies would "burn the house down over us," describing this nightmare to Mrs. Russell. Lizzie's critics later pointed out that all of these uttered forebodings were planned by Lizzie to create the illusion of strange killers who could later be blamed for the murders that she herself committed. Yet Lizzie Borden's character and personality had never shown her to be calculating and devisive. She was a much-protected child and her father doted upon her as an adult. She lived a sheltered life up to the time of the murders, and her fears were those of a child rather than a devious adult with a clever murder plan.

At 9:30 a.m. on the morning of the murders, Bridget Sullivan went to the Borden barn and got a pail and a brush and began washing the outside first-floor windows of the house. Abby Borden went upstairs to make the beds and Lizzie was somewhere in the house at the time. At 10:30 a.m. Andrew Borden arrived back home from his downtown business chores, but when he tried the front door of the house he found it locked. He knocked and rattled the doorknob which Bridget heard; the maid left her window-washing and entered the house through an unlocked side door and went to the front door. Just as she did so, she later testified, she saw Lizzie standing on the first step of the front staircase leading to the bedrooms, appearing as if she had just come downstairs. When Borden was finally let into the house, he walked into the dining room, asking for Abby.

"She's gone out," Lizzie told him. "She had a note from somebody who was sick."

Borden went upstairs to his bedroom, then he returned to the main floor and rested on a small couch in the sitting room. Bridget continued washing the windows but from inside the house, while Lizzie began ironing some handkerchiefs in the kitchen. She asked the maid if she planned to go out in the afternoon, reminding Bridget, whom she called Maggie, that there was a sale of some dress goods that day at a local store. Bridget told her that she was not feeling well, that the heavy family breakfast had upset her stomach. The meal served by Bridget that morning was extraordinary for the sweltering hot season, consisting of mutton-broth soup, johnny cakes, coffee, and cookies. The soup had been made from the mutton eaten the night before which had obviously made everyone ill, but no one thought to question the soup. The Borden household was a frugal one and nothing was thrown away if it could serve a purpose; so consuming some slightly tainted soup was part of the family's utilitarian custom.

Lizzie then told Bridget that "if you go out, make sure and lock the door, for Mrs. Borden has gone out on a sick call and I might go out too."

"Miss Lizzie, who is sick?" Bridget asked.

"I don't know. She had a note this morning. It must be in the town."

A few minutes before 11 a.m., Bridget climbed the back stairs to her attic room to take a short nap, her daily custom. She worked from 6 a.m., preparing breakfast, then working at chores until her short nap before preparing the family lunch. The maid lay back on her bed and tried to sleep but the intense heat caused her only to doze. She later testified that she could hear every noise in the old house, every creaking floorboard and that all was silent. At 11 a.m. she heard the city hall clock chime out the time. Then she heard Lizzie frantically calling her: "Maggie! Come down!"

She went to the back stairs and called down to Lizzie: "What's the matter?"

Lizzie called back with words that sent shivers of fear through the maid: "Come down! Quick! Father's dead! Somebody came in and killed him!"

Bridget flew down the stairs and found Lizzie standing at the door to the sitting room. Lizzie blocked the half-opened door to the sitting room, as if to shield the maid from the awful scene within, then said: "Oh, Maggie, don't go in. I have to have a doctor quick." She told Bridget to go to Dr. Seabury W. Bowen's home, a house diagonally across the street from the Borden house, and bring the physician. The maid raced across the street and found that Dr. Bowen was making a house call; she returned to find Lizzie in the hallway.

"Miss Lizzie," Bridget asked, "where were you when this thing happened?"

"I was in the yard," she said, "and heard a groan, and came in and the screen door was wide open." She then ordered the maid to fetch her friend and neighbor, Mrs. Russell. Bridget went next door to bring back the neighbor. At this time, Mrs. Adelaide B. Churchill, whose house bordered the Borden home on the north, looked out an open window and saw Lizzie standing at the screen door, holding on to it, trembling. "Is there anything the matter," Mrs. Churchill asked.

"Oh, Mrs. Churchill," Lizzie said, "do come over. Someone has killed Father."

Mrs. Churchill hurried to Lizzie, standing with her at the side door and holding on to her arm, as if to keep her from fainting. "Where is your father?"

"In the sitting room," Lizzie responded in a dazed voice.

"Where were you when it happened?"

"I went to the barn to get a piece of iron," she replied. She later explained that by "iron" she meant a fishing sinker as she intended to go fishing when she visited the Borden farm outside of town, a trip that had been planned for a week.

"Where is your mother?" questioned Mrs. Churchill.

"I don't know. She had a note to go see someone who is sick, but I don't know but she is killed, too, for I thought I heard her come in. Father must have an enemy for we have all been sick, and we think the milk has been poisoned."

Then Mrs. Churchill went looking for a doctor, asking neighbors to call police. Oddly, given Lizzie's remark about her mother being another possible murder victim, Mrs. Churchill did not suggest to look for Mrs. Borden. Bridget then returned to the house, meeting patrolman George W. Allen who was responding to Mrs. Churchill's alarm. Following these two was a scurrying Dr. Bowen. Both Officer Allen and Dr. Bowen entered the sitting room and found Andrew Borden sprawled on the couch, his face a river of blood, a pulpy ruin that caused even Dr. Bowen to shudder. Shaking his head, Dr. Bowen said in a near whisper: "Physician that I am, and accustomed to all kinds of horrible sights, it sickens me to look upon the dead man's face." Patrolman Allen noticed that the sitting room was undisturbed. There had been no struggle and not a stick of furniture was out of place. The dead man lay half on the couch, his legs sticking outward to the floor. His hands were unclenched and it appeared that he had been attacked while sleeping. The couch and the wall behind it were coated with Andrew Borden's blood, as if the blows he had received, from what was later determined to be a hatchet, were savagely repeated.

While Dr. Bowen and Officer Allen were inspecting the gruesome corpse in the sitting room, Lizzie sat in the kitchen, as if in a stupor, Mrs. Churchill and Mrs. Russell comforting her. She then said that someone should look for Mrs. Borden and tell her what happened. Mrs. Churchill and Bridget then decided they would search every room in the house, believing that they would find Mrs. Borden in the same condition as her husband. They were correct. As they climbed the front staircase, Mrs. Churchill looked into the guest room to see a body sprawled on the floor. She and Bridget went back downstairs and Mrs. Russell asked the ashen-faced Mrs. Churchill "is there another?"

"Yes, she is up there," replied the terrified neighbor. Officer Allen and Dr. Bowen almost bounded up the stairs to inspect the guest room where John Morse had slept the night before. Abby Borden, too, had been hacked to death, her head crushed with what looked to be numerous blows from a hatchet. She lay in an awkward position, face down, on her knees, her backside pushed upward and forward. It appeared that she had been making the bed in the guest room when attacked. Her blood had splattered the bed covers and the nearby wall. A medical examiner arrived and diligently counted nineteen head wounds to Mrs. Borden's skull, ten to Mr. Borden's head, a total of twenty-nine, not the the eighty-one "whacks" later attributed to Lizzie.

While funeral arrangements were made for the Bordens, Lizzie became the focal point of a subtle police investigation. She was repeatedly asked as to her whereabouts during the time of the murders. The answers varied. She said she was in the yard, then she said she was in the barn, then in the loft of the barn searching for sinkers, even picking pears and eating these in the barn. Why Lizzie would even enter the hot barn on such a steamy day caused great suspicion on the part of police and Fall River mayor John W. Coughlin who ordered Lizzie placed under house detention.

THE FALL RIVER MYSTERY OF LIZZIE BORDEN

Lizzie Borden, spinster, 1891, left; her father, Andrew Borden, right, hacked to pieces in the parlor, Aug. 4, 1892.

The Borden home some days after the murders.

Abby Borden, chopped to death in an upstairs bedroom.

The rear of the house, showing the barn.

Emma Borden, left, who sat through her sister's trial, was a likely suspect; at right, Lizzie is shown impatiently leaning forward to hear the jury's verdict.

Lizzie's confused conduct continued when she faced a coroner's jury. The inquest could not firmly establish just *where* Lizzie was at the time of the murders. She was then officially arrested, charged with the murder of her parents. Her trial began on June 5, 1893. She was defended by former Massachusetts governor George D. Robinson. Bridget Sullivan did a complete turn-about and offered herself as a witness for the prosecution, some later said because this would cast less suspicion in her direction. The maid had as much opportunity to murder the Bordens as did Lizzie. In fact, when she went up to take her nap that fateful morning, she could have easily gone up the backstairs, gone into the family area on the second floor and killed Mrs. Borden. The prosecution was handled by District Attorney Hosea Knowlton and he was anything but gentle with Lizzie.

Knowlton claimed that Lizzie hated her stepmother, believing they had secretly disinherited her, although Knowlton had no evidence whatsoever to support this idea. By presenting this line of argument, Knowlton also implicated Emma Borden, who was then above suspicion, in that she and Lizzie equally shared in Andrew Borden's will. (Some Lizzie Borden historians later claimed that Emma Borden could have easily murdered her parents, returning from out-of-town, slipping into the house to murder Abby and Andrew and then driving her buggy back to Fairhaven. Emma *did* rent a buggy which was reportedly seen outside the Borden house shortly before the murders, according to one report.) The district attorney then attacked Lizzie's story about the note from an anonymous sick person, a note Lizzie claimed Abby Borden had shown her but one that she did not read. There was no note, Knowlton said. This was merely a device Lizzie employed to explain her stepmother's absence when Andrew Borden's body was found. Lizzie simply invented the note, Knowlton said.

Robinson's defense was spirited and telling. With all that blood splattering after each blow, he pointed out, why was Lizzie not coated with gore? She was seen only a few minutes before and after the discovery of Andrew Borden's body, dressed in the same dress and not a blotch of blood on her. It was also claimed that Lizzie had somehow managed to wash off the blood after murdering her parents (in a ridiculous TV story about Lizzie she runs about naked to commit the murders, washes, and then puts her original dress back on). The washroom, however, had been thoroughly examined by police just after the murders and no trace of water existed; there had been no quick bath. Also, where was the murder weapon, Robinson wanted to know? He held up the hatchet that was exhibited in court, but this, the prosecution admitted, had been found in the Borden basement without a handle, rusted, and covered with cobwebs. There had not been a spot of blood on it.

The *possibility* of a strange intruder entering the house, Knowlton pointed out, was a good one. The screen door was open and there was enough time for someone to come into the Bordon house, kill both Abby and Andrew Borden, and escape undetected while both Lizzie and Bridget were out of the house. The defense attorney pointed to the recent burglaries suffered by the Bordens to prove that their property had been successfully invaded and looted earlier and where one burglar could go, a murderer could follow. Every word bantered between prosecution and defense was picked up and hurried into print by the more than forty newsmen covering the trial which captured national headlines for two weeks. Lizzie Borden herself was the reason why country wide readers were fascinated with this case. She was not a low-born, uneducated slattern from the criminal dens of America. Lizzie represented mainstream America, in fact, she was of the upper middleclass. She had money, position, and was an esteemed member of Fall River society. Lizzie was a member in good standing of the Fruit and Flower Mission, the Woman's Christian Temperance Union, secretary of the Christian Endeavor Society, and, most importantly, a Sunday school teacher. Could such a woman cold-bloodedly murder her parents? The jury thought not.

On June 20, 1893, Lizzie Borden stood before the court and was pronounced Not Guilty. She sank back into her chair, exhausted, relieved. Applause and mild cheering broke out in the courtroom, mostly from Lizzie's friends and members of her social clubs. With her sister Emma at her side, Lizzie moved out of the old Borden house and purchased a handsome mansion called Maplecroft. She spent the rest of her life here, occupying her hours with social clubs and aiding stray animals. She made small but shrewd investments and she and her sister more than doubled the $350,000 left to them by her father. Lizzie, at her death on June 2, 1927, left most of her estate to animal shelters. She died, in the eyes of the law, an innocent woman, but the public had long been convinced of her guilt, not from the results of the trial that freed her but from a bit of clever doggerel written at the time of her trial, lines that pricked the imagination of the public and were passed down from one generation to another, so that history has blurred the true facts, leaving only the following wrongful but memorable ditty:

> Lizzie Borden took an ax,
> And gave her mother forty whacks;
> And when she saw what she had done,
> She gave her father forty-one.

REF.: Boar, *The World's Most Infamous Murders;* Boucher, *The Pocket Book of True Crime Stories;* ____, *The Quality of Murder;* Brophy, *The Meaning of Murder; Case and Trial of Lizzie A. Borden; CBA;* Churchill, *A Pictorial History of American Crime;* Dunbar, *Blood in the Parlor;* Gribble, *Such Women are Dangerous;* Gross, *Masterpieces of Murder;* House, *Crimes That Shocked America;* Jones, *Unsolved!;* Lincoln, *A Private Disgrace: Lizzie Borden in Daylight;* Lunday, *The Mystery Unveiled: The Truth About the Borden Tragedy;* Lustgarten, *The Murder and the Trial;* ____, *Verdict in Dispute; Minutes of Preliminary Hearing in Second District Court;* Nash, *Almanac of World Crime;* ____, *Open Files; Official Trial Minutes;* Pearson, *Five Murders;* ____, *Masterpieces of Murder;* ____, *More Studies in Murder;* ____, *Murder at Smutty Nose;* ____, *Studies in Murder;* ____, *Trial of Lizzie Borden;* Porter, *The Fall River Tragedy;* Radin, *Lizzie Borden, The Untold Story;* Samuels, *The Girl in the House of Hate;* Scott, *The Concise Encyclopedia of Crime and Criminals;* Snow, *Piracy, Mutiny and Murders;* Spiering, *Lizzie;* Sullivan, *Goodbye Lizzie Borden;* Sutherland, *Ten Real Murder Mysteries Never Solved;* Wilson, *Encyclopedia of Murder;* (BALLET) DeMille, *Fall River Legend;* (DRAMA) Colton, *Nine Pine Street;* De La Torre, *Goodbye, Miss Lizzie Borden* (published in *Murder, Plain and Fanciful,* edited by James Sandoe); Denham, *Suspect;* Kaufman and Hart, *The Man Who Came to Dinner;* Lawrence, *The Legend of Lizzie;* Miles, *Lizzie Borden;* Reach, *Murder Takes the Stage;* (FICTION) Bierstadt, *Satan Was a Man;* Dougall, *The Summit House Mystery; or, The Earthly Purgatory;* Lowndes, *Lizzie Borden, A Study in Conjecture;* (FILM) The *Man Who Came to Dinner,* 1942.

Borelli, LaVerne, 1909- , U.S., mansl. After drinking a bottle of whiskey, LaVerne Borelli returned to her San Francisco apartment on the night of May 9, 1946, to punish her husband for his infidelity. She slipped Gene Borelli's automatic pistol out of the dresser drawer, and shot and killed him while he slept. Seeing no point in going on with her own life, she shot herself twice in the breast after swallowing some strychnine. But her suicide attempt failed, and she was tried for murder.

Even though she was defended by criminal attorney Jake Erlich, LaVerne proved to be an uncooperative client. She did not care about the outcome of the trial, and made the fact clear throughout the proceedings. Borelli was convicted of manslaughter and given a light prison sentence at the women's prison at Tehachapi, Calif. She was paroled on Mar. 10, 1953.

REF.: *CBA;* Nash, *Look For the Woman.*

Boreman, Herbert Stephenson, 1897-1982, U.S., jur. Prosecuting attorney of Wood County, W. Va., in 1928. He was appointed to the bench in 1954, to the court of the Northern District of West Virginia by President Dwight D. Eisenhower, then to the Fourth Circuit Court in 1959. REF.: *CBA.*

Boreman, Jacob Smith, 1831-1913, U.S., jur. City attorney of

City, Mo., from 1861-62 and judge of the criminal court of Jefferson City, Mo., from 1863-68. He was appointed to the bench of the territorial court of Utah in 1873 by President Ulysses S. Grant, re-appointed by President Rutherford B. Hayes in 1877, and by President Chester Arthur in 1884. REF.: *CBA.*

Borger (Texas), 1926-29, U.S., mur. The town of Borger, Texas, sprang into existence almost hours after oil was discovered there. With the boomtown that mushroomed came an army of confidence men, prostitutes, claim-jumpers, and killers. The town exploded to a population of 10,000 and became the seat of Hutchinson County. Its mayor, the sheriff, and all of its officials were notoriously corrupt, sanctioning the claim-jumping and the many murders connected with stealing oil lands. More than forty killings occured in less than three years in this boomtown, the last being that of District Attorney John A. Holmes, one of the few honest citizens in the community and one who had been actively tracking down the murderers. Following Holmes' murder, the state took drastic action, Governor Dan Moody ordering Brigadier General Jacob F. Wolters and his National Guardsmen of the 56th Cavalry Brigade into the city. Martial law was declared and Wolters jailed the city administration, running the gamblers, prostitutes, and thugs out of town. Within a week, Borger, Texas, was a tame town, all of its gambling halls, saloons, bordellos, and vice dens closed or burned down. The killings were never solved. REF.: *CBA.*

Borgia Family (or Borja), prom. 15th-16th Cent., Italy, polit. corr.-rape-mur. The Spanish-Italian Borgia family constituted a sprawling membership of stellar and infamous individuals who came to symbolize the Renaissance period. Family members were both saintly and beneficent, venal and murderous. Stemming from Spanish ancestors which may or may not have been low born, the Borgias rose to enormous prestige and power in Italy where Alfonso Borgia (1378-1458) became Pope Callistus III, creating a papal dynasty for the Borgias (or Borja in Spanish) with Rodrigo Borgia (1431-1503) establishing the Vatican as a corporal power after he became Pope Alexander VI. Rodrigo was the patriarch of the Borgia line that became infamous, although his great-grandson, Francis Borgia (1510-72) would later become a Jesuit leader of such purity and grace that he was cannonized a saint. There was little or nothing saintly about Rodrigo who, after his ordination and while a Catholic priest, conducted illicit affairs with many women, notably a Roman lady of questionable virtue, Vannozza dei Cattanei. The pair produced five illegitimate children, two of whom, Cesare (1475-1507) and Lucrezia (1480-1519) became the most celebrated and feared nobles of their colorful era—the son a power-hungry, lust-consumed mass killer, the daughter a political pawn and an intriguer who brought about the death of several persons, if not directly, through the ornate machinations of her scheming brother.

In 1492, two events occured that would radically change the politics and history of Europe. Rodrigo Borgia became pope of the Roman Catholic church and Columbus discovered America. Rodrigo, who reportedly paid 5,000 ducats for the final vote that made him Alexander VI, intended to bring all Italy and Europe under his political domination, using the office of pope to accomplish this end. He indulged himself in every conceivable vice, bringing harlots into the Vatican to cavort with his favorite court lackeys and sexually entertain him at all hours. He gave lavish, obscene fetes and banquets at which all manner of debaucheries took place, such as the infamous "Chestnut Supper," where common prostitutes performed the most lascivious acts, and an orgy ensued with Rodrigo's knowledge and tacit approval. All manner of immoral and licentious activities flourished in the Vatican at this time and corruption was the order of the day. Papal bulls, canons, and official documents were very often altered, changed, forged to permit financial swindles and marriages between nuns and laymen, allowing sub-deacons to marry. The pope's secretary, Bartolomeo Flores, archbishop of Consenza, was convicted of forging official Vatican documents, undoubtedly with Rodrigo's knowledge, and sent to prison where he confessed to countless forgeries.

To keep up appearances, the profligate Rodrigo often punished those who acted illegally on his behalf, but he continued to encourage the worst kind of behavior. One of his favorite courtesans, La Cursetta, was found to be living with a Moor who had impersonated a woman. Both were punished by having to publicly walk through the city amidst the jeers of thousands, La Cursetta wearing a trailing black gown without a girdle and the Moor wearing his woman's dress, lifted above his waist to show his privates and his true sex. The courtesan was released after this public humiliation but the Moor was executed—strangled publicly and then burned—such was the fate of any discovered transvestite in this age of "enlightenment." La Cursetta was then invited back to Rodrigo's chambers to entertain him. Many in the Church hierarchy quietly denounced such scandals. One such was Cardinal Peraudi, who had voluntarily exiled himself to Perugia. He found the morals at the Vatican appalling, stating: "When I think of the life of Pontiff and certain Cardinals, I shudder at the idea of remaining in the Curia."

The Borgia family dining—a painting by John Collier ironically entitled "A cup of wine with Cesare Borgia."

One of the offending cardinals was Cesare Borgia, son of the pope. Rodrigo doted upon his children, Cesare and Lucrezia, encouraging them to seize every opportunity to enrich themselves and obtain power, first in Rome, then through war and murder by Cesare and through marriages to ruling lords by Lucrezia. Cesare, the younger of the two, had an insatiable appetite for power, money, and beautiful women. He did as he pleased and lived for conquest. He had been given power early by his nepotistic father; Rodrigo had made Cesare archbishop of Valencia when Cesare was only seventeen. Rodrigo made him a cardinal a year later, a post from which he would resign in 1498. Rodrigo, in order to remove the stigma of illegitimacy from his son, blatantly lied in an official papal bull, dated Oct. 17, 1480, which stated that Cesare was the son of Vanozza and Domenico d'Arignano.

Handsome, clever, devious, wholly without morals, Cesare Borgia took one fuedal duchy after another, Piombino, Pesaro, Urbino, either through force of arms, or through sly murders. He often put the conquered town to the torch and ordered all the women raped by his men as an abject lesson to those who opposed him. Cesare reveled in despoiling the women of his enemies. One story had it that after conquering one town, Borgia ordered that forty of the prettiest virgins be brought to him, and he would not budge from his bed, despite the urgings of his captains, until he had sexually vanquished the forty virgins. Canard or not, this tale reveals the inexhaustible stamina and greed of this prince.

Cesare Borgia would stop at nothing to get what he wanted. He murdered countless men or had his henchmen perform the killings to obtain their fortunes, their land, and their women. When he learned that his father favored his brother Giovanni, Cesare, in 1497, arranged to have his brother murdered and his body thrown into the Tiber River. Thus, Cesare took over the wealthy duchy of Gandia which had been ceded to Giovanni Borgia by the king of Spain, undoubtedly the real motive for having his brother killed. Cesare employed all manner of guile to eliminate his enemies. On one occasion he invited captains in his command to dine with him and then, because he suspected two of them having gone over to the enemy, had the offending pair strangled as he nibbled an artichoke.

Lucrezia Borgia was the willing pawn to both her father and brother, although the claim that she slept with both or, particularly, Cesare whom she adored, has no foundation in fact. Blonde and lithe, Lucrezia was married three times, all unions of a political nature designed to strengthen the Borgia ties to powerful city-states. Lucrezia was first married at sixteen to Giovanni Sforza, lord of Pesaro, a union ordered by her father Rodrigo so that the wealthy city-state would fall under control of Cesare. This marriage was annulled by Rodrigo when he felt his daughter could better serve the Borgia interests by remarrying, this time to the nephew of the king of Naples, Alfonso of Aragon. This was a happy union but Cesare Borgia wanted Lucrezia again free to marry Alfonso de Este, son and heir to the powerful Duke of Ferrara.

To that end Cesare went to his sister and explained that Alfonso of Aragon would have to be eliminated as the pope could not annul a second marriage without appearing to be the ruthless power-broker he truly was. From most reliable reports, Lucrezia did not, as popularly thought, poison her husband (this method of murder was Cesare's specialty). She did inveigle the young man into an ambush where, on July 15, 1500, he was repeatedly stabbed but managed to survive the attack. Alfonso of Aragon staggered back to the Vatican apartments in Rome, clutching his wounded chest. He was put in Lucrezia's care and she began to nurse her husband back to health. Then she conveniently left her husband's sickbed unattended one night. Cesare and two assassins crept into the room, and the hired killers strangled the helpless Alfonso to death while Cesare stood over the bed staring down at his victim with dispassionate interest. Lucrezia, later that year, was married to Alfonso de Este by proxy and then joined her third and final husband in Ferrara where she ruled as a grand duchess, setting up a magnificent court which attracted the greatest painters, sculptors, and writers of the Renaissance.

But the time of the Borgias was waning and, on Aug. 11, 1503, Rodrigo Borgia died from a virulent fever, not a box of poisoned sweetmeats that his enemies had offered him as a gift, a popular canard. A priest attending Rodrigo, who was covered with large, black, ugly skin tumors, recorded the pope's death and wrote: "Today he is descended to hell where he was born." In fact, Cesare was ill at the time of his father's death, also from a fever, and it was also later said that he, too, had eaten from the same box of poisoned sweetmeats. Pope Julius II was elected in 1503 and Cesare Borgia was immediately informed that his presence at the Vatican was no longer encouraged. Julius II discredited his venal predecessor as well as Rodrigo's scheming children. The pope demanded the return of all estates and castles seized by the murderous Cesare, and when these vast holdings were returned to the families from which they were stolen, Cesare Borgia was arrested in Naples by Gonzalo de Córdoba who banished the intriguer to Spain in 1504. There he was imprisoned for two years, but escaped in 1506 and fled to Navarre where he raised an army and began to wage war, attempting to again relive his former military victories. This was not to be. In 1507, Cesare Borgia, while attempting to take a castle at Viana was pierced with a spear through his body and died on the battlefield. The writer Niccolò Machiavelli, a plotter and intriguer of the first rank, admired the ruthless Cesare so much that Borgia became the protagonist in his epic, *Il Principe,* or *The Prince.*

Lucrezia fared much better than her father and brother, enjoying a golden court, wealth, and comfort. Yet, for all of her past intrigues, she proved to be a loyal wife to her third husband, even selling her fabulous jewels to pay off the debts he incurred while waging wars to protect Ferrara territory. She also earned a reputation in her day for her charities to the sick, the poor, and the homeless, a reputation that would not linger much beyond her own death on June 21, 1519. Was Lucrezia Borgia the mass poisoner so many sensation-seeking writers later claimed her to be? Most probably not. She undoubtedly inherited the vile reputation her brother Cesare worked so diligently to earn. She did have her share of intrigues and was most probably guilty of helping to murder her second husband, Alfonso of Aragon. But master poisoner she was not. Cesare Borgia poisoned many of his victims, using what was later described as the "Borgia Poison," described by one historian as "a white powder of a faint and not unpleasing flavor." This poison was probably cantarella from the highly poisonous fungus of that name. Cesare's own alchemists mixed cantarella with subacetate of copper, arsenic, and crude phosphorous, a small dose of which was sure to kill anyone.

REF.: Alvisi, *Cesare Borgia;* Bellonci, *The Life and Times of Lucrezia Borgia;* Bérence, *Les Borgias;* ____, *Lucrèce Borgia;* Boulting, *Women in Italy;* Bradford, *Cesare Borgia;* Burchard, *At the Court of the Borgia;* ____, *Pope Alexander and His Court;* Burckhardt, *The Civilization of the Renaissance;* Castiglione, *The Book of the Courtier;* Catalano, *Lucrezia Borgia;* CBA; Creighton, *A History of the Papacy From the Great Schism to the Sack of Rome;* De Roo, *Materials for a History of Alexander VI;* Erlanger, *Lucrezia Borgia;* Ferrara, *The Borgia Pope;* Funck-Brentano, *Lucrèce Borgia;* Fusero, *The Borgias;* Garnett, *Rome and the Temporal Power;* Gilbert, *Lucrezia Borgia;* Gordon, *The Lives of Pope Alexander VI and His Son Caesar Borgia;* Guicciardini, *The History of Italy;* Hay, *The Italian Renaissance in Its Historical Background;* Kelso, *Doctrine for the Lady of the Renaissance;* Latour, *The Borgias;* Lucas-Dubreton, *The Borgias;* Machiavelli, *The Prince and the Discourses;* Mallett, *The Borgias;* Matarazzo, *Chronicles of the City of Perugia;* Mathew, *The Life and Times of Rodrigo Borgia;* Noyes, *Story of the Ferrara;* Pastor, *The History of the Popes;* Plumb, *The Horizon Book of the Renaissance;* Portigliotti, *The Borgias;* Putnam, *The Lady;* Rolfe, *Chronicles of the House of Borgia;* Rubinstein, *Lucrezia Borgia;* Sabatini, *The Life of Cesare Borgia;* Thompson, *The Civilization of the Renaissance;* Thompson, *Poison and Poisoners;* Woodward, *Cesare Borgia;* Yriarte, *Cesare Borgia;* (FILM) *Lucrezia Borgia,* 1937; *Bride of Vengeance,* 1949; *Prince of Foxes,* 1949; *Lucrece Borgia,* 1953; *The Nights of Lucretia,* 1960.

Borgio, Rosario, prom. 1910s, U.S., org. crime. Long a Mafia don in Akron, Ohio, Rosario Borgio operated a large general goods store as a front. He managed all his illegal operations from two large rooms in the rear of the store. His residence was above the store and it was "police proof," he claimed, having alarms on the doors leading to the front and back stairs, with several stairs that would open backward to drop intruders into pits filled with razor-sharp, foot-long spikes. Anyone falling into one of these pits was immediately impaled and killed on the spikes. If an intruder managed to get by the stairs, he would be faced with a solid steel door impossible to batter down. Behind these doors, Borgio kept an arsenal of shotguns, rifles, pistols, and submachine guns. As the top Mafia leader in Akron, Borgia controlled all the Black Hand extortionists and selected wealthy victims from his community upon whom his gangsters preyed. Moreover, Borgia controlled all gambling and most of the brothels in the city.

Although the gangster had many local officials on his payroll, he was not able to penetrate Akron's police force, its members refusing to take his bribes and payoffs. By early 1918, police began to raid aggressively Borgio's gambling dens and whorehouses, locking up the operators *and* the patrons. The Mafia don reasoned that by jailing his patrons, the Akron Police Department was intent on putting him out of business. He next decided that he, too, would declare war on the Akron police. Borgio called all the top Black Handers and killers on his extensive payroll to a meeting in his store in the fall of 1918. He then announced the most incredible decision ever made by a U.S. gang boss. He declared open war on the entire Akron Police Department. He intended to "wipe them all out, every last one of those s.o.b. cops."

Paul Chiavaro, one of Borgio's trusted lieutenants, stepped up to say: "You mean you want us to rough up every cop on the force, boss?"

"No," clarified Borgio. He stared intently at the twenty or more gangsters surrounding him. "I want you to kill every cop in Akron! You got that? Every cop out there in the city. Now, right now!" He took a wad of large bills from his pocket and waved this in the air. "Two hundred and fifty dollars a head for policemen! You kill a cop, I give you two hundred and fifty dollars, right away. Just make sure you kill him, not just hurt him. He never gets up again. Dead. All of them, dead."

The gangsters stared in disbelief, but Borgia repeated his order and his price for the death of each Akron police officer. Then, nodding, the gangsters filed out. The first killing took place on Dec. 26, 1918. Patrolman Robert Norris was walking down a residential Akron street that night, making his rounds, when someone shot him from ambush. Several bullets struck Norris in the back. He was found dead some hours later when a passerby stumbled over his body. A few days later, officers Edward Costigan and Joe Hunt, on patrol, were both shot dead. Patrolman Gethin Richards was also killed a few days after the double slaying. The killings baffled Akron detectives. There were seemingly no motive for the murders, which were committed in different parts of the city, ruling out local gangs. None of the officers were robbed after being killed. Detectives believed that they were dealing with a maniac. Then Chief of Detectives Harry Welch received a strange phone call, a tip, so to speak, from an anonymous woman who nervously told him that one of the men involved with the police murders had gone to New York. She gave no names, only a bizarre description of the man, and then hung up.

Welch called New York Police Department Lieutenant Michael Fiaschetti, who had taken over the Department's Italian Squad after its erstwhile leader, Lieutenant Joseph Petrosino, had been murdered in Palermo, Sicily, while tracking down Black Handers ten years earlier on Mar. 12, 1909. Welch told Fiaschetti the incredible story of how someone was indiscriminately killing members of the Akron police force. He told him that his tipster had informed him that one of those involved was Italian and then passed on this description: "All we have is this: Look for the man with the hole in his hand." Fiaschetti, with only this thin clue to follow, alerted his squad to the problem. All of its members were Italian and knew the Italian community in New York intimately, having plumbed its underground for a decade. They contacted all of their informants and regularly checked hoodlum hangouts. In late January 1919, one of Fiaschetti's best informants, a poolroom operator, called the detective, telling him that "he was in my place last night. Says he's coming back tonight. Looks like he has been shot through the hand."

That night, Fiaschetti went to the poolroom and found two strangers playing pool. When one of them placed his hand on the pool table, the detective saw that he bore a livid scar in the middle of his right hand. He immediately arrested the two men, Tony Manfredi, the man with the bullet wound, and his friend Pasquale Biondo. After securing an extradition order, Fiaschetti, alone, boarded an Akron-bound train with his prisoners. En route, he studied both gangsters, who had remained sullen and silent. Biondo was a savage gunsel, full of guile and hatred for the law, but Manfredi was an outgoing type who liked to sing. He gave Fiaschetti some samples of his tenor voice, and the detective decided that Manfredi would be the one to question. He locked Biondo to a steel handrail in the compartment and then took Manfredi to the lounge car, where he bought him several drinks. The gangster then began to talk freely about himself.

Fiaschetti listened as Manfredi admitted that he was walking down a lonely road outside of Akron a few weeks earlier with three friends, heading toward a roadhouse, and that he had been walking ahead, singing, when his friends suddenly began to shoot at him and he dove into some nearby woods, escaping with a wound where a bullet cleanly passed through the center of his right hand.

"Why did they do that to you, your friends?" asked Fiaschetti.

"I don't know," Manfredi replied, "some grudge maybe."

"Was Biondo with them?"

"Biondo? No. He's my friend. Had he been there he would never have let them do such a thing to me." Manfredi explained that after he escaped from his would-be killers, he returned to Akron and met with Biondo. "He told me how dirty they were," Manfredi said, proud of his association with Biondo, saying that his friend had suggested that they both leave Akron for a short time and go to New York "until this police thing dies down."

At this point, Fiaschetti, a tough, shrewd cop who had been handling gangsters for decades, decided to confront the handsome, egotistical Manfredi with what he knew and bluff his way along with the rest of the story. Said Fiaschetti: "Listen, Manfredi. I know all about those policemen killed in Akron. You were in on it and so was Biondo. The gang that tried to knock you off had planned to take you for a ride because you knew too much and they were afraid you would talk. When they made a mess of the job, what else could they do? Biondo wasn't in on the shooting so the gang knew you would trust him. He wanted you to go to New York where he planned to kill you, to get the job done right this time." Manfredi stared at the detective bug-eyed. Fiaschetti continued his lie with expert ease: "That's the tip that's come from Akron. When the word came, it was up to me to keep Biondo from sending you to the morgue. I jumped in just in time to save your life."

White-faced, Manfredi's hands gripping the lounge chair, the gangster stared at Fiaschetti. The insidious gangster plot was perfectly logical to Manfredi. Then, before he could utter a word, Fiaschetti took the cigar from his mouth, blew a puff of smoke above their heads and nonchalantly said: "Come through, Manfredi, and you won't burn. Do the right thing and you'll get away with a prison sentence instead of the electric chair." He took a long drink from his glass and feigned indifference, then pointed down the aisle toward the sleeping car. "That man in the compartment. He's only got one thing on his mind. To kill you and to do it even though you're in custody."

Manfredi let loose a screaming curse and then blurted: "And I thought he was my friend!" As the train raced through the night toward Akron, Manfredi began to talk. "It all began with Rosario Borgio," he said, and detailed the murders of Akron policemen and how Borgio paid by the body. When the train reached Akron, Fiaschetti delivered his prisoners and outlined the entire murder conspiracy to stunned Akron detectives. Borgio and his men were quickly arrested and brought to trial. Manfredi received a twenty-year sentence, but Borgio, the man who had tried to wipe out an entire American police department, went to the electric chair, as did Paul Chiavaro, Vito Mezzano, and Lorenzo Biondo (Pasquale's brother). Biondo also went to prison. Fiaschetti was give a gold medal for valor by the governor of Ohio, and was lauded by the NYPD upon returning to New York.

REF.: *CBA;* Fiaschetti, *You Gotta Be Rough;* Nash, *Murder, America.*

Bormann, Martin Ludwig, c.1900-45?, Ger., war crimes. Martin Bormann, one of the most ruthless proponents of racial and ethnic intolerance in Germany, joined Adolf Hitler in 1925, following his release from prison on a murder charge. Bormann rose quickly through the ranks of the Nazi party. His obsequious manner appealed to the Nazi hierarchy. From 1933 to 1941, Bormann served as chief of staff under Rudolf Hess. In this capacity, he contrived a compulsory accident insurance scheme whereby party members paid into a general fund. The venture seemed to be financially successful for both Hitler and Bormann.

Bormann also masterminded the "Adolf Hitler Endowment Fund of German Industry," another financial swindle that lined party coffers. His fawning upon the Führer angered party regulars. In 1941, Third Deputy Rudolf Hess inexplicably flew to

Britain to negotiate a separate peace with the British. The news of this unauthorized trip stunned Hitler, who was consoled by the ever-present Bormann. By the time Hermann Goering and Josef Goebbels arrived at the Führer's Bavarian retreat for a high-level conference, Bormann had been appointed Party Chancellor, a discouraging setback for their own political ambitions.

Hitler's top aide, Martin Bormann.

While Europe went up in flames, Bormann remained safely behind the lines, indulging Hitler's every whim and attending to the considerable fortune he had amassed over the years. In 1943, Martin Bormann prepared a memorandum appointing himself "Secretary to the Führer." His enemies soon realized that the only way to get to Hitler was through Bormann. As secretary, Bormann saw to it that the policies of racial genocide against Jews were carried out to the letter. Sequestered in the underground bunker—Fortress Berlin, Hitler called it—amidst the dying embers of the Third Reich, Bormann continued to plot against his rivals. He gleefully reported to the Führer that Goering was planning to seize control of the nation on Apr. 23, 1945. Hitler was shaken to a blind rage. He ordered Bormann, who had played his trump card masterfully, to telegraph Goering at once and order him to resign his command. Bormann notified the Obersalzburg S.S. leaders to arrest Goering on sight. In the last hours of the Reich, as the Russian mortars crashed outside the bunker, Bormann witnessed the marriage of the Führer to Eva Braun. While Hitler, Goebbels, and the rest of the Berlin entourage loftily spoke of suicide, Bormann plotted his escape.

Hitler with Bormann, 1938, who was later Secretary to the Führer.

On May 1, Bormann and four men, among them Artur Axmann, Hitler youth leader, and the Führer's personal physician, Dr. Stumpfegger, made their way through a maze of underground tunnels leading toward the railway station near Wilhelmsplatz. From there, Bormann hoped to reach Schleswig-Holstein in northern Germany. The party made it as far as the Friedrich-strasse station and was forced to split up.

What happened to Bormann after this point remains a mystery. Axmann later said that Bormann and Dr. Stumpfegger were killed on the bridge near the River Spree. After the Battle of Berlin, witnesses claimed to have found Bormann's diary on the ground near the body of a dead man, thought to be that of the Nazi leader. This claim was disputed by eminent Nazi hunter Dr. Simon Weisenthal, who explained that it was common for fleeing Nazis to place their private papers in the coats of dead men. At the War Crimes Tribunal in Nüremberg, the international jurists sentenced Bormann to death *in absentia*. They were not satisfied that he had met his death, as previously claimed, in Berlin.

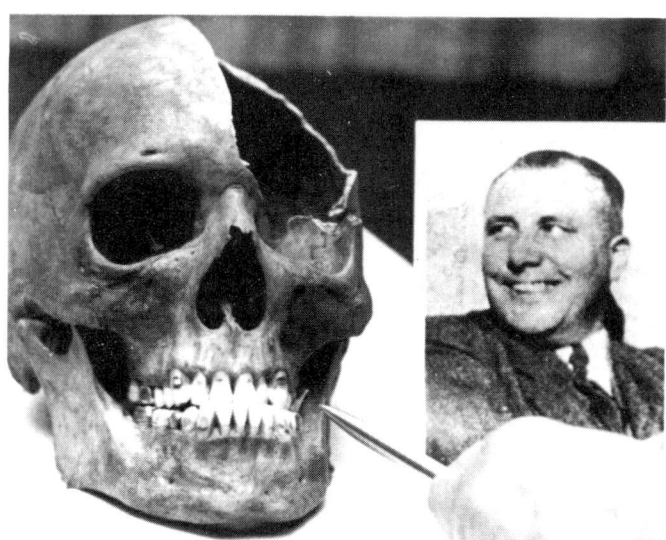

Skull found in Berlin ruins, thought to be that of Martin Bormann.

In the years to come, there were many unconfirmed reports that Bormann had made his way to Argentina, where he lived as José Perez in a colony of Nazi exiles. The village was supposedly named *Kolonie 555*, Bormann's former party identification number. In 1973, a skeleton was unearthed in Berlin, near where Axmann claimed to have seen Bormann fall. Forensic experts stated that it was Bormann's. What happened to Bormann's illicit fortune remains a mystery.

REF.: *CBA*; Sullivan, *The Bureau: My Thirty Years In Hoover's FBI*.

Born, Juan, and **Born, Jorge**, prom. 1974, Arg., kid. Two brothers who headed Argentina's largest private firm were kidnapped together by a team of professional criminals who were highly organized and actually welcomed publicity about their techniques.

Juan Born and Jorge Born, who headed Bunge Born, Argentina's largest private company, were kidnapped on Sept. 16, 1974. The brothers usually traveled to work from their home, about twenty-two miles from Buenos Aires, with their general manager in the front seat next to the chauffeur, followed by a second car carrying two bodyguards. Frequently a third car, which dropped off the Born children at school, accompanied the entourage. For the kidnapping the Monteneros Gang used nineteen terrorists, with another twenty to thirty assistants to guard the hostages. The actual kidnap group was broken down into five teams. Choosing a wide boulevard with narrow parallel service roads on both sides, the criminals closed the street off on the pretext of doing landscaping work on trees. Then they received the signal that the Borns' cars were approaching. Bringing in a portable traffic light to divert other cars to the service roads, the kidnappers used two trucks to collide with both the bodyguards' and the Born brothers' cars. Dressed as policemen, the terrorists pretended to arrest the bodyguards, beating them and handcuffing them under their own car. They then shot and killed the chauffeur and the general manager, taking the Born brothers away from the scene. As is frequent in Latin American kidnappings, the events took place on busy streets in broad daylight.

Also in keeping with other Latin American kidnappings, negotiations were prolonged—the Born brothers' case took thirty weeks to be settled. Contact was maintained throughout with the police, who tapped the telephones. The main negotiator perceived the kidnappers to be professionals, and felt confident they would not harm the hostages. Demanding daily proof of their safety and health, he received letters and tapes throughout the long bargaining. The ransom was reduced to a fraction of the original sum in the fourth month of negotiating. An unusual aspect of the Born brothers' kidnapping is the fact that a leading member of the Monteneros gang, Mario Eduardo Firmenich, gave an hour-long press conference a few days before their release, describing in detail how the kidnapping was accomplished and calling for the resignation of the country's president, Isabel Peron. The ransom payment of $60 million was delivered soon after and the Born brothers were released in June 1975.

REF.: *CBA;* Clutterbuck, *Kidnap and Ransom.*

Born, Ronald Joseph, 1935-76, U.S., mur. Wanted for driving a stolen car, a fugitive killed three policemen, then shot himself rather than be captured.

On Apr. 2, 1976, Ronald Joseph Born, a fugitive believed to have been from Blue Island, Ill., was staying at the Beach Motel in Miami, Fla. Wanted for failing to show up in the U.S. District Court of Miami on charges of interstate auto theft, he had been registered at the motel for almost a month under the name Joseph Mouload. According to officials, three policemen, acting on a hunch, went to Born's room to ask about a stolen Lincoln sedan he had been driving. When they approached him Born fired on them with a shotgun. Fatally wounded were Thomas Hodges, thirty-two, Clark Curlette, twenty-eight, and Frank Dazevedo, thirty-one. Born then fired a pistol into his own head, apparently when he realized he was trapped by other policemen. A police spokesman explained, "U.S. marshals told me this morning that he had vowed he would never be taken alive." REF.: *CBA.*

Borne, Henry, See: **Dutch Henry.**

Borno, Louis-Eustache-Antoine-François-Joseph, 1865-1942, Haiti, lawyer. Served on the Court of International Justice at the Hague from 1919-22 and was president of Haiti from 1922-30. REF.: *CBA.*

Borrow, George, 1803-81, Brit., writer. Published *Celebrated Trials* (1825) while still serving his law apprenticeship. REF.: *CBA.*

Borynski, Father Henry, prom. 1953, Brit., (unsolv.) mur. A young Polish priest working in a small English town disappeared from his parsonage after receiving a mysterious phone call.

Father Henry Borynski moved to Little Horton, near Bradford, Britain, from his native Poland to serve the thousand Polish immigrants who settled there following the war. On July 13, 1953, his housekeeper, Elizabeth Beck, answered a phone call and heard a man with a strong foreign accent on the other end. She then heard Borynski say "Now this has come...I go." The Roman Catholic priest put on his hat and overcoat, and left the house. He was seen on a nearby street corner a few minutes later and never seen again. He left papers strewn about his study and took no money or possessions beyond what he had on his person. Theories about his disappearance suggested that he had been murdered by Communists, a group he hated, that he had been killed by the elderly priest he had replaced, that he had killed himself somewhere on the isolated Yorkshire moors, or that he had returned to Poland. The last theory is the only one with any support, in that Borynski's mother wrote to him on July 26 begging her son to write her and asking what had happened to him. The fact that the mother never wrote again was the only clue that the priest might have returned to Poland.

REF.: *CBA;* Furneaux, *Famous Criminal Cases, vol. 7;* Nash, *Among the Missing.*

Bosch, Orlando, prom. 1976, Venez., terr.-mur. A Cuban pediatrician in exile was accused of terrorist activities in Venezuela and was said to be one of four people who planted a bomb that killed seventy-three persons aboard a Cuban airliner.

On Oct. 6, 1976, a bomb exploded in a Cuban plane near Barbados, killing everyone on board. Charged with first-degree murder and manufacture and use of a lethal weapon were Dr. Orlando Bosch, an exiled Cuban pediatrician said to be a leader of the Commandos of the United Revolutionary Organizations, a group of five Cuban exile organizations. Also charged were two Venezuelan photographers, Hernan Ricardo Losano and Freddy Lugo, and a former official of Venezuela's political police, Luis Posada-Carriles. Judge Delia Estaba Moreno reviewed evidence, which included questioning of the four men, for eight days before finding cause to try the suspects. Bosch had been charged several times previously with gun-running but was never convicted, and had also been acquitted in the U.S. of federal extortion charges, including bombings, shooting attacks, and death threats to Cuban exiles in Miami in 1966. He had entered Venezuela on a false passport and was wanted in the U.S. for parole violation in connection with a bazooka attack on a Polish freighter.

On Aug. 14, 1977, a bomb was thrown over a fence at the Miami International Airport, apparently intended for a Venezuelan Air Force DC-9 plane. A spokesman for the Luis Bostel Commandos, a Cuban exile group, called United Press International's Miami offices before and after the explosion to claim responsibility for the bombing as the work of anti-Communist commandos, threatening to attack a commercial plane next if Bosch were not released. Four months later, on Dec. 27, 1977, when the Venezuelan consulate-general's office on East 51st Street in New York City was bombed, an anonymous caller told the news media that the device had been planted by an anti-Castro group of Cuban exiles, Omega Seven, to protest Bosch's imprisonment. On Sept. 26, 1980, Bosch, Ricardo Losano, Posada-Carriles, and Lugo were acquitted for lack of evidence by a Venezuelan military court. REF.: *CBA.*

Boschetti, Enzo, prom. 1969, Italy, kid. In early autumn 1969 an Italian national was kidnapped in Sardinia. His release for a ransom brought to an end the first phase of Italy's modern kidnapping epidemic.

Enzo Boschetti was abducted in Cagliari, Sardinia, in September 1969. His well-organized kidnappers received $115,500 for his release. Boschetti's kidnapping marked the end of Italy's first phase of modern abductions, the rash brought on by the shepherd outlaws of Sardinia. In the latter years of the 1960s these criminals kidnapped forty-one victims, more than half of them from the small area in the central mountains of Barbagia, in the Nuoro province.

REF.: *CBA;* Moorehead, *Hostages to Fortune.*

Boshears, Willis Eugene, 1931-   , Case of, Brit., mur. Staff Sergeant Willis Boshears was feeling lonely on New Year's Eve. The U.S. airman remained in his flat at Dunmow, England, while his wife and three children visited his mother-in-law. That night, Dec. 31, 1960, Sergeant Boshears, decorated during the Korean War, met 20-year-old Jean Sylvia Constable at the Bell Hotel. She was in the company of an Englishman named David Sault, but Sergeant Boshears joined them for drinks. The airman suggested that the three of them adjourn to his flat.

Shortly after midnight Sault left the apartment alone. A neighbor said she heard a woman crying that night. Boshears later claimed that he passed out, and had no memories of what happened in the flat. When he awoke in the morning he found Jean Constable dead on the floor. In a panic, he wrapped the body in winter clothing and drove it to a deserted lover's lane. The corpse was found by Sidney Ambrose on Jan. 3.

At the Wethersfield base, dozens of servicemen were interviewed about the murder. The next night Boshears was arrested and charged with murder. His only defense was sleepwalking. Under existing NATO agreements, the British were granted the right to try Airman Boshears. The six-week ordeal that began on New Year's Eve ended with a verdict of Not Guilty. Justice Glyn-Jones reminded the jury that if Airman Boshears had strangled Jean Constable while he was asleep, it was not a voluntary act and therefore he had to be acquitted.

After the decision was announced, his wife expressed her forgiveness and the couple returned home to the U.S. In July, the Air Force dismissed Boshears under what were termed "less than honorable conditions."

REF.: *CBA;* Furneaux, *Famous Criminal Cases.*

Boston, 1928, a novel by Upton Sinclair. The sensational Sacco-Vanzetti case (U.S., 1920) served as the basis of this work of fiction. See: Sacco, Nicola. REF.: *CBA.*

Boston, Patience, 1713-35, U.S., mur. Patience Boston was executed at York, Maine, on July 24, 1735, after being found Guilty of murdering 8-year-old Benjamin Trot in Falmouth. For reasons known only to herself, Patience picked the boy up and hurled him down a well. It was the climax of her short, but dissolute life, in which she violated all the Puritan tenets by lying, swearing, and drinking.

REF.: *CBA;* Nash, *Bloodletters and Badmen.*

Boston *Globe* **Hoax,** prom. 1883, U.S., fraud. In a curious case of synchronicity, a journalistic hoax turned out to be a portent of a volcanic eruption.

An assistant telegraph editor of the *Boston Globe* invented an interview with an elderly South Seas ship captain and obtained wide circulation of his story on both sides of the Atlantic. In this fraud, the editor told of an island blown into the sky by the sudden eruption of a dormant volcano. The yarn was based on accounts from encyclopedias, with vivid descriptions of the ocean bubbling with heat, showers of ashes darkening the sun, blocks of ice floating in streams of molten lava, and the ocean surface clotted with dead fish. Critics of the young writer, named Soames, were distressed and appalled when, a short time later, the biggest volcanic explosion of modern times occurred on the Indonesian island of Krakatoa, almost totally obliterating the island.

REF.: *CBA;* MacDougall, *Hoaxes.*

The Boston Massacre, a case of jangled nerves and too much ale.

Boston Massacre, The, 1770, U.S., mob vio. On Mar. 2, 1770, riot and mob rule was fomented by the sudden appearance of British troops in Boston. That day, a British soldier of the twenty-ninth regiment named Patrick Walker stopped between Pearl and Congress streets to watch a group of rope makers at their tasks. To supplement his small army pay, Walker was looking for off-duty tasks, a not uncommon pursuit at the time.

Rope maker William Green, a radical who thought himself a wit, looked impishly up from his rope laying and said to Walker: "Soldier, do you want work?"

"Yes I do, faith," responded Walker enthusiastically.

Green smirked and bawled out, "Well, then, go and clean my outhouse."

"Empty it yourself!" the trooper yelled back.

The exchanges grew red-hot until the soldier waded into the knot of rope makers who surrounded and taunted him. He was quickly disarmed, beaten so that welts rose on his face, and sent scurrying back to his barracks in humiliation. Walker returned with at least forty soldiers and a massive brawl ensued, the soldiers eventually driven off. For three days, such outbursts occurred throughout the city of Boston. On Mar. 5, a crowd numbering between 300 and 400 persons collected on King Street and faced eight British soldiers and their commander, Captain Thomas

Preston. Their weapons loaded, the troopers withstood a barrage of insults, jeers, and snowballs hurled by the mob.

Samuel Gray, a rope maker, bustled through the crowd, slapping people on the backs and shouting: "They dare not fire! They dare not fire!" He had gulped down great quantities of liquor and was drunk. Agitators moved through the sullen crowd informing them that the British troopers could not fire upon the citizens unless directed to do so by a civil authority. Somehow, the rioters construed this to mean that no matter how they taunted and pummeled the soldiers, they would not shoot. Gone was the basic line of reason that anyone would defend himself against lethal attacks to the point of firing weapons, particularly this much-harassed patrol.

"Fire! Fire! Damn your bloods, fire!" shouted members of the mob, confident that the nervous soldiers would retreat. Some of the troopers were almost convulsive, either out of fear or anger as their muskets shook in their hands; they formed an arcing line and held up their weapons. A furious flurry of snowballs from the mob assailed the troopers. Then someone threw a heavy club that knocked trooper Hugh Montgomery off his feet and sent him sprawling in the snow.

Montgomery scrambled up, grabbed his musket, and in a blind rage shouted at no one in particular, "Damn you, fire!" And he fired the first fatal shot of the Boston Massacre. A merchant named Richard Palmes then struck the first known blow on the part of the mob, swinging a club wildly and striking Montgomery. He then smacked Captain Preston who was frantically attempting to control his men. Palmes ran off down an alley as some of the troopers pointed their weapons in his direction.

Nathaniel Fosdick jumped from the head of the mob and ran along the wavering front of the troopers, clubbing them with a large stick. They bayoneted him as he ran but his wounds were superficial. Fosdick's actions seemed to spur the crowd into a forward, headlong dash. One of those in the van of the charge was a six-foot-two-inch sailor in his mid-forties named Michael Johnson. Only a short hour before the melée broke forth, Johnson had eaten a heavy meal and swilled down several tankards of ale in the victualing-house of Thomas Symmonds. Upon hearing the commotion coming from nearby King Street, Johnson had stepped from the inn and led about thirty sailors to the scene of the riot, telling them to take along clubs.

Much has been made, and wrongfully so, of Johnson's heritage. His real name was Crispus Attucks and negligent historians insist to this day that he was black, yet most evidence proves Attucks to be either partly or entirely an Indian of the Natrick tribe located near Framingham, Mass.

Attucks/Johnson and four others were quickly shot down as they started for the British line. There was only a six-second lull between the time of Montgomery's first shot and the irregular volley that broke forth from the other troopers. First to die was the drunken Samuel Gray. John Hickling rushed to him, rolled him over in the blood-spattered snow, and found a hole "as big as my hand" in Gray's head. He was the first martyr to the American Revolution. Also sprawled before the smoking muskets of the British troops were the bodies of Attucks, James Caldwell, Samuel Maverick, and Patrick Carr.

Captain Preston looked about in amazement and then angrily addressed his soldiers: "Damn you, why did you fire?"

"We heard *someone* shout 'fire,'" came the reply from one soldier. (It was Montgomery who had shouted the command.)

As the mob fled, a militant radical, Benjamin Burdick, approached the still body of Crispus Attucks and examined it. Moments later, Attucks' body was removed to the Royal Exchange Pub where it was placed upon a table; a physician performing a hasty autopsy determined that he had been shot in the right breast, the ball making a one-inch-wide wound that ran six inches deep. Burdick looked up from the slain Attucks into the pock-marked face of Captain Preston (a victim of smallpox).

"I want to see some faces that I may swear to another day," Burdick announced grimly.

Preston, just as solemnly, replied, "Perhaps, sir, you will."

The Boston Massacre brought about the trial of the British soldiers, even though the affair was more of a military act than a criminal offense. Six of the troopers were acquitted. Two were convicted of manslaughter and, as their only punishment, were branded on the hands.

REF.: *An Account of the Military Massacre at Boston;* Bowen, *John Adams and the American Revolution;* CBA; Davidson, *Propaganda and the American Revolution, 1763-1783;* Knollenberg, *Origin of the American Revolution: 1759-1766;* Lathrop, *Innocent Blood Crying to God from the Streets of Boston;* Miller, *Origins of the American Revolution;* Preston, *A Short History of the American Revolution;* Robson, *The American Revolution; A Short Narrative of the Horrid Massacre in Boston;* Zobel, *The Boston Massacre.*

Boston Police Strike, 1919, U.S., mob vio. The Boston police strike of 1919 was a near disaster; officers left their posts and the city to the whims of thugs, who instituted a giant crap came in broad daylight to flaunt their defiance of the law. It was, as one writer termed it, "a hoodlum gesture which was interrupted by a company of militia who promptly shot the ringleader, bayoneted a couple of others, and threw the rest into jail as a reminder that there was still law of a sort in the town."

Striking for better wages (and additional bathtubs in precinct stations, according to one report), the police department walked off duty *en masse* on Sept. 9, 1919. Minutes later, bands of hoodlums who had been waiting for just such an opportunity, surged through the streets of Boston, committing wholesale thievery. Criminals broke into homes, shops, and even some

A mounted national guardsman confers with one of the few working police officers during Boston's disastrous police strike of 1919.

government buildings, stealing what they pleased, unmolested in their work. Boston Common was thronged with hundreds of gamblers for three days. Cards and dice games flourished. One shopkeeper who had boarded up his store won $1700 in one of these crap games in an hour.

Automatic rifles were distributed to privately hired watchmen, and pitched battles were fought between these private police and armed bands of hoodlums. Hundreds of women, foolish enough to go outdoors during the police strike, were chased breathless for blocks by drunken rowdies; scores were dragged into doorways and parks and openly raped. During the nights of the strike, incessant

shots were heard. In many instances, thieves breaking into offices and stores were in the secret employ of some of the disgruntled policemen who thought such acts of vandalism and theft would cause authorities to agree to police demands. Governor Calvin Coolidge called in the militia instead and looters were shot on sight.

At one corner in the South End, a company of militia, made up of professional men from Boston and teachers and students

Massachusetts governor Calvin Coolidge inspects guardsmen during Boston's police strike.

from Harvard, faced at least 100 jeering hooligans. A young lieutenant stood next to his line of troops and shouted, "Load! Aim..."

The overconfident mob, crazily draped in clothing stolen from shattered stores, refused to disperse, and one of their rowdy number sneered at the troopers and sarcastically shouted, "Fire!" Unexpectedly, they did and six hoodlums were blasted to pieces. Not until more companies marched through Boston Common and around Brimstone Corner bayoneting hundreds of seemingly crazed gamblers who would not disperse did the underworld hosts retreat back into their dark kennels.

It became evident that militiamen and private guards had not only restored order, but had reduced Boston's normal crime rate by fifty percent. When the police resumed their duties, they were publicly chastised by President Woodrow Wilson, who lectured: "A strike of the policemen of a great city, leaving that city at the mercy of an army of thugs, is a crime against civilization...The obligation of a policeman is as sacred and direct as the obligation of a soldier. He is a public servant, not a private employee, and the whole honor of the community is in his hands. He has no right to prefer any private advantage to public safety."

For Governor Coolidge, the strike proved to be an inadvertent blessing. His decisive show of force in calling out the national guard swept him into the vice-presidential post in the Harding Administration and, subsequently, the presidency.

REF.: Amory, *The Proper Bostonians;* CBA; Coolidge, *Autobiography;* Fosdick, *American Police Systems;* Murray, *Red Scare; Report of Boston Police Commissioner; Report of Citizens Committee Appointed by the Mayor to Consider the Police Situation;* Keppetto, *The Blue Parade;* Rogers, *I Remember Distinctly;* Russell, *A City in Terror;* Sann, *The Lawless Decade;* White, *A Puritan in Babylon.*

Boston Strangler, The, See: **DeSalvo, Albert Henry.**

Boston Tea Party, The, 1773, U.S., mob vio. Many of those who participated in the riot that led to the Boston Massacre were on hand for the celebrated Boston Tea Party three years later. While Samuel Adams, Josiah Quincy, Jr., and others led protests against the British tax on tea at threepence-a-pound in a massive meeting at the Old South Meeting House on Dec. 16, 1773, about seventy or eighty patriots met in the Long Room in back offices of the Edes and Gill Printing Company.

For several hours this group, composed of the most hot-headed revolutionaries in Boston, sat about drinking great draughts from a five-gallon punch bowl which was continually reinforced with a mixture of Medford rum, arrack, lime, and apple brandy. The

Patriots dressed as Indians hold the Boston Tea Party, 1773.

potent drink caused many of the more vociferous among the group to become quite silly. They began to stick feathers in their hair. A gang of burly radicals appeared with boxes of trade tomahawks taken from a warehouse and these were passed out. There was much joking and laughter as the more tipsy of the lot began to chop up the furniture.

The group suddenly adjourned and, pretending to be "Mohawks," marched to Griffin's Wharf, ordered the lone watchman on duty to run for his life, and then boarded the three British tea ships docked there, the brigs *Dartmouth, Eleanor,* and *Beaver.* The punch bowl and several more gallons of the heady punch were taken aboard the ships and the rowdy "Mohawks" drank their fill as they tore open the hatches of the ships and began to dump the large chests of tea into the ocean (342 chests in all, worth about £18,000).

Many members of this raiding band were so drunk that they stumbled about the ships, slipping and falling and scattering tea every which way. Others so agog with grog mistook the starboard for the port sides of the ships and unthinkingly dumped the heavy tea chests down upon the heads of hundreds of cheering rebels at dockside, rather than into the sea.

This most famous tea party in history lasted only a few hours, and other than tremendous hangovers suffered the following day by a good deal of the participants, no one was hurt. The last

survivor of the Boston Tea Party was Captain Henry Purkitt who died in 1846 at the age of ninety-one. He recalled little of that night. He was too drunk to remember much.

REF.: *CBA;* Knollenberg, *Origin of the American Revolution;* Miller, *Origins of the American Revolution;* Preston, *A Short History of the American Revolution;* Quincy, *Memoirs of Josiah Quincy, Junior, of Massachusetts;* Robson, *The American Revolution.*

Bothwell, Fourth Earl of (James Hepburn), c.1536-78, Case of, Scot., mur. Bothwell was a dashing adventurer, a Scottish Protestant nobleman who married Mary, Queen of Scots and became involved in a number of intrigues. In 1562, Bothwell stood accused of being involved in a conspiracy to seize Queen Mary. He was imprisoned but escaped to France from where he was recalled by Mary. She was protected by him after the murder of her chief adviser, David Rizzio, by Scottish noblemen opposed to Mary's rule. Mary's second husband, Lord Henry Stewart Darnley, was murdered in 1567 and Bothwell, it was claimed, directed the unknown assassins who carried out the killing. Bothwell was acquitted of the Darnley slaying, but many historians adamantly insisted that he was guilty of this murder. Bothwell kidnapped Mary on Apr. 24, 1567, and married her on May 15. He was made Duke of Orkney and Shetland, but an overwhelming number of Scottish nobles threatened to kill him as a usurper. He fled first to his estates, and then to Norway, where he lived out his life as a prisoner of the Danish king, dying insane in 1578. See: **Darnley, Henry Stewart; Mary, Queen of Scots; Rizzio, David.** REF.: *CBA.*

Botkin, Cordelia (AKA: Cordelia Brolon, Mrs. Curtis, Mrs. C), 1854-1910, U.S., mur. In the early 1890s, Cordelia Botkin of Stockton, Calif., abandoned her husband and moved to San Francisco to pursue a Bohemian lifestyle. There she met John Presley Dunning, bureau chief of the Associated Press, who was wed to the prim and proper Elizabeth Pennington, formerly of Dover, Del. Botkin and Dunning were an unlikely pair. She was ten years older than the journalist and was plain and unassuming in her appearance, but Dunning was enchanted and he began openly courting her.

This arrangement continued for several years, until Dunning decided to move in with Cordelia, her son Beverly, and his mistress Louise Seeley. The four of them lived off a support check sent regularly to them by the cuckolded husband Welcome A. Botkin. Dunning was soon unemployed and began earning his money in the pool halls of San Francisco. But when the Associated Press needed competent reporters to cover the Spanish-

Poisoner Cordelia Botkin.　　　**Victim Elizabeth Dunning.**

American War, Dunning left his mistress to tour the battle zones in Puerto Rico.

Cordelia imagined that when the conflict ended, her lover would return to his wife, who had moved back to Dover. To prevent this, Botkin spiked some candy with arsenic, which was readily available before the enactment of the 1907 Poison Act. She sent the candy by mail to the Pennington residence in Delaware. The confections were sampled by Elizabeth Dunning and her sister, Mrs. Joshua Deane, on Sept. 9, 1898. Elizabeth mistakenly thought that the candies had been sent to her by the kindly Mrs. Corbally. Three days later, the two women died.

Dunning returned home from Puerto Rico to identify the handwriting on the package as that of his former mistress, Cordelia Botkin, who was arrested by San Francisco chief of police Isaiah W. Less. Cordelia was sentenced to life imprisonment in December 1898, but through charm and guile she was able to secure for herself special favors and accommodations from her jailers. When the sentencing judge, Carroll Cook, spotted her on a downtown cable car, he immediately ordered her moved into a cell at the Branch County Jail and stripped of her special privileges and two-day furloughs. After the 1906 earthquake which leveled the jail, Cordelia Botkin was transferred to San Quentin where she died in 1910. See: **Blandy, Mary; Cotton, Mary Ann Robson Mowbray; DeMelker, Daisy Louisa; Jegado, Helene; LaFarge, Marie; Smith, Madeleine.**

REF.: Boucher, *The Quality of Murder;* CBA; Duke, *Celebrated Criminal Cases of America;* Gross, *Masterpieces of Murder;* Kobler, *Some Like It Gory;* Nash, *Bloodletters and Badmen;* ____, *Look For the Woman;* Rodell, *San Francisco Murders;* Smith, *Famous American Poison Mysteries;* Stevens, *From Clue to Dock.*

Bottaro, Angelo, 1939-88, Italy, org. crime. Two Mafia clans in Siracusa, Sicily, began an open war in the late 1980s. One of the most ruthless killers in this internecine struggle was Angelo Bottaro, responsible for at least twenty murders, according to Sicilian authorities. Bottaro was so bold in his killings that he was finally caught red-handed following one murder and was tried several times, convicted and sentenced to life imprisonment. Bottaro claimed, as part of his defense, that he was hopelessly insane and insisted that he receive neurological treatment. He was sent to a hospital in Siracusa and, on Dec. 3, 1988, an unknown killer slipped into Bottaro's hospital room, located on the ground floor, and knifed the mass killer to death before he could find the pistol that he kept hidden under his pillow. REF.: *CBA.*

Botting, James (AKA: Jemmy), d.1837, Brit., execut. An illiterate, surly man, James Botting was the executioner at Newgate where he began as an assistant in 1815 for ten shillings and sixpence a week, later raised to a fixed weekly wage of one pound. Known for an occasional spark of gallows humor, Jemmy, as he was known to all, once was taunted at length about his profession by several loafers as he passed a public house. An onlooker asked him why he didn't respond. The hangman replied, "Nay, nay. I never quarrel with my customers." He did, in fact, hang one of the men, Falkener, a few months later, on Apr. 12, 1817, for rape. Botting apparently enjoyed his work, and always acted out his part, never speaking to the convicted, whom he treated like animals. His most famous hanging was of five leaders of the Cato Street Conspiracy, a political group accused of treason for trying to massacre cabinet ministers. The men were executed on May 1, 1820, as several of their revolutionary companions looked on. As an additional punishment, they all were decapitated, and many in the crowd hissed and yelled as the heads were held aloft by the executioner. The beheadings were performed by a surgeon who hid behind a mask to conceal his identity.

Botting was fired not long after these hangings, given a small pension of five shillings a week, and ended up in debtors' prison for a while. After suffering two strokes he was left bedridden and eventually became entirely paralyzed. He had repeated hallucinations of ghostly processions of the 175 persons he had killed, and he would have animated, angry conversations with them. He was said to find pleasure only in following highly-publicized murder cases and other crimes, becoming excited and lively as the execution dates neared, and gloating as the hour of death came. He died on Oct. 1, 1837.

REF.: Atholl, *Shadow of the Gallows;* Bleackley, *Hangmen of England;* CBA.

Bottom, Anthony, and **Washington, Albert,** and **Bell, Herman,** prom. 1971, U.S., asslt.-terr.-mur. The Black Liberation Army, known also as the BLA, was a badly organized, suicidal group made up of 200 to 300 members, men and women, bitter, armed,

and fanatically daring. With weak leadership and little organization, their methods were haphazard and amateurish, with many of the "soldiers" usually high on drugs and a large number having extensive police records. On May 21, 1971, the police team of Jones and Piagentini answered a disturbance call from a Harlem housing development but by the time they arrived the brawl was over. As the two policemen walked back to their car they were followed by two young men who suddenly pulled pistols and fired repeatedly as the officers fell. The youths then took the policemen's revolvers and emptied these into the prone bodies. Two nights earlier a police radio car had been machine-gunned from a vehicle on 106th Street. A few days after the Harlem shooting, the Black Liberation Army sent a message to the *New York Times,* claiming responsibility for the attacks and including the police car's license number.

Three months later the organization struck in Ingleside, Cal. On Aug. 29, three young men approached a police duty sergeant's desk. One pulled out a shotgun and fired through the speaking hole in the glass partition, blasting the policeman away while the other two men began firing at random, wounding a woman clerk before running out and fleeing in waiting cars. In Jan. 1972 New York City patrolmen Gregory Foster and Rocco Laurie were gunned down on Avenue B and Eleventh Street, shot in the back by three men who repeated the BLA method of grabbing the officers' guns and emptying them into their bodies. One assailant was seen dancing and leaping over one of the dead policemen before the attackers took off. Another message sent to the press said that the BLA's "spring offensive" had begun, with "more to come." The note continued, "We also dealt with the pigs in Brooklyn. We remember Attica." The note was signed, "The George Jackson Squad of the B.L.A."

Although the Black Liberation Army read political diatribes by Chairman Mao and purported to "exhibit the potential power of oppressed peoples to acquire revolutionary justice," the members struck at civilians as well, robbing banks, stealing cars, and dealing drugs. In attacks in San Francisco, St. Louis, and on the New Jersey Turnpike, the organization began to collapse, as weapons jammed, their cars were wrecked, and several members were killed. By April 1972 they were known fugitives, many of them fingerprinted and photographed in police records. Two of the BLA's leaders, Anthony Bottom and Albert Washington, were arrested in San Francisco, and a third, Herman Bell, was captured in New Orleans. The trials, which would drag on for three years, involved multiple charges in several states. Bottom, Bell, and Washington were convicted of the murders of Jones and Piagentini, and of the attempted murder of Sergeant Kowalski in San Francisco, but many trials of other members ended in hung juries or acquittals. See: **Attica Prison Riot; McKay Commission.**

REF.: *CBA;* Godwin, *Murder U.S.A.*

Bottomley, Horatio William, 1860-1933, Brit., fraud. One of England's most colossal frauds, Horatio Bottomley, was clever enough to avoid being ruined by his own fast-crumbling confidence games for almost forty years. And when it all caught up to him in old age, the wily sharper, acting as his own lawyer, called on the jury's patriotism and God to prevent his imprisonment, a plea that was properly answered with a stiff jail sentence. Before that career-ending time, Bottomley had made millions, lived like a king, and even got himself elected to Parliament. From the beginning, Bottomley thought of himself as larger than life or, at least, equal to the tremendous financial schemes he enacted. He came to believe that he was a brilliant lawyer, a financial genius, and a national hero. That was his public pose. In private, Bottomley was a flagrant spendthrift, a libertine, an alcoholic, and an unconscionable flimflammer who gutted the savings of hundreds of thousands of gullible investors.

Bottomley's background was as empty as any worthless share of stock he ever peddled. His father, William King Bottomley, was a tailor's assistant, although Bottomley, no doubt hating his father for the poverty that placed the boy in an orphanage, later insisted that he was the illegitimate son of the famous atheist,

Charles Bradlaugh, whom he came to amazingly resemble in later years. The idea for this claim may have come to Bottomley after discovering that his mother, Elizabeth Holyoake, was the sister of Jacob Holyoake, investment broker and also a pronounced atheist like Bradlaugh. The boy's parents lived so mean a life that they could not afford to keep their son, and placed him in an orphanage at age five. William Bottomley would shortly thereafter commit suicide. Young Bottomley lived for a while with an uncle, George Holyoake, but the uncle put the boy back into the orphanage at age ten. Four years later, Bottomley escaped the Sir Joseph Mason Orphanage at Edgbaston, fleeing to London.

A fast learner, Bottomley got a job as an errand boy, and while making deliveries, he studied the offices of solicitors and lawyers, realizing that good money could be made in these occupations. He applied for a job as a lawyer's clerk and got it. Bottomley befriended a female legal reporter and, mixing romance with ambition, dated her and induced her to teach him legal shorthand. Within a few years the industrious youth was earning his living as a legal reporter with a reputation for his lightning ability to capture words on paper. It was a short step for Bottomley to start his own small newspaper in 1884, the *Hackney Hansard,* which reported political activities in Parliament. For a short time Bottomley prospered, mostly from advertisements for companies with whom Bottomley was familiar. As a court reporter, he had learned much inside information about these firms and their dubious practices. He now solicited advertising from these firms; their managers felt compelled to advertise lest Bottomley publish details about their less than honest operations. To some this was journalistic blackmail, but to Bottomley it was just another way of making a good living.

From the newspaper, Bottomley expanded into printing, establishing two companies—one a publishing operation, the other a printing firm—going to his newspaper advertisers first, then the public, to sell stock in these shaky ventures. He pocketed most of the money and began to live high, returning nothing to his investors. In 1893, the shallow companies went into receivership and Bottomley was charged with conspiracy to defraud. His ego (not to mention the money he would save by not hiring a lawyer) demanded that he defend himself. During his defense, Bottomley proved that he was a brilliant orator, one who could move a jury to his side as easily as he had convinced investors to give him money for useless stock. He won his own acquittal. Inflated with confidence, Bottomley felt he could sell anything to anyone, regardless of its worth, and never face legal consequences.

In the following year, Bottomley capitalized on the public craze to invest in newly discovered Australian gold deposits. He set up public meetings in town halls, church basements, and the backs of pubs, exhorting those who flocked to his meetings to buy his gold certificates in Australian firms, and convincing thousands to hand over lifetime savings. He made an estimated £3 million without ever returning one pound to his investors. Whenever investors complained about not receiving any return on their money, Bottomley merely shrugged and reported that the gold mine had not panned out. Those who were angry enough to file complaint found Bottomley defending himself vigorously in court and with such eloquence (as well as well-placed bribes to jurors) that the con man escaped conviction time and again.

Bottomley was now fabulously rich and he purchased a huge country estate in Sussex, a luxury flat in London, and a villa on the French Riviera. Further, his love of horses caused him to buy a sprawling horse stable in Ostend, Belg. He began a lifelong habit of drinking champagne for breakfast, and drinking glass after glass until retiring each night. He bought the best champagne available, hundreds of cases every few months, storing these in his Sussex estate where he gave lavish parties. In London, Bottomley also ingratiated himself with high society by giving sumptuous fetes. With phenomenal ease, Bottomley began one new company after another, selling stock in the almost nonexistent firm (usually a secretary in a single office and a set of books that would confuse the most astute accountant) and then collapsing

the company a short time later. Dozens of these shell companies were started and went nowhere. Before stunned investors learned of these failed companies, Bottomley filed bankruptcy. Dozens of complaints and charges of fraud were filed against him, but he evaded conviction year after year. Nothing could be made of his books and no concrete evidence proving fraud could be found.

Fame as well as fortune beckoned to Bottomley, and he soon sought public recognition to go hand-in-hand with his personal fortune. He ran for Parliament in 1905 and was elected as Liberal MP from South Hackey. Now, Horatio William Bottomley had truly arrived. He glad-handed his fellow members in Parliament who thought him an affable fellow, although a few refused to shake his hand, knowing of his unsavory reputation. To further ingratiate himself with his peers, Bottomley posed as a wealthy philanthropist, giving money to various charities, especially to orphanages, and making sure that he received heavy newspaper coverage in his newly established weekly, *John Bull.*

Juggling his many firms became confusing even for Bottomley, and he fell behind in organizing their planned collapses. Too many of these firms shattered in one year, 1909, and his entire fortune was depleted. Bottomley declared personal bankruptcy for the second time and was compelled to resign his seat in Parliament. He soon created a new fortune by organizing sweepstakes and lotteries which brought more charges of fraud, but Bottomley managed to escape conviction once again. His name was becoming synonymous with stock swindles but, astoundingly enough, there never ceased to be a supply of suckers who raced to his town-hall type meetings to be mesmerized by his oratory and invest in his schemes.

When WWI began, Bottomley seemed to have a change of heart, suddenly instilled with patriotic fever. He announced to his friends that he was going to overcome his "sordid past" by helping England in her time of need. Bottomley volunteered to recruit men for the services and was suddenly seen everywhere—at public rallies, church meetings, recruiting stations, and particularly at bond rallies, where he bounced across stages, waving his arms, smashing a fist into the palm of his hand, and shouting to the enthralled crowds that England needed men and money to destroy the kaiser's legions. He was well paid for his patriotic efforts, receiving £50 to £100 every time he opened his mouth for England. Bottomley howled his patriotic propaganda in the pages of *John Bull,* which became immensely popular during the war. His speeches were so popular that large dailies paid him a great deal of money to reprint them. This led to a series of long articles by Bottomley which appeared regularly in such publications as the *Sunday Pictorial.* For more than four years, the hustler financed himself with his war propaganda, earning almost £30,000.

So popular had Bottomley become that he was able to run for Parliament once again in 1918, winning back his old South Hackney seat but as an Independent. Shortly after his election, Bottomley developed his all-time money-making scheme, an idea that he borrowed from the British government. When the government announced the sale of Victory Bonds in 1918, Bottomley seized upon the gigantic scam that would eventually land him in prison. Victory Bonds were sold at less than £5 per bond, but could be redeemed later for larger amounts. Bottomley announced that he would buy these bonds in large numbers and allow the "little people," as he called his suckers, the opportunity of purchasing these bonds for even less than purchase price, promising that he would return top value on the bonds. Tens of thousands of patriotic citizens bought these Victory Bonds through Bottomley, or at least they thought they were buying bonds. They sent their money directly to Bottomley, who had established the Victory Bond Club which ostensibly bought the government bonds in large quantities and received additional interest because of such huge purchases. These revenues were later to be disbursed to the club members.

Of course, Bottomley bought no bonds and pocketed almost every pound he received, living higher than ever before. He did make some token bond payments to the Treasury. It appeared that the great stock swindler had invented yet another scheme that would make him unlimited millions. Yet Bottomley's own tight-wad mentality was to be his undoing. He had never paid his associates much beyond an initial retainer and they, like his invest-ors, were usually left holding the bag. One of these, Reuben Bigland, who was involved in Bottomley's Victory Bond Club, went public when Bottomley reneged on paying Bigland his fees. Bigland published a pamphlet exposing how Bottomley fleeced the public, stating that the Victory Bond Club was the con man's "latest and greatest swindle," and that Bottomley never had any intention of returning profits on the investments, let alone return the original investments.

British swindler Horatio Bottomley exhorting crowds in Trafalgar Square at a WWI recruitment rally, 1915.

Bottomley immediately denounced the pamphlet as defamatory and filed a suit of criminal libel against Bigland. Realizing that his appearance in court could open his muddled books to public inspection, Bottomley reconsidered and then dropped his suit against Bigland. The government, however, was urged to act by a public aroused by Bigland's widely read exposé. At first the courts were disinclined to go after Bottomley, who was still an MP, but public pressure soon compelled the government to bring fraud charges against the great swindler.

Mindful that their quarry was still a respected member of Parliament, the government of David Lloyd George dragged its feet, having the distinguished Horace Avory and Richard Muir prosecute, but not until the redoubtable criminal counsel, Sir Travers Humphreys, who declined to prosecute, went over the swindler's labyrinthine books. Using a bevy of accountants, Humphreys and his people spent months sifting through every shady, complicated transaction dealing with the Victory Bond Club. They finally emerged, like lost travelers out of the swamps, with what they felt would be enough evidence to convict the grand con man. Bottomley was brought to trial in 1922, acting, as usual, in his own defense. The prosecution did not minimize its oppo-nent's ability to act as his own counsel, knowing full well how Bottomley's brilliant orations had convinced hardhearted juries in the past, and how he had escaped conviction time and time again. He was a spellbinder and could confuse any logical facts, reasonable conclusions, and sound arguments against him.

Before Bottomley went to trial, however, he gave indications that his days as a shrewd legal opponent were over. He asked the court if he could take an early lunch break, at 11:30 a.m. each day, since he was "required" to have his daily portion of champagne (he referred to the bubbly as his "medicine") at that time lest he go into convulsions. He was, as his opponents then described him, "a champagne addict," drinking as much as three or four bottles during the day and an equal number at night before retiring. His appearance bespoke his alcoholic addiction. His face was puffy, sagging everywhere. Bags of flesh squeezed his eyes into slits. Heavy jowls sagged over Bottomley's high, starched collar. He was a physical, besotted wreck at sixty-two. He was also con-cerned about a female friend whose name appeared in one of the accounts Humphreys was inspecting. He practically begged Humphreys and the court not to mention the lady's name, admit-ting that he had deposited large amounts of money in her name and did not wish to "compromise" her in any way. He insisted that this obvious paramour knew nothing of his business operations and was perfectly innocent of any wrongdoings the court might determine.

The age of chivalry had not yet died in England. The court agreed to keep the woman's name out of the proceedings if Bottomley would admit that the account in her name was his own. Bottomley grinned and said he would claim the account. Then he added: "And what about my medicine?" The court understood that problem and informed the anxious drunk that the presiding judge would recess the court early and allow Bottomley to get to his bottle before noon. Pleased, the old sharper girded his considerable loins for battle. Humphreys took on the burden of attack just before the trial, agreeing to represent the government. The trial took place at the Old Bailey before Justice Salter. Humphreys' opening address to the jury detailed how Bottomley juggled and doubled his books to funnel huge amounts from the Victory Bond Club into his personal accounts. In one instance it was shown how the club paid a company £20,000 for services that really did not exist, that the firm was really Horatio Bottomley under a different name. In another instance, it was shown how the sharper paid out enormous sums from club funds for the upkeep of his Belgium racing stables.

Bit by accounting bit, the prosecution mounted a damning case against the swindler who sat glum at the defense table, slumped forward, staring straight ahead as if in a daze (or alcoholic stupor, some who were present later claimed). The prosecution brought some witnesses to the stand who claimed that Bottomley had not returned profits or even their original investments when requested by them to do so. This brought the old man jumping to his feet. He asked Judge Salter if he could bring 100,000 witnesses—all of those who had purchased bonds through his club—to refute such claims. All of these 100,000, thundered Bottomley, had not only received a return on their money but had enjoyed profits galore. The judge declined to allow a parade of 100,000 witnesses to the stand which would have taken, certainly, several decades to cross-examination. He set aside his ruling on the matter and told Bottomley that the court would consider any *reasonable* evidence he could provide. It was obvious that Bottomley was bluffing; he did not have a single satisfied customer to bolster his fast-fading, self-projected image of honest businessman, the working man's friend, the ally of the "little fellow," as Bottomley was forever calling his victims.

What undoubtedly hurt Bottomley more than any of the exact-ing paper-chase details which pinned him down as a fraud was the prosecution's questioning of his patriotic image. It was shown that he had been paid handsomely for his war lectures and bond rally appearances, so much so that he appeared to be earning money from the boys who did the fighting and dying for England in the trenches of France. This hard evidence was obviously much on his mind when he burst forth with his histrionic summation, an explosive fight for his public life as well as his private business transactions. Bottomley stormed about the courtroom, his mas-sive body seeming to tilt treacherously forward as if he were about to topple onto his face. He raised his arms akimbo, as if asking for divine intervention, and the flab of his face turned bright crimson in anger at being portrayed aswho exploited the heroic dead and the heroic veterans who had given him the wages of their bloody battles.

Bottomley, right, under indictment, leaves the Bow Street court.

To the jury Bottomley fulminated: "You may have entertained a great opinion of me and thought that, whatever my faults in days gone by, I have endeavored to do my duty to my king and country. Now you are asked to change your opinion, and to say that all the time I was an arrant humbug and scoundrel." He reminded the jury that his patriotic honor was not on trial and that his peers must only decide whether or not he had defrauded the members of the Victory Bond Club. "You have got to find that I had the intention to steal the money of poor devils such as ex-soldiers who subscribed to the Club. You have got to find that Horatio Bottomley, editor of *John Bull,* member of Parliament, the man who wrote and spoke throughout the war with the sole object of inspiring the troops and keeping up the morale of the country, who went out to the front to do his best to cheer the lads—you have got to find that that man intended to steal their money! God forbid! I swear before God that I have never fraudulently converted a penny of the club's money."

His anger gushed through a torrent of words, mounting in volume until Bottomley was delivering a cannonade. He charged about the courtroom as if he were a national legend unfairly defiled, posturing shock at the mere suggestion that he, Horatio Bottomley, England's greatest hero, no doubt, since Wellington and Nelson, could be profiled as a villain. His summation to the jury was almost a threat. Should his peers find him guilty of fraud they would face God's own wrath: "You will not convict me! The jury is not yet born that would convict me on these charges. It is unthinkable!" There was a long sword hanging on a wall behind the judge's bench and Bottomley, who had been studying this gleaming blade for days as he heard his sins recited, suddenly wheeled about and pointed to it, saying: "That sword of justice will drop from its scabbard if you give a verdict of guilty against me. I say it with a clean conscience. I say it without one thought of fear or misgiving. I know my country and my country's people, and knowing you, and knowing myself, and knowing the truth about this matter, without one atom of hesitation, one atom of fear...I know by the mercy of God and the spirit of justice you will liberate me from this ordeal!" With that, the heavy-breathing Bottomley buried his head in large, hoary hands and openly wept, his sobs sent directly toward the jury.

In the end, the jury disbelieved the fiery orator who relied upon a style of delivery that had long gone out of fashion. He was a man of bombast and hortatory exclamations. His rhetoric creaked of ancient ploys and devices that were all too obvious, even to the most unsophisticated. He tried, as in his court appearances of decades earlier, to shape the jury, to bend its collective will to his own. His roaring rage against the attacks on his image, his dignity,

rang hollow and untrue. In the end, the prosecution ground the old campaigner down with the overwhelming weight of its evidence and even he, at his nadir, had to admit that he had falsely advertised his club when claiming that it possessed £500,000. In a half hour's deliberation, the jury returned to find the defendant Guilty on all counts but one. The sword on the wall behind Judge Salter never moved an inch.

Bottomley stood mute in the dock as the court handed down its sentence. The judge delivered an unusually scathing summary to the jury's conclusions: "Horatio Bottomley, you have been rightly convicted by the jury of a long series of heartless frauds. These poor people trusted you and you robbed them of £150,000 in ten months. The crime is aggravated by your high position, by the number and poverty of your victims, by the trust which they reposed in you. It is aggravated by the magnitude of your frauds and by the callous effrontery by which your frauds were committed." The arch swindler was given, despite the rancor from the bench, a fairly light sentence—seven years in prison.

Bottomley could only scowl and frown, indignant to the last for being put upon by what he thought to be the judge's gratuitous remarks. He asked if it were not customary for a convicted person to render some remarks before being sentenced. Judge Salter reminded him that that was the case only for capital offenses. Sneered Bottomley: "Had it been so, my Lord, I should have had something rather offensive to say about your summing up!" A short time later the great fraud was shown to his cell at Wormwood Scrubs Prison. He was formally expelled from the House of Commons a few days later.

Five years later, in 1927, Bottomley was released, broken in health, ignominious, a pauper—but not for long. If he could no longer sell bogus stock, Horatio Bottomley could at least sell the story of the man who sold the bogus stock. He quickly arranged to write a series of articles about his prison days, for which a daily newspaper paid him the then-staggering sum of £12,500. Bottomley showed himself unrepentant in the series of articles which was entitled "I Have Paid...But I Did Not Owe the Debt." He contacted old partners, loan sharks for the most part, and persuaded them to invest in another newspaper he established overnight, a publication he called *John Blunt.* (Some

Bottomley after his release from prison in 1927, still hortatory.

claimed that these investors willingly came to Bottomley's financial rescue rather than risk exposure of their past sins by Bottomley, a man who knew well their dark deeds.)

There would be no meteoric rise from the ashes this time. The new publication quickly failed and Bottomley now lost everything. His wife died and he was compelled to sell his country estate, his racing stables, even the furnishings of his London apartment. Flat broke in 1930, he applied for an old-age pension but this was denied him. The old sharper grew ill and was taken in by a one-time musical comedy star, Peggy Primrose; he had backed several of her hit shows during his palmy days. Some of Ms. Primrose's friends thought to put Bottomley to work exploiting himself and they arranged for him to make stage appearances. Half tipsy with cheap champagne and dressed in soiled evening clothes, the old fraud shuffled before the footlights to talk about his sinful past. He would pathetically blather about how he was pilloried and imprisoned for trying to make money for the "little people." The "little people" in the audience only hooted and jeered in response.

Some days later, in May 1933, Horatio Bottomley was leaving the stage, the roaring ridicule of the audience in his ears. He stopped, heaved a great sigh, and his heavy body crashed to the floor. He died on May 26, 1933 in Middlesex Hospital and was placed in a common grave, an end that the determined orphan boy of the previous century could never have envisioned.

REF.: Bowker, *Behind the Bar*; CBA; *The Dictionary of National Biography*; Humphreys, *A Book of Trials*; ____, *Criminal Days*; Kingston, *Dramatic Days At the Old Bailey*; ____, *A Gallery of Rogues*; Lustgarten, *Story of Crime*; Marjoribanks, *For the Defence*; Scott, *The Concise Encyclopedia of Crime and Criminals*; Symons, *Horatio Bottomley*; Thomson, *The Story of Scotland Yard*.

Boudes, Abbé, b.c.1830, Fr., forg.-fraud-extor.-child abuse-attempt. mur.-mur. Abbé Boudes, born in France, was expelled from the Perigeux seminary for stealing candlesticks and a cassock in 1855 and a year later he was expelled from ecclesiastical college for immorality, a subject which would be a lifelong pursuit for him. Spending two years in Italy, Boudes returned to France as a priest, consecrated by an Italian bishop. When appointed curate at Lagarde by the Bishop of Rodez, Boudes extorted money from a dying man by scaring him into turning it over, used the confessional to depose rightful heirs, and robbed parishioners on their deathbeds. Throughout his life, Boudes was said to have sexually abused children of both sexes. In 1860, fearing that his priest might report his crimes, Boudes tried to murder the man by putting poison in the sacred church vessels. Upon discovery of Boudes' plot, the soft-hearted priest did not inform against him. In 1865, made curate of Viviers, Boudes procured an abortion for a young girl, lent money as a usurer, forged bills, robbed his priest, swindled clerical garment vendors, and offered 600 francs to induce heart palpitations in a young man who wanted to get out of serving in the army. Boudes was transferred to Taurines in 1871 as a priest, where he continued to steal, forge, and procure abortions.

On Mar. 1, 1875, Abbé Alvar, priest of the Saint-Cirq parish, was found dead in his home, repeatedly stabbed. Money collected for repairs to his church had been stolen. Alvar's sister, who became partly deranged after the murder, testified that she saw two men with blackened faces come into the house through a hole they made in the wall, and they chased her out of the house after killing her brother. It was proven that Boudes did not sleep at home that night. He fled from Taurines and was arrested on July 28, 1876, in Ardèche, and charged with the murder. Boudes pretended to be mad, spending the next ten years, from 1876-86, in an asylum in Montpellier to avoid standing trial and to exhaust the legal period during which he could be tried for his earlier crimes. He explained to a warden, "They think I am mad because I have committed some trifling breaches of the sixth commandment, but I am not, and I mean to get out of this." Bribing a warder, Boudes escaped in 1886, showing up in Tarn and practicing as an Alsatian priest under the name Jean Mary. Two years later, made a professor at the St. Marie school at Albi, he ingratiated himself with a wealthy elderly woman, Madame Calmels, and induced her to sell some land to him at a ridiculously low price. Recognized by a girl from France, Boudes was turned in to the authorities. When captured, he pleaded with them to do him a favor by killing him.

Sixty years old at the time of his trial on Dec. 19, 1889, Boudes faced the Cour d'Assises at Rodez. Because of the ten-year lapse, he could not be charged with the attempted poisoning of his priest at Lagarde, and the madness of Alvar's sister made it impossible to collect sufficient evidence to prosecute him on that charge. Boudes wrote to the Bishop of Rodez, swearing his innocence, claiming to be accused of "a few trifling peccadilloes which I hardly remember," and asking the Bishop's assistance to help him withdraw into a monastery. Instead, Boudes was found guilty of several crimes on Dec. 21, 1889, and sentenced to penal servitude for life.

REF.: CBA; Irving, *Studies of French Criminals of the Nineteenth Century*.

Boudin, Kathy, 1944- , U.S., terr.-mur. In 1981, a group of radicals held up a Brink's truck in Rockland County, N.Y., taking $1.6 million and killing a guard. In a shootout with police that followed, two officers were slain. Information from the incidents led police to the revolutionaries' hiding places in Mt. Vernon, N.Y., the Bronx, and other areas where, through informants and evidence brought in by an FBI conspiracy probe, they arrested several people. Among these were Samuel Brown, an ex-convict, and Kathy Boudin, notorious for her link to a 1970 bombing of a Greenwich Village Weather Underground bomb factory. A graduate of Bryn Mawr, Boudin became a leading figure in the Weather underground movement, disappearing after the 1970 explosion. Charged with multiple counts of murder and robbery in the 1981 attack, Boudin was tried in front of Judge David Ritter. Her defense team included her father, radical lawyer Leonard Boudin, and attorney Leonard Weinglass. Weinglass argued that the evidence placing Boudin at the Brink's robbery site was circumstantial, but prosecutor Kenneth Gribetz contended that there was "hard evidence consisting of eyewitness testimony, circumstantial evidence, and evidence developed by FBI laboratory experts."

Maximum sentences were given to four other defendants convicted in the Brink's robbery: Sekou Odinga and Silvia Baraldini were each sentenced to forty years in prison and fined $50,000 for conspiracy and racketeering, and Cecil Ferguson and Edward L. Joseph were sentenced to twelve and one-half years each on accessory charges on Sep. 3, 1983. Boudin pleaded guilty to all charges and was convicted in White Plains, N.Y. and on May 3, 1984, was sentenced to twenty years to life in prison for her part in the Brink's robbery. See: **Weather Underground Organization**.

REF.: Castellucci, *The Big Dance*; CBA.

Bougrat, Dr. Pierre, prom. 1927, Fr., mur. A Marseilles bank cashier, Jacques Rumèbe, was reported missing by his wife on Mar. 15, 1925. Nearly 85,000 francs were also missing, causing police to conclude that the motive for the crime was robbery. Two months later, police searched the office of Dr. Pierre Bougrat, one of the last places the cashier was seen. In a large cupboard in the physician's operating room, the police discovered the decomposing remains of Rumèbe. Dr. Bougrat explained that Rumèbe had dropped by for his daily injection on the afternoon of Mar. 15. This time, Rumèbe said that he was in dire financial difficulty. He needed to raise the equivalent of £800 or face ruin. Bougrat agreed to go into the city to try to locate the money, and when he returned he found Rumèbe dead on the floor and his poison cabinet broken into. It was a suicide to be sure, but given the incriminating circumstances, he had no other choice but to conceal the body, he said.

Bougrat was arrested on a charge of murder. His trial opened in Marseilles in March 1927, two years after the murder of Rumèbe. The prosecution contended that Bougrat, and not the murder victim, was in serious debt. Various witnesses testified to Bougrat's numerous attempts to raise money, usually through highly illegal means. It was intimated at the trial that Rumèbe was not the first victim of the physician. A Greek heiress named Odette Lepocal, who had been under Bougrat's care, vanished from her nursing home. She was found by the police bound and gagged. The story of her abduction, and Bougrat's subsequent ransom demand, led to his arrest.

Bougrat was found Guilty and was transported to Devil's Island in French Guiana for the remainder of his life. But he escaped to Venezuela in October 1928, one of only a handful of men to accomplish this feat in the long history of the penal colony

REF.: CBA; Furneaux, *The Medical Murderer*; Heppenstall, *Bluebeard and After*; Hynd, *Sleuths, Slayers and Swindlers*; Nash, *Almanac of World Crime*; Thompson, *Poisons and Poisoners*.

Boulanger, Georges Ernest Jean Marie (AKA: **The Man on Horseback**), 1837-91, Fr., consp.-suic. Led the Army of Occupation in Tunis from 1884-85 and served as Minister of War from 1886-87. He was arrested for the first time in 1877 for disobeying orders, but received the support of the people. He was often seen on horseback in the streets of Paris rallying the Royalists and Bonapartists against the Third Republic. He organized a move ment known as *Boulangism* advocating strong measures against Germany. For this he was accused of conspiracy and treason by Prime Minister Pierre Tirard and was convicted in absentia. He fled to Brussels and the isle of Jersey before taking his own life. REF.: *CBA*.

Boulay de la Meurthe, Antoine Jacques Claude Joseph, 1761-1840, Fr., treas. Member of the Council of Five Hundred and opponent of Jacobin tyranny. He was banished by Louis XVIII in 1815, but returned to France four years later. REF.: *CBA*.

Boulogne, Henri, prom. 1929, Fr., mur. Clement Pascal fancied himself a master swindler and enjoyed the nickname given him by the editors of Paris' *Le Matin:* the "Napoléon of Crooks." Pascal was released from the Loos Prison in late August 1929, but his vanity got the best of him. He decided to write his memoirs, but in order to arouse interest in such a project he needed publicity.

Clement Pascal invented a French version of the Ku Klux Klan, a secret society known as the Knights of Themis. This organization sent a series of letters to *Le Matin* describing their abduction and ritualistic torture of Clement Pascal, each one more lurid in content than the last.

The Knights of Themis letters drew considerable attention. In his last correspondence, shortly before Oct. 1, Pascal said he was going to be buried alive. He actually went through with it, recruiting an ex-convict named Henri Boulogne to help him dig the grave near the Bois de la Justice. Detailed instructions were given to Boulogne. He was to mail a last letter to the newspaper announcing that Pascal had been buried alive. An oilskin package containing copies of the letters, newspaper clippings, and other paraphernalia was buried next to the grave. In twelve hours, Boulogne was to return to make sure everything was alright.

There was only one problem. The breathing pipe connecting the coffin to the surface did not work. Pascal had tested the device in his cottage by placing himself inside the box and breathing through the pipe. The cracks in the wood provided the necessary suction to draw the air into the coffin. But under the weight of the earth the suction disappeared, and it was impossible to extract air from ground level. Pascal perished within hours.

The unwitting Boulogne told this fantastic story to the police who charged him with "murder by imprudence." He was found Guilty and was sentenced to prison for eight months.

REF.: *CBA*; Reynolds, *Murder 'Round the World*.

Boulton, Robert, prom. 1925, Brit., Case of, fraud. In a complicated case in England in 1925, involving fine points of banking and partnership law, Robert Boulton was charged, along with a Mr. Moncrieff and a third partner, of converting shares valued at £250,000 entrusted by the Alliance Bank of Simla in India to Boulton's Bank, Alliance's London agents. Boulton was the senior partner and had been a director as well as the chairman of the Alliance at the Simla Bank for three years. Moncrieff, away on vacation in India when the majority of the transactions occurred, protested immediately when he learned of the conversion. The third partner, a peer's son who took care of the Boulton Bank's Russian business, a minor concern, spent as little time as possible doing any kind of business, being more interested in his social life. The main prosecutor was an attorney named Mr. Curtiss-Bennett, and defense lawyers included Roland Oliver for Moncrieff and Henry Maddocks and Walter Frampton for Boulton. Tried before a jury in the court of Judge Rigby Swift, the prosecution had no sooner completed giving its evidence when Swift withdrew the case against Moncrieff and the Russian partner and instructed the jury to bring in a verdict of Not Guilty, explaining, "In my view there is no reflection whatever upon the character of either (of the accused)."

The case against Boulton went on for several more days. Although by Boulton's action the Bank of Simla had lost more than £250,000, the jury, angered by the prosecution's attempt to implicate Moncrieff and the Russian partner, acquitted Boulton as well, despite the fact that Boulton maintained the responsibility was his. The attorney who represented Moncrieff and Boulton's

other partner felt that all three men had been innocent and that justice was served.

REF.: *CBA*; Humphreys, *Criminal Days*.

Bounty Mutineers, See: **Mutiny on the Bounty.**

Bourbon, Cesar de (Duke of Vendome), 1594-1665, Fr., consp. Illegitimate son of Henry IV and member of the Bourbon royal family whose members sat on the thrones of France, Spain, and Italy. He earned the wrath of Cardinal Richelieu for his part in various aristocratic intrigues, and was imprisoned from 1626-30 for his role in the Chalais plot against the Cardinal. In 1640, he was exiled to England when the second intrigue was uncovered. REF.: *CBA*.

Bourbon, Charles Ferdinand (duc de Berry), 1778-1820, Fr., assass. Brother of the last dauphin of France, he lived in England during the long period of Revolution and Empire from 1789-1814. In 1814, he traveled to Ghent during the hundred day return of Napoléon I and was assassinated by a Bonapartist zealot. REF.: *CBA*.

Bourbon, François, 1616-69, Fr., consp. Son of Cesar de Bourbon. He remained in exile until the death of Cardinal Richelieu. From 1643-48, he served a prison sentence for conspiring against Mazarin, successor to Richelieu during the Thirty Years War. He returned to complete his military career. REF.: *CBA*.

Bourbon, Henri (Duc de Bordeaux, Comte de Chambord), 1820-83, Fr., consp. Pretender to the throne following the death of Charles X in 1830. He was exiled the same year but, in 1832, returned to France undercover and was later imprisoned for inciting a revolt on behalf of Henri at Vendée. REF.: *CBA*.

Bourbon, Louis-Auguste de, 1670-1736, Fr., consp. Denied a place on the council of regency and personal command of the royal guards by Philippe II, duc d'Orléans in 1715. His wife, Louise-Bénédicte de Bourbon-Condé, drew him into a plot to kidnap Philippe and place Philip V as regent for Louis XV. He was arrested for this unsuccessful attempt and imprisoned for two years from 1718-20. REF.: *CBA*.

Bourdon de l'Oise, François Louis, c.1758-98, Fr., treas. Instrumental in the execution of King Louis XVI. He renounced his former association with the radicals and helped depose Robespierre in 1794. He became a Royalist, and was sent to Guiana as punishment by the Directory. REF.: *CBA*.

Bourg, Frank, 1890-1950, U.S., (unsolv.) mur. Bourg was stricken with a heart attack and was recuperating in a New Orleans hospital when, in April 1955, an unknown man crept into his room and crushed his skull with a hand ax. The murder baffled police. Bourg was an innocuous 64-year-old bank teller with no criminal ties. It was then reasoned that Bourg had been murdered by accident, his hospital room being only a few doors distant from the room occupied by Sheriff Frank Clancy. The sheriff had recently appeared before the Kefauver Committee to testify about gambling in Louisiana. Clancy clearly implicated himself as a payoff man for the syndicate and told how he had permitted thousands of slot machines to be placed in his parish. He also admitted that he had interests in many gambling operations, and this obliquely implicated New Orleans Mafia boss Carlos Marcello. Sheriff Clancy had been hospitalized about the same time that Bourg had been wheeled into a neighboring room and it was believed that the bank clerk had been murdered in error, the syndicate killer mistaking Bourg's room for Clancy's. A hospital employee told police that she saw the killer near the room where Bourg was killed and believed she could recognize him. A few days later she called authorities and told them that she was mistaken. She could identify no one. No one was ever indicted for the Bourg killing which remains unsolved to this day. See: **Marcello, Carlos.** REF.: *CBA*.

Bourke, Patrick, and **Ellis, George,** d.1745, Brit., rob. For the crime of killing fifteen sheep, Patrick Bourke and George Ellis were hanged at Tyburn Hill on Feb. 20, 1745. The charge was serious, akin to horse stealing in the U.S. The ewes belonged to John Messenger, a Kensington farmer who found the animals ripped open, the fat around the kidneys removed. Bourke and Ellis sold the fat to a candlemaker for the sum of forty-one shillings and twopence halfpenny.

The thieves might have gone unpunished if not for their own petty squabbles. Ellis resented the two black eyes he had received from his partner. He went to Constable Joseph Agnew, and a detachment of watchmen went to Bourke's place, where they found a clasp-knife covered with animal fat.

The knife was exhibited in court, and the two sheep-killers were found guilty and sentenced to die. In his defense, Bourke accused the constable of forcing a confession out of him with alcohol, but the jury at the Old Bailey rejected this excuse and sent both men to Tyburn.

REF.: CBA; Mitchell, *Newgate Calendar*.

Bourke, Richard Southwell (Lord Mayo), 1822-72, India, assass. A momentary lapse in the security surrounding Richard Bourke, the viceroy and governor general of India, provided the opening his assassin needed. Early in 1872, Bourke, the sixth earl of Mayo, and viceroy of India since 1869, decided to make a trip to the Andaman Islands, an archipelago in the Bay of Bengal and the site of a large penal colony. Bourke's visit was in response to recent trouble in the islands where only a handful of English officials and Indian troops had charge of some 8,000 convicts.

On Feb. 8, 1872, Bourke and his party spent a long day touring the island installations. Despite Bourke's impatience with tight security, his men kept him safe throughout the day's travels. Just an hour before sunset, however, he announced his desire to climb 1,200-foot Mount Harriet, where he intended to build a malaria sanatorium. Though they disapproved, the viceroy's aides had little choice. By the time they had climbed to the top of the hill and returned, it was quite dark. When they stopped briefly at the bottom of the hill to make arrangements for the following day, the viceroy wandered away from the group. He was attacked by a convict who had followed the viceroy and his entourage since they began their climb. Shere Ali, thirty, imprisoned for the murder of a relative, stabbed the viceroy twice in the back.

Bourke soon died of his wounds. The next morning, the assassin was given a preliminary hearing during which he was committed for trial on the charge of murder. That afternoon he was tried, found Guilty, and sentenced to death by hanging. He was executed on Viper Island on Mar. 11, 1872. Bourke's body was returned to Dublin for burial.

REF.: CBA; Hyams, *Killing No Murder*; Williams, *Heyday For Assassins*.

Bousfield, William, d.1856, Brit., mur. William Bousfield was tried for the murders of his wife and three children in 1856, convicted, and sentenced to death. During his imprisonment he threw himself face first into the fire in his cell. For this reason, he was taken to the gallows seated, with his face covered in cloth. When the executioner pulled the bolt releasing the floor beneath him, Bousfield dropped through the floor of the scaffold. Apparently, his seated position interfered with the proper functioning of the noose. He swung for a few seconds and then, to the surprise and horror of the witnesses, pulled himself back up to the scaffold with his feet. Three separate times Bousfield managed to haul himself back up onto the scaffold. Each time, prison guards pushed him back down. The execution was completed only when Calcraft, the executioner, threw himself on the suspended Bousfield, holding him down until Bousfield finally strangled.

REF.: CBA; Cooper, *Lesson of the Scaffold*; Thompson, *The Story of Scotland Yard*.

Bousquet, Pierre (AKA: Pierre Delvain), prom. 1716, Fr., pir. Pierre Bousquet was one of the boisterous, brawling New Providence, Bahamas, pirates who sailed up and down the coastal colonies of the New World. The colorful Frenchman was one of a group of homosexual pirates whose profligacy and exaggerated clothing was well known to the residents of New Providence. At one time he sailed under the command of Anne Bonny who once remarked after blasting off a man's ear: "Is that a head? I thought I was shooting the handle off a mug." REF.: CBA.

Bouvier, John, 1787-1851, Italy, lawyer. Immigrated to the U.S. in 1802 where he later wrote his famous *Law Dictionary* (1839) and *The Institutes of American Law* (1851). REF.: CBA.

Bouvier, Léone, 1930- , Fr., mur. Léone Bouvier was born into a peasant family in the village of Saint-Macaire-en-Mauges. She was the victim of drunken, abusive parents who imbibed "gniole," a locally produced cider whose properties were known to induce madness if consumed in excess.

In 1951, Émile Clenet, a 22-year-old garage mechanic, seduced Bouvier with false words of love and a vague promise of marriage. They met regularly for sex on Sundays, but after Léone became pregnant, Clenet soon lost interest and ordered her to get an abortion. She agreed to his demand, but contracted an illness from the operation which prevented her from working. Bouvier was dismissed from her factory job, and when she heard no further word from Clenet, she found him at his place of employment in Nantes.

Émile Clenet told his one-time girlfriend not to bother him at the garage again. Penniless, she spent the month engaged in prostitution. With the few dollars she earned, Léone purchased a cheap .22-caliber pistol from a Nantes gunsmith. In February 1952, at a local dance, Clenet told her of his decision to move to North Africa to start all over. Marriage, Clenet said was never in the cards for them. During a farewell embrace, Léone fired a shot into the back of his head.

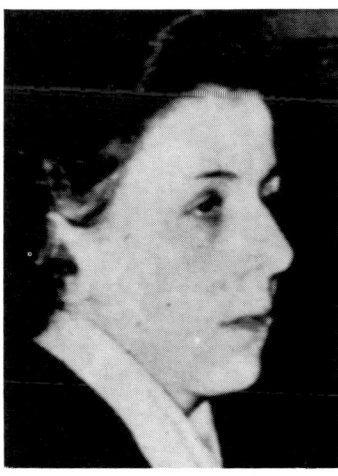

The young woman was charged with murder and placed on trial at the Assizes of Maine-et-Loire, at Angers, on Dec. 10, 1953. Defense lawyer Claude Fournier pointed to the sorrowful homelife endured by his client. Her drunken father was brought forward into the witness box

French murderess Léone Bouvier.

for everyone to see. But Léone's mother stated that her other daughter was a nun. Judge Diousidon rebuked the defendant. "You see! There was no need for you to go wrong!" he cried. "I loved him," she replied meekly. Léone was sentenced to life imprisonment, the maximum penalty under French law.

REF.: CBA; Goodman, *Crime of Passion*; Nash, *Look For the Woman*; Wilson, *Encyclopedia of Murder*.

Bouyer, Lester, prom. 1929, U.S., lynch. Lester Bouyer was arrested for allegedly murdering a white man and raping his female companion, then jailed in the Alabama State Prison near Montgomery for his safety while an angry crowd threatened mob violence. Governor Bibb Graves announced, "There will not be a lynching in Alabama if I can prevent it," and called out 200 National Guardsmen to enforce his decision to protect Bouyer "at any hazard" as the accused man traveled to Eufaula, where the crimes took place, for his trial. Security in the courtroom was so intense that it resembled an armed camp. Bouyer, who was convicted in ten minutes and sentenced to death, pleaded for a quick execution. The condemned man returned to prison on a special, high-security train, and was summarily executed. REF.: CBA.

Bouza, Anthony V., prom. 1980-88, U.S., law enfor. off. Before he became the head of the Minneapolis Police Department, Bouza worked with the New York City police force for several years. Anthony V. Bouza held positions as Deputy Chief of New York City's Transit Police Department, and as Assistant Chief of the New York City Police Department, before moving to Minneapolis to head the police department there. He brought stability to a department that had had several chiefs in a short period of time, and served from 1980-89, retiring in the spring of 1989 to work for a Minneapolis newspaper. REF.: *CBA*.

Bove, James, See: **Fay, Joseph**.

Bowden, John, 1956- , Brit., mur. In 1981 John Bowden, along with Michael Ward, a Camberwell gravedigger, and David Begley, a porter from Walworth, two other alcoholics, murdered Donald Ryan, a former ama-teur boxer. Bowden, who at twenty-four had already spent five years in jail, for crimes that included robbery, black-mail, burglary, assault, and carrying weapons, had taken to preying on derelict South Londoners. When he, Ward, and Begley met Ryan they lured him to a south London apartment, then struck him on the head, leaving him semicon-scious. The sadistic killers then immersed Ryan in a tub of scalding water where he faint-ed. Taking him to another room, they cut off his arms and legs with an electric carving knife, beheaded him with a

John Bowden, murderer.

machine and a saw, disposed of his trunk and limbs in empty lots, and stored his head in the refrigerator for a time, later dumping it in the garbage. Bowden was said to have joked and laughed as he held the head aloft. All three men went out to drink at a local pub before returning to the apartment to sleep near the grisly remains.

Justice Mars-Jones who tried the case at the Old Bailey, said, "Bowden is a man who obviously enjoyed inflicting pain and even killing." Sentenced to life imprisonment, Bowden yelled at the judge, "You old bastard, I hope you die screaming of cancer." Evidence at the trial was so dreadful that court was adjourned when four members of the jury became ill after viewing photo-graphs. Afterward, Bowden's parents said their son had been a "good boy, gentle and kind," until kept in solitary confinement for escaping when jailed on an earlier charge. A year after he began serving his sentence at the Isle of Wight maximum security prison, Bowden and another inmate, James McCaig took the assistant governor of the jail hostage, holding him at knifepoint while they called a Fleet Street newspaper to air their grievances, releasing the official after the British Home Office promised to look into their case.

REF.: *CBA*; Wilson, *Encyclopedia of Modern Murder*.

Bowdre, Charles, See: **Billy the Kid**.

Bowe, Alice Atte, d.1284, Brit., mur. Alice Atte Bowe was the mistress of Ralph Crepin, a London merchant. Their relationship was apparently a happy one. But Crepin's neighbor, Laurence Ducket, a goldsmith, became infatuated with Bowe and aggressive-ly tried to win her away from her lover. Though Bowe had no interest in Ducket, the goldsmith persisted, offering her jewels and anything she coveted if she would be his lover. When Bowe still refused, Ducket, finally realizing that she would never relent, sneaked into the merchant's house one night, fatally stabbing Crepin while he slept at Bowe's side. Bowe, awakened during the incident, recognized Ducket as he fled to Bow Church. Calling out more than twelve men, Bowe went to the church, dragged Ducket from hiding, and hanged him from a church window in such a way as to make it appear that he had committed suicide. The ruse was successful. The coroner's report listed Ducket's cause of death as self-destruction, and the dead killer's body was dragged through the streets and then thrown into a ditch, as was the custom of the time for those who died by their own hand.

Bowe and her gang might have gotten away with murder but for a hidden witness—a small boy who had been sleeping in the church belfry and had observed the hanging—who came forth to testify against the lynching. Bowe and sixteen others were

arrested, then tried at the Newgate Jail. Seven of the prisoners were hanged, drawn and quartered, and Bowe was burned at the stake. The remaining members of the gang were jailed in the Tower of London.

REF.: *CBA*; O'Donnell, *Should Women Hang?*

Bowen, Charles Synge Christopher, 1835-94, Brit., jur. Junior counsel prosecuting Arthur Orton, the celebrated Tichborne Claimant, from 1871-72. He was a judge of the Queen's Bench and knighted in 1879, and lord of appeal in Ordinary in 1893. See: **Orton, Arthur**. REF.: *CBA*.

Bowen, George, prom. 1816, Case of, U.S., mur. In 1815, an inmate at the Hampshire, Mass., prison named George Bowen suggested to his cellmate Jonathan Jewitt that the only sure way of cheating the hangman was to commit suicide. Jewett had been sentenced to death for the murder of his father. The condemned man saw the logic in this reasoning, and took his life on Nov. 9, 1815. Bowen was tried for the murder of Jonathan Jewitt in 1816, but was acquitted and returned to prison to complete his own sentence.

REF.: *CBA*; Nash, *Almanac of World Crime*.

Bowen, Nancy, prom. 1930, U.S., mur. In March 1930, Nancy Bowen walked into the Buffalo, N.Y., home of artist Henri Marchand and confronted his wife, Clothilde Marchand, asking her if she was a witch. When Mrs. Marchand facetiously replied, "Yes," Bowen beat the woman to the ground with a hammer, stuffed chloroform-soaked paper down her throat, and left her dead. Lila Jimerson, a Seneca Indian woman who had posed for Marchand's pictures, commissioned by the Buffalo Natural History Museum, was charged with instigating the killing. Also known as "Red Lilac," Jimerson had fallen in love with Mr. Marchand after he seduced her, and believed that eliminating his wife would free her lover to marry her. Jimerson had told Bowen on the reserva-tion where they both lived that Mrs. Marchand was a witch who had caused the recent death of Bowen's husband, Charley Bowen. Initially tried for first-degree murder, the consumptive Jimerson collapsed in the Buffalo courtroom. Judge F. Bret Thorn dis-missed the jury and declared a mistrial. The prosecution's main witness at the first trial was Henri Marchand, who admitted his intimacy with Jimerson but insisted it had been a matter of "professional necessity" done to get her to pose as his model.

From her Buffalo City Hospital bed Jimerson pleaded guilty to reduced charges of murder in the second degree, answering all the questions posed to her by Judge Thorn by nodding her head. Not once did she speak. She was expected to be formally sen-tenced when released from the hospital but instead she hired new attorneys who refused to withdraw her initial plea of guilt to second degree murder, arguing that the improvised sickbed courtroom had been illegal and that their client was still on trial for first-degree murder. At Jimerson's retrial, late in 1930, she contended that the artist had plotted the murder of his wife and used her to carry it out. She was acquitted by a supreme court jury on Feb. 28, 1931. On Mar. 13, 1931, Nancy Bowen, who had pleaded guilty to reduced charges of first-degree manslaughter, was sentenced by Judge Thorn to a one- to ten-year prison term. But because she had already been detained in jail for longer than the amount of her minimum sentence, she was immediately freed. REF.: *CBA*.

Bower, Elliot, prom. 1852, Fr., mur. Elliot Bower was the French correspondent for the *Morning Advertiser*, a well-known London journal in the tumultuous days following the French Revolution of 1848. Although he had several romantic affairs outside of his marriage, he grew jealous of his wife's friendship with an old Cambridge friend, a fellow journalist, Saville Morton. Morton, stationed in Paris as well, was visiting Fanny Bower, when she received a letter from Isabella Laurie, one of her husband's jilted lovers who hoped to take revenge by detailing the affair to his wife. Mrs. Bower, upset to learn of her husband's infidelity, turned to Morton for comfort and they fell in love, with Morton going so far as to inquire into possible ways that Fanny might obtain a divorce.

Then, on Sept. 2, 1852, Fanny Bower gave birth to her fourth child. Shortly after she fell victim to temporary insanity, caused by childbed fever. She was so ill that Bower, though suspicious and jealous of Morton, called him in to sit with his wife and Morton spent several days sleeping on a settee in Mrs. Bower's room, attempting to comfort her. Finally, in a lucid moment, Fanny told her husband the child was Morton's. When he refused to believe her, she called the housekeeper to confirm that Morton had spent a night with her when her husband was away—exactly nine months earlier.

Bower rushed downstairs to find Morton sitting at a table and, grabbing a knife, tried to stab him. Bower's mother, who was present, seized her son by the coat while Morton ran for the door. Bower broke free, ran after Morton, and fatally stabbed him in the neck, afterwards fleeing to London. Perhaps remorseful, he soon returned to France, surrendered, and was tried at the Seine Court of Assize on Dec. 28, 1852. Meanwhile, his wife recovered her sanity. The prosecution maintained that Bower's murder of Morton would not have occurred but for the statement of an insane woman that her child was Morton's. Attorney Chaix D'Estange, in charge of Bower's defense, contended that there was no doubt of Mrs. Bower's infidelity and that Bower's slaying of his rival was justified. Bower was acquitted. It is not known whether he and his wife reconciled, but what is certain is that they were ostracized by the Victorian society they lived in, socially ruined by the dramatic scandal.

REF.: *CBA*; Lambert, *When Justice Faltered*; Wilson, *Encyclopedia of Murder*.

Bowers, Dr. J. Milton, 1843-1904, U.S., mur. Dr. J. Milton Bowers was born in Baltimore, but with an inheritance of $20,000, he traveled to Germany to study medicine. Returning to the U.S. shortly before the Civil War, Bowers secured a staff position at the Patterson Hospital in Washington. He was permitted to care for patients despite the lack of a medical degree. Bowers remedied this situation in 1873 when he was handed a diploma from the Bennett Eclectic Medical College in Chicago. It was there that he met the first of three wives, the winsome Fannie Hammond. Their nine-year marriage ended with her death in 1874. After her Chicago home was consumed in a mysterious fire, Dr. Bowers moved to New York to open a practice. He married 17-year-old actress Teresa Sherek, whom he had met while living in Chicago.

After their marriage, Bowers changed his original plan and headed west to San Francisco. There, Teresa attained a degree of literary notoriety with the publication of her book *The Dance of Life,* an "answer" to an earlier volume published by Ambrose Bierce, titled *The Dance of Death.* Teresa Bowers' book was an ironic soliloquy to her own untimely death on Jan. 28, 1881. Six months later, Dr. Bowers found himself a third bride, 29-year-old Cecilia Benhayon-Levy, a former patient.

In Summer 1885, after four years of marriage, Cecilia became sick and died. An anonymous letter sent to the coroner two days after her burial stated that her death did not result from natural causes. The letter writer may have been Cecilia's suspicious brother Henry Benhayon. An autopsy conducted on Nov. 9 showed that Mrs. Bowers had been poisoned with phosphorous. The doctor was charged with murder, and placed on trial Mar. 11, 1886. He was found Guilty and was sentenced to death.

On Oct. 23, 1887, Henry Benyahon was found dead in a Geary Street rooming house. A bottle of potassium and a suicide note was left behind. Benhayon stated that it was he, and not Dr. Bowers, who poisoned Cecilia. Detectives soon learned that John Dimming, the husband of Bowers housekeeper, had rented the room. A check of local drug stores revealed that Dimming had purchased the bottle of potassium cyanide used to kill Benyahon. The shadowy Dimming, a purveyor of "art books" was tried for murder in December 1887. Prosecution attorneys contended that Bowers had succeeded in blackmailing Dimming into forging a suicide letter before doing away with Benhayon. The trial ended in a hung jury. Dimming was returned to jail, and Bowers was

denied a new trial.

Dimming's second trial began on Dec. 10, 1888, and continued until the following January. The jurors had trouble reaching a verdict, but this time the judge refused to release them until they decided on the fate of the accused. They acquitted Dimming, which meant that Bowers was technically free since the Not Guilty verdict implied the suicide note was genuine. Bowers was granted an unconditional release on Aug. 16, 1889. He set up a new practice in San Francisco, found himself a fourth wife, and died peacefully on Mar. 7, 1904.

REF.: *CBA*; Duke, *Celebrated Criminal Cases of America*; Dunbar, *Blood In the Parlor*; Furneaux, *The Medical Murderer*; Nash, *Open Files*; Rodell, *San Francisco Murders*; Smith, *Famous American Poison Mysteries*; Wilson, *Encyclopedia of Murder*.

Bowers, Martha, prom. 1903, U.S., mur. Born Martha Byers, the daughter of a respectable mother in Portland, Ore., the fickle Martha had been married and divorced twice when she met and married a bridge builder, Martin L. Bowers, in San Francisco in 1902. On June 5, 1903, Mrs. Bowers called a Dr. Carl Von Tiedemann to prescribe for her husband who was, she explained, ill as a result of ptomaine poisoning caused by eating ham. The doctor treated Mr. Bowers, later dropping treatment after a financial misunderstanding with Mrs. Bowers. A second physician, Dr. J.F. Dillon, prescribed for the patient and then stopped visiting him when improvement was shown after a short time. When Martin Bowers suffered a relapse, his wife called in Dr. A. McLaughlin who concurred with the diagnosis of the previous doctors but insisted that the patient be taken to the Waldeck Sanitarium for observation. Though puzzled by some of the sick man's symptoms, McLaughlin was not suspicious. After a month's stay the convalescent was returned, at his spouse's entreaty, to his home, with a doctor's instructions for the wife to give her husband a daily massage. One week later, McLaughlin made a house call and discovered that his instructions had not been followed and that the patient's condition had deteriorated. He ordered that the sick man be taken to the German Hospital, where Bowers died on Aug. 25, 1903. The widow, present at the death, flung herself on the corpse and wept copiously.

Harry Bowers, the deceased's brother, was suspicious of his sister-in-law and demanded an investigation. Four grains of undissolved arsenic were found in the dead man's stomach, and two investigating chemists determined that it was impossible for Bowers to have died from ptomaine poisoning through eating ham, since the salt and creosote found in that meat would most likely have destroyed the arsenic. The report was highly publicized and brought forth a druggist, J.C. Peterson, who recalled a woman coming to him on Aug. 20 with a prescription, written on a blank sheet of paper and signed by a Dr. McLaughlin, that called for an unspecified amount of arsenic. The description of the woman fit that of Martha Bowers' sister, Zylpha Sutton, who was positively identified by Peterson.

Found in the Bowers' home was a composition school book with a page torn out that matched that on which the fraudulent prescription was written. A handwriting expert testified that songs in the book matched the handwriting on the prescription, and that both were the work of Martha Bowers. It was also proved that the grieving widow had been in the company of her lover, Patrick Leary, within two hours of her husband's death.

The prosecution contended that Bowers murdered her husband so that she would be free of his strong objections to her involvement with Leary. Mrs. Sutton was released for lack of evidence, but Bowers was charged with murder, tried on Jan. 14, 1904, and found guilty on Jan. 20. Appropriately, the woman undone by romance was sentenced to life imprisonment on Valentine Day 1904.

REF.: *CBA*; Duke, *Celebrated Criminal Cases of America*.

Bowers, Sam H., Jr., prom. 1964-68, U.S., mur. On June 21, 1964, members of the Ku Klux Klan murdered three civil rights activists on a deserted road in Neshoba County, Miss. The slain activists, Andrew Goodman, twenty, James Chaney, twenty-one, and Michael Schwerner, twenty-four, became a media sensation, and the ensuing trial evolved into the decade's most closely followed criminal proceedings. Schwerner, a veteran field worker for the Congress of Recial Equality, had moved to the town of Meridian, Miss., six months earlier to organize voter registration within the black community. The local white racist population hated Schwerner, not only because he was Jewish, but because he represented the civil rights movement. Goodman, also Jewish, was a college student who arrived in Philadelphia, Miss., June 20. Chaney worked with Schwerner as a co-organizer in voter registration drives and was the group's link to the black community. The three were driving back to Meridian after visiting a burned-out black church near Philadelphia, Miss., when Neshoba County deputy sheriff Cecil R. Price, a secret Klan member, arrested them on trumped-up charges of speeding. He released the three around 10 p.m. that evening. Price stopped them again, after a high-speed chase through the backroads of Neshoba County, and turned them over to a lynch mob formed by the Ku Klux Klan and led by the 43-year-old Klan Imperial Wizard, Sam H. Bowers, Jr. The lynch mob shot each of the victims individually and buried them in open graves, then created an earthen dam over them the following week. Just before he was killed, Schwerner reportedly turned to his executioner and said: "Sir, I know just how you feel."

The summer of 1964 was a time of optimism and hope for the civil rights movement. It was the year of the historic "Freedom Summer," during which more than 1,000 college students came to Mississippi to aid a grass-roots movement to register black voters. They hoped their work would focus national attention on the evils of segregation. At that time, only five percent of the 500,000 blacks eligible to vote in Mississippi were registered. Mississippi was an effectively segregated state. The Ku Klux Klan, with its law enforcement connections, intimidated the black community. Fear of Klan terrorism, bombings of homes and churches, and cross-burnings kept blacks from seeking basic voting rights. Occasionally, blacks who attempted to register simply disappeared.

The FBI involved itself in the case when state authorities grew lethargic. The FBI code named the investigation "Miburn" becuase the case began with the burning of the black church. For five months, 150 agents worked on the case, piecing together evidence of the plans that culminated with the lynch mob on June 21. Spurred by the grieving families and enraged civil rights workers from around the country, the investigations became one of the most extensive in FBI history. Forty-four days after the execution, and after days of wading through swampy land, volunteers unearthed the badly decomposed bodies of the civil rights workers. With the help of an informant and one confession, the FBI learned that the Ku Klux Klan ordered and executed the lynching. Twenty-one men were initially charged with murder and conspiracy to murder, but their prosecution was thwarted when the state court refused to allow the Justice Department to introduce the testimony of Horace D. Barnette, one of the accused who confessed to his part in the crime. The case was dismissed, and the department was forced to seek a grand jury indictment. Aided by the testimony of Barnette, the FBI's star witness James E. Jordan, and Philadelphia resident Florence Mars, the grand jury indicted eighteen men on an old federal law prohibiting conspiracy against the rights of another citizen. Each of those convicted faced a ten-year maximum sentence and $5,000 in fines.

The trial, which lasted two weeks and received national coverage, was presided over by U.S. District Court Judge W. Harold Cox. Cox was decidedly unsympathetic to civil rights, and once publicly referred to several blacks registering to vote as "a bunch of chimpanzees." The all-white jury initially deadlocked when they could not convict all the defendants. Yet when Judge Cox further instructed them that they could find individual defendants guilty, they returned a verdict the following day, Oct. 20. Seven men were found Guilty of conspiracy to murder: Sam H. Bowers, Jr., Cecil R. Price, Horace Barnette, Jimmy Arledge, a 30-year-old truck driver, Billy Wayne Posey, a 30-year-old gas station operator, Jimmie Snowden, a 34-year-old laundry truck

driver, and Alton W. Roberts, a 29-year-old salesman. The jury, however, acquitted eight men, including the Neshoba County sheriff Lawrence Rainey, and came to no judgement on three of the defendants.

When the verdict was read, Judge Cox said, "I very heartily enter into this jury's verdict." The judge then denounced Roberts and Price and ordered their immediate incarceration because of the threats they made before the jury returned its verdict. On Dec. 29, the judge sentenced Bowers and Roberts to ten years' imprisonment, Price and Posey to six years, and Barnette, Arledge, and Snowden to three years' imprisonment. None of those convicted were fined. Jordan, the federal witness, received a four-year prison sentence on Jan. 13, after a separate trial.

The lynching and the trial had an enormous impact on Mississippi and on the civil rights movement. Blacks increasingly dominated the movement and abandoned nonviolence for militant action. Yet the voter registration campaigns that summer brought into the political process tens of thousands of blacks who had never attempted to register. And the town of Philadelphia, Miss., changed. The public schools eventually desegregated, and an effort was made to broaden job opportunities for blacks. Despite the tragedy, many civil rights workers echoed the sentiment of Freedom Summer volunteer Haywood Burns, who claimed, "...it was one of our finest hours."

REF.: *CBA;* (FILM) *Mississippi Burning,* 1988.

Bow Kum, d.1909, U.S., (unsolv.) mur. An uneasy peace came to New York's Chinatown in 1906 after years of street warfare between rival gangs fighting for control of the Mott Street opium trade. But when Bow Kum arrived in New York tensions flared again.

Bow Kum was born in Canton. When she was five years old a Chinese slave trader bought her for $300. When she was fifteen, her guardian sold her to a wealthy older man in San Francisco for $3,000. His name was Low Hee Tong, and Bow Kum became his servant for the next four years. But the police took her away during a general crackdown on white slavery. Mr. Tong angrily demanded a return on his $3,000 investment.

Bow Kum lived at an American mission until a wealthy young truck farmer named Tchin Len proposed marriage. When news of their wedding reached San Francisco's Chinatown, Low Hee Tong was very angry. Len traveled to New York with his bride, but he was not safe from Low Hee Tong, whose family was part of a Mott Street gang known as the Four Brothers. Tchin Len was a member of the rival On Leongs, and as the dispute escalated, the two factions decided to arbitrate the matter. It was decided that Bow Kum was Len's exclusive property, and therefore it was not necessary to compensate Low. A few nights later, on Aug. 15, 1909, Bow Kum was found dead, her throat cut.

The murder was listed as unsolved by the New York police. The Four Brothers, allied with the Hip Sings, went to war with the On Leongs in a gang war that claimed fifty lives, one of the most fearful in the history of New York's Chinatown. REF.: *CBA.*

Bowler, Tom, prom. 1812, Brit., attempt. mur. On July 2, 1812, Tom Bowler was tried for shooting and wounding William Burrowes. The defense pleaded insanity, with the prisoner's housekeeper testifying that Bowler had been brought home on July 9, 1812, in a near-lifeless state, apparently suffering an epileptic seizure. Since then, she said, her employer's appearance and conduct had deteriorated. He began to eat meat raw and frequently would lie on the grass in the rain, suffering fits of depression so acute that he was kept under watch to prevent his harming himself. The keeper of an insane asylum testified that it was a characteristic of madness resulting from epilepsy that the patient would develop violent hatreds toward people who had done him no harm, including friends and people he did not know, and that the afflicted would make up reasons for attacking them. The head of the institution for the insane said he believed Bower to be mad, a theory further supported by the June 17, 1812, findings in a report of a commission that studied lunacy. Bowler was declared insane. Nevertheless, Justice Le Blanc explained to the jury that it must decide whether the accused was incapable of telling right from wrong when he launched his attack, or whether he was under the influence of delusions regarding Burrowes. In either case, the prisoner would not be responsible under the law. If, on the other hand, Bowler could distinguish right from wrong and suffered no delusions, he would be held responsible. After long deliberation the jury brought in a verdict of Guilty.

REF.: *CBA; Keeton, Guilty, But Insane.*

Bowles, Frank, prom. 1902, U.S., mur. Frank Bowles, a Kentucky youth, had been spending time with one of the girls in the Christie family against the will of her father, Isham Christie. These two families in the Honey Creek area of Kentucky had been at odds for some time, and tensions increased when Christie found two of his steers dead in the pasture and ordered young Bowles not to carry a gun on his land. According Christie's daughter, several hogs belonging to the nearby Boyer family were discovered missing about a week after the Christie family's dead steers were found. Rumor had it that the notorious Bowles family had once again stolen hogs from their neighbors, had salted them, and hidden the meat away in a cave. The girl's uncle, Carl Boyer, went to Magistrate Tom Washam and obtained a warrant to search the Bowles farm. Two of the Christie boys were deputized to go with him. Nearing the house, they saw Frank Bowles sitting on the side of the road, a shotgun in his lap. Islam Christie and Bowles began to argue and when Christie called Bowles "a damned sheep-eyed devil," Bowles shot and killed his visitor, then ran away. He was arrested a few days later, taken to Shelltown to appear before Magistrate Dale Rigney, and released, supposedly bartering for his freedom at the cost of ten dollars and a gallon of whiskey. Learning of the payoff, the dead man's youngest son went to the grand jury and obtained an indictment against the accused, who fled to Alabama to hide out at his parents' home. Sheriff George Crutchfield and his sons went to Alabama to arrest Bowles, bringing him back to Kentucky to stand trial, where he was convicted and sentenced to a ten-year term in the state penitentiary.

REF.: *CBA; Montell, Killings.*

Bowles, Homer, prom. 1913, U.S., mur. On May 13, 1913, Cindy Curtis, a landowning black woman who had recently lost her husband, went to Ben Emory's store to collect some money for laundering work she had done for Emory's wife. After collecting, she sat on the porch of the store to rest. Also on the porch were Homer Bowles, Bess Talbot, and Lura Lee Talbot, Homer's girlfriend. According to Emory's nephew, who witnessed the slaying, "All of them was barefooted...and Bowles kept pointing his gun at the girl's feet. This old colored woman was there, and he turned the gun on her and let it go off. On purpose." Curtis' head was blown off by the force of the blast. Though Bowles maintained that the killing was an accident, it was generally believed that he had been hired to murder the woman by her nephew, who lived with Curtis and would inherit the property at her death. Bowles was convicted and sentenced to serve time in the state penitentiary at Nashville, Tenn.

REF.: *CBA; Montell, Killings.*

Bowlsby, Alice Augusta, prom. 19th Cent., U.S., (unsolv.) mur. A woman with a large trunk got out of a cab at the Hudson River Railway Station in New York City, and asked to have her trunk sent ahead to Chicago. Told there would be no train to Chicago that night, the woman immediately fled, leaving the trunk behind. Inside was the body of Alice Augusta Bowlsby, a young woman. A doctor was implicated in the case, connected to the victim through pieces of her clothing marked with her initials which were found at his house, but it was never proved that he killed her, and the case remains unsolved.

REF.: *CBA; Pearce, Unsolved Murder Mysteries.*

Bowsher, Perry, d.1878, U.S., mur. Twice confined in an insane asylum, Perry Bowsher, on the night of Oct. 26, 1877, crept up on a small tollhouse on the Columbus Pike, five miles outside of Chillicothe, operated by Edwin S. and Ann McVay. Bowsher

killed the couple, bludgeoning them to death and stealing the toll money. He was found with the money a short time later, convicted of murdering the elderly couple, and hanged.

REF.: *CBA; Life and Trial of Perry Bowsher.*

The Bow Street police office, 1800.

Bow Street Runners, 1739-1829, Brit., law enfor. agency. In 1739, Colonel Sir Thomas De Veil established Bow Street in London as the principal "headquarters" of the city's policing agency. Their meeting place was the private residence of Sir Thomas, the ambitious police magistrate, who served as detective on a force of one. In 1749, novelist Sir Henry Fielding organized an elite corps of six parish constables who performed detective duty in civilian clothing. Fielding installed his men at the same Bow Street address. In the early years, the "runners," as they were known, functioned as ordinary thief-takers. They earned only the reward money that accompanied a successful arrest. It was not until the runners had proved their worth by taking into custody vicious street gangs, that the government agreed to pay them a guinea a week—money drawn from the Secret Service Fund. There were always two runners assigned to the Bow Street address, one for the day and a second working at night. Later, a uniformed Bow Street patrol was organized to supplement the rather thinly stretched runners, but they did not engage in detective work. The patrol was readily identifiable to London citizens by their red waistcoats.

In 1786, following an unsuccessful attempt on the life of King George III, two Bow Street Runners named Townsend and Thayer were assigned to protect His Majesty. They performed these duties with alacrity for many years, earning wealth and a measure of fame. The success of Fielding's enterprise convinced the government to expand. In 1792, seven new offices were opened in London, each location staffed by six plainclothes detectives, but no patrols. The runners scored a major victory in 1820 when

George Ruthven and several of his associates captured the Cato Street Conspirators and their leader, Arthur Thistlewood, who were plotting the assassination of Lord Castlereagh and other government ministers.

Like any other policing agency, the Bow Street Runners had its share of men who were less than circumspect in their dealings. In 1816, one was arrested and found Guilty of conspiracy. The runner had induced five other persons to break into a London home, and then after catching the thieves red-handed, claimed the usual Parliamentary Reward that accompanied the apprehension of thieves.

In 1829, the Bow Street Patrols were disbanded when Sir Robert Peel organized the London Metropolitan Police Force. The runners continued to serve as the city's primary detective agency until 1839 when they too, were discontinued. There was no London detective force until 1842, when two ghastly murders aroused public feeling of the urgent situation. The first detective branch at Scotland Yard was organized that year to lend professionalism to sensitive criminal investigation. Many Londoners preferred to privately employ former Bow Street Runners to help them recover stolen property in lieu of calling on the police. See: **Peel, Robert; Scotland Yard.**

REF.: *CBA;* Potter, *The Art of Hanging;* Reppetto, *The Blue Parade;* Scott, *Concise Encyclopedia of Crime and Criminals.*

British marines manning guns on a Peking wall, 1900.

Boxers, The (I Ho Chuan), prom. 1900, China, secret crim. soc. Western powers, which for many years had carved the interior of China for their own economic advancement, were forced to confront the wrath of secret societies in June 1900. The fifty-five day Boxer Rebellion forced more than 3,000 western diplomats, missionaries, and businessmen to seek refuge in their embassies. Terrorist activities against foreigners were sparked by the Boxers, popularly known in the provinces as the *I Ho Chuan,* or "The Fists of Righteous Harmony." The Boxers found popular support among the peasants following their attack on missionary outposts in Shantung.

They found a willing ally in the dowager empress, who believed that the supernatural forces would help them drive the corrupting influences of westerners out of Imperial China. The Manchu government and Ch'ing Dynasty supplied the Boxers with military officers to direct their clandestine attacks. These moves earned the Manchus widespread support, especially in the north country. The power of magic and the reliance on supernatural faith did little good, however. Peking was placed under siege and was forced to surrender to the combined forces of Great Britain, the U.S., France, and Russia in August 1900. By year's end, China's destiny was again controlled by the West.

REF.: *CBA;* MacKenzie, *Secret Societies.*

Boyce, Arthur Robert (AKA: The Trousseau Murderer), d.1946, Brit., big.-mur. In Summer 1946, an English woman, Elizabeth McLindon, was hired by King George II of Greece to refurbish his wartime home in Chester Square, Belgravia, London. She accepted, and moved in with her fiancé, one Arthur Robert Boyce, a painter and decorator from Brighton. McLindon did not know that her man was already married and had, in fact, served a prison sentence on a bigamy charge.

The king dropped by to inspect his summer house on June 9, but was perturbed by his housekeeper's absence. Three days later, Papanikolaou, the king's private secretary paid a second visit, and still there was no sign of the 41-year-old McLindon. Police were called to investigate on June 14 and found the body of the housekeeper in a locked room. She had been shot once through the back of the head. A letter signed, "Your loving and true hubby, Arthur" was found next to the body.

A search of Arthur Boyce's lodgings in Brighton turned up a luggage label bearing the name of John Rowland, the owner of the .32-caliber Browning automatic pistol used to kill McLindon. Rowland told police that the gun had been taken from him, and he strongly suspected Boyce. A ballistics test conducted by Robert Churchill showed that the bullets extracted from the body were fired from the same gun. Boyce was put on trial in September 1946. No motive was clearly established; however, it was known that McLindon was increasingly suspicious of Boyce's background, and fearing possible scandal, he decided to murder the woman. Boyce claimed the gun was given to McLindon for her own protection, but the jury, discounting his claim, returned a Guilty verdict. Boyce was sentenced to die by Justice Morris. His execution was carried out on Nov. 1, 1946.

REF.: Brock, *A Casebook of Crime; CBA;* Cutherbert, *Science and the Detection of Crime;* Hastings, *The Other Mr. Churchill;* Shew, *A Companion to Murder.*

Boyce, Henry, 1797-1873, U.S., jur. District attorney at Washington, D.C., in 1849. He was appointed judge of the Western District Court of Louisiana in 1849 by President Zachary Taylor. REF.: *CBA.*

Boyd, Jabez, d.1845, U.S., mur. Boyd presented the image of a devout churchgoer and upstanding citizen by day. At night he practiced highway robbery. His was a sinister double life very much like that embraced by the notorious Scottish burglar and murderer, William Brodie. One night he robbed Wesley Patton in Westchester, Pa. When the victim resisted, Boyd clubbed him to death. He was seen as he left the scene of the crime and was later identified and arrested in church "with a hymn book in his hand from which he was singing with apparent composure," according to one report. He was quickly convicted, condemned, and hanged in 1845.

REF.: *An Account of the Arrest, Trial, Conviction and Confession of Jabez Boyd; CBA;* Nash, *Bloodletters and Badmen.*

Boyd, James Edmund, 1845-1935, U.S., jur. Confederate army soldier from 1864-65. He served as U.S. attorney for North Carolina from 1880-85 and was appointed judge of the Western District Court of North Carolina by President William McKinley in 1901. REF.: *CBA.*

Boyd, Jorge Eduardo, b.1886, Pan., lawyer. Foreign diplomat and served as attorney general from 1924-26. REF.: *CBA.*

Boyd, Marion Speed, 1900-   , U.S., jur. District attorney general assigned to Memphis, Tenn., from 1938-40 and appointed to the court of the Western District of Tennessee by President Franklin D. Roosevelt in 1940. REF.: *CBA.*

Boyd, Murray Allen, 1940-70, U.S., org. crime. Murray Allen Boyd had moved to Vancouver, reputedly to serve as one of the leaders in a gangland style "civil war" shaping up between the Vancouver and Montreal crime families. Detectives who had been tipped off about Boyd by Jacob Leonhard, jailed survivor of a 1955 car bombing, found Boyd on record for convictions ranging from assault with a deadly weapon to armed robbery. He had disappeared following the murder of a gangster in Vancouver in 1967, and was a suspect in several other killings as well, including that of Judy Scott, a singer and a drug addict found in July 1968 in the Fraser River with an eighty-pound rock wired to her neck. Then, in January 1969, Lucien Joseph Mayer, an ex-convict suspected of being deeply entrenched in the Montreal heroin business, was found murdered in Vancouver, his throat slit and his head smashed in with a tire iron. As the competition between the Montreal and Vancouver drug rings escalated, police expected Boyd to resurface as one of the main enforcers. Rigby Kier, a special investigator, helped assemble an investigation team that included the Royal Canadian Mounted and Vancouver police. In late 1969, they captured Boyd, who refused to talk. With thirty-five convictions, he escaped from prison on Jan. 21, 1970, on a rope made of torn canvas strips and grappling irons, taking with him another inmate. Boyd collected his teenage girlfriend soon after and disappeared.

A month after Boyd's escape, the gangland killings escalated again. A mob informer was found dead in his car, murdered by a shotgun blast that tore his head off. Shortly after, a Mr. Weber and his wife, Lieselotte Weber, were shot to death in their Vancouver kitchen. The basement of the Weber's house was set up as an exotic sex game room, and police initially suspected that the couple had been engaged in elaborate blackmail schemes. But when they cracked the code in a notebook they came across in the sex den and found a master copy of drug deal transactions, they realized that the setup was an elaborate scam—the couple were part of the narcotics ring they were after.

On Apr. 21 police received a tip that a large consignment of heroin was going to be delivered to a supermarket, and Boyd would be involved. Setting up a squad of police and detectives, officers blocked off streets around the store. Boyd arrived in a truck with his young girlfriend, who went shopping alone, then walked back to the truck, slowly loading her bags into the car as Boyd read a newspaper and the police waited. At a signal from the leader, one unmarked police car pulled in front of the truck while a second came in beside it. Boyd's girlfriend screamed and ducked under the truck. Trapped, Boyd grabbed a thirty-two automatic from his waistband and the police killed him. The girlfriend, unharmed, said afterwards, "It was just like Bonnie and Clyde," remarking that Boyd had been reading his horoscope just before the shooting began. Dead at thirty, Boyd had always carried a gun, and boasted that he would never be taken alive.

REF.: *CBA; Gribble, The Dead End Killers.*

Boyd, Payne, prom. 1925, U.S., (wrong. convict.) mur. In May 1918 in Modoc, Mercer County, W. Va., Cleveland Boyd, a miner with a reputation for aggressive behavior, was called before Squire H.E. Cook on vagrancy charges. Boyd had stood before Cook five months earlier on charges of drunk and conduct, and had vowed revenge on Cook at the sentencing. In the May hearing, Cook sentenced Boyd again, this time to thirty days' imprisonment, or road work, and a $25 fine. As deputy sheriff A.M. Godfrey and Cook were taking Boyd to the Matoaka jail, the criminal asked permission to go to his home nearby to change shoes. Cook and Godfrey waited outside Boyd's shack. Seconds later, Boyd reappeared, firing a revolver and killing Cook with two shots. Godfrey ran for his life, and Boyd took off for the hills. Because of Cook's status as a leader in the town, the murder aroused great indignation and a description of the killer was released to the police. Six years later, in 1924, police in Richmond, Va., arrested a man named Payne Boyd of Winston-Salem, N.C., for a minor infraction. In a routine check of police records it was discovered that the man matched Cleveland Boyd's description. A photograph of Boyd was mailed to Mercer County authorities, who came to Richmond to positively identify him in a jail line-up as the man who murdered Cook. Though the prisoner continued to deny that he was Cleveland Boyd, and insisted he had never been in Mercer County, he was indicted for the six-year-old murder.

Given a three-day trial on Feb. 5-8, 1925, before Judge George L. Dillard, Boyd was found guilty of first-degree murder, but the verdict was set aside on technical grounds and a second trial took place in late April, when the accused again was found guilty and sentenced to life imprisonment by Dillard. In both trials, the only issue was whether the defendant was Cleveland Boyd. Thirty-one witnesses for the defense, including Cleveland Boyd's father-in-law, the judge who married him, neighbors, coworkers, and guests at his wedding, testified with total conviction that the prisoner was not the accused murderer. But another twenty-four witnesses for the prosecution were positive in their identifications that Payne was Cleveland Boyd, noting a scar over his left eye and one under his left jaw which matched markings on the accused. An appellate court set aside Dillard's second verdict, and ordered a third trial held in Cabell County in October 1925, in Huntington, before Judge Thomas R. Shepherd. A fingerprint expert, Garfield Rose, of the Huntington Police Department, took the prisoner's fingerprints and found they matched those of Payne Boyd, on record with the War Department in Washington—Payne had served in the U.S. Army in 1917-19. On Oct. 13, 1925, the jury found Payne Boyd Not Guilty. Boyd was released from jail, having served a year and a half in custody because of his resemblance to Cleveland Boyd.

REF.: Borchard, *Convicting the Innocent; CBA.*

Boyd, William C., 1967-   , Case of, U.S., mur. On July 17, 1981, a group of teenagers held a party in the backyard of the Boyd family in Wheeling, Ill. Included in the group were 14-year-old Mary K. Kosinski, 13-year-old Barbara Boyd, 14-year-old William C. Boyd, and three other neighborhood youths. At around 2 a.m., William Boyd, father of the family, told the teenagers to be quiet or go home. The Boyd children later went inside, and three of the other teen-agers returned to their own homes. At 10 a.m. on Saturday, Barbara Boyd began to clean up the party debris from the yard. Entering the shed where the group had played, she discovered the partly-clothed, battered body of Kosinski, beaten, raped, and strangled. Police took William C. Boyd in for questioning. After several hours of interrogation he was taken to Dr. Clarence P. Trausch, a psychotherapist who put the boy under hypnosis, during which Boyd confessed to the murder. In his confession, Boyd admitted that he had placed a pillow over Kosinski's face when she rejected his attempts to fondle and kiss her during a strip-poker game in the Boyd family playhouse. During the trial Elizabeth A. Brown, defense attorney, called Dr. Edward Pavlik, an orthodontist and chief of forensic pathology for the Cook County Sheriff's department, who testified that bite marks on the girl's body had been made by Boyd. Murder charges were dropped in 1983 when Cook County Circuit Judge Nicholas Pomaro ruled that the confession had been obtained improperly, violating Boyd's Fifth Amendment right against self-incrimination.

According to Boyd's lawyer, Anthony Pinelli, his client "was arrested without probable cause and coerced to confess." The four officers involved in the questioning, John Stone, William Hoos, Edward Theriault, and Ronald Nelson, maintained they had conducted their investigation properly. "I don't think anyone can change our mind about who killed the girl," Theriault said. On Feb. 18, 1988, Boyd and his mother lost a case seeking $2.6 million in damages from the four Wheeling policemen and Dr. Trausch, alleging that Boyd's civil rights had been violated during the police investigation. Lawyers for the officers and witnesses who testified for the defense were unanimous in maintaining that Boyd was responsible for the killing. As of 1988, Boyd was a student at a Bible institute, with aspirations of becoming a missionary in Third World countries. REF.: *CBA.*

Boyer, Ernie, prom. 1932, Case of, U.S., mur. Ernie Boyer and

Bert Goins had both grown up in the Kentucky Rocky Valley area. For unknown reasons, Boyer had never liked Goins, and his animosity increased when Goins married his sister. Goins, quarrelsome and frequently drunk, was believed to have provoked Boyer on several occasions, including shooting at him as he drove in his Chevrolet roadster. It was also said that there was a long-standing boundary dispute between the two families. On June 30, 1932, Boyer, who was drunk, went to the Rocky Valley Methodist Church while it was in session and shot Goins six times with a .38 Special. As Boyer walked away to reload, Goins opened up his shirt to look at his wounds, staggered home, and stayed in bed for a week before he was transferred to a hospital, where he died a few days later. A local resident commented that even though Goins was unarmed at the time, "Somebody had to kill him. It didn't make much difference who done it, somebody had to kill him. He would get drunk and turn on his friends even." Indicted for the murder, Boyer was awarded a verdict of Not Guilty, primarily because several witnesses would not testify against him. Boyer later became a wealthy landowner.

REF.: *CBA; Montell, Killings.*

Boyer, Marie, See: **Vitalis, Leon.**

Boyington, Charles R.S., d.1834, U.S., mur. Nathaniel Frost, a businessman in Mobile, Ala., was out walking on the night of May 10, 1834, when he was attacked and killed, his purse stolen. Boyington was seen strolling with the victim a short time before the robbery-murder and he was arrested. He was convicted on slim circumstantial evidence and condemned. Before his execution by hanging, the well-educated Boyington wrote a number of verses which were sold widely to pay for the upkeep of his family. The condemned man insisted upon his innocence to the last.

REF.: *The Last Hours of Charles R.S. Boyington; A Statement of the Trial of Charles R. S. Boyington.*

Boyle, Charles Edmund, 1836-88, U.S., jur. District attorney of Uniontown, Pa., from 1862-65. He received his first judicial appointment in 1888 and was assigned to the Washington State Territorial Court by President Grover Cleveland. REF.: *CBA.*

Boyle, James H., See: **Bogle, James H.**

Boyle, Patricia Jean Ehrhardt Pernick, 1937- , U.S., jur. Assistant U.S. attorney, U.S. Department of Justice, Detroit, Mich., from 1965-70. She was appointed assistant prosecuting attorney from 1976-78 and appointed to the federal bench of the Eastern District of Michigan by President Jimmy Carter in 1978. She was cited for outstanding achievements in 1978 by the Prosecuting Attorneys Association and published "Criminal Sexual Conduct" which appeared in the *Detroit Bar Journal* (1977). REF.: *CBA.*

Boyle, Richard (First Earl of Cork), 1566-1643, Case of, Brit., embez. Founder of the House of Cork and Orrery. He was acquitted of embezzlement in 1588. He served as Irish lord justice in 1629, and while serving as lord high treasurer in 1631 he helped impeach Thomas Wentworth, Earl of Strafford, a political arch-rival. REF.: *CBA.*

Boyle, Victor James (Johnny), prom. 1950, Case of, Brit., mur. On Aug. 8, 1950, 15-year-old Patricia Beard was sent by her mother to pick up some fish. She left home eagerly, and was seen by several people on the street as she passed the fish store in the Brixton section of London, returning by the same route ten minutes later, reeling and dazed. Staggering. she held on to a wall. As she fell, she called for the police. Her throat had been cut, and she died a few minutes later on the way to the Kings College Hospital. Several neighbors mentioned seeing Beard earlier that evening, and again just minutes before her death, with Johnny Boyle, a 53-year-old ex-boxer who worked as a night watchman and lived in the area with Hilda Julia Gallagher. Boyle had disappeared, however, leaving a farewell note to his lover, explaining that he was in trouble and would be "taking care that the person responsible will not get any poor devil into the same boat." He had also left behind an empty razor case.

When questioned, Gallagher said Boyle had been very upset over charges of child molestation of two 11-year-old girls about

to be brought against him. A few days later, Boyle turned himself in to police, saying he was the man they sought, but that he knew nothing about the girl's murder, insisting that he had run away because of the molestation charges. Gallagher tried to commit suicide a few days after Boyle's arrest. When she revived, she amended her first confession, now declaring that Boyle had told her he was going to kill Beard because she had "shopped (told on) me to the police about those children."

The trial at the Old Bailey began on Oct. 23, 1950, before Mr. Justice Byrnes. Prosecuting attorney Christmas Humphreys maintained that Boyle killed Beard because he mistakenly believed she had informed on him. Defense lawyer L.J. Belcourt interrogated Gallagher, who broke down and admitted that she and Boyle had had a fight—its cause the defense attorney claimed was jealousy from Beard's crush on Boyle, a cause Gallagher strongly denied. Boyle testified he told Gallagher before the girl's death he was going to flee to Ireland with Pat to avoid the molestation charge—a lie invented by him for whimsical reasons—whereupon Mrs. Gallagher grew furious and left the house. He talked with Gallagher soon after the murder was known, and she said she told a neighborhood gang, the so-called "Brixton mob," of his planned trip. Thus Gallagher implied that the mob murdered the girl to keep her from going with him. Boyle said when he saw how bad the circumstantial evidence against them both would look, he told her that he would admit to the crime to distract the police from suspecting her.

He fled to Southport where he turned himself in to the police. At the trial Belcourt did not excuse Boyle's behavior, but three times questioned him about killing her, eliciting a firm "No, sir," each time. The attorney also emphasized that a vindictive person was determined to prevent the teenager from going to Ireland with him. The jury found Boyle Not Guilty. The gang of killers apparently was never prosecuted.

REF.: *CBA; Reynolds, Murder 'Round The World.*

Boyle, William Anthony (Tony), 1904-85, U.S., mur. Tony Boyle and Joseph Albert Yablonski were longtime members of the American United Mine Workers Union. Boyle had served a term as president and Yablonski, suspecting him of embezzlement and of publicly lying about safety violations that led to a November 1968 mine explosion in West Virginia, decided to run against Boyle in an effort to clean up the union, which had been rife with strongarm and terrorist tactics for more than a decade. Suspected in the coal mining intimidation was Albert Pass, treasurer of the East Kentucky branch of the union. William Prater, a union representative who had been one of the strong-arm members, spoke to Silous Huddleston to set in action the plan for Yablonski's murder. Huddleston contacted his son-in-law, Paul Gilly, who hired two young burglars, James Phillips and Claude Vealey, to do the job. When Phillips got drunk the night they stole guns for the killing, Aubrey Wayne (Buddy) Martin, another young burglar, replaced him for the slaying. Yablonski lost the election. Convinced that Boyle had won dishonestly, he was prepared to challenge the election results in court.

On Dec. 30, 1969, Vealey, Martin, and Gilly drove from Cleveland, Ohio, to Clarksville, Pa., breaking into Yablonski's home just after midnight and brutally slaying him along with his wife, Margaret, and daughter, Charlotte. The three men then drove back to Cleveland, throwing their guns into a river along the way. The bodies were discovered six days later when the Yablonskis' son became alarmed at getting no response to phone calls. The police had one clue: the killers had visited Yablonski two weeks before the slayings, pretending to be miners looking for work. When Yablonski did not invite them in they decided not to kill him then. Suspicious, Yablonski had written down the license plate number of their car, and police traced it to Huddleston's daughter, Annette Gilly.

Police rounded up the three killers, along with Huddleston and the daughter. Vealey was the first to talk, bargaining for his life. Martin and Gilly were tried separately and both sentenced to death, Martin's sentence later being reduced to three consecutive life terms. Prater and Pass were each found Guilty of participating in the killings and sentenced to life imprisonment. William Turnblazer, another union executive, implicated Boyle when he admitted overhearing Boyle order Yablonski's murder. Before he could be arrested, however, Boyle, already sentenced to five years in jail for embezzlement of union funds and having lost the presidency, attempted suicide. When revived, he was tried and, in April 1974, found Guilty of the murders. Sentenced to life imprisonment for his part in the crimes, he was released on Mar. 17, 1977, for a retrial when the Pennsylvania Supreme Court ruled that the trial judge had improperly refused to admit testimony that might have aided the defense. Boyle, then seventy-five, was convicted a second time in 1978, and sent back to prison. He died on May 31, 1985. REF.: *CBA*.

Boyles, Odell Carlysle, and **Boyles, Sue Zachary**, prom. 1932-33, U.S., extor. From Nov. 1, 1932, through Jan. 5, 1933, Joseph F. Cannon, a wealthy mill owner in Concord, N.C., received fourteen letters demanding ransom to prevent the kidnapping of his 2-year-old granddaughter, Ann Reynolds, and his 18-year-old son, Joseph F. Cannon, Jr. A Charlotte, N.C., police officer found a latent fingerprint—a vague, indistinct marking left by perspiration from the fingertips—on one of the letters, and sent it to his Division of Investigation. When the print was circulated, Odell Carlysle Boyles and his wife, Sue Zachary Boyles, were taken into custody in Atlanta, Ga., on Jan. 10, 1933. At first denying their extortion attempt, the couple confessed soon after facing the fingerprint evidence against them. Boyles said he was surprised, as he believed he had been careful to avoid leaving any latent prints. Tried and convicted, he was sentenced to fifteen years in prison.

REF.: *CBA*; Cooper, *Ten Thousand Public Enemies*; Robinson, *Science Catches the Criminal*.

Boynton, Charles A., 1867-1954, U.S., jur. U.S. attorney for the Western District of Texas from 1907-12. He was appointed federal judge in 1924 by President Calvin Coolidge and assigned to the court of the Western District of Texas. REF.: *CBA*.

Boynton, Edward, and **Malcolm, Vance**, and **Simmons, G.W.**, prom. 1906, Case of, U.S., mur. Herbert Tilden, a wealthy merchant known for his kindness and philanthropy, gave his time and his automobile over to the Red Cross following the quake. Working around the clock, he carried invalids to shelters. On Apr. 22, 1906, he visited his family in nearby San Mateo, accompanied by Acting Lieutenant Seamans of the Army Signal Corps. Returning to San Francisco around midnight, Tilden was driving his car, which flew a Red Cross flag. At Twenty-second Street the merchant heard several men cry out, "Halt!" but, assuming they would see his flag as he approached, he ignored the command. When someone then fired a revolver at the oncoming car, Seamans responded by shooting back. Tilden collapsed over the wheel, mortally wounded. Seamans was also hurt but survived. Arrested for the crime were Boynton, Malcolm, and Simmons. Members of the so-called "Citizens' Police," a group formed to assist the police, but with no authority as police officers, they were brought before Judge Shortall for a hearing, and Boynton and Simmons were tried before Superior Judge Cook on Sept. 20. Mayor E.E. Schmitz testified that he had given an order on Apr. 18 for all guardians of the peace to kill persons committing serious crimes, including thieves. Boynton testified that he believed that martial law had been declared, and described seeing the car coming at him and his fellow guards at great speed, with the driver ignoring their command to halt. Both Boynton and Simmons had fired as soon as Seamans began to shoot at them. The jury returned a verdict of Not Guilty against Simmons and Boynton, and the charges against Malcolm were dismissed as well.

REF.: *CBA*; Duke, *Celebrated Criminal Cases In America*.

Boynton, James, 1937- , U.S., skyjack. James Boynton, a former researcher at the Fort Custer Job Corps Center, told his father that he was traveling to Florida to find work. Instead, he chartered a small commercial plane in the Florida Keys on Feb. 18, 1968, and then ordered the pilot to fly to Cuba. With a gun

pressed against his head, the pilot of the craft radioed to ground control that he was on his way to Cuba.

Boynton found the climate and the food not to his liking. Worse yet were the suspicions of the Cubans, who believed that Boynton was a CIA operative. From time to time, he was interrogated and thrown in jail. "The boy must have been temporarily out of his head," explained his father James Boynton, a chemistry professor at Western Michigan University. "He was just eating librium to keep going."

In November 1969, James Boynton left Cuba. He arrived in Canada, where he surrendered to immigration authorities. Shortly afterward the skyjacker was returned to Miami to stand trial on charges of kidnapping and aircraft piracy. The case was heard by District Judge William Mehrtens, who sentenced Boynton to twenty years in prison on June 4, 1970. REF.: *CBA*.

Bozzeli, Peter, prom. 1953, U.S., mur. Gloria Bozelli's nude, beaten body was found floating in a duffel-bag in Iron Ore Creek, New Jersey. Known to be Peter Bozelli's favorite child among his eight offspring, Gloria, twenty-four, had been the surrogate mother for the family in the three years since her mother's death. An over-protective father, Bozelli was described by one of Gloria's boyfriends as "like one of those Spanish duennas...a chaperone." The father claimed that he and his daughter had eaten out together the night of her disappearance, but the restaurant where he said they had been at around 9:30 p.m. had closed at 7:30 p.m. When police examined Bozelli's home they found numerous traces of blood. Breaking down, Bozelli confessed to murdering his daughter, jealous of her possible marriage. "I loved my daughter...I didn't want her to leave," he said. He was sentenced to life imprisonment, dying in 1954 after a prison hunger strike.

REF.: *CBA*; Wilson, *Encyclopedia of Murder*.

Braasch, Clarence E., prom. 1973, U.S., blk.-extor. Police commander of Chicago's 18th District, Captain Clarence E. Braasch, one of the department's top-ranking officers, used his power to extort hundreds of thousands of dollars from the wealthy tavern owners in his district.

Under the supervision of then-U.S. Attorney James R. Thompson, government agents worked for more than two years building a case against the Chicago Police Department. By August 1973, twenty-three policemen from the 18th District had been charged with belonging to a "club" that demanded $100 a month protection payments from nightclub and bar owners in the Rush Street and Old Town areas known locally as "glitter gulch." The conspiracy involved around sixty taverns from between 1966 to 1971. Braasch, with many commendations on his record, was the $28,000-a-year chief of the 1,000 man traffic department in 1973 when he was indicted on charges of conspiracy to commit extortion, but he had been commander of the nightclub district between 1966 to 1970. The most important state's witness in the trial was Sergeant John Cello, also known as "Skippy," who collected the monthly payments. Describing his activities, Cello admitted that he began taking bribes his fourth day on the police force. Two other bagmen officers were Sergeant Sal Mascolino and Edward Rifkin. Both testified before a grand jury as did fifty-five tavern owners who paid the bribes.

Government prosecutors Farrell Griffin, Daniel K. Webb, and James Holderman acted as attorneys for the prosecution, calling more than fifty witnesses to testify about police corruption. The case was tried in the U.S. District Court of Judge William J. Bauer. Defense counsel for several of the policemen, David Schippers, attempted to link prosecution witness Robert W. Fischer, an ex-police lieutenant who admitted to receiving more than $40,000 from shakedowns during his seventeen years on the force, with Shirts Unlimited, a crime front used by syndicate leaders Joseph Arnold and Joseph Di Varco. Another defense lawyer, Eugene Pincham attempted to clear his clients by implying that only state's witnesses who had turned government witnesses, including Cello, Fischer, Mascolino, Rifkin, and Lowell Napier, had profited from the extortion. On Oct. 5, 1973, a federal grand jury found nineteen Chicago police officers guilty of conspiracy to commit extortion. Braasch and eight other officers also were convicted of perjury, and the former police captain received five years' imprisonment for conspiracy to extort, and one year for perjury. Of the fifty-seven policemen indicted on charges of corruption in 1973, thirty-five were convicted. REF.: *CBA*.

Brace, Philander, d.1856, U.S., mur. On June 3, 1856, Philander Brace murdered Joseph B. West, a deputy police officer and National Guard captain, on San Miguel Rancho. Brace continued his criminal career, committing several robberies, and continually evading capture. Arrested along with another thief and murderer, Joseph Hetherington, both were tried, found guilty, and hanged on July 29, 1856, from a scaffold on Davis Street, near Commercial Street in San Francisco. They had won the dubious distinction of being the last criminals to be hanged by the San Francisco Vigilance Committee, a citizens' group which held the final parade for their organization on Aug. 18, 1856.

REF.: *CBA*; Duke, *Celebrated Criminal Cases In America*.

Bracey, Joan, c.1656-85, Brit., rob. Like many young, impressionable women, Joan Bracey of Northamptonshire dreamed of a more exciting life than she experienced growing up. Though her father was a man of means, she found life dull until excitement came along in the form of Edward Bracey. When Bracey appeared at the farm to cheat and rob John Phillips, the young daughter was charmed by the highwayman's villainy and notoriety. When Bracey left, so did Joan.

Joan Phillips never married Bracey, but she took his name for her own. When they had accumulated enough money from their robberies, the Braceys opened a public inn outside Bristol.

Joan's beauty and gracious manner impressed everyone. She received offers of marriage and the promise of romance, but she rebuffed each new suitor. Her more persistent suitors were punished. A merchant named Mr. Day, for example, was invited to the house and admitted by a maid. He was told that Bracey was safely away, and invited to remove his clothes and go to the bedroom. The maid, an accomplice, urged Day to enter a dark room and locked the door behind him. After falling down a flight of stairs, he spent all night in the basement minus his clothes. In the morning he was cast into the street at the point of Bracey's sword. Day had two choices: to hide and freeze or to run through the town naked. He chose to make a break for it, dancing and prancing so that passersby would think him mad.

The swindles and robberies pulled off by the Braceys were known throughout England. More often than not, they based their crimes on the vanity and foibles of their victims. When they traveled on the highway, Joan would frequently disguise herself in men's clothing. Joan and Edward's adventures ended in 1685 in Nottinghamshire when they were captured after holding up a nobleman's coach. Edward Bracey, who had knowingly led Joan into a criminal life, was acquitted. Joan herself was condemned and hanged in April 1685. Six days later, Edward was killed when constables fired at him as he attempted to escape from an ale house. He had stopped there on his way to visit the grave of Joan, the woman he loved but never married.

REF.: *CBA*; Smith, *Highwaymen*.

Brach, Helen Voorhees, 1911-77, (unsolv.) mur. At the time of her disappearance on Feb. 17, 1977, Helen Voorhees Brach was worth about $25 million. Her husband Frank, founder of the candy empire bearing the family name, had died in 1970. He left the bulk of his estate to his wife, who donated large sums to various animal rights causes. "She had a soft spot for animals," conceded Jack Matlick, the 45-year-old chauffeur and houseman who looked after Mrs. Brach's seven-acre home in Glenview, Ill., and a farm in Schaumburg. Matlick, a devoted servant and ex-convict, catered to Mrs. Brach's every whim, and was to receive a $50,000 inheritance upon her death. Many believe that Matlick grew impatient and plotted her death.

Mrs. Brach entered the Mayo Clinic in Rochester, Minn., for a routine checkup on Feb. 17, 1977. After being given a clean bill of health, she went to the lobby and bought a small gift item using a charge card. "My chauffeur is waiting," she said impatiently.

That was the last anyone saw of her, but Matlick swore to police that he picked her up at Chicago's O'Hare Field and drove her to the Glenview estate, a distance of twelve miles. He claimed to have taken Brach back to O'Hare four days later where she was to board a plane to Miami to visit her relatives. Airline records showed that Brach was not registered on any flight, nor had her family in Fort Lauderdale been expecting her. On Mar. 9, seventeen days after she first was missed, Matlick reported her disappearance to the police.

A $250,000 reward was posted in newspapers around the country. Thousands of people, including mediums and spiritualists, came forward with hints and suggestions, but there were no tangible clues. The search for the missing heiress continued in Miami, New York, and Rio de Janeiro, spots frequented by Brach. Matlick moved to Glenshaw, Penn., soon after, and remains the most likely suspect. He underwent two lie detector tests, which, according to his attorney, he failed. Matlick and Charles Vorhees, Mrs. Brach's brother, burned some private diaries that she had been keeping. Investigators questioned their motives, but Matlick explained that it was Mrs. Brach's wish that the journals be destroyed.

Matlick cashed eleven checks totaling $15,000 bearing Helen Brach's forged signature dated Feb. 17 and Feb. 18, 1977. But handwriting experts concluded that at least two persons had signed Brach's name, and that Matlick was not one of them. In 1984, Edward Donovan, attorney for Charles Vorhees, described Helen Brach as the victim of an embezzlement to which Matlick holds the final clue. "One part of Jack Matlick's testimony can be believed," Donovan said. "He was the last person to see her alive. The corollary to that is that he was the first person who saw her dead."

In 1987, a Mississippi convict named Maurice Ferguson said he had been retained by millionaire Chicago horseman Silas Jayne to "move" Brach's remains from a gravesite in Morton Grove, Ill., to a secluded spot in Minnesota. A few months before she vanished, Mrs. Brach bought two racehorses from Paul J. Bailey, a former jockey and constant companion to the heiress during her last years. The horses were stabled in Morton Grove, which lent some credence to Ferguson's story. Even if Jayne murdered Brach, there was no hard evidence. Ferguson was driven around for hours in the Minneapolis area, but could not find the right cemetery. "The description he gives of the cemetery is similar to cemeteries all around the country," sighed Major Philip Kruse of the Illinois State Police. The truth about this baffling case may never be known. See: **Jayne, Silas**. REF.: *CBA*.

Brackenbury, Sir Robert (Robert Brakenbury), d.1485, Brit., law enfor. off. Constable of the Tower of London. In 1483, he refused a direct order from King Richard III to execute the two young sons of Edward IV, the Duke of York and Edward V, and the task was given over to Sir James Tyrrell. See: **Richard III**. REF.: *CBA*.

Bracton, Henry de (Henry de Bratton, Henry de Bretton), d.1268, Brit., jur. Wrote the first treatise on English laws during the Middle Ages. REF.: *CBA*.

Bradford, Edward Green, 1819-84, U.S., jur. U.S. district attorney for Washington D.C. from 1861-65 and 1865-66. He was named to the bench of the District Court of Delaware by President Ulysses S. Grant in 1871. REF.: *CBA*.

Bradford, Sir Edward Ridley Colborne, 1836-1911, Brit., law enfor. off. Best known for his work as commissioner of the London Metropolitan Police, a post he held for more than twelve years, Bradford also served for some time in India.

The son of a minister, Bradford was educated at Marlborough. He entered the Madras Cavalry in 1853, serving in the Persian Campaign in 1856-7, returning then to India to participate in another military campaign there, twice receiving medals for valor. In 1860 he commanded the First Central India Horse Brigade which proved to be the beginning of a long and distinguished life in political and civil service.

While serving in India in 1867, Bradford lost an arm in a tiger

He served for four years, 1874-78, as general superintendent of the operations for suppression of crime in India, and, in 1878, became chief commissioner in Ajmere. Knighted in 1885, Bradford returned to London in 1887 to become Secretary to the Secret and Political Department of the India Office, conducting Prince Albert Victor on a tour of India in 1889-90. Later in 1890 he became Commissioner of Metropolitan Police, a post whose jurisdiction extended to over six and a half million people and 16,500 policemen. Bradford led the processions of three major state ceremonies which took place during his term: the Diamond Jubilee of 1897, Queen Victoria's funeral in 1901, and King Edward's Coronation in 1902. He was appointed Baronet in 1902, Extra Equerry to King Edward in 1903, and later reappointed to the office under King George. REF.: *CBA.*

Bradford, John, c.1510-55, Brit., her. Accused of sedition when Catholic Queen Mary ascended to the throne in 1554. He was tried by Bishop Gardiner, condemned as a protestant heretic, and burned at the stake in Smithfield. REF.: *CBA.*

Jonathan Bradford discovering his intended murder victim already slain.

Bradford, Jonathan, prom. 1700s, Brit., mur. Jonathan Bradford never killed anyone. But someone else did, and Bradford paid the ultimate price. Bradford ran a modest rooming house in Oxford, where a man named Mr. Hayes, attended by his servant, secured a room for the night. Hayes was rumored to possess a large sum of money.

In the middle of the night, a rattling sound was heard by two boarders sleeping across the hall from Mr. Hayes. When they burst into the room, they found Bradford standing over the bed clutching a carving knife in one hand and a lantern in the other. On the bed lay Hayes, dead in a pool of his own blood.

There was little Bradford could say or do to establish his innocence. A jury found him Guilty and he was executed. What they did not know was that Hayes' servant had plunged the fatal dagger into his master and had stolen his money moments before Bradford had appeared to do the same thing. The innkeeper, innocent in deed but not in his soul, was left holding the bag.

REF.: *CBA; Newgate Calendar.*

Bradford, Priscilla, 1944- , and **Cummings, Joyce Lisa,** 1962- , and **Gould, Janice Irene,** 1946- , U.S., mur. John Young Bradford, Jr., a wealthy optometrist from Melbourne, Fla., suspected that his wife was trying to kill him. The 53-year-old doctor had even quickly prepared a new will. On Mar. 30, 1980, Dr. John Bradford, Jr. was found dead the kitchen of his Melbourne, Fla., home. Bradford had been beaten by his 36-year-old wife Priscilla Ann Hadley Smith, who explained that she was fighting for her life. Police Chief C.W. "Jake " Miller was at first

sympathetic to the wife, who bore the visible marks of violence. And so too, were Priscilla's companions: Joyce Lisa Cummings, eighteen, and Janice Irene Gould, thirty-four. Both worked in Bradford's optical lab.

Bradford left an estate worth $300,000 and a lucrative eyewear business that brought in $12,000 a month. Now it all belonged to Priscilla, Bradford's second wife. When police questioned the first wife Deenie, she said that in twenty-eight years of marriage, John had never struck her once. Tracy Smith and John Lockhart, two of Bradford's lab employees, told police about Priscilla's determination to push her husband out of the way to wrest control of the business.

This was mere conjecture though, until Priscilla's teenage daughter, Eden Elaine, came forward to provide substantive weight to the allegations. She told of a fiendish murder plot hatched by Priscilla Bradford with the connivance of Gould and Cummings. After failing in an attempt to poison him, they decided to ambush him as he sat down to what he thought was going to be a "reconciliation" dinner with his wife. "It's going to be his last supper," Priscilla joked. On Mar. 28, they carried out the plan, and Eden was ordered to keep the shower in the bathroom running, so that the three murderesses could wash off the blood traces. Gould and Cummings selected their murder weapons from the kitchen—Priscilla chose a frying pan. The three women beat him senseless, and then ordered Eden to "keep hitting him...everywhere!" Finally, after repeated blows to the head and face, he died.

Eden was granted immunity in the murder trial that began Apr. 10, 1980. While in jail Priscilla approached a prostitute named Ursula Mattox in hopes of finding someone to murder Tracy Smith and John Lockhart. Priscilla even brought her own mother into the plan. She was to "drop" the $2,000 down payment for the hired killer at a pizzeria. Mattox pretended to go along with the scheme but instead informed prison authorities, who notified the police. With the help of Mattox, police allowed the plan to continue, intervening when the money was actually dropped off to an undercover officer. The evidence gathered was then used to tack on additional charges of conspiracy to commit murder to the original murder indictment. Cummings, Gould, and Bradford were convicted of murder and sentenced to life imprisonment. Said Joyce Cummings at the conclusion of her trial: "All we wanted was an all-female lab."

REF.: *CBA; Nash, Look For the Woman.*

Bradford, William, 1755-95, U.S., atty. gen. Soldier in the Continental Army from 1776-77 before receiving an appointment as attorney general of Pennsylvania in August 1780. He was judge of the Supreme Court of Pennsylvania from 1791-94, and named U.S. attorney general in 1794. He authored the influential *Inquiry Into How Far the Punishment of Death is Necessary in Pennsylvania* (1793). REF.: *CBA.*

Bradlaugh, Charles (AKA: the Iconoclast), 1833-91, Case of, Brit., libel. Religious reformer, lecturer, and free thinker. He advocated, in his *National Review,* the right of a man to affirm instead of swearing on the Bible. In 1876, he was prosecuted along with Annie Besant for re-issuing the controversial *Fruits of Philosophy,* a case he won which inadvertently helped pave the way for greater freedom of the press in England. REF.: *CBA.*

Bradley, Edward E., prom. 1857, Case of, U.S., mur. Bradley was accused of murdering Lucius H. Foot who was beaten to death with a hammer, the body left in a horse stall in the Litchfield, Conn., church. The case is curiously interesting in that several crude experiments in pathology and blood identification were made. The corpse, however, was found in such an advanced stage of *rigor mortis* that, according to a local doctor, "one could end it up like a post." The bloodstains found on Bradley's clothes were not identified as having come from the victim, and he was released after a short trial and speedy acquittal.

REF.: *CBA; Report of the Trial of Edward E. Bradley.*

Bradley, James, and **Barratt, Peter Henry,** b.1853, Brit., mansl. On the morning of Apr. 11, 1861, 2-year-old George Burgess was by himself near the Star Inn in Stockport, England. His nurse, Mrs. Warren, looked in on him from time to time, but left him to his own devices and went back to her work. At three in the afternoon, George vanished from his playlot.

The next day he was found floating face down in a brook in Ford's Field, nearly a mile from his home. There was evidence of skin abrasions on his buttocks and a blow to the head. A neighbor woman named Mrs. Williams said that she had observed three boys playing in the field but had done nothing, even after she saw an older boy hit a younger boy with a stick.

Policeman William Morley identified two 8-year-old boys as the assailants: James Bradley and his friend Peter Barratt. It was Peter who undressed the small boy, just before he pushed him into the pond where he drowned. They were arrested and charged with murder—the first time children so young would be tried for so serious a crime.

Their case was tried at the Chester Assizes on Aug. 7, 1861. The defense attorney argued that the murder was caused by "boyish mischief," and that the boys were too young to distinguish between right and wrong. After only fifteen minutes of deliberation, however, both were found Guilty on a reduced charge of manslaughter. The judge sentenced them to one month in jail, and at the end of their term ordered them confined to the reformatory for five years.

REF.: *CBA*; Wilson, *Children Who Kill*.

Bradley, James, d.1982, U.S., (unsolv.) mur. When he left Roosevelt High School in East Chicago, Ind., in the late 1960s, six-foot-ten-inch James Bradley was hailed as one of the most promising athletes in the Midwest. In 1971, Bradley fulfilled prophecy as he led the Northern Illinois *Huskies* to a national college ranking. Upon completion of his studies, Bradley signed with the Kentucky Colonels of the American Basketball Association, a team of stars led by Artis Gilmore. When the league merged with the National Basketball Association (NBA) in 1976, Bradley drifted. He was released by the Denver Nuggets for missing practices and was forced to play in the European leagues and in the Philippines.

After returning to the U.S., James Bradley signed a contract with the Rochester Zeniths, an NBA farm team that won two championships during his tenure. After four successful seasons in Rochester, Bradley tried to make the jump back into the pros, this time with the Portland Trailblazers. He failed, but chose to linger behind in Portland. On Feb. 18, 1982, Bradley was arrested for selling drugs after he attempted to peddle cocaine to a pair of undercover police. Free on bond two days later, he was shot in the back as he left the Copper Penny II, a Portland disco. The murderer was never apprehended, though several theories were offered. Some believed that Bradley was silenced before he could implicate top drug kingpins, others maintain that he was shot by a jealous husband.

REF.: *CBA*; Nash, *Open Files*.

Bradley, Joseph P., 1813-92, U.S., jur. Republican Party leader and associate Supreme Court justice from 1870-92. His support of the radical Republican wing of the party earned him the loyalty of the party leaders including President Ulysses S. Grant who nominated him to take the place of Supreme Court justice James Wayne in 1870. In 1876, he served on the electoral commission to determine the victor in the Rutherford B. Hayes-Samuel Tilden presidential contest. Tilden won the popular vote, but by voting along partisan Republican lines, he cast the twenty decisive electoral votes for Hayes. REF.: *CBA*.

Bradley, Stephen Leslie (Istvan Baranyay), and **Bradley, Magda**, prom. 1960, Aus., kid.-mur. The parents of 8-year-old Graeme Thorne soon found out that winning the £A100,000 Sydney Opera House Lottery carried with it a terrible price: the loss of their son. On July 7, 1960, Mrs. Freda Thorne notified the police that her boy was missing. As she spoke to a Sydney detective, the telephone rang. A voice on the other end demanded £A25,000 of the prize money in return for the safe return of the child. This was the first child abduction in Australia, and the

local police were unsure of how to proceed with the investigation. Unlike Canada, Australia had never formed a federal police force; they had no Royal Canadian Mounted Police. R.J. Heffron, premier of New South Wales, expressed his government's frustration. "We have never thought that kidnapping a child and holding him to ransom could occur in this country."

A search for the boy commenced immediately, but there was no further ransom demand from the kidnappers. Two boys playing on a waste dump at Seaforth on Aug. 16 found the body of Graeme Thorne wrapped in a carpet. He had died from suffocation and a fractured skull. Forensic investigators established the time of death as five weeks prior. Spores found on the body were identified as coming from two species of cypress which rarely grew together.

A search of the immediate vicinity turned up the garden where two such trees grew. The owners of the house had just moved in, and they explained that the previous couple, Stephen Bradley (formerly István Baranyay of Hungary) and his wife Magda had booked passage on the ocean liner *Himalaya*, which was bound for England. The carpet used to wrap Graeme was from the house. The Bradleys were arrested at Colombo, and returned to Sydney where they stood trial on Mar. 20, 1961. They explained that the Thorne boy had died of suffocation in the trunk of the car. Attempting to curry the sympathy of the jurors, Bradley told of his troubled youth, and how he escaped a Nazi firing squad in Hungary by jumping in the Theiss River. The ploy failed. After an eight-day trial, they were found Guilty and sentenced to life imprisonment.

REF.: *CBA*; Goodwin, *Killers In Paradise*; Thorwald, *Crime and Science*.

Bradshaw, Jack, and **Ogden, Will**, and **Reynolds, Tom**, prom. 18th Cent., Brit., rob. The Dover Road in England was the site of many highway robberies in the early years of the eighteenth century, one of the most famous involving Jack Bradshaw, Will Ogden, and Tom Reynolds. Bradshaw stopped a young woman pedestrian and demanded the box she was carrying. He tore open the box. Among the items that spilled out was a hammer, which the woman quickly grabbed. She struck Bradshaw a blow to the temple, and as he lay on the ground she gored him through the neck with the claw end of the tool.

By the time a passing stranger summoned help, Ogden and Reynolds were safely away. See: **Ogden, Will; Reynolds, Tom.**

REF.: *CBA*; Pringle, *Stand and Deliver*.

Bradshaw, John, 1602-59, Brit., jur. Presided at the trial of King Charles I in 1649. He condemned the king as an unpardonable tyrant and pronounced the death sentence. See: **Charles I.** REF.: *CBA*.

Brady, Al, 1910-37, U.S., rob.-mur. Al Brady liked to think that he was another John Dillinger, and during his brief heyday as a notorious bandit who roamed and robbed the country from the Midwest to New England, he almost matched the Hoosier bank robber, at least in notoriety. Like Dillinger, Brady was born and bred in Indiana where, in his late teens, he began stealing—compiling an arrest record. He later went to prison for theft and when he was paroled, Brady put together a gang of bandits that included James Dalhover, Clarence Lee Shaffer, Jr., and Charles Geisking. These men held up nine banks in a short period of time, taking small amounts, and in the process killing a police officer in Anderson, Ind., another in Indianapolis, Ind., and a clerk in Piqua, Ohio. Trapped after committing another robbery, the gang was locked up in the Greenfield, Ind., jail but Brady, Shaffer, and Dalhover escaped on Oct. 11, 1936, and promptly robbed the bank in tiny Goodland, Ind., (pop. 978), taking $2,500. This was Brady's hometown and the savings he stole were those of neighbors he had known since childhood.

The Indiana State Police under the command of Captain Matt Leach, who had hunted Dillinger in the early 1930s, combed the state for the Brady gang, but the trail began to grow cold as the bandits moved eastward. The gang was last reported in Bridgeport, Conn., where it disappeared from sight. FBI agents continued pursuit, running down the slightest leads. The Bureau had come onto the case after the Brady gang fled with a stolen auto across a state line and also because the bank robberies the gang committed were by then federal offenses. Still, no trace of the killer bandits could be found. Then, in early October 1937, three young men, all about five-foot-five-inches tall (a peculiarity of the Brady gang) walked into Dakin's sporting goods and hardware store in Bangor, Maine. They bought two .45-caliber Colt automatics and a generous supply of ammnuition from owner Everett Hurd. The men also ordered a Winchester rifle and another .45-caliber Colt automatic which Hurd said he would get from his gun supplier and would be available within a week or so.

Hurd was suspicious of the three men. They talked with "strange accents" which, of course, was a Midwestern twang, and he had heard that some Indiana bandits had been recently sought in New England. He called the Bangor police and the FBI, in turn, was contacted. Descriptions of the three men convinced FBI agents that the men in Dakin's store had been Brady and his men. On Oct. 12, 1937, Dalhover returned to Dakin's and went to the clerk standing behind a counter, saying: "Say, where's the stuff I ordered." The clerk was Walter Walsh, an FBI agent who was a crack shot. He had been stationed in the store which had been watched round-the-clock for days by FBI agents, state troopers, from Maine and Indiana, and Bangor police.

Walsh told Dalhover that he would get his order right away. He then tried to signal the officers stationed outside but Dalhover, suddenly realizing that he had walked into a trap, whipped out an automatic, woundiung Walsh in the shoulder with a single shot. As he fired, several agents raced into the shop but Dalhover momentarily escaped, running the length of the store, then downstairs, then out a back entrance. Here he ran right into the arms of Bangor policemen who quickly disarmed and subdued him. It would be more difficult with Brady and Shaffer who were waiting in a car outside the store. They jumped from the auto and began firing wildly through the plate glass window of the store at the agents inside.

Bangor residents fled from the scene in all directions while more FBI agents, state troopers, and local police advanced down Central Street from both ends of the block, pistols barking, machine guns chattering. Brady and Shaffer jumped behind cars and began firing back in a gun battle that roared and raged for more than five minutes. Citizens looked out of windows and stepped from shops to witness a scene right out of the Old West. The shootout drew the attention of Ralph O. Brewster, one-time governor of Maine and a U.S. congressman (1925-29). He had been nibbling on a sandwich at a lunch counter in a drugstore just down the block. Brewster stepped from the store with the sandwich still in his hand, finishing it as he pointed out one of the bandits hiding behind a car to a crouching FBI agent. The agent let loose a blast from his submachine gun and the bandit staggered backward into the street, collapsing dead. It was Clarence Lee Shaffer, Jr. The second bandit then jumped into the middle of the street, surrounded by agents and officers who closed in on him. He began firing in all directions and drew a hailstorm of bullets that sent him crashing dead to the cobblestone pavement, his body sprawled between trolley car tracks. It was the end of the Brady gang. REF.: CBA.

Brady, Ian, See: **Moors Murders.**

Brady, John, See: **Smith, James.**

Brady, John (AKA: **John McGuire, Henry Williams**), prom. 1894-95, U.S., rob.-mur. On Oct. 12, 1894, two men, one tall and the other of average height, stopped a track-walker, stole his dynamite cartridges and red lantern, and used both to flag down the Omaha Overland train near San Francisco. They forced engineer Bill Scott and his firemen to take them to the Wells Fargo and Co. car and carry the contents of the safe, close to $53,000, back to the locomotive, and uncouple it from the train. The thieves got away with the loot, then sent the locomotive back the other way, where it ran out of steam as it bumped into the rest of the train cars.

On Mar. 16, 1895, two men entered the Ingleside roadhouse of Cornelius Stagg, an elderly host known for his practical jokes. The masked men told Stagg to hold up his hands. Thinking it was a joke, Stagg laughed. One of the criminals smashed him over the head, then killed him with two shots, robbing the place of $4 and fleeing.

On Mar. 30, 1895, the Oregon Express train running near Wheatland, Calif., was brought to a halt by two masked bandits who forced the engineer to lead them to the Wells Fargo Company car. Unable to open the combination safe, the two men made the engineer and the fireman precede them into the passenger cars, taking valuables from travelers as they went. A porter woke up Sheriff J.J. Bogard in his sleeping car and he rushed the bandits in the smoking car, firing his pistol and killing one of the thieves. The other masked man shot and killed the sheriff, wounded the fireman, and disappeared without the loot.

Robber and killer John Brady.   **Train robber O.S. Brown.**

The day after the failed train robbery, Sheriff Sam Inlow, of Yuba County found an abandoned bicycle near the holdup scene, and traced it to a San Francisco shop, where the owners identified a photograph of the dead bandit, O.S. Brown, saying they had rented him the bike a week prior to the robbery. Further investigation revealed that the man who got away was John Brady, also known as John McGuire and Henry Williams. The police found photographs in Brady's room of him with Brown—the men had been inseparable companions.

On July 25, 1895, a man came into a Freeport, Calif. grocery. As owner Phil Riehl wrapped his purchases, he observed the man intently reading a newspaper. The grocer glanced at the story and saw it was an article about a clue police had recently obtained regarding Brady's whereabouts. Riehl notified police, who arrested Brady two days later as he sat under a bridge near Richland, Calif., a sawed-off shotgun at his side. On July 27 Brady confessed to both train robberies and to robbing and killing Stagg. He took the officers to the spot near Sacramento where he and his cohort had buried $50,000 of the money stolen from the Omaha train. On July 29 Brady was tried in Marysville by Sheriff Inlow for the murder of Sheriff Bogard. On Nov. 27, 1895, he was convicted and sentenced to life imprisonment.

REF.: CBA; Duke, *Celebrated Criminal Cases In America.*

Brady, Mary, prom. 1889, U.S., crime&punish. As late as 1899 in Jersey City, N.J., a woman named Mary Brady was, according to a newspaper report, indicted for being "a common scold." At that time, in some parts of the U.S., the punishment for disagreeing or fighting, by a woman, was a ducking-stool, a chair or stool to which the woman was tied and then plunged into water. Used primarily in New England, the so-called Common Scold Law applied only to women and was brought from England to Connecticut by the Puritans and other settlers, and carried as far as the state of New Jersey.

REF.: Andrews, *Old-Time Punishments; CBA.*

Brady, Matthew (AKA: **Gentleman Matt**), d.1826, Brit., forg.-rob. A valet from Manchester, Brady was convicted of forgery and sentenced to serve a seven-year term. He was so insubordinate that he was immediately transferred to Macquarie Harbour, a notoriously harsh camp on Van Dieman's Land. With fourteen other prisoners, Brady escaped, fighting off wardens and taking a whaleboat to get to the Hobart estuary. Six prisoners were soon caught but Brady and the remaining eight stayed free, and began raiding and looting the area. Attacking Robert Taylor, a rich settler, three more of the escaped prisoners were caught and hanged. Moving on to Hobart with the remaining gang, Brady and his cohorts broke open the jail and locked the warders in the empty cells in Sorrell Township. Angered at the affront, Lieutenant Governor Arthur intensified his campaign against petty swindlers, also known as bushrangers, offering £25 a head for their capture. Brady's gang countered by making up a poster of Arthur, offering twenty-five gallons of rum for his capture. In 1825, one hundred bushrangers were caught. In 1826, Brady was captured and charged with more than 350 crimes. Women packed the courtroom at his trial and filled his cell with gifts of fruit and flowers. Despite his popularity, Brady was convicted, and hanged in 1826. REF.: *CBA.*

Brady, Patrick, 1893-1965, Case of, Aus., mur. Patrick Brady stood accused of murder in 1935 in one of the most bizarre killings in Australian history. James Smith, a part-time handyman in Sydney, Aus., who made most of his money smuggling, vanished on Apr. 8, 1935. Smith, a 40-year-old ex-boxer, had told his wife that he was going on a fishing expedition, but he did not name his companions in this outing. Mrs. Smith filed a Missing Person's report. Ten days later, a group of female tourists looked down into a seaside aquarian in Coogee, a Sydney suburb, and several fainted. Floating in the aquarium was a muscular human arm which had been disgorged by a recently captured fourteen-foot tiger shark. When it was inspected later, experts quickly determined that the limb had not been chewed off by a shark. It had been neatly severed. The arm bore a tattoo of two boxers, a tattoo that had been part of Mrs. Smith's description of her missing husband. The arm was so well preserved that fingerprints were taken and the limb was positively identified as having belonged to Smith, the prints checked against Smith's long police record as a forger and thief.

Shark experts then determined that the arm had been swallowed by the recently captured shark in the Coogee aquarium only a few hours earlier which was explained by the arm's well-preserved condition. After thirty-six hours, the experts stated, the shark's digestive juices would have broken down the arm. The shark had not eaten anything since its capture so it was rightly assumed that the shark had swallowed the arm at sea. A desperate search by military and police divers was conducted through the waters about Sydney, but the rest of Smith's body was never recovered. Police then learned that Smith had recently been working on a smuggling launch, *Pathfinder.* This speedy boat had been smuggling opium taken from Chinese liners. Further investigation revealed that Sydney was the center of an enormous drug smuggling operation since it was the first port of call for Oriental ships destined for the U.S.

Detectives next confronted wealthy boat builder Reginald Holmes, who had owned the *Pathfinder,* and who had gotten rich from drug smuggling. He admitted that Smith had worked for him on his launch but that the boat had been sunk and he had not seen Smith since. He later claimed that another boat builder, Patrick Brady, was blackmailing him, knowing that the *Pathfinder* was being used for drug smuggling. He also said that Smith made blackmail payments to Brady. Witnesses claimed that Smith had last been seen with Brady, but Holmes refused to support this story. The boat builder did tell his wife later that "Brady did it...He put the body in a trunk, took it out in his boat, and dumped it overboard." (These remarks were repeated by Inie Holmes after her husband's murder a short time later, but since it was ruled

hearsay in Brady's subsequent trial, they were dismissed.)

Ironically, two of the world's greatest pathologists, Sir Bernard Spilsbury and Sydney Smith, were then attending a forensic science convention in Sydney and they were consulted in what the press now historically dubbed "The Shark Arm Case." After inspecting the arm, both pathologists concluded that Smith was murdered and his body dismembered, stuffed into a trunk. Since the arm did not fit inside of the trunk, it was tied to the outside of the trunk which was then dumped overboard. The tiger shark later caught for the Coogee aquarium swallowed the arm which had somehow broken loose and disgorged it hours later when in captivity.

Based on the statements of Holmes and others, Brady was arrested and charged with Smith's murder on May 17, 1935. Three days later, a police launch chased a fast-moving speedboat about Sydney Harbor. The boat had not only failed to stop when the police boat signaled to it but it had turned about and tried repeatedly to ram the police launch. The wild, zigzagging chase between the police launch and the speedboat went on for more than four hours until the speedboat ran out of gas. When the police launch came alongside they found Reginald Holmes at the wheel, his face covered with blood from a bullet wound in the head. Since the police and Holmes had not exchanged shots, officers were baffled by the wound. Holmes was rushed unconscious to a hospital, but he regained consciousness to tell detectives that someone had shot him as he was leaving his home and he escaped the gunmen by jumping into his speedboat and heading across Sydney Harbor. He thought that the police launch was a boat powered by the pursuing gunmen which is why he at first attempted to outrun it and then sink it by ramming his own boat into the launch. This fantastic story was accepted and Holmes was allowed to return home after he recovered from his headwound.

Holmes was scheduled to appear as a star witness against Brady on June 13, 1935, but on the morning of the trial, he was found shot to death. The case against Brady was weak without Holmes's testimony. Brady's lawyer's dismissed the grisly arm on display as Exhibit A, saying that a single human arm did not constitute a body and there was no real proof that Smith was, indeed, dead. During the course of Brady's trial, two men were arrested and charged with Holmes' murder but they were later acquitted. Brady was acquitted in a bench trial, the presiding judge deciding that the circumstantial evidence against him was not enough to convict. Brady insisted for the rest of his life that he was innocent of murdering Smith and Holmes and that Smith's arm bore bullet wounds, although he failed to explain the meaning of this contention which was never supported by police and forensic experts. Brady died in an Australian hospital in 1965 and the Smith and Holmes murders remain unsolved to this day. See: **Smith, Sydney; Spilsbury, Bernard.**

REF.: *CBA;* Godwin, *Killers Unknown;* Kelly, *The Shark Arm Case;* Nash, *Open Files;* Smith, *Mostly Murder.*

Braeseke, Barry, 1957-   , U.S., mur. At twenty-five, Barry Braeseke was serving a life sentence for the 1976 killings of his mother, father, and grandfather, when, in 1982, the California Supreme Court upset the 1977 conviction, ruling that Braeseke confessed before police properly advised him of his rights. As part of the hearings for the retrial, Judge Stanley Golde of Alameda County ordered the CBS News Program "60 Minutes" to bring twenty-eight minutes of unused material from an interview it had aired with Braeseke. Golde had declared a 1980 California state law permitting reporters to withhold their sources unconstitutional on Jan. 18, 1982, calling the shield law a First Amendment privilege that must give way to the Sixth Amendment, which guarantees the right to a fair trial for the accused. The two minutes of "60 Minutes" that had been broadcast in 1977 showed Braeseke saying he was under the influence of the drug PCP when he murdered his relatives. On Jan. 26, 1982, when CBS News delivered the tape to Judge Golde, he responded by vacating his earlier ruling that called the shield law unconstitutional. CBS lawyer Edwin Heafey, Jr. said the network had "attempted to reach an accommodation to protect the rights the court was worried about." The tape was admitted as evidence for the defense in Braeseke's second trial and viewed by the jury. In February 1982, he was convicted of the murders a second time and resentenced to life in prison. REF.: *CBA*.

Bragg, Thomas, 1810-72, U.S., lawyer. Brother of General Braxton Bragg. He was attorney general for the Confederate States of America from 1861-62. REF.: *CBA*.

Brain, George, 1911-38, Brit., mur. Twenty-seven-year-old George Brain drove a van for a shoe repair business on Pancras Street, Tottenham Court Road, London. Occasionally his employer would let him take the company van home for the night. On July 13, 1938, Brain used the van to pay a social call on his bride-to-be in Kingston. However, he missed his connection. Undaunted, he drove about the city in search of something else to do. Near Wimbledon Common he recognized a familiar face: 30-year-old Rose Muriel Atkins, a street walker known as "Irish Rose."

Brain offered her a lift, but she pan-handled him for money. He refused, and Atkins threatened to tell his employer that he had been driving the van around the city for pleasure. Furious with her demands, Brain struck her repeatedly with the starting handle until she died. To cover his tracks and alleviate suspicion he placed the body curbside and drove over it, hoping to give the impression that Atkins had been the victim of a hit-and-run driver.

Witnesses reported seeing Irish Rose enter a green van, possibly an Austin Seven or Morris Minor. These were the only two vehicles that matched the tire tracks found on the dead woman. The abandoned van was found on July 16. It was eventually traced back to Brain. Police sent his photograph to the papers and requested from the public any information regarding his whereabouts. A Richmond school boy recognized Brain near the Minister Cliffs at Sheerness on July 25. The following September he was placed on trial at the Old Bailey. It took the jury only fifteen minutes to debate his fate. A Guilty verdict was returned, and Justice Wrottesley passed sentence. The sentence was carried out at Wandsworth Prison on Nov. 1, 1938.

REF.: *CBA*; Cherrill, *Cherrill of the Yard*; Henry, *Detective-Inspector Henry's Famous Cases*; Jacobs, *Aspects of Murder*; Sanders, *They Caught These Killers*; Shew, *A Second Companion to Murder*; Singer, *My Greatest Crime Story*; Wilson, *Encyclopedia of Murder*.

Bram, Thomas Mead Chambers, b.1864, U.S., mur. Thomas Mead Chambers Bram was of mixed blood and was raised to be a religious zealot, going to sea at an early age and later becoming a waiter at the Dennett res-taurants, a peculiar nationwide chain with waiters who were all religious fanatics who loud-ly chastised patrons about committing sin as they served them soup and sandwiches. There were murals on all the walls of these restaurants which depicted the fiery dam-nation of hell, the tempta-tions of the Devil and cau-tioned with fiery signs the wages of sin, as well as warn-ing customers that evil was at their elbow, right next to the breadsticks, and that everyone should watch their hats, pur-ses, gloves, and coats for thieves were probably sitting at the next table waiting to lunge for any stray belonging. Bram was one of the most

The murder ship, *Herbert Fuller,* **1896.**

zealous of Dennett waiters, going into shrieking diatribes about sin and sluts as he took lunch and dinner orders. He so impressed the owner that Dennett made him a manager of one restaurant and it promptly went broke.

Bram went to sea and rose through the ranks to become a mate, sometimes a captain of cargo vessels. In 1896, Bram was serving as first mate of the barkentine, *Herbert Fuller,* which sailed from Boston on July 3, 1896, bound for Rosario, on the Panama River, in the Argentine Republic. Captain Charles I. Nash and his wife Laura sailed on that voyage, along with a lone passenger, 20-year-old Lester Hawthorne Monks, taking the voyage for his health, and nine crew members. On the night of July 13-14, 1896, as the ship sailed silently through heavy fog, Monks was aroused from his sleep by strange "gurgling" sounds, he later said, which caused him to go on deck with his revolver in hand. He found Captain Nash in the afterhouse, his throat gashed, murdered. Mrs. Nash was in her cabin, lying dead on her back in her bunk, her clothes above her waist, her head crushed. She had also been raped. Monks raced to the deck to find Mate Bram pacing solemnly through the gloom. He informed Bram of the murders and the mate suddenly went to pieces, sobbing, his body shaking, falling to his knees and desperately holding on to Monks' legs, asking the youthful passenger to protect him against what was probably a bloody mutiny.

Monks later found August W. Blomberg, an enormous Russian Finn, murdered in his bunk in the crew's quarters, his head also crushed by blows from an ax. The ax, coated with the blood of the three victims, was later found. Mate Bram, saying that he would get rid of it lest the murderer among the crew use it again, threw the bloody ax overboard before anyone could stop him. Then Bram, alternately be-tween hysteria and euphoria at remaining alive, concluded that Blomberg had crept into Mrs. Nash's cabin and was raping her or, perhaps, had her consent, when Captain Nash entered the cabin with an ax and killed Mrs. Nash with it, thinking she had be-trayed him. Then Blomberg, Bram went on, wrested the ax away from the captain and killed him with it but received a mortal blow to the head and staggered back to his own bunk where he died. The victims had all killed each other, it was that simple.

Thomas Bram, first mate of the *Herbert Fuller* and hatchet killer.

(When this theory was later repeated in court, it caused the spectators to break into loud laughter.)

As the *Herbert Fuller* sailed for Halifax, Bram tried to convince the crew that perhaps he had been wrong and that a seaman named Charley Brown was the murderer. Brown was manacled and held prisoner for the authorities, but he told Monks and other crew members that Bram had accused him because he had been at the wheel at the time of the murders and had seen Bram kill Captain Nash with the ax through a small window of the after-house which was directly in front of the wheel. Bram was then tied to a mast and charged by Monks and the crew with the awful murders. He screamed his innocence all the way into port, the ship reaching Halifax on July 21, 1896. The bodies of victims had been placed in a longboat which was being pulled by the barkentine as the superstitious crew feared having the corpses on board. The survivors were taken to Boston, and Thomas Mead Chambers Bram, charged with murder, was tried Dec. 14, 1896.

Witnesses came forward to testify that Bram had been a mutinous crewman on board other ships. One sailor stated that Bram proposed the murder of another captain on another ship or that the sailor and Bram board a Norwegian ship and murder the captain and some of the crew. It was proved that, while a captain of other ships, Bram had sold cargoes and claimed that they had been ruined by seawater or sold cargo, then scuttled ships and reported the cargo sinking with the ship in a storm. His background was thoroughly disreputable and, with Brown's eye-witness testimony against him, Bram was convicted of murder and sentenced to death. His lawyers won him several reprieves and a second trial at which he was again convicted, but this time the jury qualified its verdict with the words "without capital punishment." Bram was sent to prison in the federal penitentiary in Atlanta on July 12, 1898 to serve a life term.

Bram would have undoubtedly died behind bars for his gruesome killings had it not been for the mystery writer Mary Roberts Rinehart who wrote a novel about the case called *The After House*. Rinehart had supposedly studied the case in depth but, in reality, her investigation was superficial. In the novel, Rinehart placed the blame for the murders on Charley Brown, claiming that he had lashed the wheel with a rope, run down to Mrs. Nash's cabin, raped and killed her, and then killed Captain Nash who had interrupted him. Blomberg was killed next, supposedly after discovering the crime, and his body dragged back to his bunk. Of course, this was all nonsense in that Brown was on deck at the wheel when Monk discovered the bodies, and that Bram was on deck, having the watch. Had Brown left the wheel, Bram would instantly have seen this, something Bram never claimed.

The Rinehart novel became a *cause célèbre* among the literati and certain politicians with avid mystery reading habits, embraced Rinehart's theory about Brown being the killer, not the least of whom was President Woodrow Wilson who, surprisingly, gave Bram a full pardon on Apr. 22, 1919. Bram walked out of the penitentiary and settled in Atlanta, becoming rich as a wholesaler in peanuts. He later went back to sea and was the captain of freighters as late as 1928. Throughout the remainder of his long life, Mate Bram never tired of talking about the murders on board the *Herbert Fuller* (sunk by a German U-boat during WWI on May 29, 1917). He reveled in his dark fame and never failed to show his presidential pardon to anyone who would listen to his own theories of the murders. Sometimes he would say Brown was the killer. On other occasions he would pinpoint Blomberg. Then he would say Captain Nash did the murders and died in the act, committing suicide by smashing his own skull with the lost ax! And Mate Bram? Why, he was at his post, loyal to his duty, bravely walking through the murk on deck, on watch, guarding in the gloom against creeping, lurking maniacs who clutched razor-sharp axes in their hands, waiting to murder.

REF.: Boar, *The World's Most Infamous Murders*; CBA; Nash, *Murder, America*; Pearson, *Five Murders*; _____, *Studies in Murder*.

Bramah, Ernest (Ernest Bramah Smith), c.1869-1942, Brit., writer. Published numerous detective stories. He invented the blind detective Max Carrados who appeared in *Max Carrados* (1914) and *The Eyes of Max Carrados* (1923). REF.: *CBA*.

Bramble, Clifford, b.1892, U.S., arson. In 1937, Clifford Bramble confessed to setting thirty-one fires in Sacramento, Calif., and five more in Salt Lake City, Utah. He said his actions "relieved the pressure" of daily living. The fires had caused $2 million in damages. Bramble was sent to an insane asylum.

REF.: *CBA*; Nash, *Almanac of World Crime*.

Brame, Lex, Jr., d.1907, U.S., (unsolv.) mur. A lawyer in his mid-thirties, Brame vanished in 1907 while sitting on the banks of the Mississippi River, in back of a Vicksburg, Miss., hotel. Originally from Jackson, Miss., Lex Brame was seen—according to one report—reading a copy of Eugène Sue's *The Wandering Jew* as he sat by the river, and this infuriated a group of Jew-baiters who bludgeoned him to death. Brame's body, however, was not found. In 1937, a skeleton was unearthed in the cellar of a Vicksburg house once belonging to a member of the racist gang suspected of murdering Brame, and these remains, according to dental charts, were identified as the missing murdered man.

REF.: *CBA*; Nash, *Among the Missing*.

Bramlet, Al, See: **Hanley, Andrew** and **Thomas**.

Bramwell, George William Wilshere, 1808-92, Brit., jur. Drafted the Common Law Procedure Act of 1852. He was ap-

pointed lord justice in 1876. REF.: *CBA*.

Bramwell, Henry, 1919- , U.S., jur. Hearing officer in New York for conscientious military objectors in 1966 and from 1969-75. He was named a judge of the Court of the Eastern District of New York in 1974 by President Gerald Ford. REF.: *CBA*.

Brancati, Dr. Charles, prom. 1928, U.S., count.-miss. per. When last seen, Dr. Charles Brancati, a wealthy Italian immigrant who rose to prominence in the 1920s, was walking slowly toward a New York City subway station. It was Nov. 19, 1928, and at Brancati's specific request, his handyman George Rheinish dropped him off at the station so that he could attend to urgent business in his Manhattan office. Turning to Rheinish, he said, "Paint the place, the whole house!" Puzzled by this, the handyman returned to the lavish estate in Throg's Neck that Brancati called home, to carry out his employer's orders, but Brancati was never seen again.

Missing counterfeiter Dr. Charles Brancati.

The Brancati brothers—Charles, Oreste, Edward, and Ernesto—arrived in the U.S. from their home in Naples, Italy, sometime around 1900. Young Charles was a thrifty immigrant who worked his way through the Columbia College of Physicians and Surgeons as a dishwasher. By the 1920s, he acquired vast real estate holdings and large blocks of stock. At the time of his disappearance, Brancati was estimated to be worth over $1 million. He never married, preferring to live alone in a mansion that once belonged to a Colonial politician in the Bronx.

During the next four months, several communiques were received from Brancati in Canada, Passaic, N.J., and finally London. Concerned, the Brancati brothers reported his disappearance to the police who entered the Morris Mansion. There they found the place in a shambles, and a cryptic note that read: "You Big Villain. If you don't put her out, I'll cut your throat like a sheep's." The police concluded that Dr. Brancati had been kidnapped. The sum of $225,000 had been withdrawn from the brokerage firm of Hardy & Company, and transferred to the private account of Luigi Romano, who like Brancati, was never found. Romano's bank account showed a deposit of $225,000, and a withdrawal of around $224,800.

The theory that Brancati had been kidnapped was disproven when it was learned that the doctor had a criminal record dating back to 1923. He had led a counterfeit ring, and had helped New York racketeer Arnold Rothstein set up a nationwide drug ring. When Rothstein was shot dead at the Park Central Hotel on Nov. 4, 1928, police surmised that Brancati was wrapped up in it. Brancati was declared legally dead in January 1932. See: **Rothstein, Arnold**.

REF.: *CBA*; Nash, *Among The Missing*.

Brancato, Rose, See: **Law, Walter**.

Branch, Elizabeth, and **Branch, Mary**, d.1740, Brit., mur. Young Mary had the same traits as her mother Elizabeth: she was cruel and sadistic toward the kitchen help, and apparently bereft of all human mercies. It was the misfortune of a kindly farmer named Branch to take Elizabeth for his wife. Sometimes, in tantrums of rage, the mother and daughter would hurl plates, forks, and other deadly objects at the domestics. Mr. Branch was all that stood between them and probable torture. When he passed away, most of the servants quit.

But Elizabeth and her equally vicious daughter soon received help in the form of a young replacement from the parish officers, a woman named Jane Buttersworth who was without family or friends. Jane tried hard to please the two but quickly ran afoul of the Branches when she failed to return from a shopping errand at the designated time. The frightened girl devised an excuse that Elizabeth considered wholly unacceptable.

To punish her, Mary pressed her face into the floor while Elizabeth battered her with sharp, sinewy branches. The girl's pleas for mercy fell on deaf ears. She broke away from her

Elizabeth and Mary Branch beating Jane Butterworth.

tormentors for an instant but was chased into the next room and cornered. Armed with brooms, they beat her senseless, and did not stop until she was dead.

The two women tried to conceal their crime, but another maidservant named Ann Somers saw the bleeding body of her friend lying on the floor. Elizabeth confined her in the house and the mother and daughter buried Jane's body that night, satisfied that their crime was foolproof.

The disappearance of two servant girls prompted speculation in the village that they had met with foul play. The coroner, armed with a warrant, quickly uncovered the body of Jane Butterworth. At the trial, defense attorneys claimed that Jane was prone to seizures and violent behavior, which resulted in her fatal injuries. But the Branches were unable to substantiate this claim, and a verdict of Guilty was returned.

Crowds of would-be watchers, avid for the unusual sight of two women being hanged at the same time, were drawn to the area. Officials, afraid of mob violence, took the mother and daughter to a sequestered location far from town. Their deaths, at 3 a.m. on May 3, 1740, were witnessed by only six people.
REF.: *CBA; Newgate Calendar.*

Branch, Mark, 1969-88, U.S., suic.-mur. The celluloid delusions of teenage videophile Mark Branch became an inescapable horror for 18-year-old Sharon Gregory, found stabbed and mutilated in her Greenfield, Mass., home on Oct. 24, 1988. Branch's fascination with horror movies may have been a contributing factor in the brutal death of Gregory, because, as he once explained, "I want to know what it's like to murder someone." His alter ego was Jason, the fictional psychopath in the 1979 film *Friday the 13th.* When Branch cut firewood in back of his parents' house at 112 Meadow Lane in Greenfield, he would sometimes don a leather mask like the one worn by the maniacal killer in *Texas Chainsaw Massacre II.* Branch was a frequent customer at Greenfield's Video Expo One, where, according to owner Bob Quesnel, he rented everything on the shelf that promised blood and gore by the minute. "I could have seen this coming," Quesnel said. "I don't think he would watch a regular movie."

But Branch attended therapy sessions and had begun working in a store. By all accounts, he seemed to be putting his life back in order. Then Sharon Gregory was killed, and Branch, who quickly became a prime suspect, was missing. Quesnel recalled a statement Branch had made nearly four years earlier. "He said that if anything really bloody ever happened around here, people would automatically think he did it because they know he's into it."

Gregory's body was found by her sister in the bathroom of the family home on South Shelburne Road, Greenfield. A medical examiner from the coroner's office concluded that the girl had suffered multiple stab wounds. Police told reporters only that witnesses had observed Branch entering the Gregory home early that day. Based on the identification of Branch's gray Chevette near the murder scene, police issued an all-points bulletin for the young man. Later that day the vehicle was found on Avery Road in Buckland, a secluded spot west of Greenfield in Franklin County. The driver of the car was gone.

Police concentrated their search in the woods near Hog Mountain, but were unable to find a trace of the suspected killer. Michael Duquette, Branch's brother-in-law, conducted his own search of the area but came up with nothing. A full month passed without any new leads, until Nov. 29 when Kevin Purinton found Branch's body while tracking deer in the woods. It was hanging from a tree on Hog Mountain, two miles from where the car had first been found. Purinton had made it his own private mission to locate the remains. "I had told my mother I was going to find him," he said to reporters. "I just had that gut feeling."

Branch was hanging by his boot laces, an apparent suicide. "He's been there awhile," Greenfield Police Chief Joseph La-Chance said, adding that police search parties had come within a hundred yards of the body when searching the densely wooded area. A final identification of the decaying corpse was made at the state police crime lab, closing the book on the "Jason" case. REF.: *CBA.*

Brâncoveanu, Constantin (or **Brincoveanu**), 1654-1714, Rom., assass. Military figure and leader of the Walachian people in what is now modern Romania. He was arrested and killed by the Turks for conducting secret negotiations with Czar Peter I of Russia. REF.: *CBA.*

Brand, Elizabeth, and **Brand, Maria,** and **Griffiths, Mrs.,** prom. 1932, Case of, South Africa, mur. On Jan. 7, 1932, Christian Pieter Brand, a 65-year-old South African farmer in Koedoesbrak, near Koopmansfontein, died after two days of violent convulsions following a dose of "bitter oil," an herbal potion administered to him by his wife, Maria Adriana Griffiths Brand. A neighbor of Brand's, Jacobus Johannes Duffue, had visited the man on the day of his death, and later testified that Brand had burst into tears, then told Duffue that the day before, on Jan. 6, Elizabeth Brand, twenty-nine years old, his wife's sister and married to his brother, had given his wife, Maria, some stomach medicine when Brand requested it. Maria herself had taken a dose, then Elizabeth poured out a generous measure for Brand, who drank it, and later that night went into convulsions. When Duffue left Brand in late afternoon of Jan. 7, his neighbor seemed to be improved. That night, Duffue learned that Brand was dead. He testified that the widow was very upset and did not want a doctor called in, but Duffue insisted that strict legal procedures be followed. Therefore, an autopsy was performed by a Dr. Murphy, who found strychnine in the stomach and liver of the corpse.

In a celebrated trial, unprecedented in the sense that women had never before been accused in a poisoning murder trial in South Africa, the sisters and their mother were charged with murder. The mother, Mrs. Griffiths, eventually was exonerated. Evidence that implicated both sisters included the testimony of two laborers on the Koedoesbrak farm. Hendrik Phillipus Fourie had witnessed many quarrels between the Brands during his several years living and working on the farm and said that after one of these fights, four years prior to Brand's death, Brand, a hypochondriac, had become ill and complained that he had been poisoned. On Dec. 23, 1931, Fourie overheard Elizabeth Brand tell her disgruntled sister, Maria, "I told you long ago, poison the old man. If you haven't the poison, I have some." A few days later, Maria said to Fourie, "I will pay you £50 if you will hide yourself and shoot the old man." When Fourie refused, Mrs. Brand replied, "I was only joking." Another native worker, Johannes Pieter Muller said Brand had told him, on Jan. 7, 1932, "Jan, I am getting the same illness that I had last night. It is the medicine that I drank just now." He did not say who had given him the dose. On Jan. 8, Muller stated, Mrs. Griffiths told him, "If the police come and ask you whether the old baas said anything to you about the medicine he drank, you must say 'no'." Four days after the murder, Elizabeth Brand made a voluntary statement to Justice of the Peace C.H. Mitchell, saying that her sister Maria had told her she was "tired" of her spouse and intended to "give him poison as he must die." Elizabeth called the statement false when she was later charged with murder and committed for trial.

The trial began on May 2, 1932, at the Kimberly Sessions before Mr. Justice Hutton. Despite the considerable evidence against both sisters, the court eventually decided that, because it was impossible to determine which woman had actually poisoned Brand, both must be released. The clinching testimony was that of Dr. John Murphy who revealed that Brand must have died from strychnine administered on Jan. 7, 1932. Although Elizabeth was known to have given him the "bitter oil" on Jan. 6, it could not be proven who gave him the fatal dose on Jan. 7. Maria Griffiths admitted to giving the earlier dose, but emphatically denied having any hand in its preparation and no knowledge of its lethal contents. Releasing the sisters, Judge Hutton explained: "it is impossible to convict either of them without making a tragic mistake, and both must therefore be acquitted."

REF.: Bennett, *Up For Murder; CBA.*

Brand, Samuel, d.1773, U.S., mur. Samuel Brand lived with his parents in their Pennsylvania farmhouse. One night, following a domestic quarrel, young Brand set fire to the residence and pointed a gun at his brother, who sat peaceably in the kitchen. "I'll shoot thee," Brand threatened. "Shoot if thou wilt," the brother replied. He took aim, and fired. Brand was arrested and charged with murder. He was hanged in Lancaster on Dec. 18, 1773.

REF.: *CBA; Nash, Bloodletters and Badmen.*

Brandebury, Lemuel G., b.1810, U.S., jur. Authored various governmental reports. He was appointed by President Millard Fillmore to the territorial court of Utah in 1851. He co-authored *Polygamy Revived In the West* (1852), a report to the President concerning the activities of Mormon polygamists. REF.: *CBA.*

Brandeis, Louis Dembitz, 1856-1941, U.S., jur. Supreme Court justice noted for his advocacy of the eight-hour day, free speech, and a fair minimum wage law. He served as special counsel handling wage and hour cases in California, Illinois, Ohio, and Oregon from 1907-14. He was appointed to succeed associate Supreme Court justice Joseph R. Lamar in 1916 by President Woodrow Wilson. He was confirmed, after four months of heated debate, to become the first Jew appointed to the high court and joined Justice Oliver Wendell Holmes as the second great dissenter. The two liberal-minded jurists were the only members of the court to vote against the majority in *Abrams vs. the United States* (1919). The court upheld the convictions of anti-war activists who had been convicted under the terms of the Espionage Act. He retired in 1939 to work for various Zionist causes and to begin a refugee organization for German exiles. REF.: *CBA.*

Brandenburg, Leopold William August, prom. 1941, U.S., abor.-fraud. On Halloween night, 1941, in Austin, Tex., police picked up a suspect who claimed to be Robert Pitts. Attempting to fingerprint him, they found he had no papillary lines on his fingertips. Tracking down his identity, they realized they were holding Robert J. Philipps, an ex-convict who had committed several robberies and spent time in an Atlanta prison and Alcatraz. Questioning Philipps' former jailmates, FBI agents found one man who remembered hearing about "Doc" Brandenburg.

In Union City, N.J., police located Brandenburg, who had been arrested several times, including once on a charge of abortion and another time for participating in a mail robbery that netted him $100,000. He had repeatedly escaped conviction. But with the new evidence against him, Brandenburg admitted that Philipps had come to him in May 1941 to have his fingerprints altered. Taking the fingers of each hand in turn, Brandenburg had done the operations in his home. Philipps had held the fingers of one hand against his skin for three weeks over transplant sites on his chest, until the skin grew over the fingers. The graft was completed when the skin was peeled away from the chest and the fingertips "modeled." Brandenburg and Philipps both were sentenced to long penitentiary terms.

REF.: *CBA;* Thorwald, *Century of the Detective.*

Brandl, John H., prom. 1982, U.S., fraud. Indicted by a federal grand jury for knowingly accepting worthless collateral in a fraudulent loan scheme that allegedly cost a bank $7 million dollars, a former suburban bank executive drew a jail term and was ordered to make restitution of $447,000.

On Nov. 29, 1982, 43-year-old former Glenview, Ill., bank president John H. Brandl was indicted on 11 counts of making false entries on bank records, mail fraud, and misapplying bank funds from the First Trust & Savings Bank of Glenview. Also charged was Chicago businessman Michael A. Poley, thirty-seven, who operated a holding company out of two penthouse apartments, the company serving as a corporate umbrella for real estate and security guard companies he ran. Allegedly collecting cash for a variety of schemes, including fraudulent condominium conversions, Poley fled from Chicago in 1980 when his businesses began to fall apart, but returned and was kept in custody by federal agents who wanted him to testify against leading crime syndicate figures. Poley fled again before testifying and is believed to be living in Paris.

In the complex scheme, Brandl accepted worthless collateral, including bogus land trusts, for loans to Poley and companies controlled by him. Pleading guilty to two counts of misapplying bank funds, Brandt was sentenced by U.S. District Court Judge Nicholas J. Bua on Mar. 23, 1983, to a six-month prison work-release program and ordered to pay the bank $447,000. As of this writing, Poley has not resurfaced. REF.: *CBA.*

Brandon, Gregory, d.c.1640, Brit., execut. Gregory Brandon, the assistant to the famous English executioner, Derrick, later succeeded him as hangman. Derrick, who had executed the Earl of Essex, his one-time benefactor, seems to have been frequently absent from his post, as Brandon often acted as a substitute for him. In December 1616 Brandon officiated when the Garter King of Arms had a practical joke played on him by York Herald, Ralph Brooke.

Brooke designed some coats of arms and took them to Sir William Segar, saying they were for Gregory Brandon, a London gentleman living in Spain. Segar was told that a waiting ship would carry the arms to Spain, and no further investigation was made into the matter. The arms were sealed after fees for them were paid. Subsequently, after they were presented to the public hangman, the Garter King of Arms was sent to prison by the King for his carelessness. Afterwards, Brandon was always called "Esquire," and the rumor got around that the post of city of London hangman carried with it the right to a coat of arms and the designation of "Gentleman" after the executioner had dispatched anyone for treason. Both Brandon and Derrick were mentioned in poems and other literature of the times. Brandon died in 1640 and was succeeded by his son. See: **Brandon, Richard.**

REF.: Atholl, *Shadow of the Gallows;* Bleackley, *Hangmen of England; CBA;* Laurence, *A History of Capital Punishment.*

Brandon, Mark, d.1944, Brit., mur. On an October evening in 1942 Beatrice Swanson put her three children to bed and walked over to snuggle with her husband, Samuel Swanson. Outside the window of their home a shot shattered the glass and Samuel Swanson slumped forward. His frantic spouse tried to drag him out to their car in an effort to reach Meadville, the nearest town, for help. As she appeared in the doorway, a man jumped her, knocking her unconscious. When she revived and staggered toward the car again, he fired two shots at her and she dropped to the ground. At 5 a.m. Morton Brown, a friend who drove Swanson to work every day, came to pick him up and saw Samuels' body sprawled in the doorway. The Swanson children were still sleeping. Finding Beatrice Swanson unconscious and wounded, Brown carried her back into the house, put her to bed, then went for the police. Officers discovered threads of heavy blue serge cloth on the ground near the house. Later, as Mrs. Swanson lay dying, she said that their hired man, Mark Brandon, had made advances to her. Her description of Brandon was similar to that of the suspect in a Meadville case that the sheriff and undersheriff were working on. Calling Meadville to report the resemblance, they were told that the murder was known to officers there, for it had been related in great detail by a young man in a cafe to an officer having breakfast there. The description of the young man matched that of Brandon again.

Around midnight officers picked up a pedestrian who claimed he was Ted Harris from Phoenix, Ariz. But relatives of Brandon's quickly identified him. When confronted with the evidence of the threads that matched those torn from clothes he had been seen wearing the day before, Brandon confessed. The trial began on Dec. 10 and Brandon was found "Guilty of murder, with the recommendation of the death penalty," on Dec. 24. Later, the case went to higher courts, and Brandon obtained one stay of execution but lost an insanity plea. He was hanged for the double murder on Aug. 10, 1944.

REF.: *CBA*; Cohen, *One Hundred True Crime Stories.*

Brandon, Richard, d.1649, Brit., execut. When his father died in 1640, Richard Brandon, often called "Little Gregory," became executioner. A year later, Richard was a prisoner in Newgate on charges of bigamy, but apparently won acquittal. On May 12, 1641, Brandon executed Stafford, an advisor to Charles I, and on Jan. 10, 1645, Laud, an English prelate accused of high treason. According to the English *Dictionary of National Biography,* Brandon also executed Charles I. He refused to carry out that sentence, but supposedly he was dragged from his bed and forced to decapitate the king, for which he was rewarded £30 as well as an orange stuck full of cloves and a handkerchief from the king's pocket. Although there is contradictory evidence that Brandon carried out the sentence against the king, he is known to have executed the Earl of Holland, the Duke of Hamilton, and Lord Capel. Brandon died on June 20, 1649. See: **Brandon, Gregory; Charles I.**

REF.: Bleackley, *Hangmen of England; CBA;* Laurence, *A History of Capital Punishment.*

Brandreth, Jeremiah, d.1817, Brit., treas. In 1817 Jeremiah Brandreth was condemned, along with two others, for high treason and executed in Nottingham. The three were carried to the place of execution on hurdles, then hanged. After their bodies had been hanging for half an hour, the corpses were cut down and decapitated. The heads were held up at the scaffold's four corners, with the words, "Behold the head of a traitor," to further underscore the shamefulness of treason.

REF.: Brock, *A Casebook of Crime; CBA;* Cooper, *Lesson of the Scaffold.*

Brandstatter, N.L., prom. 1930s, U.S., smug.-suic. Molly Wendt had a quantity of heroin in her possession when apprehended on a steamer bound for Mexico. She named N.L. Brandstatter, as the chief of an international drug smuggling ring, with most of its members in Mexico and others in China. The head of the Shanghai Machinery & Engineering Corporation, Brandstatter found himself trapped in Havana at the time Wendt informed against him. He was refused entry into Mexico, where he had already shipped thirty-seven pieces of luggage, and as he was wanted in the U.S., the narcotics smuggler booked passage on the *S.S. Oriente* heading for Spain. When U.S. secret agents in Havana alerted the government back home of Brandstatter's plan,

the ship was rerouted to Spain via New York. The morning the ship entered New York harbor, the wanted man went on deck, saw the Statue of Liberty, and realized he was caught. Brandstatter returned to his stateroom and hanged himself with the sash of his robe.

REF.: *CBA;* Roark, *Coin of Contraband.*

Brann, William Cowper, 1855-98, U.S., writer-gunman. William Cowper Brann was a frontier journalist whose invective and vituperation appearing in the newspapers and magazines he published caused him to be repeatedly attacked and finally killed in a Texas gunfight. Born Jan. 5, 1855, in Cole County, Ill., Brann became a newspaperman early in life and moved with his family in 1886 to Texas where he worked for the Galveston *Tribune.* He later worked on the Houston *Post* with such literary luminaries as O. Henry and M.E. Foster. Brann specialized in stinging, biting editorials which earned him myriad enemies. He started a magazine in Austin, Texas, in 1892 which he called *The Iconoclast.* He sold the magazine and later started it again in Waco, Texas, where his enemies beat him up many times and even wrecked his press. Yet, this outspoken journalist, whose motto was to attack "injustice, intolerance, and stupidity," saw *The Iconoclast* rise in circulation until it had more than 100,000 national subscribers. Brann dipped his pen once too often in acid and T.E. Davis, one of his most bitter enemies, read an editorial that caused him to seek out Brann on the streets of Waco on Apr. 1, 1898. The editor, who also wore a gun and had been in many close brushes, met Davis on the street. Davis, a lightning draw, pulled his pistol and shot Brann in the side. Brann, whirling, yanked his six-gun from its holster and fired off four shots, all of which struck Davis and killed him instantly. Brann died a short time later.

REF.: Bartholomew, *The Biographical Album of Western Gunfighters; CBA.*

Brannan, Joshua, prom. 1925, U.S., mur. The Kentucky sawmill camp where Joshua Brannan and Boris Beary both worked was notorious for weekends of excessive drinking and aggressive behavior. Beary was married, but had been spending a great deal of time with Brannan's eight-months pregnant wife. The level of hostility had gotten so intense that Brannan had recently purchased a new pistol. On Saturday, May 2, 1925, Beary got drunk enough to follow Brannan home, presumably after again flirting with his co-worker's wife. When Beary forced his way into their house, Brannan shot and killed him. A man who surveyed the scene of the crime just after the shooting said Brannan's wife was temporarily trapped inside the logging camp house when Beary's corpse lay in the doorway, and a plank had to be taken off the back of the lodging so she could exit, as she refused to step over the dead body.

Sentenced to life in the state penitentiary, Brannan was paroled early. His spouse divorced him not long after the murder and soon remarried, dying in 1970. Brannan also married again, dying in the late seventies.

REF.: *CBA;* Montell, *Killings.*

Branson, Edith May Olive, See: **Pinet, François.**

Branson, Sir George Arthur Harwin, 1871-1951, Brit., jur. First called to the bar by the Inner Temple in 1899, and served as judge of the King's Bench Division of the High Court from 1921-40. He presided over many well known cases including those of Alfred Arthur Kopsch, Tony Mancini, and Reginald Ivor Hinks. REF.: *CBA.*

Branson, William, prom. 1916-20, U.S., mur. Convicted in 1916 of murdering, on Oct. 8, 1915, William Booth, a rancher in Yamhill county and the husband of Anna Booth, with whom Branson apparently was involved, the young man was tried, convicted of second-degree murder in 1916, and sentenced to life in prison. The decision was later appealed and reversed on the basis of improper jury instructions. In 1917 Branson again was tried, convicted, and given a life sentence. He was sent to the state penitentiary in Salem, Ore., on Mar. 3, 1917. The state parole board became so convinced of his innocence—one of the central questions in the trial apparently had been whether he or Anna

Booth had actually pulled the trigger—that they wrote to Governor Olcott asking his release, explaining, "We...are satisfied after a full and complete investigation of this case that the accused was not guilty of the crime with which he was charged." Both the warden of the penitentiary, Louis Compton, and the state hospital superintendent, Dr. R. Lee Steiner, added their names to the parole board's recommendation for pardon. According to Olcott's statement when he paroled Branson, the accused had been (twice) convicted on "the sheerest kind of circumstantial evidence," and another man had confessed to committing the crime and was held afterwards in the insane asylum for life.

Anna Booth was paroled on Jan. 31, 1920. Branson received his unconditional pardon in September of the same year. REF.: *CBA*.

Brantley, John, d.1870, U.S., Case of, mur. John Brantley, the dissolute son of a wealthy Alabama farmer, was in his early forties when he married Minerva Brantley, a woman who was a morphine addict. Brantley despised his neighbor John Howard, who lived near their small plantation in the Selma area and who had a longtime feud with the Brantley clan. When Howard was found dead in a swamp, police arrested Brantley on suspicion of murder. Released on a technicality, he fled to the village of Shuqualak, Miss., to hide out. His wife sent him money and they decided that she should come to see him. In the early morning hours of Dec. 4, 1870, Brantley, waiting at the train station for her to arrive, had fallen asleep, when a figure on the platform shot him, killing him instantly. Deputy Sheriff Simmons found Mrs. Brantley's letter on her husband's corpse and learned from a passenger on the train that a woman had peered out at Shuqualak and asked for her husband, continuing on to Macon when there was no reply. Simmons found Mrs. Brantley, who vaguely rattled on about her many problems after he told her Brantley had been killed. According to Simmons, "She made an effort to cry but did not shed many tears." The night prior to the killing, several Shuqualak residents had noticed a stranger on a gray horse lurking about the station for some time, carrying an ill-concealed double-barreled shotgun.

Following the tracks of the horse, which had a worn shoe on one foot, Simmons rode day and night, covering thirty-four miles, to apprehend a man named Joseph Eskridge, whom he caught off guard and arrested. Eskridge and Mrs. Brantley were lovers. Because he had been friends with Eskridge, and even trusted him enough to give him power of attorney over some of his business affairs in the year he hid out, Brantley had no suspicions of their affair. Eskridge and Mrs. Brantley had taken out a $20,000 life insurance policy on Brantley. Afterward Eskridge went to the district attorney and suggested that the brother and brother-in-law of the murdered John Howard should be told they could find Brantley at a certain hotel, trying to set up a confrontation that would result in Brantley's death.

Simmons established further evidence against the couple with a postcard marked "Demopolis" sent by Mrs. Brantley to her spouse. Eskridge and Mrs. Brantley, on their way to Brantley, had stayed a night in Demopolis and had registered for two nights as a married couple in a hotel in Livingstone, where together they purchased the shotgun with which Brantley was killed.

Both Eskridge and Brantley were brought to trial. Public feeling existed in Mrs. Brantley's favor, and magistrates released her on a $1,000 bail. In an odd action, Mrs. Brantley then wrote to her lover, Eskridge, and delivered—through a police officer—a missive that called him affectionate names, in which she promised to get him released "cost what it may." Mrs. Brantley then started proceedings to collect the life insurance taken out on her late husband.

The life insurance company quickly established all the evidence against the couple and refused to pay. Mrs. Brantley disappeared. Eskridge escaped from jail, but was captured, tried, convicted, and sentenced to death. But during the Alabama governor's temporary absence, a lieutenant-governor apparently wrongfully accepted a $500 bribe for Eskridge's pardon and he was released from prison.

REF.: *CBA*; Dilnot, *Triumphs of Detection*.

Bras Coupé (AKA: Squier, The Brigand of the Swamps), d.1837, U.S., rob.-mur. A product of the ante-bellum South, Bras Coupé was a giant slave, about six-foot-six-inches, owned by General William de Buys, who also owned one of the largest plantations outside of New Orleans. First known as Squier, the giant black was a marvel to behold when he performed African tribal dances such as the bamboula and the calinda, the latter requiring incredible gyrating, leaping, and contortionist movements, all stemming from voodoo ceremonial rites. Bras Coupé would perform his wild dances with hundreds of other slaves who were brought to New Orleans' ancient Circus Square. Here, once a week, between 4 and 6 p.m., slaves were allowed to vent their frustration and anger in wild, abandoned dancing. This custom began in 1817 and continued until the Civil War. The square itself was renamed Congo Square for obvious reasons, and Bras Coupé became the star attraction. He would select a new black female slave each week and whirl, toss, and throw her about until she fell exhausted, but he would continue leaping and stomping until overseers called the curfew and ended the frenetic celebration.

Bras Coupé dancing the bamboula in Congo Square.

De Buys was tolerant of his prized possession, teaching Bras Coupé to shoot and hunt, and even loaning him his best rifles to hunt wild game in the swamps and bayous about New Orleans. He learned to fire a weapon with both hands because, he said, he had had a dream where he lost an arm. In 1834 he was shot in a swamp by whites who thought he was a runaway slave, the bullet shattering his arm which had to be amputated. The loss of his arm embittered Bras Coupé; he became moody and developed an explosive temperament. Then he tried to run away, but when he was captured and returned to his owner, the indulgent de Buys refused to have him whipped or punished. Instead, the general lectured his errant slave on the proper behavior for a favored possession. The one-armed giant stood mute, then ran away permanently to the swamps, where he formed a band of other runaway blacks who preyed on white travelers and made robbing forays into small villages and hamlets. (Bras Coupé would later serve as the role model for Robert Penn Warren's character Rau-Ru in his novel of the Old South, *Band of Angels*.)

Soon the once-esteemed slave became known as The Brigand of the Swamp. So notorious did Bras Coupé's reputation become that unruly children all over Louisiana were warned that if they did not mind their manners they would "be trimmed by Bras Coupé." The outlaw band swelled to several dozen cutthroats, and Bras Coupé led his men into New Orleans itself on raids where he attacked districts of the city, looting homes, murdering helpless whites, including women and children. More than fifty deaths were attributed to his murderous gang within three years. The outlaws, which even included some renegade whites, would strike in the middle of the night, race through houses and scoop up valuables, then torch the house and shoot and knife to death all the occupants while they slept in their beds. Bras Coupé became the most notorious black outlaw in the U.S., and it was believed that if he could call enough dissident blacks and disenfranchised whites to his banner, the South would suffer another slave revolt worse than the 1831 uprising led by Nat Turner.

To the oppressed blacks, Bras Coupé became a heroic and legendary creature. He could not be shot, it was said at their campfire meetings, since Bras Coupé's skin was as hard as iron and no bullet could penetrate it. He could not be burned since he used voodoo herbs to cover it. He could not be caught by the vigilantes and troops following him into the swamps since mystical fogs would envelope the pursuers and whisk them off to far countries. Those who hunted him through the eerie bayou country told bone-chilling tales about this fierce bandit. If they stumbled upon him in the gloom, hunters were cautioned to never look into his eyes since his stony stare could wither the limbs or even kill. Pursuers camping in the swamps could hear his booming, sinister laughter echoing through the mangroves. Worse, the brigand had turned cannibal by 1836, or so it was claimed. One eyewitness vigilante reported that while hiding in thick brush he watched Bras Coupé kill four pursuing soldiers with his one hand, then tear them limb from limb and make a meal of them, hideously devouring their uncooked flesh.

Such ghastly tales, along with very real accounts of the brigand's murders and robberies, caused New Orleans Mayor Dennis Prieur to place a $2,000 reward on Bras Coupé's head. The New Orleans *Picayune* urged the capture or killing of the outlaw, describing him in one editorial as a "semi-devil and a fiend in human shape whose life was one of crime and depravity." The myth of this outlaw evaporated on July 18, 1873. Fisherman Francisco Garcia was sitting in a boat, the *Bayou St. John,* when he was spotted by Bras Coupé who shot at him. Garcia quickly paddled ashore and, grabbing a club, attacked the giant. Bras Coupé staggered back from the blows, weakened by a bullet wound he had received on Apr. 6, 1837, when two white bounty hunters shot him. Garcia clubbed the outlaw to death, then put the huge body into a sack and rode with it to New Orleans in his cart.

Garcia uncovered the body as he entered the city so that thousands of slaves could see his trophy. The blacks wept to see their hero slain and carted to city hall. Here the fisherman jumped from the cart and ran inside to claim the $2,000 reward. After much haggling with Mayor Prieur, he was paid $250. (There was a claim that Garcia deserved no reward at all and that he should have been locked up instead; some said he had actually been a member of Bras Coupé's band and had betrayed his leader, killing the outlaw as he slept in Garcia's swamp hut.) The brigand's badly beaten corpse was taken to the Place d'Armes and dumped next to the fountain. For days the carcass rotted in the hot sun while thousands of slaves were forced to march past it in single file and view the remains. This was to teach all slaves that revolt against the white South meant death. (A similar action was taken by Mexican authorities following the 1919 assassination of the great Mexican leader Emiliano Zapata, whose body was gruesomely exhibited to dissuade his followers from continuing their struggle for independence.) The display did nothing but anger slaves, and many resolved to escape their brutal masters. The legend of Bras Coupé was passed on from one generation of blacks to another, until few of the real facts remained inside of what is now a traditional image of a black Robin Hood.

REF.: Asbury, *The French Quarter; CBA;* Nash, *Almanac of World Crime;* (FICTION) Warren, *Band of Angels.*

Brattle, Thomas, 1658-1713, U.S., witchcraft. One of the organizers of the Brattle Street Church in Cambridge, Mass., but is better known for his fierce opposition to Cotton Mather and his sons. He condemned the Salem witchcraft trials. See: **Mather, Cotton, Salem Witch Trials.** REF.: *CBA.*

Braun, Thomas Eugene (AKA: Mike Ford), 1948- , and **Maine, Leonard,** 1948- , U.S., mur. Thomas Braun was born in the state of Washington. When barely into his adolescence, he was forced to shoot the family dog because his drunken father thought the dog was "a chicken killer." On Aug. 17, 1967, Braun left his job as a gas station attendant in Ritzville, Wash., to ride off with Lenny Maine. They took with them a .22-caliber Luger

and a Frontier Colt single-action .22-caliber pistol.

Heading for Seattle, they overtook a late-model Skylark driven by 22-year-old Deanna Buse on Route 72 outside Richmond. They motioned her over to the side of the road on the pretense that her tires were going flat. When she got out of the car, Braun aimed a gun at her head and told her to get into their car. Maine got in the Skylark and followed Braun to a secluded spot near Echo Lake. There Braun shot Buse five times. He and Maine drove on to Seattle, where they abandoned their car and took the Skylark.

The next day, Braun and Maine crossed into Oregon and tried to register at a resort motel. The owner was suspicious of the unkempt strangers, and asked to see their vehicle registration. They drove off, but had a flat tire a few miles away. Samuel Ledgerwood, who had just come from his favorite fishing spot, offered to help. Braun pumped two shots into Ledgerwood's head, and then set fire to the Skylark. The two killers drove off in Ledgerwood's shiny new Buick. They continued south to Northern California. On Route 120, Braun stopped to pick up two 17-year-old hitchhikers, Susan Bartolomei and Timothy Luce.

Killer Thomas Braun, left front, with co-murderer Leonard Maine behind him.

Early the next morning, the Mease family stopped their car on the same highway to investigate what they thought was an accident. They found Susan Bartolomei lying on the side of the road, barely conscious. She said that two men named Mike and John from Oklahoma had shot them, killing Timothy. Meanwhile, searchers found the body of Deanna Buse. Oregon police reported the murder of Samuel Ledgerwood, and soon the manhunt had begun as three states pooled their resources. Several days later, Maine and Braun were captured at a motel in Jamestown, Calif., after Constable Ed Chafin noticed the green Buick with Oregon plates. The boys were barely awake in their rooms when the police broke in. Braun reached for a gun but was subdued. After being shown still photos and movies of the victims, they confessed to their crimes.

On Dec. 2, 1968, Superior Court Judge Joseph Kelly of San Jose, Calif., sentenced Braun to die in the San Quentin gas chamber. However, the sentence was later commuted to life imprisonment. Leonard Maine also received a life sentence.

REF.: *CBA;* Nash, *Bloodletters and Badmen.*

Braunsdorf, Eugene, prom. 1950, Case of, U.S., mur. Eugene Braunsdorf's daughter, Virginia Braunsdorf, was born a spastic and the father struggled to keep his child at home. Once he worked four jobs, as a music teacher, a registrar for Detroit Business University, a Ford assembly line worker, and a bass violist for the Detroit Symphony Orchestra. In 1942, Braunsdorf, under tremendous strain, became ill and decided to invest all his earnings into a flower shop in an attempt to recover his finances. Forced to sell the shop at a loss, he resigned himself to committing his child to a sanitarium where he visited her regularly, worrying constantly about her future.

Then one day in the spring of 1949 he picked up Virginia from the sanitarium, telling attendants he was taking her to the dentist. On a side road he stopped the car, placed a pillow behind his daughter's head, and fired a bullet into her skull. He then shot himself twice, passed out, came to, and shot himself twice more. Braunsdorf survived and was charged with murder, judged to be sane, and ordered to stand trial. At the end of May 1950, however, a Detroit jury found him "Not Guilty by reason of temporary insanity at the time of the killing." REF.: *CBA*.

Bravo, Florence Ricardo, 1846-78, Case of, Brit., mur. The murder of Charles Delauny Turner Bravo proved to be one of the most sensational cases of the Victorian era, creating a *cause célèbre* trial in which the victim's wife was acquitted but remained guilty in the minds of her peers. The successful, 30-year-old lawyer died on Apr. 21, 1876, following three days in which he writhed in terrible agony, poisoned, it was later determined, by antimony. Watching the wealthy Bravo die was his wife Florence, her companion, Mrs. Jane Cannon Cox, and a bevy of doctors who were baffled at his condition and helpless in recommending a cure. Doctors who originally ascribed the illness to tainted food eaten on Apr. 18, 1876, were nonplussed as to why Florence Bravo and Cox, who had eaten the same food, were not also stricken.

The Bravos lived in a fashionable home, called The Priory, on Bedford Hill Road in Belham. With them lived some servants and Cox, all occupying separate rooms in the sprawling mansion. Florence and Charles Bravo maintained separate rooms since Florence had been ill after her third miscarriage. They had been repeatedly unsuccessful in having children, which may have been a source of agitation between them. The Bravos had only been married five months, having wed on Dec. 7, 1875. Florence, though twenty-five, had a rather spectacular past. She was already a wealthy widow and was having a torrid affair with an elderly physician when Bravo met her. She had been married to Captain Alexander Ricardo, of the Grenadier Guards, but Ricardo suffered from accute alcoholism and died in a drunken stupor in 1871, leaving a fortune to his young bride, more than £40,000. The rich widow had then taken up with Dr. James Manby Gully, a 64-year-old phrenologist (a criminal science long since abandoned, one that claimed to determine criminal heredity and criminal tendencies from the shape of the human head, length of ears, thickness of lips, and other physical characteristics).

Gully was an active man, apparently having a strong sexual appetite, given the torrid love letters he exchanged with Florence Ricardo. His attraction was obviously his lofty station in life. Born in Kingston, Jam., Gully was well known for inventing the Water Cure. He was also a playwright of some note which brought him into the literary world where he was both friend and physician to such famous men as Charles Dickens, Alfred Tennyson, Thomas Carlyle, Bulwer Lyton, and British Prime Minister Benjamin Disraeli. Florence, upon her husband's death, stayed with friends, the Brooks family, who lived in Tooting. Here, in 1871, she met and befriended Jane Cox, a homely 43-year-old widow whose husband had died in 1867 and who had been forced to become a governess to raise her three sons. Oddly, before meeting Florence Ricardo, Cox had known Joseph Bravo, Charles' father. The Cox family had settled in Jamaica and met Bravo there. When Cox's husband died, she left Jamaica and returned to England and was hired by Mrs. Brooks. (The strange coincidence existed that Gully, Cox, and Bravo family members were all from Jamaica or had business interests there, a fact that later led detectives to speculate that voodoo or black magic was involved in the odd death of Charles Bravo, but this remained pure conjecture.)

When Florence met Cox she hired her as her own ladies' companion but when Charles Bravo met Florence through the Brooks family, he displayed an instant dislike for the aging governess. Florence was immediately attracted to the handsome and sophisticated Bravo and decided to end her relationship with Gully, preferring a man more her own age. She told Bravo of her ties to the elderly physician and promised she would break off the relationship. This she did, writing to Bravo on Oct. 21, 1875: "Need I tell you that I have written to the Dr. to say that I must never see his face again. It is the right thing to do in every respect, whether we marry or whether we do not." Bravo, apparently wanted Florence to certify in writing that she was finished with Gully. He himself had a mistress at Maidenhead and he broke off with her shortly before his marriage to Florence. He was very formal and not a little aloof when he informed Florence that he was "quite satisfied to make you my wife."

Bravo, though seeming to be well-to-do, had a good practice but less money in the family coffers than what most people believed. He was later accused of marrying Florence for her money and property which, under British law at the time, would become his once he and Florence were man and wife. When they were wed and honeymooning in Bravo's parents' home at Palace Green in Kensington, Charles received a vicious, anonymous letter in which the writer stated that he had married Gully's mistress for her wealth. A witness later testifying at Florence's trial stated that when Charles and Florence had been engaged, a friend of Bravo's congratulated him. Bravo's response was: "Damn your congratulations! I only want the money!"

Following the wedding, the Bravos moved to the Priory where they settled in with Cox, and assorted footmen and maids. After three miscarriages, Florence remained in fragile health but she compounded her physical problems by drinking heavily, no doubt to dull her apprehensions about not being able to have children. Charles Bravo seemed solicitous but distant. He began to suffer from neuralgia and toothaches which were later attributed to psychological problems stemming from his wife's repeated miscarriages. He began to rub laudanum on his gums to sooth his aching teeth. Both Charles and Florence seemed well enough to travel to London on Apr. 18, 1876, riding in their private coach, resplendent with coachman and footman. Florence returned to the Priory before Charles, who stayed to have lunch with friends. He was in good spirits when returning home and he spoke lightheartedly about the future when he, Florence, and Cox sat down to dinner at 7:40 p.m. They ate heartily, dining on whiting, roast lamb and anchovy eggs on toast. Following dinner, Bravo began to drink burgundy and his wife and Cox joined him, drinking heavily. In fact, the women reportedly downed two full bottles of sherry, although several reports later claimed that Cox was not feeling well and retired early. It was after 9 p.m. when the Bravos and Cox went to bed, Bravo and Florence sleeping in separate rooms due to Florence's weakened condition. Shortly before 10 p.m. Charles Bravo cried out in shrieking pain. A maid answered his call and he asked for hot water and his wife. The maid summoned Cox but by the time she entered Bravo's room, she found him unconscious. Florence was roused from a deep sleep and immediately called doctors. Bravo began to vomit repeatedly and found it difficult to keep any kind of food in his stomach. Specialists, including the famous Dr. William Gull, physician to Queen Victoria, were called in, but not one of these imminent doctors could diagnose Bravo's illness. Gull thought Bravo had somehow accidentally poisoned himself, but, according to some reports, Bravo himself told Gull that he believed that he had been poisoned. The patient was asked: "Mr. Bravo, what have you taken?"

"I rubbed my gums with laudanum," he replied.

"Laudanum won't explain your symptoms, Mr. Bravo."

On Apr. 21, 1876, after three days of terrible suffering, Charles Bravo died. Gull, who had already stated that he believed Bravo had died of "irritant poisoning," suggested that an autopsy be conducted. A post-mortem was held at St. Thomas' Hospital which revealed no natural cause of death. The large intestine was ulcerated which indicated an irritant poison. Dr. Redwood, a

The Bravos strolling across the lawns of the Priory in Balham, a residence of Victorian splendor.

Florence with first husband Alexander Ricardo.

Florence Bravo at the time of her trial.

The eccentric Charles Bravo, top left, who loved his wife from afar and encouraged another man to lavish affections upon her; Dr. James Manby Gully, Florence's doddering lover, top center, whose brilliant career was wrecked by Bravo's murder; at right, Florence and Mrs. Cox tending to the poisoned and dying Charles Bravo, April 20, 1876; bottom left, the inscrutable Mrs. Jane Cox, lady's companion, who did more harm than good when she appeared in court, below right, to testify for her dear friend Florence and almost got her convicted.

pathologist, reported that he had found antimony present in the intestine, that twenty to thirty grains had been administered or taken. Redford's report stated that "there is one form in which antimony could have been administered, and that is emetic tartar. It is soluble in water and tasteless." Following these revelations, an informal inquest was held at the Priory on Apr. 25, 1876. So relaxed was this hearing that Florence served refreshments to the jury members who quickly decided that, although antimony was, indeed, present in the body of the deceased, no blame for Charles Bravo's death could be fixed and the verdict was left open. It was widely believed by the time of the inquest that Bravo had committed suicide. Cox was later to state that Bravo had said to her, and her alone, when she first responded to his call for help that he had brought about his own end. Cox quoted Bravo as having said: "Mrs. Cox, I have taken poison...Don't tell Florence!"

After reviewing the cursory inquiry, the Lord Chief Justice quashed the inquest findings and ordered another inquest which was more or less a trial of either Florence Bravo or Cox, or both, the inquest held at the Bedford Hotel in Balham on July 11, 1876. One of the first chores of the inquest was an inspection of Bravo's remains by jurymen who visited the Lower Norwood Cemetery and here beheld, through a glass panel which had been inserted into the coffin lid, the horrid remains of the deceased. One description of those ghostly remains had it that "the face had acquired the dark hue of a mummy, and the teeth were almost entirely black." Whether or not this funereal visitation was designed to emphasize the claim Bravo had been poisoned was never made clear, although this seemed to be the implication. Bravo's past was then revealed in almost every painful detail, her marriage to the alcoholic Ricardo, her long affair with Gully and her peculiar relationship with Cox. The thrust of inquiries was apparently aimed at a collusive effort to murder Bravo by Florence, Cox, and even Gully himself, so that Florence would be free to resume her relationship with Gully.

The elderly doctor was called in to testify, or, more to the point, defend himself. He nervously admitted his affair with Florence and even one of his servants, George Griffith, came forward to state that fully six years earlier, in 1869, he had purchased two ounces of emetic tartar for Gully, saying that this was to be used as horse medicine. Gully, who said that he felt his "position most bitterly," defended himself against the unspoken accusation that he had helped Florence Bravo murder her husband. Cox then testified that Bravo had not only said to her that he had taken poison but she added at this late date that his *full* statement to her was "I have taken poison *for Dr. Gully*." The meaning here was that Charles Bravo had committed suicide so that Florence could be with her elderly physician. Said Cox: "I thought of Mrs. Bravo. It was in thinking of her that I withheld the words 'for Dr. Gully' in my statements to the coroner." Cox went on to portray a husband with a violent streak of jealousness, saying that Bravo regularly accused Florence of being attracted to other men and flirting with them. He had even struck her once, said Cox, in a fit of jealous rage. Without being too explicit in that delicate era, Bravo was also shown to be a man with a ravenous sexual appetite and that he had made demands upon an unwell wife. If nothing else, the inquiry established Charles Bravo to be a greedy, self-centered, sexually overactive, inconsiderate brute.

Reversing the earlier "open verdict" of the previous inquest, the second coroner's jury concluded that Bravo had been wilfully murdered, adding that "there is insufficient evidence to fix the guilt upon any person or persons." Florence and Cox were dismissed. The result for Gully was a ruined reputation and a badly damaged practice. The enigmatic Cox had not helped matters, implying that Gully had aided Florence in murdering Bravo. Cox, it was later rumored, had murdered Bravo herself, feeling that he was about to fire her and therefore poisoning him to secure her position with Florence. The prevalent conjecture was that *both* Florence and Cox had killed Bravo by dumping antimony into his decanter of burgundy on the night of their last family dinner, drinking with him in joyous toast after toast to make sure that he consumed enough of the tainted wine to kill him, and getting necessarily drunk in the process. This was a plan put into effect shortly after the marriage, it was said, to free Florence from a deceiving and domineering spouse and to allow her to go back to the kind, patient and understanding Gully.

Florence not only lived out the rest of her short life with the stigma of possibly having murdered Bravo, but it was said that she had poisoned her first husband, Ricardo, in a similar manner, that the dashing guards officer was not an alcoholic and that Florence had merely used this malady as a screen to her having dosed *his* wine in order to obtain his considerable money. Following the second inquest, Florence moved to Southsea where, on Sept. 13, 1878, she died of what physicians diagnosed as accute alcoholism. Some claimed she died a lonely woman, haunted by the murder or murders she had committed, or driven half mad after being condemned out-of-hand for a crime she did not commit. Black rumors did not cease following her death. One story insisted that Cox had murdered Florence in 1878 to keep her from revealing how they had both connived to kill Bravo—a wild and improbable tale since Cox had left for Jamaica after the second inquest and settled on the sun-filled island to contemplate her troubled past.

Florence Bravo's after-death image was fixed as that of a murderer, thanks to a popular parody penned by some anonymous wag, much the same way Lizzie Borden (see entry) after her was condemned through history by a memorable bit of doggerel. In Florence Bravo's case, the parody read:

When lovely woman stoops to folly
And finds her husband in the way,
What charm can soothe her melancholy
What art can turn him into clay?

The only means her aim to cover,
And save herself from prison locks,
And repossess her ancient lover
Are Burgundy and Mrs. Cox!

See: **Borden, Lizzie.**
REF.: Bridges, *How Charles Bravo Died; CBA;* Curtin, *Noted Murder Mysteries;* Dunbar, *Blood in the Parlor;* Hall, *The Bravo Mystery and Other Cases;* Hartman, *Victorian Murderesses;* Jones, *Unsolved!;* Lambton, *Echoes of Causes Celebres;* Nash, *Open Files;* Pearson, *More Studies in Murder;* Roughead, *Classic Crimes;* ____, *The Murderer's Companion;* Thompson, *Poisons and Poisoners;* Thompson, *Poison Mysteries Unsolved;* Villiers, *Riddles of Crime;* Williams, *Suddenly at the Priory;* Wilson, *Encyclopedia of Murder.* (FICTION) Lowndes, *What Really Happened;* Rickard, *Not Sufficient Evidence;* Shearing, *So Evil My Love;* (FILM) *So Evil My Love,* 1948.

Bravo, Nicolas, c.1786-1854, Mex., treas. Leader of rebellion against President Guadalupe Victoria in 1827 and was defeated and banished. He returned later to serve General Santa Anna. REF.: *CBA.*

Bravo-Murillo, Juan Gonzalez, 1803-73, Spain, lawyer. Founded the first law journal in his country, the *Boletin de Jurisprudencia* (1835). He was prime minister from 1851-52, and exiled from 1854-56. REF.: *CBA.*

Bravos, George, 1911-88, U.S., org. crime. A long-time loanshark and gambling operator for the syndicate on Chicago's North Side, George Bravos had gone into Florida retirement after local and federal officers began closing down mob gambling operations on Chicago in the early 1960s. Bravos was called back to Chicago by his superiors, Gus Alex and Dave Yarros, according to reports, and ordered to revamp and expand loan-sharking and gambling in Chicago's Near North Side. One of his victims was a contracting firm owned by three brothers who, in 1965, borrowed $165,000 from Bravos and his brutal enforcer, William Messino, at 110 percent interest or $1,500 a day. The brothers paid back $303,000 in principal and interest but Bravos still insisted they owed an additional $124,000. When they failed to pay, Messino and others kidnapped and viciously beat the brothers, who, to save their lives, went to the police. Bravos, Messino, and others were convicted of loan-sharking and sent to prison. After being released, Bravos resumed his old position as head of the bookie operations on the Near North Side. He died of natural causes on Nov. 23, 1988. REF.: *CBA*.

Brawley, Tawana, 1972- , Case of, U.S., rape. On Nov. 28, 1987, Tawana Brawley was found in the courtyard of the Pavillion apartment complex, in Wappingers Falls, N.Y., inside a plastic garbage bag, dog excrement smeared on her body, her hair crudely chopped, burn marks on her legs, and the words "KKK" and "Nigger" scrawled in charcoal on her chest. Brawley had been missing for four days. Through family members, Brawley said she had been abducted, raped, and sodomized by six white men who then put her in a bag and left her in the road. At the hospital, a black policeman asked Brawley who had assaulted her. She reached toward his badge, then scrawled "white cop" on a piece of paper.

The case immediately became the focus of a turmoil over racial politics. Actor Bill Cosby and *Essence* Magazine offered a $25,000 reward for information. Heavyweight boxing champion Mike Tyson donated a $100,000 scholarship for Brawley. Three black activists took charge of the case, lawyers Alton H. Maddox, Jr. and C. Vernon Mason, and religious leader Reverend Al Sharpton. Sharpton accused New York governor Mario Cuomo of racism and compared State Attorney General Robert Abrams to Adolph Hitler. Following her advisers' instructions, Brawley refused to give any further details.

The case became more confused, by charges of an unjust legal system. Brawley's story was inconsistent. She initially claimed to have been beaten and raped, then later said there was no rape, but that other kinds of sexual abuse had occurred. Forensic tests revealed no evidence of sexual assault or a beating. Three months after the incident, Brawley's family added a charge of theft, saying $600 worth of gold jewelry had been stolen. Her family also claimed Brawley had been left outdoors, but tests showed no signs of exposure, and several people had seen her at the Pavillion complex during the time when she said she had been left outside. Other witnesses at the Pavillion described seeing Brawley alone, on foot, the morning after she was supposed to have been abducted. Brawley's mother, Glenda, said she and her sister had tried to report Tawana's disappearance several times but that police did not respond until Saturday at 2:02 p.m., seventeen minutes after the girl was found. Charges of coverup and conspiracy were made, and there were demonstrations. Sharpton, Mason, and nine others—including folk singer Pete Seeger—were arrested at an Apr. 4, 1988, rally in Brooklyn. Sharpton served a fifteen-day jail sentence for his part in the rally.

Brawley was advised not to testify until a new special prosecutor was named. When Governor Cuomo refused to replace Abrams, Brawley remained unavailable as a witness in her own case.

By May 1988 acting police chief of Wappingers Falls, William McCord, said, "A lot of local people feel it's just a story...All these people investigating, and they keep coming up with nothing to go on. It's hard to believe six people would be involved in a crime and no one knows anything about it." By Sept. 27, 1988, a grand jury had completed a 170-page investigation of Brawley's story, finding no evidence of kidnapping, rape, or any other crime. Attorney General Abrams said, "We have the facts. We have solved the case. The allegations she (Brawley) had made are false." Abrams attributed the controversy that surrounded the trial to the "hucksterism and opportunism" of her advisers. On Apr. 2, 1989, Samuel M. McClease, who said he had proof that would discredit Brawley's advisers—claiming he had been hired by Sharpton to bug Mason and Maddox—was brought to trial on perjury charges. The ten tapes he gave federal prosecutors turned out to be blank. McClease said someone had substituted the blanks for the ones he said would have proved his charges. REF.: *CBA*.

Bray, Sir **Reginald More**, 1842-1923, Brit., jur. Appointed to the bench in 1904 and served for nineteen years. REF.: *CBA*.

Braybrook Street Massacre, See: **Roberts, Harry Maurice**.

Brazee, Andrew Washburne, b.1826, U.S., jur. District attorney of Lockport, N.Y., from 1856-59. He was appointed judge of the Colorado Territorial Court by President Ulysses S. Grant, and reappointed in 1875. REF.: *CBA*.

Brazier, Nicola, c.1950-70, Brit., mur. On Sept. 17, 1970, Nicola Brazier was found dead, shot in the back of the head, and her body bound with wire, in the woods near Broxbourne, Hertfordshire. Brazier had last been seen driving from her High Street, Whitechurch, Buckinghamshire, home to go to work at her job as a company representative in the Broxbourne area. A few days after the murder, police found several of her belongings, along with a checkbook and a pistol engraved with the number 40084, in a locker at the Euston train station. Around that same time, a young man committed suicide by throwing himself under a train near Hoddesdon, Hertfordshire, not far from where Brazier was murdered. Following routine procedure, police fingerprinted the man's corpse. There was no reason to connect the suicide with Brazier's murder.

Toward the end of December, with the Brazier case still unsolved, police rechecked all the evidence and this time found that the dead man's fingerprints matched those on the weapon that killed Brazier. Checking into the suicide's background, they realized they had found the killer. The pistol was traced to Canada and to South Africa, where it had once been owned by a merchant seaman who had sold it to the murderer.

REF.: Borrell, *Crime In Britain Today*; *CBA*.

Brazilian Carnival Murders, prom. 1980s, Braz., mur. Each year at least a dozen murders occur during the frenetic Brazilian Carnival held in Rio de Janeiro. Amidst the round-the-clock drunken revels, wild street dancing, constant parties, and fêtes, hundreds of deaths, mostly accidental, occur. It is also a time when murder victims are most public and vulnerable to their enemies. In 1982, officials recorded 282 violent deaths in Rio during the festivities. In the following year, 110 persons died during the revelry. In 1984, 171 people were killed one way or another and nineteen of these deaths, according to authorities, were murders, this number considered average by police who find it impossible to cope with killings while the entire population is in the streets and most are wearing costumes—the perfect method by which killers disguise their identities. One recent murder victim was killed while dressed in lingerie and a blonde wig. He was reportedly killed by another man dressed similarly in female clothing. REF.: *CBA*.

Brazilian Death Squad, prom. 1950s-80s, Braz., law enfor. off.-org. crime-mur. In 1976 in Nova Iguaca, Brazil, a man named Robinson da Silva watched death squad executions nightly from his roof. From the early 1950s through the mid-70s the squad was said to have killed more than 3,000 alleged petty criminals, many of whom had tried to muscle in on the gambling, drug, and prostitution rackets controlled by death squad members. Within a ten-day period in 1976 in Nova Iguaca and other working class slums known as the lowlands, the death squad murdered twenty-one people. That killing spree began when a grocer, cousin of Gilberto Gomes, a local police official, was robbed and shot by five armed men on May 22. Over the next few days all five men were captured, tortured, and killed. Innocent victims slain in the spree included Elenil Avles de Carvalho, an electrician with no criminal record, picked up by the squad as he went to work, and a 12-year-old street vendor who was shot twice in the head.

The squad was formed in the early 1950s, but its activities intensified in 1964, following the killing of Milton Le Coq, a police detective. Hundreds of policemen attended his funeral, and vows were made to kill ten criminals for every policeman slain. The death squad has long since surpassed this target.

By 1987, the death squad had grown even larger, with greater resources of guns and information than the relatively poorly equipped police. The membership included more hired killers, organized crime members, and former police officers than the decade before. As many as 500 death squad members operated in Baixada Fluminense, one of the country's most crime-ridden slums. Though police report an average of thirty victims a month, residents claim that about fifty people disappear every day, and around 200 bodies are found each month. Local cemetery workers routinely dig an extra half dozen graves to accommodate new victims. In severe contrast to the death squad, the local police force is often forced to work without radios, nightsticks, bulletproof vests, or sometimes even uniforms. One officer said, "After three months' training, they gave me handcuffs, a .38 pistol, and six bullets that were supposed to last me three months. The rule out here is to shoot to kill, because the chances are otherwise you'll never see the end of a gunfight." REF.: *CBA*.

The Richmond, Va., Bread Riot, 1863.

Bread Riot, 1863, U.S., mob vio. Rabid mobs tore down Main Street of Richmond, Va., on Apr. 2, 1863, desperately looking for food. On that morning, a large group of Oregon Hill women gathered in the Belvidere Hill Baptist Church, convening over the desperate shortage of food in Richmond, then being ravaged by the Civil War. They decided to go to Governor John Letcher and petition for food.

Letcher met the throng of women, men, and boys swelling the outer fringes of their ranks. He sympathized with their empty-cupboard plight, he told them. He understood what it meant to go hungry. His own table was bare, The women listened for a time and then Mary Jackson, later described as "a tall, daring, Amazonian-looking woman, who had a white feather standing erect from her hat," shouted down the governor and led the delegation to Capitol Square. By then, it was a food-searching mob.

Arming themselves with knives, hatchets, and even some pistols, the women stalked down Main Street where they began to smash the windows of grocery stores. They shouted: "Bread! Give us bread!" They took all the foodstuffs they could carry and then began to pillage the clothing stores, still screaming, "Bread! Bread!"

Mayor Joseph Mayo arrived and tried to calm the rioters, but they pushed him aside and continued the looting. Thomas Mumford of the YMCA on Cary Street appeared and, at the mayor's urging, offered the rioters food if they would stop their looting and go to the Y depot. Only a few followed the philanthropic Mumford from the scene of rioting.

A company of Confederate troops marched solemnly to the scene as the looters continued to smash windows and help themselves to anything they could grab and carry. Captain Gay ordered his men to load their weapons. Before he directed them to aim their rifles, a racing carriage appeared, its galloping horses wedging into the throng.

Tall, distinguished, and sad-eyed Confederate president Jefferson Davis stood up in the carriage. Davis, although booed and hissed at by the most militant of the female demonstrators, addressed the rioters with a loud, commanding voice, telling them to disperse immediately or risk being fired upon. Many looters went back to gathering foodstuffs and clothing. The president withdrew his watch and held it dramatically in his hand. Davis announced that the crowds had only five minutes to clear the street before the troops fired. He glanced at his watch and then at the crowd. Defiant, the rioters massed about him.

"When the five minutes are up, shoot to kill!" shouted Captain Gay.

Jefferson Davis stood ramrod stiff, scanning the crowd, which still stubbornly refused to move. The seconds ticked away. Davis said nothing. The rioters said nothing. The troops began to level their weapons. Almost as one person, the crowd suddenly disintegrated, its leaders grumbling curses as they moved off. The Richmond Bread Riot was over. It cost the city merchants more that $13,000 in goods and the City Hospital about 300 pounds of beef.

The incident was covered up by the Richmond press, which was eager not to present a desperate face to Union forces, but the city council privately offered a $50 reward to anyone who could provide information which led to the conviction of any rioter. Several rioters were rounded up and a few were given maximum prison sentences of three years.

REF.: Buchanan, *A Pictorial History of the Confederacy; CBA;* Stanard, *Richmond, Its People and Its Story;* Strode, *Jefferson Davis.*

Breakenridge, William Milton (Billy), 1846-1931, U.S., west. lawman. Born in Watertown, Wis., William Milton Breakenridge sold newspapers as a boy and ran away from home to join the Union army during the Civil War. Following the war, Breakenridge sought fame and fortune by moving west where he held a variety of jobs in Denver and then became a page boy in the Colorado legislature. He next enlisted in the Third Colorado Cavalry under Colonel Chivington and participated in the Sand Creek Massacre. After leaving the cavalry, Breakenridge became a train brakeman, then a storekeeper in Sidney, Neb. After wandering about the West, Breakenridge became a deputy sheriff in Phoenix, Ariz., in 1878. He later moved to Tombstone, Ariz., where he hauled lumber, then became a deputy sheriff, working for his close friend, Sheriff John Behan. On May 25, 1881, Breakenridge entered a saloon in Galeyville, Ariz., and was immediately confronted by two of the toughest gunmen and rustlers in the area, William "Curly Bill" Brocius and Jim Wallace, a hardcase gunman who had participated in the Lincoln County war. Wallace, after spotting the star on Breakenridge's vest, drew his gun and challenged him to a duel. The lawman laughed off Wallace's insults and asked everyone to join him in a drink. Brocius, admiring Breakenridge's courage, talked Wallace out of gunfighting, but when the lawman began to leave, Brocius, by then drunk, tried to pick a fight with Breakenridge.

Ignoring Curly Bill's antagonizing remarks, Breakenridge walked to his horse, but Brocius followed him and mounted his horse. Curly Bill began to shout insults at the lawman and finally, Breakenridge had had enough. He pulled his gun and fired a shot that struck Curly Bill in the neck, the bullet emerging out of his right cheek, knocking out a tooth. Brocius recovered from this ugly wound but was so unnerved by the incident that he reportedly took off his guns forever and left Arizona, a claim much contested by Wyatt Earp. In 1882, Breakenridge, John C. Gillespie, and two other lawmen named Allen and Young tracked down two outlaws, Billy Grounds (real name Boucher) and Zwing Hunt, who had committed a robbery in Charleston, a small town near Tombstone.

Breakenridge and his men located the outlaws at the Stockton ranch about ten miles from Tombstone. They rode up quietly, hid their horses, then surrounded the small cabin. Then, inexplicably, Gillespie marched toward the front door of the cabin, demanding that Grounds and Hunt surrender. The outlaws threw open the front door and fired, killing Gillespie on the spot. Next a ranch hand named Lewis came dash-

ing from the cabin, screaming that he was innocent, but the outlaws shot him in the back. Then Allen and Young were both wounded from the withering gunfire by the outlaws. Breakenridge, alone, aimed a shotgun directly at the open door and, as soon as he saw movement inside, he let loose a blast that caught Grounds in the face, sending him to the floor. He died of this wound a short time later. Hunt raced out the back door but Breakenridge and the injured Allen fired at him and a bullet struck his back, knocking him down. Hunt got up and began running once more but the law-men later found him sprawled unconscious. He was taken to

Lawman Billy Breakenridge.

jail but later escaped and disappeared. Some reports had it that Hunt was killed by Indians or went to Texas where he changed his name and lived to a ripe old age.

In 1883, Breakenridge quit his deputy sheriff's position and turned to ranching, but when this failed he went back to law enforcement, becoming a U.S. marshal. He was involved in many dramatic shootouts and was also involved in the notorious Wham case in 1889. Major Joseph Wham, U.S. Army paymaster, and a large contingent of soldiers were ambushed near Fort Thomas by thirteen outlaws who wounded eight troopers and drove off the rest of the soldiers before scooping up a payroll of $29,000. Breakenridge and other officers rounded up many suspects who were later charged with the sensational robbery, most of these being Mormons with strong political connections. The accused men were defended by Marcus Aurelius Smith, one of the most effective and successful lawyers and politicians in the territory, and when Major Wham and his men failed to identify any of the defendants in court, they were all acquitted. Breakenridge later claimed that political pressure allowed the robbers to go free.

Breakenridge was elected surveyor of Maricopa County in 1888, and he later became a special investigator for the Southern Pacific Railroad, performing guard duty and conducting detective work, retiring in 1918 at age seventy-two. Ten years after retiring, in 1928, Breakenridge published his famous book of the Old West, *Helldorado*, which made him rich and even more famous than when he hunted outlaws along dusty Arizona trails. He died at age eighty-five of a heart attack on Jan. 31, 1931, in Tucson. See: **Behan, John; Brocius, William; Earp, Wyatt.**

REF.: Adams, *A Fitting Death for Billy the Kid*; American Guide Series: *Arizona, A State Guide*; Argall, *Outlawry and Justice in Old Arizona*; Bakarich, *Gun-Smoke*; Ball, *The United States Marshals of New Mexico and Arizona Territories, 1846-1912*; Bartholomew, *The Biographical Album of Western Gunfighters*; ____, *Wyatt Earp, 1879-1882*; Bechdolt, *When the West was Young*; Boyer, *Suppressed Murder of Wyatt Earp*; Breakenridge, *Helldorado*; Breihan, *Great Gunfighters of the West*; ____,

Great Lawmen of the West; Burns, *Tombstone, An Iliad of the Southwest*; *CBA*; Chapel, *Guns of the Old West*; Chisholm, *Brewery Gulch*; Clum, *Apache Agent*; Cox, *Luke Short and His Era*; Cunningham, *Triggernometry*; Faulk, *Tombstone*; Hendricks, *The Bad Man of the West*; Holloway, *Texas Gun Lore*; Hunter and Rose, *The Album of Gunfighters*; Jaastad, *Man of the West*; Jahns, *The Frontier World of Doc Holliday*; King, *Mavericks*; ____, *Wranglin' the Past*; Lake, *Under Cover for Wells Fargo*; Lake, *Wyatt Earp, Frontier Marshal*; ____, *He Carried a Six-Shooter*; Lockwood, *Pioneer Days in Arizona*; McClintock, *Arizona*; McCool, *So Said the Coroner*; Martin, *The Earps of Tombstone*; ____, *Tombstone's Epitaph*; Miller, *Arizona, The Last Frontier*; Morgan, *Shooting Sheriffs of the Wild West*; Myers, *Doc Holliday*; ____, *The Last Chance*; O'Neal, *Encyclopedia of Western Gunfighters*; Raine, *Forty-Five Caliber Law*; ____, *Guns of the Frontier*; Rickards, *Buckskin Frank Leslie*; Rosa, *The Gunfighter*; Sloan, *History of Arizona*; Walters, *Tombstone's Yesterdays*; Waters, *Earp Brothers of Tombstone*; Wellman, *Glory, God and Gold*; ____, *The Trampling Herd*.

Breckinridge, John, 1760-1806, U.S., atty. gen. Member of the House of Representatives in 1792. He served as attorney general of Kentucky from 1795-98, U.S. senator from 1801-05, and U.S. attorney general under President Thomas Jefferson from 1805-06. REF.: *CBA*.

Breckinridge, John Cabell, 1821-75, U.S., vice-pres., treas. Grandson of John Breckinridge. He served as vice president of the U.S. from 1857-61. He was U.S. senator from Kentucky in 1860, but was expelled by senate resolution in 1861. He lost as a candidate for president on the Southern Democratic ticket in 1860. He was indicted for treason in 1861, declared a traitor against the Union for his support of the Southern cause, and fled to the South to serve in the Confederate army. REF.: *CBA*.

Brécourt, Jeanne Amenaide (AKA: **Jeanne de la Cour**), b.1837, and **Gaudry, Nathalis**, prom. 1877, Fr., blk. Born in Paris in 1837 to a humble printer and his wife, a vegetable vendor, Jeanne Brécourt was adopted at an early age by a baroness. In 1848, she was returned spoiled by luxury to her parents, by then virtual beggars. Remaining with them until her eighteenth birthday, Brécourt then implored the baroness to take her back.

Soon after returning to the baroness, Brécourt married a grocer named Gras, an older man without his young wife's refinements. The baroness provided them with enough money to open a shop, but soon Brécourt grew weary of her husband and began refusing his advances. In time Gras moved out, and with the money she received from the sale of the food store, Brécourt struck out on her own.

A few years later, Brécourt re-emerged in Paris with a new identity. The months spent as a struggling stage actress had given her the courage to pursue her ambitions. She was now Jeanne de la Cour, the courtesan. Men were but a means to an end, and in the coming months she entertained the scions of society and politics with reckless abandon. One youth committed suicide in her name. She flippantly remarked, "It was bound to happen—he had no moderation!"

In 1873, she met a wealthy young man sixteen years her junior—Georges de Saint Pierre. She quickly won his adoration, but it was not enough. A diabolical plan began to take shape in her mind upon observing a friend escorting a blind man to a social function. She would do the same to de Saint Pierre, thereby assuring herself a secure old age.

To achieve these ends, she recruited her friend Nathalis Gaudry, who, like Brécourt, was once a child of the slums. Gaudry had fought in the Italian War of 1859, and was an otherwise honest man, but he had one weakness. He was obsessed with Jeanne Brécourt, who told him that if he would do this one thing, she would be his forever. Gaudry was to throw acid in de Saint Pierre's face as they returned home from a Paris ball the night of Jan. 13, 1877. When the young man called for Brécourt at her apartment on the rue de Boulogne, he did not know that someone was hiding in the closet observing his every move.

Brécourt was taken back to her apartment at 2:30 a.m. As de Saint Pierre made his way back to his awaiting carriage, Gaudry appeared out of the shadows and doused the bottle of burning acid in the unsuspecting man's face. Brécourt held the gate open for Gaudry who fled out of the courtyard. Georges de Saint Pierre was removed to a hospital. His sight was gone, and his face was permanently disfigured, but it did not matter to him as long as he had his beloved at his side to care for him. De Saint Pierre did not even wish to contact his relatives, who notified the police of their suspicions. They believed this assault had somehow been arranged by the courtesan. Gustave Macé, who was to become one of France's greatest detectives in the next few years was put on the case.

He followed Brécourt to her secret rendezvous with Gaudry and saw her hand Gaudry a sum of money. Next, he uncovered a cache of letters written by de Saint Pierre in a leather valise. They were given to Brécourt after the accident for her to burn. But she had only pretended to destroy them in the fire of her stove. The letters were intended to blackmail an aristocratic acquaintance of de Saint Pierre. Brécourt planned to keep them in case de Saint Pierre should leave her someday. "To blind me! To torture me! And then profit by my condition to lie to me, to betray me. It's infamous! Infamous!" Detective Macé nodded sympathetically.

Brécourt was taken into custody and thrown into the St. Lazare Prison where she remained until her trial began at the Paris Assize Court on July 23, 1877. For three days her trial was front page news in the city gazettes. "I was mad for Jeanne Brécourt," Gaudry explained. "I would have done anything she told me."

Jeanne Brécourt was sentenced to fifteen years in prison. Gaudry received five. In her last years, Brécourt peddled fruit in the same streets she had once known as a child.

REF.: *CBA;* Irving, *A Book of Remarkable Criminals;* Nash, *Look For the Woman.*

Bredell, Baldwin, and **Taylor, Arthur,** and **Jacobs, William,** and **Kendig, William,** prom. 1897-99, U.S., count. In Fall 1897, a Philadelphia bank teller counting $100 silver certificates, known as "Monroe-heads" for the president's portrait on them, was surprised when the carmine seal on one bill left ink on his finger. A Washington investigation headed by Secretary of the Treasury Lyman Gage seemed to prove that the seal was false but the bills real. When Chief Clerk W. Herman Moran tested a bill in a glass of water it separated into sheets of paper, and Gage was forced to recall a $27 million issue of the certificate. Secret Service investigator William J. Burns was put on the case, along with operative Bill McManus and scores of other agents. Secret Service Chief John E. Wilkie received a letter from Burns, suggesting that someone must have perfected a method of photoengraving with steel. In March 1898, Wilkie called Burns to Washington and put him in charge of the investigation, then sent him to Philadelphia.

Help-wanted ads for engravers were placed nationally. Within two weeks every person who could photo etch was under investigation. Burns checked out dry goods stores, aware that counterfeiters use large quantities of wet muslin to press their paper before printing. A clerk remembered a well-dressed young man who had recently made a large order, recalling that he "kept winking, as if there was something in his eye." Knowing that engravers frequently get bits of grinding dust or metal in their eyes, Burns checked with local physicians, finding one who had treated a young patient with that complaint who lived in the area. Going through the list of local photoengravers, Burns found two who had recently set up as partners in a Filbert and North Streets shop, a mechanical genius, Baldwin Bredell, and an artistic engraver, Arthur Taylor.

Organizing surveillance across the street from Taylor and Bredell's company, Burns brought in the optometrist and the clerk. With the help of field glasses, both made a positive identification of Taylor. Obtaining a key from a cleaning boy, Burns searched the engraving firm, finding no signs of business, illegal or otherwise. Though the owners discouraged customers by asking ludicrously high prices, Taylor and Bredell spent extravagantly.

Within a short time several more counterfeit $100 bills showed up in Atlantic City, with several people identifying by photo Taylor

and Bredell as the passers. Nearly a year had gone by since the first bill had appeared when fresh materials were brought into the Filbert Street shop. Then Bredell and Taylor, followed by agents, took a trip to Lancaster, Pa., where they went to a cigar factory owned by William Jacobs and William Kendig, who also owned a tobacco warehouse nearby. When Chief Wilkie heard of this, he ordered a supply of the cigars, discovering that the blue revenue stamps on the box were counterfeit. Treasury Secretary Gage wanted Kendig and Jacobs arrested, but acceded to Wilkie's plea for a delay to gather evidence that would indict Bredell and Taylor as well.

On Feb. 11, 1899, Kendig and Jacobs went to the offices of two well-known Philadelphia attorneys, Ellery P. Ingham and Harvey K. Newitt. That same day, Newitt went to agent McManus and offered him a $1,500 bribe through his new clients "to make sure that any mention of (them) that comes into your office doesn't get out of your office." McManus said he would think about it, then reported the information to Wilkie, who instructed him to take the bribe, which he did, telling the suspicious lawyer not to worry about Burns, who was "just helping me" in the area to work on "government pension frauds".

In April 1899, Burns found a small locker in Taylor and Bredell's offices that had been overlooked and inside was a partially completed plate for a new $100 bill.

The raids and arrests began on Apr. 18, with twenty Secret Service men in Philadelphia and another dozen or more in Lancaster. When Taylor and Burns were arrested within minutes of each other, the locker was opened in their presence, and each began to accuse the other, telling of more plates hidden in Bredell's family's home in Camden, N.J., and Taylor's family's home in Philadelphia. Neither man had ever been in trouble with the law before. They admitted to being hired in 1896 by Jacobs and Kendig to make the counterfeit revenue stamps. They had graduated to creating their own currency the following year. When arrested in Lancaster, Jacobs attempted to bribe his way out by offering Burns and another agent, Schuyler Donella $14,000 in real currency, exploding in anger when he realized he had himself been conned by the lawyers Ingham and Newitt, who had paid out only $1,500 of the $3,000 monthly payoffs Jacobs had given them. Kendig, when captured, unwittingly turned over the plates for the $100 Monroe-head bills, as well as the revenue stamp plates. The $27 million currency issue was made secure, and a $250,000-a-year revenue stamp fraud ended.

On Oct. 10, 1899, the trial began. All the defendants pleaded guilty, with the exception of the lawyers, Ingham and Newitt, who, though they maintained that they had been framed by the Secret Service, were convicted along with the others. On Nov. 25, Taylor and Bredell were sentenced to twelve years each in the Moyamensing Penitentiary. Not long after beginning their terms, the inveterate frauds created, from their cell, a tiny printing press that made $20 bills, hoping to use the press as leverage to bargain for reduced sentences. They had passed about forty-five of the bills through Taylor's brother, Henry, instructing him to bury the pocket-sized press in the grave of Taylor's father. The scheme backfired, though. They were charged again, tried, and convicted, with an additional seven years added to their original sentences.

REF.: Caesar, *Incredible Detective; CBA.*

Breeds, John, d.1743, Brit., fraud-mur. John Breeds, a butcher, was caught cheating his customers by weighting his scales. Brought before mayor James Lamb, one of a long line of allegedly corrupt mayors who held rigged elections and passed their offices along to relatives, Breeds was convicted of fraud and sentenced to a term in the Ypres Tower jail. When released in 1743, Breed vowed revenge on Lamb. The angry butcher lived near a churchyard. As the mayor also was a merchant, he would routinely pass through the churchyard on his way to the ships to pick up goods. Hearing that Lamb would be meeting his son Thomas when he sailed on Mar. 16, Breed lay in wait for him. On the evening of the son's departure, Allen Grebell, Lamb's brother-in-law who alternated mayoral terms with his corrupt relative, had dinner with

Lamb. After dinner Lamb decided he did not want to meet his departing son and asked Grebell to go instead, offering him the signature red cloak of the mayor to ward off the evening chill. Grebell agreed. Passing through the churchyard, he was bumped into by someone, to whom he called out, "Get away, you drunken hound." When he returned to Lamb's house he mentioned the encounter, then said he would rest a while in front of the fire before going home.

The next morning Grebell lay dead in a chair by the fireplace, stabbed in the back. Not realizing that he had been wounded, he had bled to death internally. Breeds, the killer, had mistaken him for Lamb, fooled by the red cloak. He might not have been a suspect, except that after the killing, he danced half-naked in the streets, repeatedly shouting out, "Butchers must kill Lambs." A bloodstained knife from his shop was found in the churchyard where he had thrown it. Arrested and taken to Ypres Tower, after a long delay, Breeds was tried on May 25, again in front of Lamb, who apparently had decided it was not improper for him to stand in judgment of his would-be murderer. Lamb sentenced Breed to be hanged, and his body afterwards suspended in chains on Gibbet Marsh. The execution took place on June 8, 1743, and Breed's corpse stayed chained for some time after his execution. REF.: *CBA*; Laurence, *A History of Capital Punishment*; Smith-Hughes, *Eight Studies In Justice*.

Brehm, Walter, prom. 1951, U.S., polit. corr. On Apr. 30, 1951, Walter E. Brehm, a Republican from Ohio who had served in Congress for eight years, was convicted in Washington of unlawfully accepting 1948 campaign contributions of $1,000 from his office clerk, Emma Craven, but was not found guilty of taking funds from 74-year-old Clara Soliday, another clerk in the office. Brehm said the money just kept turning up no matter how often he refused it, appearing in filing cabinets where his wife found it, or dropped into copies of a newspaper. The 58-year-old politician's conviction did not affect his status as a congressman. On June 11, 1951, he was fined $5,000 and sentenced to five to fifteen months in jail. His attorney, Leo Rover, said Brehm would appeal. Federal Judge Burnita Shelton Matthews, before whom the case was tried, suspended the sentence, saying she had taken into consideration Brehm's probation reports, which indicated this was his first offense and that other violations were unlikely, and also the question of intent to do wrong. On Apr. 24, 1952, the U.S. Court of Appeals unanimously upheld the conviction. A final attempt to review the case was denied in October 1952. REF.: *CBA*.

Breitenstein, Jean Sala, 1900-   , U.S., jur. Assistant U.S. attorney of the Department of Justice from 1930-33. He participated in the U.S. Judicial Conference Commission on Administration of the Criminal Law from 1970-76. He was appointed to the federal bench in Colorado in 1954, and to the Tenth Circuit Court in 1957. REF.: *CBA*.

Brekke, Carstein, prom. 1949, Norway, mur. Odvar Eiken and Anders Muren had been the best of friends since they had served together in the Norwegian Air Force in the final days of WWII. Following their return to civilian life, they enrolled at the same medical college in Lund, Sweden, and became roommates. In the summer of 1948, Eiken visited Muren's family home in Norway, where he met and fell in love with Randi Muren, Anders' 22-year-old sister. The couple courted for nearly a year, and looked forward to announcing their engagement on Easter of 1949 when Eiken received an anonymous letter, telling him of Randi's alleged infidelities, and a newspaper clipping that announced Randi's engagement to Carstein Brekke, a fellow student and old-time friend of hers who also attended her teachers' college in Kristiansand. Randi also received several anonymous letters telling her about Eiken's affairs in Sweden. In February, Randi received a letter from a Signe Lundgren, who claimed to be Eiken's mistress and pregnant with his child. The lovers discussed these strange letters, deciding that they were practical jokes played on them by friends.

Shortly before Easter, Eiken received a parcel containing a small bottle of liquor in an old cigar box, mailed from a Kari Straume, with an indecipherable address. Both wondered vaguely who Kari Straume might be. He raised a toast to his upcoming engagement with his brother-in-law to be, and though both became mildly sick, they did not attribute it to the alcohol. One week later Eiken received another parcel, containing four matchboxes with chocolates inside, and a note from Randi, sending her love and asking him to eat them all. On Mar. 12, Eiken shared the candy with Muren, and with his landlady's 8-year-old daughter, Marianne Svendson, who in turn shared the sweets with her friend, Barbro Jakobson. That night all four were rushed to the hospital in Lund, where Marianne Svendson died in agony.

In the small town of Malmö, near Lund, Superintendent Alf Eliasson took over the investigation. Autopsy tests on Svendson revealed traces of arsenic. Randi Muren was questioned and told of the anonymous letters. Faint scribbles on the newsprint in which the lethal treats had been wrapped revealed the name Flemming Rosbörg, a Dane who had met Randi Muren at a Vraadal hotel the year before and had been strongly attracted to the coed. But it was proved that he had no connection to the parcels or letters. Investigations in Oslo and Copenhagen revealed that neither Signe Lundgren nor Kari Straume had anything to do with the case—police suspected their names had been taken from telephone directories.

Police had little to go on until Carstein Brekke came into headquarters to announce that somebody had also sent him poisoned chocolates, with the name S. Kihle on the wrapping. After eating one, he had been sick for three days and had come to the police because he was scared after hearing about Svendson's death. A model student from a good family, Brekke was courteous and cooperative. But when Randi mentioned that he had been in Oslo on both days when the parcels were postmarked, he quickly became a suspect. When Randi was also shown the cigar box in which the doctored liquor had been mailed she identified it as the same box in which Brekke once brought her fresh eggs from his family home. Detectives then found an old school notebook in the training college trash, with examples of Randi Muren's signature and practiced forgeries of her handwriting.

Five hours after his arrest Brekke admitted to poisoning the chocolates, refusing to be further cross-examined and insisting on writing out his confession in the intellectual form it required. His statement on a long, formal paper explained how unrequited love for Muren had driven him to create an elaborate scheme of revenge.

Brekke had happened to be visiting Randi at her house when she received a letter from Eiken thanking her for the liquor. She wrote him back, explaining she had not sent it. Addressing her lover, "My dear husband," she gave the missive to Brekke to mail on his way home. When Brekke opened the letter instead and read it, he later confessed to police, "Something snapped inside of me." It was then he decided to implicate Randi with the poisoned candy. Brekke was charged with two counts of attempted, premeditated murder, and with the manslaughter of Svendson. Found Guilty, he was sentenced to twelve years in prison and, according to Norwegian law, a ten-year loss of his rights as a citizen. When he appealed, a supreme court found him Guilty again. Judge Carl Kruse Jensen remarked to the jury that "the condemned's extremely serious actions disclosed an emphatic criminal disposition." In the May 1951 sentencing, an additional three years were added to Brekke's term.
REF.: *CBA*; Radin, *Headline Crimes of the Year*.

Brembar, Sir Nicholas, d.1388, Brit., consp. Sir Nicholas Brembar was executed during the reign of the so-called boy king, Richard II. Charged with conspiracy, he had been part of a group who plotted to overthrow the king. A brutal tyrant, Brembar had a pair of stocks erected in every one of London's wards, and an ax made with which "to behead all such as should be against him." This ax was used in Brembar's own execution.
REF.: *CBA*; Potter, *The Art of Hanging*.

Bremer, Arthur, See: **Wallace, George.**

Bremer, Edward G., See: **Barker Brothers.**

Brennan, Ben, prom. 1896-98, U.S., rob.-pros. Ben and Rosie Brennan's house of prostitution was located on Eldridge Court in Chicago. In 1896, Ben was arrested for burglary while crossing over a viaduct on Twelfth Street. He was wearing two suits of stolen clothes when apprehended. Though indicted, he got out of being prosecuted through money and influence, as he had several times before on arrests for stolen property. Detective Clifton Wooldridge later arrested the Brennans at another address. Finding only Rosie at home, he was attacked by her with a pan of hot grease, then one of water. When her husband returned, he threw rocks at Wooldridge. He nevertheless arrested them and locked them up. John King, a prominent criminal lawyer, defended them and each was fined $10 and court costs. On another occasion, on Oct. 28, 1898, Wooldridge came to arrest Ben Brennan, again, this time for larceny and jumping bond. With several officers, Wooldridge went to the Brennans' Wabash Avenue house, heard sounds of whispering inside, but was only able to locate Rosie. Lying in bed, the wife swore her husband was not there. When Wooldridge realized the criminal was hiding in an oversized trunk, he sat on it, smoking a cigar until both Brennans begged him to let Ben out.

REF.: *CBA;* Wooldridge, *Hands Up!*

Brennan, William Joseph, Jr., 1906- , U.S., jur. First appointed judge to the New Jersey Superior Court from 1949-50 and served as judge of the appellate division from 1950-52. He received an appointment to serve as associate justice of the New Jersey Supreme Court from 1952-56 before being nominated by President Dwight D. Eisenhower to replace Sherman Minton as associate justice of the Supreme Court in 1957. He offered the dissenting opinion in *Barenblatt vs. the United States* (1959), in which he argued for the First Amendment rights of persons appearing before the House Un-American Activities Committee. In a similar case, in 1961, he dissented with the majority in the case of the *Communist Party vs. Subversive Activities Control Board* which maintained that mandatory registration of Communist Party members did not violate their civil rights. He submitted the majority opinion in the obscenity case of *Roth vs. the United States* (1957), which held that material without any redeeming social value is not protected under constitutional guarantees. REF.: *CBA.*

Brennan, William Theodore, b.c.1898, Brit., mur. On the Rowlands farm, at Model Farm, Penyffordd, near Mold, on Mar. 5, 1925, a farm laborer named Evans noticed a man he presumed to be a poacher and told his employer, John Rowlands, about it. When Rowlands went to check into the matter, Evans heard a gunshot and ran out into the field to see a man in a light coat fleeing. Chasing after him, Evans saw the man turn around and point his gun at him, and the farm worker retreated.

Under suspicion was William Brennan, a 27-year-old Irishman who had recently returned to Penyffordd to live with his parents. With a history of fits of rage, and a strain of insanity in his family, Brennan had frequently been in trouble since leaving school, and his parents decided it would be best for him to live with them in the relative quiet of the country.

Brennan claimed to have been home all day when Rowlands was shot, and no weapon was found in his house. His coat had been recently cleaned. A few days after his arrest, Brennan admitted to the killing, explaining that Rowlands had approached him and attempted to take his gun. Brennan had offered to pay for the rabbits he had stolen, but would not release his shotgun. The two men struggled, the gun went off once harmlessly, and then an enraged Brennan had reloaded and murdered the farmer, later hiding the gun in a drain. A jury at Mold Assizes found Brennan Guilty but Insane, and he was sent to the Broadmoor Criminal Lunatic Asylum.

REF.: *CBA;* Jacobs, *Aspects of Murder;* Wilson, *Encyclopedia of Murder.*

Bresci, Gaetano, See: **Humbert, King.**

Breshkovsky, Catherine (Ekaterina Konstantinovna Breshkovskaya, AKA: Babushka), 1844-1934, Rus., treas. Born into a noble family and known as the "Grandmother of the Russian Revolution." She was imprisoned in Siberia from 1874-78 and again from 1907-10 for advocating rights of the peasants. She was released by Aleksandr Kerensky in 1917, only to be driven out of the country by the Bolsheviks. REF.: *CBA.*

Bretagna, Santo, and **Rosenberg, Willie**, prom. 1948, U.S., mur. On New York's East Side on Jan. 13, 1948, a policeman heard shots in his own First Street building and rushed to the apartment of Benjamin (Chippy) Weiner, a minor hoodlum, who lay dying on his kitchen floor. When the officer asked Weiner who shot him, the man just shook his head, following the underworld code of refusing to give information to the law. He died moments later. Neighborhood residents had heard the shots but no one could, or would, tell the police who had done it. A month later, Edward Fennessey, arrested for a holdup in Brooklyn, told the King's County District Attorney's office that Weiner's killers were Santo Bretagna and Willie Rosenberg. Although Rosenberg was captured, Bretagna disappeared.

Police questioned Bretagna's East Side acquaintances for two months until one of them, a young tough on parole, confessed that he had been sending money to Bretagna. On Mar. 13, 1948, police arrested Bretagna in Boston.

He told them he went to Weiner's apartment with Rosenberg, who wanted to collect his share of the profits form a recent hijacking. On the way up to the apartment, Rosenberg casually asked Bretagna to kill Weiner for him as a favor. Weiner invited the two in, and when he went to the kitchen to make drinks, Bretagna followed and shot him. Faced with Bretagna's confession, Rosenberg admitted his part in the murder. Both men were later executed in the electric chair.

REF.: *CBA;* Danforth, *The D.A.'s Man.*

Brethauser, G. Henry (AKA: Fred F. Beck), d.1958, Case of, U.S., embez. In 1958, a Chicago ice cream peddler named Fred Beck died without making provisions to properly dispose of his $15,000 estate. The only clue to the man's prior life was a remark he once made about his alma mater, Hillhouse High, located in New Haven, Conn. The local police there identified Beck as G. Henry Brethauser, the one-time city controller of New Haven, who had absconded with $12,647 in state funds back in 1938. This startling discovery was made in 1966, after the money from Beck's estate had been tied up in probate court for eight years.

REF.: *CBA;* Nash, *Among The Missing.*

Brett, Thomas Rutherford, 1931- , U.S., jur. Chairman of the Oklahoma Bar Association and the Committee on Correctional Institutions from 1974-75. He was appointed judge of the court of the Northern District of Oklahoma by President Jimmy Carter in 1979. REF.: *CBA.*

Brewer, David Josiah, 1837-1910, U.S., jur. Presiding judge of the probate and criminal courts of Leavenworth County, Kan., from 1863-64, judge of the first judicial district of Kansas from 1865-69, and Kansas Supreme Court justice from 1870-74. He received his appointment as associate justice of the U.S. Supreme Court in 1889 to replace Stanley Matthews. He was a moderate conservative opposed to the government's expansionist policies and political intervention in the Philippines. REF.: *CBA.*

Brewer, Morris Sutton Ramsden, 1926- , Aus., mur. Morris Brewer was a religious and dutiful son, raised in the Plymouth Brethren religion which forbade films, plays, and dancing. The intensity of his moral fanaticism probably contributed to a nervous breakdown for he had been in a mental hospital. He had been seeing a psychiatrist, Dr. Alexander John Maum Sinclair, for more than a year when in 1949 he met 18-year-old Carmen Walters when they both took a course in herd-testing at Burnley Agricultural College in Melbourne, Aust. Walters' demure and reserved demeanor belied her spirit of adventure—in the short time since she left school she had studied to be a missionary, worked as a trainee nurse and as a tax department employee, and had run away to the Northern Territory, some 2,000 miles from her home, to work as a secretary.

This unlikely couple courted, fell in love, and became engaged in February 1950, planning to marry later that year. Brewer went into herd-testing for a while in the nearby dairy district of Gippsland, and Carmen, switching work again, became a dental nurse. But Brewer began to doubt his bride-to-be, remembering discrepancies in things she had told him, finally confronting her with, "Why did you lie to me?" Walters tried to explain that she had merely fibbed about the length of her stay in the Northern Territory because she had not known how much they would come to mean to each other.

When Brewer approached retired RAAF Squadron Leader Roy Walters to ask for his daughter's hand, the father, concerned about Brewer's rigid behavior, gave his prospective son-in-law three conditions: that his daughter be allowed to visit her family after marriage, that she be free to continue seeing movies with her relatives, and that the couple not get tied down with a family right away. Brewer agreed to the first, but was vague about the other two. Although wedding plans continued, Carmen Walters began getting moody, talking more about her traveling plans rather than about the upcoming nuptials and eventually admitting to Brewer that she had been close with another man when she lived in the Northern Territory. Brewer was shocked and repulsed, and a doctor advised the distraught young man to leave his betrothed.

On Mar. 10, 1950, Brewer met Walters at a railway station and ended their affair. According to his father, Robert Charles Brewer, his son did not sleep for five weeks after that day. The couple made several tentative and unsuccessful efforts to get back together. On May 13, they had dinner in suburban Mordialloc and were walking toward Walters' home when she told Brewer his parents had been a partial cause of their breakup, adding: "I have caused my parents a lot of worry and trouble in the past, and you'll do the same." Brewer punched Walters in the face and strangled her to death.

When her body was found the next morning by a neighbor, Richard Hall, he did not recognize his longtime acquaintance. The police search for Brewer ended on May 17 in a State Electricity Camp, where he had gone to plead for food. The night of the murder, he had hitchhiked 100 miles into the bush, borrowing a razor at a workers' camp and unsuccessfully trying to cut his wrist. Confessing to Detective Cyril Currer, Brewer said: "She told me lies...she told me I would cause my parents a lot of trouble." Edward Francis Campbell, the Royal Melbourne Hospital psychologist who examined the killer, finding him to be a repressed personality with traits of schizophrenia, said Brewer had "hidden symptoms that could break out into aggressive insanity under emotional strain." A jury found Brewer Not Guilty on the grounds of insanity, and Mr. Justice Barry ordered that he be sent to an asylum for the criminally insane.

REF.: *CBA*; Gurr, *Famous Australasian Cases*.

Brewer, Richard M., 1852-78, U.S., west. lawman-gunman. Born in St. Alban's Vt., Richard M. Brewer moved with his family in 1860 to Wisconsin, and at age eighteen he left home and headed west. He moved to Lincoln County, Neb., and became a rancher, breeding horses. Brewer befriended his neighbor, John Tunstall, and later became Tunstall's foreman, keeping his horses with Tunstall's. In September 1877, several of Brewer's prized horses and a pair of mules were rustled by Jesse Evans, Frank Baker, Tom Hill, and others. Brewer, who had received a deputy sheriff's commission, raised a fifteen-man posse to track down the thieves. Evans, Baker, and the others were found hiding in a dugout and were ordered to surrender. When they refused, Brewer told them that they would all be killed if they continued to fight. The outlaws surrendered and were taken to Lincoln, Neb., where they were placed in a deep hole in the ground, the town having a jail too small to hold them for trial. Some days later, thirty-two men working for rival ranchers L.G. Murphy and James J. Dolan, rode into Lincoln and freed the outlaws.

The Murphy-Dolan faction and the McSween-Tunstall combined then squared off in what later became the infamous Lincoln County war. After Tunstall was murdered, Brewer organized a band of "regulators," deputizing Billy the Kid, Frank McNab, Charlie Bowdre, John Middleton, Henry Brown, Josiah "Doc" Scurlock, and others, and sought out Tunstall's killers. Brewer and his men captured and later murdered two of the killers, Billy Morton and Frank Baker in March 1878. On Apr. 4, 1878, Brewer and his men encountered an ally of the Murphy-Dolan faction, Andrew L. "Buckshot" Roberts, at Blazer's Mill, N.M. Bowdre pulled his gun and ordered Roberts to surrender. The tough Roberts sneered and roared: "Not much, Mary Ann!" Bowdre then shot Roberts in the stomach but the tough westerner began firing his Winchester, retreating into an outhouse, wounding Middleton and George Coe in the process.

Brewer raced forward to a pile of logs in front of the outhouse and began firing into the small structure. Inside, Roberts had found a Sharps .50-caliber buffalo gun and he carefully propped this heavy gun on a log, aiming through a knothole. Brewer let loose another barrage, then ducked. When he poked his head above the wood pile, Roberts fired a roaring blast from the buffalo gun which tore off the top of Brewer's head. Roberts yelled in triumph: "I killed the s.o.b.! I killed him!" With that, Billy the Kid and the others riddled the outhouse with dozens of bullets and then retreated, taking their wounded with them and leaving the dead Brewer. After the gunsmoke cleared, the owner of the place, Dr. Emil Blazer, cautiously opened the outhouse door to see that Roberts was dead, shot full of holes. He buried Brewer and Roberts side by side on his property. See: **Billy the Kid; Lincoln County War; McNab, Frank; Middleton, John; Scurlock, Josiah**.

REF.: Adams, *A Fitting Death for Billy the Kid*; Bartholomew, *The Biographical Album of Western Gunfighters*; ____, *Jesse Evans, A Texas Hide-Burner*; Bechdolt, *Tales of the Old Timers*; Breihan, *Great Gunfighters of the West*; ____, *Outlaws of the Old West*; Brent, *The Complete and Factual Life of Billy the Kid*; Brown and Schmitt, *Trail Driving Days*; Burns, *The Saga of Billy the Kid*; Casey, *The Texas Border*; *CBA*; Charles, *More Tales of Tularosa*; Coe, *Frontier Fighter*; ____, *Ranch on the Ruidoso*; Coolidge, *Fighting Men of the West*; Cunningham, *Famous in the West*; ____, *Triggernometry*; Durham, *The Negro Cowboys*; Ealy, *Water in a Thirsty Land*; Erwin, *The Southwest of John H. Slaughter*; Fulton, *Maurice Garland Fulton's History of the Lincoln County War*; Garrett, *The Authentic Life of Billy the Kid*; Hamlin, *The True Story of Billy the Kid*; Hendricks, *The Bad Man of the West*; Hendron, *The Story of Billy the Kid*; Hertzog, *A Directory of New Mexico Desperadoes*; Holloway, *Texas Gun Lore*; Horan and Sann, *Pictorial History of the Wild West*; Hough, *The Story of the Outlaw*; Hunt, *The Tragic Days of Billy the Kid*; Keleher, *Violence in Lincoln County*; King, *Pioneer Western Empire Builders*; ____, *Wranglin' the Past*; Leckie, *The Buffalo Soldiers*; Lovell, *A Personalized History of Otero County*; Monaghan, *The Book of the American West*; Moore, *The West*; Mullin, *The Boyhood of Billy the Kid*; ____, *A Chronology of the Lincoln County War*; Nolan, *The Life and Death of John Henry Tunstall*; Nye, *Pistols for Hire*; O'Connor, *Pat Garrett*; O'Neal, *Encyclopedia of Western Gunfighters*; Otero, *The Real Billy the Kid*; Penfield, *Western Sheriffs and Marshals*; Raine, *Famous Sheriffs and Western Outlaws*; Rennert, *The Cowboy*; ____, *Western Outlaws*; Rickards, *Blazer's Mill*; Siringo, *History of Billy the Kid*; ____, *Riata and Spurs*; Stanley, *The Duke City*; ____, *Fort Stanton*; Steckmesser, *The Western Hero in History and Legend*; Thorp, *Story of the Southwestern Cowboy*; Wellman, *The Trampling Herd*; White, *Trigger Fingers*.

Brewer, Rudolph, d.1927, U.S., mur. In September 1927, 70-year-old Charles Gundlacht, a native of Germany who continued making home brew in his adopted country after it went dry, offered a glass of beer to Rudolph Brewer, who had stopped for directions, as he did to every visitor to his small Leonardtown, Md., farm. Brewer returned later that same day when Gundlacht was out, showed Mrs. Gundlacht his credentials from the Prohibition Bureau, and then broke every bottle he could find. When he returned on Sept. 16, with three other agents, Gundlacht held a shotgun on them, saying as they flashed their badges, "I know who you are and I don't give a damn." Warning them to stay where they were, he fired as they advanced, wounding one agent in the knee. They returned fire and Gundlacht fell to the ground, wounded in the foot by their bullets. As he lay prone, begging for mercy, Brewer stood over the old man and shot him through the head. Charges against the other agents were dropped, and a federal jury accepted Brewer's plea of self-defense. Gundlacht was one of the hundreds of liquor law violators or suspects killed by agents during Prohibition.

REF.: *CBA;* Kobler, *Ardent Spirits.*

Brewster, Benjamin Harris, 1816-88, U.S., lawyer. Attorney general of Pennsylvania from 1867-68. He established his reputation when he prosecuted postal employees who participated in the Star Route swindle. He served as U.S. attorney general from 1881-85 under President Chester Arthur. REF.: *CBA.*

Breyer, Stephen Gerald, 1938- , U.S., jur. Professor of law at the Harvard Law School, Cambridge, Mass., from 1970-80, and appointed judge of the First Circuit Court by President Jimmy Carter in 1980. He was appointed assistant special prosecutor assigned to the Watergate Special Prosecution Force in 1973. REF.: *CBA.*

Briant, Elijah S. (AKA: Lige), 1854-1932, U.S., west. lawman-jur. Elijah S. Briant was a druggist who also served as the sheriff of Sonora, Texas. Briant, a mild-mannered, tall, lean man with light brown hair and a penetrating stare, was described by one of his contemporaries as "absolutely fearless" when facing outlaws who invaded his town. This was evident on the night of Apr. 2, 1901, when a youth ran into his drugstore and told him that "suspicious strangers" were in the town's bakery, and they looked as if they intended to rob the store. Briant collected two deputies and the town constable and marched into the bakery where two rough-looking gunmen faced him. Briant asked the men to identify themselves and both went for their guns. In a wild shootout, both outlaws were riddled and the lawmen escaped injury. During this fight, Briant cooly drew his weapon and fired three bullets into each man, as the men also emptied their weapons into the gunmen who fired wildly at the lawmen. Killed, with seven bullets in his body was Will Carver, infamous member of Butch Cassidy's Wild Bunch. Wounded, with fourteen bullets in him, was George Kilpatrick, brother of the notorious Ben Kilpatrick, the Tall Texan, and one of Butch Cassidy's closest lieutenants.

Briant's nerveless gunfight with Carver and Kilpatrick earned him a large slice in western folklore. He later became a county judge and then retired to San Angelo where he died on Dec. 22, 1932, at age seventy-eight. See: **Carver, William; Cassidy, Butch; Kilpatrick, Benjamin; Wild Bunch, The.**

REF.: Bartholomew, *The Biographical Album of Western Gunfighters; CBA.*

Bricker, John William, b.1898, U.S., attempt. assass. As he prepared to board the underground tram to Capitol Hill, Senator John Bricker of Ohio noticed a familiar figure lurking nearby. It was William L. Kaiser, a 49-year-old former Capitol policeman who had summoned him from the Senate chambers the day before to complain about financial losses due to the liquidation of a Columbus savings and loan fifteen years earlier, when Bricker was Ohio's attorney general. Kaiser's persistence annoyed Bricker and his staff, but the senator was assured that Kaiser was "harmless but queer."

Kaiser waited for Bricker in the Senate Office Building on July 12, 1947, and at the opportune moment drew a .22-caliber pistol and fired two shots, both of which missed their mark. Washington Metropolitan Police hustled Kaiser away. It was later learned that his job as a Capitol Hill policeman had ended with the expiration of Democratic Senator James Huffman's term several months earlier. Bricker, a Republican, had hired a former marine from Ohio to take his place.

William Kaiser was adjudged insane by a District Court on Aug. 18. Dr. Winfred Overholzer testified that Kaiser suffered from "an organic brain disease." He was placed in St. Elizabeth's Hospital, where he died on Mar. 29, 1948. Bricker later served as U.S. attorney general under President Franklin D. Roosevelt

from 1933-37.

REF.: *CBA;* Paine, *The Assassins' World.*

Brick Moron, The, See: **Nixon, Robert.**

Brides of the Bath Murderer, See: **Smith, George Joseph.**

Bridges, Harry Renton (Alfred Bryant Renton Bridges), 1901- , U.S., consp.-perj. Inspired by the works of Jack London, Harry Bridges left his native Australia in 1920 to sail to the U.S. In the coming years, however, he found more than he had bargained for. In 1922, after kicking about Mexico and California, Bridges became a longshoreman in San Francisco.

For the next two decades Bridges was a tireless labor organizer, helping to found a new San Francisco local of the American Federation of Labor (AF of L) in July 1933. However, due to his leftist leanings and accusations that he attended meetings of the American Communist party, Bridges was lebeled a subversive. As he gained stature in the Longshoreman's Union, the U.S. government tried three times to deport him to Australia as an undesirable. But on June 18, 1945, the Supreme Court ruled in his favor. Bridges then filed for U.S. citizenship.

On May 25, 1949, Bridges was indicted for perjury-conspiracy on the grounds that he had defrauded the U.S. and had violated the naturalization laws by lying about his past membership in the Communist party. He repeatedly denied any Communist affiliation, but on Apr. 4, 1950, was found Guilty of swearing falsely at his naturalization hearings in 1945. He was sentenced to five years in prison on the perjury charge, and two years for obstructing the naturalization laws. The conviction, however, was overturned by the Supreme Court on June 15, 1953. In a four-to-three ruling, the justices held that the ruling had come "too late to be effective" because the statute of limitations had run out. The applicable limit was three years.

But the much maligned Harry Bridges was not yet free from the McCarthyites, who wanted to make him a scapegoat. In 1955 a fourth attempt was made to deport him to Australia. On July 29, Federal Judge Louis Goodman refused to deny Bridges his citizenship on the grounds that the government had not proved that he had been a Communist party member before his naturalization in 1945. "This is my country," Bridges remarked in 1950. "I don't believe Russia wants to make war on us, but if she does...the people of the U.S. will fight and so will I."

REF.: *CBA;* Nash, *Citizen Hoover.*

Bridges, Jack L., b.1838, U.S., west. lawman. A peace officer in Kansas City for fifteen years, Jack L. Bridges was made a deputy U.S. marshal in 1869, working in Hays City, Kan., and later in Wichita. The most serious gunfight in which Bridges was involved occured in Wichita on Feb. 28, 1871, when he attempted to arrest infamous horse thief, J.E. Ledford. Bridges, accompanied by twenty-five soldiers, went to arrest Ledford who owned the Harris House Hotel. At the hotel, Bridges was told that Ledford was not on the premises. Bridges harbored deep resentment against Ledford who had pistol-whipped him some months earlier in an argument, and he had vowed to "get even" with the horse thief. Ledford, knowing this, realized that his life was in the balance when Bridges sought him out on the horse thieving charge. When Bridges could not locate Ledford at his hotel, he then scouted the area and saw a man run into an outhouse behind the Harris House. Bridges, military scout Lew Stewart, and an officer approached the outhouse with guns in hand. Ledford then came running from the outhouse, his pistol blazing. He shot Bridges who, along with the others, emptied their guns into the fleeing horse thief. Leford was hit four times and died a few hours later. Bridges was severely wounded and he moved back to his birthplace in Maine to recuperate from the wounds. Once healed, he headed west to Colorado and finally returned to Kansas, being appointed city marshal of Dodge City where he had numerous confrontations with hardcase cowboys and gunmen, not the least of whom was Luke Short. When William Tilghman replaced Bridges as marshal of Dodge City, the ex-lawman left town and faded into oblivion.

REF.: *CBA;* Drago, *Wild, Woolly & Wicked;* Miller and Snell, *Great*

Gunfighters of the Kansas Cowtowns; O'Neal, *Encyclopedia of Western Gunfighters.*

Bridge Table Murder, The, See: **Bennett, Myrtle.**

Brigate Rosse, prom. 1970s, Italy, terr.-kid.-mur. Violence and politics have always gone hand-in-hand in Italy, as is clearly evidenced by the epic proportions reached by terrorism in the latter half of the 1970s when extremist groups like the Brigate Rosse, and the more than one hundred smaller groups, reigned supreme. Although the Brigate Rosse did not account for all of the Italian terrorist activity—there were 702 acts of terrorism in 1975, 1,198 in 1976, and 2,128 in 1977—a considerable amount was attributed to them, especially those acts with the greatest political impact. The Brigate Rosse was neither leftist nor right wing and members preferred to attack whatever government was in power. Much of the increased violence was precipitated when police captured several Brigate Rosse leaders, including Renato Curcio, and killed Margherita Cagol Curcio in June 1975 at the farmhouse where kidnapped vermouth manufacturer Vittorio Vallarino Gancia was being held.

On another occasion, the government promised to free prisoners upon the release of a hostage, Mr. Sossi, but they failed to do so. Genoa's public prosecutor Francesco Coco, who had reneged on the kidnapping deal, and his driver and bodyguard were shot and killed on June 8, 1974. This killing greatly affected the upcoming elections, which resulted in the Communists gaining many government positions. Just over a month later, on July 10, the death of Rome's public prosecutor Vittorio Occorsio, who was machine-gunned, was blamed on the Brigate Rosse, though pamphlets from the Fascist New Order group were tossed over his body.

Violence continued and increased, though maiming or *azzoppamento*—laming in Italian—of enemies became preferable to murder. Once again, however, a kidnapping was carried out by the Brigate Rosse, this time successfully. In order to gain a bargaining chip that might free Curcio and their other imprisoned comrades, they kidnapped Aldo Moro, a leading Christian Democrat and former five-term prime minister, on Mar. 16, 1978. Moro's driver, Domenico Ricci, his bodyguard, Oreste Leonardi, and three security agents, Raffaele Iozzino, Guilio Rivera, and Mr. Zizzi, were all killed during the ambush.

The Italian government, unable to find Moro even with 15,000 police searching, continually refused to meet the demands of the kidnappers, even after repeated threats to kill Moro. Then fifty-four days later, on May 9, 1978, Moro's body with eight bullets fired into his chest, was found in the trunk of a car parked in the middle of Rome. He had been killed the day before. Numerous arrests failed to capture the kidnappers.

REF.: Bell, *Assassin!*; *CBA*; Hacker, *Crusaders, Criminals, Crazies: Terror and Terrorism In Our Term*; Laqueur, *Terrorism*; O'Ballance, *Language of Violence—The Blood Politics of Terrorism*; Sloan, *Simulating Terrorism.*

Bright, James, d.c.1850, Brit., (unsolv.) mur. As the Chartists' movement for political reform grew among the working classes in England—1.25 million people signed a petition to Parliament in 1839, and 6 million signatures were on another petition in 1848—the crowds that attended their meetings also grew, making the task of keeping law and order that much more difficult. Although meetings would sometimes attract more than 50,000 people, the movement was already dying out when a much smaller but deadlier crowd met at Ashton-under-Lynne in 1850.

When the meeting had ended, the crowd dispersed peacefully, but fifty men armed with pikes soon returned, though only three police officers remained on the scene. At the sight of the armed men, two of the officers ran off, leaving Constable James Bright to meet his death as the group literally marched over him, one man stabbing him in the leg and another shooting him to death.

REF.: *CBA*; Cobb, *Murdered On Duty*; Thomson, *The Story of Scotland Yard.*

Brighton Trunk Murder, The, See: **Mancini, Tony.**

Brimmer, Clarence Addison, 1922-   , U.S., jur. Attorney general of Wyoming from 1971-74. In 1975, he was appointed U.S. attorney of the Department of Justice, and in the same year, appointed to the District Court of Wyoming by President Gerald Ford. REF.: *CBA*.

Brinham, George, d.1962, Brit., mansl. (vict.). The death of former Labor Party Chairman George Brinham was at first believed to be murder committed by a 16-year-old boy who struck him with a decanter. At the boy's trial, however, the charge was reduced to manslaughter when the boy claimed self-defense in the killing because Brinham had made unwanted sexual advances. Upon the discovery that Brinham was indeed a homosexual, the jury was handed the case to decide, and a minute later charges were dropped. REF.: *CBA*.

Brinker, William H., b.1851, U.S., jur. Prosecuting attorney in Warrensburg, Mo., from 1876-82. He was appointed judge of the territorial court of New Mexico in 1885 by President Grover Cleveland. REF.: *CBA*.

Brinkley, Dr. **John Romulus** (AKA: **Goat Gland Brinkley**), 1885-1942, U.S., boot.-forg.-fraud. Radio station KFKB ("Kansas First, Kansas Best") first signed on in 1923, programming country music, farm reports, and revivalist sermons. A frequent advertiser was Dr. John R. Brinkley, a shifty salesman who first received a medical degree from a diploma mill in Kansas City, and after that school was discredited, bribed authorities at Italy's University of Pavia for another degree. Brinkley used the radio to pitch his amazing Compound Operation, a goat gland implant procedure supposed to rejuvenate elderly men and the sexually impotent.

Trading on superstitions about goats, Brinkley, of Milford, Kan., implanted goat gonads into the scrotums of hundreds of men during the 1920s. The price of the operation ranged from $750 to $1,500. Patients were permitted to select their own goat from the herd Brinkley kept in his backyard. With the profits from the operations, Brinkley bought four cars, a private plane, and several luxurious yachts. In 1930, the Federal Radio Commission revoked his license, but Brinkley simply phoned in his reports to a station in Mexico that then rebroadcasted his message.

Brinkley ran for governor of Kansas three times, and once nearly defeated Alfred Landon. He was a popular grassroots figure, despite his shady medical practice and his well-publicized association with William Dudley Pelley, leader of the Silver Shirts, an American fascist organization. Before his death on May 26, 1942, the thoroughly discredited Dr. Brinkley had committed a fortune to Pelley's movement.

REF.: *CBA*; Clugston, *Rascals In Democracy*; Gardner, *Fads*; Hunt, *Dictionary of Rogues*; MacDougall, *Hoaxes*; Nash, *Zanies*; Young, *The Medical Messiahs.*

Brinkley, Richard, d.1907, Brit., mur. At the death of 77-year-old Johanna Maria Louisa Blume, Richard Brinkley, one of her lodgers, presented her will and claimed possession of the deceased's money and home at Fulham, England. When the deceased lady's granddaughter contested the will, Brinkley realized that the people he had procured to witness the false will would quickly tell the truth in court. He therefore set out to kill his witnesses, beginning with Reginald Parker.

Brinkley acquired some prussic acid—in order to kill a dog, he claimed—and slipped it into some stout he took to Parker's home on Apr. 20, 1907. He left the bottle of stout in the kitchen and went to talk to Parker, not realizing that the well-liked beer might attract others. As it happened, Parker's landlords, Richard and Elizabeth Ann Beck, and their daughter drank the poisoned stout. It killed the elder Becks and left the daughter very ill. Police quickly discovered who provided the stout and Brinkley didn't help matters when he claimed to know nothing of it being poisoned before the police even brought up the subject.

Even though Brinkley's intent was to kill Parker, there still was a willful act committed in the deaths of the Becks, so he was tried at the Guildford Assizes and found Guilty of murder. The trial was noteworthy because of the use of scientific evidence to determine the different kinds of ink used. It was shown that three different pens had been used in the will. Exhumation and examination of Blume's body showed that she had not been murdered. Brinkley was hanged on Aug. 13, 1907, at Wands-worth Prison.

REF.: *CBA*; Shew, *A Companion To Murder*; Speer, *The Secret History of Great Crimes*; Wilson, *Encyclopedia of Murder*.

Brink's Armored Car Robbery of 1976, Can., rob. At noon on Mar. 30, 1976, a truck pulled into the alley outside the Royal Bank of Canada in Montreal where a Brink's armored car was parked. Simultaneously a white van pulled up in front of the car, blocking its exit. While three Brink's guards were inside the bank, the back doors of the van were flung open and two men aimed a .50-caliber WWII anti-aircraft machine gun at the armored car. A third robber with a revolver ordered driver Gilles Lachapelle to open the door, which he did. The bandits then drove off unnoticed in both truck and armored car, taking with them $2.8 million. The two vehicles were later abandoning south of Montreal at Nun's Island.

Police did not catch the robbers until June 1, 1976, when six people were arrested and $100,000 seized. This ended the biggest robbery ever in Brink's history, surpassing the $2.7 million—of which only $1.2 million was in cash—stolen Jan. 17, 1950, in Boston.

REF.: *CBA*; Nash, *Almanac of World Crime*; ____, *Open Files*.

Brink's Armored Car Robbery of 1981, U.S. rob.-mur. An attempted robbery of a Brink's armored truck in the fall of 1981 resulted in the death of three men and a trial that cost the county more than three times the $1.6 million dollars the robbers had hoped to steal. The truck was held up outside a mall in Nanuet, N.Y., some twenty miles north of New York City. After the robbers killed a Brink's guard, the police chased their car at high speed to a roadblock in Nyack, N.Y. There the robbers gunned down two police officers, Waverly Brown and Sergeant Edward O'Grady, before they were captured.

In all, nine people were tried over a period of two and a half years, with two changes of venue, and three separate trials costing about $5 million.

Kuwasi Balagoon, Judith A. Clark, and David J. Gilbert were all sentenced to seventy-five years to life in prison in 1983, while Samuel Brown, who suffered a broken neck in his jail cell while awaiting trial, received three consecutive twenty-five-year sentences for robbery and murder from Judge David S. Ritter on June 26, 1984. Brown will not be eligible for parole for seventy-five years. In April of that year, Brown's co-defendant Kathy Boudin had pleaded guilty to one count of robbery and one of murder, for which she was sentenced to twenty years to life in prison.

Four other defendants, Silvia Baraldini, Cecil Ferguson, Edward L. Joseph, and Sekuo Odinga, were found Guilty of conspiracy, racketeering, and other crimes, including several robberies and four murders. These four were sentenced in 1983 at the Federal District Court in Manhattan to twelve and a half to forty years imprisonment. All defendants except Brown and Boudin claimed to be political prisoners.

REF.: *CBA*; Harrison, *Criminal Calendar II*; Nash, *Almanac of World Crime*; Scott, *The Concise Encyclopedia of Crime and Criminals*.

Brink's Robbery, 1950, U.S., rob. Anthony "Tony" Pino, a New England petty thief who had a criminal record dating back to 1928, began to develop the idea of robbing the Brink's headquarters in Boston as early as 1948 when he noticed that he could enter the building almost at will and, because of the slack security, approach the upper level area where millions of dollars were processed behind an easily penetrated wire barrier. Pino took into his confidence Joseph F. "Big Joe" McGinnis, a Boston saloon keeper who helped organize a robbery gang, all culled from Boston's underworld and most of whom were, like Pino, small-time crooks looking to commit "the robbery of the century." These included Vincent J. Costa, who was said to be an expert getaway driver; James Ignatius Flaherty, bartender and burglar; Henry J. Baker, a lock specialist; and gunmen and professional burglars Thomas

F. Richardson, Michael V. Geagan, Adolph "Jazz" Maffie, John S. Banfield, Stanley H. Gusciora, and Joseph James "Specs" O'Keefe, a clever thief and burglar whose nickname, one he hated, came from the freckles that coated his face when he was in his teens.

The North Terminal Garage of the Brink's company was cased daily by members of the gang. They studied the comings and goings of employees from the street during the day and from rooftops with binoculars at night. This surveillance went on for eighteen months. Brink's shipment schedules were noted each day and when and where the biggest cash shipments would be made. Knowing the routines of the watchmen, gang members, in twos and threes, brazenly entered the Brink's building almost every night, going through their own routine of mock robbery, sneaking through doors, up stairways and down corridors to the money room so that all the gang members could find their ways through this building in the dark. Baker, the locksmith, removed locks from five separate doors in the Brink's building, one each night between the rounds of the watchmen, made keys for the locks and replaced a lock each night without being detected.

Then the gang practiced their robbery with the precision of a Ranger unit penetrating a high-security military operation. Seven of the men, led by O'Keefe, entered the building, went through the five doors and right up to the money room where Brink's employees were busy counting cash. Two others remained on rooftops with high-powered binoculars and a telescope to watch for police and guards. Another was at the wheel of a truck parked nearby, waiting for the loot to be thrown into the back. The robbers went through this routine twenty times but waited until Pino thought the moment was right—the moment being when the largest amount of cash would be on hand. The seven men entering the building were to look identical. Those chosen were all about five-feet-ten-inches tall, weighed between 170 and 180 pounds, and all would wear Navy pea jackets, halloween masks, rubber-soled shoes, and gloves.

Pino finally selected the night of Jan. 17, 1950, a murky, rainy night which would keep people off the streets. The seven men entered the Brink's building shortly before 7 p.m., went through the five locked doors using the keys made by Baker, walked silently upstairs and through halls until they came to the counting room. O'Keefe and the others reached the wire mesh door of this room at exactly 7:10 p.m. They had no key to this door. O'Keefe and the others pulled out guns and aimed them through the wire mesh at Thomas P. Lloyd, head cashier, as he came out of the vault. "This is a stickup," O'Keefe said in a low, menacing voice. "Open the gate and don't give us any trouble."

Only guard Charles Grell was armed; the weapons belonging to the four other men in the cage were in a gun wrack. Grell did as he was ordered and opened the gate without reaching for his weapon. Lloyd later told Boston police commissioner Thomas F. Sullivan that "it would have been sheer death for him (Grell) to reach for it." The five Brink's men were ordered to lay on the floor, faces down. They were then tied hands and feet behind their backs and adhesive tape was placed over their mouths by some of the thieves while other members of the robbery gang went directly into the vault and began filling large sacks with big bills. Each man knew his job. As one pulled the money off the shelves in the vault, another held open a sack and the sacks were passed from hand to hand from one robber to the next. The thieves scooped up $2,775,395 including $1,218,211.29 in cash and coins and $1,557,183.83 in money orders and checks. The sacks filled with all this loot weighed about 1,200 pounds and each man dragged two of these from the money room. Before leaving, the thieves looked at a large metal security box and thought to take it with them but, at the last minute, they decided it was too heavy to drag down corridors and steps. They left it behind and the more than $1 million in cash it contained.

By 7:27 p.m., the gang had left the premises with the largest cash haul in an American robbery to that time, accomplishing the massive theft within seventeen minutes. The money was thrown

The Brink's robbers under arrest in 1956, left to right, Jim Flaherty, Mike Geagan, Thomas Richardson, Joe McGinnis, Tony Pino, Vincent Costa, Jazz Maffie, Henry Baker.

Tony Pino, jovial mastermind.

Joseph "Specs" O'Keefe

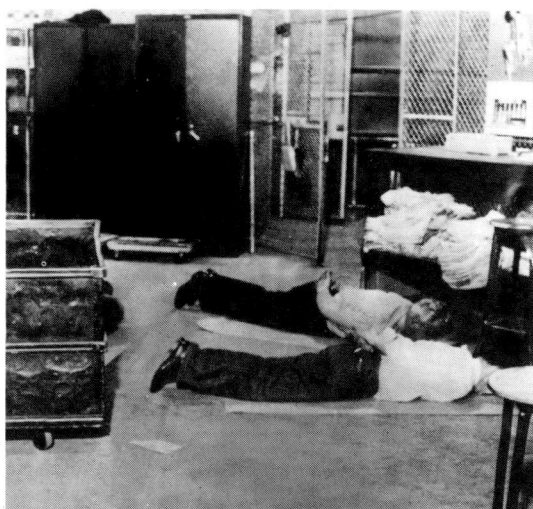

Guards on floor reenact the robbery.

Police photo: McGinnis.

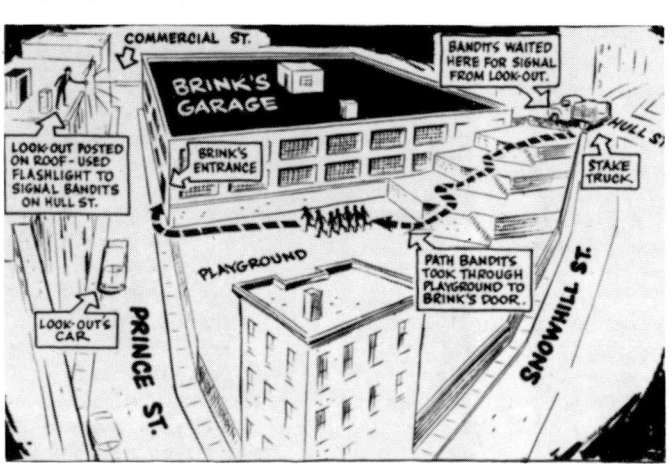

Sketch shows how thieves robbed Brink's.

Loot left behind.

into the truck which was driven to Roxbury and to the home of Adolph "Jazz" Maffie. Here the robbers destroyed more than $90,000 in new bills which the thieves suspected were marked, along with the negotiable securities. The balance was kept by Maffie to be split up later, $1,100,000. Pino and McGinnis had ordered that the money was not to be taken by anyone since any considerable spending by gang members would surely draw suspicion. They would wait until the inevitable police "heat" dissipated and then take their shares. Each gang member returned to the various jobs they held. Most of them, along with hundreds of other suspects, were pulled in for questioning since almost all the gang members had long police records. They were routinely grilled and released. State and local police, along with the FBI, had no idea where to look for the robbers. The clues left behind at the scene of the robbery were scant: two pieces of white cotton line and a visored cap with its lining and label torn from it.

A month later, the gang members took their shares of the stolen money, about $100,000. O'Keefe entrusted about $90,000 of his money to a fellow mob member, and when he was sent to prison for another robbery, he demanded but never got his money. Facing a long prison term and incensed at being stalled on getting his money, O'Keefe contacted authorities and tried to plea bargain his sentence in return for information about the celebrated Brink's robbery.

Though Banfield died of natural causes in 1955, the other thieves were arrested and given long prison sentences. Several of them were later released, and some are alive at this writing. What angered surviving gang members was the fact that a Boston *Globe* crime reporter, Joseph F. Dineen, wrote a novel about the Brink's robbery, entitled *Six Rivers to Cross* and reportedly made $150,000 on a movie sale of this book, more money than any of the robbers ever enjoyed from their elaborate and shocking robbery.

REF.: Behn, *Big Stick-Up at Brink's*; *CBA*; Harrison, *Criminal Calendar II*; Nash, *Almanac of World Crime*; ____, *Citiizen Hoover*; O'Keefe and Considine, *The Men Who Robbed Brink's*; Scott, *Concise Encyclopedia of Crime and Criminals*; Whitehead, *The FBI Story*; Williams, *The Super Crooks*; (FICTION), Dineen, *Six Bridges to Cross*; (FILM), *Six Bridges to Cross*, 1955; *The Brink's Job,* 1978.

Brinon, Fernand de, 1885-1947, Fr., treas. Advocated political reconciliation with Germany in the 1930s, and represented the Vichy government after the fall of France in 1940. In 1944, he headed the government commission established at Belfort after the fall of Marshal Pétain's collaborationist government. He fled to Germany but was caught, tried, and executed as a collaborator. REF.: *CBA*.

Brinsden, Matthias, d.1722, Brit., mur. For most of his adult life, marital happiness evaded this shopkeeper from Blackfriars. His first wife, the widow of the man under whom he had served his apprenticeship, died, leaving him the business and a modest sum of money. But then Matthias Brinsden began to court a fetching, sought-after townswoman named Hannah. For reasons known only to herself she accepted Brinsden's offer over those of her many suitors. They married and had ten children, five of whom lived to adulthood. But their domestic life was quarrelsome and further disturbed by a deadly fever which incapacitated Brinsden for a long period of time. His business suffered, and the family found itself in reduced circumstances.

When Brinsden recovered, his assets were all but gone and he had to accept menial jobs, including selling newspapers in the town. All this left Brinsden in a surly temper. After one particularly bothersome day, he returned home to have his wife ask what they were going to eat that night. "Bread and cheese," he snapped. "Can't you eat that as well as the children?"

No, she replied. She wanted some meat. He reminded her that he had no money for such an extravagance, but she continued pestering him until he seized a knife and stabbed her beneath the breast.

A surgeon was summoned, but there nothing he could do to prevent her death. Brinsden took refuge in the house of a barber in Shadwell, but was apprehended by the constable when he wrote to his children.

Matthias Brinsden in the act of murdering his wife.

During his trial he swore that his wife was drunk and had accidentally impaled herself on his knife, but the court did not believe this story, especially when his own daughter gave the most incriminating testimony. Brinsden admitted his guilt, but he said that he had only wanted to make his wife obey him, as the scriptures commanded a wife to do. To the charge that he had engaged in sexual relations with his eldest daughter, he replied, "I here solemnly declare, as I am entering into the presence of God, I never knew whether she was a man or a woman since she was a babe....I never lay with her, or carnally knew her, much less had a child by her." He was hanged at Tyburn Hill on Sept. 24, 1722. REF.: *CBA*.

Brinvilliers, Marie de, 1630-76, Fr., mur. Marie de Brinvilliers was responsible for at least fifty poison murders. Her fixation with poison was born out of personal greed. After marrying the Marquis Antoine de Brinvilliers, Marie took a lover, Gaudin de Saint-Croix, who helped her secure poison. With the help of the conniving de Saint-Croix, Marie planned to murder her wealthy father, Dreux d'Aubray, to inherit his vast estate and live a life of ease with her lover.

Before she carried out this scheme, she "experimented" with Saint-Croix's poisons. The patients of the Hotel Dieu, a hospital in Paris, became her first victims. Pretending to nurse the sick and feeble, Marie de Brinvilliers murdered at least fifty patients. She disposed of her father in 1666, and later murdered her two brothers to gain their property as well.

However, the money left behind did not satisfy her. She

The executioner displaying the head of Marie de Brinvilliers.

then turned on her peers in the French court, killing anyone that stood in her way or displeased her. Meanwhile de Saint-Croix mixed the potions as fast as he could. In a moment of carelessness, he inhaled the noxious fumes and fell over dead, and the

the true story came out. A servant confessed to her mistress' sinister activities under the threat of torture. In 1676, the beautiful but deadly Marie was ordered to issue a confession before the assembled multitudes at Notre Dame Cathedral, after which she was beheaded and burned.

REF.: Brookes, *Murder In Fact and Fiction;* Brophy, *The Meaning of Murder; CBA;* Dickson, *Murder By Numbers;* Douthwaite, *Mass Murder;* Glaister, *The Power of Poison;* Lambton, *Echoes of Causes Celebres;* Nash, *Almanac of World Crime; ___, Look For the Woman;* Thompson, *Poison and Poisoners;* Wilson, *Wncyclopedia of Murder.*

Brique, Micheline, 1954-   , and **Chamand, Jocelyne,** 1956-   , Fr., mur. It is more than likely that Jean-Michel Ray had believed himself lucky when he picked up two young, attractive, and scantily-clad female hitchhikers. Micheline Brique, eighteen, and Jocelyne Chamand, sixteen, had spent most of their adolescence in and out of trouble, finally being transferred from a juvenile delinquent home to the tighter security of a hospital. Two days after escaping form the hospital, on July 13, 1972, Brique and Chamand spent the last of their money on two butcher knives at a hardware store in Macon, Fr. The next day, Bastille Day, they began hitchhiking along Route Nationale 6, intent upon killing a driver for his money.

Ray was the fourth driver to pick up Brique and Chamand that day, the first three not being suitable victims. The women enticed him to pull off the road into a secluded glade where they savagely attacked him, stabbing him eleven times. They watched for more than half an hour as he bled to death. Brique and Chamand then caught another ride into Lyons. They were later apprehended carrying the bloodstained knives. Both women admitted their guilt and were sentenced to thirty years in prison.

REF.: *CBA;* Dunning, *The Arbor House Treasury of True Crime.*

Brisbon, Henry, Jr. (AKA: The I-57 Killer), 1956-   , U.S., consp.-rob.-mur. On the night of June 3, 1973, a car carrying four men forced a woman's car off Interstate 57, just south of Chicago. One of the men forced her from the car at gunpoint, then ordered her to strip naked and climb through a barbed-wire fence. He then shot her between the legs with a 12-gauge pump-action shotgun, leaving her in agony for several minutes before killing her with a shot to the throat. The four killers, returning to the road to seek out more victims, ran the car of a young couple off the road near Country Club Hills less than an hour later.

Dorothy Cerny and James Schmidt, both 25-years-old, were engaged to be married in six months. The couple, ordered to lie on the roadside, pleaded for mercy, but their killer shot them in the back after telling Cerny and Schmidt to "kiss your last kiss."

Henry Brisbon, Jr. was found Guilty of both conspiracy to commit murder and the murder of Cerny and Schmidt and was sentenced in November 1977 to 1,000 to 3,000 years in prison. His youth at the time of the killing—he was seventeen—and the law, which then prohibited capital punishment, prevented the judge from imposing the death penalty. At Brisbon's sentencing, Assistant State's Attorney Michael Ficaro said, "He is a wild, savage beast that should be caged ... he would gladly kill again if he got the chance." Amazingly, Ficaro proved to be quite prophetic.

On Oct. 19, 1978, the I-57 killer struck again, but this time behind bars. While serving his sentence at the Stateville Penitentiary near Joliet, Ill., Brisbon used a sharpened soup ladle to murder fellow inmate Richard E. Morgan. Brisbon was convicted of this murder on Jan. 22, 1982, and it took an all-male jury less than an hour and a half on Feb. 24 to sentence Brisbon to death in the courtroom of Herman Haase. The I-57 killer, who had instigated a prison riot and taken part in fifteen attacks on guards and inmates, declared as he was led away from the trial, "You'll never get me. I'll kill again. Then you'll have another long trial. And I'll do it again."

Indeed, another murder attempt by Brisbon took place when he broke away from his armed escort at the Menard Correctional Center's death row unit on Feb. 15, 1983. He managed to arm himself with a piece of metal wire which he used to stab two other

condemned inmates, including mass murderer John Wayne Gacy. Neither of the prisoners was seriously wounded.

Will County State's Attorney Edward Petka remarked that Brisbon was "a very, very terrible human being, a walking testimonial for the death penalty." The Illinois Supreme Court disagreed, overturning the death sentence on Apr. 19, 1985, claiming that the state had prejudiced the jury by introducing inflammatory evidence concerning the highway murders. Once again Brisbon appeared in court for sentencing, and once again, on Oct. 7, 1986, he was sentenced to death.

Brisbon continues to cause trouble in prison, even in maximum security where he is currently being held at Menard awaiting further appeal of his sentence. On Aug. 3, 1987, he threw a dumbbell at another prisoner, fracturing the skull of 34-year-old convicted murderer John Phillips. See: **Gacy, John Wayne.**

REF.: *CBA;* Godwin, *Murder, U.S.A.*

Briscoe, Ricky, 1972-88, U.S., mur. Linette West was only sixteen years old when she died on Mar. 25, 1988, in her home at 1200 Nova Avenue in the Capitol Heights district of Washington. She lived with her family and her 3-month-old child born out of wedlock. Linette's killer was Ricky Briscoe, a former boyfriend whom she had broken up with after her baby was born.

On Mar. 25, 1988, Briscoe turned up at the West residence. When Linette and Juanita, her sister, tried to send him away, Briscoe threatened Linette. "Don't go to sleep 'cause I'm going to kill you," he told her.

About 4 a.m., Juanita was awakened by the screams of her sister in the living room. Briscoe had her pinned to the floor. There was a distinct aroma of kerosene. "Help me!" cried Linette. "He's going to burn me!"

Pregnant herself, Juanita ran next door for help, but there was no answer. She ran down the street knocking on doors but there was no response. Returning to her home, she met the unspeakable horror of seeing her sister engulfed in flames. Linette fled the house and ran nearly a hundred yards to her uncle's house. She was rushed to Washington Hospital Center, where she was found to be burned over 90 per cent of her body. She died shortly before 9 a.m. on Mar. 28.

After setting Linette on fire, Briscoe was unable to escape the flames and died, after becoming entangled in some drapes. His body was found near the front door. Shocked and grief-stricken neighbors complied with the family's request and asked a local man to sing *I'm Climbing on the Rough Side of the Mountain* at Linette's funeral, the song echoing the life of one black family. REF.: *CBA.*

Brissot, Jacques Pierre (Brissot de Warville), 1754-93, Fr., treas. Author of two books on the philosophy of law in 1781 and 1782. A moderate Girondist, he was imprisoned in the Bastille, joined the mob that destroyed it in 1789, and was guillotined in Paris. REF.: *CBA.*

Bristol, 1747-63, U.S., mur. A freed black, 16-year-old Bristol attacked Elizabeth McKinstry, a total stranger, on a Taunton, Mass., street, knocking her to the ground and, in full view of many passersby, crushed her skull with an ax. When brought to trial for murder, Bristol would give no reason for the senseless attack. He was convicted and hanged before a large crowd on Dec. 1, 1763.

REF.: *The Blood of Abel; CBA.*

Bristol, Warren, 1823-90, U.S., jur. Prosecuting attorney of Goodhue County, Minn., in 1856. He was appointed judge of the New Mexico Territory in 1872 by President Ulysses S. Grant. REF.: *CBA.*

Bristol, William, 1779-1836, U.S., jur. U.S. district attorney of Connecticut in 1812. He was appointed judge of the district of Connecticut by President John Quincy Adams in 1826. REF.: *CBA.*

Bristol Reform Riots, 1831, Brit., riot. Mobs of angry protesters swept across England following the House of Lords' decision to throw out the Reform Bill that would have equalized representation in Parliament; but the mob that assembled in Bristol was by far the most destructive. The first day was relatively calm, although the carriage of the recorder, Sir Charles Wetherell was stoned and the crowd broke into fits of coughing while he gave a speech at Guildhall. But the next day, the rioters, nearly ten thousand strong, attacked the jail, released prisoners, and set fire to the building before moving on to burn down toll houses, the Gloucester county prison, the bishop's palace, the custom house, and forty-two homes. Armed troops finally brought an end to the riot.

A special commission was created on Jan. 2, 1832, by the House of Commons to investigate the matter. By Jan. 14, twenty-one people had been found Guilty of arson, and four were executed. At Nottingham, a similar proceeding took place concerning rioting in that city, ending with nine people convicted, five of whom were sentenced to death, though only three were executed.

REF.: *CBA;* Thomson, *The Story of Scotland Yard.*

Bristow, Benjamin Helm, 1832-96, U.S., lawyer. Solicitor general from 1870-72. While serving as secretary of the treasury from 1874-76, he secured valuable evidence leading to the convictions of key members of the Whisky Ring which had bilked the government out of thousands of dollars of tax revenue. REF.: *CBA.*

Britain Clothing Coupon Theft, 1943, Brit., theft. In the midst of WWII, clothing, among other things, was scarce and people whose homes had been destroyed could not afford to buy it. To alleviate this problem, the British government issued coupons to people whose clothes were destroyed by war and to discharged military personnel. On the black market, fifty of these coupons were worth £1 in September 1943, a sum which led one army major to steal five million of them.

The case was quickly solved by Chief Inspector Greeno when it was learned that the culprit must be someone working from the inside. After tailing the suspect for some time, on Sept. 18, 1943, Officer Fred Hodge finally apprehended the major red-handed, clutching a briefcase full of coupons. A trunk containing the remainder—minus the £500 worth of coupons he had already sold—was recovered from his hotel room. For the theft, the man was sentenced to five years in prison.

REF.: *CBA;* Greeno, *War On the Underworld.*

Britannicus (Claudius Tiberius Germanicus), 41-55 A.D., Roman., assass. The scion of a noble family, he was surnamed Britannicus to honor his father's (Emperor Claudius) victory in Britain in 43 A.D. He was the rightful heir to the Roman throne, but was denied by Agrippina, who placed her son Nero at the head of government. He was later poisoned by Nero. See: **Nero.** REF.: *CBA.*

Brite, Coke, and **Brite, John,** prom. 1936, U.S., (wrong. convict.) mur. Three men were shot and killed in the woods of northern California on Aug. 29, 1936. An eyewitness claimed to have seen Coke Brite and his brother John Brite shoot and kill police officers Joseph Clark and Martin Lange, and a third man, Seaborn. Not only did this account of the deaths ignore the fact that the killings took place well after midnight in a darkened forest, but the eyewitness, Baker, was a neighbor of the Brites who had a long-standing feud with the brothers.

At the December 1936 trial the jury accepted the testimony of Baker, who claimed to have accompanied the officers and his friend Seaborn to the Brites' camp where the Brites had supposedly killed the three men. Baker continually changed his story of the night's events and even made statements that could not possibly have been true. Such testimony, along with other inconsistencies, led the district attorney, James Davis, to withdraw from the prosecution because he no longer believed the men to be guilty. That did not stop the jury from finding the Brite brothers Guilty of three counts of first-degree murder, for which they were sentenced to death.

Even after the conviction of the Brite brothers the investigation continued. In 1938 California governor Culbert L. Olson commuted their sentences to life in prison and, in 1952, following inquiries made by attorney Arthur DeBeau Carr, the Brites were found to be wrongly convicted and released from prison. Carr's

investigation showed that the prosecution had withheld information, based its case on perjured testimony, and followed an inaccurate theory of the crime. REF.: *CBA.*

British Bank of the Middle East, 1976, Leb., rob. In January 1976, Lebanese insurgents blasted open the vaults of the British Bank of the Middle East in Bab Idriss, carrying off an estimated $20-$50 million from safety deposit boxes.

REF.: *CBA;* Nash, *Almanac of World Crime.*

British Soccer Riots, 1980s, Belg., riot. During the 1985 European Cup Final match between Liverpool and Juventus at Heysel Stadium in Brussels, thirty-nine people, mainly fans of the Italian team, were crushed to death when a wall collapsed under pressure from rioting British hooligans. Fourteen of the twenty-four supporters of the Liverpool team charged with inciting the crowd and participating in the stampede were found Guilty of involuntary manslaughter. Each was fined £1,000 and sentenced to three years in prison by Judge Pierre Verlynde—a sentence which was not served behind bars as all were eligible for parole after already having served more than six months while on remand.

Two officials involved with the match were found Guilty of criminal negligence. Belgian police captain Johan Mahieu, who was in charge of crowd control, was sentenced to nine months' imprisonment and former Belgian Football Union head, Albert Roosens, who failed to follow standards of the European football authority, was given six months in prison. Both sentences were suspended.

The fourteen convicted Liverpool fans were: Michael Barnes, Stanley Conroy, Gary Cooper, John Davies, Gary Evans, Kevin Hughes, Ronald O'Brien, Graham Postlethwaite, Gary Rutter, Timothy Williams, Terence Wilson, Alan Woodray, Mark Woods, and Paul Wright.

During the 1988 football season, a record 6,147 fans were arrested because of violent disruptions. The rowdy fans (known as "yobs", a slang inversion of "boys") were primarily young males. They wreaked havoc on West Germany, injuring a number of people as they rampaged through bars, broke windows, and fought with bystanders.

An attempt to curb the violence was proposed in January 1989 by the British government's Football Spectators Bill, which would limit the fans at a game to members of the respective soccer clubs involved in the match being played. The bill would also prevent soccer hooligans from traveling to the European continent to watch their teams play. REF.: *CBA.*

Britland, Mary, prom. 19th Cent., Brit., mur. Mary Britland poisoned her landlady in order to marry the woman's husband. Unfortunately for Britland, the husband did not even regard her as a friend, thus leaving her to stand trial alone.

Found Guilty of murder, Britland was sentenced to be hanged at Strangeways Jail in Manchester, England. From the time of her conviction until the executioner's release of the trap beneath her feet, Britland screamed and bemoaned her fate.

REF.: Atholl, *The Reluctant Hangman; CBA.*

Britt, Darlwin Joanne, 1963- , U.S., child abuse. A workman about to board up a ramshackle house in Gary, Ind., on Jan. 16, 1988, discovered 9-year-old Darlwin Carlisle locked inside a barricaded room in the abandoned home. When the news got out that the starving child's legs were severely frostbitten, people from across the U.S. offered their support. The child had been left in the house by her mother Darlwin Joanne Britt who had failed to support her child.

Britt was arrested for neglecting to provide her daughter with proper care. For the two- to three-day period in winter during which the girl was locked in the building with no heat, electricity, or plumbing, she suffered dehydration and such complete loss of circulation in her lower legs that both legs had to be amputated five inches below the knees.

In a plea-bargained agreement—which Britt's attorney, Lake County, Ind., public defender Daniel Toomey, tried to dissuade her from accepting—Britt agreed to plead guilty to a lesser charge carrying a reduced sentence if the state dropped two other charges. The agreement was sought by Lake County prosecutor Jack Crawford because young Carlisle was "very reluctant to testify concerning the details of her injury and to confront her mother in a courtroom context." Superior Court Judge Richard Maroc granted the plea and on May 27, 1988, sentenced Britt to fourteen years in prison, the maximum sentence she could be given. REF.: *CBA.*

Britt, Harold, c.1946- , U.S., mansl. Harold Britt was employed as a bouncer at Andrews' Triangle Pub, a lesbian bar in College Park, Ga., near Atlanta. In the fall of 1969, Britt moved in with Loraine Andrews, forty-eight, though he seldom remained faithful to the woman who was twice his age. The evening she died, the two had quarreled over Britt's seeing another woman earlier that day. During an argument in the bar, Britt fired two shots hitting no one, before Andrews escorted him from the premises. About two hours passed before Britt telephoned the bartender at the Triangle Pub to say that his boss was dead.

Britt later claimed to be innocent of murder, stating that the killing was an accident. He spent more than a year in jail awaiting trial, which was delayed eight times. On Feb. 1, 1971, Britt was found Guilty of voluntary manslaughter, for which he was sentenced to seven years in prison. REF.: *CBA.*

Brittle, William, prom. 1964-65, Brit., mur. Peter Thomas had lent William Bittle £2,000. Coincidentally, Thomas was found dead the month the loan was due to be repaid. The discovery of Peter Thomas' body in Bracknell Woods on June 28, 1964, and its state of decomposition caused by bluebottle fly larvae led pathologist Dr. Keith Simpson to conclude that Thomas had been dead for at least ten days. This estimation matched the information known to Detective Superintendent Horace Faber that Thomas had been missing from his home in Lydney since June 16 or 17. Dennis Roberts, however, claimed to have seen Thomas alive on June 20. Brittle claimed that he repaid Thomas the day he disappeared. Even with a strong witness supporting his story, a coroner's jury still named Brittle as the murderer, and he was tried at the spring assize of 1965, in Gloucester.

At the trial, Queen's Counsel Quintin Hogg represented Brittle. He had two more witnesses, Jane Charles and Gwendoline Padwick, who swore they saw Thomas alive on June 21—a minimum of three days after he was dead, according to Simpson. The prosecution, led by Ralph Cusack, could not refute the testimony of the defense witnesses, and the testimony of one defense witness, Professor McKenny-Hughes, unexpectedly corroborated Simpson's theory as to time of death. The jury decided that Thomas could not possibly have been alive when the witnesses stated and found Brittle Guilty of murder, for which he received a life sentence.

REF.: *CBA;* Simpson, *Forty Years of Murder.*

Brletic, Joseph James, 1927- , U.S., rob. Joseph James Brletic made the FBI's Ten Most Wanted list in 1948, after breaking out of the county jail in St. Louis. He was awaiting trial on charges of armed robbery. On Feb. 10, 1953, the fugitive was arrested in Lancaster, Calif., after a resident there recognized him from a photograph in a Los Angeles newspaper. Brletic was working as a pinspotter in a bowling alley at the time. REF.: *CBA.*

Broadingham, Elizabeth, and **Aikney, Thomas,** d.1776, Brit., mur. The murder of John Broadingham, planned by his wife and carried out by her reluctant lover Thomas Aikney, was cunning in design and brutal in nature. Broadingham, a smuggler, was captured and imprisoned in York for his many crimes. During his incarceration, Elizabeth Broadingham took up with Aikney and lived with him for three months—after her husband was released from prison. To rid herself of a man she didn't love, Elizabeth proposed that they kill him. Aikney, horrified at first, agreed to murder Broadingham after Elizabeth refused to elope with her lover while her husband was still alive.

On Feb.13, 1776, just eight days after Elizabeth was welcomed home by her forgiving husband, Aikney appeared on their doorstep in the dead of night, brandishing a knife. After slashing at the unsuspecting husband's thigh and stomach, Aikney dropped the knife and fled from the house. Broadingham stumbled out the door into the street, crying, "Murder, murder!" He lived through the next day, enough time for the authorities to find his murderer.

The knife was produced at the conspirators' trial as proof of their guilt. After giving a confession, the conspirators were executed on Mar. 20, 1776. Elizabeth was strangled and her body burned to ashes. Aikney was hanged for his crime and the body was sent to Leeds where it was dissected by surgeons.

REF.: *CBA;* Nash, *Look for the Woman.*

Broadwell, Richard L., See: **Dalton Brothers.**

Broadwell, William, and **Broadwell, Edward,** and **Phine, R.L.,** and **Wilson, F.,** prom. 1901, U.S., gamb. In the summer of 1901 there was one ham that was not for sale hanging behind the counter at the Chicago meat market run by gambler William Broadwell. The ham was made of wood and it concealed the bets that Broadwell, his brother Edward Broadwell, and F. Wilson had taken from customers on horseraces—the outcomes of which were received by the ticker stored in the meat freezer. Detective Clifton R. Woolridge and his men raided the store on May 31, which led to Broadwell's third gambling conviction and a fine of $50. A second raid that summer resulted in the same fine for Broadwell and a fine of $25 assessed to an associate, R.L. Phine.

REF.: *CBA;* Wooldridge, *Hands Up!*

Brody, Thomas H., Jr., c.1950- , U.S., (wrong. convict?) rob.- (wrong. convict.) mur. On June 12, 1973, restaurateur John Georgeff was murdered during a robbery. Later that year, Thomas H. Broady, Jr. was found Guilty and sentenced to ten to twenty-five years in prison. His conviction was overturned when it was discovered that police knew the identity of the real killer. According to Richard Clark, a suspect in the robbery of Georgeff's restaurant in Columbus, Ohio, Donald Boyd, who had since been killed in a police shootout, had shot Georgeff, and Broady was in no way involved. Broady's attorney, David Long, also learned that police detective Tom Jones had known this information but had chosen to suppress it. Broady was subsequently acquitted at his retrial, but he was found Guilty of another robbery in the area.

During Broady's second trial, the judge, Clifford Rader, did not allow witnesses to testify corroborating Broady's alibi, because of an Ohio criminal procedure law that permits the judge to deny all alibis not properly filed with the court a week in advance. This same judge, however, helped Broady obtain his parole in 1978 after serving five of his ten- to twenty-five-year sentence. REF.: *CBA.*

Brocius, Curly Bill (or Brosius, AKA: William Graham), prom. 1880s, U.S., west. outl. Background on this western gunman is sketchy at best. He was six foot tall with black curly hair and blue eyes, supposedly a light-hearted cowboy who was head wrangler at the McLowery ranch. He was also portrayed as a vicious, drunken gunman who would draw his six-guns at the slightest provocation. Many murders were credited to him, including that of the Haslett Brothers in 1881 in their store at Huachita after the Hasletts reportedly shot and killed two members of the Clanton-McLowery clan. A known rustler and gunman with a fast draw, Curly Bill Brocius led members of the Clanton-McLowery rustling gang into Arizona towns to "buffalo" the citizens, taking over the saloons and racing up and down the streets on their pintos, firing weapons into the air. On Oct. 28, 1880, Brocius and other cowboys entered Tombstone and were "hurrahing" the town. Drunk, the cowboys blindly fired their six-guns. This caused Fred White, Tombstone's first marshal, to deputize Virgil Earp, Wyatt Earp's brother, before both men went hunting for Brocius. They found him in an alley and when White tried to disarm Brocius, the gunman's pistol went off, mortally wounding White.

Almost immediately after the weapon went off, Wyatt Earp appeared and marched up to Brocius, pulled his foot-long Buntline

Special from its holster and crashed it down on Brocius' head, knocking him unconscious, and then dragged him to jail. Brocius was later acquitted of White's death since White himself, with his dying breath, stated that he had been accidentally shot. Brocius' next confrontation with the law occured on May 25, 1881, when he met and began an argument with tough lawman William Breakenridge. The lawman, goaded by a drunken Brocius, finally shot his antagonist in the mouth—a terrible wound from which Brocius recovered, but one that convinced him to hang up his guns, or so it was later claimed, and leave Arizona, later settling in Texas under the name of William Graham which may or may not have been his real name. According to Wyatt Earp, Brocius was involved with the Clanton-McLowery rustling gang throughout its confrontation with the Earp Brothers, and that he tracked down and killed the outlaw some time after the gunfight at the O.K. Corral. See: **Breckenridge, William; Clanton-McLowery Gang; Earp, Wyatt.**

REF.: American Guide Series: *Arizona, A State Guide*; Argall, *Outlawry and Justice in Old Arizona*; Axford, *Around Western Campfires*; Bakarich, *Gun-Smoke*; ____, *There's Treasure in Our Hills*; Bartholomew, *The Biographical Album of Western Gunfighters*; ____, *Western Hard-Cases*; ____, *Wyatt, Earp, 1879-1882*; Bechdolt, *When the West Was Young*; Bishop, *Old Mexico and Her Lost Provinces*; Blythe, *A Pictorial Souvenir*; Boyer, *An Illustrated Life of Doc Holliday*; Breakenridge, *Helldorado*; Breihan, *Great Gunfighters of the West*; ____, *Great Lawmen of the West*; Brent, *Great Western Heroes*; Brophy, *Arizona Sketch Book*; Buffum, *On Two Frontiers*; ____, *Smith of Bear City*; Burns, *Tombstone, An Iliad of the Southwest*; CBA; Chisholm, *Brewery Gulch*; Clum, *It All Happened in Tombstone*; Clum, *Apache Agent*; Cox, *Luke Short and His Era*; Cunningham, *Famous in the West*; ____, *Triggernometry*; Erwin, *The Southwest of John H. Slaughter*; Fisher and Holmes, *Gold Rushes and Mining Camps*; Francis, *Saddle and Moccasin*; Franke, *They Plowed Up Hell*; Frantz, *The American Cowboy*; Ganzhorn, *I've Killed Men*; Gardner, *The Old West*; Gaylord, *Handgunner's Guide*; Hall-Quest, *Wyatt Earp, Marshal of the Old West*; Hamlin, *The True Story of Billy the Kid*; Henderson, *Keys to Crookdom*; Hertzog, *A Directory of New Mexico Desperadoes*; Hill, *Then and Now*; Hogan, *The Life and Death of Johnny Ringo*; Holloway, *Texas Gun Lore*; Horan and Sann, *Pictorial History of the Wild West*; Hutchinson, *The Life and Personal Writings of Eugene Manlove Rhodes*; Jahns, *The Frontier World of Doc Holliday*; Jenkinson, *Ghost Towns of New Mexico*; Johnston, *The Last Roundup*; Kemp, *Cow Dust and Saddle Leather*; King, *Pioneer Western Empire Builders*; ____, *Wranglin' the Past*; Koller, *The American Gun*; Lake, *Under Cover for Wells Fargo*; Lake, *Wyatt Earp, Frontier Marshal*; ____, *He Carried a Six-Shooter*; Lesure, *Adventures in Arizona*; Lockwood, *Pioneer Days in Arizona*; McCarty, *The Enchanted West*; McCarty, *The Gunfighters*; McClintock, *Arizona*; Martin, *The Earps of Tombstone*; ____, *Tombstone's Epitaph*; Masterson, *Famous Gunfighters of the Western Frontier*; Michelson, *Mankillers at Close Range*; Miller, *Arizona, The Last Frontier*; Muir, *Old Shakespeare*; Myers, *Doc Holliday*; ____, *The Last Chance*; Nash, *Bloodletters and Badmen*; North, *The Saga of the Cowboy*; Penfield, *Dig Here!*; ____, *Western Sheriffs and Marshals*; Raine, *Famous Sheriffs and Western Outlaws*; ____, *Forty-Five Caliber Law*; Rosa, *The Gunfighter, Man or Myth?*; Santee, *Lost Pony Tracks*; Siringo, *Riata and Spurs*; Small, *The Best of True West*; Stanley, *Dave Rudabaugh, Border Ruffian*; Tilghman, *Spotlight*; Upshur, *As I Recall Them*; Walters, *Tombstone's Yesterdays*; Waters, *The Story of Mrs. Virgil Earp*; Waters, *A Gallery of Western Badmen*; Way, *Frontier Arizona*; Way, *The Tombstone Story*; Wellman, *Glory, God and Gold*; ____, *The Trampling Herd*; White, *My Texas*; Williams, *Pioneer Surveyor*; Wilson, *Out of the West*; Woods, *Ghost Towns*; Wyllys, *Arizona, The History of a Frontier State*; (FILM) *Tombstone, the Town Too Tough to Die*, 1942; *Hour of the Gun*, 1967.

Brock, Leonard Calvert (AKA: **Will Waldrip, Joe Jackson, Henry Davis, W.L. Brock**), 1860-90, U.S., west. outl. Leonard Calvert Brock was a member of the Burrow Brothers gang of train robbers. Born on July 13, 1860, Brock and his brother, W.L. Brock, joined the Burrow gang in 1888 and aided the notorious brothers in train robberies in Texas and Alabama. He was identified as one of the bandits accompanying the Burrow Brothers when they robbed a Mobile and Ohio train on Sept. 25, 1889. A substantial reward was posted for Brock, who was arrested on a train in Columbus, Miss., in July 1890. He was quickly convicted and given a long prison term, committing suicide on Nov. 10, 1890, by jumping from the fourth tier of the cell block of his prison. See: **Burrow, Reuben Houston.**

REF.: Bartholomew, *The Biographical Album of Western Gunfighters*; CBA.

Brock, Thomas, and **Pelham, John**, and **Power, Michael**, d.1816, Brit., consp.-treas. Thomas Connolly, James Quin, and Dennis Riorton were found Guilty of forging counterfeit banknotes and shillings, and they were sentenced to death, the penalty for counterfeiting at the time. The three men admitted to a Catholic priest that they were innocent but had kept silent because they had been sworn to secrecy. This oath of secrecy, however, had been made to Thomas Brock, John Pelham, and Michael Power, the same men who had employed them to cut brass into shilling-shaped pieces and then notified the police of the Irishmen's alleged wrongdoing. When the truth was made known, Brock, Pelham, and Power were soon found Guilty of high treason and took their rightful places on the scaffold in 1816. Connolly, Quin, and Riorton were given a royal pardon and provided with money to return to Ireland.

REF.: CBA; Culpin, *The Newgate Noose*; Potter, *The Art of Hanging*.

Brockway, William (AKA: **Long Bill**), prom. 1895-96, U.S. count. Rather than spend the remaining years of his life in prison and tarnish the reputation of his daughters, the notorious engraver Charlie Ulrich agreed with agent Bill Burns to become a Secret Service informant against William Brockway. Ulrich finally obtained enough information for the Secret Service to arrest Brockway and his men. The arrests began on Aug. 3, 1895, and concluded on Sept. 7. Burns provided protection for Ulrich, who had received death threats for six months until Brockway was found Guilty of counterfeiting and sentenced to ten years in prison on Mar. 8, 1896, with his accomplices receiving lighter sentences.

REF.: Bloom, *Money Of Their Own*; Ceasar, *Incredible Detective*; CBA.

Broderick, Case, 1839-1920, U.S., jur. Prosecuting attorney of Jackson County, Kan., from 1876-80, member of the U.S. House of Representatives from 1891-99, and appointed judge of the Idaho Territorial Court in 1884 by President Chester Arthur. REF.: CBA.

Broderick, David C., See: **Terry, David S.**

Broderick, Vincent Lyons, 1920-   , U.S., jur. Deputy police commissioner of New York City from 1954-56 and police commissioner from 1965-66. He was appointed judge of the District Court of the Southern District of New York by President Gerald Ford in 1976. REF.: CBA.

Brodeur, Louis Philippe, 1862-1924, Can., jur. Speaker of the House of Commons in 1901, and judge of the Supreme Court of Canada in 1911. REF.: CBA.

Brodie, James, d.1799, Brit., mur. While awaiting execution for murdering the boy who acted as his guide, James Brodie, a blind beggar, became the last person forced to wear a brank, a metal device strapped to a person's head to immobilize the tongue, for his noisy behavior in his cell. He was hanged on July 15, 1799.

REF.: Andrews, *Old-Time Punishments*; CBA.

Brodie, William (AKA: **Deacon Brodie**, Capt. **John Dixon**), 1741-88, Scot., burg. William Brodie was born in Edinburgh on Sept. 28, 1741, the son of a prosperous cabinet maker. He was well-educated and by the time he was forty, Brodie was made Deacon of the Incorporation of Wrights, a title which referred to Brodie's status as a master carpenter and had no connection with organized religion, as popularly thought by later generations unfamiliar with the details of his life. He was also a City Councilman and he lived well in a resplendent house in Lawnmarket, Edinburgh. A small, dark-haired man with large brown eyes, Brodie's shoulders were extraordinarily broad and he was nimble of foot. He was thought to be "a kind and goodly man, one of the noblest souls one could meet." He wore white during the day and was seen to carry a Bible, which he read assiduously each day, usually in public places where he could be seen to do so. He was a member of the exclusive Cape Club which counted the poet Robert Burns a member and whose members often gave receptions for such esteemed literary lights as Samuel Johnson. A confirmed bachelor, Brodie told friends that his ambition to be "the best cabinetmaker in Edinburgh, even better than my father," and such ambition left no room for marriage or romance.

That was the portrait Brodie drew for a public image. The other side of his double life was sinister, profligate, and criminal. At night, Brodie, dressed all in black, drank and gambled in the worst dens in the appropriately entitled Fleshmarket area. He maintained two mistresses, Jane Watt and Anne Grant, with whom he fathered five illegitimate children. Along with the considerable expense of supporting these households, as well as his daytime residence, Brodie's mounting gambling debts soon made financial demands on him he could never hope to meet. He had long dissipated the £10,000 inheritance left to him by his wealthy father upon the senior Brodie's death. Brodie calmly decided to pay his bills and debts by burglarizing

Brodie as a young man.

Edinburgh's government and banking houses, as well as the homes of the wealthy where he and his men worked during the day. He made skeleton keys of those buildings to which he had easy daytime access and simply let himself into the buildings at night after determining that the occupants would be gone. He began by burglarizing the banking house of Johnston and Smith in 1768, taking £800. He would continue this looting for twenty years. Brodie stole gold, silver, jewels, laces, silks, and any cash available, later fencing the goods through his underworld connections. On two occasions, he was almost caught by acquaintances who thought they recognized him wearing a mask and wielding a pistol, but in both instances, the witnesses gave up the notion that the daring burglar could have been the distinguished Brodie. These close calls, as well increased demands upon his cash because of his continued high living, caused Brodie to take accomplices into his burglarizing schemes. He put together a gang which included George Smith, Andrew Ainsle, and John Brown, and with these men began wholesale looting of government and bank buildings. Edinburgh's sheriff and his 120 guardsmen were helpless against these rampant thefts since Brodie, a member of the government, had complete schedules of the rounds made by the guardsmen and easily avoided detection.

On the night of Mar. 5, 1788, Brodie and his men entered Scotland's General Excise Office, which Brodie estimated would be bulging with tax monies recently collected. He expected to take away more than £1,500. The gang entered the main building near High Street with a skeleton key made by Brodie and then walked quietly to the cashier's door which they forced open with a pair of curling irons. Another door inside of this room had to be broken down with an iron crowbar, but once inside the revenue rooms, Brodie and his men were astounded to find but a pittance of the tax monies they expected. The burglars ransacked the place but could not find the cash, discovering only £16. Officials, alarmed at the recent burglaries committed in Edinburgh, had instituted new measures in the counting rooms: the money had been hidden in a secret drawer as a recent precaution against just such a burglary. At 8:30 p.m., with Brodie and his men desperately tearing the revenue rooms apart, James Bonar, deputy solicitor for the Excise Office, returned unexpectedly to retrieve some business papers. The gang members panicked and clambered down a rope ladder from a window, all fleeing in different directions.

When the gang met the next evening to divide the paltry loot, Brown was openly critical of Brodie, ridiculing his abilities as a master burglar. Later, Brown believed he would be paid well by the authorities if he informed on Brodie and the others. A few days later he went to the sheriff and admitted that he was part of the burglary gang that had broken into the Excise Office and that he and others had committed dozens of similar burglaries in the past. He named Ainsle, Smith, and Deacon Brodie. Smith and Ainsle were promptly arrested but Brodie, hearing of this, fled to Amsterdam. A reward of £150 was placed on his head and, through the statements of Brown and Ainsle, Brodie's double life was revealed to a shocked public. (This double life would serve as the role model for Robert Louis Stevenson when, a century later, he created his chilling novel, *The Strange Case of Dr. Jekyll and Mr. Hyde.*)

In Holland, Brodie made plans to escape to America, hoping to sail to Charleston, S.C., where he would begin a new life. He made the mistake of trying to contact one of his mistresses, Anne Grant, sending a letter to her in care of a Scottish tobacconist named Geddes. The tobacconist opened the letter and, once he saw Brodie's signature, he informed authorities in Edinburgh who sent guardsmen to the Amsterdam address on Brodie's letter. They arrived at the house and searched it thoroughly but found no one. Then they searched again and found Deacon Brodie hiding in a cupboard. He was taken back to Edinburgh and placed in Tolbooth Jail, in a cell, chained to the stone floor.

Brodie remained calm and admitted to nothing. In fact, he insisted that he was innocent of the crimes for which he stood accused, claiming that a "double" had committed these burglaries over the years and was now using him as a convenient and famous scapegoat. (The "double" concept Brodie advanced stemmed, no doubt, from his own perception of himself and the double life he had been leading for twenty years.)

Brodie's trial began at 9 a.m. on Aug. 27, 1788, in Edinburgh's Judiciary Court. He was ordered not to wear his traditional daytime white clothes, so the ever-sartorial Brodie wore a cocked hat, a lace shirt, black satin breeches, and a dark blue coat. He nodded ceremoniously to the

Brodie as criminal mastermind.

judges and then sat down in the dock, exuding confidence and projecting what he thought was an "innocent look" to the president judge, Lord Braxfield. More than two dozen witnesses came forward to detail Brodie's double life, including members of his own gang. A fifteen-man jury returned a verdict of Guilty and Lord Braxfield sentenced the criminal mastermind to death, burglary then being a capital offense. He was scheduled to hang on Sept. 30, 1788, but the ever-resourceful Brodie thought to cheat the hangman. Dr. Pierre Degravers, a French physician attending Brodie in prison, assured the master burglar that he could bring him back to life following his execution. Dr. Degravers gave Brodie a silver tube to put town his throat to prevent strangulation. He also provided "wires" that were hidden beneath Brodie's clothes and to which the rope would be secretly affixed by the reportedly bribed hangman, these wires supporting his weight once he went through the trapdoor, instead of his neck. Also, Brodie was assured, the hangman would use a rope with just the right length so that he would not be jerked about. He would take a sedative before the execution and appear to be dead but Degravers promised he could easily revive him.

So heartened by the prospect of cheating the executioner was Brodie that he made plans to begin a new life in America. In the last few weeks of his life he studied all manner of handwriting, in preparation of becoming a master forger in the New World. A lover of music, Brodie could be heard loudly singing in his cell, particularly a tune from *The Beggar's Opera* called "Let Us Take to the Road." William Brodie did not fear death. He would outsmart all the officials of Edinburgh, survive his own death, and go on to a *third* life in America. On the day of his execution, Brodie confidently mounted the stairs of the high scaffold and pompously strode about the platform, elegantly attired and oblivious to the 40,000 spectators who had come to see him hang. He waved away a chaplain who tried to give him religious comfort and insisted that the trapdoor be tested. When satisfied that it worked, Brodie looked over the ropes supplied by the hangman. He rejected several as too short or long and finally gave approval for one rope which he apparently thought was the proper length suited to his secret life-saving scheme.

The hangman, however, made no sign to Brodie that he was involved in a conspiracy to save his life. He affixed the rope about the Deacon's neck and did not bother with the wires hidden under his collar. Brodie went through the trap and was officially declared dead within minutes. He was cut down and rushed to the home of Dr. Degravers, who desperately bled Brodie and tried all manner of resuscitation but after an hour gave up. The master burglar was finally and permanently dead.

REF.: Atoll, *Shadow of the Gallows*; Birkenhead, *Famous Trials of History*; *CBA*; Hunt, *A Dictionary of Rogues*; Roughead, *Classic Crimes*; (FICTION) Stevenson, *The Strange Case of Dr. Jekyll and Mr. Hyde*.

Brogan, William F., b.1882, U.S., law enfor. off. A fight between three rival gangs—the Harlandale Gang, the South Sans, and the Tex-Mexes—in San Antonio, Texas, in June 1944, left at least seventy-five boys cut and bruised from knives, sticks, and stones. It also led to the formation of a juvenile corps of police officers.

After the fight, criminal investigator William F. Brogan convinced the youths to reconcile their differences and join together in a war on crime. He created the Junior Deputies of America, enrolling some 800 14- to 18-year-olds to fight juvenile crime in San Antonio. By the end of the year, twelve juvenile gangs had been broken up, the number of juvenile crimes had been halved, and unsolved cases were resolved. REF.: *CBA*.

Brogile, Prince Jean de, 1921-76, Case of, Fr., mur. (vict.) Prince Jean de Brogile, a prominent politician and supporter of French president Valéry Giscard d'Estaing, was shot in the neck and chest while walking along a Paris street on Dec. 24, 1976. His death was believed to have been politically motivated after a message—later proven bogus—was received from the extreme rightist Charles Martel Club. Within five days of the murder, however, police had arrested six people in connection with a plot involving two restaurateurs who planned to repay their debts with the proceeds of an $800,000 life insurance policy on Brogile. The six arrested were: the prince's business partners Patrick Allenet de Ribemont and Pierre de Varga; police detective Guy Simonet, who arranged the murder for the partners; a pimp named Gérard Frech, who had pulled the trigger; and Simon Kelkewitcz and Serge Tessedre, who assisted Frech.

The sudden arrests and solution to the case quickly erupted into a scandal concerning a possible coverup of the murder by Interior Minister Michel Poniatowski. Although the possibility of a coverup did affect the elections in France, no official misconduct was ever proved. Four men were found Guilty in the murder conspiracy; three were sentenced on Dec. 23, 1981, to ten years in prison and the fourth to five years. REF.: *CBA*.

Brogny, Cardinal de (Jean Allarmet or **d'Alouzier** or **Cardinal de Viviers** or **Cardinal d'Ostie)**, 1342-1426, Fr., jur. President of the Council of Constance from 1415-17, which condemned to death for heresy Jan Hus, Czech religious figure. REF.: *CBA*.

Bromley, Sir Thomas, 1530-87, Brit., jur. Conducted the trial of Mary Queen of Scots in 1586. REF.: *CBA*.

Bromo Seltzer Murder, See: **Molineux, Roland B.**

Bronfman, Samuel II, See: **Lynch, Mel Patrick**, and **Byrne, Dominic P.**

Brook, John, c.1943- , and **Johnson, Nicholas de Clare**, prom. 1970s, Brit., mur. Knowing he was suspected of murder, George Ince turned himself into police but maintained his innocence. Police were seeking him for the murder of Muriel Patience, who was shot and killed on Nov. 5, 1972. It took two trials before Ince was proven innocent and a third before the true murderer was convicted.

When Bob Patience, the owner of the Barn Restaurant in Braintree, Essex, refused to open the safe for robbers, they shot him and his daughter Beverly and killed his wife Muriel. Then they got into the safe and stole £900. Ince testified that he was with his fiancée Dolly Gray that night. At Ince's first trial in May 1973, at Chelmsford, no verdict was reached, while at the second trial he was found Not Guilty. Not long after his acquittal, on June 15, the murder weapon was located.

The gun that killed Patience was discovered sewn into the mattress of John Brook, and after his accomplice Nicholas de Clare Johnson admitted to the robbery and accused Brook of the shootings, the two were brought to trial. At the trial in January 1974, Brook was found Guilty of murder and attempted murder and sentenced to life in prison, while Johnson received ten years for manslaughter.

REF.: *CBA*; Cole and Pringle, *Can You Positively Identify This man?*; Fielder and Steele, *Alibi at Midnight*.

Brookings, Wilmot W., 1830-1905, U.S., jur. Compiled the civil and criminal codes for the Dakota Territory. He was appointed judge in the Dakota Territory by President Ulysses S. Grant in 1869. REF.: *CBA*.

Brookins, Louis Dwight, 1925-46, U.S., mur. The killer was as cold as ice as he recounted the exact moments leading up to the murder of a 32-year-old department store manicurist named Helen Caputo. Veteran police officers were shocked by Louis Brookins' laconic, unfeeling attitude. When he finished his story, he asked Deputy Elmer Wood of the Rochester (N.Y.) Police Department, "What do you think they will give me?" Woods' reply was unprintable.

The 20-year-old ex-soldier met his victim at a downtown Rochester restaurant on July 9, 1945. The charming young man dressed as a Marine flattered Helen Caputo, an older woman, and suggested that they go to Ontario Beach Park for a late-night swim. The suggestion appealed to the lonely woman who had been an orphan since childhood. Caputo, who was unmarried, had just been stood up by a girlfriend. She took Brookins to her rooming house at 5:15 p.m. The couple remained in the building until 8:30 p.m., when they were last seen walking near James Street.

Brookins had already decided to attack and rob Caputo, who did not know that she was being lured to the identical spot where a first victim had been assaulted twenty-four hours before. At a desolate spot near Cherry Road in the Lakedale subdivision, Brookins told his date to walk ahead. Puzzled, she complied with his request.

Knocking Helen to the ground, Brookins sexually assaulted her. A broken street light left the scene in darkness, unnoticed by passersby. She screamed, but neighbors paid no attention. He stuffed a handkerchief she had given him several hours earlier into her mouth. An autopsy later revealed that she had died of strangulation.

"Lots of people come up from the lake at night, laughing and screaming," Mrs. V.E. Lacy, who lived on Leander Road, explained later.

To conceal his crime Brookins dragged Caputo's body into a thicket next to the road. Before he fled, he removed $450 from his victim's purse, a wristwatch, and two expensive rings. The watch was later smashed. The body was found the next day by

Mrs. Russell McFarland, who was taking a shortcut through the brush when she noticed a face partially covered by a bloody handkerchief.

Satisfied with himself, Brookins walked up to Lake Avenue where he hitched a ride with three young women and their male escort. They stopped for a sandwich at Ontario Beach Park before driving back downtown. With his pocket full of cash, Brookins picked up a young prostitute on Main Street and took her to a motel where he paid her with some of the jewelry lifted from Caputo.

The next day the pair took a bus to Brookins' hometown of Syracuse where they registered in a hotel as husband and wife. In a military surplus store, he purchased a new Marine uniform and enough campaign ribbons to make a person believe that he single-handedly won the battle of Corregidor. They returned to Rochester the next day, registering in a hotel with a second man.

Based on a tip supplied by room clerk Charles Hartel, a squad of detectives led by John Rowan and Victor Raycroft burst into the hotel room where they found Brookins, the 19-year-old prostitute, and the second man. Hartel had been supplied with a physical description of the suspect several hours earlier by city detectives. His suspicions were aroused when Brookins registered under his own name, though he claimed that the girl was his wife. Brookins and the prostitute were arraigned on vagrancy charges pending a hearing. It was one of the fastest arrests of a murder suspect made by the Rochester Police in many years, because they were on his trail before he even met up with Caputo. Brookins had been linked to three other recent assaults in the city, and was identified by a woman he had accosted near the Lake Avenue bus stop. She successfully fended off her attacker by pummeling him in the face. As she ran away, she heard Brookins mutter an angry curse, adding, "You'd make a good corpse."

Brookins accompanied the detectives to the murder site, where he reconstructed the events of that night. The police also learned that their suspect had been taken into custody by the Navy Shore Patrol in Rochester a few days earlier, when he was "unable to give a good account of himself." He claimed that he had been discharged from the Marine Corps in 1944, classified as unfit for service. When they checked out his story they found out he had been discharged from the Army, not the Marines.

Brookins was convicted of first-degree murder and sentenced to die. He was on death row at Sing Sing for fourteen months before being executed in the electric chair at 11:06 p.m. on Sept. 12, 1946. REF.: *CBA*.

Brooklyn Museum of Arts and Sciences' Sargent Theft, 20th Cent., U.S., theft. The use of psychology by private detective Raymond C. Schindler not only solved the theft of some stolen golden nuggets, but also the mystery of who cut a painting by John Singer Sargent from its frame and stole it from the Brooklyn Museum of Arts and Sciences. After authorities had given up hope of solving the audacious daylight theft, another theft occurred when an ammonia tank used to clean a gallery exploded, killing one and injuring two others. In the confusion, several gold nuggets were taken from an exhibit.

Realizing that the culprit must be a museum employee, Schindler interviewed all employees, explaining to them that he had fingerprints of the culprit. However, rather than use the prints to find the guilty party, he promised that no action would be taken if the property was returned. Accepting the bargain, the man who stole the nuggets returned them by mail and even returned the painting. As Schindler had promised, fingerprint identification was not used to capture the thief. Instead, Albert S. Osborn conducted a handwriting analysis of a message on the returned package in order to determine who committed the crimes. The man was summarily fired without charges being filed by the museum.

REF.: *CBA*; Hughes, *The Complete Detective*.

Brooklyn Refinery Robbery, 1932, U.S., rob. The robbery of $50,000 worth of gold, platinum, and silver from the Brooklyn metal refinery of Kastenhuber & Lehrfeld on Oct. 25, 1932, came to a conclusion three days later when three of the five armed robbers were caught dumping the bars into the East River from the Williamsburg Bridge.

Jacob Charee, alias Jack Chadwick, twenty-eight, Frank Jandezjak, alias Frank Andrews, thirty-one, and 28-year-old Jacob Kaplan—who had also stolen $200 in cash and a rifle—were arrested by Detective William Ford and a Pinkerton man, who had been following the gang for several weeks. Four bars remained of the thirty that had been stolen. The men were dumping their prize because they had been misinformed that the bars were only made of brass. Arrested later that night was Kaplan's brother, 23-year-old William Kaplan, and 32-year-old Mr. Cohen, alias Joseph Gold. Charee and the Kaplans were named as suspects in three similar robberies earlier in the year.

All five men were found Guilty of first-degree robbery on Nov. 22, 1932. On Dec. 5, Judge Franklin Taylor sentenced Cohen, Jandezjak, and William Kaplan, who were repeat offenders, to forty years each in prison. Jacob Kaplan, a first-time offender, received fifteen to thirty-five years. Charee, who claimed he was not a repeat offender, had his sentencing deferred until Mar. 22, 1933, when he received forty years in prison as a second-time offender. REF.: *CBA*.

Brooks, Charles, 1942-82, U.S., mur. In 1976, used-car salesman David Gregory took Charlie Brooks and Woody Lourdes for a trial drive. The result was a trial for the murder of Gregory —for which each man was found Guilty and sentenced to death— and notoriety for Brooks as the first convicted killer to be executed by a lethal injection.

Lourdes was able to successfully appeal his conviction on the grounds that the jury had been improperly selected, and he received a commuted sentence of forty years in prison. Just minutes before his scheduled execution, Brooks was denied a stay of execution by the U.S. Supreme Court. Brooks' death at 12:16 a.m. on Dec. 7, 1982, also made history because he was the first man executed in Texas in eighteen years and the first black man put to death since the death penalty was reinstated by the Supreme Court in 1976. The lethal injection administered to Brooks by a medical technician—and not a physician, because the American Medical Association strongly opposed the taking of a life by a doctor—was a solution of pancurionum bromide, potassium chloride, and sodium thipental, also known as the truth drug, sodium pentothal.

REF.: *CBA*; Wilson, *Encyclopedia of Modern Murder*.

Brooks, Donald (AKA: Frank Whitney), prom. 1944, U.S., mur. Mary Finn was killed on her wedding day, July 1, 1944. The pretty young bride-to-be from Baltimore left her home the night before the wedding with $600. The money was the nest egg that Mary and her fiance Charles Rommell had been saving for their honeymoon.

When Rommell left for the graveyard shift at a nearby defense plant at 10:30 p.m., he told Mary to wait for him at her home. She was nervous about carrying the money back home again, but agreed. The next day at about 9 a.m., Rommell returned home to prepare for his wedding. He found his bride-to-be dead on the floor. There was blood everywhere. Dazed, he called a policeman.

The police questioned many friends and relatives who were on the guest list. All of them except Irene Ayres had airtight alibis. Ayres worked as a riveter at the bomber plant, and she had a boyfriend named Don Brooks who was well known to Rommell. When police talked to Irene, they discovered she had disappeared, along with her boyfriend.

A rented Buick coupe was traced to Brooks, who used the name Frank Whitney. Inside, a blood-spattered newspaper section dated June 30 was found. It was part of the same paper found in the Rommell apartment. Under direct questioning, Irene Ayres denied that Brooks had killed Mary. But when threatened with a charge of accessory to murder, she broke down and admitted that her boyfriend killed Mary Finn for the $600, which they used to pay for a weekend in New York. Brooks was convicted of first-degree murder on Oct. 6, 1944.

REF.: *CBA*; Rice, *45 Murderers*.

Brooks, Flossie, prom. 1920s, Case of, U.S., blk. Attorney William Fallon was known in his day as the "Great Mouthpiece" because of his brilliant courtroom oratory on behalf of society's "down-and-outers." Fallon was an avid theater-goer, and an intimate of gangsters, Broadway show people, and reporters from New York to Chicago. In the courtroom his great skill was tapping into the wellspring of sentiment lurking within every good citizen summoned for jury duty.

In the 1920s, Fallon defended Flossie Brooks, well-known in the New York criminal underworld as an expert blackmailer. An Armenian rug merchant was threatened with blackmail after being observed in Atlantic City with a young woman who was not his wife. The man preferred to face the anger of his wife rather than submit to the demands of a blackmailer. So the rug merchant confessed his sin to his spouse and then called the New York police. Flossie Brooks was arrested in Central Park.

When Brooks retained William Fallon as her counsel, he knew it would take all his skill for his client to beat the rap. During jury selection, he accepted several men who had cast furtive glances toward Flossie Brooks' shapely legs, believing they might be sympathetic in the end.

Fallon argued that a man who had lied to his wife about the true nature of his business in Atlantic City could not be trusted to tell the truth. And finally he accused the prosecutor of harboring ulterior motives: "I myself once had political ambitions," Fallon drawled. "And in my zeal I sent an innocent man to prison. I have vowed to the memory of my dear mother that I shall do all in my power to see that no innocent man—or lady—ever goes to prison." It took just twenty minutes for the jurors to return a verdict of Not Guilty.

REF.: *CBA*; Hynd, *Murder, Mayhem, and Mystery*.

Brooks, Gene Edward, 1931- , U.S., jur. Prosecuting attorney in Mt. Vernon, Ind., from 1959-68. He served as secretary of the Indiana Prosecutors Association from 1967-68 and was appointed federal judge to the Court of the Southern District of Indiana in 1979 by President Jimmy Carter. REF.: *CBA*.

Brooks, Henry M., 1887-1948, U.S., suic.-mur. Henry Brooks, a native of Minnesota, made his fortune on Wall Street before the stock market crash of 1929. With the money he earned from various lucrative stock investments, Brooks purchased a spacious home in Greenwich, Conn., and indulged his wife and daughter with luxuries.

In 1926, Brooks encountered the first in a long series of financial reversals when he lost $3,000,000 on Devoe & Reynolds stock. He continued to speculate, piling up a staggering debt along the way. In desperation, he turned to Joseph Watkins, an old friend from Minnesota, who, like Brooks, was a Harvard man who had enjoyed some success in the stock market. At first, Watkins eagerly invested his money in his friend's financial schemes, but he quickly pulled out when too many deals went bad.

In 1939, Watkins won a court judgment against Brooks for $72,000. By 1948, the creditors were forming lines outside the courthouse, seeking similar decisions from the judges. In the last week of August 1948, the desperate Brooks flew to Newark, N.J., where he confronted his former partner one last time.

Joseph Watkins drove up to the Princeton Inn where Brooks waited outside. In agitation, Brooks asked about the money, but his friend stalled him again. There were two quick shots from a concealed handgun, and in a second Watkins was dead at the wheel of his car.

Brooks slipped away from the restaurant unnoticed. He checked into the Albion Hotel in Asbury Park, N.J., in the wee hours of the morning. He wrote a plaintive letter to his wife Ruth, took a shower, and then slipped into his pajamas. "I had to have a definite answer to our relations problem," he said in the letter. "It was still that same maybe—mañana—perhaps, or this one little piece, until he just decided to drive away—well—the lack of anything broke up my mind." After neatly spreading out

the towels on the bathroom floor, Brooks used his gun for the last time, on himself. REF.: *CBA*.

Brooks, Hugh M. (Walter Lennox Maxwell, T.C. D'Auguier), 1861-88, U.S., mur. Hugh M. Brooks, an educated young Englishman, was convicted in 1888 for the murder of his companion, Charles Arthur Preller. Brooks, travelling under the name of Walter Lennox Maxwell, met Preller aboard a steamer bound from Liverpool to Boston. The two men became friends and agreed to meet several weeks later in St. Louis. Maxwell arrived there on Mar. 30, 1885, and checked into the Southern Hotel. Preller arrived at the hotel on Apr. 3 and took an adjoining room. During the next week, the two were seen together frequently, and the hotel staff learned that they intended to travel together to New Zealand. On Apr. 15, however, Brooks checked out of the hotel alone. When the staff noticed a strong odor from Preller's room, they called the police. Charles Preller's partly-clad body was found there, stuffed into a trunk. Attached to the corpse was a note that read "So perish all traitors to the great cause."

Police tracked Brooks to New Zealand. At his trial, Brooks claimed Preller's death was caused by an accidental overdose of chloroform administered as he was performing a medical procedure at Preller's request. The prosecution introduced the testimony of a detective who had posed as a fellow prisoner and elicited a confession from Brooks. Brooks admitted murdering Preller because he refused to pay Brooks' passage to New Zealand. Brooks was convicted, and hanged on Aug. 10, 1888.

REF.: *CBA*; Duke, *Celebrated Criminal Cases of America*; Nash, *Murder America*; Stevens, *From Clue to Dock*.

Brooks, James, and **Davis, William**, and **White, John**, prom. 1744, Brit., riot. On Mar. 10, 1744, an angry mob of London footmen gathered outside the home of Colonel de Veil, on Bow Street. Protesting the working conditions and the fact that the French were undercutting the average wages paid in the city, the footmen advanced on the Colonel's home. Positioning himself at the foot of the staircase, de Veil held off the throng and protected the lives of his wife and children with a pair of pistols and a blunderbuss for nearly three hours. Finally a troop of soldiers arrived to dispel the crowd. Three of the ringleaders escaped arrest: William Davis, James Brooks, and John White. They were never found.

REF.: Armitage, *Bow Street Runners*; *CBA*; Colby, *The California Crime Book*.

Brooks, James Abijah, 1855-1944, U.S., jur.-west. lawman. Born in Bourbon County, Ky., on Nov. 20, 1855, James Brooks moved to Collin County, Texas, in 1876 and spent some time ranching before moving to San Antonio, Texas, in 1880. Brooks joined the Texas Rangers in 1889 and served with distinction, solving widespread cattle thefts from the King Ranch in 1902 by rounding up several rustlers. Brooks resigned from the Rangers in 1906 and served in the state legislature. Brooks County was named after this upstanding lawman, who later became a county judge in the county named after him.

REF.: Bartholomew, *The Biographical Album of Western Gunfighters*; *CBA*.

Brooks, Preston (AKA: Bully Boy), 1819-57, U.S., asslt.&bat. Preston Brooks was a heavy-handed, hot-tempered U.S. congressman from South Carolina who was always ready to reach for a sword or gun to defend "Southern honor." On May 19, 1856, Senator Charles Sumner of Massachussetts, a staunch abolitionist, delivered an anti-slavery speech, condemning the slavers of Kansas, and criticizing Southern politicians, reserving his wrath for the elderly U.S. senator from South Carolina, Andrew Pickens Butler, saying that Butler had chosen "the harlot, Slavery" to be his "mistress." Brooks, who was Butler's nephew, stormed into the U.S. Senate on May 22, 1856, with the obvious intent of killing Sumner, who was seated at his desk. Brooks carried a gutta-percha cane and, without warning, he brought it crashing down on the head of the unsuspecting Sumner, whose long legs got tangled beneath the desk. He received several more vicious blows from Brooks before he managed to rip the desk away from its bolts in the floor. Unfortunately, he fell on his back and Brooks kept beating him on the head until he passed out.

No one on the Senate floor made a move to stop "Bully Boy" Brooks, even though Senator Stephen A. Douglas of Illinois and Senator Robert Tombs of Georgia were standing nearby. Brooks continued to hammer his cane down upon the head of the unconscious Sumner and quit only when he became exhausted from administering countless blows. Sumner was severely injured and took three years to recuperate from his wounds. He was nearly blind in one eye from the beating. Brooks was tried for

Congressman Brooks caning Senator Sumner.

assault and battery but was released by a Washington, D.C., judge with a $300 fine and a warning to curb his temper in the future. Brooks became an overnight hero of the South and the cause of slavery. His supporters delighted in sending him scores of expensive canes and a gold-handled cowhide whip with notes suggesting that he use these implements to administer thrashings to other abolitionists.

REF.: Butterfield, *The American Past; CBA;* Hofstadter and Wallace, *American Violence;* Donald, *Charles Sumner and the Coming of the Civil War.*

Brooks, William L. (AKA: **Buffalo Bill** or **Billy, Bully**), 1836-74, U.S., west. lawman-gunman. Elected first city marshal of Newton, Kan., in 1872, William L. Brooks, a noted Buffalo hunter, also had a reputation as a fierce gunman. On June 9, 1872, Brooks stopped several cowboys from harrassing Newton residents and was wounded in the neck for his efforts, later arresting his attackers, James Hunt and Joe Miller. He moved to Ellsworth where he served briefly as a city policeman, and then he moved to Dodge City where he quarreled frequently with other cowboys and gunslingers, getting into several shootouts, the first being on Dec. 23, 1872. He argued with a Santa Fe Railroad yardmaster named Brown and both went for their guns. Brooks was wounded, but Brown was

Buffalo Bill Brooks

killed by a single shot from Brooks' six-gun. Only five days later, on Dec. 28, 1872, Brooks took revenge on saloon keeper Matthew Sullivan, who had thrown him out of his establishment the night before. Brooks crept up on Sullivan who was standing next to an open window of his saloon, poked his six-gun through the window, and fired an almost point-blank bullet into the saloon keeper, killing him instantly. Though he was seen to commit this wanton murder, Brooks was never charged with the killing.

On Mar. 4, 1873, Brooks took issue with comments made by another Buffalo hunter, Kirk Jordan. Before he could pull his six-gun, Brooks saw Jordan leveling his buffalo gun at him and dove behind two water barrels in the street. The blast from Jordan's gun exploded the barrels and almost killed Brooks who apologized to Jordan immediately and then went nervously on his way. Brooks turned outlaw the following year and was rounded up by a huge posse which captured several horse thieves near Caldwell, Kan. On the night of July 28, 1874, a lynch mob broke into the Caldwell Jail and dragged out Brooks, L.B. Hasbrouck, and Charley Smith, all horse thieves. They promptly hanged the three men. Brooks struggled and the rope failed to break his neck. He slowly strangled to death.

REF.: Bartholomew, *The Biographical Album of Western Gunfighters; CBA;* Miller and Snell, *Great Gunfighters of the Kansas Cowtowns;* O'Neal, *Encyclopedia of Western Gunfighters;* Streeter, *Prairie Trails & Cow Towns.*

Broome, William (William Brooks), prom. 1910, Brit., mur. Following on the heels of the sensational murder trial of Dr. Hawley Crippen, the British police had another notorious killer to contend with—William Broome, an army veteran whose father owned a shop on High Street, Slough.

When an elderly woman named Mrs. Wilson was found dead in the building next door, local gossip directed Elias Bower of Scotland Yard to young William Broome, who used the name William Brooks. One Sunday morning Bower took the man in for questioning just as he was leaving the local church. Bower discovered a facial scratch running from Broome's cheek to his nose. It was the kind of wound that would be sustained during a scuffle. In coming days, three different people told three different stories about the origins of the scratch, which at the very least proved that Broome was a bad liar.

When Broome's room near Regent's Park was searched, an envelope containing £20 in gold was found. This was the precise amount that had been taken from the old lady. Dr. William Wilcox of the Home Office conducted an exhaustive examination of a slip of brown paper found in Broome's possession that connected him to the victim.

William Broome protested that on the day of the murder he had been in London applying for a job as a taxi driver. No evidence could be found to back up this assertion, so Broome was tried and duly convicted at Reading. On the day of his scheduled execution, a stiff dose of brandy helped Broome overcome a severe case of the jitters. A second before he was dropped he screamed, "I am innocent!" But it was too late.

REF.: *CBA;* Laurence, *A History of Capital Punishment.*

Brostron, Curtis, 1905-81, U.S., law enfor. off. Curtis Brostron joined the St. Louis police force in 1929, becoming its chief in 1960 and retiring in 1970 after a long career of innovative service. Brostron, a butcher before joining the police force, was trained in the FBI National Academy Program. He resigned from the force in 1952, but was reinstated in 1960, when he was made Chief of Police. In that capacity he lectured at the Southern Police Institute, the Governmental Research Institute, and the FBI National Academy. As chief, Brostron was instrumental in developing a scholarship program for police officers, as well as several new and important police techniques. On May 4, 1961, the St. Louis force became the first in the U.S. to use decoy squads of police pretending to be citizens to catch criminals; on Nov. 2, 1966, St. Louis opened the first police-run detoxification center in the world; and, on Nov. 25, 1969, it became the first law enforcement agency in the U.S. licensed to operate an educational TV channel.

In his years as chief, Brostron served on the Advisory Committee of the U.S. Attorney General's Commission on Law Enforcement and Riot Control, and was president of both the International Association of Police Chiefs and the Missouri Peace Officer's Association. Brostron retired from the department in 1970, and in 1973, he was called back to serve as Secretary of the Board of Police Commissioners. A position he held until Mar. 31, 1977.
REF.: *CBA.*

Brothers, Leo Vincent (AKA: Buster, Leo Bader), 1909-51, U.S., org. crime-mur. Leo Vincent Brothers was a professional killer for Al Capone and was loaned out as a contract killer, to mobs affiliated with Capone in the late 1920s and early 1930s. He was known as "Buster" and Leo Bader. When not on an assignment murder, Brothers busied himself with burglary, extortion, bombings, labor terrorism, and bootlegging. He lived in St. Louis and in Chicago, working both for Egan's Rats in St. Louis and Capone in Chicago. It was Brothers who was loaned out to the Maranzano faction in New York during the so-called Castellammarese War and performed several murders of Mafia sub-bosses and henchmen in 1930-31, when he was known only as "Buster" from Chicago. But the most infamous killing performed by this ruthless and systematic murderer was that of a $65-a-week newspaperman, Alfred "Jake" Lingle, star crime reporter for the Chicago *Tribune*.

Although Lingle had a sterling reputation with his editors at the *Tribune,* he lived a double life, working, in reality, for Al Capone for almost a decade, informing Capone, through his high-level police contacts, of any impending raids against Capone's breweries, stills, bordellos, and gambling dens, as well as funneling to Capone information on the operations of rival bootlegging gangs in territories Scarface did not control, chiefly the North Side gang under the leadership of Charles Dion O'Bannion, Earl "Hymie" Weiss, and George "Bugs" Moran. The chief source of Lingle's top secret information was William P. Russell, Chicago's police commissioner, a boyhood friend of Lingle's. So confident was Lingle of his position, protected as he was on one side by Capone and by Commissioner Russell on the other, that his inflated ego insisted that he, not Capone, was the real power behind the gangs since he could close or open any speakeasy or other illegal operation with a snap of his fingers. "I fix the price of beer in this town!" he once bragged to a friend.

As a reporter, Lingle never wrote a word of copy for the *Tribune*. He had been a legman or a street reporter for the paper since 1912, one who unearthed important crime facts and phoned these into the editors who had staff members write the stories. Lingle usually spent no more than a few hours a day unearthing important news on the crime front, or he appeared to be doing this, before heading off to the racetrack or his favorite gambling casinos. He was a hopeless gambler and not a good one, losing heavily, so much so that he was, by early 1930, in debt to various gamblers for more than $100,000. To pay his debts, Lingle began to use his police contacts in subtle extortion of the mobsters, going to various Capone lieutenants to demand large kickbacks for influencing his police friends to allow Capone's speakeasies, gambling dens, and brothels to continue operating. Hearing of this, Capone decided to have Lingle killed and ordered an out-of-town specialist to handle the murder. Brothers was called in St. Louis and, after he arrived in Chicago, methodically trailed the reporter as he went through his daily routines.

Capone's thinking was to have someone the astute Lingle would not recognize, knowing that Lingle was familiar with just about any gangster working in Chicago. It was soon apparent to Brothers that Lingle's predictable habits made him an easy "hit." Brothers was an expert at disguises and he changed into a different costume, a different person, so to speak, as he stalked his prey each day. One day he was a delivery man, the next a clerk, the next an executive carrying a briefcase, the next a cab driver. Almost every day, following lunch, the newsman would take the Illinois Central (IC) train to the racetrack. June 9, 1930, was no exception. On this day, according to witnesses, Leo Vincent Brothers chose a particularly impressive disguise, one which he believed would never be coupled to murder, that of a priest.

After having lunch at the Sherman House Hotel coffee shop, a hangout for underworld types and politicians, Jake Lingle began his leisurely stroll toward the IC station at Randolph and Michigan. He passed Police Sergeant Thomas Alcock of the Detective Bureau and paused for a minute to speak to the plainclothesman,

saying cryptically: "I'm being tailed, Tom." Alcock asked him what he meant, but Lingle only looked about furtively, shook his head, and moved on. Apparently the cunning Lingle had seen Brothers too many times during his daily travels and had grown suspicious. Yet he took no special precautions that day, continuing his journey to the IC Station and then, by the 1:30 p.m. train, to Washington Park racetrack in Homewood. Before entering the stairs leading down to the station, Lingle bought a copy of *The Daily Racing Form* at a newsstand in front of the public library. A car with three men wearing dark suits and hats pulled to curb, according to cab driver Armour Lapansee who was parked nearby. Lingle waved at the men, appearing to know them and one smiled and said: "Play Hy Sneider in the third, Jake."

"I've got him," Lingle replied. With that, Lingle lit up one of his $3.50 Havana cigars and began studying the racing form as he descended the stairs into the 100-foot long tunnel leading to the underground IC station. Behind him moved a blonde-haired priest, keeping pace with the slowly-moving Lingle. Another man, perhaps an accomplice, police later thought, walked slightly ahead of Brothers, also keeping pace with Lingle. Inside of Brothers' coat pocket, his hand gripped about the handle, was a snub-nosed .38-caliber Colt revolver. When Lingle was halfway through the tunnel, Brothers whipped out the pistol, rushed up behind him, while both were surrounded by hundreds of jostling train passengers, and sent a bullet crashing into the reporter's head. Lingle fell forward on his face, a bullet hole in his forehead where the slug emerged. He was dead, a large pool of blood spreading away from his face.

There were screams from women and people ran in both directions away from the fallen Lingle, many thinking a maniac or an "anarchist" was loose in the tunnel and killing people at random. Mrs. Ann Applegate, who had been walking behind both Brothers and Lingle, saw the blonde-haired young man wearing the Roman collar of a priest rush forward and shoot the man reading the paper. She pointed after Brothers who had turned around and was racing for the stairs leading back up to Randolph Street and Michigan Avenue, yelling: "Isn't anyone going to stop that man?" Her husband, Clark Applegate, ran after Brothers. Once at the street level, Applegate saw Brothers dashing across Michigan Avenue and he yelled to the traffic cop on duty, Patrolman Anthony Ruthy to "get that man!" He pointed to the running blonde-haired man and then shouted: "He's a murderer!" Ruthy drew his gun and ordered Brothers to stop, but he kept running, going West on Randolph Street, with Ruthy in pursuit. It was hopeless. Brothers dashed through the crowds, cut through an alley, went South on Wabash and then disappeared in the dense crowds.

Meanwhile, Dr. Joseph Springer, who worked in the coroner's office and who happened to be in the IC tunnel at the time of the shooting, went to the fallen man, wiped away the blood and recognized Lingle, whom Springer had known for years. The burning cigar was still clenched in his teeth and Lingle's death grip curled about the racing form. Springer pronounced him dead. Mrs. Applegate was soon joined by her winded husband who said he could not catch the killer but that the police were after him. Ann Applegate looked down at the body at her feet and said: "Poor man, he never had a chance." With that, her husband took her arm and the couple went on to Washington Racetrack. They were horseowners and had some horses running in the races that day. Neither of them realized that the slain man in the tunnel was their good friend Alfred "Jake" Lingle.

The murder weapon was found close to the body where the killer had purposely dropped it (or perhaps it was knocked from his hand by the jostling crowd). When police arrived a number of officers handled the weapon and obliterated whatever fingerprints might have been found on it. A witness, Patrick Campbell told police that a priest bumped into him after the shooting and said: "I think someone has been shot and I'm going to get out of here!" To this remark Detective William Cusack replied: "No, never! He was no priest! A priest would never do that. He

Top left, clockwise: Corrupt Chicago *Tribune* reporter Jake Lingle; Leo Brothers, Lingle's killer; the IC Station where Brothers tracked Lingle; Jake Lingle's lavish funeral in Chicago; Police Chief Russell; Lingle's body.

would have gone to the side of the stricken person."

Rewards for Lingle's killer were posted by civic groups and the *Tribune*, more than $50,000 and special investigators hired by the paper and sent out by the police combed the underworld for months. Finally, Brothers was unearthed by private detective John Hagan who had actually joined the Moran gang and later Egan's Rats to locate killer-for-hire Brothers who went to trial on Mar. 16, 1931, defended by underworld lawyer, Louis Piquett (who would later represent John Dillinger). Piquett had an uphill battle to save his client, facing a bevy of eye-witnesses who insisted he was the killer of Lingle. The jury convicted Brothers of first-degree murder on Apr. 2, 1931, but, much to the surprise of the court and the public, set a minimum sentence for the killer, a prerogative of juries at that time in accordance with existing laws. The sentence was fourteen years which meant that Brothers would be eligible for parole in eight. When the hired killer heard his sentence announced, he grinned wickedly and turned to a reporter, saying in the typical argot of the underworld: "I can do that standing on my head." The press claimed that certain jury members had been bribed by Capone's henchmen but proof was lacking and the sentence was upheld. Brothers served eight years and was released, later becoming involved in various rackets and then dying of natural causes in 1951. He never spoke one word about the killing of Alfred "Jake" Lingle. Capone was interviewed following Lingle's murder and denied having had anything to do with it, saying with a wide, pudgy smile: "Why, Jake was my pal up to the day he died. There was only one thing wrong with him—horse races." See: **Capone, Alphonse; Moran, George.**

REF.: Asbury, *Gem of the Prairie;* Bennett, *Murder is My Business;* Boettiger, *Jake Lingle;* Burns, *The One-Way Ride; CBA;* Halper, *The Chicago Crime Book;* Kobler, *Capone;* Nash, *Bloodletters and Badmen;* _____, *Murder Among the Mighty;* _____, *People to See;* Pasley, *Al Capone;* _____, *Muscling In;* Sanders, *Murder Behind the Bright Lights;* Sullivan, *Chicago Surrenders;* _____, *Rattling the Cup on Chicago Crime.*

Brotherton, Eric, prom. 1918, Brit., fraud. During WWI, Brotherton, the manager of a shipbuilding and repair company in England, took advantage of a royal contract to charge work done on his own home and garden, as well as repairs to the company's own buildings repairs, to His Royal Majesty.

Eric Brotherton was the manager of the Humber Graving Dock Company when it landed a substantial contract from the government to repair His Majesty's ships. Brotherton used this contract to charge repairs and services done on privately owned vessels and for him personally until the fraud was exposed by an honest workman who refused to be a party to the deceit. Brotherton and his colleague, Mr. Walker, were charged with "conspiring together to defraud the King of money by false representations."

The ten-day trial took place at the Old Bailey, and the lawyer for the defense, Marshall Hall, unsuccessfully used the argument that the work was done in the public interest, since, in order to keep a full-time staff available and on call night and day, it was necessary to give them regular employment and, with the royal contract alone, they would have been often idle. It was estimated that the government had been bilked of at least £25,000 and probably double that amount in the treasury fees paid out for prosecuting Brotherton. He was found Guilty and sentenced to a prison term of one year and eight months.

REF.: *CBA;* Marjoribanks, *For the Defense, The Life of Sir Edward Marshall Hall.*

Brougham, Henry, prom. 19th Cent., Case of, Brit., duel. Henry Brougham was insulted by Dandy Raikes at Brook's Club in London in front of a dozen or so other club members. Brougham sent Raikes a challenge to duel, through Sir Robert Wilson, but before he could receive a response from Raikes, Brougham was arrested, taken to Bow Street, and jailed by Sir Richard Birnie, ostensibly for his own safety. The police had been informed about the intended duel by Mr. Spring-Rice, who wanted to prevent the altercation because he needed Brougham's vote on an issue that was to be decided in the House of Commons.

REF.: Armitage, *Bow Street Runners; CBA.*

Brougham, Henry Peter (First Baron Brougham and Vaux), 1778-1868, Brit., atty. gen. In 1820, he represented Queen Caroline when the House of Lords censured her in a celebrated divorce trial. REF.: *CBA.*

Broughton, Sir Henry John Delves (AKA: Sir Jock), 1884-1942, Case of, Kenya, mur. Sir Henry Broughton, 57-year-old British aristocrat, married the ravishing young Diana Caldwell, a 27-year-old socialite, and in a pre-nuptial agreement guaranteed her an estimated yearly income of £5,000.

With his new bride, "Sir Jock," as Broughton was known to his friends in the fashionable London clubs, arrived in Kenya on Nov. 12, 1940, to begin a new life. His well-appointed home outside Nairobi held no fascination for the vivacious Lady Broughton. In this last outpost of the crumbling British empire, Diana met Josslyn Victor Hay, the dashing twenty-second Earl of Erroll.

Hay was eighteen years younger than Henry Broughton, and infinitely more interesting to Diana. Hay had many female admirers, most of them married to men of title, and was, in the words of an English divorce judge, a "very bad blackguard." On Jan. 20, 1941, less than two months after his arrival in Africa, Broughton wrote to a friend about the futility of his situation. He knew that Diana had fallen in love with Hay. "They say they are in love with each other and mean to get married," he confided. "It is a hopeless position and I am going to cut my losses. I think I'll go to Ceylon." That same day, Broughton told the police that someone had stolen two Colt revolvers from his home.

On the afternoon of Jan. 23, Hay, Broughton, and Diana discussed their situation over drinks and dinner at the Muthaiga Country Club. "Diana tells me she is in love with you," Broughton said. "She never told me that, but I'm frightfully in love with her," Hay replied curtly. Form dictated that the two aristocrats try to arrive at some understanding. Afterward, Hay would remark to his friend Lieutenant Lezard, "Jock could not have been nicer. He has agreed to everything. As a matter of fact, he has been so nice it smells bad!"

That night, Broughton had too much to drink and was driven home by a friend, leaving his wife with Hay. At 2:30 a.m., Hay brought Diana home, said his goodnight on the porch, and then climbed back into his car and drove down the Ngong Road. A short distance from the house, his car careened into a gravel pit. The next morning, a passerby found him slumped over the steering wheel. He had been shot in the back of the head. Several weeks later, Broughton was arrested and charged with murder. He was the only one with an obvious motive, and the bullet extracted from the victim's brain had been fired with a black powder propellant, which was unobtainable in Kenya. The African houseboy would later tell the court that he had seen Broughton take two pistols to his bedroom shortly after arriving home from the club.

Broughton was placed on trial May 26, 1941. The prosecution was handled by the Attorney General of Kenya, W. Harrigan. Broughton's life depended on discrediting the witnesses for the prosecution. From South Africa, H.H. Morris, one of the finest legal minds in the country, accepted his case. Morris brilliantly demonstrated to the jury that the murder bullets were not necessarily fired from his client's guns. Sir Henry John Delves Broughton was duly acquitted on July 1, 1941.

Broughton left Kenya as planned, and took up residence with Diana in Ceylon. However, Broughton soon suffered a serious fall which partly paralyzed him. Forced to return to England, Broughton sequestered himself in a Liverpool hotel, where he committed suicide in December 1942. Physicians attributed his death to an overdose of narcotics. He left a long, rambling note about the Kenya tragedy that neither affirmed nor denied his guilt. Broughton's story became the basis for the 1988 British film *White Mischief.*

REF.: Bennett, *Freedom of the Gallows;* _____, *Genius for the Defense; CBA;* Fox, *White Mischief;* Furneaux, *The Murder of Lord Erroll;* Symons, *A Reasonable Doubt.*

Broughton, William, prom. 1900, Case of, U.S., obsc. On Feb. 22, 1900, Nash R. Broyles, the city recorder of Atlanta, Ga., received a letter in the mail that maligned his moral character in an obscene manner. It was signed "Grant Jackson." The next day, the police picked up a black man named Grant Jackson, who Broyles knew; they also arrested Jackson's friend, William Broughton, a day later. The case against Jackson was dropped when it was discovered that he could not write, but further suspicion fell on Broughton when it was learned that he had several times written missives for his friend. Inducing Broughton to write a letter to his mother asking her to send him clothes in jail, the police decided his handwriting matched the letter. Broyles appeared as a witness at the trial and also qualified as a handwriting expert when he said that he had some previous experience judging writing samples when he served as U.S. commissioner in Atlanta. Dissimilarities were explained away by Broyles and two other so-called experts, one who claimed to be qualified for the task because he was a traveling auditor for Standard Oil and the other because of long experience in bank work. Broughton maintained steadfastly that he had never heard of the letter until police showed it to him. He was found guilty and sentenced to five years in prison, and was ordered to pay a fine of $500 plus the prosecution costs.

Not long after Broughton was sent to jail, Broyles received a letter from Charley Mitchell of Birmingham, Ala. Mitchell claimed that Broughton was a friend of his, and that another friend, Becky Lou Johnson, had actually written the obscene letter. When Mitchell wrote to Broyles again, Broyles invited him to come to Atlanta for a conference. The flattered Mitchell walked into Broyles' trap, and soon admitted that he had penned the letter to take revenge on Jackson after they had had a dispute over a 20 cent loan and a scarf pin. Mitchell had not known that Jackson could not write. Mitchell was found Guilty and sentenced to a five-year term and a fine of $100 plus prosecution costs. Broughton was pardoned on May 18, 1900. REF.: *CBA*.

Brown, Aaron Venable, 1795-1859, U.S., lawyer. Member of the House of Representatives from 1845-47, and postmaster general of the U.S. from 1857-59. REF.: *CBA*.

Brown, Addison, 1830-1913, U.S., jur. District judge of Southern District of New York from 1881-1901. REF.: *CBA*.

Brown, Angus (AKA: **Arapaho, Red**), prom. 1892, U.S., west. lawman. Angus Brown was the sheriff of Buffalo, Wyo., during the notorious Johnson County war. He took the side of the homesteaders against the cattlemen. Brown moved to Wyoming from Tennessee in the 1880s and was extremely well read, said to have one of the few libraries in the territory. He was later killed by two cowboys representing the cattle barons.

REF.: Bartholomew, *The Biographical Album of Western Gunfighters*; *CBA*.

Brown, Anthony Silah, 1956- , Case of, U.S., mur. On Dec. 21, 1982, James Dassinger, a 53-year-old Pensacola, Fla., gas company truck driver, was found murdered, his body lying next to his truck. Charged in the shooting were Anthony Silah Brown, then twenty-six, and Wydell Rogers. In a plea bargain agreement with state prosecutors, Rogers pleaded guilty to second-degree murder and armed robbery, both without a firearm. He was convicted and sentenced to life imprisonment.

Escambia County Sheriff's investigator Ray Rathlev called the robbery "a setup from the beginning," explaining that one of the suspects had called the Veteran's Gas Company to ask for a delivery, hoping the driver would have money. When Dassinger arrived at the Pine Forest Road address, he was killed by a shotgun blast and his wallet was taken.

Brown was found Guilty of first-degree murder and, although jurors recommended a sentence of life in prison, Circuit Court Judge Joseph Q. Tarbuck overrode the jury's suggestion and condemned Brown to be executed in the electric chair. The convicted man was sent to death row of the Florida State Penitentiary in Starke. In May 1985 Florida's Supreme Court overturned Brown's death sentence, ordering a retrial because prosecutors had erred when they took a pretrial deposition from a witness without Brown being present.

At the February 1986 retrial, key witness Rogers changed his original story, saying that he knew nothing about the 1982 murder, and explaining that he had given his first testimony under the impression that he would get reduced time and would be paroled. Now, Rogers said, "It was God that got me to testify to the truth." Rogers' new story eventually brought Circuit Judge M.C. Blanchard to declare him an adverse witness. Another witness, Clattie Frost, Jr., who had formerly been Rogers' best friend, contradicted Rogers' new testimony. Brown was found innocent of all charges, acquitted, and released from prison on June 13, 1986. REF.: *CBA*.

Brown, Arthur Ross, 1925-56, U.S., mur. On Aug. 4, 1955, Mrs. Wilma Frances Allen, a prominent Kansas City, Mo., wife and mother, left a beauty parlor at 12:30 p.m. on a rainy day and hurried to her convertible. Five hours later, concerned about not finding his wife at home, Mr. Allen, a car dealer, sent his salesman to search for her car; a few hours later, he notified the police. At 2:10 a.m. Patrolman Ronald Erhardt found Mrs. Allen's locked Chevrolet under a dark viaduct. There were bloodstains on the rear seat and floor, and in the trunk were her torn and bloodstained clothing. Finger and palm prints found by police inside the auto were too blurred to be clues. From the Allen's mileage logs, police estimated that the Chevrolet had been driven sixty to seventy miles. They blocked out an area covering parts of Missouri and Kansas, and police nationally were notified to question any violent sexual deviants in their records. Leads poured into Kansas City, but none of them yielded any clues.

On Aug. 7, a Kansas farmer, Richard A. Taylor, noticed a blue handbag in a ditch on Highway 69. When he read about the Allen case in the paper, he notified police. On Aug. 7, Clifford Erhart and his son Milton were searching for a stray cow and calf about six miles from where the handbag had been found. They discovered an open pasture gate and then saw the nude corpse of Wilma Allen. She had been shot twice in the back of the head, her hands were tied behind her back, and all her jewelry was missing. With proof that the victim had been carried across state lines, Midwestern FBI agents poured into Kansas City. But rains had washed away any footprints or other evidence, and for weeks the case dragged on with no further clues.

On Aug. 31, Arthur Ross Brown, a parole violator from California, critically wounded a sheriff in Wyoming and escaped when the officer tried to arrest him. Brown's criminal record of assaults, robberies, and attempted abductions reached back sixteen years. Soon after the Wyoming incident, Brown stole a car in Sheridan, Wyo., then robbed a liquor store in Rapid City, S.D. A man matching Brown's description stole several cars as he made his way through Florida, Texas, and Indiana, holding up liquor stores, preferring those with women clerks working alone. The FBI, still connecting him only with the charges in the shooting of the Wyoming sheriff, kept surveillance on the homes of Brown's relatives.

On Nov. 9, a Kansas City caller reported to police that his neighbor, Mrs. Arthur Ross Brown, had just been abducted at gunpoint by her estranged husband. Four hours later, the incoherent woman returned home; her spouse had disappeared. Anticipating that Brown would return to California, FBI agents interviewed his mother in San Jose. The anxious woman said that she believed her son was mad, and asked the police to stop him before he did further harm. On Nov. 13 Brown called his mother, saying he had tried to visit her, but fearing a trap, had fled. He added that he was going to kill himself. That night, he was picked up by officers outside his aunt's house in San Francisco, asleep in his car.

Initially denying his guilt, Brown soon broke down and confessed to shooting the sheriff in Wyoming, adding: "But where I'm really wanted is Kansas City." In a full confession to the murder of Wilma Allen, Brown said his motive was robbery, explaining: "I was looking for someone to rob. She looked wealthy." He had climbed in beside Allen as she got into her car in the beauty-shop parking lot, and forced her to drive at gunpoint. Finding the open pasture gate was, he told police, "just... lucky." He had shot her as she begged for mercy, then stripped the body to prevent identification before dumping her in the field. He tried to clean the car before driving it back into town. Court-appointed psychiatrists found Brown sane, and the jury found him Guilty. He was executed in the gas chamber at the Missouri State Prison on Feb. 24, 1956. REF.: *CBA*.

Brown, Barry Austin, prom. 1974, U.S., mur. In a San Mateo, Calif., Superior Court, Barry Austin Brown pleaded guilty to three first-degree murder charges. He admitted killing Lois McNamara, the mother of a high school friend; a hitchhiking, discharged sailor whom he had picked up; and Richard Pipes, a grocery store employee whom Brown murdered when he held up the Santa Cruz store. Robbery was the motive in all three slayings, and the killer had netted about $1,500 and a car from McNamara, but only a backpack from the sailor. The thoughtful slayer told a probation officer, "I don't believe murder is part of my character. I believe I can, if given the chance, offer a lot to the people around me. I want to discover why I committed those acts. I don't want to be put in prison to rot away." Brown received three concurrent life sentences.

REF.: *CBA*; Godwin, *Murder U.S.A.*

Brown, Benjamin Gratz, 1826-85, U.S., lawyer. Helped organize the Republican Party, U.S. senator from 1863-67, and vice-presidential candidate with Horace Greeley in 1872. REF.: *CBA*.

Brown, Bradford, 1947- , U.S., (wrong. convict.) mur. On Nov. 2, 1974, Rodney Frazier was shot and killed in his Washington, D.C., home when a man tried to steal drugs. In April 1975 Bradford Brown was picked up by police on a gun charge and, because he fit the description of Frazier's killer and had been picked up on Frazier's block ten months earlier, he became a suspect in the murder. An eyewitness positively identified Brown as the slayer, saying: "I am sure of this guy's face. I will never forget his face." Brown was convicted on Nov. 28, 1975, and sentenced by Judge Norma Johnson to a prison term of eighteen years to life. The convicted man continued to maintain throughout that he had been at his 6-year-old niece's birthday party at the time of the shooting.

In 1979, a police informant told police detective Robert Kanjian that he knew Frazier's killer, naming Richard Harris, a 29-year-old man with seven convictions who was serving time at Lorton Reformatory on robbery charges. When Kanjian discovered that Brown had been convicted of the crime, he reviewed the case and found a phone number written down by the killer in a message to Frazier's father and left in the house. Kanjian tracked the number back to Harris, and the case was reopened. Harris pleaded guilty to manslaughter because his court-appointed attorney, John Treanor, explained that Harris thought he had shot Frazier in the leg, not the abdomen, and didn't know he had died. Harris was convicted and given a four-to-twelve-year sentence. Brown was released after having served five years in prison. Kanjian, who had previously been in favor of capital punishment, considered changing his mind. "I kept thinking about what could have happened if Bradford had been in a state with the death penalty." REF.: *CBA*.

Brown, Bruce, prom. 1974, Brit., rob. Known as a responsible, trustworthy, and highly-cultured citizen, Bruce Brown was also the mastermind behind a gang of thieves who netted as much as £2 million in fifty-nine major robberies over a four-year period. A respected leader in his community, Brown was known as a devoted family man and an astute businessman who bought and sold properties. One of his closest friends was a Scotland Yard detective. Their families vacationed together and they were members of the same golf club. But when Derek Creighton Smalls, charged with three bank and jewel robberies totaling £170,000, decided to turn Queen's Evidence in exchange for his freedom, he named Brown as the brains behind a series of robberies that took place in the southeast of England from 1968 to 1972 and brought in loot totaling close to £2 million.

Brown was tried in 1974, along with scores of other criminals, at the biggest bank robbery trial ever to take place at the Old Bailey. By the end of the trial, with Smalls as the key witness, twenty-two men were sentenced to a total of 309 years in prison for their parts in the robberies.

REF.: Borrell, *Crime In Britain Today; CBA*.

Brown, Carrie, See: **Old Shakespeare Case**.

Brown, Charles T., prom. 1920, Case of, U.S., mur. On Feb. 23, 1920, Charles T. Brown was at Denver's Waldorf Hotel with his lover, Jessie Rodgers. That morning, Rodgers had tearfully admitted that she was married. Just that day, she had run into Edward Bell Rodgers, the husband she had separated from two years earlier because of his physical abuse and jealous threats of murder. He had been spying on the couple, and had threatened to shoot them both. Brown, who was sick in bed at the time, reassured Rodgers, calling her husband's talk a bluff, but took the precaution of putting his own gun under the pillow for protection. Edward Rodgers knocked on the door soon after, barged into the room, and began threatening them both. He brought out a gun and leveled it at Brown, who fired back in self defense, killing the irate husband.

Brown and Rodgers were tried on charges of murder at the Denver West Side Criminal Court on May 12, 1920. They were found Not Guilty, acquitted on the grounds of self defense.

REF.: *CBA*; Rodell, *Denver Murders*.

Brown, Conrad, 1935- , U.S., mur. On Mar. 23, 1977, two men came into Conrad's Food & Liquors on Chicago's South Side. They were Thomas Patzke, twenty-six, a loan specialist, and Robert Fender, fifty-two, an auctioneer; both worked for the U.S. Small Business Association. Patzke had been friendly with owner Conrad Brown for some time, and was trying to help him out with his many financial problems. Reportedly $500,000 in debt, Brown had lost his liquor license, begun bankruptcy proceedings, and was about to be evicted for non-payment of rent. When Patzke and Fender came into the store, they told the employees to leave, intending to take an inventory and padlock the place as a preliminary step in foreclosing on the SBA loan. Brown beat both men with a metal pipe, then set fire to the store. When their bodies were found in the smoldering ruins by firemen the next day, Fender's hands had been tied behind his back.

Brown was charged with murder, felony murder, and arson. Tried before Judge Frank J. Wilson, Brown admitted that he had beaten both men and started the fire. Three psychiatrists testified that Brown had lost touch with reality and was legally insane when he committed the murders, but Assistant State's Attorney Robert Quinlivan declared that the killings were premeditated because Brown was "all washed up in business." Defense Attorney Frederick Cohn said that his client "went berserk" when Patzke and Fender tried to padlock his store. On Aug. 31, 1978, Brown was found Guilty on two counts of involuntary manslaughter and one of arson. He was sentenced to to fourteen-year prison terms on each of the three counts, to be served concurrently. REF.: *CBA*.

Brown, Cordelia, See: **Botkin, Cordelia**.

Brown, Ernest, 1898-1934, Brit., arson-mur. Ernest Brown murdered his employer, Frederick Ellison Morton on Sept. 5, 1933. Morton was a well-to-do cattle farmer in Yorkshire, England. Brown was having an affair with Morton's wife, Dorothy. When Mrs. Morton tried to end the liaison, Brown intimidated her into continuing it. On Sept. 5, while Frederick was away, Brown and Mrs. Morton quarrelled because she had been swimming with another man. Brown knocked her down. While she hid in the house waiting for her husband to return, Mrs. Morton heard a gunshot. Brown appeared shortly and explained that he had been shooting at a rat in the barn. Around 3:00 a.m., there was an explosion and Mrs. Morton looked out to see the garage ablaze. She escaped with her baby and her companion, Ann Houseman, and reported the fire to the police.

When the fire was extinguished, both of Frederick Morton's cars and his badly burned body were found in the garage. The body, the cars, and garage had been doused in gasoline. Morton had been shot in the stomach before his body was set on fire. Brown was charged with murder and tried at the Leeds Assizes. He was convicted and hanged at Armley Prison on Feb. 6, 1934.

REF.: Bechhofer-Roberts, *Sir Travers Humphreys: His Career and Cases;* Butler, *Murderers' England; CBA;* Goodman, *The Burning of Evelyn Foster;* Hastings, *The Other Mr. Churchill;* Humphreys, *A Book of Trials;* Jackson, *Francis Camps;* Shew, *A Companion to Murder;* Whitelaw, *Corpus Delicti;* Wild, *Crimes and Cases of 1933.*

Brown, George, d.1819, U.S., pir.-mur. George Brown was the first mate of the *Retrieve,* a small commercial vessel bound from Cadiz to Vera Cruz. En route, Brown struck Captain John Lewis on the head and threw him overboard, sailing the schooner to a small island where he sold the cargo. One of the crew members later informed authorities, and Brown was apprehended and returned to New York, the *Retrieve*'s home port. He was convicted of piracy and murder before Judge Livingston and hanged in New York harbor on Oct. 22, 1819, on board the ship he stole. Brown was not the real name of this culprit; he took this alias to prevent his family from learning of his crime, should he be caught.

REF.: *CBA; Confession of George Brown.*

Brown, Henry Billings, 1836-1913, U.S., jur. Deputy U.S. Marshal in Michigan from 1861-63, judge of the Eastern District of Michigan from 1875-90, and associate Supreme Court justice in 1890 replacing Samuel Miller. In 1896, he wrote the majority opinion upholding the separate but equal treatment of blacks in *Plessy vs. Fergusson.* He published numerous articles and legal opinions, including "Hints About Trials" (1886), "Judicial Treatment of Criminal Offenders" (1910), and *The Lake Erie Piracy Case* (1909). REF.: *CBA.*

Brown, Henry Newton, 1857-84, U.S., west. lawman-gunman-outl. Henry Newton Brown was orphaned at an early age and raised by relatives in Rolla, Mo., until he was seventeen when he headed west to be a cowboy. He worked on Colorado ranches and then drifted southward to Texas where he killed a cowboy in a gunfight outside a Panhandle town. Brown then moved to Lincoln County, N.M., where he became involved in the Lincoln County war, fighting on the side of the McSween-Tunstall faction. He befriended Billy the Kid and helped the Kid shoot down Sheriff William Brady on Apr. 1, 1878, in Lincoln, N.M., as he, the Kid, and others hid behind an adobe wall and fired from ambush. Brown was also with Billy the Kid and others at Blazer's Mill on Apr. 4, 1878, when Andrew L. "Buckshot" Roberts shot and killed Richard Brewer, leader of the so-called "regulators" to which Brown, the Kid, and others belonged. Roberts was also killed at this shootout, Brown helping to riddle the outhouse in which Roberts had taken cover. Brown was present at

Gunman and outlaw Henry Newton Brown.

the Lincoln, N.M., siege of the McSween house in which Billy the Kid and others were trapped. Brown and two others were in a little storehouse nearby and sniped at the Murphy-Dolan men surrounding the McSween house. He managed to escape with the Kid and others.

In the fall of 1878, Brown accompanied Billy the Kid and others to the Texas Panhandle and there the band busied itself with rustling horses. When the Kid returned to New Mexico, Brown decided to stay in Texas and most probably saved his life for a few years. He tracked horse thieves and later got an appointment as a deputy sheriff in Oldham County, Texas, but he

was fired for picking fights with drunks. Next Brown worked for ranches in Oklahoma and then moved on to Caldwell, Kan., where he was first appointed deputy marshal and then city marshal. Caldwell was a tough town at the time, and Brown asked his friend Ben Wheeler (real name Ben Robertson) to work as his deputy. The two men cleaned up the town quickly. In April 1883, Brown, Wheeler, and other lawmen chased the notorious Ross gang to their hideout in Hunnewell and captured its members after shooting one of the sons of the leader. On May 14, 1883, Brown ordered a drunken Indian named Spotted Horse to leave Caldwell, but the Indian went for his gun and Brown pumped four bullets into him, killing the Indian.

Four men to hang: left to right, John Wesley, Henry Newton Brown, Bill Smith, Ben Robertson, captured after they robbed the bank in Medicine Lodge, Kan., in 1884; following the taking of this photo, the four were served meals and wrote letters to their families before their executions.

A gambler named Newt Boyce threatened to kill both Wheeler and Brown for locking him up after he cut two men in a Caldwell saloon. On the night of Dec. 15, 1883, Brown went after Boyce who met him in the street. The gambler reached inside his coat pocket, ostensibly for a derringer, but Brown fired a single shot from his Winchester and mortally wounded Boyce. Brown and Wheeler decided that their wages as peacemakers needed to be supplemented. Under the ruse of traveling to Oklahoma to look for a murderer, both men left Caldwell and joined up with two outlaws, William Smith and John Wesley. These four men then rode to Medicine Lodge, Kan., and there held up the Medicine Valley Bank. President E.W. Payne reached for his gun and Brown shot him to death. Chief Cashier George Geppert was also shot to death by the other outlaws, even though he had raised his hands. The cashier staggered to the vault and managed to close it before he fell dead to the floor.

Brown and the others fled the town with nine citizens hotly pursuing them. One of the vigilantes was Barney O'Connor, a rancher who had once employed Brown and recognized him as he rode pell-mell out of Medicine Lodge. The outlaws rode mistakenly into a box canyon and surrendered after a two-hour gun battle. The outlaws were kept prisoner in a small house and given two meals before their picture was taken. Then the prisoners were told to write letters to their loved ones and Brown wrote to his wife, which stated: "It was all for you. I did not think this would happen." Brown anticipated a lynch mob would arrive that night to string up the outlaws. He managed to get out of his handcuffs and when the mob broke into the makeshift jail at 9 p.m., Brown dashed through the open door, squirmed through the mob, and ran down an alley. A farmer fired both barrels of a shotgun as Brown raced past him and tore the gunman in half. Though Brown was already dead, several citizens fired bullets into his body, so angry were they that he had cheated them of a hanging. Wheeler also tried to escape the mob and was wounded but he was dragged with Wesley and Smith to a nearby tree and hanged. See: **Billy the Kid; Brewer, Richard; Lincoln County War.**

REF.: Adams, *A Fitting Death for Billy the Kid;* Bartholomew, *A Biographical Album of Western Gunfighters;* ____, *Jesse Evans;* Blanchard, *Conquest of Southwest Kansas;* Breihan, *Great Gunfighters of the West;* Brent, *Great Western Heroes;* Brent, *The Complete and Factual Life of Billy the Kid;* Burns, *The Saga of Billy the Kid;* Casey, *The Texas Border and Some Borderliners;* CBA; Chrisman, *Lost Trails of the Cimarron;* Coe, *Frontier Fighter;* Coe, *Ranch on the Ruidoso;* Cunningham, *Triggernometry;* Debo, *The Cowman's Southwest;* Drago, *Wild, Woolly and Wicked;* Dykstra, *The Cattle Towns;* Ealy, *Water in a Thirsty Land;* Freeman, *Midnight and Noonday;* Fulton, *Maurice Garland Fulton's History of the Lincoln County War;* Gard, *The Chisholm Trail;* ____, *Frontier Justice;* Garrett, *The Authentic Life of Billy the Kid;* Hamlin, *The True Story of Billy the Kid;* Hertzog, *A Directory of New Mexico Desperadoes;* Holloway, *Texas Gun Lore;* Horn, *New Mexico's Troubled Years;* Hough, *The Story of the Outlaw;* Hunt, *The Tragic Days of Billy the Kid;* Hunter and Rose, *The Album of Gunfighters;* Jackson, *The Life of Nellie C. Bailey;* Keleher, *Violence in Lincoln County;* King, *Pioneer Western Empire Builders;* Lake, *Wyatt Earp, Frontier Marshal;* ____, *He Carried a Six-Shooter;* McCarty, *Maverick Town;* McNeal, *When Kansas Was Young;* Metz, *John Selman, Texas Gunfighter;* Miller, Langsdorf and Richmond, *Kansas, A Pictorial History;* Miller and Snell, *Why the West was Wild;* Moore, *The West;* Mullin, *A Chronology of the Lincoln County War;* Nolan, *The Life and Death of John Henry Tunstall;* Nye, *Pistols for Hire;* O'Connor, *Pat Garrett;* O'Neal, *Encyclopedia of Western Gunfighters;* Otero, *The Real Billy the Kid;* Peavy, *Charles A. Siringo;* Penfield, *Western Sheriffs and Marshals;* Preece, *Lone Star Man;* Rayfield, *The West That's Gone;* Rennert, *Western Outlaws;* Ridings, *The Chisholm Trail;* Rosa, *The Gunfighter, Man or Myth?;* Sabin, *Wild Men of the Wild West;* Sanders, *The Sumner County Story;* Shirley, *Pawnee Bill;* ____, *Toughest of Them All;* Siringo, *History of Billy the Kid;* ____, *Riata and Spurs;* Stanley, *Desperadoes of New Mexico;* ____, *Fort Stanton;* Thorp, *Story of the Southwestern Cowboy;* Walters, *Tombstone's Yesterdays;* Warden, *Thrilling Tales of Kansas;* Wellman, *The Trampling Herd;* White, *Lead and Likker;* ____, *Trigger Fingers.*

Brown, H. Rap (Hubert Geroid Brown), 1943- , U.S., rob.-asslt. H. Rap Brown became a national figure in the late 1960s when he succeeded Stokely Carmichael as chairman of the Student Non-Violent Coordinating Committee. In 1967, Brown was charged with arson and inciting a riot following a speech he gave in racially tense Cambridge, Md. Before he was brought to trial on those charges, which could have carried a possible sentence of up to twenty years imprisonment, Brown flew home to Baton Rouge, La. After checking a rifle with the plane's pilot, he was arrested on federal charges of carrying a weapon while under indictment. He was convicted of those charges in 1968 but remained free on bail, working to quell the Maryland charges, until 1970 when, on the night of the Maryland trial, two of his friends were killed when their car exploded near the site of the trial. When Maryland officials suggested that the two men had been carrying explosives for subversive reasons, Brown disappeared, and was placed on the FBI's Ten Most Wanted list in 1970. He turned up a year later and was charged with attempted robbery in conjunction with the Red Carpet Lounge holdup in New York City. Brown was convicted of robbery and assault in April 1973, and sentenced to five to fifteen years at Attica Prison in New York.

In July 1974, the Federal Court at New Orleans was asked to set aside the five-year sentence on the grounds that the Federal Bureau of Investigation had set out to destroy Brown, along with other black leaders, during the summer of 1967. William M. Kunstler, an attorney well known in the New Left radical move-

ment, filed the request for the Center for Constitutional Rights, saying that the FBI, then under the leadership of J. Edgar Hoover, had been ordered to "use its imagination" to stop the black nationalist movement in the U.S. Instructions to agents suggested that they use fabrications and other devices, such as piling arrest upon arrest, to stop "black hate groups." The FBI's "counter-intelligence programs," aimed at such groups as the Ku Klux Klan and U.S. Socialist and Communist parties, as well as black activists, were, according to the Justice Department, discontinued in 1971. When memorandums regarding these programs were released, all names had been deleted from the documents. Attorney Kunstler showed that New Orleans lawyer James W. Lake, Jr. had sent Kunstler a letter testifying that he had heard Federal judge Lansing L. Mitchell, who had tried Brown on the federal charges in 1973, refer to Rap Brown, saying he was going to make sure to "get that nigger." Brown was paroled on Oct. 21, 1976.

REF.: CBA; Powers, *Secrecy and Power.*

Brown, Irving F., 1914- , U.S., asslt. In October 1948, Odessa Booker, a black woman, was found hiding in a farmhouse outside Tampa, Fla. She was fleeing Irving F. Brown, who had called on her, asking her to come to his house to work as a babysitter. Then he drove Booker to a deserted lane and attempted to rape her. Booker managed to escape and Brown was arrested and tried before an all-white jury, which found him guilty of assault with attempt to rape. Judge Roy Amidon said: "This is the most reprehensible case that ever came before me. It is much worse than if the races of the participants were reversed." Amidon sentenced Brown to twenty years in prison. Two weeks earlier, in Wetumpka, Ala., two white men were given 45-year prison sentences for raping black women. REF.: CBA.

Brown, James, prom. 1867, U.S., mur. The story of the Boston "vampire" received plenty of play in newspapers across the U.S. during the second half of the nineteenth century. It made good copy and helped boost circulation during the height of the great newspaper "wars." The "vampire" in question was a Portuguese sailor named James Brown who killed two crewmen on board a fishing smack sailing out of Boston Harbor. The year was 1867. Discovering that two of his men were missing from their posts, the captain of the fishing boat went into the hold where he found Brown crouched over two bodies. Holding his lantern closer, he saw Brown sucking the blood from one body. The other was stiff, and apparently devoid of blood.

Seaman Brown was tried, convicted, and sentenced to hang. However, his life was spared by President Andrew Johnson, who commuted the sentence to life imprisonment. He spent the next fifteen years in a Massachusetts prison until he was transferred to an Ohio penitentiary in 1882. There he remained until Nov. 4, 1892, when he was transferred once again, this time to the national asylum in Washington, D.C. According to an account published in the *Brooklyn Daily Eagle,* Brown "fought like a tiger" when they came to move him to a new location. Brown believed that his death warrant had been signed, and that the guards were actually taking him to his place of execution. During this period of confinement he had murdered two other men.

Charles Fort related the strange tale of Seaman Brown in his book *Wild Talents,* but he failed to add that the two sailors were not murdered for their blood, but because they had slandered the dark-skinned Portuguese with racial epithets. The blood-sucking details were probably created by newsmen. REF.: CBA.

Brown, James, 1928- , U.S., asslt. James Brown was born into a poor Georgia family, abandoned as a child, and made his way to the streets of Augusta, Ga. At sixteen he was sentenced to four to ten years in juvenile detention for stealing a battery from a car. But Brown became one of the most influential recording artists in popular music history, reigning in the music business for more than a decade, and influencing and shaping the careers of other artists. His success as a black entertainer is unparalelled, and he was a highly visible leader in the black pride movement of the late 1960s, with hits like, "Say It Loud, I'm Black and I'm Proud," and contributions of millions of dollars to charities. Brown was called in by the mayors of New York and Boston to help quell the racial violence that followed the assassination of Dr. Martin Luther King, and he performed similar services for the mayor of Augusta, Ga., two years later. In his autobiography, Brown said: "I wanted to use my position to help people, and I wanted to have something to say about the country I lived in."

But in 1987-88, rumors of drug problems and repeated cases of domestic troubles and other incidents were covered by the press. Brown's wife, Adrienne Brown, claimed her husband had abused her several times, but she never filed charges, although police were called several times. On Sept. 24, 1988, Brown, armed with a shotgun, led police on a two-state chase after interrupting a seminar to complain about people using his bathroom. A convoy of police, moving at high speeds, finally arrested and jailed the singer. The drug PCP was found in Brown's bloodstream, and there were fourteen bullet holes in his car. According to his attorney, A.H. "Buddy" Dallas, "It's an absolute miracle that James Brown is alive." Brown pleaded guilty to seven misdemeanor charges, including reckless driving, having no state license, driving with a suspended license, attempting to flee police, carrying a deadly weapon to a public gathering, simple assault, and improper lane change, as well as driving while under the influence. On Dec. 15, 1988, Brown was sentenced in an Aiken, S.C., court by Judge Hubert Long to six years in prison for failing to stop for police. On his assault charges, Brown was given the option of six months in prison or a $6,000 fine and five years of probation.

His wife, Adrienne, had pleaded no contest to charges of speeding, criminal trespass, and driving under the influence from a September 1987 incident, and received probation and a $600 fine on Jan. 23, 1989. The next day, in Augusta, Ga., James Brown was sentenced in a Richmond County State Court to a six-year prison term for failing to stop for police. Judge Gayle B. Hamrick decreed that the sentence would run concurrently with Brown's sentence from South Carolina. The sixty-year-old Brown began serving his time at the Park Correctional Center, a minimum security penitentiary where many of the 275 inmates are ill or elderly.

Brown says he is "dealing" with being in prison: "A lot of people would like to see me fall, but you can't make a winner a loser." He is flooded with visit requests; most have been turned away. In New York City, a "Free James Brown" movement was launched soon after the performer was incarcerated. Brown, who says his problems with the law stem from harassment by law enforcement officials, has released two new records since he has been in jail. The singer told a reporter, "I feel that I haven't been treated fair, no justice for the things I've done over the last four decades. I stopped the riots. I always tried to help. Had it been a man of another race, he wouldn't be where I am. There's no doubt about it. They wouldn't have allowed it." Brown will be eligible for parole in a year. REF.: *CBA.*

Brown, James W., and **Robert Leventon,** and **Isom Eades,** prom. 1901, Case of, U.S., lynch. On May 24, 1901, L.W. Leventon reported some harness stolen from his barn in Lookout, Calif. The suspects, thought responsible for several other recent thefts, were: Calvin Hall, a 74-year-old Civil War veteran; James Hall, his half-Indian son; Frank Hall, his adopted grandson, also an Indian; Martin Wilson, Hall's former wife's 13-year old son; and Daniel Yantis. On May 25, all five were arrested on burglary charges. After hearing the evidence, the court dismissed the charges against Calvin Hall. On May 30, James W. Brown, a deputy constable and four other men took Hall from his home to Meyer's Hotel at Lookout, where the other four accused thieves were being held under guard. At about 1:45 a.m., Brown and a gang of nineteen men wearing grain sacks over their faces woke the prisoners, bound and gagged them, and took them to a bridge over the Pitt River where they lynched them. The mob returned to the hotel to wake Calvin Hall, who was sleeping on a sofa, and then lynched him as well.

On June 3, Superior Judge J.W. Harrington requested that Attorney General Tirey L. Ford send a representative and a detective to assist in the grand jury investigation of the lynching. Ford sent Charles N. Post and George A. Sturtevant. With little cooperation from local residents who were either afraid of retribution from the mob or were prejudiced against the victims, the month long investigation nevertheless brought in indictments against Robert Levenson, Isom Eades, and James W. Brown for the murder of the boy, Martin Wilson. The defendants' petition to the Supreme Court to prevent Harrington from trying the cases was denied. The trial began on Nov. 21, 1901, and, despite confessions from two of participants in the lynching, John Hutton and Claude Morris, the jury of local residents found the men Not Guilty.

REF.: Carpozi, *Great Crimes of the Century; CBA;* Duke, *Celebrated Criminal Cases of America.*

Brown, J.B., prom. 1901, U.S., (wrong convict.) mur. On Oct. 17, 1901, a railroad worker found the body of an engineer, Harry E. Wesson, in the Florida Southern Railway yard. Wesson had been shot once in the head by a .38-caliber pistol, which lay a few feet from his body; his pockets were turned inside out, but $130 in a roll of bills was still hidden in his overalls. Citizens of Palatka, Fla., were enraged at the cruel murder, and Sheriff R.C. Howell brought a number of suspects into the Putnam County Jail for questioning. Jailor Hagan overheard J.B. Brown, a former brakeman on one of the trains, talking to one of the prisoners, Lucius Crawford: "Keep your mouth shut and say nothing." Within an hour, Brown was arrested.

Investigation revealed that Brown had held a grudge against Wesson since he was fired following a dispute with a conductor. Edward Ponder, a porter, said Brown had told him in September that he was going to get his pistol and kill Wesson. Brown claimed to have been in a card game until about 11:30 the night of the murder, and to have found out about the killing the next morning at a card game. According to some of the other players, Brown had seemed excited at the game, and had money; he also whispered on the side with Jim Johnson, another player. On this evidence, Brown was held as the main suspect, while the others were released. Shortly after, Brown's cellmate, Alonzo Mitchell, told the sheriff that Brown had just confessed to him that he and Jim Johnson had plotted together to murder Wesson for his money. When Henry Davis, another prisoner, corroborated that he also had heard Brown confess, the case was brought to trial.

Brown was prosecuted by State's Attorney Syd L. Carter on a charge of first-degree murder before Circuit Judge W.S. Bullock on Nov. 19, 1901. Defense attorneys were A.M. Allred and John E. Marshall. The accused man testified on his own behalf, consistently maintaining his innocence and denying that he had made a confession at the coroner's inquest. He said he did not own a pistol and had never made a threat against Wesson's life. When Bullock refused to admit Brown's alleged confession because Brown had refused to sign it, saying it was incorrect, a court reporter testified from his records about Brown's statements at the inquest.

The two-day trial ended on Nov. 20, 1901, when Bullock sentenced Brown to be hanged. An appeal to the Florida Supreme Court affirmed the conviction and sentence. As Brown was led to the gallows and a rope adjusted around his neck, the death warrant was read which had the name of one of the jurors instead of Brown's as the convicted. The hanging was cancelled, a plea was made to the governor of Florida, and the sentence was commuted to life imprisonement.

In 1902, the case against Jim Johnson, who had been jointly indicted with Brown, was dropped. In 1913, as Johnson was dying, he confessed that he had shot Wesson and that Brown had nothing to do with it. On Oct. 1, 1913, Governor Park Trammell granted Brown a full pardon. After serving twelve years in prison, a now physically disabled Brown was released. Sixteen years later, in 1929, the state of Florida granted the infirm and destitute Brown a relief fund of $2,492, to be paid in monthly installments of $25, for his "faithful service...during the period of this wrongful imprisonment." It is not known how much longer Brown lived to collect the stipends. REF.: *CBA*.

Brown, JoAnne, prom. 1974, Case of, U.S., mur. A member of a well-to-do Boston family, attorney Burr C. Hollister was known for his flamboyant courtroom style and his social conscience. Though a law secretary to a New York State Supreme Court Justice, Hollister was best known for his efforts as Long Island's foremost poverty lawyer. He lived with a former client, a black woman, Joanne Brown, and her two children, in their home in Uniondale, N.Y. Their relationship was tumultuous and erratic, and they had separated from each other many times.

In the early morning of Sept. 30, 1974, an attendant at the State Supreme Court found Hollister dead in the judge's chambers, a .22-caliber bullet in his head. With no gun in the room, suicide was ruled out, and investigators speculated that the lawyer might have been killed by an angry plaintiff. At Hollister's wake, which was well attended by both the social elite and welfare families whom Hollister had championed, JoAnne Brown knelt by the open casket, gazed into the dead man's face, and whispered to him as she laid her cheek against his. Three weeks later, she turned herself into the Nassau County police and confessed to the murder.

When Brown's lawyer informed the press that his client was insane, Brown insisted that she was rational and bitterly opposed the mental examination that her own attorney ordered her to undergo. As she was being led from the courthouse to be examined for her sanity, she shouted to waiting reporters: "I'm being framed for this. I killed Burr. I'm ready to talk about it, to tell everything. And they're trying to make me think I'm sick!" Brown's lawyer pointed to her outburst as yet another indication of her mental derangement. Brown was found "innocent of murder by reason of mental disease or defect," and ordered confined to an institution.

REF.: *CBA; Godwin, Murder U.S.A.*

Brown, John (AKA: **Brown of Priestfield**), c.1627-85, Scot., her. Shot and killed in the presence of his wife at the direction of John Graham of Claverhouse, a Royalist leader who persecuted Covenanters. REF.: *CBA*.

Brown, John (AKA: **Old Brown, Osawatomie Brown**), 1800-59, U.S., treas.-mur. A religious fanatic and an abolitionist zealot, John Brown remains an enigmatic figure in history, motivated to his bloody 1856 murders in Kansas and his equally lethal and short-lived 1859 slave revolt at Harper's Ferry, Va., by an unreasoning obsession to free the slaves of the South at any cost. To only a few northerners at that time was Brown a hero. To the South as a whole he was a "murderous fiend." To the rest of the country John Brown was a strange, obscure creature bent on self destruction and one who was probably insane. Brown was born in Torrington, Conn., to Ruth Mills and Owen Brown, a poor farmer who boasted that he was a direct descendant of Peter Brown, who had arrived on the *Mayflower* at Plymouth Rock in 1620, but research shows that Peter Brown produced no sons. The family did, however, trace back to the American Revolution in which several of its ancestors served with Washington's forces. John Brown worked his father's farm until deciding that he would become a minister, but he abandoned this notion after he received failing grades at a Massachusetts preparatory college.

In 1820, Brown returned to his father's farm and married Dianthe Lusk. The union produced seven children. The first Mrs. Brown died on Aug. 10, 1832, three days after giving birth to her last child. (She was later reported to have died insane and that insanity ran through the entire Brown family on both sides.) A year later Brown married 16-year-old Mary Anne Day who had worked for Brown and taken care of his children. Unlike Dianthe Lusk Brown, a short, frail woman, the second Mrs. Brown was a tall, large girl who had been selected by Brown as his second wife because of her "stamina." That physical strength was called upon time and again in bearing thirteen children for Brown in twenty-one years, along with the heavy farming chores she had to assume. Seven of these children died at birth and several of Brown's sons

from both marriages would later die in the carnage Brown brought about in his fanatical wars against pro-slavery forces.

John Brown was not a success in life. He tried his hand at farming, surveying, land speculating and failed. He became a postmaster and a schoolmaster and found that these positions were unsuited to his temperament. As a teacher, Brown had no more patience with his students than he did with his children. He was a severe taskmaster with his children and thrashed any of his offspring when he caught them lying or even telling fanciful stories. Though he was later called a visionary, Brown could not abide human imagination. When some of his small sons told him stories of dreams or creative ideas, he exploded, labeled such notions the "work of the Devil," and beat them severely. His rough handling of students (some said brutal, even sadistic) caused him to be removed as a teacher.

Then he briefly turned to raising racehorses, another financial disaster. He went into the tanning business with a partner, and by the mid-1850s, he had mismanaged the business and it was on the brink of bankruptcy. Only through the intervention of his partner, Colonel Simon Perkins, did Brown manage to avoid debtor's prison, with Perkins paying off the staggering debts Brown had accumulated. Then Brown entered the wool business and again failed. While attempting to make a living for his large brood, Brown became deeply involved with wealthy abolitionists in Boston, New York, and Philadelphia. Through these rich and self-indulgent men, Brown was financed piecemeal toward the abortive revoltion he would later try to create. Though these Eastern businessmen, religious leaders, and pundits thought of themselves as liberators trying to set the blacks free from slavery, they spent endless hours merely discussing their theories and reveling in their conspiracy to free the slaves. John Brown was their man of action, the man who actually put their theories into practice.

Finances flowed from this group to Brown in the mid-1850s when he was placed in charge of an abolitionist-sponsored farm in North Elba, N.Y., where runaway slaves were sheltered. It was Brown's job to turn these unschooled blacks into useful farmers, but after many months of lecturing the runaways, Brown gave up, saying that he intended to go to Kansas and fight the pro-slavers in that state. Brown and some of his sons established a settlement at Osawatomie. The state was then known as "Bleeding Kansas," one where Free State adherents opposed to slavery and pro-slavers clashed almost daily in bloody battles that subsequently left hundreds dead and thousands wounded. The Free State town of Lawrence was occupied by pro-slavery forces and sacked without any opposition from its abolitionist citizens. This lack of resistance infuriated John Brown, who called the occupants of Lawrence "cowards." A short time later, on May 22, 1856, Congressman Preston "Bully" Brooks, a virulent supporter of slavery, attacked abolitionist senator Charles Sumner on the Senate floor, beating Sumner into unconsciousness with his cane for demanding that slavery be brought to an end. This so incensed Brown, when he got the news in Kansas, that he decided to strike.

Loading a wagon with himself and six others, with one of his sons riding a horse, the Brown contingent left Osawatomie and headed, on the night of May 23, 1856, toward the pro-slavery settlement at Pottawatomie. Brown and his men were all armed to the teeth with rifles, pistols, swords, and knives. They waited until near midnight then broke into the cabin of James Doyle, dragging him outside with his two oldest sons, William, twenty-two, and Drury, twenty. Some of Brown's men were about to take out 14-year-old John Doyle, but his mother screamed: "Not him, Oh, God, not him!" John Brown, wearing a large straw hat, a light coat and holding a sabre in his hand, his face hard as stone, his piercing stare full of ice, pushed the boy into the arms of his mother. He then walked calmly outside and put a pistol to the head of James Doyle and blew off the top of his head. His men hacked William Doyle to pieces. Drury Doyle broke free and ran but was caught and also hacked to pieces, his arms and legs, and part of his head hacked away by the frenzied killers.

The murder band next went to the home of Allen Wilkinson and also dragged him from his bed, taking him outside of his cabin where the murderers slit his throat, stabbed him in the back and side, and cut his body to pieces. Then one of the killers walked back into the Wilkinson house and lied to Mrs. Wilkinson, saying that he and his coherts were members of "the Northern Army" and that they had made her husband a prisoner and that he was being taken back to their camp. She told the stranger that she was afraid to stay in the cabin alone with her two small children and asked if he would stay with her until her husband was returned to her. "I'd like to," the youth said, "but *he* won't let me." This was probably one of Brown's sons, forced to do the old man's fanatical bidding. He took two saddles and an old weapon from the mantlepiece and left the cabin.

Next was the cabin of James Harris where landowner Dutch Henry was taken out and cut to pieces with sabres, his body tossed into a nearby stream. Brown and his men then added horse stealing to the mass murders by riding away on Dutch Henry's best mounts. They had killed five men in the space of an hour, leaving two widows and many orphaned children, an apalling slaughter that nearly brought Kansas to open warfare. Brown's "army" that night consisted of his four sons, Owen, thirty-one; Frederick, twenty-five; Salmon, nineteen; Oliver, seventeen; his son-in-law, Henry Thompson; James Townsley, who was borrowed for the evening because he owned the wagon and horses that hauled the "army" to its grisly destination; and storekeeper Theodore Wiener, who, like the rest, was a dedicated abolitionist and would follow John Brown anywhere and do anything for the old man's cause. The murder party hid in some dense woods while military units searched for them. When the slaughter of the pro-slavery men was learned even the Free Staters condemned Brown. The Brown settlement in Osawatomie was burned down, and soliders were stationed in the area to arrest Brown and his men when they returned.

Informants led a detachment of cavalry to Brown's hiding place, but its commander was captured by Brown and his men while under a flag of truce and held until authorities released two of Brown's others sons who had no part in the Pottawatomie massacre. Once these sons were returned, Brown released the cavalry officer and fled with his men, never returning to Osawato-mie. He was a hunted man after that, furtively flitting between the East and Kansas where he continued to murder and steal horses. By 1859, the abolitionist cause had reached fever pitch, and Brown demanded that his secret financial backers produce enough money for him to launch the slave uprising he had planned for decades. The so-called Secret Six, who backed Brown on his revolutionary adventure and who had financed him for years through all his miserable acts of murder and mayhem in the name of abolition, were some of the wealthiest and most influential citizens in New England, the hard core of the movement: Ralph Waldo Emerson, poet and politician; the Reverend Thomas Wentworth Higginson; Dr. Samuel Gridley Howe; George Luther Stearns, millionaire liberal; Gerrit Smith, millionaire liberal; and Frank Sanborn. These men met with Brown secretly in Boston and "God's Angry Man," as Brown was called by some, insisted that these men finance his long-planned attack on the arsenal at Harper's Ferry in Virginia.

The plan was in keeping with the kind of bloody strategy he had employed in Kansas. Brown's men would spread the word to the slave populations of Virginia, Maryland, and other states that the tens of thousands of slaves were to rally to Brown at Harper's Ferry after he had seized the arsenal. They would gather at Harper's Ferry where Brown would arm them and then march on the state capitals and take over the state governments, killing and imprisoning the white populations. When the abolitionist supporters hesitated, Brown thundered at them, calling them cowards. He badly frightened them into backing his rash move. Brown had already scouted Harper's Ferry in July 1869, pretending to be a cattle buyer and using an alias. (He had often used aliases in Kansas when making his furtive plans to drive out the slavers,

at one time employing the name Shubal Morgan. Brown, a Mason, had been absorbed by the abduction and murder of William Morgan by Masons in 1826 after Morgan announced he would publish a book exposing the order's secret rites and sinister doings, and it was at that time in his life that he first became involved in conspiracies and purchased his first gun to defend himself from fellow Masons after he criticized the chastisement of William Morgan. His selection of the name Morgan years later as an alias, therefore, was a salute to his fellow Mason murdered more than two decades earlier.)

On Aug. 20, 1859, Secretary of War John B. Floyd received an anonymous letter which warned that "Old John Brown, late of Kansas," was planning to attack a federal armory in Maryland, using Harper's Ferry as a base. Floyd found that there was no federal armory in Maryland and filed the letter, dismissing it as having come from a crank. With twenty-one men, sixteen white and five black, Brown filled wagons full of hundreds of pikes and revolvers with which he would arm the rising blacks and set off for Harper's Ferry, arriving there on Oct. 16, 1859. Brown's men rounded up prominent citizens and used these men to gain entrance to the arsenal, holding these citizens as hostages. Once Brown and his men were inside the fortress-like structure, they manned the portholes and awaited the legions of blacks.

Instead of thousands of blacks rallying to his banner, the citizens of Harper's Ferry surrounded the arnsenal and began firing on it. Brown stood at a porthole and looked across the valley to see men scrambling down the hills and advancing toward the arsenal. "Here come our men," Brown said. One of his men took a good look and realized that these armed groups coming toward them were local citizens ready for battle, and he told Brown: "I'm afraid that those aren't are men, Captain."

A local militia, the Jefferson Guards, arrived and joined the citizens, and now the arsenal was under heavy fire. Brown's men began to desert. Richard Henry Kagi, one of his most loyal supporters, bolted out a back door and tried to reach the river nearby, but he was shot in the back. Billy Leeman tried to escape but was also shot. So too was John P. Copeland, a black student from Oberlin College, who had joined Brown in recent weeks. Brown's son Watson later went out with a flag of truce and was shot, dragged back into the arsenal. By 11 p.m. that night, Colonel Robert E. Lee, accompanied by his aide, Lieutenant J.E.B. Stuart, arrived at Harper's Ferry, under direct orders from President James Buchanan and Secretary of War Floyd to organize the military forces around the arsenal and recapture the building from the strange invaders. Lee ordered all the saloons closed and immediately regrouped the militia, volunteers, and guardsmen. Lee learned that the mysterious leader of the insurrectionists inside the arsenal had demanded wagons, food, and horses and to be allowed to leave with his men, promising that he would not injure remaining hostages. Lee ordered a detachment of marines to get closer to the arsenal and then decided to wait until dawn before making his next move. He had no idea of how many insurrectionists were inside the building, and he was concerned about the hostages held by them.

Inside the arsenal, Brown looked about to see that he had only four men left on their feet. All the rest were wounded or dead. Both his sons Watson and Oliver were mortally wounded, dying. Watson repeatedly called out for his father but Brown, cold-hearted, stood looking out of a porthole, not answering his son. Then the 23-year-old Watson began to beg someone to shoot him, to end his pain and agony. Finally, the old man turned and said without compassion: "Oh, you will get over it. If you must die, die like a man." He paced the wall behind the portholes until dawn, then he apparently remembered his other son, also mortally wounded and cried out in the murk: "Oliver! Oliver!" His call was greeted by silence. Then Brown said to himself: "I guess he is dead."

As dawn broke and slivers of sunlight shot through the narrow portholes, Brown turned to the hostages gathered in the arsenal, saying to them in a half-apologetic voice: "Gentleman, if you

JOHN BROWN'S RAID

Brown's financial backers, left to right, George L. Stearns, Gerrit Smith, Frank B. Sanborn.

John Brown, circa 1856.

Brown moneymen Thomas W. Higginson and Samuel G. Howe.

The farm house at North Elba.

Citizens battling Brown's men at Harper's Ferry.

Lawrence, Kansas, razed by proslavers, 1856.

Troops storming the engine house, 1859.

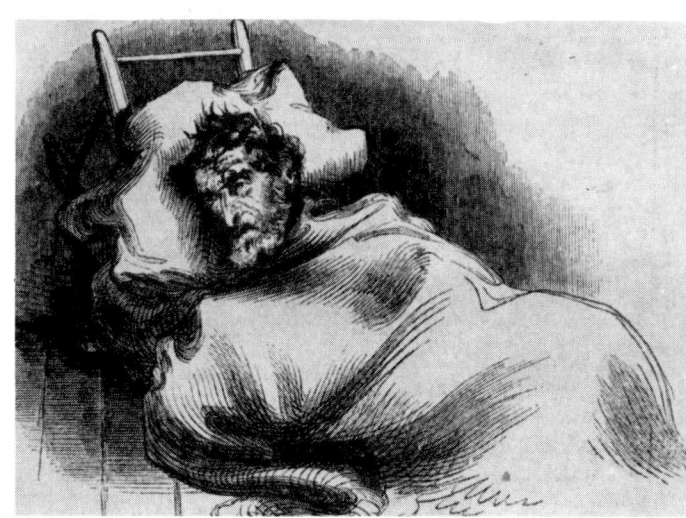

Oliver and Watson Brown, killed at Harper's Ferry.

John Brown, wounded, after being captured and jailed.

John Brown shortly before death, left, and at his hanging.

The courthouse where Brown was tried.

The grave of John Brown.

knew my history, you would not blame me...I went to Kansas a peaceable man and the pro-slavery people from Kentucky and Virginia hunted me down like a wolf. I lost one of my sons there..." He was interrupted by noise from outside. He looked out a porthole to see troops moving into position. An officer under a flag of truce was approaching the main door, and Brown went to the door to parley.

Approaching the door was Lieutenant Stuart. His orders were simple. He was to hand the leader of the insurrectionists a written demand from Lee for immediate surrender. If he proved intractable, Stuart was to leap to one side of the door and, at that moment, the marines were to charge the arsenal. The door of the engine house opened a crack as Stuart stood before it. A hoary hand reached out to take Lee's note. Stuart, who had served in Kansas and had once arrested Brown, stared in shock to see the old man, saying: "Why, aren't you old Osawatomie Brown, whom I once held prisoner."

"Yes," Brown replied without emotion, "but you didn't keep me." He read the note, then began to repeat his earlier demands to be allowed to go free with his men. Just then Stuart jumped to one side of the door and the marines charged, bayonets thrusting, other military units laying down a covering fire that sent a hailstorm of bullets pinging off the brick of the building. The marines charged forward, several carrying a large ladder. Brown had slammed the door to the engine house closed, but the marines battered it down and Lieutenant Israel Green led them into the arsenal where several of Brown's men were bayoneted to death. Green himself thrust his sword hard at Brown's middle as the old man aimed a pistol at him, pulling the trigger repeatedly, but it proved to be empty. Green's sword bent back almost double as he tried to drive it through Brown's middle, but it struck a buckle on the old man's pants, saving his life for the moment.

On Oct. 25, 1859, Brown and four of his followers were indicted in Charleston, Va., each on two charges of insurrection and two charges of murder. They were to be tried separately, and Brown's trial commenced on Oct. 27, 1859. Elsewhere, Brown's lofty backers were shocked to see their names appear in newspapers across the country, one of Brown's men, John E. Cook, to save his own skin, detailed their secret involvement with the old man. Frank Sanborn hid in Quebec. Gerrit Smith sent aides to Brown's hideouts to have his correspondence with the old man destroyed. Samuel Gridley Howe and George Luther Stearns fled to Canada. Emerson and Higginson looked forward to being called to Brown's trial (they were not), believing that Brown could now become the martyr their cause needed.

Brown's lawyers had only one course of defense since he was guilty of the charges, even by his own admissions. They pleaded him innocent by reasons of insanity and quickly pointed out the many members of his family who had been pronounced legally insane. Brown jumped up and yelled: "I looked upon this as a miserable artifice...the pretext of those who ought to take a different course." He wanted to be found Guilty and he wanted to be executed, realizing that by his death he could advance his cause further than any of the futile actions he had taken in life. The jury took forty-five minutes to find him Guilty and Judge Richard Parker, on Nov. 2, 1859, had Brown brought before him for sentencing. He asked the old man if he had anything to say. Brown stood up and let loose a flurry of self-righteous remarks, including blatant lies about not ever planning to murder anyone or lead any kind of slave revolt. He ended in eloquence: "Now, if it is deemed necessary that I should forfeit my life for the furtherance of the ends of justice, and mingle my blood with the blood of millions in this slave country whose rights are disregarded by wicked, cruel and unjust enactments, I say let it be done."

The date for the execution was set for Dec. 2, 1859, a full month which the abolitionists used to step up what was later termed "an orgy of propaganda." Brown was a martyr long before he went to his grave. Petitions from thousands of northern dignitaries poured into the offices of the governor of Virginia, most claiming that it would be wrong to kill an insane person.

Governor Henry Wise, however, believed Brown to be perfectly sane and deeply resented Brown's refusal to support Cook's statements by naming his northern sponsors. The execution would proceed as scheduled. Mrs. Brown was allowed to visit the old man the night before he was to hang. Brown exploded when his request that she be allowed to spend the night in his cell was denied. Brown was taken to his execution on a cart carrying his own black walnut coffin. He sat on top of it as the cart was driven to a scaffold in a barren field, remarking to the undertaker who rode beside him: "This is very beautiful country. I never had the pleasure of seeing it before." The site of Brown's execution had been carefully chosen so that there were no landmarks anywhere; the South intended that it would never be located by his followers and turned into a shrine.

He was taken to a high scaffold, hurried up the stairs to the platform where a black hood was immediately placed over his head to prevent a scaffold speech. The rope was placed about Brown's neck, but he was kept standing on the trapdoor for some time as large military units were marched into position. This included cadets of the Virginia Military Academy, one of its commanders being Thomas J. "Stonewall" Jackson. Militia units from Richmond drew up in long, even ranks. Among their number was a volunteer who had some reputation as an actor, John Wilkes Booth, who later was to assassinate Abraham Lincoln. When the troops were in place the executioner stepped forth with a hatchet and cut the rope that held the trapdoor. It dropped with a bang and Brown shot downward into space. The body quaked and the hands twitched. Doctors examined the body several times but the pulse continued to beat. It was thirty-five minutes before Brown was pronounced dead. Then, at the foot of the gallows, Colonel J.T.L. Preston, while on horseback, shouted to the assembled troops and the small knots of citizens in the distance: "So perish all such enemies of Virginia! All enemies of the Union! All such enemies of the human race!"

In less than two years, the Civil War began and John Brown was, in death, the anti-slavery martyr he intended to be in life. He was remembered by Union troops when they sang an old Methodist hymn with the newly added words: "John Brown's body lies a mouldering the ground...His soul goes marching on." See: **Brooks, Preston; Lincoln, Abraham.**

REF.: Abels, *Man on Fire: John Brown and the Cause of Liberty*; Adams, *America's Tragedy*; Agar, *The Price of Union*; Auchampaugh, *James Buchanan and His Cabinet*; Avey, *The Capture and Execution of John Brown, A Tale of Martyrdom*; Bagby, *John Brown and William Mahone*; Barnes, *The Antislavery Impulse*; Blackmar, *Charles Robinson*; Boyer, *The Legend of John Brown: A Biography and a History*; Brandt, *History of John Brown*; Brewerton, *The War in Kansas*; Briggs, *The Reign of Terror in Kansas*; Brooks, *The Flowering of New England, 1815-1865*; Butterfield, *The American Past*; Cash, *The Mind of the South*; CBA; Chamberlin, *John Brown*; Channing, *John Brown and the Heroes of Harper's Ferry*; Commager, *Theodore Parker: Yankee Crusader*; Connelley, *John Brown*; Cordley, *History of Lawrence, Kansas*; Curry, *The Abolitionists: Reformers or Fanatics?*; Donald, *Charles Sumner and the Coming of the Civil War*; Drew, *The John Brown Invasion*; Du Bois, *John Brown*; Durden, *The Gray and the Black*; Edelstein, *Strange Enthusiasm: A Life of Thomas Wentworth Higginson*; Edgell, *William Ellery Channing*; Fogelson, *Mass Violence in America: Invasion at Harper's Ferry*; Glasgow, *The Harper's Ferry Insurrection*; Hall, *The Religious Background of American Culture*; Harlow, *Gerrit Smith, Philantropist and Reformer*; Hawkins, *The Abolitionists: Immediatism and the Question of Means*; ____, *The Abolitionists: Means, Ends and Motivations*; Hinton, *John Brown and His Men*; Hofstadter and Wallace, *American Violence*; Hollis, *The American Heresy*; Howe, *Reminiscences, 1819-1899*; Johnson, *History of Anderson County, Kansas*; Kraus, *The United States to 1865*; Leech, *The Raid of John Brown at Harper's Ferry*; Malin, *John Brown and the Legend of Fifty-Six*; Mencken, *By the Neck*; Miller, *The Life of the Mind in America: From the Revolution to the Civil War*; Milton, *The Eve of Conflict: Stephen A. Douglas and the Needless War*; Nevins, *Ordeal of the Union*; Newton, *Captain John Brown of Harper's Ferry*; Nichols, *Bleeding Kansas*; Nichols, *The Stakes of Power, 1845-1875*; Oates, *To Purge This Land With*

Blood: A Biography of John Brown; Parker, John Brown's Expedition; Pate, John Brown as Viewed by H. Clay Pate; Perry, Radical Abolitionism: Anarchy and the Government of God in Antislavery Thought; Quarles, Blacks on John Brown; Redpath, The Public Life of Captain John Brown; Roberts, Famous American Trials; Robinson, The Kansas Conflict; Ruchames, A John Brown Reader; Rusk, The Life of Ralph Waldo Emerson; Sanborn, The Life and Letters of John Brown; _____, Recollections of Seventy Years; Scheidenhelm, The Response of John Brown; Schwartz, Samuel Gridley Howe, 1801-1876; Scott, The Secret Six, John Brown and the Abolitionist Movement; Smith, Yankees and God; Smith, The Death of Slavery: The United States, 1837-65; Steiner, Life of Roger Brooke Taney, Chief Justice of the United States; Stone, Incident at Harper's Ferry; Sumner, The Crime Against Kansas; Tharp, Three Saints and a Sinner; Thayer, A History of the Kansas Crusade; _____, The New England Immigrant Aid Society; Thomas, The Liberator: William Lloyd Garrison; Thomlinson, Kansas in Eighteen Fifty-Eight; Tuttle, History of Kansas; Villard, John Brown; Von Holst, John Brown; Warren, John Brown: The Making of a Martyr; Webb, Information for Kansas Immigrants; _____, Life and Letters of Captain John Brown; Wells, Stephen Douglas: The Last Years, 1857-1861; Welter, The Mind of America, 1820-1860; Weyl, American Statesmen on Slavery and the Negro; White, The American Judicial Tradition; Wilder, The Annals of Kansas; Williams, With the Border Ruffians; Wilson, Governor Charles Robinson of Kansas; Winkley, John Brown the Hero; Winks, The Historian as Detective: Essays on Evidence; Wright, Three Prophets of Religious Liberalism: Channing-Emerson-Parker; Zittle, A Correct History of the John Brown Invasion; Zornow, Kansas: A History of the Jayhawk State; (DRAMA) Blankfort and Gold, Battle Hymn; Gow, Gallows Glorious; Mechem, John Brown; Price, Old John Brown of Harper's Ferry; Swayze, Osawatomie Brown; (FICTION) Erlich, God's Angry Man; (FILM) Santa Fe Trail, 1940; Seven Angry Men, 1955; (POETRY) Benêt, "John Brown's Body."

Brown, John Whelan, 1933- , Aus., mur. In November 1958, the Lord family, who owned Pine Valley station near the town of Morgan, Aus., hired an extra hand to help work on their sheep ranch. John Whelan Brown, twenty-five, was quiet and shy. He was given a room adjoining that of David Stokes, another farm worker. In Stokes' room was a rifle belonging to the station, with ample ammunition nearby.

Brown had been at Pine Valley for less than a week when Gillian Lord heard the sound of a shot as she was putting her children to bed. She rushed into the master bedroom and saw her husband, Neville Montgomery Lord, lying dead on the bed. Brown came in carrying a rifle, looking "a bit bewildered" and surprised to see her. When Mrs. Lord screamed, Brown told her to be quiet and then left the room. By the time the police arrived, the .303 rifle, a pair of boots, and John Brown were missing. A large-scale search was organized, and Brown was found in the bush five days later. When asked who he was he said, "Stone. Is he dead?" Brown cooperated fully, readily admitting to shooting Lord, saying he knew he would be charged with murder and leading the police to the spot where he had left the rifle. In his statement to Constable Brian Kelly of the South Australian Criminal Investigation Branch, Brown explained: "Even though I do recall everything and I did it, I don't think I was responsible for my actions." He later added, "Yes, I know that I did it, but all the time I was hoping that it was only a dream."

Brown's trial began on Mar. 17, 1959, before Mr. Justice Abbott. The prosecutor was R.R. St. C. Chamberlain, Q.C., and the defending lawyers were N.C. Birchall and J. Elliot. Brown again maintained: "I shot Mr. Lord, but I don't know why. I had no reason to shoot him. I hardly knew him but I liked him." He described "acting in a dream," and said he had no idea of right or wrong or of any consequences. Since early youth, Brown explained, he had "Queer feelings that I was going to do something bad," and had tried to stay away from people when he felt that way. Dr. Sydney Forgan, a psychiatrist, described the accused as having "lapsed into a temporary state of simple schizophrenia." Although the question of Brown's responsibility and sanity in the case was debated at great length, the jury found him Guilty of murder in less than an hour, and Justice Abbott

sentenced him to death. Brown appealed to three other courts—the South Australian Court of Criminal Appeal, the High Court of Australia, and finally in the Privy Council. Acting upon the Criminal Appeal's judgment that Brown's "abnormality of mind" diminished his responsibility, the government of South Australia commuted his death penalty to life imprisonment. Brown is serving out his sentence at the Yatala Labour Prison.

REF.: *CBA;* Clegg, *Return Your Verdict.*

Brown, Joseph, 1918-51, and **Smith, Edward Charles,** d.1951, Brit., rob.-mur. In January 1951, Brown, thirty-three, along with his brother Frederick and Edward Charles Smith, decided to rob 79-year-old Frederick Gosling, a Surrey shopkeeper. The trio chose Gosling because it was rumored that he kept thousands of pounds in his apartment above the shop. The initial robbery attempt on Jan. 11 was foiled when some schoolgirls came into the shop while the crime was in process. The three men fled empty-handed.

The next day Joseph Brown and Edward Smith returned. This time they bound and gagged Gosling. When the police found him the next day, he had died of suffocation. About £60 had been stolen. Within days, the police arrested Brown and Smith and charged them both with the murder. They were tried in March 1951 at the Surrey Assizes. The prosecution's case was built around Frederick Brown's testimony against his brother and the identification of him by two of the schoolgirls. Both men were found Guilty and were executed at Wandsworth Prison on Apr. 25, 1951.

REF.: *CBA;* Harrison, *Criminal Calendar II.*

Dr. Lee Patrick Brown

Brown, Dr. Lee Patrick, 1937- , U.S., law enfor. off. Pursuing his goal of becoming a police chief, Lee Brown earned several advanced degrees and became a leader and an innovator in his profession. Born in Oklahoma in 1937, Lee Patrick Brown's family migrated to California during the Dust Bowl days. While attending Fresno State University, Brown became interested in criminology. Prior to receiving his bachelor's degree in the field, he joined the San Jose Police Department in 1960. Early in his career as a patrolman, Brown decided he wanted to be a police chief and pursued this goal by earning a master's in sociology and a doctorate degree in criminology.

Brown developed the first Police-Community Relations Unit in the San Jose Police Department, where he was a sergeant. In 1968, he took the position of Law Enforcement Programs Director at Portland State University in Oregon, establishing a criminal justice program at the university and becoming a full professor. In 1972, Brown relocated to Washington, D.C., to assist in developing the Institute for Urban Affairs and Research at Howard University. He returned to Portland in 1975 to become sheriff and director of Public Safety for Multnomah County, Ore. Three years later, Brown was appointed commissioner of the Department of Public Safety in Atlanta, Ga., where he gained national prominence as the director of the Atlanta Metropolitan Task Force on Missing and Murdered Children. Two months after obtaining a conviction in the child murders case in Atlanta, Brown was sworn in as chief of police in Houston, Texas, on Apr. 19, 1982.

Brown has served on several national councils and commissions, including the National Advisory Commission on Criminal Justice Standards and as national correspondent to the United Nations Program for the Prevention of Crime and Treatment of Offenders. He is co-author of a textbook, *The Police and Society: An Environment for Collaboration and Confrontation.* REF.: *CBA.*

Brown, Leslie, 1944- , U.S., mur. Leslie Brown, twenty-eight, a secretary for the Environmental Protection Agency in Chicago, Ill., was apparently tired of her husband, Clarence Brown, fifty-four. She would later tell police that her spouse forbade her to spend money and beat her. Leslie Brown hired Hubert Lewis, twenty-two, on Dec. 29, 1982, to kill Clarence, asking that the job be done during a New Year's Eve party and offering Lewis $500 on completion of the killing, with another $1,000 promised later. Obtaining a sawed-off shotgun from Emmitt Neal, eighteen, Lewis purchased gun shells from Todd Allen, twenty-seven, before coming to the party. At the celebration, Lewis asked Leslie Brown if she was sure she wanted to go through with the murder, and she said yes. She gave her husband $10 and handed Lewis her car keys so the two could buy more liquor. Brown was shot about 1:40 a.m. in an alley on his way back to the party with Lewis. The killing was Chicago's first of the New Year. Lewis returned to the New Year's event, and Mrs. Brown gave him $300, which was later found in his sock.

Indicted on charges of murder and conspiracy to murder were Brown, Lewis, Neal, and Allen. Lewis pleaded guilty to murder charges on Oct. 26, 1982, before Criminal Court Judge Earl E. Strayhorn, and was sentenced to twenty-five years in prison. Allen pled guilty to conspiracy charges and was sentenced to three years in prison, and Neal also pleaded guilty to conspiracy and was sentenced to four months of a work-release program and thirty months in jail. Brown, who was also charged with murder, was judged to be psychologically unfit to stand trial and was sent to the Mental Health Center in Elgin, Ill. REF.: *CBA.*

Brown, Nichol, d.1754, Scot., can.-mur. The people of Edinburgh knew of Captain Cook, his famous excursions to strange lands, and his encounters with cannibals. They could not imagine such things occurring in a civilized land until one of their own— drunk on ale-house rum—proved that cannibalism is not reserved exclusively for natives of distant lands.

Nichol Brown was a disagreeable man, born and reared in Cramond, a little town outside Edinburgh. He abandoned his apprenticeship in a butcher shop to go to sea on a man-of-war. Upon returning to port, Brown met a wealthy widow whom he married.

It was a loveless union, characterized by bitter, drunken quarrels. Brown frequented the pubs of Leith where he met other idle men who drank and caroused into the night. One night he boasted to his companions that he would march over to the town gibbet where the dead body of Norman Ross, a murderer, was suspended in chains. In drunken bravado, Brown promised that he would cut off a piece of flesh and eat it before their disbelieving eyes. Disgusted by the very nature of it, his friends nevertheless encouraged him to do it—if he dared.

Brown secured a ladder, climbed to the gibbet, and performed the grisly task. The story made the rounds of the village. People believed what they wanted to, but there was no doubt in anyone's

mind that Nichol Brown was a crude, vulgar man. Then he made matters worse by committing murder.

One night his long-suffering wife by this time had reached her limit over his nightly debauches at the Cannongate Ale house. When he returned, she began an argument so noisy that neighbors pounded on his door. One neighbor looked through the keyhole, and saw Brown shoving his wife into the fireplace.

"Murder! The rogue is murdering me! Help, for Christ's sake!" the woman screamed. By the time the door was battered down, Mrs. Brown lay on the floor hovering between life and death from severe burns. Meanwhile, her husband had gone off to bed.

Nichol Brown putting his wife into the fireplace.

She lingered through the night, long enough to testify against her husband. Through the trial Brown denied his guilt, but in the face of his wife's testimony and that of the witnesses, he was easily convicted. Brown was executed on Aug. 14, 1754, in Edinburgh. The next day his body was stolen from the gibbet and dumped in the nearby pond. The townsmen recovered it, and again placed it on display. The body of Nichol Brown was taken a second time, and though a reward was offered, it was never found.

REF.: *CBA; Newgate Calendar.*

Brown, Prentiss Marsh, b.1889, U.S., lawyer. City attorney for St. Ignace, Mich., from 1914-33 before his election to the House of Representatives in 1933. REF.: *CBA.*

Brown, Reese B., prom. 1928-1934, U.S., tax evas. Sarah Smith-Jordan (nee Sarah Jones) was a highly paid stenographer in Chicago when she met James R. Smith, a very wealthy copper miner from Idaho, and married him on his deathbed. She inherited from her husband most of the Hecla Mining Company with stock valued at about a half million dollars in 1908. The shrewd and financially ambitious woman first built up the Idaho company, then turned her talents to the stock and grain markets in Chicago, where she continued to amass a fortune. At the age of fifty-six, Sarah Smith married a one-time Yale football star, Mr. Wilbur, several years her junior, divorcing him a few years later, when she moved to Seattle. In 1924, at sixty-four, the now-reclusive and mentally erratic woman was pursued by a hustler named Jordan, who soon married her. He managed to extracted large amounts of her money through a variety of schemes, including a $100,000 payoff to his former fiancee, who continued to travel with him. Her third husband managed to bilk the wealthy woman of close to $2 million before she began to suspect him. When Jordan and his lover were caught by his wife, the marriage became a long and sensational divorce case in Washington State. Reese B. Brown was one of the most avid spectators at the two-year trial.

The persuasive Brown had several times sold his services as financial adviser to wealthy and gullible women, from whom he stole large amounts of money. Posing as a friend of Smith-Jordan's first husband, he began to advise her on her financial affairs. By 1929, within a year of their first meeting, he was in control of her finances. When Elmer Irey, chief of the Intelligence Unit, became suspicious of Brown and began to investigate, he discovered that Smith-Jordan had withdrawn nearly three-quarters of a million dollars from her Seattle bank on Feb. 14, 1930. On that same day, she had also taken out $500 less than a million dollars in unregistered securities from another bank. Irey made a rapid calculation of financial transactions Brown had made for Smith-Jordan in Seattle, Chicago, and Spokane banks, and realized she owed at least several hundred thousand dollars in income taxes, and that Brown also owed the government thousands of dollars in taxes. Irey would later figure that Brown actually owed back taxes in excess of $100,000, and that Smith-Jordan owed several times that much. Irey called Brown, who was belligerent and totally uncooperative, and spoke with Smith-Jordan, who was essentially incoherent. The two vanished from Seattle soon thereafter. Brown was later spotted at a Hollywood hotel, and Smith-Jordan was thought to have been a patient at a Hollywood hospital.

Both Brown and Mrs. Smith-Jordan had been indicted for criminal evasion of income-tax payments in 1931. In July 1932 Brown turned up—alone—at his home in Seattle. He seemed unconcerned about the charges, saying his high-powered lawyers would get postponements on the case until either he or the investigating tax agents died. Brown told reporters that Mrs. Smith-Jordan was "alive and well and I'm still her financial adviser. She will be produced at the proper time." True to his word, Brown got trial delays for two years. Then, on Jan. 28, 1934, he was in an automobile accident near the Yakima, Wash., Reservation and was immediately killed. Smith-Jordan was never heard from again. A rumor, which later proved to be true, related that the fabulously wealthy woman died of pneumonia, possibly contracted through neglect or criminal intention, in a Montreal Hotel.

REF.: *CBA*; Hynd, *The Giant Killers*.

Brown, Ronald, 1947- , U.S., burg.-org. crime. Ronald Brown had been a thief since he was eight years old, when he started stealing from houses in the Bridgeport neighborhood of Chicago, Ill. He spent his childhood in and out of reformatories, graduating to such adult Illinois correctional facilities as Stateville and Pontiac. With Ronald Jarrett, a burglary crime leader who operated under the patronage of organized crime leader Angelo La Pietra, also known as "the Hook", Brown became an accomplished supermarket burglar. In 1973, he was "taken for a ride" by Richard Mara and Anthony Gallichio, organized crime assailants who thought he was a stool pigeon and shot him five times, leaving him for dead. He survived and returned to his chosen trade. Brown was arrested in 1979 after an unsuccessful break-in at a Homewood suburban grocery store. When his boss, Jarrett, failed to come up with Brown's bail, the career burglar decided to turn informant. "If they'd sprung me on the second or third day," explained Brown, "I probably would have stayed a burglar." Jarrett is now serving a twenty-five year sentence as the result of Brown's testimony against him and other gang members. Brown says Jarrett's group of about thirty has stolen millions of dollars in appliances, precious metals, and other easily disposable items.

Testifying about the $1 million 1977 burglary of Levinson's Jewelers in Chicago, Brown named master burglar John Mandell, thirty-one years old, as the leader, explaining how Mandell was killed by Jarrett in 1978 when Jarrett was accused of cheating mob bosses out of their take. Mandell was found on Feb. 20, 1978, strangled with a cord, his body stuffed in a car trunk, and his throat cut in a trademark style, the same as at least four other murdered thieves. Slain in similar manner were Vincent Moretti, suspected ringleader of Mandell's gang, Donald Renno, and

Bernard Ryan. Moretti was thought to be taking goods to Las Vegas to sell, instead of disposing of them locally through syndicate fences, thereby cutting the Chicago bosses out of their portion. Saying he was most afraid of Jarrett taking revenge on him, Brown told a Chicago *Sun-Times* reporter on June 26, 1982, "I'm a walking dead man. I want to tell my story before they get me. I know I'm going to get killed. It's just a matter of time." See: **La Pietra, Angelo.** REF.: *CBA*.

Brown, Sam (AKA: **Fighting Sam, Long-Haired Sam**), d.1861, U.S., west. gunman. Mississippi born and raised, Sam Brown moved to the Nevada mining camps in the late 1850s where he reportedly killed fifteen men before he met his own violent end. Brown lived in the high timber of Sun Mountain and was a southern sympathizer just after the outbreak of the Civil War, attempting to control the mines and the unions. A large, big-boned man with long hair and a fierce look about him, Brown was habitually starting fights and encouraging gunplay, although he was not reportedly fast on the draw. As he rode down Sun Mountain he was heard to shout repeatedly: "I must have a man for supper!" This bully came to his fate on July 7, 1861, when he threatened to kill Henry van Sickles, an innkeeper at Gold Canyon, unless he was given the best room in Sickles' inn, one that was already occupied. Sickles went for his gun and the slow-drawing Brown was shot dead from his horse. A quickly convening coroner's jury concluded that Long-Haired Sam had "come to his death from a just dispensation of an all-wise Providence."

REF.: Angel, *History of Nevada*; Bartholomew, *The Biographical Album of Western Gunfighters*; Brown, *Reminiscences of Senator William M. Stewart, of Nevada*; *CBA*; Fisher and Holmes, *Gold Rushes and Mining Camps*; Jackson, *Bad Company*; Knight, *Wild Bill Hickok*; Lewis, *Suns Go Down*; Lyman, *The Saga of the Comstock Lode*; Penrose, *The Johnson County War*; Penrose, *Pots o' Gold*; Raine, *Guns of the Frontier*; Sabin, *Wild Men of the Wild West*; Wood, *Calaveras*; Wright, *History of the Big Bonanza*.

Brown, Thomas Mathieson, prom. 1906, Brit., mur. In the winter of 1906, Thomas Mathieson Brown, a retired coal mine manager, mailed an iced shortcake as a gift to his wife's aged uncle, William Lennox, of Old Cumnock, Ayrshire. The card enclosed read, "Hearty greetings to an old friend." Lennox and Grace McKerrow, his housekeeper, ate some of the shortcake and both became ill. Lennox recovered but McKerrow died. When the dessert was analyzed, it was found to contain large amounts of strychnine, as did the dead woman's body. Brown, who had called at Lennox's house to offer his condolences, was arrested and tried at the High Court of Justiciary in Edinburgh. Medical evidence revealed that Brown suffered from chronic epileptic insanity; he had been an epileptic for more than forty years and was affected with the mental deterioration that may result from extensive, severe epilepsy. Brown was found Guilty but insane, and was detained in strict custody.

REF.: *CBA*; Glaister, *The Power of Poison*; Shew, *A Companion To Murder*.

Brown, Walter Folger, b.1869, U.S., lawyer. Postmaster general from 1929-35. REF.: *CBA*.

Browne, Frederick Guy (AKA: **Leo Brown, Sydney Rhodes, Harris**), 1881-1928, and **Kennedy, William** (AKA: **William Henry Kennedy, Ginger**), 1891-1928, Brit., mur. Both Frederick Guy Browne and William Kennedy were small-time British gangsters who had criminal records dating back to their early teens. Browne had been a bicycle thief at the turn of the century, leading a gang of thugs at Oxford. He received several prison sentences for burglary and housebreaking, and when released from Dartmoor Prison in 1927, Browne vowed he would never again be taken alive to spend another moment behind bars. Kennedy, who also had a long police record, albeit one less serious than Browne's, operated a garage in Clapham. Browne joined him after leaving prison, and the two embarked on a series of car thefts, bringing the stolen autos to the Clapham garage where they were altered and later sold.

On the night of Sept. 27, 1927, the pair stole a Morris Cowley car in Billericay, Essex, from the garage of a Dr. Lovell and drove back to Clapham, going through the back roads to avoid constables they knew to be on duty in Brentwood. Between Romford and Ongar, Browne and Kennedy were flagged down by Constable George W. Gutteridge, who waved his flashlight at them. Browne ignored the signal and kept driving, but Gutteridge blew his whistle and Browne brought the car to a stop. Constable Gutteridge walked to the driver's side of the car where Browne was seated and began to question him, writing his report in a notebook. Browne drew his Webley and shot Gutteridge twice. Then he got out of the car and looked down at the constable who was either dead or dying, but whose eyes stared back up at the killer. "What are you looking at me like that for?" Browne demanded. Then, at close range, he shot out the officer's eyes. (It was later claimed that Browne believed in the old canard that a dead man's eyes photograph his murderer, and wished to eliminate the possibility of later being detected in this way. It is more likely that he performed this sadistic act through his own intense hatred for the police.)

Guy Browne and William Kennedy, killers of George Gutteridge.

Hurrying from the murder scene, Browne recklessly smashed into a tree and damaged the car's front bumper. He and Kennedy later abandoned the car on Foxley Road in Brixton. The killers then caught a train for Clapham. Gutteridge's body was found the next morning, along with the abandoned car. A thorough examination of the stolen car revealed not one fingerprint. Blood was found on the driver's side of the car, but this was assumed to be that of the slain officer. A single cartridge was found at the scene of the killing. The murder rested there, unsolved, and Scotland Yard officials believed that there was scant chance of locating the murderer. Then Browne stole another car and, while driving wildly through the streets of Sheffield, he forced a van into a wall. The irate driver wrote down the license plate number of the car Browne was driving and notified police. Detectives from Scotland Yard tracked down the car to a Clapham garage and arrested Browne, holding him for trial.

A search of the Clapham garage unearthed the Webley Browne had used to murder Constable George Gutteridge. A routine check of this weapon led to a comparison of the cartridge found after the Gutteridge murder; a ballistics expert matched the cartridge to the Webley, and Browne was charged with the policeman's murder. Kennedy, arrested in Liverpool on Jan. 25, 1928, quickly confessed to wholesale car robberies and detailed Browne's murder of Gutteridge. Both men were tried at the Old Bailey before Justice Avory on Apr. 23, 1928, with Browne represented by E.F. Lever and Kennedy defended by F.J. Powell. Solicitor General Sir Boyd Merriman prosecuted for the Crown. The defense had a doubly hard time with Browne who was offensive and bullying in court and surly in the dock. Kennedy, who tried to blame the murder of Gutteridge on Browne and therefore avoid the expected death penalty, was proved to have

the same murderous temperment as his friend Browne. When he was about to be arrested in Liverpool, officers testified, Kennedy pulled a gun and aimed it at a detective, squeezing the trigger several times, but the safety catch was on and the weapon did not go off. Officers arresting Browne told how the killer had snarled that he would have shot six of them had he been in his car and had his weapon, adding: "What I can see of it, I shall have to get a machine gun for you bastards next time!"

Ballistics expert Robert Churchill testified at great length during the Browne-Kennedy trial, demonstrating in exacting detail how Browne's Webley was matched to the cartridge and the bullets which killed Constable Gutteridge. It was this newly developed forensic science, coupled to Kennedy's testimony, that convicted both men of the murder. Churchill presented graphics in court that showed how the markings of the weapon and the bullets matched. He also pointed out how the ammunition used for the Webley revolver was an obsolete brand that had not been available since WWI; the same kind of bullets were removed from Gutteridge's corpse. The skin of the murder victim had been discolored by black powder burns which could only result from the type of ammunition employed by Browne, according to expert Churchill.

The evidence provided by Churchill was a triumph for forensic ballistics and, because of this case, established this form of police science in England as readily as it was accepted in the U.S. in the recent Sacco and Vanzetti case (see entry). Both men were quickly convicted and sentenced to death, Browne being hanged at Pentonville Prison and Kennedy at Wandsworth on May 31, 1928.

REF.: Arthur, *All the Sinners;* Berrett, *When I Was at Scotland Yard;* Brock, *A Casebook of Crime;* Browne, *The Rise of Scotland Yard;* ____, *Sir Travers Humphreys;* CBA; Cobb, *Murdered on Duty;* Cuthbert, *Science and the Detection of Crime;* Dearden, *Some Cases of Sir Bernard Spilsbury and Others;* Dilnot, *The Real Detective;* ____, *Triumphs of Detection;* Gribble, *Famous Feats of Detection and Deduction;* Hastings, *The Other Mr. Churchill;* Hibbert, *The Roots of Evil;* Humphreys, *Seven Murderers;* Humphreys, *A Book of Trials;* Hyde, *United in Crime;* Kobler, *Some Like It Gory;* Lambton, *Echoes of Causes Célebres;* Lang, *Mr. Justice Avory;* Laurence, *Extraordinary Crimes;* Leach, *On Top of the Underworld;* McConnell, *The Detectives; Notable British Trials;* Savage, *Savage of Scotland Yard;* Scott, *A Concise Encyclopedia of Crime and Criminals;* ____, *Scotland Yard;* Shew, *A Companion to Murder;* Shore, *Crime and Its Detection;* Smith, *Mostly Murder;* Thompson, *The Story of Scotland Yard;* Thorwald, *The Century of the Detective;* ____, *Marks of Cain;* "Warden", *His Majesty's Guests;* Wensley, *Detective Days;* ____, *Forty Years at Scotland Yard;* Wilson, *Encyclopedia of Murder;* Woodhall, *Secrets of Scotland Yard.*

Browne, George, See: **Bioff, Willie.**

Browne, H. Huffman, prom. 1905, U.S., forg. In December 1905, H. Huffman Browne, a real estate lawyer who had practiced at the New York bar for twenty-five years, offered a deal—two house lots on 174th Street—to Benjamin Levitan, a young architect. Because Browne had previously offered him a deal which, after investigation, proved fraudulent, Levitan researched Browne's new offer. He found that a "William R. Hubert," and not Browne, was the owner of record. Browne explained that the deed was in Hubert's name merely as a matter of convenience, and that he could either produce an unrecorded deed from Hubert to himself or simply introduce Hubert to Levitan and let him execute a direct deed himself.

Dec. 14, 1905, was set as the date for the delivery of deeds and payment. Browne produced the property deeds but not Hubert; and Levitan produced a detective who took the papers and Browne to the offices of Assistant District Attorney John W. Hart. The notary who had authorized the deeds that very day, Ella F. Braman, identified the accused lawyer as the person who had executed the papers. Arrested and jailed on charges of forgery, Browne continued to claim his innocence as he waited in the Tombs, New York City's jail, unable to raise the heavy bail, and ostensibly waiting for Hubert to show up and clear him.

At the trial, held on Mar. 12, 1906, before Judge Warren W. Foster in New York City, evidence was presented that Browne had tried to create an intricate but false paper trail that would allow him to claim a valuable piece of property and sell it to the highest bidder. In addition to this evidence, the testimony of an elderly, crippled broom-maker whom Browne had ruined by bilking him of his $800 life's savings, caused the jury to debate for only a scant five minutes before convicting Browne of first-degree forgery. Browne was sentenced to twenty years in the New York State prison.

REF.: *CBA*; Train, *True Stories of Crime*.

Browne, Robert, c.1550-c.1633, Brit., her. Founded the Brownists, a separatist movement predating the Congregationalists. After emigrating to Zeeland in 1581, he issued pamphlets that urged Independency or Congregationalism. They were banned in Britain and circulation was punishable by death. He was excommunicated in 1584 but accepted episcopal ordination in 1591. REF.: *CBA*.

Browne, William George, 1768-1813, Brit., (unsolv.) mur. Adventurer, author, and world traveler. He was murdered while en route to Samarkand in central Asian Russia. REF.: *CBA*.

Brownell, Herbert, Jr., 1904- , U.S., atty. gen. New York State assemblyman from 1933-37. He was appointed Chairman of the Republican Party from 1944-46. President Dwight D. Eisenhower selected him to be the 62nd attorney general of the U.S. in 1953 and he served until 1958. During this time Brownell reduced the backlog of cases from 75,000 in 1952 to just 53,000 four years later. A champion of civil rights, he prosecuted a number of Jim Crow cases and defended the Supreme Court's decision to declare school segregation illegal. He established a civil rights division in his own office to be run by the assistant attorney general. REF.: *CBA*.

Browning, James Robert, 1918- , U.S., jur. Served in the U.S. Department of Justice, Antitrust Division in Denver, Colo., from 1941-43. He was appointed judge of the Court of the Ninth Circuit in 1961 by President John F. Kennedy. He authored "New Death Penalty Statutes: Perpetuating a Costly Myth" and the *Gonzaga University Legal Review* (1974). REF.: *CBA*.

Browning, John Moses, 1855-1926, U.S., ballistics. Patented a breech-loading single-shot rifle in 1879, and formed a gun manufacturing company with his brother Matthew Browning. He later designed the Browning automatic pistol in 1911, a machine gun in 1917, and the Browning automatic rifle in 1918 which became the standard army shoulder weapon for nearly forty years. REF.: *CBA*.

Browning, Orville Hickman, 1806-81, U.S., lawyer. Senator from Kentucky between 1861-63, and Secretary of the Interior from 1866-69. REF.: *CBA*.

Browning, Paul Louis, Jr., 1947- , U.S., consp. The administration of Harlan County, Ky., Sheriff Paul Browning was so corrupt that when he was arrested on twenty-two charges, ranging from conspiracy to murder to counts of arson, bootlegging liquor and drugs, and illegal surveillance schemes, the county of Harlan was once again called "Bloody Harlan," a nickname it gained during the violent coal-mining labor and politics feuds of decades ago. Brown, who claimed he had tried to arrange the murders of magistrate Elijah Buell and School Board Chair Johnny Y. Blanton, to flush out hired killers in and around Harlan County, was found guilty of plotting his rivals' deaths. Evidence at the December 1982 trial included the testimony of an undercover agent for the police who revealed that Browning had given him a $313 down payment to kill Buell, plus witnesses who testified that Browning wanted Blanton killed because he had called him an incompetent and "flaky SOB." Browning backers began an "SOS—Save Our Sheriff" campaign for Browning, who appealed his case claiming to be the victim of a frame-up by his own deputies. He was sentenced to ten years in prison for conspiracy to murder. REF.: *CBA*.

Brownlee, John, 1884-1961, Can., polit. corr. John Brownlee, premier of the Canadian province of Alberta, was tried in Ed-

monton in July 1934, charged with seducing a young woman he had encouraged to come to Alberta for employment. Minister of Public Works McPherson claimed that the suit was a political frame-up, and the counsel for Brownlee filed a $10,000 countersuit against Vivian MacMillan and John Caldwell, a young medical student from Edmonton. The countersuit charged the pair with conspiracy to defame the premier's character.

MacMillan met Brownlee at a small-town picnic when she was eighteen. He soom suggested that his wife could look after her if she decided to move to Alberta for a job. MacMillan moved and became a frequent visitor to the Brownlee house where, according to her testimony, she was seduced by the premier. She claimed that he told her that "he could not go on as premier of Alberta unless I would give in to him." Caldwell had proposed to her, MacMillan explained, but, on learning of her relationship with Brownlee, offered advice instead, on how she could recover damages.

Justice Ives, before whom the sensational case was tried, slapped contempt suits on a newspaper publisher, Charles E. Campbell, and Cowper, a reporter for the Edmonton *Bulletin*. The jury debated for four hours and forty-five minutes before finding Brownlee Guilty of seduction and awarding MacMillan $10,000 in damages, with another $5,000 paid to her father. REF.: *CBA*.

Brownmiller, Roy E., prom. 1939, U.S., polit. corr. Roy Brownmiller was a key player in the notorious Pennsylvania graft ring that used state payrolls to finance the re-election campaign of Governor George Howard Earle III and other ranking Democrats in the November 1938 election. During the last days of the Earle administration, Brownmiller served as the state secretary of highways. On June 25, 1939, long after the governor had been defeated, he was convicted of fraud and conspiracy to violate the state election laws by "padding" the payroll lists to insure additional votes for the Democratic party. The prosecution charged that Brownmiller and a dozen other indicted office holders had assessed a 5 percent levy on state employees earning more than $1,200 a year, and 3 percent on those earning less. The secretary of highways was specifically accused of padding the Luzurne County payroll to the tune of $600,000.

The conviction of Roy Brownmiller was upheld on July 19, 1940, and he began serving a one-year sentence at the Dauphin County Prison in November. Because of failing health, however, he was paroled after only two months. REF.: *CBA*.

Brownrigg, Elizabeth, 1720-67, Brit., mur. Born to a family of working class people, Elizabeth Brownrigg was married at an early age to James Brownrigg, an apprentice plumber who, through hard work and considerable luck, was able to afford an elegant house on Fetter Lane, London. His fortune slowly accumulated, while Elizabeth bore sixteen children, of whom only three survived. Afterward, she became a midwife.

In 1765, Elizabeth asked the workhouse to send her an apprentice. Under the laws of the day, the children of the city's poor were placed in the homes of the wealthy to learn a trade. Mrs. Brownrigg received 14-year-old Mary Mitchell at her door. After a trial period, in which Brown-

Elizabeth Brownrigg

rigg was on her good behavior, Mary happily agreed to be bound over as an apprentice. Only then did the matron show her true colors. Brownrigg worked Mary eighteen hours a day, forced her to wear vermin-infested clothing, and ridiculed her every step. She beat her young charge unmercifully, and made her sleep under a dresser in the Brownrigg bedroom.

The girl accepted this inhuman treatment passively, no doubt afraid for her life. A second girl brought in to endure the abuse, Mary Jones slipped out the front door early one morning after James Brownrigg had failed to secure the lock. She told her story to the officials at the foundling hospital, who demanded of James Brownrigg compensation for mistreating Jones. When he failed to respond, the matter was dropped. Elizabeth Brownrigg was now forced to look elsewhere for her next apprentice. She went to the Whitefriars Parish and found Mary Clifford.

Brownrigg truly hated this girl. Elizabeth, her maniacal son John, and her doltish husband all enjoyed seeing Mary Clifford hanging from the ceiling, beaten senseless with a lead pipe. Quite by chance, Mary Clifford's stepmother paid a call on the Brownrigg residence. "We have no apprentices," Elizabeth retorted. "But I know the girl is here," the stepmother countered. "The workhouse authorities directed me to your house." Elizabeth threatened to call the police. Dejected, Mary Clifford's stepmother turned away, but a baker's wife named Mrs. Deacon told her that a servant girl did live there and was being horribly mistreated.

Brownrigg beating servant Mary Clifford.

The parish officials began an immediate inquiry. They called on Brownrigg, who said that there was no girl by that name living there. Elizabeth and her son slipped out the back door with their belongings, leaving the plumber to fend for himself. Brownrigg admitted that a Mary Mitchell lived and worked there, and Mr. Grundy demanded to speak with her. Mr. Brownrigg surrendered the emaciated girl to Grundy. She was removed to the hospital, but Grundy and his entourage soon returned with the police. Mary Clifford was found cowering in a small empty cupboard. She was near death. "Not me," Brownrigg gasped, "it was the wife who done it!" Elizabeth and her son fled to Wandsworth disguised as paupers, but an innkeeper recognized her.

On Aug. 9, 1767, Mary Clifford died of her wounds, making Elizabeth a murderess. She was brought back to London and thrown in Newgate until her trial at the Old Bailey. She stood in the dock alongside her husband and son, but in the end only Elizabeth Brownrigg would pay the price for her sins. She was found Guilty of murder, condemned, and taken to Tyburn on Sept. 14, 1767, to be hanged. The executioner was forced to act quickly, because an angry mob was about to tear her limb from limb. The body was quickly cut down, removed to Surgeon's Hall, and dissected. The skeleton remained on display near the anatomy theatre for decades.

REF.: Bleakley, *Hangmen of England; CBA;* Culpin, *The Newgate Noose;* Mitchell, *The Newgate Calendar;* Nash, *Look For the Woman;* O'Donnell, *Should Women Hang?;* Wilson, *Encyclopedia of Murder.*

Brown Sisters, The, prom. 1940-45, Int'l, kid.-mur. As part of the Nazi experiments, thousands of "Aryan-looking" children were kidnapped from countries the Germans had captured. A small fraction of these unfortunate children, most of them under five, were groomed and adopted; the rest were murdered. In pursuit of their goal of multiplying their numbers, the Nazis established, on Dec. 12, 1935, the *Lebensborn* organization, to provide maternity homes for wives and girlfriends of the SS. The babies were successfully sent out for adoption, and by 1940, a massive kidnapping program was underway. The Brown Sisters, a female counterpart to the SS, wore brown dresses with white collars and cuffs, as they scoured the schools, villages, and hospitals of occupied countries, as well as concentration camps. Given special courses in physiognomy and in abduction techniques, the Brown Sisters' prey was "racially valuable" children—those who fit the Nazi ideals of physique and attitude.

Within a few months, thousands of children were arriving in the *Lebensborn* reception centers in Poznan, Brockau, and Kaliscz, where they were measured and inspected. At least 200,000 children were stolen from Poland, 50,000 from the Hungarian Ukraine, and countless others from different areas. Of the thousands of stolen children, only about ten percent were passed, to be given new names and identities and taught German before being sent to German families. The countless others, rejected for their looks or their behavior, were murdered.

The children were usually snatched from the streets or on their way home from school. In 1942-43, it was common to see children herded into waiting trucks by SS men with dogs. A mother at Rogozno hanged her child rather than let it be taken. When villagers in Poland tried to rush a train filled with children to pull them out, the SS opened fire and slaughtered the children and the villagers. While some children managed to escape, none of them survived. When the Americans arrived in Steinhoring, Bav., in the winter of 1944-45, the model home of the *Lebensborn* was discovered. Three hundred children, all under four, were left, terrified and unable to speak, the last remanants of the tragic *Lebensborn* episode. Thirty years later, the Red Cross was still putting up posters of the missing children in Munich and Hamburg. Under the photographs were the words: "Who knows our parents and origin? Who can tell us our names and where we come from? When were we born?"

REF.: *CBA;* Moorehead, *Hostages To Fortune.*

Bruce, W.H., and **Vaughan, H.,** prom. 1940, Brit., forg. W.H. Bruce and H. Vaughan had previous convictions in Paris and London, as well as Antwerp when they were arrested in and held at the Mansion House in London for forging checks for £540, £580, and £4900. They paid the fraudulent checks into a firm's account and withdrew the money by means of another exchange check. While being held at Brixton Prison, Vaughan attempted suicide by opening a vein in his arm with a steel pen nib. Charged also with forging a will and committing perjury in connection with the probate, Vaughan and Bruce were found Guilty. Justice Darling sentenced Bruce to two terms of penal servitude of fourteen and seven years, to be served concurrently, and Vaughan, who was seventy-seven at the time, to seven years in prison.

REF.: *CBA;* Nicholls, *Crime Within The Square Mile.*

Bruce, William Cabell, 1860-1946, U.S., lawyer. Senator from Maryland between 1923-29. REF.: *CBA.*

Brucioli, Antonio, d.1566, Italy, her. Translated the Bible based on Latin of Erasmus and Pagninus in 1532. He was tried by the Inquisition in 1548, 1555, and from 1558-59 for practicing and advocating Lutheranism. He refused to recant and was imprisoned for his religious heresy. REF.: *CBA.*

Brückner, Wilhelm, b.1884, Ger., treas. Leader of the Munich Regiment during the uprising of 1923, he was imprisoned for five months for his involvement. He served as General Secretary and worked to spread German propaganda to other lands from 1924-28 before becoming a member of Adolf Hitler's elite permanent escort in 1930. REF.: *CBA.*

Brudenell-Tuckett Duel, 1840, Brit., duel. In late Summer 1840, James Thomas Brudenell, the Seventh Earl of Cardigan, found that letters maligning his character as an officer and a gentleman had been published in *The Morning Chronicle;* they were written by Lieutenant Harvey Tuckett. Through Captain Douglas, Brudenell challenged Tuckett to a duel, which was accepted. When Tuckett refused to apologize, the duel was arranged for Sept. 12, at Wimbledon Common. Their first shots missed but on the second round, Tuckett was hit in the lower rib cage, damaging his spine. Although Tuckett survived and was not in serious danger, Brudenell, under an old law, was charged with felony for shooting with intent to murder or do bodily harm.

On Oct. 21, the case was brought to a criminal court but was transferred to the House of Lords because Brudenell was a Peer of the Realm. The Parliamentary trial, which began on Feb. 16, closely examined the privileges and responsibilities of the peerage from a legal point of view, and the concepts of "intent to kill" and the question of malice, as well as homicide vs. manslaughter vs. murder. Brudenell was unanimously found Not Guilty by a jury of his peers.

REF.: *CBA;* Melville, *Famous Duels and Assassinations.*

Brudos, Jerry, 1939- , U.S., rape-mur. In 1968 and 1969 Jerry Brudos assaulted and killed four young women. Brudos' first victim was Linda Slawson, an encyclopedia saleswoman in Corvallis, Ore. Her mutilated body was found in a nearby river in January 1968.

Jerry Brudos, a 30-year-old electrician, exhibited aberrant sexual behavior at an early age. When he was seventeen, psychologists concluded that he suffered from "an adjustment reaction to adolescence with sexual deviation-fetishism." As an adult he dressed up in his wife's clothes. In April 1969, after he had committed his first two murders, two students near Oregon State University reported a man dressed as a woman to the police.

Brudos lured his victims by posing as a Vietnam War veteran. He abducted four young women: Linda Slawson, Jan Whitney, Karen Sprinker, and Linda Salee. He brought them back to his photographer's studio, raped them, and then tortured them to death. Photographs of the girls taken by Brudos were later seized by police. A fifth victim, Stephanie Vilcko, sixteen, was believed to have been killed by Brudos, but no conclusive evidence could be found. His wife Ralphene claimed to know nothing about his "other" life as a sex criminal.

Brudos was convicted on four counts of murder and sentenced to the Oregon State Prison. REF.: *CBA.*

Brühne, Vera, 1910- , and **Ferbach, Johann,** prom. 1960, Ger., mur. Each time Dr. Otto Praun of Munich found himself a new lover, he would set her up in his sprawling pleasure estate on Spain's Costa Brava. Then, after his ardor had cooled, Praun would reclaim the $250,000 villa and give it to his next girlfriend. Praun, who was rumored to have earned his fortune through rum-running, dope peddling, and by performing illegal abortions, finally met his match with Vera Brühne, an elegant 50-year-old blonde.

When the time came for her to lease the premises in 1960, she devised a little scheme. She informed Dr. Praun that she had arranged a sale of the villa to one Dr. Schmitz, who wanted to finalize the transaction at the mansion. Praun, who wanted to sell the esate, agreed to meet Schmitz. The next day, police found Otto Praun and his housekeeper dead. They concluded that Dr. Praun had suffered a nervous breakdown, killed the housekeeper, and then took his own life.

The Munich Police began receiving reports that Praun and the housekeeper were murdered. Their remains were exhumed. He had been shot twice in the head, ending the suicide theory. Vera's 14-year-old daughter supplied the missing details. She said that the killer was Johann Ferbach, a German army deserter who fled from his regiment in 1944. He became Vera Brühne's devoted love slave through her previous marriages and numerous affairs. When ordered to pose as Dr. Schmitz, the ex-Nazi readily agreed. Ferbach murdered Praun, killed the housekeeper, and then tried to make it appear that the doctor had gone berserk. But he made one mistake. Ferbach left behind the letter of introduction that Vera had written.

Handwriting samples were compared, which revealed Vera Brühne's duplicity. The twosome was found Guilty of murder and given life sentences.

REF.: *CBA;* Nash, *Look For the Woman.*

Brune, Guillaume Marie Anne, 1763-1815, Fr., assass. Marshal of France in 1804. He was killed by a Royalist throng during the period of White Terror in 1815. REF.: *CBA.*

Bruneau, Albert, 1861-92, Fr., rob.-arson-mur. At the age of twenty-five, Albert Bruneau was ordained a priest and sent to Astillé, near Laval, as a curate. A kindly old lady in the village parish left Abbé Albert 16,000 francs as a gesture of faith. This he was to give to charity, but instead the young curate satisfied some personal debts and spent the balance of the money in the local brothels. Bruneau's rectory was burgled four times and set on fire twice. The insurance money he received from these mishaps was considerable.

To further his ambitions in the church, Bruneau convinced the Bishop that Abbé Pointeau, his immediate superior, had cohabitated with women. These allegations resulted in Bruneau's transfer to the parish of Entrammes, in the province of Mayenne. There he served as curate under Abbé Fricot, preaching sermons and telling inspirational stories that he knew were blatant lies. Soon, there was a new rash of thefts in the village parish. Five hundred francs were taken from a church strong-box. Then, on the night of Jan. 2, 1894, the Abbé Fricot disappeared. He was last seen by a 9-year-old boy named Joseph. When Fricot did not return by evening, a search party was organized. Abbé Bruneau suggested that perhaps Fricot may have committed suicide, which seemed like an absurd notion to the townspeople. He mentioned the well in the garden, and the housekeeper and a neighbor named Chelle went to take a look. Under thirty-feet of water, they found Abbé Fricot.

Bruneau told the headmistress, Louise Bouvier that Fricot had committed suicide—an unpardonable sin—but logs had been thrown down on him to make it appear as if he were murdered. When the body was pulled out of the well, it was found that the head had been bludgeoned with a heavy instrument. Incriminating evidence was found in the private chambers of Abbé Bruneau, who had beaten the priest senseless and left him to die in the freezing water of the well. The keys to the organ were stained with blood, and large amounts of stolen money that had belonged to Fricot were hidden in the attic.

The Abbé Bruneau was put on trial for murder on July 9, 1894, before Judge Francis Giron. He was also charged with the 1893 murder of a Laval flower seller named Marie Bourdais as well as arson and robbery. Bruneau was found Guilty of killing Abbé Fricot but was acquitted on the charge of murdering the florist. Protesting his innocence all the way to the guillotine, Bruneau was beheaded on Aug. 29, 1894. There were 16,000 spectators present. Abbé Bruneau was one of several French clergymen convicted of murder in nineteenth-century France. In 1848, Father Léotade received a sentence of hard labor for killing a child. In 1882, the Abbé Auriol poisoned two elderly women from his parish. See: **Auriol, Joseph.**

REF.: *CBA;* Gribble, *The Deadly Professionals;* Irving, *Studies of French Criminals of the Nineteenth Century;* Wilson, *Encyclopedia of Murder.*

Brunette, Harry, 1911- , U.S., rob.-kid. In November 1936, New Jersey state patrolman William A. Turnbull stopped a speeding car near Somerville, N.J. While he was arguing with the driver, an armed couple got out of the car and stripped, bound, and gagged him. They drove the officer to a spot near Bethlehem, Pa., before dumping him. Turnbull identified his captors as Harry Brunette and Merle Vandenbush, both known bank robbers. Brunette was tracked to a New York City apartment where he was living with his new wife, Arlene Brunette, on West 102nd Street and Broadway. Because of the kidnapping charges, the FBI joined the New York city police in watching the house.

Dec. 15 was set as the day to seize Brunette, but at 1:15 a.m. on the appointed day, as the New York City officers went for coffee, about twenty-five G-men led by FBI Chief J. Edgar Hoover rapped on Brunette's door and received bullets in response. For an hour the FBI agents tear-gassed the apartment, pumping machine gun bullets into the place, and continuing to fire even after fireman arrived to put out the flames ignited by gunshots and bombs. Brunette's wife, wounded, finally staggered out of the apartment followed by Brunette, who remarked to the FBI agents, "What a brave bunch of guys."

Pleading guilty of everything on his long criminal record, the 25-year-old robber was tried at a Trenton, N.J., court in front of Judge Phillip Forman and was sentenced to life imprisonment at the federal penitentiary in Lewisburg, Pa. Arlene, also twenty-five, was sentenced to life for the kidnapping. Vandenbush, the third accomplice in the abduction, was captured on Feb. 25, 1937, along with George Rera and Joe Stuzza, twenty minutes after they robbed a Katonah, N.Y., bank of more than $17,600. For his part in the kidnapping and several bank robberies, Vandenbush was sentenced, on Mar. 16, to forty-five to seventy-five years in Sing Sing Prison by Judge Gerald Nolan. REF.: *CBA*.

Brunhilda (or **Brunhilde** or **Brunehild** or **Brunechildis** or **Brunehaut**), 534-613, queen, mur.-assass. Daughter of Athanagild, king of the Visigoths, Brunhilda was brought from Spain by her father in 567 to marry Sigebert, king of Metz, who expanded his domain into what was later known as Austrasia. (Austrasia, Neustria, and Burgundy made up the Frankish kingdoms at the time.) Following the Visigoth and Frankish union, Sigebert's brother Chilperic, ruler of neighboring Neustria, arranged to marry Brunhilda's sister, Galswintha. This act infuriated Chilperic's domineering mistress, Fredegund, who insisted that her royal lover get rid of his new bride. Chilperic had Galswintha strangled. Brunhilda, screaming revenge for her sister's death, induced Sigebert to wage war against Neustria, which caused Fredegund to send an unknown assassin to murder Sigebert in 575. Brunhilda intensified the war against Neustria and, in 584, duplicated the act of her rival Fredegund by sending an unknown assassin to murder Chilperic.

Having murdered each other's husbands, the two queens fought a seemingly endless bloody war that raged until Brunhilda's death. Hundreds, if not thousands, of persons were murdered at the orders of these two savage barbarian queens, and Brunhilda simply outlived her mortal enemy, making Austrasia the center of the Frankish empire. While she ruled Austrasia as regent for her son, Childebert II, powerful nobles ousted her from the throne. Brunhilda fled to Burgundy, where she raised new armies against Fredegund's son, Chlotar II, who captured her in 613, when she was a grandmother of eighty, and ordered her put to death. The execution of Brunhilda was undoubtedly one of the most gruesome on record. The queen was stripped naked, then tied by her hair, one arm, and one leg to a wild horse who was whipped into a frenzy, dragging Brunhilda to a painful death. REF.: *CBA*; Gregory, Bishop of Tours, *History of the Franks*.

Brunner, Heinrich, 1840-1915, Aust., jur. Member of the faculty of law in Prague, Lemberg, and Strasbourg, and noted legal scholar. REF.: *CBA*.

Bruno, Saint (**Brun** or **Bruns of Querfurt** or **Bonifacius**), c.974-1009, Ger., assass. Formed monastic community in Ravenna under Otto III. He became archbishop of missions in 1004 and preached in Hungary and the Ukraine before Prussians killed him and eighteen followers. REF.: *CBA*.

Bruno, Angelo, 1911-80, U.S., org. crime. Angelo Bruno, who referred to himself as a "commissioned salesman" for a vending corporation, was in fact a wealthy mob leader who controlled illegal gambling and loan-sharking for the Mafia in the 1960s and 1970s. Although Bruno had been pursued by police and federal agents, arrested thirteen times, and subpoenaed and indicted by grand juries regularly, his only jail term lasted two and a half years for refusing to testify in an investigation of official corruption in Atlantic City. One of the last of the old-time underworld bosses, Bruno was known as a peacemaker, and was said to have held out against the mob by opposing their involvment in drug trafficking

and truck hijacking.

One Mar. 21, 1980, Bruno, at age sixty-nine, was getting out of his car when two men fired shotguns at him, wounding John Stanfa, thirty-nine, Bruno's bodyguard, as they assassinated his boss. Bruno had recently appeared before the New Jersey State Commission of Investigation. A $250,000 contract was said to have been put out on Bruno's life following the slaying of New York crime leader Carmine Galante in July 1979. See: **Galante, Carmine**.

Mobster Angelo Bruno.

REF.: *CBA*; Demaris, *The Last Mafioso*; Gage, *The Mafia Is Not An Equal Opportunity Employer*.

Bruno, Giordano (Filippo), c.1548-1600, Italy, her. Philosopher, teacher, and traveling lecturer who was opposed to the doctrines of Aristotle. He was arrested in 1592 by the Inquisition as a heretic, and burned at the stake in 1600. REF.: *CBA*.

Bruno, John J., prom. 1934, U.S., pris. esc.-mur. On Nov. 5, 1934, gunmen opened fire on a political rally in the town of Kelayres, Pa. Three people were killed instantly, two died later, and scores were badly wounded. Indicted, tried, and convicted for the mob-style attack were John J. "Big Joe" Bruno, and several members of his family. Bruno, found Guilty on three charges each of first- and second-degree murder, he was given three life sentences. His brother, Phillip Bruno, also got life, and his sons, Alfred and James, and a relative by marriage, Tony Orlando, were each given ten to twenty years.

The Bruno family were sent to the Schuylkill County Jail, where they were apparently under loose guard. Big Joe often made spaghetti dinners for the group, and was known as the best dressed man in Schuykill County. After serving two years of his sentence, Bruno escaped from prison on Dec. 16, 1936. Pretending to have a toothache, he was driven by an unarmed guard named Irving to a Pottsville, Pa., dentist. Inexplicably, Irving allowed Big Joe to go alone to the doctor's office while he looked for a parking place. Although Pennsylvania's Attorney General Charles J. Margiotti called in the FBI, Bruno was not found for some time. He was finally located hiding out in a New York City tenement neighborhood and returned to jail.

REF.: *CBA*; Cohen, *One Hundred True Crime Stories*.

Bruno, Karl, 1911- , Yugo., war crimes. In April 1941, Hayim Kalmich was serving in the Yugoslavian army near the Albanian border when he was taken prisoner and his textile store was confiscated by the Nazis. The following year, under the German "Aryanization" program, the store was turned over to Karl Bruno, whose own fabric store in Belgrade had been destroyed by Nazi bombs. When Kalmich returned to Yugoslavia after the war, he found that his store was gone, and his wife and son had died in a concentration camp. Kalmich immigrated first to Israel, then to Canada.

While visiting friends in Chicago in 1971, Kalmich mentioned that a man named Bruno had purchased his store almost thirty years earlier, a friend exclaimed that Bruno was in Chicago and, within months, Kalmich had tracked him down, finding him working in an appliance store. Chicago attorneys Norman Handelsman and Robert Handelsman filed suit for Kamlich in 1974; it was dismissed but reinstated in 1977 when the U.S. Court of Appeals ruled that the Yugoslav law on business confiscations by Nazis was applicable to a U.S. court.

During the November 1980 trial, Bruno admitted before Justice John P. Crowley he had known that the business was confiscated because Kamlich was Jewish, and that he had purchased the store from the Nazis for about half its value. Crowley ordered Bruno to pay more than $100,000 in damages and interest to Kamlich. Bruno's attorney, James G. Meyers said his client, who was retired and living on Social Security, did not have the money. Kamlich, however, was satisfied. He told a reporter, "This has been haunting me all my life...Justice was done." REF.: *CBA*.

Brunskill, William, prom. 1786-1815, Brit., executioner. Entering his office the day after his successor died, Brunskill's first job was to execute seven criminals single-handedly. The nervous man effectively carried out his task and amazed the large crowd by taking a deep bow when he was done. In 1790, in the early days of Brunskill's reign, the barbaric custom of burning people at the stake after being strangled was abolished. It had been reserved for counterfeiters and women who had murdered their husbands. Famous persons executed by Brunskill included Governor Wall, who died in great agony because the hanging was bungled, and Colonel Despard, charged with high treason and executed with six of his colleagues. The latter party had their heads cut off and held up by Brunskill who said, "This is the head of a traitor," after each death. The executioner also hanged Captain John Sutherland, who had been sentenced for the drunken murder of his black servant, and John Bellingham, who had murdered Prime Minster Spencer Perceval. Brunskill had a stroke in 1814 and formally resigned his post in 1815.

REF.: Bleackley, *Hangmen of England; CBA*; Laurence, *A History of Capital Punishment*.

Brust, Albert (AKA: Eric), 1929-73, U.S. abduc.-tort.-suic.-mur. Nobody, not even the victim's parents, believed the story at first. According to the girl's mother, she was a "pathological liar who is continually making up bizarre stories." The anonymous victim was a 15-year-old girl who had run away from her Frankfort, Ky., home with her 16-year-old sweetheart, Mark Matson, from Ohio.

Hitchhiking outside of Fort Lauderdale, Fla., on July 14, 1973, they were picked up by 44-year-old Albert Brust, a burly psychopath who drove a shabby white panel truck. Brust, telling them to call him Eric, offered them a ride, and a chance to make some money doing odd jobs at his suburban Miami home. Reaching his home, he ordered the couple into a customized "torture chamber," where they were made to perform various sexual acts while he took pictures with a Polaroid camera.

Brust had constructed in his bedroom a four-by-eight-foot chamber lined with three-inch foam rubber and entered through a steel door. Brust spray-painted obscene words in luminous paint on the door, and had screwed various chains and leather straps into the wall to secure his victims. The ghastly torture den was illuminated by a black light. Dade County detectives later theorized that Brust was a sexual deviate who had "entertained other people with similar tastes."

When Matson attempted to wrestle his captor to the ground, Brust shot him three times and dragged him into the bathroom. Later he buried Matson under three-and-a-half feet of concrete. Brust imprisoned the girl and forced her to endure nearly twenty-two hours of sexual abuse and torture before he dragged her into the van and drove her back to Fort Lauderdale. He released her at the beach, warning her to remain quiet or he would kill her family.

She ran straight to the police department where she told Detective Sergeant Ray Eggler about her ordeal. Her estranged parents discounted the story as another in a series of fantastic stories concocted by their daughter. Police waited five more days before they moved on the case, and then did so only after receiving a report of a dead man at the same Miami address.

Brust's life of pornography, sadism, and murder ended on July 22. Dade County police found his dead body in a lawn chair in the yard of his home. Neighbors had grown suspicious when the body did not move after a thunderstorm hit the area. An autopsy revealed that he had consumed a fatal dose of strychnine shortly after returning home from Fort Lauderdale.

Brust was described by the people on the block as a loner and chronic complainer. His secret life was known only to the unwilling participants in his macabre private orgies. The fantastic story of a 15-year-old runaway was "confirmed right down the line," according to Miami police. REF.: *CBA*.

Bruys, Pierre de (Petrus Brusius; Pierre de Bruis; Peter of Bruys), prom. 1100, Fr., her. Studied under Peter Abelard. He advocated an end to infant baptism, veneration of the cross, construction of churches, and prayers for the deceased. He was captured and taken to the stake in 1126 or 1132. REF.: *CBA*.

Bryan, Henry John, 1910- , and **Saxton, John William**, 1914- , and **Wyatt, John Arthur**, 1908- , and **Wyatt, Margaret**, 1922- , and **Howells, James Thomas (AKA: Curly)**, 1906- , and **Allen, George Charles**, 1911- , and **Staggs, Robert**, 1906- , and **Staggs, Elizabeth**, 1916- , Brit., burg. In April 1951, a team of eight London safecrackers, believed responsible for over 200 burglaries during a ten-year period, were brought to trial in one of the most sensational criminal cases in British history. Their spree finally ended on Nov. 27, 1950, when police, on an anonymous tip, planted officers inside Barclays Bank in Waterlooville. James Thomas Howells and John William Saxton were apprehended as they entered the bank premises. In Saxton's pockets, police found fifty-two skeleton keys, including two that fit the bank vault. Tools commonly used to crack safes were found in their car.

With Saxton and Howells in custody, police searched the homes of suspected accomplices, John and Margaret Wyatt and Robert and Elizabeth Staggs, Margaret Wyatt's sister. The Wyatts denied any knowledge of the break-in, though a list of codes corresponding to keys to vaults throughout England was found in their home. Saxon, Howells, the Wyatts, and the Staggs were charged with conspiracy in the attempted bank robbery and linked to several other robberies that had been under investigation during the past two years.

Charles George Allen had supplied the gang with keys. A senior locksmith at a London safe manufacturing plant, he was responsible for repairing locks and making duplicate keys for safes that the company sold to businesses. Taking revenge on his employer, whom he felt had mistreated him, Allen supplied Wyatt with copies of the keys in his possession. The keys fit various locks on post office boxes, and vaults in movie theaters, restaurants, jewelry stores, and banks throughout the country. Allen admitted to Chief Inspector Daws of Scotland Yard that he had willingly given Wyatt the keys but said he did not know who the burglars were. He pleaded guilty to charges of conspiracy and theft of three keys from his employer. He was also charged with aiding Saxton and Howells in the Barclays Bank break-in, but pleaded innocent.

It was revealed that Wyatt was second in command of the group, carrying out the orders of his boss, and the "brains" of the operation, Henry John Bryan. Bryan was also apprehended and charged with conspiracy.

Following a lengthy trial at Winchester Assizes in April 1951, the jury rendered its verdicts on the eight defendants after only two hours and fifteen minutes of deliberation. Robert and Elizabeth Staggs were found Not Guilty on all charges. Margaret Wyatt was found Guilty of conspiracy in the Barclays Bank break-in. She was given only three years probation by presiding Justice Byrne because he believed her husband had influenced her to cooperate. Allen was found Guilty of conspiracy and theft. For the two offenses, Byrne sentenced him to two concurrent twelve-month terms in prison. Howells, a twelve-time previous offender, was found Guilty of conspiracy and breaking and entering, and sentenced to two concurrent four-year terms. Saxton, with three previous convictions, was found Guilty of conspiracy and breaking and entering, and sentenced to two concurrent four-year terms. Wyatt, found Guilty of conspiracy and receiving stolen goods, was sentenced to eight years in prison for each offense with the terms running concurrently. Bryan, who had seven previous convictions and had served a three-year sentence at the Old Bailey in the early 1940s, was sentenced to ten years in prison. In addition, Justice Byrne required that Bryan pay up to £2,000 toward the payment

of court costs. Bryan, who had denied his guilt throughout, appealed his conviction. His appeal was eventually overturned and his sentence carried out.
REF.: *CBA*; Harrison, *Criminal Cases II*.

Bryan, Joseph Francis, Jr., 1938- , U.S., kid.-mur. Joseph Bryan once explained that he liked to see "small boys tied up and screaming." In 1964 this former psychiatric patient traveled through the Southeast in search of youthful victims. By the time FBI agents caught up with him in New Orleans, the trail of his victims extended from New Jersey to Florida.

The search for the killer began on Apr. 1 when 8-year-old David Wulff disappeared from his home in Willingboro, N.J. The body was found May 6, in a wooded area off U.S. Highway 52 in Hillsville, Va.

Acting on a tip, FBI men traced the southward flight of Bryan through gasoline purchases he made with a stolen credit card. When he was apprehended in New Orleans, he had with him 8-year-old Dennis Burke of Humboldt, Tenn. The boy had been missing since Apr. 24 when he left a snack shop to go home for a baseball. The kidnapper's car, a stolen white Cadillac, was spotted by eyewitnesses, but the Memphis FBI and local police were baffled. "Everybody has seen that car but the law enforcement officers," said Police Chief Joe Riding of Humboldt. Five days later New Orleans FBI men found the lad in a hotel room. Unharmed by his abductor, he was returned to the arms of his tearful but happy mother. "I don't understand what this kidnapping is," Bryan muttered under his breath. "I didn't kidnap nobody."

Not so lucky were Lewis Wilson, a 7-year-old St. Petersburg, Fla., boy whose skeleton was found in a rattlesnake-infested thicket near Venice, Fla., and 10-year-old David Robinson of Mount Pleasant, S.C., whose remains were found in a swamp near Hallandale, Fla., on Mar. 31.

Bryan was returned to South Carolina on kidnapping charges stemming from his abduction of the Robinson boy. At present he is incarcerated in the federal detention facility in Minneapolis, Minn., where he will be eligible for parole in 1995. REF.: *CBA*.

Bryan, Pearl, See: **Jackson, Scott.**

Bryan, William Jennings (AKA: The Commoner), 1860-1925, U.S., lawyer. Born in Salem, Ill., a graduate of Illinois College, William Jennings Bryan served in the U.S. House of Representatives (1891-95) and was the champion of the Free-Silver advocates. He made himself famous with his "Cross of Gold" speech at the Democratic Convention in Chicago, winning the nomination for the presidency in 1896. He was defeated by William McKinley, but ran twice more for the presidency—in 1900, losing to McKinley and Theodore Roosevelt, and in 1908, when he was defeated by William Howard Taft. Bryan swung the presidential nomination for Woodrow Wilson in the 1912 Democratic Convention, and was rewarded by being named Secretary of State (1913-15), a post he resigned over Wilson's war policies following the sinking of the *Lusitania*. A strict adherent to religious fundamentalism, Bryan lectured in the popular Chautauqua circuits, preaching strict adherence to the Old Testament, a posture which later brought him into direct confrontation with his self-proclaimed nemesis, Clarence Darrow, in the sensational 1925 trial of teacher John T. Scopes in Dayton, Tenn. Bryan was one of the prosecuting attorneys against Scopes who was indicted for teaching evolution to his students. Bryan himself took the stand and was publicly humiliated under a withering cross-examination by Darrow in which his almost total lack of knowledge regarding modern science was exposed. Intellectually disgraced and emotionally wrecked by the trial, Bryan collapsed and died a few days after the Scopes trial ended, on July 26, 1925. See: **Darrow, Clarence; Scopes, John T.** REF.: *CBA*.

Bryant, Charles (AKA: Black Faced Charlie), d.1891, U.S., west. outl. Born in Wise County, Texas, Charles Bryant had been a cowboy since his teens and lived most of his life in the saddle. While still a youth, Bryant got into a gunfight and a pistol was fired at pointblank range next to his face, the grains of black powder from the shot permanently disfiguring him and resulting in his odd nickname. Bryant joined the Dalton gang in 1890 and was with the Daltons when they robbed the Santa Fe's Texas Express train near Wharton, Okla., on May 9, 1891. He was also in the Dalton band that robbed the Santa Fe train near Red Rock in the Cherokee Strip, Okla., area some weeks later, and it was reportedly Bryant who suggested to the Daltons that the passengers on this train be robbed. The Daltons refused, sneering at such a low-life notion, and telling Bryant that they did not prey upon people, only on railroads and banks. Black Faced Charlie, it was claimed, also shot a telegraph operator during this holdup.

There was a maniacal, almost suicidal, streak in Bryant, who loved gunplay of any kind. The Daltons were forever warning him to "go easy with your trigger finger," and they considered Bryant the most unreliable of their dedicated band of outlaws, believing him to be a "little crazy." After a shootout with a posse sometime in 1891, Bryant strutted about a campfire while the exhausted Dalton gang members collapsed on their bedrolls. The gunfight, in which the gang just barely managed to escape, had filled him with exhilaration and, in this manic state, Bryant yelled to his indifferent fellow thieves: "Me, I want to get killed in one hell-firing minute of smoking action!" He got his wish.

Bryant got sick while in the outlaw camp near Buffalo Springs, Okla., and gang members arranged for him to see a doctor in Hennessey, Okla. While recuperating in a hotel room in that town, Deputy U.S. Marshal Edward Short learned of Bryant's whereabouts and kicked open the door to Bryant's room, holding two six-guns. He had no trouble arresting the weakened Bryant, who had by then a $1,000 reward posted for his capture. Short then got aboard a train with Bryant on Aug. 3, 1891, intending to deliver his prisoner to the federal court district in Wichita, Kan., riding in the express car. During the trip that day, Short had to relieve himself and told the express messenger to guard the prisoner, handing him a pistol. He checked Bryant's handcuffs and then left the car. The messenger, seeing that Bryant was ill and asleep in a chair, put the pistol in a pigeonhole in his desk and went about sorting mail and other chores. Bryant was only feigning sleep. As the train neared Waukomis Station, he went to the desk when the messenger's back was turned, and grabbed the pistol just as Short reentered the car.

With his hands still manacled together, Bryant managed to snap off a shot at Short, the bullet hitting the marshal in the chest. Short lifted his rifle and pumped several bullets at Bryant, one of these ploughing into the outlaw's chest and emerging at the back, severing Bryant's spinal column. As he fell to the express car floor, the outlaw emptied the pistol in Short's direction. As he was dying, Black Faced Charlie yelled: "I can't die with my boots on! Please pull them off." Short and the messenger picked up Bryant's body and placed it on a cot. Then Short laid down on another cot and died from his wounds. When the train stopped at Waukomis, both bodies were laid out on the station platform to await the undertaker. Black Faced Charlie, curious train passengers noted, wore no boots. See: **Dalton Brothers.**

REF.: Barnard, *A Rider of the Cherokee Strip*; Bartholomew, *The Biographical Album of Western Gunfighters*; Block, *Great Train Robberies of the West*; CBA; Croy, *Trigger Marshal*; *The Dalton Brothers and Their Astounding Career of Crime* (Anon); Drago, *Outlaws on Horseback*; ____, *Road Agents and Train Robbers*; Graves, *Oklahoma Outlaws*; Hanes, *Bill Doolin, Outlaw*; Hendricks, *The Bad Man of the West*; Holloway, *Texas Gun Lore*; Horan and Sann, *Pictorial History of the Wild West*; Lake, *Under Cover for Wells Fargo*; Lamb, *Tragedies of the Osage Hills*; Newsom, *The Life and Practice of the Wild and Modern Indian*; Nix, *Oklahombres*; O'Neal, *Encyclopedia of Western Gunfighters*; Osborn, *Let Freedom Ring*; Preece, *The Dalton Gang, End of an Outlaw Era*; Raine, *Famous Sheriffs and Western Outlaws*; Rainey, *The Cherokee Strip*; Ridings, *The Chisholm Trail*; Shirley, *Heck Thomas, Frontier Marshal*; ____, *Six-Gun and Silver Star*; Shoemaker, *Missouri, Day by Day*; Sterling, *Famous Western Outlaw-Sheriff Battles*; Sutton, *Hands Up!*; Tilghman, *Outlaw Days*; Wellman, *A Dynasty of Western Outlaws*.

Bryant, Charlotte, 1904-36, Brit., mur. Charlotte Bryant married a British soldier who was part of a regiment sent into Ireland to maintain peace and order in the early 1920s. Frederick Bryant took his bride back to England where they set up housekeeping in Dorset. Though Charlotte bore her husband five children, she also engaged in many sexual liaisons with men she met in the Dorset ale houses. Charlotte often brought her lovers home to share the bed she slept in with her husband. Frederick did not seem to care about his wife's activities.

One young man in particular seemed to catch Charlotte's fancy. His name was Leonard Parsons, an itinerant gypsy who had his own wife, and several children. Yet, he moved in with the Bryants in 1933. The affair lasted until 1935, at which time Charlotte forsook the formalities of a divorce, and decided instead to poison her husband with arsenic. Bryant died on Dec. 22, 1935. Charlotte stood trial for murder the following year, but Parsons was totally unconcerned about her fate. The gypsy was drinking and cavorting in a local pub when he heard the news that Charlotte had been hanged on July 15, 1936. While awaiting her execution, the condemned woman's hair had turned white. See: **Blandy, Mary; Cotton, Mary Ann Robson Mowbrey; DeMelker, Daisy Louisa; Jegado, Helene; LaFarge; Marie; Smith, Madeline**.

REF.: Butler, *Murderers' England;* Casswell, *A Lance For Liberty; CBA;* Duff, *A New Handbook On Hanging;* Franklin, *The Woman In the Case;* Gribble, *When Killers Err;* Hoskins, *They Almost Escaped;* Huggett, *Daughters of Cain;* Jackson, *The Crime Doctors;* Jacobs, *Pageant of Murder;* O'Donnell, *Should Women Hang?;* Nash, *Look For the Woman;* Rowland, *Poisoner In the Dock;* Shew, *A Companion to Murder;* Tullett, *Strictly Murder;* Wilson, *Encyclopedia of Murder;* Wilson, *Murderess.*

Bryant, Kenneth, 1959-   , U.S., rob.-rape-mur. Before Kenneth Bryant appeared in court in 1976 on charges of murder, he had already established a long police record in his native Kentucky that began at the age of nine with his first charge of breaking and entering. By the time Bryant was seven, he was drinking whiskey and sniffing glue with his unemployed father, who had served several jail terms and was incarcerated more often than not. Bryant was convicted of breaking and entering two years later, and by the time he turned sixteen, he was an alcoholic and had committed thirty-one offenses and served six different sentences in various juvenile detention centers.

On Aug. 16, 1976, in Groveton, Va., while attempting to steal a quart of grapefruit juice to use as a mixer, Bryant fired five shots, killing the store's manager James Cox. He then stole $30 from the cash registers and fled to an adjacent gas station where he stole $70 from the attendant and shot him in the back, leaving him for dead.

After fleeing the scene, Bryant convinced his half-brother to drive him to the bus station where he boarded a bus to Washington, D.C., hoping to get a connection home to Kentucky. Bryant was apprehended at the Washington bus terminal after his half-brother notified police of his whereabouts. While awaiting trial in the Fairfax County jail, he forcibly raped his cellmate while jail officials paid no attention. A jury later convicted Bryant of murder, and he was sentenced to life imprisonment plus seventy years. Bryant will be eligible for parole in 1991.

REF.: *CBA;* Godwin, *Murder U.S.A.*

Bryant, William Perkins, 1806-60, U.S., jur. Prosecuting attorney in Indianapolis, Ind., from 1834-38. He was appointed judge of the Oregon territory in 1848 by President James Polk. REF.: *CBA.*

Bryce, James (First Viscount), 1838-1922, Brit., jur. Legal scholar, diplomat, and professor of civil law. He was a member of the Hague Tribunal in 1913. Book authored: *The American Commonwealth* (1888). REF.: *CBA.*

Bryukhanov, Viktor P., 1936- , **Nikolai M. Fomin,** 1937- , and **Anatoly S. Dyatlov,** 1930- , U.S.S.R., crim. neg. On Apr. 26, 1986, a fireball ripped open the night sky over the Ukrainian Soviet Socialist Republic, sending a radioactive cloud into the atmosphere that blanketed Europe for weeks afterward. Thirty-one people died and 135,000 villagers were evacuated from the immediate area from the explosion of reactor No. 4 of the nuclear power plant at Chernobyl. Charges of negligence were leveled at the plant's managers and six Chernobyl officials were put on trial.

The three-week trial began July 7, 1987, in a converted auditorium in Chernobyl's Culture House. Former Plant Director Viktor Bryukhanov, former Chief Engineer Nikolai Fomin, former Deputy Chief Engineer Anatoly Dyatlov, and three others were charged with systematic safety violations that led to the devastating explosion that became the world's worst nuclear disaster to date. Testimony in the trial exposed the deliberate violation of plant-operating rules by the men in order to produce larger quantities of electricity from the reactors. In addition, the defendants were accused of neglecting to warn Chernobyl residents of the danger of the excessive radiation that had been released from the reactor until thirty-six hours after the explosion.

Bryukhanov, Fomin, and Dyatlov were convicted of gross violation of safety regulations and each received the maximum sentence of ten years in a labor camp. Bryukhanov also received a second sentence of five years to run concurrently, for abuse of power. Boris V. Rogozhkin, shift chief on the night of the explosion, was also charged with violating safety rules and sentenced to five years in a labor camp. Supervisor of the Reactor Aleksandr P. Kovalenko received a three-year sentence, and Senior Engineer Yuri A. Laushkin was sentenced to two years for negligence and unfaithful execution of his duties. REF.: *CBA.*

Brzeczek, Richard, 1942-   , U.S., law enfor. off. Richard Brzeczek joined the Chicago Police Department in 1964 and held several positions before his appointment as superintendent of police by Chicago mayor Jane Byrne on Jan. 11, 1980. Brzeczek was involved in several scandals during his term as superintendent and was replaced when Harold Washington was elected mayor in 1984. Having received a law degree in 1972, Brezeczek is now practicing as an attorney. REF.: *CBA.*

BTK Strangler, prom. 1974-77, U.S., (unsolv.) mur. A letter received by KAKE-TV in Wichita, Kan., on Feb. 10, 1978, taunted the police for their lack of progress in tracking down the killer. "You guess the motives and the victims," the anonymous letter said. It was the second cryptic message from the mysterious "BTK Strangler," who killed six Wichita citizens between Jan. 15, 1974, and Dec. 8, 1977, and then was never heard from again. Officials suspect that the Strangler may be responsible for a seventh victim, but the evidence is not conclusive.

"BTK" stood for "Blind, Torture, and Kill," the signature of this homicidal maniac who stalked his victims inside their own homes. On Jan. 15, 1974, 15-year-old Charles Otero returned home from school and found his mother, father, and two siblings strangled to death in the family home on Edgemoor Avenue. Joseph Otero, thirty-eight, his wife Julie, thirty-four, and their children—Joseph, nine, and Josephine, eleven—were bound and gagged with knots that only an expert could have tied. The telephone lines had been cut, but there was no evidence of forced entry. A man in his twenties was seen driving away from the Otero residence, but police could not locate him based on a composite sketch. In October 1974, the Wichita *Eagle and Beacon* published a long, rambling message from the killer. He spoke of the "monster within": "When this monster enter my brain I will never know. But it here to stay. How does one cure himself? If you ask for help, that you have killed four people they will laugh or hit the panic button and call the cops. I can't stop it, the monster goes on, and hurt me as well as society."

The BTK Strangler may have struck again on Apr. 4, 1974, when he stabbed Kathryn Bright to death in her home on Thirteenth Street, not far from the Otero's house. Experts disagreed as to whether this murder could be linked to the Strangler. Things remained quiet for nearly three years until Mar. 3, 1977, when Shirley Vian, a 26-year-old divorcee, was bound and gagged in the presence of her two young children. Vian was strangled while the children were locked inside the bathroom. They described the killer as a paunchy, dark-haired man in his late thirties or early forties.

On Dec. 8, 1977, the Strangler claimed his final victim: 25-year-old Nancy Jo Fox, who was found strangled in her bedroom. The police were notified from a pay phone by the killer, who was seen entering a late model van. The killer then wrote a letter to the television station taking credit for the Otero, Vian, and Fox murders. Police Chief Richard LaMunyon mobilized his force to bring the BTK Strangler to justice. A special task force was organized, and an additional uniformed patrol was assigned to the neighborhoods the killer was known to frequent. Their search was relentless. Thousands of suspects were interviewed, as police checked leads across the country, but the identity of the BTK Strangler was never established. In July 1984, Wichita Police LaMunyon renewed his efforts to crack the case. A computer consultant was brought in to assist eight hand-picked detectives who employed sophisticated chemical tests and psychological profiles to try to identify a suspect. It proved futile. "I've been told by the chief that this investigation will stay open until we have no more leads to follow," promised Detective Ken Landwehr. "And that can almost be to infinity." Meanwhile, the speculation continues. REF.: *CBA*.

Bua, Nicholas John, 1925- , U.S., jur. Judge of the Northern District of Illinois, appointed by President Jimmy Carter in 1977. Author of "Experts—Some Comments Relating to Discovery and Testimony Under New Federal Rules of Evidence" (1977). REF.: *CBA*.

Buback, Siegfried, d.1977, Ger., assass. Two days after he obtained arrest warrants for two terrorists who threatened the life of Swedish Immigration Minister Anna-Grete Leijon, Chief Public Prosecutor Siegfried Buback was gunned down near a Karlsruhe, W. Ger., gas station on Apr. 7, 1977. The assassins were members of the Ulrike Meinhof Special Action Group, who demanded the release of political prisoners Jan-Carl Raspe, Gudrun Ensslin, and Andreas Baader. The three were on trial for various acts of terrorism against the state.

Buback's official limousine was stopped at a traffic light when a Suzuki motorcycle pulled up in behind it. As the light changed to green, the motorcyclist pulled out a submachine gun and sprayed the car with bullets, killing Buback and his driver and mortally wounding his bodyguard. Gang members called the West German news agency DPA to claim responsibility for the murders. Baader, Raspe, and Ensslin all received life sentences and were imprisoned at Stammheim in Stuttgart.

REF.: Bell, *Assassin!*; *CBA*.

Buccieri, Fiore (AKA: **Fifi**), 1904-73, U.S., org. crime. Beginning his career as a juvenile offender in Chicago's old 42 Gang, Fiore Buccieri then met Sam Giancana. When Giancana rose through the ranks of the underworld, Buccieri, as his top enforcer and bodyguard, rose with him, his official police record dating back to 1925 when he was first arrested for carrying a concealed weapon. At nineteen, Buccieri was then a gunman working for Al Capone and was highly active in the gang wars, reportedly killing ten or more rival gangsters for the Capone mob. He was a gravel-voiced goon, unintelligent and easily manipulated by Giancana. When Giancana took over the Chicago outfit in the mid-1960s, it was Buccieri and Felix "Milwaukee Phil" Alderisio who became his top strong-arm enforcers. Buccieri, along with Jack "Jackie the Lackie" Cerone and others, murdered the hulking loan shark, William "Action" Jackson, by placing the 300-pound mobman on a meat hook in a garage and torturing him for two days with such devices as a cattle prod, which was repeatedly inserted into Jackson's rectum. Buccieri and Cerone reveled in the agonizingly slow mob execution administered to Jackson, as an FBI tape recording of one of their conversations later revealed.

Federal investigators labeled Buccieri the "lord high executioner" of the Chicago mob in 1966. This was a time when Buccieri was most visible. He was honored that year by his fellow mobsters on his sixty-second birthday at a huge fete held at the posh Edgewater Beach Hotel. Hundreds of Chicago gangsters and mobmen representing syndicate sachems in other cities convened at this time to shower gifts and praise upon one of the worst killers in organized crime. This event, closely watched by federal and local investigators, also served as the mob summit meeting where Giancana consolidated his position as the top underworld boss in Chicago, assuming the leadership mantle worn so long by Anthony Accardo. Buccieri, as long as he was alive, made sure that Giancana would remain in control, but the aging enforcer grew ill in 1972 and died the following year of cancer. It was then that plans were made to have the flashy, limelight-bathing Giancana removed from his lofty position and, in 1975, Giancana was summarily executed in his home. This would never have happened, officials later claimed, had Buccieri been alive to protect his boss. See: **Aiuppa, Joseph; Alex, Gus; Buccieri, Frank; Giancana, Sam.**

REF.: *CBA*; Cressey, *Theft of the Nation*; Demaris, *Captive City*; Nash, *Bloodletters and Badmen*; _____, *Citizen Hoover*; Peterson, *The Mob*; Reid, *The Grim Reapers*.

Buccieri, Frank (AKA: **Frank Bruno, The Horse, Big Frank**), 1919- , U.S., org. crime. When the mob hierarchy in New York and Chicago needed someone they could trust to head California operations after the murder of Frank Bompersiero and the sellout of Aladena "Jimmy the Weasel" Fratianno, they turned to Frank Buccieri.

Frankie "the Horse" was the business manager and brother of mobster Fiore "Fifi" Buccieri, who ran the gambling and loan-shark rackets on Chicago's West Side during the 1960s. His criminal record up until 1970 was a clean one, showing only one conviction for petty larceny, and that was back in 1936. For these reasons the nine-member national commission of the Cosa Nostra was inclined to name the younger Buccieri to succeed the rebellious leaders of the West Coast crime family in June 1981.

One of a handful of surviving "old-line" Mafiosi, Buccieri was close to three of the leaders of the original five New York families: Joseph Bonnano, Vito Genovese, and Thomas Lucchese. In Chicago, Buccieri courted the favor of Anthony "Big Tuna" Accardo, the heir and successor to Sam Giancana.

After Buccieri's selection, he was allegedly assigned a capo from the Lucchese family to assist in day-to-day management of West Coast operations and his own *nostra brigata* of syndicate gunmen. "The commission wanted someone they could trust to handle the lucrative California rackets and this time it wanted to make sure nothing went wrong," explained one investigator close to the scene. See: **Accardo, Anthony; Bonnano, Joseph; Buccieri, Fiore; Genovese, Vito; Lucchese, Thomas.** REF.: *CBA*.

Buchalter, Louis (Louis Bookhouse, AKA: **Lepke, Judge Louis**), 1897-1944, U.S., org. crime. No other man in the early days of the American crime syndicate wielded more power and influence than Louis Buchalter, better known as Lepke, a diminutive, hawk-nosed creature of the Manhattan streets who began his criminal career by stealing goods from pushcarts in 1912. Lepke's far-flung criminal organization was nationwide and reached into Europe and the Orient. The illegal rackets under his control yielded more than $50 million each year, and he personally ordered dozens of men murdered—anyone who got in the way of his rackets—through the syndicate's enforcement arm, Murder, Inc., controlled by Lepke's loyal henchman, Albert Anastasia. Like his peers who came to sit with him on the board of the national crime cartel—Charles "Lucky" Luciano, Meyer Lansky, Frank Costello, and Joe Adonis—Lepke began as a lowly sneak thief, so poor at his first arrest in 1913, policemen noted, that he was wearing stolen shoes, both for the left foot.

In 1914, Lepke met another youthful thief with the torso of an ape, an apprentice thug like himself but one who could easily be controlled by the bantamweight Lepke, Jacob "Gurrah" Shapiro. Both of them were stealing from the same pushcart when they accidentally ran in the same direction. From that point on, Shapiro was Lepke's strong arm. (Shapiro's odd name stemmed from his marble-mouthed articulation; when ordering other sneak thieves out of the Lepke-Shapiro territory, he would snarl "get out of here," but the words tumbled together to sound like "gurrah.") Under Lepke's guidance, Shapiro terrorized the pushcart peddlers, hundreds of them, in their area of the lower East Side of New York, forcing them to pay weekly protection (against Shapiro and Lepke, of course). Another thug, Jacob "Little Augie" Orgen, one-time bodyguard to early day New York gangster Benjamin "Dopey Benny" Fein, heard of the Lepke-Shapiro combine and recruited them for his gang of labor sluggers which was then taking over the garment industry. While Lepke kept expanding the pushcart-protection racket, he and Shapiro went to work for Orgen, organizing strike-breaking mobs that smashed union meetings and strikes.

Orgen's gang was a polyglot assortment of Italian, Jewish, and Irish mobsters that included Lucky Luciano, Waxey Gordon, Jack "Legs" Diamond, and his brother Eddie. First Orgen worked for the company owners by breaking strikes, but then decided it was more profitable to take over the unions themselves. He and his men terrorized union leaders and, through innumerable beatings and murders, took over one local after another by having gang members named as heads of the unions. From this vantage point, Orgen easily extorted enormous amounts of money from employers under the threat of strikes. Orgen's gang battled others for the lucrative control of the garment unions, particularly the gang headed by Nathan "Kid Dropper" Kaplan who was killed in 1923 by one of Orgen's men, Louis Kushner (also known as Louis Cohen), after twenty-three known gangsters had been killed in the Orgen-Kaplan gang wars. Lepke and others had a hand in the Kaplan killing and, by 1927, Lepke had risen so high in the union and protection rackets that he decided to get rid of Orgen.

On the night of Oct. 15, 1927, Lepke, Shapiro, and Hyman "Little Hymie" or "Curly" Holtz (a brutal thug who had once worked for Orgen but who had defected to the cunning Lepke), drove along Delancey and Norfolk streets, the location of Orgen's headquarters, and spotted Orgen and his then-top bodyguard, Legs Diamond. They fired pistols and machine guns from their fast-moving roadster, cutting Little Augie in half and severely wounding Diamond. (Diamond would recover and go on to briefly become a top racketeer and bootlegger in New York, wounded so many times in gangster gun battles that he would later be dubbed by the press as "the clay pigeon of the underworld.") Diamond, once recovered, made his peace with Lepke and looked for greener pastures. Lepke was now unchallenged in the union rackets and he quickly consolidated his forces for an all-out takeover of the entire garment industry.

Lepke knew that the small cutter's union of only 1,900 workers was the pivotal labor force that controlled all garment work. Without the cutters no men's suits could be made and this affected more than 50,000 other garment workers. He strong-armed his way into control of this union and then dictated terms to the rest of the unions and the industry. Before long he was czar of this huge U.S. industry, controlling garment unions across the country. Many of the millions that rolled into Lepke's coffers went out to pay off police, judges, and officials who looked the other way when Lepke's goons went into action. Lepke's direct payroll was enormous; he supported thousands of lowly runners, thugs, and killers. Mobsters by the scores worked under his bloody banners, the most notable being Shapiro, by then a chief lieutenant, Danny Fields, Paul Berger, Mendy Weiss, and Curly Holtz. His men infiltrated the Amalgamated Clothing Workers Union, which boasted 400,000 members, and through this organization, dozens of unions in the U.S. fell under Lepke's domination. He next took over control of the Motion Picture Operators Union, and then the trucking unions (which had not yet become the Teamsters).

To keep his own forces in line, and also to chastise an occasional union leader who resisted his dictates, Lepke, through Brooklyn killer and mob man Albert Anastasia, organized several strong-arm squads—more than 250 in New York, and double that number about the country. These men had but one job, other than the petty rackets that kept them preoccupied. They were to drop all other activities when getting a "contract" on a "hit," meaning an order to kill someone. Most effective of these killing squads was Murder, Inc. in Brownsville, a seedy, crime-ridden district of Brooklyn. Here, from the late 1920s, Lepke's murder legions struck out at rival gangsters, disobedient henchmen, and ordinary citizens who had incurred Lepke's displeasure. No accurate count of the murders committed by Murder, Inc. survives, but the figures certainly reached into the hundreds, perhaps thousands.

Some of the more celebrated victims included Danny Fields, Lepke's contact man with the unions. Fields, who began drinking and talking to the wrong people, was shot to death at Lepke's orders. Curly Holtz, who was in charge of Lepke's newly developed drug-smuggling operations, was also murdered on orders from the boss for withholding huge shipments of heroin and morphine which he and Yasha Katzenburg had smuggled into the U.S. from China. (One shipment alone, brought in personally by Holtz, amounted to more than $10 million.) Holtz was stabbed to death and his body, coated with cement, was dumped into the East River.

Lepke was an enigma even to his friends and associates, and these became limited in number as he rose higher in the crime cartel. He early on befriended Lucky Luciano, as did Lepke's friend Meyer Lansky, knowing that Luciano was the key to keeping the Italian-Sicilian crime bosses from invading his union domain. It was Luciano, Adonis, Costello, and other Italian-Sicilian mob bosses that Lepke aligned himself with in 1932 to form the national crime syndicate, a loose, one-for-all organization that shared power, political protection, and, to some degree, profits from their incredibly lucrative rackets.

When Salvatore Maranzana, one of the last of the old-fashioned Sicilian gangsters, attempted to become the "boss of bosses" in New York, he first tried to take over the money-bloated union rackets from Lepke. Lepke went to Luciano, asking him for his support and telling him that if he fell, Luciano would be next, correctly assuming that Maranzano would respect no gangster, not even those of his own race. It was in Luciano's best interests to have Maranzano killed, which is exactly what happened. In return, Lepke gave Luciano huge payments from his rackets and the support of his army of gunmen. He also shared some of the pie with Luciano through the Italian's henchmen, Johnny Dio (John Dioguardi), Jimmy Doyle (James Plumeri), and Dick Terry (Dominick Didato), by allowing these hoodlums to head up the women's garments unions.

Lepke functioned as chairman of the board for the national crime syndicate, and his word was invariably law. He was known as Judge Louis, and it was he who decreed that Dutch Schultz, who had junior status with the board, be killed when Schultz told board members that New York district attorney Thomas E. Dewey, who had been energetically prosecuting Schultz and his rackets, had to be killed. Rather than allow Schultz to create enormous police pressure, which would harm all the New York racketeers by killing the crusading Dewey, Lepke decreed that Schultz himself was to die. The murder of the Brooklyn and New Jersey crime boss in a Newark restaurant in 1935 was not the work of a single mob but the execution of syndicate hit men. Not until many years later did Dewey learn that he owed his life to a man whom he would later help send to the electric chair.

Though it was Lepke's lifelong ambition to keep a low profile and let other flashier gangsters hog the limelight and the subsequent police attention, he and Shapiro came under investigation in 1933 and were indicted for labor racketeering and violating anti-trust laws. Both were fined $1,000 and given a year in jail by federal Judge John Knox, who thought this but "a slap on the wrist." Martin T. Manton, a U.S. Circuit Court of Appeals judge who later proved to be corrupt and on the syndicate payroll, allowed both gangsters bail and reversed the decisions against them. Manton had obligingly done the same for the notorious bootlegger "Big Bill" Dwyer and Frank Costello, who was later known as the "Prime Minister of the Syndicate." Police pressure against Lepke increased, and, by 1937, his life was made miserable by constant police surveillance. His phone lines were tapped and police spies were placed in his offices. He was forced to meet in

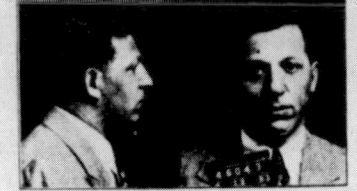

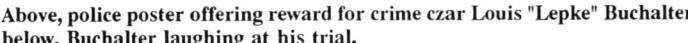

Above, a grim Lepke Buchalter en route to the death house; below, police photos of Lepke defiant and jubilant.

Above, police poster offering reward for crime czar Louis "Lepke" Buchalter; below, Buchalter laughing at his trial.

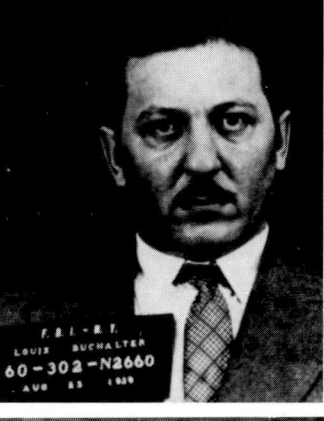

the washrooms of restaurants and on subway platforms with his lieutenants, hurrying his orders in whispers, then furtively moving on whenever he saw someone he suspected of being a detective.

Lepke went into deep hiding, first living in a hideout prepared for him by Anastasia, an apartment above the Oriental Palace, a sleazy Brooklyn dance hall, then moving to Flatbush to an apartment once occupied by Fatty Walsh, a bootlegger who had worked for Legs Diamond. The apartment had specially built secret rooms, panels leading to hidden corridors and other places where the crime czar could hide himself in case of a police raid. Ironically, Lepke used Mrs. Dorothy Walsh as a cover when secretly living here, the widow never realizing that she was playing host to the very man who had, years earlier, ordered her husband murdered. From this secret apartment, Lepke sent out scores of murder contracts on those whom he thought might cooperate with police and reveal his widespread operations, as well as the murders he had decreed in the past ten years. He still considered himself to be the top mobster in the country, if not the world. When he heard that Thomas "Three-Finger Brown" Lucchese, a Luciano ally, coveted his garment rackets, Lepke went into a tirade, telling Anastasia and Abe "Kid Twist" Reles, his top Murder, Inc. enforcer: "Nobody moved in on me when I was on the outside and nobody is gonna do it just because I am on the lam. You tell Lucky and Brown that the clothing thing is mine! There is no argument." With the looming threat of Murder, Inc., dominated by Jewish gangsters, Luciano and Lucchese had second thoughts and quickly backed away from seizing the Buchalter garment rackets.

This was but a small delay, however, since the Italian gangsters would use their usual guile and invention in getting what they wanted. Lucchese and other Italian gangsters let it be known that certain Brownsville gangsters would have plenty to say about Lepke and his operations. Several of these thugs were picked up and questioned; small-time crooks informing on others who held more important positions in the Murder, Inc. framework, until one of its leaders, Abe "Kid Twist" Reles, began to talk nonstop about Lepke, Anastasia, and other crime kingpins. Through Reles, authorities learned of on old labor slammer, Max Rubin, who had important information on Lepke. Rubin later testified that Lepke, Mendy Weiss, and Louis Capone (no relationship to Al Capone) had murdered one Joseph Rosen.

Lepke had, by that time, thought to outsmart prosecutors by surrendering to the FBI through newspaper columnist Walter Winchell on Aug. 24, 1939. He drew a fourteen-year sentence on narcotics violations and was sent to Leavenworth, anticipating parole in a few years. In this way, Lepke reasoned, he could not be tried locally in New York for murdering Rosen and others. Lepke's surrender was influenced mightily by Albert Anastasia, his top Murder, Inc. enforcer, who told him that the syndicate had "fixed" certain federal authorities. He would draw a minimum federal sentence, then be paroled, and avoid New York prosecution on more serious crimes. This was the plan that Lucchese and others had devised in order to finally get rid of Lepke and seize his enormous crime empire. He, of course, would be betrayed and eventually be turned over to New York authorities. Lepke, after taking Anastasia's suggestion, chose Walter Winchell to surrender to, having read Winchell's daily column in which the gadfly and gossip-monger regularly wrote to the crime czar, asking that he contact him and turn himself into authorities. Lepke, in dramatic fashion, contacted Winchell and told him that he would meet him on a Manhattan street, which he did. Winchell got into a cab with the gangster and drove to another location where an FBI car was waiting. Winchell and Lepke got into this car. In the back seat sat FBI director J. Edgar Hoover. Winchell was one of Hoover's friends (both of them partied in New York's Stork Club, owned by Sherman Billingsly) and took great pride in serving Hoover in this fashion, as well as getting one of the biggest scoops of the decade. "Mr. Hoover," Winchell said when he and the crime czar got into the car, "meet Lepke."

In 1940, Lepke was brought from federal custody and tried in New York for the Rosen murder. He, Weiss, and Louis Capone were convicted and sentenced to death. While fighting desperately to save his life through a barrage of appeals filed by his lawyers, Lepke, even from his cell, ran his criminal empire and ordered the deaths of those who had betrayed him. Reles was pushed out of a window of the hotel in which he was being guarded in Coney Island in 1942. Moey "Dimples" Wolinsky was shot to death in a Manhattan restaurant in 1943 because he had arranged for Lepke's 1939 surrender to Winchell and Hoover. Lepke's execution date, as well as that of Weiss and Capone, was repeatedly delayed and reset. But finally, on Mar. 4, 1944, Lepke and the two henchmen walked to Sing Sing's electric chair.

The crime czar refused to believe to the last minute that he was actually going to pay with his life for the countless crimes he had committed. He kept telling Weiss and Capone that "the fix is in, you'll see." He had important information to give to authorities, Lepke told the warden at one point when the end was near, but after he was interviewed, officials learned nothing new about the crime syndicate. Thomas E. Dewey, then governor of New York, refused to grant another stay of execution. On the night of his death, Lepke ordered roast chicken and shoestring potatoes as his last meal. Ever loyal, Weiss and Capone both ordered the same meal. The trio went to the chair as blue ribbon witnesses watched to see if any would crack at the end and reveal the dark secrets they knew. Capone entered the chamber first, at a little after 11 p.m. He said nothing as he stoically sat down in the electric chair. He was pronounced dead three minutes later. Weiss came next, asking to make a statement. He said: "All I want to say is I'm innocent. I'm here on a framed-up case. Give my love to my family and everything." With that he sat down and the current was thrown on. Mendy Weiss, chief bodyguard and killer for Lepke, died inside of two minutes.

The crime boss was saved for last. Lepke ignored the newsmen present and marched quickly to the chair, then turned and almost threw himself into it, a look of contempt on his face. He said nothing. Only the muscles of his face twitched slightly as the electrodes were placed on his head. Sing Sing's warden, William E. Snyder, raised his arm and dropped it without ceremony. More than 2,200 volts of electricity shot through the small body of Louis "Lepke" Buchalter, killing him within two minutes. Newsmen noted how saliva drooled from Lepke's lips in death, how his skin turned blue and how his 165-pound body twitched and bucked under the jolt of current and then sagged into death. One reporter ended his account with the words: "It is not a pretty sight." Thus died one of the most ruthless mass killers of the twentieth century, the only member of the national crime syndicate to ever be executed, paying with his life for the countless crimes he had personally committed or ordered to be committed. Only days after Lepke's death, Thomas Lucchese took over the garment industry rackets. See: **Adonis, Joseph; Anastasia, Albert; Costello, Frank; Dewey, Thomas E.; Diamond, Jack; Fein, Benjamin; Gordon, Waxey; Kaplan, Nathan; Lansky, Meyer; Lucchese, Thomas; Luciano, Charles; Murder, Inc.; Orgen, Jacob; Reles, Abraham; Schultz, Dutch; Shapiro, Jacob.**

REF.: Campbell, *The Luciano Project*; CBA; Cohen, *Mickey Cohen: In My Own Words*; Cressey, *Theft of the Nation*; Demaris, *Captive City*; ____, *The Last Mafioso*; Eisenberg and Landau, *Meyer Lansky*; Fried, *The Rise and Fall of the Jewish Gangster in America*; Gage, *Mafia, USA*; ____, *The Mafia Is Not an Equal Opportunity Employer*; Gaute, *MWW*; Godwin, *Murder, USA*; Gosch and Hammer, *The Last Testament of Lucky Luciano*; Katz, *Uncle Frank*; Kobler, *Capone*; Lait and Mortimer, *Chicago Confidential*; Levine, *Anatomy of a Gangster*; Lowenthal, *The Federal Bureau of Investigation*; McClellan, *Crime Without Punishment*; McPhaul, *Johnny Torrio*; Maas, *The Valachi Papers*; Messick, *Lansky*; ____, *Secret File*; ____, and Goldblatt, *The Mobs and the Mafia*; Nash, *Bloodletters and Badmen*; ____, *Citizen Hoover*; Peterson, *The Mob*; Pileggi, *Wiseguy*; Powers, *Secrecy and Power*; Reid, *The Grim Reapers*; ____, *Mafia*; Reuter, *Disorganized Crime*; Sann, *Kill the Dutchman!*; Scott, *The Concise Encyclopedia of Crime and Criminals*; Smith, *Syndicate City*; Thompson and Raymond, *Gang Rule in New York*; Toledano, *J. Edgar Hoover*; Ungar, *FBI;* Whitehead, *The FBI Story;* ____, *Border Guard;* Wicker, *Investigating the FBI;* (FILM) *The Enforcer,* 1951; *Murder, Inc.,* 1960; *Lepke,* 1975.

Buchanan, Edna Rydzik, 1939- , U.S., crime reporter. Edna Buchanan, the renowned gun-toting reporter from the Miami *Herald,* was the first woman in Dade County, Fla., appointed to a police beat, and has covered the Miami Police Department for nearly twenty years.

This gutsy female journalist is regarded as one of the nation's best crime reporters. She has covered over 5,000 deaths during her two-decade career that has spanned the 1980s when Miami became one of the nation's most violent cities sparked by the onslaught of refugees and the ever-increasing drug traffic from the Carribean and South America.

Buchanan won the Pulitzer Prize for general reporting in 1986, and in 1988 she published her memoirs in *The Corpse Had a Familiar Face.* In it she recounts many of the crimes she has covered including the deaths of several police officers with whom she had worked. REF.: *CBA.*

Buchanan, Eugene, prom. 1890s, U.S., rob. Eugene Buchanan and his gang of thieves stalked the night-shrouded streets of Chicago for several years near the end of the nineteenth century, springing from darkened alleyways to brutalize, rob, and strip unwary victims of their clothing and other valuables. Buchanan was arrested many times but managed to escape conviction until 1894. On June 6, he was arrested after ambushing Philip Schneider, who was en route to an elevated platform to catch a train to his home on the city's South Side. Schneider positively identified Buchanan as the man who had attacked him and stolen $40 and a gold watch. Buchanan was convicted and sentenced to three years in prison.

Upon his release, Buchanan returned to Chicago and pleaded with the arresting officer to write him a letter of reference in order to help him secure a job. The officer eventually agreed, but Buchanan soon returned to his familiar vocation of robbing and beating. He was arrested for the last time on Aug. 15, 1899, nearly one week after an attack on R. B. Epperson and Mrs. C. G. Kingswell. The couple was walking through Washington Park on the evening of Aug. 9, when Buchanan engaged them in a battle in which Kingswell stabbed him in the head with a hatpin. Buchanan was convicted and once again sentenced to prison. Although he pleaded leniency, he received a sentence of indeterminate length. REF.: *CBA.*

Buchanan, George, 1506-82, Scot., consp. Author, teacher, and statesman. He created a *cause célèbre* when he charged Mary, Queen of Scots with the murder of Henry Stewart, Lord Darnley in 1565. REF.: *CBA.*

Buchanan, Dr. Robert W. (or **Buckanan**), 1862-95, U.S., mur. A blatant opportunist, Dr. Robert W. Buchanan received his medical education in Edinburgh, according to one report, in Canada, according to another account. It may have been that Buchanan had no medical degree whatsoever, but had forged his degrees when he practiced in Canada without a license and was forced to flee when he was exposed. He lived for a while in Chicago, then Buffalo, N.Y., before returning to Canada to resume his unqualified practice in Halifax, Nova Scotia, where, in 1886, he married an attractive woman from a good family. It was later claimed that this woman's father, a wealthy manufacturer, supported Buchanan and even paid for the completion of his medical studies in Edinburgh. The union produced a daughter, but Buchanan's philandering soon led to a divorce when the couple moved to New York. They settled in Greenwich Village, where Buchanan spent more time in bars and with prostitutes than in his small offices at 267 Eleventh Street. Buchanan, while married, began to visit whorehouses in Newark, N.J., which were operated by a fat, ugly madam named Annie Sutherland. The little doctor with a wispish mustache and a pince-nez tried to impress his bar friends with the dubious fact that he was much sought after by females. At one point, he bragged: "There's an old dame over in Newark who is stuck on me."

The high-living doctor took to inviting his drinking companions to accompany him to a Newark whorehouse on Halsey Street owned by Sutherland where four of her girls entertained Buchanan's friends. The doctor was really functioning as a pimp in these instances, being rewarded by Sutherland with cash and her own favors. She was twice Buchanan's age and repulsive by all standards: obese, with dyed orange hair, and a huge wart adorning the tip of her large nose—the epitome of the uncouth, raucous slattern. Buchanan, as later events revealed, was not the slightest bit interested in Sutherland, but he was obsessed with her considerable fortune, and he made plans to obtain her money through what he thought was a foolproof murder plan. First, he divorced his wife, charging *her* with adultery and winning his case. He was even awarded the custody of his small daughter while his discarded wife returned to Canada.

Wife-killer, Dr. Robert Buchanan.

Madam Sutherland's considerable estate had goaded Buchanan to the divorce. He had seen the brothel owner's will, in which she had stipulated that she would leave everything to her good friend, Buchanan, but that, in the event that she married, her husband would receive all her earthly possessions at the time of her death. James Smith, who had for years acted as Sutherland's caretaker, was also close in her affections, and Buchanan feared Sutherland would marry Smith and he would be cut off from an estimated $50,000 in property and cash. He therefore brought about his own divorce on Nov. 12, 1890, marrying Sutherland on Nov. 29. Smith went to Sutherland and accused her of deserting him. The now totally reformed madam, who had been married and divorced three times before wedding Buchanan, replied to Smith with hypocritical aloofness: "I would never bind myself to a man who lives off girls."

Moving into Buchanan's Greenwich Village home, Sutherland became his receptionist and quickly alienated his carefully cultivated clientele, telling startled patients racy stories and greeting them at the desk with such inane statements as: "Hello, dearie, what'll it be? A blonde or a brunette?" At parties, she waddled her enormous frame about in loud, low-cut dresses and told ribald stories that shocked and repelled Buchanan's socialite friends. The doctor was even more embarrassed when Sutherland insulted city officials who had recently named him to a post as a police surgeon and appointed him a Lunacy Commissioner for the city.

In early 1891, Buchanan began to complain loudly about his wife to his drinking friends in his favorite saloons, chiefly to Michael Macomber, who owned Macomber's Saloon on Tenth Street, and a customer named Doria, saying that Mrs. Buchanan was ruining his business and mistreating his small daughter (who was later sent to Canada to live with her mother). He told them that he planned to go to Edinburgh to further his medical education and that his wife objected to his departure. Annie Sutherland Buchanan was also feeling morose and depressed, the doctor pointed out, and talked about ending her considerably miserable life. "Says she's going to commit suicide," Buchanan told his friends. "Says she'll swallow poison. I told her, 'Help yourself, you know where the stuff's kept.' I wish I could dump the old girl." These random remarks later came back to haunt the scheming Buchanan.

Worse, Buchanan, at that time, became fascinated with the case of Caryle Harris, a young New York medical student who had murdered his secret wife, 19-year-old Helen Potts, poisoning her with morphine. His crime was detected when examiners noticed the victim's pin-point-size pupils, a universal sign of morphine poisoning. Harris was convicted and executed. Buchanan talked endlessly about this case, scoffing at the killer. "Harris was a stupid fool," he told Macomber. "Only a bungling amateur would make such a mistake!" He added that, because of Harris' limited medical knowledge, he had no idea how to disguise the symptoms of morphine poisoning.

"Do you know of such a way?" asked the curious Macomber.

"Yes," the egotistical doctor replied, "a way has just occurred to me. Every acid has its neutralizing base and every chemical agent its reagent. If one is expert in the field, the preparation of an undetectable poison could be easily accomplished. If Harris had known enough to mix atropine with his morphine, the contraction of the pupils would have been counteracted, and nobody would have suspected morphine."

On Apr. 21, 1892, Buchanan announced to his wife, that he would be leaving for Scotland in four days, that he planned to continue his studies there. She threatened to disinherit him if he sailed. That night, in Macomber's Saloon, Buchanan made a great show of having to hurry home to attend to his wife who had become violently ill. He described how she physically shook and tremored, a malady he had yet to diagnose. He had cancelled his trip to Scotland, Buchanan announced, so that he could be near his dear wife. The next day, Buchanan called in outside medical consultants, Dr. B.C. McIntyre and Dr. H.P. Watson. Both physicians examined Mrs. Buchanan, noting how she complained of throat pains. She lapsed into a coma and then died on Apr. 23, 1892. Her demise was attributed to a cerebral hemorrhage, as a result of epilepsy, a condition Annie Sutherland Buchanan was never known to have had until the time of her death. But both Dr. McIntyre and Dr. Watson concurred in this diagnosis.

Buchanan quickly collected his dead wife's money and property and then hired a detective to watch her grave, instructing the guard to report to him if anyone disturbed it. He then sailed for Nova Scotia, not Scotland, as previously announced. His destination was the home of his first wife. He arrived as a rajah, radiating wealth and eager to share his prosperity with a woman he admitted having wronged. One florid writer described Buchanan arriving at her doorstep "wearing lavender spats, a light fawn overcoat with pearl buttons the size of poker chips, and a pale gray top hat the shade of the first, faint streaks of dawn." Within three weeks, Buchanan had remarried his first wife.

Nothing more would have come of Annie Buchanan's death had it not been for the accidental meeting of a New York crime reporter and a disgruntled whorehouse janitor. James Smith went to New York coroner Louis Schultze, whom he found working in the morgue. Smith told Schultze that he had read of Mrs. Buchanan's death in the newspapers and that he suspected her husband of poisoning her. Schultze, who, ironically, had examined the body of Helen Potts and had not detected the poison administered to her by her lover Carlyle Harris in 1891, told Smith that he was certainly mistaken, that Dr. Buchanan's wife had died of a stroke, and that two attending physicians had signed the death certificate giving that as the reason for Mrs. Buchanan's death. There was no reason whatsoever to question the decisions of qualified medical men, Schultze told Smith. The janitor went away muttering: "Buchanan murdered her just the same, to get her money, I know it."

Overhearing this startling conversation was one of the most remarkable crime reporters of the era, Isaac "Ike" White, of the New York *World*. He had been in the morgue, checking on a different story at the time, and immediately grew suspicious of Dr. Buchanan, having worked on the Harris case in 1891. He grilled Schultze, who shook his head and told him that *several* doctors had decreed that Mrs. Buchanan's death was due to a stroke. He did admit to White that Dr. Buchanan told attending physicians that he had given his wife some small doses of morphine in the past for a persistent kidney ailment, a not uncommon prescription in that day. Still, White doggedly investigated the case, and he soon learned that Buchanan had lied to his friends about his planned departure for Scotland and how he had cancelled his trip *after* his wife became ill. Checking with the steamship line, White

learned that the doctor had cancelled his reservation on Apr. 11, 1892, ten days *before* he announced his wife's sudden illness. White then learned about Buchanan's remarriage to his first wife and the detective placed on guard at Annie Buchanan's grave.

Armed with this information, White went to authorities and convinced them to exhume Mrs. Buchanan's body and make a thorough examination of the corpse. A detailed autopsy revealed that there were no lesions on the brain of the dead woman, which meant that she had suffered no cerebral hemorrhage as indicated by examining physicians McIntyre and Watson. Then Professor Rudolph Witthaus, one of the country's leading toxicologists, found one-tenth of a grain of morphine in the corpse, this being the remains of at least five or six grains that had been administered, enough to kill any human being. Witthaus unhesitatingly concluded that Mrs. Buchanan had been murdered. Yet, Witthaus admitted that he found no contraction in the dead woman's pupils, and remarked to reporter White: "Amazing, but apparently Buchanan has found a way in which to conceal the symptoms of morphine poisoning."

White continued his probe, which eventually led him to Macomber's Saloon. Here he was told by Macomber and Doria how Buchanan had described his method of disguising murder by morphine: the trick of putting drops of atropine in the eyes just after death to prevent contraction of the pupils. This, White was convinced, was exactly what Buchanan had done. (Although, other reports had it that belladonna, a drug producing the same effects as atropine, was the agent employed by Buchanan.) White took his information to local authorities, who quickly indicted Buchanan for murder.

The killer, however, had returned to New York from Nova Scotia to tie up some loose business and was warned by the detective assigned to watch his wife's grave that her body had been removed for examination. Buchanan hastily packed his bags and was leaving his Greenwich Village address when police arrived, charged him with murder, and took him to the Tombs to await trial. Buchanan's trial began on Mar. 20, 1893, before Judge Smyth. He was prosecuted by District Attorneys Delancey Nicoll, Frances L. Wellman, and James Osborne. The doctor sneered at the murder charges, telling reporters that he was being wronged by a news reporter, Ike White, who was only interested in selling papers, that the sensational charges were trumped up, and that his excellent criminal attorneys, Charles W. Brooke and William J. O'Sullivan, would prove him innocent. O'Sullivan had been specially selected by Buchanan to defend him because he was also an esteemed practicing physician.

But the web of circumstantial evidence was drawn tight about the accused. James Smith, the rejected suitor and whorehouse janitor, testified against Buchanan. Also appearing for the state were Buchanan's one-time drinking companions, Macomber and Doria. Macomber graphically told how Buchanan, while in his cups, described how atropine or belladonna could counteract the pinpointing of the pupils and dilate them so that morphine poisoning could not be detected. A great deal of forensic evidence was given relating to toxicology, and Professor Witthaus testified with devastating effect. The defense lawyers sought to avoid the mistake made by the attorneys for Carlyle Harris. They had not allowed their client to testify in that case and it was then assumed that Harris had something to hide, another point held against Harris and one that contributed to his conviction. Buchanan's lawyers thought to show their client's complete innocence and placed him on the stand. Prosecutor Nicoll savagely attacked the witness and soon had Buchanan falling over his own contradictions and outright lies. The jury took twenty-eight hours to return a verdict of Guilty. Buchanan's lawyers fought desperately to save his life, winning one stay after another while they filed appeals, but, in the end, they ran out of time and the poisoning doctor was executed on July 2, 1895. See: **Harris, Carlyle; White, Isaac.**

REF.: Carey, *Memoirs of a Murder Man; CBA;* Dunbar, *Blood in the Parlor;* Furneaux, *The Medical Murderer;* Kingston, *Dramatic Days at the Old Bailey;* Nash, *Almanac of World Crime;* ____, *Murder, America;*

Pearson, *More Studies in Murder;* Smith, *Famous American Poison Mysteries;* Thorwald, *The Century of the Detective;* (FICTION) Carr, *The Sleeping Sphinx.*

Buchmeyer, Jerry, 1933- , U.S., jur. Co-authored a chapter on Texas antitrust laws for the American Bar Association (1974), authored numerous articles and legal opinions including "Casenote, Evidence Recitals in Ancient Documents as Self-Serving Declarations" (1955) and "Constitutional Law Privi-lege: Grand Jury Witness Need Not be Warned of His Privilege Against Self-Incrimination" (1956). He was appointed judge of the Northern District of Texas in 1979 by President Jimmy Carter. REF.: *CBA.*

Buck, Norman, 1833-1909, U.S., jur. Norman Buck served as the U.S. district attorney for Idaho from 1878-80. He was was first appointed judge of the Idaho Territorial Court by President Rutherford B. Hayes in 1879, and re-appointed for a second term in 1884. REF.: *CBA.*

Buckfield, Reginald Sidney (AKA: Smiler), prom. 1940s, Brit., mur. Of the many ways that guilt overcomes accused murderers, causing them to confess their crimes, Reginald Buckfield's is one of the most original. While held in custody in an English jail, Buckfield penned a story entitled *The Mystery of the Brompton Road Murders* that provided police with complete details of the murder of Ellen Ann Symes.

Buckfield, a gunner who had deserted the British military and was commonly known as "Smiler" because of his perpetual smile, scribbled his short thriller on several scraps of paper while jailed as a deserting soldier. As police read the short story he had authored they realized that it was a factual account of the murder of Ellen Symes, who had been found dead on Brompton Road on Oct. 9, 1942. Buckfield's story related that Symes and her 4-year-old son had left her parents' home in Strood that evening to walk the twenty minutes home when they met a friendly soldier who called himself Smiler. Smiler walked with the couple a short way before stabbing her in the neck several times with a table knife.

When neighbors heard Symes' cries for help, they found the boy's stroller turned on its side, with the boy lying next to his dead mother. The child explained that his mother had been attacked by a soldier. When police noticed Buckfield nearby, they took him in for questioning. Once officers read the story, he was charged with the woman's murder.

Buckfield was tried at Old Bailey and was found Guilty of the murder and sentenced to death. Justice Hallet reviewed psychiatric tests and concluded that Buckfield was insane and remanded him into the care of doctors at Broadmoor Criminal Lunatic Asylum on Jan. 20, 1943.

REF.: Browne, *The Scalpel of Scotland Yard;* Butler, *Murderers' England; CBA; Old Bailey Trials;* Shew, *A Second Companion To Murder;* Wilson, *Encyclopedia of Murder.*

Buck Gang, prom. 1895, U.S., rape-mur. The Buck Gang, led by Rufus Buck, was made up of five illiterate Indians who terrorized the Old Indian Territory of Arkansas-Oklahoma. The Cherokee Nation was suddenly gripped by a reign of terror when Buck, an Uche Indian, accompanied by four young Creek Indians —Lucky Davis, Lewis Davis, Naomi July, and Sam Sampson— began raiding farmhouses and ranches, raping and killing as they rode wildly through a two-week crime spree, beginning on July 28, 1895. On that day, the five men gathered in tiny Okmulgee, Okla., collecting weapons for their rampage (some later said a traditional warpath was declared by Rufus Buck). They were spotted by a black U.S. deputy marshal, John Garrett, who asked them why they were so heavily armed. All five men wheeled about blazing away with their six-guns and rifles, killing the lawman. Mounting their ponies, the Indians rode out of town.

The gang struck randomly for thirteen days after that, riding to lonely ranches between Fort Smith and Muskogee, robbing stores, raping women. The first woman taken by the gang was a widow named Wilson whom they came upon as she was riding to town in her wagon. All five men raped the woman, then took her shoes away, and shot at her feet so that she fled, half dead from

fear. Next, near Berryhill Creek, the gang robbed a man named Stanley, taking his watch, horse, and $50 in cash. The Buck Gang struck the ranch of Gus Chambers, looting it of horses and riddling the Chambers house with bullets after the rancher put up a fight. Days later, they raided the farm of Henry Hassan, and while they held the rancher under guard, several gang members forced Rosetta Hassan to have sex with them, despite her pleas to remain with her children. When she resisted, Lucky Davis pushed her toward the bedroom, saying: "You must go with me or I will throw the damned brats of yours into the creek!" Later, the sadistic gang forced Hassan and one of his hired hands to fight each other and then made them dance while they shot at their feet. On the road the next day, the gang held up a drummer named Callahan. When a boy who worked for the elderly Callahan protested the rough treatment of Callahan, he was shot in the back and seriously wounded by Rufus Buck and others.

Members of the Buck Gang, all hanged for rape, 1896; left to right, Naomi July, Sam Sampson, Rufus Buck, Lucky Davis, Lewis Davis.

On Aug., 9, 1895, the gang robbed two stores, Norberg's and Orcutt's, near the town of McDermott. A huge posse of federal marshals and a company of Creek Indian police, the Creek Lighthorse, under the command of Captain Edmund Harry, was assembled and ordered to bring in the Buck Gang "dead or alive." Steve Burke, toughest of the U.S. marshals in the district, led the posse, which tracked the gang to a cave hideout near Okmulgee on Aug. 10, 1895. A wild gun battle took place, but all five outlaws were captured and taken by Marshal S. Morton Rutherford to McDermott. Here, hatred for the rapist-killers was so intense that Rutherford had to sneak his captives out of town to keep them from being lynched. The Buck Gang members, all manacled together by chain, were then taken to Muskogee and put on a train to Fort Smith, where they were quickly tried on Sept. 20, 1895, before Judge Isaac Parker. Hassan and his 30-year-old wife, as well as others, testified against the renegades, describing their perverted crimes. The jury quickly found all the gang members Guilty of rape and, on Sept. 25, 1895, Judge Parker passed sentence.

Parker asked the defendants if they had anything to say, and Lucky Davis jumped up and shouted: "Yes, suh! I wants my case to go to the Supreme Court."

"I don't blame you," replied Judge Parker sardonically. Then he stated: "I want to say in this case that the jury, under the law and the evidence, could come to no other conclusion than that which they arrived at. Their verdict is an entirely just one, and one that must be approved by all lovers of virtue. The offense of which you have been convicted is one that shocks all men who are not brutal. It is known to the law as a crime offensive to decency, and as a brutal attack upon the honor and chastity of the weaker sex. It is a violation of the quick sense of honor and the pride of virtue which nature, to render the sex amiable, has implanted in the female heart, and it has been by the lawmakers of the United States deemed equal in enormity and wickedness to murder, because the punishment fixed by the same is that which follows the commission of the crime of murder...

"Your crime leaves no ground for the extension of sympathy...You can expect no more sympathy than lovers of virtue and haters of vice can extend to men guilty of one of the most brutal, wicked, repulsive and dastardly crimes known in the annals of crime. Your duty now is to make an honest effort to receive from a just God that mercy and forgiveness you so much need. We are taught that His mercy will wipe out even this horrible crime; but He is just and His justice decrees punishment unless you are able to make atonement for the revolting crime against His law and against human law that you have committed. This horrible crime now rests upon your souls..."

Parker then sentenced all five men to hang on Oct. 31, 1895. Buck and the others "exhibited no sign" of emotion. They merely listened to their death sentences and then silently filed back to their cells. Later, Buck insisted that he could provide an alibi, that he was not present at any of the crimes committed by the gang. Judge Parker permitted a stay of execution while lawyers prepared appeals. The U.S. Supreme Court refused to hear the case and Parker's decision was affirmed without opinion. Parker rescheduled the hanging for July 1, 1896. The five men, on that day, were escorted to a large scaffold where they were to be hanged simultaneously. They stood on the large trapdoor in front of a great crowd while ropes were fixed around their necks.

None except Lucky Davis had anything to say. Davis asked for a priest and the chaplain prayed with him for a few moments. Then Davis spotted his sister in the crowd and shouted: "Goodbye, Martha!" Rufus Buck's father, a large, heavyset man, came into the courtyard and tried to walk up the stairs to the gallows. He was drunk and had to be escorted to a chair nearby and subdued by guards while he watched his son hang. Only Lucky Davis showed any signs of emotion; his face twitched and his eyes darted about furtively. At 1:28 p.m., the large trapdoor swung down and all five men fell with jerks to the ends of their ropes. Lewis Davis, Naomi July, and Sam Sampson died almost at once, their necks broken. Lucky Davis and Rufus Buck slowly strangled to death, their bodies jerking and drawing upward several times while they struggled for life.

Following the execution, a jail guard went into Buck's cell and found a photograph of Buck's mother on the wall. On the back of the photo, the rapist-killer had written the following doggerel:

> I dreamt I was in Heaven
> Among the Angels fair;
> I'd never seen none so handsome,
> That twine in golden hair.
> They looked so neat and sang so sweet
> And played the Golden Harp.
> I was about to pick an angel out
> And take her to my heart:
> But the moment I began to plea,
> I thought of you my love.
> There was none I'd ever seen so beautiful
> On earth or Heaven above,
> Goodbye my dear wife and Mother.
> Also my sister.
> Remember me, Rock of Ages.

Judge Parker, who sentenced so many men to the gallows that he later earned the sobriquet, "The Hanging Judge," had delivered his most blistering sentence to the members of the Buck Gang for the crime of rape, not murder. Parker considered this crime against females the most "intolerable" offense of all the many felonies he had to review in his so-called "court of the damned." See: **Parker, Judge Isaac.**

REF.: American Guide Series, *Tulsa, A Guide to the Oil Capital;*

Bartholomew, *The Biographical Album of Western Gunfighters; CBA;* Debo, *Tulsa, From Creek Town to Oil Capital;* Drago, *Outlaws on Horseback;* Emery, *Court of the Damned;* Harman, *Hell on the Border;* Harrington, *Hanging Judge;* Hunter and Rose, *The Album of Gunfighters;* Jones, *The Experiences of a Deputy U.S. Marshal of the Indian Territory;* McKennon, *Iron Men;* Nash, *Bloodletters and Badmen;* Shirley, *Law West of Fort Smith.*

Buckhout, Isaac Van Wart, prom. 1870, U.S., mur. Washington Irving's tale of Ichabod Crane and the headless horseman that roamed the fog-covered marshes of Sleepy Hollow pales in comparison to an actual double homicide that occurred in Sleepy Hollow, N.Y., on New Year's Day in 1870.

Isaac Van Wart Buckhout, a Sleepy Hollow farmer who lived primarily to hunt, fish, and drink, was a jealous man not much liked by his closest neighbors. Buckhout routinely accused his wife of infidelity and randomly argued with the residents of Sleepy Hollow. In a show of forgiveness, Buckhout's neighbors, Mr. and Mrs. Charles Rendall, invited Buckhout and his wife to share dinner at their home on Christmas of 1869. Following dinner, Rendall, his son, Charles Rendall, Jr., and Buckhout engaged in a friendly game of cards, which Buckhout lost. Always a poor sportsman, Buckhout became enraged at his loss and stormed from the house with his wife in tow.

Buckhout invited the Rendalls to New Year's Day dinner to apologize for his actions. They accepted, but only Rendall and his son attended as the other members of the Rendall family were ill. The Rendalls had barely sat down when Buckhout, seeking revenge for his loss at cards, shot both men with his shotgun. Mrs. Buckhout rushed into the room and he shot her, too.

Only Charles, Jr., survived the attack and lived to testify against Buckhout, who was tried three different times in a White Plains, N.Y., courtroom. He was eventually convicted of first-degree murder and hanged for the Sleepy Hollow murders.

REF.: *CBA;* Pearson, *More Studies In Murder; Speech of Henry L. Clinton, Esq. to the Jury on the Part of the Prosecution on the Trial of Isaac V.W. Buckhout.*

Buckingham, Duke of, prom. 1660s, Brit., duel. In sixteenth-century England, the most common way to settle a disagreement between two arguing parties was for one to challenge the other to a duel to the death, and the individual who remained standing would be declared the winner. Such was the case in 1667, when the Earl of Shrewsbury challenged the Duke of Buckingham to a duel over an affair the duke had with his wife.

Unknown to the earl, his wife had established somewhat of a reputation of infidelity during their marriage, and the Duke of Buckingham was simply the most recent in a long line of lovers. The duke and the earl met to settle their quarrel, the winner to receive the hand of Lady Shrewsbury. She was secretly waiting nearby, in the woods, holding the reins of her lover's horse. During the fray, the duke was wounded but the earl was killed. Lady Shrewsbury rejoiced in her husband's death and ran from her hiding place to congratulate her lover. REF.: *CBA.*

Buckingham, John William, See: **Ley, John.**

Buckley, Jerry, See: **Bommarito, Joseph.**

Buckley, Tim, 1672-1701, Brit., rob.-rape-mur. Apprenticed to a shoemaker in Lincolnshire, Tim Buckley fled from the shop one day to begin life as a footpad and highwayman. He robbed other tradesmen with wanton abandon, always claiming that his actions were justified by the greater crimes they had committed as so-called respectable businessmen.

To the innkeeper he said, "You must expect no favor from my hands, you surly son of a bitch, whose prodigality makes you lord it over the people here, like a boatswain over a ship's crew."

To the physician walking toward St. Bartholomew's he said, "Quacks pretend to honesty! There is not such a pack of cheating knaves in the nation again, in making people believe they are scholars, when they know no more of Greek or Latin than a suckling child does of Hebrew!"

To the pawnbroker of Drury Lane who had traded his items of value, Buckley said, "Hast thou so much brazen impudence as to reckon thyself an honest man, when I know thou art an unconscionable pawnbroker who lives and grows fat on fraud and oppression as a toad on filth and venom?"

And to the baker's wife he had just raped he said, "And as for conscience, I have as little of that as any baker in England, who cheats other people's bellies to fill his own. Nay, a baker is a worse rogue than a tailor, for whereas the latter commonly pinches his cabbage from the rich, the former by making his bread too light robs all without distinction, but chiefly the poor."

The highwayman's philosophical career met its untimely end two miles out of Nottingham when he attempted to rob three gentlemen riding in a coach. Determined not to surrender their guineas, they fired a blunderbuss out the coach window, which killed Buckley's horse.

The carriage rolled to a stop and the occupants continued to fire. Before Buckley was subdued, he killed a footman and his gentleman. For this, he was arrested, jailed, and executed at Nottingham.

REF.: *CBA;* Smith, *Highwaymen.*

Buckley, Will, See: **Purvis, Will.**

Buckly, William, b.1881, U.S., rob. In 1938, while Franklin Delano Roosevelt was serving as president of the U.S., a succession of minor robberies occurred in the White House. Articles of clothing, furniture, and money were stolen from Secretary Marguerite Le Hand, clerks Grace Tully, and Paula Larabee, and Chief Messenger Joseph Sheehan over a period of several months.

White House mail-room clerk, 57-year-old William Buckly, was arrested for the robberies after three marked $1 bills were found in his possession. Buckly was found Guilty and sentenced to six months in jail. REF.: *CBA.*

Buckman, prom. 1791, Haiti, arson-riot-mur. By the end of the eighteenth century, the island of Saint-Domingue was one of France's most prized colonial possessions. The African slaves who worked the lucrative plantations were abused in brutal ways by the French land owners. The slightest infringement was punished with the bullwhip.

On Aug. 22, 1791, Buckman, a slave overseer on the Turpin plantation, led a general revolt. A practitioner of voodoo, he worked his fellow slaves into a frenzy.

Slaves from all over the island began setting fire to the crops after Buckman and his followers had overrun the Turpin plantation and killed the white inhabitants. As word of the uprising spread across Saint-Domingue, French settlers fled their homes. When the Europeans returned, they carried out brutal reprisals against the leaders of the insurrection. REF.: *CBA.*

Buckminster, Fred (AKA: **The Deacon**), 1864-1943, U.S., fraud. Fred Buckminster began as a Chicago police officer and worked himself onto the bun-co squad by the 1890s. He arrested a dapper little man called Joseph Weil for pulling the pigeon drop con game sometime in the late 1890s. Weil, who was known as The Yellow Kid, and considered the most fabulous confidence man of his day, turned over his bankroll to Buckminster while the two walked toward the station house. The bunco detective was aghast at the thick wad of bills. "Where did a grifter like you get this kind of money?" Buckminster asked Weil.

The Kid smiled and told him: "That? That's just walk-about money. It's nothing. I made that in the last two

Fred "The Deacon" Buckminster

hours. Keep it."

Buckminster counted the money, hundreds of dollars, then slowly pocketed the bribe and shook the Kid's hand. "It looks like I'm off the force and into a new business," he said. For the next forty years, Weil and Buckminster proved to be the most successful team of high-class swindlers in the Midwest. The two con men, often with the help of dozens of other con men when working a "big store" swindle, concentrated on greedy financiers and crooked bankers, enticing them into what appeared to be crooked land-grabbing schemes or mining swindles in which they took the suckers for hundreds of thousands of dollars. Before he died in 1943, Buckminster claimed he had swindled $3 million from gullible marks. Buckminster spent more than ten years in prison (Weil about eight), and a few years before he died he wrote a series of articles in which he stated that no matter how smart the con man was, "the law is smarter and the con man will eventually be caught." See: **Weil, Joseph.**

REF.: *CBA;* Nash, *Hustlers and Con Men.*

Budde, Richard, prom. 1933, Case of, U.S., mur. Residents of Eagle River, Wis., were shocked when they learned on the morning of Oct. 26, 1933, that a local housewife, Virginia Budde, had burned herself alive in her bedroom closet the previous day.

Upon examination of the remains, the coroner originally ruled that Budde's death was the result of suicide, probably sparked by depression from her recent illness. However, investigators were less willing to believe that the woman had burned herself to death, and favored the idea that she had been murdered by her husband, Richard Budde. The seemingly distraught Budde had an airtight alibi, and neighbors corroborated the story that he had left for work at 8 a.m. and not returned home until his regular time in the evening.

Examining Virginia Budde's half-burnt shoes, fragments of her clothing, and the lock from the closet door, coroner P.J. Gaffney surmised that Mrs. Budde had been knocked unconscious, locked in the closet, and set on fire by her husband before he left for work. He concluded this after constructing an exact duplicate of the closet and re-enacting the crime, thus proving that Budde could very well have set the fire before leaving for work. He had the body exhumed and discovered traces of strychnine in her system. Once this evidence was reported to authorities, Budde was charged with his wife's murder.

The jury maintained that the prosecution did not prove that Mrs. Budde had not taken the poison herself, possibly to lessen the pain of the flames burning her body. They found Budde Not Guilty. Shortly afterward, Richard Budde was found dead in his home, poisoned by strychnine. His last act was to leave behind a suicide note giving a full confession to the savage murder of his wife.

REF.: *CBA;* Whitelaw, *Corpus Delicti.*

Bufalino, Russell, 1903- , U.S., org. crime. With a record that dated back to 1927, Russell Bufalino was the Mafia boss for upstate New York and controlled rackets throughout much of the state for four decades, his operations extending as far as Pennsylvania and parts of New Jersey. This Mafia don avoided the limelight at all costs and was one of the most elusive crime bosses in the U.S. He seldom saw the inside of a jail cell, despite the considerable efforts of federal agents to prove his reportedly extensive drug smuggling and jewelry fencing operations. Federal officials later insisted that Bufalino was the person responsible for ordering the

Syndicate boss Russell Bufalino.

elimination of Teamster boss James Riddle Hoffa. Bufalino was finally arrested in 1977 for extortion and sent to prison for four years. See: **Colombo, Joseph, Sr.; Apalachin Conference; Hoffa, James Riddle.**

REF.: *CBA; Cressey, Theft of the Nation;* Davis, *Mafia Kingfish;* Demaris, *The Last Mafioso;* McClellan, *Crime Without Punishment;* Nash, *Bloodletters and Badmen;* Ottenberg, *The Federal Investigators;* Reid, *The Grim Reapers;* Sondern, *Brotherhood of Evil: The Mafia;* Zuckerman, *Vengeance is Mine.*

Buffalo Bill House, prom. 1860s-70s, U.S., pros.-rob.-mur. Located at Franklin and Dryades streets in New Orleans, the Buffalo Bill House was one of the worst hellholes in the city for more than a decade until its owner and patrons, criminals and prostitutes for the most part, were driven out of the city and the dive was closed by court order. Bison Williams, who had run a lunchroom in Cincinnati, arrived in New Orleans following the Civil War and opened the Buffalo Bill House, hiring dozens of cheap strumpets to act as his waitresses. They served cheap drinks and sang obscene songs to customers who came from the ranks of the New Orleans underworld. Williams made no attempt to provide decent entertainment. He held rat and dog fights, boxing matches and butting contests. His chorus line danced lewd numbers and left nothing to the imagination in the skimpy costumes the women wore. The butting contests were bloody affairs which featured such moronic characters as a burly man known only as Looney and another called Oyster Johnny. One fight between these two behemoths lasted for almost an hour where the two giants butted heads until Looney's skull was cracked and he collapsed unconscious with permanent brain damage.

The place was packed each night with hundreds of muggers, sneak thieves, gamblers, confidence men, armed robbers, and killers-for-hire. The New Orleans Police gave the place a wide berth, and scores of naive natives and out-of-town visitors were mugged each night in the place. Those who resisted being robbed were beaten so badly that they were hospitalized and several victims were murdered. Prostitutes plied their trade by the scores here, charging no more than 25 cents a trick, $1 for those drunk enough to go off with these grotesque slatterns for a night. The city's most notorious burglars, Pierre Bertin and Jean Capdeville, used the Buffalo Bill House as their headquarters and, for years, planned all their burglaries in this dive. These two graduated to armed robbery and, in 1871, both were sent to prison for life for holding up a prominent citizen. Bertin was surprisingly pardoned by Louisiana governor H.C. Warmoth, a pardon that was revoked before Bertin left prison when the governor learned that the petition sent to him, pleading for the burglar's release, contained thousands of forged signatures.

Sam Gorman, also known as Charles Steadman, one of the most daring confidence men of his day, made the Buffalo Bill House his permanent hangout. Police arrested Gorman several times in the place, charging him with committing inventive swindles, but he was always released for lack of evidence. Gorman, a man in his seventies in 1869, was asked by a police officer why he went on swindling people when he had a large fortune in New York and New Orleans banks and owned extensive property in both cities. Replied Gorman: "Well, it's fun!" The Buffalo House was finally closed as a public nuisance by edict of the city council, following several riots in the place where both patrons and police went to the hospital in the dozens.

REF.: Asbury, *The French Quarter;* Castellanos, *New Orleans as It Was; CBA;* Dickson, *The Port of Queer Cargoes and Other Articles on New Orleans; History of New Orleans Police Department* (Anon.); Pedrick, *New Orleans As It Is.*

Buffet, Claude, prom. 1967, Fr., rape-rob.-mur. Buffet was a small-time French thief who concentrated on stealing women's handbags until he was seized by a sudden compulsion to "to see how it felt" to commit a murder. On Jan. 18, 1967, he stole a taxi and drove down the Rue de l'Assomption, Auteuil, where he picked up his first passenger, a young physician's wife, Françoise Besimensky.

He robbed the former model and then shot her to death. In order to make this crime look like the work of a sex pervert, Claude Buffet raped the corpse. He was captured and indicted, then put on trial on Oct. 8, 1970, along with a female accomplice named Marie Ansoine, who had participated in a number of his purse-snatchings. A week later, Buffet was sentenced to life in prison at Clairvaux, while Ansoine received three years.

Eleven months passed. Then, on Sept. 21, 1971, Buffet and a fellow inmate named Roger Bontems seized the prison hospital. They held the warden and a nurse hostage, demanding a supply of arms and their freedom. When French authorities refused to accede to the demands, the men killed the warden and severely stabbed the nurse. The hospital room was quickly overpowered and the prisoners recaptured.

REF.: *CBA;* Heppenstall, *The Sex War and Others.*

Buford, Thomas, See: **Elliott,** Judge **John M.**

Bug & Meyer Mob, See: **Lansky, Meyer; Siegel, Benjamin.**

Buggy, John James (AKA: Scotch Jack), d.1967, Brit., (unsolv.) mur. John James Buggy, reputed strong-arm man for a London organized crime gang, was found murdered in May 1967. Buggy had been shot and his body found floating in the water near Seaford Head. It had become detached from the concrete slab it was tied to when his corpse was dumped into the water. The gangland slaying is believed to be linked to London's illegal gambling operations. It remains an open case.

REF.: Borrell, *Crime In Britain Today; CBA;* Heppenstall, *The Sex War and Others.*

Bugliosi, Vincent, prom. 1970s, U.S., lawyer. Born in Hibbing, Minn., Vincent Bugliosi attended UCLA Law School. Upon passing the bar, he secured a position in the Los Angeles district attorney's office. When Charles Manson and members of his "family" were arrested and indicted for the 1969 murder of actress Sharon Tate, Bugliosi was chosen from among 450 trial lawyers to prosecute the case.

Despite numerous death threats from members of the California cult, Bugliosi succeeded in putting Manson and several of his followers away for life. It was a seminal case, and one that established his reputation as one of the toughest prosecutors in the business. His work on the Manson case helped secure his appointment as district attorney for Los Angeles, and also led to his authoring *Helter Skelter: The True Story of the Manson Murders* (1974). Bugliosi also was the prosecutor in the Alan Palliko murder trial, an event that was chronicled in the attorney's *Till Death Do Us Part: A True Murder Mystery* (1978). See: **Manson, Charles; Palliko, Alan.** REF.: *CBA.*

Buhl, Vilhelm, 1881-1954, Den., jur. Prime minister in 1942 and 1945, minister of justice in 1950, and member of the Danish parliament. REF.: *CBA.*

Buica, Manuel, See: **Carlos I.**

Buirmann, Franz, prom. 1630s, Ger., jur.-witchcraft. Buirmann was one of the most sadistic, relentless witchhunters of the 17th century, rivaling Matthew Hopkins of England for sheer barbarity. Franz Buirmann received his appointment to the bench from the Archbishop of Cologne. The power this rather mediocre jurist was given was absolute.

In 1631, and again in 1636, Buirmann visited the little towns of Rheinbach, Meckenheim, and Flerzheim outside Bonn. Nearly 150 persons were arrested and burned at the stake on trumped-up charges of witchcraft. Another 300 were driven from their homes. The property Buirmann seized during the persecutions made him a very wealthy man. During the first Rheinbach witchhunt, Franz Buirmann ordered the arrest of Frau Peller, the wife of the court assessor, after she had spurned his sexual advances. She was publicly humiliated and denounced as a witch, as her husband helplessly looked on. Frau Peller was raped by the torturer's assistant and then burned in a pile of dried straw.

The savage judge was denounced in the church pulpit by Father Weynhart Hartmann, who called for an immediate end to the persecutions, but he was one of only a handful of clergymen who dared cross the path of the ruthless and ambitious Buirmann, who even had his own executioner burned at the stake. See: **Hopkins, Matthew**.

REF.: *CBA;* Robbins, *Encyclopedia of Witchcraft;* Wilson, *Witches*.

Buisson, Émile (AKA: **Mimile le Dingue, Crazy Mimile**), 1902-56, Fr., rob.-mur. France's "Public Enemy No. One" sprung from humble origins. Born to a baker whose penchant was for wormwood absinthe, Émile Buisson's childhood was an exceptionally unhappy one. His mother was committed to an asylum, and Pere Buisson took to exhibiting his deaf-mute daughter in the cafés for money. He was sent to jail for lewd and indecent conduct with a minor.

Buisson experienced prison life for the first time when he was sixteen, arrested on a charge of theft. When he reached the legal age for military service, he was assigned to a penal battalion in North Africa. Under adverse conditions he fought valiantly and won the Croix de Guerre, France's highest military honor. But in France, Buisson was charged with many petty thefts which landed him in jail often. On Dec. 27, 1937, Buisson committed his first

French robber and killer, Émile Buisson.

"big score." In the company of a gangster named Charles Desgrandschamps, Émile held up two bank messengers outside of the Bank of France in Troyes. He shot and wounded one of the messengers in the thigh and began firing blindly down the street, thereby earning the nickname "Mimile le Dingue." While awaiting trial, Buisson escaped from the Troyes Prison.

By this time France was under the thumb of the Nazis. All private vehicles had been impounded by the Germans, except for Buisson's, which he had carefully stashed away in a garage before going to jail. The car came in handy when Buisson and Abel Danos, known in the French underworld as "Mammouth" decided to hold up the Crédit Lyonnais Bank in Paris on Feb. 24, 1941. They hired a room across the street from the bank, and had carefully plotted the movements of couriers who carried sacks of banknotes to the main branch each day. Buisson shot and killed one of the guards, and then loaded the money into the car and sped away. The robbers had taken nearly four million francs from the pushcart messenger. Abel Danos was picked up by the Germans on a routine identity search, and was pressed into service with the French Gestapo headed by Pierre Bony.

Madman Mimile was also arrested, but the Germans had no real use for him. He was given a life sentence and returned to the Troyes Prison. Deciding to act the part of a madman, Buisson shouted and beat on the walls of his cell, sometimes he would pace the stone floors all night. Convinced that he was truly mad, the authorities transferred him to an asylum at Villejuif on the outskirts of Paris. There in August 1947, Buisson made his plans to escape. With the help of his brother Jean, Émile scaled the walls on Sept. 3, and made his break for freedom. The very same night Buisson robbed the patrons of a crowded bar in the Montmarte. A week later he killed a policeman who had chased the gang from a restaurant on the Rue Le Sueur. The "Madman" had become France's most wanted criminal.

The police closed in on the gang at their hideout on the Rue Bichat. While Buisson outlined plans to his brother Jean, their accomplice Dekker, and two female companions, the French Sureté broke through the doors with guns blazing. In the confusion, Buisson escaped through the roof, and went into a self-imposed exile from October 1947 until February 1948. During this time he reassembled the remnants of his gang, and recruited new members from the dregs of the French underworld.

By 1950 it had become a war of wits between Émile Buisson and Charles Chenevier, director of the Sureté and responsible for bringing the killer to justice. "He is clever," Chenevier observed. "But one day I shall trick him into a mistake, and when I do I am the winner." Relying on his contacts in the French underworld, Charles Chenevier succeeded in May 1956. A tip from an ex-convict that Buisson was in need of a car and some weapons led investigators to the edge of Paris, where on June 10, 1950, the gangster was finally captured. While he was enjoying his lunch in the hotel café, two of Chenevier's men pounced on Buisson, quickly disarming him.

France's most notorious criminal of the immediate post-war era was beheaded on Feb. 28, 1956, in the courtyard of the Santé Prison.

REF.: *CBA;* Goodman, *Villainy Unlimited;* Henderson, *The Super Sleuths;* Heppenstall, *Bluebeard and After;* ____, *The Sex War and Others;* Nash, *Almanac of World Crime;* Whitehead, *Journey Into Crime;* Wilson, *Encyclopedia of Murder*.

Bukharin, Nikolai Ivanovich, 1888-1938, U.S.S.R., polit., assass. Edited *Pravda* while with Lenin in exile 1916. He was a member of the Politburo from 1918-29, expelled from the party in 1929, but re-admitted five years later. He was suspected of supporting Leon Trotsky and was expelled a second time in 1937. A year later he was executed by Josef Stalin as a dangerous subversive. REF.: *CBA*.

Bulette, Julia, prom. 1860s, U.S., pros. Known to her gentlemen admirers as the Queen of Sporting Row, Julia Bulette was the undisputed leader of the Virginia City, Nev., scarlet patch in the years following the Civil War. The notorious brothel madame was born in New Orleans to a French family, but drifted to California where she worked as a prostitute in the Angels Camp of San Francisco, not far from the seedy Barbary Coast.

Arriving in the booming frontier town of Virginia City, Bulette took up residence in the lowest, most vile houses near C Street. However, her customers spread the word where a diamond in the rough could be found. Soon the more genteel element began paying her a call. In time she *owned* the newly formed D Street. The ramshackle nests

Madam Julia Bulette.

were torn down and replaced with neatly painted white houses.

As her reputation grew, the respectable townswomen publicly shunned her, but the miners and cowpokes who drifted into town made Julia Bulette a local legend. The volunteer fire brigade elected her an honorary member, to the great consternation of the society ladies.

Then about 1868, a Frenchman named Jean Marie à Millain and two gunmen rode into Virginia City. Millain strangled Julia in her private living quarters and made off with her valuable furs and jewels. A posse was quickly deputized. Millain was captured and sent to jail while hundreds of mourners, most of them men, followed the funeral procession from the church to the cemetery. Decked out in the regalia of the fire department, brigade members feted Julia as a worthy member of the company. She was buried with full honors.

REF.: *CBA;* Drago, *Notorious Ladies of the Frontier*.

Bulgarus, d.1166, Italy, jur. First of the Four Doctors of Bologna. The others included Martinus, Hugo, and Jacobus, recognized authorities in Roman law. REF.: *CBA*.

Bulknill, Sir **Thomas Townsend** (AKA: **Sentimental Tommy**), 1845-1915, Brit., jur. Member of the House of Commons from

1892-99, and judge of the King's Bench Division of the High Court from 1899-1914. Known as a sentimentalist, Sir Thomas would frequently break down in tears when passing the death sentence. In 1911, he presided over the trial of murderers Frederick and Mary Ann Seddon. REF.: *CBA*.

Bull, prom. 1593, Brit., execut. The first British hangman to appear in public record was a man known simply as Bull, who served Queen Elizabeth in 1593. He was later succeeded by the infamous Derrick, who executed the Earl of Essex in 1601.

REF.: Bleackley, *Hangmen of England; CBA*.

Bullard, Charles (Charles Wells, AKA: Piano Charley), and Marsh, Ike, prom. 1868, U.S., rob. Charles Bullard's illustrious forebears made no impression on him, and he drifted into a world of crime following the death of his father.

It was his lifelong association with notorious international bank robber and swindler Adam Worth that brought Charley Bullard a measure of fame. Before his fateful meeting with Worth, Bullard and Ike Marsh held up the Hudson River Express train on May 4, 1868. Bullard and Marsh knocked out guard John Putnam and made off with $100,000 in cash and securities. Putnam was later identified as a conspirator in the crime and was sent to prison. Bullard and Marsh fled to Canada, but were extradited back to the U.S. and jailed in White Plains, N.Y. A week later Bullard escaped by tunneling through the wall.

Bullard's exploits attracted the attention of Adam Worth, who invited him to join a plan to rob the Boylston National Bank in Boston. The Worth

Robber Charles Bullard.

gang blew through the walls of the building and removed $450,000 from the safe. With Pinkerton agents on their trail, the gang left for Europe. In the next few years Bullard married Kitty Flynn, the toast of English cafe society, and helped Worth open the famous American Bar in Paris. In his last years, Bullard drifted through the capitals of Europe while Kitty returned to New York alone. See: **Worth, Adam.**

REF.: *CBA*; Horan, *The Pinkertons*.

Bullion, Laura (AKA: Della Rose, Clara Hays), b.1873, U.S., pros.-rob. Kentucky-born Laura Bullion moved to Texas with her family at an early age and quit school while in her teens, becoming a prostitute who later befriended and lived with many outlaws, including the brothers Tom and Sam Ketchum, and, following their capture, consorting with Wild Bunch train robbers Will Carver and Benjamin Kilpatrick. It was Ben Kilpatrick with whom Bullion became most closely associated, riding with him on raids with the Wild Bunch and accompanying him when Kilpatrick split from the gang, going his own way. Bullion was slender, five-foot-three-inches, with hazel eyes and black hair that she kept cropped close to her head, unlike the long-haired style of her day. She was not an attractive woman but much sought after by outlaws in that she was willing to share their hardships and take chances with them in their wild robberies. She was with Ben Kilpatrick when both were arrested in St. Louis on Nov. 15, 1901. Lawmen found a large amount of cash and unsigned notes in the room she shared with Kilpatrick; loot, it was later proved, from a recent train robbery committed by the Wild Bunch at Wagner, Mont. Bullion was given a five-year prison sentence in Kentucky and Kilpatrick received a fifteen-year sentence in the federal penitentiary at Atlanta. Following her release, Bullion disappeared. See: **Kilpatrick, Benjamin; Wild Bunch.**

REF.: Bartholomew, *The Biographical Album of Western Gunfighters;*

CBA; Horan and Sann, *Pictorial History of the Wild West;* Hunter and Rose, *Album of Western Gunfighters;* Nash, *Bloodletters and Badmen.*

Bullock, Sir Christopher Llewellyn, prom. 1930, Brit., polit. corr. Christopher Bullock was regarded as a fine example of the tireless British civil servant, a man who faithfully executed his duties year-in and year-out as the Permanent Secretary to the Air Ministry. Thus many observers of the British government were taken aback when Sir Bullock was suddenly discharged from his post in August 1930.

Bullock was accused of being indiscreet when he recommended that Sir Eric Campbell Geddes of Imperial Airways be granted a peerage in consideration of his work in extending the British airmail services throughout the empire. There was an ulterior motive behind this magnanimous gesture. Bullock was planning to leave the Civil Service and replace Sir Eric as chairman of the company. In essence, he was trading a peerage for the chairmanship. But as Christopher Bullock pointed out, he would have taken a $5,000 pay cut to accept the position.

What seemed like a tempest in a teapot to the outside world was taken very seriously by the staid British press. Commented the London *Times* : "The Civil Service above all is to be congratulated. It will not suffer in the end for this ruthless exposure of how high is its standard and rigorous its code." REF.: *CBA*.

Bullock, David, 1960- , U.S., mur. Openly defiant and lacking all concern for the six people he murdered, street hustler, part-time male prostitute, and armed robber David Bullock told Justice Burton Roberts of the New York State Supreme Court that killing was "fun." Bullock told of murdering Herberto Morales on Dec. 22, 1981, because he had started "messing with the Christmas tree." So he decided to shoot him. "It was in the Christmas spirit," Bullock said. "It makes me happy."

Two weeks earlier, the remorseless killer took the life of James Weber, a 42-year-old actor who was appearing in a production of Victor Herbert's "Babes in Toyland" at the 74th Street Playhouse. The body was left in Central Park.

Bullock was a criminal sociopath who derived an emotional high from the murders he committed. He used a .38-caliber pistol to extinguish the lives of five of his victims.

A special task force under the command of Lieutenant Thomas Power arrested Bullock in his apartment on Jan. 14. He confessed in a ninety-minute videotape to committing over 100 armed robberies and the murders of the six Manhattanites. It was later played back during the trial.

David Bullock pleaded guilty before Justice Roberts on Oct. 26. On Nov. 29, the defendant received six consecutive sentences of twenty-five years to life. In a lengthy prepared statement, Justice Roberts angrily denounced the defendant as "a small-time street punk, a petty thief, a shoplifter, a male prostitute." He warned the cold-hearted killer, "You are going to die in prison and then go before the Supreme Judge of us all and let Him impose whatever additional sentence He feels you so rightfully deserve."

REF.: *CBA*; Fox, *Mass Murder.*

Bullock, Jonathan Russell, 1815-99, U.S., jur. Attorney general of Rhode Island from 1849-53. He was appointed judge of the District Court of Rhode Island in 1865 by President Abraham Lincoln. REF.: *CBA*.

Bunce, Stephen, d.1707, Brit., rob. On the road to Essex one day, Stephen Bunce spied a gentleman on a mount. The horse was an exceptionally fine animal, and Bunce decided that he wanted it. He positioned himself on his knees in the center of the road, with his ear to the ground. The stranger, whose name was Bartlett, stopped to ask, "What a pox are you listening to?" Bunce looked up and said that he had heard the beautiful music of the fairies, here, in this magical place.

The astonished traveler said he didn't believe in such things, so Bunce beckoned him to dismount and hear the wondrous sound. Bartlett handed the reins to Bunce and got down on his hands and knees to see if the story was true. When his back was turned, Bunce mounted the gelding and rode away, leaving the stranger in the road, cursing his own gullibility. At the inn in Romford, Bunce explained that Bartlett was in the next town engaged in games of chance. He was losing very badly and needed fifteen guineas to cover his losses. The horse, Bunce explained, was his security deposit.

The innkeeper knew that Bartlett was as good as his word, and he said that Bunce could take one hundred guineas if he liked. No, replied Bunce, fifteen guineas was all that was required. With that, he rode off, while the duped innkeeper awaited the arrival of Bartlett who was huffing and puffing down the road—a distance of four miles.

Bunce, a cunning swindler, spent his early years as an ale-house boy. He blamed his turn to crime on his uncontrolled passions, swearing that "there was not a woman on earth but was a crocodile at ten, a whore at fifteen, a devil at forty, and a witch at threescore." Bunce spent his last shilling entertaining prostitutes, while his own wife sat home tending the house. Soon she grew tired of his wicked ways and took up with a seaman assigned to the HMS *Swiftsure*. Bunce felt betrayed by his wife but did nothing to mend his ways.

Fleeing to Spain, Bunce stole a mule from an unsuspecting peasant who would later swear that the beast was possessed by the devil. Bunce followed the peasant out of Barcelona to a lonely hilltop. When the peasant paused to rest, Bunce and his confederate slipped the bridle off the animal when its owner's back was turned. Bunce slipped the bridle over his own face, telling the disbelieving man that he was "a man real flesh and blood as you be...it being my misfortune to commit a sin against the Virgin Mary once, she resented it so heinously that she transformed me into the likeness of an ass for seven years; and now the time being expired, I assume my proper shape again. However, sir, I return you many thanks for your goodness towards me for since I have been in your custody, you put me to no more labor than what I, you, or any other ass might be able to bear."

Stephen Bunce lived for many more years, cheating and swindling the naive and unsuspecting. The authorities finally caught up with him in 1707 and, the crime of robbery being punishable by death, executed him at Tyburn alongside Jack Hall and Dick Low. See: **Hall, Jack**.

REF.: *CBA*; Smith, *Highwaymen*.

Bunch, Eugene (AKA: Capt. **J.F. Gerard**), d.1892, U.S., west. outl. Born in Mississippi, Eugene Bunch was a well-educated teacher and editor who turned to train robbery to make his fortune and wound up being shot to death by lawmen in a Louisiana swamp. Bunch, a mild-mannered man of six feet with blue eyes, earned his living as a teacher in Louisiana. He later moved to Gainesville, Texas, where he edited the local newspaper. He and a few other bandits robbed trains in Texas, Mississippi, and Louisiana in 1888, at the time the more celebrated Burrow gang was robbing trains almost every month. Introducing himself as Captain J.F. Gerard to train passengers, Bunch politely tipped his hat to ladies while refusing to take their purses, and he was just as gentlemanly when taking the wallets of male train passengers. When standing inside express cars he spoke quietly to the messengers, telling them in a soft, mellifluous voice that if they did not open the safes in their custody they would have their "brains blown out." Bunch reportedly stole more than $30,000 from six trains he robbed in 1888-92. In November 1888, Bunch robbed a New Orleans and Northwestern train of $10,000, and his biggest haul was in 1892 when he stopped a train near New Orleans and took $20,000. Shortly after this robbery, Pinkerton detectives tracked Bunch and two others to a swamp near Franklin, La., and, on Aug. 21, 1892, shot and killed Bunch and his cohorts. See: **Burrow, Reuben Houston; Pinkerton Detective Agency**.

REF.: Bartholomew, *The Biographical Album of Western Gunfighters*; *CBA*; Nash, *Bloodletters and Badmen*.

Bundy, Harry Dale, 1918-   , U.S., (wrong. convict.) mur. Harry Bundy probably regretted the day he struck up a friendship with Russell McCoy, twenty-two. It nearly cost the 39-year-old

Zanesville, Ohio, man his life.

On the evening of Feb. 9, 1957, McCoy quarreled bitterly with his sister Louise and her husband Lloyd See at their farm outside of Zanesville. The nature of the dispute was a familiar one: Russ McCoy's constant state of intoxication. About midnight McCoy shot and killed his sister and her husband, then set fire to the family home. Before the police and fire departments arrived, McCoy drove to the factory where he worked with Bundy. Thinking that his friend was drunk, Harry Bundy refused him a loan and told him to sleep it off. Angered by this, McCoy pulled a gun and told Bundy that he had just killed two people and he had better keep quiet about it.

Harry Bundy was horrified to learn the next day that the story was true. McCoy was now a fugitive from justice. Bundy called the sheriff's office and told them what he knew. By this time, the killer had already robbed three stores in Columbus and had taken off for Amarillo, Texas. At a liquor store across from the bus depot in Amarillo, McCoy purchased a bottle of vodka and conversed with the owner, Mrs. Norma Brajnovic. "I already killed four people and I'm going to kill another one, but this one will be legal," McCoy said. Brajnovic thought nothing more about the queer conversation for the next several months.

Russell McCoy returned to Ohio after his money gave out. He was arrested by the police and readily admitted to committing the two murders. He stunned law enforcement officials by confessing to robbing a grocery store in Stark County, Ohio, on Nov. 23, 1956, where the owner Reynoldo Amodio, and his clerk, Paul Cain, were killed. Then, taking revenge for what he perceived to be a deliberate betrayal, he said that Bundy had pulled the trigger.

In June 1957, Harry Bundy was convicted of murder and sentenced to die in the electric chair based on McCoy's testimony and the identification made by a 14-year-old who did not even witness the crime. Judge John Rosetti refused a motion to grant a new trial and the execution date was set for Nov. 8, 1957. Fortunately for Bundy, providence intervened.

Back in Amarillo, Mrs. Brajnovic was thumbing through a detective magazine one day when she saw a picture of McCoy, that strange young man with the phony Texas accent who had talked of murder. Seventy-two hours before the scheduled execution, she sent a special delivery letter to the prison authorities. Based on her sworn statement, a stay of execution was granted by the Ohio Court of Appeals on Nov. 8. A second trial convened in June 1958, resulting in Bundy's acquittal. See: **McCoy, Russell**.

REF.: *CBA*; Radin, *The Innocents*.

Bundy, Theodore (**Ted**, AKA: **Chris Hagen**), 1947-89, U.S., abduc.-mur. The public personality of Ted Bundy suggested nothing of the serial killer he truly was. Handsome, apparently well educated, a glib talker, Bundy struck those who met him for the first time, if they were to think ill of him, as someone who might be guilty of practicing smooth confidence games, but never one capable of violent crime. Everything in his posture and conversation smacked of culture, and his sense of humor was instant and infectious, one that won over new friends quickly and established trust on the part of the women who found him attractive. This was a fatal attraction for perhaps as many as forty young females, all of them brutally murdered. A number of pretty, young women began to suffer violent attacks from a strange intruder and others disappeared in western states in early 1974. The first of these was Sharon Clarke of Seattle, who was attacked in her bedroom while she slept, her head brutally smashed with a metal rod. She suffered skull fractures but survived and the rod was found in her room. There was no explanation for the attack and Clarke could not identify her attacker, even as to whether or not the attack was made by a male or female.

While authorities pondered this strange attack, Lynda Ann Healy, a student at the University of Washington in Seattle, who lived only a few blocks from Clarke, disappeared from her rented room on Jan. 31, 1974. Then, over the next seven months, young women began to disappear with dreadful regularity. Donna Gail Manson, a student at Evergreen State College in Olympia, Wash., went to a concert on Mar. 12, 1974, and vanished. Susan Rancourt, a Central Washington State student, disappeared in Ellensburg while going to see a foreign film on Apr. 17, 1974. Out for a late night walk on May 6, 1974, Roberta Kathleen Parks, an Oregon State University student living in Corvallis, disappeared. Brenda Ball left the Flame Tavern near the Seattle Airport with an unknown man at 2 a.m. on June 1, 1974, and vanished. On the evening of June 11, 1974, Georgann Hawkins left her boyfriend and began walking back to her sorority house at the University of Washington and she, too, disappeared.

At Lake Sammanish, Wash., on July 14, 1974, a number of attractive, young women were approached by a good-looking, dark-haired young man who called himself Ted. He had an arm in a sling and asked a number of women to help him load a sailboat on top of his car, a Volkswagen. One woman agreed and accompanied Ted to a parking lot but when he told her that they had to drive to a house on a hill to load the boat, she refused. Others did the same. Blonde-haired Janice Ott agreed to help Ted and disappeared. Some hours later Denise Naslund was seen walking toward the public washrooms at the lake and was not seen again. Other women were seen talking to the handsome young man with the arm sling and many were seen to accompany him to the parking lot that day. On Sept. 7, 1974, two hunters near the lake found the decomposed bodies of Denise Naslund and Janice Ott, along with that of another unidentified female. The remains found were in bits and pieces, scattered by wild animals, officials later concluded.

Detectives began an extensive investigation, learning from a young woman in Ellensburg that a young man wearing a sling had tried to pick her up on the night Susan Ranscourt vanished. Another Seattle woman recalled a young man wearing a sling and driving a Volkswagen who tried to pick her up. When she refused to get into his car, he shrugged and blithely took his uninjured arm out of the sling and drove off, using both hands on the wheel. Another woman reported that a man wearing an arm sling drove onto a sidewalk, attempting to block her path, in an effort to get her into his Volkswagen, but she managed to avoid him. During these investigations, the remains of two young women were found, one in northern Washington who was identified as Carol Valenzuela of Vancouver, Wash., who had vanished some months earlier. The second body, or what was left of it, was found in southern Washington State near the Oregon border. She remained unidentified. Both women had been apparently murdered. Police by then had many suspects they thought capable of having committed the abduction-murders.

One strong suspect was a depraved young man named Warren Forrest, a park employee who had picked up a Portland, Ore., woman, convincing her to pose for him. In a secluded area of the park, he tied her up, taped her mouth, stripped her naked, and fired darts at her naked breasts. Forrest sexually attacked her before strangling her and leaving her for dead. She survived, however, and identified her attacker. Another strong suspect was ex-convict Gary Taylor, who was accused of abducting Seattle females under various pretexts. Then an anonymous female caller phoned police to tell them that she believed that Ted Bundy was the man who had been abducting and killing young women in Seattle. Officers duly noted the report and filed it with the thousands of other leads they had collected. But the women continued to disappear. On Oct. 2, 1974, Nancy Wilcox vanished and, on Oct. 18, after leaving an all-night party in Midvale, Utah, Melissa Smith, daughter of the local police chief, disappeared. Her raped and strangled body was found on Oct. 27, 1974, in the Wassatch Mountains, east of Salt Lake City. In Orem, Utah, Laura Aimee went to a Halloween party after midnight on Oct. 31, and vanished.

Then, on Nov. 8, 1974, a young man pretending to be a police detective approached Carol DaRonch in a Salt Lake City shopping mall, demanding the license plate number of her car, explaining that someone had tried to break into it. She accompanied him to her car but found that it was undisturbed. The fake detective persuaded her to accompany him to police headquarters to view a suspect. She got into his Volkswagen but once they were on a quiet street, the imposter stopped the car and produced a set of handcuffs, snapping one end onto DaRonch's wrist. She let out a scream and he pulled a gun, placing this next to her head and ordering her to keep quiet. DaRonch was not the typically submissive type of woman the abductor-killer had dealt with in the past. She forced the door open and jumped out, he after her with a crowbar in his hand. He tried to smash her skull with this but she caught the bar in mid-air and struggled with him. Then DaRonch saw a car coming down the street and leaped in front of it, forcing it to come to a stop. She leaped into the auto which drove away.

The gall of the killer knew no bounds. Even with a potential victim escaping and now able to identify him, the young man tried to pick up a pretty, young French teacher outside Viewmont High School but she turned him down. A short time later Debbie Kent vanished when she went off to meet a brother at an ice skating rink. Police searching for Kent found a key to a set of handcuffs in the school playground where she disappeared. Salt Lake City police received the name of Ted Bundy from Seattle detectives, who stated that they had received an anonymous tip that Bundy had been kidnapping and killing young females. Bundy's photograph was also sent along to the Salt Lake officials and shown to Carol DaRonch, who said that Bundy was not the man who tried to abduct her. Laura Aimee, who had vanished in Orem, Utah, on Oct. 31, was found dead, her naked body having been tossed into a canyon.

The killings went on. In Snowmass Village, a Colorado ski resort, on Jan. 12, 1975, Dr. Raymond Gadowsky, staying at the Wildwood Inn, went to the room of his fiancée, Caryn Campbell, only to find her gone. Her remains were not found until Feb. 17, the naked corpse hidden in some thick underbrush. She had been raped and her skull had been crushed. In another resort town, Vail, Colo., Julie Cunningham vanished on Mar. 15, 1975, after going to meet a girlfriend in a bar. A short time later the remains of two missing women, Susan Rancourt and Brenda Ball, were found on Taylor Mountain, Wash. Then Melanie Cooley of Nederland, Colo., disappeared on Apr. 15, 1975, her body found on Apr. 23, only a dozen miles from her home. Unlike the other victims, she was fully clothed but her jeans had been slipped from her waist, showing that sex was the motive for the attack that killed her. Her head had been battered with a rock found nearby. Shelley Robertson disappeared on July 1 from her Golden, Colo., home. Three days later, Nancy Baird, a gas station attendant in Golden, Colo., vanished from her workplace. On Aug. 23, Shelley Robertson's naked body was found in a mine shaft outside of Berthoud Pass, Colo.

Then police, on Aug. 16, 1975, arrested Ted Bundy. He was stopped by a Salt Lake City patrolman who thought he was acting suspiciously, driving his Volkswagen down a street slowly as if inspecting homes for possible break-ins; the area had suffered a rash of recent burglaries. Bundy did not stop when ordered to by the patrol car and a chase ensued. His car was finally brought to the curb and Bundy was placed under arrest. His room was searched but nothing incriminating could be found, only a pile of maps and brochures of Colorado. At the station, Bundy explained that he was a psychology student who lived in Seattle. He said that he had also worked on the governor's campaign there and was presently in Salt Lake City studying law. The Colorado brochures reminded detectives that a number of girls had recently been abducted and murdered in that state, and they took particular notice of brochures about Golden, Colo., which Bundy had in his possession. The detectives knew that Shelley Robertson had been killed in that town. Forensic experts went over Bundy's car and found a hair on one of the seats that matched that of Midvale, Utah, victim, Melissa Smith. Then a witness insisted he saw Bundy at the Snowmass retreat in Colorado on the night

SOME OF
TED BUNDY'S
MURDER VICTIMS

Lynda Healy

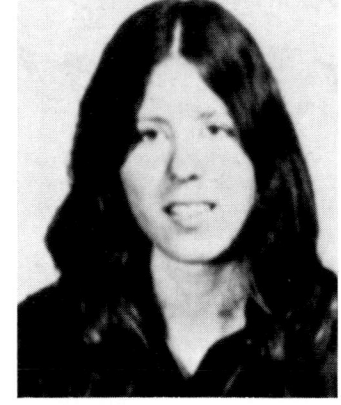

Donna Manson

Susan Rancourt

Roberta Parks

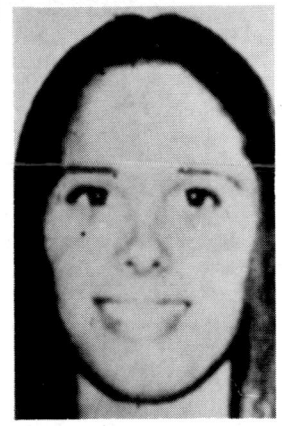

Brenda Ball

Georgann Hawkins

Denise Naslund

Janice Ott

Melissa Smith

Laura Aimee

Debra Kent

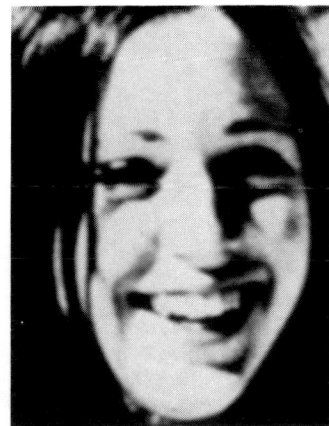

Caryn Campbell

Lisa Levy

Margaret Bowman

Kimberley Leach

Caryn Campbell disappeared.

Bundy was charged with murder and taken to Aspen, Colo., to stand trial. Here he charmed his wardens and prosecutors, affably cooperating with them, or seeming to, and giving an impression of an intelligent young man who was anything but a berserk sex slayer. He was shown every courtesy, given special health foods to eat and allowed to attend court without being manacled. Bundy insisted that he defend himself and received whatever law books he requested. Witnesses, however, showed Bundy for what he was, an inveterate liar, a cunning, crafty character who would go to any impossible lengths to get his way. Carol DaRonch, who had at first failed to recognize Bundy from a photo as the man who tried to abduct her in Salt Lake City, then came forward and identified Bundy as the man who had attacked her. As the pretrial hearings dragged on, Bundy was allowed to roam about the law library in Aspen. Even though he was under guard, Bundy managed to open a window of the library and drop twenty feet to the ground, escaping. He was tracked down eight days later at a deserted shack on Smuggler's Mountain and brought back to Aspen, where he was now kept under heavy guard.

Bundy insisted that he was a victim of circumstance, that he merely *happened* to have been in the same places where all these women disappeared and that there were many young men who bore a resemblance to him. He was also adept in using the law to create one legal motion after another to delay the case. While implementing this systematic legal stall, the insidious Bundy slowly took off weight in preparation for his next escape attempt. He somehow obtained a hacksaw and carved a hole around the light fixture of his cell, removing the fixture on Dec. 30, 1977, and squeezing through the one-foot opening—by then he had lost enough weight—Bundy made his escape. He moved to Chicago, then Ann Arbor, Mich., then on to Atlanta, and finally, he settled in Tallahassee, Fla., living only a few blocks from the sorority houses of Florida State University.

On the night of Jan. 15, 1978, Nita Neary saw a man holding a log and lurking about the front door of her sorority house. As she thought about calling the police, a student named Karen Chandler, blood flowing from wounds, staggered from her room. A madman had entered her room and had savagely beaten her on the head. Her roommate, Kathy Kleiner, had also been attacked in the same room, her jaw being broken. In another room of the sorority house police later found two other students Lisa Levy and Margaret Bowman. Both had been sexually abused. Bowman was dead, strangled with her own pantyhose. Lisa Levy had been brutally battered about the head and died en route to the hospital. Only a few hours later another female student, Cheryl Thomas, was brutally attacked in her room at another sorority house and was severely injured, but she survived the attack.

Though police began a widespread manhunt for the sorority house killer, they could find no one answering the sketchy description of the attacker. On Feb. 9, 1979, 12-year-old Kimberley Leach left her classroom in Jacksonville and disappeared. Some days later Bundy, who had been living in Tallahassee under the name of Chris Hagen and using stolen credit cards to purchase essentials, sneaked out of his Tallahassee apartment when his rent was long overdue. He stole an orange Volkswagen and drove to Pensacola, where a policeman stopped him and checked the license plates. Discovering the car was stolen, the officer arrested Bundy. Bundy bolted and the officer tackled him, struggling with him. When the officer fired a shot, Bundy meekly surrendered. He first identified himself as Chris Hagen, then admitted he was the fugitive, Theodore Bundy, wanted by Colorado authorities on charges of murder. He was held on charges of using stolen credit cards and stolen autos while detectives worked hard to tie Bundy-Hagen to the Tallahassee sorority house slayings. Meanwhile, the body of Kimberley Leach was found in the Suwannee River Park, her privates violated and mutilated; she had been strangled to death.

Still, the vain and strutting Bundy refused to admit to any murders. He claimed he was innocent. The police had made a terrible mistake. Detectives then came for Bundy on Apr. 27, 1979, and took him to an examining room. When he learned that they intended to take a wax impression of his teeth, Bundy went berserk, struggling violently so that a half-dozen men had to pin him down and hold his mouth open for the impression to be made. Bundy knew what they were after. The impressions of his teeth were later perfectly matched to the bite marks found on the buttocks of the murdered student, Lisa Levy, and it was this bizarre piece of evidence that would later, more than anything else, convict Ted Bundy of the many serial murders he had so ruthlessly committed.

Charged with the Levy and Bowman murders, Bundy was taken to Miami and placed on trial. He pled innocent, again acting as his own lawyer. He smiled at jurors, swaggering before the judge as he spouted law and precedent-setting cases of the past. He exuded confidence that he would never be convicted. His demeanor changed as he was compelled to sit quietly and listen to arresting officers tell the court how he had admitted having sexual problems, that he had begun his sexual offenses in Seattle as a voyeur and quoting Bundy as having said: "Sometimes I feel like a vampire." Dental experts then came forward to positively identify Bundy's teeth impressions with the bite marks on the body of Lisa Levy, and this convinced the jury of Bundy's guilt. He was found Guilty and sentenced to death by Judge Edward D. Cowart, who expressed regret that Bundy had gone "the wrong way" and that "you'd have made a good lawyer...I'd have loved to have you practice in front of me." Bundy was also found Guilty of the murder of the Leach girl and sentenced again to death.

Oddly, all of those around this vile and utterly cunning killer, his guards, arresting officers, the judges who heard his cases and ordered him executed, as well as most of those who later devoted tedious books to his rather unimaginative murders, especially Ann Rule, and Michaud and Aynesworth, who warmed too brightly to the man, showered him with the kind of attention given to Hollywood celebrities. The writers complained about the limelight Bundy bathed in and then flooded him with it. The killer was an actor as well as an unrepentant criminal and the portrait he drew of himself caused all about him to empathize about a future he never had, as if he deserved a future. Though various crime scribes tried to point out his talents, there was nothing redeeming about Ted Bundy and nothing to learn from him, except to recognize his pattern of serial murder as an alarmingly increasing *modus operandi* among modern killers. Like the vicious killer Jack Henry Abbott, Theodore Bundy was undeservedly a *cause célèbre,* and he played his part to the hilt, acting the pundit and even the criminologist as he waited to be executed, issuing cautionary statements to the young on how not to go wrong, to avoid pornography, to stay in school, to follow the legitimate road through life.

For a decade, this vile murderer kept himself alive with one appeal after another, reaping millions of words from the nation's press about his so-called "intellectual thought process," and his "psychological makeup," but his act finally closed when all appeals, stays, and last-minute delays were exhausted. In a last ditch stand to save his miserable life, Bundy began a recital of all the murders he committed, twenty-three in all. (At least fifteen more murders were attributed to Bundy by authorities.) The killer finally went to the electric chair at Florida's State Prison on Jan. 24, 1989. His last nervous words were: "Give my love to my family and friends." He was taken to the execution chamber, his head and right calf shaved so that the electrical conduits would work properly. He sat down in the chair and was stapped in.

Bundy gripped the arms of the chair and his head, strapped to a stationary position, could not move, but his eyes darted about wildly and, according to witnesses: "He was totally white, very scared." His eyes rolled frantically before the twenty-four witnesses gathered to observe the awful killer's end. Then, promptly at 7:07 a.m., 2,000 volts went through his body, and he was pro-

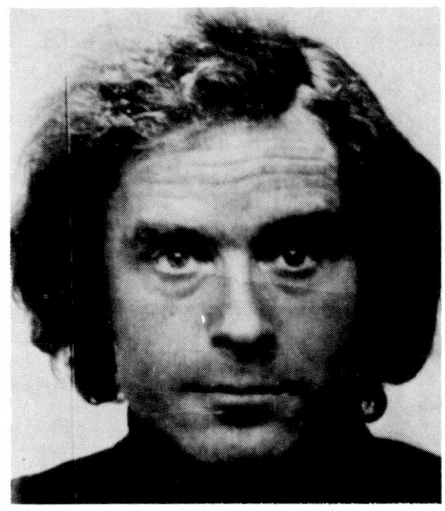 

Ted Bundy's first police photo and 1974 police sketch.

The mass killer in court.

Bundy, a prisoner in Florida and his FBI poster.

Bundy as his own lawyer, acting.

 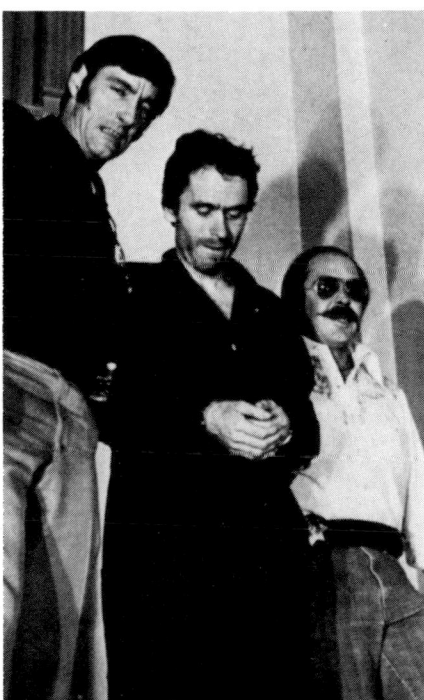

Bundy in custody, Salt Lake City, left; Florida, center and right, before his 1989 execution.

nounced dead four minutes later. Outside the prison, more than 100 reporters moved through a huge crowd that had assembled, trying to milk one more story out of Theodore Bundy. But none in the crowd protested this execution. Signs were held high that read "Buckle up, Bundy, it's the law," and "Roast in Peace!" When the black flag went up to signal the serial killer's death, the throng cheered wildly and firecrackers and other fireworks were set off in celebration. One Florida resident, hoarse from cheering the execution, told a reporter: "I waited eleven years to see that creep fry."

REF.: Boar, *The World's Most Infamous Murders*; Cartel, *Serial Mass Murder*; *CBA*; Fox, *Mass Murder*; Holmes, *Serial Murder*; Larsen, *Bundy, the Deliberate Strangler*; Michaud and Aynesworth, *The Only Living Witness*; Rule, *The Stranger Beside Me*; Wilson, *Encyclopedia of Modern Murder*.

Bunge, Friedrich Georg, 1802-97, Rus., legal historian. Specialized in the laws of Livonia, Estonia, and Kurland. REF.: *CBA*.

Bunn, Romanzo, 1829-1909, U.S., jur. Professor of law at Northwestern University. He was district attorney in Galesville, Wis., from 1857-58, and appointed judge of the Western District of Wisconsin in 1877 by President Rutherford B. Hayes. REF.: *CBA*.

Buntline, Ned (Edward Zane Carroll Judson), 1823-86, U.S., writer. After serving in the Navy, Ned Buntline became a newsman in Cincinnati, Ohio, and later established a sensational magazine, *Ned Buntline's Own*, in Nashville, Tenn., in 1845. He was arrested and charged with murder in 1846, and a lynch mob strung him up, but he was cut down alive and bore the rope burns around his neck for the rest of his life. He was subsequently found Not Guilty. Buntline traveled to the West in 1869 and gathered material for the hundreds (some reports had it at more than 1,000) of trashy short novels based on western gunmen and adventurers. He lionized William F. Cody, a

Ned Buntline

legendary cavalry scout, in many of his stories, and he introduced Cody to eastern audiences in his theatrical extravaganza, *The Scouts of the Plains*. Buntline, who dubbed Cody "Buffalo Bill," was responsible for having Cody establish his great Wild West show in later years. Buntline's tales, which preceded the dime novels of the 1880s and 1890s, also glorified such lawmen-gunmen as James Butler "Wild Bill" Hickok and Wyatt Earp. Buntline fancied himself a gun expert and he designed a foot-long six-gun for Earp which the lawman used with great effect, this weapon being forever known as the Buntline special. See: **Earp, Wyatt; Hickok, James Butler**.

REF.: Bloyd, *Jefferson County History*; Breihan, *Great Gunfighters of the West*; *CBA*; Fellows, *This Way to the Big Show*; Foote, *Letters from Buffalo Bill*; Horan, *The Great American West*; ____, *Pictorial History of the Wild West*; Monahan, *The Great Rascal, The Life and Adventures of Ned Buntline*; Russell, *The Lives and Legends of Buffalo Bill*; Sell and Weybright, *Buffalo Bill and the Wild West*; Shirley, *Pawnee Bill*; Watson, *A Century of Gunmen*; Wilstach, *Wild Bill Hickok*; (FILM) *Buffalo Bill*, 1944.

Bunton, Lucius Desha, III, 1924- , U.S., jur. Member of the Criminal Code Revisions Committee. He was appointed judge of the court of the Western District of Texas by President Jimmy Carter in 1979. REF.: *CBA*.

Bunyan, John, 1628-88, Brit., her. Joined the non-conformist church in Bedford in 1653, and authored the first pamphlets opposing the Quaker religion. He was imprisoned from 1660-72 for preaching without a license. While in jail, he preached his doctrines to the inmates and was released in 1672 by order of Charles II. Books authored: *Pilgrim's Progress* (1678, 1684); *The*

Holy War (1682). REF.: *CBA*.

Bunyon, Sidney, 1887-1909, Brit., mur. A suicide pact that went awry cost 22-year-old Sidney Bunyon his life in a way he had not planned. On the night of Aug. 23, 1909, Bunyon slit the throat of his girlfriend Lucy Smith and left the body on a public walkway known as the World's End Footpath near Enfield, Brit. Stunned and slightly dazed, Bunyon stumbled upon a night constable. He told Scotland Yard detectives that the murder was, in fact, a suicide that was Lucy's idea. He had merely carried out her wishes.

Bunyon went on trial for murder at the Old Bailey and was found Guilty on Sept. 13, 1909. Lord Justice Bernard Coleridge considered the evidence and sentenced him to die. See: **Coleridge, Bernard**.

REF.: *CBA*; Neil, *Manhunters of Scotland Yard*.

Buonarrotti (Filippo Michele), 1761-1837, Fr., consp. Revolutionary of Italian descent related to Michelangelo. He was imprisoned from 1796-1812 for his involvement in Babeuf's conspiracy. Book authored: *Histoire de la Conspiration pour l'égalité, dite de Babeuf* (1828). REF.: *CBA*.

Buondelmonte, d.1215, Italy, assass. His death on Easter Sunday in 1215 sparked a civil war between the Guelphs and the Ghibellines. REF.: *CBA*.

Buono, Angelo, See: **Bianchi, Kenneth**.

Burch, Ronald William George Arthur, d.1968, S. Afri., mur. A South African schoolteacher first discovered the remains of a human torso on Oct. 27, 1964, during an early morning jog around a lake at Boksburg in the Transvaal region. In the next few weeks, more body parts were found floating in the lake. A murderer had cut up the victim and carefully placed the remains in suitcases, which were deposited in the lake. But the cases had tore open and the body pieces rose to the surface. The Johannesburg Police surmised that the victim was a female who had been gruesomely decapitated while still alive. The unpleasant task of identifying the body still remained.

Four years passed and still the police were unable to provide positive ID to the Boksburg torso, until the daughter of Catharina Louisa Burch came forward to identify her mother based on forensic photos supplied by the District CID. A young girl at the time of Mrs. Burch's disappearance, she had been unable to offer any viable clues at the time of the disappearance. But now her testimony began to make sense. The composite drawing of the victim matched the description and photos provided by the daughter.

Suspicion fell on Mrs. Burch's second husband, Ronald William Burch, who had informed his wife's employer that she was leaving the company the same day she turned up missing. But now Ronald Burch was missing as well. Efforts to glean information from his 77-year-old mother proved fruitless. The trail led to Cape Town where Burch had moved after his wife's disappearance. He was reported to have been seen in various brothels and vice dens catering to prurient sexual tastes.

The investigation gradually shifted back to Johannesburg and the house where the elderly Mrs. Burch lived. There, on Nov. 28, 1968, police found the killer hiding in a wooden shed on the back of the property. When they burst in on Ronald Burch, he threw a light switch that activated an electric current that flowed into a pair of metal handcuffs attached to his wrist. He was dead within seconds. The aged and infirm mother went to her grave in 1974, still refusing to share any additional information with the police. Finally, after 30,000 statements had been taken and over 500 missing-person reports thoroughly investigated, the case was officially closed.

REF.: *CBA*; Gribble, *The Dead End Killers*.

Burchfield, Billy Floyd, prom. 1977, U.S., child abuse. After Judge Lloyd Simpkins of Somerset County, Md., sentenced Billy Burchfield and his wife to jail for forty years and thirty-two years respectively on May 28, 1977, he expressed the opinion that the couple deserved a "good thorough whipping from the community." But since the government doesn't allow cruel and unusual punishment he suggested they be confined in a small closet.

It was an obvious reference to the kind of treatment Burchfield had shown his 8-year-old step-daughter Patty Saunders. The child had been imprisoned in a tiny closet for weeks on end for almost four years, not even being allowed to use the washroom. Witnesses appearing for the prosecution said that Burchfield and his wife had treated Patty this way since she was four years old. REF.: *CBA*.

Burciaga, Juan Guerrero, 1929- , U.S., jur. Attended West Point from 1948-52. He served as special assistant attorney general of Santa Fe, N.M., from 1967-69, special prosecutor of the first judicial district of Santa Fe in 1975, and was appointed judge of the district court of New Mexico in 1979 by President Jimmy Carter. He authored the *New Mexico State Bar Professional Standards for Trial Practice Committee* (1972-75). REF.: *CBA*.

Burckhard, Max Eugen, 1854-1912, Aust., writer. Wrote numerous essays concerning jurisprudence. REF.: *CBA*.

Burdell, Dr. Harvey, See: **Cunningham, Emma Augusta**.

Burdett, Brian, 1932- , Brit., mur. Mrs. Moira Burdett, twenty-one, lived with her husband Brian at Appleford Road, North Kensington, London. Despite the young couple's earnest efforts, their domestic relations were not good. They had separated briefly several months earlier. Despondent, Brian Burdett stole a quantity of cyanide from his employers with the intention of killing himself so that his wife "would be better off."

Over her morning tea on Nov. 27, 1956, Moira Burdett collapsed and died. Brian said he found the empty cyanide bottle next to her and, not wanting the police to think she killed herself, he hid it. The murder trial of Brian Burdett convened at the Old Bailey in February 1957. Sir Harry Hylton-Foster, representing the prosecution, asserted that Brian poisoned Moira's tea in an act of willful murder. Brian's defense maintained that her death was a suicide, and that she could not have drunk the tea without noticing the discoloration and peculiar taste caused by the cyanide. Cited against Burdett were the facts that the dose of cyanide was exactly the fatal one, not the suicide's usual overdose, and that he waited

Poisoner Brian Burdett.

an hour after discovering the body before calling for help. Burdett was convicted and sentenced to death, but was later reprieved.

REF.: *CBA*; Furneaux, *Famous Criminal Cases, 4*; Wilson, *Encyclopedia of Murder*.

Burdett, Sir Francis, 1770-1844, Brit., libel. On Mar. 12, 1810, Sir Francis Burdett rose to make a speech in the House of Commons to protest his colleagues' treatment of John Gale Jones who had published a pamphlet that was judged to be libelous.

Mr. Jones had questioned the right of Parliament to exclude strangers from its doors and had raised various freedom-of-speech issues, resulting in his conviction for libel before the Bar of the House. Attorney General Gibbs cited various legal precedents for the action in reply to Burdett's denunciation. This did not placate Sir Francis, however, and he published an inflammatory piece in *Cobbett's Political Register*, titled "Open Letter to his Constituents."

Burdett was accused of violating the privileges of the House and was sentenced to the Tower of London, on a motion put forward by Sir Robert Salisbury. A warrant for Burdett's arrest was issued on Apr. 5, but public opinion was decidedly against Parliament on this issue. When Sir Francis refused to make himself available to be arrested, Gibbs sent military troops.

As a result, Burdett emerged as a public hero and thousands of Londoners rallied to his support in public protest. When 25,000 foot soldiers attempted to dispell the uprising and clear the streets, there were a number of minor skirmishes and injuries before order was restored. Sir Francis reaffirmed his resolve in a letter to the Sheriffs of Middlesex. "My house is at this moment beset by military force...I am resolved to resist the execution of such a warrant by every legal means in my power."

This was the most serious uprising since the Gordon Riots of 1780 and it threatened to tear the city apart at the seams. In the face of this crisis, Gibbs recalled the troops from Burdett's front yard. However, the Bow Street Runners commanded by James Read, were called on to arrest Sir Francis peaceably. He surrendered under protest and was committed to the Tower of London to await a hearing. In the House of Commons, resolutions were passed in his support, and on June 1, 1810, Burdett was freed. The matter did not end there, for it was not long afterward that Burdett instituted civil proceedings against those gentlemen who had imprisoned him. The case was heard by three judges who dismissed the complaint on Feb. 8, 1811. See: **Bow Street Runners; Gordon Riots**.

REF.: Armitage, *Bow Street Runners*; *CBA*.

Burdock, Mary Ann, 1805-35, Brit., mur. Mary Ann Burdock owned a lodging house in Bristol, England, that many wayfaring seamen called home. One of her boarders was Charles Wade, who wanted to open a small lock shop in town, but lacked the money. The 30-year-old spinster fell in love with Wade, and very much wanted to see him fulfill his ambitions. "I think I can find you a few hundred pounds for your business if you would like to settle down with me," she said. Wade, desperate for money, agreed to the scheme, lying that he would marry Burdock when he became wealthy.

Burdock had murder on her mind. Living in the house at the time was an elderly woman named Clara Smith, who was known to keep several thousand pounds in her room. Burdock, spurred on by Wade, fed the old woman some arsenic and then collected all the money she could find in the room. "She died very poor," the undertaker was told, but the woman's relatives in Portugal knew otherwise. A man named Read soon appeared at her door to demand an investigation. The body was exhumed and the cause of death was found. Meanwhile, Charles Wade had died. Burdock was condemned as a murderess and hanged in April 1835, only a block away from her former rooming house. See: **Blandy, Mary; Cotton, Mary Ann Robson Mowbrey; DeMelker, Daisy Louisa; Jegado, Helene; LaFarge, Marie; Smith, Madeline**.

REF.: *CBA*; Nash, *Look For the Woman*; O'Donnell, *Should Women Hang?*.

Bureau of Investigation, See: **Federal Bureau of Investigation**.

Burebistas (or **Burebista**), d.c.44 B.C., Roman., king, assass. King of Dacia from 60-44 B.C. He unified his kingdom through military conquest, and threatened Roman land holdings in the Balkans. He was assassinated and the short-lived empire was carved into four separate regions. REF.: *CBA*.

Burford, John H., 1852-1922, U.S., jur. State senator and later prosecuting attorney for the Twenty-second Circuit Court of Montgomery County, Ind., in 1880. He was appointed judge of the Oklahoma Territorial Court by President Benjamin Harrison, and re-appointed in 1892. He was assigned to the territorial court at El Reno, Okla., in 1898 by President William McKinley, and named to fill a vacancy on the Oklahoma territorial court at Guthrie in 1901 by President Theodore Roosevelt, and re-appointed in 1906. REF.: *CBA*.

Burger, Albert, and **Jobin, Marie**, prom. 1921, Fr., mur. Gaston Jobin worked at a large Paris hotel in the early spring months of 1921. A passive, quiet man, he was not "masculine" enough to suit his wife Marie's taste. One night he brought home co-worker Albert Burger to dine with them. He was large-boned, rugged, and self-assured; all of the qualities that Marie Jobin found attractive.

Behind Jobin's back, Marie began an illicit affair with Burger which tragically ended in murder on the night of Mar. 23, 1920. As usual, Burger dropped by the Jobin apartment. On this night, however, he was in a combative mood. When Gaston did not agree with him on a political question, Burger, aroused by strong liquor, flew at him and strangled him. When Burger realized what he had done, he dismembered the corpse into three sections using skills he learned as a butcher.

The torso was dropped into the river Seine, and the other two bundles were buried in two isolated locations in Paris. Believing she and Burger were safe, Marie sold her furniture and withdrew the remaining funds from Gaston's savings account. She told her brother-in-law Paul that Gaston had gone to Spain because he feared military conscription. It was a preposterous story, and Paul Jobin reported his suspicions to the police, who interviewed the two suspects independently.

The widow confessed to the crime and implicated Burger. At the trial, the defense played up the murderer's strong patriotic convictions, but the jury was not swayed by this ploy. Burger was convicted and executed at the guillotine. Marie Jobin was sentenced to hard labor and died in prison several years later. REF.: *CBA; Gribble, Clues That Spelled Guilty.*

Burger, Warren Earl, 1907- , U.S., jur. Member of the faculty of law at New York University, and chairman of the American Bar Association Project on Standards of Criminal Justice from 1967-69. He was assistant attorney general of the civil division of the Justice Department from 1953-56, appointed judge of the court of appeals in Washington, D.C., in 1956 by President Dwight D. Eisenhower, and appointed chief justice of the U.S. Supreme Court in 1969 by President Richard Nixon. He urged an end to partisan election of judges on the state level, and a universal system of merit selection. He voted to uphold search and seizure without a proper warrant, (*Vale vs. Louisiana 1970*), and was in favor of limiting the scope of the Miranda ruling especially in the case of *Harris vs. New York* (1971). In 1974, he ordered Richard M. Nixon to surrender the secret Watergate tapes to special prosecutor Leon Jaworski, which paved the way for the president's resignation on Aug. 9. REF.: *CBA.*

Burgess, James, See: **Great Gold Robbery, The.**

Burgess, John William, 1844-1931, U.S., writer. Published works included *Political Science and Comparative Constitutional Law* (1890) and *The Sanctity of Law* (1927). REF.: *CBA.*

Burgess, Richard (Richard Hill), d.1866, and **Kelly, Tom**, 1827-66, and **Levy, Philip**, d.1866, N. Zea., rob.-mur. On a wind sweptcliff high in the Maungatapu Mountains of New Zealand, five prospectors digging for gold were ambushed, bound and gagged, and knifed to death in May 1866. The motive was robbery, and the bodies were left to the elements near an abandoned path on the mountain Maori natives regarded as sacred.

Three convicts who had been transported from Britain were charged with the crime: Richard Burgess, Tom Kelly, and Philip Levy. A fourth man, Joe Sullivan, a hardened criminal who had arrived in the colony in 1840, attempted to save himself by turning over evidence against his cohorts.

Incensed by this sell-out, Richard Burgess admitted to having committed murder, but he pleaded not guilty so that he could have an opportunity to cross-examine Sullivan in court. Burgess blistered his one-time friend in the presence of Justice Alexander Johnston. "What I wish to do is merely to forward the ends of justice," Burgess told the judge. He then proceeded to implicate Sullivan in the murder of the miners, a charge the informer heatedly denied. "Gentlemen," Burgess said to the jury, "Sullivan's motive in giving information was to implicate others and to save himself! He is the veritable murderer, along with myself!"

After the three accused men finished questioning Sullivan, the judge instructed the jurors that even if they believed one man to have committed all five murders, the two other defendants were to be considered as accessories before the fact, and were equally guilty in the eyes of the law. The jury considered the evidence and returned a verdict of Guilty after only fifty-five minutes. Burgess, Kelly, and Levy were hanged on Oct. 5, 1866, in the prison at Nelson. Sullivan, who had hoped to avoid prosecution, stood trial for the murder of Jaime Battle, which had not been mentioned in the original indictment but was brought up by Burgess during the cross-examination.

Speaking in his own defense, Sullivan told the court that Burgess had exercised a "terror-like" influence over him, but had deliberately lied in court in order to place the rope squarely around his neck. The jury convicted Sullivan, too, of murder and he was sentenced to death. However, the court commuted his sentence to life imprisonment after recalling its earlier promise to set him free in exchange for his testimony.

Sullivan served eight years before he was released in 1874 on the condition that he leave New Zealand and never go to Australia. He returned to England for a short time, but did not linger. Joe Sullivan sneaked into Australia disguised and using an alias. He was recognized by the police and imprisoned a second time. REF.: *CBA.*

Burgh, Hubert de, d.1243, Brit., treas. Chief legal and political officer of England from 1215-32. According to the published account of Ralph of Coggeshall, he jailed Arthur, Duke of Brittany after refusing to blind and maim him, though ordered to do so by King John. He was charged with treason in 1231, outlawed, and then pardoned in 1234. He was the last British justiciar to exert strong political influence. REF.: *CBA.*

Burgman, Herbert John (AKA: **Joe Scanlon**), b.1897, U.S., treas. Herbert Burgman was born and reared in Hokah, Minn. When the U.S. entered WWI in 1917, Burgman served with the American Expeditionary Forces in Europe. There he married a German woman who bore him a son. When the war ended, Burgman stayed in Germany. In 1921, he took a post as clerk and economic statistician in the U.S. Embassy. There he remained, contented and at peace with the world for the next twenty years.

After Germany declared war on the U.S. in December 1941, however, the embassy personnel pulled out. Again, Burgman elected to remain behind. In 1942, he was hired by the Nazis to broadcast anti-U.S. propaganda over the short-wave station. Speaking from "Station Debunk" and as "The Voice of Free Americans," Burgman masqueraded as a radio commentator serving the greater Midwest. The Nazis paid him $500 a month to help undermine Allied morale.

When the war ended, Burgman went into hiding, but he was arrested in December 1948, and charged with treason. He became the twenty-fifth American to be indicted for treasonous acts against the U.S. during WWII. Burgman stated that the Gestapo forced him to betray his country, but the courts took a more narrow view of the matter. On Dec. 20, 1949, Judge Alexander Holtzoff sentenced Burgman to six to twenty years at the federal penitentiary at Lewisburg, Pa. The conviction was confirmed by the U.S. Appeals Court on Feb. 8, 1951. REF.: *CBA.*

Burgos, José, 1837-72, Phil., mut. National martyr to the Filipino people, he was an advocate of political reform and moderation of Spanish rule in his homeland. He was executed in reprisal for leading a mutiny of Filipino soldiers at Cavite. REF.: *CBA.*

Burgoyne-Watts, Walter, See: **Watts, Walter.**

Burgunder, Robert Marcus, Jr., 1917-39, U.S., mur. Declaring that his son was born with a "defective mind," Robert M. Burgunder, Sr., pleaded for the life of his son during a tense courtroom drama that began in June 1939. His namesake had been charged with the Apr. 29 slaying of two Phoenix, Ariz., automobile salesmen named Jack Peterson, thirty-five, and Ellis Koury, twenty-seven, who were bound, gagged, shot, and left for dead in a desert gulch.

Robert Burgunder, Jr. was an intelligent youth who followed his father's career as prosecuting attorney in Seattle, Wash., with great interest, carefully studying the criminal cases to see if there was such a thing as the "perfect crime." In 1936, he tested the theory by donning a Boy Scout uniform and holding up a Seattle drugstore—a crime that netted him $14.

Burgunder served twenty-three months in the Washington State

Reformatory before being released and signing up for classes at Arizona State Teacher's College in Tempe. In his sophomore year, Robert began acting strangely. He moved out of his dormitory and rented a room at a local hotel. On Apr. 29, he visited an automobile showroom and persuaded the two salesmen to give him a test ride. That was the last anyone heard of the three for the next seven days. When Burgunder, Sr. heard that two murdered men had been found in the desert, he feared the worst. "I hope," he said, "that one of them is my son."

That was not the case, however, because Burgunder drove his stolen car to Johnson City, Tenn., where he attempted to enroll at the local teacher's college. Suspicious of his credentials, the registrar phoned police and a cursory examination of his automobile turned up the murder weapon.

Citing a large gambling debt as his reason for stealing the car and fleeing to Tennessee, Burgunder admitted shooting the men to police officers before the trial, but denied it when he was on the wittness stand. He said that a fourth man, whom he refused to betray because of his respect for the criminal "code of silence," had pulled the trigger. After being convicted of first-degree murder on July 18, 1939, he amended the story. "I shot Koury first, shot him twice," he recalled. "Then I shot Peterson three times."

Burgunder said he should have the death penalty if the story about the accomplice is untrue. Judge Arthur T. La Prade accepted the jury's verdict of Guilty and sentenced the youth to die in Arizona's gas chamber on July 24. Burgunder's father accepted the verdict with weary resignation. His mother nearly collapsed in a fit of grief. REF.: *CBA*.

Burial of the Fruit, 1947, a novel by David Dotort. Murder, Inc., the organized gang of killers-for-hire (U.S., 1920s-1940s), is the basis of this novel. See: **Murder, Inc.** REF.: *CBA*.

Burk, Wayne, prom. 1940-70, U.S., burg.-rob. After years of "taking it on the lam," master thief and archswindler Wayne Burk decided to tell all in a published biography. Simply titled *The Thief*, Burk related to writer Ted Thackrey the details of his early years in Brawley, Calif., where his father, the local sheriff, showed him the nearby houses of prostitution and taught him to smoke marijuana, believing it was far safer than Prohibition moonshine.

Moving to Santa Monica, young Wayne went to work as a saloon bouncer. He pulled his first stickup before he was old enough to vote. It was a liquor-store job, and the owner asked somewhat cynically if he was of legal drinking age. By his own estimate Burk piled up a $15 million fortune from his various criminal capers. He stole valuable coin collections and rare art pieces from some of the wealthiest citizens of Hidden Valley, Calif.

Burk spent many years in West Coast jails, including a stretch at Folsom Prison, considered to be the last stop on the trail for hardened offenders. As Burk confided to his biographer, the law protects the career criminal. His prison terms became shorter and shorter the older and more experienced he became. It was a phenomenon of the age. REF.: *CBA*.

Burke, Charles, d.1933, U.S., suic.-mur. It was St. Patrick's Day 1933. The flood waters of the Ohio River had risen to a dangerous level. Officer Harry Levey of the Covington, Ky., police had strict orders to control the flow of traffic in his river town just outside of Cincinnati by whatever means necessary.

As he observed the slowly moving traffic, Levey could not help but notice a strange car with expired 1932 license plates. He pulled the vehicle over and questioned the driver, one Charles Burke of New York. The man was nervous and fidgety, and his face bore three unmistakable cut marks. Curious, Levey examined a tarpaulin sack lying on the back seat. Reaching inside, he discovered the severed remains of a human body!

Suddenly Burke pulled a straight razor and sliced his throat and wrists. He was dead before the ambulance could arrive. In his clothing police found a court order from the Hudson County Circuit Court directing Burke to pay $50 a month, beginning Mar.

15, to Ella Burke pending a divorce trial. The Covington Police later determined that Charles Burke had killed his wife on Mar. 16, 1932, after deciding not to pay alimony. He was about to begin a new life with a younger girlfriend. After cutting up his ex-wife's body into small parts, he drove to Kentucky with the package in the back seat. He never expected the flood waters of the Ohio River to be his undoing.
REF.: *CBA*; Cohen, *One Hundred True Crime Stories*.

Burke, David Augustus, 1952-87, mur. Pacific-Southwest Airlines flight 1771 took off quite routinely from Los Angeles on Dec. 7, 1987. The commuter jet was bound for San Francisco with forty-three persons on board when suddenly a cabin attendant warned the pilot that "we've got a problem here."

David Augustus Burke forced his way into the cockpit waving a .44 magnum revolver. The in-flight tape recorder picked up the unmistakable sound of gunfire, and then the ominous rush of air out of the depressurized cabin. Within two minutes the plane had spiraled to earth, crashing into a hill outside Paso Robles, in San Luis Obispo County. All 43 people aboard died in the crash.

Sifting through the wreckage, investigators from the National Transportation Safety Board found the gun and the six spent shell casings. A note written by Burke was discovered in an air sickness bag. It read:

> Hi Ray. I think it's sort of ironical that we end up like this. I asked for some leniency for my family, remember? Well I got none. And you'll get none.

The message was written to Raymond Thomson, a customer service manager for USAir at Los Angeles International Airport who was commuting to San Francisco. Police theorized that Burke slipped the note to Thomson shortly before entering the cockpit.

Burke, who had a police record in Rochester, N.Y., for drug trafficking and automobile theft was formerly employed as a ticket agent at the airport. The 35-year-old Jamaican-born hijacker had a long history of mental illness and was described by Dr. Russell Barton, former director of the Rochester Psychiatric Center as a psychopath. He had been fired in November for pilfering $69, taken from in-flight cocktail receipts.

After his dismissal, Burke had become moody and depressed. The week before the ill-fated flight, he held his girlfriend Jacqueline Camacho and her six-year-old daughter at gunpoint during a mad six-hour drive outside Los Angeles.

The ease with which he passed through airport security systems concerned the FBI. The gunman strolled by all of the routine checkpoints because airport personnel were unaware that he had been recently dismissed from his job. This latest air tragedy resulted in the Federal Aviation Administration issuing orders to tighten security checks at all passenger check-in points at U.S. airports. REF.: *CBA*.

Burke, Dell, d.1980, U.S., pros. Dell Burke ran a brothel in Lusk, Wyo., during the oil-boom years in the 1920s. She joined the local Chamber of Commerce and donated money to pay for municipal services. During those years, when the city's population exceeded 10,000, Dell Burke's fortune was estimated at $1 million. Despite her generous support of worthwhile causes over the years, the town refused to admit her to polite society.

Burke had become a prostitute in Juneau, Alaska, at the age of sixteen. At the time of her death in December 1980, Lusk, the town she had called home for nearly sixty years, contained fewer than 1,700 people. REF.: *CBA*.

Burke, Elmer (AKA: **Trigger**), 1917-58, U.S., org. crime. Orphaned at an early age, Burke was trained in crime by his older brother Charlie, a habitual criminal. He was a petty thief, living mostly in the New York streets of Hell's Kitchen. Burke was also an incorrigible truant by the age of ten. He was sent to Elmira Reformatory three times by 1941, but when WWII was declared, Burke, in an effort to escape the reformatory, volunteered for duty. He proved to be an aggressive soldier who loved handling a submachine gun. On one occasion, he stormed a German machine gun nest and killed eight enemy soldiers. An officer had to restrain Burke later when he was still pumping bullets into the dead bodies.

Following his release from the army, Burke went back to his criminal pursuits, robbing Manhattan stores and hiring himself out as a freelance killer, using machine guns on rival gangsters and earning the sobriquet of "Trigger." He was not the most intelligent of criminals. In 1946, Burke robbed a New York liquor store and then leisurely strolled from the store and stopped on the sidewalk to count his loot.

Professional killer Elmer "Trigger" Burke.

He took so much time doing this that police easily arrested him. He was sent to Sing Sing, having received a two-year sentence. While in prison, Burke's brother Charlie was killed by rival gangsters and Burke vowed revenge. When he was released, he began hunting for his brother's killer and spent years doing this, finally deciding that his murderer was gangster George Goll, even though he lacked any kind of real evidence. Burke caught Goll on a Manhattan street on Feb. 24, 1953, and shot him twice in the head, killing him.

Burke quickly developed a reputation as a berserk killer, but he was efficient and received $1,000 per murder contract. He often killed for pleasure or out of an intense rage that consumed him. One evening he fell to arguing with Joseph "Jumbo" Lancia and knocked this associate to the floor of a bar operated by Edward "Poochy" Walsh. When Walsh stopped Burke from killing his friend, he left the bar and returned a short time later, holding an automatic which he put to Walsh's head, saying: "Poochy, you shouldn't have interfered!" He pulled the trigger three times, killing Walsh on the spot.

On June 10, 1954, Burke received an assignment to murder Joseph "Specs" O'Keefe, one of the Brink's robbers who had informed on his fellow thieves, believing he had been short-changed on the split from the enormous 1950 robbery (see entry). Burke traveled to Boston carrying his submachine gun in a special case, and there he tracked down O'Keefe, shooting it out with his quarry. He managed to wound O'Keefe and leave him for dead. Burke calmly dismantled his submachine gun, placed it in its case, and walked through dozens of wailing police cars who responded to the gun battle, later boasting to friends: "Those coppers looked pretty stupid." O'Keefe, however, survived and told Boston detectives that the man they were looking for was Trigger Burke. He was later picked up and jailed but escaped.

FBI agents tracked him down a year later as he walked down a street in Charleston, S.C. Burke was extradited to New York where he was tried for killing Walsh. He complained bitterly that "it ain't fair, my reputation is being used against me." He was convicted and sentenced to death. While awaiting execution, Burke put together a large scrapbook containing 144 newspaper clippings about his sinister career, and he invited everyone on Death Row to read these but found little interest on the part of the other condemned prisoners. On the night before his death, Burke ate a huge steak dinner and smoked six cigars. This cold-hearted killer showed no emotion whatsoever when he walked into the execution chamber on Jan. 9, 1958, and sat down in the electric chair. His last request was that the warden preserve his scrapbook "for history's sake." See: **Brink's Robbery, 1950.**

REF.: *CBA;* Nash, *Bloodletters and Badmen.*

Burke, Fred (AKA: **Fred Brook, Cornbread Burchell, Frederick Dane, Killer Burke, Fred Kemp**), 1893-1940, U.S., rob.-org. crime-mur. Described by the federal government as the most dangerous man in America, Fred Burke proved to be quite timid

when simple country detectives awakened him from a deep sleep at his father-in-law's house in Milan, Mo., on Mar. 26, 1931. Fearful that rival Chicago mobsters had at last come to extract revenge for his part in the St. Valentine's Day Massacre, Burke asked the police officers if they would kindly show their badges.

The notorious triggerman and bank robber got his start with the Egan Rats, a St. Louis street gang, before being recruited by Al Capone to do away with Bugs Moran and his bothersome North Side mob in 1929. Between 1924 and 1931, Burke was accused of at least a dozen murders, two ransom kidnappings, and the theft of property worth nearly $1 million. Police departments from four different states posted rewards totaling $100,000 for his capture.

Though never formally charged with the murders of the seven Moran men in the Clark Street garage on Feb. 14, 1929, his role in this affair remains unquestioned. Calvin Goddard, a Chicago ballistics expert, testified that bullets extracted from the dead men were identical to ones found at Burke's home in St. Joseph, Mich. Police believed that the gun used during the infamous massacre may have also claimed the life of Frankie Uale, president of the Unione Siciliano, a Mafia front organization based in New York. Uale was gunned down in Brooklyn on July 1, 1928, by unidentified mobsters.

Fred "Killer" Burke, left, manacled, under arrest.

After shooting and killing patrolman Charles Skelly of St. Joseph, Mich., during a routine traffic-accident investigation, Burke went into hiding on Dec. 15, 1929. Using the alias Frederick Dane, Burke remained a fugitive from justice until he was captured at his in-laws' farmhouse in Missouri on Mar. 26, 1931. Speaking with Burke over the phone, Governor Henry Stewart Caulfield asked, "Where do you want to go? Chicago wants you. Michigan wants you."

Burke was extradited to Michigan under heavy guard. He pleaded guilty to the murder of Officer Skelly and was sentenced to life imprisonment by Marquette Circuit Court Judge Charles E. White on Apr. 27, 1931.

Killer Burke served nine years and three months at the state prison in Marquette. He died from what was described as a heart attack on July 10, 1940. See: **Capone, Alphonse; Moran, George; Yale, Frank; St. Valentine's Day Massacre.**

REF.: *CBA;* Edge, *Run The Cat Roads;* Kobler, *Capone;* Nash, *Bloodletters and Badmen;* Wellman, *A Dynasty of Western Outlaws.*

Burke, Harold P., 1895-1981, U.S., jur. Member of the judicial conference on administration of criminal law from 1958-69. He was appointed judge of the Western District of New York by President Franklin D. Roosevelt in 1937 REF.: *CBA.*

Burke, James (AKA: **Jimmy the Ger** 1931- , and **Werner, Louis**, 1933- , and **DeSimone, Thoma** 946-c.1978, U.S., rob.-mur. In the early morning hours of Dec 11, 1978, six masked men in a stolen van pulled up to the Lufthansa cargo hangar at John F. Kennedy International Airport in New York. They carried shotguns and pistols which they pointed menacingly at the Lufthansa employees who were ordered to deliver the "goods." The six men, who had been provided inside knowledge of the contents of the locked vault, left the premises with $5 million in untraceable cash and over $850,000 in pearls, gold, and jewelry.

The idea for the crime was the work of two Lufthansa freight handlers, Peter Gruenawald and Louis Werner. Gruenawald first suggested the robbery to Werner but was double-crossed by his friend who decided to deal independently with the actual robbers. Before being seized by the authorities, Werner pocketed an estimated $80,000, of which $10,000 went to Gruenawald to ensure his silence.

Lou Werner asked Martin Krugman, a well-known bookie from Nassau County, N.Y., to locate a professional who could pull the job off. Krugman, who worked as a beautician on the side, contacted Jimmy Burke, a member of the Paul Vario-Thomas Luchese organized-crime family which had masterminded a series of cargo thefts at the airport over a period of years. James Burke had a long criminal record, which included convictions for loan-sharking and fixing college basketball games involving Boston College. At the time of the robbery, he had just been released from a halfway house in Manhattan.

Witnesses described six or seven men that participated in the robbery, but Werner was the only person to be formally charged. His conviction resulted from testimony offered by Gruenawald, who was placed under the Federal Witness Protection Program.

The stolen cash and jewels were never recovered, and at least five persons were believed to have been executed by the mob for their indirect involvement in the heist including Thomas DeSimone, who the day after the robbery was released from the same halfway house Burke had been in. Richard Eaton was another associate of Burke who was silenced by the gang. After helping Burke launder the stolen money through various foreign banks, Eaton was killed and his body was dumped in a trailer truck where it was found on Feb. 18, 1980. Martin Krugman simply vanished, and 27-year-old Theresa Ferrara, part-owner of a Long Island beauty shop, was found dead near Toms River, N.J., in May 1979. Ferrara was believed to have been a girlfriend of Burke or one of his confederates.

At present, Jimmy (the Gent) Burke is serving a twenty-year sentence at a federal prison in Michigan for his part in the Boston College basketball scandal.

REF.: *CBA;* Pileggi, *Wiseguy.*

Burke, Lloyd Hudson, 1916-88, U.S., jur. Senior criminal trial deputy of Alameda County, Calif., from 1940-53, and U.S. attorney of the U.S. Justice Department from 1953-58. He was appointed judge of the district court of California in 1958 by President Dwight D. Eisenhower. REF.: *CBA.*

Burke, Thomas Henry, See: **Cavendish, Lord Frederick Charles.**

Burke, William, 1792-1829, and **Hare, William**, prom. 1820s, Scot., mur. The historically notorious William Burke and William Hare were the first body snatchers of important record who, when corpses were not available for sale to anatomists for dissection, turned to murder to replenish their dwindling supply of cadavers. They later argued that they were only providing important research material for the advancement of medical science, a point

stretched to the unbelievable. Yet in this medical dark age, the need to examine bodies to determine anatomical makeup was crucial. European anatomists, or those who studied the internal structure of the human body, found that established medical schools were neither equipped nor authorized to conduct such studies. These anatomists opened schools of their own and medical students flocked to their classes. The schools, however, were limited in bodies available for study. During this time, before the Anatomy Act of 1832, British law curtailed autopsies by stipulating that all corpses must receive Christian burial. Oc-

William Burke, left, and William Hare; body snatchers and killers.

casionally, the corpses of condemned felons were turned over to physicians for internal study, but these were limited in number. Doctors, particularly the successful anatomist Dr. Robert Knox of Edinburgh, had to rely upon body snatchers who ghoulishly roamed through unguarded graveyards in the murk of night, exhuming corpses and carting these gruesome burdens to medical schools where these nocturnal deliveries were received in secret. The most celebrated body snatchers of this era were Burke and Hare.

Burke was born in County Tyrone, Ireland, a farmer's son who received little or no education, going to work as a baker's apprentice while in his teens. He later worked as a weaver, then a cobbler, then briefly joined the British army but was released as unfit. A surly, broad-shouldered man, Burke left Ireland after repeated quarrels with his family. He went to Scotland and worked on the Union Canal, then took a room in the Beggar's Hotel in Edinburgh, a lowly, rambling boarding house for indigent Irish laborers. By that time, he had picked up a prostitute named Helen McDougal (or Nell Macdougal), and both began a clothing business of sorts, collecting discarded clothes and shoes, repairing and then reselling these shabby items. In 1826, Burke and McDougal moved to Log's boarding house in Tanner's Close, renting the basement apartment. It was here that Burke met William Hare, a lean, conniving fellow-boarder. Little of Hare's background is known. He had lived at Log's and when the owner died, he made the owner's widow, Maggie Laird, his common-law wife, and she assumed the role of boarding house proprietor.

Burke and Hare became drinking companions and would guzzle themselves into stupors while discussing get-rich-quick schemes that never materialized. Then, on Nov. 29, 1827, Hare entered Burke's quarters while Burke was repairing a shoe and told him that one of his boarders, an army pensioner named Old Donald, had died in his room, still owing £4 in rent. Hare whispered an idea to his friend Burke: Why not sell Old Donald's corpse to Dr. Knox's medical school and make a little money on a body now useless to the world? Such an act was, of course, against the law, which required that all deaths be reported to the authorities and bodies removed for Christian burial. Burke warmed quickly to the idea, and that night he and Hare carried the remains of Old

Donald to Dr. Knox who purchased the cadaver, no questions asked, for £7. To explain the absence of Old Donald, Burke and Hare built a coffin, weighted it with bags of bark, sealed it, and turned it over to officials who accepted this as the corpse of Old Donald and quickly buried the coffin. The porter at Dr. Knox's medical school informed Burke and Hare that good specimens for dissection might bring as much as £10 each and that these were in constant demand. They were invited to return often with such deliveries.

This transaction worked so smoothly that Burke and Hare resolved to continue selling bodies to Dr. Knox, except that some of the Log's boarders were reluctant to die. The body snatchers helped them along into eternity. The first of these was a boarder named Joe the Mumper who was dying of fever. Hare complained that such illnesses kept others from renting his rooms and the sick man was an inconvenience. Burke and Hare then smothered the man to death with a pillow, and his body was delivered to Knox's college in Surgeon's Square, bring £10. Burke and Hare, along with their common-law wives, then went full tilt into the murder and body-selling business. Beginning in February 1828, they waylaid street peddlers and prostitutes or got them drunk, then smothered them and sold the bodies. Such was the fate of Abigail Simpson, a hawker of salt and hearthstone, Mary Paterson, a young prostitute, Mary Haldane, an aging harlot, Haldane's half-witted daughter, and an English traveler who was suffering from jaundice. There would be between fifteen and thirty victims in all, some later claimed as many as fifty or more. In most instances, Burke and Hare took turns suffocating the victims, one holding down the feet while the other smothered the victim with a pillow in the Log's boarding house. On some occasions, Hare and Maggie Laird murdered the victims without Burke's help.

The murders were not confined to the rooms of the boarding house. Killings to obtain bodies were boldly committed in the streets of Edinburgh, especially by the cretinous and bestial Burke. He was returning to the boarding house one night with the body of an old derelict he had murdered, the body stuffed into a box carried on a cart and pulled by an ancient horse. An old Irish beggar woman made the mistake of stopping Burke to beg some money from him. He strangled her on the spot and then grabbed her grandson, a mute, and broke his back over his knee, stuffing these bodies into the box with the other corpse. The killers became obsessed with bodies and could not find victims fast enough to fill their blood-soaked trunk. One night, their broken-down cart horse refused to budge while they were en route to the medical school with a delivery. Burke and Hare had to hire a porter who used a large wheelbarrow to cart their trunk to the school where the murderers were paid £16 for two bodies. So incensed were they at their horse's refusal to move their cart that they returned to the spot where the beast still stood and cut its throat.

Dr. Knox's students began to identify the corpses brought to them for dissection. One student recognized a prostitute he had patronized but he remained silent. Knox evidently had his suspicions about Burke and Hare, but he said nothing, as long as the steady stream of bodies arrived at the door of his school. He became the most celebrated anatomist in the country and his school flourished. Meanwhile, Burke and Hare fell out, or, at least, their women took to such arguing that Maggie Laird proposed that they kill Helen McDougal and sell her corpse to Dr. Knox. Burke drew the line at this and moved out with his wife, going to live with one of McDougal's relatives at Gibbs Close. Here the Burkes actually competed with the Hares, both operating separate murder businesses and continuing to sell the bodies to Dr. Knox. Then Burke killed an idiot beggar boy known throughout Edinburgh as Daft Jamie, who was recognized by some of Dr. Knox's students. The boy's identity was pointed out to Dr. Knox, but he denied that the body was that of the beggar boy. Again, he preferred to close his eyes and stifle his suspicions as to the real activities of his suppliers, Burke and Hare.

Burke and Hare's lucrative body racket came to an end on Oct.

31, 1828. On the afternoon of that day, Burke was drinking in Rymer's pub when an old crone named Mary Docherty entered the pub and walked from table to table, begging. Burke sized her up and quickly concluded that her body would bring a considerable payment from Dr. Knox. He invited the woman to share some ale with him and the two got tipsy together. Then Burke invited Docherty to accompany him home to Gibbs Close where she would attend a "Halloween party". The woman accepted with alacrity and the pair went to Burke's boarding house where he ordered a young couple boarding there, James and Ann Gray, to leave the premises, saying a private party was to commence. Then Hare and his wife were invited, Burke and his wife having made up with their murderous friends. A drunken revel ensued with Burke dancing wildly with Docherty while she was periodically plied with heavy drink. (Because of this macabre revel, Burke was often called by writers a "dancing master.") In the middle of this raucous party, Burke suddenly pounced upon Docherty's bare feet with his hobnailed boots, grinning like a madman, and cut off her piercing screams of "murder!" (heard by the neighbors) by placing his paw-like hands about her throat and strangling her to death.

Docherty's naked body was then stuffed into the tea chest Burke used for his deliveries to Dr. Knox, and this was picked up by David Patterson, Dr. Knox's porter who gave Burke a disappointing £5 for the corpse. So accostumed was Dr. Knox of receiving bodies from Burke that he no longer waited for bodies to be delivered to his school but had his porter go to Burke for the corpses. Before this happened, however, James and Ann Gray, the momentarily evicted boarders at Burke's house, glimpsed Mrs. Docherty's legs protruding from the chest before it was quickly closed. Hare, realizing that the Grays had spotted the body, offered a great deal of money for their silence. James Gray, however, went to the police and reported the murder, along with the fact that Gray had seen Patterson collect the tea chest, hearing him state that he would be taking this grim cargo to Dr. Knox's school. Police raced to the school, barged through the back door and found the tea chest with Docherty's body in it. Burke was arrested quickly and taken to jail. Then Mrs. McDougal was captured, along with the Hares.

To save himself, William Hare turned state's evidence, detailing his many murders with William Burke, or as many as he could remember. Mrs. McDougal was charged with murder, as were the Hares. Burke's trial began on Dec. 24, 1828, but there was little to debate. He had already confessed his murders. Hare's vivid chronicle of the murders brought about a conviction for Burke but the jury felt there was insufficient evidence to convict Helen McDougal and returned the verdict of "Not Proven" against her, a unique Scottish verdict which signified that the accused was probably guilty but not enough proof was present to allow for conviction. Burke phlegmatically stood in the dock throughout his trial and said very little, except to grunt derision at his one-time partner Hare. When he heard Helen McDougal's verdict he snorted: "Nelly, you're out of the scape." The court then released William Hare and his wife. The long-nosed, tall Hare, who had not been tried but retained until Burke's trial ended, leaped from his seat in court, unable to restrain his joy at being set free; he danced a weird little jig. Burke was dragged away cursing in chains to await his execution.

While waiting for the hangman, Burke allowed artists to sketch him in his condemned cell but, ever the businessman, he charged them fees. He also complained bitterly about being cheated by Dr. Knox's porter, that many of the bodies he had turned over had been worth much more than what he had been paid. On the morning of Jan. 28, 1829, William Burke was led to a public scaffold in Edinburgh and, in a driving rain that did not thwart 25,000 people from attending, sent through the trapdoor. The huge crowd cheered his death and demanded that Hare, too, be hanged, but Hare had vanished from Edinburgh, as had Maggie Laird and Helen McDougal. Crowds hunted them for weeks but Helen McDougal was smuggled onto a ship and sailed for Australia where she reportedly died many years later. Maggie Laird was given police protection and she was escorted to a ship sailing for Ireland where she lived out her life under an assumed name. Hare fled to the Midlands where, under an assumed name, he labored in the lime pits. When his fellow workers learned who he was, one account has it, they blinded him with quicklime. He then went to London, a blind beggar last seen shaking a tin cup and begging outside the British Museum.

The hanging of William Burke in Edinburgh, 1829.

Dr. Robert Knox, who had paid for all the bodies and encouraged, willingly or not, the hard-working Burke and Hare to continue their murder spree, was in disgrace following Burke's conviction and execution. Dr. Knox's school closed and he left Edinburgh. One report had it that he became a showman with a traveling group of American Indians, but it is known that he first went to London and worked as an obstetrician and later as a general practicioner in Hackney, dying in 1862 with whatever dark memories that may have haunted him. The gloomy deeds of his servants, however, did serve one useful purpose. The acts of Burke and Hare, dubbed Resurrectionists or Resurrection Men, so appalled the country that widespread body snatching was condemned in Parliament, where liberal politicians successfully argued that the lack of legal bodies hindered the advancement of medicine and allowed beasts like Burke and Hare to flourish. Parliament passed the Anatomy Act in 1832 which permitted relatives and officials to turn over dead bodies to medical schools for dissection and study before burial. This legislation caused the gruesome business of body snatching to go into decline and eventually cease.

It was grim irony that the day following his execution, William Burke's body would follow the same route he had in life sent so many others. His corpse was taken to the medical school operated by Dr. Knox's brilliant rival, Dr. Alexander Monro. Here, before a large audience, Burke's short, thick corpse was dissected and studied, the pieces later preserved in jars and held up during anatomical lectures. His skeleton was later reassembled and placed in a glass case that can be seen to this day as a prized

exhibit at the Anatomical Museum of the University of Edinburgh. Beyond these skeletal remains, however, Burke and Hare, along with their medical mentor, Knox, would be remembered down through the annals of crime with a little ditty chanted by children for decades in the streets of Edinburgh:

> Burke's the murderer,
> And Hare's the thief,
> And Knox the boy
> Who buys the beef.

REF.: Altick, *Victorian Studies in Scarlet;* Atlay, *Famous Trials;* Ball, *The Sack-'Em Up Men;* Barzun, *Burke and Hare, The Resurrection Men;* Birmingham, *Murder Most Foul;* Bolitho, *Murder for Profit;* Brock, *A Casebook of Crime;* Brophy, *The Meaning of Murder;* Canning, *Fifty True Tales of Terror; CBA;* Cole, *Things for the Surgeon;* Dickson, *Murder by Numbers;* Dilnot, *The Real Detective;* Douglas, *Burke and Hare, The True Story;* Douthwaite, *Mass Murder;* Forster, *Studies in Black and Red;* Harrison, *Criminal Calendar II;* Hunt, *Dictionary of Rogues;* Macgregor, *The History of Burke and Hare;* Mencken, *By the Neck;* Nash, *Almanac of World Crime; Notable British Trials;* O'Donnell, *Should Women Hang?;* Parry, *Some Famous Medical Trials;* Rae, *Knox the Anatomist;* Roughead, *Burke and Hare;* ____, *Classic Crimes;* ____, *The Murderer's Companion;* Scott, *A Concise Encyclopedia of Crime and Criminals;* Sparrow, *Vintage Victorian Murder;* Turner, *The Inhumanists;* Wilson, *Encyclopedia of Murder;* (DRAMA) Bridie, *The Anatomist;* (FICTION) Stevenson, *The Body Snatcher;* (FILM) *The Body Snatcher,* 1945; *The Greed of William Hart,* 1948; *Mania* (GB: *Flesh and the Fiends;* AKA: *Psycho Killers, The Fiendish Ghouls*), 1959; *The Anatomist,* 1961; *Burke and Hare,* 1972; *The Doctor and the Devils,* 1985.

Burkitt, William (AKA: **The Iron Man**), 1886-1956, Brit., mansl. William Burkitt lived in Hull, Yorkshire, a town of heavy industry and grimy waterfront bars. These places were well known to Burkitt, a fisherman by trade, who committed his first murder in 1915 when he was twenty-nine.

His victim was Mary Jane Tyler, a married woman with whom he was having an affair. Burke killed her on Aug. 27, 1915, because she was jealous of his other women. At his trial in November, the jury found him Not Guilty of murder but convicted him on the lesser charge of manslaughter. He was sentenced to penal servitude for twelve years, but was released in 1924.

Burkitt took up with another married woman, 34-year-old Helen Spencer, whom he murdered with a kitchen knife in November 1925. After a failed suicide attempt, he was again tried for murder at the York Assizes, and again the jury convicted him of manslaughter. The other convicts at Dartmoor Prison called him the "Iron Man" for his amazing luck in escaping the hangman. In 1935 Burkitt was released for the second time. He soon met Emma Brooks, a 38-year-old woman who was separated from her husband. In February 1939, Burkitt came home from the sea and, in a fit of jealousy, murdered Brooks, who had taunted him with tales of her infidelity.

There was yet another failed suicide attempt, and another trial at the York Assizes, and for the third time the jury returned the same verdict: Guilty of manslaughter. Justice Cassels considered Burkitt's record before sentencing him to prison for life in May 1939. In 1954 he was released by order of the Home Secretary. He lived quietly thereafter, and died on Christmas Eve, 1956.

REF.: *CBA;* Jackson, *Occupied With Crime;* O'Donnell, *Cavalcade of Justice;* Shew, *A Second Companion to Murder.*

Burkley, Bluitt, 1914-34, and **Burkley, Thurman,** 1915-34, U.S., mur. The stillness of a warm summer night in Texas was punctured by sharp blasts of gunfire. The murder of a young couple was an ugly crime, made uglier by its racial overtones. When the farmers of Pleasant Mound, Tex., learned that the killers were two black men who tended crops nearby, the lobby of the tiny jail at Main and Houston Streets was filled to overcrowding. Deputy sheriffs milled through the crowd reminding people that matters were well in hand. It was Labor Day weekend, 1933. Sentiments against blacks ran deep in the South at this time, and the word "lynch" was now on everyone's lips.

Bluitt Burkley, nineteen, and his brother Thurman, eighteen, were arrested on Aug. 31, 1933, for the murder of Katheryn Prince, a 21-year-old woman, and her escort, 27-year-old Mace Carver. The pair were last seen alive as they walked home from the Oak Cliff Baptist Church. The Burkley brothers, approaching them from behind, fired into the back of their heads. Death was instantaneous for Prince. Carver was removed to Parkland Hospital in Dallas where he lingered until the next day.

The wheels of justice turned quickly. Within twenty-four hours, the two men were arrested by Deputy Sheriff Ted Hinton and brought to the home of William McCutcheon, where they were transferred under heavy guard to the Dallas city jail. Their signed confessions were taken by Captain E.V. Bunch and Lieutenant Will Fritz.

Before another day had passed, an indictment was returned by the grand jury charging the brothers with murder and assault. The case came before Judge Grover Adams of the Criminal District Court. Five months later, on Feb. 9, 1934, the Burkley brothers were executed. REF.: *CBA*.

Burleigh, Cornelius Alverson (AKA: **Con Burley**), c.1804-30, Can., mur. Had a phrenologist not shown interest in his skull after death, Cornelius Alverson Burleigh would no doubt have been completely forgotten. Executed for the murder of Constable Timothy Conklin Pomeroy on Aug. 19, 1830, in London, Ontario, "Con" Burleigh was a vagrant and drifter who allegedly killed Pomeroy after the officer pursued him for arrest on a theft charge. Held in a London jail, Burleigh might have avoided his date with the hangman had he escaped with seven other prisoners. But he believed the courts would establish his innocence if he remained behind to testify.

Burleigh was visited daily by the Reverend James Jackson—a circuit-riding Methodist preacher and cousin of President Andrew Jackson—in an effort to produce a confession. Found Guilty of murder, Burleigh was forced by Reverend Jackson to confess in his jail cell. The "Dying Confession of Cornelius Burleigh" was given wide play in the local press, but was actually paraphrased from a Methodist hymnal published in England in 1824. After the jailers had succeeded in hanging Burleigh—it took two tries—his skull was put on display by U.S. phrenologist Orson Squire Fowler, who explained to his audiences that the thickness of the cranium determined the character traits that led Burleigh to commit murder. One hundred and twenty years later in 1960, a portion of the skull was found encased in a black box in London. It is now on permanent display in a London, Ont., museum.

REF.: *CBA*; Miller, *Twenty Mortal Murders*.

Burley, Sir Simon, 1336-88, Brit., consp. Military leader and courtier to Richard II. He helped the king ascend to power in England, only to be impeached by Parliament and then beheaded. REF.: *CBA*.

Burmese Civil Riots, 1988, Burma, riot. Years of quiet desperation among the thirty-eight million Burmese who suffered under the brutal dictatorship of Ne Win finally erupted into a full-blown riot in August 1988. The people had risen up in protest against Sein Lwin, a military strong-man who replaced Ne Win when the aging despot passed away in early August. Sein Lwin was described as the "most hated man in Burma" for his oppressive tactics against Buddhist dissidents seeking a greater role in governmental affairs.

Unofficial accounts listed the death toll in excess of 1,000 during week-long rioting, as security forces clamped down on flag-waving protesters lining the streets of Sagaing and the capital city of Rangoon. Angry demonstrators asked passing motorists in Rangoon to give them gasoline so they could fashion Molotov cocktails to hurl at government troops. It was an ugly situation that threatened to escalate into a full civil war.

Since 1962, the one-time democratic republic had been subjected to the will of one man, the tyrannical Ne Win who bankrupted the economy and effectively gagged all forms of political expression. His Socialist Program Party was an unusual mixture of Buddhist thought and political isolationism. Mismanagement and fiscal waste reduced the Burmese people to a state of grinding poverty as annual per capita income dropped from $670 in 1960 to just $190 in 1987.

Sworn to uphold the policies of his predecessor, Sein Lwin announced his resignation after just seventeen days in office. In his place, General Kyaw Htin, former Burmese chief of staff and minister of defense was sworn in. The mobs in the streets were temporarily placated by this move, as they watched and waited to see if a new era of reform was about to begin. "Maybe the country has turned a corner," said one Western diplomat. "And that's a big maybe." REF.: *CBA*.

Burnes, Sir Alexander, 1805-41, Brit., mur. Renowned adventurer, author, and soldier in the Indian army, he was killed while residing in Kabul. REF.: *CBA*.

Burnet, Gilbert, 1643-1715, Brit., her. An anti-Catholic outlawed by King James II upon his accession to the throne. His unorthodox religious views resulted in condemnation by the lower house of convocation following publication of *Exposition of the Thirty-nine Articles* (1699). REF.: *CBA*.

Burnett, John, 1823-46, U.S., mur. John Burnett was born in Middleburgh, N.Y. He lived at his father's home until he was tried and convicted for murdering George Sornberger, on Mar. 24, 1846. Before he ran afoul of the law, Burnett had drifted through life working a variety of odd jobs when the mood suited him. He could barely read or write and, as he related to the court, his ear was "familiar with the sound of cursing and blasphemy."

While in the employ of a Mr. Almy, Burnett became involved in the Anti-rent movement, a grass-roots political protest against the semi-manorial system of land tenure that swept New York State over a nine-year period, 1839-48. The Antirenters were opposed to the payment of rent to the wealthy families that had been granted public lands during the original settlement of the colony in the seventeenth century.

Burnett was engaged in Almy's Anti-renter business when he arrived at the saloon of Solomon Pratt on Mar. 24, 1846. A stranger named Moses Wood entreated Burnett to buy a round of drinks for himself and his friend, George Sornberger.

When Sornberger was out of earshot, Wood suggested that Burnett help him with a joke. Sornberger needed to borrow money, and Burnett was to say he would be willing to lend it. Then when Sornberger took Burnett out to show him the land that would serve as collateral, Burnett would reveal that it was all a joke.

All went as planned, but the intoxicated Sornberger became angry at the ruse. "He said he knew better," Burnett said later, "knew that I could help him if I chose, and that I must do so. I told him again that he was mistaken, that I was poor and had no money to lend..."

When Sornberger became even more angry, Burnett threw him into the snow and, in an uncontrollable passion, stabbed him in the throat and chest with a dirk. He stripped off the dead man's clothing without searching the pockets, later finding a tobacco box, a pair of mittens, and a comforter, items used later to convict Burnett. Returning home after spending the night in Mr. Almy's saw mill, Johnny Burnett was torn by a guilty conscience. "I had laid awake all that night thinking of what I had done," he said. "I cannot believe that I am a murderer."

Arrested by the constable the next day, he confessed to the crime. During the trial, his defense counsel suggested that Burnett was insane from the ravages of liquor, and at the very worst he was guilty of manslaughter. There were no actual witnesses to the crime, only the confession—later recanted—and the small items found in Burnett's possession. "In the case of circumstantial evidence the facts are submitted to you as a jury, and you draw your inference and form your verdict from the circumstances adduced," Circuit Judge Amasa J. Parker instructed the jury. After deliberating less than an hour, a Guilty verdict was returned, and the judge sentenced the defendant to hang on July 14, 1846. The prisoner had only one request. "My father wants me to ask you to let him have my carcass after my death, that I may be decently buried," Burnett asked.

REF.: *CBA; The Confessions of John Burnett.*

Burnett, Melvin, 1955- , and **Martin, Billy**, 1959- , U.S., mur. Carl Stohn had just finished working as an extra during the filming of the movie *Thief,* when he was overtaken by four youths near his home on Chicago's Gold Coast. The 58-year-old theatrical executive who had previously worked as a producer and director at the suburban Drury Lane Theatre and Pheasant Run Playhouse, taken a bus back to his car at 1:45 a.m., Aug. 21, 1980 when he was heldup at gunpoint. Stohn grabbed one of the assailants, later identified as 20-year-old Billy Martin, by the lapels in a vain attempt to thwart the robbery. When Stohn refused to release Martin, Melvin Burnett shot and killed him. Afterwards, he made off with his cash and jewelry.

Burnett and Martin were arrested on Nov. 15, when Clay Steen and Wayne Griffin of the Chicago Police Department Gang Crimes Unit received a tip from a suspect in custody. The two killers were named as members of a South Side street gang known as the Disciples. Carl Stohn had been randomly selected, police learned. "This is just awful," said Michael Mann, director of *Thief.* "You should be able to get off a bus and get in your car and drive away without being killed." After the day's filming, the extras were driven back to their homes.

Appearing before Judge Earl Strayhorn in a bench trial that began at the Criminal Court in December 1981, Burnett claimed that he was nervous and that the gun went off accidentally. Judge Strayhorn convicted both men of conspiracy, attempted armed robbery, and murder. Melvin Burnett received a sentence of twenty years' imprisonment, followed by ninety years' imprisonment, and accomplice Billy Martin received a seventy-five year sentence. REF.: *CBA.*

Burnett, William R(iley). (AKA: **John Monahan**), 1899-1982, U.S., writer. William R. Burnett, a Chicago newsman, shot to fame with his first novel, *Little Caesar* (1929), based on Chicago's Gloriana gang, its protagonist strongly drawn from Al Capone. Burnett, who also wrote under the pseudonym of John Monahan, drew heavily from real-life criminals, as can be seen in *High Sierra* (1940), a novel loosely based on one of the last independent gangsters, the role model for which is obviously bank robber John Dillinger. Burnett, who worked in Hollywood as a top screenwriter, specialized in *film noir* scripts, and produced the classic crime caper novel (and film scenario) in *The Asphalt Jungle* (1949). REF.: *CBA.*

Burnham, Josiah, d.1806, U.S., mur. Imprisoned in the Haverhill, N.H., jail for bad debts, Josiah Burnham was confined in the same crude cell with two other deadbeats, Joseph Starkweather and Russell Freeman. Both Freeman and Starkweather continually insulted Burnham about his stupidity and eating habits. Somehow Burnham obtained a scythe and made a knife from this instrument, attacking and killing his cellmates. He later claimed that he slashed his fellow inmates to death in self-defense, a plea strongly and eloquently maintained by his defense counsel, the indefatigable Daniel Webster. But the evidence against the accused was overwhelming and he was convicted and sentenced to hang. Webster was able to obtain one reprieve just before Burnham was to hang on July 15, 1806. The condemned man, however, was ordered to the gallows on Aug. 12. Burnham suffered great agony at his execution in that he was forced to stand for more than an hour in the hot sun before 10,000 spectators while the Reverend David Sutherland delivered a fire-and-brimstone sermon on the fires below awaiting men like Burnham who committed evil acts.

REF.: *An Analysis or Outline of the Life and Character of Josiah Burnham; CBA; Pearson, Instigation of the Devil.*

Burning Car Murder, See: **Rouse, Alfred Arthur.**

Burning Court, The, 1937, a novel by John Dickson Carr. This work presents a fictional, contemporary portrait of poisoner Marie de Brinvilliers (Fr., 1676). See: **Brinvilliers, Marie de.** REF.: *CBA.*

Burns, Alfred, and **Devlin, Edward Francis**, prom. 1951, Brit., mur. Alfred Burns and Edward Devlin cut open a kitchen window pane and entered the home of Beatrice Rimmer of Cranborne Road, Liverpool, the night of Aug. 20, 1951. The two house burglars then battered the 54-year-old widow to death.

When they were arrested two months later and charged with murder, Burns told police that they were breaking into Messrs Sunblinds Limited on Great Jackson Street, Manchester, at the time of the widow's death. There had been a robbery committed that night in Manchester, but Devlin and Burns were both convicted of murdering Rimmer even though it could not be positively proved that bloodstains found on their clothing matched those of the victim.

Based on the testimony of 17-year-old Marie Milne, who was acquainted with the suspects, Burns and Devlin were sentenced to die by Justice Finnemore that same year.

REF.: *CBA; Wilson, Encyclopedia of Murder.*

Burns, Anthony, 1834-62, U.S., burg. In 1854, he was identified as a runaway slave following his arrest for burglary. The Fugitive Slave Law was challenged by angry mobs protesting his forced return to Virginia. Troops were called up to quell the disturbance. He was eventually sent back, but he was bought out of slavery and went on to study at Oberlin College. REF.: *CBA.*

Burns, Ellen Bree, 1923- , U.S., jur. Member of Commission to Study Parole Evaluation Techniques and Rehabilitation of Correctional Institutional Inmates from 1974-75. She was appointed judge of the District Court of Connecticut in 1978 by President Jimmy Carter. REF.: *CBA.*

Burns, James Milton, 1924- , U.S., jur. Member of Oregon Criminal Law Revision Commission from 1967-72, and served on the Board of Directors of Criminal Justice Research Associates Inc. from 1967-present. He was appointed judge of the District Court of Oregon by President Richard M. Nixon in 1972. Co-authored the *Sentencing Handbook,* published by the National Judicial Committee (1978). REF.: *CBA.*

Burns, John, prom. 1894, U.S., rob. In February 1894, a pickpocket named John Burns was lucky to escape with his life after an enraged mob of pedestrians chased him down Dearborn Street in Chicago, after the young man snatched the purse of Mrs. George D. Potter. The thief was overtaken by Detective Clifton Rodman Wooldridge and was safely secured behind bars at the Harrison Street lockup. For stealing seven dollars in cash, Burns was sentenced to sixty days in jail by Judge Payne on May 16, 1894.

REF.: *CBA; Wooldridge, Hands Up!.*

Burns, Louis Henry, 1878-1928, U.S., jur. U.S. attorney in New Orleans, La., from 1921-25. He was appointed judge of the Eastern District of Louisiana by President Warren Harding in 1925. REF.: *CBA.*

Burns, Owen McIntosh, 1892-1952, U.S., jur. U.S. attorney serving the Western District of Pennsylvania from 1947-49. He was appointed federal judge of the court of the Western District in 1949 by President Harry Truman. REF.: *CBA.*

Burns, Robert Elliott, 1890-1955, U.S., burg.-pris. esc. Robert E. Burns was America's modern Jean Valjean, a quiet, intelligent man who, in order to live, committed a minor crime, the only one he ever committed, and was sent to the living hell of a Georgia chain gang. Burns, a successful accountant in New York, enlisted the day after WWI was declared in 1917 and served with distinction in the medical detachment of the 14th Railway Engineers, seeing action in Flanders, at Chateau Thierry, Argonne, and St. Mihiel. Upon his return, he found it difficult to obtain a job. He drifted about the country looking for work and, while on the bum and starving in Georgia, got involved in the robbery of an Atlanta grocery store. Burns, who arrived in that city a few days before, penniless, barefoot, starving, after riding the rails from New York, went to a Salvation Army shelter where he met two men who told him that they could get him a job. He followed them to the store where one of them pulled a gun and held up the proprietor. When Burns told the others he wanted no part of the robbery and began to walk away, one of them pointed the revolver at him and told him that he was part of the robbery and would be shot unless he left with the other two thieves. The robbers took all of $5.80.

Burns was caught and sentenced in March 1922 to six to ten years and sent to the chain gang in Georgia, where he underwent unbearable living conditions, beatings, and torture. Burns resolved to escape at any price and, three months later, in June 1922, he made his escape while working on railroad repairs outside the camp compound. Burns persuaded a huge black prisoner to bring a sledgehammer down on his leg irons and break them. He then dove into a nearby swamp and got to a road where he crawled beneath a truck and rode to the state line. Burns made his way to Chicago and there got himself one job after another, working as an accountant for a lumber company, then as a real estate agent. He was able to save a considerable amount of money and, in 1924, began *The Greater Chicago Magazine,* largely devoted to real estate in Chicago.

Robert Elliott Burns while serving time on the Georgia chain gang.

By 1930, the fugitive occupied a suite of offices in a modern skyscraper, made $20,000 a year as a publisher, and was one of the leaders of the business community. But Burns' personal life was miserable. When he had arrived in Chicago in 1922, he rented a room from a Mexican divorcée, Emilia del Pino Pacheo, who later went through Burns' belongings and found a letter which talked about his being a fugitive from the chain gang. The woman, madly in love with Burns, threatened to turn him in unless he married her. He did. The marriage was an unhappy one, and, in 1929, Burns met and fell in love with cultured, young Lillian Salo. He and this woman went to Mrs. Burns and begged her for a divorce. She agreed, providing that she was given substantial alimony. Burns agreed and the papers were drawn up and signed. A short time later, Georgia officials appeared in Chicago and insisted that Burns be extradited to Georgia.

The case was widely publicized in national newspapers and editorials throughout the country encouraged the State of Georgia to give Burns a full pardon, stating that he had proven himself to be a hardworking, substantial citizen for seven years. Vivien Stanley, a member of the Georgia Prison Commission, arrived in Chicago and told Burns and his lawyers that if he waived extradition and voluntarily returned to Georgia, a full pardon would be forthcoming. (It appeared that the governor of Illinois would not approve of extradition after having received scores of letters from such distinguished citizens as Jane Addams and Carl Sandburg.) Burns, on the advice of his lawyers, accompanied Stanley back to Georgia.

In August 1929, in a small room at the state capital in Atlanta, the police commission gave Burns' lawyers a few minutes to explain the circumstances but cut off all arguments after a minute or so. The commission was made up of tight-lipped, uncompromising judges named Rainey, Johns, and Stanley. They said nothing but seemed impatient at the impassioned pleadings by Burns' attorneys and then motioned to a man named Stephens, who was asst. solicitor in Fulton County, Ga. Stephens, a short man with thick glasses and a permanent scowl, stood up and

snorted derisively at Burns: "This man is a convict. He belongs in a chain gang. He is a habitual criminal. He has violated the laws of Georgia and owes Georgia a debt. We intend to collect that debt and we expect to keep this thief in the chain gang until it is collected!" Further, Stephens held up a letter he had received from Mrs. Burns in Chicago, one in which she vilified the hapless Burns, proving that the old line was true about hell having no greater fury than a woman scorned.

Burns was summarily returned to the nightmare hell of the chain gang. The state of Georgia had reneged on its promise of a pardon. In fact, state officials were incensed at the newspapers and civic leaders of *other* states telling them what they should do with their convicted felons. Burns, Georgia authorities vowed, would serve every day of his sentence and more years added because of his 1922 escape. While his case was appealed and more understanding heads in Georgia reconsidered his case, Burns was subjected to whippings and torture. He decided that there was no hope unless he could once more escape. This Burns did in 1930, a year after he had voluntarily returned to Georgia, the only man ever to escape a chain gang twice. He somehow worked his way out of his shackles and, while working with a road repair gang, dashed into some deep woods and kept running, outdistancing bloodhounds and searchers, eventually making his way to New Jersey where he lived under an assumed name and operated an antique shop.

Robert Burns as a celebrated fugitive from the Georgia chain gang.

After writing a series of articles about the horrors of the chain gang for New York magazines, Burns put together his now classic book *I am a Fugitive from a Georgia Chain Gang.* The publication was a sensation and the book was a best-seller which was purchased by Warner Brothers Studios. The great actor Paul Muni starred in the film in 1932. During production, Burns secretly traveled to Hollywood and acted as an advisor to director Mervyn LeRoy, but all manner of precautions were taken to keep his identity a secret. Burns lived in constant fear that he would be recognized and taken back to Georgia. He was moved from one hotel room to another during his several-month stay in Hollywood, and even lived on the studio backlot for awhile, using an alias and assuming various roles, such as that of a stagehand or a technician. Finally, his nerves shattered, Burns returned to New Jersey. The film was an enormous success when released, but *I am a Fugitive from a Chain Gang* (the name of Georgia was removed from the title) was banned in Georgia. Although the film made Burns a

Burns, right, winning his pardon from Georgia's Governor Arnall, left, in 1945.

national *cause célèbre*, the state of Georgia, or its most hard-headed officials, resolved to recapture Burns at any cost. Georgia authorities felt that the film had injured the image and reputation of its state and that Burns was the cause of an undeserved stigma.

When learning that Burns was a resident of New Jersey, outraged Georgia officials demanded he be extradited back to Georgia. Hearings were held in the Trenton State House before New Jersey governor Moore, and these proved to be the most dramatic of Burns' sensational case. Clarence Darrow defended Burns at these hearings and presented petitions containing hundreds of thousands of names asking that Burns not be turned over to Georgia, a state that had already broken its sovereign word. The horrors of the Georgia penal system was exposed at these hearings and, for the first time, the nation learned of "the sweat box," a standup structure which barely allowed a prisoner to turn and one where the convict had to remain upright with little fresh air, while the heat of the day made the inside of the box unbearable. Several prisoners, it was claimed, had died in the box. Also introduced was the "barrel punishment," a small barrel with iron staves over which prisoners were tied and left to roast in the sun after being whipped. All manner of torture weapons were shown. The Georgia penal system was shown to be a bestial, dark-age organization designed to sadistically brutalize its prisoners with no thought of reform or rehabilitation. Will P. Cox, a member of the Society of Penal Information, exhibited photos of cages into which dozens of miserable convicts had been placed, cages that had been designed for half their numbers. Governor Moore denied Georgia's writ and refused to turn over Burns.

Georgia was dogged and continued its efforts to regain the fugitive. The police chief in the town where Burns lived received many telegrams, all worded the same: "Arrest escaped prisoner Robert Burns and return him to Georgia." The chief tore up the telegrams week after week. At one time, several Georgia lawmen actually tried to kidnap Burns but he managed to elude them. In 1941, Georgia's Eugene Talmadge, who had recently

been elected to the governorship on a campaign that included the return of Burns, again tried to have the fugitive brought back to the chain gang. And again New Jersey refused to turn Burns over, Governor Edison giving Talmadge a firm "no." Burns, by then remarried and the father of two children, holding a good job as a tax appraiser, seemed to weary of the hunt. "My God," he exclaimed to newsmen. "How long will they keep this up? Am I never to have any peace?"

In 1945, Georgia governor Ellis Arnall wiped out the horrid chain gang system in his state, calling it "an abomination." He also wanted to clear the record books dealing with Robert Elliott Burns. He "invited" Burns to return to Georgia, promising that if he did so, he would commute the fugitive's sentence. Burns, with no little apprehension, went to Georgia and this time, the state kept its word. Governor Arnall, an enlightened politician, commuted Burns' sentence to the time he had already served and he was a free man. He was escorted to a Pullman car and rode back to New Jersey in the luxury of his own stateroom. He noted that the last time he left Georgia, it was while riding in the back of a dump truck. The great manhunt was over, and Burns would no longer have to leap from his bed at the slightest sound in the middle of the night. He lived for another ten years, dying in a New Jersey veteran's hospital on June 5, 1955. See: **Darrow, Clarence**.

REF.: Burns, *I am a Fugitive from a Georgia Chain Gang; CBA;* Horan, *The Desperate Years;* Nash, *Among the Missing;* (FILM) *I Am A Fugitive From A Chain Gang,* 1932.

Burns, William John, 1861-1932, U.S., det. Born in Baltimore on Oct. 19, 1861, William J. Burns grew up in Columbus, Ohio, where his father had a tailor shop. His father later became police commissioner and Burns soon became interested in tracking down criminals. He began his flamboyant, spectacular career in 1885 at age twenty-four by exposing the "tally sheet" forgeries involved with Ohio election results in Columbus and Cincinnati, proving that these sheets had been altered to manipulate the outcome of elections. He obtained confessions and several persons were sent to prison as a result of his investigation. In 1890, Burns was appointed to the U.S. Secret Service and was responsible for tracking down numerous counterfeiting rings.

Burns left the Secret Service and established his own detective organization, The William J. Burns International Detective Agency, and became involved in many sensational cases which brought him into conflict with establishment forces. He unearthed land frauds in Washington, Oregon, and California in 1903. In 1906, his investigations into the corrupt San Francisco political machine led to the imprisonment of boss Abe Ruef. His brilliant investigation into the labor bombing of the Los Angeles *Times* building in 1910 caused Samuel Gompers, head of the American Federation of Labor, to accuse Burns of framing labor leaders and faking evidence. Burns, however, disproved the contentions of Gompers and others and revealed the true culprits as being the McNamara brothers, labor leaders in Los Angeles. Moreover, the detective almost brought about the ruination of the brilliant criminal lawyer, Clarence Darrow, who stood accused of jury tampering in that case and was forced to defend himself, narrowly avoiding conviction. Burns' discoveries in this case caused the New York *Times* to call him "the only detective of genius whom the country has produced."

When police corruption prevented the true facts of the 1912 slaying of New York gambler Herman Rosenthal from surfacing, Burns was brought in to gather important evidence that helped send ruthless NYPD Lieutenant Charles Becker to the electric chair. In 1913, Burns was hired by the family of Leo Frank to investigate the killing of Mary Phagan, a teenage girl who had been raped and murdered in Frank's pencil factory in Atlanta, Ga., a crime for which Frank stood accused. The Atlanta police at that time, as well as most officials in the state, took orders from populist leader Tom Watson, who had been informed that the real molester and killer of Mary Phagan was not Frank but his black janitor, Jim Conley. It was Conley, an alcoholic, who signed a statement saying that his employer was a pervert who had trysted with many of his female employees and that he had witnessed Frank's murderous attack on the helpless Mary Phagan. When boss Tom Watson was told that Frank was undoubtedly innocent and that Conley had done the deed, he reportedly said: "We can hang a nigger any time but when do we get a chance to string up a northern Jew?" Watson decreed Frank's death, as Burns later discovered, when he began working for the Frank family.

The great American private detective, William J. Burns.

Burns showed a great deal of courage in his private investigation of this case, threatened by local law enforcement officials and by a powerful group called the Knights of Mary Phagan, who were bent on lynching Leo Frank, this group later forming the nucleus of the reorganized Ku Klux Klan. On one occasion, when Burns emerged from a courthouse where he had been doing research, he was almost lynched by a group of Watson supporters. In the weeks that followed, he was shot at and threatened with death almost every day. His discoveries were ignored by the police who protected Conley. Following Frank's railroad-like conviction and sentence of death, it was Burns who went to the governor of Georgia, John Slaton, who studied the evidence the detective put before him—evidence that Burns could not convince the court to introduce during Frank's trial. Slaton concluded that Frank was innocent and he commuted his death sentence, an act he knew would be political suicide. Frank was nevertheless dragged from his prison and lynched a short time later.

Though Burns was lauded for his work on the McNamara and Frank cases, he was later accused of representing only Eastern establishment interests, but this was not true since he often took important cases involving nonentities and thought of himself as a champion of the "little people." In this regard, he was highly critical of the Pinkerton Detective Agency, his most energetic rival, accusing this firm of taking only "safe" cases and working exclusively for the interests of big business. In 1921, Burns was appointed chief of the Bureau of Investigation in the U.S. Department of Justice. Though he aggressively pursued transgressions by the Ku Klux Klan, Burns was later accused of closing his eyes to the rampant political corruption practiced by the Harding administration, notably the Teapot Dome scandals, where government lands were sold off to millionaire landgrabbers. Bribes, secret deals, and wholesale looting of government funds flourished under Burns' directorship of the Bureau of Investigation, and when Burns resigned in 1924, he left office under a cloud of criticism. His replacement was a young lawyer, J. Edgar Hoover,

who revamped the Bureau, later renamed the Federal Bureau of Investigation, and, to Hoover's considerable credit, cleansed it of political hacks and put it above corruptive influence.

In Burns' defense, it can be said that he did try to launch investigations into the activities of certain figures in the Harding Administration, but he was stymied at every turn by his own boss, U.S. Attorney General Harry Daugherty, who was part of the corrupt regime. He was also surrounded by agents in his own Bureau, such as the ubiquitous Gaston Bullock Means, who had been placed there by Daugherty to confuse and confound any investigations which Burns might order. In 1927, Burns was brought to trial, accused of having his operatives shadow the jury hearing the conspiracy trial of Albert Fall and Harry Sinclair. He was convicted of complicity in contempt of court and sentenced to fifteen days in jail. The U.S. Supreme Court, however, found him innocent of committing an overt act and he was freed. In the last five years of his life, Burns continued to direct his far-flung detective agency, which had offices in almost every major American city. He lived in semi-retirement in Sarasota, Fla., where he wrote detective stories based on his experiences. He suffered a fatal heart attack on Apr. 14, 1932. Burns, despite his failure with the Bureau of Investigation, stands today as one of America's early leading private detectives, a courageous and inventive criminologist. See: **Federal Bureau of Investigation; Frank, Leo; Hoover, J. Edgar; McNamara Brothers; Means, Gaston Bullock; Ruef, Abraham; Teapot Dome Scandal.**

REF.: Caesar, *Incredible Detective; CBA;* Churchill, *A Pictorial History of American Crime;* Logan, *Against the Evidence;* Lowenthal, *The Federal Bureau of Investigation;* Messick, *Secret File;* _____ and Goldblatt, *The Mobs and the Mafia;* Nash, *Almanac of World Crime;* _____, *Among the Missing;* _____, *Citizen Hoover;* _____, *Hustlers and Con Men;* Powers, *Secrecy and Power;* Reppetto, *The Blue Parade;* Toledano, *J. Edgar Hoover;* Ungar, *FBI;* Whitehead, *The FBI Story;* Wicker, *Investigating the FBI.*

Burnworth, Edward (AKA: Young Frazier), d.1726, rob.-mur. The son of a humble London painter, Edward Burnworth was apprenticed to a buckle-maker at a young age. It was not long before he began associating with a gang of loose and idle men who frequented the Ring at Moorfields, where carnival sideshow men and thimble-riggers congregated. Burnworth adopted the name of Young Frazier, after a skilled conman he greatly admired.

Young Frazier began his thieving career as a pickpocket, but soon took on bigger prey. He organized a gang of housebreakers and highwaymen who terrorized London and the outlying countryside. Attempts to apprehend Young Frazier often ended disastrously for representatives of the Crown. At a public drinking house near the Old Bailey, he humiliated Quilt Arnold, a thief-catcher in the employ of Jonathan Wild, who had been given the task of arresting Burnworth. Burnworth forced Arnold to his knees and made him drink a bitter mixture of brandy and gunpowder after promising never to bother Young Frazier again.

A second thief-catcher named Thomas Ball was not nearly so fortunate. Outside the Music House on Bankside, Burnworth pounced on Ball, who entertained foolish notions of collecting the prize money for bringing in the robber. Ball pleaded for his life but was given no quarter. He was shot and killed by Young Frazier.

In the end, Burnworth was betrayed by a woman who owned an alehouse near Holborn. Arrested while eating his supper, he was carted off to Newgate where he was forced to balance a 424 lb. stone on his chest. The jailer told Young Frazier that the weight would be removed if he freely admitted his guilt. After an hour of this excruciating torture, Burnworth agreed to appear before the magistrate and plead. He was tried, condemned, and hanged in 1726. See: **Wild, Jonathan.**

REF.: *CBA;* Pringle, *Stand and Deliver.*

Burr, Aaron, 1756-1836, Case of, U.S., duel.-treas. Aaron Burr, a controversial political figure from the first years of America's was a soldier, statesman, vice president, and duelist during his long career in public service. Burr was born in Newark,

N.J., and educated at what is now Princeton University. During the Revolutionary War, he rose to the rank of lieutenant colonel, serving until 1779. Three years later, he became a member of the bar, setting the stage for the turbulent events that were soon to follow.

Burr became identified with the Democratic-Republican cause, which stood in opposition to the Federalists, whose principal spokesman was Alexander Hamilton, the nation's first secretary of the treasury. In 1800, Burr ran for the presidency on the Democrat-Republican ticket. The tally of electoral votes ended in a tie between Burr and his opponent, Thomas Jefferson. Under the prevailing rules, the election was to be decided in the House of Representatives. The House chose Jefferson, who in turn selected Burr as his vice president.

By 1804, there was strong personal animosity between Aaron Burr and Alexander Hamilton. The Federalist leader had blocked Burr's bid for the New York governorship that year, and opposed his selection as Jefferson's running mate. An increasingly heated series of letters flew back and forth. When Hamilton described Burr as a "dangerous man and one who ought not to be trusted with the reins of government," the vice-president demanded retraction. Hamilton, vain and proud, refused. The matter had to be settled on the field of honor.

It was agreed that a duel of pistols was to be fought on July 11, 1804, at Weehawken, N.J., across the Hudson River from New York City. The location had become a favored place for dueling. It was widely believed that Alexander Hamilton never fired a shot. When this theory was disproven Burr's enemies charged that Hamilton had been ruthlessly shot down in cold blood after he had discharged his pistol in the air.

Historians now believe that Hamilton fired his shot a split second after Burr, just as the bullet struck his chest. Hamilton fell to the ground mortally wounded. He died thirty-one hours later. Hamilton became a political martyr, and Burr a social pariah. Murder charges were filed against the vice president in both New York and New Jersey.

Burr wanted to serve out his term, but public opinion was against him. Fearing a prison term, Burr decided to withdraw from public life. He slipped out of Washington and looked westward, toward the land recently ceded to the U.S. as the Louisiana Purchase. The triumphs of the Emperor Napoleon in Europe suggested to Burr that he too could become an emperor. The emperor of the West. Burr believed that with the connivance of the British, whose territorial ambitions west of the Mississippi River were thwarted by Jefferson's land purchase, he could "effect a separation of the western part of the United States." He recruited two other adventurers who shared his lofty vision: Senator Jonathan Dayton of New Jersey, and a rich immigrant to the Ohio Valley named Harman Blennerhassett, who put up $50,000 in cash to fund the expedition.

Burr sold the scheme to British Minister Anthony Merry, who had nothing but contempt for Jefferson, and was anxious to further his own career. On Aug. 6, 1804, he urged the Foreign Office to consider Mr. Burr's proposition. The madcap scheme swelled to continental proportions. Burr would lead an expedition into Spanish Mexico. The natives would welcome him as a "liberator," and proclaim him their emperor. His daughter Theodosia would become "empress apparent," and little "Gamp," Burr's grandson, would someday assume his place on the throne.

Aaron Burr delivered his last speech before Congress on Mar. 2, 1805. It was a brilliant oration, and there was much sympathy for him among his colleagues. He walked out of the hallowed halls for the last time. Burr headed west, informing Anthony Merry in Philadelphia that the French inhabitants of Louisiana were ready to revolt against the U.S. He urged the British to blockade the mouth of the Mississippi. In June, Burr met his old friend, Brigadier General James Wilkinson, who commanded the small army of the United States. Burr's efforts on Wilkinson's behalf led to his appointment as governor of the Territory of Louisiana. But Wilkinson lacked discretion.

On Dec. 1, 1805, a few days after Burr had dined with President Jefferson, an urgent dispatch arrived at the White House warning of traitors in the administration.

> "You admit him to your table and you held a long and private conference with him a few days ago after dinner at the very moment he is meditating the overthrow of our administration...Yes, Sir, his aberrations through the western states had no other object...Watch his connections with Mr. Merry and you will find a British pensioner and agent."

Wilkinson's loose talk around Washington had alerted the government to the growing dangers of a conspiracy. In early October 1806, Wilkinson had second thoughts. The new British foreign minister, Charles James Fox, was pro-American. As his first act, he recalled Merry to England. Wilkinson realized that support for an insurrection was fading. The Democratic movement in the country made Jefferson one of the most popular politicians of his age, and General Wilkinson decided to save his neck and inform on Burr and Dayton. Wilkinson believed that he would emerge as a national hero. Meanwhile, Burr had put his scheme into motion. Blennerhassett mortgaged what was left of his holdings to raise cash, bankrupting his family.

On Nov. 27, President Jefferson wrote to Governor Edward Tiffin of Ohio authorizing him to seize Burr's boats and supplies. The Ohio legislature drafted a bill empowering the militia to do so. The militia seized the island from which Harman Blennerhassett and his wife conducted their operations. "Blanny" escaped by pack boat in the middle of the night.

Aaron Burr firing a fatal shot in his duel with Alexander Hamilton, 1804.

On Jan. 10, 1807, Burr learned that Wilkinson had betrayed him. Judge Peter Bruin, an old friend from Natchez, Miss., showed Burr a copy of the local gazette containing the president's call for his arrest. Burr tried to bargain with acting-Governor Cowles Mead of Mississippi but he was unsuccessful. Burr and his few remaining supporters then tried to flee to Spanish dominions, but were arrested by the governor's men at Carson's Ferry. Burr was returned to Richmond, where he faced Chief Justice John Marshall for the first time on Mar. 30.

After considerable pre-trial wrangling, the deliberations finally began on Aug. 3. To convict Burr, the government had to establish his intention to wage war against the U.S. Chief Justice Marshall ruled that the treason must be proved according to the mandates of the Constitution, and because an act of Congress, by two witnesses. Marshall further ruled that "corroborative and confirmatory testimony" was inadmissible. This opinion effectively threw out the prosecution's evidence of Burr's actions up and down the Mississippi River. On Sept. 1, 1807, Burr was acquitted after only twenty-five minutes of deliberation. "We of the jury say that Aaron Burr is not proved to be guilty under this indictment by any evidence submitted to us," proclaimed the foreman, Colonel Edward Carrington. Burr was outraged by the wording of the statement. It indicated to him that the jurors were not convinced of his innocence. Chief Justice Marshall resolved the matter by suggesting that the words "Not Guilty" be inserted into the final record.

Burr was a man without a country. To escape his many creditors and political enemies, he sailed for Europe under an alias, and remained abroad for nearly four years. However, he fared no better in Europe than he had in Washington. He tried, and failed, to interest the British and French governments in hiring him as a privateer. Burr's questionable activities in England, and the large debt he had piled up in such a short time resulted in his deportation to the continent. In Sweden, he began a coded journal for the benefit of his daughter and grandson, the only two people he cared about. The journal contained a rambling summary of his life and a detailed account of his sexual profligacies in Europe.

In 1812, Burr crept back into the U.S. to resume his law practice. A year later, his beloved daughter, Theodosia Burr Alston, was lost at sea when the schooner *Patriot* went down near Cape Hatteras on its way from Charleston to New York. Many maintain that the *Patriot* was not wrecked in a storm, but boarded by pirates, and that Theodosia was forced to walk the plank to her death. See: **Marshall, John.**

REF.: *CBA;* Hurwood, *Society and the Assassin;* Parton, *The Life and Times of Aaron Burr;* Schachner, *Aaron Burr;* Smith, *Mysteries of the Missing.*

Burroughs, George, c.1650-92, U.S., (wrong. convict.) witchcraft. Wrongly accused of practicing witchcraft in Salem, Mass., he was found guilty of the charge and executed. He was the only clergyman to lose his life during the prolonged period of hysteria. See: **Salem Witchcraft Trials.** REF.: *CBA.*

Burroughs, Stephen, prom. 1780-1800, U.S., count. Stephen Burroughs was the son of a respected Presbyterian minister from Hanover, N.H. He was an intelligent but conniving lad, who was fond of racy novels and the exploits of criminals and highwaymen of yesteryear.

When he was fourteen, Burroughs enlisted as a foot-soldier in the Continental Army but was quickly discharged when he refused to cooperate with his superiors. Burroughs enrolled in Dartmouth College to study ancient languages, but after two years his money ran out and he decided to find his fortune outside the classroom.

For the next few years he wandered the roads, preaching gospel and teaching school, until he returned penniless to his home in New Hampshire. During his last months on the road, Stephen Burroughs became interested in alchemy. He experimented with copper, hoping to turn the substance into valuable silver, but he failed miserably.

Turning to counterfeiting, Burroughs attempted to pass a coin minted by Glazier Wheeler at an apothecary shop in Massachusetts. The entire transaction involved only one dollar, but the governor of the state was so incensed by the crime that he offered a large reward for Burroughs' apprehension.

Captured by the same man he attempted to rob, Burroughs was sent to the Northampton jail, which he described in his writings as "an eternity in miniature, consisting of one continued scene of gloomy horrors." Attempting to escape, he was quickly recaptured and sent to an impregnable fortress outside Boston, known as Castle Island. In a small musty cell, Burroughs worked relentlessly to tunnel through a stone wall, using only a rusty nail. After two months of sixteen hours a day labor, he finally broke through. Seizing a guard as hostage, Burroughs and the other escaped inmates set out in a small boat for the mainland.

A posse found them the next day hiding in a hayloft, and the men were returned to prison. Burroughs was severely beaten. He served three full years before being released. Reformed at last, the former counterfeiter lived out the rest of his days as a schoolteacher universally loved by his students.

REF.: *CBA;* Hamilton, *Men of the Underworld.*

Burrow, James Buchanan, See: **Burrow, Reuben Houston.**

Burrow (or Burrows), Reuben Houston (Rube, AKA: **Charles Davis**), 1854-89, U.S., west. outl. Born in Lamar County, Ala., on Dec. 11, 1854, Reuben H. Burrow owned a farm in Arkansas and tilled the soil. In 1872, he moved to Stephenville, Texas, where he maintained a ranch for fourteen years. He married a Wise County girl in 1876 and the union produced two children. He was considered to be an upstanding citizen, a cracker-barrel philosopher, and a member in good standing of the local Masonic Lodge. Burrow's first wife died in 1880 and he was left to take care of two small children. He remarried in 1884 and bought a small farm near Alexander, Texas, but his fortunes diminished when his crops failed. Some time in 1886, Burrow, who had earned a reputation as a crack marksman in local shooting meets, decided to take up train robbing. He collected a band of hard cases, including his brother Jim Burrow, W.L. and Leonard Brock, two outlaw brothers, and Nep Thornton.

Southern train robbers, Rueben and Jim Burrow.

With his brother Jim and Thornton at this side, Rube Burrow rode north to Bellevue in Clay County where, on Dec. 1, 1886, he and the others held up the Fort Worth and Denver train. While Thornton jumped into the engine's cab to hold the engineer and fireman at bay with two six-guns, Rube and Jim Burrow went through the passenger cars, robbing the startled travelers. The outlaws decided not to rob the mail car, believing this to be heavily guarded, but when they entered the last passenger car, the Burrow brothers discovered a squad of black soldiers sleeping in their seats. They disarmed these troopers and took the weapons, along with considerable ammunition. This robbery netted Burrow and his men only a few hundred dollars. The bandit chief resolved to rob the mail car of the next train they held up. With the Brock brothers and Thornton, the Burrow brothers stopped a Texas and Pacific train near Gordon, in Palo Pinto County, Texas, on Jan. 23, 1887. This time the outlaws forced the engineer and fireman to go to the mail car and order the messenger inside to open the door. When the messenger refused, Burrow fired several shots, saying that he had just killed the engineer and fireman, although he fired these shots into the air, and that he would start shooting the passengers if the messenger did not open the door. The door was opened and the bandits made off with more than $2,000.

Burrow, his brother Jim, the Brock brothers, and Thornton stopped another Texas and Pacific train near Benbrook in Tarrant County in June 1887, and the gang removed more than $3,000 from the mailcar. In September 1887, an exact duplication of this robbery occurred with the same band stopping the same train with the same crew in the same spot and getting almost the same amount of cash. On Dec. 9, 1887, Burrow and his gang stopped a train of the St. Louis, Arkansas and Texas R.R. near Genoa Station, Ark., breaking into the mailcar and forcing at gunpoint the messenger for the Southern Express Company to open the safe. They grabbed $3,500 in cash and fled just as the local sheriff arrived at the scene with a large posse, responding to an urgent call from a station-master up the line who sent out the alarm when he noted that the train was long overdue. The band continued to stop trains with such regularity that railroad detectives and lawmen came to believe that Burrow was being supplied information on cash shipments by someone working for the railroads, although this was never proven.

The Burrow gang next stopped a Fort Worth and Denver train in January 1888 and took more than $3,000 from the safe and passengers. A few weeks later the band held up a Texas and Pacific train, taking away $2,000. This time one of the outlaws made a serious mistake, leaving behind a new black raincoat. This was traced to Leonard Brock, who was arrested in his Texas home and confessed. He was given twenty years in prison but committed suicide on Nov. 10, 1890, by leaping to his death from a fourth-floor prison tier. The Burrow gang had, by early 1888, become the most infamous train robbers since Jesse James, and were sought by hundreds of lawmen throughout the South and Southwest. Scores of Pinkerton detectives searched for them at the request of their clients, the railroads. The Pinkertons barely missed capturing Jim Burrow at his ancestral Alabama home in Lamar County in January 1888, firing at him as he fled out the back door of the rickety farmhouse.

Posters describing the outlaws and showing them in drawings, were distributed to all conductors on trains. On Jan. 23, 1888, Jim and Rube Burrow were recognized by a conductor when they got aboard a Louisville and Nashville train. He wired ahead to Montgomery, Ala., and when the train came into the station, police poured into the cars, only to find that the brothers had already left their car. They were on a Montgomery street when newspaperman Neil Bray recognized them from wanted posters and called police. As he was doing so, Jim Burrow ordered him to stop. Bray kept yelling for police, who were coming down the block from the train station. When Bray continued to call for the police, Jim Burrow shot him and he and Rube escaped down an alley.

Another conductor spotted the brothers on a train as it was pulling into Nashville, Tenn., some weeks later and again police were called. This time lawmen trapped the outlaws in a passenger car, but Rube Burrow managed to shoot his way to freedom. Jim Burrow was taken into custody and bragged about the gang's exploits. William Pinkerton visited the outlaw in his cell in the Texarkana Jail and the pacing outlaw snarled to the detective: "My name is Jim Burrow, and the other man on the train is my brother Rube, and if you give us two pistols apiece we are not afraid of any two men living!" James Buchanan Burrow never got hold of another pistol. He died in his prison cell of consumption on Oct. 5, 1888. Rube Burrow was now alone and the subject of one of the most widespread manhunts in American history. Every detail known of his life and habits related in wanted posters. Americans knew that this fair-haired, six-foot-tall outlaw wore a mustache and sometimes a goatee, that he had a "lounging gait and carried his hands in his pockets in a leisurely way," that he did not smoke or chew tobacco or gamble, and that he drank only on rare occasions. He was an adept player of the game of "seven-up", and also a fascinating storyteller, "relating stories of snake, dog, and catfights."

It was also known that Reuben Houston Burrow was a cold-blooded killer. On Dec. 15, 1888, Burrow and two other men robbed an Illinois Central Train at Duck Hill, Miss. A passenger, Chester Hughes, protested the taking of his wallet and Rube Burrow shot him dead in his seat. In June 1889, an Alabama postmaster refused to give a package addressed to Burrow to one of the gang leader's relatives. The relative had been sent to retrieve the package, but the postmaster stated that unless Burrow himself arrived to sign for the package he would not release it. Burrow then rode into town, called the postmaster into the street and shot him dead in front of his horrified wife. He then tipped his hat and rode leisurely out of town. The package contained

a false beard which Burrow intended to use in his next robbery.

Burrow, like Jesse James in Clay County, Mo., was protected in his home area of Lamar County, Ala., by scores of relatives and friends. He returned constantly to his broken-down farm where he knew he would be safe since his friends would notifiy him whenever lawmen entered the wilderness area. Moreover, he had constructed a secret room in the cabin, three feet by nine, where he slept. This room was not found until years after Rube Burrow's death. Here the outlaw had dug out firing slits in the thick log walls and made pine slab ports which he could open from the inside and through which he could fire weapons, if need be.

On Sept. 29, 1889, Burrow and a new recruit, Joe Jackson, stopped a Mobile and Ohio train near Buckatunna, Ala., fleeing with $11,000. Many train robberies were then occurring in Alabama, Louisiana, Arkansas, Oklahoma, and Texas, and most of these were attributed to the infamous Rube Burrow, but some of these train holdups were committed by another wild desperado, Eugene Bunch, later killed in Louisiana. Many men were mistaken for Burrow, including one of his own cousins, who was shot and killed in Marshall County, Ala., on Nov. 17, 1889, by A.D. Scott, who attempted to collect the considerable reward on Rube Burrow's head. The man he killed, however, stated with his dying breath: "My name is Rube Smith." Rewards for Burrow totaled $7,500, a fortune for that era and and the Pinkerton Detective Agency in Chicago was flooded with "tips" from thousands of people in the South and Southwest, reporting the whereabouts of the elusive bandit. "It appears," moaned William Pinkerton, "that Rube Burrow had a thousand twins." After Joe Jackson was captured and sent to prison, Rube Burrow continued robbing trains alone. Fifty miles north of Mobile, Ala., in mid-1890, Burrow held up a Louisville and Nashville train, taking more than $4,000 from the Southern Express Company's safe in the mail car. It was his last train robbery.

On Oct. 7, 1890, Rube Burrow entered the small town of Linden, Ala., going into a store operated by C. Carter. He asked to look at some rifles on display and as he was examining the weapons, Carter, who fancied himself a detective, went into the back room and checked some Pinkerton wanted posters, identifying his customer from one of them as the infamous Reuben Houston Burrow. He came out of the back room holding a rifle on the outlaw and marched him into a storeroom where Burrow was locked up. Then Carter went to the train depot to wire the Pinkertons in Chicago that he had captured the notorious outlaw. While Carter was waiting for a reply at the train station, Burrow escaped from the storeroom and armed himself.

Instead of fleeing, the desperado was so humiliated at being captured by a mere clerk that he went looking for Carter, vowing to kill him. He spotted the shopkeeper at the depot and opened fire, striking Carter's arm. Carter drew his own six-gun and began blasting away, one shot hitting Burrow and tearing open the outlaw's stomach. Burrow, clutching his stomach and almost bent in half, backed down the street, firing as he went, while Carter, his arm wound bleeding profusely, staggered after him, also firing. Both men emptied their guns and then collapsed. Burrow died in the street. Carter recovered and was given the reward money, but not until Pinkerton agents arrived in Marengo, the county seat, and thoroughly examined and photographed the body of the big outlaw as it lay in its coffin. Then the body was put aboard a Southern Express car and taken to Burrow's relatives in Lamar County.

Thousands lined the route of this train in hopes of getting a look at the remains of the famous outlaw. When the train stopped in Birmingham, more than 1,000 persons climbed in and out of the express car to glance at the body in its open coffin. When the train reached the depot at Sulligent Station in Lamar County, Burrow's mother and father were on the platform. Detectives threw open the door of the express car and then the body, bruised and battered, was literally thrown from the car so that it spilled from the open coffin at the feet of the elderly Burrows, a horrible act by lawmen who obviously could not control their hatred even after their nemesis was dead. Moreover, the body bore horrible scars and bruises that Burrow had not received in his battle with Carter. It was easily concluded that the lawmen aboard the train had mutilated the corpse before delivering it so viciously at Sulligent Station. See: **Brock, Leonard Calvert; Bunch, Eugene; James, Jesse; Pinkerton Detective Agency.**

REF.: Agee, *Rube Burrow, King of the Outlaws and His Band of Train Robbers*; American Guide Series, *Mississippi, A Guide to the Magnolia State*; Barnum, *Rube Burrow*; Bartholomew, *The Biographical Album of Western Gunfighters*; Botkin and Harlow, *A Treasury of Railroad Folklore*; Breihan, *Badmen of Frontier Days*; ____, *Outlaws of the Old West*; Carmer, *Stars Fell on Alabama*; CBA; *Complete Official History of Rube Burrows*, (Anon.); Cushing, *The Story of Our Post Office*; Hawkeye, *Rube Burrows*; Horan, *The Pinkertons*; ____, and Swiggert, *The Pinkerton Story*; ____, and Sann, *Pictorial History of the Wild West*; Nash, *Bloodletters and Badmen*; Ray, *The Alabama Wolf*; ____, *Rube Burrow, King of Outlaws and Train Robbers*; Rennert, *Western Outlaws; Rube Burrows' Raids*; Scott, *Such Outlaws as Jesse James*; Stout, *Rube Burrows*.

Burrows, Albert Edward, 1861-1923, Brit., mur. In 1918, Albert Burrows, a 57-year-old farmer from Glossop, Derbyshire, began seeing a pretty young woman named Hannah Calladine. The 28-year-old mother of two bore him an illegitimate child.

Determined to make things right, the aging lothario married Calladine without bothering to divorce his wife. He received a six-month prison sentence for bigamy and was required to pay Hannah Calladine seven shillings a week. Balking at the payment, he was sent to prison in November 1919, for defaulting on a court order. Meanwhile Calladine moved into his house in Glossop, and the first Mrs. Burrows angrily walked out. The offended woman filed a maintenance suit against her husband. As Burrows languished in jail, he realized that he was hopelessly obligated to two women regardless of which one he chose to live with.

Recovering his wits and his freedom, Burrows resolved to do something about his problem. On Jan. 11, 1920, he took his new wife and her bastard son Albert Edward to Symondley Moor where he murdered them both. He tossed the bodies down a 105-foot air shaft into an abandoned coal mine where they remained undetected for nearly three years. To avoid any slip-up, he added a third victim the next day, Hannah Calladine's 3-year-old daughter.

On Mar. 4, 1923, a small boy named Thomas Wood disappeared from his Glossop home. Burrows became a suspect when several townspeople reported having seen him with the 4-year-old. Under steady questioning by the police, he admitted to sexually molesting the boy and dropping him down the mine shaft. A search of the area uncovered the remains of young Thomas as well as Hannah Calladine and her children.

Brought before the Derby Assizes, Burrows was pronounced Guilty by a jury that deliberated for only eleven minutes. He was hanged at Nottingham on Aug. 8, 1923.

REF.: Butler, *Murderers' England*; CBA; Humphreys, *Seven Murderers*; Shew, *A Second Companion to Murder*; Wilson, *Encyclopedia of Murder*.

Burrows, Erskine Durrant (AKA: Buck), and **Tacklyn, Larry Winfield**, prom. 1973, Ber., mur. A frantic call to Scotland Yard in London brought detectives Bill Wright and Basil Haddrell racing to Bermuda in September 1972, to investigate the mysterious shooting death of colonial police commissioner George Duckett at his suburban home.

It was the first of many politically motivated assassinations on the island that soon had the local police baffled. Duckett had been killed by a bullet from a .22-caliber revolver fired from his backyard at close range. On Mar. 10, 1973, Sir Richard Sharples, royal governor and commander in chief of Bermuda, was shot with Captain Hugh Sayers of the Welsh Guards on the terrace of the Government House by two unidentified black men.

On Apr. 6, before any viable leads could be established, two shopkeepers named Victor Rego and Mark Doe on Victoria Street, Hamilton, were killed execution style, which was apparent by the prone position of the bodies.

There were now five victims and no new clues to these

puzzling, yet seemingly related crimes. The colonial government posted a reward of $3 million for the apprehension of the killers. Eyewitness discriptions of the shopkeepers' murder led police to Larry Tacklyn. His accomplice was Erskine Burrows, who came to the attention of the police after he robbed the Bank of Bermuda on Sept. 25, 1973.

Burrows remained a fugitive for nearly a month. He was finally ambushed and captured on Oct. 18, after being knocked off his motorbike under cover of darkness by Detective John Donald of the Bermuda police. Guns belonging to the pair were found cached at various locations around the island. With the two bandits in custody, nervous residents came forward to supply evidence against them.

Tacklyn and Burrows were career criminals whose motive was robbery. They killed Sir Richard, Captain Sayers, and the police commissioner in sympathy with the aims of the Black Power movement which sought autonomy from the Crown. Erskine Burrows was convicted of killing George Duckett. Tacklyn admitted to murdering the shopowners and was found Guilty on two counts. Both men were hanged later that year.

REF.: CBA; Tullett, *Strictly Murder*.

Burrows, James Buchanan, See: **Burrow, Reuben Houston.**

Burrows, Warren Booth, 1877-1952, U.S., jur. New London County State's Attorney from 1906-16, prosecuting attorney in New London County, Conn., from 1917-27, and states attorney general from 1931-35. He was appointed judge of the district court of Connecticut in 1928 by President Calvin Coolidge. REF.: CBA.

Burrus, Sextus Afranius, d.62 A.D., Roman., (unsolv.) mur. Helped Nero ascend to the throne following the death of Claudius in 54 A.D. He served as the trusted adviser to Nero, but died under mysterious circumstances. He was allegedly poisoned. REF.: CBA.

Burt, Sir Cyril Lodowic, 1883-1971, Brit., psychologist-writer. Published works included *The Young Delinquent* (1925) and *The Subnormal Mind* (1935). He was best known for his work in test standardization, but some of his statistical measurements were eventually proven to be false. REF.: CBA.

Burton, Clara, See: **Buswell, Harriet.**

Burton, Harold Hitz, 1888-1964, U.S., jur. Mayor of Cleveland, Ohio, from 1932-35 and U.S. senator from 1941-45. He served as a member of the Truman Committee investigating fraudulent war claims against the government. He was appointed associate justice of the Supreme Court in 1945 replacing Owen Roberts. He voted with the majority in *Dennis vs. the United States* (1951), which upheld the conviction of eleven Communist party leaders in the U.S. REF.: CBA.

Burton, Lee A., 1913- , U.S., kid.-rape. Nobody, not even his wife, suspected that Lee Burton led a double life. By day he worked as an aircraft metal worker in Los Angeles, Calif., supporting his wife and young daughter. By night he led a grotesque life of fear and rape.

Fifty women who had recently been victims of sexual assaults were taken to a police station where they were asked to identify Burton. Eighteen pointed him out as the man who held a blade to their necks.

It was inconceivable to Burton's young wife that her husband could be responsible for numerous rapes in Alhambra, Pasadena, and Los Angeles. But in a tearful confession given to police on Apr. 1, 1943, Lee Burton revealed that he often cruised the streets of Los Angeles in search of women. "I knew what I did was wrong," he told police detectives Roy F. Radcliffe and Ellis Bowers, "I want to get all this cleared up."

Burton was arrested at a drive-in restaurant near Flower and Figueroa streets by Officer G.C. Moblitt, who was dining there at the time. He responded to the piercing screams of 22-year-old Eileen Thompson, never dreaming that the man he grabbed was responsible for twenty-two rape cases.

Police psychiatrist Dr. Paul De River examined the defendant but concluded that he was otherwise normal. In his book *The Sexual Criminal*, Dr. De River discussed the Burton case and its ramifications at length.

Satisfied that the evidence would sustain a conviction, the district attorney filed a complaint against Burton for kidnapping and rape. He was sentenced to prison for a period of five to 225 years. On Aug. 26, 1976, the California Department of Corrections discharged Lee Burton. He was sixty-three years old. REF.: *CBA*.

Burton, Theodore Elijah, 1851-1929, U.S., lawyer. Member of Congress 1889-1915. REF.: *CBA*.

Burton, Walter William, 1884-1913, Brit., mur. In the little town of Gussage St. Michael, there lived a 29-year-old man named Walter Burton who was employed as a rabbit catcher at the Manor Farm. He lived above the local post office with his wife who taught school and cared for their only child. His wife was quite a bit older than Burton, and he no longer found her interesting. So he gadded about town with various women and created quite a scandal.

In October 1912, Burton made the acquaintance of Winifred Mary Mitchell, a cook at the farm. She had a sophisticated beauty but was innocent in her ways. Walter Burton spent the next two months trying to seduce her. He promised her many things, including a new life in Canada. By March 1913, he had won her over, but when he suspected she was pregnant, he quickly lost his enthusiasm for the girl.

Promising to elope with her on the 29th, Burton made plans for her early death instead. He borrowed a gun to "kill a cat," and then lured Mitchell to an isolated spot near Sovel Plantation where he shot her. The body was not discovered until May 2, when the shallow grave was opened. Fragments of torn letters written by Burton were found at the Manor Farm. These hastily scrawled notes were enough to implicate him in the murder. Tried before Justice Ridley, Walter Burton was condemned to death at Dorchester Prison. He was the last man to be hanged there.

REF.: Butler, *Murderers' England*; *CBA*; Shew, *A Companion to Murder*.

Burts, Matthew (Matt), prom. 1899, U.S., west. lawman-outl. Matthew Burts was a deputy sheriff in Pearce, Ariz., in charge of prisoners, but he was really in collusion with the gang led by sometime-lawman, sometime-outlaw Burt Alvord. He reportedly participated in several train robberies with Alvord and others and allowed one of Alvord's men, Billy Stiles, to escape prison. For this and other crimes, Burts himself was given a long term in Yuma Prison. Following his release, Burts went to California, where he had a small ranch. He was allegedly killed in a gunfight as late as November 1925, but other western historians claim that he was killed about 1908 in a Wyoming gunfight.

Outlaw Matt Burts.

REF.: *CBA*; Haley, *Jeff Milton, A Good Man with a Gun*; Hunter and Rose, *The Album of Gunfighters*; Walters, *Tombstone's Yesterdays*; Way, *Frontier Arizona*.

Burundi Africa Massacre, prom. 1988, Burundi, geno. A tragedy of monstrous proportions took shape in the south-central African nation of Burundi when an estimated five thousand people were murdered in August 1988. The majority of the victims were Hutus, sworn enemies of the Tusis, who dominate both the government and the military, though they account for only 15 percent of the country's population.

Refugees fleeing into neighboring Rwanda explained that Tusi troops from the capital city were sent into the countryside to suppress a revolt by Hutu dissidents which had begun three weeks earlier. The soldiers began arresting politically active members of the Hutu community, and then systematically exterminating the people, using both machine guns and machetes. Major Pierre Buyoya, president of Burundi, imposed a dusk-to-dawn curfew and promised more government reprisals unless the Hutus cease their agitation. REF.: *CBA*.

Bury, William Henry, 1860-89, Scot., mur. One of the many suspects to emerge during the Jack the Ripper investigation was William Bury, who was hanged at Dundee Prison, Scotland, in 1889, for murdering his wife. Because he lived in the Whitechapel district at the time the Ripper was terrorizing London, and because he was trained as a butcher, the police were anxious to extract a confession out of him before he swung from the gallows.

The hangman, whose name was also Berry, was sent to interview the butcher shortly before the appointed hour of execution. "I suppose you think you are clever to hang me, but you are not going to get anything out of me," Bury said. The London police deduced that the wife-killer was covering up other crimes. It was far-fetched to think that William Bury was the notorious East End Ripper, but in those dark days of 1889, the police were almost willing to believe anything. See: **Jack the Ripper**.

REF.: Atholl, *The Reluctant Hangman*; *CBA*.

Bury St. Edmunds Witches, 1662, Brit., witchcraft. In 1662, Sir Matthew Hale, who was later appointed Chief Justice of England, presided over a landmark witchcraft case in Bury St. Edmunds, Suffolk, that established legal precedents later used in Salem, Mass.

The case involved two elderly widows named Rose Cullender and Amy Duny who had allegedly cast a spell over seven young children in the village. One of the children had died, supposedly at the hands of the witches. Their conviction was almost a foregone conclusion based on readily accepted but unsupported spectral evidence and the accusations of children. In the courtroom, the Bury St. Edmunds youngsters threw fits and exhibited wild behavior. Reports of the behavior were used by Cotton Mather, an American colonial leader, in his book *Wonders of the Invisible World* (1693). The children of Salem later conducted themselves in much the same way, suggesting that they may have been "coached" by Mather or, at the very least, were influenced by his writings on the subject.

Residents of Bury St. Edmunds corroborated the testimony of the children by recalling peculiar incidents, seemingly unrelated to the case at hand. Sir Matthew Hale accepted at face value all of the evidence brought before him. He sentenced the two women to hang after the jury returned a verdict of Guilty on all thirteen indictments presented by the prosecution. Four days later Duny and Cullender were executed to everyone's pleasure.

Perhaps a more liberal decision from Justice Hale might have staved off the Salem persecutions thirty years later. As it stood, the Bury St. Edmunds ruling stoked the flames of witchcraft hysteria for years to come. In *A Trial of Witches* (1682), Cotton Mather wrote: "In conclusion, the judge and all the court were fully satisfied with the verdict." He later added: "It was a trial much considered by the judges of New England." See: **Salem Witchcraft Trials; Mather, Cotton**.

REF.: *CBA*; Hutchinson, *An Historical Essay Concerning Witchcraft*; Kittredge, *Witchcraft in Old and New England*; Notestein, *History of Witchcraft in England from 1558 to 1718*; Robbins, *The Encyclopedia of Witchcraft and Demonology*; Summers, *The Geography of Witchcraft*.

Busacca, Thomas F., 1926- , U.S., mansl. Florence Busacca, forty-nine, was a voice teacher and former opera singer who lived with her husband Thomas in a spacious home in Baldwin, Long Island until her disappearance on Aug. 29, 1976.

According to Thomas Busacca, an unemployed photographer, his wife had become dissatisfied with married life after repeated quarrels and constant bickering. Returning home in the family car on Aug. 29, Busacca said that he found his wife in front of the garage in the arms of another man.

After chasing the unidentified man away, he beat Florence senseless and placed her unconscious body in the trunk of the family car. Busacca drove forty miles to Holbrook, where he propped his wife against a fence. She was still alive, he later assured the police, but they were unable to locate her.

Before a pretrial hearing commenced in Nassau County, an inmate who shared a cell with Busacca told authorities that the photographer had confided to him that he had dismembered Florence's body and tossed it into the Great South Bay. Assistant District Attorney Barry Grennan drew up a manslaughter indictment, even though investigators were unable to locate the remains.

Defense attorney Marvin Zevin protested this action on the part of the district attorney. "Everything is based on statements made by others," he said. "She could have gone off to Rome and is singing at La Scala." The trial began in the courtroom of Judge John Lockman and lasted three weeks. Defense witness Robert Berg recalled having lunch with Mrs. Busacca three to four weeks after Florence was reported missing.

The prosecution was unable to discredit Berg's testimony under direct cross-examination. Nevertheless, the jury found the defendant Guilty on Mar. 24, 1977. Judge Lockman sentenced Busacca to the maximum sentence of twenty-five years, which he immediately began serving at Dannemora State Prison. On Nov. 23, 1980, a forensic dentist identified skeletal remains found near Hampton Bay Beach, N.Y., as those of Florence Busacca. She had not gone to Rome or anywhere else, just to her grave. *CBA.*

Buscetta, Tommasso, prom. 1988, U.S., org. crime. Twenty-five years after Joseph Valachi spilled the secrets of the inner workings of the Cosa Nostra to a Congressional subcommittee, another Mafia foot-soldier came forward to paint a new picture of the so-called "men of honor."

Testifying before the Senate Permanent Subcommittee on Investigations, Apr. 11, 1988, Tommasso Buscetta said that drugs had changed the complexion of the modern Mafia since Valachi's time. "Along with the drugs has come more money but also more greed, more violence, and less honor," he said. "Gone are the men of honor whose word you believed in."

Buscetta turned informer after refusing to engage in drug running and fleeing to Brazil, and after the Mafia extracted revenge on ten of his relatives including two sons and a brother who were slain. Testifying in Italian, behind a screen, the former "soldier" identified and updated the structural leadership of the Cosa Nostra before Chairman Sam Nunn (D., Ga.) and a panel of U.S. Congressmen. Since 1963, several key members of the mob have moved up to positions of prominence in the hierarchy. Joseph Aiuppa, and Joseph Ferriola were listed as the leaders of the Chicago family. Both men had been low-ranking soldiers when Valachi prepared the first organizational chart.

"If the question is whether we have eradicated the Cosa Nostra, the answer is no," commented William Sessions, FBI Director. He pointed out that in 1986 alone, illicit income from the Mafia's combined activities returned an estimated $100 billion to its coffers. See: **Valachi, Joseph; Aiuppa, Joseph.**

REF.: Alexander, *The Pizza Connection;* Blumenthal, *Last Days of the Sicilians;* CBA; Servadio, *Mafioso.*

Buse, William A., d.1858, U.S., mur. William Buse was a murderous thug who had killed several men in the past before he shot and killed Thomas M'Keever in Jacinto, Miss. M'Keever made the mistake of accusing Buse of stealing a keg of whiskey from him and was promptly shot through the head by him. Buse was quickly convicted and hanged at Jacinto on Nov. 19, 1858.

REF.: CBA; *The Life, Confession and Adventures of William A. Buse.*

Busembaum, Hermann (Busenbaum), 1600-68, Ger., libel. Authored the controversial *Medulla Theologiae Moralis* (1650) which was publicly burned in 1657 for its scandalous sections dealing with regicide. REF.: *CBA.*

Bush, Edwin Albert, 1940-61, Brit., mur. Edwin Bush, a Pakistani, was brought up in London. On Mar. 3, 1961, he committed a brutal murder in a small antique shop just off Charing Cross Road. His victim was Elsie Batten, the shop assistant, who allegedly made a racist remark while Bush was negotiating the price of a dress sword that he wanted to buy.

Bush seized a dagger, stabbed the saleswoman in the neck, and fled with the sword.

Bush later appeared at a gunsmith's store across the way from Louis Meier's antique shop. He offered to sell the sword for £10, but the owner's son told him to come back later. He left the sword behind and never returned for it. By this time, however, the police were on his trail. Using a new technique in criminal identification called Identi-Kit, they developed an accurate likeness of Bush which was published in the newspapers and flashed across British TV screens within a day. The Identi-Kit System was first developed by Sheriff Hugh MacDonald of Los Angeles in 1959. Using interchangeable transparencies created from the drawing of one facial feature, police artists could quickly sketch an accurate likeness even as they spoke with eyewitnesses.

British detectives used Identi-Kit for the first time to investigate the Batten murder. When Bush was arrested by police he admitted that there was a strong resemblance. "Yes," he said, "I saw the photo in the papers. It did look a bit like me." At his trial he said he tried to sell the sword for £10 to get enough money to buy an engagement ring for his fiancée. A jury at the Old Bailey found him Guilty of murder. Bush was executed at the Pentonville Prison on July 6, 1961.

REF.: *CBA;* Furneaux, *Famous Criminal Cases #7;* Jackson, *Occupied With Crime;* Tullett, *Strictly Murder.*

Bush, Robert, d.1828, U.S., suic.-mur. Robert Bush, a resident of Westfield, Mass., murdered his wife Sally in 1828 while under the influence of opium, one of the first recorded drug-related killings in the U.S. Bush, who mixed opium with his tobacco, was in a semi-stupor when his wife ordered him to dinner. He fired a shotgun in her direction, killing her. Bush was convicted and sentenced to be hanged on Nov. 14, 1828, but he cheated the executioner by overdosing himself with opium smuggled to him in his jail cell by friends two days earlier.

REF.: *CBA; The Trial of Robert Bush.*

Busic, Zvonko, 1946- , and **Busic, Julienne,** 1949- , and **Matanic, Peter,** 1945- , and **Pesut, Frane,** 1951- , and **Vlasic, Mark,** 1947- , U.S., asslt.-terror.-kid. A TWA jet bound from New York to Chicago was hijacked to Montreal on Sept. 10, 1976, by a terrorist group calling itself the "Fighters For Free Croatia." The small armed band was seeking political autonomy for separatists who were persecuted by the Communist government of Yugoslav president Josip Broz Tito. The five terrorists were led by Zvonko Busic, a Croatian nationalist who ordered the pilot to relay a message to the Federal Aviation Administration. "We decided to undertake this particular action for many reasons. ...Our goal was to present an accurate picture of the brutal oppression taking place in Yugoslavia." Controlled by the hijackers, the plane refueled and continued to Paris, stopping in Newfoundland, Iceland, and London.

Citing the American Revolution, the United Nations, and the Atlantic Charter as inspirations, Busic typed a three-page explanation and a list of demands which were placed in a locker at Grand Central Station underneath the Bowery Savings Bank on 42nd Street. Inside locker 5713, the police found a bomb sealed in a pressure cooker. When Officer Brian Murray, a skilled electrician and demolitions expert, attempted to defuse the device, it exploded in his face, killing him instantly. The five terrorists were indicted in New York on Sept. 29, 1976.

Zvonko Busic assumed full responsibility for the group's actions, claiming that he had not intended to injure anyone. The defense attempted to portray Busic as mentally ill at the time of the killing, but Judge John Bartels disallowed testimony to this effect, stating that while insanity is a legitimate defense, mental illness is not.

On July 20, 1977, Busic and his wife received mandatory life sentences for air piracy and murder. Judge Bartels ruled that Mrs. Busic would be eligible for parole in eight years because she had fallen under her husband's Svengali-like influence. Mark Vlasic, one of the six members of the gang, received thirty years in prison after issuing a full confession. Peter Matanic and Frane Pesut were adjudged Guilty of air piracy and conspiracy by the two-man, ten-woman jury in Manhattan.

During the trial, Croatian separatists filled the courtrooms, demanding justice for their comrades. The legal fees of the defendants were paid by members of the New York-based Croatian community. The hijacking of the TWA jetliner was another in a long series of terrorist acts perpetrated by the dissidents. In 1972, the Yugoslavian ambassador to Sweden was assassinated, and his killers were granted political asylum in Spain. REF.: *CBA*.

Buss, Timothy D., 1967- , U.S., mur. Fourteen-year-old Timothy Buss was tried as an adult for the May 21, 1981, murder of Tara Sue Huffman, a young Bradley, Ill., girl whose remains were found in a landfill area outside of town. Police made the connection between Buss and the Huffman girl through the eyewitness testimony of thirty-five witnesses, and a palm print found at the dump. It was Timothy Buss who found the remains during a manhunt for the missing girl.

The case attracted more than the usual amount of attention given to child murders, because emotionally charged anti-pornography sentiments conflicted with issues of censorship and First Amendment rights. Before Buss molested and raped the 5-year-old girl, he had been observed by neighbors reading pornographic literature with his friends in a garage not far from the Huffman home. At a village board meeting, the owner of Bradley's only adult bookstore became the target of community activists and outraged parents who demanded the establishment be closed.

The trial was switched from Kankakee County to Will County because of the attending publicity in Bradley. In handing down a twenty-five-year prison sentence, Judge Robert Dannehl expressed the opinion that it was "adequate punishment for the event, for rehabilitation of the defendant, and for the protection of society." Defense Attorney Lawrence Dirksen described it as the "most outrageous verdict" he had ever heard in his life.

Meanwhile the debate about the causal relationship between pornography and violent crime continued in Bradley. "I never read it," said book store owner David Ward, "but I don't believe reading this type of material causes rape or murder or sex or drug use." REF.: *CBA*.

Bussy-d'Amboise, Seigneur **Louis de**, 1549-79, Fr., mur. Used the St. Bartholomew's Massacre of 1572 as a pretext to murder a relative whom he owed money. He was killed by the jealous husband of a woman he had seduced. REF.: *CBA*.

Buster from Chicago, See: **Brothers, Leo Vincent**.

Buswell, Harriet (AKA: **Clara Burton**), d.1873, Brit., (unsolv.) mur. Known as the Great Coram-Street Murder, this homicide occurred sometime between Christmas Eve and Christmas morning 1873, in London. Found was the body of Harriet Buswell (also known as Clara Burton), who had been seen in the company of a man only hours before. Two men from the German ship *Wangerland*, Carl Whollebe, the ship's surgeon, and Dr. Hessel, the chaplain, were arrested a short time later. Several witnesses identified Hessel as the man accompanying the victim. A waiter named William Stalker and a greengrocer, George Fleck, swore that Hessel was the man last seen with the woman. A housemaid at the hotel where Hessel had been staying was positive that he had left his room during the time Buswell was killed, and a laundress insisted that she had cleaned several of Dr. Hessel's handkerchiefs which smelled of turpentine, as if he had used this to clean away a strong stain. One of his handkerchiefs, the laundress said, "was completely saturated with blood."

Hessel was charged with the killing and appeared before Magistrate Vaughan on Jan. 29, 1874. Though the witnesses reappeared to swear that Hessel was the man, the chaplain was able to provide two persons from the ship who swore that he never left his hotel room on the night in question. Magistrate Vaughan accepted the alibis and Hessel was released. The court not only apologized but gave the chaplain a sizeable sum of money for his inconvenience. This is one of the earliest recorded cases of a wrongly identified person charged with murder in London. The killer of Harriet Buswell was never found.

REF.: *The Annual Register*, 1873; Brock, *A Casebook of Crime*; *CBA*; Pearce, *Unsolved Murder Mysteries*; (FICTION) Shearing, *Moss Rose*.

Butcher, Christine, 1944-51, Brit., (unsolv.) mur. When last seen alive, 7-year-old Christine Butcher was carrying her doll toward Stevens Meadow in Windsor Park. Earlier that afternoon, July 8, 1951, she had been part of the crowd watching U.S. prize fighter "Sugar" Ray Robinson at his training headquarters.

Two days later two passersby found her body in a field of high grass in Stevens Meadow. She had been strangled with the belt of her blue raincoat. An autopsy produced evidence of sexual assault, but no fingerprints were found. The murder was one of four child slayings in Britain that year and remains unsolved.

REF.: Butler, *Murderers' England*; *CBA*; Firmin, *Murderers In Our Midst*; Harrison, *Criminal Calendar II*; Simpson, *Forty Years of Murder*.

Butchill, Elizabeth, c.1758-80, Brit., mur. For ending the life of her newborn infant in a cruel and brutal manner, Elizabeth Butchill of Saffron Walden, Essex, was sent to the gallows at Cambridge on Mar. 17, 1780.

The unfortunate affair came to light on Jan. 7 of that year when the body of the infant was found floating in the river near Trinity College. The murder of the baby was traced to Butchill who worked as a bedmaker at the college.

On the morning of the sixth, Elizabeth's aunt, Esther Hall, found the girl in physical torment. Concluding that she suffered from colic, Hall administered some medicine before leaving for the college where she was also employed. The child was delivered by Elizabeth without the help of a midwife. When Elizabeth recovered sufficiently, she threw the baby down one of the holes feeding into the river.

The next day, the bruised, lifeless body was found, and a coroner determined that death was caused by a head wound. When William Hall learned that a child had turned up dead in the river, he notified a surgeon, who came to the house to examine his wife's niece.

Elizabeth had just delivered a child, and the baby was missing. A confession was taken to the jury and a charge of willful murder was returned. The court case was a sad one for everyone involved. Elizabeth pleaded for mercy. But, in this world, the judge said, mercy could not be granted.

REF.: *CBA*; *Newgate Calendar*.

Butler, Benjamin Franklin, 1795-1858, U.S., lawyer. Descendant of Oliver Cromwell and law partner of Martin Van Buren in Albany, N.Y. Benjamin Frnaklin Butler served as district attorney of Albany from 1821-24, and U.S. attorney general from 1833-38. He was named interim secretary of war from 1836-37. REF.: *CBA*.

Butler, Charles, 1750-1832, Brit., lawyer. Author of various legal texts. The first Roman Catholic summoned to the bar since 1688. REF.: *CBA*.

Butler, Harry Linton, d.1937, U.S., rob. Butler made a fortune speculating on Oregon real estate during the waning years of the Great Depression and instantly lost $50,000 when one of the investments failed to pan out.

Butler, a resident of Pasadena, Calif., was the former president of the local realty board and a well-respected citizen of the community before he turned to bank robbery to recoup his losses. On Jan. 7, 1937, Butler leveled a gun at George Dietzler, manager of the Colorado-Mentor branch of the Bank of America. He had already robbed the bank once before, netting over $4,000 in small bills.

Dietzler, recognizing Butler from the earlier robbery, placed a frantic call to the local police as Butler left. For unknown reasons, Harry Butler lingered outside the bank longer than he should have. When the squad cars pulled onto the street, the bandit made a quick dash for his 1929 sedan, but he was shot down before he could reach the car. Police found a .32-caliber gun in his hand. Six eyewitnesses identified the body as the former real estate mogul Harry Butler. Three suicide notes written to his wife, mother and the police lieutenant were found in his pockets. Harry Butler had reached the sad conclusion that

he was a dead man regardless of the outcome of this latest heist.
REF.: *CBA; Cohen, One Hundred True Crime Stories.*

Butler, James (Fifth Earl of Oremonde), 1420-61, Ire., treas. Member of a titled family dating back to 1328. He served as lord high treasurer of England in 1455 and 1458. After his capture by the Yorkists in 1461, he was beheaded. REF.: *CBA.*

Butler, James, c.1688-1716, Brit., rob.-mur. Born to a respectable family in Kilkenny, Ireland, Butler was a rebellious youth. Not interested in working at an honest trade, he chose instead to seek adventure and fortune in the military. After enlisting in Galway, he was sent to Spain. For purely selfish reasons, he deserted to join the Spanish army.

This new arrangement proved to be no more satisfactory than the last. So after robbing his captain's tent, James Butler abandoned the Spanish army in order to travel through the countryside as an itinerant medicine man selling potions and victuals designed to cure all manner of diseases. With a fair command of the Spanish language, Butler was able to advertise himself as the former physician of the King of Persia. After plundering the Spanish towns and villages, as well as a score of wealthy young maidens, Butler left for Italy, where the pockets of the local gentry were equally ripe. Butler was indiscriminate, guided only by the old dictum: *fallere fallentem non est fraus,* meaning "to deceive the deceivers is no deceit."

In Florence Butler made the acquaintance of a prosperous young tradesman. He found out that the man would pay five hundred pieces of gold for the murder of his uncle, so that he could inherit a sizable estate. It was a simple crime in its plan, but Butler required the help of a bandit.

The two men entered the dwelling of the old uncle and clubbed him to death while he lay sleeping. The body was carried to the appointed rendezvous where a hole was dug. Because Butler was inherently suspicious as well as greedy, he ordered his helper to murder the wealthy young nephew and take the five hundred gold coins. Then Butler killed his accomplice and threw all three bodies into the hole in the ground.

Butler eventually returned to England broke, having lost his money to a female swindler cleverer than he. With poverty staring him in the face, he became a highwayman in the company of a man named Nodes. His luck finally ran out near Holloway, where he was arrested and taken to the Old Bailey. Butler was hanged at Tyburn Hill in 1716.
REF.: *CBA; Smith, Highwaymen.*

Butler, Josephine Elizabeth, 1828-1906, Brit., pros.-wh.slav. Agitated for repeal of the Contagious Diseases Act from 1869-86, and against the licensing of commercial houses of prostitution. During this time, she proposed stronger measures to curb the flourishing white slave traffic in England. REF.: *CBA.*

Butler, Louise, prom. 1928, and **Yelder, George**, b.c.1873, U.S., (wrong. convict.) mur. On the southern bank of the sluggish Alabama River in Lowndes County, Ala., there lived a young black woman named Louise Butler who became fond of George Yelder, a 55-year-old neighbor. Louise was a jealous, possessive woman who resented the attentions that Yelder was showing Topsy Warren, her 14-year-old niece.

One day in 1928, after returning from a visit to Montgomery, Louise found Topsy chatting with Yelder, who had just given her a shiny new half-dollar. Louise marched Topsy out to the woodpile and administered a severe beating. Then the girl disappeared from the county, and rumors began to circulate that she had been murdered.

Sent to investigate, Deputy Sheriff "Buck" Meadows listened to a wild story told by Louise's 12-year-old daughter Julia, who claimed to have witnessed her mother chop up Topsy with an axe and discard the body in a burlap sack. When 9-year-old niece Anne-Mary corroborated the story, separate murder indictments were returned against Butler and Yelder for the death of Topsy Warren on Apr. 17, 1928.

The trial was held in the courtroom of Judge A.E. Gamble. Both parties maintained their innocence, but were convicted and sentenced to life imprisonment on Apr. 26, 1928. A week after they had been shipped off to the Alabama State Penitentiary, word reached the county authorities that Topsy Warren was alive and living with relatives in Dallas County. She was located and brought back to Hayneville for identification before Judge Gamble and solicitor Calvin Poole. An official pardon was granted in June, and the pair was officially released.

Sheriff Meadows later theorized that the two juvenile "eyewitnesses" had been coached into giving false testimony by a man who bore a personal grudge against George Yelder.
REF.: *Borchard, Convicting the Innocent; CBA.*

Butler, Pierce, 1866-1939, U.S., jur. County attorney of Ramsey County, Minn., from 1893-97. He was appointed associate Supreme Court Justice in 1922 by President Warren Harding, replacing William R. Day. His conservative leanings were best illustrated in the case of *Powell vs. Alabama* (1923) in which he opposed overturning the conviction of the Scottsboro Boys on the shaky grounds that the state's failure to provide them with legal counsel did not violate their Fourteenth Amendment rights. He was one of the conservative judges that President Franklin D. Roosevelt attempted to oust during his famous court-packing scheme of 1937. REF.: *CBA.*

Butler, Richard Girnt, and **Beam, Louis**, and **Pierce, Bruce Carroll**, and **Miles, Robert**, prom. 1988, Case of, U.S., consp.-treas. In February 1988, fourteen neo-Nazis and right wing extremists representing a cross-section of racial and religious intolerance in the U.S. were tried for conspiring to dump 200 pounds of deadly cyanide into the water supply of an undetermined city, either Chicago, New York, or Washington, D.C. It was to be the first step in a seditious plot to overthrow the government and replace it with a ruling triumvirate composed of Rev. Richard Girnt Butler, pastor of the neo-Nazi Church of Jesus Christ Christian in Idaho; Louis Beam, Grand Dragon of the Texas Ku Klux Klan; and Robert Miles, pastor of the Mountain Church of Cochtah, Mich.

These three men were the self-appointed "generals" of a nationwide network of right-wing terrorists, street thugs, and silent commandos sworn to avenge the death of Gordon Kahl, an anti-Semitic zealot killed by federal agents and local police in a 1983 Arkansas shootout.

The network was believed to have been responsible for the 1984 assassination of Denver radio talk show host Alan Berg and the deaths of two state troopers. A splinter group known as the Order had staged a series of commando raids that same year against three armored cars in Washington state and California that netted more than $4.4 million. Members of this group had passed large quantities of counterfeit bills from Philadelphia to Seattle.

These crimes underscored a more sinister plot hatched by Robert Miles at Butler's heavily guarded compound in Idaho. An informant named James Ellison, also known as King James of the Ozarks, explained how Miles ordered his followers to "backpack the poison to a city water supply in the Northeast or the Central U.S."

In 1981, Miles had supplied Ellison with thirty gallons of cyanide which was then stored at the Arkansas headquarters of the Covenant, the anti-Semitic faction. If the plan had been carried out, 400,000 people may have been killed, however Ellison kept the canister in storage until it was finally seized during a 1985 FBI raid.

In February, 1988, fourteen co-conspirators were tried in the courtroom of Judge Morris S. Arnold at Fort Smith, Ark. The defendants were charged with seditious conspiracy, a charge carrying with it a maximum prison sentence of twenty years each and a $20,000 fine. During the two-month trial, defense attorneys attempted to demonstrate that their clients were merely exercising their constitutional rights to free speech. Assistant U.S. Attorney Steven Snyder dismissed this as ludicrous, and painted a picture of a dangerous lunatic conspiracy responsible for many random acts of violence, including political assassination, armed robbery, and a failed attempt to blow up a string of natural-gas pipelines stretching from Texas to Chicago.

On Apr. 7, 1988, the jury found all fourteen defendants innocent of all charges. Miles, Butler, Beam and company walked out of U.S. District Court free men. According to Snyder, one of the jurors later married a defendant. See: **Berg, Alan; Ku Klux Klan.** REF.: *CBA.*

Butler, Robert (AKA: **C.J. Donelly**), 1845-1905, Aus.-N. Zea., burg.-rob.-mur. Robert Butler committed his last crime on Mar. 23, 1905, when he shot a Freemason named William Munday who was walking between Tooringa and Toowong in Queensland. The victim was a middle-aged man, only slightly younger than the killer.

Butler was born in Kilkenny, Ire., but he left his homeland in 1859 to settle in Australia where he immediately got into trouble with the law. Twelve of his next sixteen years were spent in the jails of Victoria for burglary and robbery. Butler became a voracious reader. He enjoyed the exploits of Napoléon and Frederick of Prussia, but adopted a mercenary philosophy which held "a man's life is of no more importance than a dog's; Nature respects one no more than the other; a volcanic eruption kills mice and men."

Upon his release from prison in 1876, Butler moved to New Zealand where he went to work as a schoolmaster under an alias in Cromwell, Otago, instilling his new-found knowledge in the minds of impressionable youths. He began his own "academy," but a rash of burglaries for which he was strongly suspected drove him to Dunedin. Two weeks later Butler was arrested and convicted of burglary. He received a four-year prison sentence, earning release on Feb. 18, 1880. With his employment prospects poor, a sympathetic detective named Bane tried to find him employment. Butler always had aspired to be a journalist, so he went to work for the Dunedin *Evening Star* as a crime reporter, writing a series of prison sketches. The demand of a daily job proved to be too much of a strain, however, and Butler quit.

On Mar. 14, 1880, the home of a Dunedin solicitor named Stamper was burglarized and set on fire. The next day an even worse crime was reported on the pages of the gazette. A young butcher named J.M. Dewar, his wife, and their only child were found murdered in their home on Cumberland Street. The killer had attempted to burn the house down, but failed. Detective Bain was assigned to the case, and through the chambermaid at the Scotia Hotel it was learned that Butler had hastily decamped from his room following the discovery of the tragedy.

Robert Butler was arrested the next day. He admitted to having committed the Stamper burglary, but denied any involvement in the Dewar murders. Some blood-stained clothes found in a bush outside Dunedin were proven to belong to Butler, which resulted in a criminal indictment. Placed on trial at the Supreme Court of Dunedin, Butler conducted his own defense. He earned an acquittal for himself on the murder charges. Later, he pleaded guilty to the Stamper robbery and was sentenced to eighteen years in prison by Justice Joshua Williams. He served sixteen years before being freed in 1896, at which time he was fifty-one years old and very sour on life. Butler returned to Australia and committed another robbery which earned him a fifteen-year sentence. He got out of jail in 1904, but was unable to make a decent living. He was feeble, broke, and without resources. Butler was convicted of murdering a man named Munday and received a death sentence. He was executed on June 30, 1905.

REF.: *CBA;* Irving, *A Book of Remarkable Criminals;* Wilson, *Encyclopedia of Murder.*

Butler, William, 1822-1909, U.S., jur. Served as district attorney in Harrisburg, Pa., from 1856-59, and was appointed judge of the court of the Eastern District of Pennsylvania in 1879. REF.: *CBA.*

Butler, William, d.1910, Brit., rob.-mur. Shortly after nightfall, on Nov. 11, 1909, as Charles Thomas and his wife Mary prepared to go to sleep, a housebreaker named William Butler entered their cottage at Bassaleg, near Newport, Monmouthshire.

Believing that the elderly couple possessed a large sum of money, Butler bludgeoned the couple to death with a hammer and escaped with only £3 after failing to locate their life savings. The £150 was tucked away in a drawer, out of sight.

Butler was captured, convicted at the Monmouth Assizes in 1909, and hanged the following February. REF.: *CBA.*

Butler, William, prom. 1938, Brit., mur. William Butler was identified as the assailant who had bludgeoned Ernest Percival Key to death in his jeweler's shop in Surbiton on Dec. 24, 1938.

The shopkeeper's body was examined by Sir Bernard Spilsbury and Dr. Eric Gardner, the county pathologist for Surrey. The killer left behind a black bowler hat, which was enough evidence from which the two examiners could gauge its owner's physical characteristics. Stories were planted in London and Berlin newspapers, and it was not long before the killer was flushed out. Butler was tried, condemned, and hanged for the crime. Scotland Yard received a letter from the Reichkriminal-Polizeiamt in Berlin asking for additional information about the amazing powers of the "clairvoyant" Eric Gardner. See: **Spilsbury, Bernard.**

REF.: Browne, *The Scalpel of Scotland Yard; CBA;* Shew, *A Second Companion to Murder.*

Butt, Isaac, 1813-79, Ire., lawyer. Leader of the radical Fenian movement from 1865-69, and president of the Home Rule Confederation from 1873-77. Historians credit him for coining the term Home Rule. REF.: *CBA.*

Butte, George Charles, 1877-1940, U.S., jur. Attorney general of Puerto Rico from 1925-28. He was the three-time acting governor of Puerto Rico from 1926-27 before accepting appointment to the bench of the Supreme Court of the Philippine Islands from 1932-36. Book authored: *The Reform of the Law of Contraband* (1912). REF.: *CBA.*

Butterfield, Jane, prom. 1775, Case of, Brit., mur. As a young girl, Jane Butterfield was taken by a woman from her father's home in Surrey to the private residence of William Scawen, Esq., where he tried to seduce her and then raped her.

On her release, her father collapsed, heartbroken at the thought that she was ruined for life. When he died, Scawen attempted to make amends for his crime by providing Jane with a good education and financial compensation. When Scawen himself became debilitated with a disease that required constant attention from a nurse, Jane, grateful for his financial support, took care of him.

In time his faith and trust in this woman became absolute. He lost his sight, and then miraculously recovered it, thanks to the tender care she provided. However, his regular physicians were unable to provide relief for his other ailments, so Scawen turned to quack medicines which he believed would restore his health.

Jane advised against his taking such medicines, but one day Scawen drank a glass of sarsaparilla that seemed strangely metallic in taste. He told Edmund Sanxay, a local surgeon, about the peculiar-tasting potion after he became violently ill. On June 20, 1775, he was taken to the surgeon's home where he soon died. The doctor expressed the opinion that the death was not natural, and that Scawen's collapse was brought on by mercury poisoning.

On Aug. 19, 1775, Jane was indicted for murder on the strength of the doctor's sworn testimony. In her defense, a battery of respected surgeons testified to Scawen's faith in quack medicines, which they said would be harmful to anyone who took them for a prolonged period of time.

The jury was absent for only ten minutes before deciding that the defendant should go free. It was whispered as she left the courtroom that Jane was to inherit all of Mr. Scawen's property.

REF.: *CBA; Newgate Calendar.*

Butterfield, Neale Allen (AKA: **Butterfingers**), 1933- , U.S., mur. Explaining later that he just wanted to "see someone die," 16-year-old Neale Butterfield decided to cut his classes on Nov. 16, 1949, so that he could conduct his own experiment in murder.

Frank Watson, principal of Heyburn High School in Burley, Ida., recalled how Butterfield freely joined in the murder gossip the day after the body of 7-year-old Glenda Joyce Brisbois was found in an irrigation canal outside town. "He showed no signs of worry or even of knowledge of the affair," Watson said. "He came into my psychology class and asked me calmly, 'Did you know, Mr. Watson, that they found that girl's body'?"

"Butterfingers" Butterfield was a member of the high school football team and a student leader, popular with both boys and girls. It seemed inconceivable at the time that he could wantonly take the life of a little girl. As a matter of habit, Butterfield had provided taxi service to a number of small children attending the local grammar school. He picked them up and drove them home, and none of the parents seemed to notice the peculiarity of it, or to even comprehend that the pleasant-looking high school boy was a dangerous pedophile.

The killing took place in Cassia County. The murder weapon was a tire jack, and Butterfield's motive was purely sexual. When he went home after murdering Glenda, Butterfield ate a full meal, popped some corn, and went to bed.

Arresting officers held him in the Twin Falls county jail, a distance of forty-one miles from Burley, where emotion was running high. Judge Hugh A. Baker advised Twin Falls law enforcement personnel "not to take Butterfield to Burley, or he might not be alive in the morning." Because Idaho law required that a criminal must be charged in the county where the deed was committed, Butterfield was arraigned just inside the Cassia County line in an open field.

In jail Butterfield remained dispassionate. He ate heartily and slept well. The only emotion he showed was when the sheriff denied him a package of cigarettes.

Prosecutors believed that Idaho law would permit them to seek the death penalty, though Butterfield was a minor. They cited the case of a 15-year-old boy from Idaho County who was tried as an adult and sentenced to death. However, that boy's sentence was commuted to life imprisonment by the state pardons board. In regard to Butterfield, Dr. Paul De River, in his case study *Crime and the Sexual Psychopath,* concluded that the defendant was "medically and legally sane at the time he committed the crime."

Butterfield was convicted of first-degree murder but was spared the death penalty. The prison doors slammed shut on Feb. 14, 1950. He served twelve years before receiving a parole on Nov. 14, 1962. He was granted a final discharge on Nov. 30, 1967, after meeting all of the board's requirements. At last report, Butterfield was married and had become a father. REF.: *CBA.*

Butterfield 8, 1935, a novel by John O'Hara. Starr Faithfull, a beautiful, neurotic young woman who was found mysteriously murdered (U.S., 1931), is the real-life role model for the oversexed O'Hara heroine in his lurid fictional tale. The novel was adapted for the screen in a 1960 production starring Elizabeth Taylor, who won an Academy Award for her portrayal of the troubled party girl. See: **Faithfull, Starr.** REF.: *CBA.*

Button and Badge Murder, See: **Greenwood, David.**

Butts, Thomas, prom. 1945, Case of, U.S., mur. Thomas Butts rang in the new year of 1945 by shooting and killing his son-in-law, a man named Bates, at the family home on Boyer Mountain, Md.

Bates, over sixty years old, was married to Tom Butts' young daughter. The woman decided to leave her elderly husband one day, citing irreconcilable differences. When Bates learned she had left him, he stormed off to Thomas Butts' cabin with his gun. Before he could get near the front porch, Butts shot him to death through a window.

Tom Butts was tried for murder but was acquitted. His daughter left town permanently shortly after the trial.

REF.: *CBA;* Montell, *Killings.*

Buxton, Charles Roden, b.1875, Brit., asslt. Great-grandson of Sir Thomas Fowell Buxton. He and his brother Edward Buxton were set upon by a Turkish assassin while on a mission for the British government to secure the neutrality of Bulgaria in October 1914. They escaped and later co-authored a book about the Balkans. REF.: *CBA.*

Buxton, Sir Thomas Fowell (First Baronet), 1786-1845, Brit.,

pris. reform. Advocate of prison reform and moderate treatment of convicts. He fought for the abolition of slavery in all British possessions from 1822-33. Books authored: *An Inquiry Into Prison Discipline* (1818) and *African Slave Trade and it's Remedy* (1839). REF.: *CBA.*

Buzzard Brothers, prom. 1870s-1930s, U.S., rob. For sixty years the Lancaster, Pa., area was plagued by the six Buzzard brothers, who practiced horse thieving and chicken stealing on a wide scale. Abe and Joe Buzzard led the clan in family raids on farms, inspired by a harridan of a mother who trained them in the art of stealing. Mother Buzzard was often jailed for theft, but this only encouraged her wild offspring to more robbery sprees. At one point, more than twenty members of the Buzzard family holed up in a cave near Blue Rock, Pa., rolling a huge stone across the entrance at night to prevent police from storming the place. Joe Buzzard, who stole his first horse in 1878, and his older brother Abe were both hunted fugitives for several years until Abe convinced Pennsylvania governor Robert E. Pattison that he had reformed. Both he and Joe were pardoned and Abe went about back county communities preaching sermons on "Ruin and Reform." But this was an act. Abe Buzzard was arrested for chicken stealing, and officers found a number of burglar tools in his bag, right next to his Bible and hymn book. He was sent to prison and was in and out of jail until his death in 1935 when he died in Philadelphia's Cherry Hill Prison. Joe Buzzard lasted a few more years, the last of the clan to die out. His final prison sentence was for two years at age seventy-five, in 1938. Buzzard had stolen a suitcase without ever inspecting the contents. The case held nothing but tennis shoes, all for the left foot. REF.: *CBA.*

Byng, John, 1704-57, Brit., crim. neg. John Byng, son of British naval hero Lord Torrington, was an admiral in the navy who had risen quickly through the ranks because of his father's fame and influence. He proved to be a slow, ponderous commander whose indecision and lethargy became notorious among chiefs of the admiralty. In spring of 1756, Byng was ordered to take a fleet of British warships to Minorca and lift the French siege of that port city. He approached this task with extreme reluctance, writing letters to friends that he felt the voyage was doomed to failure. At Gibraltar, Byng was denied reinforcements and, in a dejected mood, sailed to the Mediterranean island of Minorca. Arrayed before him was a huge new French fleet under the command of Admiral La Galissonière. Byng deliberated for hours while trying to decide whether or not to attack and, by the time he did, his squadron lost the element of surprise and the French fleet was aligned so as to catch his ships broadside.

Byng finally sent his ships at an angle to avoid the broadside, but his commanders botched their rather confused instructions and many of his ships sailed into a devastating broadside. Byng's own flagship, at his orders, remained out of the battle so that the admiral's own sailors labelled him a coward. Rather than attack again, Byng ordered a complete withdrawal and remained at sea while the French attacked and captured the British-held city of Minorca. Byng sailed back to England and was received in disgrace, arrested for criminal negligence and tried in December 1756. Byng pleaded with his superiors, stating that his retreat had been "the wise and humane thing," but they refused to listen, branding him a coward. So incensed by Byng's conduct was the Duke of Newcastle that he told King George II that Byng would "be tried and hanged immediately."

Testifying against Byng was General Willam Blakeney, a crusty 84-year-old campaigner who had surrendered the fortress but managed to escape. Blakeney stated that Byng should have landed his troops to help relieve the siege and that, if he had, the British garrison would have held out. This testimony, more than any other, sealed the admiral's fate. Byng was sentenced to death for criminal negligence and was taken aboard the H.M.S. *Monarch* where, on Mar. 14, 1757, he was taken to the ship's quarterdeck. A firing squad was lined up in front of him and the admiral kneeled on a velvet pillow, putting a handkerchief over his eyes.

The firing squad let loose a volley and Byng was instantly killed. This sentence was not well-received by either the British or even the French, who lambasted their enemy for taking its vengeance out on one of its own officers rather than facing the French in combat. Byng's execution was labeled "a perpetual disgrace of public justice," and remains one of the severest on record rendered to any British field commander for failing to take a military objective. REF.: *CBA*.

Byng, Julian Hedworth George (First Viscount Byng), 1862-1935, Brit., law enfor. off. Military hero in the Boer War and WWI. He served as Commissioner of the London Metropolitan Police from 1928-31, and was appointed army field marshal in 1932. REF.: *CBA*.

Byrne, Anthony, prom. 1932, Scot., burg. Byrne was indicted in December, 1932, for breaking and entering a small retail shop on West George Street, Glasgow. The crime netted him only a few pounds, but the larger issue here was the legal authority of Glasgow police to retake fingerprints to establish guilt.

On Dec. 16, a new set of fingerprints was made of the suspect while he awaited trial in the Barlinnie Jail. These were compared to fingerprints originally found on the shop's safe that contained the cash. Based on this evidence, Byrne was convicted and sentenced to eighteen months of hard labor. He appealed his case before the High Court of the Justiciary, Edinburgh, maintaining that it was illegal to take fingerprints without a warrant, because it constituted an invasion of personal liberty.

The Lord Justice-General returned a decision on May 25, 1933, upholding the right of the police to take a second set of fingerprints. Lord Clyde maintained the action was in line with other normal police procedures used to locate and identify suspects.

REF.: *CBA; Cherrill, Cherrill of the Yard.*

Byrne, Garret, and Strange, James, prom. 1779, Ire., abduc. By the late eighteenth century, abductions of wealthy young heiresses by poor men seeking an easy inheritance had ceased. During the reign of Elizabeth I, the clergy was forbidden to solemnize marriages in which the woman had been carried off against her will. Years later, such abduction became a felony crime, punishable by hanging. This was not the case in Ireland, where impoverished young men were often viewed as folk heroes by the populace.

One such case involved two men named Garret Byrne and James Strange, who kidnapped fifteen-year-old Catherine Kennedy and fourteen-year-old Ann Kennedy, heiresses to a family fortune, on Apr. 14, 1779. A reward of £100 was posted by their outraged father for their safe return. Five weeks passed.

Just before Byrne and Strange were preparing to leave the country, they were apprehended. On testimony of the two girls, the two men were found Guilty and hanged, despite having popular opinion on their side. Their crime involved theft of property, not the abduction and violation of the young girls. Had the two heiresses been impoverished, Byrne and Strange would probably have escaped the hangman.

REF.: *CBA; Moorhead, Hostages To Fortune.*

Byrne, Sir Laurence Austin, b.1896, Brit., jur. Junior treasury counsel at the Old Bailey from 1930-42. He was appointed Senior Prosecuting counsel from 1942-45, and judge of the Queen's Bench Division of the High Court from 1947-60. During his fifteen-year career at the Old Bailey, he was involved in the prosecution of Harold Dorien Trevor, Reginald Sidney Buckfield, Elvira Barney, Harry Dobkin, Karl Gustav Hulten, Thomas Joseph Davidson, and the second trial of Frederick Field in 1933. REF.: *CBA*.

Byrne, Patrick Joseph, 1932- , Brit., necro.-mansl. Patrick Joseph Byrne's blustering swagger around the boys could not disguise his anxieties toward women. The few he managed to date in Birmingham would later recall his painful shyness. Byrne, an Irish construction worker fond of strong drink and the companionship of his pub mates, was too shy to ask his dates for a goodnight kiss. Byrne's gnawing feelings of sexual inadequacy drove him to commit a heinous murder at Edgbaston YWCA

hostel on Dec. 23, 1959.

He selected his victim, 29-year-old Sidney Stephanie Baird, at random. She worked as a shorthand-typist in the city. After watching Baird undress from outside her room, Byrne summoned the necessary courage to rap on her door. "I watched her for a long time, and stood close to the window...the urge to kill her was tremendously strong. Before she could say no, I kissed her," he said. "She tried to shove me away but couldn't, and for a second I got her around the waist." Byrne stifled her screams with his hands and kissed the struggling woman until she fell over backwards, fracturing her skull. Baird was dead, but Byrne stripped to his shorts, sexually abused the corpse, then cut off its head. Byrne left behind no fingerprints, just a hastily scrawled note that read: "This was the thing I thought would never come." The police discovered Baird's remains when they investigated a complaint filed by a second female assault victim who lived in the hostel, Margaret Brown, whose loud screams saved her life when Byrne attacked her in the hostel laundry rooms.

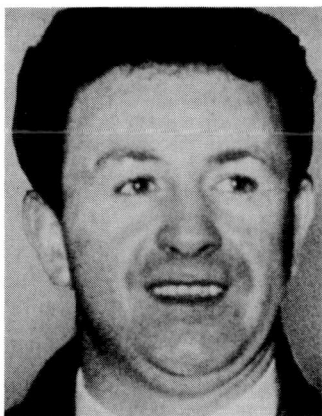 

Killer Patrick Byrne.   **Victim Sidney Baird.**

Detective Chief Superintendent Jim Haughton, head of the Birmingham CID, conducted a relentless investigation. Over 20,000 men were interviewed, before the identity of Byrne was established. Detectives were put on Byrne's trail after questioning a bus driver who had picked up a passenger near the YWCA. Drops of blood found on the seat of the bus were found to be the same type as Baird's. Byrne was traced to Warrington, and was brought in for questioning on Feb. 10, 1960. After some verbal sparring between the suspect and the detective, Byrne suddenly blurted out his confession.

Byrne was placed on trial at the Birmingham Assizes the next month before Justice Stable. He was found Guilty of murder and sentenced to life imprisonment. Following an appeal, the charge was reduced to manslaughter on the grounds of the defendant's probable insanity. The penalty however, remained unchanged.

REF.: Andrews, *Intensive Inquiries;* Butler, *Murderers' England; CBA;* Furneaux, *Famous Criminal Cases;* Lucas, *The Sex Killers;* Lustgarten, *Story of Crime;* Traini, *Murder For Sex;* Wilson, *Encyclopedia of Murder.*

Byrne, William Matthew, Jr., 1930- , U.S., jur. Attorney for the central district of California from 1966-67 and in 1970. He served on the President's Commission to investigate campus unrest in 1970, and was appointed judge to the federal court of the Central District of California in 1971. REF.: *CBA*.

Byrnes, James Francis, 1879-1972, U.S., jur. Member of Congress from 1911-41. He was appointed associate Supreme Court justice in 1941 replacing James McReynolds. He was a strong supporter of the New Deal policies by President Franklin D. Roosevelt. He served on the high court for only one year before accepting a position as director of the Office of War Mobilization. His role was a limited one but he did vote on several noteworthy cases, including *Skinner vs. Oklahoma ex rel Williamson* (1942), in which he opposed the compulsory sterilization of habitual criminals. REF.: *CBA*.

Byrnes, Thomas, d.1866, U.S., rob.-mur. George Hill of San Francisco lived an ostentatious life. His rooming house near Dupont and Sacramento Avenues was modest, but he made no secret of possessing a scarf pin valued at $1,500, often sporting his flashy jewels in public. When he disappeared on Feb. 15, 1865, few people took notice. He was a carefree type, with no family or close friends to inquire about him.

Several weeks later, a gardener named McGloin stumbled across Hill's decomposing body near a sand bog in the San Souci valley. The remains were secured by a hay rope, giving the impression that death had been caused by a runaway carriage. However, the sinister-looking head wound indicated to police that there had been foul play.

George Hill's landlady was questioned at length, and she recalled admitting an anxious young man carrying a bloody shirt into the rooming house. When the man had returned later, she had denied him entrance.

A police officer noticed that the description of the man matched that of a prisoner being held on a forgery charge. Thomas Byrnes, a butcher, was identified by the landlady. He was charged with the murder of Hill and executed in California on Sept. 3, 1866. The diamonds that Byrnes had coveted were found in a pawn shop. They were worthless fakes valued at less than three dollars.

REF.: *CBA; Duke, Celebrated Criminal Cases of America.*

Byrnes, Thomas F., 1842-1910, U.S., law enfor. off. Born in Ireland, Thomas F. Byrnes immigrated to the U.S. as a child with his family. He served in the Union Army during the Civil War and joined the NYPD in 1863, in time to survive the bloody draft riots. He was made a captain in 1870, and later rose to chief of detectives after solving several bank robberies engineered by master bank thief George Leonidas Leslie. Manhattan bankers were so grateful that a considerable amount of money was invested on behalf of Byrnes as a reward. Byrnes established a deadline at Fulton Street and let it be known

NYPD Inspector Thomas Byrnes.

in the underworld that any thief entering the banking district would be slugged and thrown into jail. He was thought of as a great detective in his day, although he was a strutting martinet

Inspector Byrnes, left, supervising the photographing of a struggling felon, 1886, a staged shot.

who enthusiastically practiced the Third Degree. He embraced the criminal identification system used by Alphonse Bertillon, and was the first to use *bertillonage* in the U.S. A famous photo

showed Byrnes and other detectives holding down a struggling felon as he was being photographed.

To his credit, Byrnes set strict regulations for his detectives, telling them that they would have no "business relationships" with underworld bosses and anyone caught taking a payoff would be summarily dismissed from the force. At least that was the story Byrnes gave out. He was publicity conscious and never failed to make a speech or be interviewed by the press. He authored a number of books, the most famous of which was *Professional Criminals of America,* which was no more than a reproduction of NYPD files on the less prominent thieves and gamblers of the city. He refrained from publishing extensive material on substantial gang bosses and bank burglars still at large in 1886 when the book was published.

Reformer Theodore Roosevelt believed that Byrnes, along with Inspector Alexander "Clubber" Williams were the most corrupt members of the NYPD hierarchy and, as one of the four police commissioners for the city at that time, he made plans to remove Byrnes from office. This proved unnecessary. Byrnes resigned from his powerful position in June 1895 after appearing before the Lexow Committee which probed police corruption. Byrnes was publicly embarrassed after admitting to the committee that he had accumulated $350,000 in cash and real estate on a $5,000-a-year salary. See: **Leslie, George Leonidas; Lexow Committee; Roosevelt, Theodore.**

REF.: Asbury, *The Gangs of New York; CBA;* Nash, *Hustlers and Con Men;* Reppetto, *The Blue Parade.*

Byrnes Hotel Burglary Gang, prom. 1893-94, U.S., burg. For nearly a year and a half, a number of swanky hotels in midtown Manhattan were plagued by a gang of burglars who crept into patrons' rooms when they were away. The ringleader of the gang was a bellboy named Byrnes, who was tracked down by detectives James McCafferty and George W. McClusky.

Byrnes had worked for all the major New York hotels in the past year. When he completed his business at one establishment, he would move on to the next, leaving the manager baffled by the thefts. McClusky finally succeeded in capturing Byrnes on Fifth Avenue, then arrested the remainder of the gang after interrogating Byrnes. REF.: *CBA.*

Byrns, Joseph Wellington, 1869-1936, U.S., lawyer. Member of the House of Representatives from 1909-36. REF.: *CBA.*

Byron, Emma (AKA: **Kitty Byron**), b.1878, Brit., mur. Emma Byron, nicknamed "Kitty," was desperately in love with Arthur Reginald Baker, who was a member of the London Stock Exchange, and married. The philandering stockbroker maintained a suite of rooms for Byron on Duke Street, but he was an abusive lover who scolded and beat the woman at the slightest provocation. The landlady of the flat, Mrs. Liard, upbraided her tenants to refrain from cursing and fighting, which went on at all hours. Madame Liard told Kitty one day in November 1902 to vacate the flat and that Baker was planning to end their affair.

This news destroyed Kitty. On Nov. 10—Lord Mayor's Day in London—she went to a small shop on Oxford Street and bought a knife. Wrapping the cleaver in her muff, she walked to the Lombard Post Office and sent a dispatch to Baker. "Dear Reg," it read. "Want you immediate, importantly. Kitty." Baker returned with the messenger to confront his mistress on the stairs of the lodging house. Their usual violent quarrel followed. With dozens of onlookers straining to see what all the commotion was about, Byron produced the knife and stabbed Baker twice—fatally. She fell on top of him, crying her eyes out before a constable led her away.

Byron was placed on trial at the Central Criminal Court a week before Christmas, 1902. Charles Matthews spoke for the Crown. Sir Henry Dickens, the son of famed Victorian novelist Charles Dickens, represented Kitty. He was assisted by Sir Travers Humphreys, who later went on to enjoy a distinguished career on the bench himself. Their defense of Byron was brilliant, given the overwhelming evidence of pre-mediated murder. The defense team collected 15,000 signatures demanding her release, including the names of 3,000 Stock Exchange clerks.

The trial lasted only one day and resulted in a Guilty verdict. The jury, however, attached a recommendation for mercy. Justice Charles Darling of the Queen's Bench sentenced her to death, but the plea for mercy was sent to the home secretary for advisement. At his discretion, the Royal Prerogative was exercised. Four days later, the death sentence was commuted to life imprisonment. Petitions calling for Byron's complete exoneration continued to be sent to the home secretary. In 1908, Kitty Bryon was granted her freedom.

REF.: Barker, *Lord Darling's Famous Cases;* Bechhofer-Roberts, *Sir Travers Humphreys: His Career and His famous Cases; CBA;* Graham, *Lord Darling and His Famous Trials;* Humphreys, *A Book of Trials;* ____, *Criminal Days;* Nicholls, *Crime Within the Square Mile;* Shew, *A Second Companion To Murder.*

Byron, George de Luna, prom. 1830s-50s, Brit., fraud. Appearing in London in the 1830s, Major George de Luna Byron claimed to be the illegitimate son of the famous poet, Lord Byron, and a Spanish aristocrat, the Countess de Luna. He made claims against Byron's publisher, John Murray, but these were rejected by the publisher. He then wrote to Byron's friends, saying that he was preparing a biography of his father, and would they be so kind as to loan him some of his father's letters. These were forwarded to him. In the same manner, he obtained original letters written by two other great British poets, Keats and Shelley. The major carefully made copies of these letters. Then, after being able to imitate the handwriting of the great poets, he began to create fake letters which were so good that they were sold for considerable cash, through agents to Byron's own publisher, John Murray, and to Mary Shelley, the wife of the dead poet. For almost a decade, the clever Major Byron supported himself on his excellent forgeries. Most of these were eventually exposed as fakes and were sent to the British Museum for exhibit, but others still remain in the possession of collectors who believe they own genuine *belles lettres* of England's finest poets.

REF.: *CBA;* MacDougall, *Hoaxes;* Wilson, *Encyclopedia of Murder.*

Byron, Lord William, prom. 1765, Brit., mansl. William, Lord Byron, a great-uncle of the famous Romantic poet, stabbed a man to death in a quarrel about who had more game on his estate.

Lord Byron was dining at the Star and Garter Tavern in Pall Mall, on the night of Jan. 26, 1765. He wagered £100 that there were more animals on his property than on that of his rival Chaworth. When the party adjourned, Lord Byron invited Chaworth into an adjoining room and commanded him to draw his sword and fight.

Byron ran his sword through Chaworth's navel, wounding him mortally, and death was pronounced by the surgeon Hawkrup. Lord Byron pleaded not guilty to murder. The House of Lords acquitted him of the more serious charge, but found him Guilty of manslaughter. Under the terms of the Statute of Edward VI, Lord Byron claimed "benefit of clergy" and was released. The statute provided that a clergyman could be tried only in an ecclesiastical court. Byron was not a clergyman, but benefited by the statute's extension to anybody who could read and write.

Years later, the poet Byron fell in love with Chaworth's great-niece Mary, who rejected him.

REF.: Brock, *A Casebook of Crime; CBA;* Melville, *Famous Duels and Assassinations;* Wilson, *Encyclopedia of Murder.*

Bywaters, Frederick, See: **Thompson, Edith.**

C

Caamaño, José Maria Plácido, 1838-1901, Ecu., consp. Exile who overthrew the military government of General José Vientemilla in a civil war fought in 1883. A year earlier, Caamaño was banished from the country for fomenting a revolt against the dictator. In 1884 he was elected president. REF.: *CBA*.

Caballero, Guadalupe (AKA: **The Owl**), prom. 1890s, U.S., west. outl. A strange little bandit, the cross-eyed Guadalupe Caballero stood only five feet tall and was a member of Vicente Silva's notorious cattle-rustling gang in Las Vegas, N.M. This runty bandit spent most of his time in a section of Las Vegas known as Old Town, squatting on the streets, pretending to be asleep but alert to lawmen or traitors who might betray Silva's operations. He was often sent by Silva to the nearby mountains to drive stolen herds to Silva's nearby ranch when they were ready for sale. Caballero was convicted of being an accessory in the murder of Pete Maes in 1894 and sent to prison for ten years.
REF.: Baca, *Vincente Silva*; Bartholomew, *The Biographical Album of Western Gunfighters; CBA*.

Cabellero, Juan, See: **Ruiz, Luis**.

Cabestant, Guillaume de, prom. late 12th Cent., Fr., mur. According to ancient legend this troubadour and poet was caught in a dalliance with Marguerite, wedded to Raymond of Château Roussillon. When Raymond learned of the affair he killed Cabestant and tore his heart from his chest. His remains were served to Marguerite, and when told what she had consumed, she vowed never to eat again, thereby killing herself. REF.: *CBA*.

Caboche, Simon (AKA: **Simon le Coustellier**), prom. 15th Cent., Fr., rebel. Led a protest movement against high taxation and government corruption in 1407. In 1413 he led a mob that stormed the Bastille, earning concessions from King Charles VI who issued the *Ordonance Cabochienne*, which provided for elections to the Council of Parliament and the Chambre des Comptes. The ordinance was later withdrawn when the rioting was suppressed. REF.: *CBA*.

Cabral, Amilcar, 1921-73, Guinea, assass. Founded the *Partido Africano da Independência da Guiné e Cabo Verde* in 1956. In 1962 he initiated a revolt against Portuguese rule, became ruler of unoccupied areas of Guinea, and was assassinated in 1973. REF.: *CBA*.

Cabranes, Jose Alberto, 1940- , U.S., jur. Appointed to the District Court of Connecticut by President Jimmy Carter in 1979. He authored "International Law and the Control of the Drug Traffic," *International Lawyer*. REF.: *CBA*.

Cabrera, Luis, b.1876, Mex., lawyer. Professor of civil law. Books authored: *El Balance de la Revolución*, and *Veinte Años Después*. REF.: *CBA*.

Cabrera, Ramón (**Conde de Morella**), 1806-77, Spain, rebel. Commanded the Carlist insurgents between 1833-40 and 1848-49. His criminal behavior resulted in his forced exile to France in 1840. He returned briefly from 1846-49, but finally retired to England in 1860. REF.: *CBA*.

Caddell, Dr. George, d.1700, Brit., mur. But for a moment's carelessness, Dr. George Caddell, an English country doctor, might have lived to a comfortable old age while held in the esteem reserved for doctors. Instead he used his surgical knife to end a life, and aborted his own.

After medical school in London, Caddell settled in with a Worcester surgeon named Randall, and married his daughter. The young woman died during childbirth, however, and Caddell moved on to Litchfield, where he worked for two years under a surgeon named Dean. In Litchfield, he again took up with the surgeon's daughter, a young woman high in the social register, and might have married her but for his attraction to Elizabeth Price, a seamstress recently jilted by a young army officer.

Caddell took advantage of her. But Price, finding herself pregnant, demanded marriage, threatening to go public with their affair if he did not comply. Weeks passed and in desperation she threatened to sabotage Caddell's future with Dr. Dean's daughter.

The only way to be rid of her, Caddell reasoned, was to kill her.

He arranged a meeting with her on the road to Burton-upon-Trent in the country, promising to discuss their impending marriage. Then at dusk, behind a hedgerow, with a surgical knife from his black bag, he stabbed her in the throat.

George Caddell murdering Elizabeth Price.

The next day the body of Elizabeth Price was discovered alongside the doctor's bag and knife. Such compelling evidence made the trial almost a matter of routine. Found Guilty, Caddell was executed at Stafford on July 21, 1700.
REF.: *CBA*; Mitchell, *Newgate Calendar*.

Cadek, Louis J., prom. 1936, U.S., fraud-corr. During the days of Prohibition, Officer Louis Cadek realized a small fortune by shaking down Cleveland bootleggers for a percentage of their profits. The burly policeman jailed anyone who refused to cooperate in his extortion scheme. It was well understood by the criminal fraternity: pay up or go to jail. On one occasion, the bootleggers threw a pig roast and clam bake for Cadek. At the end of the festive day they presented him with a prize: two beer kegs filled to the brim with currency.

Cadek escaped punishment for many years until an enterprising young reporter named Clayton Fritchey of the Cleveland *Press* began investigating the fraudulent sale of nonexistent cemetery lots to the gullible and the naive. As he examined the subpoenaed books of the Crown Hill Cemetery, one name kept popping up: a Mr. Dacek. Alerted to the possibility that Cleveland's most notorious policeman may also have been involved in a crooked scheme that netted $2 million a year, Fritchey began probing into the business affairs of Cadek, also known as Dacek. Among other things, he uncovered the existence of a hidden bank account containing $109,000.

Based on Fritchey's journalistic exposé, Captain Cadek was found Guilty of receiving bribes, and was sentenced in May 1936 to two to twenty years at the Ohio Penitentiary. When asked to comment on his sentence, Cadek told reporters: "A good guy always gets kicked around." REF.: *CBA*.

Cadière, Marie Catherine, b.1709, Fr., witchcraft. The last formal witchcraft trial to take place in France involved an elderly Jesuit priest, Father Jean-Baptiste Girard, and a 22-year-old woman from Toulon named Marie Cadière. The case was brought before the Parlement of Aix-en-Provence in 1731, and it aroused considerable debate between religious skeptics and the church clerics who maintained that the young girl had been bewitched by the old priest.

Catherine Cadière was a deeply religious woman who belonged to a spiritual order directed by Father Girard. He had served as rector of the Royal Seminary of Chaplains of the Navy at Toulon. The young woman's ambition was to become a saint, and she closely studied the behavior of other famous women who had been canonized, including St. Theresa and St. Catherine of Siena. Father Girard took Cadière under his wing, and there soon developed a strong physical attraction between them that bordered on obsession. In time though, Father Girard began to doubt the veracity of her claim of divine inspiration. He advised her to enter a retreat at the convent of Ste-Claire-d'Ollioules.

Depressed and upset by Girard's rejection, Cadière began to exhibit signs of hysteria, dementia, and hallucination. Motivated by her brother, she claimed to have been both seduced and bewitched by Girard. Two other women were persuaded to corroborate her claim, and to testify to having had similar relationships with the priest.

A hastily convened trial began on Jan. 10, 1731. The intimate details of the couple's sexual relationship scandalized the church and the townspeople. "You see here before you a young girl of twenty years, plunged into an abyss of evils, but whose heart is still unsullied," Cadière cried. *Justification de demoiselle Catherine Cadière,* published at the time of the trial, set forth her views on the matter and served as a "warning" to other young women to be on guard against the appearance of piety.

The Parlement at Aix considered the evidence for nearly ten months. A split verdict was finally returned on Oct. 11, 1731. Twelve judges declared that Father Girard should be burned at the stake, and the remaining twelve justices condemned Cadière to hang. President Lebret cast the deciding vote. He decided that Catherine should be returned to her mother, and that the charges of sorcery against Father Girard were not proven. The priest retired to his home in Dôle where he lived only two more years.

REF.: *The Case of Mistress Mary Catherine Cadière Against the Jesuit Father Jean Baptiste Girard; CBA; The Defense of Jean Baptiste Girard;* Garinet, *Historie de la magie en France;* Michaëlis, *La Socière; ____, The Witch of the Middle Ages; ____, Satanism and Witchcraft;* Robbins, *The Encyclopedia of Witchcraft and Demonology;* Summers, *The Geography of Witchcraft;*

Cadman, Josiah, d.1821, Brit., count. Josiah Cadman of London served with distinction in the British army during the Napoleonic wars, but was unable to adjust to civilian life following his honorable discharge. Finding himself in abject poverty, he resorted to printing £5 notes for his own personal use.

Put on trial at the Old Bailey on Sept. 15, 1821, Josiah Cadman entered a plea of guilty, and in an impassioned plea for mercy he described his sufferings: "...wrought upon by the piteous cries of my children, who were deprived of the necessaries of life, I fell, in an evil day, into the grief of wretchedness and misery which has brought me, as a capital felon, to the bar of my country."

Judge Baron Graham refused to grant mercy. He condemned Cadman to die. The sentence was carried out Nov. 21, 1821, despite a last-minute plea for clemency from members of the House of Commons.

REF.: *CBA;* Poynter, *Forgotten Crimes.*

Cadoudal, Georges, 1771-1804, Fr., consp.-rebel. A Royalist sympathizer during the French Revolution, Georges Cadoudal led the Chouans Revolt of 1793, which sought to overthrow the republican government. The movement failed, but Cadoudal joined the Vendé rebellion that same year. He fought in the battles of Le Mans and Savenay in December, but was arrested and imprisoned after returning to Morbihan. Cadoudal escaped and continued his Royalist intrigues. Several times he was forced to take refuge in England, but each time he returned, vainly hoping to restore the deposed heirs of the late King Louis XVI.

First Consul Napoléon offered him clemency in 1800, but Cadoudal was obdurate. He secretly plotted with Saint Régent against Napoléon's life in December 1800, and was again forced to flee to England. In 1803, Cadoudal returned to France with yet another scheme against Napoléon, but before he could put his plan in motion, he was arrested. Cadoudal and eleven co-conspirators were executed in Paris on June 10, 1804. REF.: *CBA.*

Cadwalader, John, 1742-86, U.S., duel. Appointed brigadier general of the Pennsylvania militia in 1777, John Cadwalader served on George Washington's staff during the winter of 1777-78. As the continental troops teetered on the brink of defeat he detected a political intrigue hatched by General Thomas Conway who desired to undermine Washington by placing Horatio Gates at the head of the column. He challenged Conway to a duel resulting in a severe wound and ultimate disgrace to the conspirator. The Conway Cabal was put down and its architect soon left the army. See: **Conway, Thomas.** REF.: *CBA.*

Cady, William, d.1687, Brit., rob.-mur. An artful highwayman, William Cady was one of only a few men in his chosen career to complete a college education. His father was a prominent surgeon who tried to endow his son with all the advantages of a liberal education. Instead, the young man practiced his trade on the highway where his refined manner and elegant clothes lured many unsuspecting travelers to part with their silver and gold. After he robbed the Viscount Dundee near Bagshot Heath, the London *Gazette* posted a £100 reward for his immediate capture.

Beneath the graceful facade lurked the soul of a depraved killer. One of Cady's victims was a middle-aged woman traveling in the company of her husband. When asked to hand over a gold ring that Cady wanted, she swallowed it, satisfied that the highwayman had been cheated. She paid for that gesture with her life. Cady shot her through the head, ripped open her stomach, and retrieved the ring while her husband looked on.

He was eventually captured, charged with murder, and executed in 1687.

REF.: *CBA;* Pringle, *Stand & Deliver.*

Caecina (Aulus Caecina Alienus), d.79 A.D., Italy, treas. Roman general assigned to command the military forces of Spain. At first he supported the aims of Vitellius, a political foe of Emperor Vespasian. After confronting the armies of this powerful adversary in Italy, Caecina betrayed Vitellius, inducing his men to join up with Vespasian. In 79 A.D., Caecina conspired against Vespasian and was put to death by his son Titus. REF.: *CBA.*

Caedwalla (Cadwalader, Cadwallon), d.634, Brit., assass.-mur. King of Gwynedd, North Wales, he forged a military alliance with king Penda of Mercia, against the Northumbrians and their ruler Edwin whom he killed in 633. Edwin's nephew Oswald avenged the slaying by taking the life of Caedwalla a year later. REF.: *CBA.*

Caelius (Marcus Caelius Rufus), 82-48 B.C., Roman., assass. Appointed praetor of Rome in 48 B.C. He joined the tribune Milo in a revolt against the rule of Caesar who had failed to justly reward him for his efforts against Pompey. He was killed by a group of soldiers he attempted to bribe. Cicero defended his reputation and put to rest allegations that Caelius had tried to poison the mistress of Catullus, a Roman lyric poet. REF.: *CBA.*

Caepio, Quintus Servilius, prom., 106 B.C., Roman., milit. misconduct. Roman general appointed to govern Gaul in 105 B.C. He suffered a military setback when he was defeated by the Cimbri people. As a result, he was expelled from office by the Roman Senate, convicted and imprisoned for official misconduct. REF.: *CBA.*

Caerularius, Michael, prom. 1040, Constantinople, her. Two hundred years after Photius created the schism between the Eastern (Greek) and Western (Roman) churches, Caerularius, as Patriarch of Constantinople, revived and brought to fruition the old religious controversy. In 1054 he was excommunicated by Leo IX and banished five years later by Isaac I. REF.: *CBA.*

Caesar, Julius (Gaius Julius Caesar), 100-44 B.C., Roman., gen. and statesman, assass. The most famous military leader of his day and one of the world's greatest generals, Julius Caesar was born into the patrician class. He married Cornelia, daughter of the politically powerful Lucius Cinna, in 84 B.C., immediately joining the popular party led by Cinna and his uncle, Marius. Caesar rose to prominence and was soon the rival of Lucius Cornelius Sulla, head of the oligarchic party. When Sulla triumphed, Caesar was proscribed, living in political seclusion until Sulla's death. In 60 B.C., he acted as mediator between the two leading statesmen in Rome, Pompey and Crassus, forming with them an alliance known as the first triumvirate. The following year Caesar was elected consul to the Senate and then proconsul in Gaul and Illyricum. As pontifex maximus (elected in 63 B.C.), Caesar instituted a great many reforms, notably creating the Julian calendar.

Cornelia died in 68 B.C. and Caesar remarried, wedding Pompeia who later became involved in a sex scandal with Publius Clodius, causing Caesar to divorce her, uttering the politically memorable line: "Caesar's wife must be above suspicion." He then married, in 59 B.C., his third and last wife, Calpurnia. Following this marriage, Caesar concentrated upon the military conquests in Gaul, vigorously directing the Gallic Wars (58-49 B.C.). He proved himself brilliant in strategy and tactics, defeating his enemies time and again and earning for himself the legendary reputation of an invincible commander. He outmaneuvered and defeated the huge armies of the Helvetii and was victorious over Ariovistus in 58 B.C., and the following year defeated the Belgi. He then invaded and subdued Britain (55-54 B.C.), crossed the Rhine (55-53 B.C.) to suppress a revolt led by Vercingetorix and made Roman power absolute.

Julius Caesar

Caesar's daughter Julia, who was married to Pompey, died in 54 B.C. From that time a rivalry between Caesar and Pompey increased to the point where they openly challenged each other for supreme authority; Caesar being the popular leader, Pompey the champion of the senatorial party. Then Crassus died in 53 B.C. which increased the fierce rivalry between Caesar and Pompey, and the Senate, apprehensive of Caesar's increasing power, voted to order Caesar to disband his army. This move, of course, was induced by Pompey and Caesar replied that he would comply only if Pompey disbanded *his* army. The Senate then ordered Caesar to disband his army immediately. Marc Antony and Cassius, Caesar's most devoted followers, voted against the Senate's bill and then left Rome, joining Caesar. The great general then made his fateful decision in 49 B.C. to march against Pompey and the Senate, crossing the Rubicon, the small river separating Caesar's province from Italy. As his confident armies marched into Italy, Caesar was overheard to deliver the fatalistic remark, "the die is cast."

Civil war erupted, but Caesar's powerful legions drove back Pompey's troops in disarray, and Caesar triumphantly entered Rome as the supreme ruler. He then pursued Pompey into Greece and decisively destroyed Pompey's army on the plains of Pharsala. Pompey fled to Egypt and Caesar pursued him there, only to find his old enemy assassinated by officers under the command of Queen Cleopatra as an act of appeasement to the powerful Roman general. When Caesar was shown Pompey's severed head, Caesar reportedly ordered the grisly trophy of war removed and wept over the fate of his one-time comrade. In Alexandria, Caesar dallied with the siren Cleopatra, having a brief love affair. He then secured her throne by defeating Egyptian forces pitted against her, easily destroying an Egyptian army under

the command of Pharnaces at Zela (47 B.C.), a victory so quickly won that it caused Caesar to make his vainglorious comment, "veni, vidi, vici" ("I came, I saw, I conquered"). He then wheeled his armies about and destroyed the remnants of Pompey's armies at Thapsus (46 B.C.) and Munda (44 B.C.).

By then Caesar had brought Cleopatra to Rome where he demanded she be recognized Queen of Egypt, keeping her as his mistress but living apart with his wife Calpurnia, an arrangement subtly criticized by his closest friends, Marc Antony and Cassius. In Rome, Caesar accepted the titles of dictator, first consul, and general, but refused to be named king on Feb. 15, 44 B.C., when the Senate offered him the crown. He made plans to begin a military campaign against Parthia. Meanwhile, a group of senators led by Marcus Junius Brutus, who had been a follower of Pompey and who had been pardoned by Caesar after the battle of Pharsala, were plotting his assassination. Fearing that Caesar would take the crown and become monarch of Rome, ending the powers of the Senate, Brutus joined Cassius and others in a conspiracy to murder Caesar on Mar. 15, 44 B.C. (The Ides of March).

On that day Caesar had reservations about attending the Senate meeting; his wife Calpurnia reportedly had had dreams during the night that he would be assassinated. But Decimus Brutus, whom Caesar trusted, went to his commander and convinced him that he would appear indecisive and be embarrassed in following the nightmares of his wife, then reassured Caesar that there was nothing to fear in the Senate. Decimus Brutus had been one of Caesar's most trusted officers in the Gallic wars, a brilliant admiral who had created a fleet and defeated the Veneti at sea, the first decisive naval battle to be fought in the Atlantic Ocean. And it was Decimus Brutus who was the most active of the conspirators, dragging the reluctant Marcus Brutus into the plot to murder Caesar, the latter first believing that Caesar could be persuaded by reason into not accepting absolute powers. When the crown was offered to Caesar and was rejected in February 44 B.C., Marcus Brutus came to believe that this was but a show of humility on the part of Caesar and that he would accept the crown when it was next offered.

The role played by Decimus Brutus was pivotal as he was, next to Marc Antony, the closest to Caesar. What motivated his resolve to murder Caesar is still in debate today. He was a patrician like Caesar, a trainer of gladiators, a man who felt that Rome should be ruled by a strong man and, unlike Cassius, he had little faith in the concepts of a republic or a democracy. Although generously rewarded for his bravery and victories by Caesar with titles and estates, it is possible that Decimus Brutus was prompted to his betrayal of Caesar because he resented living in the shadow of so great a man, or, perhaps, as some have also theorized, he was rebelling against a pervasive father figure. His true motives remain lost in the dark historical maw of that era. Cassius, on the other hand, had a clear view as to why Caesar had to die. He hated tyrants of all kinds and since boyhood had rebelled against the notion of absolute monarchs. As a boy he had slapped the face of Sulla's son when the youngster bragged of his father's power.

Cassius, who is historically credited as the chief conspirator, was, more so than all the others, including the highly principled Marcus Brutus, led by altruistic goals to kill Caesar. It was Cassius who argued that by killing Caesar, Rome could become a true republic. But the organizer of the assassination was certainly Decimus Brutus, who enlisted the aid of the other senators and made arrangements for Caesar's closest friends and supporters to be absent from the Senate at the time of the murder, so that only the conspirators surrounded the victim and could perform their grisly task unmolested. In this manner, the courageous Marc Antony and others were kept from defending Caesar. Other than Decimus Brutus, Marcus Brutus, and Cassius, the rest of the conspirators were of little import, adventurers and opportunists for the most part, venal rogues who could, like Casca, the one who struck first, be bought. Plutarch records that Casca was approached by another conspirator brought in at the last minute and that the senators inquired of Casca: "How came you to be so rich all of a sudden...?" The answer was that Casca had been paid—most likely by Decimus Brutus—to aid in the murder of Julius Caesar, and, like most of the others, was no more than a lowly hired assassin.

Caesar unwittingly aided the conspirators by suggesting that the Senate meeting on the Ides of March be held in the Pompeian Chamber or Portico, a somewhat closed-off area of the Senate building where the conspirators could perform their murder unseen. It was about 10 a.m. when Caesar left his villa and set off for the Senate. En route, as was then the custom, he was handed numerous petitions from those seeking all manner of political favors. Caesar bundled these under his arm, intending to read them later. One of the petitions he was handed detailed the plot to kill him that day and listed all the conspirators. This, like the rest of the petitions, went unread, its contents discovered after Caesar's murder. In this last trip of his life, Caesar also met the soothsayer Spurrina, who had warned him days earlier to "beware the Ides of March," telling Caesar that he would risk death on that day. When seeing Spurrina in the crowds about him, Caesar smiled and mocked the prophecy, saying to the augur: "The Ides of March have come." Replied the ancient Spurrina: "Aye, they have come but not yet gone."

After entering the Senate, Caesar sat down, his conspirators sitting behind him and next to him. Senator Tillius Cimber approached Caesar with another group of conspirators and pleaded the cause of his brother, who had been exiled by Caesar. With a wave, Caesar dismissed him, but Cimber, as if in desperation, reached out to clutch Caesar's cloak, the signal for the conspirators to strike. As Caesar protested and pushed Cimber away, Casca thrust a knife at Caesar from behind, the blade entering at the throat, but this was not a fatal wound and Caesar instinctively drew his own knife and stabbed Casca's arm. He then saw the entire group encircling him, blades drawn, thrusting forth. Caesar drew up his cloak so that his head was covered, but before

The assassination of Julius Caesar

he did so he saw Decimus Brutus (not Marcus Brutus, as popularly believed), and uttered the immortal line in Greek: "Kai su teknon?" ("You, too, my son?"). The famous words "Et tu Brute?" have little or no foundation in fact, and no proper authority confirms these to have been the last words of Julius Caesar or as having been directed to Marcus Brutus.

Roman historian Suetonius described how Caesar "was leaping away when another dagger caught him in the breast. Confronted by a ring of drawn daggers, he drew the top of his gown over his face, and, at the same time, ungirded the lower part, letting it fall to his feet so that he would die with both his legs decently covered. Twenty-three dagger thrusts went home as he stood there." The aim of the conspirators was for each of them to equally share in the assassination, each one obligated to make a dagger thrust so that no one conspirator would shoulder the lone responsibility for the murder. When Caesar staggered and fell to

his death—ironically near the foot of Pompey's statue—the conspirators suddenly became confused, believing that Marc Antony was arriving with troops. They had originally planned to drag the body to the Tiber and throw it in so that no corpse would serve to remind the public of the murder, then confiscate Caesar's considerable estates and treasures and destroy all his edicts. Instead, panic seized the killers and they fled to their homes.

Three of Caesar's slaves found the body some time later and carried it home on a litter with one arm hanging from the side. Here Antistius, Caesar's physician, examined the twenty-three wounds and found them all superficial; the wound that had killed him was the second dagger thrust to the heart, the thrust most likely made by Decimus Brutus. The body was cleaned and lay in state in a cemetery near the tomb of Caesar's daughter Julia, the bloody gown which Caesar had worn to his execution displayed on a high pillar above the lounge upon which the body rested. The sight of this gown incensed the thousands upon thousands of weeping mourners who passed the corpse. Many hysterically denounced the killers and the assembled throng was even more enraged at the assassins when they learned that Caesar had bequeathed in his will his vast gardens next to the Tiber to the Roman citizens as a recreation area and that he also left three gold coins to the male citizens of Rome. Marc Antony made much of this as he obliquely indicted Marcus and Decimus Brutus and the other conspirators during a short funeral oration. The crowd then, as was the custom, burned the body and women threw their jewels and the best tunics and robes of their children into the huge funeral pyre as signs of homage to the slain Caesar.

By this time the mobs called for revenge and thousands stormed about Rome seeking the conspirators. The mobs tried to burn down the homes of Marcus Brutus and Cassius, but guards managed to drive them off. A crowd of armed men, including some of Caesar's loyal guardsmen, cornered Helvius Cinna on a street, thinking him to be Cornelius Cinna, who had bitterly attacked Caesar in a speech only the day before the assassination. Despite his protests that he was not the man they were seeking, Helvius Cinna was cut to pieces and his head decapitated, then placed on a spear and carried about the streets of Rome. Caesar's nephew, Octavius (later Augustus), was named as the chief heir to Caesar's power and estates. Ironically, Decimus Brutus was also named in Caesar's will as one of his beneficiaries. Octavius joined with Marc Antony and Lepidus in the second triumvirate, pursuing the army of the conspirators and defeating Marcus Junius Brutus, Cassius, and most of the other assassins at Philippi in 42 B.C. Following this battle, Cassius and Brutus committed suicide rather than be taken prisoner and dragged through the streets of Rome in degradation. Decimus Brutus was by then dead, having fled to Gaul where he was pursued and killed in a battle forced upon him by a vengence-seeking Marc Antony.

REF.: Adcock, *The Roman Art of War under the Republic*; Africa, *Rome of the Caesars*; Balsdon, *The Romans, The People and Their Civilization*; CBA; Charles-Picard, *Augustus and Nero*; Gelzer, *Caesar: Politician and Statesman*; Gibbon, *The Decline and Fall of the Roman Empire, Vol I*; Grimal, *Hellenism and the Rise of Rome*; Hurwood, *Society and the Assassin*; Hyams, *Killing No Murder*; Johnson, *Famous Assassinations of History*; Lintott, *Violence in Republican Rome*; Nash, *Almanac of World Crime*; Oman, *Seven Roman Statesmen of the Later Republic*; Paine, *The Assassins' World*; Pearl, *The Dangerous Assassins*; Perowne, *Death of the Roman Republic*; Plutarch, *Lives: The Dryden Plutarch*; Robinson, *History of Rome*; ____, *History of the Roman Republic*; Sparrow, *The Great Assassins*; Suetonius, *The Twelve Caesars*; Syme, *The Roman Revolution*; (DRAMA) Shakespeare, *Julius Caesar*; Shaw, *Caesar and Cleopatra*; (FILM), *Cleopatra*, 1934; *Caesar and Cleopatra*, 1946; *Julius Caesar*, 1952; *Julius Caesar*, 1953; *The Story of Mankind*, 1953; *Spartacus*, 1960; *Caesar the Conqueror*, 1963; *Cleopatra*, 1963; *Julius Caesar*, 1970; *The Notorious Cleopatra*, 1970; *Antony and Cleopatra*, 1973; *Rome Wants Another Caesar*, 1974.

Caesar, Sir **Julius,** 1558-1636, Brit., jur. Descendent of an Italian noble family. He served as medical adviser to Queen Mary and Queen Elizabeth. REF.: *CBA*.

Cafe Royal Murder, The, See: **Martin, Marius.**

Caffee, William, d.1842, U.S., mur. As the frontier vanished from southwestern Wisconsin, William Caffee became a local legend as a tough-guy desperado in a world that was turning too civilized for his tastes.

While the respectable citizens of Galena, Ill., Mineral Point, Dodgeville, and other towns near the Wisconsin state line concerned themselves with lead mining and carving out a living from the earth, Caffee just drifted about. His one passion in life was dancing. Caffee would eagerly submit his name to the dance caller at the local alehouses and await his turn with the young women. One of his favorite stops on the dance-hall circuit was the ballroom adjoining the saloon of Fortunatus Berry in Gratiot's Grove, Wis. Here, early on the evening of Feb. 23, 1842, Caffee learned that the caller had mistakenly omitted his name from the dance list. Caffee ran off with the list. If he couldn't dance, then nobody would. In the clearing outside the dance hall, the manager of the evening's amusements, a man named Southwick, challenged Caffee to hand over the list, advancing on him in a threatening manner. Caffee took a step back and aimed his pistol. He fired once, dropping Southwick in his tracks.

Arraigned on a charge of first-degree murder, Caffee went on trial in Iowa County. He was found Guilty and hanged on Nov. 1, 1842. Three thousand people were in attendance in what was described as a great public holiday, made even more resplendent by a marching band.

REF.: *CBA*; Derleth, *Wisconsin Murders.*

Caffey, Francis Gordon, 1868-1951, U.S., jur. Served as U.S. attorney for the Southern District of New York from 1917-21; member of the criminal law committee of the New York City Bar Association from 1925-28, and the administration anti-trust law committee in 1927. He was nominated and appointed to sit on the court of the Southern District of New York in 1929 by President Herbert Hoover. REF.: *CBA.*

Cagliostro, Count **Alessandro di (Joseph Balsamo),** 1743-95, Brit.-Fr., fraud-blk.-rob. A flagrant and flamboyant charlatan, di Cagliostro was born Joseph Balsamo in Sicily of poor parents. His father Peter died when he was three and his mother, destitute, was supported by a kindly merchant brother. As a youth, Balsamo lived in the squalor of Palermo where he associated with the worst thieves and confidence men of the city. These underworld dregs taught the poor but intelligent youth the techniques of pickpocketing and burglary. The boy even stole from his indulgent uncle. An unaccountable curiosity led Balsamo to read, his tastes running to tales of adventure, great wealth, and power. He was also fascinated with mysticism, ancient cults, and supernatural powers. He tired of petty thievery and concluded that he would require a tool, a device by

Cagliostro, alchemist and fraud.

which to make his own great fortune. He chose the most popular of the black arts of that uninformed era, alchemy, a process of treating common metals with chemicals that would, it was claimed, change them into silver and gold.

By the time he was seventeen, Balsamo had, through trickery and guile, gained a considerable reputation as a successful alchemist. No one ever saw him perform the changing of lead into gold but he allegedly produced such minor miracles, or so the best-informed gossips had it. The youth could also call forth spirits and was reported to be a powerful medium. Of course, the legends the clever youth was building stemmed from sleight-of-

hand tricks he had learned and developed since childhood. There was some substance by then in the clever Balsamo's background. He had sought out Benedictine monks in a mountain monastery and there learned chemistry and medicine. He had also apprenticed as an apothecary, so that by the time he met a greedy goldsmith named Marano he was able to perform some basic chemical experiments that convinced the goldsmith that he could produce gold from common metals. He told Marano that he would require sixty ounces of pure gold to produce several pounds more of the precious metal. When Marano delivered the gold to Balsamo, he immediately fled to Messina where he adopted the title of Count Alessandro di Cagliostro.

With his stolen gold, Cagliostro purchased an impressive wardrobe and became the sponsor of an ancient mystic named Althotas, who dressed in Oriental robes and was always accompanied by an Albanian greyhound. It was rumored that the Greyhound aided Althotas in his performance of black magic, the so-called art of which he slowly taught to Cagliostro. To expand his perception of ancient black arts, Cagliostro toured Africa and Asia with Althotas, his guide into the realms of magic. In Egypt, Cagliostro studied the pyramids and became knowledgeable in the history of secret sects and their rites. From this he put together a loose brotherhood philosophy which he labelled Egyptian Masonry. At age twenty-three, Cagliostro sailed to the Mediterranean island of Malta. By this time the soothsayer and clairvoyant Althotas had vanished. Some later claimed that he was murdered and that Cagliostro had a hand in his violent end, wishing to rid himself of someone who might later expose his black magic and feats of alchemy.

On Malta, Cagliostro managed an introduction to the powerful Pinto, grand master of the Order of the Knights of Malta, an organization that stemmed from the crusaders of 800 years earlier and was now a Masonic sect of great political influence. Pinto was impressed with the erudite and cunning Cagliostro and not only taught him further in the occult arts of alchemy and black magic but provided him with considerable funds with which to travel to Italy as a sort of Masonic spy in high places, sending back information to his mentor in Malta. In southern Italy, Cagliostro established a lavish resort which was little more than a gambling casino. He traveled for some time, meeting the hypnotist, Franz Antone Mesmer, creator of mesmerism, and learned how to hypnotize even the most sophisticated person. (Mesmer, a charlatan of sorts himself, later denounced Cagliostro as a fraud, a clear-cut case of the pot calling the kettle black.)

In Rome, Cagliostro met a beautiful young girl, Lorenza Feliciani, the daughter of a Calabrian glovemaker. They married and she joined him in his fabulous confidence swindles. Establishing themselves in various Italian cities as nobles, renting huge villas, Cagliostro and his wife cultivated the company of aristocrats and held seances and demonstrations of his magical alchemy where he supposedly changed stones into rare gems and rope into strands of priceless silk but, of course, these "miracles" were nothing more than the magic tricks Cagliostro had perfected over the years. To raise money, the charlatan resorted to the old badger game, sending his sensual and alluring wife to lure some wealthy aristocrat to her bed and then bursting into her boudoir to shockingly "discover" the sexual betrayal which invariably resulted in Cagliostro collecting substantial blackmail payments from the aristocrat.

All during his travels through southern Europe, Cagliostro continued to establish branches of his own sect of Egyptian Masonry and these naive groups regularly sent him money to establish new chapters. His ego bloated by his own impossible claims, Cagliostro insisted that he could perform acts of astounding wizardry, such as bringing forth spirits. He claimed that he could heal all manner of illnesses by laying his hands upon sick people and pronouncing secret oaths, and that his alchemy could produce the richest metals seen on earth. He became the social rage of France and was heralded as a great healer but his so-called miracles were nothing more than demonstrations of common sense.

Cagliostro never accepted real medical challenges and only after Lorenza and other aides determined the causes of an illness, would he deign to perform his healing magic. Invariably, his patients were made up of self-indulgent nobles who were not really ill but had convinced themselves that they were suffering from some strange malady. Before a large crowd assembled in his villa or mansion, Cagliostro would simply approach his subject and state: "It is our will that your body become healthy!" The subject would usually begin to feel better and, when Cagliostro used his own planted shills, some "miracles" were seen to occur. Those imposters pretending paralyzed limbs or blindness suddenly stood and walked, astoundingly regained their sight. Cagliostro easily "cured" those aristocratic ladies who were suffering from malnutrition due to reckless diets by simply telling them to "eat a full dinner and drink one bottle of red wine."

Enormous amounts of money began to flow into Cagliostro's coffers—gifts, donations, and outright payments from the nobility for his cures, his seances, his advice on matters of health, hygiene, and even sex. He became the highest-paid oracle on earth. Coupled to this princely income were great gluts of cash he received from the dozens of Masonic sects he had established in Italy, Greece, Spain, and France. The rogue slowly withdrew from his regular private meetings and gatherings, living the life of kingly leisure. He made a great show of giving away money and food to the poor and from them he received his greatest support; in their ignorance the peasants utterly accepted Cagliostro as a true worker of magic and miracles, a man gifted with supernatural powers. His name was spread throughout Europe by the lowly-born as one of the great men of their times.

In 1776, Cagliostro was in London, celebrated and feted as the world's greatest alchemist and occultist. He and his wife Lorenza, who now called herself Serafina, lived in regal splendor in a mansion on Whitcomb Street near Leicester Square. Cagliostro's reputation preceded him to London and by the time he moved into his regal rooms, he was inundated with requests from high-born ladies who begged for audiences with him, seeking his "elixir of youth," or love philtres that were supposed to make them sexually active and alluring—all of these potions widely advertised by Cagliostro's shills before his arrival in London. He continued to claim that he could turn base metal into gold and silver and now added that he had obtained the all-powerful Philosopher's Stone, a few rubbings from which, when mixed with melted brass or copper, would produce pure gold. Those fortunate enough to buy an audience with Cagliostro entered his mansion to behold a stunning array of silk tapestries and drapes, hanging from ceiling to floor and emblazoned with occult designs and mystical symbols. Rare incense hung sweet and thick in the air. Mirrors decorated the walls of most of the larger rooms and Cagliostro often produced ghosts and apparitions in them, or so it appeared.

The great charlatan had by then enriched his lore of the occult by obtaining an obscure manuscript by one George Gaston, which ostenisbly claimed to provide answers to the Great Mysteries. Cagliostro used Gaston's gobbledygook phrases to explain the unexplainable. He had also by then studied with the enigmatic occultist and mystic, St. Germain of France and he employed this charlatan's methods to great effect, producing spectacular seances (for staggering fees, of course) which saw spirits from the dead invade rooms, float to the ceiling, drift in and out of mirrors, sink into glass goblets, and cry out messages to the living. These were the tricks of master occult frauds and swindlers which Cagliostro had carefully studied and perfected. He reveled in his riches and in his power, knowing that all feared him, including those who sat on thrones, because of his supposed control of spiritual forces. He was fond of jocularly saying to disbelievers upon first meetings: "Remember, I can afflict as well as heal."

Like P.T. Barnum a century later, Cagliostro gave a great deal of time to appearances, that of his home, his wife, and particularly himself. He strutted about London dressed in bright-colored silk coats, shoes with jeweled buckles, his hair braided and powdered, gold buttons studding his stockings, rings of diamonds, rubies, emeralds, and sapphires gleaming on his fingers. Across his frilled silk shirt was a large gold chain from which hung a gold watch, and dangling beneath this a huge diamond drop which lay atop his braided waistcoat. He adorned his head with a brilliant musketeer's hat topped with a colorful plume. He was the most sartorial resident of London.

Cagliostro took to forseeing the future, claiming impeccable clairvoyant powers and, for great sums of money, he would predict the winning numbers of lotteries, the health and sex of children to be born, and, especially for lustful noble ladies, the amorous intentions of men they admired and desired. When Cagliostro's predictions failed, he had myriad excuses which were accepted out of fear or shame. The subject had not been worthy of winning, so fates changed the winning lottery number. The subject's conspiratorial thoughts caused a wanted lover to turn away. There was no end to his fantastic apologia. Not everyone accepted Cagliostro's outlandish claims and powers. He quickly made enemies, some of whom broke into his mansion and attempted to destroy the chemicals he used in his feats of alchemy, along with the apparatus he employed to conjure spirits.

The charlatan's Masonic branches in Europe, however, continued to send him considerable funds and Cagliostro's reputation as a leader of this brotherhood impressed the London Freemasons and he was welcomed at their meetings. He agreed to represent and spread the philosophy of the Grand Lodge of England and he and his wife shortly departed for the continent. Cagliostro was glad to leave England where he was hated by an increasing number of "jealous husbands and frustrated lovers." The great charlatan toured Europe in triumph, visiting the Masonic Lodges in Belgium, Holland, and Germany, being received as a distinguished guest by Frederick II of Prussia and other monarchs. He returned to France where he became a court favorite of King Louis XVI and his tempestuous, beautiful queen, Marie Antoinette. In 1785, the powerful Cagliostro was undone in the notorious Affair of the Diamond Necklace. He was, at the time, a house guest of the cardinal-archbishop of Paris, Louis de Rohan, who had been duped through some spectacular seances into believing that Cagliostro possessed extraordinary powers. The cardinal, a capricious sort, gave over an entire wing of his palace to Cagliostro and Lorenza-Serafina and provided him with a huge laboratory in which to practice his alchemy and produce gold for his host. In return, de Rohan made sure that every important noble and lady in France met his mystical guest and profited from Cagliostro's astounding wisdom. So lofty had the charlatan become that he was now referred to as the Divine Cagliostro. One of his most devoted sponsors and patrons was the Countess de LaMotte, who intrigued with her husband and a band of sophisticated thieves to use Cardinal de Rohan in a bold swindle which would involve the cardinal and the queen herself, or someone who appeared to be the queen.

LaMotte and his wife knew that the rather naive de Rohan was deeply in love with Marie Antoinette. He was approached by an emissary of LaMotte's who told him that the queen reciprocated his affections but was forced to be discreet and not offend her ineffectual and sexually inactive husband, Louis XVI. The queen, de Rohan was informed, desired a special necklace that had been recently designed, one that boasted a fabulous collection of perfect diamonds that were worth $100,000. Marie Antoinette would be eternally grateful if de Rohan would guarantee purchase of the necklace. The cardinal asked that the queen personally make this request of him. He was given a letter reportedly signed by the queen which requested the delivery of the necklace, a clever forgery of the queen's handwriting and signature. De Rohan told the jeweler that he would guarantee payment for the necklace after it was delivered to him. The necklace was delivered and de Rohan kept a rendezvous with a woman he thought was Marie Antoinette, a night meeting in a dark palace garden where a woman named Leguet, heavily veiled, successfully impersonated the queen. The cardinal slavishly presented the necklace to the monarch he loved and she promised to reward him in the future with her "favors." With that the woman departed with the necklace, the diamonds from which were sold one by one outside of France within a few weeks, Count LaMotte and his wife receiving most of the spoils from this swindle.

A short time later, the jeweler presented his bill to the queen, saying that Cardinal de Rohan had guaranteed its payment. Marie Antoinette had no intention of paying for a necklace she had never received. When de Rohan was informed of this by the jeweler, he soon discovered that he had been swindled. Moreover, he was asked by Louis XVI to explain his actions and the embarrassed cardinal told him that he had been the victim of a giant fraud. Oddly, for his indiscretion, de Rohan was thrown briefly into the Bastille for compromising the queen and his prized house guest, Cagliostro, was seized and thrown into an adjoining cell. Though he had committed hundreds of crimes for which he deserved imprisonment, Cagliostro was entirely innocent of the diamond necklace swindle. After a six-month investigation, the great charlatan was proved innocent, as was de Rohan, and both were released. The LaMottes were exposed as the culprits but the Count LaMotte had fled. He was sentenced to the galleys for life in absentia. His wife was sentenced to be branded with a V (for *voleuse,* thief), whipped publicly, and sent to an asylum for life.

Though Cagliostro at first reveled in his exoneration, his credibility was seriously undermined by the suggestion that he was suspected of being involved in this swindle. Even the suggestion of being a fraud lent belief to the many accusations that he was a fraud. His association with de Rohan also injured him in that Marie Antonette was livid at the Cardinal for dragging her into the Affair of the Diamond Necklace and he was ostracized. Cagliostro left Paris and continued his travels but the necklace swindle tainted his image and eroded his carefully-constructed reputation. The swindle caused the French peasantry to further resent the "Austrian" monarch and this incident was one of the first to create the intense hatred for her and her overly-indulgent husband, a hatred that swept through France and eventually brought about a revolution that would end the lives of Marie Antoinette and Louis XVI.

In the very year of the French Revolution, 1789, Cagliostro returned to Rome and there purchased a lavish villa, resuming his seances and magical rites. At one of these exhibitions, the main salon teemed with nobles and distinguished visitors eager to see a demonstration of Cagliostro's powers of alchemy. One visitor described the event thusly: "At the end of the salon had been erected a kind of altar, on which were placed skulls, stuffed monkeys, serpents who writhed and coiled as in life, owls, musty parchments, amulets, crucibles, and other strange furniture. Incense was burning before the images of fantastic Chinese and Egyptian idols. Cagliostro, wrapped in a Chaldean robe, appeared followed by his wife. He passed, or pretended to pass, into a trance, and gave a lively description of the Marriage of Cana of Galilee. (By this time in his life Cagliostro had been telling his patrons that he was thousands of years old and had been a personal friend of Cleopatra and the Queen of Sheba.) He then seized a glass beaker of pure water and crying "Ero sum qui sum" poured therein two drops from a small vial he kept in his bosom, whereupon the liquid seemed to be transformed into a sparkling wine, cups of which were handed to the guests who pronounced it delicious. Pschometry and crystal-gazing followed..."

These performances were reported to members of the Inquisition and caused Cagliostro and Lorenza, and their chief aide, Fra Francesco, to be arrested on Dec. 27, 1789. Before the tribunal of the Inquisition, Cagliostro denied that he was a heretic and practiced fraud. Lorenza, however, after reported torture, confessed to these crimes and wholly implicated her husband. She was sent to the convent of Santa Appollonia in Trastevere where she remained a prisoner and died many years later. Cagliostro was sentenced to death, but Pope Pius VI commuted the sentence to life imprisonment. In the Vatican fortress prison of San Leo,

Cagliostro lived miserably in a sparsely-furnished cell, chained to the floor. He slowly went insane, some reports had it and died on Aug. 28, 1795. One account has it that he was strangled to death by his wardens who believed that followers of his Egyptian Masonic sect were planning to free him.

REF.: Burckhardt, *Alchemy;* Burland, *The Arts of the Alchemist;* Carlyle, *The French Revolution; CBA;* Faÿ, *Louis XVI;* Goran, *Fact, Fraud, and Fantasy: The Occult and Pseudosciences;* Hughes, *Witchcraft;* Hunt, *Exploring the Occult;* Hunt, *A Dictionary of Rogues;* Mossiker, *The Queen's Necklace;* Nash, *Zanies, The World's Greatest Eccentrics;* Redgrove, *Alchemy, Ancient and Modern;* Scott, *The Concise Encyclopedia of Crime and Criminals;* Seth, *Witches and Their Craft;* Summers, *The Geography of Witchcraft;* (FICTION) Dumas, *Joseph Balsamo;* (FILM), *Black Magic,* 1949.

Cagoule, La (The Hood), prom. 1937, Fr., secret soc. The Hood was an organization of French fascists founded by a right-wing journalist named Léon Daudet who railed against the breakdown of French society in the pages of his newspaper, *L'Action Française.* Between 1908 and 1944, the paper served as the voice of the ultra-right, engaging in smear tactics against liberal politicians, whom he denounced as homosexuals, and civil service administrators who did not share the publisher's extreme views.

In its heyday the Hood attracted a membership of several thousand, and was patterned after other secret societies, notably the Ku Klux Klan in the U.S. The leader of this fanatical organization was Eugène Deloncle, who was arrested in October 1937 following two bomb explosions at the offices of the industrial employers' associations in the Étoile district of Paris. The terrorist actions were designed to arouse sympathy and financial support from the leading industrial capitalists. After Deloncle was taken into custody, the warehouse of munitions that the Hood had been storing up in the event of a revolution was seized.

La Cagoule was temporarily dismantled, but it resurfaced to spread defeatist propaganda among the civilian populace when France's borders were threatened by the Nazis. When the Germans marched into Paris in June 1940, the Hood was on hand to welcome the conquering armies. Concentrated mostly in the north of France, this group of right-wing militants actively supported the Vichy government before disappearing when the war ended.

REF.: *CBA;* MacKenzie, *Secret Societies.*

Cahill, Clyde, 1923- , U.S., jur. Appointed to sit on the bench of the court of the Eastern District of Missouri, in 1980 by President Jimmy Carter. He was chairman of the criminal law division of the St. Louis Lawyers Association from 1976-78. REF.: *CBA.*

Cahn, William, prom. 1977, U.S., polit. corr. When he was at the very top of his game, Nassau County District Attorney William Cahn would explain to his associates that the reason he flew first class to his destinations was because he represented a first-class county. Cahn booked himself into the swankiest hotels and traveled first class at the state's expense.

There was an empty ring to his words following his conviction on forty-five counts of mail fraud stemming from his embezzlement of travel expense money. Cahn was accused of double billing the county and other law enforcement agencies for expense money during his twelve-year term as D.A.

His first trial in February 1976 resulted in a hung jury. The federal government expanded the case and presented a wave of new indictments, which Cahn described as a "vindictive action" on the part of the federal agents. During the trial deliberations, the Long Island resident told the jurors that the money he had squirreled away was to be used to pay an underworld informant by the name of Sam Houston who was offering valuable inside information on criminal activities in his jurisdiction.

The government claimed at the time that the informant was a figment of Cahn's imagination, invented to shield a blatant rip-off of federal monies. "I will spend the rest of my days looking for Sam Houston," Cahn vowed, "to produce him not only to the jurors but to the government of the United States." A second trial resulted on Apr. 11, 1977, in a verdict of Guilty, and Cahn began serving a one-year sentence at the Allenwood Federal Prison Camp in Pennsylvania. The 4,200-acre, minimum-security camp was home for a number of prominent white-collar criminals of the 1970s, including the major Watergate conspirators G. Gordon Liddy, Jeb Stuart Magruder, and Charles Colson. REF.: *CBA*.

Caiaphas, Joseph (Caiphas), prom. 33 A.D., Judea, jur. Jewish high priest who presided over the council that sentenced Jesus of Nazareth to death. He later sat in on the trial of the two apostles Peter and John. REF.: *CBA*.

Caifano, Marshall Joseph (John Michael Caifano, John Marshall, AKA: Michael Heale, Heels, Thomas Hynes, George Marini, Michael Monette, Johnnie Moore, Joseph Rinaldi, Frank Roberto, John Roberts, Joe Russo, Joe Russell, Shoes, John Stevens), 1911- , U.S., org. crime. Marshall Caifano and his brother "Fat Lennie" emerged as kingpins of the Chicago crime syndicate in the early 1950s. After Lennie was killed in 1951, Marshall took over Chicago gambling operations in Las Vegas. Caifano's arrest record dates back to 1929 and includes convictions for burglary, extortion, larceny, and interstate fraud. He was a prime suspect in more than ten murders, including that of Russian Louie Strauss in 1953. In his early years in Chicago, Caifano shot gambling rival Frank Quotrocci in the head at a downtown tavern.

The police arrested Matt Capone for the murder after they found a hat bearing the initials "MC" in the street. Caifano established autonomy over his gambling turf in the Uptown neighborhood of Chicago, and was a suspect in at least ten other mob-related murders, including that of Estelle Carey, a Chicago cocktail waitress involved with Nick Circella, a member of the Willie Bioff movie extortion ring. Carey was tied to a chair in her apartment and set on fire in 1941 when the mob suspected Circella of saying too much to the government. The murder was never solved. Other suspected Caifano victims were Richard Cain, Cook County sheriff's investigator turned criminal, and oil tycoon Raymond J. Ryan, who frequented syndicate-run crap tables. In the early 1960s, Caifano had threatened Ryan with abduction unless he paid $60,000 annually.

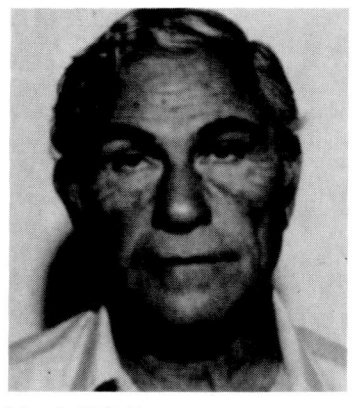

Marshall Caifano

Ryan went to the FBI in 1964, and Caifano, who had legally changed his name to John Marshall, was convicted of extortion and sentenced to ten years in prison. In 1972, Caifano was released from prison, and a year later Cain was shotgunned to death in a sandwich shop on Chicago's West Side. Ryan died in 1977 when a bomb ripped apart his automobile in Evansville, Ind.

In 1968, the mob stole a large number of stock certificates from Chicago's O'Hare Airport. Caifano agreed to help them dispose of the hot properties upon his release from jail. In 1975, he and five other men transported 2,000 Westinghouse stock certificates worth $4 million from Chicago to Florida. Caifano was arrested and convicted in West Palm Beach in March 1980 for interstate transportation of stolen securities. On May 23, 1980, a federal judge in Miami sentenced Caifano to two concurrent twenty-year sentences. Caifano is now imprisoned in the federal penitentiary in Sandstone, Minn., and is scheduled for release in 1991. See: **Cain, Richard**.

REF.: *CBA*; Demaris, *Captive City*; ____, *The Last Mafioso*; Reid, *The Grim Reapers*; Zuckerman, *Vengeance Is Mine*.

Caillaux, Henriette Claretie (Henriette Rainouard), d.1943, Case of, Fr., mur. For nearly fourteen years, editor Gaston Calmette of *Le Figaro* had published attacks on Joseph Caillaux, France's minister of finance. Caillaux bore the abuse with quiet

dignity, though his appeasement policies came under sharp scrutiny during the period of belligerence before WWI, when all of France clamored to end the German threat. Caillaux was criticized for his pacifism and for his introduction of an unpopular income tax that made him "the most hated man in France."

Henriette Caillaux, murderer of Gaston Calmette.

Caillaux was also condemned for leaving his first wife, Berthe, for 36-year-old socialite Henriette Claretie, whose unhappy marriage to a writer ended in an annulment. For some time Caillaux had conducted the affair secretly and illicitly, but wrote Henriette a series of intimate letters. Henriette's maid intercepted the letters and, out of "common decency," showed then to Berthe Gueydan-Caillaux, who began blackmailing her husband before leaving for the Riviera. She demanded a large cash settlement and continuing alimony for her granting Caillaux his freedom, a price which he was willing to pay.

Henriette's marriage to Joseph Caillaux was one of the last great social events before the war. The president of the republic threw a banquet in their honor. In February 1914, Caillaux began his own private investigation of Gaston Calmettte to determine the motives for *Le Figaro*'s endless attacks. Caillaux's investigators discovered that Calmette was associating with German financiers,

The massive funeral in Paris for Gaston Calmette.

who sat on the board of directors of *Le Figaro*. When Calmette threatened to publish Caillaux's love letters in the paper, Caillaux bought a gun.

On Mar. 16, 1914, one of Caillaux's letters to Henriette, written on the stationery of the Chambre des Désputés, appeared on page one of *Le Figaro*. Henriette Caillaux resolved to avenge the insult herself. She bought a small handgun and went to the office of *Le Figaro* on the Rue Drouot. Calmette, curious and surprisingly unafraid, ushered her into his office, where she shot him five times, then stood quietly by as police and employees rushed into the office. "Forgive me for causing a disturbance," Calmette said. He died a short time later at the hospital at Neuilly.

The murder trial of Henriette Caillaux opened on July 20, 1914. The disclosures of Calmette's alleged treason shocked Paris. Secret documents from Hungary proved that Calmette had been paid to write anti-French propaganda for the Austro-Hungarian news agency. His opposition to Caillaux's tax policies had been founded in personal greed. The case against Caillaux collapsed, and she was acquitted on July 28, 1914. Joseph Caillaux died in 1944, having said little about the Calmette murder.

REF.: Archer, *Killers In the Clear;* Boar, *The World's Most Infamous Murders;* CBA; Heppenstall, *A Little Pattern of French Crime;* Kershaw, *Murder In France;* Nash, *Look For the Woman;* Raphael, *The Caillaux Drama;* Sparrow, *Vintage Victorian Murder;* Wilson, *Encyclopedia of Murder.*

Caillol, Alain, 1939- , Fr., kid. Alain Caillol masterminded the abduction of wealthy Belgian industrialist Baron Empain outside his Paris apartment on Jan. 23, 1978. The Baron was held captive for sixty-three days while his wife and the police negotiated the ransom demand, estimated to be $20 million. However, the Baron was a brave man who had previously ordered his wife to make no deals with kidnappers. The police requested a news blackout, which angered the kidnappers. After two torturous months during which Baron Empain was moved three times, the Baron's family agreed to pay $8 million.

During this period, the police located and staked out the gang's location. On Mar. 24 they ambushed the kidnappers at the prearranged spot where the money was to be dropped. Three of the five gang members escaped. A fourth was killed, and Alain Caillol was arrested on the spot. Police learned that he was not the dangerous and desperate criminal they would have expected to commit a crime of this nature. Rather, Alain Caillol was the son of a wealthy manufacturer who owned a beautiful villa with a swimming pool. Crime was a game to this wealthy playboy, who panicked at the thought of the guillotine.

Caillol called his associates from the police inspector's office and demanded that they release Baron Empain immediately, lest they all lose their heads together. On Easter Sunday 1978, the Baron was freed on the outskirts of Paris. The other gang members were quickly rounded up and charged with complicity in the crime. Because the Baron had survived the ordeal, the kidnappers avoided the death penalty.

REF.: CBA; Clutterbuck, *Kidnap & Ransom.*

Cain, Biblical, mur. Son of Adam and Eve, Cain is infamous in the Old Testament as the world's first murderer. According to the Bible, Cain was a farmer, his younger brother Abel, a shepherd. Both made offerings to God and Abel's sacrifice was looked upon with favor, Cain's rejected. Brooding over this, Cain "rose up against Abel and slew him. And the Lord said unto Cain, 'Where *is* Abel thy brother?' And he said, 'I know not: Am I my brother's keeper?'" The Lord then drove the killer into the world and "set a mark upon Cain, lest any finding him should kill him. And Cain went out from the presence of the Lord, and dwelt in the land of Nod, on the east of Eden."

REF.: Boucher, *The Pocket Book of Crime Stories; CBA;* Genesis: iv, 1-25.

Cain, John (AKA: **Whisky Jack**), and **Rayne, Richard,** prom. 1855, Case of, Brit., mur. Robert Stirling arrived in the village of Burnopfield, Durham in October 1855, fresh out of medical school. He took a post as the personal assistant to the village physician, Dr. Watson, while awaiting military call-up. The Crimean War was waging on the continent and Stirling had requested a position in the army hospital service.

His budding medical career—and his life—were abruptly ended on Nov. 1, when he was assaulted and shot to death three miles from town on Smailes Lane. A post-mortem examination revealed the presence of a knife wound to the throat. The killer left no doubt that he wanted the young doctor dead. The Durham police, under the direction of Superintendent Jabez Squires, had very little to work with. However, a Cumberland farmer named Ralph Stobart claimed he was the last man to see the doctor alive. He told Squires that he had seen two suspicious looking men, one of them walking with a pronounced limp, lurking near a hedge.

This information led to the arrest of a Winlaton blacksmith named Richard Rayne and a Newcastle bootlegger they called "Whisky Jack Cain." Superintendent Squires searched his house and found a waistcoat with a missing button. An identical button had been found near the body of the victim, and with this evidence, the two men were bound over to the Durham Assizes to stand trial for murder on July 25, 1856. The prosecution based its case on the eyewitness testimony of Mr. Stobart who proved to be less than reliable. He assumed an air of defiance, and was obdurate in his attitudes toward the court. Other witnesses provided confusing and contradictory testimony, and it was never established that the two defendants were even on the road the day of the murder. A Not Guilty verdict was returned, and the two men were freed. In the case of Whisky Jack Cain, eleven of the twelve jurors had voted for conviction.

REF.: CBA; Lambert, *When Justice Faltered.*

Cain, Richard B. (Richard Scalzetti), 1924-73, U.S., org. crime. In 1952, at the age of twenty-six, Richard Cain joined a Miami detective agency, but was fired for stealing checks. A short time later, he was appointed to the Chicago Police Department. In 1959, Cain and his partner Gerald Shallow shot and killed an ex-convict named Harry Figel, supposedly during a gun battle. But attorneys for the Figel family charged that Cain had taken Figel downtown and murdered him. The charge was dropped, but a few months later Cain got into trouble again, this time for shaking down 68-year-old prostitute Grace Van Scoyk, who kept $30,000 in her safety deposit box. Cain persuaded her to surrender her keys, and the cash disappeared.

Cain was suspended from the police force in 1960 after he was caught using electronic surveillance devices on a top member of Mayor Richard Daley's staff. Cain then went to Miami to train anti-Castro insurgents for the Bay of Pigs invasion. In 1962, Cook County sheriff Richard Ogilvie named Cain to head his investigations unit. Despite his record, Ogilvie believed Cain could help end mob influence in the Chicago suburbs.

On Oct. 4, 1963, a truck containing drugs worth $250,000 was stolen from the Louis Zahn warehouse in Melrose Park, Ill. Four months later, Cain led a raid on the Caravelle Motel in nearby Rosemont, where some of the loot was supposedly stored. It was discovered that police officers had set up the raid. Cain, Lieutenant James Donnelly and Sergeant John Chaconas were suspended from the force and indicted for perjury, obstruction of justice, and conspiracy. It was suspected that they had set up the robbery and the raid, and then tried to sell the seized drugs back to the robbers, but this was not proven. They were found Guilty of conspiracy to commit perjury on Dec. 2, 1964, but a higher court later suspended their prison sentences. After Ogilvie fired him, Cain turned to the mob. Chicago mob boss Sam Giancana valued Cain's contacts in Mexico, South America, and the Caribbean, prime targets for syndicate gambling. Cain convinced Giancana to move to Mexico City when conditions in Chicago grew difficult.

In December 1967, Cain was indicted along with twenty-three other mobsters, including Willie "Potatoes" Daddano, for the Sept. 23, 1963, robbery of the Franklin Park (Ill.) Savings and Loan Association. The robbers were arrested a few days later, which caused Daddano to suspect that one of them was an informant. Cain used lie detector tests to find out which one it was. Guy Mendola, thought to be the traitor, was shotgunned outside his home in August 1964.

Cain's self-conducted legal defense consisted entirely of character witness testimony and newspaper clips, and in October 1967 he was sentenced to four years at the federal penitentiary in Texarkana, Texas, and fined $13,000. Upon his release in 1971, Cain returned to Giancana, whose power was already declining. Cain tried to sell the mob on the idea of gambling cruises in the Mediterranean, but Giancana staunchly refused. Cain then tried to interest younger hoods, especially disgruntled hitman Marshall Caifano in the venture. Cain told them that he soon would be the one in charge. But Giancana told him to back away. To Caifano, the message from Giancana was clear enough.

On Dec. 20, 1973, Richard Cain was murdered in Rose's snackshop on Chicago's Near Northwest Side. The gunmen were reportedly Joseph "Joey the Clown" Lombardo, Vincent "the Saint" Inserro, and Caifano himself. See: **Lombardo, Joseph; Caifano, Marshall.**

REF.: *CBA;* Demaris, *Captive City;* _____, *The Last Mafioso;* Reid, *The Grim Reapers.*

Cairns, Hugh McCalmont (First Earl Cairns), 1819-85, Ire., lawyer. Orator in the House of Lords, Cairns served the Crown as attorney general and lord justice of appeal from 1866-68. REF.: *CBA.*

Cairns, Ralph, d.1939, Palestine, law enfor. off., assass. Nine years before the founding of the state of Israel, Zionists carried out various acts of terrorism against the British occupiers of Palestine. Abraham Stern, leader of the militant Zionist faction, ordered the execution of Palestine Criminal Investigation Department (CID) Inspector Ralph Cairns in Summer 1939. The group hated Cairns for his brutal and often barbaric treatment of prisoners under interrogation. On Aug. 27, 1939, in Rehavia, located in the heart of the Jewish quarter of Jerusalem, a remote controlled land mine exploded, killing Cairns and CID Inspector Ronald Eric Barker. The CID searched for and arrested a number of terrorists suspected for the killings, but charged no one.

REF.: *CBA;* Hyams, *Killing No Murder.*

Caius, Marcus, prom. c.62 A.D., Roman., treas. Marcus Caius was put to death by Nero in a brutal, shocking manner, after he was accused of plotting the overthrow of the Emperor in 62 A.D. Caius was taken into the center ring of the Circus Maximus and placed inside a hollow bull that had been sculpted for the occasion. While thousands of bloodthirsty revelers looked on, the whipped and beaten Caius was placed inside the metal chamber and a fire was lit underneath the belly. The agonized cries of Caius shocked and delighted the assembled Roman multitudes who bore witness to this and other atrocities committed during the reign of Nero. See: **Nero.**

REF.: Bishop, *Executions; CBA.*

Cajetan of Thiene (St. Gaetano Tiene), 1480-1547, Italy, lawyer. With Pope Paul IV he helped found a religious order known as the Oratory of Divine Love, which later evolved into the Theatines. REF.: *CBA.*

Calabaza, Ariz., prom. 1870s-1880s, U.S., fugitive haven. This area, frequented by the worst criminal element in Arizona, was just across the Mexican border, near Nogales, and served as a "sheriff-proof" hideout for wanted felons, much the same as the notorious Hole-in-the-Wall or Oklahoma's Indian Territory. No lawman in his right mind would enter this area in search of wanted men as dozens, often hundreds, of gunmen were always present. The camp was destroyed when two huge outlaw factions battled each other and caused the clapboard camp to burn down in the process. The surviving residents limped across the border to resettle in Nogales. See: **Hole-in-the-Wall; Indian Territory.**

REF.: Brown, *Calabaza; CBA.*

Calamia, Leonard (AKA: Benny Leonard), 1910-   , Case of, U.S., drugs-mur. From his North Side home in Chicago, Leonard Calamia coordinated the distribution of illegal drugs on the West Coast. In 1966, the government called him one of the fifteen most influential narcotics violators in the country. Calamia was also a suspect in the 1945 murder of Carl Caramussa, racketeer turned government witness. And on May 9, 1947, the body of Chicago mobster Nick De John was found stuffed into the trunk of his new convertible in San Francisco, a penny pressed in his hand as a

message from the mob that a double-crosser had been dealt with.

Calamia, the last person believed to have seen the victim alive, was arrested on Dec. 23, 1948, and charged with murdering De John. "I knew who he was, sure," Calamia protested. "But he was a big-money man. He wouldn't pay any attention to a small-time guy like me."

Informant Anita Venza Rocchia told police that four henchmen had plotted De John's murder during a card game in San Francisco's North Beach section. De John had stolen more then $200,000 from Vincent Benevento, the boss of Chicago's Little Sicily. Calamia begged Frank Ahern and Thomas Cahill of the San Francisco Police not to arrest him because he feared retribution, but he was one of three men indicted for murder, a fourth conspirator, Frank Scappatura, having fled to Seattle.

On Feb. 1, 1949, the trial of Lenny Calamia, Michael Abati, and Sebastiano Nani began in San Francisco. But the defendants were released on Mar. 8 after District Attorney Pat Brown suspended the prosecution because of what he called "dubious" testimony.

REF.: *CBA;* Nash, *Bloodletters and Badmen;* Reid, *The Grim Reapers.*

Calamity Jane (Martha Jane Canary or Cannary), 1852-1903, U.S., pros. Much has been written about Calamity Jane, a western character who was often a mistress to lawmen and gunmen, and, periodically, a common prostitute in such western towns as Deadwood, S.D., where she met the famous lawman and gunfighter, James Butler Hickok, better known as Wild Bill. Very little of the vast amount of literature produced about this frontier character is factually reliable. Calamity Jane, as she is known in legend, was created from an illiterate, alcoholic, common prostitute. She apparently had a brief affair with Hickok but there was never a lasting relationship between these two. Calamity Jane was more man than woman, tall and muscular and wearing men's clothing. Following Hickok's death, Calamity Jane was celebrated by dime novel writers as "the White Devil of the Yellowstone" and all kinds of wild adventures were attributed to her, almost all of them pure inventions, particularly her scouting for the U.S. cavalry and fighting Indians. Calamity Jane supposedly captured Jack McCall after he shot Hickok to death, cornering the back-shooter with a cleaver in a butcher shop a short time after the killing but this, of course, is pure fiction, as Calamity Jane herself admitted some years later. She appeared in a few wild west shows but was invariably fired for being drunk. Calamity Jane briefly married but this union was ruined by her alcoholism. As late as 1900, Calamity Jane was found working in a brothel. She died in Terry, S.D., on Aug. 1, 1903, not far from Deadwood, calling out Wild Bill's name and insisting that she be buried next to the western hero, a wish that was granted. Thus, ironically, Hickok, who thought Calamity Jane a nuisance and a lowlife in life, lies next to her in eternity. See: **Hickok, James Butler.**

REF.: Abbott, *We Pointed Them North;* Adams, *Album of American History, Vol. II;* Aikman, *Calamity Jane and the Lady Wildcats;* American Guide Series: *A South Dakota Guide;* Bennett, *Boom Town Boy in Old Creede, Colorado;* Bennett, *Old Deadwood Days;* Botkin, *A Treasury of Western Folklore;* Buel, *Heroes of the Plains;* _____, *Life and Marvelous Adventures of Wild Bill;* Bullough, *Prostitution;* Burk (Calamity Jane), *Life and Adventures of Calamity Jane; CBA;* Clairmonte, *Calamity Jane was Her Name;* Cunningham, *Triggernometry;* Drago, *Notorious Ladies of the Frontier;* Godwin, *Murder, U.S.A.;* Hueston, *Calamity Jane of Deadwood Gulch;* Jenewein, *Calamity Jane of the Western Trails;* Mumey, *Calamity Jane, 1852-1903;* Sollis, *Calamity Jane;* Spencer, *Calamity Jane: A Story of the Black Hills;* (FILM), *The Plainsmen,* 1937; *Calamity Jane and Sam Bass,* 1949; *Calamity Jane,* 1953; *The Raiders,* 1964; *The Plainsmen,* 1966.

Calamy, Edmund, 1600-66, Brit., her. Opposed to religious dogma in all forms, Calamy was associated with the Calvinist party, but resigned in 1636, protesting ceremonial observances. He served as a member of the Westminster Assembly in 1643, decrying the execution of Charles I on religious and moral grounds. He declined appointment to a bishopric following the restoration of the monarch, and was subsequently imprisoned for preaching without license. REF.: *CBA.*

Calandra, Joseph, 1918- , Case of, U.S., fraud. Dr. Joseph Calandra was the founder of International Bio-Test, Inc., one of the oldest medical research and testing laboratories in the U.S., headquartered in Northbrook, Ill. The 65-year-old professor of medicine at Northwestern University was named in an indictment charging him with conspiring to defraud clients and various federal regulatory agencies by attempting to pass false test studies conducted on arthritis medicines, chemicals, and pesticides used on vegetable crops.

The Environmental Protection Agency (EPA) conducted a seven-year inquiry into the research performed at Bio-Test. Thirty-five chemicals were found to have been untested for possible health hazards. The manufacturers of the chemicals were ordered to perform safety tests or face an across-the-board ban on all U.S. sales.

The trial of Calandra and three codefendants opened in U.S. District Court on Apr. 13, 1983. U.S. Attorney William Spence described to the jury the inhumane conditions that laboratory animals were often subjected to by Calandra and his associates. Mice, rats, and other small animals were confined to an area derisively known as "the Swamp" where they frequently died from thirst and lack of food. The carcasses were often left to rot in cages.

The Northbrook, Ill., firm grew quickly in the years following the creation of the EPA. There was a need for bona fide research laboratories to conduct safety experiments on various new medicines and pesticides introduced to the U.S. markets.

Dr. Calandra escaped a possible conviction when Judge John Nordberg declared a mistrial on July 11, 1983, in order to allow the defendant to undergo triple bypass surgery at the Loyola University Medical Center. Attorney George Cotsirilos successfully argued that his client would not receive the benefits of a fair and impartial hearing following post-operative convalescence.

International Bio-Test was sold to Nalco Chemical of south suburban Oak Brook in 1976 after the investigation commenced. Experiments are no longer conducted at the Northbrook office. REF.: *CBA.*

Calas, Jean, 1699-1761, Fr., (wrong. convict.) mur. The Calas family of Toulouse, France, was part of the Protestant minority. The father, Jean Calas, clung to his faith with the hope that his children would do the same. It came as a terrible shock to him when his 28-year-old son Marc Antoine announced his intention to convert to Catholicism.

When Marc Antoine Calas was found dead in his home in 1761, the authorities assumed his father was the murderer. The evidence showed that young Calas had hanged himself. When the relatives found the body, they attempted to diguise the rope burns by affixing a tie to his neck. They were afraid of the inevitable scandal and the besmirchment of the Calas name. The police concluded that the father had merely attempted to hide his crime.

Jean Calas was tried for murder and condemned to death on the wheel. His execution was carried out, the family property confiscated, and his daughters were placed in a convent. The philosopher Voltaire became interested in the case at this point, and demonstrated to the courts that Marc Antoine had committed suicide as a result of a large gambling debt he had incurred. He had killed himself out of fear. In March 1764, the royal Councillors, meeting at the palace of Versailles, opened an official inquiry. A year later the deceased was absolved of all guilt, and the family estate was returned to its rightful owners.

REF.: *CBA;* Forster, *Studies In Black & Red;* Nixon, *Voltaire and the Calas Case.*

Calbeck, Lorene, 1922-89, U.S., suic.-mur. Thirty years after Lorene Calbeck shot and killed her three toddlers outside a trailer park in Polk County, Fla., she shot herself.

The tragedy occurred on May 24, 1956, when the 34-year-old housewife took her three children for a ride in the family car. For reasons known only to herself, she shot each of them four times in the left side of the chest, and then carried them back to the trailer. Lorene placed them side by side: Shirley, five; Pamela,

three; and Jane, aged fifteen months. She wrapped them in cellophane and then called the family doctor and asked him to come to her house in half an hour. After she hung up the phone, she fired two shots into her chest.

She left behind a suicide note explaining how to water the gardenias and giving various other instructions to her husband Mark, who was away in Michigan at the time. However, doctors were able to save Lorene Calbeck's life. She was pronounced mentally incompetent by medical investigators. A Polk County grand jury refused to return an indictment, but remanded Lorene to the care of the state mental hospital at Chattahoochee, Fla. Seemingly on the road to recovery, she was released from the doctor's care and returned to her husband Mark. On Jan. 3, 1989, Lorene Calbeck staged an eerie re-enactment of the events of that long-ago night. Armed with a .32-caliber pistol, Calbeck sat down in her lawn chair near the family plot at Lake Wales Cemetery. Despondent over the death of her husband and the direction her life had taken in the last few years, she fired a bullet into the left side of her chest, and then, in pain, drove back to her mobile home off U.S. Highway 27.

Calbeck phoned the 911 number to report the shooting. The emergency team arrived quickly, but was unable to get her to the hospital in time. She died in the ambulance. A search of her trailer turned up several notes explaining how to operate various mechanical devices, including her television and the car. The boxes on the utility shelves had been pre-arranged according to size, and her funeral had been paid in advance. In her last set of detailed instructions, Calbeck explained that she wanted to be buried beside her husband and children. REF.: *CBA.*

Calcraft, William, c.1800-79, Brit., execut. William Calcraft served as the public executioner of London for forty-five years, longer than any of his predecessors. He did not aspire to the position as a young man. Calcraft worked for a time as a shoemaker, a butler, and as a watchman at a brewery in Clerkenwell. He was recruited by John Foxen, then serving as the city's hangman. Foxen thought that a youth as robust as Calcraft might be good at administering floggings at Newgate Prison.

Calcraft went to work for Foxen at a salary of ten shillings a week. In his spare time he observed Foxen's

Hangman William Calcraft.

handling of the rope, and soon learned all the techniques of a hangman. Executions were carried out on the Monday following sentencing. The condemned prisoners were lined up in rows of three to six. Calcraft first demonstrated his hanging skills when Foxen was unable to attend to a pair of hangings in Lincoln. After Foxen died on Feb. 14, 1829, Calcraft was appointed public executioner by the Committee of the City Jails. He was sent to death many of the notable murderers of the age, including James Greenacre, Courvoisier, John Tawell, Catherine Wilson, and Margaret Walters. His first encounter with a condemned murderer was with Esther Hibber on Apr. 13, 1829. The woman had neglected and killed an innocent workhouse child. When he appeared on the scaffold, the witnesses to the execution cheered him. "Good old Calcraft!" they yelled. "Three cheers for the hangman!"

The Crown paid Calcraft a guinea for every hanging, but as his reputation for reliability spread, Calcraft was able to collect fees ranging from £10 to £15 when he was called on to leave the city. He collected additional fees from the sale of the condemned person's clothing and personal effects. It was a custom in England that these items be given to the hangman. Sections of the rope were sold for five shillings an inch if the felon had attracted a degree of notoriety.

It was Calcraft who carried out the last public execution in Britain. The victim was Michael Barrett, a member of the radical Irish Fenian movement who had masterminded the Clerkenwell explosion of 1868. Barrett was hanged in front of Newgate on May 26, 1868. The last person to die at Calcraft's hands was John Goodwin, who was hanged on May 25, 1874. Soon after, the aging executioner announced his retirement. He was given a pension of twenty-five shillings by the grateful city of London, and was replaced by William Marwood.

REF.: Atholl, *The Reluctant Hangman*; Bleackley, *Hangmen of England*; Brock, *A Casebook of Crime*; *CBA*; Cooper, *Lesson of the Scaffold*; Laurence, *A History of Capital Punishment*.

Caldclough, James, d.1739, Brit., rob.-asslt. On the gallows at Tyburn, James Caldclough admitted to the gathering that he deserved to die even though he had never murdered anyone. His last words implored all to see the error of his ways and learn from it.

Such was the lament of this failed thief of Durham. Apprenticed to a shoemaker in his youth, Caldclough fell in with hoodlums and soon quit the trade. He enlisted in a London regiment of footguards before joining up with a gang of London footpads whose petty crimes netted barely enough to a night at the local pub.

More sophisticated thievery awaited them. Stealing two horses in Kent, they could now prey on passing coaches, but not without discretion. From Enfield Chase through the woods of Epping Forest the Caldclough gang was known for its compassionate brand of thievery. One day outside Hackney, Caldclough robbed a man of his last eighteen pence. Moved by the man's pleas, Caldclough sent him off with a half-crown. He later recovered his loss, however, from a more solvent victim.

Caldclough and his cohorts spent their fortune as fast as they made it and for a long time their luck held. Then they met two wealthy gentlemen, Swafford and Banks, on the road between London and Kensington. They took five guineas from Banks and silver from Swafford, leaving him for dead on the road, before fleeing across the Thames to Westminster. But their luck had run out.

Caldclough and his accomplice, Robinson, were apprehended the next day. With Robinson's testimony against him, Caldclough was convicted and executed on July 2, 1739.

REF.: *CBA*; Mitchell, *Newgate Calendar*.

Caldecote, Thomas Walker Hobart Inskip, 1876-1947, Brit., jur. Called to the bar in 1899, he held various governmental posts, including attorney general between 1928-29 and 1932-36, and lord chief justice from 1940-46. A strict moralist when it came to cases involving religious or ethical issues, he presided over the murder trials of Thomas Henry Allaway, William Henry Podmore, Edith Thompson, and Frederick Bywaters. REF.: *CBA*.

Calderon, Rodrigo (Conde de Oliva, Marqués de Siete Iglesias), b.c.1576-1621, Spain, polit. Served the Duque de Lerma and was a court favorite of Philip III. He was imprisoned by the enemies of Philip upon the king's death in 1621. That year he was led to the gallows. His arrogance in the face of death became legend. REF.: *CBA*.

Caldwell, Arthur, prom. 1966, Brit., attempt. assass. Caldwell was a prominent member of the Labor Party of Britain in the mid-1960s. As he was driving through the streets of London one day in 1966, a deranged lone gunman named Peter Kocan pointed a sawed-off rifle at Arthur Caldwell through the glass of his car. The shot missed the mark, and Caldwell suffered only superficial facial glass cuts. Kocan was not affiliated with any radical movement, nor did it appear that the crime was politically motivated. He was captured and sentenced to life imprisonment.

REF.: *CBA*; Paine, *The Assassins' World*.

Caldwell, Charles, 1772-1853, U.S., criminol. This American physician produced *Elements of Phrenology*, published in 1824, the first textbook in the country on the subject. Elaborating upon the works of Franz Joseph Gall and John Casper Spruzheim, Charles Caldwell approached phrenology as a valid science wherein criminal tendencies and inclinations in humans could actually be determined through the measurement and study of physical shapes and proportions, chiefly the human head, a belief that found considerable support and was accepted in many forensic quarters as credible through the 1920s. As late as 1924, when phrenologists examined Richard Loeb and Nathan Leopold, killers of Bobbie Franks in Chicago, this "science" stood in good repute and experts in the field were called to testify in that case. Phrenology, since the late 1920s, however, has fallen into disrepute and is all but a discarded pursuit in modern criminology. Taking phrenological concepts to the extreme, many realized, was similar to the ridiculous Nazi propaganda that certain people could be determined to have Jewish blood simply by the shape of their noses, chins, or ears. The basic concepts of phrenology stemmed from comparing physical attributes (thick lips, long earlobes, various bumps in the skull, the setting of the eyes) to known criminals. Those who physically conformed to the physical dimensions of felons of the past were labelled rather arbitrarily to have criminal tendencies, thus rendering, on the part of phrenologists, a moral judgment relative to those who stood accused of criminal acts. See: **Gall, Franz Joseph; Leopold, Nathan; Spruzheim, John Casper**. REF.: *CBA*.

Caldwell, Henry Clay, 1832-1915, U.S., jur. Henry Caldwell was a prosecuting attorney in Des Moines, Iowa from 1859-61. He was appointed judge of the court of the Eastern District of Arkansas in 1864 by President Abraham Lincoln, assigned to the Eighth Circuit Court by President Benjamin Harrison, and reappointed in 1890. REF.: *CBA*.

Caldwell, John, b.1926, Scot., rob.-mur. Scotland was plagued by a series of murders in 1946, committed by minors or people just past the age of majority. There were at least nine deaths attributed to underage youths. One of them involved former Glasgow Detective Sergeant James Straiton, who was shot down by John Caldwell, twenty, and a 15-year-old accomplice who were breaking into a house at the time.

REF.: Brock, *A Casebook of Crime*; *CBA*.

Caldwell, Roger, 1933- , U.S., mur. Marjorie Caldwell and her husband Roger stood to inherit $8.2 million dollars upon the death of her adoptive mother, 83-year-old Elisabeth Congdon, inheritor of a Duluth, Minn., mining fortune, who lived at the thirty-nine-room family mansion on the shores of Lake Superior.

Marjorie's financial recklessness disappointed Elisabeth, and she and Roger Caldwell were always short of money. For a time they used a credit card bearing Congdon's name. In May 1977, Caldwell traveled from his home in Golden, Colo., to Duluth to ask for a $750,000 loan from the family trustees to buy a ranch. The family twice refused.

A month later, on June 27, 1977, an intruder broke into the Congdon mansion in the early daylight hours and climbed the stairs leading to Congdon's bedroom. But he was accosted by the night nurse, 65-year-old Velma Pietila. He seized a brass candlestick holder and bludgeoned the nurse to death, then smothered Elisabeth Congdon with a satin pillow. He fled from the residence and drove off in the family's 1976 Ford, which was later found at the Twin Cities Airport.

The Caldwells emerged as prime suspects in the murders. On July 5, police found a suede travel bag purchased at the Twin Cities Airport and jewelry and personal effects from the mansion in Roger Caldwell's hotel room in Bloomington. Caldwell had checked himself into a hospital in St. Louis Park, where he was arrested on July 6 and charged with murder.

The case went before a Crow Wing County jury on Apr. 10, 1978. Defense attorney Doug Thomson tried unsuccessfully to show that the Caldwells were framed by Marjorie's cousin Thomas Congdon and private detective William Furman. Strangely, Caldwell did not take the stand in his own defense.

On July 8, after eight weeks of testimony, Roger Caldwell was convicted of murdering Mrs. Congdon and her nurse. He was sentenced to two consecutive life terms in prison. Three days later, Marjorie Caldwell was charged with conspiring to murder her mother. Her trial began in March and became the longest in Minnesota history, ending on July 21, 1979, with a Not Guilty verdict.

Around the time of Roger Caldwell's 1977 arrest, a 1972 murder mystery filmed on the Congdon estate was re-released, entitled, appropriately, *You'll Like My Mother*. REF.: *CBA*.

Cale, Guillaume (Guillaume Caillet), d.1358, Fr., rebel. Led a peasant revolt of the Jacquerie in 1358. For this he was seized, tortured, and guillotined. REF.: *CBA*.

Calhoun, John, 1806-59, U.S., lawyer. President of the Kansas Territorial Constitutional Convention in 1857. He was blamed for the passage of the pro-slavery constitution drafted at LeCompton, which ultimately led to bloodshed in that region. REF.: *CBA*.

Calhoun, John Caldwell, 1782-1850, U.S., lawyer. Noted for his advocacy of southern causes in the U.S. Senate between 1832-43 and 1845-50. In 1833 his debates with Daniel Webster in the U.S. Senate brought the slavery issue into sharp focus. Articles authored: "The South Carolina Exposition," "Disquisition on Government," and a "Discourse on the Constitution and Government of the United States." REF.: *CBA*.

Calhoun, William James, 1848-1916, U.S., lawyer. Served the government as emissary to Venezuela, Cuba, and China during his twenty year career in the foreign diplomatic corps. REF.: *CBA*.

Calhoun-Williamson Duel, 1889, U.S., duel-asslt. During the nineteenth century, Atlanta, Ga., as was the case with many other southern cities in the U.S., was plagued with hot-headed gentlemen who insisted that they settle their grievances with pistols, swords, or knives. Atlanta authorities went to great lengths to prevent such slaughter on "the field of honor." This was never more evident than in the absurd clash between two tycoons whose lethal intentions toward each other caused the governors of two states to call out the militia. In August 1889, the governors of Georgia and Alabama conspired to prevent Patrick Calhoun and John D. Williamson from participating in what one writer termed "the custom of pistols for two, breakfast for one."

Both men, railroad magnates, quarreled over the sale of the C.R. & C. Railroad to the Central Railroad of Georgia. They decided to end the dispute with five-shot hammerless, Smith and Wesson pistols on the Farill plantation, just across the Georgia line near Rome. Both men left Atlanta in private cars and on different trains. Posses were ordered by Governor Gordon of Georgia and Governor Seay of Alabama to patrol the state lines and apprehend the duelists. More lawmen followed the departing trains on trains of their own. Newspapermen secreted themselves on the Calhoun and Williamson trains and were present at the place of confrontation after the participants had dodged lawmen for fifty miles.

When Calhoun's second became so nervous that he could not load one of the weapons, newspaperman Ed Bruffey volunteered to put the cartridges into the chambers. But in the semilight of dusk, Bruffey caused the weapon to fire and blew away his little finger. The antagonists finally took their positions. Suddenly, six shots were fired. When the smoke drifted away, Calhoun and Williamson were still facing each other.

There was confusion. Williamson thought they were to fire all their shots at once and did so, none of his bullets landing anywhere near Calhoun. The latter thought they were to fire one shot at a time, and his one round splinted a nearby tree, throwing a piece of bark into Williamson's face. This wound, aside from Bruffey's finger, was the only one inflicted, and the jittery men quickly reconciled their differences. They then scurried back to Atlanta before the posses closing in could arrest them. Thus ended the last great duel in Atlanta's history. REF.: *CBA*.

Calico Jim (Jim Reuben), d.c.1897, U.S., abduc. Calico Jim's Saloon at Battery Point in San Francisco was notorious in the 1890s as a place from which men simply disappeared. When a ship's captain needed sailors for a long voyage to the Orient, he saw Calico Jim. Jim was a Chilean by birth who drifted to San Francisco and became an efficient practitioner of the "Shanghai,"

the forcible impressment of men into duty aboard merchant vessels to China and Southeast Asia.

By the 1890s, the San Francisco Police were called upon to end the treachery of Calico Jim. Six police officers were sent to Calico Jim's crimping joint, but none came back. All of them had been drugged and tossed into cargo holds of sailing ships. With the law after him, Jim sold his interests and moved back to Chile. Months later, the drugged policemen returned to San Francisco one by one, swearing revenge. They allegedly tracked Jim down in Callao, Chile, and shot him six times, once for each officer he had sold into slavery. The San Francisco Police Department maintained that there was no record of six of their men being abducted, but those on the waterfront knew better. REF.: *CBA*.

Caligula (Gaius Caesar Germanicus, AKA: Little Boots), 12-41 A.D., Roman., emp. mur.-assass. Born on Aug. 31, 12 A.D., Caligula's birthplace remains in dispute, reported by Pliny the Younger to be near Trèves in the village of Ambitarvium, between the Rhine and Moselle rivers, and, according to Gnaeus Lentulus Gaetulicus, in Tivoli. Another account has Caligula's birthplace as Antium. As the son of Germanicus Caesar, nephew of Tiberius and Agrippina, Caligula was a nickname given to the boy since he was also reportedly born in a barracks of Roman soldiers on the frontier, the name meaning Little Boots, after the fact that the boy grew up with soldiers and habitually wore half boots known as *caliga*.

Caligula, assassinated in 41 A.D.

Upon the death of Tiberius in 37 A.D., Caligula, a succesful army commander and Tiberius' great nephew, was named heir to the throne jointly with his cousin Tiberius Gemellus who was Tiberius' grandson. Caligula instituted a few reforms as co-emperor and restored trials for treason in 38 A.D.

Then, after a strange illness, Caligula's personality completely changed. He tired of his cousin's authority and had him assassinated. He became inexplicably cruel and committed countless, senseless crimes, ordering wholesale murders, bloodbath shows of wild beasts, and mass executions of criminals and Christians, loosing wild beasts in the arena to devour humans for his pleasure. The emperor was fascinated by wild beasts, particularly tigers and lions, but suddenly announced that meat was too expensive to feed to them and ordered common criminals slain and their bodies thrown to these beasts as food. Caligula then turned against his own caste, selecting the young and handsome sons of noble households and having them branded, flogged, and thrown into the Tiber to drown, all for his own amusement. He had the scions of wealthy families tortured to death or thrown to his wild beasts, and compelled the parents of these victims to witness the horrid executions. When the manager of these gladitorial and wild beast shows failed to provide good performances, he had the man whipped to death with chains for days. Caligula fancied himself a writer of brilliant verse and drama. When a writer of Atellan farces was praised for his wit, Caligula had the playwright burned alive. One wealthy young patrician shouted his innocence as he was brought into the arena and thrown to the tigers. Caligula perversely saved the young man for the moment, ordering him brought to his side where the smirking emperor had Naevius Sertorius Macro, prefect of his Praetorian Guard, cut out the man's tongue and then return him to the arena where the beasts devoured him.

Caligula took mad delight in instructing his executioners in the details of their gruesome chores, insisting that his victims be tortured and then hundreds of cuts made on the flesh nowhere near vital organs so that he could take long pleasure in the victim's suffering, screaming hysterically to his executioners: "Make him feel that he is dying!" He made a great show of attending to royal business by spending hours meticulously signing death sentences and shouting to terrified scribes nearby: "I am clearing my accounts!" Caligula acted as the total tyrant, declaring to the few family members who criticized his enormous excesses: "Bear in mind that I can treat anyone exactly as I please!" When he banished his sisters after accusing them unjustly of intriguing against him, he reminded them that they were fortunate since he had "swords as well as islands" and could just as easily have had them beheaded.

Anyone who opposed Caligula incurred his wrath, and this attitude embraced the ridiculous on many occasions. On one occasion, while watching games in the amphitheater, Caligula became enraged when the crowd began cheering the wrong team, the team he opposed; he rose, screaming: "I wish you Romans had only one neck!" (So I could strangle it!) He walked through his palace constantly complaining that his reign would be forgotten since it was prosperous, with no calamities or major disasters occurring to mark the period for historical significance. He prayed madly for earthquakes, volcanic eruptions, famine, plagues, fires, or military disasters. He could not kill quickly enough. At the dedication of a bridge, the emperor invited spectators to come onto an unfinished portion of the bridge and then ordered these hundreds dumped into the river. When they attempted to swim to shore, Caligula ordered these hapless souls beaten on the head by oars wielded by his sailors. He danced and screamed with glee as this mass murder ensued.

Feasts in the emperor's court were barbaric affairs with Caligula reclining on pillows, devouring his meals while having prisoners brought before him and decapitated by his favorite headsmen. The heads of the deceased were then placed in rows before him until the marble floors were running with blood. Caligula then ordered naked female dancers to perform upon the blood-coated floor, writhing lewdly, his nobles then ordered to join these dancers in a mass orgy. On other occasions, Caligula would frolic with young men in homosexual orgies. At other times, he would invite powerful senators with attractive wives to his feasts, then take the wife into another chamber to ravish her, returning to discuss the woman's physical attributes and sexual prowess (or the lack of it) with the cowed husband. These effronteries increased as Caligula's madness deepened. He was tolerated by the Senate and the aristocracy since he was so firmly backed by the army and his powerful Praetorian Guard. But he turned against the Guard and ordered the execution of Macro, the prefect, who had the audacity to tell Caligula that he was earning a bloodthirsty reputation. Following this execution, the emperor insisted that he was a god and demanded that he be addressed as "Divinity." When Cassius Chaerea, tribune of the Practorian Guard, was too slow to acknowledge him as god, Caligula verbally insulted him for an hour, humiliating him before his best soldiers.

On Jan. 24, 41 A.D., as he was leaving a theater in Rome and selecting young male actors with which to sleep that night, Chaerea suddenly appeared behind the emperor with some of his men and shouted: "Take this!" and thrust the blade of his sword deep into Callgula's neck. The madman fell to the ground, but shouted: "I am still alive!" With that Chaerea and his guards slashed frantically away at the squirming Caligula, cutting away his genitals. Dozens of sword thrusts went into his breast and slashed his limbs and head until the body was all but unrecognizable. At the same time, a centurian, part of the widespread plot to assassinate this most brutal of emperors, killed Caligula's empress, Caesonia. His small daughter, Julia Drusilla, was also murdered by having her brains dashed out against a wall. Caligula's body was later burned. Chaerea roused the Senate and told its members that he had struck down the tyrant and that "the return of liberty" had come to Rome, demanding that they embrace the concepts of the old republic. Instead, Tiberius Claudius Drusus was named emperor. Claudius would rule for

thirteen years and prove in many ways to be a worse tyrant than his lunatic nephew Caligula.

REF.: Balsdon, *The Emperor Gaius;* _____, *The Romans;* Bishop, *Executions;* Carcopino, *Daily Life in Ancient Rome; CBA;* Charles-Picard, *Augustus and Nero;* Gibbon, *The Decline and Fall of the Roman Empire;* Grant, *The World of Rome;* Johnson, *Famous Assassinations of History;* Nash, *Almanac of World Crime;* Robinson, *The History of Rome;* Suetonius, *The Twelve Caesars;* (FILM), *The Robe,* 1953; *Demetrius and the Gladiators,* 1954.

Calinescu, Armand, 1893-1939, Rom., premier, assass. Leader of the National Peasant Party, Armand Calinescu became Romania's Minister of Interior (1937-39) and later premier (Mar. 7, 1939) and was under orders from King Carol to suppress the Iron Guardists, a pro-Nazi organization. Calinescu ruthlessly ordered wholesale arrests of Guardist gunmen, and dozens were shot while "attempting to escape." In vengeance, the Iron Guardists marked Calinescu for death and he was assassinated by Guardist thugs on Sept. 21, 1939.

REF.: *CBA;* Gaucher, *The Terrorists;* Roberts, *Rumania: Political Problems of an Agrarian State;* Wolff, *The Balkans in Our Time.*

Calkins, William Henry, 1842-94, U.S., jur. Prosecuting attorney in Indianapolis, Ind., from 1870-71. He was appointed judge of the territorial court of Washington by President Benjamin Harrison in 1889. REF.: *CBA.*

Calla, Caesar (AKA: Crispi or Cella), prom. 1911, U.S., mur. The first conviction of a suspect based solely on fingerprint evidence in New York City, was returned by a jury in May 1911. In April of that year, the owner of a millinery shop reported to police that his establishment had been burglarized. Detective Joseph Gilkerson, who had familiarized himself with the new technique of criminal identification that was slowly replacing the Bertillon Method of bone measurements, examined a piece of glass. A number of fingerprint smudges were found on the pane. The glass was dusted off and the prints were traced to Caesar Calla, who had a stock alibi. He claimed he was at the Hippodrome the night of the burglary and could not have been involved.

Calla's wife and brother confirmed his alibi, but the indictments were returned against the suspect. After weighing the evidence, a guilty plea was entered in midtrial, thus ushering in a new chapter in New York police history. REF.: *CBA.*

Callahan, Edward, d.1912, U.S., (unsolv.) assass. Edward Callahan was elected sheriff of Breathitt County, Ky., in 1902. It was a hotly contested election that commenced a bloody family feud between the Hargis faction and the Cockrells. Over 100 men were killed in a ten-year period ending in 1912.

Callahan owned and operated a general merchandise store in Crockettsville. He was regarded as a decent, well-respected citizen...as well as a dangerous man with a gun. He was closely tied in with Judge James Hargis and had been indicted for murder five times during the feud. The victims were all Cockrell men, but Callahan and Judge Hargis somehow managed to escape prosecution. To add insult to injury, Hargis was elected to the bench in the same election that placed Callahan in office.

The widow of one of the murdered mountain men, James Marcum, secured a judgment against Callahan for $8,000, which was promptly paid. After an assassination attempt on May 3, 1910, the sheriff built a stockade around his property to protect his wife and children from vengeful Cockrell men.

These precautions did not save him from the next assassin, who aimed at Callahan as he stood in his Crockettsville store on May 4, 1912. Two steel bullets pierced his chest and leg. The shots came from the same spot where a gunman had two years earlier fired on and wounded the sheriff.

REF.: *CBA;* Johnson, *Famous Kentucky Tragedies and Trials.*

Callahan, Gerald Michael (AKA: Cheesebox Callahan), 1909- , U.S., burg.-fraud-org. crime. Gerald Callahan was born and raised on the tough Lower East Side of New York. His father was a corrupt Prohibition agent who took payoffs from bootleggers operating in lower Manhattan. Through his father, who had some loose ties to Tammany Hall, Callahan received his introduction to members of the criminal underworld.

Gerry Callahan was good with his hands and proficient in electronics, talents that served him well in later life. After completing a two-year course in electronics at a small college in Texas, Callahan worked at Bell Laboratories, where he perfected his craft.

Armed with a wealth of knowledge, he quickly earned a reputation as the man to see in the underworld if you needed a wire tapped or a phone bugged. In 1931 Al Capone brought him to Chicago where he was hired to tap into the racing wire, perfected by Mont Tennes who owned the Nationwide News Service. For years, Tennes and his associates had refused to allow the Capone gang a partnership or a cut of the take.

The "wire," as it was known, disseminated race results to hundreds of poolrooms and bookie operations directly from the tracks. It was Callahan's job to tap into the phone boxes, enabling the syndicate men to disrupt Nationwide's service by sending along incorrect race results and payoff information to the poolrooms.

Another favorite technique was to hold back results long enough for the Capone men to get a bet down at the parlor even though the race had been run. "We wrecked at least twenty bookies, all of them big operators," Callahan recalled. "We took a fortune from them. The big guy in Florida (Capone) was very happy, and I went back to New York with a suitcase full of green."

Callahan completed at least 1,000 similar wiring jobs in his career and never spent a day in jail, though he was twice convicted of violating the New York wiretap law. In each instance he drew suspended sentences. In the 1950s Gerald Callahan earned the famous nickname he actually detested—Cheesebox. Working from his kitchen table in Flushing, N.Y., he invented a small electronic device resembling a cheesebox. It was a bookie's dream. The cheesebox permitted a gambler to connect two telephones and speak with his customers from a remote location. This virtually guaranteed that a horse parlor would be free of police raids. Callahan installed his cheesebox at a cost of $250 per unit and charged $100 a week in rental. In 1960 he earned revenue from sixty of these devices functioning in the New York area.

Callahan wore many hats in his day. He was a self-described card cheat, second-story man, and bookie. Though he was out of the business by 1972, the veteran wiretapper admitted that he would have enjoyed bugging the Watergate Hotel. "Only I wouldn't have used an army of men," he told a reporter in 1975. "I always worked alone. I would have taken out (tapped) every phone a distance away and set up recorders. There's no way I would have been trapped." His autobiography, *Cheesebox,* written with Paul Meskil, was published in 1975. See: **Capone, Al; Tennes, Mont.**

REF.: *CBA;* Katz, *Uncle Frank.*

Callahan, Jack (AKA: **Jack Kelly, Jack Lanahan**), prom. 1930s, U.S., burg.-pris. esc. As a boy growing up in the slums of Boston, Jack Callahan had only one ambition—to become an "A-No.1, high-grade burglar scout" like old Uncle Harry.

By the time he reached his twenty-fifth birthday, Callahan had graduated from housebreaking to bank robbery. Desperadoes like John Dillinger were making public names for themselves, so Callahan thought he would give it a try. In Littleton, N.C., he broke into a bank vault but was quickly apprehended, convicted, and sentenced to the State Prison at Raleigh for fourteen years.

The fact that no convict had successfully escaped from the "Tar Heel madhouse" did not discourage Callahan from giving it his best shot. One night he lowered himself down a rope extending from the washroom in the cellblock to the prison courtyard. Callahan had planned this escape with a lifer named Charley Melvin. What he didn't know was that Melvin had tipped off the warden, who was waiting on the bottom with a bevy of armed guards. After receiving a brutal beating that laid him up for nearly three weeks, Callahan was transferred to a prison farm at Tillery, N.C.

Reserved for only the most hardened criminals, the prison farm offered little chance of escape. The supervisor of the facility was Henry Summerfield, a brutal overseer who beat the prisoners unmercifully for the slightest provocation. Deciding that the rigors of prison life were not to his liking, Callahan made a dash for freedom, but he was cornered by Summerfield's bloodhound, a vicious animal known to all as Big Ben.

When that escape attempt failed, Callahan tried to make a friend of the dog, who was kept chained to a tree and often deprived of food and attention. For several weeks Callahan sneaked into the kitchen where he gave ham bones and pieces of meat to the dog to ensure his trust.

Satisfied that Big Ben would give him no trouble, Callahan burrowed under the wire late one night and made his way through the dense North Carolina woods. Alerted to a prison escape, guard Pat White released Big Ben, who pursued his quarry through the woods. Trusting that the bloodhound would recognize him, Callahan stopped in his tracks to greet Big Ben. The dog stopped barking and happily greeted the man who had been feeding him. Together, they proceeded to Weldon, N.C., where Jack Callahan was given new clothes and lent $2,000 in cash by his friend Jerry Sullivan.

With a new lease on life, the former prisoner and Big Ben made their way back to Boston. Six months later Callahan returned to North Carolina and stole more than $150,000 from various banks. He was determined to thumb his nose at the same men who had stripped him of his dignity and had nearly beaten him to death. With money in hand from his latest criminal operations, Jack Callahan allegedly bought himself a $10,000 pardon from the governor of North Carolina. The governor reportedly said he granted the pardon because Callahan had reformed.

REF.: *CBA;* Hamilton, *Men of the Underworld.*

Callahan, John, 1866-1934, U.S., rob. Ostensibly a junk dealer in Wichita, Kan., Callahan, a talkative, seemingly colorful type who affected a slight Irish brogue, is considered by some criminal historians as having "educated" a whole generation of thieves, bootleggers, and killers. Using his junkyard as a front for a humble but honest business, Callahan is credited with sponsoring a thieving band of ruthless killers who practiced robbery and burglary under his cunning direction. He fenced their stolen goods, harbored them when they were hunted, and financed their illegal operations.

First, Callahan began by purchasing and selling off small items taken in local robberies, until almost every sneak thief in Wichita knew he was the man to peddle their stolen goods. On the side, Callahan traveled throughout several neighboring states, occasionally robbing small banks, while operating a far-reaching burglary gang. But he was caught and imprisoned and, after serving several terms behind bars, decided to let others do the stealing. He would merely fence the stolen money, if unmarked or unrecorded, or the goods, from illegal alcohol to diamonds.

Much of Callahan's profits came from the bootlegging of illegal liquor into Kansas; the state had been voted dry since the early 1880s. Callahan lured local youths such as the identical twins, Major and Minor Poffenberger, and the wild Majors brothers, Dudley, Roy, and Ray, with promises of fast riches. He bought them old cars and taught them to drive, then mapped out back county road routes which took them to St. Louis and Joplin, Mo., where they would purchase large amounts of liquor and spirit these illegal shipments back into dry Kansas.

For more than a decade, the pipe-smoking Callahan was known as the largest, most successful bootlegger in Kansas. He accomplished this status after conferring with the local police department, making a convenient arrangement with authorities: If they did not interfere with his bootlegging and fencing operations, along with his harboring wanted fugitives, he, Callahan, would guarantee that no serious crime would occur within the city limits of Wichita. The police, after being promised a share of all stolen goods being fenced, nodded tacit approval. (This kind of arrangement between corrupt police departments and the underworld, begun by Callahan, became apparent in many cities that were to be part of the "Crime Corridor" of the 1920s and 30s.)

Many of Callahan's eager pupils graduated from bootlegging to burglary and finally bank robbing, especially the Majors brothers. On occasions, Callahan's grandiose criminal plans backfired. In 1910, his band of thieves robbed more than $6,000 in postage stamps which Callahan fenced through none other than the Wichita Chief of Police, Frank Burt, who, in turn, sold them to a corrupt bank president in town.

The scheme was uncovered when the banker was arrested. Burt immediately turned state's evidence, and was not prosecuted, although he resigned his position. Burt merely threw Callahan to the prosecutor and the fence received a prison term. The banker was also convicted and sentenced to a year in prison. He was, however, a man of considerable means and influence, and through high-positioned friends received a direct pardon from President William Howard Taft and never served a day in jail. In fact, the banker returned to his position, made a fortune, and died respected and cited in many Who's Who directories.

By 1915, Callahan became the most notorious fence for stolen bonds in the country. Almost every midwestern bandit brought stolen bonds from train and bank robberies to Callahan, and he regularly paid them twenty cents on the dollar. In this way, Callahan came into contact with some of the most infamous outlaws of the day, including Al Spencer, Frank Nash, Eddie Adams, Diamond Joe Sullivan, Jake Fleagle, the Barker-Karpis mobsters, and Charles Arthur "Pretty Boy" Floyd.

If the boys were "hot" and wanted to "cool off" in Wichita, Callahan, also for a price, put them up at a bordello run by Wichita residents Clyde and Nellie Miles. Meanwhile, Callahan would fence stolen bonds and take his cut from the receiver, deducting considerable harboring costs before paying off the bandits. He became a percentage man, taking little risk and collecting enormous profits from all kinds of illegal activities. Many a middle man studied Callahan's techniques and went into the fencing-harboring racket, like Herb Farmer of Joplin, Mo., who added another touch in the early 1930s, supplying heavy automatic weapons, from Browning Automatic Rifles to submachine guns, to the likes of the Barker Brothers, Alvin Karpis, Bonnie Parker, Clyde Barrow, Charles Arthur "Pretty Boy" Floyd and others.

In 1928, Callahan's luck ran out. He had discovered enormous profits in smuggling narcotics from Mexico, and operated a dope ring with the Miles couple. They were caught bringing in a large heroin shipment, and Callahan was implicated. All three were sent to prison, Callahan to serve twenty-five years. Sick and dying, Callahan was released so that he could die in Wichita, his stated wish. He went home to his broken-down frame house and junk yard and, before he passed on, chatted freely about his criminal past with Wichita Police Captain W.O. Lyle, outlining the careers of many a dead outlaw, particularly from the "safe" era of the Henry Starr-Al Spencer period. Callahan was always careful not to talk about those still active in criminal pursuits. In time, few came to see the old man, and he finally died without anyone listening to his banter, alone in his eerie, ramshackle house, on June 8, 1936. That was the date fixed for his death, although he was found many days later, ossified, sitting at a table, open eyes covered with dust, a handful of old pennies clenched in his fist. See: **Adams, Eddie; Fleagle, Jake; Nash, Frank; Spencer, Al.**

REF.: *CBA;* Gish, *American Bandits;* Wellman, *A Dynasty of Western Outlaws.*

Callahan, Michael, prom. 1987, U.S., lawyer. Father Michael Callahan was born in Detroit to a deeply religious family. His high regard for the parish priests he knew convinced Callahan to enter the religious life. After graduating second in his class at the Sacred Heart Seminary, he was sent by the archdiocese to Belgium, where he completed his theological studies. Awash with idealism, he returned to Detroit to accept a position as an assistant pastor.

Callahan's social convictions and a deep concern for the rights of the poor compelled him to enroll in law school in 1972. Because priests are not permitted to serve as priests in an area where they are engaged in the law or are directly involved in civil administration, Father Callahan was told that he could not act as a parish priest in any one of the six counties adjoining the Detroit metropolitan area. The archdiocese assigned him to an obscure role as the arbiter of marital annulments. Frustrated and disillusioned by the distortions and untruthfulness, Callahan said, "I was convinced that given enough time, I could annul my parents' marriage."

In 1979 he worked in the St. Clair County prosecutor's office, then served as an assistant prosecutor for the Wayne County prosecutor. On weekends, he functioned as an assistant pastor in a different diocese. Balancing two widely divergent careers has been no problem for this lawyer-priest. "I've been questioned by people in authority in the church who think my job is political, but it's public, not political. I didn't run for any office."

In his dual role, Callahan once found himself going after the murderer of a young Mexican-American boy named Tayo Guzman, whom he had hired to do odd jobs around St. Vincent's Home for Troubled Youth. At the same time, he had to look within his soul to forgive the killer for a mortal sin. "I was just as much prosecutor as priest at the funeral," he said. "I told the congregation my sentiments about law and order. And I was just as much priest as prosecutor at this trial." REF.: *CBA.*

Callahan, William H., 1927-81, and **McDade, Wendy,** 1952-81, Case of, U.S., (unsolv.) mur. Former Broadway song-and-dance man Bill Callahan wanted it all. He possessed good looks, charm, and style. All that was missing was the big bankroll.

Callahan caught his first break in 1948 when he appeared opposite Celeste Holm in the movie *Chicken Every Sunday.* In 1952 he returned to the Broadway stage where he danced with Bette Davis in *Two's Company.* His budding show business career abruptly ended when he accepted a position with a New York-based firm, Arc Electrical Construction Co., owned by wealthy industrialist Charles Rao. After marrying the boss' daughter Eleanor Rao, Callahan was elevated to the post of vice president and treasurer.

With an unlimited cash flow and time on his hands, Bill Callahan indulged himself with expensive playthings and a bevy of attractive female companions while his wife remained at home to raise his daughter Eleanor. He conducted lengthy affairs with numerous women, including model Renata Boeck, for whom he built a lavish home in the East Hamptons, and glamorous Nai Bonet, an actress he allegedly sponsored for an X-rated movie.

It was his relationship with Wendy McDade, an Ohio-born chorus girl, that drove the final wedge in the Callahans' marriage. After twenty-nine years of marriage, Mrs. Callahan hired a detective to keep track of his whereabouts while her attorneys drew up divorce papers charging him with infidelity.

In October 1980, after months of gadding about Manhattan's night spots with McDade, Bill Callahan suddenly disappeared. While detectives searched for the pair, company auditors discovered that Callahan had embezzled $1.9 million in 1977 and $2.2 million during the first eight months of 1978. The systematic drain of company funds had been going on for at least five years according to auditors.

In January 1981, a month before Mrs. Callahan filed divorce papers, Wendy McDade "married" Bill Callahan in Barbados. They traveled to Toronto and then on to Chicago, where they registered on Mar. 5 at the swank Continental Plaza Hotel as man and wife. For two weeks Callahan and wife lived opulently in their $125 a day room, always paying their bills in cash. On St. Patrick's Day, the couple informed the desk that they were going on a "sleepout." The next day, their bodies were found in a deserted strip of woods fifty miles north of Chicago, outside Kenosha, Wis. The victims were found by Phil Sander, president of the Kenosha Historical Society, who was hiking along a nature path at the time.

Callahan and McDade had been shot in the face three times

each by what ballistics experts identified as a .22-caliber automatic pistol. Expensive jewelry, $1,573 in Canadian money, and a platinum watch were left behind by the killers, but identification papers had been carefully removed. FBI agents and members of the Canadian Royal Mounted Police who were sent in to investigate concluded that the pair had been abducted and shot gangland style.

A composite drawing of the victims, which appeared in the Chicago *Tribune* and other newspapers, led night manager Thomas Nelligan of the Continental Plaza to make a preliminary identification. Relatives were then brought in to establish positive idenfication. "I can't imagine a less likely person to be murdered," said Edward McDade, former father-in-law of the slain woman. "I don't think she was anything but a girl who was carried away by a wealthy man."

Police believed that a friend of McDade named Mary Ann Barker may have inadvertently led a contract killer to their doorstep. The New York City woman had visited the couple twice in Toronto and again in Chicago just a few days before the murder. However, they were satisfied that Barker herself was not involved in any murder plot.

To end up in a dense patch of woods in rural Wisconsin was an ironic and fateful ending for the jet-setting Callahan. "The guy was top shelf. He was quiet and a great tipper," recalled a restaurant employee who had served him. "He was a sugar daddy. He sure was." REF.: *CBA.*

Callaway, Dennis, prom. 1969, U.S., mansl. Dennis Callaway of Atlanta was proud of his wife Karen Lynn—proud and very jealous. The dark-haired beauty supplemented her husband's meager earnings by working as a bunny at the local Playboy Club until November 1969, when she suddenly quit her job to go to work at Soul City, a downtown nightspot popular with Atlanta's large black population.

It was there that she became infatuated with entertainer Jackie Wilson, who was in the midst of a two-week engagement. When Callaway became aware of his wife's dalliance with the rhythm-and-blues singer, he stormed down to the nightclub determined to bring his wife back home. "Butt out, man," he was told. "If you don't leave, you're gonna get hurt."

Callaway's pride was stung. He was losing his wife to a black singer from Detroit. To make matters worse, he had come home one night and found his wife in the company of two black men. Outraged, he shouted at his wife, and then pummeled her with his fists until she left the apartment to go live with her girlfriend, Linda Joy Bartlett, a former Playboy bunny.

Several days passed before the two women returned to the apartment to pick up a few items, but Dennis Callaway was lying in wait. He had barricaded himself inside, just so he wouldn't miss Karen. Armed with a .38-caliber pistol he shot and killed her. Callaway brought the body into the apartment and had intercourse with it. Linda Joy Bartlett managed to escape.

Callaway was arrested and found Guilty of voluntary manslaughter. The prosecution had sought a verdict of first-degree murder, but the court evidently believed that there were extenuating circumstances to this case. The former carpet salesman was sentenced to nine years in prison. REF.: *CBA.*

Callender, James Thompson, prom. 1790s. U.S., libel. Anyone in Richmond, Va., who spoke vehemently against the political powers of the city and state by the late 1790s risked jail and censorship. One such individual was a notorious hack-writer named James Thompson Callender. Though well-educated, this Scotchman was a wild drunkard whose prose approached and often slipped beyond the limits of libel. To historian Mary Newton Standard, Callender was a "foul-mouthed, foul-minded creature...who had been obliged to fly his own country for political offenses."

Callender's acid pen was for hire by the highest-paying political party which happened to be the Republicans and their Richmond-based organ, *The Examiner,* which devoted most of its space to spurious attacks upon Federalists. Callender was hired by the editor of *The Examiner* specifically to defame James Monroe, who was then running for governor of Virginia.

According to some historians, Callender was also in the secret employ of Thomas Jefferson, but the vicious editorialist even turned on Jefferson after he became president, when the Federalists paid him more money. His attacks upon Jefferson consisted of fierce slandering of the President's morals. He was jailed for libel but continued his attacks for the *Recorder,* his dateline reading: "From the old Richmond Jail." Released, Callender attacked the man who sent him to prison, and for his libels against District Attorney Hay he was again jailed.

The libelist's career was finally halted by his own insatiable desire for liquor. Callender drank too much whiskey one day before taking his morning bath in the James River, and he was so intoxicated that he was unable to swim back to shore, drowning in front of startled strollers.
REF.: *CBA;* Standard, *Richmond, Its People and Its Story.*

Calley, William Laws, Jr., 1944- , U.S., war crimes. Claiming he was acted under orders of his superiors, First Lieutenant William Laws Calley, Jr. led his platoon into the South Vietnamese hamlet of My Lai, in the Quang Ngai Province, on Mar. 16, 1968, and systematically murdered at least twenty-two civilian non-combatants, though unofficial estimates place the death toll as high as 347. In the minds of many Americans the notorious My Lai Massacre symbolized the futility of a conventional land war fought in Southeast Asia against an elusive foe that was impossible to distinguish from the civilian population.

The facts of the case did not come to light until a year and a half later, which suggested a gross coverup on the part of the U.S. Army. Twenty-five individuals, including two generals, were charged with complicity in the My Lai Massacre. All except Calley were eventually acquitted, which intimated that a low-ranking lieutenant was being made a military scapegoat.

Calley was convicted of murder on Mar. 21, 1971, and was sentenced to life in prison. President Richard Nixon intervened on his behalf, and reduced the sentence from hard labor to simple house arrest at Fort Benning, Ga. Five months later, Third Army Lieutenant General Albert O'Connor further reduced the sentence to twenty years. Calley lived under house arrest in his small apartment at Fort Benning for the next three years until he was freed on bond Feb. 27, 1974, by District Judge J. Robert Elliott on a writ of habeas corpus filed by a battery of civilian lawyers. Then, on Sept. 25, a federal judge in Georgia overturned the conviction on the grounds that the army had denied Calley a fair trial during the court martial proceedings. On Sept. 10, 1975, a federal appeals court reinstated the army's court martial conviction. On Apr. 5, 1976, the U.S. Supreme Court refused to review his conviction.

Calley was set free on bail pending appeal in 1974, and a year later was transferred to parole status. Though technically free by judicial standards, the high court's refusal to reconsider the case attached a permanent stigma to Calley, who became ineligible for Army pension benefits by virtue of the decision. He returned to his home in Columbus, Ga., where he became a salesman at his father-in-law's jewelry store.
REF.: *CBA;* Fox, *Mass Murder.*

Callias, prom. 5th Cent. B.C., Gr., treas. Failing in a secret diplomatic mission to King Artaxerxes of Persia in 445 B.C., Callias returned home to Athens to face censure from his government. He was indicted on a charge of treason and fined fifty talents. REF.: *CBA.*

Callister, Marion Jones, 1921- , U.S., jur. U.S. attorney assigned to Boise, Idaho, from 1975-76. He was appointed judge of the district court of Idaho by President Gerald Ford in 1976. REF.: *CBA.*

Callisthenes, b.c.360-d.c.328 B.C., Gr., consp. Nephew of philosopher Aristotle, he joined Alexander the Great on his military expedition through Asia Minor and India from 334-324 B.C. He was one of several followers condemned for plotting against the ruler. He died in prison as a result. REF.: *CBA.*

Callistratus, d.355 B.C., Gr., milit., assass. Abandoned a career in the military to become a public orator after he successfully defended the rights of the Thebans to occupy Oropus with the promise they would relinquish all claims on demand. He was later executed. REF.: *CBA*.

Calloway, Willie, 1926- , U.S., (wrong. convict.) mur. Willie Calloway was sent to the State Prison of Southern Michigan at Jackson on July 29, 1946, for a murder he never committed. The eyewitness evidence against Calloway seemed airtight, and not even Erle Stanley Gardner and his "Court of Last Resort," which investigated wrong convictions on behalf of *Argosy* magazine, was willing to touch it. Not until journalist Ken McCormick of the Detroit *Free Press* began investigating the Calloway story did the condemned man have a chance at a hearing.

Willie Calloway was the son of a poor black sharecropper from Wetumpka, Ala. He never got past the third grade, and his mother died when he was twelve. A year later Willie was arrested for larceny and sentenced to 199 days on an Alabama chain gang. After he completed his sentence, he left Alabama forever and moved north to Detroit, where he went to work as a dishwasher and clean-up man at several restaurants in the all-black section of the city called Paradise Valley.

The murder he was charged with took place on the night of Sept. 15, 1944, when two ghetto youths attempted to rob Mrs. Victoria Len and her daughter Estelle Nanys at gunpoint as they left Grace Hospital. Nanys screamed, and one of the men fired a shot, killing her mother. Roosevelt Williams was arrested and charged with complicity in the crime. He named Willie Calloway as the gunman, and his testimony was corroborated by Mrs. Nanys, who identified him in court. A young eyewitness named James Thomas testified for the prosecution, claiming that he later observed the two men with the murder weapon in their possession. Based on what seemed to be overwhelming evidence of guilt, Williams and Calloway were sentenced to life in prison.

Digging into the story further, McCormick learned that James Thomas had confessed to a reformatory chaplain that he had given false testimony at the trial. He had been promised his freedom on an unrelated charge of robbery by the police in exchange for favorable testimony at the trial. He was only fifteen at the time. Similarly, Roosevelt Williams later recanted his original testimony against Willie, claiming that he had been tortured by the police into naming him as an accomplice.

The reporter went to interview the prisoner, who by now had served seven years of his sentence. Willie Calloway had a tough time remembering his movements that night. "I used to bum 'round at night here and there," he said. "Sometimes I just stood 'round the corner and talk (sic)."

What was puzzling to McCormick was the speed with which Calloway had been convicted. On the advice of the defense lawyers, Willie had waived a jury trial. Judge W. McKay Skillman passed sentence within one day. As he examined the transcripts, it occurred to McCormick that the defendants had not been represented by counsel during the original examination. Thus they gained no benefit from the examination process, which should have determined whether a trial was in order.

McCormick next considered the testimony of Mrs. Nanys, but concluded that the woman, badly dazed by the events of that night, had been unable to give an accurate account of the gunman. McCormick found a witness who positively stated that Willie could not have been involved in the crime in any way. Evelyn Carson, the manager of an all-night barbecue, recalled that Willie Calloway had been working in her restaurant the day of the shooting. A second restaurant manager named McKinley Cunningham had payroll records showing that Willie had been cleaning up his place from seven until ten that night.

Armed with these facts, Ken McCormick badgered Wayne County Prosecuting Attorney Gerald O'Brien for a new trial. Posters were circulated across the city announcing the forthcoming series in the newspaper. "Read the Amazing Case of Willie Calloway, by Pulitzer Prize Winner Ken McCormick. Is This Man Innocent of Murder? Starts Monday in the Detroit *Free Press*."

Warden William Bannon, of the prison at Jackson, and Dr. Garrett Heyns, warden at the Ionia reformatory where Willie Calloway had been transferred, were both convinced that he was innocent.

The ground swell on Willie's behalf resulted in a new trial. The motion was granted on Nov. 6, 1952, by Judge Martha Griffiths, who had succeeded to the bench of the Recorder's Court. When the trial opened, Prosecuting Attorney O'Brien backed down from his earlier hard-line position. In a surprise move he asked the court to enter a motion of *nolle prosequi* (a formal entry on the record that says the prosecuting officer will not prosecute further) in the case of *The People v. Willie Calloway*. Given a new lease on life, the young man settled in Grand Rapids, where he became a respected member of the community. In 1964, St. Martin's Press published McCormick's account of the case, titled *Sprung: The Release of Willie Calloway*.

REF.: *CBA*; McCormick, *Sprung: The Release of Willie Calloway*.

Calmette, Gaston, See: **Caillaux, Henriette**.

Calpurnius Bestia (Lucius Calpurnius Bestia), prom. 100 B.C., Roman., brib. Led the Roman armies into battle against Jugurtha. The internal corruption within the empire at this time was reflected by his acceptance of a bribe from his opponents to ensure favorable peace terms. When this treachery was detected by the Roman Senate, he fled the country in exile in 109 B.C. REF.: *CBA*.

Calpurnius Bestia, Lucius, prom. 63 B.C., Roman., jur., consp. Believed to be the grandson of Calpurnius Bestia, he was a tribune who entered into a secret conspiracy with Lucius Catiline to murder the consuls of Rome and sack the city in 63 B.C. The signal to begin the revolt was to be given by Calpurnius in a speech condemning Cicero. As one of the intended victims, Cicero foiled the plot. REF.: *CBA*.

Calverley, Walter, d.c.1604, Brit., mur. During the last years of Queen Elizabeth I's reign, there lived in the West Riding of Yorkshire a wealthy squire named Calverley and his young son Walter. In the eyes of his father, Walter Calverley was a good-for-nothing wastrel who squandered away his valuable years at Cambridge University in idle pursuits. When he returned home without a degree, Squire Calverley thundered, "Better wed swiftly and get money from thy wife, for I'll give thee none of mine!"

A week after he had arrived home, Walter informed his father of his intention to wed Alice Royd, the daughter of a poor but honest farmer. This enraged his father even more. For a month the debate continued. Walter was determined to marry the farmer's daughter, until Squire Calverley presented what he considered to be a suitable alternative.

Soon a marriage was arranged between Walter and Philippa Brooke, the daughter of Lord Cobham, a friend to Sir Walter Raleigh and a brother-in-law of Sir Robert Cecil. Soon after the couple's marriage was solemnized, Walter's father died, and the young couple moved into a lavish house in London provided by Lord Cobham. Calverley's mother, believing that her son had at last come to his senses, soon had her hopes dashed when she learned that Walter had mortgaged the property to satisfy a large gambling debt. Before she could prevail upon Lord Cobham to take action, the Widow Calverly died. Cobham could not have acted anyway, because his Lordship was imprisoned in the Tower of London for conspiring against the Catholic king James I.

Walter Calverley was left to care for a woman he didn't love and several hungry children. His mood became violent and ugly. Finally a kind-hearted uncle intervened and offered him a job on condition that he improve his intemperate behavior. But even then, Calverley remained defiant and ungrateful. He cursed and slandered his wife, and then fell into a deep depression when a gentleman from Cambridge lost patience and called in his debts.

On Apr. 23, a feast day for the patron saint of England, Walter was consumed with the blackest depression. When his oldest boy, a lad of six, asked him what was the matter, Walter began to shake him violently. Shouting, "Bleed, bleed, rather than beg!"

he stabbed the child repeatedly and threw him to the floor. Proceeding into the nursery, he seized the nurse and dragged her outside to a steep flight of stairs. She could offer only token resistance before falling down them.

Walter returned to the nursery where he stabbed his 4-year-old. "There are too many beggars!" he screamed, when confronted by his hysterical wife. He thrust his knife at Philippa, but her steel corset got in the way, sparing her a similar fate.

Walter fled the city on horseback but was captured outside Norton and returned to York to stand trial. The defendant refused to enter a plea. By "standing mute," he invited his own death sentence. Walter Calverley was ordered to be crushed to death under a pile of stones.

The body was buried at St. Mary's, Castlegate, in York. Generations passed, and there were rumors to the effect that the ghost of Walter Calverley haunted the churchyard. An exorcism was held by the vicar, but for years afterward daring schoolboys would challenge the ghost of old Walter to appear before them.

It was widely believed that William Shakespeare was referring to Walter Calverley when he said that "the evil that men do lives after them."

REF.: Canning, *Fifty True Tales of Terror; CBA.*

Calvert, Mrs. Louie, d.1926, Brit., mur. Mrs. Louie Calvert came to live with the recently widowed Mrs. Lily Waterhouse of Leeds, England, on Mar. 8, 1926. Calvert, a middle-aged woman, said she was in the early stages of pregnancy. She proved to be a troublesome companion for Mrs. Waterhouse. The two quarreled frequently and some bedding and silver that turned up missing were found to have been pawned by Mrs. Calvert. Mrs. Waterhouse complained to the Leeds Police, who told her to file a formal complaint the next day. Neighbors reported hearing a terrible row coming from the Waterhouse residence that night. Then they saw Calvert carrying a baby away.

Several hours later, a constable dropped by to see why Mrs. Waterhouse had not come to the station. He entered the house to find her lying dead in her bedroom. Her shoes had been removed. Mrs. Calvert emerged as the likely suspect but police wondered why she had gone to such lengths to pass off the child as her own, when the baby in fact belonged to someone else—she had borrowed it from a woman in another town. They found in her lodgings the items taken from the Waterhouse home. Police learned that Mrs. Calvert had been involved with John Frobisher, who had died in 1922. His body was found floating in the canal, and like Lily Waterhouse, his shoes had been removed. Police discovered that Mrs. Calvert had been wearing Waterhouse's boots when they arrested her. Mrs. Calvert was tried, found Guilty, and sentenced to die. From the docket she cried out that she could not die, for she was with child. A jury of matrons was summoned, but they said that it was possible that Mrs. Calvert was pregnant. The court ordered that the sentence be carried out. Mrs. Calvert was executed at Strangeways Jail, Manchester, in 1926. It was the first time in forty years that a woman had been hanged in that prison.

REF.: *CBA;* Huggett, *Daughters of Cain;* Nash, *Look For the Woman;* O'Donnell, *Should Women Hang?;* Shew, *A Companion to Murder;* Wilson, *Murderess.*

Calvert, William, and **Pine, John,** and **Pine, William,** and **Burke, John,** prom. 1839, Brit., mansl. The police were never very popular with the local gentry in the Deptford District of London, and even less so after they tried to arrest a drunken reveler named John Pine, who stumbled out of the Navy Arms Pub the night of Sept. 29, 1839.

Constable Stevens advised Pine to go on his way, but the man's mood was ugly. A second policeman named William Aldridge arrived on the scene but he had no better luck in subduing the recalcitrant Pine. When they drew out their billy clubs, the large and unruly crowd observing this street scene began to take exception.

Goaded on by William Calvert and John Burke, friends of William Pine, John's brother, the crowd tore up flagstones and

began hurling them at the officers. One stone found its mark and struck Constable Aldridge on the head. He died the next morning. Calvert, William and John Pine, and Burke were put on trial, but the Deptford jury refused to convict them of murder. Instead, they reduced the charge to manslaughter. William Pine and Burke received two years hard labor. Calvert, identified as the stone thrower, was sentenced to fifteen years in a penal colony. And because John Pine was believed to have instigated the violence, he received a life sentence.

REF.: *CBA;* Cobb, *Murdered On Duty.*

Camarena, Enrique (Enrique Camarena Salazar, AKA: Kiki), 1948-85, U.S., law enfor. off.-assass. Just three weeks before he was to leave Guadalajara, Mex., the "cocaine cowboys" abducted and murdered U.S. Drug Enforcement Administration (DEA) agent Enrique Camarena. The cocaine cowboys, a new generation of drug overlords, had made Guadalajara one of the most dangerous places in Mexico for American law enforcement officers. The abduction of Camarena on Feb. 7, 1985, drew worldwide attention to the Mexican drug trade, which until 1980 was not as well known as that in Colombia and other South American countries.

Camarena was born in Mexicali, Mex., but was raised in California. He was a seasoned police officer who was sent to Guadalahara by the DEA in 1980, about the same time that a new generation of drug manufacturers began arriving from Sinaloa in the Sierra Madre. Within a few years, the "cartel," as it came to be known, dominated the Mexican dope traffic. Meanwhile, Rafael Cáro Quintero, Félix Gallardo, and other kingpins were usurping political power and corrupting Mexican politicians. Camarena devised a plan, which he called "Operation Miracle," involving aerial reconnaissance over the marijuana fields outside Guadalajara. The Mexican government objected, but the U.S. forced them to cooperate. By January 1984, marijuana seisures along the border had increased dramatically. A May 1984 raid sanctioned by Primer Commandante Miguel Aldana Ibarra of the Mexican federales (Federal Judicial Police) resulted in the seizure of twenty tons of manicured marijuana. But the raid barely put a dent in Cáro Quintero's empire. In September 1984, Camarena heard that Aldana Ibarra had been protecting a cocaine smuggling ring. It was clear that corruption extended to the highest levels of the Mexican government, and accounted for its reluctance to mount additional raids.

In January 1985, two representatives from the U.S. House Foreign Affairs Committee investigated the situation in Guadalajara and returned to Washington to file a blistering report on the corruption there. While the documents were being printed, Camarena was abducted outside the Camelot Bar in Guadalajara. On Mar. 5, 1985, the mangled bodies of Camarena and Captain Alfredo Zavala Avelar, who had flown DEA missions, were found outside the village of Villahermosa, near the estate of Manuel Bravo Cervantes, a former legislator in the province of Michoacán. A passerby uncovered the decomposing bodies of the two men nearly a month after their disappearance. When police attempted to question Cervantes about the murders, they were shot at from inside the house. The politician, his wife, and two children were killed in a gun battle before they could shed any light on the mystery. Doctors estimated that the DEA men had been dead for at least twenty days. U.S. Ambassador John Gavin issued an angry statement, implying that the Mexican government had been lax in prosecuting drug traffickers and in searching for the abductors of Camarena and Avelar.

Commandante Jorge Armando Pavón Reyes of the Mexican police, who was in charge of the investigation, permitted Cáro Quintero to fly out of the Guadalajara airport unmolested two days after Camarena was abducted, an example of apparent negligence. Angry U.S. officials ordered a crackdown along the 2,000-mile Mexican border. Motorists were detained for up to seven hours as customs agents conducted a car-by-car search for drugs. The subsequent drop-off in tourism was intended to make the Mexican government take action against its grossly corrupt police agencies.

Mexican Federal Judicial Police director Manuel Ibarra Herrara dismissed Pavón Reyes. Raul López Alvarez, a former member of the Jalisco homicide squad, was taken into custody and questioned about the killings. In a videotaped confession, Alvarez explained that Cáro Quintero ordered the murder because he was convinced that Camarena was responsible for a raid on a marijuana depot in Chihuahua that had cost him $20 million. Three other Jalisco police officers were arrested. Group Chief Victor Manuel López Razón and homicide detective Gerardo Torres Lepe confessed to participating in the abduction.

They had lured Camarena into a Volkswagen and took him to Cáro Quintero's home, where he was tortured and killed. Three suspects were extradited to Los Angeles to stand trial: Alvarez; René Martin Verdugo-Urquidez, and Jesús Félix-Gutiérrez.

In October 1988, a federal jury in Los Angeles found Alvarez Guilty on six counts of racketeering and murder under a 1984 law that added new penalties for violence. Federal District Judge Edward Rafeedie sentenced the former policeman to 240 years plus life in prison. Verdugo-Urquidez received a nearly identical sentence in what was hailed as a milestone victory against drug trafficking in Mexico.

On Sept. 24, 1988, Rafael Cáro Quintero was sentenced in Mexico City to thirty-four years in prison for smuggling weapons into Mexico and making peasants work on a marijuana plantation. Agent Jaime Kuykendall said, "The war on drugs began on Feb. 7, 1985. Nobody did anything until Kiki Camarena was gone and a lot of people just wouldn't disappear into the mist." See: **Cáro Quintero, Rafael; Gallardo Parra, José Luis.**

REF.: *CBA;* Shannon, *Desperados.*

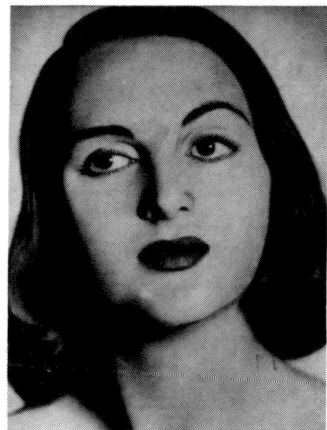

James Camb, ship's steward, and actress Gay Gibson.

Camb, James, 1916- , Brit., mur. A ship's steward on board the ocean liner *Durban Castle,* Camb was considered a shipboard Lothario and attempted to seduce many a young woman sailing the high seas. Attractive, 21-year-old Gay Gibson was no exception. She was a wide-eyed actress who had been acting in a number of plays as part of her duties with the Women's Auxiliary Territorial Service. Her full name was Eileen Isabella Ronnie Gibson. Gay Gibson was her stage name. She sailed for England from Cape Town, S. Afr., on Oct. 10, 1947, occupying Cabin 126 on B deck, a first-class berth aboard the *Durban Castle.* On the following morning, when the liner was about 150 miles off the West Coast of Africa, the actress was reported missing. Captain Arthur Patey ordered the vessel turned about and a desperate search of the shark-infested waters was made. No trace of the woman was found.

Captain Patey conducted an investigation aboard ship as it continued to steam toward Southampton. Watchman Frederick Steer reported that the service bell of Cabin 126 had been pushed several times, as if frantically, at 2:58 on the morning of Oct. 18, 1947, and he had responded to the call. He stood outside the cabin and knocked. Steer noticed that both lights, a red and a green one, positioned outside the cabin, were on, indicating that the occupant had called for *both* the steward and the stewardess. Usually passengers rang on only one or the other. The door opened a crack, and the watchman caught a brief glimpse of a man in uniform, the steward Camb, who quickly closed the door and said through the grille of the door, "It's all right." Steer went back to his duties, assuming that Camb, a steward, had answered the call. Camb, however, denied having been in Gay Gibson's cabin, insisting that Steer was mistaken. He drew suspicion, however, during the rest of the voyage by wearing a long sleeve jacket when short sleeve uniforms were commonly worn in that tropical zone. When asked to bear his arms, Camb revealed scratches on his arm which he claimed resulted from a tropical heat rash. Meanwhile, Patey had informed authorities of the Union Castle Line in London about the actress' disappearance to which he received a cable from the Criminal Investigating Department of Scotland Yard instructing him to "padlock and seal the cabin—disturb nothing—CID officers will come aboard at Cowes Roads."

When the ship docked in Cowes Roads, Southampton, officers came aboard and quickly put together background on Gay Gibson and James Camb. The actress had not had a happy experience in her most recent play, enacting the role of Lorna, the prizefight manager's trampy girlfriend in *Golden Boy,* a South African production that paid very little in salary. Witnesses were later to state that Gay Gibson was, in real life, close to the role she was playing in *Golden Boy.* She had proved to be an emotional actress subject to fits of hysteria and fainting. She also told someone before leaving South Africa that she was pregnant. One account had it that she had accepted the fare of £350 for the trip home from a less-than-reputable nightclub owner. Passengers attended a dance on the first night at sea and Gay Gibson was present, dancing with several male passengers. She caught the eye of steward Camb who remarked to another steward: "I have half a mind to take a drink to her cabin tonight."

This kind of remark was typical of the 31-year-old Camb who wore his black hair slicked back like some Latin lover from the 1920s. He thought of himself as irresistible to young women who found his Lancashire accent amusing. To his shipmates, Camb was known as "Don Jimmy," a notorious womanizer who, though married, boasted about having an affair with a female passenger on each voyage he made. Two women had accused him of rape in the past, but this did not lessen the ardor and efforts of Camb in approaching female passengers, taking great pride in attracting the prettiest women on each trip. Said one of his fellow stewards: "Jimmy was always saying that we were jealous of him."

Camb was brought before Sergeant Quinlan who interrogated him slowly, telling him that if he had any explanation for Gay Gibson's disappearance, this was the time to volunteer such information. The handsome steward seized upon this idea, volunteering the following remarks: "You mean that Miss Gibson might have died from a cause other than being murdered, she might have had a heart attack or something?" He then said that Gay Gibson had invited him to her cabin that night and he had brought her a drink. She was wearing a nightgown with nothing on beneath it and that when she removed this, he climbed into bed with her. During sexual intercourse, Camb said, her body suddenly stiffened, then went limp. He climbed out of the bed and saw that she was foaming brownish froth at the mouth and that only one eye appeared to be slightly open.

"I tried artificial respiration on her," Camb claimed. "While doing this, the night watchman knocked at the door and attempted to open it. I shut the door...I panicked. I did not want to be found in such a compromising position." He related how he went to the door of the cabin and told Steer that everything was "all right." When Steer went away, Camb returned to the actress on the bed, saying that he "could not find any sign of life...After a struggle with the limp body, I managed to lift her to the porthole and push her through." In another police interrogation, Camb was quoted as saying that the body, upon hitting the water "made a helluva splash," thus revealing his cruel, indifferent attitude toward the dead woman. In the first police interview aboard the *Durban Castle,* Camb expressed his wonder at how the service bells had been pushed. "I cannot offer any explanation as to how the bells came to be rung as I most definitely did not touch them myself." He admitted lying to the captain about being in the actress' cabin, stating that he had decided to tell the truth later. "I realized," Camb admitted, "that I was definitely incriminated by the witness Steer."

On Mar. 29, 1948, Camb was tried for murdering Gay Gibson before Justice Hilbery at the Winchester Asizzes, prosecuted by G.D. Roberts and defended by J.D. Casswell. His defense was a feeble one. He had already admitted shoving the body of Gay Gibson through a porthole for a lonely burial at sea. Camb undoubtedly and mistakenly thought that by getting rid of the body, he would be getting rid of the evidence of his crime, and that conviction was not possible without the presence of a body. (This, of course was not the case; the previous murder-without-a-body case in England was that of Thomas Joseph Davidson who was convicted of drowning his 8-year-old son in 1934 and who had been sent to prison for life for the murder.)

But there was evidence. he scatchmarks on Camb's arms had been examined by the ship's physician, Dr. Griffiths, after Captain Patey had ordered the steward to submit to a medical examination. Griffiths testified that he found these marks on Camb's shoulders and wrists and these scratches, in his opinion, had been made by a woman defending herself, not by someone undergoing some sort of seizure. Stains on the pillow in the cabin were examined by Dr. Donald Teare, a well-known pathologist and he testified that these were bloodstains. The blood was Type O. Since Camb's blood was Type A, it could be assumed that this was blood from Gay Gibson's body, not Camb's. Dr. Teare stated that these stains, along with emissions of urine could be expected from one who had been strangled to death, emissions that would not stem from someone having a heart attack. Ironically, Dr. Frederick Hocking, a defense witness, reported that, indeed, urine stains had been found on the sheets of Gay Gibson's bed.

Camb was caught in a number of untruths. He insisted that the actress had been wearing only a flimsy yellow nightgown with no undergarments when she lured him into her room. Yet Gay Gibson's black pajamas which she was known to have packed and taken with her on the sea voyage, were missing and it was concluded that she had been wearing these when Camb pushed her through the porthole which further suggested that she had not invited the steward to have sex with her. The prosecution insisted that Camb had invented the story of being invited into the cabin, that he arrived at the actress' door under the pretext of delivering a drink to her and once she opened her door he forced his way inside, and tried to rape her. She fought furiously, scratching his arms and wrists and he strangled her. Somehow, during the struggle, Gay Gibson had managed to press the service buttons and this brought Steer to Cabin 126. By the time he arrived Camb had just finished murdering the actress and pretended that nothing was amiss when he sent away the watchman. (The watchman Steer, it can be assumed, though he knew that Camb was in the cabin, did not ask to see Gay Gibson, the legitimate occupant, since he was accostumed, as it were, to the numerous "shipboard romances" occurring regularly on such voyages.)

The steward's own admission that he had callously shoved the victim's body through a porthole worked against him, along with the impressive forensic evidence provided by the prosecution. After four days of trial and following a forty-five-minute deliberation, the jury found Camb Guilty of murdering Gay Gibson. The steward, who had posed like a peacock in the dock, was stunned at the decision. Before sentence was passed by Justice Hilbery, he was asked if he had anything to say. He replied in a quavering voice: "My Lord, at the beginning of this case...I pleaded not guilty. I repeat that statement now. That is all." He was then sentenced to death. His attorneys filed an appeal and while this was being considered, the House of Commons added an amend-ment to the new Criminal Justice Bill then before Parliament, one which would abolish capital punishment. The Home Secretary, while this bill was still being debated in the House of Lords (which later rejected it), decided to commute all capital sentences still pending to life terms and Camb was one of those who benefitted from this decision.

It was after this commutation that several women came forward to tell how Camb had sexually attacked them on previous voyages of the *Durban Castle,* two of them claiming they had been raped. Another woman said that she had been attacked on deck by Camb who dragged her into a tool room where she fought desperately as he tried to strip her clothes away. He had lost patience and strangled her. She passed out, she claimed, and when she regained consciousness, she said that Camb was standing over her, grinning. Camb was paroled in 1959, changed his name to Clarke and was working as a head waiter in May 1967 when he was convicted of sexually attacking a 13-year-old girl. He was, incredibly, placed on a two-year probation. He later went to Scotland where he worked once more as a head waiter in a restaurant. A short time later he was charged with sexual misconduct with three schoolgirls and this time Camb's parole was revoked and he was returned to prison to serve out a life term.

REF.: Bennett, *Too Late for Tears;* Casswell, *A Lance For Liberty; CBA;* Cuthbert, *Science and the Detection of Crime;* Duncan, *Facts of Crime;* Firmin, *Murderers in Our Midst;* Franklin, *The Woman in the Case;* Gribble, *Murder Most Strange;* Harrison, *Criminal Calendar;* Heppenstall, *The Sex War & Others;* Humphreys, *A Book of Trials;* Jackson, *The Crime Doctors; Notable British Trials;* Roberts, *Law and Life;* Shew, *A Companion to Murder;* Simpson, *Forty Years of Murder;* Symons, *A Reasonable Doubt;* Whitbread, *The Railway Policeman;* Wilson, *Encyclopedia of Murder;* Woodland, *Assize Pageant.*

Cambacérès, Jean Jacques-Régis de (Duc de Parme), 1753-1824, Fr., jur. Held various judicial positions in the republic, including minister of justice in 1799, and second consul. Confidante of Emperor Napoléon, he was the principal architect of the famous Napoléonic Code in 1804. Following the defeat of the emperor in 1815, Cambacérès was exiled to Belgium. REF.: *CBA.*

Camberg, John F., prom. 1875, Case of, U.S., mur. John F. Camberg knew that his wife was carrying on with James S. Thompson and waited for his opportunity to surprise the pair, doing so in his home where he shot and killed Thompson after bursting through a bedroom door to find the lovers in a passionate embrace. Camberg was tried for killing Thompson in Wahoo, Neb., on Sept. 29, 1875. The jury was out only a few minutes before returning a verdict of Not Guilty, adding that Camberg had merely been defending the honor of his home.

REF.: *The Camberg Murder Case; CBA.*

Cambon, Pierre-Joseph, b.c.1756-1820, Fr., rebel. Member of the Convention 1792, he voted to execute Louis XVI. During the turbulent period preceding the empire, Cambon stabilized the French public finances and secured passage of a bill that expropriated the lands of the nobility and the church. Upon restoration of the monarch in 1815, he was exiled. See: **Louis XVI.** REF.: *CBA.*

Cambyses II, d.522 B.C., Per., king, mur. Killed his younger brother Smerdis before beginning a military expedition in 525 B.C. against Egypt, the only independent kingdom left in the east following the conquest of Asia by Cyrus. After adding major portions of the Nile Valley to the land holdings of Persia, he was turned back in Ethiopia. Upon hearing the news that a Magian usurper named Gaumata had seized the throne by posing as Smerdis, Cambyses exhibited great rage. Since the death of Smerdis was kept secret, Gaumata's claim was believed to be true by the Asian nations. Cambyses rushed back to Persia only to die along the way. REF.: *CBA.*

Camden Town Murder, The, See: **Wood, Robert.**

Cameron, Archibald, d.1753, Brit., treas. "This is a glorious day to me!" said Dr. Archibald Cameron as he stood at the gallows on the morning of his execution. Not the usual way to greet death, especially when one's death sentence is obviously undeserved. Such was the fate, however, of Dr. Cameron, who for his small part in the Scottish Jacobite uprising of July 1745 against King George II was sentenced to be hanged, disemboweled, and beheaded.

After medical studies at the University of Edinburgh and further work in Leyden, Neth., Cameron returned home to Lochaber, in the Scottish Highlands, to establish a practice, having rejected more lucrative offers elsewhere. The years ahead promised peace with his wife, seven children, and devoted patients. Little arose to mar that peace until the Pretender, Bonnie Prince Charlie, landed in Scotland with a force of 2,000 men to move on Edinburgh.

The prince immediately sent for Dr. Cameron's elder brother, who had earlier promised the support of his entire clan in whatever endeavor the Pretender might undertake. Cameron's brother would live to regret that promise, however. He saw nothing but disaster in the prince's plan and told him so. But the prince was not to be dissuaded and Cameron's brother would not renege on a promise. So he organized an army of 1200 men to fight a losing battle and also persuaded Cameron, against his instincts and the advice of his family, to attend to the wounded.

In the end the Duke of Cumberland quashed the rebellion at Culloden in 1746, and Cameron and his brother fled to France, where Cameron served as attending physician to a French regiment commanded by his brother. In 1750, lured by a relief fund for political exiles, Cameron returned to England, though only long enough to collect the money. Two years later, once more short on funds, he returned again, only to be apprehended as a treasonous Jacobite by Lord George Beauclerk. Brought before the Court of the King's Bench on May 17, 1753, Cameron admitted under oath that he had been accused of treason against the crown some years earlier. His sentence: to be hanged, disemboweled, and beheaded—a punishment far more severe than those of his fellow insurgents, whose crimes were pardoned. On June 7, 1753, as his wife, nearing the birth of her eighth child, went slowly mad with grief, Cameron was hanged at Tyburn Hill.

" 'Tis my new birthday! There are more witnesses at this birth than at my first," he said before hanging, vowing love of country and the Church of England. After twisting lifelessly in the wind for twenty minutes, his body was cut down and his heart cut out—Dr. Cameron's last but perhaps greatest indignity.

REF.: Bleackley, *Hangmen of England*; *CBA*; Mitchell, *Newgate Calendar*; Parry, *Some Famous Medical Trials*.

Cameron, Benjamin Franklin, 1890-1964, U.S., jur. District attorney serving the Southern District of Mississippi from 1929-33. He was appointed by President Dwight D. Eisenhower to sit on the bench of the U.S. Court of Appeals, Fifth Circuit Court from 1955-64. REF.: *CBA*.

Cameron, Duncan, 1764-1848, Case of, Can., rebel. Fur trapper who supervised the Red River Depot of the North West Company from 1814-16. He led a military attack against the British colonial settlement of Hudson Bay Company at Fort Gibraltar in 1816. He was captured and sent to England to stand trial, where he was eventually acquitted. REF.: *CBA*.

Cameron, John, b.c.1579-1625, Scot., asslt.-attempt. mur (vict.) Founded a moderate Calvinistic school, whose members were later known as *Cameronites*. His doctrine of passive obedience met with stiff resistance in many of the universities and churches of Scotland and France. He was assaulted and stabbed in the streets of Montauban. REF.: *CBA*.

Cammisano, William (AKA: **Willie the Rat**), prom. 1980, U.S., org. crime. A top-ranking member of the Kansas City crime family headed by Nicholas Civella, William Cammisano's role as the mob's top enforcer in Kansas City was revealed to members of a U.S. Senate subcommittee investigating organized crime in 1980.

Hidden safely behind an opaque screen, Fred Harvey Bonadonna told of Cammisano's strong-arm tactics in attempting to turn a neighborhood redevelopment project known as the River Quay into a brothel and vice section. Bonadonna's father was a former associate of Willie the Rat, but was gunned down in 1976 after his son refused to help the mob secure liquor licenses in the River Quay development. "Willie told my father that he would kill me," Bonadonna said. "My father (David) told Willie that he'd have to kill him first."

Then serving a five-year term in the federal prison in Springfield, Mo., for extortion, Cammisano refused to cooperate with the Senate committee. He was cited for contempt of Congress and sentenced to an additional term in prison on May 14, 1981. REF.: *CBA*.

Camorra, The, prom 1400s-present, Italy, secret crim. soc. Begun in Spain in 1417, the Camorra dated back to the Bourbon dynasty and was transplanted in southern Italy in the mid-1400s by the invading French armies. Unlike the Mafia of Sicily, the Camorra was never a patriotic or nationalist organization, but, from its very beginning, was a secret society dedicated to criminal pursuits. The Camorra took roots in Neapolitan society in the mid-sixteenth century but flourished in the prisons throughout Italy where young prisoners were taught the techniques of blackmail, extortion, and robbery. In the early years of its Neapolitan existence, members of the Camorra functioned as political terrorists and assassins for the Bourbons. The power of the Camorra became so widespread that by the mid-nineteenth century the society no longer recruited its members from the lowly born and traditional criminal elements of Naples but from the best families in the city. Learning the methods of ritual murder by knife and stiletto, the strangling with garrote, the young scions of wealthy families considered membership in the Camorra a distinct honor.

The Camorra was a loosely organized society, unlike the more tightly controlled Mafia in Sicily. In Italy a central committee made up of the most powerful dons from throughout the country concerned itself with the political control of provinces. Edicts issued by the reigning committee members were carried out by the society's own police force or strong-arm squads in every major city. Anyone who betrayed the directives of the committee or betrayed the society to the police were summarily murdered. Unlike the Mafia, where such betrayal might mean the extermination of an entire family for the treachery of one member, disloyal Camorristas were executed without vendetta carried out against the traitor's entire family. Like the Mafia, the initiation rites called for the letting of blood, followed by a lengthy oath of loyalty to the society, but the Camorra did not require, like the Mafia initiate, the burning of hands. Of the two secret criminal societies, the Camorra was the more religiously hypocritical, perverting the rites of the Catholic Church and holding up certain saints as sponsors of the society's evil practices.

Naples became the capital of the Camorra, the city and its officials were firmly in the grip of the society during the nineteenth century. It controlled all gambling, prostitution and fenced all stolen property. No item could be stolen without the permission of Camorra leaders who also practiced a lucrative protection racket which involved the local police. Here, officers would ignore Camorra thugs tearing apart a shop where the owner had refused to send his weekly stipend to the Camorra chief in the area. Neapolitan politics was dominated by the society and, with rare exceptions, all political candidates were Camorristas. Not until 1891 was the political stranglehold of the Camorra broken by a citizens' league which managed to defeat many of the Camorra's puppet candidates in a general election.

By the turn of the twentieth century, the Camorra controlled almost all southern Italy, its members being the top political representatives of many provinces. The only organization that stood against the powerful Camorra was the state police, the carabinieri, an elite and powerful force whose members were culled from the best families in Italy. In 1906, Enrico Alfano, the supreme Camorra leader in Italy, was displeased with the return he received from a Camorra fence and ordered this receiver of stolen goods, Angelo Cuocoloin and his wife murdered.

Following the death of this couple, the carabinieri launched a massive campaign to break the power of the Camorra, arresting Alfano, who later escaped to the U.S. New York police lieutenant Joseph Petrosino, head of the Italian Squad was contacted by carabinieri officials who sent Alfano's photo to him, asking that this infamous Camorrista be arrested and returned to Italy for prosecution. The intrepid Petrosino managed to track down Alfano and return him to Italy where he was imprisoned for thirty years.

In 1907, King Victor Emmanuel II, declared open war against the society, sending thousands of special police and armed troops into the Camorra strongholds to arrest more than 3,000 top society dons and leading assassins. The prisons filled with these and more Camorra members who promptly took control of these fortresses and jails. In retaliation for the jailings, scores of high-ranking officials who had waged war on the society were murdered. The confrontation between the government and the Camorra approached civil war by 1910 when small armies of government soldiers attacked Camorra strongholds. The society began to lose ground and prestige, especially when mass

Camorra don Carlo Filippi.

trials of its leaders took place and they were exposed as the venal killers they were. The trials were held at Viterbo in 1911, moved from Naples as being too dangerous to be held in that Camorra stronghold. More than 800 witnesses testified while the courthouse was guarded night and day by an entire regiment of heavily armed troops. The trials took sixteen months before scores of Camorristas were convicted. Long prison sentences were given to such leaders as Carlo Filippi, don of Naples, but many top Camorristas later escaped and fled Italy to the U.S. to institute Black Hand operations in New York, Chicago, New Orleans, St. Louis, and Kansas City. Here, the newly arrived Camorristas preyed upon fellow Italians, extorting millions under the threat of kidnapping, bombings, and murder.

Though the society exercised considerable power, vying with the Mafia in such places as New York and New Orleans between 1910 and 1920, it was content to maintain its ranks from those immigrating from the Old World, recruiting selectively from the families of relocated Camorrista leaders and thus limited membership expansion. The Mafia, on the other hand, broadened its base in most American cities by welcoming anyone of Sicilian descent who conformed to that society's rigorous traditions and rites. The Mafia was the better organized of the two criminal societies. Both these criminal brotherhoods, shortly before WWI, openly battled each other for supremacy in many U.S. cities, particularly New York. In 1916, Nick Del Gaudio, a top Camorrista, was shot to death in Harlem by Mafia killers. Del Gaudio's bosses Pelligrino Morano and Alessandro Vollero, decided to declare war against the Mafia. Vollero, the then reigning don of Brooklyn and boss of bosses in the U.S., summoned top members of the Camorra from all points in the U.S. The meeting was held in Morano's Coney Island restaurant, the Santa Lucia.

Attending this meeting were Camorra bosses Andrea Ricca, from Philadelphia, and from Chicago, New Orleans, and points west Leopoldo Lauritano, Salvatore Costa, Eugenio Bizzaro, Albert Esposito, Salavatore Coppolo, Luigi Terriese, Tom Corillo, and Alberto Altieri. Also in attendance were top Camorra gunmen Tony Notaro, Aniello Peretti, Alfonso "The Butch" Sgroi, and Tony "The Shoemaker" Paretti. Selected for extermination were the powerful Morello brothers, the chief Mafia leaders in Manhattan. Nicholas, Vincent, and Ciro Morello (the latter changing his name to Ciro Terranova, who was to become

infamous in the 1920s as the "Artichoke King") were to be systematically murdered. Pelligrino Morano and his men cornered Nick Morello and his top enforcer, Charles Umbriaco and shot them to death. A dozen more killings followed and, following one of these wild shootouts between at least a dozen Camorra and Mafia gunmen, Tony Notaro was caught red-handed with a smoking gun in his hand. Rather than face a death sentence for murder, Notaro turned state's evidence and implicated Morano, Vollero, and other Camorra leaders in several murders, as well as outlining the Camorra's operations in the U.S. Notaro testified at the 1918 murder trial of Morano and, during these proceedings, detailed for the first time anywhere, the Camorra's oath of membership.

Notaro's revelations were as shocking in 1918 as were those of Joseph Valachi fifty years later. The gunman stated that he had undergone the Camorra rite in the home of John Mancini on 15th Street in Manhattan shortly after Easter 1916. Testified Notaro: "Tony the Shoemaker said to me, 'Now we're going to make a Camorrista and give you a title.' He said, 'The leader of the society, the boss (for Brooklyn), is Pelligrino Morano, and Vincenzo Paragallo is the second boss.' Then Pelligrino Morano said to me, 'Do you consent to become a Camorrista and receive the title that we give you?' I answered 'Yes.' He then said to me, 'Whatever is done between us, not a word should be breathed on the outside. You have to respect the bosses. When you are ordered to do a job, or kill anybody, or whatever it is, even if you are arrested, never say a word and do not talk at all. And do not be afraid and do no speak to the police. If you speak to the police, you are discharged from this society, and you have to pay attention to what the bosses—those who have been here before—will say.' I then answered, 'Yes.' He said, 'In whatever town you might find yourself—Boston, Philadelphia, Pittsburgh, Chicago, Buffalo—in any town, simply mention my name and you will be respected, because they all know me everywhere.' I said 'Yes.'

"Then Tony the Shoemaker gave me a penknife, so big. (Notaro described the length of the knife by holding his index fingers extended at about three inches apart.) There was so much of a blade outside. There was a piece of string attached to that penknife. He had one. Tony the Shoemaker extended his arm in this fashion. (Notaro extended his naked arm in court.) He said to me, 'Strike here!' I did with the penknife and just a little blood came out. Pelligrino Morano went near the Shoemaker's arm and sucked the blood, and a little more blood came out. He said to me, 'You have gained.' The Camorra and Mafia oaths and initiation rites were similar but differed in that, with the Camorra, another's blood was let, while the Mafia drew blood from the initiate.

As a result of Notaro's statements and that of others, Morano and Vollero were both convicted and sentenced to life imprisonment. As both of these expensively dressed Camorra dons were being led from court under heavy guard, chained together, dozens of Italians rushed up to them, planting kisses on their hands and faces. One of these slavish minions was collared by an officer and explained that these Camorra followers were merely showing respect to their dons and that the kisses signified congratulations to both men for avoiding the death sentence in the electric chair. Tony The Shoemaker Paretti was not as fortunate as his bosses. He was sent to the electric chair in 1926. Paretti's last visitor at Sing Sing was Vito Genovese, who delivered a message to this Camorrista killer, informing Paretti that the informer Notaro, who had disappeared after the Morano-Vollero trial, had been summarily killed by Camorra executioners, his body dumped into the East River.

Vollero, last of the American dons of the Camorra, lived out his life in Sing Sing while serving a life term, and one of his cell mates was a young New York hoodlum named Joseph Valachi. To Valachi, the aging Camorra don spilled forth his hatred for the Mafia and Sicilian gangsters. At one point Vollero told Valachi: "If there is one thing that we who are from Naples must always remember, it is that if you hang out with a Sicilian for twenty years and you have trouble with another Sicilian, the Sicilian that you hung out with all that time will turn on you. In other words, you can never trust them. Talk to me before you get out of here, and I will send you to a Neapolitan. His name is Capone. He's from Brooklyn but he is in Chicago now." (When Valachi was released from Sing Sing, he did not go to work for Capone but joined the ranks of the New York Mafia which he was later to regret and he was also to remember the prophetic words of Alessandro Vollero.

The Camorra's power in the U.S. was broken by 1920 and the rise of the Mafia in America ensued, aided mightily by both Sicilian and Neapolitan gangsters such as Charles "Lucky" Luciano, Joe Adonis, Vito Genovese, Frank Costello, Albert Anastasia, and other young gangsters who killed off their old traditional Mafia and Camorra bosses like Joseph "The Boss" Masseria and Salvatore Maranzano. These young and rising gangsters were to join with other ambitious gang leaders in the U.S. in forming the national crime syndicate by the early 1930s. The Mafia grew with the syndicate while the Camorra diminished and eventually disappeared in the U.S., but it is still a potent underworld factor in Italy today, working hand-in-hand with its Mafia counterpart in Sicily. See: **Adonis, Joe; Anastasia, Albert; Black Hand; Costello, Frank; Genovese, Vito; Luciano, Charles; Mafia, The; Maranzano, Salvatore; Masseria, Joseph; Petrosino, Joseph.**

REF.: Asbury, *Gem of the Prairie;* Bonnano, *A Man of Honor;* CBA; Gosch and Hammer, *The Last Testament of Lucky Luciano;* Griffiths, *Mysteries of Police and Crime, Vol III;* Katz, *Uncle Frank;* Kobler, *Capone;* Lait and Mortimer, *Chicago Confidential;* MacKenzie, *Secret Societies;* Maas, *The Valachi Papers;* Nash, *Bloodletters and Badmen;* Pinkerton, *Murder in All Ages;* Reid, *Mafia;* Scott, *The Concise Encyclopedia of Crime and Criminals;* Servadio, *Mafioso;* Smith, *Syndicate City;* Thrasher, *The Gang.*

Camp, Elizabeth Annie, c.1863-97, Brit., (unsolv.) mur. Elizabeth Camp, a barmaid who had been visiting her sisters on her day off, was murdered in a second-class railway carriage, on Feb. 11, 1897, somewhere in the short distance between Hounslow and the Vauxhall Station in London. Camp, thirty-three, was about to be married to a fruit-seller named Edward Berry. He was waiting for her at the gate at Waterloo Station and saw an ambulance arrive at the train bear someone away. When Camp did not arrive, he assumed that she missed her train. Soon, though, he began to worry and went to the hospital, where he identified her body. The hospital notified the police of the death, but by then all traces of the murder had been cleaned from the carriage.

Camp had visited one sister at Hammersmith, then the other at Hounslow, and took the train for London at 7:42 p.m. She boarded an apparently empty compartment at the end of the train. At Vauxhall, where tickets were collected, the conductor glanced into the car and, seeing no one, assumed that it was empty. But Camp's dead body must have been lying near the door, half under the seat. A carriage cleaner found it there when the train reached Waterloo Station in London. Camp must have put up a fierce struggle for her life because blood was spattered throughout the compartment. Her purse lay beside her, but the contents, which may have included £15, were gone. A pair of bone cufflinks lay on the floor.

Several days later, as news of the unusual railroad murder spread, a search of the railway line uncovered a Wedgwood gold-beating pestle lying in the gravel near Putney with bloodstains and hairs on it. The hairs matched Camp's. Stories began to fly about various men hurriedly leaving the train at Wandsworth or Vauxhall. A mysterious man gulped brandy with trembling hands in a nearby pub. Another man was seen to pull a bloodstained handkerchief from his pocket, then quickly hide it. But these and other tales turned out to have no relevance. And the cufflinks were discovered to have belonged to Camp's sister.

A second-hand goods dealer in Somers Town identified the pestle as one he thought he had given to an American who had

lodged in his house. The dealer then identified Camp's body as that of a woman the American had introduced as his wife. The American was never found, and there was no evidence that Camp had ever been married.

REF.: Adam, *Murder By Persons Unknown;* Birmingham, *Murder Most Foul;* CBA; Goodman, *The Railway Murders;* Lambton, *Thou Shalt Do No Murder;* Pearce, *Unsolved Murder Mysteries;* Speer, *The Secret History of Great Crimes;* Villiers, *Riddles of Crime;* Whitbread, *The Railway Policeman.*

Camp, Eugene J., 1917-88, U.S., law enfor. off. Eugene Camp joined the St. Louis Police Department on Apr. 3, 1937, and was assigned to work as a switchboard operator. He rose quickly in the ranks, serving as the editor of the *St. Louis Police Journal,* and then as chief. With a bachelor's degree in Industrial Relations, Camp became the first college-educated man in department history to be promoted into this high office.

Eugene Camp served as chief from 1970-82. During this time he helped create the new Regional Justice Information Service (REJIS), and was able to report decreases in city crime for seven of his twelve years at the helm. REF.: *CBA.*

Campagna, Louis (AKA: **Little New York**), 1900-55, U.S., org. crime. A member of New York's Five Points gang since his teen years, Louis Campagna was imported by Al Capone from that city to Chicago in 1927, for the purpose of being Scarface's bodyguard. He was a tough, compact, and short gangster and was soon dubbed Little New York. So devoted to Capone was Campagna that he took to sleeping outside Capone's suite of rooms in the Lexington Hotel, lying on a cot with two automatics in his hands, ready to kill and die should any rival gangsters manage to get to the fourth and fifth floors of the hotel, one where invading gangsters

Chicago gangster Louis Campagna.

would have to shoot their way through at least fifty top gunmen stationed 'round the clock in the lobby and lower floors.

Campagna reportedly killed several gangster enemies of Capone's and was named as one of those responsible for murdering Joseph Aiello in 1930 after Aiello joined with George "Bugs" Moran and others in attempting to kill Capone. He survived the Prohibition era and, after Capone went to prison for tax evasion, Campagna rose in the hierarchy of the Chicago mob, becoming the top extortionist in the syndicate under Paul "The Waiter" Ricca. Campagna joined with Willie Bioff and George Browne in extorting millions from Hollywood studio bosses in the late 1930s and early 1940s, threatening to put the mob-controlled motion picture projectionist union on strike unless their demands were met. He was convicted of this extortion later after Bioff and Browne turned informant. Given a ten-year sentence, Campagna was released in three years and resumed his mob activities. He retired to a large Indiana estate in the early 1950s and died in 1955 while cruising off Miami waters. See: **Capone, Alphonse; Giancana, Sam.**

REF.: CBA; Demaris, *Captive City;* Fried, *The Rise and Fall of the Jewish Gangster In America;* Gage, *Mafia, U.S.A.;* Kobler, *Capone;* Lait and Mortimer, *Chicago, Confidential!;* Landesco, *Organized Crime in Chicago;* McClellan, *Crime Without Punishment;* McPhaul, *Johnny Torrio;* Messick, *Syndicate In the Sun;* Morgan, *Prince of Crime;* Nash, *Bloodletters and Badmen;* Pasley, *Al Capone;* Reid, *The Grim Reapers;* Smith, *Syndicate City;* Spiering, *The Man Who Got Capone;* Sullivan, *Chicago Surrenders;* ____, *Rattling the Cup on Chicago Crime.*

Campana, Giampietro (Marchese di Cavelli), 1808-80, Italy, embez. Prominent dealer in Etruscan antiques. He was arrested for embezzlement and exiled. REF.: *CBA.*

Campanella, Tommaso (Giovanni Domenico), 1568-1639,

Spain, consp. Protégé of Cardinal Richelieu and Dominican monk, he was imprisoned twice for preaching religious heresy and once for conspiring against the Spanish king between 1599-1626. While in jail, he authored *La Città del Sole*. In 1634 he was forced to leave Spain and return to France. REF.: *CBA*.

Campbell, Bertram, 1886-1946, U.S., (wrong. convict.) forg. In February 1938, police knocked on the door of Bertram Campbell, a securities salesman for several leading New York brokerage houses, and told him that he was going downtown as a suspect in a forgery case.

Five bank tellers picked Campbell out of a lineup as the man who had cashed two checks totalling $4,160 under the name of George Workmaster. Protesting his innocence, Campbell was sentenced to five to ten years at Sing Sing. Late in 1941, Campbell was paroled, but the three years in proson had taken their toll. The middle-aged man was sick, but determined to clear his name. He worked as a bookkeeper for the next three years. Then, early in 1945, he read a story about a forger whom the FBI had arrested in Kentucky and returned to New York for arraignment. The description of Alexander Thiel's crimes so perfectly matched the forgery Campbell had been charged with that he hired a lawyer to investigate. When Thiel was brought before the same five bank employees whose testimony sent Campbell to jail, they admitted their earlier error and said that Thiel was the forger. The FBI learned that Thiel was "Mr. X," a slippery forger and drug addict who bilked U.S. banks of $600,000 over a forty-year period. Bert Campbell was pardoned, and awarded a $115,000 settlement for lost earnings and personal humiliation. Just eighty-two days after winning the settlement, Campbell died of a stroke. REF.: *CBA*.

Campbell, Calif., Post Office Burglary, 1908, U.S., rob.-mur. A daring nighttime burglary was staged at the Santa Clara County post office in Campbell, Calif., the night of Jan. 2, 1908. A skilled thief, believed to be working alone, looted $3,000 worth of postage stamps.

Two days later, an Oakland police officer named James Fenton stopped a suspicious-looking man near Seventh and Pine. When asked where he was headed, the stranger replied, "San Francisco." Officer Fenton asked him to open his suitcase, but the man pulled out a loaded revolver instead. There was a brief scuffle, the sharp report of a pistol, and Fenton fell to the ground, mortally wounded. A local barber named Shields grabbed the policeman's service revolver and shot the assailant in his tracks. The stolen postage stamps were found in the suitcase, but the true identity of the killer was never learned.

REF.: *CBA; Duke, Celebrated Criminal Cases of America*.

Campbell, Cecil, prom. 1928, U.S., suic.-mur. On the morning of Feb. 6, 1928, the New York City police were notified that a murder had taken place at the Grand Hotel on Thirty-first Street. A young woman in her mid-thirties had been bludgeoned to death with a cheap dimestore hammer. A timetable listing the trains running in and out of Grand Central Station was found on the nightstand. The desk clerk informed the police that a man had signed the registry cards as Mr. T.J. James of Troy, N.Y., and that he had rented the room in the company of a woman, apparently his wife.

Using as evidence a timetable found in the hotel room and the maid's description of Mr. James, police focused their search in the vicinity of New Rochelle in Westchester County. In the sleepy little hamlet of Mamaroneck, police learned the identity of the mysterious Mr. James from an apartment-house owner. He was Cecil Campbell, reputed to be a globe-trotting soldier-of-fortune who had taught military tactics at several academies before he settled down as the headmaster of a school in New Jersey.

In 1922, Campbell had married Mary Lyle McLean while he was still wedded to a telephone operator from South Wyndham, Mass. The bigamous marriage continued until his first wife filed for divorce in 1925. When Campbell was arrested by the police, he claimed that he and his wife had grown tired of life and of poverty and had agreed on a suicide pact. They discussed various ways of killing themselves, including drowning. Campbell and

McLean boarded the Hudson River ferry but lost their nerve in the presence of a deckload of passengers. Campbell bought the ten-cent hammer at his wife's urging. He hit her over the head and prepared to jump out of the window. Campbell said that, looking down at the people in the street, he decided against it, fearing that he might injure an innocent bystander.

Against his protestations that he wanted to die, Cecil Campbell was convicted of second-degree murder and was sentenced to twenty years to life.

REF.: Carey, *Memoirs of a Murder Man; CBA*.

Major Campbell killing Captain M'Kaang.

Campbell, Colin, prom. 1764, Brit. milit.-mur. Money spilled like water through the fingers of Captain J. M'Kaarg. To pay off his debts, he embezzled his company's pay, forcing his men to go begging in the streets, but it was still not enough. M'Kaarg also had no room for gratitude. He felt only resentment, especially toward Major Colin Campbell, who helped him at this most desperate moment, yet by whose sword he would die.

Major Campbell commanded a regiment stationed on the island of Jersey while awaiting duty in Martinique. His involvement with M'Kaarg began when Britain's secretary of war, hearing word of starving troops in Jersey, ordered Campbell to investigate. Learning M'Kaarg's secret, Campbell dismissed him as paymaster, which sent money flowing to the troops, but not to M'Kaarg's creditors. M'Kaarg scoured the island for help, turning in the end to Campbell, who gave him a loan. Campbell waited for repayment, but what he received instead were rumors maligning his character, rumors he traced to M'Kaarg.

Campbell wrote to the Captain, demanding an explanation. But M'Kaarg, in writing, denied the allegations, and this so infuriated Campbell that he rushed to M'Kaarg's tent, sword drawn. "You have aspersed my characted. Turn out!" he ordered. M'Kaarg, unarmed, emerged slowly.

The men struggled. Campbell stabbed M'Kaarg with his sword and both fell to the ground. "Beg your life or you are a dead man!" cried the major. But the wound, as it turned out, was fatal, and M'Kaarg knew it. "I do beg my life," he replied. "But I am a dead man!"

In his defense Campbell tried to prove that his opponent was armed, but the claim was rejected. The court found him Guilty, but stepped back from the death penalty. Instead, Colin Campbell was court-martialed and barred from military service.

The matter did not end there, however, for Campbell brought suit against Major General Robert Monkton on Apr. 14, 1764, for obstructing justice during the trial by intimidating defense witnesses and maligning Campbell's character. In the end these charges were dropped and Campbell was reprimanded for bringing the matter before the court.

REF.: *CBA;* Humphreys, *A Book of Trials;* Mitchell, *Newgate Calendar.*

Campbell, Don, and **McGee, John,** prom. 1938, U.S., extor. In 1933, Cuyahoga County Prosecutor Frank Cullitan failed in a valiant effort to bring two suspected Cleveland, Ohio, racketeers named Don Campbell and John McGee to justice on charges of burglary and extortion.

Campbell, president of the Painter's District Council, and McGee, president of the Laborers District Council, knew they were being shadowed by a pair of plainclothes investigators so the two labor racketeers went out and hired a saxophone player, an accordionist, and a brass band to play a rousing rendition of "Me and My Shadow" while the disgusted agents were forced to swallow their pride and trail close behind.

Things weren't nearly so funny five years later when Cleveland Public Safety Director Eliot Ness concluded a four-month investigation that resulted in their indictment on charges of extorting $1,200 from a restaurant owner who had his order of plate glass delayed by the duo until the money was paid. Caught red-handed and facing a stretch in the Ohio Penitentiary, Campbell and McGee attempted to bribe a female juror with $25,000 to influence an acquittal. The jury was sequestered at the Statler Hotel and a Guilty verdict was eventually returned. The two defendants were sentenced to one to five years each at the state prison. See: **Ness, Eliot.** REF.: *CBA.*

Campbell, Gary Lee, c.1959, and **Glasder, James,** c.1958, and **Craig, Daniel,** 1957-   , and **Shine, Joseph,** 1959-   , and **Shine, John,** 1957-   , U.S., mur. A deadly prank resulted in a murder conviction for a 19-year-old Algonquin, Ill., youth named Gary Campbell. Campbell and four of his friends were attending a marijuana and beer party on Oct. 20, 1977, when they hit upon the idea of turning U.S. Highway 14 into a rock-throwing range.

Campbell, Glasder, Craig, and the two Shine brothers removed thirteen white-washed rocks weighing 20-25 pounds apiece from the nearby Stone Lake apartments in Woodstock. They dropped boulders into the oncoming lane of traffic, resulting in the decapitation death of David Klawes, 26, who was driving down U.S. 14 in McHenry County. A second victim, Arthur Engle of Sharon, Wis., was severely injured in the incident.

On Feb. 11, 1977, Joseph and John Shine, Daniel Craig, and James Glasder pleaded guilty to a reduced charge of manslaughter and were sentenced to six years in prison by Circuit Court Judge James H. Cooney. Gary Campbell was tried separately, and was convicted of murder on Apr. 1. The Campbell youth received fourteen to twenty-one years in prison for his part in the crime. REF.: *CBA.*

Campbell, Dr. Henry Colin, b.c.1870-1930, U.S., big.-mur. By all appearances, Dr. Henry Colin Campbell was a temperate, unassuming physician possessing all the desirable middle-class virtues. He resided with his lawful wife and two daughters in the pleasant neighborhood of Westfield, N.J. Then the police found the body of Mildred Mowry, a Pennsylvania woman, dumped on the side of a road outside Cranford, N.J., and the facade began to come apart.

Friends and neighbors of Mrs. Mowry explained to the police and members of the Pinkerton National Detective Agency that she had left her home in February 1928 to marry a man named Campbell, whom she had met through a Detroit matrimonial agency. Mrs. Mowry was a wealthy widow who had been persuaded by Campbell to deposit several thousand dollars in cash into a joint bank account. They were then married at Elkton, Md. Puzzled by her new husband's long absences from home, Mowry traced his movements to New York City, where she confronted him and demanded some answers. The bigamist decided to kill his second wife.

Soon he did. Police who discovered Mary's corpse beheld a gruesome scene. There was a gunshot wound in her head, and her body had been doused with gasoline and burned. The crime closely paralleled a similar murder a year before, that of Margaret Brown, a New York governess.

Detectives quickly located the marriage certificate, which listed Campbell's address as 3707 Yosemite Street in Baltimore. That was not enough to disguise the address, which was actually 3705 Yosemite Avenue. The murderer was soon located and taken into custody. It was discovered that the fast-living doctor had maintained a number of mistresses over the years, and had previously been convicted of forgery and embezzlement. No definite link was established with the widowed Margaret Brown, who had been involved with a Dr. Ross and was murdered. But with the available evidence, Colin Campbell was convicted and executed in the electric chair on Apr. 17, 1930.

REF.: *CBA;* Wilson, *Encyclopedia of Murder.*

Campbell, John (First Earl of Breadalbane), 1635-1716, Scot., corr.-mur. After King William III of England acceded to the throne in 1689, he enlisted John Campbell to go into the Scottish highlands to bribe or coerce the tribal chiefs to submit to his rule. In 1692, Campbell conspired with Archibald Argyll to massacre the Macdonald clan of Glencoe. REF.: *CBA.*

Campbell, John (First Baron Campbell), 1779-1861, Brit., jur. John Campbell served as a member of Parliament from 1830-49. During his tenure, he initiated landmark legislation and many noteworthy legal reforms including the abolition of obstructive technicalities. He was appointed attorney general from 1834-41, and chief justice of the Queen's Bench from 1850-59. Books authored: *Lives of the Lord Chancellors,* and *Lives of the Chief Justices.* REF.: *CBA.*

Campbell, John Archibald, 1811-89, U.S., jur. John Archibald Campbell was appointed associate Supreme Court justice in 1853, a position he held until until he resigned at the outbreak of the Civil War in 1861. Campbell was a compromise candidate, the third choice of Whig President Millard Fillmore. During the war, his sympathy was with the South, and he concurred with the majority opinion in the *Dred Scott* case (*Scott vs. Sandford,* 1857). He opposed secession on principal, but resigned his position when war broke out. He then accepted an appointment from Jefferson Davis to serve as assistant secretary of war for the Confederacy. REF.: *CBA.*

Campbell, John Henry, 1868-1928, U.S., jur. Attorney in the justice department from 1894-1901. He was appointed to the territorial court of Arizona in 1905, by President Theodore Roosevelt and reappointed by President William Howard Taft in 1909. REF.: *CBA.*

Campbell, John W., 1848-1918, U.S., law enfor. off. John W. Campbell joined the St. Louis Police Department in 1876. During his forty-two-year career in municipal law enforcement, he twice served as chief of police: Aug. 1, 1882-Dec. 28, 1883, and June 1, 1898-Feb. 26, 1901. In 1902, he temporarily resigned from the department to accept a position as chief of police in Hot Springs, Ark. He returned to St. Louis in 1915, to serve out his remaining days as records clerk. REF.: *CBA.*

Campbell, John Wilson, 1782-1833, U.S., jur. Prosecuting attorney for Adams County, Ohio, from 1809-17. He was appointed to the district court of Ohio by President Andrew Jackson in 1829. REF.: *CBA.*

Campbell, Melville, prom. 1932, Can., burg. In 1932, Melville Campbell became the first Canadian to be convicted of a crime based on fingerprint evidence. He was found Guilty of breaking and entering into a Toronto store and was given a two-year prison sentence. In a second trial on an unrelated robbery charge, Campbell was sentenced to seven years for receiving stolen goods. REF.: *CBA.*

Campbell, Peter, prom. 1967, Scot., mur. Peter Campbell was an incorrigible young offender who bludgeoned a woman to death when he was only sixteen. In 1967, while serving his sentence, Campbell stabbed and killed a fellow inmate. He was sentenced to life imprisonment and transferred to a penal institution at Dumfries, which was specifically reserved for youthful criminals of Scotland.

REF.: *CBA;* Heppenstall, *The Sex War And Others.*

Campbell, William Joseph, 1905- , U.S., jur. Served as U.S. attorney assigned to the Northern District of Illinois from 1938-40. He was nominated by President Franklin D. Roosevelt to serve as judge of the court of the Northern District of Illinois in 1940. Articles authored: "Improvements in the Administration of Criminal Justice," *Chicago Bar Record,* and "Eliminate the Grand Jury," *Journal of Criminal Law and Criminal.* REF.: *CBA.*

Campden Wonder, The, 1906, a play by John Masefield. The strange disappearance of William Harrison, for which four innocent people were hanged, is the basis of this short drama. See: **Harrison, William.** REF.: *CBA.*

Campi, Michel, 1850-84, Fr., mur. Who was Michel Campi? The French courts and half the city of Paris demanded to know more about the true identity of this accused killer. When asked where he lived and what his occupation was, Campi said "unknown," which fueled speculation that he was shielding higher-ups in the French government or in cafe society.

On Aug. 11, 1883, the bearded, wild-looking Campi presented himself at the residence of Ducros de Sixt, a retired lawyer who lived with his sister on the Rue du Regard. Ducros' sister answered the door and, upon learning that the servant was not at home, Campi smashed her face in with a stone-hammer. Awakened by the disturbance, the woman's brother appeared and Campi bludgeoned him in similar fashion, then slit their throats with a Spanish knife. The Ducros' concierge, hearing cries for help, summoned the police, who found Campi cowering in the attic of the elderly couple's home.

The trial of Michel Campi did not begin for seven months, during which time the accused wrote threatening letters to Judge Guillot, warning him of dire consequences. "Do your worst, but you will have to choose between killing me or seeing your detectives killed," he vowed. "I shall use every means in my power and on you will rest the moral responsibility for whatever happens."

And still the mystery about the true identity of Campi remained. In court he used every ploy to hide his past associations. There were those who believed he was a lineal descendent of Napoléon III. Whatever the case, Prosecutor Quesnay de Beaurepaire secured a Guilty verdict from the jury, and Campi was sentenced to die. He was executed on May 1, 1884, at the Place de la Roquette. It was later ascertained that Michel Campi was a rather ordinary man with no extraordinary connections to civil or military figures in France. He was merely an eccentric character who committed a hideous crime for no known reason.

REF.: *CBA;* Irving, *Studies of French Criminals of the Nineteenth Century.*

Campion, Edmund, 1540-81, Brit., treas. Edmund Campion Joined the Jesuit order in 1573 renouncing his Anglican faith. Campion accepted a professorship in Prague, but returned to England in 1580 to induce Catholics to remain true to their beliefs in the face of government repression. At the Oxford commencement in 1581 he delivered an incendiary oration against the church of England. Indicted for devising a plot to overthrow the queen, Campion was racked on three occasions and executed for treason. REF.: *CBA.*

Campos Salles, Manuel Ferraz de, 1841-1913, Braz., lawyer. Minister of justice from 1889-96, and president of Brazil from 1898-1902. REF.: *CBA.*

Camp Pendleton Attack, 1976, U.S., secret crim. soc.-asslt. Believing that a group of white Marines were holding a Ku Klux Klan meeting inside the Camp Pendleton, Calif., base, fourteen black enlisted men armed with pipes and screwdrivers assaulted them in their barracks on Nov. 13, 1976. The seven victims of the attack had been drinking beer at the time, and did not belong to the white supremacist group known to exist on the compound.

The racially-motivated attack was the culmination of years of simmering tensions between white and black Marines. In nearby Oceanside, Calif., the all-night honky-tonks and strip joints were often the site of fist fights and brawls, which accounted for the bulk of the community's crime rate.

In an effort to break up the KKK presence at Camp Pendleton, Marine officials seized a list of sixteen men purported to belong to the Klan. Corporal Daniel Bailey, the "exalted cyclops" and acknowledged leader of the Camp Pendleton chapter of the KKK, was arrested and flown to an East Coast base on Dec. 3. Bailey's father was then a retired Navy captain.

Fourteen blacks were charged with conspiracy and assault stemming from the Nov. 13 attack. In pre-trial negotiations, two Marines pleaded guilty to lesser charges. One man was acquitted, one court-martialed and eight were released on Feb. 18, 1977, by the Court of Military Appeals in Washington. Two other Marines pleaded guilty to six counts of assault and conspiracy. Corporal Dean Edwards 20, and Corporal E.F. Henry, 20, each received three months of hard labor, reduction to the grade of private, and a \$100 fine. The same day the sentences were handed down, a six-foot wooden cross was set on fire five miles from where the assaults took place. See: **Ku Klux Klan.** REF.: *CBA.*

Canada Bill, See: **Jones, William.**

Canalejas y Méndez, Jose, 1854-1912, Spain, polit., assass. Before his death, Jose Canalejas y Méndez held various cabinet posts in the Spanish government. He helped establish a separation of state and church through the passage of various anti-clerical measures. He was killed in Madrid in 1912 by an anarchist. REF.: *CBA.*

Canalizo, Valentin, 1794-1850, Mex., polit., banish. Valentin Canalizo served as president of Mexico during Santa Anna's exile from the country between the years 1843-44. Canalizo was impeached for arbitrary acts and banished in 1845. He was called back to lead an army against the U.S. between 1846-47, and was at the front of the retreating column after the battle of Cerro Gordo. REF.: *CBA.*

Canal Street, prom. 1860-1915, U.S., vice dist.-riot. Separated from the center of Buffalo, N.Y., by a forty-foot slip of water, the Canal Street vice district catered to the prurient tastes of longshoremen and the seamen of the Great Lakes for nearly half a century. In its heyday, Canal Street was as notorious as Chicago's Levee and the Storyville District of New Orleans. Within a two block radius, there were ninety-three saloons and fifteen "concert halls" which fronted brothels set back from the street for convenience. The prostitutes there attracted the men who earned their living on the Erie Canal.

The word "mugging" was said to have originated on Canal Street. If a saloon patron drank himself into a stupor and was unable to pay for his last drink, he was taken out and mugged. Like most nineteenth-century vice districts, Buffalo's Canal Street flourished through the connivance of the brothel keepers, the local police, and the magistrates. The corrupt judges instituted a "segregation" policy forbidding the prostitutes to step past the liberty pole separating the business district from the wharf areas. In 1870, Sheriff Grover Cleveland of Erie County promised to clean up Canal Street. But magistrates inevitably dismissed Canal Street cases for lack of evidence. Years later, President Cleveland called his failure to drive out the Canal Street brothel keepers his worst political setback.

In just one week in 1863, fourteen men who had refused to pay prostitutes were murdered and found floating in the canal. Among the district's colorful characters were Gallow May Moore, who carried a stiletto in her garter, Frosty Face Emma, who turned into a vicious man killer when drunk, and Fat Charley Ott, who owned a saloon, brothel, and dance hall. One night Charley Ott cheated a sailor for the last time. The drunken seaman sliced Ott's head off with the Spanish knife hidden up his sleeve.

Canal Street reached its peak in 1900, the year of the Pan-American Exhibition. By 1908, the district was in a period of eclipse. A steady influx of European immigrants, and the declining shipping traffic on the Erie Canal caused the district to die a natural death. In 1915, city officials changed the name of Canal Street to Dante Place. REF.: *CBA.*

Canaris, Wilhelm Franz, 1887-1945, Ger., consp. Naval commander placed in charge of the Abweh (the military intelligence division) from 1935-44. He was involved in Claus von Stauffenberg's unsuccessful attempt to assassinate Adolph Hitler in 1944, and was captured and executed by the Gestapo. REF.: *CBA*.

Canary, Martha Jane, See: **Calamity Jane.**

Canary Murder Case, The, 1927, a novel by S.S. Van Dine. Dot King, the so-called "Broadway Butterfly," and her unsolved murder (U.S., 1923) form the basis for this work of mystery fiction. A 1929 film, based on the Van Dine Book and with the same title, offered the beautiful Louise Brooks in a starring role as the blackmailing, vamping flapper who is murdered. William Powell, as the dapper and sophisticated Philo Vance, solves the case, unlike the real murder of Dot King. See: **King, Dot.** REF.: *CBA*.

Canazzi, Robert, and **Lucciani, Toto,** prom. 1950, Fr., pros. Before striking out on their own, Canazzi and Lucciani served the Corsican mobster Ange Salicetti as his armed bodyguards. When Salicetti was machine-gunned by rival factions during a 1950 vendetta, his two protectors were forced to seek other arrangements.

Decidedly opposed to gainful employment, Canazzi and Lucciani went into business as professional pimps along the elegant Champs Elysées in Paris. They recruited four prostitutes named Micky, Michelle, Jeanine, and Céline who strolled the boulevard in search of clients. When they failed to return a suitable profit to the Corsicans, the girls were systematically tied and beaten in a nearby apartment on the rue Germaine-Pilon.

Before the French authorities finally put an end to this ring, the two infamous gangsters had netted several million francs from the four young prostitutes. Canazzi and Lucciani were sentenced to six months each in prison for "inflicting voluntary hurt" on the four women.

REF.: *CBA*; Goodman, *Villainy Unlimited.*

Canby, Edward Richard Sprigg, 1817-73, U.S., assass. Graduate of West Point in 1839, he served in the Mexican War and the Civil War with distinction. In 1873 he was killed by Indian envoys while in private conference. REF.: *CBA*.

Cancel, Linda Louise, 1950-84, El Salvador, (unsolv.) mur. While traveling through war-torn, eastern El Salvador, American Linda Cancel, mother of two small children, was shot and killed on Jan. 26, 1984, by leftist guerrillas who had stopped their bus on the Pan American Highway leading out of Santa Rosa de Lima in La Union province.

The 23-year-old woman from Culver City, Calif., was traveling through Central America with her husband, en route to their new home in Costa Rica. The travelers were escorted by a Salvadoran customs agent named Modesto Perdomo Osorio, who had picked them up at the Guatemalan border a day earlier. Thirty miles from the Honduran border, a group of rebels dressed in quasi-military clothing tried to intercept the school bus in which they were riding. Driver Curtis Lewens, Cancel's common-law husband, attempted to speed by the roadblock and drew gunfire from the surrounding hills. Though the bus was riddled with bullets, only Cancel was shot.

The U.S. Embassy flew Lewens and his two young children, Curtis, five, and Lila, seventeen months, back to the capital city. REF.: *CBA*.

Candelaria, Nev., prom. 1860-79, U.S., vice-mur. The city officials of Candelaria, Nev., were understandably self-conscious about the unsavory image of their community. For a quarter century, the mining town was a seedbed of crime and vice, the place where drunken miners came to spend their money at the ten brothels within city limits. Gunfights were common in the 1860s and 1870s. But the anxious city managers reported only seven killings—none of which were solved. The several hundred men who died in the saloons and dusty streets of Candelaria were written off as cases of "self-defense." REF.: *CBA*.

Candra Gupta II, prom. 4th-5th Cent., India, emp. mur. Candra Gupta II was the second-generation heir to the Gupta dynasty. As emperor of Malawa from 380-415, he ascended to the throne after allegedly assassinating his older brother. The royal family spread its influence across the country through military conquest and several marriages between family members. REF.: *CBA*.

Canfield, Richard Albert, 1855-1914, U.S., gamb. Known in his heyday as "The Prince of the Flash Age," Richard Canfield was undoubtedly America's most successful and esteemed gambler, a Horatio Alger character who gambled his way to the top of a multimillion-dollar gambling empire.

"There must have been a peculiar combination of Quaker parentage, New England conscience and my own individual temperament. Among them all I became what I am. I have never felt anything to be proud of in my calling, and neither have I anything to be ashamed of. They gambled in the Garden of Eden, and I guess they will again, if there's another one." Speaking not long after his retirement was Richard Albert Canfield, the greatest gambler of his day or probably any other. New York and the rest of the world bowed to his gaming mastery and showmanship for twenty years.

Gambler Richard Canfield.

Asked to name the "biggest gambler in America," gambler Pat Sheedy, in the summer of 1903 at Saratoga, did not pause for a second. "Richard Canfield. He's not only the biggest gambler in this country, he's the biggest gambler in the world. He's in a class by himself and every gambler in this country knows it."

"Except, of course, the gamblers in Monte Carlo," a young sport put in.

"I except nobody," Sheedy corrected. "There's nobody in his class. Every gambling house in Europe is run by a corporation. Individuals are not willing to take the gambler's risk. There are a score, maybe a hundred stockholders in the Casino at Monte Carlo, and companies run the houses at Ostend and Budapest and Hamburg, while in Paris the so-called clubs take no risk whatsoever...

"Now how is it with Canfield? He is the one man back of the Saratoga Club, one of the biggest gambling houses in the world. He takes all the profits, to be sure, but there is no company back of him to stand the losses."

The greatest gambler of them all began insect small. Born in the harsh, Puritan town of New Bedford, Mass., on June 17, 1855, Richard Canfield's boyhood was awash with the adventures of whaling men. His father, William, had been a whaler and bore the marks of the cruel sea, crippled for life by frostbite before he was thirty and compelled to walk on crutches. Canfield's father set the example of determination so fastidiously illustrated by the future prince of the gaming tables. Instead of accepting the charity of friends, William Canfield entered the newspaper field, operating *The Patriot* in Fall River, which he founded (the same town where the hapless Lizzie Borden would later stand accused of chopping her parents), and later the *New Bedford Register.* After marrying Julia Ann Aiken, Canfield went into the hotel business. Richard Albert was born soon after that.

Canfield was a restless youth and, in his teens, took to periodically running away for several days to Boston and Providence. He did manage, before quitting school altogether, to graduate from the Brimmer Grammar School in New Bedford. In fact, he was a top scholar and took honors. Chosen to give one of his class' declamations upon graduation, Canfield ironically selected Josiah Quincy's *Our Obligations to the Fathers of New England.* Drunk or sober, Canfield, to the last of his days, never forgot Quincy's work and quoted freely from it when mellow in his cups.

At eighteen, Canfield made good his escape from family, moving to Providence where he and another youth named Buckley operated a ten-cent poker game in a twelve-foot-square room on the second floor of a building on Westminster Place. The furnishings of the embryonic gambling house consisted of a single, rickety table, several chairs, and three packs of cards. Yet, Canfield and Buckley made out quite well until the local cop on the beat, patrolman John A. Murray, heard of their operation and single-handedly closed them down in 1873. Canfield did not go to jail and was let off with a warning. He immediately resumed his gambling career, listing his profession in the Providence directory as an "accountant," a euphemism for gambler.

Seemingly never without money, the young wagerer built up a considerable bankroll, always thinking to move on either to Boston or New York where he might work as a faro dealer or roulette croupier, meet some of the wealthy patrons he had heard about and induce one of them to finance him in his own gambling establishment. In 1876, Canfield, then only twenty years old, had an amazing streak of good luck with the faro box in one Providence gambling house and walked away with $20,000 after a few hours of play. In prodigal fashion, he sailed for Europe, living like a rajah for a year and then returning to New York with empty pockets. He would never be broke again.

There was little of the lion in Canfield and more of the leopard. He plotted his moves carefully in New York, steering clear of the gambling dens and halls and taking a job as the night clerk in the Union Square Hotel which was operated by a cousin of Julia Canfield, one Andrew J. Dam. His lean salary would not permit any sort of gaming, but Canfield came to know through his job many of the illustrious figures of the 1870s. Maurice Barrymore and Denman Thompson of the theater came to the Union Square with attractive women on their arms. The most successful promoters and gamblers ate in the hotel's restaurant and drank at its bar.

One of these bejeweled patrons was the cultured and wealthy gambler, John F. Chamberlin. His palace of chance was, in the 1870s, considered to be the "very embodiment of Victorian sumptuousness," according to one writer who had visited the gambler's brownstone address at 8 West Twenty-fifth Street. "Fine paintings looked down on mantels crowded with gewgaws, massive furniture gave an air of elegance; and under the gaslights a crowd of men drifting from play room to supper room, to library and back to play room—men whose social and professional and business standing were of the highest. Chamberlin served the finest of foods and liquors free. Many who came to eat failed to play, but the courteous host said nothing to these deadbeats until they abused his hospitality by crowding the regular players away from the food, when they were quietly told to get out."

Chamberlin became Canfield's role model, and the young man made frequent visits to the gambler's palace, careful to make only a few small bets and observe the plungers. The future gambler watched Chamberlin move with ease through his throngs of rich customers and admired him for his manners, taste, and gaming acumen. In that period, Chamberlin, who had enlarged his operations by building the Monmouth racetrack and the Long Branch, N.J., club house, ranked slightly above the super gambler of the day, John Morrissey, and head-and-shoulders over such high rollers as Price McGrath, Charles B. Ransom, Charles Reed, Albert Spencer, and Joe Hall, whose gaming hall at 818 Broadway was the most famous gambling palace in all America until Richard A. Canfield opened his colossus next to the swanky Delmonico's Restaurant. (The one-time crony of Isaiah Rynders, Morrissey did have one undying claim to gambling fame which Canfield never equalled; he won $120,000 in a head-to-head poker game which lasted twenty-four hours with Ben Wood, editor of the New York *Daily News* and brother of Mayor Fernando Wood.)

After working a smooth stint as a day clerk and subsequently manager of Colonel L. U. Maltby's Monmouth House in Spring Lake, N.J., where he made the acquaintance of the cream of American society, Canfield married 19-year-old Genevieve Wren Martin and moved to Providence. For $5,000, accrued from his small poker parties with social lions, Canfield, at age twenty-seven, bought a piece of Thomas Sprague's faro parlor in Providence. The enterprise was profitable, but short. A raid in 1885 ended Canfield's Providence adventure, and he was sentenced to a six-month jail term in the Providence County Jail at Cranston. He served every day of his term without a word of complaint. He journeyed to New York, vowing that he would never see the inside of another cell.

"I'm through with the hotel business," Canfield told his relative Andrew Dam, who offered him another clerking job. "I know enough about gambling to become rich. That's exactly what I'm going to do."

First, Canfield applied for a dealer's job at 818 Broadway, which, although it had run down since the times of Joe Hall and John Morrissey, was still considered a first-class gaming hall. The owners, Ferdinand "Gus" Abel and Lucien O. Appleby, took his name and address and told him they'd get in touch with him if anything turned up. Canfield fielded about New York for other jobs with casinos, but finally decided to open his own operation. With only $1,000 in his pocket, he teamed up with another young sharper named William Glover, and the duo opened a small-time poker parlor on the east side of Broadway between Eighteenth and Nineteenth streets.

The place, with a half dozen bare tables and chairs and fifty-cent limit, caused Canfield to be depressed. "It's so damnably smalltime," he complained to friends. Yet, he pocketed a minimum of $150 a week from the parlor, which was open from noon to midnight.

A man named David Duff came to Canfield in the spring of 1888. He was a cousin of Glover's and had heard that Canfield wanted to open something more impressive than his nickel-dime poker parlor. Duff, who was a dealer in Charlie Reed's society gambling den at 5 West Twenty-fourth Street, told Canfield that several wealthy patrons had encouraged him to start a place of his own. Canfield promptly borrowed money from his old Providence partner, Thomas Sprague (the man from whom he had originally won the $20,000 when he was twenty years old), and his relative, Andrew Dam, who had inherited $200,000 on the death of his father in 1885.

Canfield and Duff then opened the Madison Square Club at 22 West Twenty-sixth Street, a four-story brownstone that cost the partners $600 a month in rent and, initially, $200 a month for police protection. The police payoffs went up considerably as the Madison Club prospered and began to lure the social elite. Finally, high-ranking policemen were given a percentage of the take.

Canfield's first gambling hall was not a palace, but it was comfortable. He observed all the social amenities, offering free champagne and tasty food to the customers who played roulette and faro on the first floor and poker on the second. Canfield lived on the third floor and Duff and his wife on the fourth.

The location of this club was the making of it. Delmonico's was only 100 yards distant from the front door of the gambling den and close by were the Hoffman House, the Albermarle, the Gilsey House, the Fifth Avenue Hotel, and the Brunswick, all haunts of the super rich. Methodically, Canfield built up his trade. He hired a full-time cook, a manservant, and two maids. He was careful to people the place with his own friends as dealers. Canfield had grown wary of his partner, Duff, who had taken to gambling and losing heavily in other casinos. Duff's reputation with the wealthy was also less than desirable, especially when he had too much champagne. Some patrons complained about Duff to Canfield. The ever-attentive, mild-mannered Canfield knew it was time to get rid of his partner. He first attempted to persuade Duff to give up his heavy gambling and drinking. When Duff ignored Canfield's suggestions, blunt measures were taken.

One early September morning in 1890, Duff knocked on the door of his own gambling den. David Bucklin, who acted as manager of the place, opened the door. He stood squarely in

Duff's path.

"Well, get the hell out of the way," Duff ordered.

"Mr. Canfield has asked me to inform you that you are not again to be allowed on the premises."

Duff put his hand on Bucklin's chest and gave a gentle shove. "Come now, Bucklin. Out of the way."

Bucklin gently reached up and encircled Duff's hand with a meaty grasp, forcing the hand down. "You are not permitted on the premises, Mr. Duff."

"This is my place!"

"This establishment is operated by Mr. Richard Canfield," Bucklin corrected.

Duff, in a daze, walked down the steps of the brownstone and, spying a loose brick lying nearby, grabbed it and threw it with a loud curse through the front window of the gambling den. The act severed his relationship with Richard Canfield (who paid Duff off with less than $50,000). Duff didn't quit with grace. He went to the newspapers and told reporters that his partner had stolen his club. Newsmen arrived at the casino to find a group of men smoking cigars in the front parlor. To their inquiries, Bucklin flatly stated: "This is merely a gentleman's club. Mr. Duff was a member, but had no other rights. I belong to it myself and so does Mr. Sprague. Mr. Canfield is the treasurer. We didn't like the way Mr. Duff was acting, so we asked him to resign and that's all there is to it."

After reporters poked around for a few minutes and found no evidence of gambling equipment anywhere, they raced off to the Tenderloin precinct, asking police about Canfield's operation. A Sergeant Lane blandly informed them: "Oh, that place has been closed for months. You know, boys, you wouldn't think to look at such a quiet building and figure there was gambling going on inside, but it wasn't much. Anyway, it will never happen again."

Canfield's opened again in three days, and it was jammed to the walls with wealthy plungers who considered the ousting of the obnoxious Duff as their own triumph. Canfield catered to the rich and they, in turn, lavished his tables with their money. At age thirty-five, Richard Canfield was well on his way to his first million.

A large part of the appeal of Canfield's to the power elite of his day was his discerning taste in art, cuisine, and wines. The gambler pumped tens of thousands of dollars from his profits into expensive paintings, tapestries, and antique colonial furniture (the colonial decor, in contrast to the popular heavy Victorian furniture of the day, was an original Canfield touch). The most important aspect of the rich attending the Madison Square Club was the overwhelming fact that Canfield's games were always honest. He was content to take his profits from the normal edge of odds the house always held over the plungers. The stakes were considered modest for the day, Canfield setting $50 and $100 limits on poker and faro. The more delicate patrons appreciated this type of parlor decorum play, and the conservative restrictions further enhanced Canfield's prestige.

Gathering about $2 million from his gambling profits, Canfield traveled to Europe, buying up paintings and furniture. One of his purchases, for $15,000, was six identical Chippendale chairs. He was assured by the dealer, Christie's, that the set was complete, but Canfield, though a dilettante with art, was as hardheaded a businessman with his money as he was with the rules of his gambling casinos. He later discovered that two more Chippendale chairs matched his allegedly complete six-chair set and raised so much fuss with Christie's that the esteemed firm spent years at its own cost tracking down the other four chairs that brought the set to its original twelve. This fabulous art treasure was later on display in Canfield's elegant gambling palace at 5 East Forty-fourth Street. (Marsden J. Perry bought the chairs for a fortune after Canfield died.)

The poshest gaming palace in all New York was begun by Canfield when he purchased for $75,000 the house at 5 East Forty-fourth Street. The gambler had watched carefully the march of swanky restaurants and bars into the area. Rector's, the famous lobster house, had moved to what would become the Times Square area. So had Delmonico's. This restaurant had brought good luck to the gambler in earlier years, so he moved with it; in fact, his palace was right next door to Delmonico's. Canfield shrewdly put his new property in the name of his mother-in-law, Maria Martin. The old woman knew what kind of business her son-in-law was in and made no objections. This move so confused the crusading prosecuting attorney, ironically a Tammany man, William Travers Jerome, that when he mounted his campaign against Canfield in 1902, Jerome first thought the gambling palace was "owned by a woman who is said to be traveling in the Orient...One of the Negro servants at 5 East Forty-fourth Street is named Maria Martin."

Before Canfield established his Forty-fourth Street gambling salon, he bought controlling interest in the profitable gambling palace and horse track at Saratoga, the summer retreat of the rich. The place was a bit run down after having been operated by the energetic but decidedly crude John Morrissey (and subsequently Charles Reed, Albert Spencer, and Goffried Walbaum, but Canfield invested a fortune in bringing the resort back to its former plush surroundings. He even hired a half dozen New York City detectives to quietly circulate and weed out any sharpers who attempted to mingle and play with the socialites who brought Canfield an annual profit of approximately $2,500,000 for a mere six weeks of play at Saratoga (he had paid $250,000 for the place).

Saratoga under Canfield became a dream world of quality. Gambling historian Alexander Gardiner pointed out how the impresario's pride in the Saratoga operation made him "extremely finicky about the appointments of the place. The napery, the silver, the china were the best obtainable. Woe to the head waiter who failed to throw a demitasse cup away if it had the slightest trace of a crack!" Canfield's stunning restaurant lost $70,000 each year, but the loss spent on elegance was nothing compared to what the gambler made up in his gaming profits. "Canfield was determined to have the Saratoga place the very best that money could make it. He wanted people to talk about it—not only people from all over America but the plungers from Europe, the barons and the dukes and the princes who flocked to Saratoga to help their American fathers-in-law dispose of their fortunes."

The prices one paid in the restaurant were as astronomical as the finest dining spots in New York. No one was barred from Canfield's restaurant, neither king nor common man. "If Hiram and Emma on a day's excursion to Saratoga," Gardiner illustrated, "wanted to experience the thrill of breaking the bread of the notorious Canfield, they had only to pay the stiff price and they were welcome. They might see the Vanderbilts, the Whitneys and the Goelets at tables near them..."

The common man might also see the greatest plunger of the century who played at Canfield's and for whom the sky was the limit. John W. "Bet-a-Million" Gates was a dedicated Canfield foe at the faro box. The Chicago tycoon, who made his first fortune by selling barbed wire to frontier settlers and ending the days of the open range, was in the habit of dropping enormous sums of money to gamblers. He lost a staggering $300,000 to New York bookmaker Billy Cowan in one afternoon. Gates also had fabulous wins; in 1900, he won $1,375,000 in a single race in England. In the summer of 1902, Gates, who had lost fortunes to Canfield in the past, was determined to deplete the gambler's bank account. After eating a heavy meal, Gates left Canfield's dazzling restaurant and sauntered into one of the adjacent gaming rooms, heading for the faro table. He began to play hard, betting to the limits—$500 to the cases and $1,000 to the doubles.

Gates lost. He went at the game with a vengeance and lost more—tens of thousands. The corpulent, bewhiskered plunger suddenly stopped and mopped a sweat-beaded brow. "I would like to continue the play in a private room," Gates told Canfield's manager, Billy Coe.

"Certainly," the affable Coe replied, and the party walked upstairs to a private room. It was 10 p.m. and John W. Gates had already dropped more than $150,000 into Canfield's profits for the evening. The limits were again raised for Gates' private party—$2,500 to the cases and $5,000 to the doubles. "Bet-a-Million" played furiously for an hour, but with no luck at all. He lost more and more.

"I would like to up the limit once more," Gates told Coe.

"I'm sorry, Mr. Gates," Billy Coe purred, "but only Mr. Canfield can authorize a limit beyond what you now have."

"Then I'll see Canfield," Gates said, and the heavyset man puffed his way downstairs, his sweat-stained white linen suit a mass of wrinkles. When Gates entered Canfield's office, he found the gambler coolly puffing on a cigar and discussing art with a fellow collector. "I want to shoot the works," Gates blurted out.

Ever the gentleman, the super gambler excused himself to his visitor and silently accompanied Gates to his private gaming room upstairs. Canfield had no love for Gates, and the barbed wire mogul was always less than cordial to his gambling nemesis. Gates had wanted to break Canfield's financial back for years.

"What limit have you now?" Canfield asked in front of the entire party.

"Twenty-five hundred and five thousand," Gates shot back.

"What do you want?" There was a faint smile playing about Canfield's thin lips.

"Five thousand and ten thousand."

"You may have it," Canfield said without hesitation. As "Bet-a-Million" turned back to the table, Canfield began to leave the room. Then, in a moment of deviltry, the gambler insisted on having the last word with the king of the plungers.

"Are you sure that's enough?" Canfield inquired in a mild voice.

Gates darted a quick glare at Canfield but said nothing, beginning to play wildly. Canfield confidently stepped from the room. That night Richard Canfield retired early while John Gates continued to play and sweat. He played faro until dawn, and by then his luck had changed; he had not only won back the $175,000 lost to Canfield the previous evening, but an additional $150,000.

When Gates walked weakly down the stairs to the main dining room for breakfast, he brushed the arm of Richard Canfield. He grinned triumphantly at the freshly shaven, well-rested gambler. "I've bucked you and won!" Gates announced, unable to resist voicing his victory.

With great presence, Richard Canfield patted the millionaire on the shoulder lightly. He smiled and said in a pleasant voice, "So glad, old boy." Canfield then moved off to greet other guests as if nothing serious had happened to set back his financial empire. And nothing really did. By the time Canfield retired in 1906 as a result of the investigative probes conducted by William Travers Jerome, his personal fortune exceeded $12 million. (This was a conservative estimate, advanced by gambling historian Alexander Gardiner; others estimated Canfield's estate at four to five times as much.)

Canfield's retirement was one of leisure. He retreated to his sprawling, elegant study crammed with collector's editions, for by then he had become a bibliophile. He spent moody, silent hours staring at his impressive art collection, among which James McNeil Whistler was the most prominent. (Whistler never finished the portrait he had begun of Canfield.)

Intrigued with the vagaries of Wall Street, Canfield began to gamble with stocks in 1906 and within a year had lost millions. He continued to live in comfort, even though he had sold off all of his gambling interests. For all his wealth and luxury, Richard Canfield was a lonely man; he had forsaken the gambling world to ingratiate himself with intellectuals, but he found himself shunned and ignored, except by Whistler whom he patronized.

As the Flash Age slipped away into nostalgia, Canfield spent more and more time investing in small businesses and manufacturing companies. He was returning home on the night of Dec. 10, 1914, after inspecting a prospective company and decided to take the subway. The prince of gamblers grew drowsy as the train clacked toward his Grand Central stop, a dinner of hash mixed liberally with cocktails churning in his stomach. Suddenly, he

stood up and dashed off the subway at Fourteenth Street, mistaking it for his stop. Halfway up the stairs, he realized his error and turned to go back to the trains. As he pivoted he slipped and fell, flying outward and falling almost the full length of the stairs. He landed, with an awkward crash, on his chin.

Subway employees summoned one of Canfield's friends, but the gambler refused to go to a hospital. The friend took him home in a taxi. Canfield rested that night in his study, drinking in the colorful canvases and books for which he had spent his fortune. Most of the Whistlers were gone by then, sold off to steel magnate Henry Clay Frick for $300,000. Canfield's estate had been running a little low.

At midnight, Canfield's long-time housekeeper, Virgie, looked in on him. He was propped up by a half dozen pillows in his giant four-poster. He was attempting to read, a painful expression on his face. The housekeeper asked Canfield if he wanted anything.

"I want nothing. Nothing. You just go to bed, and don't forget to call me at seven in the morning."

Those were the last words of the prince of gamblers. At seven, Virgie found her employer in a coma and called Dr. J. Clarence Sharp. Canfield's doctor could not rouse him. Two brain surgeons, Dr. Isidore Freisner and Dr. R. Foster Kennedy, were summoned and arrived in minutes. Upon examining Canfield, the brain experts determined that the gambler had fractured his skull when he had fallen on the subway stairs. An operation would have saved his life if there had been time, but Richard Canfield, age fifty-nine and with a good head of hair, died in his coma.

"Perhaps it's just as well," Dr. Kennedy remarked. "Even if the operation had proved successful, he would have been hopelessly insane for the rest of his days." See: **Hall, Joe; McGrath, Price; Morrissey, John; Ransom, Charles B.; Reed, Charles; Spencer, Albert.**

REF.: Allen, *The Lords of Creation*; Amory, *The Last Resorts*; Asbury, *Gem of the Prairie*; ____, *Gangs of the Underworld*; ____, *Sucker's Progress*; Beebe, *The Big Spenders*; Bradley, *Such Was Saratoga*; Burnley, *Millionaires and Kings of Enterprise*; Bushick, *Glamorous Days*; CBA; Chafetz, *Play the Devil*; Charles, *Gambling and Betting*; Edward, *Jack Pots*; Ezell, *Fortune's Merry Wheel*; Fetter, *The Masquerade of Monopoly*; Flynn, *Men of Wealth*; Fried, *The Rise and Fall of the Jewish Gangster In America*; Gardiner, *Canfield*; ____, *The True Story of the Greatest Gambler*; Hildreth, *The Spell of the Turf*; Logan, *Against the Evidence*; Longstreet, *Win or Lose, A Social History of Gambling in America*; McPhaul, *Johnny Torrio*; Meyers, *Great American Fortunes*; Morrell, *Diamond Jim*; Orth, *The Boss and the Machine*; Parmer, *Gold and Glory*; Peterson, *The Mob*; Quinn, *Fools of Fortune*; Reppetto, *The Blue Parade*; Sergeant, *Gamblers All*; Tully, *Era of Elegance*; Van Every, *Sins of America*; ____, *Sins of New York*; Veblen, *The Theory of the Leisure Class*; Waller, *Saga of an Imposing Era*; Warshow, *Bet-a-Million Gates*; Wendt and Kogan, *Bet a Million!*; Werner, *Tammany Hall*.

Cannaday, John Eli (AKA: **John Eli Sneedom**), d.1876, U.S., mur. John Eli Cannaday, a lowly thief, believed rumors that Marcus Louis, an elderly merchant in Holly Springs, Miss., had hoarded a great fortune. On Feb. 15, 1876, Cannaday went into Louis' store and crept up behind Louis as he was filling a sack with peas, crushing the merchant's head with an ax. The old man's reported fortune came to no more than $2. Cannaday was seen leaving the premises and was quickly arrested and tried. Convicted, he was hanged at Holly Springs on May 24, 1876.

REF.: *The Life and Confessions of John Eli Cannaday; CBA*.

Cannicott, William, b.c.1716-56, Brit. big.-mur. William Cannicott became a livery servant, though he came from a prominent family. At age twenty, he married 40-year-old Dorothy Tamlyn, another servant, set her up in a small haberdasher's shop in Boswell Court and bought her a house in which to rent out rooms. For years the couple lived together, as Cannicott later said, peaceably if not happily. Then suddenly, Cannicott was driven to bigamy and murder.

One day, when Cannicott went to dress for a special occasion, he noticed that his best suits were missing. His wife had sold them without his knowledge or permission. Her reasons for doing so were inexplicable, as she already received Cannicott's salary and all the income from the house. Cannicott was so angry about the incident that he vowed never to return to their house, a vow he kept even after tempers cooled.

He found employment with a household in Cavendish Square, though he had to pretend he was unmarried to get the position. Once this ruse was begun, it also served him in his efforts to win the heart of a servant girl he called Nanny. Aware of her many other suitors, Cannicott proposed to her, never mentioning his wife, and she accepted.

Since the master of the house did not want his domestics married, Cannicott resigned and entered into service for Lord Darnley, then promptly married Nanny on June 3, 1754. Only Hobson, a coachman, knew about Cannicott's other wife, Dorothy.

Dorothy eventually found out and she revealed everything to Nanny, who confronted Cannicott. The disappointed young woman told him not to attempt to see her again since she wanted to endure the tragedy and shame alone.

Hobson aggravated the situation by telling Dorothy that Cannicott made good wages and that he could afford to support her. So she threatened to prosecute Cannicott unless he paid up, reminding him how the law dealt with bigamists. Cannicott grew fearful and agreed to settle up with Dorothy at the Red Lion Inn at Berkeley Square. But his wife's request that night—the money for a night's lodging at the inn because of a storm—sent Cannicott into a rage. With a cord that he found hanging over a banister, Cannicott tried to strangle her, but Dorothy was strong and she broke free. Then Cannicott used a pair of sharp scissors. This time he cut her throat and stomach, killing her.

Although he fled with Dorothy's valuables, he forgot the scissors. When arrested he refused to talk, even when told that Nanny would be arrested as an accessory before the fact unless he confessed to the murder. He held out in silence until the day they imprisoned her. Only then did he confess. He was hanged at Tyburn on Sept. 20, 1756.

REF.: *CBA;* Mitchell, *Newgate Calendar.*

The trial of Elizabeth Canning for perjury.

Canning, Elizabeth, 1735-73, Brit., perj. The disappearance of housemaid Elizabeth Canning in 1753 caused little talk in London, only consternation and sadness in her family. But her reappearance turned her case into a *cause célèbre,* and the public divided into those who believed her and those who did not. Eventually the case came to the attention of Henry Fielding, author of the novel *Tom Jones.*

Canning was an 18-year-old, smallpox-scarred maiden when she disappeared on the evening of New Year's Day after visiting her aunt and uncle at Whitechapel. Four weeks later she stumbled into her mother's house, gaunt and dirty and dressed in strange

rags. When Canning could speak, she said she had been abducted by two huge men who stripped her and knocked her senseless. When she revived, she was being led to a house on the Hertfordshire Road. There three women offered her wonderful new clothing if she agreed to go into service in what was apparently a brothel. When she refused, the women stole her clothes and shoved her into a hayloft and left her there for four weeks. She had nothing to eat but a small tart she had bought for her brother, some crusts of bread, and a pitcher of water. It was not until the morning of Jan. 29 that she found she could move a board over a window and climb out.

It was suggested that Canning had been held in a brothel run by Susannah Wells. Canning recalled hearing the name and went to the alderman to ask for a warrant for Wells' arrest. The alderman reluctantly agreed to go to the house with a group of Canning's friends. At the alleged brothel, they encountered Wells, an elderly gypsy woman named Mary Squires, Squires' son and daughter, a couple named Natus, and a girl named Virtue Hall, and they found a hayloft that bore no resemblance to Canning's description. Although Mary Squires was uniquely ugly and Canning had not mentioned the fact, the housemaid claimed that she, Lucy Squires, and Hall were the three women who tempted her. The alderman, even more suspicious of the girl's story, nevertheless took the whole lot to jail.

During the ensuing trial, Hall confirmed Canning's story (though she later recanted) and Mary Squires, who Canning claimed robbed her, was quickly found Guilty of theft and sentenced to hang. Wells, found Guilty of harboring a thief, was branded with a "T" on her hand. But the Lord Mayor of London, Sir Crisp Gascoyne, disbelieved Canning's story and petitioned the king to pardon the gypsy. The public went into a frenzy of partisanship. Firstly, no one cared what happened to gypsies, or "Egyptians," as they were called. Secondly, by pardoning Squires, the Lord Mayor would proclaim Canning's whole story a lie. All of Europe eventually sided with one group or the other. Great volumes of newsprint were devoted to the case, and many influential citizens contributed to defense funds in support of Canning or the gypsy. Henry Fielding wrote in the "Case of Elizabeth Canning" that he was "firmly persuaded...that Elizabeth Canning is a poor, honest, innocent, simple girl and the most unhappy and injured of all human beings."

In March 1754, public opinion had swung against her, and Canning was tried for perjury. Thirty-six witnesses testified that Squires was elsewhere at the time of the abduction, but twenty-six others swore she had been at Wells' house. The jury hesitated, but finally found Canning Guilty. She was sentenced to be transported to America for seven years, but was sent not on a convict ship but on a regular ship with money in hand, provided by generous supporters. She settled in Wethersfield, Conn., where she soon married. In 1757, a pamphleteer in America published a fictionalized story of her travails called *Virtue Triumphant, or, Elizabeth Canning in America.* She died in 1773.

REF.: Armitage, *Bow Street Runners; CBA;* Culpin, *The Newgate Noose;* de la Torre, *Villainy Detected;* Gross, *Masterpieces of Murder;* Lustgarten, *Story of Crime;* Mitchell, *The Newgate Calendar;* Stevens, *From Clue To Dock.*

Canning, George, 1770-1827, Brit., duel. George Canning was a prominent English statesman under secretary during the administration of William Pitt the Younger from 1796-99. As the foreign secretary from 1807-10, he planned to seize the Danish fleet. When war secretary Robert Stewart, Viscount Castlereagh refused to comply with his plan, the men dueled. Canning later succeeded Stewart as foreign secretary and as leader of the House of Commons. See: **Stewart, Robert (Castlereagh).** REF.: *CBA.*

Canning, Gertrude, 1922-42, Scot., (unsolv.) mur. The bullet-riddled body of wine steward Gertrude Canning was found in a weed patch near Inverary in the summer of 1942. The Glasgow Police and Robert Churchill investigated the case for nearly a year, but found few tangible clues. The murder remains unsolved.

REF.: *CBA;* Hastings, *The Other Mr. Churchill.*

Canning, Joseph, d.1895, Brit., mur. Joseph Canning was hanged by the neck in June 1895 for the murder of his girlfriend. Affixing the noose to Canning's neck, the famous British executioner Billington listened to the condemned man's last words. "I wish to die," Canning said. "I want to join the girl I love better than life." See: **Billington.**

REF.: *CBA;* Laurence, *A History of Capital Punishment.*

Cannino, Giuseppe, prom. 1920-55, Fr., smug. Giuseppe Cannino graduated from the ranks of the Chicago bootlegging gangs of the 1920s to dope smuggling a decade later. His "China Syndicate" avoided arrest by U.S. Customs officials for many years by simply avoiding eastern U.S. ports. Cannino smuggled heroin into Montreal and then across Canada to Vancouver. From there the dope was transported into Seattle and San Francisco. The cost of these elaborate precautions was passed on to the drug addicts, of course, and Cannino became a very wealthy man.

After twenty years in the drug trade Cannino was arrested at Orly Airport in Paris in September 1955. He had tried to conceal in his luggage sixteen pounds of heroin destined for a particularly impatient client in France.

REF.: *CBA;* Goodman, *Villainy Unlimited.*

Cannon, George Quayle, 1827-1901, U.S., poly. Converted to the Mormonism in 1840 and linked up with Brigham Young, Joseph Smith, and other Mormon leaders who made the exodus from Nauvoo, Ill., to Salt Lake City, Utah, in 1847. Elected to the U.S. House of Representatives from 1873-81, he was later jailed for polygamy. REF.: *CBA.*

Cannon, James, Jr., b.1865, and **Burroughs, Ada L.,** prom. 1934, Case of, U.S., polit. corr. Bishop Cannon of the Methodist Episcopal Church was the target of a four-year government investigation into his alleged violations of the Federal Corrupt Practices Act. Cannon and Ada Burroughs, the treasurer of the Anti-Smith Committee of Virginia, were indicted in November 1931 for failing to disclose the full amount of a $65,300 campaign contribution received from Edwin Cornell Jameson, a wealthy New York insurance magnate. Burroughs had reported only $17,000 in expenditures.

Cannon and Burroughs were staunch opponents of Governor Alfred Smith, the 1928 Democratic nominee for president who ran on an anti-prohibition platform. Political allies of Governor Smith were relieved when the indictments against the pair were handed down. But, the joy in the Smith camp was short-lived. Cannon and Burroughs were acquitted in May 1934. Claiming religious persecution, Cannon succeeded in convincing the jury that the campaign funds had been spent within his home state of Virginia, and therefore he was exempt from the Corrupt Practices Act. REF.: *CBA.*

Canovas del Castillo, Antonio, 1828-97, Spain, polit., assass. High ranking government official who was banished from 1868-69. He returned to Madrid to lead the fight to restore the Bourbon King Alfonso XII to the throne in 1874. While serving as premier, he drafted a strong measure to abolish black slavery in the colonies. In 1897 he was assassinated by an anarchist. Book authored: *Problemas Contemporáneos.* REF.: *CBA.*

Cant, George, prom. 1839, Brit., rape. George Cant of High Holborn, London, was a prosperous businessman who prided himself for owning a respectable public house near Windsor Castle. So respectable was his Holborn Inn that he would not take in idlers or people of low moral character. In September 1839, Cant's wife hired the winsome 23-year-old Jane Bolland to work as a domestic at the inn.

Though she was half his age, Cant was very much taken by Bolland's beauty and delicate manner. One day he playfully slipped his arm around her and tried to force a kiss. She angrily broke free and told her employer she would be leaving the next day.

That night Bolland got drunk on Cant's liquor. She was in a near-stupor when Mrs. Cant prevailed upon the barmaid, Jane Holtier, to take her up to the servants' quarters. Early the next morning, Bolland knocked on the Cants' bedroom door. Tearfully she told about the improper advances George had made, and how during the night he had slipped into her room and raped her. This seemed preposterous to the wife, who was certain that her husband had slept soundly in their bed all night.

On Sept. 30 the police arrested the innkeeper on a charge of rape. Confident that he would be dismissed once the true facts were told, he surrendered his bail at the Old Bailey. To his horror, he learned that the court would not permit him to go into the witness box to tell his version of events. And neither would his wife be permitted to give testimony.

Bolland, an innocent-looking woman, quickly won the sympathy of the jury, who were inclined to believe the worst about Cant. She testified that she was not drunk that last night at the inn, but was suffering from a seizure, a condition that had afflicted her most of her life. Her brother, Henry Bolland, corroborated these statements, and a physician gave evidence that the young woman had recently lost her virginity.

The defense produced a lodger named Joseph Edwards, who confessed to having engaged in sex with Jane Bolland that night. "I went into her bedroom," he said. "She was awake and perfectly in her senses. I laid my hand on her and said, 'come.' She was perfectly willing. I never saw a woman more willing in my life." Edwards said that Jane Bolland desired revenge against her employer for calling her a drunken hussy.

The jury did not believe Edwards, nor did they attach much significance to the character witnesses produced on George Cant's behalf. A verdict of Guilty was returned, and the prisoner was sentenced to die. There was an appeal made to the lord mayor of London, who believed that the evidence was not sufficient to convict. The home secretary was consulted, but he would only go so far as to commute the sentence to overseas penal transportation—for life.

REF.: *CBA;* Cobb, *Trials and Errors.*

Cantelupe, Walter de, d.1266, Brit., jur. Supporter of King John and Henry III, and a bishop from 1236-66. He exercised religious dissent by supporting the cause of Simon de Montfort in opposing Henry III's request for a subsidy in 1252. He presented the case to other clerics and members of the academic community, resulting in the acceptance of the Provisions of Oxford in 1258. In 1253 he excommunicated all those who infringed upon the tenets of the Magna Carta. REF.: *CBA.*

Canter, Jack (AKA: **Charles Ostend**), prom. 1873, count.-forg. By the time Jack Canter had reached his forty-fifth birthday, he had already spent half his adult life behind the barbed wire and red-brick walls of Sing Sing prison. His fellow inmates treated him with respect, for Canter was more than just an ordinary run-of-the-mill con. He was college-educated, skilled in linguistics, chemistry, poetry, and medicine. But his greatest talents were engraving and forgery.

Canter was a notorious penman who was involved in the Central Fire Insurance Company frauds of 1873, a case that was finally cracked by the Pinkerton Detective Agency. The president of the insurance firm, W.D. Halfman, was passing forged certificates of railroad stock from the Philadelphia and Reading line. The penman had altered the valuation amounts through a delicate chemical process. One- and two-share certificates were artfully transformed into 300 to 500 shares, and circulated among "investors." Worried railroad officials retained the services of Allan Pinkerton to track down the forger. One of the arrested Central Fire executives identified Charles Ripley of New York as the man who had altered the shares of stock.

Ripley, who received $25,000 for the job, was traced to Brooklyn, where his mail was being picked up by one Charles Ostend, who resided across the street from the police station. Ostend was, of course, Jack Canter, and a nickel-plated press and other forger's paraphernalia were found in his room. Halfman and Canter were both convicted of forgery. Canter was sentenced to nine and a half years in solitary confinement at the dreaded Eastern Penitentiary at Cherry Hill. See: **Pinkerton, Allan.**

REF.: *CBA;* Rowan, *The Pinkertons.*

Cantero, Jonathan Eric, 1969- , U.S., mur. "The devil made me do it!" was a favorite gag-line of 1960s comics. It was always good for a laugh or two in those times. Twenty years later, however, it was no longer a laughing matter, for teenagers across the country were embracing Satanism, and its accompanying violence.

For Jonathan Cantero, a 19-year-old nursing student and short-order cook at a Tampa, Fla., Pizza Hut, it was the devil *and* the Geraldo Rivera television program that drove him to murder. On Oct. 6, 1988, Cantero watched a syndicated hour-long Geraldo Rivera program about Satanism and its practice by street gangs. Rivera interviewed teenagers who had, among other things, ritualistically killed animals. Cantero sat transfixed. Here were real-life stories about other youths like him from average American homes, young people who worshipped the devil.

Jonathan had been interested in devil worship for years. In recent weeks he had spent long hours in the public library, poring over every book he could find about demonic possession, the occult, and devil worship. In his bedroom he studied from a satanic bible, wrote letters of allegiance to the devil, and scrawled demonic symbols on his body, all of which terrified his mother, Patricia Cantero. She was a 38-year-old woman who worked nights as a waitress at the Toddle House Restaurant in Tampa. She also wrote religious verse in her spare time under the name "The Purple Rose," and her son's blasphemy broke her heart.

But Jonathan hated his mother and after watching the Geraldo Rivera program he summoned the courage to kill her. On Oct. 12, 1988, he drove to his mother's apartment on West Hillsborough Avenue to "just say hello," an unusual occurence, given the strained relations between the two. This strain was brought on by Patricia Cantero's despair at her inability to change her son and it led to her suicide attempt in 1986. According to a note written at the time, Jonathan had placed a spell on her.

When her son knocked on the door in 1988, however, she did what a mother would do. She let him in. Newly inspired by his demonic fantasy, Jonathan followed her into the kitchen and stabbed her forty times. He read a poem over the lifeless body and tip-toed out of the apartment, locking the door behind him.

He had completed the last item on his daily list of things to do. "Go to school. Pull up at mom's house. Enter/greet mom. Go to bathroom. Prepare knife and handkerchief. Go directly to mom. When her back is turned stab until dead. Cut off her hand." He buried the gruesome note, his bloody clothes, and a satanic poem in his grandfather's back yard, where they remained until police investigators dug them up nearly two weeks later.

David Cantero, Jonathan's 16-year-old brother, found his mother in the hallway of the apartment. Jonathan was brought to the police station for questioning, his hand heavily bandaged. He claimed the wound was caused by glass in his school parking lot, not as the attending physician at St. Joseph's Hospital later told detectives, by a knife. When confronted with the doctor's testimony, Cantero confessed. He was charged with first-degree murder, and locked up at the Hillsborough County Jail. According to the police report, Cantero said he "couldn't take it anymore because his mother got on him for not coming to see her enough." He also said he hated her for forcing Christianity on him and that demonic voices in the night ordered him to kill her.

To avoid a trial and the possibility of the death penalty, Jonathan Cantero agreed to serve a life sentence with no chance of parole for twenty-five years. He was led off to jail on Mar. 18, 1989, after embracing his aunt, the sister of Patricia Cantero. It was her wish that the boy be spared the electric chair. REF.: *CBA*.

Canton, Frank M. (Joe Horner), 1849-1927, U.S., west. lawman-gunman. Born Joe Horner near Richmond, Va., Frank M. Canton moved as a child to Texas with his family. Here, while in his teens, he became a cowboy, herding cattle from North Texas to the Kansas railheads in the late 1860s. In 1871, Canton dropped from sight, becoming a bank robber and rustler. He was next heard from when he got into a quarrel with black cavalry troopers from Fort Richardson. Canton was in a Jacksboro, Texas, saloon on Oct. 10, 1874, when one of the black soldiers made a remark about white women. Canton demanded an apology and a gunfight erupted with Canton killing one black cavalryman and wounding another. He was jailed in 1877 for robbing the bank at Comanche, Texas, but he managed to escape and returned to cattle herding. After driving a herd to Ogallala, Neb., he officially changed his name to Frank Canton and vowed to uphold law and order. To that end he hired on as the top enforcer of the Wyoming Stock Growers' Association, a group of powerful cattlemen intent upon driving out the immigrant farmers who had settled in Johnson County. Canton ran his own ranch near Buffalo, Wyo., and was later elected sheriff of Johnson County.

In 1885, Canton married and the union produced two daughters, one of them dying in childhood. He then resigned as sheriff to accept a well-paying job with his former employers, the Wyoming Stock Growers' Association. At the same time, Canton was made a deputy U.S. marshal and he enforced the law as the cattlemen wanted it enforced. One of the leaders of the opposition, the settlers, was Nathan Champion who had been branded a rustler by the cattlemen, and, thus labeled, he was ordered to be arrested. This was essentially an order to murder Champion and Canton proceed to carry out this order without questioning his employers. He rode to Champion's cabin on the Powder River on Nov. 1, 1891, accompanied by Joe Elliott, Fred Coastes, and Tom Smith, who was a friend of Champion's. Once outside the cabin, the four men drew their guns and

Lawman and gunman Frank M. Canton.

then burst inside. Champion, sick in bed, jumped up with his six-gun barking. Smith and Coates were slightly wounded as they exchanged gunfire with Champion and then Canton ordered his men to flee, all four gunmen running from the cabin, mounting their horses and riding pell mell out of the area as Champion blazed away at them with a rifle that his one-time friend Tom Smith had given to him some time earlier.

Canton then joined Frank Wolcott's Regulators, a group of more than fifty gunmen hired by the cattlemen to wipe out the settlers in Johnson County, especially the settlement at Buffalo. Wolcott, Canton, and Tom Smith led this small army toward Buffalo, Wyo., on Apr. 9, 1892, when they heard that Champion and a fellow gunman, Nick Ray, were holed up at the nearby K.C. ranch. As they approached the ranch, Canton spotted Jack Flagg driving a wagon near the ranch; this man was on the murder list of the Regulators and the gunmen fired at him. He managed to escape but left his wagon which the Regulators torched and then sent crashing into the log cabin ranch building where Champion and Ray were defending themselves. The place blazed up and Champion, his clothes smoking, dove through the front door with two six-guns firing, but fifty guns zeroed in on him and he was riddled with bullets, dying instantly.

This killing was too much for Canton to bear. In the months to come his nerves began to come apart. He had nightmares and would bolt upright from a dead sleep as he and his men slept about campfires and shout: "Do you hear them? They're coming! Get to your guns, boys!" The slightest sound, the wind, horses galloping in the distance, would cause Canton to tremble and become incoherent. He began seeing the ghosts of the dead, including James Averill and Ella "Cattle Kate" Watson, two rustlers who had defied the cattle barons and who were lynched by vigilantes, at Canton's insistence. The gunman quit the cattlemen's group and moved south to serve as a deputy U.S. marshal under Judge Isaac Parker who was headquartered in Fort Smith, Okla. Here Canton made a name for himself as a lawman who would stand up to any gunman. In Pawnee, Okla., in 1893, Canton tracked down and arrested a fugitive wanted on a murder charge, trapping him in a livery stable owned by gunman Len McCool. When McCool entered the stable and saw his friend, the fugitive, tied up and being made ready for the trip back to Judge Parker's courtroom, he slapped Canton and began to draw his gun. Canton jumped backward and produced a derringer, shooting McCool in the face, the bullet entering just under the left eye. Canton left McCool for dead and traveled back to Fort Smith. McCool, however lived, but got into a fistfight some time later and a blow to the wound inflicted by Canton brought about his death.

In the winter of 1895, Canton joined a posse that tracked down outlaws Bill and John Shelley, who had escaped from the Pawnee jail and had barricaded themselves in a cabin on the Arkansas River in Pawnee County. The posse peppered the cabin with more than 800 bullets in a five-hour gun battle but failed to dislodge the fugitives. Then Canton found a wagon filled with hay and, as he had done in the case of Nate Champion years earlier, sent this crashing into the ranch house. The resulting fire drove the outlaw brothers outside and they were quickly arrested and taken to Fort Smith. Outlaw Bill Dunn, a friend of the Shelley brothers, who was being hunted by Canton, rode into Pawnee, Okla., on Nov. 6, 1896, cornering Canton as the lawman was about to enter the courthouse. "Damn you, Canton," cried Dunn, "I've got it in for you!" He made a motion toward his gun but the lightning-fast Canton whipped out a six-gun from his wasitband and fired a single shot which struck Dunn square in the forehead. The outlaw fell backward, pulling out his gun as he fell but he died before he could fire a shot.

The restless Canton left his family in 1897 and accepted an appointment as U.S. deputy marshal in Alaska where he underwent many harrowing adventures. Canton reportedly tamed the entire lawless town of Dawson and befriended the writer Rex Beach and was used by Beach as role model for many of the frontier heroes he portrayed in his novels. Canton was snowbound in 1888 and barely survived a winter which caused him to go snowblind. He returned to Oklahoma and once more became a lawman. In 1907 Canton became adjutant general of the Oklahoma National Guard and held this post until his death in 1927. See: Averill, James; Champion, Nathan D.; Johnson County War.

REF.: Bartholomew, *The Biographical Album of Western Gunfighters;* Benedict, *The Roundup;* Burt, *American Murder Ballads;* Canton, *Frontier Trails; CBA;* Clay, *My Life on the Range;* Croy, *Trigger Marshal;* David, *Malcolm Campbell, Sheriff;* Flagg, *A Review of the Cattle Business in Johnson County;* Frink, *Cow Country Cavalcade;* Gage, *The Johnson County War is a Pack of Lies;* Gard, *Frontier Justice;* Hendricks, *The Bad Man of the West;* Holloway, *Texas Gun Lore;* Horan and Sann, *Pictorial History of the Wild West;* Horton, *History of Jack County;* Huckaby, *Ninety-Four Years in Jack County;* Hunter and Rose, *The Album of Gunfighters;* Larson, *History of Wyoming;* Lefors, *Wyoming Peace Officer;* Lloyd, *The Invaders;* McConnell, *Five Years as a Cavalryman;* Monaghan, *The Legend of Tom Horn;* Nash, *Bloodletters and Badmen;* Nix, *Oklahombres;* Paine, *Tom Horn, Man of the West;* Penfield, *Western Sheriffs and Marshals;* Raine, *Guns of the Frontier;* Rosa, *The Gunfighter, Man or Myth;* Sandoz, *The Cattlemen;* Shirley, *Henry Starr;* ____, *Six-Gun and Silver Star;* Smith, *The War on Powder River;* Strong, *My Frontier Days & Indian Fights on the Plains of Texas;* Vestal, *Queen of the Cowtowns;* Wellman, *A Dynasty of Western Outlaws;* Wister, *Owen Wister Out West;* (FILM) *Heaven's Gate,* 1980.

Cantor, Louis, prom. 1910, U.S., wh. slav. Louis Cantor was a cultured Austrian-American engaged in some very dirty work. He was a member of a New York-based gang that forced young immigrant girls into prostitution and then shipped them to various brothels in Philadelphia and Manhattan.

Brought before Judge Carr in the Quarter Sessions Court of Philadelphia on Apr. 26, 1910, Cantor pleaded not guilty to three indictments charging him with white slavery. The specific victim was a young immigrant named Dora who had been lured away from a dreary factory job in New York with the promise of greater reward in Philadelphia.

The district attorney assembled an impressive case that prompted an investigation into the white slave traffic by the Law and Order Society. Cantor was sentenced to six years in the county prison.

REF.: *CBA;* Roe, *Great War On White Slavery.*

Canute, See: **Eadric Streona.**

Canute IV, c.1043-86, Den., king, assass. Patron Saint of Denmark and the fourth of six kings who ruled Denmark from 1080-86. In 1085 he tried to invade England, but was driven back. He was murdered by a rebel band and was canonized in 1101. REF.: *CBA.*

Canute V, d.1157, Den., king, assass. Son of Magnus the Strong, and ruler of the Jutland provence of Denmark from 1147-57. He waged a civil war against Sweyn III, son of Eric the Memorable. During the course of the struggle, he was assassinated. REF.: *CBA.*

Canute Lavard (Duke of Slesvig), c.1094-1131, Den., assass. Conqueror of the Wendish tribe, he was influential in importing Germanic customs into Denmark. He was murdered by Magnus the Strong. REF.: *CBA.*

Capasso, Carl A., 1945-   , U.S., tax evas.-fraud-polit. corr. From 1978 until his indictment nine years later on charges of income tax evasion, Carl A. Capasso was one of Manhattan's most influential building contractors. His construction firm received a number of lucrative municipal projects, including street paving, sewage, and pollution control. The city of New York had awarded in excess of $150 million in contracts to his firm.

On Jan. 15, 1987, a federal grand jury in Manhattan indicted Capasso on a charge of evading $774,600 in corporate and personal taxes. Under direct questioning, the 41-year-old contractor admitted to having diverted Nanco Construction Corporation funds for his own personal use between 1980-85. "First, I categorically deny that any improper influence, bribery, or bid-rigging was involved in my obtaining contracts with New York City and New York State," he said. "I have obtained contracts with the city and the state solely because my company provides first-class quality work at the lowest bids."

Facing a nine-count indictment and a possible thirty-seven-year stretch in prison, Capasso entered a surprise plea of guilty in the Federal District Court of Manhattan on Jan. 22, 1987. By doing so, he no doubt hoped to avoid a broader indictment on racketeering charges and to divert unfavorable publicity away from his long-time paramour Bess Myerson, who served as commissioner of New York's cultural affairs.

Myerson, on an unpaid leave at the time, was facing a grand jury indictment on charges of mail fraud, obstruction of justice, and having violated state bribery laws. The former Miss America was accused of entering into a secret agreement with Justice Hortense Gabel of the state supreme court in an effort to reduce Capasso's alimony payments to his estranged wife, Nancy, in the spring of 1983. Myerson had given the judge's daughter Sukhreet a $19,000-a-year job in the cultural affairs department of the city.

While Myerson's case was preparing to go to trial, Capasso was sentenced on Mar. 30, 1987, to four years in prison for income tax evasion and assessed a $500,000 fine. His problems were compounded six months later when a state appeals court ordered Capasso, whose holdings were valued at $15.6 million, to pay his wife, Nancy, $6 million as a divorce settlement. In handing down this decision on June 11, the appellate court was tripling the amount of the settlement originally awarded by Justice Andrew R. Tyler in 1983.

Capasso won a victory in federal district court on Dec. 22, 1988, when he was cleared, along with Myerson and Justice Gabel, on charges of bribery and corruption. The former building tycoon was returned to prison to serve out the remainder of his sentence, which was scheduled to end on June 26, 1989. See: **Myerson, Bess**. REF.: *CBA*.

Capdeville, Jean, See: **Buffalo Bill House**.

Capel, Arthur (Earl of Essex), 1631-83, Brit., suic. Government official who opposed Charles II, especially his Catholic policies. When the murderous Rye House Plot of 1683 was uncovered, he was imprisoned in the Tower of London. There he was found with his throat cut, an apparent suicide. REF.: *CBA*.

Capello, Bianca, c.1542-87, Italy, assass.-mur. Mistress of Francesco de' Medici, Duke of Tuscany. To win his hand in marriage and to lay claim to a title, she faked a pregnancy and then had her co-conspirators murdered. She temporarily succeeded in this intrigue, and was proclaimed the Duchess of Tuscany. Four months later she died from a poisoning believed to have been instigated by her brother-in-law Ferdinand de Medici. REF.: *CBA*.

Capital Punishment, See: **Supplements**, Vol. IV.

Capone, Alphonse (Alphonse Caponi, AKA: Scarface, Al Brown, Alfred Caponi, A. Costa), 1899-1947, U.S., org. crime. No other American gangster rose to the international reputation of Al Capone, whose historical image is a curious blend of ruthless gangster and a distorted Horatio Alger hero who went from rags to riches to jail. Ruthless he was, hero never, not even to those with whom he robbed, racketeered, and murdered. Capone was a murderous thug without remorse. Street smart, clever, ingenious when it came to crime, Capone was also a near-illiterate who acquired countless millions and knew not where to spend a dime of it. He killed without compunction and at the whims of a mercurial and murderous temperament. He killed his enemies and his friends. He killed his employers and his own henchmen. He was responsible for perhaps as many as one thousand or more murders, certainly hundreds. Worse, for a decade the city of Chicago embraced this bragging, boasting, strutting killer, its newspapers paying homage to him and quoting his every cretinous statement, its citizens—a goodly portion of the population—nodding tolerantly, if not approvingly, in his direction.

Capone spent money lavishly on himself and those about him, projecting the image of generosity, of a philanthropist to the common man. Old-timers in Chicago still pay his bloody memory off-hand compliments about the so-called soup kitchens Capone established in Chicago during the Depression to feed the hungry, little realizing that the crime boss did this at the suggestion of attorneys attempting to improve his horrible reputation when he was being tried for income tax evasion. For decades after his death, this inhuman beast received perverse recognition from show business and film personalities who boasted of meeting Capone, of being ordered to perform for him at the Hawthorne Inn, his fortress-like headquarters in Cicero, or his Chicago bases, the Lexington and Metropole hotels, as if such performances were similar to a command performance before a czar or a president. What was Capone? He was an ignorant strong-arm thug who oozed out of New York's worst mob, The Five Points gang, graduated to flesh-peddling and more strong-arm work in Chicago, and became a billionaire through bootlegging in the 1920s. He was also, in his early years, a whoremaster who slept with his own diseased employees so regularly that he contracted syphilis which later, in the form of paresis of the brain, turned him into a raving lunatic and killed him at age forty-eight.

Unlike his Italian peers, Capone was forever proud of the fact that he was born in the U.S., not Naples, Italy, as has been claimed, and whenever he was designated an Italian immigrant, he would roar the correction: "I'm not Italian! I was born in Brooklyn." Capone's parents, Gabriel and Teresa Caponi, emigrated from Naples, Italy, in 1903, poor, speaking no English. His father plied the same trade he had in Italy; he was a barber. His shop was at 69 Park Avenue, a few doors from his home, located in Brooklyn's poverty-stricken navy yard district called Williamsburg. The Caponis (both parents naturalized in 1906) produced nine children, born in a seedy four-room flat: Vincenzo

(renamed James), Ralph (later nicknamed Bottles), Salvatore (renamed Frank), Alphonse, Amadeo Ermino (renamed John, nicknamed Mimi), Umberto (renamed Albert John), Matthew Nicholas, Rose, and Mafalda. This large family was the norm for Italians of the day who had resettled in America, naively trading, for the most part, the slums of southern Italy for the slums of New York, Chicago, New Orleans, and, to some degree, San Francisco. Here, on Jan. 17, 1899, Alphonse Capone was born. His childhood was like any other in his world, one of littered streets crowded with pushcarts and peddlers and laborers, one where the Italian immigrant was denied proper education (60 percent of Italian children born in the U.S. at that time grew up illiterate) and, because of the lack of hygiene and proper medical attention, one where newborn Italian babies died at an alarming rate—double that of all others in New York—from diarrhea, diphtheria, and respiratory diseases.

By the time he was eleven, Capone was a member of a juvenile gang which was also part of the traditional environment of this wretched community. In that year, 1910, Italians made up eleven percent of the total foreign-born population, but only seven percent of all foreign-born professional criminals, according to one survey, were Italian. Yet, it was the tradition of the first American-born generation, to either accept the menial occupations with their miserable wages and hopeless futures or, in the worst social environments, improve oneself through first petty, then serious crime. The concept of America as a land of opportunity to the then down-trodden Italian-American was translated to mean a land where the illegal was nothing more than a business adventure. Opportunity meant that one might quickly enrich oneself by ignoring laws meant for people who could afford to obey them. Authority in the form of the police was equated with the authority of ancient, unjust, and socially distant European monarchs.

Al Capone learned all this in basic terms while in his teens. He was influenced by older boys who taught him the bloody techniques of knife-fighting and the use of a revolver. One of these was Johnny Torrio, one of the tough, intelligent sub-bosses of the far-reaching Five Points gang, headed by crime czar Paul Kelly. Torrio, seventeen years older than Capone, ran myriad illegal operations out of his saloon on James Street; he was a street-smart hoodlum who had small feet, delicate hands and facial features, and a small, chubby body. He never fought battles in the streets but sent others to perform such bloody chores. He was a criminal mastermind who took over sections of Williamsburg block by block, store by store, organizing extortion through Black Hand techniques. Gambling and prostitution were his specialties. He also paid off police to ignore his rackets and, realizing the power of politics, funded political candidates for office—those who would do his bidding in the future. This racketeer opened up an office at the corner of Fourth Avenue and Union Street, which he called The John Torrio Association, a front for his many rackets.

Capone passed Torrio's headquarters every day on his way to school, where he maintained good grades until he was upbraided for his increased truancy in the sixth grade. By then Capone was a large, beefy street brawler, and he found the public chastisement unbearable. He struck the female teacher, knocking her down. The principal rushed into the classroom and thrashed young Capone. He never returned to school, taking odd jobs as a pinsetter in a bowling alley and a clerk in a candy store. He became a pool shark, champion eight-ball shooter of the neighborhood. By then Capone was an expert knife-fighter with his street gang, and he participated in many bloody battles. The gang to which Capone first swore allegiance was the Bim Booms, which also counted as a member Charles Lucania, later known as Charles "Lucky" Luciano, who had briefly attended school with Capone and befriended him. Both boys later graduated to the Five Pointers, the gang headed by Paul Kelly and Johnny Torrio. This was the most powerful gang in New York (replacing the old Whyos at the turn of the century), exceeding 1,500 thugs, all adept at burglary, extortion, robbery, assault, murder. It was while working as a strong-arm enforcer for Torrio that Capone learned all the lethal tricks of his criminal trade. He would be forever grateful to Torrio, later stating: "I looked on Johnny like my adviser and father and the party who made it possible for me to get my start."

Torrio started Capone as a goon who beat up loan-shark victims behind on their payments, then a pimp, beating up girls who were suspected of holding back part of their nightly take. He then got him a "posh" job as a bouncer in the Harvard Inn, run by Torrio's Sicilian gangster friend, Frankie Yale. Capone was by then a vicious, tenacious fighter with fists and knives. He was also an expert marksman with a revolver or automatic, having practiced shooting beer bottles for years in the basement of the Adonis Social Club, run by future crime czar, Joe Adonis.

Capone was later promoted to bartender at the Club, and it was at this time that he acquired the livid scars that would disfigure the left side of his face for life and earn him the sobriquet he hated most: Scarface. Many stories were later told as to how Capone received these scars. He liked to lie to reporters later by claiming that he had received them in WWI, saying that he had been wounded by shrapnel while serving with the legendary "Lost Battalion" of the Seventy-seventh Division. Another story has it that Capone, who now worked for Sicilians like Yale, wanted to have the special duck-tailed Sicilian-Mafia haircut then popular with thugs. He walked into a Sicilian barbershop one day, the tale goes, and asked for this type of haircut but the barber, a devout Sicilian Mafioso, refused, knowing Capone was from Neapolitan parents. This caused Capone to go berserk, attacking the barber, who had been shaving a customer. The barber slashed out wildly at the 225-pound, five-foot-ten-inch Capone, cutting him deeply on the left cheek and jaw. Another account, more believable, has Capone insulting the female companion of a Sicilian hoodlum in the Harvard Inn and the hoodlum carving Capone's face in retaliation.

Regardless of his scarred face, an Irish girl, Mae Coughlin, from a good family, was attracted to Capone, and when he proposed to her in 1918, she accepted. Capone and his bride were wed on Dec. 18, 1918, the bride being twenty-one, Capone nineteen. A short time later, a son, Albert Francis Capone, nicknamed Sonny, was born to the couple. Capone continued at the Harvard Inn and later became a union slugger for Yale and Torrio, but his prospects for the future appeared dim after he was indicted for two murders. He was released when witnesses lost their memories and evidence disappeared. By this time, Torrio had moved most of his operations to Chicago, where his uncle, James "Big Jim" Colosimo, was the crime boss of the Levee, the red light district. Torrio still maintained contact with his rackets in New York, but was gradually withdrawing control of these operations, which Joe Adonis, Lucky Luciano, and Ciro "The Artichoke King" Terranova took over. Torrio had gone to Chicago as early as 1909 or 1910 at Colosimo's request, to help the crime boss subdue the Black Handers and rival gangsters plaguing him, as well as to put his sprawling prostitution and gambling rackets in order. In 1919, Capone got into another fight and killed a man. Rather than wait to be indicted, Scarface called "Johnny Papa" Torrio, and received an invitation to join him in Chicago. Capone packed up his wife and child and took the next train West.

Arriving in Chicago, Capone immediately installed his wife and child in a small South Side apartment that one of Torrio's men had rented for him. That same day, Capone reported to Torrio at his newly-established Four Deuces at 2222 South Wabash. This four-story brick building contained a saloon on the first floor with Torrio's office in the rear, the two areas separated by a sliding steel door. The second and third floors offered gambling rooms, and the fourth floor was a brothel. That night Torrio welcomed Capone and made him his bodyguard and chauffeur, at $100 a week. There was nothing lofty about Capone's additional duties at the Four Deuces. He was a bartender on occasion and a

bouncer. In the latter capacity, Capone used his hulking body and powerful upper body strength to evict drunks and troublemakers, often beating up customers so severely that they were hospitalized with broken arms and legs, skull fractures, and, on one occasion, blood poisoning after Capone bit into a man's arm, severing an artery with his teeth. He was repeatedly arrested for assault but released without prosecution, thanks to Torrio's political and police connections.

Capone also worked as a shill for the Four Deuce's brothel, standing outside the place and hawking the fleshy wares available in the miserable cribs on the building's fourth floor. Crime writer Courtney Riley Cooper was later to state: "I saw him there a dozen times, coat collar turned up on winter nights, hands deep in his pockets as he fell in step with a passerby and mumbled: 'Got some nice-looking girls inside.'" The ruthless, bestial Capone was also used by Torrio for more sinister purposes, like murder. Torrio had on his payroll hundreds of gangsters who ran far-flung rackets for the overall crime boss of the city, Big Jim Colosimo, and those who cheated on their weekly payments to the bosses, those who went into business for themselves, and those who worked for Colosimo-Torrio and secretly for rival gangs at the same time, were brought to the Four Deuces and punished, invariably by the savage Capone. He and other goons would drag these men into the basement of the saloon and here question them while applying various tortures. When the victims had provided the information or confessions demanded, they were summarily murdered. Capone strangled at least a dozen of these disobedient racketeers to death with his hands, according to one account. The bodies were dragged through a small tunnel and brought up at the rear of the building through a trapdoor and then into an alley, where a waiting car sped away with the corpses, which were later dumped on lonely country roads.

The Chicago Capone entered was, in many respects, as volatile and cunning as he was, a political cesspool where half the city council was on the take, and aldermen received heavy bribes to protect the many red light districts, particularly the Levee on the near South Side, Colosimo's domain, glutted with gambling dens, whorehouses, and seamy saloons. The machine politicians controlling this area, and in league with Colosimo for more than a decade, were John "Bathhouse John" Coughlin and Michael "Hinky Dink" Kenna. They received enormous payoffs to make sure the district went unmolested by police raids. And they, in turn, passed on staggering amounts of money to the then mayor of Chicago, William Hale Thompson, the most venal chief executive in the city's history. Thompson not only aided the gangsters and crooked aldermen, but encouraged the expansion of the vice districts, later adopting as his blatant campaign slogan, "Chicago—a wide open city!"

In the underworld at that time, Big Jim Colosimo's word was law, often life and death. He was a gregarious, large man, bedecked with glinting diamonds. He was flashy and ostentatious, ruling his kingdom from his lavish restaurant, Colosimo's Cafe, which was only a block from the Four Deuces. Colosimo had started as a pimp and then a manager of several bordellos. After forming an alliance with Kenna and Coughlin, he began to take over other bordellos, gambling dens, and then all the rackets in the Levee until he was the supreme crime overlord in Chicago. He was a flamboyant character, a lover of Italian opera, and he reveled in the opera stars, like Enrico Caruso, who dined in his restaurant. By 1910, Colosimo's empire had become so vast that he needed the organizational abilities of his nephew in New York, so he sent for Torrio. By 1919, Torrio had ideas of becoming the supreme boss in Chicago and he sent for his most loyal assassin, Al Capone. The real reason Capone moved to Chicago was not to evade an arrest for murder in New York. He was protected there through his gang affiliations and would have, no doubt, been released, as he had been on two former occasions when charged with murder in New York. When Capone arrived in Chicago he was assigned menial jobs by Torrio as a smokescreen to disguise the real purpose of his presence—to murder Big Jim Colosimo.

Left to right: Johnny Torrio, founder of organized crime in Chicago and Al Capone's sponsor; Capone at the time he arrived in Chicago, 1919, the scars apparent on his left cheek; Al Capone, 1924, at the time he took over Torrio's crime kingdom in Chicago.

Capone, amused, as he is interrogated by CPD Captain John Stege.

Capone at Wrigley Field; Gabby Hartnett signs a ball for Sonny Capone.

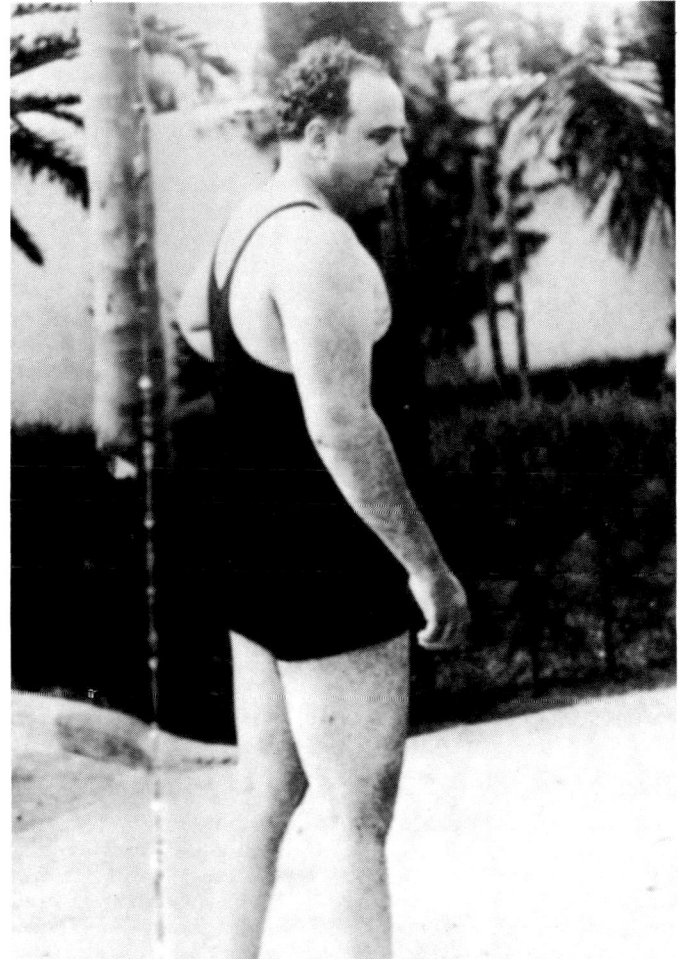

Gangster in the sun; Capone at his Palm Island, Fla., retreat.

Capone's million-dollar Palm Island, Fla., estate.

The Lexington Hotel, Capone's Chicago Headquarters, 1929.

Colosimo was an old-fashioned gangster who contentedly counted his millions from the illegal rackets he controlled. Torrio, a long-range planner, immediately saw the millions to be made from the Volstead Act, which would become law in 1920, prohibiting the manufacture, distribution, and sale of liquor. Torrio had for some time pleaded with his uncle Colosimo to set up illegal stills, to buy breweries and run them clandestinely in the future, and to establish a distribution arm which would provide beer and liquor to the thousands of saloons in Chicago. Colosimo's response was always a firm "no." He was not interested in developing this new racket, which he felt would "never amount to anything." He would leave bootlegging to the other gangs. He had enough: his lavish mansion at 3156 Vernon Avenue; his fabulous cafe; a new wife, singer Dale Winter, pretty and young, for whom he had divorced his first wife, an aging brothel operator; and his old gambling and whorehouse rackets were producing more money than he could spend. He had no intention of bringing his organization into a new and untried racket. His rejection of the Torrio proposal sealed his fate. Torrio marked Colosimo for death, and then ordered Capone to kill him on May 11, 1920.

Torrio called Colosimo in the early afternoon of that day to tell him to expect two truckloads of the best whiskey available, and that it was important for Colosimo to stock up on this now-precious commodity, which would be sorely needed for the cafe. The shipment would be delivered at 4 p.m., Torrio told Colosimo. He told Big Jim to be precise in taking the shipment at that time. Colosimo promised that he would be on hand at the cafe to take the delivery, and he arrived at the restaurant at about 3 p.m. He arrived by limousine, telling his chauffeur, Wolfson, to return to the mansion and to take his wife and her mother shopping. He strolled about the cafe, talking to employees before going to his office. A waiter noticed a dark-featured, heavyset stranger enter the vestibule of the cafe, which was closed, but then the stranger disappeared and the waiter thought that he had left, when he realized that the restaurant was not yet open.

Big Jim left his office about 4:25 p.m., walking the length of the cafe, through two large rooms, then went into the vestibule, an area closed off by glass doors. A moment later two shots were heard and Frank Camilla, Colosimo's private secretary, ran to the vestibule to find his employer face down on the tile floor, blood gushing from a bullet wound behind his ear. Big Jim Colosimo was dead, his murderer having fled out the front door of the cafe. Camilla dashed to the sidewalk and saw no one suspicious in sight. He next called Colosimo's good friend, Chief of Police John J. Garrity, who arrived a short time later with Chief of Detectives Mooney and a bevy of plainclothes officers. When they rolled Big Jim over, they marveled at the diamond shirt studs and cufflinks blazing before them. The red rose in his lapel was crushed. Inside a coat pocket they found a .28-caliber pearl-handled revolver but not a dime in his pockets, even though Big Jim was reported to have carried with him that day more than $150,000 in cash, all big bills.

Capone, by best reports, had killed Colosimo with one bullet, then fired a second bullet through the window behind the cashier's box in the vestibule. He had entered the vestibule and was seen by the waiter, but had hidden in the cloak room, and when Colosimo entered the vestibule to go to the street to check the whiskey delivery, he stepped up behind the gang boss and shot him in the head. He then took enough time to rifle the dead man's pockets and remove the considerable cash he carried, his payment for the murder, then dashed through the front door, hurriedly walked a block south to the Four Deuces, and went to the fourth floor where he climbed into bed with one of Torrio's whores. He and Torrio were quickly pulled into police headquarters for questioning, but both provided unshakable alibis. "Big Jim and me were like brothers," Torrio told police detectives, his eyes filling with tears. Capone shook his head sadly and said to officers: "Mr. Colosimo and me both loved opera. He was a grand guy." Both Torrio and Capone sent enormous floral wreaths

to Colosimo's funeral, which was the first big gangster burial, attended by hundreds of dignitaries, a lavish and gaudy display of mourning by thousands who followed the funeral cortege. Capone observed the old Italian custom of not shaving during the three days between Colosimo's death and funeral.

Immediately following Big Jim's interment, Torrio met with aldermen Coughlin and Kenna and announced that he would be running things. They agreed, and Capone was named Torrio's right-hand man, his chief lieutenant and underboss. Up to that time, Capone went by the alias Al Brown and had a seedy used funiture store as his business front. Suddenly, from bouncer, bartender, and whorehouse shill, Capone shot to a lofty position of underworld authority, the place next to Torrio's throne, a post that was also his reward for craftily killing the truculent, traditional Colosimo. Capone would employ the same kind of cunning violence in getting rid of his mentor and sponsor, Johnny Torrio, four years later.

Politically, Torrio's position as Chicago's new underworld boss was secure. He was backed by greedy, wholly amoral aldermen and a criminally-bent mayor, Thompson. Beyond Chicago, the state of Illinois was governed by crooked Len Small, who was indicted in 1921 for embezzling $600,000 while state treasurer. But, through the help of Chicago labor gangster Walter Stevens and extortionist Benjamin "Jew Ben" Newmark, Small was acquitted. Stevens and Newmark simply bribed and threatened the jurors at Small's trial. In return, Small granted pardons to all important gangsters convicted of any kind of crime, from bootlegging to murder. Stevens was on the Torrio-Capone payroll, as were the whoremaster brothers, Jake and Harry Guzik, also friends of Small's. More than 1,000 felons, mostly mobsters working for Torrio and Capone, were pardoned by Small in his first three years in office. But not all the politicians in Chicago were in Torrio's pocket. Those aldermen who represented the North Side of Chicago, the most lucrative bootlegging territory, belonged firmly to Charles Dion O'Bannion, the undisputed boss of the area.

It was with O'Bannion and his fierce lieutenants that the Torrio-Capone gang would have the most trouble. The gang was large, powerful, and lethal. Its members were of Irish and Polish descent, and made a show of practicing the Catholic religion, going to church on Sunday and on the same night hijacking booze trucks, slugging and killing rival gangsters. The leader, O'Bannion, had been a choir boy and an altar boy at Holy Name Cathedral on State Street, across from which sat a flower shop in which he owned a half interest. O'Bannion loved flowers, and spent most of his time in this shop, creating floral arrangements for weddings and funerals. He wore three guns at all times, carried in specially made pockets in his pants. Earl "Hymie" Weiss, his fierce first lieutenant, was also a dedicated killer who went to church regularly, wore a gold cross around his neck, and carried a rosary in a vest pocket, close to the shoulder holster of his gun. George "Bugs" Moran; Vincent "The Schemer" Drucci; the savage Frank and Pete Gusenberg; Louis "Two-Gun" Alterie, also called "The Cowboy" because he owned a ranch in Colorado; Samuel J. "Nails" Morton, a Jewish gangster who had served with distinction in WWI, won medals and returned to Chicago to become one of the most successful and celebrated gangsters of the early 1920s; and a host of other loyal gunmen made up this formidable gang, whose members considered Torrio and Capone low-life vipers without hope of redemption.

Before Prohibition, the Italian gangsters had centered their activities on gambling and prostitution, but O'Bannion and his men would have nothing to do with bordellos. There were some independently operated brothels on the North Side, to be sure, but these were not controlled by the O'Bannionites. According to O'Bannion, Weiss, and the others, this particular criminal profession was "against the Holy Mother, the Church," and they considered Torrio and Capone, in the words of O'Bannion, "dago pimps, making their money from diseased women." Such insults reached the ears of Capone and jarred his pride, but Torrio, ever the diplomat, ignored these remarks and sought to settle differences between the gangs through non-violent agreements. He called a meeting in 1920 which was attended by almost all the top gang leaders in the city. O'Bannion, Weiss, and Moran represented the North Side. From the West Side came the terrible Genna Brothers, six of them, all killers, Sicilians aligned with Torrio and Capone, and also from the West Side William "Klondike" Bernard, and Myles O'Donnell, who had thrown in their lot with Torrio. Terry Druggan and Frankie Lake, who controlled the Valley Gang on the Southwest Side, were fence straddlers, waiting to see who would emerge as the top crime boss. On the Northwest Side, Claude Maddox, head of the Circus Gang, and Marty Guifoyle, who led another gang in the same area, were Torrio vassals. Joseph "Pollack Joe" Saltis, who headed a large gang of bootleggers on the Southwest Side, was decidedly against Torrio and Capone and refused to attend Torrio's meeting, as did Edward "Spike" O'Donnell, who headed the large all-Irish O'Donnell gang of the far South Side, this O'Donnell gang being unrelated to the West Side O'Donnells.

Torrio played mediator and pacifier to the arguing crime bosses during this conference and managed to get everyone to agree to stay in their territories and restrain their minions. "There are millions in booze, plenty for everyone," he told the gangster enclave. "All we gotta do is respect the other guy's area and we'll make money." With that, Torrio produced a map and literally split up Chicago into sections, drawing lines on the map which gave the North Side to O'Bannion, the South Side to himself and Capone, and smaller territories to the other gangs. The two largest gangs, that of Torrio-Capone and O'Bannion, were to be separated by Madison Street. This was the "dividing line" and, other than social visits, no competing gangsters were to enter the other's territory.

At first this was an agreement all followed, but then, in 1922, encroachments began—begun by Capone. Though Torrio was well-known to government leaders and the public alike, Capone at this time was still relatively anonymous, known under his aliases Al Brown and A. Costa, names under which he had been booked for assault in the past when acting as a lowly bouncer for Torrio's Four Deuces. But in 1922, Capone came to the attention of the city's newsmen and the public under a variation of his own name. Scarface was drunk, racing his large roadster down Wabash Avenue at 60 m.p.h., his car filled with three heavily-armed bodyguards and four of his most sought-after prostitutes. Losing control of the roadster, Capone crashed his car into a taxicab. The driver, Fred Drause, holding his head, staggered from the cab and yelled at Capone: "You crazy s.o.b.! You almost killed me! Are you crazy?"

Capone jumped from his car, pulled a gun, and put it to the head of the cabbie. Cursing the driver, Capone shouted: "Don't talk that way to *me!*"

"Wait a minute, fella, how come you're pulling a gun on me?" said Drause.

The hulking gangster was silent for moment. He then produced a deputy sheriff's badge and announced: "I'm a law officer." Capone's associates, watching this charade and shocked by Capone's blatant impersonation and murderous temper, fled the scene, leaving the gang boss to face several policemen who arrived in a squad car. Drause was taken away to a hospital to have his head bandaged while Scarface was arrested for assault and impersonating a police officer. He was booked under the name of "Alfred Caponi," but he was soon released when a police captain on Torrio's payroll received a phone call at home and rushed to the precinct station, where he ordered the gang chief set free. This was to happen again and again, with Capone's political connections assuring his freedom, no matter what kind of crime he committed, including murder.

By 1924, Capone, at age twenty-five, was a multi-millionaire. In 1920, Torrio had cemented his partnership with Capone by giving him 25 percent of all profits from prostitution and 50 percent from all bootlegging operations. In the first year of this arrangement, Capone made $25,000 a month from the brothels

and ten times that amount from bootlegging. Yet he lived with his wife and child in a modest two-story brick building at 7244 South Prairie Avenue, a building which was guarded night and day by Capone gunmen sitting in cars on the street and in the alleyway. Where Torrio minded business and then retreated in the evening to his home, Capone craved nightlife and prowled through his clubs, gambling dens, and bordellos. His estimated five thousand cribs and bordellos were overseen by whoremaster Jake "Greasy Thumb" Guzik, who had become Scarface's chief accountant and bookkeeper, a short, squat little man with a florid, flabby face.

On the night of May 8, 1924, Guzik stopped at a saloon operated by Heinie Jacobs on South Wabash to talk business with some associates. As he was leaving the place, "Ragtime" Joe Howard, an aging gangster, barred Guzik's path. The drunken Howard had been regaling Jacobs at the bar with stories of the old days in Chicago when knives and guns were unnecessary. Howard had bragged that "brass knuckles to the jaw is good enough. Them wop beerboys fold up like old newspaper after one chop." Now he stood in front of Guzik, shouting to a nervous Jacobs: "This is one of them wop worker." He slapped Guzik in the face and then kicked him several times in the shins, but Guzik merely let out a yelp and then walked from the bar. Guzik was no gunman and he avoided violence at all costs. There were others to perform those chores. He nevertheless demanded the kind of respect reserved for those in the hierarchy of the Torrio-Capone mob, and the humiliation he had suffered at the hands of the old-fashioned thug Howard was intolerable. He went to Capone, who exploded and then rushed to Jacobs' saloon.

When Capone entered the bar, accompanied by several bodyguards, he walked up to Howard, who smiled affably and held out his hand, saying, "Hello, Al." Capone grabbed him by the lapel, pulling him close, snarling: "Why did you kick Jake around, Joe?"

Howard pushed Capone away, replying: "Aww, go back to your girls, you dago pimp!"

Capone drew an automatic, put it to Howard's temple and rapidly fired all six shots, which blew off the top of Joe Howard's head. Capone then turned and left the bar. Heinie Jacobs and two customers stood staring after him, and by the time police arrived were still shaking with fear. The two patrons, George Bilton and David Runelsbeck, both swore that Capone had killed Howard and said they would so testify in court. The story broke the next day, May 9, 1924, in the Chicago *Tribune,* which also ran a photo of Capone being booked for homicide, the first newspaper photo published of the gangster in Chicago, whose face the citizens of the city would see in their newspapers more often than that of the mayor or the president of the United States. Scarface would be the subject of countless newspaper stories dealing with hijackings, beatings, gang fights, murders. His would be the recognized world of the "cement overcoat," and "the one-way ride."

Though he knew he was wanted for the Howard killing, Capone hid for almost a month and then, on June 11, 1924, strolled into the Cottage Grove Avenue precinct station, saying: "I hear the police have been looking for me. What for?" Captain James McMahon put him under arrest and immediately took him to the Criminal Courts building where he was grilled by William H. McSwiggin, an energetic assistant state's attorney. Capone denied being in Jacobs' saloon on the night of Howard's death and told McSwiggin that he was a used furniture salesman and that he knew no gangsters. He was informed that, of the witnesses to the killing in the bar that night, Bilton had disappeared (frightened off by Capone killers), but Runelsbeck and Jacobs were being held as accessories after the fact and that they would swear Capone killed Howard. Scarface sneered and shrugged. "Let them," he said, "I ain't got nothing to worry about. I wasn't even there."

When the official inquest was held, Jacobs and Runelsbeck were brought before the court, but both men, visibly shaking in fright as they nervously glanced about the court, were obviously terrified. Jacobs denied ever seeing the shooting, insisting that he went into the back room of his saloon before the shooting occured. Runelsbeck said that he did not see the killer, that he ducked under a table at the first sound of gunfire. Capone sat smugly with his expensive attorneys, later to hear the coroner's verdict that "Joseph Howard was killed by one or more unknown white male persons." Capone left the inquest smiling, returning to his bastion in Cicero, the Hawthorne Inn. By then Torrio and Capone had moved their headquarters to Cicero to avoid harrassment from Chicago's new reform mayor, William E. Dever. Capone, seeking to make a strong alliance with the *Unione Siciliane*, paid a nostalgic visit to New York in December 1925, meeting with Frankie Yale, president of the New York branch of the *Unione Siciliane*. He also met with Joe Adonis and frequented the Adonis Social Club in south Brooklyn.

Here, on the night of Dec. 26, 1925, Richard "Peg Leg" Lonergan and other members of his White Hand Gang picked a fight with Capone, not knowing who he was and began insulting the almost all Italian clientele with words like "dagoes, wops, and ginzos," remarks that must have convinced Capone and his many bodyguards that Lonergan was either drunk or suicidal. When two Italian youths entered the saloon with Irish girls on their arms, Lonergan and two of his Irish friends chased the girls from the bar, shouting after them: "Come back with white men!" At 2 a.m., the lights in the Adonis Club went out and gunfire lit up the place. A short time later, police found Lonergan and two of his men dead on the floor. The killer was presumed to be Al Capone, but he had fled back to Chicago, or more specifically, Cicero, where he felt that he would be safe from lunatics, a notion soon to be disproved.

The takeover of Cicero, the sprawling blue-collar suburb west of Chicago, was accomplished with relative ease. Torrio and Capone simply ordered their satellites, the West Side O'Donnells, to instruct the local government there that they would be running their Chicago operations from the Hawthorne Inn, a popular Cicero hotel. Those rival gangsters and saloon owners who objected were quickly beaten into submission. Those who still proved truculent, like ex-boxer Eddie Tancl, were shot to death on Cicero streets.

McSwiggin was incensed at Capone's intimidation of witnesses in the Howard killing, and he resolved to convict the gangster and send him to prison. McSwiggin began to conduct investigations into Capone's activities in Cicero, and even aligned himself with rival gangsters in order to gather evidence against Scarface, or so one story had it. Two of these, Tom "Red" Duffy and James J. Doherty, along with the West Side O'Donnell Brothers, Bernard, Klondyke and Myles, had been boyhood friends of the 26-year-old McSwiggin, who had a strange and unpredictable relationship with these bootleggers. He had unsuccessfully prosecuted Doherty for the murder of Eddie Tancl, and then went on seeing Doherty socially. He also met with Capone on Apr. 17, 1926, at the Hawthorne Inn, but the nature of the discussion between mob chief and state's attorney was never disclosed. To the public, McSwiggin appeared to be a relentless fighter for justice, but to insiders, questions were raised as to his chummy relationship with Capone, the man he was supposed to be prosecuting for innumerable crimes.

On the evening of Apr. 27, 1926, as McSwiggin left a saloon on West Roosevelt Road in Cicero, a car shot down the street with a machine gunner hanging out the window and spraying the street, cutting down and killing McSwiggin, Doherty, and Duffy. All were dead before passersby reached them. A dozen persons on the street clearly saw the killer and identified him to police as Al Capone. Wild speculation about the killing was entertained by newsmen throughout Chicago, most concluding that Capone would never intentionally murder a cop, let alone a state's attorney. He had mistaken McSwiggin for a rival gangster he had personally sworn to murder, it was said, and that man was Earl "Hymie" Weiss. This, of course, was mere conjecture, and bad guessing at that, since Weiss was the sworn gang enemy of the

West Side O'Donnells, whose allegiance was to Capone. The witnesses to the McSwiggin murder vanished, lost their memories, or changed their minds when it came to identifying Capone as the killer. In the end, the gangster had the last lying word, telling a newsman: "Of course I didn't kill him. Why should I? I liked the kid. Only the day before he got killed he was up to my place and when he went home I gave him a bottle of Scotch for his old man. I paid McSwiggin and I paid him plenty, and I got what I was paying for." Scarface never specified what he was buying from the assistant state's attorney.

McSwiggin's murder was never solved, which led to an oft-repeated phrase, "Who Killed McSwiggin?", a line now classic in Chicago underworld parlance and one historically equal to "Who Killed Cock Robin?" Authorities knew that Capone was the killer, for whatever reason, but there was no evidence to convict him. It was the same story with the murder of Charles Dion O'Bannion, the fierce leader of the North Side Gang. O'Bannion's death, too, has gone down in the annals of crime as a first, one known as "the handshake murder."

Following the establishment of Madison Street as the "dividing line" in 1920, the gangsters acknowledged this border for a few years before their greedy encroachments once again caused violent confrontations. The South Side O'Donnell gang was selected by Capone as the first rival bootleg gang to be eliminated. Edward "Spike" O'Donnell and his brothers were isolated on the far South Side of the city, and Capone simply ordered his top enforcers to kill off these pesky bootleggers. Capone gunners Frank McErlane, who had been an ally of Pollack Joe Saltis before enlisting in Capone's ranks, and Danny McFall, led contingents of Capone hoodlums into the O'Donnell fiefdom, using for the first time the weapon that would later be synonymous with bootlegging, the Thompson submachine gun, a deadly, wasp-like rapid-fire gun that could cut down and kill dozens of men at close range.

The weapon was so effective that only gangleader Spike O'Donnell remained to defy Capone, saying bitterly: "I can whip this bird Capone with my bare fists any time he wants to step out into the open and fight like a man." But Capone's techniques were the ambush, the knife and the bullet in the back, a fast-moving car loaded with gangsters, firing at helpless victims on sidewalks. Capone favored the latter approach; he had used a submachine gun on McSwiggin, firing the gun from a fast-moving car. In two or three bursts from the submachine gun's chambers, he had eliminated a man whom he believed was only pretending to be a corrupt official in order to gather evidence against him. The submachine gun had been developed by Brigadier General John T. Thompson, chief of federal arsenals. Thompson intended this weapon for use in WWI, as a way of killing heavily entrenched enemy troops *en masse*. Thompson called this terrible weapon a "trench broom." The gun was completed in 1920, too late for military use, and tens of thousands stood idle in racks until sold off to commercial wholesalers to recoup government manufacturing losses. When Capone was first shown the weapon (reportedly by "Machine Gun" Jack McGurn), he marveled at its functions. At 500 yards it could penetrate a three-inch-thick pine board, and it fired 1,000 rounds of .45-caliber ammunition per minute. Capone, McGurn, McErlane, and others took the first shipment of Thompson submachine guns to a country retreat in 1923 and there practiced with it, firing at two-foot-thick trees and cutting them in half.

The government turned over the sale of the submachine gun to Auto Ordnance, a New York corporation, intending its open market sale to state and city police departments, but this plan met with little success. Police departments universally rejected the idea of arming its officers with such a deadly weapon, believing it to be hazardous to innocent bystanders. Capone had no such compunctions. He was the first to order several truckloads of these guns, equipping his 300 gunmen with them. (Capone's army of gunmen, enforcers and goon squads swelled to more than 1,000 by the end of the 1920s.) The Thompson submachine gun was used with such alacrity in Chicago that it was soon called the "Chi-

Five of Capone's top gunmen during the 1920s, left to right, William "Klondike" O'Donnell, William "Three-Fingered Jack" White, Murray "The Camel" Humphreys, Marcus Looney, and Charles Fischetti, who was Capone's cousin.

John Scalise and Albert Anselmi, Capone's favorite killers.

"Machine Gun" Jack McGurn

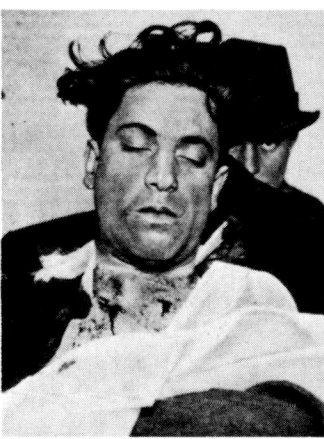

Frank Capone, dead, 1928.

Left, Capone went fishing off his Florida estate to establish an alibi while his gunmen committed the St. Valentine's Day Massacre, right.

cago typewriter," or a "Chicago piano." Other coinage, mostly from creative newsmen, labelled the weapon a "chopper," and a "tommy gun." Capone had no monopoly on the submachine gun; almost every important criminal gang purchased huge numbers of these weapons for the bootleg wars in New York, Chicago, Kansas City, St. Louis, and points South and West. But to O'Bannion, whose men were used to revolvers and shotguns, traditional gangster weapons by the turn of the 1920s, the submachine gun was a necessary tool that had to be used with prudence. His top killer, Hymie Weiss, however, became proficient with the gun and taught his men its intricacies with childish glee. Weiss would later use the submachine gun to devastating effect when raiding Capone's Cicero stronghold in 1926.

When Capone killed off and eliminated the South Side O'Donnell gang, close allies of O'Bannion's, the North Side gang leader called his sub-bosses together to tell them that it was not Torrio but Capone who was causing all the trouble, that Torrio was a gentleman who abided by agreements, but that Capone was nothing more than a mentally retarded goon with too much power and money, a gangster who would kill anyone in his way. O'Bannion pointed out that, despite the "dividing line" agreement, Capone had established, through vassals, dozens of whorehouses on the North Side, and that Capone's staunchest allies, the six terrible Genna Brothers, had been terrorizing and beating up North Side saloon owners to make them buy cheap home-made Genna liquor.

O'Bannion mourned for the dead members of the O'Donnell gang, all friends. "Those killings weren't Torrio's orders," he told Weiss, Moran, Drucci, Alterie and others. "They were all done by that dirty atheistic dago! Did you see poor Jerry O'Connor's face in the funeral home? It was all blown off. Nothing left to it. And Walt O'Donnell, too, and all those other lads. That Capone kills like a beast in the jungle!"

O'Bannion and Weiss later met Frank McErlane, one of Capone's top gunmen, as he was strolling along a North Side street, in O'Bannion territory. They stopped McErlane and reminded him of the "dividing line," and that he was north of Madison Street. McErlane smiled and said he was merely visiting a friend. Weiss then stepped close to McErlane, credited with first using the submachine gun in gang warfare, on the O'Donnell brothers. "We know it was you and some others who knocked off the O'Donnells, Frank. You can tell Capone this for me. That if he ever pulls anything like that on us, I'm gonna get him if I have to kill everybody in front of him to do it. You can tell him that, and if I see him, I'll tell him myself!" McErlane did report this conversation to his boss and Capone, for once in his violent career, paused, and then ordered the insidious infiltration of bordello and bootleg operations into the North Side to cease, at least, for a short time. He realized that the powerful North Side gang was a potent force, a large, well-organized gang with political connections equal to Torrio's. O'Bannion was no common street thug. He controlled the 42nd and 43rd wards of the city and points north, the lucrative Near North Side with its exclusive shops and swanky restaurants, the booming Rush Street area, the Gold Coast and the upper-middle class neighborhoods spreading west and north from there. His gang numbered in the hundreds, mostly Irish and Polish-Americans, with a smattering of Italian gangsters like Drucci, church-going Catholics, but killers all, fiercely loyal to their leader, O'Bannion, who was himself considered by Police Chief Morgan Collins to be "Chicago's arch criminal who has killed or seen to the killing of at least twenty-five men." O'Bannion was also as crafty and devious as his gang rivals on the South Side. By 1923, O'Bannion and Torrio had several confrontations that caused O'Bannion to rethink his association with the South Side boss.

During the Cicero elections, O'Bannion had loaned Torrio dozens of his best terrorists to make sure that Torrio-Capone candidates won and thereby secured the town for the South Siders. Torrio had never compensated O'Bannion for the use of his men. Moreover, whenever they did business on a partnership basis, the gang bosses disagreed. On one occasion, O'Bannion's men

hijacked a truckload of bonded whiskey worth $50,000. Two Chicago cops stopped the truck and demanded a payoff, holding the shipment for ransom, so to speak. O'Bannion's men called him for instructions and he, in turn called Torrio. This conversation was overheard on a police wiretap. "Those cops want $300," O'Bannion said, "and I can bump them off for half that much. To hell with them!" Torrio responded in his usual quiet manner: "Dion, we don't want no trouble. Give them the money. Take it out of my share, if you like, but give the cops the $300." O'Bannion paid the two policemen, but the payoff rankled him.

What made O'Bannion rage was the fact that the Genna Brothers, who provided the Torrio-Capone combine with most of its homemade liquor, were making serious encroachments into O'Bannion's territory, selling their beer and liquor to North Side saloon owners under threat of death. O'Bannion's men had had several shootouts with the invading Gennas in 1923. The North Side gang leader concluded that Torrio had given Capone his approval to invade O'Bannion's territory and that their former agreements meant nothing. O'Bannion resolved to teach Torrio a lesson. O'Bannion called for a meeting with Torrio and Capone in May 1924, telling them that he planned to retire from the bootleg business, that he had "all the money in the world" and would be taking his wife out West to live on the sprawling ranch owned by his good friend Louis Alterie. He wanted to sell out his third interest in the lucrative Sieben's Brewery on the North Side. This brewery had produced quality beer before Prohibition, and had been purchased by Torrio-Capone-O'Bannion as a partnership in 1920. The brewery operated at full capacity while the police on O'Bannion's payroll looked the other way, and in fact assigned officers to protect the plant from rival gangsters who might think to raid the place.

Torrio agreed to buy out O'Bannion and gave him $500,000 in cash. A few days later, on May 19, 1924, at O'Bannion's insistence, Torrio drove to the North Side to inspect his new property. Capone was not in attendance, having gone into hiding after killing Joe Howard eleven days earlier. O'Bannion took Torrio on a tour of the large brewery, but they were interrupted by Chief Morgan Collins and dozens of policemen. Collins placed Torrio and O'Bannion under arrest, along with Hymie Weiss and Louis Alterie, who were also in attendance. More then thirty brewery employees were arrested, including two of O'Bannion's bribed policemen who had been guarding the place. Chief Collins ripped their badges from their chest, on the spot. The prisoners were delivered to the Federal Building on where, Collins announced, they would be held until tried for violating the federal prohibition law. Torrio realized that he had been betrayed by O'Bannion, set up for an arrest. He had purchased a brewery that was now out of operation and, through his informants, was told while still behind bars that O'Bannion, the man in the next cell, had tipped Collins when to make the raid. Torrio then took $12,500 from his pocket and paid bail for himself and six of his own men who had been caught in the raid. O'Bannion told him he did not have any cash on him and asked that Torrio provide this. The South Side gang chief gave him a withering look and said nothing, leaving the Federal Building in smoldering silence, resolved now to listen to his protegé Capone and get rid of O'Bannion.

The occasion Capone selected as the best suited for the murder of O'Bannion was the death of Mike Merlo, president of the Chicago branch of the *Unione Siciliane,* a criminal Sicilian brotherhood with ties to almost all organized gangs in the U.S. Merlo, who had been an advocate of nonviolence, was well-liked by all the Chicago gangs, and when huge and expensive floral wreaths for his funeral were ordered by Torrio and Capone, O'Bannion received the business at the State Street flower shop he owned with William Schofield. At noon on Nov. 10, 1924, three swarthy men walked into the shop and O'Bannion came out of the back room, where he had been clipping flower stems. His janitor, William Crutchfield, went into the back room and heard O'Bannion say to the men: "Hello, boys, you want Merlo's flowers?"

"Yes," the tallest of the three said, and took O'Bannion's outstretched hand to shake it, but he held on with a vise-like grip, swinging the gangster sideways, then jerked him forward and pinioned his arms to prevent him from reaching for one of the three guns he had in his specially-built pockets. The other two men drew revolvers and fired almost point blank at O'Bannion. Six bullets were fired into him, two entering his chest, two through his larynx as he was falling, one through his right cheek and, after O'Bannion was on the floor, the man who had been holding him released his grip and pulled his own revolver, firing a *coup de grace* bullet into the gangster's head from such close range that powder burns scorched the skin. The three killers then dashed from the shop, raced across the street and jumped into a blue Jewett car, which sped north on State Street. O'Bannion was dead before he fell to the floor of his shop, landing in the middle of his own flowers, staining them red with his own blood, the victim of what was forever known as "the handshake murder."

Though his killers were never officially identified, it is fairly certain that they were Frankie Yale, the crime boss of Brooklyn, the man who held O'Bannion's hand, and Capone's two top killers, Albert Anselmi and John Scalise. Yale, a friend of Capone's from Scarface's days in the New York mobs, was brought in for the murder since O'Bannion did not know him. He also was not familiar with Scalise and Anselmi and was therefore not on guard when these three entered his shop. When Weiss heard that his boss had been killed, he exploded with rage. According to one newsman, "Hymie became a raving lunatic when he heard the news of Dion's murder. He took a solemn oath to kill Capone and Torrio and everyone else in the Syndicate he could find." In a bizarre scene, Weiss, Moran, Drucci, and the rest of the North Side gangsters faced Torrio and Capone at O'Bannion's lavish funeral, both Scarface and Torrio sending huge floral wreaths, Capone's having a large, red ribbon reading: "From Al." Weiss glared at Capone during the brief ceremonies (and again Capone showed blue stubble on his florid face, not shaving as a sign of mourning).

Torrio knew that Weiss, now the boss of the North Siders, had marked him for death. He fled the city, traveling about the country with his wife while Capone ran things, and returned to plead guilty to violating the Volstead Act on Jan. 23, 1925, a charge still standing from his arrest in connection with the Sieben Brewery the previous year. Torrio believed that the safest place for him would be in a federal prison. Judge Adam Cliffe allowed Torrio five days to take care of his business before passing sentence, and the next day the crime boss took his wife shopping. The Torrios arrived in front of their apartment building at 7011 Clyde Avenue, where they occupied the third floor, and as Ann Torrio walked toward the entrance, a Cadillac touring car moved slowly next to the Torrio limousine and stopped. Torrio was just getting out of the limousine, driven by chauffeur-bodyguard, Robert Barton, when four men in the Cadillac, holding revolvers and shotguns, began blasting him.

The four gangsters were Weiss, Moran, Drucci, and Alterie. Weiss and Moran jumped from the Cadillac and ran toward Torrio who turned toward them, packages in his arms. He was shot several times, falling to the ground; one bullet smashed his jaw, another went into his chest, another into his groin, another into his right arm. Meanwhile, Alterie and Drucci peppered Torrio's limousine with shotgun pellets which dissolved the windows and blew off the headlights and fenders. Barton, the chauffeur-bodyguard, was struck in the legs and disabled. Moran, who held two revolvers and had been firing them rapidly as he ran toward Torrio, leaned over the squirming, blood-spouting gang boss and put a revolver to Torrio's head to administer the same kind of *coup de grace* given his former boss, O'Bannion. He pulled the trigger and nothing happened. The chambers of his revolvers were empty. He started to reload but Alterie, at the wheel of the Cadillac, gave two long blasts on the horn, the signal that police were coming, and Moran and Weiss ran back and leaped inside the Cadillac, which roared away.

When police officers arrived, they found Torrio on the sidewalk, moaning to them: "bullets...tipped with garlic." He was more concerned with garlic-tipped bullets that might cause gangrene than with receiving a fatal wound. (The legend of garlic-tipped bullets began with Capone killers Anselmi and Scalise, who rubbed garlic on their bullets, believing that this would cause a lethal infection even if they failed to strike a vital organ, a mistaken belief.) There was one report that Torrio had been set up, that his time schedule detailing his daily activities in the five days before he was to begin serving his nine-month prison sentence had been given to Hymie Weiss, and that the man who had delivered this schedule through an anonymous courier was none other than Al Capone. Scarface, the report pointed out, wanted the cautious nonviolent Torrio out of the way so he could deal with his gang enemies in a way he believed effective—all-out warfare. He was also tired of taking orders from Torrio.

By some sort of miracle, Torrio survived. He refused to name his assailants. "Sure," he told newsmen from a bed in the Jackson Park Hospital, "I know all four men but I will never tell their names." Moran was the only one of the four gunmen later identified by the doorman at Torrio's building, and he was indicted for attempted murder, but the case against him was later dropped when Torrio refused to cooperate with authorities. Capone arrived and stationed four armed guards on the third floor, close to Torrio's private room. Torrio told a weeping Capone that he had made a mistake about O'Bannion. He had never realized just how loyal O'Bannion's men were to their fallen chief and how they would undertake a war of vendetta against him. On Feb. 9, with bandages wrapped about his jaw, Torrio, surrounded by Capone's gunmen, went down a back fire escape and then to court, where Judge Cliffe fined him $5,000 and sentenced him to nine months in jail, a sentence which he gladly accepted. He was, for his own safety, sent to the Waukegan Jail, where his cell was specially equipped against assassins, bullet-proof glass put into his cell window and private guards placed before his cell door. He ate catered meals as he served out his time and received Capone, his lawyers and other business associates at all hours.

During this reflective period, Torrio came to the conclusion that it was time for him to retire from the rackets. He had made untold millions in five years of ruling a huge bootleg empire. But with the killing of O'Bannion, he realized that he now faced an organization seriously threatened, and, in most parts of Chicago, under constant attack by the North Siders and their vassal gangs. He was marked for death. It was time to leave Chicago, and he told Capone that he was turning everything over to him. "It's all yours, Al," he was heard to tell his protegé. This involved thousands of speakeasies, brothels, breweries, and rackets of all sorts, that brought in an estimated $50 million a year in gross revenues. Torrio took nothing in return except Capone's undying gratitude and, after serving his time in Waukegan, Johnny Torrio packed up his wife and belongings and resettled in New York, traveling about the country as an elder statesman of crime, trying to interest gang leaders in organizing a national syndicate, an idea which Capone himself would put into reality in 1929 when calling the first national crime cartel meeting in Atlantic City, a gangster enclave at which Johnny Torrio would preside.

Capone inherited a crime empire that was exploding before his very eyes. He, like Torrio, was marked for death, and lived a furtive life, one where he and his family were guarded night and day. Capone, however, unlike Torrio, understood and accepted the street warfare being waged by Weiss and his men. Scarface surrounded himself with killers devoted to his safety and well-being, marksmen such as Louis "Little New York" Campagna, who slept outside the boss' hotel suite when he was away from his southside home; Samuel McPherson "Golf Bag" Hunt, who earned his moniker after police found him carrying a shotgun in a golf bag in his car; William "Three Fingered Jack" White, a deadly marksman who had lost two fingers on his right hand in a boyhood accident; Phil D'Andrea, Capone's favorite bodyguard, deadly with a revolver; and "Machinegun Jack" McGurn, the man who would later plan the end of the Weiss-Moran gang.

Scarface at first tried some crude diplomacy, contacting Weiss and promising him that the old Madison Street "dividing line" would be respected. Weiss' response was to tell Capone that he would make peace, but only if O'Bannion's killers, Anselmi and Scalise, were turned over to him. "What?" roared Scarface, "I wouldn't do that to a yellow dog!" He then slammed down the phone and told Louis Campagna: "Hymie's crazy. He's gotta go. Figure out something."

Weiss, however, was quickly planning to wipe out Capone's hardcore allies, the Gennas. Systematically, Weiss, Moran and others ran down Angelo, Mike, and Tony Genna, killing them and scattering their forces throughout 1925, taking over the Genna territories and moving southward, deep into Capone territory. They expanded into the Northwest Side, making an alliance with Pollack Joe Saltis, who invaded the Sheldon gang territory. Saltis and Frank "Lefty" Koncil shot John "Mitters" Foley to death, eradicating one of the top Sheldon gunman. Capone himself was unsuccessfully attacked on two occasions. The second attempt by Moran, Weiss, Drucci, and others took place in early August 1926, when the North Siders trailed Capone's car from his Prairie Avenue home to the Four Deuces. When Capone alighted from the car, the North Siders opened fire with revolvers and shotguns, killing his driver, Tony Ross, but missing Capone, who literally dove through the front door of the Four Deuces, slugs slamming into the door behind him. On Aug. 10, 1926, Capone's men struck back, a carload of Scarface's gunners catching Weiss and Drucci on Michigan Avenue as they walked toward the Standard Oil Building, where they were to have a meeting with 20th ward political boss, Morris Eller.

When Capone's men opened fire, the street was teeming with passersby, thousands of them, and people ran for cover at the first sound of gunfire, a sound with which Chicago was becoming all too familiar. Weiss and Drucci both pulled revolvers from their shoulder holsters, jumped behind a parked car and began returning fire. For several minutes, the most heavily trafficked street in the Midwest was turned into a scene out of the old Wild West, with gunmen firing at each other and through the crowds. Miraculously, only one passerby, a clerk, was slightly wounded, nicked in the thigh. The Capone men had stopped their car and stood on the street, firing into buildings, heavy plate glass windows, in an effort to pick off the dodging Weiss and Drucci. Then a police car, its alarm gonging, sped toward the scene and the Caponites raced to their car and fled, leaving behind one gunman, Louis Barko, one of Capone's top killers.

Barko, along with Weiss and Drucci, were taken to a precinct station, but they told police that they did not know each other. Drucci, who had been carrying $13,500 in cash (a payoff to Eller, newsmen later speculated), claimed that the gunmen who had fled were thieves: "It was a stickup, that's all. They were after my roll." Five days later, on Aug. 15, 1926, Weiss and Moran were once again walking down Michigan Avenue when a carload of Capone gunmen opened fire on them, almost at the same spot where the previous gunfight took place. This time the North Siders chose not to shoot it out, but drew revolvers and fired as they ran into the Standard Oil Building. In New York, reading about these two shootings, crime boss Lucky Luciano, an advocate of assassination and murder, thought Capone excessive and that Chicago was "a damned crazy place! Nobody's safe in the streets!"

This was made terrifyingly evident to Chicago residents and Capone himself on Sept. 20, 1926, when the so-called "Bootleg Battle of the Marne" exploded into the wildest gunplay ever seen in modern gang warfare, occuring outside the Hawthorne Inn, Capone's Cicero headquarters. After being shot at twice, Weiss decided that it was time to track Scarface down in his lair and kill him, keeping his promise after O'Bannion's murder to kill anyone and everyone who got in his way. Capone was having lunch that day in the rear of the Hawthorne Coffee Shop before going to the nearby Hawthorne Race Track for an idling afternoon. With him sat Frank Rio, one of his most dedicated

bodyguards and a street-smart hoodlum who had survived many a gunfight. The coffee shop was crowded with lunchtime patrons and the place was noisy, but the ever-alert Rio heard the distant sound of a "chopper." The crowd in the restaurant fell silent, petrified, as a car went by, a man hanging from a window firing a submachine gun straight at the coffee shop's windows. But no windows were shattered and not a bullet mark etched into the building. Rio realized why. When Capone got up and began to walk toward the front of shop, intending to step outside to investigate, the bodyguard ran up behind him and knocked him down, lying on top of him. "It's a decoy, boss, to draw you out."

Rio was right. The machine gunner in the first car had been firing blanks, intending to draw Capone and all his gunmen to the street so that they would be able to rake the lot of them, killing off the nucleus of the Capone mob. Ten cars, filled with Weiss' best men, at least fifty of them, all bristling with submachine guns, shotguns, rifles and revolvers, followed the advance car at a distance of a block, driving slowly and in single file past the hotel. As they reached the building, each car stopped and its occupants let loose a hellish and withering fusillade that blew away the windows of the coffee shop and most of the windows in the adjacent Hawthorne Inn. The gunners raked the building from left to right, then right to left, then up and down, to cover the three floors of the building. Louis Barko, the man who had tried to kill Weiss and Drucci earlier, was wounded in the shoulder as he was entering the lobby of the hotel when the first of the ten cars firing real bullets appeared.

Also shattered were the dozens of cars parked along the street in front of the Hawthorne Inn and its coffee shop. Inside one was Louisiana resident, Clyde Freeman, who had arrived in Cicero on vacation. Next to him sat his 5-year-old son and his wife. The family crouched inside the car when the invaders opened fire. Their car was riddled, a bullet going through Freeman's hat, one grazing his son's knee, and another ploughing into Mrs. Freeman's arm. The front window of the car was exploded by bullets and shards flew into Mrs. Freeman's right eye. Finally, the last car in the murder caravan arrived before the shot-up hotel and Pete Gusenberg, one of the most daring of Weiss' gunmen, casually got out of the car carrying a submachine gun. He knelt before the entranceway and fired directly into the lobby, raking the place in about ten seconds with more than 100 .45-caliber bullets from the drum of the weapon, firing long bursts of fire that shattered chandeliers, tore apart furniture, and ripped into walls. With that, Gusenberg strolled to the car, got in, and, as a klaxon horn let out three blasts—a signal to leave—the caravan got under way and rolled down Twenty-second Street toward Chicago.

Scarface stood up moments later to survey the damage. More than 5,000 bullets had been fired by the invading gangsters. The coffee shop was a wreck, its tables, chairs, dishes, walls, and ceiling looking like a giant sieve. Incredibly, the dozens of lunch patrons escaped injury, all lying on the floor during the five- to ten-minute attack. Capone's eyes darted about frantically, his lips twitched and his hands trembled, a visibly shaken crime czar who now realized that open war had been declared against him. The Hawthorne Inn was a shambles, but fortunately there were no fatalities. Capone made a show of paying for all the damage and even paying for more than $10,000 in hospital expenses and operations performed on Mrs. Freeman, which saved her eyesight. For the first time in his violence-strewn life, Al Capone was frightened. Weiss had reached into the heart of Capone's stronghold, a place where he felt secure, and obliterated a half block of real estate in an attempt to murder him.

But where Weiss was a lethal gangster who preferred straight ahead attacks, Capone was the master of the ambush, and this was how he planned to end the life of his chief antagonist. He consulted with his best executioners who advised killing Weiss on his own ground, right next to his headquarters located in the second-story rooms above O'Bannion's flower shop, Schofield's, across from Holy Name Cathedral on State Street. Next to the flower shop was an apartment building at 740 North State Street which was operated by Mrs. Anna Rotariu. Early in October 1926, a young man named Oscar Langdon or Lundin, rented a room in this building, asking for a room that faced State Street. None were available until Oct. 8, 1926, when a second-story room was vacated and Langdon took occupancy. On the same day, an attractive blonde, who gave her name as Mrs. Theodore Schultz, rented a second-floor room on the front of 1 Superior Street, at the southwest corner of State and Superior streets, just south of Schofield's. This room faced north, giving a clear view from a bay window of State Street and Holy Name Cathedral. Both Schultz and Oscar Langdon vanished after occupying their rooms for one night, both replaced in each of the rooms by two men—dark, swarthy men thought to be Italians, according to the managers of both buildings.

A week later, on Oct. 11, 1926, Hymie Weiss attended the trial of his friend Joe Saltis who had been charged with the murder of John "Mitters" Foley. Weiss had promised Saltis his support if he eliminated Capone allies, and he was on hand to confer with Saltis' defense attorney, William W. O'Brien, a celebrated underworld lawyer who had been shot in a Chicago saloon and then upheld the underworld code of silence by refusing to name his assailant. O'Brien had almost been disbarred after being accused of bribing two state's attorneys. Weiss had in his pocket a list of veniremen in the Saltis trial, and it would be learned later that he had spread $100,000 in bribes to assure an acquittal for Saltis. Weiss left the courthouse with Sam Peller, his chauffeur-bodyguard; Paddy Murray, another bodyguard and one of Weiss' sub-bosses in charge of beer distribution; Benny Jacobs, private legal investigator; and Saltis' lawyer, O'Brien. The five men drove up State Street, with Peller parking the Cadillac in front of Holy Name Cathedral at 4 p.m.

The five men began to cross the street to Schofield's shop and Weiss' headquarters. At that moment the two men in the second-story apartment next to the flower shop and two more men in the second-story room at 1 Superior threw up the shades covering windows and began firing submachine guns and shotguns. The cross-fire was devastating, cutting down Weiss instantly, killing him with ten bullets. Murray was killed with fifteen bullets in him. The gunfire lasted only about thirty seconds but the fusillade was so intense that it blew away several words in the cornerstore of the Cathedral. When police arrived a few minutes later, the gunmen had fled the rooms in which they had waited for days to ambush Weiss. These killers were never identified but they were reported by various sources to be Sam "Golf Bag" Hunt, William "Three-Fingered Jack" White, "Machine Gun" Jack McGurn, and Tony Accardo, who later became head of the Chicago mob, and is, at this writing, the chairman of its board.

O'Brien, Peller, and Jacobs were all seriously wounded but later recovered and, at first, it appeared that Scarface had eliminated his last serious gang rival in Chicago. Again, the underworld prepared for a lavish funeral and again there would be an enormous wreath with a red ribbon on it reading: "From Al." To the press, Capone lamented the passing of his dear old friend Weiss. "That was butchery," he clucked to newsmen, when talking about the attack on Weiss and the four other men. He sat amidst a large throng of reporters in his office suite at the Hawthorne Inn. Cigars and drinks were passed to the reporters. As cigar smoke curled about him, Capone sadly related how "Hymie was a good kid. He could have got out long ago and taken his and been alive today. When we were in business together in the old days I got to know him well and used to go to his room often for a friendly visit. Torrio and me made Weiss and O'Bannion. When they broke away and went into business for themselves, that was all right with us. We let 'em go and forgot about 'em. But they began to get nasty. We sent 'em word to stay in their own back yard. But they had the swell head and thought they were bigger than we were. Then O'Bannion got killed. Right after Torrio was shot—and I knew who shot him—I had a talk with Weiss. 'What do you want to do, get yourself killed before you're thirty?', I asked him...He could still have got along

with me. But he wouldn't listen to me. Forty times I tried to arrange things so we would have peace and life would be worth living. Who wants to be tagged around night and day by guards? I don't for one. There was, and there is, plenty of business for us all and competition needn't be a matter of murder, anyway. But Weiss couldn't be told anything. I suppose you couldn't have told him a week ago that he'd be dead today."

Then Capone sent a message to George "Bugs" Moran, who had assumed leadership of the North Side gang. "There are some reasonable fellows in his (Weiss') outfit, and if they want peace, I am for it now, as I have always been. I'm sorry Hymie was killed, but I didn't have anything to do with it. I phoned the detective bureau that I'd come in if they wanted me, but they told me they didn't want me. I knew I'd be blamed for it. There's enough business for all of us without killing each other like animals in the street. I don't want to end up in the gutter punctured by machine gun slugs, so why should I kill Weiss?"

To that last statement, Chief of Detectives William "Old Shoes" Schoemaker replied: "He knows *why*, and so does everyone else. He had them killed." But there was no way the police could arrest Capone. They had no evidence linking him to the Weiss killing. Capone's statements about his friend Weiss would make it appear that he had known the North Side gang leader for decades and that he was reflecting on "old days" that went back scores of years. He had known Hymie Weiss for six years. Weiss died at the age of twenty-eight. Capone was then twenty-seven. He looked much older. High living had turned him into a lumbering, overweight gang boss of 220 pounds. His face was flabby and the fat rippled in rolls around his thick neck. Capone's hair was falling out so rapidly that he was almost bald. He talked according to his appearance—expansive, flashy, overconfident. He was netting $5 million a year or more from his bootleg empire alone, and he was now almost the supreme power in Chicago.

Moran did read Capone's lengthy interview and concluded that a truce was necessary until he reformed the North Side Gang. On Oct. 21, 1926, he, Drucci, and other members of his gang met with Capone, Jake Guzik, Tony Lombardo, who was head of the Unione Siciliane, and others in a suite at the Hotel Sherman. Capone proposed that all grievances and feuds were ended, forgotten, and that the North Siders would continue to control the posh 42nd and 43rd wards. No one would encroach against another's territory, and all of Capone's old territory seized by Weiss would be returned. He would split up other territories for the smaller gangs. Moran agreed, and Capone later boasted to the press that he had had a conference with "all the boys" and had brought peace to Chicago. He was specifically asked about Bugs Moran and his men, and Capone replied: "They stay on the North Side and I stay in Cicero and if we meet on the street, we say 'hello' and shake hands. Better, ain't it?"

Capone had more important things on his mind. His hand-picked candidate, William Hale Thompson, who had been replaced by Mayor Dever, was again in the running for the mayoralty in the 1926 fall primary. Capone needed every goon in his ranks to fix this election, and this was one of the reasons he made peace with Moran; he planned to exterminate the North Siders later, when it was convenient. The primary in which Thompson was selected by the Republicans to run for the office of mayor has gone down in Chicago history as "the pinapple primary;" one permeated with bombs and grenades thrown into shops and homes of Thompson opponents. Voters were beaten up by Capone's goon squads, and some were even shot. When Frank Capone, Scarface's older brother, threatened some voting judges with a submachine gun, officers interrupted him and he was killed in the resulting gun battle. Thompson, with enormous funds provided by Capone, won the general election on the slogan of "a wide open city," an oblique statement that he would tolerate any kind of vice and corruption, a return of the good old days. When he was swept into office, Capone returned to the city, making his headquarters in the Metropole Hotel and later moving to the Lexington, just south of the Loop. From here, Capone reorganized his forces and began to spend millions buying up legitimate businesses, first as fronts, then as paying concerns.

Capone thought of early retirement but first he wished to amass many more millions. He bought a lavish, large estate on Palm Island, Fla., and departed Chicago during its brutal winters to fish and swim in waters lapping against his private beach on white sands. But all was not tranquil in Chicago. Moran had not for a moment trusted Capone when agreeing to the 1926 truce. Capone gunners consistently hunted down his men and killed them, and he fought back in the form of raids on Capone speakeasies and gambling joints, by hijacking Capone beer and liquor trucks. After a series of killings, Moran joined with Joey Aiello in trying to get rid of Capone, even bribing his chef to put prussic acid in his soup. Then Moran-Aiello gangsters attempted to take over the Unione Siciliane, not only in Chicago, but in New York. Aiello gangsters trained to New York and, on July 2, 1928, shot Frankie Yale to death as he drove home, an Aiello vassal taking over the Unione Siciliane there. The Chicago Unione chief, Tony Lombardo, was shot to death on Sept. 7, 1928, as he and two bodyguards, Joseph Lolordo and Tony Ferraro, were walking at the corner of Dearborn and Madison streets, the world's then-busiest corner. The killers escaped in the dense crowds.

Lombardo's death was a great blow to Capone since Lombardo was not only a close ally, but a close friend. Another Capone friend, Pasquale Lolordo, assumed the command of the Unione Siciliane but he, too, was murdered on Jan. 2, 1929, by four men—Aiello, Moran, and the Gusenberg brothers—who met with him at his home. Mrs. Lolordo served the men whiskey and wine and left the parlor. A few minutes later she heard shots and ran into the parlor to see her husband lying on the floor, bleeding from a bullet wound in his head. Joey Aiello was going out the door, putting on his hat and tossing a revolver casually onto the floor. None of these men were arrested, and Capone vowed to get rid of his enemies once and for all. He called in his top killer, Frank "The Enforcer" Nitti who had been waging war with the North Siders for two years, ordering him to plan an operation which would eradicate the North Side gang, as well as Joseph Aiello who had ultimately reached his goal—becoming president of the Unione Siciliane following Lolordo's murder.

Nitti and Machine Gun Jack McGurn planned to raid Moran's headquarters, the S-M-C Cartage Company at 2122 N. Clark Street. They picked St. Valentine's Day to deliver their message from Capone. Five men were chosen for the slaughter, three being Capone's top gunners: Jack McGurn, John Scalise, and Albert Anselmi. They would arrive in a car fixed up to look like a CPD detective car. Two more men, dressed as policemen, would enter the garage and line up Moran and his men. These two men had to be free-lance killers who would not be recognized. They were Fred "Killer" Burke and Fred Goetz, also known as Shotgun Ziegler. Capone then went to Florida to languish on the sands and await word that his worst enemies had been killed.

On Feb. 14, 1929, the fake detective car pulled up before the Moran headquarters and the two phony policemen walked inside and lined up seven men they found inside the garage. These were the Gusenberg brothers, Pete and Frank; Adam Heyer (alias John Snyder); Moran's accountant, James Clark; gunman, John May; a garage mechanic and getaway driver, Albert Weinshank; Moran's brother-in-law and beer distributor; and Dr. Rheinhardt H. Schwimmer, who had no real connection with the gang other than the fact that he enjoyed playing cards with its members. He was strangely attracted to gangsters, a fascination that would bring about his death.

Capone lookouts had watched all seven men enter the garage from windows in a rooming house across the street. When they spotted Weinshank they mistook him for Moran and made the call to McGurn that the boss of the North Side gang was inside the garage. Moran, however, was late getting to the garage that day. He and two bodyguards, Willie Marks and Ted Newbury, saw the detective car outside the garage and slipped into a coffee shop until the police raid was over, never thinking for a moment that

Capone's killers were busy slaughtering their fellow gang members. Once the phony cops Burke and Goetz had lined up the seven men in the garage facing a brick wall, they motioned for Scalise and Anselmi to enter the rear of the garage. Both killers stepped inside and drew submachine guns from beneath their long coats. Burke and Goetz put away their police revolvers and each also produced a submachine gun and a shotgun. Then all four Capone gunmen let loose a savage burst of gunfire that ripped through the bodies of the unsuspecting Moran gang members, cutting them in half and sending them to the floor. The killers continued to spray the bodies back and forth until their traumatized, quivering forms were still. Only the sound of the German shepherd chained to a truck axle could be heard as the animal began to howl. Putting the submachine guns beneath their coats, Scalise and Anselmi, dressed in civilian clothes, were marched at gunpoint to the detective car outside, as if they had been arrested by the uniformed officers. The four men got into the car and, McGurn at the wheel, roared southward down Clark Street. The killers were never completely identified, except for Burke, who fled to Michigan where he was later imprisoned for another murder. Some neighbors heard the dog howling inside the garage and went inside to discover the horror before them—seven men slaughtered, their bodies riddled with dozens of bullets, two of them with their heads blown away, their brains spilling onto the floor, these wounds administered by Goetz with his shotgun, the inevitable *coup de grace*. But one man, Frank Gusenberg, still lived. Wounded many times, he was rushed to a nearby hospital but despite pleas from friends and police, he refused to identify the killers, most likely because he did not know them. He died a short time later. Newsmen later found George "Bugs" Moran hiding out in a hospital, his bed flanked by bodyguards Marks and Newbury. He was asked about the men in the garage, his men. He denied even knowing the victims. "I didn't know those guys," he said. Who could have done such a heinous deed, he was asked. "Only Capone kills like that!" he blurted, a remark widely printed.

When Capone was confronted with this statement by newsmen in Florida, he laughed and said: "They don't call that guy 'Bugs' for nothin'." He then said: "Only Moran kills like that," in a feeble effort to shift the blame for the mass murder onto his arch enemy, but no one could believe that Moran would have his own gang members shot to pieces. The mass killing, forever after known as The St. Valentine's Day Massacre, caused an enormous public uproar and authorities were pressured into cleaning the mobsters out of Chicago. President Herbert Hoover was constantly asking his top law enforcement officials in Washington: "Have you gotten rid of that fellow Capone yet?" Federal authorities began a night-and-day campaign to put Capone behind bars, but this was no easy task. He always had an alibi whenever a killing took place. When Joseph Aiello left a friend's home at 15 North Kolmar Avenue on the night of Oct. 23, 1930, he was cut in half by machine guns set up inside two nearby apartment buildings, the same method used by Capone killers in slaying Hymie Weiss.

Following Aiello's death, all substantial gang resistance to Capone ceased. He was the supreme gang lord of Chicago but his days were marked. The federal government was closing in on his operations as its agents probed his elaborate business ventures, confiscating books and ledgers and studying his income. Meanwhile, even his most trusted aides planned to eliminate him. Before the murder of Joseph Aiello, Frank Rio came to Capone and told him that Anselmi and Scalise, in collusion with Joseph "Hop Toad" Guinta, the new Unione Sicilione president, had planned to murder him and were in league with Aiello. Capone summoned all three men to the banquet room of the Hawthorne Inn where he gave a party in their honor. At the end of a sumptuous dinner and many speeches, Capone stepped up behind the three gunmen and denounced them as traitors. He then wielded a metal bat above their heads, bringing this down repeatedly on their skulls, killing them. The bodies were then dragged to a back room, stripped and mutilated before being taken by car to a lonely road where they were dumped into a

Left, Treasury agent Frank Wilson, who got the evidence to bring Capone to trial, right, for tax evasion.

Judge James H. Wilkerson   A glum Capone after losing his case.   Capone as a federal prisoner, 1931.

Scarface en route to the penitentiary in Atlanta.   Capone's estate on Palm Island where he died in 1947.

ditch at the city limits.

In May 1929, Capone, accompanied by Jake Guzik, Frank Nitti, and Moses Annenberg, went to Atlantic City where Capone held the first national crime cartel conference with all the important crime bosses of the East Coast, including Charles "Lucky" Luciano, Joe Adonis, Frank Costello, Albert Anastasia—men who would go on to develop the crime syndicate as the most powerful organization in America next to the federal government. Presiding at this conference was Capone's old mentor, Johnny Torrio. The purpose of the gathering was to introduce Moses Annenberg to the other crime bosses and to have them place his wire service into their nation-wide book-making operations so that the crime cartel would control all racing results in the U.S., a plan that would make Annenberg and the crime bosses untold millions. Later that month, Capone, hearing that Moran had placed a $50,000 reward on his head, arranged to have himself arrested, along with his ever-loyal bodyguard, Frank Rio, as they emerged from a Philadelphia, Pa., movie theater on May 17, 1929. Both were carrying weapons and admitted that they were breaking the law.

They confessed their guilt and both men were sentenced to serve a year in prison by Judge John E. Walsh. Capone and Rio were sent to Philadelphia's Holmsburg County Prison. Both men were later transferred to the Eastern Penitentiary when news about Capone's easy life at Holmsburg was publicized. Capone and Rio were released on Mar. 17, 1930, with two months taken off their sentences for good behavior. Capone's willingness to go to jail was obvious; he felt it was the only place where he would be safe from Moran gunners.

Even Capone's political and police contacts began to shun him. His closest associate with the press, Jake Lingle, street reporter for the Chicago *Tribune,* whose connections with Police Chief William Russell, formed the conduit of high level information Capone needed, deserted him for the Moran gang, and Capone had him killed by Leon Vincent Brothers as he was going to the racetrack on June 30, 1930. Brothers, through Capone's connections and a jury that was later reported to be bribed, received a fourteen-year term and served only eight years. Then one of Capone's most trusted business associates, Edward J. O'Hare, secretly defected, providing IRS investigators with vital information needed in preparing its case against the crime czar.

Meanwhile, President Hoover plagued Secretary of Treasury Andrew Mellon daily with the same nagging question: "Have you got that fellow Capone, yet? Remember, I want that man Capone in jail." The man who got Capone was a mild-mannered tax investigator, Elmer L. Irey, chief of the IRS's Enforcement Branch. Irey and his investigators spent three years compiling evidence against Ralph Capone, Al's brother. He failed to pay about $4,000 on $70,000 declared income for the years 1922-25 and Irey managed to bring a successful case against him. Stunned, Ralph Capone was convicted of income tax evasion, fined $10,000, and sent to prison for three years. Next, Irey went after a bigger fish—Scarface himself. Edward J. O'Hare was one of the key men in providing information to Irey's agents, chiefly to Secret Service agent Frank J. Wilson. "On the inside of the (Capone) gang," Wilson later said, "I had one of the best undercover men I have ever known: Eddie O'Hare."

O'Hare was unlike any of Capone's other associates. He was cultured, well-read, a gentle man who was devoted to his son Butch who would later become a WWII pilot and national hero. O'Hare had started as a gentleman bootlegger in St. Louis and then moved to Chicago where he became a lawyer and then one of Capone's business agents, overseeing Scarface's dog and horse racing tracks, a lucrative job that made O'Hare a millionaire. (He later became president of Sportsman's Park.) He informed IRS agents where they could seize books that would reflect Capone's income and this evidence was finally obtained, along with other voluminous ledgers and documents dealing with Capone's myriad rackets and businesses.

By 1931, Irey and his agents had established Capone's income

for 1924 to be in excess of $120,000 and that taxes for this amount, about $32,000, had never been paid. For the years of 1925-29, Capone, it was proven, had earned more than $1 million and had paid no taxes on this income either. As Irey and everyone else knew, this $1 million was but a tiny fraction of what Capone had actually taken in, but it was income they could prove on paper. In fact, Capone had never paid any kind of income tax. This was his undoing. When he realized that he might share the same fate as his brother, Capone offered the federal government $400,000 to drop its case against him. This offer was rejected.

He was tried before federal judge James H. Wilkerson, a jurist who could not be intimidated or bought. The jury was another matter. O'Hare informed Irey's agents that Phil D'Andrea had obtained a list of all the jury members in the case and these were to be bribed or, if they did not find Scarface innocent, killed. Wilkinson was given this list. He first had bailiffs pull D'Andrea from his seat in the spectator's gallery and searched. A weapon was found on him and he was sent to prison for six months for carrying a concealed weapon. Then, distrusting his jury, Wilkinson had the jury in the Capone case switched completely with a jury hearing another case only a few minutes before Capone's trial began. In short order, Capone was convicted of tax evasion and Judge Wilkinson gave him the maximum sentence, a fine of $50,000, an order to pay court costs of $30,000 and eleven years in jail. Moreover, all his assets and that of his wife's were seized by the government. Much of these holdings, however, were in the names of others and dummy corporations, such as Capone's Florida estate, so they remained within the family.

Capone was stunned by the sentence and, for the first time in years, had only a few mumbling words for the press as he was hustled to jail by U.S. marshals. Judge Wilkinson had denied any form of bail while Capone's lawyers filed their expected appeals. As he was being led from the courtroom, newspaper photographers began taking pictures of the defeated crime boss. Capone sneered and then said: "Get enough boys, you won't be seeing me for a long time." He had limply accepted his fate. Capone was sent to the federal penitentiary in Atlanta, but he was treated with such deference there, creating his own fiefdom, that he was transferred in 1934 to Alcatraz as part of the first group of Public Enemies to be sent to the forlorn Rock. At Alcatraz, Capone proved to be a cooperative prisoner, although he was attacked a few times by younger men trying to make a reputation for themselves or by members of the old Chicago mobs he had once fought against. On Feb. 5, 1938, Capone entered the prison mess hall and wandered about like a man half conscious. Spittle drooled from his lips, and he seemed not to know where he was. He was taken to the prison hospital and tests revealed that he was in the advanced stages of syphilis and paresis of the brain had begun to turn his mind into jelly. This deadly venereal infection had been contracted almost two decades ago when Capone visited the diseased harlots who worked in his own infested brothels.

Paralyzed, Capone was released from Alcatraz on Jan. 6, 1939, removed to the Federal Correctional Institution at Terminal Island outside of Los Angeles and later taken to the medical center at Lewisburg, Pa., where he was ajudged insane and released to the care of his family on Nov. 19, 1939. Eleven days earlier, unknown gunmen in Chicago sought out Edward J. O'Hare, the man who had secretly provided the IRS with information that helped send Capone to prison, and shot him to death as he was driving back from Sportsman's Park. Capone was taken to his Florida resort and here, for almost a decade, Capone sat about giving orders to bodyguards who largely ignored or placated him. His mind kept drifting back to his Chicago days, and he often woke in the middle of the night screaming that rival gangsters were outside his bedroom door, coming to kill him. His empire continued to flourish under the direction of Frank Nitti, then Paul "the Waiter" Ricca, then Anthony Accardo, the present gang lord. Members of the old mob, however, continued to visit Capone up to the time of his death, pretending that he was still in charge of Chicago operations, giving him fake, often ludicrous reports on his rackets and the millions they were producing. This chore usually fell to Jake "Greasy Thumb" Guzik who was in semi-retirement, but he played out the charade almost every month. After one such visit to Florida, newsmen cornered Guzik upon his return to Chicago and asked him about the state of Capone's health. "Al?" replied the laconic Guzik. "He's as nutty as a fruitcake."

On Jan. 25, 1947, Capone, who was suffering from pneumonia, underwent a massive brain hemorrhage and died. In the words of one of his gang members at the deathbed, "Al's brain just exploded." His body was removed from the Palm Island estate and sent back to the scene of his underworld triumphs and disasters—Chicago. The city of Chicago would keep Scarface in special memory, particularly by naive generations to come. Those who were unfamiliar with his mass murders and ruthless racketeering looked briefly upon his huge and tarnished image and construed him to be some sort of subculture folk hero. In 1989, an amateur historian idiotically proposed to the National Park Service that Capone's home at 7244 S. Prairie Avenue be designated a historic landmark, complete with a bronze plaque announcing it to be the former residence of one of America's most notorious gangsters. This proposal was seriously entertained by federal officials until a storm of protest erupted in the Chicago newspapers and, especially, from Italian-American groups who rightly complained that such a move would honor and glorify a contemptible murderer. Such a move, said a spokesman for the Sons of Italy, "would assist in the stereotyping and defamation of all Italian-Americans." This sentiment was echoed by the Joint Civic Committee of Italian-Americans. The request seeking landmark status for the Capone home was withdrawn.

Immediately upon arrival in Chicago by train, the corpse of the dead crime czar was met by armed guards who escorted it to Mount Olivet Cemetery. Even in death, Capone commanded gunmen legions to protect him against unseen enemies, in this case ghouls. At Mount Olivet, the family held a quiet, unpublicized ceremony but, fearing graverobbers would abduct the corpse, the Capone family later had the body reburied in a secret plot in Mount Carmel Cemetery. Mae Capone was later offered $50,000 by a publisher for the story of her life with Scarface but she rejected the offer, saying: "The public has one idea of my husband. I have another. I will treasure my memory and I will always love him." See: **Accardo, Anthony; Adonis, Joe; Aiello, Joseph; Alcatraz; Alterie, Louis; Annenberg, Moses; Anselmi, Albert; Atlantic City Conference; Bim Boom Gang; Bloom, Isidore; Brothers, Leo Vincent; Campagna, Louis; Circus Gang; Colosimo, James; Costello, Frank; Coughlin, John; Drucci, Vincent; Druggan-Lake Gang; Five Points Gang; Genna Brothers; Guifoyle Gang; Guzik, Jake; Hecht, Ben; Heitler, Michael; Hunt, Samuel; Irey, Elmer L.; Kelly, Paul; Kenna, Michael; Luciano, Charles; Lustig, Victor; McErlane, Frank; McGurn, Jack; Moran, George; Morton, Samuel J.; Nitti, Frank; O'Bannion, Charles Dion; O'Donnell Brothers (Chicago South Side); O'Donnell Brothers (Chicago West Side); Ricca, Paul; St. Valentine's Day Massacre; Saltis, Joseph; Sheldon Gang (Chicago); Torrio, John; Weiss, Earl; White Hand Gang; White, William; Yale, Frank; Zuta, Jack.**

REF.: Allen, *Merchants of Menace—The Mafia;* Allen, *Only Yesterday;* Allsop, *The Bootleggers;* Asbury, *The Gangs of New York;* ____, *Gem of the Prairie;* ____, *The Great Illusion: An Informal History of Prohibition;* Audett, *Rap Sheet;* Barrett, *The Jazz Age;* Bartlett and Steele, *Empire: The Life, Legend and Madness of Howard Hughes;* Bennett, *Chicago Gangland;* Bennett, *I Chose Prison;* Berger, *The Eight Million;* Biddle, *In Brief Authority;* Blumenthal, *Last Days of the Sicilians;* Boettiger, *Jake Lingle;* Bonanno, *A Man of Honor;* Buell, *X Marks the Spot;* Burns, *The One-Way Ride;* Busch, *Enemies of the State;* Campbell, *The Luciano Project;* CBA; Churchill, *A Pictorial History of American Crime;* Clark, *The World of Damon Runyon;* Cohen, *Mickey Cohen, In My Own Words;* Cohn, *The Joker is Wild: The Story of Joe E. Lewis;* Cook, *Mafia!;* Cooper, *Ten Thousand Public Enemies;* Cowdery, *Capone's Chicago;* Cressey, *Theft of the Nation;* Cummings, *Selected Papers;* Davis, *Mafia Kingfish;* Dedman, *Fabulous Chicago;* Demaris, *Captive City;* ____, *The Last Mafioso;*

Dobyns, *The Underworld of American Politics;* Edge, *Run the Cat Roads;* Eisenberg and Landau, *Meyer Lansky;* Ellen, Murphy, and Weld, *A Treasury of Brooklyn;* Elliott, *My Years with Capone;* Ellis, *Alcatraz Number 1172;* Enright (Buell), *Al Capone on the Spot;* Farr, *Chicago;* Feder and Joesten, *The Luciano Story;* Fetherling, *The Five Lives of Ben Hecht;* Flynn, *Men of Wealth;* Fried, *The Rise and Fall of the Jewish Gangster in America;* Gage, *Mafia, U.S.A.;* ____, *The Mafia Is Not an Equal Opportunity Employer;* Gies, *The Colonel of Chicago;* Glazer, *Beyond the Melting Pot;* Godwin, *Alcatraz, 1868-1963;* ____, *Murder U.S.A.;* Gosch and Hammer, *The Last Testament of Lucky Luciano;* Gribble, *Murders Most Strange;* Halper, *The Chicago Crime Book;* Hamilton, *Men of the Underworld;* Harrison, *Stormy Years;* Haskins, *Street Gangs;* Healy, *Cissy;* Hecht, *Charlie;* ____, *A Child of the Century;* ____, *Gaily, Gaily;* Helmer, *The Gun That Made the Twenties Roar;* Hibbert, *The Roots of Evil;* Horan, *The Desperate Years;* Hynd, *The Giant Killers;* Irey, *The Tax Dodgers;* Johnston, *Alcatraz Island Prison;* Karpis, *The Alvin Karpis Story;* ____, *On the Rock;* Katz, *Uncle Frank;* Kefauver, *Crime in America;* Kobler, *Ardent Spirits;* ____, *Capone;* Lait and Mortimer, *Chicago: Confidential;* Landesco, *Organized Crime in Chicago;* Levine, *Anatomy of a Gangster;* Lewis and Smith, *Chicago, The History of Its Reputation;* Lindberg, *Chicago Ragtime;* Lustgarten, *The Story of Crime;* Lyle, *The Dry and Lawless Years;* Lynch, *Criminals and Politicians;* McClellan, *Crime Without Punishment;* Maas, *Deadlines and Monkeyshines;* ____, *Johnny Torrio;* ____, *The Valachi Papers;* Mariano, *The Second Generation of Italians;* Merz, *The Dry Decade;* Messick, *Lansky;* ____, *Secret File;* ____, *Silent Syndicate;* ____ and Goldblatt, *The Mobs and the Mafia;* Morgan, *Prince of Crime;* Murray, *The Legacy of Al Capone;* Nash, *Almanac of World Crime;* ____, *Bloodletters and Badmen;* ____, *Citizen Hoover;* ____, *The Dillinger Dossier;* ____, *Hustlers and Con Men;* ____, *People to See;* Navasky, *Kennedy Justice;* Ness, *The Untouchables;* Ottenberg, *The Federal Investigators;* Pasley, *Al Capone, The Story of A Self-Made Man;* ____, *Muscling In;* Peterson, *Barbarians in Our Midst;* ____, *The Mob;* Pileggi, *Wiseguy;* Powers, *Secrecy and Power;* Reckless, *Vice in Chicago;* Redston, *The Conspiracy of Death;* Reid, *The Grim Reapers;* ____, *Mafia;* Reppetto, *The Blue Parade;* Reuter, *Disorganized Crime;* Robbins, *Front Page Marriage;* Rogers, *I Remember Distinctly;* Ross, *The Trial of Al Capone;* Rudensky, *The Gonif;* St. John, *This Was My World;* Salerno, *The Crime Confederation;* Sann, *Kill the Dutchman!;* ____, *The Lawless Decade;* Scott, *The Concise Encyclopedia of Crime and Criminals;* Shannon, *Desperados;* Sinclair, *Era of Excess;* Smith, *Chicago's Left Bank;* ____, *Syndicate City;* Sondern, *Brotherhood of Evil: The Mafia;* Spiering, *The Man Who Got Capone;* Sullivan, *Chicago Surrenders;* ____, *Rattling the Cup on Chicago Crime;* ____, *The Snatch Racket;* Talese, *The Kingdom and the Power;* Thomas, *Winchell;* Thompson and Raymond, *Gang Rule in New York;* Thrasher, *The Gang;* Toland, *The Dillinger Days;* Toledano, *J. Edgar Hoover;* Toughy, *The Stolen Years;* Turkis and Feder, *Murder, Inc.;* Tyler, *Organized Crime in America;* Ungar, *FBI;* Velie, *Desperate Bargain: Why Jimmy Hoffa Had to Die;* Waldrop, *McCormick of Chicago;* Waller, *Chicago Uncensored;* Wendt, *Chicago Tribune;* ____ and Kogan, *Big Bill of Chicago;* ____, *Lords of the Levee;* Whitehead, *The FBI Story;* Whyte, *Street Corner Society;* Wicker, *Investigating the FBI;* Wilson, *Special Agent;* Wilson, *Encyclopedia of Murder;* Zorbaugh, *The Gold Coast and the Slum;* Zuckerman, *Vengeance is Mine;* (DRAMA), Nash, *Last Rites for the Boys* (orig. title, *1947*); Wallace, *On the Spot;* (FICTION), Burnett, *Little Caesar;* (FILM), *The Finger Points,* 1931; *Little Caesar,* 1931; *The Secret Six,* 1931; *Okay, America,* 1932; *Scarface,* 1932; *Special Agent,* 1935; *The Last Gangster,* 1937; *Lady Scarface,* 1941; *The Undercover Man,* 1949; *Key Largo,* 1948; *The Joker is Wild,* 1957; *Party Girl,* 1958; *Al Capone,* 1959; *The Scarface Mob,* 1962; *The Naked World of Harrison Marks,* 1967; *The St. Valentine's Day Massacre,* 1967; *Capone,* 1975; *Scarface,* 1983; *The Untouchables,* 1987.

Capone, Frank (Salvatore Capone), 1895-1924, U.S., org. crime. Frank Capone, the older brother of Chicago crime boss Al Capone, was in many ways much more ruthless. Al preferred to negotiate with an adversary before resorting to violence. Frank settled matters with bullets. As he explained, "You never get no back talk from no corpse." Had he lived, Frank Capone would have added a new dimension to Chicago's storied Prohibition era. But he died in the streets of Cicero, Ill., a suburb that the Capone mob took over after being driven into temporary exile by reform mayor William Dever of Chicago in 1923.

In just one year, Capone had the Cicero city manager, Joseph Z. Klenha, and the town committeemen in his hip pocket. In the 1924 primaries, toughs armed with machine guns and sawed-off shotguns converged on the polling places to ensure that the citizens of Cicero "voted right." Klenha, the Capone stooge, was pitted against a reform candidate, William K, Pflaum, who had pledged to drive the gangsters out of Cicero. Frank Capone led the assault against Pflaum's campaign headquarters, ransacking Pflaum's office and roughing up several campaign workers. At the polls on Apr. 1, Capone thugs accosted voters as they waited in line to vote, discreetly asking their preferences. Those who said they preferred Pflaum, or chose not to reveal who they were planning to vote for, were simply carried away. Democratic campaign worker Michael Gavin was shot in both legs and held prisoner until the election was over, along wth eight other recalcitrant Democrats.

Upon hearing of these outrages, Cook County Judge Edmund K. Jarecki swore in seventy Chicago policemen as deputy sheriffs. A squad commanded by Detective Sergeant William Cusick arrived outside a Cicero polling place near the large Western Electric Plant, where they were greeted by the Capone brothers, first cousin Charles Fischetti, and David Hedlin.

The gangsters hesitated, not sure whether they were facing Chicago police or rival gangsters from the North Side. Frank Capone, always quick on the draw, began blasting away. He shot at one of the policemen but missed, and the officers returned the volley, dropping Frank in his tracks. Al gave his brother a lavish funeral, with $20,000 worth of flowers lining the casket. The Chicago *Tribune* noted that the affair was fitting for a "distinguished statesman." Out of respect for Capone, the Cicero gambling dens and all-night saloons were ordered to close for two hours. When the votes were counted, the Klenha ticket was swept into office. See: **Capone, Alphonse; Capone, Ralph**. REF.: *CBA*.

Capone, Louis, See: **Buchalter, Louis**.

Capone, Ralph (AKA: Bottles), 1893-1974, U.S., org. crime. Ralph Capone's position in the hierarchy of the Chicago crime syndicate was largely ceremonial. When Al Capone was trying to corner the market on distilled, non-alcoholic beverages during Prohibition, he assigned his brother Ralph to manage the syndicate's bottling plants—hence Ralph's famous nickname, "Bottles." At the Chicago World's Fair in 1933, Ralph sold his drinks to the tourists. The syndicate monopoly returned a sizeable profit to the mob. It might not have been allowed to flourish had Mayor Anton Cermak lived. He was gunned down in Florida before the opening of the fair, some say by Capone torpedoes.

After Al Capone was convicted of tax evasion and sent to prison, Ralph hosted various mob conclaves at his brother's lavish estate at Palm Island, Fla. Despite these high-level meetings, Ralph Capone never became a ranking elder statesman of the Mafia, though the Senate Investigating Committee chaired by Senator Estes Kefauver of Tennessee treated him as one when he was called to testify in 1950. There was little he could tell the committee, because he was not privy to Mafia secrets.

Capone died in 1974, having outlived his son, Ralph Capone, Jr., who committed suicide in 1950. See: **Capone, Alphonse; Capone, Frank; Cermak, Anton**. REF.: *CBA*.

Caponsacchi, 1927, a play by Arthur Goodrich. This drama is drawn from Robert Browning's *The Ring and the Book*, which in turn, is based on the murder of Pompilia by her husband Count Guido Franceschini (Italy, 1697). See: **Franceschini, Count Guido**. REF.: *CBA*.

Cappas, John, 1966- , and **Bafia, Brian**, 1967- , and **Kerridan, Michael**, 1958- , U.S., drugs. John Cappas was a drug kingpin who was too smart to become personally hooked on the white powder he distributed among high school students on Chicago's southwest side and southern suburbs. Greed and a yen for the fast life, Corvette automobiles, and a $200,000 home were what motivated Cappas. "His addiction was for money and power," said Judge Charles Kocoras of the U.S. District Court.

Cappas began as a bit player, hustling small quantities of cocaine on young kids. Beginning in 1986, he struck out on his own, hiring a gang of drug runners to peddle the goods and several armed thugs to act as bill collectors. His supplier was Dante Autullo, a 33-year-old drug trafficker whose operation was fronted by a suburban restaurant and other assets. In a forty-one count indictment that described the gang's activities over a three-year period, Cappas was depicted as a cold-hearted felon who would use whatever means necessary, including murder, to gain an advantage over his competitors.

In the summer of 1986, Daniel Joyce, the 21-year-old son of Illinois State Senator Jeremiah Joyce of Chicago, moved in with Cappas. Joyce began dealing cocaine and sat in on a meeting in which the means of "eliminating" a rival drug dealer, David Avery, were discussed. Cappas offered Raymond Bonnema of suburban Worth $5,000 and Nick Ahrens, twenty-two, $10,000 to ambush Avery near a forest preserve on the southwest side. They were supplied with a .44-caliber automatic handgun and ordered to hide behind a row of bushes. But when Avery did not show up at the appointed hour, they abandoned the idea and went home.

Cappas once boasted of earning $1 million from his drug ring. He entertained lavishly, and tried to associate himself with local celebrities. Giselle Fernandez, a news reporter from the CBS affiliate in Chicago joined Cappas on his boat on Fox Lake in order to secure an interview. Afterward she remained on board for a Labor Day pleasure cruise, while officials from U.S. Attorney Anton Valukas' office were attempting to locate Cappas to arrest him on charges of drug trafficking, after he was indicted, along with eighteen others, on Sept. 2, 1988. "It was a horrible waste of federal resources," Valukas said. "There were 150 people on the street looking for Cappas all weekend." Fernandez was censured by her peers for her conduct in this manner.

After the weekend, Cappas surrendered to federal authorities and sauntered into the courtroom of Judge Charles Kocoras, confident that the system would somehow spare him from prison. Then, as the evidence against the cocaine suppliers began to mount, Cappas assumed a worried, pensive attitude. Nick Ahrens testified against his former boss in a plea-bargaining arrangement with the prosecution. Defense attorney Michael Ettinger labeled Ahrens and other members of the gang who cooperated with the government "stool pigeons." "Mr. Ettinger asks why didn't John Cappas kill David Avery himself," said Mark Prosperi, prosecuting attorney. "The reason is he insulated himself. Basically he's a coward."

After a lengthy trial, John Cappas was convicted on Feb. 21, 1989, on twenty-four counts of drug trafficking and racketeering. Convicted along with Cappas were Michael Kerridan, Brian Bafia, and several lesser offenders who were shown by the government to be sophisticated drug dealers who used electronic equipment to help peddle narcotics. Kerridan was accused of being one of the lookouts in the murder attempt on David Avery.

On May 23, 1989, Judge Kocoras sentenced Cappas to forty-five years in prison. Kerridan received twenty-five years, and Bafia, twenty. The swaggering bravado was gone. Cappas and Kerridan tearfully pleaded for mercy, but Judge Kocoras had none to give. See: **Autullo, Dante**. REF.: *CBA*.

Capriati, Antoine, d.1951, Fr., (unsolv.) assass. Early in 1951, France's most notorious gangster, Ange Salicetti, was machine gunned while driving his late-model BMW. In retaliation, Antoine Capriati was shot down on the Cours Napoléon at Ajaccio later that summer. The killer was believed to be Jean Sérini, and the motive was pure revenge. Capriati was one of the triggermen in the Salicetti hit.

REF.: *CBA*; Goodman, *Villainy Unlimited*.

Captain Jack (AKA: Keintpos), 1837-73, U.S., mur. A Modoc Indian, Captain Jack was their leader in the Modoc War in Oregon which raged between 1872-73. Captain Jack, as he was called by whites, had left the reservation near Klamath, Ore., in 1865 when Indian agents refused to acknowledge his authority, appointing others as chiefs. After an absence of four years, Captain Jack led his band back to the reservation only to find that he and his followers had been branded pariahs, and they once more left the reservation. A contingent of forty soldiers, under the command of T.B. Odeneal, superintendent of the reservation at Klamath, tracked Captain Jack and his Modocs to Lost River and there attempted to disarm them on Nov. 29, 1872. A fight ensued and several troopers and Indians were shot.

A full-scale war broke out with pitched battles being fought through 1873, the most notable of which was on Jan. 17, 1873, when fifty Modocs under Captain Jack repelled more than 300 soldiers in the Lost River area. President Ulysses S. Grant ordered a truce with the Indians and a peace settlement arranged. To that end, General Edward R.S. Canby, Methodist preacher Eleasar Thomas, and Albert B. Meacham, one-time superintendent of the Modoc Reservation at Klamath, met with Captain Jack on Apr. 11, 1873. As Canby approached the Modoc leader under a flag of truce, Captain Jack raised his rifle and shot Canby to death. Other Modocs opened fire on Meacham and Thomas, killing Thomas. Meacham managed to run back to his horse and escape. The cold-blooded murder of General Canby, a Civil War hero and the only general ever killed by Indians, caused the U.S. Army to launch full-scale attacks against the Modocs, soundly defeating the Indians at Dry Lake a short time later. On May 22, 1873, the Modocs surrendered, offering to lead the soldiers to the hideout of Captain Jack, which they did.

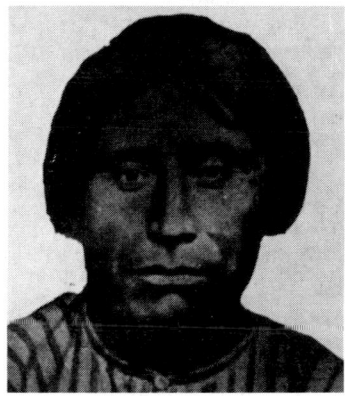

Modoc Chief Captain Jack.

Captain Jack was tried for the murders of General Canby and Thomas and, with five others, was found Guity and sentenced to death. Two of these Indians were reprieved and sent to Alcatraz for life. Captain Jack, Schonchin John, Black Jim, and Bogus Charley were hanged on Oct. 3, 1873. The Modoc tribe was transplanted to Oklahoma and held in custody until 1909 when survivors were permitted to return to Klamath. The Modoc War cost the U.S. government more than $500,000 and added another stain to the already tarnished Grant administration.

REF.: Bartholomew, *The Biographical Album of Western Gunfighters;* Bland, *The Life of Albert Meacham;* ___, *Captain Jack, The Chief of the Modocs; CBA;* Drannan, *Thirty-One Years in the Plains and in the Mountains;* Finger, *Footloose in the West;* Horan, *The Great American West;* Kirsch, *West of the West;* Maury, *Recollections;* Meacham, *Wigwam and Warpath;* Murray, *The Modocs and Their War;* Outerbridge, *Captain Jack;* Payne, *Captain Jack, Modoc Renegade;* Powers, *Redwood Country;* Riddle, *The Indian History of the Modoc War and the Causes that Led to It;* Smith, *Oregon Sketches.*

Captain Lightfoot, See: **Martin, Michael.**

Captain of Kopenick, See: **Voight, Wilhelm.**

Caracalla (Marcus Aurelius Antoninus), 188-217, Roman., emp., assass. Following the death of his father Lucius Septimius Severus in 211, he shared the throne with his brother Geta, whom he murdered a year later. Under his reign from 211-217, Germans, Gauls, and Parthians were openly oppressed. He was killed by Macrinus, a Roman prefect stationed at Edessa. REF.: *CBA.*

Caraccioli, Francesco, 1752-99, Italy, rebel. While serving in the military for the Parthenopean Republic in 1799, he blocked the combined British and Sicilian fleet from establishing a beachhead. When Naples was captured, Caraccioli was seized by Cardinal Fabrizio Ruffo, commander of the Royalist forces allied with Lord Horatio Nelson. He was taken to the British frigate *Minerva,* where he was hanged on the mast. REF.: *CBA.*

Carague, Manuel Ren, 1926-82, Guat., mayor, (unsolv.) assass.

Carague was mayor of Chichicastenango at the time of his assassination by unidentified gunmen in the city's main plaza on Feb. 7, 1982. He was the second Guatemalan mayor to be shot in as many days. Jacinto Girón Barrios, mayor of San Pedro Jacopilas, was killed Feb. 6. See: **Barrios, Jacinto Girón.** REF.: *CBA.*

Caratacus (Caractacus, Caradoc, Caradog), prom. 1st Cent., Brit., milit., war crim. Waged a strong resistance against the Roman invasion led by Emperor Claudius. He commanded the British armies with his brother Togadumnus, but was defeated by Ostorius Scapula in 50 A.D. He was taken to Rome, put on public display, and pardoned. REF.: *CBA.*

Carawan, George Washington, 1799-1852, U.S., mur. The Reverend George Carawan was ordained in 1827. A booming-voiced orator, he preached at the Pungo Church, of Goose Creek, N.C. In time, he became immensely successful, and acquired two large plantations stocked with slaves who experienced first-hand his fiery wrath.

The reverend's first wife died shortly after he had purchased some arsenic. Carawan soon remarried, and his second wife attracted an admirer named Hudson, who quickly died as well. Reverend Albin Swindell publicly accused Carawan of murder and of fathering an illegitimate child with a 16-year-old parishioner. Carawan was temporarily suspended from his duties in 1852. Armed with a shotgun, Carawan caught up with Swindell on a country road near one of the plantations. Seeing that Swindell was with another man, Carawan lost his courage. "Oh, I'm having some trouble with runaway slaves...you haven't seen any about, have you?" he stammered, as the two men furtively eyed Carawan's shotgun. That same year, Carawan murdered a young geography teacher named Clement Lassiter. A house guest, Lassiter had refused to help with the chores and was accused of making improper advances toward Mrs. Carawan. According to Carawan, Lassiter advanced on him with a knife, and Carawan drove him away at the point of a gun. Lassiter sued Carawan for slander, and won an $8,000 judgment. But Carawan and his wife chased the geography teacher through a patch of dense woods and killed him with a shotgun. There were two witnesses to this event, a slave named Seth and Carawan's nephew.

With the local authorities on his trail, Carawan fled to Tennessee, but returned to Goose Creek to dispose of his property. He was arrested and charged with three murders. Carawan said his accusers were jealous because they could not communicate with God as he had. The jurors convicted him anyway. At his sentencing, Carawan produced a small pistol from his vest and shot at the prosecutor, whose name was Warren. The bullet miraculously bounced off a metal chain Warren was wearing. Carawan then produced a second pistol, with which he killed himself.

REF.: *CBA;* Gribble, *The Deadly Professionals;* Gross, *Masterpieces of Murder;* Nash, *Murder, America;* Pearson, *Instigation of the Devil; Trial of the Rev. Geo. W. Carawan for the Murder of Clement H. Lassiter.*

Car Barn Gang, prom. 1911-14, U.S., org. crime. For a few short years, the Car Barn Gang of New York City waged war on the city police. At their headquarters on Second Avenue and East 97th Street, they posted a placard which read: Notice: Cops Keep Out! No Policemen Will Hereafter Be Allowed In This Block By Order of the Car Barn Gang.

The Car Barners were organized in 1911 by Bill Lingley ("Big Bill"), who recruited members from the tough East River docks where fighting, jack rolling, and strong arm robbery was a way of life. Skilled with guns, the Car Barn Gang mimicked the English highwaymen of old, robbing street trolleys and saloons with reckless abandon. The New York police soon found, to their dismay, that the gang were serious about their threats. Later, the police began travelling in groups of four and five, prompting one vaudeville wit to remark that "the police were insisting on police protection."

The Car Barn Gang's turf extended from East 90th Street to 100th, and from Third Avenue to the East River, but sometimes they committed saloon robberies in Lower Manhattan and the Bronx. Lingley and a cohort murdered a Bronx liquor dispenser, which resulted in a massive police crackdown. The two young bandits were arrested, tried, and executed before the outbreak of WWI. With their driving force out of circulation, the Car Barn Gang ceased operations.

REF.: Asbury, *Gem of the Prairie;* _____, *The Gangs of New York;* CBA; Fried, *The Rise and Fall of the Jewish Gangster In America;* Nash, *Bloodletters and Badmen;* Thrasher, *The Gang.*

Carbo, Frankie (Paul John Carbo), 1904-76, U.S., org. crime. When asked by a Senate investigating committee in 1960 about his connections prize fighting, Frankie Carbo answered twenty-five times, "I cannot be compelled to be a witness against myself."

A year later, he was convicted of conspiracy and extortion after muscling in on the earnings of welterweight champion Don Jordan, who had won the title in 1958.

Born on the Lower East Side of New York in 1904, Carbo's crime career began at the age of eleven when he was sent to the state reformatory for juvenile delinquents. In the next ten years he spent time in jail on charges including assault and grand larceny. At twenty, Carbo murdered a cab driver who refused to pay him protection money. Claiming he fired in self-defense,

West Coast gangster Frankie Carbo.

Carbo entered a plea of guilty on a reduced charge of manslaughter and served twenty months of a two-to-four-year prison sentence. During Prohibition he worked as a hired gun for the bootleg gangs. Carbo was indicted for the 1931 murder of Philadelphia mobster Mickey Duffy in Atlantic City, but was later released.

In the 1930s, Carbo worked for Louis "Lepke" Buchalter in Murder, Inc. In 1936, Carbo was arrested for the shooting deaths of Max Greenberg and Max Haskell, two former members of Waxey Gordon's bootleg gang. Carbo was detained for six months but the case never went to trial because witnesses were unwilling to testify.

Before he became a fight promoter, Carbo's criminal record showed seventeen arrests, five for murder, including the Thanksgiving Eve 1939 gangland slaying of Harry "Big Greenie" Greenberg, who had been talking to police on the West Coast. Brooklyn mobsters Abe "Kid Twist" Reles and Allie "Tick Tock" Tannenbaum were prepared to testify that Carbo was the killer, but at the last minute Reles threw himself out the window of the Half Moon Hotel in Coney Island and the case against Carbo collapsed.

In the 1940s, Carbo became the "underworld czar of boxing," promoting the sport through a bookie operation in New York and a "personal" interest in leading prize fighters. In 1958, Carbo was sentenced to two years on Riker's Island for managing boxers without a license. Three years later, Carbo was sentenced to twenty-five years in McNeil Island Federal Penitentiary for the Don Jordan case. Carbo was paroled early, due to ill health and died in Miami Beach, Fla., on Nov. 9, 1976.

REF.: *CBA;* Cohen, *Mickey Cohen: In My Own Words;* Eisenberg and Landau, *Meyer Lansky;* Fried, *The Rise and Fall of the Jewish Gangster In America;* Gosch and Hammer, *The Last Testament of Lucky Luciano;* Katz, *Uncle Frank;* McClellan, *Crime Without Punishment;* Messick, *Lansky;* Navasky, *Kennedy Justice;* Peterson, *The Mob;* Toledano, *J. Edgar Hoover.*

Carbo, Gaius Papirius, d.119 B.C., Roman., suic. Served as a tribune in 131 B.C., and in 130 B.C. was appointed to the land commission of Gracchus. He deserted this political faction in 122 B.C. to join the party of Optimates. He defended Lucius Optimius

for the murder of Lucius Gracchus. For this, Carbo was impeached, and he committed suicide. REF.: *CBA.*

Carbo, Gnaeus Papirius, c.139-82 B.C., Roman., milit., assass. Gnaeua Papirius Carbo led the forces of Gaius Marius into battle against Sulla. Carbo successfully blockaded Rome and forced Sulla's army to surrender in 87 B.C. Carbo usurped the consulship in 84 B.C. Two years later, he was defeated in battle by General Metellus Pius, an ally of Sulla, and was executed. REF.: *CBA.*

Carbonari, prom. 1806-30, Italy, sec. crim. soc. As the Holy Alliance's control spread from France to Italy and other areas of Europe in the early nineteenth century, a secret revolutionary society developed among the middle classes. Its primary aim was to curb the Napoleonic tendency toward monarchy. The name *Carbonari* was taken from an earlier revolutionary brotherhood of charcoal-burners, but their rites leaned toward the type used by the masonic brotherhoods, from which many of the members came. The members called each other *buoni cugini,* meaning "good cousins," and initiates, with hand upon an axe, swore secrecy and promised to "help my Good Cousins in case of need, as much as in me lies, and not to attempt any thing against the honor of their families. I consent, and wish, if I perjure myself, that my body may be cut in pieces, then burned, and my ashes scattered to the wind, in order that my name may be held up to the execration of the Good Cousins throughout the earth. So help me God."

Gradually the organization, which actively recruited from the military, spread from southern Italy throughout much of Europe, including France, Spain, Portugal, and Greece. After Napoleon's defeat in 1815, it opposed the Holy Alliance established to control Europe. The *Carbonari* had perhaps 100,000 members at its height. In whatever country a particular group was located, it generally opposed the government in power, and thus played a role in many revolutionary activities. Several assassinations were attributed to the *Carbonari,* but no specific links were ever found. Generally, the *Carbonari* were liberal republicans committed to nationalism and constitutional guarantees.

When Napoleon turned Naples over to his brother-in-law, Joachim Murat, the *Carbonari* supported him, hoping to gain benefits for Italy, but then they turned against him and supported the return of a Bourbon king. Winning that battle, they turned against the Bourbon king, who imposed strong measures against them. On July 1, 1820, the military, led by the *Carbonari,* began an uprising in Naples that turned into a successful revolution. But dissension among the democratic forces soon led to chaos, and Austria took advantage of the situation to occupy southern Italy. But the *Carbonari* did help win written constitutions for other Italian states and Spain, and helped Greece gain independence from the Ottoman Empire. Eventually, the *Carbonari,* as isolated groups of conspirators, gave way to other organizations with more general support.

REF.: *CBA;* MacKenzie, *Secret Societies;* Scott, *The Concise Encyclopedia of Crime and Criminals.*

Carbone, Paul, and **de Lussatz, Gaetan,** and **Spirito, François,** prom. 1934, Case of, Fr., mur. In the years before the Nazi occupation of France, the criminal underworld was ruled by two gangsters from Marseilles, Paul Carbone and François Spirito, who enjoyed the protection of powerful politicians and corrupt police officials like Pierre Bony. Inspector Bony, later known as commander of the feared "French Gestapo," was responsible for the arrest and execution of hundreds of resistance fighters during WWII.

In February 1934, Bony served as an ordinary police detective in the scandal-plagued Third Republic. That same year the government reeled under allegations of wrong-doing by the Mayor of Bayonne, who was implicated in illegal financial transactions with a Ukrainian named Stavisky. Stavisky specialized in "snow balling" loans to small businesses. The Mayor agreed to allow him to finance several of his pawn shops in town.

Then Stavisky was found dead, the victim of an apparent suicide attempt. The press theorized that he had been put to death in a government coverup to protect high ranking officials. To get to the bottom of the matter, Councillor Albert Prince, a High Court Magistrate was summoned to Dijon on Feb. 20 to give an accounting of his dealings with Stavisky. He died while enroute, his decapitated body found near the village of Combe-aux-Fées. Bony was ordered to make an inquiry. It was suspected that the detective knew more than he was letting on, and in fact, may have planned the murder of Prince. Bony arrested Spirito, de Lussatz, and Carbone with the promise that the trial would be a formality and acquittal was assured.

It was as he promised. The three gangsters laughed and joked through the trial, and were released. The new Minister of Justice, Henri Cheron, convened a press conference to announce that the case was closed thanks to the brilliant detective work of Pierre Bony. See: **Bony, Pierre.**

REF.: *CBA;* Goodman, *Villainy Unlimited.*

Carden, Ronald Q., 1947- , U.S., (wrong. convict.) mur. A hunter in search of game found more than he bargained for when he stumbled across the badly decomposed remains of a young woman lying in the thick underbrush in rural Pulaski County, Ark., on Sept. 12, 1981. It would take many weeks before a positive ID could be made on the woman, who came to be known as "Jane Doe."

In the small farming town of nearby Bigelow, Ron Carden was known as a hard-drinking, easy-living ex-Marine, though some would call him the "black sheep" of his family. The death of the woman infuriated the townspeople, who demanded the killer be brought to justice immediately.

Three eyewitnesses supplied the police with information that pointed to Ron Carden as the likely murderer. First, his uncle Jim Johnson said that they had picked up two female hitchhikers on Highway 113 outside Bigelow. He said that he later helped Carden drag a woman's body into the bush, but under cross-examination on the witness stand Johnson recanted this earlier statement because he said he was drunk when he gave it.

Jim Malott, who owned a nursing home in Little Rock, said that he recalled seeing Carden pick up the two women on Sept. 9, like Johnson had said, but then changed his testimony and said there was only one man, and couldn't say with certainty who that was.

Most damaging of all was the testimony of Berwin Monroe, an analyst for the crime lab, who positively stated that the hairs found on the tank top of the victim matched those from Carden's arm. Two weeks later the FBI refuted Monroe by declaring that the hair follicles were too small to identify positively.

While the trial of Carden was going on, a positive identification of the victim still had not been made. By order of Pulaski County Judge William Beaumont, the remains were cremated and the ashes spread at a Little Rock cemetery.

Arkansas *Democrat* reporter Mike Masterson became interested in this case. Through his analysis of the examination of tissue samples, fingerprints, and dental records of the victim and from information gathered from an interview with the family of Mildred Kay Honeycutt, a Pochahontas, Ark., woman who had recently been reported missing, the reporter established the victim's identity when Arkansas law enforcement agencies had given up hope. A handwriting sample of Honeycutt's contained four fingerprints that perfectly matched those of the dead woman.

Carden was convicted on May 28, 1982. Two weeks later the Reverend Marlin Howe of North Little Rock received a call from William Walter Perry, the 35-year-old boyfriend of the slain woman. "A man named Carden has already been convicted of that crime," he said, "and I do not want him to serve a life sentence for something I have done." He admitted to having an affair with Honeycutt, whose estranged husband was a friend of Perry's. The major break in the case had finally come.

Perry said an "inner voice" commanded him to strangle the woman, which he did on the morning of Sept. 10. He then took the body to a ditch off Highway 113. The prosecutor's office doubted the story at first, but forensic evidence later confirmed sperm samples as having belonged to Perry. A trial was convened, and the conviction of Ronald Carden was overturned on Dec. 20, 1982. Carden decided to leave his past behind. He settled in New Mexico where he found work as a truck driver. He told court officials that he had given up drinking for good. REF.: *CBA.*

Cardiff Giant, See: **Hull, George.**

Cardine, Mother, prom. 1566, Fr., pros. In the city of Paris during the time of King Henry III, a brothel-keeper named Mother Cardine maintained one of the largest, most elegant houses in the city, located in the Bourg l'Abbé. The Paris Edict of 1560 ordered the closing of all such houses, but Mother Cardine's money and influence helped keep the French authorities from her door until February 1566, when by Royal order she was put out of business for good.

REF.: Bullough, *Illustrated History of Prostitution; CBA.*

Cardinelli Gang, prom. 1910s, U.S., org. crime. The Cardinelli gang was headed by a towering giant, Sam Cardinelli, and its members were considered to be the most vicious and murderous in Chicago. At the dawn of Prohibition, none of the larger gangs, including the Torrio-Capone combine, dared to enter the territory controlled by Cardinelli and his top henchmen, Frank Campione and Nicholas Viana. Black Handers all, the gang specialized in extortion and banditry— robbing hotels, speakeasies and gambling dens. Viana, who was only eighteen, was called "The Choir Boy," and at least fifteen murders were credited to him. After committing more than 100 robberies and dozens of killings, Cardinelli, Viana, and Campione were convicted of murder and hanged in 1921 spelling the end of this fearsome gang. One tale told about Cardinelli's associates attempting to revive him through a medical conspiracy after he had been hanged is pure hokum. (This story originated with Chicago writer Ben Hecht who told it of another Chicago hoodlum, Frankie Piano.)

REF.: Asbury, *Gem of the Prairie; CBA;* Thrasher, *The Gang.*

Cardone, Joseph, prom. 1917, U.S., burg. Joseph Cardone was a green country boy who arrived in New York City seeking his fame and fortune during WWI. He met up with two modern-day Fagins who persuaded him to act as their "second-story man." The two thieves pointed out to their young apprentice the location of dozens of New York flats where residents were known to be gone during the day. While they waited on the street outside, Cardone climbed through windows or jimmied the doors open. At a safehouse, they would divide the loot, which typically meant ten per cent for Cardone, and ninety per cent for his criminal benefactors.

After he was arrested by detectives Daniel Curtayne and Stein, Cardone broke down and confessed that he had looted twenty-one apartments in a two-week period. By this time, the latter-day Fagins had disappeared from sight.

REF.: *CBA;* Livingston, *The Murdered and the Missing.*

Cardozo, Benjamin Nathan, 1870-1938, U.S., jur. Benjamin Nathan Cardozo was the son of Albert Cardozo, a New York City judge and notorious Tammany Hall politician who was accused of graft during the Boss Tweed scandal of 1873. Admitted to the bar in 1891, Cardozo later ran against the forces of Tammany Hall and was elected justice of the New York Supreme Court in 1914.

After serving on the bench of Court of Appeals, Cardozo was appointed associate justice of the Supreme Court in 1932 by President Herbert Hoover. He supported the New Deal policies of President Franklin D. Roosevelt and wrote the majority opinion in *Nixon vs. Condon* (1932), which held that the exclusion of blacks from primary elections by political parties was a violation of the Fourteenth Amendment. Books authored: *The Nature of the Judicial Process, The Growth of the Law,* and *The Paradoxes of Legal Science.* REF.: *CBA.*

Carew, Edith Mary Porch, b.1868, Japan, mur. When Edith Mary Porch of Glastonbury, England, married young adventurer Walter Carew, in 1889, she was the envy of all her friends. She and Carew were to leave immediately for exotic Japan, where Carew would seek his fortune and his wife would play the perfect hostess. Mrs. Carew regularly sent home news of the social life of the foreign enclave in Yokohama, in which she played a major role. But after several years she grew bored with Carew and began to eye a young bank clerk named Dickinson.

Edith Carew told Dickinson that her husband was mean, unfaithful, and spiteful. Dickinson would later testify, however, that he learned that portrayal was false and he tried to break up with Mrs. Carew so as not to interfere with her marriage. It was then that Mrs. Carew went to the local druggist and bought her first supply of arsenic. Carew became ill. His doctor diagnosed his condition as liver disease, but Carew failed to improve as he should have. When Mrs. Carew ordered Miss Jacobs, her children's governess, to buy more arsenic, Jacobs did so, but then reported the purchase to Carew's doctor. Before the doctor could move his patient, Carew died on Oct. 22, 1896.

The new widow told the doctor that Carew asked for arsenic, as it was popularly believed at the time that small doses of the poison were good for the digestion. The coroner's jury initially accepted the story, but they finally left the verdict open, finding only that Carew died of poisoning. Within a few weeks, however, the police arrested Mrs. Carew for murder.

At her trial, Mrs. Carew accused Jacobs of being "Annie Luke," Carew's lover. She produced a letter, purportedly written by Annie Luke, containing the claim, "I have bamboozled (1) the chemist, (2) the doctor, and last, but not least, that fool his wife, and I am now going to join him, my twin soul." Jacobs was arrested, but the prosecution called Dickinson, Mrs. Carew's former lover, who told his story. When his testimony was followed by that of a handwriting expert who insisted that Mrs. Carew had written the Annie Luke letter, Mrs. Carew's lawyer withdrew from the case and she was found Guilty of murder. The British ambassador commuted her death sentence to life at penal servitude. She was returned to England, where she served thirteen years in Aylesbury Prison. See: **Blandy, Mary; Cotton, Mary Ann; DeMelker, Daisy Louisa; Jegado, Helene; LaFarge, Marie; Smith, Madeleine.**

REF.: *CBA;* Curtin, *Noted Murder Mysteries;* Nash, *Look For the Woman;* Wyndham, *Feminine Frailty.*

Carey, Estelle Evelyn, d.1943, U.S., (unsolv.) mur. On Feb. 2, 1943, Chicago firemen broke into an apartment on West Addison Street and found the body of a woman who had been hacked to pieces and partially burned. Estelle Carey's unsuccessful struggle for life left blood all over the apartment and evidently involved several weapons, including a butcher knife, a broken bottle, and a blackjack. Two fur coats were missing, but a box containing money was untouched. A neighbor had seen a man leaving Carey's apartment at 2:30 p.m. carrying two fur coats.

Carey, identified as a show- **Estelle Carey; her murderer was** girl, had most recently been **never found.** unemployed. But she had previously worked at the Colony Club on Rush Street, where she was in charge of the girls who ran the illegal dice-betting game called "26." The club was owned by Nick Circella, alias Nick Dean, who was also Carey's lover. Circella, however, was out of town, in hiding to avoid a tax evasion charge. Police were convinced that Carey's death had a syndicate connection. They knew that Circella had testified to the federal government about syndicate operations, and thought that the Mafia, knowing that Circella had probably talked freely with Carey, wanted to keep her quiet.

The co-owner of the Colony Club was George Browne, who, with Willie Bioff, extorted vast sums of money from the movie industry by threatening Hollywood with labor strikes. None of the

money had made it into syndicate coffers. Circella was probably in on the huge payoffs. If so, it was likely that Carey knew where the money was hidden. Her extravagant lifestyle would have led the syndicate to go after her in hopes of finding Circella's fortune. The higher-ups did not like the underlings holding out on them, and for that reason later killed Bioff and Browne.

None of the huge number of smudged prints in the apartment could be resolved into a clear fingerprint. The gory death of the Rush Street showgirl was never solved. See: **Bioff-Browne Extortion Case.**

REF.: *CBA;* Nash, *Open Files.*

Carey, Henry (First Baron Hunsdon), c.1524-96, Brit., jur. Son of Anne Boleyn's sister. He served as commissioner of the treason trials conducted intermittently between 1585-95. In 1586 he tried Mary, Queen of Scots for her role in Babington's Plot. REF.: *CBA.*

Carey, James, See: **Cavendish, Lord Frederick.**

Carey, Joseph Maul, 1845-1924, U.S., jur. Attorney general in the territory of Wyoming from 1869-71, and appointed by President Ulysses S. Grant to sit on the bench of the supreme court of the territory of Wyoming in 1871. He was a member of the U.S. Senate from 1891-95. REF.: *CBA.*

Carey, Mary, and **Carey, Howard,** and **Carey, James,** prom. 1927-34, U.S., mur. A mother and her two sons thought they had committed the perfect crime. And for seven years it certainly seemed that way.

Mary Carey and her boys lived in the small town of Omar, Del. Shortly before the local elections were held in November 1927, Carey decided to murder her brother Robert Hitchens. He was a reserved bachelor who was content to sit back and listen to the opinions of others. Hitchens was well-liked, and it seemed inconceivable that anyone wanted to murder him. Carey's motive, though, was simple: she wanted to collect on his sizeable life insurance policy. To enlist the cooperation of her sons, she promised them a new car.

On Nov. 5, Hitchens told Mrs. Daisey, the grocery store owner's wife, that he felt ill. It was the perfect opportunity for his sister to carry out her plans. The next day when Robert did not show up at the store as he usually did, Mrs. Daisey was concerned and notified Mary Carey. They went over to his place and rapped on the door, but there was no answer. A neighbor man jimmied open a window and climbed in to see what the trouble was. He found Hitchens on the living room rug. He had been beaten and shot.

The presence of a whiskey bottle near the corpse led the police to the conclusion that perhaps it might have been the work of a gang of bootleggers. The case was later entered into the records as "unsolved."

In fact, the case was forgotten, until Dec. 5, 1934, when Mrs. Irving Powell returned to her darkened house and was accosted by an intruder. She dropped in her tracks after being winged by his errant bullet, but she had obtained a good look at the assailant before passing out. It was Mary Carey's youngest boy Lawrence. The police took him into custody and questioned him about the Powell shooting and the murder of his Uncle Robert. "I know plenty," he said, recalling the conversations he had overheard between his mother and two older brothers. As a result, Mrs. Carey, Howard Carey, and James Carey were tried and convicted of murder. Mary and Howard were hanged, and James was given life. Lawrence Carey received seven years for breaking and entering into the Powell residence.

REF.: *CBA;* Cohen, *One Hundred True Crime Stories.*

Carey, Walter Burton, III, 1949- , U.S., mur. The question of when a victim is legally dead became the central issue during the murder trial of Walter Burton Carey III, accused of killing 17-year-old Karen Ann Pomroy on the grounds of Long Island's Islip High School, Nov. 29, 1976.

The girl was on her way to a tutoring job when Carey assaulted her with a heavy railroad spike. He stole $1 from her purse and left her for dead. However, she did not lose her vital signs. Taken to the Southside Hospital in Bay Shore, Karen Ann was placed on a respirator. She was pronounced neurologically dead on Dec. 2 by Dr. William Bloom. With the consent of her parents, Pomroy was disconnected from her life-support system. Contrasting her condition to that of Karen Ann Quinlan, Bloom pointed out that Quinlan "never had a loss of electrical activity in the brain. She never had a loss of movement. She never had loss of response to painful stimuli."

District Attorney Henry O'Brien pressed for a murder indictment ment against Carey. Defense attorneys argued that Pomroy died when the respirator was cut off, not from the beating administered by the defendant. New York penal laws did not adequately define the condition of death at the time. "A court will be obligated to charge the jury...at least giving them a criterion that they can use to determine for them the question of fact, that is, when did death occur?" O'Brien said.

The case was tried before Justice George F.X. McInerney of the State Supreme Court, in Riverhead, Long Island. During deliberations, the judge sent the jury back to reconsider the matter after they reported that they were hopelessly deadlocked and unable to reach a verdict. Then, on May 27, 1977, the jury found Carey Guilty of murder. On June 20, Carey was sentenced to twenty-four years to life in prison. In passing sentence, Judge McInerney said, "If the assailant's conduct is proven to be a sufficiently direct contributing cause of death, he may be held criminally responsible for the death and his criminal responsibility is not lessened or excused by the existence of another contributing cause or factor." See: **Quinlan, Karen Ann.** REF.: *CBA.*

Carfano, Anthony (AKA: **Little Augie Pisano**), 1899-1959, U.S., org. crime. Anthony Carfano, also known as Little Augie Pisano, began as a lowly gunman for Frankie Yale (Uale) in the 1920s, but after Yale was murdered in 1928, Carfano took over many of Yale's bootlegging and gambling operations in Brooklyn. He then became a top lieutenant for Joe Adonis and Frank Costello. After Charles "Lucky" Luciano went to prison in 1936, Costello took over Luciano's New York Mafia family with Carfano as his underboss. In the late 1930s, Costello and Adonis sent Carfano to eastern Florida, where he organized widespread gambling and opened several posh spas and hotels, the most elegant being the Wofford Hotel in Miami.

By the late 1950s, Carfano was managing a multimillion-dollar gambling empire in east Florida, with Santo Trafficante controlling most of

Anthony Carfano

that state, lucrative territory which Mafia interloper Vito Genovese coveted. At the time, Genovese was battling Costello for control of the old Luciano Mafia family and the rackets it operated in New York. Genovese sent a gunman to kill Costello but the would-be killer, Vincent "The Chin" Gigante, missed his target, only wounding Costello. The "Prime Minister of the Underworld," as Costello was called, sent word to all the top Mafia leaders in his family, asking them to rally around him in his fight with the vicious Genovese. None responded except Anthony Carfano, who flew to New York and held strategy conferences with his boss, Costello.

Genovese learned of this and exploded, ordering his top killer, Anthony Strollo, better known as Tony Bender, to kill Carfano. The unsuspecting Carfano accepted a dinner invitation from Strollo on Sept. 25, 1959. Carfano, accompanied by the blonde, Janice Drake, a former Miss New Jersey, attended a dinner in a Queens restaurant which was hosted by Strollo. Also attending were Al Segal and Vincent Mauro. In the middle of the meal, Carfano received a phone call which was reportedly from Costello, who informed his aide that Strollo and Mauro planned to murder him that night. Carfano returned to the table, grabbed Janice Drake by the arm, and told Strollo that he was called away "on urgent business." Both Carfano and Drake were found in Carfano's car a few hours later, shot to death. The car was parked near La Guardia Airport, and it was believed that Carfano was attempting to fly back to Miami to escape Genovese's killers. See: **Adonis, Joe; Costello, Frank; Genovese, Vito; Luciano, Charles; Yale, Frank.**

REF.: Bonanno, *A Man of Honor;* Cohen, *Mickey Cohen: In My Own Words;* Eisenberg and Landau, *Meyer Lansky;* Fried, *The Rise and Fall of the Jewish Gangster in America;* Gage, *Mafia, USA;* Gosch and Hammer, *The Last Testament of Lucky Luciano;* Katz, *Uncle Frank;* Levine, *Anatomy of a Gangster;* Maas, *The Valachi Papers;* Martin, *Revolt in the Mafia;* Messick, *Lansky;* Messick and Goldblatt, *The Mobs and the Mafia;* Peterson, *The Mob;* Reid, *The Grim Reapers;* Thompson and Raymond, *Gang Rule in New York.*

Cargill, Donald, b.c.1619-81, Scot., treas. Spoke out against King Charles II's Declaration of Indulgence, which provoked Parliament into enacting repressive measures including the Conventicle Act. During an uprising at Bothwell Bridge in 1679, he was severely wounded by Scottish Covenanters. He joined forces with Richard Cameron, founder of a sect of Reformed Presbyterians, to declare Charles II deposed and excommunicated for his many betrayals of the faith. In 1681 he was beheaded on a charge of treason. REF.: *CBA.*

Cargin, Julia Ann, b.1834, and **Alexander, Norris,** b.1858, **Cargin, Freeman,** b. 1852, and **Smith, Mary Jane,** b.1845, U.S., mur. On the banks of the Shiawassee River a mile off the Corunna Road in Saginaw County, Mich., a farmer named Charles Smith owned forty acres of land. His wife Mary Jane was a lonely, frustrated woman who had suffered through an unhappy ten-year marriage to Smith.

In time she became infatuated with a young farmhand named Norris Alexander, who had gone to work for Smith following his discharge from the house of correction in Detroit on a conviction for larceny. Mary Jane Smith became Alexander's lover, and soon he began to suggest that they murder her husband. They talked of poisoning and shooting the man, but neither had the courage to see it through. In the early spring months of 1876, Mrs. Smith's sister, Julia Ann, came to visit from her home in New York. Anxious to see her sister content, she promised to find someone to murder Charles Smith for an agreed price of $500. In August, Julia Ann Cargin and her new husband, Freeman Cargin, turned up at the farm to visit the Smiths. They were on their honeymoon.

Mary Jane and her sister went to Corunna to take out a mortgage on a farm she owned in Maple Grove in order to raise the $500 fee. On the night of Sept. 12, Cargin and Alexander entered Smith's bedroom shortly after midnight armed with a bludgeon and a strap. Mary Jane retreated from the room seconds before her young lover assaulted her husband. There was a quick, violent struggle. Alexander struck two blows to the man's head, but then Mr. Cargin seized the club and finished Smith off. They took the body to a bed of straw in the hay barn, and started a fire. Alexander slipped back into the hotel in Chesaning, where he later claimed to have passed the night.

The charred corpse was found the next day. Traces of blood found near the body indicated that the victim died of violence. Suspicion was cast on Mrs. Smith when she began making inquiries about the status of her husband's land holdings following his death. A neighbor named Joseph Miller stated that he had observed two men leave the farmhouse to go into the barn about twenty minutes before the fire.

Alexander, the Cargins, and Mary Jane were arrested and taken to the Saginaw city jail. Each of the defendants was given a separate trial, which commenced before Justice J.M. Clark in

Saginaw City on Dec. 11, 1876. Mary Jane, who had initiated the whole affair, agreed to testify against her sister in return for a reduced sentence. She was found Guilty of second-degree murder and received fifteen years at hard labor in the Jackson penitentiary. Julia and Freeman Cargin were each sentenced to life imprisonment at hard labor, and young Alexander received just ten years.

"Can you not see the injustice?" wailed Julia Cargin. "I, who have done nothing, sentenced to life, and my sister, who has done it all, receive so paltry a sentence. I am an innocent woman and never wronged man or woman...But mark you. I swear by the living God that she will not live with him (Alexander) more than half a dozen years before he will share poor Charlie's fate! A woman who will kill one man when she tires of him, will tire of and kill another." There is no record of what awful fate, if any, befell Norris Alexander following his release from prison.

REF.: *CBA; The Chesaning Murder.*

Carigiola, Luigi, 1878-c.1930, Italy, mur. A barrel maker in Rome, Luigi Carigola learned in 1930 that he was tenth in line to inherit his uncle's business, a small manufacturing plant. With this in mind, he gave a supper for his uncle and the nine others in his uncle's will, poisoning the pasta with strychnine. The uncle and all the members of the family died in agony a short time later. When examining physicians determined that strychnine had been used and suspicion was focused upon Carigiola, the barrel maker fled, a few steps ahead of police. It was later reported that he had drowned himself in November 1930, but this was never confirmed.

REF.: *CBA.*

Caritat, Marie-Jean-Antoine-Nicolas de (Marquis de Condorcet), 1743-94, Fr., rebel. Biographer of Voltaire and a member of the Legislative Assembly from 1791-92, supporting the Girondist faction. As a consequence, he was forced into hiding by the radical Jacobins from 1792-94. He was arrested with other Girondists in 1794, and died in prison that same year. REF.: *CBA.*

Caritativo, Bart, 1906-58, U.S., mur. Many wealthy Californians employed male servants from the Philippines. Bart Caritativo, one such houseboy, worked in a large home in Stinson Beach, a suburb north of San Francisco. He became friendly with the housekeeper at the house next door, who had the good luck to marry her employer. The homeowner soon died and left her his fortune. Caritativo continued his friendship with this lady, Camille Malmgren.

Murderer Bart Caritativo.

Malmgren was soon remarried to an Englishman named Joseph Banks, an alcoholic. During the next several years she committed him to an institution for treatment a number of times. She ultimately divorced Banks, though he continued to live in her Stinson Beach house. In September 1954, Camille Banks decided to leave the country for a while. A neighbor came by to see her just before she left on her trip and found her dead in her bedroom, her skull split open. Banks lay dead in the living room, surrounded by empty liquor bottles. In his hand was the handle of a large knife which was stuck in his stomach.

Among the papers police located in the house was a suicide note signed by Banks which read, "I am responsible to what you see and find." Another was Camille Banks' will, leaving everything to Caritativo. It, too, contained grammatical errors and awkward misspellings. Don Midyett of the San Rafael sheriff's department compared Caritativo's handwriting with that on the documents and, when experts found them the same, arrested Caritativo for murder.

Caritativo's trial began in January 1955. The major evidence against him were the handwritten documents and the testimony of a pathologist that Banks, thoroughly drunk, could not have killed his wife or himself. When Caritativo saw things going against him, he fired his lawyer, telling the court, "I have lost the trust to my attorneys," misusing the word "to" as it had been misused in Banks' so-called suicide note. The jury found Caritativo Guilty of murder in the first degree. He was executed at San Quentin on Oct. 24, 1958.

REF.: Boucher, *The Quality of Murder; CBA;* de Ford, *Murderers Sane and Mad;* McComas, *The Graveside Companion;* Nash, *Bloodletters and Badmen.*

Carland, John Emmett, 1853-1922, U.S., jur. District attorney in the Dakota Territory from 1885-88. He was appointed to the Dakota Territorial Supreme Court by President Grover Cleveland in 1888; to the court of the district of South Dakota from 1896-1910; to the Commerce Court by President William Howard Taft from 1910-13; and then the U.S. Court of Appeals, Eighth Circuit in 1913. REF.: *CBA.*

Carlile, John Snyder, 1817-78, U.S., lawyer. Helped shape the statehood of West Virginia prior to his election to the Senate in 1861. REF.: *CBA.*

Carlile, Richard, 1790-1843, Brit., sedition. Disciple of the U.S. political philosopher Thomas Paine, he was imprisoned for publishing the collective works of Paine, and several newspapers considered seditious by the government, including *Political Litany* and *The Republican.* He issued the publication even though his wife, sister, and several of the printers were jailed as a consequence. From 1830-35 he was jailed for refusing to pay church taxes. REF.: *CBA.*

Carlin, Helen (AKA: Red Helen), d.1954, Brit., (unsolv.) mur. Carlin was a Pimlico prostitute found strangled in her room on Lillington Street on Sept. 6, 1954. The killer used a nylon stocking and had left behind four packages of American cigarettes, which may have indicated that he was attached to the U.S. armed services.

A street peddler named Jackie Hillsley, who sold flowers in Piccadilly, told of a U.S. soldier who bought carnations from her while in the company of Helen Carlin. Superintendent William Judge of the CID was unable to locate a suspect after touring a number of U.S. military bases located throughout Britain, and the case was filed as "unsolved."

REF.: *CBA;* Furneaux, *Famous Criminal Cases, Vol. 2.*

Carlin, William, and Flores, Tony, prom. 1910, U.S., wh. slav. The arrest of Tony Flores and William Carlin, two San Francisco men who had lured a girl into prostitution, shed new light on the West Coast white slave traffic.

The two men met the 16-year-old girl, identified in the press as "Miss Emerson," near the corner of Seventh and Market in December 1909. She was new to the city, as many girls who fell into the hands of the white slave gangs were, and she had no visible means of support. They told her to proceed to a Sixth Street "hotel" where Ethel Day would offer her meaningful employment. Emerson was advised to lie and say she was twenty years old.

Detective R.V. McSorley of the San Francisco police arrested the pair. During questioning, Flores admitted to placing the girl in the bordello, but accused Carlin of planning the abduction. The case went to trial on May 10, 1910, and the chief witness against the pair was the girl's mother, who testified that her daughter was a minor. REF.: *CBA.*

Carlisi, Sam Anthony (AKA: Wings), 1921- , U.S., fraud-org. crime. Sam Carlisi is the duly appointed "messenger of the mobsters." A one-time chauffeur and bodyguard to Chicago crime boss Joseph "Doves" Aiuppa, Carlisi has emerged as a trusted courier between the top echelons of the Chicago crime family and the armies of foot-soldiers and armed sluggers roaming the streets of the city. So good was he at disseminating information through the ranks that his associates began calling him Wings. His brother Roy is attached to the Buffalo crime family.

In 1984, Carlisi was convicted of income tax fraud. His alleged gambling activities in Cook County have caused him to be barred from the Chicago horse-racing tracks.

Carlisi's peculiarities of personality are legend. When observed in local restaurants, he is always wearing a fedora. It is said that Wings Carlisi is so tight with a dollar that he will fly economy class at three in the morning to avoid paying extra. In 1988, the Justice Department began an investigation into the activities of top Chicago mobsters including Aiuppa, John "Jacky" Cerone, John "No Nose" DiFronzo, and Sam Carlisi. See: **Aiuppa, Joseph.** REF.: *CBA*.

Carlisle, John Griffin, 1835-1910, U.S., lawyer. Member of the House of Representatives from 1877-90, and speaker from 1883-89. REF.: *CBA*.

Carlisle, William, 1890-1963, U.S., rob. Born on May 4, 1890, in Chester, Pa., William Carlisle was the last of the old western train bandits, beginning his career when such exploits were mostly legends of the past. In 1916, armed with a toy gun, Carlisle boarded a westbound luxury liner and entered the lounge car, holding up the startled passengers, leaping off the observation platform just as the train was getting up speed. His take was a little more than $50. On the night of Feb. 4, 1916, Carlisle boarded the *Portland Rose,* a luxury train of the Union Pacific, headed for Chicago. This time he carried a real gun. He placed a handkerchief over his face before entering the smoking car, poking the pistol into the back of a porter, ordered the man to pass through the car with his hat outstretched. He then shouted to the passengers: "This is a holdup. Get out your wallets and throw them into the cap." To emphasize his threat, Carlisle fired a shot into the ceiling and the passengers quickly offered their wallets. (This would be Carlisle's standard robbery procedure in the future.) When a woman frantically tried to remove her rings, Carlisle stepped forth and said: "Keep your jewelry, lady. Robbing women is something I don't do."

Carlisle moved into the next car, a Pullman, the cowed porter leading the way. The bandit ignored several women in compartments, robbing four men of their wallets. When conductor J.J. Fitzgerald saw the bandit with the gun and mask, he pulled the emergency cord and the train jerked to a halt. Carlisle jumped off the train, landed in a snow drift and disappeared in a snowstorm. The act of the conductor was providential in that a sheriff and four deputies were waiting at the next stop to board the train to apprehend a passenger suspected of being a forger.

On Apr. 4, Carlisle struck again, this time entering the lounge of a fast-moving train outside of Laramie, Wyo. He picked up wallets from male passengers who were holding up their hands, but when he came to a war veteran with an empty sleeve, he apologetically stated: "I beg your pardon," and told him to keep his money, as he did with all the female passengers present. A conductor at the end of the car wrote a desperate note explaining that the train was being robbed and threw this off at a small station. The telegraph operator there notified the next town where a large posse gathered to capture the bandit, but by then Carlisle had already jumped from the train and vanished.

William J. Jeffers, president of Union Pacific, had by then, hired several private detectives to track down the daring bandit. His own chief of detectives, John G. Gale, was ordered to capture the bandit at all costs. Gale was joined by W.J. McClements, the railway's top detective in the Denver area, and more than 300 possemen were hired to search for the train robber. Carlisle, meanwhile, was luxuriating in Denver, living with two prostitutes, taking guitar lessons and, oddly, teaching Sunday school lessons to a group of children in an impoverished area of the city. When newspapers announced that police had arrested an ex-convict and considered him a strong suspect, Carlisle sent a letter to the Denver *Post,* stating: "I plan to hold up the next Union Pacific train west of Laramie just to show the cops that they're holding the wrong man." He signed the letter: "The White Bandit." To prove that the letter was not a hoax, Carlisle enclosed a watch chain taken in his latest holdup.

Police did not act on this warning, concluding that the bandit had stipulated the Laramie area as a ruse, that he would raid elsewhere once lawmen concentrated in the Laramie district. Carlisle had correctly assumed the police would think this, and the next day he held up a train in the Laramie area, robbing the lounge car of a Union Pacific train and announcing to his victims that he was the one who had written the letter promising to rob the very train upon which they rode. Carlisle's bravado, however, was his undoing. A rancher saw the note the bandit had sent to the *Post,* reproduced on the front page, and he recognized the odd handwriting as that of a ranch hand who had worked for him in the past, a man named Will Carlisle. He gave a full description of Carlisle to the police, and plainclothes guards were placed in all the smokers and lounge cars of the Union Pacific.

A few days later, a guard was sitting next to an affable young man in one of the lounges on the fast-moving *Pacific Limited.* He began a conversation with the young man, the guard stupidly explaining why he was present, adding: "If that guy with the white mask shows up here, he'll find me ready for him." At the next stop the guard got off the train to have a smoke and then heard a women scream. He jumped back onto the train and was met by a man wearing a white mask and pointing a gun at him. The bandit said: "You're meeting Carlisle right here!" He took the guard's gun and then proceeded to rob the passengers in the lounge and in the next two Pullman cars, leaping from the train as it approached a tunnel. He landed awkwardly, however, and sprained his ankle.

When the train arrived at Walcott Station, William Haynes, town marshal, was notified, and he quickly assembled a posse, the horsemen riding back down the tracks and then following Carlisle's tracks. He was on foot, limping painfully along the banks of the North Platte River. Haynes and his men, after several days of tracking, cornered Carlisle who threw down his gun and raised his hands, limping forward.

"You Bill Carlisle?" asked Haynes.

"I'm Carlisle, all right," the bandit replied.

"The train bandit?" Haynes said, pointing his six-gun at Carlisle.

"Sure, I held up all those trains. It was good sport. I liked getting the best of you coppers, until now."

"Let's see how much good sport you have doing time in the pen," snorted Haynes, taking Carlisle into custody. The bandit was quickly tried and convicted, sentenced to life imprisonment in the Wyoming State Penitentiary at Rawlins. A model prisoner, the easy-going, compliant Carlisle quickly convinced his warders that he was repentant and intended to reform. Prison officials notified the govenor that Carlisle showed promise of complete reforming, and his sentence, after he had served two years, was reduced to twenty-five years, making him eligible for parole in ten. Yet this term seemed too long to him and, on Nov. 15, 1919, he squeazed into an empty box sitting among the boxes of goods being shipped out of the prison. He later pried open the box to see that he was on a deserted platform in Rawlins. He slipped out of the box and found a vacant cabin nearby. Inside he found clothing, food, and a revolver. Changing from his prison uniform, Carlisle hopped a freight train to Rock River.

At this stop he boarded a passenger train and drew his gun. As he entered the smoker he was startled to see it crowded with soldiers returning from duty in Europe, all of them armed with rifles. Carlisle, still the bold bandit, regained his self-confidence and announced: "I'm a train robber and I don't rob soldiers or women but don't reach for those guns." With that he turned on his heel and went into the next car where he robbed several male passengers, taking more than $500. But as the bandit leaped from the moving train, landing in a snow bank, dozens of bullets whizzed past him. The soldiers were leaning from the windows of the train, firing at him as the train sped past. One bullet struck him in the arm, another in the hand. Carlisle dove behind a snow bank and then ran into some woods. He found a farmhouse and told the farmer that he had been wounded in a hunting accident. Hundreds of possemen were now scouring the countryside for the infamous bandit, but they came up empty-handed. Then, some days later, Union Pacific officials in Cheyenne, Wyo., received a telegram which had been sent from Casper, Wyo. It read: "Thanks for the haul on your limited. Some detective force. Carlisle." Carlisle then began sending messages to several police departments, including Chicago and San Francisco. The letters contained old newspaper clippings of Carlisle's arrest, showing him handcuffed to Marshal Haynes. He wrote on the clippings: "I'll be with you bulls soon!" The letters were verified as having been sent by Carlisle when his handwriting was compared with the messages.

Carlisle never went to any of those cities but hid out with a woodsman in the Wyoming wilds. Hundreds of lawmen and militia searched for weeks for him until Sheriff A.S. Roach and his posse tracked Carlisle to the cabin where he was hiding. The bandit stepped outside and Roach promptly shot him through the chest, later claiming that the outlaw had drawn his gun. The hardy Carlisle nevertheless recovered and was sent back to the penitentiary in Rawlins where he told the warden that he was truly reformed. From that point on, Carlisle was a model prisoner. In 1932, after prison chaplain, the Reverend Gerald Schellenger wrote to the governor on his behalf, Calisle's sentence was reduced so that he was paroled on Jan. 9, 1936. He was given a full pardon in 1947 and lived out his life in Laramie, Wyo., where he operated a tourist camp.

REF.: American Guide Series, *Wyoming, A Guide to Its History, Highways, and People;* Block, *Great Train Robbers of the West;* Carlisle, *Bill Carlisle, Lone Bandit; CBA;* Howe, *Rocky Mountain Empire;* Linford, *Wyoming, Frontier State;* Mazulla, *Outlaw Album;* Winn, *The Macadam Trail.*

Carlos, See: **Sanchez, Ilyich Ramirez.**

King Carlos of Portugal, and his son, Crown Prince Luis, assassinated in 1908.

Carlos I, 1863-1908 (and Crown Prince **Luis**), King of Port., assass. Son of King Louis I and Maria Pia, Carlos was an expansive, fun-loving monarch who indulged himself in almost every extravagance and, in the process, ignored the real needs of Portugal. During his reign (1899-1908), Carlos allowed a venal and utterly corrupt government to flagrantly loot the public treasury, increase impossible taxes, and mock the very laws it was supposed to enforce. Financial speculation, bribery, and outright theft marked Carlos' administration. The king himself seemed oblivious to such corruption, spending millions on his palaces, expensive trips abroad, lavish fetes, and parties. He grew fat and more pompous with each passing day; the average citizen condemned him openly. Finally, in 1907, Carlos realized that the Cortes (the Portugese Parliament) was out of control, in the grip of landed aristocrats who refused to pay any taxes and did as they pleased, its members openly daring the king to challenge them. Carlos looked about for a strong man to bring the Cortes into line and found 52-year-old João Franco, leader of the Regenerator Party.

Franco, a rigid, uncompromising politician, became prime minister. After a year, he informed the king that there was nothing he could do with the corrupt Cortes, except to suspend it and assume the role of virtual dictator. In that capacity, he explained, he would have the power to root out all the corrupt land owners and reestablish a law-abiding Cortes. Carlos nodded his approval and Franco closed the parliament. To support the enlarged army he claimed he needed to suppress regional revolt, taxes were again increased. Moreover, Franco scandalized his administration by cancelling an enormous public debt owed by the king and increasing his own enormous salary. His police and troops suppressed all political opposition, arresting so many political dissidents that the state prisons and the Caxias Fortress were bursting with prisoners. A popular Republican uprising in Oporto was mercilessly crushed by Franco's troops but opposition and the threat of assassination were everywhere. A man pelted King Carlos with stones as he rode in his carriage through the streets of Lisbon; this man was labelled a lunatic and shut up in an asylum. The doctor who certified the assailant was assaulted and his house nearly blown up.

Queen Marie Amélie, the wealthy daughter of the Count of Paris, whom Carlos had married in 1886, became just as unpopular as her portly husband. She received threatening anonymous letters from her own palace servants. The queen confided her fears in a letter to a friend: "What an ugly business life is. What baseness surrounds us on every side! The very people who fawn upon us in our presence go out and besmirch us and try to injure us. Franco is in the right, I suppose, but he is very clumsy in his methods." Carlos, on the other hand, gave no indication that the repressive measures taken by his hand-picked dictator were bringing his country to the brink of revolution. He blithely signed, without reading, some said, all the liberty-crushing decrees Franco put before him and still insisted upon walking and riding about Lisbon as if his subjects still respected and loved him. He strode about, adorned in his magnificent uniforms, his heavily-waxed mustache turned upward in the Prussian manner, a stern look on his face, ignoring the hostile stares and angry faces that greeted him without salutation or friendship as in days of old.

The dictator Franco was also indifferent to the massive hostility he had incurred among the population. After learning that several plots to kill him were afoot, Franco snorted: "Attempts at murder prove nothing. Suppose I am assassinated. What does that prove against my ideas?" To a group of Republican extremists who were also members of the Carbonari, a secret nationalist society (see entry), assassination would release Portugal from the grip of a tyrant and an unwanted king. This group was led by 30-year-old Manuel Buica, a schoolteacher and an ex-sergeant of the 7th Cavalry. Buica, an expert rifleman who had won prizes for his marksmanship from the hands of the king, was a widower with a 7-year-old daughter. His motives for forming the assassination plot were never made clear. He was joined by several craftsmen, the most notable being Alfredo Costa, an ironmonger and editor of a small revolutionary newspaper.

There was little or no secret made of the plot to kill the king. A story later widely spread had a stranger walking the streets of Lisbon on Feb. 1, 1908, and suddenly being surprised at the sound of gunfire nearby. Asking a passerby about the shooting, he was told with a casual shrug: "Oh, they're assassinating the king." The police had broken up a Republican plot on Jan. 29, 1908, arresting several conspirators but none of these belonged to the Buica group. The assassins made plans to kill Carlos and Franco on Feb. 1, 1908, attacking him with revolvers as his cortège entered the largest and famous square, the Praça. The king and queen had just returned from a country estate and were riding in a four-horse open carriage with their two grown sons, Prince Luis and Prince Manoel. The carriage moved off on its two-mile trip toward the Necessidades Palace. Thousands of citizens lined the route but stood in strange silence as the carriage slowly went by, with few waving or cheering, almost as if the entire population of Lisbon knew that this was to be their monarch's last ride, that he would momentarily be murdered.

The assassins, perhaps as many as ten—the true number was never learned—waited beneath the huge arches at the Rua do Arsenal which faced the Praça. When the king's carriage came into the square, Costa raced from beneath an arch, a revolver in his hand, slammed through the crowds and jumped onto the footrest of the carriage. As he did so, Carlos began to stand up in the carriage, and Costa shot him point-blank in the neck. The queen then cried out so loudly that she was heard through the ranks of the horrified spectators. When Carlos began to fall, she stood up and began to beat the assassin with a large bouquet of camellias and violets she had been given upon her return to the city. The carriage began to race forward, Costa clinging to it, managing to fire a second shot which struck the king in the back. Police by then had grabbed the killer who was thrown to the ground. Costa fired a third shot which went wild and the police shot him to death.

Inside the carriage, the queen was hysterically screaming. Carlos was slumped to the floor, blood gushing from his wounds, dying. His two sons had drawn their revolvers just as Buica leaped forward, firing a rifle twice, the two bullets striking Crown Prince Luis in the head and chest, killing him. Prince Manoel fired his revolver four times at Bruica at almost the same moment, striking the assassin in the arm. Buica still managed to fire another shot from his rifle, this wounding Prince Manoel. All of the males of the royal family were now dead or wounded, lying inside the fast-moving carriage, its frightened horses stampeding. The queen bravely stood in the carriage shielding the bodies of her husband and sons with her own body.

Carriages behind the royal coach rushed forward and guard officers jumped from these, attempting to protect the monarchs by running alongside it. A lady-in-waiting raced from one of these carriages and jumped into the royal coach to help the queen who was beside herself, shouting to the young woman: "Go away! Go away! I don't want you to be killed, too!" The carriage, struck by twelve bullets from other assassins who fired from the dense ranks of the crowds, was driven wildly out of the Praça, and down the Rua do Arsenal, its passengers bloodied and dying. The royal House of Braganza lay in a heap on its floor.

Buica, the mastermind assassin, attempted to flee through the crowd but was grabbed by a soldier, Private Alvaro Siloa Valente, who held Buica by the throat as one of the king's aides, Captain Carlos Figueiro, raced forward and drew his sword, striking the assassin with it, slashing away at Buica. As he fell under these blows, the assassin managed to squeeze off two more shots from his rifle, wounding Figueiro in the leg and Valente in the thigh. A policeman ran forward and shot Buica twice but the die-hard assassin struggled with the officer for his revolver, biting the policeman so hard on the hand that he drew blood. Figueiro hacked away at him with the sword until the much-wounded Buica fell to the cobblestones unconscious. He died a few hours later.

The wounded driver of the royal carriage managed to bring the coach close to the Medical Hall where Carlos and his son Luis were quickly taken inside. Both were placed on mattresses and, within minutes, were pronounced dead by Dr. M. Moreira. Queen Amélie and her wounded son, Prince Manoel, were by then inside the nearby Weighing House and were informed of the deaths of Carlos and Luis. The queen sat holding her son whose arm was being bandaged; her face and dress were covered with blood. Both went to the Medical Hall an hour later where they were joined by the queen mother, Maria Pia. "My son, my poor child!" cried the queen mother when she saw the body of Carlos. Queen Amélie then echoed the cry, "My son, my poor child!" Queen Maria Pia turned to her and said: "*Your* son?" She looked to another area to see that her grandson Luis was also dead, and then collapsed in a faint.

Franco, who had also been marked for assassination, escaped death that day by failing to join the king's cortège, having been delayed by conversations with officials. He had dismissed his carriage and decided to walk home and, in doing so, had avoided

being murdered. Prince Manoel was declared to be the new king and the royal family, or what was left of it, departed for the palace. The body of Carlos I was propped up in an open carriage, held in a sitting position by an officer, while the body of Prince Luis was put into another open carriage and held in position by the young man's former tutor. The Queen and King Manoel followed in a closed carriage, heavily guarded by mounted cavalrymen and police. The grim procession made its way along the same route where the assassins had struck, a gruesome parade that was witnessed by thousands of startled citizens. The bodies lay in state for several days in the royal palace.

Meanwhile, police could find no trace of the half dozen or more assassins who had participated in the plot with the slain Buica and Costa. These conspirators were never found, despite an energetic search for them. It was assumed that some of these assassins were high-born men who planned to rid Portugal of a ruthless autocrat. The double assassination spelled the end for dictator Franco. He was summoned to the royal palace and there the queen mother chastised him: "You promised to release the monarchy from its tomb, and all that you have done is to dig the graves of my son and my grandson." Prince Alfonso, the dead king's brother, then stepped forward and had heated words with Franco, striking him in the face. Franco slapped the prince in response and both men tussled to the marble floor and had to be separated by guardsmen. Franco immediately resigned his post and was replaced by a liberal coalition promising immediate reform. Franco left Portugal on Feb. 5, 1908, accompanied by his wife and small son, vowing never to return. He went to France and then to Genoa, Italy, to live out his life in seclusion.

REF.: *CBA;* Corpechot, *Memories of Queen Amélie of Portugal;* Cunha, *Eight Centuries of Portugese Monarchy:* A Political Study; Gribble, *The Royal House of Portugal;* Hyams, *Killing No Murder;* Inchbold, *Lisbon and Cintra;* Nash, *Almanac of World Crime;* Salter, *Introducing Portugal;* Williams, *Heyday for Assassins.*

Carlos de Austria, Don, 1545-68, Spain, consp. Eldest son of Philip II and Maria of Portugal. Because he was thought to be unstable, his father denied him his right of succession. His father also annulled his marriage to Elizabeth of Valois, daughter of Henry II of France, so that he could marry her himself. After Carlos' plot to assassinate his father was uncovered, he fled to Spain, but was seized and imprisoned. His death in the cell remains a mystery. REF.: *CBA.*

Carlson, Gladys, d.1931, U.S., mur. In 1931, Gladys Carlson, the widow of bank robber Carl Carlson, was executed for murdering two policemen. She had been a willing accomplice with her husband in several robberies and never hesitated to draw her gun, especially when a policeman was involved. REF.: *CBA.*

Carlton, Harry (AKA: **Handsome Harry**), d.1888, U.S., mur. A legislative muddle in New York State nearly resulted in the legalization of murder for a six-month period in 1888-89. The controversy, which the U.S. Supreme Court was forced to arbitrate, involved the status of "Handsome" Harry Carlton, a convicted murderer scheduled to hang late in 1888.

The state legislature in Albany voted to substitute the electric chair for hanging as the manner of execution beginning on Jan. 1, 1889. The bill stated that convicted murderers could not be punished on the gallows after June 4, but beginning on Jan. 1, they would be executed in the chair. The legislators had unwittingly provided a six-month grace period for death row inmates, and an opportunity for Harry Carlton's attorney to save his client's life. He demanded that Carlton be freed on this technicality, which created a stir in the legal establishment, which discovered, to its horror, that the attorney had a valid point. But if Carlton were freed, all other killers slated for death would also have to be released.

The matter went before the U.S. Supreme Court, which ruled that no irregularity in the state legislature could be allowed to endanger the lives of innocent people. Death on the gallows would be permissible until the electric chair was ready for operation. On Dec. 23, 1888, Harry Carlton marched to the gallows in the courtyard of the Tombs, in New York City. One newspaper commented: "We are not at all sure that this hanging was entirely legal, but it certainly was justice." REF.: *CBA*.

Carlyle, Grace, prom. 1896, U.S., pros. An era of prosperity and unrestrained lawlessness began in 1890 in what had once been a collection of sleepy little mining towns when gold was discovered in Povery Gulch, Colo. In Cripple Creek, vice reigned supreme along Myers Avenue, and Pearl Sevan's bordello was known to all as "Old Faithful." One of the best-known residents of this bagnio was Grace Carlyle, who was said to dance naked on top of the piano in Grant Crumley's Branch Saloon, with the proper encouragement. Crumley and his brothers Sherman and Newt controlled the vice district, and were reputed to have robbed the Wells, Fargo coaches crossing the state.

The fast money and easy virtue of these free-wheeling times were best captured in the pages of the Cripple Creek *Crusher,* which noted that "such hilarious antics were nothing more than an expression of the natural ebullience of the world's richest mining camp and the increased potency of good Bourbon at high altitudes." REF.: *CBA*; Drago, *Notorious Ladies of the Frontier*.

Carmagnola (AKA: Francesco Bussone, Conte di Castelnuovo), b.c.1390-1432, Italy, treas. Commanded and led the army of Filippo Maria Visconti, the Duke of Milan. He regained the duchy of Milan shortly before his betrayal and defection to Venice. With the combined forces of Venice and Florence, he led an attack on Milan in 1436. He sustained heavy losses and was strongly suspected of collaborating with the Milanese forces. Convicted of treason by the Venetian Council of Ten, Carmagnola was put to death in 1432. REF.: *CBA*.

Carman, Mrs. Edwin, prom. 1914, Case of, U.S., mur. The mystery of the white-gloved murderer baffled Long Island police for many months, and then just faded into legend. The victim in this case was 36-year-old Louise Bailey, the beautiful wife of a wealthy New York manufacturer. She lived in Hempstead with her husband and two children.

In July 1914, Bailey paid a call on her physician, Dr. Edwin Carman. For several days she had been plagued by a condition not unlike malaria. Dr. Carman resided in the fashionable resort town of Freeport, populated by the shakers and movers of the financial world. Dr. Carman and his wife were well acquainted with the Baileys, both socially and professionally.

Louise Bailey waited in the anteroom for close to a half-hour. Then, just as the doctor emerged from his office to lead her into his examining room, there was the sound of shattering glass and a gunshot. Whirling around, Dr. Carman observed a white-gloved hand and a smoking pistol through the curtains. He tried to make his mortally wounded patient comfortable, but there was nothing he could do. Louise Bailey was shot through the heart.

A search of the grounds turned up no clues. The killer had simply vanished into air. Suspicion immediately fell on the doctor's wife, who was known to be a jealous, possessive woman. At the time of the shooting Mrs. Edwin Carman said she was fully dressed and lying on her bed upstairs. Yet her husband would swear to the fact that she was undressed when he had left her not long before.

The mystery deepened when Louise Bailey's husband said that he knew nothing about her visit to Dr. Carman. "Why was she getting treatment from him and the fact kept secret from me?" he wanted to know. There were many questions but few answers.

The police found a box of .38-caliber shells in the Carmans' attic, but the doctor said he never owned a gun. Detective William Burns arrived in Long Island to take personal charge of the case. America's foremost criminologist reconstructed the crime and concluded that Mrs. Carman had been the one to pull the trigger. The district attorney charged her with murder and produced a witness who claimed to have observed her lurking near the doctor's window at the time of the shooting. However, the testimony of this man Bardes was discredited when other witnesses said he was nowhere near the house when the shots rang out.

Mrs. Carman was arraigned on July 17. In October 1914, she went on trial for her life but was released when the jury could not reach a verdict. No one else was ever charged with the murder of Louise Bailey.
REF.: Adam, *Murder By Persons Unknown; CBA*.

Carmen, Jack Allen, 1949- , Case of, U.S., rape-mur. Fourteen-year-old Christie Lynn Mullins was beaten, raped, and killed on Aug. 23, 1975. The body of the pretty young teenager was found in a densely wooded area behind a Woolco store in the Graceland shopping mall of Columbus, Ohio. The remains were found by Henry Newell, Jr., who would later emerge as a secondary suspect. A composite police sketch was drawn from the memory of Newell and his wife who claimed to have "discovered" the corpse. Three days later, a severely retarded man named Jack Carmen, who had been a ward of the state since he was only three, was arrested and charged with murder.

Jack Carmen was charged with aggravated murder and rape after visiting the wooded area in the company of the police. He would later tell reporters that he confessed because the police "had been nice to him." Brought before Judge Frederick Williams in the Common Pleas Court on Sept. 3, 1975, Carmen entered a plea of Guilty. He was later allowed to withdraw the plea after a great public outcry against the court was registered by the Central Ohio Chapter of the American Civil Liberties Union.

Williams later withdrew from the case, and it was reassigned to Judge Fred Shoemaker, who issued a controversial ruling that declared Carmen competent to stand trial "with the benefit of extremely competent and experienced counsel." At the same time, Shoemaker ruled that Carmen's earlier confession was inadmissible. However, the Franklin County Court of Appeals in a later ruling handed down June 7, 1977, declared that Carmen's confession could be used against him in a trial. The appellate court cited an earlier precedent that said in part: "Miranda (ruling) does not mandate that a person of low intelligence may not waive his rights assuming that they have been properly explained to him."

This paved the way for the long-awaited murder trial, which began at the Franklin County Common Pleas Court in December 1977. Defense attorney David Riebel attempted to portray Henry Newell as the killer. Describing him as a "sick, vicious person," Riebel recounted Newell's past history of setting fires and then accusing someone else. It would have been easy, Riebel pointed out, for Newell to have returned home and devised an elaborate coverup scheme by enlisting his wife's support.

On Dec. 19, 1977, a Not Guilty verdict was returned by the jurors on the five-count indictment for murder filed against Jack Carmen. At the same time, the prosecution expressed its reluctance to pursue the matter any further. "Suppose we were to then try to try Henry Newell. We'd be blown out of the water in two minutes," surmised assistant county prosecutor Ronald O'Brien. The case was entered into the books as unsolved. REF.: *CBA*.

Carmody, John (AKA: John Davidson Carmen), prom. 1910, Brit., fraud. John Carmody arrived in the London financial district shortly before WWI. He was an enterprising youth of nineteen with a flair for high finance and a disposition to defraud unsuspecting investors.

He was arrested for the first time by London detectives for operating a "bucket shop" on Ludgate Hill. The business was called the "Anglo-American & Universal Exchange." Carmody would typically lure strangers into his swindle by notifying them of the recent passing of a "long-lost uncle" who had bequeathed them £1,000 in a recently filed will. The uncle's residence was usually listed as Australia. All the victim needed to do to receive the money was send Carmody a check to handle government taxes and duty.

While in the employ of a stock brokerage firm, Carmody invented his own rich uncle and drew £60 as the usual "fee" for beginning a series of financial transactions. By the time the brokers detected the swindle, £3,000 and Carmody had long since vanished.
REF.: *CBA*; Nicholls, *Crime Within the Square Mile*.

Carnera Boxing Scandal, 1930s, U.S., org. crime. In the most manly of sports, or so it was called by bare-knuckle enthusiasts, the boxer was the head-to-head hero from the 1890s to the 1930s. Yet at the beginning of the Great Depression, after Jack Dempsey had been knocked out (or was almost knocked out in the still debatable "Long Count") and Gene Tunney retired from the ring, a lackluster period enveloped boxing, and through the gloom of these lengthening shadows moved sinister mobsters who intended to take over the sport and manipulate it for gambling fortunes. They almost succeeded at forever sullying the sport. The tool employed by the gangsters was a behemoth Italian fighter who stood six-feet-seven-inches, weighed 268 pounds, and had the punch of a 10-year-old boy.

Primo Carnera with the doomed Ernie Schaaf, weighing in.

Primo Carnera (1907-67), born in Italy, was oversized from birth, and many in his village considered him a glandular freak. While still a teenager, he towered over the heads of the tallest grown men of the community. Primo was apprenticed as a mosaic-maker, but a promoter passing through his village noticed his enormous bulk—arms as thick as thighs, thighs as thick as young oak trees—and persuaded the youth that he could make a handsome living by appearing in a traveling circus as a strong man and Greco-Roman wrestler.

Carnera, a good-willed, simple-minded person, nodded grinning approval and went off with the circus, where he was trained to be a wrestler and stand on midway platforms rippling his biceps. It was while the circus was in the South of France that French boxing promoter-manager Leon See spotted the giant and immediately convinced him to become a boxer. Carnera, of course, had no natural ability as a prizefighter—no punch, no speed, no ring savvy. Yet, he was easily conned by the shrewd and wily See into believing he could become one of the world's great fighters if he boxed defensively and used his enormous size to wear down opponents.

By the late 1920s, Carnera was appearing in club fights in Paris, all of them against boxers who were woefully smaller and weighed less than the giant and with whom Leon See had apparently arranged to have their fights thrown. His first important fight was with Moise Bouquillon who weighed 174 pounds, almost ninety pounds less than the stalking Carnera.

It was obvious to those attending the fight in the underground club Salle Wagram that Carnera could not hurt or dominate the smaller fighter. He stumbled about, throwing round-house rights and lefts that were mere taps to Bouquillon's jaw. The only effective weapon Carnera had was his huge body, which he used, also ineffectively, in attempting to crowd his opponent into a corner and trap him there and club him, a technique which did not work.

On the other hand, Leon See had carefully chosen Bouquillon, as he would many another adversary, because the smaller man could not punch at all and would not hurt the awkward giant towering above him. The fight ended in a split decision, but the wise ones at ringside knew it was a setup for the giant Carnera. One of those witnessing this shameful display at the Salle Wagram was American sportswriter Paul Gallico who would, for years to come, doggedly point out the fact that Carnera was a fake fighter, that he had no punch at all.

Gallico's presence at the Paris fight was not lost on Walter "Good Time Charley" Friedman, a Broadway character who was given his sobriquet by Damon Runyon and who was on hand at the Salle Wagram to work with See in bringing Carnera to America as the new terror of the ring. Friedman was later to moan to Gallico, as quoted in *Farewell to Sport:* "Boy, was that a lousy break for us that you come walking into that Salle Wagram that night and see that the big guy can't punch! Just that night you hadda be there. Leon wanted to see if he could go ten rounds without falling down. And you hadda be there. We coulda got away with a lot more if you don't walk in there and write stories about how he can't punch." As it turned out, Friedman and a bevy of New York gangsters got away with quite a lot, including the heavyweight boxing championship of the world.

Carnera himself, it was speculated by some, never knew he was a fake boxer. The uneducated, good-natured giant was kept under close watch by See's trainers and guards, much more so when he arrived in the U.S. in 1930. He was told every moment that he had the punch of ten boxers, that he could knock out anyone, even though the years of wrestling had set his muscles so that his best punch, a right uppercut, was equal to a slap in the face with open palm by Joe Louis, if that. Carnera, it was true, was able to take incredible punishment to the body without letup and feel no pain. His massive torso was solid as concrete, which his opponents were soon to discover. His chin, however, was completely vulnerable. One good punch to the jaw, and not necessarily a powerhouse blow, would sent the giant sprawling. His managers, trainers, and controllers knew this and made sure that no boxer ever dared a blow to that part of Carnera's body.

By the time Carnera appeared in New York, Friedman and See were joined in partnership by arch hoodlums Big Frenchy DeMange and Owney "The Killer" Madden, both bootleg kingpins who sought to take over boxing through the impressive but helpless giant. Named as director for Carnera's first coast-to-coast tour was Broadway Bill Duffy, a crafty, conniving thug who put Carnera on display as one might exhibit a white elephant.

First, a whole new set of trainers were hired, all diminutive men, along with sparing partners who were also small and would make Carnera appear in press photographs to be even larger and more imposing than his actual six feet, seven inches. Photos were taken of the giant with outstretched arms as two smaller boxers perched on his biceps. He was outfitted in specially made black trunks which were emblazoned with the head of a wild boar and stitched in red silk. Carnera's impressive physique was exposed at every opportunity. Instead of wearing a boxer's robe, he wore a short, silk, sleeveless vest of glaring green and a silk, green cap with a great visor that was purposely made several sizes too small for him to also make his head and large face seem even more massive.

The press was kept at bay by Carnera's handlers who told newsmen that the giant boxer was embarrassed to talk with reporters because of his faulty English, one of the few truths his handlers ever uttered. In this respect, Carnera's ignorance of his own lack of power and ability and the fact that he was being used as a pawn by the mob did not come to light at the beginning of his American boxing career. It was highly doubtful that the giant ever really understood how he had been used, brutalized, robbed, and discarded until that disastrous career was shattered.

Carnera's U.S. career began in the heart of boxing, at Madison Square Garden, when Carnera met Big Boy Peterson, a heavyweight who was also known simply as "The Swede." This fight was a blatant tank job, obvious to even the most unsophisticated of boxing fans. Peterson did exactly what he had been told to do—throw body punches which bounced harmlessly off the lumbering Carnera. He stayed away from the giant's jaw, which became increasingly apparent in round one where Carnera seldom kept up his guard and jutted that inhuman jaw forward, inviting a tap which never came. Primo stumbled forward with an idiot's grin affixed to his face, which later became a symbol of the good-natured fighter, and landed a few blows on Peterson. He struck his opponent more with his shoulders and hips than he did with his gloved hands.

Round after round proceeded in this manner, until the entire arena was heavy with hisses and catcalls. The word "fix" was repeated so many times that patrons were at a loss to think of another word for the ridiculous charade presented to them. Half way through the play-acting, Peterson, in desperation, dropped his guard and practically invited Carnera to hit him, running up to the giant, asking to be floored, as it were. Carnera finally got the idea and *pushed* Peterson in the face, which sent the heavyweight toppling to the canvas; the Swede pretended he had been struck by a steel girder. One sports scribe later sarcastically remarked that "the Swede hit himself a punch on the jaw as he went down. Someone had to hit him."

The fraud of this Carnera win was obvious to everyone, yet the press treated the fight as a joke instead of a serious boxing swindle that promised even greater frauds to come. Moreover, the New York State Athletic Commission, fully aware of the shameful Carnera-Peterson fiasco, made no comment even though officers of this organization had the power to immediately bar Carnera and his crooked managers and handlers from the ring forever. That, of course, was the point. Madden, DeMange, and Duffy had reached certain members and paid them off, or threatened them with injury or worse, should they protest. The gangsters had moved into control of the sport to make millions, which they did.

Following the Peterson setup, Carnera began his coast-to-coast tour, heavily advertised by mobsters. He drew enormous crowds in more than twenty cities and the money, estimated between $700,000 and $2 million, flowed into the hands of Carnera's corrupt directors. The boxer himself received only a few dollars pocket money. While his managers and trainers slept and ate in the best hotels and restaurants, Carnera was boarded into small, run-down cottages, given all the spaghetti he could eat and, on rare occasions, allowed a visit from a local trollop. Yet, the gentle giant was happy, believing that his great earnings were being put aside for him so that he would eventually have a great fortune with which to return to his native Italian village, money that he intended to use to improve the lot of his peasant family.

The Carnera tour of 1930-31 saw the most disgraceful series of boxing matches in the history of the fight game. Every match was a fix, a setup, as the giant's opponents fell over themselves to make sure that the road-show fights chalked up a string of knockouts. The broken-down pugs who fought Carnera were years beyond their prime and grateful for the few dollars they were paid to take their falls. Such has-beens as K.O. Christner, Farmer Lodge, and Chuck Wiggens literally dove onto the canvas before the bumbling, floundering colossus. There were a few exceptions.

In California, Bombo Chevalier, a hulking black fighter with some talent, turned up his nose at the cash offered by mobsters for a dive. He also waved away threats, even at gunpoint, and bragged how he intended to tag Carnera's jaw and send the giant to Never-Never Land. In the first round with Carnera, Chevalier barely missed the giant's jaw, only because he had difficulty in reaching upward for it. Before the next round, his own trainer washed off the black fighter's face and, while doing so, rubbed red pepper into his eyes, causing Chevalier to stumble blindly into a push by Carnera, which sent him down to the canvas and the most

hurried count-out on record.

Another black fighter in Denver thought to knock out the giant but changed his mind when three gunmen entered his dressing room just before the fight and pulled out several weapons. "What caliber do you like?" the fighter was asked by one of the gangsters. The meaning was clear. Carnera won in the first round, by a knockout, of course.

Ace Clark, who fought Carnera in Philadelphia, changed his mind about falling before the giant's useless punches and went after him, battering Carnera about the eyes—he missed the glass jaw only by inches several times—until Carnera's eyes were almost swollen shut. When Clark sat down between rounds, his manager tapped him on the shoulder and said: "There's a fellow down there wants to who you somethin'." Clark looked down from his corner to ringside to see a man in a long overcoat which was opened slightly to reveal a mean-looking automatic. "This is for you wiseguy, after the fight," snarled the mobster. Clark nodded, the bell rang, and he dashed forward, bumping into Carnera's huge chest and then falling backward in the most ridiculous simulation of a knockout ever staged.

The gangsters manipulating Carnera's bouts had no scruples whatever in pitting physically injured fighters against their powerless giant. The most notable example of this tactic was the tragic Ernie Schaaf. The mobsters knew, as did Schaaf's manager, that the fighter had suffered serious internal injuries from previous fights and that, before he climbed into the ring to fight Carnera in 1933, he was at that moment suffering from an inflammation of the brain. (Schaaf knew this too, but, as he explained to his friends: "I need the money. I do what I have to do.") In the ring, Schaaf could barely stand up, let alone swing on the monstrous Carnera who crowded him into a corner and slapped his head a few times, sending Schaaf to the canvas for another mobster win. A short time later, Ernie Schaaf was dead, killed by a brain hemorrhage brought on by the light head slaps from Carnera. (This tragic incident was incorporated into the superb fight movie, *Body and Soul.*

The fighters kept falling under Carnera's empty onslaught, right up to June 29, 1933, when he went into the ring against the heavyweight champion of the world, Jack Sharkey, a fighter whose reputation was as oily and suspicious as that of his gangster-loving manager, Fat John Buckley. Sharkey, who was a brawler of some note, had come up through the ranks in a fashion almost identical to Carnera's, except that he could fight and had a powerful right-hand punch. He had barely won the crown from Max Schmeling on June 21, 1932, in a split, fifteen-round decision in Long Island City. (It was after this bout that Schmeling's manager, Joe Jacobs, registered the classic line, "We wuz robbed!" in a radio interview at ringside.)

The press smelled a fix from the beginning of the Carnera-Sharkey bout. When visiting the challenger's camp at Dr. Bier's Health Farm at Pompton Lakes, N.J., reporters noted that a regular who's-who of gangsterdom was in attendance. Strolling about the grounds were DeMange, Madden, and a host of other high-level mobsters from New York. In Sharkey's camp at Gus Wilson's Resort, newsmen brushed past several members of the Capone mob from Chicago and representatives of Detroit's Purple Gang.

Carnera, certainly, had no chance of winning against Sharkey, which all the smart gamblers in America knew. The odds were incredible against the possibility, fifty to one, 100 to one. Madden and company, through secret bettors, placed hundreds of thousand on the giant (which would reap them millions).

The fight was held at Garden Bowl in Long Island City, N.Y., and it was disgustingly apparent from the first round that Jack Sharkey had no intention of putting the giant out of the match. The 29-year-old Sharkey bumbled about, slipping and sliding, throwing glancing blows to Carnera's superbly toned body but little to the head, and when he did connect in this area the punches were high and away from that infamous glass jaw.

Carnera was confident that he was the better man after his

unbroken series of phony knockouts, wins he thought he had won squarely. He actually believed, or so he later stated in broken English, that *he* was carrying Sharkey. Tiring of this in the sixth round, Carnera let loose what he thought was his super punch, his right uppercut. It struck the champion *somewhere* in the head and, although it was but a slap, it looked good enough, or sounded good enough, to fall under. Sharkey collapsed to the canvas as thousands of incredulous fans gaped and gasped. The impossible had happened. Sharkey stayed down, quivering and writhing, in what many sports reporters considered the worst acting job inside of a boxing ring. He was counted out, and Primo Carnera was announced heavyweight champion of the world, which elated the mobsters collecting their millions and caused Benito Mussolini in Italy to cable congratulations.

The mob reveled in their fake champion, but used him sparingly the next year, fearful to exhibit his lack of true boxing credentials. He was pitted against Tommy Loughran in Miami, having a 100-pound advantage over the tiny Loughran, who was just barely a light-heavyweight and who had no punch at all, but who was a scrapper nevertheless and had refused to throw the fight. The gangsters found it impossible to intimidate Loughran in that, as a Catholic, he was always surrounded by priests, even in his corner.

In this Miami bout, Carnera threw everything he had at the smaller fighter, striking him flush on the jaw repeatedly, but failing to even jar the charging Loughran. Carnera himself took a terrible beating, but managed to avoid a knockout simply by keeping his adversary at bay with his enormous reach, a sort of stiff-arm defense that had the crowd howling with anger. It was a no-decision match and Carnera held onto his title.

Max Baer knocking out Carnera in the 11th round, June 14, 1934.

The belt slipped from Carnera's baby-like grasp on the night of June 14, 1934, when the mob, deciding that the duped giant had served his purposes, allowed him to get into the ring at the Garden Bowl in Long Island City with slugger Max Baer. The 27-year-old Carnera took the worst beating of his life up to that time, as Baer knocked him about the ring like a punching bag with legs. The giant crashed to the floor ten times and somehow, with his valiant heart, managed to struggle upward on wobbly legs to be punched again and again and again until, in the eleventh round, he was hit by Baer so hard that his jaw almost broke and he toppled, like a felled Redwood, to the canvas, out stone cold.

Sportswriter Damon Runyon, at ringside during the Baer-Carnera fight, described the bloody battle thusly: "In a wild, crazy brawl that is a throwback to the time of the cave man, Max Baer, of California, becomes heavyweight champion of the world tonight.

Grinning and babbling like a veritable madman and fighting with insane fury, the black-haired ex-butcher boy hammered the grotesque face and huge body of Primo Carnera, the Italian giant, until the referee, Arthur Donovan, calls a halt after two minutes and sixteen seconds of the 11th round..."

It was all downhill for Carnera after that. Joe Louis, then a top contender for the crown, met Carnera and punched him silly until his mouth was split, his nose broken, and he dripped blood with every move until he fell, unconscious and out. He took one more terrible beating from black boxer Leroy Haynes before the giant quit, realizing that he had no career left. Following the Haynes fight, Primo Carnera was a physical wreck; he lay alone in a hospital bed with a paralyzed leg, a battered body, and only a few hundred dollars to his name. The mob had used him and discarded him without pity, without compassion.

The oversized ex-champion went on to make dismal public appearances where he was ridiculed by sneering sport fans, appearing in sleazy nightclubs and burlesque houses, drifting further and further into backwater society. He made a few appearances in the wrestling ring, not unlike the protagonist of *Requiem for a Heavyweight;* these "entertainments" were nothing more than acts of muscle-bound buffoonery... In 1949, Carnera appeared in the movie, *Mighty Joe Young,* in a staged tug-of-war with a giant ape, and as in his bout with Baer, he lost.

The giant eventually returned to Italy a beaten man—he would limp forever about his hometown of Sequals, Italy, where he was thought to be a hero. But he died penniless on June 29, 1967, thirty-four years to the day when he was one of the few people in the world who thought he had actually won the heavyweight championship of the world.

REF.: *CBA;* Gallico, *Farewell to Sport;* Horan, *The Desperate Years;* Levine, *Anatomy of A Gangster;* Peterson, *The Mob;* Rogers, *I Remember Distinctly;* Sann, *Kill the Dutchman!;* Snyder and Morris, *A Treasury of Great Reporting;* Sugar, *The 100 Greatest Boxers of All Time;* (FICTION), Schulberg, *The Harder They Fall;* (FILM), *Body and Soul,* 1947; *Mighty Joe Young,* 1949; *The Harder They Fall,* 1956; *Requiem for a Heavyweight,* 1962.

Carnesecchi, Pietro, 1508-67, Italy, her. Secretary of Pope Clement VII, he violated Catholic tenets in 1540 to become a follower of the Spanish humanist Juan de Valdés. He was forced to flee to Paris in 1546 to seek the protection of Catharine de Médici. In 1558 he was condemned by Pope Paul IV, but was absolved of any guilt. After Pope Paul V acceded to the Vatican, Carnesecchi was investigated by the Inquisition, burned at the stake, and beheaded for religious heresy. REF.: *CBA.*

Carney, John, prom. 1930s, Can., mur. The murder of James Agnew, a farmer from Lindsay, Ontario, was a relatively simple matter for Canadian detectives. Agnew had been shot behind his barn during the middle of a blinding snowstorm. The unknown assailant ran off with a gold watch and a few dollars from the victim's pocket. The shots were not heard by Agnew's wife inside the farmhouse, and the killer slipped away undetected.

Detective Murray was called in to examine the evidence. The snow had covered the footprints by this time. But Murray dug deep in the snowdrifts and found impressions of a buckle and strap. The trail led to the door of Henry Logie, a neighbor who employed an 18-year-old youth named John Carney. Carney wore a pair of boots that matched the impressions in the snow near the Agnew farm. A search of Logie's wash house turned up the stolen items.

Carney was convicted on a charge of murder and sentenced to life imprisonment. He avoided the death penalty because of his tender age.

REF.: *CBA;* Kingston, *A Gallery of Rogues.*

Carnot, Joseph François Claude, 1752-1835, Fr., jur. Procurer général at Dijon and authored many law commentaries between 1812-23. REF.: *CBA.*

Carnot, Marie François Sadi, 1837-94, Fr., pres., assass. Born in Limoges, Fr., the son of Lazare Hippolyte Carnot and a member of a distinguished Burgundian family that had been prominent since

the French Revolution, Marie François Sadi Carnot began his career as an engineer. He was made prefect of the Department of Seine-Inférieure in 1871 and was a member of the National Assembly (1871-76). Carnot was a member of the Chamber of Deputies (1876-80) before being elected the fourth president of the Third French Republic (1887-94), succeeding François Paul Jules Grévy who had been forced to resign following a scandal involving his son-in-law. Carnot proved to be an able and tactful president, weathering many political storms, particularly the Panama scandal of 1892. By 1893, France was plagued by an outbreak of political violence, bombings, and attempted assassinations on the part of anarchists.

President Carnot of France.

A wave of socialism and anarchism swept through the country during the early 1890s, bringing with it death and destruction. Workers disgruntled with meager pay had flocked to the banners of the anarchists on May Day 1891, marching in almost all major French cities, threatening to bring down the local governments. The clashes between the workers and police were bloody and most serious in Clichy, a district of Paris. Here, while parading beneath a red flag, the anarchists tore through a police line, clubbing officers. Three anarchists were arrested and one was sent to prison for five years. On Mar. 11, 1892, in retaliation for the Clichy arrests and sentencing, anarchists set off a bomb in front of the home of Judge M. Benoit, who had sent the anarchist to prison. On Mar. 27, 1892, another bomb went off at the home of M. Bulot, the public prosecutor who had helped send the Clichy anarchist to prison.

On the day Bulot's home was bombed, a man named Ravachol sat down to lunch in an open air cafe on the Boulevard Magenta. A waiter named Lhérot overheard Ravachol brag to some friends that it was he who had planted the bombs at the Benoit and Bulot homes. The waiter informed police and Ravachol was arrested. Just before Ravachol was tried, the restaurant where Lhérot worked was bombed and the proprietor and one customer were killed. Alphonse Bertillon, then head of the Identification Center of the French police, took Ravachol's photograph and then compared his measurements to those of known criminals in his files, matching the measurements to a much-wanted criminal named Koeningstein, wanted for several murders. Ravachol and Koeningstein were the same person. The killer-anarchist was found Guilty of murder and was executed in July 1892.

This did not end the anarchist reign of terror. Auguste Vaillant, an uneducated, penniless 31-year-old vagrant who had wandered Algeria and South America, returned to France to embrace anarchism. He decided to murder Prime Minister M. Casimir-Périer, who, as major owner of the Anzin tin mines, represented wealth and power to Vaillant, along with president of the chamber, Charles Dupuy, an autocratic politician rumored to have the secret ambition of restoring the monarchy. Intending to kill both of these men and their colleagues in the Chamber of Deputies, Vaillant built a bomb in his miserable lodgings and took this to the Chamber on Dec. 9, 1893, climbing into the public gallery. When the deputies were assembled, Vaillant stood up and hurled his bomb, but as he did so, a female spectator bumped his arm and thus threw his aim off. The bomb hit a pillar, exploding and wounding spectators but none of the deputies were injured except for being showered by plaster and nails from the ruptured ceiling. Vaillant was seized and imprisoned, later tried and condemned. He was sent to the guillotine.

This bold attempt to murder the leaders of the French government caused severe and swift action on the part of the authorities.

Anarchists were rounded up by the scores and jailed, their newspapers shut down and their headquarters wrecked. The bombings, nevertheless, went on with devastating alacrity. A 22-year-old pacifist named Emile Henry, well-educated and from a good family, embraced anarchy and, to learn how to make bombs, apprenticed himself to a clockmaker. After making a bomb, Henry went to the sprawling cafe of the Terminus Hotel on Feb. 12, 1894, stood before the dozens dining before him and then hurled his bomb, which ripped through the unsuspecting crowd, killing one customer and seriously injuring twenty more. Henry ran from the scene, pulling a revolver, firing at gendarmes who were pursuing him. Henry stumbled and was caught. Quickly tried and condemned, Henry was guillotined on May 21, 1894.

It was in this wild atmosphere that President Sadi Carnot traveled to Lyon to officially open the Colonial Exhibition on June 24, 1894. Carnot was a well-respected leader who was considered a moderate and he had not been selected by the radicals as a target until a youth named Perrin fired a shot at him while Carnot was en route to a festival in Versailles. Perrin was judged a lunatic and placed in an asylum. Yet others had marked Carnot for assassination. A few days before the president left for Lyons, he took his daily two-hour walk through the Bois de Boulogne with one aide, Colonel Pistor, and a shadowy figure was seen to follow Carnot at a distance of about twenty yards. He disappeared when some other strollers came near. On June 23, 1894, Carnot left Paris by train and arrived late that day in Lyons. He traveled in an open carriage through the streets of France's second city while thousands lining the route cheered and waved. Carnot then attended a fete at the Hôtel de Ville and later went to the Nouvelle Prefecture where he was to remain overnight. That evening, fireworks lit up the skies over Lyons in preparation for the next day's celebrations.

Carnot's assassin, Santo Caserio.

Also in Lyons that night was 20-year-old Santo Geronimo Caserio, who had been born in Motta-Visconti, Lombardy, and who had been a dedicated anarchist for two years. Caserio had been a baker's apprentice at age thirteen and was run out of Italy for distributing anarchist pamphlets to soldiers in 1893. He traveled about Switzerland and France, obtaining a job with a baker in the town of Cette, a hotbed of anarchist activities. When learning that Carnot would visit Lyon, Caserio quit his job, taking his wages to a cutlery shop where he purchased an ornate knife with a six-inch blade. He then took a train to Lyon, planning to murder Carnot the following day. That night he waited with the crowds on the Rue de République outside the west front of the Palais de la Bourse. He learned that the president would be passing in an open carriage on his way to the Grand Théâtre at about 9 p.m., following a dinner party. The assassin wrapped his long-handled knife in a copy of the Lyons *Républicain* and patiently stood for an hour with the crowds. He heard the cheers go up when Carnot left the Palais and then saw the slowly-moving landau carriage approach him, with Carnot in the rear seat, surrounded by dignitaries. A mounted Cuirassier rode on either side of the carriage.

As Carnot's carriage came abreast of him, Caserio shoved aside several spectators and dashed into the street, carrying his knife wrapped in the newspaper. As he came to the carriage, he unsheathed the knife and threw the newspaper and sheath away.

Gripping the side of the carriage with his left hand while leaning into the carriage and lunging forward, he viciously thrust the knife blade deep into Carnot's stomach, just under the ribs. The other passengers were not fully aware of what had happened, believing Caserio to be someone who was presenting Carnot with a petition. Only when Carnot pulled his hand away from his stomach to display fingers coated with blood, did one of his aides ask: "What is wrong, Monsieur le President?"

"I'm wounded," Carnot gasped and then he fell backward, his head resting on the cushion, his eyes closed, unconscious.

Caserio stabbing Carnot to death during a parade in Lyon, France, 1894.

A crowd of officials closed in around the stationary carriage and Dr. Antonin Poncet, professor of clinical surgery in Lyon, who had attended the banquet for Carnot only hours earlier, raced from the crowd, and leaped upon the landau as its driver wheeled it about and then lashed the horses to a gallop, heading toward the Prefecture. In the carriage, Dr. Poncet grabbed Carnot's icy hand and felt no pulse. He looked down to see that the knife that Caserio had plunged into Carnot with such force, was still buried to the hilt in his stomach. Few in the festive throngs realized what had happened and many were still cheering as the president's carriage dashed past them along the route it had come only minutes earlier. Above, in the clear June night sky, fireworks lit up the night, making the scene all the more bizarre.

Meanwhile, the assassin almost made a perfect escape. He had leaped from the landau, raced ahead of its slowing horses, cut in front of it, and then run across the street diagonally. The driver of the president's carriage heard him shout: *"Vive l'Anarchie!"* He then attempted to break through the heavy crowd on the other side of the street. Only a few suspected the young man in the grey suit of having committed a crime. A young girl tried to stop him by grabbing and holding on to his sleeve. Caserio smashed his fist against her head, knocking her down. An English author, Albert Vizetelly, standing nearby, was shocked into action, as he caught the reeling girl and in the next movement, swung his own fist on Caserio's jaw, stunning the assassin for a moment. Then others began attacking Caserio, thinking him to be a pickpocket trying to escape police officers who came runing toward him. A police captain arrived and shouted to spectators around Caserio: "Hold him! He's just assassinated the president!"

When the crowd heard this, dozens surged forward to avenge the popular president, clubbing Caserio with their fists, kicking him, tearing at his clothes. He was a bloody mess when police officers finally managed to wrest him from the throng which now began to chant: "Death to the assassin, death to the assassin!"

Carnot, by then, had been taken to the Prefecture and a half dozen doctors labored to save his life. Caserio's knife wound, however, proved fatal. The blade had perforated the liver and severed a main artery. Carnot revived momentarily to tell his doctors: "I thank you for what you have done for me." He died several hours later and the nation went into mourning. Caserio was thrown into a cell where he unrepentantly announced: "I am an anarchist and I have struck the Head of State. I've done it as

I would have killed any king or emperor, of no matter what nationality."

Caserio was tried at the Assize Court of the Rône Department on Aug. 2, 1894. His lawyers claimed that he suffered from hereditary insanity and that he had been the instruments of anarchists. With that, Caserio leaped to his feet and screamed: "That's not true!" The jury deliberated this case for less than a half hour and returned a verdict of Guilty without extenuating circumstances. Caserio was condemned to death. At 5 a.m. on Aug. 16, 1894, Caserio, who had arrogantly strutted and boasted for days in his death cell, was found cowering in his cell. He trembled and quaked and went limp so that guards had to drag him from his cell and to a public square in Lyons where thousands watched as he was placed beneath the waiting blade of the guillotine. He was decapitated moments later. See: **Bertillon, Alphonse; Ravachol.**

REF.: *CBA;* Brookes, *Murder in Fact and Fiction;* Dubreuil, *Cour d'assises du Rhône;* Hyams, *Killing No Murder;* Irving, *Studies of French Criminals;* Morain, *The Underworld of Paris;* Nash, *Almanac of World Crime;* Vizetelly, *The Anarchists;* Williams, *Heyday for Assassins.*

Caroline, Amelia Elizabeth (AKA: **Caroline of Brunswick**), 1768-1821, Case of, Brit., adult. At the age of twenty-seven, Caroline, the daughter of the Duke of Brunswick-Wolfenbüttel, was forced to marry the Duke of York, the philandering son of King George III, who wanted a male heir. The prince demanded liquidation of his debts and a yearly stipend of £125,000 as his dowry for marrying his cousin Caroline. On Apr. 8, 1795, the duke and Caroline were married at the Chapel Royal, St. James. It turned out to be a loveless union, and the prince's mistresses persecuted Caroline out of spite. The duke deserted her after the birth of their

Queen Caroline of England.

daughter, Princess Charlotte Augusta, in 1796. The king took the child from her and refused to let her see the baby. In despair, Caroline left England and toured the capitals of Europe.

Parliament debating charges of Queen Caroline's adultery.

After the death of George III on Jan. 29, 1820, Caroline refused to relinquish her claim to the throne in return for a financial settlement. The Earl of Liverpool introduced a bill in the House of Lords on July 5 to strip her of all rights and privileges. Caroline was accused of committing adultery with Bartolomeo Bergami, a handsome Italian military officer she had met during her travels. On Nov. 30, Caroline's forces defeated a bill that would have granted her husband a divorce. The queen's enemies retreated after considering the implications for the new king, George IV. Popular opinion was with Caroline, and the government did not wish to offend the people just before the coronation of the new king.

On coronation day at Westminster Abbey, July 19, 1821, Caroline was excluded from the ceremonies though she had expressed her resolve to attend. Not wishing to start a riot, she returned home. Caroline became ill at the Drury Lane Theatre on July 30, and died a week later. Controversy followed her even in death. The king made known his intention to prevent her funeral cortege from passing through the city for final burial in the royal vault at Brunswick. But the citizens of London revolted, and after a brief skirmish between the Life Guards and an unruly mob at Hyde Park Corner, the procession was allowed to pass.

REF.: *CBA;* Thomson, *The Story of Scotland Yard.*

Caroline Matilda, See: **Christian VII.**

Caroline of Brunswick, See: **Caroline, Amelia Elizabeth.**

Carolla, Sylvestro (AKA: **Sam**), 1896-1972, U.S., org. crime. Sylvestro Carolla ruled the New Orleans crime family for the better part of three decades. During that time, the local Mafia made the transition from a small-time Black Hand (extortion-protection) operation ruled by Charles Matranga to a full-blown criminal enterprise raking in millions of dollars each year. Sam Carolla was born in Sicily, but emigrated with his parents to the U.S. in 1904. By age twenty-two, the ambitious young gangster had assumed a major position in the New Orleans underworld, and in a few years emerged as the number two man in the organization behind Matranga. In 1922, when Matranga retired, Carolla assumed control of the mob's fledgling bootlegging operations.

Carolla systematically eliminated his rivals, including William Bailey, who was killed during the Christmas season of 1930, when Carolla stepped from his limousine and shot Bailey with a sawed-off shotgun. Carolla emerged as the bootleg king of New Orleans. He had bought off every policeman and politician of consequence. Al Capone arrived in New Orleans in 1929 to demand that Carolla begin supplying his Chicago operation with imported liquor instead of arch-rival Joe Aiello. Carolla greeted Capone at the train station with several New Orleans policemen at his side. They relieved the Chicago gunmen of their weapons, and broke the fingers of Capone's top bodyguards. Capone quietly retreated to the train for a humbling return trip to Chicago.

In 1930, Carolla had trouble with the law for the first time after shooting federal narcotics agent Cecil Moore in a case of mistaken identity. His friends on the New Orleans police force told the courts that Carolla was in New York at the time, but the jury found him Guilty, and the judge sentenced him to two years. In 1934, Sam Carolla was back on the streets, and anxious to do business with New York mob bosses Frank Costello, Charles "Lucky" Luciano, and Meyer Lansky. They had cut a deal with Senator Huey Long of Louisiana to bring to New Orleans the slot machines that had all but disappeared from New York during the tenure of reform Mayor Fiorello La Guardia. Carolla and his top lieutenant, Carlos Marcello, learned the gambling rackets from Costello, and ran the venture undisturbed for years.

In 1938, Carolla went to prison a second time on a narcotics charge. He served two years in the Atlanta Penitentiary and faced deportation upon his release in 1940. But WWII intervened, and the government postponed further action. The campaign to drive Carolla from New Orleans resumed in 1947 when columnist Drew Pearson exposed Congressman Jimmy Morrison's attempt to push through a bill awarding Carolla citizenship, thereby making deportation impossible. In April 1947, public opinion finally forced through the deportation proceedings against Carolla. He joined "Lucky" Luciano in exile, and together they formed a criminal alliance in Mexico.

In 1949, Carolla slipped back into the U.S., but was caught and deported a second time in 1950. For the next twenty years, Marcello ran the New Orleans rackets while Carolla lived in Palermo, Italy. But the aging don returned to the U.S. in 1970, where he died in 1972, when he succumbed to illness and old age. See: **Costello, Frank; Luciano, Charles; Capone, Alphonse.**

REF.: *CBA;* Davis, *Mafia Kingfish;* Reid, *The Grim Reapers.*

Caron, René Edouard, 1800-76, Can., jur. Judge on the court of the Queen's Bench from 1853-73. REF.: *CBA.*

Cáro Quintero, Rafael (AKA: **Rafa** or **El Grenas**), 1952- , Mex., drugs-org. crime. Rafael Cáro Quintero was an illiterate peasant boy from the Sierra Madre uplands who became the head of the Guadalajara drug cartel. To the impoverished clans of Sinaloa he was a latter-day Robin Hood who built a drug empire in defiance of the "gringos" to the north.

Cáro Quintero's two uncles, Emilio and Juan José Quintero Payán had been smuggling heroin and marijuana into the U.S. for years. Rafa, as he was called, expanded the family business by offering an expensive grade of marijuana at wholesale prices. Imitating the growing techniques pioneered in the U.S., Cáro Quintero began producing sinsemilla—a seedless, potent form of marijuana that sold for $2,500 a pound in the U.S. markets. In the early 1980s, using cheap Mexican labor, he converted acres of irrigated desert into lush sinsemilla fields. Soon Cáro Quintero and his part-

Mexican drug lord Rafael Cáro Quintero, shown behind bars.

ner, Ernesto Fonseca, were trucking tons of marijuana into the U.S. over routes formerly used by produce growers.

By 1985, Cáro Quintero controlled a drug empire unmatched anywhere in Mexico. He and his lieutenants controlled all traffic and distribution through systematic payoffs to the Mexican Federal Judicial Police (MFJP), and the Federal Bureau of Social and Political Investigations (IPS). MFJP officers delivered bags of drug money to the traffickers operating near the Mexican border.

Cáro Quintero explained to reporters that he did not personally approve of drug use among young people. At the same time, his army of pushers peddled high-grade marijuana and cocaine in Southern California. In Guadalajara, U.S. Drug Enforcement Administration (DEA) agent Enrique Camarena had been waging a small but effective campaign against the drug rackets. His efforts led to the seizure of large quantities of marijuana ready for shipment. Annoyed by the persistence of this Mexican-American operative, Cáro Quintero had him abducted and killed on Feb. 7, 1985, outside Guadalajara. The U.S. State Department pressured the Mexican government to begin a crackdown against the cartel.

Cáro Quintero was forced into hiding. In March, DEA agents in Costa Rica received reports that well-known cocaine dealer Pablo Escobar had paid $500,000 cash for a villa outside San José. The free-spending Mexicans in Costa Rica aroused the suspicion of the DEA. On Apr. 4, 1985, after days of aerial reconnaissance and undercover surveillance, a crack U.S.-trained anti-terrorist team, known as the Departmento Inteligencia Seguridad (DIS), attacked the former coffee plantation and easily captured Cáro Quintero. The MFJP sent in a plane the next day to bring him back to Mexico City.

While awaiting trial, Cáro Quintero admitted bribing hundreds of politicians, judges, and police officials, including Comandante Jorge Armando Pavón Reyes, and financing a large marijuana plantation in Chihuahua. Ernesto Fonseca told police that Camarena had been abducted to avenge the cartel's loss of revenue in the DEA raids at Chihuahua and Zacatecas. Murder never entered into the equation, he said.

Rafael Cáro Quintero was convicted of arms smuggling and impressing local peasants into forced labor on his marijuana plantations. He was sentenced on Sept. 24, 1988, to thirty-four years in prison. See: **Camarena, Enrique; Fonseca Carrillo, Ernesto.**

REF.: *CBA;* Shannon, *Desperados.*

Carpenter, Mary, 1807-77, Brit., prison reform. Opened a school for indigent girls at Bristol in 1829, and became interested in prison reform during her visits to India in 1866, 1868, 1869, and 1875. She authored numerous papers and treatises on juvenile delinquency and ways to reform the youthful offender. REF.: *CBA.*

Carpenter, Oran A., prom. 1883, Case of, U.S., mur. After Zura Burns was found murdered on a lonely road outside of Lincoln, Ill., on Oct. 14, 1883, suspicion immediately fell on Oran Carpenter, her lover. The woman was found to have been pregnant and the state brought Carpenter to trial for murder, contending that Carpenter had killed the woman when he realized he was to become a father. The accused man had often in the past told friends that he did not wished to be burdened with a family. Carpenter pled not guilty and his lawyers defied the prosecution to produce evidence that their client, indeed, had murdered the hapless woman. The evidence was not forthcoming and Carpenter was acquitted. Feeling against him was so strong, however, that Carpenter was forced to leave Lincoln, relocating in the Dakotas.

REF.: *CBA;* Nash, *Almanac of World Crime; Zura Burns or the Fatal Step.*

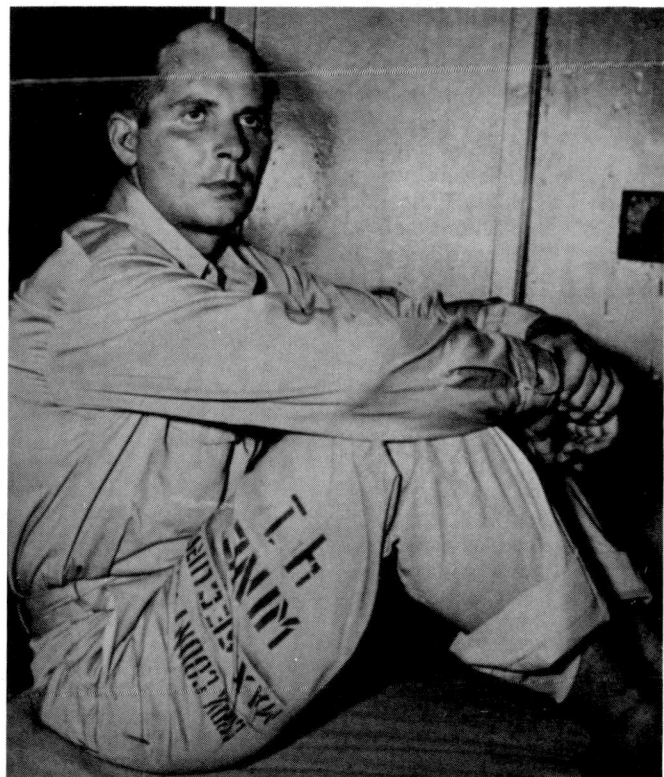

Chicago robber-murderer Richard Carpenter, executed in 1956.

Carpenter, Richard, 1929-56, U.S., mur. Richard Carpenter entered neighborhood bars and small grocery stores in Chicago as they were preparing to close, held two Western-style guns on the clerk, and demanded whatever money was in the cash register. In this way, he made a steady though precarious living for two years.

In August 1955, Police Detective Bill Murphy, who had been briefed on Carpenter, spotted the 26-year-old thief on a subway train, and immediately arrested him. When they got off the train, Murphy tried to pull an identification poster from his pocket, giving Carpenter a chance to pull his gun. Carpenter fired once, directly into the policeman's chest, killing him. Carpenter ran out of the station and hijacked a waiting limousine, telling the driver, "I've just killed a man, and I'll kill you, too, unless you drive on and keep quiet!" Carpenter got out in the Loop business district.

Carpenter could not go to any of his familiar haunts, so he slept where and when he could. He was asleep in the back row

of a downtown movie theater when he was spotted by another policeman, Clarence Kerr, who was spending an evening out with his wife. Kerr sent her out of the way, then woke the sleeping Carpenter to take him into the lobby. Carpenter pretended to trip, pulled out his gun as he rose, and shot Kerr in the chest.

As Carpenter rushed from the theater, a passing policeman shot him in the leg. Later that evening Carpenter knocked on the back door of the home of Leonard Powell, a truckdriver, and demanded to be let in. Powell and his wife calmly went about their business, held at gunpoint by the frantic murderer for more than a day. They kept their son and daughter ignorant of who Carpenter was, and Powell even went to work the next day, knowing that his family was held hostage. That evening, probably having no idea how he was going to get out of the situation, Carpenter said to the Powells, "It was a lousy life I led—but it's too late now. Either the cops will kill me or I'll go to the chair, but I hope I can see my mother before I die." Powell told Carpenter that his wife's mother would be expecting them to visit that evening, as they did every evening. Carpenter let them go, and the Powells ran for the police. Within minutes, police surrounded the building. Carpenter ran to another apartment, but soon gave himself up. Found Guilty of murder, Carpenter, after a brief visit from his mother, was sent to the electric chair at Joliet State Prison.

REF.: *CBA;* Nash, *Bloodletters and Badmen.*

Carpetbag Mystery, 1857, Brit., (unsolv.) mur. Two young boys rowing on the Thames near the Waterloo Bridge in 1857 saw a carpetbag lying on one of the bridge supports. The boys hauled in the bag to see what they had found. In it were fragments of a human body resting on bloodstained clothing badly cut as if with a dagger. There was not a whole body, nor even enough to determine how the victim died. In the following weeks, newspapers printed daily speculation, which came to nothing.

Years later, Sir Robert Anderson, assistant commissioner of Metropolitan Police, wrote a story in *Blackwood's* Magazine proposing that the body was that of an Italian police spy killed by his confederates. A journalist then claimed that a hack writer named Butterfield collected the body parts from morgues and placed them where they might be found so he would have something sensational to write about. If so, he never followed up his own story.

REF.: *CBA;* Nash, *Almanac of World Crime;* Pearce, *Unsolved Murder Mysteries.*

Carpzov, Benedikt, 1565-1624, Saxony, jur. Professor at Wittenberg and father of Benedict Carpzov. REF.: *CBA.*

Carpzov, Benedict, 1595-1666, Saxony, witchcraft. The leading authority in legal procedure and judgments on witchcraft and sorcery in Saxony, Carpzov was said to have signed the death warrants of 20,000 people.

Benedict Carpzov, "the lawgiver of Saxony" and the son of a well-known law professor at Wittenberg, became a professor himself, at Leipzig. He influenced nearly all decisions over witchcraft cases, publishing *Concerning Criminal Law* in 1635, a compendium of demonology reprinted nine times by 1723. His published verdicts controlled the laws for years throughout the Saxon witchcraft trials.

A devout man who read the Bible voraciously, Carpzov was dogmatic and bigoted in his opinions, maintaining that the heinous nature of witchcraft made the inquisitorial the only appropriate procedure to combat it, and promoting the idea that local judges should not be restricted by legal technicalities in obtaining evidence, thus giving legal and official license to cruelty and injustice. Recommending torture in witchcraft cases, Carpzov justified its use with biblical quotes and specified seventeen torture techniques to be used, including slow burning with candles and driving wedges under the fingernails and setting fire to them. According to this expert, prisoners who retracted their confessions should be tortured again, and burial of witches and sorcerers should not be allowed, as their decaying corpses lying exposed would serve as a deterrent to others.

Carpzov printed thirty-six of his legal judgments from the Leipzig Supreme Court between 1558 and 1622, which, used extensively as precedents in later trials, continued to influence witchcraft decisions for the next 100 years. REF.: *CBA*.

Carr, John, d.1750, Brit., smug.-forg. Carr's life was like that of a Charles Dickens character: packed with romance and intrigue, coupled with miserable poverty. Born in northern Ireland, John Carr was set up as a wine and brandy merchant by his father and he did quite well until he took up with thieves. He neglected his customers, who took their business elsewhere.

While he brooded about his lost chances, a former business associate persuaded him to a holiday in the country, via Kilkenny. During the coach ride Carr met an attractive young woman who captivated him. Carr asked the woman to marry him and they returned to Dublin to prepare for a voyage to England. He sold his remaining property, and turned over all his cash to the woman, who immediately stowed away on a ship bound for Amsterdam, never to be seen again.

Carr was forever shattered by this experience. He scratched out a humble existence in London, but squandered whatever money he won in the gaming houses, reverting to swindling. When his ill-gotten gains were depleted, he joined the navy. There he conceived the idea of becoming a privateer in the service of the king.

After his discharge from the navy, Carr was hired on to a fast ship and became its master-at-arms. In a short time they captured two French vessels laden with rich cargo. During one ferocious engagement with the French, the English commander was killed. Carr courted his widow, but before the marriage could be arranged she died of a violent fever. Carr sold the estate she had generously left to him and returned to London, where he became a notorious but inept smuggler. He was constantly hounded by officers from the revenue department and, seeing no hope of becoming wealthy through the black market, Carr began forging the wills of seamen, for which he was arrested and imprisoned at the Old Bailey. He was led to Tyburn hill on Nov. 16, 1750, where he was hanged.

REF.: *CBA*; Dilnot, *Triumphs of Detection*; Mitchell, *Newgate Calendar*.

Carr, Melvin, 1915-77, U.S., rape-mur. An ex-convict arrested several times on charges of molesting girls died in his garage, asphyxiated by the carbon monoxide he used to murder three victims he had locked in the trunk of his car.

Melvin Carr, sixty-two, had recently finished serving a four-year prison term for embezzlement. Indianapolis, Ind., police responded on Mar. 20, 1977, to neighbors' reports that Carr was lying dead in his garage, next to his car, and when they arrived they discovered three other bodies in the garage. According to homicide Lieutenant Patrick Stark, sex was the apparent motive. In the trunk of the car were the bodies of Sandra Harris, seventeen, Karen Mills, twenty-four, and Robert Mills, her 2-year-old son. Harris had been raped.

Carr apparently had locked the victims in his car trunk and left the engine running. He later returned with a handkerchief over his face to check on the victims and was overcome by the fumes. A .25-caliber pistol was found in the murderer's pocket. Scratch marks on the inside of the trunk indicated that the two women and the little boy had tried to claw their way out. Harris and Mrs. Mills, whose husband was in the Pendleton Reformatory on charges of breaking out of prison, lived three blocks from Carr. REF.: *CBA*.

Carr, Robert, See: **Howard, Lady Frances**.

Carr, Thomas D., d.1870, U.S., mur. Thomas Carr, a resident of St. Clairsville, Ohio, became infatuated with 14-year-old Louisa C. Fox. When she refused to marry him, Carr went berserk and strangled her. He was seen leaving the scene of the murder and was quickly convicted and sentenced to death. Carr was hanged on Mar. 24, 1870. Investigation into his felonious past revealed that he may have been involved in as many as fourteen other murders.

REF.: *CBA*; *Life and Confession of Thomas D. Carr*.

Carraher, Patrick, 1907-46, Scot., mur. An alcoholic with a history of violence, Carraher was tried twice for murder. Born in the slum district of Gorbals in Glasgow, Patrick Carraher already had a history of drunken violence in 1923 when first arrested, at age 16, for theft and assault. From then on he was continually in and out of prisons. In August 1938 he stabbed and killed James Sydney Emden Shaw, a young soldier who had interfered in a street brawl. Tried in the High Court of Justiciary in Glasgow, Carraher was found guilty of culpable homicide—the equivalent of manslaughter—and was sentenced by Lord Pittman to three years of penal servitude. On his release, he returned to his criminal career with a vengeance, his reputation as a killer giving him prestige in the underworld as he continued to steal and housebreak, often with Daniel Bonnar, his brother-in-law.

In 1943 Carraher received another prison sentence, this time for assault and slashing with a razor. On Nov. 23, 1945, he murdered John Gordon, a Seaforth Highlander soldier, in a drunken fight in the Townsend district of Glasgow. Tried before Lord Russel in February 1946, Carraher's defense lawyer argued that he had a psychopathic personality aggravated by severe alcoholism, and should be given a light sentence under the doctrine of "diminished responsibility," a concept applicable only in Scotland. But several of his cohorts testified that Carraher had often boasted about killing, and he was found Guilty, sentenced to death, and hanged at Barlinnie Prison in Glasgow on Apr. 6, 1946.

REF.: *CBA*; *Notable British Trials*; Shew, *A Second Companion to Murder*.

Carranza, Bartolomé de (AKA: **Bartolomé de Miranda**), 1503-76, Spain, her. Catholic archbishop of Toledo in 1557. In 1559 he was jailed by the Spanish Inquisition for heresy, stemming from the publication of his *Comentario Sobre el Cateqismo Cristiano*. Released in 1567, he was incarcerated again that same year, remaining in prison until 1576. REF.: *CBA*.

Carranza, Venustiano, 1859-1920, Mex., pres., assass. Born in Cuátro Ciénegas, Coahuila, as part of the landed Mexican gentry, Venustiano Carranza was educated in liberal views that brought him into conflict with the dictatorship of Porfirio Diaz. In 1893, he took part in a brief revolt in Coahuila, winning a few reforms. Carranza was later a liberal senator in the Diaz government for twelve years. When Francisco Madero called for a revolution against the tyrannical Diaz, Carranza was governor of Coahuila, one of the most influential of the northern states. Carranza, who believed in the democratic principles of Madero, joined the revolutionary leader in exile in the U.S., and became one of the most outspoken supporters of the 1910 revolution. He looked like

President Venustiano Carranza.

anything but a revolutionary, a tall patrician with white hair and a white beard, who parted both in the middle and wore blue-tinted spectacles behind which blinked weak eyes. He pontificated and fulminated, abhorring violence and preferring to back strong military men like Alvaro Obregón and Pancho Villa. He was no military leader but was an ardent politician who had a reputation for being honest. Carranza was also arrogant, egotistical, and ignorant of his country's history and social needs. Though he used to his own ends the considerable forces of the great peasant leader from Morelos, Emiliano Zapata, Carranza had little regard for Zapata as a politician and considered him beneath his own privileged class. Zapata, in turn, thought Carranza to be an aloof aristocrat who did more posing as a champion of the peons and peasants than effecting real change on their behalf.

Following Madero's assassination in 1913, Carranza became

the chief opposition to the new dictatorship of Victoriano Huerta, one of Diaz' strong men and the man who ordered Madero murdered. On Mar. 26, 1913, at the Hacienda de Guadalupe in Coahuila, Carranza published a vague document of reform and revolution which he called the *Plan of Guadalupe,* one which outlined a loose revolutionary program against Huerta and one that named its author, Carranza, as "First Chief" of the constitutionalists. The constitutionalists, with Carranza at their head, sought a return of the constitution as originally drafted by Madero and abandoned by the usurping Huerta. President Woodrow Wilson initially believed that Carranza and other Mexican revolutionaries meant to reestablish a democracy in Mexico, but the haughty Carranza proved to be unfriendly toward the U.S. Following Huerta's defeat, Carranza became the provisional president of Mexico (Oct. 1915-Mar. 1917). Because he seemingly stalled land reforms, Villa and Emiliano Zapata, formerly his strongest supporters, turned on him, sending their forces against him. Obregón became Carranza's protector and backed him as president in the 1917 election after Carranza accepted the constitution.

Carranza served as president of Mexico (1917-1920) until Obregón, who had retired, left his pea-farming and announced that he was a candidate in the 1920 election. He denounced the Carranza regime as corrupt and Carranza, in turn, put up a stooge candidate, Ignacio Bonillas who had been Carrenza's ambassador to the U.S. The "Old Badger of the Revolution," as Carranza was called, expected Bonillas to win the election with his backing and then take orders from him. Obregón then announced that he would oppose Carranza with force and several states rebelled against the Carranza regime. When General Pablo González, who had also announced his candidacy for the presidency, quit the race and retired to the country, removing himself and his troops from Carranza's banner, the president was left without military support. He decided to move his headquarters to Vera Cruz.

For several days, Carranza's men looted the palace and all government buildings in Mexico City, loading three long trains with gold, tapestries, paintings, silverware. "Carranza might have escaped with his life if he hadn't been so greedy," one historian wrote. "His train stood waiting for two or three days but there were always a few more things to be taken away...He even took the cardboard currency. He took the funds from the treasury and the light fixtures from the palace." Carranza stole more than sixty million pesos in gold and silver, packing this on his private train, including a harem of forty women. As the train finally pulled out of Mexico City on May 7, 1920, these women slipped into revealing chemises, popped the corks from champagne bottles, and began an orgy in Carranza's private cars, throwing gold and silver coins every which way as they spilled champagne down the throats of the fleeing president and his earthy followers.

There was no organization to the evacuation. No medical supplies and little water were brought along for the trip. González reentered Mexico City at the head of his troops, announcing for Obregón who arrived a few days later. Two of Carranza's trains were stopped but Carranza managed to get to Aljibes in Puebla. There the track was torn up and Carranza's thin troops were under constant attack. Carranza, his hand-picked presidential candidate Bonillas, and about seventy of Carranza's staunchest followers left the train and mounted horses, attempting to reach the headquarters of General Francisco P. Mariel who was thought to be still loyal to Carranza. The exhausted group reached one of Mariel's outposts in northern Puebla where Rudolfo Herrero, a bandit-turned-general was put in charge of the fleeing Carranza. Herrero met Carranza's bedraggled group, stating that he and his men would escort the first chief of the revolution to General Mariel's headquarters at Villa Juárez. On May 20, 1920, he guided them to a miserable little village called San Antonio Tlaxcalantongo which was made up of a ruined church and some thatched huts.

Carranza, his private secretary Pedro Gil Farias, his home secretary, Aquirre Berlanga, and two army officers were shown into a one-room hut by Herrero who told the first chief: "For now, señor, this will be the national palace." He added: "This is my country. No one shall harm you. I myself will guide you through to the coast." By then Carranza realized that his power had vanished and he resolved to flee to Cuba with as much gold his horses were able to carry. Bonillas and most of Carranza's entourage were billeted in huts far removed from the first chief, which was part of Herrero's plan. Carranza bedded down that night with a saddle for a pillow and a horse blanket thrown over his body. At about 10 p.m., General Herrero entered Carranza's hut and lit a match which caused Carranza to sit up.

"What is wanted?" Carranza said to Herrero.

"I only wished to see that you had everything you ought to have," replied his host.

Within seconds, Herrero was joined by a dozen men, guns drawn and pointed at the startled first chief. They opened fire, a dozen bullets striking Carranza as he attempted to stand up. He died in the hut, his body stripped of his watch, his glasses, and his magnificent uniform. Even the first chief's typewriter upon which he had written endless manifestos was stolen. A weeping aide covered Carranza's body with a blanket as the rest of the Carranza retinue fled in terror. Bonillas managed to escape, sliding down a treacherous ravine and then being guided by a small boy to Villa Juárez. Thirty of Carranza's men were then rounded up and ordered by Herrero at gunpoint to sign a statement that Carranza had committed suicide. The body of the first chief was taken by train to Mexico City on May 22, 1920, and buried two days later in Dolores Cemetery, placed, according to Carranza's wishes "in a third-class grave where the poor people are buried." Herrero was never punished for the brutal assassination. In fact, Obregón promoted him to the rank of brigadier general. Carranza's fabulous gold shipments, scattered throughout Puebla, are still being sought by treasure hunters. See: **Madero, Francisco; Obregón, Alvaro; Villa, Pancho; Zapata, Emiliano.**

REF.: Alba, *The Mexicans;* Alessio Robles, *Historia Politica de la Revolución;* Atkin, *Revolution! Mexico, 1910-20;* Baerlein, *The Land of Unrest;* Baker, *Woodrow Wilson, Life and Letters;* Barragán Rodriguez, *Historia del Ejército y la Revolución;* Barrera, *Villa Contra Todos;* Beals, *Porfirio Diaz, Dictator of Mexico;* Bell, *The Political Shame of Mexico;* Blasco Ibañez, *Mexico in Revolution;* Braddy, *Cock of the Walk: The Legend of Pancho Villa;* Brand, *Mexico, Land of Sunshine and Shadow;* Brenner, *The Wind That Swept Mexico;* Bulnes, *The Whole Truth About Mexico;* Calcott, *Liberalism in Mexico, 1857-1929;* Callahan, *American Foreign Policy in Mexican Relations;* CBA; Cline, *The United States and Mexico;* Creel, *The People Next Door;* Creelman, *Diaz, Master of Mexico;* Cumberland, *Mexican Revolution: The Constitutionalist Years;* ____, *Mexican Revolution: Genesis under Madero;* De la Huerta, *Memorias;* Dillon, *Mexico on the Verge;* ____, *President Obregón-A World Reformer;* Dulles, *Yesterday in Mexico;* Dunn, *The Crimson Jester: Zapata of Mexico;* Estrada, *La Revolución y Francisco Madero;* Flandrau, *Viva Mexico;* Fornaro, *Carranza and Mexico;* Fyfe, *The Real Mexico;* Gibbon, *Mexico Under Carranza;* González, *Carranza y la Revolución de México;* Grayson, *Woodrow Wilson, An Intimate Memoir;* Grieb, *The United States and Huerta;* Gruening, *Mexico and Its Heritage;* Guzmán, *Memoirs of Pancho Villa;* ____, *The Eagle and the Serpent;* Haley, *Revolution and Intervention: The Diplomacy of Taft and Wilson with Mexico, 1910-1917;* Hutton, *Mexican Images;* Inman, *Intervention in Mexico;* Johnson, *Mexico;* ____, *Heroic Mexico;* King, *Tempest Over Mexico, A Personal Chronicle;* Lansford, *Pancho Villa;* Lara Pardo, *Marcha de dictadores: Wilson contra Huerta: Carranza contra Wilson;* Moats, *Thunder in Their Veins;* Nicholson, *The X in Mexico;* O'Hea, *Reminiscences of the Mexican Revolution;* O'Shaughnessy, *A Diplomat's Wife in Mexico;* ____, *Intimate Pages in Mexican History;* Parkes, *A History of Mexico;* Parkinson, *Zapata;* Plenn, *Mexico Marches;* Quirk, *The Mexican Revolution, 1914-1915;* Reed, *Insurgent Mexico;* Regler, *A Land Bewitched;* Rippy, *The United States and Mexico;* Simpson, *Many Mexicos;* Smith, *Benighted Mexico;* Stevens, *Here Comes Pancho Villa;* Strode, *Timeless Mexico;* Taracena, *Carranza contra Madero;* Turner, *Barbarous Mexico;* Turner, *Bullets, Bottles and Gardenias;* Urquizo, *Carranza;* ____, *México-Tlaxcalantongo.*

Carrara, Francesco (AKA: Il Vecchio), d.1393, Italy, treas. Succeeded his uncle as the leader of the ruling family of Padua from 1355-88. During this period he allied his family with the powerful Viscontis of Milan against Venice. For this betrayal of a former ally, he was forced to abdicate, turning over the government to his son Francesco II. He remained a prisoner until his death. REF.: *CBA.*

Carrara, Francesco, 1850-88, Italy, jur. Opponent of capital punishment who authored *Programma del Corso di Diritto Criminale* (thirteen volumes), *Opuscoli di Diritto Criminale* (seven volumes), and *Lineamenti di Pratica Legislativa Penale* (second edition). REF.: *CBA.*

Carrasco, Fred Gomez, 1940-74, U.S., drugs-kid.-mur. A convict who barricaded himself in the Huntsville, Texas, state penitentiary library was responsible for the longest-running hostage drama in U.S. prison history. Nicknamed "El Señor" in Mexican border barrios, 34-year-old Fred Gomez Carrasco was a narcotics boss convicted of murder serving a 25-year-to-life sentence at Huntsville. On July 24, 1974, Carrasco, with two other prisoners, Rodolpho Dominguez, twenty-seven, and Ignacio Cuevas, forty-three, armed with two .38-caliber pistols and a .357 magnum, leaped up in the lunch room and shouted that they were taking over. They seized fifteen hostages: three male teachers, seven female educational aides, a prison guard, and four other convicts. The convicts released one hostage, a 51-year-old teacher who suffered a heart attack, and barricaded themselves in the windowless prison library after they shot a guard in the foot.

Ten days of death threats and negotiations for food, bedding, clothing, walkie-talkies, and bulletproof helmets followed. Guards refused their demands for ammunition, rifles, and flak jackets. Carrasco said he was prepared to die and would kill his hostages rather than surrender, explaining, "What is the sense of living when you're caged up like an animal? I'm not the type of man who can live life behind bars." As the three men continued to threaten to shoot or blow up their hostages with bombs made from library chemistry sets, one hostage, guard Bob Heard, twenty-seven, who had been shot in the shoulder, pleaded over the phone: "Give them what they want, and at least we'll know we tried, that we didn't die cooped up in here like a slaughterhouse." Convict and hostage Henry Escamilla escaped by hurling himself through the library's glass doors. The same day, Aline House, sixty-one, suffered a heart attack and was released.

Following the orders of Governor Dolph Briscoe, prison officials provided Carrusco and his cohorts with an armored car. With the help of their hostages, the convicts built an elaborate shield, nicknamed the "Trojan Horse," out of blackboards insulated with law books. On Aug. 3 at about 9:30 p.m., the prisoners moved toward the escape car with eight hostages as an additional outer shield, and the three criminals and four hostages in an inner circle.

Texas Rangers and prison guards suddenly turned high-pressure water hoses on the group and the hostages on the outside dived for cover, but a hose ruptured, giving the convicts the chance to open fire. According to Texas Department of Corrections Director W.J. Estelle, "No officer fired a shot until fired upon." At the end of the brief, bloody battle, Carrasco and Rodolfo Dominguez lay dead, while hostages Elizabeth Beseda, a 57-year-old teacher at the prison, and Judy Standley, a librarian, lay dying. Estelle told reporters that, under the circumstances, the outcome was "the best we could hope for." REF.: *CBA.*

Carrel, Nicolas Armand, 1800-36, Fr., duel. Journalist and anti-Bourbon political leader. He was critically wounded in a duel. REF.: *CBA.*

Carrera, José Miguel, 1785-1821, Chile, rebel. Soldier of Spain who served in Europe, embraced the radical right-wing movement, and returned to Chile to overthrow the ruling conservative junta in 1811. His two brothers were shot, but he succeeded in establishing a military dictatorship that lasted from 1811-13. He was replaced by Bernardo O'Higgins, and fled to Buenos Aires. In 1816 he returned to foment another coup, which failed, and he was executed in Mendoza. REF.: *CBA.*

Carrier, Jean-Baptiste, 1756-94, Fr., polit.-execut. During the bloody days of the French Revolution, a lawyer with a taste for cruelty ordered the killings of thousands of persons.

Jean-Baptiste Carrier, a lawyer who served on the revolutionary tribunal at Nantes in 1793-94, was noted for his sadistic treatment of countless French people, perhaps as many as 8,000, as he executed the tribunal's sentences. Impatient with the guillotine, Carrier crowded his victims into barges and towed them to the middle of the river Loire and drowned them, as men armed with hatchets waited on the shore to make sure none escaped; about 2,000 people were killed in the Loire, with couples often stripped and bound together, face to face, to die. The water finally became so polluted with carnage that it was forbidden to fish there.

Carrier also delighted in murdering children. Because their necks were too small to fit into the guillotine, he once ordered 500 children to be taken to fields and beaten and shot to death. One executioner working under Carrier's orders collapsed and died after beheading four young sisters. In the overcrowded prisons, 3,000 victims awaiting execution instead were killed by an epidemic. Under the reign of Maximilien Robespierre, millions of French people lived in terror, waiting to be murdered. After Robespierre's fall on July 28, 1794, the new revolutionary regime condemned his followers, and Carrier was guillotined on Nov. 16, 1794. See: **Robespierre, Maximilien.** REF.: *CBA.*

Carrillo, Braulio, 1800-45, Cos., jur., assass. Chief justice of the supreme court of Costa Rica, and president of the country from 1834-41. Exiled to Salvador in 1841, he was assassinated four years later. REF.: *CBA.*

Carrington, Henry Beebee, 1824-1912, U.S., lawyer. Admitted to the Bar in 1878. He was a military leader in the Civil War, and in the war against the Indians of the western plains from 1866-91. During the Civil War he recruited 120,000 Indiana volunteers for the Northern cause. He was instrumental in exposing the Sons of Liberty as traitors of the Union. Later he battled the Sioux in the Fetterman's Massacre in 1866. REF.: *CBA.*

Broadway producer Earl Carroll, right, shakes hands with "undesirable" Countess Vera Cathcart.

Carroll, Earl, 1893-1948, U.S., perj. The Pittsburgh-born Carroll entered show business by composing scores of popular songs (there would be more than 400), which included such ditties as "Canary Cottage," "Dreams of Long Ago," and " So Long Letty." While still in his twenties, he wrote and produced equally popular Broadway shows such as *The Land of the Lamp* and *The Love Mill,* earning so much money that he was able to finance his own continuous musical revues, which he dubbed Earl Carroll's *Vanities* (1923-35). He grew so rich, that he was able to build his own New York City theaters, one in 1923 to house the *Vanities,* and another in 1931.

Other than stints in Hollywood where he produced grade-B films (*So Long Letty,* 1929; *Murder at the Vanities,* 1934; *Love is News,* 1937; *A Night at Earl Carroll's,* 1940), Carroll concentrated on Broadway revues throughout his life. These were little more than flesh shows touched up with expensive scenery and a full-scale orchestra banging out risqué tunes. Carroll was obsessed with female pulchritude and lost no opportunity to display the bodies of his chorus line, but in 1926 he went too far, offering a scandalous private party that backfired, causing the producer to be sent to jail.

Carroll was notorious for producing extravagant, risqué shows. He personally supervised every detail of his *Vanities* productions, even the creation of the skimpiest costumes allowable on his statuesque show girls. A *Vanities* show girl always showed more of herself than her counterparts in George White's *Scandals* or Florenz Ziegfeld's *Follies*. Flesh, and plenty of it, was a Carroll hallmark. Nightclub chronicler Stanley Walker precisely described Carroll as having "a keen eye for nakedness."

Through the early twenties, Carroll flirted dangerously with the laws governing nudity and lewd, even prurient shows. He was warned dozens of times by police that his production numbers, involving almost naked women, bordered on the obscene and that he risked being closed down on morals charges. Carroll paid off the police and kept the doors to his theater wide open. The public, chiefly males, poured inside year after year to make him a millionaire.

In 1926 Carroll stepped too far over the taboo line, taunting the censors and flaunting Prohibition laws. Early that year, Carroll earned a great deal of criticism for championing Vera Cathcart who had been divorced from the Earl of Cathcart on grounds of "moral turpitude" and who was temporarily barred at Ellis Island from entering the U.S. as an undesirable. Vera, a determined and very feisty female, managed to bulldoze her way past American authorities and slip into a Manhattan hotel suite with her entourage. Earl Carroll was delighted and threw a lavish party for her at his theater on the night of Feb. 23, 1926. Most of the expense for the party was borne by Carroll's primary backer, Texas oil tycoon W.R. Edrington. Carroll offered the Countess Cathcart and his 500 or more guests all the bootleg liquor they could guzzle.

Most of those attending the party were entertainers and newsmen, but many an odd creature could be found that night among the tippling throng, including Harry K. Thaw, paroled murderer of architect Stanford White. In addition to the ample food and liquor provided guests, show girls in skimpy costumes danced with the VIPs to the strains of a full orchestra. Carroll then announced a Charleston dance contest, and a host of attractive young girls competed madly for prizes of cash and silk underwear. Writer Burton Rascoe, who was in the front row, remembered that "the first prize of $100 was won by a very pretty young girl, very fresh and innocent-looking, dressed in the ordinary street clothes of flappers of the period, in contrast with the other contestants, who wore abbreviated chorus costumes. The winner, however, wore black silk stockings and girdle with garter straps. But she had omitted to put on panties. The winner, guests were informed to their annoyance, needed the money; she was to undergo an operation for breast cancer at dawn."

The feature attraction Carroll offered that night began when he motioned a bathtub on wheels to be brought to stage center. Then, a tall, blue-eyed brunette, Joyce Hawley (real name Teresa Daughelos, a Chicago hog-butcher's daughter), all of seventeen, stepped to the tub. While Carroll held up an opera cloak in front of her, Joyce stripped stark naked and stepped into the tub, which was filled with champagne. The producer then proudly announced, as he dropped the cloak with a flair, that those wishing to drink from the tub should line up and get cups.

The guests queued and somewhat embarrassedly filled their cups as the tall, dark girl relaxed in champagne that barely covered her privates. Suddenly, there was a commotion. Joyce burst into tears at the shame of it all and then lapsed into unconsciousness. She had fainted, Carroll was told, undoubtedly from the shock of the ice-cold champagne on her naked body. Stagehands bundled up the limp girl in blankets and rushed her to a dressing room to

be revived. Carroll, disgusted by the failure of this gimmick to amuse, angrily ordered the porcelain tub wheeled off the stage.

Joyce Hawley's debacle dampened the spirits of the revelers and the party quickly broke up. The following day, Phil Payne of the New York *Mirror*, who had attended the affair, broke the story of Carroll's sleazy party, and the showman was promptly arrested for violating the Volstead Act.

Authorities seemed unconcerned about the nudity, questioning Carroll about the contents of that unspectacular tub. Did he know it was illegal to possess or even take a bath in any liquid containing more than 1.5 percent alcohol? Carroll shrugged. Was the tub indeed filled with champagne? Carroll laughed and said, "Hell no, it was full of ginger ale."

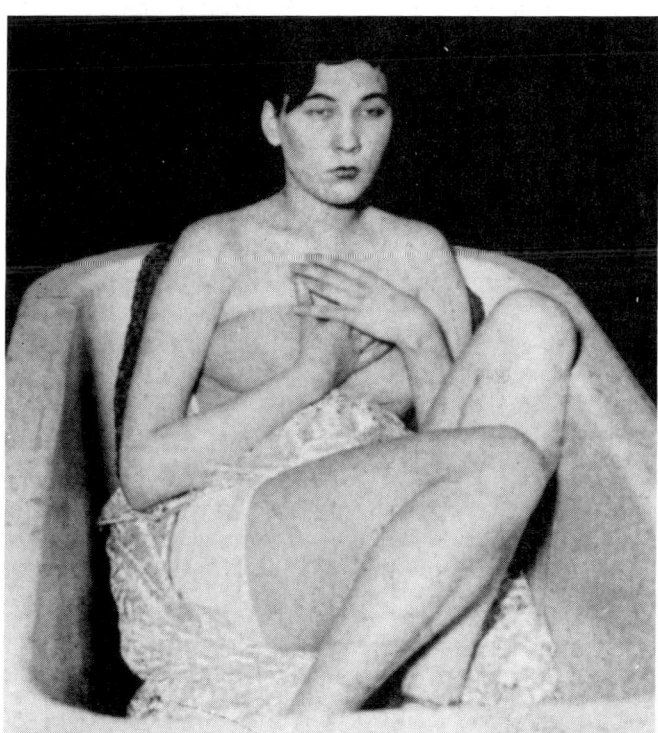

Joyce Hawley re-enacts her scandalous bathtub performance, clothed, for Carroll's notorious Cathcart party.

Untrue, said Joyce Hawley when she was brought in to testify against the producer. She was angry, as well as humiliated, she said. She stated that, yes, she had posed nude for artists as a model, but the Carroll party had been the only time when she had ever taken off her clothes in front of a non-artist crowd. And the contents of the tub, she insisted, had definitely been champagne. She had accidentally swallowed some when she slipped forward in the tub for a moment. Earl Carroll had promised to pay her $1,000 for the tawdry performance—money she sorely needed, she said—and then reneged, never paying her a dime.

Prohibition authorities pondered the case and then tried Carroll on perjury, for which he was convicted, fined $2,000, and sent to the federal penitentiary in Atlanta to serve out a year's term. He was released inside of three months after living "in very comfortable quarters where he was allowed to entertain visitors," according to one report.

Joyce Hawley went on to glean a bit more publicity when she appeared as "The Queen of the Bath" in the "Sensational Tub Tableau" at the Greenwich Village Follies in a reenactment of her bathtub performance, except that she wore a bathing suit and splashed inside of ginger ale, not champagne. The apprentice show girl capitalized on her notoriety by having cards printed up which she handed out to one and all. On these were her rates for various services—from $50 for a single photo of her in a bathtub (clothed in a bathing suit), to $1000 for what she called the "Life story and inside peeps behind the scenes of a lingerie show and nudity review."

Business must have been brisk but brief, for within a few months Joyce abandoned her meteoric show business career and returned to her mother, telling one newsman: "I'm going to help my parents now, and then I'm going to college." Joyce Hawley then exited into oblivion, while Earl Carroll went on producing musical revues and making millions.

REF.: Abel and Laurie, *Show Biz; CBA;* Churchill, *The Year the World Went Mad;* Cohen, *Mickey Cohen: In My Own Words;* Gosch and Hammer, *The Last Testament of Lucky Luciano;* Graham, *New York Nights;* McPhaul, *Johnny Torrio;* Markey, *That's New York!;* Morris, *Incredible New York;* Rascoe, *We Were Interrupted;* Rogers, *I Remember Distinctly;* Sann, *The Lawless Decade;* Walker, *The Night Club Era.*

Convicted killer Paul Dwyer, left, testifying against lawman Francis M. Carroll, 1938.

Carroll, Francis M., 1895-1956, Case of, U.S., mur. A patrolman making his rounds in North Arlington, N.J., in the early morning of Oct. 16, 1937, noticed a youth asleep behind the wheel of a large sedan parked at a curb. He leaned through an open window and shook 18-year-old Paul Nathaniel Dwyer awake. "Okay, okay," said the yawning Dwyer, "look in the trunk. The bodies are in the trunk." The policeman opened the car's trunk and stepped back. Stuffed inside were the strangled and battered corpses of Dr. James Littlefield and his wife Lydia. Carroll was immediately arrested on charges of murder and taken back to his home town of South Paris, Maine, where he was tried on Nov. 15, 1937.

Dwyer's confession to police, or rather his four versions of the murders, were revealed in court. He had consulted the 63-year-old Dr. Littlefield, Dwyer claimed, after suspecting that he had contracted a venereal disease. He said the physician had slandered his girlfriend, a waitress in South Paris, and that he had become incensed by this slur and grabbed a hammer, battering the doctor to death. He then put the body in the trunk of his car and went to Dr. Littlefield's house where he told the physician's wife, Lydia, that her husband had accidentally killed two men in a car crash and wanted to meet secretly with her in Concord, N.H. When they drove into New Gloucester, Mrs. Littlefield became suspicious of Dwyer's actions and accused him of murdering her husband. With that, Dwyer claimed, he exploded and grabbed the hammer once more, beating her to death with it. He then put Mrs. Littlefield's body next to that of her husband in the trunk. Taking his victim's money, Dwyer drove aimlessly through six states until, exhausted, he parked his car in North Arlington, N.J., where he was arrested. This was his story and he clung to it, ignoring pleas from his defense attorneys to provide motivation or even claim insanity. Dwyer was examined and pronounced sane. He was speedily convicted and sent to Maine's State Prison at Thomaston for life, Maine not having a death penalty for capital offenses.

Then suspicions about the case began to haunt Sidney Verrill, a deputy sheriff. He went to the prison at Thomaston and looked over the pasty-faced, puny Dwyer who was slender and bordered on being a weakling. Verrill found it impossible to believe that he could have carried the bodies of his victims, especially the heavyset Dr. Littlefield. Moreover, a cigarette lighter found in the driveway of Dwyer's house was identified by Verrill as one he had given to his friend Francis M. Carroll, a deputy sheriff of South Paris. Verrill reviewed Dwyer's confessions and saw that he had mumbled something about Carroll when he was arrested in New Jersey. Verrill also knew that, since Dwyer had gone to trial, Carroll had been drinking heavily.

Investigations into Carroll's movements on the night of the murder were conducted and it was learned that the deputy sheriff was a member of the American Legion, having attended each meeting for a year, except the one held on the night the Littlefields were killed. When the imprisoned Dwyer was again quizzed he provided yet another confession but this time he named Francis M. Carroll as the killer. He stated that he had seduced Carroll's 17-year-old daughter Barbara who told Dwyer that her father had had incestuous sex with her and that she hated him. Later Barbara Carroll wrote letters to Dwyer in which she obliquely referred to this incestuous relationship. Dwyer, in turn, confronted Carroll with this allegation and threatened that he would expose him if he dared to have sex with another daughter, by sending Barbara's letters to Carroll's wife.

Carroll, according to Dwyer, then wrote to him, demanding that he destroy his daughter's letters. When Dwyer refused, he said, he was almost murdered. When Dwyer was parking his car next to his home one night, a shot was fired at him by someone who quickly drove off in the darkness. Dwyer implied, of course, that Carroll had been his would-be killer. The deputy sheriff then accused Dwyer of making his daughter pregnant. Dwyer thought this to be impossible but he called Carroll's bluff by asking him to come to his house and bring his daughter Barbara. Awaiting Carroll on the night of Oct. 13, 1937, were Dwyer and Dr. Littlefield, who intended to examine Barbara Carroll to determine her pregnancy. Carroll showed up alone and Dr. Littlefield apparently confronted the deputy sheriff with having sexually molested his daughter. Dwyer had stepped outside at that moment to see if Barbara was in Carroll's car. In the meantime, Carroll exploded at Dr. Littlefield's accusation and grabbed a hammer, battering the doctor on the head and then pulling his pistol and continuing to strike Dr. Littlefield with this until he was dead.

When Dwyer reentered his house he found Dr. Littlefield's body, with Carroll standing over it. Carroll then ordered Dwyer to hand over his daughter's letters and then place the doctor's body in the trunk of his car, instructing the youth to take the body to a lonely place and dump it. Dwyer, fearful for his life, did as he was told but instead of dumping the body, Dwyer inexplicably drove to Dr. Littlefield's home, picked up Mrs. Littlefield, and told her that he was taking her to her husband. En route, Dwyer's confession went on, he told Mrs. Littlefield how Carroll had killed her husband, but he did not mention that he was driving her about in a car which contained her husband's corpse in the trunk. Mrs. Littlefield, instead of going to the police, insisted that Dwyer take her to see Carroll. Arriving at Carroll's home, he called the deputy outside. When Carroll saw Mrs. Littlefield, he clubbed and strangled her to death and ordered Dwyer to put her body, too, in the trunk of his car. This Dwyer slavishly did and then drove about in a daze for three days, living off the money he took from the dead victims.

This bizarre story constituted the case against Francis M. Carroll. Dwyer could not explain why he was at first willing to stand up to Carroll and then, following Carroll's brutal murders, was so willing to carry out the deputy's orders, stating that he was by then convinced that Carroll would kill him, too, if he failed to obey. The strange seventeen-page horror story somehow convinced Maine's special assistant attorney general Ralph M. Ingalls to reopen the case. Carroll was arrested on June 24, 1938. His trial began on Aug. 1, 1938, before Judge William H. Fisher in the Oxford County Superior Court in South Paris, Maine. Ingalls prosecuted and Clyde R. Chapman defended Carroll. The deputy pleaded not guilty and Dwyer was the chief witness against Carroll. While the trial went on, Carroll's daughter Barbara stood outside the courtroom and signed autographed pictures of herself, charging the curious 25¢ per photo. She posed in the woods nearby in a bathing suit and from her photographic fees, had a wave put into her hair. She began to receive proposals of marriage by mail. Her mother and the defendant's wife, Mrs. Ruby Carroll, walked up to her husband in court and told him: "Barbara has an offer from a New York nightclub at $1,000 a week."

"That so?" the deputy said lamely.

"Yes," his wife said sneeringly, "pretty good for a Carroll, isn't it?"

Carroll's appearance on the stand was a disaster. He was confronted with the alibi he had provided for the night of the murder and was shown that he had referred to the night before the killings. The deputy's face turned red and then he said that he had mixed up his dates. He was asked if he had had improper relations with his daughter Barbara. Carroll said nothing, merely hung his head and waited until his lawyer had the question struck from the record. Yet throughout the trial Barbara Carroll laughed, joked, and chatted with her father. She was thought to be the surprise defense witness but Barbara never took the stand. Clyde Chapman, her father's attorney, said that he would never call her as a witness because she was "moronic," and that her testimony would only "befog the issue." On the last day of the trial, Barbara got bored and absented herself from the courthouse while the jurors took five hours to come to a decision. She was sitting in the South Paris Theater watching Colin Tapley and Jane Regan in a jungle film, *Booloo,* when news was brought to her that her father had been found Guilty and had been sentenced to prison for life. She cried so that her mascara ran down her cheeks, then ran from the theater.

Carroll shown with his mother upon his 1950 release from prison.

Carroll continued to maintain his innocence and his attorneys filed endless petitions, appeals, and demands for a new trial. Finally, on Sept. 20, 1950, Carroll was released on a writ of habeas corpus which contended that the one-time lawman did not receive a fair trial and that he had been convicted on "false, perjured and manufactured evidence." He returned to South Paris, Maine, where he was a social pariah, going to work as a carpenter. Carroll died on Oct. 3, 1956, with many of his neighbors convinced of his guilt. His wife had divorced him and left the town while Carroll was in prison and had taken her two daughters with her. Dwyer, on the other hand, remained in prison, even though he appeared to be innocent.

REF.: *CBA;* Symons, *A Pictorial History of Crime;* Wilson, *Encyclopedia of Murder.*

Carroll, James, prom. 1880, Case of, Can., mur. As the result of antagonisms boiling over from a longtime feud with roots in Ireland, James Carroll and members of his clan murdered five people.

During the Irish potato famine of the early 1840s, immigrants hoping to start new lives flooded into Canada, bringing with them old feuds. James Donnelly, a Catholic who promoted cooperation with the Protestants, was the leader of a group known as the "Blackfeet." At the other end of the spectrum extremists who favored religious separatism were led by James Carroll, a local constable who formed a group of vigilantes known as the "Whiteboys."

Disregarding English law, the Whiteboys used arson and intimidation, earning the title, "Northern Ku Klux Klan." Under Carroll's leadership the vigilantes decided to destroy the Donnelly family. On Feb. 4, 1880, at Lucan in Ontario, James Donnelly, sixty-nine, and Johannah Donnelly, Thomas Donnelly, and Bridget Donnelly were awakened and viciously murdered with spades, clubs, and guns, and their home was set on fire. Later that night another Donelly relative, John, was killed at his brother's house three miles away.

The murderous gang of about twenty vigilantes had unwittingly left behind a witness—Johnny O'Connor, an 11-year-old boy who had survived the attack at the Donnelly's home by hiding under a bed. Though his father's house was mysteriously destroyed by fire, young O'Connor steadfastly identified Carroll as one of the gang leaders. The first trial in October 1880 was inconclusive, with no verdict brought in because of the jury's timidity. A second trial, in January 1881, brought in a verdict of Not Guilty for all six men charged, despite their obvious participation in the slayings.

REF.: *CBA;* Miller, *The Donnellys Must Die.*

Carroll, Janet Faye, 1940- , U.S., mur. After murdering her second husband, a North Carolina woman drove with her four children and her new lover to bury her spouse's corpse.

On June 13, 1969, Donald Carroll, recently discharged from the U.S. Army, fought with his wife, Janet, over the attention she had been paying to Jimmy D. Goins. Janet soon telephoned Goins from the Carroll's Greensboro, S.C., trailer home, saying, "I've shot my husband. Come right over and help me. I don't know what to do." At the Carroll's house Goins found Donald's body on a bloodstained mattress; Janet Carroll had killed her husband with a .22-caliber rifle while he slept. The couple put the body in the car trunk, then loaded up Carroll's children and drove to nearby Sanford to leave them with Janet's parents. Carroll and Goins took the corpse to Moore County, where they buried it and threw the rifle in Deep River.

Within a month of the murder Carroll took out a warrant charging Donald with nonsupport, claiming that he had deserted her to seek work somewhere in Tennessee, and reporting him as missing. A year later, after she and Goins had moved to New York and then back to Greensboro, Carroll divorced her husband on grounds of desertion and married Goins. All went well until they quarrelled, and an angry Goins went to the sheriff's office to complain about his wife's behavior. But Sheriff D.F. Holder of Lee County knew he had more on his mind than marital woes, "So we just kept pouring him coffee, and he just kept a-talkin'." By midnight, Goins confessed all, taking deputies to the scene of the crime and leading them to the decomposing corpse.

Condemning evidence at the trial included the bloodstained mattress on which Donald Carroll had been killed, still being used by the trailer's new tenants. Goins, convicted as an accomplice after the fact, regretted that his wife would have to do time, saying, "I wish I could do time for her." When arrested, Carroll was driving with a loaded .22-caliber rifle under the seat. At first calling the killing an accident, she later confessed to committing the murder in a fit of anger. The judge sentenced Carroll four to six years in the state penitentiary. Goins later received the same term. REF.: *CBA.*

Carroll, Mario, 1960- , and **Johnston, James,** 1959- , U.S., mur. A slow-witted boy became convinced that an elderly, crippled man had money and jewels hidden in his mattress and enlisted the help of his mother's lover to kill the old man.

Twelve-year-old Mario Carroll lived in a home with his crippled, divorced mother and admired Nazi uniforms, knives, and guns. From classmates he heard the rumor that Harry Lillywhite, also called Pops, an 82-year-old hunchback in the neighborhood, had a fortune hidden in his home. When he failed to persuade a schoolmate to help attack the old man, Carroll suggested the scheme to James Johnston, a 23-year-old laborer who was his mother's lover. When Carroll rang the doorbell Lillywhite told the pair to go away, but they forced their way in, and Johnston smashed a heavy wrench down on the elderly man's head. As Lillywhite screamed for help, Johnston bashed his skull. Searching the house, the killers found that Lillywhite had no hidden valuables, but instead lived in poverty on a small pension.

Within hours, police traced and questioned Carroll, who admitted his guilt. Carroll and Johnston were charged with murder and conspiring to rob Lillywhite. At the trial it was determined that Carroll had a low intelligence, with the reading skills of a 6-year-old. The judge, explaining that he didn't want to punish the boy, but "to insure that he will receive the education and training that he has been so lacking in life," sentenced Carroll to six years in a state school for boys. James Johnston, Carroll's accomplice, was sentenced to life imprisonment. REF.: *CBA*.

Carroll, Patrick, prom. 1835, Brit., mur. A private in the British Royal Marines, when jilted by a woman he had been courting, responded by murdering her.

Patrick Carroll met Mrs. Browning at Woolwich in 1835. He began romancing the widow, who ran an inn called the Britannia, probably with the idea of improving his finances, but she rejected him because of his excessive drinking. When she did not invite him to a tea party at the Britannia, Carroll waited until the next morning, then murdered Mrs. Browning by running her through with his bayonet. Carroll was tried and found Guilty in the Old Bailey's Central Criminal Court.

REF.: Brock, *A Casebook of Crime; CBA.*

Carroll, Thomas, b.1900, Case of, U.S., mansl. The timeless baseball cry "kill the umpire" took on new meaning on Sept. 26, 1926, when an overzealous fan rushed out of the stands to flatten an umpire. The umpire, who had just called a runner out at the plate on a close play, died a short time later.

The incident occurred in the eighth inning of a game at Degnan Oval, Long Island City, N.Y., between two semi-pro teams, the Cubs and the Centuries. With the Cubs ahead 4-1, the Centuries threatened to tie the score after putting men on first and third. As the pitcher took the sign from the catcher, the runner on third suddenly broke for the plate. The pitcher hurried his throw, and the catcher tagged the runner a split second before he slid across the plate. Umpire Patrick McTavey called the runner out.

Five hundred partisan spectators roared their disapproval. McTavey ordered play to resume when 26-year-old Thomas Carroll, brother of the Centuries' catcher ran onto the field, dealt the umpire a cruel blow, and fled. McTavey was taken to St. John's Hospital, where he died from a cerebral hemorrhage. Carroll was arrested and charged with second-degree murder. He was tried before Judge Gilbert Baker and a jury of baseball fans and ex-players at the Queens County Court on Feb. 15, 1927. After eight hours of deliberation, the jury returned a verdict of Not Guilty.

REF.: *CBA; Edge, Run the Cat Roads.*

Carrollo, Charles, prom. 1930s, U.S., org. crime-rack. In the days when Thomas J. Pendergast ruled both the political and the criminal realms of Kansas City and the state of Missouri, corruption was a fact of life. In April 1934, Kansas City's city manager Henry F. McElroy appointed Otto Higgins chief of police, and proudly announced that corruption in the police force was at an end. The previous director had been forced to resign when he hampered an investigation into the Union Station massacre, which had been directed by mobster John Lazia. Lazia's right-hand man, Charles Carrollo, did his work by intimidation.

On July 10, 1934, Carrollo drove Lazia to his hotel at 3 a.m. Lazia got out and then waited for Carrollo to emerge. Lazia was then hit by machine gun fire from two men waiting in ambush. Carrollo promptly replaced Lazia as Pendergast's man in control of the north side of Kansas City. The murder went officially unsolved, and Carrollo and Higgins became buddies.

The federal government decided to do something about Pendergast. Secretary of the Treasury Henry Morgenthau, Jr., sent treasury agents to investigate. But everywhere they turned they were subjected to Carrollo's intimidation tactics, ranging from waiters' refusals to take an agent's order in a restaurant to shots fired out of the night at an agent crossing a street. The agents continued in their work, however, and in 1939, Pendergast, Carrollo, and Higgins, were convicted of income tax evasion. See: **Pendergast, Thomas J.**

REF.: *CBA;* Hynd, *The Giant Killers;* Messick, *Secret File;* Reddig, *Tom's Town;* Smith, *Syndicate City.*

Carson, Ann, 1790-1838, U.S., count. Ann Carson was one of the first American criminals to gain notoriety in the young nation. The daughter of a naval officer, she married U.S. Army Captain John Carson. While on a military expedition against the Indians in 1810, the captain mysteriously disappeared. After two years and no further reports, he was presumed killed. In 1812, Ann Carson married another military man, Lieutenant Richard Smith, who was stationed near her home in Philadelphia. On Jan. 20, 1816, after a six-year absence, Captain Carson knocked on their door. Confused, Smith reached for a gun and shot the captain dead.

Smith was charged with murder, found Guilty, and sentenced to die. While he awaited his fate, Ann tried to kidnap Pennsylvania governor Simon Snyder, hoping to trade him for her husband. But the attempt failed, and on Feb. 4, 1816, Smith was hanged. Ann turned to a life of crime. She organized a gang of counterfeiters and cutthroats, and spent the next six years passing bad money around Pennsylvania.

By 1823, most of the Carson gang had been rounded up. Ann Carson died in Philadelphia Prison in 1838, while preparing her memoirs.

REF.: *CBA;* Nash, *Look For the Woman.*

Carson, Edward Henry (Baron Carson of Duncairn), 1854-1935, Brit., jur. Solicitor general for Ireland from 1892-1900, and member of Parliament from 1892-1921. In 1895 he successfully defended the Marquis of Queensbury against a libel suit brought by the playwright Oscar Wilde. REF.: *CBA.*

Carson, Thomas, prom. 1871, U.S., west lawman. A nephew of famous frontiersman Kit Carson, Thomas Carson was appointed a peace officer in Abilene, Kan., in June 1871. He quickly established a reputation as a man dangerous when provoked. After being reprimanded by his superiors, Carson left Abilene to accept employment in Newton, a boomtown best remembered as the site of the bloody "Newton General Massacre." Later that year, the Abilene city fathers rehired him.

Carson was again discharged after shooting bartender John Man in the hip on Nov. 22, 1871, without apparent provocation. In January 1872, Carson fired on Brocky Jack Norton, a former peace officer. The two men quarreled bitterly, and Carson settled matters the way he knew best: with pistols blazing. Norton survived the attack, but

Lawman-gunman Tom Carson.

Carson was held over for trial. Deciding that freedom was preferable to a likely prison sentence, Tom Carson made his escape before going to trial.

REF.: Bartholomew, *The Biographical Album of Western Gunfighters; CBA;* Miller and Snell, *Great Gunfighters of the Kansas Cowtowns;* O'Neal, *Encyclopedia of Western Gunfighters;* Streeter, *Prairie Trails and Cowtowns.*

Carstairs, Gilbert, prom. 1929, Brit., theft-forg. A forger who posed as a British military man stole subscription dues checks from elegant West End London clubs. Gilbert Carstairs was a convict free on probation when a series of petty thefts took place at several exclusive West End clubs and hotels in places like Mayfair and St. James. Briefcases, suitcases, and overcoats disappeared. Investigating detectives Albert Greenacre and a cohort discovered that in each case an impatient military man had come into the club around lunchtime, waited in the writing room for about an hour, then angrily left a message for his party to meet him elsewhere and left, taking a coat and briefcase with him. Warnings were sent to the clubs, and the thefts stopped. Within a few days, however, the clubs' mailboxes had been ransacked, and several annual subscription dues checks had been stolen. With the checkbooks from the earlier haul of briefcases and coat pockets, a massive forgery scam was obviously under way.

Greenacres and his partner checked the Forgery Library of the New Scotland Yard and came up with Harry Gristeller, a well-known forger, as their suspect. When they found out Gristeller was currently serving a term at Dartmouth Prison they went to his last address, Kentish Town, and kept an eye on his wife at a fish-and-chips shop known as a center for underworld activities. They also trailed Gristseller's mistress and discovered her leaving a letter for Gilbert Carstairs, a convict out on probation from Dartmoor, and realized he was working with Gristeller. The detectives caught Carstairs, disguised as an elderly army man, just as he was fleeing town, his pockets full of stolen and forged checks.

Carstairs' house in Kentish Town was set up for his operation with mapping pens, checks, and notebooks, address books, and checkbooks of West End club members. Pleading guilty to thirteen counts of forgery, larceny, and possessing a firearm with intent to endanger life (he had tried to pull a .38 revolver on the arresting detectives), Carstairs was tried at the Old Bailey and sentenced to eleven years in prison. The convicted man shrugged his shoulders at the sentencing, telling the judge, "Thank you! I expected at least fifteen!"

REF.: *CBA;* Fabian, *Fabian of the Yard.*

Carstares, William, 1649-1715, Scot., consp. Conspired with the outlawed Covenanters on behalf of William of Orange. When the Rye House Plot of 1683 was uncovered, he was imprisoned and tortured by means of the boot and thumbscrew. He survived this ordeal to become the king's chief adviser on Scottish affairs. REF.: *CBA.*

Carter, Alfred (AKA: Celluloid Alf), prom. 1944, Brit., burg. By bribing a building employee, a burglar gained access to a luxurious residential complex, rifling twenty-nine apartments in eight months. In February 1944 in the Chelsea district of London Alfred Carter, known for his ability to jimmy doors open with a small piece of celluloid, bribed a hall porter and began his burglary spree, stealing items worth £2,000 to £6,000 each time. Though police kept a careful watch on the residential block, with officers posted inside the building, they were unsuccessful until an astute detective named Fabian began to suspect the hall porter. Pretending to be short of officers, Fabian led the porter to believe that the coast was clear, hoping the man would give the go-ahead for another break-in. Within two days, another apartment was robbed.

The Criminal Investigation Department, Britain's equivalent of the FBI, reported an unusual taxi ride; the passenger had been dropped at the Park Hotel, then without entering the hotel, asked the driver to call him another cab, claiming to have forgotten something. Detectives Fabian and Bridgham were able to trace the cab and found that the address given by the mysterious rider was that of Alfred Carter and his wife Emelia Carter, both ex-

convicts. Entering their building on a pretext of visiting someone else, the detectives followed Emelia to her apartment, and discovered Alfred Carter with four buyers, the tables in his home strewn with jewelry, furs, and other valuables. Carter was sentenced to three years in jail; the building employee, Sergeant-Major Thomas Henry Burton, as his accomplice, got the same sentence.

REF.: *CBA;* Fabian, *Fabian of the Yard.*

Carter, Eliza, b.1869, Brit., miss. per. On Feb. 4, 1882, 12-year-old Eliza Carter left at about 10 a.m. for her parents' home in West Ham, England, after visiting an older sister. She never got home, but she was seen again that afternoon about 5 p.m., when she signaled to a classmate from an alley. The friend went to her and heard Eliza say that she could not go home because she was afraid of some man. Footsteps sounded just then, and Eliza ran off. That evening, her parents heard that Eliza had been seen that afternoon talking with a stout woman dressed in black. The next day, Eliza's dress was discovered, buttons torn off, in a football field. Eliza was never found.

Eliza Carter, missing in 1882.

Eliza's disappearance was not the first in the area, nor was it the last. The previous Easter, a girl named Seward disappeared without a trace. Two months after Eliza's abduction, a boy named Charles Wagner disappeared, but his body was found some time later at Ramsgate. None of the cases was ever solved, but they did stop for some years until there was another brief rash of disappearances in the 1890s.

REF.: *CBA;* Nash, *Among the Missing.*

Carter, Frank (AKA: The Phantom Sniper), 1881-1926, U.S., mur. In 1926, stores, churches, and theaters in Omaha, Neb. closed after dark during a two week period of random sniper shootings. The phantom killer fired silently, slaying a contractor, a doctor as he worked in his office, a girl sitting at a drugstore counter, and a railroad detective in the freight yards. Moving across the Missouri River to Council Bluffs, Iowa, the sniper shot at pedestrians and into people's homes.

A group of railroad workers finally captured the killer, 45-year-old Frank Carter, as he walked along the railroad ties on the outskirts of Omaha. An ex-convict paroled from the Nebraska State Prison after serving a sentence for shooting his neighbor's cows, Carter liked to brag about his skill with his silenced .22-caliber automatic, and said that he wanted to "kill, kill, kill." He was tried, convicted, and hanged shortly after his capture. See: **Bird, Jake.** REF.: *CBA.*

Carter, George, 1931- , Brit., mur. Apparently because he resented the financial burden of a family, a British laborer murdered his wife and caused permanent brain damage to his 6-year-old son. On Jan. 2, 1960, when twenty-nine-year-old George Carter came home from work for lunch, his pregnant wife, Ruby, thirty-three, lay dead in their bed, her skull fractured by three heavy blows. Carter's 6-year-old son, Alun, was severely wounded in a similar way, and would suffer permanent brain damage. Carter claimed he had gone to pick up his wife at the Cowbridge High School for Girls, where she worked, and became concerned when she didn't come out. A bureau in the Carter home was clumsily smashed, and according to Carter, £35 was missing. The wife had been dead for about six hours, so the murder had occurred at around 5:15 a.m., the time Carter left for work. The grieving but composed husband appeared on television to ask for assistance in finding his wife's slayer.

On Jan. 3 a heavy metal object was found in a field near the Carters' house. It was established as the murder weapon, and found to be from the factory where George Carter worked. On Jan. 16, he was charged with killing his wife. Although he maintained his innocence during his trial, Carter talked a great deal, presumably trying to deflect suspicion, and once claimed, "I have had to say I did not do it. But they can prove I did."

Carter was tried at Glamorgan Assizes, Cardiff, on Mar. 21 in front of Justice Barry, with W.L. Mars-Jones, Queen's Counsel as prosecuting attorney, and Norman Richards, Queen's Counsel for the defense. Evidence against him included twenty-three tiny spots of blood on his right jacket sleeve and testimony from his coworkers that he had flashed a number of banknotes at work on the morning of the murder, presumably hiding them later to give credence to his claim of burglary and a mysterious intruder. Carter's coworker, Paul Galton, testified that Carter, heavily in debt, had asked him for advice on how to end a pregnancy. Carter had been very proud of his recent purchase of a new car but was having difficulty making the monthly payments of £16, and apparently resented the financial strain of a growing family. Though all evidence was circumstantial, the jury found Carter Guilty as charged in just thirty-five minutes. He was sentenced to life imprisonment.
REF.: *CBA*; Furneaux, *Famous Criminal Cases, Vol. 6*; Wilson, *Encyclopedia of Murder*.

Carter, James Coolidge, 1827-1905, U.S., lawyer. Authored *Law: It's Origin, Growth, and Function*. REF.: *CBA*.

Carter, James Marshall, 1904- , U.S., jur. Taught in the Police School, Los Angeles Board of Education from 1934-35. He was a member of the commission to implement the Criminal Justice Act, U.S. Judicial Conference from 1965-68, and served on the subcommittee of the American Bar Association for *Minimum Standards for Criminal Justice*. President Harry S. Truman nominated him to serve on the court of the Southern District of California in 1949, and in 1967 he was named to the U.S. Court of Appeals, ninth circuit by President Lyndon B. Johnson. REF.: *CBA*.

Carter, James Y., 1916- , U.S., fraud-extor.-rack. A Chicago taxi commissioner for fifteen years, James Carter used his position for blackmail and extortion. As Chicago city public vehicle license commissioner from 1960-1975, Carter extorted almost $150,000 from five independent cab companies starting in 1962, just two years into his term. On Nov. 15, 1978, charged with nine counts of extortion, racketeering, and income tax fraud, the 63-year-old began his six-day trial in front of U.S. District Judge John F. Grady.

Initially attempting to enter a guilty plea to several charges, Carter refused to be specific about the crimes, causing Grady to refuse to accept his guilty plea. Witnesses testified that Carter had extorted funds by threats of suspension and transference of taxi licenses. He was found Guilty on Nov. 21, 1978. Prosecuting attorneys Thomas P. Sullivan and Walter Jones asked for a substantial jail term, saying Carter should be dealt with severely to set an example for other public officials tempted to abuse their power. Defense attorney Cora T. Walker requested leniency, noting Carter's ill health and the fact that a jail sentence would strip him of his right to practice law. On Jan. 10, Judge Grady sentenced Carter to a seven-year prison term, noting that he had successfully escaped punishment for fifteen years and saying, "We can't let success in this kind of conduct be rewarding to the person who engages in it." REF.: *CBA*.

Carter, John, and **Carter, Harry**, prom. 1760-80s, Brit., smug. A smuggler in Cornwall concentrated most of his criminal activity in the beach area where he and his brothers had grown up and played together. John Carter, nicknamed "The King of Prussia" as a child because he loved to play soldiers, grew up with his brothers near Prussia Cove, a beach in South Cornwall, between Marazion and Helston, hidden away from the open sea by an island. As adults, the Carters became well-known smugglers, doing most of their trading for more than thirty years in Prussia Cove. Primarily smuggling brandy and gin, the brothers preferred using the supply port of Roscoff in Brittany. They were well known by revenue officers, and were generally popular and respected as generous criminals. On one occasion, however, officers robbed the smugglers of several cases of liquor and that night the Carters retaliated by robbing the customs house, which was filled with valuables, taking only the stolen liquor.

French pirates who preyed on their boats were the Carters' worst enemies, and John Carter installed a cannon on a Prussia Cove cliff to fire at them. Seeing a sloop chasing one of his ships, Carter fired, discovering later he had attacked an English revenue boat and not one of the French privateers. The next day, Carter and his clan politely withdrew from their cove while soldiers struck back by firing on their lodgings. No one was harmed, but honor was avenged. In 1778, when war between England and France broke out, the smuggling trade suffered. Both John Carter and his brother, Captain Harry Carter were captured and held for two-year terms in the same jail. Harry was later captured again during the French Revolution and narrowly escaped the guillotine, living to old age and writing his memoirs, *The Autobiography of a Cornish Smuggler*, which told the story of Prussia Cove.
REF.: *CBA*; Scott, *The Concise Encyclopedia of Crime and Criminals*.

Carter, Nathaniel, 1951- , U.S., (wrong. convict.) mur. Convicted in the stabbing death of his former mother-in-law, Nathaniel Carter spent twenty-eight months in jail before his conviction was overturned when his wife admitted murdering her foster mother and lying in court.

On Sept. 15, 1981, Clarice Herndon, sixty, died when someone stabbed her twenty-seven times with a penknife in her Cambria Heights, Queens, home. Her adopted daughter, Delisa Carter, who lived with her, first claimed a stranger had broken into their home and attacked them both. Later, she said her former husband had killed her foster mother. Nathaniel Carter, living with his second wife, Kathy Carter, was arrested in Ossining, N.Y. Although two defense witnesses testified that he had been with them at the time of the murder, the jury convicted the former warehouse laborer of second-degree murder and he received the maximum sentence of twenty-five years in prison. Delisa Carter, the state's main witness, gained immunity from prosecution in exchange for her testimony.

Friends of Carter, a devoutly religious, former high school basketball star, refused to believe he was guilty. His current mother-in-law, Marie Parker, hired a private detective, James Nelson, who found so many gaps in the court reports that he and Police Commissioner Walter Kirkland interviewed Carter, became convinced of his innocence, and took the case to New York's Legal Aid Society. During an appeal by attorney William E. Hellerstein, Judith Cooper testified she had heard two women screaming at each other before the murder. In a secretly taped conversation between Delisa Carter and her former lover, Joseph Fife, Delisa admitted, "Carter hadn't done it."

Delisa Carter was arrested in January, 1984 at the home of relatives in Bristol, Conn. According to Queens District Commissioner John J. Santucci, she told detectives, "I killed my mother." Nathaniel Carter's conviction was overturned on Jan. 25, 1984, after Delisa Carter admitted to the murder in the State Supreme Court of Queens. Nathaniel Carter, thirty-three, had been released a week earlier after spending 28 months in prison.

Following her confession, Delisa Carter was given $20 for bus fare and released. Legal Aid Society lawyer William E. Hellerstein said, "If New York State had the death penalty, God knows what would have happened to that poor man." Further investigation into court reports and records showed that the police, prosecutors, and one of the defense lawyers made multiple errors of neglect or incompetence, including suppressing evidence and testimony, failing to call in witnesses, granting immunity to Delisa Carter despite her history of violence, and, in the case of one prosecutor, lying at the trial to make it appear as though Nathaniel Carter had admitted being at the scene the day of the murder. REF.: *CBA*.

Carter, Polk, 1906- , U.S., mur. The death of an elderly farmer in a small town in Georgia provoked so many rumors that, within a year, three of his relatives were accused of poisoning the old man. On Aug. 6, 1969, James Clark, a 77-year-old grocery store operator and farmer, died after a brief illness. He had married Effie Bell Clark less than three months earlier, and rumors that his marriage had hastened his death began to spread. Gossip also focused on Fannie Pearl Carter, Effie's 34-year-old daughter, and Fannie's husband, Polk Carter, fifty-three, who inherited most of Clark's estate. The illiterate farmer had died of a stomach ailment, and an autopsy generated whisperings that poisoning was suspected. Local law officials investigated the case for a year before they issued indictments against Effie Bell Clark Bennett, who had since remarried, and Fannie Pearl Carter and Polk Carter, charging them with poisoning Clark with arsenic from July 27 until his death.

At the trial, less than a month after the three were charged, Georgia State Crime Laboratory toxicologist Dr. June Jones testified that Clark's liver contained an arsenic concentration more than three times higher than normal, and said that he had suffered "massive liver and kidney damage." Jones also stated that all products with substantial amounts of arsenic in them were colored pink in accordance with the law. Effie Bennett, granted immunity in exchange for her cooperation, testified that she had seen her daughter and her son-in-law lace her late husband's food with "pink powder" several times.

Polk Carter, testifying in his own defense, denied preparing any food for his father-in-law and showed credit card receipts to prove he had been out of town during Clark's alleged poisoning. Despite this alibi and his claims that Clark had died of lead poisoning from tainted moonshine, the jury found Polk Carter Guilty of murder after a two-hour deliberation and sentenced him to life imprisonment. REF.: *CBA*.

Carter, Robert L., 1917- , U.S., jur. Named to the New York State Special Commission to investigate the Attica prison riot from 1971-72. He was nominated judge of the court of the Southern District of New York in 1972 by President Richard Nixon. REF.: *CBA*.

Carter, Rubin (AKA: Hurricane), 1937- , U.S., mur. In a highly publicized and controversial case that spanned more than a decade, former leading middleweight boxing contender Rubin Carter became a cause célèbre of civil rights fund-raising efforts. On June 17, 1966, at 2:30 a.m., three people were killed by shotgun blasts at the Lafayette Grill, a tavern in Paterson, N.J., during a period of racial tension in that city. The victims were James Oliver, the 52-year old bartender and part-owner of the tavern, Fred Nauykas, a patron, and Hazel Tanis, fifty-one, who died from bullet wounds a month later. Separately arrested and charged with the crime on Oct. 14 and 15, 1966, were John Artis and Rubin Carter, who claimed he barely knew Artis. The motive was said to be revenge for the killing of a black tavern owner in the same area earlier that evening; all three of the victims at the Lafayette Grill were white.

The policeman who apprehended Carter and Artis later testified that neither man had acted nervous or guilty, and that both had followed him to the scene of the crime with no reservations. A key witness at the initial trial, Alfred P. Bello, said he saw the defendants flee the tavern with guns and escape in a white car; Bello allegedly had been robbing a factory nearby when he was drawn to the scene of the murders after hearing shots. He admitted stealing money from the cash register of the Lafayette Grill soon after the shootings, and was present when police brought Carter and Artis in about half an hour after the attack. Both Bello and Arthur D. Bradley identified Carter and Artis four months after the shootings. Bello, who had served prison terms for burglary and robbery, recanted his testimony in 1974, claiming that detectives had coerced him into identifying Carter and Artis. He later disavowed his testimony a second time, offering two different versions of what he had seen. Another witness, Patricia Graham Valentine, who lived above the tavern, identified the two men although she had seen them only from the back, but she also described their escape car. And Emil DiRobbio, a homicide detective, testified that he had turned in shotgun shells found at the scene to the police property clerk's office.

In May 1967 Artis and Carter were convicted, found Guilty on three counts of first-degree murder and sentenced to life imprisonment. The case became a liberal cause, with Carter receiving support from the black community and from sports and entertainment figures. In December 1975 a "Night of the Hurricane" benefit held at New York City's Madison Square Garden helped raise money for an appeal. By March 1976, the New Jersey State Court overturned both convictions, ruling that important evidence had been withheld from the defense. Carter was freed on $20,000 bail, and Artis on $15,000 bail.

Because of prejudicial publicity against the defendants in Passaic County, the second trial was moved from Patterson to Jersey City. It began on Oct. 12, 1976, and was presided over by Judge William J. Marchese, who disqualified himself on Oct. 19 when defense lawyers protested that he might become a witness at the trial since he had sentenced Bello in an unrelated 1974 case.

Marchese was replaced by Judge Bruno L. Leopizzi. Patricia Valentine added to her testimony of ten years earlier that police had shown her a cartridge and shotgun shell they said they had found in the car Carter and Artis were driving when they were arrested. In the 1966 trial, detective Emil DiRobbio never mentioned showing the shell or cartridge to anyone but the police. The question of whether they had been found the day of the killings was a key issue in the 1966 trial. An investigation by *New York Times* reporter Selwyn Raab led to the reopening of the case.

Bello, the key prosecution witness, recanted earlier testimony which claimed that he had been "brainwashed" by police into identifying Artis and Carter as the murderers. Bello then renounced his recantation and declared in court on Nov. 15 that he had lied consistently throughout the trial and during the 1975 grand jury hearings. Asked about statements he had made in an affidavit to Assemblyman Eldridge Hawkins in 1975, Bello replied, "It's true that I said it, but it's not true." He later added, "Most of the things I said were complete lies to avoid the issue." Bello would later claim that both a television producer and an investigator from the State Public Defender's Office had offered him bribes to change his testimony.

On Nov. 22 Detective Donald LaConte corroborated Patricia Valentine's testimony when he said he, too, had seen the bullet and shell when he brought her to police headquarters so she could identify the car driven by Artis and Carter. The defense contended that the bullet and shell were planted by police to frame their clients. LaConte, the officer to whom Bello had first identified Carter and Artis as the men he had seen at the murder scene, said Bello told him later that he was "scared" because friends of Carter's had threatened him. LaConte said Bello told him, "You guys had the right men and you let 'em go," referring to Artis and Carter.

On Nov. 18 Judge Leopizzi prohibited anyone from contacting the jurors or their families about the case. The defense emphasized that the descriptions of the killers did not match either defendant, except that they were black, and that there was no strong case against the defendants until they were identified by Bello and Bradley four months after the crime. Vincent DeSimone, Jr., who had headed the initial investigation into the shootings, told a 1966 grand jury twelve days after the triple murders that the clothing worn by Carter and Artis did not fit descriptions from witnesses. DeSimone had said, "With the time element, we feel it is almost impossible that these men could have changed clothes." In the four-month interim between the incident and the arrest of Carter and Artis, DeSimone secured a positive identification of the defendants from Bello. In the 1976 trial, DeSimone, referring to a deal he made with Bello to drop charges on Bello's robbery attempt on the night of the killings, said, "If I could solve a murder by not taking action on a lesser crime, I'd do it every day of the week. I'd do it again tomorrow." William Hardney and Welton Deary, two former friends of Carter's, testified on Nov. 27 that they had been asked, prior to the 1967 trial, by Carter and his attorney at the time, Raymond Brown, to say that they had been with the former boxer at the time of the slayings. Hardney did not testify at the first trial. Deary had, and now admitted giving false testimony when he said he had been with Carter at the time of the murders.

Artis testified on Dec. 15, again telling the jury that he was not guilty. Carter declined to testify, just as he had in 1967. In final summations on Dec. 20, Passaic County Prosecutor Burrell I. Humphreys said the evidence built a "rope strong enough to bring two murderers to justice," while defense lawyers Myron Beldock and Lewis Steel, attorneys for Carter and Artis, respectively, challenged the credibility of most of the state's witnesses and focused on the uncertainty of the identifications of the defendants. On Dec. 26, 1976, Carter and Artis were found Guilty for the second time on three counts of first-degree murder. On Feb. 9, 1977, Carter was sentenced to two consecutive life terms and one concurrent life term and will not be eligible for parole until 1996. When Chicago novelist Nelson Algren died in 1981, he was working on a novel about Rubin Carter. REF.: *CBA*.

Carter, Stephen G., 1937- , U.S., consp. A ten-year veteran of the CIA was charged with conspiring to export a diesel assembly line from the U.S. to the Soviet Union.

On Jan. 5, 1983, the U.S. charged three men with conspiring to export the $5 million equipment to Russia in violation of the Export Administration Act. Charged were Stephen G. Carter, forty-six, of Palatine, Ill., Paul Sakwa of Washington, D.C., a former CIA agent from 1952 to 1962 and reportedly the chief covert activities agent in Vietnam for two years, and Gerald F. McCall of Toronto, all associates of Performance Sales and Marketing, Inc.. a commodities export business with Carter as president. They were accused of eleven counts of conspiracy against the government when they tried to export the equipment through the Arinfi Company, a fictitious business set up by federal agents and supposedly based in Paris. The assembly line was especially designed for the Russian Kama River plant, which produces military vehicles at the rate of fifty diesel engines an hour and made the trucks used in the Soviet invasion of Afghanistan.

On Jan. 10, 1983, Carter and Sakwa pleaded not guilty. McCall's lawyer, William Moffitt argued that his client was outside the jurisdiction of American courts, an argument accepted as a not-guilty plea for his client. In March all three defendants pleaded Guilty to the charges. On Apr. 1, 1983, Federal District Court Judge Richard Williams sentenced Sakwa and Carter to 300 hours each of community service and a year's probation for their roles in the plot. Williams fined McCall $1,000. Sakwa's lawyer, Mark Touhey III, had pleaded for leniency, noting Sakwa's service as a soldier and an employee of both the State Department and the CIA. Touhey maintained that Carter was the actual head of the operation, and that Sakwa became involved at Carter's request. Sakwa told Judge Williams he was sorry, saying, "I'd like to apologize for all this trouble. I do believe I was negligent." REF.: *CBA*.

Carter, Theodore H., 1932- , U.S., mur. A mildly retarded youth was discovered to be the murderer of a young woman in a small town after police spent several weeks following false leads.

On May 13, 1950, Alice Huen discovered the body of Lorraine Hess, a 17-year-old high school student, when she went to collect her son's socks from the clothesline in the backyard of her Millville, N.J. home. The socks, along with a green belt from Hess' coat, were wrapped around the neck of the strangled woman.

Heading the investigation were Public Safety Commissioner David Reid and Police Chief Samuel Fithian, later joined by State Police Lieutenant Jules Westphalen and detectives from nearby Bridgeton, the county seat. The investigators discovered that Hess had seen a play with friends the night of the murder, May 12, and had been dropped off by them about two blocks from the house of an uncle, John J. Sherman, where she planned to spend the night. Two men who had been out that evening, Charles Whilden, a college student returning from a date, and

Edward Keen, a factory worker driving home, both had seen Hess with a man on the street corner about a block from the murder scene, at around 12:30 a.m. Whilden's parents and a neighbor had heard screams, but had dismissed them.

After following several false leads, including the arrest and questioning of a local millhand and a traveling chemist with previous arrests as a Peeping Tom, police picked up Theodore Carter, an 18-year-old stockboy from Millville, who had left town shortly after the killing. Arrested in Bridgeport, Conn., where he had gone to stay with an uncle, Carter had been charged with disorderly conduct and was serving a ten-day jail sentence when turned over to New Jersey police for questioning.

On June 15, District Attorney Stanger stated that Carter had made a full confession to the slaying, saying, "I'm awfully glad to get these things off my mind. I'm full of shame." Though his mother denied that Carter had left town right after the murder, claiming her son had not gone to Connecticut until late May, Carter made five separate confessions to the crime. Since he could neither read nor write, he signed his name with an X and later declared in court that he made the confessions voluntarily. He was tried in late October 1950, in Bridgeton, N.J., in a trial that lasted two weeks and involved more than 100 witnesses. Carter's defense attorney pleaded for acquittal, saying that Carter had the mentality of an eight-year-old and that the police had dictated his statements and confessions. After several hours of deliberation the jury found Carter Guilty of first degree murder, recommending mercy based on his mental condition. On Nov. 10, 1950, Carter was sentenced to life in prison.

REF.: *CBA*; Radin, *Headline Crimes of the Year*.

Cartier, André, prom. 1936, Brit., mur. On Jan. 25, 1936, the body of a 55-year-old man was found on a quiet road in the outskirts of London, in St. Albans, Hertfordshire. The victim had been thrown out of a moving car after being shot six times. Scotland Yard detectives sent in the cleaning tag from the man's expensive coat and learned that the murdered man was Emil Haye, a jewelry salesman from Canada who lived in the Soho district of London. Sending Haye's fingerprints to the Yard, investigators discovered through American police and the French Sûreté investigations that "Haye" was actually Bull Jaw Donohue, a notorious American racketeer. When Police Constable Howard Barber, walking his regular beat in Little Newport Street, found three large glass splinters, he disposed of them by pushing them into the curb, and reported the incident to his sergeant. An inspector called Barber a few days later, showing him the photograph of Hayes, which Barber recognized from newspaper reports on the killing.

The two police officers went to the house in front of which the glass splinters were found and checked out the apartments there, discovering one, formerly occupied by a couple named Taylor, that had been abandoned in obvious haste. Sending the charwoman and the landlady to Scotland Yard, the police learned that the "Taylors" were really Yvette Constantine, who had previously operated an illegal racket in Paris, and André Cartier, a notorious gangster once sentenced to Devil's Island. In the apartment inspectors found a broken window, a half-burned slip of paper bearing the name Yvonne Ducre, with a list of wages paid for her services as a maid. Under questioning Ducre said Donohue had come to France from America to set up organized racketeering, and Cartier, his partner, had killed him in a fight over money. When Donohue was shot in Constantine's apartment, he staggered to a window, breaking the glass before falling dead. Cartier and Constantine were arrested soon after in Paris, and both were tried for Donohue's murder. Constantine was acquitted, and Cartier got a twenty-year jail term.

REF.: *CBA*; Cohen, *One Hundred True Crime Stories*.

Cartier, Sir George Étienne, 1814-73, Can., lawyer. Sir George Étienne Cartier served as attorney general of Canada from 1856- 58. In 1858, Cartier was elected joint prime minister, a duty he shared with Sir John Macdonald. Cartier held this position until 1962. REF.: *CBA*.

Cartouche (Louis Dominique Bourguignon), 1693-1721, Fr., rob. A celebrated leader of a band of thieves in Paris, Cartouche operated with wild abandon, robbing wealthy aristocrats and merchants from about 1709 until he was captured by Paris police. This colorful rogue was broken on the wheel on Nov. 28, 1721. Cartouche later became the subject of many plays and songs, in which he is portrayed as a legendary French criminal rivaling England's Robin Hood in bold adventures and extraordinary exploits. His name in French now applies to similar flamboyant felons. REF.: *CBA; Hunt, A Dictionary of Rogues.*

Cartwright, John, 1740-1824, Can., sedition. Political statesman often referred to as the father of reform for his advocacy of manhood suffrage, abolition of slavery in the colonies, and the emancipation of Greece. He served as chief magistrate of Newfoundland from 1765-70. In 1820 he was indicted for sedition, and fined. REF.: *CBA.*

Cartwright, Thomas, c.1535-1603, Brit., her. Leader of the English Puritan church, and professor of divinity at Cambridge from 1569-70. He was jailed for religious nonconformity. REF.: *CBA.*

Caruana, Salvatore Michael (AKA: Mike Bolero, Michael Carey, Mike Cassidy, T.W. Chapman, John Hurley, Mike Hurley, Sonny Face), 1938- , U.S., tax evas.-rob.-asslt. Reported to be extremely personable and outgoing, a convicted criminal with expertise in electronic surveillance is wanted for failure to appear on charges of drug smuggling.

Salvatore Michael Caruana, forty-one, has worked a variety of occupations as he pursues his real profession of crime. Convicted of bank robbery, assaulting federal agents, prison escape, and income-tax evasion, Caruana has worked as a pilot, sports shop manager, burglar alarm specialist, car salesman, and ice hockey arena operator. Known as a charmer who loves nightlife, Caruana is being sought by the FBI for failure to appear after being indicted on marijuana smuggling charges. He is reported to be heavily armed and is considered extremely dangerous. Last seen in Boston, Caruana is still at large as of this writing. The six-foot-tall criminal is of medium build, brown-eyed, with black hair. REF.: *CBA.*

Caruso, Frank T. (AKA: Skid Caruso, Frank Spino), 1911- , U.S., org. crime. Running several gambling operations inherited from his deceased father-in-law, Frank Caruso operates out of Chicago's South Side. Frequenting the area of Chicago's Near Southwest Side known as "The Patch," Frank Caruso, with a record dating back to 1935, has been arrested more than thirteen times on charges of grand larceny, gambling, and conspiracy. Operating out of Chicago's First Ward, Caruso is active in narcotics, gambling operations he inherited after Bruno Roti's death in 1956. His former legitimate business was Caruso Plumbing, in Hillside, Ill., a Chicago suburb. Caruso has a heart and the name "Viola" tattooed on his left arm, with a rose tattoo on his right. His brother, Joseph Caruso, is allegedly also connected with organized crime, as is Fred Roti, the alderman of the First Ward. REF.: *CBA.*

Caruso, Pietro, prom. 1944, Italy, war crimes. One of the most hated and feared men in Italy's fascist government, Caruso sadistically tortured victims who resisted the regime. Sent by Italian dictator Benito Mussolini to serve as chief of police in Rome, Pietro Caruso suppressed any resistance to El Duce and to WWII with a ruthlessness that made him one of the most despised men in Italy. During the last few months of Germany's occupation of Rome, Caruso kept a private apartment where he tortured those who opposed the fascists. According to London's BBC, Mussolini had movies taken of Caruso's execution of Count Galeazzo Ciano, Italy's foreign minister and Mussolini's brother-in-law, whom German dictator Adolf Hitler had condemned to death.

In June 1944 Italian partisans captured Caruso near Rome and delivered him to the Allies. Tried in Rome, Caruso told the court that he had only followed the orders of higher authorities and the Germans. Condemned to die, he was shot to death by a squad of sixteen Italian policemen as he was bound to a chair. Just before the police fired, Caruso turned his head toward them and called out, "Viva l'Italia! Aim well." See: **Mussolini, Benito; Hitler, Adolf.** REF.: *CBA.*

Carvalho, José da Silva, 1782-1845, Port., jur. Helped draft the constitution of Dom Pedro in 1842. REF.: *CBA.*

Carver, Donald (AKA: Jennie Gritz), prom. 1944, U.S., mur. At 6 a.m. on a day in December 1944, a severely battered man stumbled into the Columbia Precinct police station in Seattle, Wash., and collapsed. Taken to the hospital, Harry Lyons, a cook, died that same night. Shortly after Lyons came to the police station officers received a phone call reporting a bloody scene at a neighboring house, and the address turned out to be Lyons' house. Detectives found a number of clues, including fingerprints, a woman's glove and cosmetics, broken glasses, a beer bottle, a set of false teeth, and heel prints from a pair of women's high-heeled shoes, made by someone running. Lyons' two daughters were contacted and one identified her dying father, explaining that he lived alone and had $50 in his wallet the night before. Lyons had no money on him or in his house, and had staggered into the station with no coat or hat, despite the cold weather. It soon was discovered that Lyons' red Chevrolet also was missing.

Tracking down the clues, police received a report from a dry cleaner who told them he had received a woman's coat and a pair of suede shoes, both stained with blood, dropped off by a young man who said he or Jennie Gritz would pick them up. Then, a detective happened to observe a woman rushing to catch a bus and noticed that she ran on her toes, and realized that the heel prints had probably been made by a man—running on his heels—who had a rolling gait. After several days of looking for sailors who might know Gritz, investigators were led to Donald Carver, a young Merchant Marine. Carver was driving Lyons' red Chevrolet. Arrested in a police blockade of downtown Seattle, Carver confessed when confronted with the evidence. Needing a car to take some newlywed friends on a wedding trip, Carver had expected to borrow his foster mother's auto. When she refused him, he dressed up like a woman, picked up Lyons in order to steal his car, and murdered him in the process of the robbery. Carver was tried and convicted.

REF.: *CBA; Rice, 45 Murderers.*

Carver, William (AKA: Will, News Carver), d.1901, U.S., west. outl. William Carver was born in Texas and was a cowboy until joining up with the Ketchum gang in the early 1890s, robbing trains and banks throughout Texas and New Mexico. When the Ketchums were captured and hanged, Carver rode to Hole-in-the-Wall and joined the Wild Bunch, robbing trains and banks with Butch Cassidy, the Sundance Kid, Ben Kilpatrick, Harvey Logan, and others. When this gang broke up, Carver went on robbing banks and trains long after the heyday of the western bandit was over. He was finally trapped in 1901 in Sonora, Texas, following a robbery. Cornered by Sheriff Lige Bryant and a large posse, Carver refused to

William "News" Carver of the Wild Bunch.

surrender, preferring to shoot it out. He was shot to pieces and some reports later had it that Carver put a bullet into his own head rather than be taken prisoner. See: **Cassidy, Butch; Kilpatrick, Benjamin; Logan, Harvey; Sundance Kid, The.**

REF.: Appleman, *Charlie Siringo, Cowboy Detective;* Axford, *Around Western Campfires;* Bartholomew, *The Biographical Album of Western Gunfighters;* ____, *Kill or Be Killed;* ____, *Black Jack Ketchum;* Bechdolt, *Tales of the Old Timers;* Block, *Great Train Robberies of the West;* Burroughs, *Where the Old West Stayed Young; CBA;* Cunningham, *Trigger-*

nometry; Foster-Harris, *The Look of the Old West;* Harkey, *Mean as Hell;* Hendricks, *The Bad Man of the West;* Holloway, *Texas Gun Lore;* Horan, *Across the Cimarron;* ____, *Desperate Men;* ____, *The Great American West;* Kelly, *The Outlaw Trail;* Look, *Unforgettable Characters of Western Colorado;* Otero, *My Nine Years as Governor of the Territory of New Mexico;* Raine, *Guns of the Frontier;* Rennert, *Western Outlaws;* Sims, *Gun-Toters I Have Known;* Siringo, *Riata and Spurs;* Stanley, *No More Tears for Black Jack Ketchum;* Swallow, *The Wild Bunch.*

Casander, 350-297 B.C., Macedonia, mur. Son of Antipater, Casander was not named successor upon his father's death in 319 B.C., but he was supported by many Greek provinces. He conducted war against Macedonia and its regent Polysperchon. He ordered the kidnapping and murder of Olympias, mother of Alexander, then married Alexander's sister, Thessalonica. He fought a war with Antigonus (315-311 B.C.), then caused the murder of Roxana and her son. Eventually, Casander defeated Antigonus and ruled supreme in Macedonia, although his reign was marked by bloodbaths, murder, and endless conspiracies. REF.: *CBA.*

Casanova, Eduardo, prom. 1977, Guat., kid. A terrorist guerrilla group arranged to have its anti-capitalist message read to a meeting of international bankers after kidnapping El Salvador's ambassador to Guatemala. On May 29, 1977, a group of gunmen calling themselves the Guerrilla Army of the Poor kidnapped Eduardo Casanova, fifty-nine, an El Salvadoran ambassador. On May 30, the kidnappers' message was read to a banking conference of more than 1,200 delegates from all over the world, including U.S. Secretary of the Treasury W. Michael Blumenthal. The gunmen demanded that their message be read to "spare the life of that criminal," Casanova. The statement claimed "The millions in credits from the bank strengthen the exploiters of our people and support violence, repression, and violation of human rights."

The organization was linked to a Salvadoran guerilla group called the Popular Liberation Forces, which took responsibility for killing El Salvador's Foreign Minister Mauricio Borgonovo Pohl in early May. Casanova had been kidnapped because he headed the national police who the guerrillas held responsible for the deaths of thousands of peasants and workers. Kjell Eugenio Lauguerud, President of Guatemale and an army general, accused Cuba of financing and training the guerrilla army.

On May 31 the guerrilla army dumped Casanova by the side of the road in the southern section of Guatemala City. Casanova told reporters that he had refused to get back into his captor's car in the late afternoon of May 31, telling them, "Kill me if you want to. Liquidate me. My government is not going to negotiate with you." REF.: *CBA.*

Casanova, Giovanni Giacomo de Seingalt, 1725-98, Italy, fraud. Casanaova's career encompassed a spectrum of human endeavor. He was at various times an adventurer, a swindler, a gambler, a duelist, and a seducter. For twenty years he wandered through the capitals of Europe living as he pleased. In 1755 he was imprisoned in Venice for practicing magic, but affected a brilliant and daring escape, thanks to the wife of the Chief of Police who hid him in her home.

Casanova cheated and swindled many prominent people in his lifetime. The Marquise d'Urfe was one of many victims who fell under his spell. The aging woman wanted very badly to be young again, and enlisted Casanova, who claimed to have mystical abilities, to find a method. After several years of misleading the woman into thinking he could transform her into a youthful man, he convinced her to throw her jewels into the sea on a night with a full moon. Afterward, Casanova retrieved the precious stones and decamped.

During his lifetime, the great Italian lover rose to prominence in the court of King Louis XV where he became an intimate of many prominent French men and women of the age, including the philosopher Voltaire, and the infamous courtesan Madame de Pompadour. In Russia, Casanova fought a duel and was forced to flee the country one step ahead of the police. Later he was a police spy for the Venetian Inquisitors in 1774, and was exiled in 1782 for publishing scandalous libel. His memoirs, *Histoire de ma*

vie, renewed interest in the fascinating man when they were released for publication in 1962.

REF.: *CBA;* Hunt, *A Dictionary of Rogues;* Yeats and Brown, *Escape.*

Casares, Jose Hilario, and **Barbeito, Felix,** and **Morando, Jose,** prom. 1827, U.S., pir.-mur. Jose Casares was part of a band of pirates that boarded the brig *Crawford* in Matanzas, Cuba, as it was making its way toward New York. He, Barbeito, Morando, and others first tried to poison Captain Henry Brightman and his crew members but when this failed, the pirates attacked the crew, slew the captain, and drove the survivors into the rigging where they were eventually killed. The ship arrived in Old Point Comfort, Va., minus its crew and captain, and the pirates were identified and arrested. Several members committed suicide rather than face eventual hanging. Casares, Barbeito, and Morando were tried before Chief Justice Marshall and found Guilty. All three were condemned and hanged.

REF.: *A Brief Sketch of the Occurrences on Board the Brig Crawford; CBA; Particulars of the Horrid and Atrocious Murders Committed on Board the Brig Crawford; Piracy and Murder.*

Cascioferro, Vito, 1862-1945, Si.-U.S., org. crime-mur. One man was primarily responsible for establishing the strong connections that still exist between the Mafia in Sicily and the "Black

Hand" organization in New York that became the Cosa Nostra. A brilliant young man protected by a powerful family, Vito Cascioferro established a police record early, starting with assault in 1884. He went on to extortion, arson, and kidnapping, and was already a powerful figure in Sicily when he left for the U.S. in 1900. His backing from the Inglese family in Sicily came with him, and he quickly attained a responsible position in New York, serving as the link between the Old World and the New. He introduced the protection racket to the U.S., in which businessmen were required to pay a regular fee to stay in business. He taught the locals that the payment

Mafia don, Vito Cascioferro, shown with his son in 1902.

should never be so large that it might force the merchant into bankruptcy. Instead, the businessmen would make money and so would the protection racketeers.

Within only a few years, however, Cascioferro, already known as Don Vito, killed a man named Benedetto Madonia, then dismembered the body and hid it in a barrel. One policeman, Joseph Petrosino, was committed to destroying the Black Hand, and pursued Cascioferro until he was forced to flee the U.S. and return to Sicily.

Back in his native land, Cascioferro quickly became the head mafioso by ruling from strength, not from fear. He appears not to have killed indiscriminately to control the island. He was known for fairness and generosity, as well as for his cruelty to those he considered weaklings. Lieutenant Petrosino, who carried Cascioferro's photograph in his pocket, followed him to Italy, determined to expose the connections between the U.S. and Sicilian underworlds and to extradite certain individuals, including Cascioferro. But Petrosino was killed one night in a Palermo piazza where he had gone to meet an informer.

Within days of the execution, the police received an anonymous letter from New York naming several New Yorkers as the murderers on assignment from Cascioferro. Cavaliere Ponzi arrested Cascioferro on Apr. 3, 1909, but he had no proof of his complicity. Released, Cascioferro kept a firm hand on the Mafia in both Sicily and the U.S. for many years. In 1926, he was arrested by Benito

Mussolini's prefect, who was determined to destroy the Mafia. After he was sentenced to life imprisonment for the murders of two men, Cascioferro said that he had been guilty of many things in his life, but those two deaths were not among them. In 1945, after WWII, Cascioferro, in his eighties, asked to be pardoned and released from prison. The pardon was denied on the supposition that numerous relatives of men he had killed were waiting to take revenge. He died soon after in prison.

REF.: *CBA;* Servadio, *Mafioso.*

Case, William, 1855-1939, U.S., mur. An elderly man who had raised evergreen trees on his Ohio farm since early childhood committed murder when thieves stole more than 200 trees after a local magazine publicized him.

William Case, eighty-four, of Strogsville, Ohio, was known as "Santa Claus" for his generosity in donating an evergreen tree annually to decorate Cleveland's public square and for his tradition of handing out nickels to children at Christmastime. Since boyhood, Case had tended the trees on his farm. In December 1939, he was written up by *The American Magazine* for his charitable nature. Following the article, people came to his farm to steal trees by the truckload. On Christmas Eve Day, Case heard the sounds of yet another tree being chopped down. He picked up his shotgun, slipped up on two people tying a tree to their car, and fired twice, killing William Rousseau, thirty-seven, an unemployed man, and wounding his wife, Minnie Rousseau, twenty-nine. Case calmly explained his actions, saying: "The tree was theirs for the asking...But when people steal them it's different." After being told his arraignment was a formality, Case pleaded innocent to manslaughter and was released on bail. Later, at the request of Mrs. Rousseau, a grand jury refused to indict Case for manslaughter. He died in June 1939; his demise was withheld by relatives to avoid further publicity. REF.: *CBA.*

Casebolt, Crawford, 1934- , U.S., rob. In the fall of 1947, 13-year-old Crawford Casebolt was found Guilty in Pikeville, Ky., of using a pistol to rob a man of his car, a watch, and $4.84 in cash. Circuit Court Judge R. Monroe Fields sentenced the seventh grader "to spend the rest of his natural life at hard labor." Casebolt's sentence was the minimum punishment under Kentucky's armed robbery law at that time. REF.: *CBA.*

Case Book of Jimmy Lavender, The, 1944, a story collection by Vincent Starrett. This work of fiction contains a story ("The Raven's Claw") which is based on the murder trial of Ronald Light (Brit., 1920) which was also known as The Green Bicycle Case. See: **Light, Ronald Vivian.** REF.: *CBA.*

Casella, Louis, prom. 1910s, U.S., mur. A hit-and-run driver was tracked down through the painstaking detective work of a police sergeant who trained officers how to identify cars in the early days of the automobile.

In New York City, prior to WWI, streets held a combination of the motor car and the horse and buggy. One June evening, around Sixty-ninth Street between Park and Lexington Avenues, a speeding car hit the horse and buggy of John McHugh, a city street cleaning foreman, as he began his night inspection tour. Hugh was found by Patrolman John G. Dwyer and taken to the hospital where he died a few hours later. Dwyer assembled twenty-one broken pieces of glass from the scene of the hit-and-run and reported the incident. The next morning a street cleaner found a fragment of rubber, about three inches long, that apparently had come from a tire of the car.

Assigned to investigate the case was Sergeant John F. Brennan, instructor in the new field of car identification at the police training school. Carefully reconstructing the glass fragments, Brennan discovered that they were parts of lenses from gas and oil lights, and he uncovered patent dates showing the lenses had not been manufactured since 1912. Discerning minute fragments of gray paint on splintered wood shards the officer narrowed the make down to a gray 1909 Packard, Model 18, and surmised that it was probably in a garage for repairs that had resulted from the accident. Police checked all cars of that type, finding in a Long Island City garage a Packard of that make that belonged to Louis

Casella which had been stored in the Long Island shop but had disappeared two days earlier. Brennan went to Casella's home address, found him missing, and traced his mail to Allenhurst, N.J., fifty miles north of New York City. When he finally located Casella in Allenhurst the suspect had an airtight alibi, but Brennan managed to detach a small piece of rubber when he examined Casella's car and sent it to a chemist for analysis, where it was matched with the piece found at the crime scene.

Brennan, with the assistance of detective Edward J. Cousins, tracked down receipts for repairs to Casella's car, the evidence was assembled, and an indictment of first-degree murder was made. Casella, however, had disappeared. Brennan, presuming that the suspect would contact a lawyer, found the name of Casella's attorney and hid in a phone booth outside the law office, with the doors arranged to reflect the sun and keep him out of sight, until Casella finally appeared and was arrested.

REF.: *CBA;* Wren, *Masterstrokes of Crime Detection.*

Casement, Sir Roger, 1864-1916, Brit., treas. In 1915, at the German camp called Limburg Lahn, Sir Roger Casement offered Irish prisoners of war a chance to fight against England for the sovereignty of their own land. He promised them they would be guests of the German government until a German sea victory enabled them to land in Ireland. Even if Germany lost the war, he said, they would each get £10 or £20 and free passage to America.

Casement, Irish-born, was a retired civil servant who had spent his career working for the Foreign Office in the backwaters of Africa and South America, doing a good enough job to earn himself a knighthood in 1911. Only a few of the prisoners took Casement up on his offer. One of them went with him to Ireland,

Roger Casement shortly before his execution in 1916.

Casement himself leaving a bed in a tuberculosis sanitorium to make the trip. In his sickbed, he heard that the long-awaited Irish uprising was scheduled for Easter Sunday, 1916. He persuaded his backers in Germany—who were few because the officials disapproved of his constant companionship with a homosexual sailor—to give him arms and let him land in Ireland. They gave him an impounded Norwegian ship carrying 20,000 badly made Russian rifles, plus a submarine to sneak him into the Irish waters. Casement boarded the submarine with American-backed fighter Robert Montieth, and Daniel Bailey, the only representative of Casement's Irish Brigade. Because the Irish communications link through the U.S. failed, Casement did not know that the ship was expected on Easter Sunday evening, after the revolution had started, not on the Thursday before. Casement, Montieth, and Bailey landed at Tralee Bay, where there was no one to welcome them. Casement, weakened by his illness, chose to remain on the beach while the other two went for help. There on the beach a police constable found him the next morning. The next day, a British ship sighted the Norwegian vessel, which the crew scuttled before surrendering. Bailey was later caught, but Montieth remained free to assist the rebellion.

Casement was taken to London and tried for six separate acts of treason under a law from the year 1351. He never denied committing the actions for which he was tried, but he did claim they were committed purely for the sake of Ireland, not of Germany. He never had asked the prisoners of war to fight for Germany. But Casement could not deny that he received the enemy's assistance in his quest for Irish independence. Casement was found Guilty and sentenced to be hanged. Sentiment grew against his execution, but weakened at the publication of the "Black Diaries," which were purportedly found in Casement's home, and which described in detail a variety of homosexual acts. His lawyer's appeal was based on the language of the treason act of 1351, which, he claimed, did not include actions which took place outside the borders of the country. A panel of five judges rejected the appeal. Roger Casement was stripped of his knighthood and hanged at Pentonville Prison on Aug. 3, 1916.

Despite the fact that British law required a person hanged for murder to be buried in the prison where he was executed, the new nation of Eire made numerous efforts over the next decades to obtain Casement's remains. They were continually denied, until Feb. 23, 1965, when his body was taken to Dublin and he was reburied as a patriot.

REF.: Atholl, *Shadow of the Gallows*; Barker, *Lord Darling's Favorite Cases*; Casement, *Diaries of Sir Roger Casement: His Mission to Germany and the Findlay Affair*; *CBA*; Earl of Birkenhead, *Famous Trials of History*; Gwynn, *The Life and Death of Roger Casement*; Humphreys, *A Book of Trials*; ____, *Criminal Days*; Maloney, *The Forged Casement Diaries*; Parmiter, *Roger Casement*; Reppetto, *The Blue Parade*; Scott, *The Concise Encyclopedia of Crime and Criminals*; Spindler, *Gun-Running for Casement*.

Case of Clyde Griffiths, The, 1936, a play by Erwin Piscator and Lena Goldschmidt. Dreiser's *An American Tragedy* served as the basis of this play, the case of Chester Gillette (U.S., 1906) being at the heart of the novel. See: **Gillette, Chester**. REF.: *CBA*.

Case of the Solid Key, The, 1941, a novel by Anthony Boucher (William Anthony Parker White). This work presents a plot that is taken from the modus operandi of mass killer Herman Webster Mudgett (U.S., 1893-96) who was also known as H.H. Holmes. See: **Mudgett, Herman Webster**. REF.: *CBA*.

Caserio, Santo, See: **Carnot, Marie François Sadi**.

Casey, James P., See: **Cora, Charles; San Francisco Vigilance Committee**.

Casey, John Edward, prom. 1898, Brit., mur. A youth accused of murdering a young widow had earlier been involved in a disturbing incident with women's underclothing and a pig.

John Edward Casey, seventeen, lived with his parents at Stokesby, near Great Yarmouth. On Dec. 23, 1900, he got drunk with friends at the Horse Shoes alehouse in a nearby village and ran away in tears when the friends teased him about killing a pig two years earlier. At 10 p.m. Casey broke into the home of Thirza Isabella Kelly, a young widow he had been observing since her recent move into the area. When Kelly awakened and screamed, Casey threatened to kill her, approaching her bed from the side where her infant lay. Grabbing the child, Kelly jumped up and, in the struggle with Casey, was fatally stabbed. She survived through the night and was found the next morning, Christmas Eve Day, by her mother, whom she told of the attack before she died.

Casey was arrested and tried at Norwich Assizes, before Lord Chief Justice Alverstone. The defense maintained that Casey had killed in "an attack of mania," citing the story of the pig slaying. Two years before Kelly's murder, young Casey had broken into his employer's home and stolen some women's underwear, put it on, and then killed a pig, scattering pieces of the dead animal all over the house, finally dressing up the remaining torso of the pig in the women's underwear and hanging it up in the parlor. The Superintendent of Norfolk Lunatic Asylum pointed to this incident as an indication of a perversion that found "intense sensual pleasure in killing creatures and shedding blood." Casey was found Guilty of murder, with the jury expressing no judgment on his sanity. Sentenced to death by Alverstone, the jury recommended leniency on account of his youth and Casey's sentence was commuted to a life sentence.

REF.: Butler, *Murderers' England*; *CBA*; Shew, *A Second Companion To Murder*.

Casey, Joseph, 1814-79, U.S., jur. Joseph Casey served as a U.S. Court of Claims judge from 1861-63, and was appointed the first chief justice of the reorganized U.S. court from 1863-70. REF.: *CBA*.

Casey, Joseph E., 1890-1973, U.S., law enfor. off. Joseph Casey was a strong leader in the St. Louis, Mo., police force and served as police chief in that city for four months. A former first baseman in a semi-professional baseball league, Joseph Casey joined the St. Louis police force on Dec. 13, 1915, setting up its Mobile Reserve program and serving as Chief of Police from Sept. 17, 1959 to Jan. 15, 1960. REF.: *CBA*.

Casgrain, Philippe Baby, 1826-1917, Can., lawyer. Philippe Baby Casgrain was a lawyer and writer who authored *Notre Système Judiciare*. REF.: *CBA*.

Cash, Bailey, prom. 1938, (unsolv.) kid.-mur. During the early 1930s, there was a rash of kidnappings in the U.S. In 1934, New York kidnappings resulted in seventy-four abductors jailed that year. The *New York Times* carried a column called "The Kidnapping Box" to keep track of the arrest and conviction of kidnappers. The case of Bailey Cash, a 5-year-old who had been kidnapped and was found dead in thick undergrowth less than a mile from his home, proved to be the last kidnapping case of the 1930s.

REF.: *CBA*; Moorehead, *Hostage to Fortune*.

Cashiere, Catherine, d.1829, U.S., mur. A prostitute working lowly dives in New York City, Catherine Cashiere got drunk in a grog shop with another tart, Susan Anthony, and when Anthony made a remark about Cashiere's race (she was black of a caste called mustee), the harlot pulled a knife and slit Anthony's throat. When watchmen arrived, Cashiere handed the murder weapon to the arresting officers and laughed hysterically as she was dragged to a cell. She was tried and convicted, hanged on Blackwell's Island on May 7, 1829. A large throng gathered on the island to cheer Cashiere's execution.

REF.: *CBA*; *Trial, Conviction, Sentence, and Only True Copy of the Confession of Catherine Cashiere*; *Trial of Catherine Cashiere for the Murder of Susan Anthony*.

Cashman, John, prom. 1817, Brit., theft. During a tumultuous period of riots in England in 1816, thousands of men ransacked shops as they called for revolution. A year later, one man was hanged as a scapegoat.

On Dec. 2, 1816, London experienced the Spafields Riot. Spafields was the original meeting place of a mob attracted by handbills proclaiming protest against the conditions of society. Thousands of desperate men took to the streets, ignited by the speech of a man named Mr. Watson, who called for revolution. Gunsmiths' shops were looted as the mob called for arms, attacking the Royal Exchange, demonstrating against the Tower of London, and ransacking shops and taverns along the Strand and Fleet Street until the military was called out and the riot was quelled.

Though no lives were lost on either side, the authorities arrested, tried, and condemned a middle-aged sailor, John Cashman, a good-natured Irishman, for plundering the shop of a gunsmith, Mr. Beckwith. Cashman, who had fought in a hundred or more battles for his country, and was a genial, carefree man, was hanged on Mar. 12, 1817, in Skinner Street, Snow Hill, near the shop he had looted during the riot. Executed by hangman John Langley, who was hooted and booed by the huge crowd of spectators, Cashman, who had protested his innocence throughout, put on such a clowning performance as he was brought to execution that many doubted his sanity.

REF.: Bleackley, *Hangmen of England*; *CBA*.

Casimir-Périer, prom. 1893, Case of, Fr., assass. Because an anarchist focused on the French prime minister as the embodiment of the evils of capitalism, an assassination attempt was made on his life.

When a discontented, poverty-stricken anarchist, Auguste Vaillant, thirty-one, returned to France from his travels in Algeria and South America to try to find work at home, he could find only a poorly-paying job as a clerk. In his frustration, he decided to assassinate two important French political leaders, Prime Minister Casimir-Périer, a wealthy politician with interests in tin mines, and Charles Dupuy, the authoritarian president of the French Chamber. Vaillant made a bomb in his attic apartment and sneaked it into the Dec. 9, 1893, session of the Chamber. From his public gallery seat he tried to throw it down on the two men but, jostled by a woman next to him, Vaillant's aim was deflected and the bomb burst on a pillar, wounding several spectators. Casimir-Périer and

Dupuy were unharmed, with only a few stray nails falling down around them.

Vaillant was arrested on the spot and guillotined two months later. Astringent measures against anarchists were effected soon after, including legislation that made anarchists criminals at common law, restrictions against anarchist newspapers, stricter laws for explosives, and increased funds for the police force. The following year, sixty-four suspected anarchists were arrested. See: **Dupuy, Charles; Vaillant, Auguste.**

REF.: *CBA; Williams, Heyday For Assassins.*

Casler, Abraham, d.1818, U.S., mur. Abraham Casler, a native of Middleburgh, N.Y., had been forced to marry his wife, Catherine, in 1812 and he lived reluctantly with her for five years. Mrs. Casler suffered from fits and hysteria which also made Casler resolve, as he later claimed, to "seek peace." To that end Casler dosed his wife's food and drink with arsenic mixed with opium, poisoning her to death. The arsenic was detected and Casler was tried before Judge Yates in September of 1817. He was convicted and sentenced to death, hanged on May 29, 1818, at Schoharie.

REF.: *CBA; The Trial and Conviction of Abraham Casler.*

Cass, Lewis, 1782-1866, U.S., lawyer. Senator from 1845-48, Democratic presidential candidate in 1848, and U.S. secretary of state from 1857-60. He resigned in protest of President James Buchanan's failure to fortify the U.S. fort in Charleston Harbor. REF.: *CBA.*

Cassels, Sir James Dale (Jimmy Dale), b.1877, Brit., jur. Judge of the Queen's Bench Division of the High Court from 1939-61. He was called to the bar in 1908, and presided over the murder cases of Tony Mancini, Patrick Mahon, Norman Thorne, Daniel Raven, and the third trial of William Birkitt. REF.: *CBA.*

Cassibry, Fred James, 1918-   , U.S., jur. Member of the Louisiana Supreme Court Commission of Judicial Ethics. He was appointed judge of the court of the Eastern District of Louisiana by President Lyndon B. Johnson in 1966. REF.: *CBA.*

Cassidy, Butch (Robert LeRoy Parker, AKA: George Cassidy, William T. Phillips, Ingerfield, Lowe Maxwell), 1866-c.1908, U.S., west. outl. Butch Cassidy and his Wild Bunch members were the last of the old time western bank and train robbers, a motley group of outlaws with distinctive personalities and a flair for the flamboyant. Cassidy was no mean-minded desperado but a fun-loving, easy-going bandit who preferred to use his brains rather than his six-gun. He was backed up in most of his gun play by the lightning fast-draw artist, the Sundance Kid. His gang members included Will Carver, addicted to reading press notices about the gang; Ben Kilpatrick, the towering bandit known as the Tall Texan; and the most deadly of the group, Harvey Logan, who was also known as Kid Curry, a dead-eyed killer who vowed he would never be taken alive

The celebrated outlaw, Butch Cassidy.

by the law and kept his word. Born Robert Leroy Parker in Beaver, Utah, on Apr. 13, 1866, Cassidy was one of ten children and had no formal education. Cassidy became a cowboy while still in his teens when he met outlaw Mike Cassidy, adopting Cassidy's name after he joined him in rustling cattle in Utah and Colorado.

Cassidy taught Butch how to shoot so that he was able to hit a playing card dead center at fifty paces and his draw was much faster than historians later described. Mike Cassidy led a small band of robbers and rustlers but, after he shot a Wyoming rancher, he disappeared. Butch Cassidy took over the gang. The gang's hideout was at Robber's Roost, located in the southwest corner

of Utah, a rough, mountainous area which was difficult to find, even by the outlaws who returned again and again to the rocky haven. In early 1887, Cassidy met Bill and Tom McCarty, hard-riding outlaws who headed up their own gang which included Matt Warner (real name Willard Christiansen), Tom "Peep" O'Day, Silver Tip (Bill Wall), Gunplay Maxwell, and Indian Ed Newcomb.

When the McCarty boys suggested Cassidy join them in a train robbery, the apprentice outlaw happily agreed. On Nov. 3, 1887 Cassidy and the McCartys stopped the Denver and Rio Grande express near Grand Junction, Colo. The stubborn express guard refused to open the safe in the mail car and Bill McCarty put a six-gun to his head. "Should we kill him?" he asked.

"Let's vote," Cassidy said.

The gang members voted not to kill the guard and the train moved off leaving the bandits with not a dime in loot. Cassidy became disheartened with robbery and went back to rustling and occasional work as a cowboy or a miner in the local Colorado and Utah mines. It was almost a year and a half before Cassidy agreed to once more accompany the McCartys on another raid. This time the gang picked out the First National Bank of Denver, robbing it of $20,000 on Mar. 30, 1889. Tom McCarty approached the bank president that day and, expressing his sense of macabre humor, stated: "Excuse me, sir, but I just overheard a plot to rob this bank."

The bank president trembled so that he appeared to be undergoing an apoplectic fit, then managed to say: "Lord! How did you learn of this plot?"

"I planned it," McCarty said, pulling his six-gun. "Put up your hands."

Four men, Cassidy, Tom and Bill McCarty, and Matt Warner rode out of Denver with $5,000 each from the robbery, a fortune for those days. Warner immediately opened a saloon. Cassidy and the McCartys, however, decided to raid another bank and, on June 24, 1889, robbed the bank of Telluride, Colo., taking $10,500. Like the bank robbery in Denver, the gang never fired a shot. They merely trained guns on the bank employee, emptied the tellers' cages and looted the opened vault, then rode quietly out of town. Lawmen, however, formed huge posses and conducted wide and long searches for the bandits. This caused Cassidy and the others to go into hiding. Cassidy decided to follow the straight and narrow path and he took several jobs with ranches as a cowboy. He even worked as a butcher in Rock Springs, Wyo. which is where he earned his sobriquet "Butch." But such legitimate pursuits never worked out for Cassidy. A drunk picked a fight with him while he was serving customers and Cassidy knocked the man cold which caused his arrest. He was convicted of disturbing the peace and served a short term in the local jail. When released, Cassidy vowed he would never again work for a living.

Cassidy and Al Hainer, another cowboy, then began an extortion racket, selling Colorado ranchers protection, telling them that they would make sure that cattle was not rustled nor any of their property damaged by fire or other man-made hazards. Cassidy and Hainer were the man-made hazards, of course, and any rancher who did not pay his monthly protection fee had his cattle rustled by Cassidy and Hainer. Complaining cattlemen caused Wyoming lawmen John Chapman and Bob Calverly to hunt Cassidy and Hainer down to their cabin hideout near Auburn, Wyo. The lawmen crept up on Hainer as he was tending to the horses, wrestled him to the ground and tied him to a tree. Calverly then entered the cabin, his six-gun drawn. As soon as Cassidy spotted him he leaped for his two six-guns and gun belt, which were on a chair. Calverly fired four shots, one of which creased Cassidy's scalp and knocked him unconscious. Both men were quickly tried for extortion, sentenced to two years, and sent to the penitentiary at Rawlins, Wyo., on July 15, 1894. The man who had sworn out the arrests for Cassidy and Hainer, rancher Otto Franc, of the Big Horn Basin, was mysteriously murdered in 1903. Cassidy was released on Jan. 19, 1896, and immediately headed for a place called Hole-in-the-Wall, the last great hideout of the western outlaws. He had learned of this place behind the walls of the penitentiary and he resolved to put together the last super-bandit gang.

Hole-in-the-Wall was located in Colorado, more of a fortress than Cassidy's old Utah haven, Robber's Roost. At Hole-in-the-Wall, Cassidy was welcomed by the notorious Logan brothers, Harvey and Lonnie. Harvey Logan was the worst killer of the Wild Bunch, a brooding, small-bodied man with piercing black eyes, who had taken the name of Kid Curry, after another Hole-in-the-Wall bandit, Big Nose George Curry. Cassidy also met such gunmen and outlaws as Bob Meeks and William Ellsworth "Elzy" (or "Elza") Lay. Cassidy talked long and hard to these men about the mistakes he and others had made which resulted in imprisonment or death. He talked about how his friend Bill McCarty and another McCarty brother, Fred, had been shot to pieces in Delta, Colo., on Sept. 27, 1893, when they attempted to rob the bank there and how Matt Warner had been captured and sent to prison for a long prison term. (Warner would later reform and lecture against crime, dying in 1937.) Cassidy warned his fellow bandits that it was no good to merely ride into a town and rob the bank unless the town was scouted and it was learned whether or not a local vigilante group existed, or how strong the local sheriff's force was, how many deputies were in that town, and chiefly, how much money was really in the bank. Usually, he pointed out, such information could be easily learned by merely visiting the bank in advance and asking a few questions of its employees.

Butch Cassidy, cowboy turned outlaw.

On Aug. 13, 1896, Cassidy led Bob Meeks and Elzy Lay to the Montpelier Bank, which they successfully robbed of $7,165. Butch had scouted this bank some weeks ahead of the robbery, learning that money would be transferred to this bank a few days before he raided it. Next, Cassidy, with Elzy Lay and Joe Walker, rode to the large mining camp at Castle Gate, Utah, on Apr. 21, 1897, a camp where Butch had once worked as a miner. He knew when payrolls were received and paid and he and his fellow bandits arrived just in time to scoop up $8,000. Before the outlaws fled, Cassidy had Walker cut the telegraph wire so that the local lawmen could not be warned. Cassidy then rode to a New Mexico ranch with Lay where the two of them took jobs as cowboys. This was part of Butch's plans. He no longer drew attention to himself by freely spending the money he had robbed. He would put up a good "front" by pretending to work while posses were searching for shiftless thieves.

Cassidy and Lay left the ranch in early June, rode back to Hole-in-the-Wall and gathered more men, Harvey Logan, Walt Putney, Tom "Peep" O'Day, and Indian Billy Roberts. These men then rode to Belle Fourche, S.D., on June 27, 1897, and robbed

the bank there, taking about $5,000. On May 13, 1898, Joe Walker was killed with another man by a posse seeking cattle rustlers near Thompson, Utah. When the two bodies were brought in, the entire town of Thompson turned out to cheer, thinking that the other man was the dreaded Butch Cassidy, but the corpse was that of Johnny Herring, a lesser-known outlaw who bore some resemblance to Butch. Cassidy was far from dead. In fact he had, by then, carefully planned a train robbery at Wilcox, Wyo., on June 2, 1899.

The gang consisted of Cassidy, George "Flatnose" Curry, Elzy Lay, Harvey Logan, Lonny Logan, Ben Kilpatrick, the Sundance Kid (Harry Longbaugh or Longabaugh), and Ben Beeson. The bandits stopped the Union Pacific's Overland Flyer on a small trestle which was barricaded. When the train came to a halt, Cassidy ordered the engineer, W.R. Jones, to uncouple the express car. He refused and Harvey Logan pistol-whipped the engineer. He still refused and Lay took the controls in the engine's cab and forced the train forward. Just as it crossed the trestle the small bridge blew up. Cassidy and his men had forgotten a small charge of dynamite they had placed there. Once the train was some distance from the smashed trestle, the gang stood outside the express car and called out to the guard inside, a man who identified himself as Woodcock. He was ordered to open the express car door and come out.

"Come in and get me!" the defiant guard shouted to the bandits. A charge of dynamite was placed next to the door and the fuse lighted. The bandits dove into a nearby ditch and the resulting explosion tore the express car in half, sending Woodcock hurling outward. He was injured but alive. Harvey Logan ran up to the stubborn guard, pulling his six-gun and putting this next to the man's head. "This damned fellow is going to hell!" Logan shouted.

Cassidy ran up to him and brushed his gun aside, saying: "Now, Harvey, a man with that kind of nerve deserves not to be shot." Meanwhile the rest of the bandits ran about wildly, picking up more than $30,000 in bank notes and securities which had been blown every which way. This spectacular raid caused the Union Pacific to bring in the Pinkerton Detective Agency which sent scores of agents after the outlaws. Lawmen also, in dozens of posses led by such famous manhunters as Charles Siringo and N.K. Boswell, were on the trail of the gang. Cassidy decided that the best way for the outlaws to escape was for the Wild Bunch to split up. He, the Sundance Kid, who had become Cassidy's most loyal companion, and Ben Kilpatrick rode toward Hole-in-the-Wall while Logan, Curry, and Lay took a more circuitous route and were cornered by a large posse near Teapot Creek, Wyo.

The outlaws took refuge behind boulders while several possemen, including Sheriff Joe Hazen, charged their position. Hazen was shot off his horse, dead, by the sharp-shooting Harvey Logan. The outlaws then mounted their horses and, blazing away with their six-guns, shot their way through the ranks of the disorganized posse. Logan and Curry rode on alone while Lay joined notorious bandits, Thomas "Black Jack" Ketchum and G.W. Franks, and held up a Colorado Southern train on July 11, 1899, at Twin Mountains, N.M., stealing $30,000. The next day, the three bandits were surrounded at Turkey Creek Canyon, N.M., by a determined posse. A gunfight ensued and Lay was wounded twice and Ketchum once. The outlaws shot and killed Sheriff Edward Farr, Tom Smith, and W.H. Love before escaping. Ketchum was later captured and hanged for train robbery in a gruesome execution. Lay was trapped by lawmen in August 1899 and subdued after a desperate fight; he was sent to the New Mexico Territorial Prison on Oct. 10, 1899, given a life term. He would be paroled in 1906 and reform, living until 1934.

Despite losing some of his best riders, Cassidy put together another band of outlaws for another train raid. These bandits included Harvey Logan, who had managed to ride through several posses and return to Hole-in-the-Wall following the wild Wilcox robbery, the Sundance Kid, Ben Beeson, Ben Kilpatrick, and Laura Bullion, the Tall Texan's girlfriend. They stopped the Union

Pacific's Train Number 3 at Tipton, Wyo., on Aug. 29, 1900. Ironically, the express guard, Woodcock, was in the mail car and he again refused to open the door to the bandits. Butch shook his head in disgust and then said to the engineer: "You tell that iron-headed Woodcock that if he doesn't open the door *this* time, we're going to blow up him and the whole damned car sky high!" When the engineer pleaded with Woodcock, the plucky guard finally relented and threw open the door. The bandits blew open the safe and took more than $50,000, the largest haul taken by the gang up to that time.

The dynamited remains of the express car in Cassidy's robbery of the Union Pacific's Overland Flyer in 1899 near Wilcox, Wyo.

Joe Lefors, one of the most feared lawmen of the era, was assigned by the Union Pacific to track down Cassidy and his gang at all costs. He wore out fifty men and twice as many horses chasing the Wild Bunch across Wyoming but lost them when they slipped into their mountainous hideout, Hole-in-the-Wall. The gang rode out again to strike the bank at Winnemucca, Nev., taking $30,000 on Sept. 19, 1900. Next the gang rode far afield, all the way to Wagner, Mont., where Cassidy, Logan, Kilpatrick, the Sundance Kid, and Deaf Charley Hanks stopped the Great Northern Flyer on July 3, 1901. (The Sundance Kid had robbed a train near this spot almost ten years earlier.) Two of the men boarded the train, and as the train got up steam, Logan climbed into the engineer's cab by crawling over the coal tender, dropping down with two six-guns in his hands and ordering the engineer to stop the train. The Sundance Kid and Ben Kilpatrick raced through the passenger cars, firing their six-guns into the ceiling and shouting to the startled passengers: "Keep your heads inside the car!"

When the train came to a small trestle, it ground to a stop where Cassidy and Hanks were waiting. Cassidy planted a charge of dynamite beneath the Adams Express car and blew off its side. More than $40,000 was taken from the safe but most of it was in unsigned bank notes. This never bothered the Wild Bunch. Bill Carver or someone else with good penmanship merely signed the notes and these were quickly cashed or passed. During this holdup, Laura Bullion was present, tending to the horses. She was Ben Kilpatrick's girl, although she had been a mistress to many an outlaw before him. Following the Wagner robbery, the Wild Bunch split up for the last time. Ben Kilpatrick and Laura Bullion rode east and were later arrested in Memphis with part of the loot taken from the Wagner robbery. Both were given long prison terms. When Kilpatrick was released in 1912, he attempted another train robbery and was killed by an aggressive express car guard. Harvey Logan was later trapped by a posse and, rather than be taken captive, sent a bullet into his brain.

The fate of Butch Cassidy and the Sundance Kid after that has been much in debate. It is known that Cassidy and Sundance rode to Fort Worth, Texas, to relax in Fannie Porter's luxurious brothel. The Sundance Kid then took up with a bored teacher and housewife, Etta Place, a beautiful statuesque brunette who longed for adventure and left with Cassidy and Sundance when they decided that the West was too "hot" for them, all three going first to New York to stay in the finest hotels, eat in the best restaurants, and have their photos taken while wearing evening attire. The trio then traveled to Bolivia where they hid out by taking jobs as miners for the American-owned Concordia Tin Mine. While living in employee quarters (Sundance and Etta living as man and wife), the three went off on several raids. They reportedly took a vacation to Argentina and robbed a bank in Mercedes, San Luis Province, in 1906. Once more in Bolivia, Etta decided to leave the outlaws and returned to the U.S., where she changed her name and drifted into oblivion. Butch and Sundance, however, continued their errant ways. In Spring 1908 they robbed a Bolivian payroll in Aramayo and were trapped in the small village of San Vincente by a regiment of troops who had been looking for the "gringo" bandits. After a fierce gun battle in which Cassidy and Sundance killed a number of troopers, the bandits were finally killed, shot full of holes. A variation of this report has Cassidy wounded, looking upon his dead friend, and, rather than falling into the hands of the Bolivian soldiers, he put his six-gun to his temple and pulled the trigger.

Another story has it that only Sundance was killed in the murderous crossfire and that he gave his money belt and a letter to his best friend Cassidy, telling him to give these items to Etta Place, whom he had married. Cassidy reportedly watched the mortally wounded Sundance die and then, under the cover of darkness, escaped, returning to the U.S. There are many unsupported stories claiming that Cassidy returned to his birthplace of Circleville, Utah, and changed his name, living out his life there and dying in 1929. Another story has it that he moved to Johnnie, Nev., and lived there until 1937, running, of all things, a western curiosity shop. Still another tale insists that the celebrated outlaw survived until 1943 or 1944, dying in either California or Washington. See: **Carver, William; Curry, George; Ketchum, Thomas; Kilpatrick, Benjamin; Lay, William Ellsworth; Logan, Harvey; McCarty Brothers; Sundance Kid, The; Wild Bunch, The.**

REF.: American Guide Series, *Colorado, A Guide to the Highest State;* ____, *The Oregon Trail;* ____, *Utah, A Guide to the State;* ____, *Wyoming, A Guide to Its History, Highways, and People;* Axford, *Around Western Campfires;* Baker, *The Wild Bunch at Robbers Roost;* Bartholomew, *The Biographical Album of Western Gunfighters;* ____, *Black Jack Ketchum;* ____, *Western Hard-Cases;* Bechdolt, *Tales of the Old Timers;* Block, *Great Train Robberies of the West;* Brown, *The Plainsmen of the Yellowstone;* Burroughs, *Where the Old West Stayed Young;* CBA; Nash, *Bloodletters and Badmen;* Chapel, *Guns of the Old West;* ____, *Levi's Gallery of Western Guns and Gunfighters;* Chatterton, *Yesterday's Wyoming;* Coblentz, *Villains and Vigilantes;* Collins, *Great Western Rides;* Coolidge, *Fighting Men of the West;* Crawford, *The West of the Texas Kid, 1881-1910;* Cunningham, *Triggernometry;* Dunham and Dunham, *Our Strip of Land;* Foster-Harris, *The Look of the Old West;* Frankleton, *Sagebrush Dentist;* French, *Some Recollections of a Western Ranchman;* Gaylord, *Handgunner's Guide;* Hendricks, *The Bad Man of the West;* Hertzog, *A Directory of New Mexico Desperadoes;* Holbrook, *The Rocky Mountain Revolution;* Holloway, *Texas Gun Lore;* Hoover, *Early Days in the Mogollons;* Horan, *Desperate Men;* ____, *The Great American West;* ____, *The Wild Bunch;* ____ and Sann, *Pictorial History of the Wild West;* Howard, *This is the West;* Hunter and Rose, *The Album of Gunfighters;* Huntington, *Bill Huntington's Both Feet in the Stirrups;* Jones, *Life and Adventure of Harry Tracy;* Kelly, *The Outlaw Trail;* Look, *Unforgettable Characters of Western Colorado;* Martin, *Border Boss;* Metz, *John Selman;* Monaghan, *The Legend of Tom Horn;* Morgan, *The Humboldt Highroad;* Nash, *Bloodletters and Badmen;* Peattie, *The Inverted Mountain;* Pence, *The Ghost Towns of Wyoming;* Preece, *Lone Star Man, Ira Aten;* Provo, *Pioneer Mormon City;* Raine, *Guns of the Frontier;* Rennert, *Western Outlaws;* Reppetto, *The Blue Parade;* Rockwell, *Memoirs of a Lawman;* Sandoz, *The Cattlemen: From the Rio Grande Across the Far Marias;* Santee, *Lost Pony Tracks;* Sheller, *Bandit to Lawman;* Sims, *Gun Toters I Have Known;* Siringo, *Riata and Spurs;* Stanley, *The Alma;* Stanley, *The Mogollon;* Stegner, *Mormon Country;* Swallow, *The Wild Bunch;* Thorp, *Story of the Southwestern Cowboy;* Walker, *Stories of Early Days in Wyoming;* Waller, *Last of the Great Western Train Robbers;* Warner, *The Last of the Bandit Riders;* Wellman, *A Dynasty of Western Outlaws;* (FILM), *The Maverick Queen,* 1956; *Butch Cassidy and the Sundance Kid,* 1969; *Butch and Sundance: The Early Years,* 1979.

Cassidy, John F., and **Bishop, William Gerald,** prom. 1940, U.S., consp. J. Edgar Hoover arrested eighteen people and charged them with conspiracy to overthrow the U.S. government. Within a year, all charges had been dropped.

In mid-January 1940, J. Edgar Hoover, head of the FBI, arrested eighteen people, charging them with conspiracy against the U.S. Government. The scheme, an alleged plot to bomb a Jewish newspaper office and the Communist *Daily Worker,* seize U.S. government gold, wipe out all the police in Manhattan, then sabotage and commandeer public utilities to set up a U.S. dictatorship, involved sixteen rifles, one sword, 3,500 rounds of ammunition, and a collection of beer and soup cans intended to be turned into bombs, along with four belts of machine gun ammunition. The eighteen people arrested included a motley group of blue collar workers, a few Army and Navy reservists, and one captain in the National Guard. Several were involved with anti-Semitic Christian Front groups. Two of the Christian Front members were John F. Cassidy, thirty, and William Gerald Bishop, thirty-nine, deportees from Belgium and Britain. Bishop was said to be the leader of the group.

On June 24, 1940, nine of those charged were acquitted of the sedition plot charges, and a mistrial was declared in four other cases. The trial began on Apr. 3, at the U.S. District Court in Brooklyn under Judge Marcus B. Campbell. Claus Gunther Ernecke, thirty-six, committed suicide soon after, and George M. Kelly, twenty-four, and Edward L. Walsh, twenty-three, were discharged on May 10, after the prosecution rested. Judge Campbell ordered bail continued for Macklin Boettger, thirty-two, a traveling salesman; John Albert Viebrock, thirty-four, an elevator mechanic; Captain John T. Prout, Jr., twenty-nine, of the New York National Guard; and William D. Bushnell, Jr., eighteen. Prout was tried by a military court and cleared of charges of giving away government property and also found Not Guilty of conduct unbecoming an officer. Prout, whose father and grandfather had both served in the National Guard, had been charged with stealing government rifles and ammunition claimed that the case against him had been promoted by "certain interests" who sought "their pound of flesh" from him. The indictments against five remaining members of the Christian Front were nolle prossed in Brooklyn Federal Court before Judge Mortimer W. Byers on Jan. 2, 1941. REF.: *CBA.*

Cassini, Samuel de, prom. 1505, Italy, witchcraft. In the dark period of the Middle Ages when witchcraft trials and tortures were rampant, a few theologians stood strongly against the madness. One who adamantly opposed witchcraft, Samuel de Cassini, argued that the very belief in witches was heresy. Born in Turin and given a Parisian education, Cassini was a resident of Milan. As the idea of witchcraft developed during the fifteenth century, the demonology theories of the desert saints of Egypt were combined with ancient traditions of black and white magic to come up with a new heresy—witchcraft. With the 1486 publication of the *Malleus Maleficarum,* an inquisitor's manual detailing the specific procedures and questions for interrogating witches, wholesale license for prosecuting witches began. Writers who opposed the handbook were Cassini, Symphorien Champier, and Gianfrancesco Ponzinibio. Cassini took the position that the belief in the night-flying of witches was heresy. For several hundred years, inquisitors had to explain away this popular and pervasive belief. Cassini said the inquisitors themselves were heretical because they flouted church traditions. He further maintained that accused people should have their property and good names restored. REF.: *CBA.*

Cassius Avidius (Gaius), d.175, Roman., gen., assass. Led the Roman armies into battle against Parthia from 161-165. Through the military victories in Ctesiphon and Seleucia he was promoted to supreme commander of the eastern legions. In 175 he proclaimed himself emperor on the false rumor that Marcus Aurelius had died. He was assassinated by a cabal of his own officers. REF.: *CBA.*

Cassius Longinus (Gaius), c.20-65 A.D., Roman., jur. Au-

thored the ten-volume work titled *Libri Juris Civilis.* He was banished by Nero in 65 A.D. and was recalled by Vespasian. REF.: *CBA.*

Casswell, Joshua David, prom. 1920s, Brit., lawyer. Defense counsel in the murder trials of Neville Heath, Elizabeth Jones, and James Camb. REF.: *CBA.*

Castaing, Dr. Edmé Samuel, 1796-1823, Fr., mur. Soon after the discovery of the pain killer morphine, Dr. Edmé Castaing of Paris became the first person to use it to kill a victim. Because the properties of morphine were almost impossible to trace through chemical means, Dr. Castaing believed it was a foolproof way of eliminating the Ballet brothers, two well-to-do Parisians.

Hippolyte Ballet was a patient of Dr. Castaing's. The young man suffered from tuberculosis and was in fragile health. Through Hippolyte, the doctor met his brother Auguste. The Ballet brothers quarreled frequently and were on very bad terms. While dining together one evening, Auguste offered to gain control of Hippolyte's will if Castaing would murder him.

On Oct. 5, 1822, Hippolyte was found dead in his Paris apartment, to the puzzlement of the many doctors familiar with his condition. Nine days after the death Castaing discharged all of his many debts, advanced his mother 30,000 francs, and bought a large block of stock. No steps were taken to investigate the circumstances of Hippolyte's murder until Auguste died in the Hôtel Tête Noire in St. Cloud on June 2, 1823.

Although Auguste, who had recently signed over his fortune to Dr. Castaing, had displayed symptoms later associated with morphine poisoning, including nausea, fatigue, extreme restlessness, and a narrowing of the pupil of the eye; the medical examiners knew little about this kind of poisoning, contradicted each other about the symptoms, and had a difficult time establishing the presence of morphine in the system. During Dr. Castaing's trial, which began on Nov. 10, 1823, prosecutor General de Broe argued that the jury should not be misled by doctors unable to detect morphine, a type of vegetable alkaloid. He cited other conclusive evidence which established both motive and intent. On Nov. 17, Edmé Castaing was acquitted of Hippolyte's murder, but found Guilty of murdering Auguste Ballet. He went to the guillotine the following month still protesting his innocence.

REF.: *CBA; Furneaux, The Medical Murderer; Irving, A Book of Remarkable Criminals; Kingston, Dramatic Days at the Old Bailey; ____, Enemies of Society; Heppenstall, French Crime In the Romantic Age; Kobler, Some Like It Gory; Thorwald, The Century Of The Detective; Wilson, Encyclopedia of Murder.*

Castalas, Louis, prom. 1980, Fr., mur. A decorated and patriotic Frenchman killed his wife's lover when he realized that his 7-year-old son was sired by another man.

Louis Castalas had been a leader in the French Resistance in 1941. He was captured by the Gestapo and sent to Buchenwald and though experimented on by Nazi doctors, refused to reveal the names of his comrades. Awarded the Croix de Guerre and the Legion of Honor, Castalas continued to fight for his country against the Viet Cong in Indochina. He was again decorated with the Military Medal for gallantry. Married twice, Castalas did not tell his first two spouses that the Nazi operations left him sterile, hoping the diagnosis would prove wrong. Working as a police inspector at the age of forty-three, Castalas married a third time to Josiane, a woman seventeen years his junior. When his wife announced her pregnancy, Castalas was thrilled and became a devoted father to his son, Herve.

When Herve was seven, Casatalas came home one night and learned that his wife, visiting a nearby village, was stranded by a snowstorm, and would spend the night with her friends, the Tardes. Castalas went to pick her up the next day and found her talking with Pierre Laurent. Noticing the marked resemblance between Laurent and Herve, Castalas immediately confronted Josiane, who angrily confessed, "Yes, he is my lover and the true father of Herve!" Castalas shot Laurent, drove his wife home, then turned himself over to the police. He was tried and sentenced to a seven-year prison term by the judge who described him as "a

Frenchman of great courage and a glorious soldier of France." Castalas refused to see his wife or the boy he once called "son" again. REF.: *CBA*.

Castellammarese War, 1928-31, U.S., org. crime. Giuseppe "Joe the Boss" Masseria, one of the original members of the New York Mafia, restricted his criminal operations to his immediate neighborhood. He cloaked his activities with Sicilian "honor" and "respect," despised virtues among a younger generation of mobsters who urged him to forge alliances with the Irish and Jewish gangs threatening to take over the rackets.

However, for Masseria, Sicilian honor precluded contact with these other criminal gangs. The Mafia's "Young Turks" further questioned the wisdom of the elders in carrying on bitter power struggles and vendettas between Sicilians and Neapolitans, or between immigrants from two rival Sicilian towns. In 1928, Joe Masseria focused his attention on the threat posed by Brooklyn gangster Salvatore Maranzano who aspired to become the "boss of bosses." Maranzano, a native of the

New York's Joe "The Boss" Masseria.

Sicilian town of Castellammarese del Golfo, was one of a few townsmen to rise to power in America. Soon, Masseria realized he had a war on his hands for the control of New York.

On Masseria's side were Charles "Lucky" Luciano, Frank Costello, Albert Anastasia, Joe Adonis, Vito Genovese, Carlo Gambino, and Willie Moretti. The Maranzano camp included Joseph Bonanno, Joseph Profaci, Thomas Lucchese, Joseph Magliocco, and Gaetano Gagliano. These younger men would come to dominate the New York underworld in the years to come.

Two of Masseria's gunmen, Al Minco and Steve Ferrigno, killed in the Castellammarese War, 1930.

The Castellammarese War dragged on without a victory for either side, and certain gangsters, notably Lucky Luciano, decided to press for a peace agreement. With the support of Thomas Lucchese, Luciano plotted to eliminate Masseria, who obstinately resisted a settlement. The assassination of the aging "Don" was carried out at a Coney Island restaurant by Genovese, Adonis, Benjamin "Bugsy" Siegel, and Albert Anastasia. When the police arrived, Luciano disclaimed any involvement in the crime, saying he had been in the washroom at the time of the murder.

A peace was proclaimed with Maranzano named absolute ruler. Maranzano realized that Luciano and his contingent probably intended him for a fate similar to Masseria's, and defensively planned to eliminate Luciano, Genovese, Costello, Adonis, Dutch Schultz, and even Al Capone. Luciano, however, anticipated Maranzano's strategy, and, with the help of Meyer Lansky, hired four gunmen to pay a call on Maranzano on Sept. 10, 1931. Only hours before Vincent "Mad Dog" Coll was to carry out the purge planned by Maranzano, Luciano's gunmen, posing as police detectives, entered his office and shot and stabbed him to death.

For all practical purposes, the Castellammarese War ended with Maranzano's assassination. The days of the ethnically insulated Mafia were over. In its place stood the modern crime syndicate, which although dominated by Italians, now encompassed other ethnic groups. See: **Luciano, Charles; Bonanno Family; Genovese, Vito; Capone, Alphonse; Schultz, Dutch.**

REF.: *CBA*; Cressey, *Theft of the Nation*; Eisenberg and Landau, *Meyer Lansky*; Gosch and Hammer, *The Last Testament of Lucky Luciano*; Katz, *Uncle Frank*; Kobler, *Capone*; Maas, *The Valachi Papers*; Peterson, *The Mob*.

Castellano, Paul, 1915-85, U.S., org. crime. Shortly before Mafia boss Carlo Gambino died in 1976, he designated his brother-in-law, Paul Castellano, as his successor. Gambino had also considered Aniello Dellacroce, a member of the Gambino organization noted for his ruthlessness, for the number one position. In a conciliatory gesture, the don made Dellacroce Castellano's underboss and gave him control of the lucrative Manhattan operations. Although bitter at being passed over for the top position, Dellacroce accepted Gambino's offer.

In the next nine years, the Gambino family slipped in prestige and influence due in part to Castellano's conservative policies. Although his *capos* urged him to diversify into the airport rackets where rival mobsters were making a fortune in freight disappearances and labor racketeering, Castellano wanted to elevate Mafia business to a higher level, and chose instead to deal with legitimate businessmen like Frank Perdue, the chicken mogul. Perdue, who was having trouble getting space in New York supermarkets, moved his business to Dial Poultry, a concern run by two of Castellano's sons. Subsequent to the move, Perdue's chickens always received adequate space.

On Dec. 2, 1985, Aniello Dellacroce died of lung cancer. His death cleared the way for John Gotti, a disenchanted *capo* who had lost money under the Castellano regime. While Castellano made plans to name Thomas Bilotti underboss, Gotti plotted both of their deaths. On the night of Dec. 16, 1985, Castellano had Bilotti drive him to Sparks Steak House on East 46th Street. As they stepped out of their Lincoln limousine three men appeared and shot them. The assassins fled in a waiting car while Castellano and Bilotti, neither of whom had been armed, died in the street. As the press speculated about the rights of succession, John Gotti emerged as the new boss. See: **Gambino, Carlo; Gotti, John.**

REF.: Alexander, *The Pizza Connection; CBA*; Demaris, *The Last Mafioso*; Zuckerman, *Vengeance Is Mine.*

Castilla, Miguel Hidalgoy, 1753-1811, Mex., rebel. Member of the Catholic clergy, Castilla led the Mexican Independence Movement before he was executed. REF.: *CBA*.

Castillo, Ramon S., 1873-1944, Arg., jur. President of Argentina in 1942. REF.: *CBA*.

Castillo, Dr. Richard, 1890-1961, Brit., (unsolv.) mur. An elderly doctor answered a house call late at night and was found stabbed to death in a lonely cul de sac. The killer vanished.

On the night of May 7, 1961, 71-year-old Dr. Richard Castillo received a call at his Chelsea home. His daughter, Angela Castillo answered the phone and heard a foreign voice ask if the doctor would come and see his wife, who "has been sick, with blood," mentioning a name that sounded like "Alma." Dr. Castillo took the phone, and his daughter heard him say "Allenby," writing down the address as "3 Albert Bridge."

Castillo left to call on, he said, one of his partner's patients. By 1:30 a.m., when he still had not returned, his wife telephoned

Dr. Craig, a partner of her husband, who had never heard of a patient by the name of "Allenby" at that address, and then called the police. At the dead-end locally called "Artist's Row," off Albert Bridge Road across the river from Chelsea in Battersea, they found Castillo's body, stabbed twice by a knife. The 3 Albert Studios address had been vacated earlier that day by a woman who had lived there for a year and a half. A neighbor, Patrick Furse, had heard steps and a knock on the door of No. 3, then the sound of someone falling and crying out, "I have been attacked. Call a doctor." Another neighbor, Thomas Vaughan Welsh, rushed out to see Castillo staggering as he fell.

Detective William Montieth's only substantial clue was a report from a taxi driver who said he had picked up a fare at 11:45 p.m. the night of the murder, around fifty yards from where Castillo was killed. The case was never solved.

REF.: *CBA; Furneaux, Famous Criminal Cases, Vol. 7.*

Castillo Armas, Carlos, 1914-57, Guat., pres., assass. Right-wing political dictator supported by the U.S. government. In 1954 his military forces overthrew the government of President Guzmán Arbenz, and he was president of Guatemala from 1954-57. During his term labor unions, political dissent, and the left wing parties were vigorously suppressed, and he was assassinated. REF.: *CBA.*

Castle, Latham, 1900- , U.S., jur. Assistant attorney general in DeKalb County, Ill., from 1942-52 and attorney general of Illinois from 1952-59. President Dwight Eisenhower nominated him to the U.S. Court of Appeals, seventh circuit in 1959. He was vice-president of the State's Attorneys Association from 1928-42 and president of the National Association of Attorneys General from 1952-59. REF.: *CBA.*

Castro, Fidel, 1927- , Cuba, attempt. assass. An attempt on the life of Cuban dictator Fidel Castro was thwarted by members of the U.S. Intelligence community shortly before it could be carried off. The plot to kill Castro was hatched by Generalissimo Rafael Leónides Trujillo, the strong-arm military ruler of the Dominican Republic, and an avowed rightist who was opposed to Castro's presence in Latin America.

Trujillo located an American assassin who was to be flown secretly into Cuba to kill Castro. He was to be paid a fee not to exceed $1 million. Trujillo made his down payment, and a plan was conceived but the U.S. government stepped in to abort the operation. The would be assassin kept his down payment. In 1961, it was Rafael Trujillo, and not Castro who fell before an assassin.

REF.: *CBA; Davis, Mafia Kingfish; Kirby and Renner, Mafia Enforcer; Paine, The Assassins' World.*

Castro, Inés de (Inez de Castro; Agnes de Castro), c.1320-55, Spain, assass. Descendent of the royal house of Castile. She consorted with Dom Pedro (Peter I), son of Alfonso IV, king of Portugal, before secretly marrying him in 1354. Fearing political repercussions and the fact that their union might endanger the claim of his grandson Ferdinand, King Alfonso had Inés de Castro murdered. REF.: *CBA.*

Castro, Julie Ann, prom. 1974, Case of, U.S., mur. A young heir's taste for alcohol and firearms proved to be a fatal obsession. Bernard Castro, Jr., the moody heir to the Castro Convertible fortune, married a conservative young woman named Julie Ann. They lived in a beach house in the elite Coral Ridge section of Fort Lauderdale, Fla. which was one of their three homes. They had two children over a six-year period, during which time Castro's bouts with alcohol increased and his collection of armaments grew. The Castros boasted "his and hers" automatics, while Bernard had a second pistol and a mounted shotgun on his car, all legal in Florida state.

The couple began to quarrel and would point guns at each other in moments of anger. According to her later confession, Julie Ann Castro began to be afraid of her husband and concerned for her children's safety. When, at midnight on Oct. 29, 1974, Castro came home drunk, the couple at once resumed an earlier argument. Bernard pulled out an automatic and threatened to kill his wife. Julie Ann went into her room and returned with her

Colt pistol, then fired five shots into her husband's body, killing him. A Broward County grand jury unanimously accepted Julie Ann Castro's explanation of self-defense, and refused to indict her on any grounds.

REF.: *CBA; Godwin, Murder U.S.A.*

Casuse, Larry Wayne, prom. 1973, Case of, U.S., mur. Mystery surrounds the death of a youth civil rights leader in his Native American community. Though police admitted shooting Larry Casuse, they claim he killed himself, while his Navajo friends said suicide was contrary to his religious beliefs.

Casuse grew up in Gallup, N.M., a bright, enthusiastic student, and an officer of the high school Indian Club. With a Navajo father and an Austrian mother, Casuse, a Roman Catholic, moved easily in both the white and nonwhite societies he grew up in. At the University of New Mexico, in 1971, he became president of the Kiva Club, an Native American cultural and social organization, and gradually came to be intensely involved in political activism, joining Indians Against Exploitation and participating in protests.

Casuse spoke out at the State Commission on the Bicentennial Celebration in January, saying that money should be spent on people in need, not on celebrations. On Feb. 20, Casuse appeared before the state senate Rules Committee to criticize the appointment of Emmett Garcia, Gallup's recently elected mayor, to the post of regent at the University of New Mexico. Casuse explained that many Indians objected to Garcia's appointment because he was part owner of a tavern, the Navajo Inn, just outside the reservation, where, Casuse said, "numerous alcoholics are born."

On Mar. 1 Peter Derizotis, alcoholism coordinator for Gallup, opened the door to the mayor's office and found Casuse and another man asking to see the mayor. Though Derizotis told the men they would have to wait, the mayor shouted for them to come in. According to Derizotis' report, Casuse pulled a gun, though everyone who knew him said he had no experience with firearms, and that Navajo protest is traditionally peaceful. It was also known, however, that Casuse had been extremely upset by a recent automobile crash in which he accidentally hit and killed a young Navajo woman. A hung jury and a debate over whether Casuse had gone for help right away had recently necessitated a third trial, which was pending.

Holding the gun to the mayor's head, Casuse walked Mayor Garcia to Stearns Sporting Goods Store. There is speculation that the activist intended to hold the mayor as a hostage in order to negotiate an investigation into Gallup's treatment of Indians. At some point, police were alerted and local police chief Mr. Gonzales arrived with officers and guns and fired on the store, also shooting a tear gas bomb into the building. Casuse's companion came out with his hands up, but Larry Casuse was found inside, dying. His body was dragged outside and remained on the sidewalk for some time. A photographer for the Gallup *Independent* took a photograph of three policemen standing over the young man's corpse. Mayor Garcia was treated for cuts on his face and neck, caused when he jumped out of the window of the sporting goods store, and what police referred to as a superficial gunshot wound in his side.

Enraged at the newspaper photograph, a large group of Navajos, including many people who had no previous political involvement and were not in agreement with the activist students of Indians Against Exploitation, turned out to protest. Several thousand Native Americans attended a march four weeks after the death of Casuse. After buying controlling interests and then closing down the Navajo Inn, Frank Garcia lost his next campaign for mayor.

REF.: *CBA; Triiling, Killings.*

Catesby, Robert, 1753-1605, Brit., consp. Participated in the Rye Plot of 1603 to secure greater religious freedoms for Catholics from King James I. When this failed to achieve a result, he instigated the Gunpowder Plot of 1604-05 with Francis Tresham. However, Tresham had a change of heart and revealed the details of the plan to his brother-in-law Lord Monteagle. Catesby was killed while resisting arrest. REF.: *CBA.*

Cathars (AKA: Bogomils, Albignese, Waldenses), prom. 1208-1300s, Fr., witchcraft. A purist religious sect, disdaining the material world for the life of the spirit, so threatened wealthy church leaders that they opened a murderous crusade against them.

The beginnings of the medieval rampage against witchcraft can be traced to the church's campaign to wipe out the heretical sect called the Cathars, which, denouncing wealth and considering the church corrupt and worldly, believed the only way to salvation was to lead a godly life. In 1208, Pope Innocent III declared a drive against the Cathars. By 1209-10, 20,000 crusaders had stormed into the southern region of France known as Languedoc, massacring the inhabitants. A monk, Dominic Guzman, set up the Inquisition in 1229 in Toulouse, burning heretics and distorting the Cathars' belief that the world was created by the devil into saying that the Cathars were devil worshippers.

In 1242, the situation was further exacerbated when two of the Pope's inquisitors staying at Avignonet were killed in the middle of the night by a dozen outraged Cathars who stormed their house and slaughtered them and their servants with axes. In retaliation, the Pope escalated the crusade against the sect; in 1244, 200 Cathars were burned in a monstrous bonfire at Montségur. Survivors scattered and were pursued and murdered wherever the inquisitors found them, sometimes as far away as the Swiss valleys. It was at this time that the Cathars were loudly denounced as criminals who conspired with the devil, bringing into fashion the new crime of witchcraft, a phenomenon that would span four centuries of murder and torture. Before this time, witches were considered a benign and minor aspect of folklore, helpful crones who prescribed herbal remedies and told fortunes.

When the anti-Cathar crusaders first stormed into Béziers in 1209, the Church announced that the slaughter of the sect would not hinder the killers' salvation. Asked how the heretics should be differentiated from true believers, the papal legate said, "Kill them all; God will look after his own." Twenty thousand people were slain. In 1557, forty witches would be burned at Toulouse, then the center of the Cathars.

REF.: CBA; Wilson, Witches.

Cather, John, and Kane, Patrick, and Alexander, Daniel, prom. 1751, Brit., extor. Seeking revenge, John Cather organized a blackmail gang solely to extort money from Edward Walpole, secretary to the Duke of Devonshire when the Duke served as lord-lieutenant of Ireland.

Walpole met the gang of cutthroats when he advertised for a servant. John Cather applied for the job, but learned when he arrived at the estate that Walpole had already hired someone. Cather was nevertheless invited to spend a few days in the house as a private guest. One day, someone saw him sneaking out the back wearing one of Walpole's finest suits and, when caught, he was warned never to show his face on the grounds again.

Cather was enraged and offended that someone as lofty as Walpole should accuse him of such a low crime. After all, it was never proven that the suit actually belonged to Walpole. Cather wanted revenge.

Enlisting the support of Patrick Kane and a local attorney named Daniel Alexander, Cather concocted a blackmail scheme to smear Walpole. They underestimated Walpole's fortitude. He reported his blackmailers to the authorities, who put them on trial at the King's Bench on July 5, 1751.

Cather was sentenced to stand at the pillory at Charing Cross, Fleet Street, and Cornhill, where passersby jeered and pelted him, and then to hard labor in Clerkenwell Bridewell for four years. Attorney Alexander was sentenced to stand once at the pillory and serve three years in the King's Bench Prison, and Kane received the same sentence as Cather, spared only the ignomy of standing in three locations for all to see.

REF.: CBA; Mitchell, Newgate Calendar.

Catherine II (Sophie Augusta Frederica of Anhalt-Zerbst, Yekaterina Alekseyevna, AKA: Catherine the Great), 1729-96, Rus., adult.-morals-mur. Catherine the Great ruled Russia from 1762-96, a time when the empire expanded its borders at the expense of the peasants who were kept in misery and oppression. Catherine's reign included repeated sex scandals. Her marriage to Grand Duke Peter in 1745 was hastily arranged by Frederick of Prussia. The loveless union lasted until 1762 when Peter was deposed by Catherine and her lover, Tartar Gregory Orlov, who had him secretly poisoned. Gregory Orlov remained Catherine's lover for ten years, and she rewarded him with a gift of seven million rubles.

Catherine systematically eliminated her rivals who were perceived to be a political threat. Tzar Ivan VI, imprisoned since he was six, was killed by Basil Morovitch. It was widely believed that Empress Catherine was responsible.

At the age of forty-five, Catherine took a new lover, Prince Gregory Potemkin. He not only acted as the Queen's consort, but exercised real power in government, the military, and affairs of state. It was conceded by observers that Potemkin was little more than a high-priced male prostitute whose ostentatious lifestyle reflected the manners and morals of the imperial court. Catherine's need for continuous sexual gratification led her to organize an intimate private club known as the Little Hermitage, composed of her favorite courtiers who engaged in wild drunken orgies. See: Peter III.

REF.: Almedinggen, Catherine the Great; _____, The Romanovs; Castera, History of Catherine II; CBA; Dukes, Catherine the Great and the Russian Nobility; Grey, Catherine the Great; Gribble, The Comedy of Catherine the Great; Haslip, Catherine the Great; Henriques, Prostitution; Hyde, Empress Catherine and Prince Dashkova; Kennedy, The Palace of Leningrad; Longworth, The Three Empresses; Molloy, The Russian Court in the Eighteenth Century; Oldenbourg, Catherine the Great; Polotsoff, The Favourites of Catherine the Great; Scott-Thompson, Catherine the Great and the Expansion of Russia; Storch, Picture of St. Petersburg.

Catherine of Alexandria, b.c.307 A.D., Egypt, her. Converted the wife of Emperor Maxentius which angered the learned court philosophers. When they were unable to bring about her death on a spiked wheel, she was beheaded. REF.: CBA.

Cato, d.1803, U.S., rape-mur. Cato was a slave owned by Elijah Mount in Charleston, N.Y., who raped 17-year-old May Akins, a white girl. To cover his crime, Cato strangled the girl to death, but he was seen fleeing from the scene of the murder and quickly apprehended. Tried and convicted of murder, Cato was hanged at Johnstown, N.Y., on Apr. 22, 1803.

REF.: CBA; The Life and Confession of Cato.

Catoe, Jarvis Theodore Roosevelt, c.1905-43, U.S., rape-mur. Emma, the common-law wife of Jarvis Catoe, told police upon learning that he had murdered eight women, "He can't stay with me no more." His new residence would be death row.

Named after President Theodore Roosevelt, Catoe was born and raised in the small town of Kershaw, S.C. At twenty, he moved to Washington, D.C., where he ended up working as an undertaker's assistant and occasional police informant. Trading on his affiliation with the D.C. police, Catoe obtained a permit to drive a taxi, telling his boss that his last job had been with the metropolitan police.

First arrested in 1935 for indecent exposure, he served 135 days in jail. Arrested on the same charge in December 1935, he served 180 days more. District of Columbia police considered Catoe a minor nuisance. Little did they know that the "flasher" they held was also a sex killer.

Sixty-five-year-old Florence Dancy was Catoe's first victim, but the wrong man—41-year-old James Smith—was convicted on shaky evidence and imprisoned for life.

On Dec. 1, 1939, troubled by what he called "spells," Catoe strangled and raped 34-year-old Josephine Robinson, whose murder went undetected for nearly two years. Between Sept. 28, 1940, and Jan. 22, 1941, Catoe killed three more black women, but the police still had no strong leads. The next two D.C. killings galvanized public opinion against police ineptitude in the face of a real crime wave.

On Mar. 8, 1941, 25-year-old Rose Simons Abramowitz asked Catoe outside her 16th Street apartment if he had seen her landlord. He said that he had not. Then she asked him if he would be willing to wax her kitchen floor. He agreed, then raped and murdered Abramowitz once they were alone in her apartment. Despite hundreds of clues and the sworn statements of neighbors, Catoe still eluded police.

Three months later, on June 16, 23-year-old Jessie Elizabeth Strieff, a War Department stenographer, left her flat on 19th Street to buy some butter at Duncan's Delicatessen on Florida Avenue. Grocer Peter Duncan sold her the butter. He was the last person to see her alive.

Outside, Jessie Strieff hailed what she thought was a passing cab to get out of the rain. The driver of the car was Jarvis Catoe and he wore a chauffeur's cap. Instead of driving her home, he headed to a nearby garage and raped and killed her. He dumped the body in another garage, on Q Street, ten blocks away. The next day a maid found the body.

Despite hundreds of telephone tips to police and the assistance of the FBI, the crimes remained unsolved. Then, First Lady Eleanor Roosevelt stepped in. At a press conference, she admonished young women to be wary and suggested that more police might be the answer to Washington's crime wave. Louisiana Congressman Hebert urged Congress to act. Two police investigations were launched on Capitol Hill, resulting in major personnel shakeups.

Meanwhile, Catoe had driven north to New York City, where he murdered his eighth and final victim. At 6:20 a.m. on the morning of Aug. 4, 26-year-old Evelyn Anderson was stopped near 137th and Seventh Avenue in Harlem by a man asking directions in a 1937 coupe. He offered her a ride to work in return for the directions and she agreed. Twenty-four hours later, her body was found on Jerome Avenue.

The New York police connected Catoe to the murder when a watch belonging to Anderson turned up in a Harlem pawn shop. Catoe had given the watch to his girlfriend, Hazel Johnson, and it was then pawned by Johnson's uncle, Charles Woolfolk.

Bronx detectives Andrew O'Connor and William Carroll followed Catoe back to Washington and alerted local police about the evidence they had uncovered. Catoe was arrested on Aug. 29. Under interrogation he admitted killing Jessie Strieff and Rose Abramowitz. Then detectives took him to the Abramowitz apartment where he reconstructed the crime as reporters and police looked on. Captain Ira Keck had Catoe hold up his hands for the photographers. "Those are the hands you choked those women with?" he asked. "Yes," Catoe answered. When asked why, he said he suffered from "spells," especially after reading crime stories and looking at pornography.

Catoe confess to ten rapes, five murders, and the 1935 killing of Florence Dancy, but he later withdrew his confessions on the grounds that they had been obtained under duress and torture.

A Bronx grand jury indicted Catoe for the murder of Evelyn Anderson, but District Attorney Samuel Foley failed to have the killer extradited to New York to stand trial. Catoe was tried in Washington and found Guilty of murdering Rose Abramowitz. On Jan. 15, 1943, he was electrocuted in the D.C. district jail. As he walked the final steps to the death chamber he chanted an old Baptist hymn, *Precious Lord Take My Hand*. REF.: *CBA*.

Cato Street Conspiracy, The, prom. 1820, Brit., consp.-treas. Arthur Thistlewood, the illegitimate son of a farmer from Lincolnshire, was drafted into the British army and sent to the West Indies. But he bought himself out and traveled in the U.S. and France, where he witnessed the revolutionary terror. When he returned to England in 1817, Thistlewood was an ardent revolutionary. After he narrowly escaped the gallows in 1817 because a government witness failed to corroborate the evidence of treason against him, Thistlewood impudently challenged the home secretary to a duel, for which he was sent to jail. Upon his release, Thistlewood organized his fellow radicals into a militant political organization.

On Feb. 24, 1820, Londoners first heard the details of Thistlewood's bizarre plot when the London *Gazette* offered a reward of £1,000 for his capture. Thistlewood and twenty to thirty co-conspirators planned to assassinate fourteen ministers from the British cabinet as they dined at the Earl of Harrowby's house in Grosvenor Square. Thistlewood was to pose as a messenger and hand the butler a dispatch for one of the ministers. As the butler delivered the telegram, the conspirators were to storm the house and hurl homemade grenades into the dining hall. They planned to behead the prime minister, the Duke of Wellington, and other key officials and march with their heads on pikes through the streets, serving notice that a new "provisional government" had been established. But the government had infiltrated Thistlewood's organization with informant George Edwards, who reported the gang's every move since January.

Thirty Coldstream Guards descended on the conspirators' hideout, a loft above a stable on Cato Street, and found twenty of Thistlewood's men. During the following struggle, some of the men, including Thistlewood, escaped. Thistlewood was captured the next day at Little Moorfields. On Mar. 3, Thistlewood, the nine conspirators taken in the raids, and three conspirators found later appeared before the Privy Council where they were charged with high treason and the murder of a constable fatally wounded in the struggle. Two of these men, Robert Adams and John Monument, were allowed to trade evidence for their freedom, which allowed Edwards to leave the country to escape reprisal. On Apr. 15, 1820, the defendants' trial began at the Sessions House in the Old Bailey.

Four separate trials were held. Thistlewood, James Ings, Richard Tidd, William Davidson, and John Brunt, the second in command, were found Guilty. James Wilson, Richard Bradburn, James Gilchrist, Charles Cooper, John Shaw, and John Harrison changed their pleas to guilty, and were transported for life. On Apr. 30, Ings, Brunt, Thistlewood, Tidd, and Davidson were hanged outside Newgate. As they ascended the platform the Cato Street men were greeted like heroes. An hour after the hanging, a man in a black mask cut off the head of Arthur Thistlewood and displayed it to the crowd. REF.: *CBA*.

Catron, John, c.1778-1865, U.S., jur. First chief justice of the supreme court of Tennessee from 1831-34. President Andrew Jackson nominated him to serve as associate Supreme Court justice in 1837. He voted with the majority in denying the freedom of Dred Scott in 1857. REF.: *CBA*.

Cattanei, Vanozza dei, prom. 1480-1500, Italy, pros. Courtesans have practiced their trade throughout history. One even lived with the Roman pope and bore him four children. When Rodrigo Borgia, a native of Spain, became pope under the name of Alexander VI, he was brought to Rome by his uncle, Pope Calextus III. Borgia brought with him his mistress, Vanozza dei Cattanei, with whom he had four children, including Cesare Borgia and Lucrezia Borgia, who became important political and cultural figures, both cruel and treacherous. To cover his relationship with Cattanei, Borgia provided her with three different husbands.

As she aged, he gave her a pension. He then became involved with Giulia Farnese, a 17-year-old whom he persuaded to leave her husband and move in with him. Farnese allegedly participated in a variety of sexual orgies with the pope, including one in 1501 where fifty naked prostitutes crawled through a room filled with lighted candles. Farnese had three children with Alexander VI, and was commemorated in statues by Pintoricchio (*Madonna*), and Guglielmo della Porta (*Truth*), both of which she posed for. See: **Borgia, Cesare; Borgia, Lucrezia.**

REF.: Bullough, *Illustrated History of Prostitution; CBA*.

Cattle Kate, See: **Averill, James.**

Cauchy, Eugène-François, 1802-77, Fr., jur. Authored *Le Droit Maritime International*. REF.: *CBA*.

Caulfield, Frederick, prom. 1700s. Ire., mur. A premonition of murder led to the conviction of Frederick Caulfield, a down-and-out sailor from County Kilkenny, Ire. Adam Rogers, an innkeeper in the small village of Portlaw, near Waterford, had a strange dream in which he witnessed, in vivid detail, the murder of a large, squarely built man by his smaller traveling companion.

He told his wife and the Catholic priest of the parish, but they advised him to forget about the nightmare. He was determined to do this, until the next day, when the two men who appeared in the dream turned up at the inn seeking accommodations. They identified themselves as Hickey and Caulfield, and said they were traveling to Carrick-on-Suir.

After sizing up his guests Rogers decided that the killer-to-be was the brutish-looking Caulfield, and his victim would be Hickey, a man of refined temperament and some wealth. Rogers pulled Hickey aside and urged him to send his companion on and remain at the inn a day longer. He promised him a personal escort to Carrick if he did so. But Caulfield wanted no such arrangement and he convinced Hickey that since the two men had traveled such a great distance, from the West Indies to Ireland, there was no point in separating then. Hickey agreed.

Rogers pursued the matter no further, and as he bid them farewell, he found himself hoping that the premonition he had in his dream would come to nothing. But it was not to be. An hour's distance from the inn, Caulfield picked up a large rock and struck his companion over the head, then stabbed him to death. He fled with Hickey's money and some of his belongings, including his boots. Since shipping out from the West Indies, Frederick Caulfield deeply resented Hickey's financial advantages, advantages that he, a down-and-out sailor, could only dream about. Several times during their journey he had thought of killing Hickey, but the opportunity never presented itself until now.

Two days later, Caulfield was arrested at Waterford. He was tried and convicted on the testimony of Rogers, who recalled with amazing clarity the pair of boots that Hickey wore just before he left on his fatal journey. "Wasn't it odd that a keeper of a public house should know so much about the doings of two travelers?" Caulfield asked the court, in an effort to discredit Rogers.

The court demanded an explanation from Rogers, who reluctantly recounted his prophetic dream. It might have been dismissed as far-fetched, but Rogers' story was corroborated by the priest and several other townspeople he had told before Hickey left the inn. Frederick Caulfield was convicted and hanged. The final irony of this affair was the name of the presiding judge of the assizes—Chief Justice Caulfield.

REF.: *CBA;* Culpin, *The Newgate Noose;* Kingston, *Law-Breakers;* Mitchell, *Newgate Calendar.*

Caumont La Force, Antonin-Nompar de (Duc de Lauzun), 1633-1723, Fr., polit., treas. Imprisoned in 1665 by King Louis XIV for a dalliance with his mistress. Four years later he was again imprisoned, this time for criticizing the same woman. When he announced his intention to marry the Duchesse de Montpensier in 1671, he was imprisoned by the king for ten years. After agreeing to renounce his gifts from her, he was released, and allegedly married her a year later. REF.: *CBA.*

Caupolicán (Quepolicán), d.1558, Chile, assass. Ruled the Araucanian people in what is now Chile. He resisted Spanish colonial rule in a series of battles against Pedro de Valdivia in 1553, and against their colonial forces at Villagrán in 1557. Spanish forces led by Don Garcia Hurtado de Mendoza defeated Caupolicán in three decisive battles in 1558, forcing him to retreat to the mountains where he was captured and executed. REF.: *CBA.*

Cauty, Bill, prom. 1810-40s, Brit., rob. In a case that echoed Victor Hugo's novel, *Les Miserables,* a British police officer who had pursued a thief for years until he finally caught him successfully pleaded for the release of the criminal, who was an old man at the time of his conviction.

Bill Cauty, popularly known as "the father of all the robbers," was said to have had more than £500,000 pass through his hands during his criminal career. Starting as a bank clerk at a time when all articles of value, including bank packages, were sent through the mail, Cauty took advantage of his position to waylay consignments of great worth, leaving no trace of how they were stolen. Mr. Leadbitter of the Bow Street Runners, a group of law enforcement officials which was the precursor to the London police

department, brought in enough information against Cauty to have him thrown out of his bank position, though not enough to arrest or charge him.

Cauty then took to horse racing as a sideline, but was well enough versed in banking procedures to continue his lucrative thieving trade with the help of accomplices. When the House of Commons investigated the robberies, Leadbitter was asked if he knew any of the main culprits, and he said he did but could make no arrests because there was insufficent evidence and "it would be useless to arrest him unless we could insure a conviction." Asked to say whether Cauty was the same person then betting large amounts at the Turf, and keeping company with noblemen and gentleman, Leadbitter replied in the affirmative, explaining that the wealthy English citizens knew of Cauty's crimes but preferred betting with him "because he always pays."

So, years went by and Cauty continued to prosper in his illicit work. Eventually, however, his powers diminished, and, when an elderly Cauty stole a cash box from the London and Westminster Bank at St. James Square and walked along Haymarket with the box hidden in a bag, Leadbitter finally seized his man, along with an accomplice. Leadbitter had known of the complicated heist from its beginnings. Both Cauty and the accomplice were given life sentences to be served in penal colonies, but Leadbitter, sympathetic to Cauty's age and infirmity, pleaded for and got the old thief freed. See: **Bow Street Runners.**

REF.: *CBA;* Dilnot, *Triumphs of Detection.*

Cauvin, Louis, prom. 1891-96, Fr., (wrong convict.) mur. When the heir of an 80-year-old woman found her strangled in her bed, he was accused and convicted of the murder and the 16-year-old killer got away.

Madame Montet, an elderly woman who lived in a villa at La Blancharde, a suburb of Marseilles, disapproved of her relatives and so was leaving her land to Louis Cauvin, a neighbor she had known and been fond of for years. Montet lived with a 16-year-old maid, Marie Michel, who she had taken out of the orphanage of the Sisters of the Hospital of Toulon to work for her. Cauvin called on Mme. Montet daily to visit and talk—he had known her since early childhood. Shortly before Christmas in 1891, Montet was found dead in her bed, and a medical examination showed strangulation. The suspects were Cauvin and Michel. Cauvin had reported the death to the police, saying that Michel had awakened him around 1 a.m. to tell him she had heard her employer groaning and crying that she was choking. The girl said she was so frightened she ran to find Cauvin at once. Cauvin found Montet dead, then returned to his house. Four hours later, with his wife, mother-in-law, a servant, and Michel, he returned to Mottet's villa, then called a doctor in, telling him Montet had died of suffocation.

At first corroborating Cauvin's story, Michel, after several hours of questioning, confessed, saying that Cauvin had approached her on Dec. 16 saying he was going to murder Montet and that she had the choice of either helping him, for which he would give her 3,000 francs and guarantee her lifelong employment, or hindering him, in which case he would soon get rid of her, too. Frightened, she had hidden him in the house, later holding the old woman's hands out of the way while Cauvin choked her. Cauvin protested his innocence, but was tried, found Guilty, and condemned to a life of penal servitude. Michel was acquitted and sent back to the orphanage.

Five years later Michel, after hearing a sermon, went to the Procureur de la République and said she had given false evidence against Chauvin and that she alone had murdered Montet. The case was tried a second time, with Michel confessing that she had killed her mistress because she had "reproached me with eating too much...grumbling because I had broken a dish...(and) said if I broke anything more she would cut it out of my wages." Cauvin won an acquittal and the maid was condemned to five years in prison.

REF.: *CBA;* Morain, *Underworld of Paris;* Williamson, *Annals of Crime.*

Cavaignac, Jean Baptiste, 1762-1829, Fr., lawyer. Jean Baptiste Cavaignac was a Member of the National Convention in 1792.

He voted to execute King Louis XVI and later involved himself in the de-christianization campaign. Following the restoration of the monarch in 1815, Cavaignac was exiled for the crime of regicide. REF.: *CBA*.

Cavallotti, Felice Carlo Emmanuele, 1842-98, Italy, duel. Parliamentarian and leader of the Italian left-wing factions. Cavallotti fought with Giuseppe Garibaldi in 1860 and 1866, and against Francesco Crispi when he became a monarchist. In his thirty-third duel he was killed. REF.: *CBA*.

Cave, Alphonso, 1958- , and **Bush, John Earl**, 1958- , and **Parker, J.B.** (AKA: **Pig**), 1962- , and **Johnson, Terry Wayne**, 1957- , U.S., rob.-kid.-mur. According to her grandfather, 18-year-old heiress Frances Julia Slater, granddaughter of the famed 1940s singer and actress Frances Langford and Ralph Evinrude, the outboard motor magnate, wanted "to have the responsibility of work and see what it was all about." On Apr. 27, 1982, she was abducted from the L'il General Store, a fast-food mart in Stuart, Fla., where she was working the overnight shift. Four armed gunmen stole $35 from the till and abducted Slater. Thirteen hours later, her bullet-riddled body was found lying in a ravine thirteen miles southwest of Stuart. She had been stabbed several times and then shot in the head.

An informant's tip led to the arrest of four suspects from Fort Pierce, Fla., on May 5. Named as the ringleader was J.B. "Pig" Parker, who had chosen Slater as their victim. Unaware that Frances Slater was the heiress to a vast fortune, John Earl Bush stabbed the victim, and Parker fired the fatal shots. The four men were indicted on charges of first-degree murder, kidnapping, and armed robbery. Each was tried separately in Fort Myers, after a change of venue was granted by Lee County Circuit Judge C. Pfeiffer Trowbridge.

On Nov. 22, 1982, John Earl Bush, who said he only intended to "fake" the stab wound, was sentenced to death. Three weeks later, on Dec. 10, 1982, Alphonso Cave received two concurrent life sentences for robbery and abduction, and the death penalty for helping to carry out the murder. J.B. Parker was sentenced to two concurrent ten-year terms for robbery and kidnapping, and was sentenced to die in the Florida electric chair. At present all three men remain on death row. Twenty-six-year-old Terry Wayne Johnson, the last to be sentenced, was sentenced on June 29, 1983, to life in prison. Johnson testified that he was only joyriding with the other three and had no idea they intended to commit robbery and murder. Johnson was ordered to serve twenty-five years before parole would be considered. REF.: *CBA*.

Cave, George (Viscount Cave), 1856-1928, Brit., jur. Called to the bar in 1880, he was the king's counsel from 1904-06, a member of Parliament from 1906-18, and privy counselor in 1915. REF.: *CBA*.

Cavendish, Lord Frederick Charles, 1836-82, and **Burke, Thomas Henry**, 1829-82, Ire., assass. In the early 1880s, Ireland remained England's chief political problem. In Parliament, the Irish members were led by the formidable Charles Stewart Parnell, president of the Irish Land League, who had been jailed for agrarian sabotage in Ireland, acts over which he had no control, the burning of stored grain, the slaughter of livestock, all acts committed by Fenian extremists belonging to a militant group calling itself The Invincibles. To mollify the Irish leaders lobbying for Home Rule, British prime minister William Ewart Gladstone appointed Lord Frederick Cavendish as chief secretary of state for Ireland, replacing W.E. Forster, an extremist who had been battling Home Rule and who resigned in anger when Parnell was released from prison on May 2, 1882. Cavendish was a moderate in Ireland and was not a subject of hatred on the part of the Irish extremists. His aide and counselor, Thomas Henry Burke, however, was another matter. Burke, under secretary of the Irish Parliament, was considered a British stooge, called a "Castle rat," a derisive term reserved for those Irish Catholics loyal to the British and also meaning one who operated from the seat of government which was located in Dublin Castle.

The Invincibles, by early 1882, had been organized under the leadership of Fenian fanatics, Dublin businessman James Carey, carpenter Daniel Curley (who was the chairman of the Invincibles), shopkeeper Thomas Caffrey, and merchant James Mullet. All were family men, churchgoers, and known to be respected members of their community. None were from the criminal element but they had patriotically decided that in the national interests of Ireland, Thomas Henry Burke, not Cavendish, should be assassinated as a traitor to the Irish cause of Home Rule. There were about forty more members of the Invincibles who stemmed from the same kind of backgrounds, all devoted to the fanatical cause of assassination. On May 3, 1882, eleven Invincibles met at a tavern on Dame Street in Dublin and decided to assassinate Burke when he took his daily exercise in Phoenix Park. The fact that the park would be crowded with citizens bothered the conspirators not a bit.

Lord Frederick Cavendish, slain in 1882.

They concluded that no Irish citizen would dare inform on them, a generally correct assumption. The men selected for the killing were Joseph Brady, a giant 25-year-old laborer with extraordinary physical strength, 19-year-old Tim Kelly, another laborer, Brady's protégé Patrick Delaney, and Thomas Caffrey.

One of the conspirators was a man named Smith who was a janitor at Dublin Castle and was the only Invicibles member who could identify Burke on sight. He would point out the victim and the four assassins would rush forward and stab Burke to death with surgical knives which had recently been smuggled into Ireland from England. From May 4 to May 6, two attempts to murder Burke were foiled by the fact that his movements did not allow the assassins to get close to him. On May 6, 1882, Cavendish arrived in Dublin with Lord John Poynetz Spencer, who was the newly appointed lord lieutenant of Ireland. Both Spencer and Cavendish were sworn into office, and, following a reception, Spencer went to the Viceregal Lodge and Cavendish decided to take a stroll in Phoenix Park. Unplanned, he joined Burke who was taking his daily walk at dusk, a little after 7 p.m. Sitting on a park bench were Carey and Smith, the "finger man," who was to identify Burke. Riding up and down the nearby lane in a carriage were Brady, Delaney, Kelly, and Caffrey, the carriage being driven by a feeble-minded drunk named Kavanagh who was not a member of the Invincibles. Other members of the group sat with loaded revolvers in a parked, closed carriage. More members lay in high grass, also armed and waiting should they be needed.

Smith saw Cavendish and Burke strolling toward them and nodded that the man in the grey suit was the intended victim. Carey waved a handkerchief to the carriage containing Brady and the others and they alighted and came forward to hear Smith tell them: "Mind the man in grey." With that Brady, Kelly, Delaney, and Caffrey then walked abreast toward the two officials. Brady stooped as if to tie his shoelace just before the four assassins met the two officials and then, as Burke was almost next to him, suddenly jumped up, grabbed Burke by the right hand, swung him about and then drove the long surgical knife into his stomach. Burke gave out a groan and Cavendish sprang to Burke's defense, swinging his umbrella down on Brady's head. Delaney shouted at Cavendish: "Ah, you villain!" and with that, lunged at Cavendish. Brady, however, dropped Burke to the ground after repeatedly slashing him and grabbed Cavendish, driving his knife repeatedly into him.

As Burke fell, Kelly leaned down and cut his throat with a surgical knife. Then Brady dropped Cavendish to the ground. Both officials were dead by the time the assassins fled. It is most likely that the killers had no idea who Cavendish was since they were only interested in murdering Burke. Phoenix Park was then full of strollers and several witnessed what they later described as a "scuffle." None of these witnesses, which included a boy who was bird-watching, a drunken couple, and a captain of the Royal Dragoons, thought the double assassination had been anything more than a fight. Even when the bodies were identified as Cavendish and Burke, the shocked population of Dublin refused to believe that this had been a planned murder. The killers fled once they realized that both men were dead and the next day the newspapers were sent a notice in handwriting that was later identified as Curley's. Three plain white, black-edged cards stated: "This deed was done by The Invincibles."

Cavendish, the ranking official to be assassinated, had met his death by coincidence. He was present when Burke was attacked and tried to come to Burke's rescue, being killed in the process. The conspirators were as surprised to learn his identity as was the general population. Moreover, The Invincibles had acted as an impartial group of terrorist muderers with no personal involvement in their bloody deed. Tighe Hopkins, writing in an English publication, *Windsor Magazine* in 1896, was to state: "These men, it is to be remarked, had nothing in the nature of a private wrong to avenge. Not a man among them had ever in his lifetime suffered directly or indirectly the smallest injustice at the hands of Mr. Burke. To one and all of them he was a name and nothing more."

Dublin Police superintendent John Mallon had long been investigating the activities of the The Invincibles and he immediately launched a widespread dragnet to capture the organization's members. Most Irish leaders, including Parnell, denounced the assassination as a criminal act. The principled Parnell went to Gladstone and offered to withdraw from public life but Gladstone refused this offer. The Land League strongly denounced the killers as terrorists and assassins. A reward of £10,000 was offered for the apprehension of the killers. Parliament rushed a passage of a Prevention of Crime Act which suspended the normal judicial system in

Thomas Henry Burke, murdered with Lord Cavendish.

Ireland and gave the police absolute powers at the expense of citizen liberty. This act caused Parnell and Irish representatives to strongly oppose the Act, as well as British liberals. Hundreds of British marines were put into civilian clothes and walked about Dublin armed, expecting a general uprising. Officials also went armed and were followed everywhere by armed guards.

Superintendent Mallon was able to arrest a number of Invincibles through his well-developed system of informants, taking into custody Carey, Curley, Mullet, and lesser figures in the organization. But having no evidence to convict these men, Mallon was forced to release them. Plainclothes detectives followed these men and later trapped Delaney when he attempted to murder another official. Several Invincibles leaders were again rearrested, including James Carey. While Carey was held incommunicado, another suspect, Robert Farrel, was brought in for questioning. The questions put to him by John Adye Curran, a shrewd police official, were so adroit and pointed, all based upon Curran's suspicions and not real evidence, that Farrel was convinced that one or more of the Invincibles had turned traitor. He stated that he did not intend to be victimized while others in the secret organization went free. Farrel turned informer, detailing the

operations of The Invincibles and its membership. Mallon did not, however, have enough evidence to convict the murderers and he employed Curran's approach but with elaborate drama. He studied his prisoners and concluded that Curley was not a man who would turn state's evidence, but Carey was a nervous, apprehensive man.

Phoenix Park, Dublin, May 6, 1882: The bodies of Cavendish and Burke are discovered.

Day after day, night after night, Mallon, accompanied by several other officials made a show of walking back and forth in front of Curley's cell, carrying papers and pens, going into the next cell (these cells completely enclosed except for a small grate on the doors). Mallon made it seem as if another prisoner in the cell adjoining Carey's was giving evidence. Low murmuring talk from this cell could be heard by Carey and an occasional exclamation. Runners carrying more paper and pens and ink would scurry down the corridor outside Carey's cell until he believed that one of The Invincibles was informing on him and the others. Finally, Carey cracked, and, believing that his comrades were talking to save their own necks, volunteered information to Mallon who, at first, pretended to not need such information. Carey practically pleaded with the superintendent to take his confession.

Armed with the testimony of Farrel and Carey, twenty-six of The Invincibles were brought to trial on Apr. 9, 1883. When The Invincibles paraded into court, they counted their own number and saw that Carey was not present. Groans and curses filled the air as they instantly realized that their leader had turned informer. On the evidence provided by Farrel, Carey, Myles Kavanagh, and a few other lesser-known members of The Invincibles, Brady, Curley, Kelly, Caffrey, Delaney, and Michael Fagan were sentenced to death. At the last minute, Delaney's sentence was commuted to life imprisonment. James Fitzharris and Joseph Hanlon were also given life sentences. All five condemned men died bravely and went silently to the hangman, Marwood, executed between May 14 and June 9, 1883, at Kilmainham.

Kavanagh and Farrel were shipped to Australia. Authorities there refused to accept Farrel and he sailed to an unknown destination and was not heard from again. Kavanagh was sent to England and died an alcoholic, raving in a London lunatic asylum. Carey's fate was more direct and brutal. Sought by members of The Invincibles who were still at large, Carey was smuggled on board a ship sailing for Cape Town, the *Melrose*. He was shot to death by a fellow passenger, Patrick O'Donnell, who was claimed by The Invincibles to be one of their emissaries, assigned to wreak vengeance for Carey's betrayal. One story had it, however, that O'Donnell had no idea of who Carey was and that he shot and killed Carey whom he accused of cheating him at cards, O'Donnell later being sent to prison for life. The power of The Invincibles was broken and the organization soon disappeared.

REF.: Bussy, *Irish Conspiracies;* Cavendish, *Diary; CBA;* Corfe, *The Phoenix Park Murders;* Cosgrove, *The True History of the Phoenix Park Murders;* Curran, *Reminescences;* Hopkins, *Kilmainham Memories: Story* of the Greatest Political Crime of the Century; Hurwood, Society and the Assassin; Hyams, Killing No Murder; Laurence, A History of Capital Punishment; Macardle, The Irish Republic; MacKenzie, Secret Societies; Melville, Famous Duels and Assassinations; O'Ballance, Terror in Ireland; O'Brien, The Life of Parnell; Pollard, The Secret Societies of Ireland; Scott, A Concise Encyclopedia of Crime and Criminals; Sparrow, The Great Assassins; Tynan, The Irish National Invincibles and Their Times; Williams, Heyday for Assassins; Williams, Secret Societies in Ireland.

Cavendish, John, d.1381, Brit., jur., assass. John Cavendish was chief justice of the King's Bench (1372-81), and was arrested during the Peasant's Revolt and beheaded by Jack Staw's men. REF.: CBA.

Pirate Tom Cavendish and his crew slaying sea lions and being attacked by natives.

Cavendish, Thomas, prom. 1570-91, Brit., pir. Like Sir Francis Drake, Thomas Cavendish explored the Strait of Magellan, taking a similar route through Chile and Peru to California, and stopping at the South Sea Islands, but, unlike Drake, Cavendish burned and plundered villages and ships he came across in his travels.

A squire from Suffolk, Cavendish sailed the same routes Drake had taken in 1577-80, but the privateer made his trip during a time of war between England and Spain and left a path of destruction in his wake. Taking the great Manila galleon the Santa Ana off the California coast, Cavendish wrote to his patron, Lord Hunsdon that he had "...made great spoils. I burnt and sunk nineteen ships, both great and small. All the villages and towns that I landed at, I burnt and spoiled." A model to many buccaneers of the time, Cavendish sailed back up the Thames in 1588 with his ship decorated with gilt, gold cloths wrapping the topmasts, sails of South Sea Island silk, and his sailors and himself elegantly attired in brocades and other fine materials stolen from many countries. Despite his great haul, his wealth dissipated. Cavendish was soon in debt and had to sell and mortgage manors to outfit a second expedition in 1591. Cavendish died at sea, allegedly cursing the "insolent, mutinous mariners" he claimed had wrecked his voyage.

REF.: CBA; Mitchell, Pirates.

Cawley, Brian, prom. 1929-60, Brit., mur. An unemployed radio technician has the dubious distinction of having the shortest murder trial on record in England.

Brian Cawley, thirty, lived with his wife and three children in a New Road, Basingstoke, house owned by Rupert Steed, a retired bachelor who had befriended the Cawley family. The Cawleys lived rent free with Steed, who enjoyed giving them gifts and being their benefactor. Cawley began to drink and his wife left him, taking the children. One night, Cawley returned home and beat Steed to death for no apparent reason. Cawley was tried on Dec. 14, 1959, at Winchester Assizes. He pleaded guilty and was sentenced to life imprisonment, with the entire proceedings taking only thirty seconds.

REF.: CBA; Wilson, Encyclopedia of Murder.

Cayson, Jesse, and **Cayson, Doyle,** prom. 1958, U.S., mur. When his father was murdered by local thugs, a 12-year-old boy vowed he would find the killers. Eighteen years later he did. On Mar. 15, 1940, Les Wilson, father of six and candidate for sheriff in the Okaloosa County race, was in his Crestview, Fla., home with his wife and children, listening to the radio, when a shotgun blast through the porch window killed him. Ray Wilson, his 12-year-old son, told himself that night that he would track down whoever had murdered his father, and help clean up Okaloosa County, where gambling proliferated and illegal whiskey was sold openly, and where murders and unusual disappearances were regular occurrences. Les Wilson's life had been threatened before; as police chief of Crestview, criminals despised him, and his candidacy for sheriff threatened the gangsters' free rein.

An investigation into his murder was ordered in October 1940 by Governor Fred P. Cone and closed by Governor Fuller Warren in 1949 after there had been no results. Ray Wilson graduated from high school, served in the U.S. Army and returned to Crestview around 1950, determined to run for sheriff. With no initial support, he garnered the confidence of the public on a platform of impartial law and order and won the post in 1956, becoming, at twenty-eight, Florida's youngest sheriff and embarking on a successful campaign to clean up Crestview.

With Walter R. Steinsiek, Jr., Pensacola police superintendent of identification, Wilson began the search for his father's killer. He looked through old police files and eventually came up with Jesse and Doyle Cayson as possible suspects. The brothers had become unaccountably prosperous after Wilson's murder, and connections with organized crime were thought to be the cause. A woman who had twice changed her name was tracked to San Antonio, Texas, and interviewed by Wilson. She refused to testify but admitted that she had heard the Caysons leave with shotguns the night of the murder and had later been beaten by them and told to keep her mouth shut. She and her husband had been shot at sometime after that, and they moved from Crestview in fear for their lives. When Wilson promised her protection, "Jane" agreed to testify, saying, "I'm scared, but I've been waiting all these years to clear my mind of what happened that night."

Another witness who had overheard Jesse Cayson tell several people he had murdered Les Wilson was found, and a switchboard operator who had listened to one of the suspects call to find out if Wilson was driving a taxi that night also came forth. In June 1958, after eighteen months of intensive investigation, having questioned more than 200 people, Ray Wilson went before a grand jury to present evidence in his father's murder. The Caysons were brought to trial soon after and in November of that year, were found Guilty of the first-degree murder of Les Wilson. The killers were sentenced to life in prison. REF.: CBA.

Ceawlin, d.593, Brit., milit., exile. Ceawlin was king of West Saxons from 560-592, he defeated King Aethelberht of Kent in 568. Again in 577, he defeated their armies at Deorham, before suffering a major loss in 592 at the hands of Ceol, and was exiled. REF.: CBA.

Cecco d'Ascoli (Francesco Stabili), 1269-1327, Italy, her. Professor of Astrology at the University of Bologna in 1322, he wrote a poem attacking Dante's Divine Comedy. He was expelled for heresy in 1324, and burned at the stake three years later. REF.: CBA.

Cecil, William (Baron Burghley), 1520-98, Brit., consp. William Cecil was a member of a noble family descended from David Cyssell, sheriff of Northampton. He served Queen Elizabeth as secretary of state from 1558-72. During this time he organized a network of spies and informers to uncover plots and royal intrigues against his queen. He assumed responsibility for the planned execution of Mary, Queen of Scots in 1587. See: **Mary, Queen of Scots.** REF.: CBA.

Cedarholm, Eugenia, prom. 1927, U.S., miss. per. Eugenia Cedarholm, who ran a boardinghouse in Brooklyn, N.Y., was last seen in October 1927. It appeared that she had moved with one of her boarders, Edward Lawrence Hall, to a cottage in Freeport, on Long Island. Then, according to Hall's later story, he began to serve as her agent, cashing checks and collecting rents for her. Some months later, the New York subway system acquired Cedarholm's Brooklyn land. They condemned it, and tried to pay the woman for it, but could not locate her. Eventually the police became involved. When they picked up Hall, he claimed that he and Cedarholm had three children, but would not say where she could be found.

Three years later, Hall was charged with forgery and tried for writing checks supposedly signed by her. Authorities would have liked to charge him with murder, but there was no evidence that murder had been commited. Hall acted as his own lawyer, was found Guilty and sentenced to twenty years in Sing Sing, a longer sentence than forgery alone would usually elicit. Although his refusal to answer questions about Cedarholm probably stiffened his sentence, all the 60-year-old Hall would say was that he had married the 26-year-old Cedarholm and "taken her away."

In 1933, Hall said from prison that he had left "his wife" in Pueblo Beach, Fla., but authorities there could find no trace of her. Some years after that, Hall died in prison. Cedarholm was forgotten until 1953, when a man digging in a Long Island yard found some human bones. Because his yard was only a few doors from the house where Hall had lived, there was some speculation that the bones might have belonged to Cedarholm. But there was no proof.

REF.: *CBA;* Nash, *Among the Missing;* Woollcott, *While Rome Burns.*

Celestius, prom. 5th Cent., Roman., her. Condemned by the Council of Carthage in 412 for his religious views, and excommunicated by Pope St. Innocent in 417. After receiving a pardon from Pope St. Zosimus, he was exiled a second time by Flavius Honorius and condemned for his views by the Council of Ephesus in 431. REF.: *CBA.*

Cellini, Benvenuto, 1500-71, Italy, embez.-pris. esc. Cellini was a noted Renaissance sculptor and goldsmith who studied under Michaelangelo, Marconi, and Bandinelli. A protégé of Pope Clement VII, Cellini found himself out of favor with his successor, Paul III. In 1538, the Florentine sculptor was thrown into the Castle of St. Angelo prison in Rome on a charge of embezzlement by order of Pope Paul III.

The Pontiff charged Benvenuto with embezzling precious gems valued at 80,000 crowns. The jewels were ordered removed by the Pope during the sack of Rome. He carried out these orders faithfully, and then had to clear himself of these serious criminal charges. After he had established his innocence, Cellini discovered that his release from prison was not forthcoming. Realizing that the Pope would have him executed before allowing him to go to France where he might tell King Francis I about the duplicity, Benvenuto decided to escape. A sympathetic guard convinced him of the urgency of the matter. "Take my advice, and fly from this villain of a Pope, and from his bastard son who have sworn your destruction," he said. The goldsmith picked through the lock and made his escape. An account of the prison breakout can be found in the *Memoirs of Benvenuto Cellini,* translated in 1822.

REF.: *CBA;* Yeats and Brown, *Escape.*

Celso de Assis Figueiredo (Conde Affonso), 1860-1938, Braz., jur. Dean of the faculty of law at Rio de Janiero. REF.: *CBA.*

Celsus, Publius Juventius, c.67-c.130 A.D., Roman., jur. Although references to his legal texts exist in the papers of other prominent public men of the time, his works are lost to history. REF.: *CBA.*

Cem (Jem), 1459-95, Turk., exile. Son of Sultan Mehmed II, founder of the Ottoman Empire. He challenged his brother Bayezid II to the throne in 1481, which resulted in his forced exile to Rhodes, where he remained until his death. REF.: *CBA.*

Cenci, Beatrice, 1577-99, Italy, mur. Long the subject of fiction and poetry, this young and beautiful woman conspired with other family members to murder her tyrannical father and went to the block for her lethal acts. The father, Francesco Cenci, was a wealthy and powerful nobleman of Rome whose cruelty and sexual appetites had gained him widespread notoriety. He ignored all decent behavior and brought courtesans into his bed chamber at all hours of the day, wining and wenching before his disgusted family and his mortified wife. His sadism was rampant and he took every opportunity to punish family members, particularly Beatrice and her two brothers. It was later reported that when Francesco discovered that Beatrice was having an affair with a family servant, he threatened to have the young man killed and his daughter exposed as a common whore.

Apparently at this time, the entire family, under Beatrice's guidance, decided to rid themselves of this vicious tyrant. Beatrice Cenci, with the full aid of her mother and two brothers, hired several assassins who murdered Francesco Cenci while he slept in his bed, on the night of Sept. 9, 1598. One of the assassins later informed authorities, which led to Beatrice and her family's being arrested and tried for murder. Found Guilty, the Cencis were condemned to death but appealed for clemency from Pope Clement VIII. The pope was disinclined to spare Beatrice, her mother, and brothers, and all were beheaded on Sept. 11, 1599. Known forever after as the Beautiful Parricide, Beatrice Cenci was glorified in a famous portrait in the Barberini Palace in Rome, and became the subject of countless ballads, stories, and poems, the most famous of which was Shelly's tragedy, *The Cenci,* 1819 where the lethal lady receives empathetic treatment.

REF.: *CBA;* Thompson, *Poisons and Poisoners.*

Centralia, Wash., Riot, prom. 1919, U.S., mob vio. Patriotic feelings ran high in the U.S. in 1918, as Americans looked forward to a victorious end to WWI. There was little tolerance for the leftist views of the newly prominent International Workers of the World (IWW), or Wobblies, as they were commonly known.

When in 1918 the Wobblies appeared in Centralia, Wash., for the first time, they were denounced as traitors to the cause and enemies of the state. The newly opened IWW office was ransacked by a group of men marching in a Red Cross parade and the Wobblies were driven from town. Undaunted, they returned in September 1919 and reopened their headquarters, determined to make a stand. Businessmen who considered it their duty to drive a subversive element from their midst organized a Protective League, which conspired with the Local American Legion chapter to instigate violence against the Wobblies.

The Protective League arranged for an Armistice Day Parade to pass by the IWW headquarters. Aware of the intrigue the IWW men, led by Wesley Everest fortified their offices and braced for the coming battle. As the League turned the corner, the order to break ranks was given. Everest shot and killed one of the parade organizers, but his men were no match for the superior firepower and overwhelming numbers of Legionnaires and Protective League men. The vigilantes completely gutted the IWW office and chased Everest through town. He was finally cornered by the maddened soldiers. "You haven't got the guts to lynch a man in the daytime," Everest said, but he had underestimated their wrath. Everest was hanged from a support beam at the Chehalis River Bridge, and his corpse was mutilated by the rioters.

REF.: *CBA;* Hofstadter and Wallace, *American Violence;* Tyler, *Rebels of the Woods.*

Cepola, Bartolommeo, prom. 1400s, Italy, jur. Authored legal treatise on the technicalities of the law, which gave rise to the phrase *devices of Cepola,* meaning technical manipulation, evasive tactics, or any stratagem designed to delay or frustrate the execution of the law. REF.: *CBA.*

Ceracchi, Giuseppe, See: **Napoleon I.**

Cerchi, Vieri dei, prom. 1300, Italy, exile. Knight of the Guelf armies, he challenged his political rival Corson Donati for leadership of the Guelfs, resulting in a party split. Cerchi led the black faction, Donati the white. In 1300 the blacks were defeated and banished from Pistoia, and Cerchi was exiled. REF.: *CBA.*

Cermak, Anton Joseph, 1873-1933, U.S., mayor, assass. Born in Prague, Bohemia, Anton Joseph Cermak migrated as an infant with his family, settling in Chicago, Ill., where he became rich in the real estate business, being elected mayor in 1931, a machine candidate whose administration was marked with considerable corruption. Cermak accompanied President-elect Franklin D. Roosevelt to Miami and, on Feb. 15, 1933, was mortally wounded by a bullet fired at Roosevelt. The assassin, Joseph Zangara, meant to shoot Roosevelt, but Cermak got in the way of fire. Cermak died on Mar. 6, 1933, after doctors working around the clock failed to save his life. It was later contended that Cermak really was the intended victim of Zangara who had been sent by Chicago mobsters to murder the mayor who had been interfering in Capone-controlled rackets—but this is a canard. Cermak was simply an accidental victim. See: **Roosevelt, Franklin D.**

REF.: Bell, *Assassin!*; CBA; Demaris, *Captive City*; Gottfried, *Boss Cermak of Chicago*; Hurwood, *Society and the Assassin*; Kobler, *Capone*; Lait and Mortimer, *Chicago: Confidential*; Lynch, *Criminals and Politicians*; Morgan, *Prince of Crime*; Nash, *Almanac of World Crime*; _____, *People to See*; Ottenberg, *The Federal Investigators*; Paine, *The Assassin's World*; Pearl, *The Famous Assassins*; Reppetto, *The Blue Parade*; Smith, *Syndicate City*; (FILM), *The Man Who Dared*, 1933.

Cerny, Wenzel, prom. 1936, Czech., mur. When a prominent judge's bride took a contract out on her husband's life, the killer she hired agreed to do the job, saying the judge had sent him to jail two years earlier because he "didn't like my looks."

An upstairs neighbor called the police at about 10:20 p.m., Mar. 16, 1936, to report a commotion in the apartment of Czechoslovakian Court Judge Jan Velgo. Police officers broke in to find a man groaning on the living-room floor, shot in the forehead, after his attempt to kill himself. In the bathroom the body of Judge Jan Velgo lay submerged in the bathtub, a deep gash in his head. A medical examiner announced that he had been dead for fifteen minutes, and pronounced the cause as drowning. In the closet of one room police found Marie Havlick Velgo slumped on the floor and unconscious. The 21-year-old woman opened her eyes and asked after her husband of six weeks, saying she had been forced into the closet where she had fainted. The wounded man was identified as Wenzel Cerny, a petty criminal with a record of arson, assault and battery, robbery, and fraud dating back ten years.

Questioning the Velgo's maid and several other people, police learned that the couple had just recently married for convenience only, and that Velgo had planned to divorce his wife when he learned of a vacancy in the supreme court. Hoping to be appointed, he decided a divorce scandal would disqualify him. The distressed bride confided in her maid that she would like to get rid of Velgo and the maid procured Cerny's name. When Cerny was questioned, he was more than willing to talk, with no idea of "shielding that she-devil."

He had met with Marie Velgo in a cafe and agreed to murder her husband for a fee of $200. They had even drawn up a promissory note, which he told police to look for in the lining of his coat. The official-sounding document was dated Feb. 16, 1936, one month before Velgo's death. Tricking Marie Velgo into signing her name, police found that her signature matched that on the promissory note. Confronted with this evidence, she dropped her story of a burglary and confessed to arranging the murder, but said she had had a change of heart later and unsuccessfully begged Cerny not to go through with it. According to her testimony, the killer had brushed her off, then locked her in the closet when he heard Velgo's key in the door.

Cerny and Velgo were tried on Feb. 11, 1937. A jury took twelve minutes to find Cerny Guilty as charged and the less than bereaved widow Not Guilty "in view of irresistible force exercised upon her" by Cerny. The state's attorney called for a new trial based on improper evidence brought in by the defense. Velgo was retried in October 1937, found Guilty, and sent to jail for a twelve-year term.

REF.: CBA; Cohen, *One Hundred True Crime Stories*.

Cero, Gangi, prom. 1927-32, Case of, U.S., mur. In a convoluted case one man was found Guilty of first-degree murder and sentenced to die, obtaining a reprieve just four hours before the scheduled execution. Two years later, the man's boss was tried for the same murder and convicted. One year later, both men were retried together in an unprecedented capital trial, each trying to implicate the other. Both finally were acquitted.

On the afternoon of June 11, 1927, in Boston's Italian North End, Joseph Fantasia, thirty, was shot in the back as he walked on crowded Prince Street. Louis Smith, a passerby, noticed a man running and followed him through the crowd to a shop, where the man called for a taxi. Smith phoned the police, and Cero Gangi, a 21-year-old seaman, was arrested. As his own witness at the trial in November 1927, before Judge Louis S. Cox, Cero protested his innocence. Smith was the main witness for the prosecution. A gun found near the body was identified as the murder weapon, but could not be connected with the defendant.

Pleading mistaken identity, Cero was about to be sentenced when Smith told the court that certain parties were trying to get him to sign an affidavit saying he had erred in his testimony. Samuel Gallo, twenty-three, Gangi's boss in some ripoff scams, and Gangi's brother were arrested after police watched them take Smith to a lawyer to draw up a statement. When questioned by the district attorney, Gallo claimed not to have seen Smith before. Gallo was tried for contempt of court and sentenced to two years in jail. On Nov. 17, 1927, Cero was found Guilty of first-degree murder and in September 1928 was sentenced to death. His motivation for the crime was thought to be his previous involvement with Fantasia's sister-in-law, Philomena Romano, who had slashed Gangi's face after he became involved with another woman, and Fantasia had threatened his life in revenge as well.

Both Cero and Gallo were incarcerated at the Charles Street jail and, on Oct. 11, 1928, Cero stabbed Gallo while they were in the prison yard, seriously wounding but not killing him. With his execution date just four weeks away, Cero gave a statement that he had been employed by Gallo, that they had been walking together in Prince Street the day of the killing, and that Gallo had fired the fatal shot. Cero also denied knowing the murdered man.

With days to go before the execution, Romano came forward, telling Governor Fuller she could not watch an innocent man die and that she had seen the murder committed by Gallo. Fuller granted Cero a thirty-day reprieve. Romano disappeared for three weeks, then returned to the district attorney to repudiate her statements about Gallo, but retracting her repudiation at Gallo's trial soon afterwards, in February 1929. Cero told the same story he had from the beginning, this time admitting that Smith had told the truth at the first trial, and that he had run away after the shooting. At the end of February a jury found Gallo Guilty of first-degree murder, with Romano and Cero as witnesses against him. Judge Cox, who had tried both trials up to this point, said that the two verdicts were "inconsistent with the course of justice," and ordered a new joint trial for Cero and Gallo.

The double trial, held in September 1930, was before Judge William Adams Brown. Romano again had disappeared after the February trial, and Smith again was the sole witness. Gallo was re-convicted of murder, and Cero acquitted. On appeal, Gallo's conviction was affirmed. Yet another trial was held—this was Gallo's third—on July 5, 1932, before Judge Wilford D. Gray. Romano returned to testify but proclaimed that she could remember nothing, her mind having gone "blank." Cero, who had returned to Italy to become a marine, testified, swearing that Gallo fired the shot, but that he, Cero, had committed perjury at his own earlier trial. On July 12, 1932, the jury found Gallo Not Guilty, putting an end to five years of legal proceedings. REF.: CBA.

Cerone, Frank (Francesco Cironato, AKA: Skippy), 1913-73, U.S., org. crime. Considered a top triggerman in the Chicago outfit, Frank Cerone, a cousin of Chicago mob boss Jackie "the Lackey" Cerone, was active in gambling and drug trafficking from 1928. His criminal record included ten arrests for charges from vagrancy to robbery and rape. Cerone was convicted of bribery and conspiracy to avoid the draft, which earned him two concurrent five-year prison sentences. His mob-related activities were carefully concealed by his "legitimate" business endeavors, including the Blue

Moon Lounge and a construction firm known as Century Enterprises. REF.: *CBA*.

Cerone, John Philip (John Cironi, AKA: Jackey the Lackey), 1914- , U.S., org. crime. A U.S. Senate Subcommittee meeting in Chicago in March 1983 identified John "Jackie" Cerone as the top local mob boss in the region. It was the second time in his criminal career that Cerone had "leap frogged" past his immediate superior Joseph "Doves" Aiuppa for supremacy in the Mafia hierarchy. Cerone's penchant for killing and his unswerving devotion to duty were among the traits admired by his superiors.

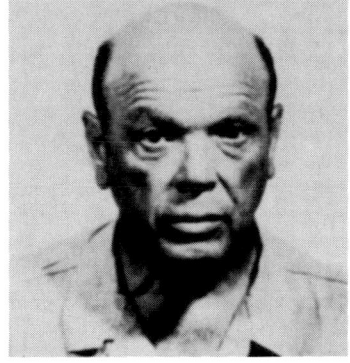

Chicago gangster "Jackey the Lackey" Cerone.

Cerone's arrest record dated back to 1932 and included arrests for robbery, gambling, and driving under the influence. He was suspected of complicity in at least four murders including the particularly gory mob execution in 1961 of the one-time juice collector and gambler, William "Action" Jackson. Cerone was the boss of three Chicago wards that comprised portions of the old "West Side Block," a syndicate domain whose elected representatives fought hard to circumvent any potentially damaging anti-crime legislation.

For years he served as the chauffeur or "pilot fish" for local mob kingpin Anthony "Big Tuna" Accardo. When Sam Giancana temporarily displaced Accardo from the top spot in the family, "Jackey the Lackey" was there to provide support and encouragement. In 1958 Cerone was called before the McClellan Senate Rackets Committee, which investigated the influence of organized crime in the U.S. He pleaded the Fifth Amendment no less than forty-five times.

By the late 1960s, the ambitious and utterly ruthless Cerone emerged as the number two man in the Mafia outfit. His career was temporarily halted in 1970 when he went to jail for running a nationwide gambling operation from his home base in the western suburbs of Chicago. Released three years later, Cerone immediately eliminated the government witness whose testimony sent him to jail. Though given a new identity and government protection in Arizona, the man was killed by a car bomb in October 1973. In 1979 Cerone's maneuvering temporarily moved him ahead of Aiuppa into the number one spot in the family. Although Aiuppa reclaimed his posisiton once he had recovered from a lingering illness, Cerone had already groomed his own number two man, Joseph Ferriola, a determined assassin every bit as unscrupulous as his mentor.

By 1985, Cerone was forced to deal with a power play within the organization as the "Young Turks," a tight clique of Chicago Mafiosi in their forties and fifties, fought for control of the outfit. This uprising occurred at a time when Cerone faced a lengthy prison sentence on charges of skimming $2 million from the Stardust Casino in Las Vegas. The Cosa Nostra had exerted their influence in the day-to-day management of the club through Allen Glick, a San Diego businessman who bought the Stardust with $62.7 million borrowed from the Teamster's Central States Pension Fund. The money they took from the untaxed casino profits was diverted to the crime families in Chicago, Milwaukee, and Cleveland. Cerone, his one-time boss Aiuppa, Joseph "the Clown" Lombardo, a former West Side crime boss, and Angelo LaPietra, a lieutenant in the First Ward, went to trial in Kansas City, Mo., on Sept. 23, 1985, nearly two years after the original indictments were handed down. On Mar. 25, 1986, Cerone was sentenced to twenty-eight-and-a-half years in prison by U.S. District Judge Joseph E. Stevens, Jr., after being found Guilty on an eight-count conspiracy indictment. The other three Chicago mobsters and Milton Rockman, the 73-year-old kingpin of the Cleveland

family, received similar sentences. See: **Aiuppa, Joseph; Giancana, Sam; Accardo, Tony; Ferriola, Joseph.**

REF.: *CBA;* Cressey, *Theft of the Nation;* Demaris, *The Last Mafioso;* Nash, *Bloodletters and Badmen;* Peterson, *The Mob;* Reid, *The Grim Reapers;* Zuckerman, *Vengeance Is Mine.*

Cerro, Luis Sanchez, d.1933, Peru, assass. A popular war hero shot sixteen times who lost three fingers while fighting for his country eventually fell from an assassin's bullet in 1933.

Luis Sanchez Cerro first came to fame in Peru in 1914, when he grabbed a machine gun muzzle with his bare hands while fighting in his country's struggle to overthrow then President Billinghurst. In 1921, Cerro captured the city of Lima in an unsuccessful effort to overthrow President Leguia. In yet another revolution in 1930, Cerro was made dictator for a brief period, only to be expelled, then returned in 1931, elected legally to serve as president.

Throughout his career, Cerro had been shot at several times, referring to such incidents as "scratches." In March 1932, he suffered another such "scratch" when would-be assassin José Melgar fired at the small but fierce president of Peru. Cerro's cohort, Colonel Rodriguez, was also wounded in the attack. Though bleeding, Cerro said, "I require no assistance, but rush Colonel Rodriguez to a hospital." About two weeks later, Melgar was tried before a court martial. He was expected to be let off lightly, since Cerro had not been badly wounded and would probably try to maintain his popularity and garner more votes through leniency. But after a long session, from 8 a.m. to 4 a.m., Melgar and Juan Seoane, his accomplice, were condemned to death, the sentence to be carried out the same day. The Aprista, or Opposition Party of Peru, flooded the government with letters of protest demanding clemency. Peru's congress responded by passing a bill permitting the president to "commute death sentences imposed on would-be murderers to penal servitude," sweetening this implied demand on Cerro by promoting him from lieutenant colonel to colonel, retroactive from Aug. 22, 1930, the date when Cerro helped to overthrow President Leguia.

Finally, in late May 1932, Cerro commuted the death sentences to a 25-year jail term. A year later, at the Santa Beatriz race track, Cerro had just completed a review of 20,000 young men, recruits for Peru's undeclared war with Colombia, when a man stepped up and shot him through the heart. In the struggle that followed, two soldiers were killed, with six more soldiers and a civilian wounded, and the assassin, Abelardo de Mendoza, a member of the Apra revolutionary party, lay dead after being both shot and stabbed. General Oscar Benavides was appointed provisional president, martial law was declared in Peru, and the entire country went into mourning for the fallen Cerro for three days. REF.: *CBA*.

Cesario, Sam, 1918-71, U.S., (unsolv.), org. crime-mob vio.-mur. Because his new wife had been involved with a high-level mob figure, a gangster from the lower ranks was murdered gangland style, despite the recent death in jail of the high-level mobster.

Sam Cesario, fifty-three, married Nan Cesario in the spring of 1971. Prior to her marriage, Nan had been the longtime friend of Felix Alderisio, an important figure in the Chicago organized crime echelons. On Oct. 19, 1971, the Cesarios were sitting on lawn chairs in front of their home when two men, faces covered with handkerchiefs, murdered the recent groom. Though Alderisio had died in jail of natural causes one month earlier, it was believed he had taken a contract out on Sam Cesario's life and his death would not have nullified the order. Nan Cesario, who had dated another gangster, Julius Grieco, in the late 1950s, earned the nickname "kiss of death woman" as a result of both Cesario's death and the gangland style slaying of William Simone, twenty-seven, a minor criminal, who was murdered in April 1974, after Mrs. Cesario became involved with him. Nan Cesario died in Chicago in September 1974, after surgery. REF.: *CBA*.

Cesaroni, Enrico, and Bolognini, Arnaldo, and Castiglioni, Eros, and Ciappina, Ugo, and DeMaria, Luciano, and Gesmundo, Arnaldo, and Russo, Ferdinando, prom. 1958, Italy, rob. A group of Italian bank robbers, under the leadership of Enrico Cesaroni, committed the largest bank robbery in Italy's history in 1958, getting away with close to a million dollars in cash and securities.

In February 1958, Enrico Cesaroni, a leader in Italian organized crime, called a secret meeting of six gangsters to outline his plan for robbing the Popular Bank of Milan. At the gathering were three ace gunmen, Arnaldo Bolognini, Eros Castiglioni, and Ugo Ciappina, and expert car thieves and getaway drivers Luciano DeMaria, Arnaldo Gesmundo, and Ferdinando Russo. From 1956-57 this same group, along with several others, had pulled in more than $78,000 in carefully planned and smoothly executed raids on banks, a jewelry shop, and a post office and had left no clues behind.

Cesaroni explained in great detail his scheme to rob the Popular Bank of Milan as it transferred money from the main office to branches throughout the city. On Feb. 26, the day before the hit, Ciappina and Cesaroni met at a Piazza Napoli bar to go over last-minute details. A truck and three cars, all stolen, were in place for the robbery, and disguises of seven pairs of blue overalls had been procured by DeMaria. Elderly Ermenegildo Rosi supplied the guns, including three machine guns, four pistols, and several hand grenades, from his home which served as the gang's armory. At 9:30 a.m. on Feb. 27, the robbery was carried out with precise timing, netting the thieves $182,400 in cash and $771,600 in money orders and negotiable securities, making the incident the biggest bank robbery in Italy's history.

At the Via Fatebenefratelli police headquarters, the chief of the police squad, the *Squadra Mobile,* Dr. Paolo Zamparelli, found no clues in the reports as he studied them with his lieutenants, Ricardo Pennetta and Mario Iovine. Zamparelli did notice a similarity between the methods of this gang and the techniques used in several other unsolved robberies over the last year. In each case, robbers struck swiftly and efficiently, covering their faces with hoods and using stolen cars which were abandoned close to the crime scene.

Although Zamparelli suspected Cesaroni as the "one man in Milan capable of organizing such disciplined operations," and brought him in for questioning, he had no proof and released him. Through a fortunate circumstance, the stagnant Olona Canal near Via Washington was drained and the pistols, hammer, and several pairs of overalls used in the theft were discovered on the muddy bottom. Tracing the overalls to an angry peddler who said, "Yes, I bought the overalls, but then some son-of-a-dog steals my car and everything in it, including the overalls," police eventually discovered a witness to the car theft who positively identified Giorgio Puccia as the thief. Puccia confessed selling the overalls to Luciano DeMaria, and, within hours, DeMaria and most of the gang were rounded up and interrogated. One of the gang finally confessed, and other admissions soon followed. In a raid on Rosi's home, the *Squadra Mobile* found an arsenal of pistols, machine guns, and hand grenades. Almost all of the money was recovered. Cesaroni and Castiglioni had fled to Venezuela. Cesaroni was captured and returned to Italy under heavy guard in the fall of 1959, tried, found guilty, and sentenced to a prison term of eighteen years and four months, and fined 439,000 lire. In absentia, Eros Castiglioni was sentenced to eleven years and ten months in prison and fined 192,000 lire. The other members of the Milan gang received terms ranging from nine to twenty years.

REF.: *CBA;* Whitehead, *Journey Into Crime.*

Cethegus, Gaius Cornelius, d.63 B.C., Roman., consp. Gaius Cornelius Cethegus was involved in Lucius Catiline's conspiracy to kill the consuls of Rome and plunder the city. Cethegus was eventually captured and was executed in 63 B.C. for his part in the plan. REF.: *CBA.*

Cevdet Pasa, Ahmed, 1822-95, Turk., jur. Ahmed Cevdet Pasa served as the minister of justice during the Ottoman Empire. Cevdet Pasa helped codify Ottoman law. REF.: *CBA.*

Chabanel, Noël, 1613-49, Can., clergy, assass. Noël Chabanel was a French Jesuit missionary assigned to live and work among the Huron Indians of Canada, spreading Christianity to the tribe. In 1649, Chabanel was murdered by a Huron tribesman. REF.: *CBA.*

Chabannes, Antoine (Comte de Dammartin), c.1411-88, Fr., jur. Antoine Chabannes was the presiding justice responsible for overseeing the commission that convicted Jacques Coeur of treason in 1451. REF.: *CBA.*

Chabot, François, 1759-94, Fr., rebel.-polit. corr. François Chabot served in the National Convention in 1792. Chabot was accused of bribery and implicated in Georges-Jacques Danton's conspiracy to curb the excesses of Robespierre and members of the Committee of Public Safety. Chabot was found Guilty and was guillotined in Paris in 1794. REF.: *CBA.*

Chabot, Saul, prom. 1951, U.S., smug. An alert customs checker responded to a man's nervousness about shipping his car to Cherbourg by notifying a customs officer. Eighty-two packages of gold were found stuffed underneath the fenders.

Saul Chabot had built up a large business in New York City dealing in used rags, but decided to expand his career into smuggling gold. In 1951, he brought a 1950 Buick sedan to the pier to be boarded for the *Queen Elizabeth's* voyage to Cherbourg. Cunard Line police officer Matthew Jake Berckman, the pier checker, inspected cars that would be shipped abroad. Berckman, a 14-year veteran of the Cunard Line, observed that, although the trunk of the car was empty except for tools and a spare tire, the car was very low in the rear. Chabot's extreme nervousness caused Berckman to inspect the car further after the owner had left, discovering that the rear fender had been newly welded though there was no other sign of damage and the paint was unmarred. Berckman reported his suspicions to Customs Inspector Howard Walter. Walter sent inspectors Mario Cozzi and James P. Dalton with three port patrol officers to examine the car. Cozzi, rapping the sides of the car and hearing a hollow sound near the rear fender, discovered and removed eighty-two packages containing sheets of gold worth a total of $171,197.

Chabot and his wife boarded the ship the next morning, went to their cabin, and were confronted by the police. Chabot protested his innocence, claiming that a man named Carl had given him money to purchase the car, and that he had no knowledge of the hidden contraband, but he was tried, found Guilty, and sentenced to five years in prison.

REF.: *CBA;* Whitehead, *Border Guard.*

Chack, Paul, 1876-1945, Fr., war crimes. A retired French navy captain with a distinguished record in WWI, who also wrote patriotic children's books, was found Guilty of being a propagandist for the Nazis in WWII and was executed.

On Dec. 18, 1944, 68-year-old Paul Chack, was tried by the Paris Court of Justice before presiding Judge Jean Pailhé. Chack was charged with contributing vicious written attacks against the Allies to Parisian newspapers, and founding, under the Nazi occupation of Paris, the Committee of Anti-Bolshevik Action.

Judge Pailhé read excerpts from Chack's anti-Allies editorials. As a hushed room listened to phrases like, "The American Army is an army of brutal gangsters," and "The Jewish gang behind the White House," Chack suddenly collapsed in the prisoner's dock. He later whispered to Pailhé, "I confess my error."

Witnesses verified that the propagandist had been subsidized by the Vichy regime with a 68,000-franc-a-month allowance, that he had founded an "Aryan club," and had instigated a traveling anti-Bolshevist exhibition. At the climax of the hearing a recording of Chack's pro-German speeches rang out in court. The chief public prosecutor directly addressed Chack, demanding the death sentence "because of your talent, because of your white hair, because of your war ribbons." The defense attorney asked for leniency, pleading "errors of judgment," but a jury of four citizens returned a verdict of Guilty. Chack was executed at dawn on Jan. 10, 1945, in Paris. REF.: *CBA.*

Chacón, Augustin (AKA: Paludo, Peledo, The Hairy One), d.1901, Mex.-U.S., west. outl. Part Indian and part Mexican, Augustin Chacón was one of the most feared outlaws to raid the

Arizona Territory in the late 1890s. He was a tall, hairy man with a fierce disposition and a decided inclination toward murder. Chacón was born and raised in Sonora, Mex., and served as a youth with the Mexican army. He attended school for a few years, which passed for a higher education in that illiterate era. By 1895, Chacón had deserted the army and had put together a ruthless band of outlaws in Sonora, raiding into Arizona. In Morenci, Ariz., Chacón and his men robbed a storeowner and when he resisted, Chacón drew a machete and hacked the man to pieces. He and his men robbed a gambling house in Jerome, Ariz., then killed two prospectors and, near Phoenix, the band shot two sheepherders to death for no apparent reason other than for the sadistic joy of killing.

Mexican bandit Augustin Chacón.

The outlaws struck next at Agua Fria, stopping and robbing a stage there. In Clifton, Ariz., a posse cornered Chacón and his men while they were freely spending their loot in the Longfellow House. A wild gunfight ensued in which Chacón shot and killed one of his old friends, Pablo Salcido, one of the deputies who had gone to the beseiged building under a flag of truce. Chacón, however, was wounded when he attempted to escape the trap and he was placed in the local jail, later removed to the stronger jail at Solomanville. He bribed a guard there and made an escape. Dozens of lawmen and vigilantes hunted Chacón who, after committing several robberies, was again captured. He was tried at Solomanville, found Guilty, and sentenced to be hanged on July 18, 1897.

Again, however, the wily Chacón escaped. He fled back to the sanctuary of Mexico. The bandit was finally caught by the indomitable Arizona Ranger captain Burton Mossman, a lawman who was one of the deadliest gunmen in the West. Mossman lost two rangers to the guns of Chacón and he vowed to track the killer down. He did, shooting it out with the bandit and wounding him several times. So powerful was Chacón that, though wounded, he leaped upon Mossman when the lawman came close and Mossman had to club him into unconsciousness with his six gun. Chacón finally kept his long overdue date with the gallows, being hanged on Nov. 21, 1902, in Solomanville. See: **Mossman, Burton**.

REF.: Bakarich, *Gun-Smoke*; Bartholomew, *The Biographical Album of Western Gunfighters*; Breihan, *Great Gunfighters of the West*; ____, *Great Lawmen of the West*; CBA; Coolidge, *Fighting Men of the West*; Erwin, *The Southwest of John H. Slaughter, 1841-1922*; Hendricks, *The Bad Man of the West*; Horan and Sann, *Pictorial History of the Wild West*; Hughes, *South from Tombstone*; Hunt, *Cap Mossman, Last of the Great Cowmen*; Hunter and Rose, *The Album of Gunfighters*; Johnson, *Famous Lawmen of the Old West*; LaFarge, *Santa Fe*; Liggett, *My Seventy-Five Years Along the Mexican Border*; Miller, *Arizona, The Last Frontier*; ____, *The Arizona Story*; O'Neal, *Encyclopedia of Western Gunfighters*; Penfield, *Dig Here!*; Raine, *Famous Sheriffs and Western Outlaws*; ____, *Forty-Five Caliber Law*; Ringgold, *Frontier Days in the Southwest: Pioneer Days in Arizona*; Rynning, *Gun Notches*; Shirley, *Buckskin and Spurs*; Small, *The Best of True West*; Walters, *Tombstone's Yesterdays*; Waltrip, *Cowboys and Cattlemen*; Way, *Frontier Arizona*; Wellman, *The Trampling Herd*.

Chadwell, William, See: **James, Jesse Woodson**.

Chadwick, Constance Cassandra (Elizabeth Bigley, AKA: Cassie, Lydia de Vere, Lydia Springsteen, Lydia D. Scott), 1859-1907, U.S., fraud. Born in Strathroy, Ontario, Can., the daughter of a railway section hand, this clever con artist was able to dupe scores of gullible suckers in swindles both simple and elaborate. Her most infamous fraud was her most daring, one that briefly netted her a fortune and involved none other than one of the world's richest men, Andrew Carnegie. At the age of sixteen, Cassie, as she was usually called, tried to cash a forged check in the amount of $5,000. She was released by the court, which

found her temporarily insane. But, as her future conduct revealed, such actions were normal for this adventuress. Traveling to San Francisco, Cassie gave herself the grand-sounding name of Lydia de Vere, claiming to be a clairvoyant. The beautiful young con lady insisted that she was a powerful hypnotist who could make any fortune for those willing to pay the high price for her seeress services, or, worse, that she could cure any illness. After several clients found themselves still afflicted by the same deformities and maladies, their savings depleted through high payments to Cassie, the con artist fled to the Midwest.

Con woman Cassie Chadwick, 1889.

There Cassie practiced the badger game, compromising wealthy married men with an accomplice ready to reveal extramarital scandals unless paid considerable cash. Cassie thus enriched herself for some years. She later began to assume the role of a wealthy society matron who would arrive in a large town and pretend to be related to socially prominent persons, renting mansions and running up huge debts on credit. She was so extravagant and acted with such authority that most of her creditors believed her to be a true member of the wealthy class, eccentric as most rich persons were expected to be. At one point, Cassie purchased twenty-seven grand pianos on credit (selling these off to fences). She entertained with the style of a Renaissance princess, hiring full orchestras to play in the ballrooms of her rented mansions, ordering table-glutted banquets from the best catering services. Members of the social set in each city were quickly convinced that Cassie was a genuine peer and she, in turn, used these new and influential acquaintences to secure more and more credit, hundreds of thousands of dollars worth. When her creditors began to demand payment, Cassie simply sold off her rented furniture and left town to assume a new identity in another location.

Cassie married several times, wedding well-to-do men and milking them of their fortunes. These included Dr. John Springsteen and Dr. William Scott. By the early 1890s, Cassie was in

Billionaire Andrew Carnegie, used by Cassie Chadwick in her fantastic flimflam.

Toledo, again practicing her clairvoyant scams which had become more sophisticated than those she had practiced in San Francisco a decade earlier. Here she hired private detectives to learn all they could about her intended victims, mostly information about their tainted pasts and, after revealing these hidden scandals to shocked clients gathered about her crystal ball, she levied heavy fees for her silence, a form of blackmail that netted Cassie an average of $50,000 a year. Finally, one angry client of her spiritualist racket threatened to take her to court, and Cassie closed her clairvoyant operation. She next obtained $20,000 in forged bills from a bank employee she compromised but she was caught, convicted of fraud and forgery, and given a nine-year sentence in 1894. She was paroled in 1897 and immediately went to Cleveland where she met and married another naive elderly man, Dr. Leroy Chadwick.

As Mrs. Chadwick, Cassie traveled to New York where she

rented an expensive suite of rooms in the Holland House, a socially elite hotel. Here she "accidentally" met James Dillon, a Cleveland lawyer who represented several Cleveland banks. In fact, she had chronicled Dillon's movements and knew he would be in New York on business, staying at the Holland House, which is why she went to New York in the first place. She had met Dillon briefly in Cleveland and he was pleased to see her in New York. Cassie then off-handedly asked if Dillon would accompany her on a small trip, she then being without a proper escort. Dillon agreed and both took a carriage, at Cassie's instructions, down Fifth Avenue. To Dillon's amazement, the carriage stopped in front of Andrew Carnegie's enormous residence, one recognized by anyone who moved in banking circles.

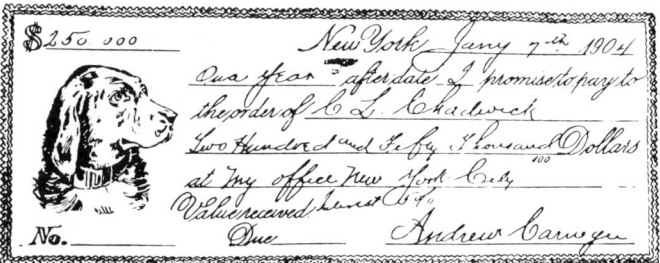

A bogus Carnegie bank draft used by Chadwick to gain fabulous credit.

Dillon then watched Cassie go into Carnegie's residence. At the entrance Cassie asked the footman to see the butler and once inside the first foyer of the sprawling mansion, she asked the butler to see Carnegie's housekeeper and the woman appeared, not knowing who she was. Cassie pretended to be a wealthy socialite who was about to hire a domestic who had given Carnegie as a former employer on her reference sheet. The housekeeper was puzzled; no such person ever worked for Carnegie, Cassie was told. But she had the application, Cassie said, and held out a letter from the supposed job applicant. Could it be that the woman had been employed at another of Carnegie's many residences? The housekeeper asked Cassie to wait, she would check in her files. It was some time before the housekeeper returned to inform Cassie that the job applicant was an imposter, that she had never worked for Carnegie. Cassie took back the letter and thanked the housekeeper for her time and effort, that she had done her a great service in revealing an untrustworthy domestic. The housekeeper was glad to be of help, she said. With that, Cassie left the Carnegie mansion. She had been inside using up time, almost a half hour, a stall which was also part of her plan.

Upon returning to the carriage where Dillon waited, Cassie climbed inside and purposely dropped a piece of paper which the lawyer retrieved. He could not help notice with gaping mouth that it was a promissory note made out to Cassie Chadwick for $2 million and it was signed by

Cassie Chadwick as Cleveland's reigning social queen.

none other than Andrew Carnegie. Dillon handed this to Mrs. Chadwick, who looked embarrassed, and then, as they rode back toward the Holland House, she revealed her family secret. She was used to receiving such payments from Carnegie since she was his illegitimate daughter. Of course, Dillon and the rest of the world knew that Carnegie had never married and was a confirmed bachelor. He was a celibate who would, one could easily imagine, do everything in his power to cover up the existence of an illegitimate child to protect his sterling reputation. Cassie sighed and said that the $2 million note was her father's way of taking care of her, that she had many more such notes in her Cleveland home, more than $7 million of such notes. Dillon was stunned, telling Cassie that such notes belonged in a safe deposit box, certainly in one of the banks he represented. She shrugged and asked if he could arrange for such business when they both returned to Cleveland. Dillon, delighted at the prospect of gaining such an affluent new client, happily agreed to make such arrangements.

When both returned to Cleveland, Cassie gave Dillon the notes and these were taken to a local bank. Dillon explained the delicacy of Cassie's position, that in no way could she be challenged lest her illegitimate status be made public. In that sorry event, Carnegie himself would be scandalized and his legal wrath might be visited upon the bank, or Cleveland as a whole, for that matter. The banker, thrilled at the prospect of increasing the assets of his bank, vowed to keep Cassie's secret and then issued a receipt for more than $7 million to Cassie which Dillon slavishly delivered to Mrs. Chadwick. The Carnegie notes, of course, were forged, but the banker never bothered to examine these, taking Dillon's word for their authenticity.

Cassie Chadwick in New York, under arrest, returning to Cleveland to stand trial.

After receiving the bank receipt, Cassie Chadwick became the biggest spender in Cleveland, buying jewelry, carriages, hiring a bevy of servants, purchasing a mansion and filling it with priceless tapestries, paintings. Meanwhile, the greedy bankers of Cleveland vied with each other in advancing hundreds of thousands of dollars to Mrs. Chadwick, all on the strength of her forged Carnegie notes. The reputation of Cassie's wealth spread through the social elite and even a Cleveland millionaire, Henry Newton, was glad to advance her $500,000, collecting enormous interest, of course, as were the banks. But unlike the patient bankers who happily watched the interest leap upward on Cassie's loans, Newton demanded payment of the interest due him. Cassie became hysterical, telling Newton that she had more than $10 million in securities in Cleveland's Wade National Bank. Instead of merely accepting her word and that of her bankers, Newton insisted on inspecting these notes. The documents were judged forgeries. Andrew Carnegie was contacted and indignantly denied ever having had a child and emphatically that he "knew no one named Mrs. Chadwick." The glorious ruse was exposed and Cassie was arrested.

Police found Cassie Chadwick in a suite of rooms in New York's Holland House on Dec. 7, 1904. She was in bed, shouting at officers who had to lift her bodily from her four-poster. A policewoman at the station house searched Cassie and found a money belt tied tightly about her waist. It contained more than $100,000 in cash. She was taken under guard by train back to Cleveland where thousands of curious citizens turned out to greet her in shocked silence. Cassie brazened her way through the crowds, telling one and all that she was innocent and being victimized because she was "a member of the upper class." Her aloof airs evaporated once she appeared in court and, following a quick trial in March 1905, where evidence of her guilt was overwhelming, she was convicted on six charges of fraud and sentenced to ten years in the Ohio State Penitentiary at Columbus. There, alone, dreaming of her grand schemes and former opulence, Cassie Chadwick died on Oct. 10, 1907.

REF.: *CBA;* Kingston, *Remarkable Rogues;* MacDougal, *Hoaxes;* Mehling, *The Scandalous Scamps;* Nash, *Bloodletters and Badmen;* ____, *Hustlers and Con Men;* ____, *Look for the Woman;* Scott, *The Concise Encyclopedia of Crime and Criminals;* Wade, *Great Hoaxes and Famous Imposters.*

Chaerea, Gaius Cassius, d.41 A.D., Roman., consp.-assass. Assassinated Emperor Caligula, and was executed by Claudius when he assumed the throne. See: **Caligula.** REF.: *CBA.*

Chafee, Zechariah, 1885-1957, U.S., lawyer. Member of the faculty at Harvard University. Books authored: *Free Speech in the United States,* and *Blessings of Liberty.* REF.: *CBA.*

Chaffers, Alexander, prom. 1872, Brit., libel-blk. In 1872, a London solicitor named Alexander Chaffers decided to blackmail the wife of Sir Travers Twiss, professor of International Law at King's College, and someone who was well-known to Queen Vicotria. The incident resulted in the passage of the 1873 statute designed to protect individuals from menaces who would extort money in return for protection from scandal. It was the first law of its kind against blackmailers enacted in the British empire.

Sir Travers married Marie Van Lynseele in 1862. She presented herself as the daughter of a respected Polish Major-General. Taking her place in British society, Lady Twiss was presented to the Prince of Wales and Queen Victoria. Not long after this, Alexander Chaffers appeared and demanded £46 as payment for legal services rendered to Lady Twiss while she was still Marie Van Lynseele. Sir Travers readily paid it. Pressing the matter further, Chaffers demanded more, and then wrote a letter to the Lord Chamberlain in which he claimed that Sir Travers' wife was a fraud. Her name, he said, was Marie Gelas, a former French prostitute. Lady Twiss said that Marie Gelas had worked as her "chaperone", a claim that could not be proven or disporven.

Chaffers was brought before the courts on a libel charge, but after eight days of deliberation, Lady Twiss inexplicibly gave up. She left London for good, and her distraught husband was forced to resign from his posts. It is conceivable that Chaffers accusations were all true, and that Lady Twiss had bribed various witnesses to provide good character references on her behalf. Then perhaps fearing criminal prosecution for perjury, Sir Travers and his wife backed down. The London *Gazette* later reported that the appearance of Lady Twiss before the Royal court had been "cancelled", meaning that it had never taken place. REF.: *CBA.*

Chagra, Jamiel Alexander (Jimmy Chagra), 1943- , U.S., tax. evas.-consp.-drugs. A gambler and convicted narcotics dealer was accused of arranging the murder of a federal judge well-known for his stringent rulings against drug dealers. Though three other defendants in the conspiracy and cover-up were found Guilty in their home state of Texas, the narcotics dealer himself was acquitted by a Florida court.

On May 29, 1979, John H. Wood, Jr., sixty-three, a San Antonio judge known as "Maximum John" because of his strict rulings and maximum sentences against drug dealers, was killed by a single shot from a rifle as he stepped out of his disabled car at around 7:50 a.m. in front of his home. He was the first federal judge to be assassinated in more than 100 years.

Attorney General Griffin Bell assembled a task force of more than forty FBI agents. According to FBI director William H. Webster, the two-and-a-half-year investigation that resulted in the indictments of Jamiel Alexander Chagra, also called Jimmy Chagra, thirty-nine, and Charles V. Harrelson, forty-four, cost $4.7 million and eventually involved more than seventy agents. Harrelson, a convicted murderer, and Chagra, a convicted gambler and narcotics dealer, were charged with the murder. Chagra was already in prison and had been scheduled to appear before Wood on drug charges in 1979. According to later FBI reports, Chagra was "the highest of high rollers," a man who often bet half a million dollars on a roll of the dice.

Judge Wood, who had once tacked twenty-nine years for contempt onto a man's fifteen-year sentence, had also sentenced an accused man to forty-five years in prison because he refused to testify in court. A conservative, he was known for never giving probation in drug-related cases—ninety per cent of the defendants before him received maximum sentences. He had several times ruled against minority cases involving the Equal Opportunity Commission, and was felt by San Antonio's Mexican-American community to give prejudiced judgments against Hispanics.

Also charged with conspiracy to murder were Chagra's brother, Joseph Salim Chagra, a lawyer who primarily defended accused drug offenders in El Paso, Elizabeth Nichols Chagra, Jimmmy Chagra's wife, and Jo Ann Starr Harrelson, wife of Charles Harrelson. Mrs. Harrelson was charged with purchasing the murder weapon, a .243-caliber hunting rifle. Joseph Chagra was accused of paying Harrelson $250,000 to murder Wood. Elizabeth Chagra, twenty-eight, accused of conspiring with her husband, reportedly wrote a letter to Wood's widow, apologizing for the killing and saying she had become a born-again Christian since the crime. She also said she had personally delivered the $250,000 fee for the assassination.

On Sept. 17, 1982, Joseph Chagra pleaded Guilty in a San Antonio court for helping to plot the murder. Federal District Judge William Sessions sealed Joseph Chagra's four-page plea agreement at the request of both prosecutor Ray Jahn and defense attorney Billy Ravkind to protect the lawyer. As part of the deal, he accepted a ten-year prison term and was not required to testify against his brother, Jamiel. On Nov. 1, Joseph Chagra testified in court, saying of Harrelson, "I asked him if he was the one who murdered Judge Wood and he said he was." On Dec. 14, after eighteen hours of deliberation, a jury found Charles Harrelson, Elizabeth Chagra, and Jo Ann Harrelson all Guilty on six counts of planning, carrying out, and trying to cover up Wood's murder. On Dec. 21, Joseph Chagra was sentenced to ten years in prison.

On Nov. 30, 1983, Jamiel Chagra, serving thirty years in an Illinois prison for drug smuggling, was indicted by a federal grand jury for conspiracy and assault in the attempted slaying of Assistant U.S. Attorney James W. Kerr, a specialist in narcotics cases, who was shot at on his way to work on Nov. 21, 1978. On Feb. 7, 1983, just seven weeks after the Harrelsons and Elizabeth Chagra were found Guilty, Jimmy Chagra was acquitted in a Jacksonville, Fla., court of plotting the assassination of Wood, but was convicted on two lesser charges of conspiracy to possess and sell marijuana and obstruct justice. He was later sentenced to fifteen years in prison and fined $120,000 with tax evasion added to the charges.

On Mar. 8, 1983, Jo Ann Harrelson was found Guilty in a Shreveport, La., courtroom of lying to a federal grand jury about purchasing the hunting rifle, and about her daughter going to pick up the $250,000 payment for the slaying. Charles Harrelson was tried in San Antonio, found Guilty, and sentenced on Mar. 18 to two life sentences for the assassination. On June 17, 1984, Jamiel Chagra pleaded guilty before Judge William Sessions of plotting to kill Wood. REF.: *CBA.*

Chain, Sir **Ernst Boris,** 1906-79, Brit., path. Researcher at the Institute of Pathology at the Charité Hospital in Berlin from 1930-33. He was awarded a Nobel Prize in 1945 for physiology and medicine. REF.: *CBA.*

Chairman, Alice Mary Heinrich, prom. 1944, U.S., abor. A trained medical professional from Hungary performed illegal abortions in New York City in the mid-1940s. Born in Hungary, Alice Chairman came from a good family and earned her medical degree from a Budapest school. In 1921 in Austria, she married Imre Czernayack, her fourth husband, and an exiled Hungarian revolutionary. Abortion was both legal and commonplace in communist countries at that time. The couple moved to the U.S. and settled in Manhattan, changing their name to Chairman, and Dr. Chairman obtained a medical license.

That license was revoked in 1940 when Chairman, married a fifth time, was put on probation in connection with an abortion case. In late February 1944 she was convicted for operating on a 19-year-old woman, the mother of twins, who was the wife of an Army man. Chairman was sentenced to one year of probation—she had previously received three months' probation on similar charges a year earlier. Chairman had the reputation of being a good practitioner, and was known as a kindly doctor. REF.: *CBA.*

Chait Singh, c.1760-95, India, polit., consp. Raja of Benares (1773-80), he became a zamindar of the British East India Company, forced to pay excessive rent to finance British military adventures in his country. In 1781 he lodged formal protests to colonial Governor Warren Hastings who had him arrested and deposed for suspected conspiracy. Hastings was recalled, and stood trial for corruption and cruelty as a consequence of this affair. REF.: *CBA.*

Chaka (Shaka, Tshka), 1787-1828, assass. Founded the Zulu empire of southeastern Africa. Under his brutal reign, the Zulus conquered many rival tribes. In 1827 he was murdered by his half-brothers. REF.: *CBA.*

Chalcraft, J., and **Chennell, George Jr.,** d.1818, Brit., mur. A grisly double murder took place in the quaint English town of Godalming on Nov. 11, 1817. Shoemaker George Chennell was bludgeoned to death with a hammer on the second floor of his home. The housekeeper, Mrs. Wilson, was also found dead, her throat slit from ear to ear. Chennell's son, George, Jr., was suspected of the murders. His questionable character and the bad company he kept led to his arrest on Aug. 12, 1818.

It was shown that on the night of the murder, George Chennell, Jr. had met his father's carriage driver, J. Chalcraft, at the Richmond Arms pub where the two agreed to do away with the old man. They used a shoemaker's hammer on George, Sr., and then killed the housemaid as she was mending a shirt by the fire.

Chalcraft and Chennell were found Guilty of murder and were hanged by Jack Ketch near Frith Hill. Twenty thousand people witnessed the execution, the last public hanging in Godalming. REF.: Butler, *Murderers' England; CBA.*

Chalinder, Jean, prom. 1956, Brit., (unsolv.) mur. On Sept. 18, 1956, in a small Welsh town, the anxious husband of Jean Chalinder, a 32-year-old bride of three months, reported his wife missing. She had left home on her bicycle to pick blackberries and had not returned. In the late evening of Sept. 20, blackberry pickers found her battered body in a ditch in the Cardiff suburb of Llanedeyrn. Her bicycle lay nearby. Her extensive head injuries led police to suspect they had been inflicted by a hooked metal object.

Chalinder had last been seen about two miles from where she was found. Witnesses reported seeing a man hurriedly bicycle away from the spot on the presumed day and around the time the murder occurred. On Jan. 18, 1957, however, a verdict of murder by person or persons unknown was recorded at the Whitchurch, Glamorgan inquest. REF.: *CBA;* Furneaux, *Famous Criminal Cases, Vol. 4.*

Chalker, Edward Poole, d.1835, Brit., (wrong. convict) mur. In March 1835, two men were wrongly convicted of murder in

England. Both were hanged.

Edward Poole Chalker, a farm laborer, was convicted in March 1835 of murdering a gamekeeper. Adamantly protesting his innocence, he was hanged within forty-eight hours. According to a 1752 act "for better preventing the horrid crime of murder," convicted killers were normally executed within two days. Seven years later, another man admitted committing the crime.

At Waterford Assizes that same month an Irish peddler known as Daniel Savage, was sentenced to die for killing his wife ten years earlier. He was positively identified by only one witness. When shaved to make the hangman's job easier, his sister visited him and, perplexed, explained, "He's not my brother...doesn't look anything like him." Soon after his death it was discovered that the man hanged was a retarded person, Edmund Pine, and not Daniel Savage. Partly in response to the deaths of Chalker and Pine, the law was eventually changed. REF.: *CBA.*

Chalkley, Dr. **Thomas,** 1934-   , U.S., Case of, pandering-child porn. For using a 16-year-old high school student in a sex video and soliciting a policewoman, a highly respected Chicago doctor was charged with child pornography and pandering.

On Apr. 11, 1988, a 17-year-old ward of the state testified that Dr. Thomas Chalkley, fifty-four, a renowned Chicago eye doctor with twenty-six years of professional credentials, awards, and appointments, had given her $500 to perform sexually explicit acts in his X-rated videos. The teenager said he paid her $200 to film a screen test on June 2 and another $300 on June 30 to participate in pornographic videos in Chalkey's Streeterville, Ill., penthouse.

Then on leave from his positions as ophthalmologist and surgeon at Northwestern Memorial Hospital and Lakeland Hospital in Elkhorn, Ill., Chalkley was charged along with Dorothy Patton, thirty-one, his live-in girlfriend and a former prostitute, and Dennis Fiorino, thirty-three, a male stripper also known as Dynamite Dennis. All three defendants were also charged with offering $150 to a female undercover officer to engage in sex with Chalkley and Fiorino.

At the April 1988 trial in Cook County Criminal Court, Chalkley insisted before Judge Earl Strayhorn that he had never offered the policewoman work in his videos, explaining: "I said I'm not going to work with her. She's too aggressive. I just don't work with aggressive women." Defense attorney James Linn charged that police had come up with the pandering charge, never before used in an Illinois trial, after they found that Chalkley was a prominent physician.

Facing up to fifteen years in prison on the child pornography charge and another three years on the pandering charge, Chalkley said he believed the high school student was eighteen or nineteen at the time. That was what she had stated on her application to model for REV (Ritzy Erotic Videos), a company he set up as a revenue source for Patton.

Playing "Hank" to Patton's character of "Maggie," Chalkley had performed in about two-thirds of the videos. At $49.85 apiece, he had sold between 1200 and 1300 of them. "Some people play golf," Chalkley explained, "I have other hobbies."

In court, assistant state's attorneys Jeanne Bischoff and Jack Murphy played videos of Chalkley performing sexual acts with the 16-year-old. But on May 4, 1988, all three defendants were acquitted of both charges. Judge Strayhorn ruled the pandering law could not be applied to activities that went on "behind closed doors" between "consenting, mature adults."

After the verdict, all three defendants promptly announced they were writing books. Saying they were looking for a publisher, Chalkley and Patton distributed a synopsis of the first half of their book to reporters. Fiorino in turn explained that his book about eight years as a stripper and porn star would be titled *Dynamite Dennis: Confessions.*

Chalkley resigned from Northwestern Hospital, saying he planned to move his medical practice and Patton to the Virgin Islands and that he was sorry REV could not market the two videos because the woman was underage. REF.: *CBA.*

Chalk-Pit Murder, See: **Ley, Thomas John.**

Challe, Maurice-Prosper-Félix, 1905-79, Fr., consp. General in command of the air force in Morocco from 1949-51, he was opposed to President Charles DeGaulle's plan to grant Algeria independence from France. He led a revolt of the military staff in 1961, and was imprisoned for five years. REF.: *CBA.*

Challoner, William, prom. 1696, Brit., count. A counterfeiter gave up his criminal career and generously offered to help his country revamp its minting procedures to prevent further fraud. William Challoner, a master counterfeiter, had a change of heart in 1696 and volunteered to help England reform its money-printing methods. He made several proposals to the chancellor of the exchequer, Charles Montagu, suggesting that counterfeiting could be stopped by raising the relief of designs to a height that could only be struck by the most powerful presses, and proposing that the royal mint's engines be increased at a small cost that would result in long-term economy.

Challoner also suggested that coins be minted with a groove in the rims making mold and cast counterfeiting impossible. The mint considered these ideas, experimented with them, and decided they were impractical. Challoner was sent to Newgate Jail. He pleaded immunity as a Parliamentary witness, was released, and captured again, then executed in 1699. Counterfeiters all over England cheered his demise. In 1933, 237 years later, several of Challoner's ideas were adopted by the royal mint.

REF.: Bloom, *Money of Their Own; CBA.*

Chalmers, George, 1742-1825, Scot., lawyer. Practiced law in the U.S. colonies until the outbreak of hostilities in 1775. He returned to London where he was appointed chief clerk to the Privy Council from 1786-1825. REF.: *CBA.*

Chalmers, James, 1841-1901, Scot., (unsolv.) mur. Ordained a Congregationalist minister in 1865, he was sent to New Guinea in 1877 where he helped establish British authority. He was murdered and eaten by cannibals at Goaribari Island. REF.: *CBA.*

Chalmers, Sir **Mackenzie Dalzell,** 1847-1927, Brit., jur. Called to the bar in 1869, he prepared legal codifications later adopted by Parliament. REF.: *CBA.*

Chamberlain, Alice Lynne (Lindy), 1948-   , Case of, Aus., mur. Michael and Lindy Chamberlain, a young couple with three children who lived in Mount Isa in western Queensland, took a camping trip in August 1980, traveling to scenic Ayers Rock in Australia's Northern Territory near Alice Springs. The family pitched a tent in the shadow of the towering, dome-shaped Ayers Rock with other tourists. On the night of Aug. 17, 1980, Lindy Chamberlain put 4-year-old Reagan and her 9-week-year-old daughter Azaria to sleep in the tent and then, with her husband and 7-year-old Aidan, went outside to help prepare supper at the campfire. At about 7 p.m., Michael Chamberlain turned to his wife and said that he thought he heard the baby crying in the tent. As Lindy approached the tent, she later stated, she saw a dingo, a breed of Australian wild dog that populated the outback, running from the tent, its head down, shaking something in its jaws. "I dashed into the tent but the carry-cot was empty," Lindy later testified. "I looked around but there was no sign of Azaria." She then realized what had happened, and Lindy turned and ran back to her husband screaming: "My God! My God! The dingo's got my baby!"

Chamberlain then ran frantically through the camp asking campers to join him in a search for his child. More than 300 campers with blazing torches began scouring the rocky, brushy area. Not a trace of the baby could be found. Lindy told her story to the local police, who also conducted an official search. A week later, some of the baby's bloodstained clothing was found near a dingo's lair. The case caused such a sensation that the inquest was televised in 1981 and Coroner Dennis Barritt of Alice Springs, determined that a dingo had, indeed, killed the child and that both Chamberlains were innocent of any wrongdoing.

A short time later, however, Paul Everingham, chief minister of the Northern Territory, ordered police to continue the investiga- tion, and forensic experts were called in to examine the child's clothing. Dr. Kenneth Brown of Adelaide reported that the holes found in the child's jumpsuit were not caused by bite marks. The esteemed London pathologist, Professor James Cameron, then examined the jumpsuit and agreed with Brown, further adding that the holes in the jumpsuit had been made by a scissors. Joy Kuhl, an Australian biologist added that there were blood stains on the front seat of the Chamberlian car and on a pair of scissors owned by the Chamberlains and that these bloodstains were from an infant less than six months old.

There were other factors that seemed to point suspicion at the couple. The parents announced their child's death long before the official search for the baby was called off and Michael allegedly tried to sell family photographs to an Adelaide publication. Moreover, gossip and rumors abounded about the Chamberlains belonging to a weird cult or sect. Chamberlain was a Sev- enth Day Adventist and this led the uninformed to believe that he might be associated with the killer cult of Jim Jones, and that the baby's name Azaria meant "sacrifice in the wilderness," a name linked to Biblical sacrifice. Coupled to that was the an- cient legend of the aborigines who believed that a giant din- go lived in the vicinity of Ay- ers Rock and that in ancient times their tribes sacrificed children to this eternal, raven- ous beast. After Professor Cameron's statements about the jumpsuit, many came to believe that the Chamberlains were baby-killers. The couple received both death and bomb threats.

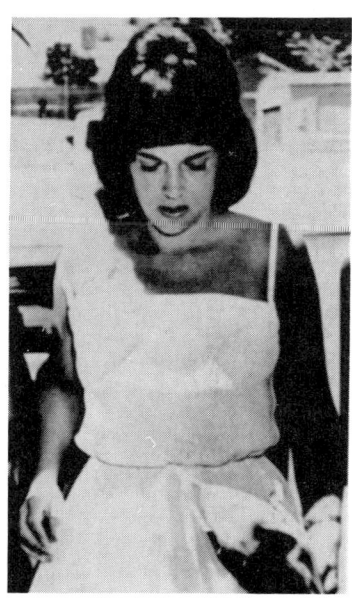

Lindy Chamberlain entering the court- house in Alice Springs.

The coroner's original ver- dict was abandoned and, in February 1982, a second coroner's inquest ordered a trial where, on Sept. 13, 1982, Lindy Chamberlain was charged with murdering her infant Azaria, and Michael Chamberlain was charged as an accessory after the fact. Prosecutor Ian Barker maintained that Lindy had cut her child's throat with a pair of scissors while she held the baby in the front seat of the family car, then hid the body in her husband's camera bag and buried the tiny corpse near Ayers Rock. To that claim, the reserved, almost unimpassioned Lindy Chamberlain finally burst forth with loud sobs and a shout of "That's not true!" This was exceptional. Lindy Chamberlain showed very little emotion when in court, she being a person of extraodinary composure. This conduct was interpreted by many to mean indifference; some beleived it indicated guilt.

Barker made some telling forensic points, saying that examina- tion of the child's jumpsuit showed that not only did it have scissor cuts instead of bite marks but that no trace of saliva was found and saliva would certainly be evident after a dingo had carried the child in its jaws for a distance of three miles, the distance from the site of the tent to where the jumpsuit was later found. More- over, Barker stated, the amount of blood found in the tent area was so small that it indicated that Lindy had sprinkled this blood in the tent *after* murdering her baby to make it appear that the dingo had attacked the child in the tent. Barker finished his summation with: "It was murder. It was her mother, and there is no room for any other reasonable hypothesis." The defense brought in its own forensic experts to undo the evidence provided by the prosecution, but these experts proved to be confusing and contradictory. At the end of a seven-week trial, the jury deliberated for six-and-a-half hours and returned a verdict of Guilty.

Lindy was sentenced to life imprisonment and was led to a cell in Darwin's Berrimah Jail. Her husband was found Guilty of being an accessory after the fact. Michael Chamberlain's counsel pleaded for him with a good deal of passion, saying that his two sons would be bereft without one of their parents to take care of them. Judge Muirhead rendered a surprising sentence in light of having sent Lindy Chamberlain to prison for life. He gave Chamberlain a suspended sentence of eighteen months at hard labor. Chamberlain was ordered to pay a bond of $A500. A short time after Lindy Chamberlain went to prison, she gave birth to a baby girl, Kahlia. Lindy was released on bail three weeks after giving birth, pending the decision on her appeal of the trial conviction. Three federal judges dismissed the appeal on Apr. 29, 1983, and she was returned to prison to serve out her life sentence.

In the next few years, support for Lindy Chamberlain grew. More than 130,000 names were gathered in petitions by the Save Lindy Campaign, headquartered in Melbourne, and these petitions demanded that Chamberlain be given a new trial. Moreover, other forensic scientists quarreled with the conclusions of the experts during Lindy's trial. Then, in February 1986, searchers looking for a lost tourist near Ayers Rock, found Azaria's jacket about 100 yards from where her jumpsuit had been located and this appeared to support Lindy Chamberlain's claims. A new inquiry was ordered but, in spite of this inquiry's outcome, announced officials of the Northern Territory, Lindy Chamberlain would be released and remain free. By then Hollywood actress Meryl Streep had already begun a film production based on the Chamberlain case, a sympathetic account which did much to bring popular support to Chamberlain. A Darwin court later declared Lindy Chamberlain innocent.

The Chamberlains moved to Cooranbong, eighty miles north of Sydney, where they filed a staggering suit against the Australian government in compensation for damages and legal fees, claiming that Lindy was wrongfully imprisoned, a suit pending at this writing. The amount of money the Chamberlains are demanding is reportedly in excess of $3 million. Lindy Chamberlain nevertheless admitted to newsmen that "some people will die believing we did it. I can live with it quite easily because I know they are wrong. The hardest person to live with is yourself and I know I didn't do it."

REF.: Brien, *Azaria: The Trial of the Century;* Bryson, *Evil Angels; CBA;* Shcrears, *Mother on Trial;* Wilson, *Encyclopedia of Modern Murder;* (FILM), *A Cry in the Dark,* 1988.

Chamberlain, Sir Robert, prom. 1686, Case of, Brit., mur. When five English servants were found Guilty of murdering a duke, they were reprieved, escaping death and mutilation afterwards.

The Duke of Gloucester was secretly murdered in 1686, and five of his servants, including Sir Robert Chamberlain, Knight Middleton, Herbert Artiz, and John Needham, were condemned to be hanged, then drawn and quartered. They were hanged at Tyburn, brought down while still alive, stripped, and marked with knives to be drawn and quartered when the Marquess of Suffolk brought them a pardon, delivering it at the place of execution and saving their lives.

REF.: Atholl, *Shadow of the Gallows; CBA.*

Chambers, Arthur, c.1678-1706, Brit., count.-rob. The poverty of his youth taught Arthur Chambers to be extremely cunning and resourceful. As a boy he converted worthless slugs into sterling and passed them as counterfeit coins. So good was his forgery that few doubted their authenticity. Occasionally arrested for his crimes, he was punished alongside older, hardened criminals. But for Chambers, doing time at Cornwall Bridewell was an opportunity to reflect on his next illegal scheme.

Upon his release, Chambers went to London where he joined a gang of housebreakers. One night he entered a room where the body of a dead child lay, wrapped in linen and ready for burial the next morning. Thinking it was a sack of linen, Chambers carried it off to a local fence. When they opened the bundle and found the body, one of the thieves volunteered to dispose of it in the Thames, but Chambers, perhaps revealing a benevolent side, responded, "As I stole the child, I'll dispose of it as I please." He placed the body in a wooden box, sealed it, and hired a livery driver to return it to the house it was taken from.

When the contents of the box were discovered by the child's parents, the livery driver was arrested and taken to Westminster. By the time the identity of Chambers was established, he and his gang were nowhere to be found.

Tricking the rich and well-heeled was Chambers' greatest pleasure. He and his cohorts had been foiled repeatedly in their attempts to rob a wealthy couple living near Huntingdon. In a final attempt, the gang decided to decoy the husband from his bedroom. Chambers outfitted a scarecrow in men's clothing and weighted it down with heavy objects, then placed a ladder against the side of the house and propped the scarecrow against the bedroom window. Hearing a supposed intruder, the husband seized his musket and fired through the window. The scarecrow fell to the ground. Chambers hid in the bush while the man ran outside and dragged away his victim, never realizing it was a scarecrow. Chambers then crawled through the window, and while her husband dug a shallow grave some distance from the house, Chambers undressed, hopped into bed, and amused himself with the half-asleep woman. In a soft, tender voice he whispered, "Perhaps this rogue's ghost may walk out of spite and come and rob us still. Pray my dear, give me your diamond rings, and your gold watch by you, into my custody."

Having secured her diamonds and gold, Chambers dressed quickly and fled, saying, "I must go and bury that wretch before dawn." Only when the husband returned from his chore and heard his wife's story did he realize that he been tricked. His loss: £1,500, and a measure of his pride.

Chambers might have continued his career in crime had he not been betrayed by Jack Hall, a chimney sweep turned criminal, who traded information as to his whereabouts in return for a reduced sentence. In 1706, Arthur Chambers marched to the gallows with two other noted felons, Dick Morris and Jack Goodwin. See: **Morris, Dick; Goodwin, Jack.**

REF.: *CBA;* Smith, *Highwaymen.*

Chambers, Ernest John, 1862-1925, Can., writer. Authored *History of the Royal Northwest Mounted Police* (1906). REF.: *CBA.*

Chambers, Isaiah, and **Davis, Charlie,** and **Williamson, Jack,** and **Woodward, Walter,** prom. 1933, U.S., (wrong. convict.) mur. Four black tenant farmers in Florida were tried, convicted, and sentenced to death for a killing they did not commit. When finally acquitted, almost nine years had gone by since the murder. One of the four went insane while on Death Row and was released to a mental hospital.

On May 13, 1933, Pompano, Fla., fish dealer Robert Darcey, a white man, was murdered in a holdup. With intense public indignation about the killing, a police dragnet brought in four young tenant farmers, all black, who were arrested on suspicion, without warrants, and were held and questioned for almost a week without counsel. Terrified of mob violence, three of the accused men, dubbed "The Pompano Boys" by the press, confessed, though Isaiah Chambers maintained his innocence throughout.

Found Guilty of the murder on the evidence of their alleged confessions were Charlie Davis, Jack Williamson, and Walter Woodward. Chambers was convicted in a separate trial in the Broward County Court after his court-appointed attorney offered a perfunctory defense, and the convicted men were sentenced to be executed in the electric chair. Their case was appealed, but the convictions were affirmed. The issue of whether the confessions had been obtained under duress continued to come up as the case went through several courts, with the four men found Guilty three more times.

On Feb. 12, 1940, Chambers, Davis, Williamson, and Woodward won a seven-year struggle to escape execution when the U.S. Supreme Court overturned their convictions. Justice Hugo Black, who delivered the opinion, condemned the Florida officials' techniques, saying "to permit human lives to be forfeited upon confessions thus obtained would make of the constitutional requirement of due process of law a meaningless symbol."

In March 1942, three of the defendants were tried again before Judge C.E. Chillingworth. Eight witnesses for the state gave testimony tending to show that sticks and a hammer had been found near the homes of the men, and a pocketbook belonging to the victim was found in a room occupied by one of the accused.

Williamson and Woodward had offered to change their pleas to Guilty of second-degree murder "to get it over with." Davis said before the bar, "I've suffered for nine years over this. I still say I'm innocent and I won't say I'm guilty." Judge Chillingworth refused to accept the pleas, and four hours later directed the jury to bring in a verdict of Not Guilty. Davis, Williamson, and Woodward were acquitted after nine years. Chambers had gone insane while on death row at Raiford Prison and was transferred to the Chattahoochee State Mental Hospital in 1940. With S.D. McGill, the Jacksonville lawyer who defended the men for the last six years, the acquitted men left for unannounced destinations. They had spent seven years on death row. The case came to be known as "Little Scottsboro" in reference to a similar highly publicized incident in Mississippi in 1931, when nine black youths were unjustly accused of raping two white women. They were later acquitted. See: **The Scottsboro Case**. REF.: *CBA*.

Chambers, Leon, prom. 1969, U.S., (wrong. convict.) mur. Although another man had confessed to the murder for which a Mississippi youth had been convicted in 1969, he later withdrew his confession and the youth was left in prison until the U.S. Supreme Court finally reversed the conviction.

Leon Chambers, a young black man from Mississippi, was convicted of killing a white police officer in that state and sentenced to life in prison. The case was appealed and the conviction upheld. Chambers had been one of dozens in a large crowd police had fired on during a thwarted attempt to make an arrest. Chambers had been shot and left for dead.

Soon after Chambers' arrest, a man confessed to the murder, both orally and in writing. Two witnesses at this man's trial testified that they had seen him shoot the officer. The confessions, however, were retracted before Chambers' case again came to court. Three witnesses who had heard the confession—which was repeated several times—were not allowed to testify in court when a trial judge ruled that their testimony would constitute hearsay evidence. The court of Mississippi upheld the trial judge's ruling, and Chambers was left in jail until the U.S. Supreme Court reversed the judgment on the grounds that Chambers had been denied a fair trial since the Fourteenth Amendment had been violated. The conviction was reversed and all charges against Chambers were dropped. REF.: *CBA*.

Chambers, Lon, prom. 1880s, U.S., law enfor. off. Lon Chambers carried his badge and enforced the law in the Texas Panhandle throughout the late 1870s. About the time that Billy the Kid was terrorizing the Southwest, Chambers left his job to join Pat Garrett's posse, bent on taking Billy dead or alive. At Fort Sumner, N.M., on Dec. 19, 1881, Garrett and Chambers got their chance. They set an ambush for The Kid.

That night, Chambers was assigned to serve as a lookout outside the post hospital where the posse had gathered to await The Kid's arrival. When Billy the Kid's gang rode into town, the posse was ready. Garrett called, "Halt!" but Tom O'Folliard and Thomas Pickett, riding in the lead, did not heed this warning. O'Folliard reached for his gun, but Chambers was faster on the draw. O'Folliard slumped, wounded and bleeding, in his saddle and tried to ride away, but the severity of his gunshot wound forced him to surrender. He died within the hour, but Billy the Kid escaped.

A year later, Chambers quit law enforcement for good and formed his own holdup gang. They pulled their biggest job at Coolidge, Kan., on Sept. 29, 1883. Three masked men boarded a westbound train that had made a brief stop at Coolidge, one of them believed to be Chambers. They ordered engineer John

Hilton to take the train out of the station, and when he was slow to comply one of the gunmen shot him through the heart. The express messenger returned the fire, which drove the robbers from the train. Chambers was eventually arrested, but was released for lack of evidence. See: **Billy the Kid**.

REF.: *CBA*; Garrett, *Billy the Kid*; Miller and Snell, *Great Gunfighters of the Kansas Cowtowns*; O'Neal, *Encyclopedia of Western Gunfighters*.

Chambers, Robert, 1967- , U.S., mansl. "Looking back on everything, I have to say yes," Robert Chambers said when a judge asked if he meant to hurt Jennifer Levin. But did he mean to kill her, or were they just two wealthy "preppies" out of control?

The former altar boy and Boston University dropout claimed the death of 18-year-old Jennifer Levin was an accident—the result of a drunken bout of rough sex in Central Park at 4:30 a.m. on the morning of Aug. 26, 1986. The handsome, square-jawed prep school alumnus had run into Levin at Dorrian's Red Hand, a trendy Upper East Side bistro. She was celebrating her upcoming departure for college with a group of friends. It was common knowledge she had a crush on Chambers, who hobnobbed with Manhattan's young jet set. She had even confided to a friend that on dates with Chambers, sex with him "was the best she ever had."

Shortly before dawn they left the bar and headed into Central Park, where, according to Chambers, Levin sexually assaulted him. He let her tie his hands behind his back, but backed off when Jennifer became more aggressive. After she grabbed his testicles, causing pain, he allegedly broke loose and flipped her over. According to Dr. Ronald Kornblum, Los Angeles' chief medical examiner and a key defense witness, a glancing blow to her neck and throat caused death within five seconds. But other interpretations of the physical evidence suggested that Levin had been strangled. Later that morning, a bicyclist riding near the Metropolitan Museum of Art found the partially clothed body. Across the road sat Chambers, watching. Within hours New York police had him in custody for Levin's murder.

Released on bond, Chambers seemed to make light of his crime. In December 1987, a friend video-taped him reenacting the killing of Levin by pretending to strangle a small doll. Staring into the camera, Chambers twisted the doll's head off. "Oops, I think I killed it," he said.

On Mar. 26, 1988, police arrested Chambers a second time. As he was led away from his swank Upper East Side town house a crowd chanted, "Murderer! Murderer!"

The trial began on Jan. 4, 1988, eighteen months after the murder. By this time victim's rights groups had become actively involved, on the lookout for an all-too-common strategy of defense attorneys: blaming the victim to secure a reduced sentence or complete acquittal. Chambers' lawyer Jack Litman had done this in defending Richard Herrin, a Yale alumnus who beat his girlfriend to death in 1978. This time Litman subpoenaed Jennifer Levin's private diary which contained proof, he said, that she was promiscuous and "kinky." A judge quashed the request as irrelevant.

"There was no sex, only death," countered Assistant District Attorney Linda Fairstein, showing photos of the facial lacerations Levin had sustained, injuries that suggested a prolonged struggle by the victim. But after nine days of deliberation and four votes, the jury was undecided. Facing a possible mistrial, Chambers at the last minute changed his plea from second-degree murder to first degree manslaughter.

The plea bargain reduced his sentence from the mandatory twenty-five years to life for second-degree murder to five to fifteen years for manslaughter. "The whole process has been unspeakably hurtful," said Dan Levin, Jennifer's uncle. "She was not a spoiled, ignored kid. She always had a job after school, then would come home and wash the dishes and talk to her parents about her day." Added one juror: "We hope that Jennifer can now rest in peace." See: **Herrin, Richard**. REF.: *CBA*.

Chambers, Robert K., 1952- , (unsolv.) mur. A human skeleton in the front yard, tales of wife swapping, and rumors that a small town police chief may have killed his wife's former husband.

This is all police had to work with as they investigated 36-year-old Robert K. Chambers, a logger turned part-time police chief. When the remains of Russell Bean were discovered in Chambers' front yard, however, the townspeople of Marlow, N.H., closed ranks around their neighbor. "Right now everyone is pulling for the Chambers family," said Ronald J. Karvosky, the town selectman. "He may be guilty of putting the body there but the circumstances around that might be debatable."

Missing since Sept. 15, 1978, after a drunken fight with Chambers, the body of Russell Bean, then a 26-year-old factory worker, was unearthed on Mar. 14, 1988. During the fight Bean had fallen backwards, hitting his head on a boulder. He died instantly. Panic-stricken, Chambers fled to his father, Clifton Chambers. Together, they buried the body under ten feet of topsoil in front of their home.

On Oct. 6, Bean's wife Sylvia moved in with Robert Chambers. In January 1979 she divorced her missing husband to marry Chambers, who finalized his own divorce in March. In 1985 Chambers became the part-time police chief for Marlow and nearby Gilsum.

All was quiet until Mar. 2, 1988, when Clifton Chambers, near death, told his granddaughter, Lorrie Wheeler, and his daughter, Melissa, what happened some ten years earlier. Sworn to secrecy until the elder Chambers was dead and buried, Melissa Chambers waited only that long. One week later Clifton Chambers died, and she went to the police of Keene, N.H. In addition to the elder Chambers' confession, she told them that months before Bean's death, he and her brother were participating in wife swapping, that Chambers' wife, Deborah, left him during that time, and that Sylvia, Bean's widow, moved in with Chambers soon after her husband's disappearance.

Mark Sisti, deputy director of the state public defender's program, described Melissa's charges as "fabricated, unreliable hearsay," adding, "He didn't do it, it's that simple." Chambers was taken into custody on a charge of second-degree murder and was held in the Cheshire County Jail until three people came forward to post bail—$75,000 in cash and $75,000 in property.

In May 1988 a grand jury sitting in Keene, N.H., refused to indict Chambers for the death of Russell Bean, sending investigators back to square one. "If I thought we were on the verge of something I'd tell you, but we're not," sighed Senior Assistant Attorney General Gregory Swope.

Sylvia Chambers, who denied the wife-swapping charges or any knowledge of the cover-up, filed for divorce shortly afterward. REF.: *CBA*.

Chambers, Whittaker (Jay David Whittaker Chambers), 1901-61, U.S., journalist. Accused Alger Hiss, a low-ranking employee of the U.S. State Department, of passing secret documents to Russian agents. Hiss was labeled a subversive because of his ties to members of the American Communist Party. Chambers had joined the party himself in 1924, but renounced all former association in 1937. Book authored: *Witness* (1952). See: **Hiss, Alger**. REF.: *CBA*.

Chamblit, Rebekah, 1706-33, U.S., mur. Rebekah Chamblit, age twenty-seven and a native of Boston, was found Guilty and sentenced to death for murder after giving birth to a bastard child who was later found dead. A recent special act had made it a capital offense in Massachusetts to conceal such births of illegitimate children who were later found dead. Chamblit was hanged in Boston on Sept. 23, 1733, after several lengthy sermons on her immoral behavior were thunderously delivered by fire-and-brimstone preachers standing next to her on the scaffold.

REF.: *CBA; The Declaration, Dying Warning and Advice of Rebekah Chamblit; Foxcroft, Lessons of Caution to Young Sinners.*

Chambre Ardente Affair, prom. 1679-82, Fr., witchcraft. When King Louis XIV set up a special investigation to look into charges of poisoning, a vicious reign of torture, headed by a sadistic police commissioner and directed primarily against lower-class men and women, was unleashed for three-and-a-half years.

As early as 1673 in France two prominent priests reported to police, without naming names, that many of their penitents had confessed to turning to murder as a solution to matrimonial problems. Parisian police commissioner Nicholas de la Reynie in 1677 discovered a well-organized international poisoning ring, led by several noblemen, a banker, and a lawyer, which distributed poisons throughout Portugal, England, and France.

Although the aristocratic leader, François Galaup de Chasteuil, escaped, Reynie began arresting local fortune-tellers, starting with Marie Bosse, also known as La Bosse, and her daughter, two sons, and La Dame Vigoreux, another soothsayer. La Bosse was overheard extolling the pleasures of her job, calling it a "lovely occupation" with "classy clients," and gloating, "Three more poisonings and I retire, my fortune made!" The case of Madame de Poulaillon, the first society woman charged, fitted a typical pattern. Bored with her wealthy, elderly husband, and having taken on a lover, Poulaillon bought poisons and attempted to murder her husband. The usual method was to soak a shirt in arsenic acid, causing an inflammation that looked like syphilis. The woman then bought allegedly soothing salves which were actually more poison. When rubbed into the skin, the poison would bring on death within a few months.

On Mar. 8, 1679, King Louis XIV created a special *commission de l'Arsenal*, or a star-chamber court, which sat "in secret" judgment, "permitting no appeal." Another fortune teller was seized, the famous Catherine Deshayes, popularly known as La Voison, who countered accusations against her by bringing new ones against La Bosse. A third woman, La Vigoreux, was condemned to be burned alive, along with La Bosse and her son, François Bosse, on May 6, 1678. Poulaillon, the only society woman charged, was only banished.

Within a year, several more society people were charged, and the French upper classes were enraged at the treatment. In January 1680, the Countess of Soissons, Madame de Tingry, the Marquise d'Alluye, Madame de Polignac, the Duchess of Bouillon, the Duke of Luxembourg, and the Marquise du Roure and Marquis de Feuquières were all imprisoned either at the Bastille or in the palace at Vincennes. The anger of the nobility and society people was encapsuled by the Marquis de Pas's statement that professional poisoners "have figured out a way to prolong their own condemned lives by denouncing...various aristocrats, whose arrest and interrogation gives these wretches a bit more time."

It was at this point that police commissioner Reynie began to use torture, including diabolical chair devices and mallets for crushing legs. La Voison, under the vicious physical harm inflicted on her, cried out in pain, repeating that she had told the truth all along. She was burned to death in a particularly sadistic manner on Feb. 22, 1680.

The element of witchcraft had by now been introduced into the Chambre Ardente Affair. With Reynie devising increasingly diabolical and repugnant ways of extracting "confessions," accounts of amatory and sacrificial masses, rites and black magic abounded, confessed to by priests and sacristans. The accusations and the admissions of guilt were made under conditions of extreme cruelty and barbarous torture, and were contradicted and retracted by many in moments of lucidity. La Filastre, accused of witchcraft, retracted her statements just before she was burned alive, explaining to the police commissioner that "everything she had said...had been only to free herself from the pain and agony of the torture and in fear lest it be continued."

King Louis XIV, under increasing pressure from French men and women who had grown disgusted with the accusations and torture, tried to suppress the scandal by suspending the Chambre Ardente in August 1680, but ordered Reynie to investigate secretly since he, himself, was the poison target of his former mistress. He wanted to keep this a secret "to conceal" the disgrace. The police commissioner continued to indiscriminately murder lower-class people accused of witchcraft and selling poisons. During three-and-a-half years of investigations, 319 people had been arrested and 104 sentenced, with thirty-six put to death; no noble was ever executed or tortured during the Chambre Ardente.

Legislation following this scandal prohibited fortune-telling, put controls on sales of poisons, and declared witchcraft a superstition. When he was seventy, in 1709, Louis XIV had the records destroyed to cover up the activities of the Chambre Ardente, but copies of transcripts survived and he failed to erase the shameful incident. See: **Black Mass; Catherine Deshayes.** REF.: *CBA.*

Chamfort, Sébastien-Roch Nicolas, 1741-94, Fr., suic. Became a Jacobin at the outbreak of the revolution, and spoke out against the Reign of Terror and the National Convention. Upon hearing that he was earmarked for arrest, he committed suicide. REF.: *CBA.*

Champion, Nathan D. (AKA: **Nate**), 1852-92, U.S., west. gunman. Born near Round Rock, Texas, Nathan Champion and his twin brother Dudley became cowboys at an early age and both helped to drive herds north to Wyoming where they settled down and began small ranches. At the outbreak of the Johnson County War, Nate and Dudley Champion sided with the homesteaders and small ranchers against the wealthy cattle barons. Nate Champion was the gunman of the family, a deadly shot and quick on the draw. He did more than his share of rustling which earned him the title of "King of the Rustlers," a sobriquet bestowed upon him by his one-time friend Frank Canton who worked as a Regulator for the cattlemen. Champion not only attacked the cattlemen verbally, but, like Jim Averill before him, he wrote letters to local newspapers denouncing the greedy, ruthless cattle barons. For this, Champion was marked for death.

On Nov. 1, 1891, Frank Canton, Fred Coates, Joe Elliot, and Tom Smith rode to the line shack owned by W.H. Hall on the Powder River where Champion and Ross Gilbertson were living. Canton and his men had but one assignment from their cattle baron employers: Kill Champion. They crept up on the shack, kicked open the door, and dashed inside, guns drawn. Shouted Canton, according to one report: "Give up, we've got you this time!" (This seemed to be an unlikely command for gunfighters sent to kill Champion, not capture him.) Champion, who was on the only bunk in the shack, bolted upright, grabbing his six gun from its holster, saying: "What's the matter, boys?" Champion and Canton fired at the same time, both shots going wild, but Champion received powder burns on the face. More shots from the invading gunmen smashed into the wall next to the bunk. Champion's next two shots were more accurate, striking one gunman in the arm, another in the side. Canton and his men, getting the worst of it, fled the shack.

The gunmen left their overcoats, a few weapons and some horses when they ran to safety. Champion dashed outside and traded shots with Joe Elliott, who was later arrested on Champion's complaint, and charged with attempted murder, but when it came time for his trial, the case collapsed since the only witness, Gilbertson, had fled Johnson County under the threat of murder. The Canton raid caused Champion to move operations to the KC Ranch, which he leased with Nick Ray. This ranch was near the famous outlaw hideout, Hole-in-the-Wall. On the night of Apr. 8, 1892, two trappers, Ben Jones and Bill Walker, visited Champion and Ray. The four pioneers spent the evening drinking and singing along with the music creaked out by Walker on his fiddle. The next morning, Jones went outside to fill a pail of water from the nearby well. He was jumped by several Regulators and dragged away; more than fifty Regulators had surrounded the ranch house before dawn, intent upon murdering Champion and Ray. When Walker stepped outside to look for Jones a half hour later, he, too, was dragged away and held prisoner.

Ray then stepped from the cabin door and dozens of shots brought him down. Champion came outside, guns blazing, shooting at Regulators positioned in the nearby stable and along the creek bed, but their firepower drove him back into the cabin. He dashed out once more to grab Ray and drag him back inside. Then began a siege where the Regulators peppered the small ranch house. Inside, both Ray and Champion were wounded but they managed to keep fighting back. During lulls of the siege, Champion recorded the attack in a small diary. Ray bled to death

by 9 a.m. but Champion continued the battle, refusing to surrender, knowing he would be shot down.

At 3 p.m., Champion, peering out of a window, saw one of his friends, Jack Flagg, riding in a wagon. Flagg fired on the Regulators, but when the fifty guns of this group were turned on him, he fled, abandoning his wagon. Frank Canton ordered the wagon filled with flammable materials, set afire, and rolled down a hill toward the cabin which blazed up when the wagon crashed into it. The fire finally drove Champion outside. He held two six guns and both blasted away at his enemies as he tried to get to a ravine some fifty yards from the cabin. The Regulators caught him in a crossfire and he was shot to pieces. He fell on his back and the Regulators, so fearful of this gunman, continued to fire bullets into Champion's dead body. Twenty-eight wounds were later found in his corpse. Champion's diary was crumpled in his dead hand and this was given to Sam Clover, a newspaperman who had accompanied the Regulators on their raid and had even helped set fire to the wagon. Clover later published excerpts of Champion's diary in his paper, the Chicago *Herald.* Before leaving, Canton pinned a note to the shirt of his old enemy, Champion, one that read: "Cattle thieves, beware." Champion's riddled body was left to be buried by his friends. This wanton murder was never called to justice and Champion's killers, most of them known, were never charged with the brutal killing. Nate Champion's twin brother Dudley was killed in 1893 by range detective Mike Shonsey, who had had several encounters with the Champion brothers in the past. See: **Averill, James; Canton, Frank; Johnson County War.**

REF.: American Guide Series, *Wyoming, A Guide to Its History, Highways, and People;* Barber, *The Longest Rope;* Bard, *Horse Wrangler;* Beals, *American Earth;* Bechdolt, *Tales of the Old Timers;* Brown, *Trail Driving Days;* Brown, *The Plainsmen of the Yellowstone;* Bruce, *Bannister was There;* Burt, *The Diary of a Dude Wrangler;* Burt, *American Murder Ballads;* Canton, *Frontier Trails; CBA;* Chaffin, *Sons of the West;* Chapel, *Guns of the Old West;* Clay, *My Life on the Range;* Clover, *On Special Assignment;* Collins, *Great Western Rides;* Cushman, *The Great North Trail;* David, *Malcolm Campbell;* Flagg, *A Review of the Cattle Business in Johnson County;* Flannery, *John Hunton's Diary;* Frink, *Cow County Cavalcade;* Gage, *The Johnson County War is a Pack of Lies;* Horan, *Desperate Men;* ____, and Sann, *Pictorial History of the Wild West;* Howard, *This was the West;* Hutchinson, *Another Notebook of the Old West;* Kelly, *The Outlaw Trail;* Larson, *History of Wyoming;* Linn, *James Keeley, Newspaperman;* Lloyd, *The Invaders;* Mercer, *Banditti of the Plains;* Monaghan, *The Book of the American West;* O'Neal, *Encyclopedia of Western Gunfighters;* Paine, *Tom Horn: Man of the West;* Penfield, *Western Sheriffs and Marshals;* Penrose, *The Johnson County War;* ____, *The Rustler Business;* Raine, *Forty-Five Caliber Law;* Rennert, *The Cowboy;* Rosa, *The Gunfighter, Man or Myth?;* Sandoz, *The Cattlemen: From the Rio Grande Across the Marias;* Small, *The Best of True West;* Smith, *War on the Powder River;* Swallow, *The Wild Bunch;* Trenholm and Carley, *Wyoming Pageant;* Waller, *Last of the Great Western Train Robbers;* Wellman, *A Dynasty of Western Outlaws;* ____, *The Trampling Herd.*

Chance, John Henry, b.c.1866, U.S., (wrong. convict.) mur. After the shooting of drugstore clerk Charles L. Russell during an attempted robbery on Apr. 4, 1898, a man wearing an overcoat ran from the store, which was inside the U.S. Hotel in Boston.

Three weeks after the crime, which no one saw, the police finally discovered the coat and duly arrested its owner, John Henry Chance, and Arthur Hagan. The latter had gone to Chicago, where he was apprehended in October. Each man was charged with second-degree murder in the indictment filed on June 11, 1898. The trial began on Feb. 8, 1899.

Hagan, who was represented by George R. Swasey, was able to provide an alibi for the night of the murder. He accused Chance of robbing a cutlery shop two nights before the murder and taking a revolver. The story he told was corroborated by a prosecution witness, Liz Nagle. Chance, unable to offer a defense, was found Guilty on Feb. 22, 1899. Hagan was acquitted. Chance's sentence of life imprisonment began on Sept. 11, 1899, after an appeal failed.

On Nov. 20, 1905, after several appeals for executive clemency, Chance wrote Massachusetts Governor William Lewis Douglas claiming that Hagan had made a confession to the murder in Chicago and that others knew of his own innocence. This plea was ignored, and it was not until 1911 that Governor Eugene Noble Foss looked into the matter. He learned that Hagan had indeed confessed and did so again to Boston authorities on the promise of immunity. Finally, on June 7, 1911, John Henry Chance was released with a full pardon.

REF.: Borchard, *Convicting the Innocent; CBA.*

Chancy, Harrison, c.1960, U.S., burg.-rob.-mur. Not only did Harrison Chancy shoot and kill a man who was on his hands and knees begging for mercy, but he even taunted the victim's widow by pretending to shoot her following his trial for murder.

On May 28, 1977, in Chicago, Ill., Chancy shot 69-year-old Emanuel Slivinski while he prayed. A jury found him Guilty on Feb. 9, 1979. When the verdict was returned, Chancy turned toward Lillian Slivinski, the 64-year-old widow of the victim, and mouthed, "Bang, bang," while pointing a finger at her. Because the crime was committed before capital punishment was reinstated, Chancy was sentenced under old felony laws which did not permit the death penalty. On Mar. 23, 1979, Criminal Court judge Frank B. Machala handed him concurrent terms of 100 to 300 years in prison for murder, twenty-five to fifty years for armed robbery, and five to fifteen years for burglary.

Before pronouncing the sentence, Machala upbraided Chancy for his brutal crime and insolent attitude, adding, "Up until this moment, this defendant has shown no signs of remorse." In reply, Chancy smiled at the judge as he was led handcuffed from the courtroom. REF.: *CBA.*

Chandler, Douglas (AKA: Lord Haw-Haw), b.c.1888, U.S., treas. American Douglas Chandler made history when he returned from Germany after WWII. He did not return as a hero, but as the first person in U.S. history to be put on trial as a traitor for broadcasting propaganda for the enemy.

Although he served as a U.S. Naval officer in WWI, Chandler left America, the country he claimed to love, in 1931, because of financial ruin and to escape what he feared was the "un-American fog spreading over the land from the swamp of imported Jewish-Bolshevik subversion." He moved to Germany in 1933, and became enthralled by the tenets of Nazism. Chandler entered into the service of the Nazis during the war, agreeing to transmit shortwave radio broadcasts to the U.S., espousing the propaganda of Joseph Goebbels. The former Baltimore, Md., newspaperman likened himself to Paul Revere, warning his country of impending doom; to his audiences he was known as America's Lord Haw-Haw. For these actions a Washington, D.C., grand jury indicted Chandler for treason in 1943. When the war ended in 1945, he was arrested and returned to the U.S.

The plane carrying Chandler and co-defendant Robert Best back to America was forced to land at Westover Field in Boston. A legal technicality concerning treason stipulates that the defendant, if brought to the U.S. from abroad, must be placed on trial where he first sets foot on U.S. soil. The two were nevertheless taken to Washington to stand trial, but only after a second indictment was obtained in December 1946.

Chandler's trial began on June 2, 1947, and lasted until June 28. During that time, thirteen of twenty-three counts in the indictment were dropped by the prosecution. He was found Guilty on the remaining counts of treason. His defense attorneys attempted to prove that the 58-year-old defendant was insane, against the wishes of Chandler, who said, "I recommended to my counsel before the trial that I should take the stand to establish the truth of my beliefs, particularly as to the danger to my country of world Jewry. My counsel thought me insane. I am, of course, not insane." In the speech Chandler delivered prior to his sentencing—a speech his defense counsel censored before allowing him to deliver it—he added, "It is the tragedy of my life that the warnings I gave my country were not and are not yet accepted. Time, however, will vindicate me. If I must die because I dared

speak the truth, then let me die." His co-defendant, Best, was eventually judged to be insane.

Judge Francis J.W. Ford, however, did not impose the death penalty. Instead, on July 30, 1947, he sentenced Chandler to life imprisonment and fined him $10,000. Ford agreed with the defendant that he was not insane but knew exactly what he was doing. Calling Chandler "a fanatic," Ford added, "The whole history of his life points out his state of mind, so far as I am concerned." See: **Joyce, William.** REF.: *CBA.*

Chandler, Raymond Thornton, 1888-1959, U.S., det. writer. Born in Chicago on July 23, 1888, to Florence and Maurice Chandler, Raymond Chandler was raised in rural Nebraska until the age of seven when his parents divorced over his father's drinking. Afterwards, Chand-
ler moved with his mother to England, living in Dulwich. He attended public schools, where he received an education in the classics. The study of literature was emphasized at the Dulwich College Preparatory School, an education that he cherished and one that was to have a profound influence on Chandler for the rest of his life. In 1905, Chandler was sent to the Continent for further studies through the aid of rich relatives on his mother's

Detective writer Raymond Chandler.

side. He lived briefly in Paris and then returned to England where, in 1907, he became a naturalized British citizen. After passing civil service examinations, Chandler went to work as a clerk for the Admiralty.

Chandler moved back to the U.S., living once again in Nebraska, then moving to Los Angeles where he worked until August 1917, when he went to Canada and joined the Canadian Army which his dual nationality permitted. He was sent to France during WWI, where during an artillery attack, his entire platoon was killed by a single shell, and Chandler, the only survivor, was taken back to a field hospital, suffering from concussion. He was returned to England to recuperate, and he later applied for service as a pilot in the Royal Air Force, but the war came to an end before his training was finished. By 1919, Chandler had returned again to the U.S. and was working for a British bank in San Francisco. He began writing stories and poems but had little luck in publishing the early efforts. He returned to Los Angeles where he briefly worked for the *Daily Express*. At this time, he met Pearl Eugenie Pascal, called Cissy, a beautiful but delicate woman who was eighteen years his senior and was twice divorced. Chandler and Cissy married in 1924. Chandler, believing his writing efforts were fruitless, abandoned any hopes of a literary career and took a job as a bookkeeper for the Dabney Oil Company. He rose to the position of auditor, then vice president.

Though he was an efficient executive, Chandler hated the oil business and began drinking heavily in the mid 1920s—an addiction he would never overcome. When compelled to attend oil banquets and conventions, Chandler would invariably remain in the background and get quietly drunk. As his wife quickly aged before his eyes and his job caused him to feel that he was being buried alive in an unimaginative business, Chandler went back to writing, completing his first short story for *Black Mask* magazine in 1933. This magazine was the leading pulp publication in the U.S., begun in 1920 by H.L. Mencken and George Jean Nathan, as a way of generating money to support their more expensive literary publications. *Black Mask* introduced not only Chandler to avid detective fiction fans but such literary luminaries as Dashiell Hammett.

Chandler's lush descriptive passages and witty, cynical dialog soon captured for him an avid following. He shortly created a detective hero that equalled Hammett's Sam Spade, a brooding, fearless, honorable detective named Philip Marlowe, whose world was shabby and shadowy, a memorable character who would dominate Chandler's entire life. After the publication of his first novel, *The Big Sleep*, in 1939, Chandler became one of the few classic writers of American detective fiction. He also began writing for Hollywood, producing memorable film noir classics such as *Double Indemnity* and Alfred Hitchcock's *Strangers on a Train*. During his heyday, Chandler moved to a modest little home in La Jolla, near San Diego, and wrote his brooding stories about Marlowe and murder. He drank heavily for the remaining years of his life while doting on his wife Cissy, who became in invalid in later years and died on Dec. 12, 1954. Chandler, who had few friends other than his editors at New York publishing houses, was desolated. He hated Hollywood and could turn to no one there. He attempted suicide, but this failed and Chandler spent his last few years attempting to finish his last novel, *Playback*, while battling alcoholism. He died on Mar. 26, 1959, embittered over what he thought to be a misspent life and a literary career that had only produced a battered detective hero who knew only the seamy side of life, an opinion not shared by his millions of fans.

Cover of *Black Mask* Magazine featuring one of Chandler's early detective stories.

Typical of Chandler's sardonic opinion of himself in relationship to Philip Marlowe, his fictional hero, was a letter he once wrote in response to a question about his own life. Wrote Chandler: "Yes, I am exactly like the characters in my books...I have fourteen telephones on my desk, including direct lines to New York, London, Paris, Rome, and Santa Rosa. My filing case opens out into a very convenient portable bar, and the bartender who lives in the bottom drawer, is a midget...I do a great deal of research, especially in the apartments of tall blondes. I get my material in various ways, but my favorite procedure consists of going through the desks of other writers after hours. I am thirty-eight-years-old and have been for the past twenty years. I do not regard myself as a dead shot, but I am a pretty dangerous man with a wet towel. But all in all, I think my favorite weapon is a twenty-dollar bill." Books authored: *The Big Sleep,* 1939; *Farewell, My Lovely,* 1940; *The High Window,* 1942; *The Lady in the Lake,* 1944; *The Little Sister,* 1949; *The Long Goodbye,* 1954; *Playback,* 1958. See: **Hammett, Samuel Dashiell.**

REF.: *CBA;* Durham, *Down These Mean Streets a Man Must Go: Raymond Chandler's Knight;* Eames, *Sleuths, Inc.: Studies of Problem Solvers;* Gardiner and Walker, *Raymond Chandler Speaking;* Gross, *The World of Raymond Chandler;* MacShane, *The Life of Raymond Chandler;* Morgan, *Prince of Crime;* Ruehlmann, *Saint With a Gun.*

Chandler, William Eaton, 1835-1917, U.S., lawyer. Leader of the Republican party and a member of the Senate from 1887-1901. REF.: *CBA.*

Chandra, Ram, d.1918, U.S., consp. In 1909, British secret agents in India discovered a plot to end British colonial occupation. But the vast underground network was poorly organized. When WWI came in 1914, the Germans exploited the situation. The "Hindu Conspiracy," in which the Germans and Hindus planned to block the Suez Canal so that British reinforcements could not reach India, was actually hatched in Berlin by Indian philosopher Har Dyal, and involved operatives in the U.S., Mexico, Switzerland, Turkey, and the Netherlands.

In the U.S., Dr. Chandra Kanta Chakravarty coordinated with the German ambassador, Count Johann von Bernstorff, to control the West Coast underground Hindu network formed by Ram Chandra, editor of the newspaper *Ghadr.* Ram Chandra's 8,000 volunteers were trained in the use of guns and explosives. Chandra took his orders from Chakravarty, and the money to finance the operation came from the German consul in San Francisco.

The San Francisco police, with help from British consular officers and private investigators from London, arrested the conspirators. Thirty-two people, including several diplomats from the German consulate in San Francisco, went to trial on Nov. 22, 1917, charged with conspiring to violate official American neutrality. Ram Chandra and his employees at the newspaper had been shipping propaganda from the German embassy to Hindu troops in India, urging rebellion. The six-month trial ended in the U.S. District Court of San Francisco in April 1918.

Thirty-one of the defendants were found Guilty, including the two German attachés, Franz Bopp and Vice-Consul Eckhart von Schaak. Both received two years in federal prison and were fined $10,000 each. On the day the attorneys presented their closing arguments one of the Indian defendants, Ram Singh, suddenly jumped to his feet and shot Ram Chandra, who died instantly. Singh then shot himself and fell over dead as frightened spectators sought cover.

REF.: Block, *Wizard of Berkeley; CBA.*

Chang Hsien-chung (AKA: the Yellow Tiger), c.1605-47, China, rebel. Following the collapse of the Ming dynasty in 1644, he entered Szechwan province to set himself up as king. He ruled as a military despot for a short time before his death at the hands of the Manchu armies. REF.: *CBA.*

Chang Hsueh-liang, 1898- , China, kid. Son of the Chinese warlord Chang Tso-lin, Chang Hsueh-liang was called "The Young Marshal," after his father's assassination in 1928 by Japanese militarists. Chang Hsueh-liang was an adept military leader, a graduate of the Mukden Military Academy, and when he assumed command of Manchuria, he immediately became subservient to Chiang Kai-shek, representing nationalist interests. He headed the northeastern frontier defense (1929-31) and, in 1933, was driven out of Manchuria by overwhelming Japanese forces. Chiang Kai-shek appointed Chang Hsueh-liang commander of the Tungpei army but instead of directing Chang Hsueh-liang to energetically attack the invading Japanese forces in northeastern China, Chiang Kai-shek insisted that the Tungpei army combat the growing Communist forces in that area.

Chang resisted this directive, pointing out to his superior that the common enemy of China was not the Communists, but Japan.

He wanted to join with the Communists in fighting Japanese troops. Chiang Kai-shek said no, destroy the red forces which the Generalissimo considered bandit armies. When Chiang heard that Chang had entrenched his army of ten divisions before Japanese forces and that he had come to an agreement with the Communists wherein they would assist his armies in fighting the Japanese, Chiang flew to the front, planning to convince his most loyal commander that attacking the Communists was the best policy. He brought along a 200,000-word manifesto which he had written and which detailed Chiang's reasons for pacifying the Japanese and eradicating the Communists, believing that once Chang had read this complicated document he would do as instructed.

Chang Hsueh-liang, Mrs. Kung, Mrs. Chang, Mrs. Chiang, and Chiang Kai-shek, 1932, four years before Chang kidnapped Chiang Kai-shek.

Chiang flew to Sian and confronted his recalcitrant commander Chang. Neither man would concede to the other, and then the unthinkable happened. Chang Hsueh-liang kidnapped his leader, Chiang Kai-shek. This was done either to force the Generalissimo to join with the Communists to fight Japan or to save his face in light of the fact that his top commander had already committed China to this military coalition. At 5 a.m., on the morning of Dec. 12, 1936, Chiang Kai-shek, asleep in a suite behind a temple, was awakened by gunshots. He leaped from his bed in his nightshirt and ran outside, scaling a ten-foot wall and dropping to the other side where, as he later claimed, he followed two white scurrying rabbits to a rocky niche where he hid from would-be assassins, these creatures serving as his mythical guides to preservation. A group of soldiers searching for Chiang found the supreme commander in his rocky hideout at noon of that day. The Generalissimo stood up proudly and courageously demanded that these soldiers either shoot him, if that was their purpose, or provide the proper escort back to the temple quarters. A battalion commander immediately kneeled and offered his broad back to Chiang, who climbed onto the officer's back and was thus carried back to his lodgings.

Once back in his quarters, Chiang took to bed and refused to leave it until his host read his manifesto. Chang kept his superior under guard and sat down to read Chiang's treatise on the evils of Communism and why China must rid itself of this political plague. Chang was also in contact with Communist officials who, then taking orders from Moscow, advised him that although Chiang Kai-shek was not a popular leader, he was the universally recognized general and politician in China and that his death would lead to chaos. He was the only person who could keep together the myriad political and military factions in China and thus present a united front against the threatening Japanese armies which also posed a threat to Russian territory to the north. Chiang began a fast, telling his commander that unless he agreed to follow his orders, he would starve himself to death, leaving China leaderless. A nervous Chang Hsueh-liang brought Chou En-lai to see the Generalissimo. Chou En-lai, later to be Foreign Minister of Communist China, pleaded the cause of his leader, Mao Tse-tung, one-time ally of Chiang Kai-shek. After much conversation, Chiang agreed to form a military coalition with the Communists. After another ten days of remaining in bed, the

Generalissimo flew back to Nanking and going with him, as an act of good faith, was his commander, Chang Hsueh-liang, who was arrested by Chiang's secret police.

Chang Hsueh-liang was not harmed, however, but kept under house arrest. He went into permanent retirement but lived comfortably and remained at Chiang Kai-shek's side for the rest of his life as an adviser and friend. When Chiang Kai-shek was driven from the mainland to Taiwan in 1948 when the Communists took over China, Chang Hsueh-liang went with him. Here was the strangest case in the annals of kidnapping, one where the kidnapper became a kidnap victim but in the inscrutable machinations of Chinese politics, the whole drama may have been a charade devised by Chiang and his loyal Chang, one where, from the onset, Chiang Kai-shek and Chang Hsueh-liang arranged the "kidnapping" to save the face of the Generalissimo, who had publicly denounced the Communists for years. He could now join with their much-needed forces to defeat the Japanese, appearing to have been forced into this unsavory alliance for the good of his country. See: **Chang Tso-lin.**

REF.: Abend, *Chaos in Asia;* ____, *My Life in China, 1926-41;* Beauvoir, *The Long March;* Bergamini, *Japan's Imperial Conspiracy: How Emperor Hirohito Led Japan Into War Against the West;* Bertram, *First Act in China: The Story of the Sian Mutiny;* Boorman et al, *Moscow-Peking Axis; CBA;* Chiang Kai-shek, *A Summing Up at Seventy: Soviet Russia in China;* Clubb, *Twentieth Century China;* Ekins and Wright, *China Fights for Her Life;* Faure, *The Serpent and the Tortoise;* Fitzgerald, *Revolution in China;* Holcombe, *The Spirit of the Chinese Revolution;* Hsiung, *The Life of Chiang Kai-shek;* Isaacs, *The Tragedy of the Chinese Revolution;* Liu, *Military History of Modern China;* Nash, *Almanac of World Crime;* Pelissier, *The Awakening of China;* Powell, *My 25 Years in China;* Snow, *Random Notes on Red China, 1936-45;* Tuchman, *Stillwell and the American Experience in China, 1911-45.*

Chang-Jen, Tjou, prom. 1983, S. Kor., skyjack.-mur. The first successful hijacking of a commercial jetliner inside the People's Republic of China resulted in a six-year prison sentence for Tjou Chang-Jen, a provisional government official and five accomplices on Aug. 18, 1983. The British-built Trident jet was commandeered in mid-air on May 5, 1983, while in route from Shenyang in Manchuria to Shanghai. The hijackers demanded to be flown to Taiwan, but landed at a U.S. Air Force base in Seoul, S. Kor. instead.

Armed gunmen shot two crew members during the incident. Chinese officials described the hijackers as "thugs," who had been previously employed at the Shenyang phsyical education school and the environmental protection department. A potentially difficult situation was avoided when Mainland China permitted the South Korean government to try the hijackers in exchange for an agreement to allow the passengers, and crew to return home unmolested.

South Korean officials found themselves caught in the middle. Taiwan demanded that the hijackers be allowed to defect. China, a country with no formal ties to the South Korean government, implied by it's actions that it might be willing to lay the groundwork for normalized relations. Weighing these considerations very carefully, Chang-Jen and his associates each only received four-to-six-year sentences. REF.: *CBA.*

Chang Soo Lee (AKA: Charley Ching, Dan Jong), 1900-37, U.S., asslt.-suic. Born in abject poverty in Korea, Chang Soo Lee was determined to flee from his homeland in order to stake a claim in America. At age thirteen, he walked 400 miles to the nearest coastal town where he boarded a boat bound for the U.S.

His journey ended in White Plains, N.Y., where Chang went to work as a houseboy and servant for Lawrence Churchill and his wife Ida. He worked hard and soon became a trusted member of the household. When Mr. Churchill died at their Florida resort home, Ida returned to her mansion in New York along with Chang. Because her health was poor, Ida Churchill invited her neice Louise Reeves and her husband George to come live with her from their home in Indiana.

Mrs. Churchill decided to change her will, leaving the bulk of the $600,000 estate to the Reeves. Simultaneously, George Reeves began complaining of stomach pains. A specialist was called in, and it was determined that Reeves was suffering from arsenic poisoning. Suspicion fell on Chang who was present when Lawrence Churchill died. The state successfully pushed for an attempted murder indictment which was handed down in October 1936. On Oct. 29, Chang Soo Lee pleaded not guilty in county court. The case was concluded on Mar. 24, 1937, with a Guilty verdict returned on a reduced charge of second-degree assault. The Korean butler was fined $2,000, sentenced to five to ten years in Sing Sing Prison, and ordered back to Korea upon completion of his sentence.

Less than three months later, on June 5, Chang threw himself from the eighth-story offices of Supreme Court Justice Sydney Syme in Yonkers, N.Y. REF.: *CBA*.

Chang Tso-lin, 1873-1928, China, assass. A burly, wily Chinese bandit, Chang was born in Fengtien Province. He began as a common laborer, but quit honest work in 1904, forming a large band of brigands in Manchuria. Joining the Chinese army in 1905, Chang rose quickly to the rank of general and then, in 1911, military governor of Fengtien Province. He was loyal to the republic of Sun Yat-sen and Japanese militarists saw in him a dangerous foe to their plans of future conquest in China, particularly long-cherished aims of seizing and controlling Manchuria. Japanese prince Kanin, after returning from an inspection tour of the crumbling Russian front during WWI, arrived at Mukden Station in Manchuria on Oct. 15, 1916, to be greeted by a cadre of Japanese officers and Chinese officials, including Chang Tso-lin. The Japanese and Chinese militarists then climbed into several carriages and headed for a local restaurant where there was to be a feast in honor of Prince Kanin. As the carriages rumbled down the dirt roads of Mukden, nearing the restaurant in the Japanese section of the city, a man darted forth and threw a bomb at the first carriage in the cavalcade, that carrying Chang Tso-lin. It fell short, exploding among the warlord's mounted troopers, blowing five of them to bits.

Chang Tso-lin immediately jumped from his carriage, doffed a cap worn by one of his dead bodyguards and mounted a horse, dashing down an alley in the disguise of a lowly guardsman. The bomb-thrower was shot to death by Chang Tso-lin's guards before he could flee. When the cavalcade proceeded, another assassin stepped forth, and, not knowing that the Chinese warlord had already escaped, threw another bomb which landed squarely on Chang Tso-lin's now empty coach, tearing it to pieces. The would-be assassins were in the employ of the Japanese officers who were following Prince Kanin's plan to murder Chang Tso-lin and then, in the resulting political confusion, Japan would bring its troops into Manchuria to restore order and gain a long-coveted toehold in Asia. After Kanin informed Japanese prime minister Terauchi that the attempt to kill the warlord had failed but that he intended to order Japanese guard units to seize Mukden anyway, a cable from the prime minister instructed him to do nothing, that the time was not yet ripe to strike.

By 1918, Chang Tso-lin had expanded his influence throughout Manchuria, controlling three provinces and ruling as a autocrat, although he brought about much reform and was generally well-liked. He often attempted to reform the Peking government and clashed with armies of Chiang Kai-shek, who had made certain secret pacts with Japan's military cabal allowing Chinese concessions to these war-plotting conspirators. Chang Tso-lin declared Manchuria independent of China while occupying the northeastern provinces in 1926, forming his own cabinet a year later and, in 1928, he governed from Peking, although he headquartered in Mukden. Chang Tso-lin was by then the absolute ruler of northern China, bestowing upon himself such lofty titles as All Highest Grand Marshal of China. He gave $7 million to charity and allowed no one to forget it. He fostered schools. He was as adamantly opposed to communism as he was to the Japanese militarists. He nevertheless made a show of protecting Russian rights in China, as he did all foreign interests.

One of these "shows," in early May 1927, involved the execution of eleven Chinese who had been seized as they tried to invade the Soviet Embassy in Peking on Apr. 6, 1927, or, at least, that was the story Chang released. U.S. senator Hiram Bingham was in Peking at the time of the executions, visiting one of his sons who was studying there. Chang invited Senator Binham to have tea with him on the porch of a government building and, less than 100 yards distant, the Chinese interlopers were brought out into an open courtyard and slowly strangled to death. When Bingham protested this barbaric act, Chang shrugged, sipped his tea and remarked: "I maintain order. I will not allow anti-foriegnism in my territory." The raid on the Soviet Embassy in Peking was, of course, planned by Chang himself and executed by his own men. Those labeled as the invaders were really Chinese Communists Chang had detected through documents his agents found in the embassy. Chang had paraded the Communists before western eyes as native Chinese who had despoiled the sanctity of a foreign nation; he would tolerate no xenophobia in his domain.

This did not apply to the Japanese, however. Chang Tso-lin had not forgotten how Prince Kanin and his cadre had tried to assassinate him in 1916, and he openly defied the Japanese to confront his powerful armies. His son, Chang Hsueh-liang, on the other hand, was sympathetic toward the Chiang Kai-shek government which leaned toward pacification of the Japanese. The Japanese military cabal, led by the young Emperor Hirohito, believed that if Chang Tso-lin was assassinated and his son assumed his command, Japan's ambitions in Manchuria could be realized. To that end, the Japanese planned the warlord's death.

Japanese general Tatekawa Yoshiji was assigned by Prince Kanin to arrange for Chang Tso-lin's murder. This was the same officer who had overseen the 1916 bungled attempt on the warlord's life; he was now given the chance to redeem himself. Tatekawa assumed a lowly role of attaché in the Japanese Embassy in Peking and watched closely the movements of Chang Tso-lin. He enlisted the aid of a Japanese dynamite expert, Colonel Komoto Daisaku, who then planned to blow up the Chinese warlord's heavily armed train which would leave Peking en route to Mukden on June 3, 1928. On board was Chang's Japanese adviser, Major Giga Nobuya, whom the warlord knew to be one of Prince Kanin's closest colleagues. The warlord thus felt that he was safe as long as Giga traveled with him. Chang was warned, however, that there was a Japanese plot to blow up his train so he sent an identical train carrying his youngest wife (number five) ahead of his own train. The ruse was discovered, however, and the Japanese bombers waiting in Mukden under Komoto's command, allowed this first train to enter Mukden without molestation.

The Japanese assassins had planted three huge cans of blasting powder beneath the tracks over which Chang's train would travel about a half mile from the town of Mukden. At dawn, on June 5, 1928, the warlord's train came barreling into view. In the lavish lounge car of the train, Chang Tso-lin sat playing mah-jongg with Major Giga, drinking beer. Suddenly, Giga begged to be excused, saying that he had to collect his bags before arriving at Mukden. Major Giga then ran to his car, grabbed a blanket and went to the observation platform of the last car, wrapping himself in the blanket and lying down. Giga's assistant, Captain Tomiya Tetsuo, was standing at an underpass, next to the plunger that would explode the barrels of black powder and, as the train slowed while coming into Mukden, he waited until the warlord's car was passing over the planted explosives before depressing the plunger. The car was blown off the tracks and shattered. Chang Tso-lin was dead, along with Governor C.C. Wu and a dozen of their retinue. Major Giga slipped from the platform of the caboose unharmed and walked to the wreckage, viewing the bodies of the warlord and his men and then exclaiming sarcastically: "Ah, how dreadful!"

The responsibility for the assassination was placed by the Japanese conspirators on two disaffected Chinese soldiers who were found dead nearby, bayoneted. They held unexploded Russian bombs in their hands. A third Chinese soldier who had escaped the Japanese killers, went to Chang's son and told him about the Japanese plot but Chang Hsueh-liang thought to keep the truth about his father's murder a secret for some weeks before revealing only brief information about the plot, fearful that if he confronted the Japanese directly, a state of war would ensue. Nine days after Chang Tso-lin's assassination, the young Emperor Hirohito gave a victory feast in Tokyo, entertaining six close friends of Colonel Komoto Daisaku, the man who had masterminded the murder of the Chinese warlord. See: **Chang Hsueh-liang.**

REF.: Abend, *My Life in China, 1926-41;* Bergamini, *Japan's Imperial Conspiracy: How Emperor Hirohito Led Japan into War Against the West;* Bisson, *Japan in China;* Byas, *Government by Assassination;* CBA; Clubb, *Twentieth Century China;* Cowan, *The Economic Development of China and Japan;* Fairbank, *The United States and China;* Holcombe, *The Spirit of the Chinese Revolution;* Hsiao-tung Fei, *China's Gentry;* Hsiung, *The Life of Chiang Kai-shek;* Isaacs, *The Tragedy of the Chinese Revolution;* Koyama, *Nagako, Empress of Japan;* Linebarger, *The China of Chiang Kai-shek;* Liu, *Military History of Modern China;* Morley, *The Japanese Thrust into Siberia, 1918;* Mosely, *Hirohito: Emperor of Japan;* Murofushi, *Nihon no teroisuto;* Pelissier, *The Awakening of China;* Powell, *My 25 Years in China;* Reischauer, *Japan, The Story of a Nation;* Scalapino, *Democracy and the Party Movement in Prewar Japan;* Sharman, *Sun Yat-sen;* Shimada, *Kanto gun;* Tawney, *Land and Labor in China;* Toland, *The Rising Sun: The Decline and Fall of the Japanese Empire;* Tsurumi et al, *Nihon no hyakunen;* Tuchman, *Stillwell and the American Experience in China;* Young, *Imperial Japan;* _____, *Japan in Recent Times, 1912-1926.*

Channel Islands Witchcraft, prom. 16th-17th Cent., Brit., witchcraft. When witch persecutions were at their height, the Channel Islands—located in the English Channel about thirty miles from France—endured, possibly, far greater brutality than the rest of Great Britain. Those convicted of witchcraft on the islands were burned. Traditionally, witches had been hanged, but with the influence of French customs, those convicted were burned. Conviction rates were also much higher. On the island of Guernsey, for example, which had a population of a few thousand during the reigns of Queen Elizabeth I, King James I, and King Charles I, seventy of seventy-eight people were found Guilty of sorcery. REF.: *CBA.*

Channell, Sir **Arthur Moseley,** 1838-1928, Brit., jur. Judge of the King's Bench Division of the High Court from 1897-1914. In 1914 he sat on the Judicial Committee of the Privy Council. He presided over several murder trials including those of Albert and Alfred Stratton and John Williams. REF.: *CBA.*

Chantrelle, Eugène Marie, 1824-78, Scot., mur. Eugène Marie Chantrelle, a Frenchman living and teaching French in Edinburgh, seduced a 15-year-old student and, after making her pregnant, married her. In the next ten years they had three children and her life became miserable, with Chantrelle increasingly drunk and violent, and often threatening her life. In October 1877, the teacher insured his wife's life—against fatal accidents only—for £1000.

On Jan. 2, 1878, the Chantrelles' servant found her mistress unconscious, with vomit stains on her pillow and nightgown. When she called Chantrelle from where he was sleeping in the nursery, he went to the bedroom and sent the maid back to tend the children. On her return to the wife's bedroom, she saw the teacher coming from the window where he had been handling something. He called attention to a smell of gas in the room. Chantrelle dressed and went for a doctor, again calling attention to the gas. The doctor sent for another doctor, Henry Littlejohn, who was also the police surgeon for Edinburgh. Elizabeth Chantrelle died soon after she was taken to a hospital. The two doctors decided that she had died not of coal-gas poisoning but of opium poisoning, probably administered in some orange slices that she had eaten. There was no opium in the body, but it was present in what she spat up. The doctors thought the opium was untraceable because Mme. Chantrelle digested it a sufficiently long time before she died.

Chantrelle was arrested and tried for the murder of his wife. A druggist in Edinburgh testified that Chantrelle bought extract of opium in November and December. A gas-company worker found a place by the bedroom window where a gas bracket had been removed and the pipe behind it freshly broken. Chantrelle was found Guilty of murder. He was hanged on May 31, 1878.

REF.: *CBA;* Glaister, *The Power of Poison;* Kingston, *Enemies of Society;* Laurence, *A History of Capital Punishment; Notable British Trials;* Wilson, *Encyclopedia of Murder.*

Chao Anou (Chao Anu, Chao Anouvong, Saya-Setha-thirath III), 1767-1835, Laos, rebel. Succeeded his brother as king of the Lao city-state of Vien Chang in 1805, and waged war along with Siamese military forces against Burma. During the rebellion of 1826-28, he was captured and tortured while leading the army of Laos toward Bangkok. REF.: *CBA.*

Chao Chi (Hui Tsung), 1082-1135, China, exile. Eighth emperor of Sung dynasty from 1110-1125. He concluded an ill-fated political alliance with the Juchen tribes of Manchuria, whereby his capital city of K'ai-feng was attacked and seized. He abdicated in favor of his son and died in exile in Manchuria. REF.: *CBA.*

Chao Huan (Chao Tan, Ch'in Tsung), 1100-60, China, exile. Son of Chao Chi, he was the ninth and last emeperor of the Sung dynasty from 1125-26. He was captured along with his father when the capital city was sacked by the Juchen tribes in 1126 and was exiled to Manchuria. REF.: *CBA.*

Chao Kao, d.207 B.C., China, consp. Concealing the death of Emperor Shih Huang Ti in 210 B.C., he conspired with foreign minister Li Ssu to deprive the rightful heir of his throne. A forged letter instructed the heir to commit suicide, leaving the government to the heir's young son Hu Hai. Instead, both Li Ssu and Hu Hai were killed. Chao Kao was later executed. REF.: *CBA.*

Chao Nan (Chao Nanthasen), d.1795, Laos, treas. Ruler of Vien Chang province from 1782-92 and conqueror of Luang Prabang in 1791. He was eventually deposed and imprisoned by Rama I of Siam. REF.: *CBA.*

Chapel, Martha, d.1802, Brit., mur. As an uneducated servant girl, Martha Chapel was unaware that she was pregnant, and the doctor who examined her was able to detect a pregnancy. Nevertheless, when her premature baby was discovered dead in Chapel's bed, she was found Guilty of murder and hanged at York Castle in 1802.

REF.: Atholl, *Shadow of the Gallows;* CBA; Potter, *The Art of Hanging.*

Chapelle, William (AKA: Chappy), prom. 1942, U.S., pros. After several months of undercover work in the Harlem and Times Square districts of New York City, Harold R. Danforth, an investigator for the District Attorney's office, finally obtained enough information to arrest William Chapelle and many others on charges of prostitution, rape, and other vice crimes, including the procuring of teenagers for sex.

The night of May 12, 1942, the New York City Police Department, under the direction of District Attorney Hogan, made one of the city's largest raids ever. In all, 205 people were arrested, and twenty-eight girls aged eleven to seventeen were also taken into custody. When statements made by Chapelle's lieutenants, "Frank the Sheik" and Blackjack, along with one by Evelyn Fox, who ran a brothel for Chapelle, were made known to Chapelle, he pleaded Guilty to a charge of compulsory prostitution. Chapelle was given a sentence of indeterminate length—most likely up to three years—though he never finished his term, as he died of syphilis at Blackwell's Island Hospital.

REF.: *CBA;* Danforth, *The D.A.'s Man.*

Chaperau, Albert Nathaniel (Shapiro, AKA: Albert Chippero, Harry Schwarz, R.L. Werner, Mr. White, Nathan Wise), prom. 1938, U.S., smug.-forg.-fraud. Albert Nathaniel Chaperau was a con man who moved among the international set. The exposure of his activities began on Oct. 7, 1938, when the SS *Ile de France* arrived in New York harbor carrying vacationers and German refugees. Mr. and Mrs. Nathaniel Chaperau went through customs with a large pile of luggage. None of it was opened for inspection because the couple carried Nicaraguan passports and a letter signed by the Nicaraguan consul general in New York declaring Chaperau to be a commercial attaché for that country.

Rosa Weber, a German maid at the Park Avenue apartment of New York Supreme Court Justice Edward J. Lauer, answered the door the next day and let Chaperau in to a warm welcome from Mrs. Lauer. He handed Weber a suitcase and a hat box, which Mrs. Lauer said contained some items purchased on their trip to Europe earlier in the summer which had not been ready when they returned home. On Oct. 21, the Lauers held a dinner party at which the guests, in their dinner table conversation, denounced Adolf Hitler. Weber flung down a plate of food and exclaimed, "Ladies and gentlemen, I am a true German. I love Adolf Hitler. If you don't stop talking against him, I will stop serving the dinner right now!" She did stop, because the Lauers instantly fired her and demanded that she pack and leave the apartment right away.

Weber got her revenge by going to customs officials in New York and accusing the Lauers of smuggling in goods from Europe, with the help of Chaperau. An investigation revealed that Chaperau had no right to use Nicaraguan credentials except to work on a movie documentary about that country. Although the consul general had given him a letter of authorization, it had nothing to do with diplomatic immunity. Customs also learned that Chapereau was wanted by the FBI as Chippero, Schwarz, and Wise, and by Scotland Yard as White for swindling and a long list of other crimes. In Chaperau's apartment, customs agents found papers indicating that he had brought in jewelry for comedians George Burns and Jack Benny.

Chaperau was charged with smuggling, to which he confessed. He also volunteered to cooperate in finding others whom he had "helped." He was fined $5,000 and sentenced to five years in prison, but President Franklin D. Roosevelt ordered Chaperau released in 1940. Justice Lauer was forced to resign, and his wife was sent to prison for three months. George Burns was given a suspended sentence of a year and a day for each of nine counts of smuggling and fined $8,000. Jack Benny received the same suspended sentence and was fined $10,000. Probably the worst part of Benny's punishment, however, was a half-hour harangue by Federal Judge Vincent Leibell. The judge said, in part, "I think it was a very poor return from you to the government and the citizens of this country who have made so much of you and so much for you, to do something like this...It was mighty small of you, and I think you were letting down your country."

REF.: *CBA*; Whitehead, *Border Guard*.

Chapin, Charles (AKA: **Rose Man of Sing Sing**), c.1858-1930, U.S., mur. As the editor of Pulitzer's New York *Evening World*, Charles Chapin made numerous enemies among the reporters for the way he used his power. Chapin invested every penny he earned for many years in speculative stocks, which provided him with a yacht, servants, and multiple homes.

When the bottom fell out of the sugar market, only a loan from a friend kept Chapin from going to jail for misusing a trust fund for which he was guardian. He swore never to speculate again, but could not keep the promise. In 1914, he lost $100,000 overnight when Germany declared war. For the next four years, he was hounded by creditors and frequently contemplated suicide. As bankruptcy neared, he decided that he could not ask his wife to live in the poverty he foresaw. He purchased a gun and, on Sept. 16, 1918, as she slept, he shot her in the chest, planning to kill himself immediately. However, she did not die at once, and by the time she did, he had lost his nerve. Chapin turned himself in to the police and asked to be electrocuted. The newsman refused to defend himself, but a volunteer lawyer managed to get the charge reduced to second-degree murder. The 60-year-old Chapin was sentenced to twenty years in Sing Sing.

Warden Lewis Lawes got Chapin interested in publishing a prison newspaper. When that was suspended, Chapin asked to be allowed to create a garden out of the prison yard, and was so successful that he earned the name "Rose Man of Sing Sing." His

gardening skills became known throughout the area, but, again, the men who were required to work for him found Chapin an arrogant slavedriver. Chapin died at seventy-two on Dec. 13, 1930.

REF.: *CBA*; Nash, *Murder Among the Mighty*.

Chapin, Kenneth R., 1936- , U.S., mur. Bernard Goldberg and his wife were out for the evening when their 4-year-old son Stephen, and his babysitter Lynn Ann Smith were brutally murdered in the family home in Springfield, Mass. The murderer later served as one of the pall bearers at the funeral.

Lynn Ann Smith was reading *Gone With the Wind* when 18-year-old Kenneth Chapin, the brother of her best friend, rapped at the window the night of Sept. 25, 1954. The teen-age babysitter had been warned about admitting strangers in the house. But Kenneth was no stranger. He was active in Boy Scouts and was a regular church-goer. Once inside the house, Chapin attempted to force himself on Lynn. When she resisted, he killed her with a knife. Fearing that Stephen would tell his parents what he had witnessed, Chapin bludgeoned the boy to death in his bedroom.

The police found a length of crocheting yarn near the Goldberg residence. Chapin had used it to tie a piece of paper around the handle of the knife. A house-to-house search revealed that the Chapin family had the only matching ball of yarn. On Oct. 8, Kenneth confessed to the double murder. In March 1955, he was convicted of first-degree murder and was sentenced to die. A day before his scheduled execution, Chapin's sentence was commuted to life imprisonment, after Dr. Frederic Wertham pronounced the young man a schizophrenic and therefore not responsible for his actions.

REF.: *CBA*; Wilson, *Encyclopedia of Murder*.

Chaplin, Charles Spencer, 1889-1977, Case of, U.S., wh. slav. Comedian Charlie Chaplin, who entertained millions with his work in silent films, was charged in October 1942 with transporting a woman across U.S. state lines for immoral purposes. The 24-year-old woman in question was alleged to have been the 54-year-old man's mistress.

Joan Berry had become Chaplin's protégé in the summer of 1941, working under a contract of $75 per week, which called for the director to give her acting lessons. Apparently, two weeks after she signed the contract, Berry became Chaplin's mistress. The love affair came to an end when the contract expired in the following summer. Berry, however, claimed that Chaplin paid for her to travel from Los Angeles to New York City to engage in sexual relations, a clear violation of the Mann Act of 1910, which prohibits transportation of a female for illicit sex.

Chaplin's defense was handled by Jerry Giesler, who attempted to show Berry as a whore, while the prosecution's case was handled by Charles H. Carr. A jury of seven women and five men before Federal Judge J.F.T. O'Connor found Chaplin Not Guilty on Apr. 4, 1944, but Chaplin's legal entanglement with Berry was far from finished.

In June 1943, Berry filed a paternity suit against Chaplin claiming that he was the father of her 4-month-old baby, Carol Ann. Chaplin's first trial resulted in a hung jury, with a vote of seven to five in his favor, in January 1945. The second jury returned a vote of eleven to one in favor of Berry on Apr. 17, 1945. Chaplin's appeals failed twice. The District Court of Appeals upheld the decision on May 27, 1946, and the California State Supreme Court denied an appeal on July 24, 1946. REF.: *CBA*.

Chaplin, Edward Royal, and **Casserley, Georgina May**, prom. 1938, Brit., mansl. Trapped in an unrewarding marriage to a man twenty-years older than herself, Georgina Casserley began an affair with Edward Royal Chaplin, a builder's foreman who had worked on a construction side adjacent to the family home in Wimbledon. When Percy Casserley was away at the nursing home where he received treatment for a nervous disorder, Mrs. Casserley would often stay with Chaplin at his place.

In March 1938 events came to a swift climax when Georgina became pregnant with Chaplin's baby. Chaplin was determined to square accounts with Georgina's 58-year-old husband. He waited for Casserley to return from the nursing home on Mar. 23, to ask him what was to be done. The husband reacted violently to the news and pulled out a revolver. Chaplin grappled with Casserley, and the gun accidentally discharged. The older man collapsed to the floor dead. Chaplin and Georgina then tried to make it look like a burglar had surprised Casserley, and shot him in the ensuing struggle.

The gambit failed, and the couple were tried separately for murder at the Old Bailey before Justice Travers Humphreys. Chaplin was found Guilty of manslaughter and was sentenced to twelve years of penal servitude. Mrs. Casserley received eleven days. On May 17, 1946, the day that Edward Chaplin was released from prison, Georgina was there waiting. They were eventually married.

REF.: Browne and Tullett, *The Scalpel of Scotland Yard;* ____, *Bernard Spilsbury: His Life and Cases; CBA;* Cuthbert, *Science and the Detection of Crime;* Hastings, *The Other Mr. Churchill;* Shew, *A Companion to Murder.*

Chapman, Annie, See: **Jack the Ripper.**

Chapman, George (Severin Antonionvitch Klosowski), 1865-1903, Brit., mur. George Chapman, born Severin Klosowski in Nargonak, Pol., on Dec. 14, 1865, the son of a carpenter. He apprenticed at age fifteen to a surgeon in Zvolen, working at a clinic for six years, but failing to be appointed to the expected post of junior surgeon. He left the clinic at twenty-one and traveled about Poland as a barber's surgeon, or *feldsher,* removing warts, performing small surgeries, even bloodletting which was still, in less sophisticated societies in the late nineteenth century, considered a form of purifying the blood system. (The red and white poles outside of barber shops originally indicated that a bloodletting expert was on the premises.) Chapman married in Poland, then

Mass poisoner George Chapman.

worked in a Prague hospital before enlisting in the Russian army where he served for almost two years. He then migrated to England, arriving in early 1888, the year that Jack the Ripper turned loose his reign of terror in London's West End. He later became one of the prime suspects in the Ripper killings and it was rumored that Chapman had decapitated a woman in Poland, but no supporting evidence could be found to support this claim.

Locating in London's West End, Chapman worked as a barber. He later moved to Tottingham to set up his own business, but when this failed he returned to his old job as a barber's surgeon and assistant. He married Lucy Baderski, but this marriage was compromised when Chapman's first wife arrived from Poland. Both women, oddly, lived with Chapman for a while until the first and legal wife returned to Poland. Chapman and Lucy went to the U.S. in 1890 but after constant quarreling, Lucy returned to London in 1891, Chapman himself arriving in London a year later. The marriage floundered when Chapman went on womanizing, taking a mistress named Annie Chapman, ironically the same name as one of Jack the Ripper's victims. Lucy left her philandering husband in 1894, taking their two children with her. Chapman, who had used his real name, Klosowski, up to this time, now took the name of his mistress, Chapman and tried to conceal his original name.

The promiscuous barber met a drunken divorcée, Mary Spinks, in 1895 in one of the many pubs he visited, and the couple lived together for two years, moving in 1897 to Hastings where they assumed the roles of man and wife. Chapman opened a hairdresser's shop and promoted "musical shaves." His mistress-wife would play the piano while Chapman shaved his customers, a notion that caught on, and so popular was Chapman's shop that he began to

turn a profit for the first time in his entrepreneurial life. He bought a sailboat and began taking his wife on sailing expeditions. A short time later the boat capsized and the Chapmans were saved by some fishermen. It was later theorized that this was the barber's first attempt at murder, since he planned to eliminate his wife. About six months later, Chapman suddenly sold his lucrative shop in Hastings and moved back to London, leasing the Prince of Wales Tavern on Bartholomew Square, near City Road.

On Apr. 2, 1897, before leaving Hastings, Chapman bought tartar emetic from a local druggist and this he would later use to murder Mary Spinks, it was concluded by police officials. Mary Spinks grew ill in late 1897 and suffered vomiting seizures. Doctors examining her could find no reason for these seizures. Chapman, meanwhile nursed her until Mary Spinks died on Dec. 25, 1897. The cause of her death was listed as consumption. A few months after Mary Spinks was buried, Chapman hired a barmaid, Bessie Taylor, a naive farmer's daughter. He married Bessie some months later. Chapman tired of Bessie and made plans to kill her. First he sold his pub and bought another tavern, The Grapes, at Bishops Stortford. Bessie was hospitalized for a small operation never disclosed. When she was released, Chapman began mistreating her, at one point threatening to shoot her with a revolver. Again, Chapman sold his pub, and bought another, The Monument, which was located on Union Street. He continued to abuse his wife and run around with other women. Bessie's health grew steadily worse and she was finally bedridden, with Chapman nursing her; she died on Feb. 13, 1901. Doctors examining her attributed her demise to "exhaustion from vomiting and diarrhea."

Maud Marsh, the daughter of a Croydon laborer, next went to work for Chapman as a barmaid in his pub. Maud was reluctant to become Chapman's mistress, even though he gave her a gold watch and chain. The young girl wrote to her mother that Chapman had threatened to send her home unless "I give him what he wants." She finally relented but grew ill in the fall of 1902, suffering from severe abdominal pains. Chapman called in doctors who had her removed to Guy's Hospital where she

Chapman with Maud Marsh, one of his murder victims; George Chapman took this photo himself.

recovered. When she returned to Chapman, he moved her into quarters above his new pub, The Crown Public House, which was also on Union Street. Here the girl grew ill again, despite constant attention from Chapman. Maud's mother and a nurse arrived one evening to attend to Maud and they found at her bedside a special drink Chapman had prepared for Maud, a brandy and soda which Maud's mother and the nurse drank. Within minutes both women became ill with vomiting and diarrhea. Mrs. Marsh went to her own physician and told him that she believed Chapman was poisoning her daughter. This doctor went to the physician attending Maud with Mrs. Marsh's suspicions. The attending doctor had no such beliefs. He and the

Marsh family physician visited the ailing girl and both men went away believing that Maud was being poisoned. Chapman, meanwhile, panicked after this visit from the doctors and he gave Maud a massive dose of his special preparation. She died on Oct. 22, 1902, the very day of Edward VII's coronation procession through the streets of London.

Maud's body was examined, and it was determined that she had been poisoned not with arsenic, as the Marsh family suspected, but with antimony. Chapman was arrested and charged with murder. He was tried before Justice Graham at the Central Criminal Court on Mar. 16, 1903. Sir Edward Carson prosecuted Chapman who was defended by George Elliott. There was very little defense. The bodies of Chapman's other two mistresses, Mary Spinks and Bessie Taylor, were exhumed and these corpses also contained antimony, enough to have killed them. Chapman was convicted in a quick trial and condemned. He was executed on Apr. 7, 1903. It was just after Chapman's arrest that Scotland Yard's Inspector Frederick Abberline approached the officer in charge of the case, Inspector Godley, telling him cryptically: "You've got Jack the Ripper at last!" Abberline believed Chapman to be the awesome Ripper since his handling of the bewildering 1888 mass murders remained unsolved. Why Abberline believed Chapman was the Ripper was never explained either by Abberline or anyone else. It is believed that Abberline had suspected Chapman or Klosowski during his original 1888 investigations but could never prove his secret suspicions about the barber.

Many experts are quick to point out that Chapman's *modus operandi* and that of the Ripper's were widely dissimilar, the Ripper using extreme violence and a surgical knife to end his victims' lives where Chapman had regularly chosen the slow, secret method of poison. It was later claimed that Chapman, as Klosowski, had even tried to obtain poison when he lived in Whitechapel during the Ripper murders, perhaps planning at the time to rid himself of his first Polish wife *and* Lucy Baderski at the same time. Another theory has it that Chapman could very well have been the Ripper and that he continued slitting throats and dismembering bodies long into the 1890s, electing to kill women he was known to associate with through poison so that the Ripper's style of murder would not be attached to him, believing that poison would allow him to go undetected.

Even more puzzling is why Chapman chose to murder three women (or more) simply because they either came to annoy him or because he tired of them. He was not necessarily a sadist, according to his character profiles, so he took no particular pleasure in slowly murdering his common-law spouses and mistresses. Moreover, he derived no money from the deaths of these women, having already bilked his first mistress of her savings to buy his first pub. There may be a link to the deaths in Chapman's consistent buying and selling of pubs, changes that were invariably made at the time of the murders. It was proposed by one crime writer that Chapman murdered his women when his pub business began to drop off, believing they were bringing him bad luck. A check of the consistent popularity of these pubs, however, disproves this contention. Chapman remains a murdering enigma, one who could possibly have been Jack the Ripper. He never confessed to his crimes, however, leaving frustrated criminologists to theorize and wonder in his wake. See: **Jack the Ripper**.

REF.: Altick, *Victorian Studies in Scarlet;* Bowen-Rowlands, *In the Light of the Law;* Brock, *A Casebook of Crime;* Brophy, *The Meaning of Murder;* CBA; Cullen, *When London Walked in Terror;* Dearden, *Some Cases of Sir Bernard Spilsbury & Others;* Dickson, *Murder by Numbers;* Ellis, *Prisoner at the Bar;* Glaister, *The Power of Poison;* Hodge, *The Black Maria;* Hyde, *Carson: The Life of Sir Edward Carson;* Knight, *Jack the Ripper, The Final Solution;* Marjoribanks, *The Life of Lord Carson;* Nash, *Almanac of World Crime;* Neil, *Manhunters of Scotland Yard; Notable British Trials;* Rumbelow, *The Complete Jack the Ripper;* Shew, *A Companion to Murder;* Thompson, *Poisons and Poisoners;* Whittington-Egan, *A Casebook on Jack the Ripper;* Wilson, *Encyclopedia of Murder;*

Woodhall, *Secrets of Scotland Yard.*

Chapman, Gerald (AKA: **G. Vincent Caldwell, Waldo W. Miller**), 1890-1926, U.S., rob.-mur. Brooklyn-born Gerald Chapman would have remained an obscure petty crook had it not been for a prison education that inspired him to commit the infamous robberies that would bring him wealth and an early death. Before he was ten, Chapman was an accomplished pickpocket and sneak thief. He was often sent to reformatories but he was just as quickly paroled. When he was sent to New York's House of Refuge in 1904 at the age of fourteen, the judge remarked that he was a likely candidate for the electric chair, a prophetic remark as it later turned out. In 1908 Chapman, at eighteen, was sent to Sing Sing Prison for the first time, after being convicted of a robbery. He was later tranferred to Auburn Prison, where he met his new cell mate and future mentor, a confirmed professional thief from Denmark named Ivan Dahl von Teller, who was known in the U.S. as George "Dutch" Anderson.

Anderson, who was highly educated, having attended the European universities at Heidelberg and Upsala, spoke five languages fluently. He so impressed Chapman that the youth began to read voraciously, improving his manner and affecting a British accent. Anderson taught his protégé the use of a "good front" to throw off suspicion, and under which criminal pursuits were best achieved. And-

erson tried to convince Chapman that non-violent crimes such as swindling and embezzlement, the crimes of which Anderson had been convicted, were preferable to armed robbery where murder was often part and parcel. When Chapman was released, however, he went back to the kind of crime he understood best and committed several robberies. With his loot, Chapman purchased expensive clothes, donned a homburg, and carried a walking cane, appearing to be every inch a gentleman. He rented an expensive apartment and began dining in better restaurants. After committing another robbery in 1912, Chapman was caught and sent back to Sing Sing. Here he met another habitual criminal, Charles Loeber, who believed that the only way to obtain fast money was with a gun.

In 1919, Chapman, Loeber, and Anderson were all paroled. At first Chapman

Celebrated robber Gerald Chapman, at right, under arrest.

followed Anderson's advice, accompanying the con man through the Midwest where several quick swindles netted the pair more than $100,000. Chapman and Anderson moved back to New York and took a lavish apartment in Gramercy Park. Here, as they planned several involved confidence games, Loeber arrived and convinced Chapman to rob a mail truck on Wall Street, explaining that he had been watching these unguarded mail trucks make pickups along Wall Street. "Inside of these trucks," Loeber announced, "are millions of dollars in money orders, securities, checks, bonds." Chapman agreed to the robbery of one of these trucks and, on Oct. 14, 1921, Chapman, Loeber, and a reluctant Anderson waited in a stolen Cleveland car. A mail truck driven by Frank Havernack shortly appeared, moving along Wall Street.

The Cleveland suddenly shot forward when the truck passed and raced alongside the truck, then swerved in front, slowing suddenly and causing Havernack to brake his vehicle. As the truck slowed down, Chapman leaped on its running board, holding a pistol in his hand which he shoved into Havernack's stomach. "Pull over and don't make any noise," the bandit ordered. Havernack brought the truck to a full stop. While Chapman held him prisoner, placing a mail sack over the driver's head and tying him with the drawropes, Anderson and Loeber opened the back doors of the truck and climbed inside, rummaging through the thirty-three regular mail sacks to find five sacks of registered mail which they dragged to the Cleveland and tossed into the back seat. Within minutes the robbers roared off on Leonard Street. Once in their hideout, they were amazed to discover that they had stolen $1,424,129—the largest mail theft in U.S. history to that date. Only $27,000 in cash was present, however, the rest being securities which the gang later fenced for 40¢ on the dollar. The return was still staggering.

Mail truck driver Frank Havernack, inset, and the truck from which Chapman stole $1,424,129 on Oct. 14, 1921.

After fencing hundreds of thousands of dollars in securities through Anderson's Midwest contacts, Chapman and Anderson, with Loeber acting as their butler and chauffeur, moved back to Gramercy Park, where they lived like drunken millionaires, spending more than $1,000 a day on lavish parties, new cars, and tall blonde chorus girls from the Follies. The Leonard Street Mail Robbery, as it came to be known, caused a sensation in the press and alarmed federal and New York law enforcement officials. Heavily armed guards were assigned to guard the mail trucks, and an intensive manhunt for the robbers ensued but their identities could not be determined. A few months later the gang again struck, taking more than $70,000 in money orders from an American Express office in Niagara Falls.

The bandits continued their high living in Gramercy Park, but Loeber proved to be their undoing. He did not have the same contacts as Anderson and Chapman had in fencing his portion of the stolen securities taken in the Leonard Street Robbery. Instead, Loeber tried to fence these highly publicized securities with some Broadway touts and was turned in to the police. Once under arrest, Loeber, to earn a lesser sentence, informed on his associates. Both Chapman and Anderson were arrested. Chapman, while awaiting trial in New York, tried to escape jail by climbing along a 75-foot ledge to freedom but was caught in the act. The bold escape attempt, coupled with the daring mail robbery, caused the tabloid newspapers of the day to make Gerald Chapman into a modern-day Robin Hood, a spectacular criminal with amazing abilities to commit holdups and make escapes. Chapman delightedly posed for newspaper photographers, dressed

in his imported tailor-made suits, puffing on a cigar and exuding a nonchalant air. He soon came to believe that he was a special kind of crook, one who could never be held long in any prison.

Following a quick trial and conviction, Chapman and Anderson were sent to the federal penitentiary at Atlanta to begin serving twenty-five-year prison sentences. Chapman arrogantly informed the warden at Atlanta that he would escape, that no prison could hold a man like him. "The publicity you have acquired recently has gone to your head, Chapman," the warden told him. "You won't be getting out of Atlanta until you've either served your time or if you die inside these walls." Chapman merely smirked. Then, once in his cell, he quickly swallowed a full bottle of disinfectant which made him violently ill and caused him to be removed to the prison hospital. Once there, he knocked a guard unconscious and, with several bedsheets tied together, managed to lower himself from a hospital window to the yard, then climbed over the wall with a handmade rope-ladder. His escape made national headlines, but he was captured two days later when police cornered him. Rather than surrender, Chapman shot it out and was wounded three times before being dragged back to Atlanta.

Undaunted, the determined Chapman recovered from his wounds and then made another escape, again employing bedsheets and ropes to get over the prison walls. Some weeks later, Anderson, who also escaped Atlanta by tunneling his way out, joined Chapman. The two began committing a series of burglaries and robberies from Boston to Savannah. In New Britain, Conn., the pair robbed a large department store but made two mistakes. The first was to take along a small-time hoodlum named Walter Shean, and the second and most important error was to shoot a policeman, Officer John Skelly, who interrupted the pair while they were cracking the safe on Oct. 12, 1924. Chapman and Anderson made good their escape, but Shean was found standing next to a Lincoln auto—waiting for the pair to show up—when police surrounded him. He boasted to police that the robbery had been masterminded by "my pal, Gerald Chapman."

With police searching every known hideout along the Eastern seaboard for Chapman, he and Anderson, both in disguises, traveled by train to Muncie, Ind., where they stayed at the home of Ben Hance, one of Anderson's underworld contacts. Somehow police learned of this hideout and closed in when Chapman was in the house alone. He was apprehended without a struggle in January 1925. Again the millions of tabloid readers were thrilled by the exploits of Chapman and most expected the "super bandit" to once again escape. But there would be no more daring flights from justice for Gerald Chapman. President Calvin Coolidge approved a commutation for Chapman on the federal conviction of the Leonard Street Mail Robbery to the time he had already served so that Chapman could be extradited to Connecticut where he would stand trial for killing Officer Skelly.

Chapman's mentor, George "Dutch" Anderson, shown in disguise.

Chapman insisted at his trial that he was in Holyoke, Mass., on the day Officer Skelly was killed, but Shean testified in court that Chapman was the man who shot and killed the officer. Ben Hance, in whose farm home Chapman had been found, appeared at the bandit's trial and also testified against him, saying that Chapman had paid him to hide out in his home. Hance provided some of the stolen money from the New Britain department store safe which clearly placed Chapman at the scene of the crime. He was convicted and sentenced to death, then sent to the state prison at Wethersfield, Conn., to await execution. Chapman's lawyers filed every appeal available, but were unable to postpone the inevitable hanging on Apr. 6, 1926.

To the time of his execution, Chapman was a model prisoner, remaining silent and always obedient and courteous. He was "the perfect gentleman," according to one report. On the day of his execution, Chapman quietly allowed guards to pinion his arms with straps and lead him into the execution chamber, the hanging room. A row of witnesses watched as he entered the room with a slight smile on his lips. His legs were tied and the rope placed about his neck, then a black hood was placed over his face. Chapman muttered a few words no one could hear since the hood muffled his voice. The warden then pulled a lever and weights shot downward, causing the rope to yank Chapman upward, jerking him to death. The bandit's body hung suspended twelve feet above the floor, dangling. Death was instantaneous, Chapman's neck being snapped. It took only fifteen seconds to execute the "super

The ever-arrogant Gerald Chapman, enjoying a cigar while prison officials dote on him only a few days before his execution for murder.

bandit" from the time he entered the death chamber. Only silence pervaded the death chamber, interrupted by the sound of pencils scratching across paper as newspapermen wrote their grim story.

When George "Dutch" Anderson read these stories of Chapman's gruesome death, he went berserk. First he attempted to kill Shean but the informer was too heavily guarded. Anderson traveled to Indiana and there confronted Ben Hance, calling him a traitor. Anderson shot and killed Hance and his wife and then burned their house down around them. He fled to Michigan and was surrounded by police in Muskegon. An officer approached the bandit cautiously, thinking him unarmed. Anderson laughed loudly, then pulled a revolver and fired at the officer just as the policeman fired. Both men fell dead, shooting each other in the heart. It was the end of the Gerald Chapman gang.

REF.: CBA; Mencken, By the Neck; Nash, Bloodletters and Badmen; Thrasher, The Gang; Twyman, The Best Laid Schemes.

Chapman, Henry, c.1878-1934, Aus., embez.-suic. Henry Chapman had a fondness for women that the English-born professor of pharmacology and physiology at Sydney University was unable to indulge on his salary alone. However, his position as president of the Linnaean Society of New South Wales, director of the Cancer Research Laboratories—a post he obtained in 1928, and honorary treasurer of the Royal Society provided considerable additional income. Chapman's illicit dealings were finally discovered in 1934 after he had embezzled some £20,000. Rather than face a prison sentence, Chapman chose to commit suicide. He injected himself with a large dose of insulin—a means of death which had gone undetected at the postmortem.

REF.: CBA; Gurr, Famous Australasian Crime.

Chapman, John T., b.1832, U.S., rob. When John Chapman, an upstanding citizen of Reno, Nev., took up with shady gambler Jack Davis in 1870, his neighbors thought he was trying to reform Davis. But Chapman was actually out to learn a new trade. He soon joined Davis along with several of his criminal friends in train robbery.

Chapman wanted to hold up the express car messenger of the Central Pacific's Train Number One, which he knew contained boxes full of cash. On Nov. 4, 1870, his gang boarded the train as it left the station in Verdi, Nev. Since there had been no train robberies in the West, security was minimal. Chapman easily overpowered the conductor and engineer. The messenger surrendered without a fight, and the gang got away with $41,600.

But the thieves began spending money extravagantly, which made the Wells Fargo detectives suspicious. Two of the Chapman gang were persuaded to confess, and to lead detectives to the buried treasure. The subsequent arrests of Davis and Chapman shocked the community. Chapman received a twenty-year sentence, and Davis got only ten years because he confessed.

Chapman led a prison break on Sept. 28, 1871, but was quickly recaptured. He served his full twenty-year sentence plus one additional year for breaking out of prison. Upon his release, he preached against the evils of train robbery, but was rumored to be involved in other holdups, including two train robberies in one day. REF.: CBA.

Chapman, Lucretia, See: **Mina, Epos Y.**

Chapman, Mark David, 1955- , U.S., mur. "We're going to live, or we're going to die. If we're dead, we're going to have to deal with that; if we're alive, we're going to have to deal with being alive." A few hours after he said those words, rock star and former Beatle John Lennon was shot to death by Mark David Chapman, a deranged fan who thought that he was Lennon.

Chapman, born in Texas and raised in Georgia, ran away from home when he was fourteen. He was away only a few weeks, but remained part of the drug scene for another two years. Becoming a Beatles fan as a teenager, he tried to emulate them with his own band. However, after Chapman became a born-again Christian, he was offended by Lennon's remark, "We're more popular than Jesus now." Thus, Chapman gave up the Beatles, as he had given up drugs, and used his spare time to work with children at the YMCA. Chapman's friends watched him become increasingly preoccupied with internal struggles concerning the sinfulness of the "Bad Mark." He moved around the country, working at various jobs and studying religions in his free time. He was arrested for armed robbery, kidnapping, and possession of drugs. He tried to commit suicide in 1977, and received psychological care. In 1979, he married a travel agent and moved to Hawaii, where he insisted that she never watch television or read newspapers. He frequently stood outside a Church of Scientology and shouted abuse, and month by month he became more irrational, although he kept that side of him hidden from most people. In 1980, he changed the name tag on his security guard's uniform to read "John Lennon," and on Oct. 23 he quit his job, signing out as John Lennon.

From that time, it became necessary for Chapman to get rid of the other Lennon. That other Lennon had dropped from the public eye and turned introspective. Chapman wanted the brash

Lennon from the old days back again, so he became that Lennon. Chapman first bought a .38-caliber pistol. Then he borrowed $2,500 from a credit union and flew to New York City on Dec. 6, 1980. He began to spend long hours stationed outside the Dakota, the apartment building where Lennon lived with his wife Yoko Ono and their son. On Dec. 8, Lennon emerged to go to a recording studio, and Chapman had him autograph his most recent album, *Double Fantasy*. Chapman stayed where he was as Lennon and Ono drove off, then turned to continue reading a copy of J. D. Salinger's *The Catcher in the Rye*. At 11 p.m. that night, Lennon and Ono returned to the Dakota. Chapman called out, "Mr. Lennon." Lennon looked up and Chapman shot him five times in the chest. Lennon died in a squad car as a patrolman tried to get him to a hospital.

After killing Lennon, Chapman sat down and returned to reading the Salinger novel. He was arrested and charged with second-degree murder. He told the police, "I have a small part in me that cannot understand the world and what goes on in it. I did not want to kill anybody, and I really don't know why I did..." His lawyer, Jonathan Marks, wanted him to plead not guilty by reason of insanity, but Chapman told the court that God had told him to confess to murder. He was sentenced on July 24, 1981, to twenty years to life in prison, with a recommendation that he be treated psychiatrically. Even his own attorney asked the judge not to sentence him too lightly. "All reports came to the conclusion that he is not a sane man. It was not a sane crime.

John Lennon's killer, Mark David Chapman.

It was...a monstrously irrational killing." Chapman's only response to the sentencing was to read aloud a passage from *The Catcher in the Rye*. He was sent to Attica State Prison in upstate New York, where he was put to work as a janitor.

REF.: *CBA*; Nash, *Murder Among the Mighty*; Wilson, *Encyclopedia of Modern Murder*.

Chappell, George Shepard, and **Ford, Corey**, prom. 1929, U.S., hoax. In the 1920s a number of American and British authors attempted to capitalize on the public's insatiable demand for books and novels about the exotic South Seas. George Chappell and Corey Ford published what purported to be a true life account of the discovery of a cluster of islands known as the Filberts. The book was titled the *Cruise of the Kawa*, and it was issued by G.P. Putnam. The news of the expedition was greated with a mixture of excitement and curiosity by the academic community. The *National Geographic* invited them to Washington for series of meetings, and a number of readers inquired about the possibility of being included on the next sailing of the *Kawa*.

A companion volume authored by Corey Ford picked right up where the earlier volume stopped. It was titled *Coconut Oil*, the "true life adventures" of June Triplett, the daughter of Captain Ezra Triplett, skipper of the *Kawa*.

In the July 1929 issue of *Vanity Fair*, Ford's article "The Adventure Racket" criticized zealous publishers for putting out books that are two-thirds false.

REF.: *CBA*; MacDougall, *Hoaxes*.

Chappleau, Joseph Ernst, 1850-1911, U.S., mur. Joseph Chappleau, a New York dairy farmer, killed his neighbor, Mr. Tabor, in 1889, when he found Tabor was having an affiar with his wife. Chappleau was found Guilty of murder, and was the first man sentenced to die in the electric chair, which had replaced hanging as the method of execution in New York state. However,

prison officials could not get the chair ready in time for Chappleau's execution date, so his sentence was commuted to life imprisonment.

Lewis Lawes, later warden of Sing Sing Prison, recalled years later that while he worked as a guard at Clinton, Chappleau saved his life during a prison riot. Lawes' opposition to capital punishment was formed by his experiences with Chappleau, who died of natural causes at Clinton in 1911. REF.: *CBA*.

Charafeddine, Mohammad, c.1964-   , U.S., forg.-theft. Ten thousand dollars worth of merchandise purchased with stolen credit cards found in the New Paltz, N.Y., apartment of a friend of Mohammad Charafeddine led to Charafeddine's arrest on Aug. 30, 1987. His arrest also created a great deal of speculation, because along with the consumer items were found a number of explosive components stolen from the defense contractor, Betatronix, in Long Island, N.Y., where Charafeddine worked.

Patrick Henry, district attorney for Suffolk County, N.Y., claimed that the 23-year-old Charafeddine was a terrorist, because of his known association with Hezbollah, a pro-Iranian Shiite faction in Lebanon, the defendant's homeland. Although it was never proved that Charafeddine had indeed stolen the military equipment for terrorist activity, he did plead guilty in New York's Supreme Court to possession of a stolen credit card, forgery in the use of the card, and theft from his employer. He was sentenced in October 1987, to spend six months in the county jail. REF.: *CBA*.

Charette de la Contrie, François-Athanase, 1763-96, Fr., rebel. French Royalist, he led the unsuccessful Vendéan revolt against the newly established Republic in 1793. He was executed at Nantes in 1796. REF.: *CBA*.

Charing Cross Trunk Murder, The, See: **Robinson, John**.

Charles (Count of Flanders, AKA: Charles the Good, Charles the Dane, Charles le Bon), c.1083-1127, Flanders, assass. Renowned for his acts of clemency toward prisoners. He was murdered at Bruges in 1127. REF.: *CBA*.

Charles I, 1600-49, Brit., treas. Son of James VI, he ruled from 1625-49. He drained the resources of Parliament to finance unsuccessful military expeditions against the Spanish and the French. When held captive at Carisbrooke Castle in 1647, he attempted to conclude a deal with the Scots that would recognize Presbyterianism in England for a period of three years in return for their military assistance. He was dispatched to London in January 1648 where he refused to plead before the House of Commons. Tried before a court of sixty-seven judges, he was condemned a tyrant and beheaded at Whitehall. REF.: *CBA*.

Charles II, 1630-85, Brit., king, assass. Claimed throne after Parliamentary forces executed his father Charles I in 1649. Charles II invaded England with Scottish help in 1651, but was routed by Oliver Cromwell and forced into exile. He intrigued with continental powers, especially Louis XIV of France. After Cromwell's death in 1658, he negotiated with Parliament for his return to the throne, which he assumed in 1660. In 1662 he issued the Declaration of Indulgence providing religious freedom for all, including Catholics. Parliament opposed the measure and enacted repressive laws against noncomformists. Charles II sold his allegiance to Louis XIV and was suspected of being a covert Catholic, which led to the foiled Rye House assassination plot in 1683. He ruled absolutely in his final years, professed Catholicism on his deathbed, and defied Parliament by naming as his successor his Catholic brother James. REF.: *CBA*.

Charles III, See: **Robert I**

Charles III (Charles of Durazzo), 1345-86, Naples-Hung., king, assass. King of Naples from 1381-86. To secure the throne in 1382, he brought about the murder of his adopted mother, Queen Joanna I. Following his accession to the throne of Hungary as Charles III in 1385, he was imprisoned as a result of a popular revolt. He was poisoned by agents of the widow of King Louis I against whom he had waged war. REF.: *CBA*.

Charles V, 1500-58, Spain, her. King of Spain as Charles I and Holy Roman Emperor as Charles V from 1516-56. He exercised tolerance toward German Protestants, but for political reasons persecuted the heretics in Spain. When he captured Rome in 1527, he imprisoned the pope. REF.: *CBA*.

Charles VII, d.1167, Swed., king, assass. King of Swedes and Goths from 1161-67, he waged a war with the Russians in 1164. Three years later he was killed by an assassin. REF.: *CBA*.

Charles IX, 1550-74, Fr., mur. Influenced by his mother, Catherine d'Medici, King Charles IX, the weak and petulant French monarch ordered the mass arrest and execution of hundreds of Protestant Huguenots on St. Bartholomew's Day in 1572. D'Medici believed the faction, led by Admiral Gaspard de Coligny, was a political threat against the Catholic King.

The massacre developed from the arranged marriage of Charles' sister Marguerite de Valois to the Protestant Henry of Navarre on Aug. 18, 1572, which was intended to be a reconciliation of the two warring factions. The occasion of their marriage led to further intrigues, for she was secretly in love with Henri de Lorraine, the powerful Duke of Guise. Guise attempted to assassinate popular military leader Admiral Coligny on Aug. 22, an event which led to the St. Bartholomew's Massacre.

The king's murder squads wore white armbands, covered at the end of the day with the blood of the Huguenots who were dragged from their homes and summarily executed. Admiral Coligny was among the casualties.

REF.: Canning, *Fifty True Tales of Terror; CBA*.

Charles, Earl, c.1953- , U.S., (wrong. convict.) mur. Without a shred of evidence against him, and possessing a rock-solid alibi, Earl Charles was still found Guilty of murdering two men he had never seen.

On Oct. 3, 1974, the 76-year-old owner of the Savannah (Ga.) Furniture Company, Max Rosenstein, and his 42-year-old son, Fred Rosenstein, were each shot in the head and killed with bullets from a .22-caliber pistol. The two assailants also struck 70-year-old Myra Rosenstein, Max's wife, in the head with a tape dispenser before making off with $1,007 in cash. While this crime was taking place, Charles and his friend Michael Williams were working at a Kwik Pep Service Station in Tampa, Fla., about 300 miles from Savannah, Charles' hometown and site of the killings.

Fingerprints at the scene of the crime did not match those on file for Charles, who had been jailed as a youth for burglary and shoplifting. Nor did either of the eyewitnesses, Myra and Bessie Corcelius, identify Charles as the killer. However, an eager detective, F.W. Wade, managed to have Charles arrested in Florida. After a police line-up that was likely rigged, he was extradited to Georgia and tried on two counts of murder, armed robbery, and aggravated assault. He was found Guilty by a jury on May 15, 1975 of all charges except aggravated assault, despite testimony by Charles' employer, Robert Zachary, that Charles was working during the shooting. For some reason, the jury chose to believe Wade's claim that Zachary had earlier said that the defendant was not working. The jury sentenced Charles to death by electrocution, which Judge George Oliver agreed to, despite his own misgivings.

The persistence of Flossie Mae Charles, Charles' mother, helped free her son. At her urging, Lemon Harvey, a Tampa police officer whom Zachary had asked to keep an eye on his new employees Charles and Williams, recalled that Zachary's statement was true since Charles had not yet been fired by the service station manager. Charles' lawyer, John Sullivan, managed to have a new trial granted, but the retrial never took place because District Attorney Andrew Ryan decided on July 5, 1978, not to reprosecute the case, and Charles was freed.

The wrong done to Charles resulted in a lawsuit against Wade for violating the defendant's rights. An April 1980 trial found the detective innocent of the charges, but a federal judge reversed this decision in 1983 and awarded the wrongly-convicted man $417,000. Charles dropped the suit when it became clear that the officer could not pay the damages, and the city of Savannah agreed to pay him $75,000 for the thirty-seven months he spent on death row. REF.: *CBA*.

Charles, Sir Ernest Bruce, 1871-1950, Brit., jur. Judge of the King's Bench Division from 1928-1947, he was called to the bar in 1896. He presided over the murder trials of Frederick Field, Elizabeth Jones and Karl Hulten, and Leonard Holmes. REF.: *CBA*.

Charles, Henri, b.c.1866, Alg., mur. What appeared to be murder and attempted suicide following a period of intimacy between a married woman and her lover may actually have been a cold-hearted, calculated murder.

On the afternoon of Jan. 25, 1888, Henri Charles and Ellen Dickson Gey arrived at Charles' villa, Sidi-Mabrouk, a half-hour's carriage ride from Constantine, Algeria. Two and one-half hours later the semi-nude woman was found dead lying on a bed with two bullet wounds to her temple. The man lay nearby with a gunshot wound to his cheek. Charles, able to talk, immediately admitted that Gey and he had been lovers for several months. He said that Gey and he had planned to run away together, leaving her home and children behind, but they had no means with which to run away—a ridiculous claim in that Gey had 1,900 francs in cash and 50,000 francs worth of securities. Therefore, Charles said, they chose death.

Gey's husband claimed that his 30-year-old wife of ten years was an honorable woman and wonderful mother of two girls, aged seven and nine, who would never think of an adulterous affair. Testimony of a number of friends supported this claim, as well as a letter Gey was writing the day she died, which showed no sign of the excitement that running away would elicit. Nor had Gey even packed any belongings. The defendant, who was represented by M. Durier, also produced letters supposedly from the dead woman supporting his claim—letters that were proven to be forgeries. With no clear evidence as to what really took place, the jury had to decide whether to believe in the dead woman's honor or in the tale told by Charles of the romance he shared with Gey.

Charles was found Guilty of premeditated murder, but the court all but ignored the jury's finding and sentenced the killer to seven years of penal servitude, a sentence which was commuted to seven years in prison by the French possession's president of the Republic, Marie-François-Sadi Carnot.

REF.: *CBA*; Russell, *Best Murder Cases*.

Charlesworth, Violet (AKA: **Margaret Cameron McLeod**), b.c.1885, and **Charlesworth, Mrs.**, prom. 1900s, Brit., fraud-consp. A ghastly car crash on Jan. 2, 1909, apparently took the life of Violet Charlesworth when she was thrown through the windshield and hurled to her death some forty feet to the base of the cliff along the North Wales coast. There was no blood on the windshield and the body could not be found. Newspaper reporters became more suspicious when they discovered that Charlesworth owed a considerable amount of money at the time of her alleged death.

Charlesworth was £400 in debt to Mrs. Martha Smith, and about £10,000 to her stockbrokers. In addition, a number of jewelers and car dealers were cheated by the honest-looking young lady, who had apparently lived beyond her means for many years. The erstwhile corpse was discovered very much alive by a newspaper reporter in Oban, Scot., where Charlesworth had taken the name of Margaret Cameron McLeod. She returned to England, and attempted to raise money and repay her creditors by making appearances at music halls. Her "entertainment" consisted of standing on stage wearing the crimson cloak she was wearing on the day she disappeared. This endeavor did not earn enough to pay her debts, nor did the mysterious Alexander MacDonald, whom she claimed had promised her £155,000, ever make an appearance. While civil suits against her were still in progress, criminal charges were filed against Charlesworth and her mother.

Mrs. Charlesworth and her daughter were arrested in Moffat, Scot., on Feb. 7, 1910, on charges of attempting to obtain money under false pretenses and conspiring to commit such a crime. On Feb. 23, 1910, the trial took place at the Assizes before Justice Darling, with Ryland Adkins and Moresby White prosecuting and Mr. Friedman defending Violet Charlesworth. Mr. H.

Maddocks defended her mother. Darling sentenced each to five years of penal servitude after a jury found the pair Guilty. The sentence caused Mrs. Charlesworth to collapse and her daughter to turn pale, likely the reason Darling reduced their sentences two days later to three years of penal servitude.

REF.: Baker, *Lord Darling's Famous Cases; CBA.*

"Charlie Chopoff" Slayings, 1972, U.S., (unsolv.) mur. In 1972, Four young boys were found dead in Manhattan, strangled and stabbed to death. The killer then hacked off their limbs and left them in alleys throughout the city. Police never found the killer, but nicknamed him "Charlie Chopoff."

REF.: *CBA;* Nash, *Open Files.*

Charlton, Porter, b.1889, Italy, mur. Porter Charlton was the son of Paul Charlton, who served as judge of the territorial court of Puerto Rico. A shy, withdrawn type who suffered from epileptic seizures, Charlton married a divorced woman named Mary Crittenden Scott Castle, the wealthy daughter of a San Francisco coal merchant who was also a minor star of the theater. The fiery Mrs. Castle was considerably older than Porter Charlton, and from the very beginning of their marriage there were quarrels and angry outbursts between them.

On June 10, 1910, a cable reached the U.S. with the news that Charlton had bludgeoned his wife to death with a crowbar while on a European tour, and the remains were found floating in a trunk on Lake Como, near the village of Moltrasio, Italy. The 21-year-old husband readily confessed to the crime, explaining that Mary's uncontrollable temper finally got the best of him. He seized a wooden mallet and had struck her over the head repeatedly. Two weeks later, police detectives arrested Charlton in Hoboken, N.J., as he stepped off the German liner and onto U.S. shores. He was taken to the Hudson County Jail in Jersey City, where he languished for the next three years, while Italian authorities and the U.S. State Department attempted to resolve the delicate matter of extradition.

The case went before the U.S. Supreme Court which ruled that Charlton had to be returned to Italy to stand trial. In August 1913, the prisoner was transported to the jail at Como, Italy, but given the numerous court delays, and the outbreak of WWI, Charlton did not go to trial until Oct. 18, 1915, when he was found Guilty of murder and was sentenced to six years and eight months imprisonment. Given his epileptic conditions, and some lingering doubts about his sanity, Charlton served just twenty-nine days before earning a final release from custody.

REF.: *CBA;* Duke, *Celebrated Criminal Cases of America;* Pearle, *Unsolved Murder Mysteries.*

Charlton Street Gang, prom. 1860s, U.S., rob.-kid. The Charlton Streeters, a gang of latter-day pirates active on the West Side of New York during the Civil War, operated on the Hudson River from Manhattan north to Poughkeepsie. They took their inspiration from the river pirates on the other side of Manhattan who plundered the small vessels crossing the East River.

In 1869, Sadie the Goat, leader of the gang, instituted a new and more ambitious policy for its members. Sadie convinced them to steal a real sailing sloop, which would fly the skull-and-crossbones. Thus equipped, the Charlton Street Gang sailed upriver where they invaded the elegant riverside mansions, sometimes holding the occupants for ransom for days on end. Sadie was a stern, utterly ruthless captain. The contemporary press reported that she made her prisoners walk the plank.

Outraged New Yorkers organized vigilante posses to deal with the pirates. After pitched gun battles claimed a number of casualties, the more timid members of the gang became disheartened. The Charlton Streeters disbanded despite recriminations from Sadie the Goat.

REF.: Asbury, *The Gangs of New York; CBA;* Haskins, *Street Gangs.*

Charmoy, Jacques-Bonaventure Collet de, prom. 1790s-1810s, Fr., execut. Following the Revolution of 1789, France was in dire need of executioners and went as far as to hire amateurs—those whose families had not undertaken the profession and those who had no training in the field. Jacques-Bonaventure Collet de

Charmoy worked as the leader of a church choir prior to the Revolution, but he gladly offered his services to operate the guillotine at La Rochelle. The residents of that town were soon repelled by his enthusiasm for his work.

In a letter to the minister of justice, Charmoy pointed out how happy he was to execute criminals, but that he would also like his name added to the list of professional executioners. Charmoy continued his supplications but to no avail. He was informed that since he had not held his post prior to June 13, 1793, he was not eligible to be a pensioned executioner.

Not only was he shunned by his employers, but he was forced to leave La Rochelle because of his lust for removing offenders' heads. He went to live with the executioner of Tours, Louis-Charles-Martin Sanson, whose brother had beheaded King Louis XVI. He became executioner at Amiens, but eventually agreed to let Constant Vermeille take his place in exchange for a lifetime annuity of 1,200 francs, an amount he never received.

REF.: *CBA;* Lenotre, *The Guillotine and Its Servants.*

Charnock, Robert (Robert Chernick), c.1663-96, Brit., consp.-assass. Member of the Catholic clergy, he conspired with Sir Robert Barclay to murder King William III. In what became known as Barclay's Plot, the conspirators were arrested in 1696 and hanged. See: **William III.** REF.: *CBA.*

Charrier, Jacques Mecislas, d.1922, Fr., rob.-mur. "I am a desperate enemy of society and my hatred will only finish with my life. I defy you, gentlemen of the jury, to take my head." That was Jacques Charrier's statement in his own defense when he was tried for the murder of a military officer. The jury found him Guilty and sent him to the guillotine. Although Charrier and his two companions thought of themselves as anarchists, it was probably pure greed that made them board the night train from Paris to Lyons on July 23, 1922. As the passengers lay sleeping, the three men moved through the train, waking the sleepers one by one with guns at their heads, and demanding their valuables. In one compartment, Captain Morel acquiesced to the demand, but Lieutenant Carabelli objected and received a bullet in the head for his effort. The three pulled the brake and leaped from the train when it slowed, disappearing into the night.

The police followed the group through several towns, but lost them as they neared Paris. However, several days later, Charrier, a former medical student, was heard boasting about their deed in a tavern. Word of the boasting reached the Paris police. Charrier had a previous record of convictions for robbery, but he readily identified his companions for the police as Thomas and Bertrand, whom he had met when he was in jail in Grenoble. He also told them that he was scheduled to meet the two men in a cafe at midnight on July 30. When the police met them instead, they drew their guns. The two robbers were killed instantly and one policeman died later. Only Charrier was left to carry the burden for the three of them, although he claimed that he had only stood lookout during the train robbery. Throughout his trial, he attempted to keep up the superior image that his dandyish clothing conveyed. But the defiance was gone when he went to the guillotine on Aug. 22, 1922.

REF.: *CBA;* Gribble, *Famous Manhunts;* Jacobs, *Pageant of Murder;* Wilson, *Encyclopedia of Murder.*

Charrière, Henri-Antoine (AKA: Papillon), 1907-73, Fr., pris. esc.-mur. On the morning of Mar. 26, 1930, 24-year-old Roland Legrand was shot dead on the Boulevard de Clichy in Montmartre, Paris. Legrand was a pork-butcher by trade, who doubled as a pimp. His assailant was Henri Charrière, commonly known as Papillon, because of a bow tie he always wore and a butterfly tattooed on his chest.

Papillon lived off the earnings of Georgette Fourel, a 19-year-old prostitute he lived with in Montmartre. He supplemented his income by receiving and selling stolen goods, and trafficking in drugs. Legrand discussed Charrière's underworld activities with the police, and so was killed. George S. Goldstein identified Papillon as the murderer. The killer was tried in October, and on the twenty-eighth was sentenced to penal servitude for life.

On Dec. 22, 1931, he married Georgette Fourel as part of a strategy to avoid deportment to French Guiana. But the plan failed. Authorities detained him for a year in prison in Caen, then shipped him to Cayenne.

He spent three years in the penitentiary there before he escaped. He hid in a leper colony, then made his way by boat to Venezuela, where he lived among the natives near Maracaibo Bay. When French authorities recaptured Papillon, they sent him to the notorious and supposedly inescapable penal colony on Devil's Island and kept him in solitary confinement for two years. On his eighth attempt, Papillon escaped from Devil's Island and paddled his raft made of dried coconuts through shark-infested waters to Venezuela. He settled there, married, and became a restaurateur and Venezuelan citizen.

In 1969, 62-year-old Charrière published *Papillon,* his memoir of his adventures and escapes. The book became a best-seller, and in 1973 the movie of the same title premiered, starring Steve McQueen as Papillon.

REF.: *CBA;* Heppenstall, *Bluebeard and After.*

Charteris, Francis, d.c.1732, Brit., gamb.-fraud-asslt. Born into a titled Scottish family, young Francis Charteris was accustomed to its accompanying privileges and comforts.

At an early age he decided upon a military career and served in the footguards under the Duke of Marlborough. His combat record indistinguishable from that of any other soldier, but far from the line of fire, in the gambling tents, Charteris excelled. After taking officers' money in rigged games of chance, he would advance loans to them at a usurious rate, sometimes as much as 100 percent, so they would stay at the table a bit longer.

When the Earl of Orkney heard that so many fine young soldiers were being financially ruined by Charteris, he placed him under house-arrest and had him court-martialed. The trial was conducted by a panel of Scottish and English officers who found him Guilty of numerous offenses. He was thrown out of the army, and ordered to make proper restitution to the swindled officers.

This disgrace did not discourage Charteris from pursuing a career as a card sharp. His infamy spread from Scotland to London, where the Duke of Queensbury, reeling from the fact that his wife the Duchess lost £3,000 to Charteris, introduced a bill in Parliament to prohibit gambling above a certain fixed sum.

With his earnings Charteris pursued a self-indulgent lifestyle, purchasing sizeable London estates and lending money to business people at exorbitant rates. His appetite for pretty young women was attended to by special agents who scoured the countryside in search of "servants" to work in his great houses. One day an innocent maiden, Ann Bond, was sent to Charteris, who used the alias Colonel Harvey. He offered her a purse of gold and a guaranteed income if she submitted to his advances. When she refused, he horsewhipped her, threatened to murder her, and turned her out onto the streets.

The matter came to the attention of a grand jury who committed Charteris to Newgate. His social position and wealth dictated better accommodations than a musty jail cell, so instead he received *lodging,* and was attended by foot servants until he secured bail through his father-in-law, Sir Alexander Swinton of Scotland.

When the case came before the justices of the Old Bailey on Feb. 25, 1730, Charteris was found Guilty. Through the intervention of the king he was granted a royal pardon in consideration of a large annuity granted the plaintiff. "Colonel" Charteris continued his profligate existence for two more years before venereal disease finally killed him.

REF.: *CBA;* Hunt, *A Dictionary of Rogues;* Mitchell, *Newgate Calendar.*

Chartists, The, prom. 1838-48, Brit., riot. The Chartist movement began in 1838 and reached its full momentum a decade later when the European continent was engulfed in revolution. The birth of the movement resulted from the failure of the Reform Bill of 1832 to address the social and economic ills of England, particularly the disenfranchised lower classes. A people's

"charter" was drawn up in 1838 calling for universal suffrage, annual parliaments, and an end to the long standing rule that only men of property could be elected to public office.

The principal spokesmen of the Chartists were Feargus O'Connor and Charles Cochrane, two fiery political leaders whose oratorical skills whipped their listeners into a frenzy. On Mar. 6, 1848, the Chartists held a massive open air rally in Trafalgar Square attended by 10,000 excited and unruly supporters in violation of the statutes that forbade political assembly within a mile of Westminster Hall.

The Chartists planned a larger meeting for Apr. 10 at Kennington Common, in which a petition containing five million signatures was to be presented to the Houses of Parliament. O'Connor predicted that 500,000 supporters would show up for the event, and the Metropolitan Police swore in 170,000 special constables to handle the crowd. The actual turnout was disappointing, and the less than 50,000 people who showed up were greatly disappointed when O'Connor and the other Chartist leaders acquiesced to police threats and led a peaceable march to the House of Commons where the petition was duly delivered. It was discovered that many of the signatures on the petition were duplicates or false. By August, the movement began to wane when the government arrested Cochrane and others for illegal assembly, and confiscated an arsenal of weapons found at the Angel Tavern in Blackfriars.

REF.: *CBA;* Thomson, *The Story of Scotland Yard.*

Chartrand, Richard, d.1968, U.S., (unsolv.) mur. The underworld generally conducts its executions in such a way that everyone knows that one took place but not who did it. The death of Richard Chartrand, the Las Vegas-area gambling chieftain, was no exception. On Aug. 27, 1968, Chartrand left his Lake Tahoe, Nev., home and stepped into his new Cadillac. He turned the ignition key, and the car blew up, Chartrand along with it.

REF.: *CBA;* Nash, *Almanac of World Crime.*

Chase, Charles, d.1867, U.S., mur. Charles Chase was a professional criminal who had committed many major crimes over several years. He attacked and murdered Mrs. Elizabeth McDonald at Brockwayville, Pa., after she had rebuffed him. He was seen near the murder site and convicted on circumstantial evidence, going to his execution at Brookville, Pa., in 1867 after admitting to many robberies, burglaries, and other crimies. He stubbornly refused, however, to admit his guilt in murdering Mrs. McDonald, despite the claims made later in publications concerned with his crimes.

REF.: *CBA; Life and Confession of Charles Chase.*

Chase, Harrie, 1889-1969, U.S., jur. State's attorney of Windham County, Vt., in 1919. President Calvin Coolidge appointed him judge of the U.S. Court of Appeals, the second circuit in 1929. REF.: *CBA.*

Chase, John Paul, prom. 1934, U.S., rob.-mur. One of Baby Face Nelson's mob, John Paul Chase began as a bootlegger in San Francisco. He fell from the top echelon in crime because scientists were learning how glass splinters when a bullet goes through it.

On Apr. 22, 1934, Chase and Nelson, whose real name was Lester Joseph Gillis, killed a former government agent named Baum. The two were on the Most Wanted list when the FBI learned that they had abandoned their pickup truck on the fringes of Chicago, stolen a car, and headed for Wisconsin. FBI agent Samuel P. Cowley called

1930s gangster John Paul Chase.

in other agents, three of whom spotted a car that they thought might be the stolen vehicle. Nelson and Chase realized they were heading into a trap and began to shoot. Nelson maneuvered and came up behind the agents, so that the lawmen had to fire out their back window into the front window of the killers' car. However, when Nelson's car died, the crooks leaped from it and began firing machine guns. Nelson and two agents, including Cowley, died in the melee, and Chase was captured in California.

Brought to trial for the murders of the agents, Chase claimed that the agents had fired out of the blue when they came up behind Chase and Nelson, and that they had fired only in self-defense. But FBI scientists had been studying shattered glass, and they were able to prove to the satisfaction of a jury that the bullet holes in the windshield of the outlaws' car could only have come from inside the car, not from outside, and that the holes could only have been made with the criminals' weapon. A surprised Chase was found Guilty and sentenced to life in prison. REF.: Block, *Science Vs. Crime; CBA;* Edge, *Run the Cat Roads;* Whitehead, *The F.B.I. Story.*

Chase, Richard Trenton, 1950-80, U.S., mur. A man who was once found with the blood of a cow covering his naked body confessed during his trial that he had drunk the blood of one of his six murder victims.

Richard Trenton Chase admitted not only to drinking blood, but also to killing six people, five by shooting them to death and then butchering them. The killing rampage occurred between Jan. 23 and 27, 1978, and Chase's five-month trial began in January 1979. It was in Palo Alto, Calif. after the venue had to be changed from Sacramento because of the widespread publicity. Farris Salamy, the public defender representing Chase, pleaded that Chase was not guilty by reason of insanity, but the jury returned a verdict of Guilty on May 8, 1979, after deliberating for six hours over two days. He was sentenced to death in the gas chamber after it was determined by the jury that Chase was not insane. REF.: *CBA.*

Chase, Salmon Portland, 1808-73, U.S., jur. Noted for his defense of fugitive slaves facing extradition back to the south. For his abolitionist sentiments he was nicknamed Attorney General for Runaway Negroes. He was elected to the U.S. Senate as a Democrat in 1849, but switched parties three years later due to his opposition to slavery. He was appointed chief justice of the U.S. Supreme Court in 1864, replacing Roger Taney. In 1868 he presided over the impeachment trial of President Andrew Johnson. REF.: *CBA.*

Chase, Samuel (AKA: Bacon Face), 1741-1811, U.S., jur. Associate Supreme Court justice impeached in 1804 for partisan conduct and tactics on behalf of the conservative Federalist party. The procedure was instigated by President Thomas Jefferson whose political support in the media was eroded by Chase. Though acquitted in 1805, it cast a shadow on some of his notable achievments, which included service in the Continental Congress from 1774-78, 1784-85. He was one of the signers of the Declaration of Independence, and in 1796 President George Washington appointed him to the High Court. He brought about his own political demise in a speech given in 1803 when he accused the Democrats of mobocracy. But when there was no evidence of job malfeasance to justify removal, he was acquitted. REF.: *CBA.*

Chastelard, Pierre de Boscosel de, 1540-64, Fr., courtier. Put to death because of his love for Mary, Queen of Scots. He followed her to back to Scotland after the death of her husband Francis II of France in 1561. His indiscreet behavior resulted in a house arrest, and he was executed in Edinburgh. REF.: *CBA.*

Chateaubriant, Françoise de, prom. 16th Cent., Fr., (unsolv.) mur. Françoise de Chateaubriant was married at the age of eleven to Jean Laval, and she gave birth to a girl a year later. Famed for her growing beauty, she attracted the attention of the king of France, Francis I, who sought to make her his mistress. Laval refused the king's first invitation to pay him court, but he did respond to the second invitation by himself. Francis was disappointed that the beautiful Chateaubriant did not join him, so he forced Laval to write a letter requesting her presence. Laval wrote, but his wife refused, just as Laval had told her to do unless

the letter was accompanied by a ring identical to the one she wore. The king learned of Laval's trick to keep Chateaubriant from his clutches and had Laval's valet steal the ring and copy it. A second letter was sent to Chateaubriant along with the phony ring. She answered Francis' request and inevitably became his mistress. Upon the king's death in 1547, Chateaubriant returned home to Brittany, only to be murdered shortly afterward. Perhaps Laval could not forgive her for her infidelity.
REF.: Bullough, *Illustrated History of Prostitution; CBA.*

Châteauneuf, prom. 16th Cent., Fr., duel. The 80-year-old Lachesnaye was the guardian of young Châteauneuf. A dispute over a lawsuit concerning Châteauneuf's property arose between them and they agreed to duel at the Isle de Louviers. When they met on the assigned day before a crowd of onlookers, Châteauneuf confronted his guardian with reports that he had spoken disrespectfully of him. Lachesnaye denied the rumors. Châteauneuf took him at his word and suggested they forget the duel. But Lachesnaye insisted that it go on so as not to disappoint the audience. Both men were armed with swords and daggers, but Châteauneuf also wore body armor. When Lachesnaye attacked his opponent's face, he left himself undefended. Châteauneuf easily ran his sword through his guardian, killing him.
REF.: *CBA;* Melville, *Famous Duels and Assassinations.*

Châtel, Jean, c.1575-94, Fr., consp.-attempt. assass. Attempted to kill King Henry IV of France in 1594, believing his actions were divinely guided by the Jesuits. As a consequence the Jesuit order was banished from the country. REF.: *CBA.*

Chatfield, Andrew Gould, 1810-75, U.S., jur. District attorney for Steuben County, N.Y., from 1845-46. He was appointed to serve on the bench of the territorial court of Minnesota by President Franklin Pierce in 1853. REF.: *CBA.*

Chatterton, Thomas, 1752-70, Brit., forg.-suic. Thomas Chatterton entered the world of literary forgery with a poetic work entitled "Elinoure and Juga." He was eleven at the time. Chatterton's greatest accomplishment was the alleged work of Thomas Rowley, a priest during the reign of King Henry II at St. John's Church, a work which he "discovered" in 1768 at the Church of St. Mary Redcliffe in Bristol, England.

Even at such a young age, Chatterton was able to convince a number of people of the authenticity of the manuscript, *A Description of the Fryars Passing Over the Old Bridge.* A surgeon named **Thomas Chatterton, prodigy forger.** William Barrett in his *History of the Antiquities of the City of Bristol* included Chatterton's works by Rowley and even used others as source material. Antiquarian Society president and Exeter dean Dr. Milles believed the Rowley poems to be genuine, as did the president of Oxford's St. John's College, Dr. Fry. The brilliant youth was so encouraged by his remarkable success that he gave Horace Walpole some manuscripts to include in Walpole's work, *Anecdotes of Painting in England.* Walpole was not easily fooled, however, and the forgery was soon found out. As a result, Chatterton killed himself by taking arsenic.

After his death, Chatterton's fame increased as many poets came to believe that he was a genius. Percy Bysshe Shelley honored Chatterton in his poem "Adonais," and John Keats dedicated his poem "Endymion" to the youth's memory. Also in Chatterton's memory is the inscription, taken from his will, on a monument in the churchyard at Redcliffe: "Reader! judge not! If thou art a Christian, believe that he shall be judged by a Superior Power. To that Power only is he now answerable."
REF.: *CBA;* MacDougall, *Hoaxes.*

Chaucer, Geoffrey, c.1340-1400, Brit., kid.-rob. A poet, while serving the crown during the Hundred Years War, he was captured by the French in 1359 and held for ransom. Chaucer lapsed into alternating periods of poverty, and was twice robbed of his money by notorious English highwaymen in 1390. Authored *The Canterbury Tales*. REF.: *CBA*.

Chaumette, Pierre-Gaspard, 1763-94, Fr., consp. Radical leader of the Paris Commune of 1793, Chaumette opposed the church, favoring the adoption of a revolutionary state religion known as the Cult of Reason. His radical stance alienated him from the more moderate Jacobin faction led by Robespierre. Chaumette was executed on the guillotine for crimes against the state. REF.: *CBA*.

Chauncey, Dr. Henry, prom. 1839, U.S., mur. Dr. Henry Chauncey, assisted by Dr. William Armstrong and William Nixon, the lover of Eliza Sowers, attempted an abortion on Sowers in Philadelphia but botched the operation, with Sowers and her child dying in the process. All three men were charged with murder and convicted of second-degree murder, receiving stiff prison sentences.

REF.: *CBA; The Life of Elizabeth Sowers*.

Chauveau-Lagarde, Claude François, 1756-1841, Fr., lawyer. Appeared as defense counsel for Charlotte Corday, Marie Antoinette, and Jacques-Pierre de Warville before the Revolutionary Tribunal. Jailed during the Reign of Terror, he was later named counselor to the Court of Cassation in 1828. REF.: *CBA*.

Chavez, Judy, prom. 1970s, U.S., pros. Cashing in on the popularity of such sex scandal ladies as Fanne Foxe and Elizabeth Ray during the late 1970s, Judy Chavez, identified as a Washington, D.C., prostitute who specialized in S&M treatments (whips, leather sex devices, and handcuffs, according to one report), publicly announced that the CIA was one of her best customers. Chavez claimed that CIA officials recruited her to sexually service Russian defector Arkady Shevchenko. She insisted that she was so persuasive in her "lovemaking" that the defector fell in love with her. Chavez also claimed in 1978 that her sexual favors were the most expensive in the nation's capital and that the CIA had paid her as much as $5,000 a month for her services to Shevchenko. REF.: *CBA*.

Cheatham, Weldon J., prom. 1929, Case of, U.S., mansl. During Prohibition in the U.S., it was perfectly legal for a police officer to shoot a felon if he attempted an escape. However, District Attorney B. Loyal O'Connell became suspicious when the officers who had shot Arthur Gordon to death in 1929 failed to write a report.

Weldon J. Cheatham and Francis L. Coveney failed to report that Gordon had been killed—the sixth shooting, though the first death, in the past ten days—when Cheatham tripped and accidentally discharged his revolver. A charge of second-degree manslaughter was filed, but no indictment was returned by the grand jury and the charge was dismissed. One year later, the two officers were convicted in a conspiracy and bribery scandal. REF.: *CBA*.

Cheever, Mary, c.1904-49, U.S., (unsolv.) mur. On returning from a Parent-Teacher Association meeting in March 1949, Mary Cheever was attacked in the alley outside her Gary, Ind., apartment by a purse snatcher who bludgeoned her over the head with a pistol and then shot her in the back. The 45-year-old teacher of French and Spanish at Lew Wallace High School died en route to the hospital ten minutes later.

Cheever's murderer was not apprehended, but her death, along with seven other killings in Gary since the first of the year, led a group of 1,500 women to march on a city council meeting to protest the city's lack of police protection and rampant crime. Promises were made by Mayor Eugene Swartz, but he had little success in curbing the violence. REF.: *CBA*.

Cheka, 1919-22, U.S.S.R., secret pol. The Cheka was the first secret police force employed by the Soviets in Russia following the Russian Revolution of 1917. The name Cheka was formed from the first letters of the first two words of its official title, the

Extraordinary Commission for Combating Counter-Revolution, Sabotage and Criminal Offenses by Officials. During its brief existence, the Cheka became as feared by the Russian populace as had its predecessor under the czars, the Okhrana. Mostly this secret police force practiced primitive torture on suspects and executed suspected royalists and white Russians out of hand, particularly during the Russian Civil War (1920-22). In 1922 the Cheka was reformed as the GPU. See: **GPU; NKVD; MVD; Okhrana**. REF.: *CBA*.

Cheke, Sir John, 1514-57, Brit., her. Seized and jailed by Queen Mary from 1553-54 for serving as the secretary of state to Lady Jane Grey. Cheke was again arrested in Belgium in 1556. Returned to England, he was held captive in the Tower of London, and brought before Cardinal Reginald Pole to publicly recant his Protestant views and join the Roman Catholic church. REF.: *CBA*.

Chekkal, Ali, c.1896-1957, Fr., assass. As he was walking toward his car following a championship soccer match at France's Colombes Stadium in the spring of 1957, 60-year-old Ali Chekkal was shot and killed by Mohammad Ben Sadok. Ali had once been Algerian National Assembly vice president and was an outspoken supporter of France in North Africa. Although Ben Sadok admitted that the killing was politically motivated, he stated that he acted on his own, and in his defense he said, "I didn't have anything against him personally...but I was against his political actions. I thought in suppressing him I would shorten the war in Algeria."

People from all walks of life came to Ben Sadok's defense, including one of his favorite authors, Jean-Paul Sartre. Sartre pleaded with the court not to condemn the assassin for his actions, arguing that there was an important difference between terrorism and political crimes. "Terrorism practiced to inspire fear, despises human life. The political killer demonstrates his respect for human life when he seeks, by killing, to avoid vast slaughter. Remember Charlotte Corday. All the French are proud of what she did," said Sartre. Corday had stabbed to death French revolutionary Jean Paul Marat while he was taking a bath on July 13, 1793.

With Ali's checkered history in Algeria—one witness claimed Ali had won a rigged election in that country—and eloquent speeches made by the defense, the prosecution had a difficult time trying to convince the jury that the death penalty should be invoked, especially when the prosecutor, Charles Dubost, who had prosecuted war criminals during the Nürnberg trials, and vowed never again to ask for the death penalty, now sought it. In December 1957, after fifty minutes of deliberation, the jury decided against capital punishment and sentenced Ben Sadok to life in prison with hard labor. REF.: *CBA*.

Chelmsford Witches, prom. 16th-17th Cent., Brit., witchcraft. A series of mass witchcraft trials were held at Chelmsford, Essex, in the sixteenth and seventeenth centuries, with many men and women hanged for allegedly bewitching people to death. Although children had to be at least fourteen to testify in other types of trials, little children were encouraged to tell what they had supposedly witnessed.

Three women were tried for witchcraft on July 26 and 27, 1566, before Reverend Thomas Cole, Sir John Fortescue, Sir Gilbert Gerard, John Southcote, and the attorney general. Elizabeth Francis, the first person tried, was found Guilty of bewitching the infant daughter of William Auger and other offenses and was sentenced to one year in prison. Her conviction for other crimes was the result of her confession in which she stated that her grandmother, Mother Eve of Hatfield Peverell, had given her a white-spotted cat named Sathan, who would apparently grant any wish she desired as long as she gave it a drop of blood. On one occasion, Francis confessed, the cat told her to sleep with Andrew Byles, which would make her desire to be Byles' wife come true. When Byles refused to marry her, she asked Sathan to kill him. Then later she asked the cat to kill the baby she was going to have by Byles. Both Byles and the baby died. Sathan again is alleged to have helped her obtain a spouse, Mr. Francis, and again to kill her child, though Francis' husband was spared the fate that Byles met when she confessed that she willed Sathan to lame the man.

The two other women tried with Francis in 1566 were 63-year-old Mrs. Agnes Waterhouse and her daughter, 18-year-old Joan Waterhouse. Agnes Waterhouse, a neighbor of Francis', allegedly borrowed Sathan the cat from Francis to do her own witchcraft. During her trial for the bewitching murder of William Fynee on Nov. 1, 1565, she confessed to crimes against livestock, saying her prayers in Latin, and attempted murder, all of which led to her conviction on July 27, 1566, and her execution by hanging on July 29. Young Joan, who was charged with bewitching 12-year-old Agnes Brown, was found Not Guilty when it was shown that her accuser had given inaccurate testimony. Agnes had charged that Joan had sent Sathan, disguised as a black dog, to kill her with a knife, one of a size that Joan did not own.

Thirteen years after the first great witch trial at Chelmsford, another was held. Elizabeth Francis was again tried for bewitching Alice Poole to death and was convicted on Nov. 1, 1578. This time she was sentenced to be hanged. Between the two trials, Francis had been found Guilty of causing Mary Cocke to become sick and was sentenced to a year's imprisonment and to be placed in the pillory four times. Also convicted and hanged along with Francis in 1579 were Alice Nokes and Ellen Smith, whose mother had met the same fate in 1574—for bewitching a child to death.

The third mass trial at Chelmsford, excluding the trial of the St. Osyth Witches held in Chelmsford in 1582, took place in 1589. At this trial, one man and nine women were tried. Four were found Guilty of bewitching others to death and hanged. Judges at the trial commended two young boys for helping to convict their unwed mother, Avice Cony, and their grandmother, Joan Cony. She, Joan Prentice, and Joan Upney were all hanged within two hours after pronouncement of their sentence. Each confessed to witchcraft on the scaffold.

At the fourth major Chelmsford witch trial in 1645 nineteen of thirty-two women charged with witchcraft were hanged, making this session the worst such trial of the century. See: **St. Osyth Witches.**

REF.: Beigel, *The Examination and Confession of Certain Witches at Chelmsford; CBA; A Detection of Damnable Drifts Practiced by Three Witches Arraigned at Chelmsford;* Ewen, *Witchcraft and Demonianism;* ____, *Witch Hunting and Witch Trials;* Hole, *A Mirror of Witchcraft;* Notestein, *History of Witchcraft in England from 1558 to 1718;* Robbins, *The Encyclopedia of Witchcraft and Demonology;* Smith, *Collections of Rare and Curious Tracts Relating to Witchcraft;* Summers, *The Geography of Witchcraft;* Williams, *Witchcraft;* Wilson, *Witches.*

Chen, Eugene (Ch'en Yu-jen), 1878-1944, China, libel. During WWI Chen was imprisoned for publishing inflammatory articles in the Peking *Gazette* against the Japanese who occupied German-leased territory in the Shantung provence. REF.: *CBA.*

Chenault, Marcus Wayne (AKA: Servant Jacob), c.1951- , U.S., mur. Just over six years after his son, Dr. Martin Luther King, Jr., was shot to death outside a Memphis, Tenn., motel, the Rev. Martin Luther King, Sr. watched, along with 400 others, as his wife, 69-year-old Alberta Williams King, was shot and killed at Ebenezer Baptist Church in Atlanta, Ga., by Marcus Wayne Chenault.

Chenault, a 23-year-old black Ohio State University dropout from Columbus, Ohio,, had traveled by Greyhound bus from Dayton, Ohio, to shoot Reverend Martin Luther King, Sr. on June 30, 1974. Instead, Chenault shot Mrs. King, daughter of the church's founder Reverend A.D. Williams, in the face as she was playing the church organ. He then shot in the neck 69-year-old deacon Edward Boykin, who died later at Grady Hospital, and wounded 65-year-old Mrs. Jimmy Mitchell. The gunman yelled, "I'm taking over, I'm taking over," before church members managed to wrestle Chenault to the floor. He had fired all the bullets in the two handguns he carried. With the shooting spree ended, it was learned that Chenault's intended victim was only the

second target on a list of ten assassinations he had hoped to commit.

In March 1973, Chenault met 70-year-old Hananiah E. Israel, who preached that only by killing all black ministers could black people be free. A month later, Chenault told the Reverend Billy Robinson that he planned to kill the Reverend Howard B. Washington in Akron, but he did not act on the threat. Two weeks prior to his rampage in Atlanta, Chenault had planned to kill the Reverend Jesse L. Jackson, whom investigators learned was number one on the gunman's hit list. A bus ticket to Chicago, where Jackson lives, was found in Chenault's apartment with the message, "Father's Day massacre canceled," written on it. Chenault, who called himself "Servant Jacob," informed the police that he was on a mission from his god to kill the Reverend King. These statements and the killer's actions led police to investigate Chenault's possible connection with the shooting deaths of Dayton, Ohio, ministers 56-year-old William Wright on May 12, 1974, and 29-year-old Eugene Johnson, Sr., on June 3, 1974. His lawyer, Randy Bacote, attempted to enter a plea of no contest, but Judge E.T. Brock entered Not Guilty pleas and Chenault stood trial.

At Chenault's trial, the defense tried to prove that the killer was insane at the time of the shooting, a contention that prosecutor Lewis Slaton was able to disprove by the testimony of two psychiatrists who stated that Chenault knew the difference between right and wrong. On Sept. 12, 1974, the jury in the court of Judge Luther Alverson took one hour and fifteen minutes to decide that Chenault was Guilty and sentence him to die in the electric chair. Upon hearing the jury's recommendation for capital punishment, Chenault blew kisses to the jurors and pointed his finger like a gun at Alverson and Slaton. REF.: *CBA.*

Cheney, Charles Edward, 1836-1916, U.S., her. Convicted of religious heresy and deposed in 1869, but the proceedings were nullified in 1874. Cheney went on to organize the Reformed Episcopal church. REF.: *CBA.*

Cheng Chih-lung, 1604-61, China, pir. Cleared the coastal waters of pirates and Dutch privateers on behalf of the Ming dynasty in 1628. After Peking fell to the Manchu tribes in 1644, he set up Chu Yü-chien the prince of T'ang as the pretender to the Ming throne in the Fukien provence. He later became a high ranking government official in the Chi'ing government of Manchus 1646. Cheng was seized, imprisoned, and executed by his son Cheng Ch'eng-kung. REF.: *CBA.*

Chénier, André Marie de, 1762-94, Fr., consp. Though in sympathy with the aims of the revolution, Chénier's articles denouncing the excesses of the Reign of Terror so enraged Robespierre that he was seized and executed at the guillotine. REF.: *CBA.*

Chennell, George, Jr., and **Chalcraft, J.,** d.1818, Brit., mur. On the night of Nov. 10, 1817, George Chennell, Jr., accompanied by J. Chalcraft, entered his father's home in Godalming and bashed him over the head with the man's own shoemaker's hammer before slitting his throat, almost severing his head. The two killers then went back downstairs and slit the throat of the housekeeper, Mrs. Wilson, who was mending the shirt of her killer at the time.

Almost ten months later, on Aug. 12, 1818, the trial of Chennell and Chalcraft took place. A verdict of Guilty was returned by the jury that same day, the damning piece of evidence being the bloodstained money found in the room where Chennell lived. A crowd of about 20,000 people showed up to watch hangman Jack Ketch perform his duty, which turned out to be Godalming's last public hanging.

REF.: Butler, *Murderers' England; CBA.*

Chenowith, Francis A., 1819-99, U.S., jur. Prosecuting attorney of the Olympia, Wash. Territorial Government in 1853, he was nominated to fill a vacancy in the territorial court of Washington by President Franklin Pierce in August 1854. REF.: *CBA.*

Chên Tu-hsiu (Ch'en Ch'ien-sheng, AKA: Shih-an, Chung-fu, Chung-tzu), 1879-1942, China, consp. Founder of the Chinese Communist Party, Chên was expelled from the central committee in 1928, tried, convicted, imprisoned, and later exiled. REF.: *CBA*.

Chernobyl, See: Bryukhanov, Viktor.

Chernozamsky, Vlada, See: Alexander I (Karageorgevic).

Chernyshevski, Nikolai Gavrilovich, c.1828-89, Rus., rebel. Led the radical dissidents against the czarist government. He was arrested in 1862 and exiled to Siberia for a period of twenty-four years where he authored a seminal account of the revolutionary movement, *What Is To Be Done?* REF.: *CBA*.

Cherokee Bill, See: Goldsby, Crawford.

Cherrill, Fred, 1892-1964, Brit., law enfor. off. Recognized as one of the foremost experts in fingerprint science, Fred Cherrill joined the London Metropolitan Police Department shortly before the end of WWI. In 1920, he was assigned to the fingerprint division, during the next fifteen years, he greatly expanded the technique, and collaborated with Superintendent Battley in founding the single fingerprint system. He described his research in a book titled *The Fingerprint System at Scotland Yard.* After his retirement, he published his memoir, *Cherrill of the Yard.* Cherrill died on Dec. 23, 1964. REF.: *CBA*.

Cherry, Noah, prom. 1878, U.S., mur. Noah Cherry, Harris Atkinson, and Robert Thompson, all black, invaded the rural home of James Worley and his wife, near Goldsboro, N.C., robbing them, and then, almost as an afterthought, killing the couple with an ax after tying them up. They were picked up a short time later when they appeared in town, spending money freely. The blood of their victims still coated their shirts and pants. At their brief trial, the accused men insisted that the stains were from oak trees they had been chopping, but local experts testified that oak does not stain in the month of February, the time of the murders. All three men were hanged.

REF.: *CBA; The Murder of the Worley Family in Wayne County, North Carolina.*

Cherry Hill Gang, prom. 1890-99, U.S., org. crime. In the 1890s, a gang of New York thieves went about their business in evening dress. Armed with metal-weighted walking sticks, members of the Cherry Hill Gang robbed and assaulted rich old gentlemen of New York. The gang inspired many imitators during their heyday.

When the Batavia Street Gang announced an elegant ball at the New Irving Hall, the Cherry Hill boys wired their acceptance and promised to show up in the latest evening wear. Intimidated, the Batavia gang robbed Segal's jewelry store on New Chambers Street of forty-four gold rings, which they sold to buy suitable attire for the evening. But when they were being custom fitted for their new suits, the police arrived to arrest the Batavia boys, who spent the evening in the Tombs while the Cherry Hill Gang enjoyed the ball.

REF.: Asbury, *The Gangs of New York; CBA;* Livingston, *The Murdered and the Missing;* Willemse, *Behind the Green Lights.*

Chesham, Sarah, d.1851, Brit., mur. Sarah Chesham's luck finally ran out. After she was tried and acquitted three times of murder by arsenic poisoning, her reputation as the professional poisoner of Clavering, England, became a reality when she killed her husband.

Two years after the deaths of two of her sons in 1845, the bodies were exhumed when a neighbor's baby died suddenly. Chesham was arrested for all three deaths. The case of the neighbor's child was dropped, however, for lack of evidence. Although arsenic was found in the Chesham boys' bodies, and she was known to have purchased arsenic in January 1845 to kill rats, no motive was ever established, and she was found Not Guilty. Her next trial proved not to have as happy an ending for Chesham.

Chesham's husband died in 1850, and an autopsy revealed that he had died from arsenic poisoning. At their home, a bag of rice was discovered to contain the poison. This time Chesham was found Guilty and sentenced to death. In March 1851, Chesham was hanged at Chelmsford.

Oddly enough, Chesham's tale does not end there. After her

death, friends removed the body to Wix, about fifty miles east of Clavering, where it mysteriously disappeared before the burial, never to be seen again. See: **Blandy, Mary; Cotton, Mary Ann; DeMelker, Daisy Louisa; Jegado, Helene; LaFarge, Marie;** and **Smith, Madeleine.**

REF.: Butler, *Murderers' England; CBA.*

Cheshire, Thomas (AKA: Old Cheese, Cheesy, Snuffy Skull-Thatcher), prom. c.1808-40, Brit., execut. Except for a brief stint as official hangman before a successor to hangman James Foxen was named, Thomas Cheshire was an assistant hangman for over thirty years, beginning in 1808. However, he did act as sole executioner at two infamous hangings.

As the assistant to Foxen from 1820 to 1829, Cheshire journeyed alone to Hertford, England, for the hanging on Jan. 9, 1824, of John Thurtell, who had brutally murdered William Weare. He also was the hangmen on Nov. 25, 1834, for William Garside and Joseph Moseley, who had shot and killed the son of their employer, Mr. Ashton. REF.: *CBA.*

Chesney, Ronald, See: Merrett, John Donald.

Chessman, Caryl (AKA: The Red Light Bandit), 1921-60, U.S., rape. A habitual criminal from an early age, Caryl Chessman was also one of the cleverest, most wily of felons, one who used his brilliant mind to educate himself with enough law to carry on a death house crusade for twelve years to save his life and, in the end, lost to the gas chamber. There was nothing redeeming about Caryl Chessman. He presented himself to the world as a martyr when, in reality, he was nothing more than a brute who committed rape, the crime for which he was executed. Had he turned his intellect to legimate pursuits, he undoubtedly would have gone far. Chessman took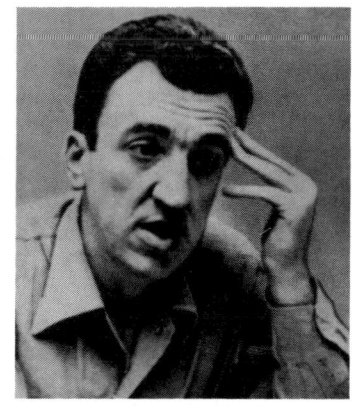

Caryl Chessman, executed in 1960.

another course—one of violence and disgusting sex crimes. At the age of sixteen, Chessman was sent to the reformatory for violent theft. He was paroled and imprisoned again, then paroled. After a number of robberies, for which he served several years in prison, he was again paroled in December 1947.

Two weeks after his parole from Folsom Prison, Chessman stole a white 1947 Ford. Affixing a red tinted screen to the car's small spotlight, Chessman was able to stop Dr. Thomas Bartle at 4:30 a.m., on Jan. 18, 1948, as the physician was driving along Pacific Coast Highway, returning from a party with Ann Plaskwitz at his side. Bartle had seen the red spotlight on his car and pulled over. Chessman, dressed in khaki pants and jacket, a hat pulled low over his eyes, demanded to see Bartle's identification. The doctor thought the lean, 30-year-old man did not look like a plainclothes police officer and demanded to see *his* identification. With that, Chessman pulled out a gun. Holding the weapon on Bartle, Chessman took all the money the doctor had, $15, and fled. Bartle went to the nearest police station and reported the robbery.

At 8 p.m. that night, Chessman struck again, finding a couple, Floyd Ballew and Elaine Bushaw, parked on a lonely road overlooking the Rose Bowl in Pasadena. He approached the car in which they sat after shining his red light on it. Ballew and his girlfriend thought he was a policeman. When Chessman was at the car, he poked a penlight into the window so that its small light shown on Ballew's face. In his other hand, he held a .45-caliber pistol. "This is a stickup," he said. "If you don't give me your money, I'll kill both of you." He took $20 from Ballew, stood about for a few minutes, as if thinking about what he might do next, then got into the stolen Ford and drove off. Ballew, suddenly bold, drove after the bandit but lost him. He reported the robbery to the police. This was the second robbery in the same day by a bandit using a red spotlight, and it caused Sheriff Eugene Biscailuz to send out a county-wide bulletin to search for the bandit who was then also called the "Lover's Lane Bandit" by the press.

Chessman found his lover's lane victims easy prey. He continued his robberies the very next night, approaching Jarnigan Lea and Mrs. Regina Johnson while the two parked near the Academy of the Sacred Heart in Altadena—a spot where they could see most of Los Angeles glimmering beneath them. The red light from Chessman's car covered Lea's car. Chessman strode over to Lea's car and said with the authority of a policeman: "I'll have to see some identification."

Lea offered identification, saying: "We were just looking at the lights." He looked up to see that the man next to the car held a gun and wore a white handkerchief over his face.

"This is a stickup," Chessman announced and grabbed Lea's wallet, which contained about $40. He ordered Johnson to hand him her purse. The married woman, who was really not on a date but merely sightseeing with her neighbor, slipped off her wedding ring and dropped it to the floor, then handed her purse to Chessman. Lea told the bandit that he could take their money but to leave the woman alone, a statement that may have acted as a suggestive thought to Chessman. He ordered Johnson to accompany him back to his own car, despite Lea's statement that Johnson had just gotten out of the hospital after suffering from infantile paralysis. Lea was ordered to face straight ahead and, to make sure that he did not drive off, Chessman took the key from the ignition.

Once Johnson, the mother of a 13-year-old child, was in the passenger seat of Chessman's car, he ordered her to take off all her clothes. He waved the automatic in her face and said that if she did not do as he told her to do, he would kill her. Johnson removed all her clothing. She told Chessman that she was menstruating. "I don't want it that way," he snorted and then ordered her to perform oral sex. The terrified woman did as she was ordered. He then told her to give him $5 from her purse which she did. Apparently, Chessman wanted to pretend that Johnson was paying *him* for the pleasure of giving him oral sex. He handed Lea's car key to the woman and sent her back to Lea's car. Lea and Johnson drove to the nearest police station and reported the robbery and rape.

On Jan. 19, 1948, Chessman found Gerald Stone and Esther Panasuk spooning in a lover's lane off Mulholland Drive. There Chessman robbed the couple of a few dollars and then drove off. Stone drove to a police station to report the "Red Light Bandit." The descriptions of the bandit varied from victim to victim. To some he was five foot, eight inches tall; others described him as six feet tall. All described him as dark, one detailing his crooked teeth. Chessman then did nothing for two days. On Jan. 22, he struck again, finding Frank Hurlburt and 17-year-old Mary Alice Meza, looking at the city's lights from a high perch off Woodrow Wilson Drive. When Chessman ordered Hurlburt to give him his money, the victim told him he was broke. "Okay," Chessman said, "I'll take the girl." Hurlburt, ordered to drive off a short distance and park, drove off down the canyon road with Chessman in pursuit. Hurlburt managed to outdistance the bandit and drove to a police station. Chessman, with the frightened girl at his side, drove to a lonely spot and tried to rape her, but when he discovered that she also was menstruating, he forced her to perform oral sex. Then he pushed the girl out onto the lonely road and drove off.

The girl returned home by 5 a.m., and by then the police were waiting for her to hear her description of the robber-rapist. The next day, Jan. 23, the LAPD sent out an all-points bulletin (APB) on the bandit. By this time, the newspapers had the details of the robbery-rapes and the horrific stories of the Red Light Bandit filled columns, shocking Los Angeles readers. Chessman, meanwhile, altered his *modus operandi* by robbing a clothier of $277 and some suits, pistol-whipping the clothier in the process so that his scalp was lacerated and later required hospital treatment. This

took place on the night of Jan. 23. The clothier told police that the bandit, accompanied by a friend, had driven off in a grey Ford or Mercury. Policemen John Reardon and Robert May spotted a car answering the description of that driven by the Red Light Bandit at the intersection of Hollywood Boulevard and Vermont Avenue.

Following the car at some distance, the officers were apparently spotted by Chessman who suddenly drove off at high speed, the police car following. Both cars screeched and roared up and down several streets until, at Sixth and Shatto, the police car caught up to the Ford and rammed it to a stop. Two men stepped out of the Ford. One, David Knowles, a 32-year-old felon, raised his hands in surrender, but Caryl Chessman ran into a back yard with May in pursuit. The policeman had to club Chessman with his revolver to force his surrender. Police, Chessman later claimed, took him to a station and handcuffed him, then took him to a locker room and mercilessly beat him, calling him a "rapist s.o.b." Chessman later insisted that confessions were beaten out of him and Knowles. Police denied the allegations.

Chessman was charged with committing no less than eighteen felonies between Jan. 3 and Jan. 23, 1948, including attempted robbery, robbery, grand theft auto, attempted rape, rape, sexual perversion, and kidnapping. On May 18, 1948, Chessman was tried before Judge Charles Fricke and convicted of seventeen counts. The conviction of "kidnapping with great bodily harm" carried with it, under what was called the "Little Lindbergh Law," a death sentence, and Judge Fricke imposed this death penalty upon Caryl Chessman. David Knowles was also convicted of the same charge and was sentenced to die in the gas chamber, along with Chessman. Knowles would later win an appeal that would commute his sentence to life in prison. This was not to be the case for Caryl Chessman. He immediately began a tenacious fight to save his life. While his lawyers filed appeal after appeal, Chessman wrote the first of four best sellers, *Cell 2445 Death Row*. It was an enormous best seller, and from its considerable royalties, Chessman financed more and more legal maneuvers to postpone, if not eliminate, his death sentence. Millions throughout the world took the unsavory Chessman as a cause, a crusade against capital punishment.

For twelve years Chessman argued his case in print and, through his lawyers, in public and in court. He became an expert jailhouse lawyer, avariciously devouring every law book in San Quentin. He outlined his appeals and found every conceivable legal loophole that would allow him to go on living. But eventually he tired of the struggle, stating in print at one point: "While I have awaited this eternity to die, one woman (Barbara Graham) and sixty-nine men have been executed in that Green Room below. Others have gone mad. A demented few have cheated the executioner by violently taking their own lives. I myself have been within hours of having my life snuffed out before desperate legal action abruptly halted the execution."

On May 5, 1960, there were no more desperate legal actions to prevent Chessman from walking into San Quentin's gas chamber. Ironically, federal Judge Louis E. Goodman instructed another delay, but the phone number at San Quentin was misdialed and by the time the call was received, the gas pellets had already been dropped into the container of acid beneath the chair in which Chessman sat. Seconds before he died, with a number of press people gaping through the glass windows of the gas chamber to see Chessman's last moments, the Red Light Bandit moved his head up and down rapidly, this being a prearranged signal to a newspaperman to indicate that there was great pain in inhaling the gas. Seconds later, Chessman was dead. When his death was announced, riots broke out throughout the world, and many U.S. embassies were attacked, windows broken, and the American flag burned. Some of these demonstrators were Communists, it was reported, using Chessman's death as a way to attack and embarrass the U.S. government.

REF.: Alix, *Ransom Kidnapping in America*; Bishop, *Executions*; CBA; Godwin, *Murder U.S.A.*; Hibbert, *The Roots of Evil*; Laurence, *A History of Capital Punishment;* Kunstler, *Beyond A Reasonable Doubt, The Original Trial of Caryl Chessman;* Nash, *Bloodletters and Badmen;* Parker, *Caryl Chessman, The Red Light Bandit;* Scott, *A Concise Encyclopedia of Crime and Criminals;* Symons, *The Pictorial History of Crime;* Wolf, *Fallen Angels;* (FILM), *Cell 2455, Death Row,* 1955.

Chester, Randulf de Gernons (Fourth Earl of Chester), c.1100-53, Brit., rebel.-assass. First supported the claim of Matilda of Germany to the British throne, but joined forces with King Stephen in return for a castle and extensive land holdings. After receiving a still larger grant from Henry, Duke of Lancaster, he defected a second time. He was believed to have been poisoned by agents of Stephen for his duplicity. REF.: *CBA.*

Chesterman, John (AKA: John Christman), prom. 1885-86, U.S., (wrong. convict.) theft. In the fall of 1885, John Chesterman, a Polish immigrant, returned to the farm of his former employer Charles P. Vokes, apparently to ask for money still owed him. The result of his visit was a conviction for a crime he never committed.

After Chesterman left the farm, Vokes informed police that the man had attempted to steal jewelry and clothing, but had been stopped in the act by the farmer himself. Chesterman was arrested by Officer Woodward of Hardwick, Mass., as he ran from his boarding house. On Nov. 16, 1885, Vokes retold his story before Judge Horace W. Bush, which led to a grand jury indictment for larceny on Jan. 21, 1886. At his trial, which began the same day at the Superior Court in Worchester, Chesterman pleaded innocent and told an entirely different version of the incident. Chesterman claimed that Vokes had shot at him when he asked the farmer for his back pay of $42, and that he had run from the police because he was afraid that Vokes had turned him in on a lie. The jury did not believe Chesterman, who spoke very halting English, and he was found Guilty and sentenced to one year in prison.

Not long after Chesterman's conviction, on Feb. 6, 1886, Vokes came forward and confessed before justice Clarence Burgess Roote to lying in court to avoid paying Chesterman his wages. Prosecutor W.S.B. Hopkins sought a pardon from Governor George D. Robinson, which was granted Feb. 12, and Chesterman was released the following day. Vokes was tried for perjury.

REF.: Borchard, *Convicting the Innocent; CBA.*

Chetwynd, William, b.c.1728, Brit., mansl. A quarrel over the division of a cake led to the murder of 19-year-old Thomas Rickets at the exclusive Soho Academy for boys in September 1743. Chetwynd had been given a cake which he was reluctant to share with his schoolmates. After finally agreeing to part with a small piece, Rickets demanded that Chetwynd give him a second. When he refused, the older boy took another piece. It was then that Chetwynd stabbed Rickets to death with the cake knife.

Given the extreme youth of the defendant, a panel of twelve judges found William Chetwynd Guilty of manslaughter. His hand was burned as punishment. The Chetwynd case is the earliest known murder trial involving an underage youth.

REF.: *CBA;* Wilson, *Children Who Kill.*

Chevallier, Yvonne, prom. 1953, Case of, Fr., mur. At the outset of WWII in 1939, Pierre Chevallier, a young doctor hurried home to Orléans, Fr., to marry his mistress of four years, Yvonne, a country midwife. During the war, Chevallier led the Resistance around Orléans and, in July 1944, before the Germans could retreat, actively threw them out of his city. The people loved him for the gesture and quickly elected him mayor. Yvonne Chevallier lost touch with him when he moved into the public arena from which her own peasant birth kept her isolated. After Chevallier was elected to the National Assembly, he began to resent her inability to serve as the attractive, intelligent hostess he needed, and she found herself increasingly left out of his life. By 1947, Chevallier took as a mistress Jeanne Perreau, the wife of a department store owner who stood calmly by as he watched them become involved. Perreau had everything that Mrs. Chevallier did not, and soon began to supplant the dowdy wife. After an episode in which one of their sons was ill and needed to be watched by his mother, Chevallier began to sleep in a separate room, never returning to his wife's bed again. She finally began to suspect that he had taken a mistress, but Mrs. Chevallier would not let him go. She wept over his increasing coldness and verbal abuse and took massive doses of tranquilizers and stimulants, plus great quantities of strong coffee and cigarettes.

In the general elections of 1951, Chevallier won by a greater margin than any other national deputy. After the celebration, at which he clearly placed higher value on Perreau than on his wife, Mrs. Chevallier confronted her husband with his infidelity and won only a request for a divorce. She refused, and also refused to take her own lover, another course he suggested. Instead, she applied for a gun license, which was granted, and purchased a 7.65mm automatic. That night, she heard on the radio that the new premier, René Pléven, had named her husband the secretary of state for technical education, youth, and sports. Knowing that he had moved far beyond her, she called a friend who was a nun and asked her to come over. She

Yvonne Chevallier

told the whole story to the nun and said that she was going to commit suicide. The nun only offered that it would be wrong to kill herself.

The nun was gone when Chevallier telephoned, saying he would be in the next morning to get fresh clothing. Mrs. Chevallier sat up the rest of the night drinking coffee, smoking, and taking stimulants. When her husband arrived in a chauffeur-driven car, he hugged his youngest son but ignored his wife. He was changing clothes in her bedroom when she confronted him.

"Can't I have an explanation?"

"I have no desire to explain anything to a whore."

The argurment went on until finally Mrs. Chevallier pulled her gun from a closet and threatened to kill herself. Chevallier's reply was a mocking, "Well, for God's sake, kill yourself, but wait until I've gone!" She raised the gun and fired at him four times. Seven-year-old Matthieu ran into the room, wondering what was wrong. Mrs. Chevallier grabbed him and took him to the cook to be looked after. Then she returned to her husband and fired a fifth shot, one which she later claimed was accidental. She then called the police and told them what she had done.

Mrs. Chevallier was indicted for murder. Newspaper captions under her unattractive photographs called her the "Assassin of Orléans." But almost immediately, she began to be regarded as the victim. Because of the local publicity, she was tried in Reims in November 1952. A psychiatrist testified, "It was an absolutely stupefying revelation for her when she discovered that her husband was deceiving her with another woman. She was seeing another world which was completely foreign to her and her subsequent actions could be compared to a bird which batters at a lighthouse, blinded by its brilliance." Perreau's husband testified that he knew about and fully approved of the affair, and Perreau herself appeared briefly when Mrs. Chevallier's defense attorney pointed at her and exclaimed, "You are the principal guilty person here; you should be ashamed to the depths of your soul." To which she replied, "My liaison with Dr. Chevallier was a private affair between myself and my conscience. I have no need for any other judge. I loved him and he loved me." The question of the fifth, and completely separate, shot was never discussed, although it might have been used by the prosecution as evidence of more emotional control than is usual for a *crime passionnel.* Instead, both the judge and the prosecution gave closing speeches that sounded as if they were written by the defense. The jury readily found Mrs. Chevallier Not Guilty of the charges. But Mrs. Chevallier regarded herself as guilty, and chose to do penance for killing her husband by going to French Guiana to run a maternity hospital.

REF.: *CBA*; Corder, *Murder My Love*; Goodman, *Crime of Passion*; Heppenstall, *The Sex War and Others*; Rowan, *Famous European Crimes*; Wilson, *Encyclopedia of Murder*.

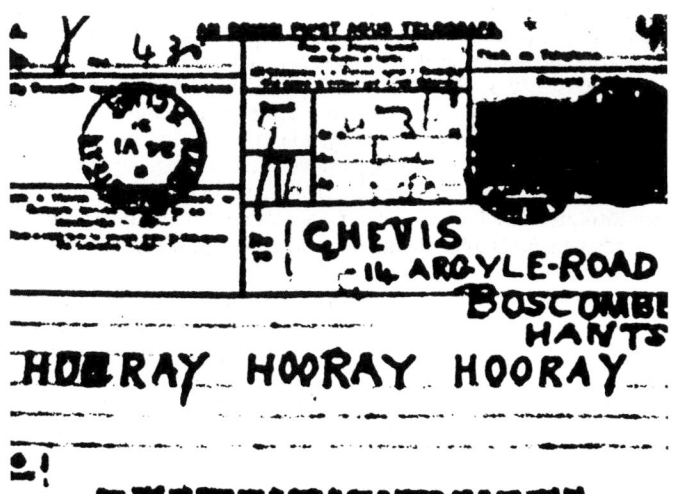

The telegram celebrating Lt. Chevis' murder.

Chevis, Hubert George, d.1931, Brit., (unsolv.) mur. "Hooray Hooray Hooray," said a telegram received by Lieutenant Chevis' father on the day his son was buried. This cruelty was unsigned but the police later found the name J. Hartigan written on the back of the telegraph form. Lieutenant and Mrs. Chevis had been served two partridges for dinner at their home at Blackdown Camp near Aldershot on June 21, 1931. They each took one bite and rejected the fowl, which had been shipped from Manchuria, saying that it "tasted horrible." The lieutenant had a servant dispose of the birds where his dog would not find them. Thus there were no birds to be examined when, fifteen minutes later, the artillery officer and his wife began to get violently ill. Mrs. Chevis, having only touched the partridge with her tongue, recovered after a few hours. Lieutenant Chevis died in the hospital the next day after long hours of agony.

The police traced the birds' progress from Manchuria to the poultry supplier to the meat safe outside the door at the Chevis's home and then to the table. They found no evidence of tampering, though it would have taken but a moment to inject the birds with strychnine. Also, they found no druggist anywhere in the area who had sold strychnine in recent months. They discovered no enemies in the officer's life. They could find no trace of a real "J. Hartigan." All they knew was that Lieutenant Chevis' death must have been murder, but they could not solve the case. Two weeks after the first telegram to the bereaved father, another one arrived. It said, "It is a mystery they will never solve. J. Hartigan. Hooray."

REF.: *CBA*; Glaister, *The Power of Poison*; Nash, *Open Files*; Shew, *A Companion to Murder*; Thompson, *Poison Mysteries Unsolved*.

Cheyney, Peter (Reginald Evelyn Peter Southouse-Cheyney), 1896-1951, Brit., writer. Authored *This Man is Dangerous* and *You Can't Keep the Change*. REF.: *CBA*.

Chiang Kai-shek, See: **Chang Hsueh-liang**.

Chiappe, Jean, 1878-1940, Fr., law enfor. off. Served the city of Paris as prefect of police 1928-34. REF.: *CBA*.

Chicago Board of Trade Bucket Shops Raid, 1900, U.S., fraud. Traffic between the Chicago police station on Central and Harrison streets and the area surrounding the Chicago Board of Trade was quite heavy on July 31, 1900. The reason was the parade of police wagons traveling back and forth carrying some 400 prisoners from the bucket shops that police raided that day.

Detective Clifton R. Wooldridge commanded the operation, organizing a simultaneous raid upon eight shops where illegal and often deceitful stock transactions took place. More than two hours were needed to bring all those arrested to the police stations for booking, and the next few days were spent in arraignment hearings. All of the illegal businesses received fines, except one when a legal technicality resulted in the case being thrown out. Later, however, the leader of that lucky bucket shop, who happened to sit on the Board of Trade, was tried by the board and expelled from his post.

REF.: *CBA*; Wooldridge, *Hands Up!*

Chicago Credit Card Case, 1966, U.S., forg.-fraud. Rather than risk losing a profitable credit-card customer market to the San Francisco-based Bank of America, banks in the Chicago area decided to mail out unsolicited credit cards to their depositors. Instead of cleaning up on the market, these banks were themselves cleaned out.

The unsolicited mailing of credit cards began before Christmas 1966, and it did not take long for the banks—especially First National Bank, which issued the "First" card, and Continental of Illinois, which issued the "Town and Country Card"—to realize their costly mistake. Apparently the banks were using outdated mailing lists and sent a number of cards to addresses without customers. These cards, if not returned by the post office, were used to purchase merchandise fraudulently by the person currently living at that address or someone else who had access to the mailbox. Often, cards were duplicated or forged by those who obtained them. A typical scheme involved the cooperation of a retail merchant who would agree to allow the fraudulent purchase of merchandise, items that he did not part with, in exchange for half of the profits from such a transaction. Although no official record of the losses incurred is known, reports speculate that at least $2 to $3 million was lost by the banks, with one report claiming that one bank lost $56,000 in a single day.

As a result of the credit-card fiasco in Chicago, a bill was introduced in the U.S. Congress that prohibits mailing unsolicited credit cards, while the legislature of Illinois passed a bill outlining penalties and laws concerning the misuse of credit cards.

REF.: *CBA*; McGuire, *The Forgers*.

Chicago Crime Commission, 1919- , U.S., citizen's group. Since 1919, the Chicago Crime Commission has functioned as an independent watchdog agency, enlisting the support of business and civic leaders to fight crime and oversee the criminal justice system. A nonpartisan volunteer organization, it was founded by journalist Henry Barrett Chamberlain, who worked closely with the Chicago Association of Commerce. The civic leaders sought to mobilize the community to demand swift punishment for offenders. The Commission also kept up-to-date records on Chicago crime and patterns of criminal behavior. In 1930, the Crime Commission published the first "Public Enemies List," containing twenty-eight names, with Al Capone's at the top. A year later, the Chicago mob boss went to jail for income tax evasion, through the efforts of the U.S. Treasury Department, the U.S. attorney's office, the Crime Commission, and its adjunct investigating unit, the "Secret Six." In 1936, Commission members drafted a new criminal code that was introduced in the Illinois General Assembly a year later.

As a result of a comprehensive organized crime study conducted by the Commission in 1959, a special unit was set up in the office of the attorney general to coordinate the work of various federal agencies in gathering evidence for the prosecution and conviction of mob racketeers in Chicago and across the country. In recent years, the Commission's focus has shifted from organized crime to drug trafficking. In 1987, the Commission reported that judges were dismissing an unacceptable number of felony narcotics charges simply because the arresting officer did not appear in court. Recommendations were presented to various public officials, and numerous reforms were implemented. REF.: *CBA*.

Chicago Eviction Riot, 1931, U.S., pol. mal. In 1931, the darkest year of the Depression, the Illinois Board of Labor reported that 624,000 people, or 40 percent of the work force in Chicago, were unemployed. In the black neighborhoods on the city's South Side, the situation was even worse, with unemployment three times worse than that among whites. Evictions of entire families were common. Sometimes there were as many as 200 evictions a week.

People began to protest the actions of the landlords. Crowds gathered in the streets, and often moved furniture back into the flats of the dispossessed. Worried landlords petitioned the Chicago Police Department for protection. On Aug. 3, 1931, 72-year-old Diana Gross was put out of her house on Dearborn Avenue on the city's South Side. The bailiff, armed with an eviction notice approved by the Municipal Court, had moved her furniture into the street.

A crowd of 5,000 formed outside the residence and demanded that Gross be let back into her building. Speaking for the displaced residents of Chicago was the Unemployment Council, a group of community activists who had recently opened offices on State Street. The Council had staged a series of marches through the South Side, which alerted city officials to the possibility of another race riot such as the city had suffered in 1919.

A squad of police dispatched to the Dearborn Street address ordered the crowd to disperse, but the leaders refused. The crowd swelled, and police called for reinforcements. Meanwhile, Officer Charles Childress fired a shot in the air, hoping to scare the demonstrators away. Patrolman Fred Graham was thrown to the ground and kicked. Police extricated Graham from the angry throng, but in the shooting that followed, three people were killed and several more were wounded. The police claimed that the crowd of blacks had been armed, but no guns were found.

The anti-eviction movement quickly spread to other cities. To ease the tense situation in Chicago, Assistant Bailiff J.M. Lee ordered a temporary halt to evictions, but they continued.
REF.: *CBA;* Hofstadter and Wallace, *American Violence.*

Chicago Fire, The, 1871, U.S., arson-loot. After the Chicago Fire of 1871, according to reporter William Walker, "the scoundrels...were inflamed with drink, and were alarmingly demonstrative in the flourishing of deadly weapons. Sometimes women and children, and not infrequently men, would be stopped as they were bearing from their homes objects of special worth, and the articles would be torn from their grasp by gangs of these wretches."

The fire that leveled three-quarters of the city began on Oct. 8, 1871, in a hay barn at the rear of the Katherine O'Leary residence on the near South Side. According to popular legend, a milk cow kicked a lantern into a haypile, which started the fire. In the next two days, the city burned as gangs looted stores and robbed fleeing residents of the few valuables they saved from the flames. The Chicago *Post* reported that looters "smashed windows with their naked hands." Gangs invaded downtown saloons and guzzled free beer and liquor, before grabbing everything they could find. When the city courthouse and jail caught fire, the police were forced to release 350 prisoners from their basement cells. The warders stood helplessly by as the thugs sacked a nearby jewelry store.

The fire burned itself out by the third day, Oct. 10. Fearing open lawlessness, President Rutherford B. Hayes ordered U.S. Army troops under General Phil Sheridan into Chicago to impose martial law. Special policemen were pressed into service, swelling the number of local law enforcement officers to 2,400 men. Seven would-be arsonists were shot while trying to start new fires. The task of rebuilding the city soon began, but as one wag observed, "no part of Chicago was rebuilt more quickly than the saloons, brothels, gambling houses, and other resorts and habitations of the underworld." REF.: *CBA.*

Chicago May, See: Churchill, May.

Chicago Police Riot, 1968, U.S., mob vio. Mayor Richard J. Daley of Chicago planned to host the 1968 Democratic National Convention and although Chicago had hosted many such gatherings during Daley's thirteen-year tenure, things were different in August 1968. The Vietnam War had created deep divisions in

American society. Draft-age college students had simply refused to serve in the military. A strong nationwide anti-war movement encouraged campus protest and confrontational politics as a means of signaling disapproval of the U.S. involvement in Southeast Asia. Among the activist groups to emerge in the late 1960s, were the Youth International Party (Yippies), Students For A Democratic Society (SDS), and the National Mobilization To End the War In Vietnam (MOBE). Through the underground press the call went out for members to meet in Chicago for a week of protests and workshops during the Democrats convention.

After the West Side Riots in April 1968 which followed the assassination of Dr. Martin Luther King, police were criticized for their restraint by Mayor Daley, who had become sensitized to the issues of riot prevention and crowd control. Fearing a possible disruption of the convention by protestors, Daley mobilized the city into an armed camp, calling up some 6,000 Illinois National Guardsmen, and 6,000 regular army troops to complement the city police force.

Requests from the hippies, Yippies, and other protestors for permits to sleep in Lincoln Park on the North Side of the city were turned down by City Hall. On Aug. 25, when the protestors camped out in the park in defiance of the 11 p.m. curfew, the Chicago Police were ordered to clear the area, and did so with few problems. The next night, many protestors refused to comply with the directive, chanting, "The parks belong to the people!" It was the opening skirmish of a three-day riot that culminated in Grant Park on Aug. 28. That night, protestors set out on a

Chicago police during the 1968 Democratic convention.

march toward the International Amphitheater where the convention was being held under tight security. Their paths were blocked by guardsmen armed with bayonets. The protestors responded by verbally taunting the police, and pelting them with various objects. The enraged police advanced on the throng, throwing tear gas bombs and beating protestors, journalists, students, and photographers. On the floor of the convention, Senator Abraham Ribicoff protested the police behavior, calling for an end to the harsh tactics. From his seat in the Chicago delegation, Mayor Daley shouted angry curses at the senator.

Daley later charged that the convention week riot was carefully planned by the leaders of the student groups: Abbie Hoffman, Rennie Davis, Jerry Rubin, and Tom Hayden. These four were among the seven later indicted for conspiracy to foment a riot. The 1970 trial of the "Chicago Seven" became the most celebrated criminal case of the anti-war era. An independent investigating committee headed by future Illinois governor Daniel Walker concluded that the police were at fault, having instigated a "police riot" through their provocative behavior. The Walker Report, *Rights In Conflict: The Violent Confrontation of Demonstrators in the Parks and Streets of Chicago During the Week of the Democratic National Convention of 1968,* was praised by some, but condemned by Daley. See: **Walker, Daniel.**

REF.: *CBA;* Hofstadter and Wallace, *American Violence.*

Chicago Race Riot, 1919, U.S., arson-loot.-mob vio. A major influx of black workers into Northern industrial cities prior to WWI contributed to a racially tense atmosphere. Blacks and whites vied for scarce jobs in the industrial sector. WWI then produced a labor shortage, black and white migration to the city, and expansion of ghetto neighborhoods. The integration of previously insulated ethnic communities often led to bloody racial confrontations. These problems resulted in a full-blown race riot in Chicago that left twenty-three blacks and fifteen whites dead.

On July 27, 1919, several black youths swimming off the segregated 29th Street beach in Lake Michigan were pelted by rocks. One of the boys, 14-year-old Eugene Williams, was struck on the head by a rock, lost consciousness, and drowned before his friends could rescue him. When a white police officer, Dan Callahan, refused to arrest the white man who had thrown the rock, angry blacks began to riot. Mayor William Hale Thompson, at first reticent to call the National Guard because of a feud with Governor Frank Lowden, was forced to put partisan political issues aside and seek help for the city.

Organized gangs of white youths from the South Side attacked public places such as trolley cars, buildings, and hotels. The gangs, which included the Ragen Colts, the Aylward Club, the Dirty Dozen, Lorraine's and Our Flag, were composed of Irish and Germans who believed it was their duty to "protect" the neighborhood. An area hospital was soon filled to capacity with the injured. The region of the South Side from Thirty-First to Thirty-Fifth Streets was virtually destroyed by arsonists and looters. The National Guard finally quelled the fighting in Chicago, but the unrest soon spread to other American cities, including Washington, D.C., Charleston, S.C., Knoxville, Tenn., Longview, Tex., and Omaha, Neb.

REF.: *CBA;* Grimshaw, *Racial Violence in the United States;* Hofstadter and Wallace, *American Violence;* Lewis and Smith, *Chicago, A History of Its Reputation;* Lindberg, *Chicago Ragtime: Another Look at Chicago 1880-1920;* Tuttle, *Race Riot: Chicago in the Red Summer of 1919.*

Chicago Seven Trial, The, 1969-70, U.S., riot. By the summer of 1968, the U.S. anti-war movement had taken shape. Resistance to the draft and the government's involvement in South Vietnam led to armed confrontation on college campuses across the U.S. By the time the Democratic National Convention opened in Chicago in August 1968, many student groups saw confrontation as the only way to end the war in Southeast Asia and launch a broad-based social revolution. A political coalition was formed. Representing the "Old Left" of the 1930s was 54-year-old David Dellinger, Chairman of the National Mobilization Committee to End the War in Vietnam (MOBE). Dellinger was a thirty-year veteran of the civil rights movement and labor struggles.

Representing the radicalized youth of the 1960s were Tom Hayden and Rennie Davis, co-founders of the Students for a Democratic Society (SDS), an outgrowth of earlier leftist movements on college campuses. Jerry Rubin and Abbie Hoffman, leaders of the Youth International Party, or Yippies, were the "clown princes" of the movement. Their irreverent behavior alarmed city officials, who saw a conspiracy forming in Chicago.

After Mayor Richard J. Daley refused to allow thousands of demonstrators to sleep in Lincoln Park after curfew, there was unrest. The ruthless crackdown by Chicago Police triggered the worst of the rioting, which culminated in an angry clash outside the Conrad Hilton Hotel in downtown Chicago on Aug. 29, 1968. Daniel Walker, a special investigator appointed to look into the causes of the violence, concluded that a "police riot" had taken place in Chicago during convention week, which Mayor Daley angrily denied.

A grand jury was empaneled on Sept. 9, 1968, to decide whether to bring the demonstration's leaders to trial. Eleven months later, on Mar. 20, 1969, the jury returned indictments against eight of the anti-war activists: Jerry Rubin, Abbie Hoffman, Rennie Davis, David Dellinger, Thomas Hayden, John Froines, Lee Weiner, and Bobby Seale of the Black Panther Party. They were charged with forming a "combine" to "conspire, confederate, and agree together on or about Apr. 12, 1968,...to travel in interstate commerce with the intent to incite, organize, promote, encourage, participate in and carry on a riot...."

The "Conspiracy Trial" began on Sept. 26, 1969, in the courtroom of 74-year-old Judge Julius Hoffman. The defendants became the "Chicago Seven" case when Bobby Seale was granted a separate trial. William Kunstler and Leonard Weinglass represented the defendants, and the prosecution was handled by Thomas Foran, a U.S. attorney and confidant of Mayor Daley, and Richard Schultz.

The divisive trial lasted nearly five months, punctuated by frequent courtroom antics by the defense and angry denunciations from the bench. The defendants, especially Hoffman and Rubin, verbally sparred with the elderly judge. On the first day of the trial, Bobby Seale accused Judge Hoffman of racism after he denied his motion for a separate trial. "Do you know you are addressing the judge who ordered the first desegregation of schools in the North?" Hoffman reminded him. After Seale's repeated outbursts, Hoffman ordered the marshals to bind and gag him, a controversial decision that called into question the judge's competence to preside in such a trial.

On Feb. 14, 1970, the jury retired to consider its verdict. While they were sequestered, Hoffman handed down contempt of court sentences. Dellinger received twenty-nine months; Davis, twenty-five; Hayden, fourteen; Hoffman, eight; Rubin, twenty-five; Froines, five; and Weiner, two. For calling the court a "medieval torture chamber," Kunstler was ordered to serve four years and thirteen days in prison. Weinglass received twenty months and nine days.

On Feb. 15, the jury acquitted the defendants of the more serious charge of conspiracy. However, Dellinger, Davis, Hayden, Hoffman, and Rubin were found Guilty of crossing state lines to incite a riot. Froines and Weiner were acquitted of the charge of conducting workshops on the construction and detonation of incendiary devices. But none of the Chicago Seven ever served time. A federal district judge overturned their convictions on May 11, 1972, because Hoffman had waited too long to impose sentencing. On Nov. 21, the convictions were permanently voided, thus ending a criminal trial that introduced radical street theater to the courtroom. See: **Chicago Police Riot.**

REF.: *CBA;* Epstein, *The Great Conspiracy Trial;* Hayden, *Trial;* Walker, *Rights In Conflict.*

Chicago White Sox Scandal, See: **Black Sox Scandal.**

Chichester Gang, prom. 1820s-70s, U.S., org. crime. A prominent New York gang centered in the Five Points area, the Chichesters operated, like other gangs of their era, out of grocery stores and warehouses, stealing goods in large lots and selling these off to fences. Their members also practiced organized gambling and sneak thievery. The Chichester gang maintained about fifty to 100 gang members throughout its fifty-year period of activity and largely sided with the powerful Dead Rabbits gang when battling for territory against the Bowery gangs. When the Whyos gang came into existence following the Civil War, the Chichesters were absorbed by this gang, which at one time numbered in the thousands. See: **Dead Rabbits; Whyos Gang.**

REF.: Asbury, *The Gangs of New York;* *CBA;* Peterson, *The Mob.*

Chicken Farm Murder, The, See: **Thorne, Norman.**

Chiesa, Carlo Alberto Dalla, c.1921-82, Italy, gen., assass. The man appointed by the Italian government to crack down on drug smuggling and Mafia control of the northwest corner of Sicily was himself gunned down, along with his wife of two months, apparently by the Mafia.

General Carlo Alberto Dalla Chiesa, the 61-year-old prefect of Palermo, Sicily, and Emanuela, his 32-year-old wife, were shot to death while driving through the downtown section of the city on Sept. 3, 1982. Machine-gun fire came from two automobiles and a motorcycle. Though extremist groups claimed responsibility, officials believe the Mafia was behind the killing of the man who had prepared a plan, read by Prime Minister Giovanni Spadolini the day before in the Italian Senate, to wipe out terrorism in Sicily. Also announced the day before by Finance Minister Rino Formica was a massive tax evasion campaign against 3,200 Mafia figures. At the time, drug smugglers in Sicily were believed to be transporting into the U.S. from between two and four tons of processed heroin, more than half of the annual U.S. supply. REF.: *CBA*.

Chifney, Samuel, c.1752-c.1807, Case of, Brit., fraud. One of England's greatest jockeys, Samuel Chifney was suspected of perpetrating one of England's great horseracing scandals, which involved the Prince of Wales, later King George IV, the owner for whom Chifney rode.

Chifney was regarded by many as being a great rider because of his remarkable ability to reserve a horse's energy until the last stretch of a race. He was retained by the prince in July 1790 for 200 guineas a year. During his short employment, he would ride what he himself felt to be the greatest horse, Escape, a 5-year-old that year. His knowledge of horses proved quite lucrative, both for the prince and the jockey. Chifney often claimed that Escape was not fit to run, while the stable manager, Warwick Lake, and others, including fellow jockey Bill Price, disagreed. Time and again Chifney proved he was correct during the race. At the Oatlands Stakes on June 28, 1791, Chifney rode Baronet, allowing Price to ride Escape because he felt the horse was not well, and he handily won the race. Escape did not even show. Chifney next rode Escape at Newmarket on Oct. 3, 1791, when the odds favored another horse, Grey Diomed, and he won. Two days later in a Subscription Stakes, Escape, mounted by Chifney, easily won again. To everyone's surprise, however, Escape lost its next race on October 20. The horse had been heavily favored going into the race but was easily defeated when Chifney eased up in mid-race. Chifney argued in his book *Genius Genuine* that Escape had not been ridden for two weeks and was in no condition to run. Escape easily distanced the field the next day and won a considerable sum for the prince, though Chifney himself bet only £20.

The Jockey Club, which at that time was more a social than a governing organization, inquired into the races held on Oct. 20 and 21. It was believed that Chifney had rigged the races by allowing Escape to lose the first, and that he had even bet against his horse in the first race. He was also accused of having been fined £300 at a past race, a fine that was allegedly paid by Vauxhall Clark, the man who often placed the jockey's bets. Called before the Jockey Club, Chifney failed to answer the questions posed by senior steward Sir Charles Bunbury and stewards Ralph Dutton and Tommie Panton. The club informed the prince that it would be wise not to employ the jockey any longer. The prince fully trusted Chifney but followed their advice, though he did continue to pay Chifney his 200 guineas per year retainer.

REF.: *CBA; Hall, The Bravo Mystery and Other Cases.*

Chigango, Chief, prom. 1923, Rhodesia, mur. In order to appease the Rain Goddess and bring an end to the drought that began in 1922, Chief Chigango ordered that his own son Mandusa be offered as a sacrifice to the great spirit Mwari. The sacrifice may or may not have ended the drought—the day after Mandusa was killed, it began to rain profusely—but it did bring an end to Chigango's reign.

Like his ancestors, Chigango, the chief of a Mtwara tribe village, believed in and followed the traditions concerning the Rain Goddess. Legend has it that the Mtwara god, Mwari, had given an earlier tribal chief a wife who was to remain a virgin throughout her lifetime. This woman became known as the Rain Goddess, and it was through her that the tribe would ask Mwari to send them rain. If no rain came even after offerings were made to Mwari, then it was a sign that someone had seduced the Rain Goddess, and that person must be sacrificed to Mwari. When the drought continued into January 1923, it was believed that Chigango's son was the man who had defiled the Rain Goddess, who was

personified by a young girl chosen at birth. Instead of trusting members of his own village to carry out the human sacrifice, Chigango called upon another chief, Chiswiti, to handle the affair. The following night Mandusa was taken in his sleep to be burned alive.

Police in Mount Darwin learned of the murder from Mandusa's younger brother, who feared for his own life in the event that rains did not come. Seven tribesmen were arrested and tried for the murder, including Chigango, Chiswiti, and Chiriseri, a tribal leader. All were found Guilty of murder except Chiswiti, who was acquitted. Because of the circumstances of the crime, the death sentences were commuted.

REF.: Bennett, *Up For Murder; CBA.*

Child, Richard Washburn, 1881-1935, U.S., lawyer. Admitted to the bar in 1906, he was ambassador to Italy from 1921-1924. Books authored: *Vanishing Man* and *Potential Russia*. REF.: *CBA*.

Childers, Jimmy, 1961- , U.S., mur. On July 9, 1978, 17-year-old Jimmy Childers of Pekin, Ill., arrived home late from a date. An argument ensued with his parents that escalated when mention was made of the boy's intention to marry the girl that winter. The fight ended with three dead at the hands of young Childers.

In a taped confession, Childers admitted killing his stepfather, 42-year-old Robert Rotramel, when the gun he was waving about went off. He then chased after his mother, 37-year-old Nora Rotramel, stabbing her to death with a knife in the kitchen, and finally using the knife to kill his 15-year-old brother, Warren Childers, as he tried to run out the front door. The confession, taken twenty-four hours after the killings, was played in court and convinced the jury to return a verdict of Guilty on Feb. 3, 1979.

Defense attorney Joseph Napoli had argued that Childers was temporarily insane, which was corroborated by two psychiatrists for the defense. However, two prosecution psychiatrists determined the boy to be perfectly capable of distinguishing right from wrong. Although tried as an adult, Childers was too young to receive the death penalty, but Judge James Heiple sentenced the youth to three terms of life imprisonment on Mar. 8, 1979. Childers burst into tears at hearing the sentence, just as he did upon hearing the jury's verdict. REF.: *CBA*.

Children of Darkness, 1929, a play by Edwin Justus Mayer. This three-act drama is based upon one of the most colorful and daring criminals in British history, Jonathan Wild (Brit., 1725). See: **Wild, Jonathan**. REF.: *CBA*.

Chilembwe, John, d.1915, Nyasaland, rebel. This South African political leader and missionary led an aborted revolt against British colonial rule in Nyasaland. He was seized and executed by the local police constables in 1915. REF.: *CBA*.

Chillingworth, Charles E., See: **Peel, Joseph, Jr.**

Chilouet, Marcel and **Lemarchand (Lagardère)**, prom. 1922, Fr., theft. Two thieves stole from their employer and fled to Athens where they lived in high style until two officers arrested them at their own masquerade party.

In March 1922, Marcel Chilouet and Lemarchand stole 600,000 francs from their employer, a money changer, and escaped to Constantinople and finally to Athens with their wives. In Athens, Chi-louet and his wife purchased a grand villa made of marble and used it as a base for entering Athenian society.

The case was cracked when two investigators of the Sûreté, sergeants Leroy and Holtzer, tracked the thieves to Athens, discovered the villa, and crashed a masquerade party being held there. After a night of revelry, when the last guests had departed, the two detectives arrested the thieves. The Chilouets handed over 100,000 francs, told police that another 120,000 francs were buried in the cellar of his parents house, and signed over the villa to Chilouet's former employer, the money changer.

REF.: *CBA; Morain, Underworld of Paris.*

Chilperic I, 539-584, Neustria, mur. Merovingian king of the Franks in Neustria from 561-584, known as the Nero of his age. He murdered his wife Galeswintha and married his mistress

Fredegund, who later murdered Sigeburt, king of Austrasia. See: **Brunhilda.** REF.: *CBA*.

Chilson, Benjamin A., prom. 1900-06, U.S., fraud. A former veterinarian and specialist in paints and dyes, Benjamin A. Chilson, called "king of the ringers" by journalists, was a swindler who altered the appearance of a fast horse, switched it for a slower horse, and collected a large sum when the fraudulent horse won on long odds. The cheat usually raced the painted horse in the last race of the day because the judges were leaving to go to the next track.

Carrying out his racing scam, Chilson's largest haul was in Morris Park when he switched McNamara for Fiddler on Oct. 3, 1903. Using McNamara and another horse, Freckman, his success continued in races all over the country. Meanwhile, detective Robert Pinkerton was beginning to inquire into reports of Chilson's ringing. And, with the aid of small cameras, Pinkerton's agents chronicled Chilson's operations.

By 1906, the Eastern Jockey Club and the California Jockey Club, powerful racetrack governing organizations, had barred Chilson from the racetracks. In addition, Pinkerton was fighting to get bills passed in New York that would outlaw ringing. REF.: *CBA*; Horan, *The Pinkertons*.

Chilson, Olin Hatfield, 1903- , U.S., jur. Served as district attorney of Loveland, Colo. 1928-54, 1940-48; president of the District Attorneys Association in 1947; member of the Commission on Administration of Criminal Law between 1964-68, and the Judicial Conference Commission to Implement the Criminal Justice Act in 1968. He was appointed to the bench of the district court of Colorado in February 1960 by President Dwight D. Eisenhower. REF.: *CBA*.

Chilton, Fred, 1865-86, U.S., west. gunman. Fred Chilton, a cowboy working for the LS ranch in Texas, was one of the participants in the LX-LS range war near Tascosa, Texas. He was shot to death in a duel with Len Woodward on Mar. 21, 1886. Chilton reportedly shot several men before meeting his violent end. REF.: Bartholomew, *The Biographical Album of Western Gunfighters*; *CBA*.

Chin, Frank, c.1929-77, U.S., (unsolv.) mur. In the late 1970s, Frank Chin was a wiretapper avidly sought by the police, the mob, those who wanted buildings bugged, those who wanted buildings debugged, and those who wanted him dead.

Chin's profession as an installer of eavesdropping devices made him a number of enemies, on both sides of the law. One of those enemies finally caught up with him on Jan. 20, 1977, and shot six bullets into his head outside his New York City workshop. The number of possible suspects in the killing far outweighed the evidence. His clientele included the CIA, United Nations officials, Communist and Nationalist Chinese, Connecticut and New Jersey police, and possibly the perpetrators of the Watergate scandal. Chin, who began surveillance work in 1964, even helped prostitute Xaviera Hollander tape conversations that became part of her book *The Happy Hooker*. It is rumored that he was a police informant as well, based on the fact that his six to eight arrests for felonies had been reduced to misdemeanor charges.

But the client who may have indirectly led to Chin's demise was a Stratford, Conn., police officer named Joseph Berke. Berke had purchased devices from Chin to bug the town hall so that he could overhear promotion hearings, a fact that Chin testified to when charges of illegal use of a wiretap were brought against the police officer. Because he testified in court, officials believed Chin's clients could no longer trust him, and one of them may have silenced the wiretap expert. REF.: *CBA*.

Chindawongse, Sihadej, 1940- , U.S., drugs. By using diplomatic pouches, which are exempt from customs inspections, Thailand's vice consul in Chicago, Sihadej Chindawongse, smuggled more than $20 million worth of 98 percent pure heroin into the U.S.

The U.S. Drug Enforcement Administration authorities, along with Chicago police and U.S. Customs officials, kept the diplomat under surveillance for several weeks. The government of Thailand also cooperated with the investigation. On Apr. 30, 1982, Chindawongse was arrested carrying three pounds of heroin; more was discovered at his apartment. Chindawongse pleaded guilty on Jan. 12, 1983, to one count each of importing and possessing drugs. A sentence of thirty years imprisonment was handed down on Feb. 18, 1983. REF.: *CBA*.

Chinese Mass Rapes, 1980, China, rape. Three Chinese youths belonging to a "gang of seven" were executed by firing squad in the northern provence of Jilin in June 1980. The condemned men were found Guilty of luring ninety-two women into an apartment house under the pretense of employment. Once inside, they were assaulted and raped. The arrest and execution of the three men was a part of a general crackdown against crime and corruption, but official government sources refused to release the names of the guilty parties. REF.: *CBA*.

Chink in the Armour, The (alt. title, *The House of Peril*), 1912, a novel by Marie Belloc-Lowndes. The killing of Emma Levin by Maria vere Goolde (Monaco, 1907) serves as the basis of this work of fiction. See: **Goolde, Marie Vere.** REF.: *CBA*.

Chin Kuei, 1090-1155, China, treas. Politician regarded as a traitor for his opposition to a military expedition to regain the northern lands lost to the Jürched tribes. He secured peace at the expense of General Yo Fei who was executed. REF.: *CBA*.

Chipman, Nathaniel, 1752-1843, U.S., jur. State's attorney of Vermont at Montpelier between 1781-85, member of the commission to revise the state statutes from 1796-97, and nominated to serve on the district court of Vermont by President George Washington in 1791. REF.: *CBA*.

Chitra, Nai, See: **Ananda, King.**

Chitty, Edward, 1804-63, Brit., lawyer. Son of Joseph Chitty, he worked for a time as a legal reporter. REF.: *CBA*.

Chitty, Joseph, 1776-1841, Brit., lawyer. Author of legal manuals. His three sons were also lawyers. REF.: *CBA*.

Chitty, Joseph D., d.1838, Brit., lawyer. Authored a book on contract law and was the eldest son of Sir Joseph Chitty. REF.: *CBA*.

Chitty, Sir Joseph William, 1828-99, Brit., jur. Justice of the High Court, Chancery Division, in 1881. He was appointed Lord Justice of Appeal in 1897 and was the son of Thomas Chitty. REF.: *CBA*.

Chitty, Thomas, 1802-78, Brit., lawyer. Served as special pleader before the court and edited standard law books. REF.: *CBA*.

Chivers, Elizabeth, c.1682-1712, Brit., mur. Poor and orphaned at the age of fourteen, Elizabeth Chivers was forced to support herself as a domestic servant in Stepney, England.

Years later, just after her thirtieth birthday, Chivers went into service for a prosperous attorney, Mr. Ward. While working for him, she became pregant with his child. Dismayed and chagrined upon hearing such news, Ward nonetheless owned up to his responsibility and promised to provide support and have the child baptized as his own.

This magnanimous gesture infuriated Ward's wife, who proceeded to spread news of the scandal throughout the town. Deeply upset, Chivers decided to do what she could to spare Ward further public disgrace.

On a day in July 1712, passersby watched as Chivers drowned the infant in a pond outside Hackney. When brought before the magistrate, who committed her to Newgate to await her execution, the griefstricken young woman cried, "Oh sir! I am lost! I cannot pray! I did commit it with deliberation and choice, and in cold blood. I was not driven to it by necessity. The father had all the while provided for me and for the child and would have done so still, had I not destroyed the child and thereby sought my own destruction."

The death sentence was carried out on Aug. 1, 1712. REF.: *CBA*; Mitchell, *Newgate Calendar*; Nash, *Look For the Woman*; O'Donnell, *Should Women Hang?*

Chivers, Thomas Holley, 1809-58, U.S., plagiarism. Following the publication of his *Eonchs of Ruby* in 1851, literary critics accused Chivers of plagiarizing from the work of the late Edgar Allen Poe. Chivers accused Poe of stealing his own material, a charge that some critics believed to be true, especially in regards to *The Raven* which may have been influenced by Chivers' own *Isadore*. REF.: *CBA*.

Chiying, d.1858, China, drugs-suic. A politician who officially ended the first Opium War in 1842 by ceding the port of Hong Kong to the British under the terms of the Treaty of Nanking. His failure to successfully conclude an agreement with the British to end the Arrow War prompted the emperor to order him to commit suicide. REF.: *CBA*.

Chlodomer, d.524, prince, assass. Son of Clovis, king of the Salian Franks. When Clovis died in 511, the realm was divided among the three sons. Chlodomer received the Loire and Garonne valleys. He waged a successful war against Sigismund of Burgundy, whose brother Godomer killed him at Vienne. REF.: *CBA*.

Chlotar II, See: **Sigebert II**.

Choate, Joseph Hodges, 1832-1917, U.S., lawyer. Led the prosecution team that secured the conviction in 1873 of the corrupt New York City political boss William Marcy Tweed. During a sixty year career which included service in the diplomatic corps and membership in the delegation to the World Court, Choate handled a number of important civil cases including Standard Oil antitrust cases and the Samuel Tilden's bequeathment of his estate to the New York Public Library. See: **Tweed, William Marcy**. REF.: *CBA*.

Choate, Pearl, 1907- , U.S., rob.-mur. "I done the decent thing. You never heard of Pearl Choate not marrying a man. Pearl Choate don't shack up!" The 59-year-old private nurse objected to being thought capable of marrying elderly men for their money, which usually came to her after only a brief marriage. Choate, a Texan, stood over six feet tall and weighed at least 250 pounds. What six men, all in their nineties, found after marrying her was a brief period of high-quality private nursing and then quiet death, preferably after writing a will leaving her their estates. The sixth man, however, died when Choate shot four bullets into him during a major argument.

Pearl Choate was tried for murder, though she claimed self-defense, and was convicted. After serving twelve years in prison, Choate was released and went to Houston, where an excursion into robbery only took her back to jail. Returning to nursing, Pearl Choate married A.O. Birch, a millionaire from Grand Prairie, Texas. He died in March 1966. Because of her past history, Choate was suspected of helping him along, but he was, after all, ninety-five. When a reporter brought up her previous six husbands, she thundered, "What's that got to do with today's love?...They were all about Mr. Birch's age when I married them. So what? I done the decent thing."

REF.: *CBA*; Nash, *Look For the Woman*.

Choate, Rufus, 1799-1859, U.S., lawyer. Considered to be the eminent jury lawyer of his day and a skilled orator. REF.: *CBA*.

Cho'e Cheu, 1824-64, Korea, rebel. Founded the Tonghak Sect in 1860, urging peasants to resist corrupting western influences. His aborted rebellion in 1864 led to his arrest and execution. REF.: *CBA*.

Cho'e Sihyong, 1826-99, Korea, treas. Following the death of Cho'e Cheu, he furthered the the influence of the Tonghak Sect by issuing the first Tonghak scriptures between 1880-81. He was arrested and executed by the government. REF.: *CBA*.

Choi, David Puilum (AKA: Choi, Tsoi Pui), c.1952- , U.S., mur. After allegedly stabbing a person to death, David Puilum Choi escaped capture and has since eluded the FBI. The one-time Chinese waiter is known for wearing flashy and trendy clothing as well as prescription glasses. Choi was last seen in San Jose, Calif., where a federal arrest warrant was issued on Nov. 18, 1985. At this writing, Choi is still at large. REF.: *CBA*.

Choice, William A., d.1876, U.S., mur. Perhaps the most blatant murder committed in boisterous antebellum Atlanta, Ga., involved William A. Choice, considered to be one of the finest actors of his day, even though he was a drunk. Choice was described as "a tall and fair-haired man of gentle blood—frame massive, yet sinewy—face fine, though reddened by debauchery—eyes of blue, blazing and melting in turn—hands smooth and white and soft—voice, deep, yet rich, even melodious—mien, proud, yet gracious."

Choice had organized the Murdock Dramatic Club in 1854, announcing to the citizens of Atlanta the lofty aims of his group: "As gentlemen, we promise that we will not pander to perverted tastes, but the noblest thoughts of noblest men shall be presented." The plays were all-male opuses such as *William Tell, The Gladiator, Pizarro*. Naturally, Choice played the lead role in all the of them.

Popularity and money surrounded Choice, but he proved himself a spendthrift and began to drink up his earnings faster than he could make them. His reputation as a surly drunk when offstage became widespread and he was involved in an increasing number of bar fights as the years fled by.

The actor was lounging at the bar of the Atlanta Hotel on the night of Dec. 30, 1858. Just as he was about to order another drink, a bailiff named Calvin Webb burrowed his way to the bar and thrust a $10 bail process owed to one of Choice's many creditors, Dr. John Dowsing.

Choice stared at the paper the diminutive Webb placed in his hands and then said: "I can't pay that sum now."

"You had better," grunted Webb.

The towering actor turned and stared down at the little bailiff. "I'll pay with my fist in a moment."

Webb was half terrier, it seemed, and put up his fists, prepared to fight the much larger Choice, only to be interrupted by Luther J. Glenn, mayor of Atlanta. Calming the actor, the mayor turned to Webb and told him he would guarantee the $10. Webb departed and Choice, his pride injured, began to guzzle all the liquor he could cadge. He passed out at the bar and was carried to his room.

Late the next morning, Choice went for a stroll in the rain, carrying high his umbrella. Whether or not he was sober was hotly debated for years. As he moved uneasily down the plank sidewalk on Pryor Street, the actor spotted Bailiff Webb across the street, walking with a companion, John Cason.

A whoop of rage came out of Choice's mouth as he drew a pistol and fired off a round in Webb's direction. He missed and the confused bailiff, who also carried an umbrella, stumbled about on the wooden planks as his friend, Cason, ran screaming down the street. Webb used the umbrella he carried as a shield, but gusts of wind tore it up and over his head. Choice then calmly kneeled, cocked his pistol, and placed it on his knee to steady it. With deliberate aim, he fired off another shot and this hit Webb squarely in the chest. The bailiff fell forward into his umbrella, quite dead.

At first, the actor hid in a shanty. He later turned himself over to constables searching for him and was taken to Milledgeville prison. By then, mobs of angry citizens were demanding his head. Webb had many friends. Choice's lawyers pleaded him insane, pointing out that he had fallen on his head eight years earlier. They also stated that he was, indeed, still drunk when he shot Webb. The arguments were ineffective. The actor was sentenced to hang the following year.

Benjamin Hill, Choice's chief lawyer, fought desperately to save the actor's life, finally convincing the state legislature that his client was certainly insane. Choice was pardoned but removed to an asylum where he was kept for a short period. The great tragedian was released in time to join the Confederate army, and he performed gallantly during the Civil War, earning several citations, not unexpectedly, as a sharpshooter.

Choice did little acting after the war, and his name finally slipped from the limelight. In 1876, newspapers announced his accidental death. William A. Choice, actor, sharpshooter, and murderer, had perished after falling from the second story of a livery stable. He was drunk at the time. REF.: *CBA*.

Choiseul-Praslin, Duc, See: **de Praslin, Duke.**

Chol Soo Lee, 1952- , U.S., (wrong. convict.?) mur. Chol Soo Lee arrived in the U.S. from Seoul, S. Kor., in 1964. He was a troubled adolescent and constantly fought in junior high school. He served thirteen months in a California Youth Authority institution, which was only a prelude to more serious crimes he would eventually commit.

In 1973, Chol Soo Lee allegedly shot and killed a rival gang leader named Yip Yee Tak on a crowded San Francisco street in broad daylight. A series of Chinatown murders plagued the Bay Area at that time, and caused Mayor Joseph Alioto many sleepless nights. There was considerable pressure on the police to come up with a suspect—any suspect. Homicide Investigator Frank Falzon soon arrested Lee after recovering a bullet lodged in the ceiling of his apartment. Ballistics tests tended to show that it was the same type of bullet used to kill Yip Yee Tak. Eyewitnesses were located by the prosecution, and their testimony helped convict Lee in 1973. The Korean immigrant received a life sentence in San Quentin.

The plight of Chol Soo Lee drew the attention of many prisoner activist groups, and the leaders of the San Francisco Asian community. There were calls for a new trial on the grounds that the defendant had been railroaded by shaky, unreliable testimony. A Chol Soo Lee Defense Committee was organized, and in 1982 a second trial was ordered.

On Sept. 3, a San Francisco jury found him Not Guilty of murdering the Chinatown gang figure. However, Lee was still in a bind. He sat on San Quentin's death row for the 1977 murder of Morrison Needham, a member of the white racist Aryan Brotherhood and a fellow prison inmate. Lee had killed Needham in a prison knife fight, for what he claimed to be a matter of self-defense. The jury disagreed, and he was sentenced to death.

This second murder conviction was overturned in 1983 when a Sacramento Appeals Court ordered a new trial on the grounds that the presiding judge had failed to inform the jurors that Lee could have been found guilty on a lesser charge of second-degree murder if they believed he acted in self-defense. In a plea bargaining arrangement, Chol Soo Lee agreed to plead guilty to one count of second-degree murder in return for a sentence of time served. The case concluded on Aug, 25, 1983. Lee was granted a final release from custody, returned to the Korean neighborhood of San Francisco and went to work in a community center. REF.: *CBA*.

Chong Yakjong (AKA: **Augustine Chong**), 1760-1801, Korea, her. First president of the Myongdo-hoe society, founded to spread Catholic doctrine throughout Korea. He was killed for his beliefs. REF.: *CBA*.

Chou En-lai, 1898-1976, China, (unsolv.) mur. Educated in France, Chou En-lai joined the Chinese Communist party in 1921 and escaped the bloody purge of Chiang Kai-shek in 1927 to become a powerful member of the Communist Central Committee and Politburo. In 1934, he led one of the greatest odysseys in recorded history—the celebrated 6,000-mile Long March to Shensi. Following the overthrow of the Nationalist government in 1949, Chou became widely known in the West as a skilled diplomat and Party leader.

In 1954, a little-known incident from his past life surfaced, suggesting that this political leader of millions was also a mass murderer.

In April 1931, the high-ranking Communist politician Koo Cheng Chang defected to the Nationalist government. He revealed the secret identities of many Communists, resulting in mass arrests and the execution of the secretary-general of the Party on June 23, 1931. Shortly after, Koo's wife, eight of his relatives, and the family cook mysteriously disappeared.

Three months later, on Sept. 28, Shanghai police arrested Wong Lau Deu Ts who confessed to being a member of the squad of assassins who strangled to death members of the Koo family. These political executions had been ordered by the newly appointed secretary-general and leader of the death squads. A search of French police records of Shanghai's International Settlement revealed that the shadowy boss of this assassination squad was Chou En-lai. Clipped to the sensitive dossier was a photograph of Chou, leaving little doubt in the minds of Western observers that this was the same man who later sat at the right hand of Mao Tse-Tung.

The final report of the British government in Shanghai concerning the Koo assassinations was submitted on Jan. 22, 1932. It revealed that the bodies of the victims were found buried in shallow graves at 33 and 37 Rue Prosper Paris and No. 6 Wuting Road. Eleven corpses, including the Koo family members, were buried at these two sites. In a seven day period between Nov. 21, and Nov. 28, 1931, the remains were exhumed and identified by police. An ad placed by Koo in the North China *Herald* on Dec. 1, 1931, offered a $3,000 reward for the suspected killers, but no one was brought to justice. REF.: *CBA*.

Chou Hsin, c.1154-c.1122 B.C., China, emp., assass. Chou Hsin was the last Shang dynasty emperor. According to legend, he taxed the people in order to build the Deer Tower Palace. His brutal reign was overthrown by Wu Wang and he was executed. REF.: *CBA*.

Chowchuilla School Bus Kidnapping, See: **Woods, Frederick.**

Chowick, William, d.1926, U.S., rob. On Aug. 24, 1926, William Chowick pulled his last bank job, blowing himself to bits. A criminal with a long record, he had stepped up to a teller in the Farmer's National Bank of Pittsburgh that day and demanded $2,000. His note to the teller said that if his demand was not met, he would drop the bomb he was carrying. The teller set off an alarm, special officers came running, and Chowick dropped the bomb. The explosion injured twenty-three people and killed a special officer and Chowick. The robber was identified by his fingerprints.

REF.: *CBA*; Robinson, *Science Catches the Criminal*.

Chrimes, Joseph, d.1959, Brit., burg.-mur. During a burglary that netted only a few small items, including a cigarette case, some spoons, and a clock, a 60-year-old widow was beaten to death with a tire iron. The crime occurred on Dec. 31, 1958, in the home of Norah Summerfield, known as the Cider Queen because she liked cider.

Joseph Chrimes, a 30-year-old stainer from Hays, and an accomplice, Ronald Hedley Charles Pritchard, stood trial. Pritchard, acquitted in the case, became a witness for the prosecution. According to Pritchard's testimony, Chrimes pried open the back door, and the widow came out of the house, commanding them to leave. Pritchard said Chrimes responded by beating her with a tire iron. The two then searched the house for valuables.

Within four months after the Cider Queen's death, Chrimes was convicted of murder, condemned to death, and executed.

REF.: *CBA*; Furneaux, *Famous Criminal Cases, Vol. 6*; Jackson, *Occupied With Crime*.

Christenberry, Herbert William, 1897-1975, U.S., jur. U.S. attorney serving the Parish of Orleans, La., 1942-47. He was law professor of Loyola University of the South law school from 1944-63, and he was nominated to the court of the eastern district of Louisiana in 1947 by President Harry Truman. REF.: *CBA*.

Christensen, William Dean (AKA: **Jeffrey Schrader**), 1945- , U.S., rape-mur. Before his 1987 murder conviction, William Christensen left a trail of mayhem. He was convicted of violent crimes in Pennsylvania, New Jersey, and Canada, and remains a prime suspect in at least a dozen unsolved murders in five other states and Canada.

The criminal odyssey of this 42-year-old drifter began in 1964, when he killed a woman in Montgomery County, Pa., by stabbing her nineteen times. Convicted of murder, Christensen was released after serving only six months of a five-year sentence. The decision to free him was made against the advice of a psychiatrist, who warned of the dangerous consequences of letting a man like Christensen back on the streets.

Christensen's next brush with the law came eight years later when, in 1972, he sexually assaulted a 21-year-old Montgomery County woman. Found Guilty, he served seven years before his parole on Apr. 1, 1980. In July, he raped and battered a 19-year-old woman in Montgomery, Md. In Montreal, New York, New Jersey, Florida, Georgia, and Kentucky, Christensen emerged as a prime suspect in several unsolved murders.

Convicted of rape, Christensen served one year of an eighteen-month sentence in Montreal, then returned to Pennsylvania, where he abducted and raped a woman in Kensington. In 1982, he assaulted and stabbed to death 23-year-old go-go dancer Michele Angiers outside her Dickerson City apartment. He remained a fugitive until Dec. 4, 1983, when Philadelphia police arrested him in a saloon for the murder of 51-year-old Joseph Connelly. A Scranton jury found him Guilty of Connelly's murder and sentenced him to life in prison.

Reflecting on the trial, attorney Daniel Preminger said it was his opinion that if the prosecution had been allowed access to Christensen's past records, the jury most certainly would have convicted him of first-degree murder and sentenced him to death.

On Aug. 24, 1989, a Maryland court sentenced Christensen to an additional forty years in prison, twenty years each on rape and battery charges for the 1980 Montgomery attack. The sentences are to be served consecutively to those in all other jurisdictions and constitute, according to Maryland Assistant State's Attorney Robert Dean, "an insurance policy" that Christensen will never be free again. REF.: *CBA*.

Christi, Frank, c.1929, U.S., (unsolv.) mur. Frank Christi, an actor who had played the role of good and bad guys on television and in films, was shot to death outside his North Hollywood, Calif., home on July 9, 1982. Police could not establish a motive, but the actor had cooperated with authorities in the prosecution's case against another man in 1973 when Christi was arrested with $100,000 in counterfeit cash in his possession. He was fined and given five years' probation. Christi had worked on such television shows as "Barnaby Jones," "Bonanza," "Cannon," "Gunsmoke," "Kojak," "Mannix," "Mission Impossible," "Mod Squad," and "The Incredible Hulk." REF.: *CBA*.

Christian (AKA: **der tolle Christian, the Mad Christian**), 1599-1626, Ger., milit. corr. Military leader who became known for pillaging when he raised and led an army on behalf of Frederick V, king of Bohemia, during the Thirty Years War. He later served King Christian IV of Denmark. REF.: *CBA*.

Christian II (AKA: **Christian the Cruel**), 1481-1559, Swed., geno. King of Sweden from 1520-23. After successfully overthrowing the Regent of Sweden in 1520, he massacred the nobility of Stockholm. The aroused citizenry rallied behind Gustavus Vasa who deposed Christian II in 1523. He was arrested and imprisoned for life. REF.: *CBA*.

Christian VII, 1749-1808, Den.-Nor., mur. King of Denmark and Norway from 1766-1808, married to Queen Caroline Matilda. Upon discovering his wife's lover, Johann Streunsee, he had him beheaded. After his marriage was dissolved, he went insane and gave up his throne to Prince Frederick. REF.: *CBA*.

Christian, Almeric Leander, 1919- , U.S., jur. U.S. attorney in the Virgin Islands from 1962-69. In a bipartisan appointment, he was nominated to serve on the bench of the district court of the U.S. Virgin Islands in 1969 by President Richard M. Nixon. REF.: *CBA*.

Christian, Fletcher, See: **Mutiny on the *Bounty***.

Christian, Will (AKA: **Black Jack, Ed Williams, 202**), d.1897, U.S., west. outl. Will Christian and his gang of Oklahoma robbers were active in New Mexico and in Arizona's Sulphur Springs Valley throughout the 1890s, when the American frontier was fast disappearing. Will and his brother, Bob, led the "High Fives," a gang that robbed stage coaches, banks, and trains. Originally nicknamed "202" because of his considerable girth, Christian's ability with a gun soon earned him the name "Black Jack."

The two Christian brothers were arrested in Guthrie, Okla., in Summer 1895 after fatally shooting a peace officer. They broke out of jail a short time later and fled to Arizona, where they remained active for the next two years. In Nogales on Aug. 6, the High Fives attempted to rob the International Bank. The attempt failed when newspaperman Frank King opened fire on Bob Hays and Jess Williams as they tried to leave town with the sack of loot, causing Williams to drop the money.

Later that month, a deputized posse from Tucson led by Sheriff Bob Leatherwood intercepted the gang near Skeleton Canyon. Deputy Frank Robson was killed in the shootout, but Christian and his men escaped across the border into Mexico. After hearing that Christian and his henchman had returned to Arizona in 1897, a second posse was organized. They ambushed the desperadoes in Black Jack Canyon. In the gun battle that followed, Christian was shot in the side and killed. The body of the dead outlaw was thrown on top of a lumber wagon and taken to town for display.

Will "Black Jack" Christian

REF.: Bartholomew, *The Biographical Album of Western Gunfighters*; ____, *Black Jack Ketchum*; Burton, *Black Jack Christian*; *CBA*; Chisholm, *Brewery Gulch*; Chrisman, *Fifty Years on the Owl Hoot Trail*; Haley, *Jeff Milton*; Hertzog, *A Directory of New Mexico Desperadoes*; Hunter and Rose, *The Album of Gunfighters*; Hutchinson, *The Life and Personal Writings of Eugene Manlove Rhodes*; Mullin, *The Boyhood of Billy the Kid*; O'Neal, *Encyclopedia of Western Gunfighters*; Rynning, *Gun Notches*; Shinkle, *Reminiscences of Roswell*; Siringo, *Riata and Spurs*; Walters, *Tombstone's Yesterdays*; Wilson, *An Unwritten History*.

Christian, William, 1608-63, Brit., embez. Accused of embezzling funds while serving as governor of the Isle of Man from 1656-58. He was captured by the Eighth Earl and shot. REF.: *CBA*.

Christiana Affair, 1851, U.S., mob vio. The Compromise of 1850 delayed the U.S. Civil War by nearly ten years. In return for California entering the Union as a free state and the abolition of slave trade in Washington, D.C., the North agreed in the 1850 Compromise to vigorously enforce the Fugitive Slave Law. By its terms, blacks accused of being runaway slaves were taken to federal commissioners who received $10 for each slave returned to the owners. The marshals, authorized by the government to track down runaway slaves, could recruit whomever they needed. Following the passage of the fugitive law, there were reports of many Northern blacks being arrested and sent into slavery.

Pro-abolition sentiment was rife in the country, and numerous vigilance committees were organized to assist blacks in their flight to freedom. In February 1851, a slave named Shadrach was saved by a racially-mixed crowd of Bostonians and delivered to the Underground Railway. A similar incident occurred in September 1851, when a Maryland slaveholder, Edward Gorsuch, discovered that several of his runaways had sought refuge in Christiana, Pa., a black settlement. Gorsuch traveled to Philadelphia where he secured a warrant to have them captured.

On Sept. 11, Gorsuch, Deputy U.S. Marshal Henry Kline, and several other slave hunters called upon William Parker, the leader of the free blacks of Christiana. When Parker refused to surrender the fugitives, the elderly Gorsuch attempted to storm into the house to look for his men. A group of field hands and local residents arrived at the Parker home armed with corn cutters, scythes, and muskets. When one of the marshals fired on Parker and missed, Parker's brother-in-law shot Gorsuch's son.

The elder Gorsuch refused to give up. He discharged both his pistols, but was quickly overpowered and clubbed to death by Parker and his neighbors. With Gorsuch dead and his son and nephew severely wounded, Kline, and the other slave hunters fled.

With Parker's help, the escaped slaves made their way to Canada. In the first jusdicial test of the fugitive law, thirty-eight people who refused to help Kline arrest the runaways were taken into custody and indicted for treason. The abolition cause prevailed when the defendants were found Not Guilty on Dec. 11. The South was furious with the outcome and a newspaper in Augusta, Ga., bitterly declared, "The Law will hereafter be a perfectly dead letter."

REF.: *CBA;* Hofstadter and Wallace, *American Violence.*

Christianson, Willard Erastus (AKA: Matt Warner, Mormon Kid), 1864-1938, U.S., west. outl. Born of hardworking immigrant parents from Sweden and Germany who came to Utah to practice the Mormon faith, Willard Christianson nearly killed a man when he was only fourteen. Without knowing his victim's fate, Christianson ran away from his parents home in Levan to become a range cowboy. He began calling himself the "Mormon Kid" and joined a band of rustlers operating in the Robber's Roost area. During these years on the run, Christianson met up with Butch Cassidy and committed several crimes with his gang.

Christianson married Rose Morgan, and together they ran a cattle ranch with Tom McCarty in Washington's Big Bend country. In 1892, Christianson and the two McCarty Brothers, Tom and Bill, held up a bank in Roslyn, Wash. The "Invincible Three" as they came to be known, escaped two lengths ahead of the furious townsmen. Shortly afterward, Christianson was captured and imprisoned in the Ellensburg, Wash., jail. While awaiting trial, Christianson and another inmate, George McCarty, attempted to escape by sawing through the wall of the jail. They were recaptured following a brief gunfight, but were freed by the courts two days later.

Christianson returned to Diamond Mountain, Utah, and lived there for the next four years. On an expedition to the Uinta Mountains in 1896, Christianson and his party were ambushed by a gang of gunslingers led by Dave Milton, and Ike and Dick Staunton. Although Christianson's horse was shot from under him, he began firing and killed Milton and Dick Staunton. Ike Staunton was shot in the knee.

When the shooting was over, Christianson sent for the sheriff. He was arrested, tried, and convicted on a charge of manslaughter in the deaths of Milton and Staunton, and sent to the Utah State Prison. After Christianson's release from prison in 1900, he was law-abiding most of the time. He moved to Carbon County where he was elected justice of the peace. He also served as a night watchman, and was involved in bootlegging. Christianson died of natural causes in 1938. See: **Cassidy, Butch; Wild Bunch, The.**

REF.: Baker, *The Wild Bunch;* Burroughs, *Where the Old West Stayed Young; CBA;* Holloway, *Texas Gun Lore;* Horan, *Desperate Men;* ____, *The Wild Bunch;* ____, *Pictorial History of the Wild West;* Kelly, *The Outlaw Trail;* Look, *Unforgettable Characters of Western Colorado;* Nash, *Bloodletters and Badmen;* O'Neal, *Encyclopedia of Western Gunfighters;* Penfield, *Western Sheriffs and Marshals;* Rockwell, *Memoirs of a Lawman;* Sheller, *Ben Snipes, Northwest Cattle King;* Swallow, *The Wild Bunch;* Warner, *Last of the Bandit Raiders;* (FICTION), Sheller, *Bandit to Lawman.*

Christie, Agatha (Agatha Mary Clarissa Miller), 1890-1976, Brit., det.-mystery writer. One of the most popular mystery writers of all time, her books selling well over 100 million copies, Agatha Christie, from appearances in her late life struck most as a pleasant but dowdy old lady whose charm belonged to a bygone age. Her detective-mystery fiction is of the average whodunit variety, constructed in a crisp literary style that is unmistakably British. Christie did, however, manage to create two memorable if unorthodox sleuths, the methodical Hercule Poirot and the lovable Jane Marple. During one rare interview Christie admitted, capriciously or not, that she created all her characters while soaking for hours in her bathtub, using a small penknife to carve out little figurines from small bars of soap and placing these along the rim of the tub, then naming these soap figures and thinking up personalities to go with them, and involving them in some sort of sudsy plot, soap mysteries, as it were. (In a 1974 interview,

Christie said she cut out apples and lined the rim of the tub with the cores and these fruity remnants formed the images of characters to come.) Then again, Christie's bathtub story may have been her own private joke or hoax since she was disinclined to give interviews in the first place and kept her private life in shadow and secret. Though she was the world's leading mystery writer, she was also a mystery herself, and she fiercely guarded her own enigma—or created that enigma—for both professional and private reasons.

Agatha Christie was born on Sept. 15, 1890, at Ashfield, a mansion in the older section of Torquay, an elegant seaside resort town in Devonshire, on the southern English coast. Her father was a well-to-do American businesmann, Frederick Alvah Miller, her mother, Clarissa Margaret Beochmer, was British. Agatha had servants waiting on her until she was sent to finishing school in Paris and, upon her return, she traveled with her mother through Egypt, her father having died when she was eleven. Upon her return to England, Agatha wrote poetry, then a first novel which she entitled *Snow Upon the Desert* which earned some interest from publishers but was scrapped.

Agatha Christie, the world's most successful mystery writer.

Then she began writing short stories in the mystery vein and these began to appear in magazines with limited circulation.

By 1912, Christie was inundated with marriage proposals, mostly from young army officers. She became engaged to Reggie Lucy, a major in the artillery, but she broke this off after meeting the handsome, young Archibald Christie, a lieutenant in the Royal Flying Corps. They were married on Christmas Eve 1914, and Christie, two days later, went off to fight in WWI. While her husband was in France, on and off for several years, Agatha Christie spent time developing her fuss-budget sleuth, Hercule Poirot, inspired by avidly devouring the stories of Sherlock Holmes by Arthur Conan Doyle. She began work on her first Poirot book, *The Mysterious Affair at Styles,* which was not published until 1920. It sold well, about 2,000 copies, and her subsequent detective-mysteries did better in the next few years, averaging about 5,000 sales. But not until the spectacular disappearance of Agatha Christie herself did her career soar into the literary stratosphere.

This vanishing act occured on the stormy night of Dec. 3, 1926. At the time, Mrs. Christie and her husband had grown distant. They had produced one child, Rosalind, born in 1919. It was later reported that Christie had begun an affair with his secretary and this caused something, perhaps a plot, to snap in the mind of Agatha Christie. On that December night, Mrs. Christie packed a bag, climbed into her car and drove away from her three-story mansion, Styles (named after her first novel), in Berkshire. Her car was found empty and deserted the next morning. By that time, hundreds of police and citizen volunteers were frantically searching for Agatha through the Berkshire woodlands and hills. Christie, by then a colonel and an important businessman, gave police little help, first saying that his wife had overworked herself while preparing her next novel and that fatigue and stress may have caused her to lose control. He remarked rather sarcastically to a newspaper reporter: "My wife said to me some time ago that she could disappear at will and defy anyone to find her. This shows that the possibility of engineering her disappearance was running through her mind." Christie was followed everywhere by the police, to and from his office and home, and they monitored his phone calls. He nervously told a business acquaintence: "They think I've murdered my wife."

As days passed, the search for Agatha Christie intensified, and substantial rewards for information leading to her whereabouts were offered. This caused thousands of amateur detectives to scour the countryside for the missing author, causing the police no end of annoyance and hindrance. Everyone had a theory about the Christie disappearance, including crime writer and playwright Edgar Wallace, who stated that the missing Christie was "a typical case of 'mental reprisal' on somebody who has hurt her. To put it vulgarly, her first intention seems to have been to 'spite' an unknown person who would be distressed by her disappearance. That she did not contemplate suicide seems evident from the fact that she deliberately created an atmosphere of suicide by abandonment of her car. Loss of memory, that is to say mental confusion, might have easily followed, but a person so afflicted could not possibly escape notice...If Agatha Christie is not dead of shock and exposure within a limited radius of the place where her car was found, she must be alive and in full possession of her faculties, probably in London. It is impossible to lose your memory and find your way to a determined destination."

But loss of memory, or specifically amnesia, was the very reason Agatha Christie would later give to explain her disappearance. She arrived on Dec. 4, 1926, at the Hydropathic Hotel in Harrogate (later called the Old Swan Hotel), then a swanky spa in Yorkshire. She carried one bag and registered under the name of Mrs. Teresa Neale and she spent a week mingling with other guests, even attending a Saturday night dance where she danced the Charleston. She chatted with guests and even discussed the disappearance of the author, Agatha Christie, with others, taking a certain interest in the case, following it in the newspapers. It should be noted that Agatha Christie, as a teenager, had been almost obsessed with the disppearance of heiress Dorothy Arnold in New York (see entry) and read every report she could find about this case. It was Bob Tappan, the banjo player in the Harry Codd Hydro Dance Band, performing at the hotel, who recognized Mrs. Christie. He went to the police in Harrogate and two detectives arrived shortly to keep "Mrs. Neale" under observation.

A report that the missing author was at the Harrogate spa brought dozens of reporters from London newspapers to Yorkshire, with Ritchie Calder of the *Daily News* being the first to arrive. He spotted Christie sitting in the hotel foyer and walked up to her, asking her if, indeed, she was the missing Agatha Christie. She remained silent for a few minutes, her face flushed. Then she admitted her identity. Ritchie then asked her how she had gotten to the hotel. She said she did not know and mentioned something about amnesia. With that, Christie abruptly stood up and went to her room, where she stayed for the rest of the day. Her husband arrived and confronted her as she was walking in a pink evening dress toward the lounge. When she looked at him, she said to some other guests: "Fancy, my brother has just arrived." Archie Christie took her by the hand and led her to the roaring fireplace in the large sitting area. Both took chairs "but several chairs apart from each other as though they had been quarreling."

The couple stayed one more night in the hotel, in a suite, not the single room Mrs. Christie had occupied. In the morning, Archibald Christie held a brief press conference with scores of anxious reporters and told them: "There is no question about the identity. It is my wife. She has suffered from the most complete loss of memory and I do not think she knows who she is. She does not know me and she does not know where she is. I am hoping that the rest and quiet will restore her. I am hoping to take her to London tomorrow to see a doctor and specialists." The matter did not end there. The newspapers, which had offered rewards for information leading to her whereabouts, were compelled to pay, and angry editors denounced the writer as staging a disappearance to create publicity for the subsequent sale of her most recent novel, *The Murder of Roger Ackroyd,* although this book was selling well before Mrs. Christie vanished. The *Daily News* sent Agatha Christie a telegram which it also published in its pages, one that did her career not a whit of good: "In view

wide-spread criticism your disappearance strongly urge desirability authentic explanation from yourself to thousands of public who joined in costly search and cannot understand your loss of memory theory."

Agatha Christie did not respond, later dealing with this sensational incident only in oblique terms in her fiction. In her autobiography, she all but ignored the disappearance. Her marriage to Christie dissolved a short time thereafter. The writer later married archeologist Max Mallowan, and settled down to a country life, producing one best-selling detective mystery after another, not the least of which was *Murder on the Orient Express,* 1934, and *Death on the Nile,* 1937, along with writing the longest-running play in London, *The Mouse Trap,* 1952.

REF.: *CBA;* Christie, *An Autobiography;* Keating, *Agatha Christie: First Lady of Crime;* Nash, *Among the Missing;* Osborne, *The Life and Crimes of Agatha Christie;* Robyns, *The Mystery of Agatha Christie.*

Christie, Avril, prom. 1971, Case of, U.S., mur. Avril Christie and his brother Hank Christie, mountain people living in the Kentucky-Tennessee area, were ruffians and troublemakers. Members of the riotous Honey Creek family, the brothers were jailed nearly every weekend by the sheriff.

The older brother, Avril, married and, according to accounts, became suspicious that Hank was paying unwanted attentions to his wife. Jealousy flared, and on Oct. 21, 1971, Avril confronted Hank about 250 yards from their homes. Hank denied the accusations but Avril refused to believe him. When Hank started to run away, Avril shot and killed him with a .22 rifle. No legal action was ever taken in the case.

REF.: *CBA;* Montell, *Killings.*

Christie, Balm, prom. 1973, U.S., mur. Balm Christie, a criminal with a long list of offenses beginning in the 1960s, shot and murdered his wife on Jan. 1, 1973. Earlier charges lodged against Christie included theft, assault and battery, and breaking and entering. Reputedly, Christie's past criminal activities and the objections of his wife's relatives were partially responsible for the friction within the household. Christie stood trial and was sentenced to prison. Balm Christie, who lived near Mattis and Bell Fort, was a cousin of Hank and Avril Christie, who lived in the Kentucky-Tennessee mountains.

REF.: *CBA;* Montell, *Killings.*

Christie, Isham Thomas, d.1902, U.S., mur. In the Mt. Gilead region of North Carolina, Isham Thomas Christie was born, lived, committed a murder, and was murdered himself.

According to one account of the murder of Peter Tripps by Christie, Christie hid in a tree and shot Tripps off his horse in an unprovoked surprise attack. In another account, Christie shot Tripps in revenge for the murder of Christie's son. While at a dance, the son, Sammy Christie, drank some whiskey that had been poisoned by the sister of a girl that both Sammy Christie and Tripps were dating. Christie reputedly went to Tripps' house, sat on the porch, and shot Tripps when he came home.

Christie himself was shot and killed by Frank Bowles on May 28, 1902. One of Christie's steers was found dead and several hogs of another family were found missing. Bowles was suspected, and Christie joined the posse, which included two of his deputized sons, to look for Bowles. Christie and Bowles began arguing, and Bowles shot Christie to death with a shotgun. See: **Bowles, Frank**.

REF.: *CBA;* Montell, *Killings.*

Christie, John Reginald Halliday (AKA: Waddingham), 1898-1953, Brit., mur. One of the most horrific killers in modern British history, Christie was half monster, half human, although in appearance he seemed to be nothing more than a meek-mannered middle-class citizen. He lived in a grimy, grubby little house at 10 Rillington Place in Notting Hill Gate, North Kensington, London. In 1948, Timothy John Evans, his wife Beryl, and baby daughter Geraldine rented the top floor of the Christie house (the Christies lived on the ground floor). On Nov. 5, 1949, Mrs. Evans' father visited with her and this was the last time she was seen alive. Police conducted a search and, on Dec. 2, 1949, the bodies of Mrs. Evans and her infant were found in a wash house in Rillington Place, both strangled to death. Evans, a 24-year-old, dim-witted truck driver, had walked into the small police station at Merthyr Tydfil, South Wales, to inform officers that he had found his wife dead in his apartment and he had placed her body down a drain. After the bodies were found, Evans was returned to London under guard and there he confessed to murdering his wife and child.

Evans was charged with murdering his child, but before he was brought to trial at the Old Bailey, he withdrew his confession. He insisted that Christie had performed the killings. Christie emphatically denied having anything to do with the deaths of Mrs. Evans and her child. Moreover, he and his wife appeared as witnesses for the prosecution and gave evidence that helped to convict Evans. He was sentenced to death and hanged at Pentonville Prison on Mar. 9, 1950. Mrs. Christie then disappeared. She was last seen alive on Dec. 12, 1952, and Christie gave nervous explanations for her absence, claiming she was visiting relatives or that she had gone on a vacation. He then left his apartment in early 1953, subletting the place to a couple named Reilly. These people were quickly evicted by the owner of the building, a Jamaican named Beresford Brown, who moved into the Christie residence.

On Mar. 24, 1953, Brown went into the kitchen of the Christie apartment and began looking for a beam behind the wall into which he could screw a bracket for a wall-mounted radio. He tore away a loose piece of wallpaper and discovered an opening in the wall, a sort of large closet that had been covered by a thin sheet of posterboard and then covered with wallpaper. Taking out the board, Brown saw that three bodies had been stuffed inside the hollow area. He immediately called the police. Another body was discovered beneath the floorboards, and officers unearthed the skeletal remains of two more corpses found in the garden. These were easy to detect when an officer noticed that a human bone was propping up a fence and the police merely dug at this spot to find the rest of the remains. All of the bodies and remains were that of women. The corpses found in the closet and the one beneath the floorboards in the front room were for the most part naked, and three had been wrapped in blankets. Contrary to most later reports, there was very little odor from the bodies and there was no "overpowering stench" which led to their discovery. All were dehydrated and the atmospheric conditions in the apartment kept the smell of the dead bodies to a minimum.

The body beneath the floorboards was Mrs. Ethel Christie, whose husband had left 10 Rillington Place three days earlier. Those in the cupboard area were all known prostitutes, Hectorina McLennan, twenty-six; Kathleen Maloney, twenty-six; and Rita Nelson, twenty-five. The remains found in the garden were subsequently identified as those of Ruth Fuerst, an Austrian girl who had been murdered by Christie in 1943, and Muriel Eady, a girl who had worked with Christie at the Ultra Radio Factory in Park Royal in 1944. The shocking story of the mild-mannered mass-murderer broke just at the time when police were conducting a nationwide search for Christie. He was found on Mar. 31, 1953, by Constable Ledger as he stood near Putney Bridge, watching a group of children at play. Christie, bald, wearing horn-rimmed glasses over weak eyes, with a flabby, middle-aged body, offered no resistance. He quickly confessed to the murders of the six women, saying that his first victim had been the Fuerst girl, followed by Muriel Eady. Christie stated that he strangled the Fuerst girl while he was having sex with her. He had not murdered for nine years but he suddenly went on a murder spree in late 1952, luring the prostitutes to his apartment when his wife was away and, after killing them, raping the corpses. He detailed his necrophiliac acts, which made him appear to be all the more inhuman. He had murdered his wife on Dec. 14, 1952, Christie said, as an "act of mercy." He could no longer bear to witness her "convulsive attacks"—she suffered from some sort of undefined malady—and so, when she went into one of her fits while they were still in bed, Christie grabbed one of her stockings, rolled

over, and strangled her with it.

Sir Francis Camps, one of England's most brilliant pathologists, examined Christie and his murders in minute detail. He learned that when Christie had brought his prostitute victims to his flat, he would ply the women with liquor. When they were drunk, get them to sit in a chair with a canopy, under which he had affixed a gas pipe. He would then turn on the gas, and, when they were unconscious, strangle the women, then rape them. The trick with the gas explained the carbon monoxide Camps found in the blood of the three women hidden in the kitchen enclosure. But there were strange sexual undertones to this case which puzzled Camps. He found that all three prostitutes were naked, but were wearing what amounted to handmade diapers. Semen had been found in them, as well as in an old pair of Christie's shoes, indicating that he had ejaculated following the murder-rapes. A tin can was found in the kitchen enclosure, and inside of this was found four separate tufts of pubic hair which Christie had plucked from his victims and preserved, but for what purpose Camps could not determine.

Camps probed deeper into the sexual mysteries of John Reginald Halliday Christie, discovering that the myopic, always frail Christie had had psychological problems rooted in childhood. Born in Boothstown, Yorkshire, in April 1898, the son of carpet designer Ernest Christie, and one of seven children, Christie was treated with unloving harshness by his martinet father. He was disciplined often for the slightest infractions. Introverted, weak, the boy was labeled a "sissy" by his classmates who made fun of his poor eyesight. He took to stealing small things which caused him to be returned home by constables. His father, at these times, responded with the typical Victorian action, a beating. At the age of fifteen in 1913, Christie quit school and took a job clerking for the Halifax Borough Police, but he was fired when he was suspected of stealing small items. About this time, Christie was seduced by an older girl who later made fun of him when he could not finish the sex act. The girl spread the story and Christie was the butt of sex jokes among his peers who called him "Can't Do It Christie." He was invalided at home for a time, ill again. Christie's confession was punctuated repeatedly by statements claiming his lifelong illnesses, and it was apparent to Camps that he was a confirmed hypochondriac.

Following a severe bout with pneumonia, Christie claimed, he went to France in 1915, serving in the trenches until he was blown out of a trench and inhaled mustard gas, which caused him to go blind for several months and lose his voice for three years. This was attributed to hysteria and not physical damage received when the artillery shell blew him out of a trench. Whenever Christie was excited after that, he would lose his voice or it would rise to a high whine. In 1920, Christie met and married his wife Ethel, a union which produced no children. Christie claimed that he did not have sex with his wife for two years following the marriage and continued to have a pervasive feeling of inadequacy. Following a quarrel with his wife in 1923, the couple separated and Christie lost his voice completely, he claimed.

Bad luck followed Christie wherever he went, he said in his confession. In 1934, a hit-and-run driver knocked him down, injuring his head, knee, and collar bone. Worse luck, most brought about by Christie himself, dogged his work life. He seldom kept a steady job, the longest being five years while working as a clerk for a transport company. He was a postal employee at one time, but it was proved that he stole money orders and he was sent to prison for seven months. During his 1923 separation from his wife, Christie was imprisoned briefly for false pretense; he had falsified documents which claimed that he was a rich man at one time but had lost his money. He went to Brixton and Battersea and there put on the air of a once-wealthy man who was down on his luck. When a woman rebuffed his advances, Christie hit her on the head with a cricket bat and was arrested and sent to prison once more.

During WWII, Christie was a member of the War Reserve Police, a blackout warden who marched about his neighborhood

Left, John Reginald Halliday Christie, British mass murderer. Right, Timothy John Evans, hanged in 1950 for murders Christie may have committed.
Below, 10 Rillingon Place, Christie's house of murder; bodies were hidden behind walls, under the floorboards, in the garden.

Left, Christie with his wife Ethel, whom he also murdered, putting her body beneath the floorboards; right, Christie in wax at Madame Tussaud's.

pumped up with authority. He delighted in turning in those who ignored blackout rules. In 1943, his wife went to visit relatives in Sheffield, and it was at this time that Christie committed his first murder, bringing Ruth Fuerst home with him and murdering her, burying her corpse in the back yard. Although Christie admitted to murdering the six women, he was contradictory about Mrs. Evans and her child. He claimed that he found Mrs. Evans unconscious in her flat after she had quarreled with her husband about "a blonde woman." She had tried to commit suicide by turning on the gas, Christie said. He gave her a cup of tea and told her to calm down.

Mrs. Evans tried to kill herself once more, Christie said, and he again came to her rescue. Then she said she was pregnant and Christie, who had no medical knowledge, offered to perform the abortion she desired. She panicked when he was applying the gas to make her unconscious prior to the operation and thus died. He varied this tale by saying that Mrs. Evans, despondent over her husband's sexual escapades, asked Christie if he would kill her since she had botched two other suicide attempts. She said he could have sexual intercourse with her, Christie claimed, if he would but help her die. He strangled her, Christie said at one point, and *then* had sexual intercourse with her corpse. When Evans returned home, Christie told him that she had gassed herself and that he had best flee since authorities would think Evans murdered his wife. Evans then reportedly murdered his child and sold off the household furniture before fleeing. His confusing statements throughout his trial concerning the death of the Evans child and his wife are impossible to decipher at this time.

Following the deaths of the three prostitutes, Christie said he sold his wife's wedding ring and the household furniture, and wandered about London with a total loss of memory. When he was arrested, he said, he had been sleeping in a cheap hotel. At the time he looked like a common tramp with dirty clothes, unshaven beard, and empty pockets. Christie was tried at the Old Bailey for three days, June 22-25, 1953, before Justice Fennemore. He was prosecuted by Sir Lionel Heald, then attorney general, and defended by Derek Curtis Bennett. Little defense could be offered on Christie's behalf, so Bennett opted to plead his client insane. Several medical experts examined Christie and testified that he was sane. The jury returned a verdict of Guilty and Christie was sentenced to death. He was hanged at Pentonville Prison on July 15, 1953.

The conviction and execution of the monster Christie left many believing that Timothy Evans' conviction and hanging was a gross miscarriage of justice, that he had been executed for a crime that Christie himself had committed, the murder of Mrs. Beryl Evans, although considerable doubt exists that Christie killed the Evans child. This is the one murder that he said he did not commit, and the one murder that Evans admitted committing. The Evans case remains a baffling mystery, which is exactly the way Christie wanted it, for he in no way cleared up the Evans murders but, through his whining statements, seemed to add even more confusion as to who was the real killer of Mrs. Evans and her child. Such were Christie's strange perversions that he would be content to go to the hangman knowing that he had created a lingering doubt in the minds of those who sent Timothy Evans to his death. From the grave, Christie would nag the consciences of good men, whereas he was without conscience altogether.

REF.: Bailey, *The Fatal Chance*; Bennett, *Why Did They Do It?*; Boar, *The World's Most Infamous Murders*; Brophy, *The Meaning of Murder*; Camps, *Camps on Crime*; ____, *The Investigation of Murder*; ____, *Medical and Scientific Investigations in the Christie Case*; CBA; Cherrill, *Cherrill of the Yard*; Cuthbert, *Science and the Detection of Crime*; deFord, *Murderers Sane and Mad*; Dickson, *Murder by Numbers*; Eddowes, *The Man on Your Conscience*; Firmin, *Murderers in Our Midst*; Furneaux, *Famous Criminal Cases, Vol. I*; ____, *The Two Stranglers of Rillington Place*; Haines, *Bothersome Bodies*; Heppenstall, *The Sex War and Others*; Hibbert, *The Roots of Evil*; Jackson, *Francis Camps*; Kennedy, *Ten Rillington Place*; Lefebure, *Murder with a Difference*; Lustgarten, *The*

Business of Murder; Maxwell, *The Christie Case*; Neustatter, *The Mind of the Murderer*; *Notable British Trials*; Page, *Hanged—And Innocent?*; Phillips, *Murderer's Moon*; Potter, *The Art of Hanging*; Scott, *The Concise Encyclopedia of Crime and Criminals*; ____, *Scotland Yard*; Shew, *A Companion to Murder*; Simpson, *Forty Years of Murder*; Traini, *Murder for Sex*; Webb, *Deadline for Crime*; Wilson, *Encyclopedia of Murder*; (FILM), *10 Rillington Place*, 1971.

Christie, Ned, 1852-92, U.S., west. outl. Ned Christie, a full Cherokee, evaded lawmen for nearly seven years. Christie worked as a blacksmith near Tahlequah, Okla., where he also sold guns, stole horses, and ran whiskey. In 1885 Christie drove away a lawman who attempted to take him into custody. For the next seven years, a state of siege existed between Christie and the government.

Subsequent assaults against his various strongholds failed to roust the determined Cherokee. However, early one morning in 1889 while Christie and his family slept, Deputy marshals L.P.

Isbel, Dave Rusk, and Heck Thomas set fire to his house in Tahlequah. Alerted by a watchdog, Christie opened fire on the lawmen. During a break in the shooting, his wife and son fled from the burning house but lawmen spotted and shot at them. Christie's son was hit in the lung and hips, but Christie managed to escape despite having his right eye put out and the bridge of his nose broken. He retreated to the mountains to build a two-story fortification that the lawmen found virtually impossible to penetrate. Various attempts to burn Christie's Fort Mountain failed. Law enforcement officials even tried to blast it open with sticks of dynamite, but failed.

Outlaw Ned Christie, dead, 1892.

On Nov. 2, Deputy U.S. Marshal Paden Tolbert and sixteen lawmen lugged a small cannon up the mountain in an all-out effort to dislodge Christie from his fortress. To Tolbert's dismay, the cannon shells merely bounced off the thick log walls. When the posse regrouped after dark, Tolbert fashioned a barricade from a burned lumber wagon that had been used in an earlier attack on the fort. A few minutes after midnight, the rolling wall was pushed close to the cabin. Inside, Christie and his companion Arch Wolf emptied a fusillade of shot into the barricade with no effect. Lawman Charley Copeland placed six dynamite sticks against the south wall, and stood back. The intensity of the blast finally pierced a hole in the structure.

With his fortress penetrated, Christie made a break for the woods but found himself confronted by Deputy Wess Bowman, who shot him in the head. Sam Maples, whose father had been killed by Christie on May 5, 1885, in Tahlequah, emptied his revolver into Christie's lifeless body.

REF.: Ballenger, *Around Tahlequah Council Fires*; CBA; Croy, *He Hanged Them High*; Drago, *Outlaws on Horseback*; ____, *Red River Valley*; Elman, *Badmen of the West*; Good, *Guns of the Gunfighters*; Harrington, *Hanging Judge*; Harrison, *Hell Holes and Hangings*; Hunter and Rose, *The Album of Gunfighters*; Jones, *The Experiences of a Deputy U.S. Marshal of the Indian Territory*; McKennon, *Iron Men*; Nash, *Bloodletters and Badmen*; O'Neal, *Encyclopedia of Western Gunfighters*; Shirley, *Heck Thomas, Frontier Marshal*; ____, *Henry Starr, Last of the Real Badmen*; ____, *Law West of Fort Smith*; ____, *Six Gun and Silver Star*; Trachtman, *Gunfighters*.

Christie-Scott Duel, prom. 1821, Case of, Brit., duel-mur. The principals of two magazines became involved in a spate of disputes when the editor of *London Magazine*, John Scott, argued with John Gibson Lockhart, Edinburgh manager of *Blackwood's Magazine*. The original dispute arose after *London Magazine* ran several articles criticizing *Blackwood's Magazine* and its managers. Christie, a friend of Lockhart, was sent to demand an explanation and public apology from Scott, but the conflict was not resolved and Christie became entangled in the fight. The friction came to a head when Scott visited Christie's house, calling for an apology or a duel. Christie accepted the duel.

The duel took place on Feb. 16, 1821, at 9 p.m. in a field near the Chalk Farm Tavern. Scott, wounded by Christie's second shot, died on March 4. Shortly thereafter, Christie, and two others who attended the duel, Trail and Patmore, stood trial for murder. Called into question during the trial was Christie's intent in firing the second shot. All men were found Not Guilty. REF.: *CBA*.

Christina, 1626-89, Swed., mur. Queen Christina ascended to the Swedish throne at the age of six. She was an aloof, unforgiving monarch who preferred the company of men, and was at ease dashing through the lush Swedish forests on her steed in pursuit of reindeer. In matters of state she held fast to her credo: "I never forgive."

The Marquis Monaldesco, her chief equerry, learned this painful lesson on Nov. 10, 1657, when he was executed by the guards. The Marquis had forged a series of letters in order to incriminate his chief rival, Count Santinelli, for the Queen's favor. He attached a vicious rumor to the documents that romantically linked the Queen to a Cardinal in Rome, and sealed his doom. It took fifteen minutes for Monaldesco to die. Queen Christina sent money to a local convent so that prayers would be said in his behalf. REF.: *CBA*.

Christison, Sir Robert, 1797-1882, Scot., toxicol. Authority on the pathology of the kidneys. He served on the faculty of Edinburgh University. Books authored: *Treatise on Poisons*. REF.: *CBA*.

Christmas, Annie, prom. 1820s, U.S., pros. Of all the evil characters who infested the Swamp, the early-day, vile district of New Orleans, none surpassed the exotic Annie Christmas, a behemoth of a woman who stood six feet, eight inches, weighed more than 250 pounds, and whose reputation certainly rivaled that of Mose the Bowery Boy in early New York. This part-time stevedore/part-time flatboat skipper was a full-time hellion, an amazon in every foreboding sense.

Wearing a trimmed mustache, Christmas could usually be spotted along the levee carrying two giant barrels of rum on either shoulder or 500 pounds of flour or the equivalent of cordwood, feats of strength that were unachievable for any man. Wild tales were told of her incredible exploits, especially by blacks, who considered her one of their few white heroes. It was said that she once towed a loaded keelboat, crew and all, singlehandedly, from Natchez to New Orleans, running all the way and making the boat literally skip on the water. Even Mike Fink, legend has it, was terrified of this towering creature. "If he (Mike Fink) ever shows his ugly face in these parts," Christmas is said to have threatened, "I'll tie him to the bottom of a flatboat and run him up to Memphis!" Fink never did appear in Christmas' domain, which was broadened considerably when she decided to give up her cargo-carrying chores in favor of more lucrative endeavors, chiefly the establishment of a floating brothel anchored off the levee.

Annie's girls were the most diseased and repulsive of the prostitute population in New Orleans, but her clientele of wharf thieves and river cutthroats was no more reputable. It was Christmas' favorite practice to offer a fine keg of whiskey to whichever of her girls could satisfy the most men in a single night. Invariably, Christmas won each and every one of these contests, sometimes taking on ten flatboat men at one time.

For those who were so foolish as to challenge Annie Christmas' strength in combat, there awaited a horrible fate. Dozens of the fiercest flatboat men, hundreds, some historians insisted, tangled with Christmas and wound up with broken bones and missing cherished parts of their anatomies. The eyes gouged out, the noses and ears chewed off by Annie Christmas, were festooned upon a grisly necklace and this the amazon wore at all times, even to bed, as a warning to the troublesome. At her death, the ghastly necklace was thirty feet long. "It would be longer," she once apologized, "but I only count the pieces of white men."

For all of her hatred of blacks, Annie Christmas was one of the great heroines of black lore. In fact, although Christmas was white, the superstitious blacks doggedly insisted that she had been born black and died a black. The real Christmas perished in a gambling den along the levee, attacked from behind by a mob of no less than fifty men. She was shot and stabbed, the story goes, more than 100 times before dying.

The black version of her death is more involved and provocative. According to slave legend, Annie Christmas was coal black and had given birth to twelve black sons all at once, like the birth of a litter, and these sons all stood more than seven feet. Christmas committed suicide over a lost love, the black legend has it, and her body was placed on a black barge as her enormous twelve sons, all dressed in black, poled the craft to the sea and disappeared forever, Annie, barge, sons, and all. Whatever dramatic end was true, both were worthy of the extravagant Miss Christmas. See: **Mose, the Bowery Boy; Swamp, The**.

REF.: Anthony, *Paddle Wheels and Pistols;* Asbury, *The French Quarter;* Buel, *Metropolitan Life Unveiled;* Cable, *Strange True Stories of Louisiana;* Castellanos, *New Orleans as It Was; CBA;* Fremaux, *New Orleans Characters; History of New Orleans Police Department;* Laughlin, *New Orleans and Its Living Past;* Spear, *Ancient and Modern New Orleans;* Tinker, *Creole City: Its Past and Its People*.

Christ Miracle Healing Center and Church, prom. 1982, U.S., riot.-assslt. An attempt to serve arrest warrants for traffic violations resulted in the deaths of two men and the wounding of nine others.

Cochise County sheriff's deputies met resistance at the Christ Miracle Healing Center and Church in Miracle Valley, Ariz., when they tried to arrest members of the church on Oct. 23, 1982. A gunfight ensued and two church members were killed—the Rev. Auguster Tate, Sr., fifty-two, and 33-year-old Bishop William Thomas, Jr.. Two other church members and seven deputies were wounded. Twenty members of the church were brought to trial.

The fundamentalist church, which had transplanted its more than 300 members from Chicago, had had a number of run-ins with the law. Church members were involved in throwing a hammer at television reporter Barbara Morse and cameraman Jamie Lopez, for which 49-year-old Georgia Tate and 41-year-old Linda Pipkins were found Guilty of assault on Feb. 5, 1983. In another incident, a church member died while allegedly carrying a bomb to a jail. Sheriff Jimmy V. Judd claimed that incidents were so frequent that he was forced to park a police trailer across the street from church property to provide better response time. Things came to a head with the gunfight.

The venue of the trial was changed to Pima County when Cochise County Superior Court Judge Matthew Borowiec felt the defendants could not receive a fair trial. In Pima County, however, no trial took place, for on Feb. 15, 1984, Superior Court Judge G. Thomas Meehan dismissed all assault and riot charges against the defendants when Cochise County officials informed the judge that they could not afford to pay the costs of the defendants' court-appointed attorneys. REF.: *CBA*.

Christofi, Styllou, 1900-54, Brit., mur. A Greek Cypriot peasant woman was charged in 1924 with murdering her mother-in-law by jamming a burning stick down her throat, but a jury acquitted her. The woman, Mrs. Styllou Christofi, continued to live with her husband and to raise her son, Stavros Christofi, in the island's matriarchal tradition.

In 1937, Stavros went to England, where he soon married a German refugee named Hella Bleicher. They had three children, and by July 1953, Mrs. Christofi had saved enough money to visit them in England. She moved into Stavros' Hampstead apartment and tried to take charge of his life. She was particularly scathing about Hella and the way she spent money. Within days, Hella, who was to take the children to visit her parents in Germany, told her husband that if his mother was there on her return, she would leave him.

That evening, July 29, 1954, Hella prepared to take a bath in the basement apartment, Mrs. Christofi grabbed a heavy ash plate from the stove and rushed into the bathroom, where she slammed it down on her daughter-in-law's head. She then dragged her unconscious into the kitchen, where she strangled her to death with a scarf. To hide the crime, she poured kerosene over the corpse and tried to set fire to it. A neighbor, a John Young, happened to look down through the glass doors into the basement entrance to the kitchen. He saw the woman working with the fire but, assuming that the waxy-looking figure on the floor was a mannequin, he went on his way. Soon thereafter, Mrs. Christofi began to fear that the flames were getting out of control. She ran out into the street and stopped a car, begging, "Please come! Fire burning, children sleeping!" Mr. and Mrs. Burstoff ran into the kitchen, saw blood on the floor, the smoldering figure, and called the police.

Mrs. Styllou Christofi, strangler.

Mrs. Christofi tried to tell the constable that she had been wakened in the night and found Hella burning, but her bed had not been slept in and she inadvertently added, "My son married Germany girl he like, plenty clothes, plenty shoes, babies going to Germany." Mrs. Christofi was charged with murder. Her attorney tried to persuade her to plead insanity, especially in light of the earlier death of her mother-in-law, but she would not. She was convicted of murder and executed on Dec. 13, 1954.

REF.: Camps, *Camps On Crime*; *CBA*; Corder, *Murder My Love*; Furneaux, *Famous Criminal Cases, Vol. 2*; Hibbert, *The Roots of Evil*; Huggett and Berry, *Daughters of Cain*; Jackson, *Francis Camps*; ____, *Occupied With Crime*; Nash, *Look For the Woman*; O'Donnell, *Should Women Hang?*; Wilson, *Encyclopedia of Murder*; Wilson, *Murderess*.

Christophe, Henri (AKA: **Henry I**), 1767-1820, Haiti, suic.-mur. Born a slave in Grenada, Christophe Henri was a lieutenant of the revolutionary leader Toussaint L'Ouverture in a Haitian native uprising against the French in 1791. He fought against Leclerc in 1802 and later joined Jean-Jacques Dessalines, who was made emperor of Haiti. Christophe assassinated Dessalines in October 1806 and became Henry I, first black king of Haiti. His reign was marked with all manner of torture and cruelty, along with murder of his political adversaries. Christophe's incredible greed, which had milked the poverty-stricken country dry, caused another rebellion in 1818. Christophe was hunted through the jungles of Haiti. He believed that he could die only if he was shot with a silver bullet. As his enemies closed in on him, Henri Christophe shot himself with a silver bullet which he had earlier made for the purpose of taking his own life. See: **Dessalines, Jean Jacques**.

REF.: *CBA*; Cole, *Christophe, King of Haiti*.

Christos, Eftihia, c.1919- , Brit., fraud. The penalty Eftihia Christos received in June 1959 for trying to earn more money to feed her starving children caused an uproar in England over that country's inhumane laws.

Christos' husband died of tuberculosis in 1953, and the money that the National Assistance Board provided was not enough to feed her four children, three of whom also had tuberculosis. She began sewing hooks and eyes on dresses, earning from £2 to £3 a week, an amount she neglected to report to the National Assistance Board. For failing to report her extra income, as required by law, Christos was sentenced by magistrate Geoffrey Rose to two months' imprisonment for fraud. By the next day, a petition had been sent to Home Secretary R.A. Butler, and a protest by more than 1,000 dock workers was held outside the Royal Albert Dock.

As a result of the case, British jurists looked into British laws, which often date back to the Middle Ages, when property was more important than human life. In 1959, the maximum penalty for maiming a person by reckless driving or having sexual intercourse with a minor was only two years in prison, while the maximum penalty for burning a haystack or blaspheming was life imprisonment. Even stealing a dog was worse than assault; the penalty for the former was eighteen months in prison, and for the latter, only one year. REF.: *CBA*.

Chubb, Edith, 1912- , Brit., mansl. Edith Chubb of Hugin Avenue, Broadstairs, was a harried woman. With only a meager salary, and nine people to care for, her resources were severely taxed. Complicating matters was her sister-in-law Lilian, who came to live with the Chubbs, but only contributed £1 and five shillings a week for room and board. According to her later statements Lilian took things for granted and refused to help around the house. Meanwhile, Chubb was forced to work three nights a week at the hospital as a night nurse in addition to her other duties.

On Feb. 7, 1958, as Lilian prepared to step outside, Chubb garroted her from behind with a scarf until she was dead. "Something just came over me. When I realized she was dead I was horror-struck," she said. She placed the body in a wheel chair and hid it in the back shed. The next morning Chubb pushed her sister-in-law to Reading Street Road and dumped the body in a culvert. Authorities found the body, and a week later she was formally charged with murder. Her trial commenced at the Old Bailey in May 1958. Defense lawyer Archie Marshall asked the jury to return a manslaughter verdict with the hope of attaining leniency.

The jury acquitted her of murder but returned a Guilty verdict for manslaughter, accepting the argument that Chubb had no real intention of killing her sister-in-law but had wrapped the sash around her neck in a moment of extreme irritation. She was given a four-year prison sentence.

REF.: Camps, *Camps On Crime*; *CBA*; Furneaux, *Famous Criminal Cases, Vol. 6*.

Chudleigh, Elizabeth, d.1796, Brit., big. The victim of an aunt's self-serving machinations, Elizabeth Chudleigh, the Duchess of Kingston, nonetheless sealed her fate by layering lies upon lies.

Born in Devon to gentle country folk, at eighteen Elizabeth became maid of honor to the Princess of Wales. Availed of many suitors, she chose the Duke of Hamilton, who proposed marriage, but only after his duties on the continent were completed.

Chudleigh's aunt, Mrs. Hammer, had other plans, however. Because she disliked the Duke of Hamilton, preferring instead that her niece marry Captain Hervey, son of the Earl of Bristol, she proceeded to sabotage the long-distance relationship between Chudleigh and the Duke by intercepting love letters and spreading lies.

Communications thus distorted, Chudleigh concluded the Duke had fallen out of love with her. She therefore reluctantly agreed to marry Captain Hervey in a private chapel near Winchester in Hampshire, not realizing her mistake until the Duke returned from abroad. With great regret, she turned him away and, not long after, left on a trip to Germany, seeking solace.

Upon returning to England, Chudleigh immersed herself in London society, playing the court favorite. Her husband, meanwhile, grew more bitter and menacing by the day. Marriage became intolerable. Chudleigh sought to nullify the nuptial record by tearing the official record out of the register book. Besides this document, there was no other evidence or witnesses: the reverend who married them had died.

By bribery and flattery, she next persuaded Mr. Merrill, at whose mansion the wedding had taken place, to strike the written record of the ceremony. Her goal thus accomplished, Chudleigh turned her attention to the Duke of Kingston, whom she married in March 1769.

Some years later, while traveling on the Continent, the Duchess met up with the Duke's nephew, Evelyn Meadows. Meadows, never really fond of his aunt by marriage, told her he knew about her marriage to Hervey. Ann Cradock, a servant who had

Elizabeth Chudleigh, the Duchess of Kingston, convicted bigamist.

witnessed it had told him, he claimed. Furthermore, Meadows intended to file suit against her for bigamy.

The trial began on Apr. 15, 1776, in Westminster Hall. The prosecution had offered to settle out of court for £10,000, but the Duchess, hoping for complete vindication, rejected the offer. Standing before the bar, she pleaded Not Guilty to the charge.

Ann Cradock, the prosecution's key witness, swore the first marriage was legal. She startled the court by implying that Chudleigh had given birth to a child while Hervey was on active duty in the navy. The defense countered by accusing Ann Cradock of having been bribed by Evelyn Meadows to lie.

What finally incriminated the Duchess, however, was the ledger she had tampered with years earlier. The book mysteriously turned up during the trial, and the reverend's widow testified that she recalled her husband mentioning the Hervey-Chudleigh wedding many times.

On Apr. 22, 1776, the court ruled against Chudleigh. After she paid her fine and had her title taken from her, she fled to Calais, Fr., faded into obscurity, and died on Aug. 26, 1796.
REF.: *CBA;* Mitchell, *Newgate Calendar;* Vincent, *Bad Women.*

Chu Hou-Chao (Wu Tsung, Cheng-te), 1491-1521, China, polit. corr. Emperor from 1505-21, largely ignored the needs of his people as he pursued scholarship and personal pleasures. The political power of the eunuchs was heightened, while taxation and corruption led to rebellions against the regime. REF.: *CBA.*

Chu Hou-tsung (Shih Tsung, Chia-ching), 1507-66, China, polit. corr. Emperor from 1521-66, his reign, like that of his cousin, Chu Hou-Chao, was characterized by self-indulgence and cruel treatment of the few competent government officials left in office. The military defense of the nation declined dramatically during his reign. REF.: *CBA.*

Chu Kichol, 1897-1944, Korea, treas. Refused to order his followers to pay homage to Japanese Shinto shrines during WWII. He was arrested and put to death. REF.: *CBA.*

Chung-Hee, Park, 1917-79, Korea, pres., assass. President Park Chung-Hee of South Korea, leader of a right wing military junta that overthrew the government of John M. Chang in 1961, was the driving force behind his nation's impressive economic growth in the 1960s and 1970s. During his sixteen years in office, 1963-79, Park maintained a hard-line approach against Communist North Korea. In 1974 he survived an assassination attempt when an errant bullet struck his wife instead.

Violent student riots in Pusan led to speculation that Kim Jae-Kyu, the head of the Korean Central Intelligence Agency was about to be dismissed. Fifty-three-year-old Kim was deeply resentful over the attentions the president was showing his bodyguard, Cha Ji-Chul. He decided to murder them both, and enlisted the aid of Kim Kae-Won, the secretary-general, and Colonel Park Heung-Joo, senior KCIA aide. They planned to kill Park on Oct. 26, 1979, at an elegant dinner party given in his honor. By prior arrangement, Kim's co-conspirators were to fire upon the other bodyguards as soon as they heard him shoot Park. The assassination was carried off according to plan. Midway through the dinner Kim excused himself from the table in order to retrieve his gun. When he returned to the dining area he pointed to Cha and said, "How can you do a good job when you use an insect like that?" Kim fired his shots at the president and the bodyguard, killing them both. His agents in the other room opened fire on the bodyguards, killing four of them and wounding a fifth man.

The attempted coup was quickly smashed, and the conspirators arrested. The U.S. placed 38,000 troops at the disposal of the new president, Choi Kyu-Hah, in the event that North Korea attempted to exploit the crisis to undermine the government. On Dec. 20, 1979, Kim Jae-Kyu, Kim Kae-Won, and Colonel Heung-Joo were sentenced to death. Four other officials who participated in the coup were also condemned.
REF.: *CBA;* Wilson, *Encyclopedia of Modern Murder.*

Chungking Fire, 1949, China, arson. The city of Chungking went up in flames on Sept. 3-4, 1949. Communist rebels were responsible for the massive blaze which killed 1,700 persons and left an additional 100,000 homeless. One of the arsonists was caught and executed on the spot.
REF.: *CBA;* Nash, *Almanac of World Crime.*

Chung Yi Miao, 1900-28, Brit., mur. Chung Yi Miao, a 28-year-old Chinese-American, married Wai Sheung Siu, the daughter of a wealthy merchant from Hong Kong, in New York in May 1928. Their whirlwind courtship and subsequent marriage ended in murder during a two month honeymoon trip abroad in June. After a brief stop in Edinburgh, the couple continued on to England where they desired to tour the English Lake District. They arrived at the Grange-In-Borrowdale Gates Hotel, Cumberland on June 18, 1928.

The next day the couple went out for a walk, but the husband returned to his hotel alone with the explanation that Wai Sheung had gone on toward Keswick to do some shopping. When she did not return that night he made inquiries with the police. By this time a local farmer had notified constables from the Southport Borough station that he had found a young woman lying dead under a tree. She was clad in a very expensive fur coat.

When questioned by police at his hotel room, Chung revealed more information than what he would have otherwise known if he had not been mixed up in her death. A search of his suitcase turned up two rolls of undeveloped film. When the contents were emptied out, Wai Sheung's diamond wedding ring and a diamond solitaire tumbled out. It was the same jewelry she had been wearing when she left the hotel. The young law student was charged with murder and placed on trial at the Carlisle Assizes on Nov. 22, 1928. The trial lasted just three days, after which a Guilty verdict was returned. Chung Miao was hanged at the Strangeways Jail in Manchester on Dec. 6, 1928. The motive for the murder, according to a published article in the *Sunday Express* of Mar. 24, 1929, was Wai Sheung's inability to bear her husband children.

REF.: Bechhofer-Roberts, *Sir Travers Humphreys: His Career and Cases;* Browne, *Sir Travers Humphreys;* Butler, *Murderers' England; CBA;* Humphreys, *Seven Murderers;* Humphreys, *A Book of Trials;* Jackson, *The Life and Cases of Mr. Justice Humphreys;* Shew, *A Companion to Murder;* Wilson, *Encyclopedia of Murder.*

Church, Harvey, 1898-1922, U.S., mur. Guards carried Harvey Church to the gallows in a kitchen chair. He could neither move nor speak, and in his last days was force-fed through a tube. Church, according to psychiatrists, became paralyzed with fear, when, on Dec. 21, 1921, Judge John R. Caverly had pronounced the death sentence. If he was trying to cheat the hangman, it did not work.

Known as the "Twin-Six" murderer, Church, at 135 pounds, seemed incapable of killing anyone—least of all the two burly car salesmen he murdered on Sept. 9, 1921. Living on the West Side with his aging mother, Church worked as a brakeman for the Chicago and Northwestern Railway.

At 4 a.m. on the morning of Sept. 10, a black Packard sedan stopped on the Lake Street bridge over the Des Plaines River between west suburban Maywood and River Forest. The driver of the car was observed dropping a large weighted object over the stone railing and into the river. Thinking it was just a prank, the pedestrians who witnessed it continued on. Later that morning, 10-year-old William Baker of nearby Melrose Park identified the mysterious object as a man. With a grappling hook, the body was fished out by suburban police.

They found a cord wrapped around the victim's neck and severe lacerations on the skull. The victim's hands were shackled. Chicago police were contacted and an effort was made to identify the large-boned man. The mystery was solved when the Chicago sales office of the Packard Automobile Company reported that two salesman—Bernard J. Daugherty and Carl Ausmus—were missing after selling a car to Harvey Church of West Fulton Street. A company employee, Edward Skelba, was sent to the bank to locate the salesmen, but all he found was a note tied to the steering wheel of a roadster. It read: "Ed, go back to office. Will come in later."

Church had just purchased a twin-six Packard for $5,400, explaining that the car was for his father in Adams, Wis. He asked the two salesmen to accompany him to the Madison-Kedzie State Bank where he would withdraw the money, but first he had to get his passbook at home.

Daugherty, a former football star and war hero, followed Church into the basement while Ausmus waited outside. In the basement, Church pulled a gun on the salesman, handcuffed him, and strangled him with a rope. He then beat him with a baseball bat.

He followed the same procedure with Ausmus, who entered the house to see about the delay. Church then buried Ausmus in a shallow grave in the garage, beneath the broken-down Harroun automobile he wanted to replace, and, early next morning, dropped the mangled body of Daugherty into the river.

When police detectives entered the Fulton Street house, Church was out joyriding with his mother. The baseball bat, a hatchet, and a trail of blood led the police to where Ausmus' body had been buried hours earlier. The salesmen's hats were found on the floor. Police worked through the night excavating the yard.

Mother and son were located in Adams, Wis. When presented with the evidence, the old woman fainted, but she would later stand by her son's alibi. "My mother was with me at the time. She saw the payment," Church said.

How such a small man alone could easily overpower two men, one a former athlete, baffled police. They were convinced Church had help in committing the crime, but he neither named accomplices nor confessed.

Back in Chicago, Church was interrogated but he refused to bend. The police, in frustration, took him back to the scene of the crime, forced him to his hands and knees, and pressed his face into the empty gravesite. Only later, upon seeing the corpse, did Church finally crack. He claimed that Leon Parks and Clarence Wilder had helped him. The two men, it turned out, were clearly not involved.

Church then said he killed the men out of fear, that a mysterious telephone caller threatened to kill his father unless he produced a new car before Sept. 10. Nonetheless, despite expert testimony that he was deranged, Harvey Church was convicted of the "twin-six" murders. During the trial, he slipped into a stupor, impervious to all efforts to rouse him—even being jabbed with needles and touched on the nose with a lighted cigar evoked no response.

Defense attorneys argued for a new trial, but Judge Kickham Scanlan sustained the death sentence. At the last minute, attorneys Frank Tyrrell and J.C. McGloon ran from court to court frantically trying to procure a written order. They found Judge Caverly and pleaded for a little more time, but the judge declined, at the moment when guards were carrying Church from his cell in a kitchen chair. REF.: *CBA.*

Church, Maple, c.1922-41, Brit., (unsolv.) mur. Within an hour of saying good-bye to her friend Vera Whymas, 19-year-old Maple Church was found dead, her naked body lying on the weakened floorboards of a bombed-out house in Camden Town, London. She had been strangled to death with a cord, and her body revealed bruises and cuts of a violent struggle, but little more was ever learned.

Investigators were unable to discover how Church ended up in such a place, nowhere near either her home in North London or Charing Cross Station, where she was last seen alive, or how the crime could have been committed on a floor that could not even support the weight of police officers. Amazingly, a fingerprint was lifted from the girl's body by Frederick Cherrill of Scotland Yard; a fingerprint obtained not because of a bloodstain, but because the victim's flesh had not sprung back to its normal level—the impression apparently being made after Church was already dead. This one clue was never enough to arrest or convict anyone for the young woman's murder.

REF.: *CBA;* Cherrill, *Cherrill of the Yard.*

Church, Richard J., 1968- , Case of, U.S., mur. After two-and-a-half years of dating Richard J. Church, 17-year-old cheerleader Colleen Ritter broke up with the 19-year-old former high-school football star at her parents' urging. Two weeks later on Aug. 21, 1988, Church allegedly broke into Colleen's home at 5 a.m. and bludgeoned and stabbed to death the girl's parents, 43-year-old Raymond Ritter and his wife, 45-year-old Ruth Ann Ritter. He also reportedly stabbed and wounded the girl's 10-year-old brother, Matthew Ritter; 15-year-old Stephen was not home at the time. Church is then believed to have attacked Colleen and dragged her into the street, while a friend, 16-year-old Amy Quinlan, hid in a closet.

Witness Chris Gehrke said that Church chased after Colleen, clubbing her until she no longer moved before running off. Although she suffered stab wounds as well, Colleen survived the attack. Church escaped from the small town of Woodstock, Ill., and fled to the Wisconsin Dells, about 120 miles to the northwest, where he was spotted later that same day. There were no more hints of his whereabouts until David Corcoran, the owner of a convenience store in Hollywood, Calif., had Church's abandoned pickup truck towed away from his parking lot. The day before, on Sept. 12, 1989, Church had told Corcoran that he would return for his truck, which he never did. At this writing Church is still at large. REF.: *CBA.*

Churchill, Deborah (AKA: **Deborah Miller**), c.1678-1708, Brit., rob.-mur. Having deftly avoided the hangman's noose in her career as a pickpocket, Deborah Churchill was hanged for a crime she witnessed but did not commit.

After the death of her first husband, John Churchill from alcoholism, Deborah turned to petty thievery in London. A few years later, after twenty-eight arrests, she was sent to Clerkenwell Bridewell, where she beat hemp from sunup to sundown. The forced labor, in time, reduced her to a mere skeleton.

One night after her release she went to Drury Lane Theatre with her lover Richard Hunt and three other men. The evening went smoothly until a violent quarrel erupted between Hunt and Martin Were. Then, on the road between King's Head Court and Vinegar Yard, the two men drew swords.

The deadly volley lasted until Churchill distracted Were long enough for Hunt to inflict a fatal wound. The man was left for dead in the road and Hunt fled, escaping to Holland. He did not look back, nor did he try to save Deborah who was taken to the magistrate and committed to Newgate until 1708. Churchill maintained her innocence, but the judges still recommended the death sentence.

Desperate to avoid execution, she feigned a pregnancy. A jury of matrons was convened and granted her time to prove her claim. But after six months and no visible sign of a pregnancy, Churchill was led to Tyburn Hill and executed on Dec. 17.

REF.: *CBA;* Mitchell, *Newgate Calendar;* Nash, *Look For the Woman;* O'Donnell, *Should Women Hang?;* Smith, *Highwaymen.*

Churchill, John (First Duke of Marlborough), 1650-1722, Brit., embez.-treas. Commanded the military forces of King James II. In 1688 he joined the forces of William of Orange who named him an earl. Four years later he conspired with James who was then living in exile in France. For this he was charged with treason and imprisoned. He involved himself in various military and court intrigues until he was dismissed from office in 1711 for embezzling the public's money. However, he resumed his military duties in 1714 when George I became king. REF.: *CBA.*

Churchill, May Vivienne (Lambert, Latimer, Sharp, AKA: Chicago May), 1876-1929, Int'l., pros.-rob.-fraud-blk.-attempt. mur. "I want to risk myself in the world. The thought of having security annoys me." With those words, May Latimer, an Irish-born, 15-year-old showgirl, ended her marriage to a wealthy army officer named Sharp. From then on, her security lay in the vast sums of money she acquired, primarily through the badger game.

May Lambert came to the U.S. from Ireland either by stealing her parents' savings to pay her fare or by performing her first badger game, seducing a wealthy young man and then demanding money from his horrified parents. In either case, her beauty won her a place in a Broadway show as soon as she arrived in New York. There she met and married Sharp, the army officer.

The money May took from Sharp when she left him set her up in finery. She collected lovers, all wealthy. She developed her own version of the badger game. She would meet a man, invite him to her apartment, then slip him something, usually chloral in champagne, to knock him out. On waking, he would find a friend of May's waiting to offer hints on how to avoid being sued by her "husband," who had supposedly found them together. The method suggested involved large sums of money, generally spread out as blackmail payments over many months. The game worked as well in South America as it did in New York. Occasionally May was taken into court for her activities, but she was usually only reprimanded and released. The police tolerated her until she helped reformer Reverend Parkhurst entrap a corrupt police officer. With the police no longer willing to turn a blind eye, May was forced to leave for Chicago, where she improved her technique by adding cameras focused on her bed to her apartment walls. Photographs were even more effective than words in eliciting blackmail. In 1900, she left for London with cohorts "Kid John" McManus and "Dutch Gus" Miller. There the trail of bankrupts and suicides she left behind grew ever wider.

In London, May met jewel thief Eddie Guerin, recently released from prison in Lyons, Fr. They became lovers as well as business partners. "Dutch Gus" Miller suggested that they join him and McManus in robbing the safe at the American Express office in Paris. They succeeded, but the watchman they tied up identified Miller to the police. Miller informed on the other men, but left Chicago May's name out of his story. As a result, May would have gotten away, but she chose to challenge fate by visiting Guerin in jail. McManus and Guerin were convicted and sent to a penal colony in French Guiana for life, while on June 29, 1902, May was sentenced to five years in prison.

Chicago May Churchill with accomplice Eddie Guerin

May won her release after three years by working her badger game on the prison physician. But she was warned never to return to France. Guerin, amazingly enough, escaped from the penal colony and persuaded the American authorities in Dutch Guiana to return him to Chicago. The two teamed up again, but not for long. Guerin left May, determined to work on his own. May threatened him with death. On June 16, 1907, in Russell Square in London, Guerin heard a taxi stop and May's voice shouting, "There he is! Shoot him!" A man named Cubine Jackson, also called Charlie Smith, but whose real name was Robert Considine, a former cellmate of Guerin's and May's current lover, chased Guerin with bullets flying. Only one struck Guerin—in the heel—before passersby prevented Jackson from shooting again. May and Jackson were tried for attempted murder. She received fifteen years in prison and he was sentenced to life.

May Churchill was released from prison in 1918. But the confidence games that depended on her beauty and skill were no longer so effective. She wrote her largely fictional memoirs in 1928, but no one showed much interest in her story. She died alone in a Philadelphia boardinghouse the following year.

REF.: Barker, *Lord Darling's Favorite Cases; CBA;* Dilnot, *Celebrated Crimes;* Hamilton, *Men of the Underworld;* Kingston, *Dramatic Days at the Old Bailey;* Morain, *Underworld of Paris;* Nash, *Look For the Woman;* Stevens, *Famous Crimes and Criminals;* Thomson, *The Criminal;* Willemse, *Secrets of Scotland Yard.*

Churchill, Winston L., 1925- , U.S., law enfor. off. Winston L. Churchill joined the Indianapolis, Ind., Police Department on May 22, 1957, becoming a permanent member of the force just one year later. He received the rank of sergeant on June 3, 1964, and the rank of lieutenant on Jan. 9, 1968. Mayor Richard G. Lugar promoted Churchill to chief of police on Feb. 23, 1968, a post that he held until Mar. 14, 1974. Churchill also was promoted to captain on Mar. 21, 1969, and major on Jan. 1, 1970. On July 22, 1977, he retired from the police force. REF.: *CBA.*

Chu Wen (Chu Ch'üan-chung), 854-914, China, emp., assass. First emperor of the Liang dynasty from 907-914. He was a rebel military leader in the armies of Huang Ch'ao, but then surrendered his own forces in return for an appointment as a territorial governor. In 907 he defeated the last T'ang emperor who was forced to abdicate the throne. He ruled for seven years before he was murdered by his eldest son. REF.: *CBA*.

Chu Yü-chien (Lung-wa, Prince of T'ang), 1602-46, China, emp., assass. Leader of the Fukien provence in southern China, enlisting the support of a pirate named Cheng Chih-lung to help him carry out a plan to gain control of the Ming dynasty. In 1645 he proclaimed himself Ming emperor, but was deposed thirteen months later. He was seized and executed by the Ch'ing forces. REF.: *CBA*.

Chu Yü-lang (Yung-li, Prince of Kuei), 1623-62, China, emp., assass. After the Prince of T'ang was forced to flee his kingdom, the Prince of Kuei moved to Canton where he named himself emperor. By 1648 he gained control of seven provinces. In 1659 the armies of the Ch'ing emperor drove him into exile in Burma. He was eventually captured and executed. REF.: *CBA*.

Cibuku, Gazi, 1947-   , U.S., mur. Numerous plastic bags strewn about a field in Detroit, Mich., led to the arrest of a 23-year-old cook from Albania. Inside the bags were the remains of 25-year-old Sandra Sue Snell, whose body was identified from fingerprints in police files taken from a check she had bounced in December 1969, the year before her death.

The cook, Gazi Cibuku, was arrested along with his roommate and fellow countryman, 21-year-old Accra Khan. Khan was arrested in New York. Cibuku admitted that he shot Snell to death after she had attacked him with a knife during a fight over money. He denied dismembering the woman's body, which he said he had placed in a closet, accusing Khan of doing so. Khan, in turn, testified that he had returned from work one evening to find Snell's body in the closet, and two nights later noticed that her body had been cut up and placed into four bags. First-degree murder charges against Khan were dismissed by the judge, but Cibuku was sentenced to forty years in prison. REF.: *CBA*.

Cicero, Ill., prom. 1920s, U.S., org. crime. When reform candidate William Dever was elected mayor of Chicago in 1923, his first priority was to crack down on the activities of the Al Capone-Johnny Torrio syndicate which had expanded its bootlegging and vice empire during the administration of his predecessor William Hale Thompson. Capone's followers responded by shifting their base of operations to suburban Cicero, Ill., located directly west of Chicago. Cicero's mayor, Joseph Z. Klenha, a former dog catcher, welcomed the gang's arrival. The suburb soon became a "honky-tonk" town, with all-night saloons operating in defiance of the Volstead Act. Eight hundred Capone gunmen protected the taverns, the gambling dens, and brothels. Once when Klenha expressed his displeasure to Capone, the gang chief knocked the mayor to the ground and kicked him in the groin while a Cicero policeman watched.

In 1924, the Democratic reform element in Cicero nominated William F. Pflaum for town clerk. Pflaum attempted to expose the Klenha-Capone alliance, but soon found this strategy hazardous. Capone thugs were sent to harass voters on election day. As the citizens of Cicero stood in line at local polling places, armed thugs asked each how they intended to vote. If they indicated a preference for Pflaum, the ballot was snatched from their hands and marked for the Capone candidate.

Poll watchers and precinct captains were abducted at gunpoint and held hostage until the election was over. When indignant Cicero residents appealed to County Judge Edmund Jarecki for help, a squad of seventy policemen and detectives were sent to restore order. Al Capone's brother Frank was shot and killed in the ensuing fight.

In 1927, Thompson regained the Chicago mayoralty and Capone's mob moved back into Chicago. The mob also held onto the Cicero stronghold which remained a base of illicit operations and racketeering for years. See: **Capone, Alphonse; Capone,**

Frank. REF.: *CBA*.

Cicero, Marcus Tullius, 106-43 B.C., Roman., statesman, assass. The great Roman orator and philosopher Cicero was born in Arpinum, Italy. He moved to Rome as a youth to study law and philosophy. He became a quaestor, or financial administrator, in Sicily in 70 B.C. and came to the public eye when he exposed the corrupt practices of the local governor, Verres, thereby causing him to be impeached in 75 B.C. Cicero became a praetor, or magistrate, in 66 B.C. and consul, a chief magistrate, in 63 B.C. Cicero was one of the most eloquent speakers in the Roman senate, but one who often made serious political mistakes. He sided with Pompey in the Civil War, but was reconciled with Julius Caesar after the battle of Pharsalus in 48 B.C. Following Caesar's assassination in 44 B.C., Cicero, a friend of Brutus and Cassius, but having no hand in Caesar's murder, attacked Mark Antony in a series of speeches he entitled *Philippics,* which earned him Antony's wrath.

After the triumvirate of Antony, Octavius, and Lepidus came to power and hunted down the assassins, Antony marked Cicero for death with the tacit approval of Octavius, who had once been Cicero's student. Cicero was proscribed and soldiers were sent to kill him. He fled Rome with his brother Quintus, intending to reach anti-triumvirate forces in Greece. Quintus turned back to retrieve some of the treasure he had left behind and was murdered by soldiers. Cicero reached the Adriatic Coast but lingered at Gaieta where he had a summer home. He felt that Octavius, his old pupil, would somehow rescind Antony's order. This was not to be. When Cicero heard that troops had entered the area and were searching for him, he leisurely packed his gold and treasures and set out by litter toward the sea and a ship waiting to take him to Greece. His litter was overtaken by Antony's soldiers on Dec. 7, 43 B.C., Cicero's retainers putting up no defense. Two officers, Herennius and Popillius, rushed up to Cicero, drawing their daggers. Cicero said nothing as they reached into the litter and cut his throat. Cicero was decapitated and his hands cut off, these grisly trophies delivered to Mark Antony. According to reports, the two Roman officers who assassinated Cicero had been successfully defended by him years earlier when they stood accused of murder. See: **Caesar, Julius.**

REF.: Boar, *The World's Most Infamous Murders;* Bury, *Cambridge Ancient History; CBA;* Plutarch, *Lives.*

Cicero Race Riot, 1951, U.S., riot. When Harvey Clark attempted to move his family into the all white suburb of Cicero, Ill., he probably realized that he was taking a chance. The racial attitudes of the ethnic Eastern European immigrant community were not tolerant ones. What Clark did not bargain for was the full scale riot that erupted on July 10, 1951.

When Clark tried to move his belongings into the apartment house he had rented from the landlord, two Cicero police officers, with the connivance of Chief Erwin Konovsky, ordered them out of town. Armed with a court injunction barring the police from interfering with his civil rights, Clark defiantly returned only to find an angry crowd of residents on his lawn. By this time he had moved his furniture into the family living quarters, but fearing for his own safety Clark drove away. Cook County Sheriff John Babb ordered the rock-throwing mob to disperse, but it was not long afterward that the angry whites regrouped. Fifty Cicero police officers stood idly by as white residents looted the house, threw the Clark's furniture on the front lawn and set it on fire. Police made no arrests.

After two nights of violence which forced the other nineteen families out of their building, the Illinois National Guard arrived. A four-hour battle with the rioters ensued, but the Guard prevailed. During three nights of periodic rioting, 119 persons were taken into custody, and twenty-three more were injured.

A series of grand jury indictments were returned against top village officials later that year. Their cases spilled over into 1952. On June 4 of that year, Federal jurists convicted Police Chief Erwin Konovsky, Sargeant Roland Brani, and Patrolman Frank Lange of denying Clark's civil rights. They were assessed fines totaling $5,250. Town President Henry Sandusky and Fire Marshal Theodore Wesolowski were cleared of any wrongdoing. The owner of the building, Mrs. Camille de Rose, was adjudged insane and ordered committed to the Kankakee State Hospital after she carried a loaded pistol into the courtroom of Judge Wilbert Crowley demanding justice. REF.: *CBA*.

Cideville Case, 1850-51, Fr., witchcraft. A civil action against the parson of Cideville, France, about eighty miles northwest of Paris, brought to light the unexplained phenomena occurring at the parsonage there. During the proceedings, thirty-four witnesses, including an expert on the occult, testified that a poltergeist was apparently inhabiting the place.

Father Tinel, the parson, apparently caused a local witch to be arrested for treating one of his parishioners without a medical license. The witch then caused Felix Thorel, a shepherd, to touch two young boys, Clement Bunel and Gustave Lemmonier, who lived at the parsonage and through whom the poltergeist acted. Thorel boasted of his ability to conjure up the entity, to which were attributed a number of noises and unexplained occurrences between Nov. 26, 1850, and Feb. 15, 1851. Thorel was fired and was attacked with a walking stick by Tinel.

Thorel brought a civil suit against Tinel and the trial began on Jan. 7, 1851, and ended on Feb. 4. During the trial, the Marquis de Mirville, an occult researcher, testified that there was indeed a poltergeist in the parsonage, and others attested that it was sent there by Thorel. The judge did not entirely believe the testimony, but he did agree that it would justify Tinel's attack, and the suit was dismissed. Eleven days after the trial ended the boys were ordered removed from the parsonage by the Archbishop of Paris, and the disturbances ceased. REF.: *CBA*.

Cienski, Ludomir, prom. 1943, Case of, Brit., mur. The contest between a husband and his wife's lover for the woman's affections ended with the shooting death of the lover. The case against the murderer ended when the inefficiency of the police was exploited.

Polish Naval Lieutenant Ludomir Cienski, stationed in London during WWII, asked his wife's lover and his fellow officer Lieutenant Jan Buchowski to come to his apartment where he was living alone. On Apr. 12, 1943, Buchowski paid a visit to Cienski. Three shots were heard, one after the other, by the landlord, who soon entered the room and saw Buchowski slumped in a chair, dead. Cienski claimed that he had offered the dead man an opportunity to shoot him because Cienski no longer desired to live without his wife. Buchowski apparently missed with his shot, and then a struggle ensued in which the second and third shot killed the man. The likelihood of death occurring in this manner was clearly refuted during Cienski's trial at the Old Bailey before Justice Humphreys.

Testimony by Sir Bernard Spilsbury, who examined the deceased, indicated that Buchowski was already dead from a shot to the heart when the second bullet entered his head, therefore making it impossible that Buchowski had pulled the trigger during a struggle. Ballistics expert Robert Churchill testified that the third bullet, lodged in a wall, was indeed fired in the direction opposite from where the body lay, supporting Cienski's claim that Buchowski had shot the gun first. Churchill added, however, that it was unlikely that a struggle had occurred—and the landlord's statement concurred—because the weapon was a .32-caliber Colt automatic pistol with a safety grip, which made firing impossible without deliberate double pressure being used. All this evidence against Cienski was rendered useless by Sir Patrick Hastings' brilliant defense. Hastings began to win the jury's sympathy by suggesting that here had been a duel between the two men, with Buchowski missing on the first shot and allowing Cienski to take the second. In questioning police officer Robert Fabian, Hastings asked whose fingerprints were on the gun. The question could not be answered because none had been taken. This seeming lack of evidence caused the jury to bring in a verdict of Not Guilty.

REF.: *CBA*; Hastings, *Cases In Court*; ____, *The Other Mr. Churchill*; Shew, *A Companion to Murder*.

Cincinnati Race Riot 1841, U.S., mob vio. Despite its official status as a free state, Ohio in the 1830s and 1840s was deeply influenced by the Southern pro-slavery forces. This was particularly true in Cincinnati, which stands directly across the river from Kentucky. An Underground Railway operated in the city as early as 1815, and the large industrial interests enjoyed close business ties with the South; by the mid-1820s, the influx of free blacks into Cincinnati became a concern to local merchants who feared their trade might suffer as a result of fugitives being harbored in the city by abolitionists. In 1829 a statute requiring blacks to post a $500 bond to ensure their "good behavior" was enforced. During the 1829 agitation, angry white mobs invaded a Negro settlement and drove more than 1,000 blacks from their homes and out of the city. In 1835 the offices of *The Philanthropist* were ransacked by gangs of white thugs. A year later the publisher, James G. Birney, was almost lynched.

The tense racial climate in the city culminated in a riot on Sept. 6, 1841, when a gang of Irishmen picked a fight with some blacks near the corner of Sixth and Broadway. The next night the Irish gang besieged a boarding house on McAllister Street demanding the surrender of a black man they wanted in connection with the previous night's hostility. An exchange of gunshots left several people wounded. Hearing about these altercations, an assembly of Kentuckians came from across the river to engage the blacks gathered along Broadway and Sixth in a rock-throwing battle.

When the mayor's pleas for a stop to the violence were ignored, the military was called in and martial law declared. Between 250-300 blacks were taken to jail for their own safety. There were sporadic outbreaks of violence during the night. The office of the *Philanthropist* was attacked, and the printing press was thrown into the river. Several more black residences were invaded before the mob dispersed from sheer exhaustion.

REF.: *CBA*; Dabney, *Cincinnati's Colored Citizens*; Hofstadter and Wallace, *American Violence*.

Cincinnati Riot 1884, U.S., mob vio. Disgusted with the leniency of the local courts when a confessed murderer, William Berner, was sentenced to twenty years in prison instead of the death penalty, an irate group of Cincinnatians staged a mass protest rally at the Music Hall on Mar. 28, 1884. An estimated 10,000 people turned out to voice their indignation against a criminal justice system that had sentenced to death only four persons out of fifty convicted of capital crimes. To the angry residents of Cincinnati, the implication was clear: the laxity of the courts indicated a conspiracy between the criminal underworld and the judicial system.

Jail officialls transferred Berner to the state prison in Columbus before the riotous mob attacked the jail. The local militia drove off the mob, but not without a significant amount of bloodshed and loss of life. The next night the crowd gathered again outside the courthouse. This time the courthouse was burned down and thousands of valuable criminal records were destroyed. Later, the mob captured the jail and lynched two prisoners. Fifty people were killed and dozens more were injured in the first three days of rioting.

No longer able to stop the mobs, the mayor prevailed upon the state to send in the militia to put down the rebellion, which by this time had caused wholesale devastation in the commercial district. Skirmishes between the rioters and the military regiments continued for the next three days. Finally the soldiers dug in on Court Street and were able to repel the advancing mobs. Soon the riot was over, but a terrible cost in lives and property had been exacted.

REF.: *CBA*; Hofstadter and Wallace, *American Violence*; Tunison, *The Cincinnati Riot: Its Causes and Results*.

Cinema Trust, prom. 1930s, Case of, U.S., consp.-fraud. Three theaters in St. Louis, Mo., almost brought the curtain down on Hollywood's three largest movie producers during a suit claiming violation of the Sherman Anti-Trust Law.

The Ambassador, the Missouri, and the New Grand Central movie theaters had been operated jointly by Paramount Pictures

Distributing Co. and Warner Brothers, until Paramount went bankrupt in 1933 and Warner Brothers was no longer able to afford sole operating costs. Then the theaters came under the control of Allen L. Snyder, who leased the buildings to Fanchon & Marco, headed by Harry C. Arthur. Arthur alleged that Paramount, Warner Brothers, and Radio-Keith-Orpheum (RKO Distributing Corp.) had refused to let any of their movies, which at the time made up almost one-half of the industry's top features each year, appear in those theaters. A St. Louis federal grand jury indicted the three motion picture companies, seven of their subsidiaries, and top executives, including Paramount vice president George Schaefer, RKO president Ned Depinet, and Warner Brothers' Gradwell Sears, Herman Starr, and president Harry Warner, on charges of breaking anti-trust laws.

Federal Judge George Moore presided over the anti-trust trial, which began on Sept. 30, 1935, and ended on Nov. 11. During the trial, the defense was represented by twenty lawyers, including former Senator James A. Reed and Frederick H. Wood, while Assistant U.S. Attorney General Russell Hardy represented the federal government. A verdict of Not Guilty was returned by the jury after only thirty-eight minutes. Attorney General Cummings filed a lawsuit on Feb. 25, 1936, accusing the three movie companies of conspiring against the St. Louis theaters. This action was ended Apr. 30, 1936, by Federal Judge John C. Knox when RKO and Warner Brothers granted Fanchon & Marco rights to show their pictures for ten years, and Paramount agreed that it would not refuse a reasonable offer made by Fanchon & Marco. REF.: *CBA.*

Cinna, See: **Antonius, Marcus.**

Cinq-Mars, Marquis de Henri Coffier de Ru'ze, 1620-42, Fr., consp. Born into the French aristocracy, Cinq-Mars was introduced into the court of Louis XIII by Cardinal Richelieu in 1638, and he became one of the king's favorites. He was full of jokes and amused the king by mimicking older courtiers, making faces in imitation of them. Cinq-Mars was then only nineteen, but Louis bestowed special honors upon him. He made him Master of the Horse so that in all parades and ceremonies, Cinq-Mars rode ahead of the King. The youth insisted that he be made a counselor to Louis but Richelieu merely laughed away this ambition as naiveté. Moreover, Cinq-Mars wanted to wed Mary of Mantua, the daughter of an Italian sovereign. Here Richelieu had to rebuke the youth, since such a marriage was for the cardinal to arrange as a political move. He reminded Cinq-Mars that such a marriage was above his position.

The youthful courtier was incensed at being put in his place and was quickly drawn into a plot against Richelieu when Louis fell ill, conspiring with Gaston d'Orleans, the king's brother, to induce the king of Spain to secretly supply the Orleans faction with money and arms to overthrow Richelieu's government. Cinq-Mars was promised high military rank by the conspirators, but he was merely being used as a spy in the court. Richelieu and Louis learned of the plot which was quickly exposed, betrayed by Gaston d'Orleans to put himself above suspicion. Marquis de Henri Coffier du Ru'ze Cinq-Mars was arrested in Lyon with another conspirator named de Toth and both were tried and condemned, going to the scaffold on Sept. 9, 1642. The king, one report had it, cynically remarked upon the death of his one-time favorite: "What sort of faces will the Master of Horse be making now?" Richelieu died the same year, on Dec. 4, 1642, Louis XIII a year later, on May 14, 1643.

REF.: Belloc, *Richelieu; CBA;* Ploetz, *Epitome of History;* Wolf, *Louis XIV.*

Cioppa, Elio, 1939- , Italy, law enfor. off. Between 1970 and 1978 the Italian kidnap-for-ransom racket grew to epidemic proportions. The spate of abductions involved $180 million in ransom money paid out to kidnap gangs, and the death of thirty-nine hostages. The assassination of Premier Aldo Moro in 1978 drew worldwide attention to the problem. The Italian government selected Elio Cioppa to head up an elite task force whose sole task was to investigate and solve these cases.

Cioppa earned a law degree from the University of Naples, and was a member of the Pubblica Sicurezza (public security police) before his appointment to the anti-kidnapping squad in 1975. His job was not an enviable one. The "Squadra Anti-Sequestro" was unpopular with much of the Italian public. "Many people," he said, "take the attitude toward victims. 'You make your money speculating, you don't pay taxes, it serves you right.' They end up hating us more than the kidnappers." See: **Moro, Aldo.** REF.: *CBA.*

Cipriani, Amilcare, 1845-1918, Italy, rebel. Twice jailed for revolutionary activity on behalf of Italian and French radical groups. He joined the leaders of the Paris Commune uprising in 1871 resulting in his imprisonment at hard labor. He was pardoned in 1888 but chose to remain in France. REF.: *CBA.*

Circus Gang, prom. 1920s, U.S., org. crime. J.E. "Screwy" Moore, alias Claude Maddox, headed up the Circus Gang in Chicago during the 1920s. Headquarters for the gang was Moore's Circus Cafe on Chicago's Northwest Side. The gang paid homage to the Torrio-Capone organization and functioned as one of Scarface's satellites, sending Capone a percentage of the bootlegging spoils in its territory in return for political and police protection arranged by Torrio and Capone. Moore and his men also provided Capone with specialists in all criminal pursuits. When Capone required a safecracker, the Circus Gang provided accomplished yegg-men such as Morris "Red" Rudensky. Most of Capone's hundreds of gunmen received weapons through Moore's Circus Gang and its suppliers, such as Peter von Frantzius. At Prohibition's end, members of the Circus Gang were absorbed by the crime syndicate.

REF.: *CBA;* Nash, *Bloodletters and Badmen.*

Cirillo, Louis, 1924- , U.S., drugs. The supplier of one-sixth of the heroin used in the U.S. annually in the early 1970s, drug smuggler Louis Cirillo claimed at his sentencing, "I'm not the monster I'm made out to be."

On Jan. 4, 1972, Louis Cirillo of the Bronx was indicted by the federal government on charges of smuggling 1,500 pounds of heroin into the U.S. Cirillo, who gave his occupation as a bagel baker and said he made $200 a week, was one of twenty-three men indicted by a federal grand jury on charges that they had smuggled the heroin, with an estimated street value of more than $200 million, into the U.S. over a two-year period.

On Apr. 10, 1972, Cirillo was held in lieu of a $1 million bail on a second indictment of obstructing justice. Assistant U.S. Attorney Walter M. Phillips, Jr. informed Judge Charles L. Brieant, Jr. that Cirillo had hired a man familiar with explosives to blow up the place where the government's key witness was being held, and that the accused drug smuggler had "no compunction against shooting agents." Also charged were James Panebianco and Carmine Pepe. A fourth man, Dennis Wedra, was being sought.

Cirillo's trial began on Apr. 18, 1972, before Judge Edward Weinfeld in New York City. Prosecuting attorney Whitney North Seymour, Jr. described the trial in summary remarks as an exceptional inside view of an international heroin smuggling operation. Testimony, much of it from principal witness Roger Preiss, a Parisian interior designer and go-between in the heroin ring, included descriptions of million-dollar negotiations, coded phone numbers, cars packed with hidden stashes of drugs, secret meetings in major metropolises, and death threats to informers. In 1967 a narcotics indictment against Cirillo had been dismissed when the state's main witness disappeared, believed to have been murdered. Cirillo, with a history of larceny, robbery, and drug smuggling charges dating to 1942, was found Guilty after the jury deliberated for about an hour.

On Apr. 28, 1972, ten federal agents armed with tools and a search warrant went to Cirillo's two-story home in the Bronx and spent five hours searching for hidden cash. Frank V. Monastero, associate director of the Bureau of Narcotics and Dangerous Drugs, said that $1,078,000 in cash, mostly in $100 bills, was found when agents discovered $900,078 in a wooden frame in a hole in the back yard, and $100,000 behind wood paneling in Cirillo's basement, the largest cash seizure ever made by the Narcotics Bureau in the U.S.

During the year in which government agents had Cirillo under surveillance, he had made several suspicious cash transactions, including a $10,000 bank deposit and a $4,500 payment for a car. On May 25, 1972, Cirillo was sentenced to a twenty-five year jail term by Judge Weinfeld who noted that the convicted man "supplies one-sixth of the six tons of heroin consumed by addicts each year in the United States."

On June 10, 1973, twenty-eight narcotics agents with a search warrant virtually dismantled the split-level ranch-style house of John Conforti, Cirillo's brother-in-law, in a fruitless search for $4 million in profits suspected hidden in the Conforti home. A crowd of about 100 neighbors watched as the agents used crowbars, hammers, and a shovel to strip shingles from the rooms, pull apart a panel truck and strip hubcaps from the Conforti's Cadillac, dig deep trenches in the back yard, and rip aluminum siding from the house. The agents found only $200,000 in bonds, which Conforti had voluntarily shown them before they began their search. The Confortis filed an $18.3 million lawsuit on charges of assault, invasion of privacy, slander, illegal trespass, and false imprisonment. They agreed, after extensive discussion with U.S. Attorney Robert A. Morse, to settle out of court in May 1973 for $160,000. REF.: *CBA*.

Cirvelo, Pedro Sanchez, c.1475-c.1560, Spain, writer. The Inquisitor at Saragossa and canon of Salamanca for over thirty years gained considerable fame with the publication of his *Opus de Magica Superstitione*, or the *Book about Belief in Magic*, which became, in 1539, the first work on witchcraft to be published in Spanish. Pedro Sanchez Cirvelo believed witchcraft should be punished as if it were a formal heresy, and that a witch's trance was a sin, whether it was real or imagined from an illusion created by the devil, as it resulted from an evil pact. REF.: *CBA*.

Vincent Ciucci, left, who murdered his family, is shown with lawyer at his 1954 trial.

Ciucci, Vincent, 1925-62, U.S., mur. Thinking to rid himself of a burdensome family, Vincent Ciucci, on the night of Dec. 4, 1953, chloroformed his wife Anne and three children, then shot each one in the head. He then set fire to the apartment, a three-room affair which was behind his grocery store. He intended to collect the insurance money and marry another woman. Ciucci remained in the burning apartment until the firemen arrived. He then stumbled outside, pretending to be overcome with smoke, feigning surprise that his entire family was dead. The murder plan was idiotic. Ciucci had ignored the basic routine of medical examiners, who soon reported that the Ciucci family members had been shot in the head. He believed that the burned flesh of his

victims would hide the bullet wounds.

Detectives confronted Ciucci, but he denied having anything to do with the killings. "I admit that I am a gambler," he blurted at police headquarters, "and I like to fool around with women, but I wouldn't do a thing like that. How could a man kill his own children? He would kill himself instead!" He stubbornly refused to admit his guilt, even stating at his trial that unknown killers had framed him by sneaking into his apartment, shooting his wife and children to death and then setting the house on fire. When asked how he could not have heard four shots being fired, Ciucci mumbled something about being a "heavy sleeper." Ciucci was convicted and given a death sentence. After a number of appeals, Ciucci was sent to the electric chair in 1962.

REF.: *CBA*; Nash, *Bloodletters and Badmen*.

Civella, Nicholas (AKA: **Mr. Nichols, Zio**), 1912-83, U.S., consp.-brib.-org. crime. Nicholas Civella may not have been one of organized crime's most powerful bosses, but in dealings between Las Vegas, Nev., and Chicago, and in Kansas City, Mo., Civella carried a lot of weight.

Federal investigators attest that Civella was at the Apalachin conference in 1957, which he denied, and he gained national notoriety when the McClellan Committee of 1963 named him and his brother Carl Civella as associates of important, but lesser, organized criminals. He was viewed as running Mafia operations in Kansas City and handling certain Las Vegas skimming conspiracies, taking casino profits prior to taxation. This final accusation was never proved in court, though he was indicted for the crime in 1981, and the FBI did obtain incriminating tape-recorded conversations Civella had with mobsters in Kansas City and Chicago.

A massive FBI wiretap of prominent mob figures led to Civella's conviction on a bribery conspiracy charge on July 18, 1980; the first major conviction from such evidence. Civella had attempted to bribe the warden of the Fort Worth, Texas, prison, Louis J. Gengler, to transfer his nephew, Anthony Civella, from a prison in Texarkana, Texas. The transaction or transfer never took place, but Civella, a second nephew, Peter Tamburello, and John Tortora were all found Guilty by a jury in the U.S. District Court of Judge Scott O. Wright. Civella was sentenced to four years in prison. While in custody, Civella was indicted on Nov. 5, 1981, for his involvement in skimming operations that netted $280,000 from the Las Vegas Tropicana Hotel from 1975 to 1979.

Civella died in prison before the trial took place in June 1983. His brother Carl, however, along with four others, was found Guilty on July 1, 1983, in the gambling conspiracy. Civella's 73-year-old brother was sentenced to seventy-five years in prison and fined $96,680; 56-year-old Carl DeLuna was sentenced to thirty years in prison and fined $221,680; 55-year-old Charles Moretina was sentenced to twenty years in prison and fined $41,680; and 50-year-old casino manager Carl Thomas was sentenced to fifteen years in prison and fined $186,680. Another Civella nephew, 64-year-old Anthony Chiavola, a former Chicago police officer, was also found Guilty.

REF.: *CBA*; Demaris, *The Last Mafioso*; Reid, *The Grim Reapers*; Zuckerman, *Vengeance Is Mine*.

Claiborne, Harry E., c.1917- , U.S., tax evas.-polit. corr. For failure to pay taxes on legal fees of $106,551 as an attorney in 1979 and 1980, the chief judge for the U.S. District Court of Nevada, Harry E. Claiborne, was sentenced to two years' imprisonment in 1984. He gained even more notoriety by his failure to step down from his post, which paid $78,700 a year.

Because he refused to resign his judgeship, the U.S. House of Representatives impeached Claiborne and the Senate removed him from office, making the judge the first public official to receive such treatment in fifty years. The U.S. Parole Commission voted eight to zero on Jan. 21, 1987, against Claiborne's appeal, citing that the judge had "seriously breached the public's trust." REF.: *CBA*.

Claiborne, William (AKA: **Billy the Kid**), 1860-82, U.S., west. gunman-outl. A cowboy who worked for the Clanton-McLowery gang, William Claiborne is often confused with the more famous Billy the Kid, because they shared the same sobriquet. Claiborne was a teenage drifter who stood only five-feet-four-inches in height. He had black hair and dark eyes. When he appeared in Tombstone, Ariz., in about 1877, he at first went to work in the mines. He later signed on as a cowhand for John Slaughter, who had been a friend of Claiborne's family. He then went on Ike Clanton's payroll, more as a rustler and gunman than a ranch worker. In October 1881, Claiborne first came to the attention of local lawmen after he shot and killed a tough saloon brawler, James Hickey (or Hicks), in Charleston, N.M., a small mining town a few miles outside of Tombstone. When Hickey refused to drink with the diminutive Claiborne, the Kid, with a lightning draw, drilled a single shot into the brawler's heart. Claiborne was arrested by the local marshal, Virgil Earp, of the famous Earp Brothers, but Claiborne managed to escape. He was later acquitted of the killing, winning a "self defense" verdict.

When the Earp Brothers faced the Clanton-McLowery gang at the O.K. Corral on Oct. 26, 1881, in Tombstone, Claiborne was present, backing the outlaw faction. When the guns went off, Claiborne, instead of going for his gun, dove to the ground and watched as Billy Clanton, and Frank and Tom McLowery were shot to death in the terrific gun battle. He saw the outlaw ringleader, Ike Clanton, his boss, run from the scene and Claiborne followed, a single bullet from Wyatt Earp's six-gun nipping at his heels. Claiborne had only a few months left to live but he spent most of that time carousing through Tombstone's saloons and berating the Earps and their friends. One Earp associate, Buckskin Frank Leslie, was in the Oriental Saloon on the night of Nov. 14, 1882, when Claiborne entered and began insulting him, condemning him for killing one of his friends, John Ringo (a gunfighter reportedly killed by Leslie's friend, Wyatt Earp).

Buckskin Frank was a noted gunfighter and he told Claiborne to shut up or go elsewhere to drink. The youth faced Leslie for a moment, then decided that back-shooting the gunman was a better course. He went outside and retrieved his rifle from the scabbard on his horse. Then he crouched behind a fruit stand, close to the saloon, waiting for Leslie to step outside, intending to shoot Leslie in the back. Buckskin Frank was an old hand at such confrontations and, suspecting a sneak attack, which was the usual ploy of the Clanton-McLowery crowd, he stepped from the Oriental via a side exit. Leslie approached Claiborne from behind and when the Kid heard him approaching in the dimly lighted street, he turned, gasped, then fired a quick shot at Leslie. The experienced gunman drew his six-gun and fired a single bullet which entered Claiborne's left side and exited from the back. Leslie marched resolutely forward and Claiborne, who was now cradled in the arms of a bystander, cried out: "Don't shoot again! I am killed!" Claiborne was taken to a private home where a doctor could only dress his wounds and watch him die. He died some six hours later, cursing the name of Buckskin Frank Leslie.

REF.: American Guide Series, *Arizona, A State Guide;* Arnold, *Thunder in the Southwest;* Axford, *Around Western Campfires;* Bakarich, *Empty Saddles;* _____, *Gun-Smoke;* Bartholomew, *The Biographical ALbum of Western Gunfighters;* _____, *Wyatt Earp, 1879-1882;* Breihan, *Great Gunfighters of the West;* _____, *Great Lawmen of the West;* Brent, *Great Western Heroes;* Burns, *Tombstone, An Iliad of the Southwest; CBA;* Chisholm, *Brewery Gulch;* Clum, *It All Happened in Tombstone;* Erwin, *The Southwest of John H. Slaughter;* Ganzhorn, *I've Killed Men;* Gard, *Frontier Justice;* Hall-Quest, *Wyatt Earp;* Harrison, *Hell Holes and Hangings;* Hendricks, *The Bad Man of the West;* Hitchcock, *Two Women in the Klondike;* Hogan, *The Life and Death of Johnny Ringo;* Holloway, *Texas Gun Lore;* Horan and Sann, *Pictorial History of the Wild West;* Johnson, *Famous Lawmen of the Old West;* King, *Mavericks;* Koller, *The Fireside Book of Guns;* Lake, *Under Cover for Wells Fargo;* Lake, *Wyatt Earp;* McClintock, *Arizona Prehistoric-Aboriginal-Pioneer-Modern;* McCool, *So Said the Coroner;* Martin, *The Earps of Tombstone;* _____, *Silver, Sex and Sixguns;* Myers, *Doc Holliday;* _____, *The Last Chance;* Nahm, *Las Vegas and Uncle Joe;* Nash, *Bloodletters and Badmen;* O'Neal, *Encyclopedia of Western Gunfighters;* Penfield, *Western Sheriffs and Marshals;* Raine,

Guns of the Frontier; Rickards, *Buckskin Frank Leslie, Gunman of Tombstone;* Sonnichsen, *Billy King's Tombstone;* Walters, *Tombstone's Yesterdays;* Waters, *The Story of Mrs. Virgil Earp;* Waters, *A Gallery of Western Badmen;* Wellman, *Glory, God and Gold;* Wilson, *Out of the West.*

Clanachan, Patrick, d.1709, Brit., theft. For stealing horses Patrick Clanachan was sentenced to death by hanging, as was customary at the time. Legend has it that on the way to the gallows on Aug. 31, 1709, he remarked to the crowd assembling to watch, "Take your time, boys; there'll be no fun till I hang." Clanachan became the last person to be hanged at Wigtown. REF.: *CBA.*

Clan-na-Gael, prom. 1860s-1880s, Ire., secret crim. soc. As the Fenian movement dissipated in mid-nineteenth century Ireland, leaders of that dissolving organization established a secret Irish society dedicated to pure terrorism in an attempt to coerce England into relinquishing its hold on Ireland. The brutal, bloody actions of this secret society were condemned by Irish statesmen such as Charles Parnell and even former Fenian leaders. The society planned to assassinate Queen Victoria, but their elaborate plans in this regard came to nothing, although six attempts upon the queen were made by others (see entry). At one point, the most ardent members of Clan-na-Gael planned to blow up British shipping by using submarines, although such underwater boats were, at that time, mere creations in the mind of futurist writer Jules Verne. Some of the terrorists busied themselves with endless drawings of submarines to accomplish the chore, and manufacture of one boat actually commenced, but ended when its makers could not figure out how to propel the ship.

Members of this secret brotherhood were mostly active in the making of bombs, which they manufactured in hidden warehouses throughout Ireland and England. In Birmingham, a group of Clan-na-Gaelers created several powerful devices made with nitroglycerin, sect leaders there planning to blow up British landmarks. They set off bombs at the House of Commons, London Bridge, and the Tower of London, but no one was injured except the bomb planters themselves when the crudely made explosives prematurely blew up and killed or injured a number of society members. To many in Ireland, the Clan-na-Gael was no more than a ruthless terrorist organization, and it was condemned by the Irish Home Rule Party and the influential Land League headed by Parnell. By the late 1880s, there were few active members in the society remaining, although one of its bombings, that of the Greenwich Observatory, occurred as late as 1894, but this terrorist act only succeeded in blowing up the anarchist who set the bomb. By then the Clan-na-Gael was politically a thing of the past. See: **Cronin, Patrick Henry; Victoria.**

REF.: Bartholomew, *The Biographical Album of Western Gunfighters;* Bussy, *Irish Conspiracies; CBA;* MacKenzie, *Secret Societies;* O'Neal, *Encyclopedia of Western Gunfighters;* Pollard, *The Secret Societies of Ireland;* Williams, *Secret Societies in Ireland.*

Clanton-McLowery Gang, prom. 1870s-80s, U.S., west. outl. The toughest cattle rustling gang of outlaws in the Southwest was without a doubt the Clanton-McLowery band which was led by Newman H. Clanton, known as Old Man Clanton, the patriarch of the Clanton family. N.H. Clanton was a crusty, tough pioneer who settled near Fort Thomas, Ariz., in 1850. He later moved to Texas, then California, then back to Fort Thomas where he settled with his large family, building the Clanton House hotel. He later sold this hotel and moved to a sprawling ranch near the San Pedro River, close to Lewis Springs and a few miles outside of the small town of Charleston, which was near Tombstone. His sons Joseph Isaac "Ike" Clanton, Finneas "Finn" Clanton, and William "Billy" Clanton, became hardworking cowboys as soon as they were old enough to ride, working for their father. N.H. Clanton led his sons into rustling until the Clanton ranch was an enormous stockpen of stolen cattle, all rustled from Mexico.

The motherless Clanton boys (their mother having died shortly after giving birth to William, the youngest child) were led by the oldest, Ike Clanton, a crafty gunfighter who had no nerve for standup gun battles but preferred the ambush and the sneak attack. Finn Clanton was an easygoing cowboy who merely went along with his brothers but he avoided gunfights. Billy Clanton, who was well over six feet when sixteen, was the wildest of the boys, a hell-raiser and a deadly shot. He was fearless and foolish, seeking confrontations with gunmen where he could best them and build a reputation as a fast gun. The McLowery Brothers, Frank and Tom, who had a small ranch adjoining the Clanton spread, worked with the Clantons in their rustling raids into Mexico and invariably backed the Clantons in their confrontations with lawmen. The McLowerys (sometimes spelled McLaury) were born in Iowa and drifted into Arizona in the late 1870s where they began two small ranches. While Tom worked these ranches, Frank hired out to the Clantons to raise money. Both brothers were soon deeply involved in cattle rustling led by Ike Clanton.

Tombstone, which was the thriving city in the area, was under the control of the Clanton family by 1878, the town sheriff, John Behan, being in their employ, receiving kickbacks from the sale of the stolen cattle the Clantons had rustled. Behan was a smug little man, vainglori-
ous and full of self-
importance, but he was in reality, nothing more than a Clanton stooge who exercised his authority only when it benefited the Clanton-McLowery faction. Regardless of the attempts by certain western writers to whitewash the rustlers for whatever reasons, the Clanton-McLowery group was nothing more than a mur-
derous band of outlaws. These men did as they pleased in Tombstone and the honest citizens there were under their criminal grip. With the coming of the Earp Brothers to Tombstone in 1879, all that changed.

Wyatt Earp had come to Tombstone at the request of his brother Virgil Earp, who was then city marshal, to act as a deputy in helping to clean up the town. To support themselves beyond the meager

Ike Clanton, leader of Tombstone's Clanton-McLowery gang.

pay they received as lawmen, the Earps, including Morgan Earp, who accompanied Wyatt to Tombstone, along with John "Doc" Holliday, Wyatt's friend, were given interests in certain gambling operations, a standard gratuity of the day, one which was extended to James Butler "Wild Bill" Hickok and other great lawmen of the Old West. It was claimed that Wyatt Earp and Ike Clanton befriended each other when Earp first arrived in Tombstone but that the two later fell out when Clanton refused to help Earp locate bandits who had been robbing the local stage line. This, of course, was impossible for Clanton, since it was he and his brothers, along with the McLowerys, who had been robbing the stages.

A feud between the two factions developed so that by 1881, a bloody confrontation was inevitable. For several days in October 1881, Ike Clanton and the McLowery brothers spent an unusual amount of time in Tombstone, confronting the Earps and Doc Holliday. On Oct. 25, Ike Clanton got into a fight with Virgil Earp and was pistol-whipped. On Oct. 26, 1881, Frank McLowery stepped from a store to see Wyatt Earp tethering McLowery's horse to a hitching post. McLowery ordered Earp to take his hands off his horse and the marshal told McLowery to keep his animal off the sidewalk. McLowery then rode to the O.K. Corral where he was joined by his brother Tom, Ike and Billy Clanton,

and Billy Claiborne who worked for the Clantons.

The outlaws then sent word to the Earps to meet them in a showdown at the corral. A short time later, Wyatt, Morgan, and Virgil Earp, accompanied by Doc Holliday, came down the street, armed with six-guns and shotguns. When they reached the corral, the Earps demanded that the rustlers throw down their guns and submit to arrest for various robberies. The outlaws fired on the lawmen who fired back, and in the space of a few minutes, Frank and Tom McLowery and Billy Clanton were shot dead. Ike Clanton, the braggart leader of the outlaws, fled at the first sound of gunfire with Billy Claiborne hot on his heels. Virgil and Morgan Earp were wounded but recovered while Wyatt Earp and Doc Holliday remained unscathed.

Claiborne was killed a few months later by Buckskin Frank Leslie in Tombstone, but Ike Clanton still headed a powerful group of gunmen, including Curly Bill Brocius, John Ringo, Frank Stilwell, Pete Spence, Florentino Cruz, and others. For months after the celebrated O.K. Corral battle, Ike Clanton schemed revenge on the Earps, arranging to have Virgil Earp ambushed in December 1881, which left him an invalid, and also employing killers to murder Morgan Earp in 1882. Wyatt Earp and others hunted down the killers and killed them one by one. Ike Clanton fled to Mexico but he returned to Arizona after the Earps and Holliday had moved away from Tombstone.

Clanton started another small ranch on Bonita Creek near Fort Grant, but when he once more took up rustling in 1887, local lawmen J.V. Brighton and George Powell confronted him at his ranch. Clanton, in an act of rare courage, went for his gun and both deputies shot him to death. N.H. Clanton was by then dead; he had been killed before his sons lined up against the Earps in the battle of the O.K. Corral. In July 1881, N.H. Clanton and several of his rustlers, ambushed a group of Mexican cowboys driving a herd through Guadalupe Canyon, killing nineteen Mexican vaqueros, a slaughter that was later known as the Guadalupe Canyon Massacre. Old Man Clanton paid for this butchery a few weeks later when he and four of his men were killed in the same canyon by Mexican cowboys seeking revenge for the earlier ambush. Finn Clanton survived in this terrible family of outlaws, dying peacefully in bed at the turn of the century. See: **Brocius, Curly Bill; Claiborne, William; Earp, Wyatt; Holliday, John; Leslie, Frank; O.K. Corral; Ringo, John.**

REF.: American Guide Series, *Arizona, A State Guide;* Arnold, *Thunder in the Southwest;* Asbury, *Sucker's Progress;* Axford, *Around Western Campfires;* Bakarich, *Empty Saddles;* ____, *Gun-Smoke;* Bartholomew, *The Biographical Album of Western Gunfighters;* ____, *Wyatt Earp, 1879-1882;* Bechdolt, *When the West was Young;* Bishop, *Old Mexico and Her Lost Provinces;* Boyer, *An Illustrated Life of Doc Holliday;* Breakenridge, *Helldorado;* Breihan, *Great Gunfighters of the West;* ____, *Great Lawmen of the West;* Brent, *Great Western Heroes;* Brophy, *Arizona Sketch Book;* Brown, *Reminiscences of Senator William M. Stewart, of Nevada;* Burns, *Tombstone, An Iliad of the Southwest;* Carr, *The West is Still Wild;* CBA; Chilton, *The Book of the West;* Chisholm, *Brewery Gulch;* Clum, *It All Happened in Tombstone;* ____, *Apache Agent;* Corle, *Desert Country;* Cox, *Luke Short and His Era;* Cunningham, *Triggernometry;* Durham, *The Negro Cowboys;* Erwin, *The Southwest of John H. Slaughter;* Forrest, *Arizona's Dark and Bloody Ground;* Ganzhorn, *I've Killed Men;* Gard, *Frontier Justice;* Gardner, *The Old Wild West;* Gregory, *True Wild West Stories;* Hall-Quest, *Wyatt Earp, Marshal of the Old West;* Hamlin, *Hamlin's Tombstone Picture Gallery;* Hayes, *Sheriff Thompson's Day;* Hendricks, *The Bad Man of the West;* Hill, *Then and Now, Here and Around Shakespeare;* Hogan, *The Life and Death of Johnny Ringo;* Holloway, *Texas Gun Lore;* Horan, *The Great American West;* ____, and Sann, *Pictorial History of the Wild West;* Hutchinson, *The Life and Personal Writings of Eugene Manlove Rhodes;* Jaastad, *Man of the West;* Jahns, *Doc Holliday;* Johnson, *Famous Lawmen of the Old West;* Keithley, *Bucky O'Neill;* King, *Mavericks;* ____, *Wranglin' the Past;* Knight, *Wild Bill Hickok;* Koller, *The Fireside Book of Guns;* Lake, *Under Cover for Wells Fargo;* Lake, *Wyatt Earp;* Lesure, *Adventures in Arizona;* Lockwood, *Pioneer Days in Arizona;* McClintock, *Arizona, Prehistoric—Aboriginal—Pi-oneer—Modern;* McCool, *So Said the Coroner;* Martin, *The Earps of Tomb-*

stone; ____, *Tombstone's Epitaph;* Masterson, *Famous Gunfighters of the Western Frontier;* Mazzanovich, *Trailing Geronimo;* Michelson, *Mankillers at Close Range;* Miller, *Arizona, The Last Frontier;* ____, *The Arizona Story;* Miller and Snell, *Why the West was Wild;* Myers, *Doc Holliday;* ____, *The Last Chance;* Nunnelley, *Boothill Grave Yard;* O'Connor, *Bat Masterson;* Olsson, *Welcome to Tombstone;* O'Neal, *Encyclopedia of Western Gunfighters;* Penfield, *Western Sheriffs and Marshals;* Raine, *Famous Sheriffs and Western Outlaws;* ____, *Guns of the Frontier;* Rickards, *Buckskin Frank Leslie;* Robinson, *The Story of Arizona;* Rosa, *The Gunfighter, Man or Myth?;* Ruth, *Great Day in the West;* Ryan, *A Skeptic Dude in Arizona;* Schmedding, *Cowboy and Indian Trader;* Schmitt, *Fighting Editors;* Sloan, *History of Arizona;* Small, *The Best of True West;* Sonnichsen, *Billy King's Tombstone;* Stanley, *Dave Rudabaugh, Border Ruffian;* Sterling, *Famous Western Outlaw-Sheriff Battles;* Train, *On the Trail of the Bad Men;* Walters, *Tombstone's Yesterdays;* Waters, *The Story of Mrs. Virgil Earp: Earp Brothers of Tombstone;* Waters, *A Gallery of Western Bad Men;* Way, *Frontier Arizona;* Way, *The Tombstone Story;* Wellman, *The Blazing Southwest;* ____, *Glory, God and Gold;* ____, *The Trampling Herd;* White, *Bat Masterson;* White, *The Autobiography of A Durable Sinner;* White, *My Texas 'Tis of Thee;* Wilson, *Out of the West;* Wister, *Owen Wister Out West;* Wyllys, *Arizona, The History of a Frontier State;* (FILM), *Tombstone, the Town Too Tough to Die,* 1942; *My Darling Clementine,* 1946.

Clanwaring, Thomas, prom. 1921, Case of, Brit., mur. A 50-year-old spinster named Alice Maud Lawn was murdered in her shop on King Street, Cambridge, on July 27, 1921. Her assailant had taken the dull side of an axe to her head. A small amount of cash missing from the till when police investigated indicated robbery as a motive.

Thomas Clanwaring, a common laborer who had been selling picture postcards in the vicinity of Lawn's shop was arrested on suspicion. Clanwaring claimed he had been drinking in the Rose and Crown pub, a considerable distance away from Lawn's shop, at the time of the crime. Clanwaring, who was something of an eccentric, was indicted for murder and placed on trial at the Cambridge Assize Court on Oct. 17, 1921. His lawyers, Frederick Levy and A.C. Fox-Davies would later describe the peculiar Clanwaring as the "greatest liar they ever met." In court, the accused murderer provided a half-hearted account of himself saying, "Only that I am innocent of the murder committed by some criminal; that my character is not good. I have been convicted five times for bicycle stealing. I heard they were looking for a Jew-looking bloke so I said I was a Jew and let them get on with it."

Clanwaring's lawyers demonstrated that it was virtually impossible for their client to have Killed Alice Lawn in view of his distance from the scene of the crime. After ninety minutes of deliberation, the jury returned a verdict of Not Guilty. Clanwaring returned to selling his post cards, Lawn's murderer was never found.

REF.: Adam, *Murder By Persons Unknown;* CBA; Shew, *A Second Companion to Murder;* Wild, *Curtis.*

Clapham, Harry, 1888-1948, Brit., fraud. Reverend Harry Clapham was ordained a minister at McGill University in Montreal. He moved to England, where he became the vicar of St. Thomas in Lambeth. It was an old and decrepit church. Lacking the funds to pay for renovation work, Reverend Harry Clapham developed the following scheme. He secured a list of people who routinely contributed to charity. He hired a small staff and sent out 200,000 letters a year asking for help. Most of the money that was received went directly into Reverend Clapham's ninety-one bank accounts. Clapham's elaborate swindle continued for nearly fourteen years.

"God has blessed me with a legacy," he replied, when asked about his expensive tailored suits and the deluxe cruises he took all over the world. It was not long before the Charity Commissioners began to take notice of Reverend Harry and his able assistant Constance Owens, known simply as "Sister Connie." Aided by the disclosures of W.A. Hewitt, who had once worked as Clapham's curate, Scotland Yard initiated an investigation.

Clapham was arrested after applying to the Cholmondeley Trust for financial help. To qualify for a grant, the recipient's income could not exceed £400.

The Reverend was arrested and charged with receiving money under false pretenses. In June 1942, he began serving a three year sentence at Parkhurst Prison after being found Guilty on twenty-one counts of fraud. Due to failing health, Clapham was eventually released from prison. Afterwards, moved to the country to live in a house with "Sister Connie." Clapham died shortly afterwards in 1948, and at the time of his death the defrocked Reverend left had an estate valued at £9,000.

REF.: *CBA;* Rose, *The World's Greatest Rip-Offs.*

Clapham Common Murder, The, See: Morrison, Steinie.

Clare, Philip, prom. 1857, Case of, Brit., mur. The body of 18-year-old Elizabeth Hopley was found floating in the Birmingham, England, canal near the Bradley arm by George Buckley on Apr. 30, 1857. The death was declared an accidental drowning. Regardless of the coroner's verdict, Philip Clare went on trial Dec. 14, 1857, at the Stafford Assizes for the girl's murder.

Clare was brought to trial solely on the weight of an accusation made by Samuel Wall, who claimed that he had seen Clare strike Hopley before midnight on Apr. 29, then carry her to the fork in the canal and toss her into the water. He added that Clare even knew Wall had seen the murder but that the alleged killer had threatened him to keep quiet. Although another person testified to hearing a man and woman arguing that night, no other evidence corroborated Wall's story. Hopley's body showed no signs of violence, Clare had a rock solid alibi, and Wall was apparently not a model witness—there was speculation that he had given false testimony before, and he had recently changed his name from George Powell for no apparent reason. Without leaving the box, the jury returned a verdict of Not Guilty.

REF.: *CBA;* Poynter, *Forgotten Crimes.*

Clarence, Duke of, 1449-78, Brit., (unsolv.) mur. King Edward IV's younger brother, George, Duke of Clarence, was popular in England. Unfortunately, he knew a secret that during Edward's reign was better left unknown.

The son of Richard, Duke of York, George was appointed Duke of Clarence in 1461 by Edward, who at the age of twenty-two secretly married 27-year-old Elizabeth Woodville on May 1, 1464. This marriage was greatly opposed by the nobility and peasantry alike, for Woodville not only was a woman of common descent, but she was also a widow with two children of her own. In addition, she was of the house of Lancaster, with which the house of York was fighting for the throne. Edward's mother, the Duchess of York, adamantly opposed the marriage because she knew that the king had already betrothed himself, more than two years earlier, to Lady Eleanor Butler before Robert Stillington, the Dean of St. Martin's and the keeper of Edward's Privy Seal. At that time a betrothal was considered equal to marriage, so regardless of Lady Eleanor's death at a Norwich convent in 1466, the Woodville marriage was void, making the son she bore Edward, Edward V, illegitimate. With no legitimate son, the Duke of Clarence would be heir to the throne. The duke's mother allegedly informed George of the secret betrothal, a secret that Woodville desired to be kept.

Woodville convinced Edward that the brother he named as Earl of Warwick and Earl of Salisbury in 1472 should be silenced. The king had his brother arrested and imprisoned in the Tower of London in 1477 on a charge of treason for allegedly seeking his throne. George was secretly put to death the following year, reportedly drowned in wine when Edward allowed him a choice in the manner of his death. An all-too-coincidental arrest of Robert Stillington, who had been made the Bishop of Bath and Wells in 1466, followed George's death. Apparently, the bishop managed to persuade the royal couple that he would remain silent and he was released after only three months in prison. REF.: *CBA.*

Clarence, Edward (Earl of Warwick), 1475-99, Brit., consp. Plantagenet nobleman, son of George Clarence, beheaded for intrigues against the king. Jailed in the Tower of London by Henry VII in 1485 for his involvement with the royal imposter Lambert Simnel, Clarence was exhibited in the streets by the king and executed when he attempted to escape from confinement. REF.: *CBA*.

Clarence, Duke George, 1449-78, Brit., necro. Accused of bringing about Henry VI's death through sorcery and black magic. He was condemned and put to death in the Tower of London. REF.: *CBA*.

Clarie, T. Emmet, 1913- , U.S., jur. Prosecutor in Danielson, Conn., in 1951. He was nominated to fill a vacancy on the district court of Connecticut in 1961 by President John F. Kennedy. REF.: *CBA*.

Clark, Bennett Champ, 1890-1954, U.S., jur. Son of Democratic presidential nominee Champ Clark, elected to the U.S. Senate from Missouri from 1933-39. He was appointed to sit on the bench of the U.S. Court of Appeals in Washington D.C., from 1945-54. REF.: *CBA*.

Clark, Charles Lee, b.c.1899, U.S., (wrong. convict.) mur. Radio stations in the U.S. often announce the names of listeners who have won money by listening to their station, but the announcement that Charles Lee Clark heard in December 1971 was one he had waited more than thirty-three years to hear, thirty of those years spent in prison.

In 1937, Clark was accused of shooting to death the owner of a Michigan store during a holdup by three men. Despite sworn affidavits from Clark's landlady claiming that Clark was home during the killing, he was convicted and sentenced to life imprisonment; Michigan had earlier done away with capital punishment. For the next three decades Clark turned down offers of a commuted sentence or parole, arguing that "If I accepted a parole, it meant I would still have that mark on my record." His determination paid off, when it was finally proven that the one eyewitness to the murder, the store owner's daughter, had been coaxed by police to identify Clark as the killer. Clark was released in 1968 after a new trial overturned the conviction. The state of Michigan agreed to pay Clark $10,000, which he was awarded on Jan. 28, 1972. REF.: *CBA*.

Clark, David, b.c.1898, Case of, U.S., mur. A case of apparent political and police corruption turned into two murders in self-defense, according to the defendant, a former Los Angeles deputy district attorney, David Clark.

Clark served in the district attorney's office after graduating from the University of Southern California's law school, only to resign eight years later in 1931, after he prosecuted reputed organized crime figure Albert Marco for assault and attempted murder. His overzealousness angered corrupt city officials, who transferred him to more menial tasks. Honest businessmen, however, liked what they saw and convinced Clark to run for municipal judge, which he agreed to do. His campaign allegedly angered some of the same people he had angered before, especially Charles Crawford, reputedly highly influential with politicians, police, and the mob, and a personal friend of Marco. Charles Crawford, and the editor of the Los Angeles magazine *Critic of Critics*, Herbert Spencer asked Clark to meet with them on May 20, 1931. Clark agreed but decided to purchase a .38-caliber revolver beforehand. During the meeting, Clark claimed, Crawford and Spencer asked him to help in defaming police chief Roy Steckel in exchange for assuring his judgeship. Clark said that after he refused, Crawford pulled a gun on him, and he was forced to shoot the man in the stomach, before turning around to shoot Spencer, who also had a gun. Both men died that day at Crawford's Sunset Boulevard office.

Clark's first trial for Spencer's murder ended in a hung jury. At the second trial, Clark was able to convince the jury that he had acted in self-defense. Mildred Rohrback, the state's star witness, was shown by the defense to be unreliable, because of a secret wedding to a member of the district attorney's office after the murders. The second charge of murder was dropped after Clark was acquitted of the first. While he was in jail between trials, Clark received 60,000 votes for judge.
REF.: *CBA*; Wolf, *Fallen Angels*.

Clark, David Scott, 1954- , U.S., pris. esc.-mur. Believing that his roommate was trying to steal his tree-trimming business from him, David Scott Clark murdered the man on Christmas Day 1978. The next day all but the torso of 27-year-old Lynn Allen Lizer was recovered from three trash containers in Lake Worth, Fla.

Clark confessed to dismembering Lizer, whose blood was discovered in the apartment and in Clark's car, under a plea-bargain agreement with prosecutors, whereby he was convicted in March 1981, of second-degree, rather than first-degree, murder. Clark was sentenced to life imprisonment, and had served more than seven and one-half years as a model prisoner before he escaped on Dec. 27, 1988.

David Scott Clark

Because of Clark's prison record, he had been transferred to the Brooksville Road Prison, designed for inmates unlikely to escape or pose a threat of danger. His escape came while he and four other prisoners, watched by an unarmed guard, were mowing the grass alongside the road. Clark ignored the guard's commands to come back and fled into the woods. REF.: *CBA*.

Clark, Dewey, 1911-42, and **Jones, Henry Earl**, 1902-42, U.S., rape-mur. Nathaniel Chinchiolo lost his girlfriend and, soon after, his life, perhaps to Ernest Striplin, who confessed to the crime, or perhaps to Dewey Clark and Henry Earl Jones, who would be executed for it. Whoever killed Chinchiolo, twenty-three, and his date Dorothy Woofter, on Apr. 28, 1940, on a road outside Stockton, Calif., picked victims both mourning recent losses—Chinchiolo, his fiancee, and Woofter, her job as a waitress.

Fixed up by Chinciolo's brother Frank, the two decided to make the best of a bad situation by drinking and dancing at the 33 Club in downtown Stockton. At 9 p.m. they left to go for a ride, saying they would be back in half an hour but it was the last anyone saw of them.

Four days later, a passing motorist found the mangled bodies of Chinciolo and Woofter on a grassy embankment between the railroad tracks and a U.S. highway not far from the Stockton Airport. The car they had driven away from the 33 Club was found abandoned in Fresno.

The bodies were securely bound, suggesting that the motive was not robbery. This was clearly a sexual crime. Woofter's dress was flung over her head and unlike Chinchiolo, her feet were untied. Death was caused by stab wounds inflicted by a small hunting knife or switchblade.

Three days after the crime, when Woofter had not returned to the apartment she shared with a girlfriend, her girlfriend called Woofter's father, Emery Woofter. Only then were the police summoned. "She could have been drugged, or it might have been the work of a white slave gang," the elder Woofter said. "I can't think of anything else."

Detectives concentrated their efforts in Fresno, where Chinchiolo's car had been found. A tip from garage mechanic Walter Guyon put them on the trail of two men recently paroled from a Folsom Prison road gang. The suspects, Henry Jones and Dewey Clark, had driven Chinchiolo's car into Guyan's service station late Sunday night to have a broken taillight repaired.

Based on the mechanic's sworn testimony, Jones was arrested at his rooming house on F Street, and Clark at his mother's home. Both men had criminal records for robbery and had served long prison sentences before their release.

Police believed the couple had parked in lover's lane southwest of Stockton, four miles from where the bodies were found. Accosted by the two killers, they were driven to the lonely stretch of highway and killed.

Indicted for murder, the two men were convicted by a jury that heard only circumstantial evidence based on the testimony of a garage mechanic in Fresno, over 100 miles away from the scene of the crime. To further confuse and muddle matters was the startling confession of Ernest Striplin, a 29-year-old convict serving time in Folsom for armed robbery. On July 12, 1940, when the fate of Clark and Jones was virtually sealed, Striplin told Folsom warden Clyde Plummer he had abducted Chinchiolo and Woofter on a Stockton street and forced them to drive to the lover's lane where he had committed the crime. Striplin then abandoned Chinchiolo's car in Fresno where it was stolen by Clark.

The Supreme Court discounted Striplin's confession, upholding the conviction of Clark and Jones despite the pardon board's recommendation that the sentence be commuted to life imprisonment. Who really killed Woofter and Chinciolo? Striplin's confession contained enough verifiable information to cast real doubt in the minds of law enforcement officers familiar with the case.

Protesting their guilt to the last, the two unlucky ex-cons nonetheless went to the gas chamber on Apr. 10, 1942. REF.: *CBA*.

Clark, Douglas Daniel (AKA: **The Sunset Slayer**), 1959- , and **Bundy, Carol**, 1943- , U.S., necro.-rape-mur. Carol Mary Bundy was anxious to please the depraved sexual fantasies of her young lover, Daniel Clark. In 1980, Clark and Bundy committed a series of grisly sex murders in Los Angeles. Bundy would cruise the Sunset Strip in search of blonde prostitutes for Clark to allegedly shoot and then engage in sexual acts with the corpse.

By his own estimate, Clark, a former factory worker, killed fifty women. According to Bundy, he hoped to double that figure before his arrest on Aug. 11, 1980. No one could say with absolute certainty just how many women he killed, but Clark was officially charged with six murders when his trial opened in Los Angeles in January 1983. On Feb. 15 the jury sentenced him to die in the electric chair. He remains on death row. Bundy, a former Burbank nurse and the mother of two children, was sentenced to fifty-two years in prison for murdering her former lover John Robert Murray in 1980, and then decapitating him.

REF.: *CBA*; Fox, *Mass Murder*.

Clark, Ephraim R., c.1925- , and **Hall, Lindberg** c.1927- , and **Kuykendall, Sceola**, c.1939- , U.S., (wrong. convict.) mur. In order to avoid a conviction for armed robbery, a woman agreed to follow police orders and testify against three men for committing a robbery and murder at a Detroit drugstore, despite the fact that the men were not near the store at the time.

On Oct. 4, 1960, three men robbed at gunpoint the drugstore owned by David Lipton. When the druggist drew his gun on the robbers, he was shot five times and died. The three ran to a waiting car and drove off.

At the trial, 24-year-old Edith Adams testified that Ephraim R. Clark, Sceola Kuykendall, and her boyfriend Lindberg Hall had committed the robbery, and that she was in the getaway car. Her statement and identification by the drugstore clerk were strong enough to convict the three, despite considerable evidence to the contrary introduced by court-appointed lawyer Harry Anbender. Anbender discovered that at the time the crime was committed Hall and Adams were on their way to Chicago with another person; Clark's car, allegedly used in the getaway, could not go in reverse as Adams claimed; and Clark's already strong alibi was corroborated by hypnosis and a lie-detector test. All of this information was ignored by the police and the prosecution. The prosecution also ignored Adams' confession that she had lied in court, as part of a deal with the police, for which robbery charges against her were to be dropped. All three men were sentenced to life imprisonment, and for eleven months, the conviction stood, until another robbery was committed and the real murderer confessed.

In November 1961, 21-year-old Gene Adams (no relation to Edith Adams) was arrested for robbery and confessed to par-

ticipating in twenty similar robberies, including one on Oct. 1, 1960, during which a clerk was shot in the leg. The bullet from that wound matched the bullets that killed Lipton, and Gene Adams admitted his guilt. A new trial was quickly held for Clark, Hall, and Kuykendall, taking place at the home of Judge Gerald W. Groat, who was recovering from surgery, at the insistence of Wayne County assistant prosecutor Max Silverman, who had handled the error-ridden case. All three were found Not Guilty of the murder. Clark was immediately released, but Hall and Kuykendall were held for a second robbery. Gene Adams and his accomplices, Joseph Kelly, twenty-five, and Ronald Gilliam, twenty-three, were tried for the drugstore murder, and the woman who gave perjured testimony was finally prosecuted for the robbery. REF.: *CBA*.

Clark, Fannie, and **Nelson, Mary**, and **Osborne, Ellen**, prom. 1896, U.S., pros. A raid at a Chicago house of prostitution on Nov. 20, 1896, ended up with two of the women and a detective lying in a garbage dump.

Fannie Clark and Mary Nelson, rather than give themselves up, climbed out the second-story window of the brothel in which they worked. The two ran across rooftops with the police in hot pursuit, until they were forced to abandon their escape with a leap into a refuse yard. Detective Clifton R. Wooldridge followed the women into the dump and landed face-down in the garbage, but somehow managing to grab hold of Clark and Nelson. Ellen Osborne, who also worked in the house, was much more easily apprehended, but the charge of prostitution and fine was the same.

REF.: *CBA*; Wooldridge, *Hands Up!*

Clark, Guy C., d.1832, U.S., mur. A native of Ithaca, N.Y., Guy Clark was forever brutalizing his wife until the woman finally threatened to have him arrested if he attacked her again. Clark, in front of witnesses, swore that he would kill her if she ever called authorities and reported his beatings of her. A short time later, he beat his wife Fanny and she summoned local lawmen who arrested him and held him in jail temporarily. When released, Clark went straight home, got an ax, and buried it in his wife's skull, keeping his lethal promise. He was quickly tried, condemned, and hanged on Feb. 3, 1832.

REF.: *CBA*; *A Sketch of the Life and Adventurers of Guy C. Clark*.

Clark, Henry Lovell William, See: **Fullam, Augusta Fairfield**.

Clark, James G., b. 1924- , U.S., drugs. In the early 1960s, Sheriff James Clark of Dallas County, Ala. became a nationwide symbol of Southern white racial intolerance. During the Selma to Montgomery freedom march in 1965, Sheriff Clark gained notoriety for using cattle prods against black civil rights activists passing through his county. When the Voting Rights Act of 1965 was passed, mewly enfranchised blacks helped defeat Clark's bud for re-election.

In 1978 Clark was arrested on smuggling charges after federal officials seized three tons of marijuana on board a DC-3 jet that landed in Montgomery. With a street value of $4.3 million, the illegal narcotic had been flown in from the drug capitals of Colombia. In December 1978, Clark was sentenced to two years in prison after pleading guilty on all counts. There were four other charges of racketeering pending against him in an unrelated case in New York City at the time. REF.: *CBA*.

Clark, James H. and **Curtis, Richard L.**, prom. 1977, U.S., brib.-polit. corr. DuPage County, Ill., treasurer James H. Clark had an agreement with Chicago's Michigan Avenue National Bank President Richard L. Curtis, whereby Clark would deposit taxpayers' money in Curtis' bank in exchange for Curtis helping Clark acquire more than $1 million in personal loans from two other banks. This agreement led to the bribery conviction of both men in DuPage County Circuit Court on Mar. 29, 1977. Clark was also convicted of official misconduct. Each defendant was sentenced to two years probation and fined $10,000 by Judge John Krause on June 10, 1977. On Apr. 8, 1977, Clark was removed from his position as treasurer, which he had held for six years. REF.: *CBA*.

Clark, Jim Cummings, 1841-95, U.S., west. outl. Missouri-born gunfighter Jim Clark committed his first criminal act at the age of seventeen when he stole his stepfather's mule, and set out to find fortune and adventure in San Antonio, Texas. Clark sold the mule there and stole $1,400 from a rancher before returning to Missouri. When the Civil War broke out, the young outlaw signed up with William Quantrill's renegade cavalry that pillaged and burned dozens of Union strongholds in Kansas and Missouri.

In the 1870s Clark drifted into Leadville, Colo., where he boxed in the ring for hundred-dollar fees. When Clark tired of boxing, he moved to Telluride and secured an appointment as city marshal. Persistent rumors that Clark consorted with outlaws when the mood suited him resulted in his eventual dismissal. He lingered in town, threatening to kill members of the city council for fifteen to twenty-five cents a head.

Clark would have been better off seeking his fortune elsewhere. On Aug. 6, 1895, he was shot outside the Colombo Saloon while in the company of a man known only as Mexican Sam. An errant bullet pierced Clark's heart, and he died within the hour.

REF.: *CBA*; O'Neal, *Encyclopedia of Western Gunfighters*; Rockwell, *Memoirs of a Lawman*.

Clark, John, 1829-80, U.S., jur. District attorney of Washington D.C., from 1872-75. He was appointed judge of the territorial court of Idaho by President Ulysses Grant in 1874 and reappointed in 1878. REF.: *CBA*.

Clark, John Willie, d.1930, U.S., lynch. In 1930, John Willie Clark had the ignominious distinction of becoming the country's seventeenth lynching victim of the year and the state of Georgia's third in one month in 1930.

The black defendant had confessed to the accidental shooting death of Cartersville police chief Joe Ben Jenkins. Clark was transferred to Atlanta under military escort because the confession greatly endangered his safety. His attorney, however, failed to convince the judge of the necessity for a change of venue, and Clark was sent back to Cartersville to stand trial, but the trial never took place. Before dawn the next day, some fifty masked residents of Cartersville overpowered the jailer and removed Clark. Police found his body hanging from a telephone pole one mile away. REF.: *CBA*.

Clark, Joseph Reginald Victor (AKA: Kennedy), c.1907-29, Brit., mur. Upon his return to England in 1927, after living with relatives in the U.S., Joseph Reginald Victor Clark became a parasite on women. He had a number of intimate relations with women who willingly gave him money. Clark persuaded one to give him money so that she could have a well-dressed escort; another, in Nova Scotia, regularly sent him cash; and at one point, he dated four sisters in Liverpool, England, without any of them knowing about the others until he tried to marry the youngest girl by using the birth certificate of the eldest sister. In fury at the failure of his plan, Clark tried to strangle the youngest sister with a pajama belt. No charges were brought for the assault.

Clark was using the last name of Kennedy when he met Alice Fontaine and became a lodger at her mother's home in Liverpool, living rent-free and constantly borrowing money. But when Fontaine discovered a letter from one of Clark's former girlfriends, she told him to leave. He returned, however, in October 1928, and strangled Alice Fontaine's mother, and again tried to use a pajama belt to murder his former sweetheart. At the Liverpool Assizes Court on Feb. 3, 1929, Clark was tried for murder. His lawyer, Basil Nield, pleaded insanity for Clark, but the defendant chose to plead guilty and the trial was over. Only four and one-half minutes had elapsed from the opening of the trial till the close when Clark was sentenced to death—one of the quickest murder trials on record.

REF.: *CBA*; Wilson, *Encyclopedia of Murder*.

Clark, Laura Ethel, c.1900- , U.S., drugs. At the age of eighty-two, Laura Ethel Clark was not exactly sure about the number of grandchildren she had—it might have been fifteen; it might have been twenty—nor, she claimed, was she aware that the plants growing in her backyard garden were marijuana.

On May 4, 1982, Houston, Texas, police arrested Clark for possession of marijuana, and after she refused to accept a plea-bargaining agreement of two years' probation for a guilty plea, she went on trial Aug. 24. During the trial, Clark's lawyer, Bill Portis, dropped to his left knee, stretched out his arms and begged the jury to be merciful. The prosecution was not so dramatic. Assistant District Attorney Glenn Gotschall asked the jury to treat her as it would any other lawbreaker, and he reminded the jurors that the state would not place Clark in prison. After deliberating twenty minutes, the jury found Clark Guilty and, true to his promise, District Court Judge Michael McSpadden sentenced her to two years of unsupervised probation, during which she would have to call him only every few months. He added this was the first and likely the last time he would hand down such a sentence. REF.: *CBA*.

Clark, Lorraine, 1926- , U.S., mur. Lorraine and Melvin Clark began to draw apart after ten years of marriage. The night of Apr. 10, 1954, Melvin came home early and found his wife in bed with another man. Lorraine had been active in a new pastime in Amesbury, Mass.—wife swapping. A group would get together, throw their house keys in a bowl, and then each chose a key and went with its owner for the evening. When Melvin found his wife with her lover, the couple quarreled. Lorraine Clark ended by stabbing her husband with a knitting needle. That gave her time to grab the gun she kept at their lakeside home, and she shot Melvin twice.

U.S. murderer Lorraine Clark.

When Lorraine realized that she had killed her husband, she set about methodically disposing of the body. She trussed it in chicken wire to make a small parcel. After transporting it by car to the Merrimack River, she tied weights to it and dumped it from a bridge. Assuming that the motion of the tidal river would carry the corpse out to sea, she pretended to friends and neighbors that her husband had left after a major quarrel. She backed up this story by suing Melvin for divorce on grounds of cruelty. But on June 2, Melvin's badly decomposed body was found in the marshlands by a birdwatcher, and it was identified by its fingerprints.

When the police asked Lorraine for an explanation of the bullet holes in her husband's body, she confessed to killing him. Although she was indicted for first-degree murder, she was found Guilty of second-degree murder and sentenced to life in prison.

REF.: *CBA*; Nash, *Look For the Woman*; Wilson, *Encyclopedia of Murder*.

Clark, Marcellus Jerome (AKA: Sue Mundy), 1845-65, U.S., rob.-mur. Near the end of the U.S. Civil War, Marcellus Jerome Clark, better known as Sue Mundy, was the scourge of the Union army. The band of more than sixty guerrillas he led with Billy Magruder attacked and murdered many northern soldiers in Kentucky during the winter of 1864 and 1865. His raiding days finally came to an end with his capture on Mar. 12, 1865.

At the age of sixteen in 1861, the son of Brigadier General Hector M. Clark joined the Confederate army. His company was forced to surrender the following year, but he managed to escape in May 1862, from Camp Morton near Indianapolis, Ind. Clark later joined another regiment but retired from duty after being wounded. It was then that he began his own war against the North. Because of his feminine features, Clark's comrades called him Sue Mundy, and under that name he undertook several attacks, until Union soldiers surrounded him at a barn not far from Brandenburg, Ky. Even so, he still managed to wound three and kill one before giving up. Clark was taken to Louisville and tried on Mar. 14, found Guilty of murder, and hanged the next day. One hour before his death he was baptized, and then at 4:30 p.m., he was choked to death when the drop failed to break his neck. REF.: *CBA*.

Clark, Marvin J. (AKA: **Big Jim; Jim Clarkson**), prom. 1929, U.S., smug.-boot. Marvin Clark was a partner of Galveston, Texas, crime boss George Musey, a slim Syrian gangster who controlled waterfront smuggling during national Prohibition. Clark was wanted in Louisiana for the hijacking of a British rum vessel at the time of his falling out with Boss Musey. It was commonly believed that Marvin Clark was the American agent for various Canadian liquor interests who smuggled contraband whiskey into the southern states.

In 1929, Clark and Musey quarreled over a woman. In retaliation, the unhappy gangster phoned Federal Agent Al Scharff in Galveston and tipped him off about a convoy of bootlegged liquor making its way to the city. When customs agents detoured the convoy into the waiting arms of the law, Musey was out $100,000.

Clark, who had been exiled from the Gulf Coast by his one-time friend, did not live long to enjoy the fruits of his revenge. He was later killed by rival gangsters. See: **Musey, George**.

REF.: *CBA*; Roark, *The Coin of Contraband*.

Clark, Mary, d.1820, Brit., mur. Mary Clark took her marriage vow of "till death do us part" literally when she helped her lover, Philip Haynes, kill her husband. Both were found Guilty of murder and hanged at Northhampton in 1820.

REF.: *CBA*; O'Donnell, *Should Women Hang?*

Clark, Michael, c.1948-65, U.S., suic.-mur. A 16-year-old boy decided to play "king of the hill" overlooking a California freeway north of Los Angeles, where Mexican bandit Solomon Pico had fired at stagecoaches over a century ago. Clark's "game," however, played in Spring 1965, involved his father's powerful Swedish Mauser deer rifle and armor-piercing bullets aimed at unsuspecting drivers.

Michael Clark stole his family's Cadillac and drove about 150 miles north along the California coastline to just outside Santa Maria, where he rammed the car into a guard rail on Route 101. From a vantage point on top of a nearby hill, Clark opened fire at 6 a.m. the next morning on the freeway below. He missed the first driver but shot the second, William Reida, through the neck, seriously wounding him. Another shot hit Reida's 5-year-old son, Kevin Reida, in the head and killed him. Reida's wife managed to flag down two passing cars, but Clark shot and killed each driver before they could help the woman. While Mrs. Reida, who did not know how to drive, steered the car down the road, Clark continued to shoot at passing motorists. No one else was killed, but three others, including a police officer, were wounded by bullets, and six others were struck by flying glass. At 8:30 a.m., the siege came to an end as police and civilians closed in on Clark. Clark yelled, "Come and get me," then pointed the rifle at his forehead and fired. It was never determined why a seemingly normal and happy youth had gone berserk. REF.: *CBA*.

Clark, Ronald E., c.1913-   , U.S., mur. Dr. Ronald Clark was granted a license to practice medicine in the state of Michigan in 1954. Four years later, his wife committed him to the state mental hospital following a series of incidents that endangered the lives of several of his female patients. The same year that Dr. Clark opened his practice, he was accused of raping two women after giving them an anesthetic. A third woman complained to the police that Clark had performed an unauthorized abortion on her.

After two and a half months in the state hospital, Clark was permitted to return to his practice in Farmington Township near Detroit, but the complaints continued. By the time of his arrest on Nov. 16, 1967, Ronald Clark had had his license revoked four times, once for what officials called "gross moral conduct," twice for "moral turpitude," and a fourth time for unspecified charges. Three patients died in Clark's office from drug overdoses, and two girls, aged eleven and fifteen, were molested. Yet the Michigan

State Board of Registration had reinstated Clark in each instance.

On Nov. 3, 1967, a policeman found the body of Mrs. Grace Neil, forty-three, in Dr. Clark's office after he noticed an illegally parked hearse outside. Neil had worked for Clark as a part-time office assistant. Her death was the result of a lethal dose of sodium pentothal that Dr. Clark administered. It was the second time in less than a year that one of Clark's female employees died under mysterious circumstances. On Mar. 20, 63-year-old Hannah Bowerbank of Detroit also died from a drug overdose.

Dr. Clark was arrested on Nov. 16, 1967, outside Port Austin, Mich., 125 miles from Detroit. He was captured in deep snow after a bloodhound was put on his trail. Oakland County prosecutor S. Jerome Bronson announced that his office would investigate six other deaths that might have been linked to "therapeutic misadventure" on the part of Dr. Clark.

Clark was charged with manslaughter and held on a $50,000 bond, but after considering the evidence in the case of Mrs. Bowerbank, the judge ordered the defendant arraigned on first-degree murder charges. In a plea-bargaining arrangement engineered by defense attorney Philip E. Rowston, Dr. Clark offered to plead guilty to manslaughter to reduce the severity of sentence. He received three to fifteen years at the state prison in Southern Michigan. REF.: *CBA*.

Clark, Thomas (AKA: **Pennsylvania Butch**), prom. 1902, U.S., rob. From an early age, Thomas Clark had been a professional thief, graduating to train robbery at the turn of the century. He and four others stopped the B&O train near Marcus, Ill., on Aug. 5, 1902, robbing the Adams Express car of $3,000. One of the gang was accidentally shot and killed by the gang leader as the bandits made their getaway, although Clark reportedly argued against this action. All the gang's members were either killed or captured within six months, with Clark being tracked down to Memphis, Tenn., where he was captured by Pinkerton detectives hired by the railroad. Clark was sentenced to life imprisonment in Joliet Prison.

Train robber Thomas Clark.

REF.: Bartholomew, *A Biographical Album of Western Gunfighters*; *CBA*.

Clark, Tom Campbell, 1899-1977, U.S., jur. District attorney in Dallas, Texas, from 1927-32. He was named special assistant to Attorney General Homer Cummings in 1943. When President Harry Truman appointed him U.S. attorney general in 1945, he reorganized the Justice Department by consolidating its seven major divisions. He actively prosecuted leaders of the American Communist Party and drew up the first attorney general's black list of known subversive organizations in 1947. In 1949 he accepted appointment as associate justice of the U.S. Supreme Court. REF.: *CBA*.

Clark, Violet (AKA: **Vicky Wright**), prom. 1956, Brit., mansl. Anchored at South Benfleet, Essex, was *Buchra*, a houseboat on which Violet Clark, her lover, and her 2-year-old twins, Colin and Reginald, lived. On Apr. 17, 1956, after Violet's lover died, she and her sons moved to the *Windmill*, the houseboat of Grace Richardson and her family. The *Buchra* was burned on May 15.

Neighbors noticed about 7 p.m. on May 16 that many of the Richardsons' and Clarks' belongings were being moved to another houseboat, the *Beta Glen*. Early the next morning, the *Windmill*, too, was destroyed by fire, and the Clark twins perished in the blaze. Richardson and Clark were brought to trial. Richardson was acquitted, but Clark, who was suspected of planning to rid herself of the twins and then join a lover, Bill Smith, was tried on murder charges. She was convicted of manslaughter, found guilty of criminal neglect. She was sentenced to two sentences of three years to be served concurrently.

REF.: *CBA*; Furneaux, *Famous Criminal Cases, Vol. 4.*

Clark, Willard, prom. 1855, Case of, U.S., mur. Willard Clark coveted an attractive young woman living in New Haven, Conn., but she rejected him, marrying Richard W. Wight. Clark then sought out Wight, finding him at work, and, without a word, shot him in the head, killing him. Clark was tried in New Haven on Sept. 17, 1855, but was acquitted on grounds of insanity.

REF.: *CBA*; McFarland, *Report of the Trial of Willard Clark.*

Clark, William Ramsey, 1927- , U.S., atty. gen. Headed a federal civilian task force during the University of Mississippi riots in 1962. He was appointed attorney general by President Lyndon Johnson in 1967, serving until 1969. He worked diligently in the movement to desegregate the public schools in the south. In the 1966 case of *Miranda vs. Arizona,* he backed the Supreme Court's decision to overturn the rape conviction of Ernest Miranda. Clark opposed capital punishment and supported a bill outlawing wiretaps in cases not involving national security. REF.: *CBA*.

Clarke, Sir Edward George, 1841-1931, Brit., lawyer. Authored *Treatise on the Law of Extradition.* REF.: *CBA.*

Clarke, Sir Edward Percival, 1872-1936, Brit., jur. Chairman of the County of London Sessions from 1932-36. He served as senior prosecuting counsel at the Old Bailey before his elevation to the bench in 1932. During this time he conducted or assisted in the prosecution of murderers Thomas Henry Allaway, Louis Voisin, William Yeldham, Henry Perry, Ernest Rhodes, Elvira Barney, Ernest Walker, Alfred Solomon, and William Holmyard. REF.: *CBA.*

Clarke, George, 1820-46, Brit., (unsolv.) mur. Constable Clarke was patrolling the Four Wants near the town of Dagenham on the Essex Coast the night of July 1, 1846. The next morning when he did not return from his rounds his fellow officers commenced a search. The ponds and waterways were dragged, but turned up nothing. Three days later, when the mutilated and battered body of the policeman was found in a potato field belonging to a farmer named Collier.

The 20-year-old patrolman's head was nearly severed from the torso, clear evidence that a fierce struggle had occurred. While the murderer was never apprehended, there was suspicion that Sergeant Parsons and other members of the police detail were somehow mixed up in it. They had provided a false report of their movements that night. Sergeant Parsons had not been on duty at all, and four other policemen assigned to the district were drinking at the home of farmer named Page.

Nearly twelve years later the widow of a man tied in with a rural farm thief named George Blewett testified that he had killed Constable Clarke after he had caught them stealing some corn. Blewett was arrested, but for lack of evidence was released.

REF.: *CBA*; Cobb, *Murdered On Duty*; Thomson, *The Story of Scotland Yard.*

Clarke, John Hessin, 1857-1945, U.S., jur. Appointed associate justice in 1916 by President Woodrow Wilson. During his six years on the bench, he upheld traditional liberal views regarding child labor, the rights of unions to organize, and freedom of speech. REF.: *CBA.*

Clarke, Mary Anne (Mary Anne Thompson), 1776-1852, Brit., fraud-libel. London-born Mary Anne Clark, born Thompson, received her education at Ham, her schooling financed by a gentleman named Day, who reportedly planned to marry the girl. At sixteen, however, the girl married a youth named Clarke and five years later, with her husband bankrupt and a drunk, she struck out on her own, becoming the mistress of Sir Charles Milner. She then became the mistress of Sir James Brudenell. The beautiful Mrs. Clarke was an expert flimflammer, bilking both of these gentlemen out of considerable money. After bilking several merchants, the alluring Mrs. Clarke began appearing on the stage, taking roles in plays produced for the Haymarket. From the audience of admiring males, she selected more victims, including Lord Barrymore and the Duke of York.

After becoming the Duke of York's mistress, Mrs. Clarke began to sell more than her body. She convinced wealthy lovers that she could secure military commissions for them through her political contacts, chiefly through the Duke of York. She sold commissions by the score at £900 each, considerably less than the average £2,500 the government charged. Most often these commissions were awarded to Mrs. Clarke's patrons. She grew rich, purchasing a mansion in London and a country estate. Then, on Jan. 27, 1809, Colonel Gwyllym Lloyd Wardle rose in the House of Commons to denounce her, stating that she had for years been selling commissions through her patron, the Duke of York. The Duke was examined and exonerated.

Mrs. Clarke was not prosecuted but she lost her political protection and her sponsoring nobles soon ignored her. She maintained her larcenous ways and high-handed lifestyle but she ran afoul when she denounced the Irish Chancellor of the Exchequer, passing certain remarks about him after he labelled her a "fallen woman." She was sued for libel and lost, serving nine months in prison. In disgrace, Mrs. Clarke left England, but took her considerable fortune with her, buying a huge estate in Boulogne where she became one of the most sought-after mistresses of her day. She died in luxury at her estate on June 21, 1852.

REF.: *CBA*; Nash, *Look for the Woman.*

Matthew Clarke murdering a servant girl, 1721.

Clarke, Matthew, d.1721, Brit., mur. Only a plough boy in his youth, Matt Clarke turned to robbery to raise the funds he needed for his wild and reckless affairs with the women of St. Albans.

When at last he found his contentment in the arms of just one woman, he proposed that they wed in London. When his future bride selected her favorite ring in a London goldsmith's shop, Clarke knew the few shillings in his pocket were not enough to buy it for her. Given the situation, his fiancee agreed to wait for him in town while he set out to raise more money.

Hiring on as a daylaborer at a nearby farm, Clarke worked for scarcely two hours before sneaking into the farmer's house to rob him. Finding a servant girl alone in the kitchen, Clarke planned to simply distract her, take what he wanted, and be on his way before the master of the house returned. When efforts to distract her failed, Clarke embraced the girl and gave her a tender, sweet kiss. He then stabbed her in the neck and watched her die in a pool of blood.

On his journey back to London he passed by Tyburn, the hanging hill. The sight of the gallows so disturbed him that he altered his route, and in doing so, he came across men who asked if he had seen a man who might be suspected of murder. When they noticed dried blood on his clothing, Clarke was taken into custody.

He was jailed at Newgate and pleaded guilty to murder. His death sentence was carried out on July 28, 1721, on Tyburn Hill, the very place he tried so hard to avoid.

REF.: *CBA; Mitchell, Newgate Calendar.*

Clarke, Morris Arthur, c.1930- , Brit., asslt.-rob.-mur. Morris Clarke, a 27-year-old truck driver, had suspected for a number of years that his wife was having an affair with her former employer, farmer Arthur Johnson of Crowtree Farm. On the night of Oct. 15, 1956, Clarke and his wife had a fight and Clarke stormed out to confront Johnson. During their discussion, Clarke picked up a piece of wood from the ground and hit Johnson over the head with it. Johnson fell to the ground, Clarke continued to strike him, and he did not rise again. Clarke used the farmer's own truck to take the body to one of the many dykes in the area. He also took Johnson's safe key. When he returned to Johnson's house, he found money hidden in various places and so never used the key to the safe.

When Johnson was reported missing, police searched his house and noticed the smell of dry rot on the whole first floor. Morris Clarke was one of the people interviewed, and the police quickly discovered that he was paying off some of his creditors with bills that had a musty smell to them. Then, on Oct. 25, the farmer's body floated to the surface. In Clarke's hayloft, police found a cake can containing more than £600 in notes, all with the pervasive smell of dry rot. Clarke was convicted of murder in 1957 and sentenced to hang, but his sentence was commuted to life imprisonment.

REF.: Butler, *Murderers' England; CBA; Furneaux, Famous Criminal Cases, Vol. 4; Heppenstall, The Sex War and Others; Jackson, Occupied With Crime; Wilson, Encyclopedia of Murder.*

Clarke, Nelly, c.1914-25, Case of, Brit., (unsolv.) mur. One evening in January 1925, Nelly Clarke's mother sent her on an errand, but the child did not come home. The 11-year-old was found the next morning, her body leaning against a telegraph pole close to her home. She had been sexually assaulted and strangled with the belt of her coat. The murderer was never caught.

REF.: *CBA; Nicholls, Crime Within the Square Mile.*

Clarke, Philmore, 1918- , U.S., mur. A rejected lover murdered his ex-girlfriend and dumped the body in the Anacostia River where it was laden with black silica slag.

Philmore Clarke, a 40-year-old carpenter, was dating a divorceé, Ruth Reeves, a 38-year-old elevator operator who worked in Washington, D.C., at the time she cut off her relationship with him and began seeing another man. Enraged, Clarke strangled Reeves on Sept. 7, 1958, left the body in her house, and then visited another girlfriend, who provided his alibi that night. Slipping out of her house, he then picked up the body, attached concrete weights to it, and dumped it in the river.

A building engineer where Reeves worked noticed a newspaper article about an unidentified body found on Sept. 8 in the Anacostia River. When she failed to show up for work, he notified police. Police found Clarke's picture at Reeves' home, and, in a search of his residence, they discovered baling wire and holes where slabs of concrete had been removed from the front of the house, materials identical to the concrete slab and wire fastened to the dead woman's leg. On Sept. 9, Clarke was arrested, but he refused to confess. However, the police case against Clarke grew stronger after black silica slag, a residue from industrial furnaces, was found on Clarke's shoes, in the car he drove, and on Reeves' clothing. Police also learned that a power company's refuse containing slag had been put on the road near where the body was found.

Clarke was tried on Dec. 9, and convicted of second-degree murder. He received a five- to twenty-five year sentence of imprisonment.

REF.: Block, *Fifteen Clues;* ____, *Science Vs. Crime; CBA; Nash, Murder, America.*

Clarke, Victor, 1946- , Brit., mur. Victor Clarke, the son of a British Army non-com stationed in West Germany in 1961, battered and strangled his 6-year-old playmate in the basement of the apartment building he lived in. The 15-year-old Clarke was brought back to England where he told the police that it had been a part of a childish game that had gotten out of hand. The younger boy had chased Clarke around in a circle, until he knocked him down. "Then I put my hands around his throat and choked him. I didn't mean to. I picked him up and put him in a hole under the stairs," Victor explained.

At his trial, Victor Clarke was found Not Guilty of murder, but Guilty of manslaughter, after the jurors received a report from the Medical Officer at Brixton Prison who cited a "degree of mental abnormality" in the boy. Under the terms of the 1960 Mental Health Act, Clarke was ordered detained in a state mental hospital until the doctors decided that he could be released.

REF.: *CBA; Wilson, Children Who Kill.*

Clarke, William, d.1802, U.S., jur. Government attorney from 1796-1800, later serving as U.S. district attorney in Kentucky. He was appointed to the bench of the territorial court of Indiana by President John Adams in 1800. REF.: *CBA.*

Clarkson, Thomas, 1760-1846, Brit., abolitionist. Attempted to persuade the king of France in 1789 and the czar of Russia in 1818 to abolish the slave trade practiced in their respective countries. He authored a number of pamphlets about the history of slavery and the case for abolition. REF.: *CBA.*

Claryngdon, Sir Roger, prom. 1402, Brit., rebel. Sir Roger Claryngdon was a supporter of King Richard II, who abdicated after being conquered by Henry IV. Throughout the early 1400s, Henry continually battled rebellions caused by Richard's supporters, including Claryngdon, who was charged with inciting mobs against Henry and with shouting out verses that mocked the king. In 1402, Claryngdon was strangled at Tyburn.

REF.: *CBA; Potter, The Art of Hanging.*

Clasper, Richard, b.c.1922, U.S.S.R., adult. A British engineer, Richard Clasper, fifty-seven, was sent to work in the U.S.S.R. After he arrived, he was seduced by a 27-year-old interpreter and then asked to spy on Soviet workers at the site of his engineering project. He refused and in July 1979, pictures of his lovemaking session with the interpreter were sent to his 54-year-old wife, who collapsed and was sent to the hospital. REF.: *CBA.*

Claude, Georges (AKA: **Edison of France**), b.c.1871, Fr., consp. The inventor of neon lights, Georges Claude, also developed a method to extract nitrogen. Angered when the pre-WWII government of France favored a German method over his, during the German occupation of France, Claude supported the Nazi-backed Vichy government. Using his own money to travel around France, he gave speeches praising National Socialism and calling for harsher treatment of French rebels. When the Allied forces landed in North Africa, he tried unsuccessfully to commit suicide. The 74-year-old Claude was convicted in early July 1945, of collaborating with the Germans and given a life sentence. REF.: *CBA.*

Claude, Jean, 1619-87, Fr., her. When the Edict of Nantes was revoked in 1685, effectively ending toleration for Huguenots, Claude was expelled from France for his defense of the faith and repeated quarrels with Catholic theologians. REF.: *CBA.*

Claudius I (Tiberius Claudius Drusus Nero Germanicus), 10 B.C.-54 A.D., Roman, emp., assass. Nephew of Tiberius, Claudius was proclaimed emperor by the Praetorian Guard after its members assassinated the vicious emperor Caligula. His reign (41-54 A.D.) was marked by an efficient administration, although he continued the barbaric traditions of gladiatorial sport, forcing at whim, all manner of Roman citizens, including his own page, to enter the arena to fight to the death. His bloodlust was considerable. He often entered the arena at daybreak and would sit until noon, after dismissing the audience, to watch hundreds of gladiators kill each other for his pleasure. If any gladiator accidentally stumbled, he was immediately killed by guards. Weak-willed and in constant fear that he would be dethroned, Claudius had all visitors to his court searched and, in the early years of his reign, he never went anywhere without his spear-carrying guards. His constant question to court advisers was: "Am I still emperor?"

Women proved to be the undoing of Claudius. He married four times, wedding the 15-year-old Valeria Messalina in 49 A.D. She was a profligate and an abandoned empress who enjoyed torturing any of those who displeased her. She plotted and intrigued not to gain power but to bring down those who had refused to show her slavish obedience. Messalina fed an insatiable sexual appetite which earned for her a fixed and deserved historical profile as a nymphomaniac. She practiced all manner of indecencies behind her husband's back, holding orgies and Bacchanalian revels in which she was the prominent player, taking on a dozen lovers at once. Claudius was either ignorant of these blatant offenses or chose to ignore them; he was sexually inactive and sixty years old at the time he married Messalina.

Yet Claudius could not ignore Messalina's most flagrant debaucheries, that of her bigamous and public marriage to Caius Silius, her favorite lover, a ceremony that shocked even Claudius.

Emperor Claudius, poisoned to death in 54 A.D.

His favorite adviser, Narcissus, prevailed upon the emperor to have Messalina executed, convincing him that she brought nothing but disgrace to his reign and, by her whoring actions, demeaned his status in history. Moreover, Narcissus pointed out that the empress was most certainly plotting Claudius' own assassination. The emperor gave orders to have his wife murdered and Narcissus sent, in 48 A.D., a centurion to Messalina's quarters in the palace, where she was promptly run through with a sword, after failing to seduce her resolute assassin.

Claudius' fourth wife was no improvement. In fact, Agrippina, his niece, lobbied for the position of empress. As a niece, Agrippina was allowed to caress and kiss the emperor and these courteous gestures she expanded into deep embraces and smoldering kisses that soon aroused Claudius' long dormant passions. Against the advice of his freedman counselors, Claudius not only married the power-hungry Agrippina but adopted her son Nero, two acts he was later to regret and openly complain about. Agrippina was a known adulteress and she had undoubtedly poisoned former husbands, yet Claudius, who occupied his later years in rewriting Roman history and was referred to by most historians as "scatterbrained," allowed Agrippina's ruthless intrigues and plots to go on unchecked, knowing she was scheming to have her son Nero assume the throne, replacing Claudius' own son Britannicus.

Slowly, Agrippina surrounded Claudius with her own retinue of allies. She brought the philosopher and teacher Seneca back from exile to tutor Nero and influence Claudius in Nero's favor. Agrippina engineered her private bodyguard and assassin, Afranius Burrus, into the position of prefect of the palace guard. Yet, the ever-present Narcissus attempted to influence Claudius against his scheming wife and her son Nero. Agrippina feared that this powerful counselor would convince Claudius to name Brittanicus as his successor, so she made plans to assassinate her husband. There are several versions relating how the Empress murdered Claudius. One report has it that she ordered the eunuch Halotus, Claudius' official taster, to poison one of his meals while he was dining in the Citadel with the priests of Jupiter.

The most reliable account has Agrippina paying the druggist Locusta to prepare a poison, most probably edible *boletus* mixed in a sauce from the same substance, that was administered to Claudius in a dish of mushrooms, his favorite delicacy. This dish was served to the emperor by Agrippina herself at a family banquet. Claudius vomited the meal and lost his ability to talk,

while suffering terrible stomach pains all night, dying at dawn on Oct. 13, 54 A.D. Another variation of this assassination reports that Claudius survived the original poisoned meal but was taken ill, and that the empress herself doctored him with a second poisoned dish of gruel, the poison being colocynth, from a wild Palestinian gourd, which was also given to Claudius as an enema by court physicians in the employ of Agrippina. Upon Claudius' death, Nero immediately appeared at the palace with Afranius Burrus at his side, announcing himself the new emperor, and instituting a mad reign that would equal and surpass the barbaric bloodletting of Caligula. See: **Agrippina the Younger; Caligula; Nero.**

REF.: Africa, *Rome of the Caesars;* Balsdon, *The Romans;* Carcopino, *Life in Ancient Rome; CBA;* Charles-Picard, *Augustus and Nero;* Charlesworth, *Cambridge Ancient History;* Dill, *Roman Society, From Nero to Marcus Aurelius;* Duff, *Freedman in the Early Roman Empire;* Gibbon, *Decline and Fall of the Roman Empire;* Grant, *The World of Rome;* Graves, *I, Claudius;* Johnson, *Famous Assassinations of History;* Momigliano, *Claudius, The Emperor and His Achievement;* Nash, *Almanac of World Crime;* Robinson, *History of Rome;* Suetonius, *The Twelve Caesars;* Syme, *Tacitus;* Tacitus, *The Annals;* (FILM), *The Robe,* 1953; *Demetrius and the Gladiators,* 1954; *Rome Wants Another Caesar,* 1974.

Claudius, Publius (Pulcher Publius Claudius), prom. 249 B.C., Roman., treas. Commanded large Roman fleet that engaged the Carthaginians in the harbor of Drepanum (Trapani). The heavy losses sustained in battle resulted in a charge of treason. He was punished with a heavy fine. REF.: *CBA.*

Claustre, Françoise, b.c.1936, S. Afri., kid. vict. A French archeologist, Françoise Claustre, thirty-eight, was involved in a field study of pre-Islamic tombs in the northern part of Chad. In April 1974, she was abducted from the Saharan site by rebel leader Hissen Habre to be used as leverage to gain financial and military aid from France to fight the Chad government. They demanded eighty tons of military equipment, excluding arms, and $800,000 cash. The situation was extremely sensitive because the Chad government, which had been battling the rebels with French aid, officially opposed France's paying the ransom.

In August 1975, Claustre's husband, Pierre, traveled to Chad to personally request her freedom, and he, too, was taken prisoner. When the archeologist was scheduled for execution on Sept. 23, 1975, France offered to parachute $2.5 million to the rebels, but the money was refused. France did gain a stay of execution and a few days later officials met some of the demands. Altogether, France gave the insurgents $800,000 in cash and $1.2 million in medical aid.

Finally, after nearly three years, the couple were released in early January 1977, following the intervention of Libyan president Muammar Gaddafi. They were taken to Tripoli and then home to France. Another hostage, Marc Combes, escaped in early 1975. REF.: *CBA.*

Clavel, John, b.c.1603, Brit., rob. A highwayman condemned to death was granted by the king one of the very few reprieves given in the seventeenth and eighteenth centuries.

John Clavel, heir and nephew of a Dorsetshire squire, was arrested in 1626, along with a soldier friend, as highwaymen. The 23-year-old Clavel was said to be an expert in mail robberies. Although the two confessed, they insisted that the crimes were never violent. Nevertheless, they were given death sentences, so Clavel begged for mercy from King Charles I, reciting his request in verse.

Perhaps because the verse pleased the ruler or maybe because his council was bribed, the king granted a pardon to Clavel and his accomplice, and reduced the sentence to imprisonment. While in prison, Clavel wrote an autobiography, *Recantation of an Ill-led Life,* which warned other highwaymen against robbery and gave advice to travelers.

REF.: *CBA;* Pringle, *Stand and Deliver.*

Clavière, Étienne, 1735-93, Fr., rebel.-suic. Fell out of favor when his Girondist faction was toppled in 1793 by the radical Montagnards. He was brought before the Revolutionary Tribunal, adjudged guilty, and sentenced to death. While in prison he committed suicide. REF.: *CBA*.

Clay, Henry, 1777-1852, U.S., lawyer. Practiced law in Kentucky until election to U.S. Senate in 1806. Known as the Great Pacificator for his key role in the passage of the Missouri Compromise, he urged moderation in dealing with southern slave interests. The 1820 measure admitted Missouri as a slave state but barred slavery in most of the remaining western territories. During the Nullification Crisis of 1833 and the Compromise of 1850, Clay presented alternatives that again staved off armed conflict between North and South. REF.: *CBA*.

Clayton, Claude Feemster, 1909-69, U.S., jur. Prosecuting attorney in Lee County, Miss., from 1935-38. Named judge of the Northern District of Mississippi in 1958 by President Dwight Eisenhower. He was appointed to the U.S. Court of Appeals, First Circuit in 1967 by President Lyndon Johnson. REF.: *CBA*.

Clayton, Henry De Lamar, 1857-1929, U.S., jur. Congressman instrumental in passage of Clayton Antitrust Act of 1914, which was a corollary to the earlier Sherman Antitrust Act of 1890. That same year he was appointed by President Woodrow Wilson district judge for the middle and northern district of Alabama. REF.: *CBA*.

Clayton, John Middleton, 1796-1856, U.S., jur. Whig politician who served as chief justice of Delaware from 1837-39. REF.: *CBA*.

Clayton, William Henry Harrison, b.1840, U.S., jur. Prosecuting attorney of Little Rock, Ark., in 1871. Nominated for the territorial court of the Indian territory by President William McKinley in 1897 and reappointed three times. REF.: *CBA*.

Clayton-Wright, Derek, 1918-   , Brit., fraud-arson. After selling a Bournemouth hotel for a large profit, Derek Clayton-Wright bought a large pleasure boat, the *Barcarolle*, for £16,000, expecting to make more profit with it. However, he was unable to sell the yacht in the U.S. because WWII was still affecting the economy. He was further discouraged when a deal to rent it to a film company collapsed, and he was still saddled with the expensive vessel.

Then, in August 1947, the boat owner increased his insurance on the boat from £14,000 to £20,000, gradually raising the coverage to £35,000 by the end of January 1948. He renewed the policy for another month on Feb. 24, 1948. The boat, now docked at Southampton, was guarded by a watchman until the end of February when Clayton-Wright directed that the guard be discharged. On the evening of Mar. 1, he visited the craft. About 1:30 a.m. on Mar. 2, fire blazed from the two ends of the ship. The fires were spotted by another night watchman who alerted the Southampton Fire Brigade. The firefighters, furnished with a plentiful supply of water by a rising tide, were able to put out the fires. Later, a police investigation revealed that Clayton-Wright had offered to pay several people to set the fires. Convicted of arson and attempted insurance fraud, he received a sentence of three years' penal servitude. REF.: *CBA*; Woodland, *Assize Pageant*.

Cleary, Joe, and **Sweeney, Jack**, and **Waldron, Tom**, prom. 1908, U.S., asslt.-rape. On a cold, dank night at the 101st Street Pier in New York on Nov. 4, 1908, Mary Jessop, the bargeman's wife, sat alone in the cabin of her husband's coal barge when suddenly three rough men entered. They were rough-hewn stevedore types who shoveled coal on the waterfront: Joe Cleary, Jack Sweeney, and Tom Waldron.

Using a silk handkerchief, Cleary gagged Mrs. Jessop while his companions raped her. Afterward, the three men rifled through the barge but could only find $7 in cash. The barge was cast off from its mooring in the East River. The three rapists believed that the swift current of the river would dash the boat against the rocks and that would be the end of it. However, providence intervened and a Harbor Launch spotted the craft careening out of control. It was towed back into port and the life of Mary Jessop was saved.

Posing as a stevedore, Detective John George Stein interviewed other harbor workers and was able to identify Cleary through his incriminating handkerchief. It bore the letter "C". By pleading guilty at the General Sessions Court, Waldron and Cleary received indeterminate six year sentences. Sweeney elected to stand trial and was sentenced to seventeen years in prison on Dec. 3.

REF.: *CBA*; Livingston, *The Murdered and the Missing*.

Cleaver, Charles (AKA: Limpy Charley), b.1874, and **Wharton, Charles S.**, 1874-1939, and **Keating, Francis L.**, b.1899, and **Holden, Thomas**, b.1897, U.S., rob. On Feb. 25, 1928 six armed bandits detonated a bomb underneath the mail car of the Grand Trunk Railway in Evergreen Park, a suburb south of Chicago. The gunmen escaped with mail sacks containing $133,000 in cash and securities. Charles Cleaver, known in criminal circles as "Limpy Charley" stored the loot in the home of former U.S. Congressman Charles S. Wharton. The former "Boy Congressman" elected from the stockyards district of Chicago in 1904 had lived in virtual obscurity when since leaving the state's attorney's office in 1923.

Wharton was prosecuted by former colleague First Assistant U.S. District Attorney John E. Northrup, who wept when the jury returned a Guilty verdict on Aug. 2, 1928. "It's like a blow to the solar plexus," Wharton said. "But I'm still fighting." Wharton received a two-year sentence in the Leavenworth Penitentiary. In 1929, he was disbarred. "Limpy" Cleaver was sentenced to twenty-five years in prison by Federal judge James H. Wilkerson. Fearing that his friends might try to free him from custody, the time of Cleaver's train departure to the penitentiary was kept secret.

The convictions of Cleaver and Wharton followed those of two accomplices: Thomas Holden and Francis Keating, who both received twenty-five-year prison sentences. Using forged passes, they escaped from Leavenworth on Feb. 28, 1930, only to be rearrested on a Kansas City golf course five months later. Their wives were casually watching the game from a parked car when federal agents arrived to bring the two men back to prison to serve out the remainder of their terms. REF.: *CBA*.

Cleaver, Eldridge, b.c.1936., U.S., asslt. Eldridge Cleaver, a former leader of the militant Black Panthers and a confessed rapist was involved in a shootout in 1968. He was arrested after the incident, but escaped to Algeria. In 1975, he returned to the U.S., declaring that he was a religious convert. Four years later, a plea bargain was arranged and the murder charges stemming from the shootout were dropped. In exchange, Cleaver pleaded Guilty to assault. Judge Winton McKibben, of the Alameda County, Calif., Superior Court placed Cleaver on probation on Jan. 3, 1980, and directed him to contribute 2,000 hours of community service.

REF.: *CBA*; Godwin, *Murder U.S.A.*; Haskins, *Street Gangs*.

Clem, Nancy E., and **Hartman, Silas W.**, prom. 1860s, U.S., bribe.-fraud-mur. A double murder was committed to keep a secret system of financial double-dealing from being revealed.

On Sept. 12, 1868, Jacob Young and his wife, Nancy J. Young, were driving in their carriage with Nancy E. Clem on a road near Indianapolis, Ind. They stopped at Cold Spring, a secluded, sandy bank that lovers frequented. Minutes later, Young was murdered with a double-barreled shotgun from behind, and his wife, standing close by, was shot in the back of the head with a pistol. Clem was then seen riding back to the town with her brother, Silas W. Hartman.

The murdered pair were well respected in Indianapolis, although at the time of the murder some speculated that Young had been involved in some underhanded enterprise. He had settled in Indianapolis five or six years before with no money and had quickly accumulated wealth. As one of several individual creditors and banks, he was linked to a scheme of Clem's in which she apparently arranged to borrow sums up to $30,000, only to use the money to pay off another loan. Young may have been murdered to keep him from revealing the transaction to Clem's husband or from upsetting her plan. Clem stood trial twice. The first one, during which she tried to bribe witnesses, ended with the jury in disagreement, and the jurors were discharged. At the second trial, she was convicted of murder in the second degree and sentenced to life imprisonment. Her brother committed suicide in his cell with a razor.

REF.: *CBA; The Cold Spring Tragedy.*

Clément, Charles (Charles Crippa), 20th Cent., Fr., suic.-mur. Charles Clément told acquaintances that he had an invalid wife who suffered from cancer and no longer recognized him, and that she was being cared for by a family near Saint-Céré. Therefore, when he met Félicie Crippa, the daughter of a wealthy Italian ribbon merchant, family and friends understood why they could not be married.

Clément and Félicie settled in Paris where Clément called himself Charles Crippa for convenience and said that he was the sales director of a prominent French perfume business. They had kept to themselves, so no one paid much attention when some time later, Clément told the landlady that his wife's legs were hurting and that she was confined to the apartment. He also changed the lock on the apartment door. Several months later, a friend, concerned about the 43-year-old Félicie, talked with detective René Chassot and requested a police investigation. About the same time, Clément's gas and electricity were shut off, and he fell behind in his rent. Meanwhile, Chassot learned that Clément had never had an invalid wife before meeting Félicie and police felt justified in breaking into his apartment. They found Félicie's body wrapped in a blanket in a water-filled bathtub. There were pressure marks on her throat and her legs had been cut off. Clément's body lay where he had shot himself in the head.

REF.: *CBA; Gribble, The Dead End Killers.*

Clementis, Vladimir, 1902-52, Czech., rebel. One of the organizers of the Communist coup that toppled the Czechoslovakian government in 1948. He was executed by Josef Stalin in 1950. REF.: *CBA.*

Clements, Emmanuel, Jr. (AKA: Mannie), d.1908, U.S., west. gunman-lawman. Following in his father's footsteps, Emmanuel Clements, Jr. also became a feared western gunman. No matter which side of the law Clements was on, he was dangerous when provoked.

In 1894, Mannie Clements arrived in El Paso, Texas, where he became deputy constable, and later, deputy sheriff. Mannie had fled Murphysville, where he had been hired to kill a local bad man named Pink Taylor. Clements had fired at Taylor through an open window, but missed and hit the wrong man. In the 1890s, Clements teamed up with his cousin, John Wesley Hardin, and his brother-in-law, "Killin'" Jim Miller. The three of them operated together on the wrong side of the law for many years.

Clements was indicted for armed robbery in 1908, but was acquitted because the jury

Emmanuel Clements, Jr.

did not dare return a Guilty verdict. Though he had been cleared, Clements' law enforcement career was ruined. He began drinking heavily, and turned to smuggling to earn a living. It is believed that his fatal shooting at the El Paso Coney Island Saloon on Dec. 29, 1908, was the result of an argument with the bartender, Joe Brown. Brown was also involved in the illegal importation of Chinese workers into the U.S. See: **Clements, Emmanuel, Sr.; Hardin, John Wesley.**

REF.: *CBA; Cunningham, Triggernometry; Hardin, The Life of John Wesley Hardin;* Horan and Sann, *Pictorial History of the Wild West;* Metz, *John Selman;* Nordyke, *John Wesley Hardin;* O'Neal, *Encyclopedia of Western Gunfighters;* Plenn and LaRoche, *The Fastest Gun in Texas;* Shirley, *Shotgun for Hire;* Sonnichsen, *Pass of the North.*

Clements, Emmanuel, Sr. (AKA: Mannen), d.1887, U.S., west. outl. Emmanuel Clements, known as Mannen, was one of four brothers brought up on a cattle ranch near Smiley, Texas. Mannen was the most notorious of the brothers, and was accused occasionally of cattle rustling. His cousin was the legendary gunman John Wesley Hardin, who came to live on the Clements ranch for a time and worked as a cowhand. Hardin took the brothers' herd on a trail drive and fought against the Sutton clan, who were feuding with the Taylors, blood relatives of the Clements family. In October 1872, Mannen repaid Hardin's many kindnesses by springing him from jail. Hardin sawed

Emmanuel Clements, Sr.

through the bars and Mannen used his lariat to pull the escapee to freedom.

The Clements clan became very wealthy as they continued to drive cattle to the Kansas railheads throughout the 1870s. But in 1877, Mannen found himself sharing a cell with Hardin, Johnny Ringo, and Bill Taylor. A decade later, Mannen ran for sheriff of Runnels County. The distinction between lawmen and outlaws frequently blurred in the Old West.

While campaigning for elective office, Clements was shot and killed at the Senate Saloon in Ballinger, Texas, on Mar. 29, 1887, by Marshal Joe Townsend. See: **Hardin, John Wesley.**

REF.: Bartholomew, *The Biographical Album of Western Gunfighters;* ____, *Kill or Be Killed;* ____, *Wyatt Earp, 1848-1880;* Boyer, *Suppressed Murder of Wyatt Earp;* Brown and Schmitt, *Trail Driving Days;* Casey, *The Texas Border and Some Borderliners; CBA;* Crawford, *The West of the Texas Kid;* Cunningham, *Triggernometry;* Drago, *Wild, Woolly & Wicked;* Gregory, *True Wild West Stories;* Haley, *Jeff Milton;* Hardin, *The Life of John Wesley Hardin;* Hendricks, *The Bad Man of the West;* Holloway, *Texas Gun Lore;* Horan and Sann, *Pictorial History of the Wild West;* Hutchinson, *The Life and Personal Writings of Eugene Manlove Rhodes;* Lake, *Frontier Marshal;* Leftwich, *Tracks Along the Pecos;* Metz, *John Selman;* Nordyke, *John Wesley Hardin;* O'Neal, *Encyclopedia of Western Gunfighters;* Plenn and LaRoche, *The Fastest Gun in Texas;* Raine, *Famous Sheriffs and Western Outlaws;* ____, *Guns of the Frontier;* Rennert, *Western Outlaws;* Ripley, *They Died with Their Boots On;* Rosa, *They Called Him Wild Bill;* Scobee, *The Steer Branded Murder;* Schoenberger, *The Gunfighters;* Shirley, *Shotgun for Hire;* Siringo, *Riata and Spurs;* Sonnichsen, *I'll Die Before I'll Run;* Stanley, *Fort Bascom;* Sutton, *The Sutton-Taylor Feud;* White, *The Autobiography of a Durable Sinner;* ____, *Lead and Likker;* ____, *Them Was the Days.*

Clements, Mark, 1964-   , U.S., arson-mur. A juvenile delinquent was tried as an adult for setting fire to an apartment building, killing four. Mark Clements, seventeen, whose tests showed a mental age of nine, set fire to a Chicago apartment house on June 17, 1981. He told police that he and three friends went to the building and became involved in an argument with someone who lived there. Clements took several empty soda bottles, poured gasoline in them, and tossed some of the gas on the tenant. Later investigators learned that the fires, ignited with gas, had been started in two stairwells.

The teenager was convicted on Sept. 3, 1982, of four counts of murder and one count of aggravated arson. Standing before Judge William Cousins, Jr., he pleaded for nearly two hours against a life sentence. "I'm seventeen years old...I know I can be somebody in my life, maybe somebody like you...I looked at the police steal my youth, and now the jury has stole my life," he told the judge. The judge sentenced Clements to life in prison without parole. REF.: *CBA*.

Clements, Dr. Robert George, 1890-1947, Brit., suic.-mur. At first, the examining physicians at the Astley Nursing Home in Southport, Lancashire concluded that the fourth Mrs. Clements died from myeloid leukemia. But Dr. Andrew Brown, the Staff Surgeon noticed the "pin-point" positioning of the pupils of her eye—an indication of mor-phine poisoning. The death of wealthy heiress Amy Vic-toria Burnett Clements on May 27, 1947 ended the mur-der spree of husband George, a Belfast doctor who belonged to the Royal College of Sur-geons.

Wife murderer Robert Clements.

During a thirty-five year span, Dr. Clements married and killed four wives, three of whom were quite wealthy. In 1912 he joined hands with Edyth Anna Mercier, who expired in 1920, about the same time as her fortune. A year later, he married Mary McLeery, who lasted until 1925 when her death was occasioned by what Dr. Clements described as endocarditis. Wife number three, Katherine Burke, was the only poor woman in the group. The third Mrs. Clements died in 1939 from cancer, which aroused the suspicion of the police. Before an autopsy could be conducted, the body was cremated.

The police concluded that Clements had turned his fourth wife into a morphine addict. A second post-mortem examination was ordered, and the examiners concluded that she had been poisoned. When the police arrived at his Southport home, they found Clements dead. He had poisoned himself with cyanide, leaving behind a note which read in part: "To whom it may concern...I can no longer tolerate the diabolical insults to which I have been recently exposed."

REF.: *CBA*; Firmin, *Scotland Yard: The Inside Story;* Firth, *A Scientist Turns to Crime;* Furneaux, *The Medical Murderer;* Heppenstall, *The Sex War and Others;* Nash, *Almanac of World Crime;* Shew, *A Companion to Murder;* Wilson, *Encyclopedia of Murder.*

Clemmons, Abel, d.1806, U.S., mur. A native of Clarksburg, Va., (later West Virginia) Abel Clemmons apparently suffered emotional problems all his life. He suddenly turned into a raving lunatic one night, grabbed an ax and killed his wife and eight children. The next morning, neighbors found him sitting amidst the bodies babbling and singing. He was undoubtedly insane but was judged Guilty and hanged on June 30, 1806, at Morgantown, Va.

REF.: *CBA; A Succinct Narrative of the Life and Character of Abel Clemmons; Murder, Horrible Murder!.*

Clémont, Jacques, See: **Henry III, King of France.**

Clench, Martin, and **Mackley, James,** prom. 1797, Brit., mur. On June 5, 1797, Martin Clench and James Mackley stood on the scaffold as hangmen William Brunskill and John Langley fitted the nooses around their necks. A Catholic priest, Reverend Villette, was ministering to the two convicted murderers when the trapdoor accidentally dropped. Although the attendants tumbled through the door, the hangmen landing on top of the priest, they were not seriously injured. The two condemned men were hanged a few minutes later. After the accident, some superstitious people believed that Clench and Mackley were innocent.

REF.: Bleakley, *Hangmen of England; CBA*.

Cleomenes I, d.498 B.C., Sparta, brib.-suic. Established Sparta as dominant kingdom in Peloponnesus through military conquest. His reign ended when he was forced to flee Sparta in 491 B.C. after he bribed a Delphian priestesses. He committed suicide in exile. REF.: *CBA*.

Cleopatra Selene, prom. 1st Cent. B.C., Egypt, queen, assass. Daughter of Cleopatra VII and Marc Antony. She was killed by the Roman Emperor Caligula. REF.: *CBA*.

Cleopatra Thea, d.121 B.C., Syria, queen, assass. According to legend this Ptolemaic queen was poisoned by her son Antiochus VIII. See: **Seleucus V.** REF.: *CBA*.

Cleophon, d.405 B.C., Athens, treas. Succeeded Cleon as leader of democratic factions, continuing aggressive war policy against Sparta. He was executed by an Athenian tribunal in 405 B.C. while under siege by Lysander. REF.: *CBA*.

Clerc, Jean Pierre, b.1888, and **Bernardon, Marc Joseph,** b.1898, Fr., mur. Speeches of political candidates are meant to inflame listeners to action, but on Apr. 23, 1925, several deaths and injuries resulted.

Three public meetings were held to express the views of candidates running for city offices. Several opposing groups, including the Communists and the Young Patriots, attended. During one meeting, speaker M. Henri Paté was annoyed by constant interruptions from the Communists, so to get rid of them, he shouted, "I speak to a portion of the audience, to my Com-munist friends, to let them know that their brothers are being assassinated at the other end of the road. We must not let them be killed!" Taking the speaker's cue, the Communists in the audience ran from that meeting to a second one, already heatedly in progress. At a third meeting, members of the Young Patriots were alerted and told that the second meeting was now in an uproar. Young Patriots and others rushed out of the third meeting to help their comrades.

In the resulting clash, several people were injured and others were killed. Police arrested two Communists, Jean Pierre Clerc, thirty-seven, an engraver, and Marc Joseph Bernardon, twenty-seven, a varnisher. Both were armed at the time of their arrests, and ballistics evidence linked them to the murders. Bernardon was acquitted because the jury was not sure if he had merely picked up a gun, as he claimed. Clerc claimed provocation, but he was found Guilty and sentenced to three years in prison.

REF.: *CBA;* Morain, *Underworld of Paris.*

Clermont-Tonnerre, Comte Stanislas Marie Adélaide de, 1757-92, Fr., assass. Served as deputy of nobility in States-General of 1789. He was murdered by a Paris mob in 1792. REF.: *CBA*.

Cleveland, Stephen Grover, 1837-1908, U.S., morals scandal. The twenty-second and twenty-fourth president of the U.S. (1885-89, 1893-97) began his professional career in 1859 as a lawyer in Buffalo, N.Y., later becoming mayor of that city (1881-82). He so thoroughly cleaned up corrupt practices in Buffalo as a thundering reformer, that he was swept into the governor's office (1883-85), his fellow Democrats hooting his fame far and wide as "Grover the Good." Yet, Cleveland's private life would later burst forth from a long-locked closet to threaten ruination and disgrace on the very eve of his greatest political triumph. Up to that time, his foes managed to ridicule only his eating habits, and even after Cleveland reached the Oval Office political opponents would make much of his appetite which was, in a word, uncontrollable.

Cleveland was an overweight and outright glutton who gorged his 260-pound, five-foot-eleven-inch body every day of his presi-dency. He would die on June 24, 1908 of gastrointestinal ailments as a result of overindulging. During his years as the chief executive, Cleveland wolfed down enormous portions of corned beef and cabbage, his favorite dish, which was served for dinner almost every other night. For breakfast he ate fish, steak, ham, and chops. The result was a corpulent body that grew to obesity and a bull neck with several chins doubling over tight collars.

Cleveland's eating habits were but teacup sensations when looking back to his first campaign for the presidency in 1884 and the scandal that almost destroyed him. "Grover the Good" was being heralded by his party as a man of impeccable morals at the time, but on July 21 of that year, the Buffalo *Evening Telegraph* let loose a scandal that should have demolished Grover Cleve-land's budding presidency. The paper announced that in the early

1870s Cleveland had seduced a widow named Maria Halpin and impregnated her. The widow gave birth to a child, and Grover admitted paternity and offered money to Halpin but refused to marry her. Halpin was forced by Cleveland's political aides to abandon the child in an orphanage, the *Evening Telegraph* said, and she herself was driven to an asylum.

Cartoon of Cleveland being tormented by his illegitimate child in the political campaign of 1884.

Republicans went berserk with joy at the prospect of dirtying their opponent with real scandal. Overnight, political cartoons appeared in which Cleveland was depicted as a roué and rake, an immoral monster abusing American womankind. In one cartoon, the presidential candidate was shown, throwing a tantrum, stomping his feet outside the White House fence, and plugging his ears to the bedeviling screams of his illegitimate child held in the arms of the sobbing Maria. To further vex "Grover the Good," some nameless, Republican-paid tunesmith devised a scathing ditty about the affair, which was soon sung sarcastically across the nation. It went:

> Ma! Ma! Where's my pa?
> Gone to the White House
> Ha! Ha! Ha!

The attacks were so vicious that they brought forth sympathy rather than condemnation, especially when it was made public that Cleveland had given the child his name, even though other men had been involved with Halpin, and that he had found a good home for the child and had set aside funds for his upbringing. Halpin had also received funds and was never driven to an asylum. Reliable reports had it that she later married and lived comfortably in upstate New York. Moreover, Cleveland's response to the slurs were typical of his straightforwardness. He wired his campaign managers: "Whatever you say, tell the truth."

Well, at least Cleveland had been a bachelor at the time of his indiscretions with Halpin, reasoned the public, and therefore it had not been an *adulterous* relationship. The public attitude changed to a "nobody's perfect" sentiment and the tide turned in favor of Cleveland. The day after he was elected to office, thousands of voters throughout the land marched triumphantly down the streets of major cities lustily singing their own jingle:

> Hurrah for Maria,
> Hurrah for the kid;
> We voted for Grover
> And we're damned glad we did!

American voters, then all male, no longer upheld the strict New England ethics and stern morality that had governed the land in earlier times. The Western notion of boldly entering wide-open frontiers carried over into the social habits of the citizenry and American males appreciated rather than condemned the strong—often ravenous—sexual appetites of politicians, especially chief executives; the more prominent the sexual peccadillo, the more supportive the voter. A wink and a knowing smile instead of wrath—that is what Cleveland got from his constituents.

REF.: Butterfield, *The American Past; CBA;* Israel, *The Chief Executive;* Johnson and Walker, *The Dynamics of the American Presidency;* Lorant, *The Glorious Burden;* Lott, *The Presidents Speak;* McElroy, *Grover Cleveland, The Man and the Statesman;* Merrill, *Bourbon Leader;* Nevins, *Grover Cleveland, A Study in Courage;* O'Brien, *Grover Cleveland As Seen By His Stenographer;* Tugwell, *Grover Cleveland.*

Cleveland Butcher Murders, prom. 1934-38, U.S., (unsolv.?) mur. For four years in the 1930s, headless corpses turned up in remote locations in and around Cleveland. The first murder occurred in September 1934 when the remains of a unknown woman were found in the Kingsbury Run section of Cleveland. The second victim, a small-time hood named Edward Andrassy, was found on Sept. 23, 1935, also in Kingsbury Run. The body had been dismembered with surgical precision, suggesting the killer might have medical exprerience. By the time the grisly remains of 36-year-old prostitute Florence Polillo were found in a bushel basket on Jan. 26, 1936, the city was in a frenzy. In June, the headless remains of another young man were found in Kingsbury Run. Fingerprints failed to identify the victim, but the body bore six unmistakable tattoos. In an effort to identify the victim, a death mask of him was displayed at the Cleveland Exposition of 1936-37, but no one could say who he was. There were three more killings in 1937. The press dubbed the fiend "The Mad Butcher of Kingsbury Run."

Private detective Lawrence "Pat" Lyons fingered former meat butcher Frank Dolezal as a likely suspect. Lyons found blood traces in Dolezal's room, and police interrogated the hard-drinking butcher for forty hours. Dolezal finally confessed to cutting up Polillo and disposing of the head, but he changed his story several times. Police believed they had a lunatic but not necessarily a murderer. Before the questions could be resolved, Dolezal hanged himself in his jail cell in September 1939.

By this time the murders in Cleveland had ended, but three similar murders were reported in Pittsburgh in 1939. Someone had severed the heads of three people in a railroad box car. A year before, a headless body had been found in Newcastle, Pa. The last such murder occurred in Pittsburgh in 1942, which convinced the Cleveland Police that the killer had moved on. Frank Dolezal's guilt or innocence remains in doubt.

REF.: *CBA;* Nash, *Open Files.*

Cleveland May Day Riot, prom. 1919, U.S., mob vio. The Socialist movement in the U.S. peaked shortly before WWI. The entry of the U.S. into the war led to a crackdown against so-called subversive groups like the International Workers of the World (IWW, or Wobblies), and various trade unions, which advocated pacifism and reconciliation with Bolshevik Russia. Congress passed the Espionage Act of June 1917 and the Sedition Act of 1918 to stifle internal subversion. Under these acts, police agencies across the country staged wholesale raids against Socialists. Many people were arrested and deported, and prominent labor leaders William Haywood of the IWW and Eugene Debs, president of the Railway Worker's Union, were arrested for their beliefs.

The anti-Socialist backlash continued after the Armistice was signed in 1918, leading to the second major "Red Scare" in U.S. history, the first having occurred during the 1877 strikes. There were outbreaks of violence across the U.S. on May Day 1919, as police and armed goons tried to break up Socialist parades. In New York City, angry mobs ransacked the offices of the newspaper the *Call* and the Russian People's House. The Boston May Day parade was disrupted, resulting in the death of one person and injuries to several others. The most serious incident occurred in Cleveland, Ohio, where a contingency of ex-soldiers, victory loan workers, and police assaulted 35,000 trade unionists and Socialist sympathizers as they marched from East 9th Street to the Public Square.

The marchers carried red silk banners, which stirred the "patriots" to action. For nearly two hours, the streets of downtown Cleveland were in chaos as club-wielding police indiscriminately attacked the Socialists, including women and children. The marchers' downtown headquarters at Prospect and Bolivar was ransacked, and the organizer of the day's events, C.E. Ruthenberg, was arrested. The police drove up and down the streets in their flivvers, scattering onlookers in every direction. When the area was cleared several hours later, Cleveland resembled a war zone. See: **B & O Railroad Strike.**

REF.: *CBA;* Hofstadter and Wallace, *American Violence.*

Clever, Daniel, prom. 1885, Case of, U.S., mur. William Martin, the 27-year-old handyman working for Daniel Clever, was apparently seduced by Clever's wife and Clever discovered their secret affair. He learned that his wife was planning to meet Martin at the home of a friend and made it easy for the handyman by giving him the day off. Clever then followed him to the rendezvous point and shot him to death just as he met with Mrs. Clever. Tried in Carlisle, Pa., Clever's lawyers pleaded him not guilty on grounds of insanity and won an acquittal.

REF.: *CBA; The Trial of Daniel Clever.*

Clichy Uprising, 1891, Fr., riot.-bomb.   France in the late 1880s was marked by civil unrest as leftist political groups sought to undermine the administration of Marie-François-Sadi Carnot, president of the Fourth Republic. The anti-Republican Boulangist Movement of 1889, together with a financial scandal following the collapse of the French Panama Canal Company, brought disgrace to the embattled leader. Anarchists used bombs against the prime minister and the president of the chamber. Labor unrest culminated in a workers' riot on May Day 1891 at Clichy-la-Garenne, a suburb north of Paris.

Police dispersing the crowd brutally clubbed five anarchists. Two people were later sentenced to prison terms for their roles in the disturbance. The Clichy affair might have been forgotten if not for an explosion at the home of the sentencing judge on Mar. 11, 1892. Sixteen days later, the public prosecutor was the victim of a second bombing. The instigator of these crimes was the half-French, half-German anarchist Ravachol, who was apprehended along with four accomplices after openly boasting of his accomplishments at a café on the Boulevard Magenta. A waiter overheard his conversation and reported it to the police. Later that night, after Ravachol was interrogated at police headquarters, one of his confederates bombed the café.

For a time Ravachol became a hero to the militant workers, who called for his release. But it was soon learned that he also had committed a number of murders. He was found Guilty, and executed in July 1892. "Long live anarchy!" he shouted, which became a rallying cry for those who carried out other acts of violence in the coming months. A bomb exploded in a Paris police station, killing six men. On June 23, 1894, President Carnot was riding through Lyon in his carriage when a young man, Italian anarchist Sante Caserio, approached him with a bouquet of flowers, then pulled a knife and stabbed the president. The next day Carnot's widow received a photograph of Ravachol, and a note which read: "He is avenged."

REF.: *CBA;* Williams, *Heyday For Assassins.*

Click, Franklin, 1919-50, U.S., kid.-rape-mur. Picked up for questioning in a 1949 kidnapping and rape case, the suspect confessed to three sex murders that had taken place five years before for which another had been previously convicted.

On Aug. 17, 1949, a 19-year-old housewife was kidnapped from her home near Fort Wayne and raped. Bargaining with his victim, the rapist said that he would buy Christmas presents for the woman and her children if she would not call police, and he returned her to her house. The woman was able to get the car's license number, and the next day Franklin Click, thirty, was picked up for questioning. During police interrogation, Click, a driver for a celery grower, confessed to three 1944 sex murders. The Fort Wayne victims included Anna Kuzeff, nineteen, Wilhelmina "Billie" Haaga, thirty-eight, and a high school student, Phyllis Conine, seventeen.

Meanwhile, convicted killer Ralph W. Lobaugh, waiting on death row, had admitted to three murders, including those of Haaga and Kuzeff. When Click confessed, Governor Henry F. Schricker gave Lobaugh another ninety-day reprieve.

During the proceedings, Click gave a confession to his wife, who tried to collect $16,500 in reward money, but police officials refused to pay. Click, the father of five, was convicted of the 1949 kidnapping and rape crime, receiving a life sentence. On Dec. 1, 1949, he was found Guilty of the 1944 sex murder of Conine, the high school student, and he was sentenced to death on Mar. 27, 1950. After two stays of execution and a confession by Lobaugh to the Conine murder in an attempt to try to keep Click from execution, Click was strapped into the electric chair at Indiana State Prison, Michigan City, on Dec. 30, 1950. REF.: *CBA.*

Clifford, John David, Jr., 1887-1956, U.S., jur. Served as U.S. attorney in Maine from 1933-47. He was appointed to the district court of Maine in 1947 by President Harry Truman. REF.: *CBA.*

Clifford, John de (Ninth Baron of Westmorland, AKA: the Butcher), c.1435-61. Brit., assass. He earned his nickname for the brutal tactics he employed while fighting for Henry VI in the Wars of the Roses. REF.: *CBA.*

Clifford, Nathan, 1803-81, U.S., jur. Member of U.S. House of Representatives from 1839-43 and U.S. attorney general under President James Polk from 1846-1848. He was appointed by President James Buchanan to the U.S. Supreme Court in 1857 and was a staunch defender of states rights. In 1866 he voted with the majority in *Ex parte Milligan* which prevented the president from declaring martial law in areas not in open rebellion. During Reconstruction he voted to overturn the practice of receiving loyalty oaths for attorneys practicing in federal courts, *Ex parte Garland. CBA.*

Clifton, Alice, prom. 1787, U.S., mur. Alice Clifton was an unwed slave who gave birth to an illegitimate child and then cut its throat. She was found cradling the murdered infant and was placed on trial in Philadelphia on Apr. 18, 1787. Clifton was found Guilty and sentenced to death, but the executive council commuted her sentence to life in prison.

REF.: *CBA; The Trial of Alice Clifton.*

Clifton, Daniel (AKA: Dynamite Dick), d.1896, U.S., west. outl. Dan Clifton was an Oklahoma cattle rustler who turned to bank robbery. In the 1890s, he joined Bill Doolin's "Oklahombres," who terrorized the Southwest for nearly a decade. Clifton supplied the firepower for the Doolin mob, who were relentlessly pursued by local posses. In Southwest City, Mo., on May 20, 1895, the gang held up the bank. With guns blazing, Clifton, Doolin, and Bill Dalton fought their way out of town. They shot and killed former Missouri state auditor J.C. Seaborn and escaped with only minor injuries.

Doolin and Clifton were arrested in Guthrie the next year, but they bribed a prison guard and made a clean escape. Dan Clifton did not live long enough to enjoy his freedom. With a posse on his trail, Clifton holed up at Sid Williams' farm sixteen miles outside Newkirk, Okla. He was trapped there on Dec. 4, 1896, by deputy marshals George Lawson and W.H.

Dan Clifton, aka: Dynamite Dick.

Bussey. When Clifton tried to escape on horseback, a bullet from Lawson's rifle shattered his arm, knocking him to the ground.

The wounded outlaw hid in a cabin deep in the woods, but his pursuers caught up with him later that night. Clifton burst out of the cabin, shooting wildly at the deputies as he ran, but they shot him in the back. Clifton died minutes later. See: **Doolin Gang.**
REF.: Bartholomew, *The Biographical Album of Western Gunfighters;* Breihan, *Great Gunfighters of the West;* Canton, *Frontier Trails; CBA;* Chambers, *The Enduring Rock;* Cunningham, *Triggernometry;* Croy, *Trigger Marshal;* Drago, *Outlaws on Horseback;* ____, *Road Agents and Train Robbers;* Gardner, *The Old Wild West;* Graves, *Oklahoma Outlaws;* Hanes, *Bill Doolin, Outlaw;* Hendricks, *The Bad Man of the West;* Horan and Sann, *Pictorial History of the Wild West;* Jones, *The Experiences of a U.S. Deputy Marshal of the Indian Territory;* Miller, *Bill Tilghman, Marshal of the Frontier;* Nash, *Bloodletters and Badmen;* Newsom, *The Life and Practice of the Wild and Modern Indian;* Nix, *Oklahombres;* O'Neal, *Encyclopedia of Western Gunfighters;* Osborn, *Let Freedom Ring;* Preece, *The Dalton Gang;* Shirley, *Buckskin and Spurs;* ____, *Heck Thomas, Frontier Marshal;* ____, *Six Gun and Silver Star;* ____, *Toughest of Them All;* Tilghman, *Marshal of the Last Frontier;* Wellman, *A Dynasty of Western Outlaws.*

Clinch, Tom, c.1600s-1700s, Brit., fictional highwayman. Tom Clinch was a fanciful character created by writer Jonathan Swift. Clinch appeared in the poem *Clever Tom Clinch Going to be Hanged* as a composite of highwaymen on their way to be hanged at Tyburn. In the poem, Tom Clinch jauntily rides through the town, stops at a pub for a drink, and bows to the ladies. As he faces the hangman, he denies any guilt, refuses any last rites, and urges others to "follow the practice of clever Tom Clinch." REF.: *CBA.*

Cline, Alfred Leonard (AKA: **F.L. Klein**), b.c.1888, U.S., theft-forg. Called "One-Man Crime, Incorporated" by a judge, this convicted forger was suspected of murdering people to defraud them of their estates.

In 1929, Alfred Cline was convicted of forgery and sent to prison after forging a widow's will. In 1933, Cline drugged Martin Frame, a traveling companion, by lacing buttermilk with narcotics, and stole $250 from him. That December, Cline was convicted by a court in San Bernardino, Calif., of grand theft and administration of narcotics with intent to commit a felony, and he was sentenced to five to fifteen years in Folsom Prison.

Between those two events, and again after 1945, Cline was linked to the deaths of several elderly people who left him substantial sums. Most of them were cremated. Among his benefactors were: Carrie May Porter, who left $20,000 in securities and jewelry to Cline, 1931; Laura Cummings, seventy-five, who supposedly eloped with Cline and lost $3,000 in bonds, 1931; Rev. E.F. Jones, sixty-eight, who left Cline his entire $11,000 estate, 1932; Bessie Ann Sickle, a widow who married Cline, 1933; Delora Krebs Cline, seventy-three, who left Cline her estate worth $250,000, 1945; Isabell Van Natta, a missing widow possibly seen with Cline, 1945; Elizabeth Hunt Lewis, who may also have been known as Elizabeth Hannah Klein, a widow seen with Cline who may have died in Kentucky, 1943; and Alice W. Carpenter, whose body was cremated by her business agent, Alfred Cline in 1945.

In 1946, Cline was found Guilty of nine counts of forgery and sentenced to a total of 126 years' imprisonment. He was never convicted of murder.
REF.: *CBA;* McComas, *The Graveside Companion;* Rice, *45 Murderers.*

Clinton, DeWitt, 1769-1828, U.S., lawyer. Member of the U.S. Senate from 1802-03, and mayor of New York City on five separate occasions. REF.: *CBA.*

Clinton, George, 1739-1812, U.S., lawyer. Vice-president of the U.S. from 1805-12 and uncle of DeWitt Clinton. REF.: *CBA.*

Clinton Prison Riot, 1929, U.S., riot. Mayhem broke out when about 1,300 convicts lounging in a prison yard began to fight and rioted out of control for five hours.

Turmoil reigned one day during the week of July 28, 1929, at Clinton Prison, known as "Siberia" by the underworld. The New York state facility located at Dannemora, N.Y., houses the state's most ruthless, depraved criminals. During the uproar, the unarmed inmates set buildings on fire, rushed the prison walls, and attacked two guards. They were finally brought under control by state police officers, prison guards, and volunteers who used tear-gas bombs, hand grenades, and riot and machine guns. Three inmates died during the fray, others were wounded, and damage was approximately $200,000. REF.: *CBA.*

Clitherow, Margaret (**Margaret Middleton**), 1556-86, Brit., her. Converted to the Catholic faith in 1574, and was arrested and imprisoned on several occasions for failing to attend Church of England services, and for hiding priests in her home. For refusing to plead before the court, she was crushed to death in 1586 and was canonized in 1970. REF.: *CBA.*

Clitus (**Cleitus,** AKA: **The Black**), prom. 328 B.C., Mac., assass. After saving the life of Alexander the Great at Grancius in 334 B.C., this trusted general was murdered by his ruler at a banquet. Intoxicated, he had criticized Alexander while extolling Philip of Macedon. See: **Alexander III.** REF.: *CBA.*

Clive, Robert (**Baron of Plassey**), 1725-1774, Brit.-India, suic. Considered the founder of the British empire in southern India, he defeated French forces there in 1751. While governor of Fort St. David, he was sent to recapture Calcutta from the Nawab of Bengal, and to avenge the atrocity known as the Black Hole. Upon returning to England in 1767 he was impeached by Parliament for misappropriating funds. Though acquitted, disgrace and opium addiction drove him to suicide. REF.: *CBA.*

Clodius, Publius (**Pulcher Clodius**), c.93-52 B.C., Roman., consp. Served as tribune of Rome in 58 B.C. His opposition to Cicero resulted in exile and confiscation of his property. He used mob rule to establish himself, and was killed in the streets in 52 B.C. during an election. REF.: *CBA.*

Cloots, Baron **Jean-Baptiste du Val-de-Grace** (**Anacharsis Cloots,** AKA: **Ali Gier-Ber**), 1755-94, Fr., rebel. Wrote and edited during the monarchy under the pseudonym Ali Gier-Ber. Attained prominence after the revolution as the self-styled Orator of the Human Race. He was guillotined along with other followers of Jacques Hébert and his Cult of Reason in 1794. REF.: *CBA.*

Close, Henry Colin (**Dr. Richard Campbell, Dr. Henry Ross**), b.c.1870, U.S., forg.-fraud-mur. Henry Close was born in Colorado, but his sinister travels took him to other areas of the country. He was imprisoned in California for forgery and then in New York for swindling his employer to support three women separately. About 1920, Close married and moved to New York, where he had two children. Virtually no criminal record existed for Close from about 1919 to 1929.

However, his trail was picked up again in 1929 by Pinkerton detective William A. Wagner, who uncovered two sizzling murders. Short of cash, Close answered a matrimonial ad placed by Mildred Mowry, a 50-year-old widow from Greenville, Pa., in July 1928. Claiming to be Dr. Richard Campbell of New York, he courted the widow, and they eloped the next month. They lived in New York for a short time before Close sent his bride back to Pennsylvania while he "attended to business," but she returned to New York on Feb. 1, 1929, to search for him. When she found him, Close, feeling trapped, drove her to a secluded place in Union County, N.J., shot her, and set her body on fire. Detective Wagner also discovered that Close had courted and murdered Margaret Brown of Salisbury, Md., and had also set her body on fire. Close was convicted and died in the electric chair.
REF.: *CBA;* Hynd, *Murder, Mayhem and Mystery.*

Clough, Joel, d.1833, U.S., mur. Mrs. Mary W. Hamilton was a widow living in Bordertown, N.J., when she attracted the attention of Joel Clough. Clough clumsily attempted to seduce Mrs. Hamilton on Apr. 6, 1833. When she refused to return his affections, Clough suddenly pulled a knife from his coat and stabbed Mrs. Hamilton several times, killing her. He was seen fleeing Mrs. Hamilton's home and was apprehended and jailed.

Clough was tried before Chief Justice Hornblower in Burlington, Pa., and found Guilty. He was sentenced to hang but he managed to escape a few days before the date of his execution. He was recaptured and hanged on time in Mount Holly, Pa., on July 26, 1833.

REF.: *The Authentic Confession of Joel Clough;* Brown, *Trial, Sentence, Confession and Execution of Joel Clough;* CBA; Clough, *The Only True and Authentic Life and Confession of Joel Clough; Confession of Joel Clough; Report of the Trial of Joe Clough;* Scarlet, *The Trial and Sentence of Joel Clough; Trial of Joel Clough.*

Clough, Jonathan, Brit., c.1600s-1700s, rob.-mur. A highwayman was arrested by a lawman eager for his capture, but the quarry slipped from his grasp through a well-orchestrated plan.

Jonathan Clough frequented Travellers' Rest Inn, run by a friend of his, near Darlington, but when the constable came to arrest him for a murder and numerous highway robberies, they found him relaxing down the road at another inn. Knowing that the constable had to pass Travellers' Rest Inn to take him to Durham Gaol, Clough sent a note to his friend, the innkeeper of Travellers' Rest Inn, asking him for help. Later that night, the innkeeper dug a ditch across the road, camouflaging it with dirt and branches.

The next morning, with his hands tied, Clough was leashed to the stirrups of the constable's horse, and he was forced to trudge along behind the rider. Nearing the Travellers' Rest Inn, the horse suddenly lurched, trying to svoid falling in the concealed ditch, throwing the constable over its head. Clough reputedly jumped on the horse's back, clenched the reins with his teeth, and rode away. The highwayman was never heard from again, and the innkeeper denied any knowledge of the affair.

REF.: *CBA;* Stevens, *From Clue to Dock.*

Clover, Billie Lee (Willie Lee Clover), b.c.1925, U.S., asslt. A hardened teenage criminal, confined in a juvenile detention facility for three days, savagely beat an assistant jailer.

In the spring of 1942, Los Angeles police arrested Billie Lee Clover on a warrant from Detroit for armed robbery. During his first three days of confinement in the Juvenile Jail, he brutally beat up two other prisoners. The third night he spent diligently working a thirty-inch metal leg off a bunk, then the next morning, he ferociously struck the assistant jailer, St. John. The middle-aged policeman was able to press an emergency buzzer and when help arrived, Clover was put in an isolation cell. Although St. John lived, he lost two teeth and the sight in one eye. Later, while serving an eighteen-month sentence, Clover escaped, but he was apprehended again.

REF.: *CBA;* Martinez, *Jigsaw John.*

Clutter, William, d.1810, U.S., mur. John Farmer, owner of a small commercial boat which operated on the Kentucky River between Pittsburgh and Kentucky, hired William Clutter as a navigator in early 1810. When Farmer went to sleep one night, Clutter bashed in his head with an ax. The next day, Clutter docked the boat near Cincinnati and was caught selling the goods on Farmer's boat while posing as Farmer. A merchant who knew the real Farmer quickly exposed the killer who was placed under arrest. Clutter was tried and convicted. While under a sentence of death, Clutter confessed to Farmer's murder. He was hanged on June 8, 1810, at Boone, Ky.

REF.: *CBA; A Concise Statement of the Trial & Confession of William Clutter.*

Clutter Family Killings, See: **Hickock, Richard E.**

Cluverius, Thomas J., d.1887, U.S., mur. One of the most sensational murder cases in the history of Richmond, Va. (or to the present for that matter), was the killing of Fannie Lillian Madison in 1885. The murder was almost an exact duplication of the Richmond slaying of Mary Emily Pitts by James Jeter Phillips in 1867.

L.W. Rose, the keeper of the old reservoir, picked up a tightly strapped bag along the James River opposite the Chesapeake and Ohio Wharf on Mar. 14, 1885. The bag contained woman's clothing. Rose looked about him and saw that the walkway had

been torn up as if a struggle had taken place. He picked up a woman's dark glove. As he stood holding these items, he pondered and looked into the water. His eyes popped. There, in front of him, floated a woman's body. Rose went screaming for constables.

The body was removed to the almshouse for identification and an inquest. A further search of the reservoir grounds unearthed another glove and a black veil. A man's footsteps were clearly marked in the muddy path where these things were found, and in the grass a gold watch key was found.

Curious people flocked to the almshouse as word of the murder spread. The body was first identified as that of Fannie Mays. A woman in the crowd screamed: "It ain't me! I'm Fannie Mays and I'm all alive!"

A woman named Dunstan arrived in the almshouse and made a positive identification of the deceased. The obviously murdered woman—there were bruises on her face indicating that she had been struck by a heavy instrument—was Fannie Lillian Madison, a farm girl from King William County. Madison was buried without ceremony in the Oakwood Cemetery, and detectives quickly went to work looking for her killer.

One of the finest sleuths in the Richmond police force, detective John Wren, discovered that Madison had been teaching school in Bath and had come to Richmond in a hurry on Mar. 12. Registering at the American Hotel under the name of F.L. Merton, Madison was given room 21. Inside that room, in a corner, Wren found a torn note addressed to "T.J.C." The scrap of paper bore the words, "I'll be there as soon as possible; so do wait for me."

Armed with these initials, Wren began to make the rounds of Richmond jewelers, showing them the watch key found at the murder site. One meticulous watch jeweler checked his files and told Wren that the key had been repaired in his shop. It belonged to a Thomas J. Cluverius, the scion of a wealthy Virginia family who, Wren had already determined, had registered under his own name at the American Hotel the day Fannie Madison arrived in Richmond.

Cluverius was arrested at his home. He was working in his shirtsleeves, tending the garden. "You must be mistaken, gentlemen," Cluverius told the officers.

"You must be surprised," one of the constables replied as they took him in tow.

Not since the Jeter Phillips' trial had Richmond been so stirred. Hundreds packed the courtroom in which the accused man was tried, and thousands more milled about outside. A special contingent of police surrounded the courtroom after several plots to lynch Cluverius were discovered. Cluverius did not help matters, renting an expensive carriage to take him back and forth between the court building and the jail.

At the trial, it was proved that Cluverius had secretly married Fannie Lillian Madison, keeping the fact from his socially prominent family. The prosecution stated that Cluverius had murdered country girl Madison to hide the marriage from his family and friends. Cluverius denied his guilt throughout the trial.

Found guilty, sentence was passed upon the convicted murderer on June 19, 1885. Judge T.S. Atkins in Hustings Court asked the prisoner if he had anything to say. Cluverius answered in a firm voice. "I would say, sir, that you will pronounce sentence upon an innocent man. That is all I have to say, sir."

"The sentence of this court," gaveled Judge Atkins, "is that on November 20, 1885, you be hanged by the neck until you are dead...and may God in his infinite goodness have mercy on your soul."

But Cluverius, like Phillips before him, used every legal avenue to escape the gallows, his execution postponed several times by the governor. Not until Jan. 14, 1887, did Thomas J. Cluverius march up the gallows stairs to meet the hangman. A local tenor, Frank Cunningham, sang several hymns as the condemned man walked to the gallows. "It was said that he (Cluverius) was never known to shed a tear," remarked one reporter.

On the scaffold, Cluverius showed no signs of emotion, telling his spiritual adviser, Dr. W.E. Hatcher: "I do not wish to say anything." Seconds later, Dr. Hatcher turned to the huge throng gathered about the gallows and announced: "I am requested by the prisoner to say that in this moment of his death he carries no ill will to anyone on earth." Hatcher excused himself, remarking that he did not wish to be present when Cluverius was hanged.

The hangman produced a silk rope. The noose was greased with olive oil. This was placed about the murderer's neck and he was quickly sent through the trap. Cluverius struggled and spun and twisted for fully ten minutes in apparent agony before he was pronounced dead. To make sure, authorities ordered that he hang for an additional twenty-six minutes.

It was feared that the killer's body would be stolen, so the corpse was shipped to a remote spot in Little Plymouth and buried in an unmarked grave. Cluverius, however, still had the last word. A small book which he had written while in prison, *My Life, Trial and Conviction,* and in which the convicted man maintained his innocence onto eternity, appeared posthumously. It was a sellout. See: **Phillips, John Jeter.**

REF.: *CBA;* Cluverius, *My Life, Trial and Conviction;* ____, *Lillian Madison's Marriage and Murder;* Stanard, *Richmond, Its People and Its Story;* ____, *The Virginia Tragedy, Trial and Conviction of Thomas J. Cluverius for the Murder of Lillian Madison.*

Coates, Edward, prom. 1680s, U.S., pir. Coates was a sailor on board the pirate ship commanded by William Mason, who had been authorized in 1689 by New York sponsors to sail to the waters near Quebec and prey upon French shipping as a privateer. In this capacity, his orders read, he was "to war as in his wisdom should seem fit." The trouble was that Mason found no French ships to attack and pillage. This bad luck vexed Mason so that he turned pirate and began raiding English ships. The spoils from his adventures were distributed to his crew members, which included Coates. At the end of one voyage, prize money amounted to 1,800 pieces-of-eight for each man.

Mason apparently withheld some of the loot, since the captain disappeared on a lonely island in the Indian Ocean and Edward Coates (long after suspected of killing Mason) assumed command of Mason's ship, sailing it back to New York. Governor Fletcher was willing to forget the disappearance of his commissioned agent Mason for the sum of £1,800, a payoff shared between the governor and his common council. This bribe assured Coates and his men that they would meet with no interference from New York authorities.

The pirate enjoyed several more years of freebooting before his capture and imprisonment. REF.: *CBA.*

Cobb, Gail A., 1950-74, U.S., law enfor. off. Officer Gail Cobb of Washington, D.C., became the first U.S. policewoman killed in the line of duty when she was shot and killed by a robbery suspect she had followed into a garage in September 1974. Not since 1910, when policewomen were first assigned to uniformed duty, had a female officer died at the hands of a criminal offender. REF.: *CBA.*

Cobb, Howell, 1815-68, U.S., rebel. Brigadier general in Confederate army in 1862 and major general from 1863. REF.: *CBA.*

Cobb, John R., prom. 1850s, U.S., mur. In 1854, John Cobb and Radford J. Crockett of Atlanta, Ga., shot and killed an old trader, Samuel B. Landrum, robbing him of $600 and his goods-laden mule on McDonough Road. Both were hanged. Crockett, an errant youth, confessed his guilt. Cobb, a hardened criminal, denied it. When the sheriff came to Cobb's cell only hours before he was taken to the gallows, he asked the condemned man if he wanted to see a minister. Sneered Cobb: "I don't want any of that damned sniveling about me." REF.: *CBA.*

Cobbett, William (AKA: Peter Porcupine), 1763-1835, Brit., libel. While in the English army from 1783-91, he secured court martial of his former officers on charges of embezzlement. He fled to Philadelphia to escape the military, who sought to prosecute him for publishing a libelous pamphlet on army abuses. In the U.S. he published the *Porcupine's Gazette,* resulting in a libel conviction. He returned to England and published the *Political Register,* reflecting his shift to radical politics. He was jailed at Newgate in 1810-12 for criticizing the flogging of militiamen by German mercenaries. In 1831 he was charged with sedition. REF.: *CBA.*

Cobham, Eleanor (Elianor Cobham), prom. 1400s, Brit., witchcraft-treas. The Duchess of Gloucester burned a likeness of Henry VI to try to sap the life from the king. Instead, she was sentenced to life in prison.

Eleanor Cobham, and her husband, Humphrey, Duke of Gloucester, had many enemies, some of whom disapproved of Eleanor's actions. Others were simply conspiring against the duke, who had angered the bishops when he accused Cardinal Beaufort, Bishop of Winchester, and the Archbishop of York of malfeasance when Henry VI was a minor.

So, primarily for political reasons, the duchess was charged with witchcraft and treason. She stood trial for directing two others to make a wax statue in the image of Henry and to put it over a slow-burning fire. The slowly melting wax was supposed to cause Henry's similar slow death. If Henry had died, her husband, as the closest heir, would have ascended to the throne.

The duchess stood trial in 1441. Found Guilty, she was sentenced on Nov. 9 to do public penance three times in London, in which she was to bring offerings to the alters of three churches. Then she was sent to an Isle of Man prison to serve a life sentence.

REF.: Andrews, *Old-Time Punishments; CBA;* Potter, *The Art of Hanging.*

Cocceius, Nerva (Marcus Cocceius), c.30-98 A.D., Roman., emp., treas. Held various governmental positions under Vespasian and Titus, and was consul to the Flavian emperor Domitian, who banished him to Tarentum in 93 A.D. REF.: *CBA.*

Cocceji, Baron Heinrich von, 1644-1719, Ger., jur. Professor at Heidelberg, Utrecht, and Frankfurt on the Oder. REF.: *CBA.*

Cocceji, Baron Samuel, 1679-1755, Ger., jur. Chief of Prussian judiciary from 1738-47 and son of Heinrich von Cocceji. REF.: *CBA.*

Cochise, c.1812-74, U.S., pris. esc.-rebel.-kid.-mur. Led the Chiricahua Apaches into battle against white settlers and U.S. army during the 1860s. In 1861 he was captured by the army for kidnapping a white child. He escaped from the territorial prison, taking with him several hostages who were later executed. He evaded capture for ten years, until brought in in 1871 by General George Crook. REF.: *CBA.*

Cochran, Ernest Ford, 1865-1934, U.S., jur. Attorney in the U.S. Justice Department from 1906-14, and U.S. attorney for the western district of South Carolina. He was appointed to the bench of the eastern district of South Carolina by President Calvin Coolidge in 1923. REF.: *CBA.*

Cochran, Garland (AKA: Bud), prom. 1970s, U.S., boot. Garland Cochran, from Elijay, Ga., was convicted of bootlegging charges and spent time in the federal prison at Eglin Air Force Base in Florida. He was later indicted and sought by police on a drug-smuggling indictment.

REF.: *CBA;* Moffitt, *Swindled.*

Cochran, Willie Grady, 1919-56, U.S., abduc.-rape-mur. At twenty-one, when other young men were setting out to find their place in society, Cochran was doing time for forgery. After serving only months of his sentence, he escaped from a chain gang on the Georgia back roads and avoided the police dragnet long enough to commit robbery and rape. He was eventually arrested, tried for the crimes, and, in the process, officially diagnosed as a dangerous psychotic. His new sentence was twenty years which he began serving in the Georgia State Prison at Reidsville, in 1940.

"The parole board investigated him very thoroughly over a long period of time, and last December (1954), the parole was granted." With these words from Rebecca Garrett, a prison official, Willie Cochran was given another chance to put his life in order. Soon after his release, he went to work at a Dallas, Ga., sawmill, and by all accounts, seemed to have renounced his criminal past.

On a Monday morning in June 1955, Cochran headed out in his green pick-up truck. Taking the day off from work, he planned to visit his parole officer in Rome, and then find a location for a business venture he hoped to pursue.

Driving toward Rome, Cochran spotted 15-year-old Patricia Ann Waters wearing a black bathing suit sitting in her front yard. "I told her I was going right by the swimming pool, and if she wanted to go there, I would drop her off," Cochran reported later, "So she put on a kind of flowered robe and got in my pick-up truck."

Patricia panicked when Cochran sped past the swimming pool but heeded his threatening orders to remain quiet. At 5:30 p.m. he stopped for cigarettes at a small country store near Stilesboro. The elderly couple tending the cash register noticed a blonde-haired girl in the cab making hand gestures, but ignored her, thinking she was just another silly teenager.

His young prisoner with him, Cochran drove down to a deserted spot in the woods where he raped and strangled her. "...I knew I was either going to kill that girl or myself, and then I decided she was going to be the one to go," he later told authorities.

By 10 p.m., Patricia's parents reported her missing to Police Chief Smith Horton. Soon after, local police were joined by the Georgia Bureau of Investigation and a battery of National Guardsmen. There were no immediate clues as to the Patricia's whereabouts. But then the name of Willie Grandy Cochran, a recent parolee from Reidsville, came to Detective Bill Terhune's mind. Cochran emerged as the prime suspect when, acting on their hunch, authorities found that he had been absent from his job on June 20, the day Waters disappeared. Shortly after, Sheriff Frank Atwood of Bartow County received a tip that two elderly people who owned a grocery store below Stilesboro had seen a girl sitting in a truck who matched the description of Patty Waters. When asked to identify the man they had seen, the ocuple believed that Cochran fit the description. As for the truck, they remembered it as gray.

All the pieces fit except for the grocers' insistence that the truck was gray. Hoping to find some answers, Detective Terhune drove back to the store in a blue squad car. When he got out of the vehicle he noticed that a filmy layer of road-dust altered the color of the car. Turhume concluded that Cochran's truck "...probably did look gray on Monday!"

Cochran was brought to the store for identification and within hours, he fully confessed. As Cochran was taken to a maximum security cell in Atlanta, Waters' body was recovered from the bottom of the Etowah River. It was bound and anchored in just the manner Cochran had described in his confession. Tried in Cartersville, Ga., Cochran was found Guilty on July 15, 1955, and executed at Reidsville on Apr. 13, 1956. REF.: *CBA*.

Cochrane, W.S., See: **White, Bob.**

Cochrane, Charles, See: **Chartists, The.**

Cochrane, Henry S., 1826-1906, U.S., burg. In the summer of 1893, the U.S. Mint in Philadelphia suffered a considerable loss of gold, officials learned following the Mint's semiannual inventory. The man responsible for this loss was none other than the Mint's chief weighing clerk, Henry S. Cochrane, who had been a trusted employee for thirty-seven years. (He would not be the only federal employee to loot a mint—Orville Harrington would rob the Denver Mint where he worked in 1919-20, the same Mint being robbed by mastermind bank caser Eddie Bentz, Harvey Bailey and others in 1922.) Cochrane had earned the trust of his superiors by turning in his predecessor for stealing many years earlier and was given the man's job as a reward. The elderly clerk lived alone and had established a chemical laboratory in the attic of his home. Then Cochrane began filching small amounts of gold from the Mint, stealing about $60,000 over several decades in such minute quantities that he could juggle the weighed amounts of gold on hand to make up the losses that might show up when inventory was taken twice each year.

Cochrane stole gold bars by simply going into the storage area where stacks of gold were stored in compartments behind floor-to-ceiling, see-through wickerwork. The doors to each compartment were fastened with combination locks and then sealed with tapes which were not removed until more gold was placed inside the compartments or inventory was taken. Inside each compartment, gold bars worth approximately $5,000 each were neatly stacked six feet high. Each compartment contained approximately $9 million in gold bars. Cochrane realized that the eight-inch open space at the bottom of the wickerwork would allow the passage of a single gold bar.

When alone in the storage room, Cochrane simply took out a wire he carried and reached through the wickerwork, pulling a single bar from the top of the pile and then dragging the bar through the eight-inch space beneath. He took two bars at a time, fastening the bars onto special suspenders he had sewn into his pants with reinforced thread. Once home with the bars, Cochrane melted them down in a crucible, forming the gold into small shapes. Then, using aliases and fake addresses, he mailed these small portions of gold to himself at the Mint. As chief weighing clerk he received the gold from himself and sent this to the refinery to be melted again into gold bars, and reimbursed himself by sending $20 gold pieces to himself in payment for the gold sent to the Mint.

Cochrane's small but systemic thefts had gone undetected for years since he himself was present to prevent any close inspection of the particular storage bin from which he had been stealing. But in the summer of 1893, an order for a complete and thorough inventory of all storage bins caused him to panic. He feared that he could not cover the loss, so he filched twenty-one bars at once and threw these through the skylight of the storage area into a small, dark space between the ceiling of the storage area and the floor above. He did this, as he would later explain, so that his original thefts would be coupled to the one big theft of the twenty-one bars, an overall theft that officials would think to be too large for a single man to commit, and thus suspicion would be diverted from himself.

This was not the case. A.L. Drummond, chief of the Secret Service in Washington, D.C., was brought into the case and, after consulting with directors of the Mint and examining the backgrounds of those responsible for the gold in the storage rooms, immediately approached the 67-year-old Cochrane. Drummond had, by a process of elimination, concluded that only Cochrane could have taken the gold. He had no idea how the elderly clerk accomplished the theft, but was convinced of Cochrane's guilt. The Secret Service chief, a nerveless, cold-eyed detective, took risks; confronting Cochrane without hard evidence was one of his greatest. "Do you know the superintendent suspects a certain person of having committed this crime?" he asked Cochrane.

"He doesn't suspect me, does he?" blurted Cochrane.

Without blinking an eye, Drummond replied, "Yes, he does, and so do I." Drummond studied Cochrane for a moment, then said, "You are an old man. You have long been in the service of the government. Your duty is to take care of the public funds that are entrusted to your keeping. A large amount of this money is missing. I know you have taken it. You know I know you have taken it. Do the best you can to make up for the wrong you have done by telling me where the money is. It is your duty—do it!"

Tears began to well up in Cochrane's eyes and soon trickled down over his wrinkled cheeks.

"Tell me where the gold is!" demanded Drummond.

"Part of it is hidden in the Mint," Cochrane sobbed, "and part of it is at home." He then showed Drummond where the twenty-one bars were hidden and took the Secret Service chief to his gold laboratory in the attic of his Darby, Pa., home, seven miles from Philadelphia. Behind the walls of one room in this house, Drummond and his agents unearthed some of the missing gold.

Quickly convicted, Cochrane was sent to prison for seven years, then released in 1900. He lived meagerly in Philadelphia until his death in 1906 and was often seen wandering outside the

U.S. Mint by guards who had to ask him to move on. The irony of Cochrane's crime was revealed after his death when shop girls in Philadelphia came forward to tell reporters writing his obituary that, during all the years of his tenure at the Mint, the old man brought them flowers and candy every week. This then, it was thought, was the reason for the systematic looting of gold. Cochrane, alone in life, stole gold from the Mint so he could buy presents for pretty young shop girls. See: **Bailey, Harvey; Bentz, Edward Wilhelm; Harrington, Orville.**

REF.: *CBA; Nash, Almanac of World Crime.*

Cochrane, Lord **Thomas (Tenth Earl of Dundonald),** 1775-1860, Brit., consp. On Feb. 20, 1814, the esteemed Lord Cochrane fell victim to a swindler. The ramifications of the fraud not only cost Thomas Cochrane his rank in society, but the reverberations of the affair set off a near panic in the London financial community.

On that day, a man named De Berenger appeared before Cochrane at Dover. He presented himself as the aide-de-camp to Lord Cathcart. De Berenger conveyed the news that Napoléon Bonaparte had been killed and that the victorious allies were soon to arrive in Paris. The unsubstantiated reports were later to be proven false, but during the interim, the news had the effect of driving up stock prices. Lord Cochrane returned to London where he sold off his stocks at an inflated price, realizing a fast profit on his initial investment. The truth of the matter was that De Berenger was a fraud, and the rumors were groundless.

Because many Londoners had lost a fortune, Cochrane was made the scapegoat and was put on trial for fraud despite evidence that showed his financial transactions were perfectly legal. He was found Guilty, sentenced to one hour in the pillory, twelve months imprisonment, and was assessed a £1,000 fine. On June 25, he was stripped of his naval rank and ten days later was expelled from the House of Commons. There was a public uproar over the injustices inflicted upon the admiral. "I shall live to bring the delinquents to justice," he vowed, believing that it was Croker, secretary of the Admiralty who conspired to bring about his downfall. In 1817, Lord Cochrane accepted appointment to command the Chilean navy.

REF.: Armitage, *Bow Street Runners;* Earl of Birkenhead, *Famous Trials of History; CBA;* Humphreys, *A Book of Trials;* Stevens, *From Clue to Dock.*

Cock, George, d.1748, Brit., rob. George Cock hated his work as a wigmaker's apprentice in Spitalfields. He quit his apprenticeship to work as an errand boy and porter to several local tradesmen. He became a thief when he met May Fair, a servant girl at a large country house. He professed his love for her to gain entry to the house where he stole a fine silver spoon.

George Cock knew that his charm could open doors. His favorite ruse for gaining admittance to the homes of the rich and well-born was to pose as the traveling companion of the master of the house. He would find out which local noblemen were out of town. Choosing one, he would knock at the door and convey warm greetings from the gallant husband far away. If admitted, he would slip a silver tankard or other small valuables under his coat.

The game ended when one of his victims described Cock to the constable. He was arrested and taken to Newgate, and later sentenced to death for burglary. He was hanged at Tyburn on June 13, 1748, casual and unrepentant to the end.

REF.: *CBA;* Mitchell, *Newgate Calendar.*

Cockburn, Sir Alexander James Edmund (Tenth Baronet), 1802-80, Brit., jur. Defense counsel for Daniel M'Naghten in 1843 trial that established legal test of insanity for those charged with murder. He served as chief justice of the common pleas from 1856-59, and as lord chief justice of England from 1873-74. He was the presiding judge in the trial of Arthur Orton, the Tichborne Claimant. See: **M'Naghten Rule; Tichborne Claimant.** REF.: *CBA.*

Cockburn, Lord **Henry Thomas,** 1779-1854, Scot., jur. Served the crown as lord of justiciary in 1837. REF.: *CBA.*

Cocklain, Matthew, prom. 1775, Brit., rob.-mur. An elderly woman was murdered and her house in the town of Derby was ransacked on Dec. 24, 1775. Matthew Cocklain, an Irishman, left town, becoming a suspect in the case. Arrested in Ireland, he was brought back to Derby, tried, and convicted. He was sentenced to be hanged and then gibbeted.

His body was still on public display the following Christmas when several people were drinking in a nearby pub late at night. One man was dared to go outside near the body. The man accepted, jokingly taking broth with to offer Cocklain. The drunken man heard a voice say, "It's hot." He responded, "Blow it, blow it," and threw the liquid on the long-dead face. Afterward, a friend conceded that he had played a trick.

REF.: Andrews, *Old-Time Punishments; CBA.*

Cockle, Sir James, 1819-95, Brit., lawyer. First chief justice of Queensland, Aus., from 1863-79. REF.: *CBA.*

Cocklyn, Thomas, and **Davis, Howell,** and **La Buze, Oliver (AKA: the Buzzard),** prom. 1719, Int'l, pir. The *Bird Galley,* an English slave ship carrying cargo out of the Netherlands and commanded by Captain William Snelgrave, was nearing her West African destination on Apr. 1, 1719. About 5:00 p.m. the ship was attacked by a flotilla of pirate ships, commanded by Thomas Cocklyn, an Englishman, Howell Davis, and Oliver La Buze. For nearly a month, the pirates controlled the *Bird Galley,* feasting, drinking, and robbing her cargo. Sated from their plundering, the pirates decided to set Snelgrave free and and to give him another ship, the *Bristol Snow,* plus the remains of his original cargo. On May 10, 1719, they parted company.

REF.: Botting, *The Pirates; CBA.*

Cockran, William Bourke, 1854-1923, U.S., lawyer. Four term member of U.S. House of Representatives from New York. REF.: *CBA.*

Cockrane, Kilso, d.1959, Brit., (unsolv.) mur. In an area where racial tensions had been mounting, a black man was stabbed to death on May 17, 1959.

Kilso Cockrane, a West Indian, was going to the hospital to have an injured thumb examined when he was accosted by a gang of white teenagers. They stabbed him and ran away. Later, the dying Cockrane said that they had asked him for money, but he did not have any. A witness to the Notting Hill murder said she thought the boys were about fifteen or sixteen years old and had been drinking. Although two suspects were questioned, no one was ever charged with the killing.

REF.: *CBA;* Furneaux, *Famous Criminal Cases, Vol. 6.*

Cockrell, Lee, b.c.1910, U.S., law enforc. off. Most of the 550 residents of Boyd, Texas, were infuriated by hotrodders who sped down Main Street every night, littering the street with beer cans. To put an end to the speeders, the town hired police officers in October 1956 to patrol Boyd, located twenty-eight miles north of Fort Worth, Texas. That solution did not work, so Lee Cockrell, who had worked in a stockyard, was named as police chief in mid-August 1958. He reportedly wrote nearly eighty tickets in one day and used his blackjack on uncooperative offenders.

The enraged hooligans confronted Mayor Willie Berle Horn, demanding that Cockrell be removed, and on Aug. 13, the unpopular sheriff was shot twice in the back and once in the arm with .22-caliber bullets. After Cockrell was taken to a Fort Worth hospital, crowds gathered outside the Boyd City Hall to celebrate, shouting, "I hope he dies." However, he quickly improved after having the bullets removed and a broken arm set. State highway patrolmen and a sheriff's deputy moved into the town to regain control and three Boyd youths in their early twenties were arrested. REF.: *CBA.*

Coco, Francesco, c.1909-76, Italy, assass. Climbing the stairs of his home around noon in June 1976, the chief prosecutor of Genoa, Francesco Coco, was gunned down with his bodyguard at close range by three assailants. The police chauffeur was shot by two other accomplices. An extreme leftist group, the Red Brigades, or Brigate Rosse, claimed responsibility for the slayings. Police sought an already wanted suspect, Giuliano Nara, twenty-nine, a member of the Red Brigades. Coco, the 67-year-old prosecutor, was well known for conducting investigations of political extremists. REF.: *CBA.*

Codarre, Edwin, 1930- , U.S., mur. When 13-year-old Edwin Codarre of New York City was led from the courtroom to begin his sentence at Sing Sing Prison, he wore long pants for the first time since the trial began.

Codarre murdered 10-year-old Elizabeth Voigt on a road near Fishkill, N.Y. Her body was found the next day partially concealed under a pile of brush. She had been sexually assaulted and bludgeoned to death.

The Voigt girl's parents owned a dairy farm near a Kiwanis Boys Farm Camp where their son Arno was spending the summer, along with boys from the city, including Edwin Codarre. John Horton, a 70-year-old neighbor, saw the Codarre boy walking along the road where the corpse was found. Horton led detectives to the camp.

Codarre was arrested on Aug. 14, 1943, after breaking down under questioning. He admitted that he sexually assaulted Elizabeth as they walked through a secluded area. A blow to the larynx with a large stone caused her death. Codarre said they were looking for Arno at the time.

When the case went to trial in November 1943, Edwin Codarre pleaded not guilty, but later changed his plea to guilty in hopes of a reduced sentence. Judge J. Gordon Flannery of Durchess County sentenced him to thirty years, of which he served nearly twenty-three before his parole on July 26, 1966. REF.: *CBA.*

Coddington, Herbert James, 1959- , U.S., abduc.-rape-mur. As a boy, Herbert Coddington of Morristown, N.J., displayed an aptitude for numbers which he later used to his advantage in the gambling casinos of Las Vegas, Nev., and Lake Tahoe, Calif. Several publishers even hired him to write pamphlets on the secret of his success.

To Maybelle "Mabs" Martin, a modeling agent, Coddington was a talented video producer who might give her pupils a boost. In 1987 he asked her for two young girls to use in an anti-drug commercial he was planning to produce in South Lake Tahoe. "Mabs" Martin suggested her two prize pupils (ages twelve and fourteen) from Showcase Modeling & Finishing School in Reno. On May 17, 1987, Coddington, accompanied by the two young models, "Mabs" Martin, and her long-time friend Dorothy Walsh, left Reno to film the commercial.

When they arrived at their destination, Coddington suggested that Dorothy and "Mabs" take the girls to his mobile home to freshen up. They followed him into the studio where he snapped the lock shut. He forced the two teenaged girls into a cramped plywood box with a small door on the outside, then strangled Dorothy Walsh and Maybelle Martin from behind with a plastic tie. Since he had soundproofed the walls of the mobile home, the screams of his victims were muted.

Three days of terror followed during which Coddington blindfolded and sexually assaulted the girls. He altered his voice with sound recordings so they would believe there were other men present.

In Reno, Assistant Chief of Police Dick Kirkland asked the FBI for help with an apparent kidnapping. But there had been no ransom demand. After two days, a part-time model gave police the license number of a car driven by a suspicious man who passed himself off as a producer of commercials. Investigations revealed the car was sold to Herbert James Coddington by a dealer in Reno who identified him from a composite sketch.

Investigators traced Coddington to the trailer park in Lake Tahoe. An FBI agent learned from neighbors that in the last few days Coddington had shaved off his mustache and dyed his hair orange.

On May 19, FBI Agent-In-Charge Terry Knowles broke down Coddington's front door, arrested him, and released the two girls. Coddington was charged with the murders of Dorothy Walsh and Maybelle Martin, whose bodies were found in the house. Forensic experts linked Coddington to the 1981 slaying of 12-year-old

Sheila Keister in Nevada. He has yet to be convicted of this crime.

The murder trial of Herb Coddington began in Placerville, Calif., on June 20, 1988. He pleaded innocent by reason of insanity, explaining that he was ordered to kill the two women by God, who sent him cryptic messages in traffic lights.

The jury rejected the insanity plea and on Aug. 11, Coddington was found Guilty of murder. On Sept. 22 he was sentenced to die in the California gas chamber. On Jan. 20, 1989, the death penalty was upheld by Judge Terrence Finney of the Superior Court. At present Coddington sits on death row. REF.: *CBA.*

Codère, Georges, b.c.1893, Brit. rob.-mur. During WWI, Lieutenant Georges Codère, a French-Canadian, was stationed at a training camp on the Hampshire-Surrey border with a Canadian infantry division. He had arrived in Britain with merely £4. Thought to be a little strange, his fellow soldiers called him "*fou*" and his superior dubbed him "bughouse." When Sergeant Henry Ozanne, in charge of regiment monies, asked Codère offhandedly if he knew where $1,000 in Canadian money could be exchanged for British money, Codère offered to change the money. Given the Canadian currency, Codère spent the money on himself in London. While dining at the Savoy Hotel, he told another member of his battalion that he planned to kill someone. Joking, the other replied that Codère should use the poison serum anti-tuberculeux, and Codère actually tried to obtain the fictitious substance.

Promising to hand over the funds, Codère met Ozanne on Dec. 8, 1915, at an unoccupied house where he murdered the sergeant. He then forced two commandant's batmen, Joe Keller and Desjourdins, to help clean up the blood. At the trial, he was defended by J. Alderson Foote, and pleaded insanity. The jury gave a verdict of willful murder. An appeal was dismissed. Codère escaped hanging, however, because of his mental condition and strong public support in Canada. He was given a reprieve and sentenced to penal servitude.

REF.: *CBA;* Shew, *A Second Companion To Murder;* Woodland, *Assize Pageant.*

Codlin, William, prom. 1802, Brit., sab. William Codlin was convicted of scuttling his ship near Brighthelmstone in 1802. (To scuttle is to bore holes in a ship to sink it.) With a rope around his neck and shoulders, Codlin said his prayers while he was transported to the Docks at Wapping on Nov. 27, 1802. He was hanged while an enormous crowd looked on.

REF.: *CBA;* Laurence, *A History of Capital Punishment.*

Codreanu, Cornelius Zelea, 1899-1938, Rom., terror.-mur.-assass. A fanatical right-wing activist, Cornelius Codreanu founded a fascist organization in 1927, the violent, anti-Communist, anti-Semitic Legion of the Archangel Michael. Its members, with Codreanu at its head, mimicked the Black Shirts of Italy under Benito Mussolini and the Brown Shirts of Germany and its leader Ernst Röhm. Codreanu was arrested several times in Bucharest and other Romanian towns for leading his thugs through the city in rampages where Jewish-owned shops and businesses were wrecked and Jews were beaten. In 1930, Codreanu's organization changed its name to the Iron Guard and its members donned green shirts to signify membership. (The organzation would later be renamed the All for Fatherland Party.)

Codreanu's green-shirted legions marched through the streets of Bucharest during the 1930s, gaining political support and influence, particularly in the ranks of the military. Its leader openly denounced any political alliance with other democratic countries lobbied for pacts with the fascist governments of Germany and Italy. So powerful did Codreanu's Iron Guard become that Romanian Prime Minister Jon Duca, in December 1933, issued an edict that proscribed the wearing of the green shirts and virtually outlawed the Iron Guard.

The response to this governmental suppression of the Iron Guard was swift. Codreanu ordered Duca assassinated. On Dec. 30, 1933, Duca was shot to death in Carpathia by Iron Guards. Anyone who stood in Codreanu's path was eliminated, even allies such as Michael Stelescu, leader of the Brothers of the Cross, another fascist organziation that had joined with the Iron Guards. Stelescu was, however, anti-German, and this brought about his execution in a hospital bed while he was recuperating from an operation on July 16, 1936, a murder dictated by Codreanu.

The Romanian government under King Carol II offered continued resistance to the Iron Guards, regularly confronting its marching legions with troops and police and harrassing its leaders. Codreanu and seventeen of his top leaders were arrested in 1938 and all were tried and convicted of terrorist activities. The Iron Guards were given stiff prison sentences, Codreanu drawing a ten-year sentence, and all were ordered to serve out their time at hard labor in the salt mines. On the night of Nov. 29-30, 1938, Codreanu and the others, while being transferred from the Ramnicu prison to the prison in Jilava, were shot and killed by a lone gunman who sprayed submachine-gunfire into their midst. Then, with pistols hanging from his belt, the gunman went from man to man, firing a *coup de grace* shot into the head of each. He emptied an entire chamber into the skull of Cornelius Codreanu, before fleeing. Obviously, the assassinations were carried out with the tacit approval of the government, whose police guards were conveniently missing from the scene of this mass execution. The lone gunman, according to the government report, remained "unknown and unapprehended." See: **Duca, Jon, Stelescu, Michael.**

REF.: *CBA;* Gaucher, *The Terrorists;* Roberts, *Rumania: Political Problems of an Agrarian State;* Wolff, *The Balkans in Our Times.*

Coe, Frank, d.1931, U.S., west. gunman. As a young man, Frank Coe worked as a farmer and ranch hand in Lincoln County, N.M., just before the infamous county war. Coe and his cousin, George, pooled their money and invested in the first thresher in Lincoln County. When the Lincoln County War started, The Coes joined the Chisum-McSween-Tunstall coalition and engaged in a series of pitched gun battles against the faction fighting for James Dolan and James Riley, owners of the powerful mercantile store, The House. On Apr. 4, 1878, George Coe and John Middleton were wounded when they sat down to lunch at Blazer's Mill, N.M., by Buckshot Rogers. Dick Brewer, leader of the McSween Regulators, and Frank Coe shot it out with Roberts. Both Roberts and Brewer were killed in the battle.

There were many more such skirmishes in the following months. On Apr. 30, Cow, Frank McNab, and Ab Sanders were ambushed by Dolan-Riley supporters near McNab's ranch. McNab was killed, Sanders seriously wounded, and Coe, his horse shot from under him, was captured. When the Lincoln County War finally ended, the Coe cousins moved to San Juan County, then left New Mexico before Frank Coe returned to Lincoln County in 1884. Coe lived there with his wife and six children until he died in 1931. See: **Billy the Kid; Coe, George Washington; Lincoln County War.**

REF.: Adams, *A Fitting Death for Billy the Kid;* Bartholomew, *The Biographical Album of Western Gunfighters;* ____, *Jesse Evans, A Texas Hide-Burner;* Bechdolt, *Tales of the Old Timers;* Brent, *The Complete and Factual Life of Billy the Kid;* Burns, *The Saga of Billy the Kid;* Casey, *The Texas Border and Some Borderliners; CBA;* Charles, *More Tales of Tularosa;* Coe, *Frontier Fighter, The Autobiography of George W. Coe;* Coe, *Ranch on the Ruidoso;* Cunningham, *Triggernometry;* Cushman, *The Great North Trail;* Ferguson, *Murder and Mystery in New Mexico;* Fitzpatrick, *This is New Mexico;* Fulton, *Maurice Garland Fulton's History of the Lincoln County War;* Garrett, *The Authentic Life of Billy the Kid;* Haley, *Jeff Milton;* Holloway, *Texas Gun Lore;* Horan and Sann, *Pictorial History of the Wild West;* Hunt, *The Tragic Days of Billy the Kid;* Hutchinson, *The Life and Personal Writings of Eugene Manlove Rhodes;* Keleher, *Violence in Lincoln County;* King, *Pioneer Western Empire Builders;* ____, *Wanglin' the Past;* Lamar, *The Far Southwest;* Nolan, *The Life and Death of John Henry Tunstall;* O'Neal, *Encyclopedia of Western Gunfighters;* Peavy, *Charles A. Siringo;* Raine, *Famous Sheriffs and Western Outlaws;* Rennert, *Western Outlaws;* Stanley, *Desperadoes of New Mexico;* ____, *Fort Stanton;* ____, *The Private War of Ike Stockton;* Steckmesser, *The Western Hero in History and Legend;* Thorp, *Story of the Southwestern Cowboy;* Wallis, *Cattle Kings of the Staked Plains;* Wellman, *The Trampling Herd;* White, *Trigger Fingers.*

Coe, George Washington, 1856-1941, U.S., west. gunman. George Coe's father was a Civil War veteran, who had moved his family from Brighton, Iowa, to Missouri. After his eighteenth birthday in 1874, Coe moved to Fort Stanton, N.M., to work on his cousin Frank's ranch. Four years later, he leased his own piece of property in Lincoln County, just when the Lincoln County War flared up. Many local ranchers were drawn into the power struggle between the Dolan-Riley faction on one side, and John Chisum, Alexander McSween, and John Tunstall on the other. Although only a bystander to these events, George Coe was arrested by William Brady, the puppet sheriff controlled by Dolan and Riley, and subjected to various physical tortures.

Coe was released, but he swore vengeance. With his cousin, Frank, Coe fought on the side of Chisum, Tunstall, and McSween. He was badly injured on Apr. 4, 1878, at Blazer's Mill, N.M. Buckshot Roberts, a member of the rival faction had just ridden into town, and Coe and his partners tried to persuade the armed gunman to surrender peacefully, but he answered them with a spray of gunfire. George Coe's hand was shattered by a stray bullet from Roberts' rifle. Buckshot Roberts was shot and killed.

George Coe led a number of armed raids against the Lincoln cow camps, and fought with reckless abandon alongside Billy the Kid and others. His activities in the Lincoln County War made Coe a wanted man. When the hostilities ceased, he petitioned Governor Lew Wallace for amnesty. In 1884, after brief stays in Nebraska and Colorado, Coe settled permanently in Lincoln County, where he operated the Golden Glow Ranch. He became a respected member of the community and lived in peace until his death. See: **Billy the Kid; Coe, Frank; Lincoln County War.**

REF.: Adams, *A Fitting Death for Billy the Kid;* Bartholomew, *The Biographical Album of Western Gunfighters;* ____, *Jesse Evans, A Texas Hide-Burner;* Bechdolt, *Tales of the Old Timers;* Brent, *The Complete and Factual Life of Billy the Kid;* Burns, *The Saga of Billy the Kid;* Casey, *The Texas Border and Some Borderliners; CBA;* Charles, *More Tales of Tularosa;* Coe, *Frontier Fighter, The Autobiography of George W. Coe;* Coe, *Ranch on the Ruidoso;* Cunningham, *Triggernometry;* Cushman, *The Great North Trail;* Erwin, *The Southwest of John H. Slaughter;* Ferguson, *Murder and Mystery in New Mexico;* Fitzpatrick, *This is New Mexico;* Fulton, *Maurice Garland Fulton's History of the Lincoln County War;* Garrett, *The Authentic Life of Billy the kid;* Hamlin, *The True Story of Billy the Kid;* Hendricks, *The Bad Man of the West;* Hendron, *The Story of Billy the Kid;* Hertzog, *A Directory of New Mexico Desperadoes;* Holloway, *Texas Gun Lore;* Horan and Sann, *Pictorial History of the Wild West;* Hunt, *The Tragic Days of Billy the Kid;* Hunter and Rose, *The Album of Gunfighters;* Hutchinson, *The Life and Personal Writings of Eugene Manlove Rhodes;* Keleher, *Violence in Lincoln County;* King, *Pioneer Western Empire Builders;* ____, *Wanglin' the Past;* Lamar, *The Far Southwest;* Lovell, *A Personalized History of Otero County, New Mexico;* Monaghan, *The Book of the American West;* Moore, *The West;* Mullin, *The Boyhood of Billy the Kid;* ____, *A Chronology of the Lincoln County War;* Nolan, *The Life and Death of John Henry Tunstall;* O'Neal, *Encyclopedia of Western Gunfighters;* Otero, *The Real Billy the Kid;* Peavy, *Charles A. Siringo;* Raine, *Famous Sheriffs and Western Outlaws;* Rennert, *Western Outlaws;* Stanley, *Desperadoes of New Mexico;* ____, *Fort Stanton;* ____, *The Private War of Ike Stockton;* Steckmesser, *The Western Hero in History and Legend;* Thorp, *Story of the Southwestern Cowboy;* Wallis, *Cattle Kings of the Staked Plains;* Wellman, *The Trampling Herd;* White, *Trigger Fingers;* Young, *Hard Knocks.*

Coe, Philip Haddox, d.1871, U.S., west. gunman. Philip Coe was an itinerant gambler who associated with the Second Texas Mounted Rifles near the Rio Grande Valley in 1862. Coe was instantly popular, and the men elected him a lieutenant, which violated military protocol. The regimental officers ordered him to enlist properly, or stop posing as an officer. When he refused, the army simply drafted him, but Coe fled to Mexico to sit out the Civil War. When the South surrendered in 1865, Coe drifted into Abilene, Kan., a fierce cow town known for its lawlessness. There he opened the Bull's Head Saloon with fellow gamblers Ben Thompson and Tom Bowles. The saloon stood on the outskirts of town, and was the first friendly place the trail hands encountered when they rode in. Coe advertised with a hanging sign that depicted the bull's anatomy in graphic detail.

Coe had sold his interests in the saloon by the time the citizens of Abilene prevailed upon their sheriff, Wild Bill Hickok, to cover the offensive portion of the sign. Coe and Hickok became bitter enemies. The situation was further complicated when Coe became involved with Hickok's former mistress.

Coe and fifty drunken cowboys from Texas ambled into Abilene on Oct. 5, 1871. They accosted townsmen in the street, and became generally disruptive. In one of many saloons, Coe and his friends ran into Marshal Hickok, who bought them a round of drinks. Later that night, when a shot was fired in the streets, Hickok ran out and asked Coe who dared endanger the lives of Abilene's citizens. Coe said he fired at a dog, whereby Hickok reached for his six-shooter. Coe fired first, but his shot passed harmlessly through the Marshal's coat. Hickok took aim and drilled Coe through the stomach.

At that moment, Deputy Mike Williams rushed to Hickok's assistance. An angry crowd had gathered in the street, but the Marshal, who suffered from poor eyesight, did not recognize Williams. He spun around and fired two shots into the young man's head by accident. Coe's life had ended, but so did Hickok's career in law enforcement. The next year he joined Buffalo Bill's Wild West Show. See: **Hickok, James Butler.**

REF.: Asbury, *Sucker's Progress*; Barkley, *History of Travis County and Austin*; Bartholomew, *Kill or Be Killed*; Brady, *Recollections of a Missionary in the Great West*; Brown and Schmitt, *Trail Driving Days*; Buel, *Heroes of the Plains*; ____, *Life and Marvelous Adventures of Wild Bill*; *CBA*; Connelley, *Wild Bill and His Era*; Cunningham, *Famous in the West*; ____, *Triggernometry*; Donoho, *Circle Dot*; Drago, *Great American Cattle Trails*; ____, *Wild, Woolly & Wicked*; Dykstra, *The Cattle Towns*; Eisele, *The Real Wild Bill Hickok*; Fielder, *Wild Bill and Deadwood*; Fisher and Holmes, *Gold Rushes and Mining Camps*; Franks, *Seventy Years in Texas*; Frantz, *The American Cowboy*; Gard, *The Chisholm Trail*; ____, *Frontier Justice*; Gardner, *The Old Wild West*; Haley, *George W. Littlefield*; Hardy, *Wild Bill Hickok*; Hart, *My Life East and West*; Hendricks, *The Bad Man of the West*; Hendron, *The Story of Billy the Kid*; Hertzog, *A Directory of New Mexico Desperadoes*; Jameson, *Heroes by the Dozen*; ____, *Miracle of the Chisholm Trail*; Johnson, *Famous Lawmen of the Old West*; Knight, *Wild Bill Hickok*; Marshall, *Swinging Doors*; Miller and Snell, *Great Gunfighters of the Kansas Cowtowns*; Milner and Forrest, *California Joe*; Monaghan, *The Book of the American West*; Moore, *The West*; Nash, *Bloodletters and Badmen*; O'Connor, *Wild Bill Hickok*; O'Neal, *Encyclopedia of Western Gunfighters*; Paine, *Texas Ben Thompson*; Parkhill, *The Wildest of the West*; Penfield, *Western Sheriffs and Marshals*; Plenn, *Texas Hellion: The True Story of Ben Thompson*; ____ and LaRoche, *The Fastest Gun in Texas*; Raine, *Famous Sheriffs and Western Outlaws*; ____, *Guns of the Frontier*; Ripley, *They Died With Their Boots On*; Roenigk, *Pioneer History of Kansas*; Rosa, *The Gunfighter, Man or Myth?*; ____, *They Called Him Wild Bill*; Sabin, *Wild Men of the Wild West*; Sandoz, *The Buffalo Hunters*; ____, *The Cattlemen, From the Rio Grande Across the Marias*; Steckmesser, *The Western Hero in History and Legend*; Sterling, *Famous Western Outlaw-Sheriff Battles*; Streeter, *Ben Thompson*; ____, *The Kaw, Heart of the Nation*; ____, *Prairie Trails and Cow Towns*; Sutton, *Hands Up!*; Walton, *Life and Adventures of Ben Thompson*; Waters, *A Gallery of Western Badmen*; Wellman, *The Trampling Herd*; White, *Lead and Likker*; White, *Trigger Fingers*; Wilstach, *Wild Bill Hickok.*

Coetzee, Jacobus Hendrik, prom. 1935, S. Afri., mur. A police officer with a bright career was sent to investigate the murder of a pregnant girl, a murder he himself had committed on Jan. 31, 1935.

The victim, Gertrina Petrusina Opperman, worked as a nurse at a farm 126 miles from Pretoria. She met Jacobus Hendrik Coetzee, a detective sergeant with the Railway Police, at a local dance in Summer 1934. One night two weeks later, on July 17, her employer discovered them together in bed. Opperman became pregnant, and Coetzee wrote her a letter two days before her death which said, "...Everything is still arranged. We will then talk."

The girl's body was found, bruised and with a bullet wound to the head, nineteen miles from Pretoria. The baby, which had been due in February, was born just before she died, but it did not survive. Alerted to the murder, Coetzee and another officer went to investigate. When Opperman's employer heard about the murder, he called the police, thinking it might be the nurse. He identified the body and turned over the damning letter. Coetzee was arrested on Feb. 3, and tried on murder charges in May 1935. During the trial, he said that although he was not the baby's father, he had offered to support it. The jury found Coetzee Guilty but recommended mercy because the girl had falsely tried to pin him with paternity. Coetzee was sentenced to imprisonment with hard labor for life. He was released on Feb. 25, 1947.

REF.: Bennett, *Famous South African Murders*; ____, *Too Late For Tears*; *CBA*.

Coeur, Jacques, c.1395-1456, Fr., (wrong. convict.) treas. Merchant who built a fortune through commercial trading and manufacturing. He became counsellor to King Charles VII and administered the royal finances. Among his many creditors were members of the aristocracy and the royal family. As a consequence he was accused of treason, wrongly convicted, and exiled to Rome. REF.: *CBA*.

Coeur d'Alene, Idaho Strike, prom. 1892, U.S., mob vio. The silver and lead mining region of Coeur d'Alene, Idaho, was the scene of several bitter labor clashes during the 1890s. Demanding better working conditions, the mine workers organized a fledgling trade union, which succeeded in winning a uniform wage.

Management organized the Mine Owner's Protective Association in 1891 to combat the growing militancy among the workers and to prevent further concessions. In January 1892, the Association tried to impose an across-the-board pay cut of 25 percent. The miners refused to accept this, were locked out, and warned that not one union man would be hired back. The Association hired scabs and armed guards to protect them. The lockout dragged on until July 11, when Pinkerton guards killed a miner.

It was the opening shot of a labor war that destroyed the Frisco Mill on Gem Creek, killing a score of non-union workers. Strikers captured the Gem Mine and seized its arsenal of weapons and explosives. The scabs were ordered to leave the state, and indeed, the country. At the Old Mission and Fourth of July Canyon, union agitators drove the scabs from their work places and then shot them as they tried to flee. A dozen men were killed at the Fourth of July Canyon.

After two days of bloody rioting, the governor of Idaho ordered in the National Guard and a regiment of federal troops. Some 600 miners were arrested and imprisoned in crudely fashioned bullpens. The squalor of these camps showed the intransigence of the Association and won sympathy for the locked-out men. Those arrested were eventually freed, and the mine owners were forced to recognize the union. The two companies that held out, the Bunker Hill and Sullivan mines, were beset by similar acts of violence in April 1899. See: **Haywood, William.**

REF.: *CBA*; Hofstadter and Wallace, *American Violence.*

Coffelt, Elijah, prom. 1947, U.S., mur. Elijah Coffelt shot his 21-year-old nephew, killing him, because they both liked the same woman. Both men were allegedly drinking at the time. Coffelt then turned himself in to police in Washington, Ky. In November 1947, he was convicted on murder charges and sentenced to life imprisonment.

REF.: *CBA*; Montell, *Killings.*

Coffelt, Winford, c.1942-75, Case of, U.S., mur. On Sept. 4, 1975, Winford Coffelt, who lived in the Kentucky-Tennessee mountain region, had been drinking heavily. When he went home, it was apparently to kill his wife. However, her brother, Alvis Tarter, was at the house with his son. Tarter was injured during the first rounds of fire by Coffelt, but then Tarter's son shot at the gunman. Both Tarters returned fire, killing Coffelt. Local police put Alvis Tarter in jail for one night and then freed him. No charges were filed.

REF.: *CBA*; Montell, *Killings.*

Coffey, William N. (AKA: **Billy Boy**), b.c.1875, U.S., forg.-big.-mur. William Coffey made a career of raising funds for religious and charitable organizations, then taking a percentage for himself. In the summer of 1926, his work took him to La Crosse, Wis., where he met Hattie Hales, a widow in her early fifties. After a short courtship she eloped with "Billy Boy," and they spent their honeymoon with her relatives, who were completely taken with him.

The relatives were soon shocked, however, when Coffey wrote that Hattie had run away with a friend of his. He also wrote that she had signed over several hundred dollars worth of stock in the Elroy Service Oil Company. Suspicious, police discovered that Hattie's signature had been forged with a rubber stamp. Coffey was arrested at a stockholder's meeting. More checking by Sheriff Lyall T. Wright of Juneau County, turned up another wife and family in Madison. Also, the sheriff found that Coffey had served time in Iowa on theft charges for withholding a greater percentage of funds than he was due. Under questioning, Coffey finally admitted that he had killed Hattie Hales with a baseball bat in Dubuque, Iowa, but buried her in Wisconsin woods. He was sentenced to life in prison with hard labor.

REF.: *CBA;* Derleth, *Wisconsin Murders;* Hynd, *Murder, Mayhem and Mystery.*

Coffin, Levi, 1798-1877, U.S., consp. Organized the Underground Railroad, which transported hundreds of fugitive slaves northward to freedom. REF.: *CBA.*

Coghlan, Sir Charles Patrick John, 1863-1927, Rhodesia, lawyer. First premier of Rhodesia after it was granted the right of self-determination by the British. REF.: *CBA.*

Cohen, Alfred Morton, 1859-1949, U.S., lawyer. Graduated Cincinnati Law School and Doctor of Hebrew Law. REF.: *CBA.*

Cohen, Arthur, 1829-1914, Brit., lawyer. First Jew to graduate from Cambridge University. REF.: *CBA.*

Cohen, Benjamin Victor, b.1894, U.S., lawyer. Helped draft the Securities Exchange Act of 1934. REF.: *CBA.*

Cohen, John, prom. 1955, Brit., rob. Three criminals, interrupted during a robbery, were caught by police after a high-speed car chase on Oct. 10, 1955.

John Cohen, twenty-five, and Ronald Thomas Parsons, twenty-two, walked into H.R. Drew & Sons, a jewelry company, at half past noon and forced the owner to open the safe. As the bandits were robbing the store, two girls looked in through the window and saw them. Taking about £450 worth of jewelry, the two fled to a waiting car driven by John Robert Cotten, twenty-nine. During the chase, by car and on foot, two police officers were shot and another one was injured.

During the previous two months, the gang had netted £52 in three other jobs. Cohen, who had eleven previous convictions, was convicted of armed robbery and shooting with intent to murder. He was sentenced to twenty years in prison. Parsons was sentenced to twelve years and Cotten to ten years. The judge, Lord Goddard, praised Detective-Sergeant Albert Chambers, Sergeant Ernest Cooke, and Police Constables Donald Wood, Donald Cameron and George Cahn.

REF.: *CBA;* Furneaux, *Famous Criminal Cases, Vol. 3;* Jackson, *Occupied With Crime.*

Cohen, Lorraine, b.c.1943, and **Cohen, Aaron,** b.c.1966, Malaysia, drugs. Lorraine Cohen, forty-four, and her son, Aaron, twenty-one, from Auckland, N. Zea., were arrested on charges of drug smuggling at Penang International Airport in 1985. Aaron Cohen, carrying 34.6 grams of heroin, was sentenced to six lashes with the cane and life imprisonment. The mother, found with 140 grams of heroin, was sentenced to be hanged on the orders of Judge Dzaiddin Abdullah, known as the "Hanging Judge." Malaysian law concerning drug smuggling became stricter in 1983 when the government decreed that convicted drug smugglers be executed. REF.: *CBA.*

Cohen, Louis, and **Coffin, Thomas,** prom. 1947, U.S., criminol. Two psychology experts examined the crimes of eighteen psychotic murderers and found several common characteristics. Dr. Louis

Cohen, who taught legal psychiatry at Yale, and Dr. Thomas Coffin, assistant professor of psychology at Hofstra College in New York, published an article about their findings that appeared in the *Journal of Criminal Law and Criminology.*

Typically, they found, the victim of the psychotic murderer was someone the killer knew well, such as a mother, wife, sister, or other relative, and the crime, usually unplanned, occurred during the day, in public, and with a makeshift weapon. The crime was never committed for financial gain, but for reasons understood only by the murderer. Additionally, the criminal usually operated alone and did not care about being arrested. Cohen and Coffin thought that the sanity of future defendants could probably be determined by analyzing the characteristics of the crime. REF.: *CBA.*

Cohen, Mickey, 1913-76, U.S., org. crime. The diminutive Mickey Cohen, a loud-mouthed, hot-headed goon, first came to prominence as a so-called bodyguard and associate of West Coast crime czar Benjamin "Bugsy" Siegel. A smalltime gambler, Cohen supposedly inherited Siegel's criminal fiefdom in Los Angeles when Siegel was murdered in the home of his mistress, Virginia Hill, in 1947. Cohen's response to his boss' murder was to enter the lobby of the Roosevelt Hotel in Hollywood, pull out two .45-caliber automatics, and empty them into the ceiling of the foyer, and demanding that Siegel's killers, whom he believed to be hiding in the hotel, meet him outside in ten minutes. When no one but the police arrived, Cohen departed. The mantle of organized crime leadership fell to Frank Carbo and the Dragna family when Siegel died,

California gangster Mickey Cohen.

but Cohen was permitted to hold onto some of the smaller gambling operations.

When Cohen's brash style began to bring state and federal attention to rackets controlled by Carbo and the Dragnas, the five-foot-five-inch gangster was marked for death. His home was bombed twice and several attempts were made on his life. He turned his Los Angeles home into a fortress, equipping it with floodlights, alarm systems, and a small arsenal, which was kept inside, next to Cohen's 200 tailor-made suits. Cohen constantly complained to the press that he was a persecuted man, that underworld enemies were trying to kill him, but he refused to identify these persons. Cohen employed John Stompanato as a bodyguard for a brief time until Stompanato was killed by Cheryl Crane, the teenage daughter of Lana Turner. When he was compelled to pay for Stompanato's funeral, the niggardly Cohen ordered a cheap coffin and angrily gave the press Lana Turner's love letters to the dead gangster.

Cohen lived in relative splendor from his gambling operations, but he was finally convicted of income tax evasion, serving four years for this offense, then was again convicted and served another ten years in prison, being released in 1972. By then Mickey Cohen was more than stir crazy; a fellow inmate had almost crushed his head with a lead pipe. Cohen still sought the limelight in old age, appearing before reporters in 1974 in a mumble-mouthed campaign against prison abuses. He died two years later of a heart attack.

REF.: Campbell, *The Luciano Project; CBA;* Cohen, *Mickey Cohen: In My Own Words;* Davis, *Mafia Kingfish;* Demaris, *The Last Mafioso;* Eisenberg and Landau, *Meyer Lansky;* Fried, *The Rise and Fall of the Jewish Gangster In America;* Messick *Lansky;* ____, *Secret File;* ____ and

Goldblatt, *The Mobs and the Mafia;* Navasky, *Kennedy Justice;* Reid, *The Grim Reapers;* Smith, *Syndicate City;* Wolf, *Fallen Angels;* Zuckerman, *Vengeance Is Mine.*

Cohen, Mitchell Harry, 1904- , U.S., jur. Prosecutor in Camden County, N.J., from 1948-58. He was named to fill a vacancy on the district court of New Jersey by President John F. Kennedy in 1962. REF.: *CBA.*

Cohen, Monty, prom. 1926, U.S., boot. A ship loaded with scrap iron actually transported illegal liquor, and its seizure ended one of the largest smuggling operations during the Prohibition era.

In early 1926, Monty Cohen arrived in Galveston, Texas, where the leader of one of the city's largest liquor smuggling gangs, George Musey, showed him around. Cohen bought an old merchant ship, the S.S. *Trader* and loaded it with scrap iron. Watching this activity was law enforcement officer Al Scharff, who heard that Cohen, actually from Detroit, Mich., was one of the Bernsteins, leaders of the infamous Purple Gang. He arrested Cohen on suspicion, but after learning nothing, released him. Scharff notified every customs office between Galveston and Maine to be alert to the ship's activities. The ship, its name changed to S.S. *Turner,* was stopped outside of New York City where officials found 5,000 cases of high-quality Scotch whiskey.

REF.: *CBA;* Roark, *The Coin of Contraband.*

Cohen, Octavus Roy, 1891-1959, U.S., det. writer. Admitted to the bar in 1913, Cohen abandoned a career in law to write dozens of detective books, articles, and plays involving blacks caught in a web of intrigue. Among his published works: *The Crimson Alibi* (1919), *Jim Hanvey Detective* (1923), *Detours* (1927), *The Townsend Murder Mystery* (1933), and *Child of Evil* (1936). REF.: *CBA.*

Cohen, Ronald John Vivian, 1929- , S. Afri., mur. Ronald Cohen was a self-made man. The 41-year-old millionaire owned and operated a lucrative finance company that bankrolled various South African building projects. In 1963, he married for the second time. His wife Susan Cohen was considerably younger, but she ran the affairs of the Cohen household in a competent manner. Seven years later, in a moment of insanity, Ronald killed his young bride.

The murder occurred on Apr. 5, 1970. Cohen roused his housekeeper from a deep sleep to tell her that a home invader had assaulted them, and that Susan was dead. The police found no signs of upheaval that bore out the presence of an intruder. Further, there were scratches on Cohen's arms which indicated that he was the assailant Susan had unsuccessfully tried to fend off.

There was no evidence of rape or robbery, therefore police concluded that Cohen's motive was purely rage. Arrested and tried in Cape Town, Cohen pleaded loss of memory and an anguished mental state for his actions. He was sentenced to twelve years in prison under the terms of the "diminished responsibility" statutes.

REF.: Bennett, *The Cohen Case; CBA.*

Cohill, Maurice Blanchard, Jr., 1929- , U.S., jur. Author of many articles and pamphlets dealing with criminal justice and penal reform. He was appointed judge to the court of the western district of Pennsylvania in 1976 by President Gerald Ford. REF.: *CBA.*

Cohn, Lenora, b.c.1909, U.S., (unsolv.) mur. Lenora Cohn, age six, was sent by her mother to the grocery store to buy milk in March 1915. When she did not return, her anxious mother searched for her and discovered her body in the hallway outside their apartment with the pail of milk sitting nearby. Lenora had been sexually molested and her body mutilated. A piece of candy she had been eating was found nearby. The case was never solved.

REF.: Carey, *Memoirs of a Murder Man; CBA.*

Coke, Arundel, and **Woodburne, John,** d.1722, Brit., asslt. Arundel Coke, a lawyer, anticipated an inheritance from his ailing brother-in-law, Edward Crispe. Coke invited Crispe to dinner on Jan. 1, 1722, and afterward the two men visited a lady friend. Coke returned home alone, and his brother-in-law arrived later,

his face gashed.

Coke was arrested after a tailor told police that Coke had asked him three years earlier to murder Crispe. Coke confessed to hiring John Woodburne for the murder, cursing him for bungling the job. Woodburne admitted that he had attacked Crispe with a billhook, a thick knife with a hooked end. The two men were tried on Mar. 13, 1722, the only defendants ever prosecuted under the Coventry Act, which allows conviction for gouging out an eye, cutting the tongue, or slitting the nose after having waited with the intent to disfigure. They were found Guilty and executed Mar. 31, 1722.

REF.: *CBA;* Wilson, *Encyclopedia of Murder.*

Coke, Sir Edward, 1552-1634, Brit., jur. A famed judge stubbornly refused to let a king meddle with judicial policies and a rival brought about his fall from power.

Sir Edward Coke was called to the bar in 1578, and he became a member of Parliament in 1589. Only forty, Coke held three influential positions as speaker of the House of Commons, solicitor general, and recorder of London, all beginning in 1592. He also became attorney general, winning the job over Francis Bacon, who was to challenge him throughout his career.

Coke helped prosecute Essex and Southampton on treason charges in 1600. He led the Crown's prosecution of Sir Walter Raleigh on charges of high treason in 1603, and of the conspirators in the Gunpowder Plot in 1605. He was appointed Lord Chief Justice of the Court of Common Pleas in 1606. While in this position, he irritated King James I by refusing to allow royal interference in judicial matters. This stance, along with the conniving of Bacon, brought about his unwilling transfer to the Court of the King's Bench in 1613. He continued to fall from favor until he was arrested and confined in prison. In the absence of any actual charges, he was freed after nine months. Elected to the Privy Council, he continued to try cases. Coke was responsible for codifying the common law into a more lucid work and his well-known works include *Institutes* and *Reports.*

REF.: *CBA;* Scott, *Concise Encyclopedia of Crime.*

Colarco, Ross, prom. 1944, U.S., rob. Ross Colarco was involved in a robbery in upstate New York that netted a large haul of furs. A former fighter for boxing clubs, Colarco fled to his old neighborhood in New York City to hide. Sheriffs from upstate requested assistance from the district attorney's office of New York County in 1944, and investigator Harold J. Danforth was placed on the case. He tracked Colarco to an apartment where he was eventually captured without gunfire in a police raid. He was sent back upstate, tried, convicted, and sentenced to a lengthy prison term in Sing Sing Prison.

REF.: *CBA;* Danforth, *The D.A.'s Man.*

Colas, André, and **Sibille, Serge,** prom. 1953, U.S., drugs. The U.S. Narcotics Bureau sent a Sicilian agent to Sicily, to crack a drug ring. The agent located Sebastien Imperiale and linked him to di Giovanni, another Sicilian mobster in Milan, Italy. The agent set up a small drug buy for two pounds of heroin and then arranged for a larger purchase. On Oct. 12, 1953, two French sailors, André Colas and Serge Sibille were arrested for drug smuggling when their ship docked in New York. They had hidden twenty pounds of heroin inside two fire extinguishers aboard the S.S. *Flandre.* The heroin was worth £20,000, and its street value in the U.S. would have been several million dollars.

REF.: *CBA;* Goodman, *Villainy Unlimited.*

Colavito, Emma, See: Kaber, Eva.

Colbert, Chunk, d.1874, U.S., west. gunman. Chunk Colbert enjoyed a modest reputation as a gunslinger, having killed at least seven men in Texas, New Mexico, and Colorado during the 1870s. In the early 1870s he shot Charles Morris dead in Cimarron, N.M., after becoming convinced that the man had been trifling with Colbert's wife.

Clay Allison proved to be a better gunman than Colbert, however. On Jan. 7, 1874, the two men went to Clifton House, an inn in Colfax County, N.M., to eat after failing to resolve their differences in a horse race. The quarter-mile trot between the two men ended in a dead heat. After finishing his meal, Allison relaxed over a cup of coffee. Colbert, meanwhile, resolved to kill his adversary. But as Colbert fingered his holstered gun nervously, the astute Allison pulled out his own revolver and blasted him through the forehead. Colbert was buried behind the inn. See: **Allison, Clay.**

REF.: Buffum, *Smith of Bear City;* CBA; Clark, *Clay Allison of the Washita;* Culley, *Cattle, Horses & Men of the Western Range;* Farber, *Texans with Guns;* Fitzpatrick, *This is New Mexico;* O'Neal, *Encyclopedia of Western Gunfighters;* Sabin, *Wild Men of the Wild West;* Schoenberger, *The Gunfighters;* Siringo, *Riata and Spurs;* Small, *The Best of True West;* Stanley, *Clay Allison;* ____, *Desperados of New Mexico;* ____, *Fort Bascom;* ____, *Fort Union;* ____, *The Grant That Maxwell Bought.*

Colby, Bainbridge, 1869-1950, U.S., lawyer. Secretary of state in Woodrow Wilson's cabinet from 1920-21, he later entered private law practice with the retired president. REF.: *CBA.*

Colby, Robert A., b.1922, Ger., mur. In June 1945, Robert Colby, twenty-three, of Geetingsville, Ind., was stationed in Germany with the U.S. Army. On June 10, he went AWOL and was found near Wiesbaden, Germany, outside his unit's restricted area. His company commander, Captain Richard J. Brown, directed that he be punished with four days at hard labor after training hours. That evening, Colby worked until 10 p.m., and then went to his tent and got a rifle. Going to the officer's area, he shot Captain Brown and First Lieutenant Donald H. Wade, firing four times at the men. Both men died within an hour. Colby then turned over his rifle to a sergeant, saying, "I shot the old man, but didn't want to shoot the lieutenant."

Colby was tried by a general court-martial on June 23 and sentenced to death. The sentence was approved by a divisional commander and by General Dwight D. Eisenhower on Aug. 29. In December 1945, Colby's sentence was commuted to life at hard labor by General Joseph T. McNarney, commander of the U.S. forces in Europe. REF.: *CBA.*

Colden, Cadwallader David, 1769-1834, U.S., lawyer. Mayor of New York from 1818-20. REF.: *CBA.*

Cole, Charles Cleaves, 1841-1905, U.S., jur. Prosecuting attorney in Puddridge County, W. Va., from 1869-70. He was nominated to serve on the bench of the supreme court of Washington, D.C., by President Benjamin Harrison and reappointed in 1892. REF.: *CBA.*

Cole, Edwin, prom. 1950s, U.S., fraud. Edwin Cole, a confidence man with a slick presentation, worked his scams for more than thirty years, making more than $1 million.

Near the end of his career, he bilked seven citizens of Wilmington, Del., of approximately $70,000. Cole then went to New York where he met a French woman and her husband and swindled them out of more than $20,000. Typical of his other schemes, he persuaded them to invest $1,600 in a gold mine and gave them a return of $200. They then invested $4,500 with a return of $3,000, and then they invested a further $18,500, including all their savings plus a $10,000 loan from his parents. This time there was no return. The couple filed a complaint with the Postal Inspection Service, and Inspector Tarpey tracked the cheat. The 68-year-old Cole was convicted. The federal judge who handed down a five-year sentence told him, "Weighing your age against what you have done, I am imposing this sentence. Your history indicates that there is not much hope of your ever being rehabilitated."

REF.: *CBA;* Kahn, *Fraud.*

Cole, Hiram, prom. 1858, Case of, U.S., mur. A native of Bainbridge, Ohio, Hiram Cole tired of his wife and reportedly attempted to poison her on several occasions, finally succeeding on Sept. 9, 1857. The poison was detected and Cole was tried for murder in Jefferson, Ohio, on Nov. 26-27, 1858, but the prosecution confused the jury by first insisting that Cole had given his wife arsenic, and then tried to prove that he had dosed her food with strychnine. Since the state could not clearly show *which* poison was used, Cole was surprisingly acquitted of what appeared to be a clear-cut case of murder. REF.: *CBA.*

Cole, James, prom. 1800s, Brit., pol. mal. A hotel porter was arrested and charged with stealing a handkerchief from a gentleman's pocket. The arresting officer, Constable James Cole, said the victim's name was Hippesley and he lived in the hotel. However, no such person existed, and witnesses said that they had seen no gentleman in the vicinity of the supposed crime, and further, they had seen Cole pull a handkerchief from his own pocket just before he arrested the porter. The porter was acquitted.

REF.: *CBA;* Thomson, *The Story of Scotland Yard.*

Cole, James, prom. 1886-87, U.S., law enfor. off. James Cole, a marshal and peace officer assigned to the Indian Territories during the 1880s, often dispensed frontier justice from the point of his gun. He and Deputy Marshal Frank Dalton were once sent to the Cherokee reservation to capture suspected horse thief Dave Smith. They tracked him to his camp near the Arkansas River, where he was joined by his brother-in-law Lee Dixon, fellow horse thief William Towerly, and Dixon's wife.

The gang spotted Cole first, and opened fire. Dalton was shot through the chest, fell to the ground, and was finished off by Towerly, who emptied his Winchester into the deputy. Cole was shot in his side by Smith, but he refused to retreat. Cole killed Dixon's wife and Smith, and wounded Dixon. Towerly managed to escape, but only temporarily. He was soon killed in a shootout. Cole brought Dixon back to Fort Smith, where he died of his wounds.

REF.: *CBA;* O'Neal, *Encyclopedia of Western Gunfighters;* Shirley, *Heck Thomas, Frontier Marshal.*

Cole, Mary, d.1812, U.S., mur. Mary Cole, a resident of Newton, N.J., tired of caring for her elderly mother, Agnes Teaurs (or Thuers), and slit her throat, hiding the body beneath the floorboards of her home. For several months, Mary Cole entertained visitors and conducted what appeared to be a normal life while her mother's body rotted beneath the floorboards. The stench from the decomposing flesh finally aroused the suspicions of neighbors and Cole was exposed. She was quickly tried, convicted, condemned, and hanged at Newton on June 26, 1812.

REF.: *CBA; The Confession of Mary Cole;* Kirn, *Sketch of the Trial of Mary Cole.*

Cole, Phyllis, 1957- , Brit., mansl. Phyllis Cole, an emotionally retarded girl of fourteen strangled 5-year-old Brenda Handley in 1971 after her mother had administered a spanking. The unhappy teenager told police that: "I felt something telling me to put my hands around her neck. It was tempting me like mad." The British courts ordered that Cole be detained for life, after she was allowed to plead guilty to manslaughter. In handing down his ruling the judge noted: "I am not punishing you. It is necessary that you should have the treatment doctors say you need. When you are better you will be able to go out into the world again putting all this behind you."

REF.: *CBA;* Wilson, *Children Who Kill.*

Cole, Thomas Charles, c.1951-76, Col., drugs-suic.-mur. Thomas Cole, twenty-five, met with officials of the U.S. Drug Enforcement Administration in Philadelphia, Pa., in November 1976 to discuss selling them information about cocaine smuggling operations in Colombia. On Dec. 13, he walked into the DEA office in Bogota, Colombia, where he shot and killed U.S. narcotics agent Octavio Gonzalez. When guards rushed to the DEA offices, Cole shot himself in the head. REF.: *CBA.*

Colebrooke, Henry Thomas, 1765-1837, Brit., jur. Assigned to India, he served as judge of the court of appeal in Calcutta in 1801. REF.: *CBA.*

Coleman, Alton, 1955- , U.S., rob.-kid.-rape-mur. Alton Coleman was given four death sentences for a series of murders, rapes, and robberies in one seven-week period in 1984. The 28-year-old Waukegan, Ill., man and his 19-year-old accomplice, Debra Brown, were captured July 20, 1984, in a park in Evanston, Ill.

Coleman's first victim was 9-year-old Vernita Wheat of Kenosha, Wis. She was kidnapped on May 29, 1984, and her strangled body was found on June 19 in the bathroom of an unoccupied building in Waukegan. FBI agents almost caught Coleman on May 30 at a relative's house in Waukegan, but he was warned and escaped through the back door. Chicago FBI chief Edward Hegarty was on the case because Coleman was charged with kidnapping and transporting Vernita Wheat across state lines for immoral purposes.

On June 18, 1984, Coleman strangled and killed 7-year-old Tameka Turks of Gary, Ind., and raped and tried to kill her 9-year-old aunt, Annie Hillard. Turks' body was discovered in a wooded region next to the Gary Sportsmen's Club the next day. Hillard was bound in the wooded area, but she had freed herself and was found a few hours later walking along a street in a confused condition. She later gave police complete descriptions of the attackers.

Coleman was also sought in connection with the June 19 disappearance of 25-year-old Gary, Ind., hairdresser, Donna M. Williams. On June 5, Coleman and Brown had rented an apartment near Williams' shop, and her car was found in Detroit on June 26.

On June 24, Coleman and Brown forced a 29-year-old Detroit woman to drive them in her car. But she intentionally ran the car into a truck and escaped unscathed. Coleman and Brown then drove the car to Inkster, a Detroit suburb, abandoned it. Later in the week, the pair were thought to have entered the Dearborn Heights, Mich., home of 62-year-old Palmer Jones and his wife, 50-year-old Maggie. The couple were eating breakfast when the intruders rushed into the kitchen and threatened them with a pistol. Coleman viciously beat by the couple and stole their car, $85, and credit cards. The car was later found abandoned about six miles from the Detroit airport.

Additionally, 15-year-old Tonnie Storey of Cincinnati, Ohio was suffocated on July 11, 1984. On July 13, Coleman and Brown murdered 44-year-old Marlene Walters, a housewife in the Cincinnati suburb of Norwood, and beat her husband, Harry. After their capture a week later, the trials of Coleman and Brown began.

On May 6, 1985, an Ohio court sentenced Coleman to death and on May 14, Brown received a life sentence in prison for the murder of Marlene Waters. Both were sentenced to death after their June 8, 1985, convictions, also in Ohio, for the murder of Tonnie Storey. Brown received an additional seven to twenty-five years for robbery in the case. The pair's last Ohio conviction came on Aug. 1, 1985, for kidnapping and added an extra twenty-year sentence each.

Coleman was convicted in Indiana on Apr. 11, 1986, of the murder of Tameka Turks and the rape of Annie Hillard, and received another death sentence plus 100 years in prison.

During his last murder trial, in Illinois, Coleman acted as his own defense lawyer and said, "I'm a dead man. I'm dead already." He later regretted his decision, saying, "I was a fool to represent myself and I admit it." Coleman was convicted, and again sentenced to death in January 1987.

Coleman, according to Illinois prosecutors, was the only man in the U.S. facing four death penalties. Held in Lake County (Ill.) Jail, Coleman asked to be baptized, but the request was denied because of security problems. Currently Coleman is waiting for his execution on Death Row in the Southern Ohio Correctional Facility in Lucasville, Ohio. He was scheduled to be executed in 1985, but his appeals delayed his death. His most recent appeal was in January 1989. REF.: *CBA*.

Coleman, Edward, d.1839, U.S., mur. Known throughout the Five Points section of New York for their style and beauty, the Hot Corn Girls were much sought after by the young toughs of the neighborhood. Clad in calico dresses and plaid shawls, the young women walked through the streets of Manhattan in the early 1800s selling hot corn on the cob from oaken buckets. Their earnings were small, and the competition was fierce. But many handsome young men would fight for the hand of a Hot Corn Girl.

Unfortunately, the Five Points had more than its share of men who were content to allow their wives to earn a living in the streets while they languished in saloons and gambling halls. Such was the case with Edward Coleman, who earned the hatred of half of New York when he murdered his Hot Corn Girl wife for failing to bring home enough money. He beat her so badly that she died from her injuries. Coleman was arrested and convicted of murder. On Jan. 12, 1839, he became the first inmate of the newly erected Tombs Prison to be hanged.
REF.: Asbury, *The Gangs of New York; CBA*.

Coleman, James Plemon, 1914- , U.S., jur. District attorney in Mississippi from 1940-46 and attorney general of Mississippi from 1950-56. He was nominated to sit on the U.S. Court of Appeals, Fifth Circuit in 1965 by President Lyndon Johnson. REF.: *CBA*.

Coleman, Jefferson, b.c.1955, U.S., rob.-burg.-pris. esc.-mur. Returning home on May 11, 1986, after a Mother's Day visit, a young Chicago couple was about to enter their front door when Jefferson Coleman appeared and demanded their money. He forced them inside, where he tied up the lawyer and took the wife to the bedroom. Coleman, thirty-two, evidently heard the husband struggling to free himself, and when he left the bedroom to check, the wife locked the door and called the police. Outside, the husband, his legs still tied, tried to take Coleman's gun away. The gun discharged into a wall, the husband fell to the floor, and Coleman left. Coleman, who had been convicted of murder in 1975, was arrested two days later when a woman partner tried to cash a stolen check at a bank. About two weeks later, on May 30, he escaped from custody when he was receiving treatment at Cook County Hospital for a bite by another inmate.

Recaptured, he was tried, and convicted for the May 11 robbery. He was sentenced on Dec. 23, 1987, to sixty years in prison. REF.: *CBA*.

Coleman, Richard, d.1749, Brit., (wrong. convict.) asslt.-rape-mur. Because of a slip of the tongue while drunk, Richard Coleman of Kingston, Surrey, was executed for a crime he did not commit.

In July 1748, while walking home late one night from a festival in Kennington Lane, young Sarah Green was raped and beaten and left for dead. Still alive, however, she crawled home to Southwark.

At St. Thomas's Hospital she told doctors she thought her assailants were connected with Taylor's brewhouse, a local pub. Two days later Richard Coleman and Daniel Trotman stopped by the Queen's Head Alehouse in Bandy-Leg Walk for a drink. Already intoxicated, Coleman was asked by a stranger if he was the rogue who assaulted Sarah Green. "If I had, you dog, what then?" he answered, in turn insulting and threatening the stranger.

Suspicious of Coleman, Trotman went to a local magistrate to incriminate him in the assault against Sarah Green. When questioned by the constable, Coleman was sober and composed. He said he had no memory of his behavior at the Queen's Head Alehouse, and if he had said such a thing it simply was not true. Still suspect, however, Coleman was twice brought before the dying woman. The first time she could not say with certainty whether this was the man or not. At the urging of her lawyer Mr. Wynne, the suspect was brought back to Sarah where she made a positive identification.

Sarah Green soon died, and Coleman was indicted for murder. Fleeing to Pinner, near Harrow on the Hill, he dispatched a message to the local newspaper. "I, Richard Coleman, seeing myself advertised in the Gazette, as absconding on account of the murder of Sarah Green, knowing myself not any way culpable, do assert that I have not absconded from justice; but will willingly and readily appear at the next [judicial inquest], knowing that my innocence will acquit me."

On Nov. 22, Coleman was arrested at Pinner and jailed at Southwark until the court convened in Kingston. The prosecution based their case on Sarah Green's shaky identification and the hearsay of Trotman.

Coleman was found Guilty and condemned to die at Kennington Common on Apr. 12, 1749. Resigned to his fate, the condemned man nonetheless bewailed the plight of his wife and children, who would henceforth be dependent on the charity of the church to survive. Coleman went to the gallows proud and defiant, protesting his guilt to the very last. More than a few people that day in Surrey believed the courts hanged an innocent man.

REF.: Brock, *A Casebook of Crime;* CBA; Cobb, *Trials and Errors;* Mitchell, *Newgate Calendar;* Potter, *The Art of Hanging.*

Coleman, Robert, b.1907, U.S., (wrong convict.) mur. On Mar. 14, 1929, Robert Coleman, twenty-two, of Clayton County, Ga., came home to find his 18-year-old wife murdered. He called the police who found the murder weapons, a block of wood, a poker, and a flat iron inside the house. They also found Coleman's overalls, recently washed, with stains that appeared to have been from human blood. Coleman suspected a man named Starks; however, Starks was never questioned. Instead, Coleman was arrested, tried, found Guilty, and sentenced to life in prison.

In 1932, an inmate named Davis in the Georgia prison told officials that another convict, Starks, had admitted killing a Clayton County woman in 1929. Following an inquiry, Coleman was granted an unconditional pardon by the governor on Apr. 14, 1933, and the Georgia legislature awarded him $25,000 in restitution on Mar. 27, 1941. REF.: *CBA.*

Coleman, Tommy, and **McNeil, Ross,** prom. 1931, U.S., rob. A prison escapee and his accomplice successfully completed a series of robberies before police, changing their tactics, apprehended them.

Tommy Coleman slipped from the confines of the Colorado State Penitentiary in the winter of 1931. He traveled to San Francisco where he and his former cellmate, Ross McNeil, were involved in ten stickups. During the spate of bank robberies, they also stole an automatic pistol from a sporting goods store.

Frustrated, the police revised their usual techniques. They replaced conventional loud alarms with silent ones that could be activated by pressing a button that was placed close to each bank employee. These alarms directly alerted police headquarters. In addition, they positioned police reinforcements where they could catch the robbers as they came out of the bank rather than during the actual robbery. With these new methods, Coleman and McNeil were captured. Coleman was sent back to complete his sentence at the Colorado State Penitentiary before serving another term in California. McNeil was given a lengthy sentence at San Quentin Prison.

REF.: *CBA;* Cohen, *One Hundred True Crime Stories.*

Coleridge, Lord Bernard John Seymour (Second Baron Coleridge), 1851-1927, jur. Judge of the King's Bench, Division of the High Court from 1907-23 and eldest son of Sir John Duke Coleridge. During his sixteen year career on the bench he heard a number of important cases, including that of the railway murderer John Alexander Dickman. REF.: *CBA.*

Coleridge, Herbert, 1830-61, Brit., lawyer. REF.: *CBA.*

Coleridge, Sir **John Duke (First Baron Coleridge),** 1820-94, Brit., jur. Appointed attorney general in 1871. Chief justice of the Queen's Bench from 1880-94. REF.: *CBA.*

Coles, Frances, d.1891, Brit., (unsolv.) mur. A man dashed out of Swallow Gardens, past startled rookie police officer Ernest Thompson, who was on his first night patrol alone, on Feb. 13, 1891. Minutes later, Thompson found the body of Frances Coles in the London garden. Although this killing took place two years after the last official Jack-the-Ripper murder, the body was disfigured in similar fashion as other Ripper slayings. See: **Jack the Ripper.**

REF.: *CBA;* Wensley, *Forty Years of Scotland Yard.*

Coles, Ronald R., b.c.1935, U.S., extor. In early 1976, popular suburban Chicago politician Ronald Coles, forty-one, was convicted on two counts of extortion that were related to the issuing of county liquor licenses and involved about $800. He was sentenced to three years' probation. At the time, Cole served as

both Lake Villa Township, Ill., supervisor and as Lake County board president. Although Cole had been removed from his offices, township officials reappointed Cole, ruling that his misdeeds were related only to the county office.

However, Lake County State's Attorney Dennis P. Ryan, a Democrat, had Coles, a Republican, discharged from office by obtaining a court order on grounds that a person convicted of some serious crimes cannot hold some positions of "honor, trust, or profit." Coles then was elected by a write-in campaign and was sworn in to the township office in April 1977. REF.: *CBA.*

Colfax, Schuyler, 1823-85, U.S., polit. corr. Ulysses S. Grant's vice-president from 1869-73. His career was cut short in 1873 when he was implicated in the Crédit Mobilier scandal. REF.: *CBA.*

Colgrove, Chester Walker, prom. 1940s, U.S., fraud. Throughout the 1940s Chester Colgrove of California marketed a suspicious potion designed to cure psoriasis, leg ulcers, eczema, and athlete's foot. Colgrove called the substance "Colusa Natural Oil," and he promoted the product in various magazine publications with "before and after" testimonials. The Food and Drug Administration (FDA) brought charges against Colgrove for misbranding, which resulted in a court-imposed $1,500 fine.

Colusa Natural Oil was a petroleum-based by-product of Colgrove's earlier, unsuccessful ventures. Before he turned his attention to skin medicine, Chester Colgrove got himself into legal trouble because of various oil and insurance schemes. Following his conviction for misbranding, Colgrove picked up where he left off, this time exercising greater care in his packaging and advertising. The FDA however, was not impressed. They brought the matter before the courts accusing Colgrove of criminal contempt for violating the earlier injunction.

Using semantics, Colgrove sought to prevail against the FDA. He contended he was not a doctor and therefore had not prescribed the substance. His ploy did not work and the original injunction was upheld.

REF.: *CBA;* Young, *The Medical Messiah.*

Coli, Eco James, 1922- , U.S., org. crime. Eco Coli has served for many years as executioner and mob enforcer for the Chicago organized crime family. His criminal record dates back to 1945, and includes arrests for assault, attempted hijacking, and sex offenses, plus convictions for contributing to the delinquency of a minor and armed robbery. This latter charge carried a prison sentence of eight to twelve years, but Coli was released by order of the Illinois Supreme Court in 1955 after having served just three years.

Resuming his former occupation of hit man for such mob bosses as Tony Accardo and Sam Giancana, Eco Coli found time to involve himself in union politics. He served for a time as secretary-treasurer of a Teamster's Local that represented Chicago's funeral home drivers, embalmers, and directors. Having attained a small measure of respectability, Coli marched proudly alongside Chicago mayor Richard J. Daley and Illinois governor Richard Ogilvie in the 1969 Columbus Day Parade.

REF.: *CBA;* Demaris, *Captive City;* Nash, *Bloodletters and Badmen.*

Coligny, Gaspard de, 1519-72, Fr., adm., assass. Renowned for his skill and bravery on the field of battle, Gaspard de Coligny became the leader of the Huguenot movement, in which French Protestants were persecuted by the Catholic monarchy. Admiral de Coligny's military exploits at St. Quentin earned him the admiration of Charles IX, the Catholic king whose every move was guided by his ambitious mother, Catherine de Medici. Her advisers had grown uneasy with the friendship between the king and the Protestant Coligny. In 1572, Catherine became particularly alarmed when Coligny urged Charles to wage war against Spain, the most powerful Catholic country in Europe. Such a war would strengthen the hand of the Protestant factions in France.

Catherine enlisted the support of Henri de Lorraine, the third Duke of Guise, who entertained notions of becoming king himself one day. The house of Guise was among the most influential Catholic dynasties in France, and the duke was not about to miss the opportunity to participate in the assassination of Admiral de Coligny. On Aug. 22, 1572, Coligny was struck by a bullet as he walked home from the Louvre. He survived the attack, but the Huguenots of Paris were whipped into a frenzy. Catherine decided that the plan to kill the admiral must proceed. King Charles threw up his hands in disgust. "If you must kill the admiral, then so be it!" he cried. "But if that is the case, then you will have to kill every Huguenot in France, so none will remain to cast the finger of reproach at me!"

The assassination of Gaspard de Coligny.

The king's ministers took the hasty remark all too literally. What had begun as an attempt to kill four or five Huguenot leaders ended in the St. Bartholomew's Day Massacre. The streets of Paris and its countryside ran red with blood. The butchery of 50,000 Protestants continued from Sept. 17 until Oct. 3 in the French provinces. Admiral de Coligny was the first to fall. See: **Charles IX.**

REF.: *CBA; Hurwood, Society and the Assassin; Soman, The Massacre of St. Bartholomew.*

Colino, Richard, b.c.1936, U.S., consp.-fraud. In 1965, Richard Colino joined Comsat, the U.S. arm of Intelsat, the company that directs global satellite communications. In January 1984, he rose to power as the first U.S. director general of Intelsat. However, after misusing his position for personal gain, Colino, fifty-one, was convicted by a Washington, D.C., district court on charges of conspiring to defraud Intelsat of $4.8 million. In late September 1987, he was sentenced to six years in prison and directed to pay $865,000 in damages to Intelsat.

In a contract kickback scheme with a construction firm, Colino arranged for Intelsat to be fraudulently charged for construction materials that did not exist. He also used monies for which he was not directly accountable to finance criminal schemes and created a phony firm that billed Intelsat for fake services. Another colleague, speculating about the former director's activities, said Colino was "ambitious and manipulative" and unhappy that he had not risen more quickly in his career. REF.: *CBA.*

Coll, Vincent (AKA: **Mad Dog**), 1908-32, U.S., kid.-org. crime. Born and raised in New York City, Vincent Coll was the son of Irish immigrants. He and his brother Peter were given little formal education and spent their childhood in the teeming squalor of Hell's Kitchen, learning to steal from pushcarts and stores at an early age. Vincent Coll proved to be one of the most adept thieves of his neighborhood. He exhibited a vicious and violent nature early in life, beating other boys senseless for the smallest insult or gangland transgression. As a teenager, Coll was tall and rangy, appearing to be much older than his years. He had mastered the use of revolvers and was involved with a number of street gang deaths. He was sent to the state reformatory at Elmira, N.Y., for robbery and when he was released went to work as a gunman and rum-runner for bootleg crime boss Dutch Schultz, at a salary of $150 a week.

In 1930, Coll went to Schultz and demanded a percentage of the bootlegging profits from the Dutchman's empire. Schultz gave him a firm "no" and Coll decided to put together his own bootlegging gang, especially after realizing that Schultz was raking in millions of dollars from his beer and liquor distribution in the Bronx and Manhattan. Coll enlisted his brother, Peter, Frank

Giodano, Arthur Palumbo, and several other young hoodlums and soon began raiding the Dutchman's territory, hijacking Schultz beer and liquor trucks and selling the stolen booze in job lots to smalltime distributors. Coll tried several times to hire Vincent Barrelli, one of Schultz's top lieutenants and one with contacts with rum-runners who sailed down from Canada, to set up better liquor distribution. Barrelli, loyal to the Dutchman, was making an enormous amount of money with Schultz, and refused. After several rebuffs, Coll sought out Barrelli and found the gangster with his girlfriend, Mary Smith. Coll shot both of them dead and drove off cursing. Next, Coll moved his headquarters to the Bronx, a half block from Schultz's headquarters on Brook Avenue, so that he could recruit the Dutchman's men to his own banner.

"The Mick," as Coll was then called, preyed upon Schultz's beer-running activities so successfully that, one day in 1931, the Dutchman walked into the Morrisania Precinct Station in the Bronx, approached three detectives in the squad room, and announced: "Look, I want the Mick killed. He's driving me out of my mind. I'll give a house in Winchester to any of you guys who knocks him off."

One detective shook his head, as if he had not heard Schultz correctly, and replied: "Arthur, do you know what you're saying? Do you know that you're in the Morrisania Station?"

Snarled the crime boss: "I know where I am. I've been here before. I just came in to tell you that I'll pay good to any cop who kills the Mick!"

This blatant murder contract verbally delivered to working NYPD detectives indicated the power wielded by crime czars such as Schultz during the early 1930s. The Dutchman, a multimillionaire from the enormously lucrative rackets he controlled, could publicly offer a fortune to anyone who would do his killing for him and walk away without being charged. As the detectives knew, arresting Schultz for proposing a murder would only be thrown out of court within hours; the gangster would merely tell the judge that he was kidding and be sent on his way. But Dutch Schultz was not kidding. He wanted Vincent Coll dead in the worst way. So did a lot of other crime bosses in New York, not the least of whom was Owney "The Killer" Madden.

On June 15, 1931, George Jean "Big Frenchy" DeMange, partner with Owney Madden in gambling and bootleg rackets and owner of dozens of nightclubs, stepped from the Club Argonaut, one of his nightspots, and was seized by Coll, who poked a gun into his ample stomach. Coll ordered DeMange into a sedan parked at curbside and the big man got in. On either side of him sat two of Coll's hoodlums, both holding guns on DeMange. Coll sat next to the driver, also aiming a gun at the racket boss. "Why, men, this is silly," DeMange told them in genuine shock. "If it's money you want, you can have it, but don't try this gun stuff."

Coll ignored the plea and stopped to make a phone call to Owney Madden, telling the big boss that he had DeMange and expected a ransom to be paid within twenty-four hours or Madden would be seeking a new partner. Within the specified time, $35,000 was paid to Coll and DeMange was released unharmed. Gangland kidnapping was unheard of at the time, but the crime set a precedent and mob kidnapping later became routine. Madden, as well as Schultz, now ordered his men to shoot down Coll on sight, but Schultz struck first by having Peter Coll kidnapped and then shot to death on a Harlem street. When Coll learned of his brother's execution he exploded, screaming at his gang members: "That yellow rat, Schultz! I'm gonna burn the Dutchman to hell!" He and his men went gunning for Schultz but found his top lieutenant, Joey Rao, who was also hunting Coll. Schultz had placed a $50,000 reward on Coll's head, for his dead body.

On July 28, 1931, Coll and two of his men went looking for Rao. As their car passed the Helmar Social Club at 208 East 107th Street, they spotted either Joey Rao, or his cousin Vincent Rao, lounging outside the club that was a Schultz gangland headquarters. Coll and his men, oblivious to passersby, opened up with their automatics and a submachine gun. The gunman

Vincent "Mad Dog" Coll

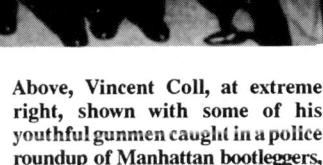

Dutch Schultz

Above, Vincent Coll, at extreme right, shown with some of his youthful gunmen caught in a police roundup of Manhattan bootleggers, 1931.

Left, the Coll gang living it up on a Coney Island set, left to right, Arthur Palumbo, Peter Coll, Lottie Kriesberger, and Vincent Coll.

Right, "Big Frenchy" DeMange, partner of gangster Owney Madden (bottom, center), kidnapped and ransomed by Coll for $35,000.

Bottom left, Vincent Coll's body being carried out of a Manhattan drugstore after he had been machine-gunned to death in a phone booth, 1932.

Bottom right, Vincent Coll with his lawyer, criminal attorney Samuel Leibowitz.

outside the club dove to the cement, as did others on the crowded street, but the gunfire tore into a group of children who were playing on the sidewalk. Wounded were Florence D'Amello, age fourteen, Samuel Divino, age five, and Michael Bevilacqua, a three-year-old in a baby carriage. Dead was little Michael Vengali, age five.

Coll was quickly identified as the baby killer, the underworld itself informing on him to the newspapers, who quickly labeled the killer "Mad Dog" Coll. The gang boss denied he had committed the ruthless killing, but he was nevertheless indicted for the Vengali killing, along with Frank Giordano. Coll hired one of the most astute criminal lawyers of the day, Samuel Leibowitz, who would become famous for his defense of the Scottsboro boys in one of the most sensational rape cases of the century. Leibowitz got his clients a bench trial and quickly shredded the case police tried to mount against Coll and Giordano. George Brecht, an underworld informer and a convicted felon, testified that he had seen Coll and Giordano gun down the children on East 107th Street. This may have been true, but Leibowitz tore into Brecht, proving that he was a highly paid witness who had made considerable money as a star witness in previous murder trials. Brecht's testimony was demolished by the incisive Leibowitz. Both his clients were acquitted for lack of evidence and released. Schultz and Madden, along with others, vowed that Coll would not live out another year.

To insulate himself against the formidable gangs of the Dutchman and that of Owney the Killer, Coll aligned himself with Jack "Legs" Diamond and Vannie Higgins, both tenacious competitors of Schultz and Madden in the bootleg wars throughout Manhattan. The battle raged on, with Coll and his men killing at least fifteen of Schultz's gunmen and beer truck drivers. In October 1931, Frank Giordano and Dominic "Toughy" Ordierno, both defectors from the Schultz legions, shot and killed Joseph Mullins, a $50-a-week handyman who did odd jobs for Schultz. This was a message to the Dutchman that Coll intended to kill everyone—whether they were important mob figures or not—who surrounded Schultz. The Dutchman was even informed that Coll meant to kill his uninvolved, dowdy wife. But Coll's men had been too bold this time.

Two electrical repairmen, peeking from beneath a manhole cover, had seen Giordano, age thirty-two, and Ordierno, age twenty-three, shoot Mullins to death. They later testified in court, and both Giordano and Ordierno were convicted and sent to the electric chair in Sing Sing. Both men were scheduled to die on June 30, 1932, but Giordano desperately made a move to save his life by telling the warden that he had important information about the killing of the Vengali boy in 1931, that the bullet that killed the child had been fired by Vincent Coll. "I know that's the truth," Giordano insisted, "since I drove the car that day, the one Coll was firing from." This information was passed on to Governor Franklin D. Roosevelt, and he called the warden, asking him to delay the execution for twenty-four hours. This was done, but Roosevelt, after reviewing the case the next day and considering Giordano's "evidence," decided that the two Bronx killers would meet their fate in the electric chair. They did. Giordano's information was quite useless by then since Coll was already dead.

After Coll had been released following his exoneration of killing little Michael Vengali, the gangster hugged his 23-year-old blonde girl friend, Lottie Kriesberger, then turned to reporters and said, grinning: "I have been charged with all kinds of crimes but baby-killing was the limit. I'd like nothing better than to lay my hands on the man who did this. I'd tear his throat out. There is nothing more despicable than a man who would harm an innocent child." The reporters said nothing in response to this. They knew what everyone knew, that Vincent Coll did indeed kill the innocent child. The state could not prove it and so he was released, free to kill again.

But Coll's killing days were over on Feb. 7, 1932. He was by then a wealthy man, raking in tens of thousands of dollars from his expanding bootleg empire. He had married Kriesberger and

they lived in an enormous apartment at the posh Cornish Arms Hotel, on the north side of West Twenty-third Street, between Eighth and Nine avenues. Across the hall lived two of his best bodyguards, and more bodyguards occupied apartments on floors below. On that February evening, Coll, as usual, stepped from his apartment building, a trusted bodyguard next to him, going a few doors down on the south side of West Twenty-third Street to the London Chemists' Shop, a drugstore with a soda fountain. Coll invariably went to the phone booth in this store to make his business calls, believing that his home phone was tapped by police. He was right. The police had also assigned two detectives to tail the killer.

As Coll entered the phone booth and began a lengthy call, his bodyguard slipped off a stool at the soda fountain where he had been sitting and walked quietly outside. He looked at a sedan parked in front of the store and saw Dutch Schultz's ace enforcer, Abraham "Bo" Weinberg. He nodded and Weinberg waved him off, a signal that he was allowing the bodyguard to live and go his own way, part of the compensation for tipping the Schultz gangsters where to find their elusive quarry. With that, either Weinberg, or one of his men got out of the car and walked into the drugstore carrying a Thompson submachine gun. At the first sight of this deadly weapon, the occupants of the store, Dr. Edward Pravner and Dr. Leo J. Latz, customers, and the clerk, Morris Kantrowitz, stood petrified. The gunmen looked at them solemnly and said: "All keep quiet. Keep cool, now."

The gunman walked to within a few feet of the phone booth, inside of which Coll was having a heated conversation. He opened up with the submachine gun, raking the booth from top to bottom, then zigzagging his fire back and forth until the booth was shredded and the man inside of it crumpled and dead, his body a human sieve. Fifteen of the fifty bullets fired in three bursts by the expert gunman tore into the 23-year-old gang boss, killing him instantly. The gunman then cradled the submachine gun and walked quietly from the scene, got into the car parked at the sidewalk and roared away. The detectives parked in a car down the block gave chase but lost the gangster's car when it turned onto Eighth Avenue and, at speeds estimated to be more than 70 m.p.h., was quickly lost from sight. When the detectives returned to the drugstore, a large crowd had assembled. A patrol wagon arrived and uniformed policemen carried the shot-up body of Vincent "Mad Dog" Coll out of the store, wrapped in a blanket, and placed it in the wagon which drove off to the morgue. Within a few hours newsboys were hawking an extra, shouting: "Baby killer slain! They got the baby killer!" See: **Diamond, Jack; Higgins, Vannie; Madden, Owen; Schultz, Dutch.**

REF.: Bonanno, *A Man of Honor;* CBA; Eisenberg and Landau, *Meyer Lansky;* Elliott, *Agent of Death;* Gage, *Mafia, U.S.A.;* Gosch and Hammer, *The Last Testament of Lucky Luciano;* Horan, *The Desperate Years;* Katz, *Uncle Frank;* Levine, *Anatomy of a Gangster: Jack "Legs" Diamond;* McClellan, *Crime Without Punishment;* Maas, *The Valachi Papers;* Messick, *Kidnapping;* Nash, *Almanac of World Crime;* ____, *Bloodletters and Badmen;* Peterson, *The Mob;* Sann, *Kill the Dutchman!;* Thompson and Raymond, *Gang Rule in New York;* Whitelaw, *Corpus Delicti;* (FILM), *Mad Dog Coll,* 1961.

Collamer, Jacob, 1791-1865, U.S., lawyer. Member of the Senate from 1855-65. REF.: *CBA.*

Collazo, Oscar, See: **Truman, Harry S.**

Collet, James, prom. 1600s, Brit., rob. During the late 1600s, England's royal family and the prostitutes they employed were the targets of a mysterious highwayman who disguised himself as a bishop. In a six-year period, the masquerading bishop robbed the real Bishop of Winchester, several members of the royal family, and attempted to rob courtesan Nell Gwynne, the Duchess of Mazarin.

But Gwynne engaged him in a game of dice. As a result of the match, Gwynne won more from him than he had attempted to steal from her. The "bishop" was later captured and exposed as James Collet, who was quickly tried and convicted of several robberies. As required by English law, Collet was hanged.

REF.: *CBA*; Pringle, *Stand and Deliver*.

Collet, John Caskie, 1898-1955, U.S., jur. County prosecutor in Chariton County, Mo., from 1925-29. Appointed judge of the court of the eastern and western district of Missouri by President Franklin Roosevelt in 1937. He was named to the U.S. Court of Appeals, Eighth Circuit Court in 1947 by President Harry Truman. REF.: *CBA*.

Colley, George (AKA: **Richard Wise, Robert Wise, The Candy Kid**), prom. 1937-42, U.S., rob.-mur. On Christmas Eve 1937, as Henry Miller walked in an isolated area of Dayton, Ohio, he was confronted by the Candy Kid, who had terrorized the city for months with a spree of gunpoint muggings. When he shot Miller with his newly purchased .38-caliber handgun, the Candy Kid graduated from robbery to murder.

His previous victims described the young mugger as slim, dark, and handsome. He taunted police with his day and night robberies, and signed the notes he left with his victims, "The Candy Kid."

Police found Miller lying wounded and unconscious in the street. They searched the area for clues and found one of the notes in a nearby gutter. When Miller died, the .38-caliber slug removed from his brain led police to a local pawnbroker. He said he had sold a .38-caliber pistol to Richard Wise on the evening Miller was shot. Further investigation of the note led police to a local restaurant owner who purchased paper cups packaged in paper identical to that on which the note was written. The restaurateur told police he had employed a young man named Bob Wise until just recently, when Wise failed to report to work. Police suspected he had fled Dayton after the murder.

Wise was apprehended several months later when he attempted to rob a New York gas station. Police determined that Wise was actually George Colley from Huntington, W. Va. Colley, who had escaped from a mental hospital in Huntington, was returned to the facility and transferred one year later to Dayton State Hospital to await trial for the murder of Henry Miller.

Five years after the murder of Miller, George Colley was tried. On Christmas Eve 1942, Colley was convicted and sentenced to life in prison at the Ohio State Penitentiary.

REF.: *CBA*; Rice, *45 Murderers*.

Thomas Colley drowning Ruth Osborne before a drunken mob.

Colley, Thomas, d.1751, Brit., mur. Fired up by liquor, and the promise of seeing an evil sorceress punished, Thomas Colley of Hertfordshire goaded the mob into action. The objects of his derision—John Osborne and his wife Ruth—had lately been rumored to be practicing witchcraft, though belief in witchcraft had all but faded during the Enlightenment.

When it was announced on Apr. 18, 1751, that Osborne and his wife were to be publicly dunked, a mob of about 5,000 descended on the workhouse where the old couple were held. Fearing that the crowd was going to turn violent, the master of the workhouse moved the couple to the local church.

When Colley demanded the surrender of the Osbornes, the workhouse master said they were not on the premises. Colley and the mob wrecked the workhouse and threatened to burn the entire town unless the Osbornes were produced. The master pointed to the church.

Colley and his drunken followers dragged the pair to a pond where they were stripped and tied for dunking. Tom Colley prodded them with a long stick, rolling them in the shallow water. John Osborne escaped with his life, but when Ruth Osborne was pulled from the water, she was dead. A coroner's inquest determined that she drowned.

While the corpse was being removed, Colley took a collection from the crowd for the entertainment he had provided. He was arrested for inciting a mob, and for the murder of Ruth Osborne. Tom Colley said he intended to save the woman, not drown her, and that the money was for the widower Osborne. The court rejected his story and sentenced Thomas Colley to die. Before his execution, he wrote a message to his fellow townsmen, urging them not to be blinded by superstition.

Colley was executed at St. Albans on Aug. 24, 1751. His corpse was taken to Gubblecut where it was hanged in chains.

REF.: Butler, *Murderers' England*; *CBA*; Mitchell, *Newgate Calendar*.

Collier, Jeremy, 1650-1726, Brit., treas. Imprisoned for his Jacobin sympathies in 1688 and 1692, he was an outspoken critic of William and Mary. He was outlawed in 1696 for absolving two conspirators who had plotted the death of William, but published several well-received histories of Britain. REF.: *CBA*.

Collier, John Payne, prom. 1852, Brit., forg. In 1852 John Collier published his *Notes and Emendations to the Text of Shakespeare's Plays* based on a portfolio of amendments, allegedly written by Perkins years earlier. The Perkins folio was given over to the British Museum in 1859 for examination. It was declared to be a worthless fraud, written in the modern era. In 1860, Nicholas Hamilton exposed the hoax in his *Inquiry*. Collier was known to have forged Shakespeare's signature to an actual letter written by the master.

REF.: *CBA*; MacDougall, *Hoaxes*.

Collier, Dr. Joseph, prom. 1790s, Case of, Brit., consp.-treas. In 1792, Dr. Joseph Collier was one of several British citizens who formed the Reformation Society. He was later charged with conspiracy to overthrow the British government. The Society was a political group which advocated expanded rights and freedoms for the masses. Collier and others formed the Society following the French Revolution and the French government's pledge to assist like revolutionaries in neighboring countries.

One member of the Society, Thomas Dunn, was arrested in Manchester for his revolutionary activities and informed on his associates, including Collier, in exchange for freedom. Dunn was the only witness for the prosecution. He testified that during Society meetings, Collier and others read the works of Thomas Paine, an act strictly forbidden by English law, and that they mocked the Royal Family and planned to unseat them. Defense attorneys brought several reputable character witnesses before the jury. Almost immediately, the jury returned a verdict of Not Guilty. Collier was released, and Dunn was charged with perjury, convicted and sentenced to two years in prison. He was also confined in a pillory to endure ridicule by Manchester residents.

REF.: *CBA*; Parry, *Some Famous Medical Trials*.

Collier, William Miller, 1867-1956, U.S., lawyer. Lecturer on international law at New York Law School and author of *The Influence of Lawyers in the Past and In the Future* in 1921. REF.: *CBA*.

Collin, Frank (AKA: **Dan Carnehan**), 1945- , U.S., porn.-sex. abuse. In 1980, Frank Collin, founder of the Chicago chapter of the National Socialist Party of America (NSPA), was arrested on charges of sexually molesting eight Chicago boys, ranging in age from eleven to fourteen, over an eight-month period in 1979. Collin was responsible for planning a Neo-Nazi march through Skokie, Ill., a Chicago suburb with a large Jewish population. Although the march never occurred, the Supreme Court ruled that the Neo-Nazi organization's right to march was protected under the First Amendment.

In December 1979, Collin was ousted as leader of the NSPA when party members discovered his sexual activities. Several young boys told police that Collin had sex with them at a North Side hotel and at the NSPA headquarters on Chicago's southwest side. Some also said that he had taken photographs of them posing nude with a military rifle. At the time of his arrest, Collin worked as a janitor under the name of Dan Carnehan at Chicago's St. Francis Hospital. When police searched the home he shared with his parents in a south Chicago suburb, they discovered pornographic photos of many young boys.

During his trial, prosecuting attorney Howard Regenbogen explained that Collin regularly cruised a neighborhood on the city's North Side searching for sexual companions, and would promise the boys money in return for sex. Collin pleaded guilty to all charges, was convicted, and sentenced to seven years in prison. REF.: *CBA*.

Collings, Benjamin P., 1893-1931, U.S., (unsolv.) mur. It was midnight when fishermen discovered the cabin cruiser *Penguin*, lights out, adrift in Long Island Sound. As they approached the boat, they heard splashes that sounded like swimming strokes in the water nearby, but when they pulled alongside, the splashing stopped. On board the *Penguin*, they found 5-year-old Barbara Collings alone, hiding in the lower decks. "I'm Barbara," she told the men. "My father went swimming with his clothes on. My mother went in swimming too. My father has lost his job."

The next morning, Mrs. Lillian Chelius Collings, Barbara's 28-year-old mother, was found alone in a lifeboat anchored near Cove Neck. She was taken to police headquarters where she was reunited with her daughter. Mrs. Collings told police that she, Barbara, and husband Benjamin Collings were on the *Penguin* the previous night when two strangers, a middle-aged man and a boy of about eighteen, boarded the boat. She said they forced her into the below-deck cabin and commandeered the boat under the pretext of taking an injured friend to get medical attention in South Norwalk, Conn. Mrs. Collings said she later heard a scuffle overhead, and went up on deck. She saw the two men dump her husband, arms and legs bound with ropes, into Oyster Bay. That was the last time she saw her husband alive.

The two men then abducted her from the *Penguin*, took her in their boat toward the shore, and left her in the anchored lifeboat where she was found several hours later. Police searched the waters off Oyster Bay, but could not find the body of Benjamin Collings. Six days later, the corpse washed up on the private beach of retail magnate Marshall Field. An autopsy concluded that Collings had been severely beaten about the head, but established that he had been alive when thrown into the water, though the head injuries had been sufficient to cause death.

The case puzzled police. They had no suspects, no motive, and no witnesses except Mrs. Collings. They began to suspect her when they learned that she had been unhappy with her husband, who had recently lost his job. Rumors of an affair with an older man ignited additional suspicion.

For several weeks, the mystery plagued authorities. They were never able to link Mrs. Collings with her husband's death, and the case remains unsolved. REF.: *CBA*.

Collings, Jack (AKA: **John Collinson**), 1672-1714, Brit., rob. Jack Collings thought his bill from the druggist who cured his venereal disease was exorbitant. Refusing to pay in full, Collings offered him a groat (four-pence), instead of the forty-eight shillings demanded.

The druggist decided the groat was all he would get, and took it. He even handled the matter amicably, and gave Collings a receipt for the coin. But Jack Collings resented having to pay the wealthy druggist at all. He followed him home and robbed

him not only of the groat, but also of twenty-four shillings and a fine silver watch.

Collings then turned to burglary. After several years of plying his trade in and around London, he entered the home of John Holloway in Chelsea by convincing Mrs. Holloway that he merely wanted a written pass into the Royal Hospital. When she went to get it, Collings searched the closets and found £194 in gold and notes totaling £237.

Collings might never have been apprehended but for the prostitute with whom he rented a room who noticed the sack full of money. When she read the newspaper story of the robbery, including a description of Collings, she called a constable. Collings was found with £70 and seventeen shillings remaining. He confessed, but refused to say how much money he had taken.

When Collings was jailed, a second victim, Mr. James Boyce, identified him as the one who robbed him near Kentish Town. On the strength of the two indictments, Collings was executed at Tyburn on Mar. 10, 1714.

REF.: *CBA*; Smith, *Highwaymen*.

Collington, John, and **Stone, John**, d.1749, Brit., arson. Young John Collington so terrorized his classmates that he was expelled from several schools and sent home to his father, the rector of Pluckley, who promptly apprenticed him to a London grocer. Collington did not mellow as he grew to manhood. He opened his own shops in Rye and Charing, but his surly attitude repelled customers.

Collington soon met and married a wealthy local woman, who bore him ten children. He beat and deprived his family, and finally killed his wife by throwing her down the stairs and stamping on her. He was never tried for assault, let alone murder.

Collington turned to wool smuggling, for which he was convicted and fined. He escaped the fine by placing his estate in another name and declaring he had no money.

He loved to hunt, but disobeyed gaming laws to such an extent that the Dowager Countess of Rockingham built a cottage nearby and had a servant spy on him. Enraged, he had Mr. Lockhurst, a servant, burn the cottage.

Although he had become affluent, Collington did not clothe or feed his children properly. He used starvation as a punishment, so that once a son was forced to beg for food. Mr. Clarke, the church warden, took the boy in. Incensed by this interference, Collington harassed and assaulted Clarke, who had him arrested. From jail he hired a laborer named John Stone and Lockhurst to burn down Clarke's barn. When Lockhurst came to the jail to collect payment, he was taken into custody and soon confessed to the crime. When convicted of arson, Collington assumed a defiant attitude, and appealed in vain to the Duke of Newcastle. Stone and Collington were hanged on Apr. 7, 1749.

REF.: *CBA*; Culpin, *The Newgate Noose*; Mitchell, *Newgate Calendar*.

Collingwood, Percy (Percy Conners), and **Kirby, Walter**, and **Manners, Arthur**, prom. 1900s, Case of, S. Afri., burg. One evening in Johannesburg, police received an anonymous report of several persons loitering. When officers arrived, they discovered a break-in at the offices of the Diamond Merchants Association. The burglars had entered the jewelry store by a rope ladder lowered through a hole in the floor of an attorney's office above. The intruders had disappeared, and nothing appeared to have been stolen.

As police were searching the area, Percy Collingwood, who had previously served a prison sentence in Port Elizabeth for robbing a jewelry store, and two other men, Walter Kirby and Arthur Manners, arrived on the scene after spending a few hours drinking in a nearby pub. Criminal Investigation Division Chief Major Theodore Etienne Mavrogordato immediately arrested Collingwood and his two companions for the break-in. Collingwood pleaded his innocence, but was quickly arraigned. Mavrogordato had little evidence, and the three men were acquitted.

After the trial, Collingwood told his defense attorney that "the police are a lot of fools. If they had not been in such a hurry and waited another half hour they would have bagged the lot of us." Collingwood explained that two days before the break-in, he made a wax impression of the key to the attorney's office. He had entered the building with his two companions intending to rob the store. After gaining entry, they decided it would be safer to finish the job later, and agreed to kill a few hours at a nearby pub before returning to complete their crime.

REF.: Bennett, *Genius For the Defense; CBA.*

Collins, Ben, d.1906, U.S., law enfor. off. Ben Collins represented law and order in the Indian Territory of Oklahoma during the 1890s. He was appointed deputy U.S. marshal in 1898, which brought him into contact with some of the most infamous characters in the vast ungoverned lands. In 1905, in Emet, Okla., Collins was ordered to arrest Port Pruitt, one of the town's leading citizens. Pruitt brandished a gun, but Collins dropped him with a single shot. As it turned out, the shot permanently crippled Pruitt, who swore revenge. Later that year, he paid an assassin $500 to kill Collins. The killer took his $200 advance and skipped the country.

On Aug. 1, 1906, Marshal Collins was ambushed near his home in Emet by "Killin'" Jim Miller, who shot him in the stomach while Collins' wife looked on. See: **Miller, James.**

REF.: *CBA;* O'Neal, *Encyclopedia of Western Gunfighters;* Shirley, *Shotgun For Hire.*

Collins, Benjamin F., b.1883, U.S., (wrong. convict.) rob. For three months in the summer of 1928, a purse-snatcher stalked female pedestrians in Sommerville, Mass. On Sept. 1, twenty minutes after one of the robberies, police arrested a hotel dishwasher matching the description of the offender. Once Benjamin F. Collins was in custody, several victims identified him as the man who had robbed them.

Somerville police repeatedly told assistant district attorney Richard S. McCabe that Collins was not the thief, and that they had arrested the wrong man. But McCabe ignored the officers and charged Collins with seven counts of larceny and two counts of robbery. Based on the testimony of Catherine Davis, Carrie M. Decker, Marion P. Jackson, Cecelia Ketter, and Mildred King, five of the purse-snatcher's victims, Collins was found Guilty and sentenced on Oct. 23 to serve between two-and-one-half and three-and-one-half years in prison. Four days later, another woman was victimized.

On Oct. 27, the purse snatcher struck again, but was apprehended after being shot by a police officer while attempting to flee. After police searched George Hill's Medford apartment and recovered many of the stolen purses, he gave a full confession.

Collins was given a second trial, acquitted of all charges, and released. Hill pleaded guilty and was sent to a state penitentiary, where he later died from an infection of the gunshot wound.

The Massachusetts Legislature later vetoed payment of reparations to Collins for his wrongful conviction. REF.: *CBA.*

Collins, Dapper Dan (or Don), See: **Toubillon, Robert Arthur.**

Collins, Ed (AKA: Chester Howard), 1911- , Case of, U.S., crucifixion. Only one month after his release from California's San Quentin Prison, Ed Collins was found screaming in agony, nailed to a homemade cross near his home in Reno, Nev.

Following his release from prison, after serving a sentence for a San Diego, Calif., robbery, Collins moved to Reno to begin a new life. He vowed never to commit another crime and started attending church regularly. In September 1938, Collins ran into two old acquaintances who tried to enlist his help in a robbery they were planning. Collins claims he told them he was going straight and wanted no part of the crime.

The two men later abducted him from the Reno Baptist Church and forced him to steal two boards from a nearby lumber yard. They drove him to the outskirts of town and fashioned the boards into a cross. They then nailed Collins' hands and feet to the cross, saying, "If you want to be a little Jesus Christ, then we'll make one out of you."

Local residents heard his screams, but once rescued, Collins refused to identify his attackers, and referred to them only as "Swede" and "Joe." REF.: *CBA.*

Collins, Francis Dignan, 1909- , Brit., mansl. On Oct. 10, 1940, British soldier Francis Dignan Collins shot and killed his commanding officer as revenge for punishing him with detention after Collins' late return from a leave of absence.

Sergeant-Major Percy Durrant ordered Collins confined for seventy-two days in detention because he had returned to the battalion two days late after a seven-day leave. Enraged, Collins threatened revenge. When he was escorted to his barracks to retrieve any necessary personal items, he also retrieved his rifle and unloaded a bullet into Durrant's abdomen.

Charged with murder, Collins claimed he had not known that the gun was loaded. He was found Guilty of the lesser crime of manslaughter and sentenced to ten years in prison.

REF.: *CBA;* Woodland, *Assize Pageant.*

Collins, George D., prom. 1900, U.S., big.-perj. In April 1905, George D. Collins and his new bride, Clarice McCurdy, traveled to Collins' hometown of San Francisco, Calif., to honeymoon in the Palace Hotel. Once settled into their rooms, Collins, a prominent San Francisco attorney, left the hotel to visit his three children and Charlotta Newman, the woman he called his housekeeper. Newman, however, had for the past six years called herself his wife.

Upon hearing of the marriage, Newman's brother William took the story to the police, who apprehended Collins for bigamy. When questioned, Collins told investigators he had married Agnes Newman, who had died four years earlier, but her name on the marriage license had been entered, by error, as Charlotte (with an 'e') Newman. Charlotta was Agnes' sister.

Refuting Collins' story, Charlotta claimed she had married Collins on May 15, 1889, and they had three children: George Jr., Consuela, and May. She further explained that her sister Agnes had lived in their house until she died while giving birth to a second baby fathered by Collins. Furious at his infidelity and false accusations, Charlotta filed for divorce and sued her husband for $200 per month child support.

Charged with bigamy, Collins failed to show up for his trial on June 12, 1905. He had fled to Victoria, British Columbia.

Although San Francisco authorities tried to extradite Collins, treaties between the United States and Canada barred extradition for bigamy. So prosecutors changed his offense to perjury, maintaining that he had perjured himself when he said Charlotta was not his wife. Eighteen months later, Canadian officials handed him over. On Oct. 24, 1905, Collins again testified that he had not married Charlotta, and was again charged with perjury.

Convicted on Mar. 10, 1906, Collins was sentenced to fourteen years in jail, a decision he appealed all the way to the U.S. Supreme Court. In 1909, the high court upheld the lower courts and Collins petitioned the California governor for a pardon. The pardon refused, Collins was immediately taken to San Quentin to begin his fourteen-year sentence.

REF.: *CBA;* Duke, *Celebrated Criminal Cases of America.*

Collins, George E., Jr., prom. 1957, U.S., kid. Eight-year-old Lee Crary of Everett, Wash., was kidnapped from his home on Sept. 22, 1957, by George E. Collins, Jr., who demanded $10,000 for his safe return. Three days later, the boy escaped and led police back to Collins' hideout, where he was arrested. Collins was sentenced to life imprisonment.

REF.: *CBA;* Nash, *Almanac of World Crime*

Collins, James Thomas, 1900- , Brit., mur. On June 13, 1926, 69-year-old grandmother Janie Tremayne Swift, her 35-year-old daughter Janie Stemp, and her 13-year-old granddaughter Peggy Stemp were picnicking in King's Woods near Ashford when a serviceman approached them with a rifle and shot all three to death. The 26-year-old army private, James Thomas Collins, picked up the body of Peggy Stemp, carried it to their car parked nearby, and dumped the corpse in a ditch several miles down the highway.

London police later received an anonymous telephone call from a man who told them they could find three badly injured bodies near the road between Ashford and Chatham. The unknown caller was James Thomas Collins. When police arrived at the picnic site, Swift still held in her hand the sandwich she had been eating the moment she died.

Collins was taken into custody in London after he pulled his gun on a policeman and engaged others in a chase and shootout. Filled with remorse, he later confessed to shooting the three women.

Collins was convicted but determined insane. Presiding Justice John Anthony Hawke sentenced him to Broadmoor hospital for the mentally insane.

REF.: Browne and Tullett, *Bernard Spilsbury: His Life and Cases;* ____, *The Scalpel of Scotland Yard; CBA;* Rentoul, *Sometimes I Think;* Shew, *A Companion to Murder.*

Collins, Joel, See: **Bass, Samuel.**

Collins, John, d.1737, Brit., mur. In the town of Harledown near Exeter, lived a roof thatcher named John Collins. Jane Upcot shared his house and his bed for many years, but little was known about the true nature of their relationship until the calamity of May 16, 1737.

On that day Collins murdered Jane Upcot with a spar-hook, severed her head, and removed her heart. Not content with mere mutilation, he affixed the body parts to the spar hook and displayed them outside his business establishment. Collins was seized, taken into custody, and put to death at Exeter that same year.

REF.: *CBA;* Mitchell, *Newgate Calendar.*

Collins, John Baptist, d.1794, U.S., pir.-mur. Three pirates, John Baptist Collins, Emanuel Furtado, and Augustus Palacha, traveled on board the brigantine *Betsy,* which was sailing to Boston in 1794, planning to take over the ship. They first attacked a wealthy passenger, Enoch Wood, killing him and taking his purse, but they were overcome by the crew. When the *Betsy* docked in Boston, all three would-be pirates were arrested and tried for Wood's murder. All three were hanged on July 30, 1794, in Boston before a large crowd. REF.: *CBA.*

Collins, John Norman (AKA: **The Ypsilanti Ripper**), 1947- , U.S., mur. Between July 1967 and July 1969, seven young women were found raped and murdered near the campus of the University of Michigan. The communities of Ann Arbor and Ypsilanti recoiled in horror. Before the identity of the killer was learned, police officials desperate for information brought in European psychic Peter Hurkos to lend his talents to the investigation.

The killing rampage began on July 10, 1967, when Mary Fleszar, a student at Eastern Michigan University, (EMU), disappeared. Her mutilated body was found on Aug. 7 by two teenagers in Superior Township. The killer struck again on July 1, 1968, when 20-year-old Joan Schell disappeared after accepting a ride from a stranger driving a red car. Her body was found five days later by construction workers in Ann Arbor. It too, bore evidence of sexual assault. In 1969, the unknown killer, no doubt encouraged by the lack of progress in the police investigation, stepped up his attacks. Between March and June, four more women were killed: Jane Mixer, a student at EMU; Maralynn Skelton, who was reputed to be a drug abuser; Dawn Basom, thirteen; and Alice Elizabeth Kalom, a recent college graduate. Peter Hurkos entered the investigation at this point. While he could not positively identify the killer, he guessed that the man was about twenty-five, heavily built, and would strike again.

He did, one more time. On July 26, Karen Sue Beineman, an 18-year-old freshman at EMU, was found near a wooded gully. Eyewitnesses reported that Karen had accepted a ride from a man on a motorcycle three days earlier. The police checked the available leads and identified 22-year-old John Norman Collins of Center Line, Mich., who attended classes at EMU. His aberrant behavior was well known. An average student, Collins was preoccupied with women. One of his girlfriends said he was oversexed. He was positively identified as the "Ripper" when police found hair clippings that matched those found in the briefs

of the last victim, Karen Beineman. The suspect had recently cut the hair of the children of State Police Sergeant David Leik. Collins was the nephew of Officer Leik's wife. He was arrested on July 31, 1969.

Described as a "bondage freak" who had fantasized about torturing women for years, Collins was convicted of murder in Ann Arbor on Aug. 19, 1970, and was sentenced to life imprisonment by Judge John W. Conlin. "I know my son didn't do it," sobbed Mrs. Loretta Collins, who had mortgaged her home to pay for her boy's defense. "I want my son back again."

REF.: Browning, *The Psychic World of Peter Hurkos; CBA;* Fox, *Mass Murder;* Keyes, *The Michigan Murders;* Wilson, *Encyclopedia of Modern Murder.*

Collins, Melvin (AKA: **Bad Boy**), 1910-48, U.S., suic.-mur. Melvin Collins had already stabbed his brother and served two terms in a Virginia state penitentiary for two shooting incidents when, in November 1948, he went on a shooting spree that wounded three people and left seven dead, including one police officer.

Collins had recently moved to Chester, Penn., where he rented a room in a downtown boarding house. One morning, he leaned out the window of his second-story room and began firing his rifle at the pedestrians below. One man was dead before police Detective Elery Purnsley returned fire from across the street. Collins gunned down Detective Purnsley as pedestrians scattered, running for cover. When curiosity seekers ran to windows to see what the commotion was about, Collins picked off additional victims from open windows and balconies.

Over seventy-five officers arrived on the scene soon after the shooting began. Collins barricaded himself in the apartment and continued firing at the officers. They responded by riddling Collins' building with heavy gunfire and lobbing some twenty canisters of tear gas through his open window. When Collins ceased firing, police entered the building. As they forced his door open, he shot himself through the roof of the mouth. REF.: *CBA.*

Collins, Robert Frederick, 1931- , U.S., jur. Nominated to the court of the eastern district of Louisiana in 1978 by President Jimmy Carter, and a member of the Board of Judges of the Criminal District Court. REF.: *CBA.*

Collins, Roosevelt, 1915-37, U.S., rape. In 1937, Roosevelt Collins, a 22-year-old black man, was accused of raping a white woman as she picked potatoes in Webster County, Ala. An armed mob and their bloodhounds caught Collins as he fled the potato field. The alleged crime shocked the county and the subsequent trial unleashed a barrage of hatred and violence.

Two hundred local residents jammed the courtroom to watch "justice" meted out. Outside, two battalions of National Guardsmen armed with machine guns guarded the courthouse.

Collins' court-appointed attorneys began the trial by explaining that they were hired by the state solely to uphold the defendant's constitutional right to an attorney, stating, "No sympathy for this defendant is implied by our actions."

The plaintiff in the case was a rugged 30-year-old farm woman, thirty pounds heavier than Collins. She testified that he accosted her in the field with a gun, then laid the gun down and forced himself on her. A woman summoning her from the distance frightened him away, she said. Why this strong woman did not overcome her weaker attacker when he dropped his gun was never asked at the trial.

Collins refused his lawyers' advice and took the stand. He had been out rabbit-hunting with a borrowed gun, he said, when he encountered the woman. He described the casual conversation he had had with her and testified that she was a willing participant. With this revelation, the courtroom erupted and the plaintiff's husband pulled a gun from under the table where he was sitting and fired at Collins on the witness stand. The judge ordered a recess until order was restored, and said he did not declare a mistrial at that point because he wanted to "get rid of this mess."

The trial concluded with Collins pleading his innocence, with no help from his attorneys and under a barrage of questions from the Attorney General. After four minutes of deliberation, the all white jury returned a Guilty verdict and the judge sentenced Collins to death. The judge later told reporters that he believed that Collins had been telling the truth and that the plaintiff had lied and several jurors questioned after the trial said they believed Collins' story. "Sure he was telling the truth," one said. "But what the hell, he deserves the chair for messing around with a white woman. Besides, if we had turned him loose, that crowd outside would have lynched us."

Roosevelt Collins was electrocuted in the Kirby Prison in Montgomery, Ala. He walked fearfully to his death, not understanding why he had been convicted. REF.: *CBA*.

Collins, Shirley, 1939-53, Aus., (unsolv.) mur. On Sept. 14, 1953, an elderly man, while walking his dog, discovered the mutilated body of Shirley Collins, the fourteen-year-old girl that Melbourne police had been searching for over the weekend. Collins had disappeared two days earlier, after her mother watched her board a bus to Regent Station. She planned to connect with a train to Richmond to meet 21-year-old Ronald Holmes for her first date. No one had seen her since.

Police conducted one of the widest searches in Melbourne history, but could find no clues. Holmes had waited at Richmond Station for over an hour and finally assumed that Collins had stood him up. Investigators questioned train conductors on both the Richmond and West Richmond lines, suspecting that she had boarded the wrong train. It was Monday morning when the man and his dog found her corpse in Mount Martha, thirty-five miles from Melbourne.

Collins' partially-nude body was lying near a vacant summer cottage, her head covered with the dress she had been wearing when she left home. She had been severely beaten, her skull crushed by hammered repeatedly with two beer bottles. Broken glass from the bottles lay nearby. Her attacker had ripped off her underclothing, several pieces of which were scattered on the ground and hanging on nearby branches. He finally dropped two fourteen-pound slabs from the cottage sidewalk onto the dead girl's head, crushing it to a pulp.

Investigators determined that Collins had not been raped, and described her killer as a sadist with a fetish for women's underwear. The largest force of plainclothes officers for any case in Melbourne history scoured the city's seedy clubs and cafes, but turned up nothing. Radio stations aired a dramatization based on available evidence of the last five hours of the girl's life to over one million listeners.

Following the broadcast, nearly 600 people called police claiming to have information on the case. None of the information led to an arrest. Today, the death of Shirley Collins remains a mystery.

REF.: *CBA*; Godwin, *Killers Unknown*; Gurr, *Famous Australasian Crimes*; Nash, *Open Files*.

Collins, William, d.1878, U.S., west. outl. A brother of the more celebrated Joel Collins, William Collins, began robbing trains after his brother Joel was killed by lawmen in 1877. Following a train robbery in Mesquite, Texas, Collins fled north on horseback, a posse tracking him through Colorado, Wyoming, the Black Hills, and then into Canada. U.S. marshal Bill Anderson alone finally cornered Collins in Pembina, Manitoba, Can. On Nov. 8, 1878, both Collins and Anderson faced each other, drawing their six-guns, advancing on each other, and emptying their revolvers at the same time. Both died from their wounds. Anderson's body was shipped back to Texas and his widow was given the $10,000 reward posted for Collins. The outlaw's body was buried in Pembina.

REF.: Armitage, *Bow Street Runners*; Bartholomew, *The Biographical Album of Western Gunfighters*; *CBA*.

Collins, Dr. W. Maunsell, b.1844, Brit., mansl. Dr. W. Maunsell Collins, a prominent physician who practiced in London's fashionable West End during the 1880s, was a back-alley abor-

tionist at a time when abortions were illegal. In June 1898, Collins performed an abortion on Mrs. Douglas Uzielli, who developed an infection and died of septic peritonitis, a condition caused by lack of proper aseptic precautions. Proper precautions, however, were next to impossible given the secrecy surrounding illegal abortions, making serious infection a risk of the shady procedure.

Charged with murder in Uzielli's death, Collins went to trial on June 27, 1898. Maintaining his innocence, he explained that he was treating Uzielli for a miscarriage and that the infection resulted from that condition rather than from an illegal abortion. After fifty minutes of deliberation, the jury returned with a verdict of Guilty on the charge of manslaughter, but urged the judge to have mercy on the doctor. The judge sentenced Collins to seven years at a penal colony.

REF.: *CBA*; Parry, *Some Famous Medical Trials*.

Collinson, William Robert, 1912- , U.S., jur. Prosecuting attorney in Springfield, Mo., from 1941-44 and president of the Missouri Prosecuting Attorneys Association in 1941. Nominated by President Lyndon Johnson to the district court of Missouri in 1965. REF.: *CBA*.

Collinsworth, Willion, 1936- , **Scarborough, Patrick**, 1939- , **Beagles, David Ervin**, 1941- , and **Stoutamire, Ollie**, 1943- , U.S., rape. That an all-white jury sentenced Willion Collinsworth, Patrick Scarborough, David Ervin Beagles, and Ollie Stoutamire—four white men—to life in prison for the violent gang rape of a 19-year-old black woman, marked a turning point in Southern justice.

In 1959, the four men abducted the woman, a Florida A&M University college student, from a car parked at a drive-in theater while she sat with her date and another couple. They drove her to a wooded area outside the city limits and, at gunpoint, raped her seven times. Throwing her onto the floorboard of their automobile, they then sped from the scene.

Notified by the woman's companions, Leon County Sheriff's police apprehended the men after a high-speed car chase in excess of 90 mph. Once in custody, however, each confessed, describing the attack in detail.

Charged with sexual assault, Collinsworth, Scarborough, Beagle, and Stoutamire appeared in a Tallahassee circuit court before Judge W. May Walker in June 1959. Although defense attorneys tried to prove the woman had willingly engaged in sexual intercourse with the four men, the jury was not convinced. After three hours of deliberation, they handed the four defendants verdicts of Guilty, recommending mercy, however, to forestall the death penalty.

On June 23, Judge Walker handed down four life sentences. A life sentence for rape in Florida, however, usually results in a minimum of ten years. For Collinsworth, Scarborough, Beagles, and Stoutamire, who were transferred to Raiford State Prison, it meant they were eligible for parole after six months, in December 1959. REF.: *CBA*.

Collot d'Herbois, Jean Marie, 1750-96, Fr., consp. An actor before the French Revolution, he became a member of the Committee of Public Safety from 1793-95, and pursued suspected Royalists. For conspiring in 1794 against Robespierre he was expelled from the Convention and exiled to French Guiana. REF.: *CBA*.

Colman, William T., 1904- , U.S., asslt. For months there were persistent allegations the Colonel William Colman, commander of Selfridge Field in Michigan was running a war-time "country club" for the benefit of his favorite non-commissioned officers. Promotions were doled out to unqualified men whose "apple-polishing" skills were far superior to those who were unable to play the game. It was further alleged that certain Air Force personnel on the base received gifts of property and real estate from families of servicemen interested in keeping their sons stateside.

Until May 5, 1943, the charges against Colonel Colman amounted to little more than hear-say. On that day he summoned a car to his office. The chauffeur, Private William McRae was a black man. Colman had a long standing policy against being driven around the base by a black driver. Without provocation, Colman pulled out a service revolver and shot Private McRae. The soldier was taken to the hospital and Colman was arrested.

The unprovoked shooting revealed the true conditions at Camp Selfridge. A court-martial was convened to investigate the irregularities, and to determine why Colman fired on McRae. Twenty-eight charges were brought against the Colonel by the Government. Described by his own counsel as a "mentally sick man," Colman was demoted to the rank of captain on September 14. He was acquitted on all other charges except for the careless use of a firearm, and drunkenness. At the discretion of the War Department, Colman was permanently retired on Nov. 9 for the good of the service. REF.: *CBA*.

Cologne Witch Trials, 1625-36, Ger., witchcraft. Seventeenth century Germany was the site of a witch-hunt so vicious that it required the intervention of the Pope. Across the countryside, women accused of witchcraft were tried at their family's expense, condemned, and killed—the mode of torture and execution left to the discretion of the executioner. The latter's methods being less than savory, the city of Cologne, alone in Germany, made executions the province of the Church while prohibiting the Church from confiscating the property of the condemned—a widespread practice in other districts.

One of Cologne's most infamous trials was that of Catherine Henot accused of bewitching the Sisters of St. Clare in 1626. Found Not Guilty when her counsel argued that the claims of those possessed by demons could not be accurate, Henot was tried a second time at the insistence of Archbishop Ferdinand of Cologne, convicted, and burned at the stake. About 1629, a second wave of witch-hunts began when Christine Plum, allegedly possessed by the devil, pointed her finger at certain Cologne residents, including the prelates who refused to believe her.

Regarding such denunciations as less than serious, the church at Cologne tried, with education, to put an end to them. Their efforts were largely successful until 1631, when Cologne became a refuge for the Abbot of Fulda, the Archbishop of Mainz, and the bishops of Bamburg, Wurzburg, Worms, and Speyer—witch-hunting church dignitaries driven from their homes to the relative safety of Cologne, where they then renewed their zealous pursuit.

Their reign of terror ended in 1636, with the intervention of the Pope when he sent Cardinals Giretti and Albizzi from Rome. Their visit increased opposition to the witch trials, and fewer women were prosecuted for witchcraft. Cologne's last witchcraft execution occurred in 1655.
REF.: *CBA; Robbins, Encyclopedia of Witchcraft and Demonology.*

Colombiere, Claude de la, 1641-82, Fr., consp. Jesuit professor who became the court attendant to Mary of Modena, the daughter of King James II of England, in 1676. He was jailed that year in connection with the Popish Plot. REF.: *CBA*.

Colombo, Joseph, Sr., 1914-78, U.S., org. crime. New York Mafia-syndicate gang boss Joseph Colombo, Sr. began his criminal career as a lowly thief, until absorbed into the Mafia family run by Joseph Bonanno. When Joe Bananas decided to take over all the Mafia families in 1964, he called his underboss, Joseph Magliocco, giving him a devastating "hit" list of the top Mafia-syndicate leaders. Magliocco, in turn, called Colombo, his top enforcer, telling him that he must murder Thomas Lucchese, Mafia don of New York and New Jersey; Carlo Gambino, Mafia don of Brooklyn; Steven Magaddino, Mafia chief of Buffalo, N.Y.; Frank DiSimone, Mafia head of California, and several others. Colombo took one look at this murder list and realized that such an assignment would mean his own death. He immediately went to those designated to be killed and informed them of Joe Bananas' insane plan.

Bonanno was himself kidnapped and later released on his promise to retire from the rackets. He ostensibly did so, but later began a full-scale war in New York after his son was nearly killed in a Mafia ambush. Colombo appeared to fight on the side of Joe Bananas but really served as an informant to the other Mafia dons so that their forces outgunned the Bonanno faction. For his betrayal, Colombo was later named head of the Joseph Profaci Mafia family in New York. He was an inept crime boss, incurring anger and resentment from his scores of gunmen and racket operators, cutting their salaries and taking from them the profits of petty rackets that had been heretofore their own. When he refused to allow the Gallo brothers a larger share of the take from the rackets they managed for him, Colombo was faced with a full-scale war that cost the lives of many of his men.

Mafia chief Joe Colombo.

In the late 1960s, Colombo again made a serious error in stepping into the limelight by creating an organization he called the Italian-American Civil Rights League. This as-sociation was supposedly or-ganized to promote Italian heritage and to combat the image that all Italians or Sicilians were members of organized crime. In effect, Colombo thought to create a smokescreen wherein his organization would be become so powerful that it would act as a shield to his Mafia-syndicate operations. It was by then ridiculous, thought the other Mafia dons, to attempt to convince the authorities and the public that the Mafia did not exist, which is essentially what Colombo attempted to do. Against the wishes of Mafia leaders, Colombo called for a giant rally in Columbus Circle on June 29, 1970, one that was sponsored by the Italian-American Civil Rights League. Surprisingly, this event was an enormous success, with more than 50,000 persons attending. Politicians suddenly became aware of Colombo's organization and many, including Governor Nelson Rockefeller, became honorary members of the group.

Colombo's thought was to reestablish the kind of fraternal organization that had been typified by the Unione Siciliane, which had been prominent in the U.S. from 1900 through the 1920s, a brotherhood that actually fronted for widespread criminal activities and was controlled by gang leaders in many major U.S. cities. To attack the gang leaders was to attack the Unione Siciliane, which was then a powerful political or-ganization. Colombo sought to neutralize the authority of the police and politicians combating organized crime by establishing a brotherhood that could eventually dictate elections. He seemed well on his way to achieving this end, but his own tightwad tenden-cies brought his group and himself to ruin. The Gallo brothers, who had revolted inside Colombo's Mafia family

Jerome Johnson, Colombo's would-be killer.

because Colombo would not share the spoils, intended to murder Colombo at the next Italian-American Civil Rights League rally.

Joey Gallo, better known as Crazy Joe, planned to gun Colombo down at this second Unity Day ceremony, but he knew full well that Colombo's guards would identify him the moment he arrived. Gallo, however, had important contacts with leaders of black organized crime in Harlem, and he borrowed one of their professional killers who was assigned to murder Colombo. In the crowds assembled on June 28, 1971, was Jerome A. Johnson, a black assassin. Johnson wore a newspaper photographer's badge and was allowed to get close to Colombo as he was haranguing the crowd. Johnson was only a few feet from the Mafia boss when he pulled out a pistol and fired three shots which struck Colombo, one bullet entering his head. Before Johnson could flee, Colombo's bodyguards shot him to death. Colombo was rushed to a

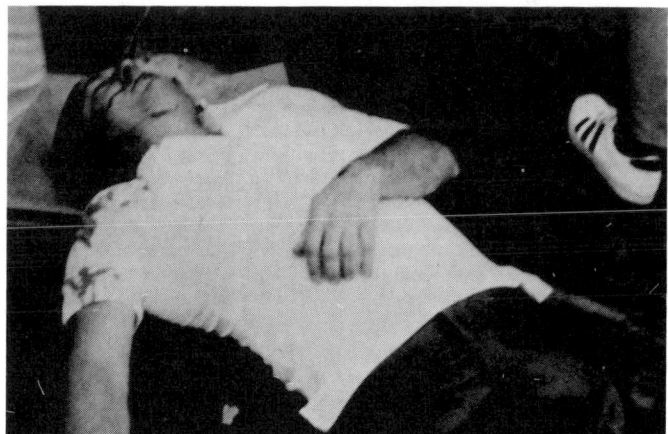

Joe Colombo, after being shot at a New York rally.

hospital where he survived, but suffered permanent brain damage. He lived for another seven years, dying in 1978. But by then Joe Colombo was no longer a potent force in the Mafia. See: **Bonanno, Joseph, Sr.; DiSimone, Frank; Gallo Brothers; Gambino, Carlo; Lucchese, Thomas; Magaddino, Steven; Magliocco, Joseph.**

REF.: Blumenthal, *Last Days of the Sicilians;* Bonanno, *A Man of Honor; CBA;* Cressey, *Theft of the Nation;* Davis, *Mafia Kingfish;* Demaris, *The Last Mafioso;* Gage, *Mafia, U.S.A.;* _____, *The Mafia Is Not An Equal Opportunity Employer;* Godwin, *Murder U.S.A.;* Haskins, *Street Gangs;* Katz, *Uncle Frank;* Maas, *The Valachi Papers;* Messick and Goldblatt, *The Mobs and the Mafia;* Peterson, *The Mob;* Pileggi, *Wiseguy;* Reid, *The Grim Reapers;* Servadio, *The Grim Reapers;* Tully, *Inside the FBI;* Ungar, *FBI.*

Colombo, Marc, 1946-   , Switz., fraud. By manipulating international funds to gain a large profit from the depreciating American dollar, foreign-exchange clerk Marc Colombo gambled away more than £32 million from Britain's Lloyds Bank.

Colombo worked at the Lugano, Switz., branch of Lloyds, and was responsible for buying foreign currency with Swiss francs. Beginning in November 1973, Colombo bought thirty-four million U.S. dollars over three months with Swiss francs from Lloyds Bank, betting that the dollar would continue to fall. Colombo lost the bet, and seven million francs in bank funds.

To recoup his losses, he set up financial transactions totalling £4,580 million over the next nine months, again gambling on the fluctuating dollar. When Colombo bet the dollar would rise, it fell, and when he wagered that it would fall, it rose. He repeatedly exceeded the bank's £700,000 daily limit on transactions.

In August 1974, Colombo's scheme was uncovered when a banker he had been dealing with mentioned the Lugano bank to a senior Lloyds official. The Lloyds banker traced Colombo to the Lugano branch and quickly relieved him of his duties. Colombo and Lugano branch manager Egidio Mombelli were flown to London for questioning by Lloyds officials.

Lloyds' accountants discovered that Colombo still owed £235 million on deals already negotiated, and that his manager had authorized transactions without knowing anything about them. Lloyds took steps to cover their expected losses and, when the dust had settled, lost £32 million on Colombo's transactions.

In 1975, Colombo and Mombelli appeared in a Lugano court on charges of criminal mismanagement, falsifying documents, and violating Swiss banking codes. Mombelli was sentenced to six months in jail and fined £300 for failing to detect Colombo's actions. Colombo got an eighteen-month suspended sentence and a £300 fine. He testified that he had gambled the money only to increase the bank's profits, and maintained that had Lloyds not

prematurely interrupted his transactions, he would have garnered the bank £11 million in profit. REF.: *CBA.*

Colonel Apis, See: **Dimitrijevic, Dragutin.**

Colonial Office Bombing, prom. 1946, Brit., smug.-attempt. bomb. Jewish extremists in Palestine stepped up terrorist attacks against the British colonial government in the months preceding the founding of the state of Israel. In 1945, a bomb obliterated the King David Hotel in Jerusalem, causing many deaths. The bombing campaign reached the British mainland on Apr. 16, 1946, when a young woman entered the Colonial Office in London. She spoke with a heavy foreign accent and wanted to use the restroom to adjust her stockings. Under her coat, the woman carried a homemade dynamite bomb wrapped in newspapers. The bomb failed to detonate because the timing device was jammed. The terrorist, a French national, quickly fled the country and was later arrested by customs officials aboard a Paris-Brussels express train. However, an extradition treaty England had signed with Belgium did not permit anyone charged with a political crime to be returned to the country where the crime originated. The woman was tried on a lesser charge of carrying imported explosives into Belgium. REF.: *CBA.*

Colony Sports Club, prom. 1960s, U.S.-Brit., org. crime. After Fidel Castro drove U.S. gangsters and gamblers out of Cuba in 1959, the Cosa Nostra considered various new locations. Legalized gambling provided a good return with minimal cash outlay. London, in particular, appealed to Meyer Lansky and other U.S. crime syndicate members.

Lansky and Philadelphia crime boss Angelo Bruno opened a number of high-toned gambling resorts in the city. They stipulated that small-time games would remain free of interference, but if a high roller appeared in the casino prepared to drop $30,000 to $40,000 in an hour, the normal rules would not apply.

British authorities eventually detected the mob cheats. Joey Napolitano and Richie Castucci were arrested and deported for their role in rigging the games at the Villa Casino. Lansky's Colony Sports Club was ostensibly fronted by Hollywood actor George Raft. Mafia informant Vinnie Teresa would later say that Raft was just there to lend legitimacy to a criminal enterprise owned by Lansky, Alfie Sulkin, and Dino Cellini.

The lure of George Raft's name brought in millions of dollars to the U.S. syndicate. After several years the British government finally ordered Raft deported. Lansky and his partners held on to their casino, however. See: **Lansky, Meyer.** REF.: *CBA.*

Colorado State Prison Riot, 1929, U.S., riot. The worst prison riot in the history of Colorado occurred at the State Penitentiary at Canon City on Oct. 3, 1929. Disgusted over the inhumane conditions at the prison, Danny Daniels, Jimmy Pardue and a handful of accomplices seized control of Cellhouse three, demanding their release in exchange for the lives of three guards and the prison hangman. Warden Francis Eugene Crawford refused to negotiate, and the hangman and two of the guards were executed. With the situation at a stalemate and over 400 prisoners trapped in the courtyard, the prison chaplain Patrick O'Neill ignited a fifty-pound box of dynamite in the cellhouse.

The walls however, did not fall and the militia was driven back behind the barricades. Reinforced by a 75-millimeter artillery piece, the soldiers cautiously advanced on the convict's stronghold. Seeing no way out, Daniels and his cohorts committed suicide.

A formal investigating commission appointed by the governor of Colorado concluded that inadequate housing, out-dated towers on the walls, and underpaid, corrupt prison guards caused the riot that claimed thirteen lives, and the loss of five buildings. REF.: *CBA.*

Colosimo, James (AKA: **Big Jim**), 1877-1920, U.S., org. crime. In 1895, 17-year-old James Colosimo emigrated with his family from Consenza, Italy. Luigi Colosimo had been a farmer and he became a laborer after arriving in Chicago. His son sought honest work, too, at first. James Colosimo worked as a bootblack, sold newspapers, and even slaved as a water boy for the railroad section workers. Through a political contact, Colosimo, at eighteen, wangled a patronage job with the sanitation department, working as a street sweeper in the vice-ridden First Ward, Chicago's notorious red light district which was called The Levee. Here Colosimo learned the art of pickpocketing and soon became so adept at stealing the wallets of drunks that he was able to quit his broom-pushing job and set himself up as a pimp, offering a string of girls who worked out of cheap cribs in the First Ward. His political sponsors were the most powerful men in Chicago at that time, two colorful, utterly corrupt aldermen, Michael "Hinky Dink" Kenna and John "Bathhouse John" Coughlin. Both represented the First Ward and protected the myriad brothels and gambling dens in that area, deriving enormous kickbacks and percentages of the nightly take from hundreds of vice spots.

The affable, easy-going Colosimo ingratiated himself with the two aldermen and they, in turn, rewarded him with management of first a poolroom, then a saloon. In 1902, Kenna and Coughlin gave "Big Jim" the important post of bagman for all their First Ward rackets. It was his job to make the daily collections from the bordellos, saloons, gambling dens, and opium houses in the district. One of the most successful whorehouses in the area at that time was operated by Victoria Moresco, an obese, decidedly ugly madam in her middle years, whose brothel was located on Armour Avenue. When Big Jim appeared at her doorstep to collect the cut of her take for Kenna and Coughlin, Moresco was immediately attracted to the burly, swarthy Colosimo, a man she later described as having "animal magnetism." Colosimo's virility notwithstanding, he was also a street-smart crook who would go places in Madam Moresco's calculations. The brothel keeper meant only one thing to Colosimo, money, and for that reason he married her. Victoria Moresco had made a fortune in her twenty-some years of peddling flesh in The Levee and she would finance, Big Jim knew, his future bordello and gambling operations.

To that end Colosimo began opening cheap cribs throughout the Levee, one-room affairs where his girls charged $1 and $2 per customer, performing dozens of "tricks" each night. By 1903 Colosimo owned more than 100 of these inexpensive whoring operations, as well as two swanky and celebrated bordellos, the Saratoga and the Victoria, the latter brothel named after his wife. Big Jim received $1.20 from every $2 trick performed by his girls, with 20¢ of this going to Kenna and Coughlin for police and political protection. He branched out, opening dozens of saloons next to his cheaper bordellos. These were connected to his whorehouses by enclosed passageways so that customers could drink themselves silly, then stagger through a passageway into the brothel without being inconvenienced by inclement weather. Big Jim next established gambling houses, and his profits soared. The gambling houses were also connected by underground tunnels to saloons and brothels he owned so that customers could easily escape occasional police raids. In these instances, Big Jim would be warned by Kenna or Coughlin that the police would be making a "show raid" just to pacify reformers, who were constantly campaigning to have The Levee closed.

The problems connected with Colosimo's prostitution business had nothing to do with the law. He, and scores like him, operated with impunity, as long as they paid off Chicago's crooked politicians. Whores were generally "used up" within five years. The young girls entering this unsavory trade, either willfully or by force through the white slave racket, aged quickly and were usually sent down from the better bordellos to the cheaper ones until they found themselves in the worst whorehouses in the Levee, along Bed Bug Row, or had to take to the streets. Disease, drunkenness, and drugs usually finished off a working prostitute in about ten years, so that they were nothing more than incoherent physical hulks, shunned by the seediest customers and their peers. To replenish his always-dwindling supply of attractive young girls, Colosimo joined forces with Maurice Van Bever, a foppish whoremaster who ran two bordellos on Armour Avenue with his wife Julia. Van Bever, from 1903 to 1909, imported hundreds of young girls for Colosimo's whorehouses, obtaining these gullible

girls, ages sixteen to twenty, from white slavers in New York, Milwaukee, and St. Louis.

These girls usually responded to advertisements offering good-paying, respectable positions. Once they were in the clutches of the white slavers, they were locked in rooms and attacked by "professional" rapists who "broke them in" for the trade. These girls were often held captive for months, forced to sexually serve near-inhuman clients, until they felt that they had been morally compromised and that there was no turning back to a respectable life. They were, in their self-estimation and in the terms of that rigidly moralistic era, "fallen women," and were not worthy of a family or home. The first notorious practitioner of the white slave racket in Chicago was Mary Hastings, a Chicago brothel-keeper. Like Hastings, Van Bever and his wife forced young girls into prostitution and then sold them to Colosimo or others for as much as $500. Truculent girls or those who were ill, frail, or uncooperative were sold for as little as $50 to the cheaper bordellos. Colosimo and other big-time bordello operators ceased working with the likes of Van Bever in 1910 when Congress passed the Mann Act or White Slavery Act, which made it a federal offense to transport women across a state line for immoral purposes, chiefly prostitution. This law was so vigorously enforced that, within a decade, white slavery was all but stamped out.

By then Colosimo had an enormous payroll, with hundreds of whores, gamblers, and saloon keepers in his employ. To keep younger, upcoming gangsters in Chicago from cutting into his rackets, Colosimo also hired scores of thugs and gunmen. He had also moved into union racketeering by then, controlling dozens of the most important unions in Chicago and taking a goodly portion of their monthly membership dues. This lucrative racket attracted many independent gangsters who began to threaten Big Jim with death and destruction, most of these threats coming from such accomplished Black Handers as James "Sunny Jim" Cosmano. To combat the nocturnal, lethal creatures who busied themselves with planting bombs in Colosimo's better saloons and gambling dens, Big Jim sent for his nephew in New York, John Torrio, one of the bosses of the notorious Five Points Gang.

Johnny Torrio arrived in Chicago in 1909, at age thirty-one, a crafty, brainy gangster who immediately hired informers who pinpointed the Black Hand operators who had been preying upon his powerful uncle. Three of these men were shot to death after meeting with Torrio and his men near Archer Avenue beneath the Rock Island Railroad overpass. Other Black Handers like Cosmano, quickly ceased their extortion of Chicago's top crime boss, Colosimo. With Torrio now managing his vast criminal empire, Colosimo, in 1910, decided to enjoy life. He opened the most fashionable dining spot in Chicago, Colosimo's Cafe, at 2126 South Wabash Avenue. Colosimo's Cafe was the most lavish nightspot in Chicago with a full orchestra, huge dance floor, and the best cuisine and chefs money could buy. Its talented entertainers were the most expensive headliners of the day, and the place drew the social elite to its tables. Here the Marshall Fields and Potter Palmers dined next to famous actors and actresses. Colosimo was an opera lover, and visiting prima donnas and great tenors were welcomed by him with open arms. It was not uncommon to see the great Italian tenor Enrico Caruso dining in Colosimo's Cafe, nor Mary Garden, Luisa Tetrazzini, Titta Ruffo, John McCormick, and Amelita Galli-Curci. Broadway entertainers such as Al Jolson, Sophie Tucker, George M. Cohan, and Gallagher and Shean also flocked to Colosimo's when playing the Chicago theaters, along with John Barrymore, and Tyrone Power, Sr.

Seated next to these luminaries would be such reporters as Ring Lardner, Ben Hecht, Charles MacArthur, and Carl Sandburg, when they could afford to eat at Colosimo's. And at other tables dined the most notorious gangsters and riffraff of the city such as gamblers Mont Tennes and Julius "Lovin Putty" Annixter, whoremasters Jake and Harry Guzik, Michael "Ike de Pike" Heitler, Charlie "Monkey Face" Genker, Dennis "The Duke" Cooney, and notorious gunmen such as Charles Dion O'Bannion, Mac Fitzpat-

"Big Jim" Colosimo

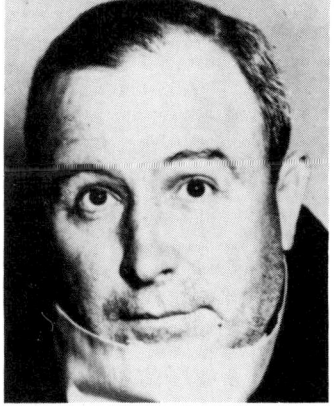

Dale Winter, "Big Jim's" widow.

Colosimo's nephew, Johnny Torrio.

Al Capone, "Big Jim's" killer.

Above, "Big Jim" with his singer-wife, Dale Winter, only weeks before his murder by Al Capone.

Left, the interior of "Big Jim's" famous cafe; right, Big Jim, dead in the foyer, 1920.

rick, Billy Leathers, "Chicken Harry" Gullet, and Joseph "Jew Kid" Grabiner. Most of the gunmen worked for Torrio as Colosimo's strong-arm enforcers, controlling Big Jim's many rackets. Of course, a special table was always reserved for the politicians who had helped Colosimo make his fortune, Kenna and Coughlin.

In 1912, religious reformers began to swarm into the Levee, demanding that the local administration clean up the red light district which was now internationally notorious. Politicians, statesmen, aristocrats, and tycoons of business and industry came from around the world to visit the most elegant bordellos in America, most of these being in Chicago and the finest being that operated by the high-minded Everleigh Sisters. Chicago's reputation as a wide-open city rankled the reformers such as Gypsy Smith, who railed against the wholesale corruption, leading massive torchlight parades into the district at night and delivering hortatory speeches against the bordello owners and gambling house operators. Pressure began to mount against the administration of Harrison Carter, who finally, in 1913, relented and ordered most of the bordellos and gambling halls in The Levee closed.

Colosimo, through Torrio's clever manipulations, opened up new brothels and gambling halls in suburbs like Burnham without losing a dime. William Hale "Big Bill" Thompson, a Republican and one of the most corrupt officials to hold office in the U.S. at any time, announced his candidacy for mayor in 1915 and he was backed by Colosimo and the other crime bosses. He was swept into office and The Levee resumed operations. The district never again approached its former days of open wickedness and sinful opulence. Big Jim was content to enjoy his millions of illicit dollars. He purchased a mansion and moved in with his whorehouse wife. He bought a fleet of chauffeur-driven cars, and adorned himself with diamonds, emulating his friend, Diamond Joe Esposito, crime boss of Chicago's West Side. Colosimo glittered and sparkled like a Christmas tree when receiving famous guests for dinner at his cafe, with diamond cufflinks, diamond studs, diamond rings, and diamond clasps on his suspenders. He reveled in his success and spent most of his time finding ways in which to spend his money while allowing Torrio to run his crime empire.

The methodical Torrio enlarged Colosimo's territory, opening bordellos, gambling houses, and saloons throughout the South and West sides of Chicago. He enforced Big Jim's rules and even directed gun battles against the police when they interfered with Colosimo's operations. Then, in 1918, Big Jim met the love of his life, Dale Winter, a young singer who was appearing in a successful musical, *Madame Sherry*. He showered expensive gifts upon her and then went to his wife, Victoria, demanding a divorce. The overweight harridan had little choice but to do as she was asked, accepting a $50,000 settlement not to contest the divorce action. "I raised one husband for another woman and there's nothing to it," she told the press, but privately, Victoria Moresco vowed revenge, or, at least that was the rumor Johnny Torrio and Al Capone later told to cover up their own assassination of Big Jim Colosimo. Almost as soon as he was divorced, Big Jim married Dale Winter and spent his waking hours seeing to her needs. He hired voice coaches to help improve her voice and financially backed shows in which she appeared. He evicted Victoria Moresco from his mansion at 3156 Vernon Avenue and refurbished the place before taking his new bride home. He even asked Dale Winter's mother to live with them—which she did.

While Big Jim played, Johnny Torrio made plans for the future. He had repeatedly beseeched his old-fashioned uncle to put together an organization that would handle bootlegging since the Volstead Act would go into effect on Jan. 17, 1920. "This will mean millions for us, Uncle Jim," he told Colosimo. "People will have nothing to drink. We'll provide the beer, the liquor. What we can't get from Canada, we'll make ourselves." But Colosimo wanted nothing to do with this new, unproven racket. He considered it "small potatoes," and "chicken feed," not for the likes of a crime czar. (Within five years bootlegging would provide

more than $50 million a year to Torrio and his protegé, Capone.) He also gave Torrio a tongue-lashing for being so presumptuous as to tell him how to run his rackets. Torrio said nothing. He made a phone call to New York and sent for a strong-arm killer whom he had known since childhood, Al Capone. The beefy Capone arrived, his face mutilated in a gang fight for which he was dubbed "Scarface" by those reckless enough to call him that. Torrio put him to work as a bouncer, a saloon manager, and an operator of a lowly whorehouse. His real purpose in Chicago was to kill Big Jim Colosimo, a man whose era was over, or so Johnny Torrio had decreed.

On May 11, 1920, Torrio called Big Jim and informed his boss that two truckloads of whiskey, intended for the deep cellars of Colosimo's Cafe, would be delivered at precisely 4 p.m. Torrio stressed this time and that his uncle should be there to pay more than $50,000 for this important shipment. Colosimo promised that he would be on hand to take delivery at the cafe. He arrived a few hours early and chatted with some of his employees. Colosimo repeatedly walked through the restaurant from his office to the vestibule where he made several calls in a telephone booth. Few employees were about. Inside the restaurant Frank Camilla, Big Jim's secretary, and Chef Caesarino were discussing the menu for the evening. The porter went into the vestibule at one point and noticed a heavyset, swarthy stranger there, but when the porter returned, the man had apparently left. This man was Al Capone, who had never met Big Jim Colosimo, and, while working for Torrio had kept out of sight (as it were) for several months, using the alias A. Costa. After entering the vestibule with a gun in his pocket, Capone had stepped into the cloak room and closed the door to a crack, waiting for Colosimo.

Big Jim reentered the vestibule and looked through the glass doors leading to the street, waiting for the liquor delivery. As he did so, Capone stepped from the cloakroom and fired a single bullet into the back of the crime boss' head, which entered the skull behind the right ear. He fired a second shot, but by then Colosimo had dropped to the floor, dead, and the second bullet slammed into a vestibule wall. Capone tore open Big Jim's shirtfront and ripped off Colosimo's money belt which reportedly contained more than $250,000. This, and the post of second-in-command to Torrio, would be Capone's payoff for executing Colosimo. He then stepped outside and calmly walked down the street to Torrio's Four Deuces, a seedy saloon and brothel, where Capone occasionally worked.

Police arrived a short time later and a rash of arrests followed. Apprehended at one of Chicago's train stations was New York gangster Frankie Yale. He was brought in for questioning, as were dozens of others. Yale proved that at the exact time Colosimo was being shot to death he was addressing a meeting of the Unione Siciliane. Yale was the president of that organization in New York. He was also present to confer with Torrio following Big Jim's assassination as to the best methods of setting up a New York-to-Chicago liquor distribution chain. (Some uninformed crime reporters have claimed that Yale was Colosimo's killer but they have never bothered to research this killing, as well as Yale's whereabouts, nor read the statement given by Colosimo's porter who first "recognized" Capone as the man in the vestibule and later withdrew this claim.) Yale was released and returned to New York. Torrio, a few days later, moved into Big Jim's offices at Colosimo's Cafe, and next to his desk was placed a smaller desk, one which would be occupied by Al Capone. The day of the old-fashioned gangster in Chicago, one that employed brass knuckles and a club instead of a submachine gun, was over. The Torrio-Capone era began that day with a murder that would eventually lead to a city-wide bloodbath that would last a decade. See: **Capone, Alphonse; Coughlin, John; Kenna, Michael; Torrio, John; Unione Siciliane; Yale, Frank.**

REF.: Asbury, *Gem of the Prairie*; CBA; Demaris, *Captive City*; Eisenberg and Landau, *Meyer Lansky*, Gosch and Hammer, *The Last Testament of Lucky Luciano*; Kobler, *Capone*; Lait and Mortimer, *Chicago: Confidential*; Landesco, *Organized Crime In Chicago*; Lustgarten,

The Story of Crime; McPhaul, *Johnny Torrio;* Messick, *Secret File;* ____ and Goldblatt, *The Mobs and the Mafia;* Morgan, *Prince of Crime;* Nash, *Bloodletters and Badmen;* ____, *Open Files;* ____, *People To See;* Peterson, *The Mob;* Reid, *The Grim Reapers;* Reppetto, *The Blue Parade;* Smith, *Syndicate City;* Spiering, *The Man Who Got Capone;* Thompson and Raymond, *Gang Rule In New York;* Willemse, *Behind the Green Lights;* Wilson, *Encyclopedia of Murder;* (FILM), *Little Caesar,* 1931.

Colquhoun, Patrick, 1745-1820, Brit., criminol.   Patrick Colquhoun was a prominent businessman before becoming Lord Provost of Glasgow, England, in 1790, a position he held for two years until 1792 when he was appointed justice of the peace in London.

Colquhoun's theories of the origins of crime, published in 1795, as *A Treatise on the Police of the Metropolis,* soon became the basis for reform within the English police force, making it a forerunner of the centralized police sys-
Early-day criminologist Patrick Colquhoun.
tem that exists today.

REF.: *CBA;* Scott, *Concise Encyclopedia of Crime.*

Colquhoun, Patrick MacChombaich de, 1815-91, Brit., lawyer. Great grandson of Patrick Colquhoin.   REF.: *CBA.*

Colquitt, Walter Terry, 1799-1855, U.S., lawyer. Member of the U.S. House of Representatives, and U.S. senator from 1839-48.   REF.: *CBA.*

Colson, David, b.c.1870, Case of, U.S., mur. On Jan. 16, 1900, in the crowded lobby of the Capitol Hotel in Frankfort, Ky., two army officers opened fire on each other in a duel to settle a long-running argument. In less than one minute, eighteen shots were fired, three men were dead, and three others were injured. Colonel David Colson, wounded in the gunfight, was charged with the murder of his rival, Colonel Ethelbert D. Scott.

Colson and Scott had been feuding since February 1899, when Colson charged Scott with incompetence and questioned his military leadership. Colson charged that Scott was often seen drunk in local bars when both officers were camped with their troops in Anniston, Ala., during the Spanish-American War. A military review board, presented with Scott's case, recommended that he be discharged. But Scott went to Washington, D.C., and used his considerable connections to stay in the army.

On Scott's return to Alabama, Colson made additional charges against him, including insubordination and disobeying orders. Colson requested yet another court martial. The next evening, the two officers inadvertently sat at the same dinner table. As Scott took a seat, Colson insulted him. Scott then stood and fired a shot that hit Colson in the groin. Colson shot back at Scott, but missed. This gunplay was the beginning of the duel that ended one year later in Frankfort.

In the Capitol Hotel shooting, Colson was acquitted of Scott's murder. It has never been determined who fired the first shot. Murder charges against Colson in the two other deaths, that of Charles Julian and 35-year-old lawyer Luther W. Demaree, were dropped.

REF.: *CBA;* Johnson, *Famous Kentucky Tragedies and Trials.*

Colson, Forrest Ray, 1925-51, Case of, U.S., rob. A man left the supermarket with a canvas bag in one hand and a shotgun in the other. He wore a gas mask to hide his identity, and a black helmet adorned with skull and crossbones and three antennae pointing skyward. Two .38-caliber revolvers were strapped to his waist. When he leveled the shotgun at the waiting police officers, they opened fire. Shot in the head, the "Man from Mars" slumped to the ground and was still alive when police removed the mask to discover that it was ex-police officer Forrest Ray Colson who had stolen more than $50,000 from Los Angeles area supermarkets

during the last ten months.

The 26-year-old Colson had been fired twice for his on-duty relationships with women, first from the Monterey Park, Calif., police force, then from the department in Glendora, Calif. He moved to Oklahoma City, Okla., to live with his mother, but took frequent trips to California, hoping that one of the two departments would hire him back.

In January 1951, a mysterious man began robbing supermarkets around Los Angeles. His bizarre attire attracted a great deal of attention but police were unable to catch him, until one evening in October, when an off-duty clerk from a San Gabriel supermarket noticed him getting out of a car parked behind the store. She notified the police, who were waiting for him when he came out. Forrest Ray Colson died two hours after police opened fire on him.   REF.: *CBA.*

Colt, John Caldwell, 1810-42, U.S., mur. Colt was a distinguished citizen of New York, a professional bookkeeper, and teacher of ornamental penmanship. His brother Samuel Colt was the nationally-known creator of the Colt revolver, an invention that reaped the Colt family a fortune. Six years after his brother had revolutionized the pistol industry, John C. Colt set about in his modest fashion to make a name for himself by authoring a work on bookkeeping, a heady tome which he felt sure would become a standard work.

The book was to be a vanity affair, published by Colt himself. The author pinched his pennies during the book's production and often argued vehemently with the printer, one Samuel Adams. On Sept. 17, 1841, Colt and Adams became so enraged with each other over a $10 charge for additional typesetting that they came to blows in Colt's elegantly appointed office at Chambers and Broadway.

During the scuffle, Colt, gentleman bred, turned to lusty murder. From Colt's confession: "He (Adams) made the remark that I meant to cheat him...Word followed word until we came to blows. The words 'you lie' were passed, and several slight blows, until I received a blow across my mouth, and more, which caused my nose slightly to bleed. I do not know that I felt like exerting myself to strong defense. I believe I then struck him violently with my fist. We grappled with each other at the time, and I was shoved against the wall, with my side next to the table. "There was a hammer on the table, which I then immediately seized hold of, and instantly struck him over the head. At this time I think his hat was nearly in my face, and I think his face was downward. I do not think he saw me seize the hammer. The seizing of the hammer and blow were instantaneous. I think this blow knocked his hat off, but will not be positive. At the time I only remember his twisting my neck handkerchief so tight that it seemed to me as if I lost all power of reason, still I thought I was striking away with the hammer. Whether he attempted to get the hammer away from me or not I cannot say. I do not think he did. The first sense of thought was, it seems, as though his hand or something brushed from my neck downward. I cannot say that I had any sense or reflection until I heard a knock at the door, yet a faint idea remains that I shoved him off from me, so that he fell over, but of this I cannot say."

Adams was sprawled quite still on the floor. Colt stood in silence in the middle of his office, staring apprehensively toward the door. The knocking had ceased. Colt took no chances and crept to the door and slowly turned the key, locking it. He felt weak, sick. Sagging into a chair, Colt attempted to regain his composure. "After sitting for a few minutes and seeing so much blood, I think I went and looked at poor Adams, who breathed quite loud for several minutes, threw his arms out, and was silent. I recollect at this time taking him by the hand, which seemed lifeless and the horrid thrill came over me that I had killed him. About this time some noise startled me. I felt agitated and frightened, and I think I went to the door to see if I had fastened it, and took the key out and turned down the slide. I think I stood for a minute or two listening to hear if the affray had caused any alarm. I believe I then took a seat near the window...

"The blood at this time was spreading all over the floor. There was a great quantity, and I felt alarmed lest it should leak through into the apothecary store (below). I tried to stop it by tying my handkerchief around his neck tight. This appeared to do no good. I then looked about the room for a piece of twine and found in a box which stood in the room, after partially pulling out some awning which was in it, a piece of cord, which I tied tight around his neck, after taking his handkerchief off, and his stock too, I think. It was then I discovered so much blood, and the fear of its leaking through the floor caused me to take a towel and gather with it all I could and rinse it in the pail which stood in the room. The pail was, I should think, at that time about one-third full of water, and the blood filled at least another third full.

"Previous to doing this I moved the body toward the box and pulled out part of the awning to rest it on, and covered it up with the remainder. I never saw his face afterward. After soaking up all the blood I could, which I did as still and hastily as possible, I took my seat near the window and began to think what it was best to do. About this time someone knocked on the door, to which, of course, I paid no attention. My horrid situation remained at this time till dark--a silent space of time, with still more horrid reflection."

Closing the packing case, Colt slipped unseen out of his office that night and walked to the City Hotel where he knew his famous brother was staying. He spotted Samuel Colt in conversation with several other men in the lobby and spoke briefly to him but could not bring himself to tell him about the murder. He nervously excused himself and spent several hours in the park pondering his dilemma. "I thought of many things, among others of going to a magistrate and relating the circumstances to him. Then I thought of the horrors of the excitement, the trial, public censure, and false and foul reports that would be raised by the many that would stand ready to make the best appear worse than the worst for the sake of a paltry pittance (the $10 over which Colt and Adams quarreled), gained to them in the publication of perverted truth and original, false, foul, calumniating lies."

Colt thought of setting fire to his office building but feared that the many people who slept there would be burned to death. He abandoned that idea. He then thought of ordering a specially made lead-lined box which would prevent more of Adams' blood from running out but gave up this project. It would take too much time. He then decided to pack up the body in the case and ship it off to some distant point. Returning to his office, Colt stripped Adams' body. Wrapping the corpse tightly in the awning, Colt hammered the case shut.

Wiping the walls where blood had splattered, Colt then went home to his mistress, a beautiful woman named Caroline Henshaw. He did not mention the killing but acted normally, even making love to her. At dawn, the murderer, dressed in his finest suit, returned to his office. He paid a cart man twelve cents to carry the case down several flights of stairs. He engaged another drayman to haul the case to the schooner *Kalamazoo,* which was docked at the foot of Maiden Lane and bound for New Orleans.

Using an alias, Colt signed a receipt for the box and then went off to Lovejoy's Hotel where he settled down to a fine breakfast. All would have gone according to his plan had not the wooden packing case containing Adams' body been cheaply constructed. The victim's blood seeped through the slats and the body was discovered before the *Kalamazoo* sailed. Authorities offered huge rewards for information regarding Adams' movements on the last day of his life and much was made of the packing case. The drayman who had hauled it from Colt's office came forward and identified the man who paid him for the job. John C. Colt was arrested and his confession followed almost immediately.

Sentenced to be hanged in the Tombs on Nov. 18, 1842, Colt told his keepers that the beauty who visited him daily, Miss Henshaw, was his common-law wife. He wanted, as a last wish, to make their union official before the courts and God and he begged them to allow him to marry the lady. Authorities thought

the request unusual but Colt was not the average criminal housed in the Tombs, and the first wedding in the prison was approved.

At 11:30 a.m. on execution day, four hours before Colt was scheduled to drop through the trap on the gallows, some of New York's most distinguished citizens filed into Colt's large cell. Samuel Colt was there. So was John Howard Payne, author and composer of "Home Sweet Home." David Graham, Robert Emmett, Justice Merritt, the Sheriff of the county. All of these powerful and rich gentlemen had fought for months to obtain a pardon for Colt and had been unsuccessful. Following this parade was Caroline Henshaw, lovelier than anyone had ever seen her, and dressed in a claret-colored cloak trimmed with red cord, a green shawl, a muff, and a straw bonnet.

The Reverend Anthon leisurely commenced with the wedding ceremony. Colt appeared to be strangely happy, too happy for a man about to be hanged in a few hours. Colt's request that he be left alone with his bride for an hour following the nuptials was granted by a chivalrous warden. What transpired inside of that cell between Caroline Henshaw and the murdering man she had officially wed has baffled criminologists for more than a century. The wedding guests and guards cluttered the hallway outside, waiting. Then Mrs. Colt emerged and the prisoner was allowed two more hours of solitude, a time of lonely reflection.

As the hour of Colt's doom approached, the warden moved solemnly toward the prisoner's cell to summon him to the gallows. Then, in the words of Tombs historian, John Josiah Munro, "the cry of fire was raised, which caused intense excitement among the officials and prisoners in their cells.

The lurid glare which came from the burning cupola, and which cast a shadow on all sides, attracted wide attention and a great crowd of people. After the fire was extinguished and order once more restored, Colt was found in his cell in a pool of blood. Many persons in the city believed that the burning of the cupola was a well-designed scheme to save Colt from the gallows, and in the midst of the excitement Colt escaped through one of the side doors by the aid of powerful friends and a dead body from one of the hospitals was substituted in his place."

The *Police Gazette* charged that the coroner had been heavily bribed by Colt's friends to pick jury members who were completely unfamiliar with the killer's appearance. Nevertheless, Colt was pronounced dead and the body, whomever it might have been, was quickly burned. Reports, for years, had Colt living in California and Mexico but nobody knew for certain. Colt's alleged disappearance was a sinister hallmark in New York's annals of crime that titillated the city's upper crust in the 1840s, an event of high scandal and black legend.

REF.: *An Authentic Life of John C. Colt;* Bartholomew, *The Biographical Album of Western Gunfighters; CBA;* Duke, *Celebrated Criminal Cases of America;* Lawson, *American State Trials;* Lewis, *Nation-Famous New York Murders; Life, Letters and Last Conversation of John Caldwell Colt;* Pearce, *Unsolved Murder Mysteries;* Pearson, *Instigation of the Devil; The Trial of John C. Colt.*

Colt, Samuel, 1814-62, U.S., firearms inventor. Invented the revolver and secured patent in 1836. He founded the Patent Arms Manufacturing Company and produced weapons for the U.S. Army during the Mexican War. REF.: *CBA.*

Columbo, Patricia, 1957-   , and **DeLuca, Frank,** 1938-   , U.S., mur. At eighteen, Patty Columbo went to work for an Elk Grove Village, Ill., pharmacy. She and the pharmacist, 38-year-old Frank DeLuca, quickly fell in love and were soon sharing an apartment, despite the fact that DeLuca had a wife and five children. But Patty wanted her parents to approve of the relationship, which they refused to do. Frank Columbo, forty-three, was so angered by the situation that he accosted DeLuca in front of his pharmacy, jammed the butt of a rifle into his mouth, and broke his teeth. Patty began to worry that perhaps her angry parents would disinherit her.

In October 1975, Patty Columbo met Lanyon Mitchell, an employee of the Cook County sheriff's office. Within days, she convinced him and his friend, Roman Sobcynski, former deputy sheriff, to kill her parents in return for sexual favors. She joined in orgies with them for several months as they continued to bring up reasons why they couldn't keep their part of the bargain. First they demanded photos of the would-be victims, then floor plans of the Columbos' house, then money that they knew she could not provide. Finally, on May 4, 1976, Patty and DeLuca went to her parents' house and did the deed themselves. Three days later, neighbors called the police, who found Frank Columbo shot four times and with his head crushed; Mary Columbo, shot between the eyes; and Patty's younger brother, Michael Columbo, stabbed eighty-four times.

The day after the murder, Frank DeLuca went to work and proudly told his employees about the deed as he washed his bloodstained clothing, but he threatened their lives and their children's lives if they told anyone. Patty told anyone who would listen that she was certain that the murders had been done by wild kids high on drugs. But the police found on the steering wheel of Frank Columbo's car the print of a three-fingered hand. Frank DeLuca had only three fingers on one hand, the result of a skydiving accident. A friend of Patty's told the police about Lanyon Mitchell, who told them the whole story. Patty Columbo and Frank DeLuca were arrested for murder. Their 1977 trial lasted six weeks, during which Patty tried to distract the jury with her attractive body. On July 1, 1977, the jury found the couple Guilty of three counts of murder. They were each sentenced to two hundred to three hundred years in prison. At the Dwight, Ill., Correctional Center, two years later, Patty Columbo was accused of arranging sexual orgies for inmates and prison officials.

REF.: *CBA*; Nash, *Look For the Woman*.

Colwell, Martin, b.1866, U.S., mur. Martin Colwell was fired from the Vallejo, Calif., Street Department in 1925, because he could not get along with co-workers. On Dec. 19, 1925, Colwell's supervisor at the Street Department, 44-year-old John McCarthy, was shot in the chest after arriving home from work one evening. Friends from the nearby Vallejo Ice Company ran to McCarthy after hearing gunshots and seeing him stumble down his sidewalk in a bloodstained shirt.

When police arrived and attempted to question the semi-conscious McCarthy, he said "I fired Colwell," a sentence he repeated over and over until he died on the way to Vallejo General Hospital. Chief of Police W.T. Stanford and Officer Beck began a search for Colwell.

By 1925, Colwell, at the age of fifty-nine, had served twenty sentences in the county jail for various offenses. He had also been sent to a state hospital from which he escaped, served two terms in a state penitentiary for assault, and one term for burglary. Colwell became violent after drinking, and was drunk when two officers caught him running down the railroad tracks toward Napa, Calif. He carried a .38-caliber revolver with one spent chamber.

When Colwell sobered up the next day, police questioned him about his whereabouts at the time of McCarthy's murder. He replied, "I was drunk and I don't remember anything I did on Saturday." Prosecutors charged him with the murder, even though they lacked any concrete evidence.

Colwell's trial began on Mar. 23, 1926, with Judge Willard T. O'Donnell presiding. This case set a legal precedent, as the prosecution maintained that all bullets fired from a gun contain rifling marks unique to that gun, much like human fingerprints. When ballistics proved the bullet that killed McCarthy came from Colwell's gun, the jury convicted him after only one hour and five minutes of deliberation.

Judge O'Donnell sentenced Colwell to life in California's San Quentin prison. He was later transferred to Folsom Prison, where he spent the rest of his life.

REF.: Block, *Wizard of Berkeley; CBA*.

Combe, Michael, 1960- , U.S., mur. Military recruits from around the country filled the U.S. Navy's Rescue Swimming Pool at the Naval Air Station in Pensacola, Fla., on Mar. 2, 1988, for a routine course on naval lifesaving techniques taught by several instructors, including 28-year-old Michael Combe. Nineteen-

year-old Airman Recruit Lee Mirecki had a diagnosed phobia of submersion in water. He feared this segment of his military training, but cooperated with instructors until the training became violent.

Combe attempted to teach Mirecki a lifesaving technique in which he grabbed him from behind and held him in a headlock underwater. Mirecki had been taught to break such a hold, but was afraid of the water and so resisted Combe's encouragement to try.

Students in the class later testified that Combe forced Mirecki back into the pool, though Mirecki repeatedly shouted requests for permission to drop the class. Witnesses said Mirecki was pried from the equipment rack he clung to and thrown back into the pool where Combe once again practiced the stranglehold on him. The private struggled to break the hold.

When Combe received the cease command from Petty Officer Richard Blevins, who stood outside the pool, he released Mirecki, who had turned pale. When Mirecki was pulled to the side of the pool, he was dead. He died in Combe's arms after suffering a heart attack caused by panic.

Combe faced a court martial on charges of manslaughter and battery. He testified that he did nothing incorrect or against Navy regulations. On Nov. 25, 1988, Combe was found Guilty of negligent homicide and conspiracy to commit battery. He was demoted a rank, reprimanded, and sentenced to ninety days in a military prison. REF.: *CBA*.

Combettes, Cécile, See: **Bonafous, Louis**.

Comeans, William, d.1980, U.S., (unsolv.) mur. "Time is short." "All have been warned." "It's time." These three short notes were sent to residents of New Rome, Ohio, after the death of 14-year-old newsboy William Comeans on Jan. 7, 1980. He had received some threatening notes himself and had told his parents about them. He also told them that two men caught him one day while he was delivering his papers and tried to strangle him, but he escaped. On Jan. 7, he was abducted from his front lawn and then strangled with his scarf. The police were unable to solve the case, and the notes panicked the little town. Parents watched their children closely, but nothing else happened in New Rome after the unsolved murder of William Comeans.

REF.: *CBA*; Nash, *Open Files*.

Comer, Jack (AKA: **Jack Spot**), 1912- , Brit., org. crime. Described in the press as "the nearest approach to the American gangster chief," Jack Comer was for many years the boss of illegal gambling and black marketeering in Britain. Born in Stepney to Polish immigrant parents, Comer rose quickly through the ranks of the British underworld. Known as "Jack Spot" for his habit of getting into a "spot of bother," Comer supervised an army of bookmakers during the 1920s and 1930s. His "Take Your Pick" straw game returned a tidy profit of £40 a day.

British gangster Jack Comer.

During the last few years before the outbreak of WWII, Comer turned his attentions to fighting the English blackshirts, led by their Fascist leader Oswald Mosley. He received six months in prison for assaulting one of Mosley's men. Jack Comer's principle rival for control of the gambling rackets was Billy Hill, whose chief enforcer was a thug named "Italian Albert" Dimes. Comer and Hill craved publicity, and welcomed the chance to publish their memoirs.

Jack Comer assaulted the reporter who was helping Hill prepare his memoirs. On Aug. 11, 1955, after Comer's memoirs appeared in print for the first time, Albert Dimes attacked Comer.

The celebrated knife fight resulted in Comer's acquittal after his wife Rita bribed a witness to testify to the fact that Dimes was the aggressor. The furor died down, and Comer soon announced his retirement. It was more important to be alive and number two, than number one and dead, he reasoned.

The murderous Hill, now seeking permanent residence in Australia, ordered another attack on Comer. It occurred on the night of May 2, 1956, when five razor-wielding men pounced on Jack Spot. They were identified and arrested. Billy Hill was himself "on the spot." He tried to persuade Victor "Scarface Jock" Russo to inflict a knife wound on himself in order to frame Comer as the assailant. He refused, so a second man named Thomas "Big Tony" Falco was ordered to take the cuts. Comer was indicted and placed on trial at the Old Bailey for allegedly slashing Falco outside the Astor Club on Berkeley Square on June 20, 1956. However, the jury saw through the frame. Comer was acquitted on July 18, ending the "affair of the knives."

REF.: *CBA;* Wilkinson, *Behind the Face of Crime.*

Comfort, Robert Anthony (Robert Comperchio), 1932-86, and **Nalo, Sam**, prom. 1972, U.S., rob. Bobby Comfort, the man who would one day rob the Pierre Hotel in Manhattan of $10 million in cash and gems, was trained to be a thief by his mother Peggy, who gained her street smarts in Prohibition Rochester. Peggy's husband, Joe, was a no-account gambler who hid his earnings in a thick wad beneath his pillow

while he slept. Joe was unwilling to provide Peggy with enough money to pay the household expenses. One night she told 7-year-old Bobby to reach under the pillow and pull $20 from the roll. The boy removed the bills without disturbing his father and repeated the procedure many times, sometimes peeling off a few bills for himself.

By the time he was twelve, Bobby Comfort was burglariz- **Bobby Comfort; he robbed New** ing homes all over Rochester, **York's Pierre Hotel of $10 million.** N.Y. The press dubbed him the "Hatless Bandit." Arrested and sent to an industrial school a year later, Bobby proved incorrigible. Not even his family could control him, though his father did teach him one rule: Never admit anything to the police. When Comfort was sixteen, a Rochester judge sentenced the teenager to the New York State Vocational Institution at Coxsackie. He spent the next two decades in and out of correctional facilities.

In 1960, Comfort received two concurrent sentences for an automobile showroom burglary and for his 1959 escape from the Monroe County Jail. At twenty-eight, he could look forward to spending the next thirty-two years of his life behind bars at the Attica State Correctional Facility. Comfort began poring over law books in search of a way out and soon found an amendment to the New York State Correction Law which ruled that a person given an indeterminate sentence could be held a maximum of five years. The amendment was passed five days before the grocery store robbery on Apr. 6, 1949, that earned him a thirty-year sentence.

In 1960, County Judge George Ogden voided Comfort's nineteen-year sentence as a parole violator. Comfort still faced five to ten years for burglary, but was granted final parole on the basis of his IQ report, which showed him to be above average in intelligence. During his time in prison from 1967 to 1969, Comfort acquainted himself with the ways of fashionable New York society. He read Suzy's column in the New York *Post,* and was soon able to chart the movements of the high and mighty from one gala event to the next. Many dignitaries stayed at the Pierre Hotel on 61st Street, where the penthouse apartment was President Richard Nixon's home away from Washington. Its small, intimate lobby made it a perfect target for a stickup.

Comfort decided robbing the Pierre would make him wealthy man and permit him to retire with his wife. In a hansom cab that rolled slowly out of Central Park on Nov. 15, 1971, Comfort outlined his plan to Sammy Nalo, an Arab thief and master of disguise.

At 3:58 a.m. on the morning of Jan. 2, 1972, a rented black Cadillac limousine pulled up in front of the Pierre. Comfort and four associates, including Sammy Nalo, got out of the car and walked past the doormen. The five were wearing tuxedos and appeared to be guests of the hotel. Moments later, they pulled out their guns and announced a holdup. The nineteen guests in the lobby at the time were relieved of their valuables while Nalo rifled through forty-seven safety-deposit boxes. Having read the society pages, Comfort recognized the names: Thomas Yawkey, owner of the Boston Red Sox; Calliope Kulkundis, Greek billionaire; Harold Uris, real estate tycoon. Boxes 154 and 194, stuffed with precious jewels, belonged to socialite and patron of the arts Gabriele Lagerwall. In less than two and a half hours, the Comfort gang fled with nearly $5 million in cash and gems. The Pierre was the fifth swank New York hotel to be robbed in eighteen months. A year earlier, Comfort had allegedly robbed the Hampshire House and made off with $700,000 worth of actress Sophia Loren's jewels, most of them uninsured. Unquestionably, the Pierre job was his masterpiece. "This job," said one detective, "was not performed by virgins."

The next day, Comfort returned to Rochester with his loot. In the New York *Post,* Comfort read Pete Hamill's account, which said the "holdup at the Hotel Pierre was beautiful. Nobody got hurt." On Jan. 7, Comfort returned to New York to rid himself of the stolen gems through the network of underworld fences. Dom Paulino and Benjamin Fradkin kept their rendezvous at the Summit Hotel. As they spread a portion of the gems across the table for appraisal—about one-quarter of the total proceeds from the heist—a squad of New York detectives led by Lieutenant Edward O'Connor broke in on them. A tip from a police informant led to the arrest of the Hotel Pierre burglars, who were taken to FBI headquarters and interrogated. In Paulino's coat, police found the name and address of Comfort's hotel, the Royal Manhattan.

On Jan. 8, the suspects were booked. Nalo and Comfort both pleaded guilty to second-degree burglary. On Dec. 27, 1972, Judge Andrew Tyler sentenced both men to seven years in prison. Stern, who pleaded guilty to possession of stolen property, received one to three years. Paulino and Fradkin were placed on one year's probation for criminal possession of stolen property. The other three thieves were never caught. Comfort served just two and a half years of his sentence at the Attica Correctional Facility. He died on June 6, 1986, in the Rochester Hospital after his second heart attack.

REF.: Berkow, *The Man Who Robbed the Pierre; CBA.*

Comines, Philippe de (Sire d'Argenton) (Philippe de Commynes), c.1447-1511, Fr., treas. Philippe de Comines served the French monarchy for forty years as counselor and ambassador to England, Brittany, and Spain. He was a member of the council of regency during the time of Charles VIII in 1489. He was arrested and exiled for ten years for political reasons. REF.: *CBA.*

Comings, William Freeman, d.1844, U.S., mur. When William Comings awoke on the morning of Sept. 10, 1842, he found his wife, Adeline T. Comings, dead. She had been tied to the bedpost with a handkerchief, brutally beaten and suffocated. Comings was arrested and charged with murder.

He appeared before Judge A.S. Woods in Haverhill, N.H., on Sept. 12, 1843. Following testimony from several witnesses, Comings was found Guilty and sentenced to death. He was hanged on Oct. 30, 1844, after a year-long reprieve during which he attempted to prove his innocence.

REF.: *CBA;* Comings, *Report of the Trial of William F. Comings.*

Commito, Angelo, 1945- , **Mattison, Carl**, 1925- , and **Wire, William**, 1937- , Case of, U.S., fraud-extor. After a three-year

FBI and U.S. Labor Department joint investigation, Angelo Commito, Carl Mattison, and William Wire were charged with conspiring to defraud a janitors' union, the Service Employees International Union (SEIU), of pension funds in a kickback scheme involving North American Life and Casualty Insurance Company.

Commito, owner of the Labor Health and Benefits Plan and Dental Health Care Alternatives, and Mattison, owner of a San Jose, Calif., firm responsible for procuring insurance for labor unions, were charged with bribing Wire, an SEIU official, to steer union officials to buy health insurance for its members from North American Life, a company Commito's firm represented. Commito and Mattison reportedly split a $150,000 commission from North American.

In January 1989, U.S. District Court Judge George Marovich in Chicago, Ill., acquitted all three defendants. At the time, Commito faced charges in Atlanta, Baltimore, and San Diego of paying off a government agent, conspiracy, mail fraud, wire fraud, money laundering, and embezzlement. Both he and Mattison also faced trial in San Francisco on charges of conspiracy, embezzlement, and taking kickbacks. REF.: *CBA*.

Commodus, Lucius Aelius Aurelius, 161-192, Roman., emp., assass. Succeeded his father Marcus Aurelius Antoninus to the throne. His reign was characterized by barbarism and self-indulgence, and he was strangled by an athlete. REF.: *CBA*.

Communist Sedition Trial, 1949, U.S., consp.-treas. In October 1949, eleven high-ranking members of the U.S. Communist Party awaited the jury's decision in a case that, at the time, was the longest legal battle in U.S. history. After nine months of litigation and testimony from fifty witnesses, the jury deliberated for seven hours, then delivered a verdict of Guilty on eleven counts of conspiring to teach and advocate the violent overthrow of the U.S. government.

The Smith Act, passed in 1940, made it a crime for any citizen to teach, advocate, or conspire to commit the overthrow of the government of the United States. Many questioned the constitutionality of the decision, citing the First Amendment guarantee of free speech.

Judge Harold R. Medina, under heavy guard during the trial, sentenced the eleven men to prison terms ranging from three to five years and fines totalling $110,000. Each defendant was fined $10,000, and ten of the eleven defendants got five-year sentences. New York State Communist Party Chairman Robert Thompson got only three years because of his celebrated WWII military record. Thompson was awarded the American Distinguished Service Cross for swimming across a flooded river in New Guinea to destroy two enemy gunnery emplacements. Following sentencing, a furious Thompson said, "I take no pleasure that this Wall Street judicial flunky has seen fit to equate my possession of the D.S.C. (Distinguished Service Cross) with two years in prison." REF.: *CBA*.

Compulsion, 1956, a novel by Meyer Levin. This work is wholly based on the Leopold-Loeb case (U.S., 1924) with Clarence Darrow as the role model for the brilliant criminal attorney whom Levin profiles. A film by the same name was produced in 1959, based on the Levin book. In this motion picture Orson Welles renders a stunning performance of the Darrow character while Dean Stockwell and Bradford Dillman moodily re-enact the roles of the neurotic Leopold and Loeb. See: **Leopold, Nathan F., Jr.** REF.: *CBA*.

Computer Crime, See: **Supplements**, Vol. IV.

Comstock, Anthony, 1844-1915, U.S., reform. Anthony Comstock's crusade against pornography, sin, and intemperance in the U.S., which lasted for five decades, prompted George Bernard Shaw to remark, "Comstockery is the world's standing joke at the expense of the U.S. It confirms the deep-seated conviction of the Old World that America is a provincial place, a second-rate country town." Comstock's crusade to purify the U.S. began in 1862 when he broke into a liquor store in New Canaan, Conn., to drain the spigots on the beer kegs. In the next few years, he took part in the Young Men's Christian Association's campaign to suppress pornography. The fight against indecent literature became his life's work. In 1873, partly because of his work, Congress passed the federal "Comstock Law" which banned obscene material and birth control devices from the U.S. mails. That same year, "special agent" Comstock organized the New York Society for the Suppression of Vice, which conducted a number of sensational raids against the purveyors of literature Comstock deemed unsuitable. What constituted indecency was largely a matter of Comstock's own taste.

George Bernard Shaw, who coined the word "Comstockery," became a target of it with the debut of his play *Mrs. Warren's Profession*. A painting by Paul Chabas titled *September Morn* came under fire from the Comstock crusaders, which only served to make the artist fabulously wealthy. President Woodrow Wilson named the famous censor the U.S. representative to the International Purity Congress in 1915. Comstock became a laughingstock when he arrested several San Francisco department store clerks for clothing a mannequin in full view of passersby. The judge who heard the case the next morning told Comstock, "I think you're nuts." Comstock died on Sept. 21, 1915, leaving two books, *Frauds Exposed*, 1880; and *Traps For the Young*, 1883.

REF.: Asbury, *The Gangs of New York*; Broun and Leech, *Anthony Comstock, Roundsman of the Lord*; CBA; Nash, *Hustlers and Con Men*; Reppetto, *The Blue Parade*.

Comyn, John (AKA: the Younger, the Red), d.1306, Scot., rebel. Member of prominent Scottish family supporting the claim of John de Baliol to the throne. He led resistance to King Edward I but was forced to disarm. He was stabbed to death by Robert Bruce following a quarrel at Dumfries. REF.: *CBA*.

Comyn, Peter, prom. 1830, Ire., arson. In 1830, England's King George IV rescued convicted arsonist Peter Comyn from the gallows, thereby initiating a movement to reform criminal sentencing.

Widely and arbitrarily applied in eighteenth-century England and throughout Europe, the death sentence was handed down for crimes heinous and minor. In 1830, English law required that arson, for example, be punished with death because of the high regard for property.

George IV, however, thought hangings should be reserved for heinous crimes, such as murder. So Comyn's neighbors, in his Clare County, Ire., village, discovering the king's stand on public execution, petitioned him to repeal Comyn's sentence. George IV did so, alone, without consulting his ministers, thereby sparking what would become a constitutional battle over sentencing reforms in England.

REF.: *CBA*; Potter, *The Art of Hanging*.

Conaboy, Richard Paul, 1925- , U.S., jur. Employed on Pennsylvania Liquor Control Board from 1959-62 and received judicial appointment to the court of the middle district of Pennsylvania by President Jimmy Carter in 1979. He served as chairman of the Pennsylvania Commission on Sentencing in 1979 and president of the Pennsylvania Joint Council on Criminal Justice Inc. in 1971. He wrote several articles including *Felony Murder* (1950), *Voiceprints: Trial Problems* (1970). REF.: *CBA*.

Conaway, Asbury Bateman, 1837-97, U.S., jur. Prosecuting attorney at Green River, Wyoming. Territory, from 1881-89. Appointed to the Wyoming Territorial Court by President Benjamin Harrison in 1890. REF.: *CBA*.

Concannon, Jack, 1944- , Case of, U.S., drugs. Having slipped from the limelight of professional football, former Chicago Bears quarterback Jack Concannon, turned to alcohol, and then, unable to meet his debts, turned to trafficking in cocaine.

On Mar. 18, 1981, Concannon was arrested on charges of selling $67,000 worth of cocaine to undercover narcotics agent Ralph Polan. Aided by Sharon Bastian, a friend of Concannon's turned informant, Polan, from Illinois' Northeastern Metropolitan Enforcement Group (MEG), took delivery of 2.2 lbs. of cocaine from the ex-Bear outside an apartment complex in the Chicago suburb of Schaumburg, Ill.

Earlier in the week, Concannon had delivered a sample of the cocaine to Bastian. She gave the sample to Polan, who then engineered the sting operation.

Almost one year later, Concannon appeared before Criminal Court Judge Earl Strayhorn facing a minimum of six years in prison. After three days of arguments, Concannon was acquitted. The judge believed MEG agents had entrapped him in the illegal deal. After Strayhorn delivered the verdict, however, he berated Concannon for drug trafficking, stressing that for thousands of Bears fans, his image was ruined.

Concannon nonetheless left the courtroom a free man. REF.: *CBA*.

Condorcet, Marquis de See: **Caritat, Marie-Jean.**

Coneys, Theodore Edward (AKA: **Matthew Cornish, Spiderman**), 1882-1967, U.S., mur. After twenty-nine years, Theodore Edward Coneys returned to Denver to haunt and inadvertently kill one of the few friends he had as a child.

Born in Petersburg, Ill., Coneys was a sickly, overprotected child. His mother, who had lost her husband when Coneys was an infant, feared a second loss and so sheltered the boy, diverting him from sports into music. At seventeen, after years of mandolin lessons, Coneys and his mother moved to Denver, where he performed for the West Moncrieff Mandolin Club.

It was there that he first met Phil Peters and his wife, Helen—regular concert-goers who admired the young Coneys and listened, often over dinner at their bungalow, to the story of his troubled young life. The relationship continued until the death of Coneys' mother in 1912.

Coneys then left Denver, and would not return for twenty-nine years. By then, Phil Peters, now seventy-three, was preoccupied with the recovery of his wife, then in the hospital. His neighbors were looking after him, inviting him for meals, but one evening he never showed up. Checking the house, and finding all the doors and windows locked, they pried open a screen and crawled inside.

Furniture was overturned, things were strewn about, blood was splattered on the walls, and Phil Peters lay dead on the bedroom floor—beaten about the head with the handle of a gun and an iron shaker, used to stoke the flames in the wood-burning stove.

Led by Captain Jim Childers, the Denver Police Department could find no clues. But had their investigation been as thorough as they thought it was, had they discovered the false plyboard ceiling in the closet, they would have turned up the only clue they needed—the murderer himself.

One year later and still no leads. Helen Peters, after learning of her husband's October 1941 murder, had since abandoned the house. It stood empty, except for the ghosts: images in the windows that could be described in no other way were sighted first by children, then by adults—sightings dismissed as superstition until Helen moved back in 1942.

Needing round-the-clock care, Mrs. Peters hired a live-in nurse. But the nurse and later her replacement both quit within weeks after seeing sights and hearing sounds they could not explain. Helen Peters moved out again soon after, having fallen and broken her hip. She said she had been startled but would not say by what.

Captain Childers began a twenty-four-hour stakeout of the now locked and vacant home. One morning, Childers and his partner saw a shadow pass behind the front window. They bolted to the porch and kicked in the front door. Hearing footsteps on the floor above, they ran upstairs just in time to glimpse a figure climbing through a tiny hole in the ceiling of the bedroom closet.

Theodore Coneys told police he had been living in the bungalow's attic since his return to Denver in September 1941. Broke and homeless, he went to the Peters for a loan. They were not at home, but he went in anyway, eventually coming upon the hole in the closet leading to the attic.

For one month Coneys lived above the Peters, lying still, when they were home, on a makeshift bed—an ironing board laid across

suitcases—and stealing food downstairs when they were gone.

In time Coneys grew brazen, climbing down from his attic hideout while Peters was home. (By then his wife was in the hospital.) He told police he would often shadow the man as he walked through the house, hiding behind doorways to avoid detection. Coneys maintained he meant no harm to Peters, that he stalked him for entertainment.

One evening in October 1941, Coneys crept down to the kitchen, thinking Peters was out. Standing at the icebox, however, he soon found himself face to face with Phil Peters, who had been asleep on the couch. Startled, Coneys grabbed a gun from a kitchen drawer and beat Peters on the head, hitting him with the iron shaker when he tried to escape.

Never knowing if Peters recognized him as the 17-year-old mandolin player he had last seen thirty years before, Coneys was nonetheless convicted for murdering him and was sentenced to life in prison at Colorado's Cañon City Penitentiary, near Colorado Springs.

REF.: *CBA*; Rodell, *Denver Murders*.

Confalonieri, Federico, 1785-1846, Italy, rebel-exile. Head of Milanese federati, seized by the Austrian government following the Piedmontese Revolt of 1821, he was sentenced to life in prison in 1824. His sentence was later commuted and he was exiled to the U.S. REF.: *CBA*.

Confessions of Artemus Quibble, The, 1911, a novel by Arthur Train. This work of fiction is based on the notorious career of criminal lawyer William F. Howe (U.S., 1860s-1990s) who, with his equally venal partner, Abraham Howe, formed the most successful and infamous criminal law firm in America. See: **Howe, William F.** REF.: *CBA*.

Confessore, Alfonse, d.1969, U.S., fraud-(unsolv.) mur. In 1967, Alfonse Confessore worked at a plastics firm that manufactured credit cards for the Diners' Club of America. He learned to operate the production equipment and began to make counterfeit Diners' Club cards while alone in the plant at lunchtime. Realizing that a large underground market existed for the cards, he contacted an organized crime family who agreed to pay $40,000 for 1500 credit cards.

With the deal, Confessore put himself in a bind between the Fraud Squad and the Mafia. In trying to fill the Mafia's order, Confessore exposed his operation. He was convicted on twenty counts of fraud for helping the Mafia bilk Diners' Club out of $621,000.

On Nov. 24, 1969, Confessore left the courthouse on bail to await sentencing. As he stepped onto the sidewalk, three men climbed from a car and shot him dead.

REF.: *CBA*; Rose, *The World's Greatest Rip-Offs*.

Congden, Robert, 1672-91, Brit., rob.-mur. Never apprehended for his many robberies on horseback, Robert Congden was finally arrested for a far more serious crime on foot.

While attending King's College in Cambridge, Bob Congden became a highwayman, having decided the £80 monthly stipend from his father was not enough to live the life he wanted.

Early one morning he attempted his first robbery. Nervous and impatient, and unable to wait while his victim fumbled for his purse, Congden shot the man in the chest and returned to school with the bag of money. Inside the bag he found a letter from his father. He had killed the messenger bringing him his monthly allowance.

Congden immediately withdrew from the university and fled to Holland hoping to escape the law. He then wired his father to confess, expressing deep regret. The elder Congden, moved by his son's plight, wired him £100 in the hope that it would dissuade him from further crimes.

After eighteen months in exile, Congden returned to England. His father's death soon thereafter ended his annuity. Impoverished, he broke into the house of the Earl of Dorset, stealing £1,000 and some silver plate. He then bought a fast horse, two pistols, and a new silver sword—the new tools of his old trade.

Congden was never apprehended for robbery. The London

authorities finally caught up with him near Brook Street in Ratcliffe after he viciously assaulted and killed his landlady with an iron bar. In a rage, he killed the woman's infant and the house maid. With £186 and a silver plate, Congden fled, but he did not get very far.

While trying to sell the plate in a pawn shop, Congdon was arrested. Imprisoned at Newgate, he was sentenced to die on Feb. 27, 1691. Gallows were erected at the door of Captain Githings, owner of the building where the three people were murdered. Afterwards, the corpse was hung in chains between Mile End and Bow.

REF.: *CBA;* Hibbert, *Highwaymen;* Smith, *Highwaymen.*

Conger, Edward, 1882-1963, U.S., jur. District attorney of Duchess County, N.Y., from 1913-16. He was appointed judge of the southern district court of New York in 1938 by President Franklin D. Roosevelt. REF.: *CBA.*

Conger, Everton Judson, 1834-1918, U.S., jur. Police magistrate of Carmi, Ill., from 1871-80. In 1880 he was appointed judge of the territorial court of Montana by President Rutherford B. Hayes. REF.: *CBA.*

Conkling, Alfred, 1789-1874, U.S., jur. District attorney for Montgomery County, N.Y., from 1819-21. He was appointed judge of the northern district of New York by President John Quincy Adams in 1825. He authored many legal treatises and digests. REF.: *CBA.*

Conkling, Roscoe, 1829-88, U.S., lawyer. Republican political boss of New York and powerhouse in Congress. He resigned his Senate seat in 1881 in protest of President James Garfield's policies. REF.: *CBA.*

Conlin, Charles William, 1906-29, Brit., rob.-mur. On Sept. 21, 1928, Charles William Conlin led his grandmother and her second husband into a vacant field where he beat them and then buried them alive.

Conlin had persuaded his grandmother, Emily Francis Kirby, and her husband, Thomas Kirby, to travel with him to his mother's house in Norton, England, on the premise that they should visit because his mother had become very ill. Taking a detour, Conlin forced the elderly couple out into a field where he bludgeoned them, stole their valuables, and dumped them into a shallow grave where they eventually suffocated to death.

A few days after the corpses were found, Conlin was taken into custody. He told investigators that he could not remember anything that had happened between Sept. 18, and the day of his capture on Sept. 22.

He was later charged with the two murders and tried before presiding Justice Roche at Durham Assizes. He was found Guilty of murder and sentenced to be executed. He was hanged Jan. 6, 1929.

REF.: *CBA;* Shew, *A Second Companion to Murder.*

Conlisk, James B., Jr., 1919- , U.S., law enfor. off. James Conlisk, Jr., a twenty-three year veteran of the Chicago Police Department, was appointed police superintendent on Aug. 1, 1967, by Chicago mayor Richard J. Daley. Conlisk began as a beat officer on the city's South Side in 1946. He rose quickly through the ranks, receiving promotions to sergeant in 1952, lieutenant in 1956, and captain in 1959.

Following their father's lead, Conlisk and his two brothers, John and William, became Chicago policemen. Their father James B. Conlisk, Sr., served the city for forty-six years, ending his career as deputy commissioner. REF.: *CBA.*

Connally, John B., See: **Kennedy, John F.**

Connecticut Witches, 1647-62, U.S., witchcraft. Before the infamous Salem witch trials, people were tried, even convicted of witchcraft all over New England. From 1647-62, in Connecticut alone, at least nine people were hanged as suspected witches.

In 1647, Mary Johnson of Wethersfield, Conn., was condemned in the state's first recorded trial. She confessed that the devil appeared before her and shared her bed.

Many of the accused were acquitted. Mary Parsons, who confessed to the murder of her child, was tried and given a reprieve in 1651. Katherine Harrison, who was found Guilty of "familiarity with Sathan {sic}," had her sentence commuted from death to banishment "for her own safety." In 1658 Elizabeth Garlick of Easthampton, N.Y., was tried in Connecticut but set free.

As was the case in Salem, many of the accusations came from adolescent girls and were often found to be spurious in the eyes of the court. In 1662 Ann Cole, a young girl from Hartford, accused two people of witchcraft during a series of fits. One of the defendants was acquitted, but Mother Greensmith, who was already in jail on suspicion of witchcraft, was not so lucky. After the girl's detailed testimony, Mrs. Greensmith and her husband were executed, even though he claimed no knowledge of witchcraft. According to reports, Ann Cole recovered from her ailment immediately after their deaths.

In 1671 16-year-old Elizabeth Knap began having seizures, "sometimes weeping, sometimes laughing, sometimes roaring hideously ...." She accused a woman in her town of Groton as being the cause, but the woman, who was in high public standing, was able to garner enough support to hold off conviction. Knap later admitted that it was not the woman, but the devil himself masquerading as the woman, who had troubled her. Cases such as this led to growing skepticism of largely unproveable witch accusations. REF.: *CBA.*

Connelly, Charles T., d.1892, U.S., west. lawman. Charles T. Connelly was the city marshal at Coffeyville, Kan., at the time when the Dalton gang raided two banks on Oct. 5, 1892. When the outlaws attacked the banks, Connelly was in an upstairs room. He ran to the street and tried to borrow a rifle from George Cubine, who was using the weapon to fire on the Daltons. Cubine told him to find a rifle of his own. Connelly finally managed to grab a rifle and he raced into the street, firing at Grat Dalton, who turned his horse about and raced down the street straight at Connelly,

Charles T. Connelly

shooting him down and killing him with a single shot at a distance of twenty feet. See: **Dalton Brothers.**

REF.: Bartholomew, *A Biographical Album of Western Gunfighters;* *CBA.*

Connelly, William C. (AKA: **Bill Condon, Bill Decker**), and **Bates, Joseph,** and **Clement, Robert**), prom. 1938, U.S., rob. The robbery of the Guarantee Loan Society in Alton, Fla., is a textbook case for young detectives. Through adept sleuthing as well as a couple of good hunches, the robbery was solved and a good portion of the stolen goods recovered in a matter of days.

Anthony Bocchini, the loan society's manager, was coming home from work when two men in a black Plymouth drove up. One of the passengers called out, "Come here, Bocchini, we want to talk about some jewelry." Bocchini was forced at gunpoint into the car. As he and his captors drove on, the men, who referred to each other as "Joe" and "Bob," forced Bocchini to reveal the combination to the loan society's safe. He was left on a deserted roadside under the watchful eye of one of the assailants. After an unsuccessful attempt to open the safe, they forced Bocchini to open it himself, revealing $125,000 in jewelry. They stole the loot, and drove with Bocchini to some woods near Larkspur Valley, where they left him bound and gagged. Bocchini eventually freed himself and found his way to a gas station, where he alerted the authorities.

Bocchini gave a detailed account of the events, and offered the wire used to secure his hands to Alton's chief of detectives, W.D. Hugo, as evidence. But Hugo was unable to uncover a useful lead, so he called in Fred Howard, a private detective.

Howard came up with their first real lead. Bocchini said the robbers had spoken of "Bill's wire," and thought they meant the wire they used to tie him up. Howard conjectured that they might be referring to a telegraph wire instead.

A search through telegraph records netted a number of communiqués between Joseph Bates of Constitution, Ind., and William Condon. One short note read: "I've got a job for you." A message from Bates to Condon read: "Arrive tomorrow." Detectives Hugo and Howard arranged to check out the Indiana address given for Joseph Bates the following day.

One hundred yards from the house, they found the black sedan that Bocchini had described. Inside the house, officers found Bates and his accomplice, Bob Clement, lunching with two women. They surrendered immediately, and about two-thirds of the loot was recovered. Bates gave a full confession, admitting that Condon had hired them for the job, and told the police that the other third of the loot had been given to Condon.

Bates mentioned that Condon had been in WWI, and with this information the detectives were able to get fingerprints and his real name, William C. Connelly, through the Veterans Administration. However, he proved difficult to capture.

Bates and Clement were found Guilty of armed robbery on Mar. 14, 1938, and were sentenced to life. Connelly was finally caught in Shreveport, La., on Mar. 26, 1940. Even though the loot had long since been disposed of, he pleaded guilty to complicity to commit robbery, and was sentenced to ten years, a lighter sentence than the men he had hired to pull off the job. REF.: *CBA; Cohen, One Hundred True Crime Stories.*

Connolly, Maurice E., prom. 1911-28, U.S., polit. corr. As president of the borough of Queens, one of Maurice Connolly's first responsibilities was to supply his electorate with a workable sewer system. As plans for the sanitation system developed, Connolly began drowning in his own ethical quagmire.

Connolly hired James Rice in 1914 as the chief engineer on the sewer project, claiming Rice had an extensive background in supervising such tasks. Rice, however, had actually had minimal experience, and he sparked controversy when he specified a rare type of piping to be used in the sewer project. It was available only through one distributor in Queens: John M. Phillips, a close friend of Connolly.

In late 1927 Governor Alfred E. Smith ordered an inquiry into the matter. Emory Roy Buckner prosecuted, and Max E. Steuer defended Connolly.

Odd things began occurring in 1928. Records that may have proved damaging to Connolly's defense were suddenly missing, allegedly burned or stolen. Connolly actually asked the taxpayers to pay for his defense, since he was a public official. The refusal of that request caused him to resign from his post. The inquiry continued, however, and led to an investigation of the ex-borough president's tax returns after his friend Phillips was arrested for income tax evasion. The indictment finally came down in June 1928: conspiracy to graft on city sewer contracts worth $29.5 million. Connolly, Phillips, and two other men faced the charges.

Phillips died before the trial, and defense attorney Steuer used this to his client's advantage, trying to pin the bulk of the blame on the dead man. "I hope that to God he has made a satisfactory reckoning," he passionately stated. The jury was not swayed: a twenty-four hour deliberation netted a verdict of Guilty, and Connolly was dealt the maximum sentence: a year in jail and a $500 fine. According to New York's law books, graft was only a misdemeanor, with a sentence no stiffer than one would get for spitting in public.

Connolly had served only two days of his sentence when Steuer secured a certificate of reasonable doubt of conviction. After posting $5,000 bail, Connolly went free. REF.: *CBA.*

Connors, Babe, 1856-1918, U.S., pros. Babe Connors, known as a patron of the arts, promoted the black spiritual as a form of popular music at her two lavishly appointed St. Louis brothels. Connors, a mulatto, became the toast of St. Louis in the 1890s, not so much for the illicit nature of her business, (her girls were said to have danced without underclothing on a mirrored floor) but because of the high level of entertainment she featured.

Her two resorts, the Palace on Chestnut Street and the Castle on Sixth, attracted music lovers as well as amorous businessmen. The star attraction was an elderly black woman named Mama Lou who sang gospel and blues. The distinguished European pianist Ignace Paderewski made a special visit to the Castle just to hear Mama Lou. Her original versions provided the melodies for such popular hits as the *Bully Song*, and a *Hot Time in the Old Town Tonight*, which was thought to have been inspired by the Chicago Fire.

Because Connors was black and the inmates for the most part of mixed race, the prevailing racial laws restricted Connors' profit margins. Nevertheless, she became one of the most famous madames of her day. Before she died in 1918, Connors converted to the Catholic faith and was permitted burial in consecrated ground. REF.: *CBA.*

Connors, Charles (AKA: **Ice-Wagon**), prom. 1933, U.S., (unsolv.) mur. A well-known Chicago thief, Charles Connors was found dead in 1933 on the outskirts of the city, shot several times with a .38-caliber gun. Connors was identified by his fingerprints. His killer was never found.

REF.: *CBA; Robinson, Science Catches the Criminal.*

Connors, David (AKA: **Daddy Connors**), d.1896, U.S., mur. While playing dice with fellow gambler James Lamon on Oct. 6, 1893, David Connors started an argument that turned into a fight that ended in murder.

At the fight's inception, the men were separated. Lamon was sent home. But Connors pursued him, pushing past those who tried to stop him. Turning round, Lamon got Connor's knife in the abdomen. Connors then fled. Lamon would die a few days later in St. Luke's Hospital.

With the help of circulars containing Connors' photo and description, Detective N.B. Wooldridge finally located and apprehended him on Apr. 10, 1894. Found Guilty of murder on Nov. 30, 1894, Connors was sentenced to twenty-one years in prison, only two of which he served before he died.

REF.: *CBA; Wooldridge, Hands Up!*

Conrad (Marquis of Montferrat, Lord of Tyre), c.1146-92, Jerusalem, assass. With troops occupied city of Tyre and held it against forces of Saladin. In 1190 he married Isabella, daughter of King Amalric of Jerusalem. He was elected king of Jerusalem but was killed by an agent of the Assassins. See: **Order of the Assassins**. REF.: *CBA.*

Conrad, Fritz, prom. 1881, Ger., mur. Fritz Conrad enjoyed the reputation of being somewhat of an intellectual despite his modest profession of drayman. Conrad had a wife, five children, and a mistress thirty years his junior that he very much wanted to be with. In 1881, Conrad decided to murder his family and disguise the crime so that it looked like a simple case of suicide. The five children were hanged from hooks inside a wardrobe closet. Mrs. Conrad was found suspended from a length of rope attached in the corner of the living room.

Fritz Conrad had succeeded in murdering his family and then had locked the doors from the inside which gave the crime the outward appearances of a suicide. Digging deeper into the available evidence, Berlin detectives found a novel entitled *Nena Sahib*, written by John Ratcliffe. Certain clipped passages from this book discussed the ways and means of affecting a murder from inside a locked room. Coupled with his mistress motive, a Berlin jury found Conrad Guilty of premeditated murder. He was eventually hanged.

REF.: *CBA; Gribble, Adventures In Murder; Wilson, Encyclopedia of Murder; Wren, Masterstrokes of Crime Detection.*

Conradin (Conrad the Younger, Conrad V), 1252-68, Jerusalem-Si., assass. Following the death of Manfred, the king of Naples and Sicily, Conradin set out to recover these lands which had been bestowed as a papal fief to Charles of Anjou by Pope Urban IV. The 16-year-old monarch was defeated and beheaded by Charles in 1268. REF.: *CBA.*

Conrad of Montferrat (Lord of Tyre), c.1146-92, Jerusalem, king, assass. Conrad occupied the city of Tyre and held it against the forces of Saladin. In 1190, he married Isabella, the daughter of King Almeric of Jerusalem. He was elected king, but was killed by the Order of Assassins while attending religious services. The murderers were disguised as Christian monks and had gained entrance to the Crusaders camp where they remained for six months before carrying out the assassination of Conrad. Alamut Ismaili policy dictated that an assassination must be carried out in full view of the public. The killers had waited for just such a moment. See: **Order of the Assassins.**
REF.: *CBA*; Hyams, *Killing No Murder.*

Conring, Herman, 1606-81, Ger., legal historian. Wrote extensively about the history of German jurisprudence. REF.: *CBA*.

Conroy, Patsy, prom. 1870s, U.S., org. crime. Patsy Conroy led a vicious gang of thugs who preyed on barge shipping off Corlear's Hook in New York's Fourth Ward. His henchmen included such underworld stalwarts as Joseph Gayles, who was known as Socco the Bracer; Johnny Dobbs, whose real name was Michael Kerrigan; Pugsy Hurley, Wreck Donovan; and Beeny Kane. This gang, led by Conroy, looted hundreds of small boats and commercial barges for several years until the notorious Conroy was caught red-handed and sent to prison to serve a long term. REF.: *CBA.*

Conroy, Teresa Miriam, 1909- , Brit., mur. A woman who was, in the words of one doctor, "of low intelligence," Teresa Miriam Conroy murdered John Conroy, her 13-year-old son, on or about Sept. 23, 1953. With the utmost care, she placed the body in the base of a divan in their home. She phoned her husband at work on Sept. 25 and told him she and John were leaving to visit a cousin and would be returning in a few days.

Mr. Conroy slept on the divan the night of Sept. 25 and discovered the body the following morning while looking for some change he thought had fallen around the mattress. When first questioned, Mrs. Conroy said her son was in the hospital, and then later admitted that she had interred him in the divan before leaving for her relative's home. She explained that John, who was an epileptic, had had a severe attack on Sept. 22 and had been discovered "drooping" next to the gas oven the following morning. According to her, he began choking soon after and died.

The coroner's report corroborated her testimony, but in addition to a high concentration of coal gas, there was also a dose of methylphenobarbitone twice as great as that considered to be fatal. Charged with murder, Mrs. Conroy pleaded not guilty on Dec. 8, 1953. She was found Guilty but insane, and was ordered to be detained.
REF.: *CBA*; Wilson, *Encyclopedia of Murder.*

Conroy, Thomas, 1903-42, U.S., mur. When 10-year-old Genevieve Connolly disappeared from her Bronx tenement house on Nov. 6, 1940, her parents suspected anyone but soft-spoken Tom Conroy, their friend from the old country.

The thin-faced Irishman worked as a janitor in an apartment building on East 138th Street. The Connollys lived nearby, on Brook Avenue in the South Bronx. From time to time they fed and entertained Conroy and his 10-year-old son, taking pity on the motherless child.

At 7:30 p.m. on Nov. 6, Genevieve left home to visit her girlfriend, who lived next door to where Conroy worked as a maintenance man. When she didn't return by 11:30, Genevieve's father, Robert Connolly, telephoned Conroy to find out if he had seen her in the neighborhood. The janitor explained that yes, she had stopped by, and he had asked the girl to run over to Frank Moran's candy shop to buy him a package of cigarettes.

That much of the story was true. Moran told police he sold the girl a pack of smokes and she skipped out of the store, seemingly carefree. Over 140 Bronx detectives and sanitation workers combed the neighborhood. The police had no leads so they returned to question Conroy. This time, they noticed he wore his shirt inside out. Detectives ordered him to remove it only to find blood stains on the inside.

"Tommy, if you know anything about Jan, I ask you for God's sake and from a mother's heart to speak up," Mary Connolly pleaded in the Alexander Street police station. When the parents left the room, Conroy confessed. He said that after Genevieve left her friend Eileen O'Brien, she made a second trip to the candy store to buy some penny chocolates. At 9 p.m., as she walked west to her tenement building, Conroy called her over. He fondled her. Then, afraid Genevieve would tell her parents, he carried her into the cellar of his building. "I threw her on the coal pile," he explained. "She made gurgling sounds. I pressed her throat and she stopped." He disposed of the corpse in the furnace, throwing in more coal to stoke the hot flames. At 1 a.m., shortly after the detectives visited him for the first time, he removed the ashes and placed them in a trash barrel for pick-up.

When the case went to trial Conroy repudiated his confession on the grounds that it had been obtained under duress. On Apr. 4, 1941, the jury convicted him of strangling Genevieve Connolly. He was put to death in the electric chair at Sing Sing Prison on Jan. 29, 1942. REF.: *CBA.*

Conspiracy of London, The, 1968, Brit., terr.-consp. Fearing that radical leftists planned to disrupt central London through violence and acts of political terror in the fall of 1968, agents from the Special Branch (SB) of Scotland Yard acted quickly to defuse a potentially dangerous situation. The SB learned that various extremists, in sympathy with the U.S. anti-war movement, planned to plant bombs in Westminster and London, targeting offices of the Bank of England, the Stock Exchange, Lloyd's, and the Ministry of Defense.

The disturbances were scheduled to coincide with U.S. anti-war demonstrations on Oct. 28. The organizers of the rally on the British side argued that there was nothing to the rumors, and the fears of the government and SB were totally unfounded. It was decided that the most effective way to curb an outbreak of violence was to arouse public opinion against the demonstrators. The SB leaked the story to the press. The newspapers ran a series of articles that pointed to the threat posed by the leftist leaders. Due to shifting public opinion, the political terrorists aborted their plans.
REF.: Borrell, *Crime In Britain Today*; *CBA.*

Constable, Sir, William, d.1655, Brit., jur.-jailer. One of the jail keepers of Carisbrooke who imprisoned King Charles I. He later sat on the court that condemned the king as an enemy of the state. See: **Charles I**. REF.: *CBA.*

Constans (Flavius Julius Constans), c.323-350, Roman., emp., assass. Youngest son of Constantine the Great who ruled the divided Roman empire of the east: Italy, Africa, and Illyricum. He waged a successful campaign against his brother Constantine in 340, but was killed by the soldiers of Magnentius, emperor of the west. REF.: *CBA.*

Constans II Pogonatus (Flavius Heraclius Constans), 630-668, Roman., assass. Son of Constantine III who ruled the Roman empire of the east, but lost Egypt to the Arabs in 643 and was forced to make concessions and sign a treaty in 659. He issued the edict of Typos in 648 which forbade debate about the true nature of Christ, and exiled Pope Martin I in 653 for nonadherence. In 660 he ordered the murder of his brother Theodosius who stood in the way of his succession to the throne at Syracuse. There he was assassinated in 668. REF.: *CBA.*

Constantine I (The Great, Flavius Valerius Aurelius Constantinus), c.280-337, Roman., mur. One of six claimants to the throne of the Roman empire, he was proclaimed emperor by his father at York, Britain, in 306. At Constantine's order, Maximian was executed in 310 for instigating a conspiracy to gain the throne. He consolidated his rule and prevented barbarian tribes from threatening the empire's borders. He renamed the city of Byzantium Constantinople in 330. REF.: *CBA.*

Constantine III (Flavius Claudius Constantinus), d.411, Roman., emp., assass. Gained control of Britain, Gaul, and Spain through military conquest, and was proclaimed emperor by his army in 407. He was defeated in Italy by Constantius and executed at Ravenna. REF.: *CBA.*

Constantine VII (Porphyrogenitus), 905-959, Roman., emp., assass. Ruled empire jointly with stepfather Romanus I Lecapenus, but was excluded from decision making. He was poisoned by his son, the successor to the throne Romanus II. REF.: *CBA.*

Constantine Asen (Constantine Tych), d.1277, Bul., 1258-77, assass. Chosen as successor to last of the Asen rulers in 1258. He was murdered by a peasant. REF.: *CBA.*

Constantine-Silvanus (Constantine of Mananali), d.c.684, Syria, assass. The likely founder of the Paulicans, a Christian dualist sect. He was seized and executed on the orders of Emperor Constantine IV. REF.: *CBA.*

Conway, Godfrey, 1945-   , Brit., mansl. Godfrey Conway was the product of a troubled home. At the age of seven or eight, he was placed in a children's home in the English Midlands. He was highly regarded by Lucinda Dean, who supervised the boys, and until August 1960, Conway seemed to get along with his schoolmates. One afternoon, Dean sent Conway outside to play until supper. He returned to the home fifteen minutes late, and by himself. Suspicion was aroused when an Anglo-Pakistani boy named Brian Ansara turned up missing at the dinner bell. The next morning his body was found in a hawthorn thicket outside the grounds. The boy had been strangled with a belt that had belonged to Godfrey Conway.

By this time Godfrey had run away. When he was overtaken by a police sergeant, Godfrey explained that he could no longer stand to work in the school garden and had decided to run away. Until the moment he strangled Ansara, Godfrey Conway bore him no personal animosity. When examined by a psychiatrist, it was determined that the youthful killer suffered from a "lack of many of the emotions which are part of the normal mind,"—in short, "a psychopathic personality." A jury found the Conway boy Guilty of manslaughter under the grounds of diminished responsibility. He was ordered detained for ten years according to the terms of the Children and Young Persons Act.

REF.: *CBA;* Wilson, *Children Who Kill.*

Conway, John, d.1891, Brit., mur. John Conway murdered 14-year-old Nicholas Martin in Liverpool. Nicholas' body was found in a carpet bag in the Sandon Basin, and many boys in the area saw Conway carrying the bag. He had scolded them when they offered to carry it for a few coins.

In his defense, Conway said he had found the body in the offices of the Seamen's and Firemen's Union where he worked. Afraid he would be held responsible, he packed the body in the bag and tossed it off St. George's Pier. The contradictory evidence was overwhelming, however, and Conway was found Guilty and sentenced to death.

From the gallows, Conway wished "all my prosecutors to be forgiven by me and by my God." After the hanging, the priest turned to the witnesses and read aloud a full confession that Conway had handed him earlier. He claimed that drunkenness caused in him a "murderous mania and a morbid curiosity to observe the process of dying."

REF.: *CBA;* Smith, *Mysteries of the Missing;* Whitelaw, *Corpus Delicti.*

Conway, Thomas, 1735-c.1800, U.S., consp. Instigator of the Conway Cabal. An Irish soldier who journeyed to the U.S. to fight the British in the Revolutionary War, Conway secured an appointment to serve as major general, against the wishes of General George Washington. He conspired to depose Washington and install General Horatio Gates as the head of the army. The plot, involving several leaders of the Continental Congress, was detected and Conway resigned his commission. He went to France and secured appointment as governor general of French colonial possessions in India in 1787. REF.: *CBA.*

Conwell, Chic, 1887-1933, U.S., pros.-fraud-theft. Involved with the mob on the East Coast for years, Chic Conwell was born in Philadelphia and began a life of crime after marrying a chorus girl. He started as a pimp, became a professional pickpocket and shoplifter, and eventually had minor success as a confidence man. He went to prison three times. At the time of his death, he had given up crime.

REF.: *CBA;* Hamilton, *Men of the Underworld.*

Conyers, James, 1960-   , U.S., mansl. James Conyers was unhappy that his grandmother, Daisy Fredericks, had to work for "white Caucasians." On Nov. 22, 1976, he broke into the Manhattan apartment of her employer, Lawrence Gerber, eighty-four, and his wife, Frances Gerber, seventy-six, and strangled both of them with a necktie from Mr. Gerber's closet. He stole $2,800 and left a message on the wall expressing his need for revenge. Fredericks discovered the bodies when she came to the apartment the following morning.

Detectives found identification cards from Mr. Gerber's wallet in a subway station in the South Bronx shortly after the murder. They had a composite sketch of a suspect from a description by Ralph Figueroa, the doorman in the Gerbers' building, but they could not find anyone matching the description.

Detectives Matthew Rosenthal and Louis de Pasquale had been investigating Conyers because of his violent background. Through interviews in Brooklyn and the Bronx, they discovered that he had boasted to friends that he killed his grandmother's employers.

By then Conyers was serving a one-year sentence for robbery on Rikers Island. He was arraigned on second degree murder charges on June 2, 1977.

But during the trial, Figueroa could not identify Conyers in two different line-ups. Justice Burton B. Roberts cited "inherent weaknesses" in the case and suggested that Conyers plead guilty to the reduced charge of manslaughter, to which Conyers and his attorney agreed.

On Apr. 20, 1978, James Conyers was sentenced to eight to twenty-five years in prison. REF.: *CBA.*

Coo, Eva, d.1935, U.S., mur. Canadian-born "Little Eva" Coo set up a combination brothel, roadhouse, and gas station outside Cooperstown, N.Y. But when the end of Prohibition caused the demise of many such houses, Eva Coo took in Harry Wright, the crippled alcoholic son of an old friend. He stayed with her for four years, until June 15, 1934, when his battered body was found in a ditch about 300 feet from her place. Police first thought he was the victim of a hit-and-run driver, but then an insurance policy on Wright's life, with Eva Coo as the beneficiary, turned up. She and her best friend, Martha Clift, were arrested as material witnesses, then interrogated by the police and insurance investigators until they incriminated each other.

Martha Clift and the prosecution held that Eva Coo had taken Harry to an empty "haunted" farm nearby and hit him over the head with the mallet. Then she had Martha Clift run over the body with her car, after which she moved it to the highway where it was found. They showed that Coo had taken an interest in the terms of Wright's life insurance, double-checking that accidents were covered. Harry Nabinger, Coo's live-in lover, testified that he had written to insurance companies for her, comparing policies and helping her determine which one to buy. Martha Clift, who said she had been promised immunity from a charge of first-degree murder, then reported that Eva had discussed ways of killing Harry Wright with her several times, and she described the murder in detail. Eva Coo was found Guilty and sentenced to die in the electric chair. She was executed on June 28, 1935.

REF.: *CBA;* Kilgallen, *Murder One;* Nash, *Look For the Woman.*

Coogler, Ovida (AKA: Cricket), 1931-49, U.S., (unsolv.) mur. Well known in the bars of Las Cruces, N.M., since she was fourteen, 18-year-old Cricket Coogler disappeared in Spring 1949. Seventeen days later, her body was found in a shallow grave twelve miles away. Without the aid of an autopsy, the sheriff of Las Cruces, A. L. (Happy) Apodaca, declared that she had been raped and murdered.

The sheriff then made a strange move: he secretly jailed a friend of his, Jerry Nuzum, as a prime suspect in the rape-murder. Nuzum, a professional football player with the Pittsburgh Steelers, denied any involvement in the crime. But Apodaca told him that if he chose to leave his "voluntary" confinement, he would be charged with murder. Nuzum stayed put until Walt Finley, a reporter with the El Paso *Herald-Post,* learned of his situation. When Texas newspapers ran the story, Apodaca had to let Nuzum go. Soon after Nuzum's release, Wesley Byrd, a local construction worker, came forward and told of his own twelve-day incarceration, during which Apodaca pressed him to admit to a crime in which he had no part.

The community was infuriated. A group of college students successfully petitioned to have a grand jury called, which indicted the sheriff with the attempted rape of Coogler and seduction of a second teenaged girl. Happy Apodaca was removed from office. The grand jury went on to indict twenty-five people, including Dan Sedillo, the chairman of the State Corporation Commission, who was accused of getting Cricket Coogler drunk and using her "for evil purposes." REF.: *CBA.*

Cook, Charles, 1818-40, U.S., mur. A native of Schenectady, N.Y., Charles Cook, at the age of twenty-two, became enamored with Mrs. Catharine Merry. Over an extended period of time, he made several sexual advances toward the woman, which she continually rebuffed.

Then, on Sept. 22, 1840, Cook broke into Merry's home and attempted to rape her. The woman fought back, but Cook slit her throat and fled. He was apprehended, and when police found the bloody knife in his possession, he confessed to the murder. Charles Cook was hanged in Schenectady on Dec. 18, 1840.

Hanging of Charles Cook.

REF.: *CBA; The Trial, Life and Confessions of Charles Cook.*

Cook, David J., 1842-1907, U.S., law enfor. off. Though not as well known as Wild Bill Hickok, Wyatt Earp, and other gunslinging legends of the Old West, David Cook attained prominence in his own right, for arresting more than 3,000 outlaws. In 1882, he published his memoirs, called *Hands Up! or Twenty Years of Detective Work In the Mountains and on the Plains.* Cook's career began in 1859, when he moved to Colorado.

He joined the Colorado Cavalry, and spent the Civil War years hunting down Confederate spies and smugglers. In 1866, Cook was appointed city marshal of Denver, and later worked as a federal marshal and private eye. Marshal Cook tracked down the dreaded Musgrove-Franklin Gang. In 1868, he put Lee Musgrove behind bars, and then lured Franklin to Denver to try to spring his partner from jail. Cook cornered Franklin in his room at the Overland Hotel. When the gunman reached for his pistol, Cook drilled him through the heart. Throughout his lengthy career in law enforcement, Cook seems to have lived by his one simple credo: "Never hit a man over the head with a pistol, because afterward you may want to use your weapon and find it disabled." REF.: *CBA.*

Cook, DeWitt Clinton, b.1919, U.S., rob.-asslt.-rape-mur. During the 1938-39 school year, Los Angeles City College was the site of a series of brutal attacks, one fatal, by a man wielding a two-by-four. Ruth Alderman, a student, escaped the first attack in October 1938.

On Feb. 24, 1939, Anna Sosoyeva, a 32-year-old dancer and drama student, was bludgeoned with a two-by-four and later died of her injuries. One month later, Delia Bogard, also a dancer at the college, was hit with a two-by-four and robbed of thirty-five cents. She recovered from the attack.

On Aug. 23, 1940, Myrtle Wagner, seventeen, who worked as a nursemaid in the area, was knocked unconscious and raped. A two-by-four was found near the scene. The following evening, the police apprehended DeWitt Clinton Cook for trespassing and found in his car a two-by-four and in his home a pair of shoes that matched a plaster cast of footprints taken near the scene of the assault on Bogard.

Cook, twenty, was on parole from an Iowa reform school. He confessed to more than 300 robberies, as well as the two-by-four attacks.

The authorities brought Cook back to the scene of Sosoyeva's murder and, with a young woman playing the part of the victim, filmed a reenactment of the murder, substituting a rolled-up newspaper for the murder weapon. The film was shown at the trial, where the all-male jury returned a verdict of Guilty after less than an hour of deliberation on Oct. 13, 1939. Four days later, Cook was sentenced to die in the gas chamber.

Cook was also given lesser sentences for various charges stemming from the attacks on Bogard and Wagner, and for three burglaries.

REF.: *CBA;* Wilson, *Encyclopedia of Murder.*

Cook, Dr. Frederick A., c.1865-1940, and **Cox, Seymour E. J.,** prom. 1923, U.S., fraud. When Dr. Frederick Cook was sentenced to prison, Federal Judge John M. Killits said angrily, "Cook, this deal of yours is so damnably rotten that it seems to me your attorneys must have been forced to hold their handkerchiefs to their noses to have represented you. It stinks to high heaven. You should not be allowed to run at large."

Cook was a physician who instead sought fame and fortune as an explorer. He did some sincere exploration of the arctic regions, but felt what he had actually done was ineffective. Initially he simply claimed that he had climbed Alaska's Mt. McKinley. Under photographs of him and some friends supposedly at the summit, he wrote, "The soul-stirring task was crowned with victory; the top of the continent was under our feet." It wasn't until the great peak was actually climbed, in 1913, that it was discovered that the scenery shown in Cook's pictures was far below the summit.

In 1891, Cook went to Greenland and spent the winter with Robert Peary and six others exploring that vast, unknown island. Two years later, he spent a winter locked in a boat in the Antarctic, keeping Roald Amundsen and the crew alive through a scurvy epidemic. On another Antarctic trip in 1899, Cook prepared, from someone else's manuscript, a grammar and

Dr. Frederick Cook

dictionary of a Patagonian language. His plagiarism was detected before the work could be published, and his academic reputation was ruined.

In 1909, after his friend Peary had reached the North Pole, Cook claimed that he had previously achieved the feat with two Eskimos. He submitted a journal to the University of Copenhagen, but they did not accept his proof. They suspected that he had spent the winter in an Eskimo village. However, he went through the rest of his life claiming the honor.

Dr. Cook became involved with confidence artist Seymour E.J. Cox, who had been in the fraud business since he was fifteen. Cox used Cook's famous name to entice investors into an oil stock swindle. This "stock reloading" swindle produced great quantities of cash for Cox and his partners. The men were tried for that scheme in 1923. Cox was fined $8,000 and sentenced to eight years in prison. Dr. Cook earned the judge's wrath, a fine of $12,000, and fourteen years and nine months in prison.

REF.: *CBA;* Hunt, *A Dictionary of Rogues;* MacDougall, *Hoaxes;* Nash, *Hustlers and Con Men.*

Cook, James, 1811-32, Brit., mur. James Cook was the last man gibbeted in England. The grotesque spectacle of his tarred corpse hanging in chains at Saffron Lane was recorded by the novelist Victor Hugo in his *L'Homme qui Rit*. Afterward, the British government permanently abolished the practice.

Cook was a bookbinder in Leicester. Because he could not pay for the tools necessary to run his shop, he accepted a loan from

a Londoner named Mr. Paas. In May 1832 payment on the loan came due. Mr. Paas informed Cook that he would collect the money on May 30. But Cook'd vices had got the better of him, and he could not pay.

When Paas called on May 30, Cook paid him twelve shillings. As Paas prepared to leave, Cook struck him repeatedly over the head. Satisfied that his creditor was dead, Cook left the shop and returned that night to cut the body into small pieces. The next night, he burned down his shop. When questioned

James Cook shortly before his execution.

about the strange odor produced by the flames, Cook explained that it was charred horseflesh. An inquest held in Leicester on June 3 established that the smoldering remains were those of a man.

Cook was arrested, but after he was given bail he tried to flee from Liverpool to America. With the help of the Bow Street Runners, he was apprehended and placed on trial Aug. 7, 1832. Three days later he was hanged at the Leicester Jail and gibbeted before hundreds of rowdy spectators. The practice of hanging the bodies of the condemned in chains was abolished by proclamation on July 25, 1834.

REF.: Andrews, *Old-Time Punishments*; Atholl, *Shadow of the Gallows*; CBA; Forster, *Studies In Black and Red*; Kingston, *Rogues and Adventuresses*; Logan, *Rope, Knife and Chair*; Mencken, *By the Neck*; Wilson, *Encyclopedia of Murder*.

Cook, Japhet (AKA: Sir **Peter Stringer**), prom. 1731, Brit., fraud. Japhet Cook was convicted of forging deeds. His sentence, carried out in June 1731, was time in the public pillory, during which the public executioner cut off both his ears, slit his nostrils and applied a hot iron to one nostril.

REF.: Andrews, *Old-Time Punishments*; CBA.

Cook, Peter, 1928-   , Brit., rape. Peter Cook spent most of his life in mental institutions. On Oct. 18, 1974, he bound and gagged a 20-year-old secretary and raped her. He was implicated in eight rapes over the next ten months, all of them in or around Cambridge. He arrived and departed the scenes of his crimes dressed as a woman and riding a bicycle. In the later rapes, he wore a black leather mask with the word "RAPIST" emblazoned in white across his forehead. On June 8, 1975, police apprehended Cook wearing a woman's dress as he rode his bike away from another rape. He was convicted and sentenced to life imprisonment on Oct. 3, 1975. REF.: CBA.

Cook, Thalis T., prom. 1895, U.S., west lawman. Thalis Cook was a God-fearing gunfighter who belonged to Company D of the Texas Rangers. His work on behalf of the church belied his reputation as a dangerous gunman. He was involved in the 1895 shootout at Marathon, Texas. Cook and his partner, Jim Putnam, were sent in to arrest Fin Gilliland for murder. Gilliland pulled his .45-caliber pistol and took aim at Cook

Lawman Thalis T. Cook.

as the men passed on horseback.

The shot hit Cook in the knee, which caused him permanent disability. Ranger Putnam shot Gilliland's horse from under him, forcing the fugitive to take cover behind the carcass. In the exchange of shots that followed, Gilliland was hit between the eyes. Neither Cook nor his partner was sure who fired the shot.

REF.: Bartholomew, *The Biographical Album of Western Gunfighters*; CBA; Martin, *Border Boss*, O'Neal, *Encyclopedia of Western Gunfighters*; Webb, *The Texas Rangers*.

Cook, William Edward, 1929-52, U.S., abduc.-mur. Within twenty-two days in 1950-51, William Cook abducted nine people and killed six of them. He reacted to the injustices that had befallen him since he was a child by having the words "HARD LUCK" tattooed on the fingers of his left hand.

Cook was one of eight children of an uneducated miner who lived outside Joplin, Mo. When Billy's mother died, W.E. Cook moved the children into an abandoned mine shaft, but soon jumped a freight train and left them to fend for themselves. Social workers found foster homes for all the children except Billy. People were repelled by his drooping right eye lid.

The courts finally agreed to pay a woman to take him in. But the relationship between Billy and his foster mother was not good. For two years in a row she gave him a bicycle for Christmas, only

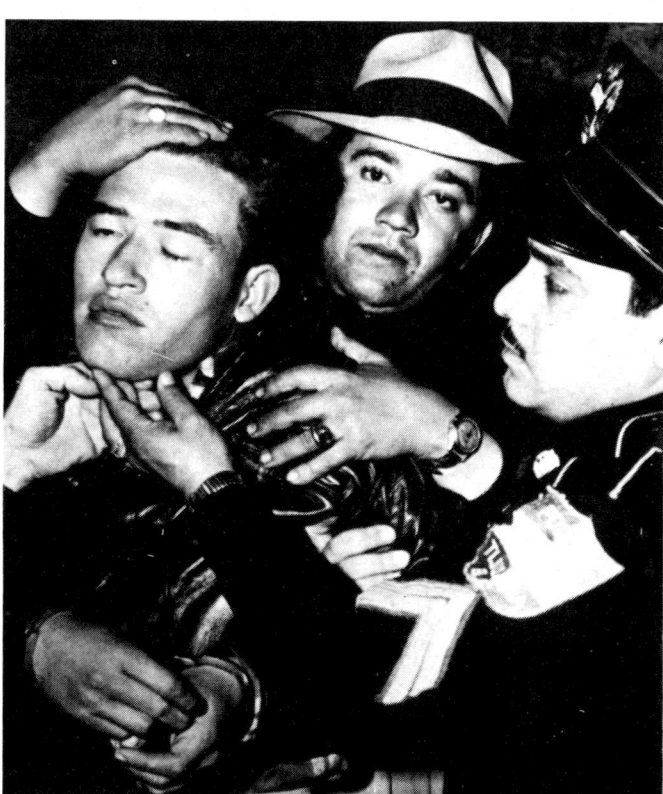

Mass murderer William Cook, being restrained by Mexican police.

to have it repossessed when she could not make the payments. By the time Cook reached his twenty-first birthday, he had served time in both of Missouri's reform schools. When he was seventeen he landed in the Missouri State Penitentiary after robbing a cabdriver of $11 and stealing a car.

Released in 1950, Cook made his way to Joplin and looked up his father. "I'm gonna live by the gun and roam," he vowed. In Blythe, Calif., Cook found a job washing dishes, the only legitimate job he ever had. Just before Christmas, Cook left his job without giving notice, and headed to El Paso, Texas, where he bought a .32-caliber pistol. Outside Lubbock on Dec. 30, Cook hitched a ride with 56-year-old mechanic Lee Archer, whom he robbed and forced into the trunk. The car broke down outside Oklahoma City, but by this time Archer had pried open the trunk's lock and escaped.

On Route 66, Cook flagged down a 1949 Chevy sedan driven by Carl Mosser, a 33-year-old farmer from Atwood, Ill. Mosser was with his wife and three small children in what started out as a vacation trip through the Southwest. For the next three days and nights, Cook drove the Chevy aimlessly. He covered 2,500 miles, crisscrossing Oklahoma, Texas, and Arkansas. When he stopped for gas in Wichita Falls, Texas, Mosser saw one last opportunity to free his family. Inside the store Mosser grabbed Cook and wrestled with him, but the frightened elderly attendant pointed a gun at the two men and ordered them outside. Cook broke free and again subdued his prisoners.

Cook ordered Mosser to drive to Carlsbad, N.M. From there they went to El Paso, Houston, and Winthrop, Ark. The journey ended back in Joplin, Mo. The three Mosser children, Ronald, seven, Pamela, three, and Gary, five, had grown restless. Thelma Mosser, had lost her composure. Cook tied up his hostages and then emptied the .32 on them. Even the family dog did not escape his vengeance.

After throwing the bodies of his victims down a mine shaft in Joplin, Cook drove to Osage County, Okla., where he abandoned the car. Five days after authorities found the car, the killer disarmed Deputy Sheriff Homer Waldrip and took his car. The lawman was found alive, but bound and gagged in the blazing Oklahoma sun. By this time, Cook had abducted his final victim, vacationing Seattle salesman Robert Dewey, who was found in the California desert with a bullet in his head. The police traced Cook to the Mexican border. He had slipped into Tijuana, where, on Jan. 15, 1951, Chief of Police Francisco Kraus Morales arrested him and freed two prospectors from El Centro, Calif., whom Cook had seized during his flight from the U.S.

Cook was extradited to Oklahoma, where federal judge Stephen Chandler sentenced him to five consecutive sixty-year terms in Alcatraz. But Justice Department officials and Judge Chandler surrendered Cook to Imperial County, Calif., where he was convicted and sentenced to death for the murder of Robert Dewey. On Dec. 12, 1952, nearly two years after his murder spree, Billy Cook entered the gas chamber in San Quentin. "I hate everybody's guts and everybody hates mine," he said.

Glan Boydstun, an undertaker in Comanche, Okla., asked Billy's father if he could bring the body back to town for burial, as a kind of memorial. W.E. Cook agreed, not knowing that the undertaker planned to use Billy to advertise his funeral home. A steady flow of people filed past the casket, and Boydstun rented a loudspeaker and hired a preacher to rail against the evils of Satan. This proved too much even for the neglectful W.E. Cook, who filed an injunction against Boydstun. Billy Cook's body was removed to Lone Elm, Kan., and quietly buried.

REF.: *CBA*; Nash, *Bloodletters and Badmen*; Steiger, *The Mass Murderer*; (FILM), *The Hitch-Hiker*, 1953.

Cook, William Tuttle (AKA: John Williams, John Mayfield), b.1873., U.S., west. outl. William Cook was born near Fort Gibson in the Cherokee Nation and was left homeless at age fourteen when his mother died in 1887. Cook served as a scout for U.S. marshals from Fort Smith, Ark., guiding them through the Indian Territory. Judge Isaac Parker in Fort Smith sentenced Cook to forty days in jail in 1893 for the illegal sale of liquor in the Indian Territory. Cook vowed that when he was released, he would put together an outlaw gang and take his revenge. In June 1894, Cook organized one of the most vicious outlaw bands in the territory. Members included Crawford Goldsby, known as Cherokee Bill; Thurman "Skeeter" Baldwin; Jess Snyder; William Farris; Curtis Dayson; Elmer "Chicken" Lucas; Jim French; George Sanders; Sam McWilliams, also known as the Verdigris Kid; Lon Gordon, and Henry Munson. The gang raided banks and trains at will, until dozens of lawmen tracked down these outlaws one by one. Gordon and Munson were trapped after the Cook gang robbed the Chandler, Okla., bank, on July 31, 1894. Both Gordon and Munson shot it out with an entire troop of the Creek Light Horse at Sapulpa, Okla., on Aug. 2, 1894. Munson and Gordon were both killed in this wild gun battle.

The gang then robbed the Kansas City and Missouri Express at Coretta, Okla., on Oct. 20, 1894. At this time Cook ordered his men to go through the coaches while the train was at a standstill, cursing the passengers and firing his six-gun into the air. Unlike Crawford Goldsby, the real killer of the band, Cook was

Bill Cook who led a notorious band of outlaws in the early 1890s.

no gunman and avoided gunplay at all costs. Following the Coretta train robbery, the Cook gang robbed a number of stores and company offices, stealing large payrolls. When the gang robbed the Schufeldt and Son store in Lenapah, Goldsby, for no apparent reason, shot and killed a prominent citizen, Ernest Melton, who was standing in the store looking out a window at the time.

The gang members rode off in different directions, but determined sheriffs and U.S. marshals tracked them down. Dayson and Lucas had been captured after the Chandler, Okla., bank robbery. Both were sent to prison to serve long terms. Then Baldwin, Snyder, and Farris were captured and they, too, were given long prison terms. French, Sanders, and the Verdigris Kid were shot to death by lawmen when they resisted arrest. Goldsby was captured and later hanged for the Melton murder. Cook himself was finally apprehended in a bloodless capture by Sheriff Thomas D. Love of Borden County, Texas, and Sheriff C.C. Perry of Chaves County, N.M., near Fort Sumner, N.M., on Jan. 11, 1895. He was tried for bank robbery before Judge Isaac Parker on Feb. 12, 1895, and found Guilty. Cook was sent to the federal prison at Albany, N.Y., to serve forty-five years. He died some time later in prison. See: **Baldwin, Thurman; Goldsby, Crawford.**

REF.: Bartholomew, *A Biographical Album of Western Gunfighters*; Bristow, *Lost on Grand River*; *CBA*; Coleman, *From Mustanger to Lawyer*; Croy, *He Hanged Them High*; Douglas, *The History of Tulsa, Oklahoma*; Drago, *Outlaws on Horseback*; Emery, *Court of the Damned*; Foreman, *Muskogee, The Biography of an Oklahoma Town*; Glasscock, *Then Came Oil*; Harrington, *Hanging Judge*; Harrison, *Hell Holes and Hangings*; Horan and Sann, *Pictorial History of the Wild West*; Hunter and Rose, *The*

Album of Gunfighters; Jones, *Fiddlefooted;* McKennon, *Iron Men;* Shipman, *Letters Past and Present;* Nash, *Bloodletters and Badmen;* Shirley, *Henry Starr, Last of the Real Bad Men;* _____, *Law West of Fort Smith;* Stansbery, *The Passing of the 3D Ranch;* Steiger, *The Mass Murderer;* Sullivan, *Twelve Years in the Saddle for Law and Order on the Frontiers of Texas;* Wellman, *A Dynasty of Western Outlaws.*

Cooke, Elisha, 1637-1715, U.S., jur. Led protest movement against despotic rule of two British colonial governors, Sir Edmund Andros and Joseph Dudley, both imprisoned in 1689 for infringing on the rights of the colonists in New York and New Jersey. He served as judge of the superior court of Massachusetts from 1694-1702. REF.: *CBA.*

Cooke, Jewey, and **Silverstein, Jack,** prom. 1907, S. Afri., (wrong. convict.) rape. A former British middleweight boxing champion trying to start a boxing career in Rand, S. Afri., Jewey Cooke was known as a proverbial tough guy. He and restaurant owner Jack Silverstein were thought capable of committing the rape they were charged with, but they probably did not.

The girl who accused them was the 14-year-old daughter of a widow who did Cooke's laundry. The girl often returned the laundry to him, and on one such occasion in 1907, she had sexual intercourse with Cooke and Silverstein, who was visiting Cooke. She later went to the police and filed charges. "You call it rape?" Cooke asked incredulously when arrested. "Why, the kid went with me of her own free will."

The trial was held in February 1907, with Justice Curlewis presiding. Attorney General E. Wingfield Douglass prosecuted, and Henry Harris Morris, King's Counsel, defended Cooke. Morris pointed out many inconsistencies in the girl's story, but she managed to evade his more pointed questions.

The jury's sympathy was with the youngster from the beginning. After only an hour of deliberation, they returned a verdict of Guilty for both men. Silverstein received a seven-year prison sentence, and ten lashes. Cooke was given eight years and eight lashes.

After Silverstein and Cooke were in prison, it came out that they had paid the girl for her services, giving her a golden "half sovereign" that was, in fact, a gilded sixpence. But Cooke never told his lawyer this, afraid of facing counterfeiting charges. Morris also mentioned in his memoirs years later that the police told him anyone called to disparage the girl's character would be arrested. It is not clear why Morris never mentioned this threat to the judge.

REF.: Bennett, *Genius For the Defence; CBA.*

Cooks, Tony, 1962- , Case of, U.S., mur. When Tony Cooks walked out of the Los Angeles County courthouse in November 1986, he had earned his acquittal. Three years before, he had been sentenced to fifteen years to life for murder.

On the night of Jan. 19, 1980, John Franklin Gould and Barbara Gould parked their car across the street from their apartment in Paramount. As Mrs. Gould locked the car, Mr. Gould crossed Orange Avenue. Mrs. Gould heard someone call out, "Let's get him," and then saw three black men attack her husband, who fell to the ground. Mrs. Gould saw one of the assailants making jabbing motions, and then heard a shot, at which point the three men ran off together. Frank Gould never regained consciousness, and died thirteen days later.

Within minutes of the attack, police stopped and questioned any young black men they saw in the neighborhood. Helen Foster, a school crossing guard who lived near the scene, said she saw one of the murderers making his getaway.

Sheriff's Detective Vernon J. Clover conducted a photo lineup at Mrs. Foster's home almost two months later. Although she didn't recognize the man from the murder scene, she pointed out that she knew a 14-year-old boy and his half-brother, Douglas Henderson. Mrs. Foster was certain Henderson was not involved in the crime, though he had been Detective Clover's prime suspect.

A few minutes later, when she returned to the crosswalk, Mrs. Foster alerted Clover that she had seen one of the killers. Police picked up three youths: Cooks, twenty-one; the 14-year-old boy identified from the photograph; and Ray Coleman, eighteen. Mrs. Foster said Cooks was the man she had seen on Jan. 19, but she did not recognize either of the other two. Coleman was later cleared and released.

On Mar. 10, while being held on another charge, the 14-year-old who had been stopped with Cooks confessed to Detective Clover that he and Cooks were two of Frank Gould's killers. But his story was inconsistent with other accounts. Four years later the boy admitted that he had made up the confession to protect his half-brother, Douglas Henderson.

Cook's first trial resulted in a hung jury. The jury at the second trial was thrown out when one of the jurors visited the scene of the crime. The third jury was also hung. The fourth jury convicted Tony Cooks of murder. But Judge Roosevelt F. Dorn was convinced that Cooks was innocent and overturned the conviction. An appeals court later overturned Judge Dorn's decision, and he was forced to sentence Cooks.

At the sentencing, Dorn made his opinions clear, calling Clover's efforts "the worst job of investigation I have ever seen." He labeled Gus T. Poole, Cooks' defense attorney, "totally incompetent." He then sentenced Cooks to fifteen years to life and freed him on bail until his appeal could be heard.

The appeal lawyers won a new trial for Cooks, which started Nov. 3, 1986. This time there was new evidence, some of it uncovered by Cooks himself. Among the new findings: Five minutes after the attack, Douglas Henderson had been questioned by police during their canvassing, but was let go. Detective Clover explained that the information on Henderson was "stuck" between the pages of the crime report, causing counsel to miss it in the earlier trials. One of the witnesses identified a photo of Henderson as Tony Cooks, proving their striking resemblance.

After six days of testimony and four hours of deliberation, the jury declared Cooks Not Guilty. Though many believed that Douglas Henderson played a part in the murder, he was not prosecuted, since, according to attorney John Yzurdiaga, Cooks' last counsel, "the identifications are too tainted and the trail too cold." REF.: *CBA.*

Cookson Hills, Okla., prom. 1870s-1930s, U.S., hideout. "A lawbreaker can get lost in those hills for all his life and live off the land without ever being caught," observed one Oklahoman of Cookson Hills. The rugged terrain has provided a safe haven for dozens of lawbreakers, since the 1870s, when the notorious Belle Starr was on the loose. In the 1930s, Pretty Boy Floyd and his gang took refuge in the Cookson Hills, and more recently a U.S. airman who went AWOL from his division in 1943 emerged from hiding there after thirty-six years. Private D.B. Benson remained undetected in the hills, living by his wits in abandoned shacks. He was fifty-seven years old when he came out of his voluntary exile in 1979. Had Benson remained in the Cookson Hills, it is likely he would never have been detected. REF.: *CBA.*

Cool, Floyd, prom. 1931, U.S., boot. Floyd Cool became a bootlegger after a career in the armed forces. In 1931 he was apprehended in the border town of Champlain, N.Y., but escaped into Canada with the man police had handcuffed to him.

He was arrested again when he checked into an Albany hospital months later. Cool was given four years of probation on the condition that he would not return to the bootlegging country in the North.

REF.: *CBA;* Everest, *Rum Across the Border.*

Cooley, Scott, 1845-c.1876, U.S., mur. Scott Cooley, a former member of the Texas Rangers, spurred the Mason County War of 1875 through an act of vengeance against Deputy Sheriff John Worley. Cooley believed that Worley was responsible for the death of his friend and benefactor Tim Williamson.

In September 1875, Deputy Sheriff Worley arrested Williamson on suspicion of cattle rustling. While he was in jail, an angry mob shot Williamson to death. That incident marked the start of the Mason County War, which petted the German cattlemen of Texas against the native-born Texans. Williamson had been killed by the Germans, and when Cooley got word of it, he went to Worley's home. He found the deputy working on his well with an assistant, who had been lowered over the side. Cooley shot Worley dead, and the well worker, who had clung to a rope, tumbled to the bottom.

Cooley cut off his victim's ears, showed them to the anti-Williamson faction, and then killed Peter Border, the second man on his death list. The war dragged on for another year, with many deaths on both sides, until the Texas Rangers restored order. Cooley escaped from a posse at

Lawman-turned-outlaw Scott Cooley.

the Llano River in 1875, and was never heard from again, though some say he died in 1876.

REF.: Bartholomew, *The Biographical Album of Western Gunfighters; CBA;* Douglas, *Famous Texas Feuds;* Gamel, *Life of Thomas M. Gamel;* Gillett, *Six Years with the Texas Rangers;* Hogan, *The Life and Death of Johnny Ringo;* Holloway, *Texas Gun Lore;* Hunter, *Peregrinations of a Pioneer Printer;* _____, and Rose, *The Album of Gunfighters;* O'Neal, *Encyclopedia of Western Gunfighters;* Polk, *Mason and Mason County;* Raht, *The Romance of Davis Mountains and the Big Bend Country;* Webb, *The Texas Rangers.*

Cooley, Thomas McIntyre, 1824-98, U.S., jur. Professor of law at the University of Michigan from 1859-84. Authored legal treatises on constitutional law. REF.: *CBA.*

Cool Hand Luke, See: **Garrison, Donald Luther.**

Coolidge, Edward H., 1937- , U.S., rape-mur. One January afternoon in 1964, Edward H. Coolidge went to Comeau's Tavern in Haverhill, Mass., to find bartender Benny Speros, who also worked with Coolidge as a bakery truck driver. Coolidge, twenty-seven, said his wife had found out he had been unfaithful, and asked Speros to give him an alibi. Speros agreed, provided it was only the wife they were trying to deceive. "It's not only my wife," Coolidge said, "it may be the police."

Overhearing the conversation, the bartender's boss called the Haverhill police. They in turn called the State Police in Concord. The authorities suddenly had a major lead in a recent murder case.

At 6 p.m. on Jan. 13, Pamela Mason, the 14-year-old daughter of Joan Mason, was picked up from her Manchester, N.H., home for a babysitting job. When Mrs. Mason returned from work at 2 a.m. the next morning, Pamela had not come home. She thought her daughter had stayed at a friend's home. But when Pamela did not appear at school the next morning, her mother went to the address Pamela had been given the day before. The couple at that address had no children and knew nothing about Pamela.

Authorities began a full-scale search, and on Jan. 21, found Pamela's partially-clothed body, schoolbooks, and pocketbook in a snowbank on Interstate 93, south of Manchester. The medical examiner found that she had been stabbed four times while undressed, and shot twice in the head with a .22-caliber gun. Her murder occurred only two to four hours after she left home. There was no sign of rape.

Inspectors Maurice LeClerc and Donald F. Glennon began the investigation by reopening a four-year-old unsolved case. Sandra Valade, eighteen, had been found in a snow bank off Derry Road in 1960, raped and shot in the head and back with .22-caliber bullets.

Two men came forward and said that on the night of Mason's disappearance they had seen a Pontiac stuck in a snowdrift where Pamela's body was found. Inspectors LeClerc and Glennon focused their investigation on Pontiac owners.

When the tavern owner gave the police Coolidge's name, they realized that he had been a suspect in the Valade case. They soon discovered that he owned a Pontiac. One of Coolidge's neighbors saw him leave his house at 5 p.m. on the night of the murder and return, his trousers soaked, after 11 p.m.

Coolidge told police several versions of his activities that night, but all were checked and disproved. Several of his acquaintances told police that Coolidge attempted to enlist their help in a false alibi. Coolidge admitted that he feared being considered a witness in the Mason case as he had been in the Valade case. He finally said he simply didn't remember what he had done on Jan. 13.

Police found a Mossberg .22-caliber rifle in Coolidge's home, and ballistics confirmed that it fired the bullets found in Pamela Mason and Sandra Valade. Coolidge was arrested on Feb. 19.

The trial opened in Manchester on May 17, 1965, with Justice Robert F. Griffith presiding. A new technique called "neuron activation analysis" had been used for the first time to identify hairs and fibers on the victim's and defendant's clothes, but when the defense called the scientist who pioneered the process he found the analysis haphazard and incomplete, and the judge rejected the entire scientific report.

Although the scientific evidence had been disallowed, Coolidge was not to go free. He took the witness stand in his own defense, but his testimony, a mass of unlikely and contradictory statements, led to a Guilty verdict on June 23, 1965. Coolidge was sentenced to life in prison.

REF.: *CBA;* Thorwald, *Crime and Science.*

Dr. Valorus P. Coolidge who murdered for profit.

Coolidge, Dr. Valorus P., d.1848, U.S., suic.-mur. Dr. Valorus Coolidge of Waterville, Maine, had a thriving practice, but it was never enough to sustain his lavish lifestyle. As he fell further into debt, Dr. Coolidge solicited loans from several wealthy townsmen. He was refused until he asked Edward Matthews, a drover who expected to sell a herd of cattle for $1,500. Dr. Coolidge promised to repay him within ten days, with $400 interest, and Matthews agreed.

Dr. Coolidge was in no position to pay back any loan. He ordered an ounce of prussic acid, poison from the druggist. On Sept. 19, 1847, he ordered more prussic acid from a Boston drug firm. Meanwhile, Dr. Coolidge kept pressing Matthews for news of the impending sale of the livestock. On Sept. 30, the deal was finalized and Matthews went to the doctor's office to complete the transaction. Handing Matthews a glass of poisoned brandy, Coolidge stood back and waited for it to take effect. With the

$1,500 in hand, he finished Matthews off with a hatchet.

Afterward, he got his trusted medical student, Thomas Flint, to hemp him carry the body to the cellar. Coolidge asked Flint when he thought the remains might be discovered. "At seven o'clock tomorrow morning by the janitor, but the cellar is as far as I go," he answered. The janitor made the discovery the next day, and a coroner's jury asked Dr. Coolidge to perform the autopsy.

Coolidge carefully removed the victim's stomach, where the poison could be found. But he was interrupted by an attendant, and left. While Coolidge was gone, a second doctor had a look, detected prussic acid, and called the police. The remaining poison was found in vials on Coolidge's shelf. Dr. Coolidge was charged with murder and was placed on trial in March 1848. He was convicted after confessing to the murder, and was sentenced to hang. Before the death sentence could be carried out, Coolidge committed suicide, using prussic acid.

REF.: *CBA*; Nash, *Almanac of World Crime;* ____, *Murder, America; Trial of Dr. Valorus P. Coolidge.*

Cooligan, Charles, and **Coveney, Francis,** and **Cheatham, Welden J.,** and **Morris, Colin,** prom. 1930, U.S., smug. Border officials responsible for enforcing U.S. smuggling laws often committed the crime they were supposed to prevent. Charles Cooligan, Francis Coveney, Walden J. Cheatham, and Colin Morris worked on the New York-Canadian border for the U.S. government, and also ran a very effective smuggling ring.

In 1930, the four patrolmen and fourteen civilians were convicted of conspiracy and bribery. Coveney drew the stiffest sentence: three terms of two years, to be served concurrently in an Atlanta penitentiary, and a $2,000 fine. Cooligan got fourteen months, and Morris one year. Cheatham was fined $2,000 and spent twenty months in Atlanta's prison.

Coveney was paroled with nine months still to serve and immediately returned to smuggling. He was arrested again, escaped, was recaptured, and was given a longer sentence.

REF.: *CBA*; Everest, *Rum Across the Border.*

Coombe, Michael, prom. 1988, U.S., negligent homicide. Airman Recruit Lee Mirecki hoped to become a Navy pilot one day, but in order to achieve this goal, the 19-year-old Wisconsin youth had to first pass rescue-training swimming at the Air Station in Pensacola, Fla. The exercise involved the "rescue" of a drowning victim. Mirecki, an otherwise good swimmer failed the drill once. Navy doctors believed he suffered from an underwater phobia. They recommended that he try to overcome these fears by going through the exercise a second time.

On Mar. 2, 1988, Airman Mirecki again failed in his attempt, but this time Petty Officer 2nd Class Michael Coombe was on hand to make sure he passed. While the other recruits stood with their backs to the pool and sang the *Star Spangled Banner,* Coombe and several other instructors threw the frightened Mirecki back into the pool and held him under water for a period of ninety seconds until he lost consciousness. He later died in the hospital.

The family of Airman Mirecki initially accepted the official Navy version that death was due to accidental drowning, but anonymous phone tips from the other recruits who were present that day, convinced them to open an investigation. Petty Officer Coombe was found Guilty of negligent homicide and conspiracy to commit battery before a Naval court martial on Sept. 23, 1988. He received a one-grade demotion, was sentenced to ninety days imprisonment, and was given an official reprimand. The rescue-swimming exercise known as "sharks and daisies" has since been banned from use in the curriculum. REF.: *CBA.*

Coombes, Robert L., 1930-49, U.S., asslt.-rape-mur. The murder of 11-year-old Jacqueline Maxwell of Malden, Mass., on Mar. 2, 1947, led to a careful examination of the laws the allowed a dangerous sex offender like Robert Coombes to be paroled repeatedly, even after his parents urged officials to reconsider.

At twelve, Coombes was charged with breaking and entering—the first, and by far, least serious of his crimes. Only one year later while on parole from reform school in December 1943, he assaulted a 10-year-old girl. He returned to reform school only to be paroled again.

Coombes had been paroled for less than one month when, on Mar. 2, he accosted his last victim, Jacqueline Maxwell. Shortly after nine that evening, a sudden and violent thunderstorm sent movie patrons exiting the Strand Theater running for cover. Perhaps that is why no one noticed Coombs running alongside little Jacqueline Maxwell, who had been to the movies alone.

In the pouring rain, he forced her into the same abandoned lot where he had once sexually assaulted a seven-year old in October 1944. It was all over in just a few minutes. He left Maxwell's strangled corpse lying in the mud where it was found the next morning by three boys on their way to school.

As she listened to the news on the radio that a little girl was missing, Elizabeth Coombes recalled how her son looked when he arrived home the night before; pants wet, streaked with mud. "I knew he had been up to something," she said, "when he refused to tell me where he had been or what he had been doing."

After his son confessed to murdering the child, Francis Coombes, said "They should have kept him in the last time. I felt there was something mentally wrong with the boy that caused him to do these things and that he should have been kept away from general society. They were using old laws in a speeded-up world."

Robert Coombes pleaded guilty to a charge of second-degree murder in Middlesex Superior Court on Oct. 21, 1947. Judge John Sullivan immediately imposed a life sentence saying, "I hope this boy never breathes the fresh air of freedom as long as he lives." Coombes was committed to the Norfolk Prison Colony where he died from tuberculosis in 1949.

Public outcry over the death of Jacqueline led Attorney General Clarence Barnes to organize a special legislative commission to investigate irregularities in the parole system, and to determine what might be done with the other 1,040 sex offenders held in Massachusetts jails and reform schools. Eventually, the Massachusetts legislature passed a bill which made it possible for sexual psychopaths to be institutionalized for life. REF.: *CBA.*

Coombs, George, prom. 1816, Case of, U.S., mur. A sailor, George Coombs had served with distinction on board the *Enterprise* and the *Constitution* during the War of 1812. He lived in Boston with a "fallen woman" named Maria Henry, who was his common-law wife. Coombs took to drinking and beat Henry regularly. One night in 1816 Coombs beat the woman so badly that he ruptured blood vessels which later caused the woman's death. Coombs had beaten her to death in full view of four other women who testified against him at his trial, which took place on June 15, 1816, in Boston. Their testimony was ignored since all four women were known prostitutes. Coombs' service record was read to the jurors, who quickly acquitted him.

REF.: *CBA*; Nash, *Almanac of World Crime; Sketch of the Trial of George Coombs.*

Cooney, Cecilia Roth (AKA: the Bobbed-Haired Bandit), b.1904, and **Cooney, Edward,** b.1899, U.S., rob. Before the police finally put Cecilia Cooney behind bars in 1924, reporters asked, "Who Is the Bobbed-Haired Bandit?" Noted for her fashionable haircut, Cooney was a perpetrator of at least ten Brooklyn robberies. Her story was typical of the reckless 1920s.

Cooney was born into very modest circumstances in the basement of a Manhattan apartment. Michael and Annie Roth were neglectful parents. Cecilia fended for herself, dropped out of high school, and went to work in the laundry of the New York Hospital. In 1923, Cecilia moved in with a man named Cherison, but left him for a garage mechanic named Edward Cooney, by whom she became pregnant. Neither of them had the money to care for a child.

They considered the possibile solutions, including suicide, but decided instead to "rob stores; take from the people who had taken from us." On Jan. 5, 1924, they held up the Roulston Store on Seventh Avenue in Brooklyn. Cecilia pointed the gun at the clerks while Ed took the money from the cash register. They fled on foot with $688.

In the next four months, the husband and wife team pulled off ten robberies in Brooklyn. Because eyewitnesses noticed Cecilia's fashionable hairdo, the press dubbed her the "Bobbed-Haired Bandit" and speculated that she might be the leader of a criminal band. "Her effrontery is amazing," the New York *Times* commented. Five-hundred Brooklyn detectives under the direction of Captain Daniel Carey combed the borough for a suspect. When an innocent woman was taken into custody, Cecilia sent a note denouncing the high-handed tactics of the police. "You dirty fish peddling bums!" she wrote. "Leave this innocent girl alone and get the right one which is nobody but us! We defy you to catch us!"

Deciding that things were getting too warm in Brooklyn, the Cooneys decided to pull one last job before heading to Florida. They hired a limousine to take them to the National Biscuit Company on Pacific Street in Brooklyn, where Ed had heard there was cash in the safe. But the cashier's cage was empty that day. Apr. 1, 1924. In frustration, Cecilia fired off a few shots, wounding an assistant cashier. The couple ran to pier thirty-six and boarded a Florida-bound boat. Cecilia and Ed arrived in Jacksonville with $50 between them. On Apr. 10, she gave birth to a sickly little girl. The infant died five days later.

New York detectives arrived in Florida on Apr. 21 after retrieving an address book that Cecilia left at the baking company. The Cooney's were returned under heavy guard to New York, and charged with ten armed robberies. Despite expert legal counsel from attorney Samuel Liebowitz, the Cooneys were each sentenced to from ten to twenty years. Celia was sent to Auburn Prison and Ed to Sing Sing. In 1931, after serving six years of the original sentence, the Cooneys were reunited. Ed was awarded a $12,000 settlement after losing his arm in an industrial accident in the prison. With this money, the couple bought a small farm in upstate New York. They later had a second child. REF.: *CBA*.

Cooney, Edward J., Jr., 1944- , U.S., abduc.-mur. Described as a "well-adjusted" honor roll student, Edward Cooney of Philadelphia, Pa., killed 3-year-old Becky Holt on June 4, 1959. Hours after the 15-year-old confessed to strangling the girl in his basement, Anatol Holt, Becky's father, wrote a letter which appeared in the Philadelphia *Bulletin* the next day. He expressed "an irrepressible wish to contribute my share of understanding to what has taken place." Holt wondered why a "well-adjusted" and "perfect child" would murder his daughter. "There is something truly terrifying about the model child," he wrote.

Cooney told police that he killed Becky Holt after she resisted his advances. Judge Sydney J. Hoffman of the juvenile division of the municipal court ordered Cooney to undergo a neuro-psychiatric examination. The psychiatrist report concluded that he was of average intelligence but emotionally disturbed. On June 19, District Attorney Victor H. Blanc announced that Cooney would not be tried for murder.

Cooney was arraigned in the juvenile division and committed to the State Industrial School at Camp Hill. He was released on his twenty-first birthday. REF.: *CBA*.

Cooney, Terence George, 1939- , Brit., mur. On the night of Feb. 24, 1958, Terence George Cooney stabbed to death Alan Godfrey Johnson at a dance hall in Barking, in the county of Essex.

A fight broke out when a group of men who had been at a nearby billiard hall arrived at the dance looking for men who were from Canning Town. Only one of the attackers reportedly carried a knife. The others were unarmed. When Johnson was approached and admitted he was from Canning Town, he was attacked and wounded fatally in the stomach. The fight spilled into the street and escalated to a small riot.

When apprehended, Cooney, a 19-year-old laborer, admitted stabbing Johnson, eighteen, but swore that he did not kill him. He claimed that he arrived after the fight began, and that Johnson had attacked him and made a move to his pocket as if fishing for a knife. Cooney said it was then that he pulled his own knife and stabbed Johnson in self-defense. Cooney admitted that Johnson did not have a knife, but said he had no way of knowing that at the time.

Four days of testimony and a twenty-minute deliberation brought the jury to a verdict of Guilty. Terence Cooney was sentenced to life imprisonment.

REF.: *CBA*; Furneaux, *Famous Criminal Cases, Vol. 6*.

Coons, William, 1838-81, U.S., lynch. (vict.)-mur. William Coons homesteaded in Lincoln County, N.M., for nearly two years before his neighbors began to suspect him of stealing cattle and hogs. In 1881, Coons quarreled with his neighbor John Flemming over water rights. In April, Coons shot Flemming on his property, claiming that he did so in self-defense. But eyewitnesses said Coons started shooting when Flemming's back was turned. However, Sheriff Pat Garrett could not find these witnesses to start a criminal proceeding.

Friends of the dead man began whispering "lynch," but the matter died down. A month later, Will Coons celebrated his forty-third birthday with a lavish party at his ranch. Mingling among the celebrants were Flemming's friends. When the party was at its height, the Flemming forces drew their guns and herded everyone into a locked room, leaving Coons to stand alone. In a mock trial, he was found guilty of murder and sentenced to die by hanging from the closest tree on his property. After the jurors drank what was left of the condemned man's whisky, they carried out the sentence. Then, an impromptu band was organized to play a death march for Coons. Those responsible for the lynching were never caught. REF.: *CBA*.

Cooper, Anthony Ashley (First Earl of Shaftesbury), 1621-83, Case of, Brit., treas. Involved with other members of the House of Commons in 1680 in attempting to place James, the Duke of Monmouth on the throne, denying James II his rightful succession. Cooper led an armed revolt on the chambers of Parliament. He was seized and sent to the Tower of London for treason. Acquitted by a grand jury in 1682, he fled to Holland. REF.: *CBA*.

Cooper, Calman, d.1955, and **Dorfman, Benny**, prom. 1940s, and **Stein, Harry**, d.1955, and **Wissner, Nathan**, d.1955, U.S., theft-mur. While serving time for murder and auto theft, Calman Cooper plotted his "perfect crime." After being paroled in 1948, he wasted no time in assembling a group of men to help him carry it out.

Careful planning and observation brought Cooper, Harry Stein, Nathan Wissner, and Benny Dorfman to the long driveway outside Reader's Digest headquarters in Pleasantville, N.Y., on Apr. 3, 1950. When the truck filled with subscriber's payments started down the drive, Cooper and his gang pulled from the side of the road in an old, beaten-up truck. Seeing the truck zig-zag toward him William Waterbury, the Reader's Digest driver, braked. Wissner approached the passenger side of the vehicle and, after trying unsuccessfully to open the door, shot through the window, mortally wounding the passenger, Andrew Petrini.

The gang then forced the driver into the back of his truck, where they bound him securely, then hid the truck among some trees on the side of a road. Taking the bag of money, the four robbers abandoned Waterbury, the dying Petrini, and the commandeered truck and loaded into a gray getaway sedan. Pulling away, they tossed guns and clothing from the windows.

From the criminals' point of view, the heist turned out to be less than perfect. Of the more than $40,000 they had stolen, over $35,000 was in checks.

It did seem, however, to be a perfectly well-hidden crime. For days, investigators watched lead after lead wither away. Then, finding the rental slip for the old truck used in the crime, they saw it had been signed by a "Walter William Comins." Checking further, they discovered that the Manhattan address indicated on the slip was a hotel where Walter William Comins had had been registered in November 1949.

Scouring their files, police found a handwriting sample in the file of William Cooper that perfectly matched the signature on the truck rental receipt. Authorities were able therefore to conclude that William Cooper and William Walter Comins were the same person. But there was still one snag: William Cooper was in prison the day of the robbery and murder.

Since criminals were prevalent in the Cooper family, it was possible, the detectives surmised, that Calman Cooper had used his brother's alias and driver's license to rent the truck. This possibility brought Calman to the forefront of the investigation and they immediately assigned round-the-clock surveillance to his home in Harlem.

Then, in June 1950, authorities set a trap. As Calman Cooper walked down the street, the man who had rented him the truck used in the crime walked toward him. Calman, obviously upset, grabbed the truck rental man and demanded to know why he was there. The trap worked—Cooper was immediately apprehended and arrested.

Shortly thereafter, Harry Stein, who had implicated himself through phone conversations with Cooper that police had tapped, was apprehended. Cooper confessed first during the interrogation, and Stein followed. Both men implicated Dorfman and Wissner, fingering Wissner as the trigger-man. Wissner was arrested soon after, though he persistently denied the charges.

On June 19 Benny Dorfman, the last member of the gang, surrendered to authorities. "I want to tell the truth and get it off my chest," he told them, paving the way toward an offer by authorities to turn state's evidence and receive a separate trial.

Cooper, Stein, and Wissner were found Guilty of first degree murder on Dec. 23, 1950. They were sentenced to the electric chair and, when the appeals finally ran out, received that sentence in Sing Sing prison on July 9, 1955. In 1952 Dorfman pleaded guilty to manslaughter, and was sentenced to ten-to-twenty years at Green Haven Prison, Stormville, N.Y. He was paroled on Dec. 24, 1957. REF.: *CBA*.

Cooper, D.B. (Dan B. Cooper), prom. 1971, U.S., skyjack. A middle-aged man giving the name D.B. Cooper or Dan B. Cooper, purchased a plane ticket for Northwest Orient Airlines flight 305, flying on Nov. 4, 1971, from Portland, Ore., to Seattle, Wash. He wore an ordinary business suit. After taking his seat, Cooper ordered a drink and, while doing so, handed the stewardess a note which read: "Miss, I have a bomb in my suitcase and I want you to sit beside me." When the girl hesitated, Cooper pulled her into the seat next to him and opened the case, revealing several sticks of dynamite connected by wires to a battery. The stewardess was ordered by Cooper to have the captain relay his ransom demand for $200,000 and four parachutes, two front- and two back-packs. The FBI complied with the demands and the parachutes and money were delivered when the plane

Police sketch of the legendary D.B. Cooper.

landed in Seattle, where it was refueled. Cooper allowed the thirty-two passengers to go free.

With a flight crew of four, the 727 Trijet took off. Once airborne, Cooper instructed the pilot to fly at 200 m.p.h. and to keep the plane at 10,000 feet, the destination being Reno, Nev. With the crew of three, and the stewardess in the cockpit, Cooper went to the back of the plane and lowered the rear stairs beneath the tail. He jumped with the money. When the plane landed in Reno, Nev., FBI agents found only one of the backpack chutes.

Agents believed that Cooper parachuted into southwest Washington. The daring skyjacking made Cooper a household name across the U.S. Scores of lawmen and FBI agents scoured the area where Cooper could have landed, but no trace of the skyjacker was found. In 1975 a skull and a parachute were found, but these proved to be the remains of another victim.

In February 1980, several thousand dollars of the ransom money was found near Vancouver, Wash. The marked $20 bills were found by children playing along the bank of the Columbia River. Whether the money had been placed there purposely by Cooper to throw pursuers off the track or it had simply washed downstream was never quite clear. Over the years, several persons claimed to possess information about the daring skyjacker. He was, at one time, identified as Jack Coffelt, a burglar and con man from Missouri, but Coffelt died in 1976 and this identification, like all the others over the years, was never confirmed. To this day, D.B. Cooper remains a criminal enigma, one that still baffles law enforcement authorities. The skyjacker, in all probability, was killed when he attempted to parachute through the heavy rainstorm and high winds surrounding him at the time he jumped. He remains a curious folk hero to some, however. An annual celebration is held in Cooper's dubious honor each year by the residents of Ariel, Wash.

REF.: *CBA*; Gunther, *D.B. Cooper*; McGrady, *Crime Scientists*; Tully, *Inside the FBI*; (FILM) *The Pursuit of D.B. Cooper*, 1981.

Cooper, Grant Burr, 1903- , U.S., lawyer. Grant Burr Cooper was one of the notable criminal lawyers of his time. He is best remembered for his defense of Sirhan Sirhan, accused of murdering Senator Robert Kennedy in the Ambassador Hotel in Los Angeles on June 2, 1968. But he also represented Dr. R. Bernard Finch and Carole Tregoff through three murder trials. The couple were accused of murdering the doctor's wife. Cooper won an acquittal for the defendants in the first two trials, but the third time the jury convicted them.

Cooper was born in New York City. He earned his law degree from Southwestern University in 1926 and was admitted to the California bar a year later. He served in the office of the Los Angeles district attorney from 1929 to 1935, and from 1940 to 1942, as deputy city attorney from 1935 to 1938, and as the chief deputy district attorney from 1940 to 1943. Grant Cooper also served as president of the Los Angeles County Bar Association in 1960 and 1961, and was a member of the board of governors for the State Bar of California. Cooper gained national notoriety for his impassioned defense of Sirhan, who was convicted and sentenced to die. As one of three defense lawyers on the case, Cooper eloquently argued against the death penalty on the grounds of diminished responsibility. "I wouldn't want Sirhan Sirhan to be turned loose because he is dangerous, especially when the psychiatrist tells us that he is going to get worse, and he is going to get worse," Cooper said in his closing remarks to the jury on Apr. 11, 1969.

On Sept. 23, 1969, Cooper was fined $1,000 by U.S. District Judge Albert Lee Stephens for unlawfully possessing a secret grand jury transcript. Cooper was defending Maurice Friedman, a Las Vegas gambler who was one of four men convicted of bilking some well-known Hollywood celebrities out of $400,000 during rigged card games at the posh Friar's Club in Beverly Hills in 1968. The list of victims included singer Tony Martin, comedian Phil Silvers, actor Zeppo Marx, and retail tycoon Harry Karl. In February, the four defendants were convicted on forty-nine counts of conspiracy and sentenced to varying terms ranging from six months to four years. A fifth man involved in the case was freed. Cooper, who was accused of lying to a federal judge about where he procured the transcript, faced a stiff penalty. He could have been fined "without limit" and imprisoned at the discretion of the judge. The judge said he considered the charge only a misdemeanor and refused to impose a prison sentence. See: **Kennedy, Robert F.** REF.: *CBA*.

Cooper, Henry Ernest, 1857-1929, U.S., lawyer. Appointed attorney general and then acting president of the Republic of

Hawaii following the deposal of Queen Liliuokalani in 1893, an event Cooper helped engineer. REF.: *CBA*.

Cooper, Herbert, d.1911, Brit., suic.-mur. A coroner's jury found Herbert Cooper Guilty of the Nov. 28, 1911, murder of 85-year-old Lord George Sanger on Sanger's farm in East Finchley. Cooper, an emotionally unstable man, was the son of the manager of Sanger's farm. He apparently felt that the lord was not lavishing enough attention on him, and, therefore, killed him with several blows of a hatchet. Soon after, Cooper committed suicide by lying on the railroad tracks between Crouch End and Highgate. He was decapitated.

Forty-five years later, the victim's grandson published a very different account of the events that took place on Nov. 28, 1911. According to the book, *The Sanger Story*, Sanger was accidentally struck on the head with a brass candlestick during a fray with Cooper. Sanger, still conscious, then went to bed and died while asleep.

REF.: *CBA*; Lukens, *The Sanger Story*; Shew, *A Second Companion To Murder*.

Cooper, Irving Ben, 1902- , U.S., jur. Associate counsel to New York Seabury Investigation from 1932-33; special counsel to the New York Department of Investigation from 1934-37; magistrate of New York City from 1938-39; and appointed judge of the court of the southern district of New York by President John F. Kennedy in 1962. REF.: *CBA*.

Cooper, James, d.1750, and **Duncalf, William**, d.1750, and **Burrell, Mr.**, prom. 1750, Brit., rob-mur. James Cooper struggled in vain to support his family with his butcher's shop. His debt were so substantial that his creditors had him imprisoned in the King's Bench Prison.

His wife maintained the shop and managed to pay a large portion of the debt. Upon his release, Cooper opened a second butcher shop which also failed. His wife died, leaving him four children to support. He married a second wife with six children of her own which only compounded his financial responsibilities. In desperation, Cooper joined William Duncalf, an Irish smuggler, and his sidekick Burrell, on a crime spree.

They roamed the countryside, looting farmhouses and robbing travelers at gunpoint. At Croydon, they robbed a prosperous farmer named Mr. Jackson who later accused two blacksmiths, one of whom was hanged for the crime.

The three thieves fled to London after killing a man near Dulwich, but the authorities suspected Duncalf. When they were finally arrested, Burrell gave evidence to save himself. He described the gang's adventures and admitted that he had planned to kill Duncalf himself. Burrell's testimony was accepted and Cooper and Duncalf were sentenced and prepared for execution. Duncalf died in prison before Cooper hanged at Kennington Common on Aug. 26, 1750.

REF.: *CBA*; Mitchell, *Newgate Calendar*.

Cooper, John L.T., prom. 1905, U.S., count. A soldier and intensely religious man, Cooper and several of his fellow soldiers were arrested and convicted of producing $10 gold coins using copper and a small amount of gold plate. He explained to the judge at his sentencing that his punishment should be light because "before I began counterfeiting I deliberately had my name stricken from the Christian Endeavor rolls."

REF.: Bloom, *Money of Their Own*; *CBA*.

Cooper, Joseph Earl, 1907- , U.S., jur. U.S. district attorney assigned to Washington D.C., in 1949; appointed to the district court of the Alaska Territory in 1953 by President Harry Truman. REF.: *CBA*.

Cooper, Paula, 1970- , U.S., rob.-mur. Paula Cooper's case brings to a boil two legal controversies: whether the execution of a 15-year-old criminal constitutes a breach of Constitutional protection from cruel and unusual punishment, and whether the age-old defense, that a criminal is a victim of an immoral or amoral environment, is valid.

Cooper, who sat on Death Row for over two years, said that her parents were "like strangers to me. I don't think they were ready to have children." If her accounts of the treatment she received at the hands of her father, Herman, are true, she understated her troubled childhood. Cooper revealed, for example, that her father whipped her and her sister with an extension cord, and forced them to watch while he raped their mother.

In this context, it is not difficult to understand her apparent callousness as she testified to the May 1985 murder of Ruth Pelke, a 78-year-old Bible teacher, in Gary, Ind. "I stood there and looked at her..." she told the court at her July 1986 trial, "...something like clicked in me...and then I remember stabbing her in the stomach. And then I stabbed her in the chest..." Pelke uttered the words to the Lord's Prayer as Cooper stabbed her thirty-three times. Cooper and some friends also robbed Pelke of some cash. Cooper was sentenced to death for the murder.

Paula Cooper's appeal of her death sentence had a wide variety of supporters, including a million Italian anti-death sentence activists who have taken up her cause, the Pope, who requested her clemency in 1987, and William Pelke, the victim's grandson. "I don't believe my grandmother would want to see her on Death Row," Pelke said.

On July 13, 1989, the Indiana Supreme Court commuted her death sentence to sixty years in prison, basing its decison on an Indiana law, passed after Cooper's conviction, that raised the minimum age that a defendant could be subject to the death penalty from ten to sixteen years old. The court also noted a 1988 U.S. Supreme Court decision which barred the death penalty for offenders under the age of sixteen.

Cooper's lawyer, William Touchette, said his client was "happy" with the court's decision. Earlier, however, Cooper had admitted, "Death means peace to me...I'm in hell right now." REF.: *CBA*.

Cooper, Ralph, and **English, Collis**, prom. 1940s, U.S., mur. Known in the media as members of the "Trenton Six," Cooper and English were originally convicted and sentenced to death along with four other black men for the murder of Fred Horner, a 72-year-old junk dealer, in Trenton, N.J. Their trial and conviction set off a flurry of legal controversy that consumed the interests of the American Civil Liberties Union, The National Association for the Advancement of Colored People, and the Communist Party.

The Trenton police force and judicial system were under intense pressure to convict someone for this crime. The year was 1948. The mayor of Trenton had recently been indicted for bribery. That, plus the failure of his administration to solve a number of other crimes had both the public and press screaming for law enforcement reform. The six men who became known as the "Trenton Six"—Ralph Cooper, Collis English, Forrest McKinlay, John McKenzie, James Thorpe, and Horace Wilson—were rounded up and arrested for the crime. They all had strong alibis, but after days of brutal police interrogation that included sleep deprivation and the refusal to grant them access to attorneys, five of the six signed vague, confusing confessions to the murder. In June 1948, on the strength of these confessions all six black men were convicted of murder by an all-white jury and sentenced to death.

The Communist Party, ACLU, and NAACP all became involved in an appeal process that eventually won the "Trenton Six" a new trial when the New Jersey Supreme Court overturned their conviction in June 1949. The defense of five of the six men was assumed by the NAACP and members of Princeton University and Princeton Theological Seminary. The second trial began on Mar. 5, 1951, and lasted for more than fifteen weeks. The result: four were acquitted; English and Cooper were once again convicted of murder and sentenced to life.

The decision was peculiar because the widow of the victim, Elizabeth Maguire, said with certainty in her first recorded statements that the men she had seen enter the store on the day of her husband's murder were light-skinned blacks. Of the six, Cooper and English were the darkest.

During the second trial, Dr. J. Minor Sullivan, III, who testified at the first trial that all the suspects had signed their confessions on their own free will, admitted that four of the six appeared to have been either drugged or bribed to sign their confessions. Sullivan was later convicted on seven counts of perjury for giving this contradictory testimony.

Another appeal was made, this time on behalf of English and Cooper. English died in prison before the appeal was heard, and Cooper eventually pleaded *non vult,* a plea equivalent to "no contest," and was released. REF.: *CBA.*

Cooper, Ray Anthony, 1954-   , U.S., rob.-rape-mur. As Detective Bernie Banahan will tell you, what a homicide detective needs, often above all else, is patience. He proved his point by cracking a case that had stumped Chicago police for months in the early 1970s.

Early on the morning of July 14, 1973, in the underground parking garage beneath Chicago's Grant Park, an electrician discovered the body of Irene Koutros, a 41-year-old elementary school teacher, in her car. She had been strangled.

A parking receipt indicated Koutros had entered the garage at 10:00 a.m. and had paid for parking at 2 p.m., but her car had never left her parking space. Witnesses said they had seen Koutros in the garage with a man at about midnight, but the report proved false. With no other leads, Detective Banahan put the case on the back burner.

In January 1974, some six months after Koutros's murder, Banahan was investigating a rape that had occurred in the women's rest room of a downtown office building. Following a hunch, he checked the job applications on file in the office and found that a man fitting the description of the rapist had applied for a job that morning. His name was Ray Anthony Cooper and he had a record of robbery and molestation convictions.

Police found Cooper, nineteen, at home that night wearing the same clothes the victim had described. They put him in a car with Detective Banahan. "You want to talk to me about that school teacher," Cooper volunteered on the way to police head-quarters. "You got my name from the police, I know." He then said he had been at the garage the day of the murder and had even been stopped by police.

Cooper continued, all but admitting to the murder, so Banahan and his co-workers decided to stall for time by treating Cooper to dinner at a downtown chili parlor. "We didn't want the guy mad at us when we were so close," he said.

Cooper asked what kind of sentence the murderer might get. Banahan explained, including the sentences for involuntary and voluntary manslaughter, and reckless homicide. Casually discuss-ing sentences and plea bargains, Banahan waited for the right moment. "Look, you're a pretty legit guy," he said to Cooper. "And you've been playing it straight with us. You know all the facts now. Is there something you'd like to get off your chest?"

With this, Cooper confessed. He repeated it later to a court reporter and signed the confession. Sentenced on Nov. 4, 1974, to twenty to sixty years for the murder of Irene Koutros, he also received a concurrent ten to thirty-year sentence for the downtown office rape. REF.: *CBA.*

Cooper, Reginald, 1942-   , Brit., mansl. In the late 1950s, the Teddy Boys were a rough and tumble English street gang, known to frequent the public houses and teen clubs that featured skiffle music. Reginald Cooper was a 15-year-old youth who ran around with the Teddy Boys. One night in October 1957 Cooper and his cohorts emerged from a pub where they had been drinking and listening to the music. The leader of the group, 19-year-old Frederick Hodges suddenly pounced on a man named Soames as the boys walked through the streets of the northern city.

Cooper attacked Hodges after the older boy refused to intervene on his behalf in a separate fight. While Hodges lay on the ground, Reginald Cooper kicked him in the face and shoulders, damaging his vertebrae and causing fatal internal bleeding. At his murder trial, the defense contended that Cooper had very little parental supervision, and because of the negative influence of the Teddy Boys, he had developed a rather severe

drinking problem. It was pointed out that on the night of the murder Reginald Cooper had downed seven pints of beer. After the jury convicted him of manslaughter, the presiding judge sentenced him to five years detention under the terms of the Children and Young Person's Act. REF.: *CBA;* Wilson, *Children Who Kill.*

Cooper, Ronald Frank, 1950-78, S. Afri., mur. "I have decided that I think I should become a homosexual murderer and shall get hold of young boys...and I shall rape them and then kill them...My first few victims shall each be killed in a different way, which shall be as follows: Victim No. 1: Strangled by hands..."

This Mar. 17, 1976, entry in the diary of Ronald Frank Cooper made it easy for the prosecution when Cooper was tried for murdering a child in Johannesburg, S. Afri.

A 26-year-old, unemployed laborer, Cooper had described at length in his diary how he would murder thirty boys and six women and possibly use human sacrifice or rape. He had, in fact, already tried to fulfill his written promises a month before by pulling a gun on Tresslin Pohl, ten, and forcing him into a park. After a few minutes, however, he lost his nerve and released the boy.

Cooper botched two more attempts but finally succeeded on the fourth try. On May 16, 1976, he trapped Mark John Garnet, twelve, in a Parktown area apartment building elevator and strangled him until the boy was unconscious. Tying a rope around Mark's neck, Cooper tried unsuccessfully to rape him. Failing at this, he loosened the rope, hoping the boy might survive. "To murder someone is not a nice thing to do, as I have now found out," he later confided to his diary. "I really am a monster."

When Tressin Pohl, Cooper's first attempted victim, found out that his friend Mark had been murdered, he went to the authorities. He told them that in April, during a Saturday matinee, he had noticed Cooper sitting in a theater filled with children. When the movie was over, Tressin had shadowed him home to the St. Kilda Hotel.

With this information, Cooper was easily apprehended. His diary did the rest. On Jan. 16, 1978, Ronald Frank Cooper was hanged.

REF.: *CBA;* Wilson, *Encyclopedia of Modern Murder.*

Cooper, Ronald John, 1938-   , Brit., mur. On the evening of July 23, 1964, Ronald Cooper shot and killed Joseph Hayes, sixty-seven, the managing director of a ship repairing company at his home in Barking, Essex. Cooper snatched £1,878 in payroll checks from the kitchen table and then fled through the hallway, shooting Mrs. Elsie May Hayes in the back. Cooper fled to New York the next day, and then continued on to the Bahamas where he went to work as a gambling casino croupier. Meanwhile, British police established the suspect's identity through fingerprints left behind on a newspaper and on a chromium stair railing.

Cooper was arrested in the Bahamas and extradited back to England where he went on trial in the Central Criminal Court on Dec. 3, 1964. Two weeks later, on Dec. 14, a Guilty verdict was returned against Cooper and the death sentence was passed. He became the first man to be convicted of a capital offense after Sydney Silverman's bill to abolish hanging was introduced into the House of Commons. Four days before the scheduled execution at Pentonville Prison on Jan. 27, 1965, Cooper was given a reprieve by the Home Office. REF.: *CBA.*

Cooper, Thomas, prom. 1842, Brit., mur. A spate of unsolved highway robberies plagued Highbury, London and Constable Timothy Daly was killed on May 5, 1842 in a vain attempt to stop the offender. Constable Charles Moss of the London Police caught up with the robber on the outskirts of Islington just as he was about to holdup a passing traveler. Before he could be taken the robber bolted across an adjacent field firing two shots from an old cavalry pistol at Moss.

One of the bullets hit the constable in the arm, but he con-tinued in hot pursuit. By this time, at least a dozen other policemen had arrived to lend support. Turning off the fields and onto a road, the fleeing robber ran into a cul-de-sac and was forced to shoot it out with police. With a gun in each hand and his back to the wall, the robber, who was later identified as a bricklayer named Thomas Cooper, killed Daly before surrendering to police. Cooper was arrested, brought to trial, and duly convicted of murder. He was sentenced to hang.

REF.: Browne, *Rise of Scotland Yard; CBA.*

Coors, Adolph, III, See: **Corbett, Joseph, Jr.**

Coote, Richard (First Earl of Bellomont), 1636-1701, Brit., pir. While serving as the colonial governor of New York, Massachusetts, and New Hampshire from 1697-1701, he was given the responsibility of clearing the coastal waters and the Indian Ocean of pirates. He retained the services of Captain William Kidd, a British seaman, who turned pirate. Coote had him arrested and sent back to England to stand trial in 1699. See: **Kidd, William.** REF.: *CBA.*

Copeland, James, 1815-57, U.S., rob.-mur. James Copeland and his gang of ruthless "land pirates" gained a popular following in Mississippi in the 1840s. Despite their reputation for depravity, the Copeland gang had dealings with the upper crust, land-owning Wage family of Augusta. The Wages used their political connections to protect Copeland from the law. In return, Copeland performed various "services," for the family, including murder.

On July 15, 1848, Copeland shot and killed James Harvey in revenge for the murder of Gale H. Wages. Gale's father paid Copeland $1,000 to carry out the murder. Copeland was quickly identified as the killer, arrested, tried, and convicted. Although it was common knowledge in Augusta that Wages had hired Copeland to kill Harvey, Copeland steadfastly refused to implicate Wages. As a testament to the family's power, Copeland stayed alive for nine years. He was hanged on Oct. 30, 1857.

James Copeland, the great western "land pirate."

REF.: Bartholomew, *The Biographical Album of Western Gunfighters; CBA;* Copeland, *Life and Confession of the Noted Outlaw, James Copeland;* Craighead, *Mobile, Fact and Tradition;* Nash, *Bloodletters and Badmen;* Pitts, *Life and Bloody Career of the Executed Criminal James Copeland, The Greatest Southern Land Pirate.*

Copeland, Michael, 1934-   , Brit., mur. Before Michael Copeland was arrested for the murders of William Elliott and George Stobbs, the police referred to these murders as the Carbon Copy Murders. Both victims frequented a tavern called the Spread Eagle, both were found dead near Chesterfield, England and both of their automobiles had been abandoned on Park Road in Chesterfield.

Elliott and Stobbs were homosexual, which Copeland later told police was "something I hated." Elliott's body was found on June 13, 1960, on Clod Hill Lane in Baslow. On Mar. 29, 1961, Stobbs' body was discovered beside a road near Wingerworth.

The trail eventually led to Copeland, a 26-year-old former soldier, whose home was near the location of the abandoned cars. He was also accused of the November 1960 murder of Guenther Helmbrecht, a young soldier, in Verden, Ger. At his trial, Copeland retracted his original confession to the murders of Stobbs and Elliott, but the evidence was overwhelming. He was found Guilty of all three murders and sentenced to death. The sentence was later commuted to life in prison when it was proven that Copeland was under mental stress at the time of the murders.

REF.: Butler, *Murderers' England; CBA.*

Coppinger, Daniel (AKA: Cruel Coppinger), prom. 18th Cent., Brit., smug. Daniel Coppinger arrived in England when his ship

sank off Cornwall during a violent storm. The Danish sailor came ashore and kidnapped a horse and its rider, young Dinah Hamlyn. They galloped to the farm where Dinah lived with her father. Coppinger took refuge there and soon became part of the household. He eventually married Dinah, and after her father died, Coppinger spent all of her inheritance frivolously.

Forced to make a living, Coppinger chose smuggling as his venture. His headquarters, located at Steeple Brink, was famous for its perilous entrance, which required tricky navigation by boat through a rocky channel and into a cave at the foot of a sheer cliff. Locals referred to the hideout as Coppinger's Cove.

Cruel Coppinger's scare tactics were infamous around Steeple Brink. He was not beyond doing anything for money, including whipping the local parson when the unfortunate man pressed the Dane for a tithe.

Coppinger's career ended as dramatically as it began: he died at sea when his ship sank.

REF.: *CBA;* Scott, *The Concise Encyclopedia of Crime and Criminals.*

Copple, William Perry, 1916-   , U.S., jur. U.S. attorney, Phoenix, Ariz., from 1965-66; appointed to the district court of Arizona by President Lyndon Johnson in 1966. REF.: *CBA.*

Coppola, Frank J., 1944-82, U.S., mur. For twenty years the oak and metal electric chair at the jail in Richmond, Va., remained unused. It stood like a silent sentry, awaiting its first victim since 1962—Frank J. Coppola, a former Roman Catholic seminarian and police officer convicted of murdering 45-year-old Muriel Hatchell during a 1978 home invasion in Newport News.

Coppola proclaimed his innocence, yet expressed a heartfelt wish to die. "I felt I owed it to myself to take control of my own destiny...they've said to me 'We're gonna take your life,' I say back to them, 'Come on, do it.' It's my decision," he said. Coppola's decision to die in the summer of 1982 was made because he wanted to spare his teenage sons the anguish and torment they would likely face when they returned to school in September. Coppola's wife, who was serving a twenty-year prison sentence for her role in the robbery said she planned to remarry after her husband was dead.

The death sentence was carried out on Aug. 10, 1982, after the U.S. Supreme Court consented to Coppola's request for a speedy execution. He became one of the first to be executed in the U.S. since the constitutionality of the death penalty was upheld by the high court in 1976.

REF.: *CBA;* Henderson, *The Super Sleuths.*

"Trigger Mike" Coppola and wife Ann whose testimony sent him to prison.

Coppola, Michael (AKA: Trigger Mike, Little Mike, Michael Russo), 1900-66, U.S., org. crime. Mike Coppola was good at making people suffer. From his first arrest in 1914, he had a reputation as one of the most vicious Mafia enforcers in New York City. In the 1930s, after Charles "Lucky" Luciano went to prison, and Vito Genovese fled to Europe to avoid a murder charge, Coppola took over the lucrative drug trafficking empire. With the addition of the artichoke racket, a legitimate business front involving the distribution of artichokes to groceries, and the Harlem numbers racket, Coppola pushed his annual profits to $1 million. In 1960, Coppola and ten other racketeers were barred from entering Nevada casinos by Nevada state gaming officials. Despite this enforced exclusion, Coppola still managed to take his cut of the profits.

Coppola's marital problems, and not the FBI or DEA, brought about his downfall. His first wife died in her hospital bed after giving birth to a child. It is believed that Coppola killed her to prevent her from testifying about the assassination of a New York political worker named Joseph Scottoriggio, which Coppola had reportedly carried out.

His second wife, Ann Coppola, learned about her predecessor's fate one night when Mike talked in his sleep. In the course of their marriage, Coppola subjected her to brutal abuse. He supplied narcotics to a daughter from her first marriage. He fired a gun at her during their honeymoon party to amuse the other guests. When she became pregnant, he forced her to undergo an abortion on the kitchen table. When she filed for divorce, Coppola sent in a team of Mafia strongmen to administer a beating. Ann recovered from her injuries and testified against Coppola in a federal tax case. Coppola was sentenced to serve a year in the Atlanta Penitentiary as a result. In 1962, Ann sent a package of information from Rome to Attorney General Robert Kennedy, and then committed suicide.

When Coppola was released from prison in 1963, he had been dropped by the Mafia inner council. An apparent inability to control his wife had made Coppola a pariah. Coppola spent his last years attending to his orchids at his home in Florida.

REF.: *CBA*; Cressey, *Theft of the Nation*; Eisenberg and Landau, *Meyer Lansky*; Fried, *The Rise and Fall of the Jewish Gangster In America*; Gage, *Mafia, U.S.A.*; ____, *The Mafia Is Not An Equal Opportunity Employer*; Katz, *Uncle Frank*; Kirby and Renner, *Mafia Enforcer*; McClellan, *Crime Without Punishment*; Maas, *The Valachi Papers*; Messick, *Lansky*; ____, *Secret File*; ____, *Syndicate In the Sun*; ____ and Goldblatt, *The Mobs and the Mafia*; Nash, *Bloodletters and Badmen*; Navasky, *Kennedy Justice*; Peterson, *The Mob*; Reid, *The Grim Reapers*; Sann, *Kill the Dutchman!*; Smith, *Syndicate City*; Thompson and Raymond, *Gang Rule In New York*.

Coppolino, Dr. Carl, 1933- , U.S., mur. Dr. Carl Coppolino, a Brooklyn-born anesthesiologist, was accused of murdering his first wife with a relaxant called succinylcholine, a drug commonly used during surgery. Used to excess, the drug was capable of paralyzing the muscles of the lungs, bringing on death. Once in the body, the drug broke down into its component parts making it difficult, if not impossible, to trace its presence.

After suffering heart problems, Dr. Coppolino abandoned his practice in New Jersey and moved to Sarasota, Fla., with his wife, the former Carmela Musetto. Although the insurance company suspected that Coppolino was faking his illness, they paid him a yearly benefit of $22,000. The couple lived comfortably in Florida from the insurance money, and the income derived from Carmela's own medical practice. Shortly before Carmela Coppolino died in 1965, her husband insured her life for $65,000. The cause of death was listed as heart failure, and the matter was pursued no further until Carl Coppolino's jilted lover Marjorie Farber informed the police and a Florida physician that she had watched him kill her husband in 1963.

Motivated by jealousy when Coppolino married a 38-year-old divorcée named Mary Gibson}, Farber told Dr. Juliette Karow that she had carried on a love affair with Collolino back in New Jersey. Coppolino became jealous of her new husband, a retired army coloner, and injected him with a chemical substance, and then smothered him with a pillow. The cause of Colonel Farber's death was listed as coronary thrombosis. Collolino was subsequently indicted for murder in both New Jersey and Florida. Confused by conflicting medical evidence, the jury found Coppolino Not Guilty in Farber's case. When Carmela's body was exhumed and re-examined it was found that the victim had been in good health and had not suffered a heart attack, as Coppolino had alleged.

Dr. Joseph Umberger, a noted toxicologist, conducted six months of intensive research before locating traces of succinic acid in the system. On the witness stand, Dr. Umberger testified that while succinic acid is naturally present in the human brain, it is in "bound" form. The evidence showed that the acid found in the victim was "unbound." This evidence and the fact that Carmella was injected immediately prior to death tended to confirm the view that she had been murdered.

Despite the efforts of defense attorney F. Lee Bailey, Dr. Collolino was convicted in 1967, of second-degree murder, and was sentenced to life imprisonment at the Avon Park Correctional Institution. At the conclusion of the trial, Bailey publicly assailed the prosecution and the battery of witnesses, behavior for which he received a one-year suspension form practicing in New Jersey. In 1977, Mary Gibson Coppolino began a fight to win her husband's freedom. She gathered reports from scientists claiming the New York City medical examiners were "out to get" Coppolino at the time. Although these statements had little effect on the parole board, Coppolino was released on Oct. 16, 1979, for exemplary behavior at the prison facility.

REF.: Bailey and Aronson, *The Defence Never Rests*; Brussel, *Casebook of a Crime Psychologist*; *CBA*; Coppolino, *The Crime That Never Was*; Halpern and Knight, *Autopsy*; Holmes, *The Trials of Dr. Coppolino*; MacDonald, *No Deadly Drug*; Wilson, *Encyclopedia of Murder*.

James P. Casey in the hands of San Francisco vigilantes.

Cora, Charles, and **Casey, James P.**, d.1856, U.S., mur. Charles Cora was a well-known San Francisco gambler and patron of the arts. He enjoyed the theatre, and was often seen in the company of his sweetheart, a brothel madame known as Belle Cora. Many of San Francisco's finer citizens were scandalized by the gambler and his mistress. One who took exception to sitting next to a denizen of the red-light district was U.S. Marshal William Richardson, whose wife was seated next to Belle Cora during an evening performance on Nov. 15, 1855.

Two days later Charles Cora ran into Richardson on Leidesdorff Street. Stung by what he perceived to be an insult against Belle's character, Cora shot Richardson down in cold blood. The gambler was tried for murder and duly convicted on Jan. 17, 1856. The matter did not end there however.

James King, editor of the San Francisco *Bulletin*, published a series of editorials decrying the lawlessness of the city. He identified one of the jurors, James P. Casey, who had served on the Cora jury as a convicted felon who had spent time in Sing Sing Prison for burglary. Enraged by the scandalous articles, Casey confronted the editor near Montgomery and Washington streets. Without a word he produced a pistol and killed King. Jim Casey was arrested and taken to the same prison where Cora resided.

The San Francisco Vigilance Committee, a group of politically influential, armed men that had been inactive since 1851 was hastily reorganized. In the days that followed the King shooting, over 3,500 citizens joined their ranks. The governor of California silently approved their methods, which left the prisoners unprotected.

On May 18, 1856, Sheriff Dave Scannell was ordered by the vigilantes to surrender the prisoners. Realizing that resistance was useless, the sheriff opened the jail and released Cora and Casey to their fate. They were given the formality of a trial, but were found Guilty and hanged five days later. Before Cora was marched to the gallows he was permitted to marry the brothel mistress in his jail cell.

REF.: *CBA;* Duke, *Celebrated Criminal Cases of America.*

Corallo, Anthony (AKA: Tony Ducks), 1914- , U.S., rack.-org. crime. For frustrating dozens of process servers over the years, New York mobster Anthony Corallo earned the nickname "Tony Ducks." By the time he was sentenced to jail in 1987 on federal racketeering charges, Corallo, a member of the Thomas Lucchese crime family, rarely had to "duck." He had been identified as a member of the ruling Mafia national commission.

Anthony "Tony Ducks" Corallo

Corallo's criminal record dates to 1929 and includes arrests for grand larceny, robbery, and violation of the narcotic laws. His conviction on drug charges resulted in a six-month prison sentence after federal authorities linked him to a cache of narcotics with a street value of $150,000. Corallo next turned his attention to labor racketeering. The McClellan Committee reported in 1958 that Corallo had infiltrated Local 239 of the Teamster's Union in New York City, and had embezzled $69,000 in funds by recording "dummy" names on the payroll. "Tony Ducks" counted Teamster's president James Hoffa among his very good friends after he supplied the muscle Hoffa needed to take control of the New York City local.

In 1962 Corallo was sentenced to two years in prison for paying $35,000 in bribes to New York Supreme Court Justice James Vincent Keogh and Assistant U.S. Attorney Elliott Kahaner to assure a light sentence for a mob associate. Six years later Corallo was sentenced to four-and-a-half years for bribing New York City Water Commissioner James L. Marcus. In return, Marcus, who was in dire financial straits at the time, awarded city contracts to various companies tied in with the Lucchese interests. Marcus, a close friend of former Mayor John V. Lindsay was sent to jail for fifteen months for his part in a scheme to shake-down a Consolidated Edison Utility Company during the awarding of city permits.

During the 1980s Corallo was implicated in several bid-rigging schemes involving garbage disposals on Long Island—a scandal that involved politicians from both major parties. When the government planted a listening device in his automobile, his fellow Mafiosi became so enraged that it was thought he might not live to see the new year. On Jan. 13, 1987, Judge Richard Owen of the Federal District Court in Manhattan gave Corallo, Anthony Salerno, and Carmine Persico 100-year sentences, coupled with heavy fines for participating in a national commission that coordinated criminal activities from coast to coast.

REF.: Alexander, *The Pizza Connection;* Blumenthal, *Last Days of the Sicilians; CBA;* Cressey, *Theft of the Nation;* Demaris, *The Last Mafioso;* Gage, *Mafia, U.S.A.;* ____, *The Mafia Is Not an Equal Opportunity Employer;* McClellan, *Crime Without Punishment;* Maas, *The Valachi Papers;* Navasky, *Kennedy Justice;* Peterson, *The Mob;* Reid, *The Grim Reapers;* Velie, *Desperate Bargain: Why Jimmy Hoffa Had To Die.*

Corbett, Joseph, Jr., 1928- , U.S., kid.-mur. Millionaire brewer, Adolph Coors III, forty-four, vanished on Feb. 9, 1960, while driving to his plant in Golden, Colo., which was twelve miles from his home. His abandoned car was found still running, the radio blaring, on a dirt road at Turkey Creek Bridge. Police found bloodstains on the front seat, along with Coors' glasses. There was also a smear of blood on the nearby bridge railing. Police organized a huge posse to look for the missing millionaire, and though the entire countryside was combed, there was no trace of Coors. Adolph Coors, Jr., the missing man's father, who had been involved as a victim in an abortive $50,000 kidnap and ransom scheme in 1933, stated that he would pay any amount demanded by the kidnappers of his son. He stated: "They have something I want to buy—my son. The price is secondary. It's like any other business transaction now. I cannot be emotional about this."

No ransom offer was ever received by the Coors family. On Sept. 16, 1960, a skull was found near Castle Rock, Colo. The Coors' family dentist, Dr. Arthur G. Kelly, examined the teeth of the skull and reported that they were identical to the dental chart of Adolph Coors III. A short time later, Joseph Corbett, Jr. was arrested and charged with Coors' kidnapping and murder. Apparently, Corbett had attempted to kidnap Coors and killed him when Coors struggled with him. He then drove to Castle Rock and dumped the body, abandoning his kidnap plan. The 31-year-old Corbett was the only suspect in the case. He was an escaped convict from Chino, Calif., who had been serving time for the murder of 22-year-old Air Force Sergeant Alan Lee Reed. Following the disappearance of Coors, Joseph Corbett vanished from Colorado where he had been living under an assumed name.

FBI agents were tipped off to Corbett's whereabouts by a resident of Toronto, Can., who happened to read about him in a *Reader's Digest* article entitled "The FBI Wants This Man." The Toronto native notified the local police that Corbett had been working in a Toronto warehouse but had left abruptly. The FBI located Corbett in Vancouver, Can., on Oct. 29, 1960. Corbett meekly surrendered to law enforcement officials and was returned to Denver to stand trial. On Mar. 29, 1961, Corbett was convicted of murdering the brewery magnate in an aborted kidnapping scheme where he had originally thought to hold the brewer for $500,000 in ransom money. On May 12, 1961, Corbett was sentenced to life imprisonment.

REF.: *CBA;* Nash, *Among the Missing.*

Corbett, Richard, prom. 1929, Case of, Fr., euth. "God is only a religious belief," declared Richard Corbett as he stood in the prisoner's docket of a cramped courtroom in Draguignan, Fr. The courtroom stirred, and the judge rebuked Corbett for deciding who should live and who should die. The young Frenchman shot his mother to death after the doctors pronounced her case hopeless. Mrs. Corbett suffered from cancer at the time of her death in November 1929.

"It was for God to consider when your mother should have died, not you," the judge said. "God might have prolonged your mother's life." Corbett explained that he could not stand to watch her suffer. After taking her life, the grieved young man turned the gun on himself, but received only minor injuries.

It took the jury only twenty minutes to return a verdict of Not Guilty. However, popular opinion was divided, and the case drew impressive attention. Corbett's supporters included Albert Einstein who said, "I am happy in his acquittal by the French court, where a healthy feeling for the spirit of justice triumphed over the dead letter of the law."

The playwright George Bernard Shaw held a different view of the matter. "It is impossible to have a state of affairs in which one person may shoot another and then allege it was a sort of suicide by deputy," he said. "Suicide cannot be permitted by deputy." REF.: *CBA*.

Corbett, Thomas P. (AKA: **Boston**), b.1832, Case of, U.S., mur. Born in England, Boston Corbett immigrated to the U.S. in 1839 with his parents, settling in New York where he later worked as a hatter. He married but his wife died in childbirth. Corbett then moved to Boston in 1857, continuing his trade as a hatter. For years Corbett had been unbalanced, if not certifiably insane. The old line "mad as a hatter" had some foundation in fact. Hatters worked with mercury and this was thought to contribute to insanity. Whether Corbett was insane before entering the trade, or that the

Thomas "Boston" Corbett, killer of John Wilkes Booth.

trade accelerated his own hereditary insanity, is not known. He was a religious zealot who, without provocation, would screech in a shrill voice at any given moment: "Amen! Glory to God!" This habit not only unnerved Corbett's fellow hatters but caused the pastors of the many churches he attended to request that he leave such exhortations to them during services. In 1858, either in self-admonishment for his wife's death or to prevent "sinful temptation by women," as one historian later claimed, Corbett castrated himself, a self-mutilation that almost cost him his life.

When the American Civil War broke out, Corbett was one of the first to rally to the Union banner, enlisting in the 12th New York Militia on Apr. 9, 1861. He served well and with great bravery, some said with fanatical fervor, reenlisting three times and rising to the rank of sergeant in Company L, 16th New York Cavalry. On June 24, 1864, Corbett was captured and sent to the notorious Confederate prison camp in Andersonville. He was later exchanged and, following the assassination of Abraham Lincoln by John Wilkes Booth, he was selected to ride after the assassin with twenty-three other troopers under the command of Lieutenant Edward P. Doherty and Lieutenant Colonel Everton J. Conger, who was in overall command of that search unit of the 16th New York Cavalry. This group tracked Booth to the Virginia farm of Richard P. Garrett where Booth and another conspirator, David Herold, were hiding.

After Herold surrendered, Booth adamantly refused to give up. Conger set fire to the barn in which the wounded Booth waited. As the fire blazed up, Corbett, behind the barn, shot Booth through a crack in the barn. The mortally-wounded Booth was then dragged out of the burning barn to gasp his last words for his mother. Conger, angry that Booth had been executed, raced up to Corbett, swearing at him and demanded to know why he had shot Booth. "Colonel," Corbett said in his unnaturally high voice, "God Almighty directed me."

"I guess He did or you couldn't have hit him through that crack in the barn," Conger replied. Corbett was arrested on murder charges and failing to obey orders, but his protector, Edwin M. Stanton, then Secretary of War in the Lincoln cabinet, ordered that the court-martial against Corbett be dropped, that Corbett was a "patriot" and that Booth was a "rebel," and this was justification enough for the killing. The slaying of Booth was nevertheless a clear-cut case of murder. Booth was not seen, but was only suspected of offering resistance after the barn was set afire, and, according to Conger, who watched Booth through the cracks of the barn after it was torched, Lincoln's assassin held a carbine. Other reports had it that he used this weapon as a crutch. He was not seen to aim or fire this weapon and, according to the reported conversations he was having with Union soldiers surrounding the barn, Booth was considering surrender.

Corbett's actions, some have claimed, were purposeful in that

he was following Stanton's direct orders to make sure that Booth did not survive, that Booth, if he had lived, could implicate powerful persons in Lincoln's own cabinet who had a hand in the conspiracy to kill the president, not the least of whom was Edwin M. Stanton himself. Corbett was given a full share of the reward money offered for Booth, $1,653.85, which every man in his unit received, but some sources claim that he was given a larger amount of money by Stanton. After being mustered out of the army in August 1865, Corbett resumed his hat-making trade in Boston but later moved to Danbury, Conn., and then to Camden, N.J.

In 1878, Corbett moved west, homesteading, and making a living as a revivalist lay preacher. In 1887, he was looked up to as a hero and was awarded the job of doorkeeper for the House of Representatives in Topeka, Kan. A short time later Corbett inexplicably rushed into the legislative hall during a session and began firing his revolver. He had to be subdued and dragged from the premises. He was examined by a number of doctors who judged him insane and confined him in a lunatic asylum in Topeka. In 1888, Corbett escaped from the asylum and went to Neodesha, Kan., where he met with an old army friend, telling him that he was going to Mexico. Corbett then vanished forever. See: **Lincoln, Abraham**.

REF.: Bates, *Lincoln in the Telegraph Office*; Borreson, *When Lincoln Died*; Bryan, *The Great American Myth*; Carter, *The Riddle of Dr. Mudd*; *CBA*; Cottrell, *Anatomy of an Assassination: The Murder of Abraham Lincoln*; Eisenshiml, *In the Shadow of Lincoln's Death*; ____, *Why Was Lincoln Murdered?*; Forrester, *This One Mad Act*; Gutman, *John Wilkes Booth, Himself*; Hanchett, *The Lincoln Murder Conspiracies*; Harris, *Assassination of Lincoln, A History of Great Conspiracy*; Johnson, *Abraham Lincoln and Boston Corbett*; Kelly, *The Crime at Ford's Theatre*; Kimmel, *The Mad Booths of Maryland*; Kunhardt, *Twenty Days*; Lorant, *Lincoln, A Picture History of His Life*; Miller, *John Wilkes Booth in the Pennsylvania Oil Region*; Neely, *The Abraham Lincoln Encyclopedia*; Roscoe, *The Web of Conspiracy*; Ruggles, *The Prince of Players*; Shelton, *Mask for Treason, The Lincoln Murder Trial*; Starkey, *Wilkes Booth Came to Washington*; Stern, *The Man Who Killed Lincoln*; Weichmann, *A True History of the Assassination of Abraham Lincoln and the Other Conspiracy of 1865*; Wilson, *John Wilkes Booth: Fact and Fiction of Lincoln's Assassination*.

Corbisiero, Carlo (AKA: **Crackshot**), 1907- , Italy, (wrong. convict.) rob.-mur. Carlo Corbisiero served nineteen years in an Italian jail for a crime he never committed.

In many respects, Corbisiero was a victim of the Fascist system of government that allowed no quarter for poets, dissenters, or, in this case, a drunken free spirit and bootlegger. In 1934 three holdup men named Corbisiero as an accomplice in a robbery in whch an innocent person died. At the time, Corbisiero was two miles away loading a consignment of bootleg liquor onto a wagon. Crackshot, as he was known to his friends in the town of Marzano di Nola, near Naples, protested his guilt, but was sentenced to life in prison. Acccording to Italian law, a suspect is guilty until proven innocent.

After a year in prison, one of the convicted gunmen confessed to a priest that Corbisiero had been framed. After the man died in prison, the priest reported his findings to Rome, but nothing was done until February 1953, long after the Fascist government had been toppled.

Corbisiero was granted a new trial and his innocence was established by famed defense attorney Giacomo Augenti, who produced thirty-five favorable witnesses. For his troubles, Corbisiero received a new suit of clothes and 10,360 lira from the government, the equivalent of $16. REF.: *CBA*.

Corbulo, Gnaeus Domitius, d.67 A.D., Roman, consp.-suic. Recalled from the battlefields of Armenia by Emperor Nero in 67 A.D., Corbulo was accused of conspiring against the legal authority. He chose suicide over prison. REF.: *CBA*.

Corcoran, Thomas Gardiner, 1900- , U.S., lawyer. Served as special assistant to the attorney general of the U.S. from 1932-35. REF.: *CBA*.

Corday, Charlotte, See: **Marat, Jean Paul.**

Corder, William (The Red Barn Murder), 1805-28, Brit., mur.
Celebrated in many ballads and dramas, Maria Marten's murder
by reluctant suitor William Corder was a calculated, cold-blooded
killing that marked Corder as one of the most horrendous slayers
in British history. Marten was a simple but attractive country
woman of twenty-five, Corder four years her junior. The woman
lived in her parents' cottage in Polstead, a village in Suffolk.
Corder met and seduced Maria Marten in 1826 and when she
became pregnant, Corder moved her into lodgings in Sudbury.
The child was stillborn and Marten moved back with her parents
who nagged Corder to marry their daughter. Corder finally
relented on May 18, 1827, telling Marten that they would wed that
day in Ipswich. He also said that she must disguise herself as a
man, wearing men's clothing, and meet him in the red barn on his
property (the building had a red tiled roof). Corder stressed
wearing the disguise, saying that his mother and the police could
not be informed that he was about to marry a woman who had
given birth to a bastard child or they would be punished. The
unsophisticated Marten went along with the strange plan, packing
her feminine clothing in a bag and donning men's clothing Corder
had provided.

**William Corder and his victim, Maria Marten, murdered in the cele-
brated Red Barn.**

Maria Marten walked to the Corder barn as instructed and
was not seen alive again. Two days later Corder was seen by
Marten's parents who asked about their daughter. He told them
that Marten was still in Ipswich, that there was some problem
about the marriage license but all would be right within a short
time. Days later, Corder told Marten's father that his daughter
was vacationing on the Isle of Wight. When others asked about
Marten, Corder told them she was in Yarmouth or in France.
Borrowing £400 from his parents, Corder then left for London,
staying at the Bull Inn in Leadenhall Street. From here he wrote
letters to the Marten family, saying that he and Marten were
married in London and living happily. Meanwhile, Corder
advertised for a wife, and a young girl responded. He married her
and made plans to open a girls' school for which he would act as
headmaster. Marten's long absence from home began to trouble
her mother, a woman who purportedly possessed psychic powers.
Mrs. Marten had a nightmare where she clearly saw Corder kill
her daughter, using an ax to crush her head, and she then saw in
this sleepy vision the killer bury her daughter's body in the earth
of the red barn.

Marten's stepbrother had earlier told the missing woman's
parents that, on the day Marten left home, he had seen Corder
walking toward his red barn with a shovel and a pickax. Marten's
father went to the barn on Apr. 19, 1828, urged on by his wife,
and began to dig up the earth. He found his daughter's body and
a warrant was issued for Corder's arrest. He was seized in Ealing
by constable James Lea and, on Aug. 8, 1828, Corder was placed
on trial at the Bury St. Edmunds Assizes. Corder pleaded not
guilty, but testimony by Marten's stepbrother and the discovery
of the body sealed his fate. Corder admitted that he had buried

Marten's body, but claimed he had not killed the woman. He
stated that she had taken a pistol from his house while they were
quarreling and had shot herself to death. He panicked, Corder
claimed, and buried the body. The jury disbelieved him and, on

The execution of William Corder, 1828.

Aug. 10, Corder was convicted and sentenced to death. He wrote
out a lengthy confession before his execution which occurred at
Bury St. Edmunds. On Aug. 11, 1828, Corder was hanged before
a large crowd.

REF.: Altick, *Victorian Studies in Scarlet;* Arnold, *Maria Marten,
Murder In the Red Barn;* Atholl, *Shadow of the Gallows;* Bleackley,
Hangmen of England; Brock, *A Casebook of Crime;* Brophy, *The Meaning
of Murder;* Butler, *Murderer's England;* CBA; Dunbar, *Blood in the Parlor;
Famous Trials;* Gibbs and Maltby, *The True Story of Maria Marten;*
Goodman, *The Correspondence of Murder;* Gribble, *Adventures in Murder;*
Lambert, *Thou Shalt Do No Murder;* Laurence, *A History of Capital
Punishment;* Logan, *Masters of Crime;* ____, *Rope, Knife and Chair;*
Mackenzie, *The Murder of Maria Marten;* McCormick, *The Red Barn
Mystery;* Mencken, *By the Neck;* Nash, *Almanac of World Crime;* Potter,
The Art of Hanging; Wilson, *Encyclopedia of World Crime.*

Cordero, Andres Figueroa, 1925-79, U.S., asslt.-attempt. mur.
On Mar. 1, 1954, four Puerto Rican nationalists unfurled the flag
of their homeland in the chambers of the House of Representatives and began shooting. During the violent outbreak that
followed, five U.S. congressmen were wounded. The attack was
intended to draw attention to the colonial "situation" of the
Puerto Rican people, according to Andres Figueroa Cordero, one
of the four gunmen. Cordero, along with Lolita Lebron, Rafael
Cancel Miranda, and Irving Rodriguez Flores were each sentenced
to twenty-five to seventy-five year terms.

In 1977 President Jimmy Carter ordered the release of Cordero,
who was suffering from cancer. The 52-year-old nationalist
returned to Aguadilla, Puerto Rico where he died on Mar. 7, 1979.
His three companions remained behind bars. REF.: *CBA.*

Cordero, José Antonio, 1936- , and **Lopez, Hector,** 1959- ,
and **Mendez, Francisco** , 1959- , U.S., arson-mur. New York
City's worst arson disaster stemmed from the jealous motives of
a 40-year-old ex-convict named José Cordero, who recruited two
teenage accomplices to set fire to a Bronx social club on Oct. 24,
1976.

Cordero, a married man with two children, was infatuated
with 18-year-old Diana Sanchez. Against his wishes, she attended
a dance at the Puerto Rican Social Club with her sister Evelyn.
Shortly before midnight, Cordero returned with Hector Lopez,
Francisco Mendez, and a gallon of gasoline. Mendez splashed
gasoline on the back stairs of the club, and then set fire to it
according to Cordero's directions. The young man was promised
marijuana, a new car, and some rum for his troubles.

The conflagration claimed the lives of twenty-five patrons.
Another twenty-four were badly injured in what Bronx District
Attorney Mario Merola described as the city's largest deliberately
set fire. Cordero and Lopez were arrested in January 1977, after
the police had conducted more than 1,000 interviews with neigh-

borhood residents.

During the four-week trial, the prosecution produced a 14-year-old witness named Julio Hernandez who told of Cordero's offers of money and liquor outside the club.

Mendez was convicted and sentenced to twenty-five years to life in prison. Cordero received a life sentence with parole possible after twenty years, and Lopez, who confessed to starting the blaze, was given life with parole eligibility after fifteen years.

The tragic fire at the social club brought into sharp focus the wanton destruction of property and loss of lives due to arson in the Bronx. A television documentary, *The Fire Next Door*, illustrated the problems facing the 1.5 million residents of the borough. According to reporter Bill Moyers, "The South Bronx has all the superlatives: highest crime, poorest people, greatest unemployment, worst blight, and the world's record for arson." REF.: *CBA*.

Córdoba, José Maria, c.1800-30, Col., assass. A general at age twenty-two, Córdoba fought with Simon Bólivar and was the victim of an assassination plot. REF.: *CBA*.

Cordova, Valdemar Aguirre, 1922- , U.S., jur. Nominated to serve on the bench of the district court of Arizona by President Jimmy Carter in 1978. He was a member of the Adult Probation and Criminal Rules Committee. REF.: *CBA*.

Cordova Davila, Felix, 1878-1938, U.S., jur. District attorney of San Juan, P.R., in 1908 and appointed justice of the supreme court of Puerto Rico by President Herbert Hoover in 1932. REF.: *CBA*.

Corens, Henry, prom. 1945, U.S., mur. When Henry Corens reported to the Bethesda, Md., police that his wife had vanished, it seemed like another routine missing-persons case—until police received two cryptic notes in the mail. "Pearl gone for good. Not returning," the first one said. It was postmarked Norfolk, Va. A few days later, a second letter arrived from Miami, Fla., that said: "Don't bother to look for Pearl."

Police ascertained that the couple had had marital problems for years. Henry Corens' affairs led Pearl's brother, Grover Walker, to surmise that she had finally run off with someone else.

The police investigation was stymied until two farmers who had dropped a fishing line into the Potomac River noticed a disembodied head in a wooded area adjacent to the bank. Dental charts confirmed that it belonged to Pearl Corens.

A young sailor who had shown an interest in Pearl was located and questioned, but it was impossible to establish a direct link to the murder. A search of the Corens' house produced a hacksaw and washtub cover with traces of human blood . A pathologist claimed that the blood was Pearl's, but it was pointed out that Henry Corens shared his wife's blood type.

A young girl that Corens had an affair with supplied the motive when she told the court that Corens had begged her to marry him. Circumstantial evidence and a batch of love letters written to his sweetheart helped convict Corens of second-degree murder. He was sentenced to eighteen years at hard labor. No clues were ever found as to who had sent the letters from Miami and Norfolk. REF.: *CBA*; Rice, *45 Murderers*.

Corey, Daniel H., prom. 1830, Case of, U.S., mur. In 1830, Matilda Nash of Sullivan, N.H., tried to stop an argument between Daniel Corey and his wife. Corey, an unreasonable man, believed there was a gold mine on his farm and killers were after it. When he was certain that his cat had been bewitched, he fashioned a silver bullet with which to kill it. And when Mrs. Nash interrupted a fight between Daniel Corey and his wife, Corey turned from his wife and battered her brains out. In one of the first "diminished capacity" decisions in American courts, Corey was found Not Guilty by reason of insanity. REF.: *CBA*; Nash, *Almanac of World Crime*; Parker, *Report on the Trial of Daniel H. Corey*.

Corey, Frank (AKA: Frank Mulleono, Wop Costello, Crecorian), prom. 1925, U.S., rob.-mur. Act One of the infamous Boston Brown Derby murder case opened on the evening of May 30, 1925, when Mae Price, a veteran wardrobe mistress, was killed in her room at the Hotel Hollis. It was the closing night of a successful engagement at the Wilbur Theatre on Tremont Street. Most of the cast members who starred in *The Brown Derby* opted to catch the midnight train back to New York, but Price stayed behind. She asked the hotel desk for a 10:00 a.m. wake-up call in order to catch her New York train. It was an appointment she never kept.

At ten the next morning, the day clerk rang her bell but got no answer. Finally the elevator operator used a pass key to get in. Price had been strangled and suffocated to death, and three pay envelopes for her staff had been stolen. Although it was thought the room had been locked, a guest told police that he had accidentally left his key in his door. The killer must have used it to open Price's door, since the locks were identical.

The police learned that a suspicious-looking man in a tan topcoat had been lurking in the hallways. The description closely matched that of Frank Mulleono, who had registered two days prior and had passed a bad $10 check. Mulleono disappeared, and the investigation petered out. Charles Marshall Drury, editor of the Boston *Herald*, kept the story alive in his newspaper and conducted an independent investigation. He uncovered the sordid past of Frank Mulleono, whose real name was Frank Corey, an ex-convict who had been sentenced to eight years in prison in 1915 for highway robbery. He had escaped in 1917, but was re-arrested and then released in 1922.

Inspector James Swan of the Worcester Police Department recognized a photo of the suspect and laid a trap for him. "I haven't been in Boston for over a year!" Corey snapped when they captured him outside his father's grocery store. Corey was transported to Boston where he was arraigned on murder charges. The first of two sensational trials ended in an acquittal for the defendant on Aug. 20, 1925, after defense attorney William Scharton had skillfully poked holes into the largely circumstantial evidence submitted by the prosecution. Playing a trump card, the state had Corey arrested and remanded to the custody of the army after it was learned that he had gone AWOL on Aug. 20, 1924. It was a gamble that bought the prosecution valuable time to prepare a bill for the grand jury charging Corey with robbery. An indictment was returned, and for the first time in Massachusetts history a defendant was to be tried for two different crimes using the same evidence.

The second Brown Derby trial convened in March 1926 in the courtroom of Judge David Lourie. The outcome was considerably different the second time around. The tan topcoat that Corey had worn on the night of the murder was produced by Inspector Harry Pierce from a rooming house near the Boston State House. A hotel desk clerk produced the ledger Corey had signed, and it was shown that the signature matched the entry at the Hotel Hollis. Frank Corey was convicted of robbery despite an emotional appeal by the defense. Defense Attorney Scharton accused a reporter from the Boston *Telegram* of jury tampering, but the judge discounted his plea, and Corey was sentenced to life in prison. Nineteen years later he was brought before the parole board, but was denied his freedom.

Frank Corey maintained his innocence. "It was never proved that the coat was mine," he said. "I never saw it till that day in court. I was convicted on my record, on circumstantial evidence." REF.: *CBA*; Rodell, *Boston Murderers*.

Corey, Giles, See: Salem Witchcraft Trials.

Corleone, Si., prom. 1870s- , Italy, org. crime. The Sicilian village of Corleone served as one of the backdrops for author Mario Puzo's *Godfather* saga. Since the 1870s, many of its male inhabitants have migrated to the East Coast of the U.S. to engage in organized crime. Corleone, has been the seedbed of the Mafia for generations, and the site of some of the most ruthless vendettas in the history of that island. Between 1944 and 1948, 153 murders were attributed to the local Mafiosi. It has been estimated at various times that 80 percent of Corleone's males were either serving prison terms or awaiting sentencing. Recent statistics show that only ten percent of the adult population are working-age males. The various Mafia wars had exacted a terrible price.

Located forty-two miles south of Palermo, the town was a Saracen settlement before a Lombard colony was introduced by Frederick II. Among the native sons to rise to prominence in the U.S. Mafia were Ciro Terranova, Ignazio Saietta (Lupo the Wolf), and the Morello clan, who for a time formed the nucleus of a New York crime family. Antonio Morella, the eldest brother of this family, was held responsible for thirty to forty murders, and Joe Morello was at one time the acknowledged leader of the New York City mafia. REF.: *CBA.*

Service photo of Dean Allen Corll, left, and his partner in mass murder, Elmer Wayne Henley, right. They killed at least twenty-seven.

Corll, Dean Allen, 1939-73, and **Henley, Elmer Wayne,** 1956- , and **Brooks, David Owen,** 1955- , U.S., mur. On Aug. 8, 1973, 17-year-old Elmer Wayne Henley called the Pasadena, Texas, Police Department and said he had just shot his friend Dean Corll. The police found Dean Corll lying face down with six slugs in his shoulder and back, and then the whole story began to come out. Henley and his friend David Brooks were accomplices to twenty-seven murders in the previous three years as Corll indulged his sado-masochistic sexual fantasies by murdering teenaged boys.

Corll was punished harshly as a child, and when his parents divorced, he and his brother Stanley were shuttled between nursery schools and baby sitters. In 1964, Corll was drafted into the army, and by 1969 his personality disorders came to concern his friends and relatives. Corll returned to Houston and went to work for the Lighting and Power Company. He began to associate with teenaged boys, and sniffed glue with two of them, Elmer Wayne Henley and David Owen Brooks.

The killing began in 1970 when Corll lured hitchhiking University of Texas student Jeffrey Konen to his house in Pasadena. But Corll usually relied on Henley, a high school dropout, to find victims from the depressed Heights section of Houston. Corll promised to pay $200 for each victim lured into the trap, but he usually reneged. Brooks, Corll's first willing recruit, said he met the man in the schoolyard and Corll gave him some candy, after which they lived together for a time. In 1970, Brooks came home and found Corll engaged in sexual acts with two young men who had been bound and gagged. Brooks was given a car to keep silent.

Brooks and Henley soon became willing participants in murder. In the next two years, the three murdered twenty-seven young boys. Victims were lured to Corll's home for drug and alcohol parties. After the victims fell unconscious, Corll tied them up, sexually molested them, and killed them. He disposed of the bodies in either a remote spot near the Sam Rayburn Reservoir or a boat shed in southwest Houston rented for the purpose.

On Aug. 8, 1973, Henley violated the "trust" by bringing 15-year-old Rhonda Williams to the apartment. "You weren't supposed to bring any girl!" Corll bellowed. The girl had run away from home and needed a place to stay for the night, and Henley said his friend Dean wouldn't mind. Varnish sniffing began, and Henley, Williams, and Timothy Kerley, sixteen, passed out. When he awoke and discovered that Corll had tied them up, Henley pleaded for his life. Corll released him when he promised to rape and kill Williams while Corll did the same to Kerley. But Henley was too upset to perform a sexual act with the girl. He seized a .22-caliber pistol and pointed it at Corll, who taunted him. Henley fired six shots, and then called the local police. Later that day he took police to shed number eleven at the Southwest Boat Storage and the excavation began. After the twenty-seventh body was removed from the shallow graves at the boathouse and near the lake, the search stopped. A "record" had been established, eclipsing the slayings of twenty-five migrant workers in California in 1971. But Mary West, Corll's divorced mother, thought there might be more victims. The Houston police were unwilling to continue, despite hundreds of parents' requests for information about their missing children.

On Aug. 11, 1973, the Houston district attorney filed murder charges against Brooks and Henley. Judge Preston Dial barred the press during jury selection. The trial opened in San Antonio in July 1974. Henley and Brooks were convicted of the murders of six of the twenty-seven victims, and were each sentenced to life imprisonment.

Jack Olsen's 1974 book about the case, *The Man With the Candy,* referred to Mary West's confectionery business, which she had operated with the help of her son in Vidor, Texas.

REF.: *CBA;* Gurwell, *Mass Murder In Houston;* Haines, *Bothersome Bodies;* McComas, *The Graveside Companion;* Olsen, *The Man With the Candy.*

Cormenin, Louis Marie de Lahaye, 1788-1868, Fr., lawyer. Member of the Chamber of Deputies from 1830-46 and in 1848. REF.: *CBA.*

Corn, Samuel Thompson, 1840-1925, U.S., jur. State's attorney of Illinois from 1872-80 and appointed judge of the territorial court of Wyoming by President Grover Cleveland in 1886. REF.: *CBA.*

Corneilison, John J., prom. 1884, U.S., asslt.&bat. In 1884, Judge Richard Reid of Mt. Sterling, Ky., seemed virtually assured of winning election to the Appellate Court of his district. He was considered to be a capable jurist, who was well liked by his constituents, with the exception of one John J. Corneilison, who attended the same church as the judge and had retained him as his legal counsel in a case before the Superior Court of Montgomery County.

Corneilison incorrectly believed that Judge Reid had secretly conspired to remove him from his position as master commissioner of the Circuit Court, and that he had betrayed his interests during the pending litigation. Judge A.E. Richards wrote the final opinion in the case of *Howard vs. Corneilison.* The blue-penciled notations in the margin were those of Richards, and not Reid, as Corneilison was led to believe. The unfavorable decision cast aspirations on the character and integrity of John Corneilison, and for these reasons he decided to punish his former friend.

Judge Reid agreed to meet his old friend in his law offices on Apr. 16, 1884. He had no idea that Corneilison was angry or upset with him. "I should like you to examine this and give me your opinion on it," Corneilison said, handing a sheaf of papers to the judge. As he looked over the documents Corneilison struck him from behind with a hickory walking stick. He rained many blows on the unsuspecting judge who escaped into the streets of Mt. Sterling with his assailant trailing close behind. Reid sought refuge in the store of John E. Bean who saw Corneilison lashing the judge with a cowhide whip.

Less than a month later, on May 15, Judge Reid committed suicide just before his election campaign concluded. There was no connection between his death and the earlier attack, but charges were immediately filed against Corneilison. The indictment charged him with assault and battery. After a brief deliberation, a Guilty verdict was returned in the matter, and John Corneilison was sentenced to three years in prison and assessed a fine of one penny.

REF.: *CBA; Johnson, Famous Kentucky Tragedies and Trials.*

Cornejo, Mariano Harlan, 1863-1942, Peru, jur. Member of the Peruvian Chamber of Deputies from 1893-1904. Cornejo later served on the Court of International Justice at the Hague from 1915-42. He authored the Code of Criminal Procedure in 1916, and drafted the constitution adopted by the constituent assembly in 1919-20. REF.: *CBA.*

Cornelys, Theresa, 1723-97, Brit., morals. Theresa Cornelys was born in Venice to a stage family. At the age of seventeen she struck out on her own, and became the mistress to a number of prominent men, while at the same time, engaging in a theatrical career of her own. Back in Venice, Madame Cornelys became the lover of the famous Italian rogue Casanova, and bore him a son. In 1759, she arrived in London and soon took the city by storm.

She purchased the Carlisle House in Soho Square a year later and gave rise to a new form of popular entertainment that shocked and scandalized the respectable elements of British society. Her masked balls, recitals, and public lyceums were assailed for their immorality.

On Feb. 24, 1771, Cornelys was brought before a grand jury and charged with keeping a disorderly house. Sir John Fielding, who was both advocate and playwright, prosecuted her for operating her establishment without a license. As a result, Cornelys was forced to sell Carlisle House at public auction in November 1772, and sent to debtor's prison, where she lived until 1779. Afterward she entered a long period of decline. Before dying in relative obscurity in 1797, Cornelys became a seller of "asses' milk" at Knightsbridge. REF.: *CBA.*

Cornero, Anthony (Anthony Cornero Stralla), 1895-1955, U.S., smug.-gamb. Anthony Cornero, born Stralla in northern Italy near the Swiss border, was raised on a sizable farm which his father lost in a card game. Before the family could emigrate to the U.S., expecting to use proceeds from their considerable grain harvest, little Tony, playing with matches, accidentally set fire to the grain bin and caused his family to arrive in New York almost penniless. Cornero went to work with his father in his early teens, vowing that he would make his family rich again. His opportunity to obtain a fortune presented itself, as it did with thousands of immigrants, with the advent of Prohibition in 1920. By then the Cornero family was living in San Francisco. Tony was driving a cab in 1922 when he decided to go into the rumrunning business.

Starting with a few small boats, Cornero smuggled bonded whiskey to most of the better nightclubs in Los Angeles and to the homes of the wealthy. As a high society bootlegger and rumrunner, Cornero soon acquired staggering profits. He was, by 1925, a millionaire many times over. Acquiring a merchant ship, the S.S. *Lily,* Cornero stocked it with more than 4,000 cases of the best liquor available and served southern Californians, running dozens of fast launches from the *Lily* each night from its anchorage many miles off Los Angeles. Millions more poured into Cornero's pockets, but federal agents sought to close down his smuggling operations in 1926, seizing the *Lily* and its storehouse of liquor.

Lawyers for the *Lily* insisted that the ship was operating far beyond U.S. coastal waters and was therefore beyond the jurisdiction of the federal authorities, an argument that failed to win Cornero's case. Cornero was not on board at the time his vessel and its cargo was impounded and his crew arrested. Hearing of the raid, he boarded a Los Angeles train en route to Seattle. Federal agents followed Cornero on board and, as the train made its way through the mountains of northern California, the rumrunner jumped off. He found an airport nearby and rented a plane which flew him to a town south of Portland, Ore., where Cornero reboarded the train to retrieve a suitcase full of money from his

stateroom, more than \$2 million, according to one report.

Agents were waiting in the stateroom, not knowing that Cornero had jumped off and reboarded the train, believing he was in hiding somewhere else on the train. As the train approached Seattle, Cornero paid a conductor for the use of his uniform and, wearing spectacles and a false mustache, Cornero entered his own stateroom, pretending to be the conductor, and retrieved his suitcase, right under the eyes of the federal Prohibiton agents. Just before the train reached Seattle, the bootlegger leaped once more from the train and vanished into the countryside. He bought a car and drove to Vancouver, British Columbia. From there Cornero traveled to Europe, and then to South America, but he longed for his home, relatives, and friends in California and he returned in 1929, voluntarily surrendering to authorities who held warrants for his arrest on smuggling charges. He was sentenced to two years' imprisonment in the federal penitentiary at McNeil Island in Puget Sound.

While in prison, Cornero formulated plans to switch his bootlegging operations to gambling, and when released in 1931, Cornero went to Las Vegas, Nev., then only a small desert resort. He used his rumrunning profits to build one of the town's first casinos, Green Meadows, which he staffed with attractive hostesses. Slot machines, poker, roulette, all the games of chance were made available to customers, who were also served the finest cuisine in the Green Meadows' elegant restaurant. Cornero invested heavily in other small gambling operations and soon began to see considerable earnings, all of this fifteen years before Benjamin "Bugsy" Siegel moved to Las Vegas to turn it into the gambling capital of America for the national crime syndicate.

East Coast gangsters representing Charles "Lucky" Luciano, Meyer Lansky, Frank Costello, and others, soon realized the profits Las Vegas could bring and they insisted that Cornero cut them in on his operations. Cornero had never been part of the Mafia, nor was he a member of the newly organized national crime syndicate. He had built his own organizations with independent West Coast bootleggers and gamblers and was, the eastern gangsters recognized, a force to be reckoned with. When Cornero rebuffed the eastern gangsters, his gambling spa, Green Meadows, was torched. Cornero realized that he could not fight the big mobs, so he sold out his interests in other small casinos like the Apache Hotel and returned to Los Angeles.

Cornero and other bootleggers purchased an old cargo ship, the *Tango,* converted it to a gambling ship and anchored it off Santa Monica. The ship was outfitted with posh gambling rooms that offered roulette, faro, craps, poker, and slot machines. A lavish dining area provided top cuisine prepared by the best chefs in Los Angeles. Fast boats picked up hundreds of gamblers each night and ferried them out to the *Tango.* Cornero's fortunes once again rose. With his enormous profits, Cornero bought another ship, a huge wooden barkentine, the S.S. *Kenilworth,* built in 1887, which had been rechristened *The Star of Scotland* in 1903. The ship had been used to ferry passengers to Catalina Island, and when Cornero found the vessel it was serving as a bait barge for fishermen.

After buying the ship and refurbishing it at a cost of \$300,000, Cornero rechristened the ship the *Rex.* In 1938, Cornero opened the great gambling ship to the public, anchoring his elegant floating gambling den more than three miles off Santa Monica. Fast launches brought hundreds of high society and movie industry gamblers to the *Rex* each night. Other gambling ships wholly or partly owned by Cornero included the *Tango,* now anchored off Venice, the *Show Boat,* anchored off Long Beach, the *Texas,* off San Diego, all part of what the press dubbed "Cornero's Navy," and he, the one-time impoverished Italian immigrant, was now "Admiral Cornero." His flagship was the *Rex,* now an elegantly appointed gambling ship. It offered 150 slot machines which lined the promenade deck and the walls of the many gaming rooms, which also featured roulette, blackjack, 21, faro, poker, bridge, chuck-a-luck, and even a Chinese lottery. There was a bingo room which seated 400.

The *Rex*, which detective writer Raymond Chandler was to describe in his fiction, was staffed by 350 crewmen, waiters, waitresses, cooks, chefs, a full orchestra, and polite gunmen in tuxedoes who gave suspicious customers a courteous frisking—Cornero was acutely aware of pirates who had raided other ships, holding up customers and looting the safe. The dining room was richly decorated and featured French cuisine. Repeal was already in force when the *Rex* went into operation, so Cornero offered the best liquor available, paying his state and federal fees for liquor seals and stamps. More than 2,000 gambling patrons could be accommodated by the *Rex* each night. The nightly payroll exceeded $3,000, but Cornero made thirty times that each night in profits. Though the millions rolled back into Cornero's pockets, the gambler inexplicably had become involved in a reform movement that would spell the ruin of his offshore gambling empire, which he felt was safe from federal prosecution because all his ships were anchored 3.1 miles off the coast, just beyond federal jurisdiction over illegal gambling.

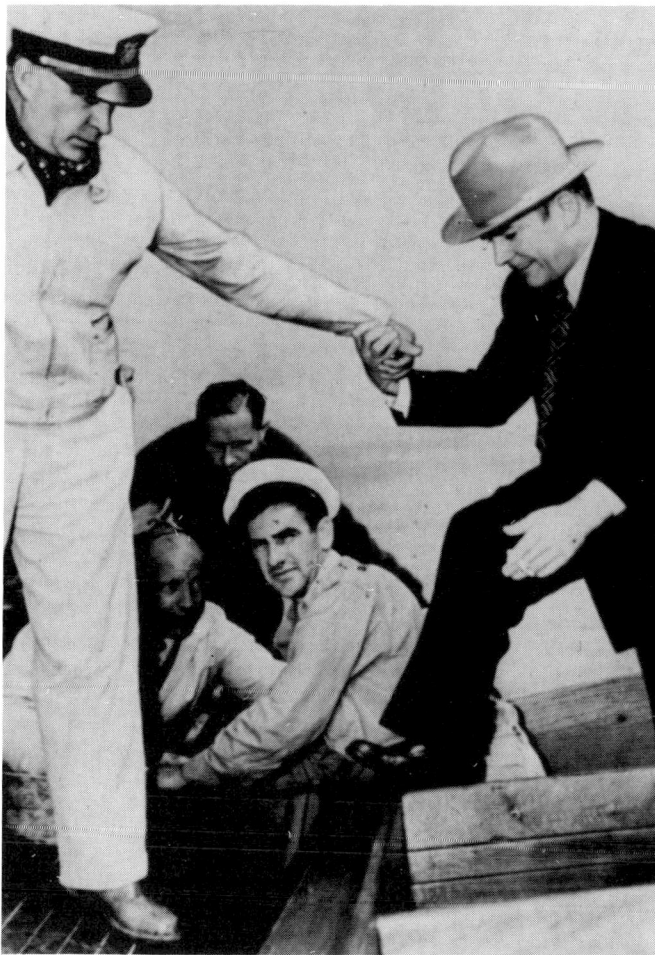

"Admiral" Tony Cornero, right, California gambling boss, is helped aboard a launch en route to his gambling ship, the *Rex,* 1938.

Prior to Cornero's establishment of his gambling ships, he had attempted to set up gambling operations in the Los Angeles area but he had run afoul of the local gamblers in league with Los Angeles mayor Frank Shaw. Cornero had opened several small gambling dens, but police in the pay of the established gamblers repeatedly raided his operations. As soon as a Cornero gambling spa opened it was closed by police. The gambler soon realized that a powerful gambling syndicate, under the direction of Mayor Shaw himself, allowed no outsiders to partake of the $20 million taken in each year from the 300 gambling houses, 600 brothels, 1,800 bookie joints, and 23,000 slot machines operating full blast almost around the clock. Everyone knew that Shaw's administration was utterly corrupt, along with most of the Los Angeles Police Department (LAPD).

Wealthy Clifford Clinton, owner of a chain of Los Angeles cafeterias which featured organ music and hymns, began a reform movement in 1937, demanding a recall of Mayor Shaw. Clinton and his candidate for mayor, Fletcher Bowron, managed to expose Earle Kynette, chief of the intelligence bureau of the LAPD, as chief enforcer for the local gamblers. Kynette resigned after he was implicated in several bombings, including that of Harry Raymond, Clinton's ace undercover investigator. Shaw was recalled and Bowron elected mayor. That still left a Los Angeles Police Department rife with corruption. Mayor Bowron wanted to learn exactly who on the LAPD was on the take. To that end, he consulted Jimmy Richardson, top crime writer for the Los Angeles *Examiner,* who had helped to expose Kynette and Shaw. Richardson suggested that Mayor Bowron talk privately with none other than Tony Cornero, knowing that Cornero hated the gambling syndicate and the crooked police officers who served it.

Cornero met with Richardson and Bowron in the mayor's home near the Hollywood Bowl. The gambler gave the mayor detailed information on the gambling syndicate and its complete operations down to the last back room behind the smallest drugstore where slot machines were available to school boys. He also named twenty-six high-ranking police officers involved with the gamblers. A short time later, all twenty-six officers, including the chief of the LAPD, resigned. The gambling syndicate was then systematically broken up. But the reform measures also included action against Cornero. Mayor Bowron, to show that he had made no deal with Cornero, ordered Attorney General Earl Warren to raid the *Rex.* On May 13, 1938, Los Angeles County prosecutor Burton Fitts raided the ship, arresting Cornero and fifty of his employees on gambling charges, but they were released the same day.

Legal battles ensued, Cornero's lawyers arguing that the *Rex* and the other ships were outside U.S. waters and therefore immune to gambling laws. Fitts, stymied by legal restrictions, then ordered all the water taxis to cease operating from Santa Monica to the *Rex.* Cornero retaliated by moving the *Rex* to an anchorage off Redondo Beach, and water taxis from that pier took up operations without delaying the hundreds of anxious gamblers wanting to reach the *Rex.* More raids ensued through 1938, but Cornero managed to fight off convictions in the courts. In early 1939, the gambler brought his boat back to the Santa Monica area, where business was so brisk that the *Rex* showed profits in excess of $300,000 a month. State and federal authorities, meanwhile, boarded the *Tango, Texas,* and *Show Boat,* smashing the gambling equipment and destroying the interior of these luxury gambling ships. The *Rex* was saved for last. Fitts and scores of lawmen raced out to the huge gambling ship and tried to board it, but Cornero's men, using high pressure hoses, repelled the boarders. The battle went on for nine hours with newsmen occupying many of the water taxis, photographing the bizarre scene. The lawmen finally gave up and returned to Santa Monica.

The state supreme court then ruled that the three-mile limit began not from the Santa Monica shore but from the headlands of the bay, which placed the *Rex* inside California waters. Cornero was beaten and he knew it. He ceased operating the gambling ship and the *Rex* went into drydock. The ship was activated during WWII and used as a cargo barge, and later sold to a private investor who planned to convert the ship into a swanky nightclub. But this never materialized and the ship was later scrapped. By then, Cornero had moved around the country, attempting to open gambling operations, but he was unsuccessful. Following WWII, the gambler purchased a Navy minelayer and converted it into a luxury gambling vessel, rechristening it the *Lux* and anchoring it six miles off Long Beach. The *Lux* featured a 100-foot bar, several dance floors, bands, posh gambling rooms, and slot machines. It opened for business on Aug. 7, 1946, and it was swamped with customers eager to lose their money.

Earl Warren, then governor of California, exploded when he heard of the gambler's new operation, saying: "Cornero has absolutely defied us. No human being in the country is big enough for that." The water taxi service was shut off by the Long Beach Port Authority on Warren's orders. Since no customers could get to the *Lux*, the last of California's great gambling ships went out of business quickly. Cornero used the ship and others he purchased for legitimate commercial shipping. Several vessels sank in maritime accidents, and the tremendous losses caused Cornero to quit the business. He opened some Los Angeles gambling dens, but Mickey Cohen and his goons soon closed these spas. Moreover, Cornero's expensive Beverly Hills home was bombed by Cohen's thugs and the gambler relocated to Las Vegas.

Here Cornero planned to build the most expensive, luxurious gambling casino in America, the Stardust. The cost was enormous, more than $6 million. Cornero tried to raise the money but fell short. He planned to make up the balance through gambling. He borrowed money and began shooting craps at the Desert Inn on July 31, 1955, playing hour after hour and losing consistently.

The marathon crapshoot was too much for the squat, overweight Cornero. While still clutching the dice, Cornero suddenly grimaced, clutched his chest and then crashed forward onto the table, dead of a heart attack. Cornero had made an estimated $25 million in his long career as a bootlegger, rumrunner and gambler. At his death, only $800 was found in his pockets. The Stardust was completed by others, becoming a great success, but not a dime of its profits went into the coffers of Tony Cornero. He was by then, in the minds of old-time gamblers, only a memory, a little man with extravagant ideas and a penchant for wild adventure. See: **Cohen, Mickey.**

REF.: *CBA;* Eames, *Sleuths, Inc.;* Gross, *The World of Raymond Chandler;* Reid, *The Grim Reapers;* Richardson, *For the Life of Me;* Wolf and Mader, *Fallen Angels.*

Cornett, Brack, d.1888, U.S., west. outl. A member of the Bill Whitley band, Brack Cornett was born and raised in Goliad County, Texas. Along with Whitley and others, Cornett robbed banks and trains in southwest Texas in the late 1880s. In 1888, Whitley, Cornett, and others robbed the bank at Cisco, Texas, taking $25,000 and, a few days later, they stopped an I&GN train near McNeill in Travis County, stealing $20,000 from the express car. Cornett's gang stopped another Southern Pacific train at Harwood, but a sheriff's posse was on board waiting for them and the gang was driven off. The band was successful in robbing another train near Flatonia. At Floresville in Wilson County, Texas, the band was finally trapped by U.S. marshals on Sept. 25, 1888. The gang members elected to shoot it out and Whitley was killed, another member was captured, and

Outlaw Brack Cornett.

Cornett escaped in a wild ride across the plains. Sheriff Alfred Allee tracked the bandit across Arizona and, at Frio, shot it out with him, killing Cornett.

REF.: Bartholomew, *The Biographical Album of Western Gunfighters;* CBA.

Cornock, Mrs. Cecil, prom. 1947, Case of, Brit, mur. Cecil George Cornock of Bristol, England, was a masochist. His wife indulged him by tying him to the tripod of an electric boiler before beating him with a cord.

Mr. Cornock's peculiar fetish formed the basis for the Crown's case against his wife when the man was found murdered in his bathtub in December 1946. He had been beaten many times over the head. Investigators found numerous injuries to his head and

limbs, and rope marks around his wrists. Further, it was alleged that Mrs. Cornock had been keeping company with a crippled man. The existence of several amorous letters confirmed these suspicions.

Mrs. Cornock was charged with murder and brought before the Briston Assizes. What was not clear to the pathologists and the attorneys was the nature of the injuries sustained by Cornock: photographs showed them as black. Pathologists dismissed them as "abrasions with bruising." Sir Bernard Spilsbury, an esteemed pathologist, now in the twilight of a long and distinguished career, was invited to examine the prosecution's evidence. He concluded that the police photos were shot on orthochromatic plates which have a tendency to make a red object appear black. The bruises, Spilsbury concluded, could have been caused by anything, weakening the case against Mrs. Cornock. Based on Spilsbury's testimony, she was acquitted after a four-day trial. See: **Spilsbury, Sir Bernard.**

REF.: Browne and Tullett, *The Scalpel of Scotland Yard;* ____, *The Life of Sir Bernard Spilsbury; CBA.*

Cornwell, Gerry, 1920- , U.S., mur. Cornwell lived with his 35-year-old girlfriend in Oakland, Calif. Several months before Christmas 1955, Alice Franklin asked him to leave the apartment: she had fallen in love with Robert Hand, a 27-year-old steel worker.

Cornwell left quietly and actually remained on good terms with his ex-girlfriend and her new love interest. Just before Christmas, Cornwell accompanied them to a party. Everyone was having a good time, and the gathering broke up quite late.

Cornwell followed Franklin and Hand home. As they prepared for bed, he lurked outside their window, suddenly possessed by an uncontrollable jealousy. He watched them having sex, which infuriated him. He proceeded to a nearby garage where he bought three gallons of gasoline. After the two had fallen asleep, Cornwell entered the bedroom and poured the fuel over them. As he left the apartment, the strong fumes were accidentally ignited by a pilot light.

The two lovers were destroyed in the flames. They were taken to an area hospital where they died several hours later. A question of criminal responsibility was immediately raised by the defense lawyers. Since Cornwell had not struck a match, could he be charged with murder? The Alameda County District Attorney proved that there was criminal intent to commit murder and, therefore, the defendant was Guilty as charged. The judge agreed and sentenced Cornwell to life in prison.

REF.: *CBA;* Wilson, *Encyclopedia of Murder.*

Corona, Juan Vallejo, 1933- , U.S., mur. Few mass murderers match the ruthlessness and systematic slaughter demonstrated by Juan Corona, a killer who murdered at least twenty-five migrant workers in the space of six weeks during 1971. Corona, a Mexican migrant worker himself, had arrived in Yuba City, Calif., in the 1950s. By the early 1970s, he was a labor contractor, hiring migrant workers to pick the various fruit crops in the Yuba City area. He was also, by that time, a man who suffered from several forms of mental illness. He had been diagnosed as suffering from schizophrenia. He was also a homosexual and a brutal sadist. As early as 1970, the Corona family was involved in violent sex. Corona's half-brother, Natividad, was charged with sexually attacking a young Mexican worker who was found bleeding in the washroom of the half-brother's Guadalajara Cafe located in Marysville, close to Yuba City. When the youth sued the half-brother and won a $250,000 settlement, Natividad fled back to Mexico.

The odd thing about Corona's murder spree which was umbilically connected to homosexual attacks was the fact that he was a married man with children. Heterosexual or not, Corona also craved sex with his own gender, an uncommon but not unheard of tendency on the part of some sex killers. As a labor contractor, Corona hired migrant workers, and housed these single men in a barracks-like building on the Sullivan ranch. These men were, for the most part, elderly alcoholics, social dropouts, and misfits. They began disappearing in early May 1971. On May 19, a Japanese fruit farmer noticed a large hole seven feet long and three and a half feet deep that had been scooped out of his land in a peach orchard. The next night he went to the same spot and saw that the earth had been packed back into the hole. He called the police who dug into what was a fresh grave. Inside of it was Kenneth Whitacre, a hobo who had homosexual literature in his back pocket. He had been sexually assaulted and then stabbed to death, his head chopped with a machete.

Mass killer Juan Corona, waving to friends, en route to prison.

Another farmer noticed what appeared to be a freshly dug grave on his land and police began digging again, this time finding an elderly man. More graves in this area yielded more men, all of them sodomized, stabbed—one was shot—and chopped viciously about the head with a machete. In one grave police found a meat market receipt made out to "Juan V. Corona." The bodies kept turning up including that of John Henry Jackson, an elderly worker who had been seen some weeks earlier riding in the back of Corona's pickup truck. The police kept digging until June 4, 1971, unearthing twenty-five bodies, along with more receipts that had the name of Juan Corona on them. Corona was arrested and charged with murder. He pleaded not guilty, but his defense lawyers, who maintained that another person had done the murders, had an uphill battle against the overpowering evidence of bodies, receipts, and eyewitnesses who had seen the murdered workers with Corona shortly before they disappeared.

There was speculation that Corona and another man had committed the murders, but no other suspect was ever found, let alone arrested. Psychiatrists ventured many theories about Corona, one claiming that as the spring deepened and the fruit ripened, Corona's madness increased until the climate drove him into a frenzy of murder and mutilation so that he was compelled to kill someone each day to satisfy his blood lust. The availability of victims increased as warmer weather set in and scores of migrant workers drifted into the Marysville-Yuba City area. Corona simply had to stop his truck at any roadside and pick up the lonely workers, social pariahs, no one would ever miss. He would work these men a few days and, when it came time to pay them, the burly, 200-pound Corona would sexually molest these men, then murder them, and bury their bodies. These included Kenneth Whitacre, Charles Fleming, Melford Sample, Donald Smith, John J. Haluka, Warren Kelley, Sigurd Beierman, William Emery Kamp, Clarence Hocking, James W. Howard, Jonah R. Smallwood, Elbert T. Riley, Paul B. Allen, Edward Martin Cupp, Albert Hayes, Raymond Muchache, John H. Jackson, Lloyd Wallace Wenzel, Mark Beverly Shields, Sam Bonafide—also known as Joe Carriveau—Joseph Maczak, and four unidentified men the court labeled "John Doe."

In several instances, the prosecution at Corona's trial was able

to prove, Corona had planned his murders in advance, digging graves days before he had any victims to put into them. Added to this were the damning bloodstained knives, machete, pistol, and Corona's blood-caked clothes found in his home, along with an equally damning ledger in which Corona had officiously listed the names of his victims and the dates of their murders. The jury in the Corona case deliberated for forty-five hours and then brought in a verdict of Guilty in the case of each of the twenty-five murdered men. In January 1973, Judge Richard E. Patton sentenced Corona to twenty-five life terms to run consecutively with no hope of parole. Corona was attacked in prison, stabbed thirty-two times. He lost the sight of one eye. He later won an appeal that claimed he had not received adequate defense, that he should have pleaded insane. He was placed in an asylum for the criminally insane.

REF.: Cartel, *Serial Mass Murder;* CBA; Cray, *Burden of Proof: The Case of Juan Corona;* Godwin, *Murder U.S.A.;* Kidder, *The Road to Yuba City;* Nash, *Murder, America;* Wilson, *Encyclopedia of Modern Murder.*

Corrie, Peter, and **Cropp, Marion,** and **Gambrill, Henry,** d.1859, U.S., mur. On the night of Sept. 22, 1858, a gang of street thugs near Pennsylvania Avenue and Biddle Street in Baltimore began creating a disturbance. The police were summoned by a concerned neighborhood resident. When the squad arrived, they were met with a volley of paving stones and other crude missiles.

When Officer Benton attempted to arrest several of the rioters, Henry Gambrill seized his pistol and shot the policeman through the neck, killing him instantly. Based on the eyewitness testimony of policeman Robert Rigdon, Gambrill was convicted of first-degree murder.

When Rigdon returned home from court on Nov. 5, two of the convicted man's associates were lying in ambush. Peter Corrie fired the shot that killed Rigdon, and Marion Cropp was implicated in the crime under direct questioning by the Baltimore police.

All three men were found Guilty and sentenced to hang. Their executions were carried out on Apr. 8, 1859 before a large throng of people that had traveled from as far away as Philadelphia and Washington, D.C, to witness the event.

REF.: CBA; Mencken, *By The Neck.*

Corrigan, Hugh, prom. 1855, U.S., mur. "By God, I will send her off or kill her," Hugh Corrigan snorted one day, referring to his wife Mary, a heavy-set Irish immigrant woman he had married a year earlier in Westmoreland County, Pa. His domestic relations with Mary deteriorated badly in that year, until finally he murdered her in 1855.

Mary Corrigan was last seen alive near their barn on Sept. 29. Of her disappearsnce Hugh said simply that she had gone to visit her relatives. A local resident named Samuel Stiffey reported hearing screams coming from the farmhouse, but the next morning the Corrigan place was the perfect picture of country serenity.

Hugh Corrigan was seen in the company of his first love, a woman known in the county as Little Mary, shortly before he left for Pittsburgh to answer a court subpoena. He returned to the farm on Oct. 2, still asserting that his wife had gone to visit her family. In fact, Corrigan had transported her body by sled to a location not far from the house.

Two days after his return, a fire was spotted in an abandoned stone quarry near the Corrigan farm. The billowing smoke and foul stench aroused the curiosity of Jacob Alters, who went to see what the trouble was. Stirring around in the smoldering pile of ashes, he was startled to discover human remains.

In a shed near the Corrigan house, investigators found blood traces on the wall. Mary's wardrobe had not been disturbed, which seemed to be convincing evidence that she had not gone on a trip as her husband claimed. Knowing that their relationship was less than ideal, the Commonwealth assembled all available evidence and filed murder charges against Corrigan.

The trial began on Feb. 12, 1856. With an air of casual indifference, the defendant pleaded not guilty and sat back to hear the charges against him. The evidence presented by the prosecution was impressive. Corrigan's domestic problems provided a suitable motive for murder. He was, after all, a wife beater, and he loved another woman. Accordingly, the jury found him Guilty and Corrigan was hanged. REF.: *CBA*.

Corrigan, Michael (AKA: Major Corrigan, Michael Cassidy), d.1946, Brit., fraud. Michael Corrigan was both charlatan and faker, an astute con-man who pulled off some of the most ingenious swindles in Britain between the two wars. It is believed he was born in Fermoy, Ireland, but he gained his wealth in Britain, posing as a wealthy tycoon who speculated in Mexican silver and oil concessions.

In 1922, Corrigan rented an office in Kingsway, but he declared bankruptcy when his investments proved to be false. When his creditors called, they found that Corrigan had vanished. A year later he borrowed £40,000 from a businessman to invest in Mexican oil stocks. He received another £35,000 from the owner of a coal mine. This was enough for him to live in the lap of luxury. He married a woman who owned a stable of fast horses in Belgium and, deciding that the nebulous title of Major was not quite up to his elitist standards, Corrigan promoted himself to Flight Commander of the Royal Naval Air Service. He claimed at the time to be a recipient of the Belgian Legion of Honor.

All this time, Corrigan was virtually unknown to the police. He was arrested in Belgium in 1926 and imprisoned for one month on a charge of fraud. After his release, he introduced himself to the mother of a wealthy young socialite as the president of the Standard Oil Company, with a corresponding rank of General in the Mexican Army. Having won her over, he persuaded the mother to give him £10,000.

Corrigan was convicted of fraud in 1930. He was sentenced to five years in prison, but survived this ordeal to return to Britain as a wealthy arms dealer. During the war, the arch-swindler continued merrily down the path of crime. He purchased large tracts of non-existent English land for South American millionaires, and secured a contract to cut and export balsa wood from the Guatemalan government. He involved himself in a range of other interesting but bogus schemes.

Corrigan was arrested for the last time in 1946. Facing another long prison sentence, he hanged himself in his jail cell at Brixton on Oct.16. It was an ignoble ending to a tainted but colorful life.

REF.: *CBA*; Jackson, *Occupied With Crime*.

Corsetti, Mirta, 1968- , Ital., kid. For a period of three months, 13-year-old Mirta Corsetti was imprisoned in a tiny seven-and-a-half by six-foot room in a coastal villa outside of Rome. The dark-haired girl was manacled to a pair of concrete weights and fed cheese, salami, and milk while her abductors negotiated the ransom demand with her father, millionaire restaurateur Alfredo Corsetti.

Mirta was abducted from her father's restaurant in Torvaianica on July 17, 1981. She was but one of twenty-six kidnap victims taken during the first ten months of that year. Abduction for ransom was fast becoming the national obsession in Italy. The press dubbed the profitable racket "Kidnap, Inc."

The Italian police freed Mirta from her captors on Oct. 24, 1981. Six people were arrested without a struggle, and the girl was found unhurt, though in a state of nervous exhaustion. Over $250,000 of ransom money was recovered at the villa. REF.: *CBA*.

Corsican Vendetta, The, prom. 1944-54, Fr., org. crime. A blood vendetta between rival Corsican families living in Marseilles and Paris mushroomed into an all-out gang war for control of the French underworld in the two cities. The feud began late in 1946, when a petty quarrel broke out between the diminutive Napoléon Corticchiato and several other men socializing at a Pigalle cafe. One of the men insulted Corticchiato by calling him "Shorty." The "Little Napoléon" responded by shooting the man dead.

The Paris shooting sparked a blood feud, and in the ensuing months the Corsican gangsters lined up behind one of two factions: the larger Marseilles contingent led by Ange Salicetti,

or the Paris mob, which controlled the dope traffic and prostitution. The gangs were interdependent: Marseilles was the source of supply, and Paris was the "retail" center where the illegal drugs were peddled.

As the instigator of the war, it was inevitable that the "Little Napoléon" should be targeted for revenge. On a February afternoon in 1946, Ange Salicetti blasted the Little Napoléon with shots from a .45-caliber automatic. François Lucchinacci had assumed control of the Paris gang in 1938. His fine manner and university education disguised his criminal nature, for "François the lawyer" had already been acquitted of murdering the keeper of a bordello in Ajaccio in August 1932. Possibly receiving inspiration from the American gangster film *Scarface,* then playing to packed houses in Paris, Lucchinacci ordered Salicetti's murder. On July 29, 1946, a fusillade of submachine gunfire ripped through the Hollandais Bar on the rue Pigalle in Paris. The shooters—four members of Lucchinacci's gang—killed Jacques Morazzini, the bar's owner, and gravely wounded Dominique Geromini, Paul Morganti, and Dominique Ventura.

Salicetti, however, escaped and fled to Corsica. In September in Corsica, Lucchinacci and three of his henchmen fired on Salicetti as he walked to mass with his uncle Pascal Pietri and girlfriend Jacqueline Dupré. Salicetti was unhurt, but Pietri was killed and Dupré was seriously injured. Soon after his return to Paris, police arrested Lucchinacci and some trusted members of his gang at the Minouche Bar, and seized a cache of hand grenades, submachine guns, and other weapons. Salicetti had given the tip to the police. On May 14, 1948, as Lucchinacci celebrated his release from prison at the Minouche Bar in Paris, Salicetti and his gunmen shot the young lawyer to death.

Control of the Paris rackets went to Mathieu Costa, who tried to resolve differences with Salicetti peacefully, hoping to end the bloody "vendetta" once and for all. Passed over for promotion to *Capitaine des Corses* (Corsican Captain), Salicetti resolved to kill Costa the same way he had eliminated Lucchinacci. In June 1949, the knife-wielding assassin, Jean Federicci, known in the French underworld as "Madman Johnny," attacked Costa in his nightclub and bar on the rue Quentin Bauchart. Costa died in the hospital on July 24, and his funeral was a gaudy affair attended by the entire Corsican underworld of Paris. A floral arrangement bore the inscription: "To our dear Boss, knifed by a Rat. Rest In Peace, for we will get him for You." The Marseilles gangsters shot up the funeral procession. Five days later, the friends of the slain Corsican captain kept their promise by shooting Madman Johnny at a sidewalk cafe in the Place Thiers, Marseilles. Ange Salicetti, the pivotal figure in the Corsican vendetta, would be the next target.

Though the vendetta escalated in the late 1940s, Salicetti had old grudges to settle as well. Before WWII, Salicetti had been a minor underworld figure living off the earnings of several prostitutes in Toulon. At the time, a Corsican gangster and brothel keeper named Henri Grazziani ran the white slave traffic in the south of France. In 1938, he abducted Salicetti's mistress, Taki, and transported her to South America to work in a brothel. One day as Grazziani drove away from a Toulon hospital, Salicetti was there waiting and shot him to death. Salicetti served eight years for the murder.

The outbreak of war temporarily interrupted the vendetta. Salicetti served the French resistance, excelling in killing Germans and their French collaborators. He became a popular hero in the South of France. One day in October 1944, Ange Fontana, known to Salicetti before the war as an ally of the Grazzianis, was playing cards in a Marseilles cafe when a camouflaged German car pulled up. On it was the emblem of the French Forces of the Interior. Salicetti's gangsters emerged, shoved a 9-mm. Schmeisser submachine gun muzzle into Fontana's back and hustled him away. Fontana, who had been involved in only minor collaboration, was taken for a ride: his kidnappers stopped along the way to buy a kerosene lamp, and then drove to Cuges Wood, a spot where Marseilles gangsters routinely executed their rivals. Accusing Fontana of shooting his cousin in the back, Salicetti tortured Fontana by scorching his skin with the flames of the lamp before shooting him in the back three times. Acting under orders from Grazziani, Ange Fontana had, in fact, murdered Salicetti's cousin, Marcel Raeffaeli, who had provided protection from the law when he served on the Nice Sûreté. Raeffaeli was shot down outside a Marseilles cabaret.

After the liberation of France, Salicetti was given a full pardon. He renewed his attacks against the Grazziani interests and sought complete control of the French drug and vice trade. But Grazziani's men had remained loyal to the Paris connection, run by Lucchinacci and the remnants of the Napoléon Corticchiato gang.

After dodging bullets most of his life, Ange Salicetti was cut down with machine gunfire as he drove away from his Equipage Bar on Dec. 3, 1950. Jacqueline Dupré, his girlfriend, witnessed the murder but was unable to identify the killers. Salicetti's death temporarily ended the gunplay between the Paris and Marseilles mobs. But in 1954, the vendetta claimed the life of 40-year-old Pierre Cuccari, captain of the Paris contingency, known as a peacemaker who had resolved many petty disputes.

French lawyer Charles Carboni said, "In my view the vendetta is a primitive form of justice. The Corsican 'bandit' who kills an adversary to avenge one of his relatives is convinced that what he does is just. In his own mind, paradoxical as it may seem, he is not a wrongdoer. He kills his enemies in cold blood, but he would not harm a fly."

REF.: *CBA;* Rowan, *Famous European Crimes.*

Cortelyou, George Bruce, 1862-1940, U.S., lawyer. Held several important government posts during two Republican administrations, including secretary of the treasury from 1907-09. REF.: *CBA.*

Cortes, See: **Cuauhtemoc.** REF.: *CBA.*

Cortes, Martin, 1532-89, Mex., consp. Son of Hernando Cortes accused of conspiracy. He was imprisoned, but after several years he was released. REF.: *CBA.*

Cortez, Gregorio, 1875-1916, U.S., west. outl. The Mexican born Gregorio Cortez migrated to Texas in 1887 where, in his teens, he worked as a ranch hand or a vaquero. He and his brother Romaldo rented a few acres of land in Karnes County where they had lived for eleven years, raising some corn crops. Cortez had never had any trouble with the law and was considered a quiet, law-abiding ranch worker. He was married and had four children. On June 10, 1901, Sheriff W.T. "Brack" Morris, a 41-year-old lawman who had seen many years service with the Texas Rangers, and who had been sheriff of Karnes County for four years, received a message from the sheriff of Atacosa County that a Mexican had recently stolen a horse and he had been trailed to Karnes County. Morris was asked to look for the horse thief. Having only a brief description, Morris went to the Cortez farm, on June 12, having heard that Cortez had recently traded, not sold, a horse.

Morris met with Romaldo and Gregorio Cortez and asked Gregorio if he had recently traded a horse. He denied having done so. Cortez' historical defenders later insisted that Cortez would have answered "yes" to that question if Morris had asked him if he had traded a *mare,* which is about the thinnest kind of hairsplitting. When Morris heard this—already having the statement from another Mexican that Cortez had, indeed, traded a horse recently—he got off his horse, stepped through the rails of a fence and told Gregorio and Romaldo Cortez that he was arresting them for horse stealing. Morris' remarks were translated into Spanish by Boone Choate, who had accompanied Morris to the ranch, a useless chore in that Gregorio Cortez spoke English but made no effort to speak the language and let Choate labor through his translations. Gregorio Cortez, who was wearing a six-gun, was about twelve feet from Morris and he spoke quickly in Spanish to the sheriff, words later interpreted by Choate to mean: "No white man can arrest me."

Cortez pulled his gun as the unarmed Romaldo "ran at Morris" as if to seize him. Morris drew his weapon and first shot Romal-

do, wounding him. He turned to Cortez and both men fired, Morris' bullets going wild. Cortez fired four bullets into Morris who reeled down the fence. When he fell, Cortez ran to him and pumped another bullet into the sheriff. The unarmed Choate jumped from a buggy and ran into a wooded area where he found a deputy, John Trimmell, who was armed. Both men thought it prudent to go to Kennedy and form a posse. This they did.

Meanwhile, Gregorio packed his wounded brother in a buckboard, along with his family, and fled, leaving Sheriff Morris to bleed to death. Gregorio took his wounded brother to Kennedy where he was left with relatives and then he struck out on foot, wearing low cut, pointed shoes, leaving his two horses behind, correctly reasoning that the posse that would be looking for him would head south toward the Rio Grande, figuring that he would head for Mexico. Cortez walked eighty miles in forty hours, finally staying with Martin Robledo near Ottine.

Robert M. Glover, sheriff of Gonzales County, went to the jail in Kennedy where the Cortez family had been locked up and talked to three women, Cortez' mother, wife, and sister-in-law. One of the women, it was never learned which, told Glover that Cortez was headed for the Robledo ranch. The sheriff and a large posse thundered after the killer. Glover and his men arrived at the Robledo ranch at night and gunfire immediately ensued. Which side fired first was never determined, but Cortez, wearing no shoes after his long walk, marched boldly toward Glover who was on horseback, trading shots with him until his bullets slammed into Sheriff Glover and knocked him dead from the saddle. Also killed was Henry Schnabel, a member of the posse and owner of the land worked by the Robledo family. He was killed by either Cortez or, as some later claimed, by bullets fired from the posse.

While the posse rounded up the Robledo family, Cortez fled, hiding in the bush. After the lawmen left the Robledo house, he returned, put on his shoes and then went to another friend, Ceferino Flores who gave him a fast mount and a six-gun. Cortez then set out for Mexico with hundreds of lawmen, militia, and vigilantes swarming all over southern Texas in search of him. He rode two horses nearly to death, hiding in small towns and pretending to be a common laborer, harbored by sympathetic Mexicans who looked upon him as a hero. The outlaw had covered an enormous amount of ground, walking almost 100 miles and riding more than 400. He was only a few miles from the Rio Grande and Mexico. By then a $1,000 reward had been posted for Cortez' capture by the governor of Texas. Jesús González spotted Cortez near the border and informed a nearby hunting party where they could find the outlaw, who was arrested without a struggle on June 22, 1901.

Cortez was jailed in San Antonio and, at that time, a campaign headed by the Miguel Hidalgo Workers' Party in San Antonio was begun to raise a huge defense fund for Cortez. Cortez was tried at Gonzalez on July 24, 1901, for the murders of sheriffs Morris and Glover and sentenced to fifty years. His lawyers filed one appeal after another, insisting that Sheriff Morris had denied Cortez his rights when arresting him for horse stealing since he had no warrant for this arrest. The legal battle for Cortez raged for several years and a number of trials were reversed and tried again while Cortez spent twelve years in prison, nine of them in Huntsville Penitentiary. He was pardoned by Texas governor Oscar Branch Colquitt and released on July 14, 1913.

Cortez later went to Mexico and fought with the despised despot General Victoriano Huerta against the revolutionaries under Pancho Villa and Emiliano Zapata. Wounded, Cortez returned to Texas to recuperate. In 1916, at Anson, while celebrating his fourth marriage (his other wives were still alive and not divorced), Cortez drank heavily, then complained of severe pains. Before the horrified eyes of his guests and new bride, he turned black and died on the spot. The life of Gregorio Cortez was lionized by writers and Hollywood wherein he was portrayed as a legendary hero, a hunted member of a persecuted minority. Although there is truth in this claim, there is also the reality of the two murders Cortez committed while resisting arrest.

REF.: Bartholomew, *The Biographical Album of Western Gunfighters;*
CBA; Dobie, *The Flavor of Texas;* ____, *The Mustangs;* King, *Ghost*
Towns of Texas; Paredes, *With His Pistol in His Hand;* Patterson,
Sensational Texas Manhunt; Sterling, *Trails and Trials of a Texas Ranger;*
Webb, *The Great Plains;* ____, *The Texas Rangers;* (FILM), *The Ballad*
of Gregorio Cortez, 1983.

Cortez, Victor, 1952- , U.S., law enfor. off. Victor Cortez, a
DEA agent from Brownsville, Texas, was transferred to Guadalajara in Summer 1986. On Aug. 13, as President Ronald Reagan
was meeting with Mexican President Miguel de la Madrid in
Washington about the "improving" drug situation in his country,
Agent Cortez was abducted by Jalisco state policemen from his
car outside a Guadalajara bowling alley. Cortez and an informant
named Antonio Garate Bustamente were driving through town
investigating the known drug hangouts when police arrested the
men on a charge that their cas was illegally registered.

Cortez was taken to the Jalisco police station and strapped
to a table in the interrogation room, where he was beaten and
tortured with cattle prods. The Mexican police demanded the
names and addresses of other DEA agents in Guadalajara, and
what they were doing. The policemen singled out Cortez for
torture because they believed him to be responsible for several
recent cocaine seizures injurious to the business of the cartel.
Four hours later, the severely beaten and dazed agent was freed.
The police told Cortez to remember what happened to DEA agent
Kiki Camarena, who disappeared and was murdered in Mexico
the previous year, and to take heed. That night, after the incident
had been reported to the U.S. Embassy and the Mexican Federales, Cortez took his wife and children back to Tucson, Ariz.

The attack on Agent Cortez convinced many U.S. politicians
that the Mexicans were not serious about ending drug corruption
in their policing agencies. A year later, in September 1987, the
Federales succumbed to U.S. diplomatic pressure and arrested five
of the eleven Jalisco policemen identified as Cortez abductors.
Mexican diplomats in Washington said that their understanding
of the matter was that Cortez had picked a fight with the policeman and had made up the story to protect himself. See: **Cama-**
rena, Enrique.

REF.: *CBA;* Shannon, *Desperados.*

Corticchiato, Napoléon, See: **Corsican Vendetta, The.**

Cortina, Juan, 1824-92, U.S., west. outl. A hero to the Mexican
peasant class, and a common rustler to U.S. landowners, Juan
Cortina was a figure of enduring controversy throughout much of
his life. Cortina was born on
the Texas side of the Rio
Grande River, and was heir to
a large ranch that spanned
both sides of the border. He
became a leader in the Mexican-American community by
virtue of his wealth and power, yet he was forced to defend his holdings against U.S.
encroachers who were taking
sections of his land as part of
a broader-based policy of discrimination. During these
years, he killed many land
grabbers, and a warrant was
issued for his arrest.

On Sept. 13, 1859, he
shoved aside the marshal of
Brownsville, Texas, as he was
beating one of Cortina's former ranch hands. The ranch

Mexican outlaw Juan Cortina.

hand escaped, which further angered the marshal, who stewed over
this insult. In response, Cortina organized 1,000 cutthroats into
an armed band that captured the city of Brownsville. According
to U.S. reports, the guerilla leader executed many people during
the siege, and held the town ransom for $100,000.

Under pressure from less militant family members, Cortina
withdrew his army from the town center, permitting a Brownsville
resident to summon the Texas Rangers. The Rangers engaged
Cortina in combat at the nearby Palo Alto, but were quickly
routed by the superior firepower of the renegade soldiers. Cortina moved on, capturing the towns of Edinburg, and Rio Grande
City, where he exacted a ransom payment of $100,000 in gold. By
Christmas Day, 1859, the Rangers had driven Cortina across the
border into Mexico, but found it impossible to circumvent his
periodic forays into U.S. territory. A full 900,000 head of cattle
were taken by the marauders over the next several years, an act
that Mexicans viewed as retribution for what they had lost to the
Yankees over several previous generations.

In later years Cortina served as a general in the army of
Mexican president Benito Juarez, and then as military governor
of the state of Tamaulipas. In 1875, Juan Cortina was imprisoned
by the new regime, headed by Porfirio Diaz. He remained behind
bars until 1890, and lived out the last two years of his life near the
U.S.-Mexican border.

REF.: Bartholomew, *The Biographical Album of Western Gunfighters;*
CBA; Hunter and Rose, *Album of Gunfighters.*

Corwin, Edward Samuel, 1878-1963, U.S., legal scholar.
Renowned expert in the study of constitutional law. Books
authored: *Doctrine of Judicial Review; Court Over Constitution;*
Liberty Against Government. REF.: *CBA.*

Corwin, Thomas, 1794-1865, U.S., lawyer. Government official
and member of the senate from 1850-53. REF.: *CBA.*

Cory, James, and **Low, George,** prom. 1893, U.S., fraud. Low
and Cory were but two of many confidence tricksters who had
arrived in Chicago in 1893 to prey upon the thousands of visitors
who had flooded the city to attend the World's Fair. The
Columbian Exposition was heralded as a wonder of the modern
age, and the "White City" fairgrounds became a haven for
pickpockets and con men. The city police were often hard pressed
to deal with the army of criminals, but they did well in the case
of Cory and his partner. Detective Clifton Wooldridge arrested
the pair on State Street in August 1893, by posing as a simple
country farmer from Posey County, Ind. Invited to join a dice
"game," Wooldridge promptly arrested both men, who were fined
and sent to Bridewell.

REF.: *CBA;* Wooldridge, *Hands Up!*

Cory Brothers Limited, prom. 1926, Case of, Brit., mansl.
Employer liability versus a responsibility to the public was the
central issue in the case of Cory Brothers Limited, a Welsh coal
manufacturing company, and the family of Brynmore Edward
John, who was killed when he touched an electric wire that
surrounded their powerhouse at Ogmore Vale, Glamorganshire.
Concerned about pilferage on the lot, the company had constructed a fence that was charged with electricity during off-
hours.

Signs were clearly posted, warning passersby of the danger.
However, John and his friends chose to ignore the signs one
night as they chased down rodents in a dangerous game of
"ratting." On the way out of the yard, John accidentally tripped
over the wire on the wet ground and was electrocuted. Charges
were brought against Cory Brothers under the guidelines of the
recently enacted Criminal Justice Act, which prohibited "setting
a man-trap calculated to destroy human life upon the trespasser
or other person(s) coming into contact with it."

A manslaughter conviction was sought by the prosecution, but
under the capable direction of Marshall Hall, who died before the
verdict was handed down, and Norman Birkett, the defense won
an acquittal for Cory Brothers. See: **Birkett, Norman; Hall, Mar-**
shall.

REF.: Bowker, *Behind the Bar;* Browne and Tullett, *The Scalpel of*
Scotland Yard; CBA; Marjoribanks, *For the Defense, The Life of Sir*
Edward Marshall Hall.

Coryell, John Russell, 1851-1924, U.S., writer. Created the
fictional detective hero Nick Carter, who appeared in hundreds
of U.S. pulp magazines and dime novels at the turn of the century.

He wrote *The Old Detective's Pupil* in 1886. REF.: *CBA*.

Cosa Nostra, prom. 1920s- , U.S., org. crime. The Cosa Nostra is an East Coast euphemism for the Mafia, one employed chiefly by Sicilian members of the Mafia who live in New York City. The translation of *cosa nostra* loosely means "this thing of ours." There is no difference between the rites, traditions, and

Mafia hit man, Joe Valachi, center, about to testify before U.S. senators, 1963; Valachi introduced the term "Cosa Nostra."

practices of the Cosa Nostra and those of the Mafia. The name was first introduced to the American press and public by Joseph Valachi during his lengthy verbal exposés of the Mafia, beginning in 1964. See: **Mafia, The; Valachi, Joseph**. REF.: *CBA*.

Cosarian, Acokis, d.1815, U.S., (unsolv.) mur. On Oct. 4, 1815, in the area that is now Detroit, Mich., an incident occurred that sparked hostilities between the British and U.S. factions who controlled the region at that time.

Several Indian youths from the Canadian side of the Detroit River crossed over to Grosse Isle to gather nuts and roots. On their way back across the narrow peninsula, around dusk, a rifle was fired from the river killing Kickapoo Indian Acokis Cosarian. Questioned later, an American settler recalled seeing an Indian canoe speeding along the Canadian shore and another long canoe, with rowing soldiers, moving upriver at about the same time with a civilian in the stern "inspecting or cleaning a gun."

The tribe's chanting of death songs that went all night did not arouse curiosity in the white settlements. The next morning, however, the governor of the Michigan Territory, Lewis Cass, received a letter from Fort Malden's British commander Lieutenant Colonel James, which detailed Cosarian's murder and ordered an inquest. Offended by the phrasing of James' letter, Cass replied angrily, and within three hours a rapidly escalating antagonism soon was in full progress.

With abusive, aggressive letters flying back and forth between the American and British sides, and conflicting testimony and charges from both, the battle heated up. When the justices of the peace in the western district of Canada learned of the murder of Cosarian, they offered a $500 reward for the apprehension of the killer or killers and this substantial amount increased the antagonism.

Governor Cass issued a proclamation, which contradicted previous evidence and claimed that Cosarian had been slain while in a canoe by a man from the island, not from another canoe. He also contended that the victim was outside the jurisdiction of either nation, being a "considerable distance" away from the boundary between the U.S. and English possessions. Chemunga, a Kickapoo man, testified at a closed inquest that while he and Cosarian, along with their friends, were about to embark in their boat to cross to the Canadian shore, a barge of about ten American soldiers pulled up alongside them, and Cosarian responded to their inquiry by saying he was British, after which they had been ordered to leave. One of the Americans had then shot Cosarian. Three other Kickapoos confirmed Chemunga's statements.

The controversy continued throughout that fall and early winter, with repeated skirmishes, thefts, and violence, including three murders. By Jan. 10, 1816, the minister to the U.S. from England, Anthony St. John Baker, wrote a firm letter to the Honorable James Monroe, serving as both secretary of state and secretary of the treasury, which named Corporal John B. Jones as the murderer. Conversations between Baker and Monroe began immediately, and a friendly understanding between the two was reached by mid-March, averting a thin but definite threat of war and easing diplomatic tensions. Despite the one-time only mention of Jones, the killer of Cosarian was never brought to justice. REF.: *CBA*.

Cosgrove, James, 1952- , and **Mendenhall, Edward J.**, 1954- , U.S., fraud. While serving on board the U.S. Navy nuclear submarine *Trepang* in 1973 and 1974, a clerk-typist named James Cosgrove concocted a far-fetched plot to hijack the underwater vessel and sell it to a foreign power for $200 million. After his discharge, Cosgrove convinced "backers" that twelve highly trained men could slip inside the submarine compound at New London, Conn., overpower the security forces, and commandeer the vessel.

Cosgrove recruited Kurtis Schmidt, a 22-year-old unemployed carpet cleaner, and Edward Mendenhall, an insurance agent from Rochester, N.Y., to help him find a prospective buyer. To finance the hijack operation, Cosgrove attempted to bilk St. Louis businessman Charles Rosene out of $250,000. James Cosgrove later claimed that the submarine hijacking story was a ruse designed to get Rosene's money.

Schmidt was arrested in a St. Louis hotel room on Oct. 4, 1978, after revealing the scheme to an undercover FBI agent. He agreed to serve as the key prosecution witness against his two confederates in exchange for immunity. Cosgrove and Mendenhall were arrested and charged with wire fraud, and placed on trial in St. Louis County in December. Both were found Guilty, and ordered to undergo psychiatric testing at the Federal hospital in Springfield, Mo., before sentencing. On Mar. 20, 1979, Cosgrove was handed a four-year prison sentence for his part in the bogus plot to steal the submarine. Earlier, Edward Mendenhall received a maximum term of five years. REF.: *CBA*.

Cossentino, Armando, c.1942- , U.S., mur. A 19-year-old man used a hammer to rid his lover of her domineering husband. New York police felt they had found a crime of passion when they examined the body of Dr. Joseph DiFede, thirty-eight, who had been hit with a hammer and stabbed repeatedly on the night of Dec. 7, 1961. An investigation of the doctor's patients led police to the stylish apartment of unemployed Armando Cossentino and his jobless roommate.

They soon learned that Cossentino's rent was paid by the doctor's wife, Jean DiFede, thirty-five, with whom he was having an affair, and interrogated the roommates. Cossentino revealed nothing, but his roommate confessed that he and Cossentino killed the doctor, who also was involved in affairs. Cossentino was convicted of murder and received the death sentence, later commuted to life imprisonment. DiFede, found guilty of manslaughter, was sentenced to life. REF.: *CBA*.

Cossgriff, Mary (AKA: **Irish Mollie**), prom. 1866, U.S., mansl. Jealous over the affections her lover had showered upon a race horse, "Irish Mollie" Cossgriff bolted into a Chicago saloon one evening in 1866 and shot the man dead. Actually, Mary Cossgriff had come to right an injustice. The prostitute had been maintaining company with George Trussell, a well-known Chicago gambler and cardsharp who operated two deluxe downtown emporiums at the time of the Civil War. Trussell was a sharp-eyed dandy who competed for underworld supremacy with Cap Hyman, boss of "Gambler's Row"—a strip of betting parlors, faro joints, and brothels along Randolph Street. It was said that Trussell would either kill Hyman, or Hyman would shoot Trussell. But in the end, Irish Mollie put a stop to the speculation after her pride had been injured by the scurrilous "Yankee from Vermont."

Trussell had purchased half interest in a prized racehorse named Dexter, the toast of the local sporting gentry. By Sept.

4, 1866, Mollie had lost patience with Trussell and the animal. Her closest friends had taunted her for the alienation of affection brought on by a horse. When Trussell failed to keep his dinner appointment that night, Mollie stormed into Seneca Wright's saloon. She fired a shot at Trussell but only managed to clip him in the side. She shot him a second time as he exited the saloon. The gambler fled into an adjacent livery stable where Mollie cornered him. She fired a third shot, and he was dead. Sick with grief, she wailed: "Oh, my George! My George!"

Mollie Cossgriff was convicted of manslaughter and was sentenced to one year in prison. However, she was pardoned by the governor of Illinois before she was transported to jail. Mollie returned to her Chicago brothel and made no claim for Trussell's considerable estate. It was believed that she had agreed to drop all claims to the estate in return for the pardon. REF.: *CBA*.

Costa, Afonso Augusto da, b.1871, Port., polit. Minister of justice from 1910-11. REF.: *CBA*.

Costa, Antone C., c.1945- , U.S., mur. An admitted drug addict failed to prove insanity in his trial for the murders of two 23-year-old women from Providence, R.I.

The dismembered bodies of Patricia H. Walsh, a second-grade teacher, and Mary Ann Wysocki, a college senior, were found in shallow graves in Truro, Mass., on Mar. 5, 1969, about six weeks after they disappeared. They were last seen, with Costa, on Jan. 25, 1969, in Walsh's car in Provincetown, Mass., en route to Truro, where Costa invited them to use drugs he had hidden in the small town. Costa was suspected of taking part in the women's disappearance because he was seen driving Walsh's Volkswagen, which he claimed she had sold him.

When the women's graves were discovered, the Provincetown resident was immediately arrested. In his room police discovered a .22 caliber revolver with bullets that matched the bullets found in the victims' bodies, bloodstains, fingerprints linking Costa to the women, and some possessions the women brought for their weekend visit in Provincetown. With so much evidence against his client, defense attorney Maurice Goldman claimed the defendant's extensive drug use—he had been taking mind-altering drugs such as LSD since 1965—had caused him to lose the ability to distinguish right from wrong. The prosecution, however, pointed to Costa's deliberate efforts to conceal his crime, such as forging a note and telegram in the dead women's names. After six-and-a-half hours of deliberation, Costa was found Guilty of both murders and sentenced to life imprisonment with no possibility of parole. REF.: *CBA*.

Costa, Gaetano, c.1916-80, Italy, (unsolv.) mur. The chief state prosecutor of Palermo, Si., was killed by five bullets shot by an unknown gunman on Aug. 6, 1980. State authorities linked the murder to a then on-going investigation of drug traffic between the island and the U.S. Fifty-six members of prominent Mafia families were arrested. REF.: *CBA*.

Costa, Mathieu, See: **Corsican Vendetta**.

Costa Cabral, Antônio Bernardo da, 1803-89, Port., jur., Judge of supreme court, Opporto and Lisbon. In 1842 Costa Cabral fomented a bloody insurrection that gave him temporary control of the government. He was deposed in 1846, and a second time in 1851 after he had claimed the prime ministership. REF.: *CBA*.

Costa e Silva, Artur da, 1902-69, Braz., consp. Led successful military coup toppling the regime of President Goulart in 1964. He was elected president by popular vote in 1966, serving until 1969. REF.: *CBA*.

Costa y Martinez, Joaquin, 1846-1911, Spain, jur. Author of several books, including *El colectivismo agrario* in 1898 and *Reconstitucion y europeización* in 1900. REF.: *CBA*.

Costello, Frank (Francisco Castiglia, AKA: Francisco Seriglia, Frank Saverio, Frank Stello, The Prime Minister), 1891-1973, U.S., org., crime. Of all the founders of the national crime syndicate in the U.S., Frank Costello was undoubtedly the most politically influential, his rackets utterly protected by American politicians, chiefly in New York City where he served as one of the elder statesmen of organized crime. Born in Calabria, Italy,

on Jan. 26, 1891, Costello immigrated to the U.S. as a child with his family in 1896, settling in New York. He was raised in East Harlem where he became a petty thief in his teens, stealing from small stores and pushcarts. On Apr. 25, 1908, Costello was arrested for assault and robbery, but discharged. On Oct. 16, 1912, he was again in court on the same charge, but was again released. In 1914, Costello and his brother Edward became part-time members of Owney Madden's vicious Manhattan gang, The Gophers, and Costello began carrying a gun. On Mar. 12, 1915, Costello was arrested as he left a barber shop, detectives alerted by an informer that he would be carrying a gun. He was taken before Judge Edward Swann, charged with carrying a concealed weapon. Judge Swann reviewed Costello's past record, noting his prior releases after being charged with serious crimes. Swann sentenced Costello to a year in prison.

After serving ten months on Welfare Island, Costello was released, vowing that he would use his wits and not a gun to make his way in the underworld. He sought political protection and became a gambler, setting up several fruit stores as fronts for gambling dens in the back rooms. Costello willingly paid police kickbacks and regularly paid politicians, who further protected his gambling operations. He became rich, wearing tailor-made suits and driving expensive cars. Costello became an associate of William Vincent "Big Bill" Dwyer, later one of New York's leading bootleggers, and through him, he met Tammany sachems like Jimmy Hines. When Costello was inducted into the Army through the draft in 1917, he managed to worm out of serving through his political contacts.

In 1919, Costello formed a novelty company with Harry Horowitz and this firm produced Kewpie dolls as prizes for punchboard players, then a craze where players punched out holes on a board to discover winning numbers, paying up to 25¢ per chance. Within a year, Costello had made $80,000 in this company, money he used in early 1920 to finance a bootlegging operation wherein he obtained the liquor through his Manhattan contacts, and his brother, a brawny character, supplied the muscle to compel saloons to buy from the Costellos. During this period, Costello, rather than enter the bootleg wars, played the diplomat and was able to carve out niches of liquor distribution as a wholesaler to the larger, better organized bootleg gangs of Waxey Gordon (Irving Wexler), Owney Madden, Charles "Lucky" Luciano, Vannie Higgins, Dutch Schultz, Joe Adonis, Jack "Legs" Diamond, and many others. He imported, through rum-runners, the best whiskey available, making special deliveries to the swanky nightclubs owned by bootleg racketeer Larry Fay. He also worked closely with Big Bill Dwyer who, within two years, went from lowly gang boss to multimillionaire.

Higgins was Dwyer's distribution boss who worked with Costello, obtaining all his Canadian whiskey through the Costello rumrunning operations. Unlike Costello, who avoided the limelight, Higgins was a flashy, loud-mouthed gangster who committed outlandish stunts to appease the army of newspapermen following him about. He once flew a private plane to upstate New York merely to have dinner with Joseph H. Wilson, warden of the Comstock Prison. Costello became an early supporter of Luciano and acted as his top adviser by the end of the 1920s, encouraging Luciano to invest his bootleg millions in several legitimate enterprises. He also encouraged Luciano, Adonis, and other New York crime bosses to attend the first national crime cartel meeting in Atlantic City in 1929, one which had been called by Al Capone of Chicago to introduce Moses Annenberg and his wire services to future syndicate leaders, a wire service which Costello convinced the East Coast gangsters to install in every gambling operation they controlled.

When bootlegging crumbled in 1933, Costello concentrated on gambling interests in New York, Miami, and with his good friend Meyer Lansky, in developing the lush and lucrative casinos in Havana, Cuba, where the mob was backed by strongman Fulgencio Batista. Millions poured into the Costello coffers which were also enriched through his overseeing of Luciano's myriad

Early police photos of Frank Costello when he was a gunman for Owney Madden in New York, 1912.

NYPD photos of Costello taken in 1936 when he was under arrest for running illegal gambling operations.

Above and right, Costello at the height of his underworld power when he was known as "The Prime Minister" of the national crime cartel.

Frank Costello as rackets boss, 1938.

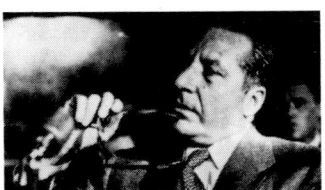

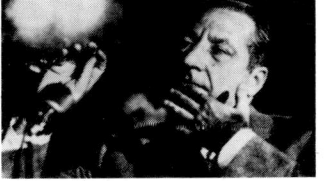

Frank Costello testifying before the Kefauver Committee in 1950, a televised appearance that earned the crime kingpin unwanted fame; he would be identified thereafter as one of the syndicate's board members.

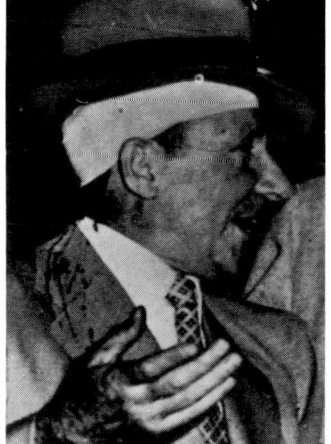

Left, Costello wounded, 1957, by syndicate gunman Vincent "The Chin" Gigante, right.

Costello's luxury home in suburban New York where he retired after almost being murdered.

rackets after Luciano was sent to prison for operating a huge prostitution ring. Costello, by the 1950s, was one of the most powerful underworld bosses in the U.S. He sat on the national board of the crime syndicate, and most disputes were arbitrated through his cool-headed decisions. He quickly earned the sobriquet, The Prime Minister. He was sent to prison for contempt in refusing to answer questions from the Kefauver Committee, receiving an eighteen-month sentence. He entered the federal prison at Atlanta on Aug. 15, 1952. Tacked on to this was another five-year sentence for income tax evasion.

While he served his brief prison stint, Costello's alliances began to fade from power. His long-time friend, Willie Moretti, was sought by the Kefauver Committee, but Costello, realizing that Moretti's mind was becoming dimmed from syphilis, kept the aging crime boss in hiding. He also knew that Vito Genovese, who coveted the Costello rackets, as well as Moretti's, was spreading the word that if Moretti ever testified before the Kefauver Committee, he was likely to blab much guarded information about the crime cartel. Genovese lobbied to have Moretti killed, but Costello hid the old man both from senatorial inquisitors and the blood-lusting Genovese. Moretti finally did testify and deftly sidestepped any probing questions. Still, Genovese engineered Moretti's murder.

There were other problems for Costello by then. He had been one of the first to develop gambling in Las Vegas, with Philip "Dandy Phil" Kastel, being one of the backers of Benjamin "Bugsy" Siegel, who had been sent to the West Coast by Louis "Lepke" Buchalter and Meyer Lansky to develop rackets there. Siegel had discovered Las Vegas for the mob in the mid-1940s and had built a lavish hotel-casino, The Flamingo, but he had failed to show profits and was murdered in 1947 when eastern gangsters felt he was skimming profits from their take. Costello was not one of these but he felt the same kind of pressure that had been applied to Siegel when his own operations in Las Vegas showed considerable profits which he refused to share with the likes of Vito Genovese. The response from Genovese was typical. On May 2, 1957, Genovese sent a hulking enforcer, Vincent "The Chin" Gigante, to kill Costello. Gigante confronted Costello as he was entering his posh apartment building in New York, shouting: "This is for you, Frank!" With that he let loose several shots, one of which grazed Costello's head. Gigante was later arrested but Costello, upholding the underworld tradition of silence, refused to identify Gigante as his assailant. (Gigante is, at this writing, one of the heads of the five Mafia families in New York.)

Costello's power in the syndicate waned following the near execution at the hands of the bumbling Gigante (although some claimed that Gigante was instructed to only wound Costello, to teach him a lesson he would not forget). The crime boss got Genovese's message loud and clear and he soon began divesting himself of his widespread gambling rackets, going into retirement in the early 1960s, although he was said to have been instrumental in the imprisonment of his arch enemy, Vito Genovese, who went behind bars in 1959 and died there ten years later.

Costello's later years were spent playing the role of the retired gangster, one in which he reveled. He spent hours in Toots Shore's nightclub, gossiping with the owner. He met J. Edgar Hoover and told him that he, Costello, "had to be careful about the people I associate with." Frank Costello died in bed of natural causes on Feb. 18, 1973. Only fifty friends and relatives were invited to the funeral. Ghouls later broke into Costello's burial crypt and disturbed the corpse, looking for jewelry reportedly buried with the dead crime czar. There was none. See: **Adonis, Joe; Annenberg, Moses; Atlantic City Convention; Batista, Fulgencio; Capone, Alphonse; Diamond, Jack; Dwyer, William; Fay, Larry; Genovese, Vito; Gopher Gang; Gordon, Waxey; Higgins, Vannie; Hines, James; Kastel, Philip; Luciano, Charles; Lansky, Meyer; Madden, Owen; Moretti, Willie; Schultz, Dutch; Siegel, Benjamin.**

REF.: Alexander, *The Pizza Connection*; Bonanno, *A Man of Honor*;

Campbell, *The Luciano Project; CBA*; Cohen, *Mickey Cohen: In My Own Words*; Cressey, *Theft of the Nation*; Davis, *Mafia Kingfish*; Demaris, *Captive City*; ____, *The Director*; ____, *The Last Mafioso*; Eisenberg and Landau, *Meyer Lansky*; Fried, *The Rise and Fall of the Jewish Gangster In America*; Godwin, *Murder U.S.A.*; Gosch and Hammer, *The Last Testament of Lucky Luciano*; Katz, *Uncle Frank, The Biography of Frank Costello*; Kobler, *Capone*; Lait and Mortimer, *Chicago: Confidential*; Levine, *Anatomy of a Gangster*; Lustgarten, *The Story of Crime*; McClellan, *Crime Without Punishment*; McPhaul, *Johnny Torrio*; Maas, *The Valachi Papers*; Martin, *Revolt In the Mafia*; Messick, *Lansky*; ____, *Secret File*; ____, *Syndicate In the Sun*; ____ and Goldblatt, *The Mobs and the Mafia*; Nash, *Bloodletters and Badmen*; ____, *Citizen Hoover*; Navasky, *Kennedy Justice*; Ottenberg, *Wiseguy*; Reid, *The Grim Reapers*; Reppetto, *The Blue Parade*; Reuter, *Disorganized Crime*; Sann, *Kill the Dutchman*; Scott, *The Concise Encyclopedia of Crime and Criminals*; Servadio, *Mafioso*; Smith, *Syndicate City*; Spiering, *The Man Who Got Capone*; Thompson and Raymond, *Gang Rule in New York*; Velie, *Desperate Bargain: Why Jimmy Hoffa Had To Die*; Wicker, *Investigating the FBI*; Wolf and DiMona, *Frank Costello, Prime Minister of the Underworld*; (FILM), *Hoodlum Empire*, 1952.

Costello, Jessie, prom. 1930s, Case of, U.S., mur. A family's fondness for cleaning the kitchen boiler saved a Peabody, Mass., housewife from a murder conviction. Captain Bill Costello of the Peabody Fire Department died of cyanide of potassium poisoning one morning in February 1933, the day after his wife, Jessie, had brought the cyanide and oxalic acid home to clean the broiler. Charged with murder, Jessie Costello denied knowing that cyanide was poisonous or even knowing what capsules containing cyanide looked like, contrary to the pharmacist's testimony that he had warned her about the poison and another witness' testimony that Costello had bought the capsules before.

The prosecution accused Costello of seeking insurance money even before her husband was buried, and of having an affair with Peabody police officer Eddie McMahon. These accusations were supported by Dr. Pomeroy's testimony that he caught her hiding in McMahon's hospital room. Costello, who strongly denied having an affair, was found Not Guilty.

REF.: *CBA*; Gross, *Masterpieces of Murder*; Pearson, *More Studies In Murder*.

Costello, John Aloysius, 1891-1976, Ire., exile. Served as attorney general from 1926-32, and later as two-term prime minister from 1948-51 and 1954-57. A fervent Irish separatist, Costello withdrew his country from the British Commonwealth of Nations in 1949. REF.: *CBA*.

Costello, Seamus, 1939-77, Ire., (unsolv.) assass. Seamus Costello was the leader of the militant Irish Republican Socialist Party. The 38-year-old Marxist advocated total revolution as a solution for Ireland's religious and social problems. In 1975, Costello survived a machine gun attack while driving through Waterford. He later recalled the bullets piercing his car, but had no recollection of the sound of gunfire. Two years later, on Oct. 5, 1977, an unknown gunman fired two shotgun blasts directly into his face in the crowded shopping district near the Dublin docks. "The gunman talked to Costello before he shot him," according to one witness on the scene. The unknown killer sped away in a grayish car driven by an accomplice.

REF.: Bell, *Assassin; CBA*.

Costello, William, d.1822, and **Fitzmaurice, Walter** (AKA: **Captain Rock**), prom. 1822, Ire., abduc.-rape. In the 1820s, young women of Cork County, Ire., were told to beware of the White Boys, whose favorite tactic was to burst into a home at gunpoint and kidnap the eldest daughter. At midnight on Mar. 4, 1822, eight of the White Boys abducted Honora Goold of Glangurt. They took her to the house of Daniel Leahy and his two brothers. Brown, the leader of the White Boys, wanted the Goold family fortune. That night he raped Honora, which only made her more defiant.

The White Boys held the 16-year-old girl prisoner for three weeks. Brown demanded her hand in marriage, and she refused him. Her captors finally left Honora in a roadside cabin, where her friends found her. Based on Honora Goold's descriptions, police arrested several White Boys including Walter Fitzmaurice, William Costello, the Leahy brothers, and John Cussen. Brown fled the country. The evidence against Costello consisted only of the uncertain recollections of Honora's brother. Though Costello admitted that he was related to Brown, he insisted he knew nothing of the crime until the next morning. But the court believed Honora's story.

On Aug. 23, 1822, Costello and Fitzmaurice were found Guilty and sentenced to die. Costello protested his innocence to the last, but Fitzmaurice pleaded guilty and was given a reprieve. John Cussen and the Leahy brothers, who provided the safe-house, were released on a technicality. Only Costello was hanged. REF.: *CBA*.

Coster, F(rank). Donald, See: Musica, Philip.

Costley, Cann, prom. 1850s, U.S., mur. On July 4, 1854, volatile John Humphries, who had murdered a man in 1853, and his behemoth brother, Asa, who weighed close to 300 pounds, were involved in an Atlanta, Ga., murder. The Humphries brothers, Dink Carlton, Cann Costley, and William Robertson, met a 16-year-old youth, Sidney Kent, during the Fourth of July festivities at the racetrack. Costley accused Kent of rocking his house at night, the building apparently a frail structure. (Kent must have had superhuman strength since he weighed less than 100 pounds.)

As the youth was denying the accusation, the five men closed in around him. One of the men hit him over the head with a club, another punched him, another kicked him, and Costley plunged a knife into him. While he was down, Asa Humphries stamped on him, crushing many bones. Kent died of these awful injuries three weeks later, and all five men were held on a murder charge.

Costley was tried separately, found guilty, and sentenced to be hanged. He escaped the gallows through legal maneuvering. Robertson and Carlton were also freed on technicalities. The Humphries brothers were locked up in the DeKalb jail until 1856 when a friend smuggled them a crowbar. With this, they pried apart the bars of a window and made their successful escape. Neither Asa or John Humphries was ever seen in Atlanta again, much to the relief of their family and Atlantans in general. See: **Humphries, John R.** REF.: *CBA*.

Cotroni Gang, prom. 1980-89, Can.-U.S., org. crime. Having had his fill of American-born toughs who promised more than they delivered, New York crime boss Carlo Gambino devised an ingenious new method of recruitment. What the crime syndicate needed was an infusion of new talent—*paisanos* from the old country who asked no questions and did as they were told. So Gambino made connections with the Cotroni Gang of Montreal to bring in Sicilian gangsters at $2,000 to $3,000 a head. Brought into Canada without a visa, the new recruits remained inside the country at a mutually acceptable location until they were assigned to street duty in New York, or as needed by the Gambino family.

The Cotronis were well versed in all forms of smuggling, and were particularly adept in the narcotics trade both in Canada and in southern Florida. REF.: *CBA*.

Cotter, Benny, prom. 1940s, U.S., rob.-mur. A tip about a criminal's removable glass eye helped lead to the arrest and conviction of a policeman's murderer.

On July 22, 1942, Bledsoe police officer Harry Barton was shot dead by a young man he had arrested for carrying a revolver—the suspect appeared to have a cataract. The youth reportedly had stolen a car at gunpoint from three frightened women, and police had heard that a suspicious-looking young man was seen at the Beacon Foundry. They investigated and there obtained information about Benny Cotter, who would remove his artificial eye after committing crimes so that he would never match a witness' description, and was wanted for robbery in nearby Lakewood, where he had also stolen a car.

The day after police learned Cotter's name he was arrested by Roland Battersbey, a motorcycle patrolman who caught him driving a stolen black sedan. He was also carrying a case for his glass eye. Cotter's trial was interrupted on Nov. 19, 1942, when he confessed to the killing of officer Barton. He was sentenced to 100 years' imprisonment by Judge Maurice V. Harte.

REF.: Cohen, *One Hundred True Crime Stories; CBA*.

Cottereau, François, c.1762-94, Fr., rebel. One of the four Chouan brothers who defied the revolutionary republic. He died from combat wounds. REF.: *CBA*.

Cottereau, Jean, 1757-94, Fr., rebel. Brother of François Cottereau, he was killed while trying to escape. REF.: *CBA*.

Cotterill, Eardley, prom. 1930, Brit., suic.-mur. The son-in-law of actor Gerald Lawrence killed his wife, Margery Cotterill by firing four bullets into her and used one on himself in their Hampstead, England, home in July 1930. Cotterill, a gramophone engineer, had grown despondent over his actress wife's loss of interest in him.

REF.: Browne and Tuttle, *The Scalpel of Scotland Yard; CBA*.

Cottington, John (AKA: Mull-Sack), 1614-59, Brit., rob.-mur. One of nineteen children of a poor haberdasher, John Cottington ran away to London at thirteen where he began his legendary career as a highwayman. Drinking cheap wine from dawn till dusk at the Devil Tavern on Fleet Street, Cottington acquired the nickname Mull-Sack, and true to his name, many a night found himself among thieves and prostitutes, sleeping off a revelry in Fleet Prison. On one of these nights, Cottington met Aniseed-Water Robin, whom he later married. However, their marriage was never consummated, for on their wedding night, Cottington discovered his wife was a hermaphrodite.

Cottington then took to pickpocketing and robbing England's most prominent citizens—even Lord Protector Oliver Cromwell whose pockets were picked as he was leaving Parliament. Cottington escaped prosecution for this crime and soon took a new profession as a highwayman. Accompanied by Captain Horne, a fellow thief, Mull-Sack victimized Cromwell a second time while travelling from Hounslow Heath to Windsor. Cromwell's soldiers chased the highwaymen, apprehending Horne, who was sent to Newgate to await execution. Cottington was able to escape.

The legend of Mull-Sack spread across England. Besides his skill as a highwayman, Cottington was adept in the art of deception. In disguise, usually as a jewelry merchant, he tricked other merchants into advancing him money, and thus acquired great wealth.

Arrested for breaking into the General-Receiver's house at Reading, Cottington stood trial in Abingdon. Notwithstanding the substantial evidence against him, Mull-Sack bribed and intimidated the jury into returning an acquittal. The jurors feared the highwayman more than the wrath of the judge and prosecutor.

Once free, Cottington resumed a long-standing love affair. Finding the woman's husband an encumbrance, he killed him, not counting, however, on the vengeance of his relatives. Fleeing prosecution, Cottington sailed to Cologne, where he promptly robbed Charles II, the exiled heir to the British throne, of a plate valued at £1,500 and some highly sensitive correspondence he thought Cromwell might find useful.

Cromwell invited Cottington back to England, but when he failed to deliver the goods as promised he was hanged at Smithfield in April 1659.

REF.: *CBA*; Hibbert, *Highwaymen*; Pringle, *Stand and Deliver*; Smith, *Highwaymen*.

Cotton, Mary Ann Robson Mowbray, c.1833-1873, Brit., big.-mur. When Mary Ann Cotton predicted that her youngest son would die, just as the other members of her family had, she revealed herself as the most deadly serial murderer England has ever known.

In 1853, Mary Ann Robson went to Cornwall with her husband, William Mowbray. There they had five children, but four of them—all boys—died of a horribly agonizing condition identified as "gastric fever." When the family moved back to Durham, the last child, a daughter, also died, apparently from the same disease. Soon another child was born and died of the fever, as did William

Mowbray, soon after taking out some life insurance. Mary Ann worked as a nurse and soon married again, but her husband, George Ward, died in 1866, leaving her to wed James Robinson, who had five children. They all died of the mysterious illness that seemed to follow Mary Ann.

Mary Ann then met Mr. Cotton, who would give her her name of lasting fame. She became nurse to his wife, who was dying of tuberculosis. When the wife died, Mary Ann bigamously wed Frederick Cotton three months before their child was born. When the Cottons' neighbors started speculating about why their pigs were dying, the Cottons moved to West Auckland, where, within a brief time, all but one of the children, as well as Frederick Cotton, died of gastric fever. When a government official expressed a desire to marry Mary Ann, she knew it was time to get rid of Charles, the only remaining Cotton stepchild. She offered him to a workhouse on condition that she get any money he earned, adding, however, that she didn't expect the boy to live much longer.

When Charles Cotton died on July 12, 1872, Thomas Riley, the government official, reported Mary Ann's comment to the police. They exhumed the body and found arsenic. Sending word throughout northern England, the police found numerous other relatives of Mary Ann whose bodies contained arsenic; she was brought to trial only for the death of young Charles. Her lawyer, Campbell Foster, tried to convince the jury that the family had died because of arsenic in a green wallpaper, but that didn't explain the other deaths. Mary Ann Cotton was found Guilty of murder and sentenced to hang. Five days before her execution, the 40-year-old murderer delivered a daughter, a child of the customs official who had wanted to marry her. This child presumably survived, and she was adopted by a childless couple. Mary Ann Cotton, after killing at least twenty people in twelve years, was hanged on Mar. 24, 1873.

REF.: Altick, *Victorian Studies In Scarlet*; Appleton, *Mary Ann Cotton*; Boar, *The World's Most Infamous Murders*; Butler, *Murderers' England*; CBA; Dunbar, *Blood in the Parlor*; Glaister, *The Power of Poison*; Lambert, *When Justice Faltered*; Nash, *Look For the Woman*; O'Donnell, *Should Women Hang?*; Wilson, *Murderess*.

Cotys I, d.359 B.C., Thrace, king, assass. Waged war against Athens, threatening grain shipments in the region with the capture of Sestos in 360 B.C. REF.: *CBA*.

Coudert, Frederic René, 1832-1903, U.S., lawyer. Represented U.S. in its maritime disputes with Venezuela; regarded as an expert on international law. REF.: *CBA*.

Coughlin, John (AKA: **Bathhouse John**), 1860-1938, U.S., polit. corr. Of all the crooked politicians and "Gray Wolves" to come out of Chicago, none possessed the personal flamboyance and audacity of the "Poet Laureate of the First Ward"—Alderman John "Bathhouse" Coughlin. Elected alderman of the graft-ridden First Ward in 1892, Coughlin held sway for over forty years. He recited bad poetry in the City Council, fought against those who sought to close the saloons, brothels, and clip joints of the South Side Levee District, and personally supervised a political spoils system that sustained Mayor Carter Harrison II through four terms.

Coughlin was the son of an Irish immigrant whose grocery business burned in the 1871 Chicago Fire. Reflecting on his father's misfortune, Coughlin would later say: "If not for that bonfire I might have been a rich man's son and gone to Yale—and never amounted to nothing!" The store was rebuilt, but Coughlin went to work as a "rubber" in a Clark Street Bathhouse—hence the nickname "Bathhouse John." Coughlin's easy-going manner appealed to the politicians, gamblers, business magnates, and criminals who frequented the saunas. He was able to cultivate valuable political connections, and with the $800 he was advanced by bathhouse members, Coughlin opened his own bathhouse and saloon.

In 1892, he became a member in good standing of the City Council, which at the time was dominated by a gang of aldermen known as the "Gray Wolves." Teaming up with his First Ward

counterpart Michael "Hinky Dink" Kenna, the two aldermen formed a graft alliance which lasted through the next forty years. Kenna and Coughlin took their cut from the owners of the South Side vice dens who gladly paid bribes to stay in business free from police interference. The First Ward Democratic organization became rich and powerful, and the two aldermen were able to dictate terms to the mayor and other council members.

The annual "First Ward Ball," held at the Chicago Coliseum, was a fundraising event that became a drunken, debauched orgy. Every notable brothel inmate, two-bit gambler, and syndicate gunman in the city attended the gala event. The spectacle continued until 1910, when the Roman Catholic archbishop and various reform groups finally demanded that Mayor Fred Busse cancel the Ball in the name of public decency. During the heyday of the Ball, Kenna acted as the collector, and made all the important political decisions, while John Coughlin attended to "public relations." He regaled the newspaper reporters and local pundits with his dry wit, and stale poetry. In 1900, Coughlin wrote a syrupy love ballad titled *Dear Midnight of Love* which he introduced to a sellout crowd at the Chicago Opera House. He hired May

The very colorful and wholly corrupt "Bathhouse John" Coughlin.

de Sousa, the daughter of a Levee police detective, to sing the latest "Bathhouse Opus." Afterward, the beaming Coughlin remarked: "I'm certainly the best there is, the best anybody ever looked at! I'm doing a stunt right here now that no alderman can touch, no alderman in the world. The orchestra's alright. The singer's alright, the song's alright, the house will be alright...Well...I ain't swelled a bit because I got it all coming to me!" During rehearsals, Kenna overheard the song and fled, shouting "Help! Help! I need a drink!" See: **Kenna, Michael**.

REF.: Asbury, *Gem of the Prairie*; Boettinger, *Jake Lingle*; *Chicago Police Problems*; CBA; Demaris, *Captive City*; Faris, *Chicago Sociology, 1920-32*; Gosnell, *Negro Politicians: The Rise of Negro Politics in Chicago*; Gottfried, *Boss Cermak of Chicago*; Harrison, *Stormy Years*; Kobler, *Capone*; Lait and Mortimer, *Chicago: Confidential*; Landesco, *Organized Crime In Chicago*; Lewis and Smith, *Chicago, A History of Its Reputation*; McPhaul, *Johnny Torrio*; Merriam, *Chicago: A More Intimate View of Urban Politics*; Morgan, *Prince of Crime*; Nash, *Hustlers and Con Men*; ____, *People to See*; ____, *Zanies*; Reckles, *Vice in Chicago*; Reppetto, *The Blue Parade*; Smith, *Syndicate City*; Wendt and Kogan, *Big Bill*; ____, *Lords of the Levee*.

Coulter, Ernest Kent, b.1871, U.S., lawyer. Helped found children's court of New York in 1902; author of *The Children in the Shadow* and the *History of Child Protection*. REF.: *CBA*.

Countryman, Alfred, d.1857, U.S., mur. Alfred Countryman was a confirmed criminal, practicing robbery and burglary in Rockford, Ill. He was finally arrested for robbery by John F. Taylor, sheriff of Winnebago County. As Sheriff Taylor was escorting Countryman to jail down a Rockford, Ill., street, the felon broke free of Taylor's grasp and ran. Taylor pursued him, revolver in hand, ordering Countryman to stop. Countryman drew a revolver he had hidden in his pants leg, and fired several times, shooting and killing the sheriff. Other deputies quickly caught Countryman and he was tried for Taylor's murder. Following a quick conviction, he was hanged, without appeal, on Mar. 27, 1857.

REF.: *CBA*; *Trial of Alfred Countryman*.

Coupon Fraud Scandal, 1984, Case of, U.S., fraud. The fraudulent use of newspaper and magazine coupons by dishonest grocers and consumers to receive small rebates on their inventories and on personal household items cost U.S. manufacturers an estimated $225 million in 1983.

About 80 percent of all Americans redeem coupons at their local grocery stores according to industry analysts. The potential for fraud is great, and it can occur in a variety of ways. Average consumers will sometimes switch a coupon from one product to another. This represents only a small percentage of fraud and is not a great concern to manufacturers. Organized "rings" sell retail outlets coupons in bulk for a discounted price. The stores will then redeem them with the manufacturer without having sold the product in question. This practice bothers the large food companies most. Still another way of bilking the coupon issuer is through the dishonest cashier who collects bundles of coupons and then exchanges them for money in the drawer or provides this "service" to friends and relatives.

The losses to manufacturers are then passed on to consumers, which is reflected in higher prices at the check-out line. In an effort to curtail this booming business, the American Society for Industrial Security devised an elaborate sting operation run in New York City in 1977. Four million coupons for a nonexistent laundry detergent known as "Breen" were dropped by the U.S. postal system. Retailers from forty-two states attempted to cash in Breen coupons with the manufacturer, resulting in 223 arrests.

A similar operation was planned for Chicago with a shampoo called "Essent." Before the mail drop could go out, however, *Advertising Age* leaked the story to the public, thus destroying the effectiveness of the sting in a marketplace that is a major base of operations for coupon rings.

According to Tom Spinelli, a private investigator who has worked on this type of fraud: "Almost any circumstances that you can imagine where coupons can be stolen, they're being stolen. It's lucrative enough that all sorts of people get into the act at all stages of the game." In recent years manufacturers have begun to number the coupons in computerized codes that allow for a thorough analysis on the back end. REF.: *CBA*.

Courbet, Gustave, 1819-77, Fr., vandal. Prominent realist painter who participated in Paris Commune of 1871. He took personal charge of the dismantling of the column in the Place Vendôme. Arrested in 1875, Courbet was jailed for six months and assessed a fine equal to the cost of erecting a new column. REF.: *CBA*.

Courci, John de, d.c.1219, Brit., milit. Led the Anglo-Norman tribe into Ireland where he captured Ulster in 1177. In 1204 he was arrested by Hugh de Lacy the younger, and jailed. REF.: *CBA*.

Courson, George W., prom. 1932, U.S., mansl. To the burly prison guards at the Sunbeam Prison Camp in Duval County, Fla., Arthur Maillefert was a troublemaker from the start. The 22-year-old New Jersey man had been convicted of stealing $30, and sentenced to nine years at the Florida camp.

Known as Jersey to his fellow inmates, Maillefert attempted to escape from the sweltering, miserable prison camp on four different occasions. Following his last unsuccessful dash for freedom, the prisoner was placed inside a three-foot-long sweatbox and denied food for a twenty-four hour period by acting guard, Captain George Courson, the 285-pound man who had it in for the brash youngster from the north.

Courson tied Maillefert's neck to the roof of the tin box, and placed his feet in stocks. On June 3, 1932, Maillefert was found strangled in the parched, airless sweatbox. At first the justice of the peace ordered that no inquest be conducted. But as the sordid details of the brutal and unusual punishment inflicted by Courson and his deputy Solomon Higginbotham began to leak out, there was a demand for an investigation.

Murder indictments were returned against the pair, and a jury trial commenced in Jacksonville in October 1932. The prisoner's mother was brought down to observe the proceedings. Her greatest fear was the so-called "Southern justice." "I am going to sit through the trial to see what kind of justice they mete out down here," she said. "I wish they'd just get one man from New Jersey on the jury."

Courson was found Guilty of manslaughter, but Higginbotham was acquitted. On Oct. 29, 1932, the corpulent prison guard was sentenced to twenty years of hard labor by Judge George Gibbs. REF.: *CBA*.

Courtenay, Edward, c.1526-56, Brit., polit. Son of Henry Courtenay, Earl of Devonshire, young Edward was jailed in the Tower of London merely because his father had attempted to usurp the throne, for which he had been put to death. He served a fifteen year sentence from 1538-53, before Queen Mary signed his release papers. REF.: *CBA*.

Courtenay, Henry (Marquis of Exeter, Earl of Devonshire), c.1496-1538, Fr., consp. Cousin of King Henry VIII, Courtenay sat in judgment of the king's adulterous wife Anne Boleyn in 1536. After a conflict with the king, he was beheaded on suspicion of attempting to usurp the throne. REF.: *CBA*.

Courtright, Timothy Isaiah (AKA: Longhaired Jim), 1848-87, U.S., west. gunman-lawman. Born in Iowa, Courtright served under General John "Black Jack" Logan during the Civil War, and continued a personal friendship with Logan for much of his life. When the war ended, Courtright moved to Texas where Logan hired him as an army scout. In 1876, he was appointed city marshal of Fort Worth, Texas, a position he held for the next three years. He then moved to Lake Valley, N.M., a mining camp where he guarded silver ore mined for the American Mining Company. Here he was reunited with Logan who retained him as ranch foreman.

Gunman Jim Courtright.

Courtright's job was little more than that of hired gun. Trespassers and cattle rustlers had been roaming Logan's property at will, and it was Courtright's duty to secure the land. In 1883, near Silver City, N.M., Courtright shot and killed two squatters, a crime that forced him to flee from the territory under threat of imprisonment. He returned to Fort Worth and opened a private detective agency, but when federal agents served extradition papers on him, he fled to western Canada. He completed his self-imposed exile in the Pacific Northwest before heading back to New Mexico to clear his name.

Returning to New Mexico around 1887, Courtright re-opened his T.I.C. Commercial Agency, which provided "protection" to gambling dens and saloons in return for a portion of their profits. On Feb. 8, Luke Short, part owner of the White Elephant Saloon, refused to pay the extortion money. Short, in the company of Bat Masterson, confronted Courtright outside a Fort Worth shooting gallery that night. A quarrel ensued, and Short drew his gun and shot Courtright to death. Short was later freed on the grounds that Courtright had fired first. See: **Short, Luke**.

REF.: Allen, *The Great Southwest Strike*; Archembeau, *Old Tascosa, 1885-1888*; Bartholomew, *The Biographical Album of Western Gunfighters*; ____, *Wyatt Earp, 1848-1880*; *CBA*; Cox, *Luke Short and His Era*; Cunningham, *Triggernometry*; Faulkner, *Roundup, A Nebraska Reader*; Foster-Harris, *The Look of the Old West*; Gard, *The Chisholm Trail*; ____, *Rawhide Texas*; ____, *Sam Bass*; Gardner, *The Old Wild West*; Gaylord, *Handgunner's Guide*; Hendricks, *The Bad Man of the West*; Hertzog, *A Directory of New Mexico Desperadoes*; Holloway, *Texas Gun Lore*; Horan, *The Great American West*; Hunter and Rose, *The Album of Gunfighters*; Knight, *Fort Worth*; Looney, *Haunted Highways*; McCarty, *The Gunfighters*; McIntire, *Early Days in Texas*; Martin, *Border Boss*; Masterson, *Famous Gunfighters of the Western Frontier*; O'Connor, *Bat Masterson*; O'Neal, *Encyclopedia of Western Gunfighters*; Paddock, *History of Texas*; Penfield, *Western Sheriffs and Marshals*; Porter, *Memory Cups of Panhandle Pioneers*;

Rosa, *The Gunfighter, Man or Myth?*; Sanders, *The Sumner County Story*; Sandoz, *The Buffalo Hunters*; Schoenberger, *The Gunfighters*; Shirley, *Heck Thomas, Frontier Marhsal*; Stanley, *Fort Bascom*; ____, *Jim Courtright, Two-Gun Marshal of Fort Worth*; ____, *The Kingston*; ____, *The Lake Valley (N.M.) Story*; Walters, *Tombstone's Yesterdays*; Waters, *A Gallery of Western Badmen*; White, *Texas, An Informal Biography*.

Courvoisier, Francois Benjamin, 1817-40, Brit., mur. The Swiss-born Francois Benjamin Courvoisier emigrated from Geneva to London in 1836, working at odd jobs until convincing 73-year-old Lord William Russell that he was an accomplished manservant. Within a week of being employed, Courvoisier had taken over the Russell household, efficiently managing the two maids and butler, but he was headstrong and refused to carry out Russell's orders. On the morning of May 6, 1940, one of the maids called Courvoisier after finding several rooms upset with turned over furniture. The manservant and the maid inspected the premises and found Lord Russell dead on his bed in the master bedroom. He had an ugly wound on his throat.

Murderer Francois Courvoisier.

Courvoisier pointed out to the maid that someone had forced open the rear entrance to the house and it was he who noted that certain valuables were missing where more priceless objects had not been touched. He brought suspicion upon himself when he repeatedly asked in front of the maid, and investigating officers who arrived later, "Oh, what shall I do? What shall I do? I shall never get another position." He was more concerned about his own plight than that of his murdered employer. A search of his rooms revealed some of the missing valuables and Courvoisier's own clothing—his gloves, shirtfront, and handkerchief—all coated with the blood of the victim. He was arrested and charged with Lord Russell's murder, his trial being held at the Old Bailey in May 1840.

While Courvoisier was being held for trial, a boarding house operator read of the case and realized that the suspected killer of Lord Russell might be the man who had brought a parcel to her house, asking that she look after it. The woman opened the parcel and discovered silver bearing Lord Russell's crest. She took the silver to the police and then identified Courvoisier as the man who had delivered the parcel to her. Despite the testimony of this woman and the incriminating evidence against him, Courvoisier staunchly insisted that he was innocent of slashing his employer's throat and robbing him.

Courvoisier was nevertheless convicted and sentenced to death. Awaiting his execution, Courvoisier wrote three separate confessions. In one, he blamed revolutionary reading matter he had obtained which urged the killing of all aristocrats. In the next confession he blamed liquor, saying that he had taken to drink and was intoxicated when he murdered his employer. In the third confession, Courvoisier blamed the Devil for urging him to commit murder. On July 6, 1840, Courvoisier was hanged at Newgate Prison.

REF.: Altick, *Victorian Studies in Scarlet*; Atholl, *Shadow of the Gallows*; Ballantine, *Some Experiences of a Barrister's Life*; Bleackley, *Hangmen of England*; Bridges, *Two Studies In Crime*; Brock, *A Casebook of Crime*; Brophy, *The Meaning of Murder*; *CBA*; Cobb, *The First Detectives*; Cooper, *Lesson of the Scaffold*; Kingston, *Dramatic Days at the Old Bailey*; ____, *A Gallery of Rogues*; Lambton, *Thou Shalt Do No Murder*; Logan, *Rope, Knife and Chair*; Mencken, *By the Neck*; Russell, *Though the Heavens Fall*.

Cousins, Walter (David Bruce Simmons), and **Gordon, Edgar (Alfred Mills) (AKA: Miles Garnham** and **Thompson Garnham)**, prom. 1910, Brit., fraud. Two con men garnered more than £35,000 through a fraudulent stock options business called the Equitable Exchange. The business, based in Bishopsgate, England, urged more than 19,000 clients to invest in certain U.S. and South African stocks, the money usually going to Cousins and Gordon instead.

Only seven customers profited from their investments, and Cousins and Gordon were charged with conspiracy to cheat in February 1912. Prominent attorney Sir Edward Marshall Hall defended them, but they were found Guilty. Cousins was sentenced to twenty-two months of hard labor by Judge Lumley Smith, and Gordon received two years' hard labor.

REF.: *CBA*; Nicholls, *Crime Within the Square Mile*.

Couthon, Georges, 1755-94, Fr., rebel. Member of the National Convention and the Committee of Public Safety from 1792-94, he was an ardent supporter of Robespierre. Together they expedited passage of the Law of 22 Prairial which ushered in the Reign of Terror. Couthon's last trip with Robespierre was to the guillotine in 1794. REF.: *CBA*.

Couturier, Delphine, prom. 1800s, Fr., adult.-pros.-suic. Unhappy with her dull marriage to prominent Dr. Eugene Delamare, Couturier engaged in extramarital affairs with a farmhand, a neighbor, and a clerk, and started charging money for sexual favors. Couturier killed herself by drinking arsenic after nine years of marriage, leaving behind a daughter and the husband, who also committed suicide after learning that his wife had been unfaithful to him and had spent too much of his money. Gustave Flaubert based his novel *Madame Bovary*, published in 1857, on Couturier's life.

REF.: Bullough, *Illustrated History of Prostitution*; *CBA*.

Couzens, John E.D., prom. 1800s, U.S., law enfor. off. As St. Louis police chief from Oct. 18, 1861, to Mar. 16, 1865, Couzens defeated a plan to reduce the police force of 255 men, and presided over the force during the Civil War, when officers had military status and the added responsibility of home guard. After resigning from office, Couzens served as U.S. customs inspector and later as U.S. marshal during the presidency of Grover Cleveland. REF.: *CBA*.

Covell, Arthur, b.c.1877, and **Covell, Alton**, c.1907- , U.S., mur. Ebba Covell of Bandon, Ore., was found dead by her husband, Dr. Fred Covell, on Sept. 3, 1923. The doctor, a chiropractor with strong hands, was charged with murdering Ebba by breaking her neck. Noted detective Luke S. May, believing the doctor innocent, ordered the body exhumed and reexamined. The neck was found intact and red marks were discovered on the dead woman's face. May called ammonia poisoning the official cause of death.

Without revealing his discovery, May focused on Arthur Covell, Fred's crippled brother who lived with the family. Covell's diary, filled with astrological signs, recorded what Covell did on the day Ebba died. He wrote about his breakfast, and articles he read in the newspaper, but did not mention the death of his sister-in-law. A further search into Covell's papers revealed plans to order Alton, his 16-year-old nephew, to kill twenty-eight others, and the victims' horoscopes and the date and time of day to kill each one.

Covell also was involved in an elaborate fraud scheme in which he charted astrologically the best day for a client to make an investment. When the day arrived, another con artist would offer the victim an appealing, though eventually worthless, opportunity. May found the nature of the uncle and nephew's relationship—the boy had been hypnotized—and discovered secret messages between the two about police investigation.

After Alton confessed to murdering his stepmother, his uncle followed suit but retracted the confession in court, explaining that he wished to protect Alton. Arthur Covell was found Guilty of murder and received the death penalty. Alton also was convicted and received life imprisonment.

REF.: Block, *Science Vs. Crime*; *CBA*.

Coventry, Sir John, d.1682, Brit., (unsolv.) asslt. Sir John Coventry was the son of a noted member of Parliament and fought on the Royalist side during the English Civil War. In 1661, following the restoration of the Stuart king Charles II to the throne, Coventry was knighted and elected to Parliament six years later.

Within three years of his election, Coventry became embroiled in a scandal. In 1670, opponents of the king sponsored a tax on English playhouses. During the Parliamentary debate, Coventry made a sarcastic reference to the king's morality. "Whether did the king's pleasure lie among the men or the women that acted?" He was slyly referring to Charles' amorous affairs with two notable actresses—Nell Gwyn and Moll Davies. Provoked by this insult, friends of the king, allegedly led by Sir Thomas Sandys, assaulted Coventry on Dec. 21, as he rode home in his carriage.

Coventry was dragged from his carriage and his nose was sliced to the bone. The savagery of the act stirred the House of Commons to action. They passed a measure which declared that nose slitting or any other similar assault was a felony. The bill came to be known as the Coventry Act. His assailants were never captured. See: **Gwyn, Nell.** REF.: *CBA.*

Coventry, Thomas (First Baron Coventry), 1578-1640, Brit., jur. Member of Parliament, and attorney general in 1621. REF.: *CBA.*

Covert, Clarice, prom. 1950s, Case of, Brit., mur. A woman sentenced to life for killing her husband with an ax was freed by a judge who rejected a controversial agreement between Britain and the U.S. empowering the latter to prosecute crimes committed by civilians accompanying the U.S. Air Force.

On Mar. 10, 1953, Master Sergeant Edward Covert was slain by his wife as he slept in their home in Heyfort, England. The country had no jurisdiction to prosecute the wife due to a section of the 1950 Uniform Code of Military Justice, and she was sent back to the U.S. where she received life imprisonment by a court-martial of the U.S. Air Force. Mrs. Covert was freed in late fall of 1955 by Federal District Judge Edward A. Tamm, who ruled that the section of the military code by which she was sent home was unconstitutional. REF.: *CBA.*

Covington, James Harry, 1870-1942, U.S., jur. State's attorney in Talbot County, Md.; appointed justice of the supreme court of Washington, D.C., by President Woodrow Wilson in 1914. REF.: *CBA.*

Cowan, Frederick W. (AKA: Second Hitler), 1944-   , U.S., suic.-mur. Frederick Cowan's pleasures in life were Nazi memorabilia, his weapons collection, and weightlifting. He bore tattoos of Nazi symbols on his arms, and expressed his hatred of Jews and blacks to anyone who would listen. He attributed his hatred of blacks to a time during the Vietnam War when a black man refused to help him. But Cowan was never in Vietnam. Then his neighbor in New Rochelle, N.Y., Theresa Schmidt, started dating a black man. On Aug. 2, 1975, when Schmidt walked by Cowan's house, he pointed her out to a nearby kid as a "nigger lover." Schmidt, overhearing,

Mass killer Frederick Cowan.

turned on him amd demanded to know what he had said. Cowan went to the trunk of his car, grabbed a rifle, and said, "Get out of there before I blow your brains out!" Schmidt ran to call the police, but the officer who answered the call expressed no interest in pursuing the matter when Cowan was not in sight on his arrival. Months later, when Schmidt passed Cowan's house again, he pointed a rifle at her and pulled the trigger, but the weapon was not loaded.

In January 1977, 33-year-old Cowan's opinions got him in trouble at his job. He was suspended after refusing to work for a man he thought was Jewish. The superior who suspended him, Norman Bing, was himself Jewish, and later said, "The guys figured he was a lot of talk. He had no history of violence. Everybody said he was a pussycat." But on Valentine's Day 1977, his first day back at work, Cowan drove to work at the Neptune Moving Company, stood in the parking lot, and armed himself as if for battle with pistols, hand grenades, bandoliers of ammunition, and a semi-automatic rifle. He walked into the main entrance searching for Bing, and immediately shot and killed two black men passing through the office. Cowan told another employee, "Go home and tell my mother not to come down to Neptune." He continued into the company cafeteria, up the stairs, killing two more people on the way. When a squad car arrived, Cowan saw it from a window and killed one policeman as he emerged from the car. Within minutes, the Neptune building was under siege, a New York City Police Department armored personnel carrier on hand to help.

The killer, moving back and forth from the offices to the roof, would not answer loudspeaker calls for several hours, even when his mother arrived and spoke to him. Once he shouted that he had "plenty of grenades and other guns to last me all day." Another time he answered a phone and said, "I'm sorry for your trouble. Tell the mayor that I'm sorry to be causing the city so much trouble." At 2:40 p.m., a single shot sounded. As the police cleared the building, they found that Fred Cowan, killer of five, had killed himself with a gunshot to the head.

REF.: *CBA; Fox, Mass Murder;* Godwin, *Murder U.S.A.;* Nash, *Murder, America.*

Cowan, John W., 1807-35, U.S., mur. John Cowan ended his unhappy marriage by killing his wife, Mary Cowan, and their children, 1-year-old Sarah Cowan and 3-year-old Thomas Cowan, with an ax on Oct. 10, 1835, in Cincinnati, Ohio. Cowan confessed that he murdered his wife because he thought she was having an affair, then killed the children to spare them shame. He was convicted of the murders and hanged on Nov. 27, 1835. REF.: *CBA.*

Cowdrey, Thomas, and **Brown, William**, prom. 1900s, Brit., mur. Two men convicted of murdering Esther Atkins near Aldershot, England, in 1903, took different approaches toward their imminent executions. While William Brown spoke only rarely to those around him, Thomas Cowdrey sang funny songs and loudly protested that he was innocent. Cowdrey apparently believed that no one would tolerate his being hanged.

REF.: *CBA;* Laurence, *A History of Capital Punishment.*

Cowell, John, 1554-1611, Brit., jur. Professor of civil law at Cambridge from 1594-1610. Enraged by the publication of *The Interpreter,* Cowell's law dictionary that upheld the king's absolute powers, the House of Commons set out to burn every copy they could find. REF.: *CBA.*

Cowland, John, d.1700, Brit., mur. Despite his early religious training, John Cowland, as a young man, loved the theater and the company of the *bons vivants* who attended it.

One of them, Sir Andrew Slanning, baronet, left the Drury Lane one night with a woman he met there. Cowland met them in the street and made what Slanning considered an improper advance toward the woman. The two men quarreled and drew swords. Passersby convinced them that the point was too trivial for bloodshed.

When Cowland, Sir Andrew, and others stopped at the Rose Tavern, the dispute flared up again. Cowland again drew his sword and this time ran it through Sir Andrew's belly.

On Dec. 5, 1700, Cowland was tried at the Old Bailey for murder, found Guilty, and sentenced to hang at Tyburn.

REF.: *CBA;* Mitchell, *Newgate Calendar.*

Cowley, James D. (AKA: Big Jim Cowley), prom. 1930s, Can.-Fr., rob.-attempt. rob. Detective Ashton-Wolfe quashed Cowley's plans to rob a casino near the Crédit Lyonnais in Monte Carlo, but was unable to capture the criminal, also wanted for robbing a bank in Canada. James D. Cowley's large size and western manner distinguished him from other revelers at the Casino which Blanchard of the Sureté patrolled and Ashton-Wolfe was visiting. Cowley's yacht, the *Mariposa*, attracted even more attention, transporting many of his friends to the gambling place. Blanchard and Ashton-Wolfe, their suspicions aroused, focused on Cowley's behavior in the casino, with Ashton-Wolfe finding the strange man carrying an intricate map of the playing room, complete with the location of cash boxes. They arrested John Franklin, one of Cowley's companions, who eventually confessed that Cowley and forty men, some of whom had participated in the Canadian bank robbery, were planning to rob the casino, and adding that Cowley threatened to kill him and his sister, Doris, Cowley's girlfriend, if they tried to run away.

Franklin, after being promised free passage for himself and his sister back to the U.S., agreed to find out when the robbery was planned. With their help, the police were ready on Feb. 25, aware that Cowley had two cars, one equipped with a Hotchkiss machine gun, to drive to the Crédit Lyonnais, and to the Casino, where, on a given signal, the electricity would fail, leaving the oil lamps above the gambling tables to illuminate the room, which was to be stormed by Cowley's pistol-waving confederates. Unfortunately, however, Cowley became aware that the gendarmes knew of the plan and escaped on his yacht, disappearing after an overnight chase by police. Some of his henchmen were arrested and sent to the U.S. where they were convicted of various crimes.

REF.: Ashton-Wolfe, *The Underworld; CBA.*

Cowper, Spencer, and **Stephens, Ellis,** and **Rogers, William,** and **Marson, John,** prom. 1699, Case of, Brit., mur. Sarah Stout, a young Quaker woman, was found floating in the pond two miles outside of Hertford in March 1699. At the formal inquest that accompanied the tragedy, the jury returned a verdict of suicide while insane. The body was laid to rest and people went about their normal business until the devout Quakers raised a protest. Suicide was not a part of their religious faith. They claimed that Sarah had been deliberately drowned and strangled by a man who had compromised her virtue: Spencer Cowper.

A charge of murder was brought against Cowper, a young barrister of thirty who had given evidence at the inquest, and three lawyers who arrived in town to attend the Hertford Assizes. The trial opened in Hertford on July 16, 1699. Cowper conducted his own defense, summoning five medical men and two seamen who testified to the fact that the bodies of murder victims dropped into the water usually sank, while the drowning victims would tend to float on the surface. To support this thesis, the physicians experimented with three dogs that were drowned the night before the trial.

Baron Matsell instructed the jury to draw their own conclusions from the testimony and evidence given. Accordingly, they returned a verdict of Not Guilty against the defendants in a case that was motivated by social and moral antagonism between the Quakers and Lawyer Cowper.

REF.: Birmingham, *Murder Most Foul;* Earl of Birkenhead, *Famous Trials of History; CBA;* Guttmacher, *The Mind of the Murderer.*

Cowper, William (First Earl Cowper), c.1665-1723, Brit., jur. Presided as lord high steward at the trial of the Earl of Winton and others implicated in the Jacobite uprising of 1715. REF.: *CBA.*

Cox, Chastine, d.1879, U.S., mur. Mrs. Jane L. de F. Hull, a wealthy New York socialite who had moved from London to Manhattan, hired Chastine Cox as a footman and butler. After a short time, Cox began pilfering Hull's silverware, selling these items through fences. She later caught him stealing some of her jewelry and Cox leaped upon the elderly woman and strangled her to death. He ran from the Hull mansion in full sight of other servants, Hull's jewelry clutched in his hands. Arrested a short time later in Boston, Cox was returned to New York where he was hanged, following a brief trial.

REF.: *CBA; Mrs. Hull's Murder.*

Cox, Edward, d.1901, U.S., mur. A source of embarrassment to the more compassionate citizens of Atlanta, Ga., was the forced convict labor, wherein convicted prisoners of the penitentiary were leased to business operations to perform manual labor. John B. Gordon was one of the major lessees until he found the system repugnant and decided to sell his interest in Penitentiary Company No. 2. He appointed his lawyer, Colonel Robert B. Alston, one of the city's most distinguished citizens, as his agent.

Alston approached several persons interested in the lease, but Edward Cox, a plantation owner who was a sub-lessee under Gordon, objected to these buyers. Alston nevertheless made arrangements with one Colonel C. B. Howard to pick up Gordon's lease. Cox, who felt cheated in the deal, stormed into Hutchins' Barber Shop on Mar. 11, 1879, and demanded that the deal be rescinded. Alston was getting a shave; he waved the livid Cox away. Cox drew a knife and waved it in front of Alston.

The lawyer wiped his face with a towel. "I am unarmed," he told the foot-stomping Cox. "I desire no difficulty with you."

"Then go and arm yourself," Cox shouted.

The two men had served with distinction in the Confederate army, Alston with Morgan's raiders, Cox in Wheeler's cavalry. Neither man was a stranger to pistols, knives, and sabres. Minutes after Alston left the barber shop, ostensibly to arm himself, Cox threw a fit, screaming abusive language about Alston and all lawyers in general. He was heard to shout: "If that man does not do right in this matter, I'll kill him before sundown!"

Cox then stormed out of the barber shop and made the rounds of friends, asking to borrow a weapon. Not finding one, the irate gentleman farmer barged into the Heinze and Berkele gun store and purchased a nickel-plated revolver with the brand name, Swamp Angel, stamped on its butt.

The one-day feud came to an unlikely end in an even more unlikely place—the office of State Treasurer John W. Renfroe in the State House at Forsyth and Marietta streets. Cox and Alston immediately began to argue. Renfroe and Captain John W. Nelms, keeper of the penitentiary, tried to calm the antagonists, but suddenly both men drew weapons and began shooting at each other. As bullets whizzed and ricocheted inside the paneled office, Renfroe and Nelms hugged the floor, Cox was hit first in the upper lip. He cursed as he spat blood and fired. He missed. Another of Alston's bullets plowed into Cox's left hand. He moved his revolver to the other hand and fired at Alston, hitting him in the head. The lawyer died a few hours later. Cox was sentenced to hard labor for life. It was his grim irony to slave alongside the very convicts he had once driven so ruthlessly on his own plantation. He died, however, a free man in 1901 and was buried in the Decatur cemetery—three feet from the man he had killed. REF.: *CBA.*

Cox, Frederick William, c.1897-1924, S. Afri., mur. A young man failed to fulfill his part in a suicide pact with his paramour, resulting in his death by execution for murder.

Frederick William Cox, who was unemployed at the time, attempted to defraud a neighbor, borrowing £15 to supposedly establish a partnership between the two. When the man threatened to press charges of theft against him, Cox denied the ruse, agreeing to meet the disgruntled partner and a detective at a bank the next day. On Feb. 21, 1924, Cox met the men, then excused himself briefly to pick up his secret girlfriend, his cousin Annie Cox, whom he called Dolly. Aghast at the thought of being separated because of Frederick's crime, and already forced to hide their feelings because of Annie's disapproving father, the couple decided they would rather die together than be apart, according to Frederick Cox' testimony at his sentencing.

As arranged, Frederick led his lover into an office where he stabbed her, surprising Annie who probably expected a quicker death, according to witnesses who observed her fight to live. Cox, apparently devastated that Annie suffered and that he had no time to kill himself, confessed to the murder.

Cox' trial started on May 19, 1924, with examining doctors calling him sane. Cox, protesting any efforts by his lawyer to help him avoid the death penalty, was found Guilty after twenty-five minutes of jury deliberation. Sentenced to die at the gallows he lost some of the composure he showed during sentencing and was hanged on July 1, 1924.

REF.: Bennett, *Too Late For Tears; CBA.*

Cox, Jacob Dolson, 1828-1900, U.S., lawyer. Dean of the Cincinnati Law School from 1881-97. REF.: *CBA.*

Cox, John, and **Pugh, James,** prom. 1827, Brit., mur. For testifying against a member of their gang, John Cox and James Pugh strangled James Harrison, who also belonged to their Shropshire gang of robbers and sheep thieves.

In an earlier attempt to avenge Mr. Ellson, their confederate, John Cox, Sr.—the Cox boys' father—Robert Cox, and Ann Harris joined the others in trying to buy arsenic to kill Harrison. When that failed, Harris, who was Ellson's mother, and the senior John Cox paid 100 shillings to have Harrison killed. Robert Cox dug the grave while his older brother and Pugh strangled Harrison.

Ellson was acquitted of sheep stealing, but told police about the murder to avoid a stiff penalty when arrested for another theft. All five members of the gang were tried, convicted, and given the death penalty, but Harris and the elder Cox were later reprieved.

REF.: Butler, *Murderers' England; CBA.*

Cox, Robert, 1772-86, Brit., (wrong convict.) mur. Fourteen-year-old Robert Cox was dragged screaming to the gallows in Holborn on Dec. 18, 1786, for a crime he probably never committed. Cox was one of three men arrested for the murder of Duncan Robinson, who was accosted by pickpockets in Holborn on Nov. 16, as he walked down the street with Michael Hunt.

The assailants were identified as Michael Walker and Richard Payne. Hunt believed Cox was the boy he saw as the two older men attempted to make their escape. The fact that the boy was associating with a gang of robbers was enough to convict him of murder in the stabbing death of Robinson. At his trial the judge conceded as much by stating that "though he had not struck a blow, yet it was a maxim in law that persons connected for a felonious purpose, if any evil consequences ensued, were all equally answerable for the guilt."

REF.: *CBA;* Wilson, *Children Who Kill.*

Cox, Samuel Sullivan (AKA: Sunset Cox), 1824-89, U.S., lawyer. Member of the U.S. House of Representatives from 1857-65 and from 1869-89. REF.: *CBA.*

Cox, Seymour Ernest J., prom. 1920s, U.S., fraud. One of the most blatant sellers of phony stock during the 1920s, when America was enamored of Wall Street, was Seymour Ernest J. Cox, a dapper, smooth-talking character who specialized in oil stock promotions. Cox, who was called "the arch pirate" of oil speculations, began his criminal career in Illinois where he was sent to jail at age fifteen for forgery. Upon his release, Cox went to Michigan where, in 1911, he was again convicted of fraud and sent to prison. In 1914, Cox served time after being convicted of using the mails to defraud. Upon his release, Cox went to Oklahoma and Texas, where he began to sell fake potash and oil stocks, bilking more than 16,000 purchasers out of an estimated $7 million, all before 1920.

Con man Seymour Cox with his wife.

This inventive hustler was, perhaps, the first con man to use an airplane in promoting his stock swindles. Cox rented a plane to fly over oil fields that were "off limits" to the public. He would take notes about those locations where he could see intense activity and large numbers of oil drilling crews, reasoning that "gushers" were soon expected. He filed reports on these oil operations to his stockholders, telling them that his companies owned portions of these oil operations. When official reports were released on the productivity of these new wells, Cox would sell his customers even more shares of phony stock in these operations, oil wells in which Cox had no business interests at all.

Cox was clever, challenging his prospective victims by writing them letters in which he would ask: "Are you sure that you would like to own an oil well? Are you absolutely certain you care to assume the responsibilities of becoming a millionaire?" Then Cox would send follow-up letters to prospects, knowing they were holders of worthless oil stock, convincing them to exchange their certificates for equally valueless stock he would issue in firms that ostensibly were beginning new oil fields, but which, in reality, had no field operations whatsoever. This was known in the parlance of con men as "stock reloading." In 1923, Cox and eleven others, including the celebrated adventurer, Dr. Frederick A. Cook, were convicted of stock swindling. Cox was fined $8,000 and sent to prison for eight years. Cook, the most famous of the group, was fined $12,000 and sent to prison for fourteen years.

REF.: *CBA;* Nash, *Hustlers and Con Men.*

Cox, Tom, 1666-91, Brit., rob.-mur. Asked to recite a last prayer at the gallows, Tom Cox instead cursed God and kicked the hangman, a fitting act for a man whose insolence knew no bounds.

Leaving home in Dorsetshire for London in his youth, Cox joined up with a gang of highwaymen who shared his penchant for the fast life. After his third arrest, trial, and acquittal, however, a wealthy woman who sat in on his last trial fell in love with him and became his benefactor. In two years, he squandered her fortune, then left for the highway.

On the road between Somerton and Shepton Mallet Cox met up with Thomas Killigrew, the court jester to King Charles II. When Killigrew asked if Cox really meant to take his money, the highwayman replied: "I am in earnest, for though you live by jesting I can't. Therefore, deliver your money, before a brace of balls make the sun shine through your body."

Inspired by his shrewdness, Cox continued to belittle his wealthy victims' misfortune. To his fellow highwaymen he was equally uncompromising. Observing two colleagues at the Inn of Coventry counting out their day's take, Cox lay in wait until morning and ambushed them out on the road. "Two of a trade cannot agree, I must make bold to do by you as you would have done by me," he said. But the two robbers resisted, so he killed one of them and made off with £120.

Tom Cox committed his last crime on Houslow Heath, stealing £20 from a farmer. His mistake was running into the farmer some time later in London, near Essex Street on the Strand. "Stop! Thief!" the man cried. Cox was apprehended soon after, tried at the Old Bailey, found Guilty, and hanged at Tyburn on June 3, 1691.

REF.: *CBA;* Smith, *Highwaymen.*

Coxey, Jacob Sechler, 1854-1951, U.S., mob vio. On May 1, 1894, a group of unemployed and homeless men, led by Populist businessman "General" Jacob Coxey, arrived in Washington to lobby for government relief in the form of a public works measure that would pay a $1.50 daily minimum wage. Known as Coxey's Army, the group became a national curiosity. The government treated the marchers as anarchists, and Coxey was arrested and charged with trespassing on the grass of the Capitol.

Jacob Coxey was an Ohio businessman who operated a successful stone quarry that made him one of the most influential citizens in his native Massillon, Ohio. In 1892, Coxey joined the Populist Party which supported the Greenback movement, and advocated agrarian land reform. The economic depression that lasted through much of the 1890s galvanized his political thinking, and by then Coxey had become a champion of the American underclass seeking their fair share of the pie.

In 1894, Coxey presented a plan to Carl Browne, a veteran labor agitator, for a march to Washington. Coxey proposed two Congressional bills that would create a country-road fund, supported by $500 million in non-interest-bearing government bonds. The road work would be performed by the unemployed for the guaranteed wage of $1.50 per day. The march on Washington began in Massillon on Easter Sunday 1894. The "Commonweal" Army numbered roughly 290 kindred souls who would be fed, according to Coxey, by plucking "ears of corn along the way." Representative Joseph Outhwaite of Ohio predicted that Coxey's followers would stir up a revolution if they succeeded in coercing Congress to grant their demands. This was the view held by a majority of legislators, who would not compromise with Coxey or anyone else with such radical notions.

Coxey's army marched through Pennsylvania and Maryland, picking up converts along the way. The national press reported their movements, and soon there were other marches scheduled across the U.S. When the marchers arrived at the steps of the Capitol Building, Coxey arose to address his followers and was told that the demonstration was against the law. When he asked if he could read a written protest, this was also denied. The "army" became unruly when it learned that Coxey was being denied the right to speak. They pushed and shoved their way forward, only to be driven back by mounted policemen. Five minutes later order was restored, and Coxey, Browne, and Christopher Columbus Jones were taken into custody. On May 8, they were found Guilty of trespassing, fined $5 each, and given a twenty-day jail sentences.

Scattered fragments of other Coxey armies were rounded up by Baltimore Police and arrested as vagrants. The movement collapsed as quickly as it had begun, but Coxey refused to give up the fight. In 1914, he led a second march on Washington with similar results. In 1932, he ran for president on the Farm-Labor ticket in Minnesota and received 5,371 votes in a losing cause. Coxey later had the satisfaction of seeing some of his ideas incorporated by President Franklin D. Roosevelt in the New Deal. REF.: *CBA*; Butterfield, *The American Past*; McMurray, *Coxey's Army*.

Coyle, Joseph William, 1954-   , U.S., rob. An unemployed longshoreman, claiming insanity, was acquitted of stealing $1.2 million that had fallen from an armored truck in Philadelphia, Pa.

On Feb. 26, 1981, two money sacks fell from an armored car owned by Purolator Armored, Inc., and were grabbed by three men traveling in a maroon 1971 Chevrolet Malibu. A week later, on Mar. 5, police arrested Joseph Coyle at John F. Kennedy Airport in New York City as he checked in for a flight to Acapulco, Mex., carrying in his socks $105,000 in 21 envelopes of $5,000 each. Francis A. Santos, charged with bringing Coyle to the airport, purchasing his plane ticket, and supplying him with identification papers, also was arrested. Coyle won acquittal on the theft charge on May 25, 1982, and was advised by Common Pleas Court Judge John Chiovero to continue private psychiatric counseling. Still missing at the time of Coyle's trial was $200,000 from the armored truck. REF.: *CBA*.

Crabb, Christopher Columbus, 1852-1935, U.S., pros. Christopher Crabb was earning $14 a week as a department store clerk when he met Chicago brothel keeper Lizzie Allen in 1878. Second only to Carrie Watson as the reigning queen of city prostitution, the 38-year-old demimonde took Crabb under her wing. He became her lover, business manager, and confidant, and the girls who worked for Lizzie Allen respected him as someone they could count on to treat them fairly. It was understood that he would help a woman find suitable employment should she decide to abandon the prostitute's life—an act of benevolence unheard of during the years of the white slave trade in Chicago.

At the same time he was attending to Allen's needs, Crabb began a secret tryst with Mollie Fitch, a competitor in the prostitution trade. When Fitch died, Crabb inherited a sizeable chunk of her estate—$150,000. In 1890, he invested $125,000 of it into the refurbishing of a double house at 2131 South Dearborn Street. Allen and Crabb called it the House of Mirrors. In 1900, the Everleigh Sisters purchased the building and turned it into one of the nation's most opulent brothels of the gaslight era.

Allen died in 1896, leaving Crabb with all of her cash and property. She was buried at Rosehill Cemetery, with the inscription "Perpetual Ease" on her tomb—which is exactly the kind of life she had bestowed on Crabb. It was estimated that her estate was valued at $300,000. By the time Christopher Crabb died on Jan. 5, 1935, he was worth $416,589.81. Three quarters of it went to the Illinois Masonic Orphans' Home. See: **Allen, Lizzie; Everleigh Sisters.** REF.: *CBA*.

Crabb, George, 1778-1851, Brit., lawyer. Published history of English law in 1829. REF.: *CBA*.

Cradlebaugh, John, 1819-72, U.S., jur. Nominated to fill vacancy on bench of territorial court of Utah by President James Buchanan in 1858. REF.: *CBA*.

Cradock, Anne, See: **Chudleigh, Elizabeth.**

Craft, Ellis, prom. 1800s, U.S., consp.-mur. The Christmastime murders of three adolescents caused the deaths of four other persons at the hands of militia guards, who were never indicted for the killings.

On Dec. 24, 1881, the bodies of Emma Carico, Fannie Gibbons, and her 17-year-old brother Robert Gibbons, were found by neighbors in the burning home of the Gibbons' family in Ashland, Ky. Initially assumed that the children had died of smoke inhalation, soon it became obvious that the adolescents had been murdered, for their heads were bashed in. The murder weapons were a blood-covered ax, discovered underneath some carpeting in the house, and a bloody crowbar, found stuck between fenceposts. The two girls had been raped. A $1,000 reward was posted for the capture of the killers and a number of detectives came to Ashland.

Nine days after the crime, George Ellis confessed to U.S. Deputy Marshall James Heflin that he had watched his two friends, Ellis Craft and William Neal, murder the teenagers. Ellis claimed that Neal and Craft threatened him with a pistol, forcing him into the Gibbons home and making him hold the girls down as they raped them. Craft then forced him to pour coal oil over the girls' bodies, and Craft set the oil on fire. Craft had earlier slain Robert with an ax when the boy ordered the two intruders to leave the girls alone. Based on Ellis' confession, Craft and Neal were arrested the next day. They denied everything.

Neal's trial began on Jan. 16. After eight days of testimony and only eighteen minutes of deliberation, the jury found him Guilty of murdering Emma Carico and he was sentenced to death. Craft, tried immediately after Neal, was found Guilty of killing Fannie Gibbons and also sentenced to death. Both men protested their innocence but neither influenced the judge, and they were scheduled to die on Apr. 14, 1882, but their cases were appealed.

On May 30, Ellis was tried for the murder of Robert Gibbons, based on testimony that he had been seen near the house during and after the fire. Found Guilty and sentenced to life, he was the first of the three men to die when several hours later eighteen men and boys wearing black masks broke into the jail at Catlettsburg, dragged Ellis out, and hanged him on a Sycamore tree near the crime scene.

Twenty Boyd County residents were indicted for the lynching following an investigation by a special grand jury convened by Circuit Court Judge George N. Brown, but no one was prosecuted. Neal and Craft's guilt was reaffirmed following a trial at the Boyd County Court, but they again appealed because Judge Brown had failed to instruct the jury that no verdict could be found on a case based on an accomplice's confession. They were granted a change of venue in Carter County. When they were being transported and escorted by 215 guards from the Kentucky state militia, followed by 200 citizens who wanted to lynch the convicted men, more than nineteen people were shot near the Ohio River, four of them killed. After a chase that attracted more than a hundred observers to the shore, a small group of men demanded that Major John R. Allen relinquish the prisoners. He refused. No one was indicted. Three months after the massacre, Craft was found Guilty and sentenced to die on May 25, 1883.

While Craft's case awaited appeal and before proceedings

against Neal commenced, Detective Alfred Burnett of West Virginia reiterated his theory that black men, and not the three whites, had killed the adolescents. He now had a suspect, William Direly, who was promptly charged and tried for the slayings but the case was dropped for lack of evidence.

The day before he was to die, Craft, who showed no signs of guilt but believed he was a victim of men anxious to receive the reward money, was baptized in a creek before an audience of guards armed with guns to prevent a mob lynching. A massive audience of more than 3,000 people gathered on Oct. 12, 1883, to witness the first use of the newly constructed gallows of Carter County. In a fifteen-minute speech, Craft repeated his declaration of innocence, saying "Soon I will swing between the heavens and earth...I would not lie now." REF.: *CBA*.

Craft, Mary Faye, 1936- , Case of, U.S., mur. Craft insisted her husband's Apr. 9, 1988, death was an accident. West Virginia State Police initially concurred, but an unavoidable question surfaced: Just how could retired Air Force Major General Robert Sadler, an expert marksman, accidentally fire a bullet into his head?

An official investigation was launched, spurred on, no doubt, by the poem Craft wrote and delivered to her stepchildren. "If your father were alive/How unhappy he would be. To hear the vicious lies/being told about me." The investigation moved quickly and Craft was indicted on a charge of first-degree murder in July 1988.

Craft, a published poet and public relations consultant, met Sadler through the personal ads in *Washington Magazine*. After a brief courtship, she became a military wife. She was familiar with the lifestyle because each of her first four husbands had also been military officers. The couple settled down on Sadler's 190-acre farm in Grant County, W. Va., 150 miles outside Washington, D.C. From the beginning, their marriage was troubled. In her journal, Craft complained about her husband's alleged flirtations with "the gals at work," and she confided to a son, James Craft, that she was intending to file for a divorce.

The murder trial of Mary Faye Craft began on Oct. 24, 1988, in the Grant County Courthouse in Petersburg, W. Va. Prosecuting Attorney Dennis DiBenedetto argued that Craft murdered her husband and made it appear an accident to collect his life insurance policy valued at $410,000, which doubled if his death was accidental.

"I am not guilty of murder!" she shouted in response. Craft then broke into tears and told yet another version of her story. What really happened, she explained this time, was that Sadler was playing with a .38-caliber handgun as he sat in his favorite wingback chair, sipping cocoa. Suddenly, according to Craft, he began to point the gun at the window, the door, and then directly at her. Nervous and scared, she tried to wrestle the handgun away from him. In the struggle, the gun discharged behind Sadler's right ear, killing him. DiBenedetto summoned expert medical witnesses who stated that the physical evidence did not support her claim that it was a "tragic accident." Sadler was shot behind the right ear from a distance of twelve to fourteen inches. Yet the weapon was found between his legs.

After five days of emotional courtroom testimony in which the jury weighed Craft's various accounts of the incident with disparate reports from medical witnesses, a decision of Not Guilty was delivered. Upon hearing the verdict, Craft jumped up from her chair shouting, "Praise the Lord! Praise the Lord!" but it was not quite over.

While conducting their investigation into the shooting of Sadler, police found items valued at $150,000 hidden behind a false wall. Two years earlier, Craft reported to her insurance company that these very items had been stolen. She was charged with fraud. At the ensuing trial, Craft accused her deceased husband of instigating the crime. "But they were your items," pointed out prosecuting attorney Elizabeth Luttig. In typical style, Craft replied, "But he was my husband!" On May 20, 1988, Fairfax Circuit Court Judge Lewis Griffith pronounced her Guilty of fraud

and imposed a three-year suspended sentence.

In reaction, Craft chortled, "I love God, I love my family, I love my country!" REF.: *CBA*.

Crafton, Paul Arthur (AKA: **Dr. Peter H. Pearse, Dr. John Byron Hext**), 1923- , U.S., forg. A technological genius established thirty-four aliases with nearly seventy credit cards, false passports, and fake letterheads, apparently to line up teaching jobs at eastern colleges.

Paul Arthur Crafton, an engineering professor at George Washington University in Washington, D.C., was arrested in March 1983, charged with forgery and theft after being caught teaching other subjects at Shippensburg State University, in Shippensburg, Pa., as Dr. John Hext from Australia, and at the University of Pennsylvania at Millersville under the name of Dr. Peter Pearse of Canada.

A widespread investigation mounted by the U.S. State Department, the Social Security Administration, Scotland Yard, the Royal Canadian Mounted Police, Interpol, and authorities from six states found no motive for Crafton's seemingly bizarre crimes. Crafton's attorney, John Pyfer, argued that Crafton needed the $90,000 he earned from the three teaching posts to pay for treatment of his daughter's cerebral palsy and curvature of the spine. Investigators, however, said Crafton did not pay significant amounts to take care of Laura, his 17-year-old daughter.

Crafton lived in Potomac, Md., with his wife Sonia, his daughter, and his 20-year-old son, Eric, but maintained an apartment near the two Pennsylvania schools in Lancaster, where officials found false birth certificates, academic records, and other papers to support his many assumed identities. Also found were papers indicating he had tried to obtain teaching jobs at more than twenty eastern colleges, and letters to and from several women Crafton apparently attracted through personal ads taken out under several different aliases, including Peter de W. Connaught of England, whose wife and child actually were killed in a car accident. A woman who grew suspicious of "Connaught" hired a detective, who found the Englishman was really Crafton. The woman alerted George Washington University, where Crafton had taught engineering since 1956. The university took no action, but Crafton eventually was caught by a professor at Shippensburg who grew suspicious after reading a magazine article by the real Professor Hext, and alerted Herb Bowers, director of campus police at Shippensburg. Bowers discovered "Hext's" car was registered under a different name, and brought the mysterious professor's picture to Millersville, some eighty miles away, where it was identified as a photo of Pearse.

Crafton, who had patents on a device to confirm the identities of credit-card users and six other inventions, baffled officials searching for a motive for his behavior. They found he owned property in Nova Scotia and apparently contemplated moving to Canada or Switzerland, based on papers found in his Lancaster apartment. He also had worked under his real name at the Naval Research Laboratory in Washington, D.C., assigned to secret research, with security clearance by the government. But with all his peculiar involvements, Crafton was only required to plead guilty to charges of forgery after agreeing to a plea-bargain that reduced the charges against him from twenty-six to four. He was sentenced on Feb. 29, 1984, to two years probation and 500 hours of community service and fined $500 by Lancaster County Judge Ronald Buckwalter for posing as Dr. Pearse at Millersville State from 1982-83. Crafton received a three-to-nine-month prison sentence from Cumberland County Judge Harold Sheely for impersonating Dr. Hext at Shippensburg. REF.: *CBA*.

Craggs, James, 1657-1721, Brit., fraud-polit. corr. While serving as joint postmaster general from 1715-21, he accepted £30,000 in illegal stock from directors of the South Sea Company. The accompanying scandal became known as the South Sea Bubble. See: **South Sea Bubble**. REF.: *CBA*.

Craig, Alvin, c.1909- , and **Hess, Walter**, c.1909- , U.S., (wrong. convict.) mur. Mistaken testimony by a dying man caused two teenagers to be wrongly convicted of murder. Virgil Romine was shot in the abdomen at about 1:30 a.m. on Jan. 7, 1929, in Herculaneum, Mo. Before being taken to the hospital where he died, Romine told Deputy Sheriff J.W. Dugan that his attackers had caused trouble at the Artesian Park Filling Station the previous month and had returned to an adjacent restaurant, where Romine was shot. Alvin Craig and Walter Hess, two boys who had stolen money from a slot machine at the filling station, were arrested and charged with murder.

Craig and Hess' trial began on Apr. 18, 1929, with defense attorney Albert S. Ennis arguing that bloody clothes, including a shirt with a bullet hole found by a crew from the State Highway Department, proved that the uninjured defendants were innocent. The jury felt otherwise, however, and Craig and Hess were convicted and sentenced to ten years.

While Craig awaited appeal, Mamie Woolem, nicknamed Babe, told police that she, Louis Taylor, Joe Muehlman, and Radford Browning were at the filling station the night of the murder, and that Taylor had shot Romine. The other three also confessed and pleaded guilty in court in May 1930.

Browning and Muehlman were sentenced to ten years in prison, while Taylor, who had a chest injury matching the bullet hole in the shirt found after the crime, received a life sentence. Woolem, who helped Taylor take care of his injury, was also found Guilty and sentenced to life on Taylor's testimony that his former girlfriend had planned the robbery of the filling station and had given Taylor the gun. Hess and Craig were pardoned by Governor Caulfield of Missouri within a year after their sentencing. REF.: CBA.

Craig, Christopher, 1936- , Brit., mur. Christopher Craig grew up in comfortable surroundings in the suburb of Croydon. His father was a bank executive, and by all accounts Christopher and his brother were never in want. Despite his obvious advantages Craig turned to a life of crime, and together with his partner Burney were trafficking in stolen furs and clothing. Both men were living in Kensington where they were cornered by police on Sept. 14, 1952. After a violent struggle, the two were arrested and charged with armed robbery. Craig and Burney were convicted and sentenced to twelve years and nineteen years in prison respectively. The matter did not end there. On the night of Nov. 2, two men broke loose from prison and holed up inside a London warehouse. The Croydon police arrived on the scene minutes later, attempting to reason with the felons. "If you want us, well come and get us!" shouted Craig. Shots rang out. Two unarmed policemen were felled by bullets: Officer P.C. Miles who was killed instantly, and Detective Constable Fairfax who sustained a shoulder wound but nevertheless managed to subdue the second man, Derek Bentley.

Bentley was convicted of murder, and summarily executed at Wandsworth Prison after the Home Secretary turned down his request for a pardon. Craig, who was only sixteen years old at the time, was ordered detained at the Queen's pleasure.

REF.: CBA; Furneaux, *Famous Criminal Cases, Vol. 1.*

Craig, Eric Roland, prom. 1932, Aus., mansl.-mur. A man's training in the army, specifically the way he learned to tie knots, led to his capture and eventual conviction for murder and manslaughter.

On Dec. 9, 1932, a 30-year-old Irish prostitute named May Miller, also known as Iris Marriott, was seen getting into an Essex automobile. The next day her naked body was found in Centennial Park, her skull crushed in by the branch of a fig tree found nearby and her clothes neatly tied together in a bundle. Four days later, 14-year-old Bessie O'Connor was taken from her home in the Sydney suburb of Redfern to National Park, also in an Essex, where she was found naked and dead the following morning, the victim of an ax attack. She died before regaining consciousness but an Aboriginal tracker found an important clue—the girl's clothes, tied in a bundle. Detective-Sergeant James Comans of the Sydney Police, who later became superintendent, recognized a similarity between the bundles—a gunner's knot, the kind he had learned to tie in the Royal Australian Artillery. From this

he deduced that the killer was also trained in the artillery, half a mile from the park where O'Connor was murdered. Eric Roland Craig, who enlisted in May 1927, was identified in group photographs of Australian soldiers by witnesses, and, though he had moved his wife and two children to Paddington and had grown a mustache, was arrested Jan. 7, 1933.

Craig confessed to killing May during interrogation, explaining that she had attacked him first because he did not have five shillings to pay for her favors, and that he had stripped her so police would be unable to identify the body. He also admitted to stealing the car, but denied murdering O'Connor.

Craig was not charged with the murder of Hilda White, found naked in Centennial Park, probably because she had been strangled. Craig was strongly suspected in the case, however, because White's clothing also was found neatly tied.

For the death of Miller, who had an unsavory reputation as a prostitute convicted of several assaults, Craig was found Guilty of manslaughter and sentenced to twenty years' imprisonment. Craig's first two trials for the murder of O'Connor ended in mistrials, but the third jury found him Guilty of murder and he received the death sentence. The New South Wales Cabinet commuted the sentence to life imprisonment with no possibility of parole on Sept. 19, 1933.

REF.: CBA; Gribble, *Clues That Spelled Guilty.*

Craig, Ernest, c.1921-49, U.S., asslt. A three-hour shootout between Chicago police and an unpopular gun collector injured seven people, including five police officers, and killed the gunman.

Ernest Craig, known to point pistols out his window at passersby, extended his habit in August 1949 by firing at Lawrence Mack, a 17-year-old trying to get money from him for a cleaning job. The bullet missed the youth and slightly injured an infant in a yard near Craig's run-down home.

Craig fired more shots at police attempting to enter his house, then ran to various windows shooting at police gathering outside. A combination of tear gas, Tommy guns, carbines, pistols, and gasoline flares failed to silence Craig, but attracted a crowd of nearly 10,000 people. A fire set with flares thrown through first-floor windows and strong streams of water aimed at the top floor by firemen only inspired Craig to dare police to invade the home. Craig shot at two entering officers, Police Commissioner John C. Prendergast and Police Chief Ray Crane, who returned a volley and ran out. After a long silence, Crane saw Craig hiding alongside the house, and ordered his men to shoot. Craig, holding two pistols, tried to fire back but was killed by a barrage of eighteen bullets. REF.: CBA.

Craig, John, c.1512-1600, Scot., her. Joined the Dominican order of friars, but after reading John Calvin's *Institutes,* he renewed his ties to the Protestant church. In 1559 he was sentenced to death by the inquisition in Rome, but managed to escape. REF.: CBA.

Craig, John H., d.1818, U.S., mur. John H. Craig shot and killed Edward Hunter from ambush near his home at Chester, Pa., believing that Hunter had persuaded an uncle of Craig's to eliminate him from his will. Craig drew suspicion to himself when he inquired of his uncle's attorney whether or not the slain Hunter had been named in the will. He was arrested for Hunter's murder and confessed to the crime. Craig was hanged at Chester, Pa., on June 6, 1818. The local sheriff allowed Craig a last request; he was allowed to walk for a mile through the woodlands he had known as a boy to the place of execution.

REF.: CBA; Rowan, *The Pinkertons; The Confession of John H. Craig.*

Craig, Robert, 1922- , and **Markert, Louis**, 1928- , U.S., fraud-polit. corr. Two Illinois lawmakers convicted of soliciting bribes from a political lobbyist were sentenced to prison on Mar. 23, 1977. Democratic State representatives Robert Craig and Louis Markert from downstate Illinois had been accused of extorting $1,500 from Doris Steigberg in exchange for their promise to "kill" a 1971 General Assembly bill. The legislation would have required car dealers to inform consumers interested in purchasing vehicles if they had been operated in the rental or leasing business. The effect of such a bill would have driven down used car prices by as much as $600.

The legislation, first introduced by Rep. Thomas Hanahan, was labeled by federal prosecutors a "fetcher bill"—one designed to solicit bribes from special interest groups, in this case the car rental industry. A top executive from Hertz reportedly mailed Ms. Steigberg a check to cover the amount of the bribe, which constituted mail fraud. The bill died in committee May 1972. Hanahan was later acquitted, but Craig and Markert were found Guilty on Feb. 9, 1977. Federal Judge Alfred Kirkland imposed a three-year sentence on Craig, a dairy farmer from Danville, and six months on Markert, a farmer representing the community of Mount Sterling. Afterward, Hanahan said he was "pleased" by the verdict. REF.: *CBA*.

Craig, Sir **Thomas**, c.1538-1608, Scot., jur. Justice Deputy of Scotland, he presided over numerous criminal trials from 1564-73. REF.: *CBA*.

Crain, **James**, 1954- , and **Berg**, **Pamela Sue**, 1957- , U.S., mansl. On Jan. 11, 1981, the body of 5-year-old Alan Madden of Quincy, Ill., was taken to pathologist Dr. Zakiah Ali, for an autopsy. Ali concluded that the boy's death was caused by a severe blow from a knee, which tended to support the testimony of Pamela Sue Berg, the boy's mother. James Crain, a 27-year-old computer programmer, accused Berg, his former girlfriend, of beating her son with a wooden stick. He denied executing a karate maneuver known as a "knee drop" on the boy. Crain said he tried to prevent the abusive Berg from hurting the boy, and called the Illinois Department of Children and Family Services.

In separate trials, Pamela Berg was convicted of involuntary manslaughter and sentenced to ten years in prison, and on Jan. 21, 1982, James Crain was handed a ten year sentence coupled with a $10,000 fine, also for manslaughter. The two defendants were also charged with embezzling $10,000 in public aid benefits in the year before Alan's death. The case led to an investigation of the Department of Children and Family services in the Quincy area. REF.: *CBA*.

Crain, **J.V.**, d.1855, U.S., mur. Susan Newnham of Ringgold, Calif., was one of the most attractive young women in El Dorado County. One of the many suitors vying for her hand in marriage was J.V. Crain who eventually became engaged to her. Newnham's parents, however, investigated Crain's background and discovered that he was already married and instructed their daughter to call off the wedding. When she did so, Crain went berserk and shot the young lady to death, shouting that "no one else will have you!" He was quickly apprehended and sentenced to death. While awaiting execution, Crain wrote his self-aggrandizing memoirs. He was then hanged on Oct. 26, 1855.

REF.: *CBA*; Crain, *The Conspirators' Victims, or, The Life and Adventures of J.V. Crain*.

Cranch, **William**, 1769-1855, U.S., jur. Served Washington, D.C., as chief justice of the district court from 1805-55. During this time he compiled dozens of collections of legal reports. REF.: *CBA*.

Crandall, **Prudence**, 1803-90, U.S., consp. Prosecuted in 1833 for her work on behalf of blacks, which intensified the already strained relations between southern sympathizers and northern abolitionists. REF.: *CBA*.

Crane, **Cheryl**, 1944- , Case of, U.S., mansl. The only child of Hollywood actress Lana Turner, Cheryl Crane was born to Turner and Stephen Crane, the actress' second husband, a marriage that lasted only a few months. Turner had already been married to Artie Shaw and, after her annulment from Crane, went on to marry Henry J. "Bob" Topping, Lex Barker, Fred May, Robert Eaton, and Ronald Dante. The marriage to Barker, it was claimed, had been broken up by Cheryl, who continued to live with her mother through her host of husbands. The girl was surrounded by her mother's enormous wealth—a mansion, servants, jewels, expensive cars, and mostly fame. Teenage jealousy of her mother prompted Cheryl, some claimed, to whisper nasty gossip to her mother about her husbands and those she

dated between marriages. One of these was the handsome, smooth-talking gangster, John Stompanato, one-time chauffeur and bagman for Los Angeles gambler and gangster Mickey Cohen.

Stompanato, born in Woodstock, Ill., in 1925, had served as a Marine during WWII. He had attended an exclusive military school and then Notre Dame briefly before enlisting in the Marines in 1944, serving three years. The rugged Stompanato had married and divorced twice by 1948 when he went to work for Cohen in Los Angeles as Cohen's bodyguard, driver, and later as bagman, collecting the profits from Cohen's gambling and extortion rackets. He then struck out on his own, operating as a Hollywood lounge lizard, picking up lonely but wealthy women who were married, then make love to them in a room where hidden motion picture cameras recorded every move. Stompanato would then sell the film to the compromised women at staggering extortion prices.

When Lana Turner's marriage to Lex Barker ended, she received a call from Stompanato, asking her for a date. He first used the name John Steele when introducing himself to Turner and her daughter Cheryl. The lonely 38-year-old Turner accepted and their tempestuous affair began. The gangster was nothing like Turner's husbands or previous lovers. He was loud, crude, gauche, a braggart and a bully, who wore shiny shirts open almost to his navel to reveal his chest. He oozed Latin charm and earthiness, but at the same time his passions were violent and menacing. Cheryl Crane was enamored by her mother's new lover; she and Stompanato spent hours horseback riding or swimming together in her mother's Olympic-sized pool. Stompanato played the older brother to her, writing her long letters when she was traveling with her mother. Turner, meanwhile, lavished Stompanato with expensive gifts, clothes, and then loaned him $10,000—money that was never repaid. When he joined her and Cheryl in London while Turner was filming *Another Time, Another Place*, Stompanato moved into the luxurious townhouse Turner and Cheryl were sharing. The gangster then asked the actress for another loan, $50,000, to secure the rights to a film script for a movie in which, he, Johnny Stompanato, would star. The gangster had long nurtured the secret ambition to become a film star.

The actress turned him down, saying that she did not have that kind of cash and that her financial advisers had ordered her not to give him any more money. Her refusal caused Stompanato to go berserk. He threatened the star, who walked out on him, going to the set of *Another Time, Another Place* where she began to rehearse with co-star Sean Connery. Stompanato suddenly appeared on the set, raging, ordering Connery to "stay away from Lana!" Connery turned his back on Stompanato, who grabbed the burly actor and swung him about, waving a gun in Connery's face. The actor's response was to land a powerful punch to the gangster's jaw, sending him to the floor in a half-conscious state. Stompanato got up and walked away, swearing revenge. Back at the townhouse, the gangster cornered Turner and shrieked: "When I say hop, you'll hop! When I say jump, you'll jump!"

The actress ordered Stompanato out of the townhouse. He yelled: "I'll mutilate you! I'll hurt you so that you'll be so repulsive you'll have to hide forever!" With that he leaped forward, grabbed the actress around the throat and began to choke her. He then threw her down to the floor and threatened her with a razor, saying that he could cut her "just a little" but he could "do worse." She pleaded with Stompanato, who then relented, but he warned her: "That's just to let you know that I'm not kidding. Don't think that you can ever get away!" Cheryl Crane had heard the commotion and expressed fears for her mother's life. The director of the film Turner was working on called Scotland Yard, and Stompanato was politely escorted to the airport and put on the next plane to the U.S. Lana Turner had successfully gotten rid of the menacing thug.

Once the film in England was completed, however, Turner and Cheryl returned to Los Angeles and the actress made the mistake of calling Stompanato, showing herself to be much more dependent upon him than she had previously admitted. Stom-

Lana Turner with Johnny Stompanato.

Return from Mexico; Lana is interviewed, Stompanato chats with Cheryl Crane.

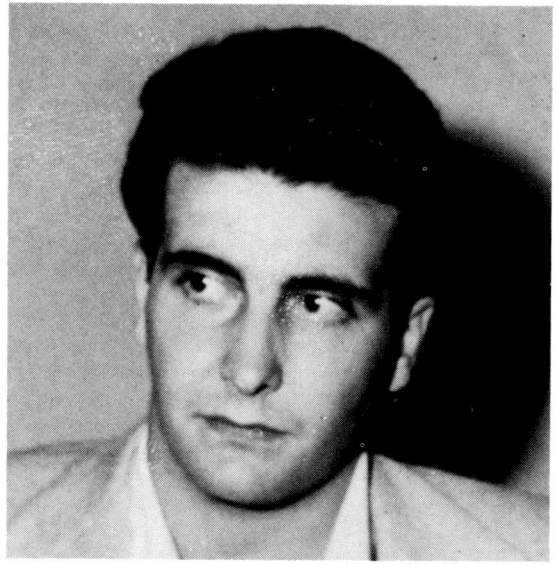

Stompanato was an accomplished blackmailer.

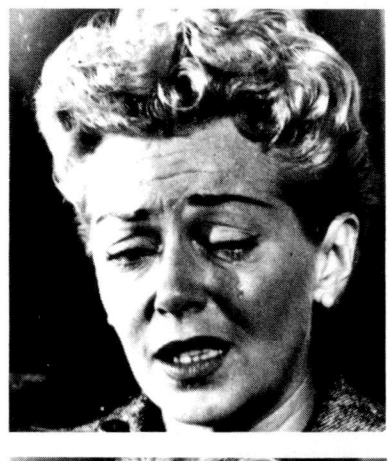

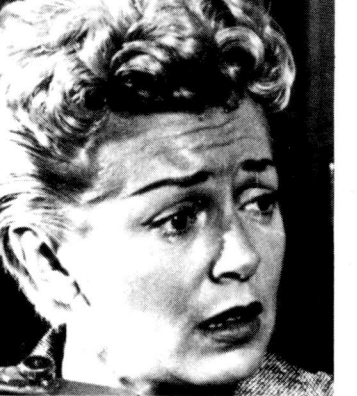
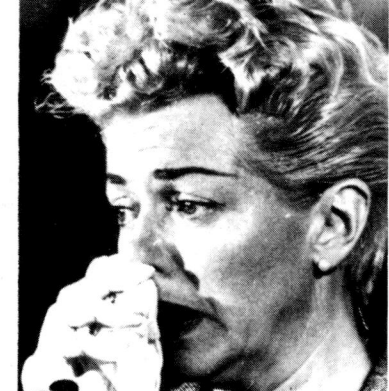

Lana Turner, on stage, testifying at her daughter's trial.

Actress Lana Turner after her daughter received a verdict of "justifiable homicide"; her lawyer, Jerry Geisler, is at right.

panato now moved into her mansion to fully enjoy Lana Turner's luxurious lifestyle, swimming in her pool, lounging in the sunray and massage rooms, watching the latest Hollywood films in her private screening room. The couple took a seven-week vacation to Acapulco, renting a suite at the Via Vera Hotel. When they returned to Los Angeles, Cheryl Crane, now a tall girl who towered over her mother, was present to welcome the pair home. The arguments began all over again, beginning with the Academy Awards. Turner had been nominated for an Oscar for her performance in *Peyton Place* (she did not win) and had decided to attend the ceremonies without Stompanato. When he learned that he was not invited, the gangster went into a raging tirade, accusing the actress of being ashamed of him, that she did not want to be seen in public with him.

More importantly, Stompanato had been gambling heavily in gambling spas owned by his former employer Mickey Cohen, and Cohen held several IOUs Stompanato had signed. On the evening of Apr. 4, 1958, Stompanato demanded that Turner pay these debts. He confronted her in her lavish bedroom and she, in turn, utterly refused to give him any more money. Again the gangster lost control and began screaming that he would use a razor to disfigure her for life. Cheryl Crane, downstairs, could hear the gangster yelling: "If a man makes a living with his hands, I would destroy his hands. You make your living with your face, so I will destroy your face. I'll get you where it hurts the most! I'll cut you up and I'll get your mother and your daughter, too...That's my business!"

Stompanato grabbed the actress by the arm and she broke away. She opened the bedroom door to see her daughter standing there. "Please, Cheryl, please don't listen to any of this," the actress told her, and closed the door. She then ordered Stompanato to return to his own room. He picked up a hanger with a jacket on it and approached her, poised it seemed, to attack her with it. The actress then told the gangster that she was finished with him and that he was to get out of her house. She again opened the door and Stompanato came rushing toward her, holding the jacket and the hanger. Cheryl Crane was there, moving past her mother into the bedroom, holding a butcher knife with a nine-inch blade which she had gotten in the downstairs kitchen. The actress was later to testify: "I swear it was so fast, I—I truthfully thought she had hit him in the stomach. The best that I can remember is that they came together and they parted. I still never saw the blade."

The gangster, holding his stomach, fell backward on the thick carpet. Lana Turner went to him and pulled back his shirt to see the deep knife wound. Stompanato tried to speak but only a gurgle came out of his throat. She grabbed a towel from the bathroom and tried to staunch the flow of blood but it was useless, her lover was dead. Her daughter stood sobbing nearby as Turner called her mother and then her lawyer, the famed Jerry Geisler. She said to Geisler: "This is Lana Turner. Could you please come to my house. Something terrible has happened." Within minutes, Geisler was driving toward the Turner mansion. Cheryl Crane then called her father and asked him to come to the house. Crane asked a patron in his restaurant to drive him to Turner's Beverly Hills home and was the first to arrive there. Cheryl met him at the door. Crane looked at Stompanato's stiffening body in the upstairs bedroom while his sobbing daughter blurted: "I did it, Daddy, but I didn't mean to. He was going to hurt Mommy. I didn't mean to, I didn't mean to."

Geisler showed up, meeting the actress for the first time, but promising her that his office would do all to protect her and her child. Clinton Anderson, Beverly Hills police chief, then arrived with several officers. Reporter Jim Bacon quickly appeared, gaining access to the house by telling uniformed officers stationed outside that he was from the coroner's office. Lana Turner was by then pleading with Anderson to put the blame on her, that her child only meant to protect her. "I don't want her involved, poor baby," Turner said through tears. "Please say that I did it." Stompanato was by this time examined and pronounced dead.

Geisler immediately introduced his defense by putting his arm around Turner and saying: "Your daughter has done a courageous thing. It's too bad that a man's life is gone but under the circumstances the child did the only thing she could do to protect her mother from harm." Geisler looked at Chief Anderson and spoke to Turner but kept his eyes on the police officer: "I understand your concern for the child's welfare. But you won't get anyplace by hiding the truth, will she, Chief?"

Lana Turner than gushed the whole sordid affair between herself and Stompanato while Bacon and other reporters took notes. Anderson sympathetically listened to her and then to Cheryl's description of how she plunged the knife into the gangster who was about to attack her mother. The chief reluctantly informed the actress that he would have to lock up her 14-year-old daughter. "Can't you arrest me instead?" Turner pleaded with him. "Poor baby's not to blame for all this mess."

Cheryl Crane was arrested and locked up in the Juvenile Section of the city jail, charged with murder. The newspapers blared the killing from coast to coast and most of the gossip columnists used the Stompanato death to parade Turner's torrid love affairs in print. She was pilloried for subjecting her daughter to a series of reckless marriages and love affairs, and some even wildly speculated that Turner herself had murdered Stompanato after finding her daughter in bed with him. Only Walter Winchell came to the defense of the movie queen, asking that fans understand the tragedy and give their hearts "to the girl with a broken heart."

Few of Turner's peers had anything to say about the killing. The outspoken Gloria Swanson, sex goddess of the silent era, did voice a scathing opinion, attacking Winchell for defending Turner, saying that his defense of the actress was "disgusting...You are trying to whitewash Lana...She is not even an actress...she is only a trollop." Gangster Mickey Cohen then suddenly appeared in the editorial offices of the Los Angeles *Herald Examiner,* dumping Lana Turner's love letters to Stompanato into the editor's hands. He had ordered his goons to go to Stompanato's apartment after hearing about the killing and obtain these gushing *billet doux,* after being stuck with the bill for Stompanato's funeral, costs he expected the actress to bear. He released the letters out of spite.

By the time Cheryl Crane appeared in court, the charge against her had been reduced to manslaughter. Geisler brilliantly placed Lana Turner on the stand and softly talked her through the nightmare killing. The actress detailed everything that occurred that evening, weeping, wiping away perspiration with her handkerchief, her face distorted in anguish, a mother's pain. Some say it was the greatest performance of her career. Then Cheryl Crane testified, repeating almost word for word the story her mother had given. The coroner's jury, relying exclusively on the testimony of the two females, ruled that Cheryl Crane had committed justifiable homicide. She was made a ward of the state and placed in her grandmother's custody. The press photographers had a field day with Lana Turner on the stand that day and reveled in taking photos of her kneeling at her mother's feet, a penitent pose that was no doubt meant to elicit sympathy.

Cheryl Crane did not adjust well. Her grandmother, Mildred Turner, could not control her. The girl ran away several times and was later placed by court order in the El Retiro School for Girls in the San Fernando Valley. She later worked for her father as a hostess in his restaurant. The American public favored Lana Turner and her daughter in this sensational killing, and the actress' next few films were box office hits. She and her daughter survived the scandal, emerging as heroines. Cheryl Crane later became a success as a San Francisco real estate broker and wrote a book about her life, detailing the Stompanato murder in terms that repeated her original statements, a book in which she revealed she was a lesbian. Only the publicity-seeking gangster Mickey Cohen angrily spoke up on behalf of Johnny Stompanato, declaring to the world: "Look, this was a great guy!"

REF.: Anderson, *Beverly Hills Is My Beat;* Anger, *Hollywood Babylon;*

Bacon, *Hollywood Is a Four Letter Town;* Carr, *Hollywood Tragedy; CBA;* Cohen, *Mickey Cohen: In My Own Words;* Crane, *Detour: A Hollywood Story;* Geisler, *The Jerry Geisler Story;* Hirsh, *Hollywood Uncensored;* Nash, *Murder Among the Mighty;* Nuetzel, *Whodunit? Hollywood Style;* (FILM) *Where Love Has Gone,* 1964.

Crane, James, 1947- , Brit., mur. Fifteen-year-old James Crane could not stand to see his mother abused by his father. In Fall 1962, Mrs. Crane told her husband of her plans to end the marriage and take her three children away. The 42-year-old dockworker was furious, and vowed to kill her if she did so. But James promised to protect her, and to kill his father.

As his father slept in the daybed on the first floor of their home, James fired a shotgun at him from a distance of three feet. When Mrs. Crane heard the shot, she ran downstairs and found her husband dead. The police were summoned and took the boy into custody. James Crane was later found Not Guilty of murder, but Guilty of manslaughter. He was ordered confined to a mental institution on the grounds of diminished responsibility.

REF.: *CBA;* Wilson, *Children Who Kill.*

Crane, Jim, d.1881, U.S., west. outl. Cattle rustler and stage coach robber Jim Crane rode with the Clanton-McLaury gang in southern Arizona until shortly before his death in 1881. Crane's most famous gunfight occurred near Contention, Ariz., when he attempted to rob a Wells Fargo shipment of bullion valued at $26,000. Twelve miles from Tombstone, Ariz., Crane, Bill Leonard, Luther King, and Harry "the Kid" Head overtook the stagecoach after Wells Fargo special agent Bob Paul had changed places with driver Budd Philpot. In a narrow ravine, the gang of robbers stepped out of the shadows and ordered Paul to stop the coach. Before he could respond, Crane fatally shot Philpot. A passenger riding in the stage, Peter Roerk, was also killed, but agent Paul relieving Philpot on the box, regained control of the frightened horse team and managed to pull away without losing his precious cargo. Wells Fargo offered a $2,000 reward for each of the four, and lawman Wyatt Earp offered Ike Clanton, an Arizona outlaw, $3,600 to lure the stage robbers into a trap.

A posse headed by Sheriff John Behan and Wyatt Earp later arrested King, who told them the names of his accomplices. Wanted by the law, Bill Leonard and "Kid" Head attempted to rob the Haslett Brothers general store in Eureka, N.M. Their holdup was thwarted by Bill and Ike Haslett who opened fire on the gunmen. Head was killed instantly, but Leonard lived long enough to implicate Crane as the murderer of Philpot. Unaware of this sellout, Crane recruited several others to help him massacre the Haslett Brothers outside of Eureka. The Hasletts killed two members of the gang and wounded three more before falling in a hail of gunfire. Crane fled across the border into Mexico where he was shot and killed.

REF.: Bartholomew, *The Biographical Album of Western Gunfighters; CBA;* Faulk, *Tombstone;* O'Neal, *Encyclopedia of Western Gunfighters;* Waters, *Earp Brothers of Tombstone.*

Crane, William (AKA: John Lawson, John Larsen), and Tracy, Christopher (AKA: Charles J. Tracy, Toppin, Topping, Charles Tompkins), and Wyatt (AKA: Fred Williams), prom. 1905, Case of, U.S., fraud. John Felix, a German-born businessman and prominent New York City gambler, was contacted him on Feb. 1, 1905, by a gentleman calling himself Nelson, who said he was an employee of the Western Union Telegraph Company, which provided New York poolrooms with race track results. But Nelson was actually one of a gang of "wire tappers" and expert con men. The wire service was manipulated by crooked bookies and swindlers who held back race results for a few minutes so poolroom operators could cheat a "sucker" out of his money. Felix was assured that he could parlay a $50,000 bet into a quarter-million-dollar windfall at the poolroom on East 22nd Street.

Nelson showed Felix a room disguised as a busy off-track betting parlor, then introduced him to McPherson, who laid out the plan. Assuming they could find someone with the right amount of cash, they could all stand to make a handsome profit by getting the bet down. Felix would place his $50,000 bet during

the three minute "delay." The next day, Feb. 2, Nelson escorted Felix to the Fifth Avenue Hotel to a room packed with gamblers placing large wages on the races. Nelson showed Felix to a telephone where McPherson's call was to arrive. After a few minutes, "Mac" called to say that the winner in the third race was Colonel *Starbottle,* and Felix soon saw the result confirmed. When Felix heard that the winner of the fourth race was *Old Stone* by a nose, he played the horse at five to one odds. Old Stone was first announced as the winner, but because the jockeys had worn the same colors, the track announcer had made a mistake, and the real winner was Calvert, with Old Stone finishing second. Mr. Felix left the building, and the conmen divided their earnings, which, after expenses, came to $48,400.

Two days later Felix identified the swindlers to police. Nelson was really confidence trickster William Crane. McPherson was Christopher Tracy, a veteran swindler, and the cashier who took the $50,000 was a man named Wyatt, who was never found. Crane and Tracy were arrested and brought before Judge Warren W. Foster in the General Sessions Court on Feb. 27, 1906. Defense attorneys cited an old statute which held that a person is not liable for the gullibility of others, and thought the jury found the two con men Guilty, Judge Foster overturned the verdict on these grounds. In the next session of the New York Legislature the penal code was amended to make wire-tapping a criminal offense. REF.: *CBA.*

Cranfield, Lionel (First Earl of Middlesex), Brit., polit. corr. Served crown as lord chancellor in 1622. He urged King James I to exercise fiscal restraint and was opposed to the costly military adventures James engaged in with the Spanish. For this and other offenses he was accused of the crime of maladministration. Impeached in 1624, he was pardoned by Charles I in 1626. REF.: *CBA.*

Cranmer, Thomas, 1489-1556, Brit., her.-treas. Archbishop of Canterbury, he won the favor of Henry VIII by arguing before the pope that Catherine of Aragon's prior marriage to Prince Arthur would nullify her union with Henry. He persecuted the Protestant clergyman John Frith, John Lambert, Cromwell's military leader in the field, and a score of others. Twice he was saved from enemy plots by his benefactor Henry VIII. When Queen Mary took her place on the throne his esteem and court influence quickly waned. He was convicted of treason by a papal commission in 1555, excommunicated on a charge of heresy and forced to sign seven recantations admitting the supremacy of the pope by Cardinal Pole. These he later renounced. He was burned at the stake, but defiantly held his offending right hand before the flames to be burned first. REF.: *CBA.*

Cranstoun, William Henry, See: **Blandy, Mary.**

Crapsey, Algernon Sidney, 1847-1927, U.S., her. In 1906 he was deprived of his Episcopal ministry upon conviction of a charge of religious heresy. REF.: *CBA.*

Crassus, Marcus Licinius (AKA: Dives; The Rich), c.115-53 B.C., Syria, governor, assass. Financed Pompey and Caesar when they organized the First Triumvirate, and became governor of Syria in 54 B.C. His military adventure against the Parthians resulted in a rout in 53 B.C. He was captured and executed. REF.: *CBA.*

Crater, Joseph Force, 1889-c.1939, U.S. mur.? Long active in Democratic politics in New York City, Joseph Crater became president of the elite and powerful Cayuga Democratic Club in the Nineteenth Assembly District in 1920, a powerful position which was the professional and political making of him. He joined the firm of Wagner, Quillinan and Rifkind, becoming its chief counsel and specializing in receiverships. Crater averaged an income of between $75,000 and $100,000 each year and spent most of his extra cash on clothes and chorus girls, discreetly financing his tall Broadway mistresses without his wife's knowledge. He and his wife Stella lived in a luxurious apartment at 40 Fifth Avenue.

When Crater learned that New York Supreme Court Justice Joseph M. Proskauer would be resigning his post in early 1930, he energetically began lobbying for the post, asking his Tammany friends to persuade Governor Franklin D. Roosevelt to appoint him. He also asked Martin J. Healy, political boss of the Nineteenth District, and Magistrate George F. Ewald to apply pressure on his behalf. On Apr. 8, 1930, Governor Roosevelt appointed Crater to fill Proskauer's vacated post. Crater, with his powerful Tammany backing, expected to be elected to the fourteen-year post, one that paid $22,500 a year, only one-fourth of Crater's annual salary as a private attorney. The post, however, carried with it tremendous influence and, in the case of other jurists at that time, one that meant enormous illegal profits.

Judge Joseph Crater.

Crater's friend and colleague, Judge Ewald was soon accused of paying Healey for his judgeship and was tried but acquitted. Ewald nevertheless resigned. This was not the case with Judge Albert H. Vitale, close friend of underworld kingpin, Arnold Rothstein. He was removed from his judgeship. It was then the common corruption to buy judgeships in the amount of a year's salary. Crater immediately went to work on paying off his appointment, according to investigators later looking into his affairs. He withdrew $7,500 from his bank account and sold off about $15,000 in stocks to make up the exact amount of his salary of $22,500 for an obvious payoff.

Investigators were already probing Crater's affairs when he and his wife left for their Maine retreat at the end of the court session in June 1930. On Aug. 3, 1930, Crater received a call at his retreat and then left for New York City after telling his wife: "I've got to straighten those fellows out." His wife never saw him again. After spending some days in his Fifth Avenue apartment, Crater busied himself by removing documents and cash from his judge's chambers on Aug. 6, 1930. He also withdrew more than $10,000 from various other accounts. It was later claimed that Crater used this money to pay off a ravishingly beautiful woman named Lorraine Fay who had met with lawyer Samuel Buchler a few days earlier, discussing the possibility of filing a $100,000 suit against Crater for breach of promise. This woman never surfaced again and Lorraine Fay may not have been her real name.

Crater met some friends, lawyer William Klein and showgirl Sally Lou Ritz, and left them shortly after 9 p.m., taking a cab on 45th Street, intending to attend a musical, *Dancing Partner*. He was never seen alive again. Crater had told his wife Stella that he would return to their retreat on Aug. 25, so it was a few days after that time that Mrs. Crater began sounding the alarm, but the newspapers, chiefly the New York *World*, announced Crater's disappearance on Sept. 3, 1930. Within the next few weeks, Crater became the most famous person in the modern annals of missing persons. Large rewards were posted for information concerning his whereabouts. Dozens of investigators searched throughout the East Coast for him. Cab drivers were canvassed and thousands of their trip tickets were examined. None remembered having Crater as a fare.

The search went on for months. Hundreds of persons were interviewed but no one could provide information beyond what was known. What was left was speculation. "Crater's disappearance was premeditated," said Police Commissioner Edward P. Mulrooney, but he did not elaborate upon this statement. Most, however, including Mrs. Stella Crater, believed Judge Crater had been murdered. Mrs. Crater, two years before her husband was officially declared dead, eloped with electrical engineer Carl Kunz, marrying in Elkton, Md., on Apr. 23, 1937. Judge James A. Foley ruled Crater legally dead on July 6, 1939, two years after the normal waiting period for such court decisions. A few days after Foley's decision, Emil K. Ellis, representing the ex-Mrs. Crater, stated that Judge Crater had met his end "by external,

violent, or accidental means."

Ellis stated that Crater was being blackmailed at the time of his disappearance by an unnamed Broadway showgirl. He met with her on the night of Aug. 6, 1930, offering her several thousand dollars to prevent her from exposing his wild sexual relationship with her. The girl turned down the payment, Ellis stated, demanding more. When Crater refused, the girl's friends, two underworld thugs, struggled with Crater, one of them hitting the judge too hard and killing him. His body was then taken to New Jersey where he was wrongly identified with a fake death certificate and quickly cremated. Mrs. Crater received insurance settlements, based on Ellis' claim, of more than $20,000 from the Mutual Life Insurance Company of New York and the Fidelity Mutual Life Insurance Company.

Was Crater murdered? Many criminologists and law enforcement officers believed so. So did one of the most astounding mediums in the world, Gerary Croiset, a Dutch seer who had solved many crimes in the Netherlands. In 1955, a photo of Crater was given to Croiset, one which was not shown to him but placed facedown in front of him. Croiset went into a trance, touched the back of the photo, and was quoted as saying: "This man is not alive...I see him sitting in a chair raised above the floor...two men sitting below him, one on each side. He has to do with criminals but not as a lawyer...He was murdered long ago, maybe twenty-four, twenty-five years ago." Croiset even drew a crude map, indicating that a house in Westchester, N.Y., was the murder site. A house which was used by Judge Ewald and Judge Crater for some of their more indiscreet parties was located and examined. Although the area was dug up, no bodies or remains were found. Judge Joseph Crater remains one of the most enigmatic disappearances on record, his name being synonymous with missing persons. In the office of the New York Bureau of Missing Persons, his file, Number 13595, remains open to this date.

REF.: *CBA*; Levine, *Anatomy of a Gangster*; Nash, *Among the Missing*; Peterson, *The Mob*; Purvis, *Great Unsolved Mysteries*.

Cravens, Ben, 1868-1950, U.S., west. outl. Ben Cravens was the last of a generation of Oklahoma gunfighters to roam the plains. Born in Lineville, Iowa, Cravens was the son of a respected farmer. He had a yen for adventure, and he ran away to the Indian Territory, where in a few short years, he became a train robber, horse thief, and whisky runner. It seemed as if there wasn't a jail secure enough to hold Cravens who had escaped from custody in three different states—Kansas, Oklahoma, and Iowa. After marrying a Missouri

Outlaw Ben Cravens.

woman, Cravens attempted to go straight. He even settled down to a life of farming before his past caught up with him. In 1896, after attempting to rob a train in Blackwell, Kan., Cravens was arrested, convicted, and sentenced to serve fifteen years in the state penitentiary. He escaped a year later after whittling the facsimile of a gun from a piece of wood. He wrapped the stick into a wad of silver tinfoil he had saved from cigarette packages, and made his escape from the prison coal mine.

Near Red Rock, Okla., on Mar. 19, 1901, Cravens murdered a postmaster at a combination store and postal agency. As he made his escape, he turned his gun on Bert Welty, a former convict who had helped him plan the heist. Welty survived the shotgun blast, and later identified Cravens as his assailant. By this time, however, Cravens was already serving a jail sentence under an alias.

REF.: Barnard, *A Rider of the Cherokee Strip*; Bartholomew, *The Biographical Album of Western Gunfighters*; Canton, *Frontier Trails*; *CBA*; Chambers, *The Enduring Rock*; Croy, *Trigger Marshal*; Dalton, *When the Daltons Rode*; Emery, *Court of the Damned*; Gordon, *I Arrested Pearl*

Starr; Hendricks, *The Bad Man of the West;* Holloway, *Texas Gun Lore;* Hunter and Rose, *The Album of Gunfighters;* Lamb, *Tragedies of the Osage Hills;* Nix, *Oklahombres;* O'Neal, *Encyclopedia of Western Gunfighters;* Rainey, *The Cherokee Strip;* Shirley, *Buckskins and Spurs;* Tillotson, *How to Be a Detective.*

Crawford, Annie, b.c.1883, Case of, U.S., mur. Despite confessing she had administered morphine capsules to a sister who died of morphine poisoning, Annie Crawford was inexplicably acquitted of killing her.

The second oldest and perhaps least attractive daughter of the Crawford family, Annie Crawford took a special interest in treating the sudden, short-lived illnesses of her relatives, and, after their deaths, arranging their funerals, eventually buying additional land to make more room in the family plot. The first to die, Mary Agnes Crawford, the oldest daughter, passed away in June 1910. Her parents, Mr. and Mrs. Robert Crawford, died the next month, forcing the three surviving daughters to move in with their aunt, Mary Crawford, and her husband.

Three sudden deaths in a month caused suspicion, but Aunt Mary was not prepared to blame nurse Annie until 25-year-old Elise Crawford suddenly fell ill on Sept. 18, 1911, complaining of nausea and stomach pains. Annie offered her sister calomel and soda capsules supposedly prescribed by Dr. Marion H. McGuire, but Elise fell in and out of consciousness, rising occasionally to give her youngest sister, Gertrude, her highly prized rings and a necklace, and complaining to her aunt that Annie was not as caring as she had appeared, sometimes abandoning her in the middle of the night.

Annie was arrested shortly after Elise died on Sept. 23, 1911, and soon confessed about the morphine to District Attorney St. Clair Adams, explaining that she had been addicted to the drug for at least three years and had accidentally confused it with calomel and soda capsules the doctor prescribed for Elise. St. Clair took note that Annie had worked six years in the narcotics department at the New Orleans Sanitarium, experience that should have warned her that her sister would fall into a coma if given an overdose of morphine. Although Annie was suspected of killing her three other relatives, their bodies were not exhumed because officials believed they would be unable to detect the cause of their deaths after they had been buried for more than a year.

Confronted with devastating evidence against her, Annie hired noted New Orleans lawyers Lionel Adams and Joseph Generelly to represent her at her trial, which began Mar. 12, 1912, with Judge Frank D. Chretien presiding. Adams and Generelly attacked Elise to deflect the facts against their client. They argued that Elise, mother of an illegitimate child, had killed herself because she was living in shame. St. Clair countered with evidence that Dr. McGuire never prescribed any capsules for Elise, and that Annie deliberately concealed her "mistake" from the family, removing all morphine capsules from the house, as she had earlier admitted. Generelly and Adams laughed away St. Clair's contention that Annie had killed for insurance money, pointing out that the cost of Elise's funeral, which Annie arranged, exceeded the amount of the woman's life insurance. On Mar. 26, Annie Crawford, dressed in her customary black mourning dress and veil, was released due to a hung jury, as only three of twelve jurors believed she could kill.

REF.: *CBA;* Tallant, *Ready to Hang;* Wilson, *Encyclopedia of Murder.*

Crawford, Ed, d.1873, U.S., west. lawman. Ed Crawford was discharged from the Ellsworth, Kan., police department along with the rest of the officers on the day Sheriff C.B. Whitney was killed in a card game by a group of carousing Texans. Crawford was soon reappointed to the force, and while lounging in front of a local store on Aug. 20, 1873, saw the same Texans appear, led by Cad Pierce and Neil Cain.

"Hello Hogue!" Pierce called to city marshal Ed Hogue. "I understand you have a white affidavit for me. Is that so?" The marshal tried to calm Pierce down, but there were angry words and then shots. Crawford, who was sitting with Hogue, wounded Pierce in the arm and then beat him to death with the butt of a

rifle. Crawford was suspended from the police force for his action, and the Texans warned him to leave town, which he did, only to return early in November. Crawford burst in on Pierce's brother-in-law, Putnam, who was with a prostitute. The drunken ex-lawman fired at Putnam, who drew his six-shooter and killed Crawford. Putnam's friends from Texas burst into the room and fired thirteen slugs into the dead man.

REF.: Bartholomew, *Wyatt Earp: The Untold Story; CBA;* Drago, *Notorious Ladies of the Frontier;* ____, *Wild, Woolly, & Wicked;* O'Neal, *Encyclopedia of Western Gunfighters;* Streeter, *Ben Thompson.*

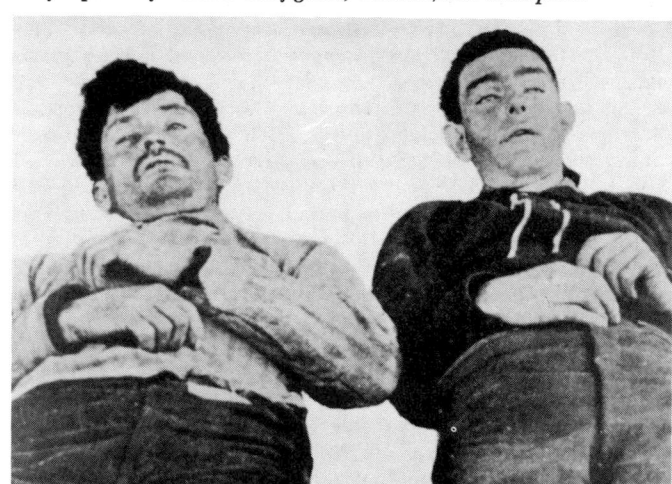

Bank robbers Foster Crawford and Elmer "Kid" Lewis, lynched, 1896.

Crawford, Foster, d.1896, U.S., west. outl. A one-time Oklahoma cowboy, Foster Crawford was reportedly a member of the Al Jennings gang before going to Texas where he teamed up with Elmer Lewis, better known as the Slaughter Kid, Kid Lewis, or The Mysterious Kid. Crawford, who had an abiding passion for French poetry and often quoted such poets as François Villon, decided with Lewis to rob the bank in Wichita Falls, Texas. He and Lewis rode into the town on Feb. 25, 1896, and walked into the City National Bank with guns drawn, demanding all the cash on hand. The cashier of this bank, Frank Dorsey, resisted opening the vault, and was killed. A clerk was also wounded by the outlaws before they fled the bank with about $2,000.

A company of Texas Rangers, led by Captain W.J. McDonald, was soon in pursuit and captured the outlaws some hours later. The two were jailed in Wichita Falls. After the Rangers left town, on Feb. 27, 1896, a mob broke into the jail and dragged Crawford and Lewis out to a telephone pole and lynched both of them. One of the witnesses to this lynching was Tex Rickard, who had worked with Crawford as a cowhand on ranches near Henrietta in Clay County, Texas. Crawford had invited Rickard to join him and Lewis in the bank raid but Rickard had refused, telling Crawford: "If you boys go and do a damned fool thing like that the Rangers will ride you down. You're asking me to join you in boot hill and I say no to that!" Rickard later went on to become the first great impresario of boxing, managing the career of Jack Dempsey and promoting the first million-dollar fight. Rickard died a multimillionaire. See: **Lewis, Elmer.**

REF.: Bartholomew, *The Biographical Album of Western Gunfighters;* Breihan, *Great Lawmen of the West; CBA;* House, *Riding for Texas;* Hunter and Rose, *The Album of Gunfighters;* Johnson, *Wagon Yard;* Morgan, *The History of Wichita Falls;* Paine, *Captain Bill McDonald, Texas Ranger;* Samuels, *The Magnificent Rube, The Life and Gaudy Times of Tex Rickard;* Sullivan, *Twelve Years in the Saddle for Law and Order on the Frontiers of Texas.*

Crawford, George, prom. 1932, U.S., mur. The murder of prominent socialite Agnes Boeing Ilsley at her estate in Loudoun County, Va., on Jan 12, 1932, was apparently motivated by revenge. Police investigators found no evidence of theft, just the mangled bodies of Mrs. Ilsley and her elderly maid, Mina Buckner, in their beds. The likely culprit was George Crawford, a young black chauffeur recently dismissed for pilfering liquor from the Ilsley wine closet. The men of the nearby village organized a posse to track down Crawford.

But Crawford had fled to Boston, where he was arrested for larceny one year later. The controversy over his extradition pitted New England liberalism against the entrenched racial attitudes of the South. U.S. District Court Judge James Lowell, a descendant of famous abolitionists, granted a writ of *habeas corpus* to Crawford in April 1933. As grounds, he cited the exclusion of blacks from Virginia juries, and ruled that any conviction returned there would be voided by the U.S. Supreme Court.

The ruling incensed Southern legislators. U.S. Representative Howard Smith of Virginia introduced impeachment proceedings against Lowell on the floor of the House, charging him with high crimes and misdemeanors. The U.S. Circuit Court of Appeals later overturned Lowell's ruling. While the House Judiciary Committee was investigating his conduct, Judge Lowell died at his home in Boston. In October, the U.S. Supreme Court refused to review the decision of the Court of Appeals. Crawford was returned under heavy guard to Leesburg, Va., where his trial began on Dec. 11.

After a five-day trial the jury returned a Guilty verdict, and Crawford was sentenced to life imprisonment. He narrowly escaped the death penalty because, as defense attorneys argued, he would eventually be needed to testify against his accomplice, Charles Johnson, who was still at large. On Feb. 12, 1934, Crawford received a second life sentence for the murder of the housemaid Mina Buckner. REF.: *CBA*.

Crawford, James (AKA: **Harry Kirby**), prom. 1922, U.S., suic.-mur. Facial reconstruction so expert it made the victim's sister faint led to the arrest and eventual suicide of the woman's killer.

On Apr. 13, 1922, a skeleton found in a shallow grave on Cheesecock Mountain in New York caused a scandal in nearby wealthy Tuxedo Park. Commissioner Richard Enright of the New York City police department, seeing an opportunity to climb the social ladder, gladly accepted the case although it was outside his force's jurisdiction. Enright relied on retired police captain Grant Williams, a skeletal expert, to identify the corpse. Williams, inspired enough by the challenge to suspend retirement, instantly set about his investigation, soon identifying the body as belonging to a woman who had suffered from curvature of the spine. Three small fractures on the left side of the woman's head were caused by blows from a hammer, Williams revealed, most likely struck by a left-handed attacker.

After treating the skull with a formaldehyde solution and covering it with a thin layer of sculptors' clay, Williams embarked on a two-day project to reconstruct the victim's face. The shape of the jaw and nose convinced him that the victim was of Irish descent, and, when a policeman gave Williams the woman's scalp, complete with hair, he added blue eyes that typically belong to the Irish. Armed with photographs of Williams' work, police stormed the area adjacent to the mountain, most notably Letchworth Village, an institution for the mentally ill, where the victim was identified as Lillian White, a waitress who quit Sept. 15, seven months before the body was found. White was Irish and had curvature of the spine. She also had a dislocated jaw, as Williams had foretold.

Mary Hamilton, the first woman to serve in the New York City police department, took over the investigation, apparently to protect the residents of Tuxedo Park from interrogations by a brusque male. Hamilton quickly learned that White had a roommate named Mabel, who gave a box of White's love letters to the policewoman. Inside were slightly illiterate notes from a man named John, who, according to handwriting experts, was right-handed. Instead of losing faith in Captain Williams' theories, Hamilton concentrated on a Robert Browning verse found in the box, written by someone other than John or White.

Letchworth Village staff members revealed that Ruby Miller, a nurse who had quit the previous September to get married, was an avid fan of Browning. Officer Hamilton found a marriage certificate linking Miller to James Crawford, an attendant at Letchworth, who had quit the same day as White. He and Miller were married on Sept. 17, but the minister who performed the service remembered the groom had an infection on his right hand, which explained the location of White's head wounds. Williams, upset that his work in reconstructing the woman's face had not led to any arrests, again sidestepped retirement to search for Crawford. He gathered fingerprints at Crawford's home in Maine, but the suspect had fled. Three years later, New York Police found the fingerprints matched those of Harry Kirby, who had fled Maine after shooting to death Aida Hayward. Crawford, or Kirby, was captured shortly thereafter and jailed in Winthrop, Maine. He killed himself after admitting he murdered White with a hammer as Williams had deduced.

REF.: *CBA*; Hynd, *Murder, Mayhem and Mystery*.

Crawford, William, 1784-1849, U.S., jur. Served as U.S. attorney assigned to Washington, D.C., from 1814-17, and as district attorney of Washington in 1817. He was nominated to the court of the northern and southern district of Alabama by President John Quincy Adams in 1826. REF.: *CBA*.

Crawford, William Harris, 1772-1834, U.S., lawyer. Presidential candidate of 1824. REF.: *CBA*.

Crazy Butch Gang, prom. 1890s, U.S., org. crime. Left to fend for himself in Manhattan, an 8-year-old boy known only as Butch organized his own street gang in the 1890s. Crazy Butch refused to acknowledge the last name of his parents, who had abandoned him. When he was thirteen, Butch found a dog, which he named Rabbi. He trained the animal to snatch handbags from women's hands and return them to the corner of Willett and Stanton Streets, where Butch was waiting.

By his late teens, Crazy Butch had organized twenty to thirty young toughs into a "snatch" racket. Butch would deliberately maneuver his bicycle into the path of a startled pedestrian. As he helped the victim up, he would scold them loudly enough to attract a crowd of onlookers. While the crowd watched Butch make a scene, his gang would lift their wallets and purses. The proceeds were divided at the gang's headquarters on Forsyth Street on the Lower East Side.

The Crazy Butch Gang linked up with the ruthless gangster Monk Eastman, who dominated the turf between the Bowery and the East River. Crazy Butch and his boys were constantly at war with the Five Points Gang, whose members included Johnny Torrio, Paul Kelly, and later, Al Capone. Butch fought a number of gun battles with these thugs. Butch was killed by Harry the Soldier after they had quarreled over a female shoplifter named the Darby Kid. Big Jack Zelig was one prominent gangster of a later era who got his start with the Crazy Butch Gang. REF.: *CBA*.

Cream, Dr. Thomas Neill, d.1892, Can.-U.S.-Brit., mur. The fact that Dr. Thomas Neill Cream committed his diabolical murders at the same time as Jack the Ripper has led many armchair detectives to speculate that the two killers were one and the same. The parallels were striking. The Ripper and Cream had a fixation for London prostitutes. Both men were in the habit of taunting the police with letters after the commission of a crime. Cream, however, disdained the use of knives and was never present at the moment of his victim's death.

Thomas Neill Cream was a short, squat, cross-eyed man who began his medical practice in London, Ontario, in 1878 after completing his medical studies at McGill University. He earned plaudits for his experiments with chloroform, a substance he would later find useful in murdering young women. A widower at an early age, Cream was forced to flee from the province after local pharmacists became suspicious about his over-reliance on chloroform. Then the body of a young chambermaid was found in back of Cream's office on Dundas Street. The inquest showed that the girl was pregnant at the time of her death, and had solicited Cream for an illegal abortion. Letters were uncovered that indicated that Cream was attempting to blackmail a prominent citizen whom he accused of murder.

Cream was freed under a cloud of suspicion. He settled in Chicago in 1880 but got into trouble with the authorities after performing an abortion on a Canadian woman. A second patient of his died from a fatal dose of prescribed medicine. Cream then tried to blackmail the druggist. While the police investigated his actions in connection with this case, a third patient fell victim to the poisoner. On June 14, 1881, Daniel Stott was given a fatal dose of strychnine by his wife who had become infatuated with Cream. For this the doctor received a sentence of life imprisonment at the Joliet Penitentiary. With time off for good behavior, Cream was on the streets again in July 1891.

Dr. Thomas Neill Cream

Rumors and allegations have since come to light that Cream may have in fact been released earlier after bribing prison officials. Those who believe that Cream was actually Jack the Ripper have subscribed to this unsubstantiated theory.

There is no doubt, however, that Cream left the U.S. and took up residence in London, England, in October 1891. Within the span of a year, he murdered four prostitutes by means of strychnine poisoning, but failed in three other attempts. Cream's undoing came when he tipped the hand of the police by writing a series of extortion letters to various citizens of London. As a result he was arrested on June 3, 1892, and charged with blackmail. The charge was later expanded to include murder and attempted murder.

His well-publicized trial was held in October 1892, and a Guilty verdict was duly returned. Thomas Neill Cream, one of the most famous gaslight murderers of Victorian England was executed at Newgate on Nov. 15, 1892. According to the story the hangman later told, Cream muttered: "I am Jack—" seconds before the trap was sprung. See: **Jack the Ripper.**

REF.: Altick, *Victorian Studies In Scarlet*; Boar, *The World's Most Infamous Murders*; Bowden-Rowlands, *In the Light of the Law*; Brice, *Look Upon the Prisoner*; Brock, *A Casebook of Crime*; Brophy, *The Meaning of Murder*; Browne, *The Rise of Scotland Yard*; *CBA*; Dewes, *Doctors of Murder*; Dickson, *Murder by Numbers*; Dilnot, *Great Detectives and Their Methods*; ____, *Triumphs of Detection*; Douthwaite, *Mass Murder*; Dunbar, *Blood in the Parlor*; Furneaux, *The Medical Murderer*; Glaister, *The Power of Poison*; Gribble, *They Had a Way With Women*; Gross, *Masterpieces of Murder*; Hodge, *The Black Maria*; Jesse, *Murder and Its Motives*; Kingston, *Enemies of Society*; Lambton, *Thou Shalt Do No Murder*; Laurence, *A History of Capital Punishment*; Lustgarten, *A Century of Murderers*; Marjoribanks, *For the Defense, The Life of Sir Edward Marshall Hall*; Miller, *Twenty Mortal Murders*; Nash, *Almanac of World Crime*; ____, *Murder, America*; *Notable British Trials*; Parry, *Some Famous Medical Trials*; Pearce, *Unsolved Murder Mysteries*; Pearson, *Murder at Smutty Nose*; Rodell, *Chicago Murders*; Stevens, *Famous Crimes and Criminals*; Thompson, *Poisons and Poisoners*; Wilson, *Encyclopedia of Murder*; Woodhall, *Secrets of Scotland Yard*; (FICTION), Burke, *A Teashop in Limehouse* (Short Story: "The Hands of Mr. Ottermole"); Cashman, *The Gentleman from Chicago*.

Creamer, James, and **Emmett, George,** and **Hacker, Larry,** and **Powell, Hoyt,** and **Jenkins, Billy,** and **Roberts, Charles,** and **Ruff, Wayne,** prom. 1973, U.S., (wrong. convict.) rob.-mur. Creamer and his six associates were convicted of murdering two Georgian pathologists, Warren Matthews and his wife Rosina during a home invasion on May 7, 1971. A year later Cobb County authorities received word from the South Carolina State Police that they had a suspect in custody with intimate knowledge of the crime.

District Attorney Ben Smith replied that he would guarantee Debbie Ann Kidd immunity from prosecution if she agreed to turn state's evidence. During the murder trial held in Cobb County in 1974, Kidd testified that she had taken part in the robbery and had been the one that shot Mrs. Matthews through the head. She implicated a second woman named Carol Sue Boling Johnson in the crime, but upon further investigation it was learned that she was in Ohio the day of the shootings. Debra Kidd was an unreliable witness. Just before the trial opened she had undergone hypnosis in order to help regain her memory. Defense attorneys argued that she should have been declared incompetent because of the strong possibility that her memory had been "altered" during these sessions. Kidd eventually admitted that she had lied on the witness stand.

On Aug. 26, 1975, following an investigation into the true facts of the case by the Atlanta *Constitution*, Cobb County Superior Court Judge Luther Hames ordered new trials for Roberts, Jenkins, Emmett, and Powell on the grounds that the prosecution had suppressed evidence that would have discredited the star witness, Debra Kidd. The two other convicted men, Creamer and Ruff, were also guaranteed new trials, but were ordered detained in prison on various other unrelated charges.

The police had obtained confessions from three other men who did not know the original defendants. They included: Billy Sunday Birt, Billy Wayne Davis, and Willie Hester. On Sept. 2, 1975, the charges against Creamer and the other five co-defendants were dropped in the wake of this new evidence uncovered by police. The long, expensive trial cost Cobb County taxpayers $750,000. REF.: *CBA*.

Creasy, Sir Edward Shepherd, 1812-78, Brit., jur. Sir Edward Shepard Creasy served as Chief justice of Ceylon, India, in 1860, during British rule of the country. REF.: *CBA*.

Crédit Mobilier, prom. 1870s, U.S., brib.-polit.corr. Little action was taken against U.S. congressmen caught making fraudulent profits from the construction of the nation's first transcontinental railroad.

The operation was established by Thomas Durant, vice president of the Union Pacific Railroad Company, who secured controlling interest in the Pennsylvania Fiscal Agency, creating the Crédit Mobilier of America in 1864. The company, brazenly named after a joint-stock company that defrauded many French investors during the 1850s, was authorized to build the railroad at a crookedly enormous cost, giving Durant and his Union Pacific colleagues who owned stock handsome profits from government bonds and land grants, nearly as large as $50 million, usually authorized by congressmen who owned stock in the company.

To prevent legislation against the Crédit Mobilier's methods, Congressman Oakes Ames of Massachusetts gave shares to his fellow congressmen, sometimes at no charge. None of the many congressmen/stockholders complained about the enormous returns they were receiving on their investments until the New York *Sun* published names of congressmen allegedly bribed by Ames, the frontman and major stockholder in the Crédit Mobilier, in the Fall of 1872.

Congress formally censured Ames for distributing the shares and also censured Congressman James Brooks of New York, probably more for being a Democrat than for illicit behavior. Both men died shortly afterward. A special Senate investigating committee voted to remove New Hampshire Senator James W. Patterson from office, but, with only five days remaining in his term, Patterson was allowed to stay. Congressional inquiries also implicated James A. Garfield, later U.S. president, Vice President Schuyler Colfax, William D. Kelley of Pennsylvania, John Bingham of Ohio, and John A. Logan. Durant was removed from the directorate of the Union Pacific on May 25, 1869. REF.: *CBA*.

Creecy, Edmund P., 1847-1913, U.S., law enforc. off. Born on a southern plantation, Edmund P. Creecy was an innovator in the police force and served as police chief in St. Louis, Mo.

Born in 1847 in North Carolina, Edmund P. Creecy was educated by private tutors on his father's plantation. An active member of the Sons of the American Revolution, he joined the St. Louis police force in 1877. Becoming chief on Sept. 19, 1906, Creecy encouraged communications by initiating an open-door policy for the public and the press. He also implemented a three-shift program to stagger hours for his officers. During Creecy's term, St. Louis purchased the world's first motorized patrol wagon in 1908. In 1910, Creecy was tried by the Board of Police Commissioners, accused of indiscretion concerning embezzlement of funds by the secretary of the Police Relief Fund. He was found Guilty and dismissed from the force, his term ending on Apr. 9, 1910. REF.: *CBA*.

Creed, Edwin Austin, 1880-1926, Brit., (unsolv.) mur. A kindly shop manager was brutally murdered in the cheese shop where he had worked for many years.

Edwin Austin Creed, forty-six, managed a cheese store on the corner of Leinster Terrace and Craven Square in Bayswater. On July 28, 1926, he stayed on in the store to wash his hands after his assistants had left. Three hours later Mr. Andrews, a chemist next door, smelled gas coming from the store and called the police. Patrolman Watts arrived and discovered Creed's battered body halfway down the cellar stairs, dead from repeated blows from a heavy weapon. For no apparent reason, three gas jets had been opened and left unlighted. Somewhere between £35-40 had been stolen from the safe. A left-handed glove and two bloodstained prints were found on the floor of the shop but could not be traced.

Scotland Yard inspectors surmised that Creed had heard a knock on the front door as he was washing up downstairs and, thinking it a late customer, opened the door only to be attacked, then thrown down the stairs. The assailant or assailants had then rifled the safe and turned on the gas jets with the idea of starting a fire to cover up the crime.

The West End coroner, H.R. Oswald, opened the inquest on Aug. 13, 1926, and shortly thereafter the police received two anonymous letters, both postmarked from Notting Hill and both in the same handwriting. They were marked "Important Urgent," and their author purported to be able to supply "important information" about the slaying. The investigation continued, headed by Chief Constable Wensley, CID, but no further clues were found and the letter-writer never responded to police requests to come forth. Though more than 100 interviews were conducted, no other evidence was found and Oswald reluctantly closed the inquest with a verdict of "Willful murder by some person or persons unknown," later writing a newspaper article calling the murder of Creed "the perfect crime."

REF.: Adam, *Murder Most Mysterious*; *CBA*; Shew, *A Second Companion to Murder*.

Creffield, Franz Edmund (AKA: Joshua the Second), b.c.1867, U.S., adult. German-born Franz Creffield appeared in Corvallis, Ore., in 1902, in the Salvation Army band. He disappeared for some months, reappearing with his earlier religious interest turned to fanaticism. He wore white robes and a long beard, and called himself the prophet Joshua the Second, head of a new church called the Church of the Bride of Christ. He was to search for "The Mother of a Second Christ." His method of carrying out that task was to have sex with as many women as he could. Soon women of all ages were attending Joshua's services, each one hoping that she was the bride, but all willing to indulge in his "soul cleansing" activities.

The husbands, fathers, and brothers of the women drawn to Creffield objected. First they drove his church to a deserted island and then, after secret photos of his religious rites were published, they arrested and tried him on charges of mass adultery. He was found Guilty and sentenced to two years in prison. After serving fifteen months, he was released, and reopened his church near Corvallis. When he took credit for the great San Francisco earthquake of Apr. 17, 1906, women flocked to him again, but he had left the group to marry a follower, Esther Mitchell. On May 7, Esther's brother, George Mitchell, saw Creffield in a drugstore, put a pistol to his ear, and shot him. George Mitchell was tried

for murder but acquitted. Esther, taking retribution into her own hands, put a pistol to her brother's ear and fired, killing him as he had killed her prophet husband. Esther Mitchell Creffield was sent to an insane asylum.

REF.: *CBA*; Hynd, *Murder, Mayhem and Mystery*; Nash, *Murder, America*.

Creighton, Mary Frances, d.1936, and **Appelgate, Everett**, 1899-1936, U.S., mur. Everett Appelgate worked as an investigator for the Veterans Unemployment Bureau of Nassau County, N.Y., and lived with his wife Ada and their 12-year-old daughter Agnes at the home of Mrs. Appelgate's parents. It was an unpleasant arrangement, and Appelgate asked his friend John Creighton if the family could live in his house until things began to turn around. In November 1934, the Creightons welcomed the Appelgates into their home.

The Creightons had two children, 15-year-old Ruth, and a 12-year-old son named Jackie. Their mother, Mary Frances Creighton, also had a skeleton in her closet. In 1923, she had been tried for murder in connection with the poisoning of her brother Raymond Avery, who left her his insurance money. There was evidence that she administered arsenic to her brother, but since there were no witnesses, she was acquitted. Mrs. Creighton was also indicted for murdering her mother-in-law, but the jury decided that the small quantity of arsenic found in the body was not enough to cause death. The Creightons left New Jersey in disgrace and settled on Long Island.

The tiny Creighton house was inadequate for two families. The girls slept in a cramped, dirty attic, while the Creightons were consigned to a small back bedroom. This overcrowding led to some peculiar sleeping arrangements. The Appelgates invited Ruth Creighton to share their bed on occasion, which led to sexual intimacy between Everett and Ruth. Mrs. Appelgate, in whom Everett had lost all interest in, apparently approved. Mrs. Creighton found out about it, but kept quiet after Appelgate threatened to expose her as a poisoner. On Sept. 25, 1935, Appelgate gave Mrs. Creighton some arsenic to place in his wife's eggnog, intending after her death to marry Ruth Creighton. At the same time, he was having an affair with Mrs. Creighton behind her husband's back.

Mrs. Appelgate became sick and eventually died in the hospital. Newspaper clippings describing the circumstances of Raymond Avery's death reached the district attorney, who, ordered an autopsy. The world-famous toxicologist Dr. Alexander Gettler was brought in to examine Mrs. Appelgate's internal organs in which traces of arsenic trioxide were found. Dr. Richard Hoffman, questioned Ruth on behalf of the district attorney's office, and she admitted having sexual relations with "Uncle Everett."

Only then did Mrs. Creighton confess her involvement in the murder. She and Appelgate were indicted for murder and placed on trial side by side on Jan. 13, 1936. The murder trial became national news. The jury returned a Guilty verdict on Jan. 30. On July 19, 1936, the two poisoners were executed in the electric chair. Mary Frances Creighton, prostrate with fear, had to be wheeled to the chair unconscious.

REF.: *CBA*; Duff, *A New Handbook On Hanging*; Elliott, *Agent of Death*; Gribble, *Compelled to Kill*; Hoffman and Bishop, *The Girl In Poison Cottage*; Hynd, *Murder, Mayhem and Mystery*; Kilgallen, *Murder One*; Nash, *Murder, America*.

Creighton, William, Jr., 1778-1851, U.S., jur. William Creighton, Jr. U.S. served as district attorney in Washington, D.C., from 1809-11. In 1828, Creighton was appointed to the bench by President John Quincy Adams and presided over the district court of Ohio. REF.: *CBA*.

Crell, Nikolaus (Nikolaus Krell), c.1551-1601, Saxony, her. Nikolaus Crell served as Chancellor of Saxony in 1589. Crell was known for his outspoken religious beliefs and was executed in 1601 for his attempt to replace Lutheranism with a modified version of Calvinism. REF.: *CBA*.

Cremonse, Francesco, prom. 1938, Fr., fraud. An unusual technique in art fraud is to bury a carefully designed and deliberately "aged" statue, with parts of it missing, expecting it to be dug up and discovered as an antique.

Francesco Cremonse, an obscure Italian sculptor, buried a statue of Venus in a French peasant's turnip patch in south central France, near St. Etienne—the statue missing one arm, the nose, and the lower parts of both legs. Plowed up in 1938, not long after it was buried, the Venus was lauded by art critics as an invaluable relic from the time of the Roman invasion of Gaul, and highly touted as an excellent example of the neo-Attican period from seventeen hundred to twenty-five hundred years earlier.

The government of France issued a decree declaring the Venus de Brizet, as the statue was named, one of that country's most priceless national art treasures, forbidding its sale without official authorization. Cremonse then came forward with the missing parts of the Venus and the nightclub performer who had posed for the statue. The value plummeted and the art world retracted its lavish praise.

REF.: *CBA;* MacDougall, *Hoaxes.*

Crespo, Santiago Domingo, 1911- , P.R., Case of, (attempt.) assass. A Puerto Rican nationalist attempted to assassinate Santiago Iglesias, U.S. resident commissioner in Puerto Rico, in 1936.

In 1901, American labor leader Samuel Gompers appointed Santiago Iglesias, a young Puerto Rican politician, to organize his country for the American Federation of Labor. Since 1933, Iglesias had been Puerto Rico's resident commissioner—a member of the United States Congress without a vote—in Washington.

In November 1936 Iglesias, sixty-four, was campaigning for re-election at Mayaguez, on Puerto Rico's western shore, for when Santiago Domingo Crespo, twenty-five, a sergeant in the militant auxiliary of the Puerto Rican Nationalists, grew angry at his speeches recommending the preservation of "loving American institutions." As Iglesias shouted, "Keep intact the union with the United States!" Crespo fired five shots and Iglesias fell. Police saved Crespo from mob violence and Iglesias was taken to a Mayaguez hospital with a minor wound in one arm.

By Nov. 16, evidence had been uncovered that suggested the assassination attempt was part of a conspiracy that would have taken the lives of Maria Luisa Arcelay, an island legislator, and M.A. Gracia Mendez, speaker of the House of Representatives, both on the campaign platform with Iglesias on the day of the shooting. Four other persons were arrested and held in the plot. Crespo was found Guilty of attempted murder and, on Dec. 5, 1938, sentenced to ten years in prison. REF.: *CBA.*

Cretan, The, 1926, U.S., boot.-smug. The *Cretan* was a large freighter purchased by New York and Philadelphia mobsters to smuggle in contraband alcohol in defiance of Prohibition. In the early months of 1926, the ship made a rendezvous with the British vessel *Herald,* off the Bay of Fundy. The entire cargo of 700 drums containing 70,000 gallons of Belgian alcohol was transferred to the cargo hold of the *Cretan.*

To hide the illegal liquor from the Coast Guard and Customs agents, crew members piled several tons of waste paper on top of the drums. The *Cretan* steamed toward Philadelphia, but was ordered to proceed to Boston to take on more baled waste paper.

A few days after the freighter was moored in Boston Harbor, several well-heeled men who did not appear to be seamen arrived. A customs agent who observed their movements reported his suspicions to Deputy Collector Thomas Finnegan who ordered the ship's cargo searched. After several unsuccessful attempts to break into the hold, Finnegan ordered that the loading of waste paper onto the vessel be halted. Breaking through a coal bunker, the Custom's men located the alcohol, and then had it impounded under federal statutes. The *Cretan* was sold at public auction and the liquor was sold to drug companies who held the necessary permits which allowed them to dispense the contents for "medicinal purposes."

REF.: *CBA;* Whitehead, *Border Guard.*

Cretzer, Joseph Paul, 1911-46, U.S., rob.-mur. The youngest of three sons, Joseph Cretzer was born in Montana of deaf mute

parents. At age ten he moved with his family to Oakland, Calif. There his older brothers committed a string of minor crimes that escalated into more serious offenses. These were the only male influences in young Cretzer's life and he aspired to follow in the footsteps of his errant brothers. He did, learning from them the methods of their awkward burglaries. He committed seven burglaries in nearby Emeryville, all industrial plants, and in each instance he was apprehended and brought back to his parents. He was not prosecuted because of his age and because authorities felt sorry for his handicapped parents.

Bank robber Joseph Paul Cretzer and wife Edna.

When Cretzer's brothers went east to commit several armed robberies in 1927, he attempted to join them, stealing a car. Outside of Livermore, Calif., police stopped and arrested him. Cretzer escaped jail while awaiting trial, but was recaptured near Lake Merritt. He was sentenced to the Preston Reformatory Industrial School at Ione. While being driven to Ione, Cretzer escaped again, leaping from the car of the parole officer taking him to the reformatory. Not until 1929 did officers track Cretzer down, finding him at his parents' Oakland home. By this time, Cretzer had nowhere else to go since his brothers had both been sentenced to long prison terms for armed robberies. Cretzer arrived at Ione at age eighteen and immediately befriended 20-year-old Arnold T. Kyle. Originally from Oregon, Kyle had moved to northern California and, while in his teens, committed a series of armed robberies. Kyle had been caught red-handed while robbing a grocery store in Galt, Calif., after slugging the owner. He had been convicted of assault with intent to kill.

Cretzer and Kyle had the same violent view of the world. They shared their hatred of authority and made plans to embark on a joint career of crime once released. This came in 1931 when both were freed from the reformatory. Almost immediately the pair stopped a car, slugged its occupants and robbed them, then drove off in the auto. They drove to Pittsburg, Calif., where Kyle's sister Edna operated a whorehouse in the Bruno Hotel on Black Diamond Street. Here Edna Kyle was known as Kay Wallace. She was an aggressive, red-headed woman with sharp features and a cunning mind. Cretzer was impressed with her wisecracking, sardonic manner, and Edna was taken with the burly youth with the black, wavy hair. The pair were soon married in Antioch, Calif.

Here Cretzer, his wife, and Arnold Kyle operated a profitable whorehouse for several years, but Edna was arrested for white slavery, in forcing a 17-year-old Mexican girl into prostitution. Released on bail, Edna agreed with her husband that they, along with her brother, should flee to avoid certain conviction. The three decided to raid small banks in northern California and Oregon. Scores of banks were robbed by the trio, forty armed robberies in the San Francicso Bay area alone, according to police estimates. Edna served as the getaway driver while Cretzer and Kyle cleaned out the cages of the banks. So successful were they, that the gang was joined by John Hertzer and James D. Courey, two notorious bank robbers wanted in several states.

Cretzer's new super gang struck the Oakland branch of the American Trust Company on Jan. 23, 1938, taking $6,000 in a bloody holdup which saw one bank officer severely wounded. The FBI placed Cretzer on its Most Wanted list, which stated that he was then one of the most dangerous bank robbers in the nation. Newspapers hungry for headlines compared Cretzer's daring bank robberies to those of John Dillinger, Charles Arthur "Pretty Boy" Floyd, and George "Baby Face" Nelson. The youthful holdup man reveled in his new notoriety, proudly pointing out to his associates that he was listed as Public Enemy Number Five. Cretzer's new status made him unbearable, and he and his wife began to argue about his bold plans to stick up larger and more heavily guarded banks. She returned alone to Oakland and got a job as an usherette in the Grand Lake Theater and while she was thus occupied, Cretzer and Kyle were arrested in Chicago and returned to California to stand trial for robbing a Pasadena bank. Newsmen interviewed Cretzer as he and Kyle headed west to stand trial and the bank robber gloried in the attention shown to him, boasting to reporters that he could escape from any prison, just as Johnny Dillinger had, and that he would soon be Public Enemy Number One.

California authorities soon realized that Cretzer and his gang were, as the prosecuting attorney in the Pasadena robbery had stated, unlike any criminals in the state's history. During his trial, Cretzer almost escaped again, using the tongue of his belt buckle to try to pick the lock on the handcuffs he wore to and from the courtroom. He would have gotten away had it not been for an alert guard. Federal authorities stepped in and took jurisdiction before the California trial got underway, claiming Cretzer and Kyle for trial in Washington state where the pair had committed three Seattle bank robberies. Both men were convicted and sent to McNeil Island on Puget Sound to serve twenty-five-year prison sentences, but Cretzer and Kyle quickly plotted another escape. They studied prison routines and carefully noted gaps in security. On May 23, 1940, both men, working on a tree-cutting detail, saw their opportunity. A prison truck arrived as usual to pick up brush and tree limbs, and as it slowed down, Cretzer and Kyle jumped into the cab, ordering the driver to keep going or be decapitated by the sharp axes they held. The truck roared down the road as guards shot up the back of the truck.

Cretzer and Kyle abandoned the riddled truck and headed into the thick woods, but they were recaptured four days later, starving and ragged. The pair went on trial again for the prison escape. Their trial was held in Tacoma, Wash., on Aug. 22, 1940. On that day, Cretzer and Kyle, manacled together, asked to go to the washroom. An elderly U.S. marshal, A.J. Chitty, accompanied them and, once in the washroom, both men turned on him, smashing his head with their manacled fists, while attempting to reach his holstered gun. Other guards heard the commotion and subdued the pair, but Chitty had taken a terrible beating and he suffered a fatal heart attack a few moments later. Now the two were tried for murder, but their expensive attorneys successfully argued that Chitty did not die of the beating the prisoners gave him but of a heart attack that would have eventually happened anyway. Federal Judge Neterer obviously came to the same conclusion, sentencing the pair to life in prison.

Because of their repeated escapes, Cretzer and Kyle were considered too dangerous to send back to McNeil Island. The Federal Bureau of Prisons decided that there was only one place that could hold them, Alcatraz. They were sent to the Rock in the fall of 1940, arriving in heavy foot chains and manacles and heralded by other prisoners as two of the toughest convicts ever to step onto that dreaded island. From that day to the hour of his death, "Dutch Joe" Cretzer, as he was nicknamed, thought of nothing but escape. He would make two violent attempts to beat the Rock, the first ending in frustration, the second in his own bloody death.

On May 21, 1941, Cretzer and Kyle tried to break out of the prison's mat shop to get to the shoreline where they expected to be picked up by Edna Kyle Cretzer. The convict's wife, who had visited Alcatraz many times and helped to plot the escape, was to rent a speedboat and anchor close to the island, pretending to be fishing until she spotted Cretzer and Kyle near the water. She was then to pick them up and they would roar away to San Francisco and freedom. But Cretzer, Kyle, and other convicts in on the break could not get through the bars of the mat shop window and Edna Cretzer never appeared in the boat; she had been detained by San Francisco police on the day she was to have rented it. The frustrated convicts gave up.

For this escape attempt, Cretzer spent almost five years in Alcatraz's D block which was where the most dangerous prisoners were kept in solitary confinement. Here he brooded and plotted his next break. He also read almost every law book in the prison library, becoming an expert jailhouse lawyer, advising other convicts on how to present petitions for their releases. When not complaining about the monotonous menu (Cretzer dreamed constantly of breaking out just to get a steak dinner and pie à la mode in one of his favorite San Francisco restaurants), Cretzer wrote endless letters to his wife and even penned lengthy poems. In one 1945 poem, he stated:

> Countless cons, with writs galore,
> A horde of deadly dingbats;
> Guilty as hell, but still they yell
> "We wanna change our habitats."

To Edna, Cretzer wrote of the awful conditions on Alcatraz, particularly expressing his repugnancy of the terrible smells that permeated the prison, the sweet-sickening odors drifting from the kitchen, after meals in particular, so offensive to Cretzer that his sensitive palate remained permanently disturbed, allowing him to eat only sparingly. He had been a fastidious man on the outside and was highly repelled by the odor of the sweating bodies around him. On hot nights, when the body odors of the prisoners clung to the cell block, Dutch Joe Cretzer got sick to his stomach. His bitterness knew no bounds and he seethed with hatred and disgust for Alcatraz, much of this finding its way into his letters to Edna. One read: "I have no quarrel with society. It ought to have none with me. I only want what's coming to me. I've been wrong all my life. But I ain't bad. Now, in this hole, I fight the atmosphere, the silence, the bodies. No one feels the hard misery inside me..."

Cretzer waited and planned and schemed another breakout. This break finally occurred on May 2, 1946, when he and Bernard Coy led four other convicts in a futile but bloody uprising that almost destroyed Alcatraz and took the lives of three convicts and two guards and left one prisoner and fourteen guards wounded. The battle that raged for forty-eight hours before the mutiny was put down is considered to this day one of the worst in American penal history, one that received more press in its day than the 1971 prison riot in Attica, N.Y. It took the life of its planner, Joseph Paul Cretzer, but, ironically, the Battle of Alcatraz was so violent that the prison structure itself sustained permanent damage that contributed to its ultimate closing.

The death of Cretzer in the 1946 Alcatraz uprising was placed at the door of the American press by FBI director J. Edgar Hoover, who later wrote: "The best way to deflate ego-maniac individuals is to tell the truth about them. Had John Dillinger been depicted for the filthy type of vermin he was, crawling through holes of our law enforcement, rather than as one series of articles portrayed him, a clever and adventurous individual given a marked degree of chivalry of Robin Hood proportions, perhaps there would not be so many stupid boys like Cretzer laying dead, naked, and unclaimed."

Cretzer's body was claimed, however, by his then ex-wife, Edna, who had remarried and was known as Kay Benedetti. She waited a week after the bloody uprising had been put down before she claimed the body which was shipped to San Francisco for cremation at the Cypress Lawn Cemetery. Newsmen swarmed about the one-time gun moll, questioning her about Cretzer, the complex, lethal convict who thought he could beat the Rock. Edna told them that she had not seen Cretzer in sixteen months and during that prison visit she claimed that she had told Cretzer that she intended to remarry and live a law-abiding life. "Even if he had made it, I wouldn't have helped him," she said. "I told Joe I was going to marry a good man and I wouldn't be seeing him anymore. I really wanted to start a new life. But because he loved me, I'll see to his burial. He was really a good man, once you came to know him. He would have meant no harm if he had gotten a few decent chances in life."

Almost immediately after the cremation services, Edna Kyle Cretzer Benedetti was arrested and charged with stealing a $19 hat from a San Francisco department store. See: **Alcatraz.**

REF.: Audett, *Rap Sheet; CBA;* DeNevi, *Alcatraz '46;* Heaney, *Inside the Walls of Alcatraz;* Howard, *Six Against the Rock;* Johnston, *Alcatraz Island Prison;* Karpis, *On the Rock.*

Crews, Paul David (AKA: Butch), 1952- , Case of, U.S., rob.-mur. An outdoorsman who likes to read, Crews is wanted in connection with the vicious slaying of a woman, whose throat was slashed several times.

Born in Union County, S.C., Paul David Crews, thirty-seven, reportedly carries a hunting knife sheathed on his belt and is considered dangerous. Distinguishing tattoos are "Casey" on his right shoulder and "C" on his left shoulder. Crews usually works as a migrant worker or a laborer, and spends time at libraries reading. A woodsman who can live off the land, he is likely to be in a rural or wooded area, but could turn up at a local bookstore or library. As of this writing, Crews was last spotted in Tampa, Fla. REF.: *CBA.*

Crime, The, 1959, a novel by Stephen Longstreet. The Hall-Mills case (U.S., 1922) is the basis for this work of fiction. See: **Hall-Mills Case.** REF.: *CBA.*

Crime of Laura Sarelle, The, 1941, a novel by Joseph Shearing (British title: *Laura Sarelle*). This work of fiction takes its story from the murder of Sir Theodosius Boughton by Captain John Donellan (Brit., 1780). See: **Donellan, Capt. John.** REF.: *CBA.*

Crimes of Honor Law, 1930-1981, Italy, mur. A law that promoted and encouraged light sentences for the murder of spouses—almost all of them wives—was introduced by fascist dictator Benito Mussolini, an infamous womanizer, in 1930, and remained the law in Italy until 1981.

In 1930 Mussolini declared that anyone murdering a spouse, daughter, or sister "when discovering an unlawful carnal relationship and in a state of anger due to the affront of his or the family's honor shall be imprisoned from three to seven years." (The minimum sentence under Italy's basic murder provision is twenty-one years.)

Article 587 of the penal code, which came to be known as the Crimes of Honor Law figured extensively in Italian murder cases for the next fifty-one years. So-called "honor killers" were frequently allowed to go free, and hundreds of husbands avoided life sentences by claiming that they had killed in the rage brought about when their wives had besmirched their honor. Until the early 1970s, when divorce was legalized in Italy, some men murdered their wives to be free to remarry, getting light sentences by claiming that their victims had committed adultery. A popular film, *Divorce, Italian Style,* was based on this situation.

In 1976-78, at least eighty people were murdered in purported "crimes of honor." A Naples truck driver who killed his wife and injured her lover was given a jail sentence of thirty-two months, and Salvatore Vitrano, a postman from Misilmeri, Si., was convicted on Mar. 17, 1981, of murdering his wife and brother when he caught them together in bed. Vitrano pulled a five-year-four-month prison term, the last person to benefit from the "license to kill" law which was abolished in 1981 after a four-year parliamentary battle. Undersecretary Giuseppe Gargani called the law "a genocidal idea that is no longer in keeping with the collective conscience of the Italian people." REF.: *CBA.*

Crime Story, A, 1981, a novel by Jay Robert Nash. The structure of this work is taken, in part, from the Constance Kent murder case (Brit., 1860), but characters and sub-plots stem from contemporary U.S. cases. See: **Kent, Constance.** REF.: *CBA.*

Crimmins, Alice, 1941- , U.S., mansl. The attractive, 26-year-old Alice Crimmins lived in Queens, N.Y., with her two children, Eddie, age five, and Alice Marie, called Missy, who was four. She had been separated from her husband Edmund, who visited regularly with the children. On the morning of July 14, 1965, Edmund Crimmins visited his children only to find them missing from their room in the ground-floor Crimmins apartment. A desperate search took place and Alice Marie was found later that day in a vacant lot, strangled to death with her pajamas. Eddie Crimmins was found a week later about a mile distant from the Crimmins home and he, too, had been strangled, although forensic experts were uncertain if this was truly the case since the little boy's body had rapidly decomposed. Mrs. Crimmins explained to suspicious investigators that a hook-and-eye fastener on the door leading to her children's room was missing, that she always fastened this apparatus to prevent them from leaving their room to raid the refrigerator.

Alice Crimmins and her two children, Alice Marie and Eddie, Christmas, 1964.

Mrs. Crimmins seemed rather unemotional at the time of her children's death. When she was taken to the barren lot at 162nd Street where her daughter's body was discovered, Crimmins appeared to go into a faint but recovered within moments. She shed not a single tear, nor was any trace of emotion present in the woman. Later, Mrs. Crimmins explained precisely what happened on the night her children left their room. She said that she had fed both her children manicotti and string beans at 7:30 p.m. She said she looked in on them at midnight and they were sleeping peacefully in their beds. Mrs. Crimmins added that she was awake until 4 a.m., and that her children must have left their room after that time or were kidnapped and later killed for inexplicable reasons after that time. Questioned repeatedly about these time periods, Alice Crimmins insisted that the times she had provided were correct, that she had checked several clocks in the house. These statements were to convict Alice Crimmins later in one of the most sensational murder trials of the 1960s.

The police suspected Mrs. Crimmins from the start, but they cautiously built their case against her. Twenty-three months later, she was charged with murdering her children, and in May 1968, placed on trial for the murder of her daughter Missy. The prosecution demonstrated how Mrs. Crimmins had led a promiscuous life and even her own lawyer described his client as "amoral." It was for this reason that her husband was suing for divorce at the time of the children's deaths. The custody battle was intense and full of vicious charges from both sides. Mrs. Crimmins, the prosecution contended, had murdered her children rather than let her husband take custody of them; an act, she felt, that would label her as an unfit mother.

Dr. Milton Helpern, one of the leading pathologists in the U.S., testified that he had examined the contents of the Crimmins daughter and that the child had, indeed, been fed manicotti and string beans. But the girl had not digested this food, Helpern said, at the time Mrs. Crimmins insisted she had fed her children, the little girl having died about two hours after eating the meal. Helpern stated that the girl had eaten the food only a short time before her murder and that Mrs. Crimmins' statements were "impossible—just impossible. If she said she saw them alive before midnight, how could the stomach of Missy show that she must have died within two hours of taking a meal at 7:30...It is patently absurd to think that death might have occurred in the predawn hours after her mother had gone to bed."

A neighbor, Mrs. Earomirski, then testified that she looked out her second-story window about 2 a.m. on the morning of the deaths, and recognized Alice Crimmins with a man, going toward a car. The man was carrying a blanket bundle and Alice Crimmins was leading a small boy by the hand. The man threw the bundle into the back seat of the car and Crimmins said to him: "My God, don't throw her like that!" Mrs. Earomirski said she then began to close the window which squeaked and caused Crimmins to look toward the window and say to the man: "Somebody's seen us!"

The guilt of Alice Crimmins was firm in the minds of the jury, who convicted her of first-degree manslaughter. She was sentenced to twenty years in the New York State Prison for women. Her lawyers, however, managed to win an appeal and the appellate court quashed the sentence, ordering a new trial which occurred in March 1971. This trial proved to be more devastating to Crimmins than the first one. One of her lovers, Joseph Rorech, a building contractor, testified that Crimmins was with him in a motel room following the deaths of her children and that she confessed that she had murdered both the little boy and girl so that their father would not get custody of them. This drew Crimmins' only emotional outburst in her long fight for freedom. She called Rorech a liar and then lapsed into silence. Crimmins was found Guilty of first-degree murder in the death of her son Eddie and of first-degree manslaughter in the death of her daughter Missy. She was sentenced to life imprisonment. After two more appeals, Crimmins was released on bail in 1975. The New York Court of Appeals dismissed the murder conviction of her son but upheld the conviction of manslaughter in the case of her daughter. Crimmins was transferred in 1976 to a release institution in Harlem where she finally took work as a secretary.

REF.: Carpozi, *Ordeal By Trial*; CBA; Gross, *The Alice Crimmins Case*; Helpern and Knight, *Autopsy*; Nash, *Look for the Woman*; Spain, *Post Mortem*; Wilson, *Encyclopedia of Modern Murder*.

Crimmins, Craig (Phantom of the Opera Case), 1959- , U.S., mur. A husky, baby-faced, young man with extraordinarily large hands, Craig Crimmins grew up in the North Bronx, N.Y. As a child he was a slow learner, and was afraid to appear stupid in front of his teachers. Withdrawn and oversized for his age, Crimmins was the favored child of three offspring. At the age of three, he began to sleepwalk, which was often a problem for his parents. One night his mother followed him out of the apartment building and through a snowswept street to return him to his bedroom; he had no recall of the event. After managing to squeak through high school, Crimmins followed his father, brother, and stepfather into stagehand work. He was employed by the Metropolitan Opera House in Manhattan, and there he was attracted to pretty Helen Hagnes Mintiks, a 30-year-old violinist who worked in the orchestra pit during regular performances. On the night of July 23, 1980, Crimmins was in a sub-level elevator when Mintiks entered. Impulsively, Crimmins leaned next to her

and suggested they have sexual intercourse. Mintiks turned crimson and slapped his face. Then, realizing she was alone in the elevator with the hulking Crimmins, the violinist panicked and hit several buttons on the elevator control board. The elevator stopped at a lower level and she got out. Crimmins followed her.

The violinist realized that the area was deserted and tried to strike up a friendly conversation with Crimmins, according to his later confession. He grabbed a hammer and ordered her to undress. She obediently disrobed. When she was naked, the stagehand attempted to rape the woman but was unsuccessful. In frustration, he marched Mintiks up the backstairs of the Met to the roof and there tied her to a pipe. He claimed later that he had no real intention of hurting her and that he told her he would "call someone" and let them know where she was. As he went to a rooftop door, Mintiks broke free of the rope which Crimmins had used to tie her up. He raced back to the pipe, caught the woman, and tied her up again with rags he found in a nearby bucket.

Again, according to his later statement, Crimmins started to leave the roof, but he turned around to see the violinist about to once more break free. "I heard her pouncing up and down," Crimmins was later quoted, "and that's when it happened. I went back and kicked her off." Crimmins, at that point, walked up to the bound woman and kicked her through an opening in an air conditioner fan shaft. Her naked, bound body was found the next day. New York police conducted an exhaustive search for the killer, combing the maze-like dressing rooms, backstairs, elevators, basements, and sub-basements for clues. More than 200 suspects were interviewed; their backgrounds examined in detail. On Aug. 14, 1980, the two chief detectives assigned to the case, Michael Struk and Jerry Giorgio, began to systematically photograph and fingerprint every Met employee. They noticed that one of them, Craig Crimmins, was extremely nervous when it came his turn to have mug shots taken and his fingerprints and palms printed. Both officers noticed that Crimmins was hyperventilating while the printing process went on. Shortly thereafter, the detectives matched Crimmins' palm print to a perfect print found on the pipe of the roof of the Met where the victim had been tied.

The two officers played a cat-and-mouse game with Crimmins, interviewing him several times but not charging him with the murder, running him about the Met as if seeking information from him. In a final marathon interrogation on Aug. 29-30, Craig blurted his confession to Giorgio. He was charged with murder and tried before Judge Richard G. Denzer the following spring. Crimmins' attorney argued that the stagehand's confession had been manipulated out of the slow-witted youth and obliquely referred to the case of George Whitmore, Jr., another dim-witted youth who had been manipulated into confessing the murder of Janice Wylie in 1963—a celebrated Manhattan slaying. (Whitmore was later released when pharmacist Richard Robles admitted killing Janice, the niece of writer Philip Wylie, and her roommate Emily Hoffert.)

Both Giorgio and Struk underwent grueling courtroom examinations but remained unruffled. Their testimony reflected proper police procedure during their investigation of the killing and their conduct concerning Crimmins. The jury believed the detectives and that the confession was legitimate. On June 4, 1981, the jury, after deliberating five-and-a-half hours, found Crimmins Not Guilty of intentional murder but Guilty of felony murder, Judge Denzer later sentenced the killer to twenty years to life, which meant that Crimmins would not be eligible for parole until serving the entire twenty-year sentence. At the turn of the next century, Craig Crimmins will be forty-one, in the prime of life, and will begin petitioning the parole board for his freedom.

REF.: Black, *Murder at the Met*; CBA.

Crippen, Dr. Hawley Harvey (AKA: John Philo Robinson), 1862-1910, Brit., mur. Dr. Hawley Harvey Crippen was a meek, inoffensive man and the last person anyone would select as a brutal murderer. For that very reason, and because of his sensational escape and capture, Crippen has found a permanent place in the annals of murder as a celebrated slayer. Born in Coldwater, Mich., Crippen attended the University of Michigan and received his medical degree from the Homoeopathic Hospital College in Cleveland, Ohio, in 1885. He then served his internship at Hahnemann Hospital in Manhattan where he met and married a student nurse, Charlotte Jane Bell, who was born in Ireland and brought up in the strict manners and morals of a convent. The first Mrs. Crippen was a moody, young woman who had to get a special dispensation to wed the doctor—he being Protestant, she having been baptized a Catholic. After making love, Crippen later complained, she would hurry to a local priest to confess her "sin." Charlotte nevertheless bore the doctor a son, Otto Hawley Crippen, and was about to give birth to another child in January 1892 when she died of apoplexy. Crippen left his son to be raised by his parents in California while he looked about for another wife in New York.

The woman who became the second Mrs. Crippen was a bosomy teenager, the daughter of a Polish grocer, named Kunigunde Mackamotzki who was then appearing on the stage under the name Belle Turner. She was being kept by a wealthy Brooklyn stove manufacturer named Lincoln, and had apparently suffered a miscarriage for which she was treated by Dr. Jeffrey who was assisted by Crippen. Young Crippen was impressed by the sensual, ambitious Belle, but he was quick to see her dominant personality. "She would never give in to anything," he later lamented from the dock when tried for her murder. Belle Turner took a liking to Crippen, and the couple married on Sept. 1, 1892. Belle had told Crippen the lie that her father had been a Polish nobleman whose vast estates she was still trying to regain. The mild-mannered Crippen soon learned that his second wife was just the opposite of the first, so sexually demanding that she "fairly exhausted" him. Moreover, she never stopped talking about how she would some day be a great opera star like the celebrated Adelina Patti who received $5,000 a performance.

There would be no children in the marriage as Belle had had an operation which prevented her from giving birth. The couple settled down to a hum-drum life, and Belle soon began complaining that Crippen's meager salary did not cover the cost of her singing lessons—an expense that her lover Lincoln had absorbed. Economic depression and the public's declining patronage of homoeopathic medicine, one which relied heavily on drugs, caused Crippen to field about for a way to make the kind of money his wife thought due their station. He and his wife opened up a patent medicine shop on East 14th Street and Sixth Avenue and they began to make considerable money selling quack drugs and cure-alls, most of which were nothing more than alcohol and opiates colored and sweetened with sugar. Crippen then came under the wing of Professor Munyon, king of the patent medicines. He was soon promoted to general manager of Munyon's widespread U.S. operations.

Though the couple saved no money from Crippen's considerable income, they began to live luxuriously, and Belle hired the best singing coaches in New York. They spent most of their money on diamonds for Belle and she would, each night, take these out and "babble to her diamonds and kiss them," according to one report. Belle also flirted with almost every man she met, and Crippen suspected her of having brief affairs when he was out of the city on business for Munyon. Crippen was sent to England in 1897 by Munyon to open a London branch of Munyon's operations with a $10,000 salary, a hefty sum for that time. When the Crippens arrived in London, they took up residence in a comfortable flat, but Belle insisted that she launch her singing career, and Crippen spent most of his money arranging for her to appear at the Old Marleybone Music Hall. She appeared as Cora Motzki in a an operetta which left the audience sitting on their hands. She was cancelled after a week and thereafter appeared occasionally in the cheaper music halls.

Belle, however, felt that her failure was due to Crippen who had meekly opposed her music hall career and that he had somehow sabotaged her future on the stage. She was forever criticizing him and his lack of vision in her talent. To vex him further and to enhance her own vanity, Belle took several lovers, including an actor named Bruce Miller, flaunting these affairs in front of her cuckolded husband. The five-foot-four-inch Crippen took these humiliations in silence. Meanwhile, he lost his job with Munyon's and began selling his own quack remedies. He muddled along year after year, abused and ignored by his wife, trying to make ends meet, especially struggling to pay for the new Crippen residence, a sprawling house at 39 Hildrop Crescent, Camden Town, in North London.

Crippen's prospects improved, however, when in 1903 he hired a new assistant, a pretty, young girl named Ethel Clara LeNeve who had large grey eyes and a sensual mouth. Her father had been a drunken brute, and she craved any type of affection. The gentle, kind-hearted Crippen provided that, and by 1905, a deep relationship had developed between the two. Crippen promised that he would rid himself of his now overweight, vain wife and marry Ethel, but he kept putting this off, making no move to finish his second marriage. His wife intimidated him so much that he feared she might resort to violence. Her lover, Bruce Miller, had returned to Chicago where he had a wife and child, and Belle, who was now using the stage name Belle Elmore, finally had enough of her do-nothing husband, informing him in December 1909 that she intended to leave him and would be drawing their life savings from the bank.

On Jan. 17, 1910, Crippen ordered five grains of hydrobromide of hyocine, a deadly drug he knew was fatal if only a few grains were ingested. On Jan. 25, 1910, Ethel LeNeve arrived at her boarding house in a state of near hysteria, and her landlady later reported that she was ill and trembling all through the night. Whether or not she was aware of Crippen's recent decision to murder his wife was never learned, but Ethel did tell her landlady that Crippen's accounts were very low and that she worried about the future. Six days later, on Jan. 21, 1910, Crippen and Belle held a small dinner party for Belle's music hall friends, Mr. and Mrs. Paul Martinetti. Following dinner, Belle "entertained" her guests for several hours, as was her usual custom, by babbling about her stage career—a career that as her friends, and silent husband, knew was practically non-existent. The guests did not leave until 1:30 a.m. Belle saw them to the door and was about to step outside as they walked down the steps of her house. Mrs. Martinetti turned and called back to her: "Don't come out, Belle, you'll catch a cold!" Belle waved goodbye and closed the door, never to be seen alive again.

Two days following the dinner with the Martinetti's, a letter from Belle was received by the Music Hall Ladies' Guild, of which Belle was a staunch member, informing the Guild that she was resigning her position and was hurrying to the U.S. to visit a dying relative. The letter was written by Crippen who informed the Guild that his wife left in such a hurry that she had no time to write the note herself. Some days later, Crippen pawned some of Belle's jewelry, receiving £80. Neighbors were then shocked to see Crippen's petite secretary, Ethel LeNeve, move into the Crippen house at 39 Hildrop Crescent. She appeared in local restaurants with Crippen, wearing Belle's furs and jewelry, and Crippen introduced Ethel as his new housekeeper. Then Crippen placed an advertisement in Era Magazine, informing its readers that his wife had died. The ad informed Belle's fans that "she passed on of pneumonia up in the high mountains of California." Crippen next appeared at the grand ball given by the Music Hall Ladies' Guild with Ethel LeNeve on his arm. Ethel was wearing a diamond brooch which had been Belle's favorite piece of jewelry. In fact, the Martinetti's had last seen the brooch on the bosom of Belle when they dined with the Crippens on Jan. 31, 1910. Then the doctor and the housekeeper packed their bags and took a vacation to Dieppe together, a trip Crippen made no pains to hide. Such scandalous conduct on the part of the otherwise proper Crippen raised more than a few eyebrows with neighbors who promptly notified Scotland Yard about their suspicions.

In response, Inspector Walter Dew, accompanied by Sergeant

Dr. Hawley Harvey Crippen, and in disguise with beard.

Above, the ambitious Belle Elmore Crippen, part-time music hall singer, full-time cuckolder who moved the mild-mannered doctor to a slaughter-house murder. There was nothing left of her except a few gruesome pieces. Left, Dr. Crippen's pretty mistress, the long-suffering Ethel LeNeve, shown here disguised in men's clothing as Crippen tried to pass her off as his son during a dramatic attempt to escape Scotland Yard in a sea chase.

Dr. Crippen, at right, hat pulled down, scarf on face, is escorted off ship by Inspector Walter Dew.

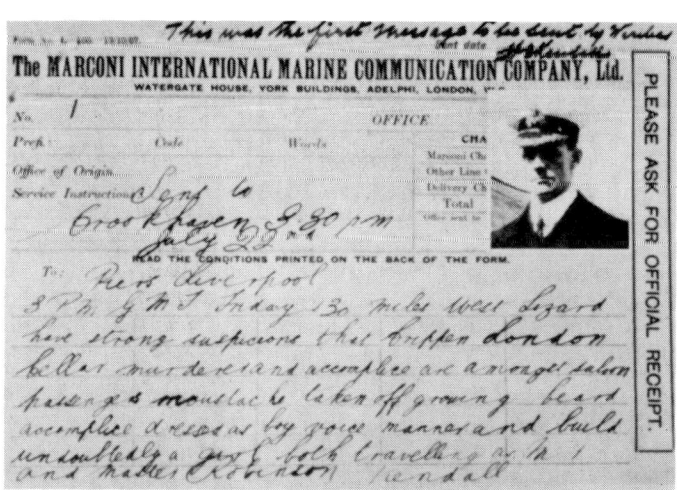

Captain Kendall's famous telegram, the first used to catch a criminal.

Arthur Mitchell, began looking into the disappearance of Mrs. Crippen. Dew was the intrepid Chief Inspector of Scotland Yard's Criminal Investigation Department (CID) but he was anything but a severe detective. He was kind-hearted, understanding, and gave the benefit of a doubt to any suspect. He visited Crippen's offices while the doctor was periodically treating some patients, asking a few polite questions concerning Belle's whereabouts. Crippen was most affable and cooperative, finally telling Dew with considerable embarrassment: "It's extremely humiliating, sir, to inform you that my wife is not visiting any ailing relative in America, nor did she die in California. I've tried to protect her reputation and my own humiliation and failure. The truth is, sir, that my wife has left me for another man, a man better able to support her than myself." Crippen then told Dew that the man was none other than the actor, Bruce Miller, who had returned to the U.S. Belle had simply followed him.

Dew's suspicions were further put to rest when Crippen suggested they have lunch the next day, which they did. Crippen then suggested that Dew inspect his home at 39 Hildrop Crescent. Dew, accompanied by the extremely cooperative Crippen, walked through every room of the house while the detective looked about rather sheepishly. Dew even inspected the cellar and garden and concluded that, aside from the absence of Belle, nothing was amiss. The matter seemed to be one of a domestic nature and Scotland Yard washed its hands of Belle Elmore Crippen and her cuckolded husband. The woman Dew was seeking was, at one point during his search of the Crippen house, directly beneath the detective's feet, buried in the cellar. Crippen had poisoned Belle with hyocine, then dragged her heavy body to the cellar where he decapitated the body, the limbs, and filleted the rest of the corpse, burning the bones in a cellar grate, a job that took several days and nights. Crippen, on hands and knees, cleaned the blood and bone chips from the grate for hours. The rest of the remains he buried in small hole in the cellar floor, wrapped in men's pajamas which were packed with quicklime.

The visit from Inspector Dew alarmed Crippen to the point that he felt he would be arrested at any moment. He and Ethel packed their bags and left for the Continent, arriving in Rotterdam. Ethel was dressed as a boy, wearing some of Crippen's clothing, and pretending to be his son to avoid detection as a couple traveling together. On July 11, Dew returned to 39 Hildrop Crescent to check the exact date Belle had left for America, but he found that the doctor and his housekeeper had left three days earlier. Dew acted immediately, ordering his men to thoroughly search the house and surrounding area. For several days, investigators tore apart cupboards, peeled back wallpaper, dug up the garden and, finally, dug up the cellar where the bundle of flesh wrapped in a man's pajama top was unearthed. There was not much to go on. The sexless remains consisted of pieces of skin, a human buttock, chest and stomach organs, and bits of muscle. One hunk of flesh revealed a scar which appeared to have been the result of an abdominal operation. This scar was checked against Belle's medical records and it was identified as an old incision made during one of Belle's many operations.

Dew swore out a warrant for Crippen and LeNeve on July 16, 1910, and a nation-wide manhunt ensued. Unaware of the search being conducted for them, Crippen and Ethel boarded the S.S. Montrose, at Antwerp on July 20, traveling as father and son. The Montrose was en route to Canada. Once in Canada, Crippen hoped to begin a new life with Ethel. No sooner was the 5,431-ton Montrose out of Antwerp harbor than its captain, Henry Kendall, looked through a porthole of his cabin to see two men on deck, standing behind a lifeboat and holding hands in what for that day was a shocking display of homosexual affection. Said Captain Kendall later in triumphant retrospect: "The younger one squeezed the other's hand immoderately. It seemed to me unnatural for two males, so I suspected them at once." Kendall did not explain exactly what it was that he suspected. Kendall encountered the pair when the Montrose reached the open sea and invited the two to have lunch with him at his table.

Crippen introduced himself as John Philo Robinson, a merchant who was taking his 16-year-old son to California for his health. At this point, Ethel, her hair pulled back and tucked beneath a cap, dutifully coughed and looked ill. (Crippen's alias was plucked from his family tree; his uncle was named Harvey Robinson and he had a cousin in Michigan named Philo Robinson.) Crippen was not wearing a beard as a disguise as later artists would draw him but was clean-shaven for the voyage. He had discarded, however, his glasses, although the tell-tale marks from his spectacles remained at the bridge of his nose. He seemed to talk incesssantly, making remarks about the weather, the speed of the ship, other passengers, the scenery. In contrast, the boy appeared to be a mute, saying little or nothing. The youth appeared to Kendall to be dressed awkwardly; some of the clothes Ethel wore drooped and sagged on her. Other garb seemed too tight, and the youth appeared to be bursting at the seams.

Captain Kendall noticed also that the youth had curves instead of angles, and that Robinson's "son" had a face that was decidedly feminine. All of these observations by Kendall were later made, some said, to enhance his image as an amateur sleuth, when, in reality, he had read about the murder of Belle Elmore before sailing and immediately identified Crippen and Ethel in their ineffective disguises. Kendall had taken pride years earlier when he exposed a number of card sharps who were traveling on board the Empress of India, for which he was then first mate. Ever since that day, Kendall had suspiciously eyed every passenger traveling on the vessels he commanded, ferreting out culprits and malefactors.

Captain Kendall did admit later that he thought about wiring Scotland Yard about his two suspicious passengers almost from the time of his first conversation with the Robinsons, but he was uncertain as to their true identities and that he would be risking his reputation, as well as that of the Canadian Pacific line if he was proven wrong. He conducted an experiment, he later pointed out, by going to his cabin and leafing through the latest Continental editions of the London Daily Mail, finding one dated July 14 which bannered the murder of Mrs. Crippen and offered a photograph of Dr. Crippen. Kendall took a piece of chalk and whited out the glasses and mustache on the Crippen photo and was satisfied that the merchant Robinson was one in the same. Before the Montrose was 150 miles from land, the longest distance where its wireless messages would be picked up, Kendall sent the following message to the directors of the ship line: "Have strong suspicions that Crippen, London cellar murderer, and accomplice are among saloon passengers. Mustache taken off, growing beard. Accomplice dressed as boy. Voice, manner and build undoubtedly a girl. Both traveling as Mr. and Master Robinson. Kendall."

The message was to electrify the world. It was forwarded by the ship owners to Scotland Yard and Chief Inspector Walter Dew. The policeman took a copy of Kendall's telegram to his superior, Sir Melville Macnaghten, asking for permission to chase Crippen across the Atlantic, saying: "I want to go after them in a fast steamer. The White Star liner Laurentic sails from Liverpool tomorrow. I believe it is possible for her to overtake the Montrose and reach Canada first."

Smiling at the thought of this daring plan, Macnaghten authorized Dew to begin the chase. Dew had already learned that the Laurentic's sailing time was only seven days but the Montrose, a much older cargo ship which also carried passengers, had a sailing time to Canada of eleven days. The code name given to Dew's assignment was Operation Handcuffs, and the chief inspector was so secretive about his mission that he told his wife only that he had "to go abroad for a few days on a matter of some urgency." Like Crippen and Ethel LeNeve, Dew chose to disguise himself, boarding the Laurentic as a simple passenger and using the alias "Dewhurst." The newspapers by this time had gotten hold of Kendall's telegram—the first time any criminal was identified and hunted down through an electronic device. They also learned that Dew was in pursuit on a faster ship and readers clamored for each day's editions to learn whether or not the chief

The Crippen case, particularly the wild sea chase to catch the murderer, caught the attention of readers on both sides of the Atlantic.

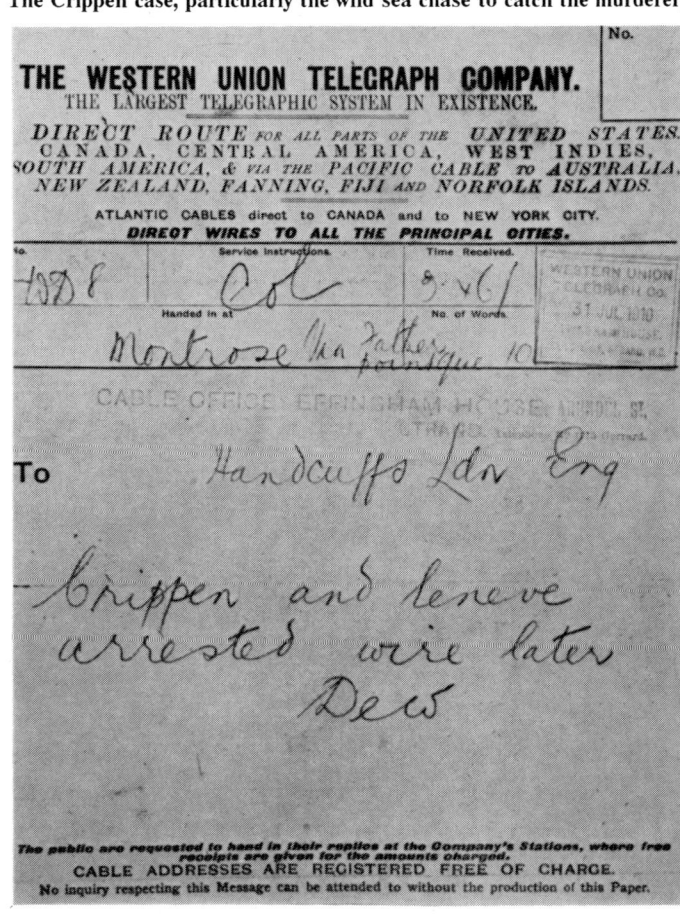

Inspector Dew's terse telegram announcing the capture of Crippen.

Dr. Crippen with Ethel LeNeve in the dock, on trial for murder.

inspector would reach Canada before the fleeing Crippen. The drama was intense, and readers on both sides of the Atlantic were held in suspense while the chase went on. There was a grim irony to it all. While Crippen and Ethel were sitting at the captain's table deciding what to order from the menu, the rest of the world, unknown to them, was reading about their flight to Canada and the dedicated detective from Scotland Yard who had vowed to apprehend them.

On board the *Montrose,* Crippen let his beard grow but shaved his upper lip. He strolled along the deck with Ethel, stoking his beard. He sat in deck chairs with her, holding her hand and cracking nuts for her. He was solicitous and attentive to her at all times, giving her half his salad at dinner. Kendall, playing his role of detective to the hilt, began to keep a diary, and whenver possible, sent off more wires to authorities, saying that he had spotted a revolver in Crippen's pocket. Here he was mistaken; the mild-mannered murderer was unarmed. Kendall also stated that he had crew members collect all newspapers that carried the story of the Crippen murder which were on board when the *Montrose* sailed so as not to alert the disguised couple to the fact that they were suspected by the captain and crew. Kendall, who had been commended for his actions by his superiors, now heightened the tension by sending out wireless messages, no matter how trivial, that dealt with the Robinsons, whom he openly identified as Crippen and Ethel. His wireless message on July 29, 1910, read: "Ethel's trousers are very tight about the hips and split a bit down the back and secured with large safety pins. Kendall."

When this was published in the next editions, the tense drama changed to comedy. That very night in a London music hall, a singer sauntered to the footlights and sang:

Oh, Miss LeNeve, Oh, Miss LeNeve,
Is it true that you are sittin'
On the lap of Dr. Crippen
In your boy's clothes
On the *Montrose*
Miss, LeNeve?

Captain Kendall enjoyed the cat-and-mouse game he played with Crippen, often joining him and Ethel in their walks about the deck. On several occasions, he would approach the pair from behind, calling after Crippin, using the alias the murderer had assumed. Crippen did not respond to the name Robinson, called out three times by Kendall, until Ethel tugged at his sleeve. Crippen turned about and said: "Excuse me, I didn't hear you. The cold air of the sea has made me a bit deaf." On another occasion, Crippen looked up at the wire stretching from the mast to the wireless shack and said to Kendall, not realizing that he was talking about the instrument that had spelled his own doom: "What a marvelous invention it is! How privileged we are to be alive in an age of such scientific miracles!"

On July 27, the *Laurentic* passed the slow-moving *Montrose.* At one point, the ships were reportedly in sight of each other. Inspector Dew wired from the *Laurentic* to the *Montrose* the following message for Kendall: "Will board you Father Point. Please keep any information till I arrive there strictly confidential. Walter Dew, Chief Inspector, Scotland Yard." Kendall testily wired back: "What the devil do you think I have been doing?"

Crippen, as the voyage neared its end, became more and more nervous, asking questions about their arrival in Canada and checking the boat chart showing the *Montrose's* progress. He and Ethel no longer attended the ship concerts and sing alongs. They kept more and more to their cabin, and when Crippen was seen on a deck chair he was absorbed by an Edgar Wallace thriller, *The Four Just Men.* He later went to Ethel and gave her all his money, telling her that she might have to go on alone without him, a statement that perplexed and troubled her. He assured her that she would like Quebec, their ultimate destination, and that she could always find work with her typing and millinery skills.

It was later believed that Crippen had planned to fake a suicide attempt, leaving a note and hiding out with a bribed ship's quartermaster who would later smuggle him ashore. In his memoirs, Dew stated that he believed Crippen honestly meant to kill himself before the ship docked, by that time believing that he was identified and would be captured. He did not want his fate to befall the woman he loved. Most British criminolgists at that time, and even the celebrated detective writer Raymond Chandler in later years, agreed that Crippen could have escaped had he not brought along his lover, Ethel LeNeve. It was her easily detected disguise which gave him away. But love ruled the passions of Crippen, and for this reason he became one of Britian's most memorable murderers. He would not give up the woman he loved to escape the hangman.

In the early hours of July 31, 1910, a Sunday, with the *Montrose* off Father Point, Inspector Dew, along with members of the Quebec Police Department, boarded the vessel from a small tugboat. Still in disguise, wearing a pea jacket and the visored cap of the pilot service, Inspector Dew and the other officers went straight to the bridge where Captain Kendall met them. Kendall pointed out a small man in a frock coat who was emerging from behind a funnel on deck. Dew went to the man, followed by the Quebec officers and Kendall. As Dew was later to write: "Presently only a few feet separated us. A pair of bulgy eyes were raised to mine. I would have recognized them anywhere." Then, in a statement certainly equal to the "Doctor Livingston, I presume" salutation of H.M. Stanley, Dew said to the fugitive: "Good morning, Dr. Crippen. I am Chief Inspector Dew of Scotland Yard. I believe you know me."

Crippen blinked his large eyes up at the tall Inspector Dew. His adam's apple worked up and down and then he replied in a low voice: "Good morning, Mr. Dew."

The chief inspector informed Crippen that he was being arrested for the murder of his wife and the doctor was taken to the stairs leading to the decks and cabins below. Crippen suddenly turned and said to Chief Constable McCarthy of the Quebec Police: "Do you have a warrant? What is the charge?"

McCarthy produced the warrant and Crippen grabbed this out of the constable's hand, reading for himself: "Murder and mutilation! Oh, God!" Crippen threw the warrant to the deck and he was moved into a cabin under arrest. Some minutes later, passengers heard Ethel LeNeve shriek as Inspector Dew burst into her cabin and he placed her under arrest. With the fugitives safely under guard, Kendall, by prearranged signal, ordered a crewman to give three blasts on the *Montrose's* siren.

The tugboat *Eureka,* which had been waiting off some distance, then came alongside and swarms of reporters poured from the tugboat onto the *Montrose,* running wildly about the deck, molesting passengers who spoke no English, to see if they might be Crippen and Ethel LeNeve. Mayhem ruled the decks of the *Montrose* as Captain Kendall gave quick interviews to dozens of reporters who jammed their scribbled stories into bottles and frantically threw these overboard to be picked up by little boats waiting to take these "scoops" to the Quebec newspapers. The *Montrose* then leisurely made its way up the St. Lawrence River to Quebec where Crippen and Ethel were taken ashore and locked up. The historic chase was over. Crippen and Ethel sailed back to England under guard, and his trial took place at the Old Bailey on Oct. 18, 1910. From the beginning, Crippen's only thought was to protect Ethel. He insisted that she had nothing to do with the killing of his wife. Crippen alone was convicted after a four-day trial, and sentenced to death.

Crippen awaited the hangman in Pentonville Prison where he pleaded with authorities to spare his lover who was being tried at the time as an accessory after the fact. One of Crippen's imploring letters to authorities read: "In this farewell letter to the world, as I face eternity, I say that Ethel LeNeve has loved me as few women love men, and that her innocence of any crime, save that of yielding to the dictates of her heart, is absolute. My last prayer will be that God will protect her and keep her safe from harm and allow her to join me in eternity." A few days later, Ethel was found Not Guilty which allowed Crippen to go to his death with some satisfaction. His last request, before being hanged on Nov. 23, 1910, was that a photo of Ethel LeNeve be placed in his coffin. This was done.

At the hour of Crippen's execution, Ethel LeNeve boarded the White Star liner, *Majestic*, which was sailing for New York. She was dressed in black and a heavy black veil covered her face. Using the alias "Miss Allen," Ethel sailed to a new life and oblivion in America. Captain Kendall later went on to become the skipper of the *Empress of Ireland* which was rammed and sunk by the collier *Storstad* on May 29, 1914, while the two ships were trying to navigate the St. Lawrence in a dense fog. The *Empress of Ireland* suffered the loss of 1,024 passengers and Kendall, once the hero of the Crippen chase, was digraced by the disaster.

The fate of the Crippen residence, 39 Hildrop Crescent, was worse. Following Crippen's hanging, the owner tried repeatedly to rent or sell the property, but no one wanted to live in a house everyone said was haunted. An entrepreneur named Sandy McNab then purchased the property. First he tried to run the place as a boarding house for elderly musical hall entertainers, but none cared to live in the place. Next, McNab turned the place into a Crippen museum of sorts, displaying press clippings of the murder and the chase, along with clothing and family artifacts. Only handfuls of the curious paid to see the place, and soon the house was again empty, except for, of course, the ghost of Belle Elmore, according to local residents who swore for years that they heard her piercing screams from the basement. Gone to ruin, the boarded up house remained empty until WWII when well-placed Luftwaffe bombs hit it squarely and demolished the landmark of murder.

REF.: Alverston, *Bar and Bench;* Birkenhead, *Famous Trials of History;* ____, *Frederick Edwin, Earl of Birkenhead;* Bishop, *From Information Received;* Block, *Science Vs. Crime;* Boar, *The World's Most Infamous Murders;* Bowen-Rowlands, *In the Light of the Law;* Bowker, *Behind the Bar;* ____, *A Lifetime with the Law;* Brock, *A Casebook of Crime;* Brophy, *The Menaing of Murder;* Brown, *Sir Travers Humphreys;* Browne and Tullett, *The Scalpel of Scotland Yard, The Life of Sir Bernard Spilsbury;* ____, *Sir Bernard Spilsbury: His Life and Cases;* Camps, *The Investigation of Murder; CBA;* Chandler, *Raymond Chandler Speaking;* Clarkson, *Red Plush and Greasepaint;* Constantine-Quinn, *Dr. Crippen;* Corder, *Murder My Love;* Cullen, *The Mild Murderer, The True Story of the Dr. Crippen Case;* Cuthbert, *Science and the Detection of Crime;* Dearden, *Some Cases of Sir Bernard Spilsbury and Others;* Dew, *I Caught Crippen;* Dewes, *Doctors of Murder;* Easton, *Famous Poison Trials;* Ellis, *Black Fame;* ____, *Blackmailers & Company;* Felstead, *Sir Richard Muir;* Furneaux, *The Medical Murderer;* Gilbert, *Dr. Crippen;* Glaister, *The Power of Poison;* Gribble, *Adventures in Murder;* Gross, *Masterpieces of Murder;* Haines, *Bothersome Bodies;* Hardwick, *Doctors on Trial;* Hastings, *The Other Churchill;* Hicks, *Not Guilty, M'Lord;* Humphreys, *A Book of Trials;* ____, *Criminal Days;* Hynd, *Sleuths, Slayers and Swindlers;* Irving, *The Trial of the Wainwrights;* Kingston, *Dramatic Days at the Old Bailey;* Kobler, *Some Like It Gory;* Lane, *Edgar Wallace, The Biography of a Phenomenon;* Laurence, *A History of Capital Punishment;* LeNeve, *Ethel LeNeve, Her Life Story;* Lustgarten, *A Century of Murderers;* ____, *Verdicts in Dispute;* Macnaghten, *Days of My Years;* Marjoribanks, *For the Defense, The Life of Sir Edward Marshall Hall;* Morland, *Hangman's Clutch;* Nash, *Almanac of World Crime;* ____, *Among the Missing; Notable British Trials;* Oddie, *Inquest;* Parry, *Some Famous Medical Trials;* Pearson, *Murder at Smutty Nose;* Randall, *The Famous Cases of Sir Bernard Spilsbury;* Rose, *Red Plush and Greasepaint;* Rowland, *Poisoner in the Dock;* Scott, *The Concise Encyclopedia of Crime and Criminals;* Shew, *A Companion to Murder;* Shore, *Crime and Its Detection;* Speer, *The Secret History of Great Crimes;* Thompson, *Poisons and Poisoners;* Thomson, *The Story of Scotland Yard;* Thorwald, *The Century of the Detective;* ____, *Dead Men Tell Tales;* Townsend, *Black Cap: Murder Will Out;* Tullett, *Strictly Murder;* Van Druten, *The Widening Circle;* Wallace, *A Short Biography;* Warner-Hooke and Thomas, *Marshall Hall;* Whitelaw, *Corpus Delicti;* Wilson, *Encyclopedia of Murder;* Woodhall, *Secrets of Scotland Yard;* Young, *The Trial of Hawley Harvey Crippen;* (FICTION),

Meadows, *Dr. Moon;* Ronald, *This Way Out;* (FILM), *The Suspect,* 1944.

Cripple Creek Explosion, 1903, U.S., bomb.-sab. On Nov. 21, 1903, the superintendent of the Vindicator Silver Mine in Cripple Creek, Colo., was killed along with an assistant during a routine check of one of the shafts on the sixth level. The bomb blast had been triggered by a single gunshot that was fired into sticks of dynamite at the precise moment Charles McCormick gripped the hand railing. The dynamite and the railing were both connected to the detonating device, a revolver. For three months there had been trouble at the Cripple Creek mines with the National Guard called in to preserve order during a general strike. The sabotage of the Vindicator Mine, one of the first incidents of industrial sabotage in the U.S., was attributed to militant union men. REF.: *CBA.*

Cripps, Charles Alfred (First Baron Parmoor), 1852-1941, Brit., lawyer. Member of Parliament from 1895-1914. REF.: *CBA.*

Cripps, Sir **Richard Stafford**, 1889-1952, Brit., lawyer. Son of Charles Cripps. He was King's counsel in 1927, and solicitor general from 1930-31. REF.: *CBA.*

Crisp, Charles Frederick, 1845-96, U.S., lawyer. Speaker of the U.S. House of Representatives from 1891-95. REF.: *CBA.*

Crispi, Charles, prom. 1910, U.S., burg. In 1907 the British police used the technique of fingerprinting for the first time in a criminal trial. By 1910, the first American criminal was convicted as a result of using the technique.

When fingerprinting was first introduced in legal cases by the British, Manhattan's French-born Lieutenant Faurot, later to be named chief inspector, fingerprinted Charles Crispi, a thief. Three years later, the only clue left behind in a Broadway loft burglary, was a fingerprint found on the doorknob. When Faurot matched these marks with Crispi's prints, the thief was convicted and sent to Sing Sing Prison, becoming the first criminal in the U.S. to be sentenced on such evidence. Although Crispi wore fawn-colored gloves after his release, he was nonetheless arrested nineteen more times and sent to prison five more times.

REF.: *CBA;* Kobler, *Some Like It Gory.*

Crispus, Flavius Julius, d.326 A.D., Roman., treas. Appointed ruler of Gaul by his father, Constantine the Great, in 317 A.D. He later was executed by his father for high treason. REF.: *CBA.*

Crittenden, John Jordan, 1787-1863, U.S., lawyer. Appointed attorney general in 1841 but only served six months due to the unexpected death of President William Henry Harrison and political differences with his successor John Tyler. He was appointed attorney general a second time by President Millard Fillmore in 1850, serving until 1853. He authored the Crittenden Compromise of 1860, a measure designed to appease the South and placate the North on the eve of the Civil War. It was defeated in committee. REF.: *CBA.*

Crittenden, Thomas, prom. 1882, Case of, U.S., mur. A man from a prominent Kentucky family known as both a fighter and a hot-tempered youth, was indicted for willful murder and convicted of voluntary manslaughter. The case was appealed and the decision reversed when the judge ruled a minor detail of testimony as incompetent evidence.

Thomas Crittenden came from a prestigious Kentucky family, with members who had served as U.S. marshals, senators, congressmen, and governors. With every advantage of education, wealth, and position, Crittenden was known as a reckless man prone to fighting. While living with his father, U.S. Marshal R.H. Crittenden in Anchorage, Ky., Thomas Crittenden, drunk, went to the railroad station on Dec. 8, 1882, and got into a fight with Philip Young, a black porter, slapping him across the face and striking him several times with his fists.

On Dec. 9 a warrant against Crittenden was issued and the trial took place on Dec. 13. The key witness, Rose Mosby, a young black man who worked as a dining room servant at the Crittenden's home gave testimony that helped find Crittenden guilty of assault, with a ruling of a one-cent fine and court costs. On his way out of the courtroom Crittenden told Mosby he would "see you later about this."

That evening Mosby and a friend, William Butler returned to their place of work and the cook warned Mosby to leave, for Crittenden had been around three times looking for him. Butler and Mosby walked to the railroad station. Crittenden came shortly after and asked Mosby, "Aren't you going up to the house and clean up the dishes?" When Mosby replied: "No, I don't think I'll go back there any more," Crittenden left only to return with a double-barreled shotgun. Calling Mosby a name and saying he had lied in court, Crittenden shot him twice, killing the youth instantly, then chased briefly after Butler, as he fled.

At the inquest it was decided that Mosby died of wounds inflicted by Crittenden, who caused them with malice aforethought, and the marshal's son was jailed without bail. In January 1883 he was indicted for willful murder and tried on that charge in April. A hung jury ended in Crittenden's release on a $2,000 bail. In February 1884 the case was tried a second time, with Asher G. Caruth as the prosecuting attorney while the attorneys defending Crittenden included Judge P.B. Muir, Isaac Caldwell, Major W.R. Kinney, and Marc Mundy. Brumbley Crittenden testified that Mosby had a large rock in his hand, but other witnesses said they saw no rock on the platform or in Mosby's hand before or after he fell, and that no rock was found anywhere on the platform. The defense presented the theory that several young black men, members of a secret order, were at the depot to assist Mosby who planned to assault Crittenden, and that the dining-room servant had been shot when he lifted a large rock to throw at his employer's son. The jury found the defendant Guilty of voluntary manslaughter and Crittenden was sentenced to eight years' imprisonment.

The case was then sent to the court of appeals where Judge W.L. Jackson reversed the judgment, citing incompetent evidence, in that the cook who had warned Mosby to stay away had said at first, "I did not think he would be killed, I did not know," and then later responded to a similar question about whether she had told someone else that Mosby might be killed, "I don't know whether I told Henry that or not." The court judged this testimony to be illegal because it showed that the witness had stated, out of court, facts which she failed to prove while in court, thereby transforming hearsay testimony into substantive evidence.

The case then moved to Spencer County where prosecuting attorney Judge James Morris fought to convict Crittenden, but the jury acquitted the defendant. Soon after this final trial the Spencer County courthouse, with all the records of the case, burned down.

REF.: *CBA;* Johnson, *Famous Kentucky Tragedies and Trials.*

Croc, Raoul (AKA: **Gottlieb Rinhalter, Armande Geraud**), prom. 1828-38, Fr., mur. A crippled man who believed in the Malthusian Principle that advocated curtailing the world's population to prevent catastrophe, murdered at least forty-four persons in his distorted pursuit of decreasing humanity's numbers.

In 1828 in the province of Languedoc near the village of Puy St. O'Stein, a single pistol shot killed a popular local farmer, Jacques Moulin. The only witness was a dwarfish man with a wooden right leg who carried a book titled, *An Essay on the Principle of Population as it Affects the Future Improvement of Society,* by Thomas Robert Malthus.

When two local men discovered Moulin's body as they rode home from the market place, they asked the man if he had seen anything. Identifying himself as Armande Geraud, the man said he had heard a shot and saw Moulin die but had no idea where the bullet came from. A grand jury at the coroner's inquest accepted his statement and he was released, and with no suspect or murder weapon, the case was closed.

Three weeks later a similar murder occurred at an inn in Clermont, fifty miles from where the farmer had been slain. Again there was no weapon and Geraud again was at the scene, saying he had seen a man with a musket but could not run after him. Three days later, a silversmith fishing late at night died in the same way, with the same single witness. Police questioned

Geraud who bragged about his extensive military service, and he received corroboration and praise from Marshal Soult.

On Aug. 15, 1836, a British couple named Stuart was vacationing at the Rhenish town of Godesberg with their Prussian valet, Karl, and Jane Simpson, a maid. Simpson and the valet went for a midnight stroll but only the valet returned. Simpson was found under an apple tree, killed by a single pistol shot. Because a gun he owned matched the type of bullet found, the valet, protesting his innocence, was tried, convicted, and hanged for the murder.

Several months later a bullet struck Mrs. Stuart in the arm. The Stuart's dog ran off into the nearby woods and, when Mr. Stuart followed, he came across a short, one-legged man, who said his name was Gottlieb Rinhalter, explaining proudly that he had fought against Bonaparte in the war. A search proved that he carried no weapon was released by the local magistrate.

In Wittenberg in March 1838 three soldiers sat in a coffee house when a bullet felled one, Gustav Grimm. Rinhalter, the fourth man at the scene, and he explained that a shot had been fired through the window. Before he died, Grimm told detectives he had seen smoke coming out of Rinhalter's wooden leg. Searching the crippled man, they found a small derringer so deeply embedded in his stump that it could not be extricated without hacking the wood. Rinhalter gave his real name, Raoul Croc, and proudly explained how he had only to rest his leg on a chair or table and then discharge the device by means of a wire in his pocket fastened to the trigger.

Croc admitted that he had never been a soldier and had lost his leg after being bitten by a rabid dog as a child. He had killed forty-four people in his quest to reduce the population according to the principles of Malthus. His first victim had been an elderly soldier named Armande Geraud, from whom he had taken papers and his identity after bludgeoning him to death. His trial was a formality and he was kept under double guard as he awaited execution. Croc requested to share a last meal with a semi-imbecile dressmaker. As he was lashed to the chair to be executed by beheading in his cell, he aimed his leg at the dressmaker's heart. The shot missed, tearing open the cell door, wounding the executioner, and blowing Croc to pieces. The dressmaker later confessed she had supplied Croc with a pound of gunpowder and a new derringer, trying to help him end his life by committing suicide, which, in fact, and by accident, she had.

REF.: *CBA;* Kobler, *Some Like It Gory.*

Crocker, Kerry, prom. 1975, U.S., child abuse. A son who grew increasingly afraid of his divorced father found he had reason to be when discovered that the man had slowly and repeatedly poisoned him with radioactive materials, effectively castrating the boy.

Barbara and Kerry Crocker had met and married in 1955 in a small Louisiana town. The petroleum engineer and the full-time housewife raised two sons, Kirk and Patrick. The perfectionist, autocratic father made harsh demands on his family and often disappeared with no explanation.

After moving to a suburb of Houston, Texas, the Crockers divorced in 1970, remarried, and divorced again within six months, sharing custody rights of their children in a bitter, ongoing struggle. In the summer of 1970 10-year-old Kirk went water-skiing with his father for the first time, not wearing a life jacket. He started to drown as his father watched, motionless. Then the rope came loose and the boy floated to the surface. Kirk now believes his father threw the boat's anchor on the tow line. That was the first time the son feared his father.

One month later both boys were camping with Kerry Crocker, who insisted Kirk sleep alone in the front of the camper. Late that night an unexplained gas explosion blew out Kirk's end of the van, severely burning him. Kirk would not stay silent when his father copied the key to his ex-wife's apartment and used it to enter against her wishes; she filed burglary charges against Crocker. Though stubborn in his defiance, Kirk realized, "I was making him mad. You didn't want to make him mad."

In Fall 1971 Crocker began to visit Sidney Morrison, an oil-well logger, asking many detailed questions about radioactive sources used to drill holes for oil wells, such as, according to Morrison, "How dangerous it was. How long you had to be around it. How close. How would it hurt you...?" On Nov. 18, 1971, Crocker applied to the Texas State Department for a license for radioactive materials and was granted one.

On Christmas Day 1971 Barbara Crocker married Harry Smith, and Kerry Crocker purchased his first curie of Cesium 137, which arrived in a minute stainless steel jacket resembling a flat-nosed bullet. By March 1972, Crocker applied for permission to possess two curies and, on Aug. 2 had his license amended to allow him four units.

On Apr. 7, 1972, Kirk's father told him to use headphones while watching TV so he wouldn't disturb the neighbors. Kirk discovered a small steel cylinder in the earphones, took it out, and didn't use them, for which he was later berated by his father. Eight days later Barbara Smith noticed peculiar bruises on Kirk's inner thighs. Over the course of the next year, Kerry Crocker continued to give his son strange instructions, and to drug him with orange juice and Valium. Several times Kirk woke to see his father "fooling with something on the ground" or near him, sometimes arranging a sock—which he saw contained the same cylinders as the earphones—to place on his body, or a pillow his father told him to use. Kirk's hair began to fall out and the lesions on his body grew worse as his unexplained sicknesses continued. In October 1972 he dropped out of school. In March 1973 he was hospitalized and put on cortisone and pain killers and diagnosed with possible herpes and other viral infections by perplexed doctors. In 1973 he saw sixteen different physicians.

Just after Christmas in 1973, plastic surgeon Dr. Thomas Cronin, came to look at Kirk Crocker's crippled body and made an immediate diagnosis of necrotic ulcers caused by radiation. When Barbara Smith told Kerry Crocker that their son's condition was the result of radiation burns, he had "no response," walking up and down the hall for a minute and then silently leaving. Soon after, one of Kirk's testicles became abscessed and sloughed off because his body no longer produced testosterone, leaving Kirk functionally castrated. A letter of inquiry to the state revealed that Crocker was licensed to possess radioactive materials.

After a complicated trial, Crocker was found Guilty of castrating his son in May 1975 and sentenced to ten years in the Huntsville, Texas, state penitentiary. He jumped bail not long before his conviction was upheld in May 1978 in an appellate court. For two and a half years Crocker hid from the law, but he continued to stay in the oil business without changing his appearance, despite FBI posters out for his arrest. By the time of his capture in January 1981 in Farson, Wyo., living under the name Pat Grant, his son's radiation ulcers had healed. Kerry Crocker, called by prosecuting state's attorney Mike Hinton "the most evil man I have ever prosecuted," received an additional five years on Jan. 14 for his flight to avoid prison, and began serving his sentence at Huntsville. He never admitted his guilt.

Kirk Crocker underwent sixteen skin graft and plastic surgery operations and twenty-three surgical procedures in a five-year period, and is now married. He will require monthly testosterone injections for the rest of his life and has filed a million-dollar damage suit against his father. He lives with the fear of developing leukemia and cataracts as a result of radiation exposure, and is intensely ambitious, hoping to "get into a good financial position" so he will be "powerful enough so he [his father] can never escape my scrutiny. So I always know where he is. I'm not ever going to be put in the position of being the hunted one again." REF.: *CBA*.

Crocker, Myron Donovan, 1915- , U.S., jur. Employed as a special agent of the FBI from 1940-1946. Nominated to sit on the district court of California by President Dwight Eisenhower and reappointed in 1959. REF.: *CBA*.

Croft, William James, d.1943, Brit., mur. The accused said his girlfriend had killed herself and that he had tried, but failed, to take his own life. The jury said he was lying, but they gave him what he said he had wanted anyway: death.

It was against the backdrop of early winter in war-torn England, 1943, that a young soldier, William James Croft, claimed that he and his beloved, Joan Lewis, had decided to make a commitment. Theirs was to be a commitment to death. Each would sit beside the other in the summer home at Camborne, in Cornwall, sharing a revolver between them, until one of them decided to make the first move. "Don't let us do it in the News of the World way. We will each shoot ourself," Lewis supposedly said.

Lewis, Croft said, made the first move, putting the revolver to her heart and pulling the trigger. The blast wasn't enough to kill the girl so Croft was running for help, when, he said, he heard a second shot. He returned to find his girlfriend lying on the floor with a fatal bullet wound to her head. Croft said it was then that he tried to shoot himself in the temple, but the gun wouldn't fire.

Neither of Lewis' wounds could have been self-inflicted, pathologist Dr. Hocking testified. Croft was subsequently found Guilty of murder at the Winchester Assizes and was sentenced to die.

The jury didn't believe Croft's story, but in England at that time, the survivor of a suicide pact was guilty of a double crime. Even if the trial's outcome had been different, the sentence would have been the same. Croft was destined to die from the moment he said he wanted to die.

REF.: *CBA*; Hastings, *The Other Mr. Churchill*.

Crofton, Sir Walter Frederick, 1815-97, Ire., penologist. Commissioner of prisons in Ireland from 1853-54 and 1869, and in England from 1866-68. He pioneered what later came to be known as the Crofton system of prison administration. REF.: *CBA*.

Croker, Richard (AKA: Boss Croker), 1841-1922, Case of, U.S., mur. Born in Ireland, Croker migrated to the U.S. at an early age and settled in New York where, in 1862, he joined the Tammany organization and rose through the political ranks. When William Marcy Tweed, boss of Tammany, went to prison, Croker took over the reins of leadership (1886-1902). He retired in 1903 and returned to Ireland as a millionaire, and he lived like a country squire until his death in 1922. Croker was the absolute boss of New York City politics for almost two decades, a period marked by great corruption, particularly in the police department, where many officers were on the payrolls of gamblers and vice-mongers. Croker received a considerable share of the graft and kickbacks for allowing the gambling dens, bordellos, and other illegal rackets to flourish.

Croker's career almost came to a dead end in 1874 when he and two other men, lobbying at election time, confronted James O'Brien and Billy Borst on the corner of Thirty-Fourth Street and Second Avenue. At the time, O'Brien was running for Congress and Croker was backing the Tammany candidate, Abraham S. Hewitt. The two factions got into a heated

New York's Boss Richard Croker, who stood accused of murder in 1874.

argument with name-calling on both sides. Fists flew and shots were fired. John McKenna, thirty-one, an O'Brien supporter, was killed by gunfire and Croker was accused of firing the revolver that took McKenna's life. In a lengthy trial, Croker stood accused of murder with several witnesses coming forward to insist that Croker had fired the weapon that took McKenna's life. An equal number testified that Croker was not the guilty party. The jury could not agree and Croker was dismissed, never to be tried again for this murder, which remained unsolved.

REF.: Barker, *Henry George; CBA;* Connable and Silberfarb, *Tigers of Tammany;* Hodder, *A Fight for the City;* Lewis, *Richard Croker;* Parkhurst, *Our Fight with Tammany;* Croker, *Some Things Richard Croker Has Done and Said;* Steffens, *The Shame of the Cities;* Stoddard, *Master of Manhattan: The Life of Richard Croker;* Werner, *Tammany Hall;* (FICTION), Lewis, *The Boss and How He Came to Rule New York.*

Crokes, Willie, prom. 1860s, U.S., mur. During the Kentucky Hills feudings that took place during the Civil War, a man accused of murdering a guerrilla fighter was lynched while awaiting trial.

Bearcat Bede, a well-known Kentucky pioneer, was the father of Elijah Bede, who lived on Bear River. Of Elijah Bede's four sons, two were northern sympathizers while two favored the South. In guerrilla skirmishes in this area, Ron Bede was killed by a Confederate gang lead by Flash Troxwell in 1863. In June 1864, Union guerrillas under the leadership of Doug Beary killed Jeff Bede. It was believed that Preston Holt, one of Beary's men, had ambushed Bede in revenge for the murder of Holt's father during the war. Preston Holt was later killed in 1866 or 1867 in retaliation when he argued with Willie Crokes, Jeff Bede's brother-in-law.

Crokes disappeared soon after Holt's murder and eventually was tracked down to a Michigan logging camp. Arrested and returned to Jessetown, Ky., to be tried, Crokes was spending his first night in the Kentucky prison when a gang broke in, tied him up, and took him to a Bear River Valley mountaintop. There they tied him to a horse's tail and shot him dead as the horse raced down the mountain with his body. See: **Beary, Doug.**

REF.: *CBA;* Montell, *Killings.*

Crome, Karl, 1859-1931, Ger., jur. REF.: *CBA.*

Cromwell, Oliver (AKA: Old Noll), 1599-1658, Brit., mur. Champion of the Puritan and Parliamentarian causes in England, Oliver Cromwell became a member of Parliament in 1628 and he fought as a cavalry captain at the outbreak of the Civil War in 1642, leading the deciding cavalry charge at Marston Moor in 1644. In the second part of the Civil War, Cromwell was victorious over usurping Scottish legions at Preston in 1648. With his roundheads he fought for Parliamentary independence against the Presbyterian aristocracy and generals backing Charles I. It was largely due to Cromwell's arguments and insistence that Charles I (Stuart) was stripped of powers and eventually executed in 1649. Though Cromwell brought many reforms to England and was considered a liberator, he was branded a regicide upon the restoration of the Stuarts and his body was exhumed, along with that of John Bradshaw, who had been president of the High Court of Justice that had condemned Charles, and Henry Ireton, Cromwell's son-in-law. These gruesome remains were publicly hanged and then gibbeted in 1661. The remains were then thrown into a ditch reserved for common felons. See: **Charles I.**

REF.: Ashley, *The Greatness of Oliver Cromwell;* Blauvelt, *Oliver Cromwell, A Dictator's Tragedy; CBA;* Firth, *Oliver Cromwell and the Rule of the Puritans in England;* Fraser, *Cromwell, The Lord Protector;* Harrison, *Cromwell;* Hill, *God's Englishman: Oliver Cromwell and the English Revolution;* Paul, *The Lord Protector; Religion and Politics in the Life of Oliver Cromwell;* Roosevelt, *Oliver Cromwell;* Simpson, *Puritanism in Old and New England;* Waylen, *The House of Cromwell;* Wedgewood, *The Trial of Charles I.*

Cromwell, Thomas (Earl of Essex), c.1485-1540, Brit., treas. Served as legal adviser to Cardinal Thomas Wolsey, but attempted to convert the Church of England to Protestantism as a means of advancing the monarchy of Henry VII. He lost the support of the king in 1539 by negotiating an unsuccessful marriage with Anne of Cleves. For this he was condemned as a traitor by the Duke of Norfolk, attainted by Parliament, and put to death. REF.: *CBA.*

Cronin, Patrick Henry, 1846-89, U.S., assass. Dr. Patrick Cronin, an esteemed Chicago physician vanished from his office on May 4, 1889, after driving off to answer a distress call at an ice factory belonging to Patrick O'Sullivan, a powerful rival in the Irish Nationalist Movement known as the Clan-Na-Gael. Nineteen days later Dr. Cronin—or what was left of him—was found stuffed in a drainage ditch north of Chicago in what was then suburban Lakeview.

The assassination of Patrick Cronin was carried out by Alexander Sullivan and other disgruntled members of the Clan-Na-Gael who believed that the doctor had betrayed their secrets to British agents. A number of clan operatives, sent to London to bomb government installations in the name of Irish freedom, had been arrested in Liverpool as they stepped off the boat. The Cronin faction had accused the Sullivanites of misappropriating funds, and in retaliation the doctor was falsely labeled a traitor to the cause.

Six indictments were returned against Clan-Na-Gael leaders who had plotted the assassination of Cronin. During the first trial, it was shown that certain Chicago Policemen working out of the East Chicago Avenue Station secretly belonged to the clan and had aided and abetted a cover-up. The conspiracy was far-flung, and only five men actually served time. In 1894 the sole surviving member who was still in prison—a Chicago police officer—received a new trial and was subsequently acquitted. See: **Clan-na-Gael.**

REF.: *Assassination of Dr. P. H. Cronin;* Bailie, *The Cronin Case; CBA; Dr. Cronin's Murder; The Great Cronin Mystery;* Hunt, *The Crime of the Century, The Assassination of Dr. Patrick Henry Cronin;* McEnnis, *The Clan-na-Gael and the Murder of Dr. Cronin.*

Crook, Japhet (AKA: Sir Peter Stranger), c.1731, Brit., forg.-fraud. Today he would get off with a steep fine and short jail term. In eighteenth-century England, because the people liked him and the court was lenient, Japhet Crook got off with public torture and life in prison.

Crook lived a life of crime. Posing as Sir Peter Stranger, he quite handily forged deeds of conveyance to swindle a couple out of 200 acres of prime Clacton-on-Sea land. The court sentenced Crook to stand in a pillory for one hour, after which hangman Jack Hooper would slice off both his ears "close to his head," then slit his nostrils and sear them with a hot iron. Crook would then forfeit all his property and live out the rest of his days in prison.

Crook used the pillory punishment as an opportunity to make new friends. He stood at Charing Cross and joked with the crowds that gathered. The villagers, who already regarded the convicted deed-forger as some kind of hero, were most impressed with his bravery. No stones, no rotten eggs, not even harsh words were thrown Crook's way. The accused man stood stolidly while his ears were removed and his nostrils slit. It wasn't until the burning iron was brought near him that Crook displayed normal human fear. At the first touch of the red-hot iron to his nostrils, he sprang from his chair with a yelp. Because Crook had proved himself brave throughout most of his punishing ordeal, authorities ended the torture and allowed the condemned man one final indulgence at the nearby Ship Tavern. Bloodied from his legal mutilation and drunk from the drinks bought him by his newly made fans, Crook stumbled into his life-long prison term, never to be seen or heard from again.

REF.: Bleackley, *Hangmen of England; CBA;* Potter, *The Art of Hanging.*

Croom-Johnson, Sir Reginald Powell, 1879-1957, Brit., jur. Judge of the Queen's Bench, Division of the High Court from 1938-54. Before receiving his appointment to the bench Sir Reginald prosecuted the cases of murderers Reginal Hinks, Alma Rattenbury, and George Percy Stoner. As a judge he presided over the murder trials of Marian Grondkowski and Henry Malinowski. REF.: *CBA.*

Crosby, Henry Grew (Harry), 1898-1929, U.S., suic.-mur. Following WWI, wealthy Americans, many of them young and purposeless, went to Europe, specifically Paris, where they embraced the expatriate life. It was a manner of living wherein that which was labelled as vice-ridden at home was an expression of art in Europe. One of the leaders of these youthful effete, dilettantes was a young man who lived only to dwell upon self, Harry Crosby. He was a sensualist and a part-time poet, a publisher for the sake of literary image and excuse for excesses, one who made a career of glorious disillusionment, and one whose fatalism was his only confidence. He was the saint of sophisticated sin, this heir to one of America's great fortunes. He was Harry Grew Crosby, nephew and godson of billionaire J. Pierpont Morgan, and his premature death would be marked by murder.

Crosby, born into great wealth on June 4, 1898, in Boston's Back Bay, could boast of a lineage (though he expressed hatred for all that was ancestral in America) that ran to the marrow of the founding fathers. He was related to Alexander Hamilton, William Floyd, and other luminaries of the American Revolution. Riches had flowed into the Crosby coffers since the early seventeenth century when another relative, General Stephen Van Rensselaer, established a fiefdom on his land (through a Dutch grant) that ran for twenty lucrative miles along the Hudson River.

Harry's father, Stephen Van Rensselaer Crosby, a pillar of Harvard and Back Bay society, was the eternal club man who became a partner in the banking investment firm of F.S. Mosely. Harry's family ties knotted tightly about the vast fortunes of the richest man in America, if not the world at that time, J. Pierpont Morgan. It was as natural as sunrise that Harry would attend the exclusive St. Mark's preparatory school and then go on to Harvard. WWI interrupted the schedule with Harry sailing to France to become an ambulance driver just after taking his entrance examinations to Harvard in 1917.

For Crosby and his schoolmates, the war in Europe was high adventure—not much more, at the beginning, than a tour similar to those European junkets taken by offspring of the rich before entering college. The difference became sharply apparent when the youthful Crosby encountered horrible, mutilating death. The shock of recognition changed his life forever, especially after his close friends, Oliver Ames, Jr., Richard Fairchild, and Aaron Davis Weld, were killed in battle.

Worse still, on Nov. 22, 1917, the 19-year-old Harry Crosby was hemmed in by a barrage as he attempted to rush his ambulance to a field hospital near Verdun with a friend bleeding to death inside. It was a brutalizing incident he was never to forget, writing ten years later in his diary (absent of almost all punctuation, a writing quirk): "The hills of Verdun and the red sun setting back of the hills and the charred skeletons of trees and the river Meuse and the black shells spouting up in columns along the road to Bras and the thunder of the barrage and the wounded and the ride through red explosions and the violent metamorphose from boy into man."

Crosby's abrupt loss of innocence was replaced by anger and resentment. He blamed God for the war and, in justifying his own slim survival, he concluded that there was a bit of the Superman about him; that he had been forged into a special human being who was, by birth and station, already special in his own mind.

He returned home with a chestful of medals, including the Croix de Guerre, which he coveted and likened to achieving an "H" grade in college. Crosby impatient to get out of the service at war's end, begged his parents to prevail upon his omnipotent uncle, J. Pierpont Morgan, to "try and get me a discharge," according to Crosby's War Letters. "Anything can be done by means of graft." Whether or not Crosby meant for Morgan to use his considerable influence or merely buy off authorities to get him released early is not known. But there certainly was a venal streak in Crosby, among myriad eccentricities and vices, all of which, in his short life, he would tax to exhaustion.

When he was mustered out, Crosby arrived in New York and immediately went to the Morgan mansion where, in the absence of his uncle, he ordered a feast which he devoured alone while servants did his bidding. (He called them "lackeys" and "menials.") Then he began to down goblet after goblet of ancient, priceless wine until he was drunk. In that state, he later arrived by train in Boston, staggering into the arms of his waiting family.

Harry's intoxication did not alarm Mr. and Mrs. Crosby; he was their only son and his ordeal in France was excuse enough for his unpredictable behavior. Crosby was quick to take up the same rationale, using his war experience for the rest of his short life as an excuse to wallow in the libertine life.

At first Crosby seemed to adjust, entering Harvard where his grades were less than spectacular. He studied literature and language, excelling in French in which, by virtue of his war experience, he was fluent. Crosby, like many other veterans of that day, was allowed to earn a "War Degree" at Harvard, which granted a shorter time of study in achieving a degree as compensation for serving overseas. He graduated in 1921.

A year earlier, Crosby had met and fallen in love with a married woman; he was to develop a habit—approaching mania—of trysting with married women for the rest of his days. The buxom, attractive female, six years older than Crosby, was Mrs. Richard Rogers Peabody (maiden name Mary Phelps Jacob), whom everybody called Polly. They met at a beach outing and both were smitten. Crosby told his parents that he intended to marry Polly, no matter what the consequences.

The Crosbys recoiled in shock. Polly would have to divorce her husband, another scion of a Back Bay fortune, to marry their son, and divorce, at that time, was inconceivable. Yet Harry persisted, telling his father that he would kill himself if he failed to have Polly as his bride. Polly reciprocated Harry's dedication. Her husband, the youthful Mr. Peabody, was a gentleman about it all. He told his wife to think it over during a trial separation. Polly did exactly that, going to New York with Crosby. At the end of six months, she still asked for a divorce and Peabody, who had taken to heavy drinking (he would later write about his alcoholism in The Common Sense of Drinking), agreed to let his wife go.

Harry and Polly married seven months after she received her divorce. Before that time, Crosby took to drink. He had accepted a desk job, arranged by his father, in the Shawmut National Bank in Boston, and hated it. He told his parents that he found Boston stifling, that the environment strangled his will to write great works. He promptly went on a six-day binge and quit his job. Next he begged uncle Jack (Morgan) to get him a job in Paris, something that would allow him and Polly to live in the "City of Light" where he could follow his artistic urges. Morgan arranged for Crosby to work in the Paris offices of Morgan, Harjes & Co. Delighted, Harry asked Polly to marry him and they were wed on Sept. 9, 1922, in New York City. Two days later, they sailed to France on the Aquitania. It was all idyllic, a fantasy come true; but then again, Harry Crosby had been born into fantasy and he always got what he wanted.

After living in expensive Paris hotels and running up staggering bills paid for by Crosby's relatives, Harry and Polly took a series of apartments, finally renting the huge flat once occupied by Princess Marthe Bibesco in St. Germain. For a year, Crosby halfheartedly worked at his uncle's banking concern, but he spent more time during each workday strolling the boulevards, drinking in bistros, and chasing women, than he did in his office.

Another rich relative, an older cousin, Walter Van Rensselaer Berry, who had been living in European luxury for more than a decade, learned of Harry's writing ambitions and suggested that he quit his job with Morgan. Crosby, using his older cousin as a sanction of the literary life, quit, and wrote his parents that he was, from that point on, dedicating his life to the muse, so would they please sell off a few thousand shares of the great amount of stock he held and forward spending money? They did—they always did.

By 1923, the Crosbys set the style of the young rich expatriates in Paris, or, at least, the mode of morality, a sort of glossy, intellectual hedonism. Harry was an artist and his temperament demanded that he seek release with women other than his wife. Among the many affairs he openly conducted was a torrid interlude with Constance Coolidge who was the niece of Frank Crowinshield, editor of *Vanity Fair*. The darkly attractive and willful Constance, divorced from diplomat Ray Atherton, had once been the scandal of China where here husband had been stationed. There she had raced horses and carried on in such a manner as to earn herself the sobriquet of "The Queen of Peking." Crosby, who met her at a racetrack in Paris, called her "The Lady of the Golden Horse." He was forever dubbing his mistresses with romantic names—Helen of Troy, The Tigress, The Lady of the White Polo Coat, The Sorceress, Nubile, The Youngest Princess, The Fire Princess. These were the names he used in his diaries in referring to his many sexual escapades.

Polly, whose name the Crosbys later changed to Caresse for alliterative, arcane reasons, seemed not to care about her husband's sexual adventures. She knew these "other" women well; they were social acquaintances and many of these ladies were introduced to her womanizing husband by none other than herself.

Yet Harry was inexplicably loyal to Caresse. Constance Coolidge insisted Harry leave Caresse for her. When he refused, she went off to marry the Comte de Jumilhac, thereby becoming a rich and landed countess. Harry continued to see her periodically, considering her part of his stable.

There were others, many of them, including petite, dark Polia Chentoff, a Russian painter who excited the Crosbys with her weird, bizarre tales of famine in Russia. On one occasion, she said that the people in her village were so hungry that they ate an American missionary who had brought them a little food.

While Harry's harem increased in numbers, Caresse was not idle. She, too, took on a series of lovers, boldly mentioned by Crosby in a letter to his over-indulgent mother. "Caresse's boy friends are," wrote Crosby casually, "the Comte Civry, the Tartar Prince, Ortiz, Frans de Geetere (the husband of a couple who had been living on a barge docked on the Seine), Lord Lymington..."

As early as 1923, Crosby had gotten the reputation of a crazy millionaire American who gave vent to any sensual urge and wrote poetry on the side. One of Harry's passions was attending the raucous Four Arts Balls which heralded the closing of the art academies in Paris each summer. These were nothing more than costume orgies into which Crosby hurled himself with glee. In 1923, Crosby attended the ball wearing a Roman toga. He returned to his apartment stripped of this garment, his underpants, and all his money. Emerging completely drunk and stark naked, he staggered down the street and into his lodgings, to the amazement of his bug-eyed neighbors. Had this been the conduct of a resident Frenchman, the police would certainly have been summoned, but Crosby was too rich to arrest. Two years later, he found a monkey at the ball and got it drunk.

In 1926, Harry and Caresse shocked even the wild students attending the ball. Crosby went as an Incan chieftain, donning a loin cloth and coating his almost naked body with red ocher. Around his neck he wore a necklace of dead pigeons. Caresse matched Harry's abandon by appearing with a turquoise wig and was naked from the waist up, displaying her large breasts to hundreds of hooting students. (Caresse Crosby consistently complained that no female undergarments served as a proper halter for her mammae and, so she later claimed, she invented the brassiere.) The ball culminated with Caresse, breasts flopping wildly, being carried about the ballroom in the mouth of a papier-mâché dragon made up of dozens of students.

These balls were held in enormous halls, where as many as three to five thousand people jammed inside. Half of the guests were whores plying their trade. The police looked the other way on these occasions, tolerating any and all excesses, except assault and battery. It was not an uncommon sight, following the closing of the ball, to see hundreds of naked men and women dancing in the streets and atop cabs, and scores more fornicating in doorways and near the hall.

Before the balls, the Crosbys invariable gave a party which became *the* pre-ball party. Hundreds flocked into their spacious apartment to guzzle their gin-laced punch and fall to the floor in amorous embrace. In 1927, Crosby threw a party that alarmed even his own sense of expansive tolerance. Males in attendance mobbed his maid and almost raped her. Ushering out most of the guests, Harry retired to the bathroom with Caresse and other close friends, and all stripped and sank into the hot water held by an enormous, specially built bathtub. Then Harry painted himself green, grabbed a bag of snakes, and headed for the ball, where he distributed the reptiles as necklaces to horrified guests.

When bored with Paris, Harry would suddenly hustle Caresse off to Athens or Africa to see the sights and sample the perversions. In 1925, Harry and Caresse traveled to Tunisia, where they both made love to an 11-year-old girl named Zara. In Constantinople, on a later trip, Harry scouted the city to find just the right kind of entertainment and one night took Caresse to an enormous whorehouse, where they paid exorbitant prices to watch couples fornicate.

In Egypt, they visited a huge brothel, one of Harry's favorite visiting spots; the Crosbys sank into utter sexual perversion, seeking out young girls with which to sleep. It was here that they (especially Harry) developed a great taste for opium and hashish, buying the drugs in great quantities. Crosby consumed so much opium on one occasion that he almost died from an overdose (he developed the habit of swallowing opium pills and mixing this with champagne).

The ancient land held a deep and morose fascination for the American millionaire. He collected strange artifacts from its crypts and tombs. On one occasion, he paid a large sum for three mummified hands of young girls, each having a blue ring on the forefinger. Another time he bought the skeleton of a young girl, which he pridefully hung in the library of his Paris apartment at 19 Rue de Lille. What cabalistic rites attended these purchases was never learned. Yet the mysteries of Egypt continued to hold Crosby in a trance throughout his short life.

His uncle, Walter Van Rensselaer Berry, had had an abiding interest in all things Egyptian, and his influence upon Harry to seek the answers to that land's mystical secrets was permanent. It was in Egypt that Harry Crosby became enamored with sun worship, following the ancient Egyptian rites to the sun god, Ra. He thought of the sun as God, and at every opportunity stripped naked and baked beneath its rays, absorbing its heat, its fire, until, toward the end of his life, the normally pale-skinned young man from Boston appeared to friends as a "red Indian."

Walter Berry further enriched Crosby's life when he died on Oct. 12, 1927, leaving to Harry most of his estate and his collection of rare books, almost eight thousand tomes. This behest infuriated author Edith Wharton, who expected not only Berry's fortune, or part of it, but also Berry's library of priceless volumes. (The two had been lovers and Berry, an aristocratic, knowledgeable intellectual, had served as Mrs. Wharton's mentor.) For weeks—after Harry supervised the cremation of his cousin and sneeringly greeted distinguished mourners at the funeral in Paris—Crosby and Wharton vied for the library. Crosby feared that Mrs. Wharton, who, under the Berry will could choose whatever books she wanted, would swallow the entire library. Harry thought of her as "a bad sort," and Mrs. Wharton, according to Geoffrey Wolf, writing in *Black Sun*, told a friend that "Walter's young cousin Crosby turns out to be a sort of half-crazy cad." In the end, Mrs. Wharton selected only a few books and Harry received the bulk of the library.

That he read any of these rare volumes is debatable. What he did do with many of the books would have caused Mrs. Wharton, had she known, to collapse with apoplexy. The Berry library caused the normally spacious Crosby apartment to overflow with books; they were everywhere—on the walls and piled high on the floors of many rooms, so that the Crosbys had to move about the place through narrow paths. Harry solved the problem by giving hundreds of books away to complete strangers, cab drivers, prostitutes, bartenders, those whose interest in ancient

THE ELEGANT PLAYBOY WORLD OF HARRY CROSBY, 1920S ILIAD WHICH ENDED IN MURDER & SUICIDE

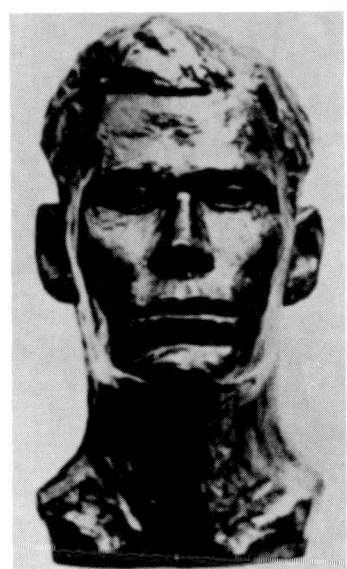

Harry Crosby in bronze.

Crosby, left, at his French estate with friends, Caresse on donkey.

Harry behind the wheel of his Bugatti, 1926.

Crosby with unidentified woman, Four Arts Ball, Paris, 1928.

Left to right, Caresse, Harry, and Crosby's sister, Kitsa, Deauville, France.

literature was considerably less than ravenous. Crosby then amused himself by donning disguises, a rag peddler, say, and slinking through the open-air book stalls lining the Seine where cheap books were sold. He would slip from a bag slung about his shoulders many of his cousin's priceless books and secretly bury them among the tawdry novels. It amused him to think that uneducated book buyers would casually pick up one of Berry's cherished volumes for a few francs, not knowing the book's true value, which would also be the case with the unschooled book dealers along the Seine.

Crosby's own literary aspirations were grossly inflated by himself, his wife, and his friends. He and Caresse started the Black Sun Press to publish their own awkward poetry and then expanded to include the most well-known writers of the day—Hemingway, Joyce, Pound, and others, but these writers merely tolerated the Crosbys, giving them fragmentary works that were expensively published and for which the authors received handsome pay. D. H. Lawrence, for instance, demanded that the millionaire playboy pay him for a short work in gold pieces, and Harry dutifully complied.

Literary figures Crosby admired repeatedly told him he was a talented poet. They should have known better, but perhaps they were merely stroking the golden goose. As a result of such boulevard flattery, Crosby began to submit his material to other publications, but not before he made substantial financial contributions to such struggling expatriate periodicals as *Transition*. In this fashion, Crosby's neurotic, erotic poetry found a wider audience than the Black Sun Press could provide. To the literary set, he quickly became known as a weird playboy poet whose work screamed out doom and death wish.

To Ernest Hemingway, Crosby was certainly nothing more than a rich social acquaintance who paid the way at the restaurant and racetrack during the author's lean years. It amused the author, once he learned of Crosby's fanatical sun-worshipping, to jibe him about it. From Cuba in 1929, Hemingway sent Harry a newspaper clipping that ridiculed sun-worshippers, but it did not daunt Crosby's belief in the ancient rite. By 1929, Harry Crosby had become hopelessly involved in himself. He lived only for pleasure. More and more, he escaped the real world to indulge in his fantasies, not unlike the time when he was on the way to a Paris bank to place Caresse's expensive jewelry in a safe deposit box. He spotted an attractive female relative, a distant cousin, and drank with her, attempting to seduce her. When Crosby departed the cafe, he left Caresse's jewels behind; they were never found. More and more, Harry sank into prolonged stupors from drugs and great quantities of absinthe (wormwood alcohol, banned even in Paris where the deadly drink had driven poet Paul Verlaine insane and killed others).

In 1928, Caresse and Harry moved into an old mill in the Ermenonville forest, near Paris, on the 9,000 acre estate of Armand de la Rochefoucauld, renting it by the year. Renovating the place to a posh spa-like quarters, the Crosbys invited phalanxes of artists, writers, and bon vivants to spend weeks with them, drinking and cavorting. Hart Crane, the distinguished poet published by Crosby, came to marvel at the luxury and flaunt his insatiable homosexuality—he seduced Crosby's chauffeur. (Crane would commit suicide in 1932 by jumping from a ship while returning from Mexico, swimming directly into the propellers.) Guests were encouraged to drink themselves blind night and day, and when not blind with booze, to amuse themselves in the gleaming, enormous pool (into which they consistently jumped fully-clothed), or participate in donkey races which Harry religiously conducted. Some of the guests stayed but briefly at Harry's wild retreat.

Writers Robert McAlmon and Kay Boyle, as recalled in *Being Geniuses Together,* left one of the wild parties late at night, going from the main building to the guest cottages after a riot erupted. "It's too damned depressing," McAlmon groaned to Boyle, "so depressing that I can't even get drunk. They're wraiths, all of them. They aren't people. God knows what they've done with their realities."

Reality had long run out on Harry Crosby. He shielded himself from it with money and the rays of the sun. Crosby was forever adorning his body with pagan symbols; in Africa he had crosses tattooed on the soles of his feet. In 1928, he paid a Hindu to tattoo a huge sun on his back in the dead of night as he lay face down in a boat wallowing on the Nile. It was also in 1928 that Harry Grew Crosby began planning his suicide and that of his wife. Caresse agreed with her husband to end their lives on Oct. 31, 1942, a date arrived at through crazy-quilt theories of Harry's own mad invention.

The year 1928 was momentous for Crosby. It was also in that year, on July 9, that he met at the Lido 21-year-old Josephine Noyes Rotch, a darkly attractive Boston socialite. He fell madly in love with her, calling her his "Fire Princess." For three weeks they carried on a torrid affair, but when Harry refused to leave Caresse for her, Miss Rotch sailed for the U.S. The following year, on June 21, she married Albert Bigelow, a wealthy member of a distinguished East Coast family.

Harry brooded over the loss of another mistress. His extravagances increased as did his erratic behavior. He leaped into a cab one night to drive down the Champs Elysee in Paris, hurling gold coins to startled passersby. He bought racehorses he never raced, and lost fortunes through reckless, stupid gambling, paying for his debts by selling off huge blocks of stock. (In 1929, Crosby wired his father: PLEASE SELL TEN THOUSAND DOLLARS WORTH OF STOCK. WE HAVE DECIDED TO LEAD A MAD AND EXTRAVAGANT LIFE. This wire came as no surprise; the Crosbys had led nothing but the life of wastrels to that time.)

Desperate to occupy his hours with something, anything, that would provide stimulation, Crosby suddenly became obsessed with flying. His mania led him to take many commercial flights between Paris and England (at a time when only a handful of passengers, at great expense, could cram aboard the small planes available, traveling at about 100 mph and at an altitude of no more than 1000 feet). Looking down from a plane on one flight, it occurred to Harry Crosby that it would "be fun to drop bombs" on the peaceful French countryside below.

Crosby took flying lessons and, in his gnawing vanity, saw himself as another Lindbergh, to whom he bore a striking resemblance. He saw himself as a hero, a pathfinder, but he never went beyond student status as a pilot. Next came fast racing cars. Crosby raced for weeks, but soon exhausted his zest for dirt tracks, sputtering engines and oil-smeared hands. For a while, the would-be literary giant decided to become the world's greatest photographer and purchased almost every known camera. He tired of this, too.

Caresse tolerated her husband's excesses and went her own way, becoming engrossed with the duties of a publisher at Black Sun Press. Harry thought only of Josephine, his fire princess, and corresponded with her. His thoughts also, more and more, turned to suicide, about which he wrote reams of poetry and talked incessantly. He had apparently little regard for his own poetry. Early in March 1929, while staying at the old mill, he dragged out eighty-some copies of his self-published book, *Red Skeletons,* and blew them to pieces with a shotgun. He then burned the remains.

On Nov. 18, 1929, Crosby received a wire from Mrs. Josephine Rotch Bigelow, urging him to come to her in America. Harry was at first reluctant to return to his native land. His last visit in 1928 produced in him a hatred for his hometown. In one poem, he called Boston a "City of Dead Semen." Worse, on that trip Harry had barraged Boston's literary bastion, *The Atlantic Monthly,* with more than fifty poems, all of which were rejected.

But Harry did return with Caresse. Keeping him company on the boat trip was an other old flame, Constance, the Comtesse de Jumilhac. After going to Boston, Harry met with Mrs. Bigelow on Nov. 28, 1929. Caresse went to New York and registered at the Savoy-Plaza Hotel on Nov. 25. Her husband showed up three days later but stayed only a week. Harry then took a train to

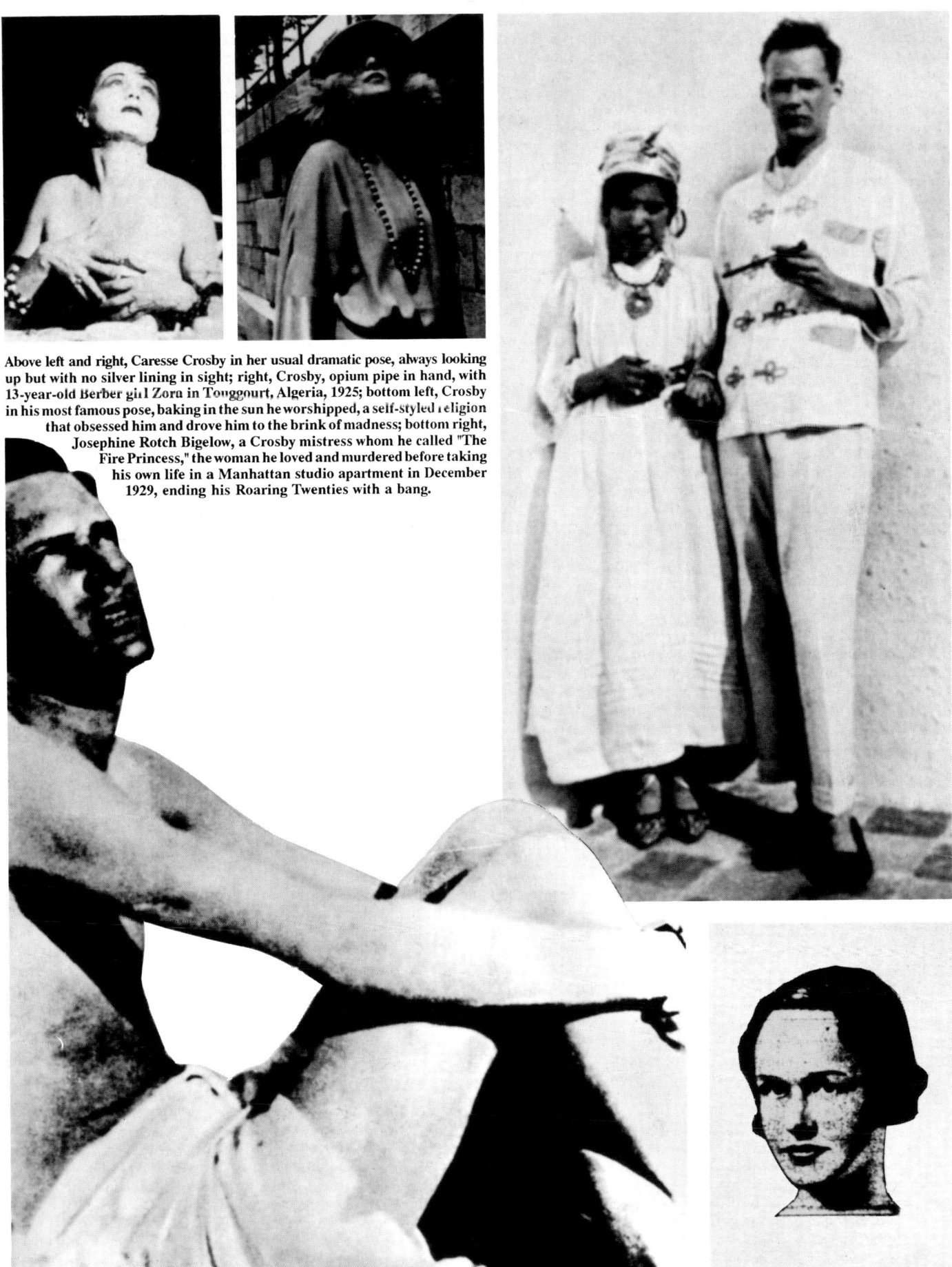

Above left and right, Caresse Crosby in her usual dramatic pose, always looking up but with no silver lining in sight; right, Crosby, opium pipe in hand, with 13-year-old Berber girl Zora in Touggourt, Algeria, 1925; bottom left, Crosby in his most famous pose, baking in the sun he worshipped, a self-styled religion that obsessed him and drove him to the brink of madness; bottom right, Josephine Rotch Bigelow, a Crosby mistress whom he called "The Fire Princess," the woman he loved and murdered before taking his own life in a Manhattan studio apartment in December 1929, ending his Roaring Twenties with a bang.

Detroit, where he had arranged to meet Mrs. Bigelow. He and Josephine registered under the name of Mr. and Mrs. Harry Crane, using the name of Crosby's poet friend, Hart Crane. The love tryst lasted for two days before both returned to New York and their spouses.

Crosby began drinking heavily in early December as he and his wife prepared to return to Paris. Hart Crane gave them a party, but Harry seemed disinterested, even when Crane let in a horde of drunken sailors whom he, Crane, attempted to seduce on the spot. Unknown to Caresse, her husband had broken more than his marriage vows; it was already settled in his mind that he would not live up to their suicide pact scheduled for 1942. He intended to end it in 1929 "with a bang, not a whimper," (Harry's convolution of T. S. Eliott's premise), and with another woman, the fire princess.

Dec. 10, 1929, was an auspicious day for the Crosbys. They were to dine in the august presence of J. Pierpont Morgan, Harry's uncle. That morning, Harry and Caresse attended an exhibition by a sculptor who had done a bronze of their dog, Narcisse Noir. Then Harry left his wife, kissing her and telling her he would see her and his mother at "uncle Jack's." From there, they would join Hart Crane for dinner and the theater.

Following a quick lunch, Crosby took a cab to 1 West 67th Street, getting out at Hotel des Artistes and going to the duplex studio occupied by his friend, Stanley Mortimer, a portrait painter. Here, he met Mrs. Josephine Bigelow. They had met several times at Mortimer's and the artist, an obliging friend, had given Harry a key to his ninth-floor abode. They arrived together at noon to be greeted by Mortimer. They had a few drinks and then Crosby led Josephine to an upstairs bedroom with an overhanging balcony. Mortimer continued painting, but the couple leaned over the balcony and "kidded me," according to Mortimer later. "Crosby gave me a signal and I got on my street clothes and went out."

While Crosby spent unknown hours in Mortimer's place with Mrs. Bigelow—described as a "strange wild girl who delighted in saying things to shock people" and who was extremely possessive of Harry—Crosby's wife and mother spent an uncomfortable tea-time with uncle Jack Morgan in the financier's behemoth mansion, trying to explain the absence of the errant Harry. Caresse and Mrs. Crosby finally left the Morgan house without waiting for Harry, returning to the Savoy, where they dressed for dinner. Still, Harry did not arrive. They went to the Caviar Restaurant and met Hart Crane. Halfway through the meal, Caresse later claimed, she had a terrible premonition, and left the table to phone Stanley Mortimer at his mother's house (this, of course, made it obvious that Caresse knew all along that her husband was not only meeting with Mrs. Bigelow, but was using Mortimer's apartment as a love nest). Mortimer told Caresse that he would go by his apartment and check on Harry.

The artist reached his studio at 9:30 p.m. and found it bolted from inside. He knocked and called, but no one answered. Desperately, he raced to the superintendent of the building and demanded that he break down the door. The man wielded an ax to batter down the door. Inside, Mortimer found Harry Grew Crosby and Josephine Rotch Bigelow—he was then thirty-one, she twenty-two—both dead on his bed. A bullet hole was in Josephine's left temple, another in Harry's right temple. Both were fully clothed, according to later newspaper reports. Their left hands were entwined and Harry's free arm was wrapped loosely about her neck, the right hand clutching a .25-caliber Belgian automatic pistol.

Police arrived to find more than $500 in cash stuffed in Harry's pockets, along with the steamship tickets which Harry and Caresse were to use on their return voyage to France. Crosby had removed a gold ring, one he called his "sun ring," which he had promised his wife he would never take off. It had been flattened, as if he had stomped on it.

Caresse learned of the suicide-murder, as it was later termed by police, late that night. She did not go to the scene of the crime, nor did the Crosbys utter a word of the disgrace their son had brought down upon the family name. It became practice for decades that none of the Crosby relatives ever mention the name of Harry Crosby again.

The bizarre end of Harry Crosby and his Bryn Mawr-trained mistress captured the nation's headlines. The Chicago *Tribune,* which bannered the deaths with the headlines, CROSBY DIED FOR A THRILL, stated that: "As a writer and publisher and a wealthy, amusing fellow besides, Crosby just about set the pace for the whole crowd of expatriates, who credit him with having 'lived more fully than any man of his generation.' None of his fast-moving crowd believe Crosby committed suicide for love, and are sure he sought death just to see what it was like..."

But for Josephine, according to Deputy Chief Medical Examiner Thomas Gonzalez of New York City, there was no such intention. Gonzalez, along with Inspector Mulrooney, stated that, from the position of the bodies and the varying states of rigor mortis, Crosby had murdered Josephine, then spent several hours alone in the apartment before killing himself. Gonzalez was quoted as saying that homicide was obvious, along with "the expression of smiling expectancy on the dead face of the beautiful young wife, indicating that she had gone to her rendezvous expecting a caress, not deadly bullets."

Albert Bigelow arrived in New York from Boston the following day, while his wife and Harry were taken to separate mortuaries to await burial. The outraged husband, a Harvard man, told a reporter from the *Daily News:* "This man lured her to his apartment and murdered her. I don't believe in any suicide pact no matter what the police or anybody else says, and I believe my wife to be the victim of a mad poet who turned murderer because he could not have the woman he wanted—and who was true to me."

Bigelow proved his loyalty to Josephine by having her remains buried in the family plot at Old Lyme, Conn. Harry's body was cremated two days later, and the remains were given to Caresse in an expensive urn which she took with her to Paris. (She would die on Jan. 24, 1970, still promoting Harry Crosby to the world as an offbeat, misunderstood rebel poet who simply happened to be rich.) Critic Malcolm Cowley further eulogized Crosby in his 1920s literary memoirs, *Exile's Return,* remarking about this supremely self-indulgent young man: "Harry Crosby, dead, had...become a symbol of change...In spite of himself he had died at the right time." It was Cowley's thought that the death of Harry Crosby signaled the close of the Roaring Twenties, the age of excess, only moments before a great night of depression and war blanketed the world.

Poet E.E. Cummings dealt with the murder-suicide as would a deadline-hounded newspaper editor, captioning the strange deaths with:

> 2 Boston
> Dolls found
> with
> Holes in each other
> 's lullaby

REF.: Beach, *Shakespeare and Company;* Beebe, *Boston and the Boston Legend;* Bell, *Edith Wharton and Henry James;* Boyle, *My Next Bride;* Callaghan, *That Summer in Paris;* CBA; Cowley, *Exile's Return;* Crawford, *Famous Families of Massachusetts;* Crosby, *The Passionate Years;* ____, *War Letters;* Farber, *The Theory of Suicide;* Glassco, *Memoirs of Montparnasse;* Hardwick, *Seduction and Betrayal;* Hemingway, *A Moveable Feast;* Hoffman, *The Twenties: American Writing in the Postwar Decade;* Horton, *Hart Crane: The Life of an American Poet;* Huddleston, *Bohemian Literary and Social Life in Paris: Salons, Cafes, Studios;* Josephson, *Life Among the Surrealists;* Kellogg, *The Two Lives of Edith Wharton: The Woman and Her Work;* Lawrence, *The Letters of D. H. Lawrence;* Lewis, *Edith Wharton, A Biography;* Lubbock, *Portrait of Edith Wharton;* McAlmon, *Being Geniuses Together;* Peabody, *The Common Sense of Drinking;* Powel, *New York, 1929;* Pritchett, *Midnight Oil;* Putnam, *Paris Was Our Mistress;* Rogers, *Ladies Bountiful;* Seaburg, *Boston Ob-*

served; Shattuck, *The Banquet Years: The Origins of the Avant-Garde in France: 1885 to World War I;* Stein, *Paris France;* Stengel, *Suicide and Attempted Suicide;* Tomkins, *Living Well Is the Best Revenge;* Unterecker, *Voyager: A Life of Hart Crane;* Weber, *The Letters of Hart Crane;* Wickes, *Americans in Paris;* Wilson, *The Twenties;* Wolff, *Black Sun.*

Cross, Edward, 1798-1887, U.S., jur. Attorney general of Arkansas at Little Rock in 1874. He received his first judicial appointment in 1830 to the Arkansas Territorial Court by President Andrew Jackson. REF.: *CBA.*

Cross, James, 1921- , Case of, Can., kid. If Canada followed to the letter its established policy concerning kidnappings, James Cross probably would have died. On Oct. 5, 1970, Canada experienced its first run-in with terrorist kidnappings. Cross, the 49-year-old British trade commissioner for Canada, was the first to be kidnapped, Pierre Laporte, Quebec minister of labor, was the first to be killed, and Prime Minister Pierre Trudeau and his colleagues were the first to make what turned out to be a life-saving, last-minute change of plans.

Front de Libération Quebec, a group that had long been threatening drastic action unless its separatist demands were met, openly claimed responsibility for Cross' kidnapping. Up until now, no one had taken the threats seriously. Faced with its first political kidnapping, Canada sought frantically for a solution. Meanwhile, the kidnappers waited for their demands to be met: more than twenty FLQ prisoners to be released from jail and flown out of Canada and more than £200,000 in gold to the kidnappers, or Mr. Cross would die.

Trudeau stood forthright, declaring, "You can't let a minority impose its view upon a majority by violence....It is a difficult decision when you have to weigh a man's life in the balance, but certainly our commitment to society is greater than anything else."

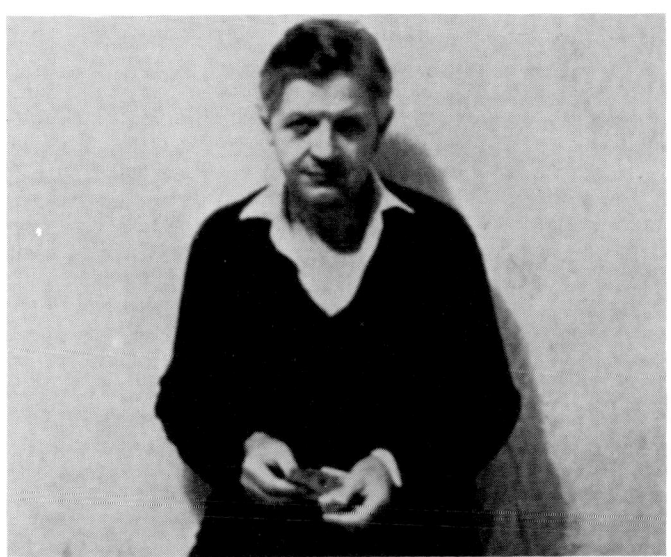

Canada's trade commissioner James Cross, photographed by his terrorist kidnappers, 1970.

And so Canada stood its ground, until the FLQ kidnapped Laporte, Quebec's minister of labor. Writing from captivity, Laporte urged his country to act quickly to avoid a "blood-bath and panic." Trudeau didn't know what else to do. On Oct. 15, the Canadian government offered to free five FLQ prisoners in exchange for the two men. On Oct. 17, Canada learned of its first political killing in more than 100 years. Laporte's body was found in the trunk of a car at St. Huberts airport. He had been shot and strangled.

Within two weeks, a deal was struck. The three kidnappers and four FLQ prisoners were flown to Cuba by orders of the Canadian government. In exchange Cross was released unharmed, Laporte was killed, and Canada was a little bit wiser.

REF.: *CBA;* Lustgarten, *Story of Crime;* Nash, *Almanac of Crime.*

Cross, Philip Henry, 1821-88, Ire., mur. Dr. Philip Cross, a retired army surgeon, lived with his wife, Laura Cross, at Shandy Hall, Dipsey, in County Cork. He led a quiet life with their four children, his sister Henrietta, and his wife. In June 1886 the family's tranquil life was disrupted when 20-year-old Mary Skinner was hired as governess to the Cross children.

Within weeks, Laura Cross began to suspect her husband of having an affair with the young woman, and dismissed her. Dr. Cross was unwilling to give up his affair and continued to see Skinner. In January 1887, Laura Cross began suffering from

Wife murderer, Dr. Philip Cross, with Mary Skinner.

vomiting, diarrhea, and thirst—the usual symptoms of arsenic poisoning. Yet she told a friend that her husband had diagnosed her condition as heart disease.

On June 1, Laura Cross died. Eight days later Cross sailed for England and married Mary Skinner. The impropriety of the event led to much speculation in the village. Cross returned to Ireland on June 21, just before the authorities exhumed the remains of Laura Cross. The subsequent examination revealed traces of both arsenic and strychnine. Dr. Cross was arrested and tried at the Munster Assizes. The four-day trial revealed that the defendant had recently purchased the poison for "sheep dipping." He was found Guilty and hanged in January 1888.

REF.: Atholl, *The Reluctant Hangman;* Brock, *A Casebook of Crime; CBA;* Duke, *Six Trials;* Furneaux, *The Medical Murderer;* Gribble, *Adventures In Murder;* Kingston, *Dramatic Days at the Old Bailey;* Lambton, *Thou Shalt Do No Murder;* Parry, *Some Famous Medical Trials;* Roughead, *The Murderer's Companion;* Sanders, *They Couldn't Lose the Body;* Wilson, *Encyclopedia of Murder;* Wyndham, *Consider Your Verdict.*

Crossman, George Albert (AKA: **Charles Seymour**), 1871-1904, Brit., poly.-suic.-mur. The honeymoon at Kensal Rise in England ended too soon for Mrs. Ellen Sampson when George Crossman murdered his bride the day after the wedding.

Because Crossman couldn't settle on just one woman, he "married," under various names, at least seven. The first three marriages were legitimate, the last four were polygamous. The fifth "Mrs. Crossman" turned out to be the unluckiest of all. Crossman, under the name Charles Seymour, took Ellen Sampson, nurse and widow, as his wife in January 1903. The two moved to Ladysmith Road to live, as Sampson no doubt believed, in wedded bliss. But the pressures of married life got to Crossman and the morning after the wedding night, he killed her by hitting her over the head. He hid the body in a room upstairs, so as not to disturb the fourth Mrs. Crossman, Edith Thompson, who was to return from a visit with friends in Peckham that day.

For more than a year, the two lived happily together. Thompson remained ignorant of the facts that downstairs, the remains of her husband's fifth "wife" were decaying in a tin box, and that her husband was, in fact, not her legal husband, and that during that year he married "wives" six and seven during occasional trips to London.

But Crossman and Thompson didn't live happily ever after. Crossman's lodger, William Dell, started to complain about smells seeping from a closet under the stairs. He continued to complain until, in March 1904, Crossman made arrangements to have the 15-month-old corpse removed. Meanwhile, the suspicious Dell had arranged to have the police come and check the house. The police found the body, and in the ensuing confusion, fearing retribution, Crossman took off at a run. Three quarters of a mile away, he pulled out a razor and slit his throat, ear to ear.

REF.: *CBA;* Logan, *Masters of Crime;* Shew, *A Second Companion to Murder;* Stevens, *Famous Crimes and Criminals.*

Crouch, Eliza Elizabeth (AKA: **Cora Pearl**), 1835-86, Fr., pros. Crouch's father ran off to the U.S. with his mistress when Eliza was a little girl. Her mother felt that the only hope of raising a proper English girl was to get her away from the family turmoil, so she sent her daughter to a French convent and then to England to live with her grandmother.

It was while returning from church one Sunday morning that the young English girl of fourteen was approached by a man who asked if she liked cakes. Unfortunately, she did. Expecting cakes but receiving gin and tonic, Crouch was raped. She woke up the following morning with an offering of £5 for services rendered. Although Crouch decided not to stay with the man, she never did go home to her grandmother. She got a place of her own and within a year had become mistress to one William Buckle. The business agreement lasted for two years, when, during a trip to Paris, Crouch decided to remain in France. She opened a shop under the name Cora Pearl and marketed herself as a spirited young girl who would do anything. She was an immediate hit and soon became mistress to Napoleon III's cousin, Prince Jerome Bonaparte.

Crouch reached the pinnacle of success when the prince gave her a mansion in the Rue de Chaillot, known as Les Petites Tuileries, which cost, according to Crouch, £80,000. When the Second Empire fell during the Franco-Prussian War, she fell, too, because the prince was forced to relocate to London and she was forbidden to visit him. Always the businesswoman and being civic-minded, Crouch returned to Paris, where she flew the British Union Jack over her house, which she turned into a hospital for wounded officers. The neighbors complained, but it wasn't until her latest lover attempted suicide after spending several million dollars on Crouch and her unrequited love that the man's family used their influence to have Crouch removed from Paris.

No longer youthful, and rebuffed by Prince Jerome, Crouch moved from London to Monte Carlo to Milan to Rome, to Nice, to Baden-Baden, hoping to recapture her past glories. She eventually returned to Paris where she died of cancer at age fifty-one.

REF.: Bullough, *Illustrated History of Prostitution; CBA.*

Crouch, John, prom. 1766, Brit., wh. slav. Appearing before the magistrate at Guildhall on Jan. 15, 1766, John Crouch claimed that the ragged, undernourished child in his custody was his daughter. There was little else he could offer in his defense. He had, after all, tried to sell the 14-year-old girl to a sea captain.

Testifying before the court, the sea captain explained that an elderly couple walking near the Royal Exchange in London had offered to sell him the girl for a fair price. He said he was struck by the girl's thin, tattered clothing, so unsuitable for January. Then, after the proposition had been made, he had the couple arrested for solicitation.

The magistrates arrested Mr. and Mrs. Crouch for vagrancy. They committed the girl to the London Workhouse and arranged for a general hearing to determine what was to be done. During the sessions held at the Guildhall on May 12, John Crouch explained that the teenaged girl was really his niece, and hearing there was a market for young girls in London, they had walked 231 miles from Bodmin, in Cornwall, to find a customer.

Crouch was sentenced to six months' imprisonment at Newgate and ordered to pay one shilling. His wife was acquitted.

REF.: *CBA;* Mitchell, *Newgate Calendar.*

Crouch, Mary Ann, 1822-41, Brit., (unsolv.) mur. It would have been better for Mary Ann Crouch to forego dessert. In September 1841, the 19-year-old died after eating a cake laced with arsenic. The whole family in Ridgmont, England, became ill, but only Crouch died. The arsenic apparently came from soda provided by the family's cook Ann Lee.

To this day, nobody knows for certain who killed the girl, but people have always suspected either Lee, who was soon dismissed as cook, or George Peppott, a worker for the family who had recently purchased arsenic. He said he needed the poison to kill rats, but he and the cook may have been romantically involved and plotted the murder.

REF.: Butler, *Murderers' England; CBA.*

Crowder, James, d.1829, U.S., mur. James Crowder was given the death penalty for slaughtering his wife and children in 1829, the first official execution in Atlanta, Ga.

Crowder attempted to cover up the mass slaying of his wife and three children by setting fire to his home. As he watched the fire mount, apparent pangs of remorse caused him to wander to the back yard, where he attempted suicide by slitting his throat. He did a poor job and was found alive. Crowder's hanging, according to the *Atlanta Constitution,* "drew an immense crowd." REF.: *CBA.*

Crowding, Elizabeth Ann, 1931-   , U.S., embez. A woman entrusted by her community to act responsibly with its finances was found Guilty of embezzling $12,523. Elizabeth Ann Crowding, former Kent County, Md., treasurer, was to pay dearly for her greed.

Calvert County Circuit Judge Perry T. Bowen, Jr. sentenced Crowding, forty-five, to ten years on each of the twenty-eight embezzlement and eleven forgery counts for which she was convicted, the terms to run concurrently. She was also ordered to repay the total amount she stole from her Prince Frederick neighbors. Crowding, touched by grief, fear, and remorse, cried as she was led away by state correctional authorities. REF.: *CBA.*

The adventuresome kidnapper Pat Crowe.

Crowe, Patrick, prom. 1900, Case of, U.S., kid. A disgruntled employee of the Cudahy Meatpacking Company of Omaha, Neb., Patrick Crowe decided to take revenge on his former employer by kidnapping 15-year-old Edward Cudahy, Jr. On the evening of Dec. 18, 1900, Cudahy was returning from a doctor's office after having delivered second-hand magazines his father no longer wanted. Barring his path, wearing masks and wielding revolvers, were Crowe and accomplice James Callahan. "We're detectives," Crowe announced to the boy, "and you're a robber named McGee.

We've been after you, McGee, and now we've got you. Come along with us."

Cudahy pushed away a revolver pointed at him and shouted: "You're crazy!" Ignoring the boy's protests, the kidnappers hustled him into a buggy, tied his arms and feet, and put a hood over his head. They then drove to an old abandoned house in the area and took Cudahy inside, handcuffing him to a chair and giving him a plate of food. Crowe and Callahan then celebrated their kidnapping feat by opening a bottle of liquor. When the boy did not return home, Edward Cudahy, Sr. phoned the doctor who told him that Eddie had delivered the magazines several hours earlier and had left for home. Cudahy then called the police, and the entire force turned out to look for the missing youth. They were joined by hundreds of Cudahy's workers, who had been ordered to help search for the meatpacking heir.

By morning, when the boy did not return home, Cudahy realized that his son had been taken and he immediately offered a sizeable reward with no questions asked if his boy was returned to him. He also called in the Pinkertons who began searching for Eddie. A ransom note delivered that day demanded $25,000 in gold. If the money was paid, the boy would be returned unharmed the note read, but if Cudahy refused to pay, the

Kidnap victim Edward Cudahy, Jr.

kidnappers vowed that they would blind the boy with acid. To instill fear within the Cudahy family, the kidnappers made mention of the fate that befell Charley Ross, a millionaire's son who had been kidnapped in 1874 and how the boy vanished forever when the ransom for him was not paid.

Cudahy put five sacks of gold into a buggy that night and delivered this money to a remote spot on the outskirts of Omaha. His son was released unharmed some hours later. Cudahy, once his son was safely back home, offered a large reward for the capture of the kidnappers, but interest in apprehending these culprits was practically nonexistent as Cudahy was not a well-liked man. He paid his employees slave wages and was a severe taskmaster who had smashed several campaigns to unionize the suffering meatpacker workers.

Police detectives studying the case and various descriptions given of the men seen with the Cudahy boy, concluded that the kidnapping had been masterminded by a colorful character named Pat Crowe, one-time Cudahy employee who had turned to train robbery and other criminal pursuits. Crowe, however, was nowhere to be found. Crowe was reported to be in China or in the South Seas, off on some adventure. The kidnapper, in February 1901, then began sending a series of letters to Cudahy, first claiming he was innocent, then offering to return $20,000 of the $25,000 in ransom money. His accomplice, Callahan, was caught in 1901 and identified by Eddie Cudahy as one of the men who had kidnapped him. Callahan was tried for the Cudahy kidnapping. Oddly, Nebraska had no fixed laws governing the crime and Callahan was acquitted. The search for Crowe went on, however.

After reportedly serving with the Boers in South Africa in their fight against the British, Crowe returned to the U.S. in 1906. He sent Cudahy's money back to him through an Omaha attorney, he claimed. Then he publicly declared that he, indeed, had kidnapped Eddie Cudahy, and submitted himself to trial. Crowe had picked an opportune time to surrender. Feeling against the meatpacking trusts was high and Cudahy represented the oppressive and unyielding owner class. Unions were organized, and the

meatpacking czar was under siege to change his employment procedures. Crowe's trial took place at the height of this crisis, and he was, not surprisingly, acquitted as had been Callahan some five years earlier. Crowe went on to become a popular lecturer, railing against the trusts. Capriciously, he sent a postcard every year for many years to Eddie Cudahy on the anniversary of the kidnapping and signed these missives, "from your old kidnapper." See: Ross, Charley.

REF.: Alix, *Ransom Kidnapping in America*; Bartholomew, *A Biographical Album of Western Gunfighters*; CBA; Crowe, *Pat Crowe, His Story, Confession and Reformation*; ____, *Spreading Evil, Pat Crowe's Autobiography*; Faulkner, *Roundup, A Nebraska Reader*; Jones, *A Review of Famous Crimes*; Jones, *The Life and Adventure of Harry Tracy*; Lait and Mortimer, *Chicago: Confidential*; Messick, *Kidnapping*; Nash, *Almanac of World Crime*; ____, *Among the Missing*; Smith, *Mysteries of the Missing*; Tillotson, *How to Be a Detective*.

Crowe, Richard H., 1909- , U.S., embez. He wasn't stupid, and the court's psychiatrist said he wasn't crazy. Richard Crowe, forty, had everything going for him in the spring of 1949, including a promising banking career at Manhattan's renowned National City Bank, a lovely wife, three great kids, two stylish cars and an eleven-room home on Staten Island. He was also very active in the community. But beneath that facade, Crowe was getting desperately in debt, so he embezzled $883,660—the largest sum, at that time, to be stolen from a Manhattan bank.

Crowe wasn't even clever about the way he went about stealing the money, and so it wasn't very difficult for authorities to figure out who had done it. Working late one Friday, he opened the vault and removed $193,660 in small bills, five U.S. $100,000 Treasury bonds, and $190,000 in smaller bonds. He gathered the money, threw it in the family car, and met his wife for dinner at a Staten Island country club. He spent a casual weekend at home and on Sunday announced he needed to go into Manhattan on a business trip.

Soon registered envelopes with Florida postmarks stuffed full of cash began arriving at various New York banks. Crowe finally had enough money to pay off the enormous debt he had incurred in maintaining his lifestyle.

On a warm April day in sunny Florida, Crowe was found and arrested in a Daytona Beach tavern. He eventually pleaded guilty as charged: violating the Federal Reserve Act, the National Robbery Act, and the National Stolen Property Act. During the trial, Irving H. Saypol, the chief assistant U.S. attorney, disclosed for the first time that Crowe had forged the names of his parents and of an aunt to apply for bank loans. Saypol said the relatives had assumed responsibility for the loans and had been impoverished as a result. Crowe ingratiated himself with the court, promising to make complete restitution and begging for mercy.

And mercy is what Crowe received. For a crime that carries a maximum penalty of forty-five years in prison and a fine of $30,000, Judge Henry W. Goddard had Crowe jailed one year, one month, and one day. When released from prison, Crowe, met by his wife, was busily deciding which of the several offers of salesmen's jobs he would accept. REF.: *CBA*.

Crowley, Aleister, 1875-1947, Case of, Int'l., blk. Aleister Crowley was born into wealth in Leamington, England. A spoiled child, he inherited a fortune, about $500,000, and proceeded to practice every known perversity. He became a member of the Rosicrucians and then perverted the traditions and practices of this sect, renovating an old abbey in Scotland where he held Black Masses and practiced what he called Magick, ceremonies that were Satanic in nature but relied on sexual orgies. He sacrificed cats and goats and went through dozens of mistresses and two wives, sending one to an insane asylum and another into chronic alcoholism. On the island of Sicily, in the 1920s, Crowley renovated another abbey and held his satanic rites there, including sex orgies, drunken revels, and bestiality of every known kind, earning a notorious reputation that soon compelled the Italian government to banish him.

Crowley bestowed upon himself a number of glorious occult

titles, including The Great Beast (after Satan), 666 (the traditional Biblical mark of the Beast and also the number of the exhibit in the Cairo Museum which housed the god Horus, a netherworld god), Baphomet, Frater Perdurabo, Master Therion, Prince Chioa Khan, and Adeptus Minor, a title derived from the Rosicrucian sect he distorted and abominated through his sex rites and use of drugs and alcohol. In the early 1920s, Crowley lived among the artists and writers who had expatriated themselves to Paris, and there he was known as "the most evil man in the world," a title in which he reveled. Noted writers such as Ernest Hemingway and Somerset Maugham wrote about Crowley as an offbeat member of the expatriate set, thus giving him credibility, intentionally or not.

In reality, Crowley was an alcoholic, drug-addicted sex maniac posing as a powerful, wise practitioner of black magic, luring countless gullible women to his lairs where he impregnated them and then abandoned them. The number of illegitimate children spawned by this demented creature was once estimated to be in the hundreds. When he had exhausted his personal fortune, Crowley took to seducing lonely society women and persuading them to participate in satanic sex orgies of his own weird creation, then later blackmailed these women for huge amounts of money. He was twice placed on trial for blackmail, but managed to escape conviction and imprisonment. In 1932, one of his old friends, Nina Hammett, published her memoirs, Laughing Torso, a book in which she described Crowley's scandalous Sicilian operations in a temple at Cefalu, detailing the satanic masses Crowley conducted, the blood sacrifices of animals, and how, "one day a baby was said to have disappeared mysteriously," implying that Crowley sacrificed the infant in one of his bloody black masses. Crowley, then down on his luck, thought to get rich by suing Hammett and her British publishers. His plan backfired. His repulsive practices and vile background were exposed by defense lawyers. Crowley arrogantly insulted the court and the jury, and instead of reaping any rewards from his lawsuit scheme, his suit was thrown out of court.

By the end of WWII, Crowley was a human derelict, his body wracked by syphilis and heroin addiction. His friends had long ago abandoned him and his cult followers had dwindled to a few old hags, themselves utterly addicted to heroin, who begged through the seaside resort of Hastings, England, to obtain enough money to support Crowley in his single room in a seedy boarding house, a room he never left. He spent his last weeks, when not in a heroin stupor, madly writing his nearly incoherent diaries. One entry read: "What an ass I am! Will heroin help me forget it?" The next day, Dec. 2, 1947, Aleister Crowley committed suicide by injecting a dozen grains of heroin into his already demolished body. He was cremated.

REF.: Cammell, Aleister Crowely: The Man, The Magic, The Poet; CBA; Crowley, The Confessions of Aleister Crowley; Hammett, Laughing Torso; Hemingway, A Moveable Feast; Hunt, A Dictionary of Rogues; Nash, Zanies; Symonds, The Great Beast: The Life and Magick of Aleister Crowley; (FICTION), Maugham, The Magician.

Crowley, Francis (AKA: Two-Gun), 1911-31, U.S., rob.-mur. Francis Crowley was the illegitimate offspring of a German housemaid who had been placed in a foster home as an infant. He grew up under severe supervision, going to work in a factory when only twelve and returning his entire paycheck to his family. He did not drink or smoke and was addicted only to hard rock candy. An uneducated and impressionable youth, Crowley read the daily newspapers, avidly following the notorious careers of such gangsters as Dutch Schultz, Jack "Legs" Diamond, Vincent Coll, Vannie Higgins, and others. He admired their lifestyles of fast cars, bankrolls, blonde mistresses, and especially their contempt for police. Since childhood, Crowley had hated policemen, his foster grandfather having served on the New York Police Department.

At age eighteen, Crowley met and befriended a heavyset, dimwitted youth named Rudolph "Fats" Duringer, whom Crowley called "Big Rudolph." The two worked together in the same plant, but after work the pair planned and committed several small robberies in Manhattan. Their take was small, but the elation Crowley felt after committing these crimes motivated him to plan more sensational crimes. In 1931, Crowley and Duringer robbed a small bank and then, after purchasing a car, robbed a series of gas stations and grocery stores. When one grocery store operator resisted, Crowley shot him to death. The two youths thought of themselves as clever, desperate men who could outsmart lawmen at every turn. With cash in their pockets, the two began to frequent dance halls where they flashed their money and quickly attracted pretty young females. An older woman, Virginia Banner, who served as a hostess in one of these dance halls, caught the eye of Fats Duringer. He asked her for a date but she refused.

Francis "Two-Gun" Crowley

A few nights later Crowley and Duringer waylaid the Banner woman as she left the dance hall, shoved her into their car and drove to a remote area where Duringer repeatedly raped her. Then Crowley dragged the semiconscious woman from the car and, using two revolvers, shot her to death. Duringer also sent several bullets into the hapless Virginia Banner. He later said: "I heard she was going to marry someone else. I was jealous of him."

Police later matched the bullets fired into the grocery store owner and the Banner woman and realized they were dealing with the same psychopathic killer. Two policemen met him head on a few months later in April 1931. Officers Frederick Hirsch and Peter Yodice, patroling a lover's lane area in North Merrick, N.Y., noticed a dirty green coupe parked in Black Shirt Lane. Hirsch got out of the squad car and walked up to the coupe, bouncing the light from his flashlight onto the pasty face of a young man behind the wheel. Next to him sat a girl, and the youth had his arm around her. Hirsch asked to see the youth's driver's license.

"Sure, sure," Francis Crowley said, but instead of reaching for his wallet, he quickly opened the car door, knocking Hirsch backward. He then pumped three bullets into the officer. Hirsch managed to get off a wild shot before collapsing. Then Crowley dashed from the car, grabbed the officer's gun, and jumped back into the car, dodging officer Yodice's bullets. He drove the coupe wildly down the road and managed to escape.

Crowley was now identified as the killer of three people and an all-points bulletin went out for his capture. Crowley, however, had found a hiding place and he remained at large while scores of officers searched for him in Manhattan. An enterprising New York Journal reporter then managed to find one of Crowley's old girlfriends, dance hall hostess Billie Dunne. When the reporter told her that he was looking for "Two-Gun" Crowley, the Dunne girl exploded, saying she never wanted to see "that crazy man again." She explained that Crowley, Duringer, and Crowley's new girlfriend, 16-year-old Helen Walsh, were holed up in a cheap apartment at 303 W. 90th Street. She knew the apartment well, she said, since it was her own and the gang had kicked her out of it a few days earlier, leaving her homeless. As the reporter and his photographer raced off to get their "scoop," Billie Dunne shouted a warning: "You better watch out, that guy would shoot his own mother!"

The reporter called the address in to his editor, who in turn called police, and detectives were soon going up the stairs to the Manhattan apartment. They stood outside the door and pounded. Crowley's voice was heard to shout: "Get out of here! We don't want any!" The door suddenly flew open and there stood Francis "Two Gun" Crowley, boy bandit and killer, except that he had five guns, not two. He held two revolvers in either hand, had another gun tucked into a shoulder holster and the legs of his trousers were rolled up. Strapped to his calves were two more guns. He began firing two weapons, emptying them at the detectives, who dove for cover. The door to the apartment then slammed shut. As the smoke from Crowley's guns began to clear, the startled officers heard Crowley snarl a line that movie gangsters had made famous: "Come and get me, coppers!"

Police roped off two blocks of city streets while preparing to lay siege to the apartment. Hundreds of officers raced to the area, training submachine guns, shotguns and high-powered rifles with telescopic sights on the apartment from the streets below and from facing buildings. They began to pepper the building. Cowley fired back, blasting away as he leaped from window to window, firing down on the officers below in the street. Machine guns answered, spraying through the windows of the apartment, shattering glass, thudding into the walls. When there was a lull, Crowley jumped up and began emptying his pistols and revolvers at the police, firing down five stories at them.

Duringer and Helen Walsh had by then taken refuge beneath the two small beds in the apartment. Crowley, after emptying his weapons at the police, would sit on one of the beds and reload, cursing Duringer, yelling: "You're yellow! Yellow!"

Rudolph "Fats" Duringer

More carloads of police arrived until 300 officers had been thrown into the battle. More than 15,000 people leaned from windows and gathered in the streets below to witness the siege, almost as if they were spectators at a New York parade. Police began firing tear gas shells into the apartment, but Crowley picked them up and threw them to the street below where several officers were overcome with the gas from their own canisters. Crowley laughed hysterically at this sight, but in dumping the canisters out the window he exposed himself to intense gunfire. He was hit time and time again, but he kept getting up and returning to the windows, firing and yelling curses at the police.

A squad of detectives finally charged the door to the apartment, knocking it down. Crowley was staggering about inside, tears from the gas running down his cheeks, half-blinded and wounded. He spotted the officers and leveled his two guns at them, squeezing the triggers, but nothing happened. Two Gun was out of ammunition. He collapsed unconscious as detectives rushed toward him. Crowley was bleeding from four bullet wounds. Duringer and Helen Walsh were dragged from beneath the beds and all three were finally taken into custody. The battle had raged for several hours and the police had fired more than 700 shots at the defiant gunman, with Crowley firing an equal number.

Helen Walsh testified against Crowley at his trial for murder. He refused to look at her when she left the witness stand, winking at him, still playing the game. Duringer also took the witness stand and attempted to pin all the murders on Crowley, but he was convicted of killing Virginia Banner along with Crowley. Two Gun was also convicted of murdering Officer Hirsch. Both he and Duringer were sentenced to death and sent to Sing Sing. Crowley, strutting for news photographers, boasted that he would "laugh all the way to the hot seat." He would show them how tough he was, and when he arrived at Sing Sing and was placed on Death Row, he attacked the guard bringing him his tray of food, kicking over the tray and tearing up his bunk. Helen Walsh wrote him a letter in which she accused him of being "yellow." This caused Crowley to tear up his cell once more. He stuffed his bedding down the toilet and flooded the cell.

Though denied matches, the killer managed to set fire to his cell and cause the guards to fight a serious blaze. Next Crowley tore a wire from his bunk and wrapped it around a magazine, using it for a club, knocking a guard unconscious in an unsuccessful effort to escape. Warden Lawes finally ordered Crowley placed in solitary confinement. He was stripped naked and the cell was also stripped. At night a mattress was thrown into the cell, but it was removed in the morning. Without other inmates to cheer him on, Crowley became docile, silent. Shortly before his execution, Crowley was offered $10,000 for a fake autobiography but he turned it down, telling Warden Lawes: "Who would I give that dough to? If my mother had that money when I was born I wouldn't have wound up here. I knew that when I bought that first gun that it would land me in the electric chair."

The newspapers were still running lurid stories about Crowley's brief but spectacular criminal career on Oct. 28, 1931, when he was led into the death chamber at Sing Sing. He had a smile on his face and waved at a guard he liked. Only a short time earlier Duringer had been electrocuted, lumbering to the chair and plopping down into it, closing his eyes before the current killed him. As Crowley approached the chair he turned to Lawes, who accompanied him, and said that he had a request. When asked what the request was, Crowley said: "I want a rag to wipe off the chair after that rat sat in it!" No rag was forthcoming. Crowley sat down in the chair and when executioner Robert Elliott fastened the electrodes, Crowley told him that he had better tighten one of the legstraps "if you want this thing to work." He then asked Lawes to give his love to his stepmother. A moment later the lever was thrown, and within seconds Two Gun Crowley was dead. Only his lethal reputation remained.

REF.: *CBA;* Elliott, *Agent of Death;* Horan, *The Desperate Years;* Marten, *The Doctor Looks at Murder;* Nash, *Bloodletters and Badmen.*

On trial, left to right, John Francis Knapp, Joseph Knapp, George Crowninshield.

Crowninshield, Richard, c.1802-30, and **Crowninshield, George,** and **Knapp, John Francis,** and **Knapp, Joseph,** prom. 1830, U.S., mur. By 1830, the Knapp brothers of Salem, Mass., thought it was time that their 82-year-old uncle, Captain Joseph White, died so that they could inherit his money. They contacted an experienced killer-for-hire named Richard Crowninshield. The three entered the old captain's room on the night of Apr. 6, 1830, and Crowninshield stabbed him to death. The murder went unsolved until a jailed pickpocket said that he knew that Richard Crowninshield killed the old man. Richard and his brother George were in jail when the Knapp brothers' father inadvertently opened a letter to the boys from Crowninshield demanding blackmail money. The Knapps, too, were arrested. Joseph Knapp agreed to testify against the others in return for immunity. When he named Richard Crowninshield, the killer strangled himself in his prison cell.

The other three men all went to trial for the death of White. George Crowninshield was acquitted after proving that he had spent the night of the murder in a three-way tryst with his mistress and her girl friend. Francis Knapp went to trial twice: the first time yielded a hung jury, the second time a conviction. He was hanged. Joseph, who had agreed to testify, lost his immunity when he refused to speak against his brother, so he, too, was found Guilty and hanged. One of the prosecutors in this case was famed lawyer Daniel Webster.

REF.: *CBA; Nash, Bloodletters and Badmen;* Wilson, *Encyclopedia of Murder.*

Crown Jewels of England, The, 1671, Brit., theft. There have been at least four attempts to steal the Crown Jewels of England, but only one was successful. Oliver Cromwell carried off the jewels during the English Civil War. Charles II later commissioned Sir Robert Vyner to make him a new crown for his coronation in 1660.

On May 9, 1671, Irish adventurer Thomas Blood seized and gagged Talbot Edwards, the keeper of the crown, and tried to make off with the treasured symbol of the British monarchy. Captain Martin Beckman and the son of Talbot Edwards pursued Blood, arrested him and brought him before the king, who pardoned the thief and restored his impounded estate in Ireland.

In 1815, a peasant woman stuck her hands behind the bars of the display case and tore the crown to pieces. It was never clear whether she intended political vandalism or theft. Guards quickly subdued the woman. The last attempt on the Crown Jewels occurred in 1851, during the five-month Exhibition at Hyde Park. An international gang of jewel thieves planned to steal the crown from its specially constructed gilt cage. However, a young servant girl overheard the plans, and the conspirators were arrested.

REF.: Brock, *A Casebook of Crime; CBA.*

Croydon Murders, 1928-29, Brit., (unsolv.) mur. On Apr. 26, 1928, in Croydon, England, Edmund Duff died after eating a chicken dinner. A coroner's jury found that his death resulted from natural causes. Nearly ten months later Duff's sister-in-law Vera Sydney, her aunt, and the family cook became violently ill after eating lunch. Two days later Mrs. Sydney passed away. Although the symptoms of poisoning were present—vomiting, stomach cramps, and severe abdominal pain—no evidence of foul play was uncovered. Vera's grieving mother, Violet Emelia Sydney, was given a sedative by Dr. Binning. After taking it, she became very ill and died on Mar. 15, 1929. Upon examination, the medicine was found to contain arsenic. The bodies of Duff and Mrs. Sydney were exhumed, and the presence of arsenic was detected in these remains also. Although the available evidence suggested that the likely poisoner was Edmund's widow, Grace Duff, she was never brought to trial.

In 1973, after the 87-year-old Grace Duff had died, an investigative reporter theorized that Duff had killed her family members to secure the family inheritance and the love of a local doctor with whom she had become involved. Despite attempts to establish a motive, the crimes remain unsolved. See: **Duff, Edmund.**

REF.: Browne, *The Scalpel of Scotland Yard; CBA;* Cuthbert, *Science and the Detection of Crime;* Dilnot, *Rogue's March;* Jackson, *Coroner: The Biography of Sir Bentley Purchase;* Morland, *Background to Murder;* Nash, *Open Files;* Rowland, *Criminal Files;* Shew, *A Companion to Murder;* Symons, *A Reasonable Doubt;* Thompson, *Poison Mysteries Unsolved;* ____, *Poisons and Poisoners;* Whittington-Egan, *The Riddle of Birdhurst Rise;* Wilson, *Encyclopedia of Murder.*

Crump, Johnny, 1940- , U.S., burg. It was a lone hair strand that led police investigators to the perpetrator of a Lone Star State killing.

Though commonplace today, in 1963 a scientific method of analyzing strands of hair was just being developed. The method was first used successfully by Texan Floyd McDonald, a crime laboratory expert well respected for his ability to discern evidence at the scene of a crime that other detectives never even noticed. This time what McDonald noticed was one strand of blond eyebrow hair.

On a Sunday morning in October 1963, a Houston couple on their way to church discovered the battered body of a well-dressed, middle-aged man near the popular Holly's Lounge bar. Near the man's arm lay an empty wallet and car keys. The dead man was easily identified as Orval F. Crain, fifty-four. But detectives were stumped over the murder scenario and who could possibly have killed the man described as mild and soft-spoken.

Clues were scarce. Holly Lounge patrons had seen Crain the night before talking with a tall man who "didn't talk like a Texan." Police took plaster casts of tire marks in the parking lot and compared them with the markings on Crain's shirt. They knew he had been run over, either dead or alive, by a lightweight pickup truck. More clues were gathered when a truck fitting the police description was found smashed into a telephone pole and abandoned on the outskirts of the city. The license plate number indicated that the truck had come from Oklahoma City.

The police were still baffled. McDonald ordered the truck moved to a garage where he could thoroughly examined it. "I think I've got something," he called out, triumphantly holding up a small blond hair he had found on the exterior. Analysis proved conclusively that the hair did indeed come from the murder victim.

The truck was traced to a dealer in Oklahoma City, who was able to steer police detectives to owner John Crump. He readily admitted that he was the tall stranger seen talking with Crain that fateful night. He said that he and Crain had gotten into a fight later that night and that he had hit Crain. But he did not kill him...or at least he didn't think he had...or at least if he did, he hadn not meant to.

Before Crump could be extradited back to Texas, he was convicted for burglary and sentenced to twelve years in Oklahoma State Penitentiary at McAlester. Eventually Houston authorities dropped the murder charge, feeling it would be too difficult to gather witnesses after twelve years.

REF.: Brock, *Fifteen Clues;* ____, *Science Vs. Crime; CBA.*

Crump, Michael Tyrone, 1961- , U.S., mur. Between October 1985 and February 1986, the bodies of six Tampa, Fla., prostitutes were found in empty fields near cemeteries. The county police could not identify the killer, but they suspected Michael Crump, a former construction worker with a criminal record for aggravated assault dating back to 1981. Crump was arrested and indicted for the Oct. 9, 1986, murder of Areba Jean Smith, a 34-year-old prostitute. When the woman became "impatient" with Crump, she pulled a knife. According to his own testimony, Crump strangled her during the fight. Following Crump's conviction in July 1987, Circuit Court Judge Donald C. Evans sentenced him to life imprisonment. On Mar. 31, 1989, Crump was found Guilty of murdering a second prostitute, Louvinia Palmore Clark, whose body was found near the Shady Grove Cemetery on Dec. 12, 1985. Citing Crump's violent history, Judge M. William Graybill imposed the death sentence. Michael Crump accepted the verdict impassively. REF.: *CBA.*

Crump, Paul, 1930- , U.S., mur. It was a question of life and death, and it took nine years and fourteen reprieves to answer. For nine years in post-slavery/pre-civil rights America, convicted murderer Paul Crump, waited while the state of Illinois decided his fate. At the very last minute, even as he watched officials test his electric chair twenty steps away, the 32-year-old black man was granted his final sentence: He would live—all of his days in prison—but he would live.

At twenty-three Crump was found Guilty of killing a guard in a March 1953 robbery of payroll clerks at Libby, McNeill & Libby's Chicago plant. Originally called "savage" and "animalistic," he had become, under the guidance of Warden Jack Johnson, thoughtful, insightful, a convert to Catholicism, and truly sorry for what he had done. His attorney, Donald P. Moore, based an appeal to the state parole board on an argument rarely attempted: that Crump had been rehabilitated. The convict read Socrates, Nietzsche, William Blake, and the *Bible.* To give his own life some meaning in the face of death, he had written a novel, *Burn, Killer, Burn.* "One ought to be ashamed to die," he said, "until he has contributed something in justification of his living." Through all those years of learning, Crump was scheduled fourteen different times to die. Finally, clergymen, newspaper columnists, penologists, politicians, and convinced citizens called for a permanent stay of execution for the young man.

Crump's salvation became a massive public cause. Even opposing Assistant State's Attorney James Thompson was moved by the eloquence of trial lawyer Louis Nizer's testimony that Crump was "a rehabilitated man, a newborn man, a transformed personality." Nizer read from fifty-seven affidavits attesting to this change of character. In the end there was no end. Illinois Governor Otto Kerner changed Crump's sentence to life in prison without parole. REF.: *CBA*.

Crump, Raymond, Jr., c.1940- , Case of, U.S., mur. Mary Pinchot Meyer, the niece of the late conservationist and governor Gifford Pinchot and good friend of Jacqueline Kennedy, was shot to death during a fall walk along the C & O Canal in Washington, D.C., on Oct. 12, 1964, two days before her forty-fourth birthday. Two men working on a stalled car near the canal heard a shot and a scream, "God, somebody help me!" One of them, Henry Wiggins, saw a man standing over a woman. The man stared at Wiggins for a moment and then ran off into the woods along the bank of the canal. Wiggins told a policeman that the man was wearing a light-colored jacket. The policeman, who had the all exits from the towpath blocked within eight minutes, saw Raymond Crump, Jr. coming out of the water in an orange sweatshirt. There was a white jacket lying on the bank almost a thousand feet upstream. Crump, twenty-five, the father of five, had a record of petty larceny and drunkenness. Higgins identified Crump as the man he had seen. Crump said he had been fishing, but had fallen asleep and lost his pole. Despite a foot-by-foot search of the entire area, including the canal itself, neither the fishing pole nor the murder weapon was ever found.

Crump was arrested and quickly indicted by a grand jury. His trial began on July 20, 1965. His attorney, Mrs. Dovey Roundtree, fifty-one, called Crump himself the "number one exhibit in the case," and emphasized the fact that Higgins had described the killer as about five feet, eight inches tall and weighing about 185 pounds. Crump was five feet, five inches tall and weighed less than 145 pounds. In her closing statement, she told the jury: "You have the life of a man in your hands—a *little* man." After an eleven-hour deliberation, the jury found Crump Not Guilty. REF.: *CBA*.

Crumpley, Ronald K., 1942- , U.S., mur. A minister's son, former New York City transit police officer, husband, and father of two stalked and killed homosexuals for the good of the nation and himself.

Ronald K. Crumpley, thirty-eight, faced his aversion to homosexuality with two automatic pistols, a magnum handgun, a machine gun, and the will to kill. He entered Greenwich Village, known for its gay nightclubs, in a black Cadillac he stole from his father, let go of all inhibition and began shooting at random. In seconds, two lay dead, four injured.

Crumpley believed that "demons in the guise of homosexuals" were after him and that he "was merely protecting the nation and himself." He was found Not Guilty on two counts of murder by reason of mental disease or defect and sentenced to a battery of psychiatric tests. In September 1981, Judge James J. Leff committed Crumpley to the Mid-Hudson Psychiatric Center in New Hampton, N.H. REF.: *CBA*.

Cruse, William, 1928- , U.S., mur. A retired librarian, who was a loving husband and son, voluntarily mowed lawns for his elderly neighbors and sat by his ailing wife's side for long months. Then he killed six people, including two policemen, and attempted to kill twenty-four more because they called him a homosexual behind his back. William Cruse, sixty-one, responsible for the above deeds, was an elderly-looking man with long gray hair and an unkempt beard, who went on a shooting spree at a Bartow, Fla., neighborhood shopping center on Apr. 23, 1987.

Cruse awaits his fate after being convicted on Apr. 5, 1989, of six counts of first-degree murder, twenty-four counts of attempted murder, kidnapping and false imprisonment. The jury of seven women and five men for this case took less than two hours to decide unequivocally that Cruse should die for his crimes.

The controversy now lies in differing opinions concerning Cruse's mental health and motives for killing. State and defense mental health experts testified that the man has been an alcoholic and severely mentally ill with incurable paranoid schizophrenia for at least the last thirty years. The prosecution contends that Cruse premeditated his actions, evident by the fact that he bought special weapons and large amounts of clips and ammunition and that his acts required his loading and packing his ammunition sacks. "The defendant essentially decided he was going to kill people for talking about him and testing his sexuality...then began his own personal war ..." assistant state attorney Wayne Holmes said.

On July 29, 1989, Brevard Circuit Judge John Antoon rejected Cruse's mental illness pleas and sentenced him to die in the electric chair for the murder of the two policemen. Cruse's twenty-six other convictions carry a total mandatory minimum prison sentence of 103 years. Cruse's lawyer plans to appeal the sentences. REF.: *CBA*.

Crutcher, Willie, d.1922, and **Murchison, John,** prom. 1920s, and **Hudson, Jim,** d.1923, and **Staten, Cleo,** d.1927, U.S., (wrong. convict.) mur. The year 1920 was not a good time to be black in Alabama, but for four black men falsely accused of murder and convicted on perjured testimony and circumstantial evidence, it was a death sentence.

On Aug. 6, 1920, John McClendon told his wife he was going to Guntersville and then to Smith's Lake to conduct business the following day. But McClendon did not show up at Smith's Lake, nor did he return home in the days that followed. Searchers were eventually directed to the crest of Brindlee Mountain by a small boy who had noticed buzzards flying overhead. There they followed uneven rubber-tired buggy tracks leading to a cave and the badly decayed body of McClendon, a white man. The boy later recalled having told John Murchison, one of the four black men later convicted of McClendon's murder, of what he had seen and having been told not to tell anyone because it might get him into trouble. This information, along with the fact that Murchison owned a rubber-tired buggy with one bent stirrup, which would make an uneven track, and that he and McClendon had on occasion played craps together, was all the police needed to know to throw Murchison in jail on charges of murder.

Even less evidence was needed to incarcerate Willie Crutcher, Cleo Staten, Jim Hudson, G.B. Staten, Alfred Staten, and Ben Nobles, all black. These men were thought to have been hunting in the Brindlee Mountain area.

At the trial, Nobles swore that he had seen Murchison shoot McClendon in the back during a craps game between Hudson, Crutcher, Murchison, and Cleo Staten. Murchison fired the first shot into McClendon's back, and Cleo Staten shot next. The body was then wrapped in a quilt and taken away. Nobles testified that he had a clear view of the scene.

According to Nobles and others, Murchison and Crutcher objected to the relationship between McClendon and Laura Bell Nobles. This was the motive jury members wanted.

In response, the defendants could do little more than tell the truth. Each denied having been at a crap game that night and having any connections with the murder whatsoever. Each had witnesses supporting his alibi.

The prosecution actually had enough information to prove the defendants not guilty. One of the searchers who helped remove the body from the cave vowed the victim had been shot in the front, not in the back, as Noble said he had so clearly seen. If Noble had lied or simply been mistaken about this point, would not it have been possible that his entire story was wrong? Further, evidence presented by witnesses indicated the accused men were hunting near Black's Gate, not Brindlee Mountain. No one on the jury raised an eyebrow over the fact that McClendon and his wife had not been getting along.

Instead, the jury based its decision on circumstantial evidence and perjury. They were taken with Nobles' description of what he claimed to have seen. They were impressed by the young boy's warning from Murchison not to tell anyone about the birds. The jury jumped when it heard that Murchison, Crutcher, and the others were acquaintances of McClendon and that he and Laura Bell Noble had a relationship, that she had a son born out of wedlock, and that Murchison had a buggy with a bent stirrup.

And so the jury jumped to a faulty conclusion. Four young men—Crutcher, Hudson, Murchison, and Cleo Staten—were found Guilty of murder and sentenced to life in prison.

Life was two years for Crutcher, who was killed by a falling rock in the mine where he was sent to work. Hudson died of tuberculosis after three and a half years. Three years after that, Otis McClendon, nephew of the murder victim, finally came forward. He confessed that he had conspired with the dead man's wife to kill McClendon in exchange for forty acres of land, a pair of mules, and Mrs. McClendon's loyalty. He became willing to tell the truth when she refused to live up to her side of the bargain.

Eventually, Staten was given a full pardon, but he died shortly before it was issued. Murchison was initially denied a pardon because of his poor behavior in prison. Eventually, five years later, eleven years after being falsely convicted, Murchison was given $750 for his troubles and sent away. The younger McClendon was murdered, apparently by Cleve King, Myrtle's new husband. REF.: *CBA*.

Cruttenden, Ann, 1696-1776, Brit., mur. Maybe she no longer believed in divorce. Details are sketchy over the 1776 domestic dispute that turned into a brutal murder, but it is known that 80-year-old Ann Cruttenden of Horsham, England, was convicted and sentenced to die for cutting the throat of her husband, a man half her age.

Although she was scheduled to be "drawn on a hurdle to the place of execution, and there to be burnt with fire until she be dead," Cruttenden, who was probably insane, was most likely strangled before the burning. If she was, it was decided by the executioner, who was authorized to use his own judgment.

REF.: *CBA*; Poynter, *Forgotten Crimes*.

Cruz, Florentino, d.1882, U.S., west. gunman. Florentino Cruz, a Mexican-American renowned for his gunplay, killed Wyatt Earp's brother, Morgan, on Mar. 18, 1882, in Tombstone, Ariz. Earp was playing a game of billiards at Campbell and Hatch's establishment when Cruz, Pete Spence, Frank Stilwell, and "Indian" Charley appeared. Wyatt was sitting near the billiard tables watching the game when Cruz suddenly fired a shot into Morgan Earp's back. A second shot narrowly missed Wyatt's head.

The two surviving Earp brothers, along with Doc Holliday, Jack Johnson, and Sherman McMasters took off after Morgan's killers. They gunned down Stilwell in Tucson, and returned to Tombstone on Mar. 22 to look for Cruz. Wyatt Earp was told by informant Theodore Judah that he could find Cruz working on a woodpile near the Pete Spence camp. When Judah returned to the woodpile, he found Cruz's bullet-riddled body. See: **Earp, Wyatt**.

REF.: *CBA*; Nash, *Bloodletters and Badmen*; O'Neal, *Encyclopedia of Western Gunfighters*.

Cruz, Robert "Fat Man", See: **McCall, Edward L.**

Crying Kid, The, prom. 1870s, U.S., fraud. The Crying Kid was a wiry little man who operated through east coast cities and invariably mulcted victims in short cons, those confidence games that take only a few hours to complete. The Kid's most effective con game dealt with providing tips on horse races, entering pool rooms, and, for a small amount of money, giving gullible bettors "inside" information on horses that were "sure to win" in that day's races. After the races, the victims soon learned that the Crying Kid had misled them and they soon tracked down the con man, prepared to teach him a lesson with their fists. At this time, the sharper earned his sobriquet. The con man would be found weeping, his body wracked with sobs as he chokingly explained that he had also bet on the losing horses he had touted with every dime he had in the world, and that now he was broke and his family, a poor, struggling wife and nine children, would go hungry. The Kid would carry on with such convincing sorrow and vows of suicide that his victims were moved to console him and even give him more money so that his family might have a few meals.

REF.: *CBA*; Nash, *Hustlers and Con Men*.

Cuauhtémoc (Guatimozin), c.1495-1522, Mex., emp., assass. Served as the last ruler of the Aztec people. He was the nephew of Montezuma II, taking his place on the throne in 1520. Under Hernán Cortés' siege of Tenochtitlán, he was captured. Despite torture, he refused to reveal the location of the Aztec treasury and was later executed by Cortés. REF.: *CBA*.

Cuban Gardens, 1920s-30s, U.S., gamb. After Kansas City, Mo., crime boss Johnny Lazia and his associates closed down their high society gaming operation, The Green Hills Club, the Kansas City kingpin fielded about for a place to establish a new, even more lavish gambling project that would serve the gambling needs of the rich. He chose the private grounds of the sprawling Riverside Race Track, a Pendergast-sanctioned dog track operation.

Political sachem Tom Pendergast, through his crime boss enforcer Lazia and political allies, had established Riverside in 1928, and the profits from this wholly illegal gambling operation had been enormous. When Lazia approached Pendergast with his idea for a new gambling operation to be called Cuban Gardens, the political boss beamed and nodded approval. The next day, Phil McCrory gave Lazia a "donation" of $12,000 with promises of more to come from the Pendergast people, McCrory being a political front man for Pendergast. Lazia and his associates gathered more subscription money until reaching a sum of about $200,000, and construction of Cuban Gardens got underway.

The place was built along the lines of a fabulous Monte Carlo casino, with dining rooms and evening-long entertainment by big bands, singers, and ballroom dancers. The overall look of the place was that of a Spanish villa with wide archways, beautifully landscaped gardens and pools, and several wings adjoining the main gambling hall, where thousands of women in expensive gowns and men in tuxedos bet tens of thousands of dollars on roulette, blackjack, and poker.

The dining room at Cuban Gardens was enormous, filigreed with plaster cherubs and a jungle motif of palm trees and exotic fake shrubbery. The cuisine was strictly continental, and French chefs, imported from Europe, offered dazzling entries. The scores of waiters, cigarette girls, band members and even burly bouncers were dressed in ornate Spanish costumes.

Cuban Gardens was a huge success, raking in weekly fortunes for its venal investors. The place became a gnawing source of aggravation, however, for the reformers of Kansas City, and especially the powerful Ministerial Alliance of Liberty, seat of Clay County, where the operation existed. The clergymen constantly complained to the local sheriff, who feared raiding the main grounds of Boss Pendergast and Lazia, also complaining that he would be making enemies among Kansas City's super-rich if he dared to arrest them while they whiled away their time at the gaming tables.

But the Alliance kept up its pressure, and no less than five raids were eventually conducted against Cuban Gardens, all of them dismal failures which resulted in zero arrests. Lawmen found the place difficult to access. By the time they did get past the front gates, no gambling or even drinking, this still being Prohibition, was in evidence. Lazia's private guards could easily warn those inside the club of the arrival of police, by alarm buttons electronically hooked up to all rooms.

All that greeted embarrassed deputies were richly attired couples dancing to "The Chant of the Jungle" and other Spanish hits of the day. It was suspected, but never proven, that the sheriff's men themselves warned the heavily-armed guards at the gates of Cuban Gardens, long in advance of any raid against this seemingly impregnable Pendergast-Lazia fiefdom. Cuban Gardens continued to flourish through the 1930s until Tom Pendergast and his allies were finally overturned by political opponents and reformers. The place died of old age when its ambiance and entertainment were no longer in vogue, passing into oblivion by 1939. See: **Green Hills Club; Lazia, John; Pendergast Machine**.

REF.: Brown, *The Politics of Reform: Kansas City's Municipal Government, 1925-1950; CBA;* Reddig, *Tom's Town.*

Cubbin, Brian, See: **Ewart-Biggs, Christopher.**

Cuccari, Pierre (AKA: **Cuc, La Médiateur**), 1914-54, Fr., (unsolv.) mur. Pierre Cuccari was just trying to help when he was sprayed with bullets in a bar called the Charivar on a July evening in 1954.

The dashing and dapper French gangster, with a reputation for armed robbery, assault, attempted murder, and carrying illegal weapons, met his match and maker while acting as self-appointed mediator between prostitutes and their pimps. Cuccari, known, among other things, as a specialist in vice and women, took it upon himself to settle disputes over who owned which prostitutes. One evening while at work he became too involved in another's vendetta. Instead of collecting his usual "fine" from the prostitute who had hooked up with the wrong pimp, he paid with his life for offering advice. See: **Corsican Vendetta.**

REF.: *CBA;* Goodman, *Villainy Unlimited.*

Cuckoos Gang, prom. 1920s, U.S., org. crime. The Cuckoos Gang of St. Louis was so named by the local press because of their audacious defiance of the powerful Mafia gang called The Green Ones, headed by Sicilian Mafia don Vito Giannola. The Cuckoos were made up of young non-Italian whites who battled for bootlegging operations in the lucrative East Side territory of St. Louis. In the war between the Cuckoos (1926-30) and the Green Ones, more than thirty people, including innocent by-standers, were killed and two dozen seriously wounded. See: **Giannola, Vita; Green Ones, The.**

REF.: *CBA;* Reid, *The Mafia.*

Cudahy, Edward A., Jr., See: **Crowe, Patrick.**

Cuenca, Miguel Cruz, 1912-79, Spain, assass. Spanish Supreme Court Justice Miguel Cruz Cuenca was the sixth victim of a bloody 1979 New Year's trend in young democratic Spain. The 67-year-old president of the sixth court chamber, known for his liberal decisions, was gunned down outside his Madrid home by Basque separatist guerrillas.

Cuenca knew his life was in danger. For several months he had received death threats, the most explicit having been the Nov. 16, 1978, killing of another supreme court judge and the killing of a military governor of Madrid Province six days earlier. As the justice walked from his front door to his car on Jan. 10, Cuenca was shot twice, as the other justice had been, once in the temple and a second time in the stomach, by a young gunman who got away. Roadblocks were established on all highways leading out of Madrid and controls were set up at railway stations and at Madrid's Barajas Airport. The same measures to catch the assassin had been followed in the previous killing but had failed.

ETA, or Basque Homeland and Liberty, guerrillas claimed responsibility for this killing and for five additional assassinations since the beginning of the new year, including the deaths of General Constantino Ortin Gil, adjutant to the military governor of the Basque Guipuzcoa Province, a police demolition expert, and a civil guard and his fiancée. Spain had experienced an ever-increasing number of assassinations since becoming a democratic nation less than two years earlier. Terrorists claimed the lives of ninety-nine people in Spain in 1978, three times more than in the previous year. Two-thirds of the victims were murdered by ETA guerrillas in their attempt to gain independence for the northern Basque provinces. REF.: *CBA.*

Cueva, Alfonso de la (**Marqués de Bedmar**), 1572-1655, Spain, consp. Served Philip II as ambassador to Venice in 1607. He was expelled by the government for allegedly instigating the Conspiracy of Venice in 1618. REF.: *CBA.*

Cujas, Jacques (**Jacobus Cujacius**), 1522-90, Fr., jur. Specialized in Roman law as professor at Valence and Bourges. Author of a definitive work on Justinian I titled *Paratitla.* REF.: *CBA.*

Culbertson, William Smith, 1884-1966, U.S., lawyer. REF.: *CBA.*

Culhane, Charles, 1946-   , and **McGivern, Gary**, 1944-   , U.S., mur. On Sept. 13, 1968, Westchester County, N.Y., Deputy

Sheriffs William Fitzgerald and Joseph Singer were driving three handcuffed inmates of the Auburn Correctional Facility to a court hearing in White Plains. When the car pulled into a rest stop on the way, prisoners Charles Culhane, Gary McGivern, and Robert Bowerman, all serving time for robbery, tried to grab Singer's gun in what appeared to be a pre-arranged escape attempt. In the ensuing struggle, Deputy Sheriff Fitzgerald, sixty-three, and an inmate, Bowerman were killed. Singer, Culhane, and McGivern were wounded.

Culhane and McGivern were tried for Fitzgerald's murder, though they contended it was Bowerman who killed him in an attempt to escape alone. After a hung jury in 1970, Culhane and McGivern were convicted in 1971 and sentenced to die in the electric chair. The two were on death row for thirty-three months, until New York's capital punishment law for the murder of police officers was ruled unconstitutional. At a third trial in 1975, Culhane and McGivern were each sentenced to twenty-five years to life in prison. REF.: *CBA.*

Cull, Clarence, prom. 1942, U.S., attempt. assass. In 1942, a U.S. Army deserter named Clarence Cull began manufacturing nitroglycerin bombs. He intended to kill President Franklin D. Roosevelt by approaching the executive limousine with bombs strapped to his waist and igniting them when he reached the car. Secret Service agents captured Cull in his rooming house before he could execute his plan.

REF.: *CBA;* Pearl, *The Dangerous Assassins.*

Cullender, Rose, and **Duny, Amy**, d.1664, Brit., witchcraft. "Real difficulties can be overcome, it's only the imaginary ones that are unconquerable." Theodore Vail said it, but Rose Cullender lived and died it in 1664. Two elderly English women represent just two of hundreds who were falsely accused and convicted of witchcraft.

The people of Lowestoft, England, attributed great powers to the frail and aging Cullender. The woman supposedly worked in association with another witch, Amy Duny, in casting spells on neighborhood children. A seventeenth-century court trial proved conclusively that Cullender knowingly and maliciously caused the children of Edmund Durent and Diana Bocking to vomit pins and nails. Witness Susan Chandler, in description graphic for any period in history, described how and where she found the "Devil's mark" on Cullender's body. Chandler also swore that her daughter had been bewitched, vomited pins, and screamed the name of Rose Cullender.

Additional testimony indicated that Cullender threatened John Soam after his harvest cart brushed her window. Strangely, the cart overturned two or three times that same day and would no longer pass through a gate it had gone through hundreds of times before.

Evidence mounted against witch Cullender when Robert Sherringham swore that she set lice in his clothes after he accidentally damaged her house with an axle-tree.

The jury was instructed by the judge to decide two key points: one, were the children (who could not attend the trial because it sent them into spellbound fits) truly bewitched and, two, was it Cullender and Duny who bewitched them?

Convinced by the apparently overwhelming evidence, the jury returned after thirty minutes with a verdict of Guilty. The children immediately recovered, and the women were executed.

REF.: *CBA;* Postgate, *Murder, Piracy and Treason.*

Culley, Robert, 1806-33, Brit., (unsolv.) mur. Much speculation still exists concerning the murder, during an 1833 London riot, of Scotland Yard Constable Robert Culley. Virtually the only thing all agree on is that this man, twenty-seven years old, a husband, and only weeks away from becoming a father, died trying to reestablish peace and protect innocent lives. No more was ever learned because the trial held to find the cause of death turned into a free-for-all of a different kind, with both working and aristocratic classes airing grievances and vying for control.

Most witnesses during the trial noted extreme police brutality, the likes of which they had never before seen. Others told of orderly and controlled police response, the likes of which they were pleased to see. Jury members, the majority of whom belonged to the lower middle class, took control of the courtroom, conducted their own cross-examinations and sought the answer, not to how Culley died, but to who was ultimately responsible for the situation. Naturally the government and favored classes contended that the crowds were at fault. The laborers maintained that the police were at fault.

The end result was one of the most unexpected, sensational verdicts in history: The jury found those arrested Guilty of *justifiable* homicide because neither the Riot Act nor any warning for the people to disperse was read. Furthermore, the jury stated that the government had not taken precautions to prevent the assembly and that the police acted brutally against the people. The decision concluded with a hope expressed by jury members that the police would be more careful about preventing such disgraceful and dangerous reactions in the future.

Crowds cheered the verdict as the coroner attempted to refuse it. He eventually gave in and accepted the jury's decision. This led to the strengthening of the National Political Union of Working People and the acquittal of several men who had been arrested during the riot on charges of inciting violence and attempted murder. Parliament eventually took up the issue and ruled that the police had acted according to instructions and that Home Secretary Lord Melbourne was the man to blame because he had tried to escape his own responsibility by blaming the commissioner, Colonel Rowan. The people and police, both satisfied with their newfound scapegoat, dropped the issue, and now no one will ever know for sure who killed Constable Culley.

REF.: *CBA*; Cobb, *Murdered On Duty*.

Culliford, Albert (AKA: **Cecil Scott, Henry Langley, Albert Stanley, Herbert Jones**), b.1842, and **Culliford, Stanley**, b.1881, and **Lovesay, Joseph John**, b.1879, Brit., fraud. With their financial savvy and success at convincing people to invest with them, T. Morton Harris & Company, Stock and Share Dealers, could have actually been a vital investment company. Instead, it was a front for fraud conducted by British swindlers Albert Culliford, sixty-eight, son Stanley Culliford, twenty-nine, and son-in-law Joseph John Lovesay, thirty-one.

The three men began their con game in 1910, six years before British law required persons trading in a name other than their own to register their proper names and place that name on all printed matter. Assuming pseudonyms, the elder Culliford and his family baited financial unsophisticates with alluring circulars promising big money for investments made in monthly profit-sharing. Then they reeled in their client/victims with literature filled with glowing testimony of T. Morton's payoffs to imaginary customers. At least £57,000 came from investors who fell for the deal hook, line, and sinker. The only expenditures of T. Morton Harris & Company were £5000 for stationery and personalized envelopes and a negligible amount as "dividends" going to the more cantankerous clients. The rest was pocketed by Culliford & Company.

Ever-innovative, Culliford, Culliford, and Lovesay devised their "Canadian Deal" to attract those who had tired, of the idea at least, of monthly profit-sharing. Contrary to what was promised investors, not one penny was invested. The swindlers instead used their take to put £10,000 down on a Birmingham theater. They used more for jewelry and even more for basic spending money. It was the wanton spending of this money that finally lead to revelation of the grim reality behind T. Morton Harris & Co.

Lovesay, during a routine banknote-to-gold transaction at a London bank, was apprehended by a London detective already wise to the Culliford crimes. With a little investigation, all three men were brought in and, in time, Justice Hamilton sentenced Culliford senior to five years' penal servitude and his son to nine months in prison for the forty-one counts of acting under false pretenses of fraud and conspiracy. Lovesay was acquitted.

REF.: *CBA*; Nicholls, *Crime Within the Square Mile*.

Cullins, Eddie, c.1903-31, Ire., mur. A native of Crete, Eddie Cullins, twenty-eight, and a Turk, Achmet Musa, twenty-six, formed a partnership to profit from a human oddity. They collected money from people who paid to see Zara Agha, said to be a 156-year-old native of the Asia Minor region.

On Sept. 4, 1931, Musa's body was found near Belfast, Ire. He had been shot in the head twice. His bloodied clothes were found in the Belfast town center, and in Britain, police recovered a suitcase containing a pistol that was linked to the murder by Scotland Yard detective Frederick Churchill. Eddie Cullins was arrested, tried, convicted, and hanged. No motive was established, but after Cullins was executed, a girlfriend alleged that the two associates were gunrunners and that Musa had threatened to reveal the scheme.

REF.: *CBA*; Hastings, *The Other Mr. Churchill*.

Cullotto, Frank, 1937- , U.S., burg.-org. crime. Frank Cullotto, a burglar, formally joined the crime syndicate in 1978, quickly rising to the position of top lieutenant for reputed Las Vegas mobster Tony Spilotro. As a member of the mob, he later admitted he was involved with three murders, sixty armed robberies, at least 200 burglaries, about twenty-five arsons, and perhaps fifteen drug sales.

His fall from mob favor began in June 1981 when Cullotto and others met at the home of Sam Romano, an FBI informant, to plan a $1 million burglary; the FBI recorded the meeting. That fall, Cullotto argued with his boss, Spilotro, and when Cullotto was arrested on burglary charges in connection with the June planning session, Spilotro would not put up bond to free him. After waiting for trial for five months, he was convicted on burglary charges, and given an eight-year prison sentence. In April 1982, Cullotto turned informant, entering the Federal Witness Protection Program. He told jury members later that federal agents told him that Spilotro had ordered him to be murdered to insure his silence.

Cullotto divulged numerous mob secrets, including detailed information about several unsolved murders, and he was the state's primary witness when he testified in 1983 against Wayne Matecki and Lawrence Neumann, who were tried on murder and armed robbery charges. REF.: *CBA*.

Cullum, Jack (AKA: **Jack Johnson**), 1689-1714, Brit., rob. When Jack Cullum's parents died, he left Suffolk County for London to work as a domestic servant. He worked several years for one man but seeking new adventures, joined the navy and served with distinction.

Honorably discharged, Jack Cullum began housebreaking shortly after returning to London. In 1713, while serving time in Bridewell at Clerkenwell—having already suffered the punishment of hand burning for his crimes—Cullum took part in a riot that ended in the murder of prison guard Edward Perry. Two confederates, Richard Keele and William Lowther, were executed for their part in the crime while Cullum escaped prison.

He returned to his former life, breaking and entering at will, until he was caught stealing three suits of clothes and some riding gear from the stable of Lord Paget on Mar. 17, 1714.

At Justice Hall in the Old Bailey, Cullum said he was an unwilling participant in the murder of Edward Perry. The court nonetheless condemned him to death for his other infamous crimes, and on Apr. 21, 1714, he was hanged.

REF.: *CBA*; Smith, *Highwaymen*.

Cummings, Homer Stille, 1870-1956, U.S., atty. gen. Born in Chicago, Homer Cummings became a lawyer and entered politics at an early age, becoming mayor of Stamford, Conn. (1900-02, 1904-05). In 1924, Cummings served as the state's attorney for Fairfield County, Conn., and prosecuted a drifter, Harold Israel, for the murder of a Catholic priest, Father Hubert Dahme. After reviewing the evidence against Israel, Cummings did a spectacular turn about and actually came to the accused man's defense, proving that Israel could not have shot the priest with the weapon claimed to have been used. He had the .32-caliber revolver found on Israel reexamined and ballistic experts showed that it was not the gun used in the killing. Doctors examined the suspect and reported that he admitted the killing vaguely at some times, denied performing the murder at other times. He was labelled "dim-witted" and subject to nervous fits by the physicians. His personality, they reported, was unpredictable.

The many Bridgeport citizens who claimed to have seen the killer shoot the priest and who identified Israel as the murderer were all separately interviewed by Cummings and he quickly realized that not one of the witnesses could positively identify Israel. Armed with exhaustive evidence from his own investigation, Cummings was convinced that the wrong man was being tried. He moved that the case against Israel be dropped.

Israel was released due to Cummings' dedicated investigation and he was undoubtedly saved from certain execution. This widely publicized investigation by Cummings, which undid his own "airtight" case and certain conviction, did not go unnoticed by Franklin D. Roosevelt, who appointed Cummings his U.S. attorney general (1933-39) after his first choice, Thomas J. Walsh of Montana, died before the first inaugural. Cummings was an effective but low-profile attorney general who fully supported the activities and programs of J. Edgar Hoover, director of the FBI, and Cummings sponsored many reforms in the U.S. Department of Justice and federal judicial system, such as new rules of civil procedure. He created an administrative office for federal courts and sponsored a juvenile delinquency act. Cummings took special pains to expand and improve the federal prison system, establishing Alcatraz as the country's leading maximum security prison.

Cummings called for the first National Conference on Crime, and secured legislation for J. Edgar Hoover's FBI to extend its authority, particularly enlarging the scope of FBI powers concerning kidnapping and interstate crime. Although Cummings, through Hoover and the FBI, did much to suppress the wave of bankrobbing and kidnapping during the turbulent 1930s, he was nevertheless unduly influenced by the doggedly persuasive Hoover to concentrate in those criminal areas and largely ignore the growing menace of organized crime in the U.S. President Roosevelt's so-called "court-packing" plan (1937) was drafted by Cummings. Books authored: *Liberty Under Law and Administration*, 1934; *Federal Justice* (with Carl McFarland), 1937; *We Can Prevent Crime*, 1937; *The Tired Sea*, 1939. See: **Alcatraz**; **Dahme, Father Hubert**; **Hoover, J. Edgar**; **Israel, Harold**.

REF.: Baker, *Back to Back*; *CBA*; Demaris, *The Director*; Edge, *Run the Cat Roads*; Gosch and Hammer, *The Last Testament of Lucky Luciano*; Hurd, *When the New Deal Was Young and Gay*; Kobler, *Capone*; Kunstler, *The Case for Courage*; Lowenthal, *The Federal Bureau of Investigation*; Nash, *Almanac of World Crime*; ____, *Citizen Hoover*; Overstreet, *The FBI in Our Open Society*; Powers, *Secrecy and Power*; Thompson and Raymond, *Gang Rule In New York*; Toledano, *J. Edgar Hoover*; Ungar, *FBI*; Wicker, *Investigating the FBI*.

Cummings, Lulu, prom. 1920s, U.S., fraud. An attractive southern belle, reportedly from Natchez, Miss., Lulu Cummings was one of the most charming con artists working hotel scams. She would call a hotel in a distant city, pretending to be her own secretary and arrange to have the best suite available for her employer, the wealthy widow Mrs. Lulu Cummings—this being during the 1920s, decades before credit cards. When Mrs. Cummings appeared, she was attended by her own servants and was accompanied by a dozen trunks. She dripped with jewels and furs and the hotel management would invariably treat her as a regal lady of social prominence. The press would be alerted and the social columns soon filled with long interviews and profiles on the beautiful, rich widow. Mrs. Cummings would then be invited to a bevy of balls, banquets, and high society functions. She would have dozens of men asking to squire her about and, with very little prompting, local jewelers and merchants sold necklaces, rings, paintings, wardrobes to her.

Cummings would purchase these items by having them charged to her hotel bill. After a few weeks, she would suddenly be called back to Mississippi or Georgia. A close relative was at death's door, she would hastily explain, and she had to go immediately to the stricken person. She would leave a check to cover her

bills and depart with maids, footman, and trunks of loot. Of course, the hotel managers soon learned that Mrs. Cummings was a flagrant fraud. Her check would bounce within a few days. Meanwhile, the con artist had made off with thousands of dollars worth of gems and goods.

Cummings was only once tracked down by a detective hired by an irate hotel owner, confronting her with a bill for $10,000 and telling her that if it was not paid within a half hour, she would be arrested. Cummings contacted some gentlemen admirers and, within twenty minutes, the amount was paid in cash. At the time, Cummings was housed in the best suite of rooms in the best hotel in Louisville, Ky., living grandly, on an imagined reputation.

REF.: *CBA*; Nash, *Hustlers and Con Men*.

Cummings, Samuel M. (AKA: **Doc**), d.1882, U.S., west. gunman-lawman. Samuel Cummings' association with Texas gunslinger Dallas Stoudenmire ultimately cost him his life. Prior to his association with Stoudenmire, Cummings had owned a hotel in San Marcial, N.M., and raised sheep in West Texas. Beginning in 1870 when Cummings' sister married Stoudenmire, the two men became partners.

Stoudenmire, who was unpopular with the local gunslingers, served as marshal of El Paso in 1881. On the night of Apr. 17, Cummings was riding with his brother-in-law through town when a hired assassin named Bill Johnson shot at the two men. When Johnson missed, Stoudenmire and Cummings killed him with a fierce volley of shots from their six-guns.

Marshal Stoudenmire believed the attack was instigated by the Manning brothers of El Paso. Tensions between the two factions continued for the next several months until Cummings ran into Jim Manning at the Coliseum Variety Theatre on Feb. 14, 1882. Cummings had been drinking heavily, and challenged Manning to a fight. Although Cummings drew first, Manning and the bartender David Kling outdrew him. Cummings staggered out of the saloon and died. See: **Stoudenmire, Dallas**.

REF.: *CBA*; Metz, *Dallas Stoudenmire*; O'Neal, *Encyclopedia of Western Gunfighters*; Sonnichsen, *Pass of the North*.

Cummins, Albert Baird, 1850-1926, U.S., lawyer. Albert Baird Cummins was a member of the U.S. Senate from 1908-26. REF.: *CBA*.

Cummins, Gordon Frederick (AKA: **the Count, the Duke**), 1914-42, Brit., mur. The British press believed they were onto a second "Jack the Ripper." Within four days in March 1942, four women were savagely mur-dered in London air raid shelters during the blackout.

Gordon Frederick Cum-mins was the illegitimate son of a member of the House of Lords. His friends called him the "Duke" or the "Count" because of his social preten-sions. When the war came, he enlisted in the RAF. On Feb. 9, 1942, the mutilated body of Evelyn Hamilton, a 42-year-old schoolteacher, was found in the central district of London known as Maryle-bone. The killer placed the body in an air raid shelter. The next day, Mrs. Evelyn Oatley was found dead in her

Gordon Frederick Cummins, hanged in 1942 for killing four women.

Soho apartment. Police found a blood-stained can opener nearby which the killer had used to rip open the lower portion of her body. Oatley, under the name of Nita Wood, had turned to prostitution to support herself. Cummins murdered his third victim, 42-year-old Margaret Lowe, on Feb. 11, but the body was not discovered until three days later. The mutilation convinced police that the same killer was responsible. Like Oatley, Lowe was a prostitute.

The body of the fourth murder victim, 40-year-old Doris Jouannet, was found just hours later in Paddington. She was in the custom of picking up servicemen in Leicester Square. Cummins assaulted two other women, Greta Heywood and Catherine Mulcahy who were fortunate to escape with their lives. Cummins left one clue near the shelter where he accosted Heywood: a gas mask bearing an easily traceable serial number. The police arrested him near St. John's Wood. Fingerprints found at the murder locations matched Cummins'. It took a jury at the Old Bailey only thirty-five minutes to find him Guilty of murder. Lord Chief Justice Humphreys dismissed his appeal, and Cummins was taken to Wandsworth Jail, where he was hanged on June 25, 1942.

REF.: Brophy, *The Meaning of Murder*; Browne, *Fingerprints*; ____, *The Scalpel of Scotland Yard*; ____ and Tullett, *Sir Bernard Spilsbury: His Life and His Cases*; *CBA*; Cherrill, *Cherrill of the Yard*; Firmin, *Murderers In Our Midst*; Greeno, *War On the Underworld*; Gribble, *They Had A Way With Women*; Higgins, *In the Name of the Law*; Jackson, *Occupied With Crime*; Lucas, *The Sex Killers*; McKnight, *The Murder Squad*; Sanders, *Murder Behind the Bright Lights*; Shew, *A Companion to Murder*; Tullett, *Strictly Murder*; Wilson, *Encyclopedia of Murder*.

Cummins, Ark., Prison Farm Escape, 1940, U.S., pris. esc. On a morning in early September 1940, numerous convicts worked in the pea fields three miles from the Cummins Prison Farm. Among them were Frank Conley, thirty-four, a robber and kidnapper serving a twenty-one-year term, and Percy Loftin, twenty-five, a murderer, robber, and kidnapper serving a life term plus fifty-two years. The prisoners stopped for lunch, during which they were watched by guards, including several armed trusties. Then, with synchronized movements, a few prisoners and inmate guards quickly took control of the camp. One guard, Claude Martin, was killed and about thirty inmates, including Conley and Loftin, escaped.

Conley and five companions forced their way into the car of Frank Horsfall and his wife, pushing the car up to eighty miles an hour. When another car crashed into them, some teenaged friends of the Horsfalls stopped to help. Gladys Diamond, sixteen, Voncille Williams, and Jerry Harrigill, both seventeen, were taken hostage in their car. When a tire blew out, Conley, Bruce Fowler, and another convict split from the group. Three other escapees forced the teenagers into a swamp to hide.

Conley was later found by a posse member shot to death. Fowler seized first one, then a second car and drove to Vicksburg, Va., where police shot him in the head. Loftin was captured by a schoolteacher and an oil driller, who knocked the fugitive unconscious. And after two days in the swamp, the other runaways sent Voncille Williams to negotiate with the posse. She led officials to the hideout where the other three criminals surrendered. Most of the others were also recaptured. REF.: *CBA*.

Cunningham, Charles, 1787-1805, U.S., mur. Born in York, Pa., Charles Cunningham was deserted by his mother at an early age and placed in a poorhouse. He was later sent to an inn operated by a man named Eichelberger to be a bond servant. With no schooling, Cunningham grew up living in a back room, his tutors being the ruffians who drank in the inn's bar. He was an alcoholic by the age of eighteen and he was nothing more than a petty thief, a brawler, responding only to the most animalistic instincts. On May 16, 1805, Cunninghman and two other teenaged boys, Joseph Rothrock and John Heckendorn, began gambling in the inn's kitchen, playing hustlecap, a game where coins were shaken and tossed into a cap. The boys continued gambling and drinking at another inn. First Cunningham won, then he lost to Rothrock and claimed he had been cheated.

Taking Rothrock to a dark alley, Cunningham, according to his later confession, drew a knife which slipped from his hands. Cunningham then jumped on the smaller youth and began strangling him until Rothrock "appeared to be dead." But the youth revived and Cunningham took a piece of rough twine from his pocket, looped this about Rothrock's neck and twisted it hard, until he strangled the boy to death. Then, his hatred seething,

Cunningham smashed Rothrock's face against a flagstone repeatedly until his face was all but unrecognizable. Cunningham later stated that he committed this murder and mutilation "at the instigation of the Devil." He then ran from the scene but was recognized by some passersby and was quickly arrested after Rothrock's body was found. Cunningham made a lengthy confession after his arrest and he was tried, condemned, and hanged in York on Sept. 19, 1805.

REF.: *CBA*; *The Dying Confession of Charles Cunningham*; Nash, *Bloodletters and Badmen*.

Mrs. Emma Cunningham, left, who stood accused of killing Dr. Harvey Burdell, right, in 1857.

Cunningham, Emma Augusta, prom. 1857, Case of, U.S., fraud-mur. In 1857, P.T. Barnum had people paying to enter his museum in New York City to see a perfectly normal baby girl and her mother. The attraction stemmed from the murder on Jan. 29 of a dentist named Dr. Harvey Burdell. The miserly man owned a large mansion, but he rented rooms to many different people while he and his dental operation occupied just one room at the front. That night, the 46-year-old man was seen to enter his quarters from the street, then heard to shout the partial word, "MURD—." The police found him dead in his room, knifed fifteen times and strangled. No weapon was found and no one was seen leaving the residence, so the police investigated the lodgers.

Several weeks after Burdell's death, Mrs. Emma Cunningham, who lived in the second floor front room, filed for his estate on the grounds that she had married him in secret, with Burdell wearing a false beard. The police, suspecting that a butcher named John Eckel had disguised himself for the wedding, arrested Mrs. Cunningham. She was tried for the murder but acquitted because of lack of evidence. Determined to get something out of the enterprise, she borrowed a baby and claimed that it was Dr. Burdell's child. While she went to jail for fraud, Barnum exhibited the child and its real mother. Dr. Burdell's murderer was never found.

REF.: *The Burdell Murder Case*; *CBA*; Duke, *Celebrated Criminal Cases of America*; Lewis, *Nation—Famous N.Y. Murders*; Nash, *Almanac of World Crime*; Pearce, *Unsolved Murder Mysteries*; Pearson, *Murder at Smutty Nose*; *Speech of Henry L. Clinton, to the Jury, on the Part of the Defense, on the Trial of Emma Augusta Burdell (otherwise Called Cunningham), for the Murder of Dr. Harvey Burdell*.

Cunningham, Evelina, 1805-25, U.S., (unsolv.) mur. On Apr. 9, 1825, Evelina Cunningham went for a walk at about 3 p.m. along Baltimore's Post Road. A young boy saw a man step from the woods and drag the 20-year-old Cunningham back among the thick underbrush. By the time the boy brought police to the site, Cunningham was dead. She had been raped and strangled to death. The victim was "a female of respectability," according to most reports. Rewards were offered for information leading to the arrest of the rapist-murderer, but the killer was never found.

REF.: *CBA*; Hanna, *$100 Reward, Stop the Murderer*.

Cunningham, Sawney, See: **Bean, Sawney**.

Cunningham, Thomas, 1811-65, U.S., jur. District attorney for Beaver County, Ohio, in 1857 and nominated to serve on the territorial court of Kansas by President Franklin Pierce in 1856. REF.: *CBA*.

Curcio, Margherita Cafol, d.1975, Italy, kid.-terr. Margherita Curcio was an Italian terrorist responsible for the 1975 abduction of wealthy Vermouth manufacturer Vittoria Vallarina Goncia, who was taken to an isolated farmhouse and held prisoner for twenty-four hours. Police stormed the building and killed Curcio in a shoot-out. REF.: *CBA*.

Curley, James, prom. 1909, Brit., mansl. James Curley and Elizabeth Watts were living together in a tenement building in Southwark. One Saturday night after a drunken argument with Curley, Watts fell out of their apartment window and died. When Curley was tried on murder charges in March 1909, the jury decided that the woman fell accidentally while calling for help or trying to get away from him. James Curley was convicted of manslaughter and received a sentence of eight years' penal servitude.

REF.: Bechhofer, *Sir Travers Humphreys*; *CBA*; Shew, *A Second Companion to Murder*.

Curley, James Michael, 1874-1958, U.S., fraud-polit. corr. About the time that the Boston police commissioner ordered his officers to shave daily (the Gillette Safety Razor Co. coincidentally being founded in Boston during the same time), there arose from the Irish rank and file a brash, swaggering politician named James Michael Curley, a second-generation Irishman who exercised the direct approach at all costs and by all means. He was to Boston's burgeoning Irish population what Cotton Mather was to the Puritans. Curley, between stints as a U.S. congressman and governor of Massachusetts (1935-37), served four terms as mayor of Boston where he was a political institution for three generations (1914-18; 1922-26; 1930-34; 1946-50).

The Irish in Boston at that time, although treated equally with old Bostonian families with regards to education, were, in the words of Robert R. Mullen, socially "as segregated as Negroes riding a Jim Crow car...they were as oppressed as they had been for seven hundred years in their native land." Curley was the first to organize his people into an effective political machine. His philosophy was built upon a patronage system of overwhelming proportions.

Curley was to state that his beginnings were romantically and soft-heartedly attached to his own people: "It was Christmas. I was walking in Jamaica Plain with some friends. We saw a line of poor folks. Children were among them. They had been standing in the cold, shivering, hungry, for hours, waiting their turn for a Salvation Army dinner.

"Right there I resolved my people would never stand in line again. We organized the Tammany Club (not to be confused with the Tammany organization of New York), and it was noted that the Salvation Army never was called upon to feed people in that district again. On Christmas a bell would ring, and before the door could be opened our basket with turkey and everything of the best would be left and the donor out of sight."

This soup-kitchen politicking went a long way in endearing Curley to his strong, Irish supporters. Even when he went to jail for sixty days for fraud, Curley was hailed as a hero. In 1903, Curley, then twenty-nine, disguised himself as an old man and took a civil-service examination under an assumed name for the position of mailman. This act, which was discovered and led to his conviction while he was a member of the Common Council, he explained, was a gesture of kindness for an old family friend whose literacy was questionable. "Pat couldn't spell Constantinople, but he had wonderful feet for a letter carrier," the future mayor of Boston liked to banter.

During his campaigns, Curley was met by the usual question about his jail term from an alleged heckler in the crowd. Curley would strike his best pose as a martyr and answer in resonant tones: "I took an examination for the sake of an old and beloved friend, brother." Humbled, the heckler would start to clap and this led to thundering ovations which Curley half-heartedly

attempted to wave down. The heckler, of course, was a plant. Curley also neglected to mention that he had been paid for his civil service impersonation.

"King Mike" was a man with a silver tongue. The tall, handsome Curley was voted by Harvard students as having one of the three best voices in the world. He seldom gave it a rest. As mayor of Boston, Curley never tired of receiving visitors in his ornate office. Inside of his desk he kept dozens of pictures of himself. At the bottom of the pile was a yard-long photo, and the sizes diminished to eight-by-ten glossies at the top. After eyeing his visitor, Curley would hand him or her an autographed picture. The size of the picture he bestowed indicated his opinion of his guest's importance. To special friends, he handed out gold medals in jeweled boxes. The medals had a bas-relief of Curley on one side and, on the other, a list of the public offices he had held during his lifetime. Also in his massive, mahogany desk reposed a vast quantity of silver dollars; the coins filled an entire drawer. These he reserved for females who particularly caught his fancy.

As his dress-rustling visitor prepared to leave, King Mike would stand up, and through a beamish face announce: "Now, madam, there are two things that are the right of woman, good looks and money. You have the beauty and now here is the money." With that, he would press a shining silver dollar into the female's palm. None of these ladies ever failed to vote for James Michael Curley.

Charming though he was, Curley's regime was one which flaunted corruption and practiced blatant graft. The mayor's cronies, Eddie (Edmund) Dolan, who had been Curley's City Treasurer, and J. Walter Quinn, conspired to steal $200,000 by selling themselves city bonds. They were indicted and sent to jail for jury fixing. As early as 1921, Curley himself was charged with shaking down film producers Hiram Abrams and Adolph Zukor following a dinner party honoring Roscoe "Fatty" Arbuckle at the Copley-Plaza Hotel in 1917. Twenty years later, Curley was charged with having taken a $35,000 bribe in a city settlement for a broken water main caused in the construction of Boston's subway. In his fourth term as mayor of Boston, Curley was sent to Danbury Prison (June 26 through Nov. 28, 1947) for using the mails to defraud, only to be pardoned by President Harry Truman who declared him innocent. (The title of Curley's autobiography was, in itself, a defiant roar at his detractors; it was entitled, *I'd Do It Again*.)

Like the reckless city administration of New York's "Gentleman Jimmy" Walker, Curley's various tenures in office provided a "wide open" city. His police department rampaged through the town taking bribes and payoffs and running illicit operations. Police commissioners like Herbert A. Wilson were involved, and were removed from office. Even patrolmen prospered greatly during the salad days of Curley's rule.

One cop, patrolman Oliver B. Garrett, began his career with only $30 in the bank in 1923. Between 1924 and 1926, Garrett banked $28,000. In 1927, he stashed another $27,000. More than $39,000 found its way into Garrett's account in 1928, and the following year industrious Garrett put away another $28,000 (1929 was a bad year). His patrolman's meager pay, Garrett early discovered, could be supplemented by operating a small dairy on the side. His modest firm supplied milk to almost every bordello in and about Boston. Gambling dens and other underworld hangouts also bought his milk at extremely inflated prices. Those who refused were raided by Oliver Garrett and some of his friends, and at no time did the officer bother with anything so obstreperous as a search warrant. It was also pointed out that Garrett was not above an occasional robbery or accepting whole-sale bribes.

Charges brought against Garrett and others who operated with the same brazenness were casually perused by high-ranking police officials, and forgotten. Superintendent of Police Crowley was one of those who ignored indictments made against Garrett. Crowley, "that great moral crusader against literature and communists," as the *Nation* once sarcastically described him, was one of the early Boston champions of censorship, joining with Mayor John "Honey Fits" Fitzgerald in banning such wicked works as Strauss' *Salome*. (The banning of plays and books in Boston became such a ritual that it would be impossible to list all the works censored; some include *Strange Interlude, The Sun Also Rises, Manhattan Transfer, Elmer Gantry, Dark Laughter*, and *Mosquitoes*.)

Other Curley cronies in on the take included Charles McGlue, former chairman of the Democratic State Committee, who went to jail for income tax evasion; Clerk of Court John Patrick Connelly, who received a three-year prison term for his misconduct; and one-time schoolhouse commissioner, James J. Egan, who had been removed from office for his illegal connections with dog-racing tracks and fined $5,000 for tax evasion. (Egan had been a silent partner with dog-track tycoon Edward J. O'Hare, who was later murdered by Chicago gangsters.)

Despite the massive corruption symbolizing Curley's political reign in Boston, his public image survived, tarnished only at the edges. His constituents knew he was and had always been a wheeler-dealer who winked at the law instead of strictly obeying it. They accepted Curley's corrupt ways as an integral element of American politics (and it was Curley and his like who purposely encouraged this public notion). It was all right to steal, the sentiment went, as long as the politician stole in moderation and did it with a smile on his face.

When Curley died in November, 1958 following an intestinal operation, his body was placed on a bier in Boston's State House amid the honored battle flags of the state's great battle regiments. It took two days for the 200,000 spectators to file past his corpse, paying him a fond farewell.

REF.: *CBA*; Curley, *I'd Do It Again*; Reppetto, *The Blue Parade*; (FICTION), O'Connor, *The Last Hurrah*; (FILM), *The Last Hurrah*, 1958.

Curly Bill, See: Brocius, Curly Bill.

Curran, Edward Matthew, 1903-   , U.S., jur. Served as a U.S. attorney assigned to the Justice Department from 1940-46 and appointed to the district court of Washington, D.C., by President Harry Truman in 1946. REF.: *CBA*.

Curran, James M., c.1925-   , U.S., extor. The Tenderloin, a notorious area of San Francisco, was known as a harbor for prostitutes, for robbers who preyed on tourists and elderly residents, and for the distribution of illegal liquor. The area was also apparently profitable for at least nineteen policemen whose activities were uncovered by a special U.S. Department of Justice team investigating organized crime.

On Mar. 24, 1977, eight police officers were indicted and eleven were named as conspirators in a scheme to extort protection money from at least eighteen Tenderloin businesses. Operating between July 1966 and January 1974, the shady officers allegedly collected between $100 and $400 per month, totaling as much as $680,000.

The eight officers under indictment by a federal grand jury included Captain James M. Curran, fifty-two, also head of the Crime Specific Task Force; Lieutenant Eugene H. Del Carlo, fifty-five, retired; Sergeant Joseph J. Cuneo, forty-seven; Sergeant Charles C. Gale, forty-six; and patrolmen Albert J. O'Keefe, forty-eight, James T. Evans, thirty-four, William T. Wasley, thirty-four, and Arthur L. Posner, sixty-four, retired. After the indictment, all of the active-duty officers were withdrawn from regular duty and reassigned to desk jobs. Captain Curran was put in charge of department communications.

On May 17, 1977, the federal charges were completely dropped by U.S. District Court Judge Robert H. Schnacke, who said that the payoffs did not interfere with interstate commerce. However, on July 26, 1977, two previous Tenderloin bar owners were fined for perjury after they admitted that they had lied when they said they never paid extortion money. Harold E. Woodward, seventy-six, was fined $10,000 and given three years' probation while Martin Hertz, forty-seven, received a $1,000 fine and two years'

probation for his involvement.

REF.: *CBA*; Shew, *A Second Companion to Murder*.

Curran, John Philpot, 1750-1817, Ire., jur. Established his reputation as a skilled orator defending Archibald Rowan and other leaders of the 1798 insurrection. REF.: *CBA*.

Curran Murder Case, See: Gordon, Ian Hay.

Currieri, Cesar, prom. 1940s, Fr., (unsolv.) mur. In a series of killings between vengeful gangsters, Ange Salicetti was suspected of shooting Sylvestre Nicolai in Paris on Dec. 6, 1944. Nicolai was the cousin of Cesar Currieri, and after Currieri identified Nicolai's body, he vowed to get even. He searched the bars, armed with several .45-caliber Colt automatics, looking for the killer. Unsuccessful, Currieri went back to Marseilles. As he disembarked from his train, Salicetti murdered him with a submachine gun.

REF.: *CBA*; Goodman, *Villainy Unlimited*.

Curry, George (AKA: Flat Nose, Big Nose), 1871-1900, U.S., west. outl. Born on Prince Edward Island, Can., George Curry moved as a young boy to a farm in Chadron, Neb. At the age of fifteen, Curry moved west and became a stock thief. After a horse kicked him in the nose he became known as "Flat Nose." Curry rode with the Wild Bunch for several years during the late 1890s. In October 1897, Curry, the Sundance Kid, and Harvey Logan rode into southern Montana where they planned to hold up a train. Their plan was thwarted by "Six-Shooter" Bill Smith and an ambitious bounty hunter. Curry and the Kid were arrested and taken to the Deadwood jail, but managed to escape. They

George "Big Nose" Curry

returned to Nevada and spent the next few months breaking horses for local ranchers.

In 1899 Curry held up a train at Wilcox Siding. A posse led by sheriffs Jesse Tyler and William Preece trailed Curry all the way to Castle Gate, Utah, where, on Apr. 17, 1900, they trapped him on a ranch. Curry ran for six miles, before he was hit in the head with a bullet from a long-range rifle. Before Curry's body was dumped into a common grave at Thompson, Utah, souvenir hunters ripped away portions of his skin. See: **Cassidy, Butch; Logan, Harvey; Sundance Kid, the; Wild Bunch, The.**

REF.: Appleman, *Charlie Siringo*; Baker, *The Wild Bunch at Robbers Roost*; Bartholomew, *The Biographical Album of Western Gunfighters*; Bechdolt, *Tales of the Old Timers*; Brown, *The Plainsmen of the Yellowstone*; Burroughs, *Where the Old West Stayed Young*; *CBA*; Coburn, *Stirrup High*; Crawford, *The West of the Texas Kid*; Cunningham, *Triggernometry*; Dunham, *Our Strip of Land*; Holloway, *Texas Gun Lore*; Horan, *Desperate Men*; ____, *The Great American West*; ____, *The Wild Bunch*; ____, and Sann, *Pictorial History of the Wild West*; Kennedy, *Cowboys and Cattlemen*; Lefors, *Wyoming Peace Officer*; Look, *Unforgettable Characters of Western Colorado*; Nash, *Bloodletters and Badmen*; O'Neal, *Encyclopedia of Western Gunfighters*; Pointer, *Butch Cassidy*; Rennert, *Western Outlaws*; Small, *The Best of True West*; Urquhart, *Roll Call: The Violent and Lawless*; Waller, *Last of the Great Western Train Robbers*.

Curry, Kid, See: Logan, Harvey.

Curtin, John Thomas, 1921-   , U.S., jur. Appointed federal judge of the court of the western district of New York, serving from 1961-67. REF.: *CBA*.

Curtis, Benjamin Robbins, 1809-74, U.S., jur. Appointed associate justice of the U.S. Supreme Court in 1851 through the efforts of his political ally Daniel Webster, who interceded on his behalf with President Millard Fillmore. Curtis was willing to compromise with the southern slave interests but drew the line when it came to the case of Dred Scott. He was one of only two justices who felt that Scott should not be returned to his owner. His disagreement with Justice Roger Taney resulted in his resignation from the court in 1857. He later served as President Andrew Johnson's chief legal counsel during the impeachment trial of 1868. REF.: *CBA*.

Curtis, Charles, 1960-   , U.S., mur. Before Charles Curtis, a drifter from Martinsburg, W. Va., confessed to the murder, the disappearance of Judith Lynne DeMaria of Sterling, Va., baffled Loudoun County Deputy Sheriff Robert Turner. After two years, everyone else had given up hope. But Turner kept the case alive and made it his own personal crusade. He even carried DeMaria's driver's license in his pocket.

Turner painstakingly reconstructed the events of the afternoon of Aug. 2, 1985, when the 27-year-old jogger disappeared from the Washington & Old Dominion bike path in rural Loudoun County. Witnesses later told police that Judith DeMaria was last seen crossing the bridge over Broad Run Creek. Blood was found in a field nearby, but there was no trace of a body.

The case might have gone unsolved if not for the killer's desire to confess to someone he trusted. Charles Curtis admired Captain John Sealock, who befriended the troubled youth in 1975. "Chuckie and I go back a long way," Sealock said.

On Sept. 9, 1987, a man called the Loudoun County Sheriff's Police to talk about the DeMaria case. He would speak only to John Sealock. In the company of Police Investigator Jay Merchant, Robert Turner, and Captain Sealock, Curtis pointed out a shallow grave near Dulles International Airport. The remains were identified as those of Judith DeMaria.

Charles Curtis told Jay Merchant that in his drug-induced state he had intended to rape DeMaria but she put up a struggle. Her death was caused by repeated slashes from a carpet razor. Curtis said that he had been on his way to a marijuana growing area where he was "going to rip off a couple of pot patches" in order to buy more PCP.

Charles Curtis claimed to have experienced visions, and to have spoken with "the Lord." "I am absolutely certain that his reason for coming forth when he did was the result of the torture he had been going through," explained his attorney Blair Howard.

Indicted on a charge of first-degree murder, Curtis pleaded guilty to Judge Thomas Horne on Feb. 22, 1988. On May 5, 1988, Curtis was sentenced to the maximum two life terms plus twelve years, which were to be served consecutively. REF.: *CBA*.

Curtis, George Ticknor, 1812-94, U.S., lawyer. Author of *History of the Origin, Formation, and Adoption of the Constitution of the United States,* published in two volumes between 1854 and 1858. REF.: *CBA*.

Curtis, John Hughes, prom. 1932, U.S., fraud. After the child of Colonel Charles A. Lindbergh and his wife was kidnapped, John Hughes Curtis contacted them, saying he had information about the case. Curtis, a boat builder and former president of the Norfolk Country Club in Virginia, said he met a man named Sam at the club shortly after the kidnapping. He was then introduced to some of Sam's friends, who claimed to have money that was part of the $50,000 ransom. Lindbergh and the police believed Curtis, and two newspapers offered to pay for the tale after the baby's safe return.

When the baby's body was found, Curtis confessed, stood trial, and was convicted of having knowingly given false information to the police and to the Lindberghs. He was given one year's suspended sentence and fined $1,000. See: **Lindbergh Kidnapping**.

REF.: *CBA; MacDougall, Hoaxes*.

Curtis, Maurice (Maurice Bertram Strelinger) (AKA: Sam'l o' Posen), b.1851, Case of, U.S., mur. Maurice Bertram Strelinger, born in London, traveled to the U.S. and became an actor. Under the stage name of Maurice Curtis he rose to theatrical success in New York with one of his characters, Sam'l o' Posen. He then retired in about 1886 to Berkeley, Calif., where he was a well-known member of the community.

On Sept. 11, 1891, several shots were heard, and officer Alexander Grant was found dying with a bullet wound in his head, Maurice Curtis, observed running away from the vicinity, was arrested. Handcuff marks were found on Curtis' wrists. Curtis claimed he and another man had been arrested by Grant, and witnesses gave conflicting testimony about the number of people at the scene. The first trial ended with a hung jury on Feb. 26, 1892, and Curtis was acquitted at the second trial. Later, a member of the jury admitted that he was supposed to have received $5,000 for a favorable vote. In addition, an eyewitness who never testified was paid $3,000 and told that a change of climate would suit him.

REF.: *CBA; Duke, Celebrated Criminal Cases of America*.

Curtis-Bennett, Sir Henry Honywood, 1879-1936, Brit., lawyer. In 1902 Henry Curtis-Bennett, twenty-three, was called to the bar. Toward the end of WWI, he became involved in counter-espionage work. Then, from 1924-25, he served in the House of Commons.

He participated in many celebrated criminal cases, usually for the defense. As defense counsel, he appeared in the trials of the Stratton brothers, 1905; one defendant of the Windell Bank Fraud, 1908; espionage cases in WWI; the Douglas-Pennant (WRAF) Enquiry, 1919; Herbert Armstrong, 1922; and Edith Thompson and Frederick Bywaters. He also defended Jean Pierre Vaquier and Lord de Clifford, and prosecuted Patrick Mahon, as well as Sidney Fox.

REF.: *CBA; Scott, The Concise Encyclopedia of Crime and Criminals*.

Cushing, Caleb, 1800-79, U.S., lawyer. Served four years as attorney general under two Democratic presidents. Appointed in 1853 by President Franklin Pierce, he continued in office until 1857. Nominated by President Ulysses Grant to sit on the U.S. Supreme Court in 1873, the appointment was voted down by the Senate. REF.: *CBA*.

Cushing, Luther Stearns, 1803-56, U.S., jur. REF.: *CBA*.

Cushing, William, 1732-1810, U.S., jur. Chief justice of the Massachusetts Supreme Court from 1777-1789. While serving on this court, he handed down one of the earliest known anti-slavery decisions, and was instrumental in putting down Shay's Rebellion. He was nominated and confirmed to serve on the U.S. Supreme Court as associate justice in 1789, one of the five original members named to the High Court by President George Washington. REF.: *CBA*.

Custine, Adam Philippe de, 1740-93, Fr., consp. Commanded the revolutionary armies into battle at Mainz, capturing, but ultimately losing the city in 1793. Suspected of conspiring with the enemy forces to bring about counter-revolution, Custine was executed in Paris in 1793. REF.: *CBA*.

Custom House Place, prom. 1880s-90s, U.S., vice dist. The Custom House Place vice district existed in the shadow of Chicago's financial district for nearly two decades before reformers forced it to move to 22nd Street on the South Side around 1900. Within a four-block area bounded by State and Clark streets, Plymouth Place and Custom House, there existed a variety of clip joints, bordellos, gambling dens, and "panel houses" in which a customer would be accosted by the prostitute's male accomplice during a sexual liaison. The assailant gained access to the room by means of a sliding panel or secret passageway.

The most famous practitioner of this infamous art was Lizzie Davenport, keeper of a brothel at 202 Custom House Place. She employed at various times Emma Ford, her sister Pearl Smith, Flossie Moore, and Mary White, who came to be known as the "Strangler." The Chicago Police estimated that the Strangler stole $50,000 from her clients in a three-year period. According to the memoirs of Chicago detective Clifton Wooldridge, who wrote about Lizzie Davenport in his book *Hands Up in the World Of Crime*, a thick oaken door was constructed to conceal a secret closet for the girls to hide in in the event of a raid. Detectives from the nearby Harrison Street lockup had to employ ingenious methods to find them. On one occasion, they put red pepper under the door to force the thieves from their chamber. See:

Ford, Emma; Moore, Flossie; Panel Houses; Wooldridge, Clifton. REF.: *CBA*.

Cutler, Lloyd, 1918-   , U.S., lawyer. A prominent lawyer in Washington, D.C., Lloyd Cutler was well-known for supporting liberal issues as well as defending the interests of corporations. He was instrumental in establishing an organization to defend Southern blacks, the Lawyer's Committee for Civil Rights Under Law in 1963. He also represented peace activists, and in a 1983 Supreme Court case, he represented the NAACP, winning an economic boycott case.

Cutler also appeared as counsel for the business world, including an antipollution case in which he advised automobile corporations, and he fought for drug companies' interests in confrontations over safety standards and pricing. REF.: *CBA*.

Cutolo, Don Raffaele (AKA: Don Raf), c.1941-   , Italy., org. crime-mur. Don Raffaele Cutolo, leader of a mob in Naples, was serving a twenty-four-year prison term for murder while continuing to direct organized crime operations from his prison cell. He was faced with a crisis in late 1980 after an earthquake and a recession hit the area when an annual take of $300 million from the organized crime business was at stake. Commanding operations from inside the prison walls, Cutolo launched an offensive to try to take control of the business, which resulted in at least 450 casualties. REF.: *CBA*.

Cutpurse, Moll (Mary Frith, AKA: Mary Markham), c.1589-1662, Brit., rob. The most notorious female criminal in British history was Moll Cutpurse, born Mary Frith on London's Aldersgate Street around 1589. Her parents were hardworking, law-abiding middle-class citizens and there is little or nothing to suggest a criminal influence in Moll's background. The little girl was, however, extremely homely and, as she aged, Cutpurse would develop a decidedly masculine-looking face. Moll's parents denied her nothing, even providing tutors for her, but from an early age she rebelled against them. One historian described her as "above breeding and instruction. She was a very tomrig, rumpscuttle, or hoyden."

Moll Cutpurse shown as a young woman wearing men's clothing.

Despairing of ever having a man find interest in her, Moll, by her early teens, took to playing with the roughest boys in her neighborhood, and standing outside of pubs and contorting her already repulsive features into hideous faces at the men entering and leaving. Physically powerful, Moll could best any boy in acrobatic feats and could run and jump faster and higher than any of her male peers. She was also feared for her ability to use her large fists and had the reputation of beating up any boy or man who displeased her. The family realized that they could not control the wild girl, so her rich uncle made arrangements to send her to the American colonies, believing that once she arrived in Virginia, the rigorous pioneer life would tame her. Moll acquiesced and boarded a ship bound for America but, as the ship pulled away from the Gravesend dock, she dove overboard and swam to shore. "I escaped the voyage," she sardonically remarked later, "alike hating Virginia and my virginity."

Donning men's clothing, Moll struck out on her own, becoming a fortuneteller and befriending the members of the lowest criminal element in London. Most of her friends belonged to the Society of Divers, a diver being one who dove into the pockets of wealthy passersby to pick wallets and purses. One of the most adept of these was Mary Jones who was later celebrated in *The Beggar's Opera* as Jenny Diver (see entry). Moll learned the art of pickpocketing so well that she soon became one of the most successful thieves in London. Those purses too difficult to pluck from a pocket, Moll learned, had to be cut away, and often as not this meant cutting away an entire pocket in the coat of a victim without being detected. Pickpockets who could successfully perform this delicate act were known as "cutpurses." Such techniques required special dexterity and skill, which Moll expertly demonstrated time and again. So adept did she become at this method of pickpocketing that she quickly earned the esteemed underworld sobriquet Moll Cutpurse.

She reveled in her legendary exploits, such as cutting away the purses of more than fifty victims in a single day, and became rich. Even law-abiding citizens looked upon Moll as a sort of cult heroine. She played the part, dressing in elegant men's apparel, brocaded breeches, doublet, plumed hat, and smoking a pipe, a habit she was addicted to until her death at age seventy-three. So rich did Moll Cutpurse become that she bought stores and property, but she never deserted her underworld friends, fencing their stolen wares for a handsome profit. Not until she decided to blatantly publicize her wicked image did she run afoul of the law. In 1605, she leaped upon the stage of London's Fortune Theatre, dressed, of course, as a man, and puffing heavily on a pipe, loudly sang bawdy songs while strumming a lute. She regaled the raucous crowd with lascivious stories until watchmen arrived to place her under arrest. The charge was a minor one, that of a female wearing the garb of a man. She was fined and released.

More serious punishment came with her being branded four times on the hands after she was somehow caught with her fingers working loose the pocketbooks of unsuspecting victims. These rare arrests and subsequent brandings were badges of honor to Moll, but as she grew older and her fingers were less adept in picking purses, she abandoned the practice. She put together a band of roughnecks and embarked on the career of highway robbery. She would ride wildly down a road in pursuit of a coach and order the driver to halt while training a brace of pistols on him. Her confederates would then order the passengers to step out and they would be robbed of their jewelry and purses. She was even bold enough to stop the coach of General Fairfax. The general resisted and Moll shot him in the arm. When he tried to flee by grabbing the reins of the horses, Moll shot two of the horses to death, then climbed onto the coach, knocked the general unconscious, took his purse bulging with gold coins, and fled.

Fairfax returned to Hounslow where a company of troopers were alerted. They pursued Moll and found her in the middle of the road, cursing her horse, which had gone lame. Surrounded by fifty guardsmen with drawn swords, Moll threw down her empty pistols and surrendered. Taken to Newgate, she was tried and sentenced to be hanged. Moll asked to see General Fairfax, who was astounded to discover that a woman had robbed and shot him. When meeting Fairfax, Moll proposed a deal. She would pay him £2,000 if he would drop the charges against her and arrange for her release. Fairfax, at the time, was in need of funds, Moll knew, because he was helping to finance Cromwell and his roundheads who were in revolt against King Charles I. The general accepted the deal, and after the money was paid, released Moll. The experience so frightened Moll that she gave up highway robbery. With her considerable fortune she retired to her lavish Fleet Street residence but kept active by opening the Globe Tavern which became the center of all criminal activities in London, the meeting place for every pickpocket, highwayman, and cutthroat in the city.

At the Globe, Moll gave advice on planned robberies and burglaries and also established herself as the most important fence in the city, buying stolen silver and gold and other valuables and then reselling them at a considerable profit, often to the original owners. She was referred to at this time in her life by the aristocrats of London as "The Queen of Misrule." Moll then established a bevy of beautiful harlots on her premises and used these women to compromise wealthy nobles, making sure the aristocrats wrote letters to her girls that Moll later used in effective and lucrative blackmail schemes. Further, because no man, not even the lowest of her criminal associates, would involve himself with Moll due to her repulsive face and body, she grew to hate all females and horribly abused her barmaids and female servants. Moll later established brothels where clients were encouraged to abuse the strumpets.

Moll's hatred for women ran so deep that she took to prowling the streets of London, picking up young girls from rural towns who had come to London to seek honest employment. She cajoled and lured these girls to her brothels where they were made white slave captives and forced into a life of prostitution. Those who resisted the powerful Moll were beaten

Moll Cutpurse shown in old age.

senseless by her and physically carried to her bordellos. If a girl proved truculent after having been held captive for more than a week and refused to service Moll's noblemen clients, Moll personally administered severe whippings. Denied the love of men, Moll perversely watched through peepholes as her captive whores were ravished by her clients, cackling with joy over each debasement and debauchery.

Moll still reveled in her role of criminal overlord, swaggering through the elegant areas of Drury Lane and St. Giles, richly bedecked in her men's clothing, puffing her pipe and roaring out ribald stories to aristocrats who squirmed at being in her company. She was once again arrested for "indecently and publicly wearing male attire." Tried and convicted in February 1612 at the Court of the Arches, Moll was sentenced to do public penance. She was forced to stand before St. Paul's Church on a Sunday morning after services, dressed only in a white sheet, making public apologies to passersby for daring to dress like a man. She wept openly, but it was later learned that these were not penitent tears. Moll had downed three bottles of rum before doing her penance and she was sloppy drunk standing in the square pretending to be a remorseful sinner. Thousands filled the square to witness this spectacle, as Moll knew they would. They hooted and jeered at her, cursing her, calling her every vile name. Meanwhile, as Moll had arranged it, scores of her best pickpockets roamed through the crowd, picking the purses of the very persons who stood about deriding her.

As the decades rolled by, Moll Cutpurse amassed one of England's great fortunes. She purchased grand manor houses, even estates. Her wealth was fabulous and her criminal career so notorious that every child in the country knew her name. She grew more hideous with each passing year, and by her late sixties, gluttony had made her obese. She never bathed and the stench of her body became so overpowering that even her closest associates crossed the street when they saw her approaching. In the next few years, Moll's once keen mind became muddled. She lost track of her affairs and her associates bled her accounts, stole her valuables, and looted her houses. At the age of seventy-three, afflicted by severe dropsy, Moll Cutpurse had but a few hundred pounds left and this money she bequeathed in her will to the three maids still working for her. She left a small amount to a distant relative, a Captain Frith. Her last wish was that she be buried face down in her coffin "as because I am unworthy to look upwards, and that, as I have in my life been preposterous, so I may be in my death." In 1662, her diseased, bloated body

relaxed into death, and she was buried in St. Bride's churchyard, face down, according to her request, so that God would not have to look upon her withering ugliness at Judgment Day. See: **Diver, Jennie**.

REF.: *CBA;* Hibbert, *Highwaymen;* Hunt, *A Dictionary of Rogues;* Nash, *Look for the Woman; The Newgate Calendar;* Pringle, *Stand and Deliver;* Scott, *The Concise Encyclopedia of Crime and Criminals;* Smith, *Highwaymen.*

Cutten, Arthur William, 1870-1936, U.S., fraud. A man who started with nothing accumulated a fortune on the Chicago grain market and was accused of trading violations by the Grain Futures Commission.

Arthur Cutten, a Canadian, traveled to the U.S. when he was eighteen, taking a job as a bookkeeper. He saved $600 and in 1897 bought a seat on the Board of Trade. He was phenomenally successful, amassing $1 million by age thirty-seven.

In 1933, the Grain Futures Commission accused him of trying to manipulate grain prices. The commission charged that during 1930 and 1931 he operated blind accounts to keep from reporting transactions involving 500,000 or more bushels of grain, and made fraudulent entries and false reports of his holdings. In February 1935, the commission found him Guilty of violating the Grain Futures Act, and he was suspended from any trading on the grain markets for four years. However, he appealed the ruling based on the wording of the act, and the punishment was reduced to two years. In November 1935, the Supreme Court overturned the decision and Cutten was allowed to return to trading.

On Mar. 10, 1936, Cutten was indicted by a grand jury on charges of tax evasion, accused of owing $229,944 on income of $414,525. The proceedings were pending at the time of his death.

Cutten and his wife were also robbery victims on Mar. 8, 1922. Nine robbers locked the couple and his brother in a vault and stole $50,000 in cash, jewelry, and liquor. Joseph Vormittag, a former servant, was arrested, convicted, and sentenced to prison. All of the other accomplices were tracked down and convicted. REF.: *CBA.*

***Cutty Sark* Tragedy**, 1880, Brit., mur.-suic. Racial tension between black seaman John Francis and white First Mate Smith aboard the clipper ship *Cutty Sark* ended in murder and suicide during a voyage to Anjer in 1880. Captain Wallace and most of the other crewmen sided with Francis. The captain ordered his first mate to apologize, but Smith refused.

Several days later Smith struck Francis over the head with a heavy object; Francis died three days later. When the *Cutty Sark* anchored in the port of Anjer, Smith slipped ashore and signed on with the American ship *Colorado.* When the *Cutty Sark* crew found out what had happened, they accused Captain Wallace of letting Smith escape. Unable to convince them otherwise, Wallace jumped overboard as the ship steamed toward Yokohama. His body was never found. Nearly two years later, Smith returned to England where he was apprehended and sentenced to seven years' penal servitude.

REF.: Brock, *A Casebook of Crime; CBA.*

Cvek, George, 1918-42, U.S., mur. George Cvek hitchhiked along U.S. Highway 1 in New Jersey and told whoever picked him up that he was the "Mayor of Boy's Town," and that he was on his way to his sister's home. Cvek panhandled for money, which the drivers were often willing to give after hearing his sad tales. Cvek asked for each driver's address so that he could send a check.

Cvek would then turn up at his benefactor's door a few days later and introduce himself to the wife as a business associate or "close friend" of the husband. After providing just enough details to be convincing, Cvek would be admitted. Once inside, he would ransack the house and often sexually assault the woman. He repeated this crime fifteen times between July 1940 and January 1941.

On the night of Feb. 4, 1941, Cvek entered a Bronx apartment house in search of a victim. He rang the doorbell of the first apartment he passed and was greeted by a middle-aged Greek woman, Mrs. Catherine Pappas. Cvek pretended to know her husband, who was away. The woman even put out a plate of cookies and some brandy for her guest. Cvek wrapped his arm around her neck and choked her. She lapsed into unconsciousness as Cvek bound her hands with his necktie and placed a cloth around her ankles. He made off with a small amount of cash, and some jewelry items that were later pawned. The police, who by this time were familiar with Cvek's technique, questioned the other robbery victims at length. They traced him to the Mills Hotel on Seventh Avenue at 36th Street. The next night Cvek was arrested. He was taken to the Bronx Police Headquarters and interrogated around the clock. The next morning Cvek broke down and confessed. The "Mayor," as the press referred to him, went on trial for his life two months later. But a mistrial was declared on Apr. 28 because adverse newspaper publicity prejudiced the jury. A second trial was held in the Bronx County Court in May, which resulted in Cvek's conviction. He was sentenced to die at Sing Sing the week of July 7. The sentence was carried out on Feb. 26, 1942, after Cvek's appeals were exhausted.

REF.: *CBA;* Radin, *Crimes of Passion.*

Cyprian (Thascius Caecilius Cyprianus), d.258, Carthage, her. Appointed Bishop of Carthage in 248 and led the Christian movement despite the brutal suppression of two Roman pagan emperors, Decius and Valerian. He frequently clashed with the constituted authority of the church in Rome, especially Bishop Stephen. During Valerian's persecution he was seized and executed at Carthage. REF.: *CBA.*

Cyrano de Bergerac, Savinien de, 1619-55, Fr., duel. A soldier in the French army from 1637-40, de Bergerac gained his real fame as a duelist in the household of Duc d'Arpajon. REF.: *CBA.*

Czolgosz, Leon F., See: **McKinley, William.**